Sunset

Western Garden Book

EDITED *by* KATHLEEN NORRIS BRENZEL

Sunset Publishing Corporation ❧ Menlo Park, California

Gardening isn't just a hobby, it's a magnificent journey of discovery.

—JOSEPH F. WILLIAMSON JR. 1925–2000

Sunset Western Garden Book
Editor: Kathleen Norris Brenzel
Managing Editor: Pamela Cornelison
Art Director, Design and Production Manager: Alice Rogers
Senior Editors: John R. Dunmire, Philip Edinger, Susan Lang, Jim McCausland, Janet Sanchez, Lance Walheim, Tom Wilhite
Writers and Contributors: John C. MacGregor, Pamela Peirce, Fred D. Rauch; Martin Grantham, Richard D. Rifkind, Marty Wingate
Consulting Editors: Suzanne Normand Eyre, Fiona Gilsenan, Kathy Musial
Copy Editors: Rebecca LaBrum (Chief), Christine Miklas
Proofreaders: Lura Dymond, Mary Roybal, David Sweet
Indexer: Pamela Evans
Assistant Editors: Emily Abernathy-Jones, Bridget Biscotti Bradley, Barbara Brown
Photo Editor: Cynthia Del Fava
Production Coordinator: Patricia S. Williams
Computer Production: Linda M. Bouchard, Elaine Holland, Joan Olson
Botanical Illustrators: Mimi Osborne, Erin O'Toole, Jenny Speckels
Map Design and Cartography: Reineck & Reineck, San Francisco

Sunset Books
VP, General Manager: Richard A. Smeby
VP, Editorial Director: Bob Doyle
Production Director: Lory Day
Director of Operations: Rosann Sutherland
Art Director: Vasken Guiragossian

Sunset Publishing Corporation
Senior Vice President: Kevin Lynch
VP, Editor-in-Chief, *Sunset* Magazine: Rosalie Muller Wright
VP, Publisher: Christopher D. Kevorkian
VP, Manufacturing Director: Lorinda Reichert
VP, Custom Publishing Director: Katie Tamony
Marketing Director: Beth Faso
Consumer Marketing Director: Christina Olsen
Business Manager: Janet Campbell

Cover photograph: 'Kaleidoscope' shrub rose, Norman A. Plate
Endpapers photograph, hardcover edition: Galium odoratum, *David McDonald*

10 9 8 7 6 5 4 3 2 1

 Library of Congress Catalog Card Number: 00-109158. Hardcover edition: ISBN 0-376-03874-8. Softcover edition: ISBN 0-376-03875-6.

Printed in the U.S.A.

For additional copies of *Western Garden Book* or any other Sunset book, call 1-800-526-5111. Or see our web site at www.sunsetbooks.com

Dedication

On the day in 1967 when an earlier edition of this book went to press, Joseph F. Williamson, then garden editor of *Sunset* magazine and "sheriff" of the *Western Garden Book* team, swaggered down the hall of our Menlo Park headquarters wearing chaps, cowboy boots, red bandanna, and a Stetson. He carried a toy cap gun in one hand, a bottle of champagne in the other. Climbing onto a desk, he pointed the gun at the ceiling and pulled the trigger. "The garden book is finished," he bellowed. A wisp of smoke drifted above as staff gathered around him to cheer and toast the occasion. Joe and his colleagues—including botanist John R. (Dick) Dunmire—had much to celebrate. After more than three years of intense work, the ultimate guide to Western gardening was about to become reality.

Sunset had published predecessors of this book in the 1930s, 40s, and 50s, but the 1967 edition broke significant new ground. Among other firsts, it introduced a refined system of 24 climate zones for 11 states west of the Continental Divide.

Subsequent editions evolved to meet the demands of an ever-changing garden marketplace. Different teams of writers and editors have worked on the book, each bringing to its pages their varied experiences and observations. After I succeeded Joe as garden editor in the 1980s, I took an expanded role in updating the book. About that time, I embarked on my first of many trips to Alaska, where I fell in love with its glaciers and mountains, forests and meadows, and with the gardeners who were succeeding brilliantly despite short seasons, permafrost, and marauding moose. I also began to spend time in Hawaii and was enchanted by the islands' sumptuous tropical blooms and treasured native plants, the fragrant plumerias and graceful palms. Numerous gardeners in both states have requested information from Sunset that addresses their unique climates.

With this New Century Edition, we introduce climate zone maps for Alaska and Hawaii, plus refined climate zones for southwestern Canada and the intermountain West. The Western Plant Encyclopedia contains listings for some 2,000 new plants that have come on the scene since the 1995 edition. Plant entries are freshly illustrated with full-color art and photographs.

At the same time, this book remains a no-nonsense garden guide for Westerners, built upon the rich legacy of previous editions. We dedicate this edition to Joseph F. Williamson. His passion for gardening and for the West has inspired many a gardener and garden writer.

And to you, Dick Dunmire, a huge thanks for once again editing the plant encyclopedia and for sharing your vast horticultural knowledge with friends, colleagues, and Sunset readers. Anyone who knows you will agree that you carry this encyclopedia in your head.

Kathleen N. Brenzel, Editor

Contents

DESIGN: Freeland Tanner, Napa, Calif.

GARDENING FOR THE NEW CENTURY

Lessons from the land

Late afternoon on a warm summer day is a magical time in the natural garden. Rosy light bathes the trees, shrubs, and colorful perennials that mingle there with joyous abandon. The setting sun shines through leaves and turns grassy seed heads to spun gold. Blossoms with the ephemeral beauty of wildflowers glow as though lit from within, while a gentle breeze stirs ornamental grasses into a lyrical dance. Mornings are special, too. That's when fattening buds, ripe with promise, sparkle with dew, and the air is fresh and still. But then any time is special where scent and motion, plants and creatures, water, serenity, and joyous informality come together.

Much has been written in recent years about turning to nature for inspiration, about creating gardens in tune with the earth's cycles and seasons, about using as models the land and its natural plant communities. Still, ideas about what a natural garden should be vary widely. For some Westerners, a "natural" garden is decidedly green—a rich tapestry of trees, shrubs, and ornamental grasses.

In wildness is the preservation of the world.

—HENRY DAVID THOREAU

For others, it's a cluster of natives with endearing names that belie their toughness: Fairy duster or pussy toes. Woolly blue curls, shooting star, or silk-tassel. Mexican hat or sugar bush. For still others, it's a carnival of colorful flowers—cosmos and catmint, sages and sunflowers—blooming together in delightful chaos. Or a backyard habitat for birds and butterflies—a nursery, grocery store, and all-night salad bar for a variety of creatures that call the garden home. The natural garden can be all of these things, or none of them. But all natural gardens do have three things in common.

DESIGN: Patti Pardi, Scottsdale, Ariz.

The natural garden is alive. Butterflies alight here to sip nectar from flowers.

Honeybees buzz and ladybugs scuttle among the leaves foraging for aphids. Look closely within the foliage and you may find a hummingbird nest woven from pine needles, lined with tiny mosses and downy feathers. Birds, frogs, dragonflies, earthworms, and lacewings are part of this magnificent microcosm.

The natural garden respects nature's priceless resources. It makes intelligent use of water, for one thing. Where the climate is arid (as in most of the West), gardeners choose plants that withstand dry summers and drought. Patios and paths are porous enough—or pavers have spaces between them—to allow rainfall to pass through to the roots of plants rather than run off to the street, to a storm drain, to a stream, to the sea.

DESIGN: Susanne Jett, Jettscapes Landscape Design, Santa Monica, Calif.

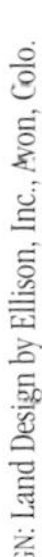

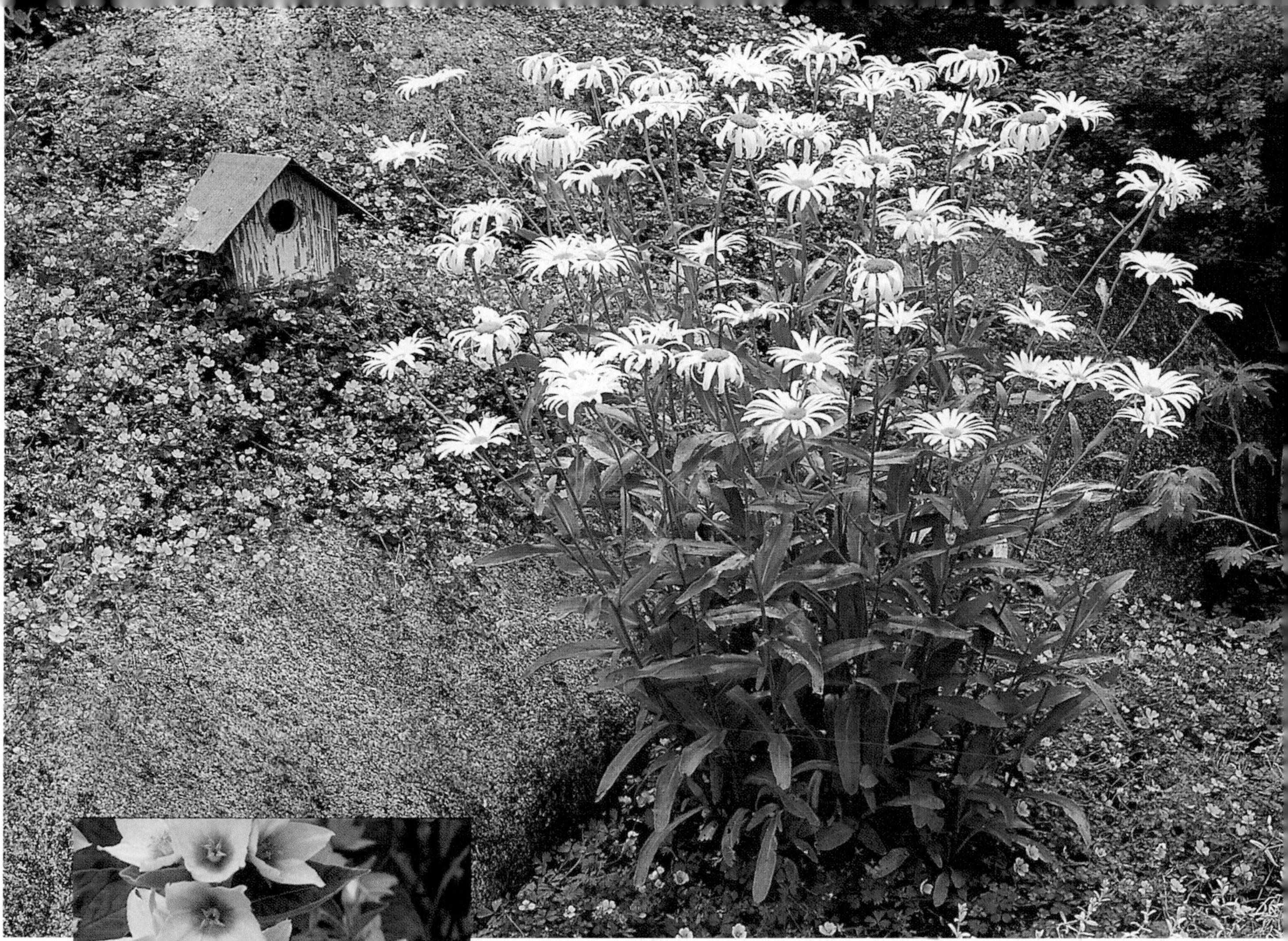

DESIGN: Land Design by Ellison, Inc., Avon, Colo.

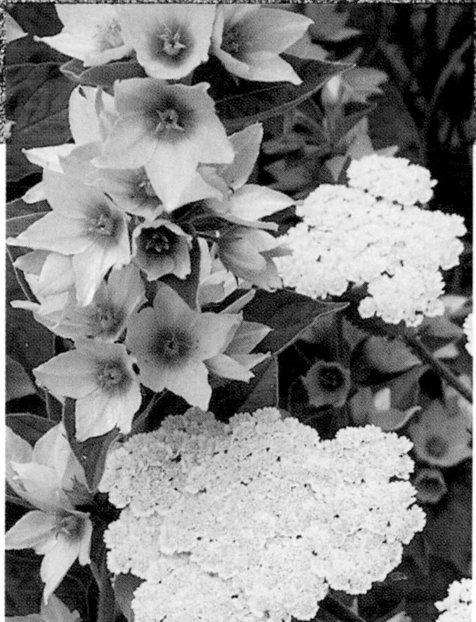

Leaf litter is turned to compost that enriches the soil. "If we feed the soil, we feed Mother Nature," writes master gardener John Jeavons, "and she in turn will feed us abundantly." Grass clippings remain on lawns, breaking down to form nitrogen. A healthy balance of predators to prey diminishes the need for heavy-duty chemical controls.

At the same time, new-generation building materials—such as wood made from recycled plastic and simulated boulders that look like the real thing—help gardeners create the look of wild habitats, while leaving those wild habitats intact.

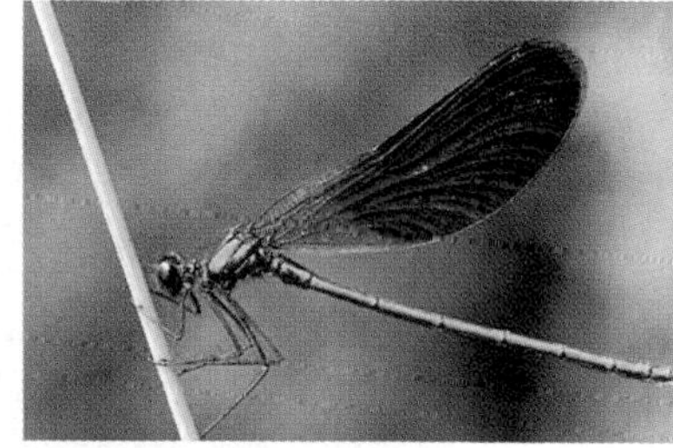

DESIGN: Phil Hedrick, Aspen, Colo.

The natural garden is appropriate to the land and the climate. It captures and reflects the essence of wild plant communities, using plants that will grow easily in the site and the soil. Native or adapted plants—it doesn't matter. If they like the conditions, they'll thrive without heavy-handed care.

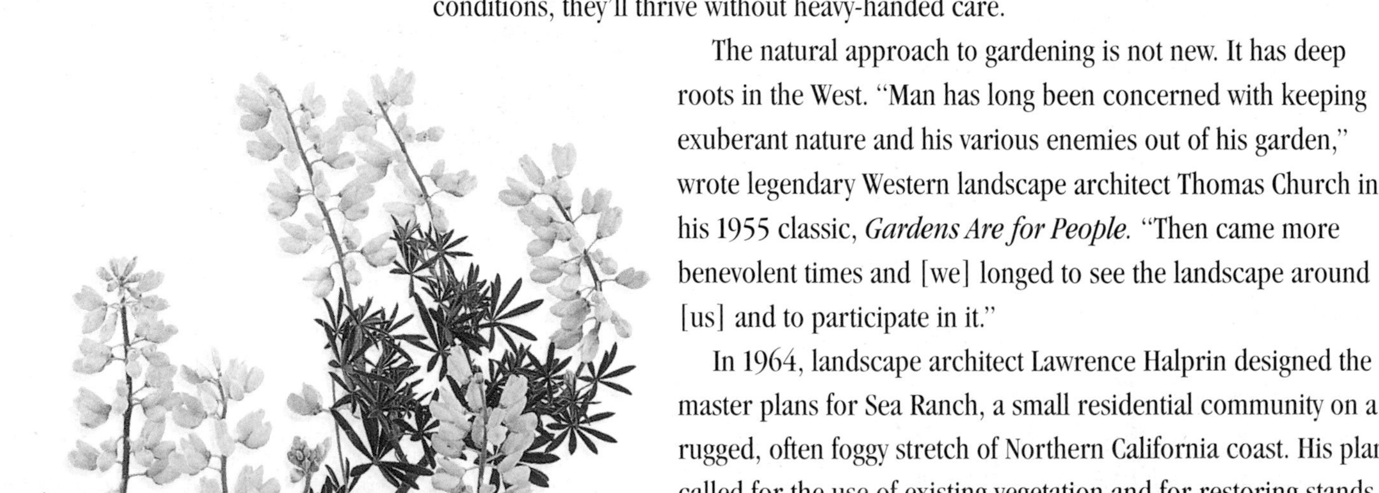

The natural approach to gardening is not new. It has deep roots in the West. "Man has long been concerned with keeping exuberant nature and his various enemies out of his garden," wrote legendary Western landscape architect Thomas Church in his 1955 classic, *Gardens Are for People.* "Then came more benevolent times and [we] longed to see the landscape around [us] and to participate in it."

In 1964, landscape architect Lawrence Halprin designed the master plans for Sea Ranch, a small residential community on a rugged, often foggy stretch of Northern California coast. His plans called for the use of existing vegetation and for restoring stands of conifers that had been cut down in the 1880s. "People are there in order to relate to the wild and natural environment—its incredible rhythms and forms—the sounds of the water, the great view up and down the coast," he wrote, adding that it is "important to maintain an indigenous north coast character."

Part of our responsibility as humans is to be good stewards of the land.

—RON PAYTON, geologist

DESIGN: Steve Chase, Rancho Mirage, Calif.

DESIGN: Tim Curry and Barry Sattels, Los Angeles

DESIGN: Marietta and Ernie O'Byrne, Eugene, Ore.

Later, in the 1970s, came Portola Valley Ranch, set among native oaks on California's golden hills. Houses there were carefully sited to preserve these majestic trees. And the landscaping, by Nancy Hardesty, was designed to blend into this oak habitat, with plants that could tolerate dry shade beneath the oaks, and moisture-lovers along creek banks.

DESIGN: Hendrikus Schraven, Issaquah, Wash.

By the 1980s and 1990s, natural gardens were turning up everywhere. In Washington State, a gardener named Joyce Moulton on a rural stretch of Whidbey Island drew inspiration from the common-sense principles of permaculture, developed by Australian ecologist Bill Mollison, to create a self-renewing garden that preserved the diverse native habitat around her home. She planted natives and a grassy wildflower meadow with hedges of flowering currants to provide nectar for bees and hummingbirds and fruit and cover for other birds. Just outside her kitchen door, the vegetable garden grew from soil enriched by composted nettles from the nearby forest edge.

DESIGN: Huberta A. Martin, Thornton, Colo.

DESIGN: Sarah Munster, Los Angeles

DESIGN: Leland Miyano, Honolulu

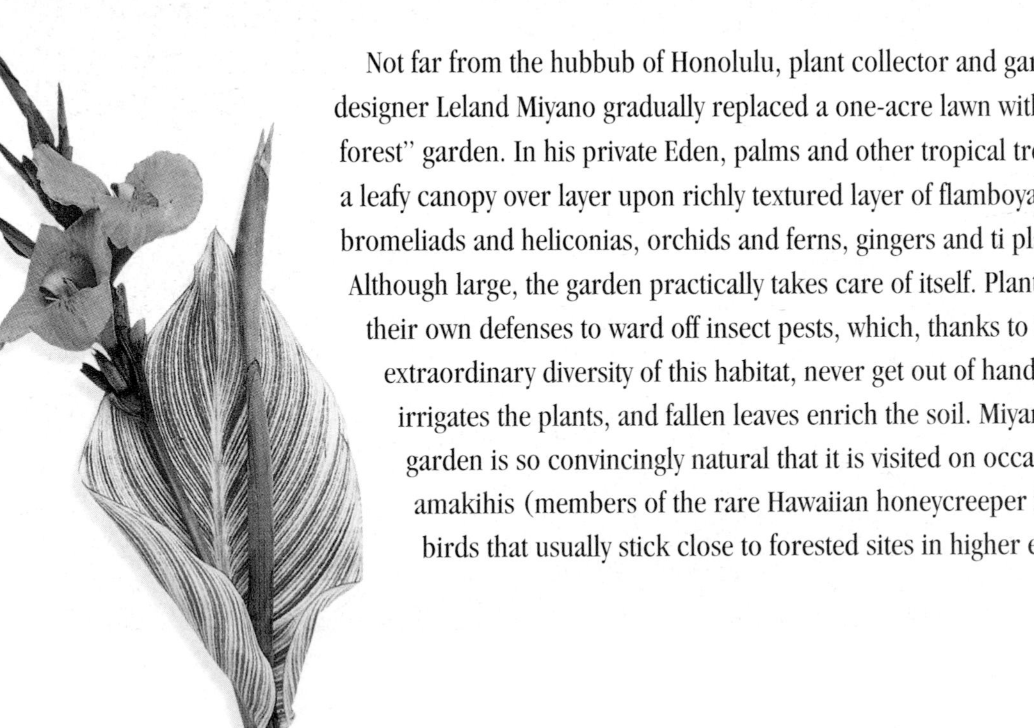

Not far from the hubbub of Honolulu, plant collector and garden designer Leland Miyano gradually replaced a one-acre lawn with a "rain forest" garden. In his private Eden, palms and other tropical trees spread a leafy canopy over layer upon richly textured layer of flamboyant plants—bromeliads and heliconias, orchids and ferns, gingers and ti plants. Although large, the garden practically takes care of itself. Plants rely on their own defenses to ward off insect pests, which, thanks to the extraordinary diversity of this habitat, never get out of hand. Rainfall irrigates the plants, and fallen leaves enrich the soil. Miyano's lowland garden is so convincingly natural that it is visited on occasion by amakihis (members of the rare Hawaiian honeycreeper family), birds that usually stick close to forested sites in higher elevations.

And in "Call of the Wild" country northwest of Anchorage, horticulturist, nurseryman, and avid gardener Les Brake carved a flower-filled garden out of a dense birch and spruce forest. Growing seasons are short here, but during the brief, long-day summers, beautiful perennials chosen to survive snow and frigid winter temperatures race into robust bloom. Daylilies and delphiniums, campanulas and glacier-blue Himalayan poppies grow in a glorious burst in free-form beds, giving the garden a natural meadow look.

DESIGN: Les Brake, Anchorage, Alaska

DESIGN: Troy Bankord, Phoenix

Now, thanks to forward-thinking gardeners and landscape designers, the natural gardening movement is gaining broader popularity. In the Southwest deserts, landscape architects match plants to the rugged cactus and brittlebush landscape, with small pools and joyously colored walls as accents. Garden designers and homeowners take pains to preserve slices of pristine wild land as they build houses that will blend into natural surroundings.

Even on postage-stamp plots in urban canyons, gardeners are finding room to grow beautiful clusters of wild-looking plants, sometimes backed by boulders. Today, most gardeners are eager to connect with nature and to create gardens that complement natural landscapes.

DESIGN: Carrie Nimmer, Phoenix

DESIGN: Julie O'Donald, Brier, Wash.

DESIGN: Kevin Casey and Ken Bowling, Tucson, Ariz.

Since we are part of nature
…we empathize deeply with its ways…
they serve us subconsciously as models
of how things should be….

—LAWRENCE HALPRIN
landscape architect

DESIGN: Val Moore, Everett, Wash.

DESIGN: Val Moore, Everett, Wash.

DESIGN: Jana Ruzicka, Laguna Beach, Calif.

Observe nature and learn from it

Aridity, and aridity alone, makes the various Wests one.

—WALLACE STEGNER

"The West is short-grass plains, alpine mountains, geyser basins, plateaus and mesas and canyons and cliffs, salinas and sinks, sagebrush and joshua tree and saguaro deserts," wrote novelist and historian Wallace Stegner in *Where the Bluebird Sings to the Lemonade Springs*. Gardeners, too, are finding ways to celebrate this land by making use of their sites' natural attributes, whether hills or sinks. They're capturing the spirit of place, planting in harmony with the surroundings. Boundaries are blurred—between paths and flower beds, between planted areas and wild land, even between pavers. Views are framed, paths meander. Plants grow in drifts or meadows, not rows.

DESIGN: Margaret de Haas van Dorsser, Portland, Ore. (left); Kevin Casey and Ken Bowling, Tucson, Ariz. (right)

Layers of plants, low to tall—perennials and shrubs to understory to tree canopy—replicate natural plant communities. The trees and shrubs provide a sense of enclosure.

Like its surrounding landscape, a Puget Sound garden might have a woodland feel with layers of ground covers, vine maples, rhododendrons, and conifers. A desert garden might showcase a mesquite or palo verde, along with Apache plumes and Mexican bird of paradise, salvias, yuccas, and spring wildflowers among sand-colored boulders. A mountain garden might grow among ponderosa pines or a grove of quaking aspens, with drifts of columbines nearby. A California garden might include natives such as ceanothus and California poppies or plants, like lavenders, adapted from Mediterranean climates.

DESIGN: Darcy Hahn and Ann Rosseau, Berkeley, Calif.

Plants in natural gardens are given the freedom to roam and ramble and sprawl as they would in the wild rather than grow up pinched or sheared, squeezed or cinched. The effect is not messy—just refreshingly informal. If a plant's form is naturally stiff and upright (cactus or agave, for instance), it's placed to show off its sculptural qualities, to capture backlighting from the sun and uplighting from lamps, or to cast shadows that wiggle and dance across adjacent paving. There is still a place for neatness—small gardens demand it—and for formality. But the exuberance of plants that is the essence of the natural garden, for many Westerners, represents a kind of breaking free from old traditions, with only climate and geography as guideposts.

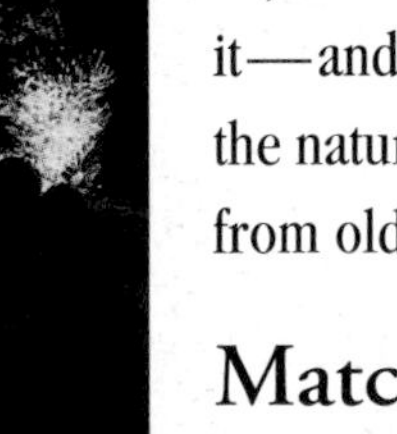
DESIGN: Steve Chase, Rancho Mirage, Calif.

Match the plants to your site

Nature's ways in the West inspire and challenge our plant choices. Along the coasts, wind and salt spray are hard on many plants. So gardeners there choose sea lavenders or Pride of Madeira, rockroses or Santa Barbara daisies that can withstand such abuse. In the grassy foothills, conifer forests, canyons, and dry coastal chaparral zones where wildfires are part of the scene, it makes sense to avoid highly flammable plants such as juniper and rosemary and to maintain an irrigated greenbelt near the house. Sun and shade, bogs and dry washes, slopes and valleys—all present challenges and opportunities. Choose the right plants and they will grow lustily, with minimal fussing on your part. Include in the mix plants that will enhance your garden's magical qualities—flowers for fragrance, grasses for motion, foliage that turns flaming hues in autumn. Encourage surprises like Johnny-jump-ups that rear their tiny purple heads in gravel paths, or lacy, white sweet alyssum that reseeds between pavers. Adopt creeping ground covers, rambling roses, pillowy perennials, and delicate wildflowers.

Plant for diversity

A manicured garden with a lawn and sheared shrubs is of little interest to birds, beneficial insects, or the host of other creatures that keep insect pests in check. However, a diverse planting where many different kinds of plants mingle together as in nature, where nectar and seed producers thrive, is wildlife heaven.

Many wild creatures, after all, are a gardener's best friends. Consider: Beneficial lacewing larvae can consume 200 to 400 aphids before becoming adults. Parasitic wasps and flies deposit eggs on or inside the bodies of aphids, caterpillars, and tomato hornworms, producing pupae or adult parasites that kill the hosts. Garden spiders include hardworking insect destroyers within their ranks.

DESIGN: Ron Lutsko Jr., San Francisco (top); Chris Moritz, Bigfork, Mont. (bottom)

Birds, too, love buggy gardens and dine on all manner of earwigs, whiteflies, and more. That's a good thing, because wild bird habitats shrink every day and many birds are declining in numbers. Honeybees, which pollinate many food crops, including apples, melons, peaches, and squash, are also losing their habitats as lawns and houses replace forage plants and nesting sites. By choosing plants with nectar, seeds, and pollen to aid birds, butterflies, bees, and other beneficial creatures, gardeners help to restore what has been lost. And in the process, the creatures they invite will become allies. "Trust in the goodness of living things," advised the late Joseph F. Williamson, former garden editor of *Sunset* magazine. "Let them go at their own pace. And the good guys among them will prevail."

Recycle plants and materials

In nature, the cycle of life and of the seasons ensures recycling, as trees drop leaves that turn to compost. Likewise, the natural garden wastes nothing. Fallen or pruned tree branches can be used to make rustic trellises and pea stakes, to build out-of-sight brush piles for birds, or to chip into mulch. Tree stumps make fine pedestals for container plants. Man-made materials, from stone pillars and concrete chunks to iron gates, that would otherwise go to landfills can find new homes among the plants.

DESIGN: Land Design by Ellison, Inc., Avon Colo.

The legacy continues

With the dawn of the 21st century, we've entered a brave new world of gardening. Biologists are tinkering with genes that may someday produce blue roses or lawn grasses that seldom need mowing. In backyards across the West today, however, we still practice the gentle art of guiding what nature gives us. "Gardeners are not magicians," wrote Elsa Uppman Knoll, a former garden editor of *Sunset* magazine, in 1949. "They know that in order to succeed, they must work in close collaboration with certain fundamental laws of nature. And so they don't attempt to grow tropical plants where temperatures fall to zero, nor alpines in the desert." That is every bit as true today as it was then. We're coming to realize that the plants and materials we choose for our gardens and the way we go about maintaining them can have consequences far beyond our back fences.

To witness change and growth and evolution and the cycle of nature in our gardens... is truly miraculous, and one of the greatest joys in life.

—HOWARD-YANA SHAPIRO
author, seedsman

DESIGN: Pat Brodie, Santa Barbara, Calif.

The earth is a garden, and each of us need only care for our own part for life to be breathed back into the planet, into the soil, into ourselves.

—John Jeavons
author, master gardener

At the same time, we're learning to appreciate the simple joys of gardening with nature. The shimmering beauty of a garden spider's web on a dewy morning or the incredible industry of countless little creatures that make their homes among the leaves. The play of the moonlight over silvery foliage and snowy flowers, the golden glow of sun shining through leaves, or the way a pond reflects light and clouds.

The natural garden teaches us to plant with the cycle of seasons, to listen to the pulse of the earth. But perhaps the greatest lesson of all is this: working *with* nature helps us to understand that every living thing in the garden—every plant, animal, bird, insect, and worm—is connected, part of an intricate web of life with built-in systems of checks and balances. They'll all work together, if we let them, to keep our gardens, the land, and, ultimately, ourselves much healthier.

The West's CLIMATE ZONES

To find your garden's climate zone, start with this locator map and then turn to the page listed for your area. And because climate zones blend into one another, it is important that you learn about adjacent zones as well.

British Columbia Pages 28 & 36
Alberta Pages 28 & 33
Washington Pages 33 & 36
Montana Pages 33 & 34
Alaska Page 30
Oregon Pages 33 & 39
Idaho Page 33
Wyoming Page 34
Northern California Page 43
California
Nevada Page 34
Utah Page 34
Colorado Page 34
San Francisco Pages 46 & 47
Central California Page 44
Los Angeles Pages 50 & 51
California Deserts Page 57
Arizona Page 61
New Mexico Page 58
San Diego Pages 54 & 55
Hawaii Page 62

In this book, we have assigned climate zones to almost every listed plant. If you have been gardening for long, you know why: some plants can't handle winter cold, while others require it; some suffer in coastal humidity, while others depend on damp air—and so it goes.

The maps on the following pages show where these numbered climate zones are. Take a few minutes to find your zone on the maps (see the locator map above for page numbers) and read the description. It will outline the conditions that combine to make your climate perfect for some plants, trouble for others.

Several important factors combine with temperature to make each of our climate zones unique.

Latitude. Generally, the farther an area is from the equator, the longer and colder are its winters. Also, as you move toward the poles, the number of daylight hours increases in summer and decreases in winter.

Elevation. High gardens get longer and colder winters, often with intense sunlight, and lower night temperatures all year.

Ocean influence. Weather that blows in off the Pacific Ocean tends to be mild and laden with moisture in the cool season.

Continental air influence. The North American continent generates its own weather, which—compared with coastal climates—is colder in winter, hotter in summer, and more likely to get precipitation any time of year. The farther inland you live, the stronger this continental influence. Incessant wind also becomes a major factor in open interior climates—in the Great Basin and the Plains, for example.

Mountains and hills. These land formations determine whether areas beyond will be influenced most by marine air or by continental air. The Coast Ranges take some

Hala trees *(Pandanus tectorius)*, native to Hawaii and the Pacific islands, fringe this black sand beach at Pailoa Bay on the island of Maui (Zone H2).

Saguaros *(Carnegiea gigantea)* march over desert terrain at the base of the Santa Catalina Mountains on the outskirts of Tucson, Arizona.

Black spruce trees *(Picea mariana)* rise from a snow-covered muskeg (grassy bog) in Alaska's interior, Zone A1. Majestic Mount McKinley dominates in the background.

marine influence out of the air that passes eastward over them. The Sierra-Cascades and Southern California's interior mountains further weaken marine influence. East of the Rocky Mountains, continental and arctic air dominate. In the opposite direction, first the Rockies, then the interior ranges, and finally the Coast Ranges reduce the westward influence of continental air. Hawaii's mountains also squeeze moisture out of clouds passing over them, giving most major islands distinct wet and dry sides.

Microclimates. Local terrain can sharply modify the climate within any zone. South-facing slopes get more solar heat than flat land; north-facing slopes get less. Slope also affects airflow: warm air rises, cold air sinks. Because hillsides are never as cold in winter as the hilltops above them or the ground below them, they're called thermal belts. Lowland areas into which cold air flows are called cold-air basins. Microclimates also exist within every garden.

Plants live or die by these elements, and we consider them all when we map climate zones. You'll read about these influences in the zone descriptions along with another important factor: the growing season.

Each zone's growing season—the average number of days between the last frost in spring and the first frost in fall—is shown below each zone description as a green band on a bar. The yellowish green color at each end of the green band indicates shoulder seasons, when light frosts could occur but wouldn't likely bother cool-season crops.

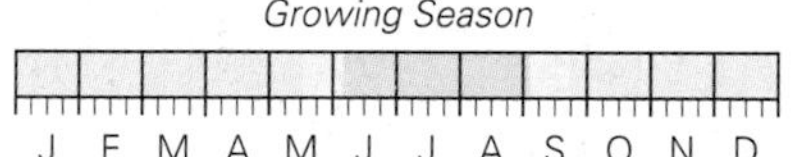

WHY DON'T WE USE OTHER CLIMATE ZONES?

The U.S. Department of Agriculture (USDA) employs a climate zone scheme based on winter minimum temperatures. It provides a useful plant hardiness index, but it has some important drawbacks. Its focus on cold-tolerance alone, for example, places the Olympic rain forest into a zone with parts of the Sonoran Desert. The American Horticultural Society (AHS) has developed a heat zone system based on the average number of days above 86°F (30°C)—the temperature at which cellular protein is damaged in many plants. Used with the USDA system, it targets optimal climates for particular plants. But this information is largely irrelevant to many Western gardeners, particularly those who live in mild coastal areas where it seldom gets that hot. Our method of zoning considers a broad range of factors, including winter minimums, summer highs, elevation, proximity to coast or mountains, rainfall, humidity and aridity, and growing season. It gives gardeners a more accurate picture of what will grow where. Our thanks to the many institutions and experts who helped us create and refine the *Sunset* climate zones.

Growing seasons, however, don't tell the whole story. For example, Zone 5 has a much longer average growing season than Zone 3a, but Zone 3a's extra heat makes it a much more favorable climate for heat-loving summer fruits and vegetables such as melons and peppers. Another influencing factor is soil.

Although soil is not a climate condition, it too can influence or limit plant growth. If your soil is heavy and slow to drain, choose plants that can tolerate those conditions. You can amend or replace enough of it to grow a fair number of favored plants. When that isn't practical, you can install raised garden beds. In any case, you will need to learn which plants can handle tough soils. See A Guide to Plant Selection (page 64) and A Practical Guide to Gardening (page 658).

Zoning in on Your Climate

With this edition of the *Sunset Western Garden Book,* we've expanded our climate zones beyond the West's contiguous states to include Alaska, southern British Columbia and southwestern Alberta, and Hawaii. In this chapter, climate zones range from the coldest (Alaska's Zone A1) to the mildest (Hawaii's Zone H2).

THE CONTIGUOUS STATES. Temperate western North America embraces a broad range of climates and terrain, from alpine and desert to seashore and plains. Here in Zones 1–24, most areas receive little to no summer rainfall, and garden plants depend on watering to survive.

As outlined later in the chapter, the coldest parts of the contiguous states and southwestern provinces (Zones 1–3) have been divided and refined. Located mostly in the mountains, the intermountain regions, and the plains, these zones are now redesignated Zones 1a, 1b, 2a, 2b, 3a, and 3b. The new zones were mapped with extensive guidance from horticulturists, climatologists, home gardeners, botanical gardens, and vast amounts of National Weather Service data collected over many decades.

CANADA'S CLIMATE ZONES

Oceans, mountains, and latitude make all the difference in southwestern Canada. The Pacific Ocean keeps the coastal area (Zones 4 and 5) mild and moist as storms move onshore every month of the year. The mountains (Zone 1a) check the ocean's influence, creating warmer summers in the valleys (Zone 2a), colder winters everywhere, and a shorter growing season. In the Canadian prairies (Zone 1b), continental air ensures more wind all year, very cold winters, mild summers, and shorter growing seasons as it moves north.

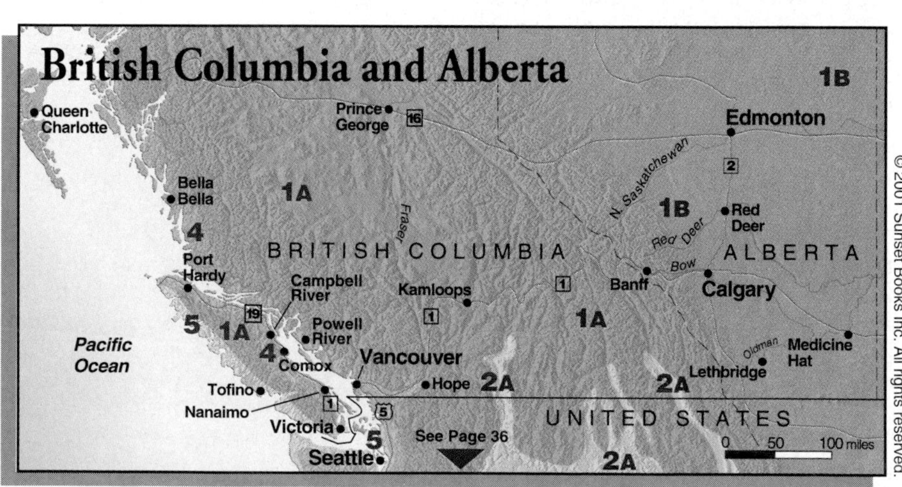

THE ALASKA DIFFERENCE. Though many may try to compare Alaska with cold-winter parts of the Lower 48, this really can't be done. With its unmatched, huge seasonal differences in day length, wild swings in temperature, permafrost (a permanently frozen layer of subsoil), Arctic desert, rain forests, warm-summer interior, and wind-scoured coasts, Alaska is a land apart.

Alaska's Zone A1 encompasses the interior climate centered in Fairbanks; Zone A2, Anchorage and areas along Cook Inlet; and Zone A3, the mild marine climate along the state's southern coast. (The mildest, southernmost part of Alaska tips into Zone 4 of the Lower 48.)

Garden successes here are striking, from the trial grounds for vegetables, annuals, and perennials at Georgeson Botanical Gardens in Fairbanks to the whopping vegetables in the Matanuska River valley, and intimate flower gardens that border southeastern Alaska's rain forests. But to grow anything in the face of permanently low soil temperatures, gardeners throughout Alaska cover annual vegetable and flower beds with infrared-transmitting (IRT) plastic sheeting at planting time, which raises soil temperatures by 10 to 30 degrees, depending on the weather. Gardeners make masterful use of microclimates, press native plants into service, and share ideas and innovation freely, contributing to Alaska's success as a gardening state.

THE HAWAII DIFFERENCE. At the opposite side of the climate scale, Hawaii, the West's southernmost state, has the only true tropical zones in the Western U.S. Its two climates include the higher-elevation H1, which is cool enough for many temperate-zone plants, and the lower-elevation H2, which is evenly warm and frost-free. Moderated by the Pacific Ocean and persistent northeasterly tradewinds, Hawaii is mild year-round with two seasons: the cool season (October through April) and the warm season (May through September). But the same sheer cliffs, deep valleys, broad slopes, ridges, high volcanic peaks, and windy points that give the islands their awesome beauty also create an array of microclimates.

Rainfall can vary immensely within a short distance—even within a neighborhood. The upper Manoa Valley on Oahu, for example, can receive 160 inches of rainfall per year, while Waikiki, just 4 miles away, gets 20 inches per year.

Below about 6,000 feet elevation, it's difficult to grow plants that need winter chill to thrive, including daffodils, temperate fruit trees, and most rhododendrons. Such plants grow better at higher elevations on Maui and the Big Island, where air temperatures are cooler. Throughout the islands, the same benign climates that nurture a wide variety of plants to lush growth also help some introduced species—unless properly managed—to escape and spread, crowding out native plants. Some plants that are well-mannered on the mainland have become tenacious wanderers in the islands. Among these are kahili ginger, *Lantana camara,* banana passion vine, princess flower, strawberry guava, and Queensland umbrella tree. Gardeners should avoid importing any plants (or pieces of plants) without proper permits or inspections.

Vibrant pink blooms of dwarf fireweed *(Epilobium latifolium)* and blue-flowered nootka lupine *(Lupinus nootkatensis)* (top) glow in evening light at Bering Glacier, Alaska. Bird's-eye view from Kalalau Lookout on Kauai (bottom) gives sweeping panorama of jagged ridges, the Kalalau Valley, and the distant Na Pali Coast.

Alaska

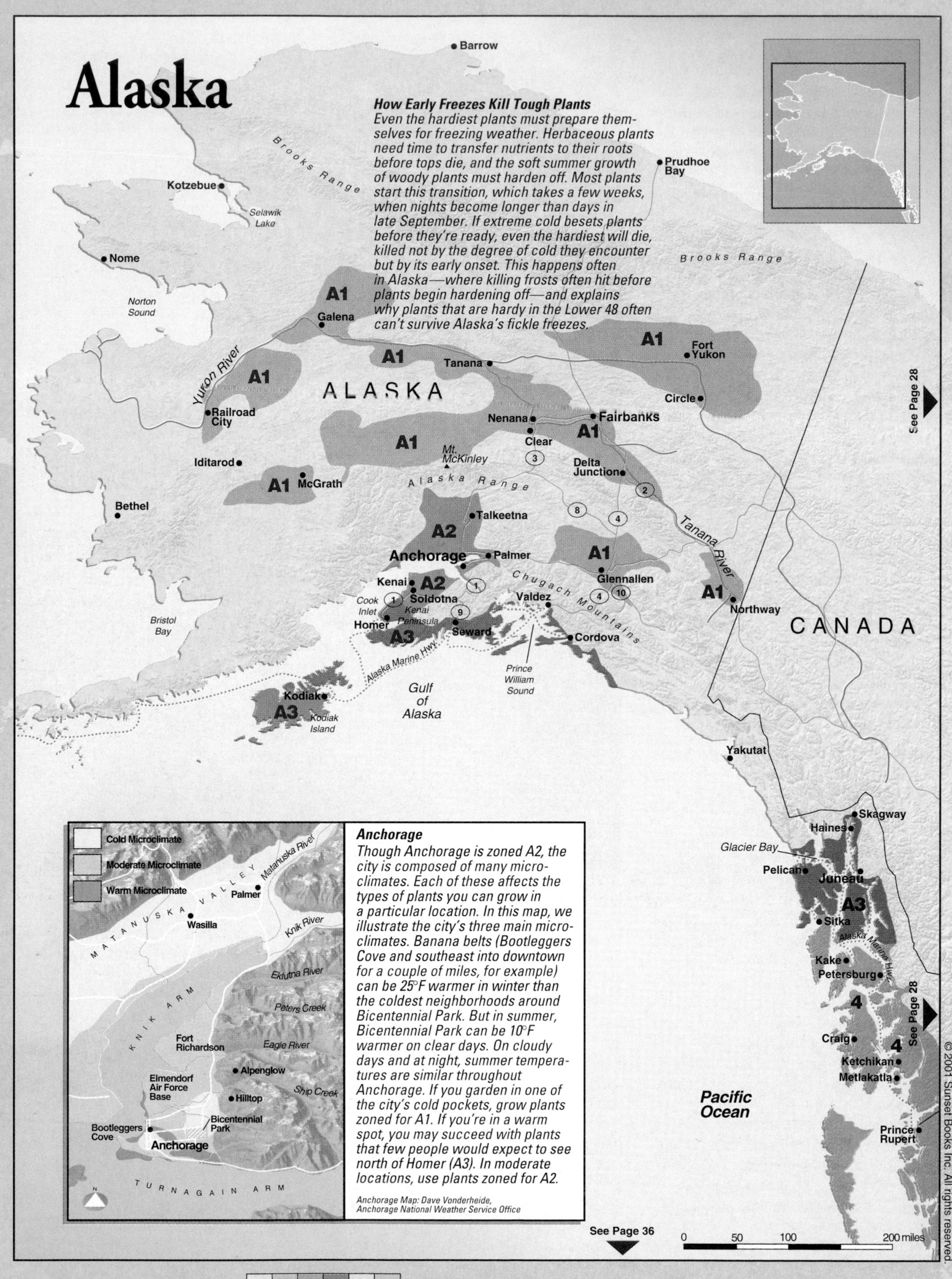

How Early Freezes Kill Tough Plants

Even the hardiest plants must prepare themselves for freezing weather. Herbaceous plants need time to transfer nutrients to their roots before tops die, and the soft summer growth of woody plants must harden off. Most plants start this transition, which takes a few weeks, when nights become longer than days in late September. If extreme cold besets plants before they're ready, even the hardiest will die, killed not by the degree of cold they encounter but by its early onset. This happens often in Alaska—where killing frosts often hit before plants begin hardening off—and explains why plants that are hardy in the Lower 48 often can't survive Alaska's fickle freezes.

Anchorage

Though Anchorage is zoned A2, the city is composed of many microclimates. Each of these affects the types of plants you can grow in a particular location. In this map, we illustrate the city's three main microclimates. Banana belts (Bootleggers Cove and southeast into downtown for a couple of miles, for example) can be 25°F warmer in winter than the coldest neighborhoods around Bicentennial Park. But in summer, Bicentennial Park can be 10°F warmer on clear days. On cloudy days and at night, summer temperatures are similar throughout Anchorage. If you garden in one of the city's cold pockets, grow plants zoned for A1. If you're in a warm spot, you may succeed with plants that few people would expect to see north of Homer (A3). In moderate locations, use plants zoned for A2.

Anchorage Map: Dave Vonderheide, Anchorage National Weather Service Office

See Page 28
See Page 28
See Page 36

A1 A2 A3 4

ZONE A1 Alaska's Coldest Climate—Fairbanks and the Interior

Encompassing most of interior Alaska in a region between the Alaska and Brooks Ranges, Zone A1 is Alaska's gardening surprise. During summer, plants benefit from long, warm days, while in winter, gardeners can usually depend on snow to insulate plants. And in areas where there's permafrost, frost usually recedes below root level during the warm months.

The keys to beating temperature extremes in Zone A1 and to gardening success—with everything from strawberries to snapdragons, beans to sweet corn—include taking advantage of microclimates (especially south and west exposures), boosting soil temperatures with mulches or IRT plastic sheeting over the soil, and choosing the right plant varieties. Many birches, for example, reach nearly unparalleled proportions in Fairbanks, as do hardy perennials and a long list of annuals.

Conifers and grasses edge a mirror-smooth tundra pond near Wonder Lake in Denali National Park, Alaska. The snow-covered peak of Mount Mather towers behind.

Average winter minimums are −10 to −20°F (−23 to −29°C), with occasional dips to −60°F (−51°C). Summer highs are in the 70s, with rare spikes to 90°F (32°C). The average growing season in Fairbanks is 113 days.

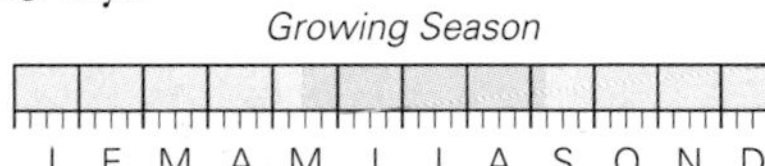

ZONE A2 The Intermediate Climate of Anchorage and Cook Inlet

The Alaska Range protects this area from continental extremes to the north, while the Kenai and Chugach Mountains strip most of the wind and moisture from storms blowing in from the Gulf of Alaska. The salt water of Cook Inlet moderates temperatures as well. However, seasons are well defined and permafrost hides here on north-facing slopes and in sheltered hollows.

Plants like showy mountain ash, late lilac, Siberian larch, Amur chokecherry, Swiss stone pine, and Colorado blue spruce do well in Zone A2. But success depends much on each area's microclimate (see Anchorage map, facing page).

Winter lows average 6°F (−14°C) at Anchorage Airport, 0°F (−18°C) in Palmer and Wasilla, with drops to −20 or−30°F (−29 or −34°C) once in a while. Summer days are usually cloudy and in the mid-60s, with occasional jumps into the high 70s. The growing season ranges from 105 days on the Kenai Peninsula to 138 days in Anchorage. When sowing seeds, take note that plants grow more slowly here than seed packets indicate.

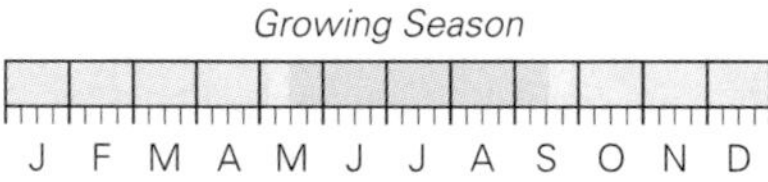

Giant cabbages, like these ready-to-harvest beauties growing in the Matanuska Valley, can reach a hefty 90 pounds apiece (or more). In summer, Alaska's long days (about 20 hours) coax many plants into robust growth.

ZONE A3 The Mild Southern Maritime Climate from Kodiak to Juneau

Prickly bright green devil's club *(Oplopanax horridus)* grows beneath Sitka spruce *(Picea sitchensis)* at Fort Abercrombie State Historical Park on Kodiak Island. These two plants often grow together along glacial rivers outside Juneau and elsewhere in southeastern Alaska, where they thrive in the moist air and soil.

This zone includes southeastern Alaska north of Sitka clear to Skagway, plus Kodiak Island, Homer, Seward, and Prince William Sound. (Zone 4, Alaska's mildest climate, covers southeastern Alaska below Sitka. See page 38 for a description.)

Summers are cool and cloudy, while winters are typically windy and rainy. Annual precipitation runs from 80 inches at Kodiak to 200 inches near Sitka. The ground freezes every winter, and repeated freeze-thaw cycles in spring play havoc with cold-hardy plants like hybrid tea roses.

Hardy rhododendrons, azaleas, Japanese maples, and dwarf conifers do well here. The easiest bedding plants to grow include pansies, violas, and snapdragons. Planting in raised beds of light, sandy soil assures good drainage in wet areas and quick warm-up of soil in spring.

Winter minimums average 20 to 30°F (−7 to −1°C), with occasional drops to −5°F (−21°C). Summer highs are in the low 60s, with occasional jumps to 80°F (27°C). The growing season runs from 113 days in Cordova to 162 days in Haines. But cool summer temperatures offset the advantages of summer day length. Plants take longer to grow than seed packets describe.

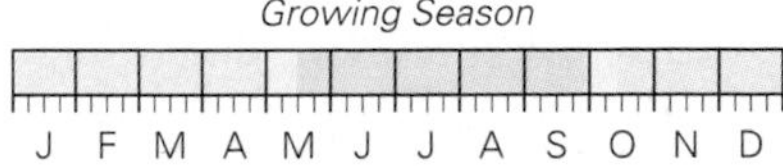

ZONE 1A Coldest Mountain and Intermountain Areas of the Contiguous States and Southwestern British Columbia

Marked by a short growing season and relatively mild summer temperatures, Zone 1a includes the coldest regions west of the Rockies, excluding Alaska, and a few patches of cold country east of the Great Divide. The mild days and chilly nights during the growing season extend the bloom of summer perennials like columbines and Shasta daisies. If your garden gets reliable snow cover (which insulates plants), you'll be able to grow perennials listed for some of the milder zones. In years when snow comes late or leaves early, protect plants with a 5- or 6-inch layer of organic mulch. Along with hardy evergreen conifers, tough deciduous trees and shrubs form the garden's backbone. Gardeners can plant warm-season vegetables as long as they are short-season varieties.

Winter lows average in the 0 to 11°F (−18 to −12°C) range; extremes range from −25 to −40°F (−32 to −40°C). The growing season is 50 to 100 days.

Growing Season

J F M A M J J A S O N D

Aspen trees *(Populus tremuloides)* with their silvery trunks cluster behind Rocky Mountain maples *(Acer glabrum)* in eastern Idaho. In autumn, the colored foliage of these trees glitters against the dark green Rocky Mountain junipers *(Juniperus scopulorum)*.

ZONE 1B Coldest Eastern Rockies and Plains Climate of Wyoming, Montana, and Southwestern Alberta

Wyoming's open plains provide plenty of good grazing for cattle, but their persistent winds and sub-zero winters test garden plants to the limit. The mountains to the west block most of the ocean influence that would otherwise temper continental weather, keeping winters cold and summers long and warm.

Centered over the plains of Wyoming and Montana, this zone sees January temperatures from 0 to 12°F (−18 to −11°C), with extremes between −30 and −50°F (−34 to −46°C). Zone 1b lies east of the Great Divide, where the continental climate reigns supreme. Arctic cold fronts sweep through 6 to 12 times a year, sometimes dropping temperatures by 30 or 40°F in 24 hours. The summer growing season tends to be warm and generous at 110 to 140 days long; but constant winds—12 miles per hour average, year-round in many places—call for windbreaks and shade trees, like hackberries and cottonwoods, whose leaves are animated by the wind. Few shrubs are better loved here than lilacs or better adapted than smoke tree. With protection, annual vegetables and flowers thrive, as do wind-tolerant perennials such as buckwheats, grasses, and penstemons. Where hail is a problem, gardeners favor small-leafed plants; where winters are dry and snow cover light, they compensate with mulch and extra water.

Growing Season

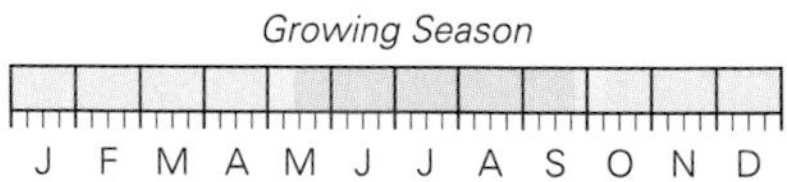

Eastern Washington, Eastern Oregon, Idaho

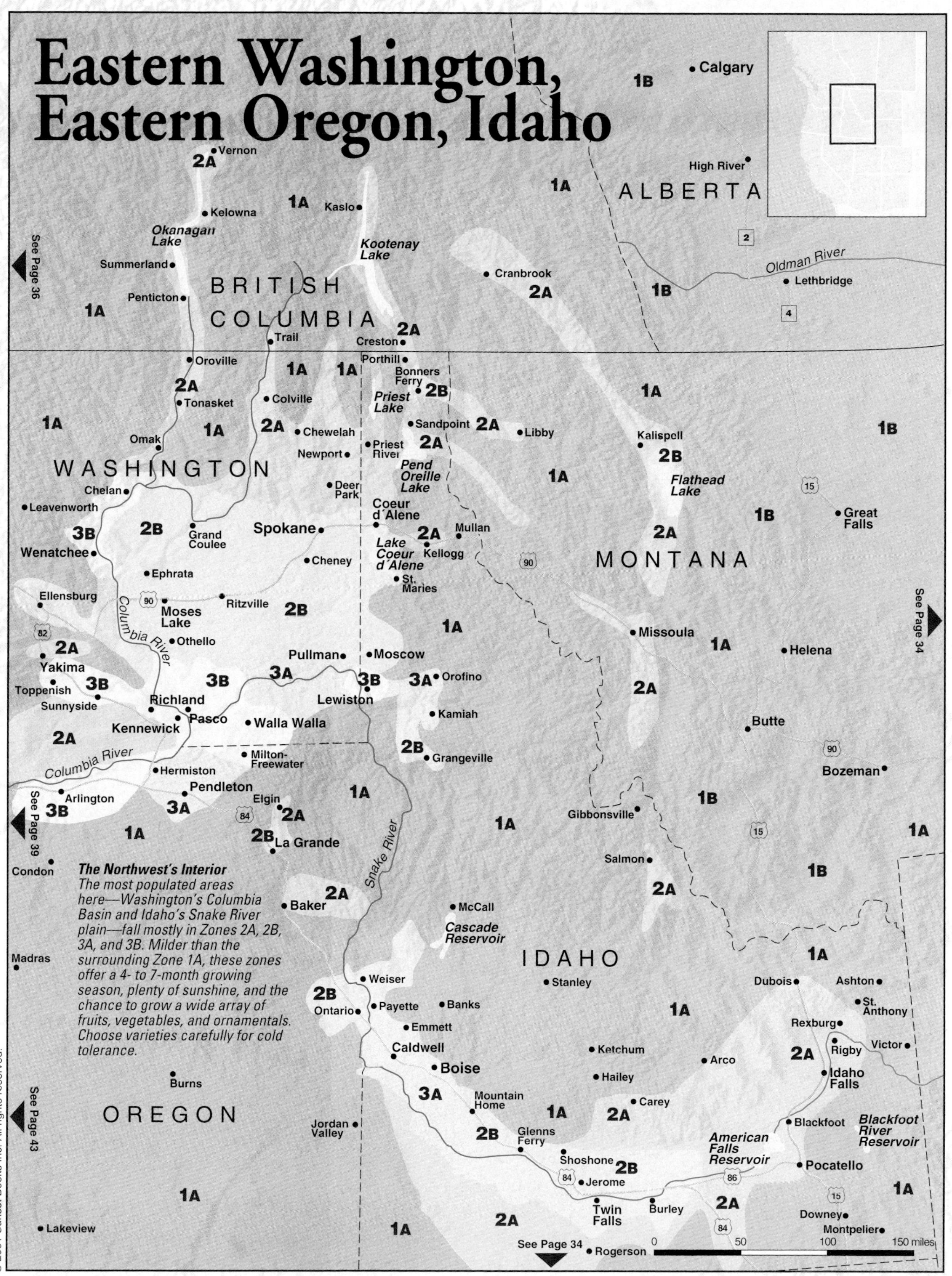

The Northwest's Interior

The most populated areas here—Washington's Columbia Basin and Idaho's Snake River plain—fall mostly in Zones 2A, 2B, 3A, and 3B. Milder than the surrounding Zone 1A, these zones offer a 4- to 7-month growing season, plenty of sunshine, and the chance to grow a wide array of fruits, vegetables, and ornamentals. Choose varieties carefully for cold tolerance.

Climate Zones 1A 1B 2A 2B 3A 3B

Nevada, Montana, Wyoming, Utah, Colorado

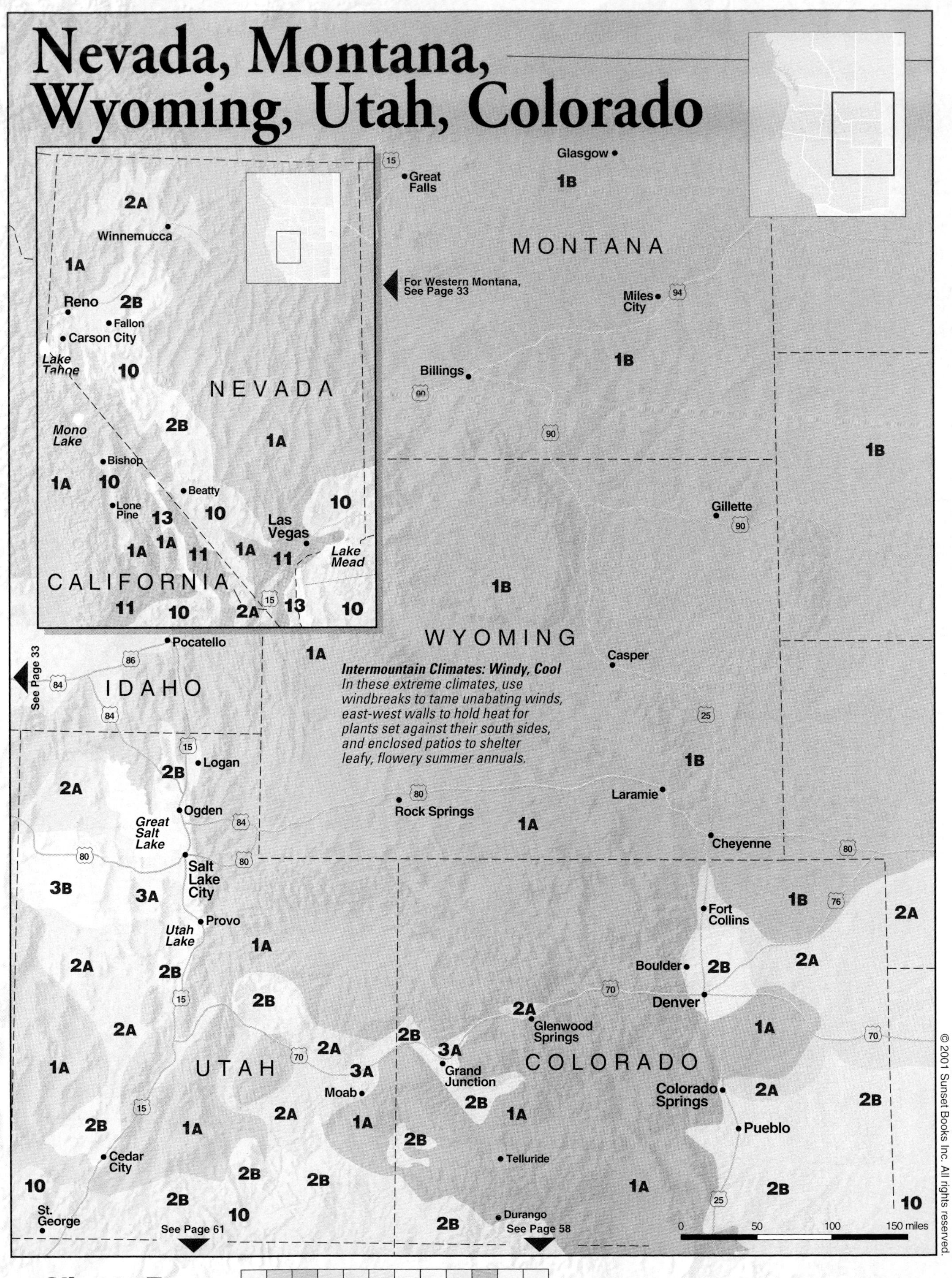

Climate Zones 1A 1B 2A 2B 3A 3B 10 11 13

ZONE 2A Cold Mountain and Intermountain Areas

Another snowy winter climate, Zone 2a covers several regions that are considered mild compared with the climates around them. You'll find this zone stretched over Colorado's northeastern plains, a bit of it along the Western Slope and Front Range of the Rockies, as well as mild parts of river drainages like those of the Snake, Okanogan, and the Columbia. It also shows up in western Montana and Nevada and in mountain areas of the Southwest. This is the coldest zone in which sweet cherries and many apples grow.

Winter temperatures here usually hover between 10 and 20°F (–12 to –7°C) at night, with drops between –20 and –30°F (–29 and –34°C) every few years. When temperatures drop below that, orchardists can lose even their trees. The growing season is 100 to 150 days.

Growing Season

J F M A M J J A S O N D

This zone, which almost invariably looks up at higher, colder Zone 1a, often inhabits river valleys like the one shown above (foreground), where aspens cluster among evergreens. Summers here are usually mild and beautiful, a perfect climate for growing long-blooming summer flowers.

ZONE 2B Warmer-Summer Intermountain Climate

This is a zone that offers a good balance of long, warm summers and chilly winters, making it an excellent climate zone for commercial fruit growing. That's why you'll find orchards in this zone in almost every state in the West. You'll also find this warm-summer, snowy-winter climate along Colorado's Western Slope and mild parts of the Front Range; in Nevada from Reno to Fallon, then north to Lovelock; in large areas of northern Arizona and New Mexico; and in mild parts of the Columbia and Snake River basins.

Winter temperatures are milder than in neighboring Zone 2a, minimums averaging from 12 to 22°F (–11 to –6°C), with extremes in the –10 to –20°F (–23 to –29°C) range.

The growing season here in Zone 2b runs from 115 days in higher elevations and more northerly areas to more than 160 days in southeastern Colorado.

Growing Season

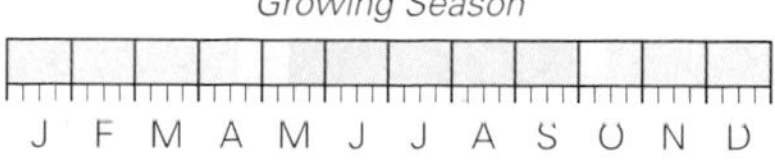

The rolling hills and amber waves of grain shown at left are familiar sights in the Palouse region of southeastern Washington and western Idaho. This rich agricultural land produces abundant crops of wheat (new wheat is emerald green; ripe wheat is golden), barley, lentils, and peas. In the photo above, corn grows tall and lush during summer's long, warm days.

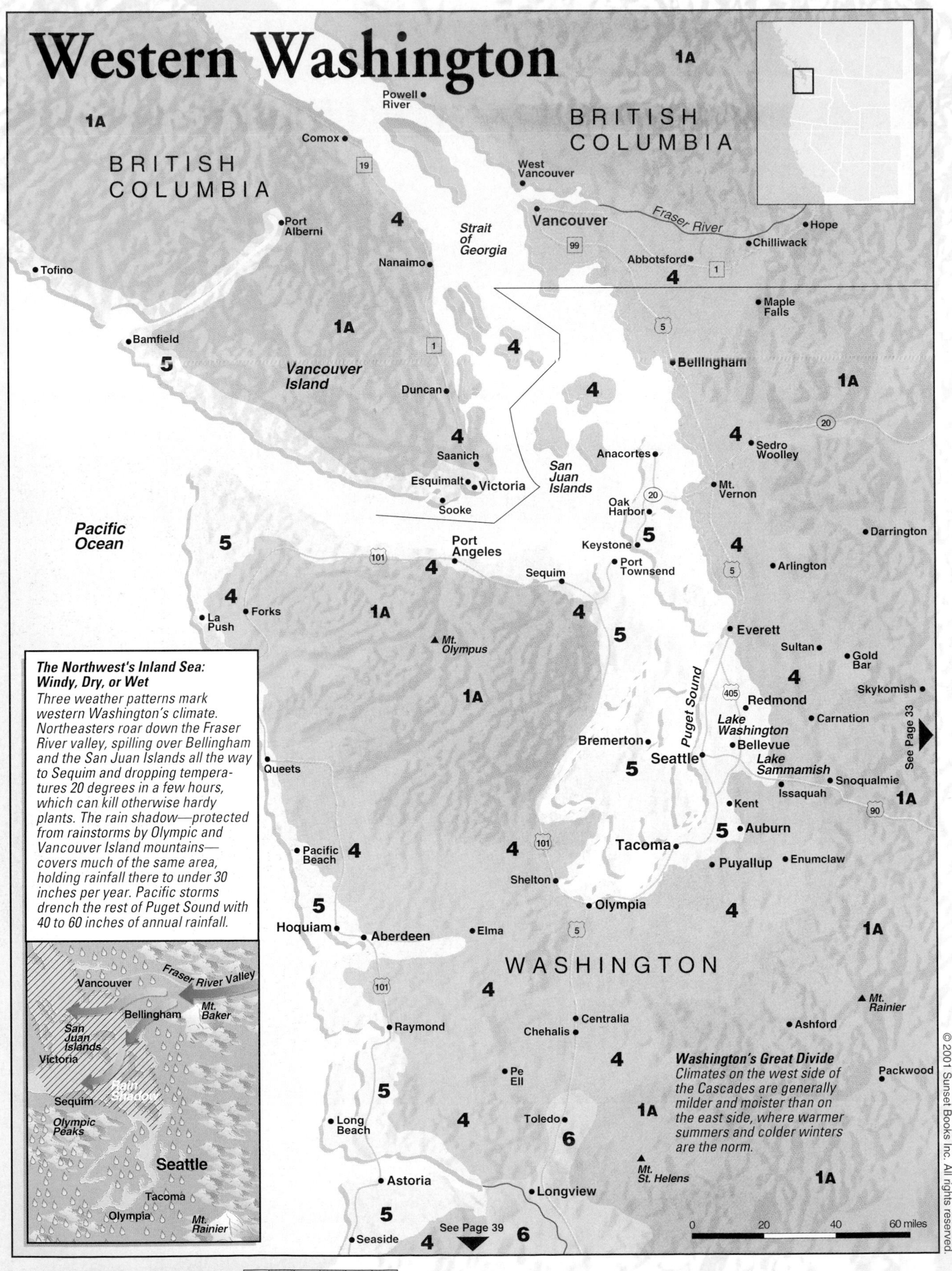

Climate Zones | 1A | 4 | 5 | 6 |

ZONE 3A Mild Areas of Mountain and Intermountain Climates

East of the Sierra and Cascade ranges, you can hardly find a better gardening climate than Zone 3a. Winter minimum temperatures average from 15 to 25°F (−9 to −4°C), with extremes between −8 and −18°F (−22 and −28°C). Its frost-free growing season runs from 150 to 186 days. The zone tends to occur at lower elevations in the northern states (eastern Oregon and Washington as well as Idaho), but at higher elevations as you move south crossing Utah's Great Salt Lake and into northern New Mexico and Arizona. Fruits and vegetables that thrive in long, warm summers, such as melons, gourds, and corn, tend to do well here. This is another great zone for all kinds of deciduous fruit trees and ornamental trees and shrubs, as long as you keep them well watered during the summer.

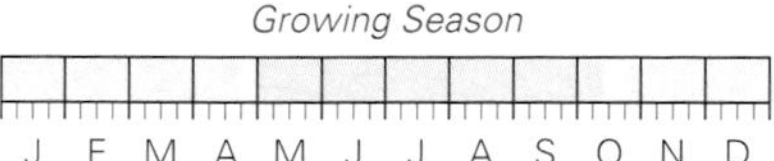

Daylilies, monardas, hollyhocks, and daisies (left) grow in this Santa Fe garden within view of New Mexico's Sangre de Cristo Mountains. Against a backdrop of deep green conifers and cinnamon-colored walls, the blooms are brilliant in the summer sun. Multicolored ears of corn (below) fill Southwest-style baskets.

3B Mildest Areas of Intermountain Climates

Zone 3b is much like Zone 3a, but with slightly milder winter averages of 19 to 29°F (−7 to −2°C) and extremes that usually bottom out between −2 and −15°F (−19 to −26°C). Summer temperatures are a bit higher than in Zone 3a—mostly in the high 80s and low- to mid-90s. Zone 3b offers one of the longest growing seasons of the intermountain climates. Gardeners here count on a growing season that averages 180 to 210 frost-free days with plenty of heat. However, it's one of the smallest zones. Most of it lies in the warmest parts of eastern Washington's Columbia Basin, with bits in Lewiston, Idaho, and parts of southern Utah, New Mexico, and Arizona. This is fabulous country for annual vegetables and flowers and a long list of perennials, trees, shrubs, and vines.

The Columbia Gorge nails down one end of mild Zone 3b, where summers become warmer, longer, and drier as you move east. Most of Zone 3b receives irrigation water from the river. That and a long growing season make this zone capital gardening country. Some of the Northwest's best watermelons come from Zone 3b.

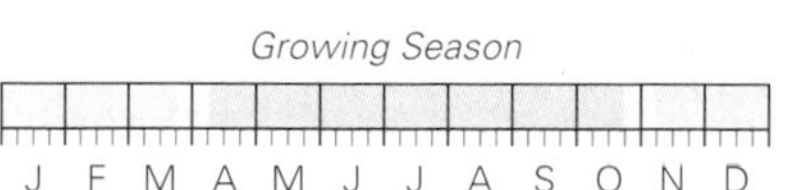

ZONE 4 Cold-Winter Areas of the North Coast and Mild-Winter Areas of Alaska and British Columbia

Multicolored ribbons of tulips in shades of cream and rose to red and pink fill this field at DeGoede Bulb Farm in Mossyrock, Washington. The many flower colors are a bright contrast with brooding spring skies.

One of the West's most narrow, linear climates, Zone 4 runs from high in the coastal mountains of Northern California to southeastern Alaska, losing elevation as it moves north. It gets considerable influence from the Pacific Ocean, but also from the continental air mass, higher elevation, or both. As it extends north, the zone first touches salt water in northern Puget Sound and is almost entirely surrounded by salt water in southeastern Alaska.

In the contiguous states, Zone 4 has more cold than neighboring Zone 5, more snow, and a shorter growing season. Compared to neighboring zones in Alaska and Canada, however, it has less winter cold and a longer growing season. No zone grows better perennials and bulbs; people who like woodland plants and rock plants love Zone 4. But beware: though you can grow winter vegetables in the southern part of Zone 4, it doesn't get enough winter sunlight in Alaska to sustain them.

Average winter lows in Zone 4 range from 34°F (1°C) down to 28°F (−2°C), with extreme lows averaging 8 to 0°F (−13 to −18°C). The growing season is 150 to 200 days long, but because Zone 4 summers are temperate (highs average from the low 60s to the 70s), plants take more time to develop. If you're sowing vegetables, for example, add at least 50 percent to the days-to-harvest figure listed on the seed package.

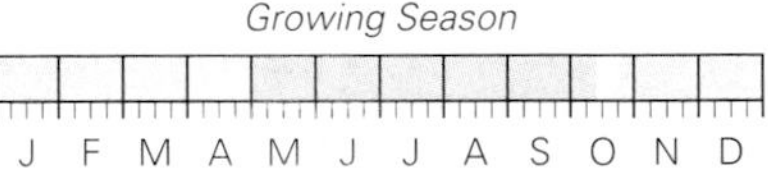

ZONE 5 Marine Influence Along the Northwest Coast, Puget Sound, and South Vancouver Island

Mild ocean air moderates winters in this area. The region produces some of the finest rhododendrons, Japanese maples, and rock garden plants anywhere.

Average January minimum temperatures here range from 37 to 33°F (3 to 1°C), with annual lows in the 20s, extremes from 17 to 10°F (−8 to −12°C). But some areas, such as parts of south Vancouver Island, almost never get a freeze. In the rest of Zone 5, big freezes do considerable damage when they come very early or very late, when plants are not conditioned for that kind of cold. And while these occasional disasters clear the slate of most borderline plants, they should not serve as a general gauge of plant hardiness here.

Many waterside areas show low heat accumulation in the summer, with July days rarely moving above the low 70s. To grow heat-loving plants, pick out the hottest spots in the garden for them—a south wall or a west wall does a good job of reflecting heat—and select peach and tomato varieties with low heat needs. The mildness in these areas favors leaf vegetables, which are slow to bolt, and flowering ornamental plants like fuchsias and calendulas. The growing season usually runs between 200 and 250 days.

The lowlands around Puget Sound and along the coast were once covered with forest, so native woodland plants like trilliums, piggy-back plant, and a host of ferns thrive here, as do forest-edge trees like vine maples and dogwoods.

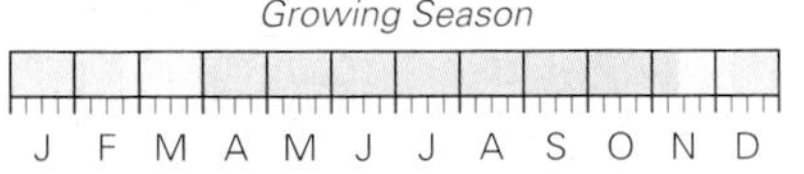

These astilbes and dogwoods thrive in a woodland garden near Lake Washington. The climate in Zone 5 is much like that of southern England, and the gardens here have benefited from England's long and successful search for more varied garden plants.

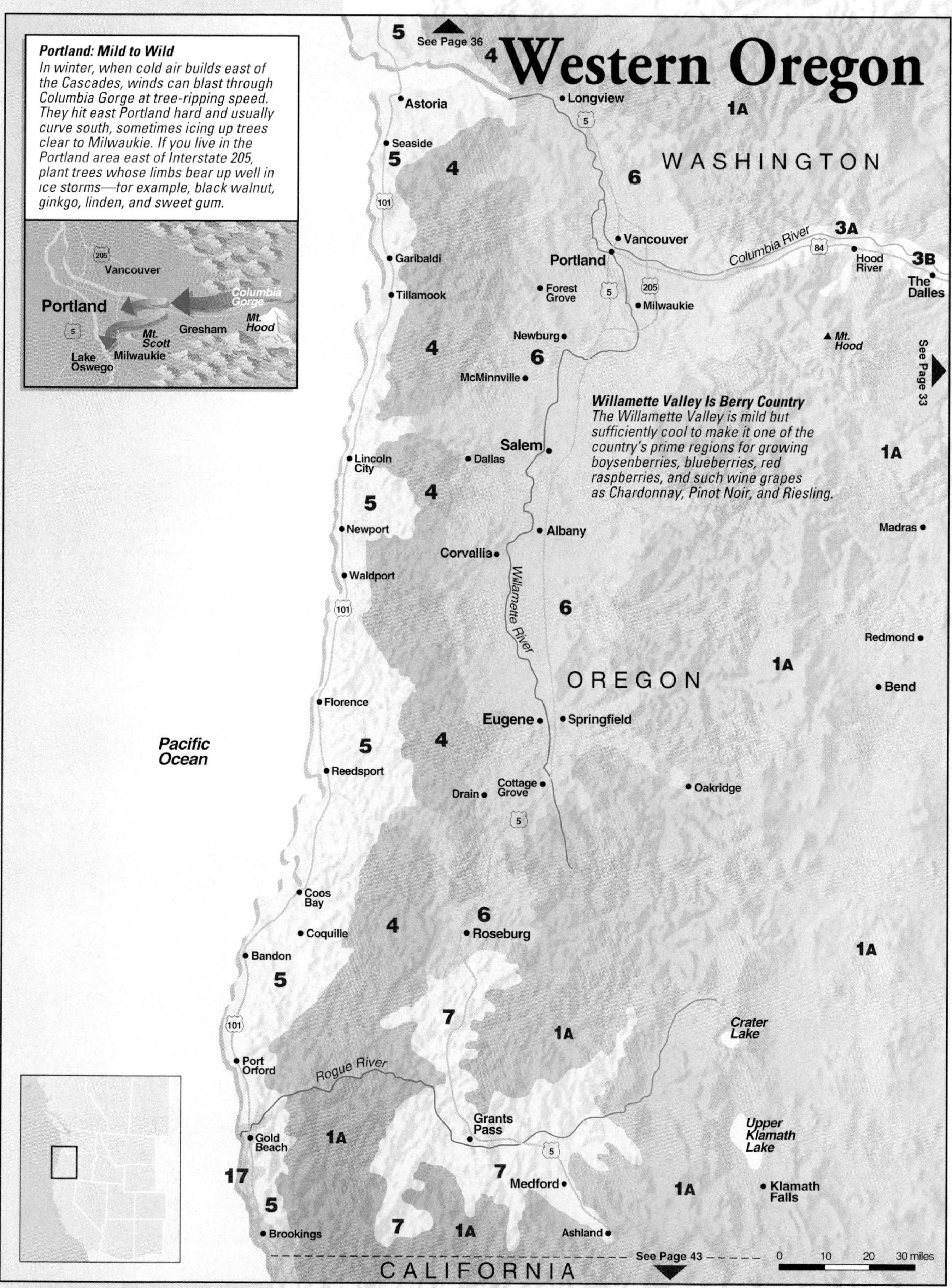

Western Oregon
Portland: Mild to Wild
In winter, when cold air builds east of the Cascades, winds can blast through Columbia Gorge at tree-ripping speed. They hit east Portland hard and usually curve south, sometimes icing up trees clear to Milwaukie. If you live in the Portland area east of Interstate 205, plant trees whose limbs bear up well in ice storms—for example, black walnut, ginkgo, linden, and sweet gum.
Vancouver
Portland
Columbia Gorge
Mt. Hood
Gresham
Mt. Scott
Lake Oswego
Milwaukie
See Page 36
Astoria
Longview
WASHINGTON
Seaside
Vancouver
Portland
Columbia River
Hood River
The Dalles
Garibaldi
Tillamook
Forest Grove
Milwaukie
Newburg
Mt. Hood
McMinnville
See Page 33
Willamette Valley Is Berry Country
The Willamette Valley is mild but sufficiently cool to make it one of the country's prime regions for growing boysenberries, blueberries, red raspberries, and such wine grapes as Chardonnay, Pinot Noir, and Riesling.
Salem
Lincoln City
Dallas
Newport
Albany
Madras
Corvallis
Waldport
Willamette River
Redmond
OREGON
Bend
Florence
Eugene
Springfield
Pacific Ocean
Reedsport
Cottage Grove
Drain
Oakridge
Coos Bay
Coquille
Roseburg
Bandon
Crater Lake
Port Orford
Rogue River
Grants Pass
Upper Klamath Lake
Gold Beach
Medford
Klamath Falls
Brookings
Ashland
See Page 43
CALIFORNIA
0 10 20 30 miles
Climate Zones 1A 3A 3B 4 5 6 7 17

ZONE 6 The Willamette and Columbia River Valleys

Warmer summers and cooler winters distinguish Zone 6 from coastal Zone 5. Tucked between the Coast Range and the Cascades, Zone 6 includes the Willamette Valley in Oregon, the Columbia River valley between Vancouver and Longview, and north of Longview 20 miles or so.

The Coast Range reduces the amount of marine weather (wind and rainfall) that reaches this area, but Zone 6 is still a maritime climate that offers a long growing season (nearly 280 days in the Portland/Vancouver area). However, Zone 6 also has the continental influence that makes its presence known in occasional ice storms created from freezing winter air that roars through the Columbia Gorge and over the eastern half of Portland.

Summer temperatures average 10 to 15°F (−12 to −9°C) higher than those along the coast—enough added heat to put sugar in 'Elberta' peaches—while winters are chilly enough to trigger good fruit set. The long, mild growing season makes the Willamette Valley one of the West's best-known growing areas for berries, hazelnuts, and nursery stock. Roses, Japanese maples, flowering fruit trees, and broadleafed evergreens like rhododendrons and pieris attain near perfection here.

Because the Willamette Valley contains many hills and small mountain ranges, it also has many microclimates. South- and west-facing slopes are warmer (most of the area's Pinot Noir grapes grow on these slopes), north- and east-facing slopes are cooler, and all the valley's slopes have better air drainage and less frost than the valley floor. If you choose plants based on these influences, you'll have far more success than if you ignore them.

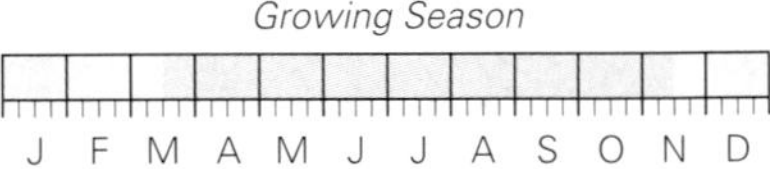

Sunrise illuminates the rows of grapevines (top left) at Dundee Hills Vineyard on the slopes of the Willamette Valley in Oregon. From mid-May through June, spectacular fields of bearded iris bloom (bottom left) in shades of gold and cream to bronze at Schreiner's Iris Gardens in the Willamette Valley. Mount Hood looms in the distance.

Pinot Noir grapes ripen on the vines at King Estate Winery in Lorane, Oregon.

ZONE 7 California's Gray Pine Belt and Oregon's Rogue River Valley

Gray pines (far left), also called foothill or digger pines, mark much of Zone 7. Often you'll find them mixed with oaks, ponderosa pines, and even knobcone pines. Valley oaks (left) dot grassy, rolling foothills in many parts of Zone 7.

Zone 7 encompasses several thousand square miles in the regions west of the Sierra Nevada and Cascade ranges. Because of the influence of latitude, this climate is found at low elevations in a valley in Oregon (the Rogue Valley) but at middle elevations in California (the low mountains, most of which can be identified by native gray pines).

Hot summers and mild but pronounced winters give Zone 7 sharply defined seasons without severe winter cold or enervating humidity. The climate pleases plants that require a marked seasonal pattern to do well—peony, iris, lilac, and flowering cherry, for example. Deciduous fruit trees that benefit from chilly winters and warm summers do well also; the region is noted for its pears, apples, peaches, and cherries.

Gardeners in a few spots around the San Francisco Bay will be surprised to find their gardens mapped in Zone 7, even though there isn't a gray pine to be seen. These are hilltop and ridge-top areas that are too high (and hence too cold in winter) to be included in milder Zones 15 and 16.

For such a large area, it is impossible to state exact low temperatures, but at weather-recording stations in Zone 7, the typical winter lows range from 23 to 9°F (−5 to −13°C), and the record lows vary from 15 to −1°F (−9 to −18°C).

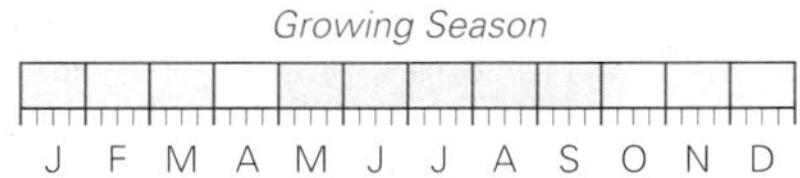

ZONE 8 Cold-Air Basins of California's Central Valley

Only a shade of difference exists between Zone 8 and Zone 9, but it's an important difference—crucial in some cases. Zone 9 is a thermal belt, meaning that cold air can flow from it to lower ground—and that lower ground is found here in Zone 8. Citrus furnish the most meaningful illustration. Lemons, oranges, and grapefruit, which flourish in Zone 9, cannot be grown commercially in Zone 8 because the winter nights are frequently cold enough to injure the fruit or the trees; the trees would need regular heating to deliver decent crops. The same winter cold can damage many garden plants.

Zone 8 differs from Zone 14, which it joins near the latitudes of north Sacramento and Modesto, in that Zone 14 occasionally gets some marine influence. Low temperatures in Zone 8 over a 20-year period ranged from 29 to 13°F (−2 to −11°C). Certain features that Zones 8 and 9 share are described under Zone 9.

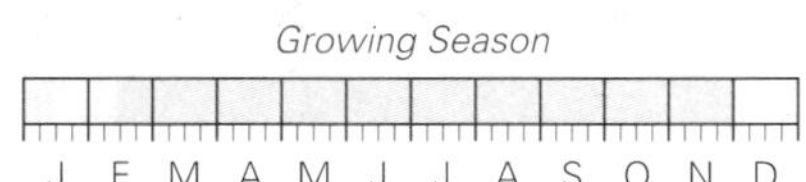

On winter nights, cold air rolls off Zone 9 hillsides and pools in Zone 8's colder flatlands (right). Fruit trees that need chill, like these apple trees near Winters, grow best in the valleys of Zone 8.

ZONE 9 Thermal Belts of California's Central Valley

For Zones 10 to 13, an area that includes the Southwest deserts, turn to pages 58–61.

Zone 9 hills rise into the clear air above the fog-shrouded flatlands of Zone 8. In winter, dense tule fogs can blanket Zone 8 and rise into Zone 9 by afternoon, closing roads throughout the Central Valley. The picture above was taken near Bakersfield.

As cited in the description of Zone 8, the biggest readily apparent difference between Zones 8 and 9 is that Zone 9, a thermal belt, is a safer climate for citrus than Zone 8, which contains cold-air basins. The same distinction, thermal belt versus cold-air basin, determines which species and varieties — hibiscus, melaleuca, pittosporum, and other plants — are recommended for Zone 9 but not for Zone 8.

Zones 8 and 9 have the following features in common: summer daytime temperatures are high, sunshine is almost constant during the growing season, and growing seasons are long. Deciduous fruits and vegetables of nearly every kind thrive in these long, hot summers; winter cold is just adequate to satisfy the dormancy requirements of the fruit trees. Fiercely cold, piercing north winds blow for several days at a time in winter, but they are more distressing to gardeners than to garden plants. You can minimize them with windbreaks.

Tule fogs (dense fogs that rise from the ground on cold, clear nights) appear and stay for hours or days during winter. The fogs usually hug the ground at night and rise to 800 to 1,000 feet by afternoon.

Heat-loving plants such as oleander and crape myrtle perform at their peak in Zones 8 and 9 (and 14). Plants that like summer coolness and humidity demand some fussing; careful gardeners accommodate them by providing filtered shade from tall trees and plenty of moisture. In Zone 9, winter lows over a 20-year period ranged from 28 to 18°F (−2 to −8°C).

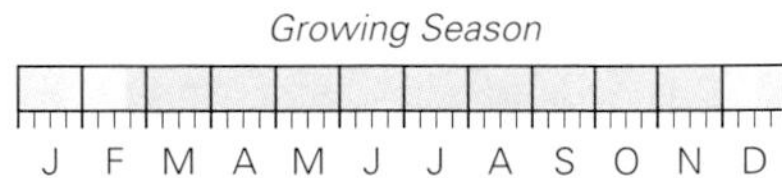

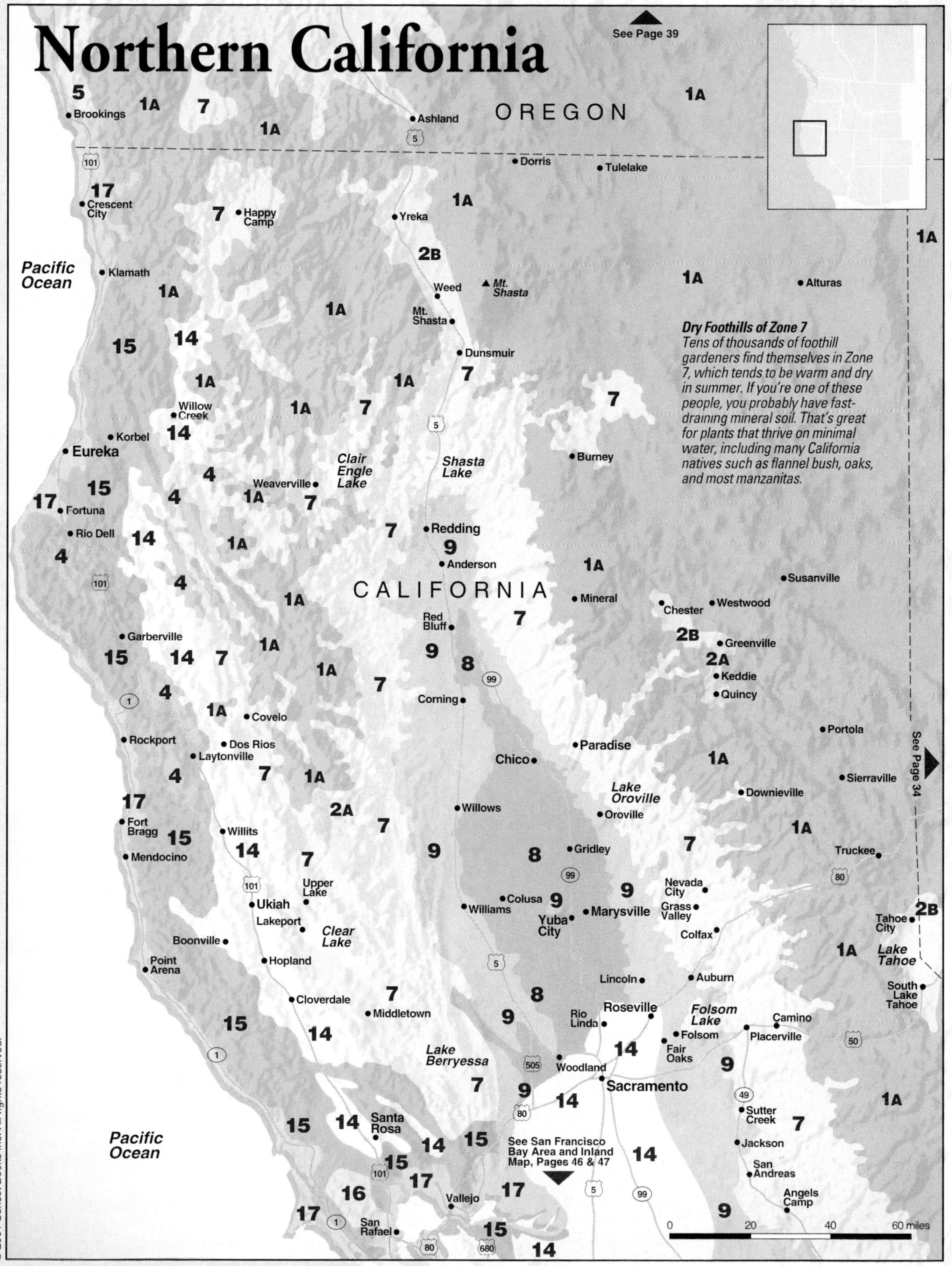

Climate Zones | 1A | 2A | 2B | 4 | 5 | 7 | 8 | 9 | 14 | 15 | 16 | 17 |

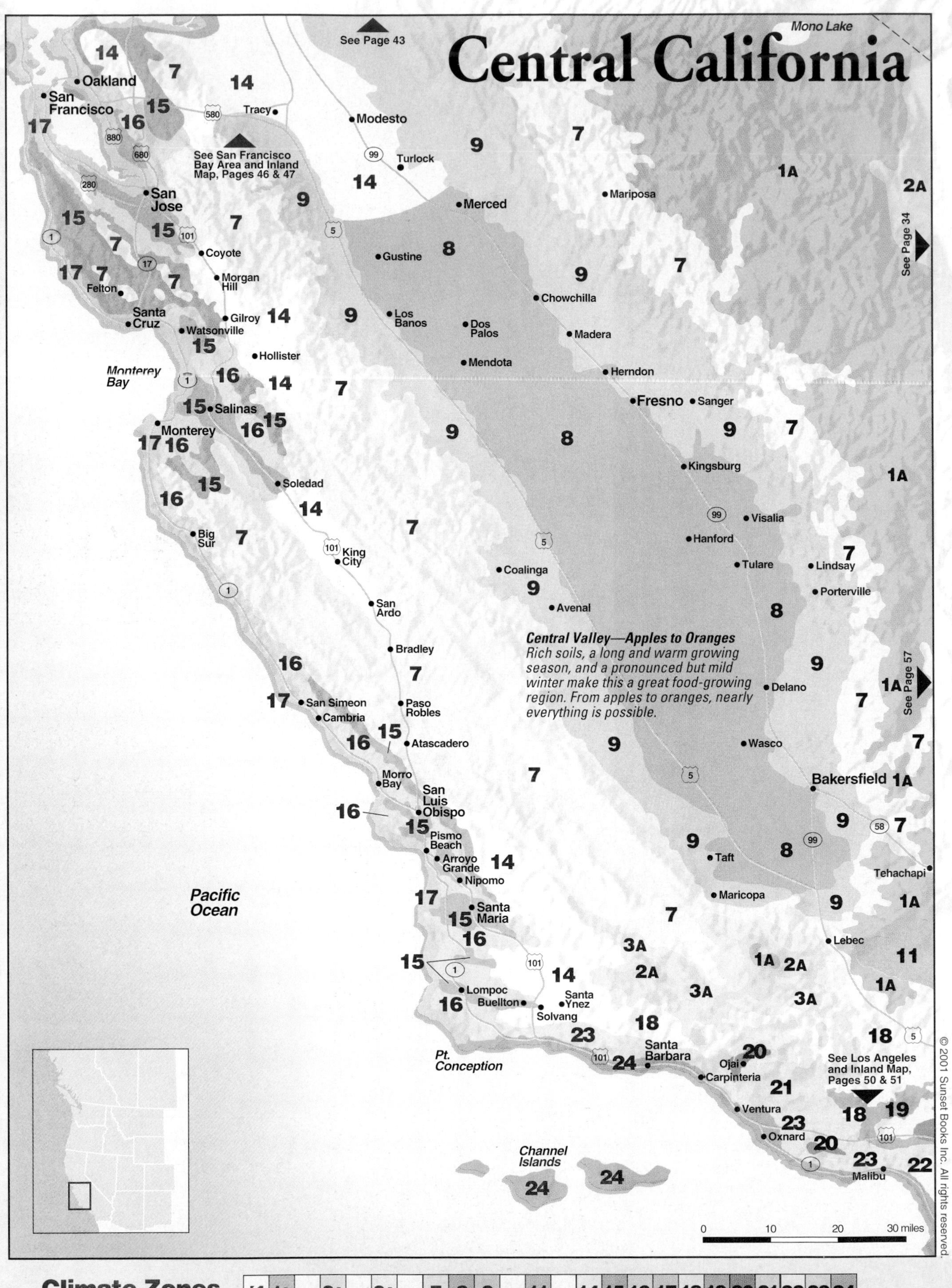
Central California
Mono Lake
See Page 43
See Page 34
See Page 57
See San Francisco Bay Area and Inland Map, Pages 46 & 47
See Los Angeles and Inland Map, Pages 50 & 51
Oakland
San Francisco
Tracy
Modesto
Turlock
Merced
Mariposa
San Jose
Coyote
Morgan Hill
Felton
Santa Cruz
Gilroy
Watsonville
Hollister
Gustine
Los Banos
Dos Palos
Chowchilla
Madera
Mendota
Herndon
Fresno
Sanger
Monterey Bay
Salinas
Monterey
Soledad
Kingsburg
Visalia
Hanford
Tulare
Lindsay
Porterville
Big Sur
King City
Coalinga
Avenal
San Ardo
Bradley
Central Valley—Apples to Oranges
Rich soils, a long and warm growing season, and a pronounced but mild winter make this a great food-growing region. From apples to oranges, nearly everything is possible.
Delano
San Simeon
Cambria
Paso Robles
Atascadero
Wasco
Bakersfield
Morro Bay
San Luis Obispo
Pismo Beach
Arroyo Grande
Nipomo
Taft
Tehachapi
Pacific Ocean
Santa Maria
Maricopa
Lebec
Lompoc
Buellton
Solvang
Santa Ynez
Pt. Conception
Santa Barbara
Ojai
Carpinteria
Ventura
Oxnard
Malibu
Channel Islands
0 10 20 30 miles
© 2001 Sunset Books Inc. All rights reserved.
Climate Zones
1A 2A 3A 7 8 9 11 14 15 16 17 18 19 20 21 22 23 24

14 Northern California's Inland Areas with Some Ocean Influence

Marine air moderates parts of Zone 14 that otherwise would be colder in winter and hotter in summer. The opening in Northern California's Coast Ranges created by San Francisco and San Pablo bays allows marine air to spill much farther inland. The same thing happens, but the penetration is not as deep, in the Salinas Valley. Zone 14 includes the cold-winter valley floors, canyons, and land troughs in the Coast Ranges from Santa Barbara County to Humboldt County.

The milder-winter, marine-influenced areas in Zone 14 and the cold-winter inland valleys within Zone 14 differ in humidity. For example, lowland parts of Contra Costa County are more humid than Sacramento.

Fruits that need winter chill do well here, as do shrubs needing summer heat (oleander, gardenia). Over a 20-year period, this area had lows ranging from 26 to 16°F (−3 to −9°C). Weather records show all-time lows from 20 down to 11°F (−7 to −12°C).

Growing Season

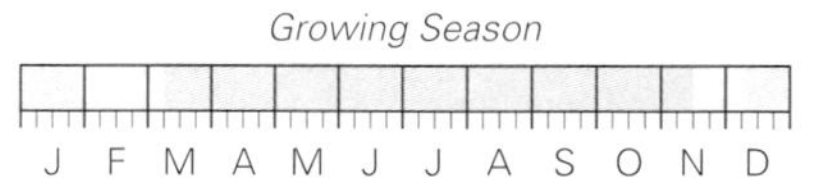

Vineyards blanket much of the land in Napa and Sonoma counties, producing hefty crops for wineries. The valley floors here are designated Zone 14, while surrounding hills are in Zones 15 and 16.

ZONE 15 Chilly Winters Along the Coast Range

Zones 15 and 16 are areas of Central and Northern California that are influenced by marine air approximately 85 percent of the time and by inland air 15 percent of the time. Also worthy of note is that although Zone 16 is within the Northern California coastal climate area, its winters are milder because the areas in this zone are in thermal belts (explained on page 28). The cold-winter areas that make up Zone 15 lie in cold-air basins, on hilltops above the thermal belts, or far enough north that plant performance dictates a Zone 15 designation.

Many plants that are recommended for Zone 15 are not suggested for Zone 14 mainly because they must have a moister atmosphere, cooler summers, milder winters, or all three conditions present at the same time. On the other hand, Zone 15 still receives enough winter chilling to favor some of the cold-winter specialties, such as herbaceous peonies, which are not recommended for Zones 16 and 17.

Most of this zone gets a nagging afternoon wind in summer. Trees and dense shrubs planted on the windward side of a garden can disperse it, and a neighborhood full of trees can successfully keep it above the rooftops. Lows over a 20-year period ranged from 28 to 21°F (−2 to −6°C), and record lows from 26 to 16°F (−3 to −9°C).

Growing Season

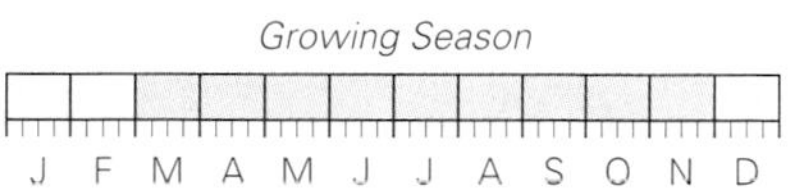

Zone 15 is moist enough for coast redwoods (above left) to thrive, yet it's warm and dry enough to grow agave and cacti (left). Both plantings were photographed at Sunset's Menlo Park headquarters; the redwoods, now towering more than 80 feet tall, were planted in 1952 from 7-gallon cans.

San Francisco Bay Area and Inland

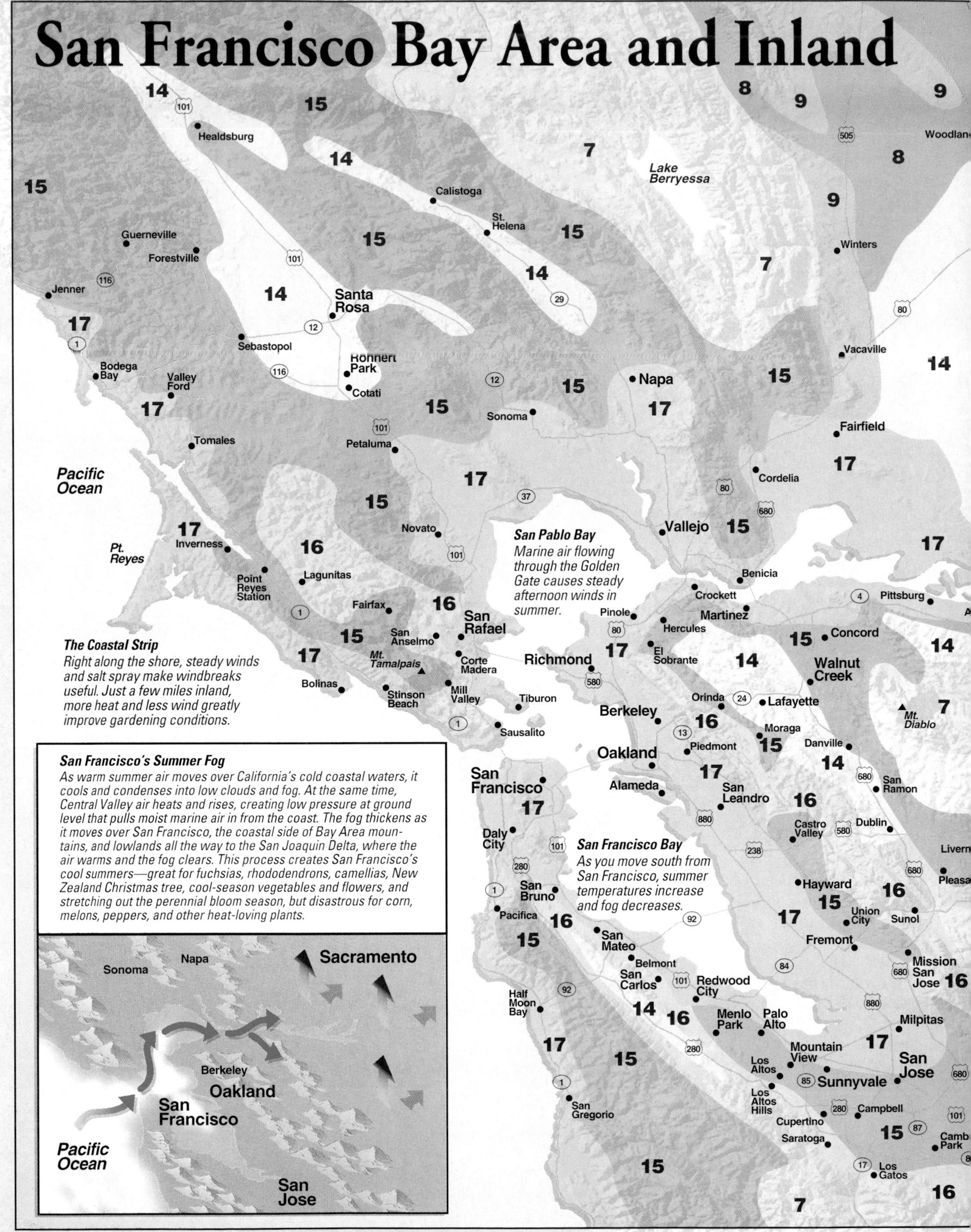

Climate Zones 7 8 9 14 15 16 17

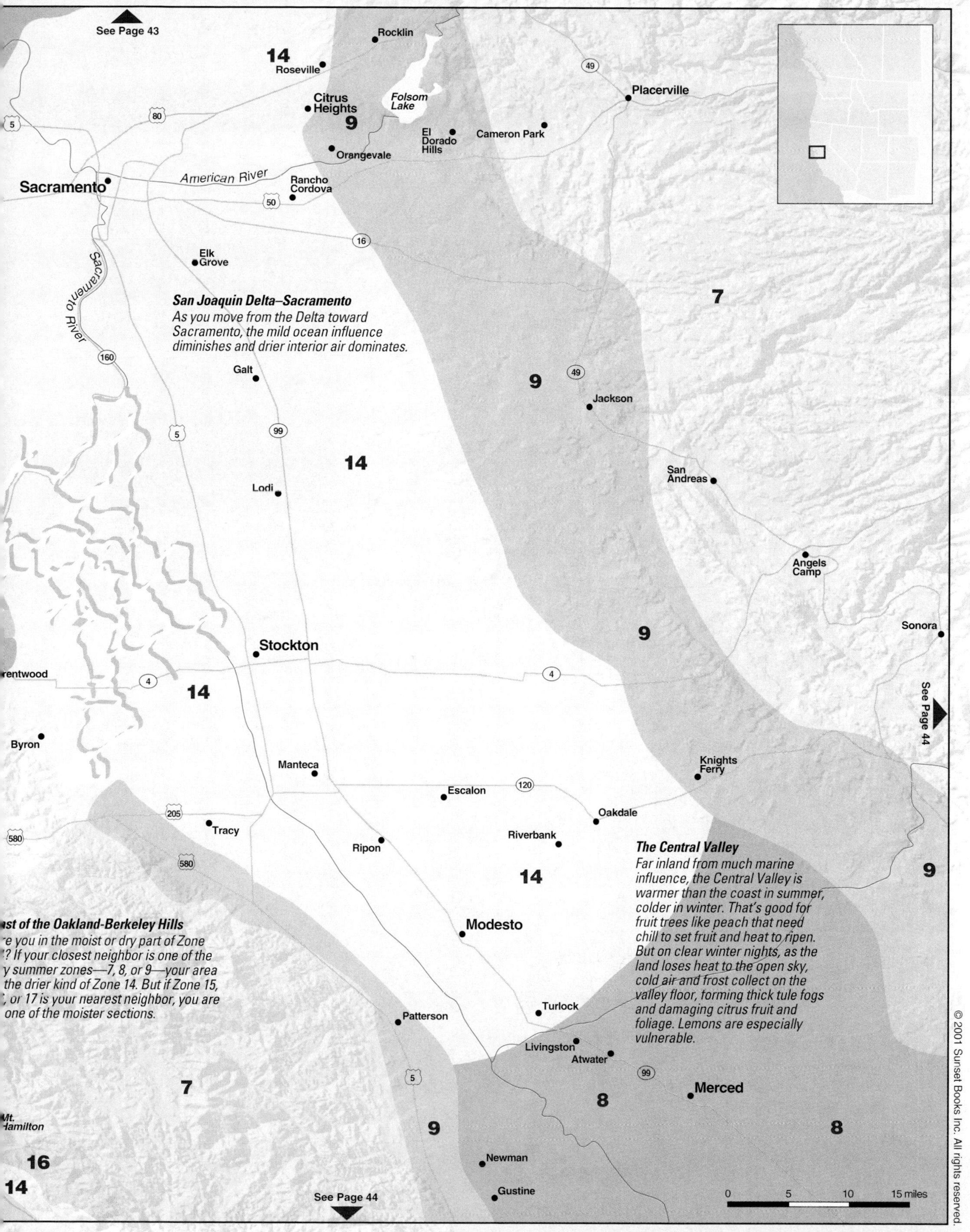

See Page 43
Rocklin
14
Roseville
49
Placerville
Citrus Heights
Folsom Lake
9
80
5
El Dorado Hills
Cameron Park
Orangevale
Sacramento
American River
Rancho Cordova
50
16
Elk Grove
Sacramento River
7
San Joaquin Delta–Sacramento
As you move from the Delta toward Sacramento, the mild ocean influence diminishes and drier interior air dominates.
160
Galt
9
49
Jackson
5
99
14
San Andreas
Lodi
Angels Camp
9
Sonora
Stockton
4
4
14
Byron
See Page 44
Knights Ferry
Manteca
Escalon
120
Oakdale
205
Tracy
580
Riverbank
Ripon
580
The Central Valley
Far inland from much marine influence, the Central Valley is warmer than the coast in summer, colder in winter. That's good for fruit trees like peach that need chill to set fruit and heat to ripen. But on clear winter nights, as the land loses heat to the open sky, cold air and frost collect on the valley floor, forming thick tule fogs and damaging citrus fruit and foliage. Lemons are especially vulnerable.
14
9
Modesto
Turlock
Patterson
Livingston
Atwater
99
5
7
Merced
8
9
8
Newman
16
14
See Page 44
Gustine
0 5 10 15 miles

ZONE 16 Central and Northern California Coast Thermal Belts

Parts of Zone 16, such as the Oakland-Berkeley hills (right), practically never see a white frost. This zone gets more heat in summer than Zone 17 and has warmer winters than Zone 15—great for subtropicals like ginger lily (above).

This benign climate exists in patches and strips along the Coast Ranges from western Santa Barbara County north to northern Marin County. It's one of Northern California's finest horticultural climates. It consists of thermal belts (slopes from which cold air drains) in the coastal climate area, which is dominated by ocean weather about 85 percent of the time and by inland weather about 15 percent.

Typical lows in Zone 16 over a 20-year period ranged from 32 to 19°F (0 to –7°C). The lowest recorded temperatures range from 25 to 18°F (–4 to –8°C). This zone gets more heat in summer than Zone 17, which is dominated by maritime air, and has warmer winters than Zone 15. That's a happy combination for gardening.

A summer afternoon wind is an integral part of this climate. Plant trees and shrubs on the windward side of your garden to help disperse it.

Growing Season

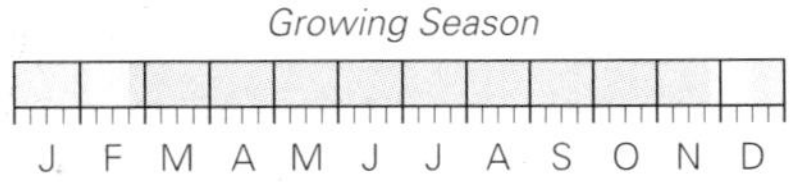

ZONE 17 Marine Effects in Southern Oregon, Northern and Central California

The climate in this zone features mild, wet, almost frostless winters and cool summers with frequent fog or wind. On most days and in most places, the fog tends to come in high and fast, creating a cooling and humidifying blanket between the sun and the earth, reducing the intensity of the light and sunshine. Some heat-loving plants (citrus, hibiscus, gardenia) don't get enough heat to fruit or flower reliably.

In a 20-year period, the lowest winter temperatures in Zone 17 ranged from 36 to 23°F (2 to –5°C). The lowest temperatures on record range from 30 to 20°F (–1 to –7°C). Of further interest in this heat-starved climate are the highs of summer, normally in the 60 to 75°F (16 to 24°C) range. The average highest temperature in Zone 17 is only 97°F (36°C). In all the other adjacent climate zones, average highest temperatures are in the 104 to 116°F (40 to 47°C) range.

Growing Season

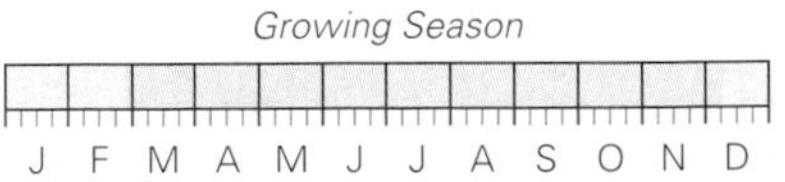

Zone 17's climate is dominated by the ocean about 98 percent of the time. You can see salt water from most areas in this zone, such as Pacific Grove (above), where mounding aloes and agaves with tall flower spikes bloom at the water's edge. This climate also favors fuchsias and commercially grown artichokes, Brussels sprouts, and Easter lilies.

18 Above and Below the Thermal Belts in Southern California's Interior Valleys

Zones 18 and 19 are classified as interior climates. This means that the major influence on climate is the continental air mass; the ocean determines the climate no more than 15 percent of the time.

Many of the valley floors of Zone 18 were once regions where apricot, peach, apple, and walnut orchards flourished, but the orchards have now given way to homes. Although the climate supplies enough winter chill for some plants that need it, it is not too cold for many of the hardier subtropicals like cymbidiums. It is too hot, too cold, and too dry for fuchsias but cold enough for tree peonies and many apple varieties, and mild enough for a number of avocado varieties. Zone 18 never supplied much commercial citrus, but home gardeners who can tolerate occasional minor fruit loss can grow citrus here.

Over a 20-year period, winter lows ranged from 28 to 10°F (−2 to −12°C). The all-time lows recorded by different weather stations in Zone 18 ranged from 22 to 7°F (−6 to −14°C).

Growing Season

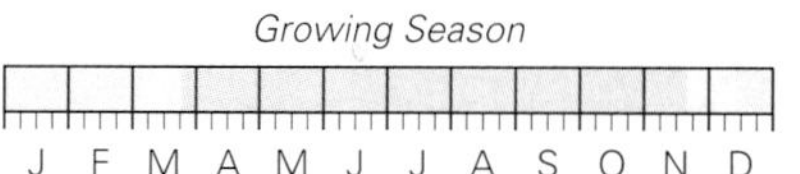

Zone 18 hilltops, like this one laced with houses, get more cold in winter and warmth in summer than the thermal belts (slopes and hillsides from which cold air drains) that make up Zone 19. Hilltops and cold-air basins get frost, while the thermal belts that connect them don't.

ZONE 19 Thermal Belts Around Southern California's Interior Valleys

Like that of neighboring Zone 18, the climate in Zone 19 is little influenced by the ocean. Both zones, then, have very poor climates for such plants as fuchsias, rhododendrons, and tuberous begonias. Many sections of Zone 19 have always been prime citrus-growing country—especially for those kinds that need extra summer heat in order to grow sweet fruit. Likewise, macadamia nuts and most avocados can be grown here.

The Western Plant Encyclopedia cites many ornamental plants that do well in Zone 19 but are not recommended for its neighbor because of the milder winters in Zone 19. Plants that grow well here, but not in much colder zones, include bougainvillea, bouvardia, calocephalus, Cape chestnut *(Calodendrum)*, flame pea *(Chorizema)*, several kinds of coral tree *(Erythrina)*, livistona palms, Mexican blue and San Jose hesper palms *(Brahea armata, B. brandegeei)*, giant Burmese honeysuckle *(Lonicera hildebrandiana)*, myoporum, several of the more tender pittosporums, and lady palm *(Rhapis excelsa)*.

Winter lows over a 20-year period ranged from 27 to 22°F (−3 to −6°C), and the all-time lows at different weather stations range from 23 to 17°F (−5 to −8°C). These are considerably higher than the temperatures in neighboring Zone 18.

Douglas iris, California poppies, and yellow meadowfoam splash the landscape with spring color at Rancho Santa Ana Botanic Garden in warm, dry Claremont, California. This garden also contains a wealth of evergreen natives, including ceanothus and manzanitas, that remain unscathed when winter temperatures drop into the 20s.

Growing Season

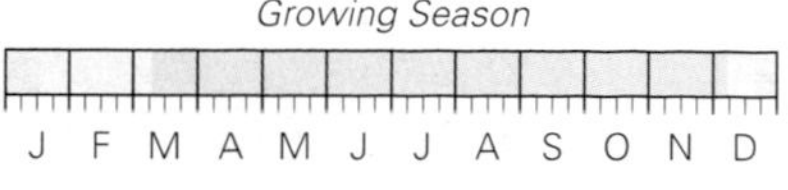

Los Angeles and Inland

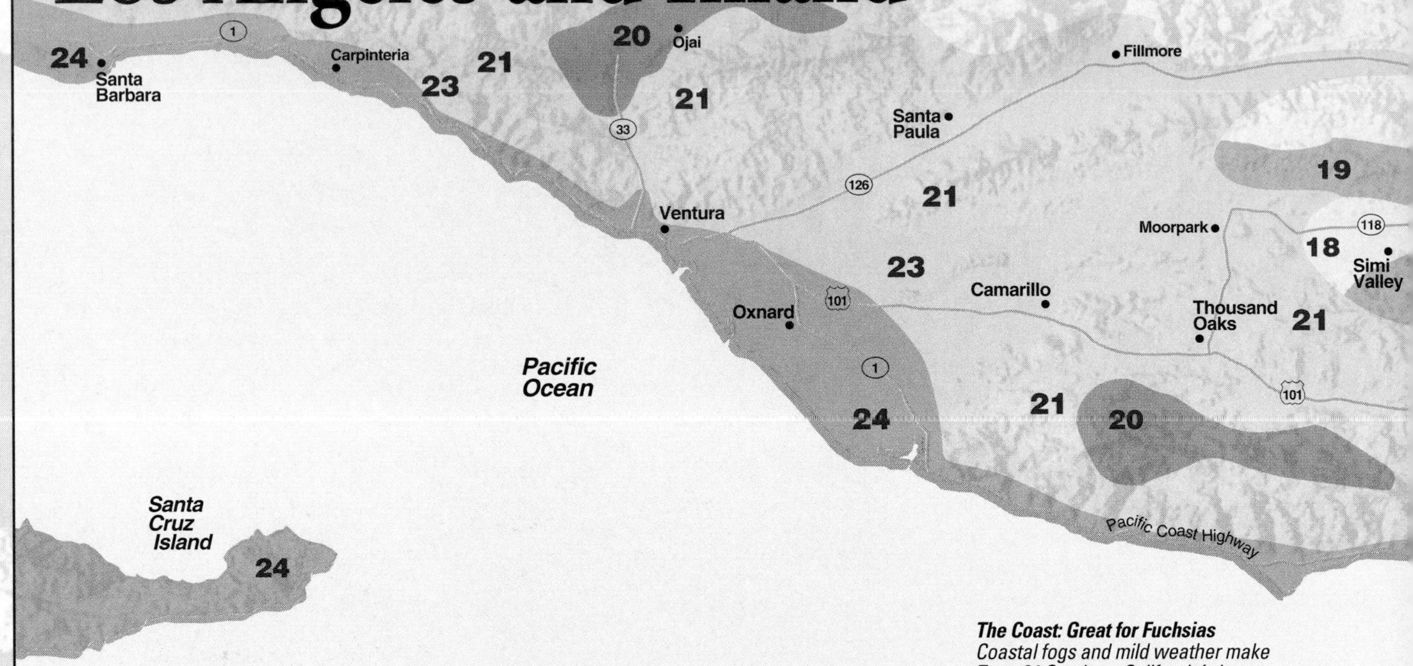

See Page 44
18
24
Santa Barbara
1
Carpinteria
23
21
20
Ojai
21
33
Fillmore
Santa Paula
19
126
21
Ventura
Moorpark
118
18
Simi Valley
23
Camarillo
101
Oxnard
Thousand Oaks
21
Pacific Ocean
1
101
24
21
20
Pacific Coast Highway
Santa Cruz Island
24

The Coast: Great for Fuchsias
Coastal fogs and mild weather make Zone 24 Southern California's best fuchsia and tuberous begonia climate. Scores of less well known plants from Chile, New Zealand, the Canary Islands, and the moister parts of South Africa do well here for the same reason.

The Santa Anas: Nature's Desiccants
Every fall and winter, the Santa Ana wind revs up as the interior's cold, heavy air flows downhill toward the Southern California coast. As this air loses elevation, it compresses, heats up, dries out, and roars ferociously through the passes behind Los Angeles and San Bernardino. Cajon Pass and Soledad Canyon are two main routes, although the wind is named for Santa Ana Canyon. When the Santa Ana winds hit the Los Angeles Basin, they're so hot and dry they can dehydrate plants to a crisp in a few hours. Sprinklers, windbreaks, and row covers help protect them. Santa Anas usually play out near the coast, though sometimes they blow all the way to Santa Catalina Island.

Soledad Canyon
Cajon Pass
San Bernardino
San Fernando Valley
Pasadena
Riverside
San Gorgonio Pass
Santa Ana Canyon
Los Angeles
Anaheim
Santa Ana
Long Beach
Temecula
Pacific Ocean
San Clemente
Santa Catalina Island

Climate Zones | 1 | 2A | | 3A | | 11 | | 18 | 19 | 20 | 21 | 22 | 23 | 24 |

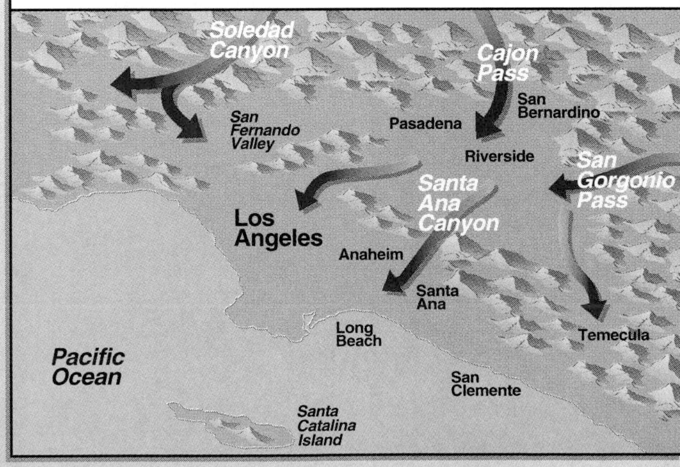

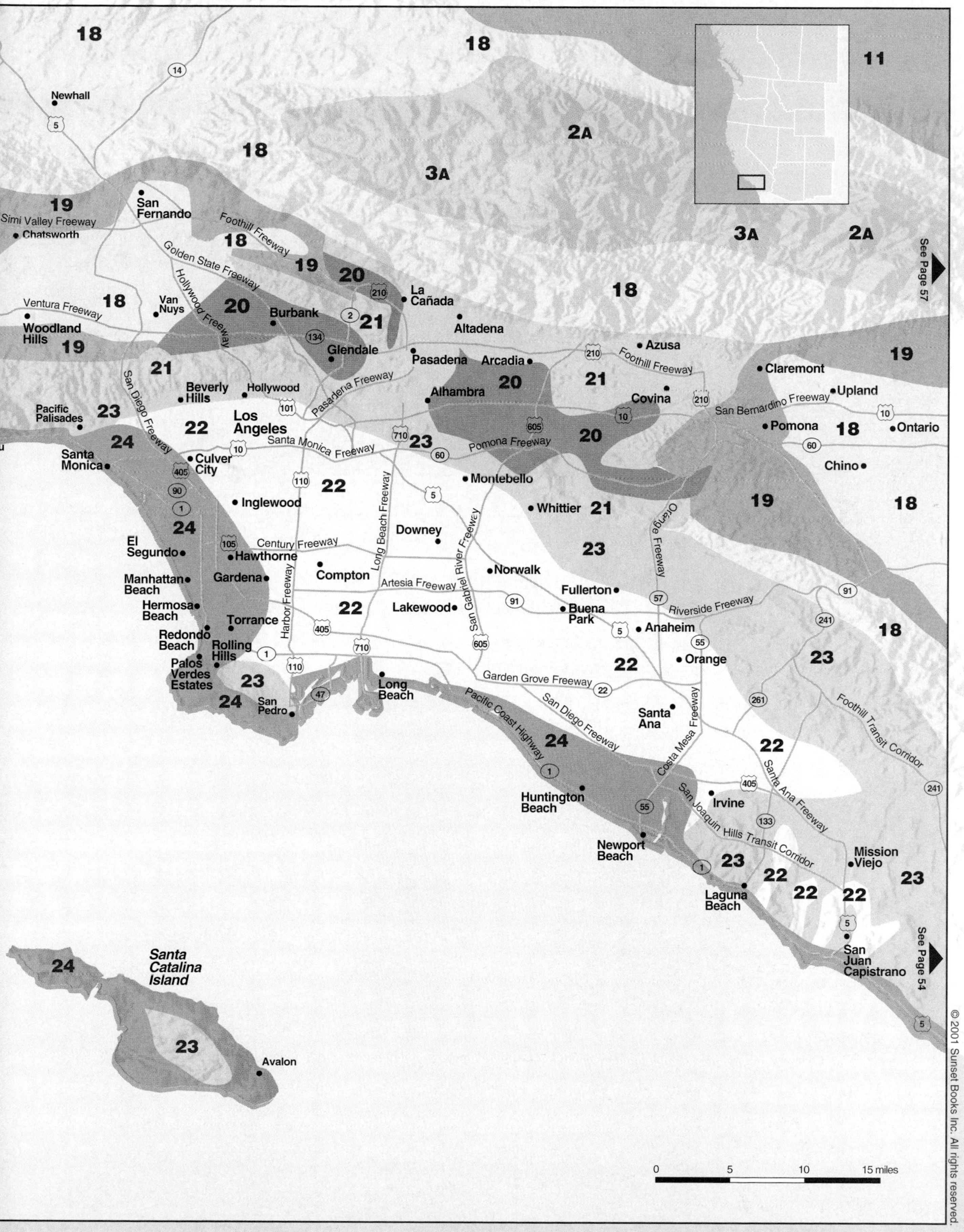

Newhall
San Fernando
Simi Valley Freeway
Chatsworth
Foothill Freeway
Golden State Freeway
Hollywood Freeway
Ventura Freeway
Van Nuys
Woodland Hills
Burbank
La Cañada
Altadena
Glendale
Pasadena
Arcadia
Azusa
Claremont
Upland
Pacific Palisades
Beverly Hills
Hollywood
Los Angeles
Alhambra
Covina
San Bernardino Freeway
Pomona
Ontario
Santa Monica
Culver City
Santa Monica Freeway
Pomona Freeway
Chino
Montebello
Inglewood
Whittier
El Segundo
Hawthorne
Century Freeway
Downey
Norwalk
Manhattan Beach
Gardena
Compton
Artesia Freeway
Fullerton
Hermosa Beach
Lakewood
Buena Park
Riverside Freeway
Redondo Beach
Torrance
Anaheim
Rolling Hills
Orange
Palos Verdes Estates
San Pedro
Long Beach
Garden Grove Freeway
San Diego Freeway
Santa Ana
Pacific Coast Highway
Costa Mesa Freeway
Foothill Transit Corridor
Huntington Beach
Irvine
Santa Ana Freeway
San Joaquin Hills Transit Corridor
Newport Beach
Mission Viejo
Laguna Beach
San Juan Capistrano
Santa Catalina Island
Avalon
See Page 57
See Page 54
0 5 10 15 miles

ZONE 20 Cool Winters in Southern California's Areas of Occasional Ocean Influence

In Zones 20 and 21, the same relative pattern prevails as in Zones 18 and 19. The even-numbered zone is the climate made up of cold-air basins and hilltops, and the odd-numbered one comprises thermal belts. The difference is that Zones 20 and 21 get weather influenced by both maritime air and interior air. In these transitional areas, climate boundaries often move 20 miles in 24 hours with the movements of these air masses.

Because of the greater ocean influence, this climate supports a wide variety of plants. You can see the range of them at the Los Angeles State and County Arboretum in Arcadia. Winter lows over a 20-year period ranged from 28 to 23°F (−2 to −5°C). Record lows at various weather stations range from 21 to 14°F (−6 to −10°C).

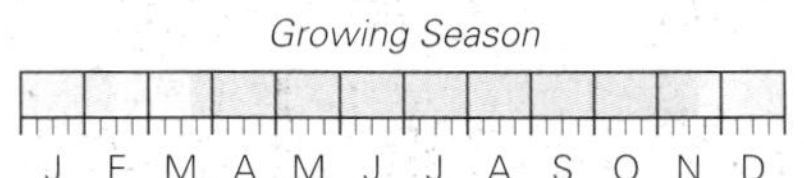

In Zone 20 (but bordering Zone 21), the Los Angeles Arboretum is influenced by both marine and interior air. The result: everything from birches to palms grows here, as do relatively tender tropical trees like the floss silk tree *(Chorisia speciosa),* jacaranda, Moreton Bay fig, and tabebuia.

ZONE 21 Thermal Belts in Southern California's Areas of Occasional Ocean Influence

Cold air drains from slopes above the Santa Clarita River near Moorpark, California, making them perfect for growing oranges (left). Thermal belts such as these make it possible to grow plants in Zone 21 that would be too tender for Zone 20. Zone 21 is just cold enough for some lilacs. Varieties bred to grow and bloom with less winter chill than most lilacs require grow at Descanso Gardens in La Cañada (below).

The combination of weather influences described for Zone 20 applies to Zone 21 as well. Your garden can be in ocean air or a high fog one day and in a mass of interior air (perhaps a drying Santa Ana wind from the desert) the next day.

Because temperatures never drop very far below 30°F (−1°C), this is fine citrus-growing country. At the same time, Zone 21 is also the mildest zone that gets sufficient winter chilling for most forms of lilacs and certain other chill-loving plants.

Over a 20-year period, winter lows at the weather-recording stations in Zone 21 ranged from 36 to 23°F (2 to −5°C), while record lows were 27 to 17°F (−3 to −8°C).

Growing Season

J F M A M J J A S O N D

ZONE 22 Cold-Winter Portions of Southern California's Coastal Climate

Areas falling in Zone 22 have a coastal climate (they are influenced by the ocean approximately 85 percent of the time). When temperatures drop in winter, these cold-air basins or hilltops above the air-drained slopes have lower winter temperatures than those in neighboring Zone 23.

Actually, the winters are so mild here that lows seldom fall below 28°F (–2°C). Annual winter lows recorded over 20 years ranged from 24 to 21°F (–4 to –6°C).

Gardeners who plant under overhangs or tree canopies can grow subtropical plants that would otherwise be burned by a rare frost. Such plants include bananas, tree ferns, and the like. The lack of a pronounced chilling period during the winter limits the use of such deciduous woody plants as flowering cherry and lilac. Many herbaceous perennials from colder regions fail here because the winters are too warm for them to go dormant.

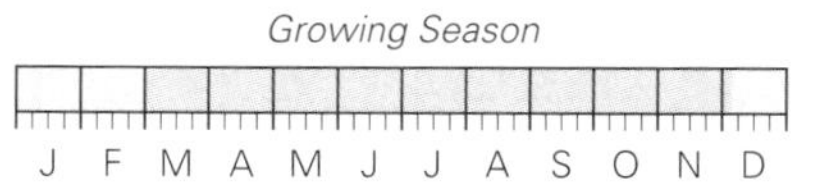

Coastal canyons—narrow, steep-sided valleys that jut inland from the coast—are numerous in Orange County. The canyon floors, where cold air settles in winter, are in Zone 22, while the higher ground on either side falls into warmer Zone 23. Plants that thrive on the slopes can freeze in the canyon below.

ZONE 23 Thermal Belts of Southern California's Coastal Climate

One of the most favored areas in North America for growing subtropical plants, Zone 23 has always been Southern California's best zone for avocados. Frosts don't amount to much here, because 85 percent of the time, Pacific Ocean weather dominates; interior air rules only 15 percent of the time. A notorious portion of this 15 percent consists of those days when hot, dry Santa Ana winds blow.

Zone 23 lacks either the summer heat or the winter cold necessary to grow pears, most apples, and most peaches. But it enjoys more heat than Zone 24. Gardenias and oleanders, for example, are recommended for Zone 23, but not for Zone 24.

Temperatures are mild here, but severe winters descend at times. Over a 20-year period, lows ranged from 38 to 23°F (3 to –5°C). In recorded history, lows range from 28 to 23°F (–2 to –5°C).

Growing Season

J F M A M J J A S O N D

Proteas are grown commercially in Zone 23, both as nursery stock and for their huge, long-lasting flowers, like the pincushions below. Cacti and fountain grass get plenty of sun in this garden in the Hollywood Hills (far left), and more warmth than they would in Zone 24.

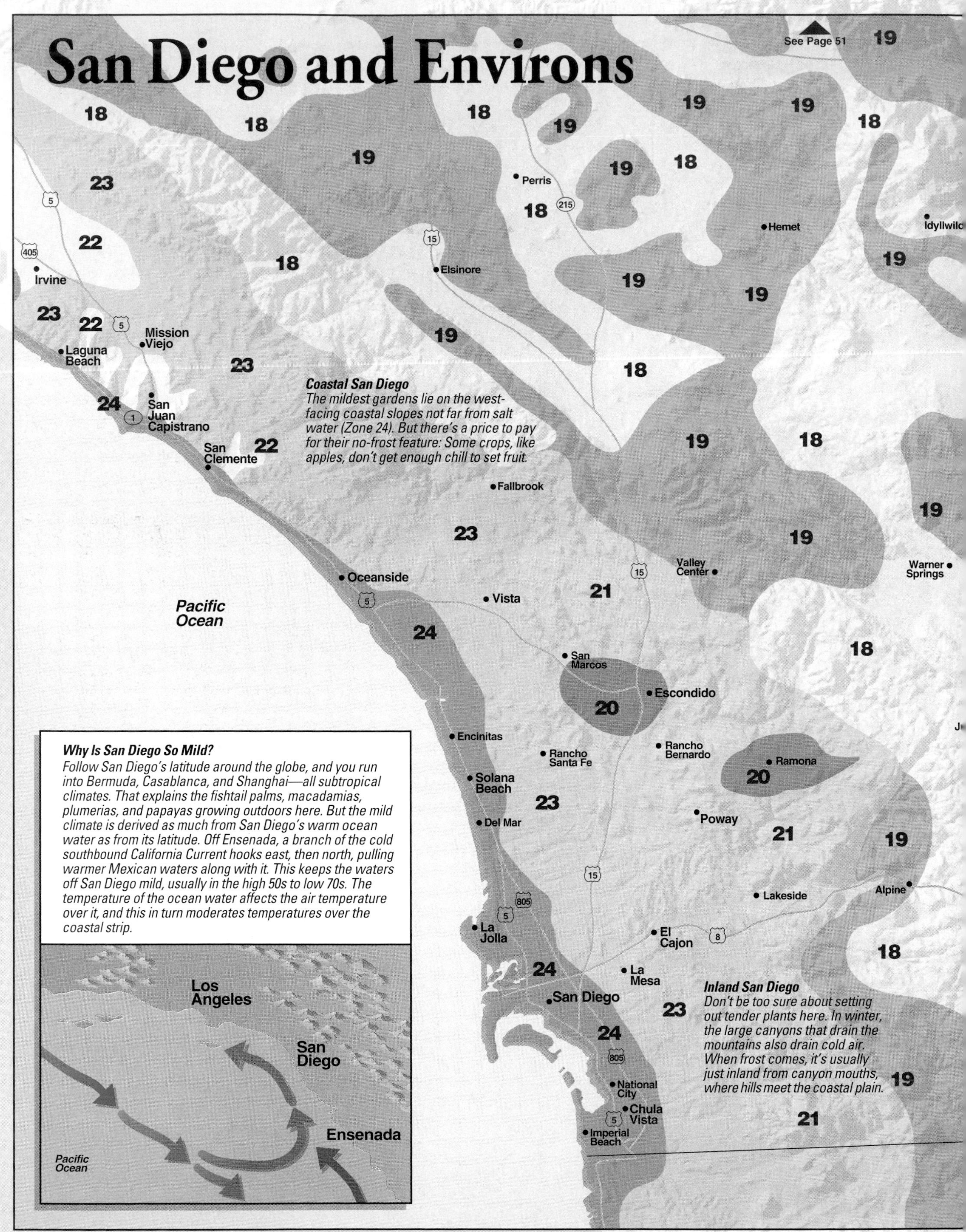

Climate Zones | 2B | | 11 | | 13 | | 18 | 19 | 20 | 21 | 22 | 23 | 24

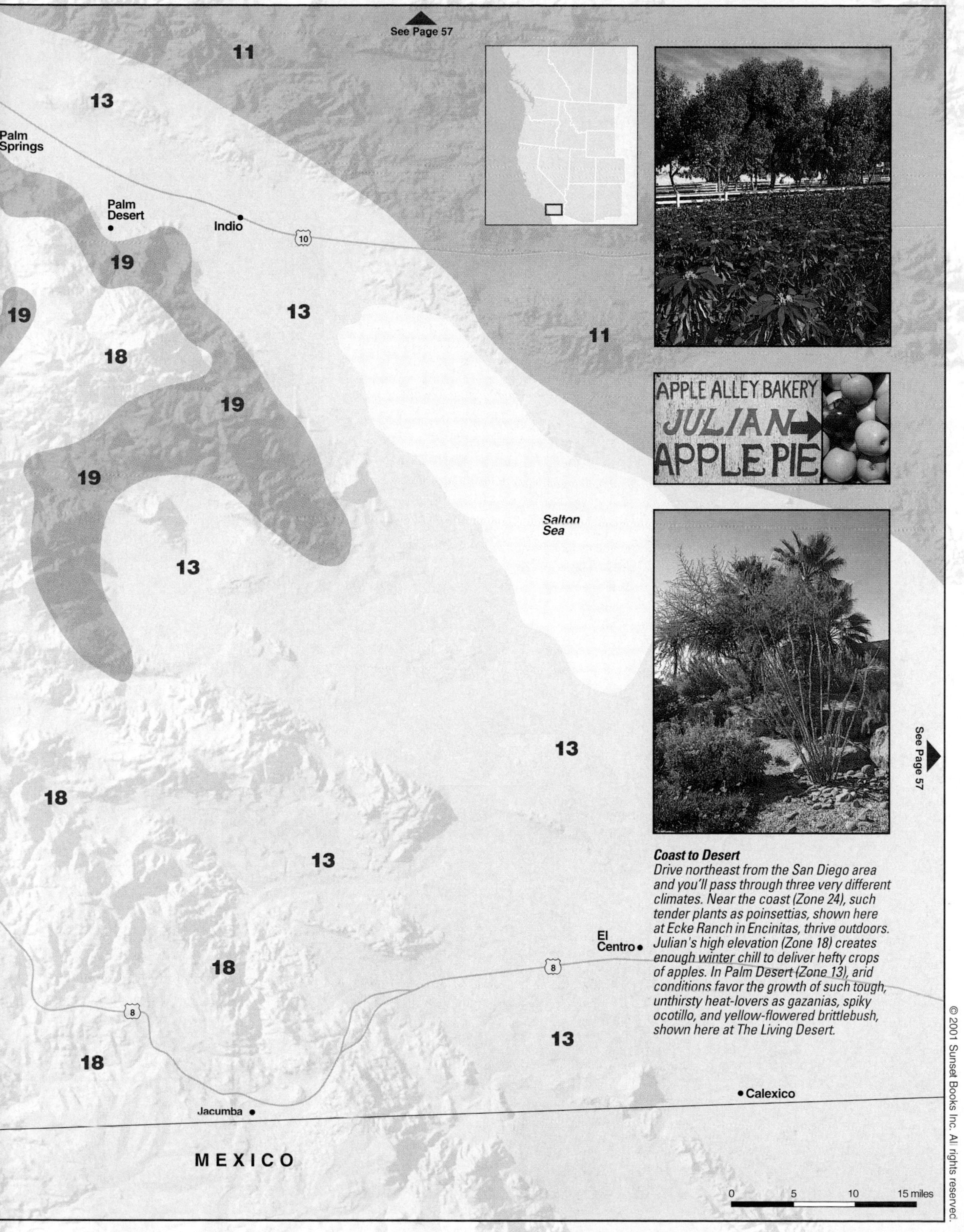

Coast to Desert
Drive northeast from the San Diego area and you'll pass through three very different climates. Near the coast (Zone 24), such tender plants as poinsettias, shown here at Ecke Ranch in Encinitas, thrive outdoors. Julian's high elevation (Zone 18) creates enough winter chill to deliver hefty crops of apples. In Palm Desert (Zone 13), arid conditions favor the growth of such tough, unthirsty heat-lovers as gazanias, spiky ocotillo, and yellow-flowered brittlebush, shown here at The Living Desert.

ZONE 24 Marine Influence Along the Southern California Coast

Stretched along Southern California's beaches, this climate zone is almost completely dominated by the ocean. Where the beach runs along high cliffs or palisades, Zone 24 extends only to that barrier. But where hills are low or nonexistent, it runs inland several miles.

This zone has a mild marine climate (milder than Northern California's maritime Zone 17), because south of Point Conception, the Pacific is comparatively warm. The winters are mild, the summers cool, and the air seldom really dry. On many days, the sun doesn't break through the high overcast until afternoon. Very tender plants like fuchsias find a good home here; they get along fine with only moderate summer heat. In this climate, gardens that include such plants as figs, rubber trees, and scheffleras can become jungles.

Zone 24 is coldest at the mouths of canyons that channel cold air down from the mountains on clear winter nights. Several such canyons between Laguna Beach and San Clemente are visible on the map. Numerous smaller ones touch the coast between San Clemente and the Mexican border. Partly because of the unusually low temperatures created by this canyon action, there is a broad range of winter lows in Zone 24. In a 20-year period, lows ranged from 44 to 24°F (7 to −4°C). The all-time lows range from 33 to 20°F (1 to −7°C). Some weather stations in Zone 24 have never recorded a freezing temperature.

The all-time high temperatures aren't greatly significant in terms of plant growth. The average all-time high of weather stations in Zone 24 is 105°F (41°C). Compare this with highest temperatures of Northern California's marine climate, Zone 17, which average 97°F (36°C), and Southern California's inland climates—Zone 22 at 111°F (44°C), Zone 20 at 114°F (46°C), and Zone 18 at 115°F (46°C).

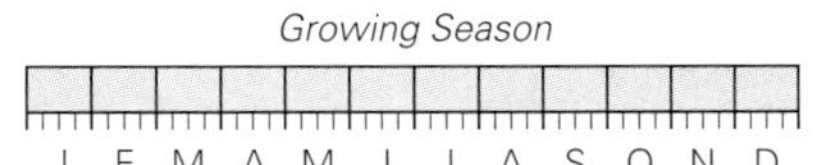

At its best in frost-free Zone 24, bougainvillea can grow rampant where conditions are good (above). This one competes for light, heat, and space with an ornamental asparagus. Both can thrive here on rainfall alone.

In summer, high fog is one of this zone's regular features, rolling in off the ocean in the morning and burning off during the day (below). It stretches the season for wildflowers, like these California poppies dotting a meadow at Santa Barbara Botanic Garden.

Southwest Deserts: Southern California

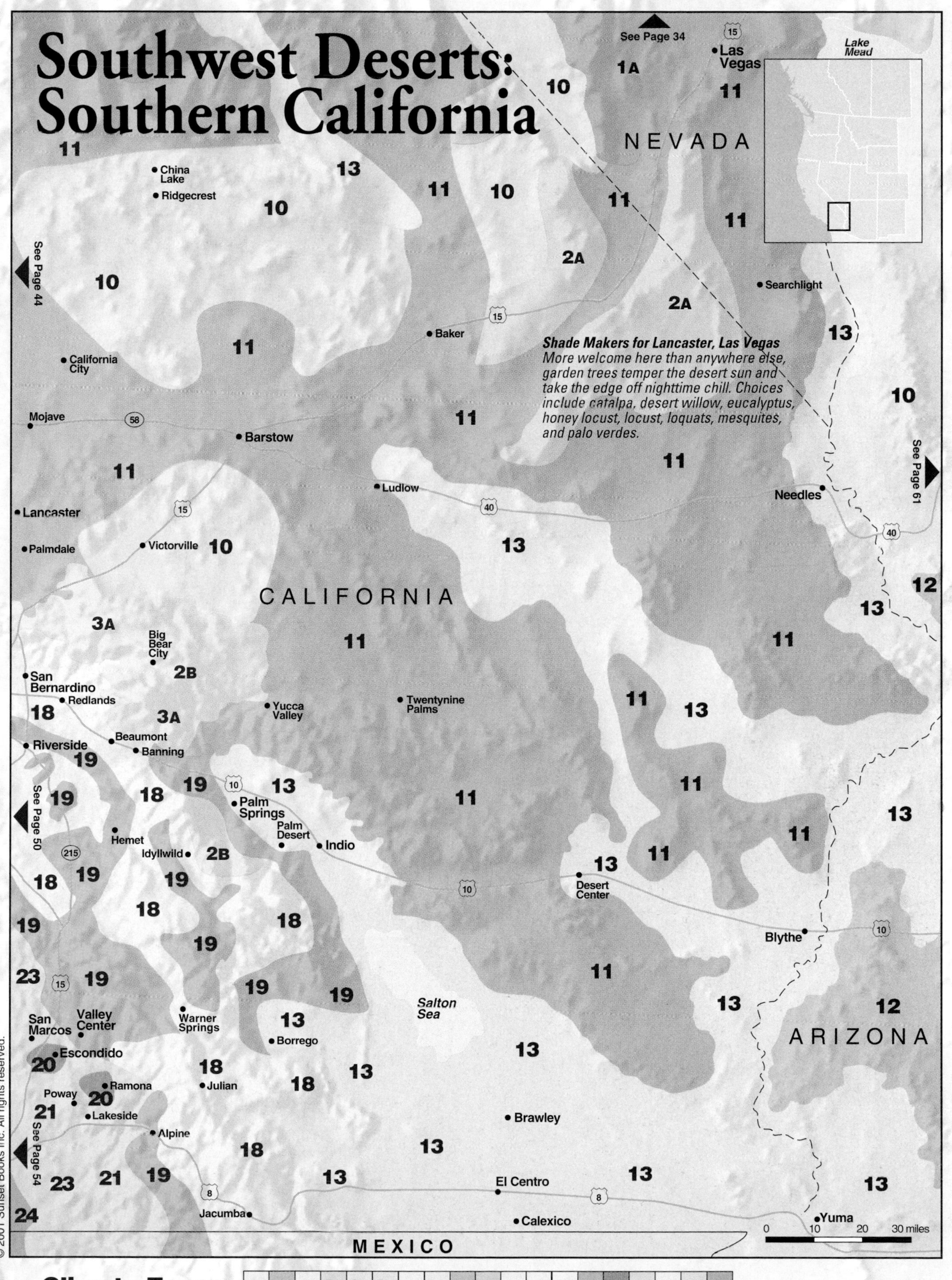

Shade Makers for Lancaster, Las Vegas
More welcome here than anywhere else, garden trees temper the desert sun and take the edge off nighttime chill. Choices include catalpa, desert willow, eucalyptus, honey locust, locust, loquats, mesquites, and palo verdes.

Climate Zones 1A 2A 2B 3A 10 11 12 13 18 19 20 21 23 24

Southwest Deserts: New Mexico

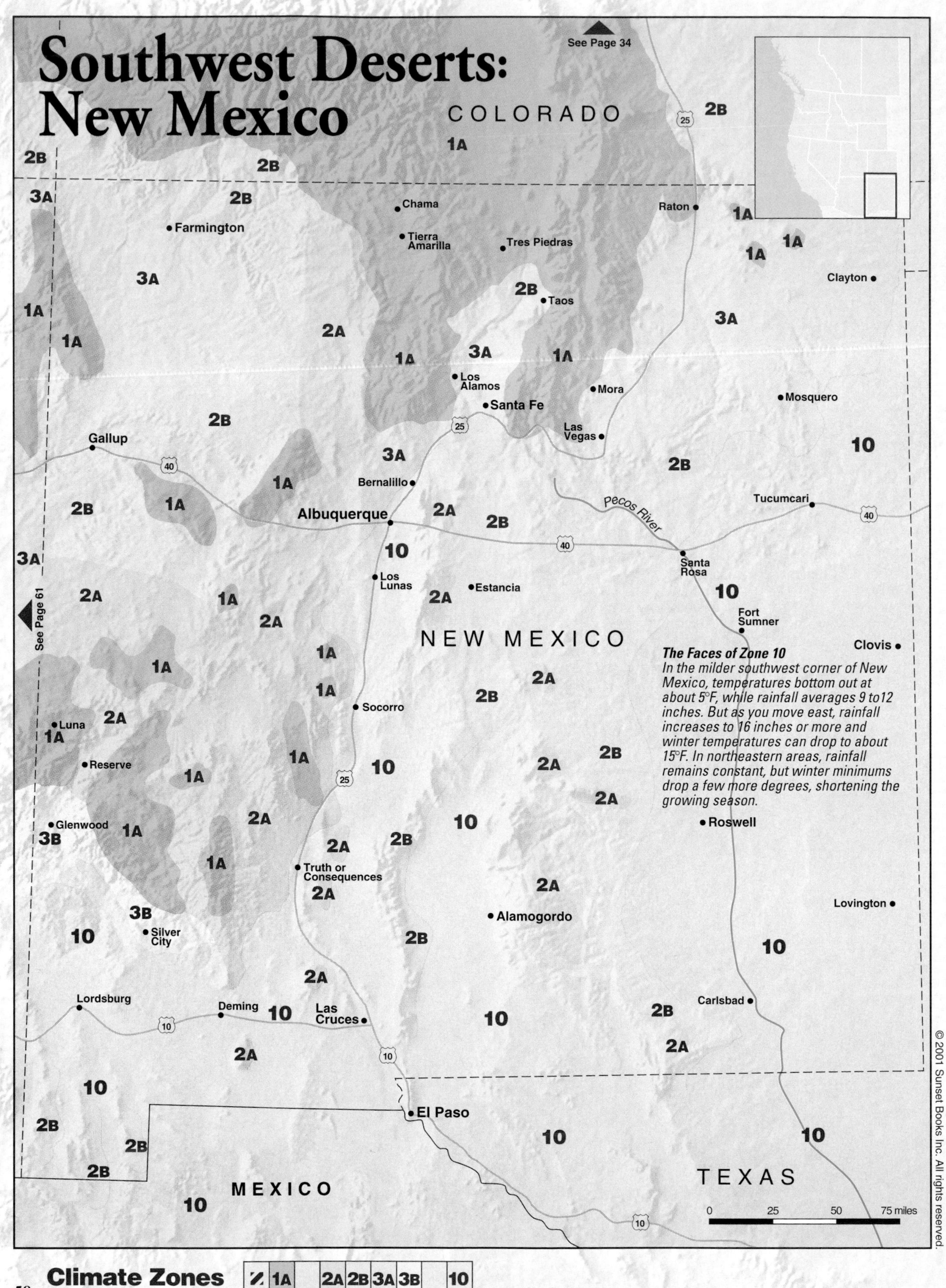

Climate Zones 1A 2A 2B 3A 3B 10

ZONE 10 High Desert Areas of Arizona and New Mexico

Zone 10 gets enough winter chill to flock pampas grass (far left) and let you grow plants that need chilling—lilacs and deciduous fruits, for example. But it also gets plenty of summer heat for growing chilies, shown at left drying in the sun on a pole.

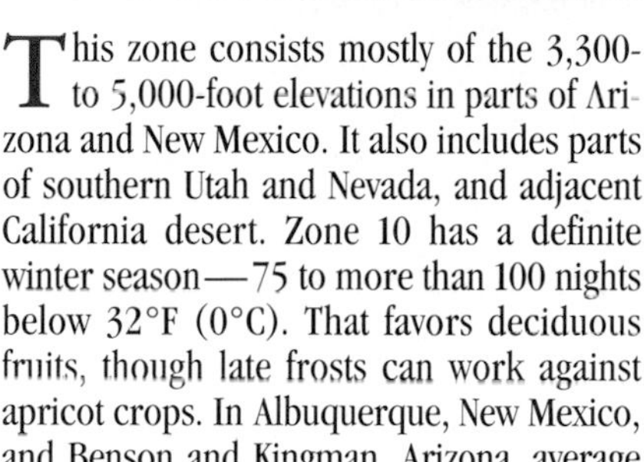

This zone consists mostly of the 3,300- to 5,000-foot elevations in parts of Arizona and New Mexico. It also includes parts of southern Utah and Nevada, and adjacent California desert. Zone 10 has a definite winter season—75 to more than 100 nights below 32°F (0°C). That favors deciduous fruits, though late frosts can work against apricot crops. In Albuquerque, New Mexico, and Benson and Kingman, Arizona, average winter minimums range from 32 to 23°F (0 to −5°C). Lows of 25 to 22°F (−4 to −6°C) often come in April, with extremes averaging 10 to −10°F (−12 to −23°C). The cold winter season calls for spring planting, unlike Zones 12 and 13 where most planting is done in fall.

More rainfall and less heat distinguish Zone 10 from Zone 11. Annual rainfall averages 12 inches, with more falling in the east, notably less in the west. Most plants in these areas benefit from the extra summer water. The Pecos River drainage receives more precipitation in summer than in winter. Growing seasons are very long, running from 185 to 225 days.

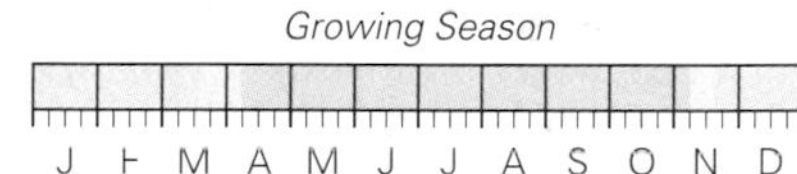

ZONE 11 Medium to High Desert of California and Southern Nevada

This climate zone shares similarities with its neighbors—the cold-winter Zones 1, 2, and 3, and the subtropical low desert, Zone 13. Like Zones 1 to 3, Zone 11 has cold winters, and like Zone 13, it has hot summers. Overall, it has wide swings in temperature. Hot summer days are followed by mild nights; near-freezing winter nights, followed by daytime temperatures near 60°F (16°C). On average, there are 110 summer days above 90°F (32°C), with the highest temperatures recorded between 111 and 117°F (44 to 47°C). About 85 nights have temperatures below 32°F (0°C), with lows between 11 and 0°F (−12 to −18°C).

If soil moisture is inadequate, the characteristic winds and bright sunlight may combine to dry out normally hardy evergreen plants, killing or badly injuring them.

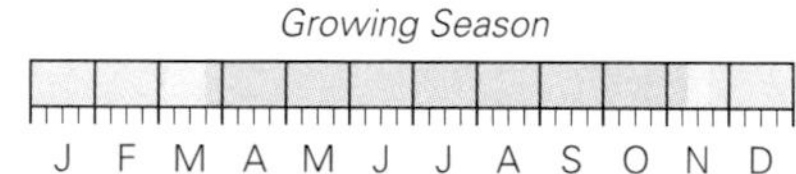

Las Vegas doesn't get much rain: only about 4 inches in an average year. But dry streambeds like the one above can help channel rainwater from downspouts to plants. At left, spring wildflowers make a dazzling appearance in Antelope Valley. Challenges for gardeners in Zone 11? Hot summer days, chilly nights, late spring frosts, hard alkaline soil, and desert winds.

ZONE 12 Arizona's Intermediate Desert

The crucial difference between Arizona's intermediate desert (Zone 12) and the low desert (Zone 13) is winter cold. But though the intermediate desert averages only 5 more freezing nights than the low desert (20 in Tucson compared with 15 in Phoenix and El Centro), it has harder frosts spread over a longer cold season. Zone 12 averages about 8 months between freezes, 9 months between killing frosts of 28°F (−2°C) or lower. Zone 13, on the other hand, averages more than 11 months between killing frosts, when it gets them at all. Extreme low temperatures of 6°F (−14°C) have been recorded in Zone 12. The mean maximums in July and August are 5 or 6°F cooler than the highs of Zone 13.

Many subtropicals that do well in Zone 13 aren't reliably hardy here, but succeed with protection against the extreme winters.

Although winter temperatures are lower than in Zone 13, the total hours of cold are not enough to provide sufficient winter chilling for some deciduous fruits.

From March to May, strong winds (to 40 miles per hour) can damage young tender growth. Windbreaks help. Here, as in Zone 13 and the eastern parts of Zone 10, summer rains are to be expected and can be more dependable than winter rains. And as in Zone 13, the best season for cool-season crops (salad greens, root vegetables, cabbage family members) starts in September or October.

Saguaro, cholla, and organpipe cacti rise up out of a sea of yellow brittlebush flowers in southern Arizona's intermediate desert. Zone 12 supports a more lush, gardenlike flora than any other desert zone.

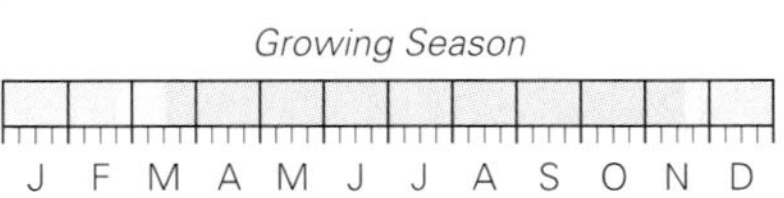

ZONE 13 Low or Subtropical Desert Areas

Ranging from below sea level in the Imperial Valley and Death Valley to an elevation of 1,100 feet around Phoenix, Zone 13 is subtropical desert. Average summer highs range from 106 to 108°F (41 to 42°C). Winters are short and mild. Frosts, anticipated from December 1 to February 15, are brief. Although the average minimum winter temperature is 37°F (3°C), with just 15 nights below freezing, lows of 19 to 13°F (−7 to −11°C) have been recorded.

The gardening year begins in September and October for most vegetable crops and annual flowers, although crops like corn and melons are planted in late winter. Fall-planted crops grow slowly in winter, pick up speed in mid-February, and race through the increasing temperatures of March and April. Spring winds and summer storms are a factor in gardening: the rains help with watering, and dense clouds shield plants from the hot sun.

Winter lows and summer highs exclude some subtropicals from this zone, but ones like bauhinia (above), date palms, and grapefruit thrive here. California fan palms and brittlebush bask in the sun in a canyon near Palm Springs (left).

Growing Season*

J F M A M J J A S O N D

*heat stops growth in summer

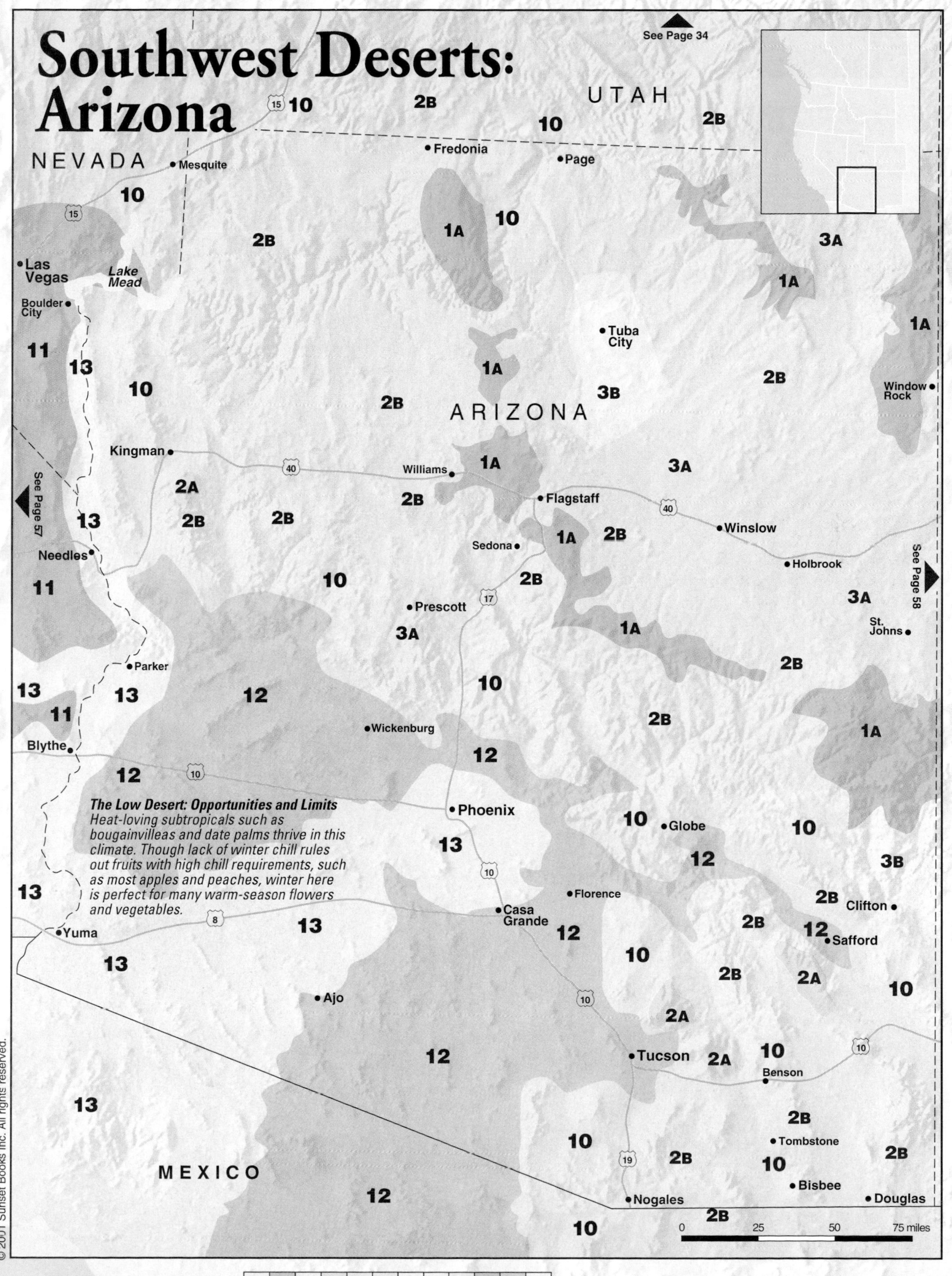

Southwest Deserts: Arizona
See Page 34
UTAH
NEVADA
ARIZONA
MEXICO
See Page 57
See Page 58
Mesquite
Fredonia
Page
Las Vegas
Lake Mead
Boulder City
Tuba City
Window Rock
Kingman
Williams
Flagstaff
Winslow
Holbrook
Sedona
Needles
Prescott
St. Johns
Parker
Wickenburg
Blythe
Phoenix
Globe
Florence
Clifton
Casa Grande
Safford
Yuma
Ajo
Tucson
Benson
Tombstone
Bisbee
Nogales
Douglas
0 25 50 75 miles
The Low Desert: Opportunities and Limits
Heat-loving subtropicals such as bougainvilleas and date palms thrive in this climate. Though lack of winter chill rules out fruits with high chill requirements, such as most apples and peaches, winter here is perfect for many warm-season flowers and vegetables.
Climate Zones 1A 2A 2B 3A 3B 10 11 12 13

Hawaii

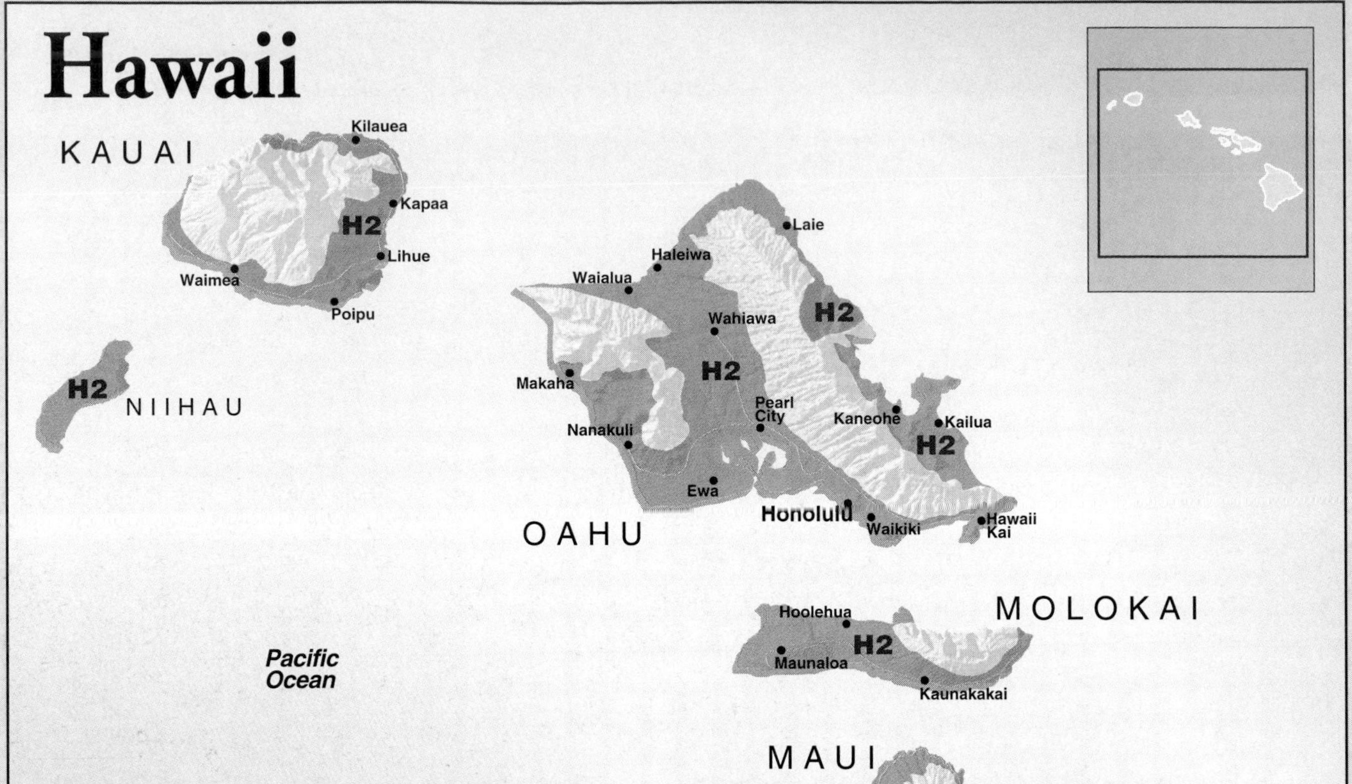

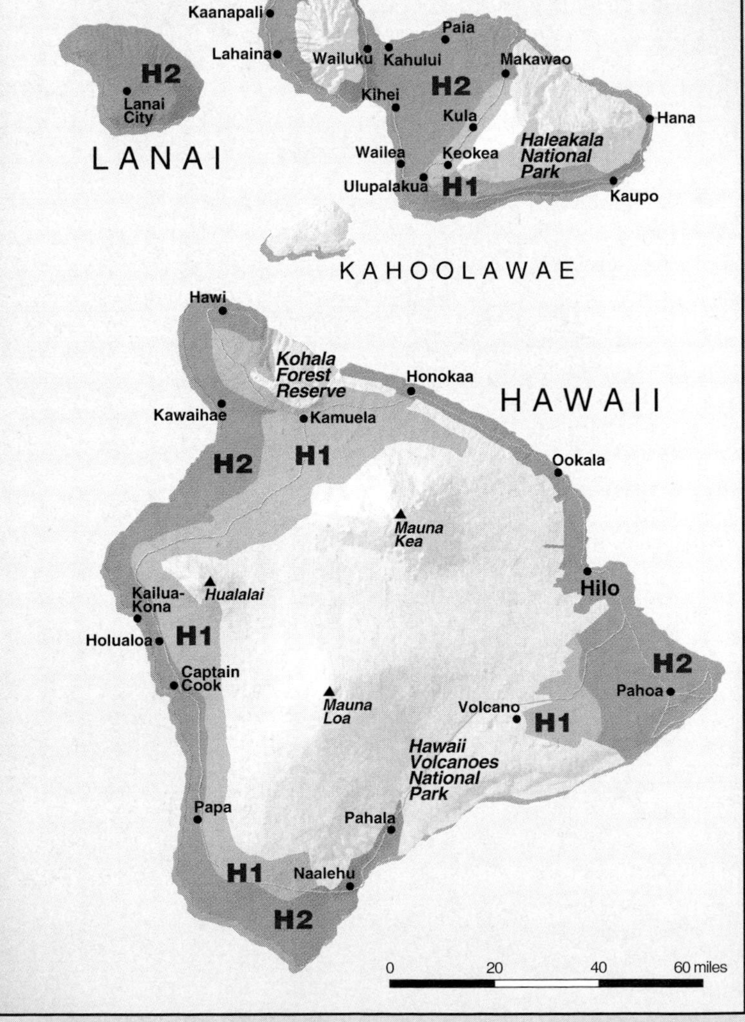

KAUAI
Kilauea
Kapaa
Lihue
Waimea
Poipu
H2

NIIHAU
H2

OAHU
Laie
Haleiwa
Waialua
Wahiawa
Makaha
Nanakuli
Pearl City
Kaneohe
Kailua
Ewa
Honolulu
Waikiki
Hawaii Kai
H2
H2
H2

MOLOKAI
Hoolehua
Maunaloa
Kaunakakai
H2

Pacific Ocean

MAUI
Kaanapali
Lahaina
Wailuku
Kahului
Paia
Makawao
Kihei
Kula
Hana
Wailea
Keokea
Ulupalakua
Kaupo
Haleakala National Park
H2
H1

LANAI
Lanai City
H2

KAHOOLAWAE

HAWAII
Hawi
Kohala Forest Reserve
Honokaa
Kawaihae
Kamuela
Ookala
Mauna Kea
Hualalai
Kailua-Kona
Holualoa
Captain Cook
Hilo
Pahoa
Volcano
Mauna Loa
Hawaii Volcanoes National Park
Papa
Pahala
Naalehu
H1
H2

0 20 40 60 miles

Oahu

Ewa
Honolulu
Waikiki
Diamond Head
LEEWARD
WINDWARD
TRADE WINDS

Wet and Dry

On all the islands except Hawaii, the north and east (windward) sides are wet, the south and west (leeward) sides are dry. From the ocean off the windward sides, evaporation rises. Carried by trade winds, this warm, moist air passes over land, increasing clouds and showers, then over mountains, where it cools. Heavy rains are the result. Leeward, the air warms as it descends, leaving these south and west sides mostly sunny and dry.

The Big Island, though, is different. Its high volcanic peaks (Mauna Loa, Mauna Kea, and Hualalai) block and deflect the trade winds, leaving local winds to drive Kona Coast weather. Here, especially in summer, upslope winds give rise to afternoon clouds and rain at elevations from 1,000 to 4,000 feet (prime for growing coffee).

Hawaii

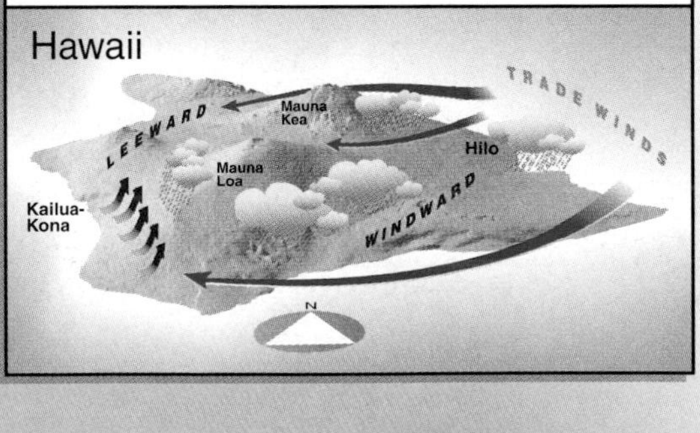

Mauna Kea
Mauna Loa
Hilo
Kailua-Kona
LEEWARD
WINDWARD
TRADE WINDS

ZONE H1 Cooler Volcanic Slopes: 2,000 to 5,000 Feet

This zone includes Kula and Ulupalakua on Maui and Kamuela and Volcano on Hawaii (the Big Island). Cooler air temperatures make these areas higher up the volcanic slopes better for growing standard cymbidiums, hydrangeas, proteas, and sweet bulbing onions (Maui onions). Low-chill varieties of apples, peaches, and plums grow throughout this zone, though they bear crops most prolifically in its highest elevations. The upper reaches of this zone and slightly higher elevations are also better for growing plants that can't abide much heat, including Douglas fir and Japanese maples. Lower soil temperatures and cooler nights, too, help some gardeners at the 4,000- to 6,000-foot elevations on the dry sides succeed with plants from Mediterranean climates that cannot tolerate warm, wet soils.

Warm-season highs range from 65 to 80°F (19 to 27°C); cool-season lows can dip to the mid-40s. Frosts can occur above this zone. The growing season is year-round.

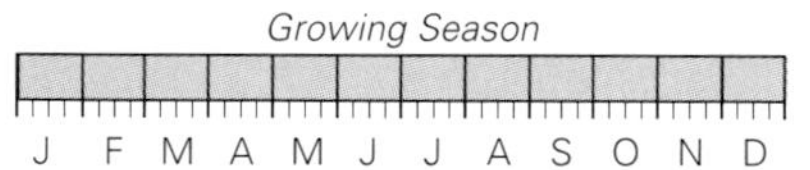

Ulupalakua Ranch (below) on the slopes of Maui's Haleakala volcano provides panoramic views of the island's distant shore. This cool, often misty upcountry area, one of the state's most prosperous agricultural regions, produces everything from sweet Kula onions, baby lettuce, and Carnelian grapes to proteas (right).

ZONE H2 Coconut Palm Belt: Sea Level to 2,000 Feet

Zone H2 includes the Ewa plain, Hawaii-Kai, Kailua, Kaneohe, Honolulu, and Waikiki on Oahu; Kahului, Kihei, and Lahaina on Maui; and the Hilo, Kailua-Kona, and Kohala coasts on Hawaii. Most lowland lees in this zone get their heaviest rains between November and March, and May through September is relatively dry. (Droughts can come when storms don't.) Sunny days urge bougainvilleas, poincianas, plumerias, and shower trees *(Cassia)* into spectacular bloom. On the wet windward sides, where rain comes from passing storms and year-round tradewind showers, moisture-loving bananas, gingers, and heliconias do particularly well.

The Kona Coast, however, gets more rain in the warm season than in the cool season. The same plants grow here as elsewhere in Zone H2 but may have slightly different cultural requirements.

Highs in this zone hover in the 80s; lows can dip to the mid-60s. The growing season is year-round.

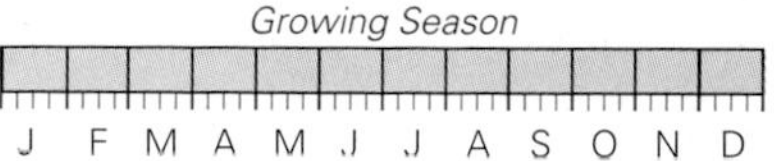

Coconut palms *(Cocos nucifera)* are at their best near the shore; they will not thrive above 2,000 feet. The elegant specimens pictured above, with fronds rustling in an early-morning breeze, fringe Oahu's Waikiki Beach.

A Guide to

PLANT SELECTION

Rhynchelytrum nerviglume 'Pink Crystals' blooming at the Denver Botanic Garden.

Choosing the right plants for your garden from among the hundreds of thousands available can be a challenge even for the most experienced gardener. But with the help of the many plant lists in this chapter, you can tackle the job with confidence. Let these lists guide you in selecting plants to achieve the result you want, whether it's a distinctive effect from flowers or foliage, an attractive planting for a problem spot, a basic garden framework of trees, shrubs, and ground covers, or something special—perhaps a butterfly garden or a tropical "jungle."

In each list, certain symbols are used to specify every plant's needs (and allow you to determine its suitability for your garden).

☼: Grows best in full sunlight all day long or almost all day—except for an hour or so of shade at the beginning or end of a summer day

◑ Needs partial shade—shade for half the day or for at least 3 hours during the hottest part of the day

● Prefers little or no direct sunlight—for example, it does best on the north side of a house or in shade cast by a broad, dense tree

Z Refers to the climate zones (explained and mapped in The West's Climate Zones, pages 27–63) where the plant typically grows best

Coreopsis verticillata 'Moonbeam'

COLOR

BASIC LANDSCAPING

SPECIAL SITUATIONS

PROBLEM SOLVERS

Perennial border

PERENNIALS

with Showy Flowers

These garden mainstays flower reliably, year after year—one trait that has long endeared them to gardeners. Unlike annuals and biennials, which live for only a year or two, perennials are semipermanent plants that need, at most, just periodic division and replanting to keep up a satisfying floral display. Some are evergreen; others die to the ground at the end of each growing season, then reappear from the roots the following year.

Anemone × hybrida

COLOR CODES: Each tint represents a range of colors, not a color match.

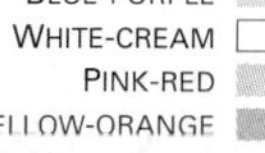

BLUE-PURPLE
WHITE-CREAM
PINK-RED
YELLOW-ORANGE

Armeria maritima

Aster novi-belgii

Astilbe × arendsii

Astilbe chinensis 'Pumila'

Achillea
YARROW
☼ ⁄ A1–A3; 1–24 **p. 170**

Aconitum
ACONITE
☼ ◑ ⁄ A1–A3; 1–9, 14–21 **p. 171**

Adenophora
LADY BELLS
☼ ◑ ⁄ A2, A3; 1–10, 14–24 **p. 172**

Agapanthus
LILY-OF-THE-NILE
☼ ◑ ⁄ 4–9, 12–24; H1, H2 **p. 174**

Agastache
☼ ◑ ⁄ ZONES VARY **p. 174**

Alstroemeria
☼ ◑ ⁄ 5–9, 14–24; H1 **p. 182**

Anemone × hybrida
JAPANESE ANEMONE
◑ ⁄ 2B–24 **p. 185**

Aquilegia
COLUMBINE
☼ ◑ ⁄ ZONES VARY **p. 195**

Arctotis (some)
AFRICAN DAISY
☼ ⁄ ALL ZONES **p. 199**

Armeria
THRIFT
☼ ⁄ ZONES VARY **p. 201**

Artemisia lactiflora
WHITE MUGWORT
☼ ⁄ 1–9, 14–21 **p. 202**

Aruncus
GOAT'S BEARD
☼ ◑ ⁄ ZONES VARY **p. 203**

Asclepias tuberosa
BUTTERFLY WEED
☼ ⁄ 1–24 **p. 204**

Aster
☼ ⁄ ZONES VARY **p. 207**

Astilbe
FALSE SPIRAEA
☼ ◑ ⁄ 1–9, 14–24 **p. 208**

Astrantia
MASTERWORT
☼ ◑ ⁄ 1–9, 14–24 **p. 208**

Aurinia saxatilis
BASKET-OF-GOLD
☼ ◑ ⁄ 1–24 **p. 210**

Baptisia
FALSE INDIGO
☼ ⁄ 1–24 **p. 218**

Bergenia
◑ ● ⁄ A1–A3; 1–9, 12–24 **p. 222**

Boltonia asteroides
☼ ◑ ⁄ 1–24 **p. 227**

Campanula (some)
BELLFLOWER
☼ ◑ ⁄ 1–9, 14–24 **p. 247**

Centaurea (some)
☼ ⁄ ZONES VARY **p. 260**

Centranthus ruber
JUPITER'S BEARD
☼ ◑ ⁄ 2–9, 12–24; H1 **p. 260**

Cerastium tomentosum
SNOW-IN-SUMMER
☼ ◑ ⁄ A1, A2; 1–24 **p. 261**

Chrysanthemum
NEEDS, ZONES VARY **p. 272**

Cimicifuga
BUGBANE
☼ ◑ ⁄ 1–7, 17 **p. 275**

Plant listings continue ▶

Campanula persicifolia

Cerastium tomentosum

Chrysanthemum maximum

Plant	Common name	Zones	Page
Coreopsis (some)		ZONES VARY	p. 290
Corydalis		2–9, 14–24	p. 294
Delphinium		ZONES VARY	p. 311
Dianthus	PINK	A2, A3; 1–24	p. 313
Diascia	TWINSPUR	ZONES VARY	p. 314
Dicentra	BLEEDING HEART	1–9, 14–24	p. 314
Dictamnus albus	GAS PLANT	1–9	p. 316
Digitalis	FOXGLOVE	NEEDS, ZONES VARY	p. 317
Echinacea purpurea	PURPLE CONEFLOWER	A2, A3; 1–24	p. 322
Echinops	GLOBE THISTLE	A2, A3; 1–24	p. 323
Epimedium		2–9, 14–17	p. 327
Erigeron	FLEABANE	ZONES VARY	p. 329
Eryngium amethystinum	SEA HOLLY	1–24	p. 334
Erysimum 'Bowles Mauve'		4–6, 14–17, 22, 23	p. 334
Eupatorium		ZONES VARY	p. 343
Euphorbia (some)		NEEDS, ZONES VARY	p. 344
Felicia amelloides	BLUE MARGUERITE	8, 9, 14–24	p. 349
Filipendula		ZONES VARY	p. 352
Gaillardia × grandiflora		1–24; H1, H2	p. 359
Gaura lindheimeri		2B–24	p. 361
Gazania		NEEDS, ZONES VARY	p. 361
Geranium	CRANESBILL	ZONES VARY	p. 363
Gerbera jamesonii	TRANSVAAL DAISY	8, 9, 12–24; H1, H2	p. 365
Geum		2–24	p. 365
Gypsophila		ZONES VARY	p. 377
Helenium autumnale	SNEEZEWEED	1–24	p. 382
Heliotropium arborescens	COMMON HELIOTROPE	15–17, 23, 24; H1, H2	p. 384
Helleborus	HELLEBORE	ZONES VARY	p. 384
Hemerocallis	DAYLILY	1–24; H1, H2	p. 385
Heuchera	CORAL BELLS	ZONES VARY	p. 387
Hibiscus moscheutos	PERENNIAL HIBISCUS	2–24; H1	p. 388
Iberis sempervirens	EVERGREEN CANDYTUFT	1–24	p. 396
Kniphofia uvaria	RED-HOT POKER	2–9, 14–24	p. 418
Ligularia		1–9, 14–17	p. 432
Limonium (some)	STATICE	ZONES VARY	p. 435
Linaria purpurea	TOADFLAX	2–10, 14–24	p. 436
Linum perenne	PERENNIAL BLUE FLAX	2–24	p. 437
Lobelia cardinalis	CARDINAL FLOWER	1–7, 14–17	p. 440

Coreopsis grandiflora 'Early Sunrise'

Delphinium elatum hybrid

Dianthus deltoides

Dicentra spectabilis 'Alba'

Erigeron karvinskianus

Gaillardia × *grandiflora* 'Goblin'

Heliotropium arborescens 'Black Beauty'

Hibiscus moscheutos

Heuchera × *brizoides*

For growing symbol explanations, please see page 64.

Lychnis chalcedonica

Oenothera speciosa 'Woodside White'

Paeonia, herbaceous hybrid

Papaver orientale

Perovskia 'Blue Spire'

Lupinus (some)
LUPINE
ZONES VARY p. 443

Lychnis chalcedonica
MALTESE CROSS
A1–A3; 1–10, 14–24 p. 444

Macleaya cordata
PLUME POPPY
A2, A3; 1–24 p. 446

Malva alcea
MALLOW
1–9, 14–24 p. 457

Mimulus
MONKEY FLOWER
NEEDS, ZONES VARY p. 469

Nepeta
1–24 p. 480

Nierembergia
CUP FLOWER
ZONES VARY p. 482

Oenothera
EVENING PRIMROSE
ZONES VARY p. 485

Osteospermum
AFRICAN DAISY
8, 9, 12–24 p. 491

Paeonia (herbaceous)
PEONY
ZONES VARY p. 493

Papaver orientale
ORIENTAL POPPY
A1–A3; 1–11, 14–21 p. 495

Pelargonium
GERANIUM
8, 9, 12–24 p. 509

Penstemon (many)
BEARD TONGUE
ZONES VARY p. 510

Perovskia
RUSSIAN SAGE
2–24 p. 512

Phlomis (some)
ZONES VARY p. 517

Phlox paniculata
SUMMER PHLOX
1–14, 18–21 p. 518

Phlox subulata
MOSS PINK
1–17 p. 518

Phygelius
CAPE FUCHSIA
4–9, 14–24; H1, H2 p. 520

Physostegia virginiana
FALSE DRAGONHEAD
A3; 1–9, 14–24 p. 521

Platycodon grandiflorus
BALLOON FLOWER
1–10, 14–24 p. 532

Polemonium
1–11, 14–17 p. 540

Primula (many)
PRIMROSE
ZONES VARY p. 545

Prunella
SELF-HEAL
2–24 p. 549

Pulmonaria
LUNGWORT
1–9, 14–17 p. 555

Rodgersia
2–9, 14–17 p. 578

Romneya coulteri
MATILIJA POPPY
4–12, 14–24; H1 p. 578

Rudbeckia
1–24 p. 589

Salvia
SAGE
NEEDS, ZONES VARY p. 592

Scabiosa
PINCUSHION FLOWER
ZONES VARY p. 600

Sedum spectabile, S. telephium
1–24 pp. 605, 606

Sidalcea malviflora
CHECKERBLOOM
2–9, 14–24 p. 609

Silene
ZONES VARY p. 609

Stokesia laevis
STOKES ASTER
2–10, 12–24 p. 620

Thalictrum
MEADOW RUE
2–10, 14–17 p. 630

Tricyrtis
TOAD LILY
ZONES VARY p. 638

Trollius
GLOBEFLOWER
A2, A3; 1–6 p. 639

Verbena
ZONES VARY p. 645

Veronica
SPEEDWELL
ZONES VARY p. 645

Platycodon grandiflorus

Penstemon ×*gloxinioides* 'Garnet'

Rudbeckia fulgida 'Goldsturm'

Stokesia laevis

Trollius chinensis

Allium giganteum

BULBS
and Bulblike Plants

Crocus 'Remembrance'

Some of the garden's showiest flowers come from plants that grow from true bulbs, corms, tubers, rhizomes, and tuberous roots. Gardeners often call all these underground structures bulbs—and all store food that keeps the plant alive through a dormant period, ready to grow again once dormancy has ended. Some bulbs (daffodil and iris, for example) thrive in most of the West; others, such as caladium, have a more restricted range. You can enjoy many bulbs outside their preferred climate zones by growing them in pots, or by digging and storing them over winter in a frostless location. A few even thrive as houseplants.

Amaryllis belladonna

Anemone blanda

Freesia hybrid

COLOR CODES: Each tint represents a range of colors, not a color match.

BLUE–PURPLE
WHITE–CREAM
PINK–RED
YELLOW–ORANGE

FALL PLANTED BULBS

Plant	Common name	Needs / Zones	Page
Allium	ORNAMENTAL ALLIUM	ZONES VARY	p. 178
Amaryllis belladonna	BELLADONNA LILY	4–24	p. 183
Anemone	WINDFLOWER	NEEDS, ZONES VARY	p. 185
Babiana	BABOON FLOWER	4–24	p. 212
Brodiaea		ZONES VARY	p. 232
Chionodoxa	GLORY-OF-THE-SNOW	1–7, 14–20	p. 270
Convallaria majalis	LILY-OF-THE-VALLEY	A1–A3; 1–7, 14–20	p. 288
Crocus		1–24	p. 300
Cyclamen persicum	FLORISTS' CYCLAMEN	15–24	p. 304
Eranthis hyemalis	WINTER ACONITE	1–9, 14–17	p. 328
Freesia		8, 9, 12–24	p. 356
Fritillaria	FRITILLARY	ZONES VARY	p. 357
Galanthus	SNOWDROP	1–9, 14–17	p. 359
Galtonia candicans	SUMMER HYACINTH	4–24; H1	p. 359
Hippeastrum	AMARYLLIS	ZONES VARY	p. 390
Hyacinthoides	BLUEBELL	ZONES VARY	p. 393
Hyacinthus orientalis	COMMON HYACINTH	ZONES VARY	p. 393
Hymenocallis		5, 6, 8, 9, 14–24	p. 395
Ipheion uniflorum	SPRING STAR FLOWER	2B–24	p. 400
Iris (some)		NEEDS, ZONES VARY	p. 401
Ixia	AFRICAN CORN LILY	7–9, 12–24	p. 406
Leucojum	SNOWFLAKE	ZONES VARY	p. 430
Lilium	LILY	ZONES VARY	p. 433
Muscari	GRAPE HYACINTH	ZONES VARY	p. 474
Narcissus	DAFFODIL	A2, A3; 1–24	p. 476

For growing symbol explanations, please see page 64.

Convallaria majalis

Hymenocallis 'Sulfur Queen'

Iris, tall bearded 'Cinderella's Coach'

Nerine sarniensis

Scilla

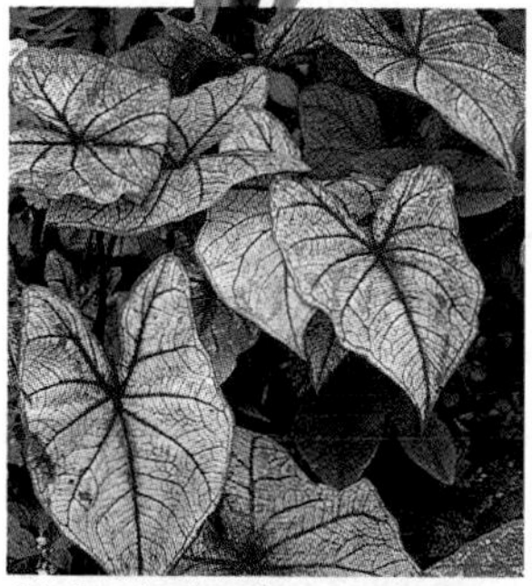

Caladium bicolor 'White Queen'

Canna hybrids

Crocosmia 'Lucifer'

Nerine
☼ ◑ 5, 6, 8, 9, 13–24 **p. 481**

Oxalis (some)
NEEDS, ZONES VARY **p. 491**

Puschkinia scilloides
☼ ◑ 1–11, 14 **p. 556**

Ranunculus asiaticus
PERSIAN RANUNCULUS
☼ ALL ZONES **p. 564**

Scilla
SQUILL
☼ ◑ ZONES VARY **p. 603**

Sparaxis tricolor
HARLEQUIN FLOWER
☼ 9, 12–24 **p. 614**

Triteleia
☼ 3–9, 14–24 **p. 638**

Tritonia crocata
FLAME FREESIA
☼ 9, 13–24 **p. 639**

Tulipa
TULIP
☼ ◑ 1–24 **p. 640**

Watsonia borbonica
☼ 4–9, 12–24 **p. 651**

Zantedeschia
CALLA **p. 655**
NEEDS VARY, 5, 6, 8, 9, 12–24; H1, H2

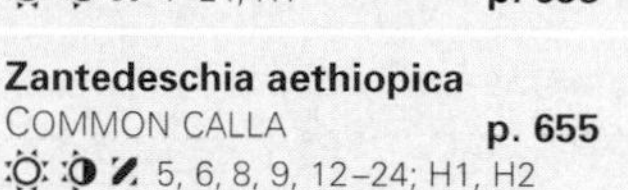

WINTER-SPRING PLANTED BULBS

Begonia, tuberous
◑ 4–9, 14–24; H1 **p. 221**

Caladium bicolor
FANCY-LEAFED CALADIUM
◑ ● H2 **p. 237**

Canna
☼ 6–9, 12–24; H1, H2 **p. 249**

Colocasia esculenta
TARO
◑ 12, 16–24; H1, H2 **p. 288**

Crocosmia
☼ ◑ 5–24 **p. 300**

Cyclamen persicum
FLORISTS' CYCLAMEN
☼ ◑ 15–24 **p. 304**

Dahlia
☼ ◑ 1–24 **p. 307**

Gladiolus
☼ 4–9, 12–24; H1 **p. 366**

Gloriosa superba 'Rothschildiana'
GLORY LILY
☼ ◑ 24; H1, H2 **p. 368**

Hippeastrum
AMARYLLIS
☼ ◑ ZONES VARY **p. 390**

Homeria collina
☼ 4–24 **p. 391**

Hymenocallis
☼ ◑ 5, 6, 8, 9, 14–24 **p. 395**

Liatris spicata
GAYFEATHER
☼ A2, A3; 1–10, 14–24 **p. 432**

Lilium, Oriental hybrids
☼ ◑ 1–9, 14–24 **p. 434**

Polianthes tuberosa
TUBEROSE
☼ 7–9, 14–24; H1, H2 **p. 540**

Schizostylis coccinea
CRIMSON FLAG
☼ ◑ 5–9, 14–24; H1, H2 **p. 602**

Tigridia pavonia
TIGER FLOWER
☼ ◑ 4–24; H1 **p. 633**

Zantedeschia aethiopica
COMMON CALLA **p. 655**
☼ ◑ 5, 6, 8, 9, 12–24; H1, H2

Zephyranthes
ZEPHYR FLOWER
☼ ◑ ZONES VARY **p. 656**

SUMMER PLANTED BULBS

Colchicum
MEADOW SAFFRON
☼ 2–10, 14–24 **p. 287**

Crocus (fall-flowering)
☼ ◑ 1–24 **p. 300**

Cyclamen (except florists' types)
☼ ◑ ZONES VARY **p. 304**

Iris (some)
NEEDS, ZONES VARY **p. 401**

Lycoris
SPIDER LILY
☼ ZONES VARY **p. 444**

Sternbergia lutea
☼ 3–10, 14–24 **p. 619**

Gladiolus × colvillei 'The Bride'

Liatris spicata 'Kobold'

Colchicum 'Waterlily'

Iris, tall bearded

Antirrhinum majus

ANNUALS

for Seasonal Color

Flowering annuals provide quick color to liven up almost any part of the garden. You can choose from a dazzling array of colors and floral styles; size varies just as widely, from ground-hugging to knee-high to towering. Cool-season annuals (such as calendula and sweet pea) prosper in cool soils and mild temperatures—fall through spring in mild-winter climates, early to late spring elsewhere. Warm-season annuals such as cosmos and zinnia are planted after the year's last frost and usually grow best between late spring and fall—though in the low desert and hot interior climates, some perform better from early to late spring.

Calendula officinalis

Campanula medium

Chrysanthemum × morifolium

COOL-SEASON ANNUALS

Plant	Common name	Needs; zones	Page
Antirrhinum majus	SNAPDRAGON	☼ ⁄ A3; 1–24	**p. 188**
Calendula officinalis	CALENDULA	☼ ⁄ 1–24; H1	**p. 239**
Campanula medium	CANTERBURY BELL	☼ ◑ ⁄ 1–9, 14–24	**p. 248**
Centaurea cyanus	CORNFLOWER	☼ ⁄ 1–24; H1, H2	**p. 260**
Chrysanthemum (several)		NEEDS, ZONES VARY	**p. 272**
Clarkia		☼ ◑ ⁄ 1–24	**p. 281**
Consolida ajacis	LARKSPUR	☼ ⁄ 1–24	**p. 288**
Cynoglossum amabile	CHINESE FORGET-ME-NOT	☼ ⁄ A2, A3; 1–24; H1, H2	**p. 305**
Dianthus (some)		☼ ◑ ⁄ A2, A3; 1–24	**p. 313**
Dimorphotheca	AFRICAN DAISY	☼ ⁄ 1–24	**p. 317**
Eschscholzia californica	CALIFORNIA POPPY	☼ ⁄ 1–24; H1	**p. 336**
Iberis umbellata	GLOBE CANDYTUFT	☼ ◑ ⁄ 1–24	**p. 396**
Lathyrus odoratus	SWEET PEA	☼ ⁄ ALL ZONES	**p. 424**
Linaria maroccana	BABY SNAPDRAGON	☼ ◑ ⁄ 1–24	**p. 436**
Matthiola incana		☼ ◑ ⁄ 1–24	**p. 463**
Myosotis sylvatica	FORGET-ME-NOT	◑ ⁄ A1–A3; 1–24	**p. 475**
Nemesia strumosa		☼ ⁄ 1–24	**p. 479**
Papaver (some)	POPPY	☼ ⁄ ZONES VARY	**p. 495**
Primula (many)	PRIMROSE	☼ ◑ ● ⁄ ZONES VARY	**p. 545**
Schizanthus pinnatus	POOR MAN'S ORCHID	◑ ⁄ 1–6, 15–17, 21–24	**p. 602**
Senecio × hybridus	FLORISTS' CINERARIA	☼ ◑ ● ⁄ 16, 17, 22–24	**p. 606**
Viola	VIOLA, PANSY	NEEDS, ZONES VARY	**p. 648**

WARM-SEASON ANNUALS

Plant	Common name	Needs; zones	Page
Ageratum houstonianum	FLOSS FLOWER	☼ ◑ ⁄ 1–24	**p. 175**
Brachyscome iberidifolia	SWAN RIVER DAISY	☼ ⁄ 1–24	**p. 230**

COLOR CODES: Each tint represents a range of colors, not a color match.

BLUE–PURPLE
WHITE–CREAM
PINK–RED
YELLOW–ORANGE

Clarkia amoena

Matthiola incana

Eschscholzia californica

For growing symbol explanations, please see page 64.

Brachyscome iberidifolia

Catharanthus roseus

Gomphrena globosa

Lavatera trimestris 'Silver Cup'

Lobelia erinus

Plant	Common name	Zones	Page
Browallia speciosa	AMETHYST FLOWER	17, 23, 24; H1, H2	p. 233
Callistephus chinensis	CHINA ASTER	1–24	p. 240
Catharanthus roseus	MADAGASCAR PERIWINKLE	1–24; H1, H2	p. 255
Celosia	COCKSCOMB	1–24; H1, H2	p. 259
Cleome hasslerana	SPIDER FLOWER	1–24	p. 283
Convolvulus tricolor	DWARF MORNING GLORY	1–24	p. 289
Coreopsis tinctoria	ANNUAL COREOPSIS	1–24; H1, H2	p. 290
Cosmos		1–24	p. 295
Eustoma grandiflorum	LISIANTHUS	1–24	p. 346
Gaillardia pulchella		1–24; H1, H2	p. 359
Gomphrena	GLOBE AMARANTH	1–24; H1, H2	p. 368
Gypsophila elegans		1–24	p. 377
Helianthus annuus	COMMON SUNFLOWER	ALL ZONES	p. 382
Helichrysum bracteatum	STRAWFLOWER	ALL ZONES	p. 383
Impatiens	BALSAM	NEEDS, ZONES VARY	p. 399
Ipomoea	MORNING GLORY	ZONES VARY	p. 400
Lavatera trimestris	ANNUAL MALLOW	ALL ZONES	p. 427
Limonium (some)	STATICE	ZONES VARY	p. 435
Lobelia erinus		ALL ZONES	p. 440
Lobularia maritima	SWEET ALYSSUM	ALL ZONES	p. 440
Mimulus × hybridus		1–24	p. 469
Moluccella laevis	BELLS-OF-IRELAND	1–24; H1, H2	p. 471
Nicotiana		ZONES VARY	p. 482
Petunia × hybrida	PETUNIA	ALL ZONES	p. 514
Phlox drummondii	ANNUAL PHLOX	A2, A3; 1–24; H1	p. 517
Portulaca grandiflora	ROSE MOSS	ALL ZONES	p. 543
Salpiglossis sinuata	PAINTED TONGUE	1–24	p. 592
Salvia splendens	SCARLET SAGE	ALL ZONES	p. 597
Sanvitalia procumbens	CREEPING ZINNIA	1–24	p. 599
Scabiosa atropurpurea	PINCUSHION FLOWER	1–24	p. 600
Silene coeli-rosa	VISCARIA	ALL ZONES	p. 609
Tagetes	MARIGOLD	ZONES VARY	p. 626
Thunbergia alata	BLACK-EYED SUSAN VINE	1–24; H1, H2	p. 631
Tithonia rotundifolia	MEXICAN SUNFLOWER	ALL ZONES	p. 634
Torenia fournieri	WISHBONE FLOWER	ALL ZONES	p. 636
Tropaeolum majus	GARDEN NASTURTIUM	ALL ZONES	p. 639
Verbena		ZONES VARY	p. 645
Zinnia		1–24; H1, H2	p. 657

Mimulus × hybridus

Nicotiana alata hybrid

Thunbergia alata

Tropaeolum majus

Verbena × hybrida

Camellia reticulata

LANDSCAPE PLANTS
with Showy Flowers

Trees, shrubs, and vines form a garden's permanent framework, but they offer more than just a neutral background for showier plants. In fact, many of these plants put on a flower show every bit as striking as that of annuals and perennials; depending on your climate, you can plant for color in two, three, or even all four seasons. In this list, plants are grouped by bloom season; the color bar for each entry shows the range of flower colors available.

Flowering rhododendrons and azaleas

COLOR CODES: Each tint represents a range of colors, not a color match.
BLUE–PURPLE
WHITE–CREAM
PINK–RED
YELLOW–ORANGE

Aesculus × carnea

Bauhinia variegata

Cornus florida 'Rubra'

SPRING
Trees

Plant	Needs / Zones	Page
Acacia (most)	ZONES VARY	p. 164
Aesculus HORSECHESTNUT	ZONES VARY	p. 173
Bauhinia ORCHID TREE	ZONES VARY	p. 218
Catalpa	3–10, 14–24	p. 255
Cercidium PALO VERDE	8–14, 18–20	p. 262
Cercis REDBUD	ZONES VARY	p. 263
Chionanthus virginicus FRINGE TREE	2–6, 15–24	p. 270
Cornus DOGWOOD	ZONES VARY	p. 291
Crataegus HAWTHORN	2–12, 14–17	p. 298
Erythrina (some) CORAL TREE	ZONES VARY	p. 334
Halesia	2B–9, 14–21	p. 378
Laburnum GOLDENCHAIN TREE	1–10, 14–17	p. 420
Magnolia (most deciduous)	ZONES VARY	p. 447
Malus FLOWERING CRABAPPLE	1–11, 14–21	p. 457
Melaleuca (some)	ZONES VARY	p. 464
Prunus (flowering)	NEEDS, ZONES VARY	p. 549
Pyrus calleryana	2B–9, 14–21	p. 558
Tabebuia chrysotricha GOLDEN TRUMPET TREE	13, 15, 16, 20–24; H1, H2	p. 626

SPRING
Shrubs

Plant	Needs / Zones	Page
Abutilon (most) FLOWERING MAPLE	8, 9, 12–24; H1, H2	p. 163
Alyogyne huegelii BLUE HIBISCUS	13–17, 20–24; H1, H2	p. 182
Berberis BARBERRY	ZONES VARY	p. 221
Brunfelsia pauciflora	12–17, 20–24; H1, H2	p. 234
Camellia (many)	4–9, 12, 14–24	p. 243
Ceanothus WILD LILAC	5–9, 14–24	p. 256

Laburnum anagyroides

Prunus (flowering plum)

Malus 'Liset'

For growing symbol explanations, please see page 64.

highlight foreground of blue-flowered bulbs.

Ceanothus thyrsiflorus

Deutzia gracilis

Fremontodendron californicum

Kalmia latifolia

Chaenomeles
FLOWERING QUINCE
2–23 p. 264

Choisya ternata
MEXICAN ORANGE
4–9, 14–24 p. 271

Cistus (some)
ROCKROSE
4–9, 14–24 p. 276

Cytisus
BROOM
ZONES VARY p. 306

Daphne
NEEDS, ZONES VARY p. 309

Deutzia
2–11, 14–17 p. 313

Enkianthus
3–9, 14–21 p. 326

Erica (most)
HEATH
ZONES VARY p. 329

Exochorda
PEARL BUSH
2–9, 14–23 p. 346

Forsythia
ZONES VARY p. 354

Fremontodendron
FLANNEL BUSH
4–24 p. 357

Grevillea (some)
NEEDS, ZONES VARY p. 375

Jasminum (some)
JASMINE
ZONES VARY p. 408

Kalmia latifolia
MOUNTAIN LAUREL
2–7, 16, 17 p. 416

Kolkwitzia amabilis
BEAUTY BUSH
2–11, 14–20 p. 419

Leptospermum
TEA TREE
14–24 p. 428

Melaleuca (some)
ZONES VARY p. 464

Michelia figo
BANANA SHRUB
6, 9, 14–24; H1, H2 p. 468

Paeonia (tree)
PEONY
2–12, 14–23 p. 493

Philadelphus (some)
MOCK ORANGE
ZONES VARY p. 516

Photinia
ZONES VARY p. 519

Pieris
ZONES VARY p. 522

Plumbago auriculata
CAPE PLUMBAGO
8, 9, 12–24; H1, H2 p. 534

Rhaphiolepis indica
INDIAN HAWTHORN p. 567
4–10, 12–24; H1, H2

Rhododendron
AZALEA, RHODODENDRON
ZONES VARY p. 568

Ribes (some)
CURRANT, GOOSEBERRY
ZONES VARY p. 577

Rosa
ROSE
ZONES VARY p. 579

Rosmarinus officinalis
ROSEMARY
4–24; H1, H2 p. 587

Sophora secundiflora
TEXAS MOUNTAIN LAUREL
8–16, 18–24 p. 613

Spiraea (some)
ZONES VARY p. 616

Syringa
LILAC
ZONES VARY p. 624

Viburnum (some)
NEEDS, ZONES VARY p. 646

Weigela
1–11, 14–21 p. 651

SPRING
Vines

Beaumontia grandiflora
HERALD'S TRUMPET p. 219
12, 13, 16, 17, 21–24; H1, H2

Bougainvillea
p. 228
5, 6, 12–17, 19, 21–24; H1, H2

Clematis (some)
ZONES VARY p. 282

Clytostoma callistegioides
VIOLET TRUMPET VINE
8, 9, 12–24 p. 285

Plant listings continue ▸

Melaleuca nesophila

Rhododendron 'Bow Bells'

Rosa 'Belle Story'

Syringa vulgaris

Clematis 'Ville de Lyon' (large-flowered hybrid)

Hibbertia scandens

Lonicera japonica

Wisteria floribunda

Calodendrum capense

Erythrina coralloides

Distictis buccinatoria
BLOOD-RED TRUMPET VINE
8, 9, 14–24; H1 — p. 318

Gelsemium sempervirens
CAROLINA JESSAMINE
4–24 — p. 362

Hardenbergia
LILAC VINE
ZONES VARY — p. 380

Hibbertia scandens
GUINEA GOLD VINE
16, 17, 21–24 — p. 388

Jasminum (some)
JASMINE
ZONES VARY — p. 408

Lonicera (some)
HONEYSUCKLE
ZONES VARY — p. 441

Macfadyena unguis-cati
CAT'S CLAW
8–24; H1, H2 — p. 446

Rosa (some)
ROSE
ZONES VARY — p. 579

Solandra maxima
CUP-OF-GOLD VINE
15–24; H2 — p. 611

Solanum jasminoides
POTATO VINE
8, 9, 12–24; H1, H2 — p. 612

Wisteria
NEEDS, ZONES VARY — p. 652

SUMMER
Trees

Albizia julibrissin
SILK TREE
4–23 — p. 177

Calodendrum capense
CAPE CHESTNUT
15, 16, 19, 21–24 — p. 242

Cassia leptophylla
GOLD MEDALLION TREE
21–24; H2 — p. 254

Catalpa
3–10, 14–24 — p. 255

Chilopsis linearis
DESERT WILLOW
3B, 7–14, 18–23 — p. 269

Chionanthus retusus
CHINESE FRINGE TREE
3–9, 14–24 — p. 270

× Chitalpa tashkentensis
3–24 — p. 270

Cornus kousa
KOUSA DOGWOOD
2–9, 14–17 — p. 292

Erythrina (some)
CORAL TREE
ZONES VARY — p. 334

Eucalyptus ficifolia
RED-FLOWERING GUM
SEE CHART — p. 339

Jacaranda mimosifolia
12, 13, 15–24; H1, H2 — p. 407

Lagerstroemia indica
CRAPE MYRTLE
2–10, 12–24; H1, H2 — p. 421

Magnolia grandiflora
SOUTHERN MAGNOLIA — p. 449
4–12, 14–24; H1, H2

Robinia × ambigua 'Idahoensis'
IDAHO LOCUST
2–24 — p. 578

Sophora japonica
JAPANESE PAGODA TREE
2–24 — p. 613

Stewartia
4–6, 14–17, 20, 21 — p. 619

Vitex agnus-castus
CHASTE TREE
4–24; H1, H2 — p. 650

SUMMER
Shrubs

Abelia
ZONES VARY — p. 162

Abutilon
FLOWERING MAPLE
8, 9, 12–24; H1, H2 — p. 163

Alyogyne huegelii
BLUE HIBISCUS
13–17, 20–24; H1, H2 — p. 182

Brunfelsia pauciflora
12–17, 20–24; H1, H2 — p. 234

Buddleja davidii
BUTTERFLY BUSH
2–24; H1 — p. 235

Caesalpinia
ZONES VARY — p. 237

Callistemon
BOTTLEBRUSH
ZONES VARY — p. 240

Calluna vulgaris
SCOTCH HEATHER
1A, 2–6, 15–17 — p. 241

For growing symbol explanations, please see page 64.

Magnolia grandiflora

Catalpa bignonioides

×Chitalpa tashkentensis

Eucalyptus ficifolia

Jacaranda mimosifolia

Buddleja davidii

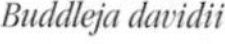

Caryopteris × clandonensis

Fuchsia triphylla hybrid 'Gartenmeister Bonstedt'

Hebe andersonii

Hydrangea macrophylla

Carpenteria californica
BUSH ANEMONE
5–9, 14–24 **p. 252**

Caryopteris
BLUEBEARD
ZONES VARY **p. 253**

Ceratostigma
ZONES VARY **p. 262**

Cistus (some)
ROCKROSE
4–9, 14–24 **p. 276**

Clerodendrum
NEEDS, ZONES VARY **p. 283**

Clethra
ZONES VARY **p. 284**

Daboecia
IRISH HEATH
ZONES VARY **p. 307**

Deutzia (some)
2–11, 14–17 **p. 313**

Escallonia
4–9, 14–24 **p. 335**

Fuchsia
ZONES VARY **p. 357**

Gardenia augusta
p. 360
7–9, 12–16, 18–24; H1, H2

Grewia occidentalis
LAVENDER STARFLOWER
8, 9, 12–24; H1, H2 **p. 376**

Hebe
14–24 **p. 380**

Hibiscus
ZONES VARY **p. 388**

Hydrangea
ZONES VARY **p. 394**

Hypericum (some)
ST. JOHNSWORT
ZONES VARY **p. 395**

Jasminum (some)
JASMINE
ZONES VARY **p. 408**

Justicia carnea
BRAZILIAN PLUME FLOWER
8, 9, 13–24; H1, H2 **p. 415**

Lavandula
LAVENDER
ZONES VARY **p. 425**

Lavatera
TREE MALLOW
ZONES VARY **p. 427**

Leucophyllum
TEXAS RANGER
7–24 **p. 430**

Melaleuca (some)
ZONES VARY **p. 464**

Nerium oleander
OLEANDER
8–16, 18–24; H1, H2 **p. 482**

Philadelphus (some)
MOCK ORANGE
ZONES VARY **p. 516**

Phlomis
ZONES VARY **p. 517**

Plumbago auriculata
CAPE PLUMBAGO
8, 9, 12–24; H1, H2 **p. 534**

Plumeria
FRANGIPANI
ZONES VARY **p. 538**

Potentilla
CINQUEFOIL
ZONES VARY **p. 544**

Punica granatum
POMEGRANATE
5–24; H1, H2 **p. 556**

Rosa (some)
ROSE
ZONES VARY **p. 579**

Salvia (several)
SAGE
NEEDS, ZONES VARY **p. 592**

Solanum rantonnetii
p. 612
12, 13, 15–24; H1, H2

Sollya heterophylla
AUSTRALIAN BLUEBELL CREEPER
8, 9, 14–24; H1, H2 **p. 612**

Spiraea (some)
ZONES VARY **p. 616**

Tecoma stans
YELLOW BELLS **p. 629**
12, 13, 21–24; H1, H2

Tibouchina urvilleana
PRINCESS FLOWER **p. 633**
14–17, 21–24; H1, H2

SUMMER
Vines

Antigonon leptopus
CORAL VINE **p. 188**
12, 13, 18–24; H1, H2

Jasminum nitidum

Lavandula angustifolia 'Hidcote'

Potentilla fruticosa

Tibouchina urvilleana

Antigonon leptopus

Plant listings continue ▶

Lonicera japonica

Passiflora mollissima

Podranea ricasoliana

Sollya heterophylla

Trachelospermum jasminoides

Beaumontia grandiflora
HERALD'S TRUMPET p. 219
12, 13, 16, 17, 21–24; H1, H2

Bougainvillea
p. 228
5, 6, 12–17, 19, 21–24; H1, H2

Campsis
TRUMPET CREEPER
ZONES VARY p. 247

Clematis (some)
ZONES VARY p. 282

Distictis
ZONES VARY p. 318

Fallopia baldschuanica
LACE VINE
A1–A3; 1–24 p. 347

Hibbertia scandens
GUINEA GOLD VINE
16, 17, 21–24 p. 388

Hydrangea anomala petiolaris
CLIMBING HYDRANGEA
A2, A3; 2–21 p. 394

Jasminum (some)
JASMINE
ZONES VARY p. 408

Lapageria rosea
CHILEAN BELLFLOWER
5, 6, 15–17, 23, 24 p. 423

Lonicera
HONEYSUCKLE
ZONES VARY p. 441

Mandevilla
ZONES VARY p. 461

Pandorea jasminoides
BOWER VINE
16–24; H1, H2 p. 495

Passiflora
PASSION VINE
ZONES VARY p. 499

Petrea volubilis
QUEEN'S WREATH
19–24; H1, H2 p. 514

Podranea ricasoliana
PINK TRUMPET VINE p. 539
9, 12, 13, 19–24; H1, H2

Rosa (some)
ROSE
ZONES VARY p. 579

Solanum jasminoides
POTATO VINE
8, 9, 12–24; H1, H2 p. 612

Trachelospermum jasminoides
STAR JASMINE
8–24; H1, H2 p. 636

FALL
Trees

Bauhinia × blakeana
HONG KONG ORCHID TREE p. 218
13, 19, 21, 23, 24; H1, H2

Chorisia
FLOSS SILK TREE
ZONES VARY p. 271

Erythrina humeana
NATAL CORAL TREE
12, 13, 20–24; H1, H2 p. 335

Eucalyptus erythrocorys
RED-CAP GUM
SEE CHART p. 339

Melaleuca (some)
ZONES VARY p. 464

Prunus × subhirtella 'Autumnalis'
2–7, 14–20 p. 551

FALL
Shrubs

Abelia
ZONES VARY p. 162

Alyogyne huegelii
BLUE HIBISCUS
13–17, 20–24; H1, H2 p. 182

Brugmansia
ANGEL'S TRUMPET p. 233
12, 13, 16–24; H1, H2

Buddleja davidii
BUTTERFLY BUSH
2–24; H1 p. 235

Caesalpinia
ZONES VARY p. 237

Camellia sasanqua
4–9, 12, 14–24 p. 246

Cassia (some)
ZONES VARY p. 254

Escallonia
4–9, 14–24 p. 335

Fuchsia
ZONES VARY p. 357

Hibiscus (some)
ZONES VARY p. 388

Lavatera
TREE MALLOW
ZONES VARY p. 427

Melaleuca nesophila

Alyogyne huegelii

Brugmansia 'Charles Grimaldi'

Fuchsia × hybrida

Lavatera thuringiaca

For growing symbol explanations, please see page 64.

Rosa 'Charmian'

Tibouchina urvilleana

Lonicera sempervirens

Bauhinia variegata 'Candida'

Chaenomeles

Melaleuca (some)
ZONES VARY p. 464

Nerium oleander
OLEANDER
8–16, 18–24; H1, H2 p. 482

Plumbago auriculata
CAPE PLUMBAGO
8, 9, 12–24; H1, H2 p. 534

Rosa (some)
ROSE
ZONES VARY p. 579

Salvia (some)
SAGE
NEEDS, ZONES VARY p. 592

Tibouchina urvilleana
PRINCESS FLOWER p. 633
14–17, 21–24; H1, H2

FALL
Vines

Antigonon leptopus
CORAL VINE
12, 13, 18–24; H1, H2 p. 188

Clematis (some)
ZONES VARY p. 282

Distictis buccinatoria
BLOOD-RED TRUMPET VINE
8, 9, 14–24; H1 p. 318

Lonicera (some)
HONEYSUCKLE
ZONES VARY p. 441

Mandevilla (some)
ZONES VARY p. 461

Millettia reticulata
EVERGREEN WISTERIA
6–9, 14–24 p. 469

WINTER
Trees

Acacia (many)
ZONES VARY p. 164

Bauhinia variegata
PURPLE ORCHID TREE
13, 18–24; H1, H2 p. 218

Erythrina (some)
CORAL TREE
ZONES VARY p. 334

Michelia doltsopa
14–24; H1, H2 p. 468

Prunus mume
JAPANESE FLOWERING APRICOT
3–9, 12–22 p. 553

WINTER
Shrubs

Acacia
ZONES VARY p. 164

Camellia (many)
4–9, 12, 14–24 p. 243

Cassia (most)
ZONES VARY p. 254

Chaenomeles
FLOWERING QUINCE
2–23 p. 264

Chamelaucium uncinatum
GERALDTON WAXFLOWER
8, 9, 12–24 p. 266

Chimonanthus praecox
WINTERSWEET
4–9, 14–21 p. 269

Corylopsis
WINTER HAZEL
ZONES VARY p. 294

Daphne (some)
NEEDS, ZONES VARY p. 309

Erica (many)
HEATH
ZONES VARY p. 329

Euphorbia pulcherrima
POINSETTIA
13, 16–24; H1, H2 p. 345

Forsythia
ZONES VARY p. 354

Hamamelis (most)
WITCH HAZEL
ZONES VARY p. 379

Jasminum mesnyi
PRIMROSE JASMINE
4–24; H1, H2 p. 408

Viburnum (some)
NEEDS, ZONES VARY p. 646

WINTER
Ground Covers, Vines

Gelsemium sempervirens
CAROLINA JESSAMINE
4–24 p. 362

Hardenbergia
LILAC VINE
ZONES VARY p. 380

Jasminum (some)
JASMINE
ZONES VARY p. 408

Daphne odora 'Aureo-marginata'

Mandevilla splendens

Forsythia × intermedia

Viburnum tinus

Hardenbergia violacea 'Happy Wanderer'

CUTTING FLOWERS

Centaurea cyanus

Bouquets of flowers beautify your home and make a satisfying reward for your gardening efforts. A wide range of plants provide lovely cut flowers, but this list focuses on those whose blossoms typically last for a week in water. Annuals and biennials must be planted every year, though a few (such as calendula and cosmos) may reseed themselves to ensure blossoms in the year to come. Perennials and most bulbs, in contrast, faithfully produce flowers for cutting year after year.

Cottage-style cutting garden features

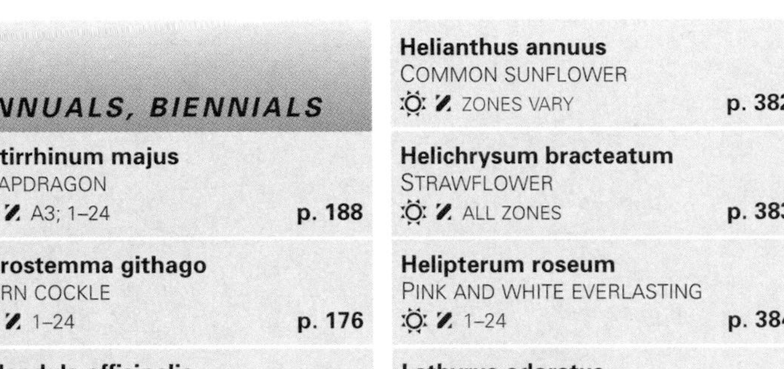
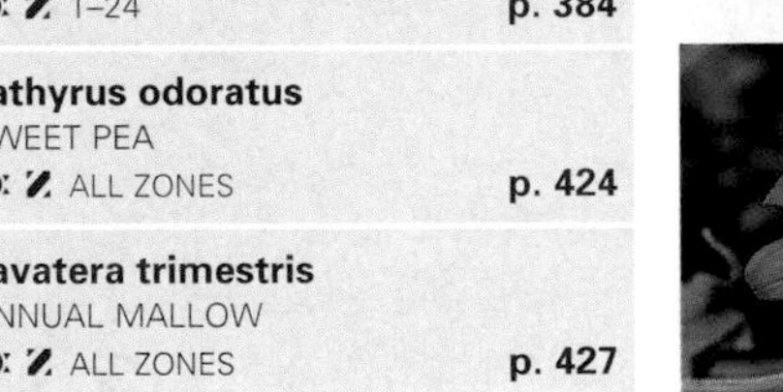
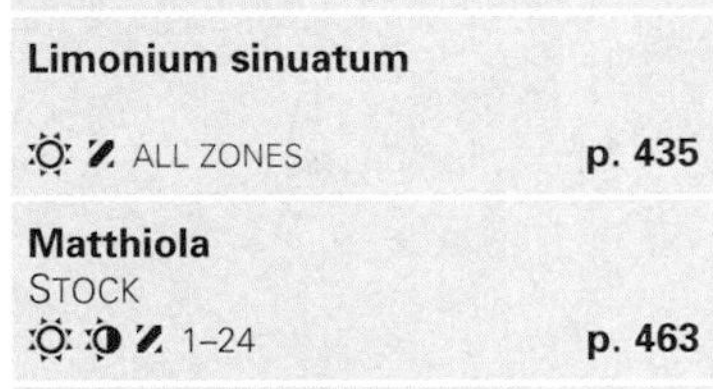
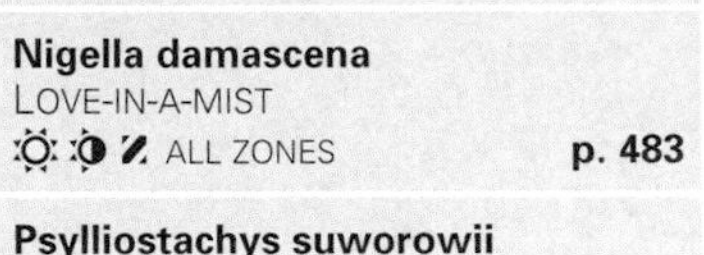
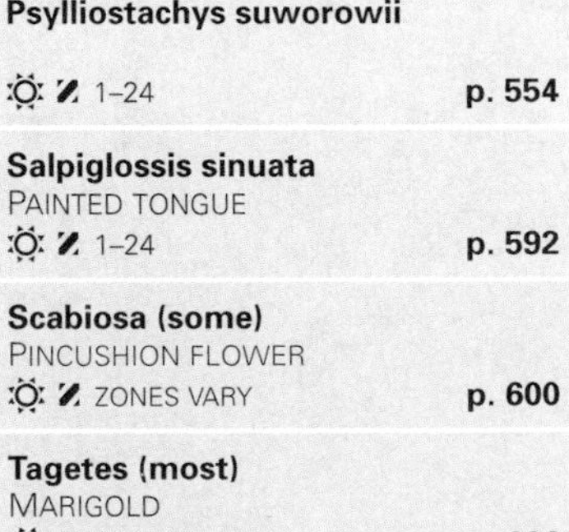
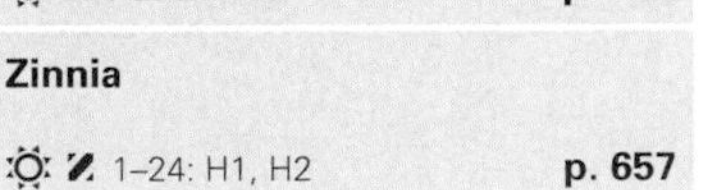

ANNUALS, BIENNIALS

Plant	Common name	Zones	Page
Antirrhinum majus	SNAPDRAGON	A3; 1–24	**p. 188**
Agrostemma githago	CORN COCKLE	1–24	**p. 176**
Calendula officinalis	CALENDULA	1–24: H1	**p. 239**
Callistephus chinensis	CHINA ASTER	1–24	**p. 240**
Centaurea cyanus	CORNFLOWER	1–24: H1, H2	**p. 260**
Clarkia amoena	FAREWELL-TO-SPRING	1–24	**p. 281**
Cleome hasslerana	SPIDER FLOWER	1–24	**p. 283**
Consolida ambigua	LARKSPUR	1–24	**p. 288**
Cosmos bipinnatus		1–24	**p. 295**
Dianthus (some)		A2, A3; 1–24	**p. 313**
Eustoma grandiflorum	LISIANTHUS	1–24	**p. 346**
Gomphrena globosa	GLOBE AMARANTH	1–24; H1, H2	**p. 368**
Gypsophila elegans		1–24	**p. 377**
Helianthus annuus	COMMON SUNFLOWER	ZONES VARY	**p. 382**
Helichrysum bracteatum	STRAWFLOWER	ALL ZONES	**p. 383**
Helipterum roseum	PINK AND WHITE EVERLASTING	1–24	**p. 384**
Lathyrus odoratus	SWEET PEA	ALL ZONES	**p. 424**
Lavatera trimestris	ANNUAL MALLOW	ALL ZONES	**p. 427**
Limonium sinuatum		ALL ZONES	**p. 435**
Matthiola	STOCK	1–24	**p. 463**
Nigella damascena	LOVE-IN-A-MIST	ALL ZONES	**p. 483**
Psylliostachys suworowii		1–24	**p. 554**
Salpiglossis sinuata	PAINTED TONGUE	1–24	**p. 592**
Scabiosa (some)	PINCUSHION FLOWER	ZONES VARY	**p. 600**
Tagetes (most)	MARIGOLD	ZONES VARY	**p. 626**
Tithonia rotundifolia	MEXICAN SUNFLOWER	ALL ZONES	**p. 634**
Zinnia		1–24: H1, H2	**p. 657**

Cleome hasslerana

Cosmos bipinnatus

Helianthus annuus

Scabiosa atropurpurea

Tagetes tenuifolia 'Lemon Gem'

Tithonia rotundifolia

Zinnia elegans

Consolida ambigua

For growing symbol explanations, please see page 64.

Cosmos bipinnatus and *Cleome hasslerana.*

Coreopsis grandiflora 'Early Sunrise'

Delphinium elatum Magic Fountains strain

Gerbera jamesonii

PERENNIALS, BULBS

Achillea (most)
YARROW
A1–A3; 1–24 **p. 170**

Alstroemeria
5–9, 14–24; H1 **p. 182**

Anemone coronaria
POPPY-FLOWERED ANEMONE
4–24 **p. 185**

Anemone × hybrida
JAPANESE ANEMONE
2B–24 **p. 185**

Aster
ZONES VARY **p. 207**

Bracteantha bracteata
BUSH STRAWFLOWER
8, 9, 14–24 **p. 231**

Campanula (some)
BELLFLOWER
1–9, 14–24 **p. 247**

Chrysanthemum (some)
NEEDS, ZONES VARY **p. 272**

Coreopsis (most)
ZONES VARY **p. 290**

Dahlia
1–24 **p. 307**

Delphinium
ZONES VARY **p. 311**

Dianthus (many)
A2, A3; 1–24 **p. 313**

Echinacea purpurea
PURPLE CONEFLOWER
A2, A3; 1–24 **p. 322**

Echinops
GLOBE THISTLE
A2, A3; 1–24 **p. 323**

Freesia
8, 9, 12–24 **p. 356**

Gaillardia × grandiflora
1–24; H1, H2 **p. 359**

Gerbera jamesonii
TRANSVAAL DAISY
8, 9, 12–24; H1, H2 **p. 365**

Gladiolus
4–9, 12–24; H1 **p. 366**

Gypsophila paniculata
BABY'S BREATH
A2, A3; 1–10, 14–16, 18–21; H1 **p. 377**

Helleborus (most)
HELLEBORE
ZONES VARY **p. 384**

Iris
NEEDS, ZONES VARY **p. 401**

Liatris spicata
GAYFEATHER
A2, A3; 1–10, 14–24 **p. 432**

Lilium
LILY
ZONES VARY **p. 433**

Limonium perezii
13, 15–17, 20–24 **p. 435**

Narcissus
DAFFODIL
A2, A3; 1–24 **p. 476**

Paeonia (herbaceous)
A1–A3; 1–11, 14–20 **p. 493**

Phlox paniculata
SUMMER PHLOX
1–14, 18–21 **p. 518**

Platycodon grandiflorus
BALLOON FLOWER
1–10, 14–24 **p. 532**

Polianthes tuberosa
TUBEROSE
7–9, 14–24; H1, H2 **p. 540**

Ranunculus asiaticus
PERSIAN RANUNCULUS
ALL ZONES **p. 564**

Rudbeckia hirta
GLORIOSA DAISY
1–24 **p. 589**

Scabiosa (some)
PINCUSHION FLOWER
ZONES VARY **p. 600**

Stokesia laevis
STOKES ASTER
2–10, 12–24 **p. 620**

Thalictrum aquilegifolium
2–10, 14–17 **p. 630**

Tulipa
TULIP
1–24 **p. 640**

Veronica spicata
A2, A3; 1–9, 14–21 **p. 646**

Zantedeschia
CALLA
5, 6, 8, 9, 12–24; H1, H2 **p. 655**

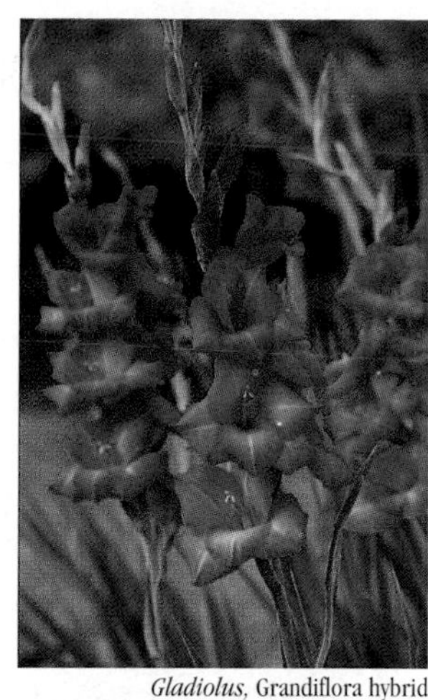
Gladiolus, Grandiflora hybrid

Helleborus orientalis

Phlox paniculata

Echinacea purpurea

Cosmos atrosanguineus

FRAGRANT

Flowering Plants

Lilac *(Syringa vulgaris)*, wisteria, and

A garden's fragrance can be as unforgettable as its appearance; the scent of a particular flower can at once evoke memories of past times and places. You can use fragrant plants in a variety of ways. En masse, they create a bathed-in-scent garden; set out in just a few spots, they provide a mystery perfume from who-knows-where. Plant them in containers to scent a deck or patio; locate them beneath a window to let fragrance waft indoors.

Elaeagnus angustifolia

Magnolia grandiflora

Brugmansia 'Charles Grimaldi'

Citrus 'Bearss' (Lime)

TREES

Plant	Growing / Zones	Page
Chionanthus virginicus FRINGE TREE	☼ ⁄ 2–6, 15–24	**p. 270**
Citrus	☼ ⁄ 8, 9, 12–24; H1, H2	**p. 276**
Cladrastis kentukea YELLOW WOOD	☼ ⁄ 2–9, 14–16	**p. 281**
Clethra arborea LILY-OF-THE-VALLEY TREE	☼ ◑ ⁄ 15–17, 21–24	**p. 284**
Elaeagnus angustifolia RUSSIAN OLIVE	☼ ◑ ⁄ A2, A3; 1–3, 7–14, 18, 19	**p. 324**
Hymenosporum flavum SWEETSHADE	☼ ◑ ⁄ 8, 9, 14–24	**p. 395**
Magnolia (many)	☼ ◑ ⁄ ZONES VARY	**p. 447**
Malus (some) FLOWERING CRABAPPLE	☼ ⁄ 1–11, 14–21	**p. 457**
Michelia	☼ ◑ ⁄ ZONES VARY	**p. 468**
Prunus, deciduous (many) FLOWERING PLUM	☼ ⁄ ZONES VARY	**p. 551**
Robinia (many) LOCUST	☼ ⁄ ZONES VARY	**p. 578**
Styrax obassia FRAGRANT SNOWBELL	☼ ◑ ⁄ 4–9, 14–21	**p. 622**

SHRUBS

Plant	Growing / Zones	Page
Acacia (several)	☼ ⁄ ZONES VARY	**p. 164**
Azara (some)	◑ ⁄ ZONES VARY	**p. 211**
Boronia	☼ ◑ ⁄ ZONES VARY	**p. 228**
Bouvardia longiflora 'Albatross'	◑ ⁄ 12, 16, 17, 19–24	**p. 230**
Brugmansia (several) ANGEL'S TRUMPET	☼ ◑ ● ⁄ 12, 13, 16–24; H1, H2	**p. 233**
Buddleja BUTTERFLY BUSH	☼ ◑ ⁄ ZONES VARY	**p. 234**
Carissa macrocarpa NATAL PLUM	☼ ◑ ⁄ 22–24; H2	**p. 251**
Carpenteria californica BUSH ANEMONE	☼ ◑ ⁄ 5–9, 14–24	**p. 252**
Cestrum (some)	◑ ⁄ ZONES VARY	**p. 264**
Chimonanthus praecox WINTERSWEET	☼ ◑ ⁄ 4–9, 14–21	**p. 269**
Choisya ternata MEXICAN ORANGE	☼ ◑ ⁄ 4–9, 14–24	**p. 271**
Clerodendrum bungei CASHMERE BOUQUET	◑ ● ⁄ 5–9, 12–24	**p. 284**

Buddleja davidii

Gardenia augusta 'Radicans'

Choisya ternata

Clethra alnifolia

For growing symbol explanations, please see page 64.

a climbing rose perfume the spring air.

Corylopsis pauciflora

Daphne × burkwoodii

Jasminum nitidum

Lonicera japonica

Clethra alnifolia
SUMMERSWEET
A2, A3; 1–6 p. 284

Corylopsis
WINTER HAZEL
ZONES VARY p. 294

Daphne (many)
NEEDS, ZONES VARY p. 309

Elaeagnus
ZONES VARY p. 324

Gardenia
ZONES VARY p. 360

Hamamelis
WITCH HAZEL
ZONES VARY p. 379

Jasminum (some)
JASMINE
ZONES VARY p. 408

Lavandula (most)
LAVENDER
ZONES VARY p. 425

Lonicera
HONEYSUCKLE
ZONES VARY p. 441

Magnolia stellata
STAR MAGNOLIA
2B–9, 14–24 p. 453

Michelia
ZONES VARY p. 468

Murraya paniculata
ORANGE JESSAMINE
21–24; H1, H2 p. 473

Osmanthus (most)
ZONES VARY p. 490

Philadelphus (most)
MOCK ORANGE
ZONES VARY p. 516

Pittosporum (several)
ZONES VARY p. 531

Plumeria
ZONES VARY p. 538

Rhaphiolepis 'Majestic Beauty'
8–10, 12–24; H1, H2 p. 567

Rhododendron 'Else Frye'
4–6, 15–17 p. 570

Rhododendron 'Fragrantissimum'
4–6, 15–17 p. 570

Rhododendron, Loderi hybrids
4–6, 15–17 p. 571

Rhododendron, Maddenii hybrids
15–17 p. 568

Rhododendron, Viscosum hybrids
DECIDUOUS AZALEAS
3–7 p. 574

Ribes odoratum
A2, A3; 1–10, 14–17 p. 577

Rosa (many)
ROSE
NEEDS, ZONES VARY p. 579

Sarcococca
SWEET BOX
4–9, 14–24 p. 599

Skimmia japonica
4–9, 14–22 p. 610

Sophora secundiflora
TEXAS MOUNTAIN LAUREL
8–16, 18–24 p. 613

Syringa (many)
LILAC
ZONES VARY p. 624

Viburnum (several)
NEEDS, ZONES VARY p. 646

VINES

Beaumontia grandiflora
HERALD'S TRUMPET p. 219
12, 13, 16, 17, 21–24; H1, H2

Clematis armandii
EVERGREEN CLEMATIS
4–9, 12–24 p. 282

Distictis laxiflora
VANILLA TRUMPET VINE
16, 22–24; H1, H2 p. 318

Gelsemium sempervirens
CAROLINA JESSAMINE
4–24 p. 362

Hoya carnosa
WAX FLOWER
15–24; H1, H2 p. 392

Ipomoea alba
MOONFLOWER
ALL ZONES p. 400

Jasminum (some)
JASMINE
ZONES VARY p. 408

Lonicera (some)
HONEYSUCKLE
ZONES VARY p. 441

Plant listings continue ▶

Philadelphus coronarius

Michelia figo

Pittosporum tobira

Rosa 'Iceberg'

Sophora secundiflora

Jasminum polyanthum

Passiflora × alatocaerulea

Crinum × powellii 'Album'

Dianthus plumarius

Iris, tall bearded

Plant	Zones	Page
Mandevilla laxa CHILEAN JASMINE	4–9, 14–24	**p. 461**
Passiflora × alatocaerulea	5–9, 12–24; H1, H2	**p. 499**
Stephanotis floribunda MADAGASCAR JASMINE	23, 24; H2	**p. 619**
Trachelospermum STAR JASMINE	ZONES VARY	**p. 636**
Wisteria	ZONES VARY	**p. 652**

PERENNIALS, ANNUALS, BULBS

Plant	Zones	Page
Amaryllis belladonna BELLADONNA LILY	4–24	**p. 183**
Centaurea moschata SWEET SULTAN	1–24	**p. 260**
Convallaria majalis LILY-OF-THE-VALLEY	A1–A3; 1–7, 14–20	**p. 288**
Cosmos atrosanguineus CHOCOLATE COSMOS	4–9, 14–24	**p. 295**
Crinum	8, 9, 12–24; H1, H2	**p. 299**
Crocus chrysanthus	1–24	**p. 300**
Dianthus (some)	A2, A3; 1–24	**p. 313**
Erysimum cheiri ENGLISH WALLFLOWER	4–6, 14–17, 22, 23	**p. 334**
Freesia (some)	8, 9, 12–24	**p. 356**
Hedychium coronarium WHITE GINGER	8, 9, 14–17, 19–24; H1, H2	**p. 381**
Heliotropium arborescens COMMON HELIOTROPE	ALL ZONES	**p. 384**
Hemerocallis lilioasphodelus LEMON DAYLILY	1–24; H1, H2	**p. 385**
Hosta plantaginea FRAGRANT PLANTAIN LILY	1–10, 14–24	**p. 392**
Hyacinthus HYACINTH	ZONES VARY	**p. 393**
Hymenocallis	5, 6, 8, 9, 14–24	**p. 395**
Iberis amara HYACINTH-FLOWERED CANDYTUFT	1–24	**p. 396**
Ipomoea alba MOONFLOWER	ALL ZONES	**p. 400**
Iris, bearded (many)	1–24	**p. 402**
Lathyrus odoratus SWEET PEA	ALL ZONES	**p. 424**
Lilium (many) LILY	ZONES VARY	**p. 433**
Matthiola STOCK	1–24	**p. 463**
Narcissus (many) DAFFODIL	A2, A3; 1–24	**p. 477**
Nelumbo LOTUS	1–24; H1, H2	**p. 479**
Nicotiana	ALL ZONES	**p. 482**
Paeonia (many) PEONY	ZONES VARY	**p. 493**
Phlox paniculata SUMMER PHLOX	1–14, 18–21	**p. 518**
Polianthes tuberosa TUBEROSE	7–9, 14–24; H1, H2	**p. 540**
Primula alpicola MOONLIGHT PRIMROSE	3–6, 17	**p. 546**
Primula vulgaris (some) ENGLISH PRIMROSE	MOST ZONES	**p. 547**
Reseda odorata MIGNONETTE	ALL ZONES	**p. 566**
Tropaeolum majus GARDEN NASTURTIUM	ALL ZONES	**p. 639**
Viola odorata SWEET VIOLET	1–24	**p. 649**

Lilium 'Stargazer'

Nelumbo nucifera

Nicotiana alata hybrids

Phlox paniculata 'Franz Schubert'

For growing symbol explanations, please see page 64.

COLOR

Celastrus scandens with mockingbird

COLORFUL FRUITS AND BERRIES

Citrus (Calamondin)

The plants listed below produce showy fruits and berries in a variety of colors—red, orange, yellow, cream, white, blue, purple, black. In some, the fruits follow an equally striking floral display; in others, the show comes as a brilliant surprise after unremarkable blossoms. Certain fruits, notably those of firethorn and toyon, are attractive to birds. And some—such as citrus and persimmon—provide the gardener with both visual and edible treats.

Malus 'Red Jade'

Persimmon

Sambucus mexicana

TREES

Plant	Common name	Exposure / Zones	Page
Acmena smithii	LILLY-PILLY TREE	☼ ⁄ 15–17, 19–24	p. 170
Amelanchier	JUNEBERRY	☼ ◑ ⁄ ZONES VARY	p. 183
Citrus		☼ ⁄ 8, 9, 12–24; H1, H2	p. 276
Cornus	DOGWOOD	☼ ◑ ⁄ ZONES VARY	p. 291
Crataegus	HAWTHORN	☼ ⁄ 2–12, 14–17	p. 298
Eriobotrya japonica	LOQUAT	☼ ◑ ⁄ 6–24; H1, H2	p. 333
Ilex (many)	HOLLY	☼ ◑ ⁄ ZONES VARY	p. 397
Koelreuteria		☼ ⁄ ZONES VARY	p. 419
Malus	FLOWERING CRABAPPLE	☼ ⁄ 1–11, 14–21	p. 457
Persimmon		☼ ⁄ ZONES VARY	p. 513
Pittosporum (most)		☼ ◑ ⁄ ZONES VARY	p. 531
Sambucus	ELDERBERRY	☼ ◑ ⁄ ZONES VARY	p. 597
Schinus	PEPPER TREE	☼ ⁄ ZONES VARY	p. 602
Sorbus	MOUNTAIN ASH	☼ ◑ ⁄ ZONES VARY	p. 613
Syzygium paniculatum	BRUSH CHERRY	☼ ◑ ⁄ 16, 17, 20–24, H1, H2	p. 626

SHRUBS

Plant	Common name	Exposure / Zones	Page
Arbutus unedo	STRAWBERRY TREE	☼ ◑ ⁄ 4–24	p. 197
Aronia	CHOKEBERRY	☼ ◑ ⁄ ZONES VARY	p. 201
Aucuba japonica	JAPANESE AUCUBA	◑ ● ⁄ 4–24	p. 209
Berberis (many)	BARBERRY	☼ ◑ ⁄ ZONES VARY	p. 221
Callicarpa bodinieri	BODINIER BEAUTYBERRY	☼ ◑ ⁄ 3–9, 14–24	p. 240
Carissa macrocarpa	NATAL PLUM	☼ ◑ ⁄ 22–24; H2	p. 251
Clerodendrum trichotomum	HARLEQUIN GLORYBOWER	◑ ⁄ 5, 6, 15–17, 20–24	p. 284
Cornus kousa	KOUSA DOGWOOD	☼ ◑ ⁄ 2–9, 14–17	p. 292
Cornus mas	CORNELIAN CHERRY	☼ ◑ ⁄ 1–6	p. 292

Sorbus aucuparia

Arbutus unedo 'Elfin King'

Carissa macrocarpa

Plant listings continue ▶

Cotoneaster lacteus

Ilex aquifolium

Mahonia lomariifolia

Heteromeles arbutifolia

Ochna serrulata

Corokia cotoneaster
4–24 — p. 293

Corylus
FILBERT, HAZELNUT
2–9, 14–20 — p. 294

Cotoneaster
ZONES VARY — p. 296

Daphne mezereum
FEBRUARY DAPHNE
2–7, 14–17 — p. 310

Elaeagnus
ZONES VARY — p. 324

Euonymus (many)
NEEDS, ZONES VARY — p. 342

Fatsia japonica
JAPANESE ARALIA
4–9, 14–24; H1, H2 — p. 348

Heptacodium miconioides
SEVEN SONS FLOWER
2B–6, 14–17 — p. 386

Heteromeles arbutifolia
TOYON
5–9, 14–24 — p. 386

Ilex (many)
HOLLY
ZONES VARY — p. 397

Kolkwitzia amabilis
BEAUTY BUSH
2–11, 14–20 — p. 419

Lonicera (most shrubby types)
HONEYSUCKLE
ZONES VARY — p. 441

Mahonia
NEEDS, ZONES VARY — p. 455

Myrtus communis
MYRTLE
8–24; H1, H2 — p. 476

Nandina domestica
HEAVENLY BAMBOO
3–24; H1, H2 — p. 476

Ochna serrulata
BIRD'S-EYE BUSH
14–24 — p. 484

Pernettya mucronata
4–7, 15–17 — p. 512

Photinia (most)
ZONES VARY — p. 519

Punica granatum (some)
POMEGRANATE
5–24; H1, H2 — p. 556

Pyracantha
FIRETHORN
ZONES VARY — p. 557

Rhaphiolepis
4–10, 12–24; H1, H2 — p. 567

Rhus typhina
STAGHORN SUMAC
A1–A3; 1–10, 14–17 — p. 576

Ribes (some)
CURRANT, GOOSEBERRY
ZONES VARY — p. 577

Rosa (many, especially rugosas)
ROSE
ZONES VARY — p. 579

Sarcococca ruscifolia
SWEET BOX
4–9, 14–24 — p. 599

Skimmia japonica
4–9, 14–22 — p. 610

Symphoricarpos
SNOWBERRY
NEEDS, ZONES VARY — p. 624

Ugni molinae
CHILEAN GUAVA
14–24 — p. 642

Vaccinium
NEEDS, ZONES VARY — p. 643

Viburnum (many)
NEEDS, ZONES VARY — p. 646

VINES

Ampelopsis brevipedunculata
PORCELAIN BERRY
2–24 — p. 184

Celastrus
BITTERSWEET
ZONES VARY — p. 259

Euonymus fortunei (some)
2B–17 — p. 343

Grape
ZONES VARY — p. 369

Lonicera (some)
HONEYSUCKLE
ZONES VARY — p. 441

Rosa (some)
ROSE
ZONES VARY — p. 579

Solanum (some)
ZONES VARY — p. 611

Punica granatum 'Wonderful'

Pyracantha

Rosa rugosa

Viburnum trilobum

Euonymus fortunei

Canna 'Pretoria'

COLORED FOLIAGE

Not all color comes from flowers or fruit. The plants listed below offer long-term garden accents in the form of colored leaves: gray or silver, bronze, red or purple, yellow or gold, blue, and variegated. They can be used to enliven the basic green of other garden foliage, to form contrasting combinations (such as gray and red) with one another, to complement flower colors in season, and to provide eye-catching focal points.

Caladium bicolor 'Florida Elise'

Elaeagnus angustifolia

Eucalyptus pulverulenta

Santolina chamaecyparissus

GRAY, SILVER
Trees

Cupressus arizonica glabra
SMOOTH ARIZONA CYPRESS
☼ ⁄ 7–24 — p. 303

Elaeagnus angustifolia
RUSSIAN OLIVE — p. 324
☼ ◐ ⁄ A2, A3; 1–3, 7–14, 18, 19

Eucalyptus (many)
☼ ⁄ ZONES VARY — p. 337

GRAY, SILVER
Shrubs

Cistus (several)
ROCKROSE
☼ ⁄ 4–9, 14–24 — p. 276

Convolvulus cneorum
BUSH MORNING GLORY
☼ ◐ ⁄ 5–9, 12–24 — p. 289

Elaeagnus 'Coral Silver'
☼ ◐ ⁄ 2B–24 — p. 324

Feijoa, Pineapple guava
☼ ⁄ 6–9, 12–24; H1, H2 — p. 348

Helianthemum nummularium (some)
SUNROSE
☼ ⁄ 2B–9, 14–24 — p. 382

Juniperus (many)
JUNIPER
☼ ◐ ⁄ ZONES VARY — p. 410

Lavandula (most)
LAVENDER
☼ ⁄ ZONES VARY — p. 425

Leucophyllum frutescens
TEXAS RANGER
☼ ⁄ 7–24; H1, H2 — p. 430

Salvia leucophylla
PURPLE SAGE
☼ ⁄ 8, 9, 14–17, 19–24 — p. 595

Santolina chamaecyparissus
LAVENDER COTTON
☼ ⁄ 2–24; H1, H2 — p. 598

Teucrium fruticans
BUSH GERMANDER
☼ ⁄ 4–24 — p. 630

GRAY, SILVER
Perennials

Achillea (many)
YARROW
☼ ⁄ A1–A3; 1–24 — p. 170

Artemisia (many)
☼ ⁄ ZONES VARY — p. 201

Centaurea cineraria
DUSTY MILLER
☼ ⁄ 8–24; H1, H2 — p. 260

Cerastium tomentosum
SNOW-IN-SUMMER
☼ ◐ ⁄ A1, A2; 1–24 — p. 261

Echeveria (many)
☼ ◐ ⁄ ZONES VARY — p. 322

Erysimum 'Bowles Mauve'
☼ ◐ ⁄ 4–6, 14–17, 22, 23 — p. 334

Helichrysum petiolare
LICORICE PLANT
☼ ⁄ 16, 17, 22–24 — p. 383

Lychnis coronaria
CROWN-PINK
☼ ◐ ⁄ 1–9, 14–24 — p. 444

Perovskia
RUSSIAN SAGE
☼ ⁄ 2–24 — p. 512

Romneya coulteri
MATILIJA POPPY
☼ ⁄ 4–12, 14–24; H1 — p. 578

Salvia chamaedryoides
GERMANDER SAGE
☼ ⁄ 8, 9, 12, 14–24 — p. 593

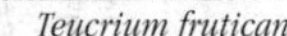

Teucrium fruticans

Cerastium tomentosum

Echeveria secunda

Achillea 'Moonshine'

Plant listings continue ▶

Helichrysum petiolare

Salvia chamaedryoides

Stachys byzantina

Acer palmatum 'Ever Red'

Cercis canadensis 'Forest Pansy'

Salvia officinalis 'Berggarten'
GARDEN SAGE 'MOUNTAIN GARDEN'
☼ ◩ 2–24; H1, H2 **p. 596**

Senecio cineraria
DUSTY MILLER
☼ ◩ 4–24; H1, H2 **p. 606**

Stachys byzantina
LAMB'S EARS
☼ ◑ ◩ 1–24 **p. 618**

Thymus (several)
THYME
☼ ◑ ◩ ZONES VARY **p. 632**

Zauschneria
CALIFORNIA FUCHSIA
NEEDS, ZONES VARY **p. 656**

BRONZE, RED, PURPLE
Trees

Acer palmatum (some)
JAPANESE MAPLE
☼ ◑ ◩ A3; 2–10, 12, 14–24 **p. 168**

Acer platanoides (some)
NORWAY MAPLE
☼ ◑ ◩ A2, A3; 1–9, 14–17 **p. 169**

Cercis canadensis 'Forest Pansy'
EASTERN REDBUD
☼ ◩ 1–24 **p. 263**

Cordyline australis 'Atropurpurea'
☼ ◩ 5, 8–11, 14–24; H1, H2 **p. 290**

Cotinus coggygria (some)
SMOKE TREE
☼ ◩ 2–24 **p. 296**

Eriobotrya deflexa
BRONZE LOQUAT
☼ ◑ ◩ 8–24 **p. 333**

Fagus sylvatica (some)
EUROPEAN BEECH
☼ ◑ ◩ A3; 2B–9, 14–21 **p. 347**

Malus (some)
FLOWERING CRABAPPLE
☼ ◩ 1–11, 14–21 **p. 457**

Prunus cerasifera (most)
CHERRY PLUM
☼ ◩ 3–22 **p. 552**

BRONZE, RED, PURPLE
Shrubs

Berberis thunbergii (several)
JAPANESE BARBERRY
☼ ◑ ◩ A3; 2B–24 **p. 222**

Corylus (several)
FILBERT, HAZELNUT
☼ ◑ ◩ 2–9, 14–20 **p. 294**

Dodonaea viscosa 'Purpurea'
PURPLE HOP BUSH
☼ ◑ ◩ 7–24; H1, H2 **p. 319**

Prunus × cistena
DWARF RED-LEAF PLUM
☼ ◩ A3; 1–22 **p. 552**

BRONZE, RED, PURPLE
Perennials

Aeonium arboreum 'Atropurpureum'
☼ ◑ ◩ 15–17, 20–24 **p. 173**

Ajuga reptans (several)
CARPET BUGLE
☼ ◑ ◩ A2, A3; 1–24 **p. 176**

Anthriscus sylvestris 'Ravenswing'
☼ ◑ ◩ 1–9, 14–24 **p. 187**

Astilbe × arendsii 'Fanal'
FALSE SPIRAEA
☼ ◑ ◩ 1–9, 14–24 **p. 208**

Bergenia (some)
◑ ● ◩ A1, A3; 1–9, 12–24 **p. 222**

Canna (some)
☼ ◩ 6–9, 12–24; H1, H2 **p. 249**

Euphorbia amygdaloides 'Purpurea'
☼ ◩ 2B–24 **p. 344**

Heuchera micrantha 'Palace Purple'
☼ ◑ ◩ 1–10, 14–24 **p. 387**

Imperata cylindrica 'Rubra'
JAPANESE BLOOD GRASS
☼ ◑ ◩ 2B–24 **p. 399**

Pennisetum setaceum 'Rubrum'
☼ ◩ 8–24; H1, H2 **p. 510**

Phormium tenax (several)
NEW ZEALAND FLAX
☼ ◑ ◩ 5–9, 14–24; H1, H2 **p. 519**

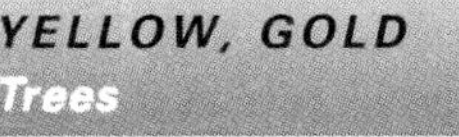

YELLOW, GOLD
Trees

Chamaecyparis lawsoniana (some)
PORT ORFORD CEDAR
☼ ◑ ◩ A3; 3–6, 15–17 **p. 265**

Gleditsia triacanthos 'Sunburst'
SUNBURST HONEY LOCUST
☼ ◩ 1–16, 18–20 **p. 367**

Robinia pseudoacacia 'Frisia'
☼ ◩ 1–24 **p. 578**

Sambucus (some)
ELDERBERRY
☼ ◑ ◩ ZONES VARY **p. 597**

Thuja plicata
☼ ◑ ◩ A3; 1–9, 14–24 **p. 631**

Cotinus coggygria 'Royal Purple'

Berberis thunbergii 'Atropurpurea'

Canna 'Tropicanna'

Heuchera micrantha 'Palace Purple'

Imperata cylindrica 'Rubra'

For growing symbol explanations, please see page 64.

Chamaecyparis lawsoniana 'Golden King'

Chrysanthemum parthenium 'Aureum'

Helichrysum petiolare 'Limelight'

Taxus baccata 'Aurea'

YELLOW, GOLD
Shrubs, Perennials

Acer shirasawanum 'Aureum'
GOLDEN FULL MOON MAPLE
3B–6, 14–16 — p. 169

Calluna vulgaris (several)
SCOTCH HEATHER
1A, 2–6, 15–17 — p. 241

Caryopteris × clandonensis 'Worcester Gold'
2B–9, 14–24 — p. 253

Chamaecyparis (some)
FALSE CYPRESS
ZONES VARY — p. 265

Chrysanthemum parthenium 'Aureum'
2–24 — p. 274

Coleonema pulchrum 'Sunset Gold'
PINK BREATH OF HEAVEN
7–9, 14–24 — p. 287

Helichrysum petiolare 'Limelight'
LICORICE PLANT
16, 17, 22–24 — p. 383

Hosta (several)
PLANTAIN LILY
ZONES VARY — p. 391

Juniperus (several)
JUNIPER
ZONES VARY — p. 410

Ligustrum 'Vicaryi'
VICARY GOLDEN PRIVET
2–24 — p. 433

Milium effusum 'Aureum'
BOWLES' GOLDEN GRASS
3B–9, 14–17 — p. 469

Spiraea japonica (several)
A2, 3; 2–10, 14–21 — p. 616

Taxus baccata (several)
ENGLISH YEW
A3; 3–9, 14–24 — p. 628

Thuja occidentalis (some)
ZONES VARY — p. 631

Thuja orientalis (several)
ORIENTAL ARBORVITAE
2–24; H1, H2 — p. 631

Viburnum opulus 'Aureum'
1–9, 14–24 — p. 647

BLUE
Trees

Cedrus atlantica 'Glauca'
ATLAS CEDAR
3B–10, 14–24 — p. 256

Chamaecyparis lawsoniana (some)
PORT ORFORD CEDAR
A3; 3–6, 15–17 — p. 265

Eucalyptus (some)
ZONES VARY — p. 337

Picea pungens (some)
COLORADO SPRUCE
A2, A3; 1–10, 14–17 — p. 521

BLUE
Shrubs, Perennials

Chamaecyparis lawsoniana (some)
PORT ORFORD CEDAR
A3; 3–6, 15–17 — p. 265

Festuca (several)
FESCUE
ZONES VARY — p. 349

Hosta (several)
PLANTAIN LILY
ZONES VARY — p. 391

Panicum virgatum (some)
SWITCH GRASS
1–11, 14–23 — p. 495

Ruta graveolens 'Jackman's Blue'
RUE
2–24 — p. 590

VARIEGATED
Trees

Acer negundo 'Variegatum'
VARIEGATED BOX ELDER
A2, A3; 1–10, 12–24 — p. 168

Cornus florida (several)
FLOWERING DOGWOOD
2B–9, 14–16 — p. 292

Fagus sylvatica 'Tricolor'
TRICOLOR BEECH
A3; 2B–9, 14–21 — p. 347

VARIEGATED
Shrubs

Aucuba japonica (several)
JAPANESE AUCUBA
4–24 — p. 209

Bougainvillea (some)
5, 6, 12–17, 19, 21–24; H1, H2 — p. 228

Buddleja davidii 'Harlequin'
BUTTERFLY BUSH
2–24; H1 — p. 235

Cotoneaster horizontalis 'Variegatus'
A3; 2B–11, 14–24 — p. 296

Daphne odora 'Marginata'
WINTER DAPHNE
4–10, 12, 14–24 — p. 310

Plant listings continue ▶

Eucalyptus perriniana

Picea pungens

Ruta graveolens 'Jackman's Blue'

Cornus florida 'Welchii'

Aucuba japonica 'Variegata'

Bougainvillea 'Hawaii'

Myrtus communis 'Variegata'

Pittosporum tobira 'Variegata'

Weigela hybrid 'Variegata'

Actinidia kolomikta

Elaeagnus pungens (some)
SILVERBERRY
☼ ◑ ⁄ 4–24 **p. 325**

Euonymus (some)
NEEDS, ZONES VARY **p. 342**

Hydrangea macrophylla (several)
BIG-LEAF HYDRANGEA
☼ ◑ ⁄ 3B–9, 14–24; H1 **p. 394**

Ilex (several)
HOLLY
☼ ◑ ⁄ ZONES VARY **p. 397**

Juniperus (several)
JUNIPER
☼ ◑ ⁄ ZONES VARY **p. 410**

Leucothoe walteri 'Rainbow'
DROOPING LEUCOTHOE
☼ ◑ ● ⁄ 4–7, 15–17 **p. 431**

Myrtus communis (several)
MYRTLE
☼ ◑ ⁄ 8–24; H1, H2 **p. 476**

Osmanthus heterophyllus 'Variegatus'
☼ ◑ ⁄ 4–10, 14–24 **p. 490**

Pieris japonica 'Variegata'
LILY-OF-THE-VALLEY SHRUB
◑ ⁄ 2B–9, 14–17 **p. 522**

Pittosporum tobira (several)
TOBIRA
☼ ◑ ⁄ 4–24; H1, H2 **p. 531**

Viburnum tinus 'Variegatum'
☼ ◑ ⁄ 4–9, 14–24 **p. 648**

Weigela hybrid 'Variegata'
☼ ◑ ⁄ 1–11, 14–21 **p. 652**

VARIEGATED Vines

Actinidia kolomikta
☼ ◑ ⁄ A1–A3; 1–9, 15–17 **p. 171**

Hedera (some)
IVY
☼ ◑ ⁄ ZONES VARY **p. 380**

Lonicera japonica 'Aureo-reticulata'
GOLDNET HONEYSUCKLE
☼ ◑ ⁄ 1–24; H1, H2 **p. 441**

VARIEGATED Perennials

Aegopodium podagraria 'Variegatum' **p. 173**
☼ ◑ ● ⁄ A1–A3;1–9, 12, 14–24

Ajuga reptans (some)
CARPET BUGLE
☼ ◑ ⁄ A2, A3; 1–24 **p. 176**

Caladium bicolor
FANCY-LEAFED CALADIUM
◑ ● ⁄ H2 **p. 237**

Coleus × hybridus
COLEUS
☼ ◑ ⁄ 24; H1, H2 **p. 287**

Gaura lindheimeri (some)
☼ ⁄ 2B–24 **p. 361**

Helichrysum petiolare 'Variegatum'
LICORICE PLANT
☼ ⁄ 16, 17, 22–24 **p. 383**

Heuchera (some)
CORAL BELLS
☼ ◑ ⁄ ZONES VARY **p. 387**

Hosta (many)
PLANTAIN LILY
◑ ● ⁄ ZONES VARY **p. 391**

Houttuynia cordata 'Variegata'
☼ ◑ ● ⁄ 2–9, 14–24 **p. 392**

Impatiens, New Guinea hybrids
◑ ⁄ 24; H1, H2 **p. 399**

Lamium (several)
DEAD NETTLE
◑ ● ⁄ ZONES VARY **p. 422**

Liriope muscari (some)
BIG BLUE LILY TURF
☼ ◑ ● ⁄ 2B–10, 14–24; H1, H2 **p. 439**

Miscanthus sinensis (several)
EULALIA
☼ ◑ ⁄ 2–24 **p. 470**

Pachysandra terminalis 'Variegata'
JAPANESE SPURGE
◑ ● ⁄ 2–10, 14–21 **p. 493**

Pelargonium (several)
GERANIUM
☼ ◑ ⁄ 8, 9, 12–24 **p. 509**

Phormium (many)
NEW ZEALAND FLAX
☼ ◑ ⁄ 5–9, 14–24; H1, H2 **p. 519**

Physostegia virginiana 'Variegata'
FALSE DRAGONHEAD
☼ ◑ ⁄ A3; 1–9, 14–24 **p. 521**

Pulmonaria (several)
LUNGWORT
◑ ● ⁄ 1–9, 14–17 **p. 555**

Salvia officinalis (some)
GARDEN SAGE
☼ ⁄ 2–24 **p. 596**

Tulbaghia violacea (some)
SOCIETY GARLIC
☼ ⁄ 13–24; H1, H2 **p. 640**

Vinca (some)
PERIWINKLE
☼ ◑ ● ⁄ ZONES VARY **p. 648**

Hedera helix 'Buttercup'

Lamium maculatum

Pelargonium 'Golden Ears'

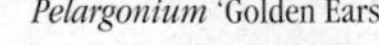

Phormium 'Yellow Wave'

Salvia officinalis 'Tricolor'

For growing symbol explanations, please see page 64.

Autumnal planting with maples

AUTUMN FOLIAGE COLOR

Liquidambar styraciflua 'Palo Alto'

Yellow, gold, russet, orange, red, burgundy: in much of the West, foliage in these warm colors means autumn has arrived. To bring these hues to your fall garden, look to the following plants. Because color can vary within a species, it's wise to shop in fall, while colors are changing—or simply to buy selected varieties with known, reliable fall color. Keep in mind that climate can affect color change; in general, it's less of a feature in mild-winter areas.

Cornus florida

Crataegus

Ginkgo biloba

Gleditsia triacanthos

TREES

Acer (many)
MAPLE
ZONES VARY — **p. 167**

Amelanchier
JUNEBERRY
ZONES VARY — **p. 183**

Betula
BIRCH
ZONES VARY — **p. 223**

Cercidiphyllum japonicum
KATSURA TREE
2B–6, 14–16, 18–20 — **p. 262**

Cercis canadensis
EASTERN REDBUD
1–24 — **p. 263**

Cladrastis kentukea
YELLOW WOOD
2–9, 14–16 — **p. 281**

Cornus (many)
DOGWOOD
ZONES VARY — **p. 291**

Crataegus (some)
HAWTHORN
2–12, 14–17 — **p. 298**

Franklinia alatamaha
3B–6, 14–17 — **p. 355**

Fraxinus (deciduous)
ASH
ZONES VARY — **p. 355**

Ginkgo biloba
MAIDENHAIR TREE
A3; 1–10, 12, 14–24 — **p. 366**

Gleditsia triacanthos
HONEY LOCUST
1–16,18–20 — **p. 367**

Halesia
2B–9, 14–21 — **p. 378**

Koelreuteria bipinnata
CHINESE FLAME TREE
8–24; H1 — **p. 419**

Lagerstroemia indica
CRAPE MYRTLE
2–10, 12–24; H1, H2 — **p. 421**

Larix
LARCH
ZONES VARY — **p. 423**

Liquidambar
SWEET GUM
ZONES VARY — **p. 437**

Liriodendron tulipifera
TULIP TREE
2–12, 14–24 — **p. 437**

Malus
FLOWERING CRABAPPLE
1–11, 14–21 — **p. 457**

Metasequoia glyptostroboides
DAWN REDWOOD
A3; 3–10, 14–24 — **p. 467**

Morus alba
WHITE MULBERRY
2–24; H1, H2 — **p. 472**

Nyssa sylvatica
SOUR GUM
2–10, 14–21 — **p. 484**

Oxydendrum arboreum
SOURWOOD
2B–9, 14–17 — **p. 492**

Parrotia persica
PERSIAN PARROTIA
2B–7, 14–17 — **p. 497**

Persimmon
ZONES VARY — **p. 513**

Plant listings continue

Lagerstroemia indica

Liquidambar styraciflua

Persimmon 'Hachiya'

Pistacia chinensis

Populus tremuloides

Pyrus calleryana

Quercus coccinea

Cotinus coggygria

Pistacia chinensis
CHINESE PISTACHE
☼ ⁄ 4–16, 18–23 — **p. 530**

Populus (some)
POPLAR
☼ ⁄ ZONES VARY — **p. 543**

Prunus (deciduous)
NEEDS, ZONES VARY — **p. 549**

Pyrus (deciduous)
ORNAMENTAL PEAR
☼ ⁄ ZONES VARY — **p. 558**

Quercus (deciduous)
OAK
☼ ⁄ ZONES VARY — **p. 558**

Salix
WILLOW
☼ ⁄ ZONES VARY — **p. 591**

Sapium sebiferum
CHINESE TALLOW TREE
☼ ⁄ 8, 9, 12–16, 18–21; H1 — **p. 599**

Sorbus
MOUNTAIN ASH
☼ ◑ ⁄ ZONES VARY — **p. 613**

Stewartia
☼ ◑ ⁄ 4–6, 14–17, 20, 21 — **p. 619**

Styrax japonicus
JAPANESE SNOWDROP TREE
☼ ◑ ⁄ 4–9, 14–21 — **p. 622**

Tilia
LINDEN
☼ ⁄ 1–17 — **p. 633**

Zelkova serrata
SAWLEAF ZELKOVA
☼ ⁄ 3–21 — **p. 656**

SHRUBS

Amelanchier
JUNEBERRY
☼ ◑ ⁄ ZONES VARY — **p. 183**

Berberis (deciduous)
BARBERRY
☼ ◑ ⁄ ZONES VARY — **p. 221**

Blueberry
☼ ⁄ ZONES VARY — **p. 226**

Cercis
REDBUD
☼ ⁄ ZONES VARY — **p. 263**

Cornus (deciduous)
DOGWOOD
NEEDS, ZONES VARY — **p. 291**

Cotinus coggygria
SMOKE TREE
☼ ⁄ 2–24 — **p. 296**

Cotoneaster (most deciduous)
☼ ⁄ ZONES VARY — **p. 296**

Enkianthus
☼ ◑ ⁄ 3–9, 14–21 — **p. 326**

Euonymus (deciduous)
NEEDS, ZONES VARY — **p. 342**

Fothergilla
☼ ◑ ⁄ 2B–9, 14–17 — **p. 354**

Hamamelis
WITCH HAZEL
☼ ◑ ⁄ ZONES VARY — **p. 379**

Hydrangea quercifolia
OAKLEAF HYDRANGEA
☼ ◑ ⁄ 2B–23 — **p. 394**

Kerria japonica
☼ ◑ ⁄ 2–23 — **p. 417**

Lagerstroemia indica
CRAPE MYRTLE
☼ ⁄ 2–10, 12–24; H1, H2 — **p. 421**

Nandina domestica
HEAVENLY BAMBOO
☼ ◑ ● ⁄ 3–24; H1, H2 — **p. 476**

Photinia villosa
☼ ⁄ 3–9, 14–17 — **p. 520**

Punica granatum
POMEGRANATE
☼ ⁄ 5–24; H1, H2 — **p. 556**

Rhododendron
AZALEA, DECIDUOUS
◑ ⁄ ZONES VARY — **p. 574**

Rhus (deciduous)
SUMAC
☼ ⁄ ZONES VARY — **p. 576**

Spiraea (most)
☼ ◑ ⁄ ZONES VARY — **p. 616**

Viburnum (many)
NEEDS, ZONES VARY — **p. 646**

VINES

Grape
☼ ⁄ ZONES VARY — **p. 369**

Parthenocissus
☼ ◑ ● ⁄ ZONES VARY — **p. 498**

Wisteria
NEEDS, ZONES VARY — **p. 652**

Euonymus alatus

Hamamelis × intermedia 'Jelena'

Viburnum opulus

Parthenocissus tricuspidata

Parthenocissus quinquefolia

For growing symbol explanations, please see page 64.

Crataegus laevigata 'Paul's Scarlet'

GARDEN TREES

Dodonaea viscosa 'Purpurea'

When you shop for a tree, carefully consider how well it will suit its intended location. Because garden size is a crucial determinant, the trees in this list are grouped in three size categories. Patio trees are generally small, as trees go, and reward close viewing of details: flowers, fruits, fall foliage, decorative bark. All produce minimal litter from flowers, fruits, leaves, branches, and have root systems not likely to crack or raise pavement. Patio trees are also fine for garden planting, but the list of garden trees includes others that may have litter or root attributes that exclude them from patios but that are not issues in a garden setting. Large landscape trees are generally too massive for small gardens but are choice candidates for planting wherever there's room for them to achieve their full majesty.

Acer griseum

Acer palmatum

Bauhinia × *blakeana*

PATIO TREES

Deciduous

Acer buergeranum
TRIDENT MAPLE
2–9, 14–17, 20, 21 — p. 167

Acer circinatum
VINE MAPLE
A3; 2B–6, 14–17 — p. 167

Acer davidii
DAVID'S MAPLE
2–6, 15–17, 20, 21 — p. 167

Acer griseum
PAPERBARK MAPLE
2–9, 14–21 — p. 168

Acer palmatum
JAPANESE MAPLE
A3; 2–10, 12, 14–24 — p. 168

Acer tataricum ginnala
AMUR MAPLE
A1–A3; 1–9, 14–16 — p. 169

Amelanchier
JUNEBERRY
ZONES VARY — p. 183

Bauhinia
ORCHID TREE
ZONES VARY — p. 218

Cercidium
PALO VERDE
8–14, 18–20 — p. 262

Cercis
REDBUD
ZONES VARY — p. 263

Chilopsis linearis
DESERT WILLOW
3B, 7–14, 18–23 — p. 269

Chionanthus
FRINGE TREE
ZONES VARY — p. 270

× Chitalpa tashkentensis
3–24 — p. 270

Chorisia speciosa
FLOSS SILK TREE
12–24; H1, H2 — p. 271

Cladrastis kentukea
YELLOW WOOD
2–9, 14–16 — p. 281

Cornus florida
FLOWERING DOGWOOD
2B–9, 14–16 — p. 292

Cornus kousa
KOUSA DOGWOOD
2–9, 14–17 — p. 292

Corylus (most)
FILBERT, HAZELNUT
2–9, 14–20 — p. 294

Cotinus coggygria
SMOKE TREE
2–24 — p. 296

Crataegus
HAWTHORN
2–12, 14–17 — p. 298

Davidia involucrata
DOVE TREE
4–9, 14–21 — p. 310

Erythrina (most)
CORAL TREE
ZONES VARY — p. 334

Franklinia alatamaha
3B–6, 14–17 — p. 355

Halesia carolina
SNOWDROP TREE
2B–9, 14–21 — p. 378

Koelreuteria
ZONES VARY — p. 419

Plant listings continue ▶

Chilopsis linearis

Chionanthus retusus

Cornus kousa

Cotinus coggygria

Erythrina falcata

Lagerstroemia indica

Nerium oleander

Prunus (flowering cherry)

Lagerstroemia (most)
CRAPE MYRTLE
ZONES VARY p. 421

Lysiloma microphylla thornberi
FEATHER BUSH
12–24; H1, H2 p. 445

Magnolia (small)
ZONES VARY p. 447

Malus
FLOWERING CRABAPPLE
1–11, 14–21 p. 457

Oxydendrum arboreum
SOURWOOD
2B–9, 14–17 p. 492

Parrotia persica
PERSIAN PARROTIA
2B–7, 14–17 p. 497

Prunus (flowering cherry)
ZONES VARY p. 550

Prunus cerasifera 'Purple Pony'
3–22 p. 552

Prunus mume
JAPANESE FLOWERING PLUM
3–9, 12–22 p. 553

Sapium sebiferum
CHINESE TALLOW TREE
8, 9, 12–16, 18–21; H1 p. 599

Stewartia (small)
4–6, 14–17, 20, 21 p. 619

Tabebuia
15, 16, 20–24; H1, H2 p. 626

PATIO TREES
Evergreen

Acacia podalyriifolia
PEARL ACACIA
8, 9, 13–24 p. 165

Brugmansia
ANGEL'S TRUMPET p. 233
12, 13, 16–24; H1, H2

Cassia leptophylla
GOLD MEDALLION TREE
21–24; H2 p. 254

Citrus
8, 9, 12–24; H1, H2 p. 276

Clethra arborea
LILY-OF-THE-VALLEY TREE
15–17, 21–24 p. 284

Cocculus laurifolius
8, 9, 12–24 p. 286

Cordia boissieri
TEXAS OLIVE
8–24 p. 289

Cupressus (some)
CYPRESS
ZONES VARY p. 303

Dodonaea viscosa
HOP BUSH
7–24; H1, H2 p. 319

Drimys winteri
WINTER'S BARK
5–9, 14–24 p. 320

Eriobotrya deflexa
BRONZE LOQUAT
8–24 p. 333

Eucalyptus formanii
SEE CHART p. 339

Eucalyptus torquata
CORAL GUM
SEE CHART p. 341

Geijera parviflora
AUSTRALIAN WILLOW
8, 9, 12–24 p. 362

Hakea laurina
SEA URCHIN
9, 12–17, 19–24 p. 378

Heteromeles arbutifolia
TOYON
5–9, 14–24 p. 386

Laurus nobilis 'Saratoga'
SWEET BAY
5–9, 12–24; H1, H2 p. 424

Leptospermum laevigatum
AUSTRALIAN TEA TREE
14–24; H1, H2 p. 428

Melaleuca quinquenervia
CAJEPUT TREE p. 464
9, 12, 13, 15–17, 20–24; H1, H2

Michelia doltsopa
14–24; H1, H2 p. 468

Nerium oleander
OLEANDER
8–16, 18–24; H1, H2 p. 482

Olea europaea (fruitless)
OLIVE
8, 9, 11–24; H1, H2 p. 486

Osmanthus fragrans
SWEET OLIVE
5–9, 12–24; H1 p. 490

Palms (some)
NEEDS, ZONES VARY p. 494

Podocarpus gracilior
FERN PINE
8, 9, 13–24; H1, H2 p. 539

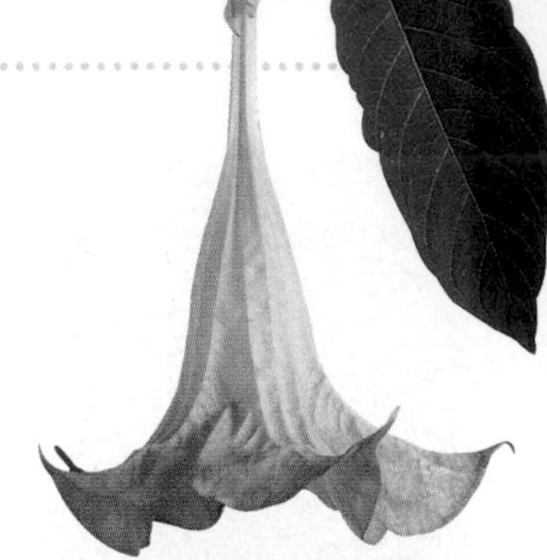
Brugmansia 'Charles Grimaldi'

Sapium sebiferum

Cassia leptophylla

Geijera parviflora

Laurus nobilis 'Saratoga'

For growing symbol explanations, please see page 64.

Albizia julibrissin

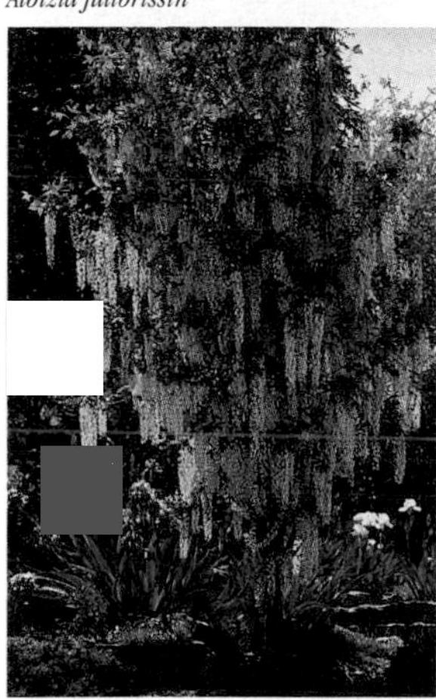
Laburnum

Magnolia × soulangiana

Malus (flowering crabapple)

Pyrus kawakamii
EVERGREEN PEAR
☼ ⁄ 8, 9, 12–24 **p. 558**

Rhaphiolepis 'Majestic Beauty'
☼ ◑ ⁄ 4–10, 12–24; H1, H2 **p. 567**

Rhus lancea
AFRICAN SUMAC
☼ ⁄ 8, 9, 12–24 **p. 576**

Schefflera
☼ ◑ ⁄ ZONES VARY **p. 601**

Schinus terebinthifolius
BRAZILIAN PEPPER TREE
☼ ⁄ 13–17, 19–24; H1, H2 **p. 602**

Sophora secundiflora
TEXAS MOUNTAIN LAUREL
☼ ◑ ⁄ 8–16, 18–24 **p. 613**

Stenocarpus sinuatus
FIREWHEEL TREE
☼ ⁄ 16, 17, 20–24 **p. 618**

Thevetia thevetioides
GIANT THEVETIA
☼ ⁄ 12, 13, 22–24; H2 **p. 630**

Tristaniopsis laurina
WATER GUM
☼ ⁄ 15–24 **p. 638**

Xylosma congestum
☼ ◑ ⁄ 8–24 **p. 654**

SMALL TO MEDIUM GARDEN TREES

Deciduous

Albizia julibrissin
SILK TREE
☼ ◑ ⁄ 4–23 **p. 177**

Alnus cordata
ITALIAN ALDER
☼ ◑ ● ⁄ 2B–9, 14–24 **p. 179**

Betula
BIRCH
☼ ⁄ ZONES VARY **p. 223**

Brachychiton
☼ ⁄ ZONES VARY **p. 230**

Calodendrum capense
CAPE CHESTNUT
☼ ⁄ 15, 16, 19, 21–24 **p. 242**

Carpinus
HORNBEAM
NEEDS, ZONES VARY **p. 252**

Celtis
HACKBERRY
☼ ◑ ⁄ ZONES VARY **p. 260**

Cercidiphyllum japonicum
KATSURA TREE
☼ ◑ ⁄ 2B–6, 14–16, 18–20 **p. 262**

Elaeagnus angustifolia
RUSSIAN OLIVE
☼ ◑ ⁄ A2, A3; 1–3, 7–14, 18, 19 **p. 324**

Erythrina (some)
CORAL TREE
☼ ⁄ ZONES VARY **p. 334**

Fraxinus angustifolia 'Raywood'
RAYWOOD ASH
☼ ⁄ 2B–9, 12–24 **p. 356**

Fraxinus greggii
LITTLE LEAF ASH
☼ ⁄ 10–13 **p. 356**

Fraxinus mandashurica 'Mancana'
MANCHURIAN ASH
☼ ⁄ A1–A3; 1–3 **p. 356**

Fraxinus velutina
ARIZONA ASH
☼ ⁄ 3B–24 **p. 356**

Gleditsia triacanthos
HONEY LOCUST
☼ ⁄ 1–16, 18–20 **p. 367**

Laburnum
GOLDENCHAIN TREE
☼ ◑ ⁄ 1–10, 14–17 **p. 420**

Magnolia (many)
☼ ◑ ⁄ ZONES VARY **p. 447**

Malus
FLOWERING CRABAPPLE
☼ ⁄ 1–11, 14–21 **p. 457**

Morus alba
WHITE MULBERRY
☼ ⁄ 2–24; H1, H2 **p. 472**

Nyssa sylvatica
SOUR GUM
☼ ◑ ⁄ 2–10, 14–21 **p. 484**

Parkinsonia aculeata
JERUSALEM THORN
☼ ⁄ 8–24; H1, H2 **p. 497**

Persimmon
☼ ⁄ ZONES VARY **p. 513**

Pistacia chinensis
CHINESE PISTACHE
☼ ⁄ 4–16, 18–23 **p. 530**

Populus tremuloides
QUAKING ASPEN
☼ ⁄ A1–A3; 1–7, 14–19 **p. 543**

Prosopis
MESQUITE
☼ ⁄ ZONES VARY **p. 547**

Prunus
FLOWERING CHERRY, PEACH, PLUM
☼ ⁄ ZONES VARY **p. 548**

Punica granatum
POMEGRANATE
☼ ⁄ 5–24; H1, H2 **p. 556**

Xylosma congestum

Nyssa sylvatica

Persimmon

Populus tremuloides

Plant listings continue ▶

Punica granatum

Pyrus calleryana

Styrax japonicus

Tilia cordata

Callistemon citrinus

Pyrus
ORNAMENTAL PEAR
☼ ⁄ ZONES VARY — **p. 558**

Sophora japonica
JAPANESE PAGODA TREE
☼ ◑ ⁄ 2–24 — **p. 613**

Sorbus aucuparia
EUROPEAN MOUNTAIN ASH
☼ ◑ ⁄ A1–A3; 1–10, 14–17 — **p. 613**

Styrax
☼ ◑ ⁄ 4–9, 14–21 — **p. 622**

Tilia (most)
LINDEN
☼ ⁄ ZONES VARY — **p. 633**

Tipuana tipu
TIPU TREE
☼ ⁄ 12–16, 18–24; H1, H2 — **p. 634**

Vitex agnus-castus
CHASTE TREE
☼ ⁄ 4–24 — **p. 650**

SMALL TO MEDIUM GARDEN TREES
Evergreen

Acacia baileyana
BAILEY ACACIA
☼ ⁄ 7–9, 13–24 — **p. 164**

Acacia cognata
BOWER WATTLE
☼ ⁄ 16–24 — **p. 164**

Acacia pendula
WEEPING ACACIA
☼ ⁄ 13–24 — **p. 165**

Acacia smallii
☼ ⁄ 8, 9, 12–24 — **p. 166**

Acacia stenophylla
SHOESTRING ACACIA
☼ ⁄ 8, 9, 12–24 — **p. 166**

Agonis
☼ ◑ ⁄ 15–17, 20–24 — **p. 175**

Arbutus 'Marina'
☼ ⁄ 8, 9, 14–24 — **p. 197**

Arbutus unedo
STRAWBERRY TREE
☼ ◑ ⁄ 4–24 — **p. 197**

Arctostaphylos manzanita 'Dr. Hurd'
☼ ◑ ⁄ 4–9, 14–24 — **p. 198**

Callistemon citrinus
LEMON BOTTLEBRUSH
☼ ⁄ 8, 9, 12–24; H1, H2 — **p. 240**

Callistemon viminalis
WEEPING BOTTLEBRUSH
☼ ⁄ 6–9, 12–24 — **p. 240**

Ceratonia siliqua
CAROB
☼ ⁄ 9, 13–16, 18–24; H1 — **p. 262**

Cornus capitata
EVERGREEN DOGWOOD
☼ ◑ ⁄ 8, 9, 14–20 — **p. 292**

Crinodendron patagua
LILY-OF-THE-VALLEY TREE
☼ ⁄ 14–24 — **p. 299**

Eriobotrya japonica
LOQUAT
☼ ◑ ⁄ 6–24; H1, H2 — **p. 333**

Erythrina falcata
☼ ⁄ 19–24; H1, H2 — **p. 335**

Eucalyptus ficifolia
RED-FLOWERING GUM
☼ ⁄ SEE CHART — **p. 339**

Eucalyptus microtheca
COOLIBAH
☼ ⁄ SEE CHART — **p. 340**

Eucalyptus nicholii
NICHOL'S WILLOW-LEAFED PEPPERMINT
☼ ⁄ SEE CHART — **p. 340**

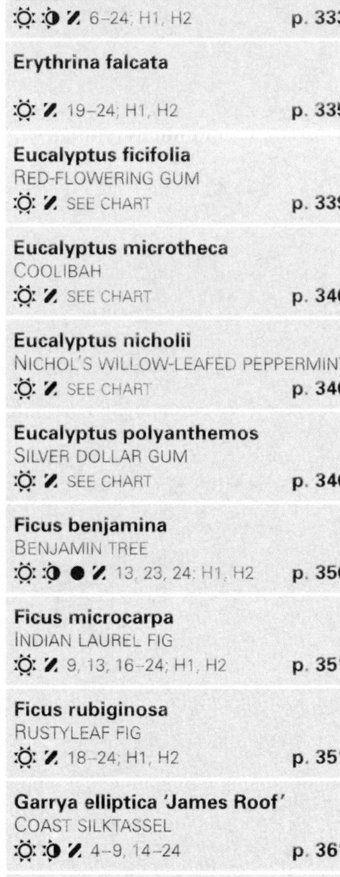

Eucalyptus polyanthemos
SILVER DOLLAR GUM
☼ ⁄ SEE CHART — **p. 340**

Ficus benjamina
BENJAMIN TREE
☼ ◑ ● ⁄ 13, 23, 24; H1, H2 — **p. 350**

Ficus microcarpa
INDIAN LAUREL FIG
☼ ⁄ 9, 13, 16–24; H1, H2 — **p. 351**

Ficus rubiginosa
RUSTYLEAF FIG
☼ ⁄ 18–24; H1, H2 — **p. 351**

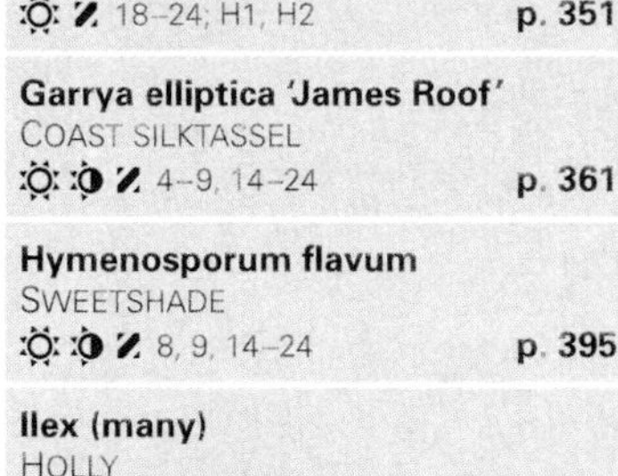

Garrya elliptica 'James Roof'
COAST SILKTASSEL
☼ ◑ ⁄ 4–9, 14–24 — **p. 361**

Hymenosporum flavum
SWEETSHADE
☼ ◑ ⁄ 8, 9, 14–24 — **p. 395**

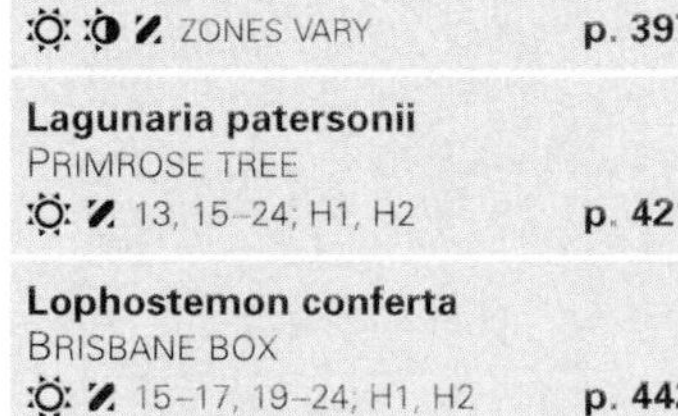

Ilex (many)
HOLLY
☼ ◑ ⁄ ZONES VARY — **p. 397**

Lagunaria patersonii
PRIMROSE TREE
☼ ⁄ 13, 15–24; H1, H2 — **p. 421**

Lophostemon conferta
BRISBANE BOX
☼ ⁄ 15–17, 19–24; H1, H2 — **p. 442**

Luma apiculata
☼ ⁄ 14–24 — **p. 443**

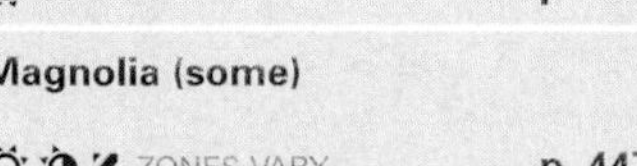

Magnolia (some)
☼ ◑ ⁄ ZONES VARY — **p. 447**

Cornus capitata

Ilex aquifolium 'Argenteo-marginata'

Eucalyptus ficifolia

Maytenus boaria

Pittosporum eugenioides

For growing symbol explanations, please see page 64.

Acer rubrum

Ginkgo biloba

Jacaranda mimosifolia

Maytenus boaria
MAYTEN
8, 9, 14–24 **p. 463**

Melaleuca (several)
ZONES VARY **p. 464**

Metrosideros excelsus
NEW ZEALAND CHRISTMAS TREE
16, 17, 23, 24; H1, H2 **p. 467**

Olneya tesota
DESERT IRONWOOD
8–9, 11–14, 18–23 **p. 486**

Pinus contorta contorta
BEACH PINE, SHORE PINE
A3; 4–9, 14–24; H1 **p. 525**

Pithecellobium flexicaule
TEXAS EBONY
10–13 **p. 530**

Pittosporum (several)
ZONES VARY **p. 531**

Prunus caroliniana
CAROLINA LAUREL CHERRY
5–24 **p. 549**

Umbellularia californica
CALIFORNIA LAUREL
4–9, 14–24 **p. 643**

LARGE LANDSCAPE TREES
Deciduous

Acer rubrum
RED MAPLE
A2, A3; 1–9, 14–17 **p. 169**

Catalpa
3–10, 14–24 **p. 255**

Fagus sylvatica
EUROPEAN BEECH
A3; 2B–9, 14–21 **p. 347**

Ginkgo biloba
MAIDENHAIR TREE
A3; 1–10, 12, 14–24 **p. 366**

Jacaranda mimosifolia
12, 13, 15–24; H1, H2 **p. 407**

Larix
LARCH
ZONES VARY **p. 423**

Liquidambar
SWEET GUM
ZONES VARY **p. 437**

Liriodendron tulipifera
TULIP TREE
2–12, 14–24 **p. 437**

Metasequoia glyptostroboides
DAWN REDWOOD
A3; 3–10, 14–24 **p. 467**

Nyssa sylvatica
SOUR GUM
2–10, 14–21 **p. 484**

Platanus
PLANE TREE, SYCAMORE
ZONES VARY **p. 531**

Quercus (many)
OAK
ZONES VARY **p. 558**

Robinia ×ambigua 'Idahoensis'
IDAHO LOCUST
2–24 **p. 578**

Robinia pseudoacacia
BLACK LOCUST
1–24 **p. 578**

Zelkova serrata
SAWLEAF ZELKOVA
3–21 **p. 656**

LARGE LANDSCAPE TREES
Evergreen

Castanospermum australe
MORETON BAY CHESTNUT
18–22 **p. 254**

Cedrus
CEDAR
ZONES VARY **p. 256**

Cinnamomum camphora
CAMPHOR TREE
8, 9, 12–24; H1, H2 **p. 275**

Elaeocarpus decipiens
JAPANESE BLUEBERRY TREE
8, 9, 14–24; H1 **p. 325**

Picea
SPRUCE
ZONES VARY **p. 521**

Pinus (many)
SEE CHART **p. 523**

Quercus agrifolia
COAST LIVE OAK
7–9, 14–24 **p. 560**

Quercus ilex
HOLLY OAK
4–24 **p. 561**

Quercus suber
CORK OAK
5–7, 8–16, 18–24 **p. 562**

Quercus virginiana
SOUTHERN LIVE OAK
4–24 **p. 562**

Sequoia sempervirens
REDWOOD, COAST REDWOOD
4–9, 14–24 **p. 607**

Tsuga canadensis
CANADA HEMLOCK
A3; 2–7, 17 **p. 639**

Liquidambar styraciflua

Robinia ×ambigua 'Idahoensis'

Cinnamomum camphora

Quercus suber

Plants for
HEDGES AND SCREENS

Plants that are densely foliaged from top to bottom are ideal for boundary plantings of various heights and styles. Large shrub-trees are good candidates for screens; if grouped close together, they can block an objectionable view or direct attention to a garden focal point. Shearing can transform some plants into formal hedges. Low-growing shrublets—knee-high or even smaller—are primarily useful for edging walks or paths; they can be clipped or left informal.

SYMBOL: ♣♣♣ indicates plants that can be clipped into formal hedges.

Chaenomeles

Weigela florida

Arbutus unedo

DECIDUOUS

Plant	Common name	Conditions and zones	Page	Hedge
Acer campestre	HEDGE MAPLE	☼ ◑ ⁄ 2–9, 14–17	p. 167	♣♣♣
Berberis (some)	BARBERRY	☼ ◑ ⁄ ZONES VARY	p. 221	♣♣♣
Carpinus betulus	EUROPEAN HORNBEAM	☼ ◑ ⁄ 2–9, 14–17	p. 252	♣♣♣
Chaenomeles	FLOWERING QUINCE	☼ ⁄ 2–23	p. 264	
Crataegus monogyna		☼ ⁄ 1–12, 14–17	p. 298	♣♣♣
Elaeagnus angustifolia	RUSSIAN OLIVE	☼ ◑ ⁄ A2, A3; 1–3, 7–14, 18, 19	p. 324	
Ligustrum (some)	PRIVET	☼ ◑ ⁄ ZONES VARY	p. 432	♣♣♣
Maclura pomifera	OSAGE ORANGE	☼ ⁄ 2, 3, 10–13	p. 447	
Rhamnus frangula 'Columnaris'	TALLHEDGE BUCKTHORN	☼ ◑ ⁄ 1–7, 10, 11	p. 566	♣♣♣
Rosa (shrub)	ROSE	☼ ◑ ⁄ ZONES VARY	p. 579	
Salix purpurea 'Gracilis'	DWARF PURPLE OSIER	☼ ⁄ A2, A3; 1–11	p. 591	
Viburnum opulus 'Nanum'	EUROPEAN CRANBERRY BUSH	☼ ◑ ⁄ A2, A3; 1–9, 14–24	p. 647	
Weigela		☼ ◑ ⁄ 1–11, 14–21	p. 651	

EVERGREEN

Plant	Common name	Conditions and zones	Page	Hedge
Abelia × grandiflora	GLOSSY ABELIA	☼ ◑ ⁄ 4–24; H1, H2	p. 162	
Arbutus unedo	STRAWBERRY TREE	☼ ◑ ⁄ 4–24	p. 197	
Bamboo (many)		☼ ◑ ⁄ ZONES VARY	p. 213	
Berberis (some)	BARBERRY	☼ ◑ ⁄ ZONES VARY	p. 221	
Buxus	BOXWOOD	☼ ◑ ● ⁄ ZONES VARY	p. 236	♣♣♣
Callistemon (some)	BOTTLEBRUSH	☼ ⁄ ZONES VARY	p. 240	♣♣♣
Calocedrus decurrens	INCENSE CEDAR	☼ ◑ ⁄ 2–12, 14–24	p. 241	
Carissa macrocarpa	NATAL PLUM	☼ ◑ ⁄ 22–24; H2	p. 251	♣♣♣
Chamaecyparis lawsoniana (several)		☼ ◑ ⁄ A3; 3–6, 15–17	p. 265	
Choisya ternata	MEXICAN ORANGE	☼ ◑ ⁄ 4–9, 14–24	p. 271	
Citrus		☼ ⁄ 8, 9, 12–24; H1, H2	p. 276	
Cotoneaster (some)		☼ ⁄ ZONES VARY	p. 296	
× Cupressocyparis leylandii		☼ ⁄ 3B–24	p. 302	♣♣♣

For growing symbol explanations, please see page 64.

Abelia × grandiflora

Buxus

Callistemon citrinus

Escallonia × exoniensis 'Fradesii'

Nandina domestica

Grewia occidentalis

Leptospermum scoparium

Ligustrum japonicum

Cupressus (most)
CYPRESS
ZONES VARY p. 303

Dodonaea viscosa
HOP BUSH
7–24; H1, H2 p. 319

Elaeagnus (some)
ZONES VARY p. 324

Escallonia
4–9, 14–24 p. 335

Euonymus (most)
ZONES VARY p. 342

Feijoa, Pineapple guava
6–9, 12–24; H1, H2 p. 348

Garrya elliptica
COAST SILKTASSEL
4–9, 14–24 p. 361

Grevillea (many)
NEEDS, ZONES VARY p. 375

Grewia occidentalis
LAVENDER STARFLOWER
8, 9, 12–24; H1, H2 p. 376

Heteromeles arbutifolia
TOYON
5–9, 14–24 p. 386

Hibiscus rosa-sinensis
CHINESE HIBISCUS
9, 12–16, 19–24; H1, H2 p. 388

Ilex
HOLLY
ZONES VARY p. 397

Juniperus (shrub, columnar)
JUNIPER
ZONES VARY p. 410

Leptospermum (most)
TEA TREE
14–24 p. 428

Leucophyllum frutescens
TEXAS RANGER
7–24 p. 430

Ligustrum (some)
PRIVET
ZONES VARY p. 432

Mahonia (tall)
NEEDS, ZONES VARY p. 455

Myrica californica
PACIFIC WAX MYRTLE
4–9, 14–24 p. 475

Myrsine africana
AFRICAN BOXWOOD
8, 9, 14–24 p. 475

Myrtus communis
MYRTLE
8–24; H1, H2 p. 476

Nandina domestica
HEAVENLY BAMBOO
3–24; H1, H2 p. 476

Nerium oleander
OLEANDER
8–16, 18–24; H1, H2 p. 482

Osmanthus (several)
ZONES VARY p. 490

Photinia
ZONES VARY p. 519

Pittosporum (several)
ZONES VARY p. 531

Podocarpus
ZONES VARY p. 538

Prunus (evergreen)
NEEDS, ZONES VARY p. 549

Pyracantha
FIRETHORN
ZONES VARY p. 557

Rhamnus (many)
NEEDS, ZONES VARY p. 566

Rhaphiolepis
4–10, 12–24; H1, H2 p. 567

Syzygium paniculatum
BRUSH CHERRY
16, 17, 20–24; H1, H2 p. 626

Taxus
YEW
ZONES VARY p. 628

Tecoma capensis
CAPE HONEYSUCKLE
12, 13, 20–24; H1, H2 p. 628

Teucrium fruticans
BUSH GERMANDER
4–24 p. 630

Thuja
ARBORVITAE
ZONES VARY p. 630

Vaccinium ovatum
EVERGREEN HUCKLEBERRY
4–7, 14–17, 22–24 p. 643

Viburnum (several)
NEEDS, ZONES VARY p. 646

Xylosma congestum
8–24 p. 654

Nerium oleander

Myrtus communis

Photinia fraseri

Tecoma capensis

Viburnum tinus

Xylosma congestum

Rosa and Clematis (large-flowered hybrid)

VINES

Vines are among the most tractable of plants. In contrast to the generally rigid and inflexible branches of trees and shrubs, their stems are fairly limber and can be guided to grow in the direction you want: upward or outward (or both) on a wall or fence, up and around a post or tree trunk, up and over an arbor or pergola. Many can also serve as ground covers. Though all vines have long, pliable stems, they climb in different ways. Some are equipped with tendrils; some twine; others cling. And some are scrambling plants with no natural means of attachment; they climb only if their stems are securely tied to a support.

Clematis, large-flowered hybrid

Lonicera sempervirens

Clytostoma callistegioides

Distictis buccinatoria

EVERGREEN

Plant	Common name	Needs / Zones	Page
Allamanda cathartica	ALLAMANDA	☼ ⁄ 23, 24; H1, H2	**p. 178**
Beaumontia grandiflora	HERALD'S TRUMPET	☼ ◑ ⁄ 12, 13, 16, 17, 21–24; H1, H2	**p. 219**
Bignonia capreolata	CROSSVINE	☼ ◑ ⁄ 4–9, 14–24	**p. 224**
Bougainvillea		☼ ⁄ 5, 6, 12–17, 19, 21–24; H1, H2	**p. 228**
Cissus		NEEDS, ZONES VARY	**p. 275**
Clematis armandii	EVERGREEN CLEMATIS	☼ ⁄ 4–9, 12–24	**p. 282**
Clerodendrum thomsoniae	BLEEDING HEART GLORYBOWER	◑ ⁄ 22–24; H2	**p. 284**
Clytostoma callistegioides	VIOLET TRUMPET VINE	☼ ◑ ⁄ 8, 9, 12–24	**p. 285**
Dalechampia dioscoreifolia	COSTA RICAN BUTTERFLY VINE	☼ ◑ ⁄ 17–24	**p. 309**
Distictis		☼ ◑ ⁄ ZONES VARY	**p. 318**
Euonymus fortunei (some)		☼ ◑ ● ⁄ 2B–17	**p. 343**
Fallopia baldschuanica	LACE VINE	☼ ⁄ A2; 8, 9, 13–24	**p. 347**
Ficus pumila	CREEPING FIG	☼ ◑ ● ⁄ 8–24; H1, H2	**p. 351**
Gelsemium sempervirens	CAROLINA JESSAMINE	☼ ◑ ⁄ 4–24	**p. 362**
Hardenbergia	LILAC VINE	☼ ◑ ⁄ ZONES VARY	**p. 380**
Hedera	IVY	☼ ◑ ⁄ ZONES VARY	**p. 380**
Hibbertia scandens	GUINEA GOLD VINE	☼ ◑ ⁄ 16, 17, 21–24	**p. 388**
Jasminum (several)	JASMINE	☼ ◑ ⁄ ZONES VARY	**p. 408**
Lapageria rosea	CHILEAN BELLFLOWER	◑ ⁄ 5, 6, 15–17, 23, 24	**p. 423**
Lonicera (several)	HONEYSUCKLE	☼ ◑ ⁄ ZONES VARY	**p. 441**
Macfadyena unguis-cati	CAT'S CLAW	☼ ◑ ⁄ 8–24; H1, H2	**p. 446**
Mandevilla		☼ ◑ ⁄ ZONES VARY	**p. 461**
Merremia	YELLOW MORNING GLORY	☼ ⁄ ZONES VARY	**p. 466**
Millettia reticulata	EVERGREEN WISTERIA	☼ ⁄ 6–9, 14–24	**p. 469**
Muehlenbeckia complexa	MATTRESS VINE	☼ ◑ ⁄ 8, 9, 14–24	**p. 473**

For growing symbol explanations, please see page 64.

Lonicera × beckrottii

Pandorea jasminoides

Passiflora caerulea

Thunbergia gregorii

Akebia quinata

Ampelopsis brevipedunculata

Clematis, large-flowered hybrid

Ipomoea indica

Pandorea
16–24; H1, H2 **p. 495**

Passiflora (some)
PASSION VINE
ZONES VARY **p. 499**

Petrea volubilis
QUEEN'S WREATH
19–24; H1, H2 **p. 514**

Podranea ricasoliana
PINK TRUMPET VINE
9, 12, 13, 19–24; H1, H2 **p. 539**

Pyrostegia venusta
FLAME VINE
13, 16, 21–24; H1, H2 **p. 557**

Rhoicissus capensis
EVERGREEN GRAPE
16, 17, 21–24; H2 **p. 575**

Solandra maxima
CUP-OF-GOLD VINE
15–24; H2 **p. 611**

Solanum (some)
ZONES VARY **p. 611**

Stephanotis floribunda
MADAGASCAR JASMINE
23, 24; H2 **p. 619**

Stigmaphyllon ciliatum
ORCHID VINE
19–24; H1, H2 **p. 619**

Tecoma capensis
CAPE HONEYSUCKLE
12, 13, 20–24; H1, H2 **p. 628**

Thunbergia
ZONES VARY **p. 631**

Trachelospermum
STAR JASMINE
ZONES VARY **p. 636**

DECIDUOUS

Actinidia kolomikta
A1–A3; 1–9, 15–17 **p. 171**

Akebia quinata
FIVELEAF AKEBIA
2–24 **p. 177**

Ampelopsis brevipedunculata
PORCELAIN BERRY
2–24 **p. 184**

Antigonon leptopus
CORAL VINE
12, 13, 18–24; H1, H2 **p. 188**

Aristolochia
NEEDS, ZONES VARY **p. 200**

Campsis
TRUMPET CREEPER
ZONES VARY **p. 247**

Celastrus
BITTERSWEET
ZONES VARY **p. 259**

Clematis (most)
ZONES VARY **p. 282**

Fallopia baldschuanica
LACE VINE
A1, A3; 1–7, 10–12 **p. 347**

Grape
ZONES VARY **p. 369**

Humulus lupulus
COMMON HOP
A2, A3; 1–10, 14–21 **p. 393**

Hydrangea anomala petiolaris
CLIMBING HYDRANGEA
A2, A3; 2–21 **p. 394**

Ipomoea
MORNING GLORY
ZONES VARY **p. 400**

Lonicera (some)
HONEYSUCKLE
ZONES VARY **p. 441**

Mandevilla laxa
CHILEAN JASMINE
4–9, 14–24 **p. 461**

Mascagnia
ORCHID VINE
12–24 **p. 462**

Parthenocissus
ZONES VARY **p. 498**

Passiflora (some)
PASSION VINE
ZONES VARY **p. 499**

Rosa (climbers)
ROSE
ZONES VARY **p. 579**

Schizophragma hydrangeoides
JAPANESE HYDRANGEA VINE
2–9, 14–17 **p. 602**

Solanum wendlandii
COSTA RICAN NIGHTSHADE
16, 21–24; H1, H2 **p. 612**

Vigna caracalla
SNAIL VINE
12–24; H1, H2 **p. 648**

Vitis
GRAPE
ZONES VARY **p. 650**

Wisteria
NEEDS, ZONES VARY **p. 652**

Parthenocissus tricuspidata

Trachelospermum jasminoides

Rosa 'Mme. Grégoire Staechelin'

Vigna caracalla

Wisteria floribunda

Ajuga reptans

GROUND COVERS

Lawn is the best-known ground cover, unsurpassed as a surface to walk and play on. But where foot traffic is undesirable or infrequent, many other plants offer much of a lawn's neatness with far less maintenance. These plants run the gamut of foliage textures and colors, and many are noted for their flowers; you can even combine different plants to form a lovely tapestry. Heights vary from virtually flat to knee-high. Some spread by rooting stems or underground runners; others form clumps and require close spacing to achieve a solid cover. Shrubby types spread from individual root systems; space them according to their expected width at maturity.

Ground cover features *Helianthemum*

SYMBOL: (foot traffic symbol) indicates plants that can take a limited amount of foot traffic.

Aegopodium podagraria 'Variegata'

Alchemilla mollis

Artemisia stellerana 'Silver Brocade'

Asarum caudatum

PERENNIALS

Plant	Common name	Zones	Page
Achillea tomentosa	WOOLLY YARROW	A1–A3; 1–24	p. 170
Aegopodium podagraria	BISHOP'S WEED	A1–A3; 1–9, 12, 14–24	p. 173
Ajuga reptans	CARPET BUGLE	A2, A3; 1–24	p. 176
Alchemilla	LADY'S-MANTLE	ZONES VARY	p. 177
Antennaria dioica	PUSSY TOES	A1, A2; 1–3, 6, 7, 14–16	p. 187
Arabis	ROCKCRESS	ZONES VARY	p. 196
Arctotheca calendula	CAPE WEED	8, 9, 13–24	p. 199
Arenaria (foot traffic)	SANDWORT	NEEDS, ZONES VARY	p. 200
Artemisia (several)		ZONES VARY	p. 201
Asarum	WILD GINGER	ZONES VARY	p. 204
Astilbe chinensis 'Pumila'	FALSE SPIRAEA	1–9, 14–24	p. 208
Bamboo (several)		ZONES VARY	p. 213
Bergenia		A1–A3; 1–9, 12–24	p. 222
Campanula (some)	BELLFLOWER	1–9, 14–24	p. 247
Carex comans	NEW ZEALAND HAIR SEDGE	2B–9, 14–24	p. 251
Carex flacca (foot traffic)	BLUE SEDGE	3–9, 14–24	p. 251
Cerastium tomentosum	SNOW-IN-SUMMER	A1, A2; 1–24	p. 261
Ceratostigma plumbaginoides	DWARF PLUMBAGO	2B–10, 14–24	p. 262
Chamaemelum nobile (foot traffic)	CHAMOMILE	2–24	p. 265
Convallaria majalis	LILY-OF-THE-VALLEY	A1–A3; 1–7, 14–20	p. 288
Convolvulus sabatius	GROUND MORNING GLORY	4–9, 12–24	p. 289
Coronilla varia	CROWN VETCH	1–24	p. 293
Cymbalaria muralis	KENILWORTH IVY	3B–24	p. 304
Dampiera diversifolia		15–24	p. 309
Diascia	TWINSPUR	ZONES VARY	p. 314

For growing symbol explanations, please see page 64.

Bergenia crassifolia

Convallaria majalis

Diascia rigescens

nummularium in foreground.

Plant	Common name	Needs; zones	Page
Dichondra micrantha ♛		☼ ◑ ⁄ 8–10, 12–24; H1, H2	p. 315
Dryas		☼ ⁄ A1–A3; 1–6	p. 320
Duchesnea indica	INDIAN MOCK STRAWBERRY	☼ ◑ ● ⁄ 1–24; H1, H2	p. 321
Dymondia margaretae		☼ ◑ ⁄ 15–24	p. 321
Epimedium		◑ ⁄ 2–9, 14–17	p. 327
Erigeron karvinskianus	MEXICAN DAISY	☼ ◑ ⁄ 8, 9, 12–24; H1, H2	p. 332
Erodium reichardii	CRANESBILL	☼ ◑ ⁄ 7–9, 14–24	p. 333
Festuca	FESCUE	☼ ◑ ⁄ ZONES VARY	p. 349
Fragaria chiloensis	BEACH STRAWBERRY	☼ ◑ ⁄ 4–24; H1	p. 355
Galium odoratum	SWEET WOODRUFF	◑ ● ⁄ A2, A3; 2–6, 15–17	p. 359
Gazania		NEEDS, ZONES VARY	p. 361
Geranium (some)	CRANESBILL	☼ ◑ ⁄ ZONES VARY	p. 363
Glechoma hederacea	GROUND IVY	☼ ◑ ● ⁄ A2, A3; 1–10, 14–24	p. 367
Gypsophila repens		☼ ⁄ 1–11, 14–16, 18–21	p. 377
Herniaria glabra	GREEN CARPET	☼ ◑ ● ⁄ 2B–24	p. 386
Houttuynia cordata		☼ ◑ ● ⁄ 2–9, 14–24	p. 392
Ice plants		NEEDS, ZONES VARY	p. 396
Lamium	DEAD NETTLE	◑ ● ⁄ ZONES VARY	p. 422
Liriope spicata	CREEPING LILY TURF	☼ ◑ ● ⁄ 3–10, 14–24; H1, H2	p. 439
Lotus		☼ ◑ ⁄ ZONES VARY	p. 442
Lysimachia (some)		☼ ◑ ⁄ ZONES VARY	p. 445
Mazus reptans		☼ ◑ ⁄ 1–9, 14–24	p. 463
Nepeta (some)		☼ ◑ ⁄ 1–24	p. 480
Nierembergia	CUP FLOWER	☼ ◑ ⁄ ZONES VARY	p. 482
Oenothera (many)	EVENING PRIMROSE	☼ ◑ ⁄ ZONES VARY	p. 485
Ophiopogon japonicus	MONDO GRASS	☼ ◑ ● ⁄ 5–9, 14–24; H1, H2	p. 439
Origanum (some)	OREGANO, MARJORAM	☼ ⁄ ZONES VARY	p. 489
Osteospermum fruticosum	TRAILING AFRICAN DAISY	☼ ⁄ 8, 9, 12–24; H1, H2	p. 491
Oxalis oregana	REDWOOD SORREL	☼ ◑ ● ⁄ 4–9, 14–24	p. 492
Pachysandra terminalis	JAPANESE SPURGE	◑ ● ⁄ 2–10, 14–21	p. 493
Pelargonium peltatum	IVY GERANIUM	☼ ◑ ⁄ 8, 9, 12–24	p. 509
Persicaria (several)	KNOTWEED	☼ ◑ ⁄ ZONES VARY	p. 513
Phlox subulata	MOSS PINK	☼ ◑ ⁄ 1–17	p. 518
Phyla nodiflora ♛	LIPPIA	☼ ⁄ 8–24; H1, H2	p. 520
Plecostachys serpyllifolia		☼ ⁄ 8, 9, 14–24	p. 532
Potentilla (several)	CINQUEFOIL	☼ ◑ ⁄ ZONES VARY	p. 544
Pratia ♛		☼ ◑ ⁄ 4–9, 14–24	p. 545
Prunella	SELF-HEAL	☼ ◑ ⁄ 2–24	p. 549

Plant listings continue ▶

Epimedium pinnatum

Festuca glauca

Fragaria chiloensis

Galium odoratum

Lysimachia nummularia

Pachysandra terminalis

Ophiopogon japonicus

Oxalis oregana

Prunella vulgaris

Phlox subulata

Potentilla neumanniana

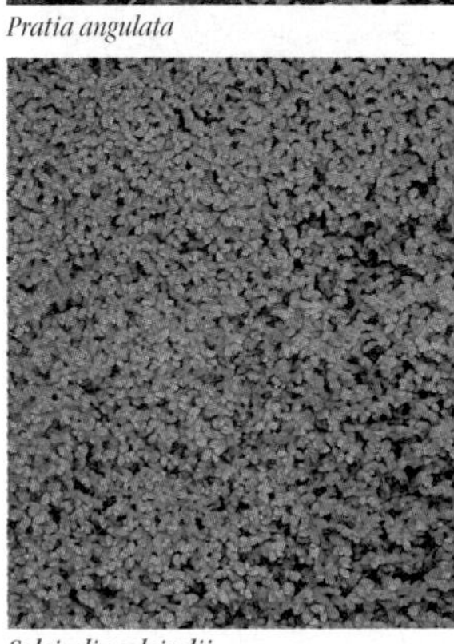
Pratia angulata

Soleirolia soleirolii

Pulmonaria (several)
LUNGWORT
◑ ● ⁄ 1–9, 14–17 — p. 555

Ranunculus repens pleniflorus
CREEPING BUTTERCUP
☼ ◑ ● ⁄ 1–10, 14–24 — p. 564

Sagina subulata ♛
IRISH MOSS, SCOTCH MOSS
☼ ◑ ⁄ 1–11, 14–24 — p. 590

Saponaria ocymoides
☼ ⁄ 1–11, 14–24 — p. 599

Saxifraga
SAXIFRAGE
◑ ● ⁄ ZONES VARY — p. 600

Scaevola
☼ ⁄ 8, 9, 14–24; H1, H2 — p. 601

Sedum (many)
STONECROP
☼ ◑ ⁄ ZONES VARY — p. 604

Senecio mandraliscae
☼ ◑ ⁄ 12, 13, 16, 17, 21–24; H1, H2 — p. 606

Senecio serpens
☼ ◑ ⁄ 16, 17, 21–24 — p. 607

Soleirolia soleirolii
BABY'S TEARS, ANGEL'S TEARS
☼ ◑ ⁄ 4–24; H1, H2 — p. 612

Teucrium (some)
GERMANDER
☼ ⁄ ZONES VARY — p. 630

Thymus (some)
THYME
☼ ◑ ⁄ ZONES VARY — p. 632

Vancouveria
◑ ⁄ ZONES VARY — p. 644

Verbena (many)
☼ ⁄ ZONES VARY — p. 645

Veronica (several)
SPEEDWELL
☼ ⁄ ZONES VARY — p. 645

Vinca
PERIWINKLE
☼ ◑ ● ⁄ ZONES VARY — p. 648

Viola (several)
VIOLA, VIOLET
NEEDS, ZONES VARY — p. 648

Zauschneria
CALIFORNIA FUCHSIA
NEEDS, ZONES VARY — p. 656

Zoysia tenuifolia ♛
KOREAN GRASS
☼ ◑ ⁄ 8, 9, 12–24; H1, H2 — p. 657

SHRUBS

Abelia × grandiflora 'Prostrata'
GLOSSY ABELIA
☼ ◑ ⁄ 4–24; H1, H2 — p. 162

Acacia redolens
☼ ⁄ 8, 9, 12–24 — p. 166

Arctostaphylos (several)
MANZANITA
☼ ◑ ⁄ ZONES VARY — p. 198

Ardisia japonica
MARLBERRY
◑ ● ⁄ 6, 15–17 — p. 199

Atriplex semibaccata
AUSTRALIAN SALTBUSH
☼ ⁄ 8–10, 12–24 — p. 209

Baccharis pilularis
DWARF COYOTE BRUSH
☼ ⁄ 5–11, 14–24 — p. 212

Calluna vulgaris (some)
SCOTCH HEATHER
☼ ⁄ 1A, 2–6, 15–17 — p. 241

Camellia sasanqua (some)
☼ ◑ ⁄ 4–9, 12, 14–24 — p. 246

Carissa macrocarpa (some)
NATAL PLUM
☼ ◑ ⁄ 22–24; H2 — p. 251

Ceanothus (some)
WILD LILAC
☼ ⁄ 5–9, 14–24 — p. 256

Cistus (some)
ROCKROSE
☼ ⁄ 4–9, 14–24 — p. 276

Coprosma (some)
☼ ◑ ⁄ ZONES VARY — p. 289

Cornus canadensis
BUNCHBERRY
◑ ● ⁄ A1–A3; 1–9, 14–16 — p. 292

Correa (some)
AUSTRALIAN FUCHSIA
☼ ◑ ⁄ 14–24 — p. 293

Cotoneaster (some)
☼ ⁄ ZONES VARY — p. 296

Erica (some)
HEATH
☼ ◑ ⁄ ZONES VARY — p. 329

Euonymus fortunei (some)
☼ ◑ ● ⁄ 2B–17 — p. 343

Forsythia (some)
☼ ⁄ ZONES VARY — p. 354

Teucrium × lucidrys

Ardisia japonica

Baccharis pilularis 'Twin Peaks'

Coprosma repens 'Marble Queen'

Vinca minor 'Bowles' Variety'

For growing symbol explanations, please see page 64.

Euonymus fortunei 'Emerald 'n Gold'

Grevillea rosmarinifolia

Rosmarinus officinalis 'Prostratus'

Juniperus sabina 'Tamariscifolia'

Lantana montevidensis

Gaultheria (some)
ZONES VARY p. 361

Genista (some)
BROOM
ZONES VARY p. 362

Grevillea (several)
NEEDS, ZONES VARY p. 375

Helianthemum nummularium
SUNROSE
2B–9, 14–24 p. 382

Hypericum (some)
ST. JOHNSWORT
ZONES VARY p. 395

Juniperus (many)
JUNIPER
ZONES VARY p. 410

Lantana (some)
8–10, 12–24; H1, H2 p. 422

Mahonia (some)
NEEDS, ZONES VARY p. 455

Myoporum (some)
ZONES VARY p. 474

Nandina domestica (some)
HEAVENLY BAMBOO
3–24; H1, H2 p. 476

Paxistima canbyi
1–10, 14–21 p. 500

Pyracantha (some)
FIRETHORN
4–9, 12–24 p. 557

Rhus aromatica
FRAGRANT SUMAC
1–3, 10 p. 576

Ribes viburnifolium
CATALINA PERFUME
5, 7–9, 14–17, 19–24 p. 577

Rosmarinus officinalis (some)
ROSEMARY
4–24; H1, H2 p. 587

Rubus pentalobus
4–6, 14–17 p. 588

Santolina
ZONES VARY p. 598

Sarcococca hookerana humilis
SWEET BOX
3–9, 14–24 p. 599

Sollya heterophylla
AUSTRALIAN BLUEBELL CREEPER
8, 9, 14–24; H1, H2 p. 612

Taxus baccata 'Repandens'
SPREADING ENGLISH YEW
A3; 3–9, 14–24 p. 628

Vaccinium vitis-idaea
COWBERRY, FOXBERRY
3–7, 14–17 p. 643

VINES

Akebia quinata
FIVELEAF AKEBIA
2–24 p. 177

Bougainvillea
p. 228
5, 6, 12–17, 19, 21, 22–24; H1, H2

Cissus (some)
NEEDS, ZONES VARY p. 275

×Fatshedera lizei
4–10, 12–24; H1, H2 p. 348

Gelsemium sempervirens
CAROLINA JESSAMINE
4–24 p. 362

Hedera
IVY
ZONES VARY p. 380

Hibbertia scandens
GUINEA GOLD VINE
16, 17, 21–24 p. 388

Jasminum (some)
JASMINE
ZONES VARY p. 408

Lonicera japonica
JAPANESE HONEYSUCKLE
1–24; H1, H2 p. 441

Macfadyena unguis-cati
CAT'S CLAW
8–24; H1, H2 p. 446

Muehlenbeckia
WIRE VINE
ZONES VARY p. 473

Parthenocissus
ZONES VARY p. 498

Rhoicissus capensis
EVERGREEN GRAPE
16, 17, 21–24; H2 p. 575

Rosa (some)
GROUND COVER ROSES
1–24 p. 584

Tetrastigma voinieranum
13, 17, 20–24; H1, H2 p. 629

Trachelospermum
STAR JASMINE
ZONES VARY p. 636

Rhus aromatica 'Gro-Low'

Akebia quinata

Bougainvillea 'San Diego Red'

Hibbertia scandens

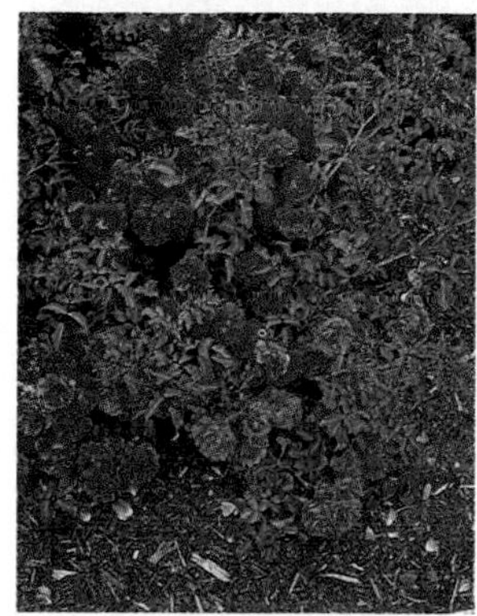
Rosa 'Flower Carpet'

Adiantum capillus-veneris

FERNS

Think of ferns and you may at once envision a lush, shady, forest nook—and many ferns are in fact woodland natives. In size, they range from forest-floor creepers to the majestic tree ferns that seem to belong to the age of dinosaurs. Foliage may be soft, thin, and silky or firm, thick, and leathery. Fronds are sometimes undivided, reminiscent of lances or spearpoints. More often, though, they're divided—either palmate, resembling a hand with outstretched fingers, or pinnate, looking more like a bird's feather. In the more elaborate sorts, the frond divisions are further divided to give the effect of green lace.

Platycerium bifurcatum

Adiantum aleuticum

Athyrium nipponicum 'Pictum'

Dicksonia antarctica

Plant	Common name	Growing symbols and zones	Page
Adiantum	MAIDENHAIR FERN	◑ ● ⁄ ZONES VARY	**p. 172**
Arachniodes simplicior		◑ ● ⁄ 4–24	**p. 196**
Asplenium		◑ ● ⁄ ZONES VARY	**p. 206**
Athyrium		◑ ● ⁄ ZONES VARY	**p. 209**
Blechnum		◑ ● ⁄ ZONES VARY	**p. 226**
Cyrtomium		◑ ● ⁄ ZONES VARY	**p. 306**
Davallia trichomanoides	SQUIRREL'S FOOT FERN	◑ ⁄ 17, 23, 24; H1, H2	**p. 310**
Dryopteris	WOOD FERN	◑ ● ⁄ ZONES VARY	**p. 320**
Humata tyermannii	BEAR'S FOOT FERN	◑ ⁄ 17, 23, 24; H1, H2	**p. 392**
Matteuccia struthiopteris	OSTRICH FERN	☼ ◑ ● ⁄ A1–A3, 1–10, 14–17	**p. 462**
Microlepia		◑ ● ⁄ 17, 23, 24	**p. 468**
Nephrolepis	SWORD FERN	◑ ● ⁄ ZONES VARY	**p. 481**
Osmunda regalis	ROYAL FERN	☼ ◑ ⁄ 1–9, 14–17	**p. 491**
Pellaea	CLIFF-BRAKE	◑ ⁄ ZONES VARY	**p. 510**
Platycerium	STAGHORN FERN	◑ ⁄ ZONES VARY	**p. 532**
Polypodium scouleri	LEATHERY POLYPODY	◑ ● ⁄ 4–6, 15–17, 24	**p. 541**
Polystichum		◑ ● ⁄ ZONES VARY	**p. 542**
Pteridium aquilinum	BRACKEN	☼ ◑ ⁄ 1–10, 14–24	**p. 554**
Pteris	BRAKE	◑ ● ⁄ ZONES VARY	**p. 554**
Pyrrosia lingua	JAPANESE FELT FERN	☼ ◑ ⁄ 14–17, 19–24	**p. 558**
Rumohra adiantiformis	LEATHERLEAF FERN	☼ ◑ ⁄ 14–17, 19–24; H1, H2	**p. 589**
Woodwardia fimbriata	GIANT CHAIN FERN	◑ ● ⁄ 2B–9, 14–24	**p. 653**
TREE FERNS			
Cibotium glaucum	HAPU'U	☼ ◑ ⁄ 17, 23, 24; H2	**p. 274**
Cyathea cooperi	AUSTRALIAN TREE FERN	☼ ◑ ⁄ 15–24; H1, H2	**p. 303**
Dicksonia antarctica	TASMANIAN TREE FERN	☼ ◑ ● ⁄ 8, 9, 14–17, 19–24; H1	**p. 315**

For growing symbol explanations, please see page 64.

Polystichum munitum

Rumohra adiantiformis

Woodwardia fimbriata

Calamagrostis × acutiflora 'Karl Foerster'

ORNAMENTAL GRASSES

Unlike the familiar lawn grasses, ornamental types (including grasslike sedges and rushes) are not for mowing. Denizens of prairie, seashore, forest, and marsh, they offer fountains and hummocks of foliage that vary widely in texture, color, and overall character. Many put on significant floral displays, bearing tall stems set with plumes or pendants of tiny blossoms that sway and shimmer in the breeze. Some even offer pleasing fall color.

Helictotrichon sempervirens

Plant	Common name	Exposure / Zones	Page
Alopecurus pratensis 'Aureus'	YELLOW FOXTAIL GRASS	☼ ◐ ∕ 2–10, 14–17, 21–24	**p. 181**
Andropogon gerardii	BIG BLUESTEM	☼ ◐ ∕ 1–9, 14–24	**p. 185**
Arrhenatherum elatius bulbosum 'Variegatum'		☼ ◐ ∕ 1–7, 15–17, 23, 24	**p. 201**
Bamboo		☼ ◐ ∕ ZONES VARY	**p. 213**
Calamagrostis	REED GRASS	☼ ◐ ∕ 2B–24	**p. 238**
Carex	SEDGE	☼ ◐ ∕ ZONES VARY	**p. 251**
Chasmanthium latifolium	SEA OATS	☼ ◐ ∕ 2–10, 14–24	**p. 266**
Cortaderia selloana	PAMPAS GRASS	☼ ∕ 3–24; H1	**p. 294**
Cyperus		☼ ◐ ● ∕ ZONES VARY	**p. 306**
Deschampsia	HAIR GRASS	☼ ◐ ∕ 2–24	**p. 312**
Elymus magellanicus	MAGELLAN WHEATGRASS	☼ ◐ ∕ 3–6, 14–17, 21–24	**p. 325**
Festuca	FESCUE	☼ ◐ ∕ ZONES VARY	**p. 349**
Hakonechloa macra	JAPANESE FOREST GRASS	☼ ◐ ● ∕ 2B–9, 14–24	**p. 378**
Helictotrichon sempervirens	BLUE OAT GRASS	☼ ∕ 1–24	**p. 383**
Imperata cylindrica 'Rubra'	JAPANESE BLOOD GRASS	☼ ◐ ∕ 2B–24	**p. 399**
Juncus	RUSH	☼ ◐ ∕ ZONES VARY	**p. 410**
Leymus	LYME GRASS	☼ ◐ ∕ ZONES VARY	**p. 431**
Milium effusum 'Aureum'	BOWLES' GOLDEN GRASS	◐ ∕ 3B–9, 14–17	**p. 469**
Miscanthus	EULALIA	☼ ◐ ∕ ZONES VARY	**p. 470**
Molinia caerulea	MOOR GRASS	☼ ◐ ∕ 1–9, 14–17	**p. 471**
Muhlenbergia		☼ ◐ ∕ ZONES VARY	**p. 473**
Panicum virgatum	SWITCH GRASS	☼ ◐ ∕ 1–11, 14–23	**p. 495**
Pennisetum	FOUNTAIN GRASS	☼ ◐ ∕ ZONES VARY	**p. 510**
Phalaris arundinacea picta	RIBBON GRASS	☼ ◐ ∕ A1–A3; 1–10, 14–24	**p. 515**
Rhynchelytrum	NATAL RUBY GRASS	☼ ∕ 2B–24; H1, H2	**p. 577**
Stipa	FEATHER GRASS	☼ ∕ ZONES VARY	**p. 619**

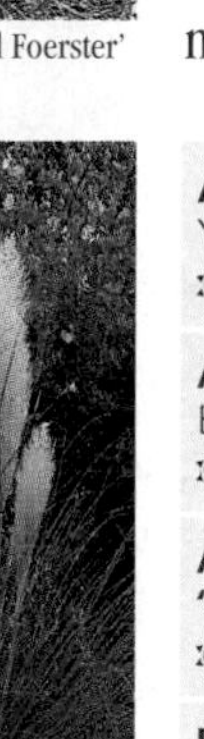

Cortaderia selloana 'Pumila'

Festuca glauca

Hakonechloa macra 'Aureola'

Helichtotrichon sempervirens

Imperata cylindrica 'Rubra'

Pennisetum setaceum 'Rubrum'

Phalaris arundinacea picta

Stipa gigantea

Archontophoenix cunninghamiana

PALMS AND CYCADS

Whether they bring to mind a desert oasis or a tropical beach, it's clear that palms are evocative plants. And not all have the classic silhouette of one straight trunk and a topknot. They may be single- or multitrunked, fan leafed or feather leafed, soft and graceful or stiff and architectural. Cycads resemble small feather palms but they're very slow growing—good choices for smaller gardens. Use palms and cycads to set a garden mood or as stylish exclamation points in the landscape.

Cocos nucifera

Butia capitata

Chamaerops humilis

Phoenix dactylifera

PALMS

Plant	Common name	Needs and zones	Page
Archontophoenix cunninghamiana	KING PALM	☼ ◑ ⁄ 21–24	**p. 197**
Brahea		☼ ⁄ ZONES VARY	**p. 231**
Butia capitata	PINDO PALM	☼ ◑ ⁄ 8, 9, 12–24; H1, H2	**p. 236**
Caryota	FISHTAIL PALM	☼ ◑ ⁄ 23, 24; H2	**p. 253**
Chamaedorea		◑ ● ⁄ 16, 17, 22–24; H2	**p. 265**
Chamaerops humilis	MEDITERRANEAN FAN PALM	☼ ◑ ⁄ 4–24; H1, H2	**p. 266**
Cocos nucifera	COCONUT PALM	☼ ⁄ H2	**p. 286**
Dypsis		NEEDS, ZONES VARY	**p. 322**
Hedyscepe canterburyana		☼ ◑ ⁄ 17, 23, 24; H1, H2	**p. 381**
Howea		◑ ⁄ 17, 21–24; H1, H2	**p. 392**
Jubaea chilensis	CHILEAN WINE PALM	☼ ⁄ 12–24	**p. 409**
Livistona		☼ ⁄ 13–17, 19–24; H1, H2	**p. 440**
Phoenix	DATE PALM	☼ ⁄ ZONES VARY	**p. 518**
Pritchardia	LOULU PALM	☼ ⁄ H2	**p. 547**
Ptychosperma		◑ ⁄ 23, 24; H1, H2	**p. 555**
Rhapidophyllum hystrix	NEEDLE PALM	☼ ◑ ● ⁄ 2–24	**p. 567**
Rhapis	LADY PALM	◑ ● ⁄ ZONES VARY	**p. 567**
Rhopalostylis		☼ ◑ ⁄ 17, 23, 24; H1, H2	**p. 575**
Roystonea	ROYAL PALM	☼ ⁄ 24; H2	**p. 588**
Sabal	PALMETTO	☼ ⁄ 12–17, 19–24; H1, H2	**p. 590**
Syagrus romanzoffianum	QUEEN PALM	☼ ⁄ 12, 13, 15–17, 19–24; H1, H2	**p. 624**
Trachycarpus fortunei	WINDMILL PALM	☼ ◑ ⁄ 4–24	**p. 636**
Washingtonia		☼ ⁄ 8–24; H1, H2	**p. 650**

CYCADS

Plant	Common name	Needs and zones	Page
Cycas		◑ ⁄ 8–24; H1, H2	**p. 304**
Dioon		◑ ⁄ ZONES VARY	**p. 318**
Zamia		NEEDS VARY ⁄ 21–24; H1, H2	**p. 655**

Trachycarpus fortunei

Washingtonia filifera

Cycas revoluta

For growing symbol explanations, please see page 64.

Native Alaskan spruces

NATIVE PLANTS

Regional native plants are wise additions to the garden. They bring diverse textures and colors to your plantings; and because they are naturally suited to the climate, they typically need less maintenance than many popular non-native plants. Where water is scarce, they're an appropriate (and thrifty) choice, likely to thrive on nothing more than natural rainfall. On these pages, we list natives for six Western regions: Alaska, the Pacific Northwest, the Rocky Mountain area, California, the Southwest, and the Hawaiian Islands. Be aware, though, that these broad areas encompass a good deal of variation. Check the descriptions in the Western Plant Encyclopedia for climate zone adaptation, exposure preference, and moisture needs; then choose the plants best suited to your climate and site. If you start with nursery-raised plants, remember that drought-tolerant natives will need dry-season watering for a year or two until they're established.

Populus tremuloides

Cornus stolonifera

Calocedrus decurrens

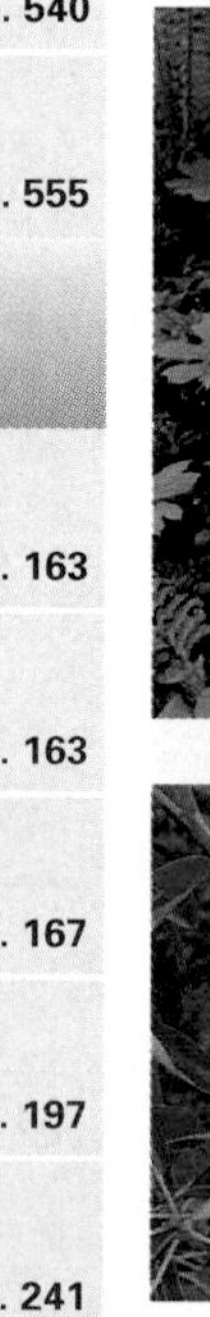

ALASKA — *Trees*

Picea glauca
WHITE SPRUCE
A1–A3; 1–7, 14–17 — p. 521

Populus tremuloides
QUAKING ASPEN
A1–A3; 1–7, 14–19 — p. 543

ALASKA — *Shrubs*

Amelanchier alnifolia
SASKATOON
A1–A3; 1–6 — p. 183

Cornus stolonifera
REDTWIG DOGWOOD
A1–A3; 1–9, 14–21 — p. 293

Elaeagnus commutata
SILVERBERRY
A1–A3; 1–3 — p. 324

Rosa rugosa
RAMANAS ROSE, SEA TOMATO
A1–A3; 1–24 — p. 587

Viburnum edule
HIGHBUSH CRANBERRY
A1–A3; 1–11 — p. 646

ALASKA — *Ground Covers*

Arctostaphylos uva-ursi
BEARBERRY — p. 199
A1–A3; 1–9, 14–24

Juniperus communis 'Effusa'
A1–A3; 1–24 — p. 411

Rubus arcticus 'Kenai Carpet'
NAGOONBERRY
A1–A3; 1–3 — p. 588

ALASKA — *Perennials, Ferns*

Allium schoenoprasum
CHIVES
ALL ZONES — p. 179

Chrysanthemum arcticum
ARCTIC CHRYSANTHEMUM
A1–A3; 1–10, 14–21 — p. 272

Iris setosa
A1–A3; 1–6 — p. 405

Matteuccia struthiopteris
OSTRICH FERN
A1–A3; 1–10, 14–17 — p. 462

Polemonium pulcherrimum
A1–A3; 1–11, 14–17; H1 — p. 540

Pulsatilla patens
EASTERN PASQUE FLOWER
A1–A3; 1–6, 15–17 — p. 555

PACIFIC NORTHWEST — *Trees*

Abies concolor
WHITE FIR
A2, A3; 1–9, 14–24 — p. 163

Abies lasiocarpa
ALPINE FIR
A2, A3; 1–9, 14–17 — p. 163

Acer circinatum
VINE MAPLE
A3; 2B–6, 14–17 — p. 167

Arbutus menziesii
MADRONE
4–7, 14–19 — p. 197

Calocedrus decurrens
INCENSE CEDAR
2–12, 14–24 — p. 241

Plant listings continue▶

Chrysanthemum arcticum

Iris setosa

Matteuccia struthiopteris

Arbutus menziesii

Chamaecyparis nootkatensis

Tsuga mertensiana

Corylus cornuta californica

Gaultheria shallon

Chamaecyparis nootkatensis
NOOTKA CYPRESS
☼ ◐ ⁄ A2, A3; 2–6, 15–17 **p. 265**

Cornus nuttallii
PACIFIC DOGWOOD
☼ ◐ ⁄ 3B–9, 14–20 **p. 292**

Fraxinus latifolia
OREGON ASH
☼ ⁄ 3–9, 14–24 **p. 356**

Pinus contorta contorta
BEACH PINE, SHORE PINE
☼ ⁄ A3; 4–9, 14–24; H1 **p. 525**

Pseudotsuga menziesii
DOUGLAS FIR
☼ ◐ ⁄ A2, A3; 1–10, 14–17 **p. 554**

Quercus garryana
OREGON WHITE OAK
☼ ⁄ 4–11, 14–23 **p. 561**

Taxus brevifolia
WESTERN YEW
☼ ◐ ● ⁄ A3; 1–7, 14–17 **p. 628**

Thuja plicata
WESTERN RED CEDAR
☼ ◐ ⁄ A3; 1–9, 14–24 **p. 631**

Tsuga mertensiana
MOUNTAIN HEMLOCK
☼ ◐ ⁄ A1–A3; 1–7, 14–17 **p. 640**

PACIFIC NORTHWEST
Shrubs

Acer glabrum
ROCKY MOUNTAIN MAPLE
☼ ◐ ⁄ 1–7, 10 **p. 168**

Amelanchier alnifolia
SASKATOON
☼ ◐ ⁄ A1–A3; 1–6 **p. 183**

Arctostaphylos columbiana
HAIRY MANZANITA
☼ ◐ ⁄ 4–6, 15–17 **p. 198**

Cornus stolonifera
REDTWIG DOGWOOD
☼ ◐ ⁄ A1–A3; 1–9, 14–21 **p. 293**

Corylus cornuta californica
WESTERN HAZELNUT
☼ ◐ ⁄ 2–9, 14–20 **p. 295**

Gaultheria ovatifolia
◐ ⁄ 3–7, 14–17 **p. 361**

Gaultheria shallon
SALAL
◐ ⁄ 4–7, 14–17 **p. 361**

Holodiscus discolor
CREAM BUSH
◐ ⁄ 1–9, 14–19 **p. 390**

Leucothoe davisiae
SIERRA LAUREL
☼ ◐ ● ⁄ 2, 4–7, 15–17 **p. 430**

Mahonia aquifolium
OREGON GRAPE
☼ ◐ ● ⁄ 2–12, 14–24 **p. 455**

Mahonia nervosa
LONGLEAF MAHONIA
◐ ● ⁄ 2B–10, 14–24 **p. 456**

Myrica californica
PACIFIC WAX MYRTLE
☼ ⁄ 4–9, 14–24 **p. 475**

Rhododendron occidentale
WESTERN AZALEA
◐ ⁄ 4–7, 14–17, 19–24 **p. 575**

Ribes aureum
GOLDEN CURRANT
☼ ◐ ⁄ A2, A3; 1–12, 14–23 **p. 577**

Ribes sanguineum
PINK WINTER CURRANT
☼ ◐ ⁄ A3; 4–9, 14–24 **p. 577**

Vaccinium ovatum
EVERGREEN HUCKLEBERRY
☼ ◐ ● ⁄ 4–7, 14–17 **p. 643**

PACIFIC NORTHWEST
Ground Covers, Vines

Asarum caudatum
WILD GINGER
◐ ● ⁄ 4–6, 14–24 **p. 204**

Cornus canadensis
BUNCHBERRY
◐ ● ⁄ A1–A3; 1–9, 14–16 **p. 292**

Fragaria chiloensis
BEACH STRAWBERRY
☼ ◐ ⁄ 4–24; H1 **p. 355**

Mahonia repens
CREEPING MAHONIA
☼ ◐ ⁄ 2B–9, 14–24 **p. 456**

Maianthemum dilatatum
FALSE LILY-OF-THE-VALLEY
◐ ⁄ A2, A3; 2–9, 14–17 **p. 456**

PACIFIC NORTHWEST
Perennials, Ferns, Grasses

Adiantum aleuticum
FIVE-FINGER FERN
◐ ● ⁄ 1–7, 14–21 **p. 172**

Aquilegia formosa
WESTERN COLUMBINE
☼ ◐ ⁄ A1–A3; 1–11, 14–24 **p. 195**

Blechnum spicant
DEER FERN
◐ ● ⁄ 2B–7, 14–19, 24 **p. 226**

Camassia quamash
CAMASS
☼ ◐ ⁄ 1–10, 14–17 **p. 243**

Dodecatheon
SHOOTING STAR
☼ ◐ ⁄ ZONES VARY **p. 318**

Mahonia aquifolium

Myrica californica

Cornus canadensis

Adiantum aleuticum

Aquilegia formosa

For growing symbol explanations, please see page 64.

Dryas octopetala

Iris, Pacific Coast

Lewisia cotyledon

Sedum spathulifolium 'Cape Blanco'

Trillium ovatum

Picea pungens

Dryas octopetala
☼ ⁄ A1–A3; 1–6 **p. 320**

Dryopteris expansa
SPREADING WOOD FERN
◑ ● ⁄ 2–7, 14–17, 19–24 **p. 321**

Erythronium revolutum
◑ ⁄ 1–7, 14–17 **p. 335**

Fritillaria camschatcensis
BLACK LILY
◑ ⁄ A1–A3; 1–7, 15–17 **p. 357**

Iris, Pacific Coast
☼ ◑ ⁄ 3–9, 14–24 **p. 404**

Lewisia
☼ ◑ ⁄ 1–7, 14–17 **p. 431**

Lilium columbianum
COLUMBIA LILY
☼ ◑ ⁄ 2–7, 14–19 **p. 435**

Linnaea borealis
TWINFLOWER
◑ ● ⁄ A1–A3; 1, 2, 4–6, 14–17 **p. 436**

Polystichum munitum
SWORD FERN
◑ ● ⁄ A3; 2–9, 14–24 **p. 542**

Sedum spathulifolium
☼ ◑ ⁄ 2–9, 14–24 **p. 605**

Smilacina racemosa
FALSE SOLOMON'S SEAL
◑ ● ⁄ 1–7, 14–17 **p. 611**

Tolmiea menziesii
PIGGY-BACK PLANT
◑ ● ⁄ 4–9, 14–17, 20–24 **p. 634**

Trillium ovatum
WAKE ROBIN
◑ ● ⁄ 2–7, 14–17 **p. 638**

Vancouveria
◑ ⁄ ZONES VARY **p. 644**

ROCKY MOUNTAIN REGION

Trees

Abies concolor
WHITE FIR
☼ ◑ ⁄ A2, A3; 1–9, 14–24 **p. 163**

Betula occidentalis
WATER BIRCH
☼ ⁄ A3; 1–7, 10 **p. 223**

Juniperus monosperma
☼ ◑ ⁄ 1–3, 10–11 **p. 414**

Juniperus scopulorum (tree form)
☼ ◑ ⁄ 1–24 **p. 414**

Picea pungens
COLORADO SPRUCE
☼ ◑ ⁄ A2, A3; 1–10, 14–17 **p. 521**

Pinus (several)
PINE
☼ ⁄ SEE CHART **p. 523**

Populus × acuminata
LANCELEAF COTTONWOOD
☼ ⁄ 1–11, 14–21 **p. 543**

Populus tremuloides
QUAKING ASPEN
☼ ⁄ A1–A3; 1–7, 14–19 **p. 543**

Prunus americana
WILD PLUM
☼ ⁄ 1–3, 10 **p. 552**

Pseudotsuga menziesii
DOUGLAS FIR
☼ ◑ ⁄ A2, A3; 1–10, 14–17 **p. 554**

ROCKY MOUNTAIN REGION

Shrubs

Acer glabrum
ROCKY MOUNTAIN MAPLE
☼ ◑ ⁄ 1–7, 10 **p. 168**

Amelanchier alnifolia
SASKATOON
☼ ◑ ⁄ A1–A3; 1–6 **p. 183**

Artemisia tridentata
BIG SAGEBRUSH
☼ ⁄ 1–3, 6–11, 14–24 **p. 202**

Ceanothus velutinus
TOBACCO BRUSH
☼ ⁄ 2–7, 15–17 **p. 258**

Cercocarpus ledifolius
CURL-LEAF MOUNTAIN MAHOGANY
☼ ⁄ 1–3, 7–10, 14–21 **p. 263**

Cercocarpus montanus
☼ ⁄ 1–3, 7–10 **p. 263**

Chrysothamnus nauseosus
RABBITBRUSH
☼ ⁄ 1–3, 10, 11 **p. 274**

Cornus stolonifera
REDTWIG DOGWOOD
☼ ◑ ⁄ A1–A3; 1–9, 14–21 **p. 293**

Corylus cornuta californica
WESTERN HAZELNUT
☼ ◑ ⁄ 2–9, 14–20 **p. 295**

Elaeagnus commutata
SILVERBERRY
☼ ◑ ⁄ A1–A3; 1–3 **p. 324**

Fallugia paradoxa
APACHE PLUME
☼ ⁄ 2–23 **p. 347**

Forestiera neomexicana
NEW MEXICAN PRIVET
☼ ⁄ 1–3, 7–24 **p. 353**

Pinus aristata

Populus × acuminata

Chrysothamnus nauseosus

Fallugia paradoxa

Plant listings continue ▶

Quercus gambellii

Ribes aureum

Antennaria dioica

Campanula rotundifolia

Holodiscus dumosus
MOUNTAIN SPRAY
1–3, 10 **p. 390**

Juniperus communis 'Compressa'
A1–A3; 1–24 **p. 414**

Philadelphus lewisii
WILD MOCK ORANGE
1–10, 14–24 **p. 516**

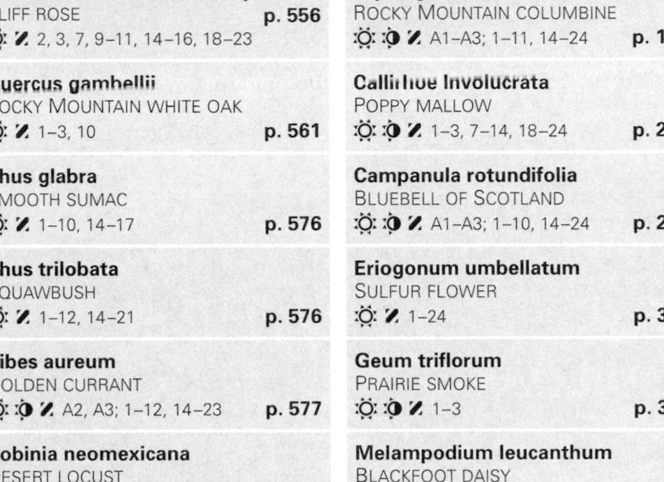

Prunus besseyi
WESTERN SAND CHERRY
A1–A3; 1–3, 10 **p. 552**

Purshia mexicana stansburyana
CLIFF ROSE **p. 556**
2, 3, 7, 9–11, 14–16, 18–23

Quercus gambellii
ROCKY MOUNTAIN WHITE OAK
1–3, 10 **p. 561**

Rhus glabra
SMOOTH SUMAC
1–10, 14–17 **p. 576**

Rhus trilobata
SQUAWBUSH
1–12, 14–21 **p. 576**

Ribes aureum
GOLDEN CURRANT
A2, A3; 1–12, 14–23 **p. 577**

Robinia neomexicana
DESERT LOCUST
2, 3, 7–11, 14, 18–24 **p. 578**

Rubus deliciosus
ROCKY MOUNTAIN THIMBLEBERRY
1–6, 10 **p. 588**

Shepherdia argentea
SILVER BUFFALOBERRY
1–3, 7, 10 **p. 609**

Symphoricarpos orbiculatus
CORALBERRY
1–11, 14–21 **p. 624**

Yucca baccata
BANANA YUCCA, DATIL
1–24 **p. 654**

ROCKY MOUNTAIN REGION
Ground Covers, Vines

Antennaria dioica
PUSSY TOES
A1, A2; 1–3, 6, 7, 14–16 **p. 187**

Arctostaphylos uva-ursi
BEARBERRY
A1–A3; 1–9, 14–24 **p. 199**

Calylophus hartwegii
SUNDROPS
1–3, 6–16, 18–24 **p. 243**

Clematis ligusticifolia
1–9, 14–21 **p. 283**

Humulus lupulus neomexicanus
COMMON HOP
A2, A3; 1–10, 14–21 **p. 393**

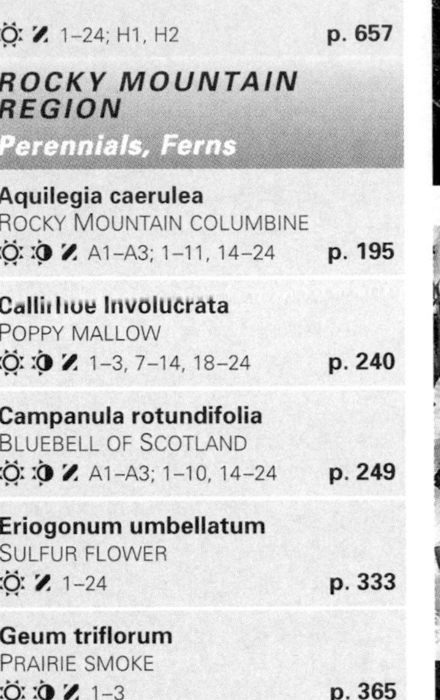

Mahonia repens
CREEPING MAHONIA
2B–9, 14–24 **p. 456**

Zinnia grandiflora
1–24; H1, H2 **p. 657**

ROCKY MOUNTAIN REGION
Perennials, Ferns

Aquilegia caerulea
ROCKY MOUNTAIN COLUMBINE
A1–A3; 1–11, 14–24 **p. 195**

Callirhoe involucrata
POPPY MALLOW
1–3, 7–14, 18–24 **p. 240**

Campanula rotundifolia
BLUEBELL OF SCOTLAND
A1–A3; 1–10, 14–24 **p. 249**

Eriogonum umbellatum
SULFUR FLOWER
1–24 **p. 333**

Geum triflorum
PRAIRIE SMOKE
1–3 **p. 365**

Melampodium leucanthum
BLACKFOOT DAISY
2, 3, 10–13 **p. 465**

Monarda fistulosa
BEE BALM
A2, A3; 1–10, 14–17 **p. 471**

Oenothera caespitosa
TUFTED EVENING PRIMROSE
1–3, 7–14, 18–21 **p. 485**

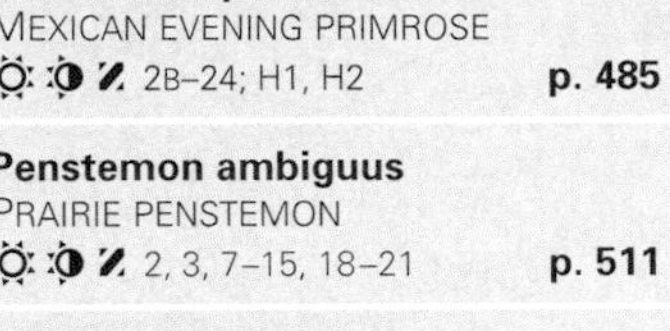

Oenothera speciosa
MEXICAN EVENING PRIMROSE
2B–24; H1, H2 **p. 485**

Penstemon ambiguus
PRAIRIE PENSTEMON
2, 3, 7–15, 18–21 **p. 511**

Penstemon barbatus
1–20 **p. 511**

Penstemon eatonii
FIRECRACKER PENSTEMON
1–3, 7–13, 18–21 **p. 511**

Penstemon palmeri
SCENTED PENSTEMON
2, 3, 10–13 **p. 511**

Penstemon pinifolius
2–24 **p. 511**

Penstemon strictus
ROCKY MOUNTAIN PENSTEMON
1–3, 10–13 **p. 511**

Oenothera caespitosa

Oenothera speciosa 'Rosea'

Penstemon ambiguus

Penstemon strictus

For growing symbol explanations, please see page 64.

Ratibida columnifera

Aesculus californica

Pinus radiata

Platanus racemosa

Ratibida columnifera
MEXICAN HAT
ALL ZONES p. 565

CALIFORNIA
Trees

Abies (several)
FIR
ZONES VARY p. 162

Aesculus californica
CALIFORNIA BUCKEYE
3–10, 14–24 p. 173

Arbutus menziesii
MADRONE
4–7, 14–19 p. 197

Calocedrus decurrens
INCENSE CEDAR
2–12, 14–24 p. 241

Cercis occidentalis
WESTERN REDBUD
2–24 p. 263

Chamaecyparis lawsoniana
PORT ORFORD CEDAR
A3; 3–6, 15–17 p. 265

Chamaecyparis nootkatensis
NOOTKA CYPRESS
A2, A3; 2–6, 15–17 p. 265

Cornus nuttallii
PACIFIC DOGWOOD
3B–9, 14–20 p. 292

Lithocarpus densiflorus
TANBARK OAK
4–7, 14–24 p. 438

Lyonothamnus floribundus
CATALINA IRONWOOD
14–17, 19–24 p. 444

Picea breweriana
BREWER'S WEEPING SPRUCE
2B, 3–7, 14–17 p. 521

Pinus (several)
PINE
ZONES VARY p. 523

Platanus racemosa
CALIFORNIA SYCAMORE
4–24 p. 532

Populus fremontii
WESTERN COTTONWOOD
1–12, 14–21 p. 543

Populus tremuloides
QUAKING ASPEN
A1–A3; 1–7, 14–19 p. 543

Quercus (many)
OAK
ZONES VARY p. 558

Umbellularia californica
CALIFORNIA LAUREL
4–9, 14–24 p. 643

CALIFORNIA
Shrubs

Arctostaphylos (many)
MANZANITA
ZONES VARY p. 198

Baccharis pilularis
DWARF COYOTE BRUSH
5–11, 14–24 p. 212

Calycanthus occidentalis
SPICE BUSH
4–9, 14–24 p. 242

Carpenteria californica
BUSH ANEMONE
5–9, 14–24 p. 252

Ceanothus (many)
WILD LILAC
5–9, 14–24 p. 256

Cercis occidentalis
WESTERN REDBUD
2–24 p. 263

Comarostaphylis diversifolia
SUMMER HOLLY
7–9, 14–24 p. 288

Cornus stolonifera
REDTWIG DOGWOOD
A1–A3; 1–9, 14–21 p. 293

Dendromecon harfordii
ISLAND BUSH POPPY
7–9, 14–24 p. 312

Eriogonum (many)
WILD BUCKWHEAT
ZONES VARY p. 333

Fremontodendron (several)
FLANNEL BUSH
4–24 p. 357

Galvezia speciosa
ISLAND BUSH SNAPDRAGON
14–24 p. 360

Garrya (several)
SILKTASSEL
ZONES VARY p. 361

Heteromeles arbutifolia
TOYON
5–9, 14–24 p. 386

Lavatera assurgentiflora
TREE MALLOW
14–24 p. 427

Lupinus arboreus
4, 5, 14–17, 22–24 p. 443

Mahonia (several)
NEEDS, ZONES VARY p. 455

Myrica californica
PACIFIC WAX MYRTLE
4–9, 14–24 p. 475

Plant listings continue ▶

Arctostaphylos uva-ursi 'Wood's Compact'

Calycanthus occidentalis

Carpenteria californica

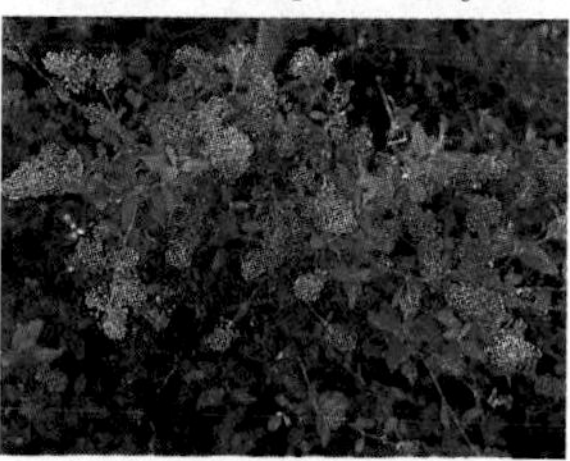
Ceanothus 'Ray Hartman'

Cercis occidentalis

Dendromecon harfordii

Salvia clevelandii

Eriogonum umbellatum

Sambucus racemosa racemosa

Philadelphus lewisii

Trichostema lanatum

Rhamnus californica 'Eve Case'

Rhus integrifolia

Ceanothus griseus horizontalis 'Yankee Point'

Aquilegia formosa

Erigeron glaucus

Iris, Pacific Coast

Lilium pardalinum

Penstemon centranthifolius
SCARLET BUGLER
7–23 **p. 511**

Philadelphus lewisii
WILD MOCK ORANGE
1–10, 14–24 **p. 516**

Prunus ilicifolia
5–9, 12–24 **p. 549**

Rhamnus californica
COFFEEBERRY
4–9, 14–24; H1, H2 **p. 566**

Rhododendron occidentale
WESTERN AZALEA
4–7, 14–17, 19–24 **p. 575**

Rhus integrifolia
LEMONADE BERRY
8, 9, 14–17, 19–24 **p. 576**

Rhus ovata
SUGAR BUSH
9–12, 14–24 **p. 576**

Ribes (several)
CURRANT, GOOSEBERRY
ZONES VARY **p. 577**

Salvia clevelandii
CLEVELAND SAGE
8, 9, 12–24 **p. 593**

Salvia leucophylla
PURPLE SAGE
8, 9, 14–17, 19–24 **p. 595**

Sambucus (some)
ELDERBERRY
ZONES VARY **p. 597**

Symphoricarpos albus
COMMON SNOWBERRY
A3; 1–11, 14–21 **p. 624**

Trichostema lanatum
WOOLLY BLUE CURLS
14–24 **p. 637**

Vaccinium parvifolium
RED HUCKLEBERRY
A3; 2–7, 14–17 **p. 643**

CALIFORNIA
Ground Covers, Vines

Arctostaphylos (many)
MANZANITA
ZONES VARY **p. 198**

Aristolochia californica
CALIFORNIA DUTCHMAN'S PIPE
5–10, 14–24 **p. 200**

Ceanothus (many)
WILD LILAC
5–9, 14–24 **p. 256**

Clematis ligusticifolia
1–9, 14–21 **p. 283**

For growing symbol explanations, please see page 64.

Mimulus aurantiacus

Penstemon heterophyllus purdyi

Romneya coulteri

Sisyrinchium bellum

CALIFORNIA
Perennials, Ferns, Grasses

Achillea millefolium
COMMON YARROW
A1–A3; 1–24 p. 170

Aquilegia formosa
WESTERN COLUMBINE
A1–A3; 1–11, 14–24 p. 195

Artemisia californica
CALIFORNIA SAGEBRUSH
7–9, 14–24 p. 202

Asarum caudatum
WILD GINGER
4–6, 14–24 p. 204

Erigeron glaucus
BEACH ASTER
4–6, 15–17, 22–24 p. 329

Heuchera (some)
CORAL BELLS
ZONES VARY p. 387

Iris, Pacific Coast
3–9, 14–24 p. 404

Leymus condensatus
LYME GRASS
7–12, 14–24 p. 431

Lilium humboldtii
HUMBOLDT LILY
3, 7, 14–24 p. 435

Lilium pardalinum
LEOPARD LILY
2–7, 14–24 p. 435

Mimulus
MONKEY FLOWER
NEEDS, ZONES VARY p. 469

Muhlenbergia rigens
DEER GRASS
4–24 p. 473

Nassella pulchra
PURPLE NEEDLE GRASS
5–9, 11, 14–24 p. 478

Penstemon heterophyllus
BEARD TONGUE
7–24 p. 511

Penstemon spectabilis
ROYAL BEARD TONGUE
7, 14–23 p. 511

Romneya coulteri
MATILIJA POPPY
4–12, 14–24; H1 p. 578

Sidalcea malviflora
CHECKERBLOOM
2–9, 14–24 p. 609

Sisyrinchium bellum
BLUE-EYED GRASS
2–9, 14–24 p. 610

Sisyrinchium californicum
YELLOW-EYED GRASS
4–9, 14–24 p. 610

Vancouveria hexandra
4–7, 14–17, 19–24 p. 644

Vancouveria planipetala
INSIDE-OUT FLOWER
4–7, 14–17, 19–24 p. 644

Zauschneria
CALIFORNIA FUCHSIA
NEEDS, ZONES VARY p. 656

SOUTHWEST
Trees

Acacia constricta
WHITE THORN
10–24 p. 164

Acacia smallii
8, 9, 12–24 p. 166

Cercidium floridum
BLUE PALO VERDE
8–14, 18–20 p. 263

Cercidium microphyllum
LITTLELEAF PALO VERDE
8–14, 18–20 p. 263

Cercidium praecox
PALO BREA, SONORAN PALO VERDE
12, 13, 18–20 p. 263

Chilopsis linearis
DESERT WILLOW
3B, 7–14, 18–23 p. 269

Cupressus arizonica
ARIZONA CYPRESS
7–24 p. 303

Lysiloma microphylla thornberi
FEATHER BUSH
12–24; H1, H2 p. 445

Olneya tesota
DESERT IRONWOOD
8, 9, 11–14, 18–23 p. 486

Pithecellobium flexicaule
TEXAS EBONY
10–13 p. 530

Platanus wrightii
ARIZONA SYCAMORE
10–12 p. 532

Prosopis (several)
MESQUITE
10–13, 18–24 p. 547

Quercus emoryi
EMORY OAK
10–13 p. 560

Washingtonia filifera
CALIFORNIA FAN PALM
8–24; H1, H2 p. 650

Vancouveria hexandra

Zauschneria californica latifolia

Cercidium microphyllum

Olneya tesota

Calliandra californica

Plant listings continue ▶

Encelia farinosa

Salvia greggii

Sophora secundiflora

Tagetes lemmonii

Tecoma stans

SOUTHWEST
Shrubs

Anisacanthus thurberi
CHUPAROSA
☼ ✓ 8–13, 18–23, H1, H2 **p. 187**

Calliandra californica
BAJA FAIRY DUSTER
☼ ✓ 10–24 **p. 239**

Calliandra eriophylla
FAIRY DUSTER
☼ ✓ 10–24 **p. 239**

Chrysothamnus nauseosus
RABBITBRUSH
☼ ✓ 1–3, 10, 11 **p. 274**

Cordia boissieri
TEXAS OLIVE
☼ ✓ 8–24 **p. 289**

Dalea frutescens
BLACK DALEA
☼ ✓ 10–13 **p. 309**

Dalea pulchra
INDIGO BUSH
☼ ✓ 12, 13 **p. 309**

Dodonaea viscosa
HOP BUSH
☼ ◑ ✓ 7–24; H1, H2 **p. 319**

Encelia farinosa
BRITTLEBUSH
☼ ✓ 8–16, 18–24; H1 **p. 326**

Fallugia paradoxa
APACHE PLUME
☼ ✓ 2–23 **p. 347**

Justicia californica
CHUPAROSA
☼ ✓ 10–14, 18–24 **p. 415**

Larrea tridentata
CREOSOTE BUSH
☼ ✓ 7–14, 18–21 **p. 423**

Leucophyllum
TEXAS RANGER
☼ ✓ 7–24 **p. 430**

Rhus ovata
SUGAR BUSH
☼ ✓ 9–12, 14–24 **p. 576**

Rhus trilobata
SQUAWBUSH
☼ ✓ 1–12, 14–21 **p. 576**

Salvia greggii
AUTUMN SAGE
☼ ✓ 8–24 **p. 594**

Salvia microphylla
☼ ◑ ✓ 7–24 **p. 595**

Simmondsia chinensis
JOJOBA
☼ ✓ 7–24 **p. 610**

Sophora secundiflora
TEXAS MOUNTAIN LAUREL
☼ ◑ ✓ 8–16, 18–24 **p. 613**

Tagetes lemmonii
COPPER CANYON DAISY
☼ ✓ 8–10, 12–24; H1 **p. 626**

Tecoma stans
YELLOW BELLS
☼ ✓ 12, 13, 21–24; H1, H2 **p. 629**

Vauquelinia californica
ARIZONA ROSEWOOD
☼ ◑ ✓ 10–13 **p. 644**

SOUTHWEST
Ground Covers, Vines

Antigonon leptopus
CORAL VINE
☼ ✓ 12, 13, 18–24; H1, H2 **p. 188**

Baccharis sarothroides
DESERT BROOM
☼ ✓ 7–24 **p. 212**

Calylophus hartwegii
SUNDROPS
☼ ◑ ✓ 1–3, 6–16, 18–24 **p. 243**

Dalea greggii
TRAILING INDIGO BUSH
☼ ✓ 10–13 **p. 309**

Mascagnia macroptera
YELLOW ORCHID VINE
☼ ✓ 12–24 **p. 462**

Merremia aurea
YELLOW MORNING GLORY
☼ ✓ 12–24 **p. 467**

Oenothera speciosa
MEXICAN EVENING PRIMROSE
☼ ◑ ✓ 2B–24; H1, H2 **p. 485**

Oenothera stubbei
SALTILLO EVENING PRIMROSE
☼ ◑ ✓ 10–14, 18–24 **p. 485**

Zinnia grandiflora
☼ ✓ 1–24; H1, H2 **p. 657**

SOUTHWEST
Grasses, Accent Plants

Agave parryi
☼ ◑ ✓ 2B, 3, 6–24 **p. 175**

Echinocactus (many)
BARREL CACTUS
☼ ◑ ✓ 12–24 **p. 322**

Echinocereus (some)
HEDGEHOG CACTUS
☼ ✓ ZONES VARY **p. 323**

Ferocactus (some)
BARREL CACTUS
☼ ✓ 8–24 **p. 349**

Calylophus hartwegii

Zinnia grandiflora

Fouquieria splendens

Hesperaloe parviflora

Opuntia basilaris

For growing symbol explanations, please see page 64.

Baileya multiradiata

Melampodium leucanthum

Penstemon eatonii

Ratibida columnifera

Verbena bipinnatifida

Fouquieria splendens
OCOTILLO
10–13, 18–20 p. 354

Hesperaloe parviflora
RED YUCCA
2B, 3, 7–16, 18–24 p. 386

Muhlenbergia dumosa
BAMBOO MUHLY
8–24 p. 473

Muhlenbergia rigens
DEER GRASS
4–24 p. 473

Opuntia (many)
ZONES VARY p. 487

Yucca (many)
ZONES VARY p. 654

SOUTHWEST
Annuals, Perennials

Baileya multiradiata
DESERT MARIGOLD
1–3, 7–23 p. 213

Melampodium leucanthum
BLACKFOOT DAISY
2, 3, 10–13 p. 465

Oenothera caespitosa
TUFTED EVENING PRIMROSE
1–3, 7–14, 18–21 p. 485

Penstemon ambiguus
PRAIRIE PENSTEMON
2, 3, 7–15, 18–21 p. 511

Penstemon barbatus
1–20 p. 511

Penstemon eatonii
FIRECRACKER PENSTEMON
1–3, 7–13, 18–21 p. 511

Penstemon parryi
PARRY'S PENSTEMON
3, 10, 12, 13 p. 511

Penstemon strictus
ROCKY MOUNTAIN PENSTEMON
1–3, 10–13 p. 511

Penstemon superbus
12, 13 p. 511

Ratibida columnifera
MEXICAN HAT
ALL ZONES p. 565

Salvia farinacea
MEALYCUP SAGE
ALL ZONES p. 594

Verbena bipinnatifida
1–24 p. 645

Verbena gooddingii
7–24 p. 645

HAWAII
Trees

Acacia koa
KOA
H1, H2 p. 165

Cibotium glaucum
HAPU'U
17, 23, 24; H2 p. 274

Erythrina sandwicensis
WILIWILI
H2 p. 335

Metrosideros polymorphus
'OHI'A LEHUA
H1, H2 p. 467

Pritchardia hillebrandii
LOULU LELO
H2 p. 547

HAWAII
Shrubs

Artemisia australis
'AHINAHINA
H1, H2 p. 202

Dodonaea viscosa
HOP BUSH
7–24; H1, H2 p. 319

Gnaphalium sandwicensium sandwicensium
H1, H2 p. 368

Hibiscus waimeae
WHITE KAUAI HIBISCUS
H1 p. 389

Scaevola taccada
BEACH NAUPAKA
H2 p. 601

Sida fallax
'ILIMA
23, 24; H1, H2 p. 609

HAWAII
Ground Covers

Alyxia oliviformis
MAILE
H1, H2 p. 183

Heliotropium anomalum argenteum
H2 p. 383

HAWAII
Perennials

Plectranthus parviflorus
'ALA 'ALA WAI NUI
22–24; H2 p. 533

Acacia koa

Cibotium glaucum

Erythrina sandwicensis

Hibiscus waimeae

Scaevola taccada

Alyxia oliviformis

Monarch butterfly and *Achillea*

Plants that Attract

BUTTERFLIES AND HUMMINGBIRDS

Coreopsis verticillata 'Moonbeam'

Butterflies and hummingbirds are welcome visitors to most gardens. Choose the right plants and you can encourage them to stay a while. Butterfly larvae (caterpillars) need food plants; adult butterflies need nectar plants. Sunny areas such as meadows that are sheltered from the wind and contain such amenities as leaf litter, rock crevices, brush piles, damp places, and even weeds are the most welcoming of gardens for butterflies. When you choose plants, keep in mind that not every plant will attract butterflies in every region. And never use pesticides, unless you can target the specific pest without harming the butterflies. Hummingbirds ingest half their weight in food every day. Flowering plants provide nectar; spiders and insects supply protein. Hummingbirds visit a huge array of plants. The ones listed are some of their favorites.

Alcea rosea

Aster novi-belgii

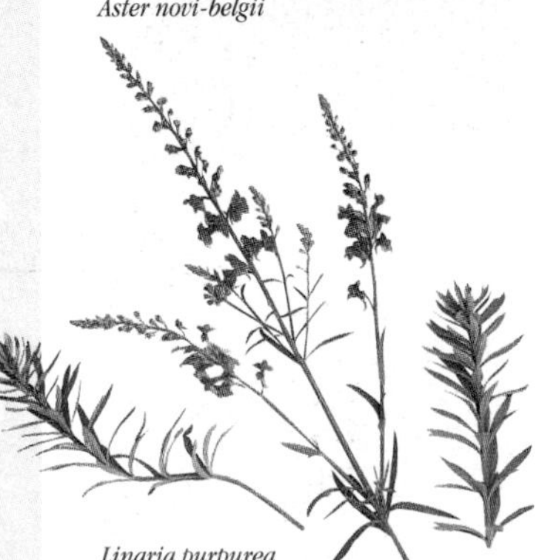

Linaria purpurea

BUTTERFLY LARVAE

Annuals, Perennials, Grasses

Achillea millefolium
COMMON YARROW
☼ A1–A3, 1–24 — p. 170

Alcea rosea
HOLLYHOCK
☼ ◑ 1–24 — p. 177

Antirrhinum majus
SNAPDRAGON
☼ A3; 1–24 — p. 188

Asclepias
☼ ZONES VARY — p. 204

Aster
☼ ZONES VARY — p. 207

Broccoli, Cabbage, Mustard
☼ ALL ZONES — pp. 232, 236, 474

Dicentra
BLEEDING HEART
◑ ● 1–9, 14–24 — p. 314

Digitalis purpurea
COMMON FOXGLOVE
☼ ◑ ● A2, A3; 1–24 — p. 317

Eriogonum
WILD BUCKWHEAT
☼ ZONES VARY — p. 333

Foeniculum vulgare
COMMON FENNEL
☼ ZONES VARY — p. 353

Helianthus
SUNFLOWER
☼ ZONES VARY — p. 382

Linaria purpurea
TOADFLAX
☼ ◑ 2–10, 14–24 — p. 436

Lobularia maritima
SWEET ALYSSUM
☼ ◑ ALL ZONES — p. 440

Lupinus
LUPINE
☼ ZONES VARY — p. 443

Malva
MALLOW
☼ 1–9, 14–24 — p. 457

Mimulus aurantiacus
STICKY MONKEY FLOWER
☼ ◑ 5–9, 14–24 — p. 469

Penstemon
BEARD TONGUE
☼ ◑ ZONES VARY — p. 510

Ruta graveolens
RUE
☼ 2–24 — p. 590

Sidalcea malviflora
CHECKERBLOOM
☼ 2–9, 14–24 — p. 609

Tropaeolum majus
GARDEN NASTURTIUM
☼ ◑ ALL ZONES — p. 639

Veronica
SPEEDWELL
☼ ZONES VARY — p. 645

Helianthus annuus

Mimulus aurantiacus

Linaria purpurea

For growing symbol explanations, please see page 64.

Wisteria floribunda

Hibiscus syriacus

Holodiscus discolor

Ribes sanguineum

Rosa 'Leander'

BUTTERFLY LARVAE
Ground Covers, Vines

Humulus lupulus
COMMON HOP
A2, A3, 1–10, 14–21 **p. 393**

Passiflora
PASSION VINE
ZONES VARY **p. 499**

Strawberry
A1–A3; 1–9, 14–24; H1, H2 **p. 620**

Wisteria
ZONES VARY **p. 652**

BUTTERFLY LARVAE
Shrubs

Cassia
ZONES VARY **p. 254**

Ceanothus
WILD LILAC
5–9, 14–24 **p. 256**

Hibiscus
ZONES VARY **p. 388**

Holodiscus discolor
CREAM BUSH
1–9, 14–19 **p. 390**

Lavatera
TREE MALLOW
ZONES VARY **p. 427**

Plumbago auriculata
CAPE PLUMBAGO
8, 9, 12–24; H1, H2 **p. 534**

Rhamnus
NEEDS, ZONES VARY **p. 566**

Ribes
CURRANT, GOOSEBERRY
ZONES VARY **p. 577**

Rosa
ROSE
ZONES VARY **p. 579**

Spiraea
ZONES VARY **p. 616**

Viburnum
ZONES VARY **p. 646**

BUTTERFLY LARVAE
Trees

Aesculus
HORSECHESTNUT
ZONES VARY **p. 173**

Betula
BIRCH
ZONES VARY **p. 223**

Citrus
8, 9, 12–24; H1, H2 **p. 276**

Cornus
DOGWOOD
NEEDS, ZONES VARY **p. 291**

Crataegus
HAWTHORN
2–12, 14–17 **p. 298**

Malus
FLOWERING CRABAPPLE
1–11, 14–21 **p. 457**

Pinus
PINE
ZONES VARY **p. 523**

Platanus
PLANE TREE, SYCAMORE
ZONES VARY **p. 531**

Populus
POPLAR
ZONES VARY **p. 543**

Prosopis
MESQUITE
10–13, 18–24 **p. 547**

Prunus
NEEDS, ZONES VARY **p. 549**

Pseudotsuga menziesii
DOUGLAS FIR
A2, A3; 1–10, 14–17 **p. 554**

Quercus
OAK
ZONES VARY **p. 558**

Salix
WILLOW
ZONES VARY **p. 591**

ADULT BUTTERFLIES
Annuals, Perennials, Grasses

Achillea
YARROW
A1–A3; 1–24 **p. 170**

Agapanthus
LILY-OF-THE-NILE
4–9, 12–24; H1, H2 **p. 174**

Antirrhinum majus
SNAPDRAGON
A3; 1–24 **p. 188**

Aquilegia
COLUMBINE
ZONES VARY **p. 195**

Armeria
THRIFT
ZONES VARY **p. 201**

Plant listings continue ▶

Platanus × acerifolia

Passiflora × alatocaerulea

Quercus robur

Salix × babylonica

Achillea millefolium

Scabiosa columbaria 'Pink Mist'

Armeria maritima

Centranthus ruber

Cosmos bipinnatus

Plant	Common name	Needs / Zones	Page
Asclepias tuberosa	BUTTERFLY WEED	☼ ⁄ 1–24	**p. 204**
Aster		☼ ⁄ ZONES VARY	**p. 207**
Astilbe	FALSE SPIRAEA	☼ ◑ ⁄ 1–9, 14–24	**p. 208**
Borago officinalis	BORAGE	☼ ◑ ⁄ A2, A3; 1–24; H1	**p. 228**
Bouvardia		◑ ⁄ ZONES VARY	**p. 230**
Catananche caerulea	CUPID'S DART	☼ ⁄ 1–10, 14–24	**p. 255**
Centranthus ruber	JUPITER'S BEARD	☼ ◑ ⁄ 2–9, 12–24; H1	**p. 260**
Chrysanthemum maximum	SHASTA DAISY	☼ ◑ ⁄ A1–A3; 1–24; H1	**p. 272**
Coreopsis		☼ ⁄ ZONES VARY	**p. 290**
Cosmos		☼ ⁄ 1–24	**p. 295**
Cynoglossum		NEEDS, ZONES VARY	**p. 305**
Delphinium		☼ ⁄ ZONES VARY	**p. 311**
Dianthus	PINK	☼ ◑ ⁄ A2, A3; 1–24	**p. 313**
Echinacea purpurea	PURPLE CONEFLOWER	☼ ⁄ A2, A3; 1–24	**p. 322**
Echinops exaltatus	GLOBE THISTLE	☼ ⁄ A2, A3; 1–24	**p. 323**
Erigeron	FLEABANE	☼ ◑ ⁄ ZONES VARY	**p. 329**
Eriogonum	WILD BUCKWHEAT	☼ ⁄ ZONES VARY	**p. 333**
Eryngium amethystinum	SEA HOLLY	☼ ⁄ 1–24	**p. 334**
Erysimum cheiri	ENGLISH WALLFLOWER	☼ ◑ ⁄ 4–6, 14–17, 22, 23	**p. 334**
Gaillardia × grandiflora		☼ ⁄ 1–24; H1, H2	**p. 359**
Heliotropium arborescens	COMMON HELIOTROPE	☼ ◑ ⁄ ALL ZONES	**p. 384**
Iberis	CANDYTUFT	☼ ◑ ⁄ ZONES VARY	**p. 396**
Lathyrus odoratus	SWEET PEA	☼ ⁄ ALL ZONES	**p. 424**
Liatris spicata	GAYFEATHER	☼ ⁄ A2, A3; 1–10, 14–24	**p. 432**
Lobelia		NEEDS, ZONES VARY	**p. 440**
Lobularia maritima	SWEET ALYSSUM	☼ ◑ ⁄ ALL ZONES	**p. 440**
Monarda	BEE BALM, OSWEGO TEA	☼ ◑ ⁄ ZONES VARY	**p. 471**
Origanum vulgare	OREGANO, MARJORAM	☼ ⁄ ZONES VARY	**p. 489**
Penstemon	BEARD TONGUE	☼ ◑ ⁄ ZONES VARY	**p. 510**
Phlox		☼ ◑ ⁄ ZONES VARY	**p. 517**
Ranunculus		NEEDS, ZONES VARY	**p. 564**
Rudbeckia hirta	GLORIOSA DAISY	☼ ⁄ 1–24	**p. 589**
Salvia	SAGE	NEEDS, ZONES VARY	**p. 592**
Scabiosa	PINCUSHION FLOWER	☼ ⁄ ZONES VARY	**p. 600**
Sedum (most)	STONECROP	NEEDS, ZONES VARY	**p. 604**
Solidago	GOLDENROD	☼ ◑ ⁄ 1–11, 14–23	**p. 612**
Tagetes	MARIGOLD	☼ ⁄ ZONES VARY	**p. 626**
Verbena		☼ ⁄ ZONES VARY	**p. 645**

For growing symbol explanations, please see page 64.

Eryngium amethystinum

Erysimum cheiri

Lathyrus odoratus

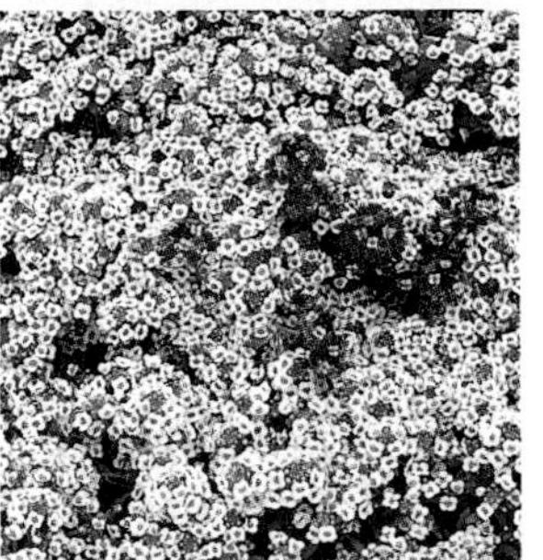
Lobularia maritima

Rudbeckia hirta 'Marmalade'

Salvia clevelandii

Buddleja davidii

Abelia × grandiflora

Heteromeles arbutifolia

Lantana camara

Zauschneria
CALIFORNIA FUCHSIA
NEEDS, ZONES VARY p. 656

ADULT BUTTERFLIES
Shrubs

Abelia
ZONES VARY p. 162

Abutilon
FLOWERING MAPLE
8, 9, 12–24; H1, H2 p. 163

Arctostaphylos
MANZANITA
ZONES VARY p. 198

Buddleja
BUTTERFLY BUSH
ZONES VARY p. 234

Calluna vulgaris
SCOTCH HEATHER
1A, 2–6, 15–17 p. 241

Caryopteris
BLUEBEARD
ZONES VARY p. 253

Ceanothus
WILD LILAC
5–9, 14–24 p. 256

Choisya ternata
MEXICAN ORANGE
4–9, 14–24 p. 271

Clethra alnifolia
SUMMERSWEET
A2, A3; 1–6 p. 284

Escallonia
4–9, 14–24 p. 335

Grewia occidentalis
LAVENDER STARFLOWER
8, 9, 12–24; H1, H2 p. 376

Hebe
14–24 p. 380

Heteromeles arbutifolia
TOYON
5–9, 14–24 p. 386

Lantana
8–10, 12–24; H1, H2 p. 422

Lavandula
LAVENDER
ZONES VARY p. 425

Lonicera
HONEYSUCKLE
ZONES VARY p. 441

Mahonia
NEEDS, ZONES VARY p. 455

Philadelphus (single-flowered)
MOCK ORANGE
ZONES VARY p. 516

Potentilla
CINQUEFOIL
ZONES VARY p. 544

Rhamnus californica
COFFEEBERRY
4–9, 14–24; H1, H2 p. 566

Rhododendron
ZONES VARY p. 568

Rhus
SUMAC
ZONES VARY p. 576

Ribes
CURRANT, GOOSEBERRY
ZONES VARY p. 577

Rosmarinus officinalis
ROSEMARY
4–24; H1, H2 p. 587

Sambucus
ELDERBERRY
ZONES VARY p. 597

Spiraea
ZONES VARY p. 616

Syringa
LILAC
ZONES VARY p. 624

Vaccinium
NEEDS, ZONES VARY p. 643

ADULT BUTTERFLIES
Trees

Acer
MAPLE
ZONES VARY p. 167

Aesculus
HORSECHESTNUT
ZONES VARY p. 173

Apple
ZONES VARY p. 189

Arbutus menziesii
MADRONE
4–7, 14–19 p. 197

Citrus
8, 9, 12–24; H1, H2 p. 276

Salix
WILLOW
ZONES VARY p. 591

Vitex
CHASTE TREE
ZONES VARY p. 650

Mahonia aquifolium

Rhododendron (Kurume azalea)

Spiraea japonica

Choisya ternata

Aesculus × carnea

Plant listings continue ▶

Gladiolus, Grandiflora hybrid

Heuchera sanguinea

Kniphofia uvaria

Leonotis leonurus

Crocosmia × crocosmiiflora

HUMMINGBIRDS
Annuals, Perennials, Bulbs

Agastache
☼ ◑ ⁄ ZONES VARY — **p. 174**

Alcea rosea
HOLLYHOCK
☼ ◑ ⁄ 1–24 — **p. 177**

Aloe
☼ ◑ ⁄ 8, 9, 12–24 — **p. 180**

Alstroemeria
☼ ◑ ⁄ 5–9, 14–24; H1 — **p. 182**

Aquilegia
COLUMBINE
☼ ◑ ⁄ ZONES VARY — **p. 195**

Asclepias tuberosa
BUTTERFLY WEED
☼ ⁄ 1–24 — **p. 204**

Clarkia
☼ ◑ ⁄ 1–24 — **p. 281**

Cleome hasslerana
SPIDER FLOWER
☼ ⁄ 1–24 — **p. 283**

Crocosmia × crocosmiiflora
MONTBRETIA
☼ ◑ ⁄ 5–24; H1, H2 — **p. 300**

Delphinium
☼ ⁄ ZONES VARY — **p. 311**

Digitalis
FOXGLOVE
NEEDS, ZONES VARY — **p. 317**

Gladiolus
☼ ⁄ 4–9, 12–24; H1 — **p. 366**

Heuchera
CORAL BELLS
☼ ◑ ⁄ ZONES VARY — **p. 387**

Impatiens
BALSAM
NEEDS, ZONES VARY — **p. 399**

Kniphofia
RED-HOT POKER
☼ ◑ ⁄ ZONES VARY — **p. 418**

Leonotis leonurus
LION'S TAIL
☼ ⁄ 8–24; H1, H2 — **p. 428**

Lobelia (red flowered)
☼ ◑ ⁄ ZONES VARY — **p. 440**

Lupinus
LUPINE
☼ ⁄ ZONES VARY — **p. 443**

Mimulus
MONKEY FLOWER
NEEDS, ZONES VARY — **p. 469**

Monarda
BEE BALM, OSWEGO TEA
☼ ◑ ⁄ ZONES VARY — **p. 471**

Pelargonium
GERANIUM
☼ ◑ ⁄ 8, 9, 12–24 — **p. 509**

Penstemon (many)
BEARD TONGUE
☼ ◑ ⁄ ZONES VARY — **p. 510**

Salvia (many)
SAGE
NEEDS, ZONES VARY — **p. 592**

Veronica
SPEEDWELL
☼ ⁄ ZONES VARY — **p. 645**

Zauschneria
CALIFORNIA FUCHSIA
NEEDS, ZONES VARY — **p. 656**

Zinnia
☼ ⁄ ZONES VARY — **p. 657**

HUMMINGBIRDS
Ground Covers, Vines

Campsis
TRUMPET CREEPER
☼ ◑ ⁄ ZONES VARY — **p. 247**

Campsis radicans
COMMON TRUMPET CREEPER
☼ ◑ ⁄ 1–21 — **p. 247**

Ipomoea quamoclit
CYPRESS VINE
☼ ⁄ ALL ZONES — **p. 401**

Lonicera
HONEYSUCKLE
☼ ◑ ⁄ ZONES VARY — **p. 441**

Pyrostegia venusta
FLAME VINE
☼ ⁄ 13, 16, 21–24; H1, H2 — **p. 557**

Tecoma capensis
CAPE HONEYSUCKLE
☼ ◑ ⁄ 12, 13, 20–24; H1, H2 — **p. 628**

HUMMINGBIRDS
Shrubs

Abelia
☼ ◑ ⁄ ZONES VARY — **p. 162**

Abutilon
FLOWERING MAPLE
☼ ◑ ⁄ 8, 9, 12–24; H1, H2 — **p. 163**

Acacia
☼ ⁄ ZONES VARY — **p. 164**

Lupinus, Russell hybrid

Monarda didyma

Salvia leucantha

Pyrostegia venusta

For growing symbol explanations, please see page 64.

Campsis radicans

Cestrum parqui

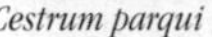

Grevillea 'Poorinda Constance'

Hibiscus syriacus 'Aphrodite'

Justicia brandegeana

Arbutus unedo
STRAWBERRY TREE
4–24 p. 197

Arctostaphylos
MANZANITA
ZONES VARY p. 198

Bouvardia (red-flowered)
8–10, 12, 14–24 p. 230

Buddleja
BUTTERFLY BUSH
ZONES VARY p. 234

Caesalpinia
ZONES VARY p. 237

Calliandra
ZONES VARY p. 239

Callistemon
BOTTLEBRUSH
ZONES VARY p. 240

Ceanothus
WILD LILAC
5–9, 14–24 p. 256

Cercis occidentalis
WESTERN REDBUD
2–24 p. 263

Cestrum
ZONES VARY p. 264

Chaenomeles
FLOWERING QUINCE
2–23 p. 264

Correa
AUSTRALIAN FUCHSIA
14–24 p. 293

Cotoneaster
ZONES VARY p. 296

Feijoa, Pineapple Guava
6–9, 12–24; H1, H2 p. 348

Fuchsia
ZONES VARY p. 357

Grevillea (red-flowered)
NEEDS, ZONES VARY p. 375

Heteromeles arbutifolia
TOYON
5–9, 14–24 p. 386

Hibiscus
ZONES VARY p. 388

Justicia (several)
NEEDS, ZONES VARY p. 415

Kolkwitzia amabilis
BEAUTY BUSH
2–11, 14–20 p. 419

Lantana
8–10, 12–24; H1, H2 p. 422

Lavandula (many)
LAVENDER
ZONES VARY p. 425

Leucophyllum
TEXAS RANGER
7–24 p. 430

Lonicera
HONEYSUCKLE
ZONES VARY p. 441

Melaleuca
ZONES VARY p. 464

Ribes
CURRANT, GOOSEBERRY
ZONES VARY p. 577

Rosmarinus officinalis
ROSEMARY
4–24; H1, H2 p. 587

Sambucus
ELDERBERRY
ZONES VARY p. 597

Syringa
LILAC
ZONES VARY p. 624

Tecoma stans
YELLOW BELLS
12, 13, 21–24 p. 629

Trichostema lanatum
WOOLLY BLUECURLS
14–24 p. 637

Weigela
1–11, 14–21 p. 651

HUMMINGBIRDS

Trees

Albizia julibrissin
SILK TREE
4–23 p. 177

Chilopsis linearis
DESERT WILLOW
3B, 7–14, 18–23 p. 269

Citrus
8, 9, 12–24; H1, H2 p. 276

Erythrina
CORAL TREE
ZONES VARY p. 334

Eucalyptus
ZONES VARY p. 337

Lavandula angustifolia

Syringa meyeri 'Palibin'

Weigela 'Newport Red'

Albizia julibrissin

Eucalyptus ficifolia

Fuchsia × hybrida 'Lord Byron'

Plants for HANGING BASKETS AND WINDOW BOXES

The charm of a garden in the air—whether it hangs suspended or perches at the edge of a window—derives from the choice of plants. You want a full (and probably colorful) show, with foliage that is lax enough to soften the edges of the container or even spill over it. Here's a selection of proven aerial artists, drawn from a variety of annuals, perennials, and woody plants

Brachyscome

Coleus × hybridus

Convolvulus tricolor

Lobularia maritima

ANNUALS

Plant	Common name	Needs, zones	Page
Asarina antirrhiniflora	CLIMBING SNAPDRAGON	☼ ⁄ 17–24; H1, H2	**p. 204**
Brachyscome	SWAN RIVER DAISY	☼ ⁄ ZONES VARY	**p. 230**
Browallia	AMETHYST FLOWER	◑ ⁄ ZONES VARY	**p. 233**
Calibrachoa	MILLION BELLS	☼ ◑ ⁄ 2–7, 10–13	**p. 239**
Coleus × hybridus		☼ ◑ ⁄ ALL ZONES	**p. 287**
Convolvulus tricolor	DWARF MORNING GLORY	☼ ◑ ⁄ 1–24	**p. 289**
Evolvulus glomeratus		☼ ◑ ⁄ ALL ZONES	**p. 346**
Hypoestes phyllostachya	FRECKLE FACE	☼ ◑ ⁄ ALL ZONES	**p. 396**
Impatiens walleriana	BUSY LIZZIE	☼ ◑ ● ⁄ ALL ZONES	**p. 399**
Ipomoea tricolor	MORNING GLORY	☼ ⁄ ALL ZONES	**p. 401**
Lobelia erinus		☼ ◑ ⁄ ALL ZONES	**p. 440**
Lobularia maritima	SWEET ALYSSUM	☼ ◑ ⁄ ALL ZONES	**p. 440**
Mimulus × hybridus	MONKEY FLOWER	◑ ● ⁄ 1–24	**p. 469**
Nemesia strumosa		☼ ⁄ 1–24	**p. 479**
Petunia × hybrida	PETUNIA	☼ ⁄ ALL ZONES	**p. 514**
Portulaca grandiflora	ROSE MOSS	☼ ⁄ ALL ZONES	**p. 543**
Sanvitalia procumbens	CREEPING ZINNIA	☼ ⁄ 1–24	**p. 599**
Schizanthus pinnatus	POOR MAN'S ORCHID	◑ ⁄ 1–6, 15–17, 21–24	**p. 602**
Sutera cordata		☼ ◑ ⁄ ALL ZONES	**p. 623**
Thunbergia alata	BLACK-EYED SUSAN VINE	☼ ◑ ⁄ ALL ZONES	**p. 631**
Torenia fournieri	WISHBONE FLOWER	☼ ◑ ⁄ 1–24; H1, H2	**p. 636**
Tropaeolum majus	GARDEN NASTURTIUM	☼ ◑ ⁄ ALL ZONES	**p. 639**
Verbena × hybrida	GARDEN VERBENA	☼ ⁄ ALL ZONES	**p. 645**
Viola	VIOLA, VIOLET, PANSY	NEEDS, ZONES VARY	**p. 648**
Zinnia angustifolia		☼ ⁄ 1–24; H1, H2	**p. 657**

For growing symbol explanations, please see page 64.

Mimulus × hybridus

Portulaca grandiflora

Viola × wittrockiana

Begonia, tuberous

Campanula isophylla

Gazania

Helichrysum petiolare 'Limelight'

Lamium maculatum 'Beacon Silver'

PERENNIALS, BULBS

Plant	Zones	Page
Achimenes	ALL ZONES	**p. 170**
Asparagus densiflorus	12–24; H1, H2	**p. 205**
Aurinia saxatilis BASKET-OF-GOLD	1–24	**p. 210**
Begonia, semperflorens	14–24; H1, H2	**p. 220**
Begonia, tuberous	4–9, 14–24; H1	**p. 221**
Campanula isophylla ITALIAN BELLFLOWER	4–9, 14–24	**p. 248**
Campanula portenschlagiana DALMATIAN BELLFLOWER	2–9, 14–24	**p. 249**
Campanula poscharskyana SERBIAN BELLFLOWER	1–12, 14–24	**p. 249**
Ceropegia woodii ROSARY VINE	21–24	**p. 264**
Chlorophytum comosum SPIDER PLANT	15–17, 19–24; H1, H2	**p. 270**
Cymbalaria muralis KENILWORTHY IVY	3B–24	**p. 304**
Diascia TWINSPUR	ZONES VARY	**p. 314**
Epiphyllum ORCHID CACTUS	8, 9, 14–24; H1, H2	**p. 327**
Erigeron FLEABANE	ZONES VARY	**p. 329**
Gazania	NEEDS, ZONES VARY	**p. 361**
Glechoma hederacea GROUND IVY	A2, A3; 1–10, 14–24	**p. 367**
Helichrysum petiolare LICORICE PLANT	16, 17, 22–24	**p. 383**
Iberis sempervirens EVERGREEN CANDYTUFT	1–24	**p. 396**
Lamium maculatum DEAD NETTLE	A2, A3; 1–11, 14–24	**p. 422**
Lotus berthelotii PARROT'S BEAK	9, 15–24; H1	**p. 442**
Lotus maculatus 'Gold Flash'	9, 15–24	**p. 442**
Lysimachia nummularia CREEPING JENNY	1–9, 14–24	**p. 445**
Nierembergia CUP FLOWER	ZONES VARY	**p. 482**
Pelargonium peltatum IVY GERANIUM	8, 9, 12–24	**p. 509**
Primula (some) PRIMROSE	ZONES VARY	**p. 545**
Saxifraga stolonifera STRAWBERRY GERANIUM	2–9, 14–24	**p. 600**
Scaevola	8, 9, 14–24; H1, H2	**p. 601**
Sedum morganianum DONKEY TAIL, BURRO TAIL	13–24; H1, H2	**p. 605**
Sedum sieboldii	2–9, 12, 14–24	**p. 605**
Senecio cineraria DUSTY MILLER	4–24; H1, H2	**p. 606**
Senecio mikanioides GERMAN IVY	14–24; H1, H2	**p. 606**
Tradescantia fluminensis WANDERING JEW	12–24; H1, H2	**p. 637**
Vinca minor DWARF PERIWINKLE	1–24	**p. 648**

SHRUBS, VINES

Plant	Zones	Page
Abutilon megapotamicum FLOWERING MAPLE	8, 9, 12–24; H1, H2	**p. 163**
Fuchsia × hybrida HYBRID FUCHSIA	4–9, 14–17, 20–24; H1	**p. 358**
Hedera helix ENGLISH IVY	3–24; H1	**p. 381**

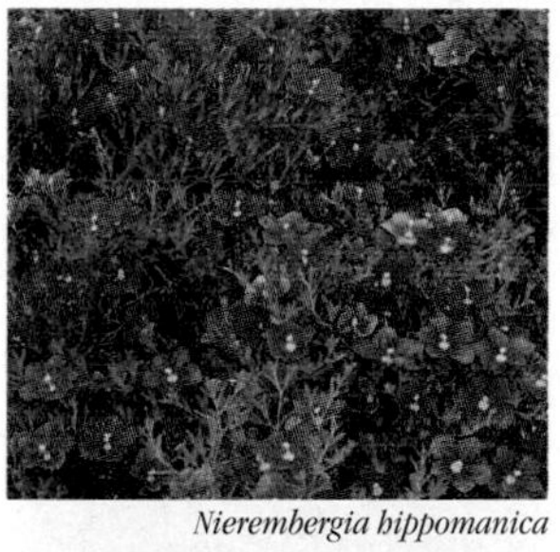
Nierembergia hippomanica

Pelargonium peltatum

Vinca minor

Abutilon megapotamicum

Hedera helix 'Needlepoint'

Acer palmatum

TREES AND SHRUBS

for Containers

Annuals, perennials, herbs, and even vegetables are standard choices for container gardening. Sometimes, however, only larger, woody plants will suit your needs. Perhaps you want a tall accent for the patio; maybe you long to grow a favorite camellia but have no available ground for planting. Perhaps you have your heart set on a lemon tree, but the climate is too chilly in winter to permit its survival in the open. The trees and shrubs on these two pages adapt well to life in larger containers.

Laurus nobilis

Citrus (Lemon)

Fig, edible

Wisteria sinensis 'Alba'

Anisodontea × hypomandarum

TREES

Acer japonicum
FULLMOON MAPLE
☼ ◑ ⁄ 2–6, 14–16 — p. 168

Acer palmatum
JAPANESE MAPLE
☼ ◑ ⁄ A3; 2–10, 12, 14–24 — p. 168

Acer shirasawanum 'Aureum'
GOLDEN FULLMOON MAPLE
◑ ⁄ 3B–6, 14–16 — p. 169

Apple (dwarf)
☼ ⁄ ZONES VARY — p. 194

Citrus
☼ ⁄ 8, 9, 12–24; H1, H2 — p. 276

Fig, edible
☼ ⁄ 4–9, 12–24; H1, H2 — p. 351

Pinus (several, see chart)
☼ ⁄ ZONES VARY — p. 523

Pseudopanax lessonii
☼ ◑ ● ⁄ 17, 22–24 — p. 553

Wisteria (trained as tree)
NEEDS, ZONES VARY — p. 652

SHRUBS

Abutilon
FLOWERING MAPLE
☼ ◑ ⁄ 8, 9, 12–24; H1, H2 — p. 163

Anisodontea × hypomandarum
CAPE MALLOW
☼ ◑ ⁄ 14–24 — p. 187

Arbutus unedo (smaller cultivars)
STRAWBERRY TREE
☼ ◑ ⁄ 4–24 — p. 197

Aucuba japonica
JAPANESE AUCUBA
◑ ● ⁄ 4–24 — p. 209

Berberis thunbergii
JAPANESE BARBERRY
☼ ◑ ⁄ A3; 2B–24 — p. 222

Bougainvillea (shrubby cultivars) — p. 228
☼ ⁄ 5, 6, 12–17, 19, 21–24; H1, H2

Bouvardia longiflora 'Albatross'
◑ ⁄ 12, 16, 17, 19–24 — p. 230

Brugmansia
ANGEL'S TRUMPET
☼ ◑ ● ⁄ 12, 13, 16–24; H1, H2 — p. 233

Brunfelsia pauciflora
◑ ⁄ 12–17, 20–24; H1, H2 — p. 234

Buxus
BOXWOOD
☼ ◑ ● ⁄ ZONES VARY — p. 236

Camellia
◑ ⁄ 4–9, 12, 14–24 — p. 243

Choisya ternata
MEXICAN ORANGE
☼ ◑ ⁄ 4–9, 14–24 — p. 271

Corokia cotoneaster
☼ ◑ ⁄ 4–24 — p. 293

Correa
AUSTRALIAN FUCHSIA
☼ ◑ ⁄ 14–24 — p. 293

Corylus avellana 'Contorta'
HARRY LAUDER'S WALKING STICK
☼ ◑ ⁄ 2–9, 14–20 — p. 295

Arbutus unedo 'Compacta'

Aucuba japonica 'Picturata'

Berberis thunbergii

For growing symbol explanations, please see page 64.

Eriobotrya deflexa

Fatsia japonica 'Variegata'

Gardenia augusta

Lavandula angustifolia

Daphne odora
WINTER DAPHNE
4–10, 12, 14–24 p. 310

Enkianthus
3–9, 14–21 p. 326

Eriobotrya deflexa
BRONZE LOQUAT
8–24 p. 333

Escallonia (smaller species and cultivars)
4–9, 14–24 p. 335

Fatsia japonica
JAPANESE ARALIA
4–9, 14–24; H1, H2 p. 348

Fuchsia
ZONES VARY p. 357

Gardenia
ZONES VARY p. 360

Hydrangea macrophylla (some)
BIGLEAF HYDRANGEA
3B–9, 14–24; H1 p. 394

Ilex (many)
HOLLY
ZONES VARY p. 397

Justicia brandegeeana
SHRIMP PLANT p. 415
12, 13, 15–17, 21–24; H1, H2

Kalmia latifolia
MOUNTAIN LAUREL, CALICO BUSH
2–7, 16, 17 p. 416

Lagerstroemia indica (dwarf forms)
CRAPE MYRTLE
2–10, 12–24; H1, H2 p. 421

Lantana
8–10, 12–24; H1, H2 p. 422

Laurus nobilis
SWEET BAY
5–9, 12–24; H1, H2 p. 424

Lavandula
LAVENDER
ZONES VARY p. 425

Ligustrum japonicum
JAPANESE PRIVET
4–24; H1, H2 p. 432

Mahonia (most)
NEEDS, ZONES VARY p. 455

Melianthus major
HONEY BUSH
8, 9, 12–24; H1, H2 p. 465

Myrsine africana
AFRICAN BOXWOOD
8, 9, 14–24 p. 475

Nandina domestica
HEAVENLY BAMBOO
3–24; H1, H2 p. 476

Nerium oleander (especially dwarf cultivars) OLEANDER
8–16, 18–24; H1, H2 p. 482

Osmanthus fragrans
SWEET OLIVE
5–9, 12–24; H1 p. 490

Peach (genetic dwarfs)
ZONES VARY p. 501

Picea glauca (smallest forms)
WHITE SPRUCE
A1–A3; 1–7, 14–17 p. 521

Pieris
ZONES VARY p. 522

Pittosporum tobira
TOBIRA
4–24; H1, H2 p. 531

Plumeria
FRANGIPANI, PUA MELIA
ZONES VARY p. 538

Podocarpus macrophyllus
YEW PINE
4–9, 12–24; H1, H2 p. 539

Podocarpus nagi
8, 9, 14–24; H1, H2 p. 539

Punica granatum (dwarf cultivars)
POMEGRANATE
5–24; H1, H2 p. 556

Rhododendron
ZONES VARY p. 568

Rosa
ZONES VARY p. 579

Skimmia japonica
4–9, 14–22 p. 610

Solanum rantonnetii
12, 13, 15–24; H1, H2 p. 612

Sollya heterophylla
AUSTRALIAN BLUEBELL CREEPER
8, 9, 14–24; H1, H2 p. 612

Sparmannia africana
AFRICAN LINDEN
15–24; H1, H2 p. 614

Taxus
YEW
ZONES VARY p. 628

Ternstroemia gymnanthera
4–9, 12–24 p. 629

Mahonia bealei

Nerium oleander 'Petite Salmon'

Rhododendron

Plumeria hybrid

Canna 'Pretoria'

Plants for TROPICAL EFFECTS

Dicksonia antarctica

You may be able to visit Honolulu or Mazatlán without going any farther than your garden. A surprising number of tropical and tropical-looking plants prosper in milder Pacific Coast climates, even in such nontropical climes as Seattle. Listed here is a rich array of trees, shrubs, vines, and perennials with flashy flowers, bold foliage, or simply that overall lushness that defines tropical vegetation worldwide.

Aralia spinosa

Catalpa bignonioides

Erythrina crista-galli

Musa acuminata

TREES AND TREELIKE PLANTS

Aralia
☼ ◑ ZONES VARY **p. 196**

Bauhinia
ORCHID TREE
☼ ZONES VARY **p. 218**

Catalpa
☼ 3–10, 14–24 **p. 255**

Chorisia
FLOSS SILK TREE
☼ ZONES VARY **p. 271**

Cyathea cooperi (tree fern)
AUSTRALIAN TREE FERN
☼ ◑ 15–24; H1, H2 **p. 303**

Dicksonia (tree fern)
☼ ◑ ● ZONES VARY **p. 315**

Ensete ventricosum
ABYSSINIAN BANANA
☼ ◑ 13, 15–24; H1, H2 **p. 326**

Erythrina
CORAL TREE
☼ ZONES VARY **p. 334**

Ficus lyrata
FIDDLELEAF FIG
☼ ◑ 22–24; H1, H2 **p. 351**

Firmiana simplex
CHINESE PARASOL TREE
☼ ◑ 5, 6, 8, 9, 12–24 **p. 353**

Musa
BANANA
☼ ◑ ZONES VARY **p. 473**

Palms
NEEDS, ZONES VARY **p. 494**

Paulownia tomentosa
EMPRESS TREE
☼ 4–9, 11–24 **p. 500**

Tabebuia
TRUMPET TREE
☼ 15, 16, 20–24; H1, H2 **p. 626**

VINES

Beaumontia grandiflora
HERALD'S TRUMPET **p. 219**
☼ ◑ 12, 13, 16, 17, 21–24; H1, H2

Bougainvillea **p. 228**
☼ 5, 6, 12–17, 19, 21–24; H1, H2

Campsis
TRUMPET CREEPER
☼ ◑ ZONES VARY **p. 247**

×Fatshedera lizei
◑ ● 4–10, 12–24; H1, H2 **p. 348**

Lonicera hildebrandiana
GIANT BURMESE HONEYSUCKLE
☼ ◑ 9, 14–17, 19–24; H1, H2 **p. 441**

Mandevilla
☼ ◑ ZONES VARY **p. 461**

Monstera deliciosa
SPLIT-LEAF PHILODENDRON
◑ 16, 17, 22–24; H1, H2 **p. 472**

Pandorea
☼ ◑ 16–24; H1, H2 **p. 495**

Passiflora
PASSION VINE
☼ ◑ ZONES VARY **p. 499**

Solandra maxima
CUP-OF-GOLD VINE
☼ 17, 21–24; H1, H2 **p. 611**

Beaumontia grandiflora

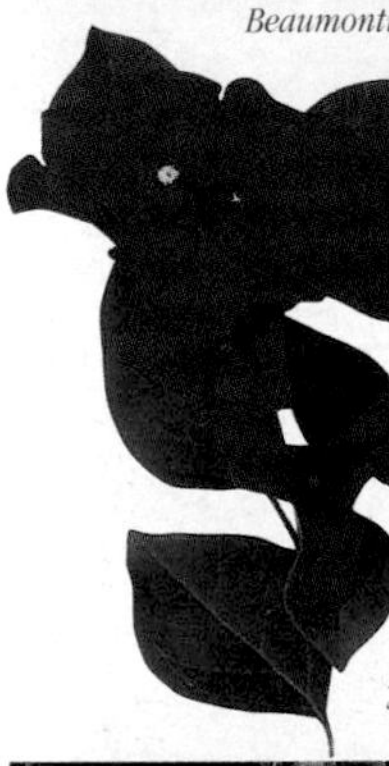

Bougainvillea 'Barbara Karst'

Campsis radicans

Lonicera hildebrandiana

For growing symbol explanations, please see page 64.

Solandra maxima 'Variegata'

Fatsia japonica

Iochroma cyaneum

Melianthus major

Tetrastigma voinieranum
13, 17, 20–24; H1, H2 p. 629

SHRUBS

Abutilon
FLOWERING MAPLE
8, 9, 12–24; H1, H2 p. 163

Brugmansia
ANGEL'S TRUMPET
12, 13, 16–24; H1, H2 p. 233

Crotalaria agatiflora
CANARY BIRD BUSH
13, 15–24; H1, H2 p. 300

Cycas
ZONES VARY p. 304

Euphorbia cotinifolia
CARIBBEAN COPPER PLANT
23, 24; H1, H2 p. 344

Euphorbia pulcherrima
POINSETTIA
13, 16–24; H1, H2 p. 345

Fatsia japonica
JAPANESE ARALIA
4–9, 14–24; H1, H2 p. 348

Ficus auriculata
20–24; H1, H2 p. 350

Hibiscus rosa-sinensis
CHINESE HIBISCUS
9, 12–16, 19–24; H1, H2 p. 388

Iochroma cyaneum
15–17, 19–24 p. 400

Melianthus major
HONEY BUSH
8, 9, 12–24; H1, H2 p. 465

Plumeria
FRANGIPANI
ZONES VARY p. 538

Schefflera
ZONES VARY p. 601

Sparmannia africana
AFRICAN LINDEN
15–24; H1, H2 p. 614

Tecoma stans
YELLOW BELLS
12, 13, 21–24; H1, H2 p. 629

Tetrapanax papyriferus
RICE PAPER PLANT
15–24; H1, H2 p. 629

Tibouchina urvilleana
PRINCESS FLOWER
16, 17, 21–24; H1, H2 p. 633

PERENNIALS

Alocasia
ELEPHANT'S EAR
22–24; H1, H2 p. 180

Alpinia
14–24; H1, H2 p. 181

Aspidistra elatior
CAST-IRON PLANT
4–10, 12–24; H1, H2 p. 206

Bamboo
ZONES VARY p. 213

Caladium bicolor
FANCY-LEAFED CALADIUM
H2 p. 237

Canna
6–9, 12–24; H1, H2 p. 249

Clivia miniata
12–17, 19–24; H1, H2 p. 285

Colocasia esculenta
TARO
12, 16–24; H1, H2 p. 288

Crinum
8, 9, 12–24; H1, H2 p. 299

Epiphyllum
ORCHID CACTUS
8, 9, 14–24; H1, H2 p. 327

Gunnera
4–6, 14–17, 20–24 p. 377

Hedychium
GINGER LILY
8, 9, 14–17, 19–24; H1, H2 p. 381

Philodendron
NEEDS, ZONES VARY p. 516

Platycerium
STAGHORN FERN
ZONES VARY p. 532

Strelitzia
BIRD OF PARADISE
ZONES VARY p. 621

Xanthosoma
12, 13, 16, 17, 21–24; H1, H2 p. 653

Zantedeschia aethiopica
COMMON CALLA
5, 6, 8, 9, 21–24; H1, H2 p. 655

Zingiber officinale
TRUE GINGER
9, 14–24; H1, H2 p. 657

Caladium bicolor

Colocasia esculenta

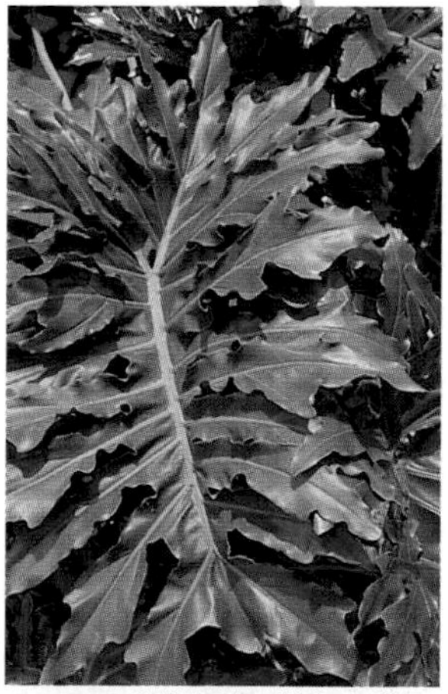

Philodendron bipinnatifidum

Zantedeschia aethiopica

Hosta sieboldiana

Plants for
DAMP SOIL AND PONDS

Whether you're planning a pond or stream garden or just deciding how best to deal with a patch of perpetually boggy ground, you'll find that most standard nursery offerings are not up to the challenge. Constantly saturated soils lack the air that most plants need for good growth—the reason why not just any plant will grow in a swamp. These two pages list the best choices for wet (even underwater) soil: true aquatics, with roots that grow beneath the water's surface; plants that take shallow water or soggy soil; and those that need the constant moisture found beside a pool or brook.

Nelumbo nucifera

Acorus gramineus 'Variegatus'

Pontederia cordata

Caltha palustris

AQUATIC (SUBMERGED ONLY)

Aponogeton distachyus
CAPE PONDWEED
☼ ◑ 4–9, 12–24 **p. 189**

Eichhornia crassipes
WATER HYACINTH
☼ 8, 9, 13–24; H1, H2 **p. 324**

Nelumbo
LOTUS
☼ ◑ 1–24; H1, H2 **p. 479**

Nymphaea
WATER LILY
☼ 1–24; H1, H2 **p. 484**

Petasites japonicus
JAPANESE COLTSFOOT
☼ ◑ ● 2B–9, 14–17 **p. 514**

Pistia stratiotes
WATER LETTUCE
☼ ◑ 24; H2 **p. 530**

Pontederia cordata
PICKEREL WEED
☼ ◑ 1–24; H1, H2 **p. 542**

DAMP SOIL OR SHALLOW WATER

Acorus gramineus
JAPANESE SWEET FLAG
☼ ◑ 3B–10, 14–24 **p. 171**

Bacopa monnieri
WATER HYSSOP
☼ 8–24; H1, H2 **p. 212**

Caltha palustris
MARSH MARIGOLD
☼ ◑ ● A1–A3; 1–9, 14–24 **p. 242**

Carex elata 'Aurea'
☼ ◑ 2–9, 14–24 **p. 251**

Chondropetalum tectorum
CAPE RUSH
☼ ◑ 8, 9, 14–24 **p. 271**

Colocasia esculenta
TARO
◑ 12, 16–24; H1, H2 **p. 288**

Cyperus
☼ ◑ ● ZONES VARY **p. 306**

Equisetum hyemale
HORSETAIL
☼ ◑ 1–24 **p. 328**

Iris, Japanese
☼ 1–10, 14–24 **p. 403**

Iris laevigata
☼ 1–10, 14–24 **p. 405**

Iris, Louisiana
☼ ◑ 3–24; H1, H2 **p. 403**

Iris pseudacorus
YELLOW FLAG
☼ ◑ 1–24 **p. 405**

Iris versicolor
BLUE FLAG
☼ ◑ 1–9, 14–17 **p. 405**

Iris virginica
SOUTHERN BLUE FLAG
☼ ◑ 3–9, 14–17 **p. 405**

Juncus
RUSH
☼ ◑ ZONES VARY **p. 410**

Oenanthe javanica
JAPANESE WATERCRESS
☼ 9, 14–24 **p. 485**

Primula florindae
☼ ◑ ● A2, A3; 3–6, 15–17 **p. 546**

Colocasia esculenta

Equisetum hyemale

Primula japonica

For growing symbol explanations, please see page 64.

Gunnera tinctoria

Hosta 'Ginko Craig'

Siberian iris 'Ego'

Ligularia dentata 'Desdemona'

Ligularia dentata

Primula japonica
:Ö: :◐ ● ⁄ A3; 2–6, 15–17 **p. 546**

Schoenoplectus tabernaemontanus 'Zebrinus'
:Ö: :◐ ⁄ 5–24 **p. 603**

DAMP SOIL ONLY

Aconitum
ACONITE
:Ö: :◐ ⁄ A1–A3; 1–9, 14–21 **p. 171**

Alocasia
ELEPHANT'S EAR
:◐ ⁄ 22–24; H1, H2 **p. 180**

Asclepias incarnata
SWAMP MILKWEED
:Ö: ⁄ 1–9, 14–24 **p. 204**

Aster novae-angliae
NEW ENGLAND ASTER
:Ö: ⁄ 1–24 **p. 207**

Astilboides tabularis
:◐ ⁄ 2B–9, 14–17 **p. 208**

Athyrium
:◐ ● ⁄ ZONES VARY **p. 209**

Chelone lyonii
TURTLEHEAD
:Ö: :◐ ⁄ 1–9, 14–24 **p. 267**

Darmera peltata
UMBRELLA PLANT
:◐ ⁄ 2–7, 14–20 **p. 310**

Eupatorium purpureum
JOE PYE WEED
:Ö: :◐ ⁄ 1–9, 14–17 **p. 343**

Farfugium japonicum
:◐ ● ⁄ 4–10, 14–24; H1, H2 **p. 348**

Filipendula (most)
:Ö: :◐ ● ⁄ ZONES VARY **p. 352**

Gunnera
:◐ ⁄ 4–6, 14–17, 20–24 **p. 377**

Hosta
PLANTAIN LILY
:◐ ● ⁄ ZONES VARY **p. 391**

Houttuynia cordata
:Ö: :◐ ● ⁄ 2–9, 14–24 **p. 392**

Iris setosa
:Ö: ⁄ A1–A3; 1–9, 14–17 **p. 405**

Iris, Siberian
:Ö: :◐ ⁄ 1–10, 14–23 **p. 404**

Ligularia
:◐ ● ⁄ 1–9, 14–17 **p. 432**

Lobelia (several)
NEEDS, ZONES VARY **p. 440**

Lysimachia
:Ö: :◐ ⁄ ZONES VARY **p. 445**

Matteuccia struthiopteris
OSTRICH FERN
:Ö: :◐ ● ⁄ A1–A3; 1–10, 14–17 **p. 462**

Milium effusum 'Aureum'
BOWLES' GOLDEN GRASS
:◐ ⁄ 3B–9, 14–17 **p. 469**

Mimulus cardinalis
SCARLET MONKEY FLOWER
:Ö: :◐ ● ⁄ 2–24 **p. 469**

Molinia caerulea
MOOR GRASS
:Ö: :◐ ⁄ 1–9, 14–17 **p. 471**

Myosotis
FORGET-ME-NOT
:◐ ⁄ A1–A3; 1–24 **p. 475**

Osmunda regalis
ROYAL FERN
:Ö: :◐ ⁄ 1–9, 14–17 **p. 491**

Panicum virgatum
SWITCH GRASS
:Ö: :◐ ⁄ 1–11, 14–23 **p. 495**

Phalaris arundinacea picta
RIBBON GRASS
:Ö: :◐ ⁄ A1–A3; 1–10, 14–24 **p. 515**

Rheum
ORNAMENTAL RHUBARB
:Ö: :◐ ⁄ 2B–7, 14–17 **p. 567**

Rodgersia
:Ö: :◐ ⁄ 2–9, 14–17 **p. 578**

Scirpus cernuus
FIBER OPTICS PLANT
:◐ ⁄ 7–24 **p. 603**

Tradescantia virginiana
SPIDERWORT
:Ö: :◐ ● ⁄ 1–24; H1 **p. 637**

Trollius
GLOBEFLOWER
:Ö: :◐ ⁄ A2, A3; 1–6 **p. 639**

Woodwardia fimbriata
GIANT CHAIN FERN
:◐ ● ⁄ 4–9, 14–24 **p. 653**

Xanthosoma
:◐ ⁄ 12, 13, 16, 17, 21–24; H1, H2 **p. 653**

Zantedeschia aethiopica
COMMON CALLA
:Ö: :◐ ⁄ 5, 6, 8, 9, 12–24; H1, H2 **p. 655**

Lobelia cardinalis

Osmunda regalis

Rheum palmatum 'Atrosanguineum'

Tradescantia virginiana

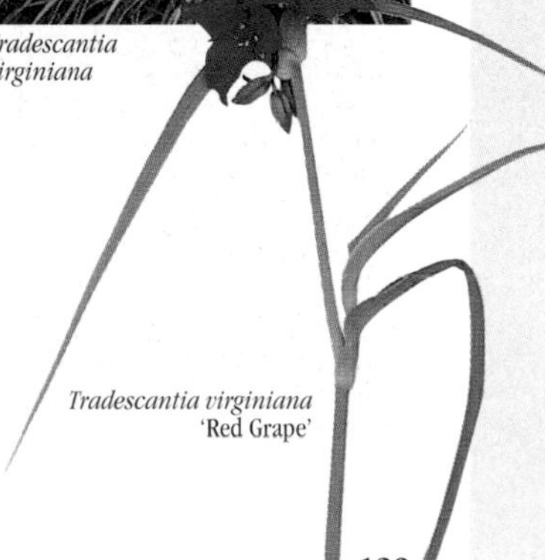
Tradescantia virginiana 'Red Grape'

Hydrangea macrophylla

Plants to Use Near
SWIMMING POOLS

When you're selecting plants to enhance a swimming pool, keep several requirements in mind. First, look for smooth branches, foliage, and flowers; anything bristly, prickly, sharp, or thorny will annoy or injure pool users. Second, choose plants that are virtually litter-free, and make sure any litter they do produce is too large to pass into the pool's filter. Finally, of course, aim for good-looking choices that are diverse in form and foliage. The plants listed here meet these specifications.

Garden pool is embraced by

Fatsia japonica

Feijoa, Pineapple Guava

Lavandula angustifolia

TREELIKE PLANTS		
Cordyline	NEEDS, ZONES VARY	**p. 290**
Dracaena	☼ ◑ ⁄ ZONES VARY	**p. 320**
Ensete ventricosum	☼ ◑ ⁄ 13, 15–24; H1, H2	**p. 326**
Eriobotrya deflexa BRONZE LOQUAT	☼ ◑ ⁄ 8–24	**p. 333**
Ferns (tree types)	NEEDS, ZONES VARY	**p. 349**
Ficus auriculata	☼ ⁄ 20–24; H1, H2	**p. 350**
Geijera parviflora AUSTRALIAN WILLOW	☼ ⁄ 8, 9, 12–24	**p. 362**
Musa BANANA	☼ ◑ ⁄ ZONES VARY	**p. 473**
Palms (some)	NEEDS, ZONES VARY	**p. 494**
Rhaphiolepis 'Majestic Beauty'	☼ ◑ ⁄ 4–10, 12–24; H1, H2	**p. 567**
Schefflera	☼ ◑ ⁄ ZONES VARY	**p. 601**
Tabebuia chrysotricha GOLDEN TRUMPET TREE	☼ ⁄ 13, 15, 16, 20–24; H1, H2	**p. 626**

SHRUBS		
Camellia	◑ ⁄ 4–9, 12, 14–24	**p. 243**
Fatsia japonica JAPANESE ARALIA	◑ ● ⁄ 4–9, 14–24; H1, H2	**p. 348**
Feijoa, Pineapple Guava	☼ ⁄ 6–9, 12–24; H1, H2	**p. 348**
Hibiscus rosa-sinensis CHINESE HIBISCUS	☼ ⁄ 9, 12–16, 19–24; H1, H2	**p. 388**
Hydrangea macrophylla BIGLEAF HYDRANGEA	☼ ◑ ⁄ 3B–9, 14–24; H1	**p. 394**
Juniperus (some) JUNIPER	☼ ◑ ⁄ ZONES VARY	**p. 410**
Lantana	☼ ⁄ 8–10, 12–24; H1, H2	**p. 422**
Lavandula LAVENDER	☼ ⁄ ZONES VARY	**p. 425**
Pittosporum tobira 'Wheeler's Dwarf'	☼ ◑ ⁄ 8–24; H1, H2	**p. 531**
Rhaphiolepis	☼ ◑ ⁄ 4–10, 12–24; H1, H2	**p. 567**
Ternstroemia gymnanthera	◑ ● ⁄ 4–9, 12–24	**p. 629**
Viburnum davidii	◑ ⁄ 4–9, 14–24	**p. 646**

For growing symbol explanations, please see page 64.

Pittosporum tobira 'Wheeler's Dwarf'

Rhaphiolepis indica

Solandra maxima

SPECIAL SITUATIONS

pool-friendly plants.

Anigozanthos flavidus

Canna hybrid

Scaevola 'Mauve Clusters'

VINES

Beaumontia grandiflora
HERALD'S TRUMPET
☼ ◐ ◪ 12, 13, 16, 17, 21–24; H1, H2 — **p. 219**

×Fatshedera lizei
◐ ● ◪ 4–10, 12–24; H1, H2 — **p. 348**

Lonicera hildebrandiana
GIANT BURMESE HONEYSUCKLE
☼ ◐ ◪ 9, 14–17, 19–24; H1, H2 — **p. 441**

Mandevilla
☼ ◐ ◪ ZONES VARY — **p. 461**

Solandra maxima
CUP-OF-GOLD VINE
☼ ◪ 15–24; H2 — **p. 611**

Tetrastigma voinieranum
◐ ◪ 13, 17, 20–24; H1, H2 — **p. 629**

PERENNIALS

Agapanthus
LILY-OF-THE-NILE
☼ ◐ ◪ 4–9, 12–24; H1, H2 — **p. 174**

Agave attenuata
◐ ◪ 13, 20–24; H1, H2 — **p. 175**

Aloe
☼ ◐ ◪ 8, 9, 12–24 — **p. 180**

Alstroemeria, evergreen hybrids
☼ ◐ ◪ 5–9, 14–24; H1 — **p. 182**

Anigozanthos flavidus
KANGAROO PAW
☼ ◪ 15–24 — **p. 186**

Artemisia 'Powis Castle'
☼ ◪ 2–24 — **p. 202**

Aspidistra elatior
CAST-IRON PLANT
◐ ● ◪ 4–10, 12–24; H1, H2 — **p. 206**

Canna
☼ ◪ 6–9, 12–24; H1, H2 — **p. 249**

Clivia miniata
◐ ● ◪ 12–17, 19–24; H1, H2 — **p. 285**

Colocasia esculenta
TARO
◐ ◪ 12, 16–24; H1, H2 — **p. 288**

Coreopsis
☼ ◪ ZONES VARY — **p. 290**

Crassula ovata
JADE PLANT
☼ ◪ 8, 9, 12–24; H1, H2 — **p. 298**

Cyperus
☼ ◐ ● ◪ ZONES VARY — **p. 306**

Dianella tasmanica
☼ ◐ ◪ 8, 9, 14–24 — **p. 313**

Dietes
FORTNIGHT LILY
☼ ◐ ◪ 8, 9, 12–24; H1, H2 — **p. 316**

Erysimum 'Bowles Mauve'
☼ ◐ ◪ 4–6, 14–17, 22, 23 — **p. 334**

Gazania
NEEDS, ZONES VARY — **p. 361**

Hedychium
GINGER LILY
◐ ◪ 8, 9, 14–17, 19–24; H1, H2 — **p. 381**

Hemerocallis
DAYLILY
☼ ◐ ◪ 1–24; H1, H2 — **p. 385**

Hesperaloe parviflora
RED YUCCA
☼ ◪ 2B, 3, 7–16, 18–24 — **p. 386**

Kniphofia
RED-HOT POKER
☼ ◐ ◪ ZONES VARY — **p. 418**

Limonium perezii
☼ ◪ 13, 15–17, 20–24 — **p. 435**

Liriope and Ophiopogon
LILY TURF
☼ ◐ ● ◪ ZONES VARY — **p. 438**

Philodendron (treelike types)
◐ ● ◪ ZONES VARY — **p. 516**

Phlomis
☼ ◪ ZONES VARY — **p. 517**

Phormium
☼ ◐ ◪ 5–9, 14–24; H1, H2 — **p. 518**

Santolina
☼ ◪ ZONES VARY — **p. 598**

Scaevola
☼ ◪ ZONES VARY — **p. 601**

Strelitzia
BIRD OF PARADISE
☼ ◐ ◪ ZONES VARY — **p. 621**

Yucca (some)
☼ ◪ ZONES VARY — **p. 654**

Hesperaloe parviflora

Kniphofia uvaria

Liriope spicata 'Silver Dragon'

Limonium perezii

Acer palmatum 'Dissectum'

Plants for
ROCK GARDENS

Phlox subulata with *Aurinia saxatilis*

Dwarf trees, tiny shrubs, miniature bulbous plants, perennials and annuals that form low tufts or creeping mats of foliage are premier rock garden plants. Favorites in all categories are listed below. Classic European alpine gardens can be replicated in cool parts of the Pacific Northwest, but to create the same effect in hotter, drier, or colder regions, you'll need a different assortment of plants. Be sure to heed climate zone adaptations and cultural needs.

Picea pungens 'Glauca'

Pinus mugo mugo

Erica cinerea

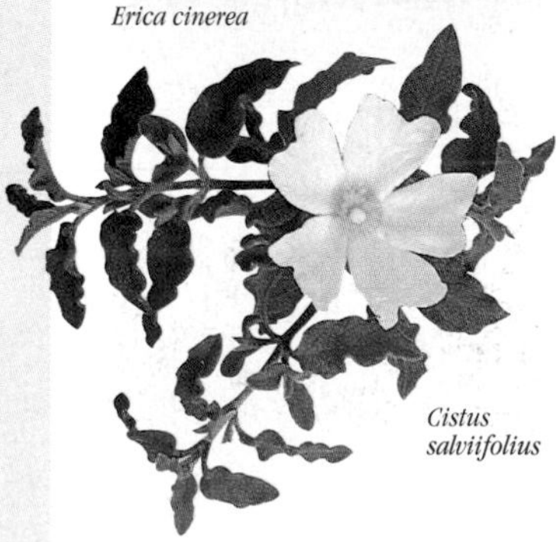

Cistus salviifolius

TREES

Abies balsamea 'Nana'
DWARF BALSAM FIR
A3; 1–7, 15–17 — **p. 162**

Acer palmatum (dwarf)
JAPANESE MAPLE
A3; 2–10, 12, 14–24 — **p. 168**

Betula pendula 'Trost's Dwarf'
A2, A3; 1–12, 14–24 — **p. 223**

Cedrus deodara (dwarf)
DEODAR CEDAR
3B–10, 14–24 — **p. 258**

Chamaecyparis obtusa (dwarf)
HINOKI FALSE CYPRESS
A3; 2B–6, 15–17 — **p. 265**

Picea (many dwarf types)
SPRUCE
ZONES VARY — **p. 521**

Pinus densiflora 'Pendula'
DWARF JAPANESE RED PINE
2–9, 14–17; H1 — **p. 525**

Pinus densiflora 'Umbraculifera'
TANYOSHO PINE
2–10, 14–17 — **p. 525**

Pinus edulis
PIÑON
1–11, 14–21 — **p. 525**

Pinus monophylla
SINGLELEAF PIÑON PINE
2–12, 14–21 — **p. 526**

Pinus mugo mugo
MUGHO PINE
A1–A3; 1–11, 14–24 — **p. 527**

Pinus strobus Nana Group
DWARF WHITE PINE
1–6 — **p. 528**

Pinus sylvestris (several)
DWARF SCOTCH PINE
A1–A3; 1–9, 14–21 — **p. 529**

Tsuga canadensis (dwarf)
CANADA HEMLOCK
A3; 2–7, 17 — **p. 639**

SHRUBS, SHRUBLETS

Berberis × stenophylla 'Corallina Compacta'
4–9, 14–24 — **p. 222**

Berberis thunbergii (smaller)
JAPANESE BARBERRY
A3; 2B–24 — **p. 222**

Calluna vulgaris (dwarf)
SCOTCH HEATHER
1A, 2–6, 15–17 — **p. 241**

Calocephalus brownii
CUSHION BUSH
16, 17, 19, 21–24 — **p. 242**

Cistus (some)
ROCKROSE
4–9, 14–24 — **p. 276**

Cotoneaster (dwarf)
ZONES VARY — **p. 296**

Daboecia cantabrica
IRISH HEATH
3B–9, 14–24 — **p. 307**

Daphne cneorum
GARLAND DAPHNE
2B–9, 14–17 — **p. 309**

Erica (dwarf)
HEATH
ZONES VARY — **p. 329**

Gaultheria (most)
ZONES VARY — **p. 361**

Gaultheria shallon

Hebe pinguifolia 'Pagei'

Rhododendron impeditum

For growing symbol explanations, please see page 64.

Teucrium × lucidrys

Aeonium urbicum

Androsace sarmentosa

Genista (several dwarf types)
DWARF BROOM
ZONES VARY p. 362

Halimium
5–9, 12–24 p. 379

Hebe (several dwarf types)
14–24 p. 380

Helianthemum nummularium
SUNROSE
2B–9, 14–24 p. 382

Hypericum coris
ST. JOHNSWORT
4–9, 14–24 p. 395

Ilex crenata (several dwarf types)
DWARF JAPANESE HOLLY
3–9, 14–24 p. 397

Jasminum parkeri
DWARF JASMINE
5–9, 12–24 p. 408

Juniperus (many dwarf types)
JUNIPER
ZONES VARY p. 410

Pieris japonica (dwarf)
LILY-OF-THE-VALLEY SHRUB
2B–9, 14–17 p. 522

Rhododendron (azalea)
MACRANTHA HYBRIDS
4–9, 14–24 p. 573

Rhododendron (dwarf types)
ZONES VARY p. 568

Teucrium (low-growing)
GERMANDER
ZONES VARY p. 630

PERENNIALS

Achillea (dwarf)
YARROW
A1–A3; 1–24 p. 170

Aeonium
15–17, 20–24 p. 173

Aethionema
STONECRESS
1–9, 14–21 p. 173

Ajuga genevensis
CARPET BUGLE
A2, A3; 1–24 p. 176

Androsace
ROCK JASMINE
1–6, 14–17 p. 185

Antennaria dioica
PUSSY TOES
A1, A2; 1–3, 6, 7, 14–16 p. 187

Aquilegia (dwarf)
COLUMBINE
ZONES VARY p. 195

Arabis
ROCKCRESS
ZONES VARY p. 196

Arenaria
SANDWORT
NEEDS, ZONES VARY p. 200

Armeria
THRIFT, SEA PINK
ZONES VARY p. 201

Aster alpinus
1–4 p. 207

Aubrieta deltoidea
COMMON AUBRIETA
1–9, 14–21 p. 209

Aurinia saxatilis
BASKET-OF-GOLD
1–24 p. 210

Campanula (smallest)
BELLFLOWER
1–9, 14–24 p. 247

Cerastium tomentosum
SNOW-IN-SUMMER
A1, A2; 1–24 p. 261

Delosperma
ICE PLANT
ZONES VARY p. 311

Dianthus (smallest)
PINK
A2, A3; 1–24 p. 313

Draba
ZONES VARY p. 319

Dryas
A1–A3; 1–6 p. 320

Echeveria (many)
ZONES VARY p. 322

Erigeron (dwarf)
FLEABANE
ZONES VARY p. 329

Eriogonum (dwarf)
WILD BUCKWHEAT
ZONES VARY p. 333

Erodium reichardii
CRANESBILL
7–9, 14–24 p. 333

Euphorbia myrsinites
2–24 p. 344

Gentiana
GENTIAN
2–6, 14–17 p. 363

Plant listings continue ▶

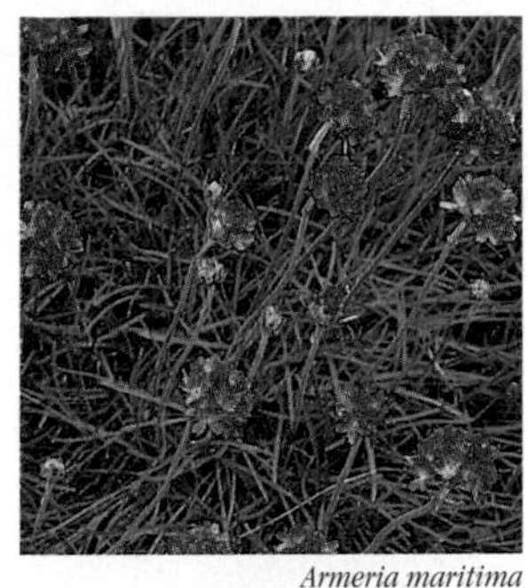

Armeria maritima

Campanula portenschlagiana

Echeveria (mixed)

Erigeron karvinskianus

Euphorbia myrsinites

Geranium

Heuchera micrantha 'Palace Purple'

Lewisia cotyledon

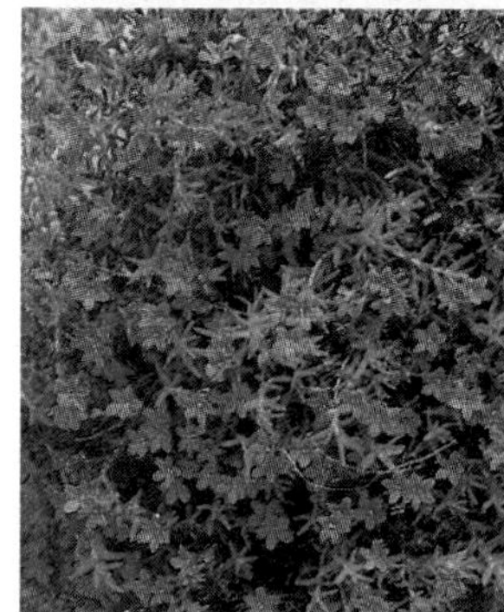
Lithodora diffusa

Geranium (smallest)
CRANESBILL
☼ ◑ ⁄ ZONES VARY — p. 363

Gypsophila (several dwarf types)
☼ ⁄ ZONES VARY — p. 377

Herniaria glabra
GREEN CARPET
☼ ◑ ● ⁄ 2B–24 — p. 386

Heuchera
CORAL BELLS
☼ ◑ ⁄ ZONES VARY — p. 387

Hosta (smallest)
PLANTAIN LILY
◑ ● ⁄ ZONES VARY — p. 391

Iberis sempervirens
EVERGREEN CANDYTUFT
☼ ◑ ⁄ 1–24 — p. 396

Lewisia
☼ ◑ ⁄ 1–7, 14–17 — p. 431

Lithodora diffusa
☼ ◑ ⁄ 5–7, 14–17 — p. 438

Origanum (low-growing)
OREGANO, MARJORAM
☼ ⁄ ZONES VARY — p. 489

Penstemon (subshrubs or mat-forming)
☼ ◑ ⁄ ZONES VARY — p. 510

Phlox (trailing or creeping)
☼ ◑ ⁄ ZONES VARY — p. 517

Pleione
◑ ⁄ 5–9, 14–24 — p. 533

Polemonium reptans
◑ ● ⁄ 1–11, 14–17 — p. 540

Potentilla (most)
CINQUEFOIL
☼ ◑ ⁄ ZONES VARY — p. 544

Primula (most)
PRIMROSE
☼ ◑ ● ⁄ ZONES VARY — p. 545

Pulsatilla vulgaris
PASQUE FLOWER
☼ ⁄ 2B–6, 15–17 — p. 555

Saponaria ocymoides
☼ ⁄ 1–11, 14–24 — p. 599

Saxifraga
SAXIFRAGE
NEEDS, ZONES VARY — p. 600

Sedum (many)
STONECROP
NEEDS, ZONES VARY — p. 604

Sempervivum
HOUSELEEK
☼ ◑ ⁄ 2–24 — p. 606

Senecio (some)
NEEDS, ZONES VARY — p. 606

Silene acaulis
CUSHION PINK — p. 609
☼ ◑ ⁄ A1–A3; 1–11, 14–16, 18–21

Sisyrinchium (smallest)
☼ ◑ ⁄ 4–9, 14–24 — p. 610

Thymus
THYME
☼ ◑ ⁄ 1–24 — p. 632

Veronica (mat-forming)
SPEEDWELL
☼ ⁄ ZONES VARY — p. 645

BULBS, BULBLIKE PLANTS

Allium (smallest)
ORNAMENTAL ALLIUM
☼ ◑ ⁄ ZONES VARY — p. 178

Chionodoxa
GLORY-OF-THE-SNOW
☼ ◑ ⁄ 1–7, 14–20 — p. 270

Crocus
☼ ◑ ⁄ 1–24 — p. 300

Cyclamen (except C. persicum)
☼ ◑ ⁄ ZONES VARY — p. 304

Freesia
☼ ◑ ⁄ 8, 9, 12–24 — p. 356

Galanthus
SNOWDROP
☼ ◑ ⁄ 1–9, 14–17 — p. 359

Iris (smallest)
NEEDS, ZONES VARY — p. 401

Muscari
GRAPE HYACINTH
☼ ◑ ⁄ ZONES VARY — p. 474

Narcissus (small)
DAFFODIL
☼ ◑ ⁄ A2, A3; 1–24 — p. 476

Sternbergia lutea
☼ ⁄ 3–10, 14–24 — p. 619

Tulipa (species only)
TULIP
☼ ◑ ⁄ 1–24 — p. 640

Zephyranthes
ZEPHYR FLOWER, FAIRY LILY
☼ ◑ ⁄ ZONES VARY — p. 656

Saponaria ocymoides

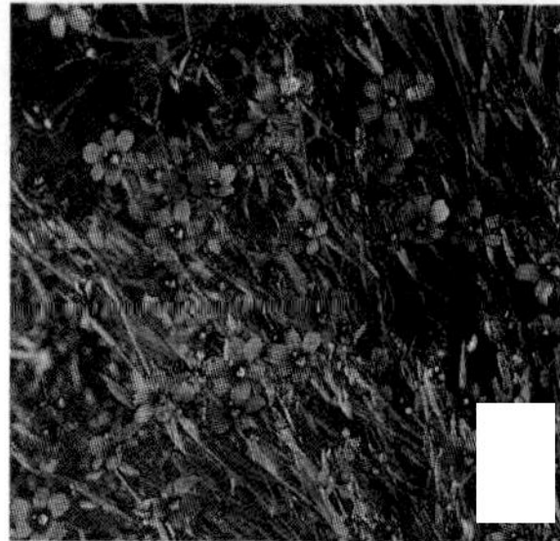
Sisyrinchium bellum

Veronica 'Waterperry Blue'

Crocus 'Mammoth Yellow'

Muscari armeniacum

For growing symbol explanations, please see page 64.

× *Cupressocyparis leylandii*

Plants for WINDY AREAS

Callistemon citrinus

Regular strong winds can wreak havoc on plants. Water stress is one common problem; constant wind pulls moisture from foliage faster than roots can draw it from the soil. And really powerful winds can virtually destroy many plants—defoliate them, uproot them, wrench off branches with such force that trunks may split. Fortunately, the plants listed below will endure high winds without much damage to health or appearance. For plants unfazed by ocean winds, see "Plants for Seacoast Gardens" (page 138).

SYMBOL: ♠♠♠ indicates plants that serve as windbreaks.

Melaleuca linariifolia

Picea abies

Olea europaea

TREES

Plant	Common name	Needs / Zones	Windbreak	Page
Acacia (some)		☼ ⁄ ZONES VARY		p. 164
Acer campestre	HEDGE MAPLE	☼ ◑ ⁄ 2–9, 14–17	♠♠♠	p. 167
Broussonetia papyrifera	PAPER MULBERRY	☼ ⁄ 3B–24; H1, H2	♠♠♠	p. 233
Calocedrus decurrens	INCENSE CEDAR	☼ ◑ ⁄ 2–12, 14–24	♠♠♠	p. 241
Casuarina	BEEFWOOD	☼ ⁄ 8, 9, 12–24; H1, H2	♠♠♠	p. 254
Chamaecyparis lawsoniana	PORT ORFORD CEDAR	☼ ◑ ⁄ A3; 3–6, 15–17	♠♠♠	p. 265
Chilopsis linearis	DESERT WILLOW	☼ ⁄ 3B, 7–14, 18–23		p. 269
×Cupressocyparis leylandii		☼ ⁄ 3B–24	♠♠♠	p. 302
Cupressus (most)	CYPRESS	☼ ⁄ ZONES VARY	♠♠♠	p. 303
Elaeagnus angustifolia	RUSSIAN OLIVE	☼ ◑ ⁄ A2, A3; 1–3, 7–14, 18, 19	♠♠♠	p. 324
Eucalyptus (most)		☼ ⁄ ZONES VARY	♠♠♠	p. 337
Fraxinus 'Fan West'		☼ ⁄ 2–14		p. 356
Fraxinus velutina 'Rio Grande'	FAN-TEX ASH	☼ ⁄ 8–24		p. 356
Lagunaria patersonii	PRIMROSE TREE	☼ ⁄ 13, 15–24; H1, H2	♠♠♠	p. 421
Ligustrum lucidum	GLOSSY PRIVET	☼ ◑ ⁄ 5–24; H1, H2	♠♠♠	p. 433
Maclura pomifera	OSAGE ORANGE	☼ ⁄ 2, 3, 10–13	♠♠♠	p. 447
Melaleuca (most)		☼ ⁄ ZONES VARY		p. 464
Melaleuca quinquenervia	CAJEPUT TREE	☼ ⁄ 9, 12, 13, 15–17, 20–24; H1, H2	♠♠♠	p. 464
Olea europaea	OLIVE	☼ ⁄ 8, 9, 11–24; H1, H2		p. 486
Palms		NEEDS, ZONES VARY		p. 494
Parkinsonia aculeata	JERUSALEM THORN	☼ ⁄ 8–24; H1, H2		p. 497
Picea abies	NORWAY SPRUCE	☼ ◑ ⁄ A2, A3; 1–6, 14–17	♠♠♠	p. 521
Pinus (many)	PINE	☼ ⁄ ZONES VARY	♠♠♠	p. 523
Pittosporum (except P. phyllyreoides)		☼ ◑ ⁄ ZONES VARY	♠♠♠	p. 531
Populus (several)		☼ ⁄ ZONES VARY	♠♠♠	p. 543

Plant listings continue ▸

Quercus virginiana

Sequoia sempervirens

Thuja plicata

Ceanothus impressus

Chamaecyparis pisifera

Cistus × hybridus

Cotoneaster microphyllus

Escallonia × langleyensis

Juniperus chinensis 'Torulosa'

Prosopis glandulosa
HONEY MESQUITE
☼ 10–13, 18–24 p. 548

Pseudotsuga menziesii
DOUGLAS FIR
☼ ◑ A2, A3; 1–10, 14–17 p. 554

Quercus ilex
HOLLY OAK, HOLM OAK
☼ 4–24 p. 561

Quercus virginiana
SOUTHERN LIVE OAK
☼ 4–24 p. 562

Schinus molle
CALIFORNIA PEPPER TREE
☼ 8, 9, 12–24; H1, H2 p. 602

Sequoia sempervirens
REDWOOD, COAST REDWOOD
☼ ◑ 4–9, 14–24 p. 607

Tamarix
TAMARISK
☼ ZONES VARY p. 627

Thuja occidentalis
AMERICAN ARBORVITAE p. 631
☼ ◑ A2, A3; 1–9, 15–17, 21–24; H1, H2

Thuja plicata
WESTERN RED CEDAR
☼ ◑ A3; 1–9, 14–24 p. 631

Ulmus pumila
SIBERIAN ELM
☼ A1–A3; 1–11, 14–21 p. 643

SHRUBS

Arbutus unedo
STRAWBERRY TREE
☼ ◑ 4–24 p. 197

Arctostaphylos
MANZANITA
☼ ◑ ZONES VARY p. 198

Artemisia
☼ ZONES VARY p. 201

Baccharis pilularis
DWARF COYOTE BRUSH
☼ 5–11, 14–24 p. 212

Berberis
BARBERRY
☼ ◑ ZONES VARY p. 221

Buxus
BOXWOOD
☼ ◑ ● ZONES VARY p. 236

Callistemon
BOTTLEBRUSH
☼ ZONES VARY p. 240

Ceanothus
WILD LILAC
☼ 5–9, 14–24 p. 256

Chamaecyparis
FALSE CYPRESS
☼ ◑ ZONES VARY p. 265

Cistus
ROCKROSE
☼ 4–9, 14–24 p. 276

Correa
AUSTRALIAN FUCHSIA
☼ ◑ 14–24 p. 293

Cotoneaster
☼ ZONES VARY p. 296

Dodonaea viscosa
HOP BUSH
☼ ◑ 7–24; H1, H2 p. 319

Elaeagnus
☼ ◑ ZONES VARY p. 324

Escallonia
☼ ◑ 4–9, 14–24 p. 335

Euonymus japonicus
EVERGREEN EUONYMUS
☼ 4–20; H1 p. 343

Griselinia littoralis
☼ ◑ 9, 14–17, 20–24 p. 376

Hakea suaveolens
SWEET HAKEA
☼ 9, 12–17, 19–24 p. 378

Juniperus
JUNIPER
☼ ◑ ZONES VARY p. 410

Lantana
☼ 8–10, 12–24; H1, H2 p. 422

Laurus nobilis
SWEET BAY
☼ ◑ 5–9, 12–24; H1, H2 p. 424

Lavandula
LAVENDER
☼ ZONES VARY p. 425

Lavatera
TREE MALLOW
☼ ZONES VARY p. 427

Leptospermum
TEA TREE
☼ 14–24 p. 428

Leucophyllum
TEXAS RANGER
☼ 7–24 p. 430

Ligustrum japonicum 'Texanum'
☼ ◑ 4–24; H1, H2 p. 432

Myrica californica
PACIFIC WAX MYRTLE
☼ 4–9, 14–24 p. 475

Lavatera thuringiaca 'Barnsley'

Leptospermum scoparium

Ligustrum japonicum 'Texanum'

Nerium oleander

Pittosporum tobira

Nandina domestica

For growing symbol explanations, please see page 64.

Prunus lusitanica

Bougainvillea

Carex elata 'Bowles Golden'

Chrysanthemum frutescens

Eriogonum umbellatum

Nandina domestica
HEAVENLY BAMBOO
3–24; H1, H2 — **p. 476**

Nerium oleander
OLEANDER
8–16, 18–24; H1, H2 — **p. 482**

Pittosporum (most)
ZONES VARY — **p. 531**

Prunus (evergreen)
ZONES VARY — **p. 549**

Pyracantha
FIRETHORN
ZONES VARY — **p. 557**

Rhamnus (some)
NEEDS, ZONES VARY — **p. 566**

Rhaphiolepis (most)
4–10, 12–24; H1, H2 — **p. 567**

Rhus (some)
SUMAC
ZONES VARY — **p. 576**

Rosmarinus officinalis
ROSEMARY
4–24; H1, H2 — **p. 587**

Westringia fruticosa
COAST ROSEMARY
8, 9, 14–24 — **p. 652**

Xylosma congestum
8–24 — **p. 654**

VINES

Bougainvillea
5, 6, 12–17, 19, 21–24; H1, H2 — **p. 228**

Fallopia baldschuanica
LACE VINE
A1–A3; 1–24 — **p. 347**

Muehlenbeckia complexa
MATTRESS VINE
8, 9, 14–24 — **p. 473**

Tecoma capensis
CAPE HONEYSUCKLE
12, 13, 20–24; H1, H2 — **p. 628**

PERENNIALS

Agapanthus
LILY-OF-THE-NILE
4–9, 12–24; H1, H2 — **p. 174**

Agave
ZONES VARY — **p. 175**

Aloe
8, 9, 12–24 — **p. 180**

Asparagus densiflorus 'Sprengeri'
SPRENGER ASPARAGUS
12–24; H1, H2 — **p. 205**

Carex
SEDGE
ZONES VARY — **p. 251**

Cerastium tomentosum
SNOW-IN-SUMMER
A1, A2; 1–24 — **p. 261**

Chrysanthemum frutescens
MARGUERITE
14–24; H1 — **p. 272**

Crassula ovata
JADE PLANT
8, 9, 12–24; H1, H2 — **p. 298**

Eriogonum
WILD BUCKWHEAT
ZONES VARY — **p. 333**

Euphorbia
NEEDS, ZONES VARY — **p. 344**

Euryops
ZONES VARY — **p. 345**

Felicia amelloides
BLUE MARGUERITE
8, 9, 14–24 — **p. 349**

Hemerocallis
DAYLILY
1–24; H1, H2 — **p. 385**

Kniphofia
RED-HOT POKER
ZONES VARY — **p. 418**

Pelargonium
GERANIUM
8, 9, 12–24 — **p. 509**

Penstemon
BEARD TONGUE
ZONES VARY — **p. 510**

Phlomis
ZONES VARY — **p. 517**

Phormium
5–9, 14–24; H1, H2 — **p. 518**

Salvia
SAGE
NEEDS, ZONES VARY — **p. 592**

Santolina
ZONES VARY — **p. 598**

Yucca
ZONES VARY — **p. 654**

Euphorbia seguierana niciana

Euryops pectinatus 'Viridis'

Kniphofia uvaria

Phlomis russeliana

Agapanthus 'Peter Pan'

Plants for
SEACOAST GARDENS

Escallonia × exoniensis 'Frades'

A walk on the beach is a pleasure in fine weather, but on less pleasant days, blustery, salt-laden winds can send you scurrying for shelter. Plants, unfortunately, have no escape: they have to tough it out. Even on the breeziest coastlines, though, the plants listed below look fresh and healthy whatever the weather.

A seacoast garden relies on specially

Eucalyptus ficifolia

Melaleuca quinquenervia

Arbutus unedo

Cistus 'Victor Reiter'

TREES

Plant	Common name	Sun/water/zones	Page
× Cupressocyparis leylandii		☼ ⁄ 3B–24	**p. 302**
Eucalyptus ficifolia	RED-FLOWERING GUM	☼ ⁄ SEE CHART	**p. 339**
Ficus rubiginosa	RUSTYLEAF FIG	☼ ⁄ 18–24; H1, H2	**p. 351**
Melaleuca quinquenervia	CAJEPUT TREE	☼ ⁄ 9, 12, 13, 15–17, 20–24; H1, H2	**p. 464**
Metrosideros		☼ ◑ ⁄ ZONES VARY	**p. 467**
Myoporum laetum		☼ ⁄ 8, 9, 14–17, 19–24	**p. 475**
Pinus (some; see chart)	PINE	☼ ⁄ ZONES VARY	**p. 523**
Quercus ilex	HOLLY OAK	☼ ⁄ 4–24	**p. 561**
Umbellularia californica	CALIFORNIA LAUREL	☼ ◑ ● ⁄ 4–9, 14–24	**p. 643**

SHRUBS

Plant	Common name	Sun/water/zones	Page
Arbutus unedo	STRAWBERRY TREE	☼ ◑ ⁄ 4–24	**p. 197**
Carissa macrocarpa	NATAL PLUM	☼ ◑ ⁄ 22–24; H2	**p. 251**
Cistus	ROCKROSE	☼ ⁄ 4–9, 14–24	**p. 276**
Coprosma		☼ ◑ ⁄ ZONES VARY	**p. 289**
Corokia cotoneaster		☼ ◑ ⁄ 4–24	**p. 293**
Correa	AUSTRALIAN FUCHSIA	☼ ◑ ⁄ 14–24	**p. 293**
Cotoneaster (many)		☼ ⁄ ZONES VARY	**p. 296**
Cytisus	BROOM	☼ ⁄ ZONES VARY	**p. 306**
Dodonaea viscosa	HOP BUSH	☼ ◑ ⁄ 7–24; H1, H2	**p. 319**
Elaeagnus		☼ ◑ ⁄ ZONES VARY	**p. 324**
Escallonia		☼ ◑ ⁄ 4–9, 14–24	**p. 335**
Euonymus japonicus	EVERGREEN EUONYMUS	☼ ⁄ 4–20; H1	**p. 343**
Genista	BROOM	☼ ⁄ ZONES VARY	**p. 362**
Griselinia		☼ ◑ ⁄ 9, 14–17, 20–24	**p. 376**
Hakea		☼ ⁄ 9, 12–17, 19–24	**p. 378**
Halimium		☼ ⁄ 5–9, 12–24	**p. 379**
Hebe		☼ ◑ ⁄ 14–24	**p. 380**

Correa 'Ivory Bells'

Dodonaea viscosa

Escallonia × exoniensis 'Frades'

Hebe 'Patty's Purple'

For growing symbol explanations, please see page 64.

adapted plants.

Lantana 'Radiation'

Phlomis fruticosa

Rosa rugosa alba

Aloe arborescens

Juniperus
JUNIPER
ZONES VARY — p. 410

Lantana
8–10, 12–24; H1, H2 — p. 422

Lavandula
LAVENDER
ZONES VARY — p. 425

Leptospermum
TEA TREE
14–24 — p. 428

Melaleuca (most)
ZONES VARY — p. 464

Nerium oleander
OLEANDER
8–16, 18–24; H1, H2 — p. 482

Phlomis fruticosa
JERUSALEM SAGE
3B–24 — p. 517

Pittosporum crassifolium
9, 14–17, 19–24 — p. 531

Pittosporum tobira
TOBIRA
4–24; H1, H2 — p. 531

Rhamnus alaternus
ITALIAN BUCKTHORN
4–24 — p. 566

Rhaphiolepis
4–10, 12–24; H1, H2 — p. 567

Rhus integrifolia
LEMONADE BERRY
8, 9, 14–17, 19–24 — p. 576

Rosa rugosa
RAMANAS ROSE, SEA TOMATO
A1–A3; 1–24 — p. 587

Rosmarinus officinalis
ROSEMARY
4–24; H1, H2 — p. 587

Viburnum (most evergreen species)
ZONES VARY — p. 646

Westringia fruticosa
COAST ROSEMARY
8, 9, 14–24 — p. 652

PERENNIALS

Achillea
YARROW
A1–A3; 1–24 — p. 170

Agapanthus
LILY-OF-THE-NILE
4–9, 12–24; H1, H2 — p. 174

Aloe arborescens
TREE ALOE
8, 9, 12–24; H1, H2 — p. 180

Armeria maritima
COMMON THRIFT
A2, A3; 1–9, 14–24 — p. 201

Artemisia
ZONES VARY — p. 201

Centranthus ruber
JUPITER'S BEARD
2–9, 12–24; H1 — p. 260

Chrysanthemum frutescens
MARGUERITE
14–24; H1 — p. 272

Convolvulus sabatius
GROUND MORNING GLORY
4–9, 12–24 — p. 289

Dianthus
PINK
A2, A3; 1–24 — p. 313

Echium candicans
PRIDE OF MADEIRA
14–24 — p. 323

Erigeron
FLEABANE
ZONES VARY — p. 329

Eriogonum
WILD BUCKWHEAT
ZONES VARY — p. 333

Euphorbia
NEEDS, ZONES VARY — p. 344

Euryops
ZONES VARY — p. 345

Felicia amelloides
BLUE MARGUERITE
8, 9, 14–24 — p. 349

Gazania hybrids
8–24; H1, H2 — p. 361

Limonium perezii
SEA LAVENDER
13, 15–17, 20–24 — p. 435

Pelargonium
GERANIUM
8, 9, 12–24 — p. 509

Phormium
5–9, 14–24; H1, H2 — p. 518

Santolina
ZONES VARY — p. 598

Yucca
ZONES VARY — p. 654

Euphorbia characias wulfenii

Dianthus chinensis 'Super Strawberry Parfait'

Euryops pectinatus

Limonium perezii

Pelargonium × hortorum

Eucalyptus ficifolia

Plants for
DRY AREAS

Much of the West has a short annual rainy season followed by many dry months in which plants receive no water other than that supplied artificially. In periodic drought years, when rainfall is far below normal, the water available for gardens may be severely limited. Fortunately, many fine plants—once they are established in the garden—thrive with little or no supplemental water during the dry season. Here are some proven performers.

Lavender, penstemon, and yarrow

Aesculus californica

Brachychiton acerifolius

Cedrus libani

Ceratonia siliqua

Lagerstroemia indica

Lagerstroemia indica

Olea europaea

Parkinsonia aculeata

TREES

Plant	Common name	Exposure, water, zones	Page
Acacia (many)		☼ ⁄ ZONES VARY	**p. 164**
Aesculus californica	CALIFORNIA BUCKEYE	☼ ⁄ 3–10, 14–24	**p. 173**
Arbutus		☼ ⁄ ZONES VARY	**p. 197**
Brachychiton		☼ ⁄ ZONES VARY	**p. 230**
Calocedrus decurrens	INCENSE CEDAR	☼ ◑ ⁄ 2–12, 14–24	**p. 241**
Cassia fistula	GOLDEN SHOWER	☼ ⁄ H2	**p. 254**
Casuarina	BEEFWOOD	☼ ⁄ 8, 9, 12–24; H1, H2	**p. 254**
Cedrus	CEDAR	☼ ⁄ ZONES VARY	**p. 256**
Celtis	HACKBERRY	☼ ◑ ⁄ ZONES VARY	**p. 260**
Ceratonia siliqua	CAROB	☼ ⁄ 9, 13–16, 18–24; H1	**p. 262**
Cercidium	PALO VERDE	☼ ⁄ 8–14, 18–20	**p. 262**
Chilopsis linearis	DESERT WILLOW	☼ ⁄ 3B, 7–14, 18–23	**p. 269**
×Chitalpa tashkentensis	CHITALPA	☼ ⁄ 3–24	**p. 270**
Cupressus	CYPRESS	☼ ⁄ ZONES VARY	**p. 303**
Elaeagnus angustifolia	RUSSIAN OLIVE	☼ ◑ ⁄ A2, A3; 1–3, 7–14, 18, 19	**p. 324**
Eucalyptus (most)		☼ ⁄ ZONES VARY	**p. 337**
Geijera parviflora	AUSTRALIAN WILLOW	☼ ⁄ 8, 9, 12–24	**p. 362**
Grevillea robusta	SILK OAK	☼ ⁄ 8, 9, 12–24; H1, H2	**p. 375**
Koelreuteria paniculata	GOLDENRAIN TREE	☼ ⁄ A2; 2–24	**p. 418**
Lagerstroemia indica	CRAPE MYRTLE	☼ ⁄ 2–10, 12–24; H1, H2	**p. 421**
Laurus nobilis	SWEET BAY	☼ ◑ ⁄ 5–9, 12–24; H1, H2	**p. 424**
Leucaena retusa	GOLDEN BALL LEAD TREE	☼ ⁄ 10–13	**p. 429**
Lophostemon confertus	BRISBANE BOX	☼ ⁄ 15–17, 19–24; H1, H2	**p. 442**
Maclura pomifera	OSAGE ORANGE	☼ ⁄ 2, 3, 10–13	**p. 447**
Olea europaea	OLIVE	☼ ⁄ 8, 9, 11–24; H1, H2	**p. 486**

For growing symbol explanations, please see page 64.

brighten a water-thrifty landscape.

Quercus rubra

Artemisia 'Powis Castle'

Baccharis pilularis 'Twin Peaks'

Olneya tesota
DESERT IRONWOOD
8, 9, 11–14, 18–23 p. 486

Parkinsonia aculeata
JERUSALEM THORN
8–24; H1, H2 p. 497

Pinus (most)
PINE
ZONES VARY p. 523

Pistacia
PISTACHE
ZONES VARY p. 530

Pithecellobium
ZONES VARY p. 530

Prosopis
MESQUITE
10–13, 18–24 p. 547

Quercus (many)
OAK
ZONES VARY p. 558

Rhus lancea
AFRICAN SUMAC
8, 9, 12–24 p. 576

Robinia
LOCUST
ZONES VARY p. 578

Schinus molle
CALIFORNIA PEPPER TREE
8, 9, 12–24; H1, H2 p. 602

Sophora japonica
JAPANESE PAGODA TREE
2–24 p. 613

Tamarix
TAMARISK
ZONES VARY p. 627

Tilia tomentosa
SILVER LINDEN
2–21 p. 633

Umbellularia californica
CALIFORNIA LAUREL
4–9, 14–24 p. 643

SHRUBS

Acacia (many)
ZONES VARY p. 164

Adenostoma fasciculatum
CHAMISE
6–9, 14–24 p. 172

Aloysia triphylla
LEMON VERBENA
4–9, 10, 12–21 p. 181

Alyogyne huegelii
BLUE HIBISCUS
13–17, 20–24; H1, H2 p. 182

Anisacanthus thurberi
CHUPAROSA
8–13, 18–23; H1, H2 p. 187

Anisodontea × hypomandarum
CAPE MALLOW
14–24 p. 187

Arbutus unedo
STRAWBERRY TREE
4–24 p. 197

Arctostaphylos
MANZANITA
ZONES VARY p. 198

Artemisia (most)
ZONES VARY p. 201

Astartea fascicularis
15–24 p. 206

Atriplex
SALTBUSH
ZONES VARY p. 209

Baccharis
ZONES VARY p. 212

Caesalpinia
ZONES VARY p. 237

Calliandra (some)
NEEDS, ZONES VARY p. 239

Callistemon (most)
BOTTLEBRUSH
ZONES VARY p. 240

Calocephalus brownii
CUSHION BUSH
16, 17, 19, 21–24 p. 242

Caragana arborescens
SIBERIAN PEASHRUB
A1–A3; 1–12 p. 250

Carpenteria californica
BUSH ANEMONE
5–9, 14–24 p. 252

Caryopteris × clandonensis
BLUE MIST
2B–9, 14–24 p. 253

Ceanothus
WILD LILAC
5–9, 14–24 p. 256

Cercis occidentalis
WESTERN REDBUD
2–24 p. 263

Cercocarpus
MOUNTAIN MAHOGANY
ZONES VARY p. 263

Chamelaucium uncinatum
GERALDTON WAXFLOWER
8, 9, 12–24 p. 266

Callistemon citrinus

Ceanothus 'Julia Phelps'

Cercis occidentalis

Cistus × purpureus

Cordia boissieri

Cytisus canariensis

Plant listings continue ▶

Dendromecon harfordii

Dodonaea viscosa

Fallugia paradoxa

Fremontodendron californicum

Cistus
ROCKROSE
4–9, 14–24 **p. 276**

Convolvulus cneorum
BUSH MORNING GLORY
5–9, 12–24 **p. 289**

Coprosma (most)
ZONES VARY **p. 289**

Cordia (some)
ZONES VARY **p. 289**

Correa
AUSTRALIAN FUCHSIA
14–24 **p. 293**

Cotinus coggygria
SMOKE TREE
2–24 **p. 296**

Cotoneaster
ZONES VARY **p. 296**

Cytisus
BROOM
ZONES VARY **p. 306**

Dalea
ZONES VARY **p. 309**

Dendromecon
BUSH POPPY
ZONES VARY **p. 312**

Dodonaea viscosa
HOP BUSH
7–24; H1, H2 **p. 319**

Elaeagnus (some)
ZONES VARY **p. 324**

Eleutherococcus sieboldianus
2B–10, 14–17 **p. 325**

Encelia farinosa
BRITTLEBUSH
8–16, 18–24; H1 **p. 326**

Eremophila (most)
EMU BUSH
8, 9, 13–24 **p. 328**

Euryops
ZONES VARY **p. 345**

Fallugia paradoxa
APACHE PLUME
2–23 **p. 347**

Feijoa, Pineapple Guava
6–9, 12–24; H1, H2 **p. 348**

Fremontodendron
FLANNEL BUSH
4–24 **p. 357**

Galvezia speciosa
ISLAND BUSH SNAPDRAGON
14–24 **p. 360**

Garrya (some)
SILKTASSEL
ZONES VARY **p. 361**

Genista
BROOM
ZONES VARY **p. 362**

Grevillea (most)
NEEDS, ZONES VARY **p. 375**

Hakea
9, 12–17, 19–24 **p. 378**

×Halimiocistus
4–24 **p. 378**

Halimium
5–9, 12–24 **p. 379**

Heteromeles arbutifolia
TOYON
5–9, 14–24 **p. 386**

Holodiscus
ZONES VARY **p. 390**

Juniperus (some)
JUNIPER
ZONES VARY **p. 410**

Justicia (some)
NEEDS, ZONES VARY **p. 415**

Lantana
8–10, 12–24; H1, H2 **p. 422**

Lavandula
LAVENDER
ZONES VARY **p. 425**

Lavatera assurgentiflora
TREE MALLOW
14–24 **p. 427**

Leonotis leonurus
LION'S TAIL
8–24; H1, H2 **p. 428**

Lepechinia
PITCHER SAGE
7–9, 14–24 **p. 428**

Leptospermum
TEA TREE
14–24 **p. 428**

Leucophyllum
TEXAS RANGER
7–24 **p. 430**

Luma apiculata
14–24 **p. 443**

Grevillea 'Poorinda Constance'

Juniperus chinensis

Lavandula angustifolia 'Hidcote'

Lavatera assurgentiflora

For growing symbol explanations, please see page 64.

Leonotis leonurus

Myrtus communis

Plumbago auriculata

Nandina domestica

Rosmarinus officinalis

Lysiloma microphylla thornberi
FEATHER BUSH
12–24; H1, H2 **p. 445**

Mahonia (many)
NEEDS, ZONES VARY **p. 455**

Melaleuca (most)
ZONES VARY **p. 464**

Myoporum
ZONES VARY **p. 474**

Myrtus communis
MYRTLE
8–24; H1, H2 **p. 476**

Nandina domestica
HEAVENLY BAMBOO
3–24; H1, H2 **p. 476**

Nerium oleander
OLEANDER
8–16, 18–24; H1, H2 **p. 482**

Osmanthus
ZONES VARY **p. 490**

Phlomis
ZONES VARY **p. 517**

Plumbago auriculata
CAPE PLUMBAGO
8, 9, 12–24; H1, H2 **p. 534**

Portulacaria afra
ELEPHANT'S FOOD
8, 9, 12–24; H1, H2 **p. 544**

Prostanthera
MINT BUSH
14–17, 19–24 **p. 548**

Prunus ilicifolia
5–9, 12–24 **p. 549**

Punica granatum
POMEGRANATE
5–24; H1, H2 **p. 556**

Pyracantha
FIRETHORN
ZONES VARY **p. 557**

Rhamnus (most)
NEEDS, ZONES VARY **p. 566**

Rhus
SUMAC
ZONES VARY **p. 576**

Ribes (most)
CURRANT, GOOSEBERRY
ZONES VARY **p. 577**

Rosa rugosa
RAMANAS ROSE, SEA TOMATO
A1–A3; 1–24 **p. 587**

Rosmarinus officinalis
ROSEMARY
4–24; H1, H2 **p. 587**

Rubus
BRAMBLE
ZONES VARY **p. 588**

Ruscus
BUTCHER'S BROOM
4–24; H1 **p. 589**

Salvia (many)
SAGE
NEEDS, ZONES VARY **p. 592**

Santolina chamaecyparissus
LAVENDER COTTON
2–24; H1, H2 **p. 598**

Simmondsia chinensis
JOJOBA, GOATNUT
7–24 **p. 610**

Sophora (some)
ZONES VARY **p. 613**

Symphoricarpos
SNOWBERRY, CORALBERRY
NEEDS, ZONES VARY **p. 624**

Taxus
YEW
ZONES VARY **p. 628**

Tecoma stans
YELLOW BELLS
12, 13, 21–24; H1, H2 **p. 629**

Teucrium
GERMANDER
ZONES VARY **p. 630**

Trichostema lanatum
WOOLLY BLUE CURLS
14–24 **p. 637**

Vauquelinia californica
ARIZONA ROSEWOOD
10–13 **p. 644**

Westringia fruticosa
8, 9, 14–24 **p. 652**

GROUND COVERS, VINES

Acacia redolens
8, 9, 12–24 **p. 166**

Arctostaphylos uva-ursi
BEARBERRY
A1–A3; 1–9, 14–24 **p. 199**

Arctotheca calendula
CAPE WEED
8, 9, 13–24 **p. 199**

Calylophus hartwegii
SUNDROPS
1–3, 6–16, 18–24 **p. 243**

Plant listings continue ▶

Salvia leucantha

Salvia leucantha 'Midnight'

Tecoma stans

Trichostema lanatum

Arctostaphylos uva-ursi

Gazania hybrids

Hypericum calycinum

Lantana montevidensis

Mahonia aquifolium 'Compacta'

Thymus pseudolanuginosus

Cissus (some)
NEEDS, ZONES VARY **p. 275**

Dalea greggii
TRAILING INDIGO BUSH
10–13 **p. 309**

Fallopia baldschuanica
LACE VINE
A1–A3; 1–24 **p. 347**

Gazania
NEEDS, ZONES VARY **p. 361**

Hypericum calycinum
AARON'S BEARD
2B–24 **p. 395**

Ice Plants
NEEDS, ZONES VARY **p. 396**

Juniperus (some)
JUNIPER
ZONES VARY **p. 410**

Lantana montevidensis
8–10, 12–24; H1, H2 **p. 422**

Macfadyena unguis-cati
CAT'S CLAW
8–24; H1, H2 **p. 446**

Mahonia (some)
NEEDS, ZONES VARY **p. 455**

Malvastrum lateritium
TRAILING MALLOW
8, 9, 14–24 **p. 457**

Mascagnia
ORCHID VINE
12–24 **p. 462**

Myoporum parvifolium
8, 9, 12–24 **p. 475**

Podranea ricasoliana
PINK TRUMPET VINE
9, 12, 13, 19–24; H1, H2 **p. 539**

Potentilla neumanniana
CINQUEFOIL
A1–A3; 1–24 **p. 544**

Ribes viburnifolium
CATALINA PERFUME
5, 7–9, 14–17, 19–24 **p. 577**

Rosa banksiae
LADY BANKS' ROSE
4–24; H1, H2 **p. 586**

Rosmarinus officinalis
ROSEMARY
4–24; H1, H2 **p. 587**

Thymus
THYME
1–24 **p. 632**

Verbena (some)
ZONES VARY **p. 645**

Wisteria
NEEDS, ZONES VARY **p. 652**

PERENNIALS, BULBS, ANNUALS

Achillea
YARROW
A1–A3, 1–24 **p. 170**

Agapanthus
LILY-OF-THE-NILE
4–9, 12–24; H1, H2 **p. 174**

Agastache
ZONES VARY **p. 174**

Agave (most)
ZONES VARY **p. 175**

Aloe
8, 9, 12–24 **p. 180**

Amaryllis belladonna
BELLADONNA LILY
4–24 **p. 183**

Armeria maritima
COMMON THRIFT
A2, A3; 1–9, 14–24 **p. 201**

Artemisia
ZONES VARY **p. 201**

Asclepias tuberosa
BUTTERFLY WEED
1–24 **p. 204**

Ballota pseudodictamnus
2, 3, 6–9, 14–24 **p. 213**

Calamintha
CALAMINT
1–9, 14–24 **p. 238**

Centaurea
ZONES VARY **p. 260**

Centranthus ruber
JUPITER'S BEARD
2–9, 12–24; H1 **p. 260**

Coreopsis (most)
ZONES VARY **p. 290**

Dasylirion wheeleri
DESERT SPOON
10–24 **p. 310**

Echium
ZONES VARY **p. 323**

Centranthus ruber

Achillea × *taygetea*

Agave vilmoriniana

Aloe

Coreopsis lanceolata

For growing symbol explanations, please see page 64.

Erigeron karvinskianus

Euphorbia characias wulfenii

Gaura lindheimeri

Linum perenne

Oenothera speciosa

Erigeron karvinskianus
MEXICAN DAISY
☼ ◑ 8, 9, 12–24; H1, H2 **p. 332**

Eriogonum
WILD BUCKWHEAT
☼ ZONES VARY **p. 333**

Euphorbia (most)
NEEDS, ZONES VARY **p. 344**

Festuca (some)
FESCUE
☼ ◑ ZONES VARY **p. 349**

Gaura lindheimeri
☼ 2B–24 **p. 361**

Hesperaloe parviflora
RED YUCCA
☼ ◑ 2B, 3, 7–16, 18–24 **p. 386**

Iris, bearded
☼ ◑ 1–24 **p. 402**

Iris foetidissima
GLADWIN IRIS
☼ ◑ ● 3–24 **p. 404**

Limonium perezii
☼ 13, 15–17, 20–24 **p. 435**

Linum
FLAX
☼ ZONES VARY **p. 436**

Lobelia laxiflora
☼ ◑ 7–9, 12–24 **p. 440**

Melampodium leucanthum
BLACKFOOT DAISY
☼ 2, 3, 10–13 **p. 465**

Mimulus aurantiacus
STICKY MONKEY FLOWER
☼ ◑ 5–9, 14–24 **p. 469**

Monardella
☼ ZONES VARY **p. 471**

Muhlenbergia
☼ ◑ ZONES VARY **p. 473**

Narcissus
DAFFODIL
☼ ◑ A2, A3; 1–24 **p. 476**

Nassella
NEEDLE GRASS
☼ ZONES VARY **p. 478**

Nolina
☼ ZONES VARY **p. 483**

Oenothera
EVENING PRIMROSE, SUNDROPS
☼ ◑ ZONES VARY **p. 485**

Pennisetum setaceum
FOUNTAIN GRASS
☼ 8–24; H1, H2 **p. 510**

Penstemon (many)
BEARD TONGUE
☼ ◑ ZONES VARY **p. 510**

Perovskia
RUSSIAN SAGE
☼ 2–24 **p. 512**

Phlomis
☼ ZONES VARY **p. 517**

Phormium
☼ ◑ 5–9, 14–24; H1, H2 **p. 518**

Romneya coulteri
MATILIJA POPPY
☼ 4–12, 14–24; H1 **p. 578**

Salvia (some)
SAGE
NEEDS, ZONES VARY **p. 592**

Santolina
☼ ZONES VARY **p. 598**

Sedum (many)
STONECROP
NEEDS, ZONES VARY **p. 604**

Sisyrinchium bellum
BLUE-EYED GRASS
☼ ◑ 2–9, 14–24 **p. 610**

Stachys byzantina
LAMB'S EARS
☼ ◑ 1–24 **p. 618**

Stipa (some)
FEATHER GRASS
☼ ZONES VARY **p. 619**

Tagetes lemmonii
COPPER CANYON DAISY
☼ 8–10, 12–24; H1 **p. 626**

Tithonia rotundifolia
MEXICAN SUNFLOWER
☼ ALL ZONES **p. 634**

Verbena (many)
☼ ZONES VARY **p. 645**

Watsonia
☼ 4–9, 12–24 **p. 651**

Yucca (most)
☼ ZONES VARY **p. 654**

Zauschneria
CALIFORNIA FUCHSIA
NEEDS, ZONES VARY **p. 656**

Zinnia grandiflora
☼ ALL ZONES **p. 657**

Pennisetum setaceum

Perovskia 'Blue Spire'

Salvia coccinea

Sedum 'Autumn Joy'

Hosta 'So Sweet'

Plants for SHADE

Shady spots, whether created by leafy trees, sun-blocking walls, or an overhead structure, are darker and cooler than sunny locations. Many plants that thrive in sunlight and warmth fail to prosper in the different environment that shade provides—either dwindling away or becoming leggy and sparse. In the lists below are trees, shrubs, ground covers, vines, perennials, bulbs, and annuals that prefer or accept some degree of shade.

Red-flowered rhododendron lights

Arbutus unedo

Abutilon hybrid

Aucuba japonica 'Variegata'

Acer circinatum

TREES

Plant	Needs / Zones	Page
Acer circinatum VINE MAPLE	☼ ◑ ⁄ A3; 2B–6, 14–17	**p. 167**
Acer palmatum JAPANESE MAPLE	☼ ◑ ⁄ A3; 2–10, 12, 14–24	**p. 168**
Arbutus unedo STRAWBERRY TREE	☼ ◑ ⁄ 4–24	**p. 197**
Cercis canadensis EASTERN REDBUD	☼ ⁄ 1–24	**p. 263**
Cornus DOGWOOD	NEEDS, ZONES VARY	**p. 291**
Davidia involucrata DOVE TREE	☼ ◑ ⁄ 4–9, 14–21	**p. 310**
Halesia	◑ ⁄ 2B–9, 14–21	**p. 378**
Laurus nobilis SWEET BAY	☼ ◑ ⁄ 5–9, 12–24; H1, H2	**p. 424**
Palms (some)	NEEDS, ZONES VARY	**p. 494**
Parrotia persica PERSIAN PARROTIA	☼ ◑ ⁄ 2B–7, 14–17	**p. 497**
Podocarpus	☼ ◑ ⁄ ZONES VARY	**p. 538**
Stewartia	☼ ◑ ⁄ 4–6, 14–17, 20, 21	**p. 619**

SHRUBS

Plant	Needs / Zones	Page
Abutilon FLOWERING MAPLE	☼ ◑ ⁄ 8, 9, 12–24; H1, H2	**p. 163**
Aucuba japonica JAPANESE AUCUBA	◑ ● ⁄ 4–24	**p. 209**
Azara	◑ ⁄ ZONES VARY	**p. 211**
Brunfelsia pauciflora	◑ ⁄ 12–17, 20–24; H1, H2	**p. 234**
Buxus BOXWOOD	☼ ◑ ● ⁄ ZONES VARY	**p. 236**
Camellia	◑ ⁄ 4–9, 12, 14–24	**p. 243**
Carpenteria californica BUSH ANEMONE	☼ ◑ ⁄ 5–9, 14–24	**p. 252**
Clethra alnifolia SUMMERSWEET	☼ ◑ ⁄ A2, A3; 1–6	**p. 284**
Cleyera japonica	◑ ⁄ 4–6, 8, 9, 14–24; H1	**p. 284**
Cocculus laurifolius	☼ ◑ ● ⁄ 8, 9, 12–24	**p. 286**
Coprosma repens MIRROR PLANT	☼ ◑ ⁄ 15–24; H1	**p. 289**
Cornus DOGWOOD	☼ ◑ ⁄ ZONES VARY	**p. 291**

For growing symbol explanations, please see page 64.

Brunfelsia pauciflora

Camellia japonica

Carpenteria californica

Cycas revoluta

up shaded garden.

Fatsia japonica

Gardenia augusta

Hydrangea macrophylla

Pieris forrestii

Cycas
◑ ◪ ZONES VARY — p. 304

Daphne odora
WINTER DAPHNE
◑ ◪ 4–10, 12, 14–24 — p. 310

Enkianthus
☼ ◑ ◪ 3–9, 14–21 — p. 326

Euonymus fortunei
☼ ◑ ● ◪ 2B–17 — p. 343

Fatsia japonica
JAPANESE ARALIA
◑ ● ◪ 4–9, 14–24; H1, H2 — p. 348

Fuchsia
☼ ◑ ◪ ZONES VARY — p. 357

Gardenia augusta
☼ ◑ ◪ 7–9, 12–16, 18–24; H1, H2 — p. 360

Gaultheria
◑ ◪ ZONES VARY — p. 361

Griselinia lucida
☼ ◑ ◪ 9, 14–17, 20–24 — p. 376

Hamamelis
WITCH HAZEL
☼ ◑ ◪ ZONES VARY — p. 379

Hydrangea
☼ ◑ ◪ ZONES VARY — p. 394

Ilex
HOLLY
☼ ◑ ◪ ZONES VARY — p. 397

Kalmia latifolia
MOUNTAIN LAUREL
◑ ◪ 2–7, 16, 17 — p. 416

Leucothoe
☼ ◑ ● ◪ ZONES VARY — p. 430

Loropetalum chinense
☼ ◑ ◪ 4–9, 14–24 — p. 442

Mahonia
NEEDS, ZONES VARY — p. 455

Nandina domestica
HEAVENLY BAMBOO
☼ ◑ ● ◪ 3–24; H1, H2 — p. 476

Osmanthus
☼ ◑ ◪ ZONES VARY — p. 490

Pieris
◑ ◪ ZONES VARY — p. 522

Pittosporum
☼ ◑ ◪ ZONES VARY — p. 531

Rhamnus (some)
NEEDS, ZONES VARY — p. 566

Rhododendron
AZALEA, RHODODENDRON
◑ ◪ ZONES VARY — p. 568

Ribes sanguineum
PINK WINTER CURRANT
☼ ◑ ◪ A3; 4–9, 14–24 — p. 577

Sarcococca
SWEET BOX
◑ ● ◪ 4–9, 14–24 — p. 599

Skimmia japonica
◑ ◪ 4–9, 14–22 — p. 610

Symphoricarpos (some)
SNOWBERRY
NEEDS, ZONES VARY — p. 624

Ternstroemia gymnanthera
◑ ● ◪ 4–9, 12–24 — p. 629

Vaccinium
NEEDS, ZONES VARY — p. 643

Viburnum (evergreen)
☼ ◑ ◪ ZONES VARY — p. 646

VINES

Cissus (some)
NEEDS, ZONES VARY — p. 275

×Fatshedera lizei
◑ ● ◪ 4–10, 12–24; H1, H2 — p. 348

Hedera
IVY
☼ ◑ ◪ ZONES VARY — p. 380

Parthenocissus
☼ ◑ ● ◪ ZONES VARY — p. 498

Trachelospermum jasminoides
STAR JASMINE
☼ ◑ ◪ 8–24; H1, H2 — p. 636

PERENNIALS, BULBS, ANNUALS

Acanthus mollis
BEAR'S BREECH
☼ ◑ ● ◪ 5–24 — p. 167

Aconitum
ACONITE
☼ ◑ ◪ A1–A3; 1–9, 14–21 — p. 171

Rhododendron 'Hino-crimson' (Kurume hybrid azalea)

Skimmia japonica

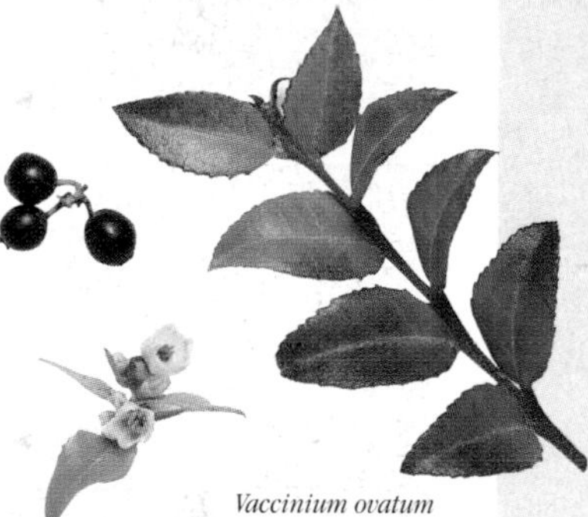

Vaccinium ovatum

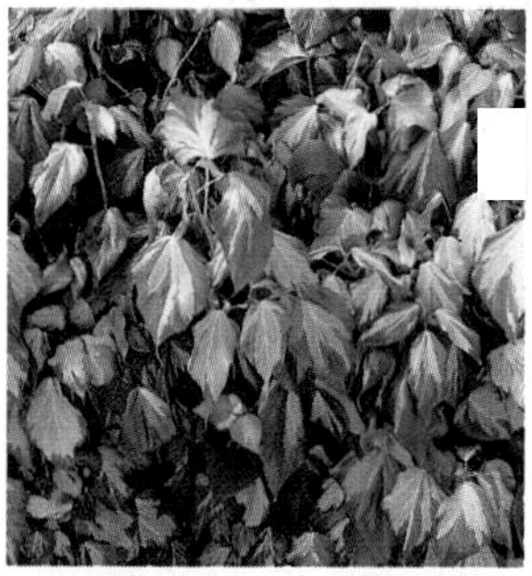

Hedera colchica

Parthenocissus tricuspidata

Plant listings continue ▶

Alchemilla mollis

Astilbe × arendsii hybrid

Begonia foliosa 'Miniata'

Brunnera macrophylla

Aconitum napellus

Ajuga
CARPET BUGLE
☼ ◑ ◢ A2, A3; 1–24 **p. 176**

Alchemilla
LADY'S-MANTLE
☼ ◑ ◢ ZONES VARY **p. 177**

Anemone (some)
WINDFLOWER
NEEDS, ZONES VARY **p. 185**

Aquilegia
COLUMBINE
☼ ◑ ◢ ZONES VARY **p. 195**

Arum
◑ ● ◢ ZONES VARY **p. 203**

Aruncus
GOAT'S BEARD
☼ ◑ ◢ ZONES VARY **p. 203**

Asarum
WILD GINGER
◑ ● ◢ ZONES VARY **p. 204**

Aspidistra elatior
CAST-IRON PLANT
◑ ● ◢ 4–10, 12–24; H1, H2 **p. 206**

Astilbe
FALSE SPIRAEA
☼ ◑ ◢ 1–9, 14–24 **p. 208**

Astilboides tabularis
◑ ◢ 2B–9, 14–17 **p. 208**

Astrantia
MASTERWORT
☼ ◑ ◢ 1–9, 14–24 **p. 208**

Begonia
◑ ◢ 14–24; H1, H2 **p. 220**

Bergenia
◑ ● ◢ A1–A3; 1–9, 12–24 **p. 222**

Bletilla striata
CHINESE GROUND ORCHID
◑ ◢ 2B–9, 12–24 **p. 226**

Browallia
AMETHYST FLOWER
◑ ◢ ZONES VARY **p. 233**

Brunnera macrophylla
BRUNNERA
☼ ◑ ◢ 1–24 **p. 234**

Caladium bicolor
FANCY-LEAFED CALADIUM
◑ ● ◢ H2 **p. 237**

Calceolaria (most)
NEEDS, ZONES VARY **p. 238**

Campanula (some)
BELLFLOWER
☼ ◑ ◢ 1–9, 14–24 **p. 247**

Cimicifuga
☼ ◑ ◢ 1–7, 17 **p. 275**

Clivia miniata
◑ ● ◢ 12–17, 19–24; H1, H2 **p. 285**

Coleus × hybridus
COLEUS
◑ ◢ ALL ZONES **p. 287**

Colocasia esculenta
TARO
◑ ◢ 12, 16–24; H1, H2 **p. 288**

Convallaria majalis
LILY-OF-THE-VALLEY
◑ ◢ A1–A3; 1–7, 14–20 **p. 288**

Corydalis
◑ ◢ 2–9, 14–24 **p. 294**

Cyclamen
☼ ◑ ◢ ZONES VARY **p. 304**

Dianella tasmanica
☼ ◑ ◢ 8, 9, 14–24 **p. 313**

Dicentra (most)
BLEEDING HEART
◑ ● ◢ 1–9, 14–24 **p. 314**

Digitalis
FOXGLOVE
NEEDS, ZONES VARY **p. 317**

Doronicum
LEOPARD'S BANE
◑ ◢ A2, A3; 1–7, 14–17 **p. 319**

Epimedium
◑ ◢ 2–9, 14–17 **p. 327**

Erythronium
◑ ◢ ZONES VARY **p. 335**

Farfugium japonicum
◑ ● ◢ 4–10, 14–24; H1, H2 **p. 348**

Ferns
NEEDS, ZONES VARY **p. 349**

Filipendula
☼ ◑ ● ◢ ZONES VARY **p. 352**

Francoa ramosa
MAIDEN'S WREATH
◑ ◢ 4–9, 14–24 **p. 355**

Galium odoratum
SWEET WOODRUFF
◑ ● ◢ A2, A3; 2–6, 15–17 **p. 359**

Gentiana
GENTIAN
☼ ◑ ◢ 2–6, 14–17 **p. 363**

For growing symbol explanations, please see page 64.

Campanula portenschlagiana

Clivia miniata

Digitalis purpurea Foxy strain

Francoa sonchifolia

Helleborus orientalis

Geranium 'Johnson's Blue'

Hosta hybrids

Lamium maculatum

Impatiens walleriana

Lilium Asiatic hybrid

Geranium (some)
CRANESBILL
☼ ◐ ⁄ ZONES VARY **p. 363**

Hedychium
GINGER LILY
◐ ⁄ 8, 9, 14–17, 19–24; H1, H2 **p. 381**

Helleborus
HELLEBORE
◐ ● ⁄ ZONES VARY **p. 384**

Heuchera
CORAL BELLS
☼ ◐ ⁄ ZONES VARY **p. 387**

×Heucherella
◐ ⁄ 1–10, 14–24 **p. 387**

Hosta
PLANTAIN LILY
◐ ● ⁄ ZONES VARY **p. 391**

Hyacinthoides
BLUEBELL
◐ ⁄ ZONES VARY **p. 393**

Impatiens (most)
BALSAM
NEEDS, ZONES VARY **p. 399**

Iris foetidissima
GLADWIN IRIS
☼ ◐ ● ⁄ 3–24 **p. 404**

Kirengeshoma palmata
YELLOW WAXBELLS
◐ ⁄ 2–9, 14–24 **p. 417**

Lamium
DEAD NETTLE
◐ ● ⁄ ZONES VARY **p. 422**

Ligularia
◐ ● ⁄ 1–9, 14–17 **p. 432**

Lilium
LILY
☼ ◐ ⁄ ZONES VARY **p. 433**

Liriope and Ophiopogon
LILY TURF
☼ ◐ ● ⁄ ZONES VARY **p. 438**

Lobelia (most)
NEEDS, ZONES VARY **p. 440**

Mertensia
◐ ● ⁄ ZONES VARY **p. 467**

Mimulus × hybridus
◐ ● ⁄ 1–24 **p. 469**

Myosotis
FORGET-ME-NOT
◐ ⁄ A1–A3; 1–24 **p. 475**

Oxalis
NEEDS, ZONES VARY **p. 491**

Pachysandra
◐ ● ⁄ ZONES VARY **p. 493**

Polemonium
◐ ● ⁄ 1–11, 14–17 **p. 540**

Polygonatum
SOLOMON'S SEAL
◐ ● ⁄ A1–A3; 1–9, 14–17 **p. 541**

Primula
PRIMROSE
☼ ◐ ● ⁄ ZONES VARY **p. 545**

Pulmonaria
LUNGWORT
◐ ● ⁄ 1–9, 14–17 **p. 555**

Rehmannia elata
CHINESE FOXGLOVE
☼ ◐ ● ⁄ 6–10, 12–24 **p. 566**

Saxifraga
SAXIFRAGE
◐ ● ⁄ ZONES VARY **p. 600**

Senecio × hybridus
FLORISTS' CINERARIA
◐ ● ⁄ 16, 17, 22–24 **p. 606**

Smilacina racemosa
FALSE SOLOMON'S SEAL
◐ ● ⁄ 1–7, 14–17 **p. 611**

Thalictrum
MEADOW RUE
◐ ⁄ 2–10, 14–17 **p. 630**

Tiarella
FOAMFLOWER
◐ ● ⁄ ZONES VARY **p. 633**

Tolmiea menziesii
PIGGY-BACK PLANT
◐ ● ⁄ 4–9, 14–17, 20–24 **p. 634**

Tradescantia
NEEDS, ZONES VARY **p. 637**

Tricyrtis hirta
TOAD LILY
◐ ⁄ 2–9, 14–17 **p. 638**

Trillium
WAKE ROBIN
◐ ● ⁄ ZONES VARY **p. 638**

Trollius
GLOBEFLOWER
☼ ◐ ⁄ A2, A3; 1–6 **p. 639**

Vancouveria
◐ ⁄ ZONES VARY **p. 644**

Vinca
PERIWINKLE
☼ ◐ ● ⁄ ZONES VARY **p. 648**

Viola
VIOLA, PANSY
☼ ◐ ● ⁄ ZONES VARY **p. 648**

Polygonatum odoratum

Rehmannia elata

Senecio × hybridus

Tradescantia virginiana

Viola × wittrockiana

Plants for
GROWING BENEATH OAKS

Nandina domestica (foreground) thrives

The West is home to a variety of oaks; much of California, in particular, features oak-dotted hillsides. Due to population growth, however, many wild oaks have become part of suburban landscapes—to their detriment, if they receive regular garden watering (see page 559). To preserve these oaks in garden settings, use only drought-tolerant plants when landscaping within the range of their root systems. The plants listed here take both drought and shade and are good choices if the area beneath the oak's canopy is shaded. Where there's considerable sun (beneath the open crown of an old oak, for example), choose from "Plants for Dry Areas" (page 140).

Daphne odora 'Aureo-marginata'

Garrya elliptica

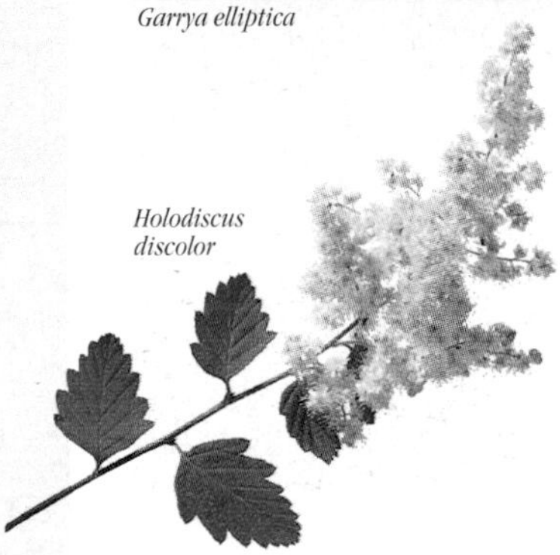

Holodiscus discolor

SHRUBS

Arbutus unedo (small forms)
STRAWBERRY TREE
☼ ◑ 💧 4–24 — p. 197

Arctostaphylos
MANZANITA
☼ ◑ 💧 ZONES VARY — p. 198

Aucuba japonica
JAPANESE AUCUBA
◑ ● 💧 4–24 — p. 209

Berberis darwinii
DARWIN BARBERRY
☼ ◑ 💧 5–9, 14–24 — p. 221

Carpenteria californica
BUSH ANEMONE
☼ ◑ 💧 5–9, 14–24 — p. 252

Cistus (some)
ROCKROSE
☼ 💧 4–9, 12–24 — p. 276

Daphne odora
WINTER DAPHNE
☼ ◑ 💧 4–10, 12, 14–24 — p. 310

Galvezia speciosa
ISLAND BUSH SNAPDRAGON
☼ ◑ 💧 14–24 — p. 360

Garrya
SILKTASSEL
☼ ◑ 💧 ZONES VARY — p. 361

Heteromeles arbutifolia
TOYON
☼ ◑ 💧 5–9, 14–24 — p. 386

Holodiscus discolor
CREAM BUSH
◑ 💧 1–9, 14–19 — p. 390

Mahonia (several)
NEEDS, ZONES VARY — p. 455

Myrica californica
PACIFIC WAX MYRTLE
☼ 💧 4–9, 14–24 — p. 475

Myrsine africana
AFRICAN BOXWOOD
☼ ◑ 💧 8, 9, 14–24 — p. 475

Myrtus communis
TRUE MYRTLE
☼ ◑ 💧 8–24; H1, H2 — p. 476

Nandina domestica
HEAVENLY BAMBOO
☼ ◑ ● 💧 3–24; H1, H2 — p. 476

Osmanthus
☼ ◑ 💧 ZONES VARY — p. 490

Rhamnus (most)
NEEDS, ZONES VARY — p. 566

Rhus integrifolia
LEMONADE BERRY
☼ 💧 8, 9, 14–17, 19–24 — p. 576

Rhus ovata
SUGAR BUSH
☼ 💧 9–12, 14–24 — p. 576

Ribes (drought-tolerant)
CURRANT, GOOSEBERRY
☼ ◑ 💧 ZONES VARY — p. 577

Ruscus
BUTCHER'S BROOM
◑ ● 💧 4–24; H1 — p. 589

Sarcococca ruscifolia
SWEET BOX
◑ ● 💧 4–9, 14–24 — p. 599

Symphoricarpos (most)
SNOWBERRY
NEEDS, ZONES VARY — p. 624

Viburnum tinus
LAURUSTINUS
☼ ◑ 💧 4–10, 12–23 — p. 647

Myrtus communis

Osmanthus heterophyllus

Rhus ovata

Symphoricarpos albus

For growing symbol explanations, please see page 64.

in shade of native oaks.

GROUND COVERS, VINES		
Achillea tomentosa WOOLLY YARROW	☼ ⁄ A1–A3; 1–24	**p. 170**
Arctostaphylos MANZANITA	☼ ◑ ⁄ ZONES VARY	**p. 198**
Ceratostigma plumbaginoides DWARF PLUMBAGO	☼ ◑ ⁄ 2B–10, 14–24	**p. 262**
Cissus (several)	NEEDS, ZONES VARY	**p. 275**
Coprosma × kirkii	☼ ◑ ⁄ 14–24; H1, H2	**p. 289**
Correa (several) AUSTRALIAN FUCHSIA	☼ ◑ ⁄ 14–24	**p. 293**
Cotoneaster (several)	☼ ⁄ ZONES VARY	**p. 296**
Duchesnea indica INDIAN MOCK STRAWBERRY	☼ ◑ ● ⁄ 1–24; H1, H2	**p. 321**
Fragaria chiloensis BEACH STRAWBERRY	☼ ◑ ⁄ 4–24; H1	**p. 355**
Hardenbergia violacea LILAC VINE	☼ ◑ ⁄ 8–24	**p. 380**
Hypericum calycinum AARON'S BEARD	☼ ◑ ⁄ 2B–24	**p. 395**
Juniperus JUNIPER	☼ ◑ ⁄ ZONES VARY	**p. 410**
Mahonia aquifolium 'Compacta' OREGON GRAPE	☼ ◑ ● ⁄ 2–12, 14–24	**p. 455**
Mahonia repens CREEPING MAHONIA	☼ ◑ ⁄ 2B–9, 14–24	**p. 456**
Persicaria capitata	☼ ◑ ⁄ 8, 9, 12–24	**p. 513**
Ribes viburnifolium CATALINA PERFUME	☼ ◑ ⁄ 5, 7–9, 14–17, 19–24	**p. 577**
Rubus pentalobus	☼ ◑ ⁄ 4–6, 14–17	**p. 588**
Sollya heterophylla AUSTRALIAN BLUEBELL CREEPER	☼ ◑ ⁄ 8, 9, 14–24; H1, H2	**p. 612**

PERENNIALS		
Aloe	☼ ◑ ⁄ 8, 9, 12–24	**p. 180**
Aspidistra elatior CAST-IRON PLANT	◑ ● ⁄ 4–10, 12–24; H1, H2	**p. 206**
Bergenia crassifolia WINTER-BLOOMING BERGENIA	◑ ● ⁄ A1–A3; 1–9, 12–24	**p. 222**
Dryopteris arguta CALIFORNIA WOOD FERN	◑ ● ⁄ 2B, 4–9, 14–24	**p. 321**
Erigeron karvinskianus MEXICAN DAISY	☼ ◑ ⁄ 8, 9, 12–24; H1, H2	**p. 332**
Heuchera CORAL BELLS	☼ ◑ ⁄ ZONES VARY	**p. 387**
Iris foetidissima GLADWIN IRIS	☼ ◑ ● ⁄ 3–24	**p. 404**
Iris, Pacific Coast	☼ ◑ ⁄ 4–9, 14–24	**p. 404**
Leymus LYME GRASS	☼ ◑ ⁄ ZONES VARY	**p. 431**
Mimulus aurantiacus STICKY MONKEY FLOWER	☼ ◑ ⁄ 5–9, 14–24	**p. 469**
Muhlenbergia rigens DEER GRASS	☼ ◑ ⁄ 4–24	**p. 473**
Nepeta × faassenii CATMINT	☼ ◑ ⁄ 1–24	**p. 481**
Nephrolepis cordifolia SOUTHERN SWORD FERN	◑ ● ⁄ 8, 9, 12–24; H1, H2	**p. 481**
Penstemon (some) BEARD TONGUE	☼ ◑ ⁄ ZONES VARY	**p. 510**
Polystichum munitum SWORD FERN	● ⁄ A3; 2–9, 14–24	**p. 542**
Sedum (many) STONECROP	☼ ◑ ⁄ ZONES VARY	**p. 604**
Sisyrinchium bellum BLUE-EYED GRASS	☼ ◑ ⁄ 2–9, 14–24	**p. 610**
Vancouveria	◑ ⁄ ZONES VARY	**p. 644**

Arctostaphylos uva-ursi

Ceratostigma plumbaginoides

Cotoneaster dammeri 'Streib's Findling'

Rubus pentalobus

Bergenia crassifolia

Heuchera sanguinea

Nepeta × faassenii

Nephrolepis cordifolia

Polystichum munitum

Crataegus laevigata 'Paul's Scarlet'

DEER-RESISTANT PLANTS

Browsing deer don't dine indiscriminately. Some plants are particular favorites; others are left more or less alone. If you live in deer country, you'll find it far simpler to build your garden from less-favored plants than to protect the choicer morsels. Deer generally ignore the plants listed below. Few are really deerproof, though: deer in different areas may have different tastes, and tastes may vary from year to year or even from season to season.

SYMBOL: 🍃 indicates plants that are eaten in some areas.

Acer palmatum 'Sango Kaku'

Ginkgo biloba

Albizia julibrissin

TREES

Plant	Common name	Needs / Zones	Page	
Abies	FIR	☼ ◑ ⁄ ZONES VARY	p. 162	
Acacia		☼ ⁄ ZONES VARY	p. 164	
Acer circinatum	VINE MAPLE	☼ ◑ ⁄ A3; 2B–6, 14–17	p. 167	🍃
Acer palmatum	JAPANESE MAPLE	☼ ◑ ⁄ A3; 2–10, 12, 14–24	p. 168	🍃
Albizia		☼ ◑ ⁄ ZONES VARY	p. 177	
Callistemon	BOTTLEBRUSH	☼ ⁄ ZONES VARY	p. 240	
Cedrus	CEDAR	☼ ⁄ ZONES VARY	p. 256	
Celtis	HACKBERRY	☼ ◑ ⁄ ZONES VARY	p. 260	
Ceratonia siliqua	CAROB	☼ ⁄ 9, 13–16, 18–24; H1	p. 262	
Cercis occidentalis	WESTERN REDBUD	☼ ⁄ 2–24	p. 263	🍃
Chamaecyparis	FALSE CYPRESS	☼ ◑ ⁄ ZONES VARY	p. 265	
Crataegus	HAWTHORN	☼ ⁄ 2–12, 14–17	p. 298	
Cupressus	CYPRESS	☼ ⁄ ZONES VARY	p. 303	
Eucalyptus (some)		☼ ⁄ ZONES VARY	p. 337	🍃
Fig		☼ ⁄ 4–9, 12–24; H1, H2	p. 351	🍃
Fraxinus	ASH	☼ ⁄ ZONES VARY	p. 355	🍃
Ginkgo biloba	MAIDENHAIR TREE	☼ ⁄ A3; 1–10, 12, 14–24	p. 366	
Magnolia		☼ ◑ ⁄ ZONES VARY	p. 447	
Maytenus boaria	MAYTEN	☼ ⁄ 8, 9, 14–24	p. 463	
Melaleuca		☼ ⁄ ZONES VARY	p. 464	
Olea europaea	OLIVE	☼ ⁄ 8, 9, 11–24; H1, H2	p. 486	
Palms		NEEDS, ZONES VARY	p. 494	
Picea	SPRUCE	☼ ◑ ⁄ ZONES VARY	p. 521	
Pinus	PINE	☼ ⁄ ZONES VARY	p. 523	
Podocarpus		☼ ◑ ⁄ ZONES VARY	p. 538	

Browsing deer

Magnolia × soulangiana

Picea pungens

For growing symbol explanations, please see page 64.

Blue-flowered *Ceanothus* 'Julia Phelps' and other deer-resistant foliage plants

Alyogyne huegelii

Anisodontea × hypomandarum

Arctostaphylos densiflora 'Howard McMinn'

Calluna vulgaris 'Spring Torch'

Pseudotsuga menziesii
DOUGLAS FIR
A2, A3; 1–10, 14–17 — **p. 554**

Quercus
OAK
ZONES VARY — **p. 558**

Sequoia sempervirens
REDWOOD, COAST REDWOOD
4–9, 14–24 — **p. 607**

Umbellularia californica
CALIFORNIA LAUREL
4–9, 14–24 — **p. 643**

SHRUBS

Abelia × grandiflora
GLOSSY ABELIA
4–24; H1, H2 — **p. 162**

Aesculus californica
CALIFORNIA BUCKEYE
3–10, 14–24 — **p. 173**

Alyogyne huegelii
BLUE HIBISCUS
13–17, 20–24; H1, H2 — **p. 182**

Anisodontea × hypomandarum
CAPE MALLOW
14–24 — **p. 187**

Arctostaphylos
MANZANITA
ZONES VARY — **p. 198**

Bamboo
ZONES VARY — **p. 213**

Berberis
BARBERRY
ZONES VARY — **p. 221**

Buddleja
BUTTERFLY BUSH
ZONES VARY — **p. 234**

Buxus
BOXWOOD
ZONES VARY — **p. 236**

Callistemon
BOTTLEBRUSH
ZONES VARY — **p. 240**

Calluna vulgaris
SCOTCH HEATHER
1A, 2–6, 15–17 — **p. 241**

Calycanthus occidentalis
SPICE BUSH
4–9, 14–24 — **p. 242**

Carpenteria californica
BUSH ANEMONE
5–9, 14–24 — **p. 252**

Cassia
SENNA
ZONES VARY — **p. 254**

Ceanothus
WILD LILAC
5–9, 14–24 — **p. 256**

Chaenomeles
FLOWERING QUINCE
2–23 — **p. 264**

Choisya ternata
MEXICAN ORANGE
4–9, 14–24 — **p. 271**

Cistus (most)
ROCKROSE
4–9, 14–24 — **p. 276**

Coleonema
BREATH OF HEAVEN
7–9, 14–24 — **p. 287**

Coprosma
ZONES VARY — **p. 289**

Corokia cotoneaster
4–24 — **p. 293**

Correa
AUSTRALIAN FUCHSIA
14–24 — **p. 293**

Cotoneaster
ZONES VARY — **p. 296**

Daphne
NEEDS, ZONES VARY — **p. 309**

Dendromecon
BUSH POPPY
ZONES VARY — **p. 312**

Dodonaea viscosa
HOP BUSH
7–24; H1, H2 — **p. 319**

Elaeagnus
ZONES VARY — **p. 324**

Erica
HEATH
ZONES VARY — **p. 329**

Eriogonum
WILD BUCKWHEAT
ZONES VARY — **p. 333**

Escallonia
4–9, 14–24 — **p. 335**

Feijoa, Pineapple Guava
6–9, 12–24; H1, H2 — **p. 348**

Fremontodendron
FLANNEL BUSH
4–24 — **p. 357**

Gaultheria shallon
SALAL
4–7, 14–17 — **p. 361**

Plant listings continue ▸

Correa 'Ivory Bells'

Quercus agrifolia

Dendromecon harfordii

Elaeagnus pungens 'Maculata'

Eriogonum umbellatum

Fremontodendron 'California Glory'

Grevillea 'Canberra Gem'

Lavatera thuringiaca

Leonotis leonurus

Lantana 'Radiation'

Nerium oleander

Plant	Common name	Zones	Page
Grevillea		NEEDS, ZONES VARY	p. 375
Hakea suaveolens	SWEET HAKEA	9, 12–17, 19–24	p. 378
Heteromeles arbutifolia	TOYON	5–9, 14–24	p. 386
Hypericum	ST. JOHNSWORT	ZONES VARY	p. 395
Ilex	HOLLY	ZONES VARY	p. 397
Juniperus	JUNIPER	ZONES VARY	p. 410
Kerria japonica		2–23	p. 417
Lantana		8–10, 12–24; H1, H2	p. 422
Lavandula	LAVENDER	ZONES VARY	p. 425
Lavatera	TREE MALLOW	ZONES VARY	p. 427
Leonotis leonurus	LION'S TAIL	8–24; H1, H2	p. 428
Leptospermum	TEA TREE	14–24	p. 428
Mahonia		NEEDS, ZONES VARY	p. 455
Myoporum		ZONES VARY	p. 474
Myrica californica	PACIFIC WAX MYRTLE	4–9, 14–17, 20–24	p. 475
Myrtus communis	MYRTLE	8–24; H1, H2	p. 476
Nandina domestica	HEAVENLY BAMBOO	3–24; H1, H2	p. 476
Nerium oleander	OLEANDER	8–16, 18–24; H1, H2	p. 482
Phlomis		ZONES VARY	p. 517
Plumbago auriculata	CAPE PLUMBAGO	8, 9, 12–24; H1, H2	p. 534
Potentilla	CINQUEFOIL	ZONES VARY	p. 544
Pyracantha	FIRETHORN	ZONES VARY	p. 557
Rhododendron (not azaleas)		ZONES VARY	p. 568
Rhus	SUMAC	ZONES VARY	p. 576
Ribes	CURRANT, GOOSEBERRY	ZONES VARY	p. 577
Rosmarinus officinalis	ROSEMARY	4–24; H1, H2	p. 587
Salvia	SAGE	NEEDS, ZONES VARY	p. 592
Sarcococca	SWEET BOX	ZONES VARY	p. 599
Sollya heterophylla	AUSTRALIAN BLUEBELL CREEPER	8, 9, 14–24; H1, H2	p. 612
Spiraea		ZONES VARY	p. 616
Symphoricarpos	SNOWBERRY, CORALBERRY	NEEDS, ZONES VARY	p. 624
Syringa	LILAC	ZONES VARY	p. 624
Teucrium	GERMANDER	ZONES VARY	p. 630
Tibouchina urvilleana	PRINCESS FLOWER	16, 17, 21–24; H1, H2	p. 633
Trichostema lanatum	WOOLLY BLUE CURLS	14–24	p. 637
Vaccinium ovatum	EVERGREEN HUCKLEBERRY	4–7, 14–17, 22–24	p. 643
Viburnum		NEEDS, ZONES VARY	p. 646
Westringia fruticosa	COAST ROSEMARY	8, 9, 14–24	p. 652

Rhododendron 'Pink Pearl'

Sollya heterophylla

Vaccinium ovatum

Ceratostigma plumbaginoides

Gazania 'Burgundy'

For growing symbol explanations, please see page 64.

Osteospermum fruticosum

Hedera helix 'Buttercup'

Acanthus mollis

Achillea millefolium hybrid

Aster × frikartii

GROUND COVERS, VINES

Ajuga
CARPET BUGLE
A2, A3; 1–24 — p. 176

Arabis
ROCKCRESS
ZONES VARY — p. 196

Bougainvillea
5, 6, 12–17, 19, 21–24; H1, H2 — p. 228

Ceratostigma plumbaginoides
DWARF PLUMBAGO
2B–10, 14–24 — p. 262

Fragaria chiloensis
BEACH STRAWBERRY
4–24; H1 — p. 355

Galium odoratum
SWEET WOODRUFF
A2, A3; 2–6, 15–17 — p. 359

Gazania
NEEDS, ZONES VARY — p. 361

Gelsemium sempervirens
CAROLINA JESSAMINE
4–24 — p. 362

Hedera helix
ENGLISH IVY
3–24; H1 — p. 381

Hibbertia scandens
GUINEA GOLD VINE
16, 17, 21–24 — p. 388

Jasminum
JASMINE
ZONES VARY — p. 408

Osteospermum fruticosum
TRAILING AFRICAN DAISY
8, 9, 12–24; H1, H2 — p. 491

Pachysandra terminalis
JAPANESE SPURGE
2–10, 14–21 — p. 493

Scaevola
8, 9, 14–24; H1, H2 — p. 601

Solanum jasminoides
POTATO VINE
8, 9, 12–24; H1, H2 — p. 612

Tecoma capensis
CAPE HONEYSUCKLE
12, 13, 20–24; H1, H2 — p. 628

Vinca
PERIWINKLE
ZONES VARY — p. 648

Wisteria
NEEDS, ZONES VARY — p. 652

PERENNIALS, BULBS

Acanthus mollis
BEAR'S BREECH
5–24 — p. 167

Achillea
YARROW
A1–A3; 1–24 — p. 170

Agapanthus
LILY-OF-THE-NILE
4–9, 12–24; H1, H2 — p. 174

Agave
ZONES VARY — p. 175

Aloe
8, 9, 12–24 — p. 180

Aquilegia
COLUMBINE
ZONES VARY — p. 195

Armeria
THRIFT
ZONES VARY — p. 201

Artemisia
ZONES VARY — p. 201

Aster
ZONES VARY — p. 207

Astilbe
FALSE SPIRAEA
1–9, 14–24 — p. 208

Begonia, tuberous
4–9, 14–24; H1 — p. 221

Brachyscome
SWAN RIVER DAISY
ZONES VARY — p. 230

Campanula poscharskyana
SERBIAN BELLFLOWER
1–12, 14–24 — p. 249

Carex
SEDGE
ZONES VARY — p. 251

Centaurea
ZONES VARY — p. 260

Centranthus ruber
JUPITER'S BEARD, RED VALERIAN
2–9, 12–24; H1 — p. 260

Cerastium tomentosum
SNOW-IN-SUMMER
A1, A2; 1–24 — p. 261

Chrysanthemum frutescens
MARGUERITE
14–24; H1 — p. 272

Plant listings continue▶

Astilbe × arendsii hybrid

Brachyscome

Aquilegia McKana Giants strain

Campanula poscharskyana

Carex comans 'Bronze'

Erodium reichardii

Eschscholzia californica

Erysimum 'Bowles Mauve'

Euphorbia × martinii

Hemerocallis hybrid

Plant	Common name	Needs / Zones	Page
Coreopsis		ZONES VARY	p. 290
Crocosmia		ZONES VARY	p. 300
Crocus		1–24	p. 300
Dahlia		1–24	p. 307
Dicentra	BLEEDING HEART	1–9, 14–24	p. 314
Dietes	FORTNIGHT LILY	8, 9, 12–24; H1, H2	p. 316
Digitalis	FOXGLOVE	NEEDS, ZONES VARY	p. 317
Echinacea purpurea	PURPLE CONEFLOWER	A2, A3; 1–24	p. 322
Echium candicans	PRIDE OF MADEIRA	14–24	p. 323
Erigeron	FLEABANE	ZONES VARY	p. 329
Erodium reichardii	CRANESBILL	7–9, 14–24	p. 333
Erysimum	WALLFLOWER	ZONES VARY	p. 334
Eschscholzia californica	CALIFORNIA POPPY	1–24; H1	p. 336
Euphorbia		NEEDS, ZONES VARY	p. 344
Euryops		ZONES VARY	p. 345
Felicia amelloides	BLUE MARGUERITE	8, 9, 14–24	p. 349
Ferns		NEEDS, ZONES VARY	p. 349
Festuca glauca	COMMON BLUE FESCUE	1–24	p. 350
Freesia		8, 9, 12–24	p. 356
Gaillardia × grandiflora		1–24; H1, H2	p. 359
Geranium	CRANESBILL	ZONES VARY	p. 363
Helichrysum		ZONES VARY	p. 383
Helleborus	HELLEBORE	ZONES VARY	p. 384
Hemerocallis	DAYLILY	1–24; H1, H2	p. 385
Iberis	CANDYTUFT	1–24	p. 396
Iris		NEEDS, ZONES VARY	p. 401
Ixia	AFRICAN CORN LILY	7–9, 12–24	p. 406
Kniphofia	RED-HOT POKER	ZONES VARY	p. 418
Lamium	DEAD NETTLE	ZONES VARY	p. 422
Leucojum	SNOWFLAKE	ZONES VARY	p. 430
Limonium	STATICE	ZONES VARY	p. 435
Liriope and Ophiopogon	LILY TURF	ZONES VARY	p. 438
Lithodora diffusa		5–7, 14–17	p. 438
Lupinus	LUPINE	ZONES VARY	p. 443
Lychnis coronaria	CROWN-PINK	1–9, 14–24	p. 444
Mimulus	MONKEY FLOWER	NEEDS, ZONES VARY	p. 469
Miscanthus sinensis	EULALIA	2–24	p. 470
Monarda	BEE BALM	ZONES VARY	p. 471

For growing symbol explanations, please see page 64.

Kniphofia uvaria

Pennisetum setaceum

Penstemon × gloxinioides

Phormium hybrid

Lupinus, Russell hybrid

Romneya coulteri

Santolina chamaecyparissus

Stachys byzantina

Tagetes lemmonii

Myosotis scorpioides
◑ ⁄ A1–A3; 1–24 **p. 475**

Narcissus
DAFFODIL
☼ ◑ ⁄ A2, A3; 1–24 **p. 476**

Nepeta
☼ ◑ ⁄ 1–24 **p. 480**

Origanum
OREGANO, MARJORAM
☼ ⁄ ZONES VARY **p. 489**

Papaver
POPPY
☼ ⁄ ZONES VARY **p. 495**

Pennisetum setaceum
FOUNTAIN GRASS
☼ ⁄ 8–24; H1, H2 **p. 510**

Penstemon
BEARD TONGUE
☼ ◑ ⁄ ZONES VARY **p. 510**

Phlomis
☼ ⁄ ZONES VARY **p. 517**

Phlox subulata
MOSS PINK
☼ ◑ ⁄ 1–17 **p. 518**

Phormium
☼ ◑ ⁄ 5–9, 14–24; H1, H2 **p. 518**

Romneya coulteri
MATILIJA POPPY
☼ ⁄ 4–12, 14–24; H1 **p. 578**

Rudbeckia hirta
GLORIOSA DAISY
☼ ⁄ 1–24 **p. 589**

Santolina
☼ ⁄ ZONES VARY **p. 598**

Saxifraga
SAXIFRAGE
NEEDS, ZONES VARY **p. 600**

Scabiosa (some)
PINCUSHION FLOWER
NEEDS, ZONES VARY **p. 600**

Scilla
SQUILL
☼ ◑ ⁄ ZONES VARY **p. 603**

Sisyrinchium
☼ ◑ ⁄ ZONES VARY **p. 610**

Stachys byzantina
LAMB'S EARS
☼ ◑ ⁄ 1–24 **p. 618**

Stipa
FEATHER GRASS
☼ ⁄ ZONES VARY **p. 619**

Tagetes lemmonii
COPPER CANYON DAISY
☼ ⁄ 8–10, 12–24; H1 **p. 626**

Thymus
THYME
☼ ◑ ⁄ ZONES VARY **p. 632**

Tulbaghia violacea
SOCIETY GARLIC
☼ ⁄ 13–24; H1, H2 **p. 640**

Verbena
☼ ⁄ ZONES VARY **p. 645**

Veronica
SPEEDWELL
☼ ⁄ ZONES VARY **p. 645**

Viola odorata
SWEET VIOLET
☼ ◑ ● ⁄ 1–24 **p. 649**

Zantedeschia
CALLA
☼ ◑ ⁄ 5, 6, 8, 9, 12–24; H1, H2 **p. 655**

Zauschneria
CALIFORNIA FUCHSIA
NEEDS, ZONES VARY **p. 656**

ANNUALS

Ageratum houstonianum
FLOSS FLOWER
☼ ◑ ⁄ 1–24 **p. 175**

Calendula officinalis
CALENDULA
☼ ⁄ 1–24; H1 **p. 239**

Campanula medium
CANTERBURY BELL
☼ ◑ ⁄ 1–9, 14–24 **p. 248**

Catharanthus roseus
MADAGASCAR PERIWINKLE
☼ ◑ ⁄ 1–24; H1, H2 **p. 255**

Clarkia amoena
FAREWELL-TO-SPRING
☼ ◑ ⁄ 1–24 **p. 281**

Impatiens
BALSAM
NEEDS, ZONES VARY **p. 399**

Myosotis sylvatica
◑ ⁄ A1–A3; 1–24 **p. 475**

Papaver rhoeas
FLANDERS FIELD POPPY
☼ ⁄ A1–A3; 1–24 **p. 496**

Scabiosa (some)
PINCUSHION FLOWER
NEEDS, ZONES VARY **p. 600**

Senecio × hybridus
FLORISTS' CINERARIA
◑ ● ⁄ 16, 17, 22–24 **p. 606**

Dahlia

Ageratum houstonianum

Catharanthus roseus

Clarkia amoena

Myosotis sylvatica

Quercus lobata

Plants that Resist
OAK ROOT FUNGUS

Oak root fungus *(Armillaria mellea)* occurs in many parts of the world. In the West, it's most prevalent in California. The fungus sustains itself on buried wood (mostly dead roots), but it will invade susceptible plants through direct contact with their roots. In time, it kills its hosts, leaving behind a dead yet infested root system—and the cycle continues. Where oak root fungus is a problem, use resistant plants such as these.

Acer palmatum 'Ever Red'

Acer palmatum 'Sango Kaku'

Ailanthus altissima

Catalpa bignonioides

TREES

Abies concolor
WHITE FIR
☼ ◑ ⁄ A2, A3; 1–9, 14–24 **p. 163**

Acacia longifolia
SYDNEY GOLDEN WATTLE
☼ ⁄ 8, 9, 14–24 **p. 165**

Acer macrophyllum
BIGLEAF MAPLE
☼ ◑ ⁄ 2–9, 14–24 **p. 168**

Acer palmatum
JAPANESE MAPLE
☼ ◑ ⁄ A3; 2–10, 12, 14–24 **p. 168**

Acer tataricum ginnala
AMUR MAPLE
☼ ◑ ⁄ A1–A3; 1–9, 14–16 **p. 169**

Ailanthus altissima
TREE-OF-HEAVEN
☼ ⁄ 2B–24 **p. 176**

Apple
☼ ⁄ ZONES VARY **p. 189**

Arbutus menziesii
MADRONE
☼ ⁄ 4–7, 14–19 **p. 197**

Avocado
☼ ⁄ ZONES VARY **p. 210**

Brachychiton populneus
BOTTLE TREE
☼ ⁄ 12–24 **p. 230**

Calocedrus decurrens
INCENSE CEDAR
☼ ◑ ⁄ 2–12, 14–24 **p. 241**

Catalpa
☼ ⁄ 3–10, 14–24 **p. 255**

Celtis australis
EUROPEAN HACKBERRY
☼ ◑ ⁄ 8–16, 18–20 **p. 260**

Celtis occidentalis
COMMON HACKBERRY
☼ ◑ ⁄ 1–24 **p. 260**

Ceratonia siliqua
CAROB
☼ ⁄ 9, 13–16, 18–24; H1 **p. 262**

Cercis occidentalis
WESTERN REDBUD
☼ ⁄ 2–24 **p. 263**

Cercis siliquastrum
JUDAS TREE
☼ ⁄ 3B–19 **p. 263**

Chamaecyparis lawsoniana
PORT ORFORD CEDAR
☼ ◑ ⁄ A3; 3–6, 15–17 **p. 265**

Cryptomeria japonica
JAPANESE CRYPTOMERIA
☼ ⁄ 4–9, 14–24 **p. 301**

Cupaniopsis anacardioides
CARROT WOOD
☼ ⁄ 16–24; H1, H2 **p. 302**

×Cupressocyparis leylandii
☼ ⁄ 3B–24 **p. 302**

Cupressus arizonica glabra
ARIZONA CYPRESS
☼ ⁄ 7–24 **p. 303**

Elaeagnus angustifolia
RUSSIAN OLIVE
☼ ◑ ⁄ A2, A3; 1–3, 7–14, 18, 19 **p. 324**

Eucalyptus camaldulensis
RED GUM
☼ ⁄ SEE CHART **p. 338**

Eucalyptus cinerea
SILVER DOLLAR TREE
☼ ⁄ SEE CHART **p. 338**

Celtis occidentalis

×Cupressocyparis leylandii

Fig 'Brown Turkey'

For growing symbol explanations, please see page 64.

Plant	Common name	Zones	Page
Fig		4–9, 12–24; H1, H2	p. 351
Fraxinus angustifolia	ASH	2B–9, 12–24	p. 356
Fraxinus uhdei	EVERGREEN ASH	9, 12–24	p. 356
Fraxinus velutina	ARIZONA ASH	3B–24	p. 356
Geijera parviflora	AUSTRALIAN WILLOW	8, 9, 12–24	p. 362
Ginkgo biloba	MAIDENHAIR TREE	A3; 1–10, 12, 14–24	p. 366
Gleditsia triacanthos inermis	HONEY LOCUST	1–16, 18–20	p. 367
Gymnocladus dioica	KENTUCKY COFFEE TREE	1–3, 7–10, 12–16, 18–21	p. 377
Ilex aquifolium	ENGLISH HOLLY	4–9, 14–17; H1	p. 397
Ilex opaca	AMERICAN HOLLY	2–9, 14–17, 19–23	p. 398
Jacaranda mimosifolia		12, 13, 15–24; H1, H2	p. 407
Juglans californica	CALIFORNIA BLACK WALNUT	5–9, 14–24	p. 409
Liquidambar	SWEET GUM	ZONES VARY	p. 437
Liriodendron tulipifera	TULIP TREE	2–12, 14–24	p. 437
Macadamia		9, 16, 17, 19–24; H1, H2	p. 446
Maclura pomifera	OSAGE ORANGE	2, 3, 10–13	p. 447
Magnolia		ZONES VARY	p. 447
Malus	FLOWERING CRABAPPLE	1–11, 14–21	p. 457
Maytenus boaria	MAYTEN	8, 9, 14–24	p. 463
Melaleuca styphelioides	BLACK TEA TREE	9, 13–24; H1	p. 464
Metasequoia glyptostroboides	DAWN REDWOOD	A3; 3–10, 14–24	p. 467
Morus	MULBERRY	ZONES VARY	p. 472
Pear, European		ZONES VARY	p. 506
Pecan		2, 3, 6–10, 12–14, 18–20	p. 506
Persimmon		ZONES VARY	p. 513
Pinus canariensis	CANARY ISLAND PINE	8, 9, 12–24	p. 524
Pinus monticola	WESTERN WHITE PINE	1–7	p. 527
Pinus nigra	AUSTRIAN BLACK PINE	A3; 2–10, 14–21	p. 527
Pinus patula	JELECOTE PINE	8, 9, 14–24; H1	p. 527
Pinus sylvestris	SCOTCH PINE	A1–A3; 1–9, 14–21	p. 529
Pinus torreyana	TORREY PINE	8, 9, 14–24	p. 529
Pistacia chinensis	CHINESE PISTACHE	4–16, 18–23	p. 530
Pittosporum rhombifolium	QUEENSLAND PITTOSPORUM	12–24; H1, H2	p. 531
Platanus	PLANE TREE, SYCAMORE	ZONES VARY	p. 531
Plum, Japanese		ZONES VARY	p. 536
Prunus cerasifera	CHERRY PLUM	3–22	p. 552
Pseudotsuga menziesii	DOUGLAS FIR	A2, A3; 1–10, 14–17	p. 554
Pyrus calleryana		2B–9, 14–21	p. 558

Fraxinus uhdei

Ilex aquifolium

Liriodendron tulipifera

Malus

Maytenus boaria

Metasequoia glyptostroboides

Quercus ilex

Plant listings continue ▶

Sequoia sempervirens 'Aptos Blue'

Carpenteria californica

Cotinus coggygria

Hibiscus syriacus

Quercus ilex
HOLLY OAK, HOLM OAK
4–24 **p. 561**

Quercus lobata
VALLEY OAK, CALIFORNIA WHITE OAK
3B–9, 12–24 **p. 561**

Quillaja saponaria
SOAPBARK TREE
8, 9, 14–24 **p. 563**

Sapium sebiferum
CHINESE TALLOW TREE
8, 9, 12–16, 18–21; H1 **p. 599**

Sequoia sempervirens
REDWOOD, COAST REDWOOD
4–9, 14–24 **p. 607**

Sophora japonica
JAPANESE PAGODA TREE
2–24 **p. 613**

Taxodium distichum
BALD CYPRESS
2–10, 12–24 **p. 627**

Ulmus parvifolia
CHINESE ELM
3–24 **p. 642**

SHRUBS

Acacia verticillata
14–24 **p. 166**

Brugmansia
ANGEL'S TRUMPET
12, 13, 16–24; H1, H2 **p. 233**

Buxus sempervirens
COMMON BOXWOOD
3B–6, 15–17 **p. 236**

Calycanthus occidentalis
SPICE BUSH
4–9, 14–24 **p. 242**

Carpenteria californica
BUSH ANEMONE
5–9, 14–24 **p. 252**

Chaenomeles
FLOWERING QUINCE
2–23 **p. 264**

Clerodendrum bungei
CASHMERE BOUQUET
5–9, 12–24 **p. 284**

Cotinus coggygria
SMOKE TREE
2–24 **p. 296**

Erica arborea
TREE HEATH
15–17, 21–24 **p. 330**

Exochorda racemosa
COMMON PEARL BUSH
2–9, 14–23 **p. 346**

Guava
ZONES VARY **p. 376**

Hibiscus syriacus
ROSE OF SHARON
2–24; H1 **p. 389**

Hypericum beanii
4–9, 14–24 **p. 395**

Ilex × aquipernyi
4–9, 14–24 **p. 397**

Lonicera nitida
BOX HONEYSUCKLE
4–9, 14–24; H1, H2 **p. 442**

Mahonia aquifolium
OREGON GRAPE
2–12, 14–24 **p. 455**

Myrica pensylvanica
BAYBERRY
1–7 **p. 475**

Nandina domestica
HEAVENLY BAMBOO
3–24; H1, H2 **p. 476**

Phlomis fruticosa
JERUSALEM SAGE
3B–24 **p. 517**

Prunus caroliniana
CAROLINA LAUREL CHERRY
5–24 **p. 549**

Prunus ilicifolia
5–9, 12–24 **p. 549**

Rhus aromatica
FRAGRANT SUMAC
1–3, 10 **p. 576**

Rhus copallina
SHINING SUMAC
2–9, 14–18 **p. 576**

Sambucus canadensis
AMERICAN ELDERBERRY
A1–A3; 1–7, 14–17 **p. 597**

Shepherdia argentea
SILVER BUFFALOBERRY
1–3, 7, 10 **p. 609**

Vitex agnus-castus
CHASTE TREE
4–24; H1, H2 **p. 650**

VINES

Hedera helix
ENGLISH IVY
3–24; H1 **p. 381**

Wisteria sinensis
CHINESE WISTERIA
3–24 **p. 653**

Mahonia aquifolium

Sambucus canadensis

Hedera helix

Wisteria sinensis

For growing symbol explanations, please see page 64.

Western Plant ENCYCLOPEDIA

Rosa banksiae 'Lutea'

Many of the myriad plants sold in Western nurseries—from tall trees to tiny succulents, from roses and poppies to ornamental grasses—are described in this chapter. Ornamental plants and herbs are listed alphabetically by their botanical names, such as Quercus *(oak) and* Ocimum *(basil). Cross-references of their common names may also appear, directing you to the botanical-name listings. Fruits and vegetables, however, are listed by common names like apple and pumpkin, for example. You'll find both botanical and common names in the index at the end of this book.*

The sample entry below illustrates the format used throughout this encyclopedia. The plant's botanical name is listed first. Where applicable, alternate botanical names (former ones that are still widely used or new ones that haven't yet taken hold) are shown in parentheses. Next is the plant's common name or names, followed by the family name. The next three lines list type of plant and cultural information. Occasionally, a final line notes toxic properties.

Climate

Refers to climate zones (see pages 27–63) where the plant grows best. "Zones 8, 9, 12–24," for example, gives the inclusive zones for which the plant is recommended. "All zones" means the plant will grow anywhere in the West. If the zone line includes "...or indoors," the plant can be grown outdoors in the designated zones and indoors there or in colder climates.

Exposure

☼ Means the plant grows best with unobstructed sunlight all or almost all day; you can overlook an hour or so of shade at the beginning or end of a summer day. ◑ means the plant needs partial shade—some shade for half the day or for at least 3 hours during the hottest part of the day. ● indicates that a plant prefers little or no direct sun—for example, it does best on the north side of a house or beneath a broad, dense-foliaged tree.

COLCHICUM

MEADOW SAFFRON, AUTUMN CROCUS

Liliaceae

PERENNIALS FROM CORMS

ZONES 2–10, 14–24; OR INDOORS

☼ FULL SUN; BRIGHT INDIRECT LIGHT

● REGULAR WATER DURING GROWTH AND BLOOM

◈ ALL PARTS ARE POISONOUS IF INGESTED

Colchicum

Some listings contain qualifications. For example, "☼ ◑ Partial shade in hottest climates" means the plant succeeds in full sun or partial shade except in the hottest areas, where it must have partial shade. If a plant can be grown indoors, outdoor exposure needs are followed by indoor light requirements. In the sample entry below left, the plant needs full sun outdoors, bright indirect light indoors.

Watering

Moisture needs are given for established plants. Bear in mind that even plants that will survive at maturity on rainfall alone need regular moisture for a time after planting—perhaps a single season for a perennial, up to 2 to 5 years for a tree. ○ indicates the most drought-tolerant plants; some require no supplemental irrigation once established, while others may need a little. ◒ means the plant needs less than regular moisture; this may mean a soaking every 2 or 3 weeks. ● means the plant requires regular moisture: soil shouldn't be too dry or too wet. ●● is reserved for plants needing ample moisture, such as bog and aquatic plants and streambed natives. Many plants show a range; for example, ● ●● means the plant can take regular moisture or wetter conditions.

Toxicity

◈ The plant or some of its parts are known to have toxic or irritant properties.

The drawings that accompany the entries illustrate one or more members of a genus. Be sure, however, to read the individual species descriptions, since not all look alike. The descriptions contain approximate plant heights and widths. Often a range is given, but the same plant may be smaller where summers are hot, dry, or short, and larger where summers are cool, moist, or long. Also note that seasons are according to the calendar, though many Westerners call all warm months "summer" and all rainy or cold ones "winter." Bloom times have been averaged for the various regions; flowering may start earlier or last longer in the mildest-winter climates, and begin later or be briefer in the coldest areas.

A

AARON'S BEARD. See **HYPERICUM calycinum**

ABELIA

Abelia ×grandiflora

Caprifoliaceae

EVERGREEN, SEMIEVERGREEN, DECIDUOUS SHRUBS

ZONES VARY BY SPECIES

BEST IN SUN, TOLERATE SOME SHADE, EXCEPT AS NOTED

REGULAR WATER

Graceful, arching branches densely clothed with oval, usually glossy leaves ½–1½ in. long; bronzy new growth. Tubular or bell-shaped flowers in clusters at ends of branches or among leaves. Though small, blossoms are plentiful enough to be showy, mostly during summer and early fall. When blooms drop, they usually leave purplish or copper-colored sepals that provide color into the fall months. Leaves also may take on bronzy tints in fall.

To keep the shrub's graceful form, prune selectively; don't shear. The more stems you cut to the ground in winter or early spring, the more open and arching next year's growth will be. Abelias are adaptable plants, useful in shrub borders, as space dividers and visual barriers, and near house walls; lower kinds are good bank or ground covers.

A. chinensis. Deciduous. Zones 4–24. Chinese native growing to 4–5 ft. tall and wide, with fragrant, pink-tinted white flowers.

A. floribunda. MEXICAN ABELIA. Evergreen. Zones 9, 12–24; with periodic damage in Zones 7, 8. Severely damaged at 20°F/–7°C. Native to Mexico. Usually 3–6 ft. tall; sometimes 10 ft. tall and up to 12 ft. wide. Arching, reddish, downy or hairy stems. Pendulous reddish purple flowers appear singly or in clusters. Heaviest bloom is in summer, with sporadic bloom during rest of year. Needs partial shade in hot climates.

A. ×grandiflora. GLOSSY ABELIA. Evergreen to semievergreen. Zones 4–24; H1, H2. This cross between two Chinese species is the best known and most popular of the abelias. To 8 ft. or taller, spreading to 5 ft. or wider. Flowers white or faintly tinged pink. Loses most of its leaves at 15°F/–9°C. Freezes to the ground at 0°F/–18°C but usually recovers to bloom the same year, making a graceful border plant 10–15 in. high. The following are among the varieties grown.

'Edward Goucher'. Zones 5–24. Less hardy, lacier, and more compact (to 3–5 ft. tall and wide) than *A. ×grandiflora.* Bears small lilac pink flowers with orange throats.

'Francis Mason'. Compact (to 3–4 ft. high and wide) and densely branched, with pink flowers and yellow-variegated leaves.

'Prostrata'. Low grower (1½–2 ft. high, spreading 4–5 ft. wide) useful as ground cover, bank planting, foreground shrub.

'Sherwoodii'. Dense, compact, refined growth to 3–4 ft. tall, 5 ft. wide.

'Sunrise'. Densely branched, with bronzy green leaves that turn red and purple in fall. To 3–6 ft. tall and wide.

ABELIA-LEAF. See **ABELIOPHYLLUM distichum**

ABELIOPHYLLUM distichum

Abeliophyllum distichum

WHITE FORSYTHIA, ABELIA-LEAF

Oleaceae

DECIDUOUS SHRUB

ZONES 1–11, 14–19

BEST IN SUN, TOLERATES SOME SHADE

REGULAR WATER

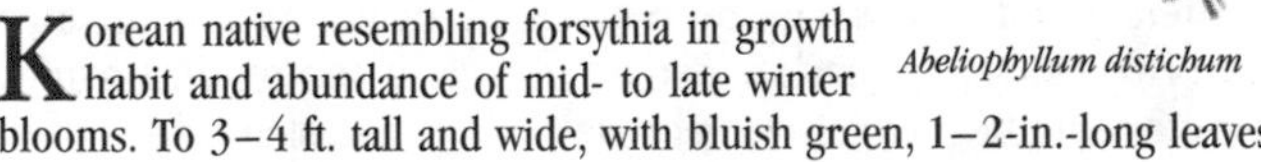

Korean native resembling forsythia in growth habit and abundance of mid- to late winter blooms. To 3–4 ft. tall and wide, with bluish green, 1–2-in.-long leaves. Pink buds along deep brown or black branches open to very fragrant white blossoms (sometimes flushed pink). 'Roseum' is a pink-flowering form. After bloom, remove some of the oldest branches at base to keep flowering wood coming. Or cut branches while in bud or bloom to use for decoration; budded branches can be forced to flower indoors.

ABELMOSCHUS

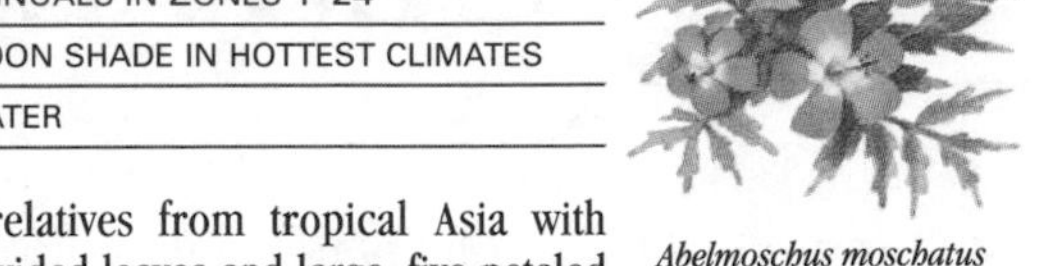

Abelmoschus moschatus

Malvaceae

PERENNIALS OFTEN GROWN AS ANNUALS

ZONE H2; ANNUALS IN ZONES 1–24

AFTERNOON SHADE IN HOTTEST CLIMATES

REGULAR WATER

Hibiscus relatives from tropical Asia with deeply divided leaves and large, five-petaled flowers. Most commonly grown as summer annuals; will bloom first year from seed sown early. Thrive in good garden soil. The annual *A. esculentus* is a vegetable; see Okra.

A. manihot (Hibiscus manihot). To 6 ft. or taller, 2–3 ft. wide. Large, coarse leaves and 3–5-in., cream to deep yellow flowers with maroon central blotch.

A. moschatus (Hibiscus moschatus). SILK FLOWER. Bushy plant about 1½ ft. high and wide, with deep green, deeply cut leaves. Five-petaled, 3–4½-in., cherry red or deep pink blooms resemble those of tropical hibiscus. Can be grown as a houseplant in 6-in. pot; set on a windowsill in bright light.

ABIES

Abies concolor

FIR

Pinaceae

EVERGREEN TREES

ZONES VARY BY SPECIES

FULL SUN OR LIGHT SHADE, EXCEPT AS NOTED

MODERATE TO REGULAR WATER, EXCEPT AS NOTED

In nature, firs are tall, erect, symmetrical trees with uniformly spaced branch whorls. Though sometimes confused with spruces *(Picea),* they have softer needles that fall directly from the stems (spruces leave short pegs behind), and their large cones grow up rather than down. Cones shatter after ripening, leaving a spiky stalk. Most (but not all) firs native to North America are high-mountain plants that do best in or near their natural environments. They grow slowly if at all in hot, dry, windy areas at low elevations, though firs from some other parts of the world do well in warm, dry climates.

Christmas tree farms grow native firs for cutting, and nurseries in the Pacific Northwest and Northern California grow a few species for the living Christmas tree trade. Licensed collectors in the Northwest dig picturesque, contorted firs at high elevations near the timberline and market them through nurseries as "alpine conifers." Use these in rock gardens; small specimens are good container or bonsai subjects. Birds are attracted by fir seeds. New growth on firs is susceptible to aphid damage.

Allow ample growing room at planting; if you later try to restrict a fir tree's size by pruning, you'll only ruin its natural shape. Pruning is rarely necessary; plants are more attractive with branches all the way to the ground.

A. amabilis. SILVER FIR, CASCADE FIR. Zones 3–7, 15–17. Native to southern Alaska south through Coast Ranges and Cascades of Washington and Oregon. Imposing tree in the wild, smaller (20–50 ft. tall and 12–15 ft. wide) in lowland gardens in the Pacific Northwest. Dark green needles, silvery beneath, curve upward along the branches.

A. balsamea. BALSAM FIR. Zones A3; 1–7, 15–17. Native to eastern North American mountains. Dwarf 'Nana' is the form most commonly sold in the West. It's an interesting rock garden subject, very slowly forming a dense, dark green cushion 2–3 ft. high and wide. Needs partial shade, regular water.

A. bracteata (A. venusta). SANTA LUCIA FIR, BRISTLECONE FIR. Zones 6–9, 14–21. From steep, rocky slopes on the seaward side of California's Santa Lucia Mountains. A tall tree (to 70 ft. in 50 years), with spreading lower branches (to 15–20 ft.) and slender steeplelike crown. Stiff, 1½–2½-in.-long needles are dark green above, with white lines beneath; needle points are unusually sharp. Roundish cones are unusual—about 4 in. long, with a long, slender, pointed bract on each cone scale. Exceptionally tolerant of heat and aridity.

A. concolor. WHITE FIR. Zones A2, A3; 1–9, 14–24. Native to mountains of southern Oregon, California, southern Rocky Mountains, Baja California. One of the big five in the timber belt of the Sierra Nevada, along with ponderosa pine, sugar pine, incense cedar, and Douglas fir. A popular Christmas tree and one of the most commonly grown native firs in Western gardens. Needs no irrigation where native; some elsewhere.

Large, symmetrical tree (80–120 ft. tall and 15–20 ft. wide) in its native range and in the Northwest. Slower growing in California gardens; has reached 30 ft. in as many years in lowland California. Best as container plant in Southern California. Bluish green, 1–2-in.-long needles. Some consider 'Candicans', with bluish white foliage, the "bluest" of all conifers.

A. grandis. LOWLAND FIR, GRAND FIR. Zones 1–9, 14–17. From British Columbia inland to Montana, southward to Northern California, where it grows near the ocean. Many Northwest gardeners live and garden successfully under this fir; they prune it high. It's one of the largest firs, reaching 300 ft. in the wild (smaller in cultivation—80–200 ft. tall, 15–25 ft. wide). Handsome, deep green, 1–1½-in.-long needles are glossy above, with white lines beneath; they grow in two rows along branches. 'Johnsonii' is suited to urban gardens, growing 65 ft. tall and 10 ft. wide.

A. koreana. KOREAN FIR. Zones 3b–9, 14–24. Native to Korea. Slow-growing, compact, pyramidal tree seldom over 30 ft. tall and 20 ft. wide. Shiny, short green needles. Sets cones on young, small trees. 'Aurea', with gold-green foliage, is even smaller, slower growing. 'Horstmann's Silberlocke' provides a dwarf silver accent; its needles turn upward, showing silvery white undersides.

A. lasiocarpa. ALPINE FIR, ROCKY MOUNTAIN FIR. Zones A2, A3; 1–9, 14–17. Native to Alaska, south through the high Cascades of Washington and Oregon; nearly throughout the Rocky Mountains. In the wild in good, moist soil, it is a narrow, steeple-shaped tree, 60–90 ft. tall and 10 ft. wide. In gardens, usually grows much shorter and loses its narrow shape; allow for 15–20-ft. spread in Northwest. Extremely slow growing in California gardens. Bluish green, 1–1½-in.-long needles.

A. l. arizonica. Zones 2–9. Native to San Francisco Peaks, Arizona, at 8,500-ft. elevation. Thick, corky creamy white bark gives the tree its common name, "cork fir." Blue, often silvery, needles. Very handsome as a youngster; good bonsai. Excellent substitute for blue spruce *(Picea pungens)* in smaller spaces; also more disease free than blue spruce.

A. magnifica. RED FIR. Zones 2–7. Native to the mountains of southern Oregon and parts of California's Sierra Nevada and Coast Ranges. This is the "silver tip" fir of the California cut Christmas tree trade. Stately (80–120 ft. tall and 15–20 ft. wide in the wild), with symmetrical, horizontal, rather short branches. New growth silvery gray. Mature needles blue green, 1 in. long. Hard to grow at low elevations.

A. nordmanniana. NORDMANN FIR. Zones 1–11, 14–24. Native to the Caucasus, Asia Minor, Greece. Vigorous, densely foliaged fir, 30–50 ft. tall and 20 ft. wide in cultivation. Dark green, shiny, ¾–1½-in.-long needles, with whitish bands beneath. More adaptable to California gardens than native firs, becoming a symmetrical, densely branched, cone-shaped tree. Needs regular water; will submit to long-term container growing.

A. pinsapo. SPANISH FIR. Zones 5–11, 14–24. Native to Spain. Very slow growing, to 25 ft. tall and 10 ft. wide in 40 years. In Southern California, good dwarf effect for years. Dense, symmetrical form; it's sometimes taken for a spruce. Stiff, deep green, ½–¾-in.-long needles are set uniformly around branches. 'Glauca' is blue gray.

A. procera (A. nobilis). NOBLE FIR. Zones 2–6, 15–17. Native to the Siskiyou Mountains of California, northern mountains of Oregon and Washington. Similar to *A. magnifica* in appearance; grown in Northwest nurseries as a living Christmas tree. Grows 90–200 ft. tall and 20–30 ft. wide in the wild, almost as tall in Northwest gardens. Short, stiff branches; blue-green, 1-in.-long needles. Large cones (6–10 in. long, 3 in. wide) with extended bracts as in *A. bracteata*.

A. sibirica. SIBERIAN FIR. Zones A1–A3; 1–3. Native to Siberia, Mongolia. Narrowly conical tree to about 30 ft. tall. Aromatic, bright green needles just over 1 in. long are arranged all around the twigs and point toward twig tips. Short cones (about 3 in. long) are bluish at first, becoming brown. Does best in cool, moist climates; valuable for tolerance to extreme cold.

ABUTILON

FLOWERING MAPLE, CHINESE BELLFLOWER, CHINESE LANTERN

Malvaceae

EVERGREEN SHRUBS

ZONES 8, 9, 12–24; H1, H2; EXCEPT AS NOTED

PARTIAL SHADE IN HOTTEST CLIMATES

MODERATE TO REGULAR WATER, EXCEPT AS NOTED

Abutilon hybrid

Native to warm regions of the world, especially South America. Planted primarily for showy flowers. Good drainage essential. Control whitefly and scale insects. In cold-winter climates, can be grown as potted plants; keep indoors in winter, put out on terrace or patio in summer.

A. hybrids. Grown in zones above and also as an annual in colder climates. The best-known flowering maples. Upright, arching growth to 8–10 ft. tall, with equal spread. Broad maplelike leaves; drooping bell-like flowers in white, yellow, pink, or red. Main bloom season is spring, but white and yellow forms seem to flower almost continuously. The following are some of the best hybrids.

'Bartley Schwartz'. Arching, weeping growth, with constant production of orange-yellow, drooping flowers. Good basket plant or standard.

'Clementine'. Compact, with red-orange bells over a long season.

'Crimson Belle'. Deep red blossoms.

'Dwarf Red'. Compact and free branching, with orange-red flowers.

'Kentish Belle'. Trailing habit, with yellow-orange flowers.

'Linda Vista Peach'. Orange petals protrude from deep pink calyxes.

'Mobile Pink'. Upright, compact growth. Large, wide-open flowers of pale pink veined deeper pink.

'Moonchimes'. Drooping, 3-in. yellow flowers on a compact plant.

A. megapotamicum. Vine-shrub from Brazil. Vigorous growth to 10 ft. and as wide, with arrowlike, 1½–3-in.-long leaves. Flowers resembling red-and-yellow lanterns gaily decorate the long, rangy branches in spring and summer. Pinch branch tips to control size, make bushier. More graceful in detail than in entirety but can be trained to an interesting pattern. Usually best as loose, informal espalier. Good hanging basket plant. 'Marianne' has better, more intense flower color; 'Variegata' has leaves mottled with yellow; 'Victory' is compact and floriferous, with small deep yellow flowers.

A. palmeri. INDIAN MALLOW. Zones 8, 9, 11–13. From low deserts of Arizona, California. To 5 ft. tall and wide. Clustered spring flowers are orange yellow, about 1 in. wide. Grown primarily for its soft, velvety, heart-shaped to roundish leaves, to 6 in. wide and 8 in. long. Little water.

A. pictum 'Thompsonii'. Variety of a Brazilian species. Similar in form to hybrids, but foliage is strikingly variegated with creamy yellow. Blooms almost continuously, bearing pale orange bells veined with red.

A. vitifolium (Corynabutilon vitifolium). Zones 5, 6, 15–17. From Chile. To 15 ft. tall, 8 ft. wide. Gray-green, maplelike leaves to 6 in. or longer. In summer, lilac blue to white flowers are borne singly or in clusters on long stalks. Needs high humidity.

A

ABYSSINIAN BANANA. See ENSETE ventricosum

ABYSSINIAN SWORD LILY. See GLADIOLUS callianthus

ACACIA

Fabaceae (Leguminosae)

EVERGREEN AND DECIDUOUS SHRUBS AND TREES

ZONES VARY BY SPECIES

FULL SUN

LITTLE OR NO WATER

SEE CHART

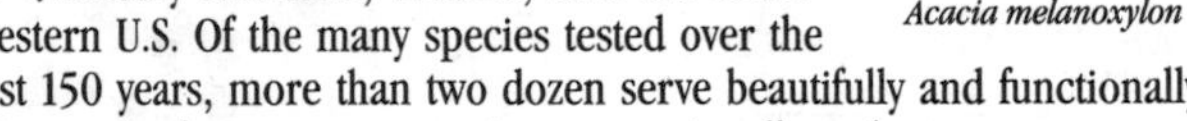

Acacia melanoxylon

Native to tropics or warm regions of world, notably Australia, Mexico, and the southwestern U.S. Of the many species tested over the last 150 years, more than two dozen serve beautifully and functionally in Western landscapes; new species are continually under test.

Of species in use today, several offer fountains of clear yellow flowers in early or midwinter. Some are quite fragrant when in bloom. Many decorate and protect hillsides, banks, freeway landscapes. Some serve well in beach plantings. All are attractive to birds. Those listed in chart are evergreen except where noted.

Most nurseries sell only a few of the many acacia species, but you can easily grow acacias from seed you collect yourself or order from a specialist.

Acacia baileyana

The acacias differ widely in foliage and growth habit. Some have feathery, much divided leaves; others have flattened leafstalks that fulfill the function of leaves. Many start life with feathery leaves and later develop leathery ones.

You can prune acacias or leave them to their own devices. Larger-growing species may end up as shrubs or trees depending on how they are treated in youth. Remove the lead shoot and the plant grows as a shrub; remove the lower branches and it will be treelike. It's best to prune trees to open up their interiors; this will reduce dieback of shaded branches and prevent wind damage. Thin by removing branches all the way to the trunk.

Many acacias are relatively short lived—20 to 30 years. But if a plant reaches 20 ft. high in 3 years, the short life can be accepted.

Acacias seldom suffer pest damage. Where water is bad and salts accumulate, many become chlorotic (as do numerous other plants in such soil).

ACACIA

NAME	ZONES	HEIGHT	SPREAD	LEAVES	FLOWERS	COMMENTS
Acacia armata KANGAROO THORN	13–24	10–15 ft.	10–12 ft.	Light green, waxy, 1-in.-long leaves on thorny branches	Yellow, single, ¼-in.-wide balls. Mid- to late winter	Blooms when young. Used as pot plant in cold areas. Thorniness makes it an excellent barrier plant
A. baileyana BAILEY ACACIA (often called "mimosa" as cut flowers)	7–9, 13–24	20–30 ft.	20–40 ft.	Feathery, finely cut, blue gray	Yellow, in clusters. Fragrant. Profuse in early to midwinter	Most commonly planted and one of hardiest. Wonderful tree on banks when grown as multitrunked shrub-tree
A. b. 'Purpurea' PURPLE-LEAF ACACIA	8, 9, 13–24	20–30 ft.	20–30 ft.	Same as above, except for lavender to purple new growth	Same as above	Cut back to encourage new growth, prolong foliage color
A. berlandieri GUAJILLO	10–24	5–12 ft.	5–20 ft.	Feathery, finely divided, light green	White, fragrant. Early spring	Thornless forms especially useful for background or screen
A. boormanii SNOWY RIVER WATTLE	8, 9, 12–24	10–15 ft.	6–15 ft.	Narrow, gray green, 2–3 in. long	Bright yellow, fragrant puffs at branch ends. Winter	Can sucker to form thickets. Tolerates winter wet
A. cognata (A. subporosa) BOWER WATTLE, RIVER WATTLE	16–24	20–30 ft.	20–30 ft.	Narrow, drooping, bright green, to 4 in. long	Paired pale yellow puffs. Spring	Graceful weeping tree. Damaged at 20°F/–7°C. Selections include 'Emerald Cascade' and 'Emerald Showers'
A. confusa FORMOSAN KOA	H1, H2	30–50 ft.	To 30 ft.	Dark green, slightly curved	Bright yellow puffs in spring, summer	Open, upright to round headed
A. constricta WHITE THORN, MESCAT ACACIA	10–24	10–18 ft.	To 18 ft.	Tiny, feathery	Yellow, fragrant. Summer	Open, spiny, deciduous shrub native Texas to Arizona. Valuable in desert for texture, summer flowers
A. cultriformis KNIFE ACACIA	13–24	10–15 ft.	10–15 ft.	Silvery gray, shaped like 1-in.-long paring knife blades	Yellow, in clusters. Early spring	Naturally a multistemmed tree. Barrier or screen. Useful on banks, slopes
A. cyanophylla (see **A. saligna**)						

ACACIA

NAME	ZONES	HEIGHT	SPREAD	LEAVES	FLOWERS	COMMENTS
A. cyclops	8, 9, 13–24	10–15 ft.	15–20 ft.	Dark green, narrow, to 3½ in. long	Bright yellow, single or clustered; inconspicuous. Spring	Screening plant along highways. Good for hedges. Pods open to show unusual seeds—black with red rings surrounding them. Very drought resistant
A. dealbata (A. decurrens dealbata)	8, 9, 14–24; borderline in 6	To 50 ft.	40–50 ft.	Feathery, silvery gray	Similar to *A. baileyana*	Twigs and young branches silvery gray; attractive. Very fast growing
A. decora GRACEFUL WATTLE	13–24	6–8 ft.	6–8 ft.	Rather narrow, 2 in. long, curved, bluish	Yellow balls in 2-in.-long clusters. Mass display in spring	Good for screening. Can be used as trimmed hedge 5 ft. high
A. decurrens (A. decurrens mollis)	8, 9, 14–24; borderline in 6	To 50 ft.	40–50 ft.	Feathery, dark green	Yellow, in clusters. Late winter	Longer lived than *A. baileyana;* more tolerant of wind and water. Invasive roots, litter rule it out for small gardens. Plants sold are often the similar *A. mearnsii,* green wattle
A. farnesiana SWEET ACACIA (see also **A. smallii**)	13–24	To 20 ft.	15–25 ft.	Deciduous, feathery, finely divided leaves on thorny branches	Deep yellow, fragrant balls in winter. May freeze in cold snaps	Needs frost-free location in Zone 13. Can freeze to stump at 28°F/–2°C. Better for desert is similar *A. smallii,* often sold as *A. farnesiana*
A. greggii CATCLAW ACACIA	10–24	15–25 ft.	15 ft.	Finely divided, feathery, dark green; carried on spiny branches	Creamy yellow. Spring and intermittently through fall	Native California to Texas. Shrubby in drought, treelike with water
A. koa KOA	H1, H2	To 60 ft.	To 60 ft.	Feathery in young trees; later leathery, curved, 6 in. long, up to ½ in. wide	Yellow, in clusters. Spring	Native Hawaiian tree produces a beautiful hardwood
A. longifolia (often sold as **A. latifolia**) SYDNEY GOLDEN WATTLE	8, 9, 14–24	To 20 ft.	To 20 ft.	Bright green, 3–6 in. long	Golden yellow, loose, 2½-in.-long spikes along branches in late winter, early spring	Usually big, rounded, billowy shrub. Very fast growing; very tolerant. Used as road screening against dust and headlights. Good soil binder near the beach (winds make it prostrate). Resists oak root fungus
A. melanoxylon BLACKWOOD ACACIA, BLACK ACACIA	8, 9, 13–24	To 40 ft.	To 20 ft.	Dark green, 2–4 in. long	Creamy to straw color, in short clusters. Spring	Fast, dense, upright growth. Aggressive roots, litter, brittle branches a problem in confined areas. Thrives in intense heat, coastal winds, poor soil, drought
A. minuta (see **A. smallii**)						
A. pendula WEEPING ACACIA, WEEPING MYALL	13–24	To 25 ft.	To 15 ft.	Blue gray, to 4 in. long, on long, weeping branches	Yellow, in pairs or clusters. Blooms erratically in spring	Beautiful weeping tree. Perfect for cascading from behind wall. Makes graceful espalier. Interesting structure in maturity. Slow grower, seldom looks good in container
A. podalyriifolia PEARL ACACIA	8, 9, 13–24	10–20 ft.	12–15 ft.	Roundish, 1½ in. long, silvery gray, soft and satiny to touch	Light yellow, fluffy, in long clusters. Late fall, winter	Grow as shrub or train as rounded, open-headed tree. Excellent for patio. Good winter color. Won't tolerate summer water. Prune heavily after flowering to keep it compact
A. pravissima OVENS WATTLE	12–24	12–20 ft	12–20 ft.	Short, triangular, gray green; tightly packed along branches	Profuse, bright yellow, scented. Winter, spring	Endures frost, heat, wind, marine exposure

ACACIA

NAME	ZONES	HEIGHT	SPREAD	LEAVES	FLOWERS	COMMENTS
A. redolens	8, 9, 12–24	Variable; 1–6 ft.	Variable; to 15 ft.	Narrow, gray green, leathery	Puffy yellow balls. Spring	Ground cover for banks, large areas of poor soil. Endures drought, heat. 'Desert Carpet' is low-growing form: 2 ft. high, spreading to 12 ft.
A. retinodes (often sold as **A. floribunda**) WATER WATTLE, FLORIBUNDA ACACIA	8, 9, 13–24; borderline in 5, 6	To 20 ft.	To 20 ft.	Yellow green, to 5 in. long	Yellow, small heads in clusters. Blooms most of year near coast	Quick screen. Can be a pendulous, see-through tree. Tends to get leggy. The only acacia with chance of survival in Seattle if mild winters come four in a row
A. rigidula BLACKBRUSH ACACIA	10–13	10–15 ft.	10–15 ft.	Deep green, rounded leaflets	Fragrant, pale yellow, 2–3-in. spikes; almost glow on a bright spring day	Slower growing than other acacias. Naturally multitrunked. To train to single trunk, pull off suckers at base
A. salicina WILLOW ACACIA, AUSTRALIAN WILLOW	8, 9, 12–24	20–40 ft.	To 15 ft.	Dark green, narrow, to 3 in. long	Cream-colored balls. Blooms most of year; heaviest in fall, winter	Fast growing, with semiweeping habit. Prune to keep open. Don't overwater
A. saligna **(A. cyanophylla)** BLUE-LEAF WATTLE	8, 9, 12–24	20–30 ft.	15–20 ft.	Narrow, blue green, 6–12 in. long	Nearly orange balls in clusters. Heavy bloom in spring	Screen for privacy or wind control. Multitrunked big shrub or tree
A. schaffneri	8, 9, 12–24	To 18 ft.	To 20 ft.	Deciduous, finely divided, closely set along branches	Yellow balls, fragrant. Spring	Exotic form with curving, nearly black branches. Prune to form trunk and shape branches. Short thorns hidden in leaves
A. smallii **(A. minuta)**	8, 9, 12–24	Variable; 10–35 ft.	15–25 ft.	Deciduous, finely divided leaves on thorny branches	Yellow, fragrant, puffy balls. Spring	Desert Southwest native often sold as *A. farnesiana,* which is cold tender. Plant *A. smallii* where frost occurs
A. stenophylla SHOESTRING ACACIA	8, 9, 12–24	To 30 ft.	To 20 ft.	Long (to 16 in.), narrow, drooping, pale green; maroon new bark	Creamy, ½-in. balls. Late winter, spring	Fast growing, open, weeping; makes good shadows on walls, provides lightest shade for underplantings
A. subporosa (see **A. cognata**)						
A. verticillata	14–24	To 15 ft.	To 15 ft.	Dark green, needlelike, ¾ in. long, in whorls	Pale yellow, in 1-in.-long spikes. Spring	Looks like an airy conifer. Good low hedge in wind. Unpruned, it develops open form with many spreading, twisting trunks. Sheared, it grows dense and full. Good at beach. Resists oak root fungus
A. willardiana PALO BLANCO	12–24	To 20 ft.	To 10 ft.	Deciduous fernlike leaves fall early, leaving narrow leaflike stalks 3–12 in. long	Pale yellow. Early spring	Striking feature is white or cream-colored, papery, peeling bark

ACALYPHA

Euphorbiaceae

EVERGREEN SHRUBS

ZONES 24; H2; OR INDOORS

PARTIAL SHADE; BRIGHT INDIRECT LIGHT

REGULAR WATER

Acalypha hispida

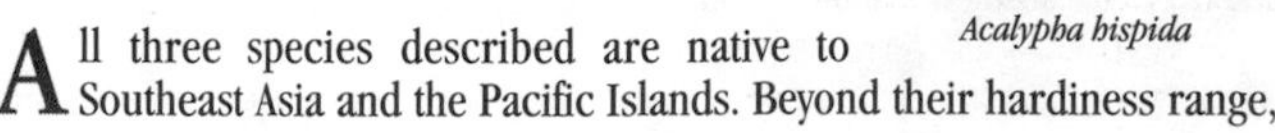

All three species described are native to Southeast Asia and the Pacific Islands. Beyond their hardiness range, they can be grown indoors; *A. wilkesiana* and *A. pendula* can be used as annuals in Zones 22 and 23. All bloom intermittently during the warm months, must have good drainage. Pinch young plants regularly to encourage bushy growth.

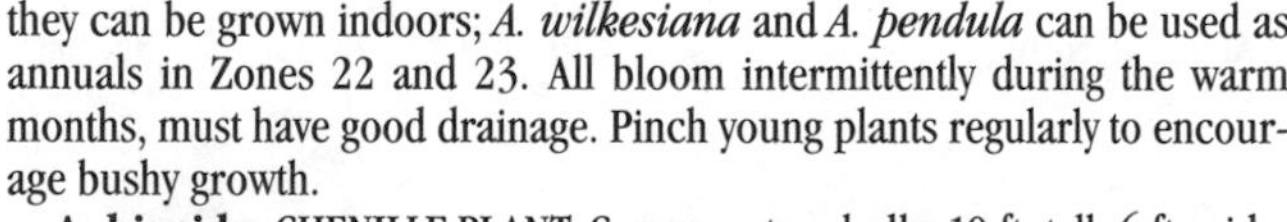

A. hispida. CHENILLE PLANT. Can grow to a bulky 10 ft. tall, 6 ft. wide. Heavy, rich green leaves to 8 in. wide. Flowers come in hanging, 1½-ft.-long clusters that resemble tassels of crimson chenille. Heaviest bloom in early summer; scattered bloom all year. Thrives in tropical climates. Can also be grown in greenhouse or enclosed patio or, with heavy pruning, as a houseplant.

A. pendula. FIRETAIL. Resembles *A. hispida* in flower form, but plant is much smaller; shorter tassels droop from trailing branches. Good in hanging basket.

A. wilkesiana (A. tricolor). COPPER LEAF. Foliage more colorful than many flowers. Often used as an annual, substituting for flowers from late summer to frost. Leaves to 8 in. long, in color combinations including bronzy green mottled with red and purple; red with crimson and bronze; and green edged with crimson and stippled with orange and red. In a warm, sheltered spot it can grow as a shrub to 6 ft. or taller, nearly as wide. Outdoor potted plants should be kept slightly dry through winter.

Acanthaceae. The acanthus family consists of herbs and shrubs, generally from warm or tropical areas. Many have showy flowers or foliage. Examples are bear's breech *(Acanthus), Aphelandra,* and *Thunbergia.*

ACANTHOPANAX sieboldianus. See ELEUTHEROCOCCUS sieboldianus

ACANTHUS

BEAR'S BREECH

Acanthaceae

PERENNIALS

ZONES VARY BY SPECIES

SUN OR SHADE

MODERATE TO REGULAR WATER

Acanthus mollis

Native to southern Europe and the Mediterranean. Large, deeply lobed, sometimes spiny leaves in clumps to about 3 ft. wide. Bloom in late spring or summer, when foliage clumps send up tall spikes of hooded whitish, rose, or purple flowers beneath spiny green or purplish bracts. Lop off the prickly spikes after bloom.

These tough plants have spreading roots and can become invasive. Give them plenty of room, or confine them with an 8-in.-deep barrier. In dry-summer regions, they will lose leaves if deprived of moisture in summer, then leaf out again with winter rains; occasional soakings will keep leaves green during hot weather. To propagate, dig and divide between midfall and early spring. Control snails and slugs. Plants are effective in shade with bamboo and large-leafed ferns but will survive in dry, sunny spots.

A. balcanicus (A. hungaricus). Zones 2–24. Somewhat smaller than *A. mollis,* with more finely cut and toothed leaves.

A. mollis. Zones 5–24. Most commonly grown species. To 4–5 ft. high in bloom. Spineless leaves to 2 ft. long are deeply lobed and cut. 'Latifolius' has larger leaves and is hardier.

A. spinosus. Zones 4–24. Similar to *A. mollis* in size, but leaves are more finely cut and armed with long spines. Foliage is silvery on the true species. Hybrids have bright green leaves and are known as the Spinosissimus Group.

ACCA sellowiana. See FEIJOA

ACER

MAPLE

Aceraceae

DECIDUOUS TREES AND SHRUBS

ZONES VARY BY SPECIES

FULL SUN OR PARTIAL SHADE

MODERATE TO REGULAR WATER

Acer palmatum

When you talk about maples, you're talking about many trees—large and midsize shade trees; smaller trees; and dainty, picturesque shrub-trees. Leaves range from simple ovals to deeply lobed and finely dissected shapes. One element common to all maples is the fruit (seed capsule), which resembles a hardware store wingnut. In general, maples are highly favored in the Pacific Northwest, in the intermountain areas, and, to a lesser extent, in Northern California; with the few exceptions noted here they are not adapted to Southern California or the Southwest's desert areas. Practically all maples in Southern California show marginal leafburn after mid-June and lack the fall color of maples in colder areas. In all regions, for good fall leaf display, look for a maple that colors well in your locale; visit nurseries while the foliage is changing hue.

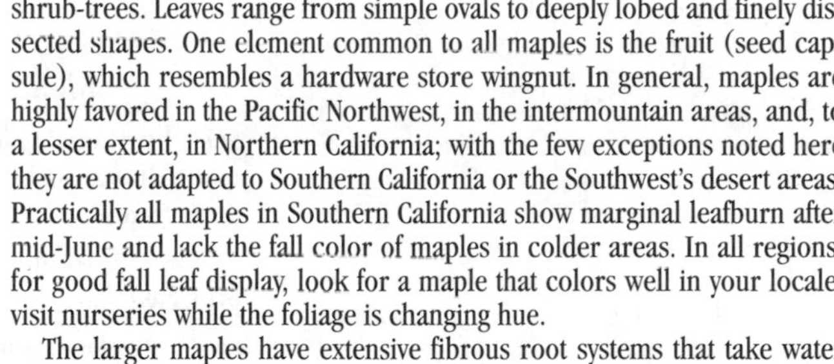

The larger maples have extensive fibrous root systems that take water and nutrients from the topsoil. The great canopy of leaves calls for a steady, constant supply of water—not necessarily frequent watering but constantly available water throughout the root zone. Occasional deep watering and periodic feeding will help keep roots deep.

Medium to large maple species need little pruning. On smaller types, prune to accentuate the natural shape. To minimize sap bleed, make any cuts in summer or early fall in mild-winter areas, or from summer to the end of January where temperatures remain below freezing.

A. buergeranum. TRIDENT MAPLE. Deciduous tree. Zones 2–9, 14–17, 20, 21. Native to China, Japan. Grows 20–25 ft. high and wide. Roundish crown of 3-in.-wide, glossy green, three-lobed leaves that are paler green beneath. Fall color usually red, sometimes orange or yellow. Attractive flaking bark on older wood. Low, spreading growth; stake and prune to make it branch high. A decorative, useful patio tree and favorite bonsai subject.

A. campestre. HEDGE MAPLE. Deciduous tree. Zones 2–9, 14–17. Native to Europe, western Asia. Slow growing to 70 ft., seldom over 30 ft. tall and wide in cultivation. Forms an especially dense, compact, rounded head in the Northwest; thinner in California. Leaves 2–4 in. wide, with three to five lobes, dull green above, downy beneath; turn yellow in fall. 'Queen Elizabeth' has glossier foliage, more erect habit.

A. capillipes. Deciduous tree. Zones 2–9, 12, 14–24. Native to Japan. Moderate growth rate to 30 ft. tall and wide. Young branches red, turning brown with white stripes with age. Shallowly three-lobed leaves are 3–5 in. long; red when new, retain red leafstalks and midribs at maturity, turn scarlet in fall. In warmer climates, does best in partial shade.

A. cappadocicum. COLISEUM MAPLE. Deciduous tree. Zones 3–6. Native to western Asia. Known in the West by its variety 'Rubrum', red coliseum maple. Grows to 35 ft. tall and wide; forms compact, rounded crown. Leaves with five to seven lobes, 5½ in. wide. Foliage is bright red when new, later turns rich dark green.

A. circinatum. VINE MAPLE. Deciduous shrub or tree. Zones A3; 2b–6, 14–17. Native to moist woods, stream banks in coastal mountains of British Columbia south to Northern California. In the forest shade, it is crooked, sprawling, and vinelike, with many stems from the base. In the open, it becomes a nearly symmetrical small tree 5–35 ft. high, with one or several trunks. Leaves nearly circular, to 6 in. across, with 5–11 lobes; red tinted when new, light green as they mature, then orange, scarlet, or yellow in fall. Tiny reddish purple spring flowers are followed by winged red seeds. 'Monroe' has deeply cut foliage.

Let it go untrimmed to make natural bowers, ideal settings for ferns and woodland flowers. Use under a canopy of tall conifers where its blazing fall color offers brilliant contrast. Can be espaliered against shady side of a wall. Its contorted leafless branches make an intricate pattern in winter.

A. davidii. DAVID'S MAPLE. Deciduous tree. Zones 2–6, 15–17, 20, 21. Native to central China. To 20–35 ft. high and wide. This maple is distinctive on several counts. Bark is shiny green striped with silvery white, particularly striking in winter. Leaves are glossy green, oval or lobed, 2–7 in. long, 1½–4 in. wide, deeply veined. New foliage bronze tinted; fall color combines bright yellow, red orange, and purple. Clustered greenish yellow flowers are showy in spring. Part shade in warmer areas.

Acer davidii

A. ×freemanii. See A. rubrum

A. ginnala. See A. tataricum ginnala

A. glabrum. ROCKY MOUNTAIN MAPLE. Deciduous shrub or tree. Zones 1–7, 10. Leaves 2–5 in. wide, three to five lobed or divided into three leaflets, borne on dark red twigs. Fruit tinged red. Fall foliage yellow. Multitrunked clumps may be only 6 ft. tall or up to 30 ft. under ideal conditions. Slender, upright branches spread one-half to two-thirds plant height. Needs well-drained soil and regular moisture. *A. g. douglasii (A. douglasii)* grows along shores of southeastern Alaska (Zones A2, A3; also succeeds in Zones 1–7, 10). It reaches 20–30 ft. tall, 20 ft. wide, has shallowly three-lobed leaves.

A. grandidentatum. See A. saccharum grandidentatum

A. griseum. PAPERBARK MAPLE. Deciduous tree. Zones 2–9, 14–21. Native to China. Grows to 25 ft. or higher; may be half as wide to equally as wide as tall. In winter it makes a striking picture with bare branches angling out and up from main trunk and reddish bark peeling away in paper-thin sheets. Late to leaf out in spring. Leaves are divided into three coarsely toothed leaflets 1½–2½ in. long, dark green above, silvery below. Inconspicuous red flowers in spring develop into showy winged seeds. Foliage turns brilliant red in fall.

A. japonicum. FULLMOON MAPLE. Deciduous shrub or tree. Zones 2–6, 14–16. Native to Japan. To 20–30 ft. high, with equal or greater spread. Nearly round, 2–5-in.-long leaves cut into 7–11 lobes. Give regular moisture, part shade in warm regions. The following varieties are small, slow growing, and best placed as shrubs.

'Aconitifolium'. FERNLEAF FULLMOON MAPLE. Leaves are deeply cut, almost to leafstalk; each lobe is also cut and toothed. Fine fall color where adapted.

'Aureum'. GOLDEN FULLMOON MAPLE. See A. shirasawanum 'Aureum'

A. macrophyllum. BIGLEAF MAPLE. Deciduous tree. Zones 2–9, 14–24. Native to stream banks, moist canyons, southern Alaska (Zone 4) to foothills of California. Dense shade tree 30–75 ft. tall, 30–50 ft. wide—too big for a small garden or a street tree. Large three- to five-lobed leaves are 6–15 in. wide, sometimes bigger on young, vigorous sapling growth; leaves turn from medium green to yellow in fall. Small, greenish yellow spring flowers are followed by tawny winged seeds hanging in long, chainlike clusters. Yellow fall color spectacular in cool areas. Resistant to oak root fungus.

Acer macrophyllum

A. negundo. BOX ELDER. Deciduous tree. Zones A2, A3; 1–10, 12–24. Native to most of U.S. The plain species is a weed tree of many faults—it seeds readily, hosts box elder bugs, suckers badly, and is subject to breakage. Fast growing to 60 ft. (usually less) and as wide or wider. Leaves divided into three to nine oval, 2–5-in.-long leaflets with toothed margins; yellow in fall. Several varieties improve on the species.

'Flamingo'. White and pink leaf markings. Some shade in warmer areas.

'Sensation'. Slower growth (to 40 ft. tall, 30 ft. wide) and better branch structure than the species. Doesn't sucker. Good deep pink fall color.

'Variegatum'. VARIEGATED BOX ELDER. Not as large or weedy as the species. Combination of green and creamy white leaves is a standout. Large, pendent clusters of white fruit are spectacular.

A. nigrum. BLACK MAPLE. Zones 1–10, 14–20. Similar to *A. saccharum* but more resistant to heat and drought. Light green leaves turn yellow in fall. 'Greencolumn' can reach 65 ft. tall, 25 ft. wide.

A. palmatum. JAPANESE MAPLE. Deciduous shrub or tree. Zones A3; 2–10, 12, 14–24. Native to Japan and Korea. Slow growing to 20 ft. with equal or greater spread; normally many-stemmed. Most airy and delicate of all maples. Leaves 2–4 in. long, deeply cut into five to nine toothed lobes. All-year interest: young spring growth is glowing red; summer leaves are soft green; fall foliage is scarlet, orange, or yellow; slender leafless branches in greens and reds provide winter pattern.

Grafted garden varieties are popular, but common seedlings have uncommon grace and usefulness: they are more rugged, faster growing, more drought tolerant, and they stand more sun and wind than named forms do. Japanese maples thrive everywhere in the Northwest, where they make good small street trees. They can be grown with success in California if given shelter from hot, dry, or constant winds. Filtered shade is best, but full sun can be satisfactory. In California, consider the local soil and water; wherever azaleas are difficult to grow and suffer from salt buildup in the soil, Japanese maples will show burn on leaf edges. Give same watering treatment as azaleas—flood occasionally to leach out salts. Resistant to oak root fungus.

Used effectively on north and east walls, in patios and entryways, as small lawn trees. Attractive in groves (like birches) as woodland planting; for natural effect, set out plants of different sizes with varying spacing. Good under oaks, as background for ferns and azaleas, alongside pools. Invaluable in tubs and for bonsai. Japanese maple is inclined to grow in flat, horizontal planes, so pruning to accentuate this growth habit is easy.

The grafted garden forms are usually smaller than seedlings, more weeping and spreading, brighter in foliage color, and more finely cut in leaf. In California, it seems that the more finely cut the leaf, the greater the leafburn problem. The following list includes some of the best.

'Atropurpureum'. RED JAPANESE MAPLE. Purplish or bronze to bronzy green leaves, brighter in sun. Holds color all summer.

'Bloodgood'. Vigorous, upright growth to 15 ft. Deep red spring and summer foliage, scarlet in fall. Blackish red bark.

'Bonfire'. Orange-pink spring and fall foliage; twisted trunk, short branches, drooping branchlets.

'Burgundy Lace'. To 12 ft. high, 15 ft. wide. Leaves more deeply cut than those of 'Atropurpureum'; branchlets bright green.

'Butterfly'. Small (to 7-ft.) shrub with small bluish green leaves edged in white. Cut out growth that reverts to plain green.

'Crimson Queen'. Small, shrubby, 9-ft. mound, with finely cut leaves that hold color all summer, turn scarlet before dropping off in fall.

'Dissectum' ('Dissectum Viridis'). LACELEAF JAPANESE MAPLE. Small shrub to 6 ft. high, 12 ft. wide, with drooping branches, green bark; pale green, finely divided leaves turn gold in autumn.

'Ever Red' ('Dissectum Atropurpureum'). A 7-ft. mound with weeping branches. Finely divided, purple-tinged, lacy foliage turns crimson in fall.

'Filiferum Purpureum'. Mounding shrub to 10 ft., with threadlike leaf segments opening dark red and aging to bronzy green.

'Garnet'. Similar to 'Crimson Queen' and 'Ever Red'; somewhat more vigorous grower.

'Ornatum' ('Dissectum Atropurpureum'). RED LACELEAF JAPANESE MAPLE. Like 'Dissectum' but with red leaves turning brighter red in autumn.

'Oshio Beni'. Like 'Atropurpureum' but more vigorous; has long, arching branches.

'Red Dragon' ('Dissectum Red Dragon'). Resembles 'Ever Red' but with deeper red-purple foliage. Holds color throughout summer; turns crimson in fall.

'Sango Kaku' ('Senkaki'). CORAL BARK MAPLE. Vigorous, upright, treelike. Yellow fall foliage. Twigs, branches striking coral red in winter.

A. pentaphyllum. Deciduous tree. Zones 4–9, 14–17. Native to China. Rare plant to 20–30 ft. tall and nearly as wide, with leaves divided down to the leafstalk into five narrow, 3-in. leaflets spread out like fingers on a

WHAT POTTED JAPANESE MAPLES NEED

Start by choosing the right variety—one that will stay small. Then pay attention to these factors:

EXPOSURE: Locate in a partly shaded, wind-protected spot.

SOIL MIX: Make sure it holds moisture but drains fast.

WATER: Give enough moisture to keep the plant good looking at all times.

FERTILIZER: Keep nutrients coming while the plant is in leaf; slow-release fertilizer will do the job well.

hand. Late to leaf out in spring. Medium green leaves turn pale orange to red in fall.

A. platanoides. NORWAY MAPLE. Deciduous tree. Zones A2, A3; 1–9, 14–17. Native to Europe, western Asia. Broad-crowned, densely foliaged tree to 50–60 ft. tall, from two-thirds as wide to equally as wide as high. Leaves five lobed, 3–5 in. wide, deep green above, paler beneath; turn yellow in fall. Showy clusters of small, greenish yellow flowers in early spring. Very adaptable, tolerating many soil and environmental conditions. Once a widely recommended street tree but now strongly objected to because of voracious roots, self-sown seedlings, and aphid-caused honeydew drip and sooty mold. Here are some of the best horticultural varieties (purple-leafed forms perform poorly in alkaline soils unless soil is conditioned).

'Cavalier'. Compact, round headed, to 30 ft.

'Cleveland' and 'Cleveland II'. Shapely, compact, well-formed trees about 50 ft. tall, 40 ft. wide.

'Columnare'. Slower grower, narrower form than the species (about 20 ft. wide).

'Crimson King'. Holds purple foliage color until leaves drop. Slower growing than the species. Fine in Northwest and California foothills.

'Deborah'. Like 'Schwedler' but faster growing, straighter.

'Drummondii'. Leaves are edged with silvery white; unusual and striking. Some shade in warm climates.

'Faassen's Black'. Pyramidal in shape, with dark purple leaves.

'Globe'. Slow growing with dense, round crown; eventually reaches 20–25 ft. high.

'Green Lace'. Finely cut, dark green leaves; moderate growth rate to 40 ft.

'Jade Glen'. Vigorous, straight-growing form with bright yellow fall color.

'Parkway'. A broader tree than 'Columnare' (about 25 ft. wide), with a dense canopy.

'Royal Red Leaf'. A good red- or purple-leafed form.

'Schwedler' ('Schwedleri'). Purplish red leaves in spring turn to dark bronzy green by summer, gold in autumn.

'Summershade'. Fast-growing, upright, heat-resistant selection.

A. pseudoplatanus. SYCAMORE MAPLE. Deciduous tree. Zones 1–9, 14–20. Native to Europe, western Asia. Moderate growth to 40 ft. high or more, and two-thirds as wide to equally as wide as tall. Leaves 3–5 in. wide, five lobed, thick, prominently veined, dark green above, pale below. No particular fall color. 'Atropurpureum' ('Spaethii') has leaves that are rich purple underneath.

A. pseudosieboldianum. Deciduous tree. Zones 2b–10, 14–18. Native to Korea, Manchuria. Rounded tree to 20 ft. tall and wide. Resembles *A. palmatum* in size, form, leaf shape, and fall color and is thought by many to be hardier to cold.

A. rubrum. RED MAPLE, SCARLET MAPLE. Deciduous tree. Zones A2, A3; 1–9, 14–17. Native to low, wet areas of eastern North America. Fairly fast growth to 60 ft. tall, 40 ft. wide (or even larger). Faster growing than *A. platanoides* or *A. pseudoplatanus.* Red twigs, branchlets, and buds; quite showy flowers. Dull red fruit. Leaves 2–4 in. long, with three to five lobes, shiny green above, pale beneath; brilliant scarlet fall color in frosty areas. Tolerates most soils. Not at its best in urban pollution. Some of the trees below, although sold as *A. rubrum,* are actually *A. ×freemanii*—hybrids between it and *A. saccharinum.*

Acer rubrum

'Armstrong' and 'Armstrong II' *(A. ×freemanii).* Very narrow (15-ft.-wide) trees. Fall color—often poor—is orange to red.

'Autumn Blaze' *(A. ×freemanii).* Dense oval, upright crown, excellent orange-red fall color.

'Autumn Radiance'. Dense oval form, orange-red fall color.

'Bowhall'. Narrow (15 ft. wide), cone shaped, with orange-red foliage in fall.

'Columnare'. Narrow (10 ft. wide), with orange-red fall color.

'Gerling'. Broadly pyramidal, to 35 ft. tall with 20-ft. spread.

'Karpick'. Narrow grower (20 ft. wide) with red twigs, yellow to red fall color.

'Northwood'. Rounded form. Extremely cold hardy.

'October Glory'. Tall, round-headed tree; last to turn color in fall.

'Red Sunset'. Upright, vigorous branching pattern.

'Scarlet Sentinel' *(A. ×freemanii).* Columnar (about 25-ft.-wide), fast-growing tree.

'Schlesingeri'. Tall, broad, fast growing, with regular form; orange-red fall color.

'Shade King'. Very fast grower. Pale green foliage turns bright red in fall.

'Tilford'. Nearly globe-shaped crown if grown in the open; pyramidal when crowded.

'V. J. Drake'. Unusual fall color; leaf borders turn red and violet while center is still green. Leaves eventually turn completely red.

A. saccharinum. SILVER MAPLE. Deciduous tree. Zones A2, A3; 1–9, 12, 14–24. Native to eastern North America. Grows fast to 40–100 ft. with equal spread. Open form, with semipendulous branches; casts fairly open shade. Silvery gray bark peels in long strips on old trees. Leaves 3–6 in. wide, five lobed, light green above, silvery beneath. In colder part of range, fall color is a mixture of scarlet, orange, and yellow—often in same leaf. Aggressive roots are hard on sidewalks, sewers.

You pay a penalty for the advantage of fast growth: weak wood and narrow crotch angles make this tree break easily. Unusually susceptible to aphids and cottony scale. Suffers from chlorosis in alkaline soils. Many rate it the least desirable of maples, but nonetheless it is often planted for fast growth and graceful habit.

'Silver Queen'. More upright form than the species, seedless. Bright gold fall color.

'Wieri' ('Laciniatum'). WIER MAPLE, CUTLEAF SILVER MAPLE. Same as species, but leaves are much more finely cut; provides open shade.

A. saccharum. SUGAR MAPLE. Deciduous tree. Zones 1–10, 14–20. Native to eastern North America. The source of maple sugar. Moderate growth to 60 ft. or taller. Stout branches with upward sweep usually form fairly compact canopy to about 40 ft. wide. Leaves 3–6 in. wide, with three to five lobes, green above, pale below. In cold-winter climates, spectacular fall color ranging from yellow and orange to deep red and scarlet. Varieties include the following.

'Arrowhead'. Erect pyramid to 30 ft. wide, with yellow to orange leaves in fall.

'Bonfire'. Bright red fall foliage.

'Commemoration'. Heavy leaf texture; orange, yellow, and red fall color.

A. s. grandidentatum (A. grandidentatum). WASATCH MAPLE, BIG-TOOTH MAPLE, ROCKY MOUNTAIN SUGAR MAPLE. Deciduous. Zones 1–3. Grows as shrub or tree, 20–30 ft. tall and wide. Leaves have three to five lobes and large, blunt teeth. Brilliant fall color in tones of yellow, orange, rose red. In nature, grows in canyons and on stream banks. In gardens, requires well-drained soil on the dry side.

'Green Mountain'. Tolerant of heat and drought; autumn leaves vary from yellow to orange to reddish orange.

'Legacy'. Fast growing, drought resistant. Fall color is red, sometimes yellow orange.

'Monumentale' ('Temple's Upright'). Narrow (15-ft.-wide), erect form with yellow-orange fall leaves.

'Sweet Shadow'. Leaves are deeply cut, with each lobe also deeply cut. Orange fall color.

A. shirasawanum 'Aureum'. GOLDEN FULLMOON MAPLE. Deciduous shrub or tree. Zones 3b–6, 14–16. Grows to 20 ft. tall and wide. Leaves open pale gold in spring and remain pale chartreuse all summer. Partial shade.

A. tataricum. TATARIAN MAPLE. Deciduous shrub or tree. Zones A2, A3; 1–6, 14–16. Native to southeastern Europe, western Asia. Reaches 20–25 ft. high and wide. Tooth-edged leaves (lobed on young plants) are 2–3½ in. long. Showy red-winged seeds appear in summer. Yellow to reddish brown fall color.

A. t. ginnala. AMUR MAPLE. Zones A1–A3; 1–9, 14–16. Native to Manchuria, northern China, Japan. Toothed leaves are three lobed, even on mature plants. Clusters of small, fragrant yellowish flowers bloom in early spring; these are followed by handsome bright red, winged seeds. Striking red fall color. 'Flame', 15–20 ft. high and wide, has especially fiery foliage in autumn. ▸

A

A. truncatum. Deciduous tree. Zones A2, A3; 1–9, 14–23. Native to China. Grows fairly rapidly to 25 ft., with equal or slightly smaller spread. Like a small *A. platanoides* with more deeply lobed leaves to 4 in. wide. Emerging leaves are purplish red, summer leaves green, autumn leaves yellow to orangish. A good lawn or patio tree.

Aceraceae. The maple family consists of deciduous, rarely evergreen, trees and shrubs with paired opposite leaves and paired, winged seeds.

ACHILLEA

YARROW

Asteraceae (Compositae)

PERENNIALS

ZONES A1–A3; 1–24

FULL SUN

LITTLE TO MODERATE WATER

Achillea tomentosa

Yarrows are among the most carefree and generously blooming perennials for summer and early fall, several being equally useful in the garden and as cut flowers (taller kinds may be cut and dried for winter bouquets). Leaves are gray or green, bitter-aromatic, usually finely divided (some with toothed edges). Flower heads are usually in flattish clusters. Yarrows need only routine care: some watering (though they endure drought once established), cutting back after bloom, dividing when clumps get crowded.

A. ageratifolia (A. serbica). GREEK YARROW. Native to Balkan region. Low, foot-wide mats of silvery leaves, toothed or nearly smooth edged. Topped by white flower clusters ½–1 in. across on stems 4–10 in. tall.

A. clavennae. SILVERY YARROW. Native to Europe. Silvery gray, silky leaves, lobed somewhat like chrysanthemum leaves, form mats about 8 in. wide. Loose, flat-topped clusters of ½–¾-in.-wide, ivory white flower heads on 5–10-in. stems. Often sold as *A. argentea.*

A. filipendulina. FERNLEAF YARROW. From Caucasus. Tall, erect plants 4–5 ft. high and to 3 ft. wide, with deep green, fernlike leaves. Bright yellow flower heads in large, flat-topped clusters. Dried or fresh, they are good for flower arrangements. Several horticultural varieties are available. 'Gold Plate' has flower clusters up to 6 in. wide. Hybrid 'Coronation Gold', to about 3 ft. high, also has large flower clusters.

A. ×kellereri. To 6 in. high, 1 ft. wide, with gray-green ferny leaves. Clusters of flower heads look like tiny white daisies with yellow centers.

A. millefolium. COMMON YARROW, MILFOIL. Native to Europe, western Asia. Erect plant with narrow green or grayish green leaves and flat-topped white flower clusters on 3-ft. stems. Spreads by underground runners. A form that grows wild on California's Channel Islands has bright pink blossoms. Many garden varieties have been selected for their flower color. 'The Beacon' ('Fanal') and 'Rosea' are bright rose pink; 'Cerise Queen' is deeper pink, 'Lavender Beauty' lavender pink, 'Weser River' rose pink fading to tan, and 'Salmon Beauty' ('Lachsschönheit') salmon pink. 'Hoffnung' is pale yellow; 'Fire King', 'Fireland', and 'Paprika' are all red (with yellow center) aging to coppery red.

Seed-grown garden strains include Garden Pastels and Debutante, with flowers ranging from white and cream to yellow and red, and Galaxy, with deeper colors. Summer Shades has both pastel and stronger colors.

A. 'Moonshine'. Resembles *A. ×taygetea,* but grows somewhat taller (to 2 ft. high) and bears deeper yellow flowers.

A. ptarmica. From Europe, Asia. Erect plant to 2 ft. high and wide. Narrow leaves with finely toothed edges. White flower heads in rather open, flattish clusters. 'The Pearl' has double flowers.

A. ×taygetea. Native to the eastern Mediterranean. Grows to 1½ ft. high and wide. Gray-green, divided leaves 3–4 in. long. Dense clusters of bright yellow flower heads fade to primrose yellow—excellent contrast in yellow until it's time to shear off old stalks. Good cut flowers.

A. tomentosa. WOOLLY YARROW. From Europe, western Asia. Makes a flat, spreading mat (to about 1½ ft. wide) of fernlike, gray-green, hairy leaves. Golden flower heads in flat clusters top 6–10-in. stems. 'Primrose Beauty' has pale yellow flowers; 'King George' has cream blooms. A good edging and a neat ground cover for small areas; used in rock gardens. Shear off dead flowers to leave attractive gray-green mat.

ACHIMENES

Gesneriaceae

PERENNIALS FROM RHIZOMES

ALL ZONES

LIGHT SHADE

REGULAR WATER

Achimenes

Group of hybrids derived from species native to Central America and the Caribbean. Related to African violet and gloxinia. To 1–2 ft. high; slender stems may be upright, spreading, or trailing. Crisp, hairy leaves are bright to dark green. Throughout summer and early fall, offer a lavish display of five-lobed, flat-faced, 1–3-in.-wide trumpets in purple, orchid, lavender, blue, white, pink, red, or orange.

Can be grown in beds as ground cover in mildest California climates and Hawaii. Even there, usually kept to containers (protected from direct sun and wind). In late winter or early spring, plant rhizomes ½–1 in. deep in moist peat moss and sand; maintain at 60°F/16°C to encourage sprouting. When 3 in. high, plant close together in pots for best show—6 to 12 plants in 6–7-in. pot or hanging basket. Use potting mix of equal parts peat moss, perlite, leaf mold. Pinch back new growth for bushy plants; leave growth unchecked in hanging baskets. In fall, when flowering ends, cut back on water so plants will die down. Leave rhizomes in dry soil over winter; or turn out of pots and store in dry perlite or vermiculite in a cool, dry place. Repot in fresh soil before spring growth begins.

ACHNATHERUM speciosum (Oryzopsis hymenoides)

INDIAN RICE GRASS

Poaceae (Gramineae)

PERENNIAL GRASS

ZONES 1–3, 10–13

FULL SUN

LITTLE OR NO WATER

Achnatherum speciosum

Native to dry regions of the Southwest and northward to Canada. Forms a clump 1–2 ft. tall and wide; tight at the base, spreading and open above. Very narrow, 6–8-in.-long leaves are bright green in cool weather, turning golden brown when summer heat comes. Open, airy flower clusters (attractive for cutting) produce seeds that were harvested by Native Americans for food. Useful plant in desert landscapes.

ACIDANTHERA bicolor. See GLADIOLUS callianthus

ACMENA smithii (Eugenia smithii)

LILLY-PILLY TREE

Myrtaceae

EVERGREEN SHRUB OR TREE

ZONES 15–17, 19–24

FULL SUN

REGULAR WATER

Acmena smithii

Australian native's big feature is its dramatic, long-lasting winter show of clustered, ¼–½-in.-wide, edible berries in white, lavender, or lavender pink. If trained, can grow as tree to 10–25 ft. high, 8–15 ft. wide.

Irregular habit improved by pruning; remove wayward growth at any time. Shiny, pinkish green to green, 3-in.-long leaves. Many small white flowers are clustered at branch tips in summer. Takes ordinary garden care but is at its best with deep, rich, moist soil. Easy to grow from seed.

ACONITUM

ACONITE, MONKSHOOD

Ranunculaceae

PERENNIALS

ZONES A1–A3; 1–9, 14–21

FULL SUN OR PARTIAL SHADE

REGULAR WATER

ALL PARTS ARE POISONOUS IF INGESTED

Aconitum napellus

Leaves, usually lobed, in basal clusters. Flowers shaped like hoods or helmets, along tall spikes. Monkshood has a definite place under trees, at the back of flower beds, or even at the edge of a shaded bog garden. Substitute for delphinium in shade.

Need some winter chill; hard to establish in warm, dry climates. Sow seeds in spring; or sow in late summer or early fall for bloom the next year. Moist, rich soil for best growth and bloom. Divide in early spring or late fall, or leave undivided for years. Die back in winter; mark site.

A. carmichaelii (A. fischeri). Native to central China. Densely foliaged plant 2–4 ft. high, nearly as wide. Leathery dark green leaves are lobed and coarsely toothed. Blooms from late summer into fall; deep purple-blue flowers form dense, branching clusters 4–8 in. long. 'Wilsonii' grows 6–8 ft. high and 1–2 ft. wide, has more open flower clusters 10–18 in. long.

A. napellus. GARDEN MONKSHOOD. Native to Europe. Upright leafy plants 2–5 ft. high to 1 ft. wide. Leaves 2–5 in. wide, divided into narrow lobes. Late summer flowers usually blue or violet, in spikelike clusters.

ACORUS

SWEET FLAG

Araceae

PERENNIALS

ZONES VARY BY SPECIES

LIGHT SHADE IN HOTTEST CLIMATES

AMPLE WATER

Acorus gramineus 'Variegatus'

Found throughout the Northern Hemisphere, these bog or aquatic plants will succeed in water or in rich, well-irrigated soil. They look like clumps or tufts of iris but are related to calla *(Zantedeschia)*. Flowers are inconspicuous. Use in damp borders, at pool edges, or in shallow water.

A. calamus. SWEET FLAG. Zones 2–10, 14–24. Sword-shaped leaves are 1½ in. wide, 4–5 ft. long, in a clump about 2 ft. wide. Foliage is fragrant when bruised, as are the thick rhizomes. 'Variegatus' has very showy white-bordered leaves. Plants die to the ground in winter.

A. gramineus. JAPANESE SWEET FLAG. Zones 3b–10, 14–24. Fans of 6–12-in., narrow, semievergreen leaves ½ in. wide rise from the ends of slowly creeping rhizomes that eventually form large clumps. Leaves of 'Licorice' are 1½ ft. long, with a licorice flavor; 'Ogon' has narrow (¼-in.), arching, 10-in.-long leaves of golden yellow. 'Variegatus' has 6–12-in.-long leaves striped with white. Dwarf 'Pusillus', 3–5 in. high, spreads very slowly and is useful between stepping-stones or as a companion plant for bonsai.

A PRACTICAL GUIDE TO GARDENING
PLEASE SEE PAGES 658–731

ACTINIDIA kolomikta

Actinidiaceae

DECIDUOUS VINE

ZONES A1–A3; 1–9, 14–17

FULL SUN OR PARTIAL SHADE

MODERATE TO REGULAR WATER

Actinidia kolomikta

Most kiwi vines are grown for delicious fruit, but this eastern Asian species is grown for its flamboyant foliage. Grows rapidly to 15 ft. or more, producing a marvelous foliage mass made up of 3–5-in.-long leaves with elongated heart shape: some in solid green, others white-splashed green, others green strikingly variegated in pink to red. Female varieties produce a bonus crop of small fruits, but male plants (which are nonfruiting) typically have better leaf color. Colors are best in cool weather and—in warmer regions—in partial shade. Clusters of small, fragrant, white flowers appear in early summer. Plants climb by twining; provide sturdy support and train new stems into place as they lengthen. Thin out growth in late dormant season.

For information on growing various types of kiwi vines for their fruit, see Kiwi.

ADENANTHOS

WOOLLYBUSH

Proteaceae

EVERGREEN SHRUBS

ZONES 8, 9, 14–24

PARTIAL SHADE IN HOTTEST CLIMATES

LITTLE TO MODERATE WATER

Adenanthos sericea

Australian natives related to and resembling grevilleas. Valued most for silvery, furry, finely divided foliage. Colorful tubular blossoms are attractive when viewed close up but are often borne sporadically. Need excellent drainage.

A. meisneri. To 3–6 ft. tall and equally broad. Foliage eventually turns smooth and green. Purplish red, 1½-in. flowers come in small clusters at branch ends; heaviest bloom in midsummer.

A. sericea. To 6–20 ft. tall and wide. Exceptionally silky, silvery foliage. Red, 1½-in. flowers are borne scantily throughout the year. Can be treated as small tree by removing bottom limbs.

ADENIUM obesum

Apocynaceae

SUCCULENT SHRUB

ZONES 23, 24; H2; OR INDOORS

FULL SUN; BRIGHT INDIRECT LIGHT

REGULAR WATER

MILKY SAP IS POISONOUS IF INGESTED

Adenium obesum

Twisted branches grow from a huge, fleshy, half-buried trunk or rootstock. Grown outdoors in the ground, can reach 9 ft. tall and half as wide. Leaves are sparse, and plant is leafless for long periods. Clustered saucer-shaped, deep pink blossoms, each 2 in. or more across, are extremely showy; plant is known as "desert rose" or "desert azalea" in eastern tropical Africa, where it is native.

This plant cannot take frost, winter chill, cold soil. Relocate potted plant to warm area when a freeze threatens. Needs heat, good light, perfect drainage, regular water during growth, dryness during dormancy—in short, this is a plant for careful enthusiasts and collectors. *A. o. swazicum* differs from the species only in technical details.

A

ADENOPHORA

LADY BELLS

Campanulaceae (Lobeliaceae)

PERENNIALS

ZONES A2, A3; 1–10, 14–24

FULL SUN OR PARTIAL SHADE

MODERATE TO REGULAR WATER

Adenophora liliifolia

Plants and flowers resemble those of medium-size campanulas. Blue or white, drooping, bell-shaped flowers in branching clusters are fragrant. Sometimes planted at woodland edge or in sunny border. Prefer fertile, well-drained soil. Long lived; resent moving once well established.

A. bulleyana. From western China. To 3 ft. tall, 1 ft. wide. Pale blue bells in autumn.

A. confusa. From western China. To 3 ft. tall, 2 ft. wide. Dark blue flowers in summer.

A. liliifolia. Native from central Europe to Siberia. To 1½ ft. high, 1 ft. wide. Pale blue or white flowers in midsummer.

ADENOSTOMA

Rosaceae

EVERGREEN SHRUBS

ZONES 6–9, 14–24

FULL SUN

NO IRRIGATION NEEDED

Adenostoma fasciculatum

These California natives resemble heather *(Calluna)* and tolerate heat, aridity, and poor, rocky soil; need good drainage in moister climates. Both of the species described below are highly flammable, so don't plant them near houses or other structures.

A. fasciculatum. CHAMISE, GREASEWOOD. Native to coastal hills of California. Tiny, needlelike, clustered leaves; tiny white flowers in dense, 2–5-in. clusters at branch tips. Ordinarily a sparse shrub 5–12 ft. tall and nearly as wide, but a prostrate form is available and makes a good ground cover for rugged slopes.

A. sparsifolium. RED SHANKS. Native to Southern California. To 6–18 ft. tall and about half as wide, with shredding red bark. Needles not clustered; flower clusters somewhat longer and more open than those of *A. fasciculatum.*

ADIANTUM

MAIDENHAIR FERN

Polypodiaceae

FERNS

ZONES VARY BY SPECIES

PARTIAL OR FULL SHADE

AMPLE WATER

Adiantum aleuticum

Most are of tropical origin; some are western natives. All form spreading clumps over time. Stems are thin, wiry, and dark. Fronds are finely cut; leaflets are mostly fan shaped, bright green, thin textured. Plants need steady moisture and soil rich in organic matter. Protect from snails and slugs. Even hardy types may die back in hard frosts. Kinds listed as indoor or greenhouse plants may succeed in sheltered outdoor spots in mild-winter areas.

A. aleuticum (A. pedatum aleuticum). FIVE-FINGER FERN, WESTERN MAIDENHAIR. Zones 1–7, 14–21. Native to North America. Fronds fork to make a fingerlike pattern atop slender stems reaching 1–2½ ft. tall. General effect is airy and fresh. Excellent choice for containers or shaded beds.

A. capillus-veneris. SOUTHERN MAIDENHAIR. Zones 5–9, 14–24; H1, H2. Native to North America. To 1½ ft. tall. Fronds are twice divided but not forked.

A. hispidulum. ROSY MAIDENHAIR. Native to tropics of Asia, Africa. Indoor or greenhouse plant. To 1 ft. tall. Young fronds rosy brown, turning medium green, shaped somewhat like those of *A. aleuticum.*

A. jordanii. CALIFORNIA MAIDENHAIR. Zones 7, 9, 14–17. Native to California, southern Oregon. Twice-divided fronds to 2 ft. tall.

A. peruvianum. SILVER DOLLAR MAIDENHAIR. Native to Peru. Indoor or greenhouse plant. To 1½ ft. or taller. Segments of leaves quite large, to 2 in. wide.

A. raddianum (A. cuneatum, A. decorum). Native to Brazil. Indoor or greenhouse plant. Fronds cut three or four times, 15–18 in. long. Many named sorts differing in texture and compactness. Grow in pots; move outdoors to a sheltered, shaded patio in summer. Commonly sold are 'Fritz-Luthii', 'Gracillimum' (very finely cut), and 'Pacific Maid'.

A. tenerum. Native to tropical America. Indoor or greenhouse plant. Long, broad fronds arch gracefully, are finely divided into many deeply cut segments ½–¾ in. wide. 'Wrightii' is similar or identical.

AECHMEA

Bromeliaceae

PERENNIALS

ZONES 22–24; H1, H2; OR INDOORS

PARTIAL SHADE; SUNNY WINDOW

KEEP CUP WITHIN LEAF ROSETTE FILLED WITH WATER

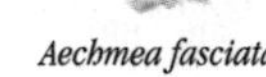

Aechmea fasciata

In frost-free areas, grow these Central and South American natives in pots, hanging baskets, or moss fastened in crotches of trees—always in shaded places with good air circulation. Indoors, need lots of light (such as east or west window) to bloom. Indoors or outdoors, soil should be fast draining but moisture retentive. Keep central tube or cup within leaves filled with water; water soil (or moss) when it's dry. Bromeliad specialists list dozens of species and varieties, and new hybrids appear frequently.

A. chantinii. Leaves 1–3 ft. long, green to gray green banded with silver or darker green. Tall flower clusters have orange, pink, or red bracts, yellow-and-red flowers. White or blue fruit.

A. fasciata. Leaves to 2 ft. long, gray green crossbanded with silvery white. From the center grows a cluster of rosy pink bracts in which nestle pale blue flowers that change to deep rose. 'Silver King' has unusually silvery leaves; leaves of 'Marginata' are edged with creamy white bands.

A. fulgens. Leaves 12–16 in. long, green dusted with gray. Flower cluster usually held above the leaves. Blossoms are red, blue, and blue violet; berries are pinkish red. *A. f. discolor* has brownish red or violet red leaves, usually faintly striped.

A. hybrids. The following are among the most commonly grown hybrid bromeliads.

'Foster's Favorite'. Bright wine red, lacquered leaves about 1 ft. long. Drooping, spikelike flower clusters are coral red and blue.

'Royal Wine'. Forms open rosette of somewhat leathery, glossy light green leaves that are burgundy red beneath. Drooping clusters of orange-and-blue flowers.

A. pectinata. Stiff rosette of leaves to 1½ ft. long, strongly marked pink or red at bloom time. Flowers whitish and green.

A. weilbachii. Shiny leaves to 2 ft. long, green or suffused with red. Dull red, 1½-ft. flower stalk has orange-red berries tipped with lilac.

FOR INFORMATION ON YOUR CLIMATE ZONE

PLEASE SEE PAGES 27–63

AEGOPODIUM podagraria

BISHOP'S WEED, GOUT WEED

Apiaceae (Umbelliferae)

PERENNIAL

ZONES A1–A3; 1–9, 12, 14–24

SUN OR SHADE

MODERATE WATER

Aegopodium podagraria 'Variegatum'

Native Europe to western Asia; naturalized in North America. Rampant ground cover, especially in rich soil. Spreads by creeping underground rootstocks; best contained by underground barrier of wood, concrete, or metal extending 8–12 in. into soil. Many light green, three-leafleted leaves make a dense mass to 6 in. high. Flat-topped clusters of inconsequential flowers rise above the leaves in summer. To neaten, mow two or three times yearly. Shear off flowering stems before they set seed to limit volunteer seedlings. Deciduous even in mild-winter areas.

'Variegatum' is the most widely planted form; commonly used in intermountain and mountain regions. Leaflets are edged white, look luminous in shade. Set plants 1 ft. apart. Pull any that revert to solid green. In warm climates, give light shade during hottest part of day.

AEONIUM

Crassulaceae

SUCCULENT PERENNIALS

ZONES 15–17, 20–24

FULL SUN IN COOLER CLIMATES ONLY

MODERATE WATER

Aeonium arboreum

Native to Canary Islands, North Africa, and the Mediterranean. Among the most useful succulents for decorative effects, in pots or in the ground. Bloom in spring, summer.

A. arboreum. To 3 ft. tall and wide. Each branch has a 6–8-in.-wide rosette of light green, lightly fringed, fleshy leaves. Yellow flowers in long clusters. 'Atropurpureum', with dark purple rosettes, is more striking and more widely grown than species. 'Zwartkop' has nearly black rosettes.

A. decorum. Bushy, rounded, many-branched plant to 10 in., each branch ending in a 2-in. rosette. Fleshy, reddish-tinted leaves with red edges. Neat, compact. Pink flowers.

A. ×floribundum. Forms 1-ft. cushion with 2–3-in. rosettes of medium green, fleshy leaves streaked with darker green. Yellow flowers.

A. haworthii. Free branching, shrubby, to 2 ft. tall and wide, with blue-green, red-edged rosettes 2–3 in. wide. White flowers.

A. 'Pseudotabulaeforme'. Smooth, flat light green rosettes to 10 in. wide. Makes offsets freely. Some gardeners remove the green flowers.

A. simsii (A. caespitosum). Low, dense, spreading, very leafy, 6 in. tall. Bright green leaf rosettes. Yellow flowers.

A. urbicum. "Dinner plate" rosettes to 8–10 in. wide. Long, narrow, light green leaves, loosely arranged, have reddish edges. White or pinkish flowers.

AESCULUS

HORSECHESTNUT, BUCKEYE

Hippocastanaceae

DECIDUOUS TREES OR SHRUBS

ZONES VARY BY SPECIES

FULL SUN

REGULAR WATER, EXCEPT AS NOTED

SEEDS OF ALL ARE SLIGHTLY TOXIC IF INGESTED

Aesculus × carnea

Leaves are divided fanwise into large, toothed leaflets. Showy spring flowers, borne at ends of branches in long, dense clusters, attract hummingbirds. In autumn, leathery fruit capsules enclose glossy seeds. Prune established horsechestnuts only to eliminate dead or damaged wood and any awkward-looking branches.

A. californica. CALIFORNIA BUCKEYE. Shrub or tree. Zones 3–10, 14–24. Native to dry slopes and canyons below 4,000-ft. elevation in Coast Ranges and Sierra Nevada foothills. Often multitrunked. Grows 10–20 ft. or taller, spreads 30 ft. or wider. New foliage is pale apple green; mature leaves have five to seven rich green, 3–6-in.-long leaflets. Striking sight in spring, when fragrant, cream-colored flower plumes make it a giant candelabra. Big pear-shaped fruits split to reveal shiny brown seeds favored for dried flower arrangements. Seeds sprout freely; seedlings make unusual bonsai subjects.

In the wild, plant drops its leaves by July, but if given moderate water will hold them until autumn. After leaf drop, silvery trunk, branches, and branchlets create an interesting silhouette.

A. ×carnea. RED HORSECHESTNUT. Tree. Zones 1–10, 12, 14–17. Hybrid between *A. hippocastanum* and *A. pavia*. To 40 ft. high, 30 ft. wide—smaller than *A. hippocastanum* and a better fit for small gardens. Round headed with large dark green leaves, each divided into five leaflets; casts dense shade. Bears hundreds of 8-in.-long plumes of soft pink to red flowers; 'Briotii' has rosy crimson flowers, 'O'Neill Red' single flowers of bright red.

A. hippocastanum. COMMON HORSECHESTNUT. Tree. Zones 1–10, 12, 14–17. Native to Europe. Reaching 60 ft. high with a 40-ft. spread, this bulky, densely foliaged plant gives heavy shade. Invasive roots can break up paved surfaces. Leaves are divided into five to seven toothed, 4–10-in.-long leaflets. Spectacular flower show: ivory blooms with pink markings are borne in 1-ft.-long plumes. 'Baumannii' has double flowers and sets no seed.

A. pavia. RED BUCKEYE. Shrub or tree. Zones 2–9, 14–24. Native to eastern U.S. Bulky growth to 12–20 ft. tall, with irregular rounded crown nearly as wide. Glossy deep green leaves with five to seven 3–6-in.-long leaflets. Narrow, erect, 10-in. clusters of bright red or orange-red (rarely yellow) flowers. Best choice for humid climates.

AETHIONEMA

STONECRESS

Brassicaceae (Cruciferae)

PERENNIALS

ZONES 1–9, 14–21

FULL SUN

LITTLE TO MODERATE WATER

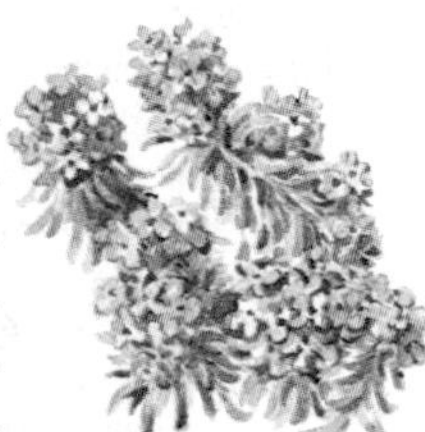

Aethionema × warleyense

Native to Mediterranean region and Asia Minor. Choice shrublets, attractive in or out of bloom. They are best adapted to colder climates and are favorites among rock gardeners. Grow best in a light, porous soil with considerable lime. Bloom late spring to summer. Deadhead flowers to extend bloom.

A. schistosum. To 5–10 in. high, 1 ft. wide. Erect, unbranched stems densely clothed with narrow, slate blue, ½-in.-long leaves. Fragrant, rose-colored flowers; petals about ¼ in. long.

A. ×warleyense (A. 'Warley Rose'). Neat, compact plant to 8 in. high and wide. Pink flowers in dense clusters. Most commonly planted stonecress in warmer climates.

AFRICAN BOXWOOD. See MYRSINE africana

AFRICAN CORN LILY. See IXIA

AFRICAN DAISY. See ARCTOTIS, DIMORPHOTHECA, OSTEOSPERMUM

AFRICAN IRIS. See DIETES

AFRICAN LINDEN. See SPARMANNIA africana

AFRICAN VIOLET. See SAINTPAULIA

A

AGAPANTHUS

LILY-OF-THE-NILE

Amaryllidaceae

PERENNIALS

ZONES 6–9, 12–24, H1, H2 FOR EVERGREEN KINDS; ZONES 4–9, 12–21 FOR DECIDUOUS KINDS

FULL SUN OR PARTIAL SHADE

LITTLE TO REGULAR WATER

Agapanthus orientalis

All of these South African natives form fountainlike clumps of strap-shaped leaves that are evergreen in some species and varieties, deciduous in others. In summer, the clumps give rise to bare stems ending in spherical clusters of funnel-shaped flowers, each cluster like a burst of blue or white fireworks. Some nursery plants are labeled only as "blue" or "white"; if you want a particular shade of blue, choose plants while they're in bloom.

Prosper in full sun or light shade where summers are mild; need some afternoon shade in hottest areas. Evergreen kinds need protective winter mulch in Zone 6. Best in loamy soil but will grow in heavy soils. Thrive with regular water, but established plants in the ground year-round can grow and bloom without irrigation during prolonged dry periods in most areas; need supplemental water in the low desert.

For mass plantings, space plants from 1 to 1½ ft. apart (use the tighter spacing for smaller varieties). Divide infrequently; every 6 years or so is usually sufficient. These are superb container plants. Good near pools. Protect from snails and slugs.

Names of species have been much confused over the years, largely because the plants hybridize so easily. It has even been suggested that all agapanthus are merely forms of one species.

A. africanus. Evergreen. Leaves shorter, narrower than those of *A. orientalis;* flower stalks shorter (to 1½ ft. high) with fewer flowers (20–50 per cluster). Blossoms are deep blue. Often sold as *A. umbellatus.*

A. campanulatus. Deciduous. To 3 ft. high, with drooping dark blue flowers. 'Albus' is white flowered.

A. inapertus. Deciduous. As tall as *A. orientalis* and nearly as many-flowered, but its deep blue blossoms are in drooping clusters.

A. orientalis (A. praecox orientalis). Evergreen. Most commonly planted. Broad, arching leaves in big clumps. Stems to 4–5 ft. tall bear up to 100 blue flowers. There are white ('Albus'), double ('Flore Pleno'), and light to fairly dark blue varieties. There are also varieties with striped leaves. Often sold as *A. africanus, A. umbellatus.*

A. selections and hybrids. Types sold by variety or hybrid name include the following. All are evergreen, except as noted.

'Elaine.' Large clusters of nodding bluish purple blossoms borne on 4-ft.-tall stems.

'Ellamae'. Large dark blue flowers on stems to 5 ft. tall.

Headbourne Hybrids. Deciduous. Flowers come in a range of blues and in white on 2½-ft.-tall stems above fairly narrow, rather upright foliage.

'Henryi'. Resembles 'Peter Pan' but has white flowers.

'Midknight Blue'. To 3–4 ft. tall, with deepest blue flowers.

'Mood Indigo'. Deciduous. Hybrid involving *A. inapertus,* with deep violet blooms on 3–4-ft. stems.

'Peter Pan'. Outstanding free-blooming dwarf variety. Foot-high foliage mass and blue flowers on 1½-ft. stems.

'Queen Anne'. Foliage clump to 1½ ft. high; blue blossoms on stems to 2 ft.

'Rancho White'. Foliage clump 1–1½ ft. high; broad leaves. Flower stalks 1½–2 ft. tall carry heavy clusters of white flowers. Also known as 'Dwarf White' and 'Rancho'. 'Peter Pan Albus' is similar or identical.

'Storm Cloud'. Evergreen in warmer part of range. Developed from deciduous 'Mood Indigo' and an evergreen agapanthus; has deep blue-violet blossoms on 4-ft. stems.

'Tinkerbell'. To 2 ft. tall, with light blue flowers and white-striped leaves.

FOR GROWING SYMBOL EXPLANATIONS
PLEASE SEE PAGE 161

AGASTACHE

Lamiaceae (Labiatae)

PERENNIALS

ZONES VARY BY SPECIES

FULL SUN OR PARTIAL SHADE

MODERATE WATER

Agastache foeniculum

Summer-blooming perennials with aromatic foliage, whorls of pink, purple, blue, red, or orange flowers in spikelike clusters. All rebloom if deadheaded. Favorites with hummingbirds. Species from Mexico and the Southwest need excellent drainage, especially in wet-winter areas.

A. aurantiaca. ORANGE HUMMINGBIRD MINT. Zones 3–24. Native to northern Mexico. To 2½ ft. tall, 2 ft. wide, with pink flowers that fade to orange. Can be grown as an annual in cold or wet regions.

A. barberi. Zones 2–24. From Arizona, New Mexico. To 2 ft. tall and wide, with reddish purple flowers.

A. breviflora. Zones 6–24. From Arizona, New Mexico, northern Mexico. To 2 ft. tall, 1½ ft. across, with spikes of purplish red blossoms.

A. cana. TEXAS HUMMINGBIRD MINT. Zones 2–24. Native to Texas, New Mexico. To 2–3 ft. tall, 1½ ft. across. Blooms heavily, bearing reddish pink flowers that smell like bubble gum. A seed-grown selection, 'Heather Queen', blooms the first year from seed sown early.

A. foeniculum. ANISE HYSSOP. Zones A3; 1–24. From north-central North America. Erect, narrow plant to 3 ft. tall and 2 ft. wide, with dense clusters of lilac blue flowers. Its anise- or licorice-scented leaves make a tasty tea. Useful and attractive in perennial borders and herb gardens. More tolerant of winter cold and wet than other species.

A. hybrids. Zones 4–24, except as noted. The following are among the many fine hybrids sold.

'Apricot Sunrise'. Zones 2b–24. To 2½ ft. tall, 2 ft. wide. Deep orange flowers fade to apricot on opening.

'Blue Fortune'. To 3 ft. tall, 1½ ft. wide, with powder blue flower spikes.

'Firebird'. To 1½–2 ft. tall, 1½ ft. wide; blooms of coppery orange red.

'Summer Breeze'. Zones 6–24. To 3 ft. tall, 2 ft. wide. Large lavender-pink flowers; dark gray-green leaves.

'Tangerine Dreams'. Zones 6–24. Forms a compact, 1½–2-ft.-wide clump; orange flowers, larger and deeper in color than those of 'Apricot Sunrise', are carried atop many 2–3-ft. stems.

'Tutti Frutti'. Zones 2b–24. To 3–4 ft. tall, 1–2 ft. wide, with purplish red blooms set off nicely by gray-green foliage.

A. mexicana. GIANT MEXICAN LEMON HYSSOP. Zones 3–24. Rangy Mexican native to 2–3 ft. (possibly to 5 ft.) tall and 1 ft. wide. Bears masses of pink flowers, starting in spring and continuing until late fall. Lemon-scented leaves can be used in tea and as a flavoring.

A. rugosa. KOREAN HUMMINGBIRD MINT. Zones 4–24. Native to Korea. To 5 ft. tall, 2 ft. wide. Licorice-scented foliage is glossy green with a purple tinge. Flowers are purplish blue. Like *A. foeniculum,* tolerates wet winters. 'Honeybee Blue' and 'Honeybee White' are compact growers 2–2½ ft. high. The species and its varieties will bloom the first year from seed sown early.

A. rupestris. LICORICE MINT, SUNSET HYSSOP. Zones 1–24. From southern Arizona, northern Mexico. To 1½–2½ ft. tall and 1½ ft. wide, with narrow, fragrant gray-green leaves and spikes of orange flowers with lavender calyxes. Outstanding garden performance.

Agastache rupestris

AGATHAEA coelestis. See FELICIA amelloides

Agavaceae. The agave family contains rosette-forming, sometimes treelike plants generally from dry regions. Flower clusters are spikelike; leaves often contain tough fibers.

AGAVE

Agavaceae

SUCCULENT PERENNIALS

ZONES VARY BY SPECIES

FULL SUN OR PARTIAL SHADE

LITTLE TO MODERATE WATER, EXCEPT AS NOTED

Agave attenuata

Succulents with large clumps of fleshy, strap-shaped leaves. The flower clusters are big but not colorful. After flowering—which may not occur for years—the foliage clump dies, usually leaving behind suckers that make new plants. The plants shrivel from serious drought but plump up again with watering or rainfall. Provide good drainage. Species listed here are native to Mexico, except as noted.

A. americana. CENTURY PLANT. Zones 10, 12–24; H1, H2. Blue-green leaves grow to 6 ft. long, and have hooked spines along the margins with a wicked spine at the tip. Be sure you really want one before planting it: its bulk (to 10 ft. wide) and spines make it formidable to remove. After 10 years or more, the plant produces a branched, 15–40-ft. flower stalk bearing yellowish green flowers. There are several varieties available with yellow- or white-striped leaves.

A. attenuata. Zones 13, 20–24; H1, H2. Leaves 2½ ft. long, soft green or gray green, fleshy, somewhat translucent, without spines. Makes clumps to 5 ft. across; older plants develop a stout trunk to 5 ft. tall. Greenish yellow flowers borne densely on arching spikes to 12–14 ft. long. Will take poor soil but does best in rich soil with regular water. Protect from frost and hot sun. Statuesque container plant. Good near ocean or pool.

A. filifera. Zones 12–24. Hardy to 17°F/–8°C. Rosettes less than 2 ft. wide; narrow dark green leaves are lined with white and edged with long white threads.

A. parryi. Zones 2b, 3, 6–24. Native to Southwest and Mexico. Gray-green 2–3-ft.-wide rosettes. Leaf tips fiercely spined. Makes offsets freely.

A. victoriae-reginae. Zones 10, 12, 13, 15–17, 21–24. Clumps only a foot or so across. The many dark green leaves are 6 in. long, 2 in. wide, stiff, thick, with narrow white lines. Slow growing; will stand in pot or ground 20 years before flowering (greenish flowers on tall stalks), then die.

A. vilmoriniana. OCTOPUS AGAVE. Zones 12–24. Pale green or yellowish green rosettes up to 6 ft. wide. Leaves 3–4 in. wide, fleshy, deeply channeled above, with a single long spine at the end. Arching, twisted leaves give plant look of an octopus or a huge spider. Handsome in pots.

AGERATINA altissima. See EUPATORIUM rugosum

AGERATUM houstonianum

FLOSS FLOWER

Asteraceae (Compositae)

ANNUAL

ZONES 1–24

FULL SUN IN COOLER CLIMATES ONLY

REGULAR WATER

Ageratum houstonianum

Reliable favorite for summer and fall color in borders and containers; can be grown as a winter annual in mild-winter climates. Native to Central America, West Indies. Hairy, soft green leaves are roundish, usually heart shaped at the base. Tiny blue flowers in dense clusters resemble powder puffs. Dwarf kinds (4–6 in. high) include 'Blue Blazer', 'Blue Danube' ('Blue Puffs'), 'Blue Surf', and 'Royal Delft'. 'Neptune', 6–8 in. high, produces its new blooms directly above and concealing older flowers. Somewhat taller (9–12-in.) types include 'Blue Mink' and 'North Sea'. 'Capri' and 'Southern Cross', to 1 ft. high, have clusters of blue flowers with white centers. 'Blue Horizon', to 2½ ft. tall, good as midborder plant and for cutting. Good varieties in other colors are 'Pink Powder-puffs' and white-blooming 'Summer Snow', both 9 in. high. Most floss flowers form foot-wide clumps.

Best in rich, moist soil. Easy to transplant even when in bloom. Low growers make excellent edgings or pattern plantings with other annuals of similar size. Taller types provide good cut flowers.

AGLAONEMA

Araceae

PERENNIALS

ZONE H2; OR INDOORS

PARTIAL SHADE; CAN TAKE VERY LOW LIGHT

REGULAR WATER

Aglaonema 'Silver King'

Tropical Asian plants valued mostly for their ornamental foliage. Flowers resemble small, greenish white callas *(Zantedeschia)*. Used in shady borders in Hawaii; elsewhere, they're houseplants. Among the best plants for poorly lighted situations. In fact, few plants can get by on as little light as aglaonema; *A. modestum* is especially tolerant of low light.

Potted plants need a rich, porous potting mix; thrive with lots of water but get by with little. Cut stems will grow for a long time in water. Exudation from leaf tips, especially of *A. modestum,* spots wood finishes.

A. commutatum. Grows to 2 ft. tall and wide. Deep green leaves to 6 in. long, 2 in. across, with pale green markings on veins. Flowers are followed by inch-long clusters of yellow to red berries. *A. c. maculatum,* with many irregular gray-green stripes on leaves, is the most common. 'Pseudobracteatum', 1–2 ft. tall, has white leafstalks and deep green leaves marked pale green and creamy yellow. 'Treubii' has narrow bluish green leaves marked with silvery gray.

A. costatum. Slow growing to 2½ ft. high and wide. Broad deep green leaves have white spots and a broad white stripe along the midrib. 'Foxii' is similar or identical.

A. crispum (A. roebelenii). To 4 ft. tall and broad. Robust plant with leathery leaves to 10 in. long, 5 in. wide, dark green with pale green markings. Sometimes sold as *A.* 'Pewter'.

A. modestum. CHINESE EVERGREEN. Easy to grow, in time forming substantial, several-stemmed clumps 2–3 ft. high and wide. Shiny dark green leaves to 1½ ft. long, 5 in. wide. Often sold as *A. simplex.*

A. 'Silver King' and **'Silver Queen'.** Both are heavy producers of narrow, dark green leaves strongly marked with silver. Both grow to 2 ft. high and wide. 'Silver King' has larger leaves than 'Silver Queen'.

AGONIS

Myrtaceae

EVERGREEN TREES OR SHRUBS

ZONES 15–17, 20–24

FULL SUN OR PARTIAL SHADE

LITTLE TO REGULAR WATER

Agonis flexuosa

Native to Australia. Very tolerant of different soil types and watering practices. Related to *Leptospermum* and *Melaleuca.*

A. flexuosa. PEPPERMINT TREE, AUSTRALIAN WILLOW MYRTLE. One of the best small trees for California gardens where temperatures stay above 27°F/–3°C. Will freeze to the ground at 25°F/–4°C but may come back from a stump if not severely frozen. Spreading, medium-fast grower to 25–35 ft. tall and 15–30 ft. wide. Narrow, willowlike leaves to 6 in. long densely clothe the weeping branches. Leaves smell like peppermint when crushed. Small white flowers bloom profusely in late spring. Use it in a lawn, train it as an espalier, or use it as a tub plant.

A. juniperina. JUNIPER MYRTLE. More open and finely textured than *A. flexuosa* but grows to about the same size. Narrow, ¼–½-in.-long, soft green leaves. Bears fluffy white flower clusters, summer into fall.

AGROPYRON

WHEATGRASS
Poaceae (Gramineae)
PERENNIAL GRASSES
ZONES 1–3, 10
FULL SUN
MODERATE WATER

Agropyron smithii

Two kinds of wheatgrass, both basically pasture grasses, make reasonably attractive lawns in Rocky Mountains and high plains. They can survive with 8–18 in. of rainfall per year, but when planted close and mowed at 2 in. they should be soaked to 18–20 in. every month. Plant 2 lbs. per 1,000 sq. ft.

A. cristatum. CRESTED WHEATGRASS. Native to Eurasia; naturalized in U.S. Bunching rather than sod-forming grass. Fairway strain, used for low-maintenance, low-irrigation lawns, is shorter, denser, and finer than common kind.

A. smithii. WESTERN WHEATGRASS. Native to western U.S. Forms sod, but slowly. Tolerates intense heat and cold; takes moderately alkaline soil.

AGROSTEMMA githago

CORN COCKLE
Caryophyllaceae
ANNUAL
ZONES 1–24
FULL SUN
MODERATE WATER
ALL PARTS ARE POISONOUS IF INGESTED

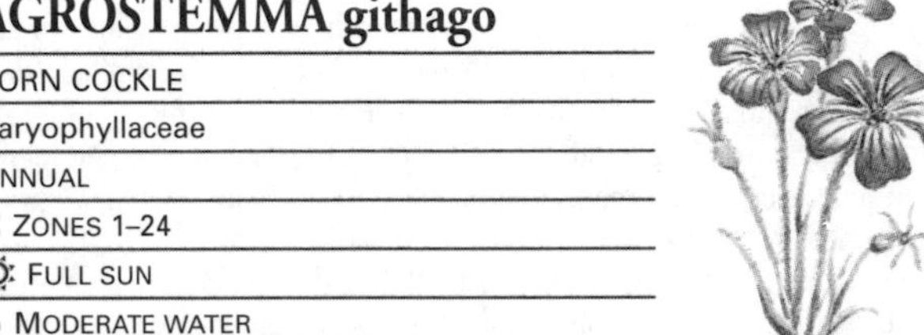
Agrostemma githago

This attractive weed of roadside and grain field is a Mediterranean species that has naturalized in North America. Several varieties offered are superior plants; they're 2–3 ft. tall and 1 ft. wide, wispy but sturdy. (Like the species, they will self-sow.) Blooms are 2–3 in. wide, on 6–12-in. stems; make good cut flowers. 'Milas' has deep purplish pink blossoms lined and spotted with deep purple and centered with a white eye; 'Purple Queen' bears deeper purple-pink blooms; 'Ocean Pearl' has white flowers with black flecks. Sow seeds in spring or early summer for summer and fall bloom (or in fall for winter-to-spring bloom in mild-winter climates). Mass at rear of border, among shrubs, or in front of fence or hedge. Self-sown seedlings of varieties tend to revert to the dark pink–flowered, plain species over time.

AGROSTIS

BENT, BENT GRASS
Poaceae (Gramineae)
PERENNIAL GRASSES
ZONES 1–10, 14–24; BEST WHERE SUMMERS ARE COOL TO MILD
FULL SUN
REGULAR TO AMPLE WATER

Agrostis stolonifera

All except *A. gigantea* make beautiful velvety lawns—and the best putting greens—under proper conditions and with constant care. They need frequent close mowing, frequent feeding, occasional topdressing, and much water. In hot weather they succumb to fungal diseases. In San Francisco Bay Area and western Oregon and Washington, bent grasses (planted intentionally or distributed by birds) tend to dominate bluegrasses and fescues.

A. gigantea. REDTOP. Coarser than other bents; not generally used in lawns. Has been used as quick-sprouting nurse grass in mixtures or for winter overseeding of Bermuda and other winter-dormant grasses.

A. stolonifera (A. palustris). CREEPING BENT. Premium lawn but requires the most care, including frequent mowing to ½ in. tall with special mower. Seed-grown strains include Emerald, Penncross, and Seaside. In some areas you can buy sprigs or sod of the choice strains Congressional, Old Orchard.

A. tenuis. COLONIAL BENT. More erect than *A. stolonifera;* somewhat easier to care for but still fussy. Astoria and Highland are best-known strains; the latter is tougher, hardier, more disease resistant. Mow to ¾ in.

AILANTHUS altissima

TREE-OF-HEAVEN
Simaroubaceae
DECIDUOUS TREE
ZONES 2B–24
FULL SUN
LITTLE OR NO WATER TO REGULAR WATER

Ailanthus altissima

Native to China, but naturalized over much of the U.S. Planted in the 1800s in California's gold country, where it now runs wild. Fast growth to 50 ft. tall and wide. Leaves 1–3 ft. long are divided into 13–25 leaflets 3–5 in. long. Flowers on male trees are smelly. On the female trees, the inconspicuous greenish flowers are usually followed by handsome clusters of red-brown, winged seedpods in late summer and fall; great for dried arrangements. Though often condemned as a weed tree because it suckers profusely and self-seeds, it must be praised for its ability to create beauty and shade under adverse conditions—aridity, hot winds, extreme air pollution, and every type of difficult soil. It is the tree that survived against all odds in *A Tree Grows in Brooklyn.*

AIR PLANT. See KALANCHOE pinnata

Aizoaceae. This family of succulent plants includes all the ice plants and most of the so-called living stones.

AJUGA

CARPET BUGLE
Lamiaceae (Labiatae)
PERENNIALS
ZONES A2, A3; 1–24
FULL SUN OR PARTIAL SHADE
REGULAR WATER

Ajuga reptans

Of the European natives listed below, one is a rock garden plant; the others are ground covers. Of the latter, the highly variable *A. reptans* is better known and more useful, though it will escape into lawns unless contained. All bloom from spring to early summer.

A. genevensis. Rock garden plant 5–14 in. high, 1½ ft. wide; does not spread by runners. Grayish, hairy stems and coarse-toothed leaves to 3 in. long. Flowers in blue spikes; rose and white forms are also sold.

A. pyramidalis. Erect plant 2–10 in. high, 1½–2 ft. wide; does not spread by runners. Stems, with long grayish hairs, have many roundish 1½–4-in.-long leaves. Violet blue flowers are not obvious among the large leaves. 'Metallica Crispa' has reddish brown leaves with a metallic glint.

A. reptans. The popular ground cover carpet bugle spreads quickly by runners, making a mat of dark green leaves in the basic species. Each oval to tongue-shaped leaf is 2–3 in. wide in full sun, to 4 in. wide in part shade; entire foliage mass tops out at around 4 in. high. Blue flowers in 6-in. spikes appear in spring and early summer. Plant 1 ft. apart in spring or early fall. Subject to root rots and fungal diseases where drainage or air circulation is poor. Mow or trim off old flower spikes. Many varieties of this species are available, some sold under several names. The following are among the best choices; all have blue flowers unless otherwise noted. Varieties with bronzy or metallic-looking leaves keep color best in sun.

'Alba'. White-blooming form.

'Burgundy Lace' ('Burgundy Glow'). Reddish purple foliage variegated with white and pink.

'Catlin's Giant'. Large, bronzy green leaves and flower spikes to 8 in. tall.

'Giant Bronze'. Deep metallic bronze leaves are larger, more vigorous, and crisper than in basic species. To 6 in. high in sun, 9 in. in part shade.

'Giant Green'. Like 'Giant Bronze' but with bright green leaves.

'Jungle Bronze'. Clumps of large, rounded, wavy-edged, bronze-toned leaves; flower spikes to 8–10 in. high.

'Jungle Green'. Large-leafed variety with green foliage. Less mounded than 'Jungle Bronze'.

'Multicolor'. Leaves are green blended with white and pinkish purple.

'Purpurea' ('Atropurpurea'). Bronze-tinted green leaves.

'Rosea'. Pink blossoms.

'Variegata'. Leaves edged and splotched with creamy yellow.

AKEBIA quinata

FIVELEAF AKEBIA

Lardizabalaceae

DECIDUOUS VINE, SEMIEVERGREEN IN MILD WINTERS

ZONES 2–24

SUN OR SHADE

REGULAR WATER

Akebia quinata

Native to Japan, China, and Korea. Twines to 15–30 ft. Grows fast in mild regions, more slowly where winters are cold. Valued chiefly for its dainty leaves on 3–5-in. stalks, each divided into five deep green leaflets 2–3 in. long, notched at tips. Clusters of quaint, dull purple, vanilla-scented flowers in spring are more a surprise than a show. The edible fruit, if produced, looks like a thick, 2½–4-in.-long, purplish sausage.

Give support for climbing. Keep plant under control to prevent it from becoming rampant. Benefits from annual winter pruning. Recovers quickly when cut to the ground. For a tracery effect on post or column, prune out all but two or three basal stems. Can also be used as ground cover in large spaces; plant 6 ft. apart.

A. trifoliata, threeleaf akebia, is like the above but with three instead of five leaflets per leaf.

ALASKA CEDAR. See CHAMAECYPARIS nootkatensis

ALBIZIA (Albizzia)

Fabaceae (Leguminosae)

DECIDUOUS AND SEMIEVERGREEN TREES

ZONES VARY BY SPECIES

FULL SUN OR PARTIAL SHADE

WATER NEEDS VARY BY SPECIES

Albizia julibrissin

These trees have twice-divided, finely textured foliage and powder-puff flowers that are attractive to birds.

A. distachya (A. lophantha). PLUME ALBIZIA. Semievergreen. Zones 15–17, 22–24. Native to Australia. Not as hardy as the better-known *A. julibrissin*. In California coastal areas, it often naturalizes. Needs no irrigation; will grow in pure sand at beach. Fast growing to 20 ft. tall, with irregular, sprawling habit. Foliage is dark velvety green and fernlike. Late spring flowers are greenish yellow, in fluffy, 2-in.-long spikes. Best as a temporary screen at beach while slower permanent planting develops. Grown inland, it gets shabby looking.

A. julibrissin. SILK TREE, MIMOSA. Deciduous. Zones 4–23. Native to Asia, ranging from Iran to Japan. Rapid growth to 40 ft., with a canopy spreading to as much as twice the tree's height. Can be headed back to make a 10–20-ft.-tall umbrella. Ferny, pale yellowish green leaves are light sensitive and fold at night. Fluffy pink flowers like pincushions bloom in summer. 'Rosea' has richer pink flowers and is considered hardier. Silk tree does best with high summer heat; it's one of the best sellers in inland valleys of Southern California. In Zones 4 and 5, plant in the warmest possible locations. With regular water grows fast; on skimpy moisture usually survives but grows slowly, looks yellowish.

Unique flat-topped, spreading canopy makes this a good patio tree, despite fallen leaves, flowers, and pods. Because of undulating form and flowers held above the foliage, it's especially beautiful when viewed from above, as from a deck or hilltop. Most attractive if allowed to assume its natural habit, as a multistemmed tree. Somewhat of a problem to get started as a high-headed tree: it must be staked and trained (any buds too low on the trunk should be rubbed out with the thumb). You'll have best success with trees planted from containers established at least 1 year.

ALCEA rosea (Althaea rosea)

HOLLYHOCK

Malvaceae

BIENNIAL OR SHORT-LIVED PERENNIAL

ZONES 1–24

PARTIAL SHADE IN HOTTEST CLIMATES

REGULAR WATER

Alcea rosea

Old-fashioned favorite from the Mediterranean region has its place against a fence or wall or at the back of a border. Old single varieties can reach 9 ft. tall; newer strains and selections are shorter. Big, rough, roundish heart-shaped leaves, more or less lobed, form a clump to about 3 ft. wide. Summer flowers are 3–6 in. wide, carried on spikes; they may be single, semidouble, or double and come in colors including white, pink, rose, red, purple, creamy yellow, apricot. Chater's Double is a fine perennial strain; 6-ft. spires have 5–6-in.-wide flowers. So-called annual strains (biennials treated as annuals) that bloom first year from seed include 5–6-ft.-tall Summer Carnival, with double 4-in. flowers, and 2½-ft.-tall Majorette, with 3–4-in. blossoms.

Sow seeds in ground in late summer for next season's bloom; seed annual strains in early spring for bloom that summer. After flowers fade, cut stalks just above the ground; continue to feed and water plants to encourage late summer or early fall rebloom. Destroy any rust-infected leaves as soon as disease appears. Watch for slugs, snails.

ALCHEMILLA

LADY'S-MANTLE

Rosaceae

PERENNIALS

ZONES VARY BY SPECIES

FULL SUN IN COOLER CLIMATES ONLY

REGULAR WATER

Alchemilla mollis

Rounded, pale green, lobed leaves have a silvery look; after rain or overhead watering, they hold beads of water on their surfaces. Summer flowers are yellowish green, in large branched clusters, individually inconspicuous but attractive as a mass. Useful for edgings in shady places, as ground cover, and as soothing contrast to brightly colored flowers.

A. alpina. Zones 1–9, 14–17. Native to northern Europe, Greenland. Mat-forming plant creeping by runners, with flowering stems 6–8 in. tall. Leaves 2 in. wide, divided into five to seven leaflets. ▸

A

A. ellenbeckii. Zones 14–24. Native to mountains of East Africa. Attractive small-scale ground cover to about 2 in. high, with creeping, rooting stems and leaves less than 1 in. wide.

A. erythropoda. Zones 1–9, 14–24. Native to mountains of Balkans, Turkey. Resembles *A. glaucescens* but has more deeply lobed leaves and red-tinted flowering stems.

A. glaucescens (A. pubescens). Zones 3–9, 14–24. Native to Europe. Dense grower, wide spreading in time. Nearly round leaves with seven to nine lobes. Flowering stems to 8 in. high.

A. mollis. Zones A2, A3; 1–9, 14–24. Native to Asia Minor. Most commonly planted lady's-mantle. Clump-forming plant to 2 ft. or taller, 2½ ft. wide. Nearly circular, scallop-edged leaves to 6 in. across. Self-sows.

A. pectinata. Zones 14–24. Native to Mexico. Miniature, creeping ground cover with inch-wide leaves.

ALDER. See ALNUS

ALDER BUCKTHORN. See RHAMNUS frangula

ALEURITES moluccana

KUKUI, CANDLENUT TREE

Euphorbiaceae

EVERGREEN TREE

ZONES 23, 24; H2

FULL SUN

REGULAR WATER

Aleurites moluccana

Native to Polynesia and southern Asia; has naturalized in Hawaii, where it has been designated the official state tree. Fast growing to 35–60 ft. high and as wide, with upright to spreading habit. Leaves are variable, often lobed, up to 8 in. long, covered with short hairs that give them a distinctive frosted appearance. Tiny white flowers, produced in branched clusters, are followed by green, 2-in. fruits. These are rich in oil used by Polynesians for fuel and cooking; the polished kernels are used in leis. Kukui is useful as a specimen or massed in a grove where litter won't present a problem. Needs well-drained soil. Moderate tolerance to wind, salt. Will take some shade.

ALEXANDRA PALM. See ARCHONTOPHOENIX alexandrae

ALGERIAN IVY. See HEDERA canariensis

ALLAMANDA

Apocynaceae

EVERGREEN VINES OR SHRUBS

ZONES 23, 24; H1, H2; ANYWHERE AS INDOOR/OUTDOOR PLANTS

FULL SUN

REGULAR WATER

ALL PARTS ARE POISONOUS IF INGESTED

Allamanda cathartica

These handsome plants from tropical South and Central America tolerate very little frost and require considerable heat for proper growth and bloom; warm nights as well as warm days seem necessary. Trumpet-shaped flowers (borne nearly year-round) and foliage are both imposing. Permanent outdoor plants only in the mildest climates. Elsewhere, grow as summer-blooming potted plants; keep indoors during cold weather.

A. blanchetii (A. violacea). PURPLE ALLAMANDA. Shrubby or with a few vining stems; usually grows 6–10 ft. tall and wide. Somewhat downy leaves up to 5 in. long. Rose purple flowers are 4½ in. across. 'Chocolate Cherry' and 'Chocolate Swirl' have pinkish purple flowers with purple-brown throats.

A. cathartica. ALLAMANDA, GOLDEN TRUMPET. Can grow to great heights (over 50 ft.) as a vine; it can clamber through trees but must be tied to other supports. Often pinched back to grow as a large freestanding shrub. Leaves are glossy, leathery, 4–6 in. long. Yellow trumpets are 5 in. wide, 3 in. long. 'Flore Pleno' has double flowers. 'Hendersonii' bears exceptionally attractive orange-yellow blooms.

ALLIUM

ORNAMENTAL ALLIUM

Liliaceae

PERENNIALS FROM BULBS

ZONES VARY BY SPECIES; OR DIG AND STORE

FULL SUN OR PARTIAL SHADE

REGULAR WATER DURING GROWTH AND BLOOM

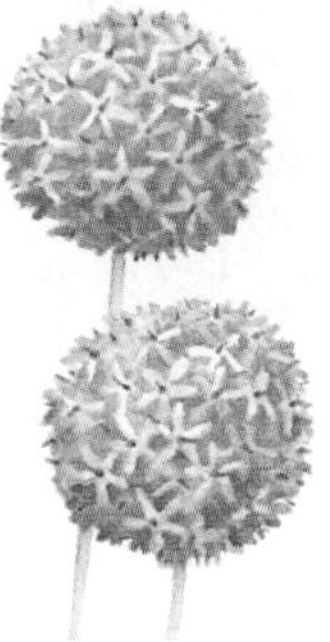
Allium giganteum

About 500 species, all from the Northern Hemisphere, many from mountains of the West. Relatives of the edible onion, they are peerless as cut flowers (fresh or dried) and useful in borders; smaller kinds are effective in rock gardens. Bear small flowers in roundish, compact or loose clusters at ends of leafless stems that range in height from 6 in. to 5 ft. or taller. Many are delightfully fragrant; those with onion odor must be bruised or cut to give it off. Bloom in spring or summer, with flowers in white and shades of pink, rose, violet, red, blue, and yellow.

All prefer well-drained soil (preferably on the sandy side), enriched before planting with organic matter. In fall or spring, plant bulbs as deep as their height or width, whichever is greater. Space smaller species 4–6 in. apart, larger ones 8–12 in. apart. Cut back on watering or let soil go dry when foliage begins to yellow after flowering. Foliage dies to the ground, even in mild-winter areas. Lift and divide only after clumps become crowded. In areas colder than stated hardiness, dig and store; or grow in pots and protect during winter.

A. aflatunense. Zones 2–24. Clusters of lilac flowers on stems 2½–5 ft. tall. Resembles *A. giganteum* but with smaller (2–3-in.) flower clusters; blooms in spring.

A. albopilosum. See A. christophii

A. atropurpureum. Zones 1–24. Stems to 2½ ft. tall carry 2-in. clusters of dark purple to nearly black flowers in summer.

A. caeruleum (A. azureum). BLUE ALLIUM. Zones 1–24. Cornflower blue flowers in dense clusters to 2 in. across on 1-ft.-tall stems. Late spring bloom.

A. carinatum pulchellum (A. pulchellum). Zones 3–24. Tight clusters of reddish purple flowers on 2-ft. stems in summer.

A. cepa. See Onion

A. christophii (A. albopilosum). STAR OF PERSIA. Zones 1–24. Distinctive. Very large clusters (6–12 in. across) of lavender to deep lilac, starlike flowers with metallic sheen, late spring. Stems 12–15 in. tall. Leaves to 1½ ft. long, white and hairy beneath. Dried flower cluster looks like an elegant ornament.

A. giganteum. GIANT ALLIUM. Zones 2–24. Summer bloomer bearing spectacular softball-size clusters of bright lilac flowers on stems to 5 ft. or taller. Leaves 1½ ft. long, 2 in. wide.

A. 'Globemaster'. Zones 2–24. Bears 6–8-in. clusters of deep violet flowers in summer, on stems rising to 2½ ft. or a little taller.

A. karataviense. TURKESTAN ALLIUM. Zones 1–24. Bears large, dense flower clusters in midspring, varying in color from pinkish to beige to reddish lilac. Broad, recurved leaves, 2–5 in. across.

A. moly. GOLDEN GARLIC. Zones 1–24. Bright, shining yellow flowers in open clusters on 9–18-in.-tall stems, late spring. Flat leaves 2 in. wide, almost as long as flower stems.

A. narcissiflorum. Zones 3–24. Foot-tall stems with loose clusters of ½-in., bell-shaped, bright rose flowers. Summer bloom.

A. neapolitanum. Zones 4–24. Spreading clusters of large white flowers on 1-ft. stems bloom in midspring. Leaves 1 in. wide. 'Grandiflorum' is larger, blooms earlier. A form of 'Grandiflorum' listed as 'Cowanii' is considered superior. Grown commercially as cut flowers.

A. oreophilum (A. ostrowskianum). Zones 1–24. Large, loose clusters of rose-colored flowers on 8–12-in. stems in late spring; two to three narrow, gray-green leaves. 'Zwanenburg' has deep carmine red flowers, 6-in. stems. Good for rock gardens, cutting.

A. porrum. See Leek

A. pulchellum. See A. carinatum pulchellum

A. rosenbachianum. Zones 2–24. Similar to *A. giganteum* but slightly smaller; blooms in late spring. 'Album' has greenish white flowers.

A. sativum. See Garlic

A. schoenoprasum. CHIVES. Zones A1–A3; 1–24; H1, H2. Clumps to 2 ft. high (usually shorter). Leaves look grasslike but are round and hollow in cross section. Clusters of rose purple spring flowers (like clover blossoms) atop thin stems. Use as edging in flower border or herb garden. Small divisions can be potted in rich soil and grown on a windowsill. Chop or snip leaves; use as garnish for delicate onionlike flavor.

A. scorodoprasum. See Garlic

A. siculum. See Nectaroscordum siculum

A. sphaerocephalum. DRUMSTICKS, ROUND-HEADED GARLIC. Zones 1–24. Tight, dense, spherical red-purple flower clusters on 2-ft. stems in summer. Spreads freely.

A. tuberosum. CHINESE CHIVES, GARLIC CHIVES, ORIENTAL GARLIC. Zones 1–24; H1, H2. Clumps of gray-green, flat leaves ¼ in. wide, 1 ft. long or less. Abundance of 1–1½-ft.-tall stalks bear clusters of white flowers in summer. Flowers have scent of violets, are excellent for fresh or dry arrangements. Leaves have mild garlic flavor, are useful in salads and cooked dishes.

A. unifolium. Zones 3–9, 14–24. California native. Extremely handsome satiny, lavender-pink flowers on 1–2-ft. stems in late spring.

Allium tuberosum

ALLOPLECTUS nummularia. See NEMATANTHUS gregarius

ALLSPICE, CAROLINA. See CALYCANTHUS floridus

ALMOND

Rosaceae

DECIDUOUS TREES

ZONES 2B, 3B, 8–10, 12–16, 19–21

FULL SUN

MODERATE WATER

Almond

Botanically known as *Prunus dulcis;* native to Asia Minor and North Africa. As a tree, it is nearly as hardy as peach (its close relative), but as a nut producer it is more exacting in climate adaptation. Trees bear best where summers are long, hot, and dry; nuts will not develop properly in areas with cool summers or high humidity. Need some winter chill yet must be spared from frosts at the wrong time. Trees bloom early (winter or early spring), and frost then will cut the crop; late frosts will destroy small nuts that are forming. To experiment in areas where frost is a hazard, choose late-blooming varieties. Unless you choose a self-fruitful type, two varieties that bloom at the same time are needed for pollination (they can be planted in the same hole if space is tight).

Nuts are borne on spurs that are productive for about 5 years; each dormant season, remove about a fifth of the oldest fruiting wood to encourage development of new spurs.

Trees reach 20–30 ft. high, erect when young, spreading and dome shaped in age. Leaves are 3–5 in. long, pale green with gray tinge; flowers are palest pink or white. Fruit looks like leathery, flattened, undersize green peach; in late summer or fall, the hull splits to reveal the pit, which is the almond. Harvest nuts after hulls have cracked open and are partially dry. You can knock or shake them from the tree; waiting for them to drop takes too long, carries risk of rotting. Peel off hulls and spread nuts in the sun for a day or two to dry. To test for adequate dryness, shake nuts—kernels should rattle.

Adapt to all soils except heavy, slow-draining ones. Need deep soil (at least 6 ft). Subject to attack by brown rot (causes fruit rot, twig dieback, cankers on trunk and branches) and mites (cause premature yellowing and falling of leaves). The following are the main varieties sold for nuts. For flowering almonds, see *Prunus triloba.*

'All-in-One'. Semidwarf tree blooms at same time as 'Mission' and 'Nonpareil'. Medium to large sweet, soft-shelled nuts. Self-fruitful. Best variety for home gardens.

'Butte'. Semihard-shelled nut, slightly smaller than 'Mission'. Very productive tree. Late bloomer, flowering just before 'Mission'. Pollinate with 'All-in-One', 'Nonpareil', or 'Mission'.

'Garden Prince'. Genetic dwarf with showy pink blooms and medium-size soft-shelled nuts. Self-fruitful.

'Hall' ('Hall's Hardy'). Hard-shelled, bitter, small nut of low quality. Pink bloom comes late, an advantage in late-frost regions. Tree may actually be a peach-almond hybrid. Partially self-fruitful but better with 'Mission' as pollenizer.

'Mission' ('Texas'). Small, semihard-shelled nut. Regular, heavy producer. Late bloomer, one of the safest for cold-winter, late-frost areas. Pollinate with 'Hall'.

'Ne Plus Ultra'. Large kernels in attractive soft shells. Pollinate with 'Nonpareil'.

'Nonpareil'. Excellent all-around variety. Easily shelled by hand. Midseason bloomer; some bud failure where summers are very hot. Pollinate with 'All-in-One', 'Mission', 'Ne Plus Ultra'.

'Titan'. Sweet, high-quality kernel in thin shell. Late bloomer. Pollinate with 'Hall' or any peach blooming at the same time.

ALMOND, FLOWERING. See PRUNUS triloba

ALNUS

ALDER

Betulaceae

DECIDUOUS TREES

ZONES VARY BY SPECIES

SUN OR SHADE

REGULAR TO AMPLE WATER

Alnus rhombifolia

Moisture-loving trees that thrive in moist or wet soils, even tolerate periodic flooding. Good near creeks and other waterways. Very fast growing. In all species, clusters of tassel-like, greenish yellow male flower catkins give interesting display before leaf-out. Female flowers develop into small woody cones that decorate bare branches in winter; these delight flower arrangers. Seeds attract birds. Alders need little pruning except to remove suckers, crossing branches, and dead wood.

A. cordata. ITALIAN ALDER. Zones 2b–9, 14–24. Native to Italy, Corsica. Young growth vertical; older trees to 40 ft. tall, spreading to 25 ft. Heart-shaped, 4-in. leaves, glossy rich green above, paler beneath. Short deciduous period. More restrained than *A. rhombifolia.* Favored in Southwest, except high desert.

A. glutinosa. BLACK ALDER. Zones 1–10, 14–24. Native to Europe, North Africa, Asia. Not as fast growing as *A. rhombifolia.* Probably best as

A

multistemmed tree. Grows to 70 ft. tall, 30 ft. wide. Roundish, 2–4-in., coarsely toothed leaves in lustrous dark green. Makes dense mass from ground up. Good for screen.

A. oregona (A. rubra). RED ALDER. Zones 3–7, 14–17. Native to stream banks and marshy places from Alaska south to Northern California; usually found in areas with maritime influence. Most common alder of lowlands in Pacific Northwest. Can grow to 90 ft. high but is usually seen at 45–50 ft. tall, 20–30 ft. wide. Attractive smooth, light gray bark. Dark green, 2–4-in. leaves, rust colored and hairy beneath; coarsely toothed margins are rolled under. Can take a surprising amount of brackish water and is useful wherever underground water is somewhat saline. This tree is generally disliked in the Pacific Northwest because it's a favorite of tent caterpillars.

A. rhombifolia. WHITE ALDER. Zones 1b–10, 14–21. Native along streams throughout most of California's foothills except along coast; mountains of Oregon, Washington, British Columbia, and Idaho. Very fast growing to 50–90 ft. tall, 40 ft. wide. Branches spread out, then droop at tips. Coarsely toothed, 2½–4½-in. leaves are dark green above, paler green beneath. Very tolerant of heat and wind. Susceptible to tent caterpillars and borers in its native range.

A. tenuifolia. MOUNTAIN ALDER, THINLEAF ALDER. Zones A1–A3; 2, 3, 7, 10. Shrub or small tree to 20–25 ft. tall, 15–20 ft. wide. Extremely hardy to cold.

ALOCASIA

ELEPHANT'S EAR

Araceae

PERENNIALS

ZONES 22–24; H1, H2, EXCEPT AS NOTED; OR INDOORS

PARTIAL SHADE; BRIGHT INDIRECT LIGHT

REGULAR TO AMPLE WATER

SAP IS POISONOUS IF INGESTED

Alocasia macrorrhiza

Native to tropical Asia. Handsome, lush plants for tropical effects. Flowers like those of calla *(Zantedeschia)*. Tropical plant specialists sell many kinds with leaves in coppery and purplish tones, often with striking white veins. Provide rich soil, frequent light feedings, and wind protection.

A. ×amazonica. AFRICAN MASK. Leathery, deep bronzy green leaves to 16 in. long have wavy edges, heavy white main veins. Plants may grow as tall as 4 ft. and about half as wide. This species is the one most commonly available as a houseplant.

A. cucullata. CHINESE TARO, CHINESE APE. Zones H1, H2. Slow-growing, clumping evergreen plant to 2 ft. high. Grown for shiny, deep green, pointed leaves to 15 in. long, 1 ft. wide. Usually massed as a ground cover; plant 1½–2 ft. apart. Requires moist, rich, well-drained soil and protection from wind. Excellent container plant.

A. macrorrhiza. Evergreen at 29°F/–2°C; loses leaves at lower temperatures but comes back in spring if frosts are not too severe. Large, arrow-shaped leaves to 2 ft. or longer, on stalks to 5 ft. tall, form a dome-shaped plant 4 ft. across. Tiny flowers on spike surrounded by greenish white bract. Flowers followed by reddish fruit, giving spike the look of corn on the cob.

A. odora. Similar to *A. macrorrhiza* but not quite as hardy. Fragrant flowers.

A. plumbea. Resembles *A. macrorrhiza,* but leaves are dark olive green or purplish green (or nearly black, in some forms).

A. sanderiana. Grows to 6 ft. tall and wide. Arrow-shaped, deeply lobed leaves about 12–16 in. long, metallic dark purplish green with silver veining on surface.

FOR INFORMATION ON SELECTING PLANTS
PLEASE SEE PAGES 64–160

ALOE

Liliaceae

SUCCULENT TREES, SHRUBS, AND PERENNIALS

ZONES 8, 9, 12–24, EXCEPT AS NOTED

FULL SUN OR LIGHT SHADE, EXCEPT AS NOTED

LITTLE TO MODERATE WATER

SAP BENEATH THE SKIN IS AN IRRITANT

Aloe arborescens

Primarily South African natives, the aloes range from 6-in. miniatures to trees; all form clumps of fleshy, pointed leaves and bear branched or unbranched clusters of orange, yellow, cream, or red flowers. Some species are in bloom every month; biggest show comes from midwinter through summer. Leaves may be green or gray green, often strikingly banded or streaked with contrasting colors. Showy and easy to grow in well-drained soil in reasonably frost-free areas; need little water but can take more. Except as noted, give full sun in cooler climates, light shade in hotter regions. Where winters are too cold for all-year outdoor culture, grow in pots and shelter from frosts. Most kinds make outstanding container plants. Highly valued as ornamentals, in the ground or in pots. Aloes listed here are only a few of the many kinds.

A. arborescens. TREE ALOE. Zones 8, 9, 12–24; H1, H2. Grows about 10 ft. tall, 6 ft. wide, though older clumps may reach 18 ft. Branching stems carry big clumps of gray-green, spiny-edged leaves. Winter flowers in long, spiky clusters, bright vermilion to clear yellow. Withstands salt spray. Tolerates shade. Foliage damaged at 29°F/–2°C, but plants have survived 17°F/–8°C. Not reliably hardy in Zone 12.

A. aristata. Dwarf for pots, edging, ground covers; just 8–12 in. tall and wide. Rosettes packed with 4-in.-long, ¾-in.-wide leaves ending in whiplike threads. Orange-red winter flowers in 1–1½-ft.-tall clusters.

A. bainesii. Slow-growing tree to 20–30 ft. or taller, with heavy, forking trunk and branches. Rosettes of 2–3-ft. leaves, spikes of rose pink flowers on 1½–2-ft. stalks. Used for stately, sculpturesque pattern in landscape. Tender to frost.

A. barbadensis. See A. vera

A. 'Blue Elf'. Dwarf hybrid with 6-in. rosettes of tooth-edged blue-green foliage. Eventually forms a dense mound 1–2 ft. high and wide. Has never been known to flower. Similar or identical to 'Walmsley's Blue'.

A. brevifolia. Low, spreading clumps of blunt, thick, gray-green, spiny-edged leaves 3 in. long. Clusters of red flowers on 20-in. stalks, intermittent all year.

A. ciliaris. Zones 8, 9, 12–24; H1, H2. Climbing, sprawling form with pencil-thick stems to 10 ft. long. Small, thick, soft green leaves. Long-stalked, 3–6-in. flower clusters with 20–30 green- or yellow-tipped scarlet flowers; intermittent bloom all year. Takes a bit more shade than the other species, little frost. In all but the mildest-winter zones, make sure plant has overhead protection in winter.

A. distans. JEWELED ALOE. Running, rooting, branching stems make clumps of 6-in., fleshy blue-green leaves with scattered whitish spots and white teeth along edges. Forked flower stems, 1½–2 ft. tall, carry clusters of red flowers in winter.

A. ferox. BITTER ALOE. Large single trunk rises 6–10 ft. high (after 10 years), topped by a single crown of gray-green, spiny, red-toothed leaves 3–4 ft. long and 6–8 in. wide. Each branched inflorescence holds hundreds of bright scarlet or orange blossoms in late winter or early spring.

A. marlothii. Large, treelike aloe with a stout trunk to 12 ft. tall, topped with a single dense foliage rosette. Leaves are green or grayish, 3–4 ft. long and up to 8 in. wide, often spined both on surfaces and margins. Old dried leaves persist on trunk. Winter flower clusters branch horizontally, holding many spikes in yellow, orange, or (rarely) red or bicolors.

A. nobilis. Dark green leaves edged with small hooked teeth grow in rosettes to 1 ft. wide and high. Clustered orange-red flowers on 2-ft. stalks in early summer. Good in pots—takes limited root space.

A. plicatilis. Slow growing, with thick, forking trunks crowned with fans (not rosettes) of smooth, gray-green, foot-long leaves. Scarlet flowers in clusters to 1½ ft. long, in winter. Sculpturesque container plant when young; reaches 3–5 ft. in 10 years. Not suited to intense summer heat; tender to frost.

A. polyphylla. Zones 15–17. Best in cool coastal areas of Northern California; will not survive summers in hot inland areas. Hardy to 10°F/−12°C. To 16 in. tall, 2–3 ft. across. Striking rosette, with five rows of leaves that all spiral in the same direction, producing a pinwheel-like or "spinning" effect when plant is viewed from above. Mature plants produce a branching, 3-ft.-tall stalk of nodding, light red to salmon pink blossoms in spring (may fail to bloom some years). Prefers slightly acidic soil. Withhold fertilizer in summer. Partial shade.

A. saponaria. SOAP ALOE. Short-stemmed rosettes a foot or more wide feature broad, white-spotted green leaves to 8 in. long. Multibranched, 1½–2½-ft. flower stalks rise in summer, topped with tight heads of nodding blossoms in scarlet, red orange, salmon pink, or yellow. Sends out suckers to form dense, expanding colonies. Dig and separate when plants become too crowded. 'Yellow Form' corresponds to *A. s. fixburgeana.* Among shrimp pink–flowered forms, the most widely grown is old hybrid 'Commutata'.

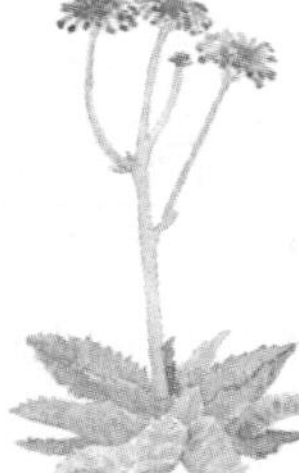
Aloe saponaria

A. ×spinosissima. Dense, compact, multibranched shrub, expanding slowly to 4–6 ft. high and wide. Leaf surfaces are not as spiny as the name would suggest. Unbranched, 1½-ft.-tall flower stalks bear coral red blossoms from late winter to early spring.

A. striata. CORAL ALOE. Broad leaves to 20 in. long are spineless, gray green, with narrow pinkish red edge. They grow in rosettes 2 ft. wide on short trunk. Brilliant coral pink to orange flowers in branched clusters, midwinter into spring. Handsome, tailored plant.

A. striatula. Scrambling shrub has glossy green leaves, each edged with a thin white margin and minute teeth; distinctly striped leaf bases surround the stem. Multiple stems form a dense mound 5–6 ft. tall and to 15 ft. across, but plant may be kept much more compact with occasional hard pruning. Single spikes of flowers in scarlet, orange, or yellow rise 6–18 in. above the foliage in summer.

A. tenuior. Dense, much-branched, climbing or scrambling shrub to 2–4 ft. tall. Lax stems to 10 ft. long (often horizontal) are tipped with rosettes of 6-in.-long, 1-in.-wide leaves edged with tiny white teeth. In late spring, 6–12-in., unbranched spikes of tiny, cylindrical yellow (sometimes red) flowers are held horizontally above the mound. Best given support of a fence or rocks or trained up a palm trunk.

A. variegata. PARTRIDGE-BREAST ALOE, TIGER ALOE. Foot-high, tight rosette of fleshy, triangular, dark green, 5-in.-long leaves strikingly banded and edged with white. Loose clusters of pink to dull red flowers, intermittent all year.

A. vera (A. barbadensis). MEDICINAL ALOE, BARBADOS ALOE. Zones 8, 9, 12–24; H1, H2. Clustering rosettes of narrow, fleshy, stiffly upright leaves 1–2 ft. long. Yellow flowers in dense spike atop 3-ft. stalk, spring and summer. Favorite folk medicine plant used to treat burns, bites, inflammation, and a host of other ills. Among best aloes for Zones 12, 13. Survives without extra water but needs some to look good.

ALOPECURUS pratensis 'Aureus'

YELLOW FOXTAIL GRASS
Poaceae (Gramineae)
PERENNIAL GRASS
ZONES 2–10, 14–17, 21–24
PARTIAL SHADE IN HOTTEST CLIMATES
REGULAR WATER

Alopecurus pratensis 'Aureus'

Golden-variegated selection of a cool-season grass native to Eurasia and naturalized in North America. May be sold as 'Variegatus' or 'Aureovariegatus'. Smaller and less vigorous than plain (green-leafed) species. To 1 ft. high; spreads slowly to form mats 1½ ft. wide or wider. Translucent foliage ranges from green striped with gold to almost entirely yellow; in part shade, it is chartreuse. When flower spikes form in midspring, shear them off to keep foliage attractive longer (as summer heat pushes it toward dormancy) and to prevent the appearance of volunteer seedlings, which would be green leafed. Fresh new growth resumes in fall and persists until the first hard freeze. Nearly evergreen in climates with cool summers and mild winters. Dislikes drought, excessive moisture, and extremes of heat. Good for border, rock garden, ground cover. Divide every 2 or 3 years in spring or fall.

ALOYSIA

Verbenaceae
DECIDUOUS OR SEMIEVERGREEN SHRUBS
ZONES VARY BY SPECIES
FULL SUN
REGULAR WATER

Aloysia triphylla

These are aromatic shrubs with tiny flowers and a sparse growth habit; they are native to warmer parts of North and South America. Provide good drainage.

A. triphylla (Lippia citriodora). LEMON VERBENA. Zones 9, 10, 12–21; marginal in Zones 4–8. Native to Argentina, Chile. Legginess is its natural state; it's the herb that grew like a gangling shrub in gardens of long ago, reaching 6 ft. or taller and sprawling to 6 ft. wide. Prized for lemon-scented leaves used to flavor teas and iced drinks; when you read of the fragrance of verbena in literature about the antebellum South, this is the plant being described. Narrow leaves to 3 in. long are arranged in whorls of three or four along branches. Bears open clusters of very small lilac or whitish flowers in summer.

Grow it among lower plants to hide its legginess; or locate it against a wall or fence and pinch-prune to create interesting tracery. Can also be trained into a standard and tolerates clipping into a hedge. Borderline hardy as far north as Seattle if planted against a warm wall. In colder climates, grow it as a houseplant (pinch frequently) and let it spend warm months outdoors.

A. wrightii. OREGANILLO, MEXICAN OREGANO. Zones 8–13, 19–24. Native to desert mountains from California to Texas and northern Mexico. Dense grower to 5 ft. high and wide, with numerous small stems and small (½-in.) leaves. From spring through fall, produces very sweet-scented white flowers that can be used as a flavoring or for tea. Performs best when it gets lots of heat. Good in natural landscape, herb garden, as informal hedge.

Often confused with *A. lycioides,* a larger plant (to 8 ft. tall and 6 ft. wide) bearing blossoms that have a more vanillalike fragrance and are sometimes tinged with purple. Plants sold under either name may be one or the other—but both are outstanding ornamentals. Both make excellent honey. *A. lycioides* is the Mexican oregano of commerce.

ALPINE STRAWBERRY. See FRAGARIA vesca

ALPINIA

Zingiberaceae
PERENNIALS
ZONES 14–24; H1, H2
LIGHT SHADE
AMPLE WATER

Alpinia zerumbet

Rhizomes produce leafy clumps that are evergreen in Zones 22–24, H1, and H2. Roots are hardy to about 15°F/−9°C. Tops die back in prolonged cool winter weather, but new shoots appear in spring. Need wind-free exposure, good soil. Must be established for at least 2 years in order to bloom. Each year, remove canes that have flowered.

A. purpurata. RED GINGER. To 9–12 ft. tall, 2–3 ft. wide, with 2½-ft.-long leaves. Blooms in late summer, producing brilliant inflorescence of red bracts and small white flowers. In California, blooms only as a greenhouse plant.

A. sanderae (A. vittata). VARIEGATED GINGER. Native to Solomon Islands. To 3–4 ft. tall, 2 ft. wide, with 8-in.-long leaves striped with white. Rarely blooms. A good container plant.

A. zerumbet (A. nutans, A. speciosa). SHELL GINGER, SHELL FLOWER. Native to tropical Asia and Polynesia. Grandest of gingers, best all-year appearance. To 8–9 ft. tall, 3–4 ft. wide. Leaves shiny, 2 ft. long, 5 in. wide, with distinct parallel veins; leafstalks are maroon at maturity. Waxy white or pinkish, shell-like, fragrant flowers marked red, purple, or brown in pendent clusters on arching stems in late summer.

ALSOPHILA australis, A. cooperi. See CYATHEA cooperi

ALSTROEMERIA

Liliaceae

PERENNIALS FROM TUBEROUS ROOTS

ZONES 5–9, 14–24; H1

AFTERNOON SHADE IN HOTTEST CLIMATES

REGULAR WATER DURING GROWTH AND BLOOM

CAN CAUSE DERMATITIS IN ALLERGIC PEOPLE

Alstroemeria aurea

These perennials fall into two horticultural classes, which might be called "deciduous" and "evergreen." Both produce masses of color in borders, bearing clustered flowers at the tops of leafy stems. The flowers, brightly colored and marked with contrasting blotches and flecks, are superb cut flowers and a favorite with florists for their lasting quality. Plants appreciate good drainage. Mulch deeply where winters are severe.

Deciduous types. For many years, deciduous alstroemerias were the only ones readily available as garden subjects. The seed-grown Ligtu hybrids and Dr. Salter's hybrids have azalealike flowers in beautiful, edible-sounding colors—orange, peach, shrimp, salmon—as well as red and near-white; all types are flecked and striped with deeper colors. They produce leafy shoots 2–5 ft. tall in late winter and into spring; as these shoots begin to brown, the flowering shoots appear, with blooms following in early to midsummer. If allowed to set seed, they will self-sow. Plants go dormant after bloom and need no water unless winter rains fail. They naturalize where winters are not severe. Sow seeds in fall, winter, or earliest spring, either where plants are to grow or in pots for later planting out.

Evergreen types. Evergreen alstroemerias include two species and a number of hybrids. The hybrids, available in various colors, were once grown only by commercial florists, who jealously guarded their plants from the gardening public. American breeders have now produced similar hybrids, which are offered as potted plants. These will produce flowering shoots as long as the soil does not get too warm; repeat bloom can be stimulated by pulling up flowering shoots from the base rather than cutting them.

A. aurea (A. aurantiaca). Grows 3–4 ft. tall, with numerous leafy flowering stems topped by yellow, orange, or orange-red flowers liberally sprinkled with dark stripes and flecks. Sometimes available in winter or spring as dormant roots; these are frail and easily broken. Plant them 8 in. deep and 1 ft. apart. Once established, the plant is vigorous, possibly even invasive.

A. hybrids. These include series such as Meyer, Cordu, Premier, and Inca. They vary in height and come in many colors, mostly in the purple–pink–red range with dark flecks. Usually sold by color; buy in bloom. Named hybrids include 'Little Eleanor', only 8 in. high, with bright yellow flowers; and 'Third Harmonic', to 4 ft. tall and almost excessively vigorous, with orange flowers marked in yellow and black.

A. psittacina (A. pulchella). Odd looking rather than beautiful. Flowering stems to 2½ ft. tall are crowned by a few dark red flowers marked with green and blotched dark purple. Travels by rhizomes but is not a pest; prefers partial to fairly deep shade.

ALTERNANTHERA tenella

JOYWEED

Amaranthaceae

PERENNIAL OFTEN TREATED AS ANNUAL

ZONES H1, H2; ANYWHERE AS ANNUAL

FULL SUN

MODERATE WATER

Alternanthera tenella

Colorful foliage plant, native from Mexico to Argentina. To 6–12 in. high; plant 4–10 in. apart for best impact. Useful as edging, ground cover, or massed for special landscape effect. Accepts most well-drained soils but is not salt tolerant; will take some shade. Grow from cuttings. Keep planting compact by shearing.

Among the many varieties are 'Bettzickiana' (known by the common names "Jacob's coat" and "calico plant"), with spoon-shaped leaves blotched yellow and red; 'Magnifica', dwarf form with red-bronze leaves; and 'Parrot Feather' and 'Versicolor', with broad green leaves marked with yellow and pink veins. A form from Thailand that is grown in Hawaii has larger green leaves with irregular white margins.

ALTHAEA rosea. See ALCEA rosea

ALUM ROOT. See HEUCHERA

ALYOGYNE huegelii (Hibiscus huegelii)

BLUE HIBISCUS

Malvaceae

EVERGREEN SHRUB

ZONES 13–17, 20–24; H1, H2

FULL SUN

LITTLE TO MODERATE WATER

Alyogyne huegelii

Australian native hardy to about 23°F/–5°C. Upright, to 5–8 ft. tall and wide, with deeply cut, rough-textured dark green foliage. Glossy-petaled flowers 4–5 in. across, lilac blue to deep purple. Blooms off and on all year; individual flowers last 2 or 3 days. Pinch or prune as needed to keep it compact. Variable from seed. 'Santa Cruz' is a good deep blue selection; 'Monterey Bay' and 'Mood Indigo' are deeper blue. 'White Swan' has white blossoms.

ALYSSUM

Brassicaceae (Cruciferae)

PERENNIALS

ZONES 1–24

FULL SUN OR LIGHT SHADE

MODERATE WATER

Alyssum montanum

Mostly native to Mediterranean region. Mounding plants or shrublets that brighten spring borders and rock gardens with their cheerful bloom. They thrive in poor, rocky soil as long as it is well drained.

A. montanum. To 8 in. high, 1½ ft. wide; leaves gray, hairy (more so on underside). Fragrant yellow flowers in dense, short clusters.

A. saxatile. See Aurinia saxatilis

A. wulfenianum. Prostrate and trailing to about 1½ ft. wide, with fleshy, silvery leaves and sheets of pale yellow flowers.

ALYSSUM, SWEET. See LOBULARIA maritima

ALYXIA oliviformis

MAILE

Apocynaceae

EVERGREEN SHRUBBY VINE

ZONES H1, H2

PARTIAL OR FULL SHADE

MODERATE TO REGULAR WATER

Alyxia oliviformis

A Hawaiian native, this plant is found in various habitats—dry to wet, sea level to high elevation—and is correspondingly quite variable in appearance. In the wild, can be seen straggling along the ground as well as twining in trees. Bears small, tubular greenish yellow flowers followed by shiny purple-black fruits. Main feature, however, is dark green, glossy foliage that is fragrant when bruised, as is bark of stems. Both foliage and stems are widely used in leis. Makes an attractive cover for a shaded trellis. Best in rich, well-drained soil.

AMARACUS dictamnus. See ORIGANUM dictamnus

Amaranthaceae. The amaranth family largely consists of herbaceous plants, many of them weedy. The small flowers are dry and papery, but often effective when massed.

AMARANTHUS

AMARANTH

Amaranthaceae

ANNUALS

ZONES 1–24; H1, H2

FULL SUN OR PARTIAL SHADE

REGULAR WATER

Amaranthus caudatus

Coarse, sometimes weedy plants native to many regions of the world; a few ornamental kinds are grown for their brightly colored foliage or flowers. Sow seed in place in early summer—soil temperature must be above 70°F/21°C for germination. Or start indoors for planting out after frost danger is past in zones where the growing season is short.

Picked when young and tender, leaves and stems of many species (even some of the weedy ones) can be used like spinach, taking its place in hot weather. Some species have seeds that look like sesame seeds, have a high protein content, and can be used as grain.

A. caudatus. LOVE-LIES-BLEEDING, TASSEL FLOWER. Sturdy, branching plant 3–8 ft. high, 1½–3 ft. wide; leaves 2–10 in. long, ½–4 in. wide. Red flowers in drooping, tassel-like clusters. A curiosity rather than a pretty plant. One of the amaranths that produce grain.

A. hypochondriacus (A. hybridus erythrostachys). PRINCE'S FEATHER. To 5 ft. high, 2 ft. wide, with leaves 1–6 in. long, ½–3 in. wide, usually reddish. Red or brownish red flowers in many-branched clusters. Some strains are grown as a spinach substitute or for grain.

A. tricolor. JOSEPH'S COAT. Branching plant 1–4 ft. high, 1–1½ ft. wide. Leaves 2½–6 in. long, 2–4 in. wide, blotched in shades of red and green. Selections such as 'Early Splendor', 'Flaming Fountain', and 'Molten Fire' bear masses of yellow to scarlet foliage at tops of main stems and principal branches. Green-leafed strains used as spinach substitute under the name "tampala."

×AMARCRINUM memoria-corsii. See CRINUM

Amaryllidaceae. The amaryllis family consists of herbaceous plants with strap-shaped leaves, bulbous or rhizomatous rootstocks, and clustered flowers (rarely a single flower) atop a leafless stem.

AMARYLLIS belladonna (Brunsvigia rosea)

BELLADONNA LILY, NAKED LADY

Amaryllidaceae

PERENNIAL FROM BULB

ZONES 4–24

FULL SUN

NO IRRIGATION NEEDED

ALL PARTS ARE POISONOUS IF INGESTED

Amaryllis belladonna

Native to South Africa. Performs best in areas with warm, dry summers. Bold, straplike leaves form fountainlike clump about 1 ft. high, 2 ft. wide in fall and winter; foliage dies back in late spring or early summer. About 6 weeks later, 2–3-ft. stalks rise from bare earth, each topped by a cluster of 4–12 fragrant, trumpet-shaped, rosy pink flowers.

Grows in almost any well-drained soil. Gets all the moisture it needs from winter rains. Plant bulbs 1 ft. apart right after bloom period ends. Where winter temperatures stay above 15°F/–9°C, keep tops of bulb necks at or slightly above ground level. In colder-winter areas, choose a protected southern exposure and set bulbs slightly below ground level. Lift and divide clumps infrequently; they may not bloom for several years if disturbed at the wrong time. Very long lived. For plants with common name "amaryllis," see *Hippeastrum.*

A. hallii. See Lycoris squamigera

AMELANCHIER

JUNEBERRY, SHADBLOW, SERVICEBERRY

Rosaceae

DECIDUOUS SHRUBS OR SMALL TREES

ZONES VARY BY SPECIES

FULL SUN OR PARTIAL SHADE

MODERATE TO REGULAR WATER

Amelanchier laevis

Graceful, airy plants grow about twice as high as wide. Bloom in early spring, just before or during leaf-out, bearing drooping clusters of white or pinkish flowers that are showy but short lived. Fruits follow in summer; they are similar to blueberries though with a somewhat musty flavor. Use them in pies and preserves—if you can get to them before the birds do (in Alaska, birds have thus far seemed uninterested in fruit). Purplish new spring foliage turns deep green in summer, fiery in fall.

Locate these plants against a dark background to show off flowers, form, fall color. Choose a site where litter from fruit and birds won't be a problem. Prune after bloom to remove crossing, crowded, diseased, or dead branches. The common name "serviceberry" is often pronounced "sarvisberry."

A. alnifolia. SASKATOON. Zones A1–A3; 1–6. Native to western Canada and mountainous parts of western U.S. To about 20 ft. tall, spreading by rhizomes. Selections grown for larger, sweeter berries than the species include 'Smoky', 'Martin', 'Northline', 'Thiessen', and dwarf 'Regent' (only 4–6 ft. tall).

A. canadensis. Zones A2, A3; 1–6. Plants offered under this name may actually belong to other species. Grows to 25 ft. tall, with short, erect clusters of flowers. ▸

A. × grandiflora. Zones 1–6. Hybrids between *A. arborea* (similar to *A. canadensis* but larger) and *A. laevis.* Many named selections are available and may be sold under any of the three names. Most grow to 25 ft. tall, with drooping flower clusters. 'Autumn Brilliance' has blue-green foliage that turns orange red in fall. 'Cole's Selection' and 'Princess Diana' are similar. Strong stems, profuse bloom, and brilliant fall color make them good choices for ornamental use.

A. laevis. ALLEGHENY SERVICEBERRY. Zones 2–6. Native to eastern North America. To 30 ft. tall, with nodding or drooping clusters of flowers. Sweet fruit. Hybrid 'Cumulus' has a narrower habit and yellow-orange to red fall color.

AMERICAN SWEET GUM. See LIQUIDAMBAR styraciflua

AMETHYST FLOWER. See BROWALLIA

AMPELOPSIS brevipedunculata

PORCELAIN BERRY

Vitaceae

DECIDUOUS VINE

ZONES 2–24

SUN OR SHADE

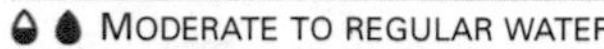

MODERATE TO REGULAR WATER

Ampelopsis brevipedunculata

Native to Asia. Rampant woody vine climbs 20–30 ft. by stem tendrils. Large, handsome, three-lobed, 2½–5-in.-wide leaves are dark green. In warm climates, leaves turn red and most drop in fall; more leaves come out, redden, and drop all winter. Many clusters of small, grapelike berries turn from greenish ivory to brilliant metallic blue in late summer and fall; attract birds. Needs strong support: superb on concrete and rock walls or on sturdy arbors. Thin out and shorten stems each winter; dig out suckers. You can cut the vine to the ground and still get berries, since it blooms and fruits on new growth.

'Elegans' has leaves variegated with white and pink. Smaller, less vigorous, and less hardy than the species, it is a splendid hanging-basket plant.

Boston ivy and Virginia creeper, formerly included in genus *Ampelopsis,* are now placed under *Parthenocissus* because, unlike *Ampelopsis,* both have disks at ends of their tendrils.

AMSONIA

BLUE STAR FLOWER

Apocynaceae

PERENNIALS

ZONES 2–24

FULL SUN OR LIGHT SHADE

MODERATE TO REGULAR WATER

Amsonia tabernaemontana

Elegant milkweed relatives from southeastern U.S. To 2–3 ft. high and wide, with narrow leaves and erect stems topped by clusters of small, star-shaped blue flowers in late spring. Bright yellow fall foliage is a bonus. Tough plants that succeed in ordinary soil and tolerate occasional lapses in watering.

A. ciliata. Crowded, needlelike (but soft) leaves to 2 in. long; exceptional fall color. Pale blue flowers.

A. illustris. Leathery, shiny green, willowlike leaves to 3 in. long. Pale blue blossoms.

A. tabernaemontana. Dull dark green, willowlike leaves to 3 in. long. Slate blue flowers.

AMUR CHOKECHERRY. See PRUNUS maackii

Anacardiaceae. The cashew family includes evergreen or deciduous trees, shrubs, and vines with small, unshowy, but often profuse flowers. Attractive foliage is colorful in fall; fruits are sometimes showy or edible. Many have poisonous or irritating sap. Mango and poison oak *(Toxicodendron)* indicate the diversity of the family.

ANACYCLUS depressus (A. pyrethrum depressus)

MOUNT ATLAS DAISY

Asteraceae (Compositae)

PERENNIAL

ZONES 2–24

FULL SUN

LITTLE TO MODERATE WATER

Anacyclus depressus

Native to North Africa, Spain. Slowly forms dense, spreading mat somewhat like chamomile *(Chamaemelum).* Grayish, finely divided leaves. Single daisylike summer flowers to 2 in. across, with yellow center disks and white rays (red on reverse side). Good in sunny, dry, hot rock gardens. May freeze in severe winters or rot in cold, wet, heavy soil. Dislikes humidity.

ANAGALLIS

PIMPERNEL

Primulaceae

ANNUALS AND PERENNIALS OR BIENNIALS

ZONES VARY BY SPECIES

FULL SUN

LITTLE TO REGULAR WATER

Anagallis monelli linifolia

Two species sometimes seen, one a weed. Less aggressive type attractive in rock gardens.

A. arvensis. SCARLET PIMPERNEL. Annual. Zones 1–24. Low-growing weed from Europe, with ¼-in., brick red flowers. *A. a. caerulea* has deep blue, larger flowers.

A. monelli. Perennial or biennial. Zones 4–9, 12–24. Mediterranean native to 1½ ft. high and wide, with ¾-in. flowers of intense blue. 'Pacific Blue' is a superior selection; 'Phillipsii' is compact, 1 ft. tall; *A. m. linifolia* has narrower leaves than the species.

ANCHUSA

Boraginaceae

ANNUALS, BIENNIALS, AND PERENNIALS

ZONES VARY BY SPECIES

FULL SUN

MODERATE TO REGULAR WATER

Anchusa capensis

Related to forget-me-not *(Myosotis)* but larger and showier. Worth growing for vibrant blue color; rate high for purest blue among relatively easy-to-grow plants. Give well-drained soil. High humidity inhibits performance.

A. azurea (A. italica). Perennial. Zones 1–24. Native to the Mediterranean region. Coarse, open, spreading; to 3–5 ft. tall, 2 ft. wide. Leaves 6 in. or longer, covered with bristly hairs. Clusters of bright blue blossoms, ½ to ¾ in. across, in summer and fall. Horticultural forms include gentian blue 'Dropmore', sky blue 'Opal', and rich blue 'Loddon Royalist'.

A. capensis. CAPE FORGET-ME-NOT, SUMMER FORGET-ME-NOT. Biennial in Zones 6–24; annual anywhere. Native to South Africa. To 1½ ft. tall, 8 in. wide. Narrow, 5-in.-long leaves about ½ in. wide. Bright blue, ¼-in.-wide flowers with white throats come in clusters about 2 in. long. Use in summer borders.

ANDROMEDA polifolia

BOG ROSEMARY

Ericaceae

EVERGREEN SHRUB

ZONES A1–A3; 1–6

FULL SUN OR LIGHT SHADE

AMPLE WATER

Andromeda polifolia

Mounding shrub to 1–1½ ft. high and 2–3 ft. wide; native to northern climates in North America, Europe, Asia. Narrow, leathery leaves ½–2 in. long, dark green above, blue gray beneath. Flask-shaped, nodding spring flowers are white to pink, carried in clusters of up to eight at top of stems. Requires strongly acid soil and protection from hottest sun. Connoisseur's plant for rock garden, pot culture, or streamside or bog garden. Varieties include 'Grandiflora', a dwarf with blue-green leaves and large, creamy, pink-shaded flowers; 'Nana', very compact and vigorous, with nearly round pink flowers; and 'Blue Ice', with powder blue foliage and profuse soft pink blooms.

ANDROPOGON gerardii

BIG BLUESTEM, TURKEYFOOT

Poaceae (Gramineae)

PERENNIAL GRASS

ZONES 1–9, 14–24

FULL SUN OR LIGHT SHADE

LITTLE TO REGULAR WATER

Andropogon gerardii

This is the classic tall prairie grass of the Midwest, where it can reach 8 ft. high. In drier climates, it's more likely to grow 3–5 ft. tall. A clump former (to about 3 ft. wide), it does not ordinarily spread by rhizomes. Thin blades are blue green in summer, turning bronzy red or coppery in fall. Flowers are unshowy but interesting: purplish spikes to 4 in. long, borne at stem ends in sets of three or more (arranged like a turkey's foot). Tolerates a range of soil and moisture conditions. Cut dried stems to base yearly before new spring growth begins. Divide clump when center starts to die. Effective screen when massed if given regular water. A single plant makes a good accent in a mixed border.

ANDROSACE

ROCK JASMINE

Primulaceae

PERENNIALS

ZONES 1–6, 14–17

FULL SUN

MODERATE WATER

Androsace lanuginosa

Choice rock garden miniatures grown mostly by alpine plant specialists. Clusters of small flowers in summer. All types require perfect drainage and are best adapted to gravelly banks in rock gardens. Protect from more aggressive rockery plants such as alyssum, rockcress *(Arabis)*, aubrieta. Rarely succeed in warm-winter areas. These species are native to the Himalayas.

A. lanuginosa. Trailing plant forms mats 3 ft. across. Silvery leaves to ¾ in. long, covered with silky white hairs. Pink flowers on 2-in. stems. *A. l. leichtlinii* has white flowers with a crimson eye.

A. primuloides. Spreads by runners. Leaves ½–2 in. long, in rosettes covered with silvery hairs. Pink flowers on 5-in. stems.

A. sarmentosa. Spreads by runners. Leaves to 1½ in. long, in rosettes, covered with silvery hairs when young. Rose-colored flowers on 5-in.-tall stems. *A. s. chumbyi* forms a dense clump, has woolly leaves.

ANEMONE

WINDFLOWER, ANEMONE

Ranunculaceae

PERENNIALS

ZONES VARY BY SPECIES

EXPOSURE NEEDS VARY BY SPECIES

REGULAR WATER

ALL PARTS ARE POISONOUS IF INGESTED

Anemone blanda 'White Splendor'

A rich and varied group of plants ranging in size from alpine rock garden miniatures to tall Japanese anemones grown in borders; bloom extends from very early spring to fall, depending on species.

Most of the anemones described below have fibrous roots or creeping rhizomes or rootstocks, but *A. blanda, A. coronaria,* and *A. ×fulgens* are grown from tubers requiring special attention. Set out *A. blanda* in fall; where winter temperatures drop below –10°F/–23°C, apply a thick mulch after first hard frost. Plant *A. coronaria* and *A. ×fulgens* in fall where they are hardy in the ground; in cooler regions, plant in early spring. In warmer climates, some gardeners soak tubers for a few hours before planting.

Plant tubers scarred side up (look for depressed scar left by base of last year's stem), setting them 1–2 in. deep and 8–12 in. apart in rich, light, well-drained loam. Or start in flats of damp sand; set out in garden when stems are a few inches tall. Keep soil moist during growth and bloom. Protect from birds until leaves toughen. In high-rainfall areas, excess moisture induces rot. Tuberous types best treated as annuals in rainy-summer or warm-winter climates, where they tend to be short lived; *A. blanda,* in particular, needs distinct winter chill for good performance. Tuberous anemones make good container plants.

A. blanda. Zones 2–9, 14–23. Native to southeastern Europe; sometimes called Greek windflower. Tubers produce spreading mat of finely divided, softly hairy leaves (clumps are wider spreading in colder climates). In spring, each 2–8-in. stem bears one sky blue flower, 1–1½ in. across. Often confused with *A. apennina,* which has more pointed leaf segments. Selections with 2-in. flowers on 10–12-in. plants include 'Blue Star', 'Pink Star', 'White Splendor', and purplish red 'Radar'. All work well as underplantings for tulips, as ground cover drifts under deciduous shrubs and trees, and naturalized in short grass. Partial shade.

A. canadensis. Zones 1–4. To 1–2 ft. tall, spreading by creeping rhizomes. Inch-wide, yellow-centered white flowers appear in twos and threes from the upper joints of divided leaves. Produces profuse bloom from late spring to early summer. Can be invasive in small gardens. Partial shade.

A. coronaria. POPPY-FLOWERED ANEMONE. Zones 4–24. Native to the Mediterranean; grows from a tuber. Species is rarely seen in gardens; it has been replaced by showy large-flowered hybrids valued for cutting and for spectacular spring color in borders or mass plantings. Blossoms are 1½–2½ in. across, borne singly on 6–18-in. stems above finely divided leaves; colors include red, blue, tones and mixtures of these colors, and white. Among the most popular strains are De Caen (single flowers) and St. Brigid (semidouble to double). Full sun or partial shade.

Anemone coronaria

A. ×fulgens. SCARLET WINDFLOWER. Zones 4–9, 14–24. To 1 ft.; grows from a tuber. Basal leaves are divided, stem leaves undivided. Spring flowers 2½ in. across, brilliant scarlet with black stamens. St. Bavo strain comes in unusual color range including pink and rusty coral. Same uses as for *A. coronaria.* Partial shade.

A. ×hybrida (A. japonica, A. hupehensis japonica). JAPANESE ANEMONE. Zones 2b–24. Long-lived, fibrous-rooted perennial indispensable for fall flower color. Graceful, branching stems 2–4 ft. high rise from clump of dark green, three- to five-lobed leaves covered with soft hairs. Single or semidouble flowers in white, silvery pink, or rose. Many named varieties. Slow to establish, but once started it spreads readily if roots are not disturbed. Space plants 2 ft. apart. May need staking. Mulch in fall where winters are severe. Increase by divisions in fall or early spring or by root cuttings in spring. Effective in clumps in front of tall shrubbery or under high-branching trees. Partial shade.

A. nemorosa. WOOD ANEMONE. Zones 1–9, 14–24. European native to 1 ft. high, with creeping rhizomes, deeply cut leaves, and inch-wide white (rarely pinkish or blue) spring flowers held above the foliage. Spreads slowly to make an attractive woodland ground cover. Many named varieties exist; 'Allenii' has large blue flowers, and there are double forms. Partial or full shade.

A. pulsatilla. See Pulsatilla vulgaris

A. quinquefolia oregana. Zones 4–7, 15–17. Native to Pacific Northwest and Northern California. Attractive woodland ground cover resembling *A. nemorosa,* with inch-wide white (sometimes blue or pink) spring flowers. Partial shade.

A. sylvestris. SNOWDROP ANEMONE. Zones 1–10, 14. European native growing from creeping rootstock to 1½ ft. tall. Fragrant, 1½–3-in., yellow-centered white flowers in spring, followed by cottony seed heads. Plant spreads readily in damp, wooded locations. 'Grandiflora' has larger blossoms; 'Flore Pleno' is double flowered. Partial or full shade.

A. tomentosa. Zones 2b–9, 14–21. Vigorous, fibrous-rooted Tibetan native often sold as *A. vitifolia* 'Robustissima'. Foliage resembles grape leaves, grows in a spreading clump that gives rise to branching, 3½-ft.-high stems bearing single pink flowers in late summer, early fall. Allow 3 ft. between plants. Partial shade.

ANETHUM graveolens

DILL

Apiaceae (Umbelliferae)

ANNUAL

ZONES 1–24

FULL SUN

REGULAR WATER

Anethum graveolens

Native to southwestern Asia and naturalized in northern U.S. To 3–4 ft. tall, with soft, feathery leaves and umbrellalike, 6-in.-wide clusters of small yellow flowers in summer (winter in the desert). Seeds and leaves have pungent aroma. Sow seeds where plants are to grow; for constant supply, sow several times in spring and summer (germinates and grows better in spring). In the desert, sow in later summer or fall. Thin seedlings to 1½ ft. apart. An easy way to grow dill in a casual garden is to let a few plants go to seed. Seedlings can be pulled and chopped for use in cooking. Use seeds in pickling and vinegar; use fresh or dried leaves in cooked dishes, salads, sauces.

ANGELICA archangelica

ANGELICA

Apiaceae (Umbelliferae)

BIENNIAL

ZONES A2, A3; 1–10, 14–24

FULL SUN IN COOLER CLIMATES ONLY

REGULAR WATER

Angelica archangelica

Native to northern Europe and western Asia. Tropical-looking plant with divided and toothed, yellow-green leaves 2–3 ft. long. When it blooms (in early summer), it sends up a thick, hollow stem to 6 ft. tall topped by a large (4-ft.-wide), umbrellalike cluster of greenish yellow flowers. Grow in moist, rich soil. Propagate from seeds as soon as they ripen in fall. Because angelica is taprooted and doesn't transplant well, sow in place. To prolong plant's life for a few years, cut out flowering stem after it has formed. Angelica leaves are a nice addition to salads; the leafstalks can be cooked and eaten like asparagus. Both leafstalks and hollow flower stems can be candied and used to decorate pastries. Seeds are used commercially to flavor wines, vermouth, and liqueurs.

ANGELICA TREE. See ARALIA elata

ANGEL'S HAIR. See ARTEMISIA schmidtiana

ANGEL'S TEARS. See NARCISSUS triandrus, SOLEIROLIA soleirolii

ANIGOZANTHOS

KANGAROO PAW

Haemodoraceae

PERENNIALS

ZONES 15–24

FULL SUN

REGULAR WATER

Anigozanthos flavidus

Native to open eucalyptus forests in western Australia. Thick rootstocks send up clumps of dark green, smooth, swordlike evergreen leaves. Spikes of striking, fuzzy, tubular flowers in red, purple, green, or yellow, curved at tips like kangaroo paws (tips split into six segments). Flowers attract hummingbirds. Intriguing in flower, otherwise not outstanding. Bloom from late spring to fall if spent flowering spikes are cut to ground. Good cut flowers. Light sandy soil or heavier soil with good drainage. Control snails and slugs.

A. flavidus (A. flavida). Branching stems to 5 ft. tall bear 1–1½-in.-long, yellow-green flowers tinged with red. Foliage clump is 2–3 ft. wide.

A. hybrids. Kangaroo paws hybridize freely in nature and in cultivation. The following are among the many superior garden plants that have been developed. Foliage clumps range from a foot across (for most dwarf varieties) to about 3 ft. wide; the smaller types make good container subjects.

'Big Red'. Extra-large bright red blossoms top 3–4-ft.-tall stems.

Bush Gems Hybrids. All resist leaf and root diseases that afflict kangaroo paws. Two of the best are 2½–3-ft., easy-to-grow 'Bush Gold', which bears clear lemon yellow flowers above lime green leaves over a long bloom season, and 1½–2½-ft. 'Bush Ranger', a long-lived variety with clear red blooms. Other good varieties include 'Bush Baby', with flowers blending red, orange, and yellow on 1½-ft. stems; 'Bush Emerald', bearing surprising green flowers with contrasting yellow throats and brilliant orange anthers on 2–2½-ft. stems; 'Bush Lantern', a bright yellow dwarf 1–2 ft. tall; and 'Bush Pearl', with bubble-gum pink blossoms on 2-ft. stems.

'Harmony'. Yellow flowers on tall (4–6-ft.) stems clothed with bright red hairs.

'Pink Joey'. Silvery pink flowers on stems 1–3 ft. high.

A. manglesii. Unbranched green stems to 3 ft. high, thickly covered with red hairs; 3-in. flowers in brilliant deep green, red at base. Foliage clump is 1½–2 ft. wide.

ANISACANTHUS

DESERT HONEYSUCKLE

Acanthaceae

EVERGREEN OR DECIDUOUS SHRUBS

ZONES 8–13, 18–23; H1, H2

EXPOSURE NEEDS VARY BY SPECIES

MODERATE WATER

Anisacanthus thurberi

Heat-loving shrubs have nectar-filled tubular flowers with two lobes above the mouth, three on the lower lip. Highly favored by hummingbirds and butterflies. Fairly drought tolerant; water deeply every 2 to 3 weeks in summer.

A. quadrifidus wrightii (A. wrightii). Deciduous. Native to southeastern Texas, northeastern Mexico. To 3 ft. tall, 4 ft. wide, with dark green leaves 2 in. long and 1 in. wide. Spikes of 2-in.-long, brilliant red-orange flowers from early summer to fall. Rabbits love new shoots; protect with

wire cage until a woody structure is established. For compact shape and prolific bloom, cut back by one-half to two-thirds before new spring growth commences. 'Mexican Flame' is a superior selection grown from cuttings. Full sun or light shade.

A. thurberi. CHUPAROSA. Mostly evergreen. Native to northern Mexico and canyons and washes of the Sonoran Desert of southern Arizona and New Mexico. In mild-winter areas grows to 4 ft. tall (or more) and as wide, with stout branches. Looks best when treated as perennial, cut to ground before spring growth begins. Valued for spikes of 1½-in.-long, yellow-orange flowers held above light green leaves 1½–2 in. long, ½ in. wide. Blooms most prolifically in spring, with occasional blossoms in summer and fall. Full sun. Plants with red or orange-red flowers sold under this name may be *Justicia spicigera.*

ANISE. See PIMPINELLA anisum

ANISE TREE. See ILLICIUM

ANISODONTEA ×hypomandarum

CAPE MALLOW

Malvaceae

EVERGREEN SHRUB

ZONES 14–24

FULL SUN OR LIGHT SHADE

LITTLE TO MODERATE WATER

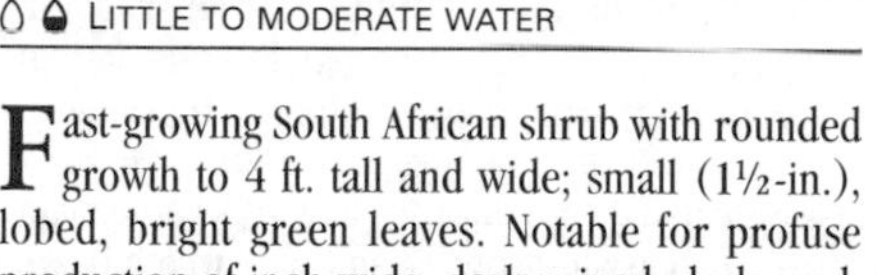

Fast-growing South African shrub with rounded growth to 4 ft. tall and wide; small (1½-in.), lobed, bright green leaves. Notable for profuse production of inch-wide, dark-veined, dark-eyed pink to purplish blooms resembling miniature individual hollyhocks; flowers come throughout warm weather, year-round in mildest climates. Good for borders, large containers. Often sold as single-trunk standard or "patio tree."

Anisodontea ×hypomandarum

'Tara's Wonder' is an open grower to 6 ft. tall and wide, freely branching, with darker, narrowly lobed leaves and very large dark pink flowers. 'Tara's Pink' is bushier, with larger, more widely lobed leaves and lighter pink blossoms.

Annonaceae. The annona family consists primarily of tropical trees and shrubs; many have edible fruit, but only a very few are hardy in the West.

ANNONA cherimola. See CHERIMOYA

ANNUAL MALLOW. See LAVATERA trimestris

ANTENNARIA dioica

PUSSY TOES

Asteraceae (Compositae)

PERENNIAL

ZONES A1, A2; 1–3, 6, 7, 14–16

FULL SUN

MODERATE TO REGULAR WATER

Native to Europe, North America. Forms inch-high mats of woolly foliage that slowly spread among rocks, between paving stones, or at front of border. Furry puffs of flowers are pinkish white in the basic species, deep pink in 'Rubra', and rose pink in 'Rosea'. Extremely hardy to cold; will withstand some light foot traffic.

Antennaria dioica

ANTHEMIS

Asteraceae (Compositae)

PERENNIALS

ZONES VARY BY SPECIES

FULL SUN

MODERATE TO REGULAR WATER

Some species are weedy, but those listed here (from southern Europe and Turkey) are good garden plants with long-lasting daisylike or buttonlike flowers. Many-segmented leaves are aromatic, especially when bruised. Provide good drainage.

Anthemis tinctoria 'E. C. Buxton'

A. carpatica (A. cretica carpatica). Zones 3b–10, 14–24. Forms low, 2-ft.-wide mounds of green to gray-green foliage. Stems about 6 in. high rise from foliage clumps in spring and summer, bearing 1½-in. white daisies with yellow centers.

A. marschalliana (A. biebersteiniana). Zones 1–9, 14–24. Rounded plant 1 ft. tall and wide, with finely cut, fernlike, silvery leaves and 1-in., brilliant yellow daisylike blooms in summer.

A. nobilis. See Chamaemelum nobile

A. punctata cupaniana. Zones 4–9, 14–24. Mound of silvery foliage 1 ft. tall and at least as wide, topped by 2½-in. long-lasting white daisies in summer.

A. tinctoria. GOLDEN MARGUERITE. Zones 1–11, 14–24. Erect, shrubby plant to 2–3 ft. tall and wide, with angular stems, light green leaves, and golden yellow, 2-in. daisies in summer and early fall. Good cut flower. Cut back lightly after first flush of bloom to keep flowers coming. Short lived; start new plants from stem cuttings in spring or divide clumps in spring or fall. Varieties include 'Beauty of Grallagh', golden orange flowers; 'E. C. Buxton', white with yellow centers; 'Kelwayi', golden yellow; and 'Moonlight', pale yellow.

ANTHRISCUS

Apiaceae (Umbelliferae)

ANNUALS AND PERENNIALS OR BIENNIALS

ZONES VARY BY SPECIES

EXPOSURE NEEDS VARY BY SPECIES

REGULAR WATER

Native to Europe, North Africa, and Asia. Though both of these plants produce many umbrella-shaped clusters of tiny flowers, they are valued for their fernlike foliage. In the first species, the leaves are used in cooking; in the second, the foliage brings deep, striking color to the perennial border.

Anthriscus cerefolium

A. cerefolium. CHERVIL. Annual. Zones 1–24. Low foliage mounds about a foot wide. Flower stems, 1–2 ft. topped with white blossoms in summer. The leaves have a parsleylike flavor with overtones of anise; use like parsley, fresh or dried. Sow seeds in place in early spring (in cold-winter areas) or in fall (where winters are mild). In the following years, volunteer seedlings will keep you supplied with new plants. Goes to seed quickly in hot weather; keep flower clusters cut to encourage leafy growth. Partial shade.

A. sylvestris 'Ravenswing'. Perennial or biennial. Zones 1–9, 14–24. Very attractive purple-black foliage in clump 1½ ft. high, 2½ ft. wide. In late spring or early summer, flowering stems to 3 ft. tall bear white blossoms with purplish pink bracts. Deadhead for best appearance and to prevent self-sowing. Full sun or light shade.

FOR DEFINITIONS OF GARDENING TERMS
PLEASE SEE PAGES 746–750

ANTHURIUM

SPATHE FLOWER

Araceae

PERENNIALS

ZONE H2, EXCEPT AS NOTED; OR INDOORS

PARTIAL SHADE; BRIGHT INDIRECT LIGHT

REGULAR WATER

Anthurium andraeanum

Native to tropical American rain forests. Exotic plants with handsome dark green leaves and lustrous flower bracts. Bloom best in moderate shade. Among species listed here, all but *A. hookeri* are usually grown as potted plants, even in tropical climates.

Anthuriums make unusual houseplants in cooler climates. As such, they are no more difficult to grow than some orchids. The higher the humidity, the better. Leaves lose shiny texture and may die if humidity drops below 50 percent for more than a few days. Keep pots on trays of moist gravel, in bathroom, or under polyethylene cover. Sponge or spray leaves several times daily. For good bloom, locate by window with good light but no direct sun. Generally grow best in 80 to 90°F/27 to 32°C temperature range but will get along at normal house temperature. Growth stops below 65°F/18°C, is damaged below 50°F/10°C. Protect from drafts. Pot in coarse, porous mix of leaf mold, sandy soil, and shredded osmunda. Give light feeding every 4 weeks.

A. andraeanum. Dark green, oblong leaves to 1 ft. long and 6 in. wide, heart shaped at base. Spreading, heart-shaped flower bracts in shades of red, rose, pink, and white shine as though lacquered. Bracts reach 6 in. long, surround yellow, callalike flower spike. Bloom more or less continuously—plant may have from four to six flowers during the year. Flowers last 6 weeks on plant, 4 weeks after cutting.

A. crystallinum. Leaves to 1½ ft. long, 1 ft. wide, deep green with striking white veining. Flowers unexciting, with small, narrow, greenish bracts. Many similar anthuriums exist in florist trade; plants offered as *A. crystallinum* may be *A. clarinervium, A. magnificum,* or some other species.

A. hookeri. Grown in the tropical landscape for handsome foot-wide "nest" of large (to 8-in.-long) leaves. Excellent accent in a wind-sheltered garden or as a tubbed specimen. Needs high humidity. Grow in well-aerated, rich, moist soil; feed regularly.

A. scandens. Climbing or trailing plant to 2 ft., with 3-in.-long, tapered oval leaves; small, fragrant, greenish flowers; translucent lilac berries.

A. scherzerianum. Zones 23, 24; H2. Slow-growing, compact plant to 2 ft. Dark green leaves 8 in. long, 2 in. wide. Flower bracts broad, 3 in. long, deep red varying to rose, salmon, white. Yellow flower spikes spirally coiled. Easier to handle than *A. andraeanum* and often thrives under good houseplant conditions.

ANTIGONON leptopus

CORAL VINE, QUEEN'S WREATH, ROSA DE MONTANA

Polygonaceae

EVERGREEN OR DECIDUOUS VINE

ZONES 12, 13, 18–24; H1, H2

FULL SUN

MODERATE TO REGULAR WATER

Antigonon leptopus

Native to Mexico. Where summers are long and hot, this tuberous-rooted perennial vine grows quickly, climbing by tendrils to 40 ft. Makes an open, airy foliage cover; leaves are bright green, 3–5 in. long, heart shaped or arrow shaped. Small rose pink flowers are carried in long, trailing sprays from midsummer to fall. Evergreen in mild-winter areas; cut back vigorous growth in late winter or early spring. In frosty areas, leaves drop in fall and most of top dies, but recovery is quick when weather warms up. Where winter temperatures dip below 25°F/–4°C, protect roots with mulch. Remove frost-killed stems from their support before new growth emerges in spring. Varieties include rare white 'Album' and hot rose pink (nearly red) 'Baja Red'; the latter's color is variable from seed, but the best are as red as 'Barbara Karst' bougainvillea.

A wonderful vine in the low deserts of California and Arizona; there, it can grow without irrigation but may die back to ground in summer. Elsewhere give it hottest place in garden; choose a warm, wind-sheltered spot in Southern California coastal gardens. Let it shade patio or terrace or drape its foliage and blossom sprays along eaves, fence, or garden wall.

ANTIRRHINUM majus

SNAPDRAGON

Scrophulariaceae

PERENNIAL TREATED AS ANNUAL

ZONES A3; 1–24

FULL SUN

REGULAR WATER

Antirrhinum majus

Among best flowers for sunny borders and cutting, at their best in spring and early summer. In regions with mild winters and hot summers, will bloom in winter and spring. Individual flower of basic snapdragon has five lobes, which are divided into unequal upper and lower "jaws"; by pinching sides of flower lightly, you can make jaws snap open. Later developments include the double flower; the bell-shaped kind, with round, open flowers; and the azalea-shaped bloom, which is a double bellflower. All available in many colors.

"Snapping" snapdragons in tall (2½–3-ft.) range include Rocket and Topper strains (single flowers) and Double Supreme strain. Intermediate (to 1–2 ft.) are Cinderella, Coronette, Minaret, 'Princess White with Purple Eye', the Ribbon series, Sprite, and Tahiti. Dwarfs (6–8 in. high) include Dwarf Bedding Floral Carpet, Kim, Kolibri, and Royal Carpet. Bell-flowered strains include Bright Butterflies and Wedding Bells (both 2½ ft.), La Bella (1½ ft.), and Little Darling and Liberty Bell (both 15 in.). Azalea-flowered strains include Madame Butterfly (2½ ft.) and Sweetheart (1 ft.). Plants range from about 6 in. across for smallest types to 2 ft. wide for tallest.

In a category of its own is the Chinese Lanterns strain, a bell-flowered snapdragon grown for its growth habit: its trailing, cascading stems make it ideal for hanging baskets.

Sow seed in flats from late summer to early spring for later transplanting or buy plants at nursery. Set out plants in early fall in mild-winter areas, spring in colder climates. If snapdragons set out in early fall reach bud stage before night temperatures drop below 50°F/10°C, they will start blooming in winter and continue until weather gets hot.

Valuable cut flowers. Tall and intermediate forms are splendid vertical accents in borders. Dwarf kinds are effective as edgings and in rock gardens and raised beds, or in pots.

APACHE PLUME. See FALLUGIA paradoxa

APHELANDRA squarrosa

Acanthaceae

EVERGREEN SHRUB

ZONES 23, 24; H2; OR INDOORS

SOME SHADE; BRIGHT INDIRECT LIGHT

REGULAR WATER

Aphelandra squarrosa

Native to Mexico, South America. Appreciated for striking foliage and flowers. Leaves are 8–12 in. long, dark green veined with white. Green-tipped yellow flowers and waxy, golden yellow flower bracts make colorful upright spikes at stem tips. In tropical climates, plant reaches

6½ ft. tall and wide, but as houseplant rarely exceeds 1–2 ft. Best-known variety is 'Louisae', but newer 'Apollo White' and 'Diana' are more compact and show more white venation.

Occasionally used as an accent in protected spots in Southern California gardens. If plant freezes, cut it to the ground; new shoots will appear when weather warms up. Indoors, provide bright filtered light or morning sun. When bracts fade, cut back their stalk to a pair of sturdy leaves to keep plants bushy. Repot annually after bloom. Propagate every few years, as older plants decline rapidly; take stem cuttings from late winter to late spring.

Apiaceae. This family, also known as Umbelliferae, comprises nearly 3,000 plants, most of them annuals and perennials. All have flowers in umbels—flat- or round-topped clusters whose individual flower stems all originate at a single point. Many are vegetables (carrot, parsnip, celery, fennel) or aromatic herbs (parsley, coriander, dill). Others are grown for ornament, such as sea holly *(Eryngium)* and blue lace flower *(Trachymene)*.

APIUM graveolens. See CELERIAC, CELERY.

Apocynaceae. The dogbane family contains shrubs, trees, and vines with milky, often poisonous sap. Flowers are often showy and fragrant, as in *Plumeria* and oleander *(Nerium)*.

Aponogetonaceae. Only the following genus is of importance in this small family of aquatic plants.

APONOGETON distachyus

CAPE PONDWEED, WATER HAWTHORN
Aponogetonaceae
AQUATIC PLANT
ZONES 4–9, 12–24
FULL SUN OR PARTIAL SHADE
LIVES IN WATER

Aponogeton distachyus

Native to South Africa. Suitable for small water gardens. Like miniature water lily, it produces floating leaves from submerged tuber. Leaves are long and narrow; ⅓-in.-long white, fragrant flowers stand above water in double-branched clusters. In hot-summer climates, blooms in cool weather and is dormant in hottest weather; where winters are cold, blooms in summer and is dormant in winter. Same culture as water lily *(Nymphaea)*.

APPLE

Rosaceae
DECIDUOUS FRUIT TREES
ZONES VARY BY VARIETY
FULL SUN
REGULAR WATER DURING FRUIT DEVELOPMENT
SEE CHART NEXT PAGE

Apple

Most widely adapted deciduous fruit. Ripens from July to early November, depending on variety. Mild winters of the low desert and the marine and coastal climates of Southern California do not provide enough cold for most standard varieties—in those areas, be sure to choose apples with low winter chill requirement (such low-chill varieties are noted in the chart). In many apple-growing areas, demand for the popular varieties seen on fruit stands often causes nurseries to sell unsuitable selections. For this reason, the chart indicates where some varieties perform best as well as where they are sold. In the coldest climates, including Alaska, rootstock is as important as variety; apples in such areas are best grown on hardy crabapple rootstocks such as *Malus antonovka, M. ranetka,* and *M. baccata.* Apple-crabapple hybrids offer another option for coldest-winter areas.

WHAT APPLES NEED

WINTER CHILL: Most varieties demand 900 to 1,200 hours of temperatures at or below 45°F/7°C. In mild-winter areas, look for low-chill varieties (100 to 400 hours).

FULL SUN: Essential for a good crop—so don't crowd an apple tree into a partially shaded site. To plant more than one variety in a small space, choose dwarf or multiple-variety trees.

WATERING: When fruit is developing, make up for any lack of rainfall with periodic deep soakings.

POLLINATION: If you have a tree that is not bearing, graft a branch of another variety onto it or place fresh bouquets of blossoms from another variety (in a can of water) at base of tree.

'Spitzenberg'

Although many apples are partially self-fruitful to varying degrees ('Golden Delicious', 'Mollie's Delicious', and 'Chehalis' are closest to self-fruitful), it is generally recommended that, unless there are apples growing nearby in your neighborhood, two or more varieties be planted for cross-pollination and good fruit set. Certain varieties (triploids) do not produce fertile pollen and will not fertilize either their own flowers or those of other apples. Don't use 'Gravenstein' or any other pollen-sterile tree to pollinate an unfruitful tree.

A standard apple tree grows about 20 ft. tall, 20–25 ft. wide. If space is at a premium, consider dwarf trees. For very small yards, multiple-variety trees provide an assortment of different apples as well as cross-pollination—all on a single tree. Available in standard and dwarf sizes, these trees have three to five varieties grafted onto a single trunk and rootstock.

In choosing varieties, remember that good apples are not necessarily red. Skin color is not an indicator of quality or taste. Make sure that eye appeal, taste preference, or name doesn't influence you to choose a difficult-to-grow variety. For example, if to your taste 'Golden Delicious' and 'Red Delicious' are nearly equal (and you live in an area where either can be grown), consider differences in growing them. 'Golden Delicious' produces fruit without a pollenizer and comes into bearing at a younger age. It keeps well, while 'Red Delicious' becomes mealy if not stored at temperatures of 35 to 40°F/12 to 4°C or lower. And it can be used for cooking, while 'Red Delicious' is principally a fresh eating apple.

If you want nearly perfect fruit, the apple tree will need much care in most regions. But even with less-than-perfect fruit, an apple tree is ornamental; it has more character, better form, and a longer life than most deciduous fruit trees. It does best in deep, well-drained soil but gets by in many imperfect situations, including heavy soils.

Codling moth is the universal insect pest of apples. Pheromone traps, trichogramma wasps, *Bt,* or horticultural oil may be enough to thwart this pest in home gardens, but proper timing of controls is critical. Synthetic pesticides such as carbaryl are also effective. Apple maggot is a problem in some areas (particularly western Washington); infested fruit is soft, rotten, and unusable. Various types of sticky traps may be of some help, but frequent insecticide sprays from midsummer to harvest are often needed for complete control. Apple scab causes hard, corky spots on the fruit, with subsequent defoliation and stunting of immature fruit. It is particularly severe in coastal areas of the Pacific Northwest. Planting disease-resistant varieties (see chart) is the best way to avoid the problem. Leaf rollers and

▶ page 194

A

APPLE

NAME	ZONES	RIPENING DATE	FRUIT	COMMENTS
'Adina'	18–24; H1	Early to midseason	Large, round, fragrant, dark red. Firm, sweet, creamy white flesh with cinnamon overtones	Low-chill variety
'Akane'	1–7, 14–16	Early to midseason	Small to medium, round to flat. Red skin, crisp white flesh	Scab and mildew resistant
'Anna'	7–24; H1	Early. Sometimes bears light second and third crops later in the season	Large, pale green blushed red. Crisp, sweet with some acid	Begins producing at a young age. Low-chill variety; useful in warmest winter areas. Good annual bearer. Good pollenizer for 'Dorsett Golden' and 'Ein Shemer'
'Arkansas Black'	1–3, 10, 11	Late	Medium size; deep dark red. Hard, crisp	Best after storage for 2 months. 'Arkansas Black Spur' is spurred variation
'Ashmead's Kernel'	4–9, 14–17	Late	Medium size; red-orange blush over rough yellow-green skin	Good disease resistance
'Beverly Hills'	18–24	Early	Small to medium. Yellow skin splashed and striped red. Tender, somewhat tart. Fair quality. Somewhat resembles 'McIntosh'	Definitely for cool areas; will not develop good quality in hot interiors. One of best for Southern California coast
'Braeburn'	1–3, 6, 14–16 18–23	Late	Medium size; orange-red blush over yellow ground. Crisp, sweet-tart flesh. Stores well	Fruit drops in hot climates. Thin fruit to prevent bearing in alternate years. Very susceptible to mites
'Breakey'	A2, A3; 1–3	Midseason	Medium size. Red to scarlet skin; white, mildly spicy flesh. Good fresh or cooked	Vigorous tree with excellent hardiness
'Chehalis'	4–6	Early	Large, yellow green, similar to 'Golden Delicious'. Soft but bakes well. Mild flavor, melting flesh; good in salads. Poor keeper	Self-fruitful. Resists scab
'Cox's Orange Pippin'	7, 14–16	Midseason	Medium size. Dull orange-red skin; yellow, firm, juicy flesh. Superb flavor. English dessert favorite	Susceptible to scab and cracking. Dense growth; thin out branches. Dislikes extreme cold, heat, low humidity. Worth trying for its unique flavor
'Delicious' ('Red Delicious')	Sold wherever apples will grow; best in 2, 3, 7	Midseason	Pointed blossom end with five knobs. Color varies with strain, climate; best with sunny, warm days, cool nights. Mildly sweet. Good finish. Often older, striped kinds taste better than highly colored commercial types	Many strains that vary in ripening season, depth and uniformity of coloring. 'Crimson Spur' and 'Bisbee Spur' are popular home varieties. All types susceptible to scab; difficult for home gardeners to grow in Zones 4–6
'Dorsett Golden'	13, 17–24; H1	Early	Medium to large, yellow or greenish yellow; sweet flavor. Good for eating fresh or cooking. Keeps a few weeks	Seedling of 'Golden Delicious' from Bermuda. Low-chill variety. Good pollenizer for 'Anna' and 'Ein Shemer'
'Ein Shemer'	13, 17–24; H1	Early	Medium size, yellow to greenish yellow. Juicy, crisp, mildly acid	Low-chill variety. Good pollenizer for 'Anna' and 'Dorsett Golden'
'Empire'	2, 3, 6, 7, 14–16	Midseason	Cross between 'McIntosh' and 'Delicious'. Small to medium size, roundish, dark red. Creamy white flesh is juicy, crisp, mildly tart	Semispur growth habit. Good tree structure. Susceptible to spring frost damage. Better adapted to hot-summer areas than 'McIntosh'
'Enterprise'	1–9, 14–16	Late	Medium size, firm; red blush. Sweet; keeps well	Immune to scab; subject to preharvest fruit drop
'Fiesta'	1–9, 14–16	Midseason to late	Firm fruit is larger and even better flavored than 'Cox's Orange Pippin' and doesn't crack. Red-striped skin	Productive; no preharvest fruit drop
'Fuji'	6–9, 14–16, 18–22	Late	Medium to large; yellow-green ground with red stripes. Firm flesh with excellent, very sweet flavor. Stores exceptionally well	Tends to bear heavy crops in alternate years. Needs a long growing season (160 days) to ripen properly. Fairly low chill requirement. 'Red Fuji' is an excellent red-skinned form

A

APPLE

NAME	ZONES	RIPENING DATE	FRUIT	COMMENTS
'Gala'	6–9, 14–16	Early to midseason	Medium size; beautiful red-on-yellow color. Yellow flesh is highly aromatic, firm, crisp, juicy, sweet. Loses flavor in storage	Vigorous, heavy bearer with long, supple branches that break easily; provide support if necessary. Very susceptible to fireblight. Several color strains are available
'Garden Delicious'	1–3, 6–9, 14–20	Midseason	Medium to large, golden green with red blush	Genetic dwarf 5–8 ft. tall and as wide
'Ginger Gold'	1–9, 14–16	Early midseason	Medium to large, yellow, firm, crisp, mild. Resembles 'Golden Delicious'. Good keeper; one of the best early yellow apples	Ripens over 2 to 3 weeks. Susceptible to mildew. Resistant to sunburn
'Golden Delicious' ('Yellow Delicious')	1–3, 6–11, 14–24	Late midseason	Medium to large. Clear yellow color, though it may develop skin russeting in some climates. Similar in shape to 'Delicious', with less prominent knobs. Highly aromatic, crisp. Excellent for eating fresh and cooking	Not related to 'Red Delicious'; different taste, habit. Long bloom season, heavy pollen production make it a good pollenizer. Self-fruitful. Various strains available. Spur types include 'Goldspur', 'Yellospur'
'Golden Russet'	1–3, 6–9, 14–16, 18, 19	Early to midseason	Medium size; greenish yellow to golden brown with heavy russeting. Creamy yellow, sweet flesh. Good fresh or cooked	Vigorous and productive. Partially self-fruitful but better crop with pollenizer
'Gold Rush'	1–3, 6–9, 14–16	Late	Medium size, yellow, often with some russeting. Best after storage	Immune to scab. Good resistance to mildew; some resistance to fireblight
'Gordon'	18–24; H1	Midseason	Large, greenish yellow blushed red. Sweet-tart flavor	Tree vigorous, upright, semidwarf. Many closely spaced spurs. Long blooming, bearing periods. Low-chill variety
'Granny Smith'	7–11, 14–16	Midseason (later in cool-summer areas)	Large, bright to yellowish green, firm fleshed, tart. Good quality. Stores well; makes good pies, sauce	Australian favorite before it came to U.S. Chancy in cold areas because of late ripening
'Gravenstein'	Widely sold in 4–11, 14–24; best in 15–17	Early to midseason	Large, with brilliant red stripes over deep yellow ground. Crisp, aromatic, juicy. Excellent for fresh eating; makes applesauce with character	Justly famous variety of California's north coast apple district. Pollen-sterile; will not pollinate other varieties. Susceptible to mildew in Zones 4–6. 'Red Gravenstein' is more highly colored
'Haralson'	1–3, 7, 14–16	Early to midseason	Medium size; red ground with deeper red stripes. Crisp, juicy, mildly tart white flesh	Hardy, vigorous, productive tree. Moderate resistance to fireblight
'Honeycrisp'	1–7, 14–16	Midseason	Medium size, red, firm, crisp; excellent sweet-tart flavor	Hardy apple from Minnesota. Resistant to fireblight; somewhat resistant to scab
'Hudson's Golden Gem'	2–6, 7, 14–16	Early to midseason	Elongated, with light brown–russeted skin and crisp, nutty flesh. Good for desserts	Productive; fruit holds well on the tree. Resistant to scab, mildew, and fireblight
'Idared'	4–6, 15–17	Late	Medium to large, bright red apple with firm white flesh, tart at picking time. Stores well, and flavor sweetens in storage	Begins bearing at a young age. Heavy producer
'Jonagold'	2–9, 14–17	Late midseason	Large; heavy red striping over yellow ground. Firm, juicy; fine mildly tart flavor. A frequent taste-test favorite	Productive medium-size tree. Pollen-sterile; won'tpollinate other varieties. Not pollinated by 'Golden Delicious'
'Jonathan'	Sold every-where; best in 2, 3, 7	Midseason	Small to medium, roundish oblong apple with bright red skin. Juicy, moderately tart, crackling crisp, sprightly. All-purpose apple, good keeper	Subject to mildew, somewhat resistant to scab
'Liberty'	4–9, 14–16	Late midseason	Medium size, heavy red blush. Crisp, with fine sweet-tart flavor, dessert quality	Productive tree. Immune to scab; can get mildew west of Cascades. Resists rust, fireblight

▶

A

APPLE

NAME	ZONES	RIPENING DATE	FRUIT	COMMENTS
'Lodi'	A2, A3; 1–3, 6–11, 14–16	Early	Medium size, greenish yellow, tart. Good for cooking, keeps well	Large, hardy tree; tends to bear heavily in alternate years
'McIntosh'	2, 3, 14–16	Midseason	Medium to large, bright red, nearly round. Snowy white, tender flesh. Excellent tart flavor	Fine choice for cooler climates if given good care. Very susceptible to scab, preharvest fruit drop
'Melrose'	1–7, 15, 16	Late	Medium to large, roundish, red ground striped deeper red. Flesh white, mildly tart, aromatic. Stores exceptionally well; good dessert apple	Cross between 'Jonathan' and 'Delicious'. Somewhat mildew resistant. Considered one of the best in Northwest
'Mollie's Delicious'	8, 9, 14–20	Early	Large, light yellow blushed red. Light yellow, aromatic, juicy, sweet flesh. Stores well	Self-fruitful; bears from an early age. Low-chill variety
'Mutsu' ('Crispin')	7–9, 15, 16	Late	Very large, greenish yellow blushed red. Cream-colored, very crisp flesh, somewhat tarter than 'Golden Delicious'. Excellent dessert and cooking apple with long storage life	Exceptionally large and vigorous tree. Pollen-sterile; won't pollinate other varieties
'Newtown Pippin' ('Yellow Newtown', 'Yellow Pippin')	1–11, 14–22.	Late	Large, green. Crisp and tart, fair for eating, excellent for cooking	Large, vigorous tree. Excellent California central coast commercial variety. Susceptible to mildew in Zones 4–6
'Norland'	A1–A3; 1–3	Early	Medium size, oblong, pinkish striped with red. Good fresh or cooked. Stores well	Hardy variety from Canada. Other Canadian introductions such as 'Noran', 'Noret', 'Norson', 'Parkland', and 'Westland' are also good in coldest-winter areas
'Northern Spy'	1–3, 6, 7, 14–16	Late	Large, red skinned. Tender, fine-grained flesh with sprightly flavor. Not attractive but excellent dessert and cooking apple. Keeps well	Slow to reach bearing age
'Oriole'	A2, A3; 1–3, 7, 14–16	Early	Large apple with yellow-orange skin striped or spotted with red. Excellent fresh or cooked	Productive tree with excellent hardiness. Susceptible to mildew
'Paulared'	2, 3, 6, 7, 14–16	Early	Large, round to flattish; solid red blush. Crisp, mildly tart flesh. One of the best early apples	Strong, upright tree. Thrives west of Cascades in Northwest. Somewhat resistant to scab
'Pettingill'	23, 24	Midseason to late	Large, thick skinned, red-blushed green to red. Firm, tasty, moderately acid white flesh	Large, upright, productive tree; regular bearer. Very low chill requirement
'Pink Pearl'	1–9, 14–16	Early	Medium size. Pale green skin, sometimes blushed red. Sweet-tart pink flesh. Makes colorful sauce. Good keeper	Very attractive in bloom; blossoms deeper pink than on most other varieties
'Pristine'	3–11, 14–16, 18, 19	Early	Medium; bright yellow skin, mildly tart white flesh. Good for eating, baking, applesauce	Immune to scab; somewhat resistant to mildew, fireblight
'Redfree'	4–9, 14–17	Early	Medium size. Red skin; firm, crisp flesh with good flavor	Heavy bearer. Immune to scab
'Rome Beauty' ('Red Rome')	3, 6, 7, 10, 11	Late	Large, round, smooth red apple with greenish white flesh. Original 'Rome Beauty' has been supplanted by more uniformly red-skinned types like 'Red Rome'. Outstanding baking apple, only fair for eating fresh	Bears at an early age
'Sierra Beauty'	2, 3, 6–9, 14–16	Late	Large, exceptionally attractive yellow apple with red stripes. Firm, sweet-tart flesh. Keeps well	Productive tree
'Spartan'	4–7, 15, 16	Midseason	Medium size. Dark red with purplish bloom; crisp flesh. Good flavor, similar to that of 'McIntosh'	Good tree habit. Heavy producer

A

APPLE

NAME	ZONES	RIPENING DATE	FRUIT	COMMENTS
'Spitzenberg' ('Esopus Spitzenberg')	1–7, 14–16; best in 1–3	Late	Medium to large, red-dotted yellow. Crisp, fine grained, tangy, spicy	Old favorite that still rates high. Subject to fireblight, mildew
'Stayman'	1–3, 7, 10, 11	Late	Large red apple with green and russet dots. Fine-grained, firm, juicy flesh with lively flavor	Pollen-sterile; won't pollinate other varieties. Old-timer that still has its devotees. Susceptible to scab
'Summerred'	A2, A3; 1–7, 15, 16	Early	Medium size, bright red; tart and good chiefly for cooking until fully ripe, then good dessert quality too	Hardy. Consistent annual bearer for western Oregon and Washington. Goes overripe too fast in hot-summer climates
'Tropical Beauty'	18–24; H1	Early	Medium to large, bright red. Juicy white flesh with mild, sweet flavor	Partially self-fruitful; production enhanced if it grows near 'Adina'
'Wealthy' ('Red Wealthy', 'Double Red Wealthy')	1–7	Early midseason	Medium to large, rough, red. Flesh white with pink veining, firm, tart, juicy. Good cooking variety	Small, cold hardy tree that tends to bear in alternate years. Not for hot climates
'William's Pride'	1–7	Early	Medium-size, dark red fruit with sweet-spicy flavor. One of the best early red apples	Immune to scab; resistant to fireblight; susceptible to mildew
'Winter Banana'	7–9, 14–24	Late midseason	Large, attractive, pale yellow blushed pink; waxy finish. Tender, tangy, aromatic	Low-chill variety. There is a 'Spur Winter Banana'
'Winter Pearmain' ('White Winter Pearmain')	20–24	Midseason	Medium to large. Pale greenish yellow skin with pink blush. Tender, fine-grained flesh; excellent flavor	Low-chill variety. Performs better than standard cold-winter varieties in Southern California
'Yellow Transparent'	A2, A3; 1–3, 7, 14–16	Early	Medium size. Thin yellow skin with tart white flesh. Good for cooking if harvested when greenish yellow	Tall, vigorous tree with excellent hardiness

'Crimson Spire'
Columnar Apple Tree

TOP: 'Gravenstein'
BOTTOM: 'McIntosh'

TOP: 'Fuji'
BOTTOM 'Pink Pearl'

'Gala' 'Braeburn' 'William's Pride' 'Pettingill' 'Anna' 'Jonagold' 'Gordon' 'Mutsu' 'Gala' 'Liberty' 'Winter Pearmain'

A

aphids are potentially troublesome. Powdery mildew and fireblight can also infect apples in some regions. For timing of sprays and other control measures for any of the above problems, consult your Cooperative Extension Office or a reliable local nursery.

Dwarf and spur apples. Dwarf apples (5–8 ft. tall and wide) are made by grafting wood from standard apple varieties onto dwarfing rootstocks such as M9, EMLA27, and P22. Dwarfs take up little room and bear at a younger age than standard apples, but they have shallow roots and need the support of a post, fence, wall, or sturdy trellis to withstand wind and heavy rain. They are not reliable in the coldest regions. They also need good soil and extra care in feeding and watering. Genetic dwarf apples, such as 'Garden Delicious', are naturally small and stay that way; even grafting them onto a standard (nondwarfing) rootstock would not produce a standard-size tree.

Semidwarf trees are larger than dwarfs but smaller than standard trees. They bear bigger crops than dwarfs and take up less space than standards. Many commercial orchards get high yields by using semidwarf trees and planting them close together. Semidwarfing rootstocks MARK, M26, and M7 reduce normal tree height by about half; the trees may be espaliered or trellised if planted 12–16 ft. apart and allowed to grow 8–12 ft. tall. Semidwarfing rootstocks MM106 and MM111 reduce height by approximately 15 to 25 percent.

Apples bear flowers and fruit on spurs—short branches that grow from wood 2 years old or older. Spurs normally begin to appear only after tree has grown in place 3 to 5 years. On spur-type apples, spurs form earlier (within 2 years after planting) and grow closer together on shorter branches, giving more apples per foot of branch. Spur apples are natural or genetic semidwarfs about two-thirds the size of standard apple trees. They can be further dwarfed by grafting onto dwarfing rootstocks; EMLA27, M9, P22, and MARK give smallest trees.

Columnar apple trees develop a single spirelike trunk to 8 ft. tall, with fruiting spurs directly on the trunk or on very short branchlets. Total width does not exceed 2 ft. Varieties include 'Crimson Spire', red fruit with tart-sweet white flesh; 'Emerald Spire', mellow, sweet green fruit with gold blush; 'Golden Sentinel', sweet, juicy yellow fruit; 'Northpole', crisp, juicy McIntosh-type apple; 'Scarlet Sentinel', large, sweet green-yellow fruit with red blush; 'Scarlet Spire', juicy red-and-green eating apple; and 'Ultra Spire', tart, tangy red apple with yellowish blush. Two varieties are needed for pollination. Columnar trees are easy to maintain and attractive as accent, screen, or container plants. Plant at least 18 in. apart.

Training and pruning apple trees. For most home use, plant dwarf or semidwarf trees for ease in maintenance and harvest. Even commercial growers favor these smaller trees, since closer spacing permits more trees to the acre and a heavier crop. Preferred style is pyramidal or modified leader, in which widely angled branches are encouraged to grow in spiral placement around the trunk. Don't worry about fruit production the first 4 or 5 years—prune to develop strong, evenly spaced scaffold branches. Keep narrow-angled crotches from developing; don't let side branches outgrow the leader or secondary branches outgrow the primary branches.

To prune mature trees (do it late in the dormant season), remove weak, dead, or poorly placed branches and twigs, especially those growing toward the center of the tree (bearing is heaviest when some sun can reach the middle). Removing such growth will encourage development of strong new wood with new fruiting spurs (on apples, spurs may produce for up to 20 years but they tend to weaken after about 3 years) and discourage mildew. If you have inherited an old tree, selective thinning of branches will accomplish the same goal.

Dwarf trees can be grown as espaliers tied to wood or wire frames, fences, or other supports. The technique requires manipulating the branches to the desired pattern and pruning out excess growth. On columnar apples, just remove any wayward growth.

For ornamental relatives, see *Malus*.

A PRACTICAL GUIDE TO GARDENING
PLEASE SEE PAGES 658–731

APRICOT

Rosaceae

DECIDUOUS FRUIT TREES

ZONES VARY BY VARIETY

FULL SUN

REGULAR WATER DURING FRUIT DEVELOPMENT

Apricot

This stone fruit, which originated in China, can be grown throughout much of the West, with some limitations. Because apricot trees bloom early in the season, they will not fruit in regions with late frosts. In cool, humid coastal areas, tree and fruit are usually subject to brown rot and blight; in mild-winter areas of Southern California, only varieties with low requirements for winter chill do well.

Standard apricot trees reach 15–20 ft. high and wide and make good, easily maintained dual-purpose fruit and shade trees; they can also be espaliered. Thin, roundish leaves to 3 in. long are reddish when new, maturing to bright green; flowers are pink or white.

Apricot trees bear most of their fruit on short spurs that form on the previous year's growth and remain fruitful for about 4 years. Most varieties ripen from late spring into summer. To get a good crop of large fruit, do this: in midspring, thin excess fruit from branches, leaving 2–4 in. between individual fruits. Prune in summer (rather than in the dormant season, as is usually recommended) to avoid Eutypa dieback, a disease characterized by sudden limb dieback and oozing cankers; it is spread by rain and can infect trees through pruning wounds.

Apricots are subject to various other diseases and insect pests. To avert some problems, consult your Cooperative Extension Office for a local timetable and directions for preventive spraying. Essential treatment dates are during dormancy, before and after flowering, and at red-bud stage.

The following is a good representation of nursery varieties; many are available on dwarf and semidwarf rootstocks. Some varieties need a pollenizer, as indicated. For ornamental relatives, see *Prunus*.

'Autumn Royal'. Zones 2, 3, 6–9, 12–16, 18–24. Resembles 'Blenheim' but fruit ripens very late; only fall-ripening apricot tree.

'Blenheim' ('Royal'). Zones 2, 3, 6–23. Standard variety in California's apricot regions. Good for canning or drying. Early to midseason.

'Chinese' ('Mormon'). Zones 1–3, 6. Late bloom, hardy tree; good production in late-frost and cold-winter regions. Midseason to late.

'Floragold'. Zones 2, 3, 6–23. Full-size fruit grows on natural semidwarf tree (about two-thirds the size of standard apricot tree). Early.

'Goldcot'. Zones 1–3. Developed for cold climates. Sweet flavor. Midseason.

'Golden Amber'. Zones 2, 3, 6–9, 12–16, 18–23. Like 'Blenheim' but blooms over month-long period; fruit ripens late.

WHAT APRICOTS NEED

CLIMATE: Ideal climate provides chilly winters, freedom from late frosts, and fairly warm, dry springs.

POLLINATION: Most varieties are self-fruitful; some need pollen from another apricot variety.

PRUNING: Moderation is the key. The goal is to conserve enough new growth to produce adequate new fruiting spurs and to remove old, exhausted spurs.

'Puget Gold' Apricot

DISEASE PREVENTION: Several rounds of preventive sprays may keep some problems at bay.

'GoldenGlo'. Zones 2, 3, 6–9, 12–16, 18–23. Only reliable genetic dwarf apricot; grows 4–6 ft. tall. Full-size, good-quality, sweet, mild fruit. Midseason to late.

'Gold Kist'. Zones 8, 9, 12–16, 18–23. Excellent sweet-tart flavor. Heavy bearing, even in mild-winter areas. Early.

'Goldrich'. Zones 2–6. Good-quality fruit on hardy, cold-resistant tree. Needs pollenizer. Midseason.

'Harcot'. Zones 1–11, 14–16. Medium to large fruit, sweet and juicy. Frost hardy, blooms late. Early.

'Harglow'. Zones 1–11, 14–16. Medium-size orange fruit, sometimes blushed red. Firm, sweet, flavorful. Late blooming; disease resistant. Early.

'Katy'. Zones 2, 3, 6–23. Large yellow fruit with red blush. Mild, sweet flavor. Favorite in mild-winter areas. Early.

'King'. Zones 8, 9, 12–16, 18–23. Very large, very highly colored. Hard to pollinate; 'Perfection' does best job. Early.

Manchurian apricot *(Prunus armeniaca mandshurica)*. Zones A2, A3; 1–3. Hardy shrub to small tree. Small, mild-flavored orange fruit, good for drying. Early.

'Moongold'. Zones 1–3. Plum-size, golden, sweet, sprightly fruit. Developed for cold-winter climates. Late.

'Moorpark'. Zones 2, 3, 6–11, 14–16. Very large fruit, fine flavor. Color develops unevenly. Good home dessert or drying variety, poor canner. Midseason.

'Newcastle'. Zones 10–12, 20–23. Good Southern California variety; needs little winter chill. Midseason.

'Perfection' ('Goldbeck'). Zones 2–9, 12–16, 18–23. Fruit very large but flavor only mediocre. Low chill requirement; hardy tree. Needs pollenizer. Early.

'Puget Gold'. Zones 4–6. Consistent bearer in Puget Sound area; fairly resistant to apricot diseases. Medium-size fruit with good flavor; low in acid. Late.

'Riland'. Zones 2, 3, 6. Highly colored, roundish fruit. Needs pollenizer. Midseason.

'Rival'. Zones 2–6. Large, oval orange fruit blushed red. Needs early-flowering pollenizer ('Perfection'). Early.

'Royalty'. Zones 2, 3, 6–9, 12–23. Extra-large fruit on heavy, wind-resistant spurs. Begins bearing at early age. Ripens early.

'Sun-Glow'. Zones 2–6. Highly colored, early fruit. Hardy tree with extra-hardy fruit buds. Midseason.

'Sungold'. Zones 1–3. Plum-size, slightly flattened, bright orange, sweet, mild fruit. Developed for cold-winter climates. Early.

'Tilton'. Zones 1–8, 10, 11, 18, 20. Higher chill requirement than 'Blenheim' but less subject to brown rot and sunburn. Midseason.

'Tomcot'. Zones 8, 9, 12–16. Large fruit with sweet orange flesh. Needs a pollenizer for best production. Early.

'Wenatchee' ('Wenatchee Moorpark'). Zones 2, 3, 6. Large fruit, excellent flavor. Midseason.

APRIUM. See PLUMCOT, PLUOT

APTENIA cordifolia (Mesembryanthemum cordifolium)

Aizoaceae

SUCCULENT SHRUBBY PERENNIAL

ZONES 12, 13, 15–17, 21–24; H1, H2

SOME SHADE IN HOTTEST CLIMATES

LITTLE TO MODERATE WATER

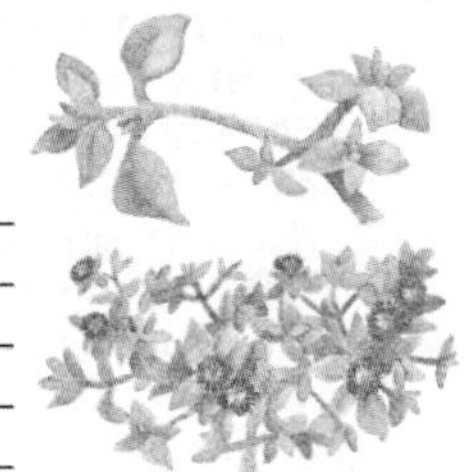

Aptenia cordifolia

South African ice plant relative. Trailing stems to 2 ft. long are profusely set with inch-wide, heart-shaped or oval, fleshy bright green leaves. Purplish red, inch-wide flowers bloom in spring and summer. Despite fleshy foliage, it looks less like ice plant than most other related plants do. Use as low trailer in rock garden, on slope or wall; plant 2 ft. apart. Also good in hanging pot. 'Variegata' has white-bordered leaves; hybrid 'Red Apple' has brighter red flowers.

Aquifoliaceae. The holly family contains evergreen trees and shrubs with berrylike fruit. *Ilex* (holly) is the only important genus.

AQUILEGIA

COLUMBINE

Ranunculaceae

PERENNIALS

ZONES VARY BY SPECIES

FULL SUN OR LIGHT SHADE

REGULAR WATER

Aquilegia McKana Giant

Lacy foliage and beautifully poised flowers in exquisite pastels, deeper shades, and white give columbines a fairylike, woodland-glen quality. Plants are erect and range from 2 in. to 4 ft. high, depending on species or hybrid. Divided leaves reminiscent of maidenhair fern *(Adiantum)* may be fresh green, blue green, or gray green. Slender, branching stems carry erect or nodding flowers to 3 in. across, often with sepals and petals in contrasting colors; they usually have backward-projecting, nectar-bearing spurs. Some columbines have large flowers and very long spurs; these have an airier look than short-spurred and spurless kinds. Double-flowered types lack the delicacy of the single-flowered sort, but they make a bolder color mass. Bloom season comes in spring and early summer.

Plants are not fussy about soil as long as it is well drained. On all columbines, cut back old stems for second crop of flowers. All kinds attract hummingbirds. Most are not long-lived and will need to be replaced every 3 or 4 years. Allow spent flowers to form seed capsules to ensure a crop of volunteer seedlings. If you're growing hybrids, the seedlings won't necessarily duplicate the parent plants, but seedlings from species (if grown isolated from other columbines) should closely resemble the originals. Leaf miners are a potential pest, especially on hybrids.

A. alpina. ALPINE COLUMBINE. Zones A1–A3; 1–9, 14–24. Native to the Alps. Grows 1–2 ft. tall, 1 ft. wide. Nodding, bright blue flowers to 2 in. across, with curved spurs to 1 in. long. Good rock garden plant.

A. caerulea. ROCKY MOUNTAIN COLUMBINE. Zones A1–A3; 1–11, 14–24. Native to the Rockies; state flower of Colorado. To 1½–3 ft. high, 2 ft. wide. Blue-and-white flowers erect, 2 in. or more across, with straight or spreading spurs to 2 in. long. An important parent of many long-spurred hybrids.

A. chrysantha. GOLDEN COLUMBINE, GOLDEN-SPURRED COLUMBINE. Zones 1–24. Native to Arizona, New Mexico, and adjacent Mexico. One of showiest species. Large, many-branched plant to 3–4 ft. tall, 1–2 ft. wide. Undersides of leaflets densely covered with soft hairs. Upright, clear yellow, 1½–3-in. flowers with slender, hooked spurs 2–2½ in. long.

A. desertorum. ARIZONA COLUMBINE. Zones 2b, 3, 6–24. Native to northern Arizona, Utah, New Mexico. To 1½ ft. high, 15 in. wide. Rich bright orange to yellow, 1½-in. flowers. Spurs are held in the same plane as the rest of the blossom and extend beyond it, giving the bloom as a whole a distinct arrowhead shape.

A. flabellata. Zones A2, A3; 1–9, 14–24. Native to Japan. Stocky plant 8 in.–1½ ft. high, 1 ft. wide, with nodding, 1½-in., two-tone flowers of lilac blue and creamy white. Hooked spurs to 1 in. long. Differs from most other columbines in having thicker, darker leaves with often overlapping segments. *A. f. minor* is a very dwarf form (just 4 in. high). Good rock garden plant.

A. formosa. WESTERN COLUMBINE. Zones A1–A3; 1–11, 14–24. Native Alaska to Northern California, Montana, Utah. Grows 1½–3 ft. high, 1½ ft. wide. Nodding red-and-yellow flowers are 1½–2 in. across, with stout, straight red spurs. Good in woodland garden. Allow it to set seeds, which are relished by song sparrows, juncos, and other small birds. *A. f. truncata* (sometimes sold as *A. californica*) has yellow-and-orange blossoms with red spurs.

A. hybrids. Zones A2, A3; 1–10, 14–24. Derived from several species. Preferred tall hybrid strains include graceful, long-spurred McKana Giants and double-flowering Spring Song (both to 3 ft. tall, 2 ft. wide). Nora Barlow Mixed, reaching 2–2½ ft. high and 2 ft. wide, has double flowers in a wide range of colors (the original 'Nora Barlow' has reddish pink blooms with white margins). About the same size is Vervaeneana Woodside Variegated Mixed, with variegated leaves and various flower colors. Lower-growing strains include Biedermeier and Dragonfly (1 ft. high and wide); long-spurred Music (1½ ft. high and wide); and single to double, upward-facing Fairyland (15 in. high and wide).

A. longissima. Zones 1–11, 14–24. Native to southwest Texas, southern Arizona, and northern Mexico. Grows 2½–3 ft. tall, 1½–2 ft. wide. Similar to *A. chrysantha.* Numerous erect, pale yellow blossoms with very narrow, drooping, 4–6-in.-long spurs.

A. saximontana. Zones 1–10, 14–24. Native to the Rocky Mountains. In effect, a miniature *A. caerulea,* just 4–8 in. high and wide.

A. sibirica. Zones A1–A3; 1–6. To 2 ft. tall and wide, with short-spurred, 1½-in., blue to dark purplish red flowers on leafless stalks.

A. vulgaris. EUROPEAN COLUMBINE. Zones A2, A3; 1–10, 14–24. Naturalized in eastern U.S. Grows 1–2½ ft. tall, 1 ft. wide. Nodding blue or violet flowers to 2 in. across; short, knobby spurs about ¾ in. long. Many selections and hybrids offer single to fully double blooms, either short spurred or spurless.

ARABIS

ROCKCRESS

Brassicaceae (Cruciferae)

PERENNIALS

ZONES VARY BY SPECIES

FULL SUN

MODERATE WATER

Arabis caucasica

Low-growing, spreading plants for edgings, rock gardens, ground covers, pattern plantings. All kinds have attractive year-round foliage and clusters of small white, pink, or rose purple flowers in spring. Give good drainage.

A. alpina. MOUNTAIN ROCKCRESS. Zones 1–7. Native to high elevations of Europe. Low, tufted, rough-hairy plant 4–10 in. high, 2 ft. wide. White flowers in dense, short clusters. 'Rosea' bears pink flowers; 'Variegata' has yellow-edged green leaves. Plants sold as *A. alpina* are often really *A. caucasica.*

A. blepharophylla. CALIFORNIA ROCKCRESS, ROSE CRESS. Zones 5, 6, 15–17. Native to rocky hillsides and ridges along Northern California coast. Tufted plant to about 8 in. high and wide. Fragrant rose purple flowers in short, dense clusters. Good in rock garden, containers.

A. caucasica (A. albida). WALL ROCKCRESS. Zones A1; 1–10, 14–24. Dependable old favorite; native Mediterranean region to Iran. Forms mat of gray-green leaves to 6 in. high, 1½ ft. wide. White flowers almost cover plant during bloom season. Excellent ground cover and base planting for spring-flowering bulbs such as daffodils and 'Paper White' narcissus. Provide some shade in hot climates. 'Variegata' has gray leaves with creamy white margins; 'Flore Plena' is double flowered; 'Rosabella' and 'Pink Charm' bear pink blooms.

A. ferdinandi-coburgi. Zones 2b–10, 14–24. Native to Bulgaria. Tight clumps to 4 in. high, 1 ft. wide. White blossoms. Most common form is 'Variegata', with leaves heavily edged and splashed with white.

A. procurrens. Zones 3–10, 14–24. Native to southeastern Europe. Creeping plant with 1½-in. leaves and white flowers clustered on 4–12-in. stems. Over time, spreads widely.

A. × sturii. Zones 1–10, 14–24. Dense, fist-size cushions of small bright green leaves eventually grow into small mats bearing clusters of white flowers on 2–3-in. stems. Some consider it among the finest rock garden plants.

Araceae. The arum family contains plants ranging from tuberous or rhizomatous perennials to shrubby or climbing tropical foliage plants. Leaves are often highly ornamental; while variable in shape, they tend to be arrow-like. Inconspicuous flowers cluster tightly on a club-shaped spadix within an often showy leaflike bract (spathe). Examples are *Anthurium,* calla *(Zantedeschia),* and *Philodendron.* Sap of many is highly irritating to mouth and throat.

ARACHNIODES simplicior

Dryopteridaceae

FERN

ZONES 4–24

PARTIAL OR FULL SHADE

REGULAR TO AMPLE WATER

Arachniodes simplicior 'Variegata'

From Japan and China; sometimes referred to as holly fern. Usually seen in its variety 'Variegata', growing 10–16 in. tall and twice as wide. Fronds are broadly triangular and once-divided, the divisions deeply cut. Each division is marked by a yellow stripe along its full length. Evergreen where winters are warm; deciduous in frosty regions.

ARALIA

Araliaceae

DECIDUOUS SHRUB-TREES

ZONES VARY BY SPECIES

FULL SUN OR PARTIAL SHADE

MODERATE TO REGULAR WATER

Aralia elata

Most are striking bold-leafed plants that may eventually grow to 25–30 ft. tall under ideal conditions. Not for small gardens. Often shrublike and multistemmed (because of suckering habit), especially in colder areas where they may grow to 10 ft. high. Clumps may be from one-half to almost as wide as they are tall. Branches are nearly vertical or slightly spreading, usually very spiny. Huge leaves, clustered at ends of branches and divided into many leaflets, have effective pattern value. White flowers, small but in such large, branched clusters that they are showy in midsummer, are followed by purplish berrylike fruit enjoyed by birds.

Grow in well-drained soil. Not good near swimming pools because of spines; even leafstalks are sometimes prickly. Protect plants from wind to avoid burning foliage. Need minimal pruning; dig out suckers to limit spread of clump.

A. elata (A. chinensis). ANGELICA TREE. Zones 1–10, 14–24. Native to Asia. Only moderately spiny. Leaves 2–3 ft. long, divided into toothed, stalkless, 2–6-in.-long leaflets. 'Variegata' has leaflets strikingly bordered with creamy white.

A. elegantissima. See Schefflera elegantissima

A. papyrifera. See Tetrapanax papyriferus

A. sieboldii. JAPANESE ARALIA. See Fatsia japonica

A. spinosa. HERCULES' CLUB, DEVIL'S WALKING STICK. Zones 3–9, 14–24. Native to eastern U.S. Puts up several spiny, usually unbranched stems, each of them crowned by 2–6-ft.-long leaves. This is one of the most tropical-looking genuinely hardy plants. Has a coarse appearance in winter.

Araliaceae. The aralia family of herbaceous and woody plants is marked by leaves that are divided fanwise into leaflets or veined in pattern like the fingers of a hand. Individually tiny flowers are in round clusters or in large compound clusters. Examples are ivy *(Hedera),* Japanese aralia *(Fatsia japonica),* and *Schefflera.*

ARAUCARIA

Araucariaceae

EVERGREEN TREES

ZONES VARY BY SPECIES

FULL SUN

REGULAR WATER

These strange-looking conifers provide a distinctive silhouette with their evenly spread tiers of stiff branches. Most have stiff, closely overlapping, dark to bright green leaves. All do well in a wide range of soils with adequate drainage.

Make impressive skyline trees and are seen in that role in many parks and old estates in California—but they become so towering that they really do need the space they have in a park or large, open property. And they are not trees to sit under—with age they bear large, spiny, 10–15-lb. cones that fall with a crash. They thrive in containers for several years, even in desert areas.

Araucaria araucana

A. araucana (A. imbricata). MONKEY PUZZLE TREE. Zones 4–9, 14–24; H1, H2. Native to Chile. Arboreal oddity with heavy, spreading branches and ropelike branchlets closely set with sharp-pointed dark green leaves. Slow growing in youth, it eventually reaches 70–90 ft. tall, 30 ft. wide. Hardiest of araucarias.

A. bidwillii. BUNYA-BUNYA. Zones 7–9, 12–24; H1, H2. Native to Australia. Probably most widely planted araucaria in both coastal and valley areas of California. Moderate growth to 80 ft. tall, 60 ft. wide; broadly rounded crown supplies dense shade. Juvenile leaves are glossy, rather narrow, ¾–2 in. long, stiff, more or less spreading in two rows; mature leaves are oval, ½ in. long, rather woody, spirally arranged and overlapping along branches. Unusual houseplant; very tough and tolerant of low light.

A. heterophylla (A. excelsa). NORFOLK ISLAND PINE. Zones 17, 21–24; H1, H2. Native to Norfolk Island near Australia. Moderate growth rate to 100 ft. tall, 60 ft. wide. Pyramidal shape. Juvenile leaves rather narrow, ½ in. long, curved, sharp pointed; mature leaves somewhat triangular, densely overlapping. Can be held in pots for years—outdoors in mild climates, indoors anywhere. Popular Christmas tree in Hawaii.

Araucaria heterophylla

Araucariaceae. Coniferous trees with symmetrical branching habit and leaves that vary from needlelike to broad and leathery. *Araucaria* is the only representative in this book.

ARBORVITAE. See THUJA

ARBUTUS

Ericaceae

EVERGREEN TREES OR SHRUBS

ZONES VARY BY SPECIES

FULL SUN, EXCEPT AS NOTED

LITTLE TO REGULAR WATER, EXCEPT AS NOTED

Arbutus unedo

All have ornamental bark, clusters of little urn-shaped flowers, decorative edible fruit, handsome foliage. Provide good drainage, especially if plant receives regular water. Thin growth of all types as needed.

A. andrachne. Zones 8, 9, 14–24. Native to eastern Mediterranean. To 20–40 ft. tall and wide. Like *A. menziesii* but is not as difficult to grow and has smaller, less shiny leaves. Peeling bark is beautiful.

A. 'Marina'. Zones 8, 9, 14–24. Hybrid of uncertain parentage. To 40 ft. tall (usually less) and equally wide. Resembles *A. unedo* but has larger leaves and rosy pink fall flowers. Good garden substitute for *A. menziesii.*

A. menziesii. MADRONE, MADRONA. Zones 4–7, 14–19. Native from British Columbia to Southern California in Coast Ranges, occasionally in middle elevations of Sierra Nevada. Mature height ranges from 20 to 100 ft. Forms broad, round head almost as wide as tall. In groves, plants are more slender. Main feature is smooth, reddish brown bark that peels in thin flakes. Leathery, 3–6-in.-long leaves are shiny dark green on top, dull gray green beneath. In spring, large clusters of white to pinkish, bell-shaped flowers appear at branch ends. These are followed in early fall by clusters of brilliant orange to red, rough-coated berries that remain on tree most of winter if birds don't get them.

If you live in madrone country and have a tree in your garden, treasure it. Its requirements in gardens outside its native area are exacting: it must have fast drainage and nonalkaline water. Water just enough to keep plants going until they are established, and then give only infrequent and deep watering.

A. unedo. STRAWBERRY TREE. Zones 4–24; damaged in severe winters in Zones 4–7 but worth risk. Native to southern Europe, Ireland. Remarkably good performance in wide range of climates and soils, from desert to seashore; tolerates wind at the beach. In California, it is one of the best lawn or raised-bed trees. Sun or part shade; needs some shade in the desert.

Slow to moderate growth to 8–35 ft. with equal spread. Normally has basal suckers, stem sprouts. Can thin branches to make open-crowned tree, or plant several and leave unpruned to make screen. Trunk and branches have rich red-brown, shredding bark; tend to become twisted and gnarled in age. Dark green, handsome, red-stemmed leaves are oblong and 2–3 in. long. Clusters of small white or greenish white, urn-shaped flowers and round, ¾-in. fruit, yellow (young) and red (mature), like strawberries in texture, appear at the same time in fall and winter; fruit is edible but usually mealy and bland in flavor. Individual plants may produce tasty fruit.

Varieties include 'Elfin King', a dwarf form (not over 5 ft. tall at 10 years old) that flowers and fruits nearly continuously; 'Compacta', seldom exceeding 10 ft. high; and 'Oktoberfest', a 6–8-ft.-tall plant with deep pink flowers.

ARCHONTOPHOENIX

Arecaceae (Palmae)

PALMS

ZONES 21–24; OR INDOORS

SUN OR PART SHADE; BRIGHT INDIRECT LIGHT

MODERATE TO REGULAR WATER

Archontophoenix cunninghamiana

Native to rain forests of eastern Australia; called bangalow or piccabeen palms in that country. Grow to 50 ft. or taller, with 10–15-ft. spread. Handsome, stately, difficult to transplant when large. Where winds are strong, plant in lee of buildings to prevent damage. Young trees can't take frost; mature plants may stand 28°F/–2°C. They tolerate shade and can grow for many years grouped under tall trees. Old leaves shed cleanly, leaving smooth green trunks. Feathery leaves on mature trees 8–10 ft. long, green above, gray green beneath. Good potted plants indoors or out.

A. alexandrae. ALEXANDRA PALM. Trunk enlarged toward base.

A. cunninghamiana (Seaforthia elegans). KING PALM. More common than *A. alexandrae.* Trunk not prominently enlarged at base. Clustered amethyst flowers are handsome. Highly recommended for nearly frost-free areas.

ARCTANTHEMUM arcticum. See CHRYSANTHEMUM arcticum

ARCTOSTAPHYLOS

MANZANITA

Ericaceae

EVERGREEN SHRUBS

ZONES VARY BY SPECIES

FULL SUN OR LIGHT SHADE

LITTLE TO MODERATE WATER

Arctostaphylos densiflora

This enormous clan of evergreen woody plants is native to the Far West. Plants vary from creeping ground covers to treelike shrubs, but all have small, urn-shaped white or pink flowers, usually in late winter to early spring, followed by berrylike red or brown fruits that attract birds. (Fruits are noted in descriptions below if they are particularly attractive.) Most are characterized by (and admired for) crooked branches with smooth red to purple bark.

Manzanitas require excellent drainage, but they can tolerate poor soil and in fact prefer rocky or sandy, acid soils to rich, heavy ones. To get quick coverage from low ground cover types, plant about 2 ft. apart, then mulch to suppress weeds and encourage rooting along stems. The first summer after planting any manzanita, water every 4 to 7 days, depending on the weather. Once established, plants in warm-summer areas generally thrive on once-a-month watering in well-drained soil; in heavy soil and where summers are cool, they need less frequent irrigation. You may get away with watering just once or twice a summer.

Regular pruning is not required. To make plants denser and more uniformly compact, pinch new spring growth to force branching. On types with interesting branch structure, remove any limbs that detract from effect. Don't cut into bare wood; plants won't send out new growth.

A. 'Austin Hill'. Zones 4–9, 14–24. Smaller (to 8 ft. tall and wide) than *A. manzanita* 'Dr. Hurd', but otherwise similar, with burgundy-colored bark and good tolerance for garden watering.

A. bakeri 'Louis Edmunds'. Zones 4–9, 14–17. Selection of a species native to Sonoma area, California. Upright shrub to 5–6 ft. tall and wide. Gray-green foliage; pink flowers in hanging clusters. Good tolerance for garden watering.

A. columbiana. HAIRY MANZANITA. Zones 4–6, 15–17. Treelike species native to low coastal mountains, central California to British Columbia. Form propagated and sold in northwestern nurseries is called 'Oregon Hybrid'. Low-growing, compact shrub about 3 ft. high and 5–7 ft. wide, with reddish brown bark and 3-in. gray-green leaves. White flowers, red-cheeked brownish fruit. Useful plant, tough enough for highway landscaping in western Oregon and Washington.

A. densiflora. VINE HILL MANZANITA. Zones 7–9, 14–21. Native to Sonoma area, California. Generally low and spreading; outer branches take root when they touch soil. Slender, crooked main stems; smooth, reddish black bark. Small, glossy, light or dark green leaves. White or pink flowers. In bank planting, low types do best on east- or northeast-facing slopes, in loose soil with good drainage.

'Howard McMinn' forms a mound to 5–6 ft. tall (usually much lower), spreading as far as 7 ft. in 5 years. If you prune branch tips (but not those of prostrate branches) after flowering, plant becomes as dense as sheared Kurume azalea. Whitish pink flowers. A similar but somewhat taller and broader variety is 'Harmony'. It's less well known than 'Howard McMinn' but considered the best form by some specialists. 'Sentinel', to 6 ft. or taller and spreading to 8 ft., has light green, downy leaves and more upright growth. Can be trained as small tree by selecting dominant stem or stems and removing others. It is sensitive to salt burn, root rots.

A. edmundsii. LITTLE SUR MANZANITA. Zones 6–9, 14–24. Foot-tall species from coastal Monterey area, California. Several named selections are good ground covers, forming broad mats to about 12 ft. wide. Fast-growing 'Carmel Sur', with neat gray-green foliage and soft pink flowers, has exceptionally good form; very garden-water tolerant. 'Danville' has light green, roundish, inch-long leaves on red stems and bears pink flowers in early to midwinter. Slow-growing 'Little Sur' has dense, flat habit, pointed leaves with reddish margins (bronze when new), and soft pink flowers; good hillside planting. 'Parvifolia' has exceptionally shiny foliage (new growth is rich bronze) and showy pink flowers in early spring.

A. 'Emerald Carpet'. Zones 6–9, 14–24. One of the greenest, most uniform ground cover manzanitas. Forms a dense carpet 8–14 in. tall, mounding slightly higher after many years. Spreads about 5 ft. Roundish oval, ½-in.-long leaves, bright green even in hottest, driest weather. Small pink flowers are not showy. In hot interior valleys, it needs deep irrigation every 2 to 3 weeks.

A. franciscana. Zones 6–9, 14–24. Native to San Francisco but nearly extinct there. Grows to 2½ ft. high, spreads slowly (in 15 years) to 7 ft. White flowers.

A. glauca. Zones 4–9, 14–24. Native California to Baja California. Spreading shrub to 15 ft. tall, 20 ft. wide, with dark reddish brown bark and 3-in., blue-gray leaves. Large, branched clusters of pink to white flowers.

A. hookeri. MONTEREY MANZANITA. Zones 6–9, 14–24. Native to Monterey, California. Slowly forms a dense mound 1½–4 ft. high, spreading 6 ft. or more. Small, glossy green leaves; white to pinkish flowers; shiny, bright red fruit; smooth, red-brown bark. Good on hillsides. 'Monterey Carpet' is a compact grower to 1 ft. high, 12 ft. wide. 'Wayside' grows 4 ft. tall, 8 ft. or wider; may be slow to fill in but eventually forms dense, attractive mound.

A. 'Indian Hill'. Zones 6–9, 14–24. Ground cover that looks like a small-leafed *A. edmundsii*. Near-white flowers in winter. Very tolerant of garden watering.

A. insularis. ISLAND MANZANITA. From Channel Islands, California. Zones 16–24. Large, dense shrub to 10–15 ft. tall and wide. Bright green leaves; large, drooping clusters of white flowers in midwinter. 'Canyon Sparkles' is a compact selection (about 4 ft. tall, 6 ft. wide).

A. 'John Dourley'. Zones 6–9, 14–24. One of the best of the newer selections, it grows to 3 ft. tall, 6–10 ft. wide, with gray-green foliage (bronze when new) and pink-tinged white flowers. Good tolerance for garden watering.

A. manzanita. COMMON MANZANITA. Zones 4–9, 14–24. Native to inner Coast Ranges, Sierra Nevada foothills; widely adapted. Tall shrub or shrub-tree 6–20 ft. high, 4–10 ft. wide. Picturesque, crooked branching habit; purplish red bark. Small, shiny, bright to dull green, broadly oval leaves. White to pink flowers in drooping clusters. Fruit starts out white, then turns deep red. 'Dr. Hurd' is a treelike form to 15 ft. tall and as wide or wider, with mahogany bark, large light green leaves, and white winter flowers.

A. × media. Zones 4–9, 14–24. May be a natural hybrid of *A. uva-ursi* and *A. columbiana.* Looks like a taller-growing *A. uva-ursi* (to 2 ft.), with brighter red branches and leathery dark green leaves; also spreads faster.

A. nummularia. FORT BRAGG MANZANITA. Zones 14–24. Dense foliage; nearly dome-shaped, low shrub, usually under 2½ ft. high. Small, almost circular bright green leaves; little white flowers. Attractive but considered difficult to grow outside its native north coastal California forests. Needs good drainage, acid soil, and some shade except near coast.

A. 'Pacific Mist'. Zones 7–9, 14–24. To 2½ ft. tall, at least 10 ft. wide. Spreading stems turn upward near ends. Deep reddish brown bark, narrow gray-green leaves, sparse white bloom. Needs pinching to force branching, but eventually forms a good, dense ground cover.

A. pajaroensis. PAJARO MANZANITA. Zones 14–24. Native to central Monterey Bay area, California. To 3–8 ft. tall, 10–12 ft. wide. New growth bronzy, maturing to bluish green. Pink to white flowers. 'Paradise' is a choice pink-flowered selection with long-lasting bronze foliage color. 'Warren Roberts' is similar, but mature leaves are more bluish color and new growth is darker bronze.

A. pumila. DUNE MANZANITA. Zones 16, 17. Native to dunes around Monterey Bay, California. Spreading, prostrate habit, to 1–2½ ft. high; branches root freely where they touch ground. Plant 6 ft. apart. Narrowish, dull green leaves. Short, dense clusters of small white to pink flowers. Good ground cover in sandy soil near coast.

A. 'Sunset'. Zones 6–9, 14–24. Natural hybrid between *A. hookeri* and *A. pajaroensis.* Foliage is coppery red when new, maturing to bright green. Makes mound 4–5 ft. tall, 4–6 ft. wide. Pinkish white flowers.

A. uva-ursi. BEARBERRY, KINNIKINNICK. Zones A1–A3; 1–9, 14–24. Native from Northern California north to Alaska; also widespread in other northern latitudes. Long a popular ground or bank cover in Pacific Northwest and intermountain areas. Plant is prostrate, spreading and rooting as it grows; eventually forms a mat 15 ft. wide. Small, glossy, leathery leaves are bright green, turning red or purplish in winter. White or pinkish flowers are followed by red fruits. Plants are slow to become established; mulch heavily between plants to suppress weeds until branches provide cover. The following named, cutting-grown varieties provide uniform appearance in large plantings.

'Alaska'. Flat grower with small, round dark green leaves.

'Massachusetts'. Small leafed, flat growing. Abundant pinkish white flowers and plentiful fruit. Good resistance to leaf spot and leaf gall in Northwest.

'Point Reyes'. Dark green leaves closely set along branches. More tolerant of heat and drought than 'Radiant'.

'Radiant'. Leaves lighter green and more widely spaced than those of 'Point Reyes'. Heavy crop of large fruit in fall, lasting into winter (but sometimes fails to fruit if pollinating insects are not active at bloom time).

'Vancouver Jade'. Flat growing like 'Alaska' and 'Massachusetts', but not as wide spreading as those two varieties. Jade green leaves turn bronzy red in winter.

'Wood's Compact'. Compact grower with red branches densely clad in dark green leaves. Pink flowers.

'Wood's Red'. Reliable crop of large berries. Small dark green leaves turn reddish in cold weather. Grows best in the Northwest and Northern California.

ARCTOTHECA calendula

CAPE WEED
Asteraceae (Compositae)
PERENNIAL
ZONES 8, 9, 13–24
FULL SUN
LITTLE OR NO WATER

Arctotheca calendula

South African native is a tough, easy-to-grow evergreen ground cover. Plants spread by runners to make a thick cover 6–12 in. high; space 1½ ft. apart for fast cover. Elongated gray-green leaves are deeply cleft. Yellow, 2-in. daisies bloom most of year, peaking in spring. Not fussy about soil. Suffers some frost damage when temperature dips just below freezing, but recovers quickly. Not for small areas, since plants can easily spread out of bounds (though they're easy to remove). Good on hillsides. Mow shaggy plantings to tidy them.

ARCTOTIS

AFRICAN DAISY
Asteraceae (Compositae)
ANNUALS AND PERENNIALS
ALL ZONES, EXCEPT AS NOTED
FULL SUN
MODERATE WATER

Arctotis acaulis

The name "African daisy" can refer to any of several plants from southern Africa, and identities are often confused, even by many seed companies and nurseries. *Arctotis* species have lobed leaves that are rough, hairy, or woolly; their flower heads usually have a contrasting ring of color around the central eye. *Dimorphotheca* species (commonly used for mass color in winter) have smooth green foliage, blooms that are white or in the yellow–orange–salmon range. Trailing ground cover African daisies and woody, shrubby white, yellow, or purple African daisies are *Osteospermum*.

In cold-winter areas, set out annuals (or perennials grown as annuals) in spring for summer bloom. Where winters are mild, plant in fall or winter for bloom from spring into early summer (with scattered bloom later). They do not withstand extreme heat and humidity.

A. acaulis. Perennial. Zones 5–9, 14–24. Spreading, stemless clumps of leaves to 1 ft. high. Yellow, 3½-in.-wide flower heads with purplish black centers. 'Magenta' has purplish red flowers.

A. breviscapa. Annual. Smaller than *A. acaulis* (to about 6 in. high), with brown-centered orange-yellow flowers.

A. hybrids. Most representatives of *Arctotis* sold in nurseries are hybrids that grow 1–1½ ft. tall and wide. The 3-in.-wide flowers come in white, pink, red, purplish, cream, yellow, and orange, usually with a dark ring around a nearly black central eye. Will self-sow but tend to revert to orange; to perpetuate colors you like, take cuttings. Plants survive as perennials in Zones 7–9, 14–24, but even there they bloom best in their first year.

A. venusta (A. stoechadifolia, Venidium fastuosum). Annual. Bushy growth to 2 ft. tall and 1½ ft. wide, with gray-green, slightly hairy leaves; white, 3-in.-wide daisies with a yellow ring surrounding a deep blue eye. In selection 'Zulu Prince', an inner ring of yellow and purple encircles a black center.

ARDISIA

MARLBERRY
Myrsinaceae
EVERGREEN SHRUBS
ZONES VARY BY SPECIES
PARTIAL OR FULL SHADE
REGULAR WATER

Ardisia japonica

This genus comprises 150 shrub species, but only the following two Asian natives are typically grown in Western gardens. Valued for handsome foliage and ornamental, beadlike, bright red berries that persist during winter. Provide rich, moisture-retentive, well-drained soil. If necessary, prune lightly before bloom period.

A. crenata (A. crenulata, A. crispa). Zones 15–24; H1, H2; or indoors. In warmest frost-free climates, often grown in the ground or in patio planters. Most familiar as a 1½-ft., single-stemmed houseplant; in a large tub, though, it can reach 4 ft. tall and almost that wide. Spirelike clusters of tiny white or pinkish flowers bloom in spring, carried above the shiny, wavy-edged, 3-in.-long leaves. Houseplants require indirect light in summer, several hours of direct sun in winter.

A. japonica. Zones 6, 15–17. Low shrub that spreads by runners to produce a series of upright branches 6–18 in. high. Makes a good-quality ground cover in shade; set plants about 2 ft. apart. Leathery, 4-in.-long, bright green leaves are clustered at tops of branches. White, ½-in. flowers, two to six in a cluster, appear in fall. Forms with white or gold foliage variegation are sometimes sold.

Arecaceae. It's difficult to generalize about any plant family as large and widespread as palms. Generally speaking, they have single, unbranched trunks of considerable height; some grow in clusters, though, and some are dwarf or stemless. The leaves are usually divided into many leaflets, either like ribs of a fan (fan palms) or like a feather, with many parallel leaflets growing outward from a long central stem (feather palms). But some palms have undivided leaves. This family was formerly called Palmae. See also Palms.

ARECA lutescens. See DYPSIS lutescens

ARECASTRUM romanzoffianum. See SYAGRUS romanzoffianum

A

ARENARIA

SANDWORT

Caryophyllaceae

PERENNIALS

ZONES VARY BY SPECIES

EXPOSURE NEEDS VARY BY SPECIES

WATER NEEDS VARY BY SPECIES

Arenaria montana

Low evergreen plants carpet the ground with dense mats of mosslike foliage, have small white flowers in late spring and summer. They are often used as lawn substitutes, between stepping-stones, or for velvety green patches in rock gardens. Can be invasive; hard to eradicate in well-watered gardens. Provide good drainage.

A. balearica. CORSICAN SANDWORT. Zones 4–9, 14–24. Mediterranean native forms a mat to 3 in. high, 1½ ft. wide. Leaves oval, thick, glossy, to ⅛ in. long. Grows best in shade with regular water. Adapted to planting in small areas—for example, to cover soil of container-grown tree.

A. montana. Zones 2–9, 14–24. Native to mountains of southwestern Europe. Grows 2–4 in. high; weak stems up to 1 ft. long, usually covered with soft hairs. Leaves grayish green, ½–¾ in. long. Good plant to let trail over rock or tumble over low wall. Full sun. Moderate water.

A. verna (A. v. caespitosa). See Sagina subulata

ARGEMONE

PRICKLY POPPY

Papaveraceae

ANNUALS OR BIENNIALS

ZONES VARY BY SPECIES

FULL SUN

LITTLE OR NO WATER

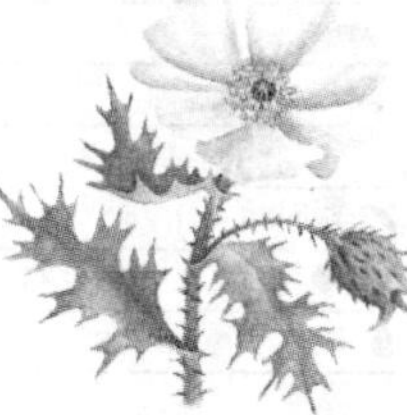
Argemone mexicana

Prickly-leafed and prickly-stemmed plants to 3 ft. tall, 1½ ft. wide, with large, showy poppies that bloom mainly in summer. Easy to grow from seeds sown in place or in pots (transplant gently). Will reseed and colonize. Provide good drainage. Seed specialists may offer other species.

A. mexicana. MEXICAN POPPY. Annual. Zones 2, 3, 7–24; H1, H2. Native to West Indies and probably Central America and Florida; naturalized in the Southwest and Hawaii. Yellow to orange, 1½–2½-in. flowers. 'Yellow Lustre' grows 1½–2 ft. tall, has lemony orange blooms.

A. polyanthemos (A. intermedia). Annual or biennial. Zones 2, 3, 7–24. Western native with white, 2½–4-in. flowers.

ARGYRANTHEMUM frutescens. See CHRYSANTHEMUM frutescens

ARISAEMA

JACK-IN-THE-PULPIT

Araceae

PERENNIALS FROM TUBERS

ZONES VARY BY SPECIES

PARTIAL OR FULL SHADE

REGULAR WATER DURING GROWTH AND BLOOM

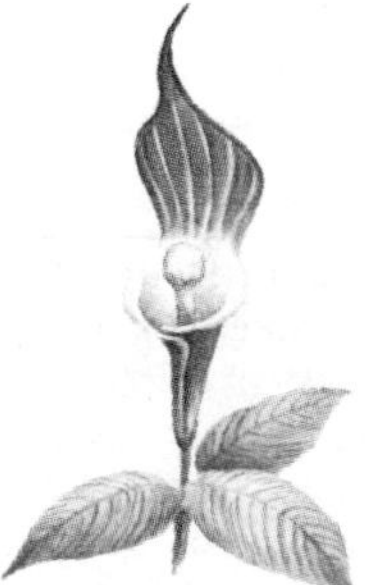
Arisaema sikokianum

Curious rather than beautiful relatives of calla *(Zantedeschia)*, attractive both to children and to fanciers of the odd. Flowers are tiny, crowded on a club-shaped spadix surrounded by an overarching spathe (flower bract) that is usually green or dull purple in color and often striped in a contrasting color. In late spring, tubers send up one to three leaves, each divided into three or more leaflets. Inflorescences appear on a separate stalk in spring or early summer. As flowers fade, spathe withers and spadix forms orange to red seeds.

These are woodland plants, appreciative of organic material in the soil. Plant in fall, setting tubers 1 ft. apart, 2 in. deep. Plants die to the ground in winter; don't let dormant tubers dry out completely. Species other than those listed below may appear from time to time in specialists' catalogs.

A. sikokianum. Zones 3–6, 14–17. From Japan. To 20 in. tall, with 6-in. leaflets. A 4–12-in. stalk supports a 6-in. spathe that is erect rather than arching. Spathe is purplish brown on the outside, yellowish white within; spadix is pure white and expanded at the tip.

A. speciosum. Zones 4–6, 14–17. Himalayan native. A single leaf grows to 2 ft., with 8–16-in.-long leaflets on a stalk marbled with dark purple. Spathe is blackish purple outside, whitish within, up to 8 in. long; spadix has a long, whiplike tip that can reach 2½ ft. long.

A. tortuosum. Zones 4–6, 14–17. Himalayan native. Can reach 4 ft. tall. Leaves have many narrow leaflets. Green or purple spathe to 6 in. long; spadix protrudes from spathe, then curves upward for several inches.

A. triphyllum. Zones 1–6. From eastern North America; the common Jack-in-the-pulpit familiar to easterners. Grows to 2 ft. tall. Both spathe and spadix are green or purple; spathe is striped in white or green.

ARISTEA ecklonii

Iridaceae

PERENNIAL

ZONES 8, 9, 12–24

FULL SUN OR PARTIAL SHADE

MODERATE WATER

Aristea ecklonii

Native to southern Africa. Swordlike evergreen leaves form clump 2 ft. tall and wide, above which rise winged, flattened, 2½-ft. branching flower stalks that bear bright blue six-petaled flowers less than an inch wide. Individual flowers are short lived, but new ones appear over a long season. Remove spent flower stems to prevent aggressive self-sowing. 'Sonja' has larger leaves and flowers than the species.

ARISTOLOCHIA

Aristolochiaceae

DECIDUOUS AND EVERGREEN VINES

ZONES VARY BY SPECIES

EXPOSURE NEEDS VARY BY SPECIES

REGULAR TO AMPLE WATER

Aristolochia littoralis

Twining vines noted for curiously shaped flowers in rather sober colors; they resemble curved pipes with flared bowls or birds with bent necks. Vigorous growers; thin out unwanted growth in late dormant season or wait until after bloom. If plant is too thick and tangled for selective thinning, cut it to the ground before spring growth begins.

A. californica. CALIFORNIA DUTCHMAN'S PIPE. Deciduous. Zones 5–10, 14–24. Native to Coast Ranges and Sierra Nevada foothills of Northern California. Will cover an 8- by 12-ft. screen with some training or climb by long, thin shoots 10–16 ft. into any nearby tree without harming it. Flower display comes before leaf-out in winter or early spring; pendulous, 1-in.-long blooms are cream colored with red-purple veins. Bright green, heart-shaped leaves to 5 in. long. Interesting and useful where many less hardy vines would freeze. Sometimes used as a ground cover. Grows from seed. Accepts any soil; needs partial shade.

A. littoralis (A. elegans). CALICO FLOWER. Evergreen. Zones 23, 24; or indoors. Native to Brazil. Grows 15–25 ft. in native habitat. Wiry, slender stems; heart-shaped leaves 3 in. long. Blooms in summer; whitish buds shaped like little pelicans open to 3-in.-wide, heart-shaped flowers of deep purple veined in creamy white. Needs rich soil, partial shade.

A. macrophylla (A. durior). DUTCHMAN'S PIPE. Deciduous. Zones 2–24; short lived in warm-winter areas. Native to eastern U.S. Easily grown from seed. Large (6–14-in.-long), kidney-shaped deep green leaves are carried in shinglelike pattern to form dense cloak on trellis; the vine will cover a 15- by 20-ft. area in a single season and was once a favorite for screening a porch. Blooms in late spring, early summer. Flowers are almost hidden by leaves; each is a yellowish green, 3-in., curved tube flaring into three brownish purple lobes about 1 in. wide. Thrives in full sun to heavy shade. Average to good soil and ample water produce the fastest growth and largest leaves. Will not stand strong winds.

Aristolochiaceae. This family includes *Aristolochia* and wild ginger *(Asarum)*. All its members display odd-shaped flowers in low-key colors.

ARMERIA

THRIFT, SEA PINK

Plumbaginaceae

PERENNIALS

ZONES VARY BY SPECIES

FULL SUN

LITTLE TO MODERATE WATER

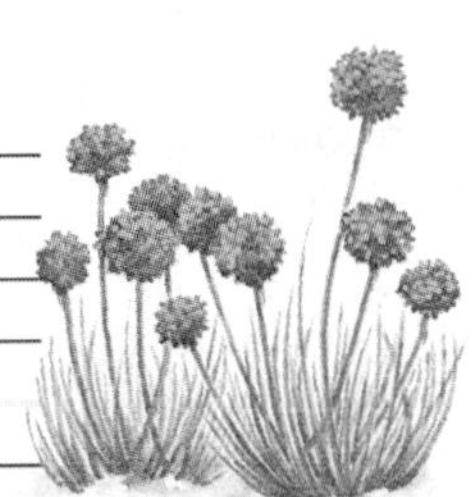

Armeria maritima

Narrow, stiff, evergreen leaves grow in compact tufts or basal rosettes; small white, pink, rose, or red flowers are carried in dense, globular heads. Main bloom period is spring to early summer, but shearing off faded flowers may prolong flowering. Sturdy, dependable plants for edging walks or borders and for tidy mounds in rock gardens or raised beds. Attractive in containers.

Good drainage is essential and permits regular watering, but safest tactic is to water moderately in dry climates, sparingly in moister regions. Tolerate seaside conditions, infertile soil. Clumps spread slowly and need dividing only when bare centers show.

A. alliacea. Zones 1–9, 14–24. From southern Europe. Clumps 2–6 in. high and 20 in. wide produce 8–16-in. blossom stalks with bright pink flowers. 'Leucantha' has white blooms.

A. caespitosa (A. juniperifolia). Zones 2b–9, 14–24. Stiff, needle-shaped leaves ½ in. long form low, extremely compact rosettes about 6 in. across. Rose pink or white flowers are carried on 2-in. stems. This little mountain native is very touchy about drainage; apply mulch of fine gravel around plants to prevent basal stem rot, especially in summer.

A. girardii (A. juncea, A. setacea). Zones 6–9, 14–24. From southern France. Narrow, needlelike foliage in dense mounds to 10–12 in. high and wide. Lavender-pink flowers.

A. maritima (Statice armeria, A. vulgaris). COMMON THRIFT. Zones A2, A3; 1–9, 14–24. Native to Europe, North America. Tufted mounds spread to 1 ft.; leaves are 6 in. long. White to rose pink flowers in tight clusters atop 6–10-in. stalks. Bloom is profuse in spring (goes on almost all year in mildest climates). 'Bloodstone' has rose red flowers, 'Cotton Tail' white blooms. 'Rubrifolia', with purplish red foliage and rosy pink blossoms, brings color to a rock garden for much of the year.

ARONIA

CHOKEBERRY

Rosaceae

DECIDUOUS SHRUBS

ZONES VARY BY SPECIES

FULL SUN OR LIGHT SHADE

MODERATE TO AMPLE WATER

Aronia arbutifolia

Native to southern Canada and the eastern U.S., chokeberries are tough, undemanding shrubs, useful as fillers or background plantings. Small white or pinkish flowers in 1–2-in. clusters are pretty but not showy—but the fruits that follow are highly decorative and last well into winter. Fall foliage is brightly colored. All chokeberries tend to spread by suckering and are somewhat leggy (good for planting beneath). Tolerate many soils. Prune oldest stems to ground in late dormant season; restrict height and increase bushiness by heading back upright stems.

A. arbutifolia. RED CHOKEBERRY. Zones 1–7. Clumping shrub to 6–8 ft. tall, with many erect stems bearing shiny leaves that are rich green above, paler beneath. Clustered, long-lasting fruits are ¼ in. wide, brilliant red. Fall foliage is likewise bright red, and plants tend to color early. 'Brilliant' ('Brilliantissima') is a selected form with especially fine fall color.

A. melanocarpa. BLACK CHOKEBERRY. Zones A2, A3; 1–7. Typically lower than *A. arbutifolia*—usually 3–5 ft. high, rarely to 10 ft. Purple-red fall foliage; shiny black fruits ½ in. wide. Can handle soils in low, wet areas as well as dry, sandy sites. Suckers profusely; may get out of hand in small gardens. 'Autumn Magic' has fragrant flowers, reliable fall color.

ARRHENATHERUM elatius bulbosum 'Variegatum'

BULBOUS OAT GRASS

Poaceae (Gramineae)

PERENNIAL GRASS

ZONES 1–7, 15–17, 23, 24

FULL SUN OR PARTIAL SHADE

REGULAR WATER

Arrhenatherum elatius bulbosum 'Variegatum'

Attractive variety of a European species, with narrow leaves boldly edged and striped in white. Good looking in a perennial border or large rock garden; useful for brightening dark places under trees or big shrubs. Makes a graceful clump about 1 ft. high and wide. Flowering stems in summer double the plant's height. Goes dormant in summer in hot climates; performs best in cool seasons and cool climates. If it flops over in heat, shear for fresh growth in fall. Bulbous structures at stem bases root on contact with soil to produce new plants; clumps may periodically need curtailing. Divide and replant as needed.

ARTEMISIA

Asteraceae (Compositae)

PERENNIALS AND EVERGREEN SHRUBS

ZONES VARY BY SPECIES

FULL SUN

LITTLE TO MODERATE WATER, EXCEPT AS NOTED

Artemisia abrotanum

Several species are valuable for interesting leaf patterns and silvery gray or white aromatic foliage (flowers are generally insignificant). Most kinds are excellent in mixed borders, where their white or silvery leaves soften harsh reds and oranges and blend beautifully with blues, lavenders, and pinks. Provide good drainage. Cut nonwoody-stemmed perennials to ground in fall to rejuvenate; prune back shrubs and woody perennials (into older wood if necessary) before first flush of spring growth. Divide perennials in spring or fall; propagate shrubs by cuttings.

A. abrotanum. SOUTHERNWOOD, OLD MAN. Woody perennial. Zones 2b–24. Native to southern Europe. To 3 ft. tall and wide. Beautiful feathery, lemon-scented gray-green foliage; yellowish white flower heads. Use for pleasantly scented leaves in shrub border. Hang dried sprigs in closet to discourage moths. Burn a few leaves on stove to kill cooking odors.

A. absinthium. COMMON WORMWOOD. Woody perennial. Zones 2–24. Native to Europe, temperate Asia. To 2–4 ft. tall, 2 ft. wide. Silvery gray, finely divided leaves with bitter taste, pungent odor. Tiny yellow flowers. Prune to shape. Divide every 3 years. Background shrub; good gray feature in flower border, particularly fine with delphiniums. 'Lambrook Silver' is a 1½-ft.-tall form with silvery white, especially finely cut leaves. ▶

A

A. arborescens. Evergreen shrub or woody perennial. Zones 7–9, 14–24. Mediterranean native to 3 ft. (sometimes 5–6 ft.) tall and 4–5 ft. wide. Silvery white, very finely cut foliage. Highly attractive but more tender than other artemisias.

A. australis. AHINAHINA, HINAHINA KUAHIWI. Evergreen shrub or woody perennial. Zones H1, H2. Native to Hawaii. To 3–4 ft. tall and wide, with lacy, silvery leaves. Thrives in rock gardens, in coastal gardens, on steep cliffs, in containers. Needs good drainage.

A. californica. CALIFORNIA SAGEBRUSH. Evergreen shrub. Zones 7–9, 14–24. Native to coastal region from Northern California to Baja California. To 1½–5 ft. tall, 4–7 ft. wide, with finely divided grayish white foliage. Drought tolerant but will drop leaves in extreme drought. 'Canyon Gray' and 'Montara' are superior selections.

A. cana (Seriphidium canum). Evergreen shrub. Zones 2, 3, 7, 14–21. Native to region east of the Sierra-Cascade divide. To 3–5 ft. tall and wide. Narrow, silvery green leaves. Very hardy to drought and cold.

A. caucasica. SILVER SPREADER. Evergreen shrublet. Zones 2–11, 14–24. Caucasus native grows 3–6 in. high, spreads to 2 ft. wide. Silky, silvery green foliage; small yellow flowers. Bank or ground cover; plant 1–2 ft. apart. Needs good drainage. Takes extremes of heat and cold.

A. dracunculus. FRENCH TARRAGON, TRUE TARRAGON. Perennial. Zones A1–A3; 2b–10, 14–24. French tarragon (may be labeled 'Sativa') is a sprawling, largely flowerless plant with shiny dark green, aromatic, flavorful leaves. Slowly spreads by creeping rhizomes, the stems becoming slightly woody and the whole plant remaining less than 2 ft. high. Makes an attractive container subject. Russian tarragon (may be labeled 'Inodorus') is a less desirable plant, lacking the characteristic flavor and aroma of true tarragon; it has upright, branching growth to about 3 ft. and small white flowers. Any seeds you find for sale will be for this culinarily inferior form.

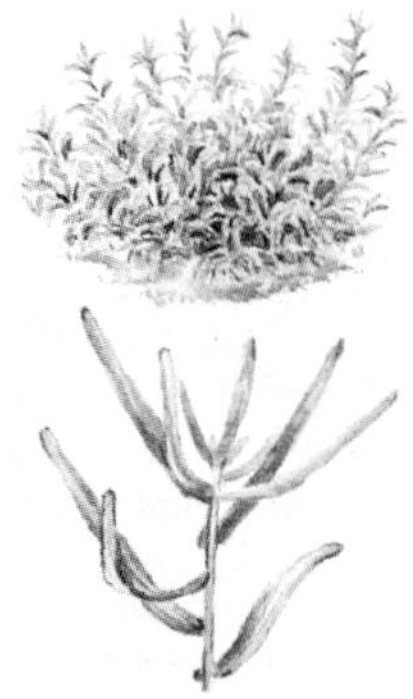
Artemisia dracunculus

Cut sprigs in early summer for seasoning vinegar. Use fresh or dried leaves to season salads, cooked dishes. Plants in all zones die to the ground in winter. Divide every 3 or 4 years to keep vigorous. Propagate by divisions or cuttings. Moderate to regular water.

A. frigida. FRINGED WORMWOOD. Perennial. Zones A1; 1–3, 7–10, 14, 18–21. Native to Southwest, interior Northwest, Alaska. To 1–1½ ft. tall and wide. Finely cut white leaves; small yellow flowers. Plants are compact when young, becoming rangy as they grow; cut back as needed.

A. 'Huntington'. Woody perennial. Zones 4–24. To 3 ft. tall and 4 ft. wide, with spreading stems covered by a thick dome of very silvery foliage. Similar to 'Powis Castle' but with bigger, softer leaves.

A. lactiflora. WHITE MUGWORT. Perennial. Zones 1–9, 14–21. Tall, straight column to 4–5 ft. tall, 2 ft. wide. This native of western China is one of the few artemisias with attractive flowers, bearing large (1½-ft.), branched sprays of creamy white blooms in late summer. Dark green leaves have broad, tooth-edged lobes. Moderate to regular water.

A. ludoviciana albula (A. albula). SILVER KING ARTEMISIA. Perennial. Zones 1–24. Native to desert Southwest and mountains. To 2–3½ ft. tall, 2 ft. wide, with slender, spreading branches and silvery white, 2-in. leaves. Lower leaves have three to five lobes; upper ones are narrow and unlobed. Cut foliage is useful in arrangements. 'Valerie Finnis' (which may be a variety of the plain species) is a compact grower to 2 ft. tall, with broader, nearly white leaves slightly lobed toward the tip.

A. pontica. ROMAN WORMWOOD. Evergreen shrub or woody perennial. Zones 2–24. Native to southeastern and central Europe; naturalized in eastern North America. Grows 2–4 ft. tall. Spreads invasively by rhizomes—makes a good ground cover if given ample room. Feathery silver gray leaves. Heads of nodding, whitish yellow flowers in long, open, branched clusters. Leaves are used in sachets.

A. 'Powis Castle'. Woody perennial. Zones 2–24. *A. absinthium* is a probable parent of this hybrid. Silvery, lacy mound to 3 ft. tall, 6 ft. wide. Makes a splendid background for bright flowers of other plants and is tough enough to use as a bank or berm cover.

A. pycnocephala. SANDHILL SAGE. Evergreen shrub or woody perennial. Zones 4, 5, 7–9, 14–17, 19–24. Native to beaches of Northern California. Rounded, somewhat spreading plant to 2 ft. tall, 3 ft. wide. Erect-growing stems are crowded with soft, silvery white or gray leaves divided into narrow lobes. Spikes of very small yellow flowers; remove them as they open to keep plant compact. Becomes unkempt after 2 years or so and should be removed and replaced at that time. 'David's Choice' is a foot-tall selection.

A. schmidtiana. ANGEL'S HAIR. Woody perennial. Zones A1–A3; 1–10, 14–24. Japanese native forms a 2-ft.-high, 1-ft.-wide dome of woolly, silvery white, finely cut leaves. 'Silver Mound' grows 1 ft. high.

A. stellerana. BEACH WORMWOOD, OLD WOMAN, DUSTY MILLER. Perennial. Zones A1–A3; 1–10, 14–24. Native to northeastern Asia; naturalized in eastern North America. Dense, silvery gray plant to 2½ ft. tall, 3 ft. wide, with lobed, 1–4-in. leaves. Hardier than *Senecio cineraria* (another dusty miller) and often used in its place in colder climates. Yellow flowers in spikelike clusters. 'Silver Brocade' is a superior, dense-growing selection.

A. tridentata (Seriphidium tridentatum). BIG SAGEBRUSH. Evergreen shrub. Zones 1–3, 6–11, 14–24. Native to Great Basin region of the West. Many-branched, silvery-looking plant to 4–15 ft. tall, 3–10 ft. wide. Narrow, very aromatic, hairy gray leaves ¾ in. long, usually with three teeth at tip. Insignificant flowers. Emits the pungent fragrance for which Western deserts are known. Grows easily in any sunny, well-drained spot. Does well with no irrigation.

ARTICHOKE

Asteraceae (Compositae)

PERENNIAL

ZONES VARY; SEE BELOW

FULL SUN

REGULAR WATER

Artichoke

Known botanically as *Cynara scolymus;* native to southern Mediterranean region. In Zones 8, 9, 14–24, grow as dependable perennial crop. In Zones 11–13, usually treated as an annual and planted in fall for spring harvest, but may hang on to be a perennial. In Zones 4–7, plant in spring when offered and hope for the best—you will get foliage, maybe flowers, and a crop if you're lucky. A big, coarse, ferny-looking plant with irregular, somewhat fountainlike form to 4 ft. high, 6–8 ft. wide. Leaves are silvery green. Big flower buds form at tops of stalks: they are the artichokes you cook and eat. If not cut, buds open into spectacular purple-blue, 6-in., thistlelike flowers that can be cut for arrangements (cut them just before blooms are fully open).

In Zone 17, where it is grown commercially, artichoke can be both a handsome ornamental plant and a producer of fine, tender artichokes from early fall to late spring. In Zones 8, 9, 14–16, 18–24, the plant grows luxuriantly at least from spring through fall; edible buds come as a dividend in early summer only.

Plant dormant roots or plants from containers in winter or early spring. Set root shanks vertically, with buds or shoots just above soil level; space 4–6 ft. apart in a full-sun location. Where roots are not available or in cold-winter areas (even Alaska), you can grow artichokes from seed. 'Imperial Star' produces the first season (150 to 180 days from seed to harvest) and can be grown as an annual; 'Green Globe' is ready to harvest the second summer after seeding. Start seeds indoors 8 to 12 weeks before last frost; set transplants outdoors in a sunny area when the soil has warmed and frost danger is past, spacing them 4–6 ft. apart.

After active growth starts, water plants thoroughly once a week, wetting the entire root system. If grown only for ornamental value, artichokes can tolerate much drought, going dormant in summer heat. Control aphids; after buds start to form, just use strong jets of water to blast off aphids. Also keep snails, slugs, and earwigs away from plants. For gopher control, plant in raised beds lined with hardware cloth at the bottom or in large containers.

Harvest buds while they are still tight and plump. To encourage a second crop, cut off main stalk an inch above ground after harvesting the last bud of the first crop; new sprouts at base will grow faster and produce sooner than uncut plant would. In all recommended climate zones, cut off old stalks near ground level when leaves begin to yellow. In cold-winter regions, cut tops to 1 ft. in fall, tie them over root crown, and mulch heavily to protect from frost.

ARTOCARPUS altilis. See BREADFRUIT

ARUGULA

ROCKET, ROQUETTE, RUGOLA
Brassicaceae (Cruciferae)
ANNUAL
ALL ZONES
FULL SUN
REGULAR WATER

Arugula

Weedy Mediterranean native known botanically as *Eruca vesicaria sativa.* Grown for its 1–4-in.-long leaves, which look like small mustard leaves and lend a nutty zing to green salads. Start from seed in winter or spring; grows best in cool weather. Thin to about 6 in. apart. Harvest tender young leaves; older, larger ones usually taste too sharp. Eventually, plants will shoot up to 3 ft. tall, then bloom; tender buds and flowers taste like the young leaves. Plants reseed.

ARUM

Araceae
PERENNIALS FROM TUBERS
ZONES VARY BY SPECIES
PARTIAL OR FULL SHADE
REGULAR WATER DURING GROWTH AND BLOOM
SAP IS AN IRRITANT IF INGESTED

Arum italicum 'Pictum'

Tubers give rise to attractively veined, arrow-shaped leaves in fall or winter. Short stalks bear curious callalike blooms featuring a bract (spathe) that half encloses a thick, fleshy spike (spadix) set with tiny flowers. These blossoms are followed by dense clusters of fruit, typically bright red, that look like little ears of corn and persist after leaves have died to the ground. Use in shady flower borders. Plant tubers in late summer or early fall (toward the end of their dormancy), setting them 8–12 in. apart and about 2 in. deep. Dormant plantings accept summer moisture but don't need it. *A. palaestinum* and *A. pictum* sometimes used as houseplants in colder climates

A. italicum. ITALIAN ARUM. Zones 2–24. Native to southern and western Europe. Leaves 1 ft. long on leafstalks of equal length appear in fall or early winter. Very short stems carry white or greenish white (sometimes purple-spotted) flowers in spring and early summer, followed by orange-red fruits. Spathe first stands erect, then folds over and conceals short yellow spadix. Leaves die to ground after bloom. In favorable situations, will naturalize by volunteer seedlings. 'Pictum' has white-veined leaves.

A. palaestinum. BLACK CALLA. Zones 14–24. Native to Israel. Leaves emerge in winter; about 8 in. long, on 1-ft. leafstalks. Spathe is 8 in. long, green outside; opens outward and curls back at tip to reveal purple interior and black spadix. Blooms spring and early summer, then leaves die back.

A. pictum. Zones 7–9, 14–24. Native to western Mediterranean. May be called black calla, like *A. palaestinum*—but unlike that species, it has an 8-in. violet spathe with a white base that encloses a dark purple spadix. Flowers appear in fall—sometimes with emerging foliage, sometimes before. Light green leaves with fine white veins reach 10 in. long and are borne on equally long leafstalks. Foliage dies to ground in hot weather.

ARUNCUS

GOAT'S BEARD
Rosaceae
PERENNIALS
ZONES VARY BY SPECIES
FULL SUN ONLY IN COOLER CLIMATES
REGULAR WATER

Aruncus dioicus

These perennials resemble astilbe, with slowly spreading clumps of finely divided leaves topped in summer by plumy, branched clusters of tiny white or cream flowers. Good in perennial borders or at edge of woodland against a dark background.

A. aethusifolius. Zones 1–9, 14–17. Native to Korea. Deep green, finely divided leaves make a mound 1 ft. tall and wide. White flower plumes reach 16 in. high. Useful in rock garden, as edging, for small-scale ground cover.

A. dioicus (A. sylvester). Zones A2, A3; 1–9, 14–17. Native to Eurasia and to southeastern and south-central Alaska. Grows to 6 (sometimes 7) ft. tall, 4 ft. wide, with foamy plumes of white flowers in 20-in., much-branched clusters. 'Kneiffii' is half the size of the species, with more finely divided, near-ferny leaves. 'Child of Two Worlds' ('Zweiweltenkind'), sometimes sold as *A. chinensis,* grows to 5 ft. tall, with gracefully drooping flower clusters.

ARUNDO donax

GIANT REED
Poaceae (Gramineae)
PERENNIAL GRASS
ZONES 3–24
FULL SUN
MODERATE TO AMPLE WATER

Arundo donax

Giant grass from the Mediterranean. Once valued for its bold effect in garden fringes and near water and for use as a fast-growing windbreak. Now, however, it has run wild in many areas, particularly in mild-winter parts of California, clogging waterways (supplanting the native waterside trees and shrubs) and even damaging bridges. Grows as tall as 30 ft., with 2-ft.-long leaves; spreads by thick rhizomes. Particularly rampant in areas where the flower clusters set fertile seeds, such as Southern California. Even where it is less invasive, its size makes it difficult to dig out or divide. In cold climates, it may die back in winter.

'Versicolor' ('Variegata') has leaves with white or yellowish stripes; it grows to about half the height of the species and is less likely to bloom, though it too can get out of bounds in warm climates. Attractive in a large, sturdy container.

ASARINA

CLIMBING SNAPDRAGON, CHICKABIDDY
Scrophulariaceae
PERENNIALS OFTEN GROWN AS ANNUALS
ZONES 17–24, EXCEPT AS NOTED;
ZONES 1–16 AS ANNUALS
ROOTS COOL, TOPS IN SUN
REGULAR WATER

Asarina antirrhiniflora

Climbing, sprawling, or trailing tender perennials have twining stems and triangular to ovate leaves. Tubular flowers, borne singly in leaf axils, flare at the mouth like snapdragon (*Antirrhinum,* a close relative). Plants from early sowings will bloom in late spring and through the summer. Grow on a trellis, in window boxes or hanging baskets, or as ground cover. Need good drainage.

A. antirrhiniflora (Maurandella antirrhiniflora). Zones 17–24; H1, H2. Native to southwestern U.S., Mexico. Grows 3–6 ft. tall, with 1-in., yellow-throated flowers in lavender, violet, blue, and red. A mixed-color seed strain offers red-and-yellow or blue-and-white flowers.

A. barclaiana (Maurandya barclayana). Native to Mexico. Vigorous, woody-based plant to 12 ft., with 2–3-in. flowers in white, pink, or purple. 'Angel's Trumpet' is a pink bloomer.

A. scandens (Lophospermum scandens). Native to Mexico. Similar to *A. barclaiana* but smaller (4–8 ft. tall), bearing somewhat smaller flowers in the same color range.

ASARUM

WILD GINGER

Aristolochiaceae

PERENNIALS

ZONES VARY BY SPECIES

PARTIAL OR FULL SHADE

REGULAR TO AMPLE WATER

Asarum caudatum

American and European species are handsome ground covers, forming a lush, lustrous carpet of heart-shaped leaves. The small, three-cornered, typically brownish red, attractive spring flowers are bell shaped, with three tapering "tails." Roots and leaves of wild gingers have a scent somewhat like that of culinary ginger but are not used as seasoning. Grow in average soil, but spread faster, look more luxuriant in rich, humusy soil. Start from divisions or container-grown plants; set about a foot apart. Watch for slugs and snails.

A few specialist nurseries offer a number of species from Japan and China. These are true collectors' plants, with ornately mottled leaves, some with flowers in odd shades of near-black and white. Expensive and difficult to grow.

A. canadense. Zones 1–6. Native to eastern North America. Deciduous, dark green, kidney-shaped leaves to 6 in. wide. Purplish brown flowers.

A. caudatum. Zones 4–6, 14–24. Native to the West Coast. Evergreen where winters are mild. Heart-shaped leaves are 2–7 in. wide. In fog belt, it makes a choice ground cover for shade and survives with just occasional water.

A. europaeum. Zones 2–6. Native to Europe. Evergreen, kidney-shaped, shiny dark green leaves 2–3 in. wide. Slow spreader.

A. shuttleworthii. Zones 3b–6. Native to the Appalachians. Evergreen, 4-in., shiny green leaves are heart-shaped or roundish and usually variegated with silvery markings. Slow growing.

Asclepiadaceae. Best-known family members are the milkweeds *(Asclepias),* but other garden plants also belong to this group, among them many succulents and some perennials and vines, including *Stephanotis.*

ASCLEPIAS

Asclepiadaceae

PERENNIALS

ZONES VARY BY SPECIES

FULL SUN

WATER NEEDS VARY BY SPECIES

ALL PARTS OF MANY SPECIES ARE POISONOUS IF INGESTED

Asclepias tuberosa

Milkweeds (so named for their milky sap) are the best-known representatives of this group of plants. Bloom in summer, typically bearing many small, starlike flowers in broad, flattened clusters at branch tips. All have inflated seedpods with silky seeds. Just a few species are cultivated in gardens.

A. curassavica. BLOOD FLOWER. Zones 8, 9, 12–24; H1, H2; all zones as annual. Native to South America. Woody-based plant with stiff stems and narrow 6-in. leaves; grows 3 ft. tall, 2 ft. wide. Clusters of vivid red flowers. 'Silky Gold' is similar but bears bright yellow to yellow-orange blooms. Moderate water.

A. fruticosa (Gomphocarpus fruticosus), A. physocarpa (G. physocarpus). SWAN PLANT, GOOSE PLANT. Zones 14–24. These two very similar woody-based plants from southern Africa sometimes volunteer in gardens. They grow upright to 3–6 ft. tall, 2–3 ft. wide, with many stems clothed in gray-green, willowlike leaves. Sometimes sold by nurseries for puffy, inflated pale green seedpods that are covered with soft, fleshy prickles and have curving stems like swans' necks; the flowers themselves are not showy. Stripped of leaves and dried, seedpod-bearing stems make striking arrangements. Provide good drainage, regular water.

A. incarnata. SWAMP MILKWEED. Zones 1–9, 14–24. Native to eastern U.S. Herbaceous perennial to 2–4 ft. tall, 2 ft. wide. Narrow, pointed leaves to 6 in. long; ball-shaped clusters of pinkish purple flowers. 'Ice Ballet' has pure white blooms. Regular to ample water.

A. tuberosa. BUTTERFLY WEED. Zones 1–24. Native to eastern U.S. From a perennial root, many herbaceous stems rise every year to form a clump about 3 ft. tall, 1 ft. wide. Clusters of bright orange flowers attract swarms of butterflies. Gay Butterflies strain features yellow, red, orange, pink, or bicolored blossoms; 'Hello Yellow' has bright yellow blooms. All make long-lasting cut flowers. Provide good drainage, moderate water.

ASH. See FRAXINUS

ASH, MOUNTAIN. See SORBUS

ASIAN GREENS

Brassicaceae (Cruciferae)

ANNUALS

ALL ZONES

FULL SUN IN COOLER CLIMATES ONLY

REGULAR WATER

Chinese Mustard Greens

The annual vegetables in this large group are mainstays of stir-fry dishes and excellent in salads. They are primarily quick-maturing cool-season crops planted at the same time as other cool-season vegetables: late winter to early spring for spring-to-summer harvest, late summer to early fall for harvest in fall and winter. In areas with short growing seasons and in mild-summer coastal regions, they can be grown all summer.

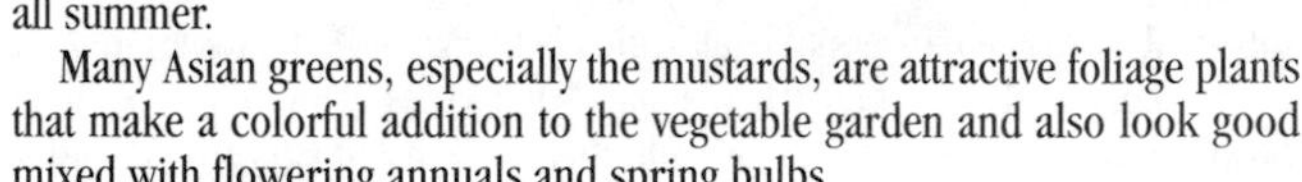

Many Asian greens, especially the mustards, are attractive foliage plants that make a colorful addition to the vegetable garden and also look good mixed with flowering annuals and spring bulbs.

Listed here are some of the most common Asian greens (specialty seed catalogs may carry additional kinds). For planting depth and row spacing, follow the instructions on the seed packet.

Broadleaf mustard (dai gai choy). Large green leaves with a pungent, somewhat bitter, mustardlike flavor that gets stronger as the plant matures. Hot weather or inadequate moisture also increases pungency. Best used in soup to tone down the sharp flavor.

Thin or transplant seedlings to 10 in. apart. Harvest plants when they are loose headed and 10–14 in. high, about 65 days after sowing.

Chinese broccoli (gai lohn). Similar in flavor and texture to standard broccoli, but with a slight pungency like that of mustard. Thin or transplant seedlings to 10 in. apart. Harvest central stalk and side shoots when stalk is 8–10 in. tall or when flower buds just begin to form, usually about 70 days after sowing.

Chinese mustard greens (gai choy). Milder member of the mustard family. Thin or transplant seedlings to 10 in. apart. Harvest the first greens when the plants are 2 in. high; continue harvesting until leaves turn tough or bitter. It usually takes 45 days after sowing for plants to reach mature height of 6–8 in.

Chinese white cabbage (bok choy, pac choi). One of the more familiar Asian greens. Tender-crisp, sweet, very mild; good alone, with meat, in soups and stir-fries. Many varieties are sold. Tat-soi is similar but more compact.

Thin or transplant seedlings to 6–12 inches apart. Harvest approximately 50 days after sowing seed, when plants are loose headed and 10–12 in. tall.

Flowering cabbage (yao choy, choy sum, ching sow sum). Tender, delicate, broccoli-type vegetable. Thin or transplant seedlings to about 6 in. apart. Harvest about 60 days after sowing, when 8–12 in. high.

Mizuna. Mild-flavored, leafy vegetable with finely cut, frilly, white-stemmed leaves. Great in salads. Thin or transplant seedlings to 8–10 in. apart. Start cutting leaves when plants are a few inches tall or wait until mature at 8–10 in. high, about 40 days after sowing.

ASIMINA triloba. See PAWPAW

ASPARAGUS

Liliaceae

PERENNIAL

ZONES A1–A3; 1–24

FULL SUN

REGULAR WATER

Asparagus

Known botanically as *Asparagus officinalis;* native to seacoasts of Europe, North Africa, Asia. One of most permanent and dependable of home garden vegetables. Plants take 2 or 3 years to come into full production but then furnish delicious spears every spring for 10 to 15 years. They take up considerable space but do so in the grand manner: plants are tall, feathery, graceful, highly ornamental. Use along sunny fence or as background for flowers or other vegetables.

Seeds grow into strong young plants in one season (sow in spring), but roots are far more widely used. Set out seedlings or roots (not wilted, no smaller than an adult's hand) in fall or winter in mild-winter climates, in early spring in cold-winter areas. Make trenches 1 ft. wide, 8–10 in. deep; space trenches 4–6 ft. apart. Heap loose, manure-enriched soil at bottom of trenches and soak. Space plants 1 ft. apart, setting them so that tops are 6–8 in. below surface; spread roots out evenly. Cover with 2 in. of soil and water again. (Where drainage is very bad, plant in raised beds.)

As young plants grow, gradually fill in the trench, taking care not to cover growing tips. Soak deeply whenever the soil begins to dry out at root depth. Don't harvest any spears the first year; the object at this time is to build a big root mass. When plants turn brown in late fall or early winter, cut stems to the ground. In cold-winter areas, permit dead stalks to stand until spring; they will help trap and hold snow, which will furnish protection to root crowns.

The following spring you can cut your first spears; cut only for 4 to 6 weeks or until appearance of thin spears indicates that roots are nearing exhaustion. Then permit plants to grow. Cultivate, feed, and irrigate heavily. The third year you should be able to cut spears for 8 to 10 weeks. Spears are ready to cut when they are 5–8 in. long. Thrust knife down at 45° angle to soil; flat cutting may injure adjacent developing spears.

Cleaning up debris from asparagus beds in fall will help get rid of overwintering asparagus beetles. Use row covers over beds in spring. If the beetles appear during cutting season, handpick them, knock them off plants with water jets, or spray them with malathion (carefully noting label precautions).

Asparagus seeds and roots are sold as "traditional" ('Martha Washington' and others) and "all-male" ('UC 157', 'Jersey Giant', and 'Jersey Knight'). The latter kinds are bred to produce more and larger spears because they don't have to put energy into seed production. Such varieties still produce an occasional female plant.

ASPARAGUS, ORNAMENTAL

Liliaceae

PERENNIALS, SHRUBS, OR VINES

ZONES 12–24, EXCEPT AS NOTED

SUN OR PART SHADE

REGULAR WATER

Asparagus densiflorus 'Sprengeri'

There are about 150 kinds of asparagus besides the edible one—all members of the lily family. Those listed here are native to South Africa. Best known is fern asparagus *(A. setaceus),* which is not a true fern. Although valued mostly for handsome foliage of unusual textural quality, some of the ornamental species have small but fragrant flowers and colorful berries. Green foliage sprays are made up of what look like leaves. Needlelike or broader, these are actually short branches called cladodes. The true leaves are inconspicuous dry scales.

Most ornamental asparagus look greenest in partial shade but thrive in sun in cool-summer climates. Leaves yellow in dense shade. Plant in well-drained soil amended with peat moss or ground bark. Because of fleshy roots, plants can go for some time without water, but they grow better when watered regularly. Feed in spring with complete fertilizer. Trim out old shoots to make room for new growth. Ornamental asparagus will survive light frosts but may be killed to ground by severe cold. After frost, plants often come back from roots.

A. asparagoides. SMILAX ASPARAGUS. Much-branched vine with spineless stems to 20 ft. or more. Often seen in older gardens. Leaves to 1 in. long, sharp pointed, stiffish, glossy grass green. Small, fragrant white flowers in spring followed by blue berries. Birds feed on berries, drop seeds that sprout at random about the garden. (Plant also self-sows readily.) Roots are clusters of fleshy thongs and are nearly immortal, surviving long drought and sprouting when rains come. Foliage sprays prized for table decoration. If it gets little water, plant dies back in summer, revives with fall rains. Becomes tangled mass unless trained. 'Myrtifolius', commonly called baby smilax, is a more graceful form with smaller leaves.

A. crispus. BASKET ASPARAGUS. Airy, graceful plant for hanging baskets. Drooping, zigzag stems have bright green, three-angled leaves in whorls of three. Often sold as *A. scandens* 'Deflexus'.

A. densiflorus. Zones 12–24; H1, H2; or indoors. The species is less commonly grown than its forms. The following are the two most popular.

'Myers'. MYERS ASPARAGUS. Several to many stiffly upright stems to 2 ft. or more, densely clothed with needlelike deep green leaves that give the plant a fluffy look. Forms a 3–4-ft.-wide clump. Performs well in containers. A little less hardy than 'Sprengeri'. Sometimes sold as *A. meyeri* or *A. myersii.*

'Sprengeri'. SPRENGER ASPARAGUS. Arching or drooping stems 3–6 ft. long. Shiny, bright green, needlelike leaves, 1 in. long, in bundles. Bright red berries. Popular for hanging baskets or containers, indoors and out. Train on trellis; climbs by means of small hooked prickles. Used as billowy ground cover where temperatures stay above 24°F/–4°C. Grows in ordinary or even poor soil. Will tolerate dryness of indoors. Sometimes sold as *A. sprengeri.* Form sold as 'Sprengeri Compacta' or *A. sarmentosus* 'Compacta' is denser, with shorter stems.

A. falcatus. SICKLE-THORN ASPARAGUS. Leaves resemble those of *Podocarpus macrophyllus;* they are 2–3 in. long, in clusters of three to five at ends of branches. Tiny, fragrant white flowers in loose clusters; these are followed by brown berries. Derives its common name from curved thorns along its stems, which it uses to clamber rapidly as high as 40 ft. in its native area (in gardens, it usually reaches about 10 ft.). Makes an excellent foliage mass to cover fence or wall or provide shade for pergola or lathhouse.

A. macowanii. See A. retrofractus

A. meyeri, A. myersii. See A. densiflorus 'Myers'

A. officinalis. See Asparagus

A. plumosus. See A. setaceus

A

A. retrofractus. (A. macowanii) Erect, shrubby, slightly climbing, very tender. Slender, silvery gray stems grow slowly to 8–10 ft. high. Leaves threadlike, 1 in. long, in fluffy, rich green tufts. Clusters of small white flowers. Handsome in containers; useful in flower arrangements. Cut foliage lasts about 10 days out of water, several weeks in water.

A. sarmentosus. See A. densiflorus 'Sprengeri'

A. scandens. BASKET ASPARAGUS. Slender, branching vine climbing to 6 ft. Deep green, needlelike leaves on zigzag, drooping stems. Greenish white flowers ⅛ in. long. Scarlet berries.

A. scandens 'Deflexus'. See A. crispus

A. setaceus (A. plumosus). FERN ASPARAGUS. Zones 12–24; H1, H2; or indoors. Branching woody vine climbs by wiry, spiny stems to 10–20 ft. Tiny threadlike leaves form feathery dark green sprays that resemble fern fronds. Tiny white flowers; purple-black berries. Dense, fine-textured foliage mass useful as screen against walls, fences. Florists use foliage as filler in bouquets; holds up better than delicate ferns. Sometimes called emerald feather. Dwarf 'Nanus' is good in containers. 'Pyramidalis' has upswept, windblown look, is less vigorous than common fern asparagus.

A. sprengeri. See A. densiflorus 'Sprengeri'

ASPEN. See POPULUS

ASPEN DAISY. See ERIGERON speciosus macranthus

ASPERULA odorata. See GALIUM odoratum

ASPHODELINE lutea

YELLOW ASPHODEL, KING'S SPEAR

Liliaceae

PERENNIAL

ZONES 3B–24

FULL SUN OR PARTIAL SHADE

REGULAR WATER

Asphodeline lutea

Mediterranean native with a rhizomatous rootstock. Forms a low clump (about 9 in. high, 1 ft. wide) of blue-green to dark green, grassy leaves to 1 ft. long. In spring, stiff, unbranched stems to 3 ft. high rise from clump, topped by narrow clusters of fragrant, 1-in., yellow flowers that peer out from shaggy buff or reddish brown bracts. Grow in well-drained soil. Divide in fall.

ASPIDISTRA elatior (A. lurida)

CAST-IRON PLANT

Liliaceae

PERENNIAL

ZONES 4–10, 12–24; H1, H2; OR INDOORS

PARTIAL OR FULL SHADE; BRIGHT TO DIM LIGHT

MODERATE TO REGULAR WATER

Aspidistra elatior

This sturdy, long-lived evergreen foliage plant from China is best known as a houseplant, but it also makes striking accent clumps outdoors. Spreads slowly by rhizomes. Tough, arching, glossy, dark green leaf blades with distinct parallel veins are 1–2½ ft. long, 3–4 in. wide; each is supported by a grooved, 6–8-in.-long leafstalk. Inconspicuous brownish flowers bloom near ground level in spring. 'Variegata' has white-striped leaves but loses its variegation if planted in too-rich soil.

True to its common name, this plant has a cast-iron constitution, thriving in conditions unacceptable to most plants. Although extremely tolerant and requiring only minimal care, it grows best in porous, organically enriched soil and responds to feeding in spring and summer. Will grow in dark, shaded areas (under decks or stairs) as well as in filtered sun—except in Zones 12 and 13, where it takes full shade only. Indoors, it prefers bright indirect light but also does well in low light. It can live for many years in the same container before repotting is necessary. To keep leaves dust free and glossy, hose them off occasionally or clean with a soft brush or cloth.

ASPIDIUM capense. See RUMOHRA adiantiformis

ASPLENIUM

Polypodiaceae

FERNS

ZONES VARY BY SPECIES

PARTIAL OR FULL SHADE

REGULAR TO AMPLE WATER

Asplenium bulbiferum

Widespread and variable group of rhizomatous ferns, once called spleenwort for alleged medicinal value. These evergreen species resemble one another only in botanical details and in their need for shade and liberal watering. Unlike many other ferns, they need a rest period from late fall to early spring when grown indoors; during that time, reduce watering and withhold fertilizer.

A. bulbiferum. MOTHER FERN. Zones 14 (protected), 15–17, 20–24; or indoors. From Australia, New Zealand. Graceful, very finely cut light green fronds to 4 ft. tall. Plant grows about 4 ft. wide. Fronds produce plantlets that can be removed and planted. Hardy to 26°F/–3°C. Watch for snails and slugs.

A. daucifolium (A. viviparum). Indoor plant. Tropical species similar to *A. bulbiferum* but smaller (to 2 ft.), with more finely divided fronds. Also produces plantlets.

A. nidus (A. nidus-avis). BIRD'S NEST FERN. Zones 23, 24; H2; or indoors. Tender fern native to many tropical regions. Showy, undivided apple green fronds to 4 ft. long, 8 in. wide, growing upright in cluster. Striking foliage plant. Grow potted plant indoors in winter, move to shady patio in summer. One snail or slug can ruin a frond.

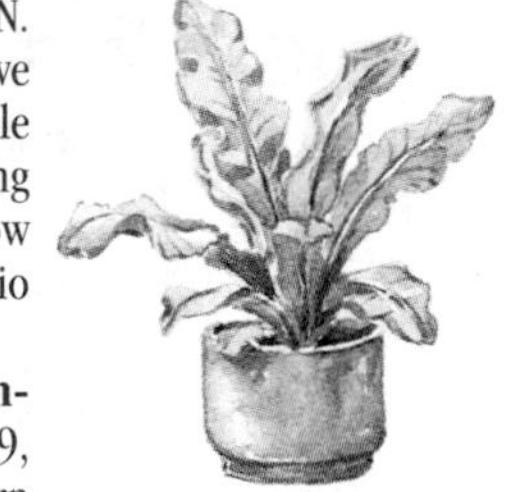
Asplenium nidus

A. scolopendrium (Phyllitis scolopendrium). HART'S TONGUE FERN. Zones 2b–9, 14–24. Native to Europe, eastern U.S. Odd fern with undivided, strap-shaped leaves 9–18 in. long; forms a clump about 2 ft. wide. Fanciers collect various dwarf, crested, or forked varieties. Needs humus; also add some limestone chips if soil is deficient in calcium. Difficult where water quality is poor. Striking in woodland or rock gardens and with rhododendrons and azaleas. Durable container plant; grows in a tight crown and can remain in the same pot for years.

A. trichomanes. MAIDENHAIR SPLEENWORT. Zones 2–6. Native to much of the Northern Hemisphere, this delicate fern grows in a clump to 6 in. high, 8 in. wide. Narrow bright green fronds are 4–8 in. long; round (or nearly so) leaflets are only ½ in. long. Likes lime. Attractive in wall crevices where it can be seen close up or in a shady rock garden.

ASTARTEA fascicularis

Myrtaceae

EVERGREEN SHRUB

ZONES 15–24

FULL SUN OR PARTIAL SHADE

NO IRRIGATION NEEDED

Astartea fascicularis

Australian native related to *Leptospermum* but with smaller leaves and flowers. Varieties more commonly grown than species. 'Bremer Bay' grows to 3 ft. or taller and is somewhat wider, with short, narrow, needlelike leaves in bundles thickly arranged along the stems. White or pinkish, ⅓-in.-wide flowers are borne in incredible profusion over a very long period, with the heaviest bloom in winter. Branches last well when cut. 'Prostrate Form' is a few inches tall, 3 ft. wide. 'Winter Pink' resembles 'Bremer Bay', but its deeper pink flowers bloom over a shorter season in winter and early spring.

ASTELIA nervosa chathamica (A. chathamica)

SILVER SPEAR

Liliaceae

PERENNIAL

ZONES 6–9, 14–17, 19–24

FULL SUN OR PARTIAL SHADE

MODERATE WATER

Astelia nervosa chathamica

Unusual New Zealand native grown for its silky, silvery evergreen foliage. Leaves are 3–4 ft. long, 2–4 in. wide; they form a 4-ft.-tall, 6-ft.-wide clump. Small, cream-colored spring flowers are borne in branched clusters 20 in. tall. On female plants (though chiefly on older ones), orange berries follow the blossoms. Offers a handsome contrast to low, mounding plants or billowing grasses and makes a striking centerpiece in a big container of mixed perennials. Must have good drainage.

ASTER

Asteraceae (Compositae)

PERENNIALS

ZONES VARY BY SPECIES

FULL SUN, EXCEPT AS NOTED

REGULAR WATER

Aster × frikartii

There are more than 600 species of true asters, ranging from alpine kinds forming compact mounds 6 in. high to open-branching plants 6 ft. tall. Flowers come in white or shades of blue, red, pink, lavender, or purple, mostly with yellow centers. Bloom time comes in late summer to early fall, except as noted. Taller asters are invaluable for abundant color in large borders or among shrubs. Large sprays effective in arrangements. Compact dwarf or cushion types make tidy edgings, mounds of color in rock gardens, good container plants. For the common annual or China aster sold at nurseries, see *Callistephus chinensis*.

True asters are adapted to most soils, but growth is most luxuriant in fertile soil. Few problems except for mildew on leaves in late fall. Strong-growing hybrids have invasive roots; they can regrow from small fragments left in soil. Divide yearly in late fall or early spring. Replant vigorous young divisions from outside of clump; discard old center. Divide smaller, tufted, less vigorously growing kinds every 2 years.

A. alpinus. Zones 1–4. Native to Alps, Pyrenees. Mounding plant to 1 ft. high, 1½ ft. wide. Leaves ½–5 in. long, mostly in basal tuft. Several stems grow from the leafy clump, each carrying one violet-blue flower 1½–2 in. across. Late spring to early summer bloom. Best in cold-winter areas. White and pink forms are uncommon.

A. amellus. ITALIAN ASTER. Zones 2–24. Native to Europe, western Asia. Sturdy, hairy plant to 2 ft. tall, 1½ ft. wide. Branching stems bear yellow-centered violet flowers 2 in. across.

A. cordifolius. BLUE WOOD ASTER. Zones 1–10, 14–21. To 6 ft. tall, 3 ft. wide, with loose, branching clusters of inch-wide lavender flowers. Native to eastern North America. Sun or light shade.

Aster × frikartii 'Wonder of Staffa'

Aster novi-belgii 'Professor Anton Kippenburg'

Aster novae-angliae 'Alma Potschke'

A. divaricatus. WHITE WOOD ASTER. Zones 1–10, 14–21. Native to eastern North America. To 3 ft. tall and wide, with a strong horizontal branching pattern and a generous show of white flowers aging to pink. Thrives in shade.

A. ericoides. HEATH ASTER. Zones 1–10, 14–24. Native to eastern North America. To 3 ft. tall and 1 ft. wide, with narrow leaves and strong horizontal branching. Flower heads are small and profusely borne, in white, pink, or blue.

A. × frikartii. Zones 2b–24. One of the finest, most useful and widely adapted perennials. Hybrid between *A. amellus* and *A. thomsonii*, a hairy-leafed, lilac-flowered, 3-ft.-tall species native to the Himalayas. Bears abundant clear lavender to violet-blue single flowers that are 2½ in. across. Open growth to 2 ft. high and wide. Blooms early summer to fall—almost all year in mild-winter areas if spent flowers are removed regularly. May be short lived. 'Wonder of Staffa' and 'Mönch' are favorites with blossoms in lavender blue.

A. fruticosus. See Felicia fruticosa

A. laevis. Zones 1–10, 14–21. Native to eastern North America. To 3½ ft. tall, 1½ ft. wide, with smooth, mildew-free foliage and clustered 1-in. flower heads of deep purplish blue.

A. lateriflorus. Zones 1–10, 14–21. North American native. Species grows to 4 ft. tall, 1 ft. wide. Garden selections are shorter (to 2 ft.), with profuse branching, tiny leaves, and a haze of small purplish pink flowers. Foliage turns a coppery purplish red in early fall. 'Prince' has blackish purple stems and leaves; its blooms are white with a red center.

A. novae-angliae. NEW ENGLAND ASTER. Zones 1–24. Native from Vermont to Alabama, west to North Dakota, Wyoming, and New Mexico. Stout-stemmed plant to 3–5 ft. tall and nearly as wide, with hairy leaves to 5 in. long. Flowers are 2 in. wide; they are violet blue in the basic form, with selections in other blue shades, white, pink, nearly red, and deep purple. Two long-time favorite varieties are still good garden plants. 'Alma Potschke' bears salmon pink single blooms on 3-ft. stems from late summer to early fall; 'Harrington's Pink' produces clear pink single flowers over a long autumn season on 3–4-ft. stems. Very tolerant of wet soils. Reseeds.

A. novi-belgii. NEW YORK ASTER, MICHAELMAS DAISY. Zones 1–24. Native to eastern North America. To 4 ft. tall and 3 ft. wide, with full clusters of bright blue-violet flowers. Similar to *A. novae-angliae* but with smooth leaves. Hundreds of selections are available, varying in height from less than a foot to over 4 ft.; flower colors include white, cream, blue, lavender, purple, rose, and pink. Among the many choices are 'Persian Rose' (rose pink) and semidouble 'Professor Anton Kippenburg' (lavender blue), both under 1 ft. high and 1½ ft. wide. Robust 'Climax' bears large sprays of single medium blue blossoms on stems to 6 ft. high.

A. pringlei. Zones 1–24. Eastern U.S. native known in cultivation through its variety 'Monte Cassino', a familiar florists' cut flower. Grows to 5 ft. tall and 1½ ft. wide; tall, narrow stems have many short side branches set with starry white, ¾-in. flowers. This plant is often sold as *A. ericoides* 'Monte Cassino'.

A. sibiricus. Zones A1–A3; 1–5. From northern parts of North America and Eurasia. To 16 in. high and as broad, with 9-in.-long basal leaves, purplish stems, and ¾-in. purple flowers borne singly or a few to the cluster.

A. tataricus. Zones 1–10, 14–21. Native to Siberia, China, Japan. Not for small gardens, this giant grows to 5–7 ft. tall and 3 ft. wide, with 2-ft.-long leaves and sheaves of inch-wide blue flowers in flat clusters in fall. Can be invasive. Takes sun or shade.

A. tongolensis (A. subcaeruleus, A. yunnanensis). Zones 3–24. From China, Himalayas. Dark green leaves in basal tufts; clumps grow to 1½ ft. high, 1 ft. wide. Each stem bears a single lavender-blue, orange-centered flower in late spring to early summer. 'Napsbury' has dark blue rays.

Asteraceae. The sunflower or daisy family, one of the largest plant families, is characterized by flowers borne in tight clusters (heads). In the most familiar form, these heads contain two types of flowers—small, tightly clustered disk flowers in the center of the head, and larger, strap-shaped ray flowers around the edge. The sunflower *(Helianthus)* is a familiar example. The family was formerly called Compositae.

ASTERISCUS

Asteraceae (Compositae)

PERENNIALS

ZONES VARY BY SPECIES

FULL SUN

LITTLE TO MODERATE WATER

Asteriscus maritimus

Leafy, evergreen, almost shrubby plants with showy yellow, 1½–2-in. daisies throughout most of the year. Shear spent flowers to neaten appearance and prolong bloom.

A. maritimus (Odontospermum maritimum). Zones 9, 15–24. Native to the Mediterranean region and the Canary Islands. Often sold as 'Gold Coin'. Attractive, silvery green–foliaged ground cover to 1 ft. tall, 4 ft. wide. Tough, tolerant plant for most soils; takes seaside conditions. 'Compact Gold Coin' is less sprawling and more mounding.

A. sericeus (Nauplius sericeus). CANARY ISLAND DAISY. Zones 16, 17, 19–24. At 3 ft. tall and wide, shrubbier and less sprawling than *A. maritimus.* Silky, silvery leaves set off bright yellow flowers for a silver-and-gold effect. The foliage has an odd odor when brushed, and old leaves tend to blacken and adhere to the stems. If groomed, makes a striking container plant.

ASTILBE

FALSE SPIRAEA, MEADOW SWEET

Saxifragaceae

PERENNIALS

ZONES 1–7, 14–17;
SHORT LIVED IN ZONES 8, 9, 18–24

FULL SUN IN COOLER CLIMATES ONLY

REGULAR WATER

Astilbe ×arendsii

Valued for light, airy quality of plumelike flower clusters and attractive foliage and for ability to provide color from late spring through summer. Leaves are typically divided, with toothed or cut leaflets, though in some species they are simply lobed, with cut margins. Small white, pink, or red flowers are carried in graceful, branching, feathery plumes held on slender, wiry stems ranging from 6 in. to 3 ft. or taller. Most plants grow 2–3 ft. wide.

Astilbes are the mainstay of the shady perennial border, although in cool-summer climates they can withstand full sun if watered adequately. Effective at the edge of pools, along shady paths, in containers. Need moist (but not boggy), rich soil with ample humus. Cut off faded flowering stems and divide clumps every 4 or 5 years. Survival in coldest areas (Zones 1a, 1b, 2a) depends on good snow cover.

A. ×arendsii. Most astilbes sold belong to this hybrid group or are sold as such. Parentage is complex, but plants often have *A. japonica, A. chinensis,* and/or *A. thunbergii* in their ancestry. The plants differ chiefly in technical details. The following are some of the best varieties.

'Amethyst'. Late. Lavender, 3–4 ft.

'Bridal Veil'. Midseason to late. Full white plumes, 3 ft.

'Deutschland'. Early. White, 1½ ft.

'Fanal'. Early. Blood-red flowers, bronzy foliage, 1½–2½ ft.

'Ostrich Plume' ('Straussenfeder'). Midseason to late. Drooping pink clusters, 3–3½ ft. Often sold as a variety of *A. thunbergii.*

'Peach Blossom'. Midseason. Light salmon pink, 2 ft.

'Rheinland'. Early. Deep pink, 2–2½ ft.

A. chinensis. Resembles *A. ×arendsii* hybrids, but generally blooms in late summer, grows taller, and tolerates dryness a little better. Varieties include the following.

A. c. davidii. Dense, narrow pink plumes to 3 ft. tall. Pink-flowered 'Finale' blooms latest, grows 18–20 in. tall.

'Pumila'. Low mats of leaves topped by lilac pink flower clusters that rise 12–15 in. high.

A. c. taquetii 'Superba'. Bright pinkish purple flowers in spikelike clusters 4–5 ft. tall. 'Purple Candles' is deeper purple, slightly shorter.

A. simplicifolia. Grows to 16 in. high. Leaves are merely cut or lobed, not divided into leaflets. Known for its garden varieties. 'Sprite' (the best known) is a low, compact plant that blooms profusely in summer, bearing drooping pink, 1-ft. spires above bronze-tinted foliage. 'Hennie Graefland' is similar but grows a few inches taller and blooms a little earlier.

A. taquetii 'Superba'. See A. chinensis taquetii 'Superba'

ASTILBOIDES tabularis (Rodgersia tabularis)

Saxifragaceae

PERENNIAL

ZONES 2B–9, 14–17

PARTIAL SHADE

AMPLE WATER

Astilboides tabularis

Large plant from China and Korea, with imposing (2-ft.-wide), nearly round leaves attached at the centers to 3-ft.-long stems. Small white flowers in large clusters appear in summer on stalks to 5 ft. high. Plants spread slowly from thick, creeping rhizomes; count on at least a 3-ft. spread. Needs plenty of water; leaves wilt quickly in hot, dry weather. Striking plant for woodland or pondside garden. Good substitute for hostas where slugs and snails cause problems.

ASTRANTIA

MASTERWORT

Apiaceae (Umbelliferae)

PERENNIALS

ZONES 1–9, 14–24

FULL SUN OR PARTIAL SHADE

REGULAR WATER

Astrantia major

Summer flowers in dense, tight clusters surrounded by papery bracts resemble pincushions or, superficially, daisies. Flowering stems rise from leafy clumps. Blossoms make attractive, long-lasting cut flowers and can also be dried for winter arrangements. Useful plants for woodland or cottage gardens—native to alpine woods and meadows of Europe. Spread by underground runners. Die back in winter, even in mild climates. Need good drainage.

A. carniolica. To 1½ ft. tall and wide, with finely divided leaves. Bracts are shorter than in other species. 'Rubra' has dark red flowers with silvery accents.

A. major. To 3 ft. high, 1–2 ft. wide, with inch-wide clusters of white-and-green or white-and-pink blossoms.

A. maxima. Similar to *A. major* but grows 2 ft. high and bears pink flowers.

ATHEL TREE. See TAMARIX aphylla

FOR INFORMATION ON YOUR CLIMATE ZONE
PLEASE SEE PAGES 27–63

ATHYRIUM

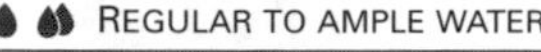

Polypodiaceae

FERNS

ZONES VARY BY SPECIES

PARTIAL OR FULL SHADE

REGULAR TO AMPLE WATER

Athyrium filix-femina

Fronds of most types turn brown after repeated frosts. Leave dead foliage on plants through winter to provide mulch and to shelter delicate emerging fronds in early spring; cut back after new fronds have appeared. All species described here prefer rich, damp soil and will tolerate full sun if grown in constantly moist soil. Propagate by dividing old clumps in early spring.

A. filix-femina. LADY FERN. Zones A1–A3; 1–9, 14–24. Native to much of North America. To 4 ft. or taller, 2–3 ft. wide. Vigorous root system can be invasive. Thin, finely divided fronds. Rootstock rises up on older plants to make short trunk. Vertical effect; narrow at bottom, spreading at top. Specialists stock many varieties with oddly cut and feathered fronds. In 'Frizelliae' (about 8 in. high, 1 ft. wide), the frond divisions are reduced to balls, giving each frond the look of a string of beads. 'Vernoniae Cristatum' (to 2½ ft. tall and wide) has crested and feathered fronds.

A. nipponicum 'Pictum' (A. goeringianum 'Pictum'). JAPANESE PAINTED FERN. Zones 1–9, 14–24. Fronds grow to 1½ ft. long, making a tight, slowly spreading clump 1 ft. high, 1½ ft. wide. Leaflets are purplish at base, then lavender, then silvery greenish gray toward end.

A. otophorum. ENGLISH PAINTED FERN. Zones 3–9, 14–24. Actually an Asian native. It resembles Japanese painted fern, but its dark green fronds have a reddish or purple midrib.

ATRIPLEX

SALTBUSH

Chenopodiaceae

EVERGREEN AND DECIDUOUS SHRUBS

ZONES VARY BY SPECIES

FULL SUN

LITTLE OR NO WATER

Atriplex hymenelytra

Unusually tolerant of direct seashore conditions and highly alkaline desert soils, saltbushes are grown for their gray or silvery foliage. Flowers and seeds attract birds. Need good drainage. Often become straggly with age; to keep them compact, cut back previous year's growth by one-third each year before the first flush of spring growth. Plants are fire resistant.

A. barklayana. Evergreen. Zones 16–24. Dwarf saltbush from Baja California forms a dense 1½-ft.-high mound 4 ft. across. Inch-long leaves are covered with white powder.

A. canescens. FOUR-WING SALTBUSH. Evergreen. Zones 1–3, 7–24. Native throughout much of arid part of West. Dense growth 3–6 ft. high, spreading to 4–8 ft. Narrow gray leaves ½–2 in. long. Often sheared into a hedge.

A. confertifolia. SHADSCALE. Deciduous. Zones 1–3, 10. Native to high plains and mesas from eastern Oregon and California to North Dakota, south to northern Arizona, western Texas, and Mexico. Mounded, woody, spiny subshrub, 8 in.–3 ft. tall and wide, with rounded, whitish leaves and pinkish or yellowish flower spikes in early summer.

A. hymenelytra. DESERT HOLLY. Evergreen. Zones 3, 7–14, 18, 19. Native to deserts of Southern California, western Arizona, southern Nevada, southwestern Utah. Compact shrub 1–3 ft. high, 3 ft. wide. Whitish branches and silvery, deeply toothed, roundish leaves to 1½ in. long. Has Christmas holly look—in silvery white; much used for decorations. Outside native range, needs very fast drainage. Can take heavy watering from midwinter into spring.

A. lentiformis. QUAIL BUSH. Deciduous. Zones 3, 7–14, 18, 19. Native to alkali wastes in California valleys and deserts and east to Nevada, Utah, Arizona, and New Mexico. Densely branched, sometimes spiny shrub, 3–10 ft. high, 6–12 ft. wide. Oval, bluish gray leaves ½–2 in. long. Useful as salt-tolerant informal hedge or windbreak.

A. l. breweri. BREWER SALTBUSH. Nearly evergreen. Zones 8, 9, 12–24. Native to California coast south of San Francisco Bay and to Channel Islands. Like *A. lentiformis* but not spiny. To 5–7 ft. high, 6–8 ft. wide. Useful gray plant on ocean front; will grow in reclaimed marine soil. Sometimes sheared into a hedge.

A. nummularia. Evergreen. Zones 15–24. Native to Australia but naturalized in parts of Southern California. Dense, rounded, nearly white shrub to 6 ft. tall, 3 ft. wide. Tolerates summer drought, winter flooding. Will grow in full sun or light shade.

A. polycarpa. DESERT SALTBUSH, CATTLE SPINACH. Evergreen to deciduous. Zones 3, 7–13, 18, 19. A tough desert shrub of alkali flats and dry lakebeds from California's Owens Valley east to Utah and south to Baja California and Sonora, Mexico. Dense covering of grayish white scales gives the densely branched, symmetrical, 3–6-ft. mound a silvery glow. Needs no irrigation but loses its leaves in extreme drought and heat.

A. semibaccata. AUSTRALIAN SALTBUSH. Evergreen. Zones 8–10, 12–24. Native to Australia but naturalized in parts of the West and Southwest. Forms a dense, foot-high mat of ½–1½-in.-long, gray-green leaves. Spreads from 1 ft. to 6 ft. or even wider. Excellent ground cover; plant 3 ft. apart.

AUBRIETA deltoidea

COMMON AUBRIETA

Brassicaceae (Cruciferae)

PERENNIAL

ZONES 1–9, 14–21

FULL SUN OR LIGHT SHADE

REGULAR WATER

Aubrieta deltoidea

Native eastern Mediterranean region to Iran. Mat-forming perennial —popular in Northwest and high-elevation rock gardens, where it blooms in early spring, with basket-of-gold, rockcress, perennial candytuft, and moss pink. Ideal for chinks in dry stone walls or between patio flagstones. Grows 2–6 in. high, 1–1½ ft. across. Small gray-green leaves with a few teeth at tips. Tiny rose to deep red, pale to deep lilac, or purple flowers. 'Novalis Blue' is a fine seed-grown variety with dark blue blossoms. 'Rokey's Purple' is a heavy producer of rich purple flowers.

Provide good drainage. Needs regular moisture before and during bloom; takes some drought later on. After bloom, shear off flowers before they set seed. Don't cut back by more than half—always keep some foliage. After trimming, top-dress with mixture of gritty soil and bonemeal. Sow seeds in late spring for blooms the following spring. Difficult to divide clumps; make cuttings in late summer.

AUCUBA japonica

JAPANESE AUCUBA

Cornaceae

EVERGREEN SHRUB

ZONES 4–24

PARTIAL OR FULL SHADE

MODERATE TO REGULAR WATER

Aucuba japonica 'Variegata'

Native from Himalayas to Japan. Seedlings vary in leaf form and variegations; many varieties offered. Standard green-leafed aucuba grows at a moderate rate up to 6–10 ft. (sometimes to 15 ft.) high and almost as wide. Plant can be kept lower by pruning. Buxom shrub, densely clothed with polished, dark green, toothed leaves 3–8 in. long, 1½–3 in. wide. ▸

Minute dark maroon flowers in earliest spring are followed by clusters of bright red, ¾-in. berries in fall and winter. Both sexes must be planted to ensure fruit crop. Green-leafed 'Rozannie' is self-fruitful, producing a heavy crop of berries without a pollenizer.

Other green-leafed varieties include 'Longifolia' ('Salicifolia'), narrow willowlike leaves (female); 'Nana', dwarf to about 3 ft. (female); 'Serratifolia', long leaves with coarsely toothed edges (female).

Variegated varieties (usually slower growing) include 'Crotonifolia', leaves heavily splashed with white and gold (male); 'Fructu Albo', leaves variegated with white, berries pale pinkish buff (female); 'Picturata' ('Aureo-maculata'), leaves centered with golden yellow, edged with dark green dotted yellow (female); 'Sulphur', green leaves with broad yellow edge (female). 'Variegata', often called gold dust plant, is the best-known aucuba. It has dark green leaves spotted with yellow; plants may be male or female. 'Mr. Goldstrike' has heavier gold splashings.

Tolerant of wide range of soils but will grow better and look better if poor or heavy soils are improved. Requires shade from hot sun, accepts deep shade. Grows well in low light under trees, competes successfully with tree roots. Tolerates sea air. Gets mealybug and mites. Prune to control height or form by cutting back to a leaf joint.

All aucubas make choice tub plants for shady patio or in the house. Use variegated forms to lighten up dark corners. Plants combine effectively with ferns, hydrangeas.

AURICULA. See PRIMULA auricula

AURINIA saxatilis (Alyssum saxatile)

BASKET-OF-GOLD

Brassicaceae (Cruciferae)

PERENNIAL

ZONES 1–24

FULL SUN OR LIGHT SHADE

MODERATE WATER

Aurinia saxatilis

Mustard relative native to mountains of central and southern Europe, Turkey. Gray, 2–5-in.-long leaves form a spreading evergreen mound 8–12 in. high. Dense clusters of tiny golden yellow flowers cover the plant in spring and early summer. Use as foreground plant in borders, in rock gardens, atop walls; plant about 1½ ft. apart. Poor soils or moderately fertile ones suit the plant perfectly—as long as drainage is good. Shear lightly (don't cut back stems by more than half) right after bloom. Generally hardy but may be killed in extremely cold winters. Self-sows readily.

Varieties include 'Citrina' ('Lutea'), with pale yellow flowers; 'Compacta', a tight-growing dwarf; 'Plena' ('Flore Pleno'), double flowered; 'Silver Queen', compact grower with pale yellow flowers; 'Sunnyborder Apricot', with apricot-shaded flowers; 'Dudley Neville', similar in flower color to 'Sunnyborder Apricot' but with white-variegated leaves; and dwarf forms 'Goldkugel' ('Gold Ball'), 6 in. high, and 'Tom Thumb', only 3 in. high.

AUSTRALIAN BLUEBELL CREEPER. See SOLLYA heterophylla

AUSTRALIAN FLAME TREE. See BRACHYCHITON acerifolius

AUSTRALIAN FUCHSIA. See CORREA

AUSTRALIAN TEA TREE. See LEPTOSPERMUM laevigatum

AUSTRALIAN TREE FERN. See CYATHEA cooperi

AUSTRALIAN WILLOW. See GEIJERA parviflora

AUSTRIAN BRIER. See ROSA foetida

AUTUMN FERN. See DRYOPTERIS erythrosora

AVOCADO

Lauraceae

EVERGREEN TREES

ZONES VARY BY VARIETY

FULL SUN

REGULAR WATER

SEE CHART

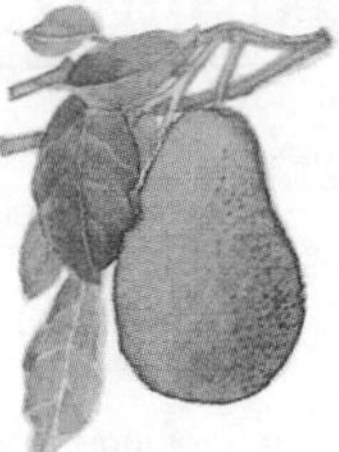

Avocado

In California, two races of avocados are grown: Guatemalan *(Persea americana)* and Mexican *(P. drymifolia)*. Widely planted 'Fuerte' is thought to be a hybrid of the two. Ideal climates for Guatemalan varieties are Zones 19, 21, 23, and 24. Mexican varieties, bearing smaller, less attractive fruit, are hardier and grow in Zones 9, 16–24, and some warmer locations in Zones 8, 14, 15. In Hawaii, Guatemalan and hybrid varieties are best adapted to (and are grown throughout) Zone H2, but away from exposure to salt spray. Avocados bloom in late winter to early spring, so even though plants are hardy to 24 to 30°F/–4 to –1°C, temperatures much below freezing will destroy crop.

Pollination is complex. In areas where avocados are common, crops are routinely heavy. Isolated trees may produce enough fruit for home consumption, but if crops are light, plant another variety nearby or graft a limb from another variety into the bearing tree. Avocado varieties have flowers categorized as either type A or type B, depending on the time of day they open and when pollen is released. For best production, combine a type A with a type B variety; flower type for each variety is noted in the chart.

When using avocados in the landscape, remember that most varieties will reach 30–40 ft. tall and spread wider (although size can be controlled to some degree by pruning). They will also produce dense shade and shed leaves constantly throughout the year. Avocado trees are resistant to oak root fungus but very susceptible to *Phytophthora* root rot and must have excellent drainage to survive. Plants take well to container culture; in marginal climates move them to protected area during cold spells.

Persea mite is a problem in Southern California; it causes small yellow and black dead spots on the foliage and excessive leaf drop. It can be controlled by releasing one of several species of predatory mites. For more information, contact your Cooperative Extension Office.

Unless otherwise noted, fruit of all varieties listed in chart has thin, pliable, smooth skin.

WHAT AVOCADOS NEED

DRAINAGE: Make sure it's good. Avoid clay soil. High water table in rainy season can kill a tree, even in well-drained soil.

WATERING: Keep soil moist but not wet with light, frequent sprinkler irrigation. Go heavy every third or fourth time to wash out excess salts. Let fallen leaves build up under the tree as mulch.

FERTILIZING: Feed young trees lightly; mature trees need 1 lb. of actual nitrogen per year, split into two applications—one in spring, one in summer. Control chlorosis with iron or zinc chelates.

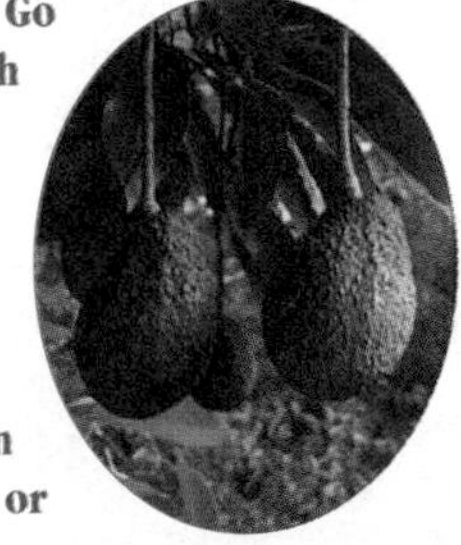

Avocado

POLLINATION: Combine type A bloomer with type B for best fruit production (see chart).

AZALEA. See RHODODENDRON

A

AVOCADO

NAME	ZONES	HARVEST PERIOD	FRUIT	COMMENTS
'Bacon'	9, 16–24	Fall and winter	Medium size, green skinned, good quality	Mexican. Upright grower. Produces when young. Type B flower
'Fuerte'	20–24	Fall through spring	Medium size, green skinned, high quality	Hybrid. Well-known variety. Large tree. Early flowers (type B) subject to frost in borderline areas
'Gwen'	19–24	Midwinter into fall	Medium size, green skinned, good quality	Guatemalan. Dwarf tree, 15–20 ft. high, narrow. Type A flower
'Hass'	16, 17, 19, 21, 23, 24	Spring into fall	Medium to large. Dark purple (almost black), pebbly skin, thick but pliable. Excellent flavor	Guatemalan. Large, spreading tree; tends to bear in alternate years. Type A flower
'Jim'	19–24	Fall into winter	Medium size, with green skin and long neck	Mexican. Bears at a young age. Type B flower
'Kahaluu'	H2	Fall into winter	Medium to large; green skin. Superb flavor	Hybrid. Light producer. Type B flower
'Mexicola'	9, 16–24	Late summer into fall	Small. Tender, dark purple skin. Outstanding, nutty flavor. Large seed	Mexican. One of the hardiest. Heavy producer. Type A flower
'Murashige'	H2	Spring to late summer	Medium to large; pebbly green skin. Very good quality, small seed	Hybrid. Heavy producer. Type B flower
'Nabal'	19–24	Summer into fall	Medium size; green skin. Excellent flavor	Guatemalan. Tends to bear in alternate years. Type B flower
'Pinkerton'	19–24	Winter into spring	Variable size. Green skin, very good quality	Guatemalan. Heavy producer. Large tree. Type A flower
'Reed'	21–24	Summer	Medium to large; green, rough skin. Fine flavor	Guatemalan. Slender, upright tree. Type A flower
'Sharwil'	H2	Fall into spring	Medium size, with pebbly green skin. Excellent flavor	Hybrid. Heavy producer. Type B flower
'Wertz' ('Wurtz')	19–24	Summer	Medium size; green skin	Guatemalan. Small tree (8–10 ft. high) with weeping branches. Good for pots or small gardens. Often sold as 'Dwarf', 'Littlecado', or 'Minicado'. Tends to bear in alternate years. Type A flower
'Whitsell'	19–24	Midwinter into fall	Medium size; green skin, very good quality	Guatemalan. Small (10–12-ft.) tree; tends to bear in alternate years. Type B flower
'Yamagata'	H2	Late spring through summer	Medium to large, with pebbly green skin and rich flavor	Hybrid. Heavy producer. Type B flower
'Zutano'	9, 16–24	Fall to midwinter	Medium size; green skin. Good quality	Hybrid. Upright grower. Type B flower

AZARA

Flacourtiaceae

EVERGREEN SHRUBS OR SMALL TREES

ZONES VARY BY SPECIES

PARTIAL SHADE

REGULAR WATER

Native to lakesides and woodland edges in Chile, Argentina. Attractive evergreen foliage; fluffy yellow flowers that smell like chocolate to some, vanilla to others. Need fast drainage, regular fertilizer, protection from hot afternoon sun. Prune after bloom to remove crowded or wayward branches.

Azara microphylla

A. dentata. Zones 5 (with shelter), 6, 15–17. To 15 ft. tall, 12 ft. wide. Toothed, rounded, shiny leaves about 1 in. across. Dense branching and rounded shape make it useful for screen or informal hedge. Tolerates considerable shade. Blooms in spring.

A. lanceolata. LANCELEAF AZARA. Zones 5 (with shelter), 15–17. Large, arching plant to 20 ft. tall, 15 ft. wide. Equal to *A. microphylla* in pattern value, but its bright yellow-green, rather narrow leaves are much larger (to 2½ in. long), producing a lusher effect. Blooms in spring.

A. microphylla. BOXLEAF AZARA. Zones 5–9, 14–24. Best-known species. Slow growing when small, faster when established. Typically reaches 12–18 ft. tall, 8–12 ft. wide, but may attain a treelike 30 ft. tall in great old age. Shiny, roundish dark green leaves are ½–¾ in. long. Flat-branching habit and neatly arranged foliage make it natural for espalier or free-standing wall plant. Blooms in late winter. ▶

A. petiolaris (A. gilliesii). Zones 15–17. Shrubby growth to 15–20 ft. tall, 12 ft. wide, but easily trained to form a single-stemmed tree. Oval to roundish, lustrous deep green leaves are 1½–3 in. long, look somewhat like those of holly; they hang from branches like aspen leaves. Blooms in late winter.

AZORELLA trifurcata. See BOLAX gummifera

AZTEC LILY. See SPREKELIA formosissima

BABACO. See PAPAYA

BABIANA

BABOON FLOWER

Iridaceae

PERENNIALS FROM CORMS

ZONES 4–24; OR DIG AND STORE

FULL SUN OR LIGHT SHADE

REGULAR WATER DURING GROWTH AND BLOOM

Babiana stricta

These natives of sub-Saharan Africa are grown for spikes of freesialike flowers in blue, lavender, purple, red, and white. In mid- to late spring, each flowering stem produces six or more blooms, each to 2 in. across. Strongly ribbed, usually hairy leaves typically grow in fans. Corms are reportedly tasty to baboons, hence the plant's common name. Plant them 4 in. deep and 4–6 in. apart—along edge of border or path, in rock garden, in deep pots. In Zones 8–24, plant in fall; in colder areas, plant in early spring, waiting until temperatures will remain above 20°F/–7°C. Cut back on water as leaves yellow. Trim off foliage after it dies back. Where corms can overwinter in ground, leave them in place for several years—they'll increase and bloom more profusely with each year. Beyond hardiness range, dig and store as for gladiolus.

B. rubrocyanea. Ruby-throated royal blue blossoms on 6-in. stems.

B. stricta. Royal blue flowers on 1-ft. stems. Varieties with purple, lavender, white, and blue-and-white blooms are sold.

BABY BLUE EYES. See NEMOPHILA menziesii

BABY'S BREATH. See GYPSOPHILA paniculata

BABY SNAPDRAGON. See LINARIA maroccana

BABY'S TEARS. See SOLEIROLIA soleirolii

BACCHARIS

Asteraceae (Compositae)

EVERGREEN SHRUBS

ZONES VARY BY SPECIES

FULL SUN

LITTLE TO MODERATE WATER

Baccharis pilularis

Main value of these plants is their toughness and ability to grow in difficult conditions: they withstand heat, wind, and poor soil. Most are densely foliaged. Male and female flowers, borne on separate plants, are inconspicuous. Female plants produce cottony seed clusters that can make a mess when blown about by wind; grow male varieties if they're available (or hoe out seedlings if they appear where you don't want them).

B. 'Centennial'. Zones 7–24; best in 10–13. Female hybrid between *B. pilularis* and *B. sarothroides.* Grows 3 ft. tall, 4–5 ft. wide, with narrow leaves and tufted tan seed capsules in spring. Tolerates desert heat; resists root rot caused by water molds.

B. pilularis. DWARF COYOTE BRUSH. Zones 5–11, 14–24. Native to Northern California coast. Remarkable climate and soil adaptation. Near the coast it thrives with no water at all; inland it looks better with monthly watering. In California's high desert, it's the most dependable of all ground covers. Everywhere, it's a very valuable, reliable bank and flatland cover for low-maintenance areas in sun.

Makes dense, rather billowy, bright green mat, 8–24 in. high and spreading to 6 ft. or more. Small (½-in.), toothed leaves are closely set on branches. Needs shearing once a year in early spring before new growth starts. Cut out old arching branches and thin to rejuvenate. Feed with a nitrogen fertilizer immediately after cutting back. The plants available in most nurseries are produced by cuttings from male plants. 'Twin Peaks' ('Twin Peaks #2') has small dark green leaves and a moderate growth rate. 'Pigeon Point' has larger leaves in a lighter green and grows faster (9 ft. wide in 4 years); can make a 2–3-ft.-high hedge.

B. sarothroides. DESERT BROOM. Zones 7–24; most useful in 10–13. Native to Southwest. Nearly leafless, but branches are bright green throughout year. Grows 5 ft. tall and wide; can be clipped to 2–3 ft. Extremely drought tolerant. Can take good or poor drainage. Useful for erosion control, replanting disturbed land, or natural landscape in desert regions.

B. 'Starn' (B. 'Thompson'). Zones 7–24; best in 10–13. Has the same size and habit as 'Centennial' but offers an improvement, since it is a male plant and won't produce seed clusters.

BACHELOR'S BUTTON. See CENTAUREA cyanus

BACOPA monnieri

WATER HYSSOP

Scrophulariaceae

AQUATIC PERENNIAL

ZONES 8–24; H1, H2

FULL SUN

AMPLE WATER

Bacopa monnieri

The true bacopa is a trailing, succulent plant native to the tropics and parts of the southeastern U.S., with ¾-in. leaves and small white or pale blue flowers. It forms mats at the water's edge, often extending its growth into the water. Grow it at a pond edge or in a pot in the water. For the familiar terrestrial bacopa seen as a hanging basket or bedding plant, see *Sutera cordata.*

BAECKEA virgata

Myrtaceae

EVERGREEN SHRUB

ZONES 15–24

FULL SUN OR LIGHT SHADE

REGULAR WATER

Baeckea virgata

Australian native with tiny needlelike leaves and profuse small white, honey-scented flowers that resemble miniature blossoms of tea tree *(Leptospermum).* Blooms in spring and summer. Reaches 8 ft. or taller, 4–4½ ft. wide. Pinch young plants to promote branching; thin out old, weak growth after flowering is over.

BAGAUAK. See CLERODENDRUM quadriloculare

FOR GROWING SYMBOL EXPLANATIONS
PLEASE SEE PAGE 161

BAILEYA multiradiata

DESERT MARIGOLD
Asteraceae (Compositae)
ANNUAL OR PERENNIAL
ZONES 1–3, 7–23
FULL SUN
MODERATE WATER

Baileya multiradiata

Western desert native grows 1–1½ ft. high, displaying inch-wide, bright yellow flowers above gray-green foliage. Basic bloom period is spring through fall, but year-round bloom is possible in low desert and other mild-winter areas if plants receive periodic moisture. Sow seed in fall or spring, rake in, and water thoroughly. Keep moist until seeds sprout, then reduce watering to once or twice weekly. Thin to 1½ ft. apart. To prolong bloom, water every week or two. Self-sows.

BALD CYPRESS. See TAXODIUM distichum

BALLOON FLOWER. See PLATYCODON grandiflorus

BALLOTA pseudodictamnus

Lamiaceae (Labiatae)
SHRUBBY PERENNIAL
ZONES 2, 3, 6–9, 14–24
FULL SUN
LITTLE TO MODERATE WATER

Ballota pseudodictamnus

Dense, rounded Mediterranean native to 1½ ft. high, 2 ft. wide, with opposite pairs of roundish, inch-wide, furry gray-green leaves. Bears whorls of unimportant small white flowers. Use in mixed perennial beds or bank plantings. Provide good drainage. Cut back hard in spring before new growth starts.

BALSAM. See IMPATIENS balsamina

Balsaminaceae. The touch-me-not family embraces herbaceous and shrubby plants with juicy stems, irregular flowers with spurs, and explosive seed capsules. *Impatiens* is the only important member.

BALSAM PEAR. See BITTER MELON

BAMBOO

Poaceae (Gramineae)
GIANT GRASSES
SEE CHART FOR HARDINESS
SUN OR PARTIAL SHADE
LITTLE TO REGULAR WATER
SEE CHART NEXT PAGE

Bambusa multiplex

Large, woody stems (culms) divided into sections (internodes) by obvious joints (nodes). Upper nodes grow buds that develop branches; these, in larger bamboos, divide into secondary branches that bear leaves. Bamboos spread by underground stems (rhizomes) that, like the aboveground culms, are jointed and carry buds. Manner in which rhizomes grow explains difference between running and clump bamboos.

In running bamboos *(Chimonobambusa, Indocalamus, Phyllostachys, Pleioblastus, Pseudosasa, Sasa, Semiarundinaria, Shibataea),* rhizomes grow rapidly to varying distances from parent plant before sending up vertical shoots. These bamboos eventually form large patches or groves. They are generally fairly hardy plants from temperate regions in China and Japan, and they are tolerant of a wide variety of soils.

In clump bamboos *(Bambusa, Chusquea, Drepanostachyum, Fargesia, Otatea),* rhizomes grow a short distance then send up stems. These form clumps that expand at edges. Most are tropical or subtropical.

See chart for hardiness. Figures indicate temperature at which leaf damage occurs. Stems and rhizomes may be considerably hardier.

Plant container-grown bamboos at any time of year. Best time to propagate from existing clumps is just before growth begins in spring; divide hardy kinds in late winter or early spring, tropical ones in mid- to late spring. (Transplanting at other times is possible, but risk of losing divisions is high in summer heat or winter chill and wet soil.) Cut or saw out divisions with roots and at least three connected culms. If divisions are large, cut back tops to balance loss of roots and rhizomes. Foliage may wilt or wither, but culms will send out new leaves.

Rhizome cutting is another means of propagation. In clump bamboos, the cutting is the rooted base of a culm; in running bamboos, it is a foot-long length of rhizome with roots and buds. Plant in rich mix with ample organic material added.

Culms of all bamboos have already attained their maximum diameter when they poke through ground; in mature plants, they usually reach their maximum height within a month. Many do become increasingly leafy in subsequent years, but not taller. Plants are evergreen, but there is considerable dropping of older leaves; old plantings develop nearly weedproof mulch of dead leaves. Individual canes live for several years but eventually die and should be cut out.

Bambusa oldhamii

Mature bamboos grow very fast during their brief growth period—culms of giant types may grow in length several feet a day. Don't expect such growth the first year after transplanting, though. Giant timber bamboo *(Phyllostachys bambusoides)* needs 3 to 5 years to build up a rhizome system capable of supporting these fast-growing culms; growth in early years will be less impressive. To get fast growth and great size, water frequently and feed once a month with high-nitrogen or lawn fertilizer; to restrict size and spread, water and feed less. Once established, plants tolerate considerable drought, but rhizomes will not spread into dry soil (or into water). The accompanying chart lists two heights for each bamboo. "Controlled height" means average height under dry conditions with little feeding, or with rhizome spread controlled by barriers. "Uncontrolled height" refers to plants growing under best conditions without confinement.

Difficult to mass-produce and little known, most bamboos are hard to find in nurseries. Inquire about specialists in your area. The American Bamboo Society has chapters in the Northwest, in Northern California, and in Southern California. Society members often propagate rare varieties for sale in connection with their meetings. Arboretum and botanical garden sales are another source. Plants may be offered under the principal name listed or under one of the synonyms. Plant names change so frequently that vendors cannot always keep up.

In the case of bamboo, disregard the rule of never buying root-bound plants: the more crowded the plant in the container, the faster its growth when planted. Both running and clump types grow well when roots are confined. To keep running bamboo from running amok in the garden, confine it with 2–3-ft.-deep barriers made from strips of galvanized sheet metal, 30-mil plastic, or poured concrete; or plant in long flue tiles, large plastic plant containers with the bottoms cut out, or bottomless oil drums. Alternatively, you can limit spread by periodically inserting a spade down to its full depth around the clump. New shoots break off easily and do not resprout. Another way to restrict large running bamboos is to dig a foot-deep trench around plant and sever any rhizomes that grow into it. The trench will eventually fill with a loose mulch of leaves; sift through leaves with gloved hands to find roving rhizomes.

▶ page 217

B

BAMBOO

For explanation of height, see page 213; for Roman numerals I, II, III, and IV, see page 217. Hardiness is temperature at which leaf damage occurs.

NAME	ALSO SOLD AS	CONTROLLED (UNCONTROLLED) HEIGHT	GROWTH HABIT	STEM DIAMETER	HARDINESS	COMMENTS (GROWTH HABIT, CHARACTERISTICS, USES)
Bambusa beecheyana BEECHEY BAMBOO	*Sinocalamus beecheyanus*	12–20 ft. (20–40 ft.)	Clump	4–5 in.	15°F/–9°C	IV. Culms arch strongly for broad, graceful effect. Tropical looking. Scarce
B. multiplex	*B. glaucescens*	8–10 ft. (15–25 ft.)	Clump	1½ in.	15°F/–9°C	II. Branches from base to top. Dense growth. Hedges, screens. Less common than its varieties described below
B. m. 'Alphonse Karr' ALPHONSE KARR BAMBOO		8–10 ft. (15–35 ft.)	Clump	½–1 in.	15°F/–9°C	II. Similar to species, but culms are brilliantly striped green on yellow. New culms pinkish and green
B. m. 'Fernleaf' FERNLEAF BAMBOO	*B. nana, B. disticha*	6–10 ft. (10–20 ft.)	Clump	½ in.	15°F/–9°C	II. Closely spaced leaves, 10–20 to twig, give ferny look. Loses this look, grows coarser with rich soil, ample water
B. m. 'Golden Goddess' GOLDEN GODDESS BAMBOO		6–8 ft. (6–10 ft.)	Clump	½ in.	15°F/–9°C	II. Golden-stemmed variety with graceful, dense, arching growth. Good container or screen plant. Give tops room to spread
B. m. riviereorum CHINESE GODDESS BAMBOO		4–6 ft. (6–8 ft.)	Clump	¼ in.	15°F/–9°C	II. Solid culms arch gracefully. Tiny leaves in lacy, ferny sprays
B. oldhamii OLDHAM BAMBOO, CLUMPING GIANT TIMBER BAMBOO	*Sinocalamus oldhamii*	15–25 ft. (20–55 ft.)	Clump	4 in.	15°F/–9°C	IV. Densely foliaged, erect clumps; good for big, dense screens. Or use single plant as imposing vertical mass. Most common big bamboo in Southern California
B. ventricosa BUDDHA'S BELLY BAMBOO		3–6 ft. (15–30 ft.)	Clump	2 in.	20°F/–7°C	II or IV. Stays small, produces swollen culms that give it its name only when grown in tubs or in poor, dryish soil. Otherwise a giant bamboo with straight culms
B. vulgaris vittata		15–25 ft. (to 50 ft.)	Clump	4 in.	30°F/–1°C	IV. Yellow culms have vertical green stripes. For Hawaii, mildest coastal climates, and well-lit interiors
Chimonobambusa quadrangularis SQUARE-STEM BAMBOO	*Bambusa quadrangularis*	10–15 ft. (20–30 ft.)	Running	1 in.	15°F/–9°C	III. Squarish culms have prominent joints, carry heavy whorls of branches. Valued for vertical effect
Chusquea coronalis		8–12 ft. (12–15 ft.)	Clump	¾ in.	28°F/–2°C	IV. Arching culms bear masses of tiny leaves on short, whorled branches. Exceptionally attractive. Sun or light shade. Rare
Drepanostachyum hookerianum (Himalayacalamus hookerianum) BLUE BAMBOO		10–15 ft. (20–30 ft.)	Clump	2 in.	20°F/–7°C	II. Culms are bluish at first, later striped in green and yellow. Arching, leafy branches
Fargesia murielae	*Sinarundinaria murielae*	6–8 ft. (to 15 ft.)	Clump	¾ in.	–20°F/–29°C	II. One of two hardiest bamboos listed here. Light, airy, narrow clump, arching and drooping at top. Best in shade. Rare
F. nitida FOUNTAIN BAMBOO	*Sinarundinaria nitida*	6–8 ft. (15–20 ft.)	Clump	¾ in.	0°F/–18°C	II. Light, airy, graceful, narrow clump, arching and drooping at top. Greenish purple culms mature to deep purplish black. Needs shade to look its best. Rare

BAMBOO

For explanation of height, see page 213; for Roman numerals I, II, III, and IV, see page 217. Hardiness is temperature at which leaf damage occurs.

B

NAME	ALSO SOLD AS	CONTROLLED (UNCONTROLLED) HEIGHT	GROWTH HABIT	STEM DIAMETER	HARDINESS	COMMENTS (GROWTH HABIT, CHARACTERISTICS, USES)
Indocalamus tessellata	*Arundinaria ragamowskii*	2–3 ft. (3–6 ft.)	Running	¼ in.	0°F/–18°C	Resembles *Sasa palmata,* but much lower growth, much longer leaves (2 ft.). Rapid spreader, best in shade. Rare
Otatea acuminata aztecorum MEXICAN WEEPING BAMBOO	*Yushania aztecorum, Arthrostylidium longifolium*	8–10 ft. (to 20 ft.)	Clump	1½ in.	15°F/–9°C	II. Extremely narrow leaves (6 in. by ⅛ in.) give lacy look. Foliage masses bend nearly to ground. Fairly drought resistant when established. Rare
Phyllostachys aurea GOLDEN BAMBOO		6–10 ft. (10–20 ft.)	Running	2 in.	0°F/–18°C	III. Erect, stiff culms, usually with crowded joints at base—good identifying mark. Dense foliage makes it good screen or hedge. Can take much drought but looks better with regular water. Good choice for growing in tubs
P. aureosulcata YELLOW GROOVE BAMBOO		12–15 ft. (15–25 ft.)	Running	1½ in.	–20°F/–29°C	III. Like more slender, more open *P. aurea.* Young culms green with pronounced yellowish groove. One of two hardiest bamboos listed here
P. bambusoides GIANT TIMBER BAMBOO, JAPANESE TIMBER BAMBOO	*P. reticulata*	15–35 ft. (25–45 ft.)	Running	6 in.	0°F/–18°C	IV. Once the most common of large, hardy timber bamboos. Most perished during blooming period in 1960s–70s. New plants from seed are available. Makes beautiful groves if lowest branches are trimmed off
P. b. 'Castillon'	*P. castillonis*	10–15 ft. (15–20 ft.)	Running	2 in.	0°F/–18°C	III. Yellow culms show green stripe above each branch cluster. Rare
P. heterocycla pubescens MOSO BAMBOO	*P. edulis*	20–40 ft. (40–60 ft.)	Running	8 in.	5°F/–15°C	IV. Largest of the running timber bamboos. Gray-green, heavy culms and small, feathery leaves. Rare and difficult to establish
P. nigra BLACK BAMBOO		4–8 ft. (10–15 ft.)	Running	1½ in.	0°F/–18°C	III. New culms green, turning black in second year (rarely olive green dotted black). Where summers are hot, does best in afternoon shade
P. n. 'Henon'		20 ft. (to 54 ft.)	Running	3½ in.	0°F/–18°C	III. Much larger than *P. nigra.* Culms whitish green, not changing to black, rough to touch
P. vivax		25–45 ft. (to 70 ft.)	Running	5 in.	–5°F/–21°C	IV. Hardiest timber bamboo and the quickest to attain large size. 'Aureocaulis' has golden yellow culms randomly striped with green
Pleioblastus argenteostriata		2–3 ft. (3–4 ft.)	Running	¼ in.	10°F/–12°C	I. Good light-colored ground cover for shade. Looks best if cut back every year. White stripes on leaves
P. chino vaginata 'Variegata'		2–3 ft. (3–4 ft.)	Running	⅜ in.	10°F/–12°C	I. Graceful and densely foliaged. Slender leaves striped in white. Takes sun or light shade
P. distichus DWARF FERNLEAF BAMBOO	*Sasa disticha*	1–2 ft. (2–3 ft.)	Running	⅛ in.	10°F/–12°C	I. Delicate in appearance. Tiny, two-ranked ferny leaves. Rampant; cut back to ground if rank or stemmy

▸

B

BAMBOO

For explanation of height, see page 213; for Roman numerals I, II, III, and IV, see page 217. Hardiness is temperature at which leaf damage occurs.

NAME	ALSO SOLD AS	CONTROLLED (UNCONTROLLED) HEIGHT	GROWTH HABIT	STEM DIAMETER	HARDINESS	COMMENTS (GROWTH HABIT, CHARACTERISTICS, USES)
Pleioblastus pygmaea	*Sasa pygmaea*	½–1 ft. (1–1½ ft.)	Running	⅛ in.	0°F/–18°C	I. Aggressive spreader; good bank holder, good for erosion control. Can be mowed every few years to keep it from growing stemmy and unattractive
P. variegata DWARF WHITESTRIPE BAMBOO	*Sasa variegata, S. fortunei*	1–2 ft. (2–3 ft.)	Running	¼ in.	5°F/–15°C	I. Fast spreader; curb rhizomes. Use in tubs or as deep ground cover. Sun or light shade
P. viridistriatus	*Arundinaria auricoma, A. viridistriatus*	1–2 ft. (to 2½ ft.)	Running	¼ in.	0°F/–18°C	I. Leaves 8 in. long, 1½ in. wide, strikingly variegated green and gold
Pseudosasa japonica ARROW BAMBOO	*Arundinaria japonica*	6–10 ft. (10–18 ft.)	Running	¾ in.	0°F/–18°C	III. Stiffly erect culms with one branch at each joint. Large leaves with long, pointed tails. Rampant thick hedge in mild-winter climates; slow spreader where winters are cold, making dense, erect clumps
Sasa palmata PALMATE BAMBOO	*S. senanensis*	4–5 ft. (8–12 ft.)	Running	⅜ in.	0°F/–18°C	In class by itself. Grows bigger in Zones 4–6 and 15–17 than in 18–24. Broad, handsome leaves (to 15 in. long by 4 in. wide) spread fingerlike from stem and branch tips. Rampant spreader; curb it
S. veitchii		2–3 ft. (2–3 ft.)	Running	¼ in.	0°F/–18°C	I. Rampant spreader with large (7- by 1-in.) dark green leaves that turn whitish buff all around the edges in autumn. Appropriate in Japanese gardens if curbed
Semiarundinaria fastuosa NARIHIRA BAMBOO		8–10 ft. (12–25 ft.)	Running	1¼ in.	–4°F/–20°C	II or III. Rigidly upright growth. Slow spreader easily kept to a clump. Planted closely, makes tall, narrow, dense hedge or windbreak
Shibataea kumasaca		2–3 ft. (5–6 ft.)	Running	¼ in.	10°F/–12°C	III. Spreads slowly, makes compact clumps of unbamboolike appearance. Leaves are short and broad (4 in. by 1 in.), distinctly stalked. Needs acid soil

Phyllostachys nigra

TOP: *Sasa veitchii*
BOTTOM: *Phyllostachys bambusoides*

Bambusa multiplex 'Golden Goddess'

TOP: *Sasa palmata*
BOTTOM: *Pleioblastus pygmaea*

Phyllostachys aurea

Scale, mealybugs, and aphids are occasionally found on bamboo but seldom do any harm; if they excrete honeydew in bothersome amounts, spray with insecticidal soap or summer oil. To control mites, release predatory mites.

The chart classifies each bamboo by growth habit, which determines its use in the garden.

Group I bamboos are the dwarf or low-growing ground cover types. These can be used for erosion control or, in small clumps (carefully confined), in border or rock garden.

Group II includes clump bamboos with fountainlike habit of growth. These have widest use in landscaping. They require no more space than the average strong-growing shrub. Clipped, they make hedges or screens that won't spread much into surrounding soil. When unclipped, they line up as informal screens or grow singly to show off their graceful form.

Group III bamboos are running types of moderate size and more or less vertical growth. Use them as screens, hedges, or (if curbed) alone.

Group IV includes the giant bamboos. Use running kinds for groves or for Oriental effects on a grand scale. Clumping kinds have a tropical look, especially if they are used with broad-leafed tropical plants. All may be thinned and clipped to show off culms. Thin clumps or groves by cutting out old or dead culms at the base.

Phyllostachys nigra

Some of the smaller bamboos bloom on some of their stalks every year and continue to grow. Others bloom partially and at erratic intervals. Some have never been known to bloom; others bloom heavily, set seed, and die. Giant timber bamboo *(Phyllostachys bambusoides)* and other species of *Phyllostachys* bloom at rare intervals of 30 to 60 years, produce flowers for a long period, and become enfeebled. They may recover very slowly or die. Very heavy feeding and watering may speed their recovery.

Bamboos are not recommended for year-round indoor culture, but container-grown plants can spend extended periods indoors in cool, bright rooms. You can revive plants by taking them outdoors, but it is important to avoid sudden changes in temperature and light.

There are several ways to eliminate unwanted bamboo. Digging it out with mattock and spade is the surest method, though sometimes difficult. Rhizomes are generally not deep, but they may be widespread. Remove them all or regrowth will occur. Starve out roots by cutting off all shoots before they exceed 2 ft. in height; repeat as needed—probably many times over the course of a year. Contact herbicide sprays that kill leaves have the same effect as removing culms. Translocation weed killers have only a temporary effect on bamboo. Full-strength glyphosate poured onto freshly cut stumps is another good control.

BAMBOO MUHLY. See MUHLENBERGIA dumosa

BAMBURANTA. See CTENANTHE compressa

BAMBUSA. See BAMBOO

BANANA

Musaceae

PERENNIAL

FOR ZONES, SEE BELOW

FULL SUN

AMPLE WATER

Banana

From Southeast Asia. Fast-growing herbaceous perennial with soft, thickish stems; spreads by suckers and underground roots to form clumps 6–10 ft. wide or wider. Spectacular broad, long (5–9-ft.) leaves are easily tattered; protect from wind. Orange-yellow spring flowers on long, drooping stalks are also striking. Bananas are attractive plants near pools or anywhere a tropical look is desired. All need ample moisture, rich soil, and heavy feeding. They are easily propagated by division.

Fruiting varieties are often grouped botanically under *Musa acuminata.* They are best adapted to Zone H2 in Hawaii and to Zones 21–24 in California, where planting near a warm, south-facing wall often results in sweet fruit. But even in warm microclimates of Zones 15, 16, 19, and 20, gardeners sometimes harvest edible bananas. In Zones 8, 9, 14, and 18, frost usually kills the tops of the plants each year, but the roots resprout each spring and plants are grown as ornamentals. Elsewhere, bananas can be grown in containers as ornamentals and brought indoors in winter. Plantains are bananas that require cooking before eating; most are tall and vigorous.

Dwarf banana varieties are the best bets for home gardens. They mature at about 7–15 ft. high and usually ripen fruit 70 to 100 days after blooming. Look for 'Dwarf Cavendish' ('Chinese'), 'Dwarf Brazilian', 'Enana Gigante', 'Goldfinger', 'Ice Cream', 'Apple', and 'Williams'.

If you want to harvest quality fruit, let only one or two stalks per clump grow; prune out all others as they emerge. Allow replacement stalks (for next year's fruit) to develop after the fruiting stalks have bloomed. Remove stalks that have fruited.

Harvest season is usually late summer into fall, or whenever the fruit at the top of the cluster starts to turn yellow. Cut the whole cluster and let it ripen at room temperature. If left on the plant, fruit will split and rot. Banana sap will permanently stain fabric, so wear old clothes when harvesting or pruning. Control ants on banana trees to help prevent scale, aphids, and sooty mold.

For ornamental species, see *Ensete* and *Musa.*

BANANA PASSION VINE. See PASSIFLORA mollissima

BANANA SHRUB. See MICHELIA figo

BANKSIA

Proteaceae

EVERGREEN SHRUBS AND TREES

ZONES 15–24; H1

FULL SUN

MODERATE WATER

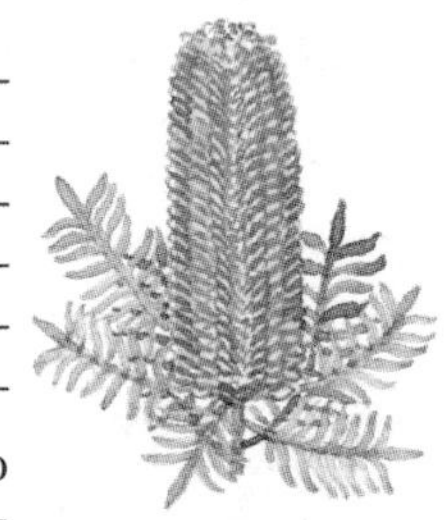
Banksia ericifolia

Few of the many banksia species (all native to Australia) are in cultivation, although botanical gardens occasionally offer some at sales. Leaves are usually long and narrow, sometimes with strikingly saw-toothed edges. Small flowers appear in dense round or cylindrical clusters (often spectacular) and are followed by long-lasting woody seed cones. Flowers are rich in nectar. Plants are subject to root rot fungi and require perfect drainage. Most can withstand long dry periods. Treat chlorosis with iron chelates. Tree species have no special pruning needs; on shrubs, shorten previous season's growth if needed to limit size. Banksias show varying tolerance to coastal conditions in California; in Hawaii, humidity is too high for them at sea level, and they are grown at higher elevations.

B. ericifolia. HEATH BANKSIA. Shrub. To 10–20 ft. tall, 6–12 ft. wide, with short, needlelike leaves and 6–8-in. clusters of orange to red flowers. Tolerates coastal conditions.

B. integrifolia. Tree. To 30–60 ft. tall, 15–30 ft. wide, with smooth-edged or slightly toothed leaves to 6 in. long, 2 in. wide. Pale yellow flower clusters can reach 6 in. long. Highly tolerant of coastal conditions.

B. speciosa. SHOWY BANKSIA. Shrub. To 10–18 ft. tall, 10–24 ft. wide. Leaves are 8–16 in. long, 1 in. wide, with strongly toothed edges. Flower cones are 6 in. tall, white opening to yellow. Can stand some coastal exposure.

BANYAN TREE. See FICUS

B

BAPTISIA

FALSE INDIGO, WILD INDIGO

Fabaceae (Leguminosae)

PERENNIALS

ZONES 1–24

FULL SUN

MODERATE WATER

Baptisia australis

Native to eastern and southern U.S. Tolerate poor, sandy soils and take some drought. Blue-green leaves have three leaflets. Small, sweet pea–shaped blooms in early summer on tall, tapering spikes. Inflated seedpods that follow are attractive in dried arrangements. Clumps gradually increase, but don't need division; also resent transplanting once established.

B. alba. WHITE FALSE INDIGO. To 2–3 ft. tall, 3 ft. wide. White or creamy white flowers.

B. australis. BLUE FALSE INDIGO. To 3–6 ft. tall, 4 ft. wide, with deep blue flowers.

BARBERRY. See BERBERIS

BARLERIA obtusa

Acanthaceae

EVERGREEN SHRUB

ZONES 13, 16–24

LIGHT SHADE IN HOTTEST CLIMATES

REGULAR WATER

Barleria obtusa

South African native to 3 ft. tall and wide, with dark green, 3-in. leaves and loose clusters of blue, 1½-in. flowers in winter and spring. It likes rich soil and regular moisture when in full growth. Pinch to keep compact. Sometimes grown as indoor/outdoor plant or houseplant in cold-winter areas.

BARREL CACTUS. See ECHINOCACTUS, FEROCACTUS

BASEBALL PLANT. See EUPHORBIA obesa

BASIL. See OCIMUM

BASKET FLOWER. See CENTAUREA americana, HYMENOCALLIS narcissiflora

BASKET-OF-GOLD. See AURINIA saxatilis

BASSIA scoparia. See KOCHIA scoparia

BASSWOOD. See TILIA americana

BAUHINIA

ORCHID TREE

Fabaceae (Leguminosae)

EVERGREEN, SEMIEVERGREEN, DECIDUOUS TREES AND SHRUBS

ZONES VARY BY SPECIES

FULL SUN, EXCEPT AS NOTED

MODERATE TO REGULAR WATER

Bauhinia forficata

These flamboyant flowering plants have a very special place in Hawaii and mild-winter areas of California and Arizona. They vary greatly by species and climate. Common to all garden bauhinias are twin "leaves," actually twin lobes. Thin out any crowded growth after bloom.

B. × blakeana. HONG KONG ORCHID TREE. Partly deciduous for short period. Zones 13, 19, 21, 23, 24; H1, H2. Umbrellalike growth habit; reaches 20 ft. high and wide. Flowers bloom from late fall to spring and are shaped like some orchids; they are much larger (5½–6 in. wide) than those of other bauhinias. Colors range from cranberry maroon through purple and rose to orchid pink, often in same blossom. Gray-green leaves tend to drop off around bloom time, but the tree does not lose all of its foliage.

B. forficata (B. candicans, B. corniculata). BRAZILIAN BUTTERFLY TREE. Evergreen to deciduous shrub or tree. Zones 9, 12–23. Native to Brazil. Probably hardiest bauhinia. To 20 ft. tall and broad, often with twisting, leaning trunk, picturesque angled branches; good canopy for patio. Short, sharp thorns at branch joints. Narrow-petaled, creamy white flowers to 3 in. wide, spring into summer. Deep green leaves have more pointed lobes than others. Give some afternoon shade in hot climates.

B. galpinii (B. punctata). RED BAUHINIA. Evergreen to semi-evergreen shrub. Zones 13, 15, 16, 18–24; H1, H2. Native to South Africa. Sprawling, half-climbing plant to about 10 ft. tall, spreading to 15 ft. Blooms from spring to fall, bearing brick red to orange flowers as spectacular as those of bougainvillea. Best as espalier on warm wall. With hard pruning, can make splendid flowering bonsai for large pot or box.

B. lunarioides (B. congesta). ANACACHO ORCHID TREE. Evergreen to semievergreen shrub or tree. Zones 10–13, 18–23. Native from western Texas into northeastern Mexico. To 8–12 ft. high, 4–5 ft. wide, with rounded, very small leaves (½ to ¾ in. long). White- and pink-flowering forms are available. Begins bloom in early spring and repeats many times over spring and summer. Open tree in afternoon shade; bushier in full sun.

B. variegata (B. purpurea). PURPLE ORCHID TREE. Semievergreen to deciduous shrub or tree. Zones 13, 18–24; H1, H2. Hardy to 22°F/–6°C. Native to India, China. Most frequently planted bauhinia. Inclined to grow as a many-stemmed shrub, but if staked and pruned, becomes an attractive tree 20–35 ft. tall and wide. Wonderful show of light pink to orchid purple, broad-petaled, 2–3-in.-wide flowers, usually winter into spring; spectacular street tree where spring is reliably and steadily warm. Light green, broad-lobed leaves generally drop in mid-winter. After bloom, it produces huge crop of messy-looking beans; trim them off if you wish (trimming brings new growth earlier). 'Candida' is white blossomed but otherwise identical to the species.

BAY. See LAURUS, UMBELLULARIA californica

BAYBERRY. See MYRICA pensylvanica

BEACH ASTER. See ERIGERON glaucus

BEACH WORMWOOD. See ARTEMISIA stellerana

BEAN

Fabaceae (Leguminosae)

ANNUALS AND PERENNIALS GROWN AS ANNUALS

ALL ZONES

FULL SUN

REGULAR WATER

Scarlet Runner Bean

Gardeners can choose from many types of beans, the most common of which are described below. Except for the broad or fava bean from the Mediterranean region, these are New World plants belonging to the genus *Phaseolus.* Most beans are frost-sensitive heat lovers, easy to grow from seed. With all, moisten soil thoroughly before planting, then do not water again until seedlings have emerged. Once growth starts, keep soil moist. Feed after plants are in active growth and again when pods start to form. Control aphids, cucumber beetles, spider mites, and whiteflies if any of these pests are problems in your garden.

Broad bean (fava bean, horse bean). Cool-season bean (actually a giant vetch, *Vicia faba*), best known in coastal climates. Cook and eat immature pods like edible-pod peas; prepare immature and mature seeds in same way as green or dry limas. Note that a very few people (mainly of Mediterranean ancestry) have an enzyme deficiency that can cause severe reactions to the beans and even the pollen.

In cold-winter areas, plant as early in spring as soil can be worked; in mild climates, plant in fall for harvest in late winter or early spring. Matures in 120 to 150 days. Space rows 1½–2½ ft. apart. Sow seeds 1 in. deep, 4–5 in. apart; thin to 8–10 in. apart. Plants produce bushy growth to 2–4 ft. high.

Dry bean. Same culture as bush form of snap bean (see below). Let pods remain on bush until they turn dry or begin to shatter; then thresh beans from pods, dry, and store them to soak and cook later as needed. 'Pinto', 'Red Kidney', and 'White Marrowfat' belong to this group.

Some varieties are particularly delicious when harvested at the green shelling stage and cooked like green limas. These include the flageolet bean (a French favorite) and 'French Horticultural Bean', also known as 'October Bean'. Heirloom varieties such as 'Aztec Dwarf White', 'Mitla White', and 'New Mexico Appaloosa' were used by Native Americans of the Southwest and are very well adapted to that region.

Lima bean. Like snap beans (which they resemble), lima beans come in either bush or vine (pole) form. They develop more slowly than snap beans—bush types need 65 to 75 days from planting to harvest, pole kinds 78 to 95 days—and do not produce as reliably in extremely hot weather. Must be shelled before cooking, a tedious chore but worth it if you like fresh limas. Grow like snap beans (see below).

Scarlet runner bean. Perennial twining vine grown as annual. Showy and ornamental, with slender clusters of vivid scarlet flowers and bright green leaves divided into three roundish, 3–5-in.-long leaflets. Use it to cover fences, arbors, outbuildings; it provides quick shade on porches. Pink- and white-flowered varieties exist.

Flowers are followed by flattened, very dark green pods that are edible and tasty when young but toughen as they reach full size. Beans from older pods can be shelled and cooked like green limas. Culture is same as for snap beans (see below).

Snap bean (string bean, green bean). The most widely planted bean type. Tender, fleshy pods, not stringy; may be green, yellow (wax beans), or purple (these turn green when cooked). Plants grow as self-supporting bushes (bush beans) or as climbing vines (pole beans). Bush types bear earlier, but vines are more productive. Plants resemble scarlet runner bean, but their white or purple flowers are not showy.

Snap Bean

Sow seeds as soon as soil is warm. Heavy seed leaves must push through soil, so be sure that soil is reasonably loose and open. Plant seeds of bush types 1 in. deep and 1–3 in. apart, allowing 2–3 ft. between rows. Pole beans can be managed in a number of ways. Set three or four 8-ft. poles in the ground and tie together at top in tepee fashion; or set single poles 3–4 ft. apart and sow six or eight beans around each, thinning to three or four strongest seedlings; or insert poles 1–2 ft. apart in rows and sow seeds as you would bush beans; or sow along sunny wall, fence, or trellis and train vines on web of light string supported by wire or heavy twine. Pods are ready in 50 to 70 days, depending on variety. Pick every 3 to 5 days; if pods mature, plants will stop bearing.

BEARBERRY. See ARCTOSTAPHYLOS uva-ursi

BEARD TONGUE. See PENSTEMON

BEAR'S BREECH. See ACANTHUS

BEAR'S FOOT FERN. See HUMATA tyermannii

BEAUCARNEA recurvata. See NOLINA recurvata

BEAUMONTIA grandiflora

HERALD'S TRUMPET, EASTER LILY VINE

Apocynaceae

EVERGREEN VINE

ZONES 12, 13, 16, 17, 21–24; H1, H2

FULL SUN OR PARTIAL SHADE

REGULAR WATER

Beaumontia grandiflora

From the Himalayas. Rampant vine that uses arching, twining branches to climb as high as 30 ft. and spread as wide. Large (6–9-in.), oval to roundish dark green leaves, smooth and shiny above, slightly downy beneath, give lush tropical look. From spring through summer, bears fragrant flowers that look like Easter lilies: trumpet shaped, 5 in. long, green-veined white.

Does best in well-drained soil enriched with organic matter; regular feeding produces most lavish display of foliage and flowers. Prune after bloom to shape or limit size; flowers are produced on wood 2 years or older, so keep a good proportion of old wood. Hardy to 28°F/–2°C. Frost kills the vine to the ground, but it usually comes back from the roots. Use as big espalier on warm, wind-sheltered wall or train along eaves of house; sturdy supports are essential, since growth is heavy. Good choice for planting near swimming pools.

BEAUTYBERRY. See CALLICARPA

BEAUTY BUSH. See KOLKWITZIA amabilis

BEE BALM. See MONARDA

BEECH. See FAGUS sylvatica

BEEFWOOD. See CASUARINA

BEET

Chenopodiaceae

BIENNIAL GROWN AS ANNUAL

ALL ZONES

FULL SUN

REGULAR WATER

European native known botanically as *Beta vulgaris.* Raised for their edible roots and tender young leaves, beets grow best in relatively cool weather. In hot-summer climates, sow in early spring or late summer so that plants will mature before extreme heat sets in. In mild-winter areas, you can also plant in late summer for fall and winter harvest. To harvest beets over a long season, sow seed at monthly intervals.

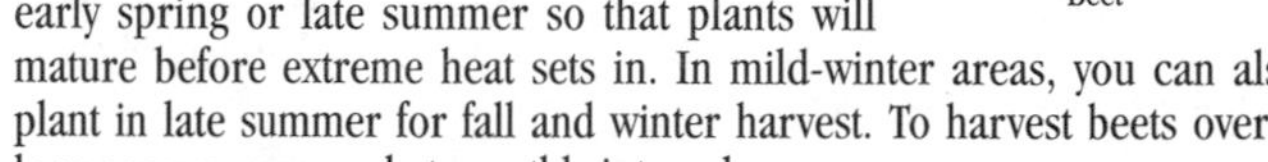

Beet

Grow in fertile, well-drained soil without lumps or rocks. Sow seed 1 in. apart and cover with ¼ in. of compost, sand, or vermiculite. Thin plants to 2 in. apart while small—the thinnings (both tops and roots) are edible. To keep roots tender, keep soil evenly moist. Begin harvesting when roots are 1 in. wide and complete it before they exceed 3 in.; they will be woody if allowed to grow bigger. In cold climates, harvest all beets before hard frosts in fall.

Types with round, red roots include 'Detroit Dark Red' and 'Crosby's Egyptian' (old favorites) as well as many newer varieties like 'Kleine Bol' and 'Sangria'. 'Bull's Blood' and 'Lutz Green Leaf' are grown for roots and edible greens. Novelties include 'Cylindra' and 'Forma Nova' (with long, cylindrical roots) and 'Chioggia' (rings of red and white); there are also varieties with golden yellow or white roots.

FOR INFORMATION ON SELECTING PLANTS
PLEASE SEE PAGES 64–160

BEGONIA

Begoniaceae

PERENNIALS

ZONES 14–24; H1, H2, EXCEPT AS NOTED; OR INDOORS; OR DIG AND STORE; OR TREAT AS ANNUALS

FILTERED SUNLIGHT; BRIGHT INDIRECT LIGHT

REGULAR WATER

Tuberous Begonia

Perennials, sometimes woody stemmed, grown for textured, multicolored foliage, saucer-size flowers, or lacy clusters of smaller flowers. Native to many tropical and subtropical regions of the world. Outdoors, most grow best in pots in the ground or in hanging baskets in filtered shade, with rich, porous, fast-draining soil, consistent but light feeding, and enough water to keep soil moist but not soggy. Most thrive as indoor plants, in greenhouse, or under lath. Some prefer terrarium conditions. Almost all require at least moderate humidity. In areas with hot, dry summers or indoors in winter, set pots in pebble-lined saucers or trays kept filled with water to below pot level.

Most can be propagated easily from leaf, stem, or rhizome cuttings. They also grow from dust-fine seed. Of the many hundreds of species and varieties, relatively few are sold widely.

Begonia enthusiasts group or classify many of the different kinds by growth habit, which coincidentally groups them by their care needs.

Cane-type begonias. They get their name from their stems, which grow tall and woody and have prominent bamboolike joints. The group includes so-called angel-wing begonias. These erect plants have multiple stems, some reaching 5 ft. or more under the right conditions. Most bloom profusely from early spring through autumn, bearing large clusters of white, pink, orange, or red flowers. Some are everblooming. When roots fill 4-in. pots, plants can be placed in large containers or in the ground. Position plants where they will get plenty of light, some sun, and no wind. They may require staking. Protect from heavy frosts. Old canes that have grown barren should be pruned back to two leaf joints in early spring to stimulate new growth.

'Bubbles'. Spotted foliage; pink flowers with apple blossom fragrance.

'Honeysuckle'. Plain green foliage and fragrant pink flowers.

'Irene Nuss'. Dark red-and-green leaves and huge drooping clusters of coral pink flowers.

Hardy begonia. Zones 3–24. Asian species *B. grandis (B. evansiana, B. grandis evansiana)* is the only begonia hardy in the continental U.S. Grows from a tuber to 2–3 ft. tall and wide, with branching red stems carrying large, smooth, coppery green leaves with red undersides. Summer flowers are pink or white, carried in drooping clusters. Tops die down after frost. In colder regions, mulch to protect roots.

Hiemalis begonias. Usually sold as Rieger begonias. Bushy, compact; profuse bloomers and outstanding outdoor or indoor plants. Flowers average about 2 in. across and appear over a long season that includes winter. On well-grown plants, green leaves and stems are all but invisible beneath a blanket of bloom. Give indoor plants plenty of light in winter. In summer, keep out of hot noonday sun. Water thoroughly when top inch of soil is dry. Don't sprinkle leaves. Plants may get rangy, an indication of approaching dormancy; if they do, cut stems to 4-in. stubs.

Multiflora begonias. Bushy, compact plants 1–1½ ft. tall and wide. Profuse bloom in carmine, scarlet, orange, yellow, apricot, salmon, pink. Includes Nonstop strain. All are essentially small-flowered, profuse-blooming tuberous begonias; for care, see Tuberous begonias.

Rex begonias. With their bold, multicolored leaves, these are probably the most striking of all foliage begonias. While many named varieties are grown by collectors, easier-to-find unnamed seedling plants are almost as decorative. The leaves grow from a rhizome; see Rhizomatous begonias for care. In addition, rex begonias should get high humidity (at least 50 percent) to do their best. Provide it by misting with a spray bottle, placing pots on wet pebbles in a tray, or keeping plants in greenhouse. When rhizome grows too far past edge of pot for your taste, either repot into slightly larger container or cut off rhizome end inside pot edge. Old rhizome will branch and grow new leaves. Make rhizome cuttings of the piece you remove and root in mixture of half peat moss, half perlite.

Rex Begonia

Rhizomatous begonias. Like rex begonias, these grow from a rhizome. Although some have handsome flowers, they are grown primarily for foliage, which varies in color and texture among species and varieties. The group includes so-called star begonias, named for their leaf shape. Rhizomatous begonias perform well as houseplants: give them bright light through a window and water only when the top inch or so of soil is dry. Plant them in wide, shallow pots. They flower from winter through summer, the season varying among specific plants. White to pink flowers appear in clusters on erect stems above the foliage. Rhizomes will grow over edge of pot, eventually forming a ball-shaped plant; if you wish, cut rhizomes back to pot. The old rhizome will branch and grow new leaves. Root the pieces of rhizome in mixture of half peat moss, half perlite.

B. masoniana. IRON CROSS BEGONIA. Large puckered leaves; known for chocolate brown pattern resembling Maltese cross on green background. Flowers insignificant.

Semperflorens begonias. Fibrous, bedding, or wax begonias. Dwarf (6–8-in.) and taller (10–12-in.) strains grown in garden beds or containers like annuals, producing lots of small flowers in a white-through-red range. Plants bloom from spring through fall (use as a winter annual in hottest-summer climates). Foliage can be green, red, bronze, or variegated. In mild-winter climates, can live for years. Thrive in full sun in cool-summer regions. Prefer broken shade in hotter climates, but dark-foliaged kinds will take sun if well watered.

Shrublike begonias. This large class is marked by multiple stems that are soft and green rather than bamboolike as in the cane-type group. Grown for both foliage and flowers. Leaves are very interesting—some are heavily textured; others grow white or red "hairs"; still others develop a soft, feltlike coating. Most grow upright and bushy, but others are less erect and make suitable subjects for hanging baskets. Flowers in shades of pink, red, white, or peach can come any time, depending on species or variety. Care consists of repotting into larger container as the plant outgrows its pot. Some shrublike begonias can get very large—as tall as 8 ft. Water when soil begins to dry on surface. Prune to shape; pinch tips to encourage branching.

'Digswelliana'. To 2–3 ft. high, with glossy leaves 2–4 in. long. Red flowers in clusters bloom almost continuously from spring to fall.

B. foliosa. Inch-long leaves packed tightly on twiggy plant give fernlike look. Stems arch or droop to 3 ft. Flowers are small, white to red, everblooming in mild weather. 'Miniata' has rose pink to rose red flowers.

'Richmondensis.' To 2 ft. or a little taller. Arching stems carry deep green, shiny, crisp leaves with red undersides. Vivid pink to crimson or white flowers develop from darker buds; nearly year-round bloom. Big and sturdy. Tolerant of sun and wind.

Trailing or climbing begonias. These have stems that trail or climb, depending on how you train them. They are suited to hanging basket culture or planting in the ground where well protected. Growing conditions similar to those for tuberous begonias, though trailing types are not lifted for storage. Sporadic bloom during warm weather.

'Potpourri'. Hybrid developed from *B. solananthera,* with strongly scented deep pink flowers.

B. solananthera. Glossy light green leaves; fragrant white flowers with red centers.

Tuberous begonias. Best in Zones 4–6, 15–17, 21–24, and H1; possible in 7–9, 14, 18–20 with attention to humidity. Among the best-known begonias in the West are these magnificent large-flowered hybrids that grow from tubers. Members of the group range from plants with saucer-size blooms and a few upright stems to multistemmed hanging basket sorts covered in blossoms. With the exception of some rare kinds, they are summer and fall blooming.

Strains are sold as hanging or upright. The former bloom more profusely; the latter have larger flowers. Colors include almost everything but blue; shapes are frilly (carnation), formal double (camellia), and tight-centered (rose). Some have petal edges in contrasting colors (picotee). Popular strains include Double Trumpet (improved rose form), Prima Donna (improved camellia), and Hanging Sensation.

Most gardeners grow tuberous begonias in containers. Buy dormant tubers (the bigger the better) in midwinter. Set them in pots filled with a rich, humusy soil mix, placing them indented side up and covering them with no more than 1/4 in. of mix. If you're planting a number of tubers, it's easiest to start them in a flat or shallow box, spacing them about 4 in. apart. Place pots or flats in a well-lit spot (but not in direct sun) where temperatures will remain above 65°F/18°C; keep soil moist but not saturated during the rooting period. When the tubers have produced two leaves, move them outside, temperature permitting (night temperature must remain above 50°F/10°C); or pot up plants started in flats. You can also plant begonias in the ground at this point; amend the existing soil, using 1 part soil to 2 parts potting mix.

Choose a spot in filtered shade, such as under lath; or plant in an open area with eastern exposure. Water enough to keep soil moist but not soggy. For best bloom, mist with water several times a day unless you live in a cool or foggy area. Watch for fuzzy white spots on leaves; these signal powdery mildew. Begin feeding with liquid fertilizer a week or two after plants reach the two-leaf stage. For largest possible blooms, you can use a half-strength solution every other week, but monthly regular-strength feedings yield fine plants.

When leaves begin to yellow and wilt in fall, reduce watering and stop fertilizing. When leaves fall off, lift tubers, shake off soil, and dry in a cool, dry spot for several days. Then store in a cool, dry place such as a shed or garage until spring; when small pink buds appear, plant the tubers once again. (You can also buy small seedling plants each year in early spring and plant them out in pots or in the ground.)

BELAMCANDA chinensis

BLACKBERRY LILY

Iridaceae

PERENNIAL FROM RHIZOME

ZONES 1–24

FULL SUN OR PARTIAL SHADE

REGULAR WATER DURING GROWTH AND BLOOM

Belamcanda chinensis

Like its iris relatives, this Asian native forms clumps of sword-shaped leaves in fanlike sheaves from slowly creeping rhizomes. In summer, zigzag 3–4-ft. stems bear sprays of 2–3-in., yellowish orange flowers dotted with red. Each flower lasts only a day, but new blossoms keep opening for weeks. As the blooms fade, rounded seed capsules develop; they split open to expose shiny black seeds that look like blackberries (hence the plant's common name). Cut seed-bearing stems for use in dried arrangements.

Effective in clumps in border. Set rhizomes 1 ft. apart, with tops just beneath soil surface. Plant in spring in Zones 1–3, in fall elsewhere. Established clumps give best display, so divide infrequently.

BELLADONNA LILY. See AMARYLLIS belladonna

BELLFLOWER. See CAMPANULA

BELLIS perennis

ENGLISH DAISY

Asteraceae (Compositae)

PERENNIAL OFTEN TREATED AS ANNUAL

ZONES 1–9, 14–24; ANYWHERE EXCEPT HAWAII AS ANNUAL

LIGHT SHADE IN HOTTEST CLIMATES

REGULAR WATER

Bellis perennis

Native to Europe, western Asia. The original English daisies are the kind sometimes seen growing in lawns. Plump, fully double ones sold in nurseries are horticultural varieties that make good edging or bedding plants; they are also effective with bulbs. Dark green, 1–2-in.-long leaves form rosettes to 8 in. wide. Pink, rose, red, or white flowers are borne on 3–6-in. stems in spring and early summer; deadhead to prolong bloom. Longer lived where summers are cool. Propagate by division.

BELLS-OF-IRELAND. See MOLUCCELLA laevis

BELOPERONE. See JUSTICIA BRANDEGEENA

BENJAMIN TREE, BENJAMIN FIG. See FICUS benjamina

BENT, BENT GRASS. See AGROSTIS

Berberidaceae. The barberry family contains shrubs and herbaceous perennials. Barberry *(Berberis)* and heavenly bamboo *(Nandina)* are typical of the former; *Epimedium* and *Vancouveria* are among the latter.

BERBERIS

BARBERRY

Berberidaceae

EVERGREEN, SEMIEVERGREEN, DECIDUOUS SHRUBS

ZONES VARY BY SPECIES

FULL SUN OR LIGHT SHADE

MODERATE TO REGULAR WATER

Berberis darwinii

These dense, spiny-stemmed plants, especially the deciduous species, tolerate climate and soil extremes. Require no more than ordinary garden care. Each year, thin out oldest wood and prune as needed to shape—after bloom for evergreen and semievergreen types, late in the dormant season for deciduous kinds. Make attractive hedges. Informal style is best for species grown for spring flowers (yellow, unless otherwise noted) and ensuing berries, which are borne on previous year's growth; species grown for foliage can be sheared. To rejuvenate overgrown or neglected plants, cut them to within a foot of the ground before new spring growth begins.

B. amurensis. Deciduous. Zones A2, A3; 1–6. Hardy to –35°F/–37°C. From northeast Asia. Dense, erect shrub to 10 ft. tall, 7–8 ft. wide, with three-pointed, 3/4-in.-long spines and 3-in. leaves divided into three leaflets. Small, fragrant flowers in hanging clusters (up to 25 blooms per cluster) are followed by bright red fruits.

B. buxifolia. MAGELLAN BARBERRY. Evergreen. Zones 4–9, 14–24. Hardy to 0°F/–18°C. Native to Chile, Argentina. Rather rigid and upright, to 6 ft. tall and as wide. Leathery 1-in. leaves. Orange-yellow flowers; dark purple berries, one or two at each leaf cluster. Dwarf 'Nana' ('Pygmaea'), to 1 1/2 ft. high and 2 ft. wide, makes a good hedge or rock garden plant.

B. × chenaultii (B. × hybrido-gagnepainii). Evergreen. Zones 3–9, 14–24. Hardy to 0°F/–18°C. Slow growing to 4 ft. tall, 5 ft. wide, with arching branches. Dark green, spiny-toothed leaves 1–1 1/2 in. long. Bluish black berries. Barrier hedge, foreground planting.

B. darwinii. DARWIN BARBERRY. Evergreen. Zones 5–9, 14–24. Hardy to 10°F/–12°C. Very showy barberry from Chile. Fountainlike growth to 5–10 ft. tall, 4–7 ft. wide. Crisp, dark green, hollylike,

1-in. leaves. Orange-yellow flowers are borne so thickly along branches that foliage is hard to see; these are followed by profuse dark blue berries, popular with birds. Spreads by underground runners to form a thicket.

B. ×gladwynensis 'William Penn'. Evergreen; drops some leaves at 0 to 10°F/–18 to –12°C. Zones 3b–24. Resembles *B. julianae* in general effect but has broader, glossier leaves and is faster growing, with denser growth, to 4 ft. tall and wide. Good floral display.

B. ×irwinii. See B. ×stenophylla 'Irwinii'

B. julianae. WINTERGREEN BARBERRY. Evergreen to semievergreen. Zones 4–24. Hardy to 0°F/–18°C, but foliage is damaged by winter cold. Chinese native. Dense, upright, to 6 ft. tall and wide; angled branches. Spiny-toothed, dark green, leathery leaves to 3 in. long; reddish fall color. Blue-black berries. One of the spiniest barberries; good as barrier hedge.

B. koreana. Deciduous. Zones 1–9, 14–17. Hardy to –35°F/–37°C. Korean native grows erect to 4–6 ft. and not quite as wide. Densely foliaged in medium to dark green leaves that turn purple in fall. Fragrant flowers in drooping, 3–4-in. clusters. Bright red fruit.

B. linearifolia 'Orange King'. Evergreen. Zones 6–9, 14–24. Hardy to 0 to 10°F/–18 to –12°C. This variety of a Chilean species has an open growth habit to 5 ft. tall and wide, with narrow, glossy, 2-in. leaves. Short clusters of deep orange flowers; bluish black fruit.

B. ×mentorensis. Evergreen to deciduous. Zones 2–24. Hardy to –20°F/–29°C but loses some or all leaves below about 0°F/–18°C. Compact growth to 7 ft. tall and wide. Dark green, 1-in.-long leaves turn a beautiful red in fall where winters are cold. Berries are dull dark red but are rarely seen. Easy to maintain as a hedge at any height. Tolerates hot, dry weather.

B. ×stenophylla. ROSEMARY BARBERRY. Evergreen. Zones 4–9, 14–24. Hardy to 0°F/–18°C. Leaves narrow, ½–1 in. long, with rolled-in edges and spiny tip. Species is 10 ft. tall, 15 ft. wide, but varieties are more commonly grown. 'Corallina Compacta', called coral barberry, reaches 1½ ft. high and wide and bears nodding clusters of bright orange flowers and bluish black fruit; effective in rock garden, as foreground plant. 'Irwinii', to 4–5 ft. tall and wide, resembles a compact-growing *B. darwinii.*

B. thunbergii. JAPANESE BARBERRY. Deciduous. Zones A3; 2b–24. Hardy to –20°F/–29°C. Graceful habit with slender, arching, spiny branches; if not sheared, usually reaches 4–6 ft. tall with equal spread. Densely covered with roundish, ½–1½-in.-long leaves that are deep green above, paler beneath; leaves turn yellow, orange, and red before they fall. Beadlike bright red berries stud branches in fall and through winter. Use as hedge, barrier planting, or specimen shrub. The following are among the many attractive varieties grown for vivid foliage.

'Atropurpurea'. RED-LEAF JAPANESE BARBERRY. Plants sold as such vary in plant size and foliage color (from bronzy red to purple red). They must have sun to develop red color (which they will hold all summer).

'Aurea'. Bright golden yellow foliage. Best color in full sun (though it can't take it in hottest climates), but plant will tolerate light shade. Slow growing to 2½–3 ft. tall and wide.

'Cherry Bomb'. Resembles 'Crimson Pygmy' but is taller (to 4 ft.), with larger leaves and more open growth.

'Crimson Pygmy' ('Atropurpurea Nana'). Selected miniature form, generally less than 1½ ft. high and 2½ ft. wide at 10 years old. Leaves are bright red when new, maturing to bronzy blood-red. Must have sun to develop color.

'Golden Ring'. Purple leaves with a thin green or golden green border.

'Helmond Pillar'. Purple-leafed form to 4–5 ft. tall, 2 ft. wide.

'Kobold'. Extra-dwarf bright green variety. Like 'Crimson Pygmy' in habit but fuller and rounder.

'Rose Glow'. To 4–6 ft. tall and wide. New foliage marbled bronzy red and pinkish white, deepening to rose and bronze with age. For best color, plant in full sun or lightest shade.

'Sparkle'. To 5 ft. tall and 6 ft. wide, with rich green foliage that turns vivid yellow, orange, and red in fall.

B. verruculosa. WARTY BARBERRY. Evergreen. Zones 4–9, 14–24. Hardy to 0°F/–18°C. Native to China. Neat, tailored-looking. Will reach 4–5 ft. tall and wide but can be kept to 1½ ft. Perky, 1-in.-long leaves glossy dark green above, whitish beneath. In fall and winter, the odd red leaf develops as a highlight here and there. Black berries with a purplish bloom. Very choice and effective on banks, in front of leggy rhododendrons or azaleas, in foreground of shrub border.

B. wilsoniae. WILSON BARBERRY. Deciduous to semievergreen. Zones 6–9, 14–24. Hardy to 5°F/–15°C. Native to China. To 6 ft. tall and wide, but can be held to 3–4 ft. Light green, roundish, ½–1-in. leaves give the plant a fine-textured look. Beautiful coral to salmon red berries. Makes a handsome barrier hedge.

BERCKMAN DWARF ARBORVITAE. See PLATYCLADUS orientalis

BERGENIA

Saxifragaceae

PERENNIALS

ZONES A1–A3; 1–9, 12–24, EXCEPT AS NOTED

PARTIAL OR FULL SHADE

REGULAR WATER

Bergenia crassifolia

Native to Himalayas and mountains of China. Thick rootstocks produce rosettes of large, ornamental, glossy green leaves that are evergreen except in coldest areas. In established plantings, foliage clumps may reach 1½ ft. high. Plants typically bloom in spring, bearing graceful, nodding clusters of small flowers on thick, leafless, 1–1½-ft.-tall stalks; colors include white and shades of pink and red. Plants lend a strong textural quality to borders and plantings under trees, make a bold-patterned ground cover. Effective with ferns, hellebores, or hostas and as foreground planting for Japanese aucuba, rhododendrons, Japanese aralia.

Perform best in shade but will tolerate sun in cool-summer climates. Will endure neglect, poor soil, and some drought, but appreciate good soil and regular watering, feeding, and grooming. Plant about 1½ ft. apart. Cut back yearly to prevent legginess. Divide crowded clumps and replant vigorous divisions in late winter or early spring. Control snails and slugs.

B. ciliata (B. ligulata). Zones 5–9, 14–24. Choicest, most elegant species, though more tender than others; foliage damaged in hard frosts. Lustrous light green, nearly round leaves to 1 ft. across, smooth on edges but fringed with soft hairs; bronzy when new. White, rose, or purplish flowers. Plants sold under this name may be garden hybrids.

B. cordifolia. HEARTLEAF BERGENIA. Glossy, roundish leaves are heart shaped at base, with wavy, toothed edges. Bears rose or lilac flowers in pendulous clusters that are partially hidden by leaves. 'Morning Red' ('Morgenrote') has bronzy-toned leaves, dark red flowers.

B. crassifolia. WINTER-BLOOMING BERGENIA. Dark green leaves to 8 in. or more across, with wavy, sparsely toothed edges. Rose, lilac, or purple flowers in dense clusters on erect stems that stand well above leaves. Blooms between midwinter and early spring, depending on climate.

B. hybrids. Many hybrids of English or German origin include 'Abendglut' ('Evening Glow'), with dark red flowers and dark reddish leaves with crimped edges, and 'Silberlicht' ('Silver Light'), with large, slightly toothed leaves and white blossoms.

BERLANDIERA lyrata

CHOCOLATE FLOWER

Asteraceae (Compositae)

PERENNIAL

ZONES 10–13, 18–23; ANYWHERE AS ANNUAL

FULL SUN

MODERATE WATER

Berlandiera lyrata

Fragrance of chocolate permeates the morning air wherever this daisy blooms. Native from summer-rainfall areas of Texas west to southeastern Arizona and northern Mexico, it's a rounded, somewhat coarse-foliaged plant to 1½–3 ft. high and wide. Blooms in spring and summer, sometimes into fall. Light yellow rays surround a maroon-and-green center. Once seed heads form, shear lightly to encourage more blooms. Native Americans used the flower heads to flavor foods; they dry well for winter bouquets. Sow seeds in place at any time. Thrives in clay soil.

BERMUDA, BERMUDA GRASS. See CYNODON dactylon

BERMUDA BUTTERCUP. See OXALIS pes-caprae

BESCHORNERIA yuccoides

Agavaceae

PERENNIAL

ZONES 8, 9, 12–24

PARTIAL SHADE IN HOTTEST CLIMATES

REGULAR WATER

Beschorneria yuccoides

From Mexico. Rosettes of 2-ft.-long, 2-in.-wide gray-green leaves increase slowly by offsets to make clumps that eventually reach 3–4 ft. wide. Resembles a yucca, but its leaves are soft and spineless. Early summer brings a spectacular flower show: a thick coral pink stalk rises to 3–6 ft. tall, its many pink branches hung with bell-shaped, yellow-tinted green flowers in yellow bracts. A good specimen plant in the ground or in a large container.

BETA vulgaris. See BEET

BETHLEHEM SAGE. See PULMONARIA saccharata

BETULA

BIRCH

Betulaceae

DECIDUOUS TREES

ZONES VARY BY SPECIES

FULL SUN

REGULAR WATER

Betula pendula

The white-barked European white birch—the tree that comes to mind when most people think of birches—has relatives that resemble it in graceful habit, thin bark peeling in layers, and smallish, fine-toothed leaves that turn from green to glowing yellow in fall. After leaf drop, the delicate limb structure, handsome bark, and small conelike fruits provide a winter display.

All birches need a regular supply of moisture and nutrients; they are generally too greedy for lawns. Nor should they be planted on a patio or where cars will be parked beneath them, since they are all susceptible to aphids that drip honeydew. Bronze birch borer can be a problem in the northern Rocky Mountain states; leaf miners in the Pacific Northwest. Prune established trees just to remove weak, damaged, or dead growth. To minimize sap bleed, prune in summer or early fall in mild-winter areas; where temperatures remain below freezing, wait until end of January. To avoid providing entry points for pests and diseases, don't make unnecessary or large cuts. If birch borer is present locally, don't prune while it is active (check timing with your Cooperative Extension Office).

B. albo-sinensis. Zones 3–11, 14–24. Native to western China. Large tree (to 100 ft. tall, 30 ft. wide) grown chiefly for beautiful bark: pinkish brown to coppery, covered with a powdery gray bloom. Oval leaves 3 in. long. *B. a. septentrionalis* has flaking, orange to orange-brown bark.

B. jacquemontii (B. utilis jacquemontii). Zones 3–11, 14–17. Native to northern India. Tall, narrow tree with brilliant white bark. Grows about 2 ft. a year to 40 ft., then more slowly to an eventual 60 ft. tall, 30 ft. wide. Seedlings vary in bark color from white to pinkish tan; for guaranteed white bark, look for grafted trees. Some borer resistance.

B. maximowicziana. MONARCH BIRCH. Zones 3–9, 14–24. Native to Japan. Fast growing; open growth when young. More stiffly upright than other birches. Can reach 80–100 ft. tall, 40 ft. wide. Flaking, orange-brown bark eventually turns gray or white. Heart-shaped leaves are the largest among birches—to 6 in. across. Reliable golden fall color even in mild-winter climates. Plants sold under this name are not always the true species.

B. nigra. RIVER BIRCH, RED BIRCH. Zones 1–24. Native to stream banks and lowlands in eastern North America. Very fast growth in early years; eventually becomes a pyamidal tree 50–90 ft. tall, 40–60 ft. wide. Trunk often forks near ground, but the tree can be trained to a single stem. Young bark is pinkish, very smooth, and shiny; on older trees, bark flakes and curls in cinnamon brown to blackish sheets. Diamond-shaped leaves are 1–3 in. long, bright glossy green above with silvery undersides. This is the most trouble-free birch. 'Heritage' is a superior, darker-foliaged selection with bark that begins peeling at an earlier age than species and remains colorful longer as the tree ages.

B. occidentalis (B. fontinalis). WATER BIRCH. Zones A3; 1–7, 10. Native to stream banks from Alaska to Oregon, east to Colorado. Shrubby; usually grows 12–15 ft. tall and wide. Smooth, shiny, cinnamon brown bark. Ovate leaves 2 in. long.

B. papyrifera. CANOE BIRCH, PAPER BIRCH. Zones A1–A3; 1–6. Native to northern part of North America. Similar to *B. pendula* but larger growing (to 50–90 ft. tall, half as wide), with larger leaves (to 4 in. long) that are less densely borne; habit is more open, less weeping. More resistant to borer, leaf miners. Creamy white bark peels off in papery layers.

B. pendula. EUROPEAN WHITE BIRCH. Zones A2, A3; 1–12, 14–24. Native from Europe to Asia Minor. Widely planted in western U.S. Delicate, lacy appearance. Upright main branches, weeping side branches. Average mature tree is 30–40 ft. tall, spreading to half its height. Bark on twigs and young branches is golden brown; as trees mature, bark on trunk and main limbs becomes white, marked with black clefts. Oldest bark (at base of tree) is blackish gray. Glossy, rich green leaves to 2½ in. long are diamond shaped, with a slender, tapered point. Often sold as weeping birch, although trees vary somewhat in habit and young trees show little inclination to weep. Very prone to borer attack. The following are some of the varieties offered.

'Crimson Frost'. Apparently a hybrid between *B. pendula* and an Asian birch, with burgundy leaf color that persists all summer. Somewhat borer resistant.

'Dalecarlica' ('Laciniata'). CUTLEAF WEEPING BIRCH. Graceful, open tree with strongly weeping branches, deeply cut leaves. Sunburns in hot, dry weather.

'Fastigiata' (*B. alba* 'Fastigiata'). PYRAMIDAL WHITE BIRCH. Branches upright; habit somewhat like that of Lombardy poplar (*Populus nigra* 'Italica'). Excellent screening tree.

'Purple Rain'. A purple-leafed variety like 'Purpurea', but it holds its color all summer.

'Purpurea' (*B. alba* 'Purpurea'). PURPLE BIRCH. Leaves are maroon purple when new, fading to purplish green in summer. Best in areas with cool summers and winter chill.

'Trost's Dwarf'. To 3 ft. tall and wide. For bonsai, container, rock garden. Needs excellent drainage.

'Youngii'. YOUNG'S WEEPING BIRCH. Decorative, dome-shaped tree with slender branches that hang straight down. Stake to desired height; branches then hang from that point. Sunburns in hot, dry weather.

B. platyphylla japonica. JAPANESE WHITE BIRCH. Zones 1–11, 14–24. Native to Japan. Fast growth to 40–50 ft. tall, about half as wide; open habit. White bark. Glossy green, diamond-shaped leaves to 3 in. long. 'Whitespire', to 30–40 ft. tall and only 15 ft. wide, is more borer resistant.

Betulaceae. The birch family includes deciduous trees and shrubs with inconspicuous flowers in tight clusters (catkins). Representatives are alder (*Alnus*), birch (*Betula*), filbert (*Corylus*), and hornbeam (*Carpinus*).

B

BIDENS ferulifolia

Bidens ferulifolia

Asteraceae (Compositae)

PERENNIAL

ZONES 16–24; ANYWHERE AS ANNUAL

FULL SUN

REGULAR WATER

Native to southern U.S., Mexico, Guatemala. The species grows to 3 ft. tall and wide, but the forms most commonly seen are trailing. Bright green leaves are divided into threadlike segments. Flower heads are bright golden yellow, an inch or so wide, with fewer ray flowers than most daisies and a light honey fragrance. Plants bloom almost continuously during mild weather. Extremely heat tolerant. Can be aggressive, clambering into or sprawling over their neighbors; when this happens, cut plants back (they will recover quickly).

Sold under a wide variety of names. Seed-grown kinds include 'Golden Eye', 10–12 in. tall and broad, and 'Golden Goddess', 1½–2 ft. high and wide, with larger (2½-in.) flowers. 'Goldie', 'Goldmarie', and 'Peter's Gold Carpet' are cutting-grown plants similar to 'Golden Eye' in size.

BIG BLUESTEM. See ANDROPOGON gerardii

BIGNONIA capreolata

Bignonia capreolata

CROSSVINE

Bignoniaceae

EVERGREEN OR SEMIEVERGREEN VINE

ZONES 4–9, 14–24

FULL SUN OR LIGHT SHADE

MODERATE TO REGULAR WATER

Native to southern states. Vigorous, woody vine climbs to a possible 60 ft. by tendrils and holdfast disks, attaching itself to almost any surface. Each shiny dark green leaf consists of two 2–6-in. leaflets and a branching tendril. Leaves turn purplish in cold weather, and some of them drop in the coldest zones. Clustered, 2-in., trumpet-shaped reddish brown to orange or scarlet flowers bloom in midspring, with intermittent bloom in summer. 'Tangerine Beauty' is a bright orange-red selection. Do any thinning or cutting back before spring growth begins.

Bignoniaceae. The bignonia family includes vines (mostly), trees, shrubs, and (rarely) perennials or annuals—all with trumpet-shaped, often two-lipped flowers. The family gets its name from the genus *Bignonia,* which once included most of the trumpet vines; though most of these have been reclassified, they are often still sold as *Bignonia*. Listed below are the older names, followed by the new.

Bignonia cherere. See Distictis buccinatoria
B. chinensis. See Campsis grandiflora
B. jasminoides. See Pandorea jasminoides
B. radicans. See Campsis radicans
B. speciosa. See Clytostoma callistegioides
B. tweediana. See Macfadyena unguis-cati
B. venusta. See Pyrostegia venusta
B. violacea. See Clytostoma callistegioides

BIG SAGEBRUSH. See ARTEMISIA tridentata

BIG TREE. See SEQUOIADENDRON giganteum

FOR DEFINITIONS OF GARDENING TERMS
PLEASE SEE PAGES 746–750

BILLBERGIA

Billbergia nutans

Bromeliaceae

PERENNIALS

ZONES 12, 13; 14 AND 15 (WITH PROTECTION); 16–24; H1, H2; OR INDOORS

FILTERED SUN; BRIGHT INDIRECT LIGHT

REGULAR WATER

These pineapple relatives are native to Brazil and other parts of tropical America, where they grow as epiphytes on trees. Plants grow in basal rosettes of stiff, spiny-toothed evergreen leaves; produce drooping clusters of showy bracts and tubular flowers. Usually grown in containers for display indoors or on patios. In desert zones, Southern California, and Hawaii, however, they are often planted under trees as an easy ground cover, used in borders, or grown on limbs of trees or bark slabs, with roots wrapped in sphagnum moss and leaf mold. Excellent cut flowers.

Need regular moisture during active growth in warm weather; reduce water as weather cools and growth slows. Plants usually hold water in the funnel-like center of the leaf rosette, which acts as a reservoir. Grow in well-drained soil; or pot in a light, porous mixture of sand, ground bark, and leaf mold. Houseplants need warmth and lots of light. Increase by cutting off suckers from base of plant. Specialists in bromeliads list dozens of varieties.

B. nutans. QUEEN'S TEARS. Most commonly grown. Narrow, spiny green leaves to 1½ ft. long. Long spikes of rosy red bracts; drooping flowers with green petals edged deep blue. Vigorous. Makes offsets freely; easy to grow and propagate.

B. pyramidalis. Leaves to 3 ft. long, 2½ in. wide, with spiny-toothed margins. Flowers with red, violet-tipped petals and bright red bracts in dense spikes 4 in. long.

B. sanderana. Leaves are leathery, spiny-toothed, dotted with white, grow to 1 ft. long. Produces loose, nodding, 10-in.-long clusters of flowers with blue petals that are yellowish green at the base; blue-tipped sepals, rose-colored bracts.

BIRCH. See BETULA

BIRCH BARK CHERRY. See PRUNUS serrula

BIRD OF PARADISE. See CAESALPINIA, STRELITZIA

BIRD OF PARADISE, FALSE. See HELICONIA brasiliensis

BIRD'S-EYE BUSH. See OCHNA serrulata

BIRD'S EYES. See GILIA tricolor

BIRD'S FOOT FERN. See PELLAEA mucronata

BIRD'S FOOT TREFOIL. See LOTUS corniculatus

BIRD'S NEST FERN. See ASPLENIUM nidus

BISHOP'S HAT. See EPIMEDIUM grandiflorum

BISHOP'S WEED. See AEGOPODIUM podagraria

BITTER MELON

Bitter Melon

Cucurbitaceae

ANNUAL VINE

ALL ZONES

FULL SUN

REGULAR WATER

Also called balsam pear or bitter cucumber, bitter melon is classified botanically as *Momordica charantia.* Widespread in tropics, naturalized in southeastern U.S. Sprawls or climbs by tendrils to 16 ft. Deeply lobed leaves; yellow to white, 1-in.-wide flowers with fringed petals. Fruit, to 8 in. long, is cylindrical with tapered ends, ridged and warty, bright yellow when ripe, splitting to show scarlet seeds. Immature fruit is cherished in Asian cooking despite its bitter flavor. Ripe fruit is showy, sometimes used in arrangements. Sow seed when soil warms, feed generously, and provide a trellis or other support.

BITTERROOT. See LEWISIA rediviva

BITTERSWEET. See CELASTRUS

BLACKBERRY

Rosaceae

BERRY-PRODUCING VINES

ZONES VARY BY VARIETY

FULL SUN

REGULAR WATER

Blackberry

Most blackberry varieties are derived from species native to North America; for ornamental relatives, see *Rubus.* The Far West has its own kinds of blackberries, most of which are trailing; these include varieties 'Boysen', 'Logan', 'Marion', and 'Olallie', often simply called boysenberry, loganberry, and so on. Midwestern and eastern blackberries are upright and stiff caned; these erect plants are generally hardier and easier to protect in winter (with a thick mulch) than trailing types. Crosses between trailing and erect blackberries are termed semierect.

All kinds of blackberries bear fruit in summer; for good crops, they need deep, well-drained soil and regular moisture throughout the growing season. (But don't locate plants where they will be standing in water during dormancy.) Blackberries can be grown with some success in the desert, though plants may be short lived—for best results, amend soil generously with organic matter, and provide frequent water, heavy mulch, and protection from wind and intense afternoon sun.

In cold-winter regions, planting is usually done after the last hard freeze, when the soil begins to warm. In these areas, blackberries are best located on slight slopes where cold air will "drain" downhill. Set new bare-root plants an inch deeper than they grew at the nursery, covering their crowns with 1 in. of soil. In mild-winter regions, gardeners can plant in spring or gain half a season by transplanting container plants.

Blackberry roots are perennial, but the canes are biennial: they develop and grow one year, bloom and fruit the next. Hence the need to distinguish first- and second-year canes when training and pruning.

Trailing and semierect types should be allowed to grow unrestricted the first year, then trained onto some kind of trellis in their second year. Train year-old canes fanwise onto the trellis; after harvest, cut to the ground all canes that have fruited. Canes of the current season—those growing beneath the trellis—should now be trained onto it. The following pruning must be done by midsummer to avoid reducing next year's crop: with trailing varieties, thin to 12–16 canes, pruning each to 6–8 ft. long; with semierect types, thin to 4–8 canes, pruning each to 5–6 ft. long. These shortened canes will produce side branches during remainder of growing season; cut them back to 1 ft. in early spring. New spring growth will produce small fruiting branches from those side branches.

Erect types don't need support, but tying them to wire helps organize the canes. In the first year, cut canes to 2½ ft. in midsummer to force side growth. Cut resulting side branches to 12–15 in. late in the dormant season. After canes bear fruit in the second year, cut them to ground. Start the process over again with new canes growing from the ground.

Blackberries are subject to many pests and diseases, including scale, borers, anthracnose, leaf spot, and powdery mildew, so start with healthy plants from a reputable supplier. Also look for resistant varieties. Because they are susceptible to verticillium wilt, do not plant blackberries where potatoes, tomatoes, eggplant, or peppers have grown in prior 3 years. To control red-berry mite (mostly affecting 'Evergreen' and 'Thornless Evergreen'), spider mites, and whitefly, apply a dormant spray containing lime sulfur in winter and again as buds are about to break.

Fertilize established plantings in the Pacific Northwest at blossom time. In California, split the yearly amount into three applications: before new growth starts, in midspring, and in midsummer. Elsewhere, fertilize just before new growth begins. Keep down weeds and pull out suckers; above all, don't let plants get away from you. These are some of the varieties available in Western nurseries. Combine early, midseason, and late varieties to get fresh fruit over the longest possible season.

'Arapaho'. Erect; midseason. Zones 1–24. Thornless, disease resistant. Big crop of medium-size, firm, tasty berries. 'Apache', 'Chickasaw', 'Choctaw', 'Kiowa', 'Navaho', and 'Shawnee' are similar varieties. All grow well in hot-summer climates.

'Boysen' and 'Thornless Boysen'. Trailing; midseason. Zones 2–24; not reliably hardy in Zone 1, but will survive winter if canes are left on ground and covered with snow or straw mulch. Popular for high yield and flavor. Very large berries are reddish, soft, sweet-tart, have a delightful aroma, and can be used fresh, cooked, or frozen. Covered with a dusty bloom that slightly dulls color. 'Nectar' is identical variety.

'Brazos'. Erect; early. Zones 4–24. Disease-resistant Texas variety well adapted to hot-summer areas. Large, fairly firm, tart fruit.

'Cascade'. Trailing; midseason. Best in Zones 4–6, 16, 17; sometimes grown in Zones 20–24; not reliably hardy in Zones 1–3. Large berries are bright, deep red—almost black (red when cooked). Classic wild blackberry flavor. Tender and very juicy.

'Cherokee'. Erect; early. Zones 1–24. Thorny. Medium-large, firm berries with excellent flavor. Resists anthracnose.

'Chester'. Semierect; late. Zones 2–9, 14–24. Thornless. Medium-size, firm berries with good flavor. Late ripener. Very cold tolerant.

'Dirkson'. Semierect; midseason. Zones 2–9, 14–24. Thornless. High yield of large, semitart berries. Resistant to anthracnose, leaf spot, and powdery mildew.

'Evergreen' and 'Thornless Evergreen'. Trailing; late. Zones 4–6, 8, 9, 12, 13, 20–24. Strong canes bear heavy crop of large, exceptionally firm, black, sweet berries with large seeds.

'Logan' and 'Thornless Logan'. Trailing; early. Same climate adaption as 'Boysen'. Large berries are light red, not darkening when ripe, with fine hairs that dull the fruit's color. Tarter flavor than 'Boysen'; excellent for canning and pies.

'Marion'. Trailing; midseason. Zones 4–9, 14–24. Rich, flavorful fruit sets the standard. 'Marion' types include late-ripening 'Waldo', with berries that maintain their shape when cooked; and 'Black Butte', 'Silvan', and 'Siskiyou', all early ripeners with excellent flavor

'Olallie'. Trailing; early. Zones 4–9, 14–24. Berries medium to large, shiny black, firm, sweeter than 'Cascade' but with some wild blackberry sprightliness.

'Tay' or 'Tayberry'. Trailing; early. Zones 4–9, 14–24. Hybrid between blackberry and raspberry. Long, thorny canes. Heavy bearer of big, mild-flavored, dark red to purple-black fruit. Bears earlier than most other blackberries.

'Triple Crown'. Semierect; late. Zones 1–9, 14–24. An improved 'Chester' type with large, very flavorful berries. Vigorous canes. Hardy. 'Hull' is similar but not as tasty.

'Young' and 'Thornless Young'. Trailing; midseason. Climate adaption same as for 'Boysen' but not as productive in all climates. Berries are same size and color as 'Boysen' but shiny and somewhat sweeter.

BLACKBERRY LILY. See BELAMCANDA chinensis

BLACK CALLA. See ARUM palaestinum

BLACK-EYED SUSAN. See RUDBECKIA hirta

BLACK-EYED SUSAN VINE. See THUNBERGIA alata

BLACK LILY. See FRITILLARIA camschatcensis

BLACK SALLY. See EUCALYPTUS stellulata

BLACK SNAKEROOT. See CIMICIFUGA racemosa

BLADDERNUT. See STAPHYLEA

BLANKET FLOWER. See GAILLARDIA grandiflora

BLAZING STAR. See MENTZELIA

BLECHNUM

Polypodiaceae

FERNS

ZONES VARY BY SPECIES

PARTIAL OR FULL SHADE

REGULAR WATER

Blechnum spicant

Evergreen ferns noted for their symmetrical, formal appearance; some form a small trunk. Plants dislike overhead watering when air is humid or still.

B. brasiliense. Zones 19, 21–24. Native to Brazil, Peru. Dwarf tree fern reaching only 4 ft. tall, 5 ft. wide. Nearly erect fronds in compact clusters; reddish when young. 'Crispum' has elegantly ruffled fronds.

B. gibbum. Zones 19, 21–24; H1, H2. Native to Fiji. Dwarf tree fern with 3-ft.-wide crown of fronds atop slender trunk that eventually reaches 3 ft. high. 'Moorei' has wider, more leathery leaflets and is more attractive in winter.

B. penna-marina. Zones 15–17, 20–24; with protection in Zones 4–6. Native to South America. Spreads slowly in cool, moist, sheltered places to make patches of refined-looking, 4–8-in. fronds. Sterile fronds have wider lobes than fertile ones. Can be used as a houseplant.

B. spicant. DEER FERN, DEER TONGUE FERN. Zones 2b–7, 14–19, 24. Native primarily to coastal forests of Northern California and Northwest. Glossy deep green fern with two strikingly different kinds of fronds: sterile ones are 1¾ in. wide, spreading or angled, 1–3 ft. tall; fertile ones are narrower and stiffly erect, with slender, widely spaced leaflets. Forms a clump to 3 ft. wide.

BLEEDING HEART. See DICENTRA

BLETILLA striata (B. hyacinthina)

CHINESE GROUND ORCHID

Orchidaceae

TERRESTRIAL ORCHID

ZONES 2B–9, 12–24

FILTERED SUN OR PARTIAL SHADE

REGULAR WATER DURING GROWTH AND BLOOM

Bletilla striata

Hardy orchid native to China and Japan. Pinkish purple, 2-in.-wide blossoms resembling cattleyas are carried up to 12 on each 1–1½-ft. stem. Bloom lasts for about 6 weeks in late spring or early summer. Pale green leaves, three to six to a plant, remain attractive into early fall. 'Alba' is a white-flowered form. *B. s. albostriata* bears light pink blossoms above leaves striped in green and white.

Grow in pots or ground, under high-branching trees or lath. Plant pseudobulbs any time during dormant period (late fall to early spring), positioning tops 1 in. below soil surface (2 in. in colder regions) and spacing 1 ft. apart. Plant in humus-rich, well-drained soil; mulch if temperatures will drop below 20°F/–7°C. Protect from slugs and snails when leaves emerge. Taper off watering when foliage begins to yellow in fall; discontinue when leaves have died back completely. Forms large clumps over time that can be divided in early spring, before growth starts. (However, blooms best when crowded.)

BLOOD FLOWER. See ASCLEPIAS curassavica

BLOODLEAF. See IRESINE herbstii

BLOOD LILY. See SCADOXUS multiflorus katherinae

BLOOD-RED TRUMPET VINE. See DISTICTIS buccinatoria

BLUEBEARD. See CARYOPTERIS

BLUEBELL. See HYACINTHOIDES

BLUEBERRY

Ericaceae

DECIDUOUS SHRUB

ZONES VARY BY TYPE

FULL SUN

AMPLE WATER

Blueberry

Native to eastern North America; for ornamental species in the same genus, see *Vaccinium.* Blueberries thrive under conditions that suit rhododendrons and azaleas, to which they are related. They need cool, moist, well-drained acid soil (pH 4.5–5.5). Where soil isn't acidic enough, either create proper conditions in garden soil or grow in containers filled with acidic potting mix.

Most blueberries grown for fruit are also handsome plants suitable for hedges or shrub borders. Leaves, to 3 in. long, are bronze when new, maturing to dark green, turning scarlet or yellow in fall. Tiny, urn-shaped spring flowers are white or pinkish. Summer fruit is decorative. Set plants about 3 ft. apart for informal hedge; as individual shrubs, space at least 4–5 ft. apart.

Blueberries are available bare-root or in containers. Plant in early spring in cold-winter regions, autumn in mild climates. Position crown so that it is no deeper than ½ in. below the ground. Blueberries have fine roots near the soil surface; keep them moist, but don't subject them to standing water. A 3–4-in.-thick mulch of sawdust, ground bark, or the like will protect roots, help conserve soil moisture, and keep weeds down. Don't cultivate around plants; roots of plants are close to surface. Use acid-forming fertilizers. California growers in particular may need to correct chlorosis with iron sulfate or iron chelate.

Prune to prevent overbearing. Plants shape themselves but often produce so many fruit buds that berries are undersize and plant growth slows down. Keep first-year plants from bearing by stripping off flowers. On older plants, cut back ends of twigs to point where fruit buds are widely spaced. Or simply remove some of oldest branches each year. Also prune out all weak shoots. Plants seldom have serious problems requiring regular control in home gardens. Netting will keep birds at bay.

The following are the major types of blueberries grown. Plant at least two varieties for better pollination, choosing kinds that ripen at different times for a long harvest. For sufficient fruit throughout the season, allow two plants for each household member.

Highbush blueberries. Selections of *Vaccinium corymbosum,* these are the blueberries found in grocery stores. Most varieties grow upright to 6 ft. or more; a few are rather sprawling and under 5 ft. The majority are northern varieties (Zones 2–9, 14–17): they require definite winter cold and ripen fruit from late spring to late summer. The relatively new southern highbush varieties (Zones 8, 9, 14–17, 18–24) are better adapted to mild-winter climates and are even finding success in Southern California; they ripen their fruit in mid- to late spring, even before rabbiteye types. Except as noted, varieties below are northern types.

'Berkeley'. Midseason. Open, spreading, tall. Large, light blue berries.

'Bluecrop'. Midseason. Erect, tall growth. Large berries. Excellent flavor. Attractive shrub.

'Blueray'. Midseason. Vigorous, tall. Large, highly flavored, crisp berries. Attractive shrub. Tolerates more heat than 'Bluecrop'.

'Cape Fear'. Southern highbush. Early midseason. Very large, light blue fruit with mild, sweet flavor. Easy-to-grow, weeping bush.

'Darrow'. Late. Vigorous, upright. Very large fruit, up to the size of a quarter. Heavy producer.

'Duke'. Early. Upright. Heavy producer of firm, mildly sweet fruit.

'Earliblue'. Early. Tall, erect. Large, heavy leaves. Large berries of excellent flavor.

'Elliott'. Late. Tall, upright. Medium to large berries of excellent flavor.

'Georgia Gem'. Southern highbush. Very early. Moderately vigorous, upright. Medium-size, firm fruit of good flavor.

'Ivanhoe'. Early to midseason. Large, dark berries—firm, crisp, tart.

'Jersey'. Late. Tall, erect. Large, light blue, very bland berries.

'Legacy'. Late. Unusual shrub that doesn't lose its leaves in winter. Will color in cold winters, but stays mostly green in mild areas. Upright, arching. Medium-size berries with fine flavor.

'Misty'. Southern highbush. Very early. Large berries with excellent flavor. Bears heavily.

'Olympia'. Midseason. Medium-size fruit with exceptional, spicy flavor. Large, vigorous, arching bush with great fall color.

'O'Neal'. Southern highbush. Very early. Large, flavorful berries.

'Patriot'. Midseason. Large, firm, tasty berries. Consistently high yields. Hardy; worth a try in warmer sites in Zone 1.

'Rubel'. Early to late. Erect, tall growth. Small, firm, tart berries.

'Spartan'. Early. Heavy bearer of large, flavorful fruit.

'Sunshine Blue'. Southern highbush. Midseason. Compact, evergreen bush tolerates higher-pH soils. Heavy crop of good-size berries with tangy flavor. Very low chill needed.

'Tophat'. Midseason. Dwarf hybrid that stays under 1½ ft.; good for pots. Small fruit with mild flavor.

'Toro'. Midseason. Compact plant with pinkish blooms. Large, firm berries with excellent, sprightly flavor.

Rabbiteye blueberries. Zones 8, 9, 14–17, 18–24. These selections of *Vaccinium ashei* are native to southeastern U.S. and can be grown in central California, Southern California, and other mild-winter areas if given acid soil conditions. Unlike most blueberries, these tolerate heat. Often taller and rangier than highbush plants, they ripen large, light blue berries from May to July. Quality is not as good as that of highbush blueberries. Varieties include 'Bluebelle', 'Southland', and 'Tifblue'.

Hardy half-high varieties. Zones A2, A3; 1–3. Highbush blueberries have been hybridized with the northeastern U.S. native lowbush blueberry *(Vaccinium angustifolium)* to create very hardy types called half-high blueberries.

'Chippewa'. Midseason. Slightly larger plant than 'Northblue'. Large, light blue fruit with excellent sweet flavor.

'Northblue'. Midseason to late. To 3–4 ft. high. Large, firm, dark blue berries with trace of wild blueberry flavor.

'Northcountry'. Early midseason. Less than 3 ft. tall. Sweet, very light blue berries. Good in containers.

'Northsky'. Midseason to late. Densely branched, to 1–1½ ft. high. Light blue berries with hint of wild blueberry flavor. Good in containers.

'Polaris'. Early. To 4 ft. tall; upright, arching. Light blue fruit with delightful flavor.

'St. Cloud'. Early. To 3–4 ft. tall. Large, firm, flavorful berries.

BLUE BLOSSOM. See CEANOTHUS thyrsiflorus

BLUE BOX. See EUCALYPTUS baueriana

BLUE BUTTONS. See KNAUTIA arvensis

BLUE DAWN FLOWER. See IPOMOEA indica

BLUE DAZE. See EVOLVULUS glomeratus

BLUE-EYED GRASS. See SISYRINCHIUM bellum

BLUE-EYED MARY. See OMPHALODES verna

BLUE FESCUE. See FESTUCA ovina 'Glauca'

BLUE GINGER. See DICHORISANDRA thyrsiflora

BLUE GRASS. See BOUTELOUA gracilis

BLUE GRAMA. See POA

BLUE GUM. See EUCALYPTUS globulus

BLUE HIBISCUS. See ALYOGYNE huegelii

BLUE LACE FLOWER. See TRACHYMENE coerulea

BLUE LYME GRASS. See LEYMUS arenarius

BLUE MARGUERITE. See FELICIA amelloides

BLUE MIST. See CARYOPTERIS × clandonensis

BLUE SPIRAEA. See CARYOPTERIS incana

BLUE STAR CREEPER. See PRATIA pedunculata

BLUE STAR FLOWER. See AMSONIA

BLUE THIMBLE FLOWER. See GILIA capitata

BOCCONIA cordata. See MACLEAYA cordata

BOG ROSEMARY. See ANDROMEDA polifolia

BOK CHOY. See ASIAN GREENS

BOLAX gummifera (B. glebaria, Azorella trifurcata)

Apiaceae (Umbelliferae)

PERENNIAL

ZONES 2–6, 14–17

FULL SUN IN COOLER CLIMATES ONLY

REGULAR WATER

Bolax gummifera

Native to Patagonia and the Falkland Islands. The name is uncertain, but the plant itself is a low, densely branching perennial with tightly packed rosettes of bright green, glossy, thick, hard leaves ½ in. or so in length. The leaves are divided into three lobes. Flowers look like tiny, greenish parsley blossoms. The plant forms a firm cushion 2 in. high and 1½ ft. across. Attractive in rock gardens or as ground cover in light shade, though it can take full sun in cool-summer climates.

BOLTONIA asteroides

Asteraceae (Compositae)

PERENNIAL

ZONES 1–24

FULL SUN OR LIGHT SHADE

REGULAR WATER

Boltonia asteroides

Native to eastern U.S. In late summer, tall stems bear airy, mounded clusters of small yellow-centered white to blue flowers that resemble Michaelmas daisies *(Aster novi-belgii)*. With regular moisture, can reach 6 ft. or taller, 3 ft. wide; may be floppy with overhead watering. 'Pink Beauty' has pink flowers. 'Snowbank' is more compact (to 5 ft. tall) and upright than the species, with larger flowers of a clearer white. Plants will survive in poor soil and with reduced water, but have reduced vigor and size (stems to just 2 ft.) and sparser bloom.

Bombacaceae. This tropical family of trees and shrubs contains a popular genus grown in the mild-winter West: *Chorisia,* both species of which have showy flowers.

B

Boraginaceae. The borage family consists of annuals and perennials (rarely shrubs or trees), most of which have small flowers in coiled clusters that straighten as bloom progresses. Forget-me-not *(Myosotis)* is a familiar example.

BORAGO officinalis

BORAGE

Boraginaceae

ANNUAL

ZONES A2, A3; 1–24; H1

FULL SUN OR PARTIAL SHADE

MODERATE WATER

Borago officinalis

Native European herb forms rounded clump to 2–3 ft. high, 1½–2 ft. wide. Bristly gray-green leaves to 4–6 in. long are edible, with a cucumberlike flavor. Blue, star-shaped summer flowers nod in leafy clusters from branched stems.

Tolerates poor soil. Seeds itself, but doesn't transplant easily because of deep taproot. Best way to start borage is to sow seeds in place in spring after frost danger is past. Good drought-tolerant ground cover and soil binder. Use small, tender leaves in salads; you can also pickle them or cook them as greens. Cut flowers for arrangements or use as a garnish.

BORONIA

Rutaceae

EVERGREEN SHRUBS

ZONES VARY BY SPECIES

FULL SUN OR LIGHT SHADE

REGULAR WATER

Boronia megastigma

Attractive, relatively short-lived shrubs from Australia. Finely divided leaves produce a wispy look. Bell-shaped blooms are good for cutting. Plants need well-drained, slightly acid, sandy or light loamy soil. Careful watering is important: they should never be completely dry or stay wet at root depth for any length of time. Prune lightly after bloom to promote bushiness and prolong life of plant.

B. crenulata. Zones 16–24. To 2–3 ft. tall, 3–4 ft. wide, with tiny dark green leaves and small pink flowers in late winter and spring. 'Shark Bay' is a compact (2-ft.-tall, 3-ft.-wide) selection with pink flowers that appear throughout the year, most profusely from winter to early summer.

B. denticulata. Zones 15–17, 20–24. To 3–8 ft. tall, 1½–4 ft. wide, with strongly aromatic leaves. Flowers in mauve, pink shades, or more rarely white, in late winter and spring; sporadic bloom otherwise.

B. heterophylla. RED BORONIA. Zones 16–24. Dense grower to 6–8 ft. tall, 4–6 ft. wide, with finely cut foliage and profuse, intensely fragrant, deep pink flowers opening from red buds in late winter and spring.

B. megastigma. BROWN BORONIA. Zones 15–17, 20–24. Only 1–2 ft. tall and wide, with nodding, ½-in., bell-shaped brown to reddish brown flowers with yellow interior; winter bloom. Powerful, pleasant scent combines freesia, orange blossom, and other fragrances. Count on replacing plant every 2 or 3 years from seed or cuttings. Lasts longer grown in light potting mix in containers.

B. molloyae (B. elatior). PINK BORONIA, TALL BORONIA. Zones 15–17, 20–24. Grows 3–12 ft. tall, 3–6 ft. wide. Clouds of ¼-in., bell-shaped pink to rose flowers in spring and summer.

BOSTON FERN. See NEPHROLEPIS exaltata 'Bostoniensis'

BOSTON IVY. See PARTHENOCISSUS tricuspidata

BO-TREE. See FICUS religiosa

BOTTLEBRUSH. See CALLISTEMON, MELALEUCA

BOTTLE PALM. See NOLINA recurvata

BOTTLE TREE. See BRACHYCHITON populnens

BOUGAINVILLEA

Nyctaginaceae

EVERGREEN SHRUBBY VINES

ZONES 5, 6, 12–17, 19, 21–24; H1, H2

FULL SUN

MODERATE TO REGULAR WATER

Bougainvillea
'San Diego Red'

Native to tropical and subtropical South America. Reliably hardy in Zones 22–24, H1, H2, yet widely and satisfyingly grown in areas of minimum frost: Zones 12–17, 19, 21. Use has extended into Zones 5, 6, thanks to low-growing shrubby types that can be purchased in full bloom and grown in containers. These are used on patios as summer annuals and moved to a protected area over winter. Where frosts are routine (as in Zones 12, 14, 19, 21), vines need a protected warm wall or warmest spot in garden. If vines get by first winter or two, they will be big enough to take most winter damage and recover. In any case, young plants bloom so readily that replacement is not a real deterrent.

Bougainvillea's vibrant colors come not from the inconspicuous true flowers, but from the large, papery, petal-like bracts that surround them. Bloom reaches its peak in summer, but in mildest-winter regions flowers may appear from spring through fall, and even into winter. Both single- and double-flowered types are sold; double kinds can look messy, because they hold faded blooms for a long time. White- and yellow-flowered varieties need light shade in the hottest climates.

Vining bougainvilleas are fast, vigorous growers, reaching 15–30 ft. depending on variety. Long, needlelike thorns arm stiff stems that are moderately to densely clothed in medium green, 2½-in., heart-shaped leaves. Vines are superb on walls and sturdy fences, trellises, arbors. Because they have no means of attachment (though the thorns help them scramble through shrubs and trees), you must tie stems to the support while basic structure is establishing.

In areas that typically have frosts, plant in early spring after frost danger has passed. Do any major pruning after flowering has ceased (in frost-free regions) or as early as possible in spring after frost danger has passed (in others). During growing season, prune as needed to direct growth.

WHAT BOUGAINVILLEAS NEED

CAREFUL PLANTING: Roots do not knit soil together in a firm root ball, and they are highly sensitive to disturbance. To minimize shock when planting, cut off container bottom; then set both plant and container in planting hole. Slide container up over the plant, filling in with soil as you go. Don't worry about damaging upper part of plant as you do so; stems are pliant, with little horizontal growth.

STRONG SUPPORT: Tie shoots to a sturdy support so they won't whip in wind. Strong gusts can shred leaves against sharp thorns along stems.

Bougainvillea
'Orange King'

NUTRIENTS: Fertilize when growing season begins and again in early summer.

MOISTURE: Water regularly in spring, moderately during bloom period.

TOP: *Bougainvillea* 'Barbara Karst'
BOTTOM: *Bougainvillea* 'Rosenka'

TOP: *Bougainvillea* 'California Gold'
BOTTOM: *Bougainvillea* 'Mary Palmer's Enchantment'

TOP: *Bougainvillea* 'Hawaii'
BOTTOM: *Bougainvillea* 'San Diego Red'

TOP: *Bougainvillea* 'Oo-La-La'
BOTTOM: *Bougainvillea* 'Texas Dawn'

Heavily pruned vines and shrubby varieties make good self-supporting container plants for terrace or patio. Without support and with occasional corrective pruning, bougainvillea becomes a broad, sprawling shrub, a bank or ground cover, or a hanging-basket plant.

All of the following are tall-growing vines unless otherwise noted.

'Afterglow'. Yellow orange; heavy bloom. Open growth, sparse foliage.

'Bangkok Red'. See 'Torch Glow'

'Barbara Karst'. Bright red in sun, bluish crimson in shade; blooms young and for long period. Vigorous growth. Likes heat of desert. Fast comeback after frost.

'Betty Hendry' ('Indian Maid'). Basically red but with touches of yellow and purple. Blooms young and for a long period.

B. brasiliensis. See B. spectabilis

'Brilliant Variegated'. Spreading, mounding shrub. Leaves variegated with gray green and silver. Brick red bracts. Good in hanging baskets, pots.

'California Gold' ('Sunset'). Deep golden yellow. Blooms young.

'Camarillo Fiesta'. Hot pink to gold blend.

'Cherry Blossom'. Double-flowered rose pink, with white to pale green centers.

'Crimson Jewel'. Vigorous shrubby, sprawling plant. Good in containers, as shrub, or as sunny bank cover. Lower growth, better color than 'Temple Fire'. Heavy bloom, long season.

'Crimson Lake'. See 'Mrs. Butt'

'Don Mario'. Large, vigorous vine with huge clusters of deep purple-red bracts.

'Hawaii'. ('Raspberry Ice'). Shrubby, mounding, spreading. Leaves have golden yellow margins. Red-tinged new leaves. Red bracts. Good hanging basket plant. Despite its tropical name, it's one of the hardiest.

'Indian Maid'. See 'Betty Hendry'

'Isabel Greensmith'. Red-orange to crimson bracts with pointed tips.

'Jamaica White'. White bracts veined in light green. Blooms young. Moderately vigorous.

'James Walker'. Big reddish purple bracts on big vine.

'La Jolla'. Bright red bracts; compact, shrubby habit. Good shrub or container plant.

'Lavender Queen'. An improved *B. spectabilis,* with bigger bracts, heavier bloom.

'Manila Red'. Many rows of magenta red bracts make heavy clusters of double-looking bloom.

'Mary Palmer's Enchantment'. Very vigorous, large-growing vine with pure white bracts.

'Mrs. Butt' ('Crimson Lake'). Old-fashioned variety with good crimson color. Needs lots of heat for bloom. Moderately vigorous.

'Oo-La-La'. Dwarf plant 1½ ft. tall, 6–8 ft. wide, with magenta red color over a long season. Good ground or bank cover, hanging basket plant.

'Orange King'. Bronzy orange. Open growth. Needs long summer, no frost.

'Pink Tiara'. Abundant pale pink to rose bracts over long season.

'Purple Queen'. Deep purple bracts. Compact grower that can reach 15 ft. if supported; as a trailer, it grows 1½ ft. tall, 6–8 ft. wide.

'Raspberry Ice'. See 'Hawaii'

'Rosea'. Large rose red bracts on large vine.

'Rosenka'. Can be held to shrub proportions if occasional wayward shoot is pruned out. Gold bracts age to pink.

'San Diego Red' ('San Diego', 'Scarlett O'Hara'). One of best on all counts: large, deep green leaves that hold on well in cold winters; deep red bracts over long season; hardiness equal to old-fashioned purple kind. Vigorous, high climbing. Can be trained to tree form by staking and pruning.

'Southern Rose'. Rosy lavender to pink bracts.

B. spectabilis (B. brasiliensis). Hardy and vigorous. Blooms well in cool summers. Purple bracts. Good choice for Zones 16, 17.

'Sunset'. See 'California Gold'

'Tahitian Dawn'. Big vine with gold bracts aging to rosy purple.

'Tahitian Maid'. Extra rows of blush pink bracts give double effect.

'Temple Fire'. Shrublike growth to 4 ft. high, 6 ft. wide. Partially deciduous. Bronze red.

'Texas Dawn'. Choice, vigorous plant among selections with bracts in pink shades. Purplish pink bracts in large sprays.

'Torch Glow' ('Bangkok Red'). An oddity: an erect, multistemmed plant to 6 ft. It needs no support. Reddish pink flowers close to stems are partially hidden by foliage.

'White Madonna'. Pure white bracts.

BOULDER RASPBERRY. See RUBUS deliciosus

BOUNCING BET. See SAPONARIA officinalis

BOUTELOUA

GRAMA GRASS

Poaceae (Gramineae)

PERENNIAL GRASSES

ZONES 1–3, 7–11, 14, 18–21

FULL SUN

LITTLE WATER

Bouteloua gracilis

These natives of dry North American grasslands form clumps of narrow gray-green leaves. Tough, heat- and drought-tolerant plants characterized by oddly attractive flowering stems that carry their summer flowers on one side only. One or a few plants are pretty in a border or large rock garden. Massed, they are useful for creating meadows. Grow from seed or division. ▸

B. curtipendula. SIDE-OATS GRAMA. To 1–2 ft. tall, 2 ft. wide. Flowering stems vary from arching to nearly horizontal, with the purple-tinted green flowers dangling underneath. These, like the leaves, turn yellow in fall, then white in winter.

B. gracilis. BLUE GRAMA, MOSQUITO GRASS. To 1½–2 ft. high, 1 ft. wide. Flowering stems have odd inflorescences springing out at right angles, said to resemble hovering mosquitoes. Reddish in summer, they bleach to white. Tolerates sunny, arid, alkaline conditions in the High Plains and Rocky Mountain areas. Makes a fair low-water-use lawn if mowed to 1½ in. high. Sow seed at 1 lb. per 1,000 sq. ft. in fall to take advantage of winter rain and snow. Irrigate to depth of 1 ft. until established; thereafter, it needs virtually no irrigation.

BOUVARDIA

Rubiaceae

EVERGREEN SHRUBS

ZONES VARY BY SPECIES

PARTIAL SHADE

WATER NEEDS VARY BY SPECIES

Bouvardia longiflora 'Albatross'

Valued for showy clusters of tubular flowers. Plants have loose, often straggling growth habit. One type has fragrant blossoms, but it is also the most tender and looks poorest after flowers are gone. The nonfragrant red-flowered species are hardier, easier to grow. All appreciate well-drained soil, midday shade. To encourage compact growth, prune hard annually after bloom.

B. glaberrima. Zones 8–10, 12, 14–24. Native to mountain canyons in southern Arizona, New Mexico. To 3 ft. tall and wide. Shrubby, but top growth dies back in cold weather. Smooth green leaves 1–3 in. long. Clustered 1-in., red (rarely pink or white), unscented flowers. Little water.

B. longiflora 'Albatross' (B. humboldtii 'Albatross'). Zones 12, 16, 17, 19–24. Variety of a Mexican species. Jasmine-scented, 3-in. snow white flowers appear at almost any time; excellent in bouquets. Plant is 2–3 ft. high and 2 ft. wide, with paired 2-in. leaves. Pinch out stem tips to make bushier. If soil is poor, grow in tubs or raised beds in rich, fast-draining soil mix. 'Stephanie' is more compact and floriferous. Regular water.

B. ternifolia (B. jacquinii). Zones 8–10, 12, 14–24. Native to Texas, Mexico. To 3 ft. tall, 2½–3 ft. wide; 2-in. leaves in whorls of three or four. Unscented, inch-long red flowers in loose clusters at branch ends in summer and early fall. Forms have pink, rose, or coral blossoms. Little water.

BOWER VINE. See PANDOREA jasminoides

BOWLES' GOLDEN GRASS. See MILIUM effusum 'Aureum'

BOX, BOXWOOD. See BUXUS

BOX ELDER. See ACER negundo

BOXTHORN. See LYCIUM chinense

BOYSENBERRY. See BLACKBERRY

BRACHYCHITON

Sterculiaceae

EVERGREEN AND PARTLY OR WHOLLY DECIDUOUS TREES

ZONES VARY BY SPECIES

FULL SUN

LITTLE TO MODERATE WATER

Brachychiton populneus

Native to Australia. All have woody, canoe-shaped fruits that delight flower arrangers but are merely litter in the view of some gardeners. Grow in well-drained soil. Tend to form strong central leader; require minimal pruning.

Blooming habit and leaf drop in the two deciduous species listed here can be most erratic. Young trees often bloom only in sections of the tree rather than all over it; those parts will drop their leaves while nonblooming areas retain their foliage. Older trees tend to produce blooms on all branches and drop all their leaves before flowers appear. Bloom is best after a dry winter.

B. acerifolius (Sterculia acerifolia). FLAME TREE, AUSTRALIAN FLAME TREE. Deciduous for brief period. Zones 15–24; H1, H2. Hardy to 25°F/–4°C. At its best, a spectacular red-flowering tree reaching 60 ft. or taller, 30 ft. wide. Strong, heavy, smooth trunk, usually green. Handsome leaves are glossy bright green, 10-in.-wide fans, deeply lobed. Showiest flowering season usually comes in late spring to early summer, when all or part of tree is covered with clusters of ¾-in., tubular red or orange-red bells.

B. discolor (Sterculia discolor). QUEENSLAND LACEBARK, PINK FLAME TREE. Deciduous for brief period. Zones 15–24. To 40–60 ft. tall; pyramidal in youth but more spreading (to about 30 ft.) in maturity. Ornamental bottle-shaped trunk. Leaves, only 6 in. wide, are narrower than those of *B. acerifolius* and are blue green rather than bright green, with whitish undersides. Leaves on young trees are deeply lobed; lobes become shallower as tree ages. Large, bell-like, deep rose pink flowers in summer; fallen flowers can be messy. Blossoms and subsequent fruit are densely covered with rusty wool on outside.

B. populneus (Sterculia diversifolia). BOTTLE TREE. Evergreen. Zones 12–24. Moderate growth to 30–50 ft. tall, 30 ft. wide. Common name refers to very heavy trunk, which is broad at base, tapering toward top. Leaves (2–3 in. long) are fresh green year-round, shimmer in breeze like those of aspens. Clusters of small, bell-shaped white flowers in late spring only noticeable close up. Appreciated in low and intermediate deserts, where it is frequently used as a shade tree and as a screen or high, wide windbreak. Susceptible to Texas root rot.

B. rupestris (Sterculia rupestris). QUEENSLAND BOTTLE TREE. Evergreen. Zones 13, 21, 23, 24. To 25 ft. tall, 15 ft. wide, often much smaller. Leaves on young trees are deeply lobed (like fingers of a hand); on mature trees they are undivided, to 6 in. long. Flowers are small and yellowish. Conspicuous feature is the trunk, which is swollen and bulbous; may measure 5–6 ft. in diameter. Young plants confined to containers often produce grotesquely twisted trunks.

BRACHYSCOME

SWAN RIVER DAISY

Asteraceae (Compositae)

ANNUALS AND PERENNIALS

ZONES VARY BY SPECIES

FULL SUN

REGULAR WATER

Brachyscome iberidifolia

Neat, charming Australian daisies make mounds 1 ft. tall, 1½ ft. across, with finely divided leaves and a profusion of inch-wide daisies in spring and summer. Use in rock garden, at front of border, in containers or raised beds.

B. hybrids. Perennials. Zones 14–24. Choices include 'City Lights', with light lavender-blue flowers; 'New Amethyst', dark purple; and 'Toucan Tango' ('Ultra'), deep lavender blue.

B. iberidifolia. Annual. Zones 1–24. Flowers are blue, white, or pink. In spring, sow seed where plants are to grow.

B. multifida. Perennial. Zones 14–24. Very similar to *B. iberidifolia.* Blue flowers most common. Propagate by cuttings.

BRACKEN. See PTERIDIUM aquilinum

A PRACTICAL GUIDE TO GARDENING
PLEASE SEE PAGES 658–731

BRACTEANTHA bracteata (Helichrysum bracteatum)

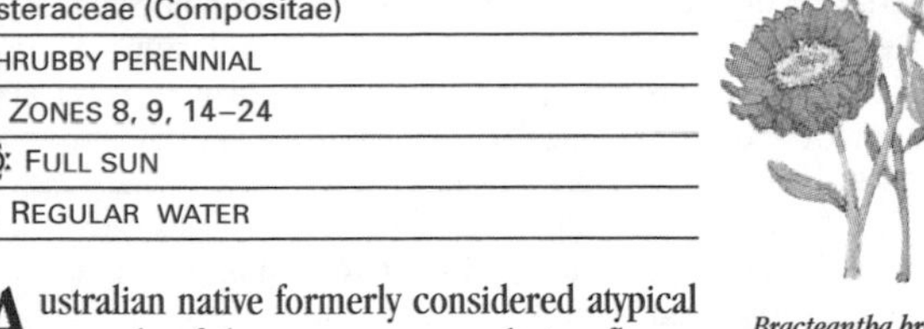

BUSH STRAWFLOWER
Asteraceae (Compositae)
SHRUBBY PERENNIAL
ZONES 8, 9, 14–24
FULL SUN
REGULAR WATER

Bracteantha bracteata

Australian native formerly considered atypical example of the common annual strawflower *(Helichrysum bracteatum)* has now been given a genus of its own. Flowers, held well above the foliage, resemble those of strawflower in having many rows of papery bracts; narrow leaves are gray green. 'Diamond Head' grows 8 in. high and 1½ ft. wide, with 1½-in., golden yellow flowers. 'Dargan Hill Monarch' is larger overall at 2½ ft. tall and 3–6 ft. wide, with leaves to 6 in. long and golden yellow flower heads to 3½ in. across. 'Cockatoo' resembles the latter but has light yellow blossoms. Newer Sundaze series includes selections with bronzy gold, golden yellow, lemon yellow, pink, or white blossoms on plants 10–14 in. high and wide. Flower heads of all types may be dried for arrangements. Plants need good drainage.

BRAHEA (Erythea)

Arecaceae (Palmae)
PALMS
ZONES VARY BY SPECIES
FULL SUN
LITTLE OR NO WATER TO MODERATE WATER

Brahea armata

These fan palms from Mexico are somewhat like the more familiar washingtonias in appearance. Need some summer water in desert regions.

B. armata. MEXICAN BLUE PALM. Zones 10, 12–17, 19–24; H1. Hardy to 18°F/–8°C. Grows slowly to 20–40 ft. tall, top spreading 12–25 ft. Silvery blue, almost white leaves. Conspicuous creamy flowers. Takes heat and wind.

B. brandegeei. SAN JOSE HESPER PALM. Zones 13, 19, 21–24; H1, H2. Hardy to 26°F/–3°C. Slow grower to 40 ft. tall and 15 ft. wide, with slender, flexible trunk. Trunk sheds leaves when old. Leaves are 3 ft. long, light gray green.

B. edulis. GUADALUPE PALM. Zones 12–24. Hardy to below 20°F/–7°C. From Guadalupe Island off Baja California. Like *B. armata,* but leaves are light green, flowers less conspicuous. Slow grower eventually reaches to 30 ft. tall and 15 ft. wide. Old leaves drop, leaving a naked, elephant-hide, stout trunk ringed with scars. Will take beach as well as desert conditions.

B. elegans. FRANCESCHI PALM. Zones 13–17, 19–24. Hardy to 22°F/–6°C. Slowest growing of braheas. Develops a trunk very slowly and reaches only 15 ft. tall; top spreads 15 ft. Gray-green leaves.

BRAKE. See PTERIS

BRAMBLE. See RUBUS

BRASSAIA actinophylla. See SCHEFFLERA actinophylla

Brassicaceae. The mustard, or cress, family contains many food plants and ornamentals as well as a number of weeds. Shared characteristic of all is a four-petaled, cross-shaped flower. Familiar members include the cabbage group, radish, turnip, stock *(Matthiola),* and sweet alyssum *(Lobularia).* This family was formerly called Cruciferae.

BRAZILIAN BUTTERFLY TREE. See BAUHINIA forficata

BRAZILIAN FLAME BUSH. See CALLIANDRA tweedii

BRAZILIAN PLUME FLOWER. See JUSTICIA carnea

BRAZILIAN SKY FLOWER. See DURANTA stenostachya

BREADFRUIT

Moraceae
EVERGREEN TREE
ZONE H2
FULL SUN
REGULAR WATER

Breadfruit

A distinctly beautiful tropical fruit tree (known botanically as *Artocarpus altilis*) native to the South Pacific region and Malaysia; its Hawaiian name is *'ulu.* This impressive evergreen eventually reaches to 40–60 ft. high and just as wide, with huge (to 3-ft.-long), deeply lobed, leathery, shiny deep green leaves. Yellow male catkins and prickly-looking female flowers appear on the same tree but are borne in different clusters.

Bumpy, thin-skinned, round to oblong fruit is 8–12 in. long. Each fruit weighs from 2 to 9 lb., and usually contains large seeds (seeded types are called breadnuts).

Fruits in all stages of development are present on the tree throughout the year, as fruiting occurs more or less continuously; peak fruiting time in Hawaii is from summer to midwinter. Green fruit can be peeled and the white pulp boiled, roasted, fried, or baked as a vegetable. It can also be used in soups and stews much as potatoes are. If left to mature, the rind of the fruit turns brownish green. The flesh is sweet, soft pulp that can be baked or steamed as dessert.

'Ma'afala' and 'Maopo' are good seedless varieties. To fruit abundantly, breadfruit requires heat and moist, fertile soil with excellent drainage. In the greenhouse, plants need high humidity and minimum night temperatures of 60 to 70°F/16 to 21°C.

BREATH OF HEAVEN. See COLEONEMA

BREYNIA nivosa (B. disticha)

SNOW BUSH
Euphorbiaceae
EVERGREEN SHRUB
ZONES 22–24; H2; OR INDOORS
FULL SUN OR LIGHT SHADE; BRIGHT INDIRECT LIGHT
REGULAR WATER

Breynia nivosa 'Roseopicta'

Native to Melanesia. Delicate, open growth to 3–4 ft. tall and wide, with gracefully arching branches in zigzag pattern. Thin, roundish leaves nearly opposite each other along the branches are rich green variegated with white. Flowers insignificant. Tends to produce suckers from the roots; can naturalize in humid tropical or subtropical regions. More commonly seen is 'Roseopicta', sweet pea bush or calico plant, with leaves mottled red, pink, white, and green. Colorful houseplant, though prone to mites in dry atmosphere.

BRIDAL VEIL BROOM. See GENISTA monosperma

B

BRIMEURA amethystina (Hyacinthus amethystinus)

Liliaceae

PERENNIAL FROM BULB

ZONES 1–10, 14–24

FULL SUN

REGULAR WATER DURING GROWTH AND BLOOM

Brimeura amethystina

European native for rock gardens or naturalizing. In bulb and leaf, resembles small hyacinth, but 10-in. spikes of pendent, bright blue flowers in spring to summer look like bluebells. A pure white form is available. Plant in mid- to late fall (before ground freezes), 2 in. deep and 3 in. apart. In Zones 1 and 2, mulch soil after first hard frost. Keep soil moist after planting; continue to water regularly until foliage yellows after bloom. Needs no moisture during dormancy.

BRISBANE BOX. See LOPHOSTEMON confertus

BRITTLEBUSH. See ENCELIA farinosa

BRIZA maxima

RATTLESNAKE GRASS, QUAKING GRASS

Poaceae (Gramineae)

ANNUAL GRASS

ZONES 1–24

FULL SUN

NO IRRIGATION NEEDED

Briza maxima

Native to Mediterranean region. Ornamental grass of delicate, graceful form, used effectively in dried arrangements and bouquets. Grows 1–2 ft. high. Leaves are ¼ in. wide, to 6 in. long. Clusters of nodding, ½-in. or longer, seed-bearing spikelets, papery and straw colored when dry, dangle on threadlike stems. Spikelets resemble rattlesnake rattles. Scatter seed where plants are to grow; thin seedlings to 1 ft. apart. Self-sows; often grows wild along roadsides, in fields. *B. media* is similar but perennial.

BROCCOLI

Brassicaceae (Cruciferae)

BIENNIAL GROWN AS ANNUAL

ALL ZONES

FULL SUN

REGULAR WATER

Broccoli

Among cole crops (cabbage and its close *Brassica* relatives), broccoli is best all-around choice for the home gardener: bears over long season, is not difficult to raise. Thought to be a Mediterranean native. Grows 2–3 ft. tall, with a branching habit. Sends up a central stalk that bears a cluster (to 6 in. wide) of green or purple flower buds. When central cluster is removed, side branches will lengthen and produce smaller clusters. Varieties that produce tight heads include 'Packman', 'Green Comet', 'Bonanza', and 'Premium Crop'. Sprouting broccoli forms many small florets that are harvested when size of buttons. Broccoli raab (broccoli rabe), an Italian relative of broccoli, has slightly stronger flavor. 'Romanesco' broccoli produces light green heads that resemble sea coral and have the flavor and texture of cauliflower. For Chinese broccoli, see Asian Greens.

All types of broccoli are cool-season plants that tend to bolt into flower at high temperatures, so plant them to mature during cool weather. In mild climates, plant in late summer, fall, or winter for crops in winter or early spring. In cold-winter areas, set out young plants 2 to 4 weeks before last frost (young plants resist frost but not hard freezes).

Good guide to planting time is availability of plants in nurseries. Seedlings ready to be planted develop in 4 to 6 weeks from sowing. One pack of seed will produce too many plants for even the largest home garden, so save surplus seed for later plantings. A dozen plants will supply a family.

Space plants 1½–2 ft. apart in rows and leave 3 ft. between rows. Keep plants growing vigorously with regular deep irrigation during dry periods and one or two feedings of commercial fertilizer before heads start to form. Harvest 50 to 100 days after setting out plants. Cut heads before clustered buds begin to open. Include 5–6 in. of edible stalk and leaves. Subject to same pests as cabbage.

BRODIAEA

Liliaceae

PERENNIALS FROM CORMS

ZONES VARY BY SPECIES

FULL SUN

NO IRRIGATION NEEDED

Brodiaea elegans

Many are natives of the Pacific Coast, where they bloom in sunny fields and meadows in spring and early summer. Plants have a few grasslike leaves; a cluster of funnel-shaped or tubular, ½–2-in.-long flowers tops the stem during bloom. Good cut flowers. After bloom, plants die to the ground.

In nature, these plants are often found in adobe soil, in areas where rainfall is heavy in winter and early spring and corms dry out completely in summer. They appreciate similar conditions in gardens; if you can't keep corms dry in summer, plant in sandy or gritty soil. Set corms 2–3 in. deep and 2–4 in. apart. In cold-winter areas, grow in containers or mulch to protect from freezing and thawing.

Brodiaea includes many plants now listed under different names. Cross-references below will guide you to appropriate entries.

B. coronaria (B. grandiflora). HARVEST BRODIAEA. Zones 4–9, 14–24. Clusters of dark blue, inch-long flowers on 6–10-in. stems.

B. elegans. HARVEST BRODIAEA. Zones 2–9, 14–24. Like *B. coronaria* but to 16 in. tall. Often sold as *B. grandiflora* or *B. coronaria.*

B. grandiflora. See B. coronaria. Another plant known by same name is *Triteleia grandiflora.*

B. hyacinthina. See Triteleia hyacinthina

B. ixioides. See Triteleia ixioides

B. lactea. See Triteleia hyacinthina

B. laxa. See Triteleia laxa

B. lutea. See Triteleia ixioides

B. minor. Zones 7–9, 14–17, 19–24. Dark blue flowers on stems that may be 3–4 in., rarely 1 ft., long.

B. 'Queen Fabiola'. See Triteleia 'Queen Fabiola'

B. tubergenii. See Triteleia tubergenii

B. uniflora. See Ipheion uniflorum

BROMELIA balansae

HEART OF FLAME

Bromeliaceae

PERENNIAL

ZONES 13, 19–24; H1, H2

FULL SUN

REGULAR WATER

Bromelia balansae

Pineapple relative from South America grows to 4 ft. tall, 4–6 ft. across. Forms impressive cluster of 30–50 arching, saw-toothed leaves, glossy dark green above, whitish beneath. Center leaves turn bright scarlet in spring or early summer. From this center rises a stalk bearing a spike of rose-colored flowers margined with white. Needs warm nights to perform satisfactorily. Takes almost any soil but needs excellent drainage. Grow in light shade in Zone 13. Feed lightly once or twice in summer.

Bromeliaceae. In the bromelia, or pineapple, family, all members are called bromeliads. Most bromeliads are stemless perennials with clustered leaves and showy flowers in unbranched or branched clusters. Leaves of many kinds are handsomely marked, and the flower clusters gain beauty from colorful bracts. Pineapple is the best-known example.

In most areas of the West, bromeliads are considered choice houseplants. Kinds most often grown indoors are, in their native homes, epiphytes: plants that perch on trees or rocks and gain their sustenance from rain and from whatever leaf mold gathers around their roots. These often have cupped leaf bases that hold water between rains. In mildest areas of the West, many of these epiphytes grow well outdoors in sheltered places.

A few bromeliads (*Puya* is the best known) are desert plants that resemble yuccas and thrive in the same conditions.

BROOM. See **CYTISUS, GENISTA, SPARTIUM junceum**

BROUSSONETIA papyrifera

PAPER MULBERRY, WAUKE

Moraceae

DECIDUOUS TREE

ZONES 3B–24; H1, H2

FULL SUN

LITTLE TO REGULAR WATER

Broussonetia papyrifera

Native to China, Japan. Common name comes from inner bark, used for making paper and Polynesian tapa cloth. Has been sold as *Morus papyrifera.* Valuable as shade tree where soil and climate limit choices. Tolerates heat, strong winds, city pollution, and stony, sterile, or alkaline soils. Drought tolerant except in Zones 11–13, where it is considered a high-water-use tree.

Moderate to fast growth to 50 ft. tall, with dense, broad crown to 40 ft. across. Often considerably smaller and more shrublike in gardens. Suckering habit can be problem in rainy climates or highly cultivated gardens. Good in rough bank plantings. Smooth gray bark can become ridged and furrowed with age. Heart-shaped, 4–8-in. leaves are green and rough on upper surface, gray and velvety beneath; leaf edges are toothed, often lobed when young. Blooms in spring. Flowers on male trees are catkins; on female trees, rounded flower heads are followed by red fruits (in early summer) if a male tree is nearby. Needs minimal pruning (done in dormant season).

BROWALLIA

AMETHYST FLOWER

Solanaceae

ANNUALS AND PERENNIALS

ZONES VARY BY SPECIES

PARTIAL SHADE

REGULAR WATER

Browallia speciosa 'Marine Bells'

Choice plants for connoisseurs of blue flowers. Bear one-sided clusters of lobelia-like blooms in brilliant blue, violet, or white; blue and violet flowers are more striking because of contrasting white eye or throat. Bloom profusely in warm shade or filtered sunlight. Graceful in hanging baskets or pots. Fine cut flowers.

Sow seeds in early spring for summer bloom, in fall for winter color in warmest-winter areas or indoors. You can lift vigorous plants in fall, cut back, and pot; new growth will produce flowers through winter in warm spots. Usually sold as seeds.

B. americana (B. elata). Annual. All zones. Branching, 1–2 ft. high and wide; roundish leaves. Violet or blue flowers ½ in. long, ½ in. across, borne among leaves. 'Sapphire', dwarf compact variety, dark blue with white eye, is very free blooming.

B. speciosa. Perennial in Zones 17, 23, 24; H1, H2; can be grown as annual anywhere. Sprawling, to 1–2 ft. high, nearly a foot wide. Flowers dark purple above, pale lilac beneath, 1½–2 in. across. 'Blue Bells Improved', lavender blue, grows 10 in. tall, needs no pinching to make it branch. 'Marine Bells' has deep indigo flowers, 'Silver Bells' white flowers.

BRUGMANSIA (Datura)

ANGEL'S TRUMPET

Solanaceae

EVERGREEN TO SEMIEVERGREEN SHRUBS

ZONES 12, 13, 16–24; H1, H2

SUN OR SHADE

REGULAR WATER

ALL PARTS ARE POISONOUS IF INGESTED

Brugmansia × candida

South American natives related to the annual or perennial jimsonweeds. All are large shrubs that can be trained as small trees. With their oversize leaves and big, tubular flowers that bloom mainly in summer and fall, they are imposing plants that will astonish your visitors. Blooms of all species except *B. sanguinea* are fragrant, especially in the evening.

Provide a sheltered spot; wind tatters the foliage. In colder part of range, expect frost damage and unattractive winter appearance. In desert zones, they need shade. Before spring growth starts, remove all weak, dead, and crowded stems. Tubbed plants can overwinter indoors with low light and very little water.

B. arborea. Plants sold under this name are often either *B. × candida* or *B. × insignis.* The true *B. arborea* has smaller flowers than the plant commonly in cultivation.

B. × candida. Fast growing to 10–12 ft. tall and wide; dull green leaves to 1 ft. long. Sweet-scented, 8–12-in.-long cream to white trumpets hang straight down from the branches. 'Double White' has creamy white double blossoms, distinctly grayish green foliage.

B. 'Charles Grimaldi'. Vigorous California hybrid between *B. × insignis* 'Frosty Pink' and another variety. Fast growing to 10–12 ft. tall and 10 ft. wide. Huge (15-in.), golden yellow to golden orange, powerfully fragrant trumpets cover the plant during bloom season.

B. × insignis. To 10–12 ft. tall and wide. Flowers are large, flaring trumpets that point outward at 45° angle from plant; they have a spicy-sweet fragrance and come in white, pink, yellow, and orange. 'Frosty Pink' has 8–10-in., salmon pink blooms. 'Jamaica Yellow' has light yellow flowers. 'Betty Marshall' bears white blossoms on a compact plant 6–8 ft. high.

B. sanguinea. MOUNTAIN ANGEL'S TRUMPET. To 8–12 ft. tall, 6–8 ft. wide. Wavy-edged, narrow green or gray-green leaves to 6–8 in. long; narrow trumpet-shaped blooms to 8 in. long. In the typical form, flowers are orange red with yellow veins; other varieties have orange to yellow or sometimes pink flowers. Doesn't bloom well in hot summers.

B. suaveolens. Plants offered as this species are usually *B. × insignis.*

B. versicolor. The most treelike species, to 15 ft. tall and wide. Huge (15-in.) flowers are a peachy apricot color; they hang straight down from the branches, covering the plant during bloom time. Blossoms are sweetly fragrant at night and in the morning. Pink- and white-flowered varieties are also sold.

FOR INFORMATION ON YOUR CLIMATE ZONE
PLEASE SEE PAGES 27–63

BRUNFELSIA pauciflora (B. calycina)

Solanaceae

EVERGREEN TO SEMIEVERGREEN SHRUB

ZONES 12–17, 20–24, H1, H2, EXCEPT AS NOTED

PARTIAL SHADE

REGULAR WATER

ALL PARTS ARE POISONOUS IF INGESTED

Brunfelsia pauciflora 'Floribunda'

Tropical American native grown for showy clusters of white-throated, rich dark purple, tubular flowers opening to flat disks; bloom comes in spring and early summer. In all but warmest locations, loses most of foliage for a short period. These handsome plants deserve extra attention—give them rich, well-drained soil and regular feedings through the growing season. (Where soil tends to be alkaline, as in Zones 12 and 13, add iron to prevent chlorosis.) Prune in spring to remove straggly growth and to shape. Choose a planting location where you can admire the flower show. Performs well in containers. The following forms are available.

'Floribunda'. YESTERDAY-TODAY-AND-TOMORROW. Common name comes from quick color change of blossoms: they turn from purple ("yesterday") to lavender ("today") to white ("tomorrow"). Flowers, several in a cluster and each opening to 2 in. wide, are borne profusely all over plant. Oval leaves, 3–4 in. long and 1½ in. wide, are dark green above, pale green below. Plant will reach 10 ft. or taller with several stems from base, but it can be held to about 3 ft. high by pruning. Has a rather spreading habit, with width nearly equal to height.

Brunfelsia pauciflora 'Floribunda'

'Floribunda Compacta'. About two-thirds the size of the more widely planted 'Floribunda'. Flowers a bit smaller but even more generously produced.

'Macrantha' ('Magnifica'). Zones 12, 13, 16, 17, 20–24; H1, H2. In addition to being less cold hardy, differs from 'Floribunda' in having fewer but larger flowers, 2–4 in. across. Also has a more slender habit and bigger leaves (to 8 in. long, 2½ in. wide).

BRUNNERA macrophylla

BRUNNERA

Boraginaceae

PERENNIAL

ZONES 1–24

FULL SUN IN COOLER CLIMATES ONLY

REGULAR WATER

Brunnera macrophylla

Eastern European woodland plant to 1½ ft. tall, 2 ft. wide. Leaves heart shaped, dark green, 3–4 in. wide. Variegated forms also available. Airy clusters of tiny, yellow-centered, clear blue flowers reminiscent of forget-me-nots *(Myosotis)*. Blooms in spring—often into summer, especially in shade.

Brunnera is useful as an informal ground cover under high-branching deciduous trees; among spring-flowering shrubs such as forsythia, deciduous magnolias; as filler between newly planted evergreen shrubs. Freely self-sows once established. Seeds you plant may not germinate easily (try freezing them before sowing). Needs well-drained, moisture-retentive soil. Increase by dividing clumps in fall.

BRUNSVIGIA rosea. See AMARYLLIS belladonna

BRUSH CHERRY, AUSTRALIAN BRUSH CHERRY. See SYZYGIUM paniculatum

BRUSSELS SPROUTS

Brassicaceae (Cruciferae)

BIENNIAL GROWN AS ANNUAL

ALL ZONES

FULL SUN

REGULAR WATER

Brussels Sprouts

A cabbage relative (in genus *Brassica*) of unusual appearance. Mature plant has crown of fairly large leaves, and its tall stem is completely covered with small sprouts. Fairly easy to grow where summers are not too hot, long, or dry. 'Jade Cross Hybrid' is most heat tolerant; 'Valiant' has excellent flavor. 'Prince Marvel' is the earliest to harvest in Alaska. You may have to grow your own from seed. In cold-winter climates, set out seedlings you start yourself or nursery transplants in spring for summer-to-fall harvest; in mild-winter areas, plant in late summer and fall for winter-to-spring production.

Treat the same as broccoli. When big leaves start to yellow, begin picking. Snap off little sprouts from bottom first—best when slightly smaller than golf ball. Leave little sprouts on upper stem to mature. After picking, remove only leaves below harvested sprouts. A single plant will yield from 50 to 100 sprouts. Subject to same pests as cabbage.

BUCHLOE dactyloides

BUFFALO GRASS

Poaceae (Gramineae)

PERENNIAL GRASS

ZONES 1–3, 10, 11

FULL SUN

LITTLE WATER

Buchloe dactyloides

Grass native from central Montana south to Arizona makes a low-maintenance, low-water-need lawn. Slow to sprout and fill in, it spreads rapidly by surface runners once established and makes matted, reasonably dense turf that takes hard wear and looks fairly good with little summer water. Gray green from late spring to hard frost, straw colored through late fall and winter. Runners can invade surrounding garden beds. Given minimal water, it grows to 4 in. tall and requires little or no mowing. More water means higher growth, some mowing.

To start from seed, sow 2 lb. per 1,000 sq. ft. Soak occasionally to 1 ft. while grass is getting started. To start from sod, plant 4-in.-wide plugs in prepared soil 3–4 ft. apart in spring; expect coverage in two seasons.

BUCKEYE. See AESCULUS

BUCKTHORN. See RHAMNUS

BUCKWHEAT. See ERIOGONUM

BUDDLEJA

BUTTERFLY BUSH

Buddlejaceae

EVERGREEN, SEMIEVERGREEN, OR DECIDUOUS SHRUBS

ZONES VARY BY SPECIES

FULL SUN OR LIGHT SHADE

MODERATE TO REGULAR WATER

Buddleja davidii

Of the many selections—all notable for flower color, fragrance, or both—these are among the most commonly available. Grow in well-drained soil. Blossoms attract butterflies.

B. alternifolia. FOUNTAIN BUTTERFLY BUSH. Deciduous. Zones 2b–24. Native to China. To 12 ft. tall and as wide, with arching, willowlike branches rather thinly clothed with 1–4-in.-long leaves, dull dark green above, gray and hairy beneath. Profuse small clusters of mildly fragrant, lilac purple flowers make sweeping wands of color in spring. Tolerates many soils; thrives in poor, dry gravels. Prune after bloom: remove some of oldest wood to within a few inches of ground. Or train up into single- or multitrunked small tree. So trained, it somewhat resembles a small weeping willow. 'Argentea' has silvery gray foliage.

B. asiatica. Evergreen. Zones 8, 9, 14–24; H1, H2. From East Indies. To 10–15 ft. tall and wide. Tiny flowers are carried in narrow, erect spikes to 10 in. long in winter and spring; powerful fragrance suggests that of freesia. Prune after bloom. Freezing weather kills it to the ground, but it recovers to bloom the same year, behaving like a perennial.

B. crispa. Deciduous. Zones 5–7, 14–17. Native to Himalayas. To 6–10 ft. tall and wide, with silvery gray foliage and 4-in. clusters of fragrant lilac flowers with orange or white throats. Peak bloom comes in late summer. For best blooms and to keep plant neat, cut back nearly to ground in late winter. In cold-winter regions, grow in large pots or tubs and protect over winter.

B. davidii. BUTTERFLY BUSH, SUMMER LILAC. Semievergreen to deciduous. Zones 2–24; H1. Native to China, Japan. Fast, rank growth each spring and summer to 3, 4, or even 10 ft. tall and as wide. Tapering leaves are 4–12 in. long, dark green above, white and felted beneath. In midsummer, branch ends are adorned with small, fragrant flowers (lilac with orange eye) in dense, arching, spikelike, slender clusters 6–12 in. long or more. Needs good drainage and enough water to maintain growth. Cut back heavily before spring growth begins. May die to the ground in freezing weather but will regrow from roots like a perennial and bloom the same year.

The many varieties include 'Harlequin', with deep purple-red flowers and white-edged leaves, and *B. davidii nanhoensis,* which grows only 3–5 ft. tall and wide and comes in forms with white, deep blue, or reddish purple flowers.

B. globosa. ORANGE BUTTERFLY BUSH. Evergreen or semievergreen. Zones 5–9, 14–24. Native to Chile. To 10–15 ft. tall and wide. Dark green leaves are downy beneath. Late-spring or early-summer flowers are tightly clustered into ¾-in. orange balls arranged in spikelike clusters that are 6–8 in. long. Prune as for *B. alternifolia.*

Buddleja globosa

B. 'Lochinch'. Deciduous (retains its leaves in mildest-winter climates). Zones 3b–9, 14–24. Hybrid between *B. davidii* and another Asian species. Grows 5–8 ft. (or taller) and as broad, with gray foliage and light lavender-blue flowers over a long season in late summer and fall. Prune as for *B. davidii.*

B. marrubiifolia. WOOLLY BUTTERFLY BUSH. Zones 10–13, 18–24. Native to southwest Texas and northern Mexico. Densely foliaged shrub to 5 ft. tall and broad, with soft, silvery, woolly foliage and small, ball-shaped, orange flower clusters in spring and summer. Prune after bloom.

B. × weyeriana. Zones 4–24. This hybrid between *B. davidii* and *B. globosa* resembles latter parent but is deciduous (except in mildest-winter climates) and hardier, with more elongated orange-yellow flower clusters in late spring or early summer. Flowers of 'Sungold' are deeper orange, those of 'Honeycomb' a buttery yellow. Prune as for *B. alternifolia.*

BUFFALOBERRY. See SHEPHERDIA

BUFFALO GRASS. See BUCHLOE dactyloides

BUGBANE. See CIMICIFUGA

FOR GROWING SYMBOL EXPLANATIONS
PLEASE SEE PAGE 161

BULBINE frutescens (B. caulescens)

Liliaceae

SUCCULENT SHRUBBY PERENNIAL

ZONES 8, 9, 12–24

PARTIAL OR FULL SHADE IN HOTTEST CLIMATES

LITTLE TO REGULAR WATER

Bulbine frutescens

Native to South Africa. Branching, barely woody stems sprawl to make clump 1 ft. high, 2–3 ft. wide. Leaves are fleshy, bright green, and shaped like slender, pointed pencils. Produces spikelike 6–12-in. clusters of tubular bright yellow flowers resembling those of aloe or red-hot poker *(Kniphofia)* most of the year. 'Hallmark' has orange flowers with fuzzy yellow stamens; plant is more compact, less heat tolerant than species. Useful as ground or bank cover in dry, well-drained soil. Don't locate them where they will be stepped on; leaves are slippery when crushed.

BULBINELLA floribunda (B. robusta, B. setosa)

Liliaceae

PERENNIAL

ZONES 14–24

PARTIAL OR FULL SHADE IN HOTTEST CLIMATES

REGULAR WATER DURING GROWTH AND BLOOM

Bulbinella floribunda

Native to South Africa. Easy to grow from seed sown in well-drained soil in spring. In fall, forms large clump of narrow, 2-ft.-long, floppy leaves; these are topped in winter with 4-in. spikes of pure yellow flowers, splendid for cutting. Similar to red-hot poker *(Kniphofia),* but flower spikes are shorter and less pointed, and blossoms are bell shaped, not tubular. Foliage dies to the ground after bloom; pull off old, dry leaves. Keep soil on dry side during spring and summer dormancy. Good for low-maintenance borders—makes colonies quickly. Divide crowded clumps in fall.

BULL BAY. See MAGNOLIA grandiflora

BUNCHBERRY. See CORNUS canadensis

BUNNY EARS. See OPUNTIA microdasys

BUNYA-BUNYA. See ARAUCARIA bidwillii

BUPLEURUM fruticosum

SHRUBBY HARE'S EAR

Apiaceae (Umbelliferae)

EVERGREEN SHRUB

ZONES 5–9, 14–24

SUN OR SHADE

LITTLE TO REGULAR WATER

Bupleurum fruticosum

Tough Mediterranean native and unusual shrub in the parsley family. Grows 5 ft. tall and wide, clothed in thick, smooth, narrowly oval, sea green leaves 4 in. long. In summer, unbranched stems are topped by 4–5-in., rounded clusters of chartreuse flowers resembling those of parsley or dill. These last a long time and are followed by brown seeds. Can be trimmed as a hedge. Cut flowering branches make unique arrangements.

BURMESE PLUMBAGO. See CERATOSTIGMA griffithii

BURRO TAIL. See SEDUM morganianum

C

BUSH ANEMONE. See CARPENTERIA californica

BUSH MORNING GLORY. See CONVOLVULUS cneorum

BUSH POPPY. See DENDROMECON

BUSH STRAWFLOWER. See BRACTEANTHA bracteata

BUTCHER'S BROOM. See RUSCUS aculeatus

BUTIA capitata

PINDO PALM

Arecaceae (Palmae)

PALM

ZONES 8, 9, 12–24; H1, H2

FULL SUN OR LIGHT SHADE

REGULAR WATER

Butia capitata

Native to Brazil, Uruguay, Argentina. Very hardy (to 15°F/–9°C), slow-growing palm to 10–20 ft. tall, with a crown of feathery gray-green, arching leaves spreading 10–15 ft. wide. Heavy trunk is patterned with stubs of old leaves; tree is more attractive if stubs are all trimmed same length. Long spikes of small flowers are followed by showy clusters of yellow to red edible fruits in summer.

BUTTERFLY BUSH. See BUDDLEJA

BUTTERFLY FLOWER. See SCHIZANTHUS pinnatus

BUTTERFLY LILY. See HEDYCHIUM coronarium

BUTTERFLY WEED. See ASCLEPIAS tuberosa

BUTTERNUT. See JUGLANS cinerea

BUTTONBUSH. See CEPHALANTHUS occidentalis

BUTTONWOOD. See PLATANUS occidentalis

Buxaceae. The boxwood family comprises principally evergreen shrubs with inconspicuous flowers (fragrant in *Sarcococca*). Other members include boxwood *(Buxus)* and *Pachysandra*.

BUXUS

BOXWOOD, BOX

Buxaceae

EVERGREEN SHRUBS

ZONES VARY BY SPECIES

SUN OR SHADE

REGULAR WATER

Buxus microphylla japonica

Widely used for edging and hedging. When not clipped, most are soft and billowing. Flowers quite inconspicuous. All are easy to grow where adapted and therefore are often neglected. Extra care with watering, feeding, and controlling mites and scale will pay off in better color and greater vigor.

B. microphylla. The species is rarely planted. Its widely used varieties include the following.

B. m. japonica. JAPANESE BOXWOOD. Zones 3b–24, except as noted. Hardy to –10°F/–23°C but has poor winter appearance in cold-winter areas. Takes dry heat and alkaline soil, but struggles in intense heat, saline soils of desert. Compact; ½–1-in., round-tipped leaves are a lively bright green in summer, brown or bronze in winter in many areas. Grows slowly to 4–6 ft. high and wide if not pruned. Most often clipped as hedge or shaped into globes, tiers, pyramids in containers. Can keep to 6 in. tall as border edging. The following are commonly grown varieties.

'Compacta'. Slow-growing extra-dwarf plant to 1 ft. tall and wide, with tiny leaves. Good rock garden plant.

'Green Beauty'. Holds its deep green color in coldest weather and is considerably greener than *B. m. japonica* in summer heat.

'Morris Midget'. Dense, rounded, slow-growing; to 1 ft. tall and broad.

'Winter Gem'. Zones 3–24. Hardiest of Japanese boxwoods.

B. m. koreana. KOREAN BOXWOOD. Zones 2b–24. Hardy to –20°F/–29°C. Noted for its hardiness and ability to survive where others freeze. Slower growing and lower (to 2½ ft. high) than *B. m. japonica,* with smaller leaves (¼–½ in.).

B. sempervirens. COMMON BOXWOOD, ENGLISH BOXWOOD. Zones 3b–6, 15–17, except as noted. Native to southern Europe, North Africa, western Asia. Dies out in alkaline soils, hot-summer areas. Will grow to height of 15–20 ft. with equal spread. Densely foliaged with medium-size, lustrous dark green, oval leaves.

'Graham Blandy'. Narrow, columnar growth to 7–9 ft. tall, 1 ft. wide.

'Suffruticosa'. TRUE DWARF BOXWOOD. Slower growing than the species; to 4–5 ft. high but generally clipped lower. Small leaves, dense form and texture. A variegated form with silver-edged foliage is available.

'Vardar Valley'. Zones 2b–6, 15–17. To 2–3 ft. tall, 6 ft. wide. Macedonian native; considered hardiest common boxwood.

CABBAGE

Brassicaceae (Cruciferae)

BIENNIAL GROWN AS ANNUAL

ALL ZONES

TOLERATES LIGHT SHADE IN HOT CLIMATES

REGULAR WATER

Cabbage

Early varieties mature in 7 to 8 weeks from transplanting into garden; late varieties require 3 to 4 months. Many good types available. In Alaska, 'O.-S. Cross' is standard variety for giant cabbage; use a floating row cover for an early start. In addition to green cabbage, you can find red and curly-leafed (Savoy) types. For Chinese cabbages, see Asian Greens and Chinese Cabbage.

To avoid overproduction, set out a few plants every week or two, or plant both early and late kinds. Time plantings so heads will form either before or after hot summer months. Sow seeds ½ in. deep about 6 weeks prior to planting-out time. Transplant to rich, moist soil, spacing plants 2–2½ ft. apart. Give frequent light applications of nitrogen fertilizer. Never let plants wilt. Mulch helps keep soil moist and cool. Light frost doesn't hurt cabbage, but harvest and store before heavy freezes occur. In low and intermediate desert, grow as a winter crop in full sun.

To avoid soil-borne pest buildup, plant in different site each year. Row covers will protect plants from some pests such as aphids, cabbage loopers, imported cabbageworms, root maggots. Alternatively, prevent root maggots by ringing base of plant with a tar-paper collar; or cover with a cone fashioned from window screen. Collars made from paper cups or metal cans (with ends removed) also deter cutworms, which chew seedlings off at the base. *Bt* can be applied to control young larvae of cabbageworms and loopers on plants.

CABBAGE AND KALE, FLOWERING

Brassicaceae (Cruciferae)

BIENNIALS GROWN AS ANNUALS

ALL ZONES

BEST IN SUN, TOLERATE SOME SHADE

REGULAR WATER

Flowering Cabbage

Flowering cabbage and flowering kale are grown for their highly ornamental, highly colored leaf rosettes, which look like giant, deep blue-green peonies marbled and edged with white, cream, rose, or purple. Kale differs from cabbage in that its head is slightly looser and its leaf edges are more heavily fringed. Both are spectacular in the cool-season garden and appreciate the same soil, care, and timing as conventional cabbage. Plant 15–18 in. apart in open-ground beds, singly in 8-in. pots, or several in a large container. Colors are strongest after first frosts. Single rosette cut and placed on a spike holder in a decorative bowl makes a striking harvest arrangement. Foliage is edible raw or cooked and is quite striking as a salad garnish. For the edible flowering cabbage typically used in Chinese cooking, see Asian Greens.

CABBAGE PALM. See SABAL palmetto

Cactaceae. The cactus family contains a huge number of succulent plants (see also Succulents). Generally leafless, they have stems modified into cylinders, pads, or joints that store water in times of drought. Thick skin reduces evaporation, and most species have spines for protection against browsing animals. Flowers are usually large and brightly colored; fruit may also be colorful and is sometimes edible.

Almost all are native to the Americas—from Canada to Argentina, from sea level into high mountains, from deserts to dripping tropical rain forests. Many are native to drier parts of the West.

Cacti range in height from a few inches to 50 ft. tall. Larger species are used to create desert landscapes. Smaller species are grown in pots or, if sufficiently hardy, in rock gardens. Many are easy-care, showy house- or greenhouse plants. Large landscaping types require full sun, well-drained soil. Water newly planted cacti very little; roots are subject to rot before they begin active growth. In 4 to 6 weeks, when new roots are active, water thoroughly; then let soil dry before watering again. Reduce watering in fall to allow plants to go dormant. Feed monthly in spring and summer. For some larger kinds appropriate for garden use, see *Carnegiea gigantea, Cephalocereus senilis, Cereus peruvianus, Echinocactus, Echinocereus, Espostoa lanata, Ferocactus, Opuntia, Stenocereus thurberi.*

Smaller cacti for pot or rock garden culture usually have interesting forms and brightly colored flowers. Feed and water plants well during warm weather for good display; taper off on fertilizer to encourage winter dormancy. Use fast-draining planting mix. See *Coryphantha vivipara, Echinopsis, Mammillaria.*

Showiest in flower are tropical cacti that grow as epiphytes on trees or rocks. These need rich soil with much humus, frequent feeding and watering, partial shade, and protection from frost. Can be grown outdoors all year in Hawaii; elsewhere, grow in lathhouse or greenhouse, or handle as outdoor/indoor plants. See *Epiphyllum, Rhipsalidopsis, Schlumbergera.*

CAESALPINIA (Poinciana)

Fabaceae (Leguminosae)

EVERGREEN AND DECIDUOUS SHRUBS AND TREES

ZONES VARY BY SPECIES

FULL SUN

LITTLE TO MODERATE WATER

PODS AND SEEDS ARE POISONOUS IF INGESTED

Caesalpinia gilliesii

Ferny-leafed plants grown for branch-end clusters of colorful blossoms featuring (except in the case of *C. platyloba*) protruding stamens. Blooms attract hummingbirds. Plants grow quickly and easily in hot, sunny locations if given light, well-drained soil and infrequent, deep watering. Prune before first flush of spring growth to remove any dead or damaged wood and wayward branches; remove lower limbs for treelike shape in shrubby species.

C. cacalaco. CASCALOTE. Evergreen tree. Zones 12, 13, 21–24. Mexican native grows slowly to 20 ft. tall and wide, with thorny branches and bright green foliage, coarser than that of *C. pulcherrima.* Very showy, large yellow flowers carried well above branches in winter.

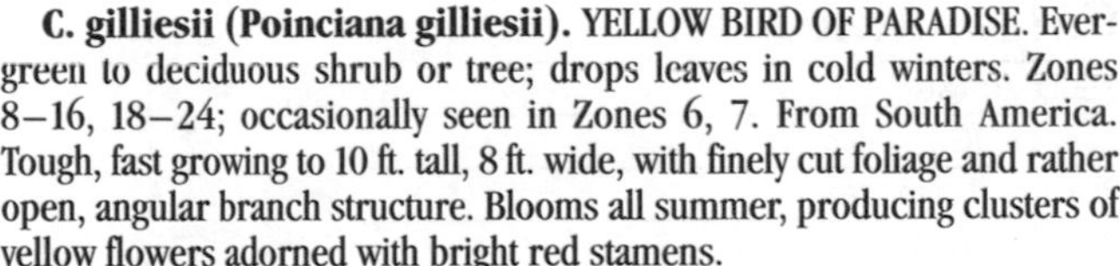

C. gilliesii (Poinciana gilliesii). YELLOW BIRD OF PARADISE. Evergreen to deciduous shrub or tree; drops leaves in cold winters. Zones 8–16, 18–24; occasionally seen in Zones 6, 7. From South America. Tough, fast growing to 10 ft. tall, 8 ft. wide, with finely cut foliage and rather open, angular branch structure. Blooms all summer, producing clusters of yellow flowers adorned with bright red stamens.

C. mexicana. MEXICAN BIRD OF PARADISE. Evergreen shrub or tree. Zones 12–16, 18–24. Moderately fast growth to 10–12 ft. tall and wide; can be kept to 6–8 ft. with pruning. Leaves are coarser than those of *C. pulcherrima.* Blooms throughout year except in coldest months, bearing 6-in. clusters of lemon yellow flowers.

C. platyloba. Evergreen tree. Zones 12, 13, 21–24. From Mexico. To 20 ft. tall and wide. Narrow, elongated clusters of tiny yellow flowers in spring lack the long, protruding stamens of other caesalpinias. Best feature is airy appearance due to open branching habit and relatively few leaflets. Leaves turn rust red in fall.

C. pulcherrima (Poinciana pulcherrima). RED BIRD OF PARADISE, DWARF POINCIANA, PRIDE OF BARBADOS. Deciduous shrub; may be evergreen in mild winters. Zones 12–16, 18–23; H1, H2. Native to tropical America. Fast, dense growth to 10 ft. tall and wide. Dark green leaves with many ¾-in. leaflets. Blooms throughout warm weather, bearing clusters of orange or red flowers with red stamens. 'Phoenix Bird' has bright yellow blooms. Various other yellow-flowered forms (including *P. c. flava*) as well as salmon-colored kinds are available in Hawaii. All are useful for quick screening.

Plants freeze to ground in colder part of range but rebound quickly in spring. In milder climates, you can cut them to ground in early spring to make more compact mound.

CAJEPUT TREE. See MELALEUCA quinquenervia

CALADIUM bicolor

FANCY-LEAFED CALADIUM

Araceae

PERENNIAL FROM TUBER

ZONE H2; OR DIG AND STORE; OR GROW IN POTS

SOME VARIETIES TOLERATE SOME SUN

REGULAR TO AMPLE WATER

SAP CAN CAUSE SWELLING IN MOUTH, THROAT

Caladium bicolor

Tropical American natives grown for foliage: large (to 1½-ft.-long), arrow-shaped, long-stalked, almost translucent leaves colored in bands and blotches of red, rose, pink, white, silver, bronze, and green. Most varieties sold in nurseries derive from *C. bicolor*—usually 2 ft. (occasionally to 4 ft.) high and wide. Most require shade. Newer varieties tolerating some sun include 'Fire Chief', 'Rose Bud', 'Red Flash', and 'White Queen'.

Caladiums need rich soil, high humidity, and heat (above 70°F/21°C during days and rarely below 60°F/16°C at nights). In Hawaii, tubers can remain in the ground all year. Elsewhere, dig and store after leaf dieback, or grow in pots and bring indoors during cold weather.

To grow in ground, plant tubers when days lengthen in spring; place them with knobby side up so tops are level with soil surface. Protect from snails and slugs. Keep well watered and feed lightly throughout growing season. Foliage may be cut back in autumn. Where freezes are likely, dig tubers; remove most of soil; dry tubers for several days in a shaded, dry location; and store in dry peat moss at 50 to 60°F/10 to 16°C.

To grow in pots, start tubers indoors in late winter, outdoors in spring. Use a soil mix made from equal parts coarse sand, leaf mold, and ground bark or peat moss. Use 5-in. pot for a 2½-in. tuber, 7-in. pot for one or two large tubers. Fill pot halfway with mix; stir in a heaping teaspoon of fish meal. Add 1 in. of potting mix, place tuber on top, cover with 2 in. of mix. Water thoroughly and keep moist until tubers sprout.

C

CALAMAGROSTIS

REED GRASS

Poaceae (Gramineae)

PERENNIAL GRASSES

ZONES 2B–24

FULL SUN OR PARTIAL SHADE

REGULAR WATER

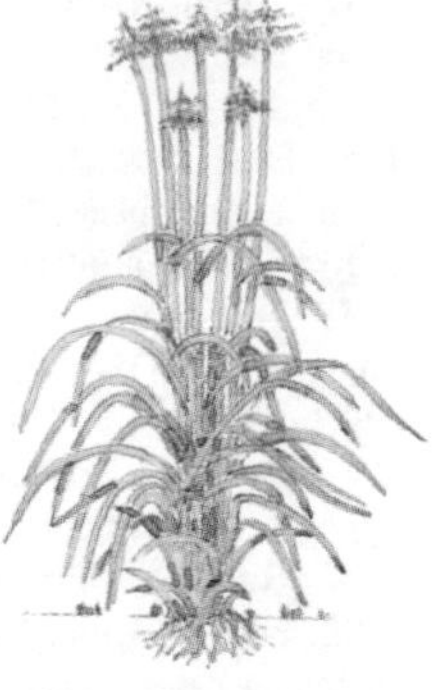

Calamagrostis × *acutiflora* 'Karl Foerster'

These Eurasian natives are sturdy, clumping grasses with feathery flower plumes that fade from purple-tinted green to yellow, then buff. These persist into winter and can be used for fresh or dried arrangements. Cut back clumps low to the ground in late winter, before new growth begins.

C. × **acutiflora.** FEATHER REED GRASS. Known mainly through these evergreen to semievergreen selections. 'Karl Foerster' ('Stricta') forms an erect, somewhat arching clump of narrow, bright green leaves 2–3 ft. tall, somewhat broader. Upright flowering stems increase the height to 6 ft. when they first appear in late spring or early summer. 'Overdam' is similar, but its foliage is variegated with white; needs partial shade in hot-summer regions.

C. brachytricha (C. arundinacea brachytricha). FALL-BLOOMING REED GRASS. Deciduous. Upright, arching clump to 1½–2½ ft. tall, 2 ft. wide. In late summer or early fall, broad flower spikes bring plant height to 4 ft.

CALAMINT. See CALAMINTHA

CALAMINTHA

CALAMINT

Lamiaceae (Labiatae)

PERENNIALS

ZONES 1–9, 14–24

FULL SUN OR LIGHT SHADE

MODERATE WATER

Calamintha grandiflora

Perennials in the mint family with pleasant-scented foliage and pretty, two-lipped flowers in clusters. Herb fanciers brew tea from the leaves. Plants need well-drained soil, winter protection in coldest zones.

C. grandiflora. Native from Mediterranean region to Iran. Creeping rhizomes produce clump 2 ft. tall and wide, with slender stems and 1½-in. pink summer flowers. Better with some shade.

C. nepeta (C. nepetoides). Native from Mediterranean region to Great Britain. To 1½ ft. high, 2½ ft. wide. Many tough, slender stems grow outward, then erect. Upper portion of the plant carries a profusion of ½-in. pale lilac to white flowers in late summer and fall.

CALAMONDIN. See CITRUS, Sour-Acid Mandarin

CALATHEA

Marantaceae

PERENNIALS

ZONE H2; OR INDOORS

PARTIAL SHADE; BRIGHT INDIRECT LIGHT

REGULAR WATER

Calathea zebrina

Native to tropical America. Ornamental leaves, beautifully marked in various shades of green, white, and pink, are arranged in basal tufts. Flowers of most are inconspicuous. Need high humidity and warm temperatures (not under 55°F/13°C). Succeed outdoors in Hawaii; elsewhere, they are indoor plants that can be brought outside in summer. Need porous soil and perfect drainage; if air is dry, also mist plants frequently. Repot as often as necessary to avoid root-bound condition. Calatheas are often mistakenly called marantas.

C. crocata. ETERNAL FLAME. To 1 ft. high, 1½ ft. wide. Leaves 6 in. long, 1–1½ in. wide, dark green above, purple beneath. Spikes, 2 in. long, consist of bright orange flower bracts that look like little torches. Leaf rosette has several shoots; each dies after blooming, but new ones appear to keep up the show. Variable performance as houseplant; subject to mites in low humidity. Does better in greenhouse.

C. lancifolia (C. insignis). To 1½–2½ ft. tall, 2 ft. wide. Long (1–1½-ft.), narrow, wavy-edged leaves are yellow green banded with dark olive green.

C. louisae. To 3 ft. tall, 1½ ft. wide. Foot-long dark green leaves heavily feathered with gray green along midrib.

C. majestica (C. ornata). To 6 ft. tall, 3 ft. wide. Leaves 2–3 ft. long, rich green above, purplish red beneath. Juvenile leaves usually pink striped between veins; intermediate foliage striped white. 'Roseolineata' has pink and white stripes at angle to midrib.

C. makoyana. Showy plant to 2 ft. high, 2½ ft. wide. Foliage colors include pale olive green, cream, and purple in featherlike, blotchy patterns, with a broad darker green border along leaf margins.

C. zebrina. ZEBRA PLANT. Compact plant to 3 ft. high, 2 ft. wide. Ellipse-shaped leaves reach 1–2 ft. long, almost half as wide. Upper surfaces are velvety green with alternating bars of pale yellow green and olive green extending outward from midrib; undersides are purplish red.

CALCEOLARIA

Scrophulariaceae

PERENNIALS

ZONES VARY BY TYPE

EXPOSURE NEEDS VARY BY TYPE

REGULAR WATER

Calceolaria Herbeohybrida

Native from Mexico to Chile. Loose clusters of small pouchlike or slipperlike flowers, usually yellow but sometimes red bronze or spotted with red or orange-brown. Bloom in spring and summer. Plants are many branched, with dark green, crinkly leaves.

C. Herbeohybrida Group. Zones 14–24; anywhere as annuals or houseplants. This is the florists' calceolaria that produces masses of velvety, inch-long yellow or red flowers, often spotted and marbled. Plants are usually grown from seed sown in spring or summer in light, porous soil; they are ready for final potting or planting out in fall. Calceolaria can reach a height of 2½ ft., but the two most popular strains are lower-growing Multiflora Nana and Multiflora, which reach only 9–15 in. high, 6–12 in. wide. Even where plants winter over, they are usually discarded after flowering. The Anytime strain tolerates high temperatures better than others; start indoors in late winter for summer bloom. Give bedding and outdoor pot plants partial or full shade. Houseplants need a sunny spot.

C. integrifolia. Zones 14–24. Woody-based plant to 3 ft. tall, 1 ft. wide. Leaves about 3 in. long, 1 in. wide. Clusters of yellow to red-brown, unspotted flowers ½ in. across. Good cut flower. 'Golden Nugget' has pure golden yellow flowers from spring to fall, 'Russet' and 'Kentish Hero' orange-red to brown blooms. Use in borders, pots, hanging baskets. Best bloom comes when root-bound. Full sun except in hottest climates, where it prefers part shade.

FOR INFORMATION ON SELECTING PLANTS
PLEASE SEE PAGES 64–160

CALENDULA officinalis

CALENDULA, POT MARIGOLD

Asteraceae (Compositae)

ANNUAL

ZONES 1–24; H1

FULL SUN

MODERATE WATER

Calendula officinalis

Mediterranean native provides sure, easy color from late fall through spring in mild-winter areas, from spring to midsummer in colder climates. Besides familiar daisylike, orange and bright yellow double blooms 2½–4½ in. across, calendulas come in subtler shades of apricot, cream, and soft yellow. Plants somewhat branching, 1–2 ft. high, 1–1½ ft. wide. Leaves are long, narrow, round on ends, slightly sticky, and aromatic. Plants are effective for masses of color in borders and parking strips, along drives, in containers. Long-lasting cut flowers.

Sow seed in place or in flats in late summer or early fall in mild-winter climates, spring elsewhere. Or buy seedlings at nurseries. Will self-sow to some degree. Adapts to most soils if drainage is fast. Remove spent flowers to prolong bloom. Although it is an excellent pot plant, the common name is actually derived from the plant's earlier use as a "pot herb"—a vegetable to be used in the cooking pot.

Dwarf strains (12–15 in. high) include Bon Bon (earliest), Dwarf Gem, and Fiesta (Fiesta Gitana). Taller (1½–2 ft. high) are Kablouna (pompon centers with looser edges), Pacific Beauty, and Radio (quilled, "cactus"-type blooms).

CALIBRACHOA

MILLION BELLS

Solanaceae

PERENNIAL OFTEN GROWN AS ANNUAL

ZONES 8, 9, 14–24 AS PERENNIAL;
ZONES 2–7, 10–13 AS ANNUAL

FULL SUN OR LIGHT SHADE

REGULAR WATER

Calibrachoa

This petunia relative is probably native to Brazil; its garden forms are the result of hybridization. Plants are smaller than petunias, with more wiry, slender stems and tiny, closely set leaves—but not all botanists believe they differ significantly enough from petunias to merit a separate genus. There are two basic types. The trailers, low and flat growing, with leaves ½ in. long and ⅛ in. wide, are called Liricashower and have white, pink, or purplish blue flowers an inch wide. A more compact and mounding, less trailing series is called Colorburst; it has somewhat larger leaves and cherry, rose, red, or violet flowers. Another grower offers both compact types and trailers under the common name "million bells"; the trailing types come in selections with blooms in blue, pink, terra-cotta, white, or yellow.

Wiry stems make the plants less subject to breakage than petunias, and tobacco budworms seem uninterested in foliage and flowers. Plants are self-cleaning (spent flowers drop off cleanly). Blooms are produced all season long and plants behave as perennials where frosts are nonexistent or light. Use them in hanging baskets, flower boxes, or as bedding plants (plant 1½ ft. apart).

CALICO FLOWER. See ARISTOLOCHIA littoralis

CALICO PLANT. See ALTERNANTHERA tenella 'Bettzickiana', BREYNIA nivosa 'Roseopicta'

CALIFORNIA BAY. See UMBELLULARIA californica

CALIFORNIA FAN PALM. See WASHINGTONIA filifera

CALIFORNIA FUCHSIA. See ZAUSCHNERIA

CALIFORNIA GERANIUM. See SENECIO petasitis

CALIFORNIA LAUREL. See UMBELLULARIA californica

CALIFORNIA NUTMEG. See TORREYA californica

CALIFORNIA POPPY. See ESCHSCHOLZIA californica

CALLA. See ZANTEDESCHIA

CALLIANDRA

Fabaceae (Leguminosae)

EVERGREEN AND DECIDUOUS SHRUBS

ZONES VARY BY SPECIES

FULL SUN, EXCEPT AS NOTED

WATER NEEDS VARY BY SPECIES

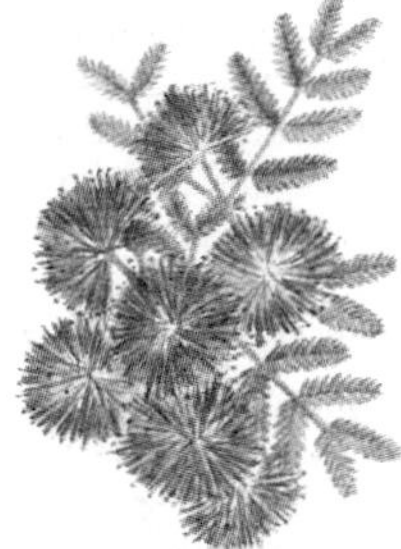

Calliandra tweedii

Group of about 200 species grown mainly for their flowers' long, silky stamens (the blossoms look like feather dusters or powder puffs) and for their ferny foliage. Prune out any dead or damaged wood after bloom.

C. californica. BAJA FAIRY DUSTER. Evergreen. Zones 10–24. Native to Baja California and Sonora, Mexico. To 5 ft. high, 5–6 ft. wide. This species is sometimes likened to *C. eriophylla,* but it's bigger, with more luxuriant foliage and bright deep red stamens.

Both the species and its hybrid 'Maricopa Red' are favorites of hummingbirds. Take little to moderate water. With moderate water, both bloom nearly year-round in Zone 13 (production drops off somewhat in midsummer and earliest winter), and close to that in Zone 12. Blooms throughout the warm parts of the year in other areas.

C. emarginata. DWARF POWDER PUFF. Evergreen. Zones 22–24; H2. Native from southern Mexico to Honduras. To 3–4 ft. tall, 4–5 ft. wide. Cerise pink flowers provide color during warmest months—or all year, if exposed to enough heat. Can be grown as annual in other climates with hot summers. Full sun or partial shade. Regular water.

C. eriophylla. FAIRY DUSTER, FALSE MESQUITE. Deciduous. Zones 10–24. Native from Southern California east to Texas and south into Baja California. Open growth to 3 ft. tall, 4–5 ft. wide. Leaves finely divided into tiny leaflets. Flower clusters show pink to white stamens in fluffy balls to 1½ in. across in late winter or early spring. No irrigation needed, but blooms and leaves (plant is summer-deciduous) will last longer with some summer water.

C. haematocephala. PINK POWDER PUFF. Evergreen. Best in Zones 22–24 and H2; will grow in Zones 13, 16–21 if protected by overhang or trained to a warm, sunny wall. Native to Bolivia. Big puffs (2–3 in. across) of watermelon red stamens from fall to early spring. There is also a white-flowered form. Leaflets are glossy copper when new, turning dark green; they are longer and broader than those of other species described here. Sprawler, growing quickly to 10 ft. high and wide—or more. Lax growth makes it very well suited to espaliering. Grow in light soil and provide regular water.

C. tweedii. BRAZILIAN FLAME BUSH, TRINIDAD FLAME BUSH. Evergreen. Best in Zones 22–24; satisfactory in Zones 15–21; freezes back but recovers in Zones 7–9, 12–14.

Native to Brazil and Uruguay, though often sold as the true Trinidad native *C. guildingii.* Graceful, picturesque growth to 6–8 ft. tall and wide. In mild-winter climates, can be pruned up to form a handsome small tree, to 15 ft. tall, with a wide, horizontal crown. Lacy, finely divided, fernlike leaves barely hide branching structure. Flower clusters, bright scarlet pompons at branch tips, are highly attractive to hummingbirds. Best flower show comes in early spring and fall, with occasional blossoms in between, but plant will bloom all winter if it gets enough heat. A white-flowered form is rarely offered. Little or no water.

C

CALLICARPA

Callicarpa bodinieri

BEAUTYBERRY

Verbenaceae

DECIDUOUS SHRUBS

ZONES VARY BY SPECIES

FULL SUN OR LIGHT SHADE

MODERATE TO REGULAR WATER

These graceful shrubs with arching branches are cultivated for their pleasing fruit display. Small lilac or pink flowers in summer are followed by tight clusters of little, round violet to purple fruits that persist well into winter. Effective in woodland gardens or massed in shrub borders. Bloom and fruit occur on current season's growth, so in late winter remove about a third of oldest stems or lop whole plant low to ground. In coldest regions, may freeze to ground but come back from roots.

C. americana. AMERICAN BEAUTYBERRY. Zones 3–9, 14–24. Native to eastern U.S. To 6 ft. tall, 5 ft. wide. Leaves to 6 in. long turn purplish in fall. Biggest, coarsest foliage of the species listed here.

C. bodinieri. BODINIER BEAUTYBERRY. Zones 3–9, 14–24. Native to China. Grows to 6 ft. or more and nearly as wide, with willowlike leaves that turn pink or orange to purple in fall. 'Profusion' is a heavy bearer.

C. dichotoma. PURPLE BEAUTYBERRY. Zones 2b–9, 14–24. Native to China, Korea, Japan. About 4 ft. tall and slightly wider, with slender branches that sweep the ground. Resembles a smaller, finer-textured *C. bodinieri.* 'Issai' bears abundant purple fruits. *C. d. albifructus* has white fruit.

C. japonica. JAPANESE BEAUTYBERRY. Zones 2b–9, 14–24. Native to China, Taiwan, Japan. To 5 ft. tall and wide, with deep reddish purple fall foliage. 'Leucocarpa' bears white fruit.

CALLIOPSIS. See COREOPSIS tinctoria

CALLIRHOE involucrata

Callirhoe involucrata

POPPY MALLOW, WINE CUPS

Malvaceae

PERENNIAL

ZONES 1–3, 7–14, 18–24

PARTIAL SHADE IN HOTTEST CLIMATES

LITTLE TO MODERATE WATER, EXCEPT AS NOTED

Native from Missouri to Wyoming, south to Texas. Thick, fleshy root produces a spreading plant 6 in. tall and 2–3 ft. wide, with roundish, deeply cut leaves and a profusion of 2-in., purplish red, mallow-type flowers during hot weather. Needs good drainage but survives in infertile soil and intense heat. Except in desert regions, useful on hot slopes and in areas that get little attention. In hot desert, provide some shade and regular summer water.

CALLISTEMON

Callistemon citrinus

BOTTLEBRUSH

Myrtaceae

EVERGREEN SHRUBS OR TREES

ZONES VARY BY SPECIES

FULL SUN

MODERATE TO REGULAR WATER

Fast growing, with colorful flowers carried in dense spikes or round clusters consisting mainly of long, bristlelike stamens—hence the common name "bottlebrush." Attractive to hummingbirds. Flowers are followed by woody capsules that can last for years and may resemble rows of beads pressed into bark.

Some bottlebrushes are naturally dense and compact (making good informal hedges); others are sparse and open (can be pruned up to become small trees). Those with pliant branches can be grown as informal espaliers. Very little routine pruning is needed—just remove any weak or dead branches after bloom or before spring growth flush. Don't cut into bare wood beyond leaves—plant may not send out new growth. Generally found in moist ground in their native Australia, they can withstand waterlogged soil. Normally tolerant of saline or alkaline soils but sometimes suffer from chlorosis. Often severely damaged at 20°F/–7°C.

C. citrinus (C. lanceolatus). LEMON BOTTLEBRUSH. Zones 8, 9, 12–24; H1, H2. Most commonly grown bottlebrush; most tolerant of heat, cold, and poor soils. Massive shrub to 10–15 ft. tall and wide, but with staking and pruning in youth easily trained into narrowish, round-headed, 20–25-ft. tree. Nurseries offer it as shrub, espalier, or tree. Narrow, 3-in.-long leaves are coppery when new, maturing to vivid green. Bruised leaves smell lemony. Bright red, 6-in.-long brushes appear in waves throughout the year.

Variable plant when grown from seed. Cutting-grown selections with good flower size and color include 'Improved' and 'Splendens'. 'Compacta' makes a 4-ft. mound with smaller spikes. 'Violaceus' ('Jeffersii'), about 6 ft. tall and 4 ft. wide, has stiffer branching; narrower, shorter leaves; and reddish purple flowers fading to lavender. 'Mauve Mist' is the same but can reach 10 ft. 'Perth Pink', 10 ft. tall, has pink flower clusters.

C. rigidus. STIFF BOTTLEBRUSH. Zones 8, 9, 12–24; H1, H2. Rigid, sparse shrub or small tree to 20 ft. with 10-ft. spread. Leaves sharp pointed, gray green (sometimes purplish). Spring and summer red flower brushes are 2½–4½ in. long. Produces prominent seed capsules. Least graceful of the bottlebrushes.

C. salignus. WHITE BOTTLEBRUSH. Zones 8, 9, 12–24. Shrub or tree to 20–25 ft. tall, 10–15 ft. wide. Dense crown of foliage. New growth bright pink to copper. Willowlike leaves 2–3 in. long. Pale yellow to cream-colored flowers appear in 1½–3-in. clusters in spring, early summer. Train as small shade tree or plant 4–5 ft. apart as hedge.

C. viminalis. WEEPING BOTTLEBRUSH. Zones 6–9, 12–24. Shrub or small tree with pendulous branches. Fast growing to 20–30 ft. tall, with 15-ft. spread. Leaves narrow, light green, 6 in. long. Bright red brushes from late spring into summer, scattered bloom rest of year. Not for windy, dry areas. As tree, needs staking, thinning to prevent tangled, top-heavy growth. Leaves tend to grow toward ends of long, hanging branches.

Callistemon viminalis

'Little John' is a superior dwarf form to 3 ft. tall and wide, with dense growth pattern and blood red flowers in fall, winter, and spring. 'Captain Cook' is a dense, rounded form to 6 ft. tall and wide, suitable for border, low hedge, or screen. 'McCaskillii' has even denser habit than others, is more vigorous (to 20 ft. tall), and has better flower color and form.

CALLISTEPHUS chinensis

Callistephus chinensis

CHINA ASTER

Asteraceae (Compositae)

ANNUAL

ZONES 1–24

FULL SUN

REGULAR WATER

Chinese native is a splendid cut flower and an effective bedding plant when well grown and free of disease. Plants are from 8 in. to 3 ft. high, 10–18 in. wide. Some kinds are branching; others (developed mainly for florists) have strong stems and no side shoots. Leaves are deeply toothed or lobed.

Bloom comes in summer. Many different flower forms: quilled, curled, incurved, ribbonlike, or with interlaced rays; some have crested centers. Varieties are classified as peony flowered, pompon, anemone flowered, and ostrich feather. Colors range from white to pastel pink, rose pink, lavender, lavender blue, violet, purple, crimson, wine, and scarlet.

Plant in rich, loamy or sandy soil. After danger of frost is past, sow seed in place or set out plants started in flats. Keep growth steady; sudden checks in growth are harmful. Subject to aster yellows, a viral disease carried by leafhoppers. Discard infected plants; control leafhoppers. All but wilt-resistant types are subject to aster wilt or stem rot, caused by a parasitic fungus that lives in soil and is transmitted through roots into plants. Overwatering produces ideal condition for diseases, especially in heavy or poorly drained soil. Never plant in same location in successive years.

CALLUNA vulgaris

SCOTCH HEATHER

Ericaceae

EVERGREEN SHRUB

ZONES 1A, 2–6, 15–17

FULL SUN

REGULAR WATER

Calluna vulgaris

This, the true and only Scotch heather, which is native from Europe to Asia Minor, has crowded, tiny, scalelike, dark green leaves and spikes of bell-shaped, rosy pink flowers. Garden varieties (far more common than wild species) range from dwarf ground cover and rock garden plants only a couple of inches high to kinds reaching 3 ft. tall. Taller varieties make good backgrounds for lower sorts and are attractive cut flowers. Blossom colors include white, pale to deep pink, lavender, and purple. Foliage—paler and deeper greens, chartreuse, yellow, gray, or russet—often changes color in winter. Most bloom in mid- to late summer; a few bloom into late fall. To prune, shear off faded flowers and pinch tips immediately after bloom (with types blooming into late fall, delay pruning until late winter).

Heathers thrive in sandy, peaty, fast-draining soil. In the Northwest, they are especially well adapted and require little or no fertilizing. Where watering must be frequent, light feeding with acid plant food—once in late winter, again in early summer—will encourage good growth and bloom.

Here are some of the many varieties available from specialists. All begin blooming in summer, except as noted.

'Aurea'. Spreading, twiggy, to 1 ft. tall, 1½ ft. wide. Gold foliage turns russet in winter. Sparse purple bloom.

'Aureafolia'. Upright, to 1½–2 ft. high, 2 ft. wide. Chartreuse foliage, tinged gold in summer. White flowers.

'Blazeaway'. To 14 in. high, 2 ft. wide. Pale foliage with apricot tints, emerging bronzy. Lavender flowers.

'Corbett Red'. Compact grower to 10 in. high, 1½ ft. wide, with dark green foliage. Violet-red flowers.

'County Wicklow'. Mounding, to 10 in. high, 14 in. wide. Medium green foliage; pink double flowers from white buds.

'Cuprea'. Compact, to 1 ft. high, 15 in. wide. Coppery yellow foliage; mauve flowers.

'Dainty Bess'. Tiny gray leaves form a foot-wide, 2–4-in.-tall mat that shapes itself to rocks, crevices. Lavender flowers.

'David Eason'. Spreading mound, 1 ft. tall, 2 ft. wide. Light green foliage; reddish purple flowers. Fall bloomer.

'Else Frye'. Erect plant to 2 ft. tall and wide. Medium green foliage; double white flowers.

'Foxii Nana'. Small mound to 4 in. high, 1 ft. wide. Dark green foliage; purple flowers.

'Goldsworth Crimson'. Mounding, 1½–2 ft. high, 2 ft. wide. Dark or smoky green foliage; crimson flowers. Fall bloomer.

'H. E. Beale'. Loose mound to 2 ft. tall and wide. Dark green foliage; soft pink double flowers. Long spikes are good for cutting.

'J. H. Hamilton'. Prostrate, bushy, to 4 in. high, 1 ft. wide. Deep green foliage; profuse double pink blooms.

'Kinlochruel'. Mounding, to 10 in. tall, 20 in. wide. Bright green foliage, double white flowers.

'Mair's Variety'. Erect, 2–3 ft. tall and wide. Medium green foliage; white flowers. Easy to grow; good background plant.

'Martha Hermann'. Compact, to 1 ft. high, 14 in. wide. Lime green leaves; white flowers.

'Minima Prostrata'. Nearly flat habit, spreading about 1½ ft. wide. Foliage dark green in summer, turning bronze in winter. Produces light rose purple flowers.

'Mrs. Pat'. Bushy, to 8 in. high, 15 in. wide. Light green foliage; pink new growth. Light purple flowers.

'Mrs. Ronald Gray'. Creeping mound to 2 in. high, 14 in. wide. Dark green foliage; reddish purple flowers. Excellent ground cover.

'Mullion'. Tight mound to 10 in. high, 20 in. wide. Dark green foliage, rosy purple flowers. Fine ground cover.

'Nana'. Low, spreading, to 4 in. high, 1 ft. wide. Dark green foliage; purple flowers. Often called carpet heather.

'Nana Compacta'. Tight mound to 4 in. high, 6 in. wide. Medium green foliage. Purple flowers. Pincushion heather for rockery.

'Peter Sparkes'. Mounding, to 15 in. tall, 20 in. wide. Dark green foliage; double deep pink flowers.

'Robert Chapman'. Spreading, to 10 in. high, 2 ft. wide. Greenish to reddish orange foliage; mauve flowers.

'Serlei'. Bushy, 1–1½ ft. high, 1½ ft. wide. Yellow-green feathery foliage; white flowers.

'Silver King', 'Silver Knight', 'Silver Queen'. Varieties with light gray-green foliage and pink flowers. All grow 1½ ft. high, 20 in. wide.

'Spring Torch'. Spreading, to 1 ft. tall, 20 in. wide. Red-tipped green foliage and pink flowers.

'Tib'. Rounded, bushy, to 1 ft. high, 15 in. wide. Medium green foliage; deepest rosy purple double flowers.

'Wickwar Flame'. Mounding, to 1½ ft. tall, 2 ft. wide. Yellow to red foliage, lavender flowers.

CALOCEDRUS decurrens (Libocedrus decurrens)

INCENSE CEDAR

Cupressaceae

EVERGREEN TREE

ZONES 2–12, 14–24

FULL SUN OR LIGHT SHADE

NO IRRIGATION TO MODERATE WATER

Calocedrus decurrens

Native to the mountains of central and southern Oregon, California, western Nevada; also to northern Baja California. Unlike most of its native associates—white fir, Douglas fir, sugar pine—it adapts to many other Western climates. Symmetrical tree to 75–90 ft. tall with dense, narrow, pyramidal crown; give it room for a 10–15-ft. spread at base. Reddish brown bark on trunk. Rich green foliage in flat sprays. Tree gives pungent fragrance to garden in warm weather. Bears small, yellowish brown to reddish brown cones that, when open, look like ducks' bills.

Although slow growing at first, it may grow 2 ft. per year when established. Takes blazing summer heat and tolerates poor soils. No supplemental water needed in Zones 2, 4–7, 15–17; give moderate water elsewhere. Good tree to make green wall, high screen, windbreak. No pruning required.

FOR DEFINITIONS OF GARDENING TERMS
PLEASE SEE PAGES 746–750

C

CALOCEPHALUS brownii (Leucophyta brownii)

CUSHION BUSH

Asteraceae (Compositae)

EVERGREEN SHRUB

ZONES 16, 17, 19, 21–24

FULL SUN

MODERATE TO REGULAR WATER

Calocephalus brownii

Native to Australia, Tasmania. Silvery white throughout, this unusual mounding plant to 3 ft. high and wide thrives when buffeted by winds and exposed to salt air and spray. (Grows best in Zones 17, 24.) Tiny threadlike leaves, ⅛ in. long, are pressed tightly against wiry, branching stems. Flower heads are button shaped, ½ in. across, in clusters. Stunning high ground cover or rock garden plant. Effective in large planters with succulents. Fresh or dried foliage is attractive in arrangements. Provide sandy or gravelly soil, fast drainage. Cut out dead wood on older plants.

CALOCHORTUS

Liliaceae

PERENNIALS FROM BULBS

ZONES VARY BY SPECIES

FULL SUN OR LIGHT SHADE

REGULAR WATER DURING GROWTH AND BLOOM

Calochortus

Beautiful Western natives, most common in California. One type, sego lily *(C. nuttallii),* is the state flower of Utah. Among the more challenging bulbs for the garden, as they demand the long, warm, dry summers of their native habitats. Sparse, grassy foliage is common to all types, but there are three distinct flower forms. Globe tulips or fairy lanterns have nodding flowers, the petals turning inward to form a globe. Star tulips have upward-facing, cup-shaped flowers, with petal tips often rolled outward; those with long, straight hairs on the inner flower parts are called "cat's ears" or "pussy ears." Mariposa lilies are generally the tallest, with striking cup- or bowl-shaped flowers. Flower colors include yellow, purple, lavender, red, pink, and white. Bloom time for most is spring or early summer.

May be difficult to find; check bulb specialists or local plant sales. It's best to plant kinds indigenous to your area; at least one type or another is available in Zones 1–9, 14–24. All can be grown in rock gardens or naturalized on sunny, grassy hillsides if they can be kept dry in summer. Or you can grow them in containers that you bury, then lift after bloom and store. Plant in fall, setting bulbs 3–4 in. deep and about 6 in. apart in well-drained soil.

CALODENDRUM capense

CAPE CHESTNUT

Rutaceae

BRIEFLY DECIDUOUS TREE

ZONES 19, 21–24; WORTH RISKING IN 15, 16

FULL SUN

REGULAR WATER

Calodendrum capense

Native to South Africa. Slow growing to 25–40 ft. tall and wide, with light to medium green, oval leaves to 6 in. long. Seldom flowers before the age of about 5 years, but the show is noteworthy when it does come: profuse spikes of rosy lilac, 1½-in.-long flowers. Whole flower cluster measures 10–12 in. high by as much across, and extends well above foliage, giving effect of candelabra. Generally blooms from late spring into summer, but time of flowering and deciduous period varies, depending on where tree is planted. Locate out of prevailing wind. Light, sandy soils are not to its liking.

CALONYCTION aculeatum. See IPOMOEA alba

CALTHA palustris

MARSH MARIGOLD

Ranunculaceae

PERENNIAL

ZONES A1–A3; 1–9, 14–24

SUN OR SHADE

AMPLE WATER

ANY PART CAN CAUSE INFLAMMATION, PAIN IF INGESTED

Caltha palustris

Native from Alaska to Newfoundland. To 2 ft. tall and wide; well adapted to edges of pools, ponds, streams, other moist situations. With sufficient water it can be grown in borders but must not dry out in summer. Good with bog irises, moisture-loving ferns. Lush, glossy green leaves 2–7 in. across give an almost tropical effect. Clusters of 2-in., vivid yellow flowers in spring; a double-flowered form is available. Marsh marigold is vigorous; increase by divisions or sow seed in boggy soil.

Calycanthaceae. The calycanthus family contains shrubs with paired opposite leaves and flowers that somewhat resemble small water lilies—each bloom has an indefinite number of segments not easily defined as petals or sepals. *Calycanthus* and wintersweet *(Chimonanthus praecox)* are typical.

CALYCANTHUS

Calycanthaceae

DECIDUOUS SHRUBS

ZONES VARY BY SPECIES

SUN OR SHADE

REGULAR WATER

SEEDS CAN PRODUCE CONVULSIONS

Calycanthus occidentalis

Both species described here are bulky, clump-forming shrubs with lush foliage and flowers valued for their fragrance and form. Blossoms are produced at ends of current season's growth. Remove twiggy or crowded stems annually, but for best appearance don't prune further.

C. floridus. CAROLINA ALLSPICE. Zones 3–9, 14–17. Native from Virginia to Florida. Stiffly branched to 6–10 ft. tall and as wide or wider; suckering, fast spreading. Oval leaves to 5 in. long are glossy dark green above, grayish green beneath. Flowers—2 in. wide, reddish brown, with heady, strawberrylike fragrance—are carried at ends of leafy branchlets in late spring or early summer. Blooms are followed by brownish, pear-shaped capsules, fragrant when crushed. Plant in shrub border or around outdoor living space where flower scent can be appreciated. Aroma varies, so buy plants in bloom. 'Athens' has yellow flowers.

C. occidentalis. SPICE BUSH. Zones 4–9, 14–24. Native along streams, moist slopes in California's Coast Ranges and Sierra Nevada foothills. To 4–12 ft. high and wide. Bright green leaves are 2–6 in. long, 1–2 in. wide, turn yellow in fall. Brownish red flowers to 2 in. across, resembling small water lilies, appear in mid- to late spring or summer, depending on climate. Both flowers and bruised leaves have fragrance of an old wine barrel. Can be trained into multistemmed small tree, but is most useful as a background shrub or medium to tall screen. Easily grown from seed.

CALYLOPHUS

SUNDROPS

Onagraceae

PERENNIALS

ZONES 1–3, 6–16, 18–24

FULL SUN OR LIGHT SHADE

LITTLE TO MODERATE WATER

Calylophus hartwegii

Western natives related to and much resembling evening primrose *(Oenothera),* with bright yellow, four-petaled flowers over a long summer bloom period. In Zone 13, flowering declines in summer heat, and plants flower in spring and from late summer to fall. Spread by rhizomes and are useful for summer color in difficult climates. Shear just before spring growth begins. Plant in well-drained soil. Tolerate regular water if drainage is superb.

C. drummondianus. To 1½ ft. high, 2 ft. wide, with narrow, tooth-edged, somewhat drooping leaves and inch-wide flowers. This species blooms for a longer period than *C. hartwegii* in spring, but it does not rebloom as well in fall.

C. hartwegii. To 1 ft. high, 2 ft. across, with inch-wide flowers; those of 'Sierra Sundrop' are larger. *C. h. lavandulifolius (C. lavandulifolius)* has narrow, gray leaves. Excellent in hot, dry locations and when mixed with desert perennials.

C. serrulatus. Prairie wildflower found from Saskatchewan to Texas. To 1½ ft. high and wide, with ¾-in. flowers.

CALYTRIX

Myrtaceae

EVERGREEN SHRUBS

ZONES 15–24

FULL SUN OR LIGHT SHADE

MODERATE WATER

Calytrix alpestris

These Australian shrubs have tiny evergreen leaves and a profusion of small but showy star-shaped flowers from late winter into summer. They need excellent drainage and should be kept compact by pruning after bloom. They can be used for low-maintenance plantings or for screening.

C. alpestris. SNOW MYRTLE. Graceful, open growth to about 5 ft. tall, 5–6½ ft. wide. Pink buds open to white flowers.

C. tetragona. FRINGE MYRTLE. To 3–6 ft. tall and wide, with white or pink flowers followed by calyxes that age to deep red or purple for prolonged color. Choice cut flower.

CAMASSIA

CAMASS

Liliaceae

PERENNIALS FROM BULBS

ZONES 1–9, 14–17, EXCEPT AS NOTED

FULL SUN OR LIGHT SHADE

AMPLE WATER DURING GROWTH AND BLOOM

Camassia quamash

Most are native to moist meadows, marshes, fields in Northern California and Pacific Northwest. Rosettes of grasslike leaves send up slender spikes of loosely spaced, starlike blossoms in spring. Plant in fall after weather cools, setting bulbs 3–4 in. deep, 6 in. apart in good, moisture-retentive soil. Locate bulbs where they can remain undisturbed for many years. Because plants die down completely after bloom, set them where other plants will hide their yellowing leaves and fill in when leaves are gone. Bulbs can get by with less water during summer dormancy.

C. cusickii. Dense clusters of pale blue flowers on stems to 3 ft. tall.

C. leichtlinii. Large, handsome clusters of creamy white flowers on stems to 4 ft. tall. *C. l. suksdorfii* (often sold as *C. l.* 'Coerulea') has blue to deep blue-violet flowers. This subspecies' variety 'Blue Danube' is deep blue. Varieties of the species include 'Alba' *(C. l. leichtlinii),* white with bluish tinge, and 'Semiplena', with creamy white semidouble blooms.

C. quamash (C. esculenta). Zones 1–10, 14–17. Loose clusters of blue flowers on 1–2-ft. stems. Flowers of 'Orion' are deeper blue, those of 'San Juan Form' deeper still.

CAMELLIA

Theaceae

EVERGREEN SHRUBS OR TREES

ZONES 4–9, 12, 14–24, EXCEPT AS NOTED

BEST OUT OF STRONG SUN

MODERATE TO REGULAR WATER

Camellia hiemalis

Native to eastern and southern Asia. There are over 3,000 named kinds, and the range in color, size, and form is remarkable.

The following pages briefly discuss the cultural requirements of camellias and describe some of the lesser-known species as well as the widely distributed old favorites and new varieties. The plant descriptions include cultural needs unique to individual species and varieties, beyond the general requirements detailed in this introduction.

Exposure and watering. Though camellias grow and bloom best when protected from strong sun, some kinds are more sun tolerant than others. Tall old plants prove that camellias can thrive in full sun when they are mature enough for their roots to be shaded by heavy leaf canopy. Young plants will grow better and bear more attractive flowers if grown in partial shade under tall trees, under lath cover, or on north side of a building. (Grow in deep shade in desert.) A few camellias need shade at any age.

Established plants (over 3 years old, vigorous, and shading their own roots) can get by with little supplemental water. If you give them regular water, be sure soil is well drained.

Fertilizing. Fertilize with a commercial acid plant food. Generally, the time to feed is in weeks and months following bloom; read fertilizer label for instructions. Don't use more than recommended; better to cut suggested amounts in half and feed twice as often. Never feed sick plants.

WHAT CAMELLIAS NEED

SOIL: Give them well-drained soil rich in organic material. Never plant so trunk base is below soil line, and never let soil cover base. Keep roots cool with 2-in.-thick mulch (kept away from base).

WATERING: Though camellias appreciate regular water (as long as drainage is good), established older plants can survive—even thrive—on fairly little supplemental moisture.

FERTILIZING: Feed with a commercial acid plant food, being sure not to overfertilize plants.

SHELTER: Protect plants from strong, hot sun and drying winds.

PRUNING: Some judicious pruning right after flowering or during summer and fall will improve plant appearance and next year's flower display.

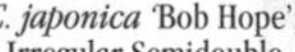

C. japonica 'Bob Hope'; Irregular Semidouble

C

Camellia problems. Poor drainage and water or soil containing excess salts are the main troublemakers for camellias. Best cure is to move plant into aboveground bed of pure ground bark or peat moss until it recovers. If you irrigate your camellias with water high in salts, leach out accumulated salts with deep soaking—twice in summer—to dissolve harmful salts and carry them deep below the root zone.

Scorched or yellowed areas in center of leaves are usually due to sunburn. Burned leaf edges, excessive leaf drop, or corky spots usually indicate overfertilizing. Yellow leaves with green veins are signs of chlorosis; treat with iron or iron chelates.

One disease may be serious: camellia petal blight. Flowers rapidly turn an ugly brown. Browning at edges of petals (especially on whites and pale pinks) may be caused by sun or wind, but if brown rapidly runs into center of flower, suspect petal blight. Sanitation is the best control. Pick up all fallen flowers and petals, pick off all infected flowers from plants, and dispose of them in covered trash bin; encourage neighbors to do the same. Remove any mulch, haul it away, and replace with fresh materials; a deep mulch (4–5 in.) helps keep spores of the fungus from reaching the air.

In the Pacific Northwest, *C. japonica* is very susceptible to cottony camellia scale and soft brown scale; worst symptom is sooty mold on foliage and stems. This damage, along with frequent browning of blossoms in rainy spring weather, has dampened the enthusiasm of gardeners in the Northwest for growing camellias.

Some flower bud dropping in all regions may be natural; many camellias set more buds than they can open. Bud drop can be caused by overwatering, but more often by underwatering, especially during summer. It can also be caused by spells of very low humidity.

Pruning. Prune away dead or weak wood and thin when growth is so dense that flowers have no room to open properly. Prune at will to get form you want; shorten lower branches to encourage upright growth, or cut back top growth to flatten lanky shrubs. Make cut just above scar that terminates previous year's growth (often a slightly thickened, somewhat rough area where bark texture and color change slightly). A cut just above this point will usually force three or four dormant buds into growth.

Some varieties bear too many flowers. To get nicest display from them, remove buds in midsummer like this: from branch-end clusters remove all but one or two round flower buds (leaf buds are more slender); along stems, remove enough to leave a single flower bud for each 2–4 in. of branch.

Camellias in containers. Camellias make outstanding container plants—especially in wooden tubs and half-barrels. As a general rule, plant gallon-size camellias into 12–14-in.-wide tubs, 5-gallon ones into 16–18-in. tubs. Fill with a planting mix containing 50 percent or more organic material.

Flower forms. The American Camellia Society defines six basic camellia flower forms; these are illustrated by the photographs below.

Single. One row (a single layer) of up to eight petals surrounding a conspicuous cluster of stamens.

Semidouble. Two or more rows (layers) of regular, irregular, or loose petals surrounding a conspicuous cluster of stamens.

Anemone form. One or more rows (layers) of petals, flat or undulating, surrounding a central mound of intermingled petaloids and stamens.

Peony form. Mounded to nearly ball-shaped flower consisting of petals in no regular arrangement, forming a sort of powder-puff effect. In loose peony form, blossoms contain loose petals (some irregular) intermingled with stamens. In full peony form, flowers are a tighter mass of petals, petaloids, and stamens, or petals and petaloids with no stamens visible.

Rose-form double. Multiple layers of regularly overlapping (imbricated) petals revealing a central cluster of stamens when flowers are fully open.

Formal double. Flowers consisting of multiple layers of imbricated petals, never showing stamens even when fully open.

C. chrysantha. GOLDEN CAMELLIA. Tall, vigorous, open grower to 6–16 ft. tall, 10–12 ft. wide, with large (6-in. or longer), glossy, net-veined leaves and 2–2½-in., golden yellow flowers. Hybridizers use it to expand the camellia color palette.

C. granthamiana. Becomes a big shrub or small tree of rather open growth to 10 ft. tall, 6 ft. wide, with leathery, glossy, heavily veined, and crinkled leaves 2–6 in. long. Flowers are large (to 6 in. or more), white, single, often with fluted or folded ("rabbit ear") petals and a heavy central tuft of bright yellow stamens. Flowers open in autumn from large, brown, scaly, silky-haired buds. A cross between this species and *C. reticulata* produced 'China Lady', which looks like a big pink *C. granthamiana.* It has been the parent of several other remarkable seedling camellias. Needs excellent drainage; avoid overwatering.

C. hiemalis. Includes a number of varieties formerly listed as sasanquas but differing in their later, longer bloom and heavier-textured flowers. Four good examples follow.

'Chansonette'. Vigorous, spreading growth to 6 ft. high, 8 ft. wide. Large, bright pink, formal double flowers with frilled petals.

'Shishi-Gashira'. One of the most useful and ornamental shrubs. Low growing (3 ft. high and 6 ft. wide), with arching branches that in time pile up tier on tier to make a compact, dark green, glossy-leafed plant. Leaves rather small for camellia, giving medium-fine foliage texture. Flowers rose red, semidouble to double, 2–2½ in. wide, heavily borne over long season—fall through winter in a good year. Full sun or shade.

'Showa-No-Sakae'. To 3 ft. high, 6–8 ft. wide. Faster growing, more open than 'Shishi-Gashira'; willowy, arching branches. Semidouble to double flowers of soft pink, occasionally marked with white. Try this as espalier or in hanging basket.

'Showa Supreme'. Very similar to above but has somewhat larger flowers of peony form.

C. japonica. Zones 4–9, 12, 14–24; H1. This is the plant most gardeners have in mind when they speak of camellias. Naturally a large shrub or small tree but variable in size, growth rate, and habit. Hundred-year-old plants in California reach 20 ft. high and equally wide, and even larger specimens exist. However, most gardeners can consider japonicas to be shrubs 6–12 ft. high and wide. Many are lower growing.

Higo camellias are a category of japonicas that has been bred for more than 200 years in Japan. Generally compact plants, they have dense, heavy foliage and thick-petaled single flowers with a broad, full brush of stamens in the center. In the ideal Higo camellia, mass of stamens should be at

Camellia Flower Forms

Camellia sasanqua 'Apple Blossom'; Single

Camellia japonica 'C. M. Wilson'; Anemone Form

Camellia japonica 'Alba Plena'; Formal Double

Camellia japonica 'Purity'; Rose-Form Double

Camellia japonica 'Debutante'; Peony Form

Camellia hiemalis 'Shishi-Gashira'; Semidouble to Double

least half the diameter of flower. Colors include white, pink, and red—both solid and variegated, as with regular japonicas.

The following list describes japonica varieties that are favorites among Western gardeners. Included here are a number of old standbys whose beauty belies their age. Some of them are among the oldest varieties still in commerce, having been brought to Europe and the U.S. from China and Japan in the 19th century or even earlier (these venerable camellias are noted by date of introduction in the text).

The list specifies season of bloom as early, midseason, or late. In California, early means October to January; midseason, January to March; late, March to May. In the Southwest, early means October to December; midseason, January and February; late, March and April. In the Northwest, early means December to February; midseason, March and April; late, May. Flower size is also noted for each variety. Very large blooms are over 5 in. wide; large, 4–5 in.; medium-large, 3½–4 in.; medium, 3–3½ in.; small, 2½–3 in.; and miniature, 2½ in. or less.

'Adolphe Audusson' (1877). Midseason. Very large, dark red semidouble flowers, heavily borne on a medium-size, symmetrical, vigorous shrub. Hardy. 'Adolphe Audusson Variegated' is identical, but its blossoms are heavily marbled with white on red.

'Alba Plena' (1792). Early. Brought from China over two centuries ago and still a favorite. Large white formal double. Slow, bushy growth. Early bloom is a disadvantage in cold or rainy areas; protect blossoms from rain and wind.

'Berenice Boddy'. Midseason. Medium light pink semidouble blooms with deeper shading. Vigorous, upright growth. One of the most cold hardy.

'Betty Sheffield'. Midseason. Large white semidouble to loose peony-form blossoms striped and blotched with red and pink. Upright, medium-size plant. The parent of many sports identical save for flower color. 'Betty Sheffield Supreme' has white petals bordered in deep rose red; 'Betty's Beauty' has a narrower pink border. 'Betty Sheffield Blush' is pale pink with a few red marks. 'Betty Sheffield Coral' is coral pink.

'Bob Hope'. Midseason. Large to very large semidouble blooms in deepest red with prominent golden stamens. Large, vigorous plant.

'Carter's Sunburst'. Early to late. Large to very large flowers, semidouble to peony form to formal double, in pale pink striped with deeper pink. Medium-size, compact plant.

'C. M. Wilson'. Early to midseason. Sport of 'Elegans' and identical to it except for its pale pink flower color. 'C. M. Wilson Variegated' has white petal markings; many plants sold as 'C. M. Wilson' are actually the variegated form.

'Covina' (1888). Midseason to late. Medium, rose red semidouble to rose-form double flowers on a compact plant. Highly sun tolerant.

'Daikagura' (1891). Early to late. Large, rose red peony-form blooms on a dense, upright bush. Very long bloom season. 'Daikagura Variegated' is similar but has rose red blossoms marbled in white.

'Debutante'. Early to midseason. Medium-large, light pink peony-form flowers. Profuse bloomer. Vigorous upright growth. Takes some sun.

'Drama Girl'. Midseason. Very large semidouble flowers of deep salmon rose pink. Vigorous, open, pendulous growth.

'Elegans' (Chandler); also sold as 'Francine' ('Chandleri Elegans Pink'). 1831. Early to midseason. The founder of a large and growing family of sports. The original plant is slow growing and spreading, bearing large anemone-form blossoms in rose pink; center petaloids are often marked with white. More frequently grown is 'Elegans Variegated', identical except for white variegation on all petals; it is often known simply as Chandleri Elegans. 'Elegans Supreme' is like 'Elegans' with the addition of deep serrations on petal edges. 'Elegans Champagne' is a white sport of 'Elegans Supreme' with creamy central petaloids. 'Elegans Splendor' has white-margined pale pink petals with fringed edges. For other sports in the 'Elegans' family, see 'C. M. Wilson', 'Hawaii', 'Shiro Chan'.

'Finlandia'. Early to midseason. Pure white, medium-large semidouble blooms with swirled, fluted petals. Compact, medium-size plant. 'Finlandia Variegated' has red streaks and dashes on white petals.

'Glen 40' ('Coquetii'). Midseason to late. Large, deep red formal double. One of the best reds for corsages. Slow, compact, upright growth. Handsome even out of bloom. Hardy; very good in containers.

'Grand Slam'. Midseason. Large to very large semidouble to peony-form flowers in glowing deep red. There is a variegated form.

'Guilio Nuccio'. Midseason. Considered by many to be the world's finest camellia. Coral rose, very large semidouble flowers of unusual depth and substance have inner petals fluted in "rabbit ear" effect. Vigorous upright growth. Forms with variegated, fringed blossoms are available.

'Hawaii'. Early to midseason. A sport of 'C. M. Wilson' with the same plant habit and light pink flower color, but in a full peony form with fringed petals. 'Kona' is a white sport.

'Herme' ('Jordan's Pride'). 1875. Midseason. Medium-large, pink semidouble flowers irregularly bordered in white and streaked with deeper pink. Sometimes bears solid pink blooms on certain branches. Free blooming and dependable.

'Kramer's Supreme'. Midseason. Very large full peony-form flowers in deep, clear red. Some people can detect a faint fragrance. Compact, upright, unusually vigorous. Takes some sun.

'Kumasaka' (1896). Midseason to late. Medium-large, rose pink rose-form double to peony-form flowers. Vigorous, compact, upright growth and remarkably heavy flower production make it a choice landscape plant. Hardy. Takes morning sun.

'Magnoliiflora' (1886). Midseason. Medium, pale pink semidouble flowers. Heavy bloomer; good cut flower. Medium-size plant with compact yet spreading form. Hardy.

'Mathotiana' (1840s). Midseason to late. Very large rose-form double to formal double blooms in deep crimson, sometimes with purplish cast. Vigorous, upright grower. Takes cold and stands up well in hot-summer areas. Does not grow very well along Southern California coast.

'Mrs. Charles Cobb'. Midseason to late. Large, deep red semidouble to peony-form flowers. Free blooming. Compact plant with dense foliage; best in warmer areas.

'Mrs. D. W. Davis'. Midseason. Spectacular blossoms in palest blush pink: very large, somewhat cup shaped, opening from egg-size buds. Vigorous, upright, compact plant with very handsome, broad leaves.

'Nuccio's Gem'. Midseason. Medium to large, white, perfectly formed formal double. Strong-growing, full, upright plant.

'Nuccio's Jewel'. Midseason to late. Large flowers in loose to full peony form are white with pink petal edges.

'Nuccio's Pearl'. Midseason. Medium full formal double blossoms are white with a rim of deep pink outer petals.

'Prince Eugene Napoleon' ('Pope Pius IX'). 1859. Midseason. Cherry red, medium-large formal double. Medium-size, compact, upright plant.

'Purity' (1887). Late. Medium white flowers, rose-form double to formal double, usually showing a few stamens. Vigorous, upright plant. Late bloom means it often escapes rain damage.

'Shiro Chan'. Early to midseason. A sport of 'C. M. Wilson' with identical habit and flower form. Blossoms may open palest pink, fading to white blushed with pink at petal bases. 'Snow Chan' is a pure white sport.

'Silver Waves'. Early to midseason. Large white semidouble blooms with wavy petal edges.

'Swan Lake'. Midseason to late. Very large white flowers with formal double to peony form. Vigorous, upright growth.

'Tiffany'. Midseason to late. Very large blossoms in warm pink; rose-form double to loose, irregular semidouble. Vigorous, upright shrub.

'Tom Knudsen'. Early to midseason. Medium to large blooms in dark red with deeper red veining. Formal double to peony form to rose-form double.

'Tomorrow'. Early to midseason. Very large strawberry red blossoms may be semidouble with petaloids mixed among stamens, or they may have full peony form. Strong, open, slightly pendulous plant. The parent of numerous sports. 'Tomorrow Variegated' is variously marked in white. 'Tomorrow Park Hill' has lightly variegated pale pink petals shading to darker pink at edges. 'Tomorrow's Dawn' reverses the effect, shading from deeper color in petal centers to white at margins. 'Tomorrow's Tropic Dawn' has red-streaked white flowers aging to blush pink.

'Ville de Nantes'. Midseason to late. Large semidouble flowers have white-blotched deep red petals with fringed edges. Bushy, slow-growing plant. 'Lady Kay' is a sport with full peony form. ▸

'Wildfire'. Early to midseason. Medium orange-red semidouble flowers on a vigorous, upright plant.

C. lutchuensis. Limber-branched shrub to 10 ft. tall, 12 ft. wide, with tiny (1½-in.-long, ½-in.-wide) leaves and profusion of tiny white flowers with strong, pleasant fragrance. Used as parent to introduce fragrance to larger camellias. Long, pliant branches make it an easily trained espalier.

C. oleifera. Shrub or small tree 10–20 ft. tall, 6–12 ft. wide, with open growth habit and somewhat weeping branches. Leaves are 1–3 in. long, glossy green. Flowers are small (1½ in.), white or cream, fragrant. Possibly the hardiest of all camellia species and a parent of hardy hybrids.

C. reticulata. Some of the biggest and most spectacular camellia flowers occur in this species, and likely as not they appear on some of the lankiest and least graceful plants.

Camellia reticulata

Plants differ somewhat according to variety, but generally speaking they are rather gaunt and open shrubs that eventually become trees of considerable size—possibly 35–50 ft. tall. In gardens, consider them 10-ft.-tall shrubs, 8 ft. wide. Leaves are also variable but tend to be dull green, leathery, and strongly net veined.

Culture is quite similar to that of other camellias, except that plants seem intolerant of heavy pruning. This, in addition to their natural lankiness and size, makes them difficult to place in garden. They are at their best in light shade of old oaks, where they should stand alone with plenty of room to develop. They are good container subjects while young but are not handsome out of bloom. They develop better form and heavier foliage in open ground. In Zones 4–6, grow them in containers so you can move them into winter protection, or plant beneath overhang or near wall.

Best-known varieties have very large semidouble flowers with deeply fluted and curled inner petals. These inner petals give great depth to flower. All bloom January to May in California, January to April in Southwest, March to May in Northwest. The following varieties are the best choices for garden use.

'Buddha'. Rose pink flower of very large size; inner petals unusually erect and wavy. Gaunt, open; fast growth.

'Butterfly Wings'. Loose semidouble flower of great size (reported up to 9 in. across), rose pink; petals broad and wavy. Growth open, rather narrow.

'Captain Rawes'. Reddish rose pink semidouble flowers of large size. Vigorous, bushy plant with good foliage. Hardiest of reticulatas.

'Chang's Temple'. True variety is large, open-centered, deep rose flower, with notched and fluted center petals. 'Cornelian' (see below) is sometimes sold as 'Chang's Temple'.

'Cornelian'. Large, deep, irregular peony-form flowers with wavy petals, rosy pink to red, heavily variegated with white. Vigorous plant with big leaves that are usually marked with white. This variety is often sold as 'Chang's Temple' (see description above) or as 'Lion Head'. The true 'Lion Head' is not found in North American gardens.

'Crimson Robe'. Very large, bright red semidouble flowers. Petals firm textured and wavy. Vigorous plant of better appearance than most reticulatas.

'Purple Gown'. Large, purplish red peony-form to formal double flowers. Compact plant with best growth habit and foliage in the group.

'Shot Silk'. Large, loose semidouble flowers of brilliant pink with iridescent finish that sparkles in sunlight. Fast, rather open growth.

'Tali Queen'. Very large, deep reddish pink, loose semidouble flowers with heavily crinkled petals. Plant form and foliage very good. Often sold as 'Noble Pearl'; true 'Noble Pearl' is not available in North America.

C. rusticana. SNOW CAMELLIA. To 6–12 ft. tall, 3–10 ft. wide. A class of small-flowered camellias from a cold, extremely snowy part of Japan. Flowers may be white, pink, or red, and single to double in form. Plants tend to be spreading, and branches are remarkably supple. They are no hardier than *C. japonica* and are generally considered to be a subspecies *(C. j. rusticana)*.

C. saluenensis. Shrub of dense, leafy growth to 10–15 ft. tall and wide. Leaves elliptic, rather narrow, pointed, thick textured, 1½–2½ in. long and half as wide. Early spring flowers are bell shaped and rather small, varying in color from white to fairly deep pink. Not of great value in itself, it has brought floriferousness, hardiness, and graceful appearance to a large group of its hybrids.

C. sasanqua. Useful broad-leafed evergreens for espaliers, ground covers, informal hedges, screening, containers, and bonsai. Plants vary in form from spreading and vinelike to upright and densely bushy; sizes range from 1½ ft. high and 6 ft. wide to 12 ft. tall and wide. Leaves are dark green, shiny, 1½–3½ in. long, a third as wide. Flowers, heavily produced in autumn and early winter, are short lived, rather flimsy, but so numerous that plants make a show for months. Some are lightly fragrant.

Most sasanquas tolerate much sun, and some thrive in full hot sun with right soil and regular water. They take drought very well. The sasanquas are hardy in camellia areas of Pacific Northwest, but flowers are too often damaged by fall and winter rains and frost to call them successful.

'Apple Blossom'. Single white flowers blushed with pink, from pink buds. Spreading plant.

'Cleopatra'. Rose pink semidouble flowers with narrow, curving petals. Growth is erect, fairly compact. Takes clipping well.

'Hana Jiman'. Large white semidouble flowers with pink edges. Fast, open growth; good espalier.

'Jean May'. Large double, shell pink. Compact, upright grower with exceptionally glossy foliage.

'Kanjiro'. Large semidouble flowers of rose pink shading to rose red at petal edges. Erect growth habit.

'Mine-No-Yuki' ('White Doves'). Large, white, full peony-form flower. Drops many buds. Spreading, willowy growth; effective espalier.

'Momozono-Nishiki'. Large semidouble flowers are rose, shaded white. Twisted petals.

'Narumi-gata'. Large, cupped single flowers, white tinged pink.

'Setsugekka'. Large, white semidouble flowers with fluted petals. Blossoms have considerable substance; cut sprays hold well in water. Upright and rather bushy shrub.

'Tanya'. Deep rose pink single flowers. Tolerates much sun. Good ground cover.

'Yuletide'. Profusion of small, single, bright red flowers on dense, compact, upright plant.

C. sinensis (Thea sinensis). TEA. In the West, the tea plant grows as a dense round shrub to 15 ft. tall and wide, with leathery, dull dark green leaves to 5 in. long. White, 1½-in.-wide, fragrant fall flowers. Takes well to pruning. Can be trimmed as hedge. Tea can be grown in California but has never been a major crop for economic reasons. 'Blushing Maiden' bears pink flowers, 'Teabreeze' especially fragrant white ones.

C. ×vernalis. Certain camellias once classed as sasanquas have been placed here because they bloom later, are denser in growth, shinier in leaf, and have firmer-textured flowers. They are generally sold as sasanquas. The best-known varieties, both to 9 ft. tall and 6 ft. wide, are the following two.

'Dawn'. Single to semidouble, small white flowers blushed pink. Dense, upright shrub of unusual hardiness.

'Hiryu'. Deep red, small, rose-form double blooms on a dense, upright plant. 'Hiryu Nishiki' has white markings on flowers.

Hybrid camellias. This term refers to camellias resulting from crosses between two or more species. Several categories of hybrids, described here, have been produced.

Medium-flowered hybrids. The first wave of hybridizing involved *C. japonica* and *C. saluenensis.* The resulting hybrids, most of them medium to large shrubs, are of generally good garden form, with foliage like that of *C. japonica* and abundant flowers. See *C. japonica* for explanations of bloom season and flower-size terminology.

'Coral Delight'. Midseason. Coral pink semidouble flowers form garlands along the branches. Slow grower.

'Donation'. Midseason. Large semidouble flowers of orchid pink borne all along stems. Blooms young and heavily on vigorous, upright, compact plant with slightly pendulous branches. Quite resistant to cold and sun. Appreciates a little shade in hot, dry areas. There is a form with variegated flowers.

'E. G. Waterhouse'. Midseason to late. Medium formal double of excellent form. Light pink flowers heavily produced on vigorous, upright shrub.

'Fragrant Pink'. Midseason. An exception in that it is a cross between *C. j. rusticana (C. rusticana)* and *C. lutchuensis*. Loose peony-form flowers on spreading bush. Flowers are small, deep pink, very fragrant.

'Freedom Bell'. Midseason. Small to medium semidouble, bell-shaped blooms of dark red open beneath branches.

'J. C. Williams'. Early to late. Medium single, cup-shaped flowers of purplish pink over very long season. Vigorous, upright shrub with rather pendulous branches. This and the similar 'Mary Christian' and 'St. Ewe' are good plants for the Pacific Northwest.

'Jury's Yellow'. Early to late. Medium anemone-form blooms with ivory white outer petals, creamy yellow central petaloids. Compact, upright.

'Taylor's Perfection'. Midseason. Profuse light pink semidouble flowers.

Large-flowered hybrids. A second wave of hybridizing, involving *C. japonica* and *C. reticulata*, produced plants that are more spectacular in blossom than the hybrids described above. See *C. japonica* for explanations of bloom season and flower-size terminology.

'Dr. Clifford Parks'. Midseason. Very large blossoms in an orange-toned rich red are semidouble to loose peony form to anemone form. Vigorous, upright plant.

'Flower Girl'. Early to midseason. Large to very large, semidouble to peony-form flowers of bright pink. Vigorous, upright growth. Profuse flowering and small leaves come from its sasanqua parent, big flowers from its reticulata ancestor.

'Francie L.'. Midseason to late. Very large semidouble flowers with upright, wavy petals. Deep rose pink.

'Valentine Day'. Midseason to late. Large to very large, salmon pink formal double flowers. Fast, upright grower.

'Valley Knudsen'. Midseason to late. Large to very large, deep orchid pink blooms, semidouble to loose peony form. Compact upright growth.

Hardy hybrids. These camellias, bred from *C. oleifera*, are probably the hardiest of all; they will withstand temperatures to −10°F/−23°C given an overhead tree canopy and protection from cold, drying winds. Most produce semidouble flowers; bloom period is fall and winter. Pink varieties include 'Winter's Beauty', 'Winter's Charm', 'Winter's Dream', 'Winter's Fire', 'Winter's Interlude', 'Winter's Peony', and 'Winter's Rose'; white ones include 'Polar Ice', 'Snow Flurry', 'Winter's Hope', and 'Winter's Waterlily'. 'Winter's Star' is purplish red.

CAMPANULA

BELLFLOWER

Campanulaceae (Lobeliaceae)

MOSTLY PERENNIALS; SOME BIENNIALS OR ANNUALS

ZONES 1–9, 14–24, EXCEPT AS NOTED

FULL SUN IN COOLER CLIMATES ONLY

MODERATE TO REGULAR WATER

SEE CHART NEXT PAGE

Campanula isophylla 'Alba'

Vast and varied group (about 300 species) encompassing trailers, creeping or tufted miniatures, and erect kinds 1–6 ft. or taller. Usually, flower stalks rise above basal leaf rosettes; basal leaves often differ from stem leaves. The perennial species tend to spread indefinitely from the root; width depends mainly on vigor of their rootstocks and time they have been in one spot. Flowers are generally bell shaped, though some are star shaped, cupped, or round and flat. Bloom comes at some time from spring to fall, depending on species. Native throughout the Northern Hemisphere. Kinds featured here come mostly from southern Europe, Turkey, the Caucasus, and northern Asia. *C. lasiocarpa* is a Rocky Mountain and Alaskan native. *C. rotundifolia* is also found in the wild in Alaska.

Uses are as varied as the plants. Gemlike miniatures deserve special settings—close-up situations in rock gardens, niches in dry walls, raised beds, containers. Trailing kinds are ideal for hanging pots or baskets, wall crevices; vigorous, spreading growers serve well as ground covers. Upright growers are valuable in borders, for cutting, occasionally in containers.

Campanulas grow best in good, well-drained soil. Most species are grown fairly easily from seeds sown in spring or early summer. Set out in fall for bloom the following year. Also may be increased by divisions or cuttings. Divide clumps in fall, every 3 or 4 years; some may need yearly division. Some species seed freely, and a few have invasive tendencies; may be difficult to remove when entwined with roots of shrubs, trees, or other perennials. For these species, choose sites carefully. Some campanulas are attractive to slugs and snails. Watch for spider mites in hot, dry weather.

Campanulaceae. The campanula, or bellflower, family contains perennials and biennials, typically with bell-, star-, or saucer-shaped flowers in shades of blue to purple, lilac, and white. This family includes plants formerly grouped under Lobeliaceae.

CAMPHOR TREE. See CINNAMOMUM camphora

CAMPSIS

TRUMPET CREEPER, TRUMPET VINE

Bignoniaceae

SEMIEVERGREEN TO DECIDUOUS VINES

ZONES VARY BY SPECIES

FULL SUN OR PARTIAL SHADE

MODERATE TO REGULAR WATER

Campsis radicans

Vigorous climbers used for large-scale effects, quick summer screens. All bear radiant, orange-toned blossoms shaped like flaring trumpets, in clusters at branch tips midsummer to fall. Glossy leaves are divided into 2½-in., ovate leaflets. Stems have aerial rootlets, cling to wood, brick, stucco, and other surfaces. Unless pruned and tied to supporting surface, old plants can become top-heavy and pull away. Each dormant season, shorten some branches and thin others. Pinch back shoot tips in summer to keep plants bushy. Plants spread by suckering roots; pull any that appear. If older plants become unmanageable, cut to ground before spring growth begins and train a few strong new stems.

C. grandiflora (Bignonia chinensis). CHINESE TRUMPET CREEPER. Zones 4–24. Not as vigorous, large, or hardy as the American native *C. radicans*, but flowers are slightly larger and redder. Each leaf has up to nine leaflets. Grows to 30 ft. under ideal conditions. 'Morning Charm' has peach-colored flowers.

C. radicans (Bignonia radicans). COMMON TRUMPET CREEPER. Zones 1–21. Native to eastern U.S. Most widely used in cold-winter areas. Deep freeze will kill it to ground, but new stems grow quickly. Each leaf has up to 11 leaflets. Flowers are 3-in.-long orange tubes with scarlet lobes flaring to 2 in. wide. Grows fast to 40 ft. or more, bursting with health and vigor. 'Flava' has yellow blossoms and somewhat lighter green leaves.

C. × tagliabuana. Zones 3b–24. Hybrid between above two species. 'Mme Galen', best-known variety, has salmon red flowers. 'Crimson Trumpet' bears pure red blooms.

CANARY BIRD BUSH. See CROTALARIA agatiflora

CANARY BIRD FLOWER. See TROPAEOLUM peregrinum

CANARY ISLAND BROOM. See GENISTA canariensis

CANARY ISLAND DAISY. See ASTERISCUS sericeus

CANDELILLA. See EUPHORBIA antisyphilitica

CANDLE BUSH. See SENNA alata

CANDLENUT TREE. See ALEURITES moluccana

CANDOLLEA cuneiformis. See HIBBERTIA cuneiformis

CANDY LILY. See × PARDANCANDA norrissii

CANDYTUFT. See IBERIS

C

C

CAMPANULA

NAME, TYPE	GROWTH HABIT, SIZE	FOLIAGE	FLOWERS	USES, COMMENTS
Campanula carpatica (C. turbinata) TUSSOCK BELLFLOWER Perennial	Compact, spreading, leafy tufts, to 6 in. tall. Flower stems upright, branching; usually about 8 in. tall, but may rise 1–1½ ft.	Smooth, bright green, with wavy, toothed edges, 1–1½ in. long. Basal leaves round, often drying up before bloom; stem leaves oval to triangular	Profuse, upward facing, bell or cup shaped, 1–2 in.; light blue, violet, or white. Late spring	Rock gardens, foreground in borders, edging. Variable in flower size and color. 'Blue Chips' and 'White Chips' good dwarf varieties. Easily grown from seed; sometimes sold as 'Blue Clips', 'White Clips'
C. cochlearifolia FAIRY THIMBLES Perennial	Dainty, ground-hugging mat of rosettes from spreading roots. Wiry, erect stems rise 3–6 in. high	Shiny, ¾ in., heart shaped or almost round with 3 large teeth on each side. Stem leaves narrow, lance shaped	Solitary, ½ in., nodding, thimble shaped. 'Bavaria Blue', deep blue; 'Alba', pure white; 'Elizabeth Oliver', multiple powder blue bells, one inside another. All summer in cooler areas	Rock crevices, troughs, between paving stones, edging. Easy to grow, spreads and seeds vigorously
C. collina Perennial	Slow-spreading clump sends up 9–15-in. flowering stems	Basal leaves downy, scallop edged, and heart shaped, on long stems. Stem leaves narrower, smaller	One-sided clusters, each with 1–5 large (1–1½-in.), flaring, deeply cut, nodding bells, usually deep violet blue. Late spring to early summer	Well-behaved garden subject for near front of border, rock garden. Likes moisture, some shade
C. garganica (C. elatines garganica) Perennial Zones 1–9, 14–24	Tight mat, 3–6 in. high, with spreading or trailing flower stems to 6 in.	Small, gray or green, sharply toothed, kidney or heart shaped	Upward-facing, flat, ½-in. stars in violet blue with white centers. One or several atop each stem. 'Baby Blue' is tiny, light blue. Late spring to fall	Rock gardens, troughs, edging. Somewhat like miniature, prostrate *C. poscharskyana*. 'Dickson's Gold' has golden foliage given enough sun. *C. g. fenestrellata* is similar to species, but flowering stems incline upward
C. glomerata Perennial Zones A1, A2; 1–10, 14–24	Upright, with erect side branches to 1–2 ft.	Basal leaves broad, wavy edged. Stem leaves broad, toothed. Both somewhat hairy	Narrow, 1-in. bells, flaring at the mouth, in violet, blue, white. Tightly clustered at tops of stems. Spring through summer	Shaded borders or large rock gardens. Plants have proportionately more foliage than flowers. Seed-grown strains include Superba (deepest purple) and Alba (white)
C. isophylla ITALIAN BELLFLOWER, STAR OF BETHLEHEM Perennial Zones 4–9, 14–24	Trailing or hanging soft stems to 2 ft. long, becoming woody at base	Round or heart shaped, light green, toothed, 1–1½ in. long and wide	Loose clusters of upward-facing, light blue, 1-in.-wide stars. 'Alba' has larger, pure white blooms. 'Stella Blue' and 'Stella White' are selections from seed-grown Kristal strain: vigorous, compact, with larger flowers. Late summer, fall (nearly all year in mildest climates)	Hanging baskets, wall pots, tops of walls, rock gardens in filtered shade. Choice ground cover for small areas on slopes in mild-winter climates. In Southern California, best near coast. Indoor/outdoor plant where winters are cold
C. lactiflora Perennial Zones 1–9, 14–24	Erect, branching, leafy, 3½–5 ft. tall	Oblong, pointed, finely toothed, 2–5 in. long	Broadly bell shaped to star shaped, 1 in.; violet to pale blue, white, pink. 'Loddon Anna' is lilac pink. Summer	Rear of border in sun or part shade. Endures even dry shade and is long-lived. 'Pouffe' forms dwarf (10-in.-high) mound covered with lavender blooms
C. lasiocarpa Perennial Zones A1–A3; 1–9, 14–24	Basal tuft to 3 in. high, with flowering stems rising 3–4 in. above foliage	Lower leaves spoon shaped, upper leaves narrow	Usually solitary, 1-in. bells, erect or nearly; violet blue. Summer	Native to Rocky Mountains and Alaska. Rock garden, low carpet plant, in sandy or rocky soil with good drainage
C. longistyla Biennial or short-lived perennial Zones 3b–9, 14–24	Wide (2-ft.) leaf rosettes send up flowering stems 2–3 ft. tall, branched from base	Large (6–8-in.), thick, rough-textured, fine-toothed, egg-shaped basal leaves. Stem leaves narrower	Spikelike clusters of nodding, slightly hairy, typically dark violet-blue, 1½-in. bells cut into lobes a third of their length. Summer	Excellent border plant, used like *C. medium.* Usually dies after blooming, but sometimes lives over to flower again second year. Isabella strain is dwarf (6–8 in. tall) with medium blue flowers; sold as bedding plant, blooming first year from seed
C. medium CANTERBURY BELL, CUP-AND-SAUCER Biennial or annual	Sturdy, hairy, leafy, with erect stems 2½–4 ft. tall. To 1 ft. wide	Lance-shaped, wavy-edged basal leaves 6–10 in. long; stem leaves smaller (3–5 in.)	Bell shaped or urn shaped, 1–2 in.; single or double, held upright in long, loose, open clusters. Purple, violet, blue, lavender, pink, white. Late spring or early summer	Sow seed in late spring for bloom following year, or set out plants from nursery 15–18 in. apart. Good for cutting. 'Calycanthema', commonly called cup-and-saucer, is very popular. Annual variety with bell-shaped (not cup-and-saucer) flowers blooms in 6 months from seed

C

CAMPANULA

NAME, TYPE	GROWTH HABIT, SIZE	FOLIAGE	FLOWERS	USES, COMMENTS
C. persicifolia PEACH-LEAFED BLUEBELL Perennial	Strong-growing, slender, erect stems 2–3 ft. tall. Plants leafy at base	Basal leaves smooth edged, green, 4–8 in. long. Stem leaves 2–4 in. long, shaped like leaves of peach tree	Open, cup shaped, about 1 in. across, held erect by short side shoots on sturdy stems. Blue, pink, or white. Summer	Choice plant for borders. Easy to grow from seed sown in late spring. 'Telham Beauty', old but still popular, has 3-in. blue flowers. 'Blue Gardenia' and 'White Pearl' have double flowers
C. portenschlagiana (C. muralis) DALMATIAN BELLFLOWER Perennial Zones 2–9, 14–24	Low, leafy, mounding or trailing mats 4–6 in. high. Semierect, branching flower stems to 8 in. high	Roundish, heart-shaped, deep green with deeply toothed, slightly wavy edges	Flaring bell shaped, violet blue or grayish white to 1 in. long; several to each stem. Late spring into summer, sometimes blooming again in fall	Fine plant for edging or as small-scale ground cover. Spreads moderately fast; is sturdy, permanent, and not invasive. Easily increased by dividing. 'Resholt' has larger, darker blue flowers
C. poscharskyana SERBIAN BELLFLOWER Perennial Zones 1–12, 14–24	Spreading, mounding, leafy clump to 8 in. high. Branching, semi-upright flower stems to 1 ft. or more	Elongated heart shape, irregularly toothed, slightly hairy, 1–3½ in. long, ¾–3 in. wide	Star-shaped, ½–1-in. wide blooms in blue lilac, lavender, or grayish white. Spring to early summer	Very vigorous. Shaded border near pools, partially shaded rock gardens, with fuchsias and begonias. Good ground cover for small areas. Needs little water
C. punctata Perennial	Flat basal rosette spreads rapidly by underground runners. Wiry 1–1½-ft. flower stems arch over at tip	Dark green, toothed, 4–5 in., heart shaped; leaves narrower on upper stems	Long (2–2½-in.), tubular, waxy, drooping bells; cream through pink to deep maroon, inside paler and spotted with crimson. 'Cherry Bells' is bright, deep rose. Late spring to early summer (scattered bloom until frost)	Forms dense, weed-suppressing mat among shrubs, but too invasive for mixed borders. Some dwarf forms exist
C. pyramidalis CHIMNEY BELLFLOWER Biennial or short-lived perennial Zones 2–9, 14–24	To 2 ft. wide. Sturdy upright stems, unbranched or branched at base, 4–6 ft. or taller	Basal leaves nearly heart shaped, 3–6 in. long with long stalks. Upper leaves lance shaped, stalkless	Dense spikes of 1-in., flat saucers in blue or white. Summer	Back of perennial borders, bays in big shrubbery borders, containers. Stake early to keep stems straight. In cold-winter climates, mulch around plants
C. raddeana Perennial Zones 2–9, 14–24	Spreading, low mat with reddish, 9–12-in., branched flower stems	Small, shiny, sharp-toothed, long-stemmed, dark green	Nodding, ¾-in., flaring, dark violet-blue bells, with lobes that curl back. A bloom in each leaf axil. Summer	Good in rock gardens or border foreground. Needs good drainage and some lime in acidic soils
C. rotundifolia BLUEBELL OF SCOTLAND, HAREBELL Perennial Zones A1–A3; 1–10, 14–24	Slowly spreading clump, 2–3 in. high. Slender, upright flower stems, some branched, 6–18 in. tall	Green or gray. Basal leaves roundish, long stalked, 1 in.; may dry before bloom. Stem leaves grasslike, 2–3 in.	Broad, bell-shaped bright blue, lavender, or white flowers 1 in. long. One or a few nodding in open clusters	Rock gardens, borders, naturalized under deciduous trees. Self-sows under favorable conditions. 'Olympica' has broader, medium blue bells; dark green, toothed leaves
C. takesimana Perennial	Habit like *C. punctata,* to which it is closely related	Similar to *C. punctata,* but rounder, glossier	Long (2-in.), pendent, pale lilac bells, spotted maroon inside. 'Elizabeth' is deep rosy red with lighter edges. 'Beautiful Trust' has white, deeply split bells, with segments curled back. Early summer	Vigorous, spreading ground cover. Like *C. punctata,* too invasive for mixed borders

CANNA

Cannaceae

PERENNIALS FROM RHIZOMES

ZONES 6–9, 12–24; H1, H2; OR DIG AND STORE

FULL SUN

REGULAR WATER DURING GROWTH AND BLOOM

Almost all cannas in nursery trade are hybrids descended from species native to American tropics and subtropics. Large, lance-shaped leaves that may be rich green, bronzy red, or variegated resemble those of banana or ti plants *(Cordyline fruticosa)*. Spikes of large, showy, irregularly shaped flowers reminiscent of ginger lilies *(Hedychium)* in red, orange, yellow, pink, cream, white, or bicolors bloom in summer, fall. Old-fashioned garden favorites reach 4–6 ft. tall; lower-growing, more compact strains include Grand Opera (2 ft.), Pfitzer's Dwarf (2½–3 ft.), Seven Dwarfs (1½ ft.).

Canna

Among the many cannas featuring brilliant foliage as well as showy flowers are the following 4–6-ft.-tall varieties: 'Minerva' has yellow-striped green leaves and yellow flowers opening from red buds; 'Pretoria' ('Bengal Tiger') has similarly variegated leaves coupled with orange blossoms; 'Tropicanna' ('Phaison') has hot orange blooms over purple foliage that becomes striped with green, yellow, pink, and red. Two 4-ft. selections with dark foliage are 'Red King Humbert', with reddish bronze leaves and orange-scarlet to red flowers, and 'Wyoming', with bronzy purple foliage and bright orange blooms.

Cannas are most effective in groups of single colors against plain backgrounds. Grow in borders, near poolside, in large pots or tubs on terrace or patio. Leaves useful in arrangements; cut flowers do not keep well. Best adapted to warm- to hot-summer climates; in areas where soil freezes deeply, lift and store over winter. Where hardy in the ground, plant in spring after danger of frost is past. Set rhizomes in rich, loose soil, 2–4 in. deep, 1½–2 ft. apart. For a good head start on bloom in colder regions, start rhizomes indoors 4 to 6 weeks before last frost date; then plant out. Cut each stem to ground after it finishes blooming; new stems will continue to grow into early fall. Divide clumps every 3 or 4 years.

CANTALOUPE. See MELON, MUSKMELON, CANTALOUPE

CANTERBURY BELL. See CAMPANULA medium

CAPE CHESTNUT. See CALODENDRUM capense

CAPE COWSLIP. See LACHENALIA

CAPE FORGET-ME-NOT. See ANCHUSA capensis

CAPE FUCHSIA. See PHYGELIUS

CAPE HONEYSUCKLE. See TECOMA capensis

CAPE MALLOW. See ANISODONTEA × hypomandarum

CAPE MARIGOLD. See DIMORPHOTHECA, OSTEOSPERMUM

CAPE PONDWEED. See APONOGETON distachyus

CAPE PRIMROSE. See STREPTOCARPUS

CAPER. See CAPPARIS spinosa

CAPE RUSH. See CHONDROPETALUM tectorum

CAPE WEED. See ARCTOTHECA calendula

Capparidaceae. The caper family includes the caper plant *(Capparis spinosa)* and spider flower *(Cleome hasslerana)*.

CAPPARIS spinosa

CAPER

Capparidaceae

DECIDUOUS SHRUB

ZONES 8, 9, 12–24

FULL SUN

LITTLE TO MODERATE WATER

Native to Mediterranean. Habit varies from sprawling semivine to dense, rounded shrub to 5 ft. tall and wide. Leaves deep green, nearly round, up to 2 in. across (usually less) on vinelike, sometimes spiny branches. In late spring through summer, white, 2–3-in. flowers with showy brushes of lavender stamens rise on long stalks from every leaf base, open at dawn and close in late afternoon. The pickled unopened buds are commercial capers.

Capparis spinosa

Propagate from cuttings or seed (seeds are slow to sprout and grow). Tolerates poor soil but needs good drainage. Grow as garden curiosity; use sprawling types as ground cover or let spill over a wall.

Caprifoliaceae. The honeysuckle family of shrubs and vines contains many ornamentals in addition to honeysuckle *(Lonicera)*; among them are *Abelia, Viburnum,* and *Weigela.*

CARAGANA

PEASHRUB

Fabaceae (Leguminosae)

DECIDUOUS SHRUBS OR SMALL TREES

ZONES A1–A3, 1–12, EXCEPT AS NOTED

FULL SUN

MODERATE WATER

Caragana arborescens

Very thorny, spiny plants native to Russia, Manchuria, Siberia. Leaves divided into small leaflets. Spring flowers shaped like bright yellow sweet peas. Useful where choice is limited by cold, heat, wind, bright sun; nearly indestructible in desert, mountain climates. Use as windbreak, cover for wildlife. On the larger species, occasionally prune out old wood to rejuvenate; these can also be clipped as a hedge.

C. arborescens. SIBERIAN PEASHRUB. Fast growing to 20 ft. tall and 15 ft. across; weeping varieties also exist. Leaves to 3 in. long, each with four to six pairs of leaflets.

C. frutex. RUSSIAN PEASHRUB. To 10 ft. tall, 8 ft. wide. Leaves have one or two pairs of 1-in. leaflets.

C. pygmaea. Zones A2, A3; 1–12. May form a 3-ft. mound or grow flat and sprawling to 3–4 ft. wide. Leaves have four ½–¾-in.-long leaflets. No pruning required.

CARAWAY. See CARUM carvi

CARDINAL CLIMBER. See IPOMOEA quamoclit

CARDINAL FLOWER. See LOBELIA cardinalis

CARDIOCRINUM giganteum

Liliaceae

PERENNIAL FROM BULB

ZONES 4–6, 14–17

LIGHT SHADE

REGULAR WATER

Cardiocrinum giganteum

Blossoms of this Himalayan native resemble oversize Easter lilies; glossy dark green leaves are broadly oval to heart-shaped, 1½ ft. long. In summer, foliage rosette gives rise to a leafy stem, 6–12-ft. tall. Stem is flowerless for the first few years, dying back to the ground each fall, but after 3 or 4 years bears up to 20 fragrant, 6–8-in., white trumpets with dark reddish throats. Flowers set seed, then the whole plant dies—but not before producing many small offset bulbs that grow to flowering size within several years. Set out bulbs (or dig and separate offsets) in early spring or, in mild-winter regions, in fall. Space 2 ft. apart, planting so tops are just beneath soil surface. You can also start new plants from seed, but seedlings may take up to 7 years to reach blooming size. In frost-prone areas, mulch in winter.

CARDOON

Asteraceae (Compositae)

PERENNIAL

ZONES 4–9, 12–24

FULL SUN

REGULAR WATER

Cardoon

Mediterranean native classified botanically as *Cynara cardunculus.* Closely related to artichoke but grown for edible leafstalks rather than flower buds. For climate, soil, and other requirements, see Artichoke.

To prepare leaves for harvest, blanch them by gathering them together, tying them up, and wrapping with paper to exclude light in late summer to early fall, 4 to 5 weeks before harvesting. To cook, cut heavy leaf midribs into 3–4-in. lengths, parboil until tender, then sauté; or serve boiled with butter or a sauce.

Grown as an ornamental, cardoon is a striking gray-green plant to 5 ft. tall and 4 ft. wide. Size, spininess rule it out in small gardens. Purple flowers like those of artichoke attractive cut and dried. Naturalizes in mild-winter climates; can escape and become a weed.

CAREX

SEDGE

Cyperaceae

PERENNIALS

ZONES VARY BY SPECIES

SOME SHADE IN HOTTEST CLIMATES

WATER NEEDS VARY BY SPECIES

Carex buchananii

Large group of grasslike, clumping plants found worldwide and grown for foliage effect in borders, rock gardens, containers, water gardens (flowers are generally insignificant). Long, narrow evergreen leaves are often striped or oddly colored. Specialists offer many varieties. Although characteristically found in damp soils, many sedges will grow under relatively dry conditions in cultivation.

C. barberae. SANTA BARBARA SEDGE. Zones 4–9, 14–24. A coastal species native from Southern California to Oregon. Rich green leaves 1 ft. long, ½ in. wide form a slowly spreading clump to 1–3 ft. tall. Good plant for erosion control. Little or no summer water.

C. buchananii. LEATHER LEAF SEDGE. Zones 2b–9, 14–24. From New Zealand. To 3 ft. tall, 2–2½ ft. wide. Curly-tipped, erect blades form clump of striking reddish bronze. Use with gray foliage or with deep greens. Moderate water.

C. comans. NEW ZEALAND HAIR SEDGE. Zones 2b–9, 14–24. Dense, fine-textured clumps reach 1–1½ ft. high. Narrow, silvery green leaves are usually 1 ft. long but may reach 6 ft.; beyond a length of about 2½ ft., they are utterly limp. On flat ground, foliage mounds look about 2½ ft. wide; same is true in areas where foot traffic is common, since leaves often catch on shoes of passersby and snap off. Where leaves are undisturbed on slopes or over ledges, they maintain their length and look like flowing water. 'Bronze' is similar but has coppery brown leaves. Green-leafed selection sold as 'Frosted Curls' or 'Frosty Curls' is usually variety of another sedge, *C. albula.* Moderate water. Occasionally invasive (by self-sowing) in moist areas.

C. conica 'Snowline' ('Marginata'). Zones 3–9, 14–24. Variegated selection of a species native to Japan, Korea. To 2 ft. wide and a little over a foot high, with white-margined dark green leaves. Regular water.

C. elata 'Aurea' ('Bowles Golden'). Zones 2–9, 14–24. Clump to 2½ ft. high, 1½ ft. wide, with narrow leaves that emerge bright yellow in spring and hold some color until late summer. Needs ample moisture; will grow in standing water.

C. flacca (C. glauca). BLUE SEDGE. Zones 3–9, 14–24. From Europe. Many forms of this creeper are in cultivation, ranging from 6 in. to 2 ft. high and wide; foliage may be blue or green. Plant is evergreen only in mildest climates. Not invasive but spreads slowly and can be clipped like a lawn. Endures light foot traffic, moderate shade, competition from tree roots. Tolerates many soils and irrigation schemes; does best with moderate water.

C. flagellifera. Zones 4–9, 14–24. From New Zealand. Closely related to *C. buchananii* and distinguished from it only by small botanical details. It is not quite as erect, and leaves are reddish brown and wider spreading. Moderate water.

C. morrowii expallida (C. m. 'Variegata'). VARIEGATED JAPANESE SEDGE. Zones 3–9, 14–24. To 1 ft. high, 1½ ft. wide, with drooping leaves striped with green and white. Good edging plant; individual clumps attractive among rocks. 'Goldband' ('Aurea-variegata') has yellow-striped leaves. Regular water.

C. spissa. SAN DIEGO SEDGE. Zones 7–9, 14–17, 19–24. Native to boggy areas in Southern California. Forms slowly spreading clumps. Coarse, upright blue-green leaves to 5 ft. tall. Light golden brown clusters of grass-type flowers appear in spring; cut back after bloom to avoid self-seeding. Needs ample moisture and will grow in standing water.

C. testacea. Zones 4–9, 14–24. From New Zealand. To 2 ft. tall, 5 ft. wide. Widely arching clumps of light green and reddish brown foliage; leaves develop red and orange highlights in good light. Some tendency to self-seed and spread under moist conditions. Moderate water.

CARICA. See PAPAYA

CARISSA macrocarpa

NATAL PLUM

Apocynaceae

EVERGREEN SHRUB

ZONES 22–24; H2; AND SEE BELOW

BEST IN SUN; TOLERATES SOME SHADE

LITTLE TO REGULAR WATER

Carissa macrocarpa

Natal plum's best climates are Zones 22–24 and H2, but so many gardeners find this South African native appealing that it is also grown in Zones 12, 13, 16–21—far beyond safe limits. Fast-growing, strong, upright, rounded shrub of rather loose habit to 5–7 ft. tall and wide (occasionally much larger). Oval, leathery, 3-in. leaves are lustrous rich green. Spines along branches and at end of each twig discourage trespassers.

Blooms throughout the year, bearing white flowers almost as fragrant as those of star jasmine *(Trachelospermum jasminoides)* and with the same five-petaled star shape, but larger (to 2 in. across). Blossoms followed by oval, 1–1½-in., fleshy red or purple fruits. Flowers, green fruit, and ripe fruit often appear together. Fruit has cranberrylike flavor and can be eaten fresh or used in jelly, sauce, pie.

Natal plum is easy to grow and accepts a variety of soils. Excellent in ocean wind, salt spray. Prune to control erratic growth (milky sap oozes from cut stems). Used mainly as screen or hedge in Zones 22–24 and H2; tolerates clipping as formal hedge. In less favorable zones, give it the same protected spot you'd give bougainvillea: warm wall facing south or west, preferably with overhang to keep off frost. Keep it away from walkways—spininess is a hazard to passersby. Can also be grown as indoor plant in good light.

'Boxwood Beauty'. Exceptionally compact, thornless growth to 2 ft. high and wide. Deep green leaves like those of large-leafed boxwood *(Buxus).* Good for hedging and shaping.

'Fancy'. More upright growth than species, with unusually large fruit.

'Green Carpet'. Low grower to 1–1½ ft. high, spreading to 4 ft. or wider. Smaller leaves than those of species. Excellent ground cover.

'Horizontalis'. To 1½–2 ft. high, spreading, trailing. Dense foliage.

'Minima'. Slow growth to 1–1½ ft. high, about 2 ft. wide. Tiny leaves and flowers.

'Prostrata'. Vigorous spreader to 2 ft. high; good ground cover. Prune out any upright growth. Can be trained as espalier.

'Ruby Point'. Grows more upright than species. New leaves hold their red color throughout growing season.

'Tomlinson'. Thornless. Compact, slow growth to 2–2½ ft. high, 3 ft. wide. Good tub or foundation plant.

'Tuttle' ('Nana Compacta Tuttlei'). Compact, dense growth to 2–3 ft. high, 3–5 ft. wide. Heavy production of flowers and fruit. Effective as a ground cover.

CARMEL CREEPER. See CEANOTHUS griseus horizontalis

CARNATION. See DIANTHUS caryophyllus

C

CARNEGIEA gigantea

SAGUARO
Cactaceae
CACTUS
ZONES 12, 13, 18–21
FULL SUN
NO IRRIGATION NEEDED

Carnegiea gigantea

Long-lived desert native grows very slowly to 50 ft. tall; in the wild, may be a column only 3 ft. high after 30 years. Typically produces branches after attaining 12–15 ft. Prominent ribs give fluted appearance. Light brown, ½–3-in.-long spines. Mature plants bloom in late spring; 3–5-in.-long, single white blossoms (state flower of Arizona) open at night and remain open until next afternoon. Edible oval fruits, sometimes mistaken for flowers, split open to show red pulp.

This is a protected species. When buying a mature specimen, be sure it was collected legally. When choosing a nursery-grown plant, look for one with a good root system. Adapted to dry conditions, but regular water and fertilizer will speed growth. Provide good drainage.

CAROB. See CERATONIA siliqua

CAROLINA ALLSPICE. See CALYCANTHUS floridus

CAROLINA JESSAMINE. See GELSEMIUM sempervirens

CAROLINA LAUREL CHERRY. See PRUNUS caroliniana

CARPENTERIA californica

BUSH ANEMONE
Philadelphaceae
EVERGREEN SHRUB
ZONES 5–9, 14–24
PARTIAL SHADE IN HOTTEST CLIMATES
LITTLE TO MODERATE WATER

Carpenteria californica

Native to a very restricted area in foothills of southern Sierra Nevada in California's Central Valley. Attractive, formal-looking shrub grows slowly to 4–6 ft. tall and wide; many stems rise from base. Older bark light colored and peeling; new shoots, purplish. Thick, narrow, 2–4½-in.-long leaves, dark green above, whitish beneath. In late spring and summer, clusters of scented, 1½–3-in., yellow-centered white flowers like anemones appear at branch ends. Cutting-grown variety 'Elizabeth' is similar.

Accepts ordinary garden conditions. Inspect occasionally for aphid or mite infestation. Resistant to oak root fungus. If pruning is necessary to shape or restrain growth, do so after flowering.

CARPET BUGLE. See AJUGA

CARPINUS

HORNBEAM
Betulaceae
DECIDUOUS TREES
ZONES VARY BY SPECIES
EXPOSURE NEEDS VARY BY SPECIES
REGULAR WATER

Carpinus betulus

Well-behaved, relatively small shade trees. Long life and good habits as street trees. Slow to moderate growth rate. Very hard, tough, heavy wood. Dark green, sawtooth-edged leaves color up in cold-winter climates; leaves hang on late in the season. Fruits (small, hard nutlets in leaflike bracts) that follow are carried in attractive drooping clusters to 5 in. long. Mature trees need little or no pruning.

Carpinus betulus

C. betulus. EUROPEAN HORNBEAM. Zones 2–9, 14–17. Native Europe to Iran. Dense, pyramidal tree to 40 ft. high and eventually as broad as tall, with drooping outer branches. Handsome, furrowed gray bark somewhat similar to that of *C. caroliniana.* Leaves are 2–5 in. long, turn yellow or dark red in fall. Best in full sun but tolerates light shade. Sometimes clipped into a hedge or screen. Subject to infestation by scale insects. 'Fastigiata' is the variety commonly sold; despite the name (which implies very upright growth), it develops an oval-vase shape with age.

C. caroliniana. AMERICAN HORNBEAM. Zones 1–9, 14–17. Native to eastern North America. Round headed, to 25–30 ft. tall and wide, sometimes larger; can be grown as single- or multitrunked tree. Smooth blue-gray trunk with undulations that look like muscles flexing beneath the surface. Leaves are 1–3 in. long, turn mottled yellow and red (sometimes mostly yellow) in fall; drop before those of *C. betulus.* Does well in exposures from full sun to heavy shade.

CARPOBROTUS

ICE PLANT
Aizoaceae
SUCCULENT WOODY-BASED PERENNIALS
ZONES VARY BY SPECIES
FULL SUN
LITTLE TO MODERATE WATER

Carpobrotus chilensis

Trailing plants with coarse, succulent leaves and summer blooms; useful for covering sunny banks (but not steep banks, since their weight when waterlogged could cause the soil to slide). Plant about 1½ ft. apart. Can rot in very wet conditions; can suffer dieback if severely stressed by lack of water or nitrogen during growth season. Scale insects can cause problems.

C. chilensis (Mesembryanthemum aequilaterale). Zones 12–24. Probably from South Africa; naturalized along coast, Oregon to Baja California. Straight, three-sided, fleshy leaves are 2 in. long; flowers lightly fragrant, rosy purple.

C. edulis (Mesembryanthemum edule). HOTTENTOT FIG. Zones 12–24; H1, H2. From South Africa. Curved, 4–5-in.-long leaves; pale yellow to rose flowers. Fruit edible but not particularly tasty.

CARROT

Apiaceae (Umbelliferae)
BIENNIAL GROWN AS ANNUAL
ALL ZONES
FULL SUN
REGULAR WATER

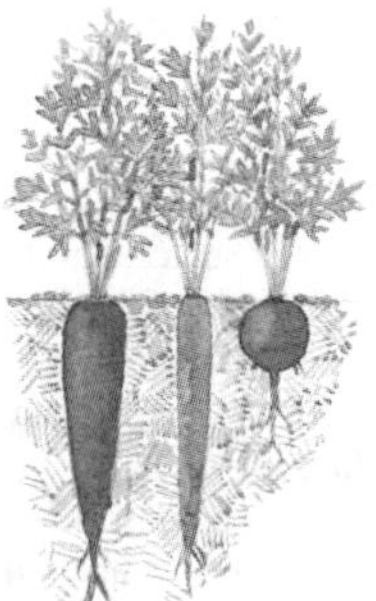
Carrot

Botanically known as *Daucus carota sativus;* probably native to Afghanistan. The variety to plant depends on the soil: carrots reach smooth perfection only in light-textured soil that is free of stones and clods. Plant long market kinds only if you can give them a foot of this ideal soil. If you can provide only a few inches, plant half-long varieties such as 'Nantes' and 'Chantenay' or miniature types like 'Lady Finger', 'Short 'n Sweet', or 'Thumbelina' (a short, round carrot). Miniature carrots are also ideal for growing in a container vegetable garden.

Sow lightly in rows at least 1 ft. apart. Soil should be fine enough for root development and loose enough so crusting can't check sprouting of seeds. If crust should form, keep soil soft by sprinkling. Too much nitrogen or manure will result in excessive top growth and cause forking of roots. Maintain even soil moisture: alternating dry and wet conditions cause split roots. To grow successive plantings, sow seed when previous planting is up and growing; in cold-winter climates, make last sowing 70 days before anticipated killing frost. When tops are 1–2 in. high, thin plants to 1½ in. apart; thin again if roots begin to crowd. Use thinnings in salads or steamed in butter. After first thinning, work in narrow band of commercial fertilizer 2 in. out from the row. Begin harvest when carrots reach finger size, usually 30 to 40 days after sowing; most types reach maturity in 60 to 70 days. In mild-winter climates, carrots store well in the ground; dig as needed.

CARROT WOOD. See CUPANIOPSIS anacardioides

CARTHAMUS tinctorius

SAFFLOWER, FALSE SAFFRON
Asteraceae (Compositae)
ANNUAL
ZONES 1–24; H1, H2
FULL SUN
MODERATE WATER

Carthamus tinctorius

This thistle relative (probably an Asian native) is ornamental as well as useful. To 3 ft. tall, 1–1½ ft. wide, with erect, spiny-leafed stems. In summer, bears orange-yellow flower heads above leafy bracts; inner bracts are spiny. Durable cut flower, fresh or dried. Popular in Hawaii for use in leis. Grown commercially for oil extracted from the seeds. The dried flowers have been used for seasoning in place of true saffron, which they somewhat resemble in color and flavor. Sow seeds in place in spring after frost danger is past. An ornamental spineless form is also available.

CARUM carvi

CARAWAY
Apiaceae (Umbelliferae)
BIENNIAL
ZONES 1–24
FULL SUN
REGULAR WATER

Carum carvi

From Asia Minor. Mound of carrotlike leaves grows from taproot to 1–2 ft. high in first year. In second spring, umbrellalike clusters of white flowers rise above foliage; after seeds ripen in midsummer, plant dies. Start seeds in place in fall or early spring; thrives in well-drained soil. Thin seedlings to 1½ ft. apart. To harvest and dry caraway seeds, see page 672. Use for flavoring pickles, vegetables, baked goods.

CARYA illinoensis. See PECAN

Caryophyllaceae. This is the pink family, including many garden annuals and perennials as well as a few weeds. Leaves are borne in opposite pairs at joints that are often swollen; leaves are often joined together at their bases. Pinks and carnations *(Dianthus)* are typical representatives, along with snow-in-summer *(Cerastium)* and *Lychnis*.

A PRACTICAL GUIDE TO GARDENING
PLEASE SEE PAGES 658–731

CARYOPTERIS

BLUEBEARD
Verbenaceae
DECIDUOUS SHRUBS
ZONES VARY BY SPECIES
FULL SUN
MODERATE WATER

Caryopteris × clandonensis

Asian natives valued for contribution of cool blue to flower borders from midsummer to frost. Bear dense stalked clusters of small flowers on current season's growth. Erect form. Generally grown as woody-based perennials—if plants don't freeze back in winter, cut them nearly to ground before spring growth flush to ensure good base for new season's growth. Trim after each wave of bloom to encourage repeat flowering. Provide good drainage, since plants can rot in wet soil.

C. × clandonensis. BLUE MIST. Zones 2b–9, 14–24. Low-growing mound (to 2 ft. tall and wide) of narrow, 3-in.-long leaves. Clusters of small flowers top upper parts of stems. 'Azure' and 'Heavenly Blue' bear deep blue blossoms. 'Dark Knight' and 'Longwood Blue' have deep blue flowers and silvery foliage; 'Worcester Gold' has yellow leaves, lavender-blue blooms.

C. incana (C. mastacanthus). COMMON BLUEBEARD, BLUE SPIRAEA. Zones 4–9, 14–24. Taller than *C. × clandonensis,* with looser, more open growth to 3–4 ft. tall, 5 ft. wide. Lavender-blue flowers appear in leaf joints.

C. odorata. HIMALAYAN BLUEBEARD. Zones 6–9, 14–24. To 8 ft. tall, 5 ft. wide, with shiny green foliage and purplish pink flower clusters at branch ends.

CARYOTA

FISHTAIL PALM
Arecaceae (Palmae)
PALMS
ZONES 23, 24; H2; OR INDOORS
SUN OR PART SHADE; BRIGHT INDIRECT LIGHT
REGULAR WATER

Caryota ochlandra

These Southeast Asian natives are feather palms with huge, finely divided leaves made up of leaflets flattened and split at tips like fish tails. Plant in humus-rich soil that provides good drainage.

C. mitis. CLUSTERED FISHTAIL PALM. Slow grower to 10–40 ft. tall, spreading 10–22 ft. Basal offshoots eventually form clustered trunks. Foliage light green. Very tender; thrives only in ideal environment.

C. ochlandra. CANTON FISHTAIL PALM. Will probably reach 25 ft. and spread half as wide. Medium dark green leaves. Hardiest of the caryotas, it has survived to 26°F/–3°C.

C. urens. FISHTAIL WINE PALM. Handsome single-stemmed palm grows to 100 ft. tall and 30 ft. wide in Asia, to 40 ft. tall and 15 ft. wide in Southern California as long as it has careful protection. Should temperature drop below 32°F/0°C, it's certain the palm will die. Arching, dark green leaves. Avoid handling fruit with bare hands; invisible crystals can cause severe itching.

CASCALOTE. See CAESALPINIA cacalaco

CASCARA sagrada. See RHAMNUS purshiana

CASHMERE BOUQUET. See CLERODENDRUM bungei

CASIMIROA edulis. See WHITE SAPOTE

C

CASSIA

Fabaceae (Leguminosae)

EVERGREEN, SEMIEVERGREEN, DECIDUOUS TREES

ZONES VARY BY SPECIES

FULL SUN

WATER NEEDS VARY BY SPECIES

Cassia × nealiae

The genus *Cassia* once included many yellow-flowered trees and shrubs now reclassified as *Senna* (see that entry), though some are still sold under their old names. These cassias are showy flowering trees that brighten landscapes in the warmest climates—not just with yellow blossoms but also with pink, cerise, and white ones. Flowering dates are approximate, since plants may bloom at any time or bloom intermittently over a long period. Most have long, round seedpods that can present a litter problem. Grow in well-drained soil. Plants are best pruned when young (to develop a strong framework) and as needed after flowering.

Cassia fistula

C. fistula. GOLDEN SHOWER, YELLOW SHOWER, INDIAN LABURNUM. Semievergreen to deciduous. Zone H2. From India. To 30–40 ft. high and 35 ft. wide. Prized for long, pendent yellow flower clusters borne from spring to fall. Medium green leaves divided into 4–8 pairs of leaflets. A specimen for garden, park, street planting. Good drought tolerance; flowers best in hot, dry locations. Takes little water.

C. grandis. PINK SHOWER, CORAL SHOWER. Deciduous. Zone H2. From tropical America. Fast growing to 20–50 ft. tall and 30 ft. wide. Abundant coral pink flowers in early spring. Leaves divided into 8–20 pairs of small leaflets, pink when young. Use for color accent or as shade, street, or park tree. Somewhat drought tolerant but blooms best with regular water.

C. javanica. PINK AND WHITE SHOWER. Deciduous. Zone H2. From Indonesia. To 30–35 ft. high and 25 ft. wide, with irregular habit. Masses of light pink flowers along branches from spring to fall, peaking in early summer. Leaves divided into 5–15 pairs of oval, 1–2-in.-long leaflets. Useful as color accent or shade, street, or park tree. Good wind tolerance; moderate drought and salt tolerance. Best with moderate water.

C. leptophylla. GOLD MEDALLION TREE. Nearly evergreen. Zones 15, 16, 20–24; H1, H2. Native to Brazil. Open-headed, fast-growing tree to 20–25 ft. tall, 30 ft. wide; low spreading with tendency to weep. Very shapely and graceful when pruned to single trunk (otherwise, becomes sprawling). Deep yellow flowers to 3 in. wide come in 6–8-in.-long spikes; main bloom in summer; sporadic bloom later. Little to moderate water.

C. × nealiae. RAINBOW SHOWER. Semievergreen to deciduous. Zone H2. A sterile hybrid between *C. fistula* and *C. javanica,* originating in Hawaii. Moderately fast grower to 30–40 ft. high and 35 ft. wide. Dark green foliage. Thrives in any well-drained soil. Withstands drought well but has only moderate wind tolerance and poor salt tolerance.

Several named varieties are available in a range of flower colors from pale yellow through golden yellow to orange and cerise—the "rainbow" of the common name. Some may produce occasional seedpods.

'Lunalilo Yellow'. Flowers open a bright yellow orange, then age to bright yellow. Late spring to fall bloom.

'Nii Gold'. A sport of 'Wilhelmina Tenney'. Blooms any time from spring to fall; deep gold buds open to blooms that age to strong yellow.

'Queen's Hospital White'. Flowers open pale yellow, fade rapidly to very light yellow to white. Blooms in spring to late summer.

'Wilhelmina Tenney'. Spectacular blossom clusters from spring to fall. Petal exteriors are deep cerise aging to paler shades; interiors are yellow. Adopted as the official tree of Honolulu.

CASTANEA. See CHESTNUT

CASTANOPSIS cuspidata

JAPANESE CHINQUAPIN, COPPER FALSE CHESTNUT

Fagaceae

EVERGREEN TREE

ZONES 7–9, 14–24

FULL SUN OR LIGHT SHADE

MODERATE TO REGULAR WATER

Castanopsis cuspidata

This subtropical relative of oaks and chestnuts is native to Japan (where it is widely grown in gardens and parks) and China. Fairly slow growing to 25–45 ft. tall, 20–25 ft. wide. Drooping branches bear glossy, leathery, slender-tipped oval leaves that are deep green above, bronze below. Bark is gray and narrowly grooved. Inconspicuous flowers are carried in erect catkins. Clusters of edible acornlike nuts, covered with downy husks, take 2 years to ripen. Requires well-drained soil. Resistant to chestnut blight. Handsome tree for garden or parking strip. 'Shogun' is a cutting-grown variety.

CASTANOSPERMUM australe

MORETON BAY CHESTNUT

Fabaceae (Leguminosae)

EVERGREEN TREE

ZONES 18–22

FULL SUN

REGULAR WATER

RAW SEEDS ARE POISONOUS IF INGESTED

Castanospermum australe

Native to Australia. Beautiful in foliage; spectacular in flower. To 50–60 ft. tall, nearly as wide. Large, shiny, dark green leaves are divided into 11–15 leaflets about 1½ by 5 in. Bright red-and-yellow flowers in stiff spikes about 8 in. long; they grow from twigs, branches, and main trunk in summer. Seeds look like chestnuts but are toxic raw; they may be eaten safely if roasted but don't taste very good. Good lawn or waterside shade tree. Little pruning required.

CAST-IRON PLANT. See ASPIDISTRA elatior

CASTOR ARALIA. See KALOPANAX septemlobus

CASTOR BEAN. See RICINUS communis

CASUARINA

BEEFWOOD, SHE-OAK

Casuarinaceae

EVERGREEN TREES

ZONES 8, 9, 12–24; H1, H2

FULL SUN

LITTLE TO REGULAR WATER

Casuarina stricta

Native primarily to Australia; *C. equisetifolia* is also a Pacific Island native. Long, thin, jointed, green branches look like long pine needles; true leaves are inconspicuous. Tolerate many tough conditions: dry or wet soil, salinity, heat, wind. Hardy to 15°F/–9°C. Particularly useful in desert areas, where they are often confused with Athel tamarisk *(Tamarix aphylla)* because of similar foliage—but the casuarinas have conelike fruit. Cones range from ¼ to 1 in. long in species described here; those of *C. stricta* are largest. Little pruning required.

C. cunninghamiana. RIVER SHE-OAK. Tallest and largest species. To 70 ft. tall, 30 ft. wide. Finest texture, with dark green branches.

C. equisetifolia. HORSETAIL TREE. Fast grower to 40–60 ft. tall, 20 ft. wide. Has pendulous gray-green branches. Plants sold under this name may be *C. cunninghamiana* or hybrids between *C. cunninghamiana* and *C. glauca*.

C. stricta (C. verticillata). MOUNTAIN or DROOPING SHE-OAK, COAST BEEFWOOD. Fast grower to 20–35 ft. tall and wide. Darkest green foliage and largest cones. Makes beautiful silhouette against sky. Attractive street tree. Good at seashore.

CATALINA CHERRY. See PRUNUS lyonii

CATALINA IRONWOOD. See LYONOTHAMNUS floribundus

CATALINA PERFUME. See RIBES viburnifolium

CATALPA

Bignoniaceae

DECIDUOUS TREES

ZONES 3–10, 14–24, EXCEPT AS NOTED

FULL SUN OR LIGHT SHADE

MODERATE TO REGULAR WATER

Catalpa speciosa

Catalpas are among the few hardy deciduous trees that can compete in flower and leaf with subtropical species. Large, upright clusters of trumpet-shaped, 2-in.-wide flowers are pure white, with stripes and markings in yellow and soft brown. These are displayed in late spring and summer above large, bold, heart-shaped leaves. Flowers are followed by long, bean-shaped seed capsules sometimes called "Indian beans."

Unusually well adapted to extremes of heat and cold and to soils throughout the West. Where winds are strong, plant in lee of taller trees or buildings to protect leaves from wind damage. Some gardeners object to litter of fallen flowers in summer and seed capsules in autumn. Plants need shaping while young, seldom develop a well-established dominant shoot. Shorten side branches as tree grows. When branching begins at the desired height, remove lower branches. On established trees, head back or thin out any branches that look out of balance.

For the tree sometimes called desert catalpa, see *Chilopsis linearis*. Another tree sometimes mistakenly called catalpa is the very similar *Paulownia tomentosa,* or empress tree, with lavender flowers. Empress tree shows flower buds in winter; catalpa does not.

C. bignonioides. COMMON CATALPA, INDIAN BEAN. Native to southeastern U.S. Generally smaller than *C. speciosa.* Grows to 30–40 ft. tall, with an equal spread. Leaves are 5–8 in. long, often arranged in whorls, give off odd odor when crushed. Becomes chlorotic in alkaline soil. Resistant to oak root fungus. Yellow leaves of 'Aurea' are showier where summers are cool.

'Nana'. UMBRELLA CATALPA. A dense globe form usually grafted high on *C. bignonioides;* almost always sold as *C. bungei.* It never blooms. Usually around 6 ft. high, 5 ft. wide; cut it back to keep it in scale.

C. × erubescens 'Purpurea'. Selection of a hybrid between *C. bignonioides* and a Chinese species; resembles *C. bignonioides.* Young leaves and branchlets are deep blackish purple, turning purplish green in summer.

C. speciosa. Zones 2–24. Native to central U.S. Most widely distributed catalpa in the West. Round-headed tree to 40–60 ft. tall, 20–40 ft. wide. Leaves 6–12 in. long, odorless when crushed. Fewer flowers per cluster than for *C. bignonioides.*

Catalpa speciosa

FOR INFORMATION ON YOUR CLIMATE ZONE
PLEASE SEE PAGES 27–63

CATANANCHE caerulea

CUPID'S DART

Asteraceae (Compositae)

PERENNIAL

ZONES 1–10, 14–24

FULL SUN

MODERATE WATER

Catananche caerulea

Wispy, free-flowering plant from Europe, good for summer borders and fresh or dried arrangements. Gray-green, grassy leaves form a clump to 1 ft. high and wide. Lavender-blue, 2-in. flower heads, reminiscent of cornflowers and surrounded by strawlike, shining bracts, appear atop leafless stems to 2 ft. high. Remove faded flowers to prolong bloom. 'Alba' has white blossoms, 'Major' deep blue-violet blooms. Plants will flower first year from seed sown in early spring. Rather short lived, but volunteer seedlings usually provide replacements.

CATHARANTHUS roseus (Vinca rosea)

MADAGASCAR PERIWINKLE

Apocynaceae

PERENNIAL USUALLY GROWN AS ANNUAL

ZONES 1–24; H1, H2

FULL SUN OR PARTIAL SHADE

MODERATE WATER

Catharanthus roseus

Native to Madagascar. Good for summer-to-fall color in hot climates; thrives in dry or humid heat. Glossy green, 1–3-in.-long leaves cover bushy plant 1–2 ft. high and wide. Phloxlike, 1½-in. flowers in pure white, white with rose or red eye, blush pink, or bright rose. Blooms all summer and keeps flowering after zinnias and marigolds have finished—until Thanksgiving if weather stays mild. Lives over in frost-free areas but may look ragged in winter. In desert regions, may also look poor in late summer. Self-sows readily. Provide good drainage and avoid overwatering.

Pacific and Cooler series are compact 15-in. plants with large (2-in.) flowers. The Little series grows 8–10 in. high. Creeping strains, including the Carpet series, grow 4–8 in. tall, 1½ ft. wide. The Mediterranean series, featuring apricot, pink, rose, lilac, or white blooms, grows 5–6 in. high and can spread 2½ ft. wide; it's useful as temporary ground cover or in hanging baskets. All types will bloom first season from seed sown early indoors or in a greenhouse or cold frame. Tropicana series blooms in only 60 days from seed, bears blooms in shades of pink and coral on 1-ft. plants. Nurseries sell plants of the many varieties in late spring.

CATMINT. See NEPETA faassenii

CATNIP. See NEPETA cataria

CAT'S CLAW. See MACFADYENA unguis-cati

CAT'S EARS. See CALOCHORTUS

CATTLEYA

Orchidaceae

EPIPHYTIC ORCHIDS

ZONE H2; OR INDOORS

LIGHT SHADE; BRIGHT INDIRECT LIGHT

REGULAR WATER

Cattleya

Native to tropical America. Among most popular and best known of orchids. Showy flowers are used for corsages. ▸

Species, varieties, and hybrids are too numerous to list here. All have pseudobulbs 1–3 in. thick, bearing leathery leaves and a stem topped with one to four or more flowers. Plants range in size from a few inches tall to 2 ft. or more. Commercial growers offer a wide range of flower colors, including lavender and purple, white, and semialbas (white blossoms with colored lip). Also available are novelties in yellow, orange, red, green, and bronze (many of these are crosses between *Cattleya* and other genera).

Cattleyas are widely grown outdoors year-round in Hawaii, either in containers or naturalized on trees. Elsewhere, they are indoor plants that can be brought outdoors during warm weather. They grow best in a greenhouse where temperature, humidity, and light can be readily controlled. However, they can be grown successfully as houseplants if the following needs are satisfied: (1) warm temperatures (55 to 60°F/13 to 16°C at night, 65 to 80°F/18 to 27°C or higher during the day); (2) relatively high humidity (50 to 60 percent or more); (3) bright indirect light with protection from hot midday sun. Leaves should be light green and held erect; if light intensity is too low, they turn dark green and new growth becomes soft. See also Orchidaceae.

CAULIFLOWER

Brassicaceae (Cruciferae)

ANNUAL OR BIENNIAL GROWN AS ANNUAL

ALL ZONES

FULL SUN

REGULAR WATER

Cauliflower

Related to broccoli and cabbage; all three are members of the genus *Brassica* and are thought to have originated in the Mediterranean region. All share similar cultural requirements, but cauliflower is more difficult to grow. Easiest in cool, humid regions; where summers are hot, grow it to harvest well before or well after midsummer, and select heat-tolerant varieties. Home gardeners usually plant one of the several 'Snowball' varieties or choose hybrids such as 'Early White Hybrid' and 'Snow Crown Hybrid'. An unusual variety is 'Purple Head', a large plant with a deep purple head that turns green when cooked.

Start with small plants. Space them 1½–2 ft. apart in rows and leave 3 ft. between rows. Water and fertilize as for broccoli. Be sure to keep plants actively growing; any check in growth is likely to cause premature setting of undersize heads. When heads first appear, tie up the large leaves around them to keep them white. (Leaves of self-blanching varieties curl over developing heads without assistance.) Harvest heads as soon as they reach full size. Most varieties are ready to cut 50 to 100 days after transplanting; overwintering types may take 6 months. Cauliflower is subject to same pests as cabbage.

CEANOTHUS

WILD LILAC

Rhamnaceae

EVERGREEN SHRUBS

ZONES 5–9, 14–24, EXCEPT AS NOTED

FULL SUN

LITTLE OR NO WATER

SEE CHART

Ceanothus gloriosus

Some species grow in eastern U.S., Rocky Mountains, the Northwest, and Mexico, but most are native to California. In flower color, they range from white through all shades of blue, from pale powder blue to deep violet blue. Typically flower in spring; bloom time is not indicated in chart unless it is unusual. Plants vary greatly in habit: some are low and spreading, others compact and bushy, still others upright and angular. Generally evergreen; a couple listed here lose leaves in cold weather. Only types with small leaves tend to be deer resistant. New varieties (most of them propagated from selected wild plants) appear frequently in nurseries, while old ones disappear. For the widest choice, deal with a specialist in Western natives. In Zones 1–3, 8, 9, stay with varieties tested and sold locally.

Ceanothus sometimes get aphids and whiteflies, but these are easy to control. As a group, plants don't live very long; 5 to 10 years is typical.

Ceanothus griseus horizontalis

WHAT CEANOTHUS NEED

DRAINAGE: In the wild, plants grow on rocky slopes. Give them light, well-drained soil in your garden.

WATERING: Some demand total dryness, but others (particularly coastal ground cover types) need occasional summer water if grown away from the fog belt. A few tolerate more frequent summer moisture.

PRUNING: Wait until after blooms have faded; avoid cutting off branches that are more than an inch in diameter. Control plant growth by pinching back shoot tips during the growing season.

Ceanothus 'Concha'

CEDAR. See CEDRUS

CEDAR, INCENSE. See CALOCEDRUS decurrens

CEDAR, WESTERN RED. See THUJA plicata

CEDAR OF LEBANON. See CEDRUS libani

CEDRELA sinensis. See TOONA sinensis

CEDRUS

CEDAR

Pinaceae

EVERGREEN TREES

ZONES VARY BY SPECIES

FULL SUN

MODERATE WATER

Cedrus atlantica

These, the true cedars, are among the most widely grown conifers in the West. Cedars bear needles in tufted clusters. Cone scales, like those of firs *(Abies)*, fall from tree, leaving a spiky core behind. Male catkins produce prodigious amounts of pollen that may cover you with yellow dust on a windy day. Plant in deep, well-drained soil. All species are deep rooted and drought tolerant once established. Some botanists contend that the several Mediterranean species are just geographic variants of a single species.

C. atlantica (C. libani atlantica). ATLAS CEDAR. Zones 3b–10, 14–24. Native to North Africa. Slow to moderate growth to 60 ft. or taller. Open, angular growth in youth. Branches usually get too long and heavy on young trees unless tips are pinched out or cut back; branches of any age tend to break in heavy snows. Growth naturally less open with age. Less spreading than other true cedars, but still needs 30-ft. circle. ▶page 258

CEANOTHUS

SPECIES OR VARIETY	SIZE	FOLIAGE	FLOWERS	COMMENTS
Ceanothus 'Blue Jeans'	7–9 ft. tall and wide	Small, dark green leathery leaves	Profuse, pale powder blue clusters	Tolerates heavy soil, drought, summer water. Shear after bloom for low-water-use hedge
C. 'Centennial'	2 ft. tall, 10 ft. wide	Small, shiny dark green leaves	Very dark blue, in short clusters	More heat resistant than *C. griseus horizontalis*
C. 'Concha' Zones 6–9, 14–24	6–7 ft. tall, 6–8 ft. wide	Densely clad in dark green 1-in. leaves	Dark blue 1-in. clusters	One of the best for gardens. Tolerates summer water. Hardy to 15°F/–9°C
C. 'Dark Star'	5–6 ft. tall, 8–10 ft. wide	Tiny (¼-in.), dark green leaves	Dark cobalt blue 1½-in. clusters	Similar to *C.* 'Julia Phelps', maybe better
C. × delilianus 'Gloire de Versailles' Zones 3b–9, 14–24	15 ft. tall and wide	Dark green leaves to 3 in. long, evergreen in mild-winter regions, deciduous elsewhere	Fragrant, profuse, light blue	Hybrid of blue-flowered Mexican species with hardy, white-flowered, deciduous eastern U.S. native. Open, rangy; can be espaliered. Only one of this hybrid group to attain popularity
C. fendleri Zones 1–3	From prostrate to 6 ft. tall; to 6 ft. wide	1-in. gray-green leaves, partially evergreen or deciduous	Bluish white	Native to Rocky Mountains
C. 'Frosty Blue'	6–9 ft. tall, 8–10 ft. wide	Dark green ½-in. leaves. Dense	Deep blue, white-frosted, 2½–3-in. spikelike clusters	White "frosting" makes flowers shimmer. Sturdy stems. Can be shaped as small tree
C. 'Gentian Plume'	10–20 ft. tall, 12–20 ft. wide	Dark green 2½-in. leaves	Dark blue, 10-in. spikelike clusters	Leggy when young; pinching helps. If stems get so long that plants "fall apart," prune them
C. gloriosus POINT REYES CEANOTHUS	1–1½ ft. tall, 12–16 ft. wide	Dark green, oval, 1-in. leaves, tough and spiny	Typically light blue, in 1-in. clusters	Much used in Zones 4–6. Does not do well in summer heat of Zones 7, 14, 18–21
C. g. 'Anchor Bay'	1–1½ ft. tall, 6–8 ft. wide	Very dense	Somewhat deeper blue than above	Dense foliage holds down weeds. 'Heart's Desire' is similar but has smaller, shiny leaves
C. g. exaltatus 'Emily Brown'	2–3 ft. tall, 8–12 ft. wide	Dark green, hollylike, 1-in. leaves	Dark violet-blue 1-in. clusters	Tolerates heavy soil, summer water near coast
C. g. porrectus MOUNT VISION CEANOTHUS	3–4 ft. tall, 6–8 ft. wide	Dark green, hollylike, ½-in. leaves	Medium dark blue 1-in. clusters	Dense growth but sparse bloom
C. griseus horizontalis CARMEL CREEPER Zones 5–9, 14–17, 19–24	1½–2½ ft. tall, 5–15 ft. wide	Glossy, oval, 2-in., bright green leaves	Light blue 1-in. clusters	Some sold under this name may be 'Hurricane Point'. Sometimes suffers winter damage in Zones 5–7, 14
C. g. h. 'Hurricane Point'	2–3 ft. tall, to 36 ft. wide	Glossy, oval, 2-in. leaves	Pale blue 1-in. clusters	Very fast, somewhat rank grower. Deer love this and the other forms of *C. griseus*
C. g. h. 'Yankee Point'	2–3 ft. tall, 8–10 ft. wide	Glossy dark green 1½-in. leaves	Medium blue 1-in. clusters	One of best ground-covering kinds. Looks refined
C. g. 'Louis Edmunds'	5–6 ft. tall, 9–20 ft. wide	Bright glossy green 1-in. leaves	Medium sea blue 1-in. clusters	Tolerates heavy soil, summer water
C. g. 'Santa Ana'	4–5 ft. tall, 10–15 ft. wide	Rich dark green ½-in. leaves	Dark midnight blue 1-in. clusters	Somewhat brushy stems, but beautiful flowers
C. hearstiorum	6 in. tall, 6–8 ft. wide	Puckered 1½-in. leaves	Medium blue 1-in. clusters	One of flattest, but lets in weeds. Spreads from center like a star. Variable performance; not dependable

C

CEANOTHUS

SPECIES OR VARIETY	SIZE	FOLIAGE	FLOWERS	COMMENTS
C. impressus SANTA BARBARA CEANOTHUS	6–9 ft. tall, 10–15 ft. wide	Dense mass of dark green ½-in. leaves	Lovely dark blue 1-in. clusters	Temperamental; does best near coast. Performs quite well in Pacific Northwest
C. 'Joan Mirov'	4 ft. tall, 10 ft. wide	Very dark green, shiny, ½-in. leaves	Profuse deep blue flowers	Good bank cover; considered one of the more disease-resistant selections
C. 'Joyce Coulter'	2–5 ft. tall, 10–12 ft. wide	Medium green 1-in. leaves	Medium blue, 3–5-in. spikelike clusters	Grows as mound rather than ground cover
C. 'Julia Phelps'	4½–7 ft. tall, 7–9 ft. wide	Small (½-in.), dark green leaves	Dark indigo 1-in. clusters	One of best colors, best bloomers
C. maritimus	1–3 ft. tall, 3–8 ft. wide	Blue-green to grayish ½-in. leaves, typically gray or white beneath	White to pale lavender ½-in. clusters	Height and color vary greatly. 'Frosty Dawn' has darker blue flowers. 'Point Sierra' is more tolerant of interior heat
C. 'Owlswood Blue'	8–10 ft. tall, 10–12 ft. wide	Dark green, oval, 2½-in. leaves	Dark blue, 4–6-in. spikelike clusters	Reliable, heavy bloom
C. prostratus SQUAW CARPET, MAHALA MATS Zones 2–6, 14–16, 18	Prostrate; to 8 ft. wide	Leathery, toothed, light green leaves, ½–1 in. long	Deep to light blue clusters	Useful in native range (higher elevations in northern Sierra Nevada), nearly impossible elsewhere. *C. p. occidentalis,* from northern Coast Ranges, is rare, difficult
C. 'Ray Hartman'	12–20 ft. tall, 15–20 ft. wide	Big (2–3-in.), dark green leaves	Medium blue, 3–5-in. spikelike clusters	Can be trained as small tree
C. rigidus 'Snowball'	6 ft. tall, 12–16 ft. wide	Dark green ½-in. leaves	White puffs, ¾ in. wide	Handsome, dense, mounding
C. 'Sierra Blue'	10–12 ft. tall, 8–10 ft. wide	Glossy, medium green 1½-in. leaves	Bright medium blue, 6–8-in. spikelike clusters	Very fast grower; weedy first few years
C. thyrsiflorus BLUE BLOSSOM	6–21 ft. tall, 8–30 ft. wide	Glossy green leaves to 2 in.	Light to dark blue, 3-in. spikelike clusters	One of the hardiest ceanothus. *C. t. repens* is a prostrate form
C. t. 'Skylark'	3–6 ft. tall, 5 ft. wide	Glossy medium green 2-in. leaves	Dark blue clusters; profuse bloom over a long season	Tolerates summer water
C. t. 'Snow Flurry'	6–10 ft. tall, 8–12 ft. wide	Rich green 2-in. leaves	Profuse pure white clusters	
C. velutinus TOBACCO BRUSH Zones 2–7, 15–17	3–8 ft. tall and wide	Glossy, aromatic leaves 3 in. long	White, late in season	Useful in native plantings in cold climates

Needles, less than 1 in. long, are bluish green. Varieties include 'Aurea', needles with yellowish tint; 'Glauca', silvery blue; 'Glauca Pendula', weeping form with blue needles; 'Pendula', vertically drooping branches. Untrained, spreading, informally branching plants are sold as "rustics."

C. brevifolia. CYPRUS (or CYPRIAN) CEDAR. Zones 5–10, 14–24. Native to Cyprus. Resembles *C. libani* but is smaller (to 50 ft. tall and 40 ft. wide) with shorter needles (¼–½ in.) and smaller cones. Sometimes considered variety of *C. libani.* Very slow growing.

C. deodara. DEODAR CEDAR. Zones 3b–10, 14–24. Native to the Himalayas. Fast growing to 80 ft., with 40-ft. spread at ground level. Lower branches sweep down to ground, then upward. Upper branches openly spaced, graceful. Nodding tip identifies it in skyline. Softer, lighter texture than other cedars. Planted in small lawn, it soon overpowers area. You can control spread of tree by cutting new growth of side branches halfway back in late spring. This kind of pruning also makes tree denser.

Cedrus deodara

Although deodars sold by nurseries are very similar in overall form, many variations occur within a group of seedlings—from scarecrowlike types to low, compact shrubs. Following variations are propagated by cuttings or grafting.

'Aurea'. New foliage is yellow, turning to golden green in summer.

'Pendula' ('Prostrata'). Grows flat on ground or will drape attractively over rocks or wall.

'Prostrate Beauty'. To 1½–2 ft. tall; may spread 7–8 ft. in 10 years.

'Silver Mist'. Similar to 'Snow Sprite', but tips are white.

'Snow Sprite'. To 12 ft. tall and broad in 10 years. Foliage is silvery green with cream-colored tips.

'White Imp'. Very dwarf—only 3 ft. tall and wide.

C. libani. CEDAR OF LEBANON. Zones 3–10, 14–24. Native Lebanon to Turkey. To 80 ft., but slow growing—to 15 ft. in 15 years. Variable in growth habit. Usually a dense, narrow pyramid in youth. In young trees, needles, less than 1 in. long, are brightest green of the cedars; in old ones, they are dark gray green. Spreads picturesquely as it matures to become majestic skyline tree with long horizontal limbs and an irregular shape; the tree is ultimately about as broad as high. Rather scarce and expensive because of time to reach salable size. Routine garden care. No pruning needed. 'Sargentii' ('Pendula Sargentii') grows even more slowly, has a short trunk and crowded, weeping branches; choice container or rock garden plant. 'Pendula' is a slow-growing, weeping form.

Celastraceae. This family of evergreen and deciduous woody plants has undistinguished flowers, but fruit is often brightly colored. Bittersweet *(Celastrus)* and *Euonymus* are examples.

CELASTRUS

BITTERSWEET
Celastraceae
DECIDUOUS VINES
ZONES VARY BY SPECIES
FULL SUN
REGULAR WATER

Celastrus scandens

Grown principally for clusters of ornamental summer fruit—yellow to orange capsules that split open to display brilliant red-coated seeds. Branches bearing fruit are much prized for indoor arrangements. Since birds seem uninterested in fruit, display extends into winter. To get fruit, you need to plant male and female plants close to each other, but unfortunately nursery plants are not always labeled. Self-fruitful forms of *C. orbiculatus* are available. Foliage turns yellow in fall.

Vigorous and twining, with ropelike branches; need support. Don't allow these vines to climb shrubs or small trees—they can kill them by girdling the stems. Prune tangled or intertwined branches before new spring growth begins; prune as needed during summer to manage growth. Growing in poorer soils helps keep vines to more manageable size.

C. orbiculatus. CHINESE BITTERSWEET. Zones 2b–7, 10. Native to Asia. Aggressive grower to 30–40 ft. Leaves roundish, toothed, to 4 in. Fruit on short side shoots is partially obscured until leaves drop.

C. rosthornianus (C. loeseneri). Zones 3b–7, 10. Chinese native. Grows to 20 ft., with oval leaves to 5 in. long. Similar to *C. orbiculatus,* but not as rampant.

C. scandens. AMERICAN BITTERSWEET. Zones A3; 2–7, 10. Native to eastern North America. To 20 ft. or more. Oval, tooth-edged leaves to 4 in. long. Fruit appears in scattered dense clusters; these are held above leaves, making *C. scandens* showier than other two species.

CELERIAC

Apiaceae (Umbelliferae)
BIENNIAL GROWN AS ANNUAL
ALL ZONES
FULL SUN
REGULAR WATER

Celeriac

Known botanically as *Apium graveolens rapaceum.* A form of celery grown for its large, rounded, edible roots rather than for leafstalks, this is the "celery root" sold in markets. Roots are peeled, then cooked or used raw in salads.

Growth requirements are same as for celery. Grow plants 6–8 in. apart in rows spaced 1½–2 ft. apart. Harvest when roots are 3 in. across or larger—about 100 to 120 days after transplanting. 'Brilliant' and 'Mentor' are among several improved varieties.

CELERY

Apiaceae (Umbelliferae)
BIENNIAL GROWN AS ANNUAL
ALL ZONES
FULL SUN
REGULAR WATER

Celery

Botanical name is *Apium graveolens dulce;* native to Europe and Asia. Needs long period of warmth but not high heat. Plant seeds in flats in early spring; where winters are mild, start in summer for winter crop. (Celery plants started from seed are slow to reach planting size; to save time, you can purchase small nursery plants.) Plant seedlings in rich soil, spacing 6 in. apart in rows 2 ft. apart. Every 2 to 3 weeks, apply liquid fertilizer with irrigation water. To keep plants upright, work some soil up around them as they grow. For whitened stalks, set bottomless milk carton, tar paper cylinder, or similar device over plants to exclude light from stalks (leaves must have sunlight). Or grow self-blanching varieties. Harvest 105 to 130 days after transplanting. Row covers will keep out many pests.

CELERY ROOT. See CELERIAC

CELOSIA

COCKSCOMB, CHINESE WOOLFLOWER
Amaranthaceae
ANNUALS
ZONES 1–24; H1, H2;
BEST IN ZONES 8–14, 18, 19; H1, H2
FULL SUN
MODERATE WATER

Celosia

Richly colored tropical plants, some with flower clusters in bizarre shapes. Although attractive in cut arrangements with other flowers, in gardens celosias are most effective by themselves. Cut blooms can be dried for winter bouquets. Sow seed in place in late spring or early summer, or set out started plants.

There are two kinds of cockscombs, both derived from a silvery white–flowered species, *C. argentea,* which has narrow leaves 2 in. long or more. One group, the plume cockscombs (often sold as *C.* 'Plumosa'), has plumy flower clusters. Some of these, like Chinese woolflower (sometimes sold as *C.* 'Childsii'), have plumy flower clusters that look like tangled masses of yarn. Flowers come in brilliant shades of pink, orange red, gold, crimson. You can get forms that grow 2½–3 ft. high and 1½ ft. wide. Dwarf, more compact varieties grow about 1 ft. high and half as wide; they bear heavily branched plumes.

The other group is the crested cockscombs (often sold as *C.* 'Cristata'). These have velvety, fan-shaped flower clusters, often much contorted and fluted. Flower colors include yellow, orange, crimson, purple, and red. Tall kinds grow to 3 ft. tall and 1½ ft. wide, dwarf varieties to 10 in. high and 6 in. wide.

FOR GROWING SYMBOL EXPLANATIONS
PLEASE SEE PAGE 161

CELTIS

HACKBERRY

Ulmaceae

DECIDUOUS TREES

ZONES VARY BY SPECIES

FULL SUN OR PARTIAL SHADE

MODERATE WATER

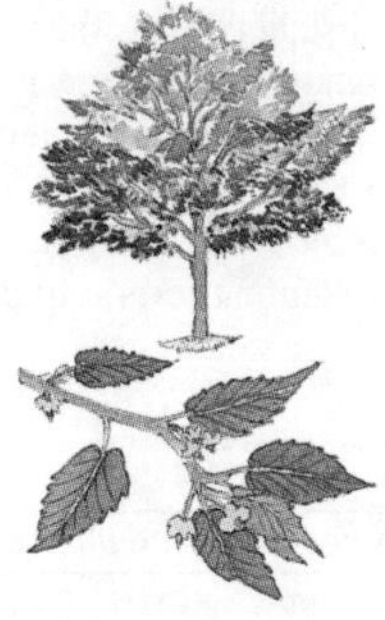

Celtis occidentalis

Related to elms *(Ulmus)* and similar to them in most details, but smaller. All have virtue of deep rooting; old trees in narrow planting strips expand in trunk diameter to nearly fill strips without producing surface roots or heaving sidewalk or curb. Good choice for street or lawn tree, even near buildings or paving. Canopy casts moderate shade in spring and summer; leaves turn yellow in fall. Mature trees have picturesque bark with corky warts and ridges. Small berrylike fruits attract birds.

Hackberry is exceptionally tough, tolerating strong winds (stake young trees until well established), desert heat, and dry, alkaline soils. Leaf gall caused by psyllids may disfigure hackberry leaves in some regions (especially in the Rocky Mountain states and Pacific Northwest), but the trees are not harmed. Little pruning required. Bare-root plants, especially in larger sizes, sometimes fail to leaf out. Buy in containers or try for small bare-root trees with big root systems.

C. australis. EUROPEAN HACKBERRY. Zones 8–16, 18–20. Mediterranean native grows at moderate rate to 40 ft. high in 14 or 15 years. Eventually can reach 70–80 ft. tall, 30–35 ft. wide. In youth, branches are more upright than those of other hackberries. Dark green, 2–5-in.-long leaves, more coarsely toothed and sharper tipped than those of *C. occidentalis;* also has shorter deciduous period. Resistant to oak root fungus.

C. occidentalis. COMMON HACKBERRY. Zones 1–24. Native to eastern North America. To 50 ft. or taller and nearly as wide, with rounded crown and spreading, sometimes pendulous branches. Bright green, oval leaves, 2–5 in. long, with finely toothed edges. Tree does not leaf out until mid-spring. Resistant to oak root fungus. In Zones 10–13, lives longer than and is superior to commonly planted "Chinese elm" (actually the Siberian elm, *Ulmus pumila*).

C. pallida. DESERT HACKBERRY, GRANJENO. Zones 10–13. Native to southwestern U.S. and northern Mexico. Small tree or shrub with dense, spiny growth to 18 ft. tall; variable in width, sometimes growing wider than tall. Leaves 1 in. or shorter. Small orange berries. Useful in desert as honey source or bird food, for screen or barrier planting, for erosion control.

C. reticulata (C. douglasii). WESTERN HACKBERRY. Zones 2–24; best in 2, 3, 7–13, 18–21. Native to eastern Washington, northern Oregon, Idaho, through intermountain area to Utah, and in mountains of Arizona and Southern California. To 25–30 ft. tall and wide, with somewhat pendulous branches. Oval, tooth-edged leaves to 2½ in. long, pale beneath, strongly veined.

C. sinensis. CHINESE HACKBERRY, YUNNAN HACKBERRY. Zones 8–16, 18–20. From East Asia. Similar in growth habit to *C. occidentalis,* but smaller (to 40 ft. tall and wide). Leaves to 4 in. long, smoother and glossier than those of other hackberries, with scalloped edges.

CENTAUREA

Asteraceae (Compositae)

ANNUALS, BIENNIALS, AND PERENNIALS

ZONES VARY BY SPECIES

FULL SUN

MODERATE WATER, EXCEPT AS NOTED

Centaurea cineraria

Out of some 500 species, only a dozen or so are widely cultivated. Of these, annuals are grown mainly for cut flowers; perennial kinds are valued for soft, silvery foliage. All are relatively easy to grow. For best performance, add lime to acid soils. Sow seeds of annuals or set out plants of perennial kinds in spring or fall. (In desert regions, plant all in autumn for winter and spring bloom.)

C. americana. BASKET FLOWER. Annual. Zones 1–24; H1, H2. Native to central and southwestern U.S. To 5–6 ft. tall, 3 ft. wide. Leaves rather rough, oval, to 4 in. long. Summer flowers to 4 in. wide are rose pink, paler toward center. Good in fresh or dried arrangements.

C. cineraria (C. candidissima). DUSTY MILLER. Perennial in Zones 8–24, H1, H2; annual in Zones 1–7. (This common name is used for many plants with whitish foliage; see Dusty Miller, page 321.) From Italy. Compact growth to 1 ft. wide, 1 ft. or taller. Velvety white, strap-shaped leaves with broad, roundish lobes, mostly in basal clump. Solitary 1-in. flower heads (purple, occasionally yellow) in summer. Trim back after bloom. Attracts bees.

C. cyanus. CORNFLOWER, BACHELOR'S BUTTON. Annual. Zones 1–24; H1, H2. From northern temperate regions. A common weed in some areas, such as the Pacific Northwest. To 1–1½ ft. tall, less than a foot wide, branching if given enough space. Narrow gray-green leaves, 2–3 in. long. Spring to midsummer flowers are 1½ in. across, in blue, pink, rose, wine red, or white; blue varieties are traditional favorites for boutonnieres. 'Jubilee Gem' is a bushy, compact 1-footer with deep blue flowers; Polka Dot strain has all cornflower colors on 16-in. plants.

C. gymnocarpa. DUSTY MILLER. Perennial. Zones 8–24. Italian native considered a form of *C. cineraria.* To 1–3 ft. tall, 1 ft. wide. White, feltlike leaves are more finely divided than those of *C. cineraria.* Usually two or three purple flowers at ends of leafy branches in summer. Trim plants after bloom. Very drought tolerant but can take regular irrigation.

C. hypoleuca 'John Coutts'. Perennial. Zones 2–9, 14–24. Variety of species from Asia Minor. Resembles *C. montana* but has more deeply lobed leaves and deep rose flowers.

C. macrocephala. Perennial. Zones 2–9, 14–24. From the Caucasus. Attractive, coarse-foliaged, leafy plant 3–4 ft. tall, 2 ft. wide. Blooms in summer, bearing 2-in. clusters of yellow flowers tightly wrapped at the base with overlapping, shiny, papery brown bracts. Flower heads resemble thistles. Use in fresh or dried arrangements.

C. montana. Perennial. Zones 2–9, 14–24. Native to mountains of central Europe. Forms clump 1½–2 ft. tall and wide; grayish green leaves reach 7 in. long. Flowers resembling ragged 3-in. cornflowers top the stems in late spring to midsummer. Protect from snails. Divide every other year. Regular water.

C. moschata (Amberboa moschata). SWEET SULTAN. Annual. Zones 1–24. From Asia Minor. Erect, branching at base, to 10 in. wide, 2 ft. tall (Imperialis strain reaches 3 ft.). Green, deeply toothed leaves. Fluffy, thistlelike, 1-in. flowers from spring to fall, mostly in shades of lilac through rose, sometimes white or yellow. Musky fragrance. Splendid cut flower. Sow seed directly on soil in spring or set out as transplants. Needs lots of heat; no overhead water.

C. rothrockii. Annual or biennial. Zones 1–24. Southwest native to 4–6 ft. tall, 2 ft. wide, with 4-in.-long leaves. Flowers like soft thistles bloom from midsummer into fall; these are 5 in. wide, with pink outer rays and a creamy white to yellow center. Frost sensitive; start seeds indoors in cold-winter areas and transplant after last frost. Good for arrangements if cut just before flowers open.

CENTRANTHUS ruber (Valeriana rubra)

JUPITER'S BEARD, RED VALERIAN

Valerianaceae

PERENNIAL

ZONES 2–9, 12–24; H1

FULL SUN OR PARTIAL SHADE

LITTLE TO MODERATE WATER

Centranthus ruber

Mediterranean native is a weed in many parts of the West. Self-sows prolifically, thanks to small dandelion-like parachutes on seeds. When used in fringe areas of garden, though, it's hard to beat for long, showy bloom. Forms a bushy clump to 3 ft. high and wide, with bluish green, 4-in.-long leaves. Small (about 1½-in.-long) flowers, in dense terminal clusters in late spring, early summer. In cool-summer climates, blooms sporadically throughout summer, sometimes into fall. Typical colors range from deep crimson to pale pink; 'Albus' has white blooms. Plants grow in poor, dry soils and tolerate almost any condition except damp shade. Cut off old flowering stems to shape plants and prevent self-seeding.

CENTURY PLANT. See AGAVE americana

CEPHALANTHUS occidentalis

BUTTONBUSH, BUTTON WILLOW

Rubiaceae

DECIDUOUS SHRUB OR TREE

ZONES 2–10, 14–21

FULL SUN OR LIGHT SHADE

REGULAR TO AMPLE WATER

Cephalanthus occidentalis

Remarkable for wide distribution—eastern Canada to Florida, Minnesota south through Oklahoma and west to California, with outposts in Cuba, Mexico, and Asia. Grows 3–15 ft. or taller and equally wide, with rounded, rather open habit and bright green, paired or whorled leaves 2–6 in. long. Leafs out late in spring. Creamy white, slender-tubed flowers crowded in rounded, 1–1½-in.-wide heads in late summer. Projecting stigmas give blossom clusters the look of a pincushion. Blossoms attract butterflies. Useful for naturalizing in wet areas. *C. o. californicus* is very similar.

CEPHALARIA gigantea

Dipsacaceae

PERENNIAL

ZONES 2–10, 14–24

FULL SUN

REGULAR WATER

Cephalaria gigantea

Native to the Caucasus. Giant perennial (to 6–8 ft. tall, 2 ft. wide) with coarse, deeply cut leaves to 16 in. long. Pale yellow summer flower heads to 2½ in. wide appear atop long, sparsely branched stems; they resemble those of pincushion flower (in fact, plant was once called *Scabiosa gigantea*). Useful in the wild garden or at the back of a border. Despite its height, seldom requires staking.

CEPHALOCEREUS senilis

OLD MAN CACTUS

Cactaceae

CACTUS

ZONES 13, 21–24; H1; OR INDOORS

FULL SUN; BRIGHT LIGHT

LITTLE OR NO WATER

Cephalocereus senilis

Native to Mexico. Slender, columnar cactus growing slowly to 45 ft. tall in great old age; usually much smaller. Covered with long, grayish white hairs and 1½-in. yellow spines. Only old, quite large (over 15-ft.-tall) plants bloom; they flower in spring, bearing 2-in.-long, rose-colored flowers that open at night. Grow in rocky or loose soil. Supplemental water, fertilizer will speed growth of garden plants. Protect from hard frosts. In Zone 13, provide some shade. Indoors, give southern exposure.

CEPHALOPHYLLUM 'Red Spike'

RED SPIKE ICE PLANT

Aizoaceae

SUCCULENT PERENNIAL

ZONES 8, 9, 11–24

FULL SUN OR PARTIAL SHADE

MODERATE TO REGULAR WATER

Cephalophyllum 'Red Spike'

South African native forms a clump 3–5 in. high, slowly spreading to 15–18 in. wide. Spiky green to bronzy red leaves point up. Bright red, 2-in. flowers in winter or early spring, sporadic bloom in other seasons. Blooms attract bees. Grow in well-drained soil. Plant 6–12 in. apart for ground cover. Provide supplemental irrigation during active growth and bloom; cut back watering in summer. In the desert, needs afternoon shade. Sometimes sold as *Cylindrophyllum* 'Red Spike'.

CEPHALOTAXUS harringtonia

PLUM YEW

Cephalotaxaceae

EVERGREEN SHRUB OR TREE

ZONES 4–9, 14–17

PARTIAL SHADE IN HOTTEST CLIMATES

MODERATE WATER

Cephalotaxus harringtonia

Slow-growing conifer from Asia. Related to yew *(Taxus)* but differs in having larger, brighter green needles 1–2½ in. long and (on female plants only) larger fruits that resemble small green or brown plums. This species is best known through its selections. 'Fastigiata' ('Stricta') is a broadly columnar form that can reach 10 ft. tall, 6–8 ft. wide. The name 'Prostrata' is given to plants propagated from side branches; these do not form a strong leader and remain 2–3 ft. tall, somewhat wider. Plum yew tolerates much pruning and will resprout after being cut back into older wood. You may find these plants labeled *C. fortunei,* but that is a different species with longer, more slender leaves.

CERASTIUM tomentosum

SNOW-IN-SUMMER

Caryophyllaceae

PERENNIAL

ZONES A1, A2; 1–24

LIGHT SHADE IN HOTTEST CLIMATES

MODERATE TO REGULAR WATER

Cerastium tomentosum

Low-growing European native performs equally well in mild and cold climates, coastal and desert areas. Forms dense, tufty mats of silvery gray, ¾-in. leaves; grows 6–8 in. high, spreads 2–3 ft. in a year. Bears masses of small snow-white flowers in early summer. Use as ground cover on slopes or level ground, as bulb cover, in rock gardens, for edging along paths, between stepping-stones. Plant is not long lived, so avoid extensive planting in prominent situations.

Takes any soil as long as drainage is good. Set divisions or plants 1–1½ ft. apart, or sow seed. To speed growth, water regularly and feed two or three times a year. After bloom ends, shear off faded flower clusters or mow planting. May look a bit shabby in winter but revives rapidly in spring. When bare patches show, divide and replant in fall or early spring.

FOR INFORMATION ON SELECTING PLANTS
PLEASE SEE PAGES 64–160

C

CERATOIDES lanata (Krascheninnikovia lanata)

WINTER FAT

Chenopodiaceae

SHRUB

ZONES 2, 3, 7–14, 18–24

FULL SUN

LITTLE TO MODERATE WATER

Ceratoides lanata

Native to much of the arid West. To 1½–3 ft. tall and equally wide, with tiny linear leaves. In autumn, produces spikelike, woolly white seed heads, 1½–7 in. long; these attract birds and can be used in dried arrangements. Tolerates alkaline soil. It has also been known as *Eurotia lanata.* Common name derives from plant's usefulness as winter browse.

CERATONIA siliqua

CAROB, ST. JOHN'S BREAD

Fabaceae (Leguminosae)

EVERGREEN SHRUB OR TREE

ZONES 9, 13–16, 18–24; H1

FULL SUN

LITTLE TO REGULAR WATER

Ceratonia siliqua

Native to eastern Mediterranean region. Often multistemmed, it maintains bushy form with branches to ground when allowed to grow naturally. Use this way as big hedge, informal or trimmed. Trained as tree, with lower branches removed, it grows at moderate rate to become dense and round headed, to 30–40 ft. tall and wide. Will reach 20 ft. in 10 years. As street tree it needs more than normal space since roots will break sidewalks.

Foliage is glossy dark green, unusually dense. Leaves are divided into four to ten round leaflets averaging about 2 in. long. Small red flowers in spring. Female trees produce (and drop) abundant 1-ft.-long flattened, dark brown, leathery pods. Rich in sugar, the pods are milled to a fine powder and sold in health food stores as chocolate substitute.

Hardy to 18°F/–8°C; give young trees winter protection first year or two. Resistant to oak root fungus. Avoid overwatering in heavy or poorly drained soils, since carob is subject to root-crown rot. Very drought tolerant. If raised for fruit crop, needs regular moisture.

CERATOSTIGMA

PLUMBAGO

Plumbaginaceae

EVERGREEN AND DECIDUOUS SHRUBS AND PERENNIALS

ZONES VARY BY SPECIES

FULL SUN OR PARTIAL SHADE

MODERATE TO REGULAR WATER

Ceratostigma plumbaginoides

Valued for clusters of intense blue, phloxlike flowers that bloom in summer to late fall, when cool hues are often especially welcome in the garden. (For pale blue–flowered Cape plumbago, see *Plumbago auriculata.*) Tolerate inconsistent watering. Shrubby species are usually treated like perennials in colder zones; cut them back after bloom and apply a thick mulch.

C. griffithii. BURMESE PLUMBAGO. Evergreen shrub. Zones 4–9, 14–24. Himalayan native similar to *C. willmottianum* in general appearance, but it has rounder leaves and more compact, somewhat lower growth (to 2½–3 ft. high and wide). Also blooms somewhat later. Growth often nipped back by frost.

C. plumbaginoides (Plumbago larpentae). DWARF PLUMBAGO. Perennial. Zones 2b–10, 14–24. Native to China. Wiry-stemmed ground cover to 6–12 in. high. Bronzy to dark green, 3-in.-long leaves turn reddish brown with frosts. Blooms well only in areas with long growing season. Most striking in early or midautumn, when blue blossoms contrast with red fall foliage. In loose soil and where growing season is long, spreads rapidly and (eventually) widely by underground stems. Plant 1–1½ ft. apart for quick cover. Shear or mow annually before spring growth begins. When plants show signs of aging, dig up and replace with rooted stems.

C. willmottianum. CHINESE PLUMBAGO. Deciduous shrub. Zones 4–9, 14–24. Grows as airy mass of wiry stems 2–4 ft. high and wide. Deep green, 2-in.-long leaves are somewhat diamond shaped, with tapering tips; turn yellow or red and drop quickly after frost.

CERCIDIPHYLLUM japonicum

KATSURA TREE

Cercidiphyllaceae

DECIDUOUS TREE

ZONES 2B–6, 14–16, 18–20

FULL SUN OR LIGHT SHADE

REGULAR WATER

Cercidiphyllum japonicum

Native to China, Japan. A specimen tree of many virtues if given regular moisture (especially during youth) and sheltered from intense sun and drying wind. Light, dainty branch and leaf pattern. Foliage changes color during growing season: emerges reddish purple, becomes bluish green in summer, then turns yellow to apricot in autumn. To enhance fall color, water less frequently in late summer. Trees grown in acid soil will have best color. Foliage of some katsura trees smells like brown sugar on warm autumn days when leaves are falling.

Rather slow growing, eventually reaching 40 ft. or taller. Pyramidal form when young; tree may remain fairly pyramidal or become more rounded (and as wide as tall) with maturity. Some specimens have single trunk, but multiple trunks are more usual. Brown bark, somewhat shaggy on old trees. Nearly round, 2–4-in. leaves neatly spaced in pairs along arching branches. No serious pest or disease problems. Mature trees need little pruning. There is a weeping form known as 'Pendulum' or 'Pendula'.

CERCIDIUM

PALO VERDE

Fabaceae (Leguminosae)

DECIDUOUS TREES

ZONES 8–14, 18–20, EXCEPT AS NOTED

FULL SUN

LITTLE TO MODERATE WATER

Cercidium floridum

Tough, trouble-free desert trees valued for floral display, shade, colorful bark. Clusters of small, bright yellow flowers nearly hide the spiny branches in spring. Lightly filtered shade is cast by intricate canopy of twigs rather than by tiny leaves, which are shed early. These trees attract birds. Prune only to enhance form, removing crossing, wayward, or too low branches; hold off on pruning when temperatures rise above 100°F/38°C.

C. 'Desert Museum'. This tree carries genes from *Parkinsonia aculeata, Cercidium microphyllum,* and *C. floridum* and combines the best traits of all three. It grows to 20 ft. tall and as wide in 3 to 5 years. Large (1-in.) blossoms appear over a long period; flowering is most profuse in spring, with rebloom possible in summer. Light green stems and leaves. This is a clean, thornless tree that produces few seedpods and scant litter.

C. floridum. BLUE PALO VERDE. Native to deserts of Southern California, Arizona, Baja California. In gardens, grows fast to 35 ft. tall, 30 ft. wide. Bright pure yellow flowers in 2–4½-in. clusters; earliest of these palo verdes to bloom in spring. Bluish green leaves with one to three pairs of smooth, tiny leaflets; bluish green branches.

C. microphyllum. LITTLELEAF PALO VERDE, FOOTHILLS PALO VERDE. Native to parts of Southern California, Arizona's Sonoran Desert, Baja California. Slow growth to 20 ft. tall and wide. Leaves (with 4–12 pairs of hairy leaflets) and bark are yellowish green. Pale yellow flowers in 1-in. clusters.

C. praecox (C. plurifoliolatum). PALO BREA, SONORAN PALO VERDE. Zones 12 (warmer parts), 13, 18–20. Native Sonoran Desert to South America. Moderate growth to 20 ft. tall and wide. Umbrella form; lime green bark and leaves divided into 12–14 pairs of ¼-in. leaflets.

CERCIS

REDBUD

Fabaceae (Leguminosae)

DECIDUOUS SHRUBS OR TREES

ZONES VARY BY SPECIES

FULL SUN OR LIGHT SHADE

MODERATE TO REGULAR WATER, EXCEPT AS NOTED

Cercis occidentalis

Valued for flowers, fruit, foliage. Clusters of small, sweet pea–shaped, rosy to purplish pink blossoms in early spring; where plant is adapted, blooms are borne in great profusion on bare twigs, branches, sometimes even on main trunk. Flowers are followed by clusters of flat, beanlike pods that persist into winter. Attractive broad, rounded leaves are heart shaped at base. All provide fall color with first frost and are attractive in naturalized settings. Do any pruning in dormant season or after bloom.

C. canadensis. EASTERN REDBUD. Zones 1–24. Native to eastern U.S. Largest (to 25–35 ft. tall and wide) and fastest growing of the redbuds, and the most apt to take tree form. Round headed but with horizontally tiered branches in age. Rich green, 3–6-in.-long leaves have pointed tips. Needs some winter chill for profuse display of rosy pink flowers. Effective as specimen or understory tree. Varieties include 'Alba' (white flowers); 'Flame' (double rose pink flowers); 'Forest Pansy' (purple foliage, needs some shade in hot climates); 'Rubye Atkinson' (pure pink flowers); and 'Silver Cloud' (leaves marbled with white).

C. c. mexicana (C. mexicana). Zones 4–24. Includes plants from many sources in Mexico. Most widely distributed is a single-trunked form to 15 ft. tall, with leathery blue-green leaves and pinkish purple flowers.

C. c. texensis 'Oklahoma' (*C. reniformis* 'Oklahoma'). Wine red flowers and thick, glossy, heat-resistant leaves.

C. chinensis. CHINESE REDBUD. Zones 4–24. Native to China, Japan. Form most often seen is light, open shrub to 10–12 ft. tall, 10 ft. wide. Flower clusters (3–5 in. long) are deep rose, almost rosy purple. Leaves are sometimes glossier and brighter green than those of *C. canadensis,* with transparent line around the edge. Spectacular in high deserts of Arizona. 'Avondale' is a superior form with deep purple flowers.

C. occidentalis. WESTERN REDBUD. Zones 2–24. Native to California, Arizona, Utah, but predominantly found in California foothills below 4,000 ft. Shrub or small tree 10–18 ft. tall and wide; usually produces several trunks from base. Provides all-year interest. Magenta flowers bloom in spring; handsome blue-green, 3-in. leaves, notched or rounded at tip, and newly forming magenta seedpods adorn branches in summer. Foliage turns light yellow or red in fall, and bare branches holding reddish brown seedpods are picturesque in winter. Best floral display comes in areas with some winter chill. Resistant to oak root fungus. Very drought tolerant; excellent for seldom-watered banks. 'Alba' is a shrub 3–6 ft. tall and somewhat broader, with white flowers and leaves to 2½ in. wide.

C. reniformis. Zones 3–24. Native to north-central Texas into Oklahoma. Leathery blue-green leaves 2–3 in. wide, with rounded or notched tips. Flowers like those of *C. canadensis;* 'Alba' has white blossoms.

C. siliquastrum. JUDAS TREE. Zones 3b–19. Native to Europe and western Asia. Generally of shrubby habit to 25 ft. tall and wide; occasionally a taller, slender tree with single trunk. Purplish rose flowers. Large (3–5-in.) leaves, deeply heart shaped at base, rounded or notched at tip. Performs best with some winter chill. Occasionally damaged by late frosts in Northwest. Resistant to oak root fungus.

CERCOCARPUS

MOUNTAIN MAHOGANY

Rosaceae

EVERGREEN AND DECIDUOUS SHRUBS AND TREES

ZONES VARY BY SPECIES

FULL SUN

LITTLE OR NO WATER

Cercocarpus betuloides

Natives of Western mountains and foothills. Several have a most attractive open structure and branching pattern. Distinguished in fall by long-lasting small fruit topped by a long, twisted, feathery, tail-like plume that sparkles in sunlight. About 20 kinds are native to the West, but the following are most widespread.

C. betuloides. HARDTACK, MOUNTAIN IRONWOOD, SWEET BRUSH. Evergreen shrub or tree. Zones 3, 5, 7–10, 13–24. Native to dry slopes and foothills below 6,000-ft. elevation, southwestern Oregon, California, northern Baja California. Generally a shrub 5–12 ft. high and wide. Can form small tree with wide-spreading crown of arching branches to 20 ft. Wedge-shaped, ½–1-in. leaves cluster on short spurs; leaves are dark green above, pale beneath, with feathery veining and toothed edges.

C. intricatus (C. ledifolius intricatus). Evergreen shrub. Zones 2, 3, 7, 9–11, 14–16, 18–24. Native from eastern California to Utah, Arizona. Slow growth to 3–9 ft. tall and wide, with intricate branching and tiny inrolled leaves, green above, gray underneath.

C. ledifolius. CURL-LEAF MOUNTAIN MAHOGANY. Evergreen shrub or tree. Zones 1–3, 7–10, 14–21. Native to dry mountain slopes throughout the West, from eastern slopes of Sierra Nevada–Cascade divide to Rockies. In warmer western part of its range, it is about the same size as *C. betuloides;* in highest, coldest part of range, it is a very slow growing, excellent hedge or small tree. Leaves leathery, ½–1 in. long, resinous, dark green above, white beneath, with inrolled edges.

C. montanus. Deciduous shrub. Zones 1–3, 7–10. Native to western U.S. mountains. Usually 4–6 ft. tall and as wide, rarely to 8–9 ft. Leaves 1–2 in. long, white beneath. Useful in dry places, coldest climates.

CEREUS peruvianus (C. uruguayanus)

Cactaceae

CACTUS

ZONES 13, 16, 17, 21–24; H2

BEST IN SUN, TOLERATES SOME SHADE

MODERATE TO REGULAR WATER

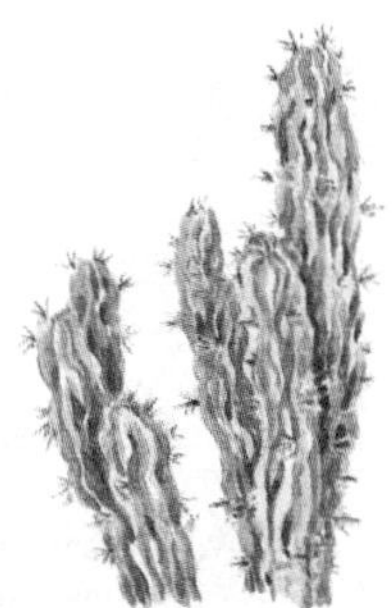

Cereus peruvianus 'Monstrosus'

Native to South America. Tall, treelike cactus, branching from base, can form bushes to 10 ft. tall with eventual spread of 15 ft. Striking bluish green color, especially when young; ribbed with scattered spines. Large white flowers—6–7 in. long, 5 in. across—open at night in late spring. Big, egg-shaped red fruits split open when fully ripe to reveal white pulp and black seeds. Striking outline; effective in ground or in large containers. Protect from hard frosts. Tolerates much drought, but better appearance with some irrigation and fertilizer during hot, dry months. Propagate by large cuttings (2–6 ft. long) any time of year. 'Monstrosus' is smaller and slower growing than species, with ribs irregularly broken up into knobs and crests.

C

CERINTHE major

HONEYWORT

Boraginaceae

ANNUAL

ZONES 1–24

FULL SUN OR LIGHT SHADE

REGULAR WATER

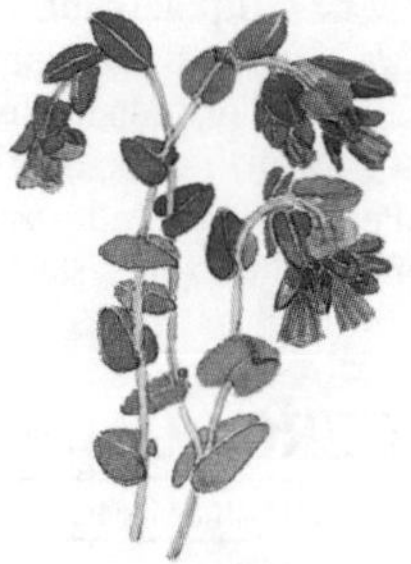

Cerinthe major 'Purpurascens'

Mediterranean native to 2 ft. tall and approximately as wide. Lower parts of stems bear 2½-in., gray-green leaves; upper parts carry leaflike bracts that partially conceal the flowers, which consist of inch-long purple tubes opening to a yellow interior. Bloom period runs from spring to fall. Though not conspicuous, flowers are rich in nectar and attract honeybees. The species is rarely grown. More often seen is variety 'Purpurascens'; its bracts and upper leaves are purplish blue, making the top of the plant look as if it's been dipped in blue dye. Easy to grow from seed and can self-sow (though not enough to become a pest). In mild-winter climates, seedlings may appear in late summer and bloom the following spring, behaving like biennials or short-lived perennials.

CEROPEGIA woodii

ROSARY VINE

Asclepiadaceae

SUCCULENT VINE

ZONES 21–24; OR INDOORS

PARTIAL SHADE; BRIGHT LIGHT

REGULAR WATER

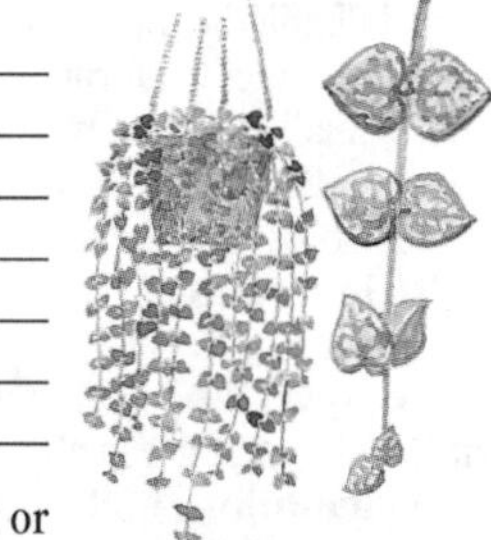

Ceropegia woodii

From South Africa. Little vine with hanging or trailing thin stems growing from tuberous base. Paired heart-shaped leaves—thick and succulent, ⅔ in. long, dark green marbled with white. Little tubers that form on stems can be used to start new plants. Small, dull pink or purplish flowers, not showy but interesting in structure. Best grown in pots; stems may trail in thin curtain or be trained on small trellis. Other species are available from specialists. Some are shrubby, some vining, and others stiffly succulent, but all of them have fascinating flower structure.

CESTRUM

Solanaceae

EVERGREEN SHRUBS

ZONES VARY BY SPECIES

PARTIAL SHADE, EXCEPT AS NOTED

REGULAR WATER

FRUIT AND SAP ARE POISONOUS IF INGESTED

Cestrum elegans

All native to the American tropics. Those in cultivation have showy clusters of tubular flowers attractive to hummingbirds. Showy fruit that follows can also attract birds. Fast growing with an arching, lax growth habit that benefits from consistent pruning and pinching back. Best in warm, sheltered spots. May be cut back severely after flowering or fruiting. Responds well to feeding and organic soil amendments. Frost damage with quick recovery possible in climates specified below.

C. aurantiacum. ORANGE CESTRUM. Zones 16, 17, 21–24; H1, H2. Native to Guatemala. To 8 ft. tall and wide (in frost-free areas may become much larger). Brilliant show of orange flowers in late spring and summer, followed by white berries. Deep green, oval, 4-in. leaves. Good for espalier. May spread by suckers. Loses leaves with cold weather.

C. elegans (C. purpureum). RED CESTRUM. Zones 13, 17, 19–24; H1, H2. Vining shrub from Mexico. To 10 ft. or greater in both height and width, with deep green, 4-in. leaves. Masses of purplish red blossoms in spring and summer are followed by red berries. 'Smithii' has pink flowers.

C. fasciculatum. Zones 13, 17, 19–24. Mexican native similar to *C. elegans* but larger in all its parts.

C. 'Newellii'. Zones 13, 17, 19–24. Resembles *C. fasciculatum* but has bright crimson flowers. Some plants listed as *C.* 'Newellii' may in fact be *C. fasciculatum.*

C. nocturnum. NIGHT JESSAMINE. Zones 13, 16–24; H1, H2. Native to West Indies. To 12 ft. tall and wide, with 4–8-in.-long leaves and creamy white summer blossoms. White berries. Powerfully fragrant at night—too much so for some people. Give full sun for best bloom.

CHAENOMELES

FLOWERING QUINCE

Rosaceae

DECIDUOUS SHRUBS

ZONES 2–23

FULL SUN

MODERATE TO REGULAR WATER

Chaenomeles 'Apple Blossom'

These are among the first shrubs to bloom each year. As early as January you can take a budded stem indoors, place it in water in a sunny window, and watch buds break into bloom. Blossoms are 1½–2½ in. across, single to semidouble or double, in colors ranging from soft to vibrant. Leaves red tinged when young, maturing to shiny green. Growth habit varies: some selections grow to 10 ft. and spread wider, while others are compact and low growing. Most are thorny, but a few are thornless or nearly so. Some bear small quincelike fruit. All are useful as hedges and barriers.

Flowering quince is easy to grow and virtually indestructible: tolerates extremes of cold and heat, takes light to heavy soil. May bloom sparsely or sporadically in warm-winter areas. Prune to shape or to limit growth at any time—but bud and bloom season is a good time for the job, since cut branches can be used for indoor arrangements. New growth that follows will bear next year's flowers. Blossoms attract birds.

The following list of choice varieties notes both height and flower color. Tall types are 6 ft. and over; low are 2–3 ft. high. All are garden hybrids (some formerly called *Cydonia*); specialists can furnish even more varieties.

'Apple Blossom'. Tall. White and pink.
'Cameo'. Low, compact. Double, soft apricot pink.
'Contorta'. Low. White to pink. Twisted branches; good as bonsai.
'Corallina' ('Coral Glow'). Tall. Reddish orange.
'Coral Sea'. Tall. Large, coral pink.
'Enchantress'. Tall. Large, shell pink.
'Falconet Charlot'. Tall, thornless. Double, salmon pink.
'Hollandia'. Tall. Large red flowers, reblooms in fall.
'Jet Trail'. Low. Pure white.
'Low-n-White'. Low, spreading. White.
'Minerva'. Low, spreading. Cherry red.
'Nivalis'. Tall. Large, pure white.
'Orange Delight' ('Maulei'). Low, spreading. Orange to orange red.
'Pink Beauty'. Tall. Purplish pink.
'Pink Lady'. Low. Rose pink blooms from deeper-colored buds.
'Red Ruffles'. Tall. Almost thornless. Large, ruffled, red.
'Rowallane'. Darkest red flowers on a 3–4-ft. shrub.
'Snow'. Tall. Large, pure white.
'Stanford Red'. Low, almost thornless. Tomato red.
'Super Red'. Tall, upright. Large, bright red.
'Texas Scarlet'. Low. Tomato red.
'Toyo Nishiki'. Tall. Pink, white, pink and white, red all on same branch.

CHAIN FERN. See WOODWARDIA fimbriata

CHAMAEBATIARIA millefolium

FERNBUSH

Rosaceae

EVERGREEN TO DECIDUOUS SHRUB

ZONES 1–3, 7, 14–21

FULL SUN

LITTLE TO MODERATE WATER

Chamaebatiaria millefolium

Native to Rocky Mountains. To 6–8 ft. tall and wide, freely branching from base. Very finely divided, fernlike, aromatic foliage is evergreen in warmer regions, semievergreen or deciduous elsewhere. Midsummer flowers are white, less than ½ in. wide, in many-blossomed upright clusters to 4 in. long. Cut off spent clusters when bloom ends in late summer. Needs good drainage.

CHAMAECEREUS sylvestri. See ECHINOPSIS chamaecereus

CHAMAECYPARIS

FALSE CYPRESS

Cupressaceae

EVERGREEN SHRUBS AND TREES

ZONES VARY BY SPECIES

FULL SUN OR PARTIAL SHADE

REGULAR WATER

Chamaecyparis lawsoniana

Conifers ranging from rock garden shrublets to timber trees. Sometimes mistaken for arborvitae *(Thuja)*, but arborvitae's leaves are entirely green, while false cypresses have white lines on leaf undersides. Most have two distinct types of foliage: juvenile and mature. Juvenile leaves are short, needlelike, soft but often prickly; they appear on young plants and some new growth of larger trees. Mature foliage consists of tiny, scalelike, overlapping leaves. Cones are small and round.

All of the many varieties sold are forms of five species—two from western U.S., two from Japan, one from eastern U.S. New varieties appear each year, while older ones lose market share. Mislabeling is common, since many of these plants closely resemble one another. Numerous dwarf and variegated kinds are available, providing a rich array of choices for bonsai and rock gardens. Pinch out or cut back tips of new growth to control size, shape; don't cut back into old, leafless wood. All types, including trees, can be sheared into hedges. All need good drainage and protection from wind.

C. lawsoniana. PORT ORFORD CEDAR, LAWSON CEDAR. Zones A3; 3–6, 15–17. Pyramidal, 60-ft. Western timber tree with lacy, drooping foliage. Species is seldom seen in gardens, but its varieties are used there. Blue-green forms include 'Allumii', a slow grower to 30 ft.; 'Ellwoodii', dense, compact to 6–8 ft.; and narrowly conical, 15–18-ft. 'Wisselii', with twisted, irregular growth. Golden-leafed forms include 'Lutea' and 'Stewartii', both conical trees to 30 ft. or more.

C. nootkatensis. NOOTKA CYPRESS, ALASKA CEDAR. Zones A2, A3; 2–6, 15–17. Native Alaska to California. Pyramidal tree to 80 ft. tall, 25 ft. wide at base. Is coarser than *C. lawsoniana* and stands greater cold, poorer soil. 'Green Arrow' is a narrow selection, reaching 35 ft. tall, only a few feet wide. 'Pendula', to 30 ft., has weeping branches. Twisted branches of 'Torulosa' make a striking silhouette; it grows slowly to 9 ft. tall.

C. obtusa. HINOKI FALSE CYPRESS. Zones A3; 2b–6, 15–17. Native to Japan. There are dozens of golden, dwarf, and fern-leafed forms, but a few varieties are particularly important in landscaping. These include 'Gracilis', slender hinoki cypress, a slender, upright tree to 20 ft. with nodding branch tips; 'Nana Gracilis', a miniature of the former, reaching 4 ft. in height; and 'Nana Lutea', a 4-ft. dwarf with bright yellow foliage.

C. pisifera. SAWARA FALSE CYPRESS. Zones A3; 2b–6, 15–17. Japanese native to 20–30 ft., rarely seen except in its garden varieties. Silvery blue-green 'Cyano-Viridis' ('Boulevard') is a dense, slow-growing bush to 6–8 ft. high and wide. 'Filifera', a dense mound to 8 ft., has drooping, threadlike branchlets; 'Filifera Aurea' has similar branchlets in yellow. 'Mops', has threadlike branchlets, forms a 1–2-ft. mound; 'Golden Mops' is similar but has yellow foliage.

C. thyoides. WHITE CEDAR. Zones 1–6, 15–17. Eastern U.S. timber tree is represented in Western gardens by varieties 'Andelyensis', a dense, columnar, gray-green shrub to 10 ft., turning bronze in cold weather; and 'Heather Bun', broader than the above, with leaves that turn intense plum purple in winter.

CHAMAEDOREA

Arecaceae (Palmae)

PALMS

ZONES 16, 17, 22–24; H2, EXCEPT AS NOTED; OR INDOORS

SOME SHADE; BRIGHT INDIRECT LIGHT

REGULAR WATER

Chamaedorea elegans

Generally small, slow-growing, feather-type palms from Central and South America. Some have single trunks, others clustered trunks. Leaf shape is variable. Good in pots on shaded patio or lanai, in ground on north side of buildings. Some types do well as houseplants. The following are among the most widely grown; other species are also sold.

C. cataractarum. CASCADE PALM, CAT PALM. Native to Mexico. Forms a dense clump to 6 ft. tall, 9 ft. wide. Does best in a moist, partially shaded location with protection from drying winds. Good as hedge, screen, border, or understory plant; fine tubbed specimen, indoors or out.

C. costaricana. If well fed and liberally watered, develops fairly fast into bamboolike clump 8–10 ft. tall and wide. Lacy, feathery leaves 3–4 ft. long. Good potted palm; will eventually need good-size container.

C. elegans. Single-stemmed species. Outdoors, grows 6–10 ft. tall, 3–6 ft. wide. Often called parlor palm, this is the best indoor chamaedorea, growing very slowly to an eventual 3–4 ft. as a houseplant. Tolerates crowded roots, poor light. Douse tops with water occasionally, feed regularly, groom by removing old leafstalks. Repot every 2 or 3 years, carefully washing off old soil and replacing it with good potting mix. Plant three or more in one container for effective display. Often sold as *Neanthe bella.*

C. seifrizii. Zones 13, 16, 17, 22–24; H2. Forms clump to 8–10 ft. tall, 6–8 ft. wide. Stems may be somewhat vining on large, established plants. Narrow leaflets.

CHAMAEMELUM nobile (Anthemis nobilis)

CHAMOMILE

Asteraceae (Compositae)

PERENNIAL

ZONES 2–24

FULL SUN OR PARTIAL SHADE

MODERATE WATER

Chamaemelum nobile

Soft-textured, spreading, 3–12-in.-high mat of bright light green, finely cut, aromatic leaves. Blooms in summer (sometimes continuing into fall in cool climates); blooms winter to spring in hot desert regions. Blossoms of the most commonly grown form look like small yellow buttons, while those of other types resemble little daisies. Makes good lawn substitute if planted 1 ft. apart, mowed or sheared occasionally. Also useful between stepping-stones or as a low edging along path. 'Treneague' is a nonflowering variety that needs no mowing; 'Flore Pleno' has double daisylike flowers.

The fragrant, sweet, and flavorful chamomile tea comes from the dried flowers of *Matricaria recutita (M. chamomilla).*

CHAMAEROPS humilis

MEDITERRANEAN FAN PALM

Arecaceae (Palmae)

PALM

ZONES 4–24; H1, H2

FULL SUN OR PARTIAL SHADE

MODERATE TO REGULAR WATER

Chamaerops humilis

From western Mediterranean. Probably one of hardiest palms; has survived brief (but not prolonged) temperature drops to 0°F/–18°C or a bit lower. Clumps slowly develop from offshoots, curving to height of 20 ft.; may also reach 20 ft. wide. Growth extremely slow in northern part of range. Green to bluish green leaves on spiny leafstalks. Use in containers, mass under trees, grow as impenetrable hedge. Tolerates poor soil, strong winds.

CHAMELAUCIUM uncinatum

GERALDTON WAXFLOWER

Myrtaceae

EVERGREEN SHRUB

ZONES 8, 9, 12–24

FULL SUN

MODERATE WATER

Chamelaucium uncinatum

Australian native that is sometimes sold as *C. ciliatum.* Needlelike bright green leaves; showy sprays of pale pink or rosy, ½-in. winter flowers cherished for arrangements of long-lasting beauty. Fast growth to 6–8 ft. (perhaps taller when staked) with equal spread. Light and airy, loose and sprawling in appearance; looks somewhat like open-growing heather *(Calluna).* Very old plants have interesting twisted trunks and shaggy bark. Plant on dry, sunny bank or in cutting garden in fast-draining soil. Cut blooming stems freely for arrangements; or cut back after bloom. Seedling plants vary; select in bloom to get color you want. Named varieties include 'Chinchilla' (small, light pink flowers), 'Eric John' (pink), 'Escondido Rose' (reddish purple), 'Purple Pride' (deep rosy purple), 'University' (reddish purple), and 'Vista' (pink). Hybrid 'Lady Stephanie' has light rose blossoms.

CHAMISA. See CHRYSOTHAMNUS

CHAMISE. See ADENOSTOMA fasciculatum

CHAMOMILE. See CHAMAEMELUM nobile, MATRICARIA recutita

CHARD. See SWISS CHARD

CHASMANTHE

Iridaceae

PERENNIALS FROM CORMS

ZONES 13, 15–24; OR DIG AND STORE

FULL SUN OR PARTIAL SHADE

NO IRRIGATION NEEDED

Chasmanthe aethiopica

South African natives with irislike fans of bright green, 2-ft. leaves that appear shortly after first autumn or winter rains. Narrow, 3–3½-ft.-tall spikes of bright orange-red flowers follow in late winter or early spring, putting on a striking show at a dull time of year. Plants are fairly hardy, but late frosts may damage flower buds. Cut spent flower spikes to prevent self-sowing. In fall, plant corms in well-drained soil; set them 4 in. deep and 8–12 in. apart. Corms multiply rapidly; dig and divide every 2 or 3 years. During summer dormancy, plants tolerate irrigation (not too much in hot desert regions) but do not need any.

C. aethiopica. Unbranched flower spikes hold blossoms on just one side of spike.

C. floribunda. Once-branched or unbranched spikes bear blossoms along both sides; each spike carries 12–28 flowers. *C. f. duckittii* has yellow flowers.

CHASMANTHIUM latifolium (Uniola latifolia)

SEA OATS, BAMBOO GRASS

Poaceae (Gramineae)

PERENNIAL GRASS

ZONES 2–10, 14–24

PARTIAL SHADE IN HOTTEST CLIMATES

REGULAR WATER

Chasmanthium latifolium

Ornamental grass from moist woodlands of eastern U.S. Broad, bamboolike leaves form 2-ft.-wide clump topped in midsummer by arching, 2–5-ft. flowering stems carrying showers of silvery green spikelets that resemble flattened clusters of oats (or flattened armadillos). These turn copper in fall, look good through winter; they dry to a greenish straw color and are attractive in dried arrangements. Clumps widen slowly and are not aggressive. Leaves turn brown in winter, when plants should be cut back almost to ground. Divide clumps when they become overgrown and flowering diminishes. Stake if flowering stems sprawl.

CHASTE TREE. See VITEX

CHAYOTE

Cucurbitaceae

PERENNIAL VINE OFTEN GROWN AS ANNUAL

ZONES 14–16, 19–24; H1, H2; ANYWHERE AS ANNUAL

FULL SUN

REGULAR WATER

Chayote

Known botanically as *Sechium edule,* this tropical American native belongs to the same family as squash and resembles a typical squash vine, though its flowers are inconspicuous. Grown for edible fruit: 3–8 in. long green or yellow green, irregularly oval, grooved, with a large edible seed surrounded by solid, meaty flesh. Flavor similar to that of summer squash. Eat young fruit raw or cooked; boil or bake mature fruit. Large, fleshy tuberous roots can also be eaten—though you cannot, of course, grow the plant as a perennial and consume its roots as well. Chayote is also known as mirliton or christophine.

Needs rich soil. Climbs by tendrils; provide fence or trellis. In areas where fruit is sold in stores, buy in fall and allow to sprout in cupboard; then plant whole fruit edgewise and slanted, with sprouted end at lowest point, narrow end exposed. If shoot is long, cut it back to 1–2 in. Plant two or more vines to ensure pollination. In mild climates, plant in late winter; in areas where roots may freeze, pot in 5-gallon container and store in a dark, cool spot until frost danger is past. Plant can produce 20–30-ft. vine in first year, reach 40–50 ft. in second. Tops die down in frost. Bloom starts when day length shortens in fall; fruit is ripe within a month. A well-grown plant can produce 200 or more fruits.

CHECKERBERRY. See GAULTHERIA procumbens

CHECKERED LILY. See FRITILLARIA meleagris

CHEIRANTHUS. See ERYSIMUM

CHELONE lyonii

TURTLEHEAD

Scrophulariaceae

PERENNIAL

ZONES 1–9, 14–24

FULL SUN OR LIGHT SHADE

AMPLE WATER

Chelone lyonii

Leafy, clump-forming perennial native to the eastern U.S. Related to penstemon—but unlike penstemon it is accustomed to life in damp, even boggy, ground. Grows to 4 ft. tall, 2 ft. wide, with 2–6-in. leaves. Short (2-in.) terminal spikes of baggy, inch-long purplish pink flowers with a yellow beard appear in late summer and fall.

CHENILLE PLANT. See ACALYPHA hispida

Chenopodiaceae. The goosefoot family contains many annuals and perennials (some of them weeds) and a few shrubs. Flowers are inconspicuous. Many will tolerate salty or alkaline soil, and some (notably beet and spinach) are useful food plants.

CHENOPODIUM

Chenopodiaceae

ANNUALS AND PERENNIALS

ZONES VARY BY SPECIES

FULL SUN

REGULAR WATER

Chenopodium quinoa

Most are weeds; some species are used as food. The plants often have a strong odor. Individual flowers are greenish and insignificant.

C. album. PIGWEED, LAMB'S QUARTERS. Annual. Zones 1–24. Tall weed with leaves to 4 in. long, whitish underneath, smooth pale green above. Leaves can be cooked like spinach.

C. ambrosioides. EPAZOTE, MEXICAN TEA. Perennial. Zones 8, 9, 14–24; H1, H2; Zones 1–7 as annual. Strongly scented leaves to 5 in. long, deeply cut or toothed. Sometimes grown in gardens or collected from the roadside as seasoning for Mexican dishes.

C. quinoa. QUINOA. Annual. Zones 1–24, but see below. To 5 ft. tall, with dense flower and seed clusters. A traditional grain of the Andes. Individual seeds look like sesame seeds; they are rinsed to remove surface bitterness, then cooked like rice. Protein content is high. Can't take high heat at blooming or seed setting. Needs short days to bloom; takes light frost. Plant in late spring and harvest in fall. Excellent production in high valleys in the Rocky Mountains. Strains that yield at sea level are available.

CHERIMOYA

Annonaceae

BRIEFLY DECIDUOUS SHRUB OR TREE

ZONES 21–24; H1, H2

FULL SUN

REGULAR WATER

Cherimoya

Known botanically as *Annona cherimola;* native to high elevations in tropics. In Hawaii, grows best above 1,000-ft. elevation. Hardy to about 25°F/–4°C. Grows fast first 3 to 4 years, then slows; eventually forms a tree 15 ft. tall, spreading 15–20 ft. wide. (Unpruned, can reach 30 ft. tall and spread at least as wide.) Leaves are 4–10 in. long, dull green above, velvety-hairy beneath; they drop in late spring, but tree remains leafless only for a brief time. Thick, fleshy, 1-in., hairy brownish or yellow flowers with a fruity fragrance begin opening about time of leaf drop and continue forming for 3 to 4 months.

Large fruits weigh ½–1½ lb. Harvest fruit in late fall or winter, when it turns yellowish green. Skin of most varieties resembles short overlapping leaves; some show knobby warts (skin is tender and thin, so handle carefully). Let fruit ripen indoors at room temperature; when ripe, it turns a dull brownish green (some varieties show tan freckles) and yields to gentle pressure like a ripe peach. Refrigerate ripe fruit. Creamy white flesh contains large black seeds and is almost custardlike, with a flavor something like pineapple crossed with banana; eat it with a spoon. Tastes best cold. Specialty nurseries offer several improved varieties, including exceptionally flavorful 'El Bumpo', 'Honeyhart', 'Pierce', and 'Sabor' in California, 'Spain' in Hawaii. 'McPherson' is popular everywhere due to its self-fruitful nature.

Locate tree where you can enjoy fragrance. After it has developed for 4 or 5 years, begin pruning yearly to produce fruiting wood. To ensure fruit set, gather freshly opened flowers and place in a small jar or film canister. Keep in a cool place 12 to 24 hours, by which time the pollen will shed. Use a small paintbrush to pollinate freshly opened flowers.

CHERRY

Rosaceae

DECIDUOUS FRUIT TREES

ZONES VARY BY TYPE

FULL SUN

REGULAR WATER

Cherry

Both sweet and sour cherries are attractive, productive trees in the home garden. For strictly ornamental relatives, including flowering cherry trees, see *Prunus.*

Sweet cherries. Most common market type and most widely known in the West. Trees 30–35 ft. tall, as broad as high in some varieties; at their best in deep, well-drained soil in Zones 2, 6–9, 14, 15. They have high chilling requirement (need many winter hours below 45°F/7°C) and are therefore not adapted to mild-winter areas of Southern California or low desert. Can't take extreme summer heat or intense winter cold; frosts or rain in spring can damage crop.

Two trees are usually needed to produce fruit, and second tree must be chosen with care. No combination of these will produce fruit: 'Bing', 'Lambert', 'Royal Ann' (they will not pollinate each other). The following varieties will pollinate any other cherry: 'Angela', 'Black Tartarian', 'Republican', 'Sam', 'Stella' (though 'Stella' will not pollinate 'Bing' in mild-winter climates), and 'Van'. However, because 'Lambert' blooms late, it is pollinated best by 'Republican'. 'Craig's Crimson', 'Glacier', 'Lapins', 'Stella', and 'Sweetheart' are self-fruitful (a lone tree will bear).

Cherry trees are easier to grow and harvest when grown on a dwarfing rootstock, such as the Giessen 148 series. Such trees can easily be maintained at less than half the size of those growing on standard rootstocks.

Fruiting spurs are long lived, do not need to be renewed by pruning. Prune trees only to maintain good structure and shape. Fruit appears in late spring to early summer. Use netting to keep birds from eating the crop. For control of brown rot and blossom blight, apply a copper spray just as leaves drop in autumn, then a fungicide when first blooms appear and weekly during bloom. Resume fungicide program about 2 weeks before harvest or if fruit rot begins to appear. Good sanitation will also help limit disease—remove any mummified fruit and prune out and discard diseased twigs as soon as you see them. Horticultural oil spray during the dormant period will control various pests, including scale insects and mites.

These are among the best varieties.

'Angela'. Small, glossy black fruit with excellent flavor. Resists cracking. Midseason to late.

'Bing'. Top quality. Large, dark red, meaty fruit of fine flavor. Midseason.

'Black Tartarian'. Fruit smaller than that of 'Bing', purplish black, firm, sweet. Early.

'Craig's Crimson'. Medium to large, deep red to black; superb flavor. Naturally dwarf (about two-thirds normal size). Self-fruitful. Midseason.

'Early Burlat'. Like 'Bing'; ripens 2 weeks earlier.

'Early Ruby'. Dark red, purple-fleshed early cherry that performs well in all sweet cherry areas. 'Black Tartarian', 'Royal Ann', 'Van' are all good pollenizers. Early.

'Emperor Francis'. Medium-size, light red fruit with fine flavor. Favorite in the Northwest. Early.

'Glacier'. Large dark cherry; ripens a few days ahead of 'Bing' and tastes even better. Self-fruitful.

'Hardy Giant'. Dark red fruit resembles 'Bing'. Good pollenizer, especially for 'Lambert'. Midseason.

'Kristin'. Large black fruit resists cracking. One of the hardiest sweet cherries; worth a try in Zones A2, A3, 1. Midseason.

'Lambert'. Very large, very firm black fruit. Flavor sprightlier than 'Bing'. Late.

'Lapins'. Resembles 'Bing' but is self-fruitful. Early to midseason.

'Mona'. Resembles 'Black Tartarian' but is larger. Very early.

'Rainier'. Has yellow skin with pink blush; fruit ripens a few days before 'Bing'.

'Republican' ('Black Republican', 'Black Oregon'). Large, spreading tree. Small, round, purplish black fruit with dark juice, tender yet crisp texture. Good flavor. Late.

'Royal Ann' ('Napoleon'). Large, spreading tree; very productive. Light yellow fruit with pink blush; tender, crisp. Sprightly flavor. Midseason.

'Sam'. Vigorous tree. Large, firm black fruit. Excellent flavor. Midseason to late.

'Stella'. Dark fruit like 'Lambert'; ripens a few days later. Self-fruitful and a good pollenizer for other cherries. 'Compact Stella' is similar, but tree is half the size.

'Sweet Ann'. Medium-size fruit is yellow with a red blush. Excellent flavor. Midseason.

'Sweetheart'. Large, bright red; excellent flavor. Self-fruitful and heavy bearing. Late.

'Utah Giant'. Ripens with 'Bing' but is larger, sweeter; develops sweetness even before fully ripe. Holds color when processed. Pollinate with 'Van' or 'Stella'.

'Van'. Heavy-bearing tree. Shiny black fruit, firmer and slightly smaller than 'Bing'. Good flavor. Ripens earlier than 'Bing' in Northwest, right with it in California.

Sour cherries. Also known as pie cherries. These are spreading trees to 20 ft. tall, best grown in well-drained soil in Zones A2, A3; 1–9, 14–17. They are self-fruitful but poor pollenizers for sweet cherries. There are far fewer types of sour cherries than sweet cherries; these are the most widely grown. The category name notwithstanding, a few varieties are sweet enough to enjoy fresh.

'Early Richmond'. Small, bright red fruit is soft, juicy, sweet-tart. Early.

'English Morello'. Darker, tarter fruit than that of 'Early Richmond'. Red juice. Late.

'Kansas Sweet' ('Hansen'). Large, semisweet red fruit. Late.

'Meteor'. Fruit like that of 'Early Richmond', but tree is smaller. Late.

'Montmorency'. Like 'Early Richmond'. Midseason to late.

'North Star'. Red to dark red skin and sour yellow flesh. Small, very hardy tree. Midseason.

'Surefire'. Bright red skin and flesh; sweet flavor. Late.

CHERRY, FLOWERING. See PRUNUS

CHERRY OF THE RIO GRANDE. See EUGENIA aggregata

CHERRY PLUM. See PRUNUS cerasifera

CHERVIL. See ANTHRISCUS cerefolium

FOR DEFINITIONS OF GARDENING TERMS
PLEASE SEE PAGES 746–750

CHESTNUT

Fagaceae

DECIDUOUS TREES

ZONES 2–9, 14–17, EXCEPT AS NOTED

FULL SUN

MODERATE WATER

Chinese Chestnut

The American chestnut *(Castanea dentata)* has become nearly extinct in its native range as a result of chestnut blight, but other species and hybrids are available. They make wonderful, dense shade trees where there is space to accommodate them and where their litter and rank-smelling pollen won't be too obtrusive. All have handsome dark to bright green foliage. Small, creamy white flowers in long (8–10-in.), slim catkins make quite a display in summer. The large edible nuts are enclosed in prickly burs. Nuts fall to the ground when ripe. Gather daily, remove from burs, and dry in the sun (shade in hot climates). Plant two or more trees to ensure cross-pollination and a substantial crop; single trees bear lightly or not at all. Give occasional deep irrigation.

C. hybrids. Zones 2–9, 14–24. These are mostly offspring of Japanese and European chestnuts (*C. crenata* and *C. sativa*). Trees usually grow 40–60 ft. tall and wide. They do not tolerate alkaline soils. Varieties include 'Colossal', 'Nevada' (small-nutted variety; the proven pollenizer for 'Colossal'), 'Schrader', and 'Skioka'.

Chestnut

C. mollissima. CHINESE CHESTNUT. Native to China, Korea. To 35–40 ft. tall with rounded crown that may spread to 20–25 ft. Leaves 3–7 in. long, with coarsely toothed edges. Most nursery trees are grown from seed, not cuttings; hence, nuts are variable but generally of good quality. Intolerant of alkaline soil.

C. sativa. EUROPEAN CHESTNUT. Native to southern Europe, North Africa, western Asia. Larger, broader than *C. mollissima:* can reach 100 ft. tall with greater spread, but typically grows 40–60 ft. high in gardens. Leaves 4–9 in. long, with sharply toothed edges. Large nuts of excellent quality—the nuts usually sold in markets. Resistant to oak root fungus.

CHICKABIDDY. See ASARINA

CHICORY and RADICCHIO

Asteraceae (Compositae)

PERENNIALS

ALL ZONES

FULL SUN

REGULAR WATER

Chicory

Botanically known as *Cichorium intybus.* Native to Mediterranean region; wild form grows as perennial roadside weed 2–4 ft. tall in much of the West and is recognized by its pretty sky blue flowers. Different chicories are grown for three purposes: for salad greens (small-rooted varieties); for roots to make a coffee substitute (large-rooted varieties); and for Belgian or French endive ('Witloof' chicory). To grow 'Witloof', sow seeds in spring or early summer; plants will mature by fall. In winter, trim the greens to an inch of stem; then dig the roots, bury them diagonally in moist sand, and set in dark, cool room until pale, tender new growth has been forced. (For the standard salad green called endive, see Endive.)

Radicchio is the name given to red-leafed chicories grown for salads. 'Rossa de Verona' ('Rouge de Verone'), 'Red Treviso', and 'Rossana' are good varieties. Radicchio makes lettucelike heads that color to a deep rosy red as weather grows cold in fall or winter; its slight bitterness lessens as color deepens. Best sown in mid- to late summer to mature in cool autumn months, though variety 'Giulio' can be sown in spring to harvest in summer. Sow green-leafed chicory starting in early spring (up to early summer where summers are not too hot); in areas with mild winters, you can also plant in mid- to late summer for fall and winter harvest (or, in the desert, in fall for winter harvest). Sow both green and red types ¼–½ in. deep; thin seedlings to 6–12 in. apart.

CHILEAN BELLFLOWER. See LAPAGERIA rosea

CHILEAN FIRE BUSH. See EMBOTHRIUM coccineum

CHILEAN GUAVA. See UGNI molinae

CHILEAN JASMINE. See MANDEVILLA laxa

CHILEAN WINE PALM. See JUBAEA chilensis

CHILOPSIS linearis

DESERT WILLOW, DESERT CATALPA

Bignoniaceae

DECIDUOUS SHRUB OR TREE

ZONES 3B, 7–14, 18–23

FULL SUN

LITTLE TO MODERATE WATER

Chilopsis linearis

Native to desert washes and streambeds below 5,000 ft. from California to Texas, south into Mexico. To 15–30 ft. tall, 10–20 ft. wide; grows fast at first (as much as 3 ft. in a season), then slows. With age, develops shaggy bark and twisting trunks. Narrow, willow-type leaves 2–5 in. long. Spring to fall, produces fragrant trumpet-shaped blossoms with crimped lobes, similar to those of catalpa; blooms are like small cattleya orchids and attract hummingbirds. Flower color varies among seedlings—may be reddish purple, lavender, rose, pink, or white, often marked with purple and gold. Nurseries select for good color, large size, ruffled form. Gallon-size plants can bloom first year. Drops leaves early; holds a heavy crop of catalpa-like seedpods through winter and can look messy. Thin growth to enhance picturesque shape.

'Burgundy' ('Burgundy Lace'). Deep purplish red flowers.

'Dark Storm'. Lower lip of flower is deep wine red, upper one lavender; lips are usually curved inward. Slow grower to 12–15 ft. high and wide.

'Hope'. White flowers with a pale yellow throat. Wispy, open growth.

'Lois Adams'. Profuse two-tone blooms in pale lavender and magenta; no seedpods. Compact, upright growth.

'Lucretia Hamilton'. Dark purple flowers in large clusters. To 15–18 ft. high and wide.

'Regal'. Combination of lavender and wine red like that of 'Dark Storm', but display is better, since blooms are flat faced and open throated.

'Rio Salado'. Large, ruffled, deep burgundy flowers. Vigorous growth.

'Warren Jones'. Large, ruffled blossoms in pure, unshaded pink with paler throat. Holds its leaves longer; evergreen in warm-winter climates.

CHIMONANTHUS praecox (C. fragrans, Meratia praecox)

WINTERSWEET

Calycanthaceae

DECIDUOUS SHRUB

ZONES 4–9, 14–21

AFTERNOON SHADE IN HOTTEST CLIMATES

MODERATE WATER

Chimonanthus praecox

Native of China, Japan. Needs some winter cold. Winter-blooming shrub with spicy-scented blossoms. Slow, open growth to 10–15 ft. high, 6–8 ft. wide, with many stems from base. Flowers appear on leafless branches in winter or spring and may last for a month or more if not hit by frost. Blossoms are 1 in. wide, translucent pale yellow, with darker centers marked in shades of purple, chocolate or maroon. Tapered leaves, 3–6 in. long and half as wide, are rough to the touch, medium green; turn yellow green in fall.

In colder part of range, plant in sheltered site to prevent frost damage. In all areas, locate plant where its winter fragrance can be enjoyed. Restrict size by pruning while in flower; shape as a small tree by removing excess basal stems. To rejuvenate a leggy plant, lop it to within a foot of the ground in late winter. Needs good drainage.

CHIMONOBAMBUSA. See BAMBOO

CHINA ASTER. See CALLISTEPHUS chinensis

CHINABERRY. See MELIA azedarach

CHINA FIR. See CUNNINGHAMIA lanceolata

CHINESE BELLFLOWER. See ABUTILON

CHINESE CABBAGE

Brassicaceae (Cruciferae)

BIENNIAL GROWN AS ANNUAL

ALL ZONES

FULL SUN

REGULAR WATER

Chinese Cabbage

Makes head somewhat looser than ordinary cabbage, its close relative. Sometimes called celery cabbage. Raw or cooked, it has more delicate flavor than cabbage. There are two kinds: pe-tsai, with tall, narrow heads; and wong bok (Napa cabbage), with short, broad heads. Favored pe-tsai variety is 'Michihli'; wong bok varieties include 'Springtime', 'Summertime', and 'Wintertime' (early to late maturing). Definitely cool-season crop; very prone to bolt to seed in hot weather or in the long days of spring and early summer. In Zones 1–6, 10, 11, plant seeds directly in open ground in midsummer; in other areas, sow in late summer. Sow seeds thinly in rows 2–2½ ft. apart and thin plants to 1½–2 ft. apart. Heads should be ready in 70 to 80 days. Tolerates light shade in hot climates. Subject to same pests as cabbage.

For Chinese White Cabbage (bok choy), see Asian Greens.

CHINESE CHIVES. See ALLIUM tuberosum

CHINESE ELM. See ULMUS parvifolia

CHINESE EVERGREEN. See AGLAONEMA modestum

CHINESE FLAME TREE. See KOELREUTERIA bipinnata

CHINESE FORGET-ME-NOT. See CYNOGLOSSUM amabile

CHINESE GOOSEBERRY VINE. See KIWI

CHINESE GROUND ORCHID. See BLETILLA striata

CHINESE HOUSES. See COLLINSIA heterophylla

CHINESE LANTERN. See ABUTILON

CHINESE LANTERN PLANT. See PHYSALIS alkekengi

CHINESE PARASOL TREE. See FIRMIANA simplex

CHINESE PARSLEY. See CORIANDRUM sativum

CHINESE PLUMBAGO. See CERATOSTIGMA willmottianum

CHINESE REDBUD. See CERCIS chinensis

CHINESE SCHOLAR TREE. See SOPHORA japonica

CHINESE SWEET GUM. See LIQUIDAMBAR formosana

CHINESE TALLOW TREE. See SAPIUM sebiferum

CHINESE TARO. See ALOCASIA cucullata

CHINESE WINGNUT. See PTEROCARYA stenoptera

CHINESE WOOLFLOWER. See CELOSIA

CHINQUAPIN. See CHRYSOLEPIS chrysophylla

CHINQUAPIN, JAPANESE. See CASTANOPSIS cuspidata

CHIONANTHUS

FRINGE TREE

Oleaceae

DECIDUOUS SHRUBS OR TREES

ZONES VARY BY SPECIES

FULL SUN

MODERATE TO REGULAR WATER

Chionanthus retusus

Spectacular flowering plants requiring some winter chill. Common name refers to narrow, fringelike white petals on flowers that are borne in impressive, ample, lacy clusters. Male and female plants are separate; males have larger flowers. If both plants are present, females produce clusters of small, dark olivelike fruit favored by birds. Broad leaves turn bright to deep yellow in fall. Give good drainage. Minimal pruning needed.

C. retusus. CHINESE FRINGE TREE. Zones 3–9, 14–24. To about 20 ft. tall, not quite as wide spreading as *C. virginicus.* Usually seen as a big multistemmed shrub but can be trained as a small tree. Leaves 2–4 in. long. Pure white blossom clusters to 4 in. long appear in late spring or early summer, 2 to 3 weeks before *C. virginicus* comes into flower. A magnificent plant when in bloom, something like a tremendous white lilac. Handsome gray-brown bark (sometimes golden on young stems) provides winter interest.

C. virginicus. FRINGE TREE. Zones 2–6, 15–24. Native to southeastern U.S. Leaves and flower clusters often twice as big as those of *C. retusus;* blooms appear a few weeks later. Lightly fragrant, greenish white flowers. Can reach 30 ft. tall, but in gardens usually grows 12–20 ft. high with equal spread. Habit varies from very shrubby and open to more treelike. In Zones 2–6, where it grows very slowly (the most you can hope for is 12 ft. in 10 years), it is best used as an airy shrub; blooms profusely when just 2–3 ft. tall. In those zones, it is one of the last deciduous plants to leaf out in spring.

Chionanthus virginicus

CHIONODOXA

GLORY-OF-THE-SNOW

Liliaceae

PERENNIALS FROM BULBS

ZONES 1–7, 14–20

FULL SUN DURING BLOOM, LIGHT SHADE AFTER IN HOT CLIMATES

REGULAR WATER DURING GROWTH AND BLOOM

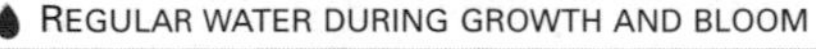

Chionodoxa luciliae

Charming little bulbous plants native to alpine meadows of Crete, Cyprus, and Turkey are among first to bloom in spring. Each bulb produces a stem to 6 in. high, with six-pointed, starlike blossoms in blue, white, or pink spaced along upper part. Straight, narrow leaves are a little shorter than flower stem. In fall, plant bulbs in rich, well-drained soil, setting them 2–3 in. deep and 3 in. apart. In very hot, dry climates, may need some moisture during summer dormancy. When bloom quality declines, dig and divide clumps in early fall. Plantings may also increase from self-seeding.

C. luciliae. Most commonly grown chionodoxa; often confused with other species. Stems typically bear one to four 1½-in., violet-blue blooms. 'Alba' has white flowers larger than those of the species; 'Gigantea' has larger leaves and larger blooms of violet blue; 'Pink Giant' and 'Rosea' bear pink flowers.

C. sardensis. Inch-wide violet-blue flowers with a very small white eye, carried 4–12 to a stem.

×CHITALPA tashkentensis

Bignoniaceae

DECIDUOUS TREE

ZONES 3–24

FULL SUN

LITTLE TO MODERATE WATER

×Chitalpa tashkentensis

Growing rapidly to 20–30 ft. tall and wide, this tree combines the larger flowers of its *Catalpa bignonioides* parent with the desert toughness and flower color of *Chilopsis linearis,* its other parent. Leaves are 4–5 in. long, 1 in. wide. Erect clusters of frilly, trumpet-shaped flowers in pink, white, or lavender appear from late spring to fall. 'Pink Dawn' has pink blooms, 'Morning Cloud' white ones.

CHIVES. See ALLIUM schoenoprasum

CHLOROPHYTUM

Liliaceae

PERENNIALS

ZONES VARY BY SPECIES; OR INDOORS

PARTIAL SHADE; BRIGHT INDIRECT LIGHT

REGULAR WATER

Chlorophytum comosum

Frost-tender lily relatives form clumps of attractive evergreen foliage, bear small white flowers in long clusters. In most areas, they are grown as houseplants.

C. bichetii. Indoor plant. West African native grows slowly to 8–10 in. high, 1½ ft. across. Dark green leaves with white stripes, shorter and broader than those of *C. comosum,* gracefully recurved. Flowers carried on 8-in. stalks. Does not produce runners.

C. comosum. SPIDER PLANT. Zones 15–17, 19–24; H1, H2. From South Africa. Forms 1–3-ft.-high clumps of soft, curving leaves like long, broad grass blades. Both 'Variegatum' and 'Vittatum' have white-striped leaves. Flowers about ½ in. long, in loose, leafy-tipped spikes held above foliage. Greatest attraction: miniature duplicates of mother plant, complete with root, at end of curved stems (as with offsets of strawberry plants). These can be cut off and potted individually.

Spider plant is a good choice for hanging baskets. To use as ground cover, set 2 ft. apart in diamond pattern; plants will fill in area in same year. Often sold as *C. capense.*

CHOCOLATE FLOWER. See BERLANDIERA lyrata

CHOCOLATE LILY. See FRITILLARIA camschatcensis

A PRACTICAL GUIDE TO GARDENING
PLEASE SEE PAGES 658–731

CHOISYA ternata

MEXICAN ORANGE

Rutaceae

EVERGREEN SHRUB

ZONES 6–9, 14–24; BORDERLINE IN ZONES 4, 5

FULL SUN ONLY IN COOLER CLIMATES

MODERATE WATER

Choisya ternata

Mexican native hardy to 15°F/–9°C. Fast growing to 6–8 ft. high and wide. Lustrous, rich green leaves held toward ends of branches are divided into fans of three leaflets to 3 in. long. Fans give shrub a dense, massive look—but with highlights and shadows. Clusters of fragrant white flowers, somewhat like small orange blossoms, open in late winter or early spring and bloom continuously for a couple of months, then intermittently through summer. Appealing to bees. Sometimes called mock orange. Foliage of 'Sundance' is yellow when young, gradually turning green.

Attractive informal hedge or screen. During growing season, thin out older branches in plant's center to force leafy new interior growth. Cut freely for decoration when in bloom. Touchy about soil conditions—difficult to grow in alkaline soils or where water is high in salts. Under such conditions, amend soil as for azaleas. Prone to root rot and crown rot if drainage is poor. Subject to damage from sucking insects and mites.

CHOKEBERRY. See ARONIA

CHOKECHERRY. See PRUNUS virginiana

CHONDROPETALUM tectorum

CAPE RUSH

Restionaceae

PERENNIAL

ZONES 8, 9, 14–24

FULL SUN OR PARTIAL SHADE

REGULAR TO AMPLE WATER

Chondropetalum tectorum

Striking accent plant makes an elegant kinetic sculpture in the ground or in a pot, moving in the breeze to provide a play of light and shadow. Rushlike 3–4-ft.-tall stems radiate in all directions from the roots. Papery bracts at each stem joint turn from tan to dark brown, then drop off. Narrow clusters of dark brown flower heads (male and female blossoms are on separate plants) top each shoot. Native to South African marshes, it likes to grow with its feet in water, but it is also happy in the ground with regular watering; will even tolerate considerable drought once new growth is complete. Resents high fertility. Cut old growth to the ground just as new sprouts show in spring; or prune out old stems individually if new shoots are already established. Clump expands slowly by rhizomes. Propagate by seed, since roots do not like to be disturbed.

CHORISIA

FLOSS SILK TREE

Bombacaceae

EVERGREEN TO BRIEFLY DECIDUOUS TREES

ZONES VARY BY SPECIES

FULL SUN

MODERATE WATER

Chorisia speciosa

Native to South America. Heavy trunk is studded with thick spines; it is green in youth, turns gray with age. Leaves divided into leaflets like fingers of a hand, drop during autumn flowering or whenever temperatures fall below 27°F/–3°C. Large, showy flowers somewhat resemble narrow-petaled hibiscus blooms. Fast drainage and controlled watering are keys to success. Water established trees about once a month during growing season; ease off in late summer to encourage more flowers. Need little pruning except to remove wayward or dead growth.

C. insignis. WHITE FLOSS SILK TREE. Zones 12, 13, 15–24. To 50 ft. tall and wide. White to pale yellow, 5–6-in. flowers. Blooms from fall into winter; stopped by frost.

C. speciosa. Zones 12–24; H1, H2. Grows 3–5 ft. a year for first few years, then more slowly to an eventual 30–60 ft. tall and wide. Pink, purplish rose, or burgundy flowers are 4 in. or more across. Grafted varieties include 'Los Angeles Beautiful', with wine red flowers, and 'Majestic Beauty', a thornless variety bearing rich pink blooms.

CHORIZEMA

FLAME PEA

Fabaceae (Leguminosae)

EVERGREEN SHRUBS

ZONES 15–17, 19–24

FLOWER COLOR MORE INTENSE IN PART SHADE

MODERATE WATER

Chorizema cordatum

Native to Australia. Hardy to 24°F/–4°C. Both species produce showy clusters of sweet pea–shaped flowers in a blend of orange and purplish red, late winter through spring. A lighter crop often blooms in fall. Fast growing, with slender, graceful branches. Left to go their own way, they are attractive spilling over wall, on banks, in containers or hanging baskets. To keep compact, pinch regularly and cut back after flowering.

C. cordatum. HEART-LEAF FLAME PEA. Grows 3–5 ft. high and wide. Dark green, 1–2-in.-long leaves with small, prickly teeth along the edges. Sometimes erroneously sold as *C. ilicifolium.*

C. ilicifolium. HOLLY FLAME PEA. To 2–3 ft. high and wide. Oval, ¾–1-in. leaves are similar to those of *C. cordatum,* but edges are wavy and have long, prickly teeth; vaguely resemble leaves of holly *(Ilex).*

CHRISTMAS BERRY. See HETEROMELES arbutifolia

CHRISTMAS CACTUS. See SCHLUMBERGERA × buckleyi

CHRISTMAS CHOLLA. See OPUNTIA leptocaulis

CHRISTMAS FERN. See POLYSTICHUM acrostichoides

CHRISTMAS ROSE. See HELLEBORUS niger

CHRYSACTINIA mexicana

DAMIANITA

Asteraceae (Compositae)

EVERGREEN SHRUB

ZONES 10–13, 18–24

FULL SUN

LITTLE TO MODERATE WATER

Chrysactinia mexicana

Native to Mexico. Heavily branched shrub to 2 ft. tall and wide, with tiny, needlelike, dark green leaves that are strongly aromatic. Golden yellow, 1-in. daisies are borne singly at tips of 2–3-in.-long flowering stems over a long period. Heaviest bloom in spring and fall; eases off in summer in intense heat. A tough plant, enduring extreme heat as well as winter lows to 0°F/–18°C. Tolerant of various soils but does best with reasonably good drainage. Very drought tolerant, but supplemental water in summer encourages more blooms. Valued in folk medicine. Shear annually in early spring; cut back more severely if plant becomes too woody.

CHRYSALIDOCARPUS lutescens. See DYPSIS lutescens

CHRYSANTHEMUM

Asteraceae (Compositae)

PERENNIALS AND ANNUALS

ZONES VARY BY SPECIES

FULL SUN, EXCEPT AS NOTED

REGULAR WATER, EXCEPT AS NOTED

Chrysanthemum ×morifolium

There are about 160 species of chrysanthemum, mostly native to China, Japan, and Europe. Included are some of the most popular and useful of garden plants—top favorite being *C.×morifolium,* whose modern descendants are known as florists' chrysanthemums. Taxonomists have split *Chrysanthemum* into a number of new genera—and, in certain cases, changed their minds and returned some species to the original genus. In the following descriptions, former names are given first, followed by new names in parentheses.

C. arcticum (Arctanthemum arcticum). ARCTIC CHRYSANTHEMUM. Perennial. Zones A1–A3; 1–10, 14–21. Native to Alaska. Very hardy fall bloomer. Forms foot-wide clump of spoon-shaped, leathery, usually three-lobed leaves 1–3 in. long. Stems 6–12 in. high bear white or pinkish, 1–2-in. flowers. A group of hybrids known as Northland daisies has been developed from this species; they bear single flowers 3 in. or wider, in shades of pink, rose, rosy purple, and yellow. *C. arcticum* itself is primarily a rock garden plant. Taller-growing hybrids reach 16–20 in. and are best in borders.

C. balsamita (Tanacetum balsamita). COSTMARY. Perennial. Zones 2–24. Native Europe to central Asia. Weedy, rhizomatous plant grown for its sweet-scented foliage (used in salads and sachets) rather than its tiny daisies. Leggy stems reach 3 ft. high; if these are cut back, the gray-green, finely scallop-margined basal leaves can make a nice edging for an herb garden. Divide clumps and reset divisions in late summer or fall.

C. carinatum (Glebionis carinatum). SUMMER CHRYSANTHEMUM, TRICOLOR CHRYSANTHEMUM. Annual. Zones 1–24; H1, H2. Moroccan native grows wild in sand dunes along parts of Southern California coast. To 1–3 ft. high and 3 ft. wide, with deeply cut foliage. Showy bloom in summer and fall: 2-in. single daisies in purple, orange, scarlet, salmon, rose, yellow, or white, with contrasting bands around dark center. Long-lasting cut flowers. Sow seeds in spring, either in pots or open ground. In mild-winter areas, can be sown in fall for winter and spring bloom. Takes light or heavy soil. Court Jesters is an excellent strain.

C. coccineum (Tanacetum coccineum, Pyrethrum roseum). PYRETHRUM, PAINTED DAISY. Perennial. Zones A1; 1–24. Native to Iran, Caucasus. Bushy plant to 2–3 ft. high, 1½ ft. wide, with very finely divided bright green leaves. Bears long-stemmed single daisies in pink, red, or white in spring; if cut back, may bloom again in late summer. Also available in double- and anemone-flowered forms. Excellent for cutting, borders. Needs summer heat to perform well (except in extreme heat of low and intermediate deserts, where it is treated as a winter annual). Sow seeds or divide clumps in spring. Double forms may not come true from sown seed, may revert to single flowers.

C. coronarium (Glebionis coronarium). CROWN DAISY. Annual. Zones 1–24; H1, H2. Mediterranean native; sometimes seen naturalized on roadsides. To 2½ ft. high and 1½ ft. wide, with coarsely cut light green leaves and yellow daisies in spring, summer. One variety of this species is the vegetable known as shungiku, chop-suey greens, or edible chrysanthemum; it can be cooked like spinach.

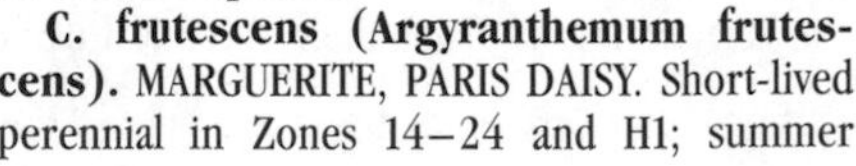

C. frutescens (Argyranthemum frutescens). MARGUERITE, PARIS DAISY. Short-lived perennial in Zones 14–24 and H1; summer annual in Zones 3–11; winter annual in Zones 12, 13. Canary Island native has bright green, coarsely divided leaves and woody-based, 3-ft. stems bearing abundant 1½–2½-in. daisies in white, yellow, or pink. Blooms most of the year in mild climates. 'Snow White', double anemone type, has pure white flowers, more restrained growth habit; 'White Lady' and 'Pink Lady' produce buttonlike flower heads; 'Silver Leaf' has gray-green leaves and masses of very small white blooms. Dwarf varieties are also available.

Chrysanthemum frutescens

All marguerites are splendid in containers and for quick effects in borders, mass displays. A small plant set out in spring can form a 4- by 4-ft. mound by summer. When buying plants, avoid large, vigorous-looking ones with big leaves—they will bloom sparsely. Also avoid plants showing signs of fasciation (flattening or widening of stems) near root crown (at plant's base). Plant in well-drained soil. Grows exceptionally well near coast; also succeeds inland if given sufficient water and good drainage, but may freeze in cold winters. For continued bloom, prune lightly at frequent intervals. In mild-winter areas, do not prune severely, since plants seldom produce new growth from hardened wood; replace every 2 or 3 years. Subject to leaf miner and thrips (which reduce flower quality); old plants are also susceptible to root galls and nematodes.

C. gayanum (Pyrethropsis gayana). Perennial. Zones 14–24. Native to Morocco and Algeria. Woody-based plant to 1½ ft. high, 4 ft. wide, with finely cut gray-green foliage and 1½-in. pink daisies with dark centers. Long bloom season; flowering is heaviest in late winter, early spring. Little water.

C. hosmariense (Pyrethropsis hosmariensis). Perennial. Zones 14–24. Native to Morocco. To 8 in. high, 2 ft. wide, with silvery, finely cut foliage. White daisies bloom over a long season; show is most profuse in winter. Little water.

C. leucanthemum (Leucanthemum vulgare). OX-EYE DAISY, COMMON DAISY. Perennial. Zones A2, A3; 1–24; H1. European native naturalized in many places; spreads by rhizomes and self-seeding. To 2 ft. high, 1 ft. wide, with bright green foliage and yellow-centered daisies from late spring to fall. 'May Queen' begins blooming in early spring.

C. maximum (C.×superbum, Leucanthemum maximum, L.×superbum). SHASTA DAISY. Perennial. Zones A1–A3; 1–24; H1. To 2–4 ft. tall, 2 ft. wide. Original plant with coarse, leathery leaves and gold-centered, 2–4-in.-wide white flowers has been largely superseded by longer-blooming varieties with larger, better-formed flowers. Available in single, double, quilled, and shaggy-flowered forms. All are white, but some show a touch of yellow. All bloom in summer; some start in late spring and continue into fall. All are splendid in borders and as cut flowers.

Among the most popular varieties are 'Esther Read', long-blooming double; 'Marconi', a large, frilly double, and the similar 'Aglaya', a long bloomer; 'Alaska', old-fashioned single variety with large flowers; 'Horace Read', with big, frilly double blossoms; 'Majestic', large single; 'Snowcap', with single blooms on a compact (14–18-in.-high) plant; 'Thomas Killin', extra-large (6-in.) single with yellow anemone-type center (with rays) that gives it the look of a double.

'Cobham's Gold' has distinctive flowers in a yellow-tinted off-white shade. 'Canarybird', another yellow, is a dwarf with attractive dark green foliage.

Shasta daisies are easy to grow from seed. Catalogs offer many strains, including Roggli Super Giant (single) and Diener's Strain (double). 'Marconi', also available in seed, nearly always blooms double. 'Silver Princess' ('Little Princess', 'Little Miss Muffet') is a 12–15-in. dwarf single. 'Snow Lady', an All-America winner, is a 10–12-in. dwarf single that begins to bloom in 5 months from seed, then blooms nearly continuously.

Set out container-grown plants at any time, divisions in fall or early spring (divide established clumps every 2 or 3 years). Thrive in moist, well-drained, fairly rich soil. Fertilize before and during bloom to encourage large flowers. Prefer sun but do well in partial shade in hot-summer climates; double-flowered kinds hold up better in very light shade. In coldest regions, mulch around plants but do not smother foliage. Shasta daisies are generally easy to grow but have a few problems. One of these is gall, a disease that causes root crown to split into many weak, poorly rooted growing points that soon die. Dig out and discard affected plants and do not replant Shasta daisies in the same spot. When buying plants, avoid those with signs of fasciation (flattening or widening of stems) near root crown. Control slugs and snails.

Florists' Chrysanthemum Flower Forms

TOP: 'Firewheel'; Spoon
BOTTOM: 'Apricot'; Single

TOP: 'Kelvin Mandarin'; Pompon
BOTTOM: 'Fireflash'; Decorative

TOP: 'Penny Lane'; Anemone Form
BOTTOM: 'Crimson Tide'; Irregular Incurve

TOP: 'Dorridge King'; Reflex
BOTTOM: 'Pink Miss Olympia'; Laciniated

TOP: 'Super Yellow'; Quill
BOTTOM: 'Virginia'; Spider

C. × morifolium. FLORISTS' CHRYSANTHEMUM. Perennial. Zones 2–24; H1. The most useful of all autumn-blooming perennials for borders, containers, and cutting, and the most versatile and varied of all chrysanthemum species, available in many flower forms, colors, plant sizes (from under a foot to 6 ft. tall), flower sizes, and growth habits. Colors include white, yellow, red, pink, orange, bronze, purple, and lavender, as well as multicolors. The following list describes flower forms as designated by chrysanthemum hobbyists.

Anemone form. One or more rows of rays with large raised center disk or cushion. Center disk may be same color as rays or different.

Brush. Narrow, rolled rays give brush or soft cactus dahlia effect.

Decorative. Long, broad rays overlap like shingles to form broad, full flower. *Laciniated* is fully double, with rays fringed and cut at tips in carnation effect.

Incurve. Big double flowers with broad rays curving upward and inward.

Irregular incurve. Like above, but with looser, more softly curving rays.

Pompon. Globular, neat, compact, with flat, fluted, or quilled rays. Usually small but can reach 5 in. if buds are thinnned to one or two per cluster.

Quill. Long, narrow rolled rays; like spider but less droopy.

Reflex. Big double flowers; rays curl in, out, and sideways, creating shaggy effect.

Semidouble. Somewhat like single or daisy, but with two, three, or four rows of rays around a yellow center.

Single or daisy form. Single row of rays around a yellow center. May be large or small, with broad or narrow rays.

Spider. Long, curling, tubular rays ending in fish-hook curved tips.

Spoon. Tubular rays flattened at tip to make little disks, sometimes in contrasting colors.

WHAT FLORISTS' MUMS NEED

SOIL: Dig organic matter and a complete fertilizer into good, well-drained garden soil 2 to 3 weeks before planting.

PLANTING: Set out young pot plants, rooted cuttings, or vigorous single-stem divisions in early spring. When dividing clumps, take divisions from outside; discard the woody centers.

FERTILIZING: Feed plants in ground two or three times during the growing season. Make last application with low-nitrogen fertilizer not less than 2 weeks before bloom.

PINCHING: Frequent pinching produces sturdy plants with big flowers. Begin at planting time by removing plant tip. Lateral shoots will form; select one to four of these for continued growth. Keep pinching all summer, nipping top pair of leaves on every shoot that reaches 5 in. long. Stop pinching earlier in coldest regions. For huge blooms (on large-flowered sorts), disbud (remove all flower buds except one or two per cluster).

'Carrousel'; Quill

Garden culture. It's easy to grow chrysanthemums, not so easy to grow prize-winning chrysanthemums. The latter need more water, feeding, pinching, pruning, grooming, and pest control than most perennials.

Plant in early spring, in an area away from large trees or hedges with invasive roots. In hot climates, choose a spot shaded from afternoon sun. Water deeply at intervals determined by your soil structure—frequently in porous soils, less often in heavy soils. Too little water causes woody stems and loss of lower leaves; overwatering causes leaves to yellow, then blacken and drop. Stems are attacked by borers in desert areas. Aphids are the only notable pest in all areas. One way to avoid them is to feed plants with systemic insecticide/fertilizer combination. Stake taller plants as needed to keep them upright.

After bloom, cut back plants to within 8 in. of ground. Where soils are heavy and likely to remain wet in winter, dig clumps with soil intact and set on top of ground in inconspicuous place. Cover with sand or sawdust if you wish (a good idea in Zones 2, 3, and 10). Take cuttings from early to late spring (up until May for some varieties) or when shoots are 3–4 in. long. As new shoots develop, you can take additional cuttings from them. In cold-winter areas, store in cold frame or mulch with light, noncompacting material like excelsior.

Pot culture. Pot rooted cuttings midwinter to early spring, using porous, fibrous, moisture-holding planting mix. Move plants to larger pots as growth requires—don't let them become root-bound. Pinch as directed in "What Florists' Mums Need" (at left); stake as required. Plants need water daily in warm weather, every other day in cool conditions. Feed with liquid fertilizer every 7 to 10 days until buds show color.

Off-season, potted chrysanthemums. Florists and even grocery stores sell potted chrysanthemums in bloom every day of the year, though by nature a chrysanthemum blooms in late summer or fall. Growers force these plants to bloom out of season by subjecting them to artificial day lengths, using lights and dark cloths. You can plunge the potted flowering plants right into a garden bed or border for an immediate (but expensive) display, or enjoy them in the house while the flowers remain fresh and then plant them out. Either way, they will not bloom again at the same off-season time the next year. Instead, they will revert to their natural inclination and commence fall bloom once again.

To pot off-season mums after bloom, cut off flowers when they fade, leaving stems 6–8 in. long. Remove soil clump from pot and break apart the several individual plants that were grown in the pot. Plant these individual plants. When new growth shows from the roots, cut off remainder of old flower stems.

C. multicaule (Coleostephus myconis). Annual. Zones A1–A3; 1–24. Native to southern Europe. Blooms in spring, when broad-rayed, buttery yellow daisies 2½ in. across rise above 6–8-in.-wide mats of bright green, fleshy foliage. Blooms best in cool weather; usually sold in fall, winter, or early spring in cell-packs or pots. In Alaska, blooms all summer until frost. In cool-summer/mild-winter climates, plants may live over a second year. 'Moonlight' has lemon yellow flowers.

C. nipponicum (Nipponanthemum nipponicum). Perennial. Zones 3–24. Japanese native resembling large, rounded, shrubby Shasta daisy (to 3 ft. tall and 2 ft. wide) with a dense mass of nearly succulent bright green leaves. Long-stemmed white daisies bloom in fall. To maintain compactness, cut back after bloom in mild-winter regions; in colder climates, cut back partway after plants put on strong new growth in spring.

C. pacificum (Ajania pacifica, Pyrethrum marginatum, Dendranthema pacificum). GOLD AND SILVER CHRYSANTHEMUM. Perennial. Zones 3–24. Prohibited in some areas as a host to white rust of chrysanthemum. Semitrailing, woody-based perennial from Japan; to 1 ft. tall, 3 ft. wide. Stems are densely clad in lobed dark green leaves that seem rimmed with white; in fact, woolly white leaf undersides show at edges. Broad clusters of yellow flowers appear in fall; lacking rays, they resemble bunches of brass buttons. Use as bank or ground cover or at the front of perennial border. A tough plant, but lower leaves will die off without regular summer water. Maintain compactness as for *C. nipponicum.* 'Pink Ice' is a pale pink–flowered variety with short rays.

C. paludosum (Leucanthemum paludosum, Melampodium paludosum). Annual. Zones A1–A3; 1–24. Western Mediterranean native forms about 8-in.-wide clumps of dark green, deeply toothed leaves. In summer, bears white flowers resembling miniature Shasta daisies on 8–10-in. stems. Sometimes lives over for a second bloom season. Popularly grown as an annual in Alaska.

C. parthenium (Tanacetum parthenium). FEVERFEW. Perennial. Zones 2–24. Native to southern Europe, Caucasus. Compact, leafy, aggressive, spreading by volunteer seedlings; once favored in Victorian gardens. Leaves have strong peppery scent that some people find offensive. Varieties range from 1 to 3 ft. tall. 'Golden Ball' has bright yellow flower heads and no rays; 'Silver Ball' is fully double, with only the white rays showing. In 'Aureum' (commonly sold in flats as 'Golden Feather'), chartreuse foliage is main attraction. To propagate, divide clumps in spring; or sow seeds in spring for bloom by midsummer.

C. ptarmiciflorum (Tanacetum ptarmiciflorum). DUSTY MILLER, SILVER LACE. Perennial in Zones 16, 17, 19–24; annual in Zones 1–15, 18. Canary Island native grows to 10 in. high and wide. Very finely cut, silvery white leaves. Where winter-hardy, produces white daisies on 1½-ft. stems in summer. Somewhat drought tolerant. (For other plants with the common name "dusty miller," see that entry.)

C. ×rubellum. Perennial. Zones 1–24. To 2 ft. high and wide, with finely cut leaves and 2–3-in. daisies over a long season beginning in late summer. 'Clara Curtis' has bright pink flowers; 'Mary Stoker' has blooms of soft yellow touched with apricot.

C. weyrichii. Perennial. Zones 2–6. From Japan. Rock garden plant with finely cut leaves; forms a mat to 1–1½ ft. high and 1 ft. wide. Single, 2-in., white to pink daisies with yellow centers appear just above foliage in fall. 'Pink Bomb' has rosy pink rays, 'White Bomb' creamy white ones.

FOR INFORMATION ON YOUR CLIMATE ZONE
PLEASE SEE PAGES 27–63

CHRYSOLEPIS chrysophylla

CHINQUAPIN
Fagaceae
EVERGREEN TREE OR SHRUB
ZONES 4–7, 14–17
FULL SUN OR PARTIAL SHADE
NO IRRIGATION NEEDED

Chrysolepis chrysophylla

Native primarily to Coast and Cascade Ranges from central California to Washington. Habit varies, depending on growing conditions; plant is seen both as a large tree (to 90 ft. tall, 50 ft. wide) and a big shrub. Narrowly oval, 2–6-in. leaves are rich glossy green above, golden beneath from a coating of tiny yellow scales. Fragrant spring flowers in erect or nodding white to creamy white catkins. Fruit a prickly 2-in. bur containing small, sweet-kerneled nuts. Bark is gray and furrowed. Handsome but difficult to grow even in its native range—and extremely difficult elsewhere. Needs excellent drainage, acid soil.

CHRYSOTHAMNUS

RABBITBRUSH, CHAMISA
Asteraceae (Compositae)
DECIDUOUS SHRUBS
ZONES 1–3, 10, 11
FULL SUN
LITTLE OR NO WATER

Chrysothamnus nauseosus

High desert, Rocky Mountain natives. Erect, freely branching shrubs to 6 ft. tall, 3 ft. wide; branches are white, with greenish upper surfaces. Gray-green, narrow leaves often drop by bloom time in late summer or fall, when branching, flat-topped or somewhat rounded clusters of fluffy flowers appear at stem ends. Leaves and stems are strongly aromatic. Useful for roadside or natural plantings, revegetation, low-care or no-care borders. Numerous subspecies of both plants described below exist; some are better suited than others to the coldest zones.

C. nauseosus. Differs from species below mainly in that its flowers are yellow.

C. viscidiflorus. Flowers are greenish yellow and somewhat sticky.

CHUPAROSA. See ANISACANTHUS thurberi, JUSTICIA californica

CIBOTIUM glaucum

HAPU'U, HAWAIIAN TREE FERN
Dicksoniaceae
TREE FERN
ZONES 17, 23, 24; H2
FULL SUN OR PARTIAL SHADE
MODERATE WATER

Cibotium glaucum

Native to Hawaii and the most common tree fern found there; creates a tropical effect in the garden. Very slow grower to 20 ft. tall, with crown spreading 15 ft. wide. Arching, intricately divided, 3–9-ft.-long fronds are medium green above, lighter green beneath. Silky, fawn-colored wool *(pulu)* shrouds the leaf bases and densely covers the frond buds at the trunk tip. Needs protection from strong winds. Best with moderate water but tolerates dry or moist conditions. Give some shade in hot, dry areas. Prune to remove old or injured fronds.

Another tree fern found in lesser numbers in Hawaiian forests is *C. chamissoi.* It has a stout trunk to about 15 ft. tall, covered with blackish, woolly hairs.

CICHORIUM intybus. See CHICORY

CIDER GUM. See EUCALYPTUS gunnii

CIGAR PLANT. See CUPHEA ignea

CILANTRO. See CORIANDRUM sativum

CIMICIFUGA

BUGBANE

Ranunculaceae

PERENNIALS

ZONES 1–7, 17

FULL SUN ONLY IN COOLER CLIMATES

REGULAR WATER

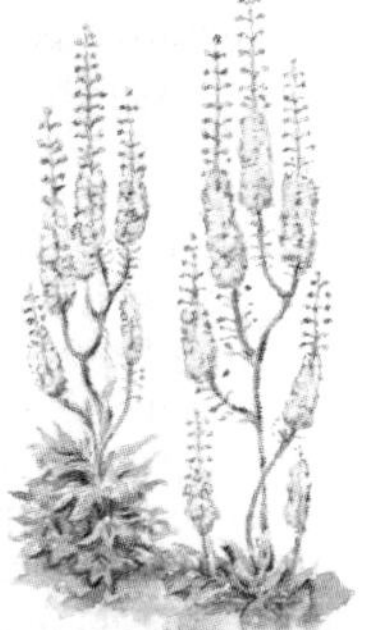

Cimicifuga racemosa

Stately, upright, slim spikes of small white flowers like elongated bottlebrushes rise from clumps of shiny, dark green leaves divided into many deeply toothed, 1½–3-in. leaflets; overall effect is delicate and airy. The various species bloom midsummer to fall; dried seed clusters are used in flower arrangements. All are handsome among large ferns in woodland gardens; tallest types are also good back-of-border plants. Best in rich, well-drained soil. Will take considerable sun if given adequate moisture. Need some winter chill for best bloom. Clumps can remain undisturbed for many years. In cold-winter areas, divide in early spring before growth starts; in milder climates, divide in fall.

C. japonica. Native to Japan. White autumn flowers on purplish black, leafless stalks. In bloom, plant is 3–4 ft. tall, 2 ft. wide. *C. j. acerina* has white flowers opening from pink buds.

C. racemosa. BLACK SNAKEROOT. Native to eastern North America. Leafy clump to 3–4 ft. tall, 3 ft. wide. Flowering stalks are typically branched and carry dense spikes of white flowers that increase plant height to 7 ft. Blooms between midsummer and early fall.

C. simplex. KAMCHATKA BUGBANE. Native to Siberia and Japan. Foliage clump to 2 ft. tall and wide, with 3–4-ft. flower stalks in fall. 'Atropurpurea' has purplish leaves and pink-tinted flower buds on 5-ft. stems. 'Brunette' and 'Hillside Black Beauty' have even darker foliage and pinkish flowers. 'Prichard's Giant' *(C. ramosa)* has foliage clumps to 4 ft. tall and wide; erect stems to 7 ft. high carry foot-long, narrow spikes of white flowers.

CINERARIA. See SENECIO × hybridus

CINNAMOMUM camphora

CAMPHOR TREE

Lauraceae

EVERGREEN TREE

ZONES 8, 9, 12–24; H1, H2

FULL SUN OR LIGHT SHADE

LITTLE TO REGULAR WATER

Cinnamomum camphora

Native to China, Japan. Grows slowly to 50 ft. or taller, 60 ft. wide. Typically a strong-structured tree with heavy trunk and heavy, upright, spreading limbs. Beautiful in rain, when trunk looks black. Aromatic, 2½–5-in.-long leaves smell like camphor when crushed. New foliage in early spring is pink, red, or bronze; matures to shiny yellow green. Inconspicuous but fragrant yellow flowers bloom profusely in late spring, followed by small blackish fruits.

Drops leaves quite heavily in early spring; flowers, fruits, and twigs drop later. Plant where litter will not be a problem. Competitive roots also make this tree a poor choice near garden beds and paved areas; roots may invade sewer and drainage lines as well. In desert zones, sometimes affected by salt burn. Subject to verticillium wilt. Symptoms are wilting and dying of twigs, branches, center of tree, or entire tree; wood in twigs or branches shows brownish discoloration. Most susceptible after wet winters or if planted in poorly drained soil. No cure is known, though trees often outgrow the problem. To treat, cut out damaged branches. Apply nitrogen fertilizer and water it in well.

CINNAMON FERN. See OSMUNDA cinnamomea

CINQUEFOIL. See POTENTILLA

CISSUS

Vitaceae

EVERGREEN VINES

ZONES VARY BY SPECIES

EXPOSURE NEEDS VARY BY SPECIES

WATER NEEDS VARY BY SPECIES

Cissus antarctica

These relatives of Virginia creeper, Boston ivy, and grape are valued for their foliage; flowers are inconspicuous. Most climb by tendrils, and most will double as ground covers in mild-winter climates. Easy to grow; not fussy about soil, water, or fertilizer. Prune any time to remove tangled or weak stems or to restrict size. Grown as houseplants, they prefer bright reflected light, moderate water.

C. antarctica. KANGAROO TREEBINE. Zones 16–24; or indoors. Native to Australia. Graceful, densely foliaged vine to 10 ft., vigorous once established. Glossy, spear-shaped leaves reach 3½ in. long; toothed edges and prominent veins are subtly decorative. In the ground, needs little or no irrigation. Good plant for climbing up or tumbling down—on trellis, wall, or hillside. Sun or shade.

C. capensis. See Rhoicissus capensis

C. discolor. Zone H2; or indoors. Native to Southeast Asia. Can climb to 6–10 ft. but is usually grown in hanging pots. Oval, 4–6-in.-long, toothed leaves resemble those of rex begonia in color and texture; they have showy pink and silver markings, maroon undersurfaces. Needs partial shade, humidity, regular water.

C. hypoglauca. Zones 13–24. Native to Australia. Rapid growth to 15 ft. in one season; eventually to 30–50 ft. Climbs by means of flexible stems rather than tendrils. Highly polished, bronze-tinted leaves are divided into five rounded, leathery, 3-in.-long leaflets. New growth is covered with rust-colored fuzz. Use as climber or erosion-controlling bank cover. Sun or light shade. Little or no water.

C. quadrangula (C. quadrangularis). Zones 24; H2; or indoors. Odd-looking succulent vine, usually grown in hanging baskets. Generally leafless, with thick, jointed, four-angled or winged stems that climb or trail several feet. Leaves occasionally appear; they are oval or three lobed, 2 in. long. Easy to grow if given regular water, quick drainage, full sun.

C. rhombifolia. GRAPE IVY. Zones 13, 15, 16, 21–24; H1, H2; or indoors. Native to South America. Beautiful dark green leaves divided into diamond-shaped, toothed leaflets 1–4 in. long. Veins on leaf undersides have reddish hairs, giving foliage a bronzy overtone. Popular houseplant; tolerates low light. Outdoors, it grows to 20 ft. and can be trained on a support. Full sun to fairly deep shade; moderate water. 'Mandaiana' is more upright and compact than species, with larger, more substantial leaflets. 'Ellen Danica' is smaller than species, with lobed leaflets.

C. striata. Zones 13–24; or indoors. Native to South America. Handsome vine reaching 20 ft. Looks very similar to a miniature Virginia creeper *(Parthenocissus quinquefolia),* with small, leathery leaves divided into three to five 1–3-in.-long leaflets. Foliage contrasts with reddish stems. Train it to make a tracery against a wall surface, let it spill over wall, or use as ground cover. Sun or shade. Moderate water.

C. trifoliata. GRAPE IVY. Zones 10–13; evergreen only in the warmest locations. Native to the Southwest and Mexico. Climbs by simple or forked tendrils to 30 ft., or sprawls along the ground. Smooth dark green leaves are typically divided into three 3–4-in. leaflets but are sometimes merely three lobed. Flowering stalks are reddish; inconspicuous flowers are followed in summer by black berries on bright red stalks. Useful for covering chain-link fences or trellises. Contact with plant may cause a skin rash in sensitive people. Full sun. Little to moderate water.

C. voinieriana. See Tetrastigma voinierianum

Cistaceae. Members of the rockrose family grown in the West are evergreen shrubs with flowers that look something like single roses—small in sunrose *(Helianthemum)*, large in rockrose *(Cistus)*. Individual flowers are short lived but appear over a long season.

CISTUS

ROCKROSE

Cistaceae

EVERGREEN SHRUBS

ZONES 6–9, 14–24; BORDERLINE IN ZONES 4, 5

FULL SUN

LITTLE OR NO WATER

Cistus × purpureus

Mediterranean natives; hardy to 15°F/–9°C. In their favored dry-summer climate, they are carefree shrubs bearing a profusion of showy flowers for a month or more from spring into early summer; may also bloom sporadically at other times. In some rockroses, leaves are coated with a perfumed resin; others have foliage covered with gray wool. When plants are out of bloom, their soft green, silver, or grayish foliage and mounded form add subtle color and texture to the landscape.

Sun loving, fast growing, tolerant of aridity. Accept poor soil, cold ocean winds, salt spray, desert heat. Often planted in fire-hazard areas. Good erosion-control cover for dry banks. Useful in big rock gardens, in rough areas along drives, in wild plantings. Taller kinds make attractive informal hedges. Give plants well-drained soil if they will be watered. When locating in an area that won't be irrigated, take particular care not to plant root-bound plants; cut circling roots and spread out the mass so roots can grow down to lower soil levels. Most rockroses resent hard pruning. To keep plants vigorous and neat, periodically cut out a few old stems. Tip-pinch young plants to thicken growth, or give a light overall summer shearing to new growth and stems that have not become woody. If plants become sparse and woody after several years, it is often easiest to replace them.

C. albidus. WHITE-LEAVED ROCKROSE. To 4 ft. tall, 8 ft. wide, with furry gray leaves. Bright purplish pink, 2-in. flowers. Repeat bloom in fall is common.

C. 'Brilliancy'. See C. 'Sunset'

C. × corbariensis. See C. × hybridus

C. crispus. To 3 ft. tall, 5 ft. wide, with furry, wavy-edged gray-green leaves and 2–2½-in. purplish pink flowers. 'Santa Cruz' is a compact, dense selection or hybrid with fuzzy gray foliage and 3-in. blossoms in deeper purplish rose. 'Descanso' grows 1 ft. tall and 4 ft. wide, bears a profusion of 1½-in. cerise flowers; often mistakenly labeled 'Warley Rose'.

C. 'Doris Hibberson'. Compact grower to 3 ft. tall and wide. Oval gray-green leaves; clear pink, 3-in. flowers with crinkled, silky petals.

C. × hybridus (C. × corbariensis). WHITE ROCKROSE. Widely grown. To 3–4 ft. tall, 4–8 ft. wide. Gray-green, crinkly, 2-in.-long leaves are fragrant on warm days. White flowers 1½ in. across, yellow centers.

C. incanus (C. villosus). Bushy plant to 3–5 ft. tall and wide. Oval, 1–3-in. leaves are densely covered with down. Purplish pink flowers, 2–2½ in. wide. 'LASCA Select' grows 3 ft. high and 5–8 ft. wide, with deep mauve blooms among soft grayish green leaves with white undersides. *C. i. creticus (C. creticus)* is similar but has wavy-edged leaves.

C. ladanifer (C. ladaniferus maculatus). CRIMSON-SPOT ROCKROSE. Compact growth to 3–5 ft. high with equal spread. Fragrant leaves to 4 in. long are dark green above, lighter beneath; 3-in.-wide flowers are white with a dark crimson spot at each petal base. 'Cordoba' is a choice selection, 'Albiflorus' an unspotted form. *C. l. latifolius (C. palhinhae)* is a lower grower (to 2 ft.) but has larger blooms (3–4 in. across). Hybrids include 'Maculatus', to 6 ft. tall, 4–5 ft. wide; and 'Blanche' (to 8–12 ft. high, 6–8 ft. wide) and 'Frank Birch' (to 6–8 ft. tall and wide), both bearing 4-in. pure white blossoms.

C. laurifolius. Stiff, erect growth to 4–6 ft. high and wide. Dark green, 5-in. leaves with pale undersides. White, 2–2½-in. flowers come in long-stalked clusters of three or more. 'Bennett's White' has 3–4-in. flowers resembling those of Matilija poppy *(Romneya coulteri)*, with wavy, crepe paper–textured petals around a large cluster of yellow stamens. Good hedge or background shrub for dry areas.

C. 'Peggy Sammons'. To 3–6 ft. tall and wide, with gray-green leaves and 2½ in. pink flowers.

C. × purpureus. ORCHID ROCKROSE. Compact grower to 4 ft. tall and wide, often shorter and wider when subjected to constant ocean winds. Leaves 1–2 in. long, dark green above, gray and hairy beneath. The 3-in., reddish purple flowers have a red spot at each petal base. Very fine where cool winds and salt spray limit choice of plants.

C. salviifolius. SAGELEAF ROCKROSE. Often sold as *C. villosus* 'Prostratus'. Wide-spreading shrub to 2 ft. high, 6 ft. wide. Light gray-green leaves about 1 in. long, crinkly, veined, crisp looking. Very profuse show of 1½-in.-wide flowers, white with yellow spot at base of each petal. Good bank or ground cover for rough situations.

C. × skanbergii. To 3 ft. tall, 8 ft. wide. Gray-green leaves; great profusion of 1-in., pure pink flowers.

C. 'Sunset' ('Brilliancy'). Dense, spreading growth to 2 ft. tall, 6–8 ft. wide, with resinous gray-green leaves and 2-in.-wide flowers in dark magenta pink.

C. 'Victor Reiter'. Stiffly erect plant to 3–4 ft. high and wide. Gray-green leaves; 2½–3½-in.-wide blossoms in hot pink with paler pink center. Sister seedling of 'Doris Hibberson' but superior to it.

C. villosus. See C. incanus

C. villosus 'Prostratus'. See C. salviifolius

CITRON. See CITRUS, CITRON

CITRUS

Rutaceae

EVERGREEN TREES AND SHRUBS

ZONES 8, 9, 12–24, H1, H2; OR INDOORS

FULL SUN; BRIGHT LIGHT

REGULAR WATER

Orange

As landscaping plants, citrus offer year-round attractive form and glossy deep green foliage; also bear fragrant flowers and decorative fruit in season. If you want quality fruit, your choice of varieties will depend on the total amount of heat available through the fruit-developing period (need varies according to type) and on the winter cold in your zone. Citrus flowers attract bees.

Heat requirements. Generally, sweet-fruited varieties need moderate to high heat to form sugars, sour types less heat. Lemons and limes require the least warmth and will produce usable fruit in cool-summer areas (as long as winter temperatures are not too low). 'Valencia' orange has a higher heat requirement and greater frost tolerance; it is adapted to areas near Southern California coast. Navel oranges demand even more warmth and are better suited to inland regions; their fruit development period is shorter than that of 'Valencia', so trees will produce palatable fruit between winter frosts if summer heat is high. Mandarins (tangerines) require high heat for top flavor and are best adapted to inland areas. Grapefruit develops full flavor only where trees receive prolonged high heat, as in the low desert. (In cooler areas, you're better off growing grapefruit-pummelo hybrids 'Oroblanco' and 'Melogold', which produce sweet fruit in more moderate temperatures.)

Heat is the factor that causes pigmented grapefruit and pummelos to develop red color; without enough heat, the flesh looks white. The exact reasons for coloration in blood oranges are not fully understood, but both color and quality are usually better in warmer inland areas with cooler night temperatures.

WHAT CITRUS NEED

CLIMATE: Most kinds of citrus flourish in areas with warm to hot summers and mild winters.

SOIL: Citrus trees are quite tolerant, as long as the soil is well-drained.

WATERING: Be consistent; don't let the soil dry out completely or get soggy.

FERTILIZING: Keep the nitrogen coming—citrus demands a fairly large amount every year. Apply micronutrients—iron, zinc, and manganese.

RIPENING: Citrus fruit ripens only on the tree. Don't go by rind color; taste to determine ripeness.

'Valencia' Sweet Orange

Hardiness. Citrus plants of one type or another are grown outdoors all year round in regions with warm to hot summers and mild winters. Lemons, limes, and citrons are most sensitive to freezes. Sweet oranges, 'Improved Meyer' lemon, grapefruit, and most mandarins and their hybrids are intermediate in cold resistance. Kumquats, satsuma mandarins, sour oranges, and calamondin are the most cold resistant, with kumquats—the hardiest of all—withstanding temperatures in the high teens.

Other factors affecting a tree's cold tolerance include preconditioning to cold (it has greater endurance if exposed to cold slowly and if first freeze comes late), type of rootstock, and location in garden. Prolonged exposure to freezing weather is more damaging than a brief plunge in temperature. All citrus fruit is damaged at several degrees below freezing—hence the importance of choosing early-ripening varieties in freeze-prone areas. For information on protecting plants from cold, see page 671.

Growing citrus in Hawaii. Home gardeners in Hawaii can grow many of the varieties grown on the mainland, plus some specialty types adapted only to the islands (these are included in the variety descriptions). However, citrus grows differently in Hawaii, and the resulting fruit often looks and tastes quite a bit different from the same variety grown in California or Arizona. The trees tend to bloom almost year-round, so the harvest is nearly continuous. The lack of cool nights results in a rind that's thinner and more greenish than the thicker, brightly colored skin of fruit grown in California. Lack of cool nights also reduces acid content—so Hawaiian citrus tastes sweeter. The fruit is very juicy as well.

Standard or dwarf. Practically all citrus plants sold have been budded or grafted on an understock. Grafted trees begin bearing fruit in just a few years, contrasted to 10 to 15 years for seedling trees. Standard trees (20–30 ft. tall and as wide) are grown on a variety of understocks. Dwarf trees are grown on understocks of trifoliate orange *(Poncirus trifoliata)* or 'Flying Dragon'; the latter is a naturally dwarf, contorted, spiny form of trifoliate orange. Ordinary trifoliate orange understocks produce trees 8–10 ft. tall (some may reach 15–20 ft.). 'Flying Dragon' produces even smaller trees (5–7 ft. at 13 years). Check citrus trees periodically for suckers (branches that arise below the graft line) and remove them before they compete with (or overwhelm) the desired variety. Some tender citrus, such as limes, are grown from cuttings; if such trees are killed to the ground by severe cold, they will resprout from the roots true to type.

Harvest periods. Most citrus varieties ripen their fruit from late fall into winter, but some varieties, such as 'Valencia' orange, ripen into spring and summer. In addition, many types can hold their fruit on the tree for extended periods without loss of quality. By growing both 'Washington' navel and 'Valencia' oranges, for example, you can have fresh fruit almost 10 months of the year. Everbearing citrus like lemons and limes can produce throughout the year, though they fruit most heavily in winter and spring.

Citrus fruit ripens only on the tree. The best way to judge ripeness is to pick a fruit and taste it; rind color is a poor indicator, since many varieties are fully colored before they are edible.

Drainage. Fast drainage is essential. If soil drains slowly, don't attempt to plant citrus in it regardless of how you condition it. Instead, plant above soil level in raised beds or on a soil mound. Drainage in average soil (and water retention in sandy soil) will be improved by digging in a 4–6-in. layer of organic matter (such as garden compost or ground bark) to a depth of about 1 ft.

Watering. Citrus trees need moist soil, but never standing water. They also need air in the soil. Danger from overwatering is greatest in clay soil where air spaces are minute. In soil with proper drainage, water newly planted trees almost as frequently as trees in containers—twice a week in normal summer weather, more frequently during hot spells. Water established trees every other week during summer. In clay soils, space watering intervals so top 4–6 in. of soil dries between irrigations. Don't let tree reach wilting point. Be sure to water consistently. Fluctuating soil moisture can aggravate fruit splitting—a problem that can affect all citrus, but especially navel oranges (typically in autumn).

If you build basins, make them wider than spread of branches. Citrus roots extend out twice as far as the distance from the trunk to branch ends. Keep trunk dry by starting basin 6 in. or more from trunk. When you water, be sure to wet entire root zone (that is, wet to a depth of 3–4 ft.).

Mulching. Since citrus roots grow near the surface as well as deeper, a mulch over the soil is beneficial. Use a 2–3-in. layer of compost or other organic matter to help maintain soil moisture. In mild-summer areas, large pebbles or gravel will increase reflected heat and hasten ripening. Don't allow grass to grow near the trunks of citrus trees. Instead, maintain a grass-free, mulched area under the canopy.

Fertilizing. Nitrogen is the main nutrient that must be supplied in all regions. If you garden in sandy soil, choose a complete fertilizer containing a full range of nutrients. Apply 2 oz. actual nitrogen the first year after a newly planted tree puts on new growth; then increase the amount by 4 oz. each year for the next few years. After the fifth year, apply 1–1½ lb. yearly. (Depending on tree size, give plants growing in raised beds or with restricted root space as well as trees grafted onto 'Flying Dragon' rootstock about a third to half the recommended amount after the fifth year.) To determine weight of actual nitrogen, multiply percentage of total nitrogen (as stated on fertilizer label) by total weight of fertilizer.

Divide total fertilizer into several feedings throughout the growing season. In freeze-prone areas, start feeding in late winter and stop in late summer. Make sure trees are well watered before feeding. Spread the fertilizer beneath and a foot or two outside the branch spread of the tree; then water it in deeply.

Citrus trees that receive too much or too little nitrogen show the evidence in leaf color. Dark green, lush leaves with burned tips or edges indicate too much nitrogen; yellowish leaves are a sign of nitrogen deficiency.

Citrus may suffer from chlorosis due to iron, manganese, or zinc deficiency. In iron chlorosis, leaves turn yellow from edges inward; veins remain dark green. (Same symptom may be caused by overwatering, so check your irrigation practices.) Manganese deficiency shows up as fine mottling, usually on young leaves, and as pale or yellowish areas between dark green veins. Signs of zinc deficiency are yellowish blotching or mottling between leaf veins. Manganese and zinc deficiencies may occur together and be difficult to distinguish from each other. Commercial products containing chelates of all three nutrients are available as foliar sprays.

Pests and diseases. Citrus can get aphids, mites, scale insects, and mealybugs. If these pests' natural enemies fail to handle the infestations, and if jets of water fail to keep the pests in check, spray with appropriate chemicals. If scale remains troublesome, spray with horticultural oil in early spring. Control snails and slugs whenever necessary, especially during warm-night spells in winter and spring.

Copper bands, available in some areas, will keep snails out of trees. Where it is legal to do so (in Southern California), colonize citrus groves with decollate snails, which prey on the garden snail.

The citrus bud mite causes weirdly deformed fruit (especially lemons). Control with horticultural oil spray in spring and in fall; spray only in fall in hot-summer areas. Reduce harmful insect populations by keeping ants out of trees with sticky bands on trunks. (Ants prey on natural insect predators of the mites.)

The few fungal ailments of citrus occur in poorly drained soil. Water molds, causing root rot, show up in yellowing and dropping foliage. Best control is to correct your watering schedule.

Brown rot gummosis usually occurs in older trees at base of trunk. Keep base of trunk dry; trim and clean the oozing wounds, removing decayed bark to a point where discolored wood does not show. Paint areas with Bordeaux paste mixture.

Sunburn. Citrus bark sunburns in hot-sun areas. Trunks should be wrapped (paper trunk bands are available commercially). When heavy pruning exposes trunks or limbs, protect bark with whitewash or latex paint diluted by half with water.

Pruning. Commercial trees are allowed to carry branches right to ground. Production is heaviest on lower branches. Growers prune only to remove twiggy growth and weak branches or, in young plants, to nip back wild growth and balance the plant. You can prune garden trees to shape as desired; espaliering is traditional, though espaliered citrus is not very productive. Lemons and sour oranges are often planted close and pruned as hedges. 'Lisbon' and 'Eureka' lemons should be pruned to keep the trees within bounds and the fruit easily reachable. Many citrus are thorny, so wear gloves and a long-sleeved shirt when picking fruit or pruning. In freeze-prone areas, don't prune in fall or winter. Wait until late spring or summer to prune frost-damaged trees—new growth will make it clear which wood is dead. If you're growing a multiple-variety citrus tree, you must continuously cut back the vigorous growers (lemon, lime, pummelo, grapefruit) so the weaker ones (sweet orange, mandarin) can survive. On all citrus, remove fruit from newly planted trees so that energy will be channeled into new growth rather than fruiting.

Citrus in containers. In general, containers should have a diameter of at least 1½ ft., though calamondin and 'Chinotto' sour orange can stay in 8–10-in. pots for years. Plant in light, well-drained soil mix. Daily watering may be necessary in hot weather. Fertilize monthly from midwinter to midautumn with high-nitrogen liquid fertilizer containing chelated zinc, iron, and manganese.

Potted citrus can stay outdoors all year in mild-winter climates, but plants should be moved to a protected location if a freeze is predicted. In cold-winter regions, shelter plants in winter; a cool greenhouse is best, but a basement area or garage with good bright light is satisfactory. Most container-grown citrus will need to be root-pruned and repotted in fresh soil every 4 or 5 years to remain healthy.

Citrus as houseplants. No guarantee of flowering or fruiting indoors, though plants are still appealing. 'Improved Meyer' and 'Ponderosa' lemons, 'Bearss' lime, kumquats, calamondin, and 'Rangpur' sour-acid mandarin are most likely to produce good fruit. Locate no farther than 6 ft. from a sunny window, away from radiators or other heat sources. Ideal humidity level is 50 percent. Increase moisture by misting tree; also ring tree with pebble-filled trays of water. Water sparingly in winter.

SWEET ORANGE

The commercial oranges of the West are typified by 'Washington' navel and 'Valencia'. In the following list, 'Washington' and the other navel varieties are described first, then 'Valencia' and its counterparts, and finally the other, lesser-known oranges.

'Washington' navel. Widely adapted except in desert regions; best in warm interiors. Standard tree is 20–25-ft. globe. On dwarf stock, it grows 8–12 ft. high. Bears early to midwinter. 'Tabata' is identical (or nearly so) to 'Washington'; it is grown in Hawaii, as is the standard 'Washington'.

'Cara Cara'. First rosy-fleshed navel; bears about the same time as 'Washington'. Rich flavor.

'Lane Late'. Late-ripening navel, extending the season well into summer. 'Summernavel' is also late ripening, but fruit quality is not as good.

'Robertson'. Variant of 'Washington'. Fruit identical but earlier by 2 to 3 weeks. Tends to carry fruit in clusters. Tree generally smaller in size than 'Washington'. Has same climate adaptation. Dwarf trees produce amazing amounts of fruit.

'Skaggs Bonanza'. Another variant of 'Washington'. Fruit colors and ripens earlier; tree produces fruit at young age. Very heavy bearing.

'Valencia'. The juice orange of stores. Most widely planted orange in the world. Widely adapted in California but a poor risk in Arizona; if you plant it there, select a warm location or provide some protection to fruit, which must overwinter on tree. One of Arizona Sweets (see below) would be a safer selection. 'Valencia' oranges mature in summer and store on tree for months, improving in sweetness. Vigorous tree, fuller growing than 'Washington', both as standard and dwarf.

'Campbell', 'Delta', and 'Midknight' are early-ripening, nearly seedless selections of 'Valencia'.

Arizona Sweets. A group of varieties grown in Arizona. 'Diller', 'Hamlin', 'Marrs', and 'Pineapple' are the principal ones.

'Diller'. Small to medium oranges with few seeds, high-quality juice. Ripen in late fall (before heavy frost). Vigorous, large, dense tree with large leaves.

'Hamlin'. Similar to 'Diller', with medium-size fruit; not as hardy.

'Marrs'. Tasty, low-acid, early-ripening fruit on a naturally semidwarf tree. Bears young.

'Pineapple'. Rich flavor, seedy fruit. Tends to bear in alternate years.

'Shamouti' ('Palestine Jaffa'). Originated in Israel and considered there to be finest orange. Large, seedless, no navel. Not a commercial orange in California because not sufficiently superior to 'Washington' navel. Grown on dwarf rootstock for home gardeners because of beauty in form and foliage. It is wider than tall. Larger leaves than those of navel oranges. Heavy crop of fruit in early spring. 'Pera' is a 'Shamouti' relative grown in Hawaii.

'Trovita'. Originated from seedling of 'Washington' navel. Thin skinned and about navel size, but without navel. Ripens in early spring. Apparently requires less heat than other sweet oranges and develops good-quality fruit near (though not on) coast. Nevertheless, it tolerates heat well enough to pass as one of the Arizona Sweets. Dwarf tree has 'Washington' navel look, with handsome dark green leaves.

Blood oranges. These are characterized by red pigmentation in flesh, juice, and (to a lesser degree) rind. Flavor is excellent, with raspberry overtones. Generally, they thrive wherever sweet oranges produce good fruit. Pigmentation varies with local microclimates and weather.

'Moro'. Deep red flesh with touch of red on rind. No rind pigmentation near coast. Bears early winter to early spring.

'Sanguinelli'. Red-skinned fruit; flesh inside streaked with red. Bears late winter to midspring.

'Tarocco'. Red or red-suffused pulp, pink to red juice. Color varies from year to year. Good quality in cooler areas. Ripens early to midwinter. Tree is very vigorous and open growing, with long, willowy, vinelike branches. Dwarf makes ideal espalier.

C

Citrus Types

TOP: 'Minneola' Tangelo
BOTTOM: 'Sanguinelli' Blood Orange

TOP: 'Oroblanco' Grapefruit
BOTTOM: 'Chandler' Pummelo

TOP: 'Nagami' Kumquat
BOTTOM: 'Valencia' Orange

TOP: 'Bearss' Lime
BOTTOM: 'Dancy' Mandarin

TOP: 'Etrog' Citron
BOTTOM: 'Improved Meyer' Lemon

SOUR ORANGE

Very ornamental trees with attractive leaves and big, perfumed, waxy white flowers. Clusters of deep red-orange, tart fruits ripen midfall to winter, hold for a year. For all citrus-growing regions.

'Bouquet de Fleurs' ('Bouquet'). Big shrub or small tree to 8–10 ft. Graceful, dark green foliage. Use as hedge or windbreak. Flowers unusually large, very fragrant. Small, bitter fruit used only in marmalade.

'Chinotto' (myrtle-leaf orange). Dense, bushy, round headed, with closely set, small, almost myrtlelike leaves. Very slow grower to 7–20 ft. tall. Formal appearance; often rounded high on stem and clipped. Makes an ideal tub plant. Decorative small, round, bright orange fruit is used in Europe for candying.

'Seville'. Thorny, upright to 20–30 ft. high. Used as a street tree in Arizona and Southern California. Good specimen plant or for hedge or tall screen. Seedy fruit makes superior marmalade.

MANDARIN

Large and diverse group of citrus that includes many varieties and hybrids. Varieties with orange-red peel are usually called tangerines. Many mandarins tend to bear heavily in alternate years. Some are always seedless, while others produce more seeds; the latter give seedier fruit if pollinated by another mandarin or mandarin hybrid or by 'Valencia' orange.

'Clementine' (Algerian tangerine). Fruit a little larger than 'Dancy', with fewer seeds. Ripens late fall into winter; remains on tree for months, staying juicy and sweet. Seems to develop full flavor in areas too cool for a good 'Dancy'. Tree reaches 12 ft., semiopen with vertical, spreading, somewhat willowy branches. Usually bears light crops without another variety for pollination.

'Dancy'. Standard tangerine in markets before Christmas. Smaller and seedier than other mandarins. Best flavor in Zones 12 and 13 but good in Zones 21–23. Ripens late fall into winter; holds well on tree. Upright tree with erect branches. Dwarf tree handsome in container or as espalier.

'Encore'. Light orange, thin-skinned fruit ripens in summer (latest of all mandarin varieties), holds until fall. Good quality. Erect tree with slender branches and narrow leaves.

'Fairchild'. Hybrid between 'Clementine' mandarin and 'Orlando' tangelo. Medium-size, deep orange fruit peels easily, is seedy but juicy and tasty. Ripens late fall into winter. Small, compact tree bears every year. Needs another variety for pollination. Best in desert areas.

'Fremont'. Medium-size, bright orange fruit ripens late fall into winter. Good flavor. Tends to bear in alternate years; thin fruit when crop is unusually heavy.

'Honey'. Small, seedy fruit with rich, sweet flavor; matures winter into spring. Typically bears heavily in alternate years. Vigorous tree. Not the same as 'Murcott', a tangor often sold in markets as 'Honey'.

'Kara'. Large fruit (2½ in. wide) for mandarin. Tart-sweet, aromatic flavor when ripened in warm interior climates. Ripens winter to spring. From one season to another may be very seedy or nearly seedless. In form, tree resembles 'Owari' satsuma, one of its parents. Spreading, often drooping branches with large leaves. Grows to a rounded 15–20 ft., half that size as dwarf.

'Kinnow'. Medium-size fruit with rich flavor and fragrance. Stores well on tree. Ripens winter to early spring. Handsome tree—columnar, dense, very symmetrical to 20 ft. (dwarf will reach 10 ft.). Densely foliaged with slender leaves. Good in any citrus climate.

'Mediterranean' ('Willow Leaf'). The important mandarin of the Mediterranean region. Sweet, aromatic fruit ripens in spring. Spreading tree with thin, willowy branches and narrow leaves.

'Page'. Hybrid between 'Clementine' mandarin and 'Minneola' tangelo. Many small, juicy, sweet fruits autumn into winter. Few seeds, even with another variety for pollination.

'Pixie'. Delicious, seedless, easy-to-peel fruit, usually with a bumpy rind. Ripens late. Upright tree.

Satsuma. This group of mandarins is the source of imported canned "mandarin oranges." Sweet, delicate flavor; nearly seedless, medium to large fruit. Loose skin. Earliest mandarin to ripen—early fall to late December. Quickly overripens if left on tree but keeps well in cool storage. Standard trees are spreading, to 10–15 ft. high. Dwarf trees can be used as 6-ft. shrubs. Open, angular growth when young, becoming more compact with age. Not suited to the desert. 'Owari' is the main satsuma grown in the West.

SOUR-ACID MANDARIN

These fairly compact plants produce usable fruit (and are everbearing in mild climates), but their best feature is good looks. They thrive outdoors in the ground or in pots in all citrus-growing areas; indoors, they fruit reliably and are very decorative.

Calamondin. Fruit looks like tiny (¾–1½-in.) orange. Hundreds hang from tall, columnar plant (8–10 ft. tall and about half as wide, even as dwarf). Flesh is tender, juicy, sour, with a few small seeds. Skin and flesh good in marmalades.

'Otaheite' (Tahiti orange). Despite the common name, not a true orange. Natural dwarf only a few feet tall. Usually grown indoors as decorative pot plant. Will bear very young. Orange to reddish orange fruit is small, round, rough skinned, insipid in flavor. ▸

'Rangpur'. Commonly called Rangpur lime, but probably not a lime at all: fruit looks and peels like a mandarin, does not have lime flavor. Less acid than lemon but with flavor overtones that make it a rich, interesting base for punches and mixed drinks. Good landscape tree: vigorous, sturdy, bushy, growing quickly to 15 ft. tall and wide (as dwarf to 8 ft.). Dense when pruned, open otherwise. Fruits are colorful and ornamental, hang on tree throughout year.

PUMMELO

Forerunner of the grapefruit. Bears clusters of enormous round to pear-shaped fruits with thick rind and pith. Once peeled, fruit is just slightly bigger than a grapefruit. Different varieties range in flavor from sweet to fairly acidic. Need a little less heat than grapefruit. Ripen starting in winter in warmest areas. To eat, peel fruit; separate segments and remove membrane surrounding them. Because fruit is so heavy, prune pummelo trees to encourage strong branching.

'Chandler'. Most widely grown variety. Pink fleshed, flavorful, moderately juicy, usually seedless.

'Reinking'. White fleshed, seedy. Not as sweet as 'Chandler'.

'Tahitian' ('Sarawak'). Greenish white flesh; moderately acidic flavor with lime overtones.

GRAPEFRUIT

Trees can reach 25–30 ft. tall (most are shorter), with large, dark green leaves. True grapefruit needs heat for sweet-tart fruit; best in the desert, where fruit ripens in 9 months (can take a year or longer where there's less heat). Elsewhere, pummelo-grapefruit hybrids 'Oroblanco' and 'Melogold' are better; they will ripen in 9 to 12 months, depending on climate. At the end of the following list is a variety ('Cocktail') sold as a grapefruit, though it really isn't one.

'Flame'. Seedless red flesh similar to that of 'Rio Red'; slight rind blush.

'Marsh' ('Marsh Seedless'). Main white-fleshed commercial variety. Large, light yellow fruit.

'Melogold'. Grapefruit-pummelo hybrid developed by the University of California. Needs less heat than true grapefruit, but fruit doesn't hold as well on the tree. Fruit is bigger, heavier, and thinner skinned than 'Oroblanco', and its seedless white flesh has more of a sweet-tart flavor.

'Oroblanco'. Sister fruit to 'Melogold', with sweeter seedless white flesh. Has same low heat requirement but is smaller and thicker skinned.

'Redblush' ('Ruby', 'Ruby Red'). Seedless grapefruit with red-tinted flesh. Red internal color fades to pink, then buff by end of season.

'Rio Red'. Seedless grapefruit with good rind blush and flesh nearly as red as that of 'Star Ruby'. More dependable producer than 'Star Ruby'.

'Star Ruby'. Seedless grapefruit with reddest color. Tree is prone to cold damage, erratic bearing, and other growing problems. Doesn't withstand desert heat.

'Cocktail'. Labeled a grapefruit, but actually a mandarin-pummelo hybrid. Large fruit with greenish orange (or mottled green-and-orange) skin and pale orange, very seedy flesh. Sweeter than grapefruit, with distinctive flavor. Best quality in warm-summer areas, but worth growing in cooler regions.

LEMON

Low heat requirement makes lemons widely adapted and especially appreciated in regions where sweet oranges and grapefruit won't ripen. Do best year-round near the coast, though some varieties are very successful in the desert. Standard varieties like 'Eureka' and 'Lisbon' are best pruned every year or two to maintain size.

'Eureka'. Standard lemon of markets. Bears all year. Not as vigorous as 'Lisbon'. To 20 ft. tall, with somewhat open growth; branches have few thorns. As a dwarf, it is a dense tree with large, dark leaves. New growth on both standard-size and dwarf plants is bronzy purple.

Lemon

'Improved Meyer'. The word "improved" refers to fact that it is a disease-free form, the only one that can be sold in California (neither original nor improved forms can be sold in Arizona). This is the best lemon for Hawaii. Fruit is quite different from commercial lemon—rounder, thinner skinned, orange yellow in color. Tangy aroma but less acidic flavor than standard lemon; very juicy. Bears fruit year-round and starts bearing at an early age. Tree is not a dwarf on its own roots, though it is sometimes sold as an own-root plant that can reach 12 ft. tall, 15 ft. wide. On a dwarf rootstock, it's half that size.

'Lisbon'. Vigorous, upright, thorny tree to 20–25 ft. tall; denser than 'Eureka'. Can be trimmed up into highly decorative small tree. Fruit practically identical to 'Eureka'. Ripens mostly in fall but has some ripe fruit all year. More resistant to cold than 'Eureka' and better adapted to high heat; best lemon for Arizona. There is also a seedless form.

'Ponderosa'. A novelty. Bears huge, rough lemons with thick, coarse skin; 2-lb. fruits are not unusual. Mild lemon flavor. Bears at early age, frequently at gallon-can size. Main crop in winter, with some fruit through year. Open, angular branching; large, widely spaced leaves. To 8–10 ft. tall; dwarf reaches 4–6 ft.

'Sungold'. Attractive semidwarf lemon (to 14 ft. tall, 8 ft. wide) with green-striped yellow fruit and leaves mottled with white and cream. Main crop in fall and winter.

'Variegated Pink' ('Pink Lemonade'). Sport of 'Eureka' with green-and-white leaves and green stripes on immature fruit; everbearing like 'Eureka'. Light pink flesh doesn't need heat to develop color. Handsome landscape tree.

'Villa Franca'. Generally similar to 'Eureka', but tree is larger and more vigorous, with denser foliage and thornier branches. Fruit is similar to 'Eureka'; comes mainly from fall through winter. Sold in Arizona to grow in Zones 12, 13; not common in California.

LIME

The various limes range from moderately to extremely cold sensitive; they are most reliable in areas where hard frosts are uncommon. Can succeed in colder areas if grown in pots and protected in winter. Depending on variety, fruit may be intensely sour or nearly devoid of acid.

'Bearss'. Best lime for California and Hawaii gardens. It is a type of the "Persian" or "Tahitian" lime commonly grown in Florida. Tree is quite angular and open when young but forms a dense, round crown when mature; reaches 15–20 ft. (half that size on dwarf rootstock). It is thorny and inclined to drop many leaves in winter. Fruit is green when immature, light yellow when ripe, almost the size of a lemon; it is especially juicy when fully ripe. Seedless. Main crop comes from winter to late spring, though some fruit ripens all year.

'Kieffer'. Leaves are used in Thai and Cambodian cooking, as is bumpy, sour springtime fruit. Available mainly in California.

'Mexican'. Sometimes called key lime in Hawaii. Small, green to yellow-green fruit; standard bartender's lime. Main harvest fall to winter, though you'll get some fruit all year. Very thorny tree to 12–15 ft., with upright, twiggy branches (there is also a thornless form). Very cold sensitive; best suited to Zones 21–23. Can be grown in Hawaii but is subject to viral diseases there.

'Palestine Sweet' (Indian lime). Shrubby plant with acidless fruit resembling that of 'Bearss'. Used in Mideastern, Indian, and Latin American cooking. Ripens fall or winter.

TANGELO

Early citrus-breeding experiments produced the tangelo, a cross between a mandarin and a grapefruit. A cross between a tangelo and a grapefruit ('Wekiwa') is sometimes called a tangelolo. All these hybrids produce their best fruit in warm-summer areas.

'Minneola'. Hybrid of 'Dancy' mandarin and a white-fleshed grapefruit. Large, smooth, bright orange-red fruit tastes much like a mandarin. Few seeds. Ripens mid- to late winter; stores on tree for 2 months. Tree not as large or dense as grapefruit.

'Orlando'. Same parents as 'Minneola'. Medium-large fruit looks like a flattened orange. Both rind and flesh are orange; rind adheres to flesh. Very juicy, mildly sweet, matures early in season. Tree is similar to 'Minneola' but with distinctly cupped leaves; less vigorous but more resistant to cold.

'Wekiwa' (pink tangelo, 'Lavender Gem'). A cross between a tangelo and a grapefruit; looks like a small grapefruit but is eaten like a mandarin. Juicy, mild flesh tastes like a mix of sweet orange, grapefruit, and mandarin; color is purplish rose in hot climates. Fruit ripens from late fall into winter.

TANGOR
Hybrid between mandarin and sweet orange; often labeled as an orange—or, in the case of 'Murcott', as a tangerine—when sold in grocery stores. These three tangors are thought to be naturally occurring hybrids rather than breeder-developed varieties. 'Temple' is widely grown in low desert; 'Murcott' and 'Ortanique' are sometimes grown in Hawaii.

'Murcott'. Bears more heavily in alternate years. Vigorous, upright tree bears very sweet, seedy, yellowish orange fruit from late winter into spring. Marketed in stores as Honey tangerine (no relation to 'Honey' mandarin).

'Ortanique'. Sweet, juicy, variably seedy fruit ripening from spring to summer. Sometimes has a small navel. Large, spreading tree.

'Temple'. Flattened, deep bright orange fruit is loose skinned and easy to peel. Tender-textured, juicy pulp is flavorful but not too sweet. Fruit has best quality in Zone 13; it is too acidic in more temperate climates. Ripens in early spring. Bushy, thorny tree to 12 ft. high with greater spread; 6–8 ft. wide on dwarf stock. More cold sensitive than other tangors.

KUMQUAT
Shrubby plants to 6–15 ft. or taller, with yellow to red-orange fruits that look like tiny oranges. Eat whole and unpeeled—spongy rind is sweet, pulp is tangy. Best in areas with warm to hot summers and chilly nights during fall or winter ripening. Hardy to at least 18°F/–8°C.

'Fukushu'. Large, oval fruit with a prominent neck. Skin and juice are sweet, but not as sweet as 'Meiwa'. Compact, thornless, very attractive tree.

'Marumi'. Slightly thorny plant with round fruit. Sweeter peel than 'Nagami', but the slightly seedy flesh is more acidic.

'Meiwa'. Round fruit is sweeter, juicier, and less seedy than that of other varieties. Performs better than other types in cool-summer areas. Considered the best kumquat for eating fresh. Nearly thornless.

'Nagami'. Main commercial variety. Oval, slightly seedy fruit is more abundant and sweeter in hot-summer climates. Thornless plant.

KUMQUAT HYBRIDS
These were the results of early experiments by the citrus industry to produce cold-tolerant kinds of citrus. Fruit has never been a commercial success, but it's good for home gardens. Plants tend to be fairly small even as standards; on dwarfing rootstocks, they reach only 3–6 ft.

Limequat. These hybrids of 'Mexican' lime and kumquat are more cold tolerant and need less heat than their lime parent. Good lime substitutes; edible rind like kumquat parent. Some fruit all year, but main crop comes from fall to spring. 'Eustis' bears fruit shaped like a big olive. 'Tavares' has elongated oval fruit on a more compact, better-looking plant than 'Eustis'.

Orangequat. Most commonly grown is 'Nippon', a cross between 'Meiwa' kumquat and satsuma mandarin. It is cold tolerant and has a fairly low heat requirement. Small, round, deep orange fruit with sweet, spongy rind and slightly acidic flesh. Sweeter than kumquat when eaten whole. Ripens winter and spring, but holds on the tree for months.

CITRON
Citron was the first type of citrus to be cultivated. Plant is small, thorny, irregular in shape; grown for big, fragrant, unusual fruit. Very sensitive to cold.

'Buddha's Hand'. Fruit is divided into "fingers" that contain all rind and no pulp. Bears some fruit all year round. This plant has absolutely no tolerance for frost.

'Etrog'. Fruit resembles a big, warty-skinned lemon with dry pulp; the peel is sometimes candied. Used in Jewish Feast of the Tabernacles.

FOR GROWING SYMBOL EXPLANATIONS
PLEASE SEE PAGE 161

CLADRASTIS kentukea (C. lutea)

YELLOW WOOD
Fabaceae (Leguminosae)
DECIDUOUS TREE
ZONES 2–9, 14–16
FULL SUN
REGULAR WATER

Cladrastis kentukea

Native to Kentucky, Tennessee, and North Carolina. Slow-growing tree to 30–50 ft. tall, with broad, rounded head half as wide as tree is high. Leaves are 8–12 in. long, divided into many (usually 7–11) oval leaflets resembling those of English walnut (See Walnut). Foliage is yellowish green when new, turning bright green in summer and brilliant yellow in fall. Bark is gray in maturity; the common name "yellow wood" refers to the color of the freshly cut heartwood.

May not flower until 10 years old and may skip bloom some years, but the late spring display is spectacular when it comes: clusters of fragrant, wisterialike white flowers (those of 'Rosea' are pink) to 14 in. long. Blooms followed by flat, 3–4-in.-long seedpods. Attractive as terrace, patio, or lawn tree even if it never blooms. Deep rooted, so you can grow other plants beneath it. Tolerates alkaline soils; withstands some drought.

Prune when young to shorten side branches or correct narrow, weak branch crotches, which are susceptible to breakage in storms. Usually low branching; you can remove lower branches entirely when tree reaches desired height. Prune in summer, since cuts made in winter or spring bleed profusely.

CLARKIA (includes Godetia)

Onagraceae
ANNUALS
ZONES 1–24
LIGHT SHADE IN HOTTEST CLIMATES
REGULAR WATER

Clarkia amoena

Native to western South and North America; especially numerous in California. Plants grow during cool times of year, bloom in spring and early summer. Attractive in mixed borders or in mass displays. Cut branches keep for several days; cut when top bud opens (others open successively). Sow seed in place in fall (in mild-winter areas) or spring. Seedlings are difficult to transplant, but volunteer seedlings grow very well. Best in sandy soil without added fertilizer. Keep soil moist from seeding to flowering.

C. amoena (Godetia amoena, G. grandiflora). FAREWELL-TO-SPRING, GODETIA. Native California to British Columbia. Two wild forms: one is coarse stemmed and sprawling, 4–5 in. high; the other is slender stemmed, 1½–2½ ft. high. Tapered leaves are ½–2 in. long. On both forms, upright buds open into cup-shaped, 2-in.-wide, slightly flaring pink or lavender flowers, usually blotched or penciled in crimson. Although seeds of named varieties are rarely sold in the U.S. (more available in England), strains of mixed colors are easy to find. Dwarf Gem grows 10 in. tall; Tall Upright reaches 2–3 ft.

C. concinna. RED-RIBBONS. California native. To 1½ ft. tall. Deep pink to lavender flowers with three-lobed, fan-shaped petals. Rounded leaves are ½–2 in. long. May be found in wildflower seed mixes.

C. pulchella. Native to Pacific Northwest. Slender, upright, mostly unbranched, 1–1½ ft. high. Reddish stems; narrow, 1–2-in.-long, sparse leaves. Flowers are single and four petaled; petals have a three-lobed tip and taper to a clawlike base. There are semidouble and dwarf forms. Some garden clarkias are probably hybrids between *C. pulchella* and *C. unguiculata.*

C. unguiculata (C. elegans). CLARKIA, MOUNTAIN GARLAND. California native. Erect, to 1–4 ft. Reddish stems, 1–1¾-in.-long leaves,

1-in. flowers in rose, purple, white. Some varieties have double flowers in white, orange, salmon, crimson, purple, rose, pink, or creamy yellow. Double-flowered kinds are the ones usually sold in seed packets.

CLEMATIS

Ranunculaceae

DECIDUOUS AND EVERGREEN VINES AND PERENNIALS

ZONES VARY BY SPECIES

ROOTS COOL, TOP IN SUN

REGULAR WATER, EXCEPT AS NOTED

Clematis armandii

Most of the 200-odd species are deciduous vines; the evergreen *C. armandii* and a few interesting freestanding or sprawling perennials are exceptions. Flowers are attractive in all kinds, spectacular in many. The true flowers are tiny and inconspicuous; the showy part consists of petal-like sepals that surround the clustered true flowers. Blossoms are followed by fluffy clusters of seeds with tails, often quite effective in flower arrangements. Leaves of vining kinds are dark green, usually divided into leaflets; leafstalks twist and curl to hold plant to its support.

Clematis are not demanding, but their few specific requirements should be met. Plant vining types next to trellis, tree trunk, or open framework to give stems support for twining. Provide rich, loose, fast-draining soil; add generous quantities of organic matter such as decomposed ground bark. Add lime only where soil tests indicate calcium deficiency.

To provide cool area for roots, add mulch, place large flat rock over soil, plant shallow-rooted ground cover over the root area, or plant in shade of low shrubs (with noncompetitive roots). Put in support when planting and tie up stems at once. Stems are easily broken, so protect them with wire netting if child or dog traffic is heavy. Clematis need constant moisture and nutrients to make their great rush of growth; apply a complete liquid fertilizer monthly during the growing season.

When planting a deciduous vine, cut stems to 6–12 in. from ground, or to two or three pairs of growth buds, whichever is lower. Late in next dormant season, cut back first year's growth to two or three pairs of buds; train shoots emerging that second spring. Don't prune evergreen vines at first; just start training shoots after planting.

Subsequent yearly pruning sounds complicated but it need not be—plants are forgiving and will quickly repair mistakes. Do remember that dormant wood can look dead. Watch for healthy buds at leaf bases and preserve them. The basic objective is to get the greatest number of flowers on the shapeliest plant.

The type of pruning you do depends on when your plants flower. If you don't know what kind you have, watch them for a year to see when they bloom; then prune accordingly.

Spring-blooming clematis (their blooms may start in winter in mild-winter climates) flower only on stems produced the previous year. After bloom, cut back shoots that have flowered to about half their length; thin out weak and tangled stems.

Summer- or fall-blooming clematis bloom only at ends of new stems produced in spring. Cut back to 1–2½ ft. in late fall after bloom is over or in early spring as buds swell.

Twice-flowering clematis bloom on last year's stems in spring, then on the current year's shoots in summer or fall. In late fall or early spring, prune lightly to thin out excess shoots or untangle stems. After spring flowers fade, prune more heavily so that new shoots will develop for second round of flowers.

Cut flowers are choice for indoors (float in bowl). Burn cut stems with match to make flowers last longer. Unless otherwise specified, flowers are 4–6 in. across.

C. alpina. Deciduous vine. Zones A2, A3; 1a, 2–6, 15–17. European native. To 8–12 ft., with dangling flowers borne singly on long stalks in spring. Flowers may be blue, white, purple, pink, or red, depending on variety; they have four spreading, pointed, petal-like sepals and an inner cup of smaller modified stamens. 'Willy' has pale pink blooms, 'Helsingborg' dark blue flowers; 'Pamela Jackman' is lavender blue.

C. armandii. EVERGREEN CLEMATIS. Zones 4–9, 12–24. Native to China. Fast-growing vine to 20–35 ft. Leaves divided into three glossy dark green, 3–5-in.-long leaflets; they droop downward, creating a strongly textured look. Glistening white, 2½-in., fragrant flowers in large, branched clusters in spring. 'Hendersonii Rubra' is a pink-flowered form.

Leaves burn badly at tips in areas where soil or water contains excess salts. Train along substantial frames such as sturdy fence tops or roof gables; or allow to climb tall trees. Makes privacy screen if not allowed to become bare at base. Slow to start but races when established. Needs relentless pruning after flowering to prevent tangling and buildup of dead thatch on inner parts of vine. Keep and tie up stems you want; cut out all others. Frequent pinching will hold foliage to eye level.

C. chrysocoma. Deciduous vine. Zones 4–9, 14–24. Native to western China. Grows to 6–8 ft. or more in height; fairly open. Young branches, leaves, and flower stalks covered with yellow down. Clusters of long-stalked, 2-in.-wide blossoms in white shaded pink on old wood in spring; later flowers follow from new wood. Will take considerable shade.

C. davidiana. See C. heracleifolia davidiana

C. 'Durandii' (C. integrifolia 'Durandii'). Perennial. Zones 1–9, 14–17. Hybrid between *C. integrifolia* and *C. ×jackmanii.* Sprawling, nonclimbing plant with simple, undivided leaves; 4-in., deep blue flowers with white anthers in summer. Use it to weave through shrubs or sturdy perennials. It can be staked or tied to a support to reach 4–6 ft. high, 3 ft. wide.

C. florida 'Sieboldii' ('Bicolor'). Deciduous vine. Zones 3b–9, 14–17, 21–23. Variety of an Asian species. To 8–12 ft. Not as rugged as other clematis vines, but summer flowers are striking: 3–4 in. across, with a central puff of purple petal-like stamens. 'Alba' ('Alba Plena') is similar but has a creamy to greenish white central puff.

C. 'Hendersonii' (C. integrifolia 'Hendersonii'). Perennial. Zones 2–9, 14–17. Hybrid between *C. integrifolia* and *C. viticella.* A nonclimbing plant somewhat like *C.* 'Durandii' but with smaller violet flowers.

C. heracleifolia davidiana (C. davidiana). Woody-based perennial. Zones 1–9, 14–17. Native to China. To 4 ft. high, 3 ft. wide. Deep green leaves divided into three broad, oval, 3–6-in. leaflets. Dense clusters of 1-in.-long, tubular, medium to deep blue, fragrant flowers in summer. Use in perennial or shrub border.

C. integrifolia. Woody-based perennial. Zones A1–A3; 1–9, 14–17. Native to Europe and Asia. To 3 ft. tall, 2 ft. wide, with dark green, undivided, 2–4-in.-long leaves and nodding, urn-shaped, 1½-in. blue flowers in summer. Provide twigs for the plant to sprawl over. For two popular hybrids often sold as selections of this species, see *C.* 'Durandii' and *C.* 'Hendersonii'.

C. ×jackmanii. Deciduous vines. Zones A2, A3; 1–9, 14–17, 19–23; freeze to ground in cold-winter areas. Series of hybrids between forms of *C. lanuginosa* and *C. viticella.* All are vigorous plants that grow rapidly to 10 ft. or more in one season. The best known of the older large-flowered hybrids, sold simply as *C. ×jackmanii,* is a profuse bloomer bearing 4–5-in., rich purple blossoms with four sepals; it flowers from early summer through fall, with heaviest bloom coming early in season. Newer hybrids have larger flowers with more sepals, but none blooms as lavishly. 'Comtesse de Bouchard' has silvery rose pink flowers; 'Mme Edouard André' bears purplish red blossoms. 'Jackmanii Superba' ('Jackmanii Purpureus Superba') has broader segments that open a deeper purple, fading as they age. (For more on large-flowered hybrid clematis, see page 283.)

C. lanuginosa. Deciduous vine. Zones 2–9, 14–17. Chinese species is best known as a parent of many of the large-flowered hybrids. Its variety 'Candida' has breathtaking 8-in.-wide white blooms on a vigorous but small (6–10-ft.) vine. Blooms in spring, again in summer.

C. lasiantha. PIPESTEMS. Deciduous vine. Zones 7–9, 14–24. This native of the California chaparral is not as showy as *C. ligusticifolia* but blooms earlier in spring. Little water.

C. ×lawsoniana. Deciduous vine. Zones 2–9, 14–17. Thought to be hybrid of *C. lanuginosa* and another species. To 6–10 ft., with 6–9-in., rosy purple, dark-veined flowers in summer. Its best-known form is 'Henryi', which bears 8-in. white flowers with dark stamens.

C. ligusticifolia. Deciduous vine. Zones 1–9, 14–21. Native to much of the West. To 20 ft. or more. Much like *C. terniflora* in habit and in color and profusion of bloom, but blossoms are only slightly fragrant and appear in spring and summer. Attractive seed heads.

C. macropetala. DOWNY CLEMATIS. Deciduous vine. Zones A2, A3; 1–9, 14–17. Native to China, Siberia. Variable in size; may reach 6–10 ft. Lavender to powder blue flowers that look double—resembling a ballerina's tutu—appear in early spring. Blooms are followed by showy bronzy pink, silvery-tailed seed clusters. 'Blue Bird' has soft blue flowers, 'Markham Pink' lavender pink blossoms.

C. montana. ANEMONE CLEMATIS. Deciduous vine. Zones 3b–9, 14–17, 21–23. Native to Himalayas, China. Vigorous grower to 20–30 ft. Massive early spring display of 2–2½-in., anemone-like flowers that open white, then turn pink. 'Elizabeth' has pale pink flowers and bronzy foliage that matures to green; 'Grandiflora' produces 3-in. white flowers. *C. m. rubens* has crimson new leaves maturing to bronzy green; the fragrant flowers are pink to rose red. Among its selections are 'Odorata', notable for fragrance, and 'Tetrarose', known for bronze foliage and 3-in., thick-textured floral segments.

Clematis montana

C. paniculata. See C. terniflora

C. recta. Perennial. Zones A2, A3; 1–6, 15–17. To 3–6 ft. tall and wide, with dark green, divided leaves and clouds of starlike, inch-wide white flowers with fragrance of vanilla; blooms from midsummer to early fall. Some forms have purple foliage that gradually fades to green. Give support to keep plants from flopping over onto their neighbors.

C. tangutica. GOLDEN CLEMATIS. Deciduous vine. Zones A1–A3; 1–9, 14–17, 19–23. Native to Mongolia, northern China. To 10–15 ft., with finely divided gray-green leaves. Nodding, lantern-shaped bright yellow flowers, 2–4 in. across, in great profusion from midsummer into fall. Blossoms are followed by handsome, silvery, mop-headed seed clusters.

C. terniflora (C. dioscoreifolia). SWEET AUTUMN CLEMATIS. Deciduous vine. Zones 2–9, 14–24; H1. Native to Japan. Tall and vigorous (some would say rampant), producing billowy masses of 1-in.-wide, fragrant, creamy white flowers in late summer, fall. Dark green, glossy leaves divided into three to five oval, 1–2½-in.-long leaflets. Good privacy screen, arbor cover. Often erroneously sold as *C. paniculata,* a little-grown species from New Zealand.

C. texensis. SCARLET CLEMATIS. Deciduous vine. Zones 2b–9, 14–17. Native to Texas. Fast growing to 6–10 ft. Dense bluish green foliage; bright scarlet, urn-shaped flowers to 1 in. long from early summer until frost. More tolerant of dry soils than most clematis. Doesn't do as well in cool coastal climates as in warm-summer areas. 'Duchess of Albany', a hybrid of this species with a large-flowered clematis, has upward-facing, cup-shaped, 2-in. deep pink flowers with pointed segments.

C. viticella. Deciduous vine. Zones A3; 2b–9, 14–17. Native to southern Europe, western Asia. To 12–15 ft. Purple or rose purple, 2-in. blooms in summer. Varieties include 'Mme Julia Correvon', with rosy red flowers, and 'Polish Spirit', bearing deep purple-blue blooms with a red center.

Large-flowered hybrid clematis. Zones 1–9, 14–17, 19–23. Although well over a hundred varieties of large-flowered hybrid clematis are being grown today, your local nursery is not likely to offer more than a dozen of the old favorites. Mail-order catalogs remain the best source for collectors seeking the newest. Flowers on some of these may reach 10 in. across.

Following is a list of old-favorite and newer varieties:

White. 'Henryi' is standard. 'Marie Boisselot' ('Mme Le Coultre'), with large, round, flat flowers, and 'Gillian Blades' (huge, star-shaped blooms) are newer. Also worth mentioning in this group is long-time favorite *C. lanuginosa* 'Candida'.

Pink. 'Comtesse de Bouchard', the standard pink, has these rivals: 'Charissima' (veined pink with deeper bars); 'Hagley Hybrid' ('Pink Chiffon'), shell pink with pointed sepals; and 'Lincoln Star' (pink with paler edges).

Red. Red clematis have deep purplish red flowers that are best displayed where the sun can shine through them, as on the top of a fence. 'Mme Edouard André', 'Ernest Markham', and 'Red Cardinal' are standards. 'Ville de Lyon' has full, rounded, velvety flowers; 'Niobe' has the darkest red blossoms of all.

Blue. Medium blue 'Ramona', is always popular. Other varieties include 'Edo Murasaki' (deep blue); 'General Sikorski' (huge, with faint red bar), 'Lady Betty Balfour' (dark blue), 'Mrs. Cholmondeley' (big, veined sky blue), 'Piccadilly' (purplish blue), 'Prince Philip' (huge purplish blue with ruffled edges), and 'Will Goodwin' (lavender to sky blue).

Purple. Classic *C. ×jackmanii* is the most popular. Others include 'Gypsy Queen' (deepest purple), 'Mrs. N. Thompson' (deep bluish purple with red bar), and 'Richard Pennell' (rosy purple).

Bicolor. 'Nelly Moser' (purplish pink with reddish center bar) is deservedly one of the most popular clematis. 'Carnaby' (white with a red bar) and 'Dr. Ruppel' (pink with red bar) are newer, splashier.

Double. Fully double, roselike blooms in early summer on old wood are usually followed later by single or semidouble flowers on new wood. Varieties include silvery blue 'Belle of Woking', white 'Duchess of Edinburgh', deep blue 'Mrs. P. T. James', lavender 'Teshio'. 'Vyvyan Pennell' has deep blue flowers centered in lavender blue; 'Arctic Queen' bears fully double white flowers on both old and new wood.

CLEOME hasslerana (C. spinosa)

SPIDER FLOWER

Capparidaceae

ANNUAL

ZONES 1–24

FULL SUN

MODERATE TO REGULAR WATER

Cleome hasslerana

Shrubby, branching South American native topped in summer and fall with many open, fluffy clusters of pink or white flowers with extremely long, protruding stamens. Slender seed capsules follow the blossoms. Stems have short, strong spines; lower leaves are divided, upper ones undivided. Leaves and stems feel clammy to the touch; they have a strong but not unpleasant smell.

Plant grows 4–6 ft. tall, 4–5 ft. wide; especially vigorous in warm, dry inland areas. Grow in background, as summer hedge, against walls or fences, in large containers; or—since plants self-sow to a fault—naturalize in fringe areas of garden. Flowers and dry seed capsules useful in arrangements.

Sow seeds in place in spring; they sprout rapidly in warm soil. A number of varieties can be grown from seed. In most cases color is indicated by variety name: 'Cherry Queen', 'Mauve Queen', 'Pink Queen', 'Purple Queen', 'Rose Queen', 'Ruby Queen'. 'Helen Campbell' is snow white.

CLERODENDRUM

Verbenaceae

EVERGREEN AND DECIDUOUS SHRUBS AND VINES

ZONES VARY BY SPECIES

EXPOSURE NEEDS VARY BY SPECIES

REGULAR WATER

Clerodendrum thomsoniae

Diverse group of plants grown for big clusters of showy, brightly colored flowers that are fragrant in some species. Bloom comes on current season's growth. Provide support for climbing species. Grow in well-drained soil. Good greenhouse plants in areas beyond their hardiness limits. ▸

C. buchananii fallax (C. speciosissimum). PAGODA FLOWER. Evergreen to deciduous shrub. Zones 24; H2. From Indonesia. Erect growth to 12 ft. tall, 6 ft. wide. Plant produces brilliant scarlet flowers much of the year. Densely pubescent, large heart-shaped leaves to 1 ft. long. Suitable shrub for mass plantings, hedges, or colorful screens; also makes a good container plant. Prune to improve appearance and shape as needed. Full sun or partial shade.

C. bungei (C. foetidum). CASHMERE BOUQUET. Evergreen shrub. Zones 5–9, 12–24. Native to China. Plant grows rapidly to 6 ft. tall and wide; spreads rapidly by suckers, eventually forming a thicket if not restrained. Big (to 1-ft.), coarse, broadly oval leaves with toothed edges are dark green above, with rust-colored fuzz beneath. Leaves smell unpleasant when bruised or crushed. Loose clusters of delightfully fragrant rosy red flowers in summer, sometimes into fall. Plant where its appearance (except during bloom time) is not important. Prune severely in spring and pinch back throughout the growing season to make a compact, 2–3-ft. shrub. Resistant to oak root fungus. Deer resistant. Provide deep shade in desert regions, partial shade elsewhere.

C. chinense pleniflorum (C. fragrans pleniflorum). Evergreen to semievergreen shrub. Zones 8, 9, 12–24. Native to southern China. Coarse plant to 5–8 ft. tall, spreading freely by root suckers unless controlled or confined. Its 10-in. leaves resemble those of *C. bungei* but are not malodorous when bruised or crushed. (This species may also be called cashmere bouquet, a name more often applied to *C. bungei.*) Pale pink double flowers with a sweet, clean fragrance are carried in broad clusters resembling florists' hydrangea. Partial shade.

C. myricoides 'Ugandense'. Evergreen shrub. Zones 9, 14–24; H1, H2. Native to tropical Africa. Grows to 10 ft. tall and about half as wide, though often much smaller in California. Glossy dark green leaves to 4 in. long. Each five-petaled blossom has one violet-blue petal and four pale blue ones; pistil and stamens arch outward and upward. Partial shade; can take full sun in Hawaii.

C. quadriloculare. BAGAUAK. Evergreen shrub. Zone H2. From the Philippines. To 15 ft. tall, spreading by root suckers. Has an upright habit; can be trained to tree form. Clusters of fragrant pink flowers in fall and spring enhance the deep purple of the leaf undersides. Use as color accent, hedge, screen, or tubbed specimen for the lanai. Protect from harsh winds. Prune to shape. Full sun.

C. ×speciosum. CLERODENDRUM VINE. Evergreen shrubby vine. Zones 22–24; H2. Hybrid between *C. splendens* and *C. thomsoniae.* A vine of fairly rapid growth to 30 ft. Produces terminal clusters of flowers in winter and spring. Bicolored blooms have a dull pink or red calyx surrounding a short tube in deep crimson with violet shades; calyxes hang on. Full sun.

C. splendens. RED CLERODENDRUM. Evergreen vine. Zones 23, 24; H2. From tropical Africa. Climbs rapidly to 30 ft. Large clusters of brilliant red flowers bloom profusely during winter. Protect from strong winds. Best in sun on vertical supports such as a fence or trellis, and can be trained along eaves.

C. thomsoniae (C. balfouri). BLEEDING HEART GLORYBOWER. Evergreen vine. Protected spots in Zones 22–24; H2; or indoor/outdoor potted plant. Native to West Africa. Restrained and mannerly growth to no more than 12 ft. Distinctly ribbed, oval, shiny dark green leaves, 4–7 in. long. Blooms from summer to fall, bearing flattish, 5-in. clusters of up to 20 flowers. White calyxes reminiscent of paper lanterns surround scarlet flowers, giving a striking two-tone contrast. Use it on sheltered patio walls or arbor posts. Grows well in large containers; move it to a frost-free shelter in winter. Partial shade.

C. trichotomum. HARLEQUIN GLORYBOWER. Deciduous shrub. Zones 15–17, 20–24. Plant can be grown in Zones 5 and 6 but may periodically freeze to the ground and come back from roots. Native to Japan. Shrub reaches 10–15 ft. tall and as wide, with many stems growing from base. Can be trained as a small tree. Soft, hairy, oval dark green leaves to 5 in. long. Fragrant blossoms—each a white tube almost twice as long as the prominent, fleshy, scarlet calyxes surrounding it—come in late summer. Calyxes hang on and contrast pleasingly with metallic-looking turquoise or blue-green fruit. Give this shrub plenty of room to spread at top; add plants underneath it to hide its legginess. *C. t. fargesii,* from China, is somewhat hardier and smaller; it has smooth leaves and green calyxes that turn pink. Partial shade.

CLETHRA

Clethraceae

DECIDUOUS SHRUBS AND EVERGREEN TREES

ZONES VARY BY SPECIES

BEST IN PARTIAL SHADE BUT ADAPTABLE

REGULAR WATER

Clethra arborea

These attractive plants are grown for the small, five-lobed, sweet-scented white or pink flowers that cluster at branch tips in mid- to late summer. Fairly soil tolerant but do best in moist, organic, slightly acid, well-drained soil. Plants prefer partial shade but can adapt successfully to less light as well as to full sun, though they need some shade where summers are very hot. On deciduous shrubs, remove some old wood from base annually before spring growth begins. Evergreen tree described below *(C. arborea)* doesn't need routine pruning.

C. alnifolia. SUMMERSWEET, SWEET PEPPERBUSH. Deciduous shrub. Zones A2, A3; 1–6. Eastern U.S. native grows 4–10 ft. tall and wide; spreads slowly by suckers. Thin, strong branches form vertical pattern. Dark green, tooth-edged, 2–4-in.-long leaves appear late in spring, turn golden yellow to brownish in fall. During bloom season, each branch tip carries several 4–6-in.-long spires of tiny, gleaming white flowers with a spicy perfume.

'Hummingbird' is a white-flowered dwarf to 1½ ft. tall, 2 ft. wide.

'Pink Spires' (to 4 ft.) has deep pink blooms.

'Rosea' has pale pink flowers.

'Ruby Lace' (to 5 ft.) bears deep pink blooms.

C. arborea. LILY-OF-THE-VALLEY TREE. Evergreen tree. Zones 15–17, 21–24. Native to Madeira. Rather stiff upright growth to 20 ft. tall and about half as wide. Plant is densely clothed with 4-in. leaves in glossy, bronzy green. White flowers in upright, branched clusters resemble lily-of-the-valley *(Convallaria majalis)* in looks and even in fragrance. Leaf tips burn with frost, but plant comes back from old wood or from roots when damaged. You may need to control spider mites in summer. For another lily-of-the-valley tree, see *Crinodendron patagua.* For lily-of-the-valley shrub, see *Pieris japonica.*

C. barbinervis. JAPANESE SWEET SHRUB. Deciduous shrub. Zones 5–9, 14–24. Slow-growing plant reaches 15–18 ft. tall and about one-half to two-thirds as wide. Shrub has attractive, peeling, glossy gray to brown bark when plant matures. Produces drooping, 4–6-in. clusters of fragrant, bell-shaped white flowers. Heavily veined, sharply toothed leaves turn bright yellow in fall.

CLEYERA japonica (Eurya ochnacea)

Theaceae

EVERGREEN SHRUB

ZONES 4–6, 8, 9, 14–24; H1

PARTIAL SHADE

MODERATE TO REGULAR WATER

Cleyera japonica

Native to Japan, southeast Asia. Handsome but not widely known bushy shrub related to camellia. Similar in character to *Ternstroemia gymnanthera.* Grows at moderate rate to 15 ft. tall and as wide, with graceful, spreading, arching branches. New leaves are beautiful deep brownish red. Mature leaves are 3–6 in. long, glossy dark green with reddish midrib. Plant produces small clusters of fragrant creamy white flowers in early fall that are followed by small, dark red, puffy berries; fruit lasts through winter. Flowers and berries are attractive but not showy; they don't form on young plants. No routine pruning needed. 'Tricolor' *(C. fortunei)* has yellow-and-rose variegation on its young leaves.

CLIANTHUS puniceus

PARROT BEAK

Fabaceae (Leguminosae)

EVERGREEN SHRUBBY VINE

ZONES 8, 9, 14–24; H1

FULL SUN ONLY IN COOLER CLIMATES

REGULAR WATER

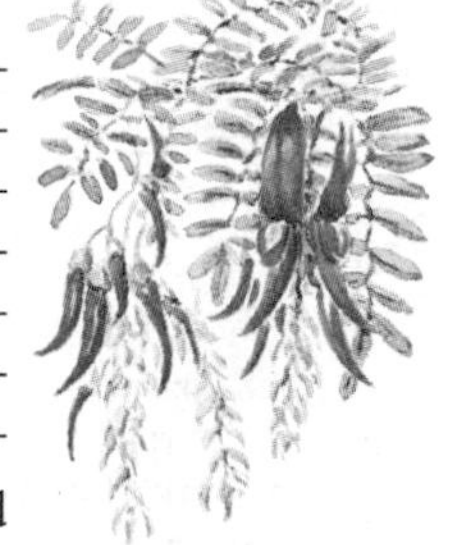

Clianthus puniceus

New Zealand native grows to 12 ft. high and nearly as wide. Sprays of 3–6-in., glistening dark green leaves divided into many narrow leaflets hang gracefully, forming an open foliage pattern. In late spring or early summer, bright red, sweet pea–shaped flowers with 3-in. keels resembling parrot beaks swing downward between the leaves. Pods that follow are 3 in. long. Forms with pink or white flowers are also available. To display beauty of leaves and flowers, train as espalier or on a support. Mix an organic soil amendment into heavy soil. Watch for slugs, snails, spider mites.

CLIFF-BRAKE. See PELLAEA

CLIFF ROSE. See PURSHIA mexicana stansburyana

CLIMBING LILY. See GLORIOSA rothschildiana

CLIVIA miniata

Amaryllidaceae

PERENNIAL FROM TUBEROUS ROOTS

ZONES 12–17, 19–24 (SEE BELOW); H1, H2; OR INDOORS

SOME SHADE; BRIGHT INDIRECT LIGHT

REGULAR WATER

Clivia miniata

Native to South Africa. Showy and striking member of the amaryllis family for garden borders, beds, or containers. Plant produces brilliant, large clusters of funnel-shaped orange flowers on 2-ft. stalks that appear above dense clumps of dark green, strap-shaped, 1½-ft.-long evergreen leaves; flowering period ranges from early winter to midspring, but most are spring bloomers. Ornamental red berries follow flowers. French and Belgian hybrids have very wide leaves and yellow to deep red-orange blooms on thick, rigid stalks. 'Flame' is an exceptionally hot orange red. Solomone Hybrids have pale to deep yellow flowers.

Clivias are damaged by freezing temperatures (32°F/0°C) and will survive only to about 25°F/–4°C. In frostless areas or well-protected parts of garden, they are handsome in borders with ferns, azaleas, other shade plants. Set them 1½–2 ft. apart; let clumps grow undisturbed for years. In areas too cold for year-round outdoor culture, grow in pots and move to shelter or bring indoors in winter. Container plants bloom best with regular fertilizing, crowded roots.

CLOVE PINK. See DIANTHUS caryophyllus

CLOVER. See TRIFOLIUM

FOR INFORMATION ON SELECTING PLANTS
PLEASE SEE PAGES 64–160

CLYTOSTOMA callistegioides

VIOLET TRUMPET VINE

Bignoniaceae

EVERGREEN VINE

ZONES 8, 9, 12–24

FULL SUN OR PARTIAL SHADE

MODERATE TO REGULAR WATER

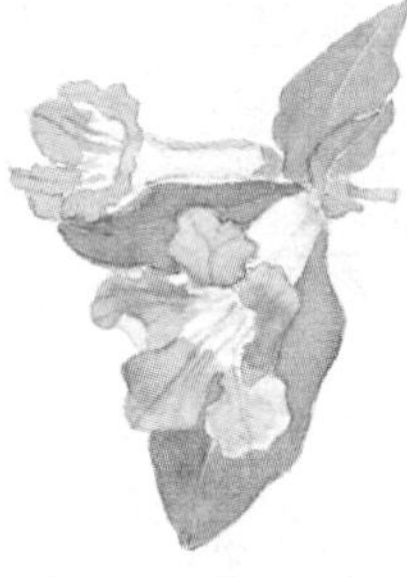

Clytostoma callistegioides

Formerly classified as *Bignonia violacea, B. speciosa.* Strong-growing vine from Brazil and Argentina will clamber over anything by tendrils; needs support on walls. Each leaf divided into two glossy dark green leaflets with wavy margins. Extended terminal shoots hang down to give a curtainlike effect. Blooms from late spring to fall, when sprays of trumpet-shaped violet, lavender, or pale purple flowers, 3 in. long and nearly as wide at the flare, appear at ends of shoots. Top is hardy to 20°F/–7°C, roots to 10°F/–12°C. Prune in late winter to discipline growth and prevent tangling. At other times of year, remove unwanted long runners and spent flower sprays.

CNEORUM tricoccon

SPURGE OLIVE

Cneoraceae

EVERGREEN SHRUB

ZONES 14–24

FULL SUN

LITTLE WATER

Cneorum tricoccon

Western Mediterranean native. Twiggy growth to 2 ft. tall and broad, with 1–2-in., shiny green or gray-green leaves set closely on stems. Looks something like boxwood *(Buxus)*. In early summer, small bright yellow flowers open at branch ends; these are followed by small, dry red fruits that resemble three little berries pressed together. Fruits eventually turn black. Tough, undemanding plant for hot, dry places. Can be used in rock garden or as edging. Thin out older wood before spring growth begins.

COBAEA scandens

CUP-AND-SAUCER VINE

Polemoniaceae

PERENNIAL VINE USUALLY GROWN AS ANNUAL

ZONES 24, H1, H2 AS PERENNIAL; ZONES 3–23 AS ANNUAL

FULL SUN

REGULAR WATER

Cobaea scandens

Native to Mexico. Extremely vigorous growth to 25 ft. in a single season. Bell-shaped flowers are first greenish, then violet or rose purple; there is a white-flowered form. Called cup-and-saucer vine because 2-in.-long cup of petals sits in large, green, saucerlike calyx. Leaves divided into two or three pairs of oval, 4-in. leaflets. At ends of leaves are curling tendrils that enable vine to climb rough surfaces without support.

The hard-coated seeds may rot if sown outdoors in cool weather. Start indoors in 4-in. pots; notch seeds with knife and press edgewise into moistened potting mix, barely covering seeds. Keep moist but not wet; transplant seedlings to warm, sunny location when weather warms. Protect from strong winds. Blooms first year from seed. May not bloom until very late summer in coolest climates. In mildest-winter areas, lives from year to year, eventually reaching over 40 ft. long and blooming heavily in midsummer the first year, from spring to fall in subsequent years.

COCCOLOBA uvifera

SEA GRAPE

Polygonaceae

EVERGREEN SHRUB OR TREE

ZONES 24; H2

FULL SUN OR LIGHT SHADE

LITTLE TO MODERATE WATER

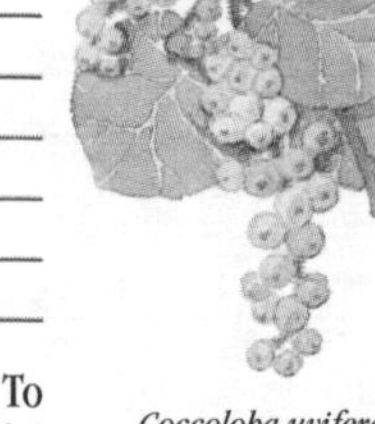

Coccoloba uvifera

From tropical America; hardy to 30°F/–1°C. To 20–40 ft. high and spreading to 20 ft. wide. Excellent for seaside planting; tolerant of wind, sand, salt, and drought. Can be grown as large, bushy shrub or trained to form a single-trunked tree. Withstands severe pruning and can be espaliered. Its rounded glossy green leaves have reddish veins and grow to 8 in. wide; coppery when young. Small white blossoms in winter and spring are followed by clustered fruits, green maturing to purple, that can be made into jelly.

COCCULUS laurifolius

Menispermaceae

EVERGREEN SHRUB OR TREE

ZONES 8, 9, 12–24

SUN OR SHADE

REGULAR WATER

Cocculus laurifolius

Himalayan native useful as screen, background plant. Grows slowly at first, then moderately fast to 25 ft. or more. Usually multistemmed shrub with arching, spreading growth as wide as high, though it can be kept smaller with pruning. Staked and trained as a tree, it takes on an umbrella shape. Long, willowy branches are as easy to train as vines; fastened to a trellis, they make an effective screen. Can also be espaliered. Shiny, leathery, oblong leaves to 6 in. long have three strongly marked veins running from base to tip.

COCKSCOMB. See CELOSIA

COCKSPUR CORAL TREE. See ERYTHRINA crista-galli

COCKSPUR THORN. See CRATAEGUS crus-galli

COCONUT PALM. See COCOS nucifera

COCOS nucifera

COCONUT PALM, NIU

Arecaceae (Palmae)

PALM

ZONE H2

FULL SUN

MODERATE WATER

Cocos nucifera

One of the world's best-known, most economically important palms. Solitary trunk rising 60–100 ft. is topped with a majestic crown of glossy, feathery fronds. Requires pruning of old fronds and removal of mature coconuts (which can become a hazard). Many varieties are known, with large edible fruit varying in size, shape, and color (green, yellow to orange). Tolerates many different soil conditions; has excellent salt and drought tolerance and can also be found growing in brackish water. Superb for large gardens, parks, or avenues. Dwarf forms are available and more suitable for the medium-size garden; some of these reach 10–15 ft. tall, with a feathery crown about equally wide. For queen palm, formerly called *C. plumosa,* see *Syagrus romanzoffianum.*

CODIAEUM variegatum 'Pictum'

CROTON

Euphorbiaceae

EVERGREEN SHRUB

ZONES 24; H2; OR INDOORS

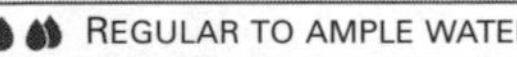

SOME FORMS TAKE SUN, OTHERS SHADE

REGULAR TO AMPLE WATER

Codiaeum variegatum 'Pictum'

Native to the tropics. Grown outdoors in a frost-free climate, it can reach 6 ft. or taller, with equal spread; elsewhere, it's usually seen as single-stemmed houseplant to about 2 ft. high. Grown principally for its large, leathery, glossy leaves, which may be green, yellow, red, purple, bronze, pink, or almost any combination of these colors. Leaves vary in shape; they may be oval, lance shaped, or very narrow, with smooth or lobed margins. Dozens of named forms are available.

Outdoor exposure depends on the variety. Give bright light, regular misting indoors; does well in a warm, humid greenhouse. Can be brought outdoors during warm times of year. Contact with croton leaves can cause a skin rash in some people.

COFFEA arabica

COFFEE

Rubiaceae

EVERGREEN SHRUB

ZONES 21–24; H1, H2; OR INDOORS

SOME SHADE; BRIGHT INDIRECT LIGHT

REGULAR WATER

Coffea arabica

Native to east Africa. The coffee tree of commerce can be grown as a specimen or in shrub borders in the mildest-winter regions; it's also a handsome container plant for patios, lanais, and large well-lit rooms in any climate. Upright shrub to 15–20 ft. tall and about half as wide outdoors; rarely more than 4–6 ft. high indoors. Evenly spaced tiers of branches are clothed with shiny, dark green, oval leaves to 6 in. long. Small (¾-in.), fragrant white flowers are clustered near leaf bases. They are followed by 1½-in. fruits that turn from green (when they first appear) to purple or red. Each contains two seeds—coffee beans. Grow in rich, well-drained soil. Protect from frosts.

COFFEEBERRY. See RHAMNUS californica

COFFEE FERN. See PELLAEA andromedifolia

COIX lacryma-jobi

JOB'S TEARS

Poaceae (Gramineae)

ANNUAL GRASS

ZONES 12–24; H1; COLDER ZONES AS NOTED BELOW

FULL SUN OR PARTIAL SHADE

REGULAR WATER

Coix lacryma-jobi

A curiosity from Southeast Asia, grown for its ornamental beadlike seeds. Leaves are 1½ in. wide, to 2 ft. long, growing in loose, sprawling clumps to 1½ ft. across. Smooth, prominently jointed stems to 6 ft. long bear separate male and female flower spikelets in autumn. Outside coverings of female flowers harden as seeds ripen, turning to shiny, ¼–½-in. "beads" in pearly white, gray, or violet; these can be strung like actual beads. For use in dried arrangements, cut stems before seeds dry and shatter.

Sow seeds in place in early to midspring. Plants need heat and a long growing season to flower. In zones colder than those listed, start seeds indoors and set out plants after danger of frost is past. Where summers are short and cool, give plants the warmest spot in the garden—even reflected heat next to wall.

COLCHICUM

MEADOW SAFFRON, AUTUMN CROCUS

Liliaceae

PERENNIALS FROM CORMS

ZONES 2–10, 14–24; OR INDOORS

FULL SUN; BRIGHT INDIRECT LIGHT

REGULAR WATER DURING GROWTH AND BLOOM

ALL PARTS ARE POISONOUS IF INGESTED

Colchicum

Native to Mediterranean region. Many species; sometimes called autumn crocus, but not true crocuses. Shining, brown-skinned, thick-scaled corms send up clusters of long-tubed, flaring lavender-pink, rose purple, or white flowers to 4 in. across in late summer or early autumn, whether corms are sitting in dish on windowsill or planted in soil. When corms are planted out, broad leaves 6–12 in. long emerge in spring, last for a few months, and then die long before flower cluster rises from ground. Best planted where they need not be disturbed more often than every 3 years or so.

Corms are available during a brief dormant period in the summer. Hybrids include 'The Giant', single lavender, and 'Waterlily', double violet. Plant corms 3 in. deep and 6–8 in. apart. Cut back on watering during dormancy but don't let the soil dry out. To plant in bowls, set upright on 1–2 in. of pebbles or in special fiber sold for this purpose, and fill with water to the base of the corms.

COLEONEMA

BREATH OF HEAVEN

Rutaceae

EVERGREEN SHRUBS

ZONES 7–9, 14–24

FULL SUN OR LIGHT SHADE

REGULAR WATER

Coleonema pulchrum

Native to South Africa. Plants of filmy appearance and delicate character, with slender branches and narrow, heathlike leaves that are fragrant when brushed or bruised. Tiny flowers are borne freely over long season in winter and spring. Plants can continue with scattered bloom at any other time.

You may find plants in nurseries under either *Coleonema* or their former name, *Diosma*. Actually, your choice amounts to a white- or a pink-flowering breath of heaven.

Good on banks or hillsides, along paths where you can break off and bruise a twig to enjoy the foliage's fragrance. Frequently used next to buildings, though a little wispy for such use. Plant in light soil; fast drainage is a must. To control size and promote compactness, shear lightly after main bloom is over. For even more filmy look, thin out some interior stems.

C. album (Diosma alba). WHITE BREATH OF HEAVEN. To 5 ft. or taller and as wide, with white flowers. Often sold as *Diosma reevesii;* once known as *D. ericoides.*

C. pulchrum. PINK BREATH OF HEAVEN, PINK DIOSMA. Grows to 5 ft. tall and as wide, occasionally to 10 ft. Bears tiny pink flowers. Species often sold as *Diosma pulchra.* 'Sunset Gold' has yellow foliage, grows 1½ ft. tall, 4 ft. wide.

COLEUS × hybridus (Solenostemon scutellarioides)

COLEUS

Lamiaceae (Labiatae)

PERENNIALS USUALLY GROWN AS ANNUALS

ZONES 24; H1, H2; ANYWHERE AS ANNUAL; OR INDOORS

SOME TYPES ARE SUN TOLERANT

REGULAR WATER

Coleus × hybridus

Group of tropical plants (they may be sold as *C. blumei*) grown for brilliantly colored leaves. Blue flower spikes are attractive, but they spoil the plant's shape and are best pinched out in bud (pinching also encourages more vigorous leafy growth). Large-leafed strains grow 1½–2 ft. tall and wide, with 3–6-in.-long leaves; dwarfs reach 1 ft. high and wide, have 1–1½-in.-long leaves. Colors include green, chartreuse, yellow, buff, salmon, orange, red, purple, and brown; a single leaf often shows many colors. The more red pigment the foliage has, the more sun tolerant the plant tends to be; 'Plum Parfait' and 'Burgundy Sun' are examples. Most coleus perform best in strong indirect light or thin shade.

Giant Exhibition and Oriental Splendor are large-leafed strains. Dwarf strain Carefree is self-branching, with deeply lobed and ruffled leaves. Salicifolius, another dwarf, has long, narrow leaves crowded along the stems; it resembles a foot-high feather duster. Named cutting-grown varieties exist, but most plants are grown from seed.

All types of coleus are useful for summer borders, indoor and outdoor containers, and hanging baskets. They are perennial in frost-free regions, but you'll typically get the best performance by starting new plants annually from seed or cuttings—which is easy to do. Plant in spring. Sow seeds indoors or, with frost protection, outdoors when weather is warm. Cuttings will root in water as well as other media. Started plants need warm temperatures and rich, loose, well-drained soil. Feed plants regularly with high-nitrogen fertilizer. Be sure to pinch stems often to encourage branching and compact habit.

COLLARDS. See KALE AND COLLARDS

COLLINSIA heterophylla (C. bicolor)

CHINESE HOUSES

Scrophulariaceae

ANNUAL

ZONES 1–24

PART SHADE IN HOTTEST CLIMATES

REGULAR WATER

Collinsia heterophylla

Native to California. This is a rather uncommon plant in nature; blooms from spring to early summer, with 1-in.-long blossoms that resemble snapdragons *(Antirrhinum).* Flowers are held in tiers at top of 1–2-ft.-tall, somewhat hairy stems. The upper lip of the flower is white, the lower one rose or violet. Plant produces oblong leaves to 2 in. long. Gives light, dainty effect in front of borders, scattered under deciduous trees, or as bulb cover. Sow seed in place in fall or early spring in rich, moist soil. Can also be sown in late spring for early fall bloom. Self-sows under favorable conditions.

FOR DEFINITIONS OF GARDENING TERMS
PLEASE SEE PAGES 746–750

COLOCASIA esculenta

TARO, ELEPHANT'S EAR

Araceae

PERENNIAL FROM TUBER

ZONES 12, 16–24; H1, H2; OR DIG AND STORE

BEST IN WARM, FILTERED SHADE

AMPLE WATER

ALL PARTS MAY CAUSE INDIGESTION IF INGESTED RAW; CONTACT WITH SAP MAY IRRITATE SKIN

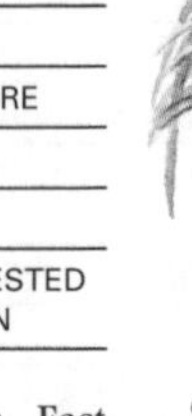

Colocasia esculenta

Native to tropical Asia and Polynesia. Fast growing to 6 ft. tall. Leathery green to gray-green, heart-shaped leaves are mammoth in size (to 2½ by 3 ft.), carried at ends of succulent stalks from spring through fall. Sometimes available are varieties with foliage marked in various purple shades; most striking among these is 'Black Magic', with solid purple leaves. All create a lush effect in the course of a single season. Flowers resembling greenish callas *(Zantedeschia)* appear only in the warmest climates. The starchy tubers were once a staple food of Polynesians, who ate other parts of the plant as well. In Hawaii, where nearly 300 forms of wetland and upland (dry) taro are recorded, the plant is still grown commercially for the edible roots.

Enrich soil with organic matter before planting. Set tubers 1–1½ ft. apart and about 2 in. deep. Tops die down at 30°F/–1°C. In zones listed above, tubers can be left in ground all year; in Zones 14 and 15, a thick mulch will allow in-ground survival over the average winter. Elsewhere, lift and store tubers after foliage is killed by frost; or grow in containers (good in any zone) and shelter over winter. Effective with tree ferns and other large-leafed tropical plants. Handsome in large tubs, in raised beds, near swimming pools. Protect plants from wind, which tears leaves. Feed lightly once a month during growing season. When clumps become overcrowded, divide them in early spring.

COLONIAL BENT. See AGROSTIS tenuis

COLUMBINE. See AQUILEGIA

COMAROSTAPHYLIS diversifolia

SUMMER HOLLY

Ericaceae

EVERGREEN SHRUB OR TREE

ZONES 7–9, 14–24

FULL SUN IN COOLER CLIMATES ONLY

MODERATE WATER

Comarostaphylis diversifolia

Native to coastal Southern California, Baja California. Rather formal growth to 6–18 ft. high, 4–8 ft. wide. Gray bark. Leathery, 1–3-in.-long leaves are shiny dark green above, white and hairy beneath, with inrolled margins. (Variety *C. d. planifolia* has flat leaves.) Small, white, bell-shaped flowers in spring, followed by clusters of red, warty berries similar to those of madrone *(Arbutus menziesii)*. Needs little pruning, but some thinning improves appearance.

COMFREY. See SYMPHYTUM officinale

Commelinaceae. The spiderwort family is composed of herbaceous perennials that are often fleshy, mostly tropical or subtropical. Wandering Jew *(Tradescantia albiflora* and *Zebrina pendula)* and spiderwort *(Tradescantia virginiana)* are familiar examples. Flowers generally have three rounded petals.

COMPASS BARREL CACTUS. See FEROCACTUS cylindraceus

Compositae. See Asteraceae

CONFEDERATE ROSE. See HIBISCUS mutabilis

CONSOLIDA ajacis (Delphinium ambiguum)

LARKSPUR, ANNUAL DELPHINIUM

Ranunculaceae

ANNUAL

ZONES 1–24

FULL SUN

REGULAR WATER

ALL PARTS, ESPECIALLY SEEDS, ARE POISONOUS IF INGESTED

Consolida ajacis

Native to southern Europe. Upright plants grow 1–4 ft. tall, 1 ft. wide, with deeply cut, almost ferny leaves. Blossom spikes densely set with 1–1½-in.-wide flowers (most are double) in white or shades of blue, lilac, pink, rose, salmon, carmine; there are also blue-and-white bicolors. Best bloom in cooler spring and early summer months. Giant Imperial strain has many 4-ft., compactly placed vertical stalks. Regal strain has 4-ft. base-branching stems, thick spikes of large flowers similar to perennial delphiniums. Super Imperial strain is base branching, has large flowers in 1½-ft. cone-shaped spikes. Steeplechase is base branching, has biggest double flowers on 4-ft. spikes; it is heat tolerant. Sow seed where plants are to grow; fall planting is best except in heavy, slow-draining soils. Thin plants to avoid crowding, get biggest flowers. Nursery transplants are also available for early-spring planting.

CONVALLARIA majalis

LILY-OF-THE-VALLEY

Liliaceae

PERENNIAL FROM RHIZOME

ZONES A1–A3; 1–7, 14–20

PARTIAL SHADE

REGULAR WATER

ALL PARTS ARE POISONOUS IF INGESTED

Convallaria majalis

Native to many northern regions of the Old World; naturalized in U.S., Canada. Graceful, creeping, 6–8-in.-high ground cover. Blooms for a short period in early spring, sending up arching stems that bear small, nodding, sweet-scented, waxy white bells along one side. Broad, glossy green, deciduous leaves are attractive throughout growing season. Bright red berries (poisonous, like the rest of the plant) may appear in fall. Double- and pink-flowered forms are sold, as are types with variegated leaves. All are charming as carpet between camellias, rhododendrons, or pieris, under deciduous or high-branching evergreen trees. Can become invasive where well adapted.

Plant single rhizomes (called pips) or clumps in rich soil in fall before ground freezes. Set 1½ in. deep; space clumps 1–2 ft. apart, single pips 4–5 in. apart. Mulch planting each year before new growth emerges. Large, prechilled pips for forcing are available in winter (even in mild climates) and can be potted for bloom indoors. After bloom, plunge pots in ground in a cool, shaded area. Once plants are dormant, remove them from pots and set out in garden; or wash soil off pips, enclose them in plastic bags, and refrigerate them (in vegetable bin) until time to repot in December or January.

A PRACTICAL GUIDE TO GARDENING
PLEASE SEE PAGES 658–731

Convolvulaceae. The morning glory family contains climbing or trailing plants, usually with funnel-shaped flowers. Morning glories *(Convolvulus* and *Ipomoea)* are typical examples.

CONVOLVULUS

Convolvulaceae

ANNUALS, PERENNIALS, AND EVERGREEN SHRUBS

ZONES VARY BY SPECIES

BEST IN SUN, TOLERATE SOME SHADE

MODERATE WATER

Convolvulus cneorum

Mediterranean natives with funnel-shaped morning glory flowers. Common vining morning glories *(Ipomoea)* are sometimes sold as *Convolvulus.*

C. althaeoides tenuissimus. Perennial. Zones 7–9, 14–24. To 6 in. high, 2–3 ft. wide. Two kinds of foliage. Basal leaves are less than 1 in. long, oval to arrow shaped, sometimes lobed; leaves on trailing or creeping flowering stems are divided into narrow segments. Summer flowers are pink, 1–1½ in. wide. Spreads by rhizomes and can be invasive. Good in rock gardens, hanging baskets.

C. cneorum. BUSH MORNING GLORY. Evergreen shrub. Best in Zones 7–9, 12–24; marginal in Zones 5, 6. Grows fast to 2–4 ft. tall and as wide. Silky-smooth, silvery gray, lance-shaped leaves 1–2½ in. long. White or pink-tinted morning glories with yellow throats open from pink buds in late spring and summer. Give light soil and fast drainage. Prune severely to renew plant; can get leggy if left alone.

C. sabatius (C. mauritanicus). GROUND MORNING GLORY. Perennial. Zones 4–9, 12–24. Grows 1–2 ft. high with branches trailing to spread 3 ft. or more. Soft, hairy, gray-green, roundish, evergreen leaves ½–1½ in. long. Lavender-blue, 1–2-in.-wide flowers bloom from early summer into fall. Grows well in light, gravelly soil with good drainage but will take clay soil if not overwatered. Tends to become woody; prevent by trimming in late winter.

C. tricolor. DWARF MORNING GLORY. Annual. Zones 1–24. Bushy, branching, somewhat trailing plant to 1 ft. high and 2 ft. wide. Small, narrow leaves. Summer flowers, 1½ in. across, variable in color but usually blue with yellow throat. Nick tough seed coats with knife and plant in place when soil has warmed up. In mild-winter climates, can be planted in fall for spring bloom. Use as edging or at top of wall. 'Blue Flash' and Ensign series (red, blue, rose, white) grow 6 in. tall.

COOLIBAH. See EUCALYPTUS microtheca

COPPER LEAF. See ACALYPHA wilkesiana

COPROSMA

Rubiaceae

EVERGREEN SHRUBS

ZONES VARY BY SPECIES

FULL SUN OR PARTIAL SHADE

LITTLE TO REGULAR WATER

Coprosma repens

Native to New Zealand. Where hardy, all are valued for ease of maintenance in difficult situations and for handsome, glossy foliage. Male and female flowers are borne on separate plants; female plants bear attractive small fruits when a male is nearby for pollination.

C. 'Coppershine'. Zones 8, 9, 14–24. Male hybrid. Rounded growth to 6 ft. high and wide; fast growing while young. Leathery leaves are 1–1¾ in. long, less than half as wide, polished bright green heavily shaded with coppery brown. New growth is even more heavily tinted; entire plant is bright copper in winter. Good hedge, screen.

C. × kirkii. Zones 14–24; H1, H2. To 1–3 ft. high or nearly prostrate; spreading 4–6 ft. wide. Long, straight stems slant outward from base. Small (½–2-in.), narrow yellow-green leaves are closely set on stems. White fruits speckled red. Tough ground cover or bank cover; prune regularly to keep dense. Grows in wide range of soils; tolerates coastal winds, salt spray. Slightly drought tolerant near coast. Give part shade inland. 'Variegata', 6–24 in. high and up to 5 ft. wide, has white-edged gray-green leaves and translucent white berries; good trailing plant for wall pot, hanging basket.

C. petriei (C. pumila). Zones 8, 9, 14–24. Spreading, mounding plant to 2–2½ ft. high, eventually 6–8 ft. wide. Small, roundish oval leaves are bright shiny green. Set 2–2½ ft. apart for ground cover in 3 years. Cut out upward-growing branches. Tolerates more cold, heat than *C. × kirkii.* Egg-shaped fruits are translucent purplish red or blue. 'Verde Vista' (*C.* 'Prostrata'), a natural hybrid, is an improvement on the parent.

C. repens (C. baueri). MIRROR PLANT. Zones 14–24; H1. Rapid growth to 10 ft. tall, 6 ft. wide; much lower and more compact when subjected to seacoast conditions. Inland, an open, straggly shrub if neglected—but beautiful, dense form if pruned twice yearly (at any height desired). Oval or oblong leaves are 3 in. long, 1½ in. wide, dark to light green, almost unbelievably shiny and glossy. Yellow or orange fruits. Use as hedge, screen, informal espalier

Variegated forms include 'Argentea', with green leaves flecked silvery white; 'Marble Queen', to 2–3 ft. tall, with creamy white leaves irregularly splashed and dotted with green; 'Marble King', slow grower with cream-colored leaves heavily speckled in lime green; 'Picturata', green leaves blotched creamy yellow in the middle; 'Exotica', female version of 'Picturata' with orange-yellow fruits; 'Marginata', with green leaves irregularly edged in creamy white; 'Pink Splendor', green leaves with yellow margin that takes on a pink edging with maturity.

CORAL BELLS. See HEUCHERA sanguinea

CORAL BERRY. See SYMPHORICARPOS orbiculatus

CORAL GUM. See EUCALYPTUS torquata

CORAL TREE. See ERYTHRINA

CORAL VINE. See ANTIGONON leptopus

CORDIA

Boraginaceae

EVERGREEN SHRUBS AND TREES

ZONES VARY BY SPECIES

FULL SUN

WATER NEEDS VARY BY SPECIES

Cordia boissieri

These members of the forget-me-not family are grown for their showy flowers. Some species are at home in the desert Southwest, others in more tropical climates.

C. boissieri. TEXAS OLIVE. Shrub or tree. Zones 8–24. Native to New Mexico, Texas, Mexico; adapted to low and intermediate deserts. To 12 ft. tall, 8–10 ft. wide. Oval, grayish green, rough-surfaced leaves to 5 in. long. Clustered, 2½-in. white flowers with yellow throats begin bloom in midspring and continue over a long season; repeat bloom is possible in autumn. Can be kept pruned as a low (3–5-ft.) shrub or trained as a small tree. Moderate water.

C. parvifolia. LITTLE-LEAF CORDIA. Shrub. Zones 8–14, 18–24. Native to Baja California. Similar to *C. boissieri* but somewhat smaller, with smaller leaves (most are ½ in. or less) and flowers (to 1½ in. wide). Plant 8–9 ft. apart for informal hedge or barrier. Little to moderate water.

C. sebestena. GEIGER TREE, KOU HAOLE. Shrub or tree. Zones 24; H1, H2. Native to the Caribbean Islands and tropical America. A popular street tree in Hawaii's dry lowlands. To 10–25 ft. high and 15 ft. wide, with dense, round head. Dark green leaves are 9–12 in. long and half as wide, so rough surfaced they are almost sandpapery. Clusters of brilliant orange-red flowers are produced much of the year at branch tips. Good wind and salt tolerance; takes drought but does best with regular water.

C. subcordata. KOU. Tree. Zones H1, H2. From seashores of East Africa to Polynesia. A good shade tree in Hawaii's hot coastal areas. Dense growth to 25–35 ft. high, 25 ft. wide. Smooth, thin, oval leaves, 4–8 in. long. Clusters of crepey light orange flowers much of year. Regular water.

CORDYLINE

Agavaceae

EVERGREEN PALMLIKE SHRUBS OR TREES

ZONES VARY BY SPECIES; OR INDOORS

EXPOSURE NEEDS VARY BY SPECIES

WATER NEEDS VARY BY SPECIES

Cordyline australis

Woody plants with swordlike leaves, related to yuccas and agaves but usually ranked with palms in nurseries and landscapes. Good next to swimming pools. As houseplants, prefer bright indirect light but tolerate low light; rarely bloom indoors. To keep indoor plants from getting too big, grow them in undersize pots and repot annually in fresh potting soil. Cordyline is often sold as *Dracaena;* for true *Dracaena,* see that entry.

C. australis (Dracaena australis). Zones 5, 8–11, 14–24; H1, H2. From New Zealand. Hardiest of cordylines, surviving to at least 15°F/–9°C. In youth, forms a fountain of narrow (2–5-in.-wide), 3-ft.-long leaves. Upper leaves are erect; lower ones arch and droop. In maturity, a tree to 20–30 ft. tall, 6–12 ft. wide, branching high on trunk; rather stiff looking (like Joshua tree, *Yucca brevifolia*). Fragrant, ¼-in. flowers in long, branching clusters in late spring. For more graceful plant, cut back when young to force multiple trunks. Grows fastest in soil deep enough for big, carrotlike root. Used for tropical effects, with boulders and gravel for desert look, near seashore. Full sun. Moderate to regular water.

Colorful varieties include 'Atropurpurea', known as bronze dracaena, with bronzy red leaves; 'Pink Stripe', bronze with pink margins; 'Red Star', purplish red; and 'Sundance', green with a pink midrib.

C. baueri. Zones 8, 9, 14–24. From New Zealand. To 8–10 ft. high, 3 ft. wide, with 2-ft.-long leaves in deep purple red. Fragrant white flowers in summer. Full sun, moderate water.

C. fruticosa (C. terminalis). TI PLANT. Zones 21–24; H1, H2. Frequently used as houseplant. From tropical Southeast Asia. Many named forms with red, yellow, or variegated leaves. White or red, foot-long flower clusters in summer or sporadically throughout year. Plants are usually started from "logs"—small sections of mature stems imported from Hawaii. Lay logs flat in mixture of peat moss and sand, covering them to about one-half their diameter. Keep moist. When shoots grow out and root, cut them off and plant them. In frost-free locations where it receives regular water and soil stays warm, reaches 6–15 ft. high, 3–8 ft. wide. Full sun or partial shade (types with colorful leaves show more intense hues in sun).

C. indivisa. BLUE DRACAENA. Zones 16, 17, 20–24. Hardy to 26°F/–3°C. From New Zealand. Trunk grows to 25 ft. tall and is topped with 8–10-ft.-wide crown of huge (6-ft.-long, 6-in.-wide), rather stiff leaves. White summer flowers in 4-ft.-long clusters. Tolerates seaside conditions. Give full sun, moderate water.

C. stricta. Zones 13, 16, 17, 20–24; H1, H2. Hardy to 26°F/–3°C. From Australia. Slender, erect stems clustered at base or branching low. Leaves are 2 ft. long, dark green with hints of purple. Very decorative during spring bloom, bearing fragrant lavender flowers in large, branched clusters. Reaches 15 ft. high and 6 ft. wide but can be kept lower by cutting tall canes to ground; new canes replace them. Long cuttings stuck in ground will root quickly. Fine container plant indoors or out; good for tropical-looking background in narrow areas, lanais, side gardens. Needs some shade except in cool-summer climates. Regular water.

C. terminalis. See C. fruticosa

COREOPSIS

Asteraceae (Compositae)

PERENNIALS AND ANNUALS

ZONES VARY BY SPECIES

FULL SUN

LITTLE TO MODERATE WATER, EXCEPT AS NOTED

Coreopsis grandiflora

Easy-to-grow members of the sunflower family yielding a profusion of yellow, orange, maroon, or reddish flowers. Deadhead for longer bloom; use hedge shears to remove large numbers of spent blooms. Both annual and perennial kinds are easy to propagate—annuals from seed sown in place or in pots, perennials from seed or division. Plants tend to self-sow; seeds attract birds. The following species are from the eastern and southern U.S. unless otherwise noted.

C. auriculata 'Nana'. Perennial. Zones 1–24. Makes 5–6-in.-high mat of 2–5-in.-long leaves. Under ideal conditions, it will spread by underground runners to form a 2-ft.-wide clump in a year. Bright orange yellow, 1–2½-in. flowers rise well above foliage; blooms profusely over a long season (from spring to fall) if you deadhead faithfully. Best used in front of taller plants, in borders, as edging.

C. gigantea. Perennial. Zones 14–17, 19–24. Native to coastal Southern California, Baja California. Grows to 3 ft. (occasionally 10 ft.) tall, with asymmetric form. Succulent trunks to 4 in. across hold a few branches of varying lengths tipped with clusters of fernlike leaves. Clusters of 3-in. yellow daisies in spring. Showy in seaside plant collection; rarely sold in nurseries.

C. grandiflora. Perennial. Zones 2–24; H1, H2. To 1–2 ft. high, spreading to 3 ft. Narrow dark green leaves with three to five lobes. Bright yellow, 2½–3-in. single flowers bloom all summer, carried high above foliage on long, slender stems.

'Sunburst' has semidouble flowers; it will bloom the first year from seed sown early in spring, then spread by self-sowing. 'Early Sunrise' is similar and blooms even earlier. 'Sunray' is a dense, compact selection with double and semidouble flowers. All are tough enough for use in roadside beautification.

C. lanceolata. Perennial. Zones 1–24; H1, H2. Grows 1–2 ft. high, 1–1½ ft. wide. Narrow, somewhat hairy foliage, mostly in tuft near plant's base; some leaves on lower part of flower stems have a few lobes. Yellow, 1½–2-in. blossoms on pale green stems bloom in late spring and summer, make excellent cut flowers. When well established, persists year after year. Has naturalized in Hawaii.

C. maritima. Perennial. Zones 14–24. Native to coast of Southern California. Sometimes called sea dahlia. Grows from a tuberous taproot to reach 1–3 ft. high, 1–2 ft. wide. Stems are hollow; leaves are somewhat succulent, divided into very narrow lobes. True yellow, 2½–4-in. blossoms on 9–12-in. stems in spring; make striking cut flowers. Use in borders, for naturalizing.

C. rosea. Perennial. Zones 2b–24. Fine-textured plant 1½–2 ft. tall, 1 ft. wide, with pink, yellow-centered daisylike flowers from summer to fall. Unlike other species, prefers moist soil.

C. tinctoria. ANNUAL COREOPSIS, CALLIOPSIS. Annual. Zones 1–24; H1, H2. Native to much of North America. Slender, upright, 1½–3 ft. tall, 1–1½ ft. wide, with wiry stems; much like cosmos in growth habit. Smooth leaves and stems. Summer-to-fall flowers in yellow, orange, maroon, bronze, and reddish, banded with contrasting colors; purple-brown centers. There are dwarf and double varieties. Sow seed in place in dryish soil.

C. verticillata. Perennial. Zones 1–24. To 2½–3 ft. tall, half as broad. Many erect or slightly leaning stems carry many whorls of finely divided, very narrow leaves. Bright yellow, 2-in. daisies are freely borne at stem tips over a long bloom season—from summer through autumn. One of the most tolerant of drought, neglect. 'Moonbeam', 1½–2 ft. tall, has pale yellow flowers; 'Zagreb', 1 ft. tall, has golden yellow flowers.

CORIANDRUM sativum

CORIANDER, CHINESE PARSLEY, CILANTRO

Apiaceae (Umbelliferae)

ANNUAL

ALL ZONES

LIGHT SHADE IN HOTTEST CLIMATES

REGULAR WATER

Coriandrum sativum

Mediterranean native grows 1–1½ ft. high, 9 in. wide. Delicate fernlike foliage; flat clusters of pinkish white flowers in summer. Both fresh leaves (cilantro) and seeds (coriander) are widely used as seasoning. Leaves are popular in salads and many cooked dishes; crush the aromatic seeds for use in sausage, beans, stews, baked goods. Grow in good, well-drained soil. Start from seed (including coriander seed sold in grocery stores) in early spring after all danger of frost is past. In low-desert areas, plant in autumn; goes to seed and dies in late spring heat. Sow in place; plant is taprooted and transplants poorly. Grows quickly, self-sows.

CORN

Poaceae (Gramineae)

ANNUAL

ALL ZONES

FULL SUN

REGULAR WATER

Sweet Corn

Sweet corn is the one cereal crop that home gardeners are likely to grow; it requires considerable space but is still well worth planting. Once standard sweet corn is picked, its sugar changes to starch very quickly; by rushing ears from garden directly to boiling water, you can capture full sweetness. Sugar-enhanced and supersweet varieties of corn are actually sweeter than standard kinds, and they maintain their sweetness longer after harvest because of a gene that increases the quantity of sugar and slows its conversion to starch. A very few people consider these varieties overly sweet.

Corn needs heat, but suitable early hybrid varieties will grow even in cool-summer areas. In Alaska, grow short-season varieties; plant seeds you have pregerminated and grow with black plastic mulch and row covers. In Hawaii, try varieties developed especially for Island gardens, such as supersweet kinds 'Waimanolo SS' and 'UH-10'.

Corn grows in various soils but does best in deep, rich ones; good drainage is important. Sow seed 2 weeks after average last-frost date, then make three or four more plantings at 2-week intervals; or plant early, midseason, and late varieties. In Hawaii, you can plant corn year-round. Plant in blocks of four or more short rows rather than in single long row; pollination is by wind, and unless a good supply of pollen falls on silks, ears will be poorly filled. Don't plant popcorn near sweet corn; pollen of one kind can affect characteristics of other. For the same reason, some supersweet varieties must be grown at a distance from standard sweet kinds.

Plant in rows 3 ft. apart and thin seedlings to 1 ft. apart. Or plant in "hills" (actually clumps) spaced 3 ft. apart on all sides. Plant six or seven seeds in each hill and thin to three strongest plants.

Give plants plenty of water. Feed with high-nitrogen fertilizer when stalks are 12–15 in. tall, again when they are 2–2½ ft. high. Just as tassel emerges from stalk, give good deep watering that thoroughly wets entire root zone; repeat when silks form. Don't remove suckers that appear. Check your crop when ears are plump and silks have withered; corn is usually ready to eat 3 weeks after silks first appear. To check, pull back husks and try popping a kernel with your thumbnail. It should squirt milky juice; watery juice means that corn is immature, while doughy consistency indicates overmaturity.

Corn earworm is the principal insect pest. There is no simple control. Most gardeners expect some harvested ears to show worm damage at the silk ends, and they just cut off those ends. The prevention (it's tedious) goes like this: 3 to 7 days after silks appear, use a medicine dropper to put two drops of mineral oil just inside the tip of each ear.

Baby corn. Special varieties that are harvested very early, when the ears are only a few inches long. The tender ears are eaten whole, often pickled or used in salads or Asian cuisine. Plant seeds 1–2 in. apart; thin seedlings to 4 in. apart. Harvest shortly after the first silks appear, which may be only a few weeks after sowing.

Ornamental corn. Some kinds of corn are grown for the beauty of their shelled ears rather than for eating. Calico, Indian, Squaw, and Rainbow are some names given to strains with bright-colored kernels—red, brown, blue, gray, black, yellow, or mixed colors. 'Indian Summer' has brightly colored, edible kernels. Grow ornamental corn well away from sweet corn; mix of pollen can affect the latter's flavor. For ornamental display, grow like sweet corn, but let ears ripen fully; silks will be withered, husks will turn straw color, and kernels will be firm. Cut ear from plant, including 1½ in. of stalk below ear; pull back husks (leave attached to ears) and dry thoroughly.

Ornamental Corn

Zea mays japonica includes several kinds of corn grown for ornamental foliage. One occasionally sold is 'Gracilis', a dwarf corn with bright green leaves striped white.

Popcorn. Grow and harvest just like ornamental corn. When ears are thoroughly dry, rub kernels off cobs and store in dry place. White, red, and yellow kinds of popcorn look like other types of corn.

Strawberry popcorn, grown either for its ornamental value or for popping, has stubby, fat, strawberry-like ears packed with red kernels.

Popcorn

Cornaceae. The dogwood family consists of trees and shrubs with clustered inconspicuous flowers (sometimes surrounded by showy bracts) and berrylike fruit. *Aucuba* and dogwood *(Cornus)* are examples.

CORNELIAN CHERRY. See CORNUS mas

CORNFLOWER. See CENTAUREA cyanus

CORN PLANT. See DRACAENA fragrans

CORNUS

DOGWOOD

Cornaceae

DECIDUOUS AND EVERGREEN SHRUBS AND TREES AND A PERENNIAL

ZONES VARY BY SPECIES

FULL SUN OR LIGHT SHADE, EXCEPT AS NOTED

REGULAR WATER, EXCEPT AS NOTED

Cornus florida 'Rubra'

All dogwoods offer attractive foliage and blossoms; some have spectacular fruit or winter bark. Leaves of many types turn brilliant colors in fall. What appear to be flower petals in many dogwoods are actually bracts—petal-like modified leaves. These surround the inconspicuous true flowers.

C. alba. TATARIAN DOGWOOD. Deciduous shrub. Zones A2, A3; 1–9, 14–24. Native to Siberia, northern China, Korea. In cold-winter areas, its bare, blood red twigs are colorful against snow. Wide spreading, eventually producing thicket of many upright stems to about 10 ft. tall. Branches densely foliaged with leaves to 2½–5 in. long, 2½ in. wide; leaves are deep rich green above and paler beneath, turn red in fall. Spring bloom; small, fragrant, creamy white flowers in 1–2-in., flattish clusters. Small bluish white to white fruits. In species and following varieties, new wood is brightest; cut back in late dormant season to force new growth.

'Argenteomarginata' (*C.* 'Elegantissima'). Showy green-and-white leaves on red stems.

'Gouchaultii'. Leaves have yellow borders suffused with pink.

'Sibirica'. SIBERIAN DOGWOOD. Smaller and not as wide spreading as species; grows to about 7 ft. high, 5 ft. wide. Gleaming coral red branches.

C. alternifolia. PAGODA DOGWOOD. Deciduous shrub or tree. Zones 2–6. Native to eastern North America. Multitrunked plant to 20 ft. high and wide. Strong horizontal branching pattern provides attractive winter silhouette. Light green leaves turn red in fall. Creamy spring flowers come in small clusters, are not showy. Blue-black fruit follows. Foliage of 'Argentea' has white markings.

C. canadensis. BUNCHBERRY. Perennial. Zones A1–A3; 1–7; difficult but possible in Zones 8, 9, 14–16. Native from Northern California to Alaska and eastward. Ground cover 6–9 in. high, found in the wild under trees by lakes and streams. Creeping rootstocks send up stems topped by whorls of oval or roundish, 1–2-in.-long, deep green leaves that turn yellow in fall, die down in winter. In late spring or early summer, plants bear small, compact clusters of tiny flowers surrounded by (usually) four oval, ½–¾-in., pure white bracts. Clusters of small, shiny red fruits follow in late summer.

Best performance in part or full shade in cool, moist climates, in acid soil with generous amounts of organic matter. Set out small plants from pots about 1 ft. apart. Small rooted pieces gathered from the woods may not establish easily. Excellent with rhododendrons, ferns, trilliums, lilies.

C. capitata. EVERGREEN DOGWOOD. Shrub or tree. Zones 8, 9, 14–20. Himalayan native hardy to 15°F/–9°C. Not reliably evergreen; may drop all its leaves in cold weather, and often loses half of them in mild winters. To 20–30 ft. tall and wide, with 2–4-in.-long, gray-green leaves; some turn red or purplish in fall. Unless grown from cuttings, trees don't flower until 8 to 10 years old—but when they do bloom, they are delightful. Small springtime clusters of flowers are surrounded by four to six 1½–2-in., creamy to pale yellow bracts. Large (1-in.), showy, strawberry-like crimson fruit in fall can be a litter problem, though birds may do some of the cleanup for you.

C. c. emeiensis. Zones 4–9, 14–17. From China; hardier than the species. To 35 ft. tall and wide. Foliage in upper portion of tree turns purple, while lower leaves remain green. New leaves replace the old ones in spring. Usually sold as *C. omeiense* 'Summer Passion'.

C. controversa. GIANT DOGWOOD. Deciduous tree. Zones 4–9, 14, 18, 19. From Asia. Resembles typical big shrubby dogwoods in leaves, flowers, and fruit, but grows rapidly into a magnificent tree 40–60 ft. tall and wide, with picturesque horizontal branches. Luxuriantly foliaged with oval, 3–6-in.-long leaves that are dark green above, silvery green beneath, glowing red in fall. Creamy white spring flowers in fluffy, flattish, 3–7-in. clusters are not spectacular, but so abundant they give a good show. Blossoms are followed in late summer by ½-in., shiny blue-black fruit enjoyed by birds. Full sun for best bloom, brightest fall color. Foliage of 'Variegata' is edged white.

C. 'Eddie's White Wonder'. Deciduous tree. Zones 3–9, 14–20. Hybrid between *C. florida* and *C. nuttallii.* A little taller and more erect than *C. florida,* twiggier and easier to transplant than *C. nuttallii.* Midspring bloom. Clusters of tiny true flowers are surrounded by four to six white bracts.

C. florida. FLOWERING DOGWOOD, EASTERN DOGWOOD. Deciduous tree. Zones 2b–9, 14–16. Native to eastern U.S. May reach 40 ft. high and wide, but more commonly seen at 20–30 ft. Trees tend to branch low, the branches building up in horizontal layers (with gray twigs pointing upward at branch ends). Mature trees—often wider than tall—have a gently rounded to flat crown. Small flower clusters are surrounded by four roundish, 2–4-in. bracts with notched tips. The species has white bracts, but selections offer bracts in pink shades to nearly red (as well as white). Bracts form in fall; tips may wither in harsh, dry winters, preventing inflorescence from opening fully. Flowers almost cover tree in midspring before leaves expand. Oval, 2–4-in.-long leaves are bright green above, lighter beneath; turn glowing red in fall. Clusters of small, oval scarlet fruit last into winter or until birds eat them. Subject to anthracnose, a fungus that can cause leaf damage, stem cankers, and decline or death of the tree. Avoid injury to bark from mowers and string trimmers; try to keep the tree healthy with adequate feeding, watering, and air circulation.

The following are among the varieties offered. (*C. florida* has been bred with *C. kousa* to produce more disease resistant hybrids; for those, see *C.* ×*rutgersensis.*)

'Cherokee Chief'. Deep rosy red bracts, paler at base.

'Cherokee Princess'. Unusually heavy display of white blooms.

'Cloud Nine'. White-bracted selection blooms young and heavily. Gives better bloom in cold climates than other *C. florida* varieties; also tolerates heat and lack of winter chill better than other varieties.

'Pendula'. Drooping branches give it a weeping look. White bracts.

'Pink Flame'. Leaves green and cream, maturing to dark green and red. Pink bracts.

'Rubra'. Long-time favorite for its pink or rose bracts.

'Welchii'. TRICOLOR DOGWOOD. Leaves about 4 in. long, variegated in creamy white, pink, deep rose, and green throughout spring and summer; turn solid deep rose to almost red in fall. Rather inconspicuous pinkish to white bracts are not profuse. Best with some shade.

C. kousa. KOUSA DOGWOOD. Deciduous shrub or tree. Zones 2–9, 14–17. Native to Japan and Korea. Can be a big multistemmed shrub or—with training—a small tree to 20 ft. tall and wide (or even larger). Dense, spreading, horizontal growth habit and delicate limb structure. Lustrous medium green leaves, 4 in. long, have rusty brown hairs at base of veins on undersurface. Flowers along tops of branches show above leaves in late spring or early summer (later than other flowering dogwoods). Creamy white, rather narrow, 2–3-in.-long bracts with slender, sharp-pointed tips turn pink along edges. In late summer and fall, inch-wide red fruits appear, resembling large raspberries hanging below branches. Yellow or scarlet autumn leaf color. Less susceptible to anthracnose than *C. florida* and *C. nuttallii.* Except as noted, the following selections bear white bracts.

Cornus kousa

'Autumn Rose'. To 20 ft. tall, 25 ft. wide. Leaves are light green when new, pink to red in fall.

'Bonfire'. Bright red fall foliage.

C. k. chinensis. Larger leaves and bracts than species.

'Gold Star'. To 12 ft. tall and wide, with yellow-centered green leaves.

'Milky Way'. More floriferous than species.

'National'. To 25–30 ft. tall, 12–15 ft. wide, with earlier bloom than species and bright red fall color.

'Satomi' ('Satomi Red', 'Rosabella'). Reaches 20 ft. tall and wide. Rose red bracts.

C. mas. CORNELIAN CHERRY. Deciduous shrub or tree. Zones 1–6. Native to southern Europe, Asia. Usually an airy, twiggy shrub but can be trained as small tree (15–20 ft. high and wide). One of earliest dogwoods to bloom, bearing clustered masses of small, soft yellow blossoms on bare twigs in mid- to late winter. Oval, 2–4-in.-long leaves turn from shiny green to yellow (or red, in some forms) in autumn. Fall color is enhanced by clusters of cherry-size, bright scarlet fruits that hang on until birds get them. Fruit can be used for preserves. In winter, flaking, mottled gray-and-tan bark provides interest. Tolerates alkaline soils. Leaves of 'Variegata' are marbled creamy white.

C. nuttallii. PACIFIC DOGWOOD, WESTERN DOGWOOD. Deciduous tree. Zones 3b–9, 14–20. Native to Pacific Northwest and Northern California. To 50 ft. tall, 20 ft. wide, with one trunk or several. Gray branches in pleasing horizontal pattern. Spectacular when it shows off its gleaming white bracts on bare branches in spring; there is often a second flowering in late summer, when tree is in full leaf. Flowers ringed by four to eight large (to 3-in.-long), rounded or pointed bracts; may be white or pink-tinged white. Oval, 3–5-in. green leaves turn yellow, pink, and red in autumn. Decorative red fruit in knoblike clusters in fall.

Dislikes routine garden watering, fertilizing, pruning; injury to tender bark provides entrance for insects and diseases. For better chance of success, give exceptionally good drainage and infrequent summer water, and plant under high-branching trees so bark will not sunburn. In Northwest, however, planting under larger trees is not advisable. *C. nuttallii* is very susceptible to anthracnose in this region, and a location under larger trees creates conditions that favor the disease—reduced air circulation and shadiness that extend time for wet foliage to dry.

Named varieties are more tolerant of garden conditions. 'Colrigo Giant' is vigorous and heavy trunked, with low-branching but erect habit; bears profusion of 6-in. flower heads. 'Goldspot' has leaves splashed with creamy yellow; because it is grafted, it blooms from an early age (when only 2 ft. high).

C. omeiense 'Summer Passion'. See C. capitata emeiensis

C. × rutgersensis. STELLAR DOGWOOD. Deciduous trees. Zones 3–9, 14–17. These disease-resistant single-trunked hybrids between *C. florida* and *C. kousa* grow to about 20 ft. tall, 25–30 ft. wide. Bloom comes between midspring bloom of *C. florida* and late-spring or early-summer bloom of *C. kousa.* Blossoms appear along with the leaves. 'Aurora', 'Celestial', and 'Ruth Ellen' have broad white bracts; 'Constellation' and 'Stardust' have narrow white ones, giving a starlike effect. 'Stellar Pink' produces pink bracts. All have brilliant fall color.

C. sanguinea. BLOODTWIG DOGWOOD. Deciduous shrub. Zones 1–7. From Europe. Grows as large multistemmed shrub to 12 ft. high, about 8 ft. wide. Big show comes in fall, thanks to dark blood red foliage, and in winter, when bare, purplish to dark red twigs and branches are on display. Prune severely in late dormant season to produce new branches and twigs for winter color. Dark green, 1½–3-in.-long leaves; greenish white late-spring flowers in 2-in. clusters. Black fruit. 'Midwinter Fire' has brilliant orange-red fall color and red berries.

C. stolonifera (C. sericea). REDTWIG DOGWOOD, RED-OSIER DOGWOOD. Deciduous shrub. Zones A1–A3; 1–9, 14–21. Like *C. sanguinea,* this one is grown for brilliant red fall foliage and winter twigs, and it too should be cut back severely in late dormant season. Native to moist places, Northern California to Alaska and eastward. Thrives not only in coldest mountain areas of West but also throughout California—even in intermediate valleys of Southern California if given frequent water. Grows rapidly to form a big multistemmed shrub 7–9 ft. high; spreads to 12 ft. or wider by creeping underground stems and rooting branches. Oval, 1½–2½-in.-long, fresh deep green leaves. Small, creamy white flowers in 2-in. clusters appear among leaves throughout summer; white or bluish fruits follow.

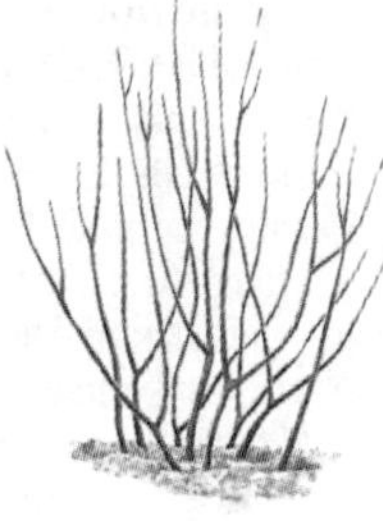
Cornus stolonifera

Use as a space filler on moist ground (good for holding banks) or plant along property line as a screen. Shade tolerant. To control spread, use a spade to cut off roots; also trim branches that touch ground.

C. s. baileyi. To 6–8 ft. tall; exceptionally bright red twigs.

C. s. coloradensis. COLORADO REDTWIG. Native from Yukon to New Mexico and California. To 5–6 ft. high, with brownish red stems. Its selection 'Cheyenne' is redder.

'Flaviramea'. YELLOWTWIG DOGWOOD. Yellow twigs and branches.

'Isanti'. Compact grower to 5 ft. tall, with bright red stems.

'Kelseyi' ('Nana'). Dwarf form seldom exceeding 1½ ft. tall. Stems not as red as those of species.

'Silver and Gold'. Yellow branches and cream-edged green leaves.

FOR INFORMATION ON YOUR CLIMATE ZONE
PLEASE SEE PAGES 27–63

COROKIA

Cornaceae
EVERGREEN SHRUBS
ZONES 4–24
FULL SUN OR PARTIAL SHADE
MODERATE WATER

Corokia cotoneaster

New Zealand natives grown for zigzag branching habit; small, starlike yellow flowers; and red, orange, or yellow fruits. Night lighting from below emphasizes bizarre branch pattern and casts interesting shadows. Sculptural form is enhanced by selective removal of a third or more of the branches and by heading back strong new shoots to maintain a compact outline. If intertwining branches are left intact, plants make dense hedges. Need good drainage. Thrive in containers.

C. cotoneaster. Slow growing to 8–10 ft. high and wide, but usually seen as a 2–4-ft. container plant. Slim, contorted, reddish to nearly black branches. Sparse, oval leaves to ¾ in. long, dark glossy green above, white beneath. Yellow, ½-in. flowers are followed on older plants by small orange or red fruit. 'Little Prince' grows 4 ft. high, has bright red fruit.

C. × virgata. A series of hybrids with more erect growth habit than *C. cotoneaster;* eventually reach 10 ft. tall, 6 ft. wide. Most have spoon-shaped leaves up to 1½ in. long. Use in containers, as accent plants in garden, as hedge or screen. 'Red Wonder' and 'Yellow Wonder' are named for the color of their showy fruits. 'Bronze King' has tiny, bronze-tinged leaves; 'Bronze Lady' has darker bronze foliage (of the usual size) and bright red fruit. 'Sunsplash' has bronzy stems and bright green leaves margined with creamy yellow.

CORONILLA varia

CROWN VETCH
Fabaceae (Leguminosae)
PERENNIAL
ZONES 1–24
FULL SUN
MODERATE WATER

Coronilla varia

Weedy European native related to peas, beans, and clovers. Creeping roots and rhizomes make it a tenacious ground cover. Sprawling stems to 2 ft. long are set with leaves divided into 11–25 oval, ½–¾-in.-long leaflets. Lavender-pink flowers in 1-in. clusters bloom from summer into fall; these are followed by bundles of brown, fingerlike seedpods. Dies to the ground in winter, even in mild climates. Too invasive and rank for flower beds; use it for covering erosion-prone banks and at garden fringes. Mow, feed, and—in absence of rainfall—irrigate in early spring for best appearance. Difficult to eliminate once established. 'Penngift' takes sun or shade.

CORREA

AUSTRALIAN FUCHSIA
Rutaceae
EVERGREEN SHRUBS
ZONES 14–24
PARTIAL SHADE IN HOTTEST CLIMATES
MODERATE WATER

Correa pulchella

These Australian natives may resemble fuchsia in their flower form, but in all other ways they are far from fuchsialike. Plants range from low growing to tall, are usually dense and spreading. Roundish, 1-in. leaves, densely felted underneath; gray or gray-green color contrasts subtly with other grays, distinctly with dark greens. All are valued for their long flowering season, usually late fall into spring (*C. alba* is a summer bloomer). Small (½–¾-in.) flowers hang from branches like little bells; they are individually handsome but not showy.

Need fast drainage; do well in poor, rocky soil. Easy to kill with kindness (overwatering, overfertilizing). Should not get reflected heat from wall or pavement. Use as ground cover on banks or slopes. Attractive in large containers placed where flowers can be enjoyed close up.

C. alba. To 8 ft. high and wide, with rusty-haired stems and dark green leaves. Flowers are white, more open and star-shaped than those of other correas. Withstands seashore conditions. Apparently not relished by deer.

C. backhousiana. Upright and rather sprawling growth to 4–5 ft. tall and wide. Chartreuse flowers. More successful in Southern California than *C. pulchella.* Often sold as *C. magnifica.*

C. 'Dusky Bells' ('Carmine Bells'). Low growing (2–2½ ft.), spreading as wide as 8 ft. Deep red flowers.

C. 'Ivory Bells'. Resembles 'Dusky Bells' but has creamy white flowers.

C. pulchella. To 2–2½ ft. high, spreading as wide as 8 ft. Leaves green above, gray green below; flower color ranges from light pink to reddish orange. Most widely grown correa in Northern California. 'Mission Bells' has deep pink to red flowers; 'Orange Flame' has somewhat smaller orange blossoms.

C. reflexa. Variable species, with many forms ranging from 1 to 9 ft. tall, 3 to 9 ft. wide. Flowers are 1–1½ in. long, tubular, red with yellow tips. 'Yanakie' is 4 ft. tall and wide, with large red flowers tipped green.

CORTADERIA selloana

PAMPAS GRASS
Poaceae (Gramineae)
PERENNIAL GRASS
ZONES 3–24; H1
FULL SUN
ANY AMOUNT OF WATER

Cortaderia selloana

Native to Argentina. Grows very fast in rich soil in mild climates—from gallon-can size to 8 ft. in one season. Established plants may reach 20 ft. tall, up to about 13 ft. wide. Each plant is a fountain of saw-toothed, grassy leaves; long stalks bearing 1–3-ft., white to chamois or pink flower plumes rise above the foliage in late summer. 'Pumila' ('Ivory Feathers') is smaller (to 3 ft. tall, 4 ft. wide), with white plumes rising to 6 ft. 'Sun Stripe' has yellow-striped foliage in clumps to 4 ft. tall, 5 ft. wide, with white flower plumes to 6 ft. high.

This well-known landscaping form of *Cortaderia*—like its truly weedy and noxious cousin *C. jubata*—may send its seeds into the wind under certain circumstances to germinate and grow wherever they land. For that reason, nurseries in some areas no longer sell *Cortaderia* at all. Many horticulturists recommend against further landscaping with *C. selloana* and suggest removing it from gardens that border wild lands. Be sure to grub out volunteer *Cortaderia* seedlings whenever they appear.

CORYDALIS

Fumariaceae
PERENNIALS
ZONES 2–9, 14–24
PARTIAL SHADE
REGULAR WATER

Corydalis lutea

Handsome clumps of dainty divided leaves like those of bleeding heart (*Dicentra,* to which it is closely related) or maidenhair fern *(Adiantum).* Clusters of small, spurred flowers. Plant in rich, moist soil. Effective in rock crevices, in open woodland, near pool or streamside. Divide clumps or sow seed in spring or fall. Plants self-sow. Tend to be short lived in mild-winter Southern California zones.

C. cheilanthifolia. Chinese native, 8–10 in. high and wide, with fernlike green foliage. Clusters of yellow, ½-in.-long flowers in spring.

C. flexuosa. From western China. Typically to 1 ft. high, 8 in. wide, but under favorable conditions it rapidly spreads wider from bulblets on the roots. Finely divided foliage and spikelike clusters of blue flowers in early spring, often continuing into summer. May go dormant in summer, especially in hot climates, but will reappear the following spring. Selections include 'Blue Panda', with gentian blue flowers; 'China Blue', pure sky blue; 'Nightshade', blue-and-lavender blossoms; 'Père David', lavender to light blue blooms. 'Purple Leaf', the earliest bloomer, has purplish blue flowers and green leaves blotched purple.

C. lutea. Native to southern Europe. To 15 in. tall, 1 ft. wide. Masses of delicate foliage on many stems. Golden yellow, ¾-in.-long, short-spurred flowers throughout summer. Self-sows and can become somewhat weedy.

C. solida. From northern Europe, Asia. To 10 in. high, 8 in. wide. Blooms in spring, producing spikes containing up to 20 purplish red flowers. Grow from fall-planted tubers.

CORYLOPSIS

WINTER HAZEL
Hamamelidaceae
DECIDUOUS SHRUBS
ZONES VARY BY SPECIES
FULL SUN OR PARTIAL SHADE
REGULAR WATER

Corylopsis spicata

Asian natives valued for sweet-scented, bell-shaped, soft yellow flowers that hang in short, chainlike clusters on bare branches in early spring. New foliage that follows is often tinged pink; it later turns bright green. Toothed, nearly round leaves somewhat resemble those of hazelnut *(Corylus);* fall color varies from none to poor to a good clear yellow. Rather open structure with attractive, delicate branching pattern. Give same soil conditions as you would rhododendrons. Grow in wind-sheltered location in shrub border or at edge of woodland.

C. glabrescens. FRAGRANT WINTER HAZEL. Zones 2–7, 14–17. Hardiest species. To 8–15 ft. high and wide. Can be trained as a small tree. Flower clusters are 1–1½ in. long.

C. pauciflora. BUTTERCUP WINTER HAZEL. Zones 4–7, 14–17. Dainty habit to 4–6 ft. high and wide. Blossom clusters are 1¾ in. long, each containing two or three blooms.

C. sinensis. Zones 4–7, 14–17. A variable species. The typical form is a spreading shrub to 15 ft. tall and wide, bearing crowded flower spikes to 2 in. long. *C. s. sinensis (C. willmottiae)* has velvety blue-green leaves, hairy leafstalks, and flower clusters to 3 in. long. Its selection 'Spring Purple' has purplish young stems that mature to green. *C. sinensis calvescens (C. platypetala)* has smooth leaf surfaces and largely hairless leafstalks.

C. spicata. SPIKE WINTER HAZEL. Zones 3b–7, 14–17. To 8 ft. high, 10 ft. wide. New growth is purple, maturing to bluish green; 6–12 blossoms in each 1½-in.-long flower cluster.

CORYLUS

FILBERT, HAZELNUT
Betulaceae
DECIDUOUS SHRUBS AND TREES
ZONES 2–9, 14–20, EXCEPT AS NOTED
FULL SUN OR PARTIAL SHADE
REGULAR WATER, EXCEPT AS NOTED

Corylus avellana 'Fusco-rubra'

Although these are usually thought of as trees grown for their edible nuts (see Filbert, Hazelnut), the following make pleasing ornamentals. The plants have separate female and male flowers. Female blossoms are inconspicuous; male ones are showy, appearing in pendent catkins on bare branches in winter or early spring. Leaves are roundish to oval, with toothed margins. Thin branches as needed in late winter; remove suckers when you see them.

Oregon currently prohibits the planting of all *Corylus* species in home gardens, in an effort to stop the spread of eastern filbert blight. Though Western native *C. cornuta californica* (described below) is blight resistant, it too is banned because of difficulty in distinguishing it from blight-prone *C. avellana.* Before planting any of these trees, check to see if the ban is still in effect.

C. avellana. EUROPEAN FILBERT. Shrub. To 10–15 ft. high and wide. One of the species grown commercially for nuts. The following are widely grown ornamental varieties.

'Contorta'. HARRY LAUDER'S WALKING STICK. Rounded to 8–10 ft. tall and wide. Grown for fantastically gnarled and twisted branches and twigs, revealed after its 2–2½-in. leaves turn yellow and drop in autumn. Branches are used in flower arrangements. Plants are almost always grafted, so suckers arising from the base below the graft should be removed; they won't have contorted form.

'Fusco-rubra' ('Atropurpurea'). Grows to 10–15 ft. high and wide, with 3–4-in., reddish purple leaves.

C. colurna. TURKISH HAZEL. Tree. Zones 2b–9, 14–20. From southeast Europe into western Asia. Pyramidal in form; usually 40–50 ft. (possibly to 75 ft.) tall and about half as wide, with leaves to 6 in. long. Can be grown as a single- or multitrunked tree. Flaking, mottled bark provides winter interest. Produces small clusters of edible nuts. Flourishes in areas with hot summers and cold winters. Attractive tree in its own right, and a parent (with *C. avellana*) of hybrids called trazels. Quite drought tolerant once established.

C. cornuta californica. WESTERN HAZELNUT. Shrub. Native to damp slopes below 7,000-ft. elevation, northern Coast Ranges and Sierra Nevada of California, north to British Columbia. Open, multistemmed, to 5–12 ft. high and wide. Roundish, somewhat hairy, coarsely toothed, 1½–3-in. leaves turn bright yellow in fall. Small nuts with flavorful kernels are enveloped in a leafy husk with a long, attenuated beak.

C. maxima. Shrub or tree. Zones 2b–9, 14–17. Native to southeastern Europe. One of the species grown commercially for nuts. Suckering shrub to 12–15 ft. high and wide; can be trained as a small tree. Most widely grown ornamental form is 'Purpurea', with rich dark purple leaves to 6 in. long and heavily purple-tinted male catkins. Leaf color fades to green in hot climates.

CORYMBIA. See EUCALYPTUS

CORYNABUTILON vitifolium. See ABUTILON vitifolium

CORYNOCARPUS laevigata

NEW ZEALAND LAUREL
Corynocarpaceae
EVERGREEN SHRUB OR TREE
ZONES 16, 17, 20–24; H1, H2; BEST IN ZONES 17, 24, H1, H2
FULL SUN OR PARTIAL SHADE
REGULAR WATER
FRUIT IS EXTREMELY POISONOUS IF INGESTED

Corynocarpus laevigata

Handsome, upright, 20–40 ft. high, 5–15 ft. wide. Beautiful oblong, dark green, very glossy, leathery leaves, to 7 in. long by 2 in. wide. (Leaves of 'Variegata' have a showy yellow border.) Flowers noticeable but of no importance—tiny, whitish, in 3–8-in.-long upright clusters. Orange, oblong fruit to 1 in. long. Good in containers. Slow growing; keeps attractive form for years. Needs only minimal pruning. Use as screen or large hedge, background. Good in sheltered areas, entryways, beneath overhangs. Has naturalized in Hawaii.

CORYPHANTHA vivipara

Cactaceae
CACTUS
ZONES 1–24; OR INDOORS
FULL SUN; BRIGHT SUNNY WINDOW
LITTLE TO REGULAR WATER

Coryphantha vivipara

Native from Alberta to north Texas, west to Arizona, Utah, Nevada, and deserts of California. Has single or clustered globular, 2-in. bodies covered with little knobs bearing white spines. Showy pink to purple flowers to 2 in. long. Wide spreading. One of the hardiest cacti; subspecies from the coldest zones will take temperatures far below zero. Also thrives as a houseplant; cut back on moisture during winter. Usually sold as *Mammillaria vivipara.*

COSMOS

Asteraceae (Compositae)
PERENNIALS AND ANNUALS
ZONES 1–24, EXCEPT AS NOTED
FULL SUN
MODERATE WATER

Cosmos bipinnatus

Native to tropical America, mostly Mexico. Showy summer- and fall-blooming plants, open and branching in habit, with bright green divided leaves and daisylike flowers in many colors and forms (single, double, crested, and frilled). Heights vary from 2½ to 8 ft. Use for mass color in borders or background, or as filler among shrubs. Useful in arrangements if flowers are cut just after they open and placed immediately in deep, cool water. Sow seed in open ground where plants are to grow or set out transplants from spring to summer. Plant in not-too-rich soil. Plants self-sow freely, attract birds.

C. atrosanguineus. CHOCOLATE COSMOS. Perennial from tuberous roots. Zones 4–9, 14–24. Where winters are colder, dig and store as for dahlias. Grows 2–2½ ft. tall, 1½ ft. wide, with coarsely cut foliage. Blooms in late summer and fall, with deep brownish red, nearly 2-in.-wide flowers with a strong perfume of chocolate (or vanilla). Attractive companion for silvery-foliaged plants. Provide well-drained soil. Winter mulch is prudent in all but mildest regions (where plant tends to be rather short lived).

C. bipinnatus. Annual. Heights up to 8 ft., widths to 1½–2½ ft. Blossoms are 3–4 in. wide, with tufted yellow centers and rays in white and shades of pink, rose, lavender, purple, or crimson. Among the many types are 3–4-ft.-tall 'Candystripe', with white-and-rose flowers; 'Picotee', to 2½ ft. high, white flowers edged red; Sensation strain, 3–6 ft. tall, including 'Dazzler' (crimson) and 'Radiance' (rose with red center); and Seashell, to 3 ft. tall, grown for quilled ray flowers that look like long, slender cones. Sonata is a dwarf strain 1½–2 ft. high; 'Sweet Dreams' reaches 3 ft. tall and has pale pink to white blossoms with rose centers; Versailles strain, bred for cut flowers, reaches 3½ ft. and bears its blossoms on long, strong stems.

C. sulphureus. YELLOW COSMOS. Annual. To 7 ft. tall, 1½–2½ ft. wide, with yellow-centered, yellow or orange-yellow single flowers. Tends to become weedy looking at end of season. Two 3–4-ft.-tall, semidouble-flowering strains are Bright Lights, with 3½-in. flowers in yellow, gold, orange, and orange red; and Klondike strain, with 2-in. flowers ranging from scarlet orange to yellow. Dwarf Klondike or Sunny strain is 1½ ft. tall, bears 1½-in. flowers. Foot-tall semidouble bloomers include Ladybird mix, with 2½-in. scarlet, yellow, and orange flowers; and 'Sunny Red', with orange-red blooms.

COSTMARY. See CHRYSANTHEMUM balsamita

COTINUS

SMOKE TREE

Anacardiaceae

DECIDUOUS SHRUBS OR TREES

ZONES 2–24

FULL SUN

MODERATE WATER

Cotinus coggygria 'Royal Purple'

Unusual and colorful shrub-trees creating broad, urn-shaped mass usually as wide as high. Naturally multistemmed, but can be trained to a single trunk. Common name derived from dramatic puffs of "smoke" from fading flowers: as the tiny greenish blooms wither, they send out elongated stalks clothed in a profusion of fuzzy lavender-pink hairs.

Plants are at their best under stress in poor or rocky soil. In cultivated gardens, give them fast drainage and avoid overly wet conditions. Resistant to oak root fungus. For another plant with the common name "smoke tree," see *Psorothamnus spinosa*.

C. coggygria. Native from southern Europe to central China. Typically 12–15 ft. high and wide, though it may eventually reach 25 ft. The roundish, 1½–3-in. leaves are bluish green in the species, but purple-leafed types are more commonly grown. Leaves of 'Nordine' ('Nordine Red') and 'Purpureus' emerge purple and gradually turn green; 'Notcutt's Variety', 'Royal Purple', and 'Velvet Cloak' hold their purple color through most of the summer. Those with purple foliage have richer purple "smoke puffs" than the species. 'Pink Champagne' is a green-leafed selection with pinkish tan puffs. Leaves of all types change in fall, taking on colors ranging from yellow to orange red.

C. 'Grace'. Hybrid between *C. coggygria* and *C. obovatus.* To 15 ft. tall and wide, with blue-green foliage shaded purple, large deep pink puffs. Orange and purple-red fall foliage.

C. obovatus. From eastern U.S. To 20–30 ft. tall and wide. Bluish to dark green leaves turn yellow, orange, and reddish purple in fall.

COTONEASTER

Rosaceae

EVERGREEN, SEMIEVERGREEN, DECIDUOUS SHRUBS

ZONES VARY BY SPECIES

FULL SUN, EXCEPT AS NOTED

LITTLE TO MODERATE WATER

Cotoneaster glaucophyllus

Native to China, Himalayas, northern India. Plants range from low types used as ground covers to small, stiffly upright shrubs to tall (25-ft.) shrubs of fountainlike growth with graceful, arching branches. White or pinkish springtime flowers resembling tiny single roses are pretty because of their abundance, though not especially showy. Berries (typically red or orange red) follow the blossoms in fall and winter. All cotoneasters grow vigorously and thrive with little or no maintenance. In fact, they look better and produce better crops of berries if planted on dry slopes (where they can reduce erosion) or in poor soil rather than in rich, moist garden soil.

While some medium and tall growers can be sheared, they look best when allowed to maintain natural fountain shapes. Prune only to enhance graceful arch of branches. Keep medium growers looking young by pruning out portion of oldest wood each year. Prune ground covers to remove dead or awkward branches. Give flat growers room to spread. Don't plant near walk or drive where branch ends will need stubbing.

Cotoneasters are useful, if not striking, shrubs and can be good looking in the proper setting. Some are especially attractive in form and branching pattern *(C. congestus, C. horizontalis),* while some others *(C. lacteus, C. microphyllus)* are notable for colorful fruit that is long lasting if birds don't get it. Trailing varieties make excellent ground covers. Low horizontal kinds die out in desert heat.

C. acutifolius. PEKING COTONEASTER. Deciduous. Zones A1–A3; 1–3. To 10 ft. tall and as wide, with glossy green foliage turning red in fall. Fruit is black. Useful as hedge or screen.

C. adpressus praecox. Deciduous. Zones 2–24. To 1½ ft. tall, 6 ft. wide, with shiny leaves turning maroon red in fall and a profusion of bright red, ½-in. fruit. Bank or ground cover. Takes some shade. *C. adpressus* is similar, somewhat smaller.

C. apiculatus. CRANBERRY COTONEASTER. Deciduous. Zones A3; 2–24. Best in cold-winter climates. Dense grower to 3 ft. tall, 6 ft. wide, with small, round leaves turning deep red in autumn. Clustered fruits about the size of large cranberries. Can take some shade. Use as bank cover, hedge, background planting. 'Tom Thumb' is a miniature mound 4–6 in. high, 10 in. wide.

C. congestus (C. microphyllus glacialis). PYRENEES COTONEASTER. Evergreen. Zones 3b–24. Slow grower reaches to 3 ft. tall and as wide, with dense, downward-curving branches and tiny dark green leaves. Plant produces small, bright red fruit. Use in containers, in rock gardens, and above walls.

C. dammeri (C. humifusus). BEARBERRY COTONEASTER. Evergreen. Zones 2–24. Fast, prostrate growth to 8 in. high, 10 ft. wide. Branches root along ground. Leaves are bright glossy green, fruit bright red. 'Coral Beauty' is 6 in. tall; 'Eichholz' grows 10–12 in. high, shows a scattering of red-orange leaves in fall; 'Lowfast' is 1 ft. high; 'Skogsholmen' grows 1½ ft. tall. 'Streib's Findling' (which may be a hybrid with *C. procumbens* or a selection of that species) grows 4–6 in. high, has dark bluish green foliage. All are good ground covers in sun or partial shade and can drape over walls, cascade down slopes.

C. divaricatus. SPREADING COTONEASTER. Deciduous. Zones 1–24. Stiff growth to 6 ft. tall and wide. Dark green leaves closely set on branches turn orange red in fall. Egg-shaped, bright red fruits are ½ in. long. Informal hedge, screen, bank planting.

C. franchetii. Evergreen. Zones 3b–9, 14–24. Arching growth to 10 ft. tall, 6–9 ft. wide. Leaves are grayish green when new, maturing to bright green; undersides are fuzzy. Pink-tinged white flowers in clusters of up to 20 are followed by orange-red berries.

C. glaucophyllus. Evergreen. Zones 11–14, 18–20. To 6–8 ft. tall and broad, with gracefully arching branches clothed in gray-green foliage. Dense clusters of white flowers are followed by dark red berries. Attractive in shrub beds or as informal hedge.

C. horizontalis. ROCK COTONEASTER. Deciduous. Zones A3; 2b–11, 14–24. Can be 2–3 ft. tall, 15 ft. wide, with stiff horizontal branches and many branchlets set in herringbone pattern. Leaves are small, roundish, bright green; turn orange and red before falling. Leafless period may be brief. Showy red fruit. Effective when given enough room to spread; ugly when branches must be cut short to accommodate traffic. Fine bank cover or low traffic barrier. 'Variegatus' has leaves edged in white. *C. h. perpusillus* is smaller, more compact.

Cotoneaster horizontalis

C. lacteus (C. parneyi). Evergreen. Zones 4–24. Graceful, arching habit to 8 ft. or taller, 10 ft. or wider, with 2-in. leaves that are dark green above, whitish green underneath. White flowers in 2–3-in. clusters followed by a heavy crop of long-lasting red fruit. Best as informal hedge, screen, or espalier. Can be clipped as formal hedge, but form suffers.

Cotoneaster lacteus

C. microphyllus. ROCKSPRAY COTONEASTER. Evergreen. Zones A3; 2–9, 14–24. Its horizontal branches trail and root, forming a mass 6 ft. across; secondary branches grow erect to 2–3 ft. Leaves are very small (⅓ in.), dark green, gray beneath. Fruit is rosy red. *C. m. thymifolius,* 2–3 ft. high and wide, has even tinier leaves, with edges rolled under. Both are effective in rock gardens or on banks. 'Cooperi', a miniature mound-forming selection to 1 ft. across, is a good rock garden plant.

C. multiflorus. Deciduous. Zones 1–12, 14–21. To 6–10 ft. tall, 12–15 ft. wide, with graceful arching and trailing branches. Let grow as spreading shrub or train as small tree. Dark green leaves are 2½ in. long. Showy clusters of white flowers, pinkish red fruits.

C. salicifolius. WILLOWLEAF COTONEASTER. Evergreen or semi-evergreen. Zones 3b–24. Shrub to 15–18 ft. tall and wide, with narrow, dark green leaves 1–3½ in. long and bright red fruits. Graceful screening or background plant but can be invasive. Some shade in low desert.

Better known are the trailing forms used as ground cover. 'Emerald Carpet' is 12–15 in. tall, to 8 ft. wide, with compact habit and small leaves. 'Herbstfeuer' ('Autumn Fire') grows 2–3 ft. high and up to 8 ft. wide. 'Repens' is similar in appearance; it is sometimes grafted to a tall stem of some other cotoneaster species and used as a weeping tree.

C. × watereri. Evergreen. Zones 4–9, 14–24. A group of large hybrids (to 25 ft. tall and wide) that resemble haystacks. Leaves to about 4 in. long; large clusters of long-lasting fruit. Examples are 'Cornubia' and 'John Waterer', both with red fruit, and 'Rothschildianus', with bright yellow fruit.

COTTONWOOD. See POPULUS

COTYLEDON

Crassulaceae

SUCCULENT SHRUBS

ZONES VARY BY SPECIES; OR INDOORS

BEST IN LIGHT SHADE; SUNNY SPOT

LITTLE TO MODERATE WATER

Cotyledon orbiculata

South African natives vary in size and appearance. Easily grown from cuttings and handsome in containers, raised beds, or open ground beds.

C. orbiculata. Zones 12, 13, 16, 17, 21–24. To 3 ft. tall, 2 ft. wide. Opposing pairs of fleshy leaves are 2–3 in. long, rounded, gray green to nearly white, narrowly edged red. Green-leafed forms are available. Flower stems rise above plant and carry clusters of orange, bell-shaped, drooping flowers in summer. Good landscaping shrub in mild climates and well-drained soils. Splendid container plant.

C. undulata. Zones 17, 23, 24. Striking 1½-ft. plant with broad, thick leaves dusted with white powder. Wavy leaf edges. Orange, clustered flowers in spring and early summer. Overhead watering washes off powder.

COWANIA mexicana. See PURSHIA mexicana

COWBERRY. See VACCINIUM vitis-idaea

COYOTE BRUSH, DWARF. See BACCHARIS pilularis

COYOTE MINT. See MONARDELLA

CRABAPPLE

Rosaceae

DECIDUOUS FRUIT TREES

ZONES A1–A3; 1–9, 11–21

FULL SUN

REGULAR WATER DURING FRUIT DEVELOPMENT

Crabapple

Crabapple is a small, usually tart apple, typically used for jelly and pickling. For the many kinds grown for their springtime flowers and small, typically inedible, colorful fruit, see flowering crabapple, described under *Malus.*

Of the crabapple varieties grown for fruit, one of the most popular is 'Transcendent', with 2-in., red-cheeked yellow crabapples that ripen in summer. Others include 'Centennial' and 'Dolgo', both with 1½-in. fruit; that of 'Centennial' is sweet. The red-fruited 'Maypole' is a newer columnar dwarf crabapple variety. 'Rescue' and 'Trailman' are very hardy apple-crabapple hybrids that can be eaten fresh or cooked. To fruit well, crabapple trees need about 600 hours of temperatures at 45°F/7°C or lower. In coldest areas, crabapples should be grafted onto hardy rootstocks (for more information, see Apple).

CRAB CACTUS. See SCHLUMBERGERA truncata

CRAMBE

Brassicaceae (Cruciferae)

PERENNIALS

ZONES A2, A3; 2–9, 14–17

FULL SUN OR LIGHT SHADE

REGULAR WATER

Crambe cordifolia

Cabbage relatives; both are ornamental, one edible. They produce large, smooth blue-green leaves like those of cabbage and large, loose heads of small, honey-scented, white flowers in summer. Leaves turn yellow and fade after bloom, leaving an empty space which can be planted with annuals. Watch out for cabbage worms on foliage.

C. cordifolia. From the Caucasus. Forms a 2–3-ft. mound of long-stalked, 1–3-ft.-long leaves. Intricately branched flowering stems bear huge, billowing cloud of blossoms. When in bloom, it may occupy a space 6 ft. high, 4–6 ft. wide.

C. maritima. SEA KALE. From coastal northern Europe; naturalized on the Oregon coast. To 2 ft. tall and wide, with blue-green leaves a foot wide. In Europe (but apparently not in the U.S.), plants are blanched in late winter or early spring by covering with pots or a deep mulch; the pale sprouts are harvested like asparagus. Grow from seed.

CRANBERRY BUSH. See VIBURNUM trilobum

CRANESBILL. See ERODIUM reichardii, GERANIUM

CRAPE MYRTLE. See LAGERSTROEMIA indica

CRASPEDIA globosa

DRUMSTICKS

Asteraceae (Compositae)

PERENNIAL

ZONES 8, 9, 14–24; ANNUAL IN OTHER ZONES

FULL SUN

REGULAR WATER

Craspedia globosa

Odd, attractive, offbeat Australian daisy. Silvery leaves form 8–12-in.-wide clumps, send up 2-ft. stalks, each topped by a 1-in. globe of tiny yellow flowers. Bloom may occur at any time of year. Flowers are useful, fresh or dry, in arrangements.

CRASSULA

Crassulaceae

SUCCULENT PERENNIALS

ZONES 8, 9, 12–24, EXCEPT AS NOTED; OR INDOORS

FULL SUN, EXCEPT AS NOTED; BRIGHT LIGHT

LITTLE TO NO WATER

Crassula ovata

Most are from South Africa. All have succulent foliage, and many have strange geometric forms. Need good drainage. May not survive winter without overhead protection in Zones 8, 9, 12–15, 18–21. To cope with extreme summer heat in Zones 12 and 13, grow in pots or coolest sites (such as a northern exposure).

C. arborescens. A shrubby, heavy-branched plant much like jade plant *(C. ovata),* but with gray-green, red-edged, red-dotted leaves. Produces summer flowers (usually seen only on old plants) that are star shaped, white aging to pink. Good change of pace from jade plant; smaller and slower growing.

C. capitella thyrsiflora (C. corymbulosa). To 6–30 in. high and a little wider than tall. Slightly branched, with rosettes of long, triangular, fleshy leaves; leaves are dark red when plant is grown in intense sunlight and poor soil. Tiny white flowers in summer.

C. falcata. Zones 8, 9, 12–24; H1, H2. Grows to 4 ft. high, 2½ ft. wide. Thick, fleshy, gray-green, sickle-shaped leaves are vertically arranged in two overlapping columns on erect stems. Dense clusters of scarlet flowers are held well above the leaves in late summer.

Crassula falcata

C. lactea. Spreading, semishrubby plant grows 1–2 ft. tall and 3 ft. wide, with fleshy dark green leaves. Bears white flowers in 4–6-in. clusters during fall. Grows in shade, even dense shade. Fine rock garden plant.

C. lycopodioides. Leafy, branching, erect stems to 1 ft. high and wide, closely packed with tiny green leaves in four rows; effect is that of braided chain or of some strange green coral. Very small, inconspicuous greenish flowers. Easy to grow and useful in miniature and dish gardens.

C. 'Morgan's Pink'. Fine miniature hybrid. Densely packed, fleshy leaves in tight cluster to 4 in. high and wide. Big, brushlike clusters of pink flowers are nearly as big as the plant; spring bloom.

C. multicava. Zones 8, 9, 12–24; H1, H2. To 1–1½ ft. high, 3 ft. wide. Dark green, spreading ground cover or hanging plant. Loose clusters of light pink flowers that resemble mosquitoes bloom in late winter and spring. Rampant grower in sun or shade, in any soil.

C. ovata (C. argentea). JADE PLANT. Zones 8, 9, 12–24; H1, H2. Sometimes sold as *C. portulacea.* Top-notch houseplant, large container plant, landscaping shrub in mildest climates. Use only as potted plant in hottest desert regions. Stout trunk, sturdy limbs even on small plants—and plant will stay small in small container. In time, can reach 9 ft. high, half as wide, but is usually smaller. Leaves are thick, oblong, fleshy pads 1–2 in. long, glossy bright green, sometimes with red-tinged edges. 'Crosby's Dwarf' is a low, compact grower; variegated kinds are 'Sunset' (yellow tinged red) and 'Tricolor' (green, white, and pinkish). Clusters of pink, star-shaped flowers bloom in profusion, fall into spring. Good near swimming pools.

C. pyramidalis. Interesting oddity grows to 3–4 in. high and wide; flat, triangular leaves closely packed in four rows give plant a squarish cross section.

C. schmidtii. Mat-forming, spreading plant to 4 in. tall, 1 ft. wide, with long, slender, rich green leaves. Clusters of small dark rose or purplish flowers put on a show in winter and spring. Good choice for pots or rock gardens.

C. tetragona. Upright plants with treelike habit, 1–2 ft. high and a little narrower. Leaves narrow, 1 in. long. Inconspicuous white flowers. Widely used in dish gardens to suggest miniature pine trees.

Crassulaceae. This large family of usually herbaceous (rarely shrubby) plants is familiar through *Sedum, Sempervivum,* and a host of other popular succulents. Leaves are often in rosettes, as in the familiar hen and chicks *(Echeveria).*

FOR GROWING SYMBOL EXPLANATIONS
PLEASE SEE PAGE 161

CRATAEGUS

HAWTHORN

Rosaceae

DECIDUOUS TREES

ZONES 2–12, 14–17, EXCEPT AS NOTED

FULL SUN

MODERATE WATER

Crataegus laevigata

These members of the rose family are known for clusters of pretty, usually white flowers after leaf-out in spring and for showy fruit resembling tiny apples in summer and fall (and often into winter). Typically multitrunked, with thorny branches that need some pruning to thin out excess twiggy growth. Many hawthorns produce water sprouts, which should be pruned out. Attract bees, birds.

Hawthorns will grow in any soil as long as it is well drained. It's best to grow them under somewhat austere conditions, since good soil, regular moisture, and fertilizer promote succulent new growth that is particularly susceptible to fireblight. The disease makes entire branches die back quickly; for controls, see page 665. Aphids and scale are potential pests.

C. ambigua. RUSSIAN HAWTHORN. Zones 1–10, 14. Native to southeastern Russia, Turkey, Iran. Extremely cold hardy. To 15–25 ft. tall and as wide or wider. Vase-shaped form and twisting branches give attractive silhouette. Leaves to 2½ in. long, deeply cut. Profuse small red fruit.

C. 'Autumn Glory'. Dense, twiggy hybrid grows vigorously to 25 ft. with 15-ft. spread. Dark green leaves similar to those of *C. laevigata* but more leathery. Very large, glossy, bright red fruit, autumn into winter. Highly susceptible to fireblight.

C. crus-galli. COCKSPUR THORN. Native to eastern U.S. and Canada. Zones 1–12, 14–17. To 20–30 ft. high, 20–35 ft. wide. Stiff thorns to 3 in. long. Smooth-textured, tooth-edged leaves are glossy dark green, turning orange to red in fall. Dull orange-red fruit. *C. c. inermis* is a thornless variety.

C. laevigata (C. oxyacantha). ENGLISH HAWTHORN. Zones A2, A3; 2–12, 14–17. Native to Europe and North Africa. To 18–25 ft. high, 15–20 ft. wide. Leaves are similar to those of *C. monogyna* but have toothed lobes. Best known through its varieties, among them 'Paul's Scarlet', with clusters of double rose to red flowers; 'Double White' and 'Double Pink', double-flowered forms that set little fruit; and 'Crimson Cloud' ('Superba'), with white-centered, bright red single flowers and vivid red fruit. All have toothed, lobed, 2-in. leaves that lack good fall color. In Northwest, susceptible to a leaf spot fungus that can defoliate trees in late spring to early summer.

C. × lavallei (C. carrierei). CARRIERE HAWTHORN. Zones 3–12, 14–21. To 25 ft. with 15–20-ft. spread. More erect and open branching than other hawthorns, with less twiggy growth. Dark green, leathery, toothed leaves are 2–4 in. long, turn bronze red after first sharp frost and hang on well into winter. Loose clusters of ¾-in. orange to red fruit last all winter. Fruit makes a mess on walks.

C. mollis. DOWNY HAWTHORN. Zones 1–12, 14–17. Native to central North America. Big, broad tree to 30 ft. tall, 35 ft. wide; looks like mature maple tree. Lobed, toothed leaves to 4 in. long, covered with down. Red, 1-in.-wide fruit is also downy; it doesn't last very long on tree but has value in jelly making.

C. monogyna. Zones 1–12, 14–17. Native to Europe, North Africa, western Asia. Classic hawthorn of English countryside for hedges and boundary plantings. Represented in Western nurseries mainly by upright variety 'Stricta', 30 ft. tall and 8 ft. wide. Plant 5 ft. apart for dense, narrow screen. Leaves 2 in. long, with three to seven deep, smooth-edged lobes. Clusters of small red fruit are rather difficult to see.

C. oxyacantha. See C. laevigata

C. phaenopyrum (C. cordata). WASHINGTON THORN. Native to southeastern U.S. Moderate growth to 25 ft. with 20-ft. spread. Graceful, open limb structure. Glossy, 2–3-in.-long leaves with three to five sharp-pointed lobes (like some maples); foliage turns beautiful orange, scarlet, or purplish in fall. Shiny red fruit hangs on well into winter. More graceful and delicate than other hawthorns, preferred street or lawn tree. One of the least prone to fireblight.

C. pinnatifida. Native to northeastern Asia. To 20 ft. high, 10–12 ft. wide. Leaves lobed like those of *C. laevigata* but bigger and thicker; turn red in fall. Slightly smaller fruit than that of *C.* ×*lavallei.*

C. 'Toba'. Zones A3; 1–10. Canadian hybrid with great cold tolerance. To 20 ft. tall and a bit wider. Leaves similar to those of *C.* ×*lavallei.* White flowers age to pink. Sparse crop of large fruit.

C. viridis. GREEN HAWTHORN. Native to eastern U.S. To 25–30 ft. high and wide, with broad, spreading crown. Leaves turn yellowish in fall; they aren't showy. Clustered white flowers are followed by red fruit. 'Winter King' is vase shaped, with silvery stems and larger red fruit that lasts all winter; it's an attractive and trouble-free hawthorn.

CREAM BUSH. See HOLODISCUS discolor

CREEPING BENT. See AGROSTIS stolonifera

CREEPING BUTTERCUP. See RANUNCULUS repens 'Pleniflorus'

CREEPING JENNY. See LYSIMACHIA nummularia

CREEPING WIRE VINE. See MUEHLENBECKIA axillaris

CREEPING ZINNIA. See SANVITALIA procumbens

CREOSOTE BUSH. See LARREA tridentata

CRESS, GARDEN

Brassicaceae (Cruciferae)

ANNUAL

ALL ZONES

FULL SUN OR PARTIAL SHADE

REGULAR TO AMPLE WATER

Garden Cress

Sometimes called pepper grass; tastes like watercress. Easy to grow as long as weather is cool. Sow seed as early in spring as possible. Plant in rich, moist soil. Make rows 1 ft. apart; thin plants to 3 in. apart (eat thinnings). Cress matures fast; make successive sowings every 2 weeks up to middle of May. Where frosts are mild, sow through fall and winter. Try growing garden cress in shallow pots of soil or planting mix in sunny kitchen window. It sprouts in a few days, can be harvested (with scissors) in 2 to 3 weeks. Or grow it by sprinkling seeds on pads of wet cheesecloth; keep damp until harvest in 2 weeks.

CRINODENDRON

Elaeocarpaceae

EVERGREEN SHRUBS OR TREES

ZONES VARY BY SPECIES

FULL SUN

AMPLE WATER

Crinodendron patagua

Little-known evergreen shrub-trees from Chile with leathery leaves, somewhat stiff growth habit, and attractive flowers. Thrive in wet spots; take regular lawn watering but should be watered deeply once a month to encourage deep rooting. Need good drainage.

C. hookerianum. Zones 5, 6, 16, 17. To 12–15 ft. tall and about as wide. Stiff branches clothed with narrow, sharply toothed leaves; in late spring or early summer, drooping, 1-in.-long red flowers open from buds resembling cherries. Easy to root from cuttings but hard to raise to maturity. Needs cool summers, high humidity. Spider mites are a constant problem.

C. patagua (C. dependens, Tricuspidaria dependens). LILY-OF-THE-VALLEY TREE. Zones 14–24. Somewhat like evergreen oak in general appearance; sometimes called flowering oak. To 25 ft. tall and almost as wide, with upright branching and a rounded crown. Leaves 2½ in. long, dark green above, gray green beneath, with irregular toothed edges. Bears hundreds of ¾-in.-long, bell-shaped white flowers in summer, sometimes into fall. Blossoms are followed by attractive cream-and-red seed capsules that drop and can be messy on paving. Tends to be shrubby; or some branches may turn down while others stick up. Early staking and pruning are important in training as tree. Prune any time to thin out brushy growth in center and remove branches that hang down. For another lily-of-the-valley tree, see *Clethra arborea.*

CRINUM and ×AMARCRINUM

Liliaceae

PERENNIALS FROM BULBS

ZONES 8, 9, 12–24, H1, H2, EXCEPT AS NOTED; OR INDOORS

SOME SHADE IN HOTTEST CLIMATES; BRIGHT FILTERED LIGHT

REGULAR TO AMPLE WATER

ALL PARTS ARE POISONOUS IF INGESTED

Crinum ×*powellii*

Native to many warm and tropical parts of the world. Lush foliage and lilylike flowers of impressive size. Each bulb tapers to an elongated, stemlike neck, from which radiate long, broad, strap-shaped leaves. Evergreen in mild-winter climates if given year-round moisture. Thick stems to 4 ft. or taller rise from the foliage, each bearing a cluster of long-stalked flowers. Blossoms resemble those of belladonna lily *(Amaryllis belladonna),* but they're twice as big and open out a bit wider. Many are highly fragrant; colors include white and many shades of pink, from light to dark. Most bloom in spring or summer; flowering goes on all year in Hawaii.

Bulbs generally are available year-round, but spring and fall are best times to plant. Amend soil with plenty of humus. Set bulbs 2–4 ft. apart, with tops of necks even with soil surface. Divide infrequently. Protect from snails and slugs. In colder part of range, mulch heavily in winter; move plants in containers to a frostproof location. These plants (especially *C.* ×*powellii* and ×*Amarcrinum*) are grown as houseplants in most areas.

C. asiaticum. SPIDER LILY, GRAND CRINUM, ST. JOHN'S LILY. Zones 20–24. From Southeast Asia. Can form a mass 4–6 ft. high, 7 ft. wide. Clusters of large, spidery-looking, fragrant white flowers, 6–8 in. across. Tolerant of poor soils, salt, drought, light shade.

C. augustum. QUEEN EMMA LILY. Zones 20–24. From Mauritius and the Seychelles. Similar to *C. asiaticum* but slightly larger, with wider white flower segments and dark red markings.

C. bulbispermum (C. longifolium). From South Africa. Long, narrow, twisting gray-green leaves tend to lie on the ground. Fragrant flowers are deep pink.

C. 'Ellen Bosanquet'. Broad bright green leaves. Fragrant flowers are deep rose, nearly red.

C. moorei. From South Africa. Large (6–8-in.-wide) bulbs with stemlike necks to 1 ft. or longer. Long, thin, wavy-edged bright green leaves. Fragrant, bell-shaped flowers typically are soft pink, though colors run from white to pinkish red.

C. ×**powellii.** Resembles *C. moorei* (one of its parents) but has fragrant flowers on shorter (2-ft.) stems. Range of flower colors is similar to that of *C. moorei.* 'Album' is a pure white form, vigorous enough to serve as a tall ground cover in shade.

×**Amarcrinum memoria-corsii (Crinodonna corsii).** Hybrid between *Amaryllis belladonna* and *C. moorei.* Resembles *Crinum* in growth habit and foliage, but its soft pink, very fragrant flowers look more like those of *Amaryllis belladonna,* with narrower funnel shape than blooms of most crinums.

CROCOSMIA

Iridaceae

PERENNIALS FROM CORMS

ZONES VARY BY SPECIES; OR DIG AND STORE

SOME SHADE IN HOTTEST CLIMATES

REGULAR WATER DURING GROWTH AND BLOOM

Crocosmia ×crocosmiiflora

Native to tropical and southern Africa. Formerly called tritonia; related to freesia, ixia, sparaxis. Sword-shaped leaves in basal clumps. Small orange, red, or yellow flowers bloom in summer (spring in hottest areas) on branched stems. Useful for splashes of garden color and for cutting.

Plant in well-drained, enriched soil; set corms 2 in. deep, 3 in. apart. Where winter temperatures remain above 10°F/–12°C, needs no winter protection. Where lows range from 10 to –5°F/12 to –21°C, provide winter mulch. In colder areas, dig and store over winter. Divide clumps only when vigor, flower quality begin to decline.

C. ×crocosmiiflora (Tritonia crocosmiiflora). MONTBRETIA. Zones 5–24; H1, H2. A favorite for generations, montbretias can still be seen in older gardens where they have spread freely, as though native to those sites, producing orange-crimson flowers 1½–2 in. across on 3–4-ft. stems. Sword-shaped leaves grow to 3 ft. tall, ½–1 in. wide. Many once-common named forms in yellow, orange, cream, and near-scarlet are making a comeback. Good for naturalizing on slopes or in fringe areas. Montbretia has established itself in wild lands throughout the Hawaiian Islands.

C. hybrids. Zones 4–24. Among 2-ft.-high choices are 'Citronella', light yellow flowers with dark eye; 'Emily McKenzie', orange with red eye; and 'Solfatare', bronze foliage and yellow flowers. 'Jenny Bloom' grows 2–3 ft. tall and bears yellow flowers; 'Lucifer' reaches 4 ft. tall, has bright red blossoms.

C. masoniorum. Zones 5–24. Leaves 2½ ft. long, 2 in. wide. Flowers flaming orange to orange scarlet, 1½ in. across, borne in dense, one-sided clusters on 2½–3-ft. stems that arch over at the top. Buds open slowly from base to tip of clusters, and old flowers drop cleanly from stems. Flowers last about 2 weeks when cut.

Crocosmia masoniorum

CROCUS

Iridaceae

PERENNIALS FROM CORMS

ZONES 1–24; BEST IN COLD-WINTER AREAS

FULL SUN DURING BLOOM, LIGHT SHADE AFTER IN HOT CLIMATES

REGULAR WATER DURING GROWTH AND BLOOM

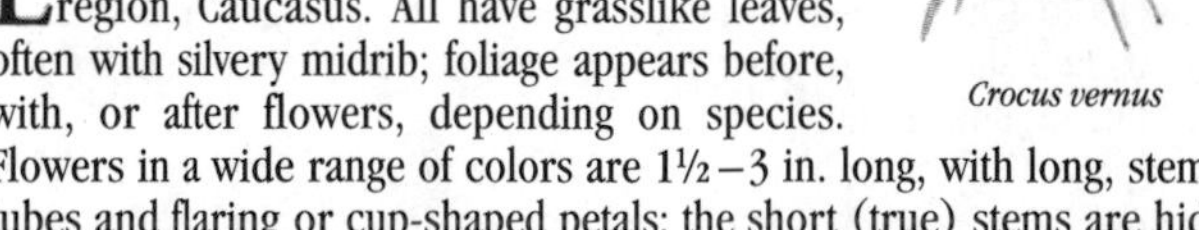

Crocus vernus

Low growers, mainly from Mediterranean region, Caucasus. All have grasslike leaves, often with silvery midrib; foliage appears before, with, or after flowers, depending on species. Flowers in a wide range of colors are 1½–3 in. long, with long, stemlike tubes and flaring or cup-shaped petals; the short (true) stems are hidden underground.

Most crocuses bloom in winter or earliest spring, but some bloom in fall, the flowers rising from bare earth weeks or days after planting. Mass them for best effect. Attractive in rock gardens, between stepping-stones, in containers. Set corms 2–3 in. deep, 3–4 in. apart, in light, porous soil. Protect from gophers. Divide every 3 or 4 years. Won't naturalize where winters are warm.

C. ancyrensis. Small golden yellow flowers in early winter.

C. angustifolius. CLOTH OF GOLD CROCUS. Formerly *C. susianus.* Orange-gold, starlike flowers with dark brown center stripe. Early winter blooming.

C. biflorus. SCOTTISH CROCUS. White flowers with yellow throat, striped purple on the outside. Late winter bloom. Highly variable in the wild; some forms are fall blooming.

C. chrysanthus. Orange-yellow, sweet-scented blooms. Hybrids and selections of species range from white and cream through yellows and blues, often marked with deeper colors. Usually even more free-flowering than *C. vernus,* but with smaller flowers. Spring bloom. Popular varieties include 'Blue Pearl', palest blue; 'Cream Beauty', pale yellow; 'E. P. Bowles', yellow with purple featherings; 'Ladykiller', outside purple edged white, inside white feathered purple; 'Princess Beatrix', blue with yellow center; and 'Snow Bunting', pure white.

C. goulimyi. Plant produces deep lavender-blue flowers during fall. Needs warmth, excellent drainage; tolerates warm winters of Southern California.

C. imperati. Bright lilac inside, buff veined purple outside, saucer shaped. Early spring.

C. korolkowii. Bright yellow to bronze-yellow flowers in late winter. Very cold tolerant.

C. kotschyanus (C. zonatus). Pinkish lavender or lilac flowers in early fall.

C. sativus. SAFFRON CROCUS. Lilac flowers in fall. Interesting rather than showy. Orange-red stigma is true saffron of commerce. To harvest saffron, pluck the stigmas as soon as flowers open, dry them, and store them in glass or plastic vials. Stigmas from a dozen flowers will season a good-size paella or similar dish. To get continued good yield of saffron, divide corms as soon as leaves turn brown; replant in fresh or improved soil. Mark planting site with low-growing ground cover so you won't dig up dormant bulbs.

C. sieberi. Delicate lavender blue with golden throat. One of earliest to bloom in winter.

C. speciosus. Showy blue-violet flowers in early fall. Lavender and mauve varieties available. Fast increase by seed and division. Showiest autumn-flowering crocus.

C. tomasinianus. Slender buds; star-shaped, silvery lavender-blue flowers, sometimes with dark blotch at tips of segments. Blooms very early in the year.

C. vernus. DUTCH CROCUS. Familiar crocus in shades of white, yellow, lavender, and purple, often penciled and streaked. Late winter or early spring bloom. This is the most vigorous crocus (and the only one widely sold in all areas).

CROTALARIA agatiflora

CANARY BIRD BUSH

Fabaceae (Leguminosae)

EVERGREEN SHRUB

ZONES 13, 15–24; H1, H2

FULL SUN OR PARTIAL SHADE

REGULAR WATER

ALL PLANT PARTS ARE POISONOUS IF INGESTED

Crotalaria agatiflora

Native to East Africa. Fast, rank growth to 12 ft. tall and wide unless pruned frequently (should be pruned two or three times a year). Common name is well earned: unique 1½-in. flowers are strung along flower spike (to 14 in. long) like so many chartreuse birds. Blossoms harmonize with most colors. Heaviest bloom in summer or fall, but in frost-free areas it blooms intermittently for 10 months. Foliage is a pleasing gray green, with leaves divided into 3-in.-long leaflets. Recovers quickly after frost damage.

CROTON. See CODIAEUM variegatum 'Pictum'

CROWN IMPERIAL. See FRITILLARIA imperialis

CROWN OF THORNS. See EUPHORBIA milii

CROWN VETCH. See CORONILLA varia

Cruciferae. See Brassicaceae

CRYPTANTHUS zonatus

Bromeliaceae

PERENNIAL

ZONES 17, 23, 24; H1, H2; OR INDOORS

SOME SHADE; BRIGHT INDIRECT LIGHT

MODERATE WATER

Cryptanthus zonatus

Native to Brazil. Bromeliad grown for showy leaves in spreading, low-growing clusters to 1½ ft. wide, usually less. Individual leaves wavy, dark brownish red, banded crosswise with green, brown, or white. Unimportant little white flowers grow among leaves. Pot in equal parts coarse sand, shredded osmunda, and ground bark or peat moss. Most effective in mass or mixed plantings, terrariums.

C. bivittatus is similar to *C. zonatus* in cultural needs and general appearance but has green leaves with lengthwise stripes of creamy white. Many other striped and banded species and hybrids are available from specialists.

CRYPTOMERIA japonica

JAPANESE CRYPTOMERIA

Taxodiaceae

EVERGREEN TREE

ZONES 4–9, 14–24

FULL SUN

REGULAR WATER

Cryptomeria japonica

Graceful conifer, fast growing (3–4 ft. a year) in youth. Eventually skyline tree to 100 ft. tall, 30 ft. wide at base. Straight columnar trunk; thin red-brown bark peels off in strips. Foliage soft bright green to bluish green in growing season, brownish purple in cold weather. Slightly pendulous branches are clothed in ½–1-in.-long, needlelike leaves. Roundish, red-brown cones ¾–1 in. wide. These trees are sometimes used in closely planted groves for a Japanese garden effect. Resistant to oak root fungus.

'Elegans'. PLUME CEDAR, PLUME CRYPTOMERIA. Quite unlike species. Feathery, grayish green, soft-textured foliage turns rich coppery red or purplish in winter. Grows slowly into dense pyramid, 20–60 ft. high, about 20 ft. wide. Trunks on old trees may lean or curve. For Oriental effect, prune out some branches to give tiered look. For most effective display, give it space.

'Lobbii Nana' ('Lobbii'). Upright dwarf grows very slowly to 4 ft. high and wide. Dark green foliage.

'Pygmaea' ('Nana'). DWARF CRYPTOMERIA. Bushy dwarf 1½–2 ft. high, 2½ ft. wide. Dark green, needlelike leaves; twisted branches.

'Tansu'. An extreme dwarf, seldom exceeding 15 in. high and wide.

'Vilmoriniana'. Slow-growing dwarf to 1–2 ft. high and wide. Fluffy gray-green foliage turns bronze during late fall and winter. Rock garden or container plant.

'Yoshino'. Resembles the species but is smaller (to 30–40 ft. tall and 20 ft. wide), with bluish green foliage that takes on reddish tones in winter.

FOR INFORMATION ON SELECTING PLANTS
PLEASE SEE PAGES 64–160

CTENANTHE

Marantaceae

PERENNIALS

ZONES 23, 24; H1, H2; OR INDOORS

PARTIAL SHADE; BRIGHT INDIRECT LIGHT

AMPLE WATER

Ctenanthe compressa

Native to Brazil. Leaves are the big feature; they may be short stalked and set along stems, or long stalked and rising from plant's base only. Insignificant white flowers form under bracts in spikes at ends of branches. Use with other tropical foliage plants such as philodendron, alocasia, tree ferns. Plant in rich, moist soil; feed regularly.

C. 'Burle Marx'. Grows to 2 ft. tall, 1½ ft. wide. Leaves are gray green feathered with dark green on their upper surfaces, maroon undersides; leafstalks are also maroon. Tender and best grown as a houseplant, except in Hawaii.

C. compressa. BAMBURANTA. To 2–3 ft. high, 1½ ft. wide. Leathery leaves are oblong, lopsided, to about 15 in. long, waxy green on top, gray green beneath, held at angle on top of wiry stems. This plant is often sold as *Bamburanta arnoldiana*.

C. lubbersiana (Maranta lubbersiana). To 2½ ft. tall and wide. Yellow, 8-in. leaves with green markings.

C. oppenheimiana. GIANT BAMBURANTA. Compact, branching plant, 3–5 ft. high, 3 ft. wide. Narrow, leathery leaves, dark green banded with silver above, purple beneath, set at angle on downy stalks. 'Tricolor' has showy cream patches with its other colors.

CUCUMBER

Cucurbitaceae

ANNUAL VINE

ALL ZONES

FULL SUN

REGULAR WATER

Cucumber

Each vine needs at least 25 sq. ft., but you can use a fence or trellis to conserve space. Requires warm soil to sprout seeds and warmth for pollination.

There are long, smooth, green, slicing cucumbers; numerous small pickling cucumbers; and roundish, yellow, mild-flavored lemon cucumbers. Novelties include Asian varieties (long, slim, very mild), Armenian cucumber (actually a long, curving, pale green, ribbed melon with cucumber look and mild cucumber flavor), and English greenhouse cucumber. The last type must be grown in greenhouse to avoid pollination by bees, with subsequent loss of form and flavor; when well grown, it's the mildest of all cucumbers. 'Sweet Success' is a mild, seedless cucumber with the flavor and character of a greenhouse cucumber; plant is female, but flowers do not require pollination.

Bush cucumbers—varieties with compact vines—take up little garden space. Burpless varieties resemble hothouse cucumbers in shape and mild flavor but can be grown out-of-doors. Pickling cucumbers should be picked as soon as they have reached the proper size—tiny for sweet pickles (gherkins), larger for dills or pickle slices. They grow too large very quickly.

Plant seeds in sunny spot 1 to 2 weeks after average date of last frost. To grow cucumbers on trellis (the best way to keep them straight), plant seeds 1 in. deep and 1–3 ft. apart and permit main stem to reach top of support. Pick while young to ensure continued production.

Row covers will protect seedlings from slugs, snails, and various insect pests, including cucumber beetles and flea beetles; remove covers when flowering begins so that pollination can occur. Whiteflies are a potential pest late in season; hose off plants regularly or hang yellow sticky traps. Misshapen fruit is usually due to uneven watering or poor pollination; bitter fruit is usually a result of uneven irrigation.

CUCUMBER TREE. See MAGNOLIA acuminata

Cucurbitaceae. The gourd family as seen in Western gardens consists of annual vines with yellow or white flowers and large, fleshy, seedy fruits—cucumbers, gourds, melons, pumpkins, and squash.

CULANTRO. See ERYNGIUM foetidum

CUNNINGHAMIA lanceolata

CHINA FIR
Taxodiaceae
EVERGREEN TREE
ZONES 4–6, 14–21
FULL SUN
MODERATE WATER

Cunninghamia lanceolata

Native to China. Picturesque conifer with heavy trunk; stout, whorled branches; and drooping branchlets. Grows at moderate rate to 30 ft. tall with 20-ft. spread. Stiff, needlelike, sharp-pointed leaves are 1½–2½ in. long, green above, whitish beneath. Brown, 1–2-in. cones are interesting but not profuse. Among palest of needled evergreens in spring and summer; turns red bronze in cold winters. Needs protection from hot, dry wind in summer and cold wind in winter. Becomes less attractive as it ages. Prune out dead branchlets. 'Glauca', with striking gray-blue foliage, is more widely grown and hardier than the species.

CUP-AND-SAUCER. See CAMPANULA medium

CUP-AND-SAUCER VINE. See COBAEA scandens

CUPANIOPSIS anacardioides

CARROT WOOD
Sapindaceae
EVERGREEN TREE
ZONES 16–24; H1, H2
FULL SUN
ANY AMOUNT OF WATER

Cupaniopsis anacardioides

Native to Australia. Slow to moderate growth to 40 ft. tall, 30 ft. wide; glossy dark green leaves divided into six to ten leathery, 4-in.-long leaflets. Tolerates seacoast conditions, heat, drought, poor soil. Generally neat, never chlorotic in appearance. As trees approach maturity, they may produce marble-size, leathery, yellow to orange fruit that splits but does not squash or stain. Some trees fruit heavily enough to be an annoyance, while others never fruit, for reasons not understood. Some feel that young trees selected for unusual vigor and broader-than-usual leaflets will produce less fruit than others; another theory is that trees under stress tend to develop more female flowers, hence more fruit. It is also believed that thinning out the tree every 2 years or so will result in production of young, nonfruiting wood. In its younger years, at least, an attractive, well-behaved tree. Consider underplanting with a ground cover deep enough to swallow the fruit drop. If you do so, be prepared to pull volunteer seedlings when they appear. Many landscape architects feel that the tree's virtues outweigh its faults.

CUP FLOWER. See NIEREMBERGIA

CUPHEA

Lythraceae
EVERGREEN SHRUBS OR WOODY PERENNIALS
ZONES 16–24, H1, H2, EXCEPT AS NOTED; ANNUALS ANYWHERE
FULL SUN OR PARTIAL SHADE
REGULAR WATER

Cuphea ignea

Native to Mexico, Central America. Provide color throughout warm months; use in small beds, as formal edging for borders, along paths, in containers. Flowers attract hummingbirds. Pinch tips of shoots for compact growth; severely cut back older plants in late fall or early spring. Reliably perennial only in frost-free areas, though they may survive light frosts in Zones 16, 17, 21–23. Easy to grow from cuttings. *C. hyssopifolia* and *C. ignea* have both naturalized on Hawaii (Big Island).

C. hyssopifolia. FALSE HEATHER, HAWAIIAN HEATHER, MEXICAN HEATHER. Grows 1–2 ft. tall, to about 2½ ft. wide. Flexible, leafy branchlets clothed in very narrow, ½–¾-in.-long leaves. Tiny flowers (scarcely half as long as leaves) in pink, purple, or white.

C. ignea. CIGAR PLANT. Zones 11–13, 16–24; H1, H2. Leafy, compact plant to 1 ft. or taller, as wide as tall. Narrow dark green leaves, 1–1½ in. long. The flowers explain the "cigar" of the common name: they're tubular, ¾ in. long, bright orange red with white tip and dark ring at end.

C. llavea (C. × purpurea). BAT-FACED CUPHEA. Zones 11–13, 21–24; H1, H2. To 2–3 ft. tall, 3 ft. wide. Leaves to 3 in. long. Red-and-purple, 1½-in.-long flowers are said to look like a bat's face. Occasionally spreads by seed in gardens. Though cultivated in the desert, it is not drought tolerant—in nature, it grows along stream banks in Mexico.

C. micropetala. To 4 ft. tall, 3–4 ft. wide. Arching stems closely set with narrow, 5-in. leaves and topped by a slender, spikelike cluster of 1½-in., bright red flowers tipped with yellow. Deciduous in cold weather.

CUPID'S DART. See CATANANCHE caerulea

CUP-OF-GOLD VINE. See SOLANDRA maxima

Cupressaceae. The cypress family differs from the pine and yew families (Pinaceae, Taxaceae) in having leaves that are usually reduced to scales and in having cones with few scales. Cones may even be berrylike, as in juniper *(Juniperus)*.

× CUPRESSOCYPARIS leylandii

Cupressaceae
EVERGREEN TREE
ZONES 3B–24
FULL SUN
MODERATE TO REGULAR WATER

× Cupressocyparis leylandii

Hybrid between *Chamaecyparis nootkatensis* and *Cupressus macrocarpa.* Grows very fast—from cuttings to 15–20 ft. high in 5 years. Most often planted as quick screening. In gardens, usually reaches 60–70 ft. tall, 8–15 ft. wide; can be pruned into tall (10–15-ft.) hedge but will quickly get away from you without regular maintenance. Long, slender, upright branches with flattened gray-green foliage sprays give youthful trees a narrow, pyramidal form, though they can become open and floppy. Produces small cones composed of scales. Will accept a wide variety of soils and climate conditions; takes strong wind. In warm-summer regions, loses stiff, upright habit and is subject to coryneum canker fungus; may reach only 30–40 ft. tall before dying from the disease (see *Cupressus macrocarpa* for information on this fungus). 'Naylor's Blue' has grayish blue foliage; 'Castlewellan' has golden new growth and narrow, erect habit; 'Emerald Isle' has bright green foliage on a plant 20–25 ft. tall, 6–8 ft. wide.

CUPRESSUS

CYPRESS

Cupressaceae

EVERGREEN TREES

ZONES VARY BY SPECIES

FULL SUN

LITTLE TO MODERATE WATER

Cupressus arizonica

These conifers have tiny scalelike leaves that are closely set on cordlike branches and bear interesting globular, golf ball–size cones made up of shield-shaped scales. Need little pruning.

C. arizonica. ARIZONA CYPRESS. Zones 7–24. Native to central Arizona. To 40 ft. tall, 20 ft. wide. Seedlings variable, with foliage from green to blue gray or silvery. Rough, furrowed bark. *C. a. glabra* (often sold as *C. glabra*) is virtually identical to the species but has smooth cherry red bark. Other forms include 'Blue Pyramid', a dense blue-gray pyramid to 20–25 ft. high; 'Gareei', with silvery blue-green foliage; and compact, symmetrical 'Pyramidalis'. Mass for windbreak or screen.

C. forbesii. TECATE CYPRESS. Zones 8–14, 18–20. Native to coastal mountains of Southern California. Low-branching tree to 10–25 ft. tall and 20 ft. wide, with cherry red bark and green foliage. Very fast growing. In fact, it may get too top heavy for size of root system; keep on the dry side to slow growth, thus lessening likelihood that tree will topple in strong winds. Useful as hedge or screen.

C. macrocarpa. MONTEREY CYPRESS. Best in Zone 17. Native to California's Monterey peninsula. Beautiful tree to 40 ft. or taller, with rich bright green foliage. Narrow and pyramidal in youth, spreading as wide as high as it grows older; picturesque in age, especially in windy coastal conditions. Away from cool coastal winds, it is very subject to coryneum canker fungus, for which there is no cure. Look for foliage that first turns yellow, then deep reddish brown, and falls off slowly. Destroy infected trees. A fast-growing windbreak tree in coastal conditions.

C. sempervirens. ITALIAN CYPRESS. Zones 4–24; H1, H2; best in Zones 8–15, 18–21. Native to southern Europe, western Asia. Species has horizontal branches and dark green foliage, but variants are more often sold. 'Stricta' ('Fastigiata'), columnar Italian cypress, and 'Glauca', blue Italian cypress (blue green in color), are classic Mediterranean landscaping plants; both are dense, narrow trees to 60 ft. high, 5–10 ft. wide at maturity. 'Swane's Golden' is a narrowly columnar form with golden yellow new growth.

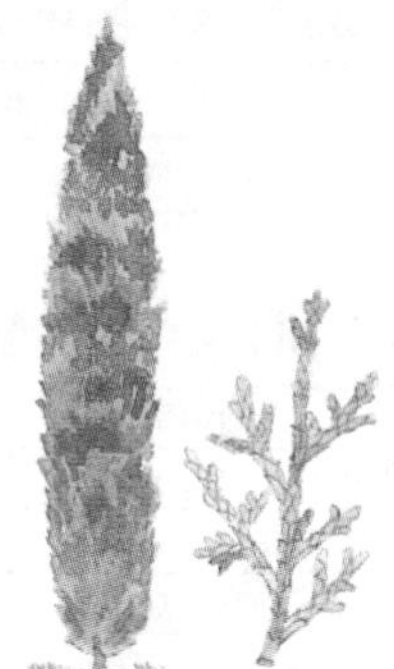

Cupressus sempervirens

CURCUMA alismatifolia

SIAM TULIP

Zingiberaceae

PERENNIAL FROM RHIZOMES

ZONES 14–24; H1, H2; OR DIG AND STORE

FULL SUN OR LIGHT SHADE

AMPLE WATER DURING GROWTH AND BLOOM

Curcuma alismatifolia

From Thailand. Not unlike a tulip in appearance (hence the common name), but it's actually a ginger rather than a tulip. Grows 2 ft. tall, with foliage like small canna leaves. Flowering stem is topped by a cluster of pink, rose, or white bracts that hide tiny flowers. The inflorescence is shaped a bit like a flaring pinecone. Plant in spring, setting rhizomes 1 in. deep, 6 in. apart. Blooms from early summer to early fall. Each blossom lasts for several weeks and is replaced by others as new plants arise from the rhizome. Plant goes dormant in winter. Beyond its hardiness range, dig and store over winter, being careful not to damage the bulbous storage organs on the roots.

C

CURRANT

Grossulariaceae (Saxifragaceae)

DECIDUOUS SHRUB

ZONES A1–A3; 1–6, 15–17

SOME SHADE IN HOTTEST CLIMATES

REGULAR WATER

Currant

Many-stemmed, thornless shrub to 3–5 ft. high and wide, depending on vigor and variety. Attractive lobed, toothed leaves to 3 in. wide drop early in fall, sometimes turning bright red, orange, or yellow first. Drooping clusters of white or yellowish flowers bloom in early spring, followed in summer by fruit used for jellies, jams, preserves. For ornamental relatives, see *Ribes.*

Currant worm can defoliate plants; control with *Bt.* Like other members of *Ribes,* currant may be host to white pine blister rust and is still banned in some areas where white pines grow; check with your Cooperative Extension Office or a local nursery for regulations in your area. Black currant, derived from *R. nigrum* or *R. odoratum* (see descriptions under *Ribes*), is favored host. Rust-immune black currant hybrids include 'Consort', 'Coronet', 'Crusader', and 'Titania'; all have rich, pungent flavor and are good in jams and preserves. Red and white currants, derived from *R. sativum,* are less likely to be hosts to the rust; they are tart flavored and used mainly for jelly. Red-fruited varieties include 'Cherry', 'Jonkheer Van Tets', 'Perfection', 'Red Lake', and 'Wilder'; white types include 'Primus' and 'White Imperial'.

Generally self-fruitful. Do not grow where water or soil is high in sodium. Mulch well. Prune during dormant season. On red and white currants, cut stems older than 3 years to the ground; on black currants, remove stems older than 2 years. Older canes are often darker and peeling.

CUSHION BUSH. See CALOCEPHALUS brownii

CUSHION PINK. See SILENE acaulis

CYATHEA cooperi

AUSTRALIAN TREE FERN

Cyatheaceae

TREE FERN

ZONES 15–24; H1, H2

PARTIAL SHADE IN HOTTEST CLIMATES

REGULAR WATER

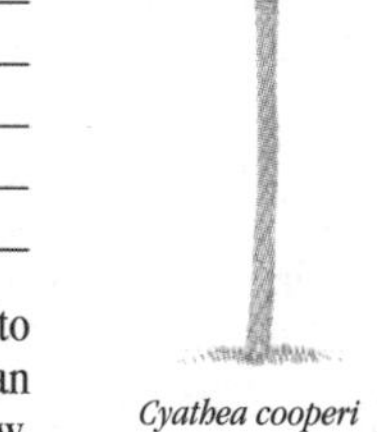

Cyathea cooperi

Fastest growing of the fairly hardy tree ferns (to 20°F/–7°C, but with damage to fronds). To an eventual 20 ft. tall, 12 ft. wide. Starts out as a low, wide clump (can spread from 1 ft. to as much as 6 ft. in a year) before growing upward. Broad, bright green, finely cut fronds. Brownish hairs on leafstalks and leaf undersurfaces can irritate skin; wear long sleeves, hat, and neckcloth when grooming plants. Reasonably certain to survive in sheltered places along coast and in warm coastal valleys of California. Becoming a pest in Hawaiian rain forests. Often sold as *Alsophila australis, A. cooperi,* or *Sphaeropteris cooperi.*

A PRACTICAL GUIDE TO GARDENING
PLEASE SEE PAGES 658–731

Cycadaceae. *Cycas* is the sole genus in this family; closely related plants in the family Zamiaceae are *Dioon* and *Zamia.* Collectively, these plants (all in the order Cycadales) are known as cycads, though the general public may consider them to be types of palms. They are slow-growing evergreen plants with large, firm, palmlike or fernlike leaves and conelike fruit. Most are native to tropical regions. Some are subtropical, and among these, certain ones are hardy enough to grow outdoors in mild-winter climates.

CYCAS

Cycadaceae

CYCADS

ZONES VARY BY SPECIES

PARTIAL SHADE

REGULAR WATER

Cycas revoluta

Neither ferns nor palms, these evergreen plants are primitive, cone-bearing relatives of conifers, excellent for tropical effects. A rosette of dark green, feathery leaves grows from a central point at the top of a single trunk (sometimes several trunks). Eventually as wide as tall. Female plants bear conspicuous, egg-shaped red to orange seeds.

C. circinalis. QUEEN SAGO. Zones 23, 24; H1, H2. Native to Old World tropics. Beautiful specimen plant to 20 ft. tall. Graceful, drooping leaves to 8 ft. long atop unbranched trunk. Protect from frost.

C. revoluta. SAGO PALM. Zones 8–24; H1, H2; hardy to 15°F/–9°C. Native to Japan. As a 2–3-ft.-tall youngster, has an airy, fernlike appearance; with age (grows very slowly to as high as 10 ft.), looks more like a palm. Leaves are 2–3 ft. long (larger on very old plants), divided into many narrow, leathery segments. Tough, tolerant house- or patio plant; also good subject for bonsai.

CYCLAMEN

Primulaceae

PERENNIALS FROM TUBERS

ZONES VARY BY SPECIES

FULL SUN OR PARTIAL SHADE

REGULAR WATER

Cyclamen persicum

Native to Europe, Mediterranean region, Asia. Grown for pretty flowers carried atop attractive clump of basal leaves; blossoms resemble shooting stars or butterflies, typically come in white and shades of pink, rose, red. Most go through near-leafless or leafless dormant period at some time during summer.

Large-flowered florists' cyclamen *(C. persicum)* is most often seen as a container-grown gift plant, though it can be used as a bedding plant in favorable climates. The other species described here are smaller-flowered, hardier plants better adapted to outdoor culture. Use them in rock gardens, in naturalized clumps under trees, or as carpets under camellias, rhododendrons, and large noninvasive ferns; hardy types also grow well under native oaks. All are good container plants if grown out of direct sun.

All cyclamens grow best in fairly rich, porous soil with lots of humus. Plant tubers 6–10 in. apart, ½ in. deep. (Florists' cyclamen is an exception: upper half of tuber should protrude above soil level.) Best planting time for tubers is dormant period in summer—except for florists' cyclamen, which is always sold as a potted plant and can be planted out anytime. Top-dress annually with light application of potting soil with complete fertilizer added (being careful not to cover top of florists' cyclamen tubers). Do not cultivate around roots.

Plants grow readily from seed. Small-flowered hardy species take several years to bloom; older strains of florists' cyclamen need 15 to 18 months from seed, while newer strains can bloom in as little as 7 months. Grown outdoors in open ground, plants often self-sow.

C. ×atkinsii. Zones 4–9, 14–24. Crimson flowers on 4–6-in. stems in winter. Deep green, silver-mottled leaves. There are also varieties with pink or white blooms.

C. cilicium. Zones 3–9, 14–24. Fragrant pale pink flowers with purple blotches on 2–6-in. stems, fall into winter. Leaves are mottled. 'Album' has white blossoms.

C. coum. Zones 2–9, 14–24. Deep crimson rose flowers on 4–6-in. stems in winter and early spring. Round deep green leaves. Varieties with pink or white flowers are available.

C. europaeum. See C. purpurascens

C. hederifolium (C. neapolitanum). Zones 2–9, 14–24. Large light green leaves marbled silver and white. Rose pink flowers bloom on 3–4-in. stems in late summer, early fall. One of the most vigorous and easiest to grow; very reliable in cold-winter climates. Set tubers a foot apart. There is a white-flowered variety.

C. persicum. FLORISTS' CYCLAMEN. Zones 15–24. Original species has 2-in., fragrant, deep to pale pink or white blooms borne on 6-in. stems. Selective breeding has resulted in large-flowered florists' cyclamen (the old favorites) and newer, smaller strains; with rare exceptions, fragrance has disappeared. Plants typically have heart- or kidney-shaped dark green leaves, often with silvery mottling. They bear crimson, red, salmon, purple, pink, or white flowers on 6–8-in. stems from late fall to spring. Good choice for color in place to be occupied by tuberous begonias in summer. Must have shade in warm-summer climates. Plants lose leaves and go dormant in hot weather, but usually survive if drainage is good and soil not waterlogged. Protect from slugs and snails; plants are especially vulnerable because tops of tubers and growing points are exposed.

Dwarf or miniature florists' cyclamens are replicas of standards with half- or three-quarter–size leaves and blossoms. Can bloom in 7 to 8 months from seed. Miniature strains (profuse show of 1½-in. flowers on 6–8-in. plants) include Miracle and Laser, both with fragrant blossoms.

C. purpurascens (C. europaeum). Zones 4–9, 14–24. Distinctly fragrant crimson flowers on 5–6-in. stems, late summer or early fall. Bright green leaves mottled silvery white; almost evergreen.

C. repandum. Zones 4–9, 14–24. Bright crimson flowers with long, narrow petals on 5–6-in. stems in spring. Rich green, ivy-shaped leaves are marbled silver, toothed on edges.

CYDONIA. See CHAENOMELES

CYDONIA oblonga. See QUINCE, FRUITING

CYLINDROPHYLLUM 'Red Spike'. See CEPHALOPHYLLUM 'Red Spike'

CYMBALARIA

Scrophulariaceae

PERENNIALS

ZONES 3B–24

PARTIAL OR FULL SHADE

REGULAR WATER

Cymbalaria muralis

European natives related to snapdragons *(Antirrhinum).* Not showy, but they have their uses as small-scale ground covers in cool, shady places or as decorations for terrarium or hanging basket. In ground, can be invasive.

C. aequitriloba. Inch-deep mat that looks like small-scale dichondra. Leaves have three to five shallow lobes. Purple, snapdragon-shaped flowers are pretty but too tiny to make a show. Use as moss substitute.

C. muralis (Linaria cymbalaria). KENILWORTH IVY. Usually grown as annual. Dainty creeper that may appear uninvited in shadier parts of garden, sometimes even sprouting in chinks of stone or brick wall. Trailing stems root at joints. Smooth leaves 1 in. wide or less, with three to seven toothlike lobes. Blooms mainly in spring, with small lilac blue flowers carried singly on stalks a little longer than leaves.

CYMBIDIUM

Orchidaceae

TERRESTRIAL ORCHIDS

ALL ZONES—SUBJECT TO CONDITIONS BELOW

PARTIAL SHADE

REGULAR WATER

Miniature Cymbidium

Native to high altitudes in Southeast Asia. Very popular because of their relatively easy culture. In areas subject to frost, grow in containers in lathhouse, greenhouse, or beneath overhang or high-branching tree. You can bring indoors when in flower. Excellent cut flower. Long, narrow, grasslike foliage forms sheath around short, stout, oval pseudobulbs. Long-lasting flowers grow on erect or arching spikes. Standard types usually bloom from midwinter to midspring. Bloom season for miniatures starts in earliest fall, is heaviest late fall into winter.

For best bloom, give as much light as possible without burning foliage. Plants do well under shade cloth or lath. Plants with yellow-green leaves generally flower best; dark green foliage means too much shade. During flowering period, give plants shade.

To set buds, plants need 50 to 55°F/10 to 13°C night temperatures. Daytime temperatures of 60 to 75°F/16 to 24°C (or even as high as 80 to 90°F/27 to 32°C) suit them. They will stand temperatures as low as 28°F/−2°C for short time only; where there's danger of harder frosts, cover plants with polyethylene film. Flower spikes are more tender than other plant tissues.

Potting mix for cymbidiums should drain fast yet retain moisture. Many commercial orchid mixes are available. Keep potting medium moist when new growth is developing and maturing—usually spring through summer. In winter, water plants just enough to keep bulbs from shriveling. On hot summer days, mist foliage early in day. Watch for slugs and snails at all times.

Feed with complete liquid fertilizer every 10 days to 2 weeks. Use a high-nitrogen formula winter to early summer, a low-nitrogen product from late summer through fall. Transplant potted plants when bulbs fill pots. When dividing plants, keep minimum of three healthy bulbs (with foliage) in each division. Dust cuts with sulfur or charcoal to discourage rot.

Most cymbidium growers list only hybrids—large-flowered varieties with white, pink, yellow, green, or bronze blooms. Most have yellow throat, dark red markings on lip. Large-flowered forms produce 12 or more 4½–5-in. flowers per stem. Miniature varieties, about a quarter the size of large-flowered forms, are popular for their size, free-blooming qualities, flower color. A growing class of intermediate-climate cymbidiums (the only types suited to Zone H2) will thrive alongside cattleyas in a greenhouse or in climates where night temperatures are too warm for standard cymbidiums. Many bloom in summer and fall; some are fragrant.

CYMBOPOGON citratus

LEMON GRASS

Poaceae (Gramineae)

PERENNIAL

ZONES 12, 13, 16, 17, 23, 24; H1, H2

FULL SUN

REGULAR WATER

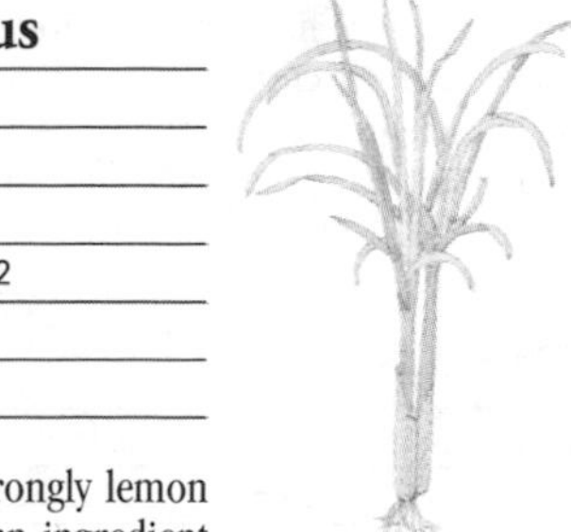

Cymbopogon citratus

From India. All plant parts are strongly lemon scented and are widely used as an ingredient in Southeast Asian cooking. Clumps of inch-wide leaves grow 3–4 ft. tall (or more) and 3 ft. wide. Base of clump, composed of overlapping leaf bases, is nearly bulbous in appearance. Occasionally grown in gardens. It can live over in the mildest-winter regions, but it's safer to pot up a division and keep it indoors or in a greenhouse over winter.

CYNARA. See ARTICHOKE, CARDOON

CYNODON dactylon

BERMUDA GRASS, BERMUDA

Poaceae (Gramineae)

PERENNIAL GRASS

ZONES 5–10, 12–24; H1, H2

FULL SUN

MODERATE TO REGULAR WATER

Cynodon dactylon

Subtropical fine-textured grass that spreads rapidly by surface and underground runners. Tolerates heat and looks good if well maintained. It turns brown in winter; some varieties stay green longer than others, and most stay green longer if well fed. Can be overseeded with cool-season grasses for winter color. Needs sun and should be cut low; 1 in. for common Bermuda, ½–¾ in. for hybrid Bermuda is desirable. Needs dethatching—removal of matted layer of old stems and stolons beneath the leaves—to look its best.

Common Bermuda is good minimum-maintenance lawn for large area. Needs feeding, careful and frequent mowing to remove seed spikes. Roots invade shrubbery and flower beds if not carefully confined. Can become extremely difficult to eradicate. Plant from hulled seed or sprigs.

Hybrid Bermudas are finer in texture and better in color than common kind. They crowd out common Bermuda in time but are harder to overseed with rye, bluegrass, or red fescue. Help them stay green in winter by feeding in early fall and by removing thatch. Useful in areas with short dormant season. Grow from sprigs (stolons), plugs, or sod.

'Santa Ana'. Deep green, coarse, smog resistant. Takes hard wear; holds color late.

'Tifdwarf'. Extremely low and dense; takes very close mowing. Slower to establish than others, but slower to spread where it's not wanted. Useful as small-scale ground cover on banks, among rocks.

'Tifgreen'. Fine textured, deep blue green, dense. Few seed spikes, sterile seeds. Takes close mowing; preferred for putting greens.

'Tifway'. Low growth; dense, fine texture. Stiff dark green blades. Wear resistant. Slow to start. Sterile (no seeds).

'U-3'. Finer in texture than common Bermuda but with obvious and unattractive seed spikes. Very tough. Grow from sprigs; not dependable from seed, tending to revert to mixture of many types. Not up to other hybrids in quality.

CYNOGLOSSUM

Boraginaceae

PERENNIALS AND BIENNIALS GROWN AS ANNUALS

ZONES VARY BY SPECIES

EXPOSURE NEEDS VARY BY SPECIES

WATER NEEDS VARY BY SPECIES

Cynoglossum amabile

Bedding, border, or wild garden plants with little blue, white, or pink flowers like forget-me-nots *(Myosotis)*, to which they are related.

C. amabile. CHINESE FORGET-ME-NOT. Biennial grown as annual. Zones A2, A3; 1–24; H1, H2. East Asian native reaching 1½–2 ft. tall, 1 ft. wide. Lance-shaped leaves are soft, hairy, grayish green. Loose sprays of rich blue, pink, or white flowers (larger than forget-me-nots) appear in spring, continue into summer where weather is cool. Widely available 'Firmament', the most popular variety, has rich blue blooms on compact plants about 1½ ft. high. All varieties bloom from seed sown in fall or early spring, preferably in location where plants are to grow. Hardy except in most severe winters. Give full sun, regular water.

C. grande. WESTERN HOUND'S TONGUE. Perennial. Zones 4–9, 14–24. Native to Oregon and California Coast Ranges and to Sierra Nevada slopes below 4,000 ft. Hairy, mostly basal leaves 6–12 in. long. Blue spring flowers with white centers. Plants reach 1–2½ ft. tall and 1 ft. wide; die back in summer to a heavy underground root. Choose a shaded, woodsy site with cool soil; provide little or no summer water.

Cyperaceae. Members of the sedge family superficially resemble grasses, but their stems are usually three-sided and their leaves are arranged in three ranks. They generally grow in wet places. *Carex* and *Cyperus* are examples.

CYPERUS

Cyperaceae

PERENNIALS

ZONES VARY BY SPECIES

SUN OR SHADE

AMPLE WATER

Cyperus papyrus

These African natives are sedges—grasslike plants distinguished from true grasses by three-angled, solid stems and very different flowering parts. Valued for striking form, silhouette, shadow pattern.

Most cyperus grow in rich, moist soil or with roots submerged in water. Keep plants groomed by removing dead or broken stems; divide and replant vigorous plants when the clump becomes too large, saving smaller, outside divisions and discarding the overgrown centers. Beyond their hardiness range, pot up divisions and keep them over the winter as houseplants.

C. albostriatus (C. diffusus). Zones 14–24. Resembles *C. alternifolius,* but tends to be less hardy, shorter (to 20 in.), with broader leaves and lusher, softer appearance. Vigorous, invasive plant; best used in contained space.

C. alternifolius. UMBRELLA PLANT. Zones 8, 9, 12–24; H1, H2. Narrow, firm, spreading leaves arranged like ribs of umbrella at tops of 2–4-ft. stems. Flowers in dry greenish brown clusters. Grows in water or moist soil. Effective near pools, in pots or planters, or in dry stream beds or small rock gardens. Self-sows. Can become weedy and take over a small pool. Naturalized in parts of Hawaii. 'Gracilis' ('Nanus') is a dwarf form to 1½ ft. high.

C. papyrus. PAPYRUS. Zones 16, 17, 23, 24; H1, H2. Tall, graceful, dark green stems 6–10 ft. high, topped with clusters of green threadlike parts to 1½ ft. long (longer than small leaves at base of cluster). Will grow quickly in 2 in. of water in shallow pool, or can be potted and placed on bricks or inverted pot in deeper water. Protect from strong wind. Also grows well in rich, moist soil out of water. Naturalized on Kauai. Used by flower arrangers.

C. prolifer (C. isocladus). DWARF PAPYRUS. Zones 16, 17, 23, 24; H1, H2. Flowers and long, thin leaves combine to make filmy brown and green clusters on slender stems about 1½ ft. high. Use in Asian-style gardens; sink in pots in water gardens where delicate design of slender, leafless stems will not be lost among larger and coarser plants.

CYPHOMANDRA betacea. See TREE TOMATO

CYPRESS. See *Cupressus.* True cypresses are all *Cupressus;* many plants erroneously called cypress are under *Chamaecyparis* and *Taxodium.*

CYPRESS VINE. See IPOMOEA quamoclit

Cypripedium. For tropical and subtropical orchids sold under this name, see *Paphiopedilum.* True cypripediums, the hardy lady's slipper orchids, are rare or endangered in the wild and extremely difficult to maintain in gardens. Most are collected from wild stands and seldom survive.

FOR INFORMATION ON YOUR CLIMATE ZONE
PLEASE SEE PAGES 27–63

CYRTANTHUS

Amaryllidaceae

PERENNIALS FROM BULBS

ZONES 16–24

LIGHT SHADE

REGULAR WATER

Cyrtanthus mackenii

South African natives with glossy, strap-shaped, evergreen leaves that remain attractive all year. Flowers appear in clusters at ends of stems that rise just above the leaves. Plants are frost sensitive; give sheltered spot in Zones 18–22. Plant in spring, in well-drained, enriched soil; set bulbs 1–1½ ft. apart, with tips just beneath soil surface. Give less water during semidormant period (winter and spring for *C. elatus,* summer for *C. mackenii*), but don't let plants dry out. To increase your planting, remove bulblets that form around larger bulb and plant separately. Good potted plants.

C. elatus (C. purpureus, Vallota speciosa). SCARBOROUGH LILY. Looks like a more delicate version of Dutch hybrid amaryllis *(Hippeastrum).* Leaves 1–2 ft. long. In summer and early fall, each thick flower stalk is topped with up to ten 3–4-in., funnel-shaped orange-red blooms. (White- and pink-flowered forms are less common.) Succeeds in competition with tree roots. Excellent houseplant.

C. mackenii. Foot-long, narrow leaves, somewhat wavy edges. Each stem holds up to five tubular, curved, 2-in.-long, fragrant white blooms in spring. There are also cream- and yellow-flowered forms and hybrids in coral, orange, and red shades. If in pots, will need annual repotting.

CYRTOMIUM

Polypodiaceae

FERNS

ZONES VARY BY SPECIES

PARTIAL OR FULL SHADE

REGULAR WATER

Cyrtomium falcatum

Coarse-textured but handsome ferns with firm-textured, glossy fronds 2–3 ft. long. Provide soil with high organic content; do not plant too deeply.

C. falcatum. JAPANESE HOLLY FERN. Zones 5–9, 14–24; H1, H2; or indoors. Native to Asia, South Africa, Polynesia; naturalized in Hawaii. Fronds to 10 in. wide, with 3–11 pairs of divisions. Takes houseplant conditions well.

C. fortunei. Zones 4–9, 14–24. From China, Japan, Korea. Fronds to 6 in. wide; more finely cut and with more divisions (12–26 pairs) than those of other species.

C. macrophyllum. Zones 7–9, 13–24. From China, Himalayas. Fronds (to 10 in. wide) are the coarsest among the species listed here, with three to eight pairs of divisions.

CYTISUS

BROOM

Fabaceae (Leguminosae)

EVERGREEN, SEMIEVERGREEN, DECIDUOUS SHRUBS

ZONES VARY BY SPECIES

FULL SUN

LITTLE OR NO WATER

Cytisus × spachianus

Most widely planted brooms belong here, but look for Spanish broom under *Spartium junceum*, other choice shrubs under *Genista.* Sweet pea–shaped flowers, often fragrant. Plants tolerate wind, seashore conditions, and rocky, infertile soil. Where soil is highly alkaline, give them iron sulfate. Prune after bloom to keep to reasonable size, lessen production of unsightly seedpods.

C. battandieri. ATLAS BROOM. Semievergreen or deciduous. Zones 4–6, 14–17. Moroccan native puts on fast growth to 12–15 ft. high and as wide. Can be trained as small tree. Leaves divided into three roundish leaflets to 3½ in. long, 1½ in. wide, covered with silvery, silky hairs. Fragrant, pure yellow flowers in spikelike 5-in. clusters at branch ends in summer.

Cytisus battandieri

C. canariensis (Genista canariensis). CANARY ISLAND BROOM. Evergreen. Zones 8, 9, 12–24. Damaged at 15°F/–9°C but recovers quickly. Many-branched, upright shrub to 6–8 ft. high, 5–6 ft. wide. Bright green leaves divided into ½-in. leaflets. Bright yellow, fragrant flowers bloom in short clusters at branch tips in spring, summer. Aggressive; has escaped from gardens.

C. ×kewensis. KEW BROOM. Evergreen. Best in Zones 2–6; less vigorous but satisfactory in Zones 16, 17. Low (less than 1 ft. high) and spreading, with trailing, cascading branches to 4 ft. or more. Creamy white, ½-in. flowers in spring. Tiny leaves.

C. lydia. See Genista lydia

C. ×praecox. WARMINSTER BROOM. Deciduous. Zones 2–9, 14–22. Compact growth to 3–5 ft. high and 4–6 ft. wide, with many slender stems. Mounding mass of pale yellow to creamy white flowers in spring. Small leaves fall early. Effective as informal screen or hedge, along drives, paths, garden steps. 'Allgold', slightly taller, has bright yellow flowers; 'Hollandia' has pink ones. 'Moonlight', formerly considered *C. ×praecox* variety, is now thought to be form of *C. scoparius.*

C. purgans. PROVENCE BROOM. Deciduous. Zones 1–7. From Europe, North Africa. Dense, mounding growth to 3 ft. high and wide. Roundish, silky, hairy leaves are ¼–½ in. long. Fragrant chrome yellow flowers in late spring, early summer. 'Spanish Gold' grows 4 ft. tall, 6 ft. wide; it is hardy in the Colorado Rockies to an elevation of 8,000 ft.

C. racemosus. See C. ×spachianus

C. scoparius. SCOTCH BROOM. Evergreen. Zones 2–9, 14–22; H1. This aggressive European species has given all brooms a bad name. Upright-growing mass of wandlike green stems (often leafless or nearly so) may reach 10 ft. Golden yellow, ¾-in. flowers, spring and early summer. A tenacious weed from Seattle to San Diego and in Hawaii, especially on the Big Island.

Much less aggressive are lower-growing, more colorful forms. Most of these grow 5–8 ft. tall and wide. 'Burkwoodii' has red blooms touched with yellow; 'Carla', pink-and-crimson flowers lined in white; 'Dorothy Walpole', rose pink and crimson; 'Lena', lemon yellow and red; 'Lilac Time', lilac pink blooms on a compact plant; 'Lord Lambourne', scarlet and cream; 'Minstead', white flushed lilac and deep purple; 'Moonlight', pale yellow blossoms, compact grower; 'Pomona', orange and apricot; 'St. Mary's', white; 'San Francisco' and 'Stanford', red.

C. ×spachianus (C. racemosus, Genista racemosa). Evergreen. Zones 7–9, 11–24. Similar in growth habit to *C. canariensis* but with larger leaflets and longer, looser spikes of fragrant yellow flowers in late spring. Naturalizes where adapted. Often sold as *Genista fragrans*.

DABOECIA

IRISH HEATH

Ericaceae

EVERGREEN SHRUBS

ZONES VARY BY SPECIES

FULL SUN ONLY IN COOLER CLIMATES

REGULAR WATER

Daboecia cantabrica

These members of the heath family bear 1½-in.-long, egg-shaped flowers in spikelike clusters. They need fast-draining, acid soil and are most useful on hillsides and in rock gardens or natural landscapes.

D. azorica. Zones 8, 9, 14–24. Native to the Azores. Forms a mound to 6–10 in. high, 16 in. wide. Closely set, bright green leaves are ¼ in. long, broader than those of other heaths and heathers. Rosy red flowers in 2-in. clusters bloom in spring or early summer, occasionally in autumn.

D. cantabrica. Zones 3b–9, 14–24. From western Europe. Erect stems make slightly spreading plant 1½–2 ft. tall. Larger leaves than those of *D. azorica.* Pinkish purple flowers in narrow, 3–5-in.-long clusters, late spring to early autumn; in warmer part of range, bloom begins earlier in spring. Varieties include white-flowered 'Alba', pure pink 'Praegerae', and deep pink 'Rosea'. 'Cinderella' has bicolor flowers (white with a touch of pink) and gray-green foliage. 'William Buchanan' is a prostrate grower with reddish purple blossoms; 'William Buchanan Gold' is similar but shows some yellow variegation in the foliage.

Daboecia cantabrica

DAFFODIL. See NARCISSUS

DAHLBERG DAISY. See THYMOPHYLLA tenuiloba

DAHLIA

Asteraceae (Compositae)

PERENNIALS FROM TUBEROUS ROOTS

ZONES 1–24, EXCEPT AS NOTED

LIGHT SHADE IN HOTTEST AREAS

REGULAR WATER

Native to Mexico, Guatemala. Through centuries of hybridizing and selection, dahlias have become tremendously diversified, available in numerous flower types and flower sizes (from 2 to 12 in. across) and all colors but true blue.

Dahlia Hybrid

Bush and bedding dahlias range from 1 ft. to over 7 ft. tall. The tall bush forms are useful as summer hedges, screens, and fillers among shrubs; lower kinds give mass color in borders and containers. Modern dahlias, with their strong stems, long-lasting blooms that face outward or upward, and substantial, attractive foliage, are striking cut flowers. Leaves are generally divided into many large, deep green leaflets.

Dahlia flower forms. Dahlia flowers are composite (daisylike) blooms containing many individual flowers called florets. One type of dahlia flower is composed of ray florets (which look like petals) surrounding a central cluster of petal-less disk florets. A second type has ray florets only. The American Dahlia Society has classified dahlias according to the flower forms described below. Blooms range in size from giant (over 10 in.), large (8–10 in.), and medium (6–8 in.) to small (4–6 in.), miniature (2–4 in.), and mignon (under 2 in.).

Anemone form. Single or multiple layers of rays surround tubular disk florets that form a "pincushion" center.

Collarette. One layer of long rays and a second, inner layer of shorter ones that form a "collar" around the center of the flower.

Orchid form. A single layer of rays with inrolled margins for two-thirds or more of their length, giving the flower a pinwheel appearance.

Peony form. Central disk florets are surrounded by two or more rows of rays; innermost rays may be curled or twisted.

Single. One layer of rays arranged in a plane around a central cluster of disk florets.

The following forms are composed of ray florets only.

Ball. Flower looks spherical, though it's flattish in profile. Rays have inrolled margins for at least half their length. *Pompon* form is similar, but rays are inrolled along their entire length, giving them a tubular look.

Cactus form. Ray margins roll downward; tips are pointed. *Straight cactus* rays radiate in all directions from center; may be straight or curved downward, margins rolled for over half their length. *Incurved cactus* rays are similar, but they curve upward. *Semicactus* flowers have broad-based

D

Dahlia Flower Forms

'Elvira'; Peony Form — 'Star Lite'; Cactus Form — 'Red Velvet'; Waterlily Form — 'Tasagore'; Peony Form — 'Corvette'; Anenome Form

'Dizzy'; Single — 'Mrs. Santa Claus'; Informal Decorative — 'Winnie'; Pompon — 'Candy Cane'; Formal Decorative — 'Ace of Hearts'; Collarette — 'Apache'; Fimbriated

rays with margins rolled along outer half (portion farthest from center); the rays may be straight or curve upward or downward.

Decorative. Full flowers of two types. *Formal decorative* has many overlapping layers of symmetrically arranged, fairly flat rays that tend to curve downward. *Informal decorative* is just as full, but rays are curved, curled, or twisted and are often arranged in a more irregular pattern.

Fimbriated. All rays split at tips with split portions twisted, giving the flower a fringed appearance.

Waterlily form. Rays broad, curving slightly upward; flower profile is flat to saucer shaped, resembling a waterlily bloom.

Novelty. Any flower form not covered in previous categories.

Planting. Most dahlias are started from tuberous roots planted in spring after frost is past and soil is warm. Several weeks before planting, dig soil to a foot deep and work in organic matter such as garden compost or ground bark. Dig deep planting holes, incorporate fertilizer, and insert stakes (for tall varieties) as described in "What Most Dahlias Need," at right. Cover roots with 3 in. of soil. Water thoroughly. As shoots grow, gradually fill hole with soil.

Dahlias can be started from seed. For tall types, start seeds early indoors; transplant seedlings into garden beds after frost danger is past. For dwarf dahlias, sow seed in place after soil is warm, or buy and plant started seedlings from the nursery. Dwarf dahlias are usually replaced each year, though they can be lifted and stored.

Thinning, pinching. On tall-growing dahlias, thin out shoots when they're about 6 in. high, leaving only the strongest one or two. When remaining shoots have three sets of leaves, pinch off tops just above upper set; smaller-flowered dahlias, such as pompons, singles, and dwarfs, need only this first pinching. For best show of larger-flowered types, pinch again by removing all but terminal flower buds on side shoots.

Plant care. After shoots are aboveground, start watering regularly to a foot deep; continue throughout active growth. Dahlias planted in enriched soil shouldn't need additional food, but if your soil is light or if roots stayed in the ground the previous year, apply a granular low-nitrogen fertilizer when the first flower buds show. Mulch to discourage weeds and to eliminate cultivating, which may injure feeder roots.

WHAT MOST DAHLIAS NEED

GOOD SOIL: Plants grow best in well-drained soil that is liberally enriched with organic matter.

PLANTING: Dig 1-ft.-deep planting holes—1½ ft. wide for larger dahlias (over 4 ft. tall), 9–12 in. wide for smaller types. Space roots of larger varieties 4–5 ft. apart, those of smaller ones 1–2 ft. apart.

FERTILIZING: Incorporate about ¼ cup of granular low-nitrogen fertilizer into the soil at the bottom of the planting hole, then add 4 in. of plain soil.

STAKING: When planting a tall variety, drive a 5–6-ft. stake into the hole just off center; place the root horizontally in bottom of hole, 2 in. from the stake and with growth bud pointing toward it.

'Deniska'; Novelty

Cutting flowers. Pick nearly mature flowers in early morning or evening. Immediately place cut stems in 2–3 in. of hot water; let stand in gradually cooling water for several hours or overnight.

Lifting, storing. In climates where ground freezes in winter, dig and store tuberous roots in fall. In other regions, roots may remain in place as long as drainage is excellent and winter temperatures remain above 20°F/−7°C. In borderline climates, mulch with 4-in. layer of straw or similar material. Gardeners in most areas, however, prefer to dig the roots annually.

To lift the roots, cut stalks to 4 in. above ground after the tops turn yellow or are frosted. Dig a 2-ft.-wide circle around each plant; carefully pry up clump with spading fork, shake off loose soil, and let the clump dry in sun for several hours. From that point, follow either of the following methods.

Method 1: Divide clumps immediately. Freshly dug roots are easy to cut, and eyes (growth buds) are easy to recognize at this time. To divide, cut the stalks with a sharp knife, leaving 1 in. of stalk attached to each section; make sure each division has an eye, so it will produce a new plant. Dust cut surfaces with sulfur to prevent rot; bury in dry sand, sawdust, peat moss, or perlite and store over winter in a cool (40 to 45°F/4 to 7°C), dark, dry place.

Method 2: Leave clumps intact. Cover them with dry sand, sawdust, peat moss, or perlite and store in cool, dark, dry place as directed in method above. With Method 2, roots are less likely to shrivel.

About 2 to 4 weeks before planting in spring, separate intact clumps, cutting them apart as described under Method 1. Then place all roots—whether fall- or spring-divided—in moist sand to plump them up and encourage sprouting.

D. imperialis. TREE DAHLIA. Zones 4–6, 8, 9, 14–24. Multistemmed tree grows each year from permanent roots to a possible 10–20 ft. tall, 4–6 ft. wide. Daisylike, 4–8-in.-wide lavender flowers with yellow centers bloom at branch ends in late fall. Leaves divided into many leaflets. Frost kills tops completely; cut back to ground afterward. If tree dahlia were longer blooming or evergreen, it would be a valued landscape plant, but annual dieback relegates it to tall novelty class. Available from specialists; seldom sold in nurseries. Grow from cuttings taken near stem tops (or from side shoots) in fall; root in containers of moist sand kept in a protected place over winter. Or dig root clump and divide in fall. Give full sun or partial shade. *D. excelsa, D. maxonii* are similar.

DALBERGIA sissoo

ROSEWOOD

Fabaceae (Leguminosae)

SEMIEVERGREEN TREE

ZONES 13, 19, 21–24; H1, H2

FULL SUN OR PARTIAL SHADE

REGULAR WATER

Dalbergia sissoo

Soft, green, thornless growth makes rosewood look more like a tropical tree than a desert native. Rapid growth to 25–50 ft. tall, 35–50 ft. wide. Handsome leaves divided into three to five 3-in., oval or roundish leaflets with narrow, elongated tips. Short clusters of pendulous, cream-colored, very fragrant flowers in spring. From India, where it is an important timber tree.

DALEA

Fabaceae (Leguminosae)

EVERGREEN AND DECIDUOUS SHRUBS

ZONES VARY BY SPECIES

FULL SUN

LITTLE TO MODERATE WATER

Dalea greggii

Extremely useful and attractive desert shrubs from the southwestern states and northern Mexico. All have finely divided foliage and clusters of small sweet pea–shaped flowers. The taller shrub types should be cut back by half during their first 3 or 4 years to encourage dense growth. Overwatering or summer drought can result in partial leaf drop.

D. bicolor. INDIGO BUSH. Deciduous. Zones 10–13. To 6–8 ft. tall, 5–6 ft. wide. Silvery leaves; deep blue autumn flowers. Rapid regrowth from hard winter pruning brings a quick crop of fresh foliage. 'Monterrey Blue' is a cutting-grown selection with especially good flower color.

D. capitata. Evergreen. Zones 10–13. Ground cover to 8 in. high and 3 ft. wide. Finely divided light green foliage has a lemon scent. Bears yellow flowers during spring and autumn. Control whiteflies. Requires some water in summer and survives regular irrigation. 'Sierra Gold' is a cutting-grown variety.

D. frutescens. BLACK DALEA. Evergreen. Zones 10–13. Mounded growth to 3 ft. tall, 4 ft. across, with silvery green, lacy foliage. Purple flower clusters appear from fall to spring. A cutting-grown form is called 'Sierra Negra'.

D. greggii. TRAILING INDIGO BUSH. Evergreen. Zones 10–13. Bush has mounding habit to 1½ ft. high and spreading 6 ft. wide. Pearl gray foliage and clusters of lavender to purple flowers in spring and early summer. Good desert ground cover.

D. lutea. Evergreen. Zones 12, 13. To 6 ft. tall and wide, with deep green leaves and clustered yellow flowers in late fall. 'Sierra Moonrise' is a selected form.

D. pulchra. INDIGO BUSH. Evergreen. Zones 12, 13. To 8 ft. high and 5 ft. wide. Silvery foliage; purple flowers in spring.

D. spinosus. See Psorothamnus spinosus

DALECHAMPIA dioscoreifolia

COSTA RICAN BUTTERFLY VINE

Euphorbiaceae

EVERGREEN VINE

ZONES 17–24

FULL SUN OR LIGHT SHADE

REGULAR WATER

Dalechampia dioscoreifolia

From Central and South America. Twining vine to 16–25 ft., with oval, pointed leaves to 3 in. long and 1 in. wide; leaves are dull dark green above, paler green and fuzzy beneath. Blossoms measure up to 6 in. across and are thought by some to resemble purple butterflies, with tiny yellow flowers appearing between two violet bracts. With adequate warmth and moisture, growth is rapid and blooms abundant. Heaviest bloom comes from early summer to late fall, but vine can flower nearly year-round.

DAMIANITA. **See CHRYSACTINIA mexicana**

DAMPIERA diversifolia

Goodeniaceae

PERENNIAL

ZONES 15–24

FULL SUN

REGULAR WATER

Australian ground cover to 3 ft. high, 6 ft. wide. It spreads steadily in loose, well-drained soil by suckering and by roots that sprout from trailing stems, but it is not invasive or weedy. Evergreen, narrowly oval leaves to 1 in. long. In spring and summer, many small dark blue flowers appear at ends of new growth.

Dampiera diversifolia

DAPHNE

Thymelaeaceae

EVERGREEN, SEMIEVERGREEN, DECIDUOUS SHRUBS

ZONES VARY BY SPECIES

EXPOSURE NEEDS VARY BY SPECIES

MODERATE WATER, EXCEPT AS NOTED

ALL PARTS, ESPECIALLY FRUITS, ARE POISONOUS IF INGESTED

Daphne odora 'Aureo-marginata'

Of the many kinds, three *(D. × burkwoodii, D. cneorum, D. odora)* are widely grown in the West; most of the others are choice rock garden subjects with limited distribution in the nursery trade. Although some daphnes are easier to grow than others, all require fast-draining soil and careful summer watering. They are generally more temperamental in California than in the Northwest. Plants respond to heavy pruning but rarely need more than the occasional snip to correct their shape. Cut back to lateral branches or to just above obvious growth buds. You can cut budded branches of deciduous types for forced bloom indoors.

D. × burkwoodii. Evergreen or semievergreen to deciduous. Zones 2b–6, 14–17. Erect, compact growth to 3–4 ft. tall and wide, densely foliaged with narrow leaves. Abundant small clusters of fragrant flowers (white fading to pink) appear at branch ends in late spring and again in late summer. 'Briggs Moonlight' has pale yellow leaves with a narrow green border; 'Carol Mackie' has gold-edged green leaves. 'Somerset' is larger (to 4 ft. tall and 6 ft. wide) and bears pink flowers. Use all in shrub borders, at woodland edges, as foundation plantings. Full sun or light shade.

D. cneorum. GARLAND DAPHNE. Evergreen. Zones 2b–9, 14–17. From mountains of central and southern Europe. Matting and spreading;

D

less than 1 ft. high and 3 ft. wide. Good container plant. Trailing branches covered with narrow, 1-in.-long, dark green leaves. Clusters of fragrant rosy pink flowers appear in spring. Choice rock garden plant; give it light shade in warm areas, full sun in cool-summer areas. After bloom is through, top-dress with mix of peat moss and sand to keep roots cool and induce additional rooting of trailing stems.

Varieties include 'Eximia', lower than the species (to 8 in. high) and with larger flowers; 'Pygmaea Alba', 3 in. tall, 1 ft. wide, with white flowers; 'Ruby Glow', with larger, more deeply colored flowers than the species and with late-summer rebloom; and 'Variegata', with gold-edged leaves.

D. genkwa. LILAC DAPHNE. Deciduous. Zones 4–6, 16, 17. From China. Erect, open growth to 3–4 ft. high and wide. Before leaves expand, clusters of lilac blue, scentless flowers wreathe branches, making foot-long wands of blossoms. White fruit follows flowers. Leaves oval, 2 in. long. Use in rock garden, shrub border. Full sun or light shade.

D. mezereum. FEBRUARY DAPHNE. Deciduous. Zones 2–7, 14–17. From Europe, Caucasus, Siberia. Rather gawky, stiff-twigged, erect growth to 4 ft. tall and 3 ft. wide, with thin, roundish, 2–3-in.-long leaves; should be planted in groups for best appearance. Fragrant reddish purple flowers in short, stalkless clusters are carried along branches in mid- or late winter before leaf-out and continue into spring. May go dormant in summer. Clustered red fruit follows flowers. Full sun or light shade. 'Alba' has white flowers and yellow fruit and is not as rangy as the species.

D. odora. WINTER DAPHNE. Evergreen. Zones 4–10, 12, 14–24. From China, Japan. So prized for its pervasive floral perfume that it continues to be widely planted despite its unpredictable behavior—it can die despite the most attentive care, or flourish with little attention until you invite all your gardening friends over to admire it, at which point it promptly succumbs without warning just to show you who's in charge. Very neat, handsome plant, usually to about 4 ft. high (occasionally 8–10 ft. high) and 6 ft. wide. Rather narrow, 3-in.-long leaves are thick and glossy. Nosegay clusters of charming, intensely fragrant flowers—pink to deep red on outside, with creamy pink throats—appear at branch ends in winter. 'Alba' has white flowers; terminal growth sometimes distorted by fasciation (growths resembling cockscombs). 'Leucanthe' is relatively disease resistant, with white-throated pale pink blooms; 'Aureo-marginata' ('Marginata'), more widely grown than species, has yellow-edged leaves.

This species needs much air around its roots, so plant in porous soil (as you would rhododendrons). Always set plant a bit high, so the juncture of roots and stems is 1–2 in. above soil grade. Where soil is heavy and poorly drained, grow in porous, organic soil mixture in raised bed or container.

In Zones 18–24, transplanting an existing *D. odora* often fails—digging cuts roots, the plant suffers, and water molds get at it. Transplanting has a better chance of success in Zones 4–9, 14–17.

Plant this daphne where it can get at least 3 hours of shade each day around midday. If possible, shade soil around roots with living ground cover. A soil pH of 7.0 is right for it (important in Zones 4–6). Feed right after bloom with complete fertilizer but not acid plant food.

During dry season, water as infrequently as plant will allow. Little or no water in summer increases flowering next spring and helps prevent death from water molds.

DARMERA peltata (Peltiphyllum peltatum)

UMBRELLA PLANT, INDIAN RHUBARB

Saxifragaceae

PERENNIAL

ZONES 2–7, 14–20

PARTIAL SHADE

AMPLE WATER

Darmera peltata

Native to mountains of Northern California and Oregon. Large, round clusters of pink flowers appear on bare stalks to 6 ft. tall in spring. Shield-shaped, 1–2-ft.-wide leaves appear later on 2–6-ft. stalks. Each plant spreads 4–8 ft. wide. Stout rhizomes to 2 in. thick grow in damp ground or even into streams. A spectacular plant for pond, stream, or damp, cool woodland site.

DASYLIRION

Agavaceae

EVERGREEN SHRUBS

ZONES VARY BY SPECIES

FULL SUN OR LIGHT SHADE

LITTLE OR NO WATER TO MODERATE WATER

Dasylirion wheeleri

Native to deserts and mountains of the Southwest and Mexico. Clumps of narrow, grassy leaves spring from a woody base that can, with age, grow into a treelike trunk. Tiny flowers are tightly clustered on a tall, narrow spike. Provide good drainage. Very drought tolerant, but some irrigation will speed growth. Definitely need summer water in Zone 13.

D. quadrangulatum (D. longissima). MEXICAN GRASS TREE. Zones 12–24. Green leaves in fountainlike clump to about 5 ft. high and wide. Trunk is slow to form, but may reach 10 ft. tall. Eventually bears white to cream-colored flowers in early summer.

D. wheeleri. DESERT SPOON, SOTOL. Zones 10–24; most widely used in 10–13. Forms a near-spherical clump 3–5 ft. high, 4–5 ft. wide. Spiky bluish gray leaves to 3 ft. long; stiffer than those of *D. quadrangulatum.* Leaves slowly form a trunk to 3 ft. tall, covered with dried, drooping shag of old leaves. Base of each leaf broadens where it joins the trunk to form a long-handled "spoon" prized in dried arrangements. Eventually produces white flowers on 9–15-ft.-tall spike in early summer.

DATE PALM. See PHOENIX

DATURA. See BRUGMANSIA

DAVALLIA trichomanoides

SQUIRREL'S FOOT FERN

Polypodiaceae

FERN

ZONES 17, 23, 24; H1, H2; OR INDOORS

PARTIAL SHADE; BRIGHT INDIRECT LIGHT

MODERATE TO REGULAR WATER

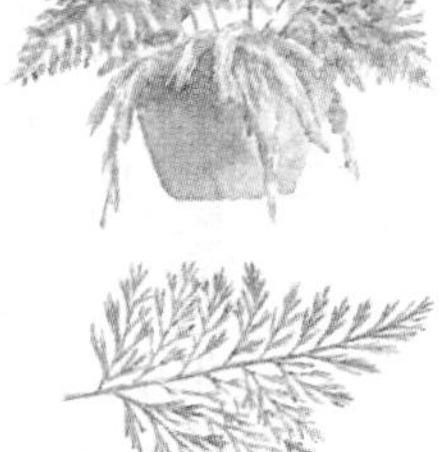

Davallia trichomanoides

Asian native. Very finely divided evergreen fronds to 1 ft. long, 6 in. wide, rise from light reddish brown, furry rhizomes (like squirrel's feet) that creep over soil surface. Hardy to 30°F/–1°C; can be used in mild-winter areas as small-scale ground cover in partly shaded areas. Best use in any climate is as hanging basket plant. Use light, fast-draining soil mix. Feed occasionally. For a similar fern, see *Humata tyermannii*.

DAVIDIA involucrata

DOVE TREE

Nyssaceae

DECIDUOUS TREE

ZONES 4–9, 14–21

PARTIAL SHADE IN HOTTEST CLIMATES

REGULAR WATER

Davidia involucrata

Native to China. Grows to 35–65 ft. tall, with strong branching pattern and a rounded crown 15–40 ft. wide. Has a clean look both in and out of leaf. Roundish to heart-shaped, 3–6-in.-long leaves are vivid green.

Comes into bloom in spring; general effect is that of white doves resting among green leaves—or, as some say, like handkerchiefs drying on branches. Small, clustered, red-anthered flowers are carried between two large white or creamy white bracts that are unequal in size—one is 6 in. long, the other about 4 in. Because leaves are already present at bloom time, the large blossoms aren't as showy as smaller flowers of many deciduous fruit trees. Trees often take 10 years to come into flower, and then may bloom more heavily in alternate years. Brown fruits about the size of golf balls persist on tree well into winter, sometimes until spring. Plant this tree by itself; it should not compete with other flowering trees. Looks pleasing in front of dark conifers, where its vivid green and white stand out.

DAWN REDWOOD. See METASEQUOIA glyptostroboides

DAYLILY. See HEMEROCALLIS

DEAD NETTLE. See LAMIUM maculatum

DEER FERN, DEER TONGUE FERN. See BLECHNUM spicant

DEERHORN CEDAR. See THUJOPSIS dolabrata

DELONIX regia

ROYAL POINCIANA, FLAMBOYANT TREE

Fabaceae (Leguminosae)

PARTIALLY OR WHOLLY DECIDUOUS TREE

ZONE H2

FULL SUN

LITTLE WATER

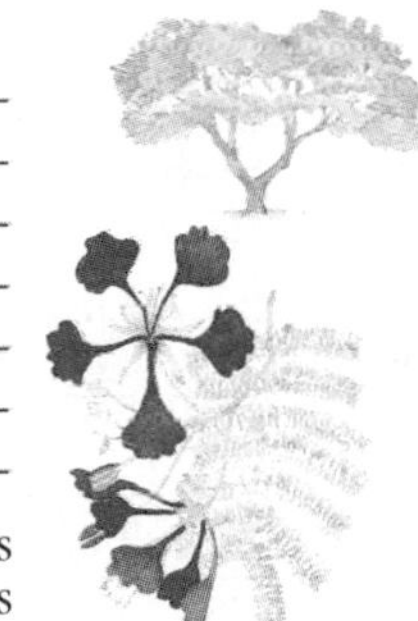

Delonix regia

This native of Madagascar, which Hawaiians call *ohai'ula,* is as flamboyant as it is shapely. Its large trusses of 4-in., orange to scarlet flowers with white or yellow markings put on a spectacular display in late spring or early summer. The blooms are followed by 2-ft.-long black seedpods that hang on the bare winter branches. Rapidly attains 30–40 ft. tall and as wide, with umbrella-shaped silhouette. Fernlike leaves, finely cut into many tiny leaflets, give filtered shade. Good drought tolerance; moderate tolerance to wind and salt. A form with pure yellow flowers, called yellow royal poinciana, is also grown in Hawaii.

DELOSPERMA

ICE PLANT

Aizoaceae

SUCCULENT PERENNIALS

ZONES 2–24, EXCEPT AS NOTED

LIGHT AFTERNOON SHADE IN HOTTEST CLIMATES

LITTLE TO MODERATE WATER

Delosperma 'Alba'

This group of ice plants includes a useful California ground cover (*D.* 'Alba') and several unusually hardy South African rock garden plants. With the latter, withhold water in fall to harden off plants for winter; they also appreciate a gravel mulch to keep crowns dry. All species thrive with just enough water to keep them looking bright and fresh. Except as noted, fleshy leaves are rich green.

D. 'Alba'. WHITE TRAILING ICE PLANT. Zones 12–24. Spreading dwarf plant, rooting freely from stems. Roundish leaves; small white summer flowers that attract bees. Good ground and bank cover; plant 1 ft. apart for quick cover.

D. congestum. Zones 1–24. Grows ½ in. high, 9 in. wide, with roundish leaves and inch-wide, daisylike bright yellow flowers with white central zones. Summer to early fall bloom.

D. cooperi. Reaches to 3 in. tall, 1½ ft. wide, with cylindrical leaves and a summer-long display of rich purple flowers.

D. nubigenum. Only 1 in. tall, spreading to 3 ft. The cylindrical leaves turn red in fall and winter, green up again in spring. Bright golden yellow, 1–1½-in. flowers cover the plant in late spring.

D. sphalmanthoides. Only ½ in. high and 8 in. wide, with tiny, plump gray-green leaves and an early spring show of pinkish purple flowers.

DELPHINIUM

Ranunculaceae

PERENNIALS, SOME TREATED AS BIENNIALS OR ANNUALS

ZONES VARY BY SPECIES

FULL SUN, EXCEPT AS NOTED

REGULAR WATER

Delphinium elatum

Most people associate delphiniums with blue flowers, but colors also include white and shades of red, pink, lavender, and purple. Leaves are lobed or fanlike, variously cut and divided. Taller hybrids offer rich colors in elegant spires. All kinds are effective in borders and make good cut flowers; lower-growing kinds serve well as container plants. Blossoms attract birds. For an annual delphinium (larkspur), see *Consolida ajacis.*

All kinds of delphiniums are easy to grow from seed. In mild-winter areas, sow fresh seed in flats or pots of light soil mix in summer; set out transplants in early fall for bloom in late spring and early summer. (In mild-winter climates, most perennial forms are short lived, often treated as annuals.) In cold climates, refrigerate summer-harvested seed in airtight containers until time to sow. Sow seed in spring and set out transplants in early summer for first bloom by late summer; plants will live over and bloom again earlier in the following summer.

Delphiniums need rich, porous soil and regular fertilizing. Improve poor or heavy soils by blending in soil conditioners. Add lime to strongly acid soils. Work small amount of superphosphate into soil around the root ball. Be careful not to cover root crown with soil. Protect from snails, slugs. In Alaska, the delphinium defoliator eats the plants' leaves in its green caterpillar stage; handpick caterpillars or spray with *Bt.*

D. ambiguum. See Consolida ajacis

D. × belladonna. Zones 1–9, 14–24. Sturdy and bushy, to 3–4 ft. tall, 2 ft. wide. Deeply cut leaves and short-stemmed, airy flower clusters. Varieties include light blue 'Belladonnna', dark blue 'Bellamosum', white 'Casablanca', and deep turquoise blue 'Cliveden Beauty'. All have flowers 1½–2 in. wide; longer lived than tall hybrids listed under *D. elatum.*

D. cardinale. SCARLET LARKSPUR. Zones 7, 14–23. Native to California coastal mountains. To 3–6 ft. tall and 2 ft. wide, with erect stems growing from deep, thick, woody roots. Leaves 3–9 in. wide, with deep, narrow lobes. Flowers 1 in. across, with scarlet calyx and spur and yellow, scarlet-tipped petals. Sow seed early for first-year bloom.

D. elatum. CANDLE DELPHINIUM, CANDLE LARKSPUR. Zones A1–A3; 1–10, 14–24. Siberian native to 3–6 ft. tall, 2 ft. wide, with small flowers in dark or dull purple. This species is among the parents of modern delphinium strains, with flower colors including shades of lilac pink to deep raspberry rose, clear lilac, lavender, royal purple, and darkest violet.

Pacific strain (also called Pacific Giants, Pacific Hybrids, and Pacific Coast Hybrids) grows 5–8 ft. tall. Available as seed-raised mixed-color plants and in named series that produce specific colors, including light blue 'Summer Skies'; medium blue 'Blue Bird'; medium to dark blue 'Blue Jay'; 'Galahad', clear white with white center; 'Percival', white with black center. Additional purple, lavender, and pink selections are sold.

Like Pacific strain but shorter (2–2½ ft. tall) are Blue Fountains, Blue Springs, and Magic Fountains strains. Even shorter is Stand Up strain (15–20 in. high). These lower-growing types seldom require staking.

Centurion is a long-stalked (4–5-ft.-tall), large-flowered hybrid strain similar to the Pacific strain. It too will bloom the first year from seed, but it's more reliably perennial. ▶

English Delphinium Mix grows 6–8 ft. tall, produces double flowers of blue, purple, mauve, pink, and white. The spikes are much denser looking than those of Pacific strain. English types may be sold under other names such as 'English Seedlings'.

D. grandiflorum (D. chinense). CHINESE or BOUQUET DELPHINIUM. Short-lived perennial treated as biennial or annual. Zones A1–A3; 1–10, 14–24. Bushy, branching, to 1 ft. tall or less and about as wide as high. Varieties include 'Dwarf Blue Mirror', 1 ft. tall, upward-facing flowers of deep blue; and 'Tom Thumb', 8 in. tall, pure gentian blue flowers. Blue Butterfly strain grows 14 in. high, has deep blue blooms.

D. nudicaule. SCARLET LARKSPUR. Zones 5–7, 14–17. Native of Northern California, southwestern Oregon. Slender plant to 1–3 ft. tall and less than a foot wide. Long-stalked, mostly basal leaves are broadly divided. Sparse show of long-spurred red flowers. Sun or part shade; best in woodland situations.

DENDRANTHEMA pacificum. See CHRYSANTHEMUM pacificum

DENDROBIUM

Orchidaceae

EPIPHYTIC ORCHIDS

ZONES VARY BY TYPE; OR INDOORS

LIGHT SHADE; BRIGHT INDIRECT LIGHT

REGULAR WATER

Dendrobium nobile

This huge genus (it may include as many as 1,400 species and even more hybrids) ranges from Japan and the Himalayas to Australia and the Pacific islands. Many are grown by orchid fanciers in greenhouses (outdoors in the tropics or mildest subtropical and Mediterranean climates); many are also commercially grown for the cut flower trade. Some have thin, canelike pseudobulbs (see Orchidaceae), others short, fat ones. Only a few of the more widely grown are mentioned here. Culturally they fall into two classes. Intermediate-climate types are evergreen; they need water throughout the year (somewhat less in winter) and temperatures similar to those required by cattleyas. Cool growers drop some or all of their leaves during a period of winter dormancy, at which time they need very little water (only enough to keep pseudobulbs from shrinking) and temperatures suitable for green-leafed paphiopedilums.

D. bigibbum phalaenopsis (D. phalaenopsis). Intermediate grower. Zone H2. Native to Australia, New Guinea. Blooms throughout the year, with canes up to 3 ft. tall producing arching spikes that carry as many as ten 3-inch purple flowers. The parent of many hybrids.

D. hybrids. Zone H2. A bewildering number of hybrids have been produced in Hawaii and elsewhere, both for ornamental pot plants and for cut flowers and leis. Most are intermediate growers. Buy plants in bloom to get desired flower color and bloom season.

D. kingianum. Cool grower. Zones 16, 17, 22–24; H1. Native to Australia. Makes large clumps of 2–20-in. pseudobulbs topped by 4-in. leaves. In late winter or early spring, erect spikes to 8 in. long carry a few or up to as many as 20 fragrant, inch-wide flowers in pink, white, or red. Thrives outdoors along California coast if protected from frost.

D. nobile. Cool grower. Zone H1. Himalayan native. Canes 12–20 in. tall carry two ranks of 2–3½-in. leaves; leaves last for about 2 years. Short inflorescences borne on leafy and leafless canes carry two to four fragrant, 1½-in., white to purplish pink flowers with a yellow or white zone surrounding a dark purple eye. Blooms almost any time of year. The parent of many colorful hybrids.

D. speciosum. Cool grower. Zones 16, 17, 22–24; H1. From Australia. Large masses of 4-in. to 3-ft. pseudobulbs topped with 1½–10-in.-long leaves. Blooms in late winter or early spring. Inflorescences are crowded spikes of fragrant, creamy to yellow flowers; they resemble bushy foxtails, can reach 2–2½ ft. long.

DENDROMECON

BUSH POPPY

Papaveraceae

EVERGREEN SHRUBS

ZONES VARY BY SPECIES

FULL SUN

NO IRRIGATION NEEDED

Dendromecon harfordii

Both species described below give showy display of bright yellow, 2-in.-wide, poppylike flowers. Use on banks and roadsides, with other native shrubs.

D. harfordii (D. rigida harfordii). ISLAND BUSH POPPY. Zones 7–9, 14–24. Native to Santa Cruz and Santa Rosa islands off coast of Southern California. Rounded or spreading large shrub or small tree 8–20 ft. tall and as wide. Deep green leaves to 3 in. long, half as wide. Free flowering from spring into early summer, with scattered bloom throughout year. Prune to thin or shape after bloom.

D. rigida. BUSH POPPY. Zones 4–12, 14–24. In Zones 4 and 5, grows best as a south-wall shrub. Native to dry chaparral in lower elevations in California. Untidy growing wild. Freely branched shrub 4–8 ft. tall and 4–6 ft. wide, with shredding yellowish gray or white bark. Thick, veiny, gray-green leaves 1–4 in. long. Flowers in spring. Prune back to about 2 ft. after bloom.

DEODAR CEDAR. See CEDRUS deodara

DESCHAMPSIA

HAIR GRASS

Poaceae (Gramineae)

PERENNIAL GRASSES

ZONES 2–24, EXCEPT AS NOTED

FULL SUN OR PARTIAL SHADE

WATER NEEDS VARY BY SPECIES

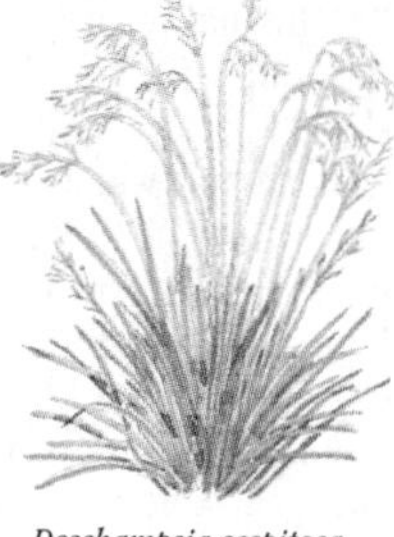

Deschampsia cespitosa vivipara

Hair grasses are grown for their graceful clumps of arching foliage and airy clouds of flowers. Although they grow over much of North America, most garden selections are imports from Europe. Use in mass plantings.

D. cespitosa. TUFTED HAIR GRASS. Clumps of narrow dark green leaves to 1–2 ft. tall and 2 ft. wide, evergreen except in colder climates. Airy inflorescences in late spring or early summer can increase plant height to 4 ft. or taller; they are green to greenish gold, turning straw color in winter. Good subject for planting under native oaks. 'Bronzeschleier' ('Bronze Veil') has bronzy yellow inflorescences; those of 'Goldgehänge' and 'Goldstaub' are golden yellow. *D. c. vivipara,* also known as 'Fairy's Joke', produces plantlets instead of seeds; these droop to the ground and may take root. All of the above forms of *D. cespitosa* take regular water.

D. c. holciformis, Pacific hair grass, grows in Zones 4–9, 14–24. It has darker green foliage than the species and dense, narrow, relatively coarse inflorescences. Takes marshy, even brackish conditions.

D. flexuosa. CRINKLED HAIR GRASS. Smaller than *D. cespitosa* (usually less than 2 ft. tall and about a foot wide in bloom), with more open, bronze to pale greenish yellow inflorescences in midsummer. Succeeds in dry woodland shade as well as in sunnier or moister situations.

DESERT BROOM. See BACCHARIS sarothroides

DESERT HOLLY. See ATRIPLEX hymenelytra

DESERT HONEYSUCKLE. See ANISACANTHUS

DESERT IRONWOOD. See OLNEYA tesota

DESERT LAVENDER. See HYPTIS emoryi

DESERT MARIGOLD. See BAILEYA multiradiata

DESERT OLIVE. See FORESTIERA neomexicana

DESERT SPOON. See DASYLIRION wheeleri

DESERT WILLOW. See CHILOPSIS linearis

DEUTZIA

Saxifragaceae

DECIDUOUS SHRUBS

ZONES 2–11, 14–17, EXCEPT AS NOTED

FULL SUN OR LIGHT SHADE

REGULAR WATER

Deutzia × rosea

These shrubs are best used among evergreens, where they can make a show when in flower, then blend back in with other greenery later on. Bloom season coincides with that of late-spring bulbs such as tulips and Dutch iris. Prune shrubs after bloom. With low- or medium-growing kinds, cut some of oldest stems to ground every other year. Prune tall-growing kinds severely by cutting back wood that has flowered. Cut to outward-facing side branches.

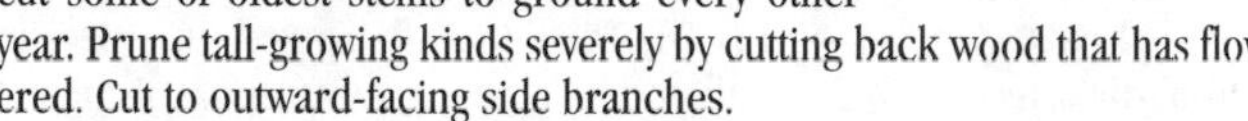

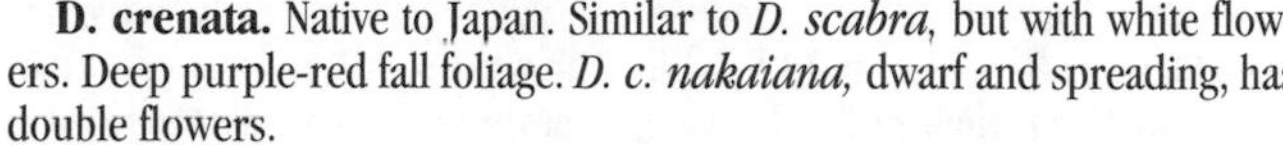

D. crenata. Native to Japan. Similar to *D. scabra,* but with white flowers. Deep purple-red fall foliage. *D. c. nakaiana,* dwarf and spreading, has double flowers.

D. × elegantissima. Grows to 6 ft. tall and wide, with pink flowers. 'Rosealind', 4–5 ft. tall and wide, has deep rose flowers.

D. gracilis. SLENDER DEUTZIA. Native to Japan. To 2–4 ft. (possibly 6 ft.) tall, 3–4 ft. wide. Many slender stems arch gracefully, carry bright green, 2½-in., sharply toothed leaves and clusters of snowy white flowers. 'Nikko' grows only 1–2 ft. by 5 ft. and can be used as a ground cover.

D. hybrids. Zones 2b–9, 14–23. These include 'Pink-a-Boo', an erect grower to 6–8 ft. tall and 6 ft. wide, with large clusters of pink flowers; and 'Magicien', similar but with dark red flowers.

D. × rosea. To 3–4 ft. tall and wide, with finely toothed, 1–3-in.-long leaves. Short clusters of pinkish flowers with white interiors.

D. scabra. Native to Japan, China. To 7–10 ft. by 6 ft. Oval, scallop-toothed, 3-in.-long, dull green leaves are roughish to touch. White or pinkish flowers in narrow, upright clusters. 'Pride of Rochester' has large clusters of small, frilly, double white flowers tinged pink. 'Codsall' ('Codsall Pink') bears double pink blooms. Leaves of 'Variegata' are marked with white.

DEVIL'S WALKING STICK. See ARALIA spinosa

DIANELLA tasmanica

Liliaceae

PERENNIAL

ZONES 8, 9, 14–24

FULL SUN IN COOLER CLIMATES ONLY

REGULAR WATER

Dianella tasmanica

From southeastern Australia, including Tasmania. Grows 3–4 ft. high; narrower than tall when young, but can spread by rhizomes. Long, sturdy, swordlike green leaves (striped white in 'Variegata'). Loose clusters of small blue summer flowers on straight, slender stalks are followed by glistening turquoise blue berries that last for 2 months or longer. Drought tolerant but looks better with regular moisture. Provide rich, porous soil and routine fertilizing. Attractive near swimming pools.

DIANTHUS

PINK

Caryophyllaceae

PERENNIALS, BIENNIALS, AND ANNUALS

ZONES A2, A3, 1–24, EXCEPT AS NOTED

LIGHT SHADE IN HOTTEST CLIMATES

REGULAR WATER

Dianthus caryophyllus

Over 300 species and extremely large number of hybrids, many with high garden value. Most kinds form attractive evergreen mats or tufts of grasslike green, gray-green, blue-green, or blue-gray leaves. Single, semidouble, or double flowers in white and shades of pink, rose, red, yellow, and orange; many have rich, spicy fragrance. Main bloom period for most is spring into early summer; some kinds rebloom later in season or keep going into fall if faded flowers are removed.

Among dianthus are appealing border favorites such as cottage pink and sweet William, highly prized cut flowers such as carnation (clove pink), and rock garden miniatures. Many excellent named varieties not mentioned here are available locally.

All kinds of dianthus thrive in light, fast-draining soil. Carnations, sweet William, and cottage pinks need fairly rich soil; rock garden or alpine types require a gritty growing medium, with added lime if soil is acid. Avoid overwatering. Sow seed of annual kinds in flats or directly in garden. Propagate perennial kinds by cuttings made from tips of growing shoots, by division or layering, or from seed. Carnation and sweet William are subject to rust and fusarium wilt.

D. 'Allwoodii'. Perennial. Group of pinks derived from crossing carnation *(D. caryophyllus)* and cottage pink *(D. plumarius)*. Plants vary in size, but most are 12–15 in. high and 2 ft. wide, with gray-green foliage and two blossoms per stem. Strongly clove-scented flowers may be pink, white, or red. Long bloom period if deadheaded regularly. More compact and floriferous than their *D. plumarius* parent.

D. arenarius. Perennial. From Europe. Tufted plant to 1½ ft. tall and wide, with narrow, grass green leaves and 1½-in.-wide, fringed white flowers sometimes marked with green or purple. Highly fragrant; can tolerate some shade.

D. barbatus. SWEET WILLIAM. Vigorous biennial often grown as annual. From southern Europe. To 20 in. tall and 1 ft. wide, with sturdy stems. Leaves are flat, light to dark green, 1½–3 in. long. Dense clusters of white, pink, rose, red, purplish, or bicolored flowers, about ½ in. across, set among leafy bracts; not very fragrant. Sow seed in late spring for bloom the following year. Double-flowered and dwarf strains are obtainable from seed. Indian Carpet is only 6 in. tall. Roundabout and Summer Beauty strains (1 ft.) bloom the first year from seed.

D. caryophyllus. CARNATION, CLOVE PINK. Perennial. Zones A2, A3; 1–24; H1. Highly bred Mediterranean species. Two distinct categories exist: florists' and border types. Both have double flowers, bluish green leaves, and branching, leafy stems that often become woody at base.

Border carnations are bushier and more compact (12–14 in. high and wide) than florists' type. Fragrant, 2–2½-in.-wide flowers are borne in profusion. Effective as shrub border edgings, in mixed flower borders, and in containers. Hybrid carnations grown from seed are usually treated as annuals but often live over. 'Juliet' makes compact, foot-tall clumps and bears 2½-in. scarlet flowers over a long season; 'Luminette', 2 ft. tall, is similar. Pixie Delight strain also is similar but includes full range of carnation colors. Knight series has strong stems, blooms in 5 months from seed; Bambino strain is a little slower to bloom. There is also a strain called simply Hanging Mixed, with pink- or red-flowered plants that sprawl or hang from pot or window box. Newer varieties include bright red 'Cinnamon Red Hots', to 1 ft. tall; rose pink 'Pinkie', reaching 6 in. high; and foot-tall 'Velvet 'n Lace', with frilly dark red flowers edged in white.

Florists' carnations are grown commercially in greenhouses, outdoors in gardens in mild-winter areas, including higher-elevation gardens in

Hawaii. Greenhouse-grown plants reach 4 ft., have fragrant flowers 3 in. wide in many colors—white, shades of pink and red, orange, purple, yellow; some are variegated. For large flowers, leave only terminal bloom on each stem, pinching out all other buds down to fifth joint, below which new flowering stems will develop. Stake to prevent sprawling. Start with strong cuttings taken from the most vigorous plants of selected named varieties. Sturdy plants conceal supports, look quite tidy.

D. chinensis. CHINESE PINK, RAINBOW PINK. Biennial or short-lived perennial; most varieties grown as annuals. Erect plant to 6–30 in. high and 6–10 in. wide; stems branch only at top. Stem leaves narrow, 1–3 in. long, ½ in. wide, hairy on margins. Basal leaves are usually gone by flowering time. Flowers about 1 in. across, rose lilac with deeper-colored eye; lack fragrance.

Modern strains are compact domes (1 ft. tall or less) covered with bright flowers in white, pink, red, and all variations and combinations of those colors. 'Fire Carpet' is a brilliant solid red, 'Snowfire' white with a red eye. Telstar is a bushy, extra dwarf (6–8-in.) strain with dark green leaves. Petals are deeply fringed on some, smooth edged on others. Some flowers have intricately marked eyes. Sow directly in ground in spring, in full sun, for summer bloom. Pick off faded flowers with their bases to prolong bloom.

D. deltoides. MAIDEN PINK. Perennial (even though it blooms in just a few weeks from seed). From Europe and Asia. To 8–12 in. high, forming a loose mat to 1 ft. wide. Blossoms about ¾ in. wide, with sharp-toothed petals, are borne at ends of forked flowering stems with short leaves. Colors include white and light or dark rose to purple, spotted with lighter colors. Blooms in summer, sometimes again in fall. Useful, showy ground or bank cover. Can tolerate half-day shade.

Varieties include white 'Albus', deep red 'Vampire', bright scarlet 'Zing', and rose red 'Zing Rose'. Microchip is a mixture including pinks, reds, and white, often with a contrasting eye.

D. gratianopolitanus (D. caesius). CHEDDAR PINK. Perennial. From Europe. Neat, ground-hugging, foot-wide mat of blue-gray foliage. Stems 6–10 in. high bear small, typically pink to rose, single blossoms (less than an inch across) that are very fragrant. Bloom season lasts from spring to fall if plants are deadheaded regularly. Effective as ground cover or edging or in rock garden.

'Bath's Pink'. Fringed, soft pink blooms on 12–15-in. stems.

'Little Boy Blue'. Foot-high stems bearing white flowers dotted with pink; foliage is intense blue gray.

'Little Joe'. Crimson flowers on 6-in. stems.

'Rose Bowl'. Cerise rose blossoms on 6-in. stems.

'Spotty'. Looks much like 'Rose Bowl', but flowers are heavily spotted with white.

'Tiny Rubies'. Dwarf selection with double ruby red flowers on 4-in. stems; clump spreads 4 in. wide.

D. plumarius. COTTAGE PINK. Perennial. Zones A1; 1–24. Charming, almost legendary European species, cultivated for hundreds of years and used in developing many hybrids. Typically has loosely matted gray-green foliage in clump to 2 ft. wide. Flowering stems 10–18 in. tall; spicily fragrant, dark-centered flowers in rose, pink, or white, with more-or-less fringed petals. Highly prized are old laced pinks, with white flowers in which each petal is outlined in red or pink. Cottage pinks bloom from summer to fall if deadheaded. Indispensable edging for borders or for peony or rose beds. Perfect addition to small arrangements and old-fashioned bouquets.

Choice selections include 'Dad's Favorite', which bears red-edged double white flowers on 10-in. stems; 'Essex Witch', with semidouble rose pink flowers on 5-in. stems; and 'Musgrave's Pink', a foot-tall classic that is at least 200 years old and bears intensely fragrant, single white blooms with a green eye.

Diapensiaceae. The diapensia family contains a few perennials and tiny shrubs native to northern parts of the globe. Some, such as *Shortia,* are useful in shady gardens or rock gardens.

DIASCIA

TWINSPUR

Scrophulariaceae

PERENNIALS AND ANNUALS

ZONES VARY BY SPECIES

PARTIAL SHADE IN HOTTEST CLIMATES

MODERATE TO REGULAR WATER

Diascia barberae

South African natives related to snapdragon *(Antirrhinum).* The coral to purplish pink flowers each have two prominent spurs on the back; these bear oils attractive to pollinating bees. Blooms are carried in spikelike clusters at stem ends from spring through early summer and often into fall. At their best used in rock gardens, borders, or containers. With the exception of *D. barberae,* all of the species listed here are perennial, though these perennials may die in winter if planted in heavy, wet soil.

D. barberae. Annual. Zones 1–10, 14–24. Mat-forming plant to 10 in. tall, 20 in. wide, with rose pink blossoms. 'Blackthorn Apricot' bears apricot-colored flowers.

D. cordata. Zones 7–9, 14–24. Low green mat to 6 in. high and 20 in. wide, with 10-in. sprays of salmon pink blossoms.

D. fetcaniensis. Zones 4–9, 14–24. To 10 in. high and 20 in. wide, with rose pink blooms.

D. hybrids. Zones 4–9, 14–24. These include 'Emma', an especially cold-hardy selection to 2 ft. tall and 4 ft. wide, with raspberry-colored blossoms; 'Langthorn's Lavender', to 1 ft. tall, with lavender blooms; and 'Red Start', to 8 in. high and 1 ft. wide, with watermelon red flowers. 'Ruby Field', to 10 in. high and 2 ft. wide, bears salmon pink blossoms; it is similar to *D. cordata,* one of its parents, but has a longer bloom season. A group of new hybrids from England (all 7–10 in. high and 1½ ft. wide) includes coral pink 'Coral Belle'; 'Little Charmer', pink with a dark red eye; rosy red 'Red Ace'; and deep pink 'Strawberry Sundae'.

D. integerrima. Zones 2–9, 14–24. To 1½ ft. tall, creeping to 3–4 ft. wide. Small, linear leaves to 1 in. long. Loose spikes of rich purplish pink flowers. 'Coral Canyon' grows 12–15 in. high and 1½ ft. wide, bears salmon pink flowers.

D. rigescens. Zones 7–9, 14–24. To 1 ft. high. Sprawling stems form clumps to 1 ft. tall, 2 ft. wide, turn up at ends to display 6–8-in. spikes of rich pink flowers. Cut out old stems.

D. vigilis. Zones 4–9, 14–24. To 20 in. high and slightly wider, with fleshy green leaves and light pink flowers.

DICENTRA

BLEEDING HEART

Fumariaceae

PERENNIALS

ZONES 1–9, 14–24, EXCEPT AS NOTED

PARTIAL OR FULL SHADE

REGULAR WATER, EXCEPT AS NOTED

Dicentra spectabilis

Delicate-looking plants. Graceful, divided, fernlike foliage. Dainty pendent flowers, usually heart shaped, in pink, rose, yellow, or white on leafless, horizontal to arching stems. In general, dicentras need rich, light, moist, porous soil. Never let water stand around roots. Foliage dies down even in mild-winter climates; mark clumps to avoid digging into roots in dormant season. Short lived in mild-winter areas.

D. chrysantha. GOLDEN EARDROPS. Native to inner Coast Ranges and Sierra Nevada foothills of California. Erect plant with sparse, blue-gray, divided leaves on stout, hollow, 4–5-ft. stems. Golden yellow, short-spurred flowers, held upright in large clusters. Plant grows 1½ ft. wide.

Requires warmth. Unlike many dicentras, this species needs soil that is not too rich; make sure drainage is good. Plant has deep taproot and does not need irrigation during its flowering in spring and summer. Seed available from wildflower specialists.

D. eximia. FRINGED BLEEDING HEART. Native to northeastern U.S. Forms tidy clump 1–1½ ft. high and wide. Blue-gray basal leaves are more finely divided than those of *D. formosa.* Deep rose pink flowers with short, rounded spurs bloom from midspring into summer. Cut back for second growth and occasional repeat bloom. Does not spread by rhizomes but may extend itself by self-sowing.

D. formosa. WESTERN BLEEDING HEART. Native to moist woods along Pacific Coast. To 1½ ft. tall, 3 ft. or wider. Blue-green foliage. In spring, leafless flower stalks hold clusters of pendulous pale or deep rose flowers on reddish stems. Spreads freely by rhizomes and seeding, forming large colonies. 'Zestful' is everblooming, with deep rose flowers. *D. f. oregana* grows to 1 ft. tall, has silvery green leaves and cream-colored flowers that are tipped with purple.

D. hybrids. *D. eximia* and *D. formosa* cross freely to yield hybrids, many of which have been named. The following are among the most commonly cultivated; they grow 1–1½ ft. high and 1½–2 ft. across (eventually spreading more widely) and bloom from spring into summer.

'Bacchanal'. Finely cut, gray-green leaves and dark red flowers.

'Bountiful'. Dark blue-green foliage and purplish pink to dusky red flowers.

'Langtrees'. Silvery green foliage and white flowers shaded pink.

'Luxuriant'. Zones A1–A3; 1–9, 14–24. Medium to dark green leaves and red flowers.

D. spectabilis. COMMON BLEEDING HEART. Zones A1–A3; 1–9, 14–24. Native to Japan. Old garden favorite; showiest and largest leafed of all bleeding hearts. To 2–3 ft. high, 3 ft. wide; stems are set with soft green leaves. Blooms in late spring, bearing flowers on one side of arching stems—rose pink, pendulous, heart shaped, with protruding white inner petals. 'Alba' ('Pantaloons') is a pure white form.

Plants generally die down and become dormant by midsummer, but they'll keep going longer in cool-summer climates if given adequate moisture. Plant summer-maturing perennials nearby to fill the gap. Dormant roots—fleshy and sometimes even woody—are available at nurseries from late fall to earliest spring; plant as soon as they become available in your area. In the Southwest, you can sometimes establish plants permanently in a cool, moist spot in foothill canyons, but usual practice in these areas is to plant new roots in ground or container each year and discard plants in early summer after blooming. In Southern California, plants usually last for only one season. Best in partial shade.

DICHONDRA micrantha

Convolvulaceae

PERENNIAL

ZONES 8–10, 12–24; H1, H2

FULL SUN OR PARTIAL SHADE

REGULAR WATER

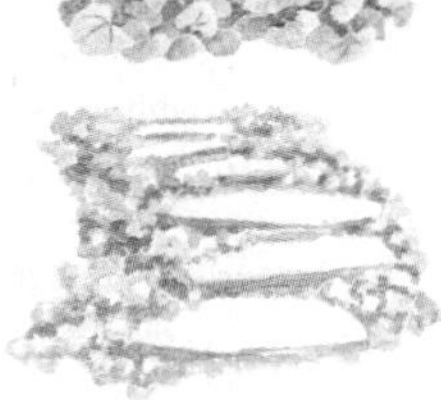

Dichondra micrantha

Ground-hugging plant that spreads by rooting surface runners. Its small, round leaves look like miniature water lily pads. In shade and with regular moisture and nutrients it can grow to 6 in. high and require frequent mowing. Once favored and commonly used as a lawn, but large plantings were so often devastated by flea beetles that it is now used mainly in limited spaces. Good in small areas that are subject to foot traffic—as between stepping-stones—where it stays low and seldom (if ever) needs trimming or mowing. Often sold as *D. carolinensis* or *D. repens.*

FOR GROWING SYMBOL EXPLANATIONS
PLEASE SEE PAGE 161

DICHORISANDRA thyrsiflora

BLUE GINGER

Commelinaceae

PERENNIAL

ZONES 23, 24; H1, H2; OR INDOORS

LIGHT SHADE; BRIGHT INDIRECT LIGHT

AMPLE WATER

Dichorisandra thyrsiflora

This Brazilian native is not a true ginger but rather a robust and upright-growing relative of wandering Jew *(Tradescantia, Zebrina).* Fleshy, unbranched or sparsely branched stems to 6–8 ft. rise from a fleshy rhizome. Deep green, oval, 6–12-in.-long, evergreen leaves are spirally arranged around the stem, forming a 3-ft.-wide foliage clump. Flowers are deep violet blue, in 6-in. spikes at tops of stems throughout the year. Best in moist soil enriched with organic matter. Easy to propagate by cuttings. As a houseplant or in greenhouse, grows 3 ft. tall in an 8-in. pot, taller in a large container.

DICKSONIA

Dicksoniaceae

TREE FERNS

ZONES VARY BY SPECIES

FULL SUN IN COOLER CLIMATES ONLY

REGULAR WATER

Dicksonia antarctica

Hardy, slow growing, from Southern Hemisphere. Easy to transplant and establish. See Ferns for culture.

D. antarctica. TASMANIAN TREE FERN. Zones 8, 9, 14–17, 19–24; H1. Native to southeastern Australia, Tasmania. Hardiest of tree ferns; well-established plants tolerate 20°F/–7°C. Thick, red-brown, fuzzy trunk grows slowly to 15 ft. Many arching, 3–6-ft. fronds grow from top of trunk; mature fronds are more finely cut than those of Australian tree fern *(Cyathea).*

D. squarrosa. Zones 17, 23, 24; H1. Native to New Zealand. Slender, dark trunk grows slowly to 20 ft. tall. Flat crown of 8-ft.-long, stiff, leathery fronds. Much less frequently grown than *D. antarctica.*

Dicksoniaceae. The dicksonia family of tree ferns differs only in technical details from the other tree fern family, Cyatheaceae. One representative is *Dicksonia.*

DICLIPTERA

Acanthaceae

PERENNIALS

ZONES VARY BY SPECIES

FULL SUN OR PARTIAL SHADE

WATER NEEDS VARIES BY SPECIES

Dicliptera suberecta

Tender perennials with narrow, tubular, two-lipped blossoms. Where stems are not killed to ground by frost, shear to about 6 in. high in late winter.

D. resupinata. Zones 13, 18–23; root hardy to about 22°F/-6°C. Native to washes and rocky slopes from southeastern Arizona and southwestern New Mexico into Mexico. Open, sparse growth to 2 ft. tall, 2–3 ft. wide. Elongated heart-shaped, 1-in.-long leaves are dark green, with an attractive purplish cast in cool weather. Slender, rosy purple, ¾-in.-long flowers from late spring to fall. Sometimes reseeds but is not invasive. Little or no water.

D. suberecta (Jacobinia suberecta, Justicia suberecta). Zones 12, 13, 15–17, 19, 21–24. Native to Uruguay. Woody-based perennial 2 ft. tall,

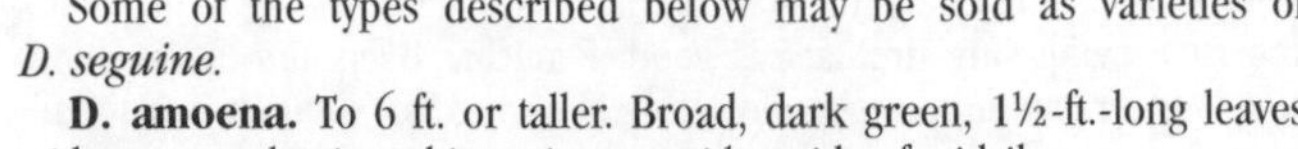

1½ ft. wide, with grayish green, softly downy leaves 1½–3 in. long and half as wide. Summertime clusters of bright orange-red, 1½-in.-long flowers attract hummingbirds. Moderate to regular water.

DICTAMNUS albus

GAS PLANT, FRAXINELLA

Rutaceae

PERENNIAL

ZONES 1–9

FULL SUN OR LIGHT SHADE

MODERATE TO REGULAR WATER

OIL FROM IMMATURE SEED CAPSULES MAY CAUSE AN ALLERGIC SKIN REACTION

Dictamnus albus 'Albiflorus'

Native Europe to northern China. Sturdy, long lived, extremely permanent in colder climates, needing little care once established. Forms clumps 2½–4 ft. high, 3 ft. wide. In early summer, produces loose spires of blossoms at branch tips; each flower resembles a wild azalea, with narrow petals and prominent greenish stamens. Pink is the basic color, but nurseries offer lilac purple 'Purpureus' and white 'Albiflorus'. Seedpods that follow can be left in place for fall interest. Glossy olive green leaves with 9 to 11 leaflets, each 1–3 in. long, are handsome throughout the growing season.

Plant emits strong lemony scent when rubbed or brushed against. In warm, humid weather, oils from immature seed capsules may briefly ignite if you hold a lighted match immediately beneath a flower cluster—hence the common name "gas plant" (this "ignition test" does not harm plant).

Effective in borders; good cut flower. Divide infrequently, since divisions are difficult to establish and often take 2 or 3 years to bloom well. Propagate from seed sown in fall or spring; or take root cuttings in spring.

DIDISCUS coeruleus. **See TRACHYMENE coerulea**

DIEFFENBACHIA

DUMB CANE

Araceae

PERENNIALS

ZONES 24; H1, H2; OR INDOORS

SUN OR SHADE; BRIGHT INDIRECT LIGHT

MODERATE WATER

SAP BURNS MOUTH, MAY PARALYZE VOCAL CORDS

Dieffenbachia amoena

From forests of tropical America. Grown for their strikingly variegated evergreen foliage—in colors varying from dark green to yellow green and chartreuse, with variegations in white or pale cream. In warmest climates, will grow year-round outdoors, either potted or in the ground as accent plants. Elsewhere, use them indoors. Small plants generally have single stems, while older ones may develop multiple stems. Taller than wide; those listed here are 1½–2 ft. wide. Mature plants bear flowers resembling odd, narrow callas *(Zantedeschia)*.

Give container plants fast-draining potting mix and feed with half-strength liquid fertilizer bimonthly in spring and summer. Underfed, underwatered plants show amazing endurance, recovering from severe wilting when better conditions come. Repotting is necessary when roots begin pushing plant up out of pot. Once repotted, plants usually send out new basal shoots. Sudden change from low to high light level will burn leaves, but you can move houseplants to a sheltered patio or lanai in summer. If plants get leggy, you can cut them back to 6 in. above the soil line; gangly specimens cut back in this way will usually resprout with multiple stems. Or start new plants by air layering or taking stem cuttings; discard the original, overly leggy looking plant.

Some of the types described below may be sold as varieties of *D. seguine.*

D. amoena. To 6 ft. or taller. Broad, dark green, 1½-ft.-long leaves with narrow, slanting white stripes on either side of midrib.

D. × bausei. To 3 ft. or taller. Greenish yellow, 1-ft.-long leaves have deep green blotches and white flecks.

D. 'Exotica'. To 3–4 ft. tall, with small leaves featuring dull green edges and extensive creamy white variegation. Midrib is creamy white.

D. maculata (D. picta). Grows to 6 ft. or taller. Broad, oval, green leaves reach 10 in. or longer, have greenish white dots and patches. Variety 'Rudolph Roehrs' has pale chartreuse foliage blotched with ivory and edged with green. Foliage of 'Superba' is thicker and slightly more durable than that of species and is more generously marked with creamy dots and patches.

DIERAMA

FAIRY WAND

Iridaceae

PERENNIALS FROM CORMS

ZONES 4–24

FULL SUN

REGULAR WATER

Dierama pulcherrimum

Native to South Africa. Evergreen; will die to the ground in extreme cold. Swordlike leaves to 2 ft. long; slender, tough, arching stems 4–7 ft. tall, topped in late spring or early summer with pendulous flowers that range in color from purplish pink to other pink shades to white. Blooms of *D. pendulum* are bell shaped, those of *D. pulcherrimum* more funnel shaped. Effective against background of dark green shrubs or at end of pool where graceful form can be displayed. Plant in spring, setting corms 3–5 in. deep and about 2 ft. apart. When dividing clumps, include several corms in each division.

DIETES

FORTNIGHT LILY, AFRICAN IRIS

Iridaceae

PERENNIALS FROM RHIZOMES

ZONES 8, 9, 12–24; H1, H2

FULL SUN OR PARTIAL SHADE

MODERATE TO REGULAR WATER

Dietes iridioides

Irislike plants with fans of stiff, narrow evergreen leaves; form dense, long-lasting clumps. Flowers resembling small Japanese irises consist of three outer and three inner segments; they appear on branched stalks throughout spring, summer, and fall, sometimes well into winter in mild climates. Bloom bursts seem to occur at 2-week intervals, hence the common name "fortnight lily." Flowers come in solid colors—white, cream, yellow; each of the three outer segments features a small blotch of contrasting orange, yellow, or brown. Each flower lasts only a day (with one exception), but supply of flowers on a stem is seemingly endless. Excellent in permanent landscape plantings with pebbles and rocks, shrubs and other long-lived perennials.

Plant from containers (bare rhizomes are not sold) at any time of year, setting plants about 2 ft. apart. All types look best with good soil and regular watering, but once established will perform satisfactorily even in poor soil or with infrequent or erratic watering. Clumps can remain undisturbed for years; when you need to divide, do so in fall or winter.

D. bicolor. From South Africa. Stems 2–3 ft. tall. Flowers about 2 in. wide and circular in outline, light yellow with dark brown to maroon blotches. Flower stems last only one year.

D. grandiflora (D. iridioides 'Johnsonii'). From South Africa. In general aspect, this is a somewhat taller (up to 3-ft.), larger version of *D. iridioides* and is usually sold as a variety of that species. Other differences include brown markings at the bases of inner segments and, on outer segments, yellow blotches that are actually bearded. Unlike all others, this species has flowers that last for 3 days before folding; flower stems are perennial (see *D. iridioides*).

D. hybrids. 'Lemon Drops' and 'Orange Drops' are hybrids of *D. bicolor* and resemble it save for flower color. 'Lemon Drops' is ivory with yellow blotches, 'Orange Drops' ivory with orange blotches. As is true for their other parent, *D. iridioides,* these hybrids' flower stems last more than a year; see below for care.

D. iridioides (D. vegeta, Moraea iridioides). From East Africa. Stems to 3 ft. tall. Waxy white flowers to 3 in. across have yellow-orange blotches, a few orange marks at bases of inner three segments; three style arms—appendages radiating from flower's center—are usually pale violet. To prevent self-sowing and prolong bloom, break off blossoms individually. Don't cut flower stems (they last for more than a year) until they clearly have stopped producing blooms; then cut back to lower leaf joint near base of stem. For the plant sold as *D. iridioides* 'Johnsonii', see *D. grandiflora.*

DIGITALIS

FOXGLOVE

Scrophulariaceae

PERENNIALS AND BIENNIALS

ZONES VARY BY SPECIES

EXPOSURE NEEDS VARY BY SPECIES

REGULAR WATER, EXCEPT AS NOTED

ALL PARTS ARE POISONOUS IF INGESTED

Digitalis purpurea

Mainly from Europe, Mediterranean region. Erect plants 2–8 ft. high form low clumps of hairy gray-green leaves topped by spikes of tubular flowers shaped like fingertips of a glove; colors include purple, yellow, white, pastels. Blossoms attract hummingbirds. Common foxglove *(D. pupurea)* is widely grown for height and color display in shaded gardens, though it will thrive in full sun in cool-summer regions. In parts of California and the Pacific Northwest, it has escaped from gardens to decorate roadsides. Other, less well known species are deserving subjects for borders, woodland edges, and larger rock gardens. Most tend to be biennials, but some can be coaxed into a second year of bloom if spent flowers are removed before they set seed.

Foxgloves need moist, well-drained soil, appreciate enrichment. Set out plants in fall for bloom the following spring and summer. Sow seed in spring. Control snails and slugs. After first flowering, cut off main spike; side shoots will develop and bloom late in the season. In hottest climates, plants will usually die out in summer heat. Plants self-sow freely; blooms of volunteers are often white or light colored.

D. ferruginea. RUSTY FOXGLOVE. Biennial or short-lived perennial. Zones 1–10, 14–24. To 4 ft. tall, 1½ ft. wide, with stems densely clothed in deeply veined leaves. Long, dense spikes of ¾–1¼-in.-long, yellowish flowers netted with rusty red. Full sun or light shade.

D. grandiflora (D. ambigua). YELLOW FOXGLOVE. Biennial or short-lived perennial. Zones 1–10, 14–24. To 3 ft. tall, 1½ ft. wide. Toothed leaves wrap around stem. Flowers are 2–3 in. long, yellowish marked with brown. 'John Innes Tetra' is a choice selection to 20. in. tall, with gray-green leaves and pale yellow flowers richly netted with gold and brown. Full sun or light shade.

D. laevigata. Perennial. Zones 3b–10, 14–24. To 3 ft. high, 1½ ft. wide, with smooth, narrow dark green leaves and inch-long, creamy yellow flowers speckled with purplish brown. Full sun; tolerates light shade.

D. lanata. GRECIAN FOXGLOVE. Biennial or short-lived perennial. Zones 2b–10, 14–24. To 2 ft. high and 1 ft. wide, with cream to light tan flowers netted with brown. Full sun or light shade.

D. lutea. Perennial. Zones 1–10, 14–24. Mediterranean native. To 2–2½ ft. tall, 15 in. wide, with narrow, tightly packed spires of pale yellow flowers dotted with brown. Partial or full shade; can take full sun in cool-summer climates.

D. × mertonensis. Perennial. Zones 1–10, 14–24. Spikes to 2–3 ft. high, bearing attractive coppery rose blooms above a foot-wide clump of furry leaves. Though a hybrid, it comes true from seed. Partial or full shade; can take full sun in cool-summer climates.

D. obscura. NARROW-LEAF FOXGLOVE. Woody-based perennial. Zones 2–10, 14–24. To 1½ ft. tall, 1 ft. wide, with lance-shaped leaves and spikes of drooping brown-and-yellow bells. Takes full sun or light shade, well-drained but not rich soil, and occasional deep watering.

D. purpurea. COMMON FOXGLOVE. Biennial or short-lived perennial. Zones A2, A3; 1–24. Variable, appearing in many garden forms. Bold, erect growth to 4 ft. or taller, with stems rising from clumps of large, rough, woolly light green leaves. Short-stalked stem leaves become smaller toward top of plant; these are the source of digitalis, a valued but highly poisonous medicinal drug. Pendulous flowers 2–3 in. long, borne in one-sided, 1–2-ft.-long spikes, purple with darker spots on lower, paler side. Partial or full shade; can take full sun in cool-summer climates.

Garden strains include 5-ft.-tall Excelsior, with fuller spikes than species and flowers held more horizontally to show off interior spotting; 3-ft. Foxy, which performs as an annual and blooms in 5 months from seed; 4-ft. Gloxiniiflora, bearing flowers that are larger and open wider than those of species; 3-ft.-high Peloric Mixed, with topmost flower of each spike open or bowl shaped and 3 in. wide; and Shirley, a tall (6-ft.), robust strain with a full range of colors.

D. thapsi. Perennial. Zones 2–10, 14–24. From Spain. To 1 ft. tall and wide, with furry foliage and short spires of drooping purplish pink flowers. Thrives under the same conditions as *D. obscura.* 'Spanish Peaks' is a selection chosen as outstanding by the Denver Botanic Garden.

DILL. See ANETHUM graveolens

DIMORPHOTHECA

AFRICAN DAISY, CAPE MARIGOLD

Asteraceae (Compositae)

ANNUALS

ZONES 1–24; BETTER IN WARM-SUMMER CLIMATES

FULL SUN

MODERATE WATER

Dimorphotheca sinuata

Gay, free-blooming South African natives with daisy flowers, unsurpassed for winter and spring color in dry-summer, warm-winter areas. In those regions, broadcast seeds in late summer or early fall where plants are to grow (preferably in light soil). In colder climates, sow in spring for summer bloom. Flowers close when shaded, on heavily overcast days, and at night. Use in broad masses as ground cover, in borders and parking strips, along rural roadsides, as filler among low shrubs. For other plants known as African daisy, see *Arctotis* and *Osteospermum fruticosum.*

D. barberae. See Osteospermum barberae

D. ecklonis. See Osteospermum ecklonis

D. fruticosa. See Osteospermum fruticosum

D. pluvialis (D. annua). Branched stems 4–16 in. high. Leaves to 3½ in. long, 1 in. wide, coarsely toothed. Yellow-centered, 1–2-in.-wide flower heads, with rays that are white above, violet or purple beneath. Variety 'Glistening White', dwarf form with flower heads 4 in. across, is especially desirable.

D. sinuata (D. aurantiaca). Best known of annual African daisies. To 4–12 in. high. Narrow, 2–3-in.-long leaves with a few teeth or shallow cuts. Flowers 1½ in. wide with yellow centers or dark centers with flecks of yellow, and orange-yellow rays sometimes deep violet at base. Hybrids between this species and *D. pluvialis* come in white and shades of yellow and light orange, often with contrasting dark centers.

Widely used for winter-to-spring color in Zones 10–13, where plantings reseed yearly. Provide some supplemental water if winter rains don't come; leave dry over summer. Highly invasive in hot desert regions; should not be used near parks, preserves, natural areas.

DIOON

Zamiaceae

CYCADS

ZONES VARY BY SPECIES

PARTIAL SHADE

REGULAR WATER

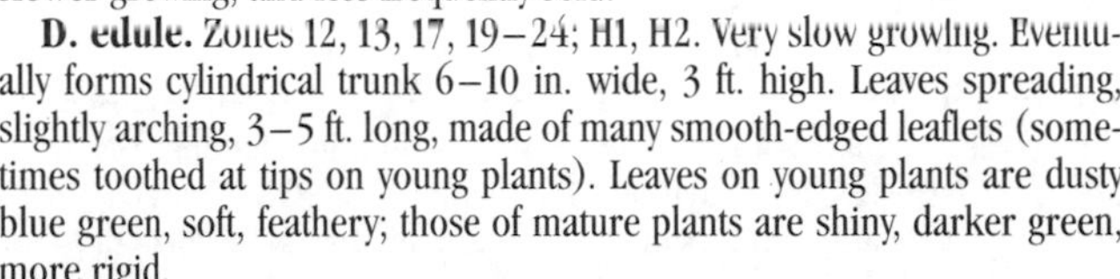
Dioon edule

In general, resemble *Cycas revoluta* and take same culture. Dioons are more tender, even slower growing, and less frequently sold.

D. edule. Zones 12, 13, 17, 19–24; H1, H2. Very slow growing. Eventually forms cylindrical trunk 6–10 in. wide, 3 ft. high. Leaves spreading, slightly arching, 3–5 ft. long, made of many smooth-edged leaflets (sometimes toothed at tips on young plants). Leaves on young plants are dusty blue green, soft, feathery; those of mature plants are shiny, darker green, more rigid.

D. spinulosum. Zones 21–24; H1, H2. Slow growth to 12 ft. high. Leaves to 5 ft. long, with up to 100 narrow, spine-toothed, dark green, 6–8-in.-long leaflets. Protect from frosts.

DIOSMA. See COLEONEMA

DIOSPYROS. See PERSIMMON

DIPLACUS. See MIMULUS

DIPLADENIA splendens. See MANDEVILLA splendens

DIPLOPAPPUS fruticosus. See FELICIA fruticosa

DIPOGON lignosus. See DOLICHOS lignosus

DISANTHUS cercidifolius

Hamamelidaceae

DECIDUOUS SHRUB

ZONES 4–7, 14–17

LIGHT SHADE IN HOTTEST CLIMATES

REGULAR WATER

Disanthus cercidifolius

Native to Japan. Slender-branched shrub to 10–12 ft. tall and wide, grown for magnificent fall color. Nearly round, smooth, 2–4-in.-wide leaves turn from bluish green to shades of deep red with orange tints at the onset of colder weather. Tiny, purplish fall flowers are mildly scented. Provide rich soil and protection from wind. No special pruning needed.

DISTICTIS

Bignoniaceae

EVERGREEN VINES

ZONES VARY BY SPECIES

FULL SUN OR PARTIAL SHADE

REGULAR WATER

Distictis buccinatoria

These Mexican natives are spectacular vines for milder climates, reaching heights of 20–30 ft. Glossy leaves consist of two leaflets with a central, three-part tendril that plants use for climbing. All bear long-lasting, trumpet-shaped flowers. Plant in good, well-drained soil; provide sturdy support, since growth is dense and heavy. Prune in winter to thin stems, control size.

D. buccinatoria (Bignonia cherere, Phaedranthus buccinatorius). BLOOD-RED TRUMPET VINE. Zones 8, 9, 14–24; H1. Oblong to oval leaflets 2–4 in. long. Clusters of 4-in.-long, yellow-throated flowers in orange red fading to bluish red; blossoms stand out well from vine. Blooms in bursts throughout year when weather warms. Give protected site in interior valleys of California.

D. laxiflora (D. lactiflora, D. cinerea). VANILLA TRUMPET VINE. Zones 16, 22–24; H1, H2. More restrained than most trumpet vines and requires less pruning. Oblong, 2½-in.-long leaflets. Vanilla-scented, 3½-in.-long trumpets appear in generous clusters throughout warmer months, sometimes giving 8 months of bloom; they are violet at first, fading to lavender and white.

Distictis 'Rivers'

D. 'Rivers'. ROYAL TRUMPET VINE. Zones 16, 22–24; H1, H2. Plants sold under this name are nearly a match for *D. buccinatoria* in vigor and foliage and have flowers of about the same size that are mauve to purple with a yellow to orange throat. Sometimes labeled *D. riversii.*

DITTANY OF CRETE. See ORIGANUM dictamnus

DIZYGOTHECA elegantissima. See SCHEFFLERA elegantissima

DODECATHEON

SHOOTING STAR

Primulaceae

PERENNIALS

ZONES VARY BY SPECIES

FULL SUN OR PARTIAL SHADE

REGULAR WATER DURING GROWTH AND BLOOM

Dodecatheon hendersonii

Mostly native to the West. Form basal rosette of pale green leaves (which later dry up in summer heat). Spring flowers somewhat like small cyclamen blooms, few to many in a cluster on leafless stems ranging from a few inches to 2 ft. tall. Rarely available in nurseries; buy seed for types native to your area (not all are hardy everywhere) from specialists in native plant seeds. Give porous, rich, well-drained soil. Let soil dry out after bloom.

Many species with flower colors ranging from white to pink, lavender to magenta. Western *D. hendersonii* (Zones 7–9, 14–24), for example, bears blossoms in white, pink shades, or magenta, carried 3–15 to each 1½-ft. stalk. Plant has 6-in. leaves, forms a clump just under a foot wide.

DODONAEA

HOP BUSH, HOPSEED BUSH

Sapindaceae

EVERGREEN SHRUBS

ZONES VARY BY SPECIES

FULL SUN OR LIGHT SHADE

LITTLE TO REGULAR WATER

Dodonaea viscosa 'Purpurea'

Tough shrubs mostly from Australia, although the most common species, *D. viscosa,* is native to the American Southwest and Hawaii as well as to many other parts of the world. All tolerate wind, poor soil, heat. Foliage is finely divided and fernlike in some, undivided in others. Flowers are insignificant, but seedpods are often showy and long lasting.

D. adenophora, D. microzyga. Zones 8, 9, 12–24. Plants sold under these names are probably forms of *D. tenuifolia.* Spreading shrub 3–10 ft. tall and somewhat wider, with finely cut leaves and very showy red fruits.

D. boroniifolia. Zones 8, 9, 14–24. Grows 1½–6 ft. tall, 3–9 ft. wide, with spreading branches and shiny, dark green, finely cut leaves 1½ in. long. Fruiting capsules are pink to purplish red, ¾ in. wide.

D. multijuga. Zones 8, 9, 14–24. Shrub to 6 ft. tall, 8–9 ft. wide, with finely cut leaves and showy red fruits.

D. viscosa. Zones 7–24; H1, H2. Native to many warmer regions, such as Arizona and Hawaii (where it is called *'a'ali'i*). Fast-growing shrub with many upright stems; reaches 10–15 ft. high and spreads almost as wide (can be trained to tree form by cutting out all but single stem). Willowlike green leaves to 4 in. long. Inconspicuous flowers followed in late spring or summer by ornamental, papery seed capsules that may be red, pink, tan, yellow, or green. In Hawaii, the capsules are used in leis.

'Purpurea', purple hop bush, is a selected form with strongly bronze-tinted foliage that darkens in winter; seedlings can vary greatly in color. Cutting-grown 'Saratoga' is uniformly deep purple. Seed capsules cream to pinkish in color. Plant purple-leafed kinds in full sun to retain rich foliage color; they will turn green in shade.

You can prune all members of this species into a hedge or espalier or plant 6–8 ft. apart and leave unpruned for a big informal screen. Takes any kind of soil, ocean winds, dry desert heat. Quite tolerant of aridity when established but will also take regular water (grows well in flower beds).

DOG-TOOTH VIOLET. See ERYTHRONIUM dens-canis

DOGWOOD. See CORNUS

DOLICHOS

Fabaceae (Leguminosae)

PERENNIAL VINES

ZONES VARY BY SPECIES

FULL SUN

REGULAR WATER

Dolichos lablab

These twining vines produce dense cover of light green leaves divided like fans into three leaflets.

D. lablab (Lablab purpureus). HYACINTH BEAN. Perennial vine usually grown as annual. All zones. Fast growing to 10 ft. Broad, oval leaflets to 3–6 in. long. Sweet pea–shaped purple or white flowers in loose clusters on long stems stand out from foliage. Flowers followed by velvety, beanlike magenta purple pods to 2½ in. long. Grow like string beans for quick screening. Needs good drainage. Naturalized in Hawaii.

D. lignosus (Dipogon lignosus). AUSTRALIAN PEA VINE. Zones 16, 17, 21–24; H2. Somewhat woody vine to 10 ft. or more, with small, triangular, 1½-in.-long leaflets and small rose purple flowers clustered at ends of long stalks. Evergreen in mild winters. Grow from seed and train on trellis or frame for summer screen.

DORONICUM

LEOPARD'S BANE

Asteraceae (Compositae)

PERENNIALS

ZONES A2, A3; 1–7, 14–17

PARTIAL SHADE

REGULAR WATER

Doronicum cordatum

Summer is the season for most yellow daisies, but these European natives bear a profusion of showy daisylike flowers in early to midspring. Blossoms are carried on long, slender, branching stems that rise from low, spreading, dense clumps of tooth-edged dark green leaves that are rounded to heart-shaped at base. Good cut flowers. Mark location of plants before they die back, and provide some moisture during dormancy. Young plants bloom best; divide clumps every 2 or 3 years in early autumn. Tolerate full sun in cool-summer climates; light, dappled, or partial shade otherwise.

D. cordatum (D. caucasicum, D. columnae, D. orientale). Flower heads to 2 in. wide, borne singly on 1–1½-ft. stems above a foot-wide foliage clump. Usually dies back in summer. 'Magnificum' and 'Finesse' are a little taller, with bigger blossoms.

D. plantagineum. PLANTAIN LEOPARD'S BANE. Larger, coarser-leafed plant than *D. cordatum,* suitable for a wild garden. Stout stems 2½–4 ft. tall rise above a 2-ft.-wide clump, each bearing a few 2–4-in. flowers. Goes dormant in summer.

DOROTHEANTHUS bellidiformis

LIVINGSTONE DAISY

Aizoaceae

SUCCULENT ANNUAL

ZONES A2; 1–24

FULL SUN

MODERATE WATER

Dorotheanthus bellidiformis

This ice plant—unlike most others—is an annual. Pretty and useful temporary carpet. Trailing, basally branching plant a few inches high, with fleshy, bright green leaves and daisylike, 2-in. flowers in white, pink, orange, red. Sow seed in warm weather. Comes into bloom quickly. Attracts bees. Tolerates poor, dry soil.

DOUBLE BRIDAL WREATH. See SPIRAEA cantoniensis

DOUGLAS FIR. See PSEUDOTSUGA menziesii

DOVE TREE. See DAVIDIA involucrata

DOXANTHA unguis-cati. See MACFADYENA unguis-cati

DRABA

Brassicaceae (Cruciferae)

PERENNIALS

ZONES VARY BY SPECIES

FULL SUN

REGULAR WATER

Draba aizoides

Some 300 species native to mountainous and subarctic regions of the world. All are low mat- or cushion-forming plants with tightly clustered, tiny leaves in rosettes and four-petaled yellow (rarely white) flowers in short, spikelike clusters. Rock garden plants that require perfect drainage, dislike soggy soil. Can endure great cold. The following are two of the most commonly planted species.

D. aizoides. Zones 2–7. Tufts of tiny rosettes form clumps 2–4 in. across. Flowering stems to 4 in. hold four to ten or more bright yellow flowers.

D. oligosperma. Zones 1–7. One of more than a dozen species native to the Rocky Mountain area. Makes silvery mats up to 1 ft. wide topped with loose clusters of yellow flowers carried on 4-in. stems.

FOR INFORMATION ON SELECTING PLANTS
PLEASE SEE PAGES 64–160

DRACAENA

Agavaceae

EVERGREEN PALMLIKE TREES

ZONES VARY BY SPECIES; OR INDOORS

SUN OR PART SHADE; BRIGHT INDIRECT LIGHT

MODERATE WATER

Dracaena draco

Foliage plants most widely grown indoors or on patio or lanai. Some show graceful, fountain-like form with broad, curved, ribbonlike leaves, occasionally striped with chartreuse or white. Others have very stiff, sword-shaped leaves. Outdoors, give all but *D. draco* a wind-protected site. In containers, water only when top ½–1 in. of soil is dry. Almost never bloom as houseplants. For other plants often called dracaena, see *Cordyline*.

D. australis. See Cordyline australis

D. deremensis. Zones 24; H2. Native to tropical Africa. Most commonly sold is variety 'Warneckii'; erect, slow growing to an eventual 15 ft. tall, 3 ft. wide, with 2-ft.-long, 2-in.-wide leaves in rich green striped white and gray. 'Bausei' is green with white center stripe; 'Longii' has broader white center stripe; 'Janet Craig' has broad, dark green leaves. Compact versions of 'Janet Craig' and 'Warneckii' exist.

D. draco. DRAGON TREE. Zones 16, 17, 21–24; H1, H2. Native to Canary Islands. Stout trunk with upward-reaching or spreading branches topped by clusters of heavy, 2-ft.-long, sword-shaped leaves. Grows slowly to 20 ft. high and as wide. Makes odd but interesting silhouette. Clusters of greenish white flowers form at branch ends. After blossoms drop, stemmy clusters remain. Trim them off to keep plants neat.

D. fragrans. CORN PLANT. Zones 21, 23, 24; H2. Native to West Africa. Upright, eventually to 20 ft. high and 5 ft. wide, but slow growing. Heavy, ribbonlike, blue-green leaves to 3 ft. long, 4 in. wide. (Typical plant in 8-in. pot will bear leaves about 1½ ft. long.) 'Massangeana' has broad yellow stripe in center of leaf. Other striped varieties are 'Lindenii' and 'Victoriae'.

D. marginata. Zones 21, 23, 24; H2. Very easy to grow, very popular. To 12 ft. tall, 5–6 ft. wide. Slender, erect, smooth gray stems carry chevron markings where old leaves have fallen. Stems topped by crowns of narrow, leathery leaves to 2 ft. long, ½ in. wide. Leaves are deep glossy green with narrow margin of purplish red. If plant grows too tall, cut off crown and reroot it. New crowns will appear on old stem. 'Tricolor' ('Candy Cane') adds narrow gold stripe to green and red.

Dracaena marginata

D. sanderana. Zones 21, 23, 24; H2. Native to West Africa. Neat and upright, to a possible 6–10 ft. tall, 2 ft. wide, somewhat resembling young corn plant. Strap-shaped, 9-in.-long leaves striped with white.

DRIMYS winteri

WINTER'S BARK

Winteraceae

EVERGREEN TREE

ZONES 5-9, 14-24

FULL SUN IN COOLER CLIMATES ONLY

REGULAR WATER

Drimys winteri

Native to southern Chile and Argentina. Slender tree to 25 ft. tall, 20 ft. wide; distinguished chiefly by its attractive foliage and dignified presence. Stems and branches, which tend to droop gracefully, have aromatic, mahogany red bark. Leathery, fragrant, bright green leaves are elliptical, 5–10 in. long. Small clusters of jasmine-scented, inch-wide, creamy white flowers appear in winter and spring. Usually multi-stemmed but easily trained to a single trunk. May require pruning from time to time to maintain a pleasingly symmetrical outline. Provide frost-sheltered location in Zones 5–7. Requires good drainage.

DROPWORT. See FILIPENDULA vulgaris

DROSANTHEMUM

Aizoaceae

SUCCULENT PERENNIALS

ZONES 14–24; H1

FULL SUN

LITTLE TO MODERATE WATER

Drosanthemum floribundum

The two South African ice plants described here are often confused with each other, although they are quite different. In both, leaves are covered by glistening dots that look like tiny ice crystals; both have typical ice plant flowers with many narrow petals, bloom in late spring and early summer, and endure poor soil.

D. floribundum. ROSEA ICE PLANT. Grows to 6 in. tall, but stems trail to considerable length or drape over rocks, walls. Best ice plant for reducing erosion on steep slopes (plant 1½ ft. apart). Pale pink, ¾-in.-wide flowers form sheets of bloom, attract bees. Often sold as *D. hispidum*.

D. hispidum. To 2 ft. tall, 3 ft. wide, less inclined to stem-root than *D. floribundum*. Showy, 1-in. purple flowers.

DRUMSTICKS. See ALLIUM sphaerocephalum, CRASPEDIA globosa

DRYAS

Rosaceae

PERENNIALS

ZONES A1–A3; 1–6

FULL SUN

MODERATE WATER

Dryas octopetala

Choice plants for rock gardens. Evergreen or partially so; somewhat shrubby at base, forming a carpet of leafy, creeping stems. Oblong leaves look like little oak leaves. Bloom from late spring into summer, bearing shiny white or yellow flowers that resemble strawberry blossoms. Ornamental seed capsules with silvery white tails follow the blooms.

D. drummondii. To 4 in. high, spreading 3 ft. or wider. Leaves 1½ in. long, white and woolly beneath. Nodding, ¾-in. yellow flowers.

D. octopetala. To 2–3 ft. high and 3 ft. wide, with 1-in. leaves and erect, 1½-in. white flowers.

D. × suendermannii. Hybrid between the two species above. To 4 in. high, 3 ft. wide. Leaves 1–1½ in. long. Nodding, 1¼-in. flowers are yellowish in bud, white in full bloom.

DRYOPTERIS

WOOD FERN

Polypodiaceae

FERNS

ZONES VARY BY SPECIES

PARTIAL OR FULL SHADE

REGULAR WATER, EXCEPT AS NOTED

Dryopteris expansa

Over 100 species from many parts of the world; only a few are generally offered by nurseries. Use in shade or woodland gardens. Grow in organically enriched soil.

D. arguta. COASTAL or CALIFORNIA WOOD FERN. Zones 2b, 4–9, 14–24. Native Washington state to Southern California. To 2½ ft. tall, 4 ft. wide. Dark green, finely cut, airy fronds. Not easy to grow in gardens; best naturalized in woods. Moderate water.

D. erythrosora. AUTUMN FERN. Zones 2–9, 14–24. Native to China and Japan. Erect growth to 2 ft. tall, 1½ ft. wide. One of the few ferns with seasonal color variation. Expanding fronds in spring are a blend of copper, pink, and yellow; they turn green in summer, then rusty brown in fall. Bright red spores, produced on leaf undersides, are an attractive winter feature.

Dryopteris erythrosora

D. expansa (D. dilatata). SPREADING WOOD FERN. Zones 2–7, 14–17, 19–24. Native to much of Northern Hemisphere, including western U.S. To 1–3 ft. tall, 3 ft. wide. Fronds even more finely cut than those of *D. arguta.* Named varieties sometimes seen in nurseries in the Northwest. In Southern California, does best in pots.

DUCHESNEA indica

INDIAN MOCK STRAWBERRY
Rosaceae
PERENNIAL
ZONES 1–24; H1, H2
SUN OR SHADE
MODERATE WATER

Duchesnea indica

Native to Japan, eastern Asia, India. Grows like strawberry, with trailing stems that root firmly along ground. Bright green, long-stalked leaves with three leaflets. Yellow, ½-in. flowers are followed by red, ½-in., nearly tasteless fruit that stands above foliage rather than under leaves as in true strawberry. Grows readily without much care. Best used as ground cover among open shrubs or small trees. Plant 1–1½ ft. apart. In a well-watered garden, it can become a rampant invader. Fruit attracts birds.

DUDLEYA

Crassulaceae
SUCCULENT PERENNIALS
ZONES VARY BY SPECIES
FULL SUN
MODERATE WATER

Dudleya brittonii

Native to California, Arizona, coastal Oregon, Baja California. About 40 species are known, and some of these are common on California's coastal cliffs or inland hills. Best known in cultivation is Baja California native *D. brittonii* (Zones 16, 17, 21–24), with 1½-ft.-wide leaf rosettes on stems that gradually lengthen into 1–2-ft. trunks; these lean or become prostrate as the plant ages. Fleshy leaves are covered with a heavy coat of chalky powder that can be rubbed off. When plants flourish, they produce reddish stalks that bear little yellow flowers in spring. Striking plant when well grown; needs bright light and shelter from rain, hail, and frost. Best under glass or plastic roof to keep powder from being washed off. Others are valued for use in containers, rock gardens, low borders. *D. caespitosa* (from Southern California; grows in Zones 9, 14–17, 19–24) and *D. farinosa* (Northern California and southern Oregon coast; succeeds in Zones 5, 7, 14–17, 19–24) are familiar sea-cliff plants; both are sometimes called cliff lettuce.

DUMB CANE. See DIEFFENBACHIA

DURANTA

Verbenaceae
EVERGREEN SHRUBS
ZONES VARY BY SPECIES
FULL SUN
REGULAR WATER
D. ERECTA BERRIES ARE POISONOUS IF INGESTED

Duranta erecta

Glossy green leaves arranged in pairs or whorls along stems. Attractive blue flowers in clusters attract butterflies in summer, are followed by bunches of berrylike yellow fruit. Plants sold as *D. stenostachya* are often actually *D. erecta;* distinguishing characteristics are described below. Use as quick, tall screen. Thrive in hot-summer areas. Need continual thinning and pruning to stay under control.

D. erecta (D. repens, D. plumieri). SKY FLOWER, GOLDEN DEWDROP, PIGEON BERRY. Zones 13, 16, 17–24; H1, H2. Native to southern Florida, West Indies, Mexico to Brazil. Fast growing to 10–25 ft. tall, 6–10 ft. wide. Tends to form multistemmed clumps; branches often drooping and vinelike. Stems may or may not have sharp spines. Oval to roundish leaves are 1–2 in. long, rounded or pointed at tip. Tubular violet-blue flowers flare to less than ½ in. wide. Waxy yellow berries in clusters 1–6 in. long. 'Alba' has white flowers.

D. stenostachya. BRAZILIAN SKY FLOWER. Zones 13, 16, 21–23; H2. Not as hardy as *D. erecta;* seems to require more heat. Makes neater, more compact shrub than *D. erecta,* growing to about 4–6 ft. tall, 3–5 ft. wide (under ideal conditions, 15 ft. high). Stems are spineless. Leaves are larger (3–8 in. long) than those of *D. erecta* and taper to long, slender point. Lavender-blue flowers are also somewhat larger; fruit clusters grow to 1 ft. long.

DUSTY MILLER. This name is given to a number of plants with gray foliage. The dusty miller of one region may be unknown in another. Among many dusty millers are *Artemisia stellerana, Centaurea cineraria, C. gymnocarpa, Chrysanthemum ptarmiciflorum, Lychnis coronaria, Senecio cineraria,* and *S. vira-vira.*

DUTCHMAN'S PIPE. See ARISTOLOCHIA macrophylla

DYMONDIA margaretae

Asteraceae (Compositae)
PERENNIAL
ZONES 15–24
FULL SUN OR LIGHT SHADE
MODERATE TO REGULAR WATER

Dymondia margaretae

Ground cover native to South Africa. Forms a tight mat 2–3 in. high, spreading slowly by offsets to 20 in. wide. Narrow (⅛-in.), evergreen leaves are 2–3 in. long, deep grayish green above, rolled in at the edges to show cottony white undersides. Summer flowers are yellow, 1–1½-in.-wide daisies half-buried in the foliage. Deep roots give established plants considerable drought tolerance, but they'll spread faster if watered. Use between paving blocks and stepping-stones, in rock gardens; can take light foot traffic.

FOR DEFINITIONS OF GARDENING TERMS
PLEASE SEE PAGES 746–750

DYPSIS (Neodypsis, Chrysalidocarpus)

Arecaceae (Palmae)

EVERGREEN TREES

ZONES VARY BY SPECIES; OR INDOORS

EXPOSURE NEEDS VARY BY SPECIES

WATER NEEDS VARY BY SPECIES

Dypsis lutescens

Madagascar natives better known by the alternative botanical names shown above. Both of these tropical species are rather tender, small to medium-size feather palms with graceful foliage and attractive trunks. Good container plants for patio, lanai. Give indoor plants bright filtered light.

D. decaryi (Neodypsis decaryi). TRIANGLE PALM. Zones 20–24; H2. Slow growing, single-trunked palm reaches 18–20 ft. tall, 12–15 ft. wide. Trunk is triangular in cross section because heavily keeled leafstalks grow in three ranks about the stem. Gray green fronds to 15 ft. long are strongly upright but arching at tips. Native to arid parts of Madagascar and requires little water. Full sun or light shade.

D. lutescens (Chrysalidocarpus lutescens, Areca lutescens). CANE PALM. Zones 23 (light shade), 24; H1, H2 (full sun). Clumping palm with slender yellowish trunks, yellow-green leaves, and clusters of golden yellow fruit. Slow growth to 28 ft. tall, 20 ft. wide; unlikely to reach that size in California. Protect from hot, dry wind. Drought tolerant but does best with regular water. Moderate salt tolerance.

DYSSODIA. See THYMOPHYLLA

EASTER CACTUS. See RHIPSALIDOPSIS gaertneri

EASTER LILY VINE. See BEAUMONTIA grandiflora

ECHEVERIA

Crassulaceae

SUCCULENT PERENNIALS

ZONES VARY BY SPECIES

FULL SUN OR PARTIAL SHADE, EXCEPT AS NOTED

MODERATE WATER, EXCEPT AS NOTED

Echeveria agavoides

Mexican natives that form rosettes of fleshy green or gray-green leaves, often marked with deeper colors. Long, slender, sometimes branched clusters of bell-shaped, nodding flowers, usually pink, red, or yellow. Good in rock gardens. Those that grow in Zone 12 need cool spot, partial shade there. Those suitable for Zone 13 need extra attention to grow outdoors in that area. Some types make good houseplants.

E. agavoides (Urbinia agavoides). Zones 8, 9, 12–24. Rosettes 6–8 in. across. Stiff, fleshy, sharp-pointed leaves are smooth and bright green, marked deep reddish brown at tips and edges. Flower stalks to 1½ ft. bear small red-and-yellow blooms.

E. crenulata. Zones 17, 21–24; or indoors. Loose rosettes, 1½ ft. across, on short, thick stems. Pale green or white-powdered leaves grow to 1 ft. long and 6 in. wide, with wavy, crimped, purplish red edges. Flower clusters to 3 ft. high, with a few yellow-and-red flowers. Striking plant. Shelter from hottest sun; water frequently during warm weather.

E. elegans. HEN AND CHICKS. Zones 8, 9, 12–24. Tight grayish white rosettes to 4 in. across, spreading freely by offsets. Pink flowers lined in yellow, in clusters to 8 in. long. Useful for pattern planting, edging, containers. Can burn in hot summer sun.

E. hybrids. Zones 8, 9, 12–24; or indoors. Generally have large, loose rosettes of big leaves on single or branched stems; plant size varies by hybrid. Leaves are crimped, waved, wattled, or heavily shaded with red, bronze, or purple. All are splendid potted plants; they do well in open ground in mild-summer areas. Among them are 'Arlie Wright', with large, open rosettes of wavy-edged, pinkish leaves; 'Cameo', with large blue-gray leaves, each centered with a large raised bump of the same color; and 'Perle von Nürnberg', with pearly lavender-blue foliage. 'Doris Taylor' is smaller, with short, close-set leaves densely covered with short hairs. Showy, nodding flowers are red and yellow.

E. × imbricata. HEN AND CHICKS. Zones 8, 9, 12–24. Rosettes 4–6 in. across, saucer shaped, gray green. Loose clusters of small, bell-shaped, orange-red flowers. Makes offsets very freely. Probably most common hen and chicks in California gardens.

Echeveria × imbricata

E. secunda. HEN AND CHICKS. Zones 8, 9, 14–24. Gray-green or blue-green rosettes to 4 in. across. Makes offsets freely. *E. s. glauca (E. glauca)* leaves faintly edged purple red; blue-green rosettes have a purplish tinge.

E. setosa. Zones 17, 23, 24. Dense rosettes to 4 in. across are dark green, densely covered with stiff white hairs. Red flowers are tipped with yellow. Good choice for rock gardens, shallow containers. Very tender.

ECHINACEA purpurea

PURPLE CONEFLOWER

Asteraceae (Compositae)

PERENNIAL

ZONES A2, A3; 1–24

FULL SUN

MODERATE TO REGULAR WATER

Echinacea purpurea

Native to central and eastern North America. Bristly, oblong, 3–4-in.-long leaves form 2-ft.-wide, dense foliage clump from which rise sparsely leafed flowering stems to 4 ft. tall. Blooms over long period in summer (may start in spring in mild-winter climates), bearing showy, 4-in. flowers with drooping rosy purple rays and a central orange-brown cone that resembles a beehive. Flowering may continue until frost. If faded flowers are left in place, bristly seed heads hang on into winter; seeds are favored by finches.

'Magnus' has deep purplish pink, orange-centered flowers to 7 in. wide. 'Bravado' is a 2-ft.-high selection with rosy purple blooms. 'White Lustre' (2½ ft. tall) and 'White Swan' (1½–2 ft. tall) have white rays and orange-yellow cones.

Use on outskirts of garden or in wide borders with other robust perennials. Generally does not need staking. Performs well in summer heat (though not in hottest desert areas, where it is mainly spring blooming). Good cut flower. Clumps spread slowly, become crowded after 3 or 4 years. Fleshy rootstocks can be difficult to separate; divide carefully, being sure each division has a shoot and roots. Or increase plantings by taking root cuttings, seeding, or transplanting self-sown seedlings.

ECHINOCACTUS

BARREL CACTUS

Cactaceae

CACTI

ZONES 12–24

PARTIAL SHADE IN HOTTEST CLIMATES

MODERATE WATER

Echinocactus grusonii

Numerous kinds of large, cylindrical cacti with prominent ribs and stout thorns. Many are native to Southwest. Best known in gardens is *E. grusonii,* golden barrel, a Mexican cactus of slow growth to 4 ft. high, 2½ ft. in diameter. With age, often produces offsets to form clumps 6 ft. across. Showy, stiff, yellow 3-in. spines; yellow, 1½–2-in. flowers at top of plant in summer. Protect from hard frosts. Water every couple of weeks in summer.

ECHINOCEREUS

HEDGEHOG CACTUS

Cactaceae

CACTI

ZONES VARY BY SPECIES

FULL SUN

MODERATE WATER

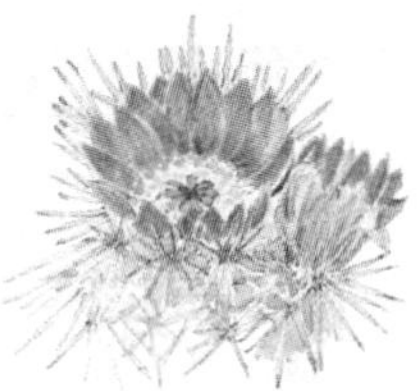
Echinocereus engelmannii

Nearly 50 species of hedgehog cactus grow in the southwestern U.S. and northern Mexico, with some growing at fairly high elevations in Utah and Colorado, where they are subject to freezing temperatures. All have cylindrical, ribbed bodies in clumps; showy red, yellow, purple, or white flowers with many rows of petals; and fleshy fruit, edible in some species. Although cold hardy in most zones, and often seen in collections, they are used in landscaping chiefly in desert or interior mountain gardens.

E. engelmannii. Zones 2, 3, 7, 10–24. Clumps 1–2 ft. tall, 3 ft. wide, with 3–4-in.-thick stems. Lavender to deep purplish red flowers 2–3 in. wide. Inch-long red fruits are edible.

E. triglochidiatus. CLARET CUP. Zones 2, 3, 10–14, 18–23. Dense clump, up to 3 ft. wide, sometimes with hundreds of 2–3-in.-diameter stems to a foot tall. Flowers are 3½ in. wide, orange to red; inch-long fruits (not edible) are pink to red.

ECHINOPS

GLOBE THISTLE

Asteraceae (Compositae)

PERENNIAL

ZONES A2, A3; 1–24

FULL SUN

MODERATE WATER

Echinops exaltatus

Well-behaved, decorative thistle relative for the perennial border. Rugged-looking, erect, rigidly branched plant 2–4 ft. tall and 2 ft. wide, with coarse, prickly, deeply cut gray-green leaves to 1 ft. long. Distinctive flower heads are spherical, about the size of golf balls; they look like pincushions stuck full of tubular metallic blue pins. Bloom midsummer to late fall.

Plants may be offered as *E. exaltatus, E. humilis, E. ritro,* or possibly *E. sphaerocephalus.* Whatever name you encounter, you're likely to get a plant closely resembling the general description above. 'Taplow Blue' has bright blue blossoms on 3–4 ft. stems. 'Veitch's Blue' has darker blue flowers on a plant 2½–3 ft. high.

Grow from divisions in spring or fall, or sow seed in flats or open ground in spring. Provide average, well-drained soil and moderate water. (With enriched soil and regular moisture, may grow too robustly and require staking.) Clump can be left in place, undivided, for many years. Flowers are excellent for dried arrangements; cut them before they open and dry them upside down.

ECHINOPSIS

Cactaceae

CACTI

ZONES 8–10, 12–24, EXCEPT AS NOTED; OR INDOORS

FULL SUN; BRIGHT SUNNY WINDOW

REGULAR WATER

Echinopsis chamaecereus

Small, spiny cacti from South America, generally grown in pots. Enormous number of species, hybrids, and selections; genus now includes plants formerly named *Lobivia* and *Lobivopsis* and still often sold under those names. All are showy and easy to grow, with many-petaled flowers in white and shades of yellow, pink, red, and orange. Free blooming during warm months if given good light, regular moisture from spring to fall, and fast-draining soil. Give little or no water in winter.

E. bruchii (Lobivia bruchii). SOUTH AMERICAN GOLDEN BARREL. Single, nearly round stem is 1 ft. tall and thick, with yellow spines and red, 3-in. flowers.

E. caespitosa (Lobivia caespitosa). Clustered cylindrical bodies, each 6 in. high and 2 in. thick, have dark, inch-long spines and orange, 3-in. flowers.

E. chamaecereus (Chamaecereus sylvestri). PEANUT CACTUS. To 4 in. high, 1–2 ft. wide. The cylindrical, ribbed, 2–3-in. joints fall off easily and root just as easily; even tiny ones produce flowers. Blooms are bright scarlet, nearly 3 in. long. Great favorite with children.

E. chrysantha (Lobivia chrysantha). Single stem is 2½ in. high, 3 in. wide. Orange-yellow, 2-in.-wide flowers with purple center.

E. eyriesii. Zones 16, 17, 21–24. Cylindrical, dark-spined cactus to 6–12 in. high and 2–4 ft. wide. Very large white flowers 8–10 in. long, 2–4 in. wide. Eventually forms clumps.

E. haageana (Lobivia haageana). Single stem grows 1 ft. tall, 3 in. thick. Flowers are 3 in. long, yellow with red throat.

E. hamatacantha. Zones 16, 17, 21–24. Rounded, to 4 in. high and 2 in. thick, with red to yellow, 3-in. flowers.

E. pentlandii (Lobivia boliviensis). Clustered round stems to 4 in. high and wide. Red, 2½-in.-long flowers.

ECHIUM

Boraginaceae

BIENNIALS, PERENNIALS, AND SHRUBS

ZONES VARY BY SPECIES

FULL SUN

LITTLE TO MODERATE WATER

E. VULGARE IS POISONOUS IF INGESTED

Echium candicans

Grown for striking form and flower clusters. All do well in dry, poor soil but need good drainage. All are excellent for seacoast gardens. Flowers attract bees. Give little or no water in mild-summer climates, weekly irrigation during summer in hotter areas.

E. candicans (E. fastuosum). PRIDE OF MADEIRA. Shrub. Zones 14–24. From Madeira, as its common name indicates. Large, picturesque plant to 5–6 ft. tall, 6–10 ft. wide, with many coarse, heavy branches. Narrow, hairy, gray-green leaves form roundish, irregular mounds at ends of stems. Great spikelike clusters of ½-in., bluish purple flowers stand out dramatically, well above foliage, in spring. Branch tips and developing flower spikes may be killed by late frosts. Use for bold effects against walls, at back of wide flower borders, on slopes. Prune lightly to keep bushy. Cut off faded flower spikes.

E. pininana. Woody-based perennial. Zones 16, 17, 22–24. From the Canary Islands. Sparsely branched, to 18 ft. tall, 2–3 ft. wide. Stems packed with long, narrow, bristly gray-green leaves and topped with long, spikelike clusters of blue flowers. Typically short lived and rarely sold but occasionally seen in old gardens near California coast.

E. vulgare. Biennial grown as annual. Zones 4–9, 14–24. European native blooms first year if sown between early fall and earliest spring. To 1–3 ft. tall, 1 ft. wide. Leaves covered with stiff white bristles; blue, white, or pink flowers in spikelike clusters. Endures aridity, poor soil. Seeds freely and can become a pest if seedlings are not hoed out.

E. wildpretii. TOWER OF JEWELS. Biennial. Zones 15–17, 21–24. Striking oddity from the Canary Islands spends its first year as an attractive, roundish mass of long, narrow leaves covered with silvery gray hairs. In its second year, it starts to grow. By mid- or late spring, it forms a column of countless little rose to rose red flowers 6–10 ft. high and a foot or more in diameter. When all flowers have faded, the plant dies, leaving behind a vast amount of seed. The resulting seedlings may grow and bloom the next year if they are not hoed out.

EDELWEISS. See LEONTOPODIUM alpinum

EDGEWORTHIA chrysantha (E. papyrifera)

PAPER BUSH

Thymelaeaceae

DECIDUOUS SHRUB

ZONES 5–9, 14–24

FULL SUN OR LIGHT SHADE

REGULAR WATER

Edgeworthia chrysantha

Native to China. Daphne relative grown in Asia for its bark, used in the manufacture of fancy paper. To 6 ft. tall and wide, with pliable stems produced freely from the base and 4-in. leaves that cluster toward branch tips. In winter or earliest spring, many small, fragrant pale yellow flowers in tight clusters to 2 in. across open from interesting-looking silky whitish buds formed the previous fall. Protect blossoms from late spring frosts. Little pruning required.

EGGPLANT

Solanaceae

ANNUAL

ALL ZONES

FULL SUN

REGULAR WATER

Eggplant 'Black Beauty'

Few vegetable plants are handsomer than eggplant, a Southeast Asian native known botanically as *Solanum melongena.* Resembles a little tree, 2–3 ft. high and equally wide. Big leaves (usually lobed) are purple tinged; drooping violet flowers are 1½ in. across. And, of course, big purple fruits are spectacular. Effective in large containers or raised beds; a well-spaced row of eggplant makes a distinguished border between vegetable and flower garden.

Most gardeners plant large roundish or oval varieties such as 'Black Beauty', 'Burpee Hybrid', 'Dusky', or 'Early Beauty'. The Japanese, who prefer their eggplant small and very tender, prefer long, slender varieties sold under a number of names, such as 'Ichiban'. Specialists in imported vegetable seeds offer numerous colored varieties, including the full-size 'White Beauty' and a host of smaller varieties in a range of sizes (down to ½ in.) and colors—white, yellow, red, green. Some of the smaller ones genuinely resemble eggs. All are edible as well as attractive.

Can be grown from seed (sow indoors 8 to 10 weeks before date of last expected frost), but starting from nursery-grown plants is much easier. To produce a crop, eggplant needs 2 to 3 months of warm days and nights (night temperatures no lower than 65°F/18°C). Set plants out in spring when frost danger is past and soil is warm. Space 3 ft. apart in loose, fertile soil. Feed once every 6 weeks; control weeds.

If you enjoy tiny whole eggplants, allow plants to produce freely. If you prefer larger fruits, keep too much fruit from setting by pinching out some terminal growth and some blossoms; three to six large fruits per plant will result. Harvest fruits after they develop some color, but don't wait until they lose their glossy shine. A second crop for late summer and fall harvest can be grown in warmest climates.

Flea beetles can be a problem on young plants; grow under row covers until big enough to tolerate leaf damage. Control aphids and whiteflies.

EGLANTINE. See ROSA rubiginosa

A PRACTICAL GUIDE TO GARDENING
PLEASE SEE PAGES 658–731

EICHHORNIA crassipes

WATER HYACINTH

Pontederiaceae

AQUATIC PLANT

ZONES 8, 9, 13–24; H1, H2; ANNUAL IN COLDER CLIMATES

FULL SUN

LOCATE IN PONDS OR POOLS

Eichhornia crassipes

Native to tropical America. Feathery roots; floating leaves ½–5 in. wide, nearly circular, on inflated stems. Showy 2-in. flowers, carried many to a spike, are lilac blue; upper petals have a yellow spot in center. Needs warmth to flower profusely. Where it is perennial, it can become an extremely serious, ineradicable pest; do not turn it loose in natural or large bodies of water.

Elaeagnaceae. This family contains trees and shrubs with a coating of tiny silvery or brown scales on leaves (and sometimes on flowers) and with small, tart-tasting, single-seeded fruits. Most are tough plants from arid or semiarid climates.

ELAEAGNUS

Elaeagnaceae

DECIDUOUS AND EVERGREEN SHRUBS AND TREES

ZONES VARY BY SPECIES

FULL SUN OR PARTIAL SHADE

LITTLE TO REGULAR WATER

Elaeagnus pungens

All are splendid screen plants. All grow fast when young, becoming dense, full, firm, and tough—and they do it with little upkeep. All tolerate seashore conditions, heat, and wind.

Foliage is distinguished in evergreen forms by silvery (sometimes brown) dots that cover leaves, reflecting sunlight to give plants a special sparkle. Deciduous kinds have silvery gray leaves. Small, insignificant, but usually fragrant flowers are followed by decorative fruit, usually red with silvery flecks. Evergreen kinds bloom in fall; in addition to their prime role as screen plants, they are useful as natural espaliers, clipped hedges, or high bank covers.

E. angustifolia. RUSSIAN OLIVE. Deciduous tree. Zones A2, A3; 1–3, 7–14, 18, 19. Native Europe to Asia. To 20 ft. high and wide, but can be clipped to make a medium-height hedge. Angular trunk and branches (sometimes thorny) are covered with shredding dark brown bark that is picturesque in winter. Bark contrasts with narrow, willowlike, 2-in.-long silvery gray leaves. Small, very fragrant, greenish yellow flowers in early summer are followed by fruit that resembles miniature olives. Can take almost any kind of punishment, including hot summers, bitterly cold winters, drought, poor soil. Has naturalized in many areas east of the Cascades in the Pacific Northwest. Doesn't do as well in mild-winter, cool-summer climates. Good background or barrier plant. Resistant to oak root fungus. 'Red King' ('King Red') has fruit in a bright rust red shade.

E. commutata. SILVERBERRY. Deciduous shrub. Zones A1–A3; 1–3. Native to Alaska, Rocky Mountains, northern plains of U.S. and Canada. Upright to 12 ft. tall and 6 ft. wide, with open form and slender, spineless, red-brown branches that become coated with silvery scales. Oval leaves are silvery gray on both surfaces. Tiny, fragrant spring flowers followed in early fall by dry, mealy, ⅓-in.-long, oval fruits, also silver coated and a favorite of birds. Plant spreads by suckers to form colonies.

E. 'Coral Silver'. Shrub. Zones 2b–24. Evergreen in Zones 19–24, deciduous or partially deciduous elsewhere. Has unusually bright gray foliage, coral red berries in fall.

E. × ebbingei. Evergreen shrub. Zones 4–24. More upright (to 10–12 ft. high and wide) than *E. pungens,* with thornless branches. Leaves 2–4 in. long, silvery on both sides when young, later dark green above and silvery beneath. Tiny, fragrant silvery flowers. Red fruit makes good jelly. 'Gilt Edge' has striking yellow margins on its leaves.

E. multiflora. Deciduous shrub. Zones 2b–24. From China, Japan. To 6–10 ft. high and wide. Leaves silvery green above, silvery brown below. Small, fragrant spring flowers followed by attractive, ½-in.-long, bright orange-red berries on 1-in. stalks. Fruit is edible but tart, loved by birds.

E. pungens. SILVERBERRY. Evergreen shrub. Zones 4–24. Has rather rigid, sprawling, angular habit of growth to 10–15 ft. high and wide; can be kept lower and denser by pruning. Even tolerates shearing into a hedge. Grayish green, 1–3-in.-long leaves have wavy edges and brown tinting from rusty dots. Branches are spiny, also covered with rusty dots. Overall color of shrub is olive drab. Oval fruit, ½ in. long, red with silver dust. Tough container plant in reflected heat, wind. Forms listed below are more commonly planted than the plain olive drab variety and have a brighter, lighter look in the landscape, but they are less hardy (grow in Zones 5–24). All make effective barriers, thanks to dense, twiggy, spiny growth.

'Fruitlandii'. Large silvery leaves.

'Maculata'. GOLDEN ELAEAGNUS. Leaves have large gold blotch in center.

'Marginata'. SILVER-EDGE ELAEAGNUS. Silvery white leaf margins.

'Variegata'. YELLOW-EDGE ELAEAGNUS. Yellowish white leaf margins.

ELAEOCARPUS decipiens (E. sylvestris ellipticus)

JAPANESE BLUEBERRY TREE

Elaeocarpaceae

EVERGREEN TREE

ZONES 8, 9, 14–24; H1

FULL SUN

REGULAR WATER

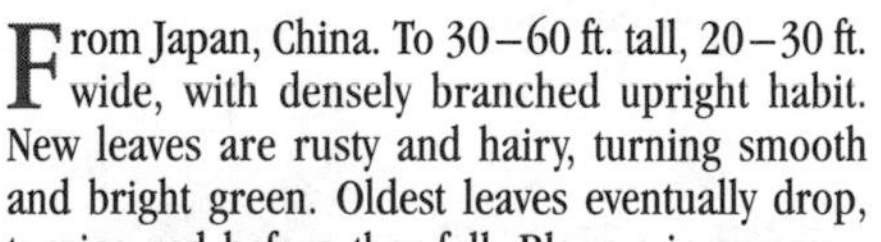

Elaeocarpus decipiens

From Japan, China. To 30–60 ft. tall, 20–30 ft. wide, with densely branched upright habit. New leaves are rusty and hairy, turning smooth and bright green. Oldest leaves eventually drop, turning red before they fall. Blooms in summer, producing tiny, scented white flowers in 1½–3-in.-long clusters; these are followed by blue-black fruits that look like small olives. Attractive street or lawn tree. Grow in rich, well-drained soil. Needs little pruning.

ELDERBERRY. See SAMBUCUS

ELEPHANT'S EAR. See ALOCASIA, COLOCASIA esculenta

ELEPHANT'S FOOD. See PORTULACARIA afra

ELEUTHEROCOCCUS sieboldianus (Acanthopanax sieboldianus)

Araliaceae

DECIDUOUS SHRUB

ZONES 2B–10, 14–17

SUN OR SHADE

ANY AMOUNT OF WATER

Eleutherococcus sieboldianus 'Variegatus'

Native to China, Japan. Grows 8–10 ft. tall and wide; erect, eventually arching stems have short thorns below each leaf. Bright green leaves have five to seven 1–2½-in.-long leaflets arranged like fingers on a hand. Small, inconspicuous white flowers are borne in clusters; these are rarely followed by clusters of small black berries. This plant's virtues are its somewhat tropical appearance, adaptability (takes rich or poor soil, any exposure, any amount of irrigation), and high tolerance for difficult conditions, including air pollution. 'Variegatus', a 6–8-ft. shrub with white-bordered leaflets, is more widely grown than the species.

ELM. See ULMUS

ELYMUS arenarius. See LEYMUS arenarius

ELYMUS magellanicus (Agropyron magellanicus)

MAGELLAN WHEATGRASS

PERENNIAL GRASS

ZONES 3–6, 14–17, 21–24

PARTIAL SHADE IN HOTTEST CLIMATES

REGULAR WATER

Elymus magellanicus

Botanists have moved some species formerly in this genus to *Leymus* (see that entry for other blue-leafed grasses). Of the species remaining in *Elymus,* this clump-forming native of South American mountains is the most ornamental. Grows 1½ ft. high and wide, with metallic blue leaves (probably the bluest of all grasses). Cool-season grass, nearly evergreen in mild climates; grown for its foliage rather than the flower spikelets produced in summer. Likes humidity along the California coast and well-drained soil. To increase your planting, divide in spring. Good container plant.

EMBOTHRIUM coccineum

CHILEAN FIRE BUSH

Proteaceae

EVERGREEN OR DECIDUOUS SHRUB OR TREE

ZONES 5, 6, 14–17, 21–24

FULL SUN OR LIGHT SHADE

REGULAR TO AMPLE WATER

Embothrium coccineum

From many altitudes and latitudes in Chile. Sometimes a large, suckering shrub of variable habit, sometimes a tree to 50 ft. tall and half as wide. It may be evergreen or deciduous; the latter forms are hardier. All have shiny green leaves that are oblong to narrow, up to 4½ in. long; all put on a showy floral spectacle in late spring or early summer, bearing clusters of long, narrow, brilliant red flowers. *E. c. lanceolatum* is a narrow-leafed semi-evergreen form.

Needs good drainage, acid soil, nonalkaline water, cold-wind protection.

EMPRESS TREE. See PAULOWNIA tomentosa

ENA'ENA. See GNAPHALIUM sandwicensium sandwicensium

ENCELIA

Asteraceae (Compositae)

DECIDUOUS SHRUBS

ZONES VARY BY SPECIES

FULL SUN

LITTLE OR NO WATER

Encelia farinosa

Much-branched shrubs to 3 ft. high and 4 ft. wide, with typically sparse foliage that tends to drop in times of drought. Loose clusters of yellow daisies bloom in spring; after bloom, cut back by at least a third to encourage repeat flowering. Useful for out-of-the-way places out of reach of irrigation. Be especially careful not to overwater in summer in hot desert regions.

E

E. californica. Zones 7–16, 18–24. Native to Southern California. Bright green leaves to 2½ in. long; brown-centered flowers to nearly 3 in. across.

E. farinosa. BRITTLEBUSH, INCIENSO. Zones 8–16, 18–24; H1. Native to the Southwest. Rounded, aromatic, stiff-branched shrub (sap is fragrant) with silvery, woolly leaves to 3 in. long in dense clusters. Shrub bears a profusion of yellow- or brown-centered daisies that are somewhat smaller than those of *E. californica.*

ENDIVE

Asteraceae (Compositae)

BIENNIAL OR ANNUAL

ALL ZONES

FULL SUN

REGULAR WATER

Endive

Mediterranean native known botanically as *Cichorium endivia.* This species includes curly as well as broad-leafed endive (escarole), both of which form a rosette of leaves. Tolerates more heat than lettuce, grows faster in cold weather. Matures in 90 to 95 days from seed. In cold-winter areas, sow seed from spring into summer; in mild-winter climates, sow so that plants mature after summer heat is past.

Plant in rows 15–18 in. apart. Be sure to thin plants to 10–12 in. apart. When plants have reached full size (a foot across), pull outer leaves over center and tie them up at top (but not when they're wet, as that may cause decay). Covered center leaves will blanch to yellow or white. Endive can be used unblanched by cutting outer leaves, as for Swiss chard. 'Green Curled' is standard curly endive; 'Broad-leaved Batavian' is a good full-leafed variety.

Belgian or French endives are the blanched sprouts of a kind of chicory; see Chicory.

ENDYMION. See HYACINTHOIDES

ENGLISH DAISY. See BELLIS perennis

ENGLISH LAUREL. See PRUNUS laurocerasus

ENGLISH PAINTED FERN. See ATHYRIUM otophorum

ENKIANTHUS

Ericaceae

DECIDUOUS SHRUBS

ZONES 3–9, 14–21, EXCEPT AS NOTED

FULL SUN ONLY IN COOLER CLIMATES

REGULAR TO AMPLE WATER

Native to Japan. Upright stems with tiers of nearly horizontal branches; plants are narrow in youth, broader in age, but always attractive. Leaves are clustered or crowded near branch ends, turn orange or red in autumn. Clusters of nodding, bell-shaped flowers bloom in spring. Like rhododendrons, require moist, well-drained acid soil enriched with plenty of organic matter such as peat moss or ground bark. Prune only to remove dead or broken branches. Plant in location where silhouette, flowers, and fall color can be enjoyed close up.

Enkianthus campanulatus

E. campanulatus. Zones 2–9, 14–21. Slow-growing shrub to 10–20 ft. tall and half as wide. Bluish green, 1½–3-in.-long leaves turn brilliant red in fall. In late spring, pendulous clusters of yellow-green, red-veined, ½-in.-long bells hang below leaves. 'Albiflorus' bears white blooms; 'Red Bells' has red flowers and notably deep red fall color. *E. c. palibinii* bears deep red blossoms.

E. cernuus. Seldom over 10 ft. tall and wide, with 1–2-in.-long leaves. White flowers. Not as well known as *E. c. rubens,* which has translucent deep red flowers in late spring.

E. perulatus. To 6–8 ft. high and wide. Roundish, 1–2-in.-long leaves; exceptionally good scarlet fall color. Small white flowers open in early spring before leaves emerge.

ENSETE ventricosum (Musa ensete)

ABYSSINIAN BANANA

Musaceae

PERENNIAL

ZONES 13, 15–24; H1, H2

FULL SUN OR PART SHADE

REGULAR WATER

Ensete ventricosum

African native is grown for its lush, attractive tropical-looking foliage. For fruit-bearing banana trees, see Banana. Fast growing to 15–20 ft. high, 10–15 ft. wide. Dark green leaves with stout midribs grow out in arching form from a single vertical stem; each leaf is 10–20 ft. long, 2–4 ft. wide. 'Maurelii' has dark red leafstalks and leaves tinged with red on upper surface, especially along edges. Bloom typically occurs 2 to 5 years after planting, when inconspicuous flowers form within a cylinder of bronzy red bracts at end of stem. Plant dies to roots after flowering; it's possible then to grow new plants from shoots that sprout from the crown, but easier to simply discard the old plant and replace it with a new one from the nursery.

Leaves are easily shredded by wind, so plant in a wind-sheltered location. Evergreen in mildest climates. In Zones 13, 15, 16, 18, will die back in a cold winter, regrow in spring. Attractive near swimming pools. Good container subject to grow outdoors in summer, move indoors or into a greenhouse over winter.

EPAULETTE TREE. See PTEROSTYRAX hispidus

EPAZOTE. See CHENOPODIUM ambrosioides

EPHEDRA

MORMON TEA, JOINT FIR

Ephedraceae

EVERGREEN SHRUBS

ZONES VARY BY SPECIES

FULL SUN

LITTLE OR NO WATER TO MODERATE WATER

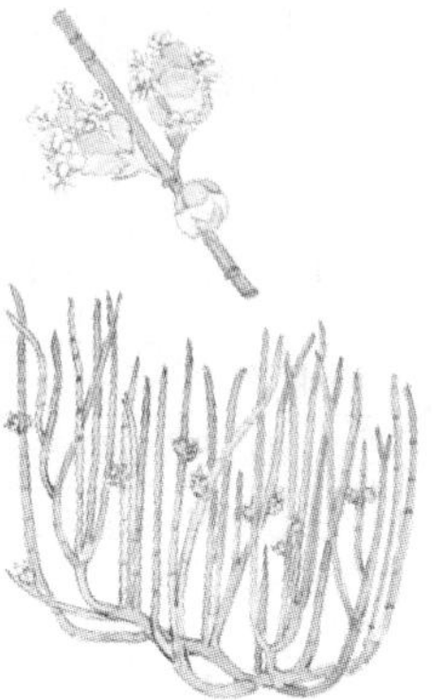

Ephedra nevadensis

Shrubby plants from arid parts of the West. Leaves are insignificant and soon drop; interest lies in slender, jointed, much-branched stems that come in various shades of green and turn yellow with age. Male and female flowers are borne on separate plants. The many species include upright-growing as well as clambering types, but those listed here are erect and densely branched. Some have papery cones, others fleshy and colorful ones. Tough plants that will tolerate dry, exposed conditions and poor soils. Must have good drainage.

E. nevadensis. Zones 3, 7, 9–14, 18–23. To 3 ft. high and wide, with pale green stems. Round yellow-green cones, sometimes tinged with pink, in late winter to midspring.

E. trifurca. Zones 3, 7–16, 18–23. To 15 ft. tall (though 6 ft. or so is common) and 8–10 ft. wide. Blue-green stems have thorny tips. Papery, translucent reddish brown cones appear in late winter to early spring.

E. viridis. Zones 1–3, 7–24. To 3–4 ft. high and wide, with bright green to yellow-green stems. Membranous or papery yellowish cones produced in spring.

EPIDENDRUM

Orchidaceae

EPIPHYTIC OR TERRESTRIAL ORCHIDS

ZONES VARY BY SPECIES

FULL SUN OR PARTIAL SHADE

REGULAR WATER

Epidendrum × obrienianum

All are easy to grow and bear large clusters of blooms. The genus formerly included a number of plants with hard, round pseudobulbs and thick, leathery leaves, but most of those species have been reassigned to *Encyclia.* Described below are reed-stemmed epidendrums with thin, stemlike pseudobulbs.

The first two species listed below are cool growers. They need plenty of sun to flower but also coolness and shade at roots. Mulch plants growing in the ground. If sun is too hot, foliage turns bright red and burns. Tip growth damaged at 28°F/–2°C; killed at about 22°F/–6°C. In cold-winter areas, grow plants in pots and move them indoors in winter.

All three species listed grow well in ground bark or other orchid media. Feed with diluted high-nitrogen liquid fertilizer during the growing season. Feed plants grown in ground bark at every other watering; plants in other media monthly. When blooms fade, cut flower stems back to within one or two joints above soil. For more information, see Orchidaceae.

E. ibaguense (E. radicans). Zones 17, 21–24; H1, H2; or indoors. Native to Colombia. Erect, leafy stems are 2–4 ft. high. Globular clusters of 1–1½-in., orange-yellow flowers with fringed lips held at tips of slender stems well above foliage. Blooms almost continuously in warm weather. Hybrids available in shades of yellow, orange, pink, lavender, and white.

E. × obrienianum. Zones 17, 21–24; H1, H2; or indoors. Best-known of these hybrids. Stems rise 1–2 ft. above foliage; clusters of vivid red flowers look like tiny cattleyas. Nearly continuous bloom in warm weather.

E. pseudepidendrum. Zone H2; or greenhouse plant. Native to Costa Rica, Panama. Intermediate grower. Erect stems to 3 ft. tall, with narrow, 8-in.-long, dark green leaves on upper half. Clusters of shiny apple green blooms (to 3 in. wide) with intense orange lip, in winter and spring.

EPILOBIUM angustifolium

FIREWEED

Onagraceae

PERENNIAL

ZONES A1–A3; 1–7, 14–21

FULL SUN

MODERATE WATER

Epilobium angustifolium

Native to northern regions of North America (including Alaska, Northwest) and Eurasia. To 2–5 ft. tall, 1½–3 ft. wide; narrow leaves to 10 in. long. Loose clusters of pink to rosy purple, four-petaled flowers in early summer. ('Album' has white flowers.) Seeds itself freely in open spaces, especially after forest fires. Attractive but generally considered weedy.

EPIMEDIUM

Berberidaceae

PERENNIALS

ZONES 2–9, 14–17, EXCEPT AS NOTED

PARTIAL SHADE

MODERATE WATER

Epimedium grandiflorum

Low growers with creeping underground stems. Thin, wiry leafstalks hold leathery leaves divided into heart-shaped leaflets 3–4 in. long. Foliage is bronzy pink in spring, green in summer, bronze in fall; even in deciduous species, leaves last late into the year. In spring, plants bear loose spikes of small, waxy flowers in pink, red, creamy yellow, or white. The flowers have four petals, which may be spurred or hooded, and eight sepals—four inner ones resembling petals and four (usually small) outer ones.

Use as ground cover under trees or among rhododendrons, azaleas, camellias; set out plants 1 ft. apart. Good in large rock gardens, containers. Tolerate heavy shade. Foliage and flowers are long lasting in arrangements. Cut back in late winter before new growth resumes. Divide large clumps in spring or fall by cutting through tough roots with a sharp spade. Keep your eyes open for interesting new species coming in from China and Japan.

E. alpinum. Zones 1–9, 14–17. From southern Europe. Evergreen, 6–9 in. high. Small flowers have red inner sepals and yellow petals. Spreads faster than other epimediums.

E. × cantabrigiense. To 8–12 in. tall, with olive-tinted semievergreen foliage and small red-and-yellow flowers.

E. grandiflorum. BISHOP'S HAT, LONGSPUR EPIMEDIUM. From China, Korea, Japan. Deciduous epimedium to about 1 ft. high. Relatively large blooms (to 2 in. across) are shaped like a bishop's mitre, with red outer sepals, pale violet inner sepals, and white petals with long spurs. There are varieties with white, pinkish, or violet flowers. 'Rose Queen' bears crimson flowers with white-tipped spurs; 'White Queen' has silvery white blooms.

E. × perralchicum. Evergreen hybrid between *E. perralderianum* and *E. pinnatum colchicum.* To 16 in. high; ¾-in. yellow flowers. Yellow blooms of 'Frohnleiten' and yellow-and-bronze ones of 'Wisley' are 1 in. across.

E. perralderianum. From North Africa. To 1 ft. tall, with shiny evergreen leaves and ¾-in., bright yellow flowers.

E. pinnatum. Zones A2; 2–9, 14–17. From northern Iran. To 8–12 in. high, with nearly evergreen foliage. Flowers have yellow sepals and very short reddish brown spurs. *E. p. colchicum* is taller (to 16 in.), with larger flowers.

E. × rubrum. This semievergreen hybrid between *E. alpinum* and *E. grandiflorum* grows to 1 ft. high. Flowers, borne in showy clusters, have crimson inner sepals, pale yellow or white petals, and upward-curving spurs. Selections include rosy pink 'Pink Queen' and white 'Snow Queen'.

E. × versicolor. Best known of several selections is 'Sulphureum', 12–20 in. tall, with light yellow flowers and semievergreen leaves marked with brownish red.

E. × warleyense. Evergreen hybrid to 1½ ft. tall, with light green foliage and clusters of small, coppery orange-red flowers.

E. × youngianum 'Niveum'. Deciduous; to 8–12 in. high. Bears pure white flowers.

EPIPHYLLUM

ORCHID CACTUS

Cactaceae

CACTI

ZONES 8, 9, 14–24; H1, H2; OR INDOORS

PARTIAL SHADE, BRIGHT INDIRECT LIGHT

REGULAR WATER

Epiphyllum Hybrid

Growers use the name "epiphyllum" to refer to a wide range of plants—both the genus *Epiphyllum* itself and a number of crosses with related plants. All are tropical (not desert) cacti, and most grow on tree branches as epiphytes, like some orchids. In California zones above, protect by growing under lath or trees. Plants need rich, quick-draining soil with plenty of sand and leaf mold, peat moss, or ground bark. Cuttings are easy to root in spring or summer. Let the base of the cutting dry for a day or two before potting it up. Overwatering and poor drainage cause bud drop.

In winter, epiphyllums need frost protection. Most have arching (to 2 ft. high), trailing stems and look best in hanging pots, tubs, or baskets. Stems are long, flat, smooth, quite spineless, and usually notched or scalloped along edges. Spring flowers vary in size from medium to very large (up to 10 in. across); color range includes white, cream, yellow, pink, rose, lavender, scarlet, and orange. Many varieties have blends of two or more colors. Feed with low-nitrogen fertilizer before and after bloom.

EPIPREMNUM pinnatum 'Aureum' (Pothos aureus)

POTHOS
Araceae
EVERGREEN VINE
ZONES 24; H2; OR INDOORS
SUN OR SHADE; BRIGHT INDIRECT LIGHT
REGULAR WATER

Epipremnum pinnatum 'Aureum'

Philodendron relative from the Solomon Islands. Oval, pointed, 2–4-in.-long, leathery dark green leaves splashed or marbled with yellow. Best known as a houseplant. Commonly used as an attractive trailer in pots, window boxes, larger terrariums; requires same care as vining philodendrons. Outdoors and in greenhouses where it is given ample room, the plant becomes a big, tropical-looking vine with deeply cut leaves 2–2½ ft. long. It's capable of climbing the tallest trees and is sometimes used as a ground cover at the base of trees. Grows well in shade but has better foliage color in sun.

EPISCIA

FLAME VIOLET
Gesneriaceae
PERENNIALS
ZONE H2; OR INDOORS
FULL SHADE; BRIGHT INDIRECT LIGHT
AMPLE WATER

Episcia cupreata viridifolia

Low-growing tropical American natives spread by runners that form new plants at their tips; excellent display in hanging pots. Leaves are 2–5 in. long, 1–3 in. wide; typically oval, velvety, and beautifully colored. Flowers that look something like African violets *(Saintpaulia ionantha)* come in red, pink, orange, yellow, lavender, or white, appear at scattered intervals throughout the year. Plants bloom well in high humidity of greenhouse but will also succeed as houseplants. Can grow outdoors year-round in Hawaii. In mild-winter areas on the mainland, potted plants can stay outside most of the year if given a warm, shady, wind-protected location.

E. cupreata has red flowers. *E. c. viridifolia* has green leaves with creamy veins; 'Metallica', olive green leaves with pale stripes, red edges; 'Chocolate Soldier', chocolate brown, silver-veined leaves; and 'Silver Sheen', silver leaves with darker margins.

EQUISETUM hyemale

HORSETAIL
Equisetaceae
PERENNIAL
ZONES 1–24
FULL SUN OR PARTIAL SHADE
LOCATE IN MARSHY AREA OR POOL

Equisetum hyemale

Rushlike survivor of Carboniferous Age in Europe, North America. There are several species, but *E. hyemale* is most common. Slender, hollow, 4-ft. stems are bright green, with a ring of black and ash gray at each joint. Spores are borne in conelike spikes at stem ends. Miniature *E. scirpoides* is similar, but only 6–8 in. high. The common name "horsetail" refers to the bushy look produced by the many whorls of slender, jointed green stems that radiate out from joints of main stems on some of the other species.

Although horsetail is effective in some garden situations, especially near water, use it with caution: it is extremely invasive and difficult to get rid of. Best confined to containers. In open ground, root-prune or dig out unwanted shoots rigorously and constantly.

ERANTHIS hyemalis

WINTER ACONITE
Ranunculaceae
PERENNIAL FROM TUBER
ZONES 1–9, 14–17
FULL SUN DURING BLOOM, PART SHADE DURING REST OF YEAR
REGULAR WATER DURING GROWTH AND BLOOM

Eranthis hyemalis

Native to Europe, Asia. Charming plant that reaches 2–8 in. high, blooming in late winter or early spring. Single yellow flowers resembling buttercups are about 1½ in. wide, with five to nine petal-like sepals; each bloom sits on a single, deeply lobed, bright green leaf that looks like a ruff. Round basal leaves divided into narrow lobes emerge immediately after the flowers bloom. All traces of the plant disappear by the time summer arrives. The species *E. cilicica* is similar but blooms later, bears slightly larger flowers, and has bronze-tinted new leaves.

Plant tubers in late summer; if they look dry or shriveled, plump them up in wet sand before planting. Plant 3 in. deep and 4 in. apart, in moist, porous soil. Reduce water in summer but don't let soil dry out completely. Divide clumps infrequently; when doing so, separate into small clumps rather than single tubers.

EREMOPHILA

EMU BUSH
Myoporaceae
EVERGREEN SHRUBS
ZONES 8, 9, 13–24
FULL SUN
LITTLE TO MODERATE WATER, EXCEPT AS NOTED

Eremophila laanii

Of the more than 200 species of these Australian shrubs, just a few are grown in warmer parts of California and the Southwest. All tolerate aridity, heat, wind, and poor soil but like good drainage. All have slender stems that change direction abruptly and interlace to form dense growth. Some may become leggy, but all respond well to pruning. Common name comes from the flightless bird that eats the small fruits of some species. In North America, fruits are food for many birds and animals. Hummingbirds visit the flowers.

E. decipiens. Compact, spreading mound 3 ft. high and wide. Leaves are about 1 in. long and seem to clasp the stems. Brilliant scarlet, slender-tubed blossoms to 1 in. long provide winter color for 2 to 3 months. Thrives without irrigation.

E. glabra. COMMON EMU BUSH. Variable species with creeping or upright growth to 5 ft. tall, 3–10 ft. wide. Narrow leaves to 2 in. long; tubular, 1¼-in.-long flowers in red, orange, yellow, or green from early spring to autumn. 'Murchison River' grows 3 ft. high and wide, has silvery foliage and bright red flowers.

E. laanii. Spreading shrub 3–6 ft. tall and 4–10 ft. wide, with narrow, 2-in. gray-green leaves. White, pink, or light red flowers to 1 in. long. White-flowered form reputedly is more vigorous and may sucker. Very adaptable species. Tolerates dappled shade.

E. maculata. SPOTTED EMU BUSH. Most widely grown type occurs naturally on flood plains; more tolerant of moisture and humidity than other species. Variable in habit. Most forms grow 3 ft. tall and twice as wide, but some are much larger. Narrow leaves are often hairy when young. Heavy winter and spring crop of flowers, with a scattering at other times of year. Blossoms are 1–2 in. long and come in dark red, yellow, orange, or pink, often with dark spotting inside. 'Aurea' has lighter green leaves and bears 1-in.-long, unspotted yellow flowers; it grows 3–6 ft. tall and to 10 ft. wide with irrigation. 'Pink Beauty' grows 10–12 ft. tall (to 6 ft. tall even without irrigation) and 4–6 ft. wide, bears profuse bluish pink, 1½-in. blossoms in late winter.

E. 'Valentine'. Upright growth 6–8 ft. tall and 5 ft. wide. Brilliant rose red, 1-in.-long blossoms in late winter almost hide the foliage. Leaves have a purplish cast that makes this shrub particularly handsome even when out of bloom. 'Rosea' is similar, if not identical.

EREMURUS

FOXTAIL LILY, DESERT CANDLE

Liliaceae

PERENNIALS FROM TUBEROUS ROOTS

ZONES 2–10, 14–16, 18–21

FULL SUN

REGULAR WATER DURING GROWTH AND BLOOM

Eremurus himalaicus

Imposing lily relatives from western and central Asia, grown for 3–9-ft.-tall spires of blooms. Bell-shaped, ¼–1 in.-wide white, pink, or yellow flowers are massed closely in graceful, pointed spikes on upper one-third to one-half of stem. Plants bloom in late spring, early summer; need winter cold to bloom well. Rosettes of strap-shaped basal leaves appear in early spring, fade away after bloom in summer. Magnificent in large borders against background of dark green foliage, wall, or solid fence. Dramatic in arrangements; cut when lowest flowers on spike open.

Handle the thick, brittle roots carefully; they tend to rot when bruised or broken. Plant them in rich, fast-draining soil, setting crown just below surface in mild-winter climates, 4–6 in. deep in colder ones. Space roots 2–4 ft. apart. When leaves die down, mark spot; don't disturb roots. Don't let soil dry out completely during dormancy. Provide winter mulch in coldest areas.

E. himalaicus. To 4–8 ft. tall, with white flowers. Leaves to 1½ ft. long.

E. ×isabellinus. Probably best known in this group are the Shelford Hybrids, 4–5 ft. tall, with blossoms in mixed colors (white, yellow, pink, orange). 'Cleopatra' is a 3–6-ft.-tall, orange-and-red selection of the Ruiter Hybrids, a Dutch strain featuring bright, clear flower colors.

E. robustus. To 6–9 ft. tall, with pink flowers lightly veined with brown. Dense basal rosettes of leaves to 2 ft. long.

E. stenophyllus (E. bungei). To 3–5 ft. tall, with bright yellow flowers aging to orange brown. Leaves to 1 ft. long.

ERICA

HEATH

Ericaceae

EVERGREEN SHRUBS

ZONES VARY BY SPECIES

PARTIAL SHADE IN HOTTEST CLIMATES

REGULAR WATER

SEE CHART NEXT PAGE

Erica carnea 'Springwood'

Grown for small, needlelike leaves and abundant, usually small flowers that may be bell shaped, urn shaped, or tubular. By choosing varieties of both heaths and their close relative heather *(Calluna)* carefully, you can have color year-round.

WHAT HEATHS NEED

SOIL: All heaths demand excellent drainage, and most need acid soil. Sandy soil amended with organic matter such as peat moss and compost is ideal; heavy clay is usually fatal.

FERTILIZING: An annual sifting of compost may be enough. If plants lose color, feed lightly with acid plant food in early spring.

WATERING: Be careful and consistent—heaths won't tolerate standing water or absolute dryness.

PRUNING: Shear or cut off faded flower spikes. Don't cut back into leafless wood, because new growth may not sprout.

Erica cinerea

The hardiest heaths, native to northern and western Europe, are widely used as shrubs or ground cover plants in cool-summer, humid regions of California and the Pacific Northwest. Fanciers sometimes plant the shortest types in masses for a multicolored Persian-carpet effect. Good on slopes. South African species are tender to frost and about as hardy as fuchsias; where temperatures dip below 28°F/–2°C, it is safest to grow them in containers and provide shelter. A third group of heaths, native to the Mediterranean and southern Europe, is intermediate in hardiness. Taller heaths can be used as screens. All attract bees.

Ericaceae. The heath family contains shrubs and trees with rounded, bell-shaped, tubular, or irregular flowers, often showy, and fruits that are either capsules or berries. All share a preference, if not always a need, for acid soil with plenty of water and excellent aeration (a few plants from dry-summer climates are exceptions). Many are fine garden plants; azalea and rhododendron *(Rhododendron)*, blueberry, heath *(Erica)*, and heather *(Calluna)* are examples.

ERIGERON

FLEABANE

Asteraceae (Compositae)

PERENNIALS

ZONES VARY BY SPECIES

FULL SUN OR LIGHT SHADE

MODERATE WATER

Erigeron speciosus

Free-blooming plants with daisylike flowers. Similar to closely related Michaelmas daisy *(Aster novi-belgii)*, except that erigeron's flower heads have threadlike rays in two or more rows rather than broader rays in a single row. White, pink, lavender, or violet flowers, usually with yellow centers. Cut back after flowering to prolong bloom. Grow best in sandy soil. Rock garden species need especially fast drainage.

E. glaucus. BEACH ASTER, SEASIDE DAISY. Zones 4–6, 15–17, 22–24. Native to California, Oregon coast. Burns in hot sun inland. Forms a clump to 1 ft. high and 1½ ft. wide, with blue-green foliage and stems. Stout, hairy stems are topped by lavender, 1½–2-in.-wide flower heads in spring, summer. 'Sea Breeze' has large pink flowers. 'Arthur Menzies' is a compact selection to 8 in. high with lavender-pink blooms. 'Wayne Roderick' ('W. R.'), also grows to 8 in. high, bears large lavender blooms in summer; possibly a hybrid, it's similar to *E. glaucus* but has larger leaves and does better in warmer areas.

▶ page 332

E

ERICA

NAME, ZONES, ORIGIN	GROWTH HABIT, SIZE	LEAVES	FLOWER COLOR, SEASON	COMMENTS
Erica arborea TREE HEATH Zones 15–17, 21–24 Southern Europe, North Africa	Dense shrub or tree to 10–20 ft. tall, 8–10 ft. wide. One or many trunks, often heavy burl at base	Bright green; new growth lighter green	White, fragrant. Spring	Slow growing. Performs well enough in Zones 4–6 in years between big freezes. Burls are the "briar" used for making pipes
E. a. alpina	Dense, upright shrub to 6 ft. tall, 3–4 ft. wide	As above	White. Spring	Slow to reach blooming age, then free blooming. Slightly hardier than *E. arborea;* a surer bet in Zones 4–6
E. australis SOUTHERN HEATH Zones 5–9, 14–24 Spain, Portugal	Upright, spirelike, 6–10 ft. tall, 3–5 ft. wide	Dark green	Rosy or red. Clustered at ends of shoots. Spring	Needs frost protection in Northwest. 'Mr. Robert' is a white form
E. canaliculata (usually sold as **E. melanthera** and often called Scotch heather) Zones 15–17, 20–24 South Africa	Bushy, spreading, but with general spired effect. To 6 ft. tall, 4 ft. wide	Dark green above, white beneath	Pink to rosy purple. Fall, winter	Sometimes called Christmas heather because of winter bloom. Pink-flowered form is sold as 'Rosea', reddish purple form as 'Rubra'. One of the best for Southern California. Cut flowers last for weeks, whether stems are immersed in water or not
E. c. 'Boscaweniana' (sometimes sold as **E. melanthera 'Rosea'**)	Upright bush or small tree to 18 ft. tall, 10–12 ft. wide	Same as above	Pale lilac pink to nearly white. Winter, spring	Like *E. canaliculata,* good source of cut flowers
E. carnea **(E. herbacea)** Zones A3; 2–10, 14–24 European Alps	Dwarf to 6–16 in. high, 2 ft. wide. Upright branchlets rise from prostrate main branches	Medium green	Rosy red. Winter, spring	Unsightly unless pruned every year. This species and its varieties tolerate neutral or slightly alkaline soil
E. c. 'Ruby Glow'	To 8 in. high, 1½ ft. wide	Dark green	Deep ruby red. Winter, spring	One of richest in color
E. c. 'Springwood' **('Springwood White')**	To 8 in. high, 14 in. wide	Light green	White; open from creamy buds. Winter, spring	Toughest, fastest-growing heath; one of neatest looking
E. c. 'Springwood Pink'	To 10 in. high, 16 in. wide	Bright green	Pure pink. Winter, spring	New growth pinkish rust
E. c. 'Vivellii'	To 1 ft. high, 1½ ft. wide	Dark green; bronzy red in winter	Carmine red. Winter, spring	Relatively tidy. Interesting for seasonal change in foliage color as well as for bloom
E. c. 'Winter Beauty' **('King George')**	To 15 in. high, 1½ ft. wide	Dark green	Deep, rich pink. Winter, spring	Often in bloom at Christmas
E. ciliaris DORSET HEATH Zones 4–6, 15–17 England, Ireland	Trailing, 6–12 in. high, 20 in. wide	Pale green	Rosy red. Summer	Good for massing

Erica arborea

Erica arborea alpina

Erica australis

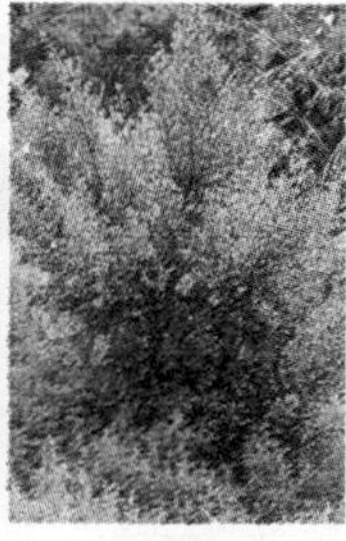
Erica canaliculata

Erica carnea 'Springwood'

Erica carnea 'Winter Beauty'

ERICA

NAME, ZONES, ORIGIN	GROWTH HABIT, SIZE	LEAVES	FLOWER COLOR, SEASON	COMMENTS
E. c. 'Mrs. C. H. Gill'	To 1 ft. high, 20 in. wide	Dark green	Deep red. Summer, early fall	Showy, bell-like flowers
E. c. 'Stoborough'	Same as above, but taller, to 1½ ft.	Medium green	White. Summer, early fall	Free blooming, showy
E. cinerea TWISTED HEATH Zones 4–6, 15–17 British Isles, northern Europe	To 1 ft. high, 2½ ft. wide. Forms low mat	Dark green, dainty	Purple. Summer	Good ground cover
E. c. 'Atrosanguinea'	To 9 in. high, 2½ ft. wide	Dark green, dainty	Scarlet. Summer, early fall	Dwarf, slow growing
E. c. 'C. D. Eason'	To 10 in. high, 20 in. wide	Dark green	Red. Late spring, summer	Outstanding; good summer flower display
E. c. 'P. S. Patrick'	To 15 in. high, 20 in. wide	Dark green	Purple. Summer	Long, sturdy spikes of large flowers
E. × darleyensis 'Darley Dale' (E. mediterranea hybrida) Zones 2–10, 14–24	Bushy grower to 1 ft. tall, 2 ft. wide	Medium green	Shell pink to light rosy purple; darken with age. Fall to midspring	Tough, hardy plant that takes both heat and cold surprisingly well. Tolerates neutral soils. In Northern California, most foolproof heath
E. × d. 'Furzey'	Bushy, 14–18 in. high, 2 ft. wide	Dark green	Deep rose pink. Winter, early spring	Spreading, vigorous plant
E. × d. 'George Rendall'	Bushy, 1 ft. high, 2 ft. wide	Medium bluish green	Deeper purple than 'Darley Dale'. Fall to early spring	New growth gold tinted
E. × d. 'Silberschmelze' ('Molten Silver', E. × d. 'Alba', 'Mediterranea Hybrid White')	Vigorous, 1½–2 ft. high, 2½ ft. wide	Medium green	White, fragrant. Winter, spring	Easy to maintain
E. 'Dawn' Zones 4–9, 14–24	Spreading mound, 1 ft. tall, 2–3 ft. wide	Green; new growth golden	Deep pink. Summer, early fall	Excellent ground cover. Easy to grow. Hybrid between *E. ciliaris* and *E. tetralix*
E. lusitanica (E. codonodes) SPANISH HEATH Zones 5–9, 14–24 Spain, Portugal	Upright feathery shrub, to 6–12 ft. high, 2–4 ft. wide	Light green	Pinkish white, slightly fragrant. Winter	Remarkably profuse bloom. Needs frost-sheltered spot in Northwest. One of best in Zones 20–24
E. mediterranea BISCAY HEATH Zones 4–9, 14–24 Ireland, France, Spain	Loose, upright, 4–7 ft. tall, 2–3 ft. wide	Deep green	Lilac pink. Winter, early spring	Good background. Tolerates neutral soil. 'W. T. Rackliff' is a pure white form with brown anthers

Erica cinerea 'Atrosanguinea'

Erica × darleyensis 'Darley Dale'

Erica vagans

Erica 'Dawn'

Erica tetralix

ERICA

NAME, ZONES, ORIGIN	GROWTH HABIT, SIZE	LEAVES	FLOWER COLOR, SEASON	COMMENTS
E. mediterranea hybrida (see E. ×darleyensis 'Darley Dale')				
E. melanthera (see E. canaliculata)				
E. quadrangularis Zones 15–17, 20–24 South Africa	Stiff, upright shrub to 2 ft. tall, 1½ ft. wide	Bright green	Tiny, rose or white. Late winter, early spring	Offered as potted plants or sold as cut branches. Often sold as *E. persoluta*
E. tetralix CROSS-LEAFED HEATH Zones 4–6, 15–17 England, northern Europe	Upright, to 1 ft. tall, 2 ft. wide	Dark green, silvery beneath	Rosy pink. Summer, early fall	New growth yellow, orange, or red. Best if given moist, acid, well-drained soil, afternoon shade
E. t. 'Alba Mollis'	Upright, slightly spreading, to 1 ft. high and wide	Silvery gray	Pure white. Summer, early fall	Foliage sheen pronounced in spring, summer
E. t. 'Darleyensis'	Spreading, open growth to 8 in. high, 1 ft. wide	Gray green	Salmon pink. Summer	Good color. Do not confuse with *E. × darleyensis,* which blooms at some point from fall to midspring, depending on variety
E. vagans CORNISH HEATH Zones 3b–6, 15–17, 20–24 Cornwall, Ireland	Bushy, open, to 2–3 ft. high and wide	Bright green	Purplish pink. Summer	Robust and hardy
E. v. 'Lyonesse'	Bushy, rounded, to 1½ ft. high and wide	Bright, glossy green	White. Summer, early fall	Best white Cornish heath
E. v. 'Mrs. D. F. Maxwell'	Same as above	Dark green	Cherry pink or red. Summer, early fall	Outstanding for color and heavy bloom; widely grown
E. v. 'St. Keverne'	Same as above	Light green	Rose pink. Summer, early fall	Heavy bloom. Compact if pruned annually
E. ventricosa Zones 15–17, 20–24 South Africa	To 3 ft. tall and wide	Medium green, needlelike	Pale to medium pink, shiny. Late spring, early summer	Heavy flower spikes at tips of branches. Occasionally sold as small pot plant in spring

E. karvinskianus. MEXICAN DAISY, SANTA BARBARA DAISY. Zones 8, 9, 12–24; H1, H2. Native to Mexico. Graceful, trailing plant 10–20 in. high, 3 ft. wide. Leaves 1 in. long, often toothed at tips. Dainty flower heads ¾ in. across with numerous white or pinkish rays. Rarely out of bloom. Use as ground cover in garden beds or large containers, in rock gardens, in hanging baskets, on dry walls. Drought tolerant. Naturalizes easily (a pest in Hawaii); invasive unless controlled. 'Moerheimii' is more compact, with slightly larger leaves and lavender-tinted flower heads.

E. speciosus. Zones 1–9, 14–24. Native to Pacific Northwest. Erect, leafy stemmed, 2 ft. high and wide. Summer flowers are 1–1½ in. across, with dark violet or lavender rays. Widespread through Rocky Mountain area is *E. s. macranthus,* aspen daisy, which bears three to five flowers on each stalk; stalks nod near top. Hybrids between *E. speciosus* and other species are available; they have larger flowers and come in white and pink as well as blue shades. Some of the best are azure blue 'Blue Beauty', violet-blue 'Darkest of All', light violet 'Strahlenmeer', 'Pink Jewel' (with blooms in various pink shades), carmine pink 'Förster's Liebling' (Förster's Darling'), and white 'Schneewittchen' ('Snow White').

ERIOBOTRYA

LOQUAT

Rosaceae

EVERGREEN TREES OR SHRUBS

ZONES VARY BY SPECIES

FULL SUN OR PARTIAL SHADE

MODERATE TO REGULAR WATER

Both species described here (one of which bears edible fruit) are Chinese natives with large, prominently veined, sharply toothed leaves that can be cut and used for indoor decoration. Both can be espaliered on fence or trellis (but not in reflected heat) and make good container plants. Attractive to birds. Plant in well-drained soil. Subject to fireblight. Moderate water for ornamental plants; regular moisture for a good fruit crop.

Eriobotrya japonica

E. deflexa. BRONZE LOQUAT. Zones 8–24. Fast-growing, shrubby plant. Though easily trained into small tree similar in size to *E. japonica*, it is often espaliered. New leaves emerge bright copper and hold that color for a long time before turning green. The leaves are shinier, more pointed, less leathery, and less deeply veined than those of *E. japonica*. Garlands of creamy white flowers in spring. No edible fruit.

E. japonica. Zones 6–24; H1, H2. Though this loquat produces edible fruit, it's most often used as an ornamental. Grows 15–30 ft. tall; spreads as wide as it is high in sun, grows narrower in shade. Leathery, crisp, stoutly veined and netted leaves are 6–12 in. long, 2–4 in. wide, deep glossy green above, woolly and rust colored beneath. New branches are woolly. Small dull white flowers, fragrant but not showy, appear in woolly 3–6-in. clusters in fall. Orange to yellow, 1–2-in.-long fruit with seeds (usually big) in the center ripens in winter or spring. Flesh may be sweet, sweet-tart, or tart, depending on tree and variety. Eat fresh or use in preserves, pies.

Most trees are sold as seedlings, good ornamental plants with unpredictable fruit quality. If you want to harvest a crop, look for a grafted variety such as 'Champagne' (best in warm areas), 'Gold Nugget' (best in cooler regions), or 'MacBeth' (exceptionally large fruit). For good fruit, thin the branches somewhat to let light into tree's interior. If the tree sets fruit heavily, remove some while it's small to increase size of remaining fruit and to prevent limb breakage.

ERIOGONUM

WILD BUCKWHEAT
Polygonaceae
SHRUBBY PERENNIALS
ZONES VARY BY SPECIES
FULL SUN
LITTLE TO MODERATE WATER

Eriogonum arborescens

Native to most areas of the West (the few sold at nurseries are mostly native to California coast). Individual blossoms are tiny but grow in long-stemmed or branched clusters—usually domed, flattish, or ball-like. Flowers age to an attractive tan or reddish brown and persist for a long time; good in dried arrangements. Flowers attract butterflies; birds enjoy the seeds.

Grow best in well-drained, loose, gravelly soil. Useful for covering dry banks, massing among rocks; smaller forms make good specimens in rock gardens. May self-sow; transplant when they're small to extend planting or replace overgrown plants. Shrubby kinds get leggy after several years. You can do some pruning to shape if you start when plants are young, but if they have had no attention, it's better to replace them. Most buckwheats withstand wind and heat. In hottest climates, plants look best with deep watering twice monthly in summer.

E. arborescens. SANTA CRUZ ISLAND BUCKWHEAT. Zones 5, 7–9, 14–24. Native to Santa Cruz, Santa Rosa, and Anacapa islands, Southern California. Grows 3–4 ft. (sometimes 8 ft.) high, spreading to 4–5 ft. or more. Trunk and branches with shredding gray to reddish bark make attractive open pattern. Rather narrow, ½–1½-in.-long, gray-green leaves cluster at ends of branches. Long-stalked, flat clusters of pale pink to rose flowers, late spring through summer.

E. cinereum. ASHYLEAF BUCKWHEAT. Zones 5, 14–17, 19–24. Native to coastal bluffs and canyons of Southern California. Grows 2–5 ft. tall and 3 ft. wide, with ash-colored, 1-in. leaves and pale pink flowers in ball-shaped clusters in summer. Best planted in groups.

E. crocatum. SAFFRON BUCKWHEAT. Zones 14–24. Native to Southern California. Low, compact plant to 1½ ft. high, 2 ft. wide. Stems and roundish, 1-in.-long leaves are covered with white wool. Sulfur yellow flowers in broad, flattish clusters, early spring to late summer.

E. fasciculatum. CALIFORNIA BUCKWHEAT. Zones 7–9, 12–24. Native to foothills of California (from Santa Clara to San Diego) and to desert mountain slopes of Southern California. Forms a clump 1–3 ft. high, spreading to 4 ft. Leaves narrow, ½–¾ in. long; may be dark green above, white and woolly beneath, or gray and hairy. White or pinkish flowers in headlike clusters, late spring to early fall. Good for erosion control. 'Theodore Payne' is lower growing, makes an attractive green ground cover.

E. f. polifolium. ARIZONA BUCKWHEAT. Native to inland mountains and deserts of California into western Utah, Arizona, and northwest Mexico. Differs from the species only in minor botanical details.

E. giganteum. ST. CATHERINE'S LACE. Zones 5, 7–9, 14–24. Native to Santa Catalina and San Clemente islands, Southern California. Differs from *E. arborescens* in its more freely branching habit; grayish white, broadly oval, 1–2½-in.-long leaves; and longer period of bloom.

E. grande rubescens (E. rubescens, E. latifolium rubescens). RED BUCKWHEAT. Zones 5, 14–24. Native to San Miguel, Santa Rosa, and Santa Cruz islands, Southern California. Woody based; branches tend to lie on ground, spreading to 1–1½ ft., with upright tips about 10–12 in. high. Gray-green, oval leaves 1–3½ in. long. Branch tips and sturdy upright branchlets are topped by headlike clusters of rosy red flowers in summer.

E. umbellatum. SULFUR FLOWER. Zones 1–24. Plants grow to timberline and above. Low, broad mats of woody stems set with 1-in. leaves that are green above, white and felted beneath. In late spring or early summer, 4–12-in. stalks carry clusters of tiny yellow flowers that age to rust. 'Shasta Sulfur' makes a silvery green mound 1½ ft. high and 3 ft. wide, adorned in spring with sulfur yellow flowers. 'Sierra' (grown from seed and somewhat variable) forms a dome 1–2 ft. high and 3–4 ft. wide, above which rise golf ball–size clusters of bright yellow flowers.

E. wrightii. WRIGHT'S BUCKWHEAT. Zones 7–11, 14–24. Widely distributed species native from eastern and southern California to western Texas and northern Mexico. Selections from higher elevations and northern part of range take more cold. Wandlike stems form a mound 1½ ft. high by 2 ft. wide. Silvery green, felted leaves, ½ in. long and ¼ in. wide, narrow to a point. Tiny white or pinkish flowers appear in clusters along stalks from midsummer through fall.

ERODIUM reichardii (E. chamaedryoides)

CRANESBILL
Geraniaceae
PERENNIAL
ZONES 7–9, 14–24
FULL SUN OR PARTIAL SHADE
REGULAR WATER

Erodium reichardii

Native to Balearic Islands and Corsica. Dainty-looking but tough plant, forming dense foliage tuft 3–6 in. high, 1 ft. across. Long-stalked, dark green, roundish, ⅓-in.-long leaves with scalloped edges. Profuse, cup-shaped, ½-in.-wide flowers with white or rose pink, rosy-veined petals notched at tips, early spring into fall. Good small-scale ground cover, rock garden plant. A double-flowered pink and a single-flowered white form exist. Plant in porous soil.

E. chrysanthum has silvery foliage and pale yellow flowers, and *E. petraeum crispum (E. foetidum)* has white flowers with lavender veins and a conspicuous purple spot on one petal.

ERYNGIUM

SEA HOLLY, AMETHYST ERYNGIUM
Apiaceae (Umbelliferae)
ANNUALS, BIENNIALS, AND PERENNIALS
ZONES 2–24, EXCEPT AS NOTED
FULL SUN
WATER NEEDS VARY BY SPECIES

Eryngium amethystinum

Mostly spiny-leafed, rosette-forming plants that produce erect, thistlelike, leafy stalks bearing tight, silvery or blue-tinted flower heads surrounded by showy bracts. Bloom in summer (sometimes into fall). Upper leaves, leafstalks, bracts, and flowers may all be frosted with silver or tinted in shades of blue or amethyst.

Sea hollies from dry, rocky areas in Europe, North Africa, Turkey, central Asia, China, and Korea tend to be taprooted; prefer dry, well-drained, poor to moderately rich soils; need protection from excessive winter water. Those from wet grasslands in Mexico, Brazil, and Argentina have fibrous root systems, prefer moist, well-drained soils. Taprooted forms are difficult to divide but may be propagated by root cuttings. If seeding, sow in place. Some species reseed vigorously. Watch out for snails and slugs. Useful in rock gardens and for long displays in borders. Good choice for dried arrangements.

E. alpinum. ALPINE SEA HOLLY. Perennial. From southeastern Europe. To 2½ ft. high, 1½ ft. wide, with taproot. Spiny, heart-shaped basal leaves 3–6 in. long. Upper leaves and stems are tinged with soft blue to steel blue near top. The conical, 1½-in. flower heads are surrounded by purplish blue, intricately cut bracts. Tolerates very light shade. Moderate water.

E. amethystinum. Perennial. Zones 1–24. From Italy and the Balkans. To 2½ ft. high, 1½ ft. wide, with taproot. Spiny, medium green leaves to 6 in. long. Silvery blue stems and conical, 1-in. amethyst flower heads surrounded by 2-in., silvery blue bracts. Moderate water.

E. foetidum. CULANTRO. Biennial grown as an annual where temperatures drop below 0°F/–18°C. Zones 4–9, 12–24; H1, H2. Native to American tropics. To 2 ft. tall and wide. Rosettes of green, spiny, lance-shaped leaves to 5 in. long; foliage has aroma similar to coriander or cilantro. Succulent new leaves can substitute for true coriander and are produced long after the latter has gone to seed. Flowering stems bear dark green, ¾-in., egg-shaped flower heads. Fertile soil, regular water.

E. giganteum. MISS WILLMOTT'S GHOST. Biennial to short-lived perennial. From the Caucasus and Iran. To 3–4 ft. or taller, 2½ ft. wide. Oval or heart-shaped, medium green leaves to 6 in. long. Three-lobed stem leaves. In late summer, bears blue or pale green, conical flower heads surrounded by silvery, 2½–4-in. bracts; the plant dies after flowering ends. Reseeds well. Fertile soil, regular water.

E. planum. FALSE SEA HOLLY. Perennial. From southeast Europe to central Asia. To 3 ft. tall, 1½ ft. wide, with taproot. Oblong to heart-shaped, deep green leaves to 4 in. long. Stem leaves are blue tinted, with three to five lobes or sections. Rounded, ½–¾-in.-wide, light blue flower heads are surrounded by narrow blue-green bracts. Moderate water.

E. varifolium. MOROCCAN SEA HOLLY. Perennial. Zones 4–9, 14–24. From Morocco. To 1½ ft. high, 10 in. wide, with taproot. Oval, tooth-edged, spiny, somewhat fleshy leaves are 2 in. long, heart shaped at base, dark green marbled with white veins. Stiff, silvery blue, branching stems bear 1-in. blue-gray flower heads surrounded by silvery blue bracts to ½ in. Moderate to regular water.

E. yuccifolium. RATTLESNAKE MASTER, BUTTON SNAKEROOT. Perennial. From central and eastern U.S. To 4 ft. tall, 2 ft. wide. Sword-shaped, spiny-edged, blue-gray leaves to a little over 3 ft. long. Strong, branched stems. Cylindrical, whitish green to pale blue flower heads are 1½ in. across, lack showy bracts. Fertile soil, regular water.

ERYSIMUM

WALLFLOWER

Brassicaceae (Cruciferae)

PERENNIALS, SOME GROWN AS BIENNIALS OR ANNUALS

ZONES VARY BY SPECIES

FULL SUN OR LIGHT SHADE

WATER NEEDS VARY BY SPECIES

Erysimum × allionii

This genus swallowed up *Cheiranthus,* which included the old-fashioned biennial bedding-plant wallflowers and several choice perennials. All have the typical clustered four-petaled flowers that give the crucifers their name, but their habits and uses differ widely.

E. × allionii. SIBERIAN WALLFLOWER. Perennial, often grown as biennial or annual. Zones A3; 1–9, 14–24. Branching plants 1–1½ ft. tall and somewhat wider are covered in spring with fragrant flowers in rich orange or yellow. In mild-winter climates, sow seed in fall; elsewhere, sow in spring for well-established plants by fall. Full sun, moderate water. Sometimes sold as *E. asperum* or *E. hieraciifolium.*

E. 'Bowles Mauve'. Perennial. Zones 4–6, 14–17, 22, 23. To 3 ft. tall, 4–6 ft. wide. Massed erect stems with narrow gray-green leaves, each topped by 1½-ft.-long, narrow, spikelike clusters of mauve flowers. Best in areas with cool summers and mild winters, where bloom is practically continuous. Plants may bloom themselves to death after several years. 'Compact Bowles Mauve' is about half the size. 'Wenlock Beauty', to 2 ft. high and wide, has flowers varying from buff to purple in a single spike. All types take moderate water.

E. cheiri (Cheiranthus cheiri). ENGLISH WALLFLOWER. Perennial in Zones 4–6, 14–17, 22, 23, but usually grown as a biennial or annual. From southern Europe. Best in cool, moist regions. Branching, woody-based plants 1–2½ ft. tall, 1–1½ ft. wide, with narrow bright green leaves and broad clusters of showy, sweet-scented flowers in spring. Blossoms are yellow, cream, orange, red, brown, or burgundy, sometimes shaded or veined with contrasting color. Main bloom period falls between that of primroses and summer bedding plants. Under ideal conditions in coastal Pacific Northwest may bloom year-round. Sow seeds in spring for bloom the following year (some strains flower the first year if seeded early); or set out plants in fall or earliest spring. May self-sow. Regular water.

E. insulare suffrutescens (E. suffrutescens). Perennial. Zones 14–17, 22–24. Native to central and southern California coasts. Woody-based growth 6–24 in. high, 4–12 in. wide, with narrow leaves and fragrant orange-yellow flowers in spring. Little water.

E. kotschyanum. Perennial in Zones 3b–11, 14–21; often treated as a winter annual in hot-summer climates. Light green leaves form a mat 6 in. high and a foot wide; in spring, fragrant deep yellow flowers appear on 2-in. stems. Use in rock garden or with other small perennials between paving stones. If plants hump up, cut out central portion, transplant it, and press original plant flat again. Divide clumps in fall. Moderate water.

ERYTHEA. See BRAHEA

ERYTHRINA

CORAL TREE

Fabaceae (Leguminosae)

DECIDUOUS OR NEARLY EVERGREEN TREES AND SHRUBS

ZONES VARY BY SPECIES

FULL SUN

MODERATE WATER

SEEDS ARE POISONOUS IF INGESTED

Erythrina caffra

Many species; known and used chiefly in Southern California. Some are also cultivated in Hawaii, and a few are grown in Arizona. Valued for brilliant flowers in colors ranging from greenish white through yellow to light or vivid shades of orange and red. The flat, beanlike pods following bloom contain poisonous seeds. Leaves are divided into three leaflets. These are typically thorny plants with strong structural value, both in and out of leaf. To eliminate too rapid, succulent growth and limb breakage in larger species, give little or no irrigation during dry weather and prune after flowering.

E. × bidwillii. Deciduous shrub. Zones 8, 9, 12–24. To 8 ft. tall and as wide; sometimes treelike to 20 ft. or taller. Spectacular spring-to-winter display of 2-ft.-long clusters of pure red flowers on long, willowy stalks; main show in summer. Cut back flowering wood after blossoms fade. Very thorny; plant away from paths and use long-handled pruners when trimming.

E. caffra (E. constantiana). CORAL TREE. Briefly deciduous tree. Zones 21–24; H2. Native to South Africa. To 24–40 ft. tall, 40–60 ft. wide. Drops leaves in early winter; then angular bare branches produce big clusters of deep red-orange, tubular flowers that drip nectar. In late winter or earlier, flowers give way to fresh, light green foliage.

E. coralloides. NAKED CORAL TREE. Deciduous tree. Zones 12, 13, 19–24. Native to Mexico. To 30 ft. high and as wide or wider, but easily contained by pruning. Fiery red blossoms like fat candles or pinecones bloom at tips of naked, twisted, black-thorned branches in spring. At end of flowering season, 8–10-in. leaves develop; they give shade in summer, turn yellow in late fall, then drop—revealing a bizarre branching structure that's almost as valuable as spring flower display. Sometimes sold as *E. poianthes.*

E. crista-galli. COCKSPUR CORAL TREE, COMMON CORAL TREE. Nearly evergreen (in Hawaii) to deciduous tree. Zones 7–9, 12–17, 19–24; H1, H2. Shrub or tree to 15–20 ft. tall and as wide in nearly frostless areas; perennial to half that size in colder part of range. Native to South America. Many-stemmed, rough-barked plant, with 6-in. leaves divided into 2–3-in.-long leaflets. First flowers form after leaves unfurl in spring, when each branch tip flaunts a big, loose, spikelike cluster of velvety, birdlike blossoms in warm pink to wine red (color varies with the plant). Depending on environment, there may be as many as three distinct flowering periods, spring through fall. Cut back old flower stems after each wave of bloom.

Erythrina crista-galli

E. falcata. Nearly evergreen tree. Zones 19–24; H1, H2. Native to Brazil and Peru. Upright habit to 30–40 ft. high. Must be in ground several years before it flowers (may take 10 to 12 years). Rich deep red (occasionally orange-red), sickle-shaped flowers in hanging, spikelike clusters at branch ends in winter, early spring. Some leaves drop at bloom time.

E. humeana. NATAL CORAL TREE. Normally deciduous tree (sometimes almost evergreen). Zones 12, 13, 20–24; H1, H2. Native to South Africa. May grow to 30 ft. tall, but begins blooming when only 3 ft. high. Flowers continuously from late summer to late autumn, carrying bright orange-red blossoms in long-stalked clusters at branch ends well above the leaves (unlike many other types). Dark green foliage. 'Raja' is shrubbier and has leaflets with long, pointed "tails."

E. lysistemon. Deciduous tree. Zones 13, 21–24; H2. Native to South Africa. Similar to *E. caffra* in size but slower growing. Light orange (sometimes shrimp pink) flowers. Time of bloom varies greatly; may bloom intermittently from early fall to late spring, occasionally in summer. Many handsome black thorns. A magnificent tree of great landscape value. Very sensitive to wet soil. Sometimes erroneously sold as *E. princeps.*

Erythrina humeana

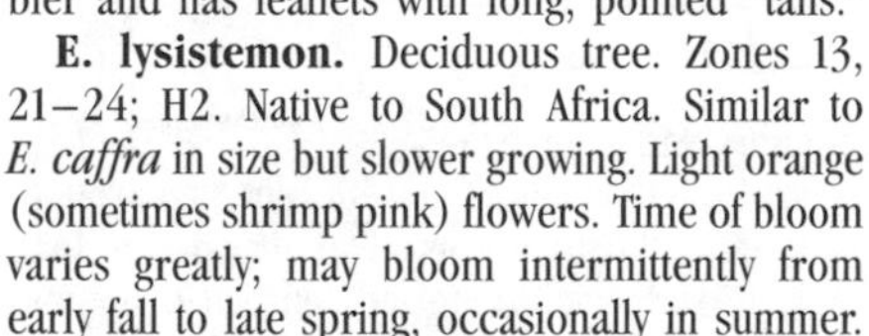

E. sandwicensis. WILIWILI, HAWAIIAN CORAL TREE. Deciduous tree. Zone H2. Hawaiian native to 20–45 ft. high and as wide. Masses of white to chartreuse, coral, orange, red, or bicolored flowers bloom in late summer to winter, preceding the flush of new foliage. Extremely drought tolerant; good selection for xeriscape gardens.

E. × sykesii. Deciduous tree. Zones 19–24. Hybrid from Australia. To 24–30 ft., with spreading habit. Showy red flowers appear in winter before leaves emerge. Unlike the other species, does not form pods.

E. variegata. INDIAN CORAL TREE, TIGER'S CLAW. Deciduous tree. Zone H2. Native from India to southern Polynesia. To 60 ft. tall, 25–35 ft. wide, with a prickly trunk and branches and leaves consisting of three broad, triangular leaflets to 6 in. long. Large clusters of brilliant coral red flowers are produced in winter before new leaves develop. Forms are available with white flowers and variegated leaves. All types are adapted to wide range of soil conditions.

'Tropic Coral'. TROPIC CORAL TALL ERYTHRINA. Columnar, evergreen to semievergreen form of *E. variegata* to 50 ft. high, 10–15 ft. wide. Bright orange flowers appear at the top of the tree in spring. Used as a windbreak or screen and near tall buildings when space is limited.

ERYTHRONIUM

Liliaceae

PERENNIALS FROM BULBS

ZONES VARY BY SPECIES

LIGHT SHADE

REGULAR WATER DURING GROWTH AND BLOOM

Erythronium tuolumnense

Spring-blooming plants with dainty, nodding, lily-shaped flowers 1–1½ in. across, on stems usually 1 ft. high or less. All have two (rarely three) broad, tongue-shaped basal leaves; these are mottled in many species. Set out in groups under deciduous trees, in rock gardens, beside pools or streams; give rich, porous soil. Plant bulbs in fall, as soon as you receive them; don't let them dry out. Set 2–3 in. deep, 4–5 in. apart. Western species need no water during dormancy, but give *E. dens-canis* moisture year-round. Divide clumps infrequently—only when vigor and bloom quality decline.

E. californicum. FAWN LILY. Zones 4–7, 14–17. Native to Northern California. Leaves mottled with brown. Creamy white or yellow flowers with deeper yellow band at base, on 6–10-in. stems.

E. dens-canis. DOG-TOOTH VIOLET. Zones 1–7, 15–17. From Europe. Leaves mottled brown and white. Deep pink to purple flowers on 6–12-in. stems. Specialists can supply named varieties with white, pink, rose, or violet blossoms. Needs some shade during hot afternoon hours.

E. hendersonii. Zones 4–7, 15–17. Native to Northern California and southern Oregon. Foot-tall stems carry light to deep lavender flowers that are dark maroon at base, deeply curled back at tips. Dark green leaves are mottled with brown.

E. revolutum. Zones 1–7, 14–17. Western native quite similar to *E. californicum,* but foliage and flowers are larger; stems up to 16 in. Blossoms are usually pink marked yellow in the center, but varieties 'Pink Beauty' (pure pink without yellow center) and 'White Beauty' are available.

E. tuolumnense. Zones 2–7, 14–17. Native to California. Robust plant with solid green leaves and 12–15-in.-tall stems. Golden yellow flowers, greenish yellow at base. 'Kondo' and 'Pagoda' are extra-vigorous selections.

ESCALLONIA

Escalloniaceae

EVERGREEN SHRUBS

ZONES 4–9, 14–24

PARTIAL SHADE IN HOTTEST CLIMATES

REGULAR WATER

Escallonia rubra

Native to South America, principally Chile. Wind tolerant, clean looking, with glossy leaves. Clusters of flowers in summer and fall (nearly year-round in mild climates). May freeze badly at 10 to 15°F/–12 to –9°C, but will recover quickly. Will take direct coastal conditions and coastal winds. Tolerant of most soils but damaged by high alkalinity. Drought tolerant, but look better with regular water. Prune taller ones by removing one-third of old wood each year after bloom, cutting to the base; or shape into multitrunked trees. Tip-pinch smaller kinds to keep them compact. Can be sheared as hedges, but this may sacrifice some bloom. Fast growing; good screen plants. Attractive to bees. Foliage of some exudes resinous fragrance.

E. 'Apple Blossom'. See E. × langleyensis

E. 'Balfouri'. See E. × exoniensis

E. bifida (E. montevidensis). WHITE ESCALLONIA. As shrub, can be kept to 8–10 ft. high and wide, useful as big screening plant; can also grow as multitrunked small tree to 25 ft. tall. Glossy dark green leaves are 3–4 in. long. White flowers in large, rounded clusters at branch ends. Many plants sold under this name are *E. illinita,* a plant to 10 ft. tall with smaller flower clusters and a pronounced resinous odor. ▸

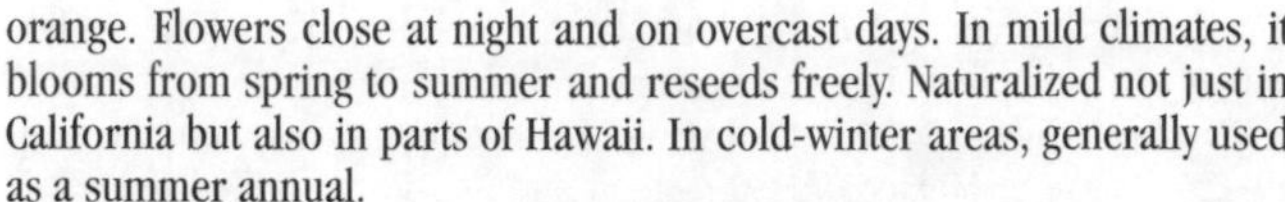

E. 'C. F. Ball'. See E. rubra

E. 'Compakta'. To 3 ft. high and wide, with rose red flowers.

E. × exoniensis. Name given to hybrids between *E. rosea* and *E. rubra.* Best selections are 'Balfouri', a graceful plant up to 10 ft. tall and wide, with drooping branchlets and narrow clusters of pink-tinted white flowers; and 'Frades' (*E.* 'Fradesii'), compact growth to 5–6 ft. high (lower with pinching) and wide. 'Frades' resembles *E. laevis,* but has smaller, glossy green leaves and prolific show of pure pink to rose flowers. Both are good as espaliers.

E. 'Fradesii'. See E. × exoniensis

E. 'Ingramii'. See E. rubra macrantha

E. 'Jubilee'. Compact-growing, 6-ft. shrub that is densely leafy right to the ground. Clustered pinkish to rose flowers. Set 4 ft. apart for informal hedge or screen.

E. laevis (E. organensis). PINK ESCALLONIA. Leafy, dense-growing shrub to 12–15 ft. tall and wide. Bronzy green leaves. Pink to red buds open into white to pink flowers in short, broad clusters. Use as a large screen or train as a small tree. Leaves burn in seacoast wind and salt as well as in high heat.

E. × langleyensis. Known as the Donard Hybrids, these are crosses between *E. rubra* and *E. virgata.* Best-known selection is 'Apple Blossom', a dense-growing shrub to 5 ft. high and wide, sprawling unless pinched back. Pinkish white flowers open from pink buds. 'Pride of Donard', a dense, rounded shrub 5 ft. high and 8 ft. wide, has glossy dark green leaves and pink flowers.

E. montevidensis. See E. bifida

E. 'Newport Dwarf'. Grows 2½ ft. tall, 4 ft. wide, with deep pink to red flowers.

E. organensis. See E. laevis

E. 'Red Elf'. Dense, spreading shrub to 8 ft. tall, 12 ft. wide, with inch-long, dark glossy green leaves and short clusters of deep red flowers.

E. rubra. Upright, compact shrub 6–15 ft. tall and wide. Leaves smooth, very glossy dark green. Red or crimson flowers in 1–3-in. clusters. Much used as screen or hedge, especially near coast. Compact varieties are 'C. F. Ball', 5–6 ft. high and wide (to 3 ft. with some pinching), and 'William Watson', to 4 ft. tall and wide, with ruddy cerise flowers, spindly habit unless pruned. *E. r. macrantha* ('Ingramii') resembles the species but has larger flowers.

E. virgata. Partially deciduous shrub grows to 6 ft. tall and 8 ft. wide, with ¾-in. leaves. Plant produces short clusters of pale rose or white flowers. This is the hardiest escallonia; does well in frostiest parts of these plants' hardiness range.

ESCHSCHOLZIA

Papaveraceae

PERENNIALS AND ANNUALS

ZONES 1–24; H1

FULL SUN

LITTLE TO REGULAR WATER

Eschscholzia californica

Poppy relatives with upward-facing, four-petaled yellow or orange blooms above finely cut foliage. Individual plants grow about 6 in. wide. Of the several species native to western North America and Mexico, *E. californica* is the most outstanding and the most widely used; it is the state flower of California. All are drought tolerant, but giving them summer water will extend the flowering season.

E. caespitosa. Annual. Native to California and southwestern Oregon. Smaller plant than *E. californica;* garden variety 'Sundew', for example, has densely tufted growth to 6 in. high. Plants bear bright yellow, 1-in. flowers. Use for edging, in containers.

E. californica. CALIFORNIA POPPY. Perennial often grown as annual. Native to California, Oregon. Free branching from base, with slender, 8–24-in.-long stems and blue-green, finely divided leaves. Single, satiny-petaled flowers about 2 in. wide; color varies from pale yellow to deep orange. Flowers close at night and on overcast days. In mild climates, it blooms from spring to summer and reseeds freely. Naturalized not just in California but also in parts of Hawaii. In cold-winter areas, generally used as a summer annual.

California poppy is not the best choice for important beds viewed close up—unless you trim off dead flowers regularly, plants go to seed and all parts turn straw color. It can't be surpassed, however, for naturalizing on sunny hillsides, along drives, or in dry fields, vacant lots, parking strips, or country gardens.

Sow seeds where plants are to grow; seedlings don't transplant well. Sow in fall in mild-winter areas, in spring in colder regions. Broadcast on cultivated, well-drained soil; if rain is absent, water to keep ground moist until seeds germinate. For large-scale sowing, use 3–4 lb. of seeds per acre. Birds are attracted to the seeds.

There are also garden forms with blooms of yellow, pink, rose, flame orange, red, cream, and white. Sunset strain has single flowers, Mission Bells semidouble flowers, and Ballerina semidouble blooms with frilled and fluted petals. Thai Silk strain has bronze-tinted foliage, semidouble flowers in full color range. Among the many California poppy selections are 'Apricot Flambeau', yellow with orange-pink borders; 'Carmine King', a blend of deep pink and white; 'Dalli', orange-red blooms with yellow eye; and 'Inferno', orange scarlet. Names of 'Cherry Ripe', 'Milky White', and 'Purple Cap' describe flower color. 'Champagne and Roses' has heavily frilled flowers in rose or light pink. 'Golden Tears' bears single golden yellow blooms on trailing stems to 2 ft. long. Garden forms usually revert to orange or yellow when they reseed.

E. mexicana. Annual. Native Arizona to west Texas, southern Utah, Mexico. Very similar to *E. californica* but generally a smaller plant (to 8 in. high) with less finely divided leaves. Sun Shades strain has brilliant orange flowers.

ESPOSTOA lanata

PERUVIAN OLD MAN CACTUS

Cactaceae

CACTUS

ZONES 12–24; OR INDOORS

SUN OR LIGHT AFTERNOON SHADE; BRIGHT LIGHT

LITTLE TO MODERATE WATER

Espostoa lanata

Columnar cactus, branching with age. Slow growing in pots, fairly fast (to 8 ft. tall and 2 ft. wide) in open ground. Light brown, bristly, ½–2-in.-long thorns are usually concealed in long white hair that covers plant. Hair is especially long and dense near summit. Tubular, pink, 2-in.-long flowers in spring. Protect from hard frosts.

ETLINGERA elatior (Phaeomeria magnifica)

TORCH GINGER

Zingiberaceae

PERENNIAL

ZONE H2

FULL SUN OR PARTIAL SHADE

REGULAR WATER

Etlingera elatior

Malaysian and Indonesian jungles are home to this herbaceous, clump-forming plant to 20 ft. high and as wide (spreading wider over time). One of Hawaii's best-loved gingers. Canelike stems are clothed with dark green, pointed leaves, each 12–28 in. long and 4–6 in. wide. Plant blooms most of the year, producing striking bright red or pink, conelike inflorescences on 2–5-ft.-long stalks that rise directly from the ground. Best in rich, organic soil with protection from wind.

EUCALYPTUS

Myrtaceae

EVERGREEN TREES AND SHRUBS

ZONES 5, 6, 8–24; H1, H2 (SEE HARDINESS IN CHART)

FULL SUN

LITTLE OR NO WATER, EXCEPT AS NOTED

SEE CHART NEXT PAGE

Eucalyptus nicholii

With few exceptions, these plants are native to Australia. More than 600 different species grow there, ranging from sprawling shrubs (many of them bearing the common name "mallee") to skyline trees. About 150 species have been grown in areas of California and Arizona that have climates similar to the plants' native Australian habitats; many have been grown as solitary representatives in arboretums. Eucalypts are the most widely planted non-native trees in these two Western states—for several hundred miles in parts of California, you never lose sight of one. The first eucalypts were planted in this country in 1856, and from 1870 on they were widely grown for windbreaks, firewood, and shade. From 1904 to 1912, thousands of acres were planted in an ill-advised hardwood timber scheme.

California and Arizona do not have a monopoly on eucalypts, however. Many can be grown in western Washington and Oregon, and gardeners in the mildest parts of Vancouver Island have also experimented with them. Safest for beginners in these milder-winter areas of the Pacific Northwest are *E. gunnii,* cider gum, and *E. pauciflora niphophila,* snow gum. Other choices include *E. perriniana,* spinning gum, and *E. stellulata,* black Sally.

Eucalyptus ficifolia

The two species most commonly used in Hawaii are *E. citriodora (Corymbia citriodora),* lemon-scented gum, and *E. deglupta,* Mindanao gum (native to jungles of the Philippines and Indonesia). *E. robusta,* swamp mahogany, is a less common landscape choice; it is used mainly in reforestation.

The chart on the following pages describes more than 40 different eucalypts. These trees are appealing on several levels: depending on the species, they may show attractive form, striking bark, good-looking foliage, or some combination of these features. Some even have showy blossoms, though flowers of many are unimportant. Note that juvenile and adult leaves differ; when juvenile foliage is significantly different, it is noted in the chart. Also pay attention to plant size; many species are best suited to larger properties.

Hardiness. The chart gives approximate hardiness for each species, but these temperatures are not absolute. In addition to air temperature, take into account the plant's age (older plants are generally hardier) and its condition, as well as the date of frost (a freeze is more damaging in November than it would be in January, after the plant has experienced weeks of low temperatures) and its duration. If temperatures in your area are likely to fall within the frost-damage range for a certain species, plant it as a risk. If they regularly drop below the given range, don't plant it.

Planting. A few species grow as much as 10 ft. annually in their early years. Such a growth rate is typically associated with short-lived trees, but not in this case—fast-growing tree eucalypts can live for at least a century if given proper care from the start.

WHAT EUCALYPTS NEED

PLANTING: Given a proper start, even fast-growing types will live a long time. Choose small, sturdy-looking plants that are not root-bound, and plant them carefully.

WATERING: Most eucalypts are supremely tolerant of dryness and thrive on rainfall alone; irrigate a little in the low desert.

FERTILIZING: Forget about regular feedings. The only nutrient gardeners sometimes must supply, especially in the desert, is iron chelate to treat chlorosis.

CUT FOLIAGE: For the types grown for their decorative foliage, trim frequently to encourage a steady supply of handsome leaves.

Eucalyptus polyanthemos

Generally, the best way to grow eucalypts is from seed—it's as easy as starting many annuals and perennials. Sow seeds in a flat in spring or summer; keep shaded and water sparingly. When seedlings are 2–3 in. tall, lift gently, separate, and transplant to another flat of prepared soil, spacing 3 in. apart. Or transplant into gallon cans or other large pots. Plant in ground in 2 to 3 months, when seedlings are 6–12 in. high.

When buying plants, select the most vigorous looking ones, not the biggest. Avoid those with many leafless twigs or evidence of hard pruning. If possible, do not buy root-bound plants. If such plants are all you can get, do this: wash soil off roots and cut off any kinked roots that cannot be straightened; then spread remaining roots out as straight as possible (in a fan shape) in premoistened planting hole, with stem's old soil line ½–1 in. below grade. Immediately fill in around roots with moistened soil and irrigate heavily. If plants are top-heavy, cut back and stake (chart prescribes staking for certain species).

Eucalyptus sideroxylon

Fertilizing and watering. Complete fertilizer is seldom needed, although iron often is required for eucalypts whose leaves chronically turn yellow between veins (chlorosis). In the desert, plants are especially subject to chlorosis in dense or shallow soils. Iron chelate applied in spring and fall is helpful for young trees. Overwatering can cause chlorosis. Newly planted trees may need water every day for their first week if weather is hot and dry, once or twice a week for rest of first growing season. Once established, most eucalypts need no watering at all, except in low desert.

Foliage. Most eucalypts have two conspicuously different kinds of foliage: soft, variously shaped juvenile leaves, found on seedlings, saplings, and new branches that grow from stumps; and (typically) tougher adult or mature foliage. Where a species' juvenile foliage is significant, it is mentioned in chart. Almost all eucalyptus leaves, juvenile and adult, have a distinctive pungent aroma, though foliage must sometimes be crushed to release its scent. Beyond the fragrance common to all types, some are accented with lemon or other perfumes.

Eucalyptus rhodantha

Pruning. Many eucalypts need pruning to improve shape or to remove dead or dying growth. The ideal time for the job is between March and August. (Where eucalyptus longhorn beetle is a problem—see "Pests," next page—avoid pruning from May to October.) Some descriptions in the chart recommend that you cut back plants to make them bushier or stouter. Wait until plant has been in the ground at least a year, then cut back to just above a side branch or bud. If there are no side branches or visible buds, cut back trunk to desired height—if plant is established, new growth will break out beneath cut. Later, remove all excess new branches that form; keep only those that are well placed.

Occasional deep or prolonged freezes may kill even large trees. Don't be too quick to remove them; they can sprout new growth from trunk or large branches, though heavy freeze damage may alter their appearance. Delay removal or heavy pruning until summer (late fall or earliest spring in areas where beetle is present). ▶

Pests. Eucalyptus was pest-free until 1984, when the eucalyptus longhorn beetle—one of the tree's native attackers in Australia—was observed in Southern California. Without natural predators to keep it in check, the beetle has become a serious pest, especially on stressed trees. Signs of infestation include oval holes made by the beetle in the plant's wood, and individual branches or the whole plant dying with leaves still attached. The best control is good management. Freshly cut wood attracts the pest, so avoid pruning during its active period (May to October). If you see tunnels under bark of firewood, immediately burn or bury the wood. Remove dead or dying trees; bury logs or cover tightly with tarpaulins for at least 6 months. Tightly cover eucalyptus firewood and do not transport it.

Another pest, the red gum lerp psyllid, is a more recent arrival from Australia. Discovered in Southern California in 1998, the tiny insect has spread throughout the state, attacking many eucalyptus species in addition to red gum *(E. camaldulensis)*. It sucks sap from leaves, excreting honeydew in the process; foliage may look black due to sooty mold growing on the honeydew. If present in high numbers, the pest can cause severe leaf drop. Infested plants are more susceptible to attack by other pests, including borers. Minimize stress by irrigating deeply (but not near the trunk) during long dry spells; don't fertilize. Don't spray with any kind of insecticide—a parasitoid wasp has been released to control the psyllid.

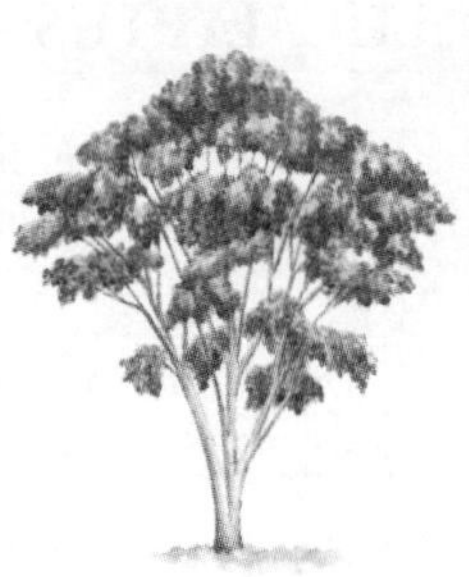

Eucalyptus citriodora

EUCALYPTUS

NAME, HARDINESS	HEIGHT	SPREAD	LEAVES, BARK	FLOWERS, FRUIT	COMMENTS
Eucalyptus albens WHITE BOX 22°F/–6°C	45–75 ft.	30–45 ft.	Large, pale gray-green juvenile leaves. Pale bark	Clusters of small white flowers from whitish buds. Small fruits	Casts fairly dense shade. Juvenile leaves are good for cut foliage. Stronger growth than *E. polyanthemos* in desert
E. baueriana BLUE BOX 10 to 18°F/ –12 to –8°C	35–75 ft.	25–45 ft.	Gray-green, nearly round juvenile leaves, broader and rougher than those of *E. polyanthemos*. Adult leaves may be slightly longer, broader, less sharply pointed	Unimportant whitish flowers	Fuller-bodied substitute for *E. polyanthemos*. Attractive round tree when young; becomes tall and straight with age
E. camaldulensis (E. rostrata) RED GUM 12 to 23°F/ –11 to –5°C	45–150 ft.	45–105 ft.	Long, slender, lance-shaped, pendulous green leaves. Tan, mottled, curved trunk	Unimportant white to pale yellow flowers, small capsules	Large tree with spreading crown, weeping branches. For highways, broad streets, parks, skylines. Gets chlorosis in desert
E. cinerea SILVER DOLLAR TREE 14 to 17°F/ –10 to –8°C	20–55 ft.	20–45 ft.	Roundish gray-green juvenile leaves, 1–2 in. long. Long, narrow green mature leaves	Unimportant small white flowers, small capsules	Cut back often for a supply of decorative foliage. Withstands wind. Best in dry site or with fast drainage. Can be used as perennial in borderline climates
E. citriodora (Corymbia citriodora) LEMON-SCENTED GUM 24 to 28°F/ –4 to –2°C	45–90 ft.	15–45 ft.	Leaves long (3–7 in.), golden green, lemon scented. Trunk white to pinkish	Small white flowers, little urn-shaped capsules	Attractive, narrow tree; can grow close to walls, walks. Lower half to two-thirds of tree is bare trunk. Trunk is weak when young; stake stoutly. Cut back and thin often to strengthen. Can take much or little water
E. cladocalyx (E. corynocalyx) SUGAR GUM 23 to 28°F/ –5 to –2°C	45–90 ft.	45–75 ft.	Shiny, reddish, 3–5-in. leaves, oval or variably shaped. Tan bark peels to show creamy patches	Unimportant creamy white flowers, small capsules	Planted for structure. Skyline tree on Southern California coast with characteristic puffy clouds of foliage separated by open spaces. Tough. 'Nana' is a small grower to 20–25 ft.
E. conferruminata (usually sold as **E. lehmannii)** BUSHY YATE 25 to 28°F/ –4 to –2°C	12–27 ft.	15–30 ft.	Elongated oval, light green, 2-in. leaves; some turn red in fall	Green flowers in 4-in. clusters open from horn-shaped buds. Large woody capsules remain on branches	Fast-growing, flat-topped, dense tree for windbreak or seashore. Left unpruned, branches touch ground
E. deglupta MINDANAO GUM 24 to 26°F/ –4 to –3°C	75–200 ft.	30–75 ft.	Dark green leaves. Flaking bark strikingly colored in blue, green, yellow, red, purple	Flowers, fruit inconspicuous	Fast-growing, erect tree from jungles of Indonesia, Philippines, New Guinea. Trunk is the spectacular feature. Regular water

EUCALYPTUS

NAME, HARDINESS	HEIGHT	SPREAD	LEAVES, BARK	FLOWERS, FRUIT	COMMENTS
E. erythrocorys RED-CAP GUM 23 to 26°F/ −5 to −3°C	12–30 ft.	9–25 ft.	Thick, shiny, deep green, lance-shaped leaves, 4–7 in. long. White trunk	Bright red caps tilt up and fall off to reveal yellow flowers in clusters like brushes. Blooms any time of year, heaviest from fall to early spring	Best with multiple trunks; sprawling but attractive. To make dense, head back main shoots several times. Can take much water if drainage is good. Can be grown in lawn. Attractive in desert
E. ficifolia (Corymbia ficifolia) RED-FLOWERING GUM 25 to 30°F/ −4 to −1°C	18–45 ft.	15–60 ft.	Deep green, leathery, 3–7-in.-long leaves; look like rubber plant foliage	Showy foot-long clusters of red flowers (sometimes white, cream, pink, or orange) all year, peaking in summer. Heavy 1-in. seed capsules like dice cups	Usually single trunked, round headed. Unpredictable flower color from seed. Prune seed capsules from young trees to avoid weighing down branches, spoiling form. Seldom thrives in lawns or hottest climates
E. formanii 15°F/−9°C	12–18 ft.	12–18 ft.	Needlelike, silvery to tan leaves to 2½ in. long. Rough gray bark	Small creamy white flowers. Small, rounded fruits	Bushy, billowy big shrub or small tree. Good in desert
E. globulus BLUE GUM 17 to 22°F/ −8 to −6°C	45–165 ft.	30–75 ft.	Oval, silvery juvenile leaves; mature leaves are sickle shaped, dark green, 6–10 in. long	Flowers white to yellowish. Warty seed capsules	Good as a windbreak, but not the best choice for gardens due to greedy roots, brittle wood, messiness—produces considerable litter from falling leaves, bark, capsules. Smaller form 'Compacta' is just as greedy, almost as messy
E. gunnii CIDER GUM 5 to 10°F/ −15 to −12°C	30–75 ft.	18–45 ft.	Silvery blue-green young foliage. Dark green, 3–5-in.-long mature leaves. Green-and-tan bark	Small creamy white flowers. Clusters of tiny capsules	One of the fastest-growing, hardiest eucalypts. Dense form good for shade, windbreak, or screen. May take temperatures a few degrees colder than indicated, if not for an extended period
E. kruseana KRUSE'S MALLEE 25 to 28°F/ −4 to −2°C	6–18 ft.	9–18 ft.	Round, silvery blue, 1-in. leaves like smaller version of *E. pulverulenta*	Small, pretty yellow flowers along stems between leaves	Attractive foliage and flowers on slow-growing, open, angular, "conversation piece" shrub. Cut back frequently. Useful in desert gardens
E. largiflorens BLACK BOX 15 to 20°F/ −9 to −7°C	To 50 ft.	To 50 ft.	Narrow gray-green leaves to 6 in. long. Dark green bark	Masses of white flowers are a good honey source	Tolerates heavy, poorly drained, and alkaline soils. Good in desert
E. lehmannii (See **E. conferruminata**)					
E. leucoxylon WHITE IRONBARK 14 to 18°F/ −10 to −8°C	30–90 ft.	18–60 ft.	Gray-green, sickle-shaped leaves, 3–6 in. long. Trunk brownish or bluish gray, shedding to reveal white new bark	Flowers variable—white to cream, pink, or reddish. Little goblet-shaped capsules	Habit somewhat variable; usually slender, upright, open, with pendulous branches. Tolerates adverse conditions, including heat, wind, and heavy soils or light, rocky ones
E. l. megalocarpa LARGE-FRUITED YELLOW GUM 14 to 18°F/ −10 to −8°C	12–27 ft.	15–20 ft.	Gray-green leaves vary in shape and size, depending on tree. Gray to pinkish trunk	Bears abundant deep reddish pink flowers from an early age. Goblet-shaped capsules	Much branched, shrublike, ornamental. Good in most soils, most sites, even near beach or in desert
E. macrocarpa 8 to 12°F/ −13 to −11°C	6–12 ft.	9–36 ft.	Light gray-blue leaves, 2–5 in. long, in pairs close to stem. Greenish white bark	Golf ball–size gray buds open to round, fluffy, flat-topped pink, red, or white flowers 4–7-in. across; blossoms are stalkless, "sit" on branches. Followed by 3-in. capsules	Sprawling and awkward, but showy. For dry places. Can be espaliered on sunny fence or wall

▶

EUCALYPTUS

NAME, HARDINESS	HEIGHT	SPREAD	LEAVES, BARK	FLOWERS, FRUIT	COMMENTS
E. mannifera maculosa RED-SPOTTED GUM 20 to 25°F/ −7 to −4°C	20–50 ft.	12–36 ft.	Narrow, 4–6-in.-long, light grayish green leaves. Powdery, pink to red new bark flakes off, leaving powdery white surface	Unimportant white flowers, small capsules	Attractive tree with graceful pendent branches. Colorful bark with powdery bloom is main feature
E. megacornuta 20 to 23°F/ −7 to −5°C	15–36 ft.	15–24 ft.	Shiny, bronzy green, lance-shaped leaves 2–5 in. long. Smooth gray to tan bark	Clusters of 1½-in. green flowers like brushes open from bronzy green buds like warty fingers. Clawlike capsules	Spindly big shrub or small tree; usually poor form for landscaping. Flower arrangers use the buds, flowers, and seed capsules
E. melliodora 18 to 20°F/ −8 to −7°C	30–90 ft.	24–75 ft.	Boat- or sickle-shaped grayish green leaves, 2–6 in. long. Old bark scaly, flaky, tan	White flowers in late winter or early spring; not showy but have a sweet honey fragrance and are attractive to bees. 'Rosea' has pink blooms	Upright with slightly weeping branches. Produces very little litter. Shade tree, street tree, windbreak
E. microtheca COOLIBAH 5 to 10°F/ −15 to −12°C	30–60 ft.	24–54 ft.	Blue-green, ribbonlike leaves to 8 in. long	Insignificant creamy white flowers. Tiny capsules create no litter	Bushy, round-headed, single- or multitrunked tree. Wind resistant. One of the best eucalypts for Arizona
E. nicholii NICHOL'S WILLOW-LEAFED PEPPERMINT 12 to 15°F/ −11 to −9°C	36–48 ft.	15–36 ft.	Narrow, 3–5-in.-long, light green leaves. Furrowed, rich reddish brown bark	Inconspicuous whitish flowers, tiny capsules	Graceful, weeping garden or street tree. Crushed leaves said to smell like peppermint. Too much water can cause chlorosis
E. papuana (Corymbia papuana) GHOST GUM 22°F/−6°C	30–54 ft.	20–45 ft.	Lance-shaped, 2–5-in., light green leaves, tinted purplish by frost. Smooth white bark	Small white flowers. Fruit inconspicuous	Semiweeping growth. White bark is most striking feature. Produces only sparse litter. Does well in desert soils
E. parvifolia SMALL-LEAVED GUM 0 to 10°F/ −18 to −12°C	18–30 ft.	18–30 ft.	Thick dark green leaves to 3 in. long	White flowers, tiny fruits	Branches to the ground. Useful as screen or windbreak. Good in desert
E. pauciflora GHOST GUM 10 to 15°F/ −12 to −9°C	24–60 ft.	18–45 ft.	Narrow gray-green leaves, 3–6 in. long. White trunk	Insignificant flowers, fruit	White trunk and branches and open crown make it a good specimen tree. Good in lawns. Takes wet or dry soil. Very little litter. In youth, remove erratic branches
E. p. niphophila (E. niphophila) SNOW GUM 0 to 10°F/ −18 to −12°C	26–40 ft.	18–30 ft.	Silvery blue, lance-shaped leaves 1½–4 in. long. Smooth white bark peels off in patches. Smallest branches cream colored (reddish under ideal conditions)	Creamy white flowers followed by silvery capsules	Hardy, picturesque tree with attractive foliage and trunk. Slow growing, wind tolerant. Good on slopes. Will not withstand protracted cold at low end of temperature range
E. perriniana SPINNING GUM 10 to 15°F/ −12 to −9°C	12–30 ft.	12–30 ft.	Round, silvery juvenile leaves form circle around stem, spin on stem when dry	Small white flowers, cup-shaped fruit	Silvery foliage useful in fresh and dried arrangements. Cut often to retain juvenile growth (mature leaves are long). Use as silver-leafed accent in border
E. polyanthemos SILVER DOLLAR GUM 14 to 18°F/ −10 to −8°C	30–75 ft.	15–45 ft.	Gray-green, nearly round, 2–3-in. juvenile leaves; dark green, lance-shaped mature leaves	Unimportant whitish flowers	Young leaves used in fresh and dried arrangements. Select young trees carefully; some have leaves less round and gray than others. Specimen, street tree. Can be used as perennial in borderline climates

EUCALYPTUS

NAME, HARDINESS	HEIGHT	SPREAD	LEAVES, BARK	FLOWERS, FRUIT	COMMENTS
E. pulverulenta SILVER MOUNTAIN GUM 15 to 21°F/ −9 to −6°C	18–30 ft.	6–15 ft.	Silver-gray, shish kebab–style juvenile foliage (stems appear to pierce leaves). Mature leaves usually long and pointed. Ribbony bark	Small, fuzzy, creamy white flowers sandwiched between round leaves along stems, fall to spring. Cup-shaped capsules	Garden curiosity. Source of branches for arrangements. Cut back often to encourage juvenile foliage
E. rhodantha ROSE MALLEE 8 to 12°F/ −13 to −11°C	6–12 ft.	9–18 ft.	Nearly round, 2–4-in., light gray-blue leaves, sometimes with greenish cast. Greenish white bark	Resembles *E. macrocarpa* in buds, flower shape, capsules. Flowers 3–5 in. wide, usually red; unlike those of *E. macrocarpa*, they have stems	Sprawling, with horizontal branching. Use for almost continuous flower display in dry site. Better for spilling down slope than *E. macrocarpa*. Good espalier
E. robusta SWAMP MAHOGANY 11 to 15°F/ −12 to −9°C	60–75 ft.	30–75 ft.	Dark green, leathery, shiny leaves 4–7 in. long. Stringy, dark red-brown bark	Pink-tinted, creamy white flowers anytime, mainly winter	Densely leafed, ultimately round headed. Strong tree; good windbreak. Performs well in moist or saline soil. Darkest green eucalypt in desert
E. rudis FLOODED GUM 12 to 18°F/ −11 to −8°C	30–60 ft.	24–40 ft.	Gray-green to green, 4–6-in., lance-shaped leaves. Rough bark	White flower clusters (not showy). Small fruit	Often weeping. Use as shade or street tree. Takes coastal conditions, wind, much or little water, sandy or saline soil. Not good in desert unless in deep, gravelly, well-drained soil
E. saligna SYDNEY BLUE GUM 18 to 20°F/ −8 to −7°C	60–150 ft.	30–75 ft.	Medium green, 4–8-in., lance-shaped leaves. Red to pinkish bark peels off	Pinkish to cream flowers (not showy)	Probably fastest-growing species; can grow 10 ft. first year. Best in cooler-summer areas. Can grow in lawns
E. salmonophloia SALMON GUM 20 to 25°F/ −7 to −4°C	To 40 ft.	To 40 ft.	Narrow, glittering bright green leaves. Salmon-colored bark	Flowers white to cream, capsules inconspicuous	Slow growing; eventually flat-topped. Bark is main feature. Tolerates drought, some salt in soil. Good choice for home landscape in desert
E. salubris GIMLET 20 to 25°F/ −7 to −4°C	20–25 ft.	20–25 ft.	Glossy deep green leaves to 4 in. long. Smooth, shiny, ridged red-brown bark	Flowers rather large, creamy white, conspicuous. Fruits inconspicuous	Can be single- or multitrunked. Like a smaller *E. salmonophloia*. Withstands heavy soils. Good in desert
E. sargentii SALT RIVER MALLET 22°F/−6°C	30–40 ft.	30–40 ft.	Narrow green leaves to 4 in. long. Dark gray, peeling bark	Cream-colored flowers open from slender buds with long horns	Stout single or multiple trunks. Exceptionally tough, very salt tolerant. Good in desert
E. sideroxylon RED or PINK IRONBARK 20 to 25°F/ −7 to −4°C	30–90 ft.	30–60 ft.	Slim blue-green leaves turn bronze in winter. Furrowed, nearly black trunk	Fluffy light pink to crimson flowers in pendulous clusters, mainly fall to late spring. Small capsules	Variable: open or dense, slender or squat, weeping or upright. Use as specimen, screen, street tree. Gets chlorotic in wet, heavy soils
E. stellulata BLACK SALLY 12 to 18°F/ −11 to −8°C	18–45 ft.	15–30 ft.	Broadly elliptical leaves. Smooth bark is grayish, olive green, or brownish	Unimportant white to cream flowers. Clusters of small fruit	Unusual colored bark is main feature. Spreading tree with pendulous branches. Good as screen, shade tree
E. torquata CORAL GUM 17 to 22°F/ −8 to −6°C	18–36 ft.	15–30 ft.	Light green to yellow-green leaves, long and narrow or blunt and round	Flower buds like tiny Japanese lanterns, opening to flowers of coral red and yellow, on and off all year	Grown for bloom (good cut flowers) and small tree size. Stake and prune or head back to make graceful. Branches often droop from weight of flowers, seed capsules. Good in desert
E. viminalis MANNA GUM 12 to 15°F/ −11 to −9°C	30–150 ft.	24–45 ft.	Light green, narrow, 4–6-in. leaves. Whitish trunk with shedding bark	Small white flowers, fruit usually too high to be seen	Needs plenty of room—good for parks, highways. Best in good soil but can take poor soil. Creates debris

EUCOMIS

PINEAPPLE FLOWER
Liliaceae
PERENNIALS FROM BULBS
ZONES 4–9, 14–24; H1, H2
FULL SUN OR LIGHT SHADE
REGULAR WATER DURING GROWTH AND BLOOM

Eucomis comosa

Unusual-looking plants from tropical southern Africa. Thick spikes closely set with ½-in.-long flowers are topped with clusters of leaflike bracts that resemble pineapple tops. Make good cut flowers. Bloom in summer; persistent purplish seed capsules carry on the show even longer. Need rich soil with plenty of humus. Plant in ground in fall, setting bulbs 4–6 in. deep, 1 ft. apart. Also fairly easy to grow from seed sown in spring. In areas where ground freezes, mulch to protect plantings. Divide every 5 or 6 years. Interesting potted plants; set bulbs with tips just beneath soil surface and repot yearly in fresh soil mix.

E. bicolor. Spikes to 2 ft. tall; green flowers with purple-edged petals. Attractive, wavy-edged leaves to 1 ft. long, 3–4 in. wide.

E. comosa (E. punctata). Thick spikes 2–3 ft. tall are set with greenish white flowers tinged pink or purple. Stems are spotted purple at the base. Leaves grow to 2 ft. long and are less wavy than those of *E. bicolor.*

EUCOMMIA ulmoides

HARDY RUBBER TREE
Eucommiaceae
DECIDUOUS TREE
ZONES 3–10, 14–21
FULL SUN
MODERATE TO REGULAR WATER

Eucommia ulmoides

From central China. Rubber can be made from this tree's sap, but the process isn't economically feasible—instead, the plant is grown for its ornamental qualities. Attractive rounded habit; can reach 40–60 ft. tall, with equal or greater spread. Leaves resemble those of elm *(Ulmus)* but are glossier and more leathery. When a leaf is slowly torn in two, sap from the veins congeals into threads of rubber, holding the two halves together. Fall color is negligible; flowers and fruit are not conspicuous. Tolerates a wide variety of soils but requires good drainage. Not troubled by pests.

EUCRYPHIA

Eucryphiaceae
EVERGREEN OR SEMIEVERGREEN SHRUBS OR TREES
ZONES 5, 6, 15–17
BEST IN SUN, TOLERATE SOME SHADE
REGULAR WATER

Eucryphia × nymansensis

Many attractive species and varieties. The kinds most frequently sold in the West have shiny evergreen leaves and 2½-in.-wide, pure white flowers with big tufts of yellow stamens in center. Give them neutral or slightly acid soil and shelter from strong winds. In Zones 5 and 6, protect young plants from temperatures below 15°F/–9°C.

E. lucida. Native to Tasmania. To 20–30 ft. tall, half as wide. Smooth-edged, glossy leaves 1½–3 in. long. Fragrant blooms in early summer. 'Pink Cloud' has red-centered rosy pink blossoms. In Zones 5 and 6, plants may be damaged in coldest winters; those that are sheltered (growing at woodland edges, for example) fare better.

E. × nymansensis. Group of hybrids between two species from Chile. Best known is 'Mount Usher', to about 20 ft. tall and 8 ft. wide, with toothed leaves—some simple, some divided into three to five 2–4-in.-long leaflets. Often bears double flowers. 'Nymansay', to 15 ft. tall and 10 ft. wide, is somewhat faster growing. Both bloom in late summer.

EUGENIA

Myrtaceae
EVERGREEN SHRUBS OR TREES
ZONES VARY BY SPECIES
FULL SUN OR PARTIAL SHADE
REGULAR WATER

Eugenia uniflora

Grown for attractive foliage, white flowers, edible "cherries." Perform best with rich, well-drained soil, moist atmosphere, sheltered planting location. Some species have been reclassified. For *E. myrtifolia* and *E. paniculata,* see *Syzygium paniculatum;* for *E. smithii,* see *Acmena smithii.*

E. aggregata. CHERRY OF THE RIO GRANDE. Zones 23, 24. Native to Brazil. To 15 ft. tall and 10 ft. wide, with bark peeling in thin layers. Narrow, elliptical, glossy dark green leaves to 3 in. long. Fruit to 1 in. long ripens from orange red to deep purplish red, is said to taste like cherries. Eat fresh or use for jams, jellies.

E. uniflora. SURINAM CHERRY, PITANGA. Zones 21–24; H1, H2. From tropical America. Very slow, open growth to 15–25 ft. tall and 10–15 ft. wide, though it's commonly seen at 6–8 ft. tall with equal spread. Glossy coppery green leaves reach 2 in. long, deepen in color to purplish or red in cold weather. Fragrant, showy, ½-in.-wide white flowers with prominent stamens. Fruit is about 1 in. in diameter, ripens from yellow to orange to deep red; edible when fully ripe. Fruit of seedlings ranges from quite sweet and cherrylike to very sour. 'Lolita' has sweet black fruit and is far superior in flavor to seedlings. Good for jams, jellies. Grafted varieties are sometimes available. Good screen. Can be sheared into a hedge, but by doing so you'll sacrifice fruit.

EULALIA. See MISCANTHUS sinensis

EUONYMUS

Celastraceae
EVERGREEN AND DECIDUOUS SHRUBS AND VINES
ZONES VARY BY SPECIES
EXPOSURE VARIES BY SPECIES
MODERATE TO REGULAR WATER

Euonymus fortunei 'Emerald 'n Gold'

Deciduous and evergreen euonymus species are distinct: the characteristic squarish "hatbox" fruit common to both offers the only hint that they're related. Deciduous types are valued for fall leaf color or showy fruit. Evergreen sorts, used mainly for landscape structure (background and foundation plants, hedges, dividers), include some of the most cold-tolerant broad-leafed plants. Most species take a range of exposures, from full sun to fairly deep shade; deciduous kinds with fall color give best display in a sunny location. Some species are very susceptible to mildew. Scale can be a problem on any euonymus.

E. alatus. WINGED EUONYMUS. Deciduous shrub. Zones A3; 2–10, 14–16. From China, Japan. Though nursery tags may indicate a much smaller plant, the species can reach 15–20 ft. high and wide. Dense, twiggy, flat-topped shrub with horizontal branching. Twigs have flat, corky wings that disappear on older growth. Though fruit is smaller and less profuse than that of *E. europaeus,* fall color is impressive: the dark green leaves turn flaming red. (On plants grown in shade, fall color is pink.) 'Compacta', a smaller plant (to 6–10 ft. high and a little narrower) with smaller corky wings, isn't quite as hardy as the species (Zones A3; 2b–10, 14–16). 'Timber Creek', to 8 ft. high and wide, is an extra-hardy selection that succeeds in Zones A3, 1–10, 14–16. All make good screens or specimen plants; set them off against dark evergreens for greatest color impact. 'Compacta' is also excellent as an unclipped hedge.

E. americanus. STRAWBERRY BUSH. Deciduous shrub. Zones 3b–9, 14–17. From eastern U.S. To 4–6 ft. tall and wide, with tough, leathery dark green leaves that turn yellow in autumn. Plentiful fall crop of scarlet fruits that open to show orange seeds. Tolerates much shade; good in woodland plantings.

E. europaeus. SPINDLE TREE. Deciduous shrub or tree. Zones 1–9, 14–16. From Europe, western Asia. Can reach 20 ft. tall and 15 ft. wide but is usually smaller. Green branches bear shiny green leaves to 3 in. long; fall color varies from yellowish green to yellow to red. Inconspicuous flowers mature into showy pink to red fruits that split to reveal white seeds with a fleshy bright orange appendage. 'Aldenham' ('Aldenhamensis') is a vigorous selection with bright pink-and-orange fruits and red fall foliage. Full sun or partial shade.

E. fortunei. Evergreen vine or shrub. Zones 2b–17. From China. One of the best broad-leafed evergreens where temperatures drop below 0°F/–18°C. Trails or climbs by rootlets. If plant is used as a shrub, its branches will trail and sometimes root; if allowed to climb, it will form a spreading mass to 20 ft. or more. Prostrate forms can be used to control erosion. Rich deep green leaves are 1–2½ in. long, with scallop-toothed edges; flowers are inconspicuous. Mature growth (like that of ivy) is shrubby and bears fruit; cuttings taken from this shrubby wood produce upright plants. Sun or shade. In desert, takes full sun better than ivy.

The varieties of *E. fortunei,* some of which are listed here, are better known than the species itself. Many nurseries still sell them as forms of *E. radicans,* once thought to be the species but now considered another variety (see *E. f. radicans,* below).

'Canadale Gold'. Compact growth to 4 ft. high, 3–3½ ft. wide, with light green leaves edged in yellow.

'Colorata'. PURPLE-LEAF WINTER CREEPER. To 2 ft. high, 6–8 ft. wide. Same sprawling growth habit as *E. f. radicans,* though it makes a more even ground cover. Leaves turn dark purple in fall and winter.

'Emerald Gaiety'. To 4–5 ft. high, 3 ft. wide. Dense-growing, erect shrub with deep green leaves edged in white.

'Emerald 'n Gold'. Similar to above but with gold-edged leaves.

'Golden Prince'. To 4 ft. high and wide. New growth tipped gold; older leaves turn solid green. Extremely hardy; good hedge plant.

'Greenlane'. To 3–4 ft. high, 4–5 ft. wide, with erect branches, deep green foliage, orange fall fruits.

'Ivory Jade'. To 3 ft. high, 6 ft. wide. Resembles 'Greenlane' but has creamy white leaf margins that show pink tints in cold weather.

'Moonshadow'. To 3 ft. high, 4 ft. wide. Bright yellow leaves with dark green margins.

E. f. radicans. COMMON WINTER CREEPER. Zones 4–9, 14–17. Tough, hardy, trailing or vining shrub from Korea, Japan. Dark green, thick-textured, 1-in. leaves. Given no support, it's a sprawling, foot-high ground cover. Given a wall to cover, it does the job completely.

'Sunspot'. To 3–6 ft. high and wide. Dark green leaves have a central bright yellow spot.

E. japonicus. EVERGREEN EUONYMUS. Evergreen shrub. Zones 4–20; H1. From China, Korea, Japan. Upright grower to 8–10 ft. high, 6 ft. wide; usually kept lower. Inconspicuous flowers. Older shrubs are attractive trained as trees, pruned and shaped to show their curving trunks and umbrella-shaped tops. Can be grouped to form a hedge or screen. Very glossy, leathery deep green leaves are 1–2½ in. long, oval to roundish.

Though the species and its varieties are very tolerant of heat, unfavorable soil, and seacoast conditions, they tend to suffer from various problems. They are prone to scale, thrips, and spider mites. They are notorious for susceptibility to powdery mildew; to lessen likelihood of mildew infection, give a full-sun location with good air circulation.

Variegated forms are the most popular and are among the few shrubs to maintain their variegation in full sun in hot summer climates. (There may be some confusion in nursery labeling of these varieties.)

'Aureo-Variegatus'. To 10 ft. tall, 6 ft. wide. Green leaves with a brilliant yellow central blotch.

'Chollipo'. Narrow, erect plant to 12 ft. tall, 2–3 ft. wide. Green leaves bordered with white.

'Grandifolius'. To 6–8 ft. high, 4–6 ft. wide, with shiny dark green leaves larger than those of species. Compact, well branched, good for shearing into pyramids, globes.

'Microphyllus' *(E. j. pulchellus).* BOX-LEAF EUONYMUS. Compact, small-leafed shrub to 1–2 ft. high and half as wide. Formal looking; usually trimmed as low hedge.

'Microphyllus Variegatus'. Like 'Microphyllus', but with white-splashed leaves.

'Silver King'. To 6 ft. tall and about half as wide, with green leaves edged silvery white.

'Silver Princess'. Like 'Microphyllus Variegatus' but larger (to 3 ft. tall, 2 ft. wide), with larger leaves.

E. kiautschovicus (E. patens). Zones 3–10, 14–19. From China. To 8 ft. tall and as wide or wider. Fully evergreen in mild-winter climates and nearly so in harsh winters where there's no snow cover. May lose leaves or suffer leaf damage at around 0°F/–18°C. Glossy dark green, rather thin-textured leaves. Fruit is pink with orange seeds, not very conspicuous. 'Manhattan' is a selection from Manhattan, Kansas—testimony to its toughness. Full sun or partial shade.

EUPATORIUM

Asteraceae (Compositae)

PERENNIALS

ZONES VARY BY SPECIES

LIGHT SHADE IN HOTTEST CLIMATES

WATER NEEDS VARY BY SPECIES

Eupatorium purpureum maculatum 'Gateway'

These are generally large plants with big domes of small flower heads that are rich in nectar and pollen. Blossoms attract butterflies. Most of the species (including two of the three described here) are wild plants of eastern U.S. meadows, little noted until recently but now popular in perennial borders and naturalistic meadow plantings.

E. greggii. Zones 3, 10–13. Native to Arizona, Texas. Weak-stemmed plant to 1½–2½ ft. tall, 2–3 ft. wide, with clusters of fluffy lavender flowers that are similar in form to those of floss flower *(Ageratum).* Spring to fall bloom. Lacy, divided leaves are somewhat hairy and usually sparse. Excellent for attracting butterflies. Native to dry, hot, rocky places but prefers some shade in low desert. Drought tolerant but looks best with occasional water. 'Boothill', first found near Tombstone, Arizona, is a choice form.

E. maculatum. See E. purpureum maculatum

E. purpureum. JOE PYE WEED. Zones 1–9, 14–17. From eastern U.S. To 3–9 ft. tall, 1–3 ft. wide, with clump of hollow stems set with tiered whorls of strongly toothed leaves to a foot long. Leaves have a vanilla scent when bruised. Big domes of pale purple flowers in late summer or fall. *E. p. maculatum* is similar but somewhat smaller (to 6 ft.), with purple-spotted stems. Most common in gardens is 5-ft.-tall 'Gateway', with reddish purple stems topped by mauve to dusky purple flowers. All put on best show with rich soil, ample water.

E. rugosum (Ageratina altissima). WHITE SNAKEROOT. Zones 1–10, 14–17. From eastern U.S. To 4 ft. tall, 2 ft. wide. Stems and lance-shaped leaves to 5 in. long are heavily marked with deep brownish red; 'Chocolate' has especially deep color. Fluffy white flowers in late summer and early fall. Give rich soil, ample water.

EUPHORBIA

Euphorbiaceae

ANNUALS, BIENNIALS, PERENNIALS, AND EVERGREEN AND DECIDUOUS SHRUBS OR TREES

ZONES VARY BY SPECIES

EXPOSURE NEEDS VARY BY SPECIES

MODERATE TO REGULAR WATER, EXCEPT AS NOTED

SAP IS IRRITATING OR POISONOUS IN MANY SPECIES

Euphorbia characias wulfenii

Large genus of about 2,000 species. What is called a "flower" is technically a cyathium, consisting of fused bracts that form a cup around the much-reduced true flowers. Cyathia may appear singly or in clusters. In some cases, as with poinsettia *(E. pulcherrima),* additional bracts below provide most of the color. Fruit is usually a dry capsule that releases seeds explosively, shooting them up to several feet away. Many euphorbias are succulents; these often mimic cacti in appearance and are as diverse in form and size. Only a few succulent types are listed here, but specialists in cacti and succulents can supply scores of species and varieties. All euphorbias have milky white sap that is irritating on contact or toxic if ingested (degree of irritation or toxicity varies, depending on species). Before using cut flowers in arrangements, dip stems in boiling water or hold in a flame for a few seconds to prevent sap bleed. Plant all in well-drained soil.

E. amygdaloides. Perennial. Zones 2b–24. From Europe and Turkey. To 3 ft. tall, 1 ft. wide, with reddish green stems. Evergreen, 1–3-in.-long, dark green leaves have red undersides that turn darker red in winter. Greenish yellow flowers in clusters to 8 in. long at stem ends in midspring to early summer. Best in sun but tolerates some shade. 'Purpurea' has foliage heavily tinted purple, bright green inflorescences.

E. a. robbiae. MRS. ROBB'S BONNET. Shorter (to 1 ft. tall) and more shade tolerant than the species; also more spreading, expanding its territory by rhizomes and sometimes becoming invasive. It has interbred with the plain species, and intermediates are often sold as this variety.

E. antisyphilitica. CANDELILLA. Succulent shrub. Zones 12, 13, 18–21. Native to southwestern U.S., Mexico. Erect plant to 3 ft. high, spreading by underground stems. Cylindrical pale green stems are covered with wax used commercially in making candles. Inflorescence consists of red bracts and white petal-like appendages in a star shape. Good for rock gardens, containers. Withstands light frosts. Full sun, little water.

E. characias. Perennial. Zones 4–24. Mediterranean native. Upright stems crowded with narrow blue-green leaves form a dome-shaped bush 4 ft. high and wide. Chartreuse or lime green flowers in dense, round to cylindrical clusters appear in late winter, early spring. Color holds with only slight fading until seeds ripen; then stalks turn yellow and should be cut out at base, since new shoots have already made growth for next year's flowers. 'Humpty Dumpty' is a shorter (to 2½-ft.-high), vigorous selection. *E. c. wulfenii (E. veneta),* the most commonly grown form, has broader clusters of yellow flowers. All are fairly drought resistant and perform best in full sun.

E. cotinifolia. CARIBBEAN COPPER PLANT. Shrub or tree. Decidious in Zone 23; evergreen in Zones 24, H1, H2. From tropical America. Usually a multistemmed shrub 9–10 ft. high and wide, though it can become a small tree to 18 ft. tall if grown in a warm, frost-free spot. Long-stalked leaves to 4 in. long, 3 in. wide, usually borne in threes, are similar to those of smoke tree *(Cotinus);* 'Atropurpurea', the form most commonly grown, has wine red leaves. Loose flower clusters have small white bracts, are not showy. Likes full sun, heat, good drainage; can't take frost. For a similar plant sometimes sold under this name, see *Synadenium grantii.*

E. cyathophora. See E. heterophylla

E. cyparissias. CYPRESS SPURGE. Perennial. Zones 2–24. European native forms feathery clump to 8 in. (possibly to 16 in.) high; spreads vigorously by rhizomes, often becoming invasive. Slender, erect stems branch toward tips. Crowded blue-green, needlelike leaves. Terminal clusters of yellow-green flowers appear in late spring to early summer; these may turn orange in poor soils. Plant may go dormant in winter. Full sun or light shade. Little to moderate water.

E. dulcis 'Chameleon'. Perennial. Zones 2b–24. Forms a mound to 2 ft. high and wide. New spring growth is burgundy, maturing to dark bronzy green. Greenish yellow flower heads with a purplish tint appear at stem ends in early summer. Leaves and bracts turn rich purple in fall. Spreads by self-sowing; comes true from seed. Full sun. Tolerates dry soil.

E. epithymoides. See E. polychroma

E. griffithii. Perennial. Zones 2–10, 14–24. Erect-stemmed Himalayan native to 3 ft. tall and wide; spreads by creeping roots but is not aggressive. Narrow, medium green leaves are red tinged when new. Reddish orange to red bracts in early summer; those of 'Fireglow' are vivid orange red. Full sun or light shade.

E. heterophylla. FALSE POINSETTIA, MEXICAN FIRE PLANT, PAINTED SPURGE. Annual. Zones 1–24; H1, H2. Plants labeled as this species are almost always *E. cyathophora,* a native of eastern U.S. and Mexico. To 3 ft. tall, 1 ft. wide. Bright green leaves of varying shapes, larger ones resembling those of poinsettia *(E. pulcherrima);* flowers unimportant. In summer, upper leaves are blotched bright red and white, giving the appearance of a second-rate poinsettia. Useful in hot, dry borders in poor soil. Sow seed in place after danger of frost is past. Heavy reseeder in desert gardens. Full sun.

E. lambii. Deciduous shrub. Zones 14–24. From Canary Islands. Reaches 3–7½ ft. tall and almost as wide; spreads slowly by self-seeding. Single trunk branches slowly, first in two, later in threes, creating an inverted cone shape. Each branch is topped with a rosette of bluish- to yellow-green leaves. Terminal clusters of chartreuse flowers in early spring. Tolerates various soil types. Full sun. Give regular water during growth and bloom; doesn't need any during summer dormancy but can take some.

E. lathyris. GOPHER PLANT, MOLE PLANT. Biennial. Zones 2–10, 14–24. From Europe, northwest Africa. Legend claims that it repels gophers and moles. Stems have poisonous, caustic milky juice; keep away from skin and especially eyes, as painful burns can result. Juice could conceivably bother a gopher or mole enough to make it beat a hasty retreat. Single-stemmed plant to 5 ft. tall and 1 ft. wide. Stem is densely set with large leaves growing at right angles to the stem and to each other (forming four longitudinal rows along stem). In second summer, produces short-lived cluster of unspectacular yellow flowers at top of stem. Flowers soon go to seed, after which the plant dies. Start from seed; plant will keep going by self-sowing. Sun or shade. Little to regular water.

E. marginata. SNOW-ON-THE-MOUNTAIN. Annual. Zones 1–24. From central North America. To 2 ft. high, 1 ft. wide. Oval light green leaves; upper ones striped and margined white, sometimes even solid white. Summer flowers are variegated in green and white. Good for contrast with bright-colored bedding plants. Sow seeds in place in spring, in sun or partial shade. Thin to only a few inches apart, since plants are somewhat rangy.

E. × martinii. Perennial. Zones 3–24. Hybrid between *E. amygdaloides* and *E. characias.* To 2–3 ft. tall and wide. Resembles a compact *E. characias,* with dense clusters of brown-centered chartreuse flowers in late winter, spring. Evergreen leaves often tinged purple when young. Stems are red in winter. Full sun. Fairly drought resistant. 'Red Martin' has leaves held nearly upright, showing off red color of stems and new foliage.

E. milii (E. splendens). CROWN OF THORNS. Woody shrub; evergreen but sparsely leafed. Zones 13, 21–24; H1, H2; or indoors. Some frost damage below 28°F/–2°C. From Madagascar. To 1–4 ft. high, 1½ ft. wide. Stems armed with long, sharp thorns. Roundish, thin light green leaves are usually found only near branch ends. Clustered pairs of bright red bracts put on a show nearly all year. Many varieties and hybrids varying in form, size, and bract color (yellow, orange, pink). Train on small frame or trellis against a sheltered wall; or grow in container. Salt tolerance makes it an ideal choice for seaside plantings. Grow in porous but not rocky soil, in full sun or light shade (needs afternoon shade in Zone 13). Indoors, give bright light.

E. myrsinites. Perennial. Zones 2–24. Native from southern Europe to central Asia. To 6 in. high, 1 ft. wide. Evergreen plant with stems that trail outward from central crown, then rise toward tips. Stiff, roundish blue-gray leaves set closely in spirals around stems. Flattish clusters of chartreuse to yellow flowers top stem ends in late winter, early spring. Cut out old stems as they turn yellow. Withstands cold, heat, and aridity but is short lived in warm-winter areas. Use in sunny rock garden with succulents and gray-leafed plants.

E. obesa. BASEBALL PLANT. Succulent perennial. Zone 24; or indoor/outdoor plant. South African native forms a solid, fleshy, gray-green sphere (or short cylinder) to 8 in., with brownish stripes and brown dots that resemble the stitching on a baseball. Flowers unimportant. Give bright light, warmth, no sudden temperature changes. Little to moderate water; keep dryish in winter.

E. palustris. Perennial. Zones 2b–9, 14–17. From Europe, western Asia. Forms robust clump to 3 ft. high and wide, with many medium green, 2–3-in. leaves that turn yellow and orange in fall. Wide-branching clusters of yellow flowers in spring, early summer. Dies back in winter. Self-sows. Full sun or partial shade. One of the few euphorbias that will grow in damp or boggy conditions; also does well in ordinary garden soil, whether dry or moist.

E. polychroma (E. epithymoides). Perennial. Zones A2; 1–24. From Europe. Neatly rounded hemisphere to 1½ ft. high, 2 ft. wide, with deep green leaves symmetrically arranged on closely set, hairy stems. From midspring to midsummer, plant is covered with rounded clusters of bright yellow flowers surrounded by whorls of yellow-green bracts. Effect is of a gold mound suffused with green. Displays good fall color (yellow to orange or red) before going dormant. Use in rock gardens, perennial borders. Needs some shade in hottest climates. Short lived but reseeds.

E. pulcherrima. POINSETTIA. Evergreen, semievergreen, or deciduous shrub. Zones 13, 16–24; H1, H2; or indoors. Native to Mexico. Leggy plant to 10 ft. or taller, 6 ft. wide. Coarse leaves grow on stiffly upright canes. Showy part of plant consists of petal-like bracts; true flowers in center are yellowish, inconspicuous. Red single form is the most familiar; less well known are double-bracted red sorts and forms with white, yellowish, pink, or marbled bracts. Plants bloom only when they experience long nights—in winter and into spring, though bracts of paler kinds often last until later in spring. Milky sap is not poisonous; most people find it either completely harmless or at most mildly irritating to skin or stomach.

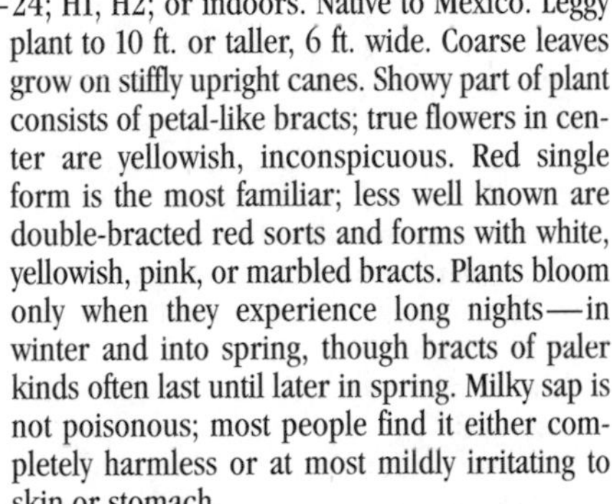

Euphorbia pulcherrima

Useful garden plant in well-drained soil and full sun (light shade in Zone 13). Where adapted outdoors, needs no special care. Grow as informal hedge in frost-free areas; where winter weather is frosty (but not severely cold), plant against sunny wall, in sheltered corner, under south-facing eaves (east-facing ones in Zone 13). Thin branches in summer to produce larger bracts; or prune them back at 2-month intervals for bushy growth (but often smaller bracts). To improve red color, feed every 2 weeks with high-nitrogen fertilizer, starting when color begins to show.

To care for holiday gift plant, keep in a sunny window and avoid sudden temperature changes. Keep soil moist but don't let water stand in pot saucer. When leaves drop in late winter or early spring, cut stems back to two buds and reduce watering to minimum. Store in a cool place until danger of frost is past; then set plant out in garden or keep in pot in a sunny spot on the patio. Potted plant will probably grow too tall for indoor use the next winter, but may survive winter if well sheltered. Start new plants by making late-summer cuttings of stems with four or five eyes (joints).

To get potted plant to bloom at Christmas time (earlier than in nature), do this: starting in early October, move it to a completely darkened closet each night for 14 hours; then, in the morning, move it into light for a maximum of 10 hours. Continue the process for 10 weeks.

E. rigida (E. biglandulosa). Perennial. Zones 4–24. Mediterranean native forms a 3–5-ft.-wide clump of stems that angle outward, then rise up to 2 ft. high. Fleshy gray-green leaves to 1½ in. long are narrow and pointed, their bases set tightly against stems. Broad, domed flower clusters in late winter or early spring are chartreuse yellow fading to pinkish. After seeds ripen, stems die back and should be removed; new stems take their place. Reseeds in mildest-winter areas, but not enough to become a pest. Showy display plant in borders, rock gardens, containers. Full sun. Tolerates drought.

E. robbiae. See E. amygdaloides robbiae

E. seguierana niciana. Perennial. Zones 4–24. From Balkans to Pakistan. Resembles a delicate, fine-textured *E. characias.* To 1½ ft. high and wide, with narrow, inch-long blue-gray leaves and chartreuse inflorescences. Full sun. Tolerates aridity.

E. tirucalli. MILKBUSH, PENCILBUSH, PENCIL TREE. Succulent tree or shrub. Zones 13, 23, 24; H1, H2; or indoors. From tropical eastern Africa. Grown for striking pattern of silhouette or shadow. Fast growing to possible 30 ft. tall and 6 ft. wide, usually much smaller. Single or multiple trunks support tangle of light green, pencil-thick, succulent branches with tiny leaves present only on actively growing tips. Flowers are unimportant. 'Sticks on Fire' has pale pink to fiery salmon pink stems; new growth has the most intense color in bright light. Both species and variety very tolerant of seacoast conditions. Full sun. Be sure to keep milky sap away from eyes, as it can cause severe damage. As houseplant, thrives in driest atmosphere; needs all the light you can give it, well-drained potting mix, routine watering and fertilizing.

E. veneta, E. wulfenii. See E. characias

Euphorbiaceae. The euphorbia family contains annuals, biennials, perennials, shrubs, and an enormous number of succulents. Most have milky sap, and many have small, unshowy flowers made decorative by larger bracts (often colorful) or bractlike structures. Poinsettia *(Euphorbia pulcherrima)* is the best-known example.

EURYA emarginata

Theaceae

EVERGREEN SHRUB

ZONES 4–6, 15–17, 21–24

LIGHT SHADE

REGULAR WATER

Eurya emarginata

Native to Japan. Slow growing to 6 ft. tall and wide, with branches rising at a 45° angle from base of plant. Easily kept to 3–4 ft. by pruning to side buds or branches. Grown for refined foliage—teardrop-shaped, dark green, leathery, ½-in.-long leaves closely set on branches. (*E. e. microphylla* has even tinier leaves—just ¼ in. long.) Young plants don't bloom, but old ones bear small greenish yellow flowers in late spring; most people consider the blossoms malodorous. Grow in organically enriched, acid, moist, well-drained soil.

EURYOPS

Asteraceae (Compositae)

EVERGREEN SHRUBS

ZONES VARY BY SPECIES

FULL SUN

LITTLE TO REGULAR WATER

Euryops pectinatus

Native to South Africa. Leaves are finely divided; flower heads are daisylike. Long bloom season; keep old flowers picked off. Plants require excellent drainage. They thrive on buffeting ocean winds but are damaged by sharp frosts. Take well to container culture.

E. acraeus. Zones 5–9, 12–24. Mounded growth to 2 ft. high and wide. Silvery gray leaves to ¾ in. long. Inch-wide, bright yellow daisies cover plant in spring. Mountain native and thus hardier to frost than *E. pectinatus* and its varieties. Has been used as a rock garden plant in western Washington and Oregon. May not survive winters in colder zones unless protected from excess moisture. ▸

E. pectinatus. Zones 8, 9, 12–24; H1, H2. To 3–6 ft. high and wide. Easy care and extremely long flowering season make it a good filler, background plant, or low screen. Gray-green, deeply divided, 2-in.-long leaves. Bright yellow, 1½–2-in.-wide daisies on 6-in. stems bloom most of the year. Cut back in late spring or early summer to maintain compactness and limit size. 'Viridis' is like species in all but leaf color; its foliage is deep green. 'Munchkin', with gray-green foliage, grows to 3 ft. tall, 4 ft. wide.

EUSTOMA grandiflorum (Lisianthus russellianus)

LISIANTHUS, TULIP GENTIAN, TEXAS BLUEBELL

Gentianaceae

BIENNIAL OR SHORT-LIVED PERENNIAL GROWN AS ANNUAL

ZONES 1–24

FULL SUN OR LIGHT SHADE

REGULAR WATER

Eustoma grandiflorum

Native to high plains of the West, but garden forms introduced from Japan. Plants grow better and have longer stems where nights are warm; best cut flowers are produced in greenhouses. In summer, a foot-wide clump of gray-green foliage sends up 1–3-ft. stems topped by tulip-shaped, 2–3-in. flowers in purplish blue, pink, or white; bloom lasts all summer if old blossoms are cut off. Fully double flowers of Double Eagle and Echo strains resemble roses. Color range of single-flowered Heidi strain includes a so-called yellow (actually ivory). 'Red Glass' has rose red single flowers. Mermaid and Lizzy are dwarf (8-in.) strains.

Start with nursery plants or, with much care, from dust-fine seeds. Sprinkle seeds on surface of potting soil; don't cover with soil. Soak well, then cover the pot with glass or plastic until seedlings emerge. At four-leaf stage (about 2 months), transplant three or four plants into each 6-in. pot; plant out in beds after plants put on some growth. Needs good garden soil, good drainage. Use in pots, borders, cutting gardens.

EVENING PRIMROSE. See OENOTHERA

EVERGREEN CANDYTUFT. See IBERIS sempervirens

EVERGREEN GRAPE. See RHOICISSUS capensis

EVERGREEN PEAR. See PYRUS kawakamii

EVERGREEN WISTERIA. See MILLETTIA reticulata

EVERLASTING. See HELIPTERUM

EVOLVULUS glomeratus

Convolvulaceae

PERENNIAL USUALLY GROWN AS ANNUAL

ZONES 24; H2; ANYWHERE AS ANNUAL

FULL SUN OR LIGHT SHADE

REGULAR WATER

Evolvulus glomeratus 'Blue Daze'

Native to Brazil. Small trailing morning glory with stems to 20 in. long and oval leaves ⅓–1¼ in. long. Half-inch-wide blue flowers in summer; they close in the evening and on dark, cloudy days. Plants most widely offered are labeled 'Blue Daze', 'Hawaiian Blue Eyes', or *E. g. grandiflorus;* or they may simply bear the common name "blue daze." These plants vary somewhat: foliage may be green or gray, blossoms bright blue or powder blue. Stems of all root where they touch the ground, and cuttings root very easily in water or moist soil. Use in hanging baskets, beds, borders.

EXACUM affine

PERSIAN VIOLET

Gentianaceae

ANNUAL OR SHORT-LIVED PERENNIAL GROWN AS ANNUAL

ALL ZONES; OR INDOORS

SOME SHADE; BRIGHT INDIRECT LIGHT

REGULAR TO AMPLE WATER

Exacum affine

Native to Socotra, an island off the Horn of Africa. Small, rounded plant with egg-shaped, inch-long leaves and blue, sweet-scented, star-shaped flowers centered with tufts of bright yellow stamens. (A white variety is also available.) Five plants in a 5-in. pot make attractive showing. Needs rich soil, high humidity. Deadhead to prolong bloom. Good plant for house or cool greenhouse.

EXOCHORDA

PEARL BUSH

Rosaceae

DECIDUOUS SHRUBS

ZONES 2–9, 14–23

FULL SUN

REGULAR WATER

Exochorda racemosa

From China. Loose, spikelike clusters of 1½–2-in. white flowers open from a profusion of buds resembling pearls. Flowers bloom in spring, at about the same time the roundish, 1½–2-in.-long leaves expand. Foliage and arching growth suggest the related spiraea, but pearl bush has larger individual blossoms. Prefers well-drained, acid soil; will take considerable neglect. Prune after bloom to control form, size. To make larger kinds fit small gardens, you can remove the lower branches to create upright, airy, multistemmed small trees.

E. giraldii. To 9 ft. tall and somewhat wider. Red tints in leaf veins and flower stalks.

E. × macrantha. 'The Bride', the only generally available form of this hybrid group, is a compact shrub 6 ft. tall and wide.

E. racemosa (E. grandiflora). COMMON PEARL BUSH. Loose, open, slender shrub to 10–15 ft. tall and wide. Resistant to oak root fungus.

Fabaceae. Previously called Leguminosae, the pea family is an enormous group containing annuals, perennials, shrubs, trees, and vines. Many are useful as food (beans, peas), while others furnish timber, medicines, pesticides, and a host of other products. Many are ornamental.

The best-known members of the pea family—sweet pea *(Lathyrus)*, for example—have flowers shaped rather like butterflies. Others have a more regular flower shape *(Caesalpinia, Cassia);* still others have tightly clustered flowers that appear to be puffs of stamens, as in acacia and silk tree *(Albizia)*. All bear seeds in pods (legumes). Many have on their roots colonies of bacteria that can extract nitrogen from air spaces in the soil and convert it to a form usable by plant roots; clover *(Trifolium)* is a familiar example.

Fagaceae. The beech family contains evergreen and deciduous trees characterized by fruit that is either a nut enclosed in a cup, as in oak *(Quercus)* and tanbark oak *(Lithocarpus)*, or a bur, as in beech *(Fagus)* and chestnut *(Castanea)*.

FOR INFORMATION ON YOUR CLIMATE ZONE
PLEASE SEE PAGES 27–63

FAGUS

BEECH

Fagaceae

DECIDUOUS TREES

ZONES VARY BY SPECIES

FULL SUN OR LIGHT SHADE

MODERATE TO REGULAR WATER

Fagus sylvatica

Of the beeches described here, European beech (*F. sylvatica*) is by far the most widely grown. The species differ very little except in leaf details. Capable of growing 90 ft. tall and 60 ft. wide, but usually much smaller. Typically have a broad cone shape, with wide, sweeping lower branches that can reach the ground unless pruned off. Smooth gray bark contrasts well with the glossy dark green foliage. In fall, leaves first take on a bronze to red-brown color, then turn brown; many hang on the tree well into winter. Lacy branching pattern and pointed leaf buds provide an attractive winter silhouette. New foliage has a silky sheen. Little three-cornered nuts enclosed in spiny husks are edible but too small to be of value; they often fail to fill, especially on solitary trees.

All beeches cast heavy shade and have a dense network of fibrous roots near soil surface, inhibiting growth of lawn or other plants beneath. Transplant from containers or, if moving an in-ground tree, dig with a substantial ball of earth. Give any good garden soil. Salts in soil or water stunt growth, turn leaves brown. Woolly beech aphids cause little trouble except for dripping honeydew. Trees withstand heavy pruning; they can be planted close together and trimmed to form a dense, impassable hedge as low as 4 ft.

F. crenata. JAPANESE BEECH. Zones 2b–6. From Japan. Scallop-edged leaves are somewhat smaller than those of other beeches. Reddish brown fall color.

F. grandifolia. AMERICAN BEECH. Zones 1–6. From eastern North America. Toothed leaves 3–6 in. long; golden bronze fall color.

F. sylvatica. EUROPEAN BEECH. Zones A3; 2b–9, 14–21. Native from central Europe to Caucasus. Glossy green leaves to 4 in. long, turning russet and bronzy in autumn. Many varieties, including the following.

'Asplenifolia'. FERNLEAF BEECH. Large, robust, spreading tree with delicate foliage: narrow leaves are deeply lobed or cut nearly to midrib.

'Atropunicea'. COPPER BEECH, PURPLE BEECH. To 50–60 ft. high, 35–45 ft. wide. Deep reddish or purple leaves. Good in containers. Often sold as 'Riversii' or 'Purpurea'. Seedlings of copper beech are usually bronzy purple, turning bronzy green in summer.

'Dawyck Gold'. Columnar tree to 60 ft. tall, 22 ft. wide. New leaves emerge yellow, mature to light green, turn yellow again in fall.

'Dawyck Purple'. Columnar, to 70 ft. tall, 15 ft. wide, with purple foliage.

'Fastigiata'. DAWYCK BEECH. Narrow, upright tree, like Lombardy poplar (*Populus nigra* 'Italica') in form; 8 ft. wide when 35 ft. tall. Broader in great age, but still narrower than the species.

'Laciniata'. CUTLEAF BEECH. Narrow, deeply cut green leaves.

'Pendula'. WEEPING BEECH. Irregular, spreading form. Long, weeping branches reach to ground. Green leaves. Without staking to establish vertical trunk, it will grow wide rather than high.

'Purpurea Pendula'. WEEPING COPPER BEECH. Purple-leafed weeping form. Usually no larger than 10 ft. high and wide. Splendid container plant.

'Red Obelisk'. Columnar tree with dark purple-red foliage. Some leaves are deeply cut, others smooth edged.

'Rohan Gold'. Leaves with wavy scalloped edges open yellow and gradually fade to green, then turn gold again in fall.

'Rohanii'. Similar to the above but with brownish purple leaves maturing to dark green; unimpressive fall color (reddish or purplish brown).

'Tricolor'. TRICOLOR BEECH. Green leaves marked white and edged pink. Slow to 24–40 ft. tall, usually much less. Foliage burns in hot sun or dry winds. Choice container plant.

'Zlatia'. GOLDEN BEECH. Young leaves yellow, aging to yellow green. Subject to sunburn. Slow grower; good container plant.

FAIRY DUSTER. See CALLIANDRA eriophylla

FAIRY LANTERN. See CALOCHORTUS

FAIRY LILY. See ZEPHYRANTHES

FAIRY THIMBLES. See CAMPANULA cochlearifolia

FAIRY WAND. See DIERAMA

FALLOPIA baldschuanica (F. aubertii)

LACE VINE, SILVER LACE VINE

Polygonaceae

EVERGREEN OR DECIDUOUS VINE

ZONES A1–A3; 1–24

FULL SUN

LITTLE TO REGULAR WATER

Fallopia baldschuanica

Formerly known as *Polygonum,* this extremely vigorous vine from Asia can cover a large space (to 40 ft.) in a short time. Heart-shaped, waxy-edged, glossy green leaves are 1½–2½ in. long. Plant is deciduous in Zones A1, A3, 1–7, 10–12; evergreen elsewhere. From spring to fall, it's covered in a frothy mass of creamy white flowers, sometimes tinged with pink; these develop into papery pinkish white fruits. Use to cover a fence or arbor or as a rough bank cover. Tolerates seacoast conditions; succeeds in desert only if given deep soil and regular watering. Prune severely to keep in bounds; can be cut back to ground in winter, but bloom will be delayed until late summer.

FALLUGIA paradoxa

APACHE PLUME

Rosaceae

SEMIEVERGREEN SHRUB

ZONES 2–23

FULL SUN

NO IRRIGATION NEEDED

Fallugia paradoxa

Native to mountains of medium and high deserts of California, southwestern U.S., northern Mexico. Grows 4–6 ft. tall, 5 ft. wide, with straw-colored branches and flaky bark. Small, lobed leaves are deep green on top, rusty beneath; carried in clusters. Flowers resembling single white roses just 1½ in. wide bloom in spring, summer. Large, showy clusters of feathery seedheads follow; greenish at first, later turning pink or taking on reddish tinges, they create a soft-colored, changing haze through which you can see the shrub's rigid branch pattern. Needs gritty, well-drained soil. Pruning usually not needed.

FALSE BABY'S BREATH. See GALIUM mollugo

FALSE BIRD-OF-PARADISE. See HELICONIA

FALSE CYPRESS. See CHAMAECYPARIS

FALSE DRAGONHEAD. See PHYSOSTEGIA virginiana

FALSE HEATHER. See CUPHEA hyssopifolia

FALSE INDIGO. See BAPTISIA

FALSE LILY-OF-THE-VALLEY. See MAIANTHEMUM dilatatum

FALSE MESQUITE. See CALLIANDRA eriophylla

FALSE POINSETTIA. See EUPHORBIA heterophylla

FALSE SOLOMON'S SEAL. See SMILACINA racemosa

FALSE SPIRAEA. See ASTILBE, SORBARIA

FANCY-LEAFED CALADIUM. See CALADIUM bicolor

FAN PALM. See WASHINGTONIA

FAREWELL-TO-SPRING. See CLARKIA amoena

FARFUGIUM japonicum (Ligularia tussilaginea)

Asteraceae (Compositae)

PERENNIAL

ZONES 4–10, 14–24; H1, H2; OR INDOORS

SOME SHADE; BRIGHT INDIRECT LIGHT

AMPLE WATER

Farfugium japonicum 'Aureo-maculatum'

From China, Japan. Forms a clump to about 2 ft. tall and wide. Glossy bright green, kidney-shaped, scalloped, or shallowly lobed leaves are 7 in. long, 15 in. wide, carried on long (1–2-ft.) leafstalks. Flower stems are 1½–2 ft. tall, each carrying several 1½–2-in. yellow daisy flowers. The species is not as popular or widely grown as its selections.

'Argenteum' has somewhat smaller deep green leaves marbled with gray green and white. 'Aureo-maculatum', also known as leopard plant, has thick, leathery leaves that are heavily, evenly speckled with yellow. 'Crispatum', sometimes called pie crust ligularia, has thick, ruffle-edged gray-green leaves.

All are choice container plants for shady beds or entryways. Tops hardy to 20°F/–7°C. Plants die back to roots at 0°F/–18°C, put on new growth in spring. Control snails and slugs.

×FATSHEDERA lizei

Araliaceae

EVERGREEN SHRUB OR VINE

ZONES 4–10, 12–24; H1, H2

PARTIAL OR FULL SHADE

REGULAR WATER

×Fatshedera lizei

Hybrid between Japanese aralia *(Fatsia japonica)* and English ivy *(Hedera helix)*, with characteristics of both parents. Highly polished, 4–10-in.-wide leaves with three to five pointed lobes look like giant ivy leaves; plant also sends out long, trailing or climbing stems like ivy, though without aerial holdfasts. This hybrid inherited shrubbiness from its Japanese aralia parent, though its habit is more irregular and sprawling. Leaves of 'Variegata' are bordered in white; those of 'Media-Picta' have a central yellow blotch.

Leaves are injured at 15°F/–9°C, tender new growth at 20 to 25°F/–7 to –4°C. Seems to suffer more from late frosts than from winter cold. Give it protection from hot, drying winds. Watch out for slugs and snails. Good near swimming pools.

This plant tends to grow in a straight line, but it can be shaped if you work at it. Pinch tip growth to force branching. Two or three times a year, guide and tie stems before they become brittle. If plant gets away from you, cut it back to ground; it will regrow quickly. If you use it as ground cover, cut back vertical growth every 2 or 3 weeks during growing season. Grown as vine or espalier, plants are heavy, so give them strong supports. Even a well-grown vine is leafless at base.

FOR GROWING SYMBOL EXPLANATIONS
PLEASE SEE PAGE 161

FATSIA japonica (Aralia sieboldii, A. japonica)

JAPANESE ARALIA

Araliaceae

EVERGREEN SHRUB

ZONES 4–9, 14–24; H1, H2

PARTIAL OR FULL SHADE

REGULAR WATER

Fatsia japonica

From Korea, Japan. Tropical-looking shrub with long-stalked, big, glossy dark green, deeply lobed, fanlike leaves to 16 in. wide. Moderate growth to 5–8 ft. high and wide (rarely more); sparsely branched. Many roundish clusters of small, creamy white flowers in fall and winter, followed by clusters of small, shiny black fruit.

Grows in nearly all soils except soggy ones. Adapted to containers. If leaves are chronically yellow, add iron to soil. During prolonged dry spells, wash occasionally with hose to clean leaves and to lessen insect attack. Control slugs and snails. Established plants sucker freely; keep suckers or remove them with spade. Rejuvenate spindly plants by cutting back hard in early spring. Plants that set fruit often self-sow.

A natural landscaping choice where bold pattern is wanted. Most effective when thinned to show some branch structure. Provides year-round good looks for shaded entryway or patio. Useful near swimming pools. 'Moseri' has compact habit. 'Variegata' has leaves edged golden yellow to creamy white.

FAVA BEAN. See BEAN, BROAD

FAWN LILY. See ERYTHRONIUM californicum

FEATHER BUSH. See LYSILOMA microphylla thornberi

FEATHERED HYACINTH. See MUSCARI comosum 'Monstrosum'

FEATHER GRASS. See STIPA

FEATHER REED GRASS. See CALAMAGROSTIS acutiflora

FEIJOA, PINEAPPLE GUAVA

Myrtaceae

EVERGREEN SHRUB OR TREE

ZONES 6 (MARGINAL), 7–9, 12–24; H1, H2

FULL SUN

REGULAR WATER

Feijoa

South American native known botanically as *Feijoa sellowiana (Acca sellowiana)*. Hardiest of so-called subtropical fruits. Normally a large multistemmed plant; reaches 18–25 ft. with equal spread if not pruned or killed back by frosts. Can take almost any amount of training or pruning (late spring is the best time) to shape as espalier, screen, hedge, or small tree. Oval, 2–3-in.-long leaves are glossy green above, silvery white beneath. Blooms in spring, bearing unusual inch-wide flowers with big central tufts of red stamens and four fleshy white petals tinged purplish on inside; blossoms attract bees and birds. Flowers are edible and can be added to fruit salads or used for jams and jellies. Plant is drought tolerant, but give it regular water for best fruiting.

Fruit ripens 4 to 5½ months after flowering in warmest regions, 5 to 7 months after bloom in cooler areas. Oval, grayish green, 1–4-in.-long fruit has soft, sweet to bland pulp with flavor somewhat like pineapple. The best way to harvest is to wait until first fruit drops, then spread a tarp underneath and give the tree a shake. Repeat every few days. Fruit is sometimes sold in markets; it may be labeled "feijoa" or "pineapple guava."

Improved varieties 'Beechwood', 'Coolidge', 'Mammoth', 'Nazemetz', and 'Trask' are self-fruitful, although cross-pollination will produce a better crop. Single plants of seedlings or other named varieties may need cross-pollination.

FELICIA

Asteraceae (Compositae)

SHRUBS, PERENNIALS, AND ANNUALS

ZONES VARY BY SPECIES

FULL SUN

WATER NEEDS VARY BY SPECIES

Felicia amelloides

Daisy relatives, typically with blue flowers; native to South Africa. Though more than 80 species are known, only a few are commonly cultivated in Western gardens.

F. amelloides (F. aethiopica, Agathaea coelestis). BLUE MARGUERITE. Woody perennial in Zones 8, 9, 14–24; treated as winter annual in Zone 13 and summer annual elsewhere. Despite the common name, not the true marguerite *(Chrysanthemum frutescens)*. About 1½ ft. tall and spreading 4–5 ft. wide, with roughish, oval, rather aromatic green leaves about 1 in. long. Produces an abundance of 1¼-in., yellow-centered sky blue daisies. As a perennial, blooms almost continuously if dead flowers are picked off; prune back hard in late summer to encourage new blooming wood. Grow in pots or containers, let spill over wall or edge of raised bed, or plant in any sunny spot. Regular water.

F. bergeriana. KINGFISHER DAISY. Annual. Zones 1–24. Freely branching plant with grayish, 1½-in. leaves makes mat 4–6 in. high, up to a foot across. Bright blue, inch-wide flowers appear all summer long. Sow in early spring (in fall where winters are warm). Good in pots, window boxes, borders, edgings. Regular water.

F. fruticosa (Aster fruticosus). SHRUB ASTER. Evergreen shrub. Zones 8, 9, 14–24. Bushy, densely branched growth to 2–4 ft. tall, 3 ft. wide. Narrow, ½–¾-in.-long, dark green leaves. Profuse, inch-wide lavender flowers in spring. Prune after bloom. Needs no irrigation.

FELT PLANT. See KALANCHOE beharensis

FENNEL, COMMON. See FOENICULUM vulgare

FERNBUSH. See CHAMAEBATIARIA millefolium

FERNLEAF YARROW. See ACHILLEA filipendulina

FERN-OF-THE-DESERT. See LYSILOMA microphylla thornberi

FERN PINE. See PODOCARPUS gracilior

FERNS. Large group of perennial plants grown for their lovely and interesting foliage. They vary in height from a few inches to 50 ft. or more and are found in all parts of the world; most are forest plants, but some grow in deserts, in open fields, or near the timberline in high mountains. Most have finely cut leaves (fronds). They do not flower but reproduce by spores that form directly on the fronds.

Ferns are divided into several families, according to botanical differences. Such technical differences aside, these plants fall into several groups based on general appearance.

Most spectacular are tree ferns, which display their finely cut fronds atop a treelike stem. These need rich, well-drained soil, moisture, and shade (except in Zones 4–6, 17, 24, where they can take sun). Most tree ferns are rather tender to frost, and all suffer in hot, drying winds and in extremely low humidity. Frequent watering of tops, trunks, and root area will help pull them through unusually hot or windy weather. For the various kinds of tree ferns, see *Blechnum, Cibotium, Cyathea, Dicksonia.*

Native ferns do not grow as high as tree ferns, but their fronds are handsome and they can perform a number of landscape jobs. Naturalize them in woodland or wild gardens, or use them to fill shady beds, as ground cover, as interplantings between shrubs, or along a shady house wall. Many endure long, dry summers but look lusher if given regular summer water. Some ferns native to eastern North America grow well in the Northwest, Northern California, and Alaska; these take extreme cold and are usually deciduous. For native ferns, see *Adiantum, Asplenium, Athyrium, Blechnum, Dryopteris, Onoclea, Osmunda, Pellaea, Phyllitis, Polypodium, Polystichum, Pteridium, Woodwardia.*

Many ferns from other parts of the world grow well in the West; although some are house, greenhouse, or (in mildest climates) lathhouse subjects, many are fairly hardy. Use them as you would native ferns, unless some peculiarity of habit makes it necessary to grow them in baskets or on slabs. Some exotic ferns will be found under *Adiantum, Asplenium, Cyrtomium, Davallia, Humata, Microlepia, Nephrolepis, Pellaea, Platycerium, Polypodium, Polystichum, Pteris, Pyrrosia, Rumohra, Woodwardia.*

All ferns look best if groomed. Cut off dead or injured fronds near ground or trunk—but don't cut back the more tender deciduous outdoor ferns until new growth begins, since old fronds protect growing tips. Natives growing outdoors don't need it, but feed others frequently during growing season, preferably with light applications of organic fertilizer such as blood meal or fish emulsion. Mulch with organic matter such as peat moss occasionally, especially if shallow fibrous roots are exposed by rain or irrigation.

FEROCACTUS

BARREL CACTUS

Cactaceae

CACTI

ZONES 8–24

FULL SUN

NO IRRIGATION NEEDED

Ferocactus cylindraceus

Medium to large cacti. Ribbed and formidably spiny; globular when young, cylindrical with increasing age.

F. cylindraceus (F. acanthodes). COMPASS BARREL CACTUS. Native to Southern California, Nevada, Arizona, Baja California. Grows slowly to 8–9 ft. tall, 3 ft. wide. Yellow to orange, bell-shaped flowers, 3 in. across, bloom midspring into summer. Plant grows faster on its shady side than on sunny side, producing curve toward the south.

F. wislizenii. FISHHOOK BARREL CACTUS. Native to Arizona, Texas, Mexico. Similar to above, with yellow or yellow-edged red flowers in summer.

FESTUCA

FESCUE

Poaceae (Gramineae)

PERENNIAL GRASSES

ZONES VARY BY SPECIES

BEST IN SUN, TOLERATE SOME SHADE

MODERATE TO REGULAR WATER

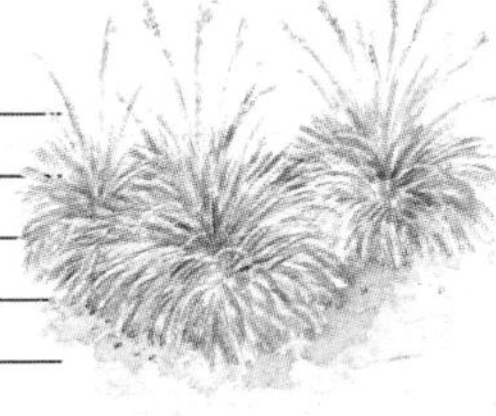

Festuca glauca

Some of these grasses are ornamental; others are used for lawns, erosion control, or pasture. All need good drainage, can withstand dry conditions and severe frosts. Clumps can be divided in fall.

F. amethystina. Zones 2–10, 14–24. From the Alps and southern Europe. To 1½ ft. high, 10 in. wide. Extremely fine-textured, threadlike leaves are blue green to intensely blue gray. Drooping, violet-tinged flower spikes held above foliage in late spring, early summer. Use like *F. glauca.*

F. arundinacea. TALL FESCUE. Zones A1–A3; 1–10, 14–24. From Europe, northern Asia; naturalized in cooler parts of North America. Clumping, tall-growing pasture grass (to 4 ft.) also used for moderately low-water-use lawns. Tough blades, tolerance of compacted soils make it a good turf for playing or sports; finer-textured strains are used alone or mixed with bluegrass. Check locally for best-adapted varieties. Forms no runners, so plants must be close together to make dense turf; sow 8–10 lb. of seed per 1,000 sq. ft. Sow in fall in mild-winter areas, in spring in colder part of range. After grass is 2–3 in. high, soak deeply if rains fail; soak again to 1 ft. when blades begin to fold or curl. Feed lightly—monthly in summer, three times during fall, winter. Mow to 2–3 in. Left unmowed, it makes an excellent, deep-rooted erosion control cover on slopes, banks.

F. californica. CALIFORNIA FESCUE. Zones 4–9, 14–24. Native to the Coast Ranges from Northern California to Oregon. Grows as loose clump of blue-green or blue-gray leaves to 2–3 ft. high, 1–2 ft. wide; topped by airy flowers in late spring, early summer. Flower spikes are green at first, later turning purple and finally maturing to deep yellow. Long lived and does well in various soil types. Tolerates summer drought in its cooler climate zones. Use as specimen plant or massed as ground cover. 'Serpentine Blue' has intensely blue-gray foliage.

F. glauca (F. cinerea). COMMON BLUE FESCUE. Zones 1–24. From Europe. To 1 ft. high, 10 in. wide. Dense tuft of extremely fine leaves; color varies from blue gray to silvery white. Summer flowers in spikes. Use as edging or ground cover. Center of clump commonly dies out after several years. Sometimes sold as *F. ovina glauca.* 'Blausilber' ('Blue Silver') is one of the best silver-leafed selections. 'Elijah Blue' forms an 8-in.-high clump of intensely silver-blue leaves and is one of the tougher, longer-lived selections. 'Siskiyou Blue', to 1–2 ft. high, has luminous blue leaves.

F. idahoensis. Zones 1–10, 14–24. Native from British Columbia to Alberta, south to central California and Colorado. Blue-green to silvery blue foliage in dense clump to 14 in. high, 10 in. wide. Longer lived than *F. glauca,* and clumps are less likely to die out in center. May also be more tolerant of wet winter soils. Good slope stabilizer.

F. rubra. RED FESCUE, CREEPING RED FESCUE. Zones A2, A3; 1–10, 14–24. From Europe, North America. Spreads by rhizomes. Principal use is in blends with bluegrass or other lawn grasses; also used to overseed Bermuda lawns in winter. Narrow dark green blades. Not fussy about soil. Can be used alone (many varieties available); mow to 1½–2 in. high. One of most shade tolerant of good lawn grasses. Unmowed, all types of red fescue make attractive meadow on slopes too steep to mow. Need regular water for good growth. For drought-tolerant red fescues, look for blue-leafed California selections.

F. trachyphylla. SHEEP'S FESCUE. Zones 1–24. From many temperate-climate areas of the world. Forage and meadow grass producing dense, foot-high tufts of fine-textured, green to gray-green leaves and small purple-tinged flowers in mid- to late summer.

F. valesiaca. WALLIS FESCUE. Zones 2b–10, 14–24. European native to 1½ ft. high and wide. Similar to *F. glauca.* Winter dormant. Known largely in its selection 'Glaucantha', which has fine-textured blue-green leaves in a clump under 6 in. high.

FEVERFEW. See CHRYSANTHEMUM parthenium

FIBER OPTICS PLANT. See SCIRPUS cernuus

FICUS

Moraceae

EVERGREEN AND DECIDUOUS TREES, SHRUBS, VINES

ZONES VARY BY SPECIES

EXPOSURE NEEDS VARY BY SPECIES

REGULAR WATER

Ficus auriculata

The average gardener would never expect to find the commercial edible fig, small-leafed climbing fig, banyan tree, and potted rubber tree under one common heading—but they are classed together because they bear small or large figs (inedible in most species). Ornamental types are discussed here; for sorts grown for tasty fruit, see Fig.

Many ornamental species make good houseplants. Generally, they thrive on rich, steadily moist (not wet) soil, frequent light feedings, and bright, indirect light.

F. auriculata (F. roxburghii). Briefly deciduous shrub or small tree. Zones 20–24; H1, H2. Native to India. To 25 ft. high and wide. Leaves have sandpapery texture, are unusually large—broadly oval to round, about 15 in. across. New growth is mahogany red, turning to rich green. Large figs are borne in clusters on trunk and framework branches. Can be shaped as small tree or espaliered. Beautiful in large container; good near swimming pools. Grow in wind-protected, sunny location.

F. benghalensis. INDIAN BANYAN. Evergreen tree. Zones 23, 24; H2. Native to India and Pakistan. On the mainland, it grows very slowly. In Hawaii, it is a very large, fast-growing tree to 80 ft. tall and initially as wide, spreading (potentially up to several acres) by accessory trunks developing from aerial roots. This is the most spectacular of the many banyans grown in Hawaii, but it should be used with extreme caution and only in large spaces. Full sun.

F. benjamina. BENJAMIN TREE, BENJAMIN FIG, WEEPING FIG. Zones 13, 23, 24; H1, H2; or indoors. From India and Malaysia. In Hawaii, fast growing to 60 ft. tall with an even greater spread. Good shade or specimen tree for larger gardens or parks, since it requires space for its invasive surface root system. In Southern California and Arizona, plant reaches about half the size it does in Hawaii and is often used as entryway or patio tree; also good as screen, espalier, or clipped hedge. Leathery, 5-in.-long, shiny green leaves densely clothe drooping branches. 'Exotica' has wavy-edged leaves with long, twisted tips; often sold simply as *F. benjamina.* New plants are easy to start from semihardwood cuttings taken between late spring and early summer. Give a frost-free, wind-protected location in sun or shade.

Ficus benjamina

One of the most popular houseplants. Sudden leaf shedding is a common problem, often resulting from plant being moved to a new location. If shedding begins shortly after a move, be patient; leaves usually grow back. If leaves that fall are green, insufficient water is another possible cause; try to keep soil evenly moist. If fallen leaves are yellow, overwatering may be to blame. If shedding is accompanied by sweet smell and sticky leaves, look for and control scale insects. For an indoor tree that is similar in size and habit to *F. benjamina* but doesn't drop its foliage (leaves are long, resembling those of many eucalyptus), try *F. binnendijkii* 'Alii'.

F. carica. See Fig

F. deltoidea (F. diversifolia). MISTLETOE FIG. Evergreen shrub. Zones 19–24; H1, H2; or indoors. Native to Southeast Asia. Grows very slowly to 8–10 ft. high, about half as wide. Interesting open, twisted branch pattern. Thick, dark green, roundish, 2-in. leaves are sparsely stippled with tan specks on upper surface and a few black dots below. Attractive, small greenish to yellow fruit borne continuously. As outdoor plant, most often grown in container on patio. Part shade.

Ficus deltoidea

F. elastica. RUBBER TREE. Evergreen shrub or tree. Zones 13, 16, 17, 19–24; H1, H2; or indoors. Native to India and Malaysia. In Hawaii, it is a wide-spreading tree 60–80 ft. high (up to 100 ft. in damp, tropical forests), but not commonly seen in landscapes. On the mainland, it can become a 40-ft. tree in mildest frost-free zones; often seen as a small tree or shrub in shaded "tunnel" garden entrances in cooler part of range. Comes back quickly if killed to ground by frost. Narrow, leathery dark green leaves are 8–12 in. long. New leaves unfold from rosy pink sheaths that soon wither and drop. Partial or full shade.

One of most foolproof indoor pot subjects; can take less light than most big houseplants. If potted plant becomes too tall and leggy, you can cut off the top and select a side branch to form a new main shoot. Or get a new plant by air layering the top section; when roots form, cut branch section with attached roots and pot it up. The following are among the best varieties.

'Abidjan' ('Burgundy'). West African selection made from 'Decora'. New growth, leaf sheaths, and leaf midribs are red. On plants grown in bright light, older leaves are dark maroon.

'Asahi'. Selection from Japan. Similar to 'Doescheri' with slightly smaller leaves and more extensive creamy yellow variegation.

'Decora' ('Belgica'). The common rubber plant sold for indoor use is usually this variety. Superior to the species because of its broader, glossier leaves. Foliage is bronzy when young.

'Doescheri'. Leaves are marbled in green and gray green, with green margins, creamy yellow midribs, and pink leafstalks.

'Rubra'. New leaves are reddish and retain a red edge as rest of leaf turns green. Sometimes grown as shrub or small tree in Zones 22–24.

'Schrijveriana'. Broad leaves on red leafstalks are variegated in green, gray green, creamy yellow, and white.

Ficus elastica 'Decora'

'Variegata'. Long, narrow leaves variegated in yellow and green. Variegation is interesting when leaves are viewed close up in container—but as an outdoor tree, plant has a sickly look.

F. lyrata (F. pandurata). FIDDLELEAF FIG. Evergreen tree or shrub. Zones 22–24; H1, H2; or indoors. Native to tropical Africa. Dramatic structural form with prominently veined, fiddle-shaped, huge leaves (to 15 in. long, 10 in. wide) in glossy dark green. In Hawaii, forms a dense, round-headed tree 35–50 ft. tall and about 35 ft. wide. In California, can grow to 20 ft. high and as wide, with trunks 6 in. thick. Good near swimming pools. To increase branching, pinch back when plant is young. Full sun or light shade. Highly effective as a houseplant.

Ficus lyrata

F. macrophylla. MORETON BAY FIG. Evergreen tree. Zones 17, 19–24; H1, H2. Native to Australia. Grows to enormous dimensions. A tree in Santa Barbara, California, planted in 1877 is about 75 ft. tall and 150 ft. wide, with massive buttressed trunk and surface roots. Blunt, oval, leathery leaves, 10 in. long and 4 in. wide, glossy green above, brownish beneath. Rose-colored leaf sheaths appear like candles at branch ends. Inch-long figs are purple spotted with white. Although plant is tender when young, it acquires hardiness with size. Shows damage at 24 to 26°F/–4 to –3°C. Be sure to give it plenty of room. Full sun.

F. microcarpa (F. retusa). INDIAN LAUREL FIG, CHINESE BANYAN. Evergreen tree. Zones 9, 13, 16–24; H1, H2. Native from Malay peninsula to Borneo. One of the more common banyans in Hawaiian landscapes, where it grows quickly to 60 ft. high, with a dense canopy spreading to about 75 ft. wide; produces multiple aerial roots in wet areas. In California and Arizona, it grows at a more moderate rate to 25–30 ft. high, 35–40 ft. wide. Beautiful weeping form, with long, drooping branches thickly clothed with blunt-tipped, 2–4-in.-long leaves. Light rose to chartreuse new leaves, produced almost continuously, give pleasing two-tone effect. Plants sold as *F. m. nitida* (a name with no botanical standing) may have the same weeping form as the species or may have upright-growing branches.

Prune at any time of year to shape as desired. Remove lower branches to reveal slim, light gray trunk. Responds well to shearing into formal hedge as low as 5 ft. Where pest free, makes a highly satisfactory tree or tub plant. Unfortunately, subject to thrips damage in California; hard to control, since the pest quickly curls new leaves (thus protecting itself from sprays). Afflicted leaves show stippling, then drop. 'Green Gem' has thicker, darker green leaves and is apparently unaffected by thrips. Full sun.

F. m. crassifolia. WAX FIG, TAIWAN FIG. To 10–12 ft. high and sprawling as wide. Tolerates salt, wind, drought, various soil types. In Hawaii, more likely to be used for hedges or containers than the species. Easily pruned to maintain size and shape. Full sun or partial shade.

F. pumila (F. repens). CREEPING FIG. Evergreen vine. Zones 8–24; H1, H2; or indoors. Native to China, Japan, Australia. Has a most unfiglike habit; it is one of few plants that attaches itself securely to wood, masonry, or even metal in barnacle fashion. Because it is grown on walls and thus protected, it is found in colder climates more often than any other evergreen fig. Grows in sun or shade; not for hot south or west wall.

Looks innocent enough in youth, making a delicate tracery of tiny, heart-shaped leaves. Neat little juvenile foliage ultimately develops into big (2–4-in.-long), leathery leaves borne on stubby branches that bear large oblong fruits. In time, stems will envelop a three- or four-story building so completely that it becomes necessary to keep them trimmed away from windows. It's safe to use on house walls if you cut it to the ground every few years; also control by removing fruiting stems from time to time as they form. Roots are invasive. 'Minima' has shorter, narrower leaves than species. Small, lobed leaves of 'Quercifolia' look like miniature oak leaves. 'Variegata' has standard-size leaves with creamy white markings.

F. religiosa. PEEPUL, BO-TREE. Briefly deciduous tree. Zones 13, 19, 21, 23, 24; H1, H2. Native India to Southeast Asia. In Hawaii, to 80–100 ft. tall with almost equal spread. On mainland, may reach 40 ft. high and wide after 25 years or more. Foliage is quite open and delicate, revealing structure of tree at all times. Bark is warm, rich brown. Pale green, 4–7-in.-long leaves are thin textured and rather crisp, roundish in shape but with a long, tail-like point. They move easily even in the slightest breeze, giving the foliage mass a fluttering look. Leaves drop completely in late spring or early summer—a frightening experience for the gardener who has bought an "evergreen" fig. Full sun.

F. retusa. See F. microcarpa

F. roxburghii. See F. auriculata

F. rubiginosa. RUSTYLEAF FIG. Evergreen tree. Zones 18–24; H1, H2. Native to Australia. Single- or multitrunked, densely foliaged tree to 20–50 ft. tall, with broad crown 30–50 ft. wide. Leaves about 5 in. long, deep green above, generally rust colored and woolly beneath. May develop hanging aerial roots characteristic of many of the evergreen figs that grow in tropical environments. A small-leafed form has been sold as *F. microphylla.* Full sun.

F. r. australis is virtually identical to the species but may vary in having leaf undersides with a less pronounced rust color. Its selections 'El Toro' and 'Irvine' have exceptionally dark green leaves; 'Florida' has lighter green leaves. 'Variegata', with leaves mottled green and cream, is sometimes sold as a houseplant.

FIG

Moraceae

DECIDUOUS FRUIT TREES

ZONES 4–9, 12–24; H1, H2; OR IN POTS

FULL SUN

REGULAR WATER

Fig

Native to western Asia, eastern Mediterranean, *Ficus carica* is grown for edible fruit; for ornamental relatives, see *Ficus.* Grow fairly fast to 15–30 ft. tall; generally low branched, spreading at least as wide as high. Where hard freezes (below 10 to 15°F/–12 to –9°C) are common, fig wood freezes back severely and plants act like big shrubs. Can be held to 10 ft. in a large container; can also be trained as espalier along fence or wall.

Heavy, smooth, gray trunks are gnarled in really old trees, picturesque in silhouette. Rough bright green leaves with three to five lobes are 4–9 in. long and nearly as wide. Casts dense shade. Winter framework, tropical-looking foliage, strong trunk and branch pattern make fig a top-notch ornamental tree, especially near patio where it can be illuminated from beneath. Fruit drop is problem immediately above deck or paving. Protect container plants in winter.

Not particular about soil. In colder part of range, trees planted near south walls or trained against them benefit from reflected heat. Cut back tops hard at planting. As tree grows, prune lightly each winter, cutting out dead wood, crossing branches, and low-hanging branches that interfere with traffic. Pinch back runaway shoots in any season. Avoid deep cultivation (which may damage surface roots) and high-nitrogen fertilizers (which stimulate leafy growth at the expense of fruit). Gophers love fig roots; if they or other burrowing animals are a problem in your garden, plant fig trees in ample wire baskets. Ripe fruit may need protection from birds.

Home-garden figs do not need pollinating, and most varieties bear two crops a year. The first comes in early summer on last year's wood; the second, more important one comes in late summer or early fall from the current year's growth. When figs are ripe, they detach easily when lifted and bent back toward the branch. Keep fruit picked as it ripens; protect from birds if you can. In late fall, pick off any remaining ripe figs and clean up fallen fruit.

Varieties differ in climate adaptability. Most need prolonged high temperatures to bear good fruit, while some thrive in cooler conditions. Familiar dried figs from the market are usually 'Calimyrna' or imported Smyrna figs. These require special pollenizers (male trees called caprifigs) and a special pollinating insect and are not recommended for home gardens.

'Black Jack'. Purple skin with sweet pink flesh. Similar to 'Mission'. Widely adapted to California climates. Easily kept small by pruning.

'Brown Turkey' ('Black Spanish', 'San Pedro'). Brownish purple fruit. Adaptable to most fig-growing climates. Good, small garden tree.

'Celeste' ('Blue Celeste', 'Celestial'). Violet-tinged bronzy skin, rosy amber flesh. Good fresh; resists spoilage. Dries well on tree in California.

'Conadria'. Choice thin-skinned white fig blushed violet; white to red flesh with fine flavor. Best in hot areas; takes intense heat without splitting.

'Desert King'. One late-summer crop of green-skinned, red-fleshed fruit. Adapted to all fig climates but better in cooler areas like Northwest.

'Genoa' ('White Genoa'). Greenish yellow skin, strawberry-colored to yellow flesh. Good quality; good in coastal valleys, California coast.

'Italian Everbearing'. Resembles 'Brown Turkey' but has somewhat larger fruit with reddish brown skin. Good fresh or dried.

'Kadota' ('White Kadota'). Tough-skinned fruit is greenish yellow. One of the best figs for Hawaii; in California, grows best in hot interior valleys. Commercial canning variety. Strong grower, needs little pruning. If pruned severely, it will bear later, with fewer, larger fruits.

'Lattarula'. Also known as Italian honey fig. Green skin, amber flesh. Grown in Northwest, where it can ripen in summer and produce fall crops in good seasons.

'Mission' ('Black Mission'). Large tree; purple-black figs with pink flesh; good fresh or dried. Widely adapted; popular in California.

'Osborn Prolific' ('Neveralla'). Dark reddish brown skin; amber flesh, often tinged pink. Very sweet; best eaten fresh. Best in Northern California coastal areas and Pacific Northwest. Light bearing in warm climates.

'Panachée' ('Striped Tiger', 'Tiger'). Greenish yellow skin with dark green stripes. Strawberry-colored flesh is sweet but dry. Best eaten fresh. Requires long, warm growing season. One crop late in summer.

'Peter's Honey' ('Rutara'). Greenish yellow skin, amber flesh. Needs hot exposure in Northwest and coastal areas.

'Texas Everbearing'. Mahogany to purple skin, strawberry-colored flesh. Bears at a young age. Produces well in short-season areas of Southwest.

FILBERT, HAZELNUT

Betulaceae

DECIDUOUS NUT TREES

ZONES 2–7

AFTERNOON SHADE IN HOTTEST CLIMATES

REGULAR WATER

Filbert

These plants are selections of European species *Corylus avellana* and *C. maxima* that are grown for nut production (their nuts are the commercial ones sold in stores). To 10–18 ft. high and wide; look more like trees than the ornamental species (see *Corylus*). Handsome and nicely structured, good choice for garden or terrace. From spring to fall, the roundish, ruffle-edged leaves cast a pleasant spot of shade. Showy catkins (male flowers) hang long and full on bare branches in winter.

Plant in late winter or early spring in deep, well-drained soil. Trees tend to sucker; clear these out three or four times a year if you wish to maintain a clean trunk. For a boundary hedgerow, plant mixed varieties 4 ft. apart and let suckers grow.

Eastern filbert blight, a destructive bark disease, has devastated old standby varieties 'Butler', 'Du Chilly', 'Ennis', and 'Daviana'; they are no longer recommended in the prime filbert-growing areas of Oregon and Washington. To protect commercial orchards, filberts and hazelnuts (including ornamentals) are quarantined in Oregon and can no longer be planted in home gardens.

The blight is evident as raised, oval black bumps in vertical lines on infected branches and twigs. Individual branches die out, and the entire plant can succumb. To protect existing plants, spray with copper and horticultural oil together at bud break (usually late March), again in mid-April, and a third time in early May. Remove dead branches, cutting 2 ft. back into healthy growth. Burn or bury prunings. Severely infected trees should be removed entirely.

Filberts ripen in late summer and drop in early fall; the roundish or oblong nuts form inside frilled husks. A 10-year-old tree may yield up to 20 lb. of nuts per year. Harvest by picking up nuts from the ground, then dry them in the sun for a few days. Squirrels and jays are a nuisance, often picking the nuts before they fall. Handpicking when the nuts are tree-ripe (when they separate easily from the hulls) will thwart animal thieves.

Since cross-pollination is necessary, plant at least two varieties. Best crops in cold-winter areas. The following are blight resistant to varying degrees; none is totally immune.

'Barcelona'. Fine flavor. Some resistance to blight.

'Casina'. Thin-shelled nuts with excellent flavor. Intermediate blight resistance.

'Hall's Giant'. Flavorful. Good resistance to blight.

'Lewis'. Good-quality nut. Highly resistant to blight.

'Tonda di Giffoni'. Excellent flavor. Highly resistant to blight.

Two types of hybrids called filazels and trazels can be grown into Zone 1. They vary in blight resistance and cannot be planted in Oregon. Filazels—hardy, 10–15-ft. producers of good-quality nuts—are hybrids between *C. avellana* and the native beaked hazelnut *(C. cornuta)*. Trazels—upright, 20–30-ft. trees producing sweet, fine-flavored nuts—are crosses between *C. avellana* and Turkish hazel *(C. colurna)*. Plant two of the same type for cross-pollination.

FILIPENDULA

Rosaceae

PERENNIALS

ZONES VARY BY SPECIES

FULL SUN IN COOLER CLIMATES ONLY

REGULAR TO AMPLE WATER

Filipendula rubra 'Venusta'

Like *Astilbe,* these bear plumes of tiny flowers above large, coarsely divided leaves. Bloom in summer. Dormant in winter, even in mild-winter areas. Most species prefer moist to constantly damp soil. Use in borders, naturalistic landscapes, beside ponds.

F. hexapetala. See F. vulgaris

F. purpurea. Zones 3b–9, 14–17. Pink, 3–4-ft. plumes rise above a 2-ft.-wide foliage clump. Leaves are 5–7 in. long, look like maple leaves.

F. rubra. QUEEN OF THE PRAIRIE. Zones A1–A3; 1–9, 14–17. Given plenty of moisture and rich soil, can reach 8 ft. high in bloom; bears pink plumes above 4-ft.-wide clump of jagged-edged leaves with big, lobed leaflet at tip. 'Venusta' has purplish pink flowers and is a little shorter (4–6 ft. high).

F. vulgaris (F. hexapetala). DROPWORT. Zones A1–A3; 1–9, 14–17. White plumes on 3-ft. stems rise above a 1½-ft.-wide mound of ferny leaves divided into inch-long leaflets. Double-flowered 'Flore Pleno' has heavier-looking plumes. Needs less water than other species; also prefers full sun in all but the warmest regions.

FINOCCHIO. See FOENICULUM vulgare azoricum

FIR. See ABIES

FIRETAIL. See ACALYPHA pendula

FIRETHORN. See PYRACANTHA

FIREWEED. See EPILOBIUM angustifolium

FIREWHEEL TREE. See STENOCARPUS sinuatus

FIRMIANA simplex (F. platanifolia)

CHINESE PARASOL TREE

Sterculiaceae

DECIDUOUS TREE

ZONES 5, 6, 8, 9, 12–24

FULL SUN OR PARTIAL SHADE

REGULAR WATER

Firmiana simplex

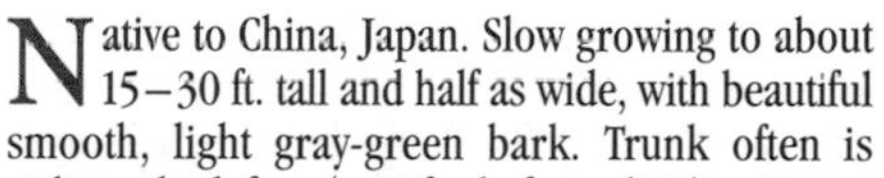

Native to China, Japan. Slow growing to about 15–30 ft. tall and half as wide, with beautiful smooth, light gray-green bark. Trunk often is unbranched for 4–5 ft. before dividing into three or more slender, upright, slightly spreading branches that carry lobed, tropical-looking, 1-ft. leaves. Each stem looks as if it could be cut off and carried away as a parasol. Tree bears large, loose, upright clusters of greenish white flowers at branch ends in summer. Interesting fruit looks like a green pea pod opened out flat, with seeds on pod margins. Goes leafless for long period in winter (unusual for tropical-looking tree). Tolerates all soil types. Does well in patios and courtyards protected from wind. Good choice near swimming pools.

FISHTAIL PALM. See CARYOTA

FIVE-FINGER FERN. See ADIANTUM aleuticum

Flacourtiaceae. This family of evergreen trees and shrubs (most of them tropical or subtropical) includes *Azara* and *Xylosma.*

FLAG. See IRIS

FLAMBOYANT TREE. See DELONIX regia

FLAMEGOLD. See KOELREUTERIA elegans

FLAME OF THE WOODS. See IXORA coccinea

FLAME PEA. See CHORIZEMA

FLAME TREE. See BRACHYCHITON acerifolius

FLAME VINE. See PYROSTEGIA venusta

FLANNEL BUSH. See FREMONTODENDRON

FLAX. See LINUM

FLAX, NEW ZEALAND. See PHORMIUM

FLAXLEAF PAPERBARK. See MELALEUCA linariifolia

FLEABANE. See ERIGERON

FLOSS FLOWER. See AGERATUM houstonianum

FLOSS SILK TREE. See CHORISIA

FLOWERING ALMOND, CHERRY. See PRUNUS

FLOWERING CRABAPPLE. See MALUS

FLOWERING CURRANT. See RIBES

FLOWERING DOGWOOD. See CORNUS florida

FLOWERING MAPLE. See ABUTILON

FLOWERING NECTARINE, PEACH, PLUM. See PRUNUS

FLOWERING QUINCE. See CHAENOMELES

FOAMFLOWER. See TIARELLA

FOENICULUM vulgare

COMMON FENNEL

Apiaceae (Umbelliferae)

PERENNIAL, SOMETIMES TREATED AS ANNUAL

ZONES VARY BY FENNEL TYPE

FULL SUN

MODERATE WATER

Foeniculum vulgare

Two forms of this Mediterranean native are commonly grown—one as a perennial for its flavorful seeds and young leaves, the other as an annual for its edible leaf bases.

The plain species, which is cultivated for licorice-flavored seeds and young leaves, is a perennial in Zones 2b–11, 14–24, H1, H2; it is treated as a winter annual in Zones 12, 13. Grows 3–5 ft. tall. Similar in appearance to dill *(Anethum graveolens),* but its yellow-green foliage, though finely cut, is coarser than that of dill. Plant produces flat clusters of yellow flowers in summer. Bronze fennel ('Purpurascens', 'Smokey') reaches 6 ft. tall, has bronzy purple foliage. Start from seed where plants are to be grown. Sow in light, well-drained soil; thin seedlings to 1 ft. apart. Use seeds to season baked goods; use young leaves as garnish for salads, fish, and other dishes. Common fennel often grows as a roadside or garden weed (in Hawaii and parts of California, it can be invasive); it's attractive until tops turn brown, and even then birds like the seeds. New stems grow in spring from perennial root.

F. v. azoricum, Florence fennel or finocchio, is grown as a summer annual in all zones except 12 and 13, where it is used as a winter annual. It is lower growing than the species (to 2 ft. high), with larger, thicker leafstalk bases that are used as a vegetable, cooked or raw. Its feathery leaves are used as a garnish and seasoning.

FORESTIERA neomexicana

NEW MEXICAN PRIVET, DESERT OLIVE

Oleaceae

DECIDUOUS SHRUB

ZONES 1–3, 7–24

FULL SUN

LITTLE TO MODERATE WATER

Forestiera neomexicana

Native to New Mexico, Colorado, Arizona west to California. Little used outside arid regions. To 12–18 ft. tall, 12 ft. wide. Smooth, medium green leaves to $1\frac{1}{2}$ in. long turn yellow in fall. Inconspicuous flowers. Small ($\frac{1}{4}$-in.-long), egg-shaped fruits, blue-black when mature, are not always produced (some plants do not have both male and female flowers); when they do appear, they attract birds. Fairly fast growth makes it a good screen plant; can be trained as a small multitrunked tree.

FORGET-ME-NOT. See MYOSOTIS

FOR INFORMATION ON SELECTING PLANTS
PLEASE SEE PAGES 64–160

FORSYTHIA

Oleaceae

DECIDUOUS SHRUBS

ZONES A2, A3, 2B–11, 14–16, 18, 19, EXCEPT AS NOTED

FULL SUN

MODERATE TO REGULAR WATER

Forsythia × intermedia

Native to China, Korea. From late winter to early spring, these fountain-shaped shrubs' bare branches are covered with ¾–1½-in. yellow flowers; budded branches can be forced for indoor bloom. During rest of growing season, foliage—medium green, rounded leaves with pointed tips—blends well with other background shrubs. Use as screen, espalier, or bank cover; or plant in shrub border. Tolerate most soils. Prune after bloom by cutting to ground a third of the branches that have flowered; also remove oldest branches and weak or dead wood. In coldest-winter climates, flower buds may be destroyed by temperatures of −15 to −20°F/−26 to −29°C. The hardiest varieties are noted below. For white forsythia, see *Abeliophyllum distichum.*

F. 'Arnold Dwarf'. Grows to about 1½–3 ft. tall, 6 ft. wide. Flowers are sparse and not especially attractive, but plant is a useful, fast-growing ground cover for cold climates.

F. hardy hybrids. Zones A2, A3; 1a, 2–11, 14–16, 18, 19. Recent introductions have extended the range of forsythia into regions formerly too cold for successful flowering—or even for the plant's survival.

'Meadowlark'. To 6–9 ft. tall and 10 ft. wide, with semiarching habit. Bright yellow flowers open from buds hardy to −35°F/−37°C.

'New Hampshire Gold'. Mounding habit to 5 ft. tall and broad, with drooping yellow flowers. Buds are hardy to −35°F/−37°C.

'Northern Sun'. Erect grower to 8–10 ft. tall and slightly narrower; reliably bud-hardy to −30°F/−34°C.

F. × intermedia. This group of hybrids between parents *F. suspensa* and *F. viridissima* includes the following selections.

'Beatrix Farrand'. Upright to 10 ft. tall, 7 ft. wide. Branches thickly set with deep yellow flowers marked with orange.

'Fiesta'. To 3–4 ft. tall and somewhat broader, with deep yellow flowers and yellow-variegated leaves.

'Goldtide'. To 20 in. high and 4 ft. wide, with profuse yellow blooms.

'Goldzauber'. Erect growth to 6–8 ft. tall and slightly narrower. Deep yellow blooms.

'Karl Sax'. Resembles 'Beatrix Farrand' but is lower growing (to about 8 ft.), neater, and more graceful.

'Lynwood' ('Lynwood Gold'). Stiffly upright to 7 ft., with 4–6-ft. spread. Profuse tawny yellow blooms survive spring storms.

'Spectabilis'. Dense, upright, vigorous shrub to 10 ft. high, 6 ft. wide. Deep yellow flowers.

'Spring Glory'. To about 6 ft. tall and wide, with heavy crop of pale yellow flowers.

F. mandshurica 'Vermont Sun'. Zones A2, A3; 1–11, 14–16. Erect, extremely bud-hardy shrub to 8 ft. tall, 6 ft. wide; lemon yellow flowers appear before those of other forsythias.

F. ovata. KOREAN FORSYTHIA. To 4–6 ft. high, 10 ft. wide. Early bloomer (about a week after *F. mandshurica* 'Vermont Sun') bearing a profusion of bright yellow flowers. 'Tetragold' is lower growing (about 3 ft. high), has deep yellow blooms.

F. suspensa. WEEPING FORSYTHIA. Dense, upright shrub reaches to 8–10 ft. tall, 6–8 ft. wide; bears golden yellow blossoms. Drooping, vine-like branches root where they touch damp soil. Useful as a large-scale bank cover. Plant can also be trained as a vine; if you support main branches, branchlets will cascade.

F. viridissima. GREENSTEM FORSYTHIA. Zones A2, A3; 2b–11, 14–16, 18, 19. Stiff-looking shrub 6–10 ft. tall and wide, with deep green foliage, olive green stems, greenish yellow flowers. 'Bronxensis' is a slow-growing dwarf to 1 ft. high, 2–3 ft. wide; use as ground cover or in borders.

FORSYTHIA, WHITE. See ABELIOPHYLLUM distichum

FORTNIGHT LILY. See DIETES

FOTHERGILLA

Hamamelidaceae

DECIDUOUS SHRUBS

ZONES 2B–9, 14–17

PARTIAL SHADE IN HOTTEST CLIMATES

REGULAR WATER

Fothergilla major

Native to southeastern U.S. Grown mainly for fall foliage color, but spring bloom is pretty: small, honey-scented white flowers in 1–2-in., brushlike clusters on zigzagging stems. Blossoms may appear before or with leaves. Performs best in moist, well-drained, acid soil.

F. gardenii. DWARF FOTHERGILLA. Typically 2–3 ft. high (though it can grow considerably taller) and as wide or wider, with 1–2½-in.-long, dark green leaves. Foliage turns intense yellow to orange to scarlet in autumn, often with all three colors in same leaf. 'Blue Mist' is a blue-foliaged variety that doesn't color up as well in fall.

F. major (F. monticola). Erect shrub to 9 ft. tall and 6 ft. wide, with roundish, 2–4-in.-long leaves turning yellow to orange to purplish red in autumn. 'Mount Airy' is smaller (3–5 ft. high and wide), with abundant bloom, good dark green leaf color, and consistently superb fall color in yellow, orange, and scarlet.

FOUNTAIN GRASS. See PENNISETUM setaceum

FOUQUIERIA

Fouquieriaceae

DECIDUOUS SHRUBS OR TREES

ZONES VARY BY SPECIES

FULL SUN

LITTLE TO MODERATE WATER

Fouquieria splendens

Desert natives with grooved, spiny branches. Drop leaves during hot, dry periods, then resprout and bloom quickly after rains, bearing tubular flowers to 1 in. long. They can survive on rainfall but grow and bloom best if soaked deeply once a month. Need excellent drainage, intense summer heat. Easily propagated from softwood cuttings in warm weather; cut branches stuck in ground will grow.

F. macdougalii. MEXICAN TREE OCOTILLO. Zones 11–13. Native to Mexico. Brown branches covered with gray spines rise from a short, smooth, yellowish green trunk. In frost-free climates, plant can reach 20 ft. tall (with trunk making up 3 ft. of height) but is more typically seen around 6–8 ft. high, 4 ft. wide (trunk about a foot high, often less). Lance-shaped light gray leaves to 1½ in. long. Deep red flowers come in open sprays reminiscent of exploding skyrockets. In frost-prone areas, grow in container and move indoors in winter.

F. splendens. OCOTILLO. Zones 10–13, 18–20. Native to Colorado and Sonoran deserts east to Texas and south into Mexico. Forms a 5–10-ft.-wide clump of stiff, whip-thin, gray stems 8–25 ft. high, heavily furrowed and covered with stout thorns. Fleshy, roundish, ½–1-in.-long leaves. Attractive foot-long clusters of flowers; color ranges from bright to deep red orange (occasionally yellow). Use as screen, impenetrable hedge, living fence for animal enclosures; or grow for silhouette against bare walls.

FOUR O'CLOCK. See MIRABILIS

FOXGLOVE. See DIGITALIS

FOXTAIL LILY. See EREMURUS

FRAGARIA

ORNAMENTAL STRAWBERRY
Rosaceae
PERENNIALS
ZONES VARY BY SPECIES
AFTERNOON SHADE IN HOTTEST CLIMATES
REGULAR WATER

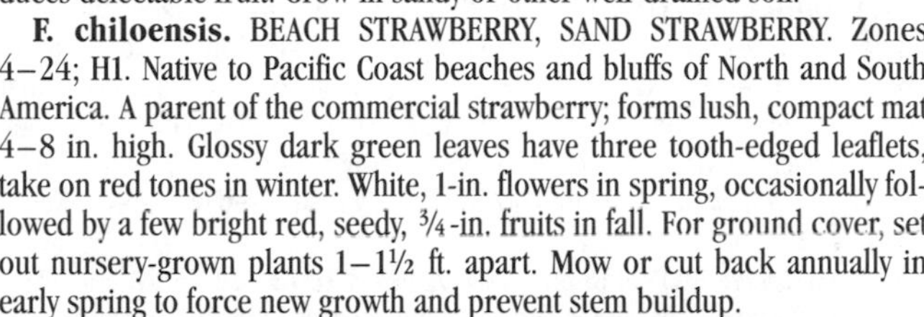
Fragaria chiloensis

For strawberries grown strictly for their edible fruit, see Strawberry; the plants described here are grown for their ornamental qualities, though *F. vesca* also produces delectable fruit. Grow in sandy or other well-drained soil.

F. chiloensis. BEACH STRAWBERRY, SAND STRAWBERRY. Zones 4–24; H1. Native to Pacific Coast beaches and bluffs of North and South America. A parent of the commercial strawberry; forms lush, compact mat 4–8 in. high. Glossy dark green leaves have three tooth-edged leaflets, take on red tones in winter. White, 1-in. flowers in spring, occasionally followed by a few bright red, seedy, ¾-in. fruits in fall. For ground cover, set out nursery-grown plants 1–1½ ft. apart. Mow or cut back annually in early spring to force new growth and prevent stem buildup.

F. 'Lipstick'. Zones 2b–24. Results from a cross between *Fragaria* and *Potentilla.* Similar to *F. chiloensis* in general appearance but bears rich rosy red flowers in spring and intermittently through summer. Use in borders, edgings, rock gardens. Produces very few fruits.

F. 'Pink Panda'. Zones 4–24. Resembles *F.* 'Lipstick' and is used in the same way, but it bears pink flowers from spring to fall.

F. vesca. ALPINE STRAWBERRY, FRAISE DU BOIS, WOOD STRAWBERRY. Zones 2b–9, 14–24; H2. This one bears a small crop of tiny but fragrant, delicious berries over a long summer season, but it's usually grown as an edging for flower or herb beds (space plants 8–12 in. apart). Does not produce runners but may be grown from seed; bears the first year from seed sown early. Varieties include red-fruiting 'Alexandria', 'Baron Solemacher', 'Improved Rügen', and 'Semperflorens'; there are also yellow- and white-fruiting selections.

FRAISE DU BOIS. See FRAGARIA vesca

FRANCESCHI PALM. See BRAHEA elegans

FRANCOA ramosa

MAIDEN'S WREATH
Saxifragaceae
PERENNIAL
ZONES 4–9, 14–24
PARTIAL SHADE
MODERATE TO REGULAR WATER

Francoa ramosa

Native to Chile. Large, wavy-edged leaves to 6 in. long in a basal clump 1–2 ft. high, 3 ft. wide (and spreading wider by rhizomes). Graceful, almost leafless flowering stems 2–3 ft. long appear in midsummer, with upper portions carrying spikes of many tiny pure white (occasionally pinkish) blossoms. Good cut flowers. Plants are distributed mainly by neighborliness—more of them pass over back fences than through nurseries. Grows in rich soil. In just a few years, one plant increases sufficiently in size to let you divide and replant fresh new segments from clump's outside edges. Best in dappled shade all day or with sun for half the day. *F. sonchifolia* is similar but bears pink flowers.

FRANGIPANI. See PLUMERIA

FRANKLINIA alatamaha (Gordonia alatamaha)

Theaceae
DECIDUOUS TREE
ZONES 3B–6, 14–17
PARTIAL SHADE IN HOTTEST CLIMATES
REGULAR WATER

Franklinia alatamaha

Though once native to Georgia, this tree has apparently been extinct in the wild since before 1800. Open, airy form; may grow 30 ft. tall but more typically reaches 10–20 ft. high. When grown with single trunk, tends to be fairly slender; grown with multiple trunks, spreads wider than high. Attractive gray bark has faint white vertical striping. Glossy green 4–6-in.-long leaves turn orange and red in fall. In late summer, round white buds open to fragrant white blossoms resembling single camellias: 3 in. wide, five petaled, with central clusters of yellow stamens. Bloom may coincide with fall foliage color. Small, woody capsules follow the flowers. Tree blooms shyly during wet autumns in Northwest. Provide well-drained, rich, light, acid soil. Easy to grow from seed, flowering in 6 or 7 years. Makes an unusual lawn or patio tree; good for contrast in azalea and rhododendron plantings.

FRAXINELLA. See DICTAMNUS albus

FRAXINUS

ASH
Oleaceae
DECIDUOUS AND EVERGREEN TREES
ZONES VARY BY SPECIES
FULL SUN
WATER NEEDS VARY BY SPECIES

Fraxinus velutina coriacea 'Modesto'

Fairly fast-growing trees, most of which tolerate hot summers, cold winters, and many kinds of soil, including alkaline sorts. Chiefly used as street, shade, lawn, and patio shelter trees. In most cases, leaves are divided into leaflets. Male and female flowers (generally inconspicuous, in clusters) grow on separate trees in some species, on the same tree in others. In the latter case, flowers are often followed by clusters of single-seeded, winged fruit, often in such abundance that they can be a litter problem. When flowers are on separate trees, you'll get fruit on female tree only if a male tree grows nearby.

Ashes are prone to borers in the Northwest. In some parts of California, ash whitefly is a problem; the chalky white, ⅛-in.-long insects colonize in patches on leaf undersides. Outbreaks are usually controlled by natural enemies; avoid spraying with broad-spectrum insecticides, which are likely to wipe out these beneficial predators.

F. americana. WHITE ASH. Deciduous. Zones 1–11, 14–17. Native to eastern U.S. Grows to 80 ft. or taller, with straight trunk and oval-shaped crown to 50 ft. wide. Leaves 8–15 in. long with five to nine dark green, oval leaflets, paler beneath; turn purplish in fall. Leaf edges burn in hot, windy areas. Regular water.

Male and female flowers are on separate trees, but plants sold are generally seedlings, so you don't know what you're getting. If you end up with both male and female trees, you will get a heavy crop of seed; both litter and seedlings can be a problem. Seedless selections include 'Autumn Applause', 'Autumn Purple', and 'Royal Purple', all with exceptionally good, long-lasting purple fall color; 'Champaign County', a dense grower; 'Rosehill', with bronzy red fall color; 'Skyline', an upright, somewhat narrow oval with brown and purple fall color; and 'Greenspire', another upright and narrowish oval with orange-red fall color. ▸

F. angustifolia (F. oxycarpa). Deciduous. Zones 2b–9, 12–24. Mediterranean native. Fairly compact, small-leafed, fine-textured ash with delicate, lacy look. Species is apparently not grown in the West, except in its variety 'Raywood' (Raywood ash or claret ash), a round-headed, compact, fast-growing tree 25–35 ft. tall, 25 ft. wide, with purple-red fall color, no seeds. Moderate water.

F. 'Fan West'. Deciduous. Zones 2–14. Seedless hybrid between *F. pennsylvanica* and *F. velutina coriacea* 'Modesto'. Resembles the latter in size and habit. Light olive green leaves, good branch structure; tolerates cold, desert heat, and wind. Best with regular water but tolerates some aridity.

F. greggii. LITTLE LEAF ASH. Evergreen. Zones 10–13. Native Arizona to Texas. To 25 ft. tall and 20 ft. wide, with leaves divided into three to seven ¾-in., leathery leaflets. Useful desert tree. Little water.

F. latifolia (F. oregona). OREGON ASH. Deciduous. Zones 3–9, 14–24. Native to Sierra Nevada and west of the Cascades from Northern California to British Columbia. To 40–80 ft. tall, 30–50 ft. wide. Leaves 6–12 in. long, divided into five to seven oblong to oval, light green, hairy or smooth leaflets; end leaflet to 4 in. long, larger than side leaflets. Male and female flowers on separate trees. Will grow in standing water during winter months. Needs no dry-season irrigation. Subject to many pests and diseases; not a first-rate tree.

F. mandshurica 'Mancana'. MANCHURIAN ASH. Deciduous. Zones A1–A3; 1–3. Very cold-hardy, seedless, cutting-grown variety to 35 ft. tall and 25 ft. wide, with a dense, oval crown. Original tree was grown from a seed collected in Manchuria. Foot-long, yellowish green leaves have up to 11 coarsely toothed leaflets to 5 in. long; take on good yellow color in fall. Thrives on regular water but tolerates drought.

F. ornus. FLOWERING ASH. Deciduous. Zones 3–9, 14–17. Native to southern Europe and Asia Minor. Grows rapidly to 40–50 ft., with broad, rounded crown 20–30 ft. wide. Supplies luxuriant mass of foliage. Leaves 8–10 in. long, divided into 7–11 oval, medium green, 2-in.-long leaflets with toothed edges. Foliage turns to soft shades of lavender and yellow in fall. In spring, displays quantities of fluffy, branching, 3–5-in.-long clusters of fragrant white to greenish white blossoms followed by unsightly seed clusters that hang on until late winter unless removed. Moderate water.

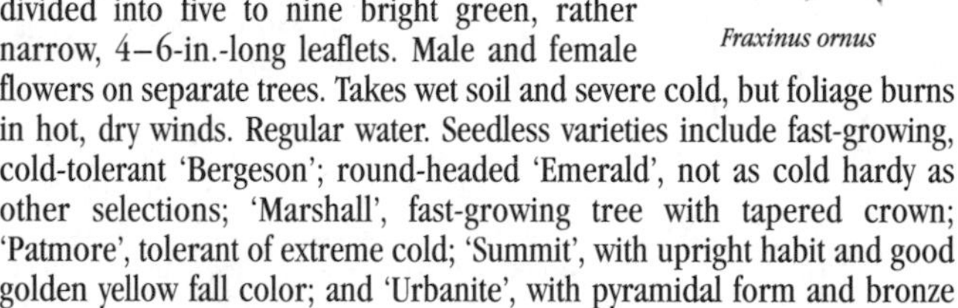

Fraxinus ornus

F. pennsylvanica (F. lanceolata). GREEN ASH, RED ASH. Deciduous. Zones A2, A3; 1–6. Native to eastern U.S. To 30–40 ft. tall and wide, with compact, oval crown. Gray-brown bark; dense, twiggy structure. Leaves 10–12 in. long, divided into five to nine bright green, rather narrow, 4–6-in.-long leaflets. Male and female flowers on separate trees. Takes wet soil and severe cold, but foliage burns in hot, dry winds. Regular water. Seedless varieties include fast-growing, cold-tolerant 'Bergeson'; round-headed 'Emerald', not as cold hardy as other selections; 'Marshall', fast-growing tree with tapered crown; 'Patmore', tolerant of extreme cold; 'Summit', with upright habit and good golden yellow fall color; and 'Urbanite', with pyramidal form and bronze fall color.

F. quadrangulata. BLUE ASH. Deciduous. Zones 2–6. Native to central U.S. Grows rapidly to 60–80 ft. tall with crown to about 40 ft. wide. Branches distinctly square in cross section, usually with flanges along edges. Oval dark green leaflets (7–11 per leaf) are 2–5 in. long and have toothed edges. Foliage turns purplish in fall. Fruit may become a litter problem if you have both female and male trees. Regular water.

F. uhdei. EVERGREEN ASH, SHAMEL ASH. Evergreen to semievergreen. Zones 9, 12–24. Native to Mexico and a favorite in Southern California and low-elevation deserts. Grows fast to 25–30 ft. tall in 10 years; reaches 40 ft. in 20 years and may eventually attain 70–80 ft. or taller. Upright, narrow tree about 15 ft. wide when young; eventually takes on a spreading form as it grows older (may spread 60 ft. wide at maturity). Leaves divided into five to nine glossy dark green, finely tooth-edged leaflets about 4 in. long. Foliage may burn if subjected to hot winds. In mildest climates, leaves hold on through winter; in colder areas, tree loses most or all of its foliage, but leafless period often lasts only for a short time. Sharp frosts may kill branch tips; tree suffers serious damage at 15°F/–9°C or lower.

Cut back any long, unsightly branches when tree is young. Eliminate deep crotches by pruning out weaker branches. Texas root rot sometimes causes dieback and will kill young trees, but established ones usually survive. Resistant to oak root fungus. Tolerates aridity but does best with regular water and an occasional deep soaking.

'Majestic Beauty'. Has exceptionally large leaves and is more reliably evergreen than species.

'Sexton'. Very compact, rounded crown. Larger, deeper green leaflets than those of species.

'Tomlinson'. Grows more slowly than species (to 18 ft. in 10 years) and is more upright and dense when young. Leaflets are more leathery, with wavy-toothed margins.

F. velutina. ARIZONA ASH. Deciduous. Zones 3b–24. Native to southwestern U.S. and Mexico. Withstands hot, dry conditions; cold hardy to about –10°F/–23°C. Grows about 30 ft. (possibly to 50 ft.) tall. Pyramidal when young, spreading to 30–40 ft. wide when mature, with more open form. Leaves divided into three to five narrow to oval, 3-in.-long leaflets; turn bright yellow in fall. Male and female flowers on separate trees. Regular water.

F. v. coriacea. MONTEBELLO ASH. Zones 8, 9, 12–24. Native mostly to Southern California. Broader, more leathery leaves than the species.

'Modesto'. MODESTO ASH. Zones 3–24. Originated in Modesto, California. Vigorous form growing to about 50 ft. tall, with 30-ft. spread. Leaflets are medium green, glossier than those of species; bright yellow fall color. Resistant to oak root fungus but subject to numerous other problems that have caused many communities to remove it from their lists of recommended trees. In many areas, leaves get a scorched look due to anthracnose fungus if springtime weather is wet. In agricultural regions, verticillium wilt is prevalent (there is no control for it; young trees may die once infected, but established trees often survive). In some areas, mistletoe—an evergreen parasitic plant—can infest Modesto ash so heavily that the trees seem to be in leaf in winter. Control is difficult; the best defense is to prune out the mistletoe as soon as you notice it. In desert, tree is subject to ash decline syndrome, an ailment of unknown origin. Keep tree vigorous; if it succumbs, replace with 'Rio Grande' (described below), *F. angustifolia* 'Raywood', or *F. uhdei.*

'Rio Grande'. FAN-TEX ASH. Zones 8–24. Thrives in hot, dry climates and alkaline soils. Has larger, darker green, more succulent leaflets than 'Modesto'; they turn golden yellow in late fall. Foliage resistant to wind burn.

FRECKLE FACE. See HYPOESTES phyllostachya

FREESIA

Iridaceae

PERENNIALS FROM CORMS

ZONES 8, 9, 12–24

FULL SUN OR PARTIAL SHADE

REGULAR WATER DURING GROWTH AND BLOOM

Freesia hybrids

South African natives prized for the rich perfume of their flowers. In spring, wiry, 1–1½-ft. stems bear spikes of tubular flowers that reach 2 in. long, flare to 2 in. across. Each stem bends at nearly a right angle just beneath lowest bud. Narrow, sword-shaped leaves to 1 ft. tall grow in irislike fans. In the past, the most widely available freesia was creamy white, powerfully sweet-scented *F. alba,* which naturalized in its preferred climates. Today, though, the most popular freesias are hybrids (Dutch and Tecolote hybrids represent the majority of those sold) with larger, single or double blossoms in yellow, orange, red, pink, lavender, purple, blue, and white—mixed or in single-color varieties. Volunteers tend to revert to cream marked with purple and yellow. These newer freesias are generally not as fragrant as the old-fashioned type.

Hardy to 20°F/–7°C. Plant in fall, setting corms 2 in. deep and 2 in. apart in well-drained soil. Cut back on watering when leaves start to yellow in late spring; withhold moisture during summer dormancy. In dry-summer regions, corms can be left in ground; in rainy-summer climates, it's best to dig them when foliage yellows and store the corms until it's time to replant them in early fall. Plantings will increase rapidly; dig and divide when vigor and quality of bloom decline. In cold-winter areas, freesias can be grown in pots in sunny window; keep room temperature as cool as possible at night. Flowering potted freesias (grown from chilled and stored corms) are available all year. In subsequent years, they will bloom at the normal time in spring.

FREMONTODENDRON (Fremontia)

FLANNEL BUSH

Sterculiaceae

EVERGREEN SHRUBS OR TREES

ZONES 4–24

FULL SUN

NO IRRIGATION NEEDED

Fremontodendron 'California Glory'

Native to California; *F. californicum* is also native to parts of central Arizona. Fast-growing plants with a typically irregular shape, reaching 20 ft. tall and 12 ft. wide except as noted. Leathery leaves are dark green above, felted beneath. Very showy, typically saucer-shaped yellow blossoms in spring. Flowers are followed by persistent conical seed capsules covered with bristly, rust-colored hairs; some people consider them unsightly, and they can irritate skin. Plants are completely drought tolerant and will accept occasional moisture during their normally dry period in summer only if drainage is excellent (hillside planting is recommended). Roots are shallow, so stake plants while young. Pinch young growth to encourage branching; prune off overly long shoots. Remove lower branches to shape into small trees. Locate in front of a sunny wall in marginal climates. Usually short lived.

F. 'California Glory'. Hybrid between *F. californicum* and *F. mexicanum.* Rich yellow flowers to 3 in. across have red-tinged backs. Prolific bloom over long period.

F. californicum. COMMON FLANNEL BUSH. Eye-catching show of lemon yellow, 1–1½-in. flowers; tend to bloom all at once. Roundish, 1-in.-long, unlobed or three-lobed leaves.

F. 'Ken Taylor'. Hybrid between *F.* 'California Glory' and a lower-growing species. To 4–6 ft. tall and 12 ft. wide, bearing somewhat cup-shaped golden flowers with orange backs.

F. mexicanum. SOUTHERN FLANNEL BUSH. Brilliant display of orange-tinted yellow blossoms to 2½ in. across. Blooms less profusely than *F. californicum,* but flowers appear over a longer period. Leaves reach 3 in. long, have three to five distinct lobes.

F. 'Pacific Sunset'. Hybrid between *F. californicum* and *F. mexicanum.* To 12–15 ft. tall and wide. Deep orange-yellow, 3½–4-in.-wide flowers. Bloom peaks in spring, is sporadic later.

F. 'San Gabriel'. Looks much like 'California Glory' and has the same parentage, but its leaves are more deeply cut, resembling maple leaves.

FRINGE BELLS. See SHORTIA soldanelloides

FRINGE CUPS. See TELLIMA grandiflora

FRINGED WORMWOOD. See ARTEMISIA frigida

FRINGE HYACINTH. See MUSCARI comosum

FRINGE TREE. See CHIONANTHUS

FRITILLARIA

FRITILLARY

Liliaceae

PERENNIALS FROM BULBS

ZONES VARY BY SPECIES

LIGHT SHADE, EXCEPT AS NOTED

REGULAR WATER DURING GROWTH AND BLOOM

Fritillaria imperialis

In spring, unbranched stems ranging from 6 in. to 3 ft. high are topped by bell-shaped, nodding flowers, often unusually colored and mottled. Use in woodland gardens, rock gardens, or borders. In fall, plant bulbs in porous soil with ample humus. Set smaller bulbs 3–4 in. deep and 6 in. apart; set largest ones *(F. imperialis)* 4–5 in. deep, 8–12 in. apart. Bulbs sometimes rest for a year after planting or after blooming, so put in enough for yearly display. All appreciate some winter chill and tend to perform poorly where summers are hot and dry. Reduce watering as foliage dies back in summer. Once it is gone, withhold water from *F. biflora* until fall. *F. meleagris* needs moderate to regular water during dormancy; the others require some summer moisture. Clumps seldom need dividing.

F. biflora. MISSION BELLS. Zones 7, 14–21. California native to 6–16 in. high, with one to six brownish, 1½-in. bells on each blossom stalk. 'Martha Roderick' has rusty orange flowers with a white center.

F. camschatcensis. BLACK LILY, CHOCOLATE LILY. Zones A1–A3; 1–7, 15–17. Native near Pacific coast, Japan to northwestern U.S. Grows 9–18 in. high, with whorls of leaves around the stem. Flowering stem carries one to eight 1¼-in.-long, deep purple to nearly black bells.

F. imperialis. CROWN IMPERIAL. Zones 1–7, 14–17. Native to Europe. Stout stalk to 3 ft. tall, clothed with broad, glossy leaves and crowned by circle of large (2–3-in.-long) bells in red, orange, or yellow; a tuft of leaves tops the flowers. Bulb and plant have musky odor that some people find offensive. Can take full sun in cooler climates.

F. meleagris. CHECKERED LILY, SNAKESHEAD. Zones 1–7, 15–17. Native to damp meadows in Europe, Asia; tolerates occasional flooding. One to three showy, 2-in. bells top each 1–1½-ft. stem; blossoms are checkered and veined with reddish brown and purple. Lance-shaped, 3–6-in.-long leaves. There is a white-blossomed form.

F. michailovskyi. Zones 2–7, 14–17. From Turkey. To 6 in. high. Each stem bears one to six 1–1½-in. bells that are purplish brown at base, bright yellow toward tip.

F. pallidiflora. Zones A1–A3; 1–7. From northern China, Siberia. Each 2–3-ft. stem carries one to six 1¼-in. bells in pale yellow tinted with green.

F. persica 'Adiyaman'. Zones 2–7, 14–17. Variety of a species from western Asia. Stems 2–3 ft. tall carry up to 30 deep plum purple, inch-long flowers on upper half. Foliage is grayish. Plant is hardy and easy to grow, but emerging stems need protection from late frosts in colder regions. Can take full sun in cooler climates.

FUCHSIA

Onagraceae

EVERGREEN AND DECIDUOUS SHRUBS

ZONES VARY BY SPECIES

FULL SUN OR PARTIAL SHADE (SEE NEXT PAGE)

REGULAR WATER

Fuchsia × *hybrida,* Double Type

From wet, mountainous areas, mainly in tropical America. Most fuchsias bloom from late spring to first frost (and some bloom even longer), bearing unscented flowers frequented by hummingbirds. Popular showy-blossomed fuchsias are forms of *F.* ×*hybrida* and are discussed under that heading. Some species fuchsias have blooms that are smaller overall than those of hybrids; others bear large, tubular flowers in unusual colors. ▸

Fuchsias grow best in cool-summer areas with much moisture in atmosphere and soil. Plant in-ground fuchsias in full sun in the Northwest; give potted ones there and all fuchsias farther south either morning sun or all-day dappled shade. If you live where fog rolls in on summer afternoons, any place in your garden will supply ideal conditions. Where summers are warm, windy, or dry, seek or create favorable exposure protected from wind and hot afternoon sun. A heavy mulch (1½–3 in. thick) helps keep soil moist in hot climates. Frequent overhead sprinkling is beneficial in several ways: it keeps leaves clean, discourages some pests, and counteracts low humidity.

Blooms appear on new wood, so do any pruning before spring growth begins. In addition to removing broken or crossing branches, you can prune as little or as much as desired to maintain size or to shape the plant. In colder areas, wait to cut out frost-damaged stems until all danger of frost is past.

Fuchsia gall mite has caused serious problems for fuchsia growers primarily in California. Most hybrid fuchsias sold today have susceptible parentage and are prone to infestation, but many species fuchsias are resistant. The tiny mites, visible only under magnification, cause large, unsightly masses of distorted leaves, usually covered with reddish hairs. Cut off and destroy all distorted tissue. The pest can live on some resistant species and hybrids without producing any symptoms, allowing reinfection of susceptible fuchsias nearby. In the Northwest, aphids are the main pest. Spider mites and whiteflies are other common pests of fuchsias, though in the Northwest they tend to cause trouble primarily on potted plants.

F. boliviana. Evergreen. Zones 17, 22–24. From South America. Woody, erect growth to 12 ft. or taller and 8 ft. wide, with softly hairy pale green leaves to 7 in. long. Blooms throughout the year, producing large, pendent clusters of red flowers with slender tubes to 3 in. long. Pinkish red fruit. May spread by seed in moist gardens. Resistant to fuchsia gall mite. 'Alba' has two-tone flowers in white and pinkish red; fruit is white.

F. campos-portoi. Deciduous. Zones 3b–9, 14–24. From Brazil. Similar to *F. magellanica* and bears very similar blossoms, but has a denser habit and smaller leaves. Inflated buds with rounded teardrop shape; profuse bloomer. Can be grown as a dense shrub or allowed to clamber up into trees. Resistant to fuchsia gall mite.

F. denticulata. Evergreen. Zones 17, 22–24. From Peru, Bolivia. Parent of many new mite-resistant hybrids. Best known of these is 'Fanfare', which produces strong canes to 10 ft. or longer if given support of a tree or garden structure; excellent trained on trellis or as espalier. Dark green, 2–7-in.-long leaves. Blooms in summer and fall. Flowers are up to 3 in. long; petals orange red, sepals and slender floral tubes red. Resistant to fuchsia gall mite.

F. fulgens. Deciduous. Zones 15–17, 22–24. From Mexico. To 5 ft. tall and wide, with heart-shaped, light green leaves 5–8 in. long (or longer). Blooms from winter into spring, bearing pendent clusters of orange-red flowers to 3 in. long. Resistant to fuchsia gall mite.

F. glazioviana. Evergreen. Zones 16, 17, 22–24. From Brazil. Vigorous, fast-growing plant to 6–12 ft. tall and wide. Grow it as a dense shrub or let it scramble into trees. Small, shiny leaves and single pink-and-purple flowers just under an inch long. Resistant to fuchsia gall mite.

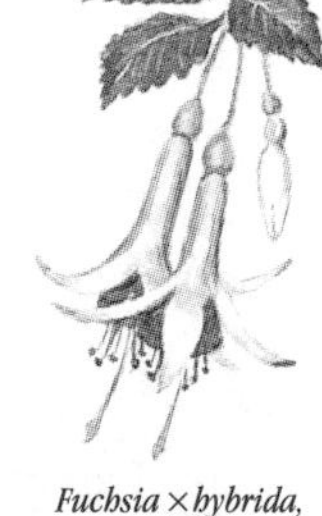
Fuchsia × hybrida, Single Type

F. × hybrida. HYBRID FUCHSIA. Zones 4–6 (with protection), 15–17, 22–24, H1; can also be grown with more difficulty in Zones 7–9, 14, 20, 21. Where frosts are light, plants lose their leaves, and tender growth may be killed. Where freezes are hard, most plants die back to hard wood, sometimes to the ground.

The vast majority of fuchsias with showy flowers fall into this hybrid group. Many hundreds of selections are sold in the West, offering a wide variety of combinations of all colors in the range. Sepals (top parts that flare back) are always white, red, or pink. Corolla (inside part of flower) may be almost any color in range of white, blue violet, purple, pink, red, and shades approaching orange. Flowers range from shelled-peanut size to giants as big as a child's fist. Some flowers are single, with just one layer of closely set petals in corolla; some are very double, with many sets of ruffled petals in corolla. Small-flowered types often have small leaves, while big-flowered sorts have large leaves.

Plant form varies widely; choices range from erect-growing shrubs 3–6 ft. high and wide to trailing types grown in hanging baskets. You can also train (or buy) fuchsias as espaliers and standards (miniature tree forms).

Gardeners in California should note that, due to susceptible parentage, many if not most hybrids are susceptible to mite damage. Mite-resistant selections include 'Carnival', 'Mrs. Victor Reiter', and 'Trumpeter'.

Main concern in Northwest is winter protection. Most hybrid fuchsias there are grown in containers and brought into a garage or basement in winter; if container-grown plants are left outdoors, roots will freeze and the plants will die. In-ground fuchsias will have a better chance of survival if planted deeper than normal. Dig hole deep enough so you can place juncture of roots and stems 4–5 in. below soil level; gradually fill in soil as plant grows. Most hybrids need the insulation of a thick mulch in winter; mounding a 5–6-in. layer of sawdust over roots is effective. Hardier selections, however, will survive winters unmulched. These include 'Cardinal', 'Jingle Bells', 'June Bride', 'Mrs. Popple', 'Phyllis', 'Rufus', 'Santa Cruz', 'Speciosa', 'Surprise', 'Tessie', 'Voltaire', 'Whiteknights Amethyst', and 'Whiteknights Pearl'.

Fuchsias in all regions—whether in containers or beds—need porous, water-retentive soil rich in organic matter. Remember that those in hanging baskets need more watering than any other form. To keep blooms coming, apply light doses of complete fertilizer frequently.

Prune potted fuchsias severely before spring growth begins, cutting back each stem of last year's growth to one or two pairs of buds. Let about three pairs of leaves develop, then pinch off stem tips to stimulate branching. Continue pinching new growth for several weeks. Pick off old flowers as they start to fade. Prune in-ground fuchsias mainly to remove dead growth and to shape as desired; pinching is unnecessary.

You can take cuttings of favorite hybrids and grow them into flowering plants in a few months to a year. Cut 2–3-in. pieces of stem (preferably tips) and stick lower halves into damp sand to root.

F. magellanica. Zones 3b–9, 14–24; H1. Deciduous where frosts are light. Top dies back with first hard frost; protection of a mulch is needed in coldest-winter areas. Native to Chile, Argentina. In virtually frost-free areas, attains 10 ft. or taller and as wide or wider. In the Northwest, will reach 5–6½ ft. tall and wide if not frozen back; can grow 4–5 ft. in a season after being frozen back. Profuse production of drooping, 1½-in.-long, red-and-violet flowers. Oval, ½–1-in.-long leaves in groups of two or three. Very vulnerable to fuchsia gall mite. Parent of most hybrid fuchsias, which have inherited its mite susceptibility.

F. paniculata. Evergreen. Zones 16, 17, 22–24. From Mexico and Central America. Woody, erect growth to 12–14 ft. tall and 8 ft. wide (or larger), with small-toothed, somewhat shiny leaves to 8 in. long. Each lavender-pink flower is tiny, but blooms are massed in clusters to 10 in. across. Resistant to fuchsia gall mite. Often confused with and difficult to distinguish from *F. arborescens,* which is not reliably mite resistant.

F. procumbens. Deciduous. Zones 4–6, 15–17, 21–24. From New Zealand. Prostrate, spreading growth to about 6 in. high and 3–4 ft. wide. Heart-shaped, half-inch-long leaves. Small, petal-less flowers in summer have pale orange sepals with green markings and purple tips; anthers and pollen are blue. Showy, ¾-in. red berries. Good in shady rock gardens and containers. Resistant to fuchsia gall mite.

F. thymifolia. Deciduous. Zones 14–17, 20–24. From Mexico. Erect grower 3–9 ft. tall and wide, with ½–1-in.-long leaves and profuse, dangling white to pink flowers that age to deeper pink. Attractive close up; good for bonsai. Pollinated by bees rather than hummingbirds. Resistant to fuchsia gall mite.

Fuchsia triphylla 'Gartenmeister Bonstedt'

F. triphylla. Evergreen. Zones 14–17, 20, 24. From the West Indies. The species is seldom seen, but hybrid 'Gartenmeister Bonstedt' is well known. Somewhat more tender than most fuchsia hybrids but said to be more tolerant of heat. To 1½–2 ft. tall and wide. (Many plants sold are actually 'Thalia', nearly identical to 'Gartenmeister Bonstedt' but reaching about 3 ft.) Leaves are reddish bronze above, purplish beneath. Drooping clusters of intense orange-red, long-tubed flowers. Blooms all year in mildest climates. Protect from frost. Susceptible to fuchsia gall mite.

Fumariaceae. This family consists of annuals and perennials, usually with irregularly shaped flowers. *Corydalis* and bleeding heart *(Dicentra)* are examples. This family is considered by many to be included in the poppy family (Papaveraceae).

GAILLARDIA

Asteraceae (Compositae)

PERENNIALS AND ANNUALS

ZONES 1–24; H1, H2

FULL SUN

MODERATE WATER

Gaillardia ×grandiflora

Native to central and western U.S. Low-growing summer bloomers with daisylike flowers in warm colors—yellow, bronze, scarlet. Thrive in heat, need good drainage. Easy to grow from seed and fine for cutting and borders; often reseed.

G. aristata. Perennial. Parent of popular hybrid *G. ×grandiflora.* Has been largely replaced in garden culture by its many offspring, but the wild form is still much used in revegetation and wildflower mixes. Grows to 2–2½ ft. tall and 2 ft. across. Flower heads to 4 in. wide are yellow to red; the most common form has red rays with a jagged yellow border. 'Indian Yellow' has pure golden yellow flowers.

G. ×grandiflora. Perennial. Hybrid of *G. aristata* and *G. pulchella.* Grows to 2–4 ft. high, 1½ ft. wide, with roughish gray-green foliage and single or double flowers 3–4 in. across. Much variation in flower color; range includes various warm shades of red and yellow, with orange or maroon bands. Exceptionally long bloom period for perennial—early summer until frost. Plants flower first year from seed.

Many strains and varieties are available, including dwarf kinds and types with extra-large flowers. 'Goblin' is a good compact variety (1 ft. tall) with large deep red flowers bordered in bright yellow. 'Goblin Yellow' is similar but has yellow blooms. 'Baby Cole', another red-and-yellow type, grows 7–8 in. high. Among 2½-ft.-tall varieties are deep red 'Burgundy'; pure orange 'Tokajer'; and 'Torchlight', bearing yellow blooms bordered with red.

G. pulchella. Annual. To 1½–2 ft. high, 1 ft. wide, with soft, hairy leaves and long, whiplike stems carrying 2-in. flowers in warm shades of red, yellow, gold. Easy to grow; sow seeds in warm soil after danger of frost is past (in Zones 12 and 13, sow in fall). 'Red Plume' and 'Yellow Plume' are double flowered, with 2-in. blossoms on uniform 12–14-in. plants.

GALANTHUS

SNOWDROP

Amaryllidaceae

PERENNIALS FROM BULBS

ZONES 1–9, 14–17

FULL SUN DURING BLOOM, LIGHT SHADE AFTER

REGULAR WATER

BULBS ARE POISONOUS IF INGESTED

Galanthus nivalis

These natives of Europe and Asia Minor perform best in cold-winter climates. Closely related to and often confused with *Leucojum* (snowflake). Among the first bulbs to bloom as winter ends. Nodding, bell-shaped white flowers are borne one per stalk; inner flower segments are infused or marked with green, while larger outer segments are pure white. Plants have two or three strap-shaped basal leaves. Use in rock gardens or under flowering shrubs, naturalize in woodland, or grow in pots. Plant in fall, setting bulbs 3–4 in. deep and 3 in. apart in moist soil with ample humus. Prefer year-round moisture. Do not divide often; when division is necessary, do the job right after bloom.

G. elwesii. GIANT SNOWDROP. Foot-high stems carry 1½-in. flowers; inner segments are heavily infused with green. Better adapted to mild-winter climates than *G. nivalis.*

G. nivalis. COMMON SNOWDROP. More delicate version of *G. elwesii.* Stems 6–9 in. high bear inch-long flowers, their inner segments marked at tips with a green crescent. 'Flore Pleno' has double blooms.

GALIUM

Rubiaceae

PERENNIALS

ZONES 1–6, 15–17, EXCEPT AS NOTED

PARTIAL OR FULL SHADE

REGULAR TO AMPLE WATER

Galium odoratum

All have whorls of narrow leaves at intervals along thin, usually sprawling stems. Flowers are tiny, often profuse. Plants are not showy, but one *(G. odoratum)* is a useful ground cover for a shady site, while others have been grown for medicine, food, or dye. Can become invasive.

G. boreale. NORTHERN BEDSTRAW. Zones A1–A3; 1–6, 15–17. From Alaska, Canada, northern Europe, Asia. To 2½ ft. tall and wide, with 2-in. leaves. Clusters of tiny white flowers appear in profusion in summer. Nice wildflower for shade.

G. mollugo. FALSE BABY'S BREATH. From North America, Europe. Sprawling, weak-stemmed plant to 5 ft. tall and wide. Tiny leaves; loose, open clusters of tiny white flowers in summer and fall. Roots were once used to make red dye, and leaves in curdling milk for cheese.

G. odoratum (Asperula odorata). SWEET WOODRUFF. Zones A2, A3; 2–6, 15–17. Attractive low spreader that brings to mind deep, shady woods. Slender, square stems encircled every inch or so by six to eight aromatic, bristle-tipped leaves. Clusters of tiny white flowers appear above foliage in late spring and summer. When dried, leaves and stems give off a fragrance like hay; they are used to make May wine. In shade gardens, best used as a ground cover or pathway edging. Spreads rapidly in rich soil with abundant moisture and can become a pest if allowed to grow unchecked. Self-sows freely; can also be increased by division in fall or spring.

G. verum. LADY'S BEDSTRAW. Much like *G. mollugo* and also blooms in summer and fall, but is somewhat smaller (to 3½ ft. high and wide) and bears yellow rather than white flowers.

GALTONIA candicans

SUMMER HYACINTH

Liliaceae

PERENNIAL FROM BULB

ZONES 4–24; H1

LIGHT SHADE IN HOTTEST CLIMATES

REGULAR WATER DURING GROWTH AND BLOOM

Galtonia candicans

Native to South Africa. Strap-shaped leaves, 2–3 ft. long. In summer, the stout, 2–4-ft. stems are topped with loose, spikelike clusters of 1–1½-in.-long, sweet-scented white flowers—drooping, funnel shaped, the three outer segments often tipped green. Plant in fall where winter lows won't fall below 10°F/–12°C, in spring in colder regions; set bulbs 6 in. deep and 1 ft. apart, in organically enriched soil. Floral display is best if clump is not disturbed from one year to the next. Where winter lows range from 10 to –20°F/–12 to –29°C, mulch planting after foliage dies down. In colder regions, dig annually and store as for gladiolus. Control slugs and snails.

GALVEZIA speciosa

ISLAND BUSH SNAPDRAGON

Scrophulariaceae

EVERGREEN SHRUB

ZONES 14–24

LIGHT SHADE IN HOTTEST CLIMATES

NO IRRIGATION NEEDED

Galvezia speciosa

Native to Catalina, San Clemente, and Guadalupe islands (off the coast of Southern California). Usually grows to 3 ft. high and 5 ft. wide, but can climb or lean on other shrubs and reach 8 ft. Leaves are about 1 in. long, half as wide. Scarlet, tubular, 1-in.-long flowers cluster toward tips of branches. Bloom is heaviest in midspring but intermittent throughout year. Endures light or heavy soils if drainage is adequate. 'Firecracker' is a compact form (2–3 ft. high and 3 ft. wide) with bright red flowers.

GARDENIA

Rubiaceae

EVERGREEN SHRUBS

ZONES VARY BY SPECIES

FULL SUN OR PARTIAL SHADE

REGULAR TO AMPLE WATER

Gardenia augusta

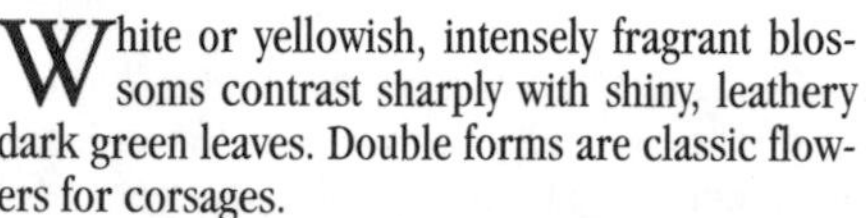

White or yellowish, intensely fragrant blossoms contrast sharply with shiny, leathery dark green leaves. Double forms are classic flowers for corsages.

G. augusta (G. jasminoides). Zones 7–9, 12–16, 18–24, H1, H2, except as noted. Native to China, Taiwan, Japan. Glossy bright green, lance-shaped leaves and intensely fragrant, single or double white flowers. Hardy to 20°F/–7°C or even lower but must have summer heat to thrive and bloom well. Hard to grow in adobe or alkaline desert soils. Give northern or eastern exposure in desert.

Provide fast-draining but moisture-retentive soil conditioned with plenty of organic matter such as peat moss or ground bark. Plant gardenias high (like azaleas and rhododendrons) and avoid crowding from other plants and competing roots. To help suppress weeds, mulch plants instead of cultivating around them. Unless water is high in salts (residue from salt in water may burn leaves), mist plants in early morning except during bloom time. Where water is poor, leach salts monthly. Feed every 3 to 4 weeks during growing season with acid plant food, fish emulsion, or blood meal. Prune to remove dead wood, straggling branches, faded flowers. To control aphids and brown scale, wash plants frequently with jet spray from hose or spray plants with light horticultural oil. (In hot weather, spray in the evening—though not if temperatures exceed 90°F/32°C—then wash foliage off next morning.)

Plants are useful in containers or raised beds, as hedges, espaliers, low screens, or specimens. Named varieties include the following.

'Aimée' ('First Love', 'Amy Yoshida'). Upright grower to 4–6 ft. tall and wide. Very large, very double, 4-in.-plus, roselike blossoms with elegantly spiraled form. Starts blooming in spring and continues well into summer.

'August Beauty'. Erect growth to 4–6 ft. high, 3–4 ft. wide. Loosely double, 2–3-in.-wide flowers produced primarily in early summer.

'Belmont' ('Hadley'). Vintage estate variety to 5 ft. high (or taller) and wide, with 4-in., roselike blossoms. Bulk of bloom comes from late spring to early summer. Large leaves (to 6 in. long).

'Chuck Hayes'. Zones 6–9, 12–16, 18–24; H1, H2. Extra-hardy variety; possibly as cold tolerant as 'Kleim's Hardy'. To 4 ft. high and wide. Double, 3-in. flowers in summer, with heavy rebloom in autumn. Very heat tolerant.

'Kimura Shikazaki' ('Four Seasons'). Compact growth to 2–3 ft. tall and wide. Flowers similar to those of 'Veitchii' but slightly less fragrant. Extremely long bloom season, from spring to fall.

'Kleim's Hardy'. Zones 6–9, 12–16, 18–24; H1, H2. Slow growing, forming a mound 2–3 ft. high and wide. Intensely fragrant single, star-shaped flowers are 1–3 in. wide. Blooms profusely in early summer, sporadically through rest of growing season. Reportedly has survived to 0°F/–18°C, suffering only damage to foliage.

'Miami Supreme'. To 6 ft. tall and wide, with large (4-in. or wider), very double flowers in spring; periodic rebloom through summer.

'Mystery'. Grows 6–8 ft. high and wide, even larger in time. Pure white, formal, 4–5-in. blossoms are the standard variety for florists' corsages. Blooms from midsummer through early fall—longer if warm weather continues. Intense fragrance carries through the air, even in dry climates. Rangy growth needs pruning to keep it neat and within bounds.

'Radicans' ('Prostrata'). True miniature gardenia. Grows 6–12 in. high and 2–3 ft. wide, with inch-long dark green leaves and many inch-wide double flowers, mainly in early summer. Good small-scale edging, ground cover, container plant. 'Radicans Variegata' ('Prostrata Variegata') has medium green leaves irregularly edged or splashed with creamy yellow and white; same habit as 'Radicans' but somewhat less vigorous.

'Veitchii'. Sometimes sold as "everblooming gardenia." Compact form 3–4½ ft. high, to 6 ft. wide; leaves to 2½ in. long. Oldest variety, but still most reliable bloomer. Roselike, 1½–2-in.-wide, pure white blossoms from late spring to fall; bloom may continue during a warm winter.

'White Gem'. Dense, compact dwarf to 1–2 ft. high and wide. Rounded, five- or six-petaled, 1½–2-in. single flowers bloom continuously from spring through summer. Sweet, carrying fragrance. Good in containers, foreground of borders.

G. taitensis. TIARE TAHITI, TAHITIAN GARDENIA, KIELE. Zone H2. Dense-crowned large shrub or small tree to 18 ft. tall and wide. Shiny dark green leaves to 8 in. long, 4 in. wide. White, 4-in.-wide, pinwheel-shaped flowers are produced throughout the year; they are powerfully fragrant and a favorite for leis. Plants can be pruned into small trees or planted as an informal hedge. Best in full sun; will tolerate shade. Withstands beach conditions if protected from salt, winds.

G. thunbergia. Zones 16, 17, 21–24; H1, H2. Native to South Africa. Winter-blooming shrub to 10 ft. tall, 20 ft. wide. Angular branches; dark green leaves to 6 in long. Single, 3–4-in. flowers have a long tube and typically eight overlapping, petal-like lobes. Somewhat more tolerant than *G. augusta* of cool conditions and less-than-perfect soil, but tender to frost. With age, becomes more vigorous and blooms more profusely. Rough, brownish gray, elliptical fruits to 5 in. long remain on plant for 2 or 3 years.

GARLAND FLOWER. See HEDYCHIUM coronarium

GARLIC

Liliaceae

PERENNIAL

ALL ZONES EXCEPT A1

FULL SUN

REGULAR WATER

Garlic

Classified botanically as *Allium sativum;* not known in the wild. Seed stores and some mail-order seed houses sell disease-free mother bulbs ("sets") for planting—and some gardeners have had good luck planting bulbs from grocery stores. In mild-winter areas, plant in fall for early summer harvest; where winters are cold, plant in early spring. Break up bulbs into cloves and select largest ones. Plant in rich, well-drained soil, setting cloves pointed end up, 1 in. deep, 3–6 in. apart, in rows 15 in. apart. Harvest when leafy tops fall over; lift out with garden fork rather than pulling. Air-dry bulbs, cut off most of tops and roots, and store in cool, well-ventilated place out of sunlight. Giant or elephant garlic *(A. scorodoprasum)* has unusually large (fist-size) bulbs and mild garlic flavor. Grow as for regular garlic, but space 8–12 in. apart. For ornamental relatives, see *Allium.*

GARLIC CHIVES. See ALLIUM tuberosum

GARRYA

SILKTASSEL
Garryaceae
EVERGREEN SHRUBS
ZONES VARY BY SPECIES
FULL SUN OR PARTIAL SHADE
WATER NEEDS VARY BY SPECIES

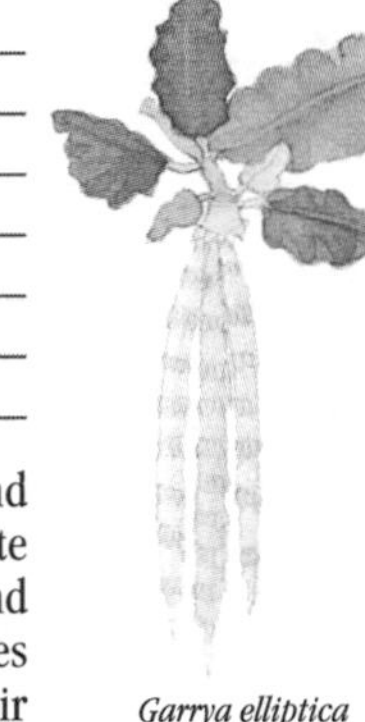
Garrya elliptica

Grown mainly for their pendulous male and female catkins, which appear on separate plants; male catkins are longer, more slender, and more decorative than female ones. Both sexes must be present for female plants to produce their grapelike clusters of fruit.

G. elliptica. COAST SILKTASSEL. Zones 4–9, 14–24. Native to Coast Ranges from southern Oregon to Southern California. Densely foliaged plant reaches 10–20 ft. high and as wide. Plant can be trained as a small tree. Elliptical, wavy-edged leaves to 2½ in. long are dark green above with gray and woolly undersides. Clustered flower tassels appear in winter. Male catkins are yellowish to greenish yellow, 3–8 in. long; female ones are pale green, rather stubby, 2–3½ in. long. Clustered purplish fruits on female plants hang on all summer—even longer if not eaten by birds. Excellent foliage plant; use as screen, informal hedge, or specimen. For unusually long catkins, plant male varieties 'Evie' (10 in.) or 'James Roof' (1 ft.). Moderate water.

G. fremontii. FREMONT SILKTASSEL. Zones 3–10, 12, 14–17. Native to mountains of Washington, Oregon, California, Arizona. To 9 ft. tall and wide. Differs from *G. elliptica* in its leaves, which are glossy, smooth edged, and lively yellow green on both upper and lower surfaces. Yellowish or purple catkins; purple or black fruit. Takes heat and cold better than *G. elliptica.* No irrigation needed.

GAS PLANT. See DICTAMNUS albus

GAULTHERIA

Ericaceae
EVERGREEN SHRUBS
ZONES VARY BY SPECIES
PARTIAL SHADE
REGULAR WATER

Gaultheria shallon

These shrubs bear urn-shaped flowers and fleshy, berrylike fruit. They all need moist, acid soil rich in organic matter. Smaller kinds are favored for rock gardens and woodland plantings. Larger kinds are good companions for other acid-loving shrubs such as rhododendrons and azaleas.

G. mucronata. See Pernettya mucronata

G. ovatifolia. Zones 3–7, 14–17. Native to the mountains in Northern California to British Columbia, east to northern Idaho. Plant is spreading and trailing, with upright branches to about 8 in. high. Oval, leathery, dark green leaves about ¾–1½ in. long and nearly as wide. Bears tiny white to pinkish flowers in summer and bright red, ¼-in.-wide berries in fall and winter that are edible, have a wintergreen flavor. Small-scale ground cover in woodland.

G. procumbens. WINTERGREEN, CHECKERBERRY, TEABERRY. Zones 1–7, 14–17. Native to eastern North America. Creeping stems send up erect branches to 6 in. high, with oval, 2-in., glossy dark green leaves clustered toward tips. Foliage emits a strong wintergreen odor when bruised, turns reddish with winter cold. Small pinkish white summer flowers are followed by scarlet berries. Both berries and foliage have flavor of wintergreen (or teaberry). Use as ground cover; plant 1 ft. apart. 'Macrocarpa' is a compact variety bearing a heavy crop of fruit.

G. shallon. SALAL. Zones 4–7, 14–17. Native from central California coast north to British Columbia. In good growing conditions, can reach 4–10 ft. tall and slightly wider; in poor, dry soil and full sun, it's a tufted plant only 1–2 ft. high (makes a good low bank cover in these circumstances). Glossy bright green leaves are nearly round, 1¾–4 in. long. Loose, 6-in.-long clusters of white or pinkish flowers on reddish stalks bloom in spring. Edible black fruits resembling large huckleberries follow the blossoms; they're bland flavored, but birds like them. Only neglected plantings need pruning; cut back in spring, remove dead wood, and mulch with organic material such as leaf mold or peat moss. Cut branches of this plant are sold by florists as "lemon leaves."

G

GAURA lindheimeri

Onagraceae
PERENNIAL
ZONES 2B–24
FULL SUN
MODERATE WATER

Gaura lindheimeri

Native to Texas and Louisiana. Airy growth to 2½–4 ft. high, 2–3 ft. wide. Leaves are 1½–3½ in. long and stalkless, growing directly from stems. Branching flower spikes bear many closely set, 1-in.-long white blossoms that open from pink buds. Long bloom period (often from late spring into fall), with only a few flowers opening at a time. Blossoms age to a rosy shade, then drop off cleanly, but seed-bearing spikes should be removed to improve overall appearance, prolong bloom period, and prevent overly enthusiastic self-sowing. Long-lived plant. Division not necessary—and difficult in any case, since gaura grows from a deep taproot (which makes it very drought tolerant). For additional plants, let a few seedlings grow.

Selected forms include 2–2½-ft. 'Corrie's Gold', featuring gold-edged foliage; 2-ft. 'Siskiyou Pink', with maroon-mottled leaves and deep maroon buds opening to rose pink flowers; and 'Whirling Butterflies', with slightly larger white flowers on a 3-ft. plant.

GAYFEATHER. See LIATRIS

GAZANIA

Asteraceae (Compositae)
PERENNIALS, SOME GROWN AS ANNUALS
ZONES VARY BY SPECIES
EXPOSURE NEEDS VARY BY SPECIES
MODERATE TO REGULAR WATER

Gazania hybrid

Native to South Africa. Low, clumping or spreading plants grown for colorful daisies over long bloom season. Tolerate seacoast conditions. Grow well in enriched or unamended soil, and with regular or only occasional water.

G. hybrids. Zones 8–24, H1, H2 as perennials; in colder climates, carry plants through winter by taking cuttings in fall as you would for pelargoniums. Dazzling color display during peak bloom in late spring, early summer. In mild-winter climates, they continue to bloom intermittently through the rest of year. Grow in full sun. There are basically two types: clumping and trailing.

Clumping gazanias (complex hybrids between a number of species) form a mound of evergreen, typically lobed leaves that are dark green above with gray and woolly undersides. Flowering stems are 6–10 in. tall, bearing 3–4-in.-wide blossoms in colors including yellow, orange, white, and rosy pink; undersides of rays are reddish purple. Blossoms often have dark centers. You can also get a mixture of hybrids (as plants or seeds) in different colors. Flowers open on sunny days and close at night and in cloudy weather.

Among seed-grown kinds is the Daybreak series—low-growing, spreading plants that bloom in 12 weeks from seed (good choice for areas with short growing season) and feature blossoms in orange, bronze, yellow, yellow striped with red, and mixed colors. Harlequin Hybrids are 12–15 in. tall and offer a full range of colors; blossoms have striking zones in contrasting colors. Other seed-grown sorts are Sundance Mixed, with 4–5-in. flowers on 10–12-in. plants; Sunshine Mix, to 10–12 in. tall, displaying several zones of color on each 4-in. flower; and 8-in.-tall Talent Mix, showing off 2½-in. blossoms against silvery foliage.

Named hybrids of special merit include 'Aztec Queen' (multicolored), 'Burgundy', 'Copper King', and 'Fiesta Red'; these are best used in small-scale plantings, though the last is sturdy enough for large expanses. 'Moonglow' is double-flowered bright yellow of unusual vigor; unlike most gazanias, it has blooms that stay open even on dull days.

Use clumping gazanias in parking strips, as edging along sunny paths, in rock gardens. Good temporary fillers between young shrubs or as replaceable ground cover for relatively level areas not subject to severe erosion.

Trailing gazanias are derived from *G. rigens leucolaena,* formerly sold as *G. uniflora* or *G. leucolaena.* They grow about as tall as clumping types but spread rapidly by long, trailing stems. Foliage is a clean silvery gray; flowers are yellow, white, orange, or bronze. Newer, larger-flowered hybrids include 'Sunburst' (orange with black eye) and 'Sunglow' (yellow). 'Sunrise Yellow' has large, black-centered yellow flowers; leaves are green instead of gray. These newer hybrids are superior to older kinds in length of bloom, resistance to dieback. Trailing gazanias are useful on banks as well as level ground. Or grow them at top of a wall and let them drape over the edge. Attractive in hanging baskets.

G. linearis 'Colorado Gold'. Zones 2–9, 14–19. Unlike other gazanias, this is a hardy perennial in much of the cold-winter West. One of the many surprisingly hardy plants brought back from the high mountains of South Africa, it has succeeded in Denver and northern New Mexico. Grows 4 in. high, 15 in. wide. Strap-shaped leaves are dark green above, woolly white beneath. Bright yellow flowers to 3 in. wide bloom all summer. Self-sows. Full sun or partial shade.

GEIGER TREE. See CORDIA sebestena

GEIJERA parviflora

AUSTRALIAN WILLOW, WILGA
Rutaceae
EVERGREEN TREE
ZONES 8, 9, 12–24
FULL SUN
LITTLE TO MODERATE WATER

Geijera parviflora

Graceful, fine-textured tree from Australia. To 25–30 ft. tall and 20 ft. wide, with main branches sweeping up and out, little branches hanging down. Distant citrus relative; called a willow because its narrow, drooping, 3–6-in.-long leaves give a weeping willow effect. Casts light shade. With age, produces loose clusters of unimportant small, creamy white flowers in early spring and early fall. Has much of willow's grace and eucalyptus's toughness. Trouble-free patio, street, or grove tree. Deep, noninvasive roots. Grow in well-drained soil. Needs pruning only to correct form (much less pruning than true willow).

FOR DEFINITIONS OF GARDENING TERMS
PLEASE SEE PAGES 746–750

GELSEMIUM sempervirens

CAROLINA JESSAMINE
Loganiaceae
EVERGREEN VINE
ZONES 4–24
FULL SUN OR PARTIAL SHADE
REGULAR WATER
ALL PARTS ARE POISONOUS IF INGESTED

Gelsemium sempervirens

Native to southeastern U.S. Shrubby, twining vine grows at a moderate rate to about 20 ft. Pairs of shiny light green, 1–4-in.-long leaves are borne on long branches that look almost like streamers. Fragrant, tubular yellow flowers to 1–1½ in. long bloom in late winter, early spring. Sometimes blooms sporadically in fall. 'Pride of Augusta' ('Plena') is a double-flowered form.

On trellis, vine will cascade and swing in wind; on house wall, makes delicate green curtain of branches. Often trained onto fences and mailboxes. Can get top-heavy; if this happens, cut back severely. Also used as ground cover, especially on banks; keep trimmed to 3 ft. high. Blooms most profusely in full sun.

GENISTA

BROOM
Fabaceae (Leguminosae)
DECIDUOUS AND EVERGREEN SHRUBS
ZONES VARY BY SPECIES
FULL SUN
LITTLE TO MODERATE WATER

Genista lydia

Leaves are often small and short lived. Green branches give deciduous plants an evergreen look. Flowers are yellow (rarely white or pink) and sweet pea shaped. Less aggressive than other brooms *(Cytisus, Spartium);* will not run wild. Smaller kinds are attractive in rock gardens and bank plantings. These shrubs tolerate rocky or infertile soil. Need good drainage.

G. aetnensis. MT. ETNA BROOM. Leafless or nearly so. Zones 5–9, 14–24. Large shrub or small tree to 18 ft. or more, with graceful arching, weeping green branchlets, bare or with a very few tiny leaves during growing season. Branches are covered with blooms in summer. Not likely to survive temperatures below 5°F/–15°C.

G. canariensis (Cytisus canariensis). CANARY ISLAND BROOM. Evergreen. Zones 8, 9, 14–24. Damaged at 15°F/–9°C but recovers quickly. Many-branched, upright shrub 6–8 ft. tall, 5–6 ft. wide. Bright green leaves divided into ½-in. leaflets. Fragrant flowers at ends of branches in spring and summer. The genista of florists. Grows like a weed and spreads by self-sown seedlings.

G. fragrans. This white-flowered species is not in the nursery trade. Plants sold under this name are *G. spachiana.*

G. hispanica. SPANISH BROOM. Deciduous. Zones 4–22. Mass of spiny stems to 1–2 ft. high, up to 5 ft. wide; stems set with ½-in.-long leaves. Clusters of flowers at stem tips in spring.

G. lydia. Nearly leafless. Zones 2b–6, 14–17. Often erroneously sold as *Cytisus lydia.* Shrub grows to 2 ft. tall and 3 ft. wide; makes a good ground cover. Bears profuse show of blossoms at tips of shoots in late spring. Sets few seeds.

G. monosperma. BRIDAL VEIL BROOM. Nearly leafless. Zones 16, 17, 22–24. Upright growth to 20 ft. high, 10 ft. wide, with slender, graceful gray-green branches. Fragrant white flowers in winter, spring.

G. pilosa. Deciduous. Zones 2b–22. Fairly fast growing prostrate shrub, ultimately to 1–1½ ft. tall with 7-ft. spread. Intricately branched gray-green twigs. Roundish, ¼–½-in.-long leaves. Blooms in spring. 'Vancouver Gold' is a good selection.

G. racemosa. See G. spachiana

G. sagittalis. Leafless. Zones 2–22. Rather rapid grower to 1 ft. high and 3 ft. wide. Upright, flattened bright green branchlets appear jointed. Makes a sheet of bloom in late spring and early summer.

G. spachiana (G. racemosa). Evergreen. Zones 7–9, 14–24. Similar to *G. canariensis,* but with larger leaflets and longer, looser spikes of fragrant flowers in late spring. Naturalizes where adapted. Often sold as *G. fragrans.*

G. tinctoria. DYER'S GREENWEED, WOADWAXEN. Deciduous. Zones 2–24. To 6 ft. tall and wide, with undivided leaves to 2 in. long. Upright flower spikes in late spring or early summer. 'Royal Gold' is a compact selection 2 ft. tall and wide.

GENTIANA

GENTIAN

Gentianaceae

PERENNIALS

ZONES 2–6, 14–17, EXCEPT AS NOTED

FULL SUN OR LIGHT SHADE, EXCEPT AS NOTED

REGULAR WATER

Gentiana acaulis

Low, spreading, or upright plants, generally with tubular flowers in intense blue shades. Most are difficult to grow, but they are prized by rock garden enthusiasts. Need perfect drainage. Most require lime-free soil. If they thrive, they are worth the care because they produce some of the richest blues in the garden.

G. acaulis. From Europe. Leafy-stemmed rosette to 4 in. high, 1 ft. wide, with inch-long, glossy dark green leaves. Rich blue flowers to 2 in. long in summer. Grows well but often fails to bloom.

G. asclepiadea. WILLOW GENTIAN. Native to Europe and western Asia. Forms a clump of arching stems to 2 ft. tall, 1½ ft. wide. Dark green, 2–3-in.-long leaves. Blooms in late summer and early fall, when deep blue, 1½-in. flowers that open into stars appear singly or in twos or threes in joints of upper leaves. Not difficult to grow. Partial shade.

G. clusii (G. acaulis clusii). Similar to *G. acaulis* but bears larger flowers.

G. cruciata. CROSS GENTIAN. From Europe, Turkey, Siberia. Foot-wide basal rosette of thick, glossy, medium green, 4–8-in.-long leaves sends up leafy, 12–16-in. stalks bearing clustered 1-in., dark blue flowers. Blooms in summer and early fall. Easy to grow.

G. septemfida. Zones A1–A3; 1–6, 14–17. From Turkey, Iran to central Asia. Arching or sprawling stems 9–18 in. long form a spreading mass about 8 in. high, 1 ft. wide. Medium green, oval leaves to 1½ in. long. Clusters of 2-in., dark blue flowers in late summer. Easy to grow. *G. s. lagodechiana,* the form commonly sold, is similar but has more widely spaced flowers.

G. sino-ornata. From China, Tibet. Bright green foliage rosette to 7 in. high and somewhat wider sends out trailing stems that end in 2-in. flowers of brightest blue in early fall. Fairly easy to grow in half shade.

G. verna. SPRING GENTIAN. From mountains of Europe. Dark green leaves to 1 in. long form a rosette to 2 in. high, 4 in. wide. Bright blue, 1-in. flowers in spring. Not a good competitor against sturdier plants; grow in pots or troughs. Needs some lime.

Gentianaceae. The gentian family includes annuals and perennials from many parts of the world. Many plants in this family have blue or purple flowers, including gentian *(Gentiana),* Persian violet *(Exacum),* and lisianthus *(Eustoma).*

Geraniaceae. The cranesbill family of annuals and perennials (the latter sometimes shrubby) includes true geranium as well as *Erodium* and *Pelargonium.*

GERANIUM

CRANESBILL

Geraniaceae

PERENNIALS

ZONES VARY BY SPECIES

AFTERNOON SHADE IN HOTTEST CLIMATES

REGULAR WATER, EXCEPT AS NOTED

Geranium pratense

The common indoor/outdoor plant most people know as geranium is, botanically, *Pelargonium.* Considered here are true geraniums, which are mostly hardy plants. Many types bloom over a long period, bearing flowers that are attractive though not always as showy as those of pelargoniums. Carried singly or in few-flowered clusters, blossoms have five overlapping petals that look alike. (Pelargonium flowers also have five petals, but two point in one direction, the other three in the opposite direction.) Colors include blue, purple, magenta, and bluish rose; some are pure pink or white. Beaklike fruit that follows the flowers accounts for the common name "cranesbill." Leaves are roundish or kidney shaped, lobed or deeply cut; plants may be upright or trailing. Good in rock gardens, perennial borders; some are useful as small- or large-scale ground covers. A few shrubby species are good for holding slopes.

Best climates for most geraniums are cool- and mild-summer regions, where plants can grow in full sun or light shade. In hot-summer areas, give afternoon shade. South African species are less cold hardy but more tolerant of heat, afternoon sun. All species appreciate moist, well-drained soil. Clumps of most types can be left in place for many years before they decline due to crowding; at that point, divide in early spring. Increase by transplanting rooted portions from a clump's edge; or take cuttings. Many produce lots of seedlings, and some can become naturalized pests.

G. 'Ann Folkard'. Zones 2b–9, 14–24. Mounding, billowing plant (1 ft. high, to 5 ft. wide) with chartreuse leaves that age to light green. Saucer-shaped, 1½-in.-wide blossoms are rich magenta purple suffused with pink and blue, centered and veined in black. Blooms from spring into fall. Effective planted at edge of patio and sprawling onto it.

G. argenteum. Zones 3–6. From the Alps. Foliage rosette 3–5 in. high, 6 in. wide. Inch-wide basal leaves are five to seven lobed, densely covered with silvery, silky hairs. Pale pink or white, 1½-in. flowers with dark veins and notched petals bloom from late spring to early summer.

G. × cantabrigiense. Zones 1–24. Excellent ground cover, 6–8 in. high, spreading slowly but widely. Dark green leaves 1½–2½ in. wide, deeply cut with multiple lobes. 'Cambridge' has bright bluish pink flowers, ¾–1 in. wide. Those of 'Biokovo' are white blushed pale pink, slightly larger. Both bloom from late spring to early summer.

G. cinereum. Zones 1–24, but very short lived where summers are hot. From the Pyrenees. Forms wide, 8–12-in.-tall mats composed of 1–1½-in., soft gray-green leaves—rounded, bluntly lobed, and deeply cut. In early to midsummer, slender, trailing stems bear many cupped, 1–1½-in.-wide flowers in pale pink with dark veins. 'Ballerina' is pinkish lilac with dark veins radiating from a wine-colored center; continues blooming into fall. The slightly larger 'Laurence Flatman' has light lavender blossoms with reddish center blotches between red veins.

G. clarkei 'Kashmir White'. Zones 2b–9, 14–24. From Kashmir. To 2 ft. tall when in bloom; spreads widely by rhizomes. Medium green, deeply cut, 2–6-in.-wide leaves with seven narrow lobes are carried on 1½-ft. leafstalks. White, 1½-in.-wide flowers with pale pink veins from late spring to early summer.

G. dalmaticum. Zones 1–24. From the Balkans. Low (4–5-in.) carpeting plant, creeping slowly by rhizomes to 2 ft. or wider. Glossy, 1½-in., deeply cut dark green leaves. Soft pink, 1-in. flowers in late spring. Red fall leaf color. Good in rock gardens.

G. endressii. Zones 1–9, 14–24. From southern Europe to southwest Asia. Bushy, 1–1½-ft.-high mound, spreading by rhizomes to 2 ft or wider. Light green, 2–3-in.-wide leaves are deeply cut in fine lobes; evergreen in mild climates. Funnel-shaped blossoms with notched petals are rose pink with a silvery sheen, about 1 in. across. Blooms late spring into fall in mild-summer areas; peters out in early summer where summers are hot.

G. 'Frances Grate' ('Silver Sugar Plum'). Zones 14–24. Billowy, woody, scrambling plant 1½ ft. tall by 5 ft. or wider. Finely cut 2-in.-wide leaves are gray green above, silvery beneath. Saucer-shaped, wide-petaled lilac mauve flowers to 1 in. across, early spring through fall. Takes hot afternoon sun. Seeds profusely and can be invasive; seedlings vary widely.

G. harveyi. Zones 5–9, 14–24. From South Africa. Woody-based mound to 8 in. high by 2 ft. or wider. Deeply five-lobed, silky, 1-in. leaves are gray green above, silvery underneath. Magenta, 1¼-in.-wide flowers from late spring through fall. Tolerates hot sun. Good on slopes or trailing among rocks.

G. himalayense (G. grandiflorum). Zones 1–24. Himalyan native to 1½ ft. high, spreading by rhizomes. Long-stalked, medium green, 2½-in.-wide leaves are roundish, with prominent veins and five broad, deeply divided lobes. Blooms from late spring into summer; 1-ft. stems bear clusters of 1½–2-in.-wide blue flowers with reddish veins and purple eye. Excellent deciduous small-scale bulb cover; plant 1–1½ ft. apart. 'Gravetye' is a dependable selection typical of the species. 'Baby Blue' has larger light blue flowers. 'Plenum' ('Birch Double') is less vigorous, with double light lavender blossoms.

G. ibericum. Zones 2–9, 11–24. From Turkey and the Caucasus. To 2 ft. tall and 3 ft. wide, with medium green, hairy, 4-in.-wide, deeply divided leaves with 9–11 lobes. Bowl-shaped, 2-in. lavender-blue flowers with purple veins in late spring.

G. incanum. Zones 14–24. From South Africa. To 6–10 in. high, spreading fast to form a 2-ft.-wide cushion of finely cut leaves. Inch-wide light magenta flowers appear from spring to fall. Cut to ground every 2 or 3 years to keep neat. Endures heat and drought better than most geraniums, but needs some summer water. Self-seeds profusely and can be invasive.

G. 'Johnson's Blue'. Zones 2–9, 14–24. Hybrid resembling its *G. himalayense* parent, but leaf divisions are narrower. Mounds 1½–2 ft. wide and spreads by rhizomes; excellent summer ground cover. Abundant 2-in., blue-violet flowers in loose clusters from spring to fall. Blossoms are sterile. Much of material sold under this name is 'Gravetye' or another *G. himalayense* form, with a shorter bloom season and fertile flowers.

G. macrorrhizum. Zones 1–24. From southern Europe. To 8–10 in. high, spreading fast by underground rootstocks and fleshy rhizomes that root on soil surface. Thick, hairy, sticky, five- to seven-lobed leaves 3–4 in. across; foliage has a strong, musky fragrance and attractive autumn coloring ranging from dull yellow to orange and scarlet. Inch-wide flowers in white, pink, or magenta. Blooms late spring through early summer; some repeat in fall. Good ground cover for small areas, though it can overwhelm smaller plants. 'Bevan's Variety' has vibrant combination of deep magenta petals and red sepals. 'Ingwersen's Variety' has soft bluish pink flowers, longer blooming season. 'Album' is white flushed pale pink, with pink sepals and stamens.

G. maculatum. WILD CRANESBILL, SPOTTED CRANESBILL. Zones 1–24. Native to moist woodlands and meadows of eastern North America; the only commonly cultivated U.S. native cranesbill. To 1½ ft. tall, 2 ft. wide, with deeply divided, five- to seven-lobed leaves. Profuse lilac pink, 1–1½-in. flowers in spring to early summer. 'Album' has white blossoms.

G. maderense. Zones 14–24. Dramatic native of Madeira likes moist conditions, shade. Largest of all geranium leaves (to 8 in. across)—overlapping, glossy, deeply divided, shaped like giant snowflakes. Reddish brown leafstalks help buttress the 3–4-ft. "trunk" supporting hundreds of densely packed, fuzzy buds and magenta-eyed deep pink blossoms. Blooms early spring through midsummer. Biennial or short-lived perennial; dies after blooming but spawns many seedlings.

G. × magnificum. Zones 1–9, 14–24. Vigorous sterile hybrid has been cultivated for more than a century. Spreads steadily, forming broad clumps 2–2½ ft. high and wide. Rounded, quilted, 3-in. leaves are divided into broad segments. Profuse 2-in. violet blossoms heavily veined in deep purple; blooms in late spring and early summer.

G. × oxonianum. Zones 2–9, 14–24. Among best selections is 'Claridge Druce', which forms a vigorous clump 2–3 ft. tall, 3 ft. wide. Rounded, 3–4-in. leaves are deeply cut between broad, toothed lobes. Funnel-shaped, broad-petaled, 1½–1¾-in., cool pink flowers with purplish veins bloom late spring to summer. Good large-scale ground cover but can overwhelm adjacent plants. Self-sows profusely; seedlings resemble parent, but blossoms often have narrower petals. 'Wargrave Pink' is similar in habit but a little less vigorous, with glossy warm pink blossoms that resemble those of *G. endressii* (one of the parents).

G. phaeum. MOURNING WIDOW, DUSKY CRANESBILL. Zones 2b–9, 14–24. Shade-loving native of southern and central European mountains. To 2 ft. high, 1½ ft. wide. Leaves are basal, 3–4 in. across, shallowly cut into seven to nine tooth-edged lobes, often with brown markings. Clusters of dusky purple or maroon blossoms bloom from spring to fall. 'Lily Lovell' has purplish maroon blooms with a white eye. 'Samobor' has light maroon flowers and leaves heavily marked with maroon.

G. 'Philippe Vapelle'. Zones 3–9, 14–24. Tight clump 1 ft. tall and 1½ ft. wide. Medium green, 3-in., rounded leaves are quilted, shallowly cut into scalloped lobes. Violet-blue flowers with darker veins have deeply notched petals. Blooms spring through midsummer.

G. 'Pink Spice'. Zones 3b–9, 14–24. Compact mound 8–10 in. tall, to 1 ft. wide. Reddish bronze, 1½-in. leaves form a dark background for 1-in.-wide pink blossoms on long, trailing stems. Blooms from late spring through fall. Foliage color is best with at least half-day direct sun.

G. platypetalum. Zones 3b–9, 14–24. From Turkey and the Caucasus. Clump 1½ ft. high and wide with rounded, quilted leaves, shallowly cut into seven to nine scalloped lobes. Saucer-shaped, 1½–1¾-in. summer flowers with notched petals are deep violet blue with paler center and dark veins.

G. pratense. MEADOW CRANESBILL. Zones 2–7, 14–24. Native from Ireland to Siberia and Japan. Forms a clump 1½–2 ft. tall, 2–3 ft. wide. Hairy, 3–6-in. leaves on upright stalks are deeply cut into seven narrow, pointed, divided lobes. Flowers about 1 in. wide, typically blue with reddish veins; bloom from spring through summer. Self-seeds profusely; cut to ground when flowers fade to prevent seedlings and encourage rebloom. 'Mrs. Kendall Clark' has pale blue flowers with lighter veins. 'Striatum' has white blossoms irregularly splashed, streaked, or spotted with violet blue.

G. psilostemon (G. armenum). Zones 2b–9, 14–24. Native to Armenia, Turkey. Large clump—to 4 ft. tall and wide—with big, deeply cut leaves and an early summer show of 1–1½-in. magenta flowers with black centers and veins. Leaves turn brilliant flame color in fall.

G. renardii. Zones 2b–9, 14–24. From the Caucasus. Compact grower to 1 ft. high and wide. Velvety gray-green leaves have deeply etched veins and scalloped lobes. Early to midsummer flowers are white with violet veining; overall effect is pearly gray.

Geranium renardii

G. × riversleaianum. Zones 2b–9, 14–24. Forms wide-spreading, foot-high mat of silky, silvery green leaves. Continuous show of rounded, ¾-in. blossoms on long, trailing stems from late spring through fall. 'Mavis Simpson' has soft shell pink blossoms with dark veins. 'Russell Prichard' is brilliant magenta rose.

G. robustum. Zones 14–24. Shrubby species from South Africa grows 3 ft. high, 4 ft. wide. Finely divided leaves to 3 in. across are silky gray green above, silvery below. Summer flowers 1 in. across, light purple with a white eye. Survives with little water. Use on slopes with other drought-tolerant plants like lavender *(Lavandula)*, rockrose *(Cistus)*. Self-sows profusely.

G. sanguineum. BLOODY CRANESBILL. Zones A2, A3; 1–9, 14–24. Native from western Europe to the Caucasus and Turkey. Forms dense clump 8–18 in. high, spreading by rhizomes to 2½ ft. or wider. Dark green, 1–2-in.-wide leaves are deeply divided into five to seven lobes, each with three narrow segments; turn blood red in fall. Typical forms have deep purple to almost crimson flowers 1½ in. wide; bloom late spring well into summer and will rebloom if cut to ground. Good 1–1½-ft.-tall selections include white 'Album'; 'John Elsley', pink with deeper pink veins; reddish purple 'Max Frei'; and 'New Hampshire', reddish magenta petals with magenta veins. 'Vision', a variable seed-grown strain, has magenta flowers with purple veins. *G. s. striatum (G. s. lancastriense)* is a compact form only 5–6 in. high. It bears light pink flowers heavily veined with red (its seedlings may vary somewhat) and makes an excellent rock garden or foreground plant.

G. subcaulescens (G. cinereum subcaulescens). Zones 3–24, but short lived where summers are hot. Native to the Balkans, Turkey. Like *G. cinereum,* but with darker green leaves and brilliant crimson-magenta flowers with black centers and veins.

G. sylvaticum. WOOD CRANESBILL. Zones 2–9, 14–24. Native from Ireland to Siberia, south to Turkey. Shade- and moisture-loving plant to 2½ ft. tall and wide. Late spring to early summer flowers are 1 in. across, range in color from white through pink to reddish purple.

G. wallichianum. Zones 2–9, 14–24. Himalayan native of low, sprawling or trailing but not rooting habit, 1 ft. tall and 3 ft. wide. Blooms from early summer until fall, bearing 1–1½-in.-wide flowers in lilac or purplish blue with a white eye. 'Buxton's Variety' has pure blue flowers with large white eye. Stout taproot is not easy to divide; propagate from seed.

G. wlassovianum. Zones A2, A3; 1–7. Native to Siberia, Mongolia, northeastern China. Clump-forming plant to 1½ ft. high, 2 ft. wide. Velvety, 2-in., divided leaves emerge pinkish bronze, mature to dusky green tinged with brown, and then turn cinnamon brown in fall. Reddish purple, 1¼-in.-wide flowers with small white eye and deep violet veins. Blooms midsummer to early fall.

GERBERA jamesonii

TRANSVAAL DAISY

Asteraceae (Compositae)

PERENNIAL OFTEN GROWN AS ANNUAL

ZONES 8, 9, 12–24; H1, H2; ANYWHERE AS ANNUAL

PARTIAL SHADE IN HOTTEST CLIMATES

REGULAR WATER

Gerbera jamesonii

This South African native is among the most elegant and sophisticated of daisies. Clump of tongue-shaped, lobed, 10-in.-long leaves sends up slim yet sturdy stems to 1½ ft. high, each bearing one slender-petaled, 4–5-in. daisy. Colors are pure, unshaded, glowing; include cream through yellow to coral, orange, flame, and red. Basic flower has single ring of rays surrounding prominent central disk. Hybrid forms may have two rows of long rays, or an outer ring of long rays and a central ring of short, tufted ones; or they may be fully double, with a fluffy look. Many strains are sold, including dwarf types only 7 in. tall. As perennial, can bloom any time of year, with peaks in early summer and late fall. Beyond hardiness range, treat as summer annual. In Zones 12 and 13, best as winter annual (may last longer during a cool spring).

Needs organically enriched soil with excellent drainage (if soil drains poorly, grow in raised bed). Plant 2 ft. apart; to avoid rot, keep root crown slightly above soil level. Protect from snails and slugs. Water deeply and let soil become nearly dry before watering again. For best flowering, fertilize monthly. Divide (in late winter) only when clump is crowded and flowering declines. When cutting flowers for arrangements, slit the bottom inch of the stem before placing in water.

GERMANDER. See TEUCRIUM

GERMAN IVY. See SENECIO mikanioides

GERMAN STATICE. See GONIOLIMON tataricum

Gesneriaceae. The gesneriads are perennials, usually tropical or subtropical, grown for attractive flowers or foliage. Although a few are rock garden perennials, most are grown as houseplants. African violet *(Saintpaulia)* and gloxinia *(Sinningia)* are examples.

GEUM

Geum chiloense

Rosaceae

PERENNIALS

ZONES 2–24, EXCEPT AS NOTED

PARTIAL SHADE IN HOTTEST CLIMATES

REGULAR WATER

Double, semidouble, or single flowers in bright orange, yellow, or red over long season (spring to late summer) if dead blooms are removed. Handsome foliage, with leaves divided into many leaflets; evergreen except in coldest winters. Good in borders and for cut flowers. Ordinary garden soil; need good drainage. Grow from seed sown in early spring, or divide plants in autumn or early spring.

G. chiloense. Native to Chile. Foliage mounds to 15 in. high, 2 ft. wide. Leafy flowering stems to 2 ft. high carry flowers about 1½ in. across. Varieties include 'Fire Opal', with semidouble orange-scarlet blooms; double yellow 'Lady Stratheden'; double scarlet 'Mrs. Bradshaw'; and double copper 'Princess Juliana'. Hybrid 'Georgenberg', to 12–15 in. high and wide, has light yellow-orange blooms.

G. coccineum. From the Balkans, Asia Minor. To 12–20 in. tall and wide, with coarsely divided foliage and brick red, 1½-in. flowers. 'Borisii' is a compact (1- by 1-ft.) variety with bright orange-red flowers. Use in rock garden or front of border. 'Red Wings', to 28 in. tall and broad, has semidouble scarlet flowers.

G. 'Starker's Magnificum'. To 1½ ft. high and wide, with double flowers in tangerine orange over a long season.

G. triflorum. PRAIRIE SMOKE, OLD MAN'S WHISKERS. Zones 1–3. Native to North America. Foot-wide leafy mound produces stems to 20 in. tall, each bearing clusters of nodding maroon flowers. Entire plant is often furry. Seeds have long, feathery gray "tails."

GHOST GUM. See EUCALYPTUS papuana, E. pauciflora

GIANT GARLIC. See GARLIC

GIANT MEXICAN LEMON HYSSOP. See AGASTACHE mexicana

GIANT REED. See ARUNDO donax

GIANT SEQUOIA. See SEQUOIADENDRON giganteum

GILIA

Gilia capitata

Polemoniaceae

ANNUALS

ZONES 1–24

FULL SUN

LITTLE TO MODERATE WATER

Western natives related to phlox. Slender plants with finely cut leaves and colorful flowers from late spring to early fall. Useful in wild garden or borders. In fall or early spring, sow seeds in well-drained soil where plants are to grow. Thin seedlings to avoid crowding.

G. aggregata. See Ipomopsis aggregata

G. capitata. BLUE THIMBLE FLOWER. Native from British Columbia to California. Grows 8–30 in. tall, to 8 in. wide. Pale blue to violet-blue flowers with blue pollen are carried in dense, ½–1½-in.-wide clusters that look like pincushions.

G. rubra. See Ipomopsis rubra

G. tricolor. BIRD'S EYES. Native to California. To 10–20 in. high, 8 in. wide. Flowers, carried singly or in clusters of two to five, are ½ in. wide or wider; pale to deep violet with yellow throat spotted purple; blue pollen.

GINGER. See ZINGIBER officinale

GINGER, WILD. See ASARUM

GINGER LILY. See HEDYCHIUM

GINKGO biloba

MAIDENHAIR TREE

Ginkgoaceae

DECIDUOUS TREE

ZONES A3; 1–10, 12, 14–24

FULL SUN

MODERATE TO REGULAR WATER

Ginkgo biloba

Ancient survivor from prehistoric times (200 million years ago), when it grew worldwide; now native only to two small areas in China. Graceful tree, attractive in any season, especially in fall when leathery light green leaves of spring and summer suddenly turn gold (they practically glow when backlit by the sun). Leaves hang on for a time, then drop quickly and cleanly to make golden carpet where they fall. Related to conifers but differs in having broad (1–4-in.-wide), fan-shaped leaves rather than needlelike foliage. In shape and veining, leaves resemble leaflets of maidenhair fern, hence tree's common name. Can grow to 70–80 ft. tall, but most mature trees are 35–50 ft. May be gawky in youth, but becomes well proportioned with age—narrow to spreading or even umbrella shaped. Typical width is no more than one-half to two-thirds of height. Usually grows slowly, about 1 ft. a year, but under ideal conditions can grow up to 3 ft. a year.

Plant male trees (grafted or grown from cuttings of male plants); female trees produce messy, fleshy, ill-smelling fruit in quantity. Named varieties listed below are male. Use as street tree, lawn tree. Plant in deep, loose, well-drained soil. Be sure nursery plants are not root-bound. Young growth may be brittle, but wood becomes strong with age. In general, ginkgos are not bothered by insects or diseases, and they're very tolerant of air pollution, heat, and acid or alkaline conditions. Resistant to oak root fungus. Water young trees regularly until they reach about 20 ft. tall, then cut back to occasional irrigation. On young trees, cut back any awkward branches and vertical shoots growing parallel to central leader. Older trees need minimal pruning; just remove weak, broken, or dead branches.

'Autumn Gold'. Upright to 40 ft., eventually rather broad and spreading to about 30 ft.

'Fairmount'. Fast-growing, pyramidal form similar to 'Princeton Sentry'.

'Princeton Sentry'. Erect to 50 ft. high; 20-ft. spread at base, tapering toward top.

'Saratoga'. Similar to 'Autumn Gold', with a distinct central leader.

GLADIOLUS

Iridaceae

PERENNIALS FROM CORMS

ZONES 4–9, 12–24, H1, EXCEPT AS NOTED; OR DIG AND STORE

FULL SUN

REGULAR WATER DURING GROWTH AND BLOOM

Gladiolus callianthus

All have sword-shaped leaves and tubular, often flaring or ruffled flowers in unbranched or branching, usually one-sided spikes. Extremely wide color range. Bloom from spring to fall, depending on kind of gladiolus and planting time. Superb cut flowers. Good in borders or beds behind mounding plants that cover lower parts of stems, or in large containers with low annuals at base.

Plant corms of baby gladiolus in fall or early spring for flowers in late spring. Plant all others from midwinter (in mildest regions) into spring, after soil has warmed. Grandiflora hybrids will flower about 100 days after planting; the smaller hybrids and species will bloom in about 80 days. For an extended flowering season, plant at 1- to 2-week intervals over a period of 4 to 6 weeks. Where growing season is long enough, gardeners often time plantings so that bloom will be over before onset of hottest weather, when thrips can seriously disfigure the flowers. That means planting from January through March in Zones 7–9, 14–24, H1; April through June in Zones 4–6; and November through January in Zones 12, 13.

Start off with corms that are high crowned for their width; broad, flat ones are older and less vigorous. Best planted in rich, sandy loam. Set corms about four times deeper than their height; plant somewhat more shallowly in heavier soils. Space big corms 6 in. apart, smaller ones 4 in. apart. You can cut flower spikes when lowest buds begin to open; keep at least four leaves on plants to build up corms.

Corms can be left in the ground from year to year where plants are perennial. After blossoms fade, trim off stems beneath lowest flower—uncut stems will set seeds, diverting energy from food storage. In colder areas, dig after foliage yellows completely (in rainy areas, dig while leaves are still green to avoid botrytis infection). Dry corms on a flat surface in a dark, dry area for 2 to 3 weeks; then store over winter in a single layer in flats or ventilated trays in a cool place (40 to 50°F/4 to 10°C).

Baby gladiolus. Zones 4–9, 12–24, H1 for most; also Zones 2b, 3 for winter-hardy types. Hybrid race resulting from breeding red-flowered *G. colvillei* with other species. Flaring, 2½–3¼-in. flowers in short, loose spikes on 1½-ft. stems in late spring. Flowers may be white, pink, red, or lilac, either solid or blotched with contrasting color. When left in the ground in borders or among shrubs, these glads will form large clumps.

Butterfly gladiolus. See Primulinus and butterfly hybrids

G. callianthus (Acidanthera bicolor). ABYSSINIAN SWORD LILY. Native to Africa. In late summer and fall, each 2–3-ft. stem bears two to ten fragrant, creamy white flowers with chocolate brown markings on lower segments. Blossoms are 2–3 in. wide, 4–5 in. long. 'Murielae' is taller, with purple-crimson blotches.

G. communis byzantinum (G. byzantinus). BYZANTINE GLADIOLUS. From southern Europe. Summer bloom of mainly maroon, sometimes reddish or coppery, 1–3-in. flowers in groups of 6–12 on 2–3-ft. stems. Narrower leaves than grandiflora hybrids.

Grandiflora hybrid Gladiolus

Grandiflora hybrids. GARDEN GLADIOLUS. These are the best-known gladiolus, producing spikes that reach from 3 to 6 ft. high depending on variety and growing conditions. Late spring and summer flowers (up to 30 per spike) are widely flaring, up to 8 in. across; colors include white, cream, yellow, orange, apricot, salmon, red, rose, lavender, purple, smoky shades, buff, and even green. More diminutive selections from grandiflora breeding are grouped as small and miniature gladiolus; these grow 3–4 ft. high, stand upright without staking, and bear up to eighteen 2½–3-in.-wide flowers per spike. Though perennial, grandiflora hybrids are usually dug and stored yearly even in mild-winter regions.

Primulinus and butterfly hybrids. These summer bloomers derive in part from *G. dalenii* (formerly *G. primulinus*), an African species with hooded (rather than funnel-shaped), primrose yellow flowers. Named varieties grow 3–4 ft. tall, each spike carrying up to 18 widely spaced, somewhat hooded blossoms in a wide range of colors. Group known as butterfly gladiolus has 2–3-ft. stems bearing more closely spaced

Butterfly hybrid Gladiolus

blossoms; distinct throat markings or blotches of contrasting color give butterfly appearance.

G. tristis. Native to South Africa. Dainty species with 2½–3-in. flowers on slender, 1½-ft. stems in summer. Creamy to yellowish white blossoms are veined with purple, fragrant at night. *G. t. concolor* has soft yellow to nearly white flowers.

GLAUCIUM

HORNED POPPY, SEA POPPY

Papaveraceae

BIENNIALS AND PERENNIALS, OFTEN GROWN AS ANNUALS

ZONES VARY BY SPECIES

FULL SUN

MODERATE WATER

ROOTS ARE POISONOUS IF INGESTED

Glaucium flavum

Gray-green leaves are lobed or finely cut. Cup-shaped, four-petaled, 2-in. flowers are individually short lived, but they keep coming during summer bloom season. Flowers are followed by unusually long (to 1 ft.), slender seed capsules. Sow seeds in place in fall or early spring.

G. corniculatum. Biennial grown as annual. Zones 2–24. From Europe, southwest Asia. Grows 1–1½ ft. high and as wide. Orange-red flowers with dark spot at base.

G. flavum. Perennial or biennial. Zones 8–24; anywhere as annual. From Europe, Canary Islands, North Africa, Turkey. Grows 1–3 ft. tall, 1½ ft. wide. Orange to brilliant yellow flowers look varnished. Cut back to new basal leaves yearly.

GLECHOMA hederacea (Nepeta hederacea)

GROUND IVY

Lamiaceae (Labiatae)

PERENNIAL

ZONES A2, A3; 1–10, 14–24

SUN OR SHADE

REGULAR WATER

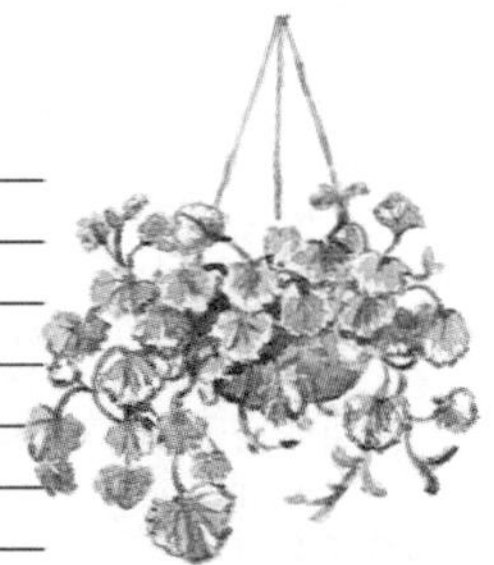

Glechoma hederacea

From Europe; naturalized in North America. Trailing plant with neat pairs of round, scallop-edged bright green or white-bordered leaves 1½ in. across, spaced along stems. Small, trumpet-shaped blue flowers in spring and summer are not especially showy. Sometimes planted as small-scale ground cover or used to trail from hanging baskets. To 3 in. high, with stems trailing to 1½ ft., rooting at joints. Can become a pest in lawns.

GLEDITSIA triacanthos

HONEY LOCUST

Fabaceae (Leguminosae)

DECIDUOUS TREE

ZONES 1–16, 18–20

FULL SUN

MODERATE TO REGULAR WATER

Gleditsia triacanthos

Native to central and eastern North America. Fast growing to 35–70 ft. tall and 25–35 ft. wide, with upright trunk and spreading, arching branches. Bright green, fernlike leaves to 10 in. long are divided into many oval, ¾–1½-in.-long leaflets. Late to leaf out; leaves turn yellow before dropping early in autumn. Inconspicuous flowers followed by broad, 1–1½-ft.-long pods filled with sweetish pulp (edible but insipid) and hard, roundish seeds.

Gleditsia triacanthos

Foliage casts filtered shade, allowing growth of lawn or other plants beneath tree's canopy. Small leaflets dry up and filter into grass, decreasing raking chores. Not good in narrow area between curb and sidewalk, since roots on old plants will heave pavement. Tolerant of acid or alkaline conditions, salt, drought, cold, heat, wind. Does best in areas with sharply defined winters, hot summers. Prune out any wayward or crossing branches. Mimosa webworm (chews leaves) and pod gall midge (deforms foliage) are main pests. Additionally, honey locust borer (tunnels into limbs and trunks) may attack stressed tree.

Trunks and branches of the species are formidably thorny, and its pods make a mess. Selections of its thornless form *G. t. inermis* are better choices for gardens, normally have few or no pods.

'Halka'. Fast growing. Forms sturdy trunk early, has strong horizontal branching pattern. Can bear a heavy crop of seedpods.

'Imperial'. Tall, spreading, symmetrical tree to about 35 ft. More densely foliaged than other forms; gives heavier shade.

'Moraine'. MORAINE LOCUST. Best-known garden selection. Graceful, spreading, and fast-growing tree with branches angled upward, then outward. Subject to wind breakage.

'Rubylace'. Deep red new growth. Subject to wind breakage.

'Shademaster'. More upright and faster growing than 'Moraine'—to 24 ft. tall, 16 ft. wide in 6 years.

'Skyline'. Pyramidal and symmetrical.

'Sunburst'. Golden yellow new foliage; showy against background of deep green. Defoliates easily in response to temperature changes, drought. Subject to wind breakage.

'Trueshade'. Rounded head of light green foliage.

GLOBE AMARANTH. See GOMPHRENA

GLOBEFLOWER. See TROLLIUS

GLOBE THISTLE. See ECHINOPS

GLOBE TULIP. See CALOCHORTUS

GLOBULARIA

GLOBE DAISY

Globulariaceae

EVERGREEN SHRUBS

ZONES VARY BY SPECIES

FULL SUN

MODERATE WATER

Globularia × indubia

Globe daisies are mat-forming or mounding plants with leathery dark green leaves. Their small lavender-blue flowers are gathered into tight, round heads on stalks standing above the foliage mound. They are not true daisies, although the flower heads resemble rayless daisies or small powder puffs.

G. cordifolia. Zones 3–9, 14–24. From mountains of central and southern Europe. To 5 in. tall and a foot wide, with creeping, rooting stems. Summer bloom. Good in rock gardens.

G. × indubia. Zones 8, 9, 14–24. To 1–2 ft. tall, 5 ft. wide. Blooms in summer and fall. Tough plant; good for hot, dry banks.

GLORIOSA DAISY. See RUDBECKIA hirta

A PRACTICAL GUIDE TO GARDENING
PLEASE SEE PAGES 658–731

GLORIOSA superba 'Rothschildiana' (G. rothschildiana)

GLORY LILY, CLIMBING LILY

Liliaceae

PERENNIAL FROM TUBER

ZONES 24; H1, H2; OR GROW IN POTS

LIGHT SHADE IN HOTTEST CLIMATES

REGULAR WATER DURING GROWTH AND BLOOM

ALL PARTS ARE POISONOUS IF INGESTED

Gloriosa superba 'Rothschildiana'

Lily relative native to tropical Africa and Asia. A tendril at the tip of each tapering, lance-shaped, 5–7-in. leaf wraps around any handy support, helping plant climb to 6 ft. In summer, top part of plant bears flashy 4-in. blossoms, each with six recurved, wavy-edged segments in brilliant red banded with yellow.

Can survive outdoors all year in completely frost-free areas, but even there is best grown in pots. For appearance of permanent planting, sink containers into garden bed. Set tubers horizontally, one to a container (pot should be at least 8 in. in diameter), about 4 in. deep in rich, loose soil mix. Start indoors or in greenhouse in winter; set out after frosts. Give climbing stems support from trellis, wires, string, or even loose-growing shrubs. Feed with liquid fertilizer every 3 weeks. Withhold water and fertilizer when leaves begin to yellow and die back in fall. Sever dead stems and move pots to dry, cool spot for winter. In late winter, knock tubers out of containers; repot in fresh soil mix. Or dig tubers from pots in fall and store.

GLORYBOWER. See **CLERODENDRUM**

GLORY-OF-THE-SNOW. See **CHIONODOXA**

GLOXINIA. See **SINNINGIA speciosa**

GNAPHALIUM sandwicensium sandwicensium

'ENA 'ENA

Asteraceae (Compositae)

PERENNIAL

ZONES H1, H2

FULL SUN

MODERATE WATER

Gnaphalium sandwicensium sandwicensium

Native to nearly every island of Hawaii, this herbaceous, clumping perennial grows from sea level to high elevations. Valued for silvery green, hairy leaves to about 4 in. long and for small size of foliage clumps (4–5 in. high and wide). Foliage has a strong balsamlike fragrance. Clusters of brownish flowers with yellow bracts are unremarkable; some gardeners pinch off stalks (which can reach 1½ ft. tall) as they appear to keep plant looking neat. Needs well-drained soil. Good in borders and rock gardens.

GOAT'S BEARD. See **ARUNCUS**

GODETIA. See **CLARKIA**

GOLD DUST PLANT. See **AUCUBA japonica 'Variegata'**

GOLDEN BALL LEAD TREE. See **LEUCAENA retusa**

GOLDEN BRODIAEA. See **TRITELEIA ixioides**

GOLDENCHAIN TREE. See **LABURNUM**

GOLDEN CUP. See **HUNNEMANNIA fumariifolia**

GOLDEN DEWDROP. See **DURANTA erecta**

GOLDEN EARDROPS. See **DICENTRA chrysantha**

GOLDEN FLEECE. See **THYMOPHYLLA tenuiloba**

GOLDEN GARLIC. See **ALLIUM moly**

GOLDEN GLOBES. See **LYSIMACHIA congestiflora**

GOLDEN LARCH. See **PSEUDOLARIX amabilis**

GOLDEN MARGUERITE. See **ANTHEMIS tinctoria**

GOLDENRAIN TREE. See **KOELREUTERIA paniculata**

GOLDENROD. See **SOLIDAGO**

GOLDEN SHOWER. See **CASSIA fistula**

GOLDEN TRUMPET. See **ALLAMANDA cathartica**

GOLDEN TRUMPET TREE. See **TABEBUIA chrysotricha**

GOLDEN WONDER SENNA. See **SENNA splendida**

GOLDFISH PLANT. See **NEMATANTHUS**

COLD FLOWER. See **HYPERICUM × moserianum**

GOLD MEDALLION TREE. See **CASSIA leptophylla**

GOMPHRENA

GLOBE AMARANTH

Amaranthaceae

ANNUALS AND PERENNIALS GROWN AS ANNUALS

ZONES 1–24; H1, H2

FULL SUN OR PARTIAL SHADE

MODERATE WATER

Gomphrena globosa

Stiffly branching plants to 2 ft. tall, 1 ft. wide, covered in summer and fall with rounded, papery, cloverlike heads ¾–1 in. wide. These may be dried quickly and easily, retaining color and shape for winter arrangements. Narrow oval leaves are 2–4 in. long.

G. globosa. Annual. From Central America. White, pink, lavender, or purple flower heads on 1–2-ft. stems. 'Strawberry Fields' has hot red, ½-in. blossoms on 2-ft. stems. Dwarf varieties for use as edging or bedding plants include 9-in. 'Buddy' (purple) and 'Cissy' (white). All types can be planted closely in large containers—six to a shallow 10-in. pot—for a long-lasting living bouquet.

G. haageana. Perennial treated as annual. From southern U.S., Mexico. Heads of tightly clustered bright orange bracts resembling inch-wide pinecones are borne on 2-ft. stems. Tiny yellow flowers peep from the bracts. Often sold as 'Haageana Aurea' or orange gomphrena.

GONIOLIMON tataricum (Limonium tataricum)

GERMAN STATICE

Plumbaginaceae

PERENNIALº

ZONES 2–21

FULL SUN, EXCEPT AS NOTED

MODERATE WATER

Goniolimon tataricum

From southern Russia, Caucasus. Dense clumps of dark green, narrowly oval leaves grow from a woody rootstock. In summer, leafless flower stalks rise to 1½ ft., forking repeatedly to form a broad, domed cluster to 1½ ft. wide. Tiny flowers are light purplish to white. Entire inflorescence can be dried for winter arrangements. Plant withstands both cold and heat. Best where summers are hot and dry. Needs partial shade in Zone 13.

Goodeniaceae. Members of this small family of perennials and shrubs—principally from the Southern Hemisphere, most notably Australia—have irregularly lipped flowers. Two of the more commonly grown members are *Dampiera* and *Scaevola.*

GOOSEBERRY

Grossulariaceae (Saxifragaceae)

DECIDUOUS SHRUBS

ZONES A1–A3, 1–6, 15–17, EXCEPT AS NOTED

SOME SHADE IN HOTTEST CLIMATES

REGULAR WATER

Gooseberry

Multistemmed plants to 3–5 ft. high and wide; varieties range from thorny to nearly spineless. Lobed, somewhat maplelike leaves usually turn bright colors in fall. Fruit is often decorative, marked with longitudinal stripes; ripens from late spring to summer and is used for pies, canning. Needs same growing conditions as currant; prune as for red and white currants. Like currant, prohibited in some areas where white pines grow; also subject to currant worm. Generally self-fruitful. Derived from several *Ribes* species; for strictly ornamental relatives, see *Ribes.*

Selection 'Captivator' has large, teardrop-shaped, sweet pink fruit on an extra-hardy, mildew-resistant, nearly thornless plant. 'Fredonia' is a fairly open grower producing large dark red fruit. 'Invicta' has large green fruit and is resistant to mildew. 'Oregon Champion' bears a heavy crop of green fruit. Pink-fruited 'Pixwell' is an extremely hardy, nearly thornless variety. 'Poorman' has red fruit sweet enough to eat off bush, though skin is tart. 'Welcome' bears medium-large, dull red, tart fruit on a productive, nearly spineless plant.

Jostaberries are disease-resistant black currant–gooseberry hybrids. Their black fruit tastes like currants but isn't as astringent; it makes great jams and jellies. Plants are less hardy than currants or gooseberries; they grow in Zones A3, 1–6, 15–17.

GOOSE PLANT. See ASCLEPIAS fruticosa

GOOSE PLUM. See PRUNUS americana

GOPHER PLANT. See EUPHORBIA lathyris

GORDONIA alatamaha. See FRANKLINIA alatamaha

GOSSYPIUM tomentosum

HAWAIIAN COTTON, MA'O

Malvaceae

EVERGREEN SHRUB

ZONE H2

FULL SUN

LITTLE WATER

Gossypium tomentosum

Native to Hawaii and adapted to hot, dry areas. Spreading shrub grows to 3–6 ft. high and equally as wide. Pure yellow, 2–3-in.-wide flowers are produced much of the year and show off nicely against the attractive silvery green, maplelike leaves. Seed capsules have brown fuzzy seeds with short cottony hairs. This plant is not grown commercially for cotton fiber but used in breeding of disease- and insect-resistant commercial cotton plants. Good as specimen shrub, informal hedge, or high ground cover. Performs best in well-drained soil.

FOR INFORMATION ON YOUR CLIMATE ZONE
PLEASE SEE PAGES 27–63

GOURD

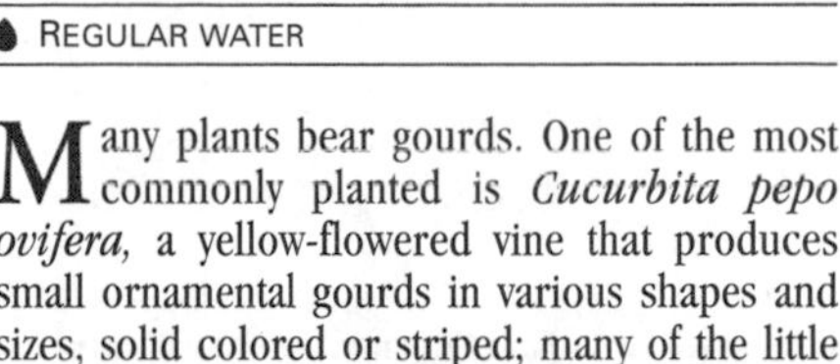

Cucurbitaceae

ANNUAL VINES

ALL ZONES

FULL SUN

REGULAR WATER

Gourd

Many plants bear gourds. One of the most commonly planted is *Cucurbita pepo ovifera,* a yellow-flowered vine that produces small ornamental gourds in various shapes and sizes, solid colored or striped; many of the little gourds you see in stores likely come from this plant. *Luffa cylindrica (L. aegyptiaca),* called dishcloth gourd or vegetable sponge gourd, is another yellow-flowered plant; it bears cylindrical, 1–2-ft.-long fruits with a fibrous interior that, when dried, may be used in place of a sponge or cloth for scrubbing or bathing. *Lagenaria siceraria (L. vulgaris),* white-flowered gourd, produces fruits from 3 in. to 3 ft. long, in round, crooknecked, coiled, bottle, dumbbell, or spoon shapes.

All gourd vines grow fast and will reach 10–15 ft. Sow seeds when ground is warm; start indoors if growing season is short. Gourds need all the summer heat they can get to develop fruit by frost. If planting for ornamental gourd harvest, give vines wire or trellis support to hold ripening fruits off ground. Set out transplants or thin seedlings to 2 ft. apart. You can harvest gourds when tendrils next to their stems are dead, but it's best to leave them on the vine as long as possible—until the gourds turn yellow or brown. They can even stay on the vine through frosts, but a heavy frost can discolor them. Cut each gourd with some stem attached, so you can hang it up to dry slowly in a cool, airy spot. When thoroughly dry, preserve with coating of paste wax, lacquer, or shellac.

GOUT WEED. See AEGOPODIUM podagraria

GRAMA GRASS. See BOUTELOUA

Gramineae. See Poaceae

GRANJENO. See CELTIS pallida

GRAPE

Vitaceae

DECIDUOUS VINES

ZONES VARY BY VARIETY

FULL SUN

MODERATE WATER

▶ SEE CHART PAGE 372

Grape

Grown for fresh fruit, wine, shade, and fall color. (For strictly ornamental types, see *Vitis.*) A single grapevine can produce enough new growth every year to arch over a walk, roof an arbor, form a leafy wall, or provide an umbrella of shade over deck or terrace. Grape is one of the few fruiting vines that offer bold textured foliage, colorful edible fruit, and a dominant trunk and branch pattern for winter interest. To produce good-quality fruit, you must choose a variety that suits your climate well, train it carefully, and prune it regularly.

There are several basic grape types. European grapes *(Vitis vinifera)* have tight skin, a generally high heat requirement, and cold tolerance to around 5°F/–15°C. These are the table grapes of the market, including 'Thompson Seedless'. The classic wine grapes, such as 'Cabernet', 'Chardonnay', and 'Pinot Noir', are also European in origin. Production of European wine grapes has greatly increased in the Northwest, but the bulk of the crop is grown in California. For information on growing wine grapes, consult your local Cooperative Extension Office.

▶ page 371

GRAPE PLANTING AND TRAINING

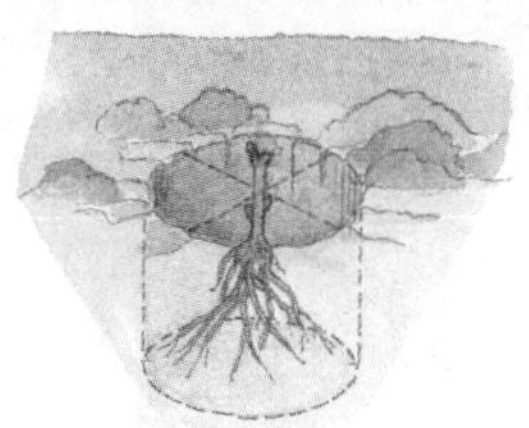

Planting. Set bare-root grapevine in front of a post at same depth as it grew in the nursery; cut the stem back to two buds. (In some areas, planting deeper and cutting to one bud are recommended; check locally.)

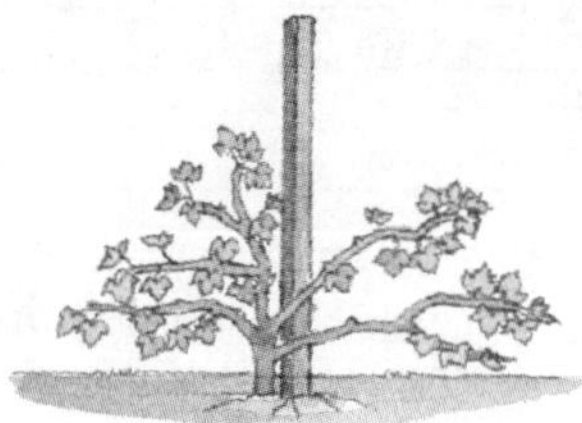

First Summer. Let the vine grow unchecked; don't try to train its growth. The more leaves, the better the root development.

First Winter. Select the sturdiest shoot for the trunk; remove all other shoots at their base. Tie the trunk to the post; then shorten trunk to the three or four lowest buds.

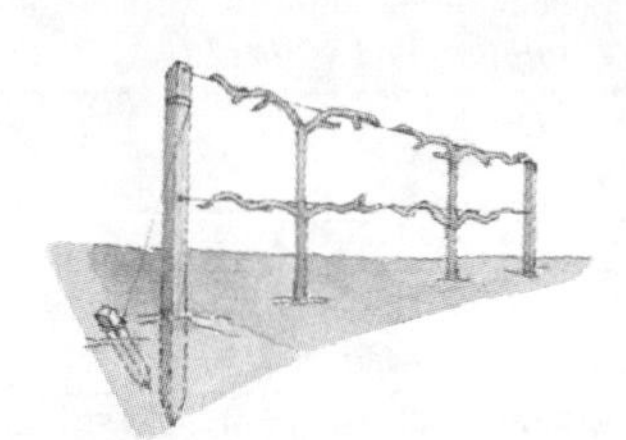

Two-wire Trellis. Set stout posts in the ground 15–20 ft. apart (farther apart for the more vigorous grapes, such as muscadines) so that their tops are 5 ft. above the ground. String sturdy galvanized wire across the post tops and also at the 2½-ft. level.

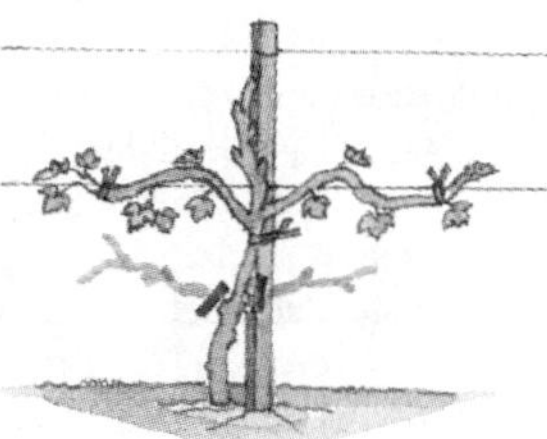

Second Spring. From the vigorous new shoots choose the strongest upright one for the continuation of the trunk; tie it to the post. Select two strong lower shoots for arms and tie them to the first wire. (If you don't have branching where you want it, pinch the trunk as needed to let new shoots develop.) Cut off all other shoots.

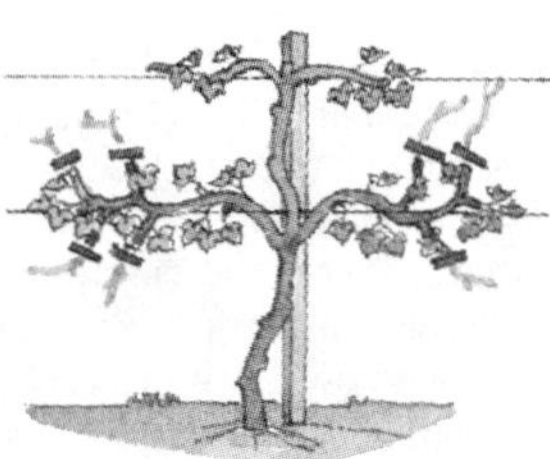

Second Summer. When the trunk reaches the top wire, pinch it back to force branching. Train the two strongest shoots along the top wire; remove any others. Tie the lower arms along the lower wire; pinch back any lateral shoots developing from those arms to about 10 in.

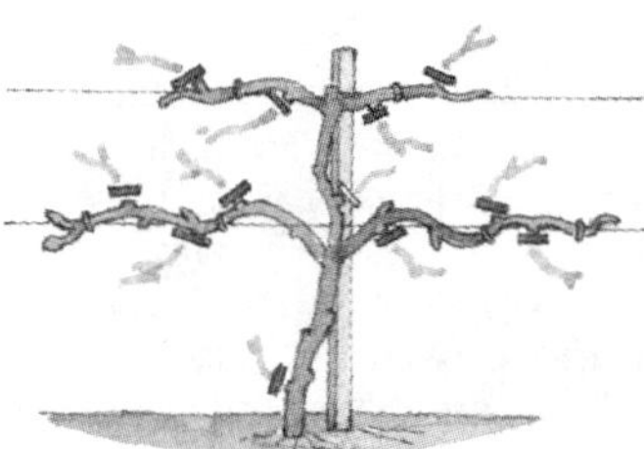

Second Winter. Cut back all growth on the trunk and arms; make sure both sets of arms are loosely tied to the wire. Don't prune yet for fruit production; vines are too immature.

Third Summer. Allow the vine to grow, but remove any shoots sprouting on the trunk. Cane pruning and spur pruning differ from here on.

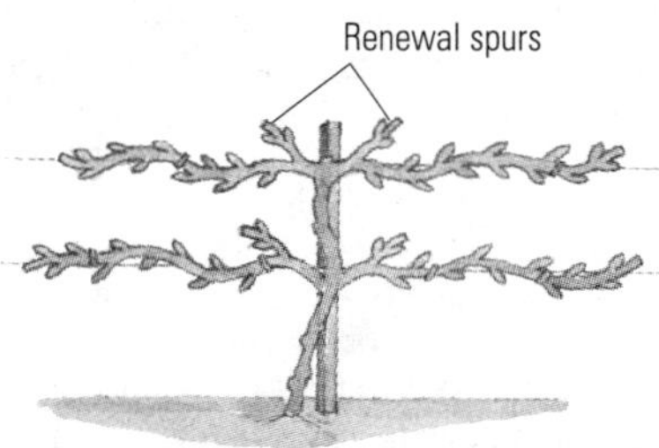

Cane Pruning from Third Winter. Cut back each arm to 12 buds; these will bear fruit the next summer. Select two strong lateral shoots near the trunk and cut each to two buds; these are the renewal spurs. During next winter and every winter thereafter, remove the fruiting canes at their base. The renewal spurs will have produced several new shoots from which new fruiting canes can be selected. Choose the two longest and strongest shoots and cut each to 12 buds; tie these shoots to the wire. Select the two next best shoots as renewal spurs and cut each to two buds.

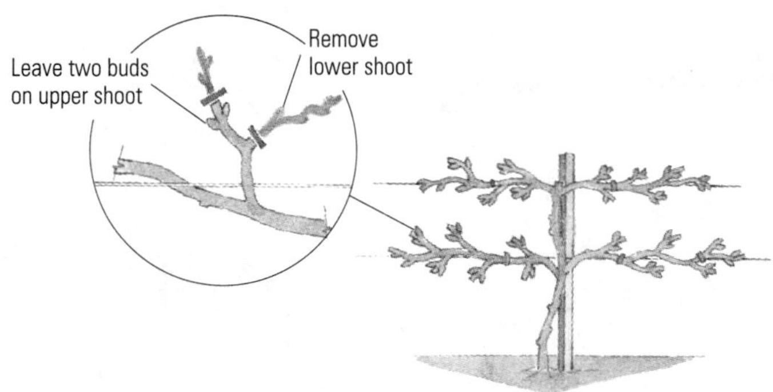

Spur Pruning from Third Winter. Remove weak side shoots from the arms. Leave the strongest shoots (spurs) spaced 6–10 in. apart, and cut each to two buds. Each spur will produce two fruit-bearing shoots during the next growing season. During next winter and every winter thereafter, remove the lower shoot on each spur and cut the upper stem to two buds. Those buds will develop into stems that bear fruit the following summer.

American grapes stem from *V. labrusca,* with some influence from other American native species. These are slipskin grapes of the 'Concord' type, which have a moderate summer heat requirement (as opposed to high heat needs of European table grapes) and tolerate temperatures well below 0°F/–18°C. American grapes are used in jelly, in unfermented grape juice, and as a flavoring for soft drinks; some wine, usually sweet, is also made from these grapes.

Hybrid grape varieties have characteristics intermediate between those of their parents. In general, these vines are almost as disease resistant and hardy as American species (most will need protection below –15°F/ –26°C), but the fruit is more like that of European grapes. Varieties called French hybrids—examples include 'Aurore', 'Seyval Blanc', 'Foch', and 'Baco Noir'—can be used for making wine in cold-winter climates. Consult your Cooperative Extension Office for varieties that will grow best locally.

Almost all grapes are self-fruitful and do not require pollination from another variety to bear fruit—but since they differ greatly in hardiness and heat requirements, choosing the right type and variety is important. Varieties listed in the chart, beginning on the following page, are widely available and of high quality where adapted, but they represent only a small portion of what can be grown.

The Pacific Northwest is primarily American grape country, but there are many opportunities to grow European grapes as well; the warmest parts of the Columbia River basin are the best European grape–growing areas there. Regions of California and Arizona with a long warm season favor European varieties; California's coastal and inland valleys offer an ideal climate for most types. In short-season, high-elevation areas, choose either American or hardy European varieties, and plant in warm microclimates. If your climate is cooler or growing season shorter than is desirable for grape growing, look for early-ripening varieties.

The popularity of European grapes, especially wine varieties, has led to their being tried beyond their normal range. In cold-winter climates, the crop may be ruined by spring frosts and summer rains in some years, but vines that are protected or planted in warm microclimates can produce harvestable fruit in other years. Even in Hawaii, European wine grapes are being successfully grown in some high-elevation areas. At lower elevations, where grapes are ravaged by the hard-to-control Chinese rose beetle, crops are rarely successful.

Once they are established, grape vines grow rampantly. If all you want is a leafy cover for an arbor or patio, you need only train a strong vine up and over its support and thin out entangling growth each year. But most people plant grapes for the fruit, even if they want shade as well. To prepare vines for good fruit production, you will need to follow more careful pruning procedures.

Grapes are produced on stems that develop from 1-year-old wood—stems that formed in the previous season. These 1-year-old stems have smooth bark, whereas older stems have rough, shaggy bark. The purpose of pruning is to limit the amount of potential fruiting wood to ensure that the plant doesn't produce too much fruit and that the fruit it does bear is of good quality.

There are several pruning methods for grapes. The two most widely used are spur pruning and cane pruning; see chart for recommended method for each variety. Either technique can be used for training grapes on arbors. Whichever method you choose, the initial steps (planting and creating a framework) are the same; see illustrations on the opposite page for details. Pruning should be done in the dormant season—that is, in winter or earliest spring before the buds swell.

Pierce's disease, caused by a bacterium spread by the sharpshooter insect, is a serious threat to grapes in California. It causes afflicted vines to lose productivity, wilt, and die in a matter of only a season or two. For more information, contact your Cooperative Extension Office.

The grape leafhopper may cause leaf drop on grapevines in California. Get rid of nearby weeds, which may harbor the pest. Spraying with insecticidal soap is somewhat effective; grape leafhopper infestations are rarely serious enough to warrant a stronger pesticide. Grape mealybug may infest vines in the Northwest and parts of California; control with horticultural oil spray in late winter.

Powdery mildew is a serious disease of European grapes (most American varieties are immune). To control, dust vines with sulfur when shoots are 6 in. long, again when they are 12–15 in., then every 2 weeks until harvest. Vines growing near lawns may need additional dustings.

WHAT GRAPES NEED

SOIL: Deep, fertile, well-drained sandy loam is ideal.

AIR CIRCULATION: Free air movement is important. If you're on hilly terrain, it's better to plant on a slope than in a low-lying basin, where trapped air increases danger from frost or mildew.

PRUNING: High-quality crop depends on initial training and regular dormant-season pruning (see opposite page).

HARVESTING: Cut bunches from vines in late summer or fall, when grapes are sweet and fully colored.

'Black Monukka', European

GRAPEFRUIT. See **CITRUS**

GRAPE HYACINTH. See **MUSCARI**

GRAPE IVY. See **CISSUS rhombifolia, C. trifoliata**

GRASSES. The grasses in this book are either lawn or ornamental plants—except for corn, the only cereal commonly grown in home gardens. They are described under entries headed by their botanical names; to find these, check lists below. (Bamboos, which are grasses, are charted under Bamboo.)

Lawn grasses include *Agropyron,* wheatgrass; *Agrostis,* bent grass, redtop; *Bouteloua,* blue grama; *Buchloe,* buffalo grass; *Cynodon,* Bermuda grass; *Festuca,* fescue; *Lolium,* ryegrass; *Paspalum,* seashore paspalum; *Poa,* bluegrass; *Stenotaphrum,* St. Augustine grass; *Zoysia,* zoysia.

Ornamental grasses include *Achnatherum,* Indian rice grass; *Alopecurus,* yellow foxtail grass; *Andropogon,* big bluestem, turkeyfoot; *Arrhenatherum,* bulbous oat grass; *Arundo,* giant reed; *Bouteloua,* grama grass; *Briza,* rattlesnake grass; *Calamagrostis,* reed grass; *Chasmanthium,* sea oats; *Coix,* Job's tears; *Cortaderia,* pampas grass; *Deschampsia,* hair grass; *Elymus,* wheatgrass; *Festuca,* fescue; *Hakonechloa,* Japanese forest grass; *Helictotrichon,* blue oat grass; *Imperata,* Japanese blood grass; *Leymus,* lyme grass; *Milium,* golden grass; *Miscanthus,* eulalia, silver grass; *Molinia,* moor grass; *Muhlenbergia,* including bamboo muhly, deer grass; *Nassella,* needle grass; *Panicum,* switch grass; *Pennisetum,* fountain grass; *Phalaris,* ribbon grass; *Rhynchelytrum,* ruby grass; *Spartina,* prairie cord grass; and *Stipa,* feather grass.

GRASS NUT. See **TRITELEIA laxa**

GRASS TREE. See **NOLINA, XANTHORRHOEA**

GREASEWOOD. See **ADENOSTOMA fasciculatum**

GRECIAN LAUREL. See **LAURUS nobilis**

GREEN CARPET. See **HERNIARIA glabra**

GREEN LAVENDER. See **LAVANDULA viridis**

FOR GROWING SYMBOL EXPLANATIONS
PLEASE SEE PAGE 161

G

G

GRAPE

VARIETY	ZONES	SEASON	PRUNING	COMMENTS
AMERICAN and AMERICAN HYBRID VARIETIES				
'Alden'	6–22	Early midseason	Spur	Large, firm, seeded reddish blue grape with light muscat flavor. Good for fresh eating, juice, wine. Very productive. Good fall leaf color
'America'	7–22	Midseason	Cane or spur	Seeded blue grape with intense flavor. Good for juice, fresh eating, wine. Resistant to Pierce's disease
'Black Spanish' ('Lenoir')	7–9, 11–24	Late midseason	Spur	Very old black grape. Small seeded fruit is fine for eating but best for wine and juice. Resistant to Pierce's disease
'Bluebell'	2–7	Early	Cane or spur	Seeded blue grape with a flavor like that of 'Concord'. Excellent for juice, good for eating fresh. Very hardy (to –35°F/–37°C). Grows in warm-summer areas but may taste flat there
'Buffalo'	2–7	Early	Cane or spur	Seeded black fruit with spicy flavor. Good for fresh eating or juice. Can produce secondary crop if frosted in spring
'Campbell Early'	5–22	Early midseason	Spur	Large, seeded black grape of 'Concord' type for fresh eating, juice. Colors before achieving full flavor
'Canadice'	2b–9, 11–21	Early	Spur	Seedless red fruit. Excellent for fresh eating or juice. Ripens in very cool areas, such as around Puget Sound. Overcrops easily; must be pruned hard or have crop thinned. Hardy to –20°F/–29°C if well pruned
'Champanel'	7 (warmer parts), 8, 9, 11–16, 18–24	Midseason	Cane	Seeded black grape. Good for juice, fresh eating. Tolerant of alkaline soil; resistant to Pierce's disease
'Concord'	2b, 3, 6–9, 14–23	Midseason	Cane or spur	Seeded blue fruit. Standard American slipskin for cooking, juice, jelly
'Edelweiss'	2–9, 14–21	Early	Cane or spur	Seeded white grape. Fresh eating or juice. Milder flavor than 'Niagara', but vine is more manageable. Flavor goes flat in hot-summer areas
'Golden Muscat' American hybrid	3b, 6–24	Late	Spur	Very large, juicy, seeded green-yellow fruit. Flavor is citruslike, not true muscat; good for eating fresh. Ripens 2 weeks after 'Concord'. Cracks in wet weather
'Himrod' American hybrid	3–9, 11–21	Very early	Cane	Seedless white fruit with spicy flavor. For fresh eating. Very vigorous, suited to arbors. Hardy to –15°F/–26°C

'Buffalo', American

'Canadice', American

'Concord', American

'Golden Muscat', American hybrid

GRAPE

VARIETY	ZONES	SEASON	PRUNING	COMMENTS
'Interlaken' American hybrid	2–9, 14–21	Very early	Cane or spur	Firm, seedless green or yellow grape with fruity flavor. Ripens a week earlier than 'Himrod'. One of few that matures in the coolest areas of Pacific Northwest. Excellent for fresh eating; only one for raisins in cool-summer areas
'Lakemont'	3, 6–22	Early	Cane or spur	Seedless white fruit with mild flavor; very productive. Fine table grape; keeps well in cold storage
'Mars'	4–9, 14–21	Early midseason	Cane or spur	Blue fruit; large for a seedless grape. Fine for fresh eating, juice, wine, raisins. Flavor improves after harvest
'New York Muscat'	2b–9, 14–21	Early	Cane or spur	Seeded blue grape with sweet muscat flavor. Excellent for fresh eating, juice, wine. Less vigorous than other varieties. Can be tried in hotter areas, but quality may suffer
'Niabell'	7–9, 14–16, 18–22	Early	Cane or spur	Large black grape similar to 'Concord' at its best. Excellent for arbors. Vigorous and productive in wide range of climates. Succeeds in hot interiors where 'Concord' fails
'Niagara'	2, 3, 6–10, 14–21	Midseason	Cane	Seedless green to pale yellow fruit. Good for fresh eating, juice, wine
'Price'	2–9, 14–21	Very early	Spur	Seeded blue grape. Sweet and juicy, with refined 'Concord'-type flavor. Very good for eating fresh and fine for juice. Ripens in coolest areas of range, even around Puget Sound. May even succeed in Zone 1 with cold protection
'Reliance' American hybrid	2b–9, 14–21	Early midseason	Spur	Seedless red grape with mild, sweet flavor. Good for fresh eating or juice. Dependably productive
'Swenson Red'	2–9, 14–21	Early	Spur	Firm, meaty, seeded red or red-blue grape with unique fruity flavor. Excellent for fresh eating, juice, wine
'Valiant'	A2, A3; 1–9	Early	Spur	Seeded blue fruit with 'Concord'-like flavor. Makes very good juice and jelly. Hardy to –50° F/–46°C
'Vanessa'	2–9, 14–21	Early	Cane	Firm, seedless red grape with fruity flavor. Resists cracking. Good replacement for European variety 'Flame' in cool-summer areas. Use for fresh eating or raisins
'Venus'	3–9, 14–21	Early midseason	Cane or spur	Seedless blue grape. Fruity, muscatlike flavor; fine choice for fresh eating or juice. Excellent fall color

'Himrod', American hybrid

'Lakemont', American

'Niagara', American

'Reliance', American hybrid

GRAPE

VARIETY	ZONES	SEASON	PRUNING	COMMENTS
EUROPEAN VARIETIES				
'Autumn Royal'	6–9, 11–16, 18–21	Midseason to late	Cane or spur	Large, seedless purplish black grape. Good for fresh eating or raisins
'Autumn Seedless'	6–9, 11–16, 18–21	Midseason	Cane or spur	Seedless pale green to golden grape. Good for fresh eating or raisins
'Black Monukka'	3, 6–16, 17 (warmer parts), 18–24	Early midseason	Cane or spur	Seedless purplish black fruit in large, loose clusters. Popular home variety. One of hardiest European grapes
'Crimson Seedless'	6–9, 12–16, 18–22	Late	Cane	Large, seedless red grape with excellent flavor. For fresh eating, raisins
'Delight'	6–9, 12–16, 17 (warmer parts), 18–24	Early	Spur	Large, seedless, dark greenish yellow. Good for fresh eating, raisins. Succeeds in mild-winter areas
'Early Muscat'	6–9, 11–16, 18–24	Early midseason	Spur	Seeded green fruit in large clusters. Excellent muscat flavor. Used for muscat wine in Northwest
'Fantasy'	6–9, 11–14, 18–21	Midseason	Cane	Large, seedless bluish black fruit with sweet, rich flavor. Good fresh or for wine. Vigorous; leave six to eight canes when pruning
'Flame'	6–9, 11–16, 17 (warmer parts), 18–24	Early midseason	Cane or spur	Seedless red grape. For fresh eating, raisins. Very vigorous. Keep on dry side to reduce vigor, encourage ripening
'Muscat' ('Muscat of Alexandria')	6–9, 11–16, 18–21	Late midseason	Spur	Large, rounded, seeded green to amber fruit. Renowned for sweet, musky, aged-in-the-vat flavor. Fine for fresh eating, juice, wine, raisins
'Muscat Hamburg'	6–9, 11–16, 18–21	Late midseason	Spur	Seeded black grape. Intense, almost orangelike muscat flavor. Good fresh or for wine
'Perlette'	6–9, 11–16, 17 (warmer parts), 18–24	Early	Spur	Pale yellow, seedless fruit. Earlier, larger, less sweet than 'Thompson Seedless'. Excellent fresh. Needs less heat than most European varieties
'Ribier'	7–9, 11–16, 18–21	Early midseason	Spur	Very large, seeded black grape with mild flavor. Good for fresh eating
'Ruby Seedless' ('King's Ruby')	7–9, 12–16, 18–24	Late midseason	Cane or spur	Large clusters of seedless red to reddish black fruit. Sweet dessert grapes. Very susceptible to powdery mildew
'Thompson Seedless'	7–14, 18, 19	Midseason	Cane	Big clusters of small, sweet, seedless greenish amber fruit. For fresh eating, raisins. Widely planted but does best in hot, dry areas

'Crimson Seedless'

'Flame'

'Perlette'

'Ribier'

'Ruby Seedless'

GREVILLEA

Proteaceae

EVERGREEN SHRUBS AND TREES

ZONES VARY BY SPECIES

EXPOSURE NEEDS VARY BY SPECIES

LITTLE OR NO WATER, EXCEPT AS NOTED

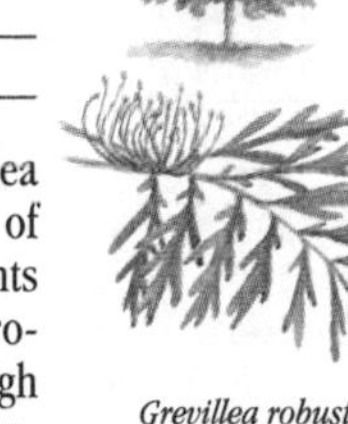

Grevillea robusta

Australia is home to a multitude of grevillea species (over 250) and hybrids; many of these have great garden merit, including plants not described here. Also watch for new introductions that often show up in nurseries. Though grevilleas vary in size and appearance, they generally have fine-textured foliage and long, slender, curved flowers, usually borne in dense clusters. Many cannot tolerate salt-laden soils, poor water quality, heavy summer irrigation, or heavy frost, but all are attractive enough to warrant some risk taking. Like other members of the protea family, they are sensitive to high levels of phosphorus in the soil. Fertilize lightly and avoid high-phosphorus fertilizers.

G. alpina. MOUNTAIN GREVILLEA. Shrub. Zones 15–24. Highly variable in size and form. Among most widely distributed is 'East Grampians', a low spreader (to 2½ ft. high and 5 ft. wide) with inch-long bright green leaves and masses of red-and-yellow flowers from fall through spring. Full sun or light shade.

G. asplenifolia. Shrub. Zones 15–24. To 9–15 ft. tall, 9–20 ft. wide, with foot-long leaves less than ½ in. wide. Deep red, 2½-in.-long flower clusters appear in late winter and spring. Showy in bloom and useful for screening. Takes sun but prefers partial shade.

G. australis. ALPINE GREVILLEA. Shrub. Zones 15, 16, 23, 24. Spreading or erect habit; reaches 1–7 ft. tall, 4–9 ft. wide. Narrow dark green to olive green leaves are ½–1 in. long. Cream-colored flowers—not showy, but powerfully fragrant—bloom in winter and spring. Full sun or partial shade.

G. banksii. Shrub or tree. Zones 16–24; H1. Often sold as *G. b.* 'Bushy Form' or 'Forsters'. To 9 ft. tall and 12 ft. wide, with 4–10-in.-long leaves deeply cut into narrow lobes. Erect, 3–6-in.-long clusters of dark red flowers appear sporadically all year but are most profuse in late spring. Showy used singly against high wall, near entryway, or grouped with other large-scale shrubs. Freezes at 24°F/–4°C; takes wind. Full sun. Little to regular water.

G. 'Boongalla Spinebill'. Shrub. Zones 15–24. Sprawling growth to 3–5 ft. high, 15 ft. wide. Deeply cut, 6-in.-long leaves are coppery when new, later turn deep green. Toothbrushlike clusters of red flowers bloom nearly all year, most heavily in late winter. Full sun or partial shade.

G. 'Canberra Gem' ('Canberra'). Shrub. Zones 8, 9, 12–24. Open, graceful growth to 8 ft. tall, 12 ft. wide. Needlelike, bright green, 1-in. leaves. Clusters of red flowers in spring (and intermittently at other times). Has been sold as 'Pink Pearl'. Full sun or partial shade.

G. 'Constance'. See G. 'Poorinda Constance'

G. curviloba. Shrub. Zones 14–24. Often sold as *G. tridentifera* or *G. biternata.* Variable habit; may reach 6 ft. high and 10–15 ft. across or grow as a low (2-ft.) spreader, also to 10–15 ft. wide. Finely divided bright green leaves; cream-colored, honey-scented blossoms in winter and spring. To use as ground or bank cover, prune out any stems that grow upright. Full sun or partial shade.

G. × gaudichaudii. Shrub. Zones 15–24; H1. Prostrate plant spreading 10–15 ft. wide. Lobed leaves resembling oak leaves are bronzy when they emerge, then mature to dark green. Toothbrushlike clusters of dark red flowers in winter and spring. Provide good drainage, moderate water. Takes sun but prefers partial shade. Tolerates extended wet periods.

G. 'Ivanhoe'. Shrub. Zones 14–24. Dense grower to 6–15 ft. tall and 9–15 ft. wide. Finely divided leaves to 6 in. long. Pinkish red flowers in toothbrushlike clusters form at branch tips in late winter, spring. Full sun or light shade.

G. lanigera. WOOLLY GREVILLEA. Shrub. Zones 15–24. Spreading, mounding growth to 3–6 ft. tall, 6–10 ft. across. Closely set, narrow, ½-in.-long leaves are covered with hairs that give foliage a grayish cast. Clusters of narrow, curved, crimson-and-cream flowers profuse in summer; attractive to hummingbirds. Good bank cover in hot, sunny area; good transition beween garden and wild area. 'Mt. Tamboritha' is a compact variety 2 ft. high and 4 ft. wide. Full sun or partial shade. Plants tolerate extended wet periods.

G. lavandulacea. LAVENDER GREVILLEA. Shrub. Zones 15–24. Variable, but all forms are dense growers with half-inch-long gray leaves. 'Billywing', to 2½ ft. high and 6 ft. wide, has red-and-cream flowers in winter and spring. 'Penola', to 5 ft. tall and 8 ft. wide (or larger), bears deep rose red blossoms fall through spring. 'Tanunda' is 1½–3 ft. high, 3–6 ft. wide, with profuse coral pink flowers; main show comes in winter, with occasional repeat bloom in midsummer. Tolerates light shade.

G. 'Long John'. Shrub. Zones 15–24. To 10 ft. tall and 15 ft. wide, with 8-in. leaves divided into many narrow lobes. Early spring brings a heavy display of pink-and-red flowers. Useful for screening. Full sun or partial shade.

G. 'Noellii'. Shrub. Zones 8, 9, 12–24. To 4 ft. tall, 4–5 ft. wide. Densely clad with narrow, 1-in.-long, glossy medium green leaves. Clusters of pink-and-white flowers bloom in spring. Full sun. Moderate water.

G. 'Poorinda Constance' ('Constance'). Shrub. Zones 8, 9, 12–24. Resembles 'Canberra Gem' in size and habit, but has broader leaves that are deep green above, almost white beneath. Bears large clusters of orange-red flowers in spring, often again in fall. Full sun.

Grevillea 'Noellii'

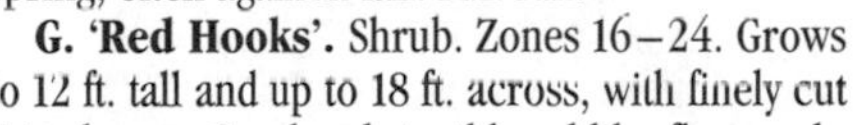

G. 'Red Hooks'. Shrub. Zones 16–24. Grows to 12 ft. tall and up to 18 ft. across, with finely cut 5-in. leaves. Coral red, toothbrushlike flower clusters from late winter to late spring, with a scattering at other times of year. Full sun or light shade.

G. robusta. SILK OAK. Tree. Zones 8, 9, 12–24; H1, H2. Weedy in parts of Hawaii. Fast growing to 50–60 ft. (rarely 100 ft.) tall. Young trees are symmetrical and pyramidal. Old ones are broad topped (30–35 ft. wide), usually with a few heavy, horizontal limbs; picturesque against skyline. Ferny leaves are golden green to deep green above, silvery beneath. Heavy leaf fall in spring, sporadic leaf drop throughout year. Large clusters of bright golden orange flowers in early spring. Wood is brittle and easily damaged in high winds. For sturdier branches, cut central leader back hard at planting time and shorten branches to well-balanced framework. Thrives in heat; one of lushest greens for low desert. Useful as quick, tall screen; can be clipped as tall hedge. Full sun. Grows in poor, dense soils if not overwatered; can take regular water in fast-draining soils. Young trees damaged at 24°F/–4°C; older ones hardy to 16°F/–9°C. Beyond hardiness range, sometimes grown as potted plant or houseplant and discarded when it gets too big.

G. 'Robyn Gordon'. Shrub. Zones 16–24. To 6–7 ft. tall and wide. Large (6–8-in.) light green leaves divided into many narrow segments. Pendent 6-in. clusters of bright red flowers are showy most of year. Full sun.

G. rosmarinifolia. ROSEMARY GREVILLEA. Shrub. Zones 8, 9, 12–24. To 6 ft. tall, nearly as broad. Narrow, 1½-in.-long leaves are dark green on top, silvery beneath; look somewhat like those of rosemary. Red-and-cream flower clusters (rarely pink or white) in fall and winter; scattered bloom in other seasons. Use as clipped or informal hedge in dryish places. Impervious to heat and aridity. A dwarf form, 3 ft. high and 6 ft. wide, bears pink-and-cream flowers in waves throughout the year, most heavily in spring and fall. 'Scarlet Sprite', another dwarf, is similar but bears blooms in bright red and cream. Full sun or partial shade.

G. 'Ruby Clusters'. Shrub. Zones 14–24. Dense growth to 6 ft. tall and broad, with narrow, 3-in.-long dark green leaves. Deep red flowers appear nearly nonstop throughout the year, with the heaviest show in early spring. Full sun or partial shade.

G. thelemanniana. HUMMINGBIRD BUSH, SPIDER-NET GREVILLEA. Shrub. Zones 9, 14–17, 19–24. Graceful, rounded habit 5–8 ft. high and wide. Dark green, 1–2-in.-long leaves divided into narrow segments. Clusters of bright red flowers tipped yellow can appear in any season. Airier, more open, less adapted to hedge and screen use than *G. rosmarinifolia.* Among the many forms is a dwarf gray-leafed selection 6 in. high and 6 ft. wide, useful for trailing over a wall or down a bank. Can be temperamental in Northern California; prefers dry, warm winters of Southern California. Full sun or partial shade.

G. victoriae. Shrub. Zones 8, 9, 14–24. Variable in size; the form most commonly seen is 6 ft. or taller and as wide, with gray-green, narrowly oval, 4-in. leaves and orange-red flowers in drooping clusters during spring and summer. Occasional summer water will prevent bud drop. Takes sun but prefers partial shade.

G. 'White Wings'. Shrub. Zones 15–24. To 6 ft. tall and spreading 10–15 ft. wide, with finely divided, 2-in.-long bright green leaves. Masses of fragrant white flowers appear in spring, with a scattering at other times. Good for bank or slope planting. Full sun or partial shade.

GREWIA occidentalis

LAVENDER STARFLOWER

Tiliaceae

EVERGREEN SHRUB

ZONES 8, 9, 12–24; H1, H2

FULL SUN

REGULAR WATER

Grewia occidentalis

Fast-growing, sprawling South African native can be used in various ways. Tends to branch freely in flat pattern, making a natural espalier if given the support of a warm, sunny wall or fence. Becomes dense with pinching and pruning. Unstaked, it grows 6–10 ft. tall (sometimes higher) with equal spread. Can be planted 4 ft. apart and used as tall clipped hedge or screen. If plant is allowed to sprawl and upright stems are removed, it can serve as a bank cover. Can be trained as a single-trunked tree or tied in place to cover arbor or trellis.

Dark green, oblong, finely toothed leaves 3 in. long. Star-shaped, inch-wide flowers are lavender pink with yellow centers. Blooms in late spring and sporadically into fall, especially if cut back lightly after first heavy bloom. Do any major pruning in fall after flowering is over. Tolerates wind.

GRISELINIA

Cornaceae

EVERGREEN SHRUBS

ZONES 9, 14–17, 20–24

FULL SUN OR PARTIAL SHADE

MODERATE TO REGULAR WATER

Griselinia littoralis

Native to New Zealand. Upright form and thick, leathery, lustrous green leaves. Flowers and fruit are insignificant. Always look well groomed. Good near swimming pools.

G. littoralis. A 50-ft. tree in New Zealand, but usually seen in the West as 10-ft.-high shrub of equal spread. Leaves roundish, to 4 in. long. With regular moisture, it can reach 8 ft. in 3 years. Dense, compact screen or windbreak. Fine beach plant, good espalier. 'Variegata' has leaves marked with cream.

G. lucida. Slower growing, a little smaller, more open and slender than *G. littoralis,* with larger (to 7-in.-long) leaves. Excellent foliage plant for partial shade. Thrives in containers. 'Variegata' has white markings on leaves.

GROUND CHERRY. See POHA

GROUND IVY. See GLECHOMA hederacea

GROUND MORNING GLORY. See CONVOLVULUS sabatius

GUADALUPE PALM. See BRAHEA edulis

GUAIACUM

Zygophyllaceae

EVERGREEN TREES OR SHRUBS

ZONES VARY BY SPECIES

FULL SUN OR LIGHT SHADE

MODERATE WATER

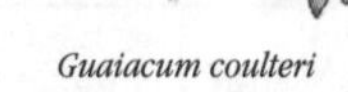

Guaiacum coulteri

Related to creosote bush *(Larrea tridentata)* and puncture vine (the weed *Tribulus terrestris*), the guaiacums belong to a small genus noted for hard, heavy wood and for producing resin.

G. coulteri. Zones 13, 23, 24. This Mexican native has light gray bark and dark green leaves divided into six to ten narrow, ½–1-in. leaflets. Clusters of deep blue-violet, ¾-in. flowers appear sporadically from spring through summer. Tolerates drought, but irrigation during dry periods will promote heavier bloom. Needs good drainage. Where subject to light frosts, plant tends to be shrubby, around 5–12 ft. high and wide. In a frost-free site, it can become a multitrunked tree to 20 ft. high and nearly as wide. Leaves and branch tips may be damaged by temperatures just below freezing point; prune out only after new growth appears in spring.

G. officinale. LIGNUM-VITAE. Zones H1, H2. From dry coastal areas of Central America and the West Indies. A very slow growing, bushy tree that can be trained to single or multiple trunks. With time, it may reach 25–35 ft. high and 20–25 ft. wide, but it is often seen at half that size or smaller. Attractive medium green leaves to 3½ in. long are composed of two or three pairs of leathery, oval leaflets. Masses of lavender-blue flowers are produced in late spring; these are followed by heart-shaped, yellow-orange, about ¾-in.-long capsules that may split to show bright red fruit. Adapted to wide range of soils; has good wind and drought tolerance. Only light pruning required to shape. Useful in entry court or as accent or screen in the landscape; does well in a container.

GUAJILLO. See ACACIA berlandieri

GUAVA

Myrtaceae

EVERGREEN SHRUBS OR TREES

ZONES VARY BY SPECIES

FULL SUN OR PART SHADE

REGULAR WATER

Guava

Native to tropical America; known botanically as *Psidium.* Plants bear white flowers composed mainly of a brush of stamens. The blossoms develop into round to pear-shaped, berrylike fruits that mature from late summer into fall, though some may be produced year-round. Though guavas are self-fruitful, trees may yield a heavier crop with another variety of the same species to pollinate them. Grow best in rich soil. Drought tolerant but need regular moisture for good fruit quality. Fruit is best picked when skin is fully colored, though it can be harvested when still greenish and ripened at room temperature (placing green fruit in bag with an apple or a banana will hasten ripening). Good eaten fresh or used in jellies, purées, juice drinks. Plants take pruning well; they can be sheared into a hedge (but at expense of fruit).

Common or tropical guava *(P. guajava)* grows in Zones 23, 24, H1, H2 (it is weedy throughout Hawaii, where it is choking out native species). To 25 ft. tall and nearly as wide, with strongly veined leaves to 6 in. long. May lose some of its leaves briefly in spring; new growth is an attractive salmon color. Yellow-skinned, 1–3-in.-wide fruit has white, pink, or yellow flesh and a musky, mildly acid flavor. 'Holmberg', 'Indonesian Seedless', and 'Ruby × Supreme' are sweeter dessert varieties grown mostly in Hawaii. 'Beaumont', 'Ka Hua Kula', and 'Waiakea', tarter and used mainly for juice, are also grown primarily in Hawaii.

Strawberry guava or purple strawberry guava (*P. cattleianum* or *P. littorale longipes*) is hardier to cold than common guava, growing in Zones 9 and 14 (sheltered locations), 15–24, H1, H2 (it has naturalized throughout Hawaii but is less invasive than common guava). In Hawaii, it is usually grown as single-trunked tree to 20 ft. tall and wide; in California, it is more often seen as a shrub to 8–10 ft. high and wide, though it is sometimes trained as a multitrunked tree 10–15 ft. tall. Especially beautiful reddish to golden brown bark. Leaves to 3 in. long are bronze when new, maturing to glossy green. Fruit is dark red (nearly black when fully ripe), 1½ in. wide, with white flesh and a sweet-tart, slightly resinous flavor. Yellow strawberry guava or lemon guava (*P. cattleianum lucidum*) differs in its more open, taller growth habit (to 30 ft. tall by 15 ft. wide in Hawaii), greenish gray to golden bark, and larger, yellow-skinned fruit.

GUERNSEY LILY. See NERINE sarniensis

GUINEA GOLD VINE. See HIBBERTIA scandens

GUM. See EUCALYPTUS

GUNNERA

Gunneraceae

PERENNIALS

ZONES 4–6, 14–17, 20–24

PARTIAL SHADE

AMPLE WATER

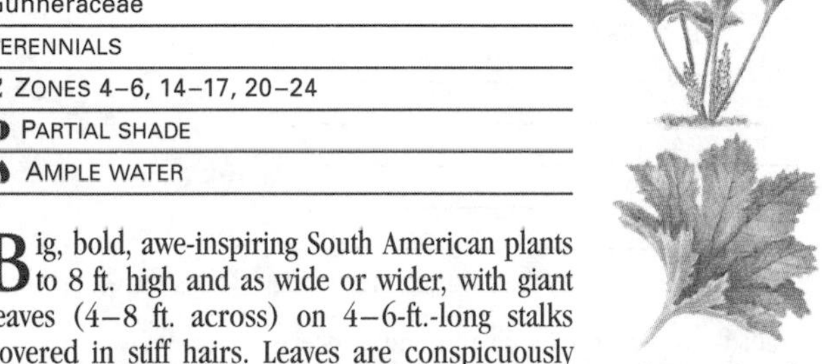

Gunnera tinctoria

Big, bold, awe-inspiring South American plants to 8 ft. high and as wide or wider, with giant leaves (4–8 ft. across) on 4–6-ft.-long stalks covered in stiff hairs. Leaves are conspicuously veined, with lobed and cut edges. Given space (they need plenty) and the necessary care, these plants can be the ultimate summertime conversation pieces. New sets of leaves grow each spring. In mild-winter areas, old leaves remain green for more than a year. Elsewhere, leaves die back completely in winter. Flower clusters to 1½ ft. long resemble corncobs, form close to roots. Tiny fruits are red.

Soil must be rich in nutrients and organic material. Feed three times a year, beginning when new growth starts, to keep leaves maximum size. Give overhead sprinkling when humidity is low or drying winds occur. Use plants where they can be focal point in summer—beside a pool or dominating a bed of low, fine-textured ground cover.

G. manicata. Native to Brazil, Colombia. Leaves carried fairly horizontally. Spinelike hairs on leafstalks and leaf ribs are red. Leaf lobes are flatter than those of *G. tinctoria* and do not have frilled margins.

G. tinctoria (G. chilensis). From Chile. Most common species. Leaf margins are lobed, toothed, somewhat frilled. Leaves are cupped and flaring, held more vertically than those of *G. manicata.*

GYMNOCLADUS dioica

KENTUCKY COFFEE TREE

Fabaceae (Leguminosae)

DECIDUOUS TREE

ZONES 1–3, 7–10, 12–16, 18–21

FULL SUN

REGULAR WATER

Gymnocladus dioica

Native to eastern U.S. Grows very fast as a sapling but slows once it hits 8–10 ft. Give it plenty of room, since it will ultimately reach 60–100 ft. tall and 45–50 ft. wide. Provides year-round interest. Attractive leaves 1½–3 ft. long, divided into many 1–3-in. leaflets; pinkish when emerging late in spring, deep bluish green by summer. In leaf, the tree casts light shade. Fall color usually not effective, but foliage sometimes turns bright yellow. The relatively few, heavy, contorted branches and stout twigs make bare tree picturesque in winter.

Gymnocladus dioica

Male and female plants are separate. Narrow, creamy to greenish white flower panicles at ends of branches in spring are up to 1 ft. long (and fragrant) on female trees, to 4 in. long on males. Blossoms on female trees are followed by flat, 6–10-in.-long, reddish brown pods containing hard black seeds. Pods persist through winter. Early settlers roasted the seeds to make a coffee substitute, hence the tree's common name. Grows best in moist, rich, deep soil but adapts to poor soil, drought, city conditions. Can take much heat and cold. Needs minimal pruning.

GYPSOPHILA

Caryophyllaceae

ANNUALS AND PERENNIALS

ZONES VARY BY SPECIES

FULL SUN

MODERATE WATER

Gypsophila repens

Slender-stemmed, much-branched plants are upright or spreading, ranging from 3 in. to 4 ft. tall. Bloom profusely in summer, covering themselves in clusters of tiny single or double flowers in white, pink, or rose. Leaves (sparse when plants are in bloom) are typically blue green. Use for airy look in borders and bouquets and for contrast with large-flowered, coarse-textured plants. Dwarf kinds are ideal for rock gardens, for trailing from pockets in walls or over tops of dry rock walls.

Add lime to strongly acid soils before planting. Perennial kinds are not always easy to transplant (especially *G. paniculata,* which has deep, carrotlike roots). If possible, do not disturb them often. Protect roots from gophers; protect tender new growth from snails and slugs. To encourage repeat bloom on perennial sorts, cut back flowering stems before seed clusters form.

G. cerastioides. Perennial. Zones 2–10, 14–21. Native to the Himalayas. Gray foliage forms a mat to 3 in. high and twice as broad; clustered flowers vary from pink-veined white to pure pink. Use in rock garden, between stepping-stones.

G. elegans. Annual. Zones 1–24. Native to Asia Minor, Caucasus, southern Ukraine. Upright grower to 1½ ft. high and wide. Lance-shaped, rather fleshy leaves to 3 in. long. Profuse single white flowers to ½ in. wide or wider; pink and rose forms are also available. Plants live only 5 to 6 weeks; for continuous bloom, sow seed in open ground every 3 to 4 weeks from late spring into summer. Excellent cut flower.

G. paniculata. BABY'S BREATH. Perennial. Zones A2, A3; 1–10, 14–16, 18–21; H1. Native to central Asia, central and eastern Europe. This is the classic filler in bouquets. To 3 ft. or taller and as broad. Slender, sharp-pointed leaves 2½–4 in. long. Single white flowers about 1/16 in. across, hundreds in a spray. 'Bristol Fairy' is an improved, more billowy form to 4 ft. high, covered with double blossoms ¼ in. wide. Florists' favorite is 'Perfecta', which bears even larger flowers (to about ½ in. wide). Dwarf varieties include 'Compacta Plena', 1½ ft. high, double white flowers; and 'Viette's Dwarf', 12–15 in. high, double pink blooms.

G. repens. Perennial. Zones 1–11, 14–16, 18–21. Alpine native 6–9 in. high, with trailing stems 1½ ft. long. Leaves narrow, less than 1 in. long. Clusters of small white or pink flowers. To propagate, take cuttings in midsummer. Varieties include 'Alba' (white) and 'Rosea' (pink).

FOR INFORMATION ON SELECTING PLANTS
PLEASE SEE PAGES 64–160

HABRANTHUS

Amaryllidaceae

PERENNIALS FROM BULBS

ZONES 8, 9, 12–24

FULL SUN OR LIGHT SHADE

REGULAR WATER DURING GROWTH AND BLOOM

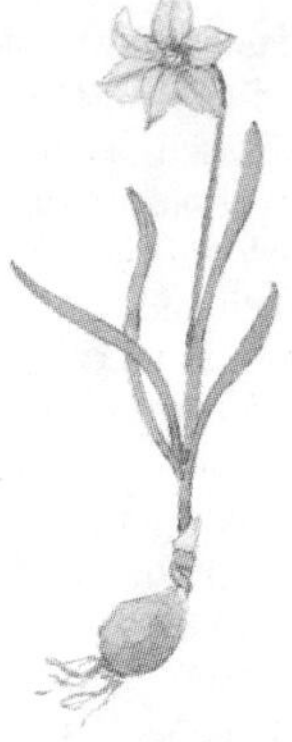

Habranthus robustus

Native from Texas to Argentina, where they sprout and flower almost immediately after ground has been moistened by summer rainfall. Grassy foliage and trumpet-shaped to funnel-shaped blossoms similar to those of fairy lily *(Zephyranthes)*, a close relative. Usually one blossom per stem. Plant in spring, in well-drained soil; set bulbs with tops at soil level and space 3 in. apart. If you live in a frost-free climate and can withhold moisture for about a month after flowering is over, you may get another bloom cycle in fall. Use in rock gardens or naturalize. Plantings don't need dividing for many years. Where soil freezes, grow in pots.

H. robustus. Flowers—sometimes two to a stem—usually bloom before leaves emerge. Light pink, 3-in. blossoms with green throats and deeper pink veining are carried on 9-in. stems.

H. tubispathus (H. andersonii). Flowers 1½ in. long, yellow veined in red on exterior of petals. Stems and leaves about 6 in. high. 'Cupreus' is coppery orange. A bright yellow form on slightly taller stems, known in Texas as copper lily, is probably a naturally occurring variety.

HACKBERRY. See CELTIS

HAEMANTHUS katherinae. See SCADOXUS multiflorus katherinae

HAIR GRASS. See DESCHAMPSIA

HAKEA

Proteaceae

EVERGREEN SHRUBS

ZONES 9, 12–17, 19–24

FULL SUN

NO IRRIGATION NEEDED

Hakea laurina

Native to Australia. Especially good for seacoast. Tougher than many other Proteaceae family members; adapt to a wide variety of soil types (including poor soils). Fertilizer is usually not needed; if you do apply it, make sure it is low in phosphorus.

In addition to the species described below, other hakeas are offered from time to time by experimentally minded nurseries. Remarkably diverse in foliage and flower, all are high-quality shrubs for difficult sites.

H. laurina. SEA URCHIN, PINCUSHION TREE. Dense, rounded habit to 10–25 ft. high and 9–30 ft. wide; often trained as single-trunked tree. Narrow, gray-green, 6-in.-long leaves are often red margined. Showy flower clusters look like round crimson pincushions stuck with golden pins. Blooms in winter, sometimes in late fall. Good small patio tree.

H. suaveolens. SWEET HAKEA. Dense, broad, upright plant to 10–20 ft. tall and wide. Stiff, dark green, 4-in. leaves, branched into stiff, needlelike, stickery segments. Small, fragrant white flowers in dense, fluffy clusters, fall and winter. Useful, fast-growing barrier plant, background, or screen. Good with conifers. Can be pruned into tree form.

H. victoria. ROYAL HAKEA. Erect, narrow plant to 6–15 ft. high and 5–9 ft. wide. Leathery leaves to 8 in. long and 5 in. wide, flat or slightly cupped, stemless, toothed, deep green beautifully netted with yellow and variegated with cream and orange. Flowers insignificant. Cut foliage dries well, lasts well in arrangements.

HAKONECHLOA macra

JAPANESE FOREST GRASS

Poaceae (Gramineae)

PERENNIAL GRASS

ZONES 2B–9, 14–24

FULL SUN IN COOLER CLIMATES ONLY

REGULAR WATER

Hakonechloa macra 'Aureola'

Clumps of gracefully arching leaves characterize this choice grass from Japan. To 1–3 ft. tall, somewhat wider. Spreads slowly by underground runners; never invasive. Tolerates full sun in fog belt or cool northwestern gardens. Prefers rich, moist, well-drained soil. Choice for shade garden, cool rock garden, containers. All-green leaves of species turn coppery orange in fall. Variegated-leaf selections more widely grown.

'Albostriata' ('Albovariegata'). To 3 ft. high. Green leaves with longitudinal white stripes.

'Aureola'. Most widely grown variety. To 14 in. high. Green leaves have longitudinal yellow stripes. In dense shade, the yellow turns to chartreuse; in full sun in cool climates, it may become paler, turning to creamy yellow. Foliage is sometimes suffused with pink in cool fall weather.

HALESIA

Styracaceae

DECIDUOUS TREES

ZONES 2B–9, 14–21

PART SHADE

REGULAR WATER

Halesia carolina

Elegant flowering trees native to southeastern U.S.; put on best floral show in cold-winter areas. Bell-shaped white flowers bloom in spring, usually just as leaves begin to appear. Because blossoms are pendent, they show off best when you can look up into tree. Leaves turn yellow in fall. Brown, winged fruits hang on almost all winter—or even into spring or summer. Plants grow best in cool, deep, humus-rich soil. Attractive in woodland gardens, with rhododendrons and azaleas planted beneath.

H. carolina (H. tetraptera). SNOWDROP TREE, SILVER BELL. To 30–40 ft. tall, with 20–35-ft. spread. Clusters of ½–¾-in. bells. Oval, finely toothed, 2–5-in.-long leaves. Fruit has four wings. Train plant to single trunk when young or it will grow as large shrub.

H. diptera. To 20–30 ft. tall and as wide, often with multiple trunks. Deeply lobed bells are ½–¾ in. long; appear 2 to 3 weeks later than those of other species. Leaves and fruits are similar in size to those of *H. carolina,* though fruits have two rather than four wings. Larger and more profuse blooms appear on *H. d. magniflora.*

H. monticola. MOUNTAIN SILVER BELL. Similar to *H. carolina* but taller (eventually to 60–80 ft.), with bigger leaves (3–6 in. long) and flowers (1 in.). Four-winged fruits are also somewhat larger. 'Rosea' has pale pink blooms.

×HALIMIOCISTUS

Cistaceae

EVERGREEN SHRUBS

ZONES 4–24

FULL SUN

LITTLE OR NO WATER TO MODERATE WATER

×Halimiocistus sahucii

These mound-forming, densely foliaged hybrids between *Halimium* and *Cistus salviifolius* combine the good qualities of both parents, offering abundant bloom and tolerance for considerable sun and heat. They need excellent drainage and cannot live in wet soil; water from lawn sprinklers can kill them. Use in rock gardens, on dry banks, spilling over a wall. Or plant on sunny side of the house under eaves where rains seldom reach.

×H. sahucii. To 1–2 ft. high, 3–4 ft. wide, with narrow dark green leaves to 1½ in. long. Profuse, 1½-in., white flowers with central puff of yellow stamens in spring.

×H. wintonensis. To 2 ft. high, 4–5 ft. wide, with furry gray-green leaves to 2 in. long. Sheets of 2-in. white flowers with pronounced dark reddish purple central blotch in spring and early summer.

HALIMIUM

Cistaceae

EVERGREEN SHRUBS

ZONES 5–9, 12–24

FULL SUN

LITTLE WATER

Halimium lasianthum

From southwestern Europe. Closely related to sunrose *(Helianthemum)* and sometimes sold under that name; cultural requirements and uses are the same. Halimiums have gray-green, ½–1½-in.-long leaves, bear loose clusters of flowers in spring.

H. lasianthum. To 3 ft. tall and 5 ft. wide, with ¼-in.-wide leaves. Flowers are 1½ in. across, bright yellow with brownish purple blotch near petal bases.

H. ocymoides. To 2 ft. tall, 3 ft. wide. Leaves slightly narrower than those of *H. lasianthum.* Inch-wide flowers are bright yellow with black-and-purple blotch at base of petals.

H. umbellatum. To 1½ ft. high and 2 ft. wide, with very slender leaves resembling those of rosemary. White, ¾-in.-wide flowers with yellow blotch at petal bases.

Hamamelidaceae. The witch hazel family contains deciduous (rarely evergreen) trees and shrubs. Some have showy flowers; these include *Fothergilla,* witch hazel *(Hamamelis),* and *Loropetalum.* Many have brilliant fall color, such as sweet gum *(Liquidambar)* and *Parrotia.*

HAMAMELIS

WITCH HAZEL

Hamamelidaceae

DECIDUOUS SHRUBS OR TREES

ZONES VARY BY SPECIES

FULL SUN OR PARTIAL SHADE

REGULAR WATER

Hamamelis mollis

Medium-size to large shrubs, sometimes treelike, usually with spreading habit and angular or zigzag branches. Valued for bright fall foliage and nodding clusters of interesting yellow to red blooms that typically appear in winter. Flowers consist of many narrow, crumpled petals and are said to resemble shredded coconut, mop heads, or spiders. Most witch hazels are fragrant and bloom over a long period. They appreciate rich, organic soil. Prune only to guide growth, remove poorly placed branches and suckers, or obtain flowering stems for scented winter bouquets.

H. ×intermedia. Zones 3–7, 15–17. Group of winter-blooming hybrids between *H. mollis* and *H. japonica.* Big shrubs (12–15 ft. high and wide). Often grafted; remove any growth originating from below graft. The following varieties are among the best.

'Allgold'. Deep yellow flowers with red sepals; yellow fall foliage.

'Arnold Promise'. Bright yellow flowers. Yellow, orange, and red fall foliage.

'Carmine Red'. Light red flowers; red-orange fall foliage.

'Diane'. Dark red flowers aging to orange red. Red-purple fall foliage.

'Hiltingbury'. Coppery red flowers; orange-yellow fall color.

'Jelena' ('Copper Beauty', 'Orange Beauty'). Coppery orange flowers. Fall foliage in orange, red, and scarlet.

'Magic Fire' ('Fire Charm', 'Feuerzauber'). Flowers in coppery orange blended with red. Fiery red fall foliage.

'Moonlight'. Pale yellow blooms marked red at base; yellow fall foliage.

'Pallida'. Luminous light yellow blossoms; yellow fall foliage.

'Primavera'. Broad-petaled light yellow flowers. Yellow-orange autumn foliage.

'Ruby Glow'. Coppery red flowers; bright red fall foliage.

'Sunburst'. Heavy clusters of radiant yellow, unscented flowers. Yellow fall foliage.

'Westerstede'. Unshaded yellow-orange flowers. Orange-red fall foliage.

H. japonica. JAPANESE WITCH HAZEL. Zones 2b–7, 15–17. From Japan. Much like *H. ×intermedia,* though perhaps somewhat more erect and treelike (to 12–20 ft. tall and broad). Fairly small, lightly scented yellow flowers in late winter or earliest spring. Chief draw is fall foliage in shades of red, purple, and yellow. *H. j. flavopurpurascens* has yellow-orange flowers, purple at the base, and reddish yellow fall foliage. *H. j.* 'Arborea' grows 20–25 ft. tall, has yellow blossoms and yellow autumn leaves.

H. mollis. CHINESE WITCH HAZEL. Zones 2b–7, 15–17. From China. Moderately slow-growing shrub to 8–10 ft. tall and wide, or small tree that may reach 30 ft. Roundish, 3½–6-in.-long leaves are dark green and rough above, gray and felted beneath, turning good pure yellow in fall. Sweetly fragrant, 1½-in.-wide, rich golden yellow flowers with red-brown sepals bloom on bare stems in winter. Flowering branches are excellent for cutting. Selections include 'Coombe Wood', a very heavy bloomer with especially fine fragrance, and 'Early Bright', earliest to bloom.

H. vernalis. OZARK WITCH HAZEL. Zones 2–7, 15–17. Native to central and southern U.S. Multistemmed, suckering shrub 6–10 ft. tall, spreading even wider. Rather small, fragrant yellow to orange flowers from winter to spring. Medium to dark green, 2–5-in.-long leaves turn bright yellow in fall and hold for several weeks in favorable weather. 'Lombart's Weeping' is a 5–6-ft. tree with somewhat drooping branches. 'Sandra' bears yellow spring flowers of no great distinction, but it has reddish purple new growth and brilliant red fall foliage.

H. virginiana. COMMON WITCH HAZEL. Zones 1–9, 14–16, 18–21. Native to eastern North America. Sometimes reaches 25 ft. tall but usually grows 10–15 ft. high and wide. Open, spreading, rather straggling habit. Moderately slow growing. Bark is the source of the liniment witch hazel. Roundish leaves similar to those of *H. mollis* but not gray and felted beneath; turn yellow to orange in fall. Small, fragrant golden yellow blossoms appear in fall but tend to be lost in colored foliage.

HAMELIA patens

SCARLET BUSH

Rubiaceae

EVERGREEN OR DECIDUOUS SHRUB OR TREE

ZONES 13, 23, 24; H1, H2

FULL SUN

REGULAR TO AMPLE WATER

Hamelia patens

Relative of gardenia and coffee; native from southern Florida to South America. Grows 6–10 ft. tall (possibly much taller) and 5–6 ft. wide. Whorls of 6-in., oval gray-green leaves; red leafstalks and flower stems. Clusters of ¾-in., tubular, orange to bright red flowers form at branch tips all summer long. Thanks to flower shape and color, the plant is also known by the names "firecracker shrub" and "fire bush." Flowers are followed by small dark red, purple, or black fruits that are much relished by birds. Give lots of water while in active growth, regular water at other times. Needs good drainage. Tolerant of salt and heat. Evergreen in Zones 24 and H1; loses its leaves in colder areas. In Zone 13, it will die to the ground without overhead shelter or other cold protection.

HAPU'U. See CIBOTIUM glaucum

HARDENBERGIA

LILAC VINE

Fabaceae (Leguminosae)

EVERGREEN SHRUBBY VINES

ZONES VARY BY SPECIES

PARTIAL SHADE IN HOTTEST CLIMATES

MODERATE WATER

Hardenbergia comptoniana

Native to Australia. Grow at moderate rate to 10 ft., climbing by twining stems. Attractive flowers shaped like sweet peas bloom from late winter to early spring, carried in clusters of several to many. Need light, well-drained soil. Provide support for climbing and cut back after bloom to prevent tangling. Good against trellises in large containers (use soil mix rich in organic matter). Subject to spider mites, nematodes; otherwise fairly free of pests and diseases.

H. comptoniana. Zones 15–24. Light, delicate foliage pattern; leaves divided into three to five dark green, narrow, 2–3-in.-long leaflets. Violet-blue, ½-in.-long flowers in long, narrow clusters. Where temperatures drop below 24°F/–4°C, plant beneath overhang.

H. violacea (H. monophylla). Zones 8–24. Coarser textured than *H. comptoniana;* leaves usually undivided, 2–4 in. long. Flowers are lilac or violet to rose or white. 'Happy Wanderer' is a tough, vigorous selection with pinkish purple blooms; 'Icicle' has pure white blossoms, 'Rosea' pink ones. 'Mini-Ha-Ha' is a shrubby dwarf form growing 3 ft. tall and wide.

HARDY RUBBER TREE. See EUCOMMIA ulmoides

HAREBELL. See CAMPANULA rotundifolia

HARE'S FOOT FERN. See POLYPODIUM aureum

HARRY LAUDER'S WALKING STICK. See CORYLUS avellana 'Contorta'

HART'S TONGUE FERN. See ASPLENIUM scolopendrium

HAU. See HIBISCUS tiliaceus

HAWAIIAN TREE FERN. See CIBOTIUM glaucum

HAWTHORN. See CRATAEGUS

HAZELNUT. See CORYLUS; FILBERT, HAZELNUT

HEART OF FLAME. See BROMELIA balansae

HEATH. See DABOECIA, ERICA

HEATHER, SCOTCH. See CALLUNA vulgaris

HEAVENLY BAMBOO. See NANDINA domestica

HEBE

Scrophulariaceae

EVERGREEN SHRUBS

ZONES 14–24, EXCEPT AS NOTED

PARTIAL SHADE IN HOTTEST CLIMATES

REGULAR WATER

Hebe 'Autumn Glory'

New Zealand natives closely related to *Veronica* and often sold under that name. Most types are grown mainly for attractive form and foliage (neat pairs of opposite leaves); some give good flower display in summer. Most are fast growing. All do best in cool-summer, mild-winter climates—in the San Francisco area, for example. Dry summer heat and winter frosts shorten their lives. Very prone to root rot if drainage is anything less than excellent. Take seacoast conditions. Prune after bloom, shortening stems that have flowered by about half to keep plants compact and bushy. Rejuvenate ragged plants by cutting back severely; they'll resprout easily from old, leafless wood.

H. 'Amy'. Zones 5, 6, 14–24. To 5 ft. high and wide, with 2–3-in.-long, dark green leaves tinged purple on top, purplish red beneath. Foliage is dark bronzy purple when new and takes on that color in winter as well. Short, dense spikes of reddish purple flowers. Summer is the main bloom season, but plants produce a scattering of flowers throughout the year.

H. × andersonii. Mounding, compact plant to 5–6 ft. tall and wide. Fleshy deep green leaves to 4 in. long. Flowers are white at base, violet at tip, carried in 2–4-in. spikes. 'Variegata' has white-bordered leaves.

H. 'Autumn Glory'. Zones 5, 6, 14–24. Compact grower to 2 ft. high and wide. Dark green, 1½-in.-long leaves. Many 2-in., deep lavender-blue flower spikes in late summer, fall.

Hebe 'Autumn Glory'

H. buxifolia. BOXLEAF HEBE. Rounded and symmetrical, to an eventual 5 ft. high and wide; easily shaped into 3-ft. hedge. Deep green, ⅓-in.-long leaves densely cover branches. Small white flowers in dense clusters.

H. carnosula. To 1 ft. high and 2–3 ft. wide, thickly foliaged in ½-in., rounded grayish green leaves. Small white flowers in dense spikes.

H. 'Coed'. Compact shrub to 3 ft. high and wide. Reddish stems densely clothed with 1½-in. dark green leaves. Profuse spikes of small pinkish purple flowers.

H. elliptica. Much-branched shrub 5–6 ft. high. Medium green leaves 1½ in. long. Clusters of fragrant bluish flowers.

H. glaucophylla. Zones 5–7, 14–24. Compact, rounded, about 2 ft. high and wide. Half-inch-long, roundish blue-green leaves. White flowers in short, dense clusters. Good low foundation plant or divider between walkway and lawn.

H. imperialis. See H. speciosa 'Imperialis'

H. 'Lake' ('Veronica Lake'). Dense growth to 3 ft. high and wide, with 1½-in. dark green leaves and abundant short spikes of lilac flowers.

H. 'Patty's Purple'. Dense, to 3 ft. high and wide. Wine red stems; tiny dark green leaves. Purple flowers on slender spikes. Use in masses, flower borders. Can be sheared.

H. pinguifolia. Zones 5–7, 14–17, 22–24. To 3 ft. tall and wide. Blue-gray leaves (sometimes with a pinkish edge) are 1½-in.-long ovals, very closely set or even overlapping. White flowers are tiny but profuse. 'Pagei' is a prostrate form that can grow 9 in. high and 4 ft. across in 5 years; it is easily increased by cutting off and planting branches that have rooted.

H. speciosa. SHOWY HEBE. Zones 14–24; H1. Dense shrub to 5 ft. high, 4 ft. wide. Stout stems bear glossy dark green, 2–4-in.- long leaves. Reddish purple flowers in 3–4-in. spikes. 'Imperialis' has reddish foliage, magenta flowers.

HEDERA

IVY

Araliaceae

EVERGREEN VINES

ZONES VARY BY SPECIES

SOME SHADE IN HOTTEST CLIMATES

MODERATE TO REGULAR WATER

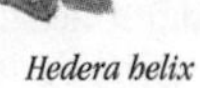

Hedera helix

Ivy is appreciated by some gardeners for its ability to cover quickly, reviled by others for its invasive tendencies. Spreads horizontally over the ground; also climbs on walls, fences, trellises. Sometimes a single planting does both: wall ivy spreads to become a surrounding ground cover, or vice versa. Climbs almost any vertical surface by aerial rootlets—a factor to consider in planting against surfaces that must be painted. A chain link fence planted with ivy soon becomes a wall of foliage. As a ground cover, it holds the soil, discouraging erosion and slippage on slopes. Roots grow deep and fill soil densely; branches root as they grow, further knitting soil.

Thick, leathery leaves are usually lobed. Mature plants will eventually develop stiff branches that bear round clusters of small greenish flowers followed by black berries. These branches have unlobed leaves; cuttings taken from them will also have unlobed leaves and will produce shrubby rather than vining plants. Such shrubs taken from variegated Algerian ivy (*H. canariensis* 'Variegata') are known by the name "ghost ivy." Plain green *H. helix* 'Arborescens' is another variety of this shrubby type.

Plant ivy in spring; where winters are not excessively cold, you can also plant in fall. Ivy can be grown from cuttings, but planting from pots is more dependable and gives faster growth. Standard spacing is 1½–2 ft. apart. Amend soil (to depth of 8–12 in. if possible) with organic matter such as ground bark or peat moss. Before planting, thoroughly moisten soil; also make sure transplants' roots are moist and their leaves and stems full of moisture (not wilted). Feed with high-nitrogen fertilizer after planting (for spring-planted ivy) or, for fall-planted ivy, in first spring after planting. Feed again in midsummer. For best growth, continue to feed every year in early spring and midsummer.

Most ivy ground covers should be trimmed around edges two or three times a year (use hedge shears or a sharp spade). Fence and wall plantings likewise need shearing or trimming two or three times a year. When ground cover builds up higher than you want, mow it with rugged rotary power mower or cut it back with hedge shears. Do this in spring so ensuing growth will quickly cover bald look.

Many trees and shrubs can grow compatibly in ivy ground cover, but small, soft, or fragile plants will be smothered. Ivy ground covers can be a haven for slugs and snails and can also harbor rodents, especially if the ivy is never cut back.

H. canariensis. ALGERIAN IVY. Zones 5–9, 12–24. Shiny, rich green leaves 5–8 in. wide with three to five shallow lobes. Leaves are more widely spaced along stems than those of *H. helix*. Coarse-looking plant; aggressive grower. 'Variegata' ('Gloire de Marengo') has dark leaves marbled with gray green and irregularly margined in creamy white; it does not take extreme heat.

H. colchica. PERSIAN IVY. Zones 3b–24. Oval to heart-shaped leaves are largest among all ivies: 3–7 in. wide, to 10 in. long. 'Dentata' has slightly toothed leaves; 'Dentata Variegata' is marbled with deep green, gray green, and creamy white. 'Sulphur Heart' ('Paddy's Pride') has central gold variegation.

H. helix. ENGLISH IVY. Zones 3–24, H1, except as noted. Dull dark green, three- to five-lobed leaves with paler veins are 2–4 in. wide at base and as long. Not as vigorous or large growing as *H. canariensis.*

Many small- and miniature-leafed forms of English ivy are good choices for pots and hanging baskets, for training into intricate patterns on walls, and for small-scale ground covers. These varieties are also used to create topiary shapes on wire frames. In general, their leaves are about half as large as those of the species, and some are even smaller. Leaf shapes vary widely: they may be deeply lobed and cleft, ruffle edged, narrow and elongated, arrow shaped, or divided into distinct leaflets. 'Baltica', with whitish-veined leaves, is often considered the hardiest variety of English ivy (Zones 2b–24); its leaves take on purplish tones in winter. 'Hahn's Self Branching' is a dense-branching form with light green leaves that does best in part shade. 'Conglomerata' is a slow-growing dwarf; 'Minima' has especially small leaves (½ to 1 in. wide). Other varieties include 'Buttercup', 'California', 'Fluffy Ruffles', 'Gold Dust', 'Gold Heart', 'Heart', 'Needlepoint', 'Ripple', 'Shamrock', and 'Star'; select for leaf color and shape.

HEDGE LAVENDER. See LAVANDULA × intermedia

FOR DEFINITIONS OF GARDENING TERMS
PLEASE SEE PAGES 746–750

HEDGE MAPLE. See ACER campestre

HEDYCHIUM

GINGER LILY

Zingiberaceae

PERENNIALS

ZONES 8, 9, 14–17, 19–24; H1, H2

LIGHT SHADE

AMPLE WATER

Hedychium gardnerianum

Native to tropical Asia, India, Himalayas. Leaves grow in a single plane along stems rising from stout rhizomes. Foliage is especially handsome in tropical conditions, as in Hawaii. Dense spikes of richly fragrant flowers are produced in late summer or early autumn.

Do best in rich soil high in organic matter. To encourage fresh new growth, remove old stems after flowers fade. Plants spread indefinitely from rhizomes and in time can outgrow even generous garden spaces. Frost can kill them to ground, but new stalks appear in early spring. Good near swimming pools, at the beach, in shade gardens, in big borders. Useful in large containers but will not grow as tall there as in open ground. Potted plants can be moved out of sight when unattractive.

H. coccineum. RED GINGER LILY, SCARLET GINGER LILY. To 6–9 ft. tall, with leaves to 20 in. long and 2 in. wide. Particularly showy, bearing orange-scarlet flowers with prominent red stamens on blossom spikes to 10 in. long.

H. coronarium. WHITE GINGER, BUTTERFLY LILY, GARLAND FLOWER. To 3–7 ft. high, with leaves 8–24 in. long and 2–5 in. wide. White flowers in 6–12-in.-long clusters are especially fragrant; good cut flowers. Naturalized in Hawaii, where the flowers are used in leis. In California, it looks best where humidity is moderate to high (in coastal areas, for example).

H. densiflorum. To 9 ft. or taller, with leaves to 14 in. long and 4 in. wide. Orange-yellow flowers are produced in dense spikes to 8 in. long.

H. flavescens. YELLOW GINGER. To 6 ft. or taller, with oblong leaves 4–22 in. long and 1–4 in. wide. Heavily perfumed yellow flowers to 3 in. across are produced in oval heads with many broad, overlapping green bracts. Naturalized in Hawaii.

H. flavum. Similar to *H. flavescens* but a little shorter (to about 5 ft.) and with yellow or orange flowers in slightly smaller heads.

H. gardnerianum. KAHILI GINGER. Plant grows to 8 ft. high, with leaves 8–18 in. long, 4–6 in. wide. Pure yellow flowers with red stamens are borne in 1½-ft.-long spikes. Naturalized in Hawaii and considered a pest on the Big Island.

H. greenei. To 5 ft. tall. Leaves 8–10 in. long, 2 in. wide; orange-red flowers in 5-in. spikes.

H. spicatum acuminatum. Grows to 3 ft. high. Leaves reach 16 in. long and 4 in. wide, have downy undersides. Bears purple flowers in loose spikes to 8 in. long.

HEDYSCEPE canterburyana

Arecaceae (Palmae)

PALM

ZONES 17, 23, 24; H1, H2

FULL SUN OR LIGHT SHADE

REGULAR WATER

Hedyscepe canterburyana

From Lord Howe Island in the South Pacific. Related to better-known kentia palms (see *Howea*) but smaller, broader, and lower growing, with broader leaf segments and more arching, lighter green feather-type leaves. To 30 ft. tall, with fronds spreading 15 ft. wide.

HELENIUM

SNEEZEWEED

Asteraceae (Compositae)

PERENNIALS

ZONES VARY BY SPECIES

FULL SUN

REGULAR WATER, EXCEPT AS NOTED

Helenium autumnale

Rather coarse looking, but valuable for profuse late summer and autumn bloom. Numerous leafy stems yield great sheaves of daisylike, typically brown-centered blossoms with yellow, orange, red, or coppery rays. In many sneezeweeds, the ray flowers are reflexed. Trim off faded blossoms to encourage long bloom. Perform best in hot-summer areas. Can survive an occasional missed irrigation but look better with regular moisture. Give good drainage. Need little fertilizer. Taller kinds require staking and are best in the back of borders. All need division and replanting every few years.

H. autumnale. Zones 1–24. Native to much of North America. To 5 ft. tall and 1½ ft. wide. Yellow, 2-in.-wide flowers with reflexed rays. Most plants sold under this name are really hybrids; see *H.* hybrids.

H. bigelovii. Zones 1–10, 14–24. From California, Oregon. To 2–3 ft. tall, 1 ft. wide. Yellow blossoms to 2½ in. across have reflexed rays.

H. hoopesii. Zones 1–3, 6–24. From mountains of the West. To 3 ft. tall, 1½ ft. wide. Yellow to orange flowers are 3 in. across, with reflexed rays.

H. hybrids. Zones 1–24. Most types of sneezeweeds sold are hybrids—even if often sold as *H. autumnale.* Flowers are 2–3 in. across, come in shades of yellow, orange, red, rust, copper, and blends of these colors. Tall types (4–5 ft. high, 2 ft. wide) include 'Baudirektor Linne', brownish red with a brown center; 'Butterpat', light yellow with a deeper yellow center; and 'Waldtraut', with coppery brown rays around a dark central disk. Compact varieties (about 3 ft. high, 1½ ft. wide) include 'Crimson Beauty', dusky deep red with a brown disk; 'Moerheim Beauty', coppery red with a brown center; and 'Wyndley', butter yellow with a yellow-brown central disk.

HELIANTHEMUM nummularium

Helianthemum nummularium

SUNROSE

Cistaceae

EVERGREEN SHRUBS

ZONES 2B–9, 14–24

FULL SUN

MODERATE WATER

Commonly sold under this name are a number of forms of this species, as well as hybrids between it and other species. All grow 6–8 in. high and spread to 3 ft. Leaves are ½–1 in. long; they may be gray on both surfaces, or glossy green above and fuzzy gray beneath. Midspring to early summer display of 1-in.-wide, single or double flowers in bright or pastel colors—flame red, apricot, orange, yellow, pink, rose, peach, salmon, or white. Each blossom lasts only a day, but new buds continue to open. Shear plants back after flowering to encourage repeat bloom.

Specialists offer many named varieties. Especially noteworthy is one sold as *H. apenninum roseum* or merely as 'Wisley Pink', with relatively large pure pink flowers that contrast nicely with the furry gray foliage.

Let sunroses tumble over rocks, set them in niches in dry rock walls, or grow them in planters on a sunny patio. Use them at seashore or in rock gardens; let them ramble over gentle slopes. If used as ground cover, set out 2–3 ft. apart. In cold-winter areas, lightly cover plants with evergreen boughs to keep foliage from dehydrating. Plants will be hardier if soil is not too rich and is kept on the dry side (good drainage is essential). The object is to encourage hard, nonsucculent growth.

HELIANTHUS

Helianthus annuus

SUNFLOWER

Asteraceae (Compositae)

ANNUALS AND PERENNIALS

ZONES VARY BY SPECIES

FULL SUN

REGULAR TO AMPLE WATER

Coarse, sturdy plants with bold blooms. Most are prime subjects for cut flowers. Plants are tough and widely adapted. Perennial kinds spread rapidly, may become invasive. Tall kinds are not for tidy gardens; may need staking. All bloom in summer and fall.

H. annuus. COMMON SUNFLOWER. Annual. All zones. The wild ancestor of today's familiar sunflowers is a coarse, hairy plant with 2–3-in.-wide flowers, native to much of the central U.S. and southward to Central America. It is the state flower of Kansas and the only plant native to the lower 48 states to have become an important agricultural commodity. It has been bred to produce giant plants as well as a host of smaller (but still significant) varieties for garden decoration and cut flowers.

Best known among the giant forms are 'Mammoth Russian' and 'Russian Giant'. They grow 10 ft. (possibly 15 ft.) tall and 2 ft. wide and typically produce a single huge head (sometimes over a foot across) consisting of a circle of short yellow rays with a brown central cushion of seeds. Newer variety 'Kong' is as large as the older varieties. 'Sunspot' carries flower heads 10 in. wide on 2-ft.-high plants. For children, annual sunflowers are easy to grow and bring a sense of great accomplishment. Sow seeds in spring where plants are to grow. Large-flowered kinds need rich, moist soil. People eat the roasted seeds; birds enjoy the raw ones in fall and winter.

Sunflowers for cutting come on compact, branching plants and bear 4–8-in.-wide blooms in a rich variety of colors. They fall into two basic categories: pollen-bearing types and pollenless ones. Kinds with pollen include 'Del Sol', early-blooming yellow, 5 ft. tall; 'Indian Blanket', red with yellow tips, 4–5 ft.; 'Italian White', creamy yellow to near white, 5 ft.; 'Lemon Eclair', light yellow, 4–6 ft.; 'Moonshadow', pale yellow to cream, 4 ft.; and Parasol Mix, lemon, orange, red, and bicolor, 4–5 ft. 'Teddy Bear', only 1½ ft. high, has fully double, 6-in.-wide flowers that look like pompons.

Kinds without pollen, classified as *H.* ×*hybridus,* have the advantage of not shedding on tabletops. They include Large Flowered Mix, yellow, red, and bronze, 6–10 ft. tall; 'Bright Bandolier', yellow-and-mahogany bicolor, 5–7 ft.; 'Cinnamon Sun', cinnamon bronze, 4–7 ft.; 'Prado Red', deep garnet, 3½–4 ft.; 'Valentine', light yellow, 4–5 ft.; and 'Velvet Queen', combination of bronze, burgundy, chestnut red, and mahogany, 6–8 ft.

H. maximilianii. Perennial. Zones 1–24. From central and southwestern U.S. Forms a clump 3 ft. wide, with 10-ft.-tall stems clothed in narrow, 8–10-in.-long leaves and topped by a narrow spire of 3-in. yellow flowers. Often seen peering over adobe walls in the Southwest.

H. ×multiflorus. Perennial. Zones 1–24. To 5 ft. tall and 3 ft. wide, with thin, tooth-edged, 3–8-in.-long leaves and many yellow, 3-in., yellow-centered blossoms. Excellent for cutting. 'Loddon Gold' ('Flore Pleno') is double flowered. 'Capenoch Star' single, but disk flowers are quilled (rolled into long, slender tubes), giving a pincushion effect.

H. salicifolius (H. orgyalis). Perennial. Zones 1–24. Native to central U.S. To 6–8 ft. tall, 3 ft. wide, with narrow, gracefully drooping leaves to 8 in. long. Stems are topped by sheaves of 2-in. yellow flowers with purplish brown centers.

H. tuberosus. JERUSALEM ARTICHOKE. Perennial. Zones 2–24. From eastern and central North America. To 6–7 ft. tall, 3 ft. wide; oval leaves to 8 in. long. Bright yellow flowers to 4 in. across. Grown as commercial crop; tubers are edible, sold in markets as "sunchokes." Harvest tubers every year; save two or three for replanting. Plant can become a pest. If controlled, makes a good, quick temporary screen or hedge.

Helianthus tuberosus

HELICHRYSUM

Asteraceae (Compositae)
ANNUALS AND PERENNIALS
ZONES VARY BY SPECIES
FULL SUN
MODERATE WATER

Helichrysum petiolare 'Limelight'

Best known is *H. bracteatum,* the annual strawflower used in fresh and dried arrangements. Others, though less familiar, are choice plants for landscape use.

H. angustifolium. See H. italicum

H. bracteatum. STRAWFLOWER. Annual. All zones. From Australia. To 2–3 ft. tall, 1 ft. wide, with straplike, 2–5-in.-long, medium green leaves. Blooms from summer until frost, bearing many papery, 2½-in. flowers that look like prickly pompons. Colors include yellow, orange, red, pink, and white. Known as "everlasting" because its blossoms last indefinitely when dried. Sow in place in late spring or earliest summer (at same time as zinnias). Dwarf forms are also available.

For shrubby perennial forms (such as 'Cockatoo', 'Dargan Hill Monarch', 'Diamond Head') previously included with annual strawflower, see *Bracteantha bracteata.*

H. italicum (H. angustifolium). CURRY PLANT. Perennial. Zones 13–24. From southern Europe. To 2 ft. high and wide, with woody base and crowded, narrow, nearly white leaves to 1½ in. long. Leaves emit a strong fragrance of curry powder when bruised or pinched. Not used in curry, but a few can add a pleasant aroma to a salad or meat dish. Bright yellow, ½-in. flowers in clusters 2 in. across appear from midsummer to autumn.

H. petiolare. LICORICE PLANT. Perennial in Zones 16, 17, 22–24; annual elsewhere. From South Africa. To 1½–3 ft. high, with trailing stems to 4 ft. White, woolly, inch-long leaves; insignificant flowers. A licorice aroma is sometimes noticeable—in hot, still weather, for example, or when leaves are dry. 'Limelight' has luminous light chartreuse leaves; 'Licorice Splash' has variegated yellow-green foliage; 'Variegatum' has leaves with white markings. All are useful for their trailing branches, which thread through mixed plantings or mingle with other plants in large pots, hanging baskets. For the so-called dwarf form, see *Plecostachys serpyllifolia.*

HELICONIA

LOBSTER-CLAW, FALSE BIRD-OF-PARADISE
Heliconiaceae
PERENNIALS
ZONES 24, H1, H2, EXCEPT AS NOTED; OR GROW IN POTS
FULL SUN OR LIGHT SHADE
AMPLE WATER

Heliconia angusta

More than 100 species of tropical American plants grown for big, showy, waxy flower clusters that consist of brightly colored bracts; small true flowers peep out from the bracts. Clusters may be erect or drooping, from a few inches to several feet in length; used in spectacular tropical flower arrangements. In growth habit, plants resemble banana or canna. Oblong to spoon-shaped evergreen leaves are large (sometimes very large), and plants form sizable clumps that keep increasing with age. Best with rich soil, heavy feeding, and plenty of water—all of which will keep clump expanding. Stems that have flowered should be cut away to make room for new growth. In areas with frosts, grow plants in tubs and shelter from winter cold. Potted plants can bloom any time; those in the ground flower in spring and summer.

H. angusta. To 4–10 ft. tall, with leaves to 3 ft. long. Erect flower clusters to 2½ ft. long. Yellow or orange to vermilion or scarlet bracts; white or yellow-tipped green flowers.

H. bihai (H. humilis). To 6–15 ft. tall, with 2–6-ft.-long leaves. Erect blossom clusters 1½–3½ ft. long. Reddish orange bracts with green margins; white to pale green flowers.

H. brasiliensis (H. farinosa). To 3–5 ft. tall, with 2½-ft. leaves. Erect clusters of red bracts enfold white or red flowers.

H. caribaea. WILD PLANTAIN. To 6–15 ft. tall, with 5-ft.-long leaves and erect flower clusters to 1½ ft. Bracts are red or yellow, often marked with contrasting colors; flowers are white with green tips.

H. latispatha. Can reach 10 ft. tall, with leaves to 5 ft. long. Erect flower clusters to 1½ ft. tall, with spirally set orange, red, or yellow bracts and green-tipped yellow flowers.

H. pendula (H. collinsiana). To 6 ft. tall; 2–3-ft.-long leaves. Pendulous 2-ft. inflorescence with spirally arranged red bracts, yellow flowers.

H. psittacorum. PARROT HELICONIA. Highly variable species; more vigorous than other heliconias. Grows 4–8 ft. tall, with leaves to 20 in. long, blossom clusters to 7 in. long. Bracts spread upward at a 45° angle. They vary in color; may be red, sometimes shading to cream or orange, and are often multicolored. Flowers are yellow, orange, or red, usually tipped in dark green or white. Many named selections are available.

H. rostrata. To 4–6 ft. tall, with 2–4-ft.-long leaves. Hanging inflorescences to 1–2 ft. long contain red bracts shading to yellow at the tip; flowers are greenish yellow.

H. schiedeana. Zones 21–24; H1, H2. To 6–10 ft. tall, with leaves to 5 ft. long. Upright, 1½-ft.-long blossom clusters feature red or orange-red, spiraling bracts that enclose yellow-green flowers.

H. wagneriana. To 6–12 ft. tall, with 4–6-ft.-long leaves. Erect flower clusters 6 in.–1½ ft. long. Heavy, overlapping, green-edged bracts are deep pink to pale crimson, shading to cream at base; flowers are white.

HELICTOTRICHON sempervirens (Avena sempervirens)

BLUE OAT GRASS
Poaceae (Gramineae)
PERENNIAL GRASS
ZONES 1–24
FULL SUN
REGULAR WATER

Helictotrichon sempervirens

Native to western Mediterranean region. Bright blue-gray, narrow leaves in fountainlike clump 2–3 ft. high and wide; resembles giant clump of blue fescue *(Festuca glauca)* but is more graceful. In spring, stems to 2 ft. or taller rise above foliage, bearing wispy, straw-colored flower clusters. Grows best in rich, well-drained soil. Attractive in borders or with boulders in rock garden. Pull out occasional withered leaves. Evergreen in mild-winter climates; semievergreen in colder areas.

HELIOTROPE. See HELIOTROPIUM arborescens, VALERIANA officinalis

HELIOTROPIUM

Boraginaceae
PERENNIALS, ONE USUALLY TREATED AS ANNUAL
ZONES VARY BY SPECIES
EXPOSURE NEEDS VARY BY SPECIES
REGULAR WATER
ALL PARTS OF H. ARBORESCENS ARE POISONOUS IF INGESTED

Heliotropium arborescens

Both species produce clusters of tiny flowers with a sweet, delicate fragrance. Foliage is handsome. Provide well-drained soil.

H. anomalum argenteum. HINAHINA. Zone H2. Native Hawaiian coastal ground cover. Rosettes of succulent gray-green to silvery leaves form a mat 3 in.–1 ft. high; in winter and spring, clusters of white flowers are held well above the foliage. Set out plants 6–8 in. apart. Both blossoms and leaf rosettes are used in leis. Thrives in coastal gardens with wind and saturating salt spray. Tolerates drought but does better with regular moisture. Full sun.

H. arborescens. COMMON HELIOTROPE. From Peru. This old-fashioned favorite grows to 4 ft. tall, 2 ft. wide as a perennial (Zones 15–17, 23, 24; H1, H2), but it's typically treated in all regions as a summer bedding annual to 1½–2 ft. high, 1–1½ ft. wide. Dark violet, purple, blue, or white blossoms are densely set in curved, one-sided spikes that form rounded, 3–4-in. clusters. Veined leaves have a darkish purple cast. 'Black Beauty' and 'Iowa' are varieties with deep purple flowers; there are also dwarf forms under 1 ft. high. All are good in containers (in cold climates, overwinter them in a frost-free spot). They can take full sun in cooler climates but need partial shade in warmer ones.

HELIPTERUM

EVERLASTING, SUNRAY

Asteraceae (Compositae)

ANNUALS AND PERENNIALS

ZONES VARY BY SPECIES

EXPOSURE NEEDS VARY BY SPECIES

REGULAR WATER

Helipterum roseum

This large Australian genus contains primarily annuals but also includes some perennials. All have daisylike flower heads with papery rays that retain their color and form when dried. Useful for winter arrangements and for garden color.

H. anthemoides. CHAMOMILE SUNRAY. Perennial. Zones 8, 9, 14–24. Forms a compact gray-green mound 1 ft. tall, 2 ft. wide. Foliage has a chamomile scent when bruised. Blooms in late winter and early spring, with scattered bloom later; bright red buds open to white, ½–1-in.-wide daisies. Give full sun in cool-summer climates, partial shade in hotter regions.

H. roseum (Acroclinium roseum). PINK AND WHITE EVERLASTING, PINK PAPER DAISY. Annual. Zones 1–24. Top-notch flower for cutting, drying. Grows 2 ft. tall, with scanty, narrow leaves and 1–2-in., pink or white daisy flowers. Grow in full sun in warm soil, sowing seeds where plants are to grow after danger of frost is past. Thin to 6–12 in. apart.

HELLEBORUS

HELLEBORE

Ranunculaceae

PERENNIALS

ZONES VARY BY SPECIES

SHADE OR PARTIAL SHADE

WATER NEEDS VARY BY SPECIES

ALL PARTS ARE POISONOUS IF INGESTED

Helleborus argutifolius

Distinctive, long-lived plants that add color to the garden for several months in winter and spring, hellebores are also appreciated for their attractive foliage. Each leaf consists of a long leafstalk ending in large, leathery leaflets grouped together like fingers on an outstretched hand.

All hellebores form tight clumps of many growing points, but species differ in their manner of growth. Some have stems that rise from the ground, bearing leaves all along their length; stems produce flowers at their tip in their second year, then die to the ground as new stems emerge to replace them. In other species, leaves are not carried on tall stems but arise directly from growing points at ground level; separate (typically leafless) flower stems spring from the same points.

Flowers are usually cup or bell shaped (those of *H. niger* are saucer shaped), either outward facing or drooping; they consist of a ring of petal-like sepals ranging in color from white and green through pink and red to deep purple (rarely yellow). Flowers of all hellebores persist beyond the bloom periods listed below, gradually turning green. Blossoms are attractive in arrangements: after you cut them, slice the stems lengthwise or seal cut ends by searing over a flame or immersing in boiling water for a few seconds. Then place in cold water. Or simply float flowers in a bowl of water.

Plant in good, well-drained soil amended with plenty of organic matter. Plants prefer soil that is somewhat alkaline but will also grow well in neutral to slightly acid conditions (*H. niger* is an exception; it must have alkaline soil). Feed once or twice a year. Don't disturb once planted; they resent moving and may take 2 or more years to re-establish (if they survive at all). If well sited, however, they may self-sow, and young seedlings can be transplanted in early spring. Offspring may not exactly resemble the parent, but all are attractive. Mass under high-branching trees, on north or east side of walls, or in beds. Not damaged by deer or rodents.

In addition to the following, a half-dozen or more other species are sometimes available. Species here have leafy stems unless otherwise noted.

H. argutifolius (H. corsicus). CORSICAN HELLEBORE. Zones 3b–9, 14–24. From Corsica, Sardinia. Erect or sprawling, to 2–3 ft. tall and wide. Substantial enough to use as a small shrub. Blue-green, 6–9-in. leaves divided into three sharply toothed leaflets. Leafy stems carry clusters of 2-in., pale green flowers from winter into spring. Best hellebore for Southern California; more sun tolerant than others. Moderate water. Two varieties with white-marbled leaves are 'Janet Starnes' (which has a touch of pink in the foliage) and 'Pacific Frost'. Seedlings of these plants, sold as Janet Starnes strain and Pacific Frost strain, closely resemble the parents.

H. foetidus. BEAR'S-FOOT HELLEBORE. Zones 2b–9, 14–24. From western and central Europe. To 2½ ft. high and wide, the stems clothed with dark green leaves divided into seven to ten narrow, leathery leaflets to 8 in. long. Clusters of inch-wide flowers are light green with purplish red edges, bloom winter to spring. Plant parts are malodorous if crushed or bruised (don't smell bad otherwise). Tolerates sun in cool, humid areas. Self-sows freely where adapted. Moderate water. Wester Flisk strain has stems, flower stems, and leafstalks infused with purplish red, with the color extending into leaf bases.

H. hybrids. Zones 2b–10, 14–24. Leaves have no obvious stems. Hybrid plants generally resemble principal parent *H. orientalis,* but flower color range has been extended and superior parents selected for seed production. Some are sold under the breeder's name *(H. ×ballardiae),* some as strains (Royal Heritage strain), some merely as color groups (Ballard Red Group, *H. ×hybridus* Purple Group, Pink Group, Picotee Group). Regular water.

H. lividus. Zones 5 (with protection), 6–9, 14–24. From Majorca. To 1½ ft. high and twice as wide. Leaves resemble those of *H. argutifolius* but lack noticeable teeth and have purplish undersides and a network of pale veins above. Winter-to-spring flowers in clusters of up to ten are pale green washed with pinkish purple. Moderate water.

H. niger. CHRISTMAS ROSE. Zones 1–7, 14–17. From Europe. Leaves have no obvious stems. Elegant plant to 1 ft. tall, 1½ ft. wide, blooming Christmas time into spring. Often planted in warm-winter climates but seldom thrives there. Plants of *H. orientalis* are often mislabeled Christmas rose. Lustrous dark green leaves are divided into seven to nine lobes with a few large teeth; they seem to rise directly from the soil. White, 2-in. flowers appear singly or in groups of two or three on a stout stem about the same height as the foliage clump. Blooms turn pinkish with age. Less tolerant of light than other hellebores; needs more definite shade. Needs alkaline soil, regular water. 'White Magic' is a large-flowered variety.

H. orientalis. LENTEN ROSE. Zones 2b–10, 14–24. Greece, Turkey, Caucasus. Leaves have no obvious stems. Much like *H. niger* in growth but more tolerant of warm-winter climates. Basal leaves with 5–11 sharply toothed leaflets; branched flowering stems to 1 ft. tall, with leaflike bracts at branching points. Blooms in late winter and spring; flowers are 2–4 in. wide, in colors including white, pink, purplish, cream, and greenish, often spotted with deep purple. Easier to transplant than other hellebores. A widely variable plant, but all forms are attractive. Encourage self-sowing and keep the colors you like. Hybridizes freely with many other species; many nursery plants may be hybrids. Regular water.

H. ×sternii. Zones 4–9, 14–24. Hybrid between *H. argutifolius* and *H. lividus,* with bluish green foliage netted with white or cream. Greenish flowers suffused with pink bloom from winter to spring. Variable from seed. Moderate water.

HELXINE soleirolii. See SOLEIROLIA soleirolii

HEMEROCALLIS

DAYLILY

Liliaceae

PERENNIALS FROM TUBEROUS ROOTS

ZONES 1–24, H1, H2, EXCEPT AS NOTED

PARTIAL SHADE IN HOTTEST CLIMATES

REGULAR WATER

Hemerocallis hybrid

Tuberous, somewhat fleshy roots give rise to large clumps of arching, sword-shaped leaves—evergreen, semievergreen, or deciduous, depending on daylily type. Deciduous types go completely dormant in winter and are the hardiest, surviving without protection to about −35°F/−37°C; where winters are very mild, however, they may not get enough chill to perform well. Evergreen kinds succeed in mild-winter regions as well as in colder areas, but they need a protective mulch (such as a 4–6-in. layer of hay) where temperatures dip below −20°F/−29°C. Semievergreen sorts may or may not retain their leaves, depending on where they are grown.

Clusters of flowers like lilies appear at the ends of generally leafless stems that stand well above foliage. Older yellow, orange, and rust red daylilies have in most part been replaced by newer kinds in an expanded range of colors and patterns; both tall and dwarf varieties are available. Many species daylilies exist, but only a few are offered by nurseries; most of those available are hybrids.

Use in borders, mass on banks under high-branching deciduous trees or along driveways and roadsides in country gardens, or group among evergreen shrubs near pools, along streams. Plant dwarf daylilies in rock gardens or as edgings or low ground covers. All are good cut flowers. Cut stems with well-developed buds; these open on successive days, though each flower is slightly smaller than the preceding one. Arrange individual blooms in low bowls.

Few plants are tougher, more persistent, or more trouble free. Daylilies adapt to almost any kind of soil. You can set out bare-root plants at any time during the growing season; spring and summer are better in cold-winter zones, while fall and winter are preferred where winters are warm. Plant from containers at any time from early spring through midautumn (year-round in mild-winter areas). For best results, provide well-drained soil amended with organic matter and give regular moisture from spring through fall. When clumps become crowded (usually after 3 to 6 years), divide them in fall or early spring in hot-summer areas, during summer in cool-summer regions or where growing season is short.

H. fulva. TAWNY DAYLILY, COMMON ORANGE DAYLILY. Deciduous. From China or Japan. To 3–5 ft. high and 4 ft. wide; may spread into colonies. Leaves are 2 ft. or longer. Tawny orange-red, 3–5-in., unscented flowers in summer. A tough, persistent plant suitable for holding banks; rarely sold but commonly seen in old gardens and along roadsides. Double-flowered 'Kwanso' ('Kwanso Flore Pleno') is sometimes seen in the same locales.

H. hybrids. Deciduous, evergreen, and semievergreen. Standard-size hybrids generally grow 2½–4 ft. tall, 2–3 ft. wide; some selections reach 6 ft. high. Dwarf types grow just 1–2 ft. tall and wide. Flowers of standard kinds are 4–8 in. across, those of dwarfs 1½–3½ in. wide. Some have broad petals, others narrow, spidery ones; many have ruffled petal edges. Colors range far beyond the basic yellow, orange, and rusty red to pink, vermilion, buff, apricot, plum or lilac purple, cream, and near-white, often with contrasting eyes or midrib stripes that yield a bicolor effect. Many varieties are sprinkled with tiny iridescent dots known as diamond dust. Selections with semidouble and double flowers exist. Tetraploid varieties have unusually heavily textured petals.

Bloom usually begins in midspring, but early and late bloomers are also sold. By planting all three types, you can extend bloom period. Scattered bloom may occur during summer, and reblooming types put on second display in late summer to midautumn. Some varieties bloom throughout warm weather. These include 3-ft.-tall Starburst series, which comes in a variety of colors, as well as 2-ft.-high dwarf varieties 'Black-eyed Stella' (yellow with red eye), bright yellow 'Happy Returns' and 'Stella de Oro', and red 'Pardon Me'.

New hybrids appear in such numbers that no book can keep up. To get the ones you want, visit daylily specialists, buy plants in bloom at your local nursery, or study catalogs. Look for varieties that have won awards from the American Hemerocallis Society. AM stands for Award of Merit, given to ten varieties each year. HM means Honorable Mention, awarded to any plant receiving ten votes from the selection committee. SM stands for Stout Medal, the highest award a daylily can receive. Past SM winners include the long-blooming 'Stella de Oro' and the free-blooming yellow tetraploid 'Mary Todd'. An old variety that has maintained its popularity is 'Hyperion', a 4-footer with exceptionally fragrant yellow blooms.

H. lilioasphodelus (H. flava). LEMON DAYLILY. Deciduous. From China. Reaches to 3 ft. high and wide, with 2-ft.-long leaves and 4-in., fragrant, pure yellow flowers in mid- to late spring. Newer hybrids may be showier, but this species is still cherished for its delightful perfume and early bloom time.

H. minor. GRASS-LEAF DAYLILY. Deciduous. Zones A1–A3; 1–9, 14–17. From eastern Asia. To 2 ft. high and wide, with narrow (¼-in.-wide) leaves. Blooms for a relatively short time in late spring or early summer, when fragrant, bright golden yellow flowers are held just above the foliage. This is among the few daylilies hardy enough to succeed in Alaska's interior.

HEMLOCK. See TSUGA

HEN AND CHICKENS. See SEMPERVIVUM tectorum

HEN AND CHICKS. See ECHEVERIA

HEPATICA

LIVERLEAF

Ranunculaceae

PERENNIALS

ZONES 1–6, 14–17

PARTIAL OR FULL SHADE

REGULAR WATER

Hepatica americana

These low-growing woodland plants (reaching 6–9 in. high and 6 in. wide) with evergreen or nearly evergreen leaves resemble the smaller anemones (and were formerly considered anemones). Leaves were once thought to resemble the liver in shape, hence the common name. Flowers appear in early spring, each rising on its own stalk above the clump of last year's leaves. A new crop of leaves follows bloom. Flowers have numerous narrow, petal-like sepals arranged around a central mass of yellow stamens. These are choice plants for woodland gardens and shaded rock gardens. Though little known in North America except among wildflower fanciers, they are popular with plant collectors in Japan, where many varieties are cultivated.

H. acutiloba. Native to eastern and central North America. Leathery, 4-in. leaves are divided into three sharp-pointed lobes. Flowers are lilac and white, ½–1 in. across, on stems to 9 in. high.

H. americana. Native to eastern and central North America. Leathery, 4-in. leaves with three rounded lobes. Flowering stems are usually just 6 in. high. Flowers are typically light blue, but sometimes pink or white, ½–1 in. wide.

H. nobilis (H. triloba). Native to Europe. Very similar to species *H. americana*. Bears flowers that are usually bluish purple but are sometimes white or pink.

A PRACTICAL GUIDE TO GARDENING
PLEASE SEE PAGES 658–731

HEPTACODIUM miconioides

SEVEN SONS FLOWER
Caprifoliaceae
DECIDUOUS SHRUB OR TREE
ZONES 2B–6, 14–17
FULL SUN OR LIGHT SHADE
REGULAR WATER

Heptacodium miconioides

From China. Fountain-shaped shrub to 15–20 ft. tall, 8–10 ft. wide. Large, narrowly heart-shaped leaves are shiny green, deeply veined. Fragrant, creamy white flowers in large clusters at branch ends open over a long bloom season in late summer and fall. Blooms are succeeded by even showier masses of small fruits with bright purplish red calyxes. Common name derives from the number of flowers in each of the clusters forming part of the larger inflorescence. Picturesque even in winter, when bark is on show: thin, pale tan strips peel away to reveal dark brown bark beneath. Not fussy about soil; not bothered by pests or diseases. Some consider it a worthy substitute for crape myrtle *(Lagerstroemia)* where that plant does not succeed. Can be trained as a single- or multitrunked tree.

HERALD'S TRUMPET. See BEAUMONTIA grandiflora

HERB-OF-GRACE. See RUTA graveolens

HERCULES' CLUB. See ARALIA spinosa

HERNIARIA glabra

GREEN CARPET, RUPTURE WORT
Caryophyllaceae
PERENNIAL SOMETIMES TREATED AS ANNUAL
ZONES 2B–24; ANNUAL ELSEWHERE
SUN OR SHADE
REGULAR WATER

Herniaria glabra

From Eurasia and North Africa, especially the Mediterranean area. Trailing plant 1–3 in. high, with crowded, tiny (less than 1/4-in.-long) bright green leaves. Bloom negligible. Where temperatures remain above −20°F/−29°C, grown as an evergreen perennial; foliage turns bronzy red in winter. In colder areas, treated as an annual. Spreads well by rooting stems but won't grow out of control. Use it between stepping-stones, on mounds, among rocks, or in parking strips. Plant 1 ft. apart. Endures the occasional footstep but not constant traffic. Provide well-drained soil.

HESPERALOE

Agavaceae
PERENNIALS
ZONES VARY BY SPECIES
FULL SUN OR LIGHT SHADE
LITTLE TO MODERATE WATER

Hesperaloe parviflora

Clumps of narrow evergreen leaves with threadlike fringe along edges give rise to tall, branching inflorescences set with many tubular flowers. Foliage clumps resemble yucca or coarse grass. Plants require little maintenance aside from removal of spent flower clusters. Established plants can get by with little summer water, but they look and bloom better with a soaking every 2 weeks or so during warm weather.

H. funifera. Zones 12, 13. From northern Mexico. Clumps to 6 ft. tall, 6–8 ft. wide. Stems to 15 ft. high bear inch-wide, greenish white flowers in late spring or early summer.

H. nocturna. Zones 12, 13. From northern Mexico. Foliage clump 5 ft. tall, 6 ft. wide. Flowers in late spring and early summer, producing blossom spikes up to 12 ft. high that bear many 1-in., night-blooming, slightly fragrant greenish lavender flowers.

H. parviflora. RED YUCCA. Zones 2b, 3, 7–16, 18–24. From Texas and New Mexico. Leaf clumps 3–4 ft. tall and wide produce 5-ft. stalks carrying many rose red to bright red flowers from late spring through midsummer, sometimes into early fall. Especially heat tolerant; can take full sun, even reflected heat. Excellent container plant. There is a yellow-flowered form.

HESPERIS matronalis

DAME'S ROCKET
Brassicaceae (Cruciferae)
PERENNIAL OR BIENNIAL
ZONES A2, A3; 1–24
FULL SUN OR LIGHT SHADE
REGULAR WATER

Hesperis matronalis

Old-fashioned cottage garden plant from central and southern Europe; naturalized in North America. Free-branching, to 3 ft. tall and wide, with 4-in., tooth-edged leaves. From late spring into summer, bears rounded clusters of 1/2-in., four-petaled lilac to purple flowers similar to those of stock *(Matthiola)*; blossoms are fragrant at night. Grows readily from seed and often self-sows. When plants get old and woody, replace them with young seedlings. White- and double-flowered forms exist.

HETEROCENTRON elegans (Schizocentron elegans)

SPANISH SHAWL
Melastomataceae
PERENNIAL
ZONES 15–24
PARTIAL SHADE
MODERATE TO REGULAR WATER

Heterocentron elegans

Native from Mexico to Guatemala. To 2–4 in. high, 1½ ft. wide, with creeping, vinelike habit. Glossy, oval evergreen leaves to 1/2 in. wide, each with three well-marked veins. Leaves and stems often take on reddish tones as the season advances. In summer, inch-wide magenta flowers appear among the leaves; calyxes remain after blossoms have withered. When used as a ground cover, blooming plants look like a carpet of bright bougainvillea. Good subject for hanging baskets. Needs frost protection in Zones 15, 16, 18–20. Best in partial shade but tolerates full sun (in cooler climates) and full shade. Protect from snails and slugs.

HETEROMELES arbutifolia

TOYON, CHRISTMAS BERRY, CALIFORNIA HOLLY
Rosaceae
EVERGREEN SHRUB OR TREE
ZONES 5–9, 14–24
FULL SUN OR PARTIAL SHADE
MODERATE WATER

Heteromeles arbutifolia

Native to California Coast Ranges, Sierra Nevada foothills, Baja California. Grows as a dense shrub to 6–10 ft. tall and broad or a multitrunked small tree 15–25 ft. tall and spreading almost as wide (can be pruned to form a single-trunked tree). Thick, leathery, glossy dark green leaves are 2–4 in. long, edged with bristly, pointed teeth. Small white flowers in flattish clusters appear in summer; these are followed in fall to winter by pea-size bright red (rarely yellow) berries, much relished by birds. Flowers attract bees. *H. a. macrocarpa,* from Southern California's Channel Islands, has larger berries.

Toyon improves under cultivation. If trimmed to give abundance of year-old wood, it produces even more berries than in the wild. Valuable as screen or bank planting. Subject to fireblight. Tolerates drought but looks better if watered.

HEUCHERA

CORAL BELLS, ALUM ROOT

Saxifragaceae

PERENNIALS

ZONES VARY BY SPECIES

FULL SUN IN COOLER CLIMATES ONLY

MODERATE TO REGULAR WATER

Heuchera sanguinea

Compact evergreen clumps of roundish leaves with scalloped edges. Slender, wiry, 1–2½-ft. stems bear loose clusters of nodding, bell-shaped flowers, typically ⅛ in. or less across. Dainty blossoms consist of colorful fused sepals and are often petal-less; they are long lasting in cut arrangements, attractive to hummingbirds. Color range includes carmine, crimson, red, coral, rose pink, greenish, and white. The various types bloom at some point between early spring and late summer; some kinds continue into fall. Many recent introductions are grown more for leaf color than floral display.

Use in rock gardens or as ground cover; mass in borders or in front of shrubs; use as edging for beds of taller perennials. Grow in well-drained, humus-rich soil. Will take full sun in cool climates, but in warmer regions they do best with afternoon shade or a northern exposure with open sky above. Divide clumps every 3 or 4 years in spring (or in fall, in mild-winter climates). Use young, vigorous, rooted divisions; discard older, woody rootstocks. Easy to propagate from cuttings started in sand in spring or from seed sown in spring. In mild climates, watch for coral bells' worst enemy—mealybugs—at base of plants.

H. americana. Zones 1–9, 14–24; often short lived in warm-summer areas. From central U.S. Foliage mound 1–2 ft. high and wide. Leaves 1½–4½ in. wide, marbled and veined brown or purple when young, maturing to green mottled with white. Flower stalks to 3 ft. high bear tiny greenish white blossoms in early summer.

The following are varieties grown for handsome foliage (a few also have somewhat more attractive flowers than the basic species).

'Chocolate Ruffles'. Leaves dark chocolate above, burgundy below; burgundy color also shows in the ruffles on leaf edges. Purple blossom spikes and flowers.

'Chocolate Veil'. Chocolate-colored leaves with maroon undersides; top surfaces of leaves are marbled with light purple and silver between veins. Purple flowers tinged lime green.

'Garnet'. Deep red winter foliage; brighter new foliage in spring.

'Lace Ruffles'. Ruffled, scalloped green leaves mottled silvery white.

'Persian Carpet'. Silver leaves with dark purple veins and leaf edges.

'Pewter Moon'. Purple leaves centered with silver.

'Pewter Veil'. Shining silvery leaves; small purple flowers.

'Ring of Fire'. Silvery, purple-veined leaves that develop a red rim in fall.

'Ruby Veil'. Large (8-in.) silvery leaves; veins red near leaf base.

'Velvet Night'. Deep bluish purple leaves.

H. ×brizoides. Zones 1–10, 14–24. Diverse group of hybrids between *H. sanguinea* and other species. To 1–2½ ft. tall, 1–1½ ft. wide, with spring or summer bloom. Seed-grown strain called Bressingham Hybrids offers flowers in white and shades of pink and red. Selected cutting-grown varieties include 'Firefly' ('Leuchtkäfer'), with fragrant, fiery scarlet bells; 'Freedom', profuse rosy pink blooms; 'Bressingham White', long-blooming white; 'June Bride', large pure white blossoms; 'Snowstorm', deep reddish pink flowers above white-variegated foliage.

H. Canyon Series. Zones 2–11, 14–24. Spring-blooming group of mat-forming hybrids. Foliage mounds are 3–6 in. high, 1–2 ft. or more wide, with rounded, medium green, ¾–1½-in. leaves. Three choices with sprays of ½ in. flowers on 16–20 in. stems are rose red 'Canyon Delight', medium pink 'Canyon Pink', and rich red 'Canyon Belle'. The following are smaller, with more diminutive blossoms on stems topping out at 8–12 in.: 'Canyon Chimes', dark pink calyx with slightly protruding white petals; 'Canyon Duet', strongly bicolored pink and white; and 'Canyon Melody', medium pink calyx with protruding white petals.

H. maxima. ISLAND ALUM ROOT. Zones 15–24. Native to Channel Islands off coast of Southern California. Foliage clumps 1–2 ft. tall, spreading 3–4 ft. or more in time. Lobed dark green leaves have a roundish heart shape. Hundreds of small whitish or pinkish blossoms appear on each narrowly branched, 1½–2½-ft. stem in early spring. Good casual ground cover.

H. micrantha. Zones 1–10, 14–24. Native to California, Washington, Oregon, Idaho. Adapts easily to garden conditions. Plant in protected spot in coldest part of range; in desert, give full shade but good light. Long-stalked, roundish, gray-green, 1–3-in.-wide leaves are toothed and lobed, hairy on both sides. Late spring to early summer flowers are whitish or greenish, about ⅛ in. long, carried in loose clusters on leafy, 2–3-ft. stems. Hybrid forms developed from *H. micrantha* are more adaptable than the species itself. Seed-grown (hence variable) varieties include 'Palace Purple', with maplelike, rich brownish or purplish leaves that retain their color all year if given adequate sunlight; and 'Ruffles', with leaves that are deeply lobed and ruffled around the edges.

Heuchera micrantha 'Palace Purple'

H. sanguinea. Zones A1–A3; 1–11, 14–24. Native to New Mexico and Arizona. Round, 1–2-in. leaves with scalloped edges form neat foliage tufts. From spring into summer, slender, wiry, 1–2-ft. stems bear open clusters of nodding, bell-shaped bright red or coral pink flowers. Varieties with white, pink, or crimson flowers are available. 'Cherry Splash' and 'Frosty' display red flowers above variegated foliage—the former has white-and-gold variegation, the latter silvery variegation.

H. 'Santa Ana Cardinal'. Zones 14–24. Outstanding hybrid between garden forms of *H. sanguinea* and *H. maxima.* Unusually vigorous and free-flowering. Foliage clump grows 3–4 ft. wide, with light green leaves 3–4 in. across. Stems to 2 ft. tall carry vibrant rose red flowers, as many as a hundred on a spike. Long bloom season—from late spring through summer, nearly all year in mild-winter areas. Does well with only twice-monthly summer watering.

H. 'Wendy'. Zones 14–24. Resembles 'Santa Ana Cardinal' in plant size, foliage, length of bloom season, and ability to thrive on less summer water than other kinds of coral bells. Stems to 2 ft. tall bear dozens of light peachy pink blossoms.

×HEUCHERELLA

Saxifragaceae

PERENNIALS

ZONES 1–10, 14–24

LIGHT SHADE

REGULAR WATER

×Heucherella alba 'Bridget Bloom'

These hybrids combine the flowering habit of coral bells *(Heuchera)* with the heart-shaped leaves of foamflower *(Tiarella cordifolia).* All produce foliage clumps 4–5 in. high and about 1 ft. wide; good in shaded rock gardens or as woodland ground cover. All types described here produce plumes of small pink flowers. Require well-drained, humus-rich soil.

×H. alba 'Bridget Bloom'. Flowering stems to 16 in. high. Blooms from spring to midsummer.

×H. 'Pink Frost'. Plumes rise to 2 ft. Blooms from spring to fall.

×H. tiarelloides. Sprays of flowers to 1½ ft. high. Blooms from spring to midsummer, often with repeat flowering in autumn.

HIBBERTIA

Dilleniaceae

EVERGREEN SHRUBS AND VINES

ZONES VARY BY SPECIES

FULL SUN OR PARTIAL SHADE

REGULAR WATER

Most are native to Australia, including those described below. All types have bright yellow flowers resembling wild roses. Low-growing species for rock gardens are worth seeking out; these include *H. vestita,* to 6 in. high and 2–3 ft. wide, with tiny dark green leaves and comparatively large (1½-in.) blossoms. The following species are more widely grown.

Hibbertia cuneiformis

H. cuneiformis (Candollea cuneiformis). Shrub. Zones 12, 13, 15–24. Grows to 4 ft. tall and to 6 ft. wide. Polished green, 1-in.-long leaves are tapered at base, toothed at tip. Flowers carried all along new growth in spring. Prune after flowering to control outline. Requires exceptionally fast drainage. Tolerates wind.

Hibbertia scandens

H. scandens (H. volubilis). GUINEA GOLD VINE. Zones 16, 17, 21–24. Fast-growing vine climbs by twining stems to 8–10 ft. In ideal climate, foliage is handsome all year—narrow, waxy dark green leaves to 3 in. long. Blooms from spring into early fall. Good for small garden areas if trained on trellis or against low fence; can be grown as ground cover. Do any significant thinning in late fall or winter; remove errant stems as needed during bloom time. Recovers quickly from light frosts.

HIBISCUS

Malvaceae

PERENNIALS, ANNUALS, AND EVERGREEN AND DECIDUOUS SHRUBS OR TREES

ZONES VARY BY SPECIES

FULL SUN

REGULAR WATER

Among the showiest flowering plants seen in Western gardens; some are very tender tropical species grown in Hawaii. Plants typically bear funnel-shaped blossoms, often with prominent stamens. The many species offer a wide range of flower colors. The giant whitefly is a relatively new pest of hibiscus in coastal Southern California, but a parasitoid wasp has been released to control it.

Hibiscus schizopetalus

H. arnottianus. HAWAIIAN WHITE HIBISCUS. Shrub or tree. Zones 23, 24; H1, H2. Native to Hawaii, island of Oahu. To 30 ft. high, 25 ft. wide. Blooms almost year-round, producing slightly fragrant white flowers with central column of magenta stamens. Beautiful for small entryway tree or as landscape accent.

H. brackenridgei. Shrub or tree. Zones 23, 24; H1, H2. Native to Hawaii—and the official state flower there. Plant grows to 8–15 ft. high and about half as wide, with a profusion of large, pure yellow flowers borne in spring and early summer. Somewhat short lived (4 to 6 years in the wild).

H. calyphyllus (H. rockii). Woody-based perennial or shrub. Zones 23, 24; H1, H2. Native to tropical Africa. Sprawling growth to 3–9 ft. high and as wide. Flowers are 3–4 in. wide, sulfur yellow marked brownish red to maroon at the base.

H. huegelii. See Alyogyne huegelii

H. manihot. See Abelmoschus manihot

H. moschatus. See Abelmoschus moschatus

H. moscheutos. PERENNIAL HIBISCUS, ROSE-MALLOW. Perennial. Zones 2–24; H1. Largest flowers of all hibiscus, some reaching 1 ft. across, on a plant 6–8 ft. high and 3 ft. wide. Bloom starts in late spring or early summer and continues until frost. Oval, toothed leaves are deep green above, whitish beneath. Plants die down in winter, even in mild climates. For most spectacular bloom, feed at 6- to 8-week intervals during growing season. Protect from wind.

Seed-grown strains often flower the first year if sown indoors and planted outdoors early. Southern Belle grows 4 ft. tall; Disco Belle, Frisbee, and Rio Carnival reach 2–2½ ft. tall. All have 8–12-in.-wide flowers in red, pink, rose, or white, often with red eye. The many cutting-grown selections and hybrids include these 4-footers: 'Blue River', 10-in. pure white flowers; 'George Riegel', 10-in. ruffled pink blooms with red eye; 'Lady Baltimore', with 6–8-in. glowing pink flowers with a large red center; 'Lord Baltimore', 10-in. deep red; 'The Clown', 6–8-in. light pink with red eye; and 'Turn of the Century', 5–10-in. blooms with red eye and bicolor petals of pink and white.

H. mutabilis. CONFEDERATE ROSE. Deciduous shrub. Zones 4–24; H1, H2. In warmest climates, shrubby or treelike to 15 ft. tall, 8 ft. wide. Behaves more like perennial in colder part of range, growing flowering branches from woody base or short trunk. Broad, oval leaves with three to five lobes. Summer flowers are 4–6 in. wide, opening white or pink and changing to deep red by evening. 'Rubrus' has red flowers. Double-flowered forms exist.

H. rosa-sinensis. CHINESE HIBISCUS, TROPICAL HIBISCUS. Evergreen shrub. Zones 9, 12–16, 19–24; H1, H2. Provide overhead protection where winter lows frequently drop below 30°F/−1°C. Where temperatures go much lower, grow in containers and shelter indoors over winter; or treat as annual, setting out fresh plants each spring. Also makes a good houseplant.

Hibiscus rosa-sinensis

One of most flamboyant flowering shrubs. Reaches 30 ft. tall and 15–20 ft. wide in Hawaii, but more typical size on mainland is 8–15 ft. tall, 5–8 ft. wide. Glossy leaves vary somewhat in size and texture depending on variety. Growth habit may be dense and dwarfish or loose and open. Summer flowers are single or double, 4–8 in. wide. Colors range from white through pink to red, from yellow and apricot to orange. Individual flowers last only a day, but the plant blooms continuously.

This shrub requires excellent drainage; if necessary, improve soil for best drainage or set plants in raised beds or containers. Can be used as screen, espalier, or specimen. To develop good branch structure, prune poorly shaped young plants when you set them out in spring. To keep a mature plant growing vigorously, prune out about a third of old wood in early spring. Pinching out tips of stems in spring and summer increases flower production. All varieties susceptible to aphids. There are thousands of selections; the following are some of those sold in the West. None will take hard frosts, but some (described below as "hardy") are a little hardier than the average.

'Agnes Galt'. Large, single pink flowers. Vigorous plant; prune to prevent legginess. Hardy.

'All Aglow'. Large, single flowers with broad, gold-blotched orange petals, pink halo around a white throat.

'Bridal Veil'. Large, pure white single flowers last 3 or 4 days.

'Bride'. Very large, single, palest blush to white flowers. Slow or moderate growth to open-branched 4 ft.

'Brilliant' ('San Diego Red'). Bright red single flowers in profusion. Vigorous, hardy.

'Butterfly'. Small, single bright yellow flowers. Slow, upright growth to 7 ft.

'California Gold'. Heavy yield of single flowers in yellow with red center. Slow to moderate growth to a compact 7 ft.

'Cooperi'. Bears small, single deep red flowers, but principal attraction is the foliage—narrow leaves variegated with white.

'Crown of Bohemia'. Double gold flowers; petals shade to carmine orange toward base. Moderate or fast growth to 5 ft. Bushy, upright. Hardy.

'Diamond Head'. Large double flowers in deepest red (nearly black red). Compact growth to 5 ft.

'Ecstasy'. Large, single bright red flowers with striking white variegation. Upright growth to 4 ft.

'Fiesta'. Large, single bright orange flowers with white central eye edged in red. Ruffled petal edges. Strong, erect growth to 6–7 ft.

'Fullmoon'. Pure yellow double flowers. Moderately vigorous growth to a compact 6 ft.

'Golden Dust'. Bright orange single flowers with yellow-orange centers. Compact, thick-foliaged plant 4 ft. tall.

'Hula Girl'. Large, single canary yellow flowers have deep red eye. Flowers stay open several days. Compact growth to 6 ft.

'Itsy Bitsy Peach', 'Itsy Bitsy Pink', and 'Itsy Bitsy Red' all have small leaves and small (2–3-in.) single flowers.

'Jason Okumoto'. Semidouble scarlet-throated flowers have a cup-and-saucer look, with thick central group of shorter orange petals surrounded by collar of large pink petals.

'Kate Sessions'. Large, broad-petaled single flowers are red, with gold tinge on petal undersides. Moderate growth to 10 ft. Upright, open habit.

'Kona'. Ruffled double pink flowers. Vigorous, upright, bushy; prune regularly. 'Kona Improved' has fuller flowers of richer pink color.

'Kona Princess'. Small double pink flowers on a 6–7 ft. shrub.

'Morning Glory'. Single blush pink flowers changing to warmer pink with white petal tips. Grows 8–10 ft. tall.

'President'. Large, single flowers in intense red shading to deep pink in throat. Upright, compact, 6–7 ft. tall.

'Red Dragon' ('Celia'). Small to medium, double dark red flowers. Upright, compact, 6–8 ft. tall.

'Ross Estey'. Flowers very large, single, with broad, overlapping pink petals shading to coral orange toward tips. Heavy-textured flowers last 2 or 3 days on bush. Leaves are unusually large, ruffled, polished dark green. Vigorous grower to 8 ft.

'Vulcan'. Large, single red flowers with yellow on back of petals open from yellow buds. Flowers often last more than a day. Compact grower, 4–6 ft. tall.

'White Wings'. Profuse, narrow-petaled, single white flowers with small red eye. Vigorous, open, upright; prune to control legginess. A compact form with smaller flowers is available.

All of the above varieties are what might be called landscape hibiscus. They are plants sturdy enough to survive reliably in open ground wherever hibiscus are hardy, and they bloom reliably with routine good care. Plants of another group—one that might be called show or connoisseur's hibiscus—are becoming available. These have large (8–10-in.), single or double flowers with striking colors, including novel shades such as gray, tan, brown, and blue. Most show blends of two or three colors. Plants are grafted onto sturdy rootstocks. They grow to about 6 ft. high and wide in the ground; can also be grown indefinitely in pots as small as 10 in. in diameter. To bloom, they need night temperatures in the 60s or higher, warmer temperatures by day, and at least 1 hour of direct sun daily. The following selections, all with single flowers, are a few of the many varieties that are available.

'Fifth Dimension'. Gunmetal gray edged with orange yellow; white lines radiate from the center toward the edges.

'Georgia's Pearl'. Pure light yellow blossoms have a dark red eye surrounded by a narrow zone of pink.

'Rainbow Christie'. Pink with a dark red eye and a wide white border.

'Silver Memories'. Unusual combination of silvery white blending to cream.

H. sabdariffa. ROSELLE, JAMAICA SORREL, JAMAICA FLOWER. Annual. Zones 1–24; H1, H2. Narrowish plant reaches 4–7 ft. high. Oval, 3-in.-long leaves with three to five lobes. Grown for fleshy red calyxes that surround bases of yellow flowers. These calyxes are used for making sauce, jelly, cool drinks, or teas; dried, they are known as Jamaica flowers. Their flavor is reminiscent of cranberry or currant. Plants need long, hot summer to ripen flowers. Bloom begins as days shorten; early frosts prevent harvest. Grow like tomatoes; space plants 1½–2 ft. apart in rows. Can be used as narrow temporary hedge.

H. schizopetalus. FRINGED HIBISCUS, CORAL HIBISCUS. Evergreen shrub. Zones 23, 24; H1, H2. From tropical East Africa. To 9–15 ft. high, 6–12 ft. wide, with a weeping habit. Throughout most of the year, produces unusual pink flowers with fringed petals. There are a number of hybrids with pure white, pink, red, or yellow blossoms. Plants are sometimes kept small and grown in hanging baskets.

H. syriacus. ROSE OF SHARON, SHRUB ALTHAEA. Deciduous shrub. Zones 2–24; H1. To 10–12 ft. tall and 6 ft. wide. Upright and compact when young, spreading and open with age. Easily trained to single trunk with treelike top or as an espalier. Sometimes trimmed as a hedge. Leaves to 4 in. long, often three lobed, coarsely toothed. Leafs out later in spring than most other deciduous shrubs; foliage drops in fall without coloring. Blooms from mid- or late summer until frost, resembling a bush covered with hollyhocks. Blossoms are single, semidouble, or double, 2½–3 in. across; some have a conspicuously contrasting red to purple throat. Single flowers are slightly more effective, opening somewhat wider, but they tend to produce many unattractive capsule-type fruits—which in turn produce many unwanted seedlings.

Hibiscus syriacus
'Diana'

Easy to grow. Prefers heat, tolerates some drought. Prune to shape; for bigger flowers, cut back previous season's growth in winter, cutting down to two buds. Where winter temperatures drop to –10°F/–23°C or lower, protect young plants with a winter mulch for first few years. The following, some of them hard to find, are among the best varieties.

'Albus'. Single pure white blooms to 4 in. across.

'Anemoniflora' ('Paeoniflora'). Semidouble red blossoms with a deeper crimson eye.

'Ardens'. Double purple.

'Blue Bird'. Single blue with deep red eye.

'Blushing Bride'. Double bright pink.

'Boule de Feu'. Double deep violet pink.

'Coelestis'. Single violet blue with reddish purple throat.

'Collie Mullens'. Double purplish lavender.

'Lucy'. Double deep rose with red eye.

'Purpurea'. Semidouble purple with red eye.

'Red Heart'. Single white with red eye.

'Woodbridge'. Single deep rose with red eye.

Newer selections are sterile triploids, which have a long blooming season and set few or no seedpods. They include 'Aphrodite', rose pink with deep red eye; 'Diana', pure white; 'Helene', white with deep red eye; and 'Minerva', ruffled flowers of lavender pink with reddish purple eye.

H. tiliaceus. TREE HIBISCUS, HAU, MAHOE. Evergreen tree. Zones 23, 24; H1, H2. Native to Old and New World tropics. To 30 ft. tall and at least as wide, with broad, leathery, unlobed green leaves to 6 in. long. The 4-in. flowers, each lasting a day, open yellow and deepen to orange by day's end. Excellent tolerance of salt, wind, drought and heat. Tangled mess in the wild; requires heavy pruning to shape into suitable tree form and regular pruning to maintain form.

H. waimeae. WHITE KAUAI HIBISCUS, KOKIO KEOKEO. Evergreen shrub or tree. Zone H1. Native to Kauai. To 18–25 ft. tall and about half as wide. Blooms much of the year. Each fragrant, 5–8-in. flower lasts just one day; blossoms open white in the morning, turn light pinkish by afternoon. Rounded, downy light green leaves to 7 in. long. Use singly as a specimen or mass as a screen. Protect from wind. Full sun or light shade.

HIMALAYAN POPPY. See MECONOPSIS betonicifolia

HINAHINA. See HELIOTROPIUM anomalum argenteum

FOR INFORMATION ON YOUR CLIMATE ZONE
PLEASE SEE PAGES 27–63

HIPPEASTRUM

Hippeastrum hybrid

AMARYLLIS

Amaryllidaceae

PERENNIALS FROM BULBS

ZONES VARY BY TYPE; OR INDOORS

LIGHT SHADE IN HOTTEST CLIMATES; BRIGHT LIGHT

REGULAR WATER DURING GROWTH AND BLOOM

Almost all amaryllis sold are hybrids; they can be grown outdoors year-round in Zones 13, 15–17, 21–24, H1, H2, and (with some shelter) in Zones 8, 9, 14, 18, 20. Usually marketed as giant amaryllis or Royal Dutch amaryllis (though developed by hybridizers around the world from species native to Central and South America). Named varieties or color selections are available in reds, pinks, salmon, near-orange, and white, some striped and variously marked. Two to several flowers, often 8–9 in. across, form on a stout, 2-ft. stem. Newer forms include double-flowered varieties in white (some with picotee edges), creamy yellow, and pink, miniatures with 3–5-in. flowers topping 12–15-in. stems; and an unusual evergreen Brazilian species, *H. papilio* (Zones 8, 9, 13–24), with 5-in. greenish white flowers heavily patterned in dark red.

Where amaryllis are grown outdoors, flowers bloom in spring, appearing either before or with the broad, strap-shaped leaves. Indoors, they bloom just a few weeks after planting.

Where hardy in the ground, they can be planted in large clumps or drifts. In fall, set bulbs 1 ft. apart in organically enriched, well-drained soil; keep tops of bulb necks even with soil surface. Protect from slugs and snails. Water thoroughly, then keep soil barely moist until leaves emerge. Once plants have sprouted, increase watering, giving enough to keep soil moist but not soggy. Leaves will grow through summer and disappear in fall if plants are dried off; otherwise, some foliage will remain. Divide infrequently.

Even where they are hardy, amaryllis are usually grown in containers. Plant them from midautumn through winter in a rich, sandy potting mix amended with bonemeal or superphosphate. Allow a 2-in. space between the bulb and the edge of the pot; set upper half of bulb above soil surface. Firm soil, water well, and then keep soil barely moist until plant growth begins. When flowers fade, cut off stem; keep up regular watering and feeding until late summer. At this point, cut back on watering. When leaves are completely yellow, withhold water and let plants dry out. Repot in late fall or early winter.

HIPPOPHAE rhamnoides

Hippophae rhamnoides

SEA BUCKTHORN

Elaeagnaceae

DECIDUOUS SHRUB OR TREE

ZONES A2, A3; 1–6

FULL SUN

MODERATE TO REGULAR WATER

Native from Europe to Mongolia. Usually seen as an open, mounding shrub 8–10 ft. tall and wide, but it can grow much taller and spread by suckering from the roots. Thorny branches carry narrow (¼-in.-wide), 3-in.-long, silvery green to grayish green leaves. Flowers are inconspicuous, but fruits on female plants are showy—bright orange, round or oval, to ⅓ in. long. Fruit persists on the plant into winter—apparently it is too acidic to appeal to birds. High in vitamin C, it can be made into sauces or jam. You need both male and female plants to get fruit.

Sea buckthorn tolerates cold, wind, poor soil (as long as it is well drained), and salt spray. Good screen plant for difficult situations.

HOGAN CEDAR. See THUJA plicata 'Fastigiata'

HOHERIA

Malvaceae

EVERGREEN AND DECIDUOUS TREES OR SHRUBS

ZONES VARY BY SPECIES

FULL SUN OR PARTIAL SHADE

REGULAR WATER

Native to New Zealand. Leaves are bright green, leathery, toothed, 3–5 in. long, 1½–2 in. wide. Pure white flowers about 1 in. wide form in clusters among leaves.

Hoheria glabrata

H. glabrata. MOUNTAIN RIBBONWOOD. Deciduous shrub or tree. Zones 4–6, 15–17. To 35 ft. tall, 20 ft. wide. Summer bloom. Attractive with azaleas and rhododendrons.

H. populnea. NEW ZEALAND LACEBARK. Evergreen tree. Zones 4–6, 15–17, 21–24. Rarely seen but worth seeking out for coastal gardens. As graceful as birch *(Betula)* in growth habit; also puts on good show of flowers from late summer into fall. Grows fast to 20–30 ft. and remains at that height for many years; eventually attains 50–60 ft. in old age. Slender tree—about half as wide as tall. Inner bark is interestingly perforated. Like birch, ideal for multiple planting and groves. Has deep, well-behaved root system. Self-sows where adapted; seedling volunteers may present a problem where tree is growing in ground cover.

HOLLY. See ILEX

HOLLY FERN. See ARACHNIODES simplicior, CYRTOMIUM falcatum

HOLLYHOCK. See ALCEA rosea

HOLLYLEAF CHERRY. See PRUNUS ilicifolia

HOLLYLEAF REDBERRY. See RHAMNUS crocea ilicifolia

HOLLYLEAF SWEETSPIRE. See ITEA ilicifolia

HOLLYWOOD JUNIPER. See JUNIPERUS chinensis 'Torulosa'

HOLODISCUS

Rosaceae

DECIDUOUS SHRUBS

ZONES VARY BY SPECIES

PARTIAL SHADE

LITTLE TO REGULAR WATER

Both species described here are Western natives, similar in appearance to the related *Spiraea.* Nodding, branched clusters of many small, creamy white flowers at branch tips in late spring or early summer make quite a show and attract birds. Flowers age to tannish gold, remain attractive for a long time. Prune by thinning after flowers have turned brown and clusters have withered. Use these shrubs in native plantings or rural low-maintenance gardens where they can fend for themselves.

Holodiscus discolor

H. discolor. CREAM BUSH, OCEAN SPRAY. Zones 1–9, 14–19. Native to Coast Ranges, Sierra Nevada; north to British Columbia, east to Rocky Mountains. May reach 20 ft. tall and 15 ft. wide in moist, rich soil. In dry, sunny situations, such as east of Cascades in Oregon and Washington, may grow just 3 ft. tall and 4 ft. wide. Triangular leaves to 3 in. long are deep green above, white and hairy beneath; edges are coarsely toothed. Flower clusters to 1 ft. long.

H. dumosus. MOUNTAIN SPRAY, ROCK SPIRAEA. Zones 1–3, 10. Native to eastern slopes of the Cascades of Oregon and to shady canyons in the Rockies from Wyoming southward. Generally smaller than *H. discolor* (may reach 15 ft. tall in good conditions), with narrower, shorter flower clusters (to 7 in. long). Coarsely toothed leaves less than 1 in. long.

HOMERIA collina

Iridaceae

PERENNIAL FROM CORM

ZONES 4–24; OR DIG AND STORE

FULL SUN

REGULAR WATER DURING GROWTH AND BLOOM

Homeria collina

Native to South Africa, where it is often found growing on slopes from low to high altitudes. First comes one floppy, grasslike leaf. It is followed by branching or unbranched, 1½-ft. stems bearing 2½–3-in.-wide flowers in soft yellow or muted orange. Soon after bloom, the foliage yellows and dies down. Where adapted, plant anytime from fall through winter, setting corms 2 in. deep, 3 in. apart; in such regions, corms can be left in the ground and allowed to multiply freely. If they are to receive moisture during their long dormancy, however, soil must be very well drained. If drainage is less than excellent and you can't keep planting area dry, dig after leaves have died down and store over summer; or grow in pots. In areas beyond hardiness range, plant in spring (as soon as soil can be worked) for summer flowers; lift corms in late summer or early fall and store over winter. In areas where the species has escaped gardens and naturalized, it has been found toxic to livestock.

HONEY BUSH. See MELIANTHUS major

HONEY LOCUST. See GLEDITSIA triacanthos

HONEYSUCKLE. See LONICERA

HONEYWORT. See CERINTHE major

HONG KONG ORCHID TREE. See BAUHINIA × blakeana

HOP. See HUMULUS

HOP BUSH, HOPSEED BUSH. See DODONAEA

HOREHOUND. See MARRUBIUM vulgare

HORNBEAM. See CARPINUS

HORNED POPPY. See GLAUCIUM

HORSE BEAN. See BEAN, BROAD

HORSECHESTNUT. See AESCULUS

HORSERADISH

Brassicaceae (Cruciferae)

PERENNIAL

ALL ZONES

FULL SUN

REGULAR WATER

Horseradish

Botanically known as *Armoracia rusticana.* Native to southeastern Europe. Large (to about 3-ft.), coarse, weedy-looking plant grown for its large white roots, which are peeled, grated, and mixed with vinegar or cream to make a condiment. Does best in rich, moist soils in cool regions. Grow it in some sunny, out-of-the-way corner. In late winter or early spring, set root horizontally in 3–4-in.-deep trench and cover with 2 in. of soil. One plant should provide enough horseradish for a family of four. For multiple plants, space 2½–3 ft. apart. Through fall, winter, and spring, harvest pieces of horseradish roots from the outside of the root clump as you need them—that way you'll have your horseradish fresh and tangy.

HORSETAIL. See EQUISETUM hyemale

HORSETAIL TREE. See CASUARINA equisetifolia

HOSTA

PLANTAIN LILY

Liliaceae

PERENNIALS

ZONES VARY BY SPECIES

PARTIAL OR FULL SHADE

REGULAR WATER

Hosta 'Great Expectations'

These plants' real glory is in their foliage—the thin spikes of blue or white trumpet-shaped flowers that last for several weeks in summer are a dividend. Leaves may be heart shaped, lance shaped, oval, or nearly round, carried at the ends of leafstalks that rise from the ground and radiate from the center of a clump. They overlap to form symmetrical, almost shingled-looking foliage mounds ranging in size from dwarf (as small as 3–4 in. across) to giant (as broad as 5 ft.). Leaves may be glossy or dull, with smooth, quilted, or puckery texture and smooth or wavy edges. Foliage colors range from light to dark green to chartreuse (sometimes almost yellow), gray, and blue. There are also color combinations, including variegations in white, cream, or yellow. (Color of variegation may differ with climate and soil type.)

New varieties enter the scene in ever-increasing numbers. Few plants have undergone so many name changes; to be sure you are getting the one you want, buy the plant in full leaf or deal with an expert. Many hostas are available only from mail-order specialists. All are native to eastern Asia.

Generally, hostas are shade lovers, though some will tolerate sun (those with considerable white or yellow in leaves are least sun tolerant), and most will take considerable sun in cool-summer zones. Plants grown in sun will be more compact and will produce more flowers. Hostas grow most luxuriantly in good, organically enriched soil, with regular feeding during the growing season. All go dormant in winter (even in mild climates), collapsing to almost nothing. Clumps expand in size over the years and shade out weeds; remain vigorous without division—clumps become more beautiful as they grow larger. To increase a planting, carefully remove plantlets from a clump's perimeter. Or cut a wedge-shaped piece from a clump and transplant it; the clump will fill in quickly. Protect from slugs and snails (hostas with heavily textured or waxy leaves are said to be less attractive to the pests). Good in containers.

H. fortunei. Zones A1–A3; 1–10, 14–21. Variable plant known mainly for its many varieties, which offer a wide range of foliage colors. Two choices, both to 2 ft. tall and 3 ft. wide, are *H. f. aureomarginata,* with distinctly veined, deep olive green leaves irregularly rimmed in yellow, and *H. f. hyacinthina,* with slightly puckered gray-green leaves edged with a fine white line. Both bear lavender blooms.

H. hybrids. Zones 1–10, 14–21; some succeed in Zones 22–24. The following list represents just a few of the many hundreds of possibilities. Size given at the start of each listing is for foliage clump. Performance in Zones 22–24 will vary, but all are worth a try in these areas.

'Blue Angel'. To 2½ ft. tall, 6 ft. wide. Blue leaves; near-white flowers on 4-ft. stalks.

'Francee'. To 15 in. tall, 3 ft. wide. Dark green leaves with a sharply defined white border; light lavender flowers on 2½-ft. stalks.

'Frances Williams'. To 20 in. tall, 3 ft. wide. Heavily corrugated blue leaves are bordered with yellow. White flowers on 2-ft. stalks.

'Great Expectations'. To 2 ft. tall, 2½ ft. wide. Leaves are creamy yellow in center, surrounded by a wide blue-green edge. White flowers on 3-ft. stalks.

'Honeybells'. To 2½ ft. high, 4 ft. wide. Wavy-edged yellow-green leaves; lightly scented pale lilac flowers on stalks 3 ft. tall.

'Krossa Regal'. To 2½ ft. high and wide, with big, leathery, frosty blue leaves that arch upward and outward to form a vase-shaped plant. Lavender flower spikes can reach 5–6 ft. tall.

'Patriot'. To 15 in. tall, 3 ft. wide. Resembles 'Francee', but leaves have a wider white border. Lavender flowers on 2½-ft. stems.

'Sagae'. To 2 ft. tall, 3 ft. wide, with upswept foliage forming a vase shape. Blue-gray leaves with a wide creamy white border. Lavender flowers on 4½-ft. stalks. ▶

H. plantaginea. FRAGRANT PLANTAIN LILY. Zones 1–10, 14–24. To 2 ft. high, 3 ft. wide. Glossy bright green leaves to 10 in. long, broadly oval with parallel veins and quilted surface. Large, noticeably fragrant white flowers on 2½-ft. stalks. 'Venus' forms a slightly shorter clump and has double flowers.

H. sieboldiana. Zones 1–10, 14–21. To 3 ft. high, 4 ft. wide. Blue-green, broadly heart-shaped leaves, 10–15 in. long, heavily veined and puckered. Many slender pale lilac flowers nestle close to leaves. Foliage of 'Elegans' is covered in a blue-gray bloom.

H. ventricosa (H. caerulea). BLUE PLANTAIN LILY. Zones 1–10, 14–24. To 2 ft. high, 3 ft. wide. Common name refers to violet-blue blossoms on 3-ft. stalks, not to foliage color: leaves are glossy deep green, broadly heart shaped, prominently veined, to 8 in. long. Leaves of 'Aureo-maculata' are yellowish green with a green border. 'Aureo-marginata' ('Variegata') has green leaves edged with creamy white.

HOTTENTOT FIG. See CARPOBROTUS edulis

HOUSELEEK. See SEMPERVIVUM

HOUTTUYNIA cordata

Saururaceae

PERENNIAL

ZONES 2–9, 14–24

SUN OR SHADE

REGULAR TO AMPLE WATER

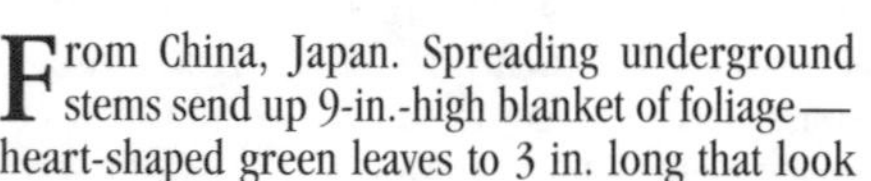

Houttuynia cordata 'Chameleon'

From China, Japan. Spreading underground stems send up 9-in.-high blanket of foliage—heart-shaped green leaves to 3 in. long that look very much like those of English ivy *(Hedera helix)*. Foliage emits an odd scent when crushed, reminiscent of orange peel. Inconspicuous clusters of white-bracted flowers like tiny dogwood *(Cornus)* blossoms. Unusual ground cover that disappears completely in winter, even in mild climates. Most commonly grown form of species is 'Chameleon' ('Tricolor', 'Variegata'), with showy splashes of cream, pink, yellow, and red on foliage; colors are most intense in sun.

Can spread aggressively in wet ground. For ground cover, plant 1½–2 ft. apart; curb growth with wood, concrete, or metal barrier extending 8–12 in. into the soil. Attractive in containers.

HOWEA

Arecaceae (Palmae)

PALMS

ZONES 17, 21–24; H1, H2; OR INDOORS

PARTIAL SHADE; BRIGHT INDIRECT LIGHT

REGULAR WATER

Howea forsteriana

Feather palms native to Lord Howe Island in the South Pacific. Slow growing; reach full height in tropics but only perhaps half as tall in California, where they are typically planted under other trees for frost protection. With age, finely divided leaves drop to show clean, green trunk ringed with leaf scars. These are the kentia palms of florists' shops (usually sold there under the name "kentia") and make ideal potted plants—the classic parlor palms. To minimize spider mite problems, keep fronds clean and dust free. Indoor plants withstand drafts, some watering neglect.

H. belmoreana. SENTRY PALM. Less common than *H. forsteriana.* Tends to be smaller than the latter (grows to 25 ft. tall and 15 ft. wide), with 6–7-ft.-long leaves.

H. forsteriana. PARADISE PALM. To 60 ft. tall, 20 ft. wide, with leaves to 9 ft. long; leaflets are long and drooping.

HOYA

WAX FLOWER, WAX PLANT

Asclepiadaceae

PERENNIALS

ZONES VARY BY SPECIES; OR INDOORS

PARTIAL OR FULL SHADE; BRIGHT LIGHT

REGULAR WATER

Hoya carnosa

Tropical plants with thick, waxy, evergreen leaves and tight clusters of small, waxy flowers that appear in leaf joints during summer. These plants prefer rich, loose, well-drained soil. When grown as container plants, they bloom best when pot-bound. Do not prune out the short stalks that bear flowers, because new flower clusters will develop on them. Specialists list dozens of available species and hybrids, with growth habit varying from vining to shrubby.

H. carnosa. WAX FLOWER, WAX PLANT. Zones H1, H2; with overhead protection, also in Zones 15–24 (but even there it is quickly damaged by temperatures much below freezing). From India, Burma, southern China. Vining plant grows to 10–20 ft., with green, oval, 2–4-in.-long rigid leaves. Fragrant (more pronounced at night) flowers in big, round, convex clusters; each ½-in. blossom is creamy white, centered with a five-pointed pink star. Red young leaves give extra color. Attractive trained on a pillar or trellis. Indoors, traditionally trained on wire in a sunny window. In cool climates, allow plant to go dormant in winter, giving only enough water to keep it from shriveling.

'Variegata' has leaves edged in white suffused with pink; it is not as vigorous or hardy as the plain species. 'Exotica' shows yellow-and-pink variegation. 'Krinkle Kurl' has crinkly leaves closely spaced on short stems; it is often sold as 'Compacta' or as Hindu-rope plant.

H. lanceolata bella. Zones H1, H2; indoor/outdoor plant elsewhere. Native from Himalayas to Burma. Shrubby growth to 1½–3 ft. high and wide, with fleshy green leaves to 1½ in. long and sweetly aromatic clusters of ½-in., purple-centered white flowers. Slender, upright branches droop as they grow older. Best used in hanging basket.

HUCKLEBERRY. See VACCINIUM ovatum, V. parvifolium

HUMATA tyermannii

BEAR'S FOOT FERN

Polypodiaceae

FERN

ZONES 17, 23, 24; H1, H2; OR INDOORS

PARTIAL SHADE

REGULAR WATER

Humata tyermannii

Native to China. This small fern has furry, creeping rhizomes that look something like bear's feet. Fronds 8–10 in. long, very finely cut, rising at intervals from the rhizome. Like squirrel's foot fern *(Davallia)* in appearance and uses, but slower growing.

HUMBOLDT LILY. See LILIUM humboldtii

HUMMINGBIRD BUSH. See GREVILLEA thelemanniana

HUMMINGBIRD FLOWER. See ZAUSCHNERIA

HUMMINGBIRD MINT. See AGASTACHE

FOR GROWING SYMBOL EXPLANATIONS PLEASE SEE PAGE 161

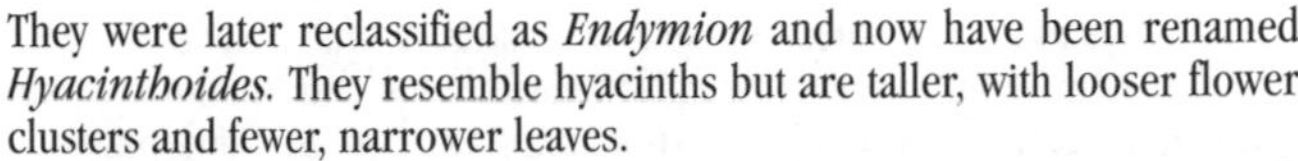

HUMULUS

HOP

Cannabaceae

PERENNIAL VINES

ZONES A2, A3; 1–10, 14–21

FULL SUN

REGULAR WATER

Humulus lupulus

Extremely fast-growing perennial vines with large, deeply lobed, toothed leaves to 6 in. long are attractive for summer screening on trellises or arbors—and one species yields the hops used in beer. Bloom in late summer. Male plants produce flower panicles; females bear blossoms in greenish spikes resembling pinecones. Squarish, hairy stems twine vertically; to get horizontal growth, twine stem tips by hand. Cut stems to ground after frost turns them brown; regrowth comes the following spring.

H. japonicus. JAPANESE HOP. From eastern Asia. Grows to 20–30 ft. Bears ¾-in. female flower spikes. Dark green leaves have five to seven lobes; 'Variegatus' marked with white. Sow seeds in place in spring.

H. lupulus. COMMON HOP. From many northern temperate regions of the world. This species produces the traditional flavoring for beer. The hops—female flowers—are soft, flaky, 1–2-in., light green cones of bracts and blossoms that emit a fresh, piny fragrance. Bright green leaves have three to five lobes. Tender top shoots can be cooked as a vegetable. Plants sold in nurseries are typically female; no pollenizer needed. May be offered as potted plants or as dormant roots. The roots should be planted in rich soil in early spring; set just below soil surface with thick end up. Many varieties are available, including 'Aureus', which has attractive chartreuse foliage. *H. l. neomexicanus (H. americanus),* native to central and southern Rockies, differs from the plain species only in botanical details.

HUNNEMANNIA fumariifolia

MEXICAN TULIP POPPY, GOLDEN CUP

Papaveraceae

PERENNIAL USUALLY TREATED AS ANNUAL

ZONES 1–24; H1, H2

FULL SUN

LITTLE OR NO WATER TO MODERATE WATER

Hunnemannia fumariifolia

Mexican native related to California poppy *(Eschscholzia).* Bushy, open grower to 2–3 ft. high; finely divided blue-green leaves. Cup-shaped, pure yellow blooms, 3 in. across with crinkled petals, in summer, early fall. If cut in bud, blooms last for a week in water. Plant from containers or start from seed, sowing seed in place in warm, sunny location and thinning seedlings to 1 ft. apart. Showy when massed. Reseeds. Needs excellent drainage.

HYACINTH BEAN. See DOLICHOS lablab

HYACINTHOIDES

BLUEBELL, WOOD HYACINTH

Liliaceae

PERENNIALS FROM BULBS

ZONES VARY BY SPECIES

FILTERED SUN OR LIGHT SHADE

REGULAR WATER DURING GROWTH AND BLOOM

BULBS MAY CAUSE AN ALLERGIC SKIN REACTION

Hyacinthoides non-scripta

These spring-blooming bulbs were once classed in the genus *Scilla* and are still popularly known by that name; some bulb dealers continue to list them as such. They were later reclassified as *Endymion* and now have been renamed *Hyacinthoides.* They resemble hyacinths but are taller, with looser flower clusters and fewer, narrower leaves.

Climate will determine which species is better for your area. Spanish bluebell *(H. hispanica)* is the better choice for warmer regions. The English species *(H. non-scripta)* definitely prefers colder winters and moderate to cool summers. When grown near each other, the two species sometimes hybridize, producing intermediate forms. Plant bulbs in fall, setting them 3 in. deep in mild climates, as deep as 6 in. where winters are severe. Space about 6 in. apart. Propensity for reseeding makes these good subjects for naturalizing; lovely in informal drifts among tall shrubs, under deciduous trees, among low-growing perennials. Need regular moisture from planting time until foliage dies and at least some moisture in summer. Divide infrequently; when division is needed, do it in fall. Plants thrive in pots, and flowers are good for cutting. Bulbs (like those of hyacinth) can cause allergic reactions on contact.

H. hispanica (Scilla campanulata, S. hispanica). SPANISH BLUEBELL. Zones 1–11, 14–24. From Spain, North Africa. Prolific and vigorous, with inch-wide, strap-shaped leaves and sturdy, 20-in. stems bearing 12 or more nodding, unscented bells about ¾ in. long. Blue is the most popular color, 'Excelsior' (deep blue) the most popular variety. There are also white, pink, and rose forms. Leaves can look a trifle ratty before dying back.

H. non-scripta (Scilla non-scripta). ENGLISH BLUEBELL, WOOD HYACINTH. Best in Zones 2b–6, 15. From western Europe. Fragrant blue flowers are narrower and smaller than those of *H. hispanica,* on 1-ft. stems that nod at the tip. Leaves are also narrower—only about ½ in. wide. 'Alba' is white flowered; 'Rosea' has pink blooms.

HYACINTHUS

HYACINTH

Liliaceae

PERENNIALS FROM BULBS

ZONES VARY BY TYPE

FULL SUN

REGULAR WATER DURING GROWTH AND BLOOM

BULBS MAY CAUSE AN ALLERGIC SKIN REACTION

Hyacinthus orientalis

Springtime bloomers grown for spikes of bell-shaped, fragrant flowers that rise from basal bundle of narrow bright green leaves. Two of the species formerly sold as *Hyacinthus* have been reclassified; remaining is the common hyacinth.

H. amethystinus. See Brimeura amethystina

H. azureus. See Muscari azureum

H. orientalis. COMMON HYACINTH. To most gardeners, hyacinths are the highly fragrant, fat-spiked Dutch hybrids derived from this species. They grow to 1 ft. tall, with straplike leaves that may be erect or arching. Large flower spikes are tightly packed with waxy blooms in white, cream, buff, yellow, pink, salmon, red, blue, or purple. Largest bulbs (called exhibition size) produce largest spikes and are the best choice for containers and forced flowers. Next largest size is good for massing in beds and borders. Smallest bulbs produce smaller, looser flower spikes—same results you'll get from larger bulbs left in the ground year to year. Dutch hybrids can be grown in all zones outside of Hawaii, but bulbs left in the ground will persist only in regions with distinct winter cold. Best treated as annuals in Zones 8, 9, 11–24.

Roman or French Roman hyacinth *(H. o. albulus),* native to south of France, is smaller than the Dutch hybrids and blooms earlier. Each bulb usually produces several slender, foot-tall stems, each with loose spikes of white, pale blue, or pink flowers. Good for naturalizing and informal drifts. Thrives in regions with little or no winter chill; will persist year after year in Zones 4–24.

Both Dutch hybrids and Roman hyacinth must be planted early enough to establish roots before ground freezes. Where winter temperatures drop below 20°F/–7°C, set out bulbs in earliest fall; in warmer regions, delay until mid- to late fall (keep bulbs cool until then). Plant in organically enriched, sandy, well-drained soil. Set largest Dutch hybrid bulbs 4–5 in. deep, 5 in. apart; set smaller hybrid bulbs and Roman hyacinth bulbs 3 in. deep, 4–5 in. apart. (Hyacinth bulbs have invisible barbs on their surfaces that can cause some people's skin to itch; after handling, wash hands before touching face or eyes.) If bulbs will remain in the ground, fertilize just as blossoms fade, remove spent spikes, and keep watering regularly until foliage yellows.

Choice container plants. Pot in porous mix with tip of bulb near surface. Cover potting mix with thick mulch of sawdust, wood shavings, or peat moss to keep bulbs cool, moist, and shaded until top growth shows; remove mulch and place in full light. You can also grow hyacinths in water in a special hyacinth glass. Keep in a dark, cool place until rooted, then give light when top growth appears; place in sunny window when leaves have turned uniformly green.

HYDRANGEA

Hydrangeaceae (Saxifragaceae)

DECIDUOUS SHRUBS AND VINES

ZONES VARY BY SPECIES

PARTIAL SHADE IN HOTTEST CLIMATES

REGULAR WATER

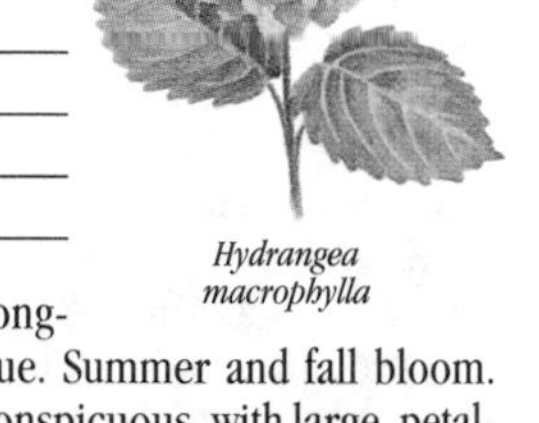

Hydrangea macrophylla

Big, bold leaves and large clusters of long-lasting flowers in white, pink, red, or blue. Summer and fall bloom. Flower clusters may contain sterile flowers (conspicuous, with large, petal-like sepals) or fertile flowers (small, starry petaled); or they may feature a cluster of small fertile flowers surrounded by ring of big sterile ones (these are called lace cap hydrangeas). Sterile flowers last for a long time (often holding up for months), gradually fading in color.

In some hydrangea varieties, blue or pink flower color is affected by soil pH—bluest color is produced in strongly acid soils (below pH 5.5), pink or red in neutral to alkaline soils (pH 7.0 and higher). Florists control flower color of potted hydrangeas by controlling soil mix; blue-flowered florists' plants may show pink blossoms when planted out in less acid soil. Flowers can be made (or kept) blue by applying aluminum sulfate to the soil, kept red (or pink) or made redder by liming the soil or applying superphosphate in quantity. Flower-color treatment is not effective unless started well ahead of bloom.

Hydrangeas are good looking as single plants, massed, or in tubs on the patio. Easy to grow in rich, porous soil. Fast growing. Prune as needed to control form—in late dormant season for those producing blooms on new growth, after bloom for those flowering on previous year's growth. To get biggest flower clusters, reduce number of stems; for numerous medium-size clusters, keep more stems.

H. anomala petiolaris (H. petiolaris). CLIMBING HYDRANGEA. Vine. Zones A2, A3; 2–21. From Russia, Korea, Japan. Climbs high (as far as 60 ft.) by clinging aerial rootlets; shrubby and sprawling without support. Green, 2–4-in.-long leaves have a rounded heart shape. Mature plants develop short, flowering branches with flat, white, 6–10-in.-wide lace-cap flower clusters. Becomes woody with age. Prune out overly vigorous growth only after vine is well established and climbing. Can be rejuvenated by cutting back to framework in late dormant season.

H. arborescens. SMOOTH HYDRANGEA. Shrub. Zones A3; 1–21. Native from New York to Iowa, south to Florida, Louisiana. Upright, dense growth to 10 ft. tall and wide. Oval, grayish green, 4–8-in. leaves; white flowers. In basic species, most flowers in a cluster are fertile; the few sterile ones are not plentiful enough for full lace cap effect. Much showier is 'Annabelle', which produces enormous (to 1-ft.) globular clusters of sterile flowers on a plant about 4 ft. tall and wide. 'Grandiflora' is another 4-footer; its flower clusters are 6 in. across. Prune in late dormant season.

H. aspera. Shrub. Zones 4–9, 14–24. From eastern Asia. Imposing shrub to 10–12 ft. tall, spreading nearly as wide. Dark green, somewhat hairy leaves to 10 in. long, 4 in. wide. Rather flat, 10-in. flower clusters contain purplish white to pink fertile flowers surrounded by 1-in. white, pink, or purple sterile blooms. Prune in late dormant season. To make a broad, many-stemmed plant, cut back hard for first 3 years; flowering will be delayed, but plant form will be improved.

H. a. sargentiana (H. sargentiana) has broader, more heavily furred leaves. Fertile flowers are light purple; sterile outer ones are pinkish white, about 1½ in. across.

Villosa Group *(H. villosa)* has blue or purple fertile flowers and 1-in.-wide, pale pinkish purple sterile flowers.

H. macrophylla (H. hortensia, H. opuloides, H. otaksa). BIGLEAF HYDRANGEA, GARDEN HYDRANGEA. Shrub. Zones 3b–9, 14–24; H1. From Japan. Symmetrical, rounded habit; grows to 4–8 ft. high (or more) and as wide. Thick, shiny, coarsely toothed leaves to 8 in. long; white, pink, red, or blue flowers in big clusters. Great performer in areas where winters are fairly mild; disappointing where plants freeze to ground every year (they may never bloom under these conditions, since flower buds are produced on old wood). Protect in colder zones by mounding soil or leaves over base of plants. Prune after bloom.

There are hundreds of named varieties, and plants may be sold under many names. Florists' plants are usually French hybrids, shorter (1–3 ft. tall) and larger flowered than old garden varieties. Two old garden selections are unmistakable: 'Domotoi', with clusters of pink or blue double sterile flowers, and 'Tricolor' ('Variegata'), a lace cap, grown for dark green leaves strongly marked with cream and light green.

Newer varieties include 'Ayesha', with light purplish pink cupped flowers (like little buttons); 'Blue Wave', lace-cap variety with light blue to pink sterile flowers and darker fertile ones; 'Buttons 'n Bows', 3–4 ft. high and wide, bearing deep pink flowers with white-edged petals; 'Lanarth White', 3–4-ft. lace cap with white sterile flowers and pink or blue fertile blooms; 'Nikko Blue', with large, round, blue blossom clusters; and 'Pia' ('Pink Elf'), 1½ ft. high and 2 ft. wide, with deep pink flowers. Unlike other bigleaf hydrangeas, 'All Summer Beauty' produces its dark blue or pinkish flower heads on current season's growth; prune this one in late dormant season.

H. paniculata 'Grandiflora'. PEEGEE HYDRANGEA. Shrub. Zones A2, A3; 1–21. Selection of a species native to Japan, eastern China. Upright and coarse textured; can be trained as 25-ft. tree but performs best as a shrub 10–15 ft. high, 8 ft. wide. Leaves are 5 in. long, turning bronzy in fall. Large (10–15-in.-long), upright clusters of mainly sterile flowers are white, slowly fading to pinky bronze. *H. p.* 'Tardiva' is similar but blooms later, in early and midautumn. Prune in late dormant season.

H. petiolaris. See H. anomala petiolaris

H. 'Preziosa'. See H. serrata 'Preziosa'

H. quercifolia. OAKLEAF HYDRANGEA. Shrub. Zones 2b–23. From southeastern U.S. Broad, rounded shrub to 6 ft. tall and 8 ft. wide, with handsome, deeply lobed, 8-in.-long leaves that resemble those of oaks, turn bronze or crimson in fall. Elongated clusters of white flowers in late spring and early summer turn pinkish purple as they age; fertile flowers are usually concealed by larger sterile flowers. 'Alice' has foliage that turns rich red in fall; 'Snow Queen' has larger flower clusters than the species; 'Snowflake' bears double flowers. Prune after bloom. Stems and flower buds may be damaged where temperatures go much below −10°F/−23°C; in these areas, oakleaf hydrangea is best grown for its handsome foliage.

Hydrangea quercifolia

H. sargentiana. See H. aspera sargentiana

H. serrata. Shrub. Zones 3b–9, 14–24. From Korea, Japan. Resembles *H. macrophylla.* To 4–6 ft. tall and wide. 'Bluebird' is a lace-cap variety with deep blue fertile flowers surrounded by pale blue sterile flowers. 'Preziosa' (*H.* 'Preziosa') has round clusters of white sterile flowers that age to red, blue, or mauve. Prune after bloom.

H. villosa. See H. aspera Villosa Group.

Hydrangeaceae. The hydrangea family includes several woody-stemmed plants formerly listed under Saxifragaceae. *Hydrangea* and mock orange *(Philadelphus)* are examples.

Hydrophyllaceae. The waterleaf family, largely but not entirely native to North America, includes annuals, perennials, and a few shrubs. Baby blue eyes *(Nemophila)* and California desert bluebells *(Phacelia)* are among the few members of this family sometimes grown in gardens.

HYLOTELEPHIUM. See SEDUM

HYMENOCALLIS

Amaryllidaceae

PERENNIALS FROM BULBS

ZONES 5, 6, 8, 9, 14–24; OR DIG AND STORE

FULL SUN OR PARTIAL SHADE

REGULAR WATER DURING GROWTH AND BLOOM

BULBS ARE POISONOUS IF INGESTED

Hymenocallis narcissiflora

To picture this summer bloomer, imagine a cross between a belladonna lily *(Amaryllis belladonna)* and a daffodil. Like belladonna lily, it has strap-shaped, 2-ft.-long leaves and thick flower stems carrying several large, fragrant flowers—though leaves and flowers appear together in hymenocallis. Like daffodils, the flowers have two sets of segments: inner ones form a funnel, while outer ones are longer, spidery, and recurved.

Plant in rich, well-drained soil—in late fall or early winter in frostless areas, after frost danger is past in colder climates. Set bulbs with tips 1 in. below surface; space 1 ft. apart. Foliage keeps all summer if watered, dies in fall. Dig bulbs after leaves have yellowed (do not cut off fleshy roots), dry with roots facing up, and store in open trays in cool, dry, dark place.

H. ×festalis. Each stem bears about four horizontally held flowers. Outer segments are very spidery, resembling curled white ribbons; these surround a broadly chalice-shaped cup with fringed lobes.

H. narcissiflora (Ismene calathina). BASKET FLOWER, PERUVIAN DAFFODIL. From Peruvian Andes. Most commonly grown hymenocallis, with green-striped white flowers in clusters of two to five. 'Advance' has pure white flowers faintly lined with green in throat.

H. 'Sulphur Queen'. Soft primrose yellow blossoms with green stripes in the throat; they have a more circular cup surrounded by broader, less spidery segments than other hymenocallis described here.

HYMENOCYCLUS. See MALEPHORA

HYMENOSPORUM flavum

SWEETSHADE

Pittosporaceae

EVERGREEN SHRUB OR TREE

ZONES 8, 9, 14–24

FULL SUN OR LIGHT SHADE

MODERATE WATER

Hymenosporum flavum

Native to Australia. Slow to moderate growth to 12–40 ft., with 9–20-ft. spread. Graceful, upright, slender, open habit. Narrow, glossy dark green leaves, 2–6 in. long. In early summer, bears yellow flowers with pronounced fragrance of orange-blossom honey. Early training is necessary to correct two problems. First, branches spread out in almost equal threes, creating weak crotches that are likely to split; second, leaves tend to cluster near ends of twigs and branches. Frequent pinching and shortening of growth in early years will result in stronger, denser plant. Best located away from strong winds. Grow in well-drained soil.

HYMENOXYS. See TETRANEURIS

HYPERICUM

ST. JOHNSWORT

Hypericaceae

EVERGREEN, SEMIEVERGREEN, DECIDUOUS SHRUBS OR PERENNIALS

ZONES VARY BY SPECIES

PARTIAL SHADE IN HOTTEST CLIMATES

MODERATE TO REGULAR WATER

Hypericum calycinum

All bear yellow flowers resembling single roses with prominent sunburst of stamens in center. Shallowly cup-shaped, five-petaled blooms range in color from creamy yellow to gold; flowers may be solitary or in clusters. Neat, fresh green foliage. Various species used for mass plantings, ground covers, informal hedges, borders. Grow especially well in mild, moist regions.

A difficult-to-control rust is extensively infecting plantings (especially those of the species *H. calycinum*) in the Pacific Northwest. Remove and destroy blighted leaves and any leaf litter; avoid overhead watering of plants in the evening.

H. androsaemum. Semievergreen shrub. Zones 3b–24. Shade-tolerant native of Europe, western Asia. To 3 ft. tall and wide, with stems arching toward the top. Leaves are medium green above, paler beneath, to 4 in. long and 2 in. wide. Clusters of ¾-in., golden yellow flowers in summer. Blossoms are followed by inedible berrylike fruits that turn from red to purple to black as they age. Useful as tall ground cover at edge of woods, on shaded slopes, in a wild garden.

H. beanii (H. patulum henryi). Evergreen shrub or perennial; more perennial-like in the cooler part of its range. Zones 4–9, 14–24. From China. Grows to 4 ft. tall and slightly wider, with oblong light green leaves on graceful, willowy branches. Brilliant golden yellow, 2-in.-wide flowers bloom summer to early fall. Good for low, untrimmed hedges, mass plantings. Looks shabby in winter.

H. calycinum. AARON'S BEARD, CREEPING ST. JOHNSWORT. Evergreen to semievergreen shrub; tops often killed in cold winters but come back in spring. Zones 2b–24. From Bulgaria, Turkey. Grows to 1 ft. high and spreads by vigorous underground stems. Short-stalked leaves to 4 in. long are medium green in sun, yellow green in shade. Bright yellow blossoms about 3 in. across throughout summer. Tough, dense ground cover that competes successfully with tree roots, takes poor soil. Fast growing; will control erosion on hillsides. May invade other plantings unless confined. Plant from flats or as rooted stems; set 1½ ft. apart. Clip or mow every 2 or 3 years during dormant season.

H. coris. Evergreen shrub. Zones 4–9, 14–24. From Europe. To about 6–12 in. or taller and about 1 ft. wide. Narrow, medium green, ½–1-in.-long leaves in whorls of four to six. Bears loose clusters of yellow, ¾-in.-wide flowers in spring or early summer. Good choice as ground cover or rock garden plant.

H. frondosum. Deciduous shrub; evergreen in mildest climates. Zones 2b–24. From southeastern U.S. Grows 1–3 ft. tall, with mounding form. Blue-green leaves set off clusters of 1½-in., bright yellow flowers that bloom from midsummer to early fall. 'Sunburst' forms a tight mound to 3 ft. tall and wide.

H. 'Hidcote' (H. patulum 'Hidcote'). Evergreen to semievergreen shrub; perennial that dies to the ground in coldest part of range. Zones 3–9, 14–24. To 4 ft. tall and 5 ft. wide in mildest climates; in cold areas, freezes keep plant to about half that size. Dark green leaves 2–3 in. long. Yellow, 3-in. flowers all summer.

H. ×moserianum. GOLD FLOWER. Evergreen shrub; perennial that dies to the ground in coldest part of range. Zones 3–9, 14–24; H1. Mounding habit to 3 ft. tall and wide, with arching, reddish stems. Leaves 2 in. long, medium green above, blue green beneath. Golden yellow, 2½-in.-wide blossoms are borne singly or in clusters of up to five. Blooms in summer, possibly into fall. Cut back in early spring. 'Tricolor' has gray-green leaves edged in white and tinged with pink.

H. patulum henryi. See H. beanii

H. patulum 'Hidcote'. See H. 'Hidcote'

H. reptans. Evergreen shrub. Zones 3b–6, 15–17. Himalayan native only about 2 in. high, 1½ ft. or wider; roots along ground. Medium green, ¼–½-in.-long leaves crowded along stems; golden summer blooms to 1¾ in. wide. Good in rock gardens. Protect from frosts in colder regions.

H. 'Rowallane'. Evergreen to semievergreen shrub; perennial that dies to the ground in coldest part of range. Zones 4–9, 14–24. Upright, rather straggly growth to 6 ft. tall and 3 ft. wide. Profuse show of bright yellow flowers, 2½–3 in. wide, in late summer and fall. Dark green leaves 2½–3½ in. long. Remove older branches annually.

HYPOESTES phyllostachya (H. sanguinolenta)

FRECKLE FACE, PINK POLKA-DOT PLANT

Acanthaceae

PERENNIAL OFTEN GROWN AS ANNUAL

ZONES 23, 24; H1, H2; ANNUAL ANYWHERE; OR INDOORS

FULL SUN OR LIGHT SHADE; BRIGHT LIGHT

REGULAR WATER

Hypoestes phyllostachya

This South African native is actually a perennial, but outside of Hawaii it is almost always used as a summer bedding annual or houseplant. Grows 1–2 ft. tall, about 1 ft. wide. Slender stems bear oval, 2–3-in.-long leaves spotted irregularly with pink or white. Selected form 'Splash' has larger spots. Plants bloom very rarely. Tip-pinch to make bushy. For indoor use, plant in loose, peaty mixture in pots or planters. Growth can be cut to within an inch or so of the soil in early spring to renew; plants tend to become woody and need replacing every few years.

HYPTIS emoryi

DESERT LAVENDER

Lamiaceae (Labiatae)

EVERGREEN SHRUB

ZONES 8–14, 18–24

FULL SUN

LITTLE TO MODERATE WATER

Hyptis emoryi

Native to desert Southwest. Erect or spreading shrub 3–10 ft. tall, 3–8 ft. wide. Woolly gray, roundish leaves to 1 in. long, with scalloped and toothed edges. Numerous tiny blue-violet flowers crowded into short spikes near branch ends can appear at any time throughout year, but bloom is heaviest in spring. Plant gives off pleasant lavender fragrance following rains or when brushed against. May die back to roots at about 25°F/–4°C. Needs excellent drainage. Drought tolerant but looks better with irrigation.

HYSSOP. See AGASTACHE, HYSSOPUS officinalis

HYSSOP, WATER. See BACOPA monnieri

HYSSOPUS officinalis

HYSSOP

Lamiaceae (Labiatae)

PERENNIAL

ZONES 1–24

FULL SUN OR LIGHT SHADE

MODERATE TO REGULAR WATER

Hyssopus officinalis

From southern Europe. Compact growth to 1½–2 ft. tall, 3 ft. wide. Narrow, glossy dark green leaves on woody-based stems; foliage has pungent scent. Profusion of dark blue flower spikes throughout summer and into autumn; not a dramatic show but pleasant looking. Selections with white, pink, or lavender blooms exist.

Start from seed sown in early spring or stem cuttings in late spring or early summer. Once established, it may self-sow. Tolerates some drought but will thrive with regular moisture if drainage is good. Tolerates trimming as a low hedge or as border for a knot garden. Peppery-tasting leaves are sometimes used in cooking.

IBERIS

CANDYTUFT

Brassicaceae (Cruciferae)

PERENNIALS AND ANNUALS

ZONES 1–24, EXCEPT AS NOTED

FULL SUN OR PARTIAL SHADE

REGULAR WATER

Iberis sempervirens

Free-blooming plants from southern and western Europe with clusters of white, lavender, lilac, pink, rose, purple, carmine, or crimson blossoms. Perennial candytufts flower from early spring to summer. Annual species bloom in spring and summer; they are most floriferous where summer nights are cool. Use all kinds in borders, containers, for cutting. Perennials are also good as edgings, in rock gardens, as small-scale ground covers.

All types need well-drained soil. In spring or (in mild climates) fall, sow seeds of annuals in place or in flats for later transplanting. Set out perennial plants in spring or fall. Shear lightly after bloom to stimulate new growth.

I. amara. HYACINTH-FLOWERED CANDYTUFT, ROCKET CANDYTUFT. Annual. To 12–15 in. high, 6 in. wide. Fragrant white flowers in tight, round clusters that elongate into spikes resembling those of hyacinth. Narrow, slightly fuzzy leaves.

I. gibraltarica. Perennial. Zones 4–9, 14–24. Resembles *I. sempervirens* but bears flatter clusters of light pinkish or purplish flowers, which may be white near the center.

I. sempervirens. EVERGREEN CANDYTUFT. Perennial. To 8–12 in. (or even 1½ ft.) high, spreading about as wide. Narrow, shiny dark green leaves are attractive all year. Pure white flower clusters carried on stems long enough to cut for bouquets. Lower, more compact varieties include 'Alexander's White', a 6-in.-high plant with fine-textured foliage; 'Kingwood Compact', also 6 in. high; 'Little Gem', 4–6 in. tall; and 'Purity', 6–12 in. tall and wide spreading. 'Snowflake', 4–12 in. high and 1½–3 ft. wide, has broader, more leathery leaves than the species; also has larger flowers in larger clusters on shorter stems. It is extremely showy in spring, with sporadic bloom through summer and fall. 'Autumnale' and 'Autumn Snow' bloom in spring and again in fall.

I. umbellata. GLOBE CANDYTUFT. Annual. Bushy plants 12–15 in. high, 9 in. wide. Lance-shaped leaves to 3½ in. long; flowers in pink, rose, carmine, crimson, salmon, lilac, and white. Lower-growing strains Dwarf Fairy and Magic Carpet, available in the same colors, reach 6 in. high.

ICE PLANTS. These low-growing, succulent perennials (and a few annuals) were once conveniently lumped together as *Mesembryanthemum,* but they are now classified under several names. Where hardy, they are among the most useful and colorful of flowering ground covers. In colder climates, grow them as summer bloomers in window boxes or hanging baskets; or treat as houseplants. All take most soils; none will tolerate foot traffic. Feed lightly in fall, again after bloom. The various perennial genera include *Aptenia, Carpobrotus, Cephalophyllum, Delosperma, Drosanthemum, Lampranthus,* and *Malephora. Dorotheanthus* is an annual genus. *Mesembryanthemum*—the original, all-encompassing genus—now contains only annuals of little ornamental value; one species is sometimes seen as a naturalized roadside planting in California.

ILEX

HOLLY

Aquifoliaceae

EVERGREEN AND DECIDUOUS SHRUBS AND TREES

ZONES VARY BY SPECIES

FULL SUN OR PARTIAL SHADE

REGULAR WATER

Ilex aquifolium

English holly *(I. aquifolium)* is the most familiar in song and legend (and in Christmas wreaths), but this species is entirely satisfactory only in the Pacific Northwest and in coastal Northern California. Many other hollies are better adapted to other parts of the West. In size, they range from foot-high dwarfs to trees 40–50 ft. tall. Many hundreds of species and hybrids exist. Smaller kinds are attractive as foundation plantings or low hedges; larger evergreen sorts make attractive and impenetrable tall hedges or screens.

Nearly all holly plants are either male or female, and as a rule both sexes must be present in order for female plants to set fruit. Best bet is to plant a male of the same species as fruiting females; if you use a different species, berries will form only if both plants flower at the same time. Varieties described below are female unless otherwise noted. A few are self-fruitful; these also are noted.

Most hollies prefer rich, slightly acid garden soil with good drainage. (A few exceptions are noted.) All appreciate a mulch to deter weeds and keep soil cool and moist. Though plants will grow in sun or part shade, choose a sunny spot for best berry production and most compact growth. Scale can cause problems in all holly-growing areas. Holly bud moth and leaf miner need attention on English holly in the Northwest; for control, employ only products currently registered for use against those pests. Diseases are rarely a problem for home gardeners.

Most hollies tend to be dense and symmetrical. Prune mainly to remove poorly placed, broken, or dead branches. Winter holiday season is good time to prune, because clipped branches can be used for indoor decoration. You can restore a holly that has become too open or ragged by severely shortening its branches and allowing new growth to fill in. Small-leafed hollies can be sheared into formal hedges or topiary figures.

I. ×altaclerensis 'Wilsonii' (I. wilsonii). WILSON HOLLY. Evergreen shrub or tree. Zones 3b–24. Hybrid between *I. aquifolium* and a species from the Canary Islands. One of the best hollies, especially in warmer regions. Takes wind, almost any soil. Usually a shrub 6–8 ft. high and wide, but easily trained as single-stemmed tree 15–20 ft. high, 10–12 ft. wide. Evenly spine-toothed, rich green leaves are thick, leathery, 5 in. long, 3 in. wide. Heavy producer of bright red berries. Makes a good espalier, screen, or informal or clipped hedge.

I. aquifolium. ENGLISH HOLLY. Evergreen shrub or tree. Zones 4–9, 14–17; H1 (above 4,000 ft.). Native to southern and central Europe, Great Britain. Slow growth to 40 ft. tall and 25 ft. wide, usually much less. Highly variable in leaf shape, color, and degree of spininess. Some varieties produce seedless berries without a pollenizer, but these berries are usually small, slow to develop, and quick to drop. Needs protection from sun in hot, dry areas and soil conditioning where soils are alkaline. Resistant to oak root fungus. The following varieties are among the best known.

'Balkans'. Hardiest of English hollies, this variety was originally grown from seed collected in the mountains of the Balkan region. Upright plants with smooth dark green leaves. Male and female (fruiting) forms are available.

'Big Bull'. Very ornamental male with large, nearly smooth-edged leaves.

'Boulder Creek'. Typical English holly with large leaves. Brilliant red berries.

'Ciliata Major'. Vigorous, erect plant with purple bark on young shoots. Large, olive-tinged dark green leaves are flat, long spined, very glossy. Good berry producer.

'Ferox'. HEDGEHOG, PORCUPINE HOLLY. Male with sterile pollen. Twisted, fiercely spined leaves give it its common names.

'Fertilis'. Sets light crop of seedless berries without pollination.

'Gold Coast'. Male selection grown for bright yellow edging on its leaves. Dense growth to 6–8 ft. high and wide.

'J. C. Van Tol' ('Van Tol'). Glossy green leaves. Produces large dark red berries at young age. Sometimes sold as a variety of *I. ×altaclerensis.*

'San Gabriel'. Bears seedless berries without pollination.

'Sparkler'. Strong, upright grower to about 12 ft. tall, 8 ft. wide. Heavy crop of glistening red berries at an early age.

'Teufel's Deluxe'. Exceptionally dark green leaves. Large, early-ripening red berries.

'Teufel's Zero'. Upright with long slender branches, weeping. Dark red berries ripen early. Unusually hardy.

Varieties with variegated leaves are also sold. Types with silver-edged leaves are 'Argenteo-marginata', 'Silvery', 'Silver Queen' (male), 'Silver King'. Types with silver-centered leaves: 'Argentea-mediopicta', 'Silver Star', 'Silver Milkmaid'. Gold-edged leaves: 'Aureo-marginata', 'Golden Queen' (male), 'Lily Gold'. Gold-centered leaves: 'Golden Milkmaid', 'Pinto'.

I. ×aquipernyi. Evergreen shrub or tree. Zones 4–9, 14–24. Hybrid between *I. aquifolium* and *I. pernyi.* To 20 ft. tall (or more), 12 ft. wide, with cone-shaped habit and dense foliage. Spiny-edged, 2–4-in.-long leaves are closely set on branches. 'San Jose' and 'Brilliant' produce small red berries without a pollenizer. Resistant to oak root fungus.

I. cornuta. CHINESE HOLLY. Evergreen shrub or tree. Zones 4–24, but needs long warm season to set fruit. In desert climates, give protection from hot sun; grow in eastern or northern exposure. From China, Korea. Dense or open growth to 10 ft. or taller, often wider in maturity. Leaves are typically glossy, leathery, nearly rectangular, with spines at the four corners and at tip. Exceptionally large, long-lasting bright red berries. Selections show great variation in fruit set, leaf form, spininess. In the following list, those setting fruit do so without a male variety.

'Berries Jubilee'. Dwarf, dome-shaped plant to 4–6 ft. high and wide, with large leaves and heavy crop of large bright red berries. Larger, spinier leaves than those of 'Burfordii', on a much smaller plant.

'Burfordii'. BURFORD HOLLY. To 15 ft. tall, 10 ft. wide. Widely planted in low-elevation California. Leaves nearly spineless, cupped downward. Useful as espalier.

Ilex cornuta 'Burfordii'

'Carissa'. Dwarf, dense grower to 3–4 ft. high and 4–6 ft. wide, with small leaves. Use for small containers, low hedge. Female, but no berries.

'Dazzler'. Compact, upright growth to 8–10 ft. high and wide. Glossy leaves have a few stout spines along wavy margins. Loaded with berries.

'Dwarf Burford' ('Burfordii Nana'). Resembles 'Burfordii' but is much smaller—to 6 ft. high and wide. Branches densely set with small (1½-in.), light green, spineless leaves.

'Rotunda'. DWARF CHINESE HOLLY. Compact low grower to 3–4 ft. high, 6–8 ft. wide. Female, but does not produce berries. A few stout spines and rolled leaf margins between spines make the medium-size light green leaves nearly rectangular.

'Willowleaf'. Large shrub or small tree to 15 ft. tall and wide, with dense growth. Long, narrow, dark green leaves. Good crop of dark red berries.

I. crenata. JAPANESE HOLLY. Evergreen shrub. Zones 3–9, 14–24. From Russia, Japan, Korea. Looks more like boxwood *(Buxus)* than holly. Dense, erect, usually to 4–10 ft. high and wide, sometimes much larger. Narrow, finely toothed, ½–¾-in.-long leaves. Black berries. Extremely useful where winter cold limits choice of polished evergreens for hedges, edgings. Varieties include the following.

'Compacta'. Rounded shrub to 6 ft. high and wide, with dense habit. Many different plants sold under this name.

'Convexa'. Compact, rounded shrub to 4–6 ft. high and somewhat wider. Leaves are roundish, cupped downward at the edges. Use clipped or unclipped. Many different plants sold under this name.

'Glory'. Small, dense, round grower to 5 ft. tall, 8 ft. wide. Extremely hardy. Male.

'Green Island'. Open, spreading; to 3 ft. tall and twice as wide.

'Helleri'. Remains very small (about 1 ft. high, 2 ft. wide) for many years. May reach twice that size in 30 years. ▸

'Hetzii'. Like 'Convexa' but with larger leaves and more vigorous growth.

'Mariesii'. Very slow-growing columnar holly with dense, tiny, round leaves. To 2 ft. high, 4–6 in. wide in about 10 years; eventually to 6 ft. tall, 16 in. wide. Good plant for rock garden, bonsai, containers.

'Northern Beauty'. To 4 ft. high, 4–5 ft. wide, with lustrous leaves.

'Sky Pencil'. Columnar plant to 6 ft. tall and only 10 in. wide.

I. dimorphophylla. OKINAWAN HOLLY. Evergreen shrub. Zones 16, 17, 19–24. From Japan. To 5 ft. tall, 3 ft. wide. Leaves less than 1 in. long, closely set with short spines. Small red berries. Tender to frost.

I. 'Ebony Magic'. Evergreen shrub. Zones 3–9, 12–24. Pyramidal form. Typically grows 8–12 ft. tall and 6–8 ft. wide, though may reach 20 ft. tall and half as wide. Blackish purple bark; shiny dark green, spiny-edged leaves. Large orange-red berries last through spring. 'Ebony Male' often used for pollination.

I. glabra. INKBERRY. Evergreen shrub. Zones 2b–24. Native to eastern North America. To 10 ft. tall and wide, with thick, spineless dark green leaves and black berries. More widely available is the dwarf form 'Compacta', which grows to 4 ft. high and wide but can be sheared to make a 2-ft. hedge.

I. latifolia. Evergreen tree. Zones 4–7, 15–17, 20–24. Native to China, Japan. Slow-growing, stout-branched plant to 25 ft. tall, 15 ft. wide. Dull dark green leaves are 6–8 in. long (largest of all hollies), thick and leathery, fine toothed. Big clusters of large dull red berries.

I

I. ×meserveae. Evergreen shrub. Zones 3–9, 14–17. Most plants in this category are hybrids between *I. aquifolium* and a cold-tolerant species from northern Japan. Dense, bushy plants; apparently the hardiest of hollies with the true holly look. To 10 ft. high and wide, though more commonly seen 3–5 ft. tall and broad. Purple stems and spiny, glossy blue-green leaves. Red-fruiting female varieties include 'Blue Angel', 'Blue Girl', and 'Blue Princess'; male pollenizers include 'Blue Boy' and 'Blue Prince'. 'Golden Girl' has yellow berries. 'China Boy' and red-fruited 'China Girl' are crosses between *I. cornuta* and the northern Japanese species; slightly hardier and more tolerant of summer heat than the other hybrids.

I. 'Nellie R. Stevens'. Evergreen shrub or tree. Zones 4–9, 14–24. Hybrid between *I. cornuta* and *I. aquifolium.* Fast growing, densely conical to 15–20 ft. tall, 10 ft. wide. Glossy, leathery, sparsely toothed leaves to 3 in. long. Self-fruitful but forms a heavier crop if pollinated by male variety of *I. cornuta.*

I. opaca. AMERICAN HOLLY. Evergreen tree. Zones 2–9, 14–17, 19–23. Native to eastern U.S. Slow growing to 40–50 ft. tall, 20–40 ft. wide; pyramidal or round-headed. Dull or glossy green, 2–4-in.-long leaves with spiny margins. Red berries; not quite as numerous as on *I. aquifolium.* Resistant to oak root fungus. Some of the many varieties are occasionally available in the West. They include 'Cardinal', 'Old Heavy Berry', and 'Torchbearer'.

I. pedunculosa. Evergreen shrub or tree. Zones 2b–9, 14–17. From China, Japan. To 15–20 ft. tall, 12–15 ft. wide; has awkward shape when young. Narrow, smooth-edged leaves 1–3 in. long. The ¼-in., bright red berries dangle like cherries on 1–1½-in. stalks in autumn.

I. pernyi. Evergreen tree. Zones 4–9, 14–24. Native to China. Slow growth to 20–30 ft. tall, 10 ft. wide. Glossy, 1–2-in.-long, triangular leaves with one to three spines on each side; closely packed against branchlets. Red berries set tightly against stems.

I. 'San Jose Hybrid'. Evergreen shrub or tree. Zones 4–9, 14–24. Resembles *I. ×altaclerensis* 'Wilsonii' but has somewhat longer, narrower leaves. Upright growth; heavy berry production.

I. 'September Gem'. Evergreen shrub. Zones 4–9, 14–24. Dense, conical dark green plant to 6 ft. tall, 3 ft. wide, with sparsely spined, 2-in.-long leaves. Early crop of bright orange-red fruit.

I. 'Sparkleberry'. Deciduous shrub or tree. Zones 1–7. Hybrid between *I. serrata* and *I. verticillata.* Upright growth to 12–15 ft. high and wide. Tooth-edged dark green leaves to 4 in. long persist until early winter before dropping. Masses of bright red berries from fall into spring. 'Apollo' is a male pollenizer.

I. verticillata. WINTERBERRY, CHRISTMAS BERRY. Deciduous shrub. Zones 1–7. Native to eastern North America. Unlike most hollies, will thrive in boggy soils, although it also succeeds in any moist, organic soil. Grows 6–10 ft. tall and spreads wider by suckering. Oval leaves to 3 in. long. Enormous crop of bright red berries ripens in early fall and lasts all winter (unless eaten by birds). 'Afterglow' has orange-red berries on a globe-shaped plant. 'Cacapon', 'Fairfax', and 'Winter Red' have dark red berries. 'Red Sprite' is a dwarf (to 3 ft. high and wide) with larger red fruit. Plant a male variety for pollination—good choices include 'Dwarf Male' (to 2 ft. tall); 'Jim Dandy' and 'Late Male' (both to 4 ft.); and 'Southern Gentleman' (to 6 ft.).

I. vomitoria. YAUPON. Evergreen shrub or tree. Zones 4–9, 11–24; H1, H2. Native to southeastern U.S. Takes extremely alkaline soils better than other hollies. To 15–20 ft. tall and 10–15 ft. wide, with narrow, inch-long, shallowly toothed dark green leaves. Often trained as standard or sheared into columnar form; good topiary plant. Pea-size scarlet berries borne in profusion. Varieties include the following.

'Nana'. DWARF YAUPON. To 3–5 ft. high and slightly wider. Refined, attractive; formal appearance when sheared. Fruit often hidden among leaves.

'Pendula'. Weeping branches show to best effect when plant is trained as standard. Male and female forms available.

'Pride of Houston'. Upright, freely branching plant to 15 ft. tall, 5–10 ft. wide. Profuse berry production. Good screen or hedge.

'Stokes' ('Stokes Dwarf', 'Schillings'). To 3–4 ft. high and wide, with closely set dark green leaves. Male.

'Will Fleming' ('William Fleming'). Columnar; 10 ft. tall, 2 ft. wide. Male.

'ILIMA. See SIDA fallax

ILLICIUM

ANISE TREE

Illiciaceae

EVERGREEN SHRUBS OR TREES

ZONES 4–9, 14–24

PARTIAL OR FULL SHADE

AMPLE WATER

ALL PARTS OF I. ANISATUM ARE POISONOUS IF INGESTED

Illicium anisatum

Little-used but attractive clan of shrubs or small trees noted for thick, leathery, glossy leaves (anise-scented when crushed) and spring flowers with many petal-like segments reminiscent of small magnolia blossoms. Fruits that follow are small, one-sided pods arranged in a ring. The star anise of Chinese cookery is the fruit of the tropical tree *I. verum,* apparently not grown in North America. All like rich soil with abundant organic material. Big, bold foliage gives the impression of rhododendrons. Seldom need pruning.

I. anisatum (I. religiosum, I. japonicum). ANISE SHRUB, JAPANESE ANISE. Native to Japan, South Korea, Taiwan. To 6–10 ft. (possibly 15 ft.) tall, 6–8 ft. wide; conical growth habit. Oval to lance-shaped, blunt-tipped, glossy leaves to 5 in. long, 2 in. wide. Inch-wide, scentless flowers on short, nodding stalks cluster in leaf axils; they open yellowish green, then fade to creamy white. Much planted in Buddhist cemeteries; cut branches are used to decorate graves. Highly fragrant wood used for incense. Seeds, wood, and foliage are toxic if ingested.

I. floridanum. FLORIDA ANISE TREE. Native Florida to Louisiana. Reaches 6–10 ft. or taller, equally wide. Pointed oval leaves 6 in. long and 2 in. wide, with prominent midribs. Waxy, nodding maroon flowers 1–2 in. across on 1½–2-in.-long stalks; most people find scent unpleasant. 'Halley's Comet' is more compact, with larger, redder flowers than the species; often blooms into fall. 'Album' is white flowered; 'Variegatum' has maroon purple flowers with subtle green-on-green leaf variegation. 'Woodland Ruby' is a hybrid with ruby pink, 2-in. flowers shaped like starfish; flowering period extends through summer.

IMMORTELLE. See XERANTHEMUM annuum

IMPATIENS

BALSAM, TOUCH-ME-NOT, SNAPWEED

Balsaminaceae

PERENNIALS AND ANNUALS

ZONES VARY BY SPECIES

EXPOSURE NEEDS VARY BY SPECIES

REGULAR WATER

Impatiens walleriana

Of the hundreds of species, only the following are usually seen in gardens. Most of these are annuals or tender perennials treated as annuals; all are valuable for long summer bloom. When lightly touched, ripe seed capsules burst open and scatter seeds.

I. balfourii. Annual. All zones. From the Himalayas. To 20 in. high and broad, with 4–5-in. leaves and loose clusters of inch-wide, pink-tinted white flowers. Seldom planted but often pops up unannounced. It can become a pest by reseeding, but it is attractive in shady, informal plantings.

I. balsamina. BALSAM. Annual. All zones. From Southeast Asia. Erect, branching plant reaches 8–30 in. high and 6–8 in. wide. Sharp-pointed, 1½–6-in.-long leaves with deeply toothed edges. Large, spurred flowers borne among leaves along main stem, branches. Solid colored or variegated, in white or shades of pink, rose, lilac, or red. Compact, double camellia–flowered forms are most frequently grown. Sow seeds in flats or pots in early spring; after frost danger is past, set out young plants (or purchased transplants) in full sun (light shade in hottest climates).

I. glandulifera (I. roylei). Annual. All zones. From the Himalayas. To 3–6 ft. tall, with thick, juicy stems and leaves to 8 in. long. Abundance of yellow-spotted purple to white flowers. Like a larger *I. balfourii* and just as likely to self-sow all over the place. Light to full shade.

I. holstii. See I. walleriana

I. New Guinea hybrids. Perennials in Zones 24, H1, H2; can be grown as annuals in all zones. A varied group of striking plants developed from a number of species native to New Guinea, especially *I. hawkeri.* Plants can be upright to spreading; most are 1–2 ft. tall and as wide or wider (though some are smaller, such as 8-in.-high Baby Bonita series). Leaves are typically large, often variegated with cream or red. Flowers usually large (2½ in. wide) though not profuse, held well above foliage; colors include lavender, purple, pink, red, orange, and white. Once considered primarily pot plants, they may also be grown in the open ground; provide ample fertilizer and give somewhat more sun than you would common impatiens (*I. walleriana*).

Popular strains include Celebration (with 3-in. flowers), Paradise, and Pure Beauty. Most New Guinea hybrids are cutting-grown plants, but Spectra (Firelake) and Java strains can be grown from seed. Spectra offers a mix of flower colors and has leaves variegated with cream or white; bronze-leafed Java is available in single or mixed colors. 'Tango', also seed-grown, has bright orange blooms and bronze-green foliage.

I. sodenii (I. oliveri). POOR MAN'S RHODODENDRON. Perennial in Zones 15–17, 21–24; indoor/outdoor plant elsewhere. From eastern tropical Africa. To 4–8 ft. tall, 10 ft. wide, with woody-based stems clothed in whorls of 8-in.-long, glossy dark green leaves. Produces many 2½-in., slender-spurred flowers in lilac, pale lavender, or pinkish shades. Tolerates seacoast conditions. Frosts kill it to ground, but it regrows in spring. Blooms in partial or deep shade; takes sun in cool-summer areas.

I. sultani. See I. walleriana

I. walleriana. BUSY LIZZIE. Perennial in Zones 17, 24, H1, H2; can be grown as an annual in all zones. Includes plants formerly known as *I. holstii* and *I. sultani.* Rapid, vigorous growth; tall types to about 2 ft. high, dwarf kinds 6–12 in. high. Narrow, glossy dark green, 1–3-in.-long leaves on juicy pale green stems. Flowers 1–2 in. wide, in all colors but yellow and true blue. All types are useful for many months of bright color in partial or full shade. Grow plants from seed or cuttings; or buy them in cell-packs or pots. Space taller types 1 ft. apart, dwarfs 6 in. apart. If plants overgrow, cut them back as low as 6 in. above ground—it's a tonic. New growth emerges in a few days, and flowers cover it in 2 weeks. Plants often reseed in moist ground.

Among the many strains and varieties are the following, all bearing the typical five-petaled blooms.

Accent. To 10 in. high. Popular, in numerous individual colors or a mix.

Accent Star. Variation of Accent strain, with white central star extending across the petals.

Bruno. To 10–12 in. Tetraploid strain (double the usual number of chromosomes), with large (2½-in.) flowers on extremely sturdy plants. Available in single or mixed colors.

Butterfly. To 10 in. high. Blossoms show contrasting central patch in butterfly form.

Mosaic. To 12–14 in. Irregular splashes of white against base color of several lilac or rosy shades.

Pride. To 10–16 in. Flowers are larger than usual (to 2½ in. across), in single or mixed colors.

Stardust. To 12–14 in. Central white star tapers off into a dusting of white.

Super Elfin. To 8–10 in. Comes in an exceptionally wide range of individual colors and blends of harmonizing hues. One example is 'Blue Pearl', with flowers in an unusual bluish lilac shade.

Swirl. To 10–12 in. Pastel shades with picotee edges of deeper color.

Many novelty strains and selections are available. They include Firefly, dwarf series to 6–8 in. high, with ½-in. flowers in the full range of impatiens colors; Confection, 10–12 in., producing high percentage of double and semidouble flowers from seed; and 'Victorian Rose', 10–12 in., with frilly rose pink semidouble flowers. Other double impatiens with flowers resembling rosebuds include cutting-grown Fiesta and Tioga strains. The double-flowered types are best used as pot plants, located where flower detail can be observed close up.

IMPERATA cylindrica 'Rubra' ('Red Baron')

JAPANESE BLOOD GRASS

Poaceae (Gramineae)

PERENNIAL GRASS

ZONES 2B–24

FULL SUN OR PARTIAL SHADE

REGULAR WATER

Imperata cylindrica 'Rubra'

From Japan. Forms upright clump 1–2 ft. tall, 1 ft. wide. In spring, leaves emerge medium green at base, red at tip; red color extends along leaf and intensifies in summer and fall. Top half or more of each leaf may be brilliant red. Striking in borders, especially where sun can shine through blades. Rarely (if ever) flowers. Turns straw colored in winter; best cut to the ground yearly. Spreads slowly by underground runners.

INCARVILLEA

Bignoniaceae

PERENNIALS

ZONES VARY BY SPECIES

LIGHT SHADE IN HOTTEST CLIMATES

REGULAR WATER

Incarvillea delavayi

These plants from the Himalayas and China have showy trumpet-shaped flowers like their trumpet vine relatives (*Bignonia, Campsis,* and the like). Flowers are large for the size of the plant. Many species are coming into cultivation, but only the following two have reached North American gardens in any numbers. Leaves are 2–8 in. long, divided featherwise into leaflets. Plants are deep rooted and need reasonably deep soil and excellent drainage. In cold-winter regions, mulch plants after ground has frozen (to prevent ground from heaving). Protect from slugs and snails.

I. arguta. Zones 4–6, 15–24; can be treated as annual elsewhere, since it will bloom first year from seed if started in earliest spring. Erect plant to 5 ft. tall and 3 ft. wide, or sprawling to 3 ft. tall and 5 ft. wide; somewhat shrubby at base. Leaves divided into 4–12 leaflets, each up to 2 in. long. Blooms in spring and summer; inflorescences have 5–20 pink or white, 1½-in.-long flowers. Effective leaning over walls or spilling down slopes. Self-sows but does not become a pest.

I. delavayi. Zones 2–24. To 2 ft. high, 1 ft. wide. Like *I. arguta,* has divided leaves and trumpet-shaped flowers—but in other respects, it is entirely different. Grows from a carrot-shaped perennial root and forms a rosette of foot-long leaves, each divided into many leaflets. The foot-long flower stalk is topped by 2–12 flowers that are 3 in. long and wide, rosy purple outside, yellow and purple within. Blooms late spring, early summer. Division is difficult.

INCENSE CEDAR. See CALOCEDRUS decurrens

INDIA HAWTHORN. See RHAPHIOLEPIS indica

INDIAN LABURNUM. See CASSIA fistula

INDIAN MOCK STRAWBERRY. See DUCHESNEA indica

INDIAN RHUBARB. See DARMERA peltata

INDIAN RICE GRASS. See ACHNATHERUM speciosum

INDIGO BUSH. See DALEA pulchra INDIGOFERA

INDIGOFERA

INDIGO BUSH

Fabaceae (Leguminosae)

DECIDUOUS SHRUBS

ZONES 2B–9, 14–21

FULL SUN

REGULAR WATER

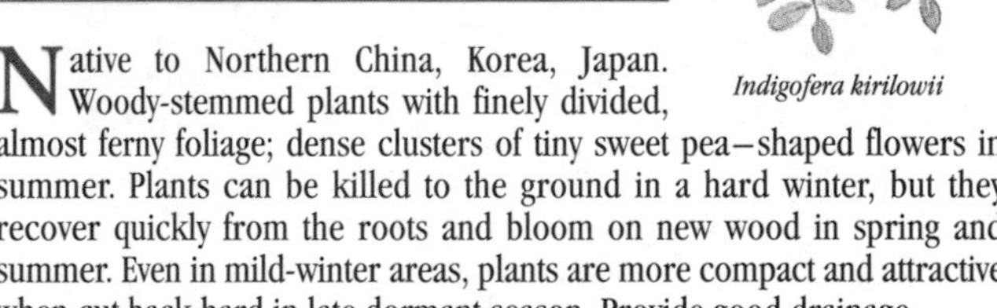

Indigofera kirilowii

Native to Northern China, Korea, Japan. Woody-stemmed plants with finely divided, almost ferny foliage; dense clusters of tiny sweet pea–shaped flowers in summer. Plants can be killed to the ground in a hard winter, but they recover quickly from the roots and bloom on new wood in spring and summer. Even in mild-winter areas, plants are more compact and attractive when cut back hard in late dormant season. Provide good drainage.

I. decora. To 1–2½ ft. tall and 3 ft. wide, with arching branches. Narrow, somewhat drooping blossom clusters to 8 in. long hold as many as 40 small white blooms suffused with pink.

I. kirilowii. To 2½–3 ft. tall, 3 ft. wide, with upright shoots and erect, 5-in. clusters of rose pink flowers.

INKBERRY. See ILEX glabra

INSIDE-OUT FLOWER. See VANCOUVERIA planipetala

IOCHROMA

Solanaceae

EVERGREEN VINING SHRUBS

ZONES 15–17, 19–24

FULL SUN OR PARTIAL SHADE

REGULAR WATER

Iochroma cyaneum

From Central and South America. Fast-growing, soft-wooded, vining shrubs with drooping tubular or trumpet-shaped flowers in clusters of up to 20 near ends of branches. Blooms from early spring through fall—or year-round in frost-free areas. Leaves 5–8 in. long, 1½–3 in. wide. Lax growth is best staked up, espaliered, or draped over a fence or wall. For continuity of bloom, prune selectively to maintain size and shape, but not when cold weather approaches. Hard pruning is all right otherwise, though it will delay bloom. Protect from hard frosts. Cucumber beetles love to eat the leaves.

I. cyaneum. To 8 ft. or more, with dull dark green leaves. Stems and new shoots covered with soft, grayish down. Narrow trumpets are 2–3 in. long. Seedling blossom colors vary from blues through violets and deep reds to purplish rose and pink, all with a metallic sheen. Buy plants in bloom to get the color you want; or select named varieties. 'Burgundy' is wine red to crimson. 'Indigo' is glossy violet blue, 'Royal Blue' a lighter, more brilliant blue; 'Sky King' is a pure light blue.

I. fuchsioides. To 10 ft. or more, with glossy bright green leaves. Brilliant orange-scarlet, tubular flowers with yellow throats; look like fuchsia flowers.

IPHEION uniflorum (Brodiaea uniflora, Triteleia uniflora)

SPRING STAR FLOWER

Liliaceae

PERENNIAL FROM BULB

ZONES 2B–24

FULL SUN OR PARTIAL SHADE

REGULAR WATER DURING GROWTH AND BLOOM

Ipheion uniflorum

Spring-blooming Argentine native with wildflower charm. Each bulb produces several slender stems, each bearing a single half-inch blossom with six overlapping petals. Usual color is white tinged with blue, but variants include white 'Album', bright blue 'Rolf Fiedler', and dark blue 'Wisley Blue'. All have narrow, nearly flat, bluish green leaves that smell like onions when bruised.

Use in borders or under deciduous shrubs; or naturalize in woodland areas or among low grasses. In fall, set bulbs 2 in. deep and 2 in. apart. Prefers dry conditions during summer dormancy but will accept water if drainage is good. Divide infrequently—plantings become more attractive over the years as bulbs multiply.

IPOMOEA

MORNING GLORY

Convolvulaceae

PERENNIAL AND ANNUAL VINES

ZONES VARY BY SPECIES

FULL SUN

MODERATE TO REGULAR WATER

Ipomoea tricolor 'Heavenly Blue'

Native to tropical and subtropical regions of the world. This genus includes many ornamental twining vines as well as the edible sweet potato (see Sweet Potato); it does not include the weedy plant known as wild morning glory or bindweed *(Convolvulus arvensis)*. The plants described here may self-sow, but they do not spread by nearly ineradicable underground runners as does wild morning glory. Plants tend to have hard seeds; to encourage faster sprouting, nick the coating or soak overnight in water before planting. For annual display, sow seeds in place after frost danger is past; or, for an earlier start, sow seeds indoors, then set out plants 6–8 in. apart. Use morning glory vines on fence or trellis or as ground cover. Or grow in containers; provide stakes or a wire cylinder for support, or let plant cascade. For cut flowers, pick stems with buds in various stages of development and place in deep vase; buds open on consecutive days.

I. alba (Calonyction aculeatum). MOONFLOWER. Perennial in Zones 15–17, 23, 24, H1, H2; annual elsewhere. Fast growing (20–30 ft. in a season), providing quick shade for arbor, trellis, or fence. Luxuriantly clothed in heart-shaped leaves to 8 in. long, closely spaced on stems.

Blooms in the evening, showing off fragrant, 6-in., funnel-shaped white blossoms after sundown and into the night (flowers also open on cloudy or dark days). Needs heat to bloom.

I. batatas. SWEET POTATO. Perennial from tuberous roots. Zones 13, 21–24; H1, H2; or indoor/outdoor plant. For the edible sort, see Sweet Potato; the following fancy-leafed forms are grown for ornament. Trailing in habit, they have leaves that vary in size from 2 to 4 in. long, range in shape from heart shaped to deeply lobed. 'Blackie' has deep blackish purple leaves; 'Marguerite' (alternate spellings include 'Margurite' and 'Margarita') has golden green foliage. A variety variously called 'Tricolor' and 'Pink Frost' has green leaves with white and pink variegation. All are attractive in hanging baskets.

I. indica (I. acuminata, I. learii). BLUE DAWN FLOWER. Perennial. Zones 8, 9, 12–24; H1, H2. Vigorous, rapid growth to 15–30 ft. Dark green, heart-shaped or three-lobed leaves. Clusters of 3–4-in., funnel-shaped flowers from spring into fall; blooms open bright blue, then fade to pinkish purple by day's end. Use to cover large bank, wall, or unsightly fence or other structure. Blooms in 1 year from seed; can also be grown from cuttings, divisions, and layering of established plants.

I. nil. MORNING GLORY. Annual. All zones. Summer bloomer resembling *I. tricolor.* The large-flowered (to 6-in.-wide) Imperial Japanese strain belongs to this species; other selections include rosy red 'Scarlet O'Hara', odd pinkish tan 'Chocolate', and mixed-color Early Call strain (useful where summers are short).

I. quamoclit (Quamoclit pennata). CYPRESS VINE, CARDINAL CLIMBER. Annual. All zones. To 20 ft., with 2½–4-in.-long leaves finely divided into slender threads. Summer flowers are 1½-in.-long tubes that flare at mouth into a five-pointed star; they are usually scarlet, rarely white.

I. tricolor. MORNING GLORY. Annual. All zones. Vigorous growth to 10–15 ft., with large, heart-shaped leaves. Showy, funnel-shaped to bell-like flowers are single or double, in solid colors of blue, lavender, pink, red, or white, often with throats in contrasting colors; some are bicolored or striped. Most types open only in morning, fade in afternoon. Bloom from summer until frost. Among the most popular selections is 'Heavenly Blue', to 15 ft., bearing 4–5-in., pure sky blue flowers with yellow throat. 'Tie Dye', to 6–8 ft., bears 6-in.-wide lavender blooms marked with deep purple swirls, stripes, and flecks; its foliage is splashed silvery white. Dwarf strain with white markings on the leaves (known as Spice Islands or simply as Variegated) grows only 9 in. high and spills to 1 ft. across; flower colors include red, pink, blue, and bicolors.

I. tuberosa. See Merremia tuberosa

IPOMOPSIS

Polemoniaceae

BIENNIALS OR PERENNIALS

ZONES VARY BY SPECIES

FULL SUN

NO IRRIGATION NEEDED

Ipomopsis aggregata

Erect single stems, finely divided leaves, and tubular red (or yellow-and-red) flowers. Individual plants are narrow and somewhat startling in appearance; best massed. Good in wild garden, where they survive on rainfall—but can take irrigation if grown in watered border. Sow seeds in spring or early summer for bloom the following summer.

I. aggregata (Gilia aggregata). Biennial. Zones 1–3, 6–14, 18–21. Native from California to British Columbia, east to Rocky Mountains. To 2½ ft. tall and 1 ft. wide. Flowers are red marked yellow (sometimes pure yellow), an inch or so long; borne in long, narrow clusters.

I. rubra (Gilia rubra). Biennial or perennial. Zones 2, 3, 7–9, 14–24. Native to southern U.S. To 6 ft. tall and 1 ft. wide. Flowers red outside, yellow marked red inside.

IRESINE herbstii

BLOODLEAF

Amaranthaceae

PERENNIAL

ZONES 22–24; H1, H2; OR INDOORS

FULL SUN; BRIGHT LIGHT

REGULAR WATER

Iresine herbstii

From Brazil. Tender, upright plant to 1–3 ft. high and wide, grown for attractive leaf color; flowers are inconspicuous. Leaves are 1–2 in. long, oval to round, usually notched at tip. Leaf color may be purplish red with lighter midrib and veins, or green or bronze with yellowish veins. Stems may be green, purple, or red. Pinch plant tips for bushiness. Good in containers. Beyond hardiness range, bring indoors for winter, treat as annual, or grow as houseplant. Easy to propagate from cuttings taken in fall and grown for spring and summer display. Similar to *I. herbstii* is *I. lindenii,* bearing deep red leaves with prominent dark or light red veins; they are pointed rather than notched at the tips.

Iridaceae. The large iris family includes many familiar (and unfamiliar) garden bulbs, corms, and fibrous-rooted perennials. Leaves are swordlike or grasslike, often in two opposing rows. Flowers may be simply arranged with six equal segments (as in *Crocus,* for example) or highly irregular in appearance (as in *Iris*).

IRIS

Iridaceae

PERENNIALS FROM BULBS AND RHIZOMES

ZONES VARY ACCORDING TO SPECIES OR TYPE

EXPOSURE NEEDS VARY BY SPECIES

WATER NEEDS VARY BY SPECIES

Japanese Iris

A large and remarkably diverse group of 200 to 300 species, varying in flower color and form, cultural needs, and blooming periods (although the majority flower in spring or early summer). Leaves are swordlike or grasslike. Flowers (fragrant, in many kinds) are showy and complex in structure. The three inner segments (the standards) are petals; they are usually erect or arching but, in some kinds, may flare to horizontal. The three outer segments (the falls) are petal-like sepals; they are held at various angles, from nearly horizontal to drooping.

Irises grow from bulbs or rhizomes. In floral detail, there are three categories: bearded (each fall bears an adornment resembling a fuzzy caterpillar); beardless (each fall is smooth); and crested (each fall bears a comblike ridge instead of a full beard).

Described here are the irises most available in the West. Tall bearded irises (and other bearded classes) are the most widely sold; many new hybrids are cataloged every year. Specialty growers abound. A smaller number offer various beardless classes and some species. Retail nurseries carry bulbous irises for fall planting; more and more nurseries are also selling Pacific Coast irises.

BULBOUS IRISES

Irises that grow from bulbs have beardless flowers. Bulbs become dormant in summer and can be lifted and stored until planting time in fall.

Dutch and Spanish irises. Zones 2b–24. The species that parented this group come from Spain, Portugal, Sicily, and northern Africa. (Dutch irises acquired their name because the hybrid group was developed by Dutch bulb growers.) Flowers are borne atop slender stems that rise up from rushlike foliage. Standards are narrow and upright; oval to circular falls project downward. Colors include white, mauve, blue, purple, brown, orange, yellow, and bicolor combinations—usually with a yellow blotch on falls. Dutch iris flowers reach 3–4 in. across, on stems 1½–2 ft. tall; these are the irises sold by florists. Bloom period is early spring in warm-winter climates, late spring in colder climates. Spanish irises are similar but have smaller flowers that bloom about 2 weeks after Dutch irises.

Dutch Iris

Plant bulbs in autumn, setting them 4 in. deep, 3–4 in. apart; give full sun. Bulbs are hardy to about –10°F/–23°C, but in coldest adapted zones, apply a mulch in winter. Give regular water during growth. Bulbs can be left in the ground for several years where summers are dry; elsewhere, they should be lifted. After bloom, let foliage ripen before digging; store bulbs in a cool, dry place for no more than 2 months before replanting. Dutch and Spanish irises are good in containers; plant five bulbs in a 5–6-in. pot.

The widely sold 'Wedgwood' is a Dutch hybrid hardy only in Zones 4–24. Large flowers are lavender blue with yellow markings, blooming earlier than others (generally coinciding with 'King Alfred' daffodils). Bulbs are larger than those of average Dutch hybrid. Vigorous foliage dies down after bloom and is best masked by bushy annuals or perennials that will mature later in the season.

English irises. Zones 3–6, 15–17, 21–24. The species *(I. latifolia)* from which named selections were made is native to the Pyrenees, where it grows in moist meadows. Early botanists first noticed the iris growing in southern England, where it had been taken by traders. Flowers are similar in structure to Dutch and Spanish irises, but falls are broader and decorated with a hairline stripe of yellow. Colors include bluish purple, wine red, maroon, blue, mauve, white. Bloom comes in early summer. Plant bulbs in fall, 3–4 in. deep, 4 in. apart, in cool, moist, acid soil. Choose a partly shaded location in warm-summer areas, full sun where summers are cool. Because English irises don't need complete dryness after flowering, they can be left in the ground in suitable climates (bulbs are hardy to about –10°F/–23°C). Or they can be lifted and replanted.

Reticulata irises. Zones 3–24; safer in pots in colder zones. The netted outer covering on the bulbs gives the group its name. These are classic rock garden and container plants, the flowers (like small Dutch irises) appearing on 6–8-in. stems in early spring (midwinter in mild areas). Narrow blue-green leaves appear after bloom. Available species include *I. reticulata,* with 2–3-in. violet-scented flowers (purple, in the usual forms), and bright yellow–flowered *I. danfordiae.* Pale blue–flowered *I. histrio* and large-flowered, blue-and-yellow *I. histrioides* may be carried by some specialists. Far more common are named hybrids such as 'Cantab' (pale blue with orange markings), 'Harmony' (sky blue marked yellow), 'J. S. Dijt' (reddish purple).

Bulbs are hardy to about –10°F/–23°C and need some subfreezing winter temperatures to thrive. Plant in autumn, in well-drained soil in a sunny location; set bulbs 3–4 in. deep and 3–4 in. apart. Need regular moisture from fall through spring. Soil should be kept dry during summer dormant period; in rainy climates, lift bulbs in summer or grow in pots so you can control moisture. Divide only when vigor and flower quality deteriorate. Watch for slugs and snails.

RHIZOMATOUS IRISES

Irises that grow from rhizomes (thickened, modified stems) may have bearded, beardless, or crested flowers; among this group are the most widely grown types. Leaves are swordlike, overlapping each other to form flat fans of foliage.

Bearded irises. Zones 1–24. The most widely grown irises fall into the bearded group. More than a century of breeding has produced a vast array of beautiful hybrids. All have upright standards and flaring to pendent falls that have characteristic epaulettelike beards. Tall bearded irises are the most familiar of these, but they represent just one subdivision of the entire group.

July to October is best planting period; in regions with mild winters and cool to moderate summers, you can plant throughout this time. In cold-winter zones, plant during July or August; where summer temperatures are high, plant in September or October.

Bearded irises need good drainage. They'll grow in soils from sandy to claylike, but in clay soils plant in raised beds or on ridges to assure drainage, avoid rhizome rot. Plant in full sun in cool climates; in hottest regions, they'll accept light shade during the afternoon. Space rhizomes 1–2 ft. apart; set with tops barely beneath soil surface, spreading roots well. Growth proceeds from the leafy end of rhizome, so point that end in direction you want growth initially to occur. For quick show, plant three rhizomes 1 ft. apart—two with growing ends pointed outward, the third aimed to grow into the space between them. On slopes, set rhizomes with growing end facing uphill. Water to settle soil and start growth. Thereafter, water judiciously until new growth shows plants have rooted; then water regularly until fall rains or frosts arrive. If weather turns hot, shade newly planted rhizomes to prevent sunscald, possible rot. Where winters are severe, mulch new plantings to prevent heaving from alternate freezing, thawing.

From the time growth starts in late winter or early spring, water regularly until about 6 weeks after flowers fade; increases and buds for next year's flowers form during postbloom period. During summer, plants need less water. In heavy soil, it may be sufficient to water every other week in hot climates, monthly in cool ones. In lighter soils, try watering weekly in hot areas, every other week in cool ones. For best performance, feed plants with moderate-nitrogen commercial fertilizer as growth begins in spring, then after bloom has finished. In cool, moist spring, leaf spot may disfigure foliage; use appropriate fungicide at first sign of infection. Remove old and dry leaves in fall.

Clumps become overcrowded after 3 or 4 years; quantity and quality of bloom decrease. Lift and divide crowded clumps at best planting time for your area. Save large rhizomes with healthy leaves; discard old and leafless ones from clump's center. Break rhizomes apart or use a sharp knife to

Dutch Irises

Reticulata Irises

Standard Dwarf Bearded Iris
'Sarah Taylor'

Border Bearded Iris
'Brown Lasso'

separate. Trim leaves, roots to about 6 in.; let cut ends heal for several hours to a day before replanting. If replanting in the same soil, amend it with organic matter.

Dwarf and median irises. These irises generally have flowers shaped like the familiar tall beardeds, but flower size, plant size, and stature are smaller. Median iris is a collective term for the categories standard dwarf, intermediate and border bearded, and miniature tall bearded.

Miniature dwarf bearded irises. Grow to 8 in. tall; flowers large for size of plant. Earliest to bloom of bearded irises (about 6 weeks before main show of tall beardeds). Hardy, need winter chill. Plants multiply quickly. Shallow root systems need regular moisture and periodic feeding.

Standard dwarf bearded irises. Grow 8–15 in. tall. Flowers and plants are larger than miniature dwarfs. Profuse bloom. Easier to grow than miniature dwarfs in Western gardens but perform best with some winter chill.

Intermediate bearded irises. Grow 15–28 in. tall, bear flowers 3–5 in. across. Flower later than dwarfs but 1 to 3 weeks before tall bearded irises. Most are hybrids between standard dwarfs and tall bearded varieties and resemble larger standard dwarfs rather than border beardeds. Some give second bloom in fall.

Border bearded irises. Grow 15–28 in. tall—proportionately smaller versions of tall beardeds in the same wide range of colors and patterns. Bloom period is same as for tall bearded.

Miniature tall bearded irises. Grow 15–28 in. high and flower with tall beardeds. Their small flowers (2–3 in. wide), narrower foliage, and pencil-thin stems give them appearance of tall bearded irises reduced in every proportion. Good for cutting and arrangements—hence their original name, "table irises."

Tall bearded irises. Among choicest perennials for borders, massing, cutting. Easy to grow. Midspring flowers, on branching stems 2½–4 ft. high. All colors but pure red and green; patterns of two colors or more, blends produce infinite variety. Countless named selections are available. Modern hybrids often have elaborately ruffled, fringed flowers. Available variegated-foliage selections include 'Pallida Variegata' (often cataloged as 'Zebra'), with green leaves striped with cream; and 'Argentea', producing green leaves with white stripes. Both bear smallish blue-lavender flowers on stems to 2 ft. high.

Tall Bearded Iris
'Beverly Sills'

Remontant (or reblooming) tall bearded irises flower in spring, again in mid- to late summer, fall, or winter, depending on variety and climate. In mild climates, some are nearly everblooming. Plants need fertilizer, regular moisture for best performance. Specialists' catalogs offer increasing numbers of remontant tall beardeds.

Aril and arilbred irises. The aril species and interspecies hybrids (characterized by an aril, or collar, on their seeds) offer strange and often remarkably beautiful flowers on unattractive plants. Exacting cultural requirements. Most species come from semidesert areas of the Near East and central Asia; they need limy soil, perfect drainage, full sun, and no summer water (and thus do best in areas with scant or no summer rain). There are two main groups: *Oncocyclus* and *Regelia. Oncocyclus* group includes a number of species with huge, nearly globular flowers in lavender, gray, silver, maroon, and gold, often intricately veined and stippled with deeper hues. *Regelia* group has smaller, narrower-petaled flowers, veined or unmarked; they come in brighter shades than *Oncocyclus,* often with a lustrous sheen. *Oncocyclus* are more difficult to grow; somewhat easier are *Regelia* group and hybrids between the two *(Oncogelia).*

Arilbreds—hybrids between the arils and bearded irises—offer some of the arils' exotic beauty on plants nearly as easy to grow as tall beardeds, given well-drained, neutral to alkaline soil. Amount of aril ancestry can determine ease of culture: hybrids containing half aril ancestry or more usually are more demanding than those of one-quarter or three-eighths aril ancestry. Specialists' catalogs often state hybrid ancestries for this reason.

Beardless irises. Flowers in this group all have smooth, "beardless" falls but otherwise differ considerably in appearance from one type or species to another. Rhizomes have fibrous roots (unlike fleshy roots of bearded types); most prefer or demand more moisture than bearded irises. Many can perform well from crowded clumps but will eventually need division. Timing varies; dig and replant quickly, keeping roots moist until planted.

The following five hybrid groups contain the most widely sold beardless irises. Also described are individual species (and their named selections) available from growers of specialty irises and perennials.

Japanese irises. Zones 1–10, 14–24. Derived solely from *I. ensata* (formerly *I. kaempferi*), these irises feature sumptuous blossoms 4–12 in. across on slender stems to 4 ft. high. Flower shape is essentially flat. "Single" types have three broad falls and much-reduced standards, giving triangular flower outline; "double" blossoms have standards marked like the falls and about the same size and shape, resulting in circular flower outline. Colors are purple, violet, pink, rose, red, white—often veined or edged in contrasting shade. Plants have graceful narrow, upright leaves with distinct raised midribs.

Plants need much moisture during growing, flowering period. Acid to neutral soil and water are required. If soil or water is alkaline, apply aluminum sulfate or iron sulfate (1 oz. to 2 gallons water) several times during growing season. Plant rhizomes in fall or spring, 2 in. deep and 1½ ft. apart; or plant up to three per 12-in. container. Use in moist borders, at edge of pools or streams, or even in boxes or pots plunged halfway to rim in pond or pool during growing season. Full sun except in hottest areas.

Louisiana irises. Zones 3–24; H1, H2. Approximately four species from the lower Mississippi region and Gulf Coast compose this group of so-called swamp irises. Graceful, flattish blossoms on stems 2–5 ft. tall, carried

I

Miniature Tall Bearded Iris
'Rosemary's Dream'

Tall Bearded Iris
'Cinderella's Coach'

Arilbred Iris
'Jeweled Veil'

Japanese Iris

above and among leaves that are long, narrow, and unribbed. The range of flower colors and patterns is extensive—nearly the equal of tall beardeds.

Specialists offer a vast array of named hybrids; some may carry the basic species as well. *I. brevicaulis (I. foliosa)* has blue flowers with flaring segments carried on zigzag stems among the foliage. *I. fulva* has coppery to rusty red (rarely yellow) blossoms with narrow, drooping segments. *I. giganticaerulea* is indeed a "giant blue" (sometimes white) with upright standards and flaring falls; stems may reach 4 ft. or more, with proportionally large leaves. *I. hexagona* also comes in blue shades with upright standards, flaring falls. *I. ×nelsonii,* a natural hybrid population derived from *I. fulva* and *I. giganticaerulea,* resembles the *I. fulva* parent in flower shape and color (but also including purple and brown tones) and approaches the *I. giganticaerulea* parent in size.

Plants thrive in well-watered, rich garden soil as well as at pond margins; soil and water should be neutral to acid. Locate in full sun where summer is cool to mild; choose light afternoon shade where summer heat is intense. Plant in late summer; set rhizomes 1 in. deep, 1½–2 ft. apart. Mulch for winter where ground freezes.

Pacific Coast irises. Best in Zones 4–9, 14–24, grown with mixed success in Zone 3. Eleven species native to Pacific Coast states constitute a homogeneous group within the genus *Iris.* From several species, breeders have developed hybrids in a broad range of colors and patterns; flowers may be white, blue shades, pink, copper, brown, maroon, violet—many with elaborate veining or patterning. Foliage is narrow; clumps are like coarse grass. Slender flower stems reach 8–24 in., depending on variety.

Best conditions are sun to light shade, well-drained soil, moderate to scant water in summer. Intense heat coupled with water and poor drainage can be fatal; in clay soil, grow in raised beds in organically amended soil. Plant from containers any time, though spring and fall are best. Timing is critical in digging and replanting. Best moment is when new roots are starting to form (scrape away soil at plant base to check); this ranges from early fall in colder regions to midwinter in mild-winter areas.

Specialists sell several species prominent in the ancestry of hybrids. *I. douglasiana* is native to California coast from Santa Barbara into Oregon. Evergreen leaves 1½–2 ft. long; stems 1–2 ft., sometimes branched, with flowers in purple and blue shades to white, cream. Tolerates less-than-perfect conditions. *I. innominata* comes from northwestern California and southwestern Oregon. Evergreen leaves; 8–12-in. stems bear flowers in yellow, orange, lavender, purple, brown, many attractively veined. Best in mild-summer regions, in woodland or rock garden. *I. tenax,* from Washington and Oregon, makes grassy clumps of foot-tall deciduous leaves. Flowers may be white, blue, purple, pink, cream, often veined in purple or brown. Best with mild summers, some winter chill.

Siberian irises. Zones 1–10, 14–23. The most widely sold members of this group are named hybrids derived from *I. sibirica* and *I. sanguinea* (formerly *I. orientalis*)—species native to Europe, Asia. Clumps of narrow, almost grasslike leaves (deciduous in winter) produce slender stems to 4 ft. high (depending on variety), each bearing two to five blossoms with upright standards and flaring to drooping falls. Colors include white and shades of blue, lavender, purple, wine, pink, and light yellow.

Siberian Iris

Give plants full sun (partial or dappled shade where summer is hot), neutral to acid soil. Set rhizomes 1–2 in. deep, 1–2 ft. apart. In cold-winter regions, plant in early spring or late summer; in milder regions, plant in autumn. Water liberally from onset of growth until several weeks after bloom. Divide infrequently—when clumps show hollow centers—at best planting time for your region.

Specialists may offer various Sino-Siberian species. Most feature drooping falls and erect to flaring standards. Predominantly yellow colors are found in *I. forrestii* and *I. wilsonii;* predominantly purple to violet flowers occur in *I. chrysographes, I. clarkei, I. delavayi,* and *I. dykesii.* These species and their hybrids perform best in Zones 4–6, 15–17, where climate is moist and relatively mild. Give plants good, acid soil, regular moisture. Interesting hybrids between these species and Pacific Coast irises are called Cal-Sibes; flowers resemble the Siberian parents but have expanded color range. Garden needs are the same as for Sino-Siberian types.

Spuria irises. Zones 2–24. In flower form, the spurias resemble Dutch irises. Older members of this group had primarily yellow or white-and-yellow blossoms; *I. orientalis* (universally known as *I. ochroleuca*) has naturalized in many parts of the West, its 3–5-ft. stems bearing white flowers with yellow blotches on the falls. Dwarf *I. graminea* bears narrow-petaled, fragrant blue-and-maroon blossoms on foot-high stems. Modern hybrids show a great color range: blue, lavender, gray, orchid, tan, bronze, brown, purple, earthy red, and near black—often with a prominent yellow spot on the falls. Flowers are held closely against 3–6-ft. stems, rising above handsome clumps of narrow dark green leaves. Flowering starts during latter part of tall bearded bloom and continues for several weeks beyond.

Plant rhizomes in late summer or early fall, in rich, neutral to slightly alkaline soil; set them 1 in. deep, 1½–2 ft. apart. Plants grow well in full sun but will also take light shade for part of the day. They need ample moisture from onset of growth through bloom period but little moisture during summer. Divide clumps (not an easy task) infrequently; mulch clumps for winter where temperatures drop to −20°F/−29°C or lower.

I. foetidissima. GLADWIN IRIS. Zones 3–24. Native to Europe. Glossy evergreen leaves to 2 ft. make handsome foliage clumps. Stems 1½–2 ft. tall bear subtly attractive flowers in blue gray and dull tan; specialists may offer color variants in soft yellow and lavender blue, as well as a form with white-variegated leaves. Real attraction is large seed capsules that open in fall to show numerous round, orange-scarlet seeds; the cut stems with seed capsules are attractive in arrangements. Grow in sun to shade in cool-summer regions, light or partial shade to full shade elsewhere. Extremely tolerant of aridity.

Louisiana Iris 'Inner Beauty'

Pacific Coast Iris 'Fairy Chimes'

Siberian Iris

Spuria Iris 'Barbara's Kiss'

Iris laevigata

I. laevigata. Zones 1–10, 14–24. Native to China, Korea, Japan. Smooth, glossy leaves reach 1½–2½ ft. high, to 1 in. wide. Flower stems grow to about the same height, bearing violet-blue blossoms with upright standards and drooping falls enlivened with yellow central stripes. Bloom period comes after that of tall bearded irises. Named color variants include kinds with white, magenta, and patterned purple-and-white blooms. There also are varieties whose standards mimic falls in shape, pattern, and carriage, producing the effect of a double blossom. This is a true bog plant, growing best in constantly moist, acid soil—even in shallow water. Full sun.

I. missouriensis. WESTERN BLUE FLAG, ROCKY MOUNTAIN IRIS. Zones 1–10, 14–24. Native to extensive Western area—from western Nebraska and Dakotas into Sierra Nevada/Cascade mountain ranges and mountains of Southern California, from the Yukon southward into northern Mexico. Elevation range is also extensive—from 2,000 to about 12,000 ft. In zones where plant is adapted, local forms are more likely to succeed. Narrow, flat, bluish green, winter-deciduous leaves range from 12 to 22 in. high. Blooms in late spring and summer, bearing blossoms with narrow, upright standards and semiflaring to drooping falls, on stems a bit higher than the foliage clump. Colors range from white to lavender, with veins in darker lavender to purple; the darker colors are found in the more southerly and westerly forms. Give a sunny location and neutral to alkaline, water-retentive soil that is kept moist throughout growth and bloom, dry thereafter. Best time to plant or transplant is from early spring into the flowering period.

A similar species, *I. longipetala,* is considered by some botanists to be a form of *I. missouriensis.* It differs from *I. missouriensis* in its nativity (northern and central California Coast Ranges, up to about 1,200 ft.) and in having evergreen foliage and an early spring bloom period. Cultural preferences are the same as for *I. missouriensis.*

I. prismatica. Zones 2–6. Native to eastern North America. Foliage and flowers suggest a small Siberian iris. Typical form grows about 1 ft. high, bearing dainty purple-and-white blossoms on branching, sinuous stems. A pure white form exists. *I. p. austrina,* native to the southern Appalachians, is a bit taller and coarser, with lilac-blue blossoms. Give plants full sun and moist (but not boggy), acid soil. Rhizomes spread widely, forming loose colonies rather than tight clumps.

I. pseudacorus. YELLOW FLAG. Zones 1–24. Native to Europe but now found worldwide in temperate regions; seeds float, aiding plant's dispersal. Impressive foliage plant; under best conditions, upright leaves may reach 5 ft. tall. Flower stems grow 4–7 ft. (depending on culture), bear bright yellow flowers 3–4 in. across. Selected forms offer ivory and lighter yellow flowers, double flowers, variegated foliage, and plants with shorter and taller leaves. Plant in sun to light shade. Needs acid soil and more than average moisture; thrives in shallow water and can become invasive where running water disperses seeds.

Several hybrids are excellent foliage plants with distinctive blossoms. All prefer ample water (but not pond conditions), sun to light shade. 'Holden Clough' perhaps has *I. foetidissima* as its other parent. Flowers, 3–4 in. across, are soft tan heavily netted with maroon veins; stems grow to 4 ft.; leaves reach 4–5 ft. but tips arch over. Two of its seedlings are similar but larger. 'Phil Edinger' grows to 4½ ft. with arching foliage; 4–5-in. flowers are brass colored, heavily veined in brown. 'Roy Davidson' is similar, but flowers are dark yellow with fine brown veining and maroon thumbprint on falls.

I. setosa. Zones A1–A3; 1–6. Native to Siberia (extending to Kamchatka), Alaska, eastern Canada, and New England. Leaves are a slightly grayed green, ½–1 in. wide; plants vary from less than 1 ft. to about 2 ft. high, with flower stems taller than leaves. Blooms in late spring and summer, bearing typically blue-purple to red-purple flowers with broadly rounded falls, standards reduced to mere bristles. Form sold as 'Nasuensis' is larger in all parts than species, reaches about 3 ft. high; will also grow in Zones 7–9, 14–17. Garden culture as for Siberian irises: moist, well-drained, neutral to acid soil; full sun except in hottest areas. Will grow where buffeted by salt-laden ocean spray. Plant in late summer, early fall.

I. unguicularis (I. stylosa). WINTER IRIS. Zones 4–9, 14–24. Native to Greece, the Near East, northern Africa. Dense clump of narrow dark green leaves. Depending on variety and mildness of winter, flowers appear from November to March. Typical form has violet-tinted blue blossoms elevated on 6–9-in. tubes that serve as stems. Named selections vary in flower color (lighter and darker lavender, orchid pink, white) and coarseness and length of foliage. Plants need neutral to acid soil, heat, and scant water during summer (but will take moderate water if soil is very well drained). In Zones 4 and 5, grow against sunny wall or house foundation to increase summer heat and to lessen winter cold. Divide overcrowded clumps in early fall (mild regions) or in late winter after flowering (colder regions). Slugs and snails are attracted to the flowers.

I. versicolor. BLUE FLAG. Zones 1–9, 14–17. Widely distributed North American species, found in bogs and swamps from Mississippi Valley to eastern Canada. Grows 1½–4 ft. tall; narrow leaves are thicker in the center but not ribbed. Shorter-growing forms have upright leaves, but foliage of taller types may recurve gracefully. The typical wild flowers are a light violet blue, but lighter and darker forms exist; a wine red variant has been sold as 'Kermesina'. Named selections include pink 'Rosea' and 'Vernal', as well as others with flowers in violet red. Like *I. pseudacorus,* this species thrives in sun to light shade, in moist, acid soil or shallow water.

Specialty growers offer hybrids between *I. versicolor* and other species such as *I. ensata, I. laevigata,* and *I. virginica.* Violet-flowered 'Gerald Darby', a hybrid with *I. virginica,* has striking wine red stems.

I. virginica. SOUTHERN BLUE FLAG. Zones 3–9, 14–17. Native to Eastern seaboard, from Virginia south and west to Mississippi River and Gulf Coast. Similar to *I. versicolor* in form and flower; distinguishing floral feature is longer standards. Flower colors include light to dark blue, wine red, pink, lavender, and white. A plant sold as 'Giant Blue' is distinctly larger in all parts, approaching *I. pseudacorus* in size. Plant in moist, acid soil or grow in shallow water. In deep ponds, plant in large pots barely submerged beneath the surface. Sun to light shade.

Crested irises. Though these are botanically placed with beardless irises, they represent a transition between beardless and bearded: each fall bears

Iris pseudacorus

Iris unguicularis 'Walter Butt'

Iris setosa

Iris tectorum

a narrow, comblike crest where a beard would be in bearded sorts. Slugs and snails are especially attracted to foliage and flowers.

I. cristata. Zones 2b–6. Leaves 4–6 in. long, ½ in. wide; slender greenish rhizomes spread freely. Flowers white, lavender, or light blue with golden crests. Give light shade, organically enriched soil, regular water. Divide just after bloom or in fall after leaves die down.

I. tectorum. ROOF IRIS. Zones 3–9, 14–24; H1, H2. Native to Japan, where it is planted on cottage roofs. Foliage fans to 1 ft. tall look like those of bearded irises, but leaves are ribbed and glossy. Flowers suggest an informal bearded iris with fringed petals and crests in place of beards. Colors are violet blue with white crests or white with yellow crests; standards are upright at first, opening to horizontal as flower matures. Provide organically enriched soil, light shade, regular water. Short lived in regions where summers are hot and dry. 'Paltec', a hybrid of *I. tectorum* with a bearded iris, will grow with bearded irises; it reaches about 1 ft. high, with lavender flowers suggesting a bearded iris with beards superimposed on crests.

Tender crested irises. Several tender species and hybrids form bamboo-type stems carrying foliage fans aloft; flower stems to 2 ft. are widely branched, orchidlike sprays of fringed flowers in lavender to white with orange crests. These include *I. confusa, I. japonica, I. wattii,* and hybrids such as 'Nada' and 'Darjeeling'. Grow in sun where summer is cool, light shade elsewhere; plant in organically enriched soil. Regular water during growth. Reliable outdoors in Zones 17, 23, 24; in other zones, grow in containers and move to shelter over winter.

IRISH MOSS. See SAGINA subulata

IRONBARK. See EUCALYPTUS

ISLAND BUSH SNAPDRAGON. See GALVEZIA speciosa

ISMENE calathina. See HYMENOCALLIS narcissiflora

ISOPOGON formosus

ROSE CONEFLOWER
Proteaceae
EVERGREEN SHRUB
ZONES 15–24
FULL SUN OR LIGHT SHADE
MODERATE WATER

Isopogon formosus

From Australia. Slender, erect habit to 4–9 ft. high, 3–6 ft. wide. Stems are densely clothed with finely divided leaves and topped by dense, 2½-in., conelike clusters of long, slender rosy purple florets in late winter or spring. Excellent cut flower—and cutting in bloom stimulates denser growth. Tip-pinching also makes plants bushier. Like most proteas, this species cannot tolerate high phosphorus levels and should be fertilized lightly with nitrogen. Avoid watering in hot weather (above 90°F/32°C).

ISOTOMA fluviatilis. See PRATIA pedunculata

ITEA

SWEETSPIRE
Escalloniaceae
EVERGREEN, SEMIEVERGREEN, DECIDUOUS SHRUBS
ZONES VARY BY SPECIES
FULL SUN, EXCEPT AS NOTED
REGULAR WATER

Only a few of the ten or so species are seen in gardens. One feature they have in common is small, scented flowers in long, narrow, tightly packed clusters. Little pruning required.

Itea ilicifolia

I. ilicifolia. HOLLYLEAF SWEETSPIRE. Evergreen. Zones 4–9, 14–24. Native to China. Shrub has graceful, arching, open habit to 10–15 ft. tall and 10 ft. wide. Leaves are oval, spiny-toothed, to 4 in. long; new foliage is bronzy red, matures to glossy dark green. Lightly fragrant greenish white flowers in nodding or drooping clusters to 1 ft. long in autumn; blooms sparsely where winters are mild. Not striking, but a graceful plant of distinction. Attractive near water or espaliered against a wall. Needs partial shade in hottest climates.

I. japonica 'Beppu'. Semievergreen. Zones 4–6. Native to Japan. Dwarf shrub to 2½ ft. tall and suckering widely. Leaves and flowers resemble those of *I. virginica,* under which name this shrub is often mistakenly sold. Foliage turns reddish purple in fall.

I. virginica. Deciduous. Zones 2b–6, 15–17. Native to eastern U.S. To 3–15 ft. tall, spreading by suckers to form large patches where well adapted. Narrow, oval, 4-in.-long, dark green leaves turn purplish or bright red in fall, hang on the plant for a long time—possibly all winter. Fragrant, creamy white summer flowers in erect clusters to 6 in. long. 'Henry's Garnet', a superior selection, grows 3–4 ft. tall, 4–6 ft. wide, has brilliant purplish red fall foliage. 'Little Henry' is a more compact variety, reaching just 2 ft. high.

ITHURIEL'S SPEAR. See TRITELEIA laxa

IVA hayesiana

POVERTY WEED, SAN DIEGO MARSH-ELDER
Asteraceae (Compositae)
SHRUBBY PERENNIAL
ZONES 17, 23–24
FULL SUN OR PARTIAL SHADE
NO IRRIGATION NEEDED

Iva hayesiana

Native to alkaline flats from San Diego to Baja California. To 1 ft. high, 5 ft. wide. Fleshy, grayish green, 1–2½-in.-long leaves have three conspicuous veins from base to tip. Flower heads are inconspicuous. Not an especially attractive plant (and bears an unlovely common name), but it makes a useful ground cover under difficult conditions—takes heat, sun, drought, alkaline soil. Good for controlling erosion, naturalizing.

IVY. See HEDERA

IXIA

AFRICAN CORN LILY
Iridaceae
PERENNIALS FROM CORMS
ZONES 7–9, 12–24; OR DIG AND STORE
FULL SUN
REGULAR WATER DURING GROWTH AND BLOOM

Ixia maculata hybrid

Clump of narrow, almost grasslike leaves sends up wiry, 18–20-in. stems topped by short spikes of 2-in. flowers in late spring. Each six-petaled blossom opens out nearly flat in full sun but remains cup shaped or closed on overcast days. Colors include cream, yellow, red, orange, and pink, typically with dark centers. Most ixias sold are hybrids of the South African species *I. maculata.*

Grow in well-drained soil. Where winter lows usually stay above 20°F/–7°C, plant corms in early fall, setting them 2 in. deep and about 3 in. apart. In climate zones where temperatures may drop down to 10°F/–12°C, plant them in late fall, setting the corms 4 in. deep; cover planting with mulch. In colder areas, plant in spring for flowers in early summer. Let soil go dry when foliage yellows after bloom. Where corms won't be subject to rainfall or irrigation during dormant period, they can be left undisturbed until the planting becomes crowded or flowering declines. When this occurs, dig corms in summer and store as for gladiolus until recommended planting time in your area. Where corms will receive summer moisture, dig and store them after foliage dies back; or treat as annuals. Potted corms (planted close together and about 1 in. deep) can be stored in pots of dry soil.

IXIOLIRION tataricum (I. montanum)

Amaryllidaceae

PERENNIALS FROM BULBS

ZONES 2 AND 3 (WITH SHELTER), 4–11, 14–21; OR DIG AND STORE

FULL SUN

MODERATE WATER DURING GROWTH AND BLOOM

Ixiolirion tataricum

Native to central Asia. Wiry, 12–16-in. stems rise from a clump of narrow gray-green leaves, bearing loose clusters of 1½-in. flowers in late spring. Each blue-violet blossom has six narrow petals marked with a darker central line. Foliage dies down in summer, not to reappear until following spring. Bulbs accept moderate summer moisture but don't need any.

Plant in fall, setting bulbs 3 in. deep, 3 in. apart. Beyond hardiness range, however, plant in early spring; dig in fall and store until planting time the next year. Where bulbs are hardy in the ground, they can remain in place for many years. Dig and divide clumps in fall when they become crowded.

IXORA

Rubiaceae

EVERGREEN SHRUBS

ZONE H2, EXCEPT AS NOTED

FULL SUN OR LIGHT SHADE

REGULAR WATER

Ixora coccinea

Large group of tropical plants with handsome, leathery, medium to dark green leaves and showy clusters of flowers that bloom throughout much of the year. These shrubs thrive in well-drained, fertile, acid soil. Require little pruning but will tolerate heavy pruning. Use as specimen shrub, hedge or screen, or tubbed plant for lanai or patio. Beyond the hardiness range, can be grown only in greenhouse.

I. casei 'Super King'. SUPER KING IXORA. Native to the Caroline Islands of the western Pacific. To 12 ft. tall, 8–10 ft. wide, with bright red flower clusters to 6 in. across.

I. chinensis 'Nora Grant'. NORA GRANT IXORA. Native from south China into the Malay peninsula. To 6 ft. high and about 4 ft. wide, with large clusters of coral flowers.

I. coccinea. FLAME OF THE WOODS, JUNGLE FLAME. Zones 24; H2. Native to Sri Lanka and southern India. Long in cultivation in southern Florida and Hawaii; many selections are available, featuring blossoms in shades of red, orange, pink, or yellow. Grows 7–10 ft. high and about 6 ft. wide but is often kept lower by tip pinching.

I. 'Thai Dwarf'. THAI DWARF IXORA. A group of compact dwarf ixoras introduced into Hawaii from Thailand. Growing 4 ft. high and wide, they provide abundant, dense clusters of small flowers in a range of brilliant colors—red, orange, gold, pink, yellow.

FOR INFORMATION ON SELECTING PLANTS
PLEASE SEE PAGES 64–160

JACARANDA mimosifolia

Bignoniaceae

DECIDUOUS OR SEMIEVERGREEN TREE

ZONES 12, 13, 15–24; H1, H2

FULL SUN

MODERATE WATER

Jacaranda mimosifolia

Often sold as *J. acutifolia.* Brazilian native to 25–40 ft. high, 15–30 ft. wide, with open, irregular, oval-headed habit; sometimes multitrunked or even shrubby. Finely cut, ferny leaves usually drop in late winter. New leaves may emerge quickly, or branches may remain bare until tree comes into bloom—typically in mid- to late spring, though blossoms may appear earlier or open at any time throughout summer. Flowers are lavender blue, tubular, 2 in. long, carried in profuse 8-in.-long clusters. White-flowered 'Alba' is sometimes sold; it has lusher foliage and sparser bloom over a longer season. All forms have flat, roundish seed capsules, quite decorative in arrangements.

Tree is fairly hardy after it gains some mature, hard wood. Young trees are tender below 25°F/–4°C but often rebound from freezes to make multistemmed, shrubby plants. Takes wide variety of soils but does best in sandy soil. Often fails to flower in path of ocean winds or where heat is inadequate. Resistant to oak root fungus. Established trees need little pruning; cut any awkward limbs back to strong laterals.

JACK-IN-THE-PULPIT. See ARISAEMA

JACOBEAN LILY. See SPREKELIA formosissima

JACOBINIA carnea, J. ovata. See JUSTICIA carnea, J. candicans

JACOBINIA suberecta. See DICLIPTERA suberecta

JACOB'S COAT. See ALTERNANTHERA tenella

JACOB'S LADDER. See PEDILANTHUS tithymaloides smallii; POLEMONIUM caeruleum

JADE PLANT. See CRASSULA ovata

JAMAICA FLOWER or SORREL. See HIBISCUS sabdariffa

JAPANESE ARALIA. See FATSIA japonica

JAPANESE BLOOD GRASS. See IMPERATA cylindrica 'Rubra'

JAPANESE BLUEBERRY TREE. See ELAEOCARPUS decipiens

JAPANESE CHINQUAPIN. See CASTANOPSIS cuspidata

JAPANESE COLTSFOOT. See PETASITES japonicus

JAPANESE FALSE OAK. See PASANIA edulis

JAPANESE FELT FERN. See PYRROSIA lingua

JAPANESE FLOWERING APRICOT, JAPANESE FLOWERING PLUM. See PRUNUS mume

JAPANESE HOLLY FERN. See CYRTOMIUM falcatum

JAPANESE LACE FERN. See POLYSTICHUM polyblepharum

JAPANESE PAGODA TREE. See SOPHORA japonica

JAPANESE SILVER TREE. See NEOLITSIA sericea

JAPANESE SNOWBALL. See VIBURNUM plicatum plicatum

JAPANESE SNOWBELL, JAPANESE SNOWDROP TREE. See STYRAX japonicus

JAPANESE SPURGE. See PACHYSANDRA terminalis

JAPANESE SWEET SHRUB. See CLETHRA barbinervis

JAPANESE WATERCRESS. See OENANTHE javanica

JAPAN PEPPER. See ZANTHOXYLUM piperitum

JASMINUM

JASMINE

Oleaceae

EVERGREEN, SEMIEVERGREEN, DECIDUOUS SHRUBS AND VINES

ZONES VARY BY SPECIES

FULL SUN OR LIGHT SHADE

MODERATE TO REGULAR WATER

Jasminum laurifolium nitidum

When one thinks of fragrance, jasmine is one of the first plants that comes to mind. Yet not all jasmines are fragrant; and despite its common name, the intensely sweet star jasmine is not a true jasmine at all, but a member of the genus *Trachelospermum.* Growth habits of jasmines range from vining to vining-shrubby to decidedly shrubby. True vining types climb by twining stems. Vining shrubs do not twine, but rather put out long, slender, lax stems that must be tied into place if the plants are to function as vines. Otherwise, they'll flop over to make green haystacks of foliage. To grow these plants as shrubs, shorten any shoots that become too long. Only one of the species listed below, *J. parkeri,* is a true shrub; its dwarf size suits it to rock gardens.

Jasmines grow more rapidly in good soil and bloom more profusely in sunny sites, but all adapt well to less-than-perfect conditions. When plants become tangled or untidy, cut them back heavily just before spring growth begins. Pinch and prune as needed throughout the year to control growth.

J. angulare. SOUTH AFRICAN JASMINE. Evergreen vining shrub. Zones 16–24; H1. From South Africa. Vigorous grower with stems 10–20 ft. long. Rich green leaves are divided into three leaflets. Summer-blooming white flowers over 1 in. wide are borne in groups of three; some gardeners detect a subtly sweet scent, others no fragrance at all.

J. azoricum. Evergreen vining shrub. Zones 17–24; H1, H2. From the Azores. To 10–15 ft. high, with dark green leaves divided into three leaflets and clusters of fragrant white flowers in summer. Plants sold under this name may be the very similar *J. fluminense* or *J. tortuosum,* both African species.

J. floridum. Evergreen or semievergreen vining shrub. Zones 4–9, 12–24; H1. From China. To 5 ft. high. Dark green leaves divided into three (rarely five) small (½–1½-in.-long) leaflets. Clusters of golden yellow, ½–¾-in., scentless flowers bloom primarily from spring into fall.

J. humile. ITALIAN JASMINE. Evergreen vining shrub. Zones 5–10, 12–24; H1, H2. From the Mideast, Myanmar, and China. Erect, willowy shoots reach 20 ft., arch to make 10-ft. mound. Light green leaves with three to seven 2-in.-long leaflets. Clusters of ½-in., fragrant bright yellow flowers all summer. Can be trained as a shrub or clipped into a hedge. 'Revolutum' has larger flowers (to 1 in. wide) and larger, darker green leaves than the species.

J. laurifolium nitidum (J. nitidum). SHINING JASMINE, ANGELWING JASMINE. Evergreen or semievergreen vine. Zones 12, 16, 19–24; H1, H2. From Admiralty Islands in the southwest Pacific. Requires long, warm growing season to bloom satisfactorily. Not reliably hardy below 25°F/–4°C. Moderate growth to 10–20 ft. Undivided glossy green leaves to 2 in. long. Very fragrant flowers shaped like 1-in. pinwheels open from purplish buds in late spring and summer. Flowers are white above, purplish beneath, borne in clusters of three. Can be used as ground cover or container plant. Often sold as *J. magnificum.*

J. leratii. PRIVET-LEAFED JASMINE. Evergreen vine. Zones 22–24; H1, H2. From New Caledonia. To 15 ft., with glossy dark green leaves to 2 in. long that resemble those of privet *(Ligustrum).* Slightly fragrant white flowers in spring.

J. magnificum. See J. laurifolium nitidum

J. mesnyi (J. primulinum). PRIMROSE JASMINE. Evergreen vining shrub. Zones 4–24; H1, H2. From China. Long, arching branches 6–10 ft. long. Dark green leaves with three lance-shaped, 2–3-in. leaflets. Bright lemon yellow, unscented flowers to 2 in. across are semidouble or double, produced singly rather than in clusters. Main bloom in winter or spring; may flower sporadically at other times. Needs space. Best tied up at desired height and permitted to spill down in waterfall fashion. Use to cover pergola, bank, large wall, or clip as 3-ft.-high hedge. In any form, may need occasional severe pruning to avoid brush pile look.

Jasminum mesnyi

J. multiflorum. DOWNY JASMINE, PIKAKE-HOKU. Evergreen vining shrub. Zones 21–24; H1, H2. From India. Leaves (to 2 in. long) and stems have a downy coating, producing an overall gray-green effect. Clustered white flowers in early spring; not strongly scented. Often called star jasmine in Hawaii, where it is commonly used as a hedge.

J. nudiflorum. WINTER JASMINE. Deciduous vining shrub. Zones 2–21; best adapted to cooler climates. From China. If unsupported, reaches 4 ft. or higher and 7 ft. wide; if trained on a trellis or wall, can grow to 15 ft. Slender, willowy green stems stand out in winter landscape. Unscented, bright yellow, 1-in. flowers appear in winter or early spring, before handsome, glossy green, three-leafleted leaves unfurl. Good bank cover; spreads by rooting where stems touch soil. Attractive planted at the top of retaining walls, with branches cascading over side. Can also be trained like *J. mesnyi* (tie plant at desired height and let branches spill down like a waterfall).

J. officinale. COMMON WHITE JASMINE, POET'S JASMINE. Semievergreen or deciduous vine. Zones 5–9, 12–24; H1. From Himalayas, Caucasus. To 30 ft. Very fragrant white flowers to 1 in. across; blooms throughout summer and into fall. Rich green leaves have five to nine leaflets, each to 2½ in. long.

J. o. affine (J. grandiflorum). SPANISH JASMINE. Main difference from basic species is size—this form climbs only to 15 ft. but bears larger (1½-in.) blooms.

J. parkeri. DWARF JASMINE. Evergreen shrub. Zones 5–9, 12–24. From India. Dwarf, twiggy, tufted shrub to 1 ft. high, 1½–2 ft. wide. Bright green, ½–1-in.-long leaves with three to five tiny leaflets. Small, scentless yellow flowers borne profusely in spring. Good choice in rock garden or as container plant.

J. polyanthum. Evergreen vine. Zones 5–9, 12–24; H1. From China. Fast-climbing, strong-growing vine to 20 ft. Bright to dark green leaves are slightly paler on undersides, have five to seven leaflets with the terminal leaflet slightly longer than the rest. Highly fragrant blossoms are white inside, rose colored outside, borne in dense clusters. Blooms in late winter and spring; sporadic flowers rest of year. Can be used as ground cover; sometimes grown in large containers or hanging baskets. 'Variegatum' has leaves with pale yellow margins.

J. primulinum. See J. mesnyi

J. sambac. ARABIAN JASMINE, PIKAKE. Evergreen vining shrub. Zones 13–21, 23, 24; H1, H2. Thought to be native to tropical Asia. To 6–10 ft. Undivided glossy green leaves to 3 in. long. Blooms in summer, bearing clusters of powerfully fragrant, ¾–1-in. white flowers. 'Grand Duke' has double flowers. In Hawaii, blossoms of this species are a favorite for leis and are used in making perfume. In Asia, they're used in jasmine tea.

J. × stephanense. Evergreen or deciduous vine. Zones 5–9, 14–24. To 15–20 ft., with dull green foliage that persists year-round in Southern California. Leaves may be undivided and about 2 in. long or divided into five 2-in.-long leaflets. Pale pink, ½-in., fragrant flowers in clusters of five or more appear in late spring and summer.

JERUSALEM ARTICHOKE. See HELIANTHUS tuberosus

JERUSALEM CHERRY. See SOLANUM pseudocapsicum

JERUSALEM SAGE. See PHLOMIS fruticosa

JERUSALEM THORN. See PARKINSONIA aculeata

JEWEL MINT OF CORSICA. See MENTHA requienii

JICAMA

Fabaceae (Leguminosae)

ANNUAL VINE

BEST IN ZONES H1, H2; MAINLY ORNAMENTAL IN ZONES 8, 9, 12–14, 18–24

FULL SUN

AMPLE WATER

SEEDS ARE POISONOUS IF INGESTED

Jicama

This tropical American native's scientific name is *Pachyrhizus erosus*. In Hawaii, it is commonly known as chop suey potato. Edible part is actually an enlarged taproot; it develops underground like a beet and tastes something like a sweet water chestnut. Very attractive vine, twining to 14 ft. high or more; has luxuriant deep green foliage and upright spikes of pretty, sweet pea–shaped purple or violet flowers in summer. Leaves have three leaflets.

Cultivate jicama for edible root in Hawaii and as an ornamental elsewhere. Plants produce poor-quality roots in Southern California, and you'll usually get only foliage and flowers in Northern California. Grow on trellis or on the ground as a trailing mound. Plant in spring, after danger of frost is past. Sow seeds 2 in. deep and 4 in. apart; thin seedlings to 8–12 in. apart. Needs long, warm growing season and rich soil. Apply high-nitrogen fertilizer monthly. Flowers should be pinched off for maximum root production (each vine yields one edible root weighing from 1 to 6 lbs.), but you can allow seed for next year's crop to form on one or two plants. Roots enlarge in fall as days begin to grow shorter, but weather must stay warm to produce a good crop; harvest them before first frost in regions where frosts are likely (if you're fortunate enough to get a crop). In frost-free areas, you can leave them in the ground until they're needed. Peel off the rough brown skin and eat the white flesh raw or cooked.

JOB'S TEARS. See COIX lacryma-jobi

JOE PYE WEED. See EUPATORIUM purpureum

JOHNNY-JUMP-UP. See VIOLA tricolor

JOINT FIR. See EPHEDRA

JOJOBA. See SIMMONDSIA chinensis

JONQUIL. See NARCISSUS jonquilla

JOSEPH'S COAT. See AMARANTHUS tricolor

JOSHUA TREE. See YUCCA brevifolia

JOYWEED. See ALTERNANTHERA tenella

JUBAEA chilensis

CHILEAN WINE PALM

Arecaceae (Palmae)

PALM

ZONES 12–24

FULL SUN

LITTLE OR NO WATER

Jubaea chilensis

From Chile. Slow-growing single-stemmed palm to 50–60 ft. tall, 25 ft. wide. Massive trunk may grow to 3 ft. thick; patterned with scars of leaf bases. Feather-type leaves; insignificant flowers. Hardy for a palm (to 20°F/–7°C).

JUDAS TREE. See CERCIS siliquastrum

Juglandaceae. The walnut family consists of nut-bearing trees with leaves divided into many paired leaflets. Pecans and hickories *(Carya)*, walnuts *(Juglans)*, and wingnuts *(Pterocarya)* are examples.

JUGLANS

WALNUT

Juglandaceae

DECIDUOUS TREES

ZONES VARY BY SPECIES

FULL SUN

WATER NEEDS VARY BY SPECIES

Juglans nigra

Usually large and spreading; leaves are divided into many leaflets and have a featherlike appearance. Bear oval or round nuts enclosed in a fleshy husk. English walnut is a well-known orchard tree (see Walnut). American native species are sometimes planted as shade trees (with a bonus of edible nuts) or used as an understock for grafting English walnut. Nuts of these species typically contain little meat, and the shells are very thick and hard to crack.

J. californica. CALIFORNIA BLACK WALNUT. Known chiefly through the following two geographic variants. Both produce roundish nuts with rich flavor; they are resistant to oak root fungus and require no irrigation.

J. c. californica. Zones 18–24. Native to Southern California. Grows 15–30 ft. high and wide, usually with several stems from ground level. Leaves are 6–12 in. long, with 9–19 leaflets (each 2½ in. long). Tree is not grown commercially but is worth saving if it grows as a native.

J. c. hindsii. Zones 5–9, 14–20. Native to scattered localities in Northern California. To 30–60 ft. high and wide, with a single trunk. Leaves have 15–19 leaflets, each 3–5 in. long. Widely used as a rootstock for English walnut in California.

J. cinerea. BUTTERNUT. Zones 1–9, 14–17. Native to eastern North America. To 50–60 ft. tall, 40–50 ft. wide. Butternut resembles black walnut *(J. nigra)*, but tree is smaller, leaves have fewer leaflets, and the flavorful nuts are elongated or oval instead of round. Regular water.

J. major (J. rupestris major). NOGAL, ARIZONA WALNUT. Zones 10–13. Native to Arizona, New Mexico, northern Mexico. Broad-headed tree to 50 ft. tall and wide. Leaves have 9–13 leaflets. Small, round nuts are enclosed in husks that dry on the tree; nuts drop still in the husk. Rich flavor like that of *J. nigra.* Takes desert heat and wind. Needs deep soil, moderate water.

J. nigra. BLACK WALNUT. Zones 1–9, 14–21. Native to eastern North America. High-branched tree to about 100 ft. tall and 70 ft. wide, with round crown and furrowed blackish brown bark. Leaves have 11–23 leaflets, each 2½–5 in. long. Round, 1½-in.-diameter nuts have rich flavor. Big, hardy shade tree for large sites. Don't plant near flower or vegetable gardens, rhododendrons, or azaleas; black walnut curbs these plants either by secreting a growth-inhibiting substance or by root competition. Long dormant season. Moderate water.

J. regia. See Walnut

JUJUBE

Rhamnaceae

DECIDUOUS TREE

ZONES 6–16, 18–24; H1

BEST IN SUN, TOLERATES SOME SHADE

MODERATE TO REGULAR WATER

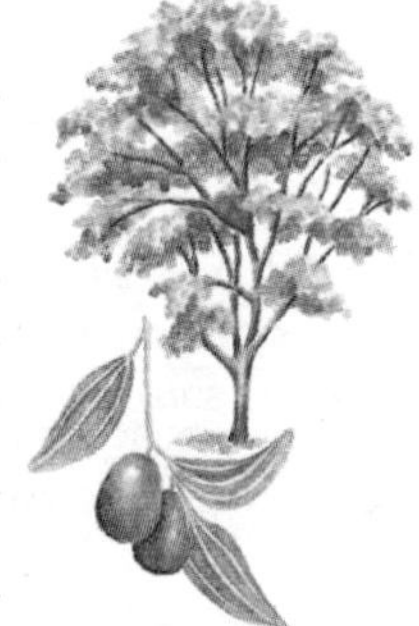

Jujube

Native to temperate regions of Asia and known botanically as *Ziziphus jujuba*. Slow to moderate growth to 15–20 ft. tall (possibly 30 ft.) and 10–15 ft. wide. Spiny, gnarled, somewhat pendulous branches. Glossy bright green, 1–2-in.- long leaves with three prominent veins; good yellow fall color. Clusters of small yellowish flowers in late spring or summer. Round to oval fruit with a central pit matures in fall; it can be eaten fresh from the tree or dried. Harvest fruit for fresh eating when it begins to turn from yellow green to reddish brown; it has a crisp texture and tastes like a sweet apple. If allowed to turn completely brown and become mushy, fruit is better for drying. The dried fruits look and taste like dates—for that reason, the plant is sometimes called Chinese date. Fruit may not ripen fully on tree in cool-summer areas; pick at half-brown stage and ripen indoors. Fruit of seedling trees is ½–1 in. long. The two most common cultivated varieties are 'Lang', with 1½–2-in., elongated fruit, and 'Li', bearing 2-in., round fruit with a very small pit. 'Lang' needs 'Li' as pollenizer; 'Li' is more productive with 'Lang' nearby, though it will produce some fruit if planted alone.

Jujube is deep rooted and takes well to desert conditions. The tree is very cold hardy but not productive in short-summer areas. Tolerates drought. Takes saline and alkaline soils but grows better in good garden soil and thrives in lawns if there is adequate drainage (though suckering from roots can be a problem, particularly in moist soil). Has no serious pests but is subject to Texas root rot in deserts. Prune in winter to shape, encourage weeping habit, or reduce size. Attractive silhouette, foliage, fruit, and toughness make it a good decorative tree, especially for high desert.

J

JUNCUS

RUSH

Juncaceae

PERENNIALS

ZONES VARY BY SPECIES

FULL SUN OR LIGHT SHADE

AMPLE WATER

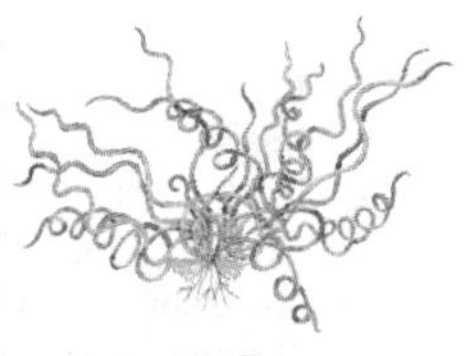

Juncus effusus 'Spiralis'

Rushes somewhat resemble grasses, with leaflike, cylindrical stems and tiny, inconspicuous flowers clustered near stem tips. Specialists usually suggest planting them with grasses or aquatic plants at the edge of a pond or stream, in water, or among stones and pebbles.

J. effusus. SOFT RUSH. Zones 1–24; H1. Native to many temperate regions of the world. To 2½ ft. high and wide. Medium green stems are ⅛–¼ in. thick; erect at first, they arch somewhat toward tips. Stems turn brown with frost. 'Spiralis' has stems that coil in spirals.

J. patens. CALIFORNIA GRAY RUSH. Zones 4–9, 14–24. Native to California and Oregon. To 2 ft. high and wide, with stiffly upright green or gray-green stems. Tolerates more heat and drought than *J. effusus* but thrives best in moist soil or even shallow water. 'Carman's Gray' and 'Elk Blue' are good gray-stemmed selections.

J. polyanthemos. AUSTRALIAN SILVER RUSH. Zones 14–24; H1, H2. Native to mainly coastal areas of Australia. Grows to 4 ft. tall, 3 ft. wide. Erect gray-green stems are easily moved about by breezes, lending motion to the garden.

JUNGLE FLAME. See IXORA coccinea

JUNIPER MYRTLE. See AGONIS juniperina

JUNIPERUS

JUNIPER

Cupressaceae

EVERGREEN SHRUBS AND TREES

ZONES VARY BY SPECIES

FULL SUN OR PARTIAL SHADE; SEE CARE BOX AT RIGHT

LITTLE OR NO WATER TO REGULAR WATER; SEE CARE BOX AT RIGHT

SEE CHART

Juniperus chinensis 'Torulosa'

Ranging from low ground covers to large trees, these widely grown plants are conifers, though they produce fleshy, berrylike fruits instead of woody cones. Foliage may consist of small, prickly needles (juvenile foliage) or tiny overlapping scales (mature foliage); or the same plant may show both types. Leaf colors include green shades as well as silvery blue, gray, and creamy yellow.

In the chart opposite, junipers are grouped by form: ground covers, shrubs, columnar types, and trees. Look for the general size and shape that will serve your purpose in the landscape, so that you won't later be forced to lop off branches to make the juniper fit the spot. Be aware, however, that many of the shrub junipers can become small trees in time.

The ground cover group includes plants from a few inches to a few feet high; the lower sorts are particularly useful in rock gardens. In the first few years after planting, a mulch will help keep soil cool and suppress weeds as the junipers fill in.

Shrub types range from low to quite tall. Shapes include mounding, gracefully spreading, irregularly twisted, and spirelike. In the chart, the latter type of shrubs—the columnar sort—is listed separately, since these narrow, upright plants perform a distinct function in the landscape. They're excellent accents and perfect for tight spots where you want some height, offering you a wider variety of choices than other plants do. Tree junipers (grown more rarely than shrubs) are valued for picturesque habit. Their height and form vary greatly, depending on growing conditions; plants are lower and shrubbier in poor soil and arid climates, much larger if given good soil and more moisture. Many of the larger junipers serve well as screens or windbreaks in cold-winter areas.

Though junipers are extremely tolerant of various soil types, you can expect root rot if the soil is waterlogged (plants will turn yellow and collapse). Avoid planting junipers so close to lawn sprinklers that their roots stay wet. Pests to watch for include spider mites (symptoms are gray or yellow, dry-looking plants with fine webbing on twigs); aphids (look for sticky deposits, falling needles, sooty mold); twig borers (browning and dying branch tips). Juniper blight causes twigs and branches to die back; control with copper sprays in summer.

WHAT JUNIPERS NEED

EXPOSURE: In cool-summer areas, junipers grow best in full sun (but do tolerate light shade). In warmer climates, they prefer partial shade.

SOIL: They will grow in virtually any soil—light to heavy, acid to alkaline—as long as drainage is good.

WATERING: In cool-summer areas, junipers may get by with no supplemental irrigation if they're growing in loam or clay soils; in lighter soils, give them little to moderate water. Where summers are warm to hot, plants in lighter soils should have moderate to regular water, while those in heavier soils will do well on little to moderate water. Wherever drainage is slow, be careful to avoid overwatering—when junipers fail, the cause is usually too much moisture.

PRUNING: Very little trimming is needed if you choose a plant of the right size and shape to fill the allotted space.

Juniperus communis 'Effusa'

JUPITER'S BEARD. See CENTRANTHUS ruber

FOR DEFINITIONS OF GARDENING TERMS
PLEASE SEE PAGES 746–750

JUNIPERUS

NAME	ZONES	HEIGHT	WIDTH	COMMENTS
GROUND COVERS				
Juniperus chinensis 'Parsonii' (J. prostrata)	1–24	To 1½ ft.	8 ft. or more	Slow growing. Dense, short twigs on flat, rather heavy branches. Blue-green new leaves mature to dark green
J. c. 'San Jose'	1–24	To 2 ft.	6 ft. or more	Slow growing and heavy trunked. Dark sage green, with both needle and scale foliage
J. communis 'Effusa'	A1–A3; 1–24	To 1 ft.	6–10 ft.	Sparsely foliaged, showing off reddish brown stems
J. c. saxatilis	1–24	To 1 ft.	6–8 ft.	Prostrate and trailing, with upturned branches like tiny candles. Color varies from gray to gray green
J. conferta SHORE JUNIPER	3–9, 14–24; H1, H2	To 1 ft.	6–8 ft.	Native to Japan. Prostrate and trailing, with soft bluish green needles. Excellent for seashore but will stand warmer climates if given moist, well-drained soil
J. c. 'Blue Pacific'	3–9, 14–24	To 1 ft.	6–8 ft.	Denser, bluer, more heat tolerant than *J. conferta*
J. c. 'Emerald Sea'	3–9, 14–24	To 1 ft.	6–8 ft.	Bright green–leafed form of *J. conferta*
J. horizontalis 'Bar Harbor' BAR HARBOR JUNIPER	A1–A3; 1–24	To 1 ft.	8–10 ft.	Fast growing. Feathery blue-gray foliage turns plum color in winter. As plant ages, foliage dies back in center to expose limbs, especially in hot climates
J. h. 'Blue Chip'	A1–A3; 1–24	To 1 ft.	6–8 ft.	Silvery blue foliage
J. h. 'Blue Rug' (see **J. h. 'Wiltonii'**)				
J. h. 'Douglasii' WAUKEGAN JUNIPER	A1–A3; 1–24	To 1 ft.	To 10 ft.	Steel blue foliage turns purplish in fall. Rich green new growth
J. h. 'Glomerata'	1–24	To 6 in.	To 10 ft.	Deep green, turning plum color in winter. Scale foliage gives it a soft look
J. h. 'Hughes'	A1–A3; 1–24	To 1 ft.	6–8 ft.	Showy silvery blue foliage
J. h. 'Huntington Blue'	1–24	9–12 in.	6–7 ft.	Dense foliage in bright blue gray
J. h. 'Mother Lode'	1–24	To 4 in.	8–10 ft.	Similar to 'Wiltonii' but with yellow foliage that turns bronze in winter
J. h. 'Plumosa' ANDORRA JUNIPER	1–24	To 1½ ft.	To 10 ft.	Feathery foliage is gray green in summer, turns plum color in winter. Flat branches with upright branchlets
J. h. 'Prince of Wales'	A1–A3; 1–24	To 8 in.	8–10 ft.	Medium green foliage turns purplish in fall
J. h. 'Wiltonii' ('Blue Rug') BLUE CARPET JUNIPER	A1–A3; 1–24	4–6 in.	6–8 ft.	Very flat juniper. Dense, short branchlets on long, trailing branches. Foliage is an intense silver blue. Similar to 'Bar Harbor' but denser; it rarely exposes limbs with age
J. h. 'Youngstown'	1–24	To 1 ft.	To 6 ft.	Resembles 'Plumosa' but is flatter, more compact
J. h. 'Yukon Belle'	A1–A3; 1–24	To 6 in.	6–8 ft.	Silvery blue foliage
J. procumbens JAPANESE GARDEN JUNIPER	1–24	1–2½ ft.	To 12 ft.	Feathery yet substantial blue-green foliage on strong, spreading branches
J. p. 'Green Mound'	1–24	To 8 in.	To 6 ft.	Mounding habit; will trail over walls. Light green foliage

J

JUNIPERUS

NAME	ZONES	HEIGHT	WIDTH	COMMENTS
J. procumbens 'Nana'	1–24	To 1 ft.	To 6 ft.	Curved branches radiating in all directions. Shorter needles and slower growth than *J. procumbens*. Can be staked into upright, picturesque shrub. Give it some protection from sun in hot climates
J. sabina 'Arcadia'	1–24	To 1 ft.	6–8 ft.	Lacy bright green foliage
J. s. 'Blue Danube'	1–24	To 1½ ft.	To 5 ft.	Blue-green foliage
J. s. 'Broadmoor'	A2, A3; 1–24	2–3 ft.	To 10 ft.	Dense, mounding habit. Soft bright green leaves
J. s. 'Buffalo'	A2, A3; 1–24	8–12 in.	To 8 ft.	Soft, feathery bright green foliage
J. s. 'Calgary Carpet'	A2, A3; 1–24	6–9 in.	10 ft.	Soft green foliage
J. s. 'Moor-Dense'	1–24	To 1 ft.	To 8 ft.	Resembles 'Broadmoor' but is denser. Has layered look
J. s. 'Scandia'	A2, A3; 1–24	To 1 ft.	6–8 ft.	Dense bright green foliage
J. s. 'Tamariscifolia' (J. tamariscifolia) TAMARIX JUNIPER, TAM	A2, A3; 1–24	1½–2½ ft.	10 ft. or more	Symmetrically spreading, with dense blue-green foliage. Widely used, probably overused. More pest problems than other junipers
J. sargentii SARGENT JUNIPER, SHIMPAKU	A2, A3; 1–24	To 2½ ft.	6–10 ft.	Feathery gray-green or green foliage. Classic bonsai plant
J. s. 'Glauca'	1–24	1½–2 ft.	6–10 ft.	Blue-green version of *J. sargentii*
J. s. 'Saybrook Gold'	1–24	2–3 ft.	To 6 ft.	Like *J. sargentii* but with rich yellow foliage
J. s. 'Viridis'	1–24	1½–2 ft.	6–10 ft.	Bright green version of *J. sargentii*
J. scopulorum 'Blue Creeper'	A2, A3; 1–24	To 2 ft.	6–8 ft.	Spreading, mounding habit. Bright blue-green foliage
SHRUBS				
J. chinensis 'Armstrongii' ARMSTRONG JUNIPER	1–24	4–5 ft.	4–5 ft.	Upright, with medium green foliage. More compact than 'Pfitzeriana'
J. c. 'Aurea' ('Gold Coast')	1–24	To 4 ft.	To 4 ft.	Compact shrub with rich golden yellow foliage. More upright than 'Pfitzeriana'; more arching than 'Armstrongii'
J. c. 'Blauw' BLAUW'S JUNIPER, BLUE SHIMPAKU	1–24	To 4 ft.	To 3 ft.	Vase shaped, dense, compact. Blue foliage
J. c. 'Hetzii' HETZ BLUE JUNIPER	1–24	To 15 ft.	To 15 ft.	Inverted pyramid, with branches spreading outward and upward at 45° angle. Blue-gray foliage

Juniperus chinensis 'San Jose'

Juniperus conferta

Juniperus horizontalis 'Wiltonii'

Juniperus sabina 'Buffalo'

Juniperus sabina 'Tamariscifolia'

JUNIPERUS

NAME	ZONES	HEIGHT	WIDTH	COMMENTS
J. c. 'Kaizuka' (see **J. c. 'Torulosa'**)				
J. c. 'Maneyi'	1–24	To 10 ft.	To 10 ft.	Semierect, with steeply angled, spreading branches. Blue-gray foliage
J. c. 'Mint Julep'	1–24	4–6 ft.	6–8 ft.	Vase shaped, with arching branches. Mint green foliage
J. c. 'Pfitzeriana' PFITZER JUNIPER	A2, A3; 1–24; H1, H2	5–6 ft.	10–12 ft.	Arching, with sharp-needled, feathery gray-green foliage
J. c. 'Pfitzeriana Aurea' GOLDEN PFITZER JUNIPER	1–24; H1, H2	4–5 ft.	8–10 ft.	Blue-gray foliage; current season's growth is golden yellow. 'Old Gold' is similar or identical
J. c. 'Pfitzeriana Compacta' NICK'S COMPACT PFITZER JUNIPER	A2, A3; 1–24; H1, H2	To 2 ft.	4–6 ft.	Compact, densely branched gray-green variety
J. c. 'Pfitzeriana Glauca'	1–24; H1, H2	5–6 ft.	6–8 ft.	Arching branches; silvery blue foliage
J. c. 'Sea Green'	1–24	4–5 ft.	4–5 ft.	Compact dark green selection with fountainlike, arching branches
J. c. 'Torulosa' ('Kaizuka') HOLLYWOOD JUNIPER	1–24; H1, H2	To 15 ft.	To 10 ft.	Irregular and upright, with twisted appearance. Rich green foliage
J. c. 'Torulosa Variegata' VARIEGATED HOLLYWOOD JUNIPER	1–24; H1, H2	8–10 ft.	To 6 ft.	Irregular cone, though growth is more regular than that of 'Torulosa'. Green foliage variegated with creamy white
J. sabina SAVIN JUNIPER	A2, A3; 1–24	4–6 ft.	5–10 ft.	Creeping or shrubby dark green plant. Exceedingly tough
J. scopulorum 'Table Top Blue'	1–24	To 5 ft.	7–12 ft.	Flat-topped gray plant
J. squamata 'Blue Star'	1–24	2–3 ft.	3–4 ft.	Uniform branching; silver blue foliage
J. s. 'Holger'	1–24	To 6 ft.	To 6 ft.	Dense, broad, flat topped. Yellow-tipped new growth
J. s. 'Meyeri' MEYER OR FISHBACK JUNIPER	A3; 1–24	6–8 ft.	2–3 ft.	Upright, with stiff, oddly angled branches. Broad needles in blend of colors: green, gray, and reddish
COLUMNAR TYPES				
J. chinensis 'Blue Point'	1–24	To 12 ft.	To 8 ft.	Densely branched blue-green cone
J. c. 'Columnaris' CHINESE BLUE COLUMN JUNIPER	1–24	12–15 ft.	To 6 ft.	Narrow blue-green cone

Juniperus scopulorum 'Blue Creeper'

Juniperus chinensis 'Hetzii'

Juniperus chinensis 'Pfitzeriana'

Juniperus chinensis 'Robusta Green'

Juniperus communis 'Compressa'

JUNIPERUS

NAME	ZONES	HEIGHT	WIDTH	COMMENTS
J. chinensis 'Hetz's Columnaris'	1–24	To 15 ft.	To 5 ft.	Dense rich green column. Largely mature (scalelike) leaves; little juvenile foliage. Threadlike branchlets
J. c. 'Robusta Green'	1–24	12–16 ft.	3–5 ft.	Brilliant green, dense column
J. c. 'Spartan'	1–24	To 15 ft.	3–5 ft.	Dense rich green column
J. communis 'Compressa'	A1–A3; 1–24	To 2 ft.	To 6 in.	Dwarf column; for rock gardens
J. c. 'Stricta' (J. c. hibernica) IRISH JUNIPER	A1–A3; 1–24	12–20 ft.	3–4 ft.	Very narrow dark green pillar with closely compact branch tips
J. scopulorum 'Cologreen'	1–24	To 15 ft.	5–7 ft.	Narrow bright green column
J. s. 'Gray Gleam'	1–24	To 15 ft.	5–7 ft.	Slow growing, attaining full height in 30–40 years. Symmetrical blue-gray column
J. s. 'Green Ice'	1–24	To 15 ft.	7–10 ft.	Dense habit makes it a good windbreak. Gray-green foliage is paler when new
J. s. 'Medora'	1–24	To 10 ft.	To 2½ ft.	Slow growing, narrow, dense, bluish green
J. s. 'Pathfinder'	1–24	To 25 ft.	To 12 ft.	Gray-blue cone
J. s. 'Skyrocket'	A2, A3; 1–24	15–20 ft.	2–3 ft.	Very narrow blue-gray spire
J. s. 'Wichita Blue'	A2, A3; 1–24	10–15 ft.	4–6 ft.	Broad silver blue cone
J. virginiana 'Cupressifolia' HILLSPIRE JUNIPER	A3; 1–24	10–15 ft.	6–8 ft.	Compact dark green cone
TREES				
J. californica CALIFORNIA JUNIPER	3, 6–12, 14–24	10–40 ft.	10–40 ft.	Native to desert regions of California and Southwest. Yellowish to rich green foliage
J. deppeana pachyphlaea ALLIGATOR JUNIPER	1–3, 10–12	10–60 ft.	10–60 ft.	Native to Southwest and Mexico. Blue-gray foliage; striking checked bark (like alligator hide)
J. monosperma (J. erythrocarpa)	1–3, 10–11	10–40 ft.	10–40 ft.	Native to southwestern U.S. Similar to *J. osteosperma;* bluish green foliage
J. occidentalis WESTERN JUNIPER	1–10, 14, 18–21	50–60 ft.	30–50 ft.	Massive, long-lived native of Sierra Nevada and intermountain regions from central Washington to Southern California. Fragrant green foliage
J. osteosperma UTAH JUNIPER	1–3, 10, 11	10–30 ft.	10–30 ft.	Native to arid West, mainly Great Basin Mountains. Adapted to high desert landscapes. Yellowish green foliage
J. recurva (J. recurva coxii)	4–6, 15–17	20–50 ft.	12–25 ft.	Native to Himalayas. Erect, with strongly weeping branches. Less hardy than other junipers
J. scopulorum 'Tolleson's Blue Weeping' ('Repandens')	1–24	To 20 ft.	To 10 ft.	Drooping branchlets clothed in blue-green foliage make a graceful, weeping tree
J. s. 'Tolleson's Green Weeping'	1–24	To 20 ft.	To 10 ft.	Like 'Tolleson's Blue Weeping' but with dark green foliage
J. virginiana EASTERN RED CEDAR	A3; 1–24	40–50 ft. or more	15–30 ft.	Native to eastern North America. Conical dark green tree; turns reddish in cold weather

JUSTICIA

Acanthaceae

EVERGREEN, SEMIEVERGREEN, DECIDUOUS SHRUBS

ZONES VARY BY SPECIES

EXPOSURE NEEDS VARY BY SPECIES

WATER NEEDS VARY BY SPECIES

Justicia brandegeeana

Group of plants grown chiefly for their tubular, tightly clustered flowers—or, in the case of *J. brandegeeana,* for showy spikes of bracts. Blossoms of all species attract hummingbirds. Leaves are paired, opposite each other on the stems.

J. brandegeeana (Beloperone guttata). SHRIMP PLANT. Evergreen. Zones 12, 13, 15–17, 21–24; H1, H2; elsewhere as annual or indoor/outdoor plant. Native to Mexico. To 3–4 ft. high and wide. Apple green, oval to elliptic leaves to 2½ in. long. Tubular white flowers spotted with purple are enclosed in overlapping coppery bronze bracts to form compact, drooping, jointed-looking spikes 3 in. long (eventually lengthening to 6–7 in.). Spike formation somewhat resembles a large shrimp. Blooms produced mainly from spring to fall, sporadically rest of year. 'Chartreuse' has chartreuse yellow bracts that sunburn more easily than the coppery kind.

Good in pots or tubs and for close-up planting near terraces, patios, entryways. To shape, pinch young plants continuously until compact mound of foliage is obtained, then let bloom. To encourage bushiness, cut back stems when bracts turn black. Leaves often drop in cold weather or if soil is too wet or dry. Give moderate water. Takes full sun, but bracts and foliage fade unless plant is grown in partial shade. Give at least half-day shade in hottest climates.

J. californica. CHUPAROSA, CALIFORNIA BELOPERONE. Semievergreen or deciduous. Zones 10–14, 18–24. Native from edges of southeastern California's Colorado Desert to Arizona and northern Mexico. To 6 ft. high and wide, with arching, grayish branches and sparse, ¼-in., roundish light green leaves. Clusters of tubular, bright red, 1½-in.-long flowers give a good show from fall through spring. ('Yellow' has yellow blossoms.) Often freezes to ground in winter but comes back quickly in spring. Full sun or light shade. Little to moderate water. Summer-deciduous but will maintain much of its foliage if irrigated during long dry periods.

J. candicans (J. ovata, Jacobinia ovata). Evergreen. Zones 12, 13, 21–24. Native to southern Arizona, Mexico. Erect growth to 3 ft. high and wide, with gray branchlets and dark green, heart-shaped leaves to 3 in. long. Clusters of 1-in., tubular, vivid red flowers from fall to early summer, with intermittent bloom later in summer. Full sun or light shade. Regular water.

J. carnea (Jacobinia carnea). BRAZILIAN PLUME FLOWER. Evergreen. Zones 8, 9, 13–24, H1, H2; elsewhere as annual or indoor/outdoor plant. From South America. Erect, soft-wooded shrub to 4–6 ft. high, 2½–3 ft. wide. Medium green, prominently veined leaves to 10 in. long. Dense clusters of pink to crimson, tubular flowers from midsummer to fall. 'Huntington Form' is a more compact plant (3–4 ft. high) with deeper pink flowers and leaves that are bronze colored on lower surfaces. Cut back plants in early spring to encourage strong new growth. Upper portions of branches freeze at 29°F/–2°C. Give partial or full shade, rich soil, regular to ample water.

Justicia carnea

J. ghiesbreghtiana. See J. spicigera

J. spicigera. MEXICAN HONEYSUCKLE. Evergreen. Zones 12–24. From Mexico and Central America. To 3 ft. tall, 4 ft. wide, with light green, smooth or velvety leaves. Few-flowered clusters of 1½-in. orange or orange-red flowers appear nearly year-round, peaking in spring and fall. Full sun or partial shade. Little to regular water. Often sold as *J. ghiesbreghtiana* or, in Arizona, as *Anisacanthus thurberi.*

J. suberecta. See Dicliptera suberecta

KAHILI GINGER. See HEDYCHIUM gardnerianum

KALANCHOE

Crassulaceae

SUCCULENT PERENNIALS

ZONES VARY BY SPECIES; OR INDOORS

FULL SUN OR PARTIAL SHADE; BRIGHT LIGHT

MODERATE TO REGULAR WATER

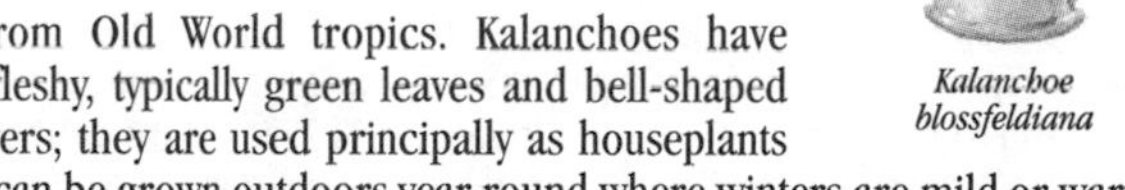

Kalanchoe blossfeldiana

From Old World tropics. Kalanchoes have fleshy, typically green leaves and bell-shaped flowers; they are used principally as houseplants but can be grown outdoors year-round where winters are mild or warm. In Zone 13, grow in a shady spot. In borderline climates, give protection of lath, eaves, or other overhead structure.

K. beharensis. FELT PLANT. Zones 13, 21–24; H1, H2. Stems usually unbranched, to 4–5 ft. (sometimes 10 ft.) tall. Very narrow plant—just 1–2 ft. wide. Thick, triangular to lance-shaped leaves (usually six to eight pairs) at stem tips. Leaves are 4–8 in. or longer, half as wide as long, strikingly waved and crimped at edges, covered with dense, feltlike coating of white to brown hairs. Flowers not showy. Hybrids between this and other species differ in leaf size, color, and degree of felting and scalloping. Striking in big rock garden, raised bed.

K. blossfeldiana. Zones 17, 21–24; H1, H2. To 1½ ft. high and wide. Shiny, red-edged dark green leaves to 2½ in. long, 1–1½ in. wide; may be smooth edged or slightly lobed. Small bright red flowers in big clusters held above leaves. Hybrids and named varieties come in various sizes and flower colors, including yellow, orange, and salmon. 'Pumila' and 'Tetra Vulcan' are choice dwarf (6-in.) seed-grown selections. Species and all selections bloom in winter, early spring. Popular houseplant at Christmas. Oftened summered outdoors and brought in before the first frost.

K. daigremontiana. MATERNITY PLANT. Zones 13, 23, 24; H2. Upright, single-stemmed plant 1½–3 ft. tall, 1 ft. wide. Gray-green leaves spotted in red, 6–8 in. long, 1¼ in. or more wide. Leaf edges are notched; young plants sprout in notches and may root on the plant. Clusters of small, drooping, grayish purple flowers in winter.

K. manginii. Zones 23, 24; H2. Hanging basket plant. Stems spreading or trailing, to 1 ft. long. Thick, 1-in.-long leaves. Drooping, inch-long, bright red flowers in spring.

K. pinnata (Bryophyllum pinnatum). AIR PLANT. Zones 23, 24; H2. Naturalized throughout Hawaiian Islands. To 2–3 ft. tall and about as wide. First leaves to form are undivided and scallop edged; later ones are divided into three to five leaflets, these also scalloped. Produces many plantlets in indented parts of leaf edges. Indoors, leaves are sometimes removed and pinned to a curtain, where they will produce plantlets until they dry up. Greenish white to reddish flowers in clusters to 3 in. long; not particularly attractive. Likes moisture.

K. tomentosa. PANDA PLANT. Zones 13, 23, 24; H2. Branching plant eventually reaches 3 ft. high, 8 in. wide. Leaves 2 in. long, with dense, feltlike coating of white hairs. Leaf tips and shallow notches in leaves are strongly marked dark brown. Yellowish green flowers in spring.

K. uniflora. Zones 23, 24; H2. Trailing plant 6 in. high, 2 ft. wide; good in hanging pots. Thick, 1-in.-long leaves have a few scallops near rounded tips. Inch-long summer flowers; color ranges from red to purple.

KALE and COLLARDS

Brassicaceae (Cruciferae)

BIENNIAL GROWN AS ANNUAL

ALL ZONES

FULL SUN OR LIGHT SHADE

REGULAR WATER

Kale

These cool-season cabbage relatives (members of the genus *Brassica*) are grown for their leaves, which can be steamed, stir-fried, sautéed, or added to soups. Curly-leafed kales (such as 'Dwarf Blue Curled' and 'Dwarf Siberian') form compact clusters of tightly curled leaves. 'Toscano' is a noncurly green kale, 'Red Russian' a noncurly red kale (its leaves are actually gray green with purple veins). So-called flowering kale is similar to flowering cabbage, with brightly colored, decorative foliage; it too is edible and is sometimes sold in markets under the name "salad savoy." The type of kale known as collards is a large, smooth-leafed plant that does not form a head. Collard varieties include 'Champion', 'Georgia', and 'Vates'.

Sow seeds in place and thin to 1½–3 ft. apart; or set out transplants at the same spacing. Plant kale in late summer for a fall crop; in cool-summer areas, it can also be planted in early spring for a summer crop (intense sun in hotter climates makes leaves turn bitter). Plant collards in summer for fall and winter harvest; or plant in early spring for a spring-into-summer crop (collards are heat tolerant). Well-grown plants can reach 2–3 ft. high. Harvest leaves by removing them from outside of clusters; or harvest entire plant. Light frost sweetens flavor. Plants suffer far fewer pest and disease problems than most other cabbage-family crops.

KALMIA

Ericaceae

EVERGREEN SHRUBS

ZONES VARY BY SPECIES

EXPOSURE NEEDS VARY BY SPECIES

REGULAR WATER

LEAVES AND FLOWER NECTAR ARE POISONOUS IF INGESTED

Kalmia latifolia

Elegant flowering shrubs related to rhododendron, with somewhat similar showy flower clusters. Notable difference is that each long flower stalk bears a small bud resembling a fluted turban; the buds open to chalice-shaped blooms with ten starlike points. Plants share rhododendron's need for moist atmosphere and moist, acid, humus-rich soil.

K. latifolia. MOUNTAIN LAUREL, CALICO BUSH. Zones 2–7, 16, 17. Native to eastern North America. Slow growing to 6–8 ft. or taller, with equal spread. Glossy, leathery, oval leaves are 3–5 in. long, dark green on upper surface, yellowish green beneath. Blooms in late spring, bearing blossom clusters to 5 in. across. Flowers are typically 1 in. wide, light pink or white opening from darker pink buds—but blossoms often have subtly different color in their throats and may have contrasting stamens. Hardy well below 0°F/–18°C. Partial shade. Has proved difficult to grow in the ground in Zones 16, 17; seems to do better in containers there. In Zones 2 and 3, give plants protection from winter sun and winds, which could cause dehydration.

Many named varieties are available. Those with flowers marked in contrasting colors include 'Carousel', light pink blooms with intricate pattern of white and purplish red inside; 'Kaleidoscope', red with a white center and white rim; 'Keepsake', burgundy red with a white edge; 'Peppermint', white with red banding from center to edge; and 'Pinwheel', red with scalloped white border. 'Bullseye' has cream-colored blossoms with white and purple-red markings in throat, white edge, and broad, purple-red band around the inside; new foliage is reddish.

Red-budded selections include 'Nipmuck' and 'Olympic Fire', both with pink flowers; 'Ostbo Red', with blossoms that open pink and deepen in color with age; 'Raspberry Glow' and 'Richard Jaynes', deep pink blooms; and 'Sarah', reddish pink flowers.

'Pristine' is a white-flowered selection. Dwarf varieties (to 3 ft. in 10 years) include 'Elf', with pink buds opening to white flowers; 'Little Linda', red buds opening to pink flowers; 'Minuet', light pink buds opening to white flowers with a maroon ring inside; and 'Tiddlywinks', pink buds opening to pink flowers.

K. polifolia microphylla (K. microphylla). WESTERN LAUREL, ALPINE LAUREL. Zones A2, A3; 1–7, 16, 17. Native from Alaska to Northern California. To 1 ft. high and 8 in. wide, with spreading branches and erect branchlets. Small (to ¾-in.) leaves are dark green above, whitish beneath. Rounded clusters of ½-in., rose to purple flowers bloom in summer. Partial shade; where summers are cool, can also be grown in full sun.

KALMIOPSIS leachiana

Ericaceae

EVERGREEN SHRUB

ZONES 4–6, 14–17

PARTIAL SHADE

REGULAR WATER

Kalmiopsis leachiana

Rhododendron relative native to mountains of southwest Oregon. Slow growing to 1 ft. tall, with 2-ft. spread. Many branches densely clothed with thick, dark green leaves. Blooms early spring, with leafy clusters of profuse, ½-in., rose pink flowers. May rebloom. Same culture as rhododendron, but fussier; needs perfect drainage, higher organic content in soil. Good rock garden plant.

KALOPANAX septemlobus (K. pictus)

CASTOR ARALIA, TREE ARALIA

Araliaceae

DECIDUOUS TREE

ZONES 2–6, 14–17

FULL SUN

REGULAR WATER

Kalopanax septemlobus

Native to eastern Asia. Unusual in being the only cold-hardy large tree in its family. Also notable for the tropical look conferred by big (7–10-in.) leaves with five to seven lobes. On young trees, leaves may exceed 1 ft. in width. In maturity, tree is 40–60 ft. tall and equally wide, with a spiny trunk and relatively few coarse, spiny branches. With age, spines eventually disappear from trunk and larger branches. Open and gaunt in youth but eventually develops an attractive, rounded habit. Tiny white flowers appear in flattish, 1–2-ft. clusters at branch ends in summer. Tiny black fruits follow the blossoms; they are quickly consumed by birds.

KANGAROO PAW. See ANIGOZANTHOS

KANGAROO THORN. See ACACIA armata

KANGAROO TREEBINE. See CISSUS antarctica

KATSURA TREE. See CERCIDIPHYLLUM japonicum

KECKIELLA

Scrophulariaceae

EVERGREEN OR DECIDUOUS SHRUBS

ZONES 7–9, 12–24

EXPOSURE NEEDS VARY BY SPECIES

LITTLE TO REGULAR WATER

Keckiella cordifolia

These woody-stemmed Southern California natives with tubular, lipped flowers were once listed as shrubby penstemons. They are extremely drought tolerant but will drop their leaves in summer unless watered. Need excellent drainage.

K. antirrhinoides. Erect to spreading habit to 4 ft. tall, 3 ft. or wider; leaves less than 1 in. long. Abundant show of fragrant yellow flowers in late spring and summer. Full sun.

K. cordifolia. Previously sold as *Penstemon cordifolius.* To about 5 ft. tall and wide, sprawling. Behaves almost like a vine when growing among taller shrubs. Dark green leaves are 1–2½ in. long. Red, 1–2-in.-long, unscented flowers from late spring into early summer; attract hummingbirds. A yellow-flowered variety is available. Full sun or partial shade.

KENILWORTH IVY. See CYMBALARIA muralis

KENTIA PALM. See HOWEA

KENTUCKY COFFEE TREE. See GYMNOCLADUS dioica

KENYA IVY. See SENECIO macroglossus

KERRIA japonica

Rosaceae

DECIDUOUS SHRUB

ZONES 2–23

FULL SUN IN COOLER CLIMATES ONLY

MODERATE TO REGULAR WATER

Kerria japonica 'Pleniflora'

Native to China. Open, graceful, rounded shrub to 6 ft. high, with 8-ft. spread. Slender stems are yellowish green to bright green in winter, providing welcome color in cold climates. Toothed, heavily veined bright green leaves somewhat triangular, 2–4 in. long. They unfold early in spring, turn yellow in fall. Flowers are similar to small (1¼–2-in.), single, yellow roses and appear in spring. Plant continues to bloom sporadically into early summer. 'Golden Guinea' has larger (2–2½-in.) flowers. 'Picta' has white-edged leaves. 'Pleniflora', the most commonly grown kerria, is a vigorous grower to 8–10 ft. tall and wide; it has double yellow, 1¼-in. blossoms that appear throughout the summer and sometimes into early fall. Flower color of all forms fades in strong sunlight.

Allow room for plant to display its arching form. Plants produce clumps of stems from roots; 'Pleniflora' in particular is likely to spread freely. Cut out any unwanted shoots to keep clumps more compact. Prune heavily after bloom, cutting out branches that have flowered and all dead or weak wood. The green branches are a favorite subject in Japanese wintertime flower arrangements.

KEY LIME. See CITRUS, Limes, Mexican

KIELE. See GARDENIA taitensis

KINGFISHER DAISY. See FELICIA bergeriana

KING PALM. See ARCHONTOPHOENIX cunninghamiana

KING'S SPEAR. See ASPHODELINE lutea

KINNIKINNICK. See ARCTOSTAPHYLOS uva-ursi

KIRENGESHOMA palmata

YELLOW WAXBELLS

Hydrangeaceae (Saxifragaceae)

PERENNIAL

ZONES 2–9, 14–24

PARTIAL SHADE

REGULAR WATER

Kirengeshoma palmata

Native to Japan, Korea. A perennial of great elegance. Reaches 2–4 ft. high, 1 ft. wide, with dark purplish stems carrying deeply lobed and toothed leaves to 8 in. across. Pale yellow flowers, borne in clusters of three, appear in joints of upper leaves and at tops of stalks in late summer and early autumn. Blossoms are drooping, narrowly bell shaped, 1½ in. long. Lovely in partially shaded border or woodland garden. Needs ample organic matter in soil.

KIWI, ORNAMENTAL. See ACTINIDIA kolomikta

KIWI

Actinidiaceae

DECIDUOUS VINES

ZONES VARY BY SPECIES

FULL SUN OR PARTIAL SHADE

REGULAR WATER

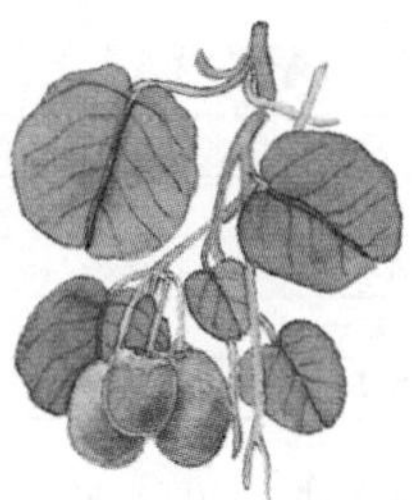

Kiwi

From eastern Asia. Fast-growing, twining vines grown for fruit with flavor that is a combination of melon, strawberry, and banana. Fuzzy-skinned kiwifruit (the type sold in markets) has a delicious piquancy; the other kinds are sweeter. Unless you have a self-fruitful variety, you will need to grow a male plant nearby to pollinate the female (fruit-bearing) plant. Supply sturdy supports, such as a trellis, an arbor, or a patio overhead. You can also train kiwi vines to cover walls and fences; guide and tie vines to the support as necessary. These vines prefer good, well-drained soil and regular applications of nitrogen fertilizer. Plants are sensitive to salt burn in alkaline soils. In fall, harvest fruit while it is firm and let it ripen off the tree; fruit left on the vine too long will spoil or be eaten by birds. Start harvesting when the first fruits just start to soften or when fuzzy kiwis turn from greenish brown to fully brown.

During dormant season, prune for form and fruit production. Cut back to one or two main trunks and remove closely parallel or crossing branches. Fruit is borne on shoots from year-old or older wood; cut out shoots that have fruited for 3 years and shorten younger shoots, leaving three to seven buds beyond previous summer's fruit. In summer, shorten overlong shoots and unwind any shoots twining around main branches. Because male pollenizer's sole purpose is flower production, you can prune it back drastically after bloom.

Fuzzy-skinned kiwi *(Actinidia deliciosa or A. chinensis)* grows and fruits best in Zones 4–9, 12–24 (note, however, that a vine can take up to 5 years from planting to flower or set fruit). Sometimes called Chinese gooseberry vine, it twines to 30 ft. if not curbed. Roundish, 5–8-in.-long leaves are rich dark green above, velvety white below. New growth often has rich red fuzz. Spring flowers are 1–1½ in. wide, opening cream colored and fading to buff. Fuzzy, brown-skinned, green-fleshed fruit is the size and roughly the shape of an egg. 'Hayward' is the most common fruiting variety. 'Saanichton', a female variety from Vancouver Island, Canada, is a good choice for cooler areas. Use 'Chico Male' or plants sold simply as "male" to pollinate 'Hayward' and 'Saanichton'. 'Vincent' needs little winter chill and is a good variety for warmest-winter climates; use 'Chico Male' as a pollenizer for it. Male hardy kiwi varieties can also supply pollen for female fuzzy-skinned kiwis.

Hardy kiwi *(A. arguta)* grows and produces well in Zones A1–A3; 1–10, 12, 14–24. It is much like fuzzy-skinned kiwi vine in appearance but has smaller leaves (which are smooth and fuzzless), flowers, and fruit. The 1–1½-in.-long, fuzzless fruit can be eaten skin and all. Green-fruited female varieties 'Ananasnaja', 'Jumbo', and 'Hood River' need a male variety (may be sold simply as "male") for pollen. 'Issai', also with green fruit, is a self-fruitful variety. Female 'Ken's Red' is a hybrid with red fruit; it needs a pollenizer.

Arctic beauty kiwi *(A. kolomikta)* is best suited to Zones A2, A3; 1–9, 14–17. Male plants are ornamental vines grown for their splashy, heart-shaped foliage (see description under *A. kolomikta*). Female plants typically have somewhat less colorful leaves than males, but they produce small green fruit about the size of hardy kiwi fruit; a male vine must be planted nearby to supply pollen. Plants typically grow to 15 ft. or more. Prefers partial shade, especially in hotter climates. 'September Sun' has sweet fruit and the best foliage variegation among female varieties.

KLEINIA. See SENECIO

A PRACTICAL GUIDE TO GARDENING
PLEASE SEE PAGES 658–731

KNAUTIA

Dipsacaceae

PERENNIALS

ZONES 2–10, 14–24

FULL SUN

REGULAR WATER

Knautia macedonica

Related to pincushion flower *(Scabiosa),* with blossoms that are similar in structure—clustered in tight heads above ruffs of leafy bracts on bare stems. Basal leaves are barely lobed, but those on upper stems are deeply divided. These are meadow plants that make few demands on the gardener; they are at home in cottage gardens, wild gardens, perennial borders, roadside plantings. Cut flowers are good for fresh or dried arrangements.

K. arvensis. BLUE BUTTONS. From Europe, Caucasus, Mediterranean region. To 1–5 ft. tall, 1½ ft. wide. Blue, 1½-in. flower heads in summer.

K. macedonica. From central Europe. To 1½–3 ft. tall and as wide. Deep purplish red flower heads bloom from early summer to fall.

K. Melton Pastels. To 1½–3 ft. or taller, 1½ ft. wide. Flower heads in tones of blue, mauve, pink, rose, salmon pink, and crimson from late spring to fall.

KNIPHOFIA

RED-HOT POKER, TORCH LILY

Liliaceae

PERENNIALS

ZONES VARY BY SPECIES

FULL SUN OR PARTIAL SHADE

MODERATE TO REGULAR WATER

Kniphofia uvaria

Dense clumps of grasslike, finely toothed foliage produce bare stems topped by nodding, tubular flowers in tight, overlapping clusters. Flowering stems look like glowing pokers or torches, hence the common names. Blossoms open from bottom to top over the course of several days, changing color as they mature. Increasing numbers of species—mostly from South Africa—are now grown in gardens and hybridized. The old 3-ft.-high forms of *K. uvaria* in shades of coral orange and yellow have given way to kinds with blooms ranging from coral red through every conceivable shade of orange, peach, and yellow to near-white and light green, on plants varying in size from 1½-ft. dwarfs to 6-ft. giants. The flowers attract hummingbirds.

Red-hot pokers require adequate moisture when blooms are forming and will fail to flower if conditions are too dry then. In summer, they'll tolerate even marshy conditions—but for winter survival, well-drained soil is essential. Most of these plants flower in summer, but some start in late spring and repeat throughout the growing season; others bloom all winter in mild climates. Where winter temperatures drop to 0°F/–18°C or below, tie foliage over clumps in fall to protect growing points (or at least leave all foliage in place over winter). In milder climates, cut or pull out any ratty-looking leaves in fall; new leaves will replace them by spring. Crowns increase slowly, forming clumps 2–3 ft. or more wide at base; you will get the best show if clumps are left in place for several years. Increase plantings by division in spring except for types still blooming then; for these, wait until summer to divide. New strains are available as seed (be aware that seelings will vary in color and quality). Protect from slugs and snails.

K. caulescens. Zones 4–9, 14–24. Blue-green leaves (purple at base) are 3–4 ft. long, 2–3 in. wide; they are produced in rosettes on short, branching, woody stems like trunks. Stalks 2 ft. tall bear heads of coral red to terra-cotta buds that open to pale yellow flowers. Blooms from midsummer into fall.

K. citrina. Zones 2–9, 14–24. Smallish species with narrow, dark bluish green leaves and globular flower heads in various yellow shades on 2–2½-ft.-tall stems. Summer to fall bloom. 'Lime Select' has bright lime green buds that open chartreuse and fade to cream.

K. hybrids. Zones 2–9, 14–24, except as noted. Although they involve several species, these hybrids generally share the narrow leaves and summer bloom season of *K. uvaria.* A distinct departure is 'Christmas Cheer', a hybrid of vigorous species *K. rooperi.*

'Bee's Sunset'. Stems to 3 ft. high, with glowing yellow-orange buds opening light yellow.

'Border Ballet'. Buds are a soft, dusty coral pink opening to cream blooms. Stems reach 4–4½ ft.

'Christmas Cheer'. Zones 19–24. Brilliant orange buds open to deep gold flowers on 4–5-ft. stems. Blooms fall through late spring in mild-winter areas, fall until frost elsewhere. Give it room; leaves (to 5 ft. long and 2 in. wide) become lax and collapse on the ground, smothering any plants in their way. Clump increases rapidly to 6–8 ft. or more across. Divide in early summer after flowering stops.

'Flamenco'. Seed-grown strain that blooms first year in early fall, in subsequent years in summer. Flower colors range from coral through orange and yellow to creamy white. Stems to 2½ ft. tall.

'Gold Mine'. Glowing orange-yellow buds opening golden amber on 3–3½-ft. stems.

'Little Maid'. Thin, grassy leaves and narrow flower stems to 2 ft. tall. Creamy white blossoms open from buds in buff-tinted pale yellow.

'Malibu Yellow'. Stems 5–6 ft. tall bear 8–10-in.-long heads of lime green buds that open primrose yellow.

'Peaches and Cream'. Stems about 4 ft. high bear peach-colored buds opening to cream blossoms.

'Percy's Pride'. To 4 ft. tall, with green-tinted yellow buds opening cream.

'Primrose Beauty'. To 3 ft. tall, with blossoms in clear light yellow.

'Shining Scepter'. Plant sold in North America under this name is 3 ft. tall, with tangerine orange flowers; the English original is 4 ft. tall, with pale yellow buds opening ivory.

'Vanilla'. Stems 2–2½ ft. tall; buds are light yellow, opening cream.

K. northiae. Zones 4–9, 14–24. Very large, dramatic-looking species with solitary rosette of broad bluish green leaves (up to 6 in. wide at base, 5 ft. long) on a woody, trunklike stem 1–3 ft. tall. Does not form clumps. Thick blossom stalks rise 1–2 ft. above foliage in summer, bearing large, oblong heads of orange buds opening light yellow.

K. uvaria. Zones 2–9, 14–24. Leaves to 1 in. wide, 2 ft. long. Oblong flower heads on stems 3–3½ ft. tall. Coral red buds open to orange or deep yellow blossoms in summer (in fall, in cold-winter climates). Most varieties sold under this name are hybrids (see *K.* hybrids, above).

KNOTWEED. See PERSICARIA

KOA. See ACACIA koa

KOCHIA scoparia (Bassia scoparia)

SUMMER CYPRESS

Chenopodiaceae

ANNUAL

ALL ZONES

FULL SUN

REGULAR WATER

Kochia scoparia

Native to Eurasia. To 3 ft. high and 2 ft. wide. Branches are so thickly clothed in soft, narrow light green leaves that plant is too dense to see through. Grow individually for its gently rounded form; or group plants for low, temporary hedge or edging. Can be sheared into any shape. Grow from seed sown in early spring or (in mild-winter climates) in fall. Tolerates high heat, performs well in short-summer areas.

K. s. trichophylla (Bassia scoparia trichophylla). MEXICAN FIRE BUSH, BURNING BUSH. Same as above, but foliage turns red in fall. Can reseed profusely enough to become a pest; hoe out unwanted seedlings when they're small.

KOELREUTERIA

Sapindaceae

DECIDUOUS TREES

ZONES VARY BY SPECIES

FULL SUN

MODERATE TO REGULAR WATER

Koelreuteria paniculata

Small trees native to Asia noted for large, loose clusters of yellow flowers followed by fat, papery fruit capsules resembling little Japanese lanterns. Capsules are used in both fresh and dried arrangements. Good patio, lawn, or street trees. Very adaptable to different soils as long as drainage is fairly good. Control self-sown seedlings.

K. bipinnata (K. integrifoliola). CHINESE FLAME TREE. Zones 8–24; H1. To 20–40 ft. tall and wide, eventually flat topped. Leaves 1–2 ft. long, divided into 7–12 oval leaflets; turn yellow for short time before dropping. Late-summer flower clusters are like those of *K. paniculata,* but 2-in. capsules are more colorful, in shades of orange, red, or salmon. Capsules come quickly after flowers and persist into fall. Prune tree to develop high branching. Roots are deep but not invasive; good tree to plant under.

K. elegans (K. formosana). FLAMEGOLD. Zones 14–24; H1, H2. Round-headed tree 20–30 ft. tall and equally broad. Leaves about 1½ ft. long, with 9–16 leaflets. Bright yellow fall flowers in tall, erect clusters are followed by especially showy clusters of long-lasting, puffy orange-red to salmon fruits. Fall foliage is yellow but not consistent; show is often poor.

K. paniculata. GOLDENRAIN TREE. Zones A2; 2–24. To 20–35 ft. tall, 25–40 ft. wide. Open branching, giving slight shade. Leaves to 15 in. long with 7–15 oval, toothed or lobed leaflets, each 1–3 in. long. New leaves are purplish, maturing to bright green in summer; may turn yellow to gold in fall, but fall foliage color is unreliable. Very showy, 8–14-in.-long flower clusters in early to midsummer. Fruit capsules are red when young, maturing to buff and brown shades; last well into autumn. Tree takes cold, heat, drought, wind. Prune to shape; can be gawky without pruning. 'Fastigiata' is 25 ft. tall, only 3 ft. wide.

KOHLRABI

Brassicaceae (Cruciferae)

BIENNIAL GROWN AS ANNUAL

ALL ZONES

FULL SUN

REGULAR WATER

Kohlrabi

Cool-season cabbage relative and, like cabbage, a member of the genus *Brassica.* Leaves and leafstalks are edible, but edible part most commonly associated with kohlrabi is the enlarged, bulblike portion of the stem formed just above the soil surface. Standard varieties are 'Early White Vienna' and 'Early Purple Vienna'—similar in size and flavor, differing only in skin color. Other white varieties include 'Triumph' and early-maturing 'Grand Duke'. 'Kolibri' is a popular purple-skinned variety. Plants are very fast growing, ready to harvest in 50 to 60 days from seed. Sow seed ½ in. deep in rich soil about 2 weeks after average date of last frost. Follow first planting with successive sowings 2 weeks apart. In areas with warm winters, plant again in late fall and early winter. Space rows 1½ ft. apart; thin seedlings to 4–6 in. apart. Plants are not usually bothered by pests or diseases. Harvest bulbous part when 2–3 in. wide. Peel, slice, and serve raw; or steam or sauté slices or chunks. Steam young leaves and leafstalks.

KOLKWITZIA amabilis

BEAUTY BUSH

Caprifoliaceae

DECIDUOUS SHRUB

ZONES 2–11, 14–20

FULL SUN OR PARTIAL SHADE

REGULAR WATER

Kolkwitzia amabilis

Native to China. Graceful, upright growth to 10–12 ft. tall and about as wide. If grown in partial shade, it has an arching form; in full sun, it's denser and shorter. Gray-green leaves to 3 in. long sometimes turn reddish in fall. Blooms heavily in mid- to late spring, bearing clusters of 1-in.-long, yellow-throated pink flowers. Blossoms are followed by conspicuous pinkish brown, bristly fruits that prolong color display. Brown, flaky bark gradually peels from stems during winter.

Adapts to many soils and climates. Blooms on wood formed the previous year. Thin out oldest stems after blossoms have faded; or, to enjoy the fruit, wait until early spring to prune, then do so lightly. Plant can be renewed by cutting to ground after bloom.

KOREAN FORSYTHIA. See FORSYTHIA ovata

KOREAN GRASS. See ZOYSIA tenuifolia

KOU, KOU HAOLE. See CORDIA subcordata, C. sebestena

KOWHAI. See SOPHORA tetraptera

KUKUI. See ALEURITES moluccana

KUMQUAT. See CITRUS

KUNZEA

Myrtaceae

EVERGREEN SHRUBS

ZONES 16–24

FULL SUN

LITTLE OR NO WATER

Kunzea baxteri

Native to Australia. These shrubs are related to tea tree *(Leptospermum)* and bottlebrush *(Callistemon).* Small flowers with fluffy stamens appear individually or crowded into bottlebrush clusters. Needlelike foliage. All species must have good drainage; they prefer sandy soil but will tolerate well-drained clay.

K. affinis. Airy, open, spreading habit to 6 ft. tall, 10 ft. wide, with bright green leaves. Blooms in winter and spring, putting on a big display of small (¼-in.), deep pink blossoms with tiny dark yellow stamens. Good cut flower.

K. baxteri. SCARLET KUNZEA. Fast growing to 8 ft. tall, 10–20 ft. wide, with open habit. Dark red flowers with yellow-tipped stamens in 4-in. bottlebrush clusters. Blooms from fall into spring, with sporadic bloom at other times. Leaves are light green when new, mature to dark green.

K. parvifolia. Highly variable plant—mat-forming or erect (1½–8 ft. high, 3–9 ft. wide), with dense or open growth, light to dark green foliage. Small pinkish mauve blossoms with tiny dark yellow stamens bloom in winter and spring.

Labiatae. See Lamiaceae

FOR INFORMATION ON YOUR CLIMATE ZONE
PLEASE SEE PAGES 27–63

LABURNUM

GOLDENCHAIN TREE

Fabaceae (Leguminosae)

DECIDUOUS TREES OR SHRUBS

ZONES 1–10, 14–17

AFTERNOON SHADE IN HOTTEST CLIMATES

MODERATE TO REGULAR WATER

ALL PARTS, ESPECIALLY SEEDPODS, ARE HIGHLY POISONOUS IF INGESTED

Laburnum × watereri

Upright growth. Usually pruned into single-trunked tree, but it can be shrubby if permitted to keep basal suckers and low branches. Green bark; bright green leaves divided into three leaflets (like clover leaves). Handsome during bloom in mid- to late spring, when it bears yellow, sweet pea–shaped flowers in hanging clusters similar to those of wisteria. Use as specimen in lawn or border, plant in groups in front of neutral background, or space regularly in long border of perennials, rhododendrons, or lilacs. Flexible branches make it easy to espalier.

Provide well-drained soil. Prune regularly after bloom to keep tidy; remove dead or crowding branches in tree's center (avoid large cuts, because cut areas callus over slowly). Remove seedpods if possible—not only are they toxic, but a heavy crop drains the plant's strength.

L. alpinum. SCOTCH LABURNUM. To 30–35 ft. tall, 20–25 ft. wide. Flower clusters 10–15 in. long. 'Pendulum' has weeping branches.

L. anagyroides. COMMON GOLDENCHAIN. To 20–30 ft. tall, 15–20 ft. wide. Flower clusters 6–10 in. long. Like *L. alpinum,* it has a weeping variety, 'Pendulum'.

L. × watereri. Hybrid between above two species. To 15–30 ft. tall, 10–20 ft. wide, with 10–20-in.-long flower clusters. 'Vossii' is the most widely grown, most graceful variety, with flower clusters near 20 in. long.

LACE FERN. See MICROLEPIA strigosa

LACE VINE. See FALLOPIA baldschuanica

LACHENALIA

CAPE COWSLIP

Liliaceae

PERENNIALS FROM BULBS

ZONES 16, 17, 23, 24; OR INDOORS

LIGHT SHADE IN HOTTEST CLIMATES; BRIGHT LIGHT

REGULAR WATER DURING GROWTH AND BLOOM

Lachenalia bulbifera

South African natives resembling hyacinths. Each bulb usually produces just two broad, succulent, strap-shaped leaves, often spotted with brown. Spikes of pendent, typically tubular blossoms appear at tops of thick flowering stems in late winter or early spring.

Planted in the ground, cape cowslip does best in mild-winter, dry-summer regions. In other areas, grow in pots in house or greenhouse. Plant in late summer or early fall. Set bulbs in well-drained soil, 1–1½ in. deep, 3 in. apart. Water sparingly until growth starts, then give regular moisture until foliage yellows after bloom. Gradually let soil dry out and keep as dry as possible until next fall. Protect from slugs and snails.

After planting for indoor bloom, water thoroughly and keep in a cool, dark place until leaves appear; then bring into light, provide cool night temperatures (50°F/10°C), and feed when flower spikes show. Store bulbs dry in pots over summer.

L. aloides (L. tricolor). Stems 10–12 in. high, with yellow flowers tipped in red and green. Inch-wide leaves. 'Aurea' has bright orange-yellow blossoms; 'Nelsonii' bears bright yellow blooms tinged with green. 'Pearsonii' has yellow-orange flowers with red-orange bases; stems are slightly taller than those of species.

L. bulbifera (L. pendula). Stems to 15 in. high, with coral red and yellow flowers tipped in purple. Leaves are 2 in. wide. 'Superba' has orange-red blooms.

L. contaminata. Stems and narrow (less than ⅛-in.-wide), upright leaves both reach 9 in. high. Tight spikes of nearly spherical bells are red to brown with white tips. Reminiscent of grape hyacinth *(Muscari).*

LADY BELLS. See ADENOPHORA

LADY FERN. See ATHYRIUM filix-femina

LADY PALM. See RHAPIS

LADY'S BEDSTRAW. See GALIUM verum

LADY'S-MANTLE. See ALCHEMILLA mollis

LADY'S SLIPPER. See PAPHIOPEDILUM, PEDILANTHUS macrocarpus

LAELIA

Orchidaceae

EPIPHYTIC ORCHIDS

ZONES VARY BY SPECIES; OR INDOORS

LIGHT SHADE; BRIGHT LIGHT

REGULAR WATER

Laelia anceps

More than 60 species belong to this genus, which is closely related to and resembles *Cattleya.* Pseudobulbs may be plump (like those of cattleya), with plants bearing large flowers; or they may be slender and canelike, with plants bearing clusters of smaller flowers. All have fleshy leaves. Laelias cross freely with cattleyas. A few are hardy enough to grow outdoors along the California coast as far north as San Francisco. Outdoor plants are usually grown on tree trunks or in pots on the patio; indoor plants can be brought outdoors at warm times of year. For cultural needs, see *Cattleya.*

L. anceps. Zones 16, 17, 21–24; H1, H2. From Mexico. Plump pseudobulbs carry thick 6-in. leaves. Flower spikes range from 6 in. to 2 ft. long, carry three to six fragrant, 4-in. pinkish lilac flowers in winter. Some varieties have pink, white, purple, or lavender-blue blossoms.

L. autumnalis. Zones 16, 17, 21–24; H1, H2. From Mexico. This species is similar to *L. anceps,* but its scented flowers bloom in autumn. Rosy purple flowers have a pinkish white lip with purple and yellow markings.

L. cinnabarina. Zone H2. From Brazil. Narrow, canelike pseudobulbs to 20 in. tall bear narrow, foot-long leaves and spikes of up to 12 bright red-orange, 3–4-in. flowers in spring.

L. purpurata. Zone H2. From Brazil. Plump pseudobulbs produce 12–16-in.-long leaves. Flower spikes to 3 ft. high carry three to eight 8-in. flowers, typically white with a purple lip. Forms with pink or blue lips exist. Blooms in late spring or early summer.

LAGENARIA. See GOURD

LAGERSTROEMIA

CRAPE MYRTLE

Lythraceae

DECIDUOUS SHRUBS AND TREES

ZONES VARY BY SPECIES

FULL SUN

MODERATE WATER

Lagerstroemia indica

The crape myrtles are among the most satisfactory of plants for hot-summer regions; showy summer flowers, good-looking bark, and (in many cases) brilliant fall color make them attractive all year round. Long, cool autumns yield the best leaf display; the first hard frost ends the show. (In cool-summer regions, these plants flower less, and mildew is a more serious problem among susceptible varieties.)

Most crape myrtles seen in gardens are varieties of *L. indica* or hybrids of that species with *L. fauriei.* The latter species has attracted some attention for its hardiness and exceptionally showy bark, although it is scarcely grown in the West.

All crape myrtles bloom on new wood and should be pruned in winter or early spring to increase next summer's flowers. On small, shrubby forms, remove spent flower clusters and thin out small, twiggy growth; to maintain compactness and avoid a leggy look, cut branches nearly to the ground in spring. On large shrubs or trees, shorten branches by 1–1½ ft. in spring if you need to limit their size. Heavy watering and any fertilizing in summer can significantly decrease hardiness in marginal climates. Where adapted, plants perform best with infrequent but deep watering.

L. fauriei. JAPANESE CRAPE MYRTLE. Tree. Zones 7–10, 12–14, 18–21. Native to Japan. To 20–30 ft. tall and as wide, with upright habit and outward-arching branches. Leaves are light green, 4 in. long, 2 in. wide, turning yellow in fall. Smooth gray bark flakes away to reveal shiny cinnamon bark beneath. White flowers are carried in 4-in. clusters. Highly mildew resistant; the parent of many resistant hybrids.

L. hybrids. Introductions of the U.S. National Arboretum, these hybrids between *L. indica* and *L. fauriei* have been selected for hardiness and mildew resistance. Grown as shrubs or train into small trees.

'Acoma'. To 10 ft. tall, 11 ft. wide, with pendulous branches. White flowers, dark red fall color.

'Biloxi'. To 20 ft. tall, 12 ft. wide. Pale pink flowers, dark red fall color.

'Chickasaw'. True dwarf—just 20 in. high, 26 in. wide. Lavender flowers.

'Comanche'. To 12 ft. tall, 13 ft. wide. Deep coral pink flowers and orange-red to purple-red fall color.

'Hopi'. To 8 ft. tall and 10 ft. wide. Medium pink flowers, orange-red autumn color.

'Lipan'. Grows to 13 ft. high and as wide. Lavender flowers, orange to red fall color.

'Muskogee'. To 25 ft. tall, 12 ft. wide. Lavender flowers, red fall color.

'Natchez'. Reaches 25 ft. tall and 12 ft. wide. White flowers, orange-red autumn color.

'Pecos'. To 8 ft. tall, 6 ft. wide. Pink flowers, maroon fall color.

'Sioux'. Reaches 8 ft. tall, 5 ft. wide. Deep pink flowers; autumn color from maroon to red.

'Tonto'. To 15–20 ft. tall and wide. Large clusters of red flowers; red autumn color.

'Tuscarora'. To 22 ft. tall, 12 ft. wide. Pinkish red flowers. Orange-red autumn color.

'Tuskegee'. To 15 ft. tall by 18 ft. wide. Deep pink blooms, orange-red fall color.

'Yuma'. To 13 ft. tall, 12 ft. wide. Lavender flowers; fall color from yellow to russet.

'Zuni'. To 9 ft. tall, 8 ft. wide. Lavender flowers, orange-red fall color.

L. indica. CRAPE MYRTLE. Tree or shrub. Excellent performance in Zones 7–10, 12–14, 18–21; H1, H2. Mildew is a serious problem in Zones 15–17, 22–24. Hardy in Zones 4 and 5 but seldom flowers well there except in hottest summers. Thrives in Zone 6 but flowers very late. Sometimes treated as perennial in Zones 2 and 3; will come back from roots if frozen to the ground.

Native to China. To 25 ft. tall and wide. Dark green leaves are 1–2½ in. long and somewhat narrower, often tinged red on opening and frequently turning brilliant orange or red in the fall. Crinkly-petaled, crepelike, 1–1½-in. flowers in dense clusters range from white through pink to red and purple. Trained as a tree, develops an attractive trunk and branch structure. Smooth gray or light brown bark peels off to reveal smooth, pinkish inner bark. Winter trunk and branches look polished.

The following list includes many of the best selections. Some are trees, some large shrubs, some dwarfs. Mildew can be a problem; best solution is to plant mildew-resistant hybrids (see *L.* hybrids).

'Catawba'. Roundish, dense growth to 6–10 ft. high and wide (can be trained as a 15-ft. tree). Dark purple flowers, orange-red fall color.

'Centennial'. Dwarf, rounded plant to 3–5 ft. tall and wide. Lavender flowers, orange fall color.

'Centennial Spirit'. Multistemmed large shrub or small tree to 20 ft. tall and as wide or nearly so. Dark red flowers, orange-red fall color.

'Chica Pink' and 'Chica Red'. Compact, dense, 3–4 ft. tall and wide. Bright pink or rosy red flowers, yellow fall color.

Dixie series. Dwarf, weeping shrubs for border, ground cover, or hanging basket. Varieties include deep red 'Beverly' ('Baton Rouge') and lavender 'Louisa' ('Cordon Bleu'), both to 3 ft. high and wide; purple-flowered 'Passion', to 3 ft. high, 5 ft. wide; and pink-blossomed 'Pink Blush' ('Delta Blush'), to 2 ft. high and 4 ft. wide.

Dwarf series. These grow 3–6 ft. tall and wide. Colors are indicated by variety names: 'Dwarf Pink', 'Dwarf Purple', 'Dwarf Red', 'Dwarf White'.

'Glendora White'. As a shrub, grows erect to 9 ft. tall and 6–7 ft. wide. With training, makes a tree to 25 ft. tall and 20 ft. wide. Bears white flowers. Red fall foliage.

'Near East' ('Shell Pink'). Rounded growth to 15–20 ft. tall and wide, with soft pink flowers. Orange-red fall color.

'Peppermint Lace'. Erect shrub 6–7 ft. tall and wide, or tree to 15–20 ft. tall and wide. Deep pink flowers with a white picotee edge. Red fall color.

Petite series. To 5 ft. tall and 4 ft. wide, with names that describe their flower color: 'Petite Embers', 'Petite Orchid', 'Petite Pinkie', 'Petite Plum', 'Petite Red Imp', 'Petite Snow'. All have yellow fall foliage.

'Prairie Lace'. To 6 ft. tall and 5 ft. wide, but otherwise quite similar to 'Peppermint Lace' in upright habit, flowers, and fall color. (It does not take well to training as a tree, however.)

'Seminole'. To 6–12 ft. tall and wide. Bright pink flowers, red fall color.

'Watermelon Red'. Rounded habit to 20–25 ft. tall and wide. Bright red flowers, yellow fall color.

L. speciosa. GIANT CRAPE MYRTLE. Tree. Zones H1, H2. Native from India to Australia. To 80 ft. tall, 30 ft. wide, with leaves 8–12 in. long, 4 in. wide. White to purple flowers are borne in clusters to 16 in. long. Sometimes planted as street tree in Hawaii.

LAGUNARIA patersonii

PRIMROSE TREE, COW ITCH TREE

Malvaceae

EVERGREEN TREE

ZONES 13, 15–24; H1, H2

FULL SUN

MODERATE WATER

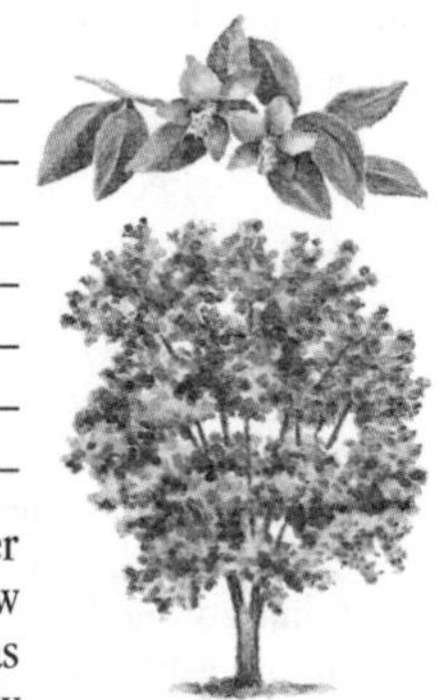

Lagunaria patersonii

Native to South Pacific and Australia. Rather fast growth to 20–50 ft. Young trees narrow and erect; old ones sometimes spreading to as wide as 40 ft., with flat-topped look. Densely foliaged in thick, oval, 2–4-in.-long leaves that are olive green above, gray beneath. Pink to rose, 2-in.-wide summer blossoms resemble hibiscus flowers, fade almost to white with age. 'Royal Purple' has purple blossoms. Brown seed capsules, popular with flower arrangers, hang on for a long time; they split into five sections, revealing bright brown seeds. Handle pods carefully, since they contain short, stiff fibers that can irritate skin and eyes.

Tolerates wide variety of soils and growing conditions. Resists ocean wind, salt spray; tolerates intense heat. Foliage is damaged at 25°F/–4°C but recovers quickly. Blooms best in coastal conditions. Use as specimen tree; or plant in groups as a showy windbreak or screen.

LAMB'S EARS. See STACHYS byzantina

LAMB'S QUARTERS. See CHENOPODIUM album

FOR GROWING SYMBOL EXPLANATIONS
PLEASE SEE PAGE 161

Lamiaceae. Members of the mint family of herbaceous plants and shrubs are easily recognized by their square stems, leaves in opposite pairs, and whorled flowers in spikelike, sometimes branched, clusters. Many of the group are aromatic; the family contains most of the familiar kitchen herbs, including basil *(Ocimum)*, mint *(Mentha)*, oregano *(Origanum)*, and sage *(Salvia)*. Many have attractive foliage or flowers (*Coleus*, sage). This family was previously called Labiatae.

LAMIASTRUM galeobdolon. **See LAMIUM galeobdolon**

LAMIUM

DEAD NETTLE

Lamiaceae (Labiatae)

PERENNIALS, SOMETIMES GROWN AS ANNUALS

ZONES VARY BY SPECIES

PARTIAL OR FULL SHADE

REGULAR WATER

Lamium maculatum

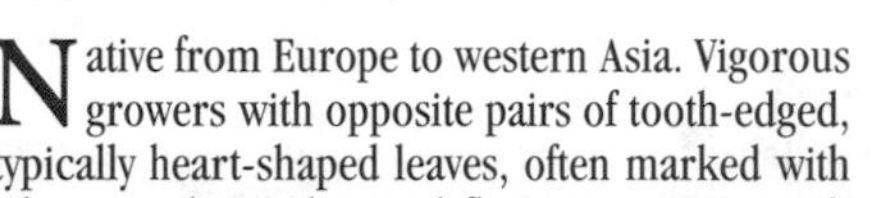

Native from Europe to western Asia. Vigorous growers with opposite pairs of tooth-edged, typically heart-shaped leaves, often marked with silver or white. Clustered flowers come in pink, white, or yellow. Most of these plants are used as ground covers. Evergreen in mild-winter climates.

L. galeobdolon (Lamiastrum galeobdolon). DEAD NETTLE, YELLOW ARCHANGEL. Perennial in Zones 2–11, 14–24; winter annual in Zones 12, 13. Trailing or clump-forming plant with roundish or heart-shaped leaves to 2½ in. long. Blooms in late spring, bearing yellow flowers (not showy). One popular variety is 'Hermann's Pride', a clump former to 2 ft. tall and wide, with 1¼-in.-long, sharply tapered leaves that are evenly and symmetrically marked with white spots and streaks. Also commonly sold is *L. g. montanum* 'Florentinum' (*L .g.* 'Variegatum'), a trailing plant with stems that root as they spread. Dull medium to dark green leaves are edged in green and marbled with silvery gray in the center. Attractive plant in hanging baskets, where it will trail to 2–3 ft., or as an informal ground cover (it can be invasive but is easily curbed).

L. maculatum. DEAD NETTLE, SPOTTED NETTLE. Perennial in Zones A2, A3; 1–11, 14–24; winter annual in Zones 12, 13. To 8 in. high; spreads by rhizomes and stolons to 3 ft. wide but is not a rampant grower. Leaves are 1–3 in. long, green with a central white stripe or zone. Pink or white flowers in late spring and early summer. Choice varieties include 'Beacon Silver', with pink flowers and green-edged, silvery gray leaves; 'White Nancy', like a white-blossomed 'Beacon Silver'; 'Chequers', with pink flowers and green leaves with a white center stripe; and 'Pink Pewter', with pink blooms and silvery leaves edged in greenish gray. All bloom from spring to midsummer and make excellent ground covers for shady spots, nicely lighting up darker garden areas. They are also useful in hanging baskets. They need some grooming to remove old, shabby growth.

LAMPRANTHUS

ICE PLANT

Aizoaceae

SUCCULENT PERENNIALS

ZONES 14–24, EXCEPT AS NOTED

FULL SUN

LITTLE OR NO WATER

Lampranthus spectabilis

From South Africa. Most of the ice plants with large, brilliant flowers belong to this genus, which includes plants formerly called *Oscularia*. Plants are fleshy, erect or trailing, woody at base. Select in bloom for the color you want. Cut back lightly after bloom to eliminate fruit capsules, encourage new leafy growth. Good at seashore. Flowers attract bees.

L. aurantiacus. To 10–15 in. tall. Gray-green, inch-long, three-sided leaves. Flowers 1½–2 in. across, bright orange; midwinter to spring bloom. 'Glaucus' has bright yellow flowers; those of 'Sunman' are golden yellow. Plant 15–18 in. apart for bedding, borders, low bank cover.

L. deltoides (Oscularia deltoides). Stems to 2 ft. long; they grow erect to 1 ft., then begin to lean and trail. Triangular blue-green leaves with a pink flush are short (less than 1 in. long), very thick and fleshy, closely set on stems. Fragrant, purplish rose, ½-in.-wide flowers in late spring, summer. Attractive trailing over walls or in hanging baskets.

Lampranthus deltoides

L. filicaulis. REDONDO CREEPER. Thin, creeping stems; fine-textured, glistening green foliage. Spreads slowly to form mats about 3 in. high. Small pink flowers bloom in early spring. Use for small-scale ground cover, mound, or low bank cover. Plant 3 ft. apart.

L. pedunculatus (Oscularia pedunculata). Like *L. deltoides* but with fragrant flowers in pale pinkish mauve.

L. productus. To 15 in. high, spreading 1½–2 ft. wide. Gray green leaves tipped bronze. Profuse show of inch-wide purple flowers from early winter into spring; scattered bloom at other times.

L. spectabilis. TRAILING ICE PLANT. Zones 12–24. Sprawling or trailing to 1 ft. high, 1½–2 ft. wide. Three-sided gray-green leaves. Planting becomes a carpet of gleaming color from late winter to spring, when the 2–2½-in.-wide, pink, rose pink, red, or purple flowers are in bloom.

LANTANA

Verbenaceae

EVERGREEN SHRUBS

ZONES 8–10, 12–24; H1, H2; ANNUALS ELSEWHERE

FULL SUN

MODERATE WATER

Lantana montevidensis

Fast-growing tropical American natives with tiny flowers in tight clusters that look like miniature nosegays. Valued for profuse show of color over long season—every month of the year in frost-free areas. Light frosts merely keep plants in check. Heavier freezes (possible in Zones 8–10, 14) may seriously damage or kill plants in some but not all winters. In colder zones, lantana is grown as a summer annual, typically used in pots, hanging baskets, and window boxes.

Prone to mildew in shade or during prolonged overcast weather. Prune hard in spring to remove dead wood and prevent woodiness. Too much water and fertilizer cuts down on bloom. Shrubby kinds are used as low hedges or foundation plants or as substitutes for annuals in beds or containers. Spreading kinds are excellent bank covers and will control erosion. Effective spilling from raised beds, planter boxes, or hanging baskets. Crushed foliage has a pungent odor that some people find objectionable.

L. camara. One of the two species used in hybridizing. Coarse, upright grower to 6 ft. tall and wide. Rough dark green leaves; yellow, orange, or red flowers in 1–2-in. clusters. In lowland areas of Hawaii, this species long ago escaped from cultivation and is considered a noxious weed; various insects that attack it have been imported in attempts to control it.

L. montevidensis (L. sellowiana). The other species used in cross breeding. This one is sold at nurseries. A little hardier than *L. camara*, it's a ground cover to about 2 ft. high, with branches trailing to 3 or even 6 ft. Dark green, 1-in.-long, coarsely toothed leaves are sometimes tinged red or purplish, especially in cold weather. Rosy lilac flowers in 1–1½-in.-wide clusters. 'White Lightnin'' is a form with white flowers. 'Lavender Swirl' has flowers clusters in pure white, solid purple, and white-and-purple.

L. selections and hybrids. In the following list, some of the selections are forms of *L. camara* or hybrids between those forms; others, hybrids between *L. camara* and *L. montevidensis.*

'Christine'. To 6 ft. by 5 ft. Cerise pink. Can be trained into small patio tree.

'Confetti'. To 2–3 ft. by 6–8 ft. Blossoms mix yellow, pink, purple.

'Cream Carpet'. To 2–3 ft. by 6–8 ft. Cream with bright yellow throat.
'Dwarf Pink'. To 2–4 ft. by 3–4 ft. Light pink. Rather tender.
'Dwarf White'. To 2–4 ft. by 3–4 ft.
'Dwarf Yellow'. To 2–4 ft. high and wide.
'Gold Rush'. To 1½–2 ft. by 4–6 ft. Rich golden yellow.
'Irene'. To 3 ft. by 4 ft. Compact. Magenta and lemon yellow clusters.
'Lemon Swirl'. Slow growing to 2 ft. tall, 3 ft. wide. Bright yellow band around each leaf; yellow flowers.
'Miss Huff'. To 3–5 ft. by 10 ft. Orange and pink. Hardier than other lantanas, surviving sharp frosts.
'New Gold'. To 2–3 ft. by 6–8 ft. Golden yellow.
'Radiation'. To 3–5 ft. high and wide. Rich orange red.
'Rainbow' ('Patriot Rainbow'). Compact plant to 1 ft. by 15 in. Flowers combine yellow, orange, and fuchsia pink.
'Spreading Sunset'. To 2–3 ft. by 6–8 ft. Vivid orange red.
'Spreading Sunshine'. To 2–3 ft. by 6–8 ft. Bright yellow.
'Sunburst'. To 2–3 ft. by 6–8 ft. Bright golden yellow.
'Tangerine'. To 2–3 ft. by 6–8 ft. Burnt orange.

LAPAGERIA rosea

CHILEAN BELLFLOWER
Liliaceae
EVERGREEN VINE
ZONES 5, 6, 15–17, 23, 24
PARTIAL SHADE
REGULAR WATER

Lapageria rosea

The national flower of Chile. Likes high humidity, moderate summer temperatures. Slender stems twine to 10–20 ft. Glossy, leathery, oval leaves to 4 in. long. Blooms off and on through late spring, summer, and fall. Beautiful, 3-in.-long, rosy red, pendent, bell-shaped flowers (frequently spotted with white) have unusually heavy, waxy texture; hold up as long as 2 weeks after cutting. Good vine for post, trellis, or tree trunk. Give it wind protection and loose, well-drained, organically enriched soil. Protect from snails and slugs.

LARCH. See LARIX

LARIX

LARCH
Pinaceae
DECIDUOUS TREES
ZONES VARY BY SPECIES
FULL SUN
REGULAR WATER

Larix decidua

These conifers form slender pyramids with horizontal branches and drooping branchlets. Needles are ½–1½ in. long, in fluffy tufts; except as noted, those of the following species are soft to the touch. Woody, roundish, ½–1½-in.- long cones are scattered all along branchlets. Notable for color in spring and fall and for winter silhouette. In spring, shows off pale green tufts of new needles, bright purple-red new cones. In fall, needles turn brilliant yellow and orange before dropping. Winter interest is enhanced by the many cones, which turn brown with age and hang on to create a polka-dot pattern against the sky. Best in regions with relatively cool summers and cool to cold winters. Not particular about soils. Plant with dark evergreen conifers as background or near water for reflection. Larches attract birds.

L. decidua (L. europaea). EUROPEAN LARCH. Zones A1–A3; 1–9, 14–17. From mountains of Europe. Moderate to fast growth to 30–60 ft. tall, 10–25 ft. wide. Grass green summer foliage. In 'Pendula', branches arch out and down and branchlets hang nearly straight down. Plants sold under this variety name may actually be *L. kaempferi* 'Pendula'.

L. gmelinii. DAHURIAN LARCH. Zones A1–A3. Native to eastern Siberia. Tall tree to 100 ft. high and 30 ft. wide; shrubby in extremely cold or very windy regions. Summer leaves are light green. Cones are brown, oval, 1 in. long.

L. kaempferi. JAPANESE LARCH. Zones 1–9, 14–19. Native to Japan. Most frequently planted larch in the West. Fast growing to 60 ft. or taller, 20–30 ft. wide, but can be dwarfed in containers. Summer foliage is bluish green. There is a weeping form, 'Pendula', often sold as a variety of *L. decidua.*

L. occidentalis. WESTERN LARCH, TAMARACK. Zones A3; 1–7. Native to Cascades of Washington and Oregon, eastern Oregon, northern Rocky Mountains. Grows 150–200 ft. tall as timber tree, but usually just 30–50 ft. tall, 10–15 ft. wide in gardens. Sharp, stiff needles are blue green to gray green in summer.

L. sibirica (L. russica). Zones A1–A3; 1, 2. Native from northeastern Europe to Siberia. Narrowly conical tree to 30–90 ft. tall and 15 ft. wide, with horizontal or upward-angled branches and yellow twigs. Needles are bright green in summer. Tolerates extreme cold but can be damaged by spells of early warming followed by hard freezes. 'Pendula' has weeping branches.

LARKSPUR. See CONSOLIDA ajacis

LARREA tridentata

CREOSOTE BUSH
Zygophyllaceae
EVERGREEN SHRUB
ZONES 7–14, 18–21
FULL SUN
LITTLE OR NO WATER TO MODERATE WATER

Larrea tridentata

One of the most common native shrubs in deserts of southeastern California, Arizona, southern Utah, Texas, northern Mexico. Grows 4–8 ft. tall and wide, with many upright branches. Straggly and open in shallow, dry soil; attractive, dense, rounded but spreading where water accumulates. Leathery yellow-green to dark green leaves divided into two tiny, ⅜-in.-long crescents; gummy secretion makes them look varnished and yields distinctive creosote odor, especially after rain. Small yellow flowers off and on all year, followed by small roundish fruit covered with shiny white or rusty hairs. With water and fertilizer, grows taller and denser with larger, shiny dark green leaves. Use as wind or privacy screen, or trim into formal hedge. Sometimes sold as *L. divaricata.*

LATHYRUS

SWEET PEA
Fabaceae (Leguminosae)
ANNUALS AND PERENNIALS
ZONES VARY BY SPECIES
FULL SUN
WATER NEEDS VARY BY SPECIES

Lathyrus odoratus

In this group is one of the best-known garden flowers—the delightfully fragrant and colorful sweet pea. Throughout this book you will find flowers described as "sweet pea shaped." The flower of the sweet pea is typical of the many members of the pea family (Fabaceae). Each flower has one large, upright, roundish petal (banner or standard), two narrow side petals (wings), and two lower petals that are somewhat united, forming a boat-shaped structure (keel). ▸

L. latifolius. PERENNIAL SWEET PEA. Zones 1–24. Native to Europe. Strong-growing vine to 9 ft., with blue-green foliage. Flowers are usually mixes of reddish purple, white, and pink; single colors may be sold. Blooms all summer if not allowed to go to seed. Grows with little care, tolerates aridity (give moderate water). May escape and become naturalized, even weedy. Use as bank cover, as trailer over rocks, on trellis or fence.

L. odoratus. Annual. All zones. Native to the Mediterranean region. Blooms in winter, spring, or summer, bearing many spikelike clusters of crisp-looking flowers with a clean, sweet perfume. Blossoms come in single and mixed colors. Mixes include deep rose, blue, purple, scarlet, white, cream, salmon, bicolors. Vining types grow to 5 ft. or more; bush kinds grow 8 in. to 3 ft. tall. Sweet peas make magnificent cut flowers in quantity.

To hasten germination, soak seeds for a few hours before planting. In less-than-perfect soil, prepare ground by digging a 1–1½-ft.-deep trench. Mix 1 part peat moss or other organic soil amendment to 2 parts soil, also adding a complete fertilizer according to label directions; backfill trench with mix. Sow seeds 1 in. deep and 1–2 in. apart. When seedlings are 4–5 in. high, thin to at least 6 in. apart. Pinch out tops to encourage strong side branches. Where climate prevents early planting or soil is too wet to work, start three or four seeds in each small peat pot, indoors or in a protected place, and set out when weather has settled. Plant peat pots 1 ft. apart, thinning each to one strong plant. This method is ideal for bush types. Protect young seedlings from birds and control slugs and snails. Never let vines lack for water; soak heavily. To prolong bloom, cut flowers at least every other day and remove all seedpods. Regular monthly feeding will keep vines vigorous and productive.

For vining sweet peas, provide trellis, strings, or wire before planting. Seedlings need support as soon as tendrils form. Freestanding trellis running north and south is best. When planting against fence or wall, keep supports away from wall to ensure good air circulation.

The following entries describe vine-type sweet peas (heirloom types first, then in groups by time of bloom) and bush types.

Heirloom varieties. Not as large and showy as modern hybrids, these old spring-blooming varieties (some dating back hundreds of years) are notable for powerful fragrance.

'America'. Crimson to scarlet with white stripes.

'Blanche Ferry'. Carmine rose standard, pink wings. Similar to 'Painted Lady' but with more intense color.

'Cupani'. Deep blue standard, purple wings. More vigorous than 'Matucana'.

'Matucana'. Same coloring as 'Cupani'. This and 'Cupani' are very close to the original wild *L. odoratus.*

Old Spice Mix. A mixture of eight old-fashioned varieties with flowers in white and in shades of pink, red, and purple.

'Painted Lady'. Dates from the 18th century; bears small rose-and-white flowers.

Early flowering (Early Flowering Multiflora, Early Multiflora, formerly called Early Spencers). The name "Spencer" once described a type of frilled flower (with wavy petals) that is now characteristic of almost all varieties. "Multiflora" indicates that the plants carry more flowers per stem than the old Spencers did.

The value of early-flowering varieties is that they will bloom in midwinter when days are short. (Spring- and summer-flowering types will not bloom until days have lengthened to 15 hours or more.) Where winter temperatures are mild (Zones 12, 13, 17, 21–24; H1, H2), sow seeds in late summer for winter bloom. Use these varieties for forcing in greenhouse. They are not heat resistant. Generally sold in mixed colors.

Spring flowering (Spring-Flowering Heat-Resistant Cuthbertson Type, Cuthbertson's Floribunda, Floribunda-Zvolanek strain). Both mixtures and single-color named varieties are available in seed packets. Wide color range: pink, lavender, purple, white, cream, rose, salmon, cerise, carmine, red, blue. Royal or Royal Family are somewhat larger flowered, more heat resistant than the others. In Zones 7–9, 12–24, plant between early fall and earliest winter. Elsewhere, plant just as soon as soil can be worked.

Summer flowering (Galaxy, Plenti-flora). Available in named varieties and mixtures in wide color range. Bloom from early summer on. Large flowers, five to seven on each long stem. Heat resistant, but not enough so for Zones 7–15, 18–21.

Bush type. The so-called bush-type sweet peas are strong vines with predetermined growth, heights. Unlike vining kinds, these stop their upward growth at 8 in. to 3 ft. high. Some kinds are completely self-supporting; others need support of a few sticks or pieces of brush (similar to what you would provide for many perennials). Suitable for all regions. Flowers come in full range of colors. Most are early or spring blooming; follow planting dates given for early- or spring-flowering vining types.

Bijou. To 1 ft. Available in single or mixed colors. Four or five flowers on each 5–7-in. stem. Self-supporting plants are spectacular in borders, beds, window boxes, containers. Not as heat resistant or as long stemmed as Knee-Hi; performs better in containers.

Cupid. To 4–6 in. by 1 ft. Trails on ground or hangs from containers.

Jet Set. Bushy plants grow 2–3 ft. tall; need some support.

Knee-Hi. To 2½ ft.; need some support. Large, long-stemmed blooms are carried five or six to the stem. Has all the virtues and color range of Cuthbertson's Floribunda, but on bush-type plants. Good for mass display in beds, borders. Growth will exceed 2½ ft. where planting bed joins a fence or wall; keep in the open for uniform height.

Little Sweethearts are rounded bushes to about 8 in. tall; they need no support, bloom over a long season. Snoopea (12–15 in.) and Supersnoop (2 ft.) need no support.

L. splendens. PRIDE OF CALIFORNIA. Perennial. Zones 14–24. Native to chaparral in San Diego County and adjacent Baja California. To 8–10 ft. Each stem bears clusters of three to ten deep red blooms in early spring. Start from seed in pots in fall or spring; plant out in fall or winter. Long lived in dry, well-drained soil.

Lauraceae. The laurel family contains evergreen and deciduous trees and shrubs with inconspicuous flowers and (usually) aromatic foliage. Fruits are fleshy, containing a single seed. Examples are avocado, camphor tree *(Cinnamomum),* sweet bay *(Laurus),* and California laurel *(Umbellularia).*

LAUREL. See LAURUS nobilis, PRUNUS, UMBELLULARIA californica

LAURENTIA fluviatilis. See PRATIA pedunculata

LAURUS nobilis

SWEET BAY, GRECIAN LAUREL

Lauraceae

EVERGREEN SHRUB OR TREE

ZONES 5–9, 12–24; H1, H2; OR INDOOR/OUTDOOR PLANT

FULL SUN OR PARTIAL SHADE

MODERATE WATER

Laurus nobilis

This Mediterranean native grows slowly to 12–40 ft. tall and wide. Natural habit is compact and multistemmed, with broad base; plant often resembles a gradually tapering cone. Leathery, aromatic leaves are the traditional bay leaves of cookery—oval, 2–4 in. long, dark green. Clusters of small yellow spring flowers are followed by black or dark purple, ½–1-in. fruit. 'Saratoga' has broader leaves and a more treelike habit than the species.

Not fussy about soil but needs good drainage. Subject to black scale and laurel psyllid ('Saratoga' is resistant to psyllid). Tends to sucker heavily. Dense habit makes it a good large background shrub, screen, or small tree (though trees will eventually be large). Takes well to clipping into standards, hedges, or topiary shapes such as globes and cones. A classic formal container plant. In areas too cold for growing sweet bay in the ground, grow it in a container and move to a greenhouse or cool, well-lighted room when temperatures drop to about 20°F/–7°C.

LAURUSTINUS. See VIBURNUM tinus

LAVANDULA

LAVENDER
Lamiaceae (Labiatae)
EVERGREEN SHRUBS
ZONES VARY BY SPECIES
FULL SUN
MODERATE WATER

Lavandula angustifolia

Native to Mediterranean region. Prized for fragrant lavender or purple flowers, often set off by colorful bracts. Blossom spikes of some species are used for perfume, aromatic oil, soap, medicine, sachets. Aromatic gray, gray-green, or yellowish green foliage. Use as informal hedge or edging, in herb gardens, or in borders with plants needing similar cultural conditions—sunrose *(Helianthemum)*, catmint *(Nepeta)*, rosemary, santolina, verbena. Where winters are too cold for year-round growth outdoors, lavenders are good container plants for sunny windows. When they are grown outside in marginal climates, self-sown seedlings often show up in summer after parent plants die from winter cold. Most lavenders attract bees and butterflies.

Lavenders need well-drained soil and little or no fertilizer. They will succeed in cool coastal or mountain climates or inland valleys and deserts but succumb to root rot in areas where heat is accompanied by humidity. Fernleaf sorts *(L. canariensis, L. multifida)* as well as *L.* ×*allardii*, *L.* 'Goodwin Creek Grey', and *L.* ×*heterophylla* are tender, but they're more resistant to heat and humidity than English lavenders and lavandins *(L. angustifolia, L.* ×*intermedia)*. Give good air circulation. If mulching around lavenders, use pea gravel, decomposed granite, or sand rather than organic materials. To keep plants neat and compact, shear back by one-third to one-half (even by two-thirds) every year immediately after bloom. If plants become woody and open in center, remove a few of the oldest branches; take out more when new growth comes. If this doesn't work, dig and replace.

For sachets and potpourri, cut flower spikes or strip flowers from stems just as blossoms show color; dry in a cool, shady place. Dried spikes make fragrant wreaths, swags, wands. Dried flowers can be used to scent water or soap. To flavor ice cream, pastries, salads, you can use fresh flowers of *L. angustifolia* and *L.* ×*intermedia* varieties; other species contain harmful chemicals that should not be ingested.

Since lavenders have been in cultivation for centuries and some species cross easily, many varieties and hybrids have arisen. Names are often confused, so some of the variety names that follow may not agree with those you see on nursery labels. Be aware that only cutting-grown stock is truly uniform. Several varieties originally propagated by cuttings are now grown from seed (for example, plants labeled Hidcote Strain and Munstead Strain); seedlings vary in color and growth habit.

L. ×**allardii.** Zones 8, 9, 12–24. A natural hybrid of *L. dentata* and *L. latifolia*—and the real identity of most lavenders sold in the U.S. as *L.* ×*heterophylla*. Fairly open growth to 3–3½ ft. tall, 3 ft. wide. Dull gray-green leaves vary from entirely smooth edged to toothed near the tip, all on the same plant. Bright violet-blue flower spikes are slender, interrupted (that is, with blossom clusters separated on the stem rather than massed together), carried on long, wiry, sometimes branched stems. Blooms from mid- to late summer. Scent is more medicinal than sweet. More tolerant of heat and humidity than English lavenders and lavandins.

L. angustifolia (L. officinalis, L. vera). ENGLISH LAVENDER. Zones 2–24. This is the sweetly fragrant lavender used for perfume and sachets. Common name notwithstanding, it is native not to England but to mountains of southern Europe. It's the hardiest, most widely planted species. In Zones 2 and 3, it is shorter lived, lasting only 3 to 5 years. Most varieties are fairly low growing, forming mounds of foliage from 8 in. to 2 ft. high and wide. Narrow, smooth-edged, gray-green or silvery gray leaves to 2 in. long. Unbranched flower stems rise 4–12 in. above foliage, topped with 1–4-in.-long spikes of flowers in white, pink, lavender blue, or various shades of purple. Blooms mainly from early to midsummer, but some varieties repeat in late summer or fall. Named selections include the following.

'Alba'. To 1½–2 ft. high and wide. Pure white flowers, gray-green foliage.

'Blue Cushion'. To 1½ ft. tall, 2 ft. wide. Profuse bright violet-blue flowers above medium green foliage.

'Compacta'. To 1½ ft. high and wide; good dwarf hedge plant. Light violet flowers; gray-green leaves.

'England'. To 1 ft. high, 15 in. wide. Light violet-blue flowers; downy, silvery foliage.

'Gray Lady'. To 1½–2 ft. tall and wide. Lavender-blue flowers; silvery gray foliage.

'Hidcote'. The original had deep violet flowers and medium green foliage on a plant 1½–2 ft. tall. The plants sold under this name today are frequently grown from seed; they may bear gray foliage and/or vary in size from the original.

'Irene Doyle' ('Two Seasons Lavender'). To 1½–2 ft. high and wide, with gray-green leaves. Light violet flowers bloom in early summer and give a repeat performance in late summer.

'Jean Davis'. To 1½–2 ft. high and wide. Flowers in pale lilac pink; gray-green foliage.

'Lady' ('Lavender Lady'). Seed-grown strain that blooms in 3 months from spring-sown seed. Gray-green foliage. Very short spikes of lavender-blue flowers on a plant 1–1½ ft. high and wide; some variation in flower color and growth habit.

'Martha Roderick'. Compact growth to 1½–2 ft. high and wide. Dense gray foliage. Bright violet-blue blossoms in great abundance from late spring to early summer.

'Melissa'. Dense, compact grower to 1½ ft. high and wide. Good pink flower color, fading to white in hottest sun. Gray-green leaves.

'Mitcham' ('Mitcham Grey'). Named for the former center of English perfume production. Semi-open habit to 2 ft. high and wide. Bright violet-blue flowers; gray foliage.

'Munstead'. The original is 1½ ft. tall, 2 ft. wide, with bright lavender-blue flowers and medium green foliage. Long bloomer; makes a good low hedge. Quite variable when grown from seed.

'Nana' ('Dwarf Blue'). Slow growing to 1 ft. high, 16 in. wide. Stiff lavender-blue flower spikes in midsummer; gray foliage. Ideal for rock garden or edging. Somewhat hardier than most other English lavenders.

'Nana Alba'. White-flowered version of 'Nana'.

'Rosea'. To 1½–2 ft. high and wide. Light mauve pink flowers; light green foliage.

'Sharon Roberts'. Semi-open growth a little over 2 ft. high and to 2 ft. wide. Profuse show of bright violet-blue flowers begins in late spring, often repeats in fall. Medium green to gray-green foliage.

'Skylark'. To 20 in. high and wide. Deep violet-blue spikes in profusion; gray-green foliage.

'Twickel Purple'. To 2–2½ ft. high, 3 ft. wide. Heavy, dense spikes of light violet flowers on long, wiry stems, fanning out around an open mound of gray-green foliage.

L. canariensis. CANARY ISLAND LAVENDER. Zones 16–24. Bushy, rounded habit to 3–4 ft. high and wide. Divided, ferny-looking light green leaves 3 in. long, 2 in wide. Spikes of bright lavender-blue flowers are held on branched stems well above foliage. Blooms from early spring to late fall (all year in warm-winter areas). Resents hard pruning; remove faded bloom stems to keep tidy.

L. dentata. FRENCH LAVENDER, TOOTHED LAVENDER. Zones 8, 9, 12–24. To 3–4 ft. tall, 4–6 ft. wide. Narrow green or gray-green leaves are 1½ in. long, ½ in. wide, with square-toothed edges. Purple flowers in short, rounded spikes, each topped with a pair of flaglike bracts that look like rabbit ears. Long spring-into-summer flowering period; almost year-round in mild-winter areas. 'Linda Ligon' has smaller leaves with irregular creamy white variegation. *L. d. candicans* ('French Gray') has grayer, somewhat larger leaves than the species, with dense grayish white down on young foliage. ▸

L. 'Goodwin Creek Grey'. Zones 8, 9, 12–24. Most likely a hybrid between *L. lanata* and *L. dentata.* This densely foliaged plant grows to 2½–3 ft. high and 3–4 ft. wide, with silvery leaves that are toothed at tips. Deep violet-blue flowers from spring to late fall; virtually year-round in mild-winter climates. Similar to *L. ×allardii* in scent and tolerance for heat and humidity.

L. ×heterophylla. SWEET LAVENDER. Zones 8, 9, 12–24. The original is probably a cross between *L. dentata* and *L. angustifolia,* occurring wild in southern France. Most plants labeled as this lavender are actually *L. ×allardii.* Both *L. ×heterophylla* and *L. ×allardii* hybrids have dull gray-green leaves, but the true *L. ×heterophylla* has upper leaves that are mostly smooth edged, while those near the plant's base are usually toothed in the middle and near the tip. *L. ×heterophylla* is also a shorter plant (grows to about 1½–2 ft. tall) with shorter, unbranched spikes of bright violet flowers—and the spikes are less interrupted, having one whorl of blossoms below the main flower spike. Bloom starts in midsummer. Similar to *L. ×allardii* in fragrance and tolerance for heat and humidity, but slightly hardier to cold.

L. ×intermedia. LAVANDIN, HEDGE LAVENDER. Zones 4–24. This group of sterile hybrids between parents *L. angustifolia* and *L. latifolia* is distinguished from the English lavenders by larger growth and by branching stems topped with interrupted flower spikes; blooms from mid- to late summer. Long used in the perfume and soap industries, lavandins are vigorous, fragrant plants. Almost as hardy as English lavender parent and more tolerant of warm, humid summers. They include the following selections.

'Albrialii'. Once the mainstay of the French lavender oil industry. To 2½ ft. high, 3 ft. wide, with gray-green foliage. Dark violet-blue blossoms in narrow, conical, 3½–5-in.-long spikes are excellent for drying.

'Dutch' ('Hortensis'). To 3 ft. tall and 2–2½ ft. wide, with gray foliage. Few-branched stems topped with narrow, conical, 2–3-in. spikes of flowers in deep blue violet.

'Fred Boutin'. To 3–4 ft. tall and wide. Dense, silvery gray foliage topped in early to midsummer with 1½–3-in.-long spikes of violet-blue blossoms on unbranched stems.

'Grappenhall'. To 3 ft. tall and wide (or larger). Profuse, slightly fragrant, blue-violet flower spikes; medium green foliage.

'Grey Hedge'. To 3 ft. or more in height and width. Dense foliage in a very silvery gray; profuse lavender-blue flowers on few-branched stems. Excellent rounded or square-sheared hedge; set plants 2 ft. apart.

'Grosso' ('Fat Spike'). Widely planted commercial variety in France and Italy; possibly the most fragrant lavandin of all. Compact growth to 2½ ft. high and wide. Silvery foliage; large (2–3½-in.-thick), conical spikes of violet-blue flowers with darker calyxes. Often gives repeat bloom in late summer. Excellent flower for drying.

'Hidcote Giant'. To 2½ ft. high and 3 ft. wide, with gray-green foliage. Stout stems topped by fat spikes of vivid violet-blue flowers.

'Provence'. Though it is often described as a traditional perfume lavandin, this selection does not produce the kind of oil that is used in perfumery. Grows to 2 ft. high, 3 ft. wide, with fragrant light violet flower spikes that dry well. Good hedge plant.

'Super'. Superb, sweet perfume, close to that of the English lavender parent; yields high-quality essential oil. To 3 ft. high and wide, with gray-green foliage. Lavender-blue flower spikes on long, graceful, laterally branched stems.

'White Spikes' ('Alba'). To 2½ ft. high and wide, with silvery leaves. Spikes of white blossoms and sage green calyxes are 1½–2 in. long, bloom from early summer through fall. Becomes woody with age.

L. lanata. WOOLLY LAVENDER. Zones 8, 9, 12–24. To 1½–2½ ft. high, 2–3 ft. wide. Thickly woolly, near-white leaves are broad (¼–⅜ in. wide), 1½–2 in. long. Widely branching stems that are 10–18 in. long support 1–4-in.-long, interrupted spikes of deep violet blossoms in late summer. Very slow growing; do not cut back hard. This shrub needs perfect drainage; more subject to root rot than English lavenders and lavandins. Difficult to propagate. Many plants sold under this name are varieties of *L. ×intermedia.*

L. lanata hybrids. Zones 4–24. The following crosses of *L. lanata* with forms of *L. angustifolia* bloom in mid- to late summer.

'Lisa Marie'. Compact growth to 12–15 in. high and 1½–2 ft. wide, with silvery leaves that have the color but not the woolly texture of *L. lanata.* Short spikes of deep violet blossoms with distinct white base, giving bicolor effect. Has cold hardiness and resistance to root disease of *L. angustifolia.*

'Richard Gray'. Dense growth to 15 in. high and wide. Silvery gray foliage. Flower stems 4–8 in. long carry short (1–1¼-in.) spikes of vivid violet blossoms; both buds and calyxes are deep violet blue, with a woolly coating.

'Silver Frost'. Semi-open plant 1½ ft. high and wide, with bright silvery foliage. Flower stems radiate in all directions, bear 2-in. spikes of deep violet blossoms with silvery blue calyxes.

L. latifolia (L. spica). SPIKE LAVENDER, BROADLEAF LAVENDER. Zones 4–24. Compact growth to 3 ft. tall and 1½–2 ft. wide, with gray-green leaves to 3 in. long, ¼ in. wide; resembles *L. angustifolia.* Slender, widely branching flower stems support interrupted spikes 1½–4 in. long; blossoms range from soft mauve to bright violet blue, with woolly gray calyxes tipped in violet. Blooms in late summer.

L. multifida. FERNLEAF LAVENDER. Zones 16–24. Sprawling growth to 1½ ft. tall and 2–3 ft. across. Gray-green to silvery foliage is finely divided into branched segments that are heavily felted with fine hairs. Wiry, branching flower stems rise 10–14 in. above the leaves, with deep blue-violet flowers arranged spirally around a 3–4-in. spike. Blooms spring to fall (all year in mild-winter areas). Remove faded bloom stalks and oldest stems to keep it neat. Has a strong, earthy, medicinal scent.

L. stoechas. SPANISH LAVENDER. Zones 4–24. Includes several subspecies, all stocky plants 1½–3 ft. tall and wide, with narrow gray or gray-green, ½–1-in.-long leaves. Small flowers are typically blackish maroon, borne on short, fat, 2-in. spikes topped by two to four flaglike bracts resembling rabbit ears; bracts come in assorted shades of purple and pink. Blossoms open first in four vertical rows around the spike; then rest of spike fills in with flowers. Blooms spring into summer; often repeats if sheared. Flower stem length varies from 1½ in. to 8 in. or more. Very drought resistant. Seeds profusely; can be invasive. Named forms include the following.

'Leucantha' ('Spanish White', 'Snowman'). To 1½–2 ft. high and wide, with pale gray-green foliage and stems. White flowers and creamy white bracts with green veining.

'Otto Quast' ('Quasti'). To 2 ft. high or a bit more, 2½–3½ ft. wide. Flower stems 2–3 in. long, with maroon blossoms and red-purple bracts. Medium green to gray-green leaves. Plants sold under this name are usually grown from seed and often are shorter than the plant just described, with shorter flower stalks.

Lavandula stoechas 'Otto Quast'

L. s. pedunculata. Taller than other forms, with longer flower stems. Green or gray-green foliage. Its selection 'Atlas' grows 2½–3 ft. tall, about as wide, with 7–14-in. flower stalks and vibrant red-violet bracts.

'Willow Vale'. Vigorous, upright, to 1½ ft. tall and wide. Wispy gray-green leaves; deep blue-violet flowers and bluish purple bracts. Short (1–2-in.) flower stems.

'Wings of Night'. Heavy bloomer that resembles 'Otto Quast' but has a broader habit.

L. viridis. GREEN LAVENDER, YELLOW LAVENDER. Zones 8, 9, 12–24. To 2–3 ft. high and wide, with bright green, pine-scented foliage. Short, densely packed, cylindrical flower heads are carried on 1–2-in.-long stems in spring. White or creamy flowers; bracts vary in color from cream through light yellow to bright chartreuse or pale green. Closely related to *L. stoechas,* with which it crosses readily, producing hybrids with foliage in gray, gray green, or yellow green; flowers and bracts come in white, cream, yellow, shrimp pink, salmon, magenta, rose pink, shades of red violet and blue violet, and various greens.

LAVATERA

TREE MALLOW

Malvaceae

ANNUALS AND EVERGREEN SHRUBS

ZONES VARY BY SPECIES

FULL SUN, EXCEPT AS NOTED

REGULAR WATER, EXCEPT AS NOTED

Lavatera assurgentiflora

These easy-to-grow plants bear blossoms resembling single hollyhocks *(Alcea)*.

L. assurgentiflora. Evergreen shrub. Zones 14–24. Native to Southern California's Channel Islands but naturalized on the coastal mainland. Erect growth to 12 ft. tall and wide. Maplelike leaves 3–5 in. long, lobed and toothed. Rosy lavender, white-striped, 2–3-in.-wide flowers bloom almost throughout the year, heaviest from midspring to late summer. Resists wind, salt spray. Use as fast-growing windbreak hedge. Will reach 5–10 ft. and bloom first year from seed. Shear to keep dense. Little to moderate water.

L. maritima (L. bicolor). Evergreen shrub. Zones 6–9, 12–24. Native to western Mediterranean. Grows quickly to 6–8 ft. tall and 4 ft. wide, with gray-green, 2½-in. maplelike leaves and a summer-long show of light pink, 2–3-in. flowers with dark rose veining and a deep purple center. Open grower; cut back hard to keep it compact. Needs partial to full shade in Zones 12 and 13.

L. thuringiaca. Evergreen shrub. Zones 2–9, 14–24. Native to central and southeastern Europe. Resembles *L. maritima* but has denser growth, greener leaves. Flowers are purplish pink, 3 in. across, nearly everblooming (except in colder-winter zones). 'Barnsley' has lighter pink flowers with deep pink centers. 'Rosea' has pink blossoms. Plants need winter protection in Zones 2 and 3.

L. trimestris. ANNUAL MALLOW. All zones. Mediterranean native reaches 3–6 ft. tall and wide from spring-sown seed. Satiny flowers up to 4 in. across. Species is seldom seen in gardens; more commonly grown are named varieties with blossoms in white, pink, rosy carmine. Bloom extends from midsummer to frost if spent flowers are removed to halt seed production. Thin seedlings to allow each plant ample room to spread. Makes a colorful, fast-growing summer hedge or background planting. In mild-winter regions, can also be sown in fall for winter-to-spring bloom. Compact (2–3-ft.) varieties include 'Mont Rose', rose pink; 'Mont Blanc', white; and 'Silver Cup', bright pink. 'Ruby Regis', to 2 ft. high and wide, has 3½-in. flowers of deep rose veined in a deeper shade. 'Loveliness' has similar blossoms but grows 3–4 ft. tall and wide.

LAVENDER. See LAVANDULA

LAVENDER COTTON. See SANTOLINA chamaecyparissus

LAVENDER MIST. See THALICTRUM rochebrunianum

LAVENDER STARFLOWER. See GREWIA occidentalis

LAYIA platyglossa

TIDYTIPS

Asteraceae (Compositae)

ANNUAL

ZONES 1–10, 14–24

FULL SUN

LITTLE OR NO WATER

Layia platyglossa

California native usually obtained in mixed wildflower seed packets or from specialists dealing in native plant seeds. Rapid growth to 5–16 in. high and wide. Narrow, softly hairy, gray-green leaves to 1¼ in. long; lower leaves toothed or lobed, upper ones smooth edged. Flowers are about 2 in. across, with light yellow rays neatly marked white at the tips. Blooms in spring; in cool-summer climates, flowering continues into early summer.

Takes poor and rather heavy soils (though it won't tolerate standing water). To give seedlings a good start, however, prepare soil as for any garden bed. Seeds are usually sown in fall but can also be planted in early spring. Self-sows and will naturalize on banks or in other well-drained sites as long as competition from grasses is minimal. Very drought tolerant; give occasional water if winter rains fail.

LEATHERLEAF FERN. See RUMOHRA adiantiformis

LEEK

Liliaceae

BIENNIAL GROWN AS ANNUAL

ZONES A3; 1–24; H1, H2

PARTIAL SHADE IN HOTTEST CLIMATES

REGULAR WATER

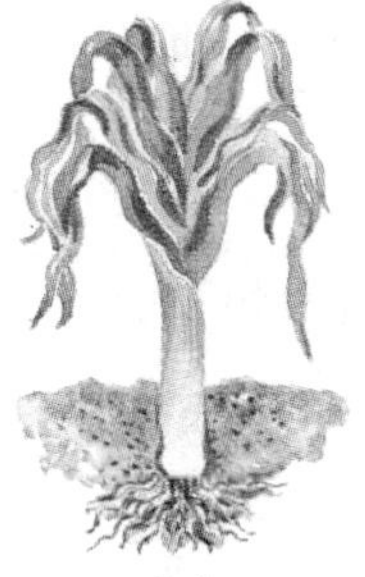

Leek

Botanically speaking, the leek is *Allium porrum*, an onion relative that doesn't form a distinct bulb. To 2–3 ft. tall, with an edible, mild-flavored stem that resembles a long, fat green onion. Give very rich soil. Performs best in cool-summer climates, but may also do well in hotter areas if given some shade. In cold-winter regions, set out plants in spring. In mild-winter areas, set them out from spring through fall where summers are cool, in fall where summers are hot. Sow seeds in containers (½ in. deep, 1 in. apart) 6 to 8 weeks before you intend to set out plants. When planting out, space seedlings 2–4 in. apart in a 5-in.-deep furrow. As plants grow, mound soil around stalks to blanch them (makes the stem bottoms white and mild), keeping mounded soil just below leaf joints.

Harvest when stems are ½–2 in. thick, usually about 4 to 7 months after setting out plants. In cold-winter climates, harvest before ground freezes. (Where ground doesn't freeze, you can leave leeks in place and harvest as needed.) Lift out with spading fork. Any offsets may be detached and replanted. If leeks bloom, small bulbils may appear in flower clusters; plant these for later harvest. To prepare leeks for cooking, slice off the roots and all but 2–3 in. of the green leaves; rinse thoroughly, separating layers. Leeks are not bothered by many of the pests and diseases that attack onions.

Leguminosae. See Fabaceae

LEMAIREOCEREUS thurberi. See STENOCEREUS thurberi

LEMON. See CITRUS

LEMONADE BERRY. See RHUS integrifolia

LEMON BALM. See MELISSA officinalis

LEMON BOTTLEBRUSH. See CALLISTEMON citrinus

LEMON DAYLILY. See HEMEROCALLIS lilioasphodelus

LEMON GRASS. See CYMBOPOGON citratus

LEMON-SCENTED GUM. See EUCALYPTUS citriodora

LEMON THYME. See THYMUS citriodorus

LEMON VERBENA. See ALOYSIA triphylla

LENTEN ROSE. See HELLEBORUS orientalis

FOR INFORMATION ON SELECTING PLANTS
PLEASE SEE PAGES 64–160

LEONOTIS leonurus

LION'S TAIL
Lamiaceae (Labiatae)
EVERGREEN SHRUB
ZONES 8–24; H1, H2
FULL SUN
LITTLE OR NO WATER

Leonotis leonurus

Mint-family member from South Africa. Branching to 4–6 ft. tall and wide. Hairy, square stems carry opposite pairs of narrow, toothed, 2–5-in.-long leaves. Blooms summer into fall with showy, dense whorls of tubular, deep orange, 2-in. flowers covered with furlike coat of fine hairs. Striking if well groomed. If frost hits, cut plant back to live growth in spring. Naturalized in Hawaii.

LEONTOPODIUM alpinum

EDELWEISS
Asteraceae (Compositae)
PERENNIAL
ZONES 1–9, 14–17
FULL SUN
REGULAR WATER

Leontopodium alpinum

Short-lived perennial from mountains of Europe. Rock garden plant growing 6–12 in. high and 1 ft. wide, with woolly white stems, leaves, and bracts. Small white flower heads are crowded at stem tips; a collar of slender leaves radiates out from below each flower head like the arms of a starfish. Tiny bracts of flower heads are tipped with black. Blooms in early summer. Needs excellent drainage.

LEOPARD LILY. See LILIUM pardalinum

LEOPARD PLANT. See FARFUGIUM japonicum 'Aureo-maculatum'

LEOPARD'S BANE. See DORONICUM

LEPECHINIA

PITCHER SAGE
Lamiaceae (Labiatae)
EVERGREEN SHRUBS
ZONES 7–9, 14–24, EXCEPT AS NOTED
PARTIAL SHADE IN HOTTEST CLIMATES
LITTLE OR NO WATER TO MODERATE WATER

Lepechinia calycina

These aromatic members of the mint family are attractive in wild gardens. They reach 6 ft. tall and nearly as wide; once established, they can do without irrigation except in the hottest regions. All have opposite pairs of 1½–5-in.-long leaves and short, spikelike clusters of tubular, 1¼-in. flowers with a gaping mouth and prominent calyx. Except as noted, species listed here are from California's Coast Ranges and bear white to pale pink or lavender blooms.

L. calycina. Lance-shaped to narrowly egg-shaped leaves. Blooms in late spring.

L. fragrans. Furry gray-green leaves, somewhat squared off at base. Blooms in spring and summer.

L. hastata. Zones 7–9, 14–24; H1. From Mexico; possibly native to Hawaii, where it is called pakaha. Spreads by rhizomes. Arrow-shaped leaves; reddish purple flowers. Main bloom comes in summer, with sporadic flowering during the rest of the year.

LEPTOSPERMUM

TEA TREE
Myrtaceae
EVERGREEN SHRUBS OR TREES
ZONES 14–24, EXCEPT AS NOTED
FULL SUN
LITTLE OR NO WATER TO MODERATE WATER

Leptospermum scoparium 'Ruby Glow'

Native to Australia, New Zealand. Called tea tree because Captain Cook brewed a tea from the leaves and gave it to his crew as a scurvy preventive. Substantial and useful plants year round; soft and casual looking (never rigid or formal). Most make a display of five-petaled single flowers (somewhat like tiny wild roses) along stems among the small leaves. Petals surround a hard central cone or cup that matures to a woody seed capsule that hangs on for a long time after the petals drop. Flowers typically white, pink, or red.

If planted in well-drained, slightly acid soil, tea trees are long-lived plants requiring little care. Where drainage is poor, they sometimes succumb quickly to root rot. Need minimal pruning, though you may want to thin growth to emphasize a picturesque habit. When clipping or shearing into hedges, don't cut into bare wood—new growth is unlikely to sprout. Old shrubs that become overgrown or bare at the base can be limbed up into small trees. Plants thrive in seacoast conditions.

L. horizontalis. See L. scoparium 'Horizontalis'

L. laevigatum. AUSTRALIAN TEA TREE. Zones 14–24; H1, H2. Large shrub or small tree 10–30 ft. high and wide, with oval or teardrop-shaped, dull green to gray-green leaves to 1 in. long. Blooms in spring, bearing white flowers to ½ in. across. Solitary plants allowed to grow to full size develop picturesque character, with shaggy, gray-brown, muscular-looking trunks that twist and curve gracefully, reach 2 ft. across at base. Equally handsome branches range out from trunk and carry canopies of finely textured foliage; some weeping branches hang down from the foliage canopies. To make a windbreak, screen, or clipped hedge, set the plants 3–6 ft. apart, depending on ultimate size of selection. Used in these roles, plants do not develop any visible branching character, but they do form a solid bank of fine-textured foliage.

'Compactum', to 5–8 ft. high and 6 ft. wide, is somewhat more open and sparser blooming than species; 'Reevesii' grows only 4–5 ft. high and wide, has rounder, slightly larger, more densely set leaves. Neither of these varieties develops the picturesque form of the species.

L. macrocarpum (L. nitidum 'Macrocarpum'). To 3–8 ft. high and wide. Tiny, narrow leaves (½ in. long, ⅛ in. wide) are reddish when new, maturing to purplish bronze. Spring flowers nearly 1 in. wide, charteuse yellow with dark green central disk.

L. petersonii. LEMON-SCENTED TEA TREE. To 9–20 ft. tall, 6–15 ft. wide. Erect, somewhat open growth with arching or weeping branchlets. Medium green leaves are 1–2 in. long, ⅛ in. wide, give off strong lemon scent when bruised; Australians occasionally use the dried leaves to make tea. Flowers are small, white, inconspicuous.

L. polygalifolium. Variable size and habit; ranges from 3 to 18 ft. tall, 1½ to 9 ft. wide, and can be upright or spreading. Narrow deep green leaves are less than 1 in. long. Showy, very profuse bloom from late spring into summer, when stems are densely set with white, honey-scented, ¾-in.-wide flowers. Attractive cut flowers and foliage. 'Yarra River' has red leaves.

L. rotundifolium. Variable in size and habit, but usually reaches about 6 ft. high and 9 ft. wide, with spreading, arching branches. Tiny roundish leaves. Spring flowers to 1 in. across vary in color from white to deep purplish pink. Extremely showy in bloom but has a shorter flowering period than *L. scoparium.* 'Manning's Choice' has deep lavender pink blossoms.

L. scoparium. NEW ZEALAND TEA TREE, MANUKA. Zones 14–24; H1, H2. Basic species is rarely seen, but its many varieties are valuable garden plants. Not as bold in form or as serviceable in hedges and screens as *L. laevigatum,* but its half-inch flowers are showier: single or double, in white, pink, or red, profuse in spring and summer. Branches densely set with needlelike green leaves, ¼–½ in. long. Good in containers.

'Gaiety Girl'. Slow growing to 5 ft. tall, 4 ft. wide. Double flowers are pink with lilac tint. Reddish foliage.

'Helene Strybing'. Seedling of 'Keatleyi'; resembles parent but has somewhat smaller, much deeper pink flowers.

'Horizontalis'. Fast growing to 3–4 ft. tall, 12 ft. wide, with horizontal branches and drooping branchlets. Single white flowers. Good bank cover.

'Keatleyi'. To 6–10 ft. tall, 5–8 ft. wide. Rangiest, most inclined to picturesque habit. Single pink flowers, pale edges, nearly an inch wide.

'Nanum Tui'. Low, rounded growth to 2 ft. high, 3 ft. wide. Light pink single flowers, darker at center.

'Pink Cascade'. To 1 ft. tall, 3–4 ft. wide. Single pink flowers on sprawling, weeping branches. Attractive trailing over walls, among rocks.

'Pink Damask'. Dense habit to 6–8 ft. tall, 4–5 ft. wide. Double ruby red flowers; red-tinged leaves.

'Pink Pearl'. To 6–10 ft. tall, 5–8 ft. wide. Pale pink buds open into double blush pink to white flowers.

'Ruby Glow'. Compact, upright growth to 6–8 ft. tall, 4–5 ft. wide. Dark foliage and 3/4-in. double blooms in oxblood red; entire shrub looks red.

'Snow White'. Spreading, compact growth 2–4 ft. high, 4–5 ft. wide. Double white flowers with green centers.

LETTUCE

Asteraceae (Compositae)

ANNUAL

ALL ZONES

PARTIAL SHADE IN HOTTEST CLIMATES

REGULAR WATER

Lettuce

Classified botanically as *Lactuca sativa.* A short browse through a seed catalog, seed display rack, or selection of nursery seedlings will reveal enough variety to keep your salad bowl crisp and colorful throughout the growing season. There are four principal types of lettuce: crisphead, butterhead or Boston, loose-leaf, and romaine.

Crisphead is the most exasperating for home gardeners to produce. Heads form best when monthly average temperatures are 55 to 60°F/13 to 16°C. In mild climates, this type of lettuce does well over a long season, but in hot-summer areas, timing of planting becomes critical. Best varieties include 'Great Lakes', 'Summertime', and 'Nevada'.

Butterhead or Boston type has a loose head with green, smooth outer leaves and yellow inner leaves. Good varieties include 'Bibb' ('Limestone'), 'Buttercrunch', and 'Tom Thumb'. 'Mignonette' ('Manoa') stands heat without bolting to seed.

Loose-leaf lettuce makes a rosette rather than a head. It stands heat better than other types. Choice selections are 'Black-seeded Simpson', 'Green Ice', and 'Oak Leaf' (all with green leaves); 'Salad Bowl' (with deeply cut green leaves); and 'Prizehead' and 'Ruby' (red-tinged leaves).

Romaine lettuce has an erect, cylindrical head of smooth leaves; outer leaves are green, inner ones whitish. Stands heat moderately well. Try 'Medallion', 'Olga', or 'Parris Island'.

Lettuces with bronzy to pinkish red leaves add color to a salad. 'Freckles', 'Marveille des Quatre Saisons', and 'Perella Red' are butterheads; 'Lollo Rosso', 'Red Oak Leaf', 'Red Sails', and 'Ruby' are loose-leaf varieties; 'Rouge d'Hiver' and 'Sierra' are romaines.

Various loose-leaf and romaine lettuce varieties are typically included in mesclun mixes—mixtures of fast-growing, tender salad greens (usually some mild and some tangy) that may include mustards, arugula, cress, chicory, radicchio, and/or mizuna.

All lettuces need loose, well-drained soil. Sow in open ground; barely cover seeds. Loose-leaf lettuce can be grown as close as 4 in. apart; thin all other types to 1 ft. apart. Grow mesclun in blocks 4 in. wide and don't thin.

For prolonged harvest, sow at 2-week intervals. In cold-winter regions, begin sowing seed for all types after frost, as soon as soil is workable; where summers are very short, sow indoors, then transplant seedlings outdoors after last frost. In mild-winter, cool-summer regions, sow in early spring for spring and summer harvest, then make further sowings in late summer or early fall for winter harvest. In mild-winter, hot-summer areas, grow only as a winter and early spring crop.

Feed plants lightly and frequently. Control snails, slugs, earwigs. Harvest when heads or leaves are of good size; once lettuce reaches maturity, it rapidly goes to seed, becoming quite bitter. With loose-leaf lettuce, you can clip off just the outer leaves as you need them. Likewise, snip off young leaves of mesclun mix for salads.

LEUCADENDRON

Proteaceae

EVERGREEN TREES AND SHRUBS

ZONES 16, 17, 20–24; H1

FULL SUN

MODERATE WATER

Leucadendron argenteum

South African native related to *Protea;* see that entry for culture. Male and female flowers are borne on separate plants. Inflorescences form at stem tips. In some shrubby species, conelike male flower clusters sit above showy colored bracts and have the look of giant daisies. Those of *L. discolor* and *L. tinctum* make striking cut flowers that dry well. Female flower clusters are less showy and develop into conelike seed clusters.

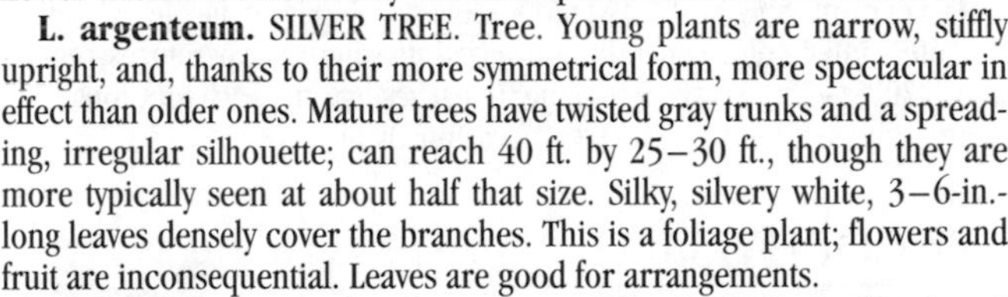

L. argenteum. SILVER TREE. Tree. Young plants are narrow, stiffly upright, and, thanks to their more symmetrical form, more spectacular in effect than older ones. Mature trees have twisted gray trunks and a spreading, irregular silhouette; can reach 40 ft. by 25–30 ft., though they are more typically seen at about half that size. Silky, silvery white, 3–6-in.-long leaves densely cover the branches. This is a foliage plant; flowers and fruit are inconsequential. Leaves are good for arrangements.

Needs fast-draining soil; will not thrive in clay or alkaline soil or in soil amended with animal manure. Needs humid air; takes ocean winds but not dry winds. Hard to use, due to cultural problems and striking appearance—it doesn't blend well with most plants. Small plants are picturesque container subjects for 3 or 4 years; larger ones are effective on slopes (good way to provide them with the excellent drainage they need) when combined with boulders, succulents, and pines in sheltered seaside gardens. Use singly or in groups.

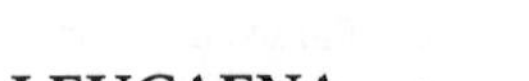

L. discolor. Shrub. Upright, slightly spreading growth to 4–8 ft. tall and wide. Stems densely set with gray-green leaves. Red-centered gold inflorescences in early fall or winter.

L. tinctum. Shrub. Upright, slender habit to 8 ft. tall and 3–4 ft. wide. Dark green foliage. Spring inflorescences are rose to red, sometimes yellow.

LEUCAENA retusa

GOLDEN BALL LEAD TREE

Fabaceae (Leguminosae)

EVERGREEN OR DECIDUOUS SHRUB OR TREE

ZONES 10–13

FULL SUN

LITTLE TO MODERATE WATER

Leucaena retusa

Native to Texas, northern Mexico. Grows 12–20 ft. tall and wide, with light green leaves twice divided into many tiny leaflets. Showy spring flowers are fluffy yellow balls 1 in. across; they are followed by flattened, beanlike pods 6–10 in. long. Useful tree for mini-oasis or transition between cultivated garden and native desert. Good choice for small patio tree. Evergreen in milder winters; deciduous otherwise.

LEUCANTHEMUM. See CHRYSANTHEMUM

LEUCOJUM

SNOWFLAKE

Amaryllidaceae

PERENNIALS FROM BULBS

ZONES VARY BY SPECIES

FULL SUN DURING BLOOM; LIGHT SHADE AFTER IN HOT CLIMATES

REGULAR WATER DURING GROWTH AND BLOOM

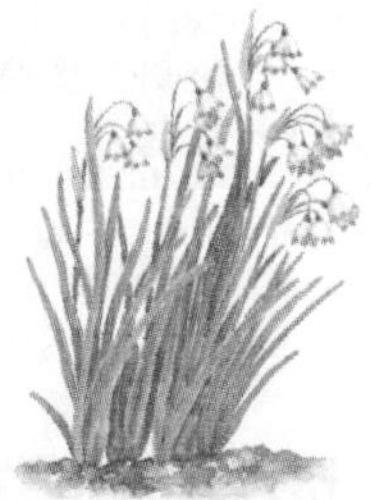

Leucojum aestivum

Native to Europe. Easy-to-grow, permanent plants with strap-shaped leaves and nodding, bell-shaped white flowers with green-tipped segments. Good naturalized under deciduous trees, in shrub borders or orchards, or on cool slopes. Plant in fall, setting bulbs 3–4 in. deep, 4 in. apart. Give some water during summer dormancy; *L. aestivum* can get by without any if soil is shaded. Do not disturb clumps until they are really crowded. When this occurs, dig clumps after foliage dies down, then divide and replant immediately.

L. aestivum. SUMMER SNOWFLAKE. Zones 1–10, 14–24. Leaves 1–1½ ft. long. Stems are 1½ ft. tall, each carrying three to five inch-long flowers. 'Gravetye Giant' is a bit taller and larger flowered than the species and bears as many as nine flowers per stem. Common name "summer snowflake" is misleading—in mild-winter areas, plants bloom from late fall through winter; in colder regions, blossoms appear in midspring.

L. vernum. SPRING SNOWFLAKE. Zones 1–6. Flourishes in areas with definite winter cold; generally unsuccessful where temperatures remain above 20°F/–7°C. Leaves 9 in. long. In earliest spring, each foot-long stem bears a single large white flower (occasionally two).

LEUCOPHYLLUM

TEXAS RANGER, SILVERLEAF

Scrophulariaceae

EVERGREEN SHRUBS

ZONES 7–24, EXCEPT AS NOTED

FULL SUN

LITTLE TO MODERATE WATER

Leucophyllum frutescens

Native to the Southwest and northern Mexico, these compact, slow-growing shrubs are highly useful and attractive in desert gardens. Most have silvery foliage and a good show of ½–1-in.- wide flowers with an open bell shape. Flowering may occur at varying times of the year, often after summer showers. Need very good drainage. Tolerate heat, wind, and alkaline soil. Use as informal or clipped hedges, massed as tall ground cover, or in mixed dry-country gardens. Unless formally hedged, plants require little pruning. Old, straggling plants can be rejuvenated by cutting close to the ground.

L. candidum. VIOLET SILVERLEAF. To 5 ft. high and wide, with small (½-in.), silvery leaves and deep purple flowers. 'Silver Cloud' is a heavy bloomer with very white foliage. 'Thunder Cloud' is smaller than the species (to 3–4 ft. high and wide) and has deeper purple, more closely spaced blossoms.

L. frutescens. TEXAS RANGER, TEXAS SAGE, CENIZO. Zones 7–24; H1, H2. To 6–8 ft. tall and wide, with gray foliage and light purple flowers. 'Green Cloud' has bright green foliage and dark rose or magenta flowers; it may be deciduous in coldest winters. 'White Cloud' has gray foliage and white flowers. 'Compacta', with gray foliage and pink flowers, grows 5 ft. high and wide.

L. laevigatum. CHIHUAHUAN SAGE. Open, angular growth to 4 ft. tall, 5 ft. wide. Tiny dark green leaves; profuse lavender flowers.

L. langmaniae. Dense grower to 5 ft. high and wide, with bright green leaves and lavender flowers.

L. pruinosum. Open growth habit to 6 ft. tall and wide, with silvery foliage. Purple flowers have a strong fragrance of grape bubble gum.

L. 'Rain Cloud'. Hybrid derived from *L. frutescens.* Erect growth to 6 ft. tall, 3–4 ft. wide. Small, silvery leaves; violet-blue flowers.

L. revolutum. Slow growth to about 4 ft. tall, 4–5 ft. wide, with light green, somewhat succulent foliage. Bears purple flowers that appear in fall, later than for other leucophyllums. 'Houdini' has larger, showier blossoms than the species.

L. zygophyllum. To 3 ft. tall and wide, with gray-green, cupped leaves and light blue flowers.

LEUCOSPERMUM

PINCUSHION

Proteaceae

EVERGREEN SHRUBS

ZONES 15–17, 21–24; H1

FULL SUN

MODERATE WATER

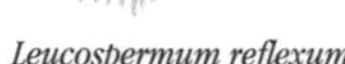

Leucospermum reflexum

South African shrubs related to *Protea;* see that entry for culture. Like proteas, these shrubs are difficult to grow, but extra effort is rewarded with spectacular clusters of many long, slender tubular flowers in a large, thistlelike head. These make stunning cut flowers that last for a month in water. Leaves are narrow, stalkless ovals, crowded along stems. Bloom peaks in late winter and early spring, but can start earlier and last up to 6 months in mild winters. Well-established plants can take several degrees of frost; side buds will produce flowers even if main flower buds freeze. Prune only to shape or remove dead flowers.

L. cordifolium (L. nutans). NODDING PINCUSHION. Compact habit to 4 ft. tall and wide. Medium green leaves. Best species for cut flowers: blossom clusters are 4 in. across, with individual tube-shaped, yellow-tipped coral flowers that curve gracefully outward, then inward again. Selections in varying colors include 'Flame Spike' (salmon red), 'Red' (orange red), and 'Yellow Bird' (light yellow).

L. reflexum. ROCKET PINCUSHION. Sprawling growth to 12 ft. tall and wide, with attractive gray foliage. Orange-rose, 4-in. flower heads. As the flowers age, the "pins" curl downward, giving blossom a shaggy look.

LEUCOTHOE

Ericaceae

EVERGREEN SHRUBS

ZONES VARY BY SPECIES

FULL SUN IN COOLER CLIMATES ONLY

WATER NEEDS VARY BY SPECIES

LEAVES AND NECTAR ARE POISONOUS IF INGESTED

Leucothoe walteri

Relatives of *Pieris,* with leathery leaves and clusters of small, urn-shaped creamy white flowers. Need deep, acid, humus-rich soil; well-suited to woodland gardens. Keep out of drying winds. Best used in masses; not especially attractive individually. Good planted in front of taller broad-leafed evergreens that will hide the leucothoes' legginess. All have suckering growth; for shape and neatness, prune oldest stems to the ground occasionally.

L. axillaris. COAST LEUCOTHOE. Zones 4–7, 15–17. Native to southeastern U.S. Spreading, arching plant 2–4 ft. tall, 3–6 ft. wide. Leaves to 4 in. long are bronze when they emerge; they mature to dark green, then turn red in winter. Drooping, 1-3-in.-long flower clusters along stems in midspring. Regular water.

L. davisiae. SIERRA LAUREL. Zones 2, 4–7, 15–17. Native to bogs and wet places in Siskiyou and Sierra Nevada mountains. Upright shrub to 3 ft.

high and 5 ft. wide. Glossy rich green leaves to 3 in. long are bronze-tinted in winter. Flowers in erect, 2–4-in.-long clusters bloom in early summer. Ample water.

L. walteri (L. fontanesiana, L. catesbaei). DROOPING LEUCOTHOE. Zones 4–7, 15–17. Native to eastern U.S. Grows slowly to 3–6 ft. high and wide, spreading by underground stems. Branches arch gracefully. Leaves are 3–6 in. long, turn bronzy purple in fall (remain greener in deep shade). Drooping, 1½–2½-in.-long clusters of flowers in mid-spring. Moderate water.

'Lovita'. To 2 ft. high and 4 ft. wide. Leaves are smaller and darker green than those of species; turn mahogany in winter.

'Nana'. To 2 ft. high, spreading to 6 ft. wide. Leaves turn bronzy red in winter.

'Rainbow'. To 5 ft. high and 6 ft. wide, with green leaves marbled cream and pink.

'Scarletta'. To 2 ft. high and 4 ft. wide. Leaves are bright red when new; they turn green by summer, then deep red in fall and winter.

LEVISTICUM officinale

LOVAGE

Apiaceae (Umbelliferae)

PERENNIAL

ZONES 4–9, 12–24

LIGHT AFTERNOON SHADE IN HOTTEST CLIMATES

REGULAR WATER

Levisticum officinale

From the eastern Mediterranean region. Ornamental herb with divided, glossy deep green leaves to 2½ ft. long. Hollow stems rise from the foliage clumps in summer, crowned by sprays of flat-topped greenish yellow flower clusters. Flowering plants may reach 6 ft. tall under ideal conditions, but more usual size is 3 ft. high and wide. Plant has a history of culinary uses; seeds are valued for their celery flavor, leaves are added to salads and soups. Grow from seeds sown in place in fall; or start seeds in containers and transplant into garden in spring. You can also divide an established clump in early spring. Volunteer seedlings are another source of extra plants.

LEWISIA

Portulacaceae

PERENNIALS

ZONES 1–7, 14–17, EXCEPT AS NOTED

FULL SUN OR LIGHT SHADE

LITTLE TO MODERATE WATER

Lewisia tweedyi

Beautiful plants for rock gardens, collections of alpine plants. Often difficult to grow. All need excellent drainage; plant with fine gravel around crowns. Of the many offered by specialists, the following are outstanding.

L. cotyledon. Native to Northern California and southern Oregon. To 1 ft. high, 10 in. wide. Rosettes of narrow, fleshy, evergreen leaves bear 10-in. stems topped by large, extremely showy clusters of 1-in., white or pink flowers often striped with rose or red. Blooms from spring to early summer. *L. c. howellii* is similar but has wavy-edged leaves and somewhat larger flowers. Prune out side growth to maintain air circulation around root crown. Can be grown in pots of fast-draining sterilized soil or growing mixes.

L. rediviva. BITTERROOT. Native to mountains of the West. To 2 in. high, 4 in. wide. State flower of Montana. Fleshy roots; short stems with short, succulent, strap-shaped leaves to 2 in. long that usually die back before flowers appear (seemingly from bare earth) in spring. Flowers, borne singly on short stems, look like 2-in.-wide water lilies in rosy pink or white. Not difficult if drainage is excellent; risky otherwise.

L. tweedyi. Zones A2, A3; 1–7, 14–17. Native to mountains of south central Washington. To 8 in. high, 1 ft. wide. Stunning big, satiny, salmon pink flowers, one to three to a stem, bloom above fleshy, evergreen, 4-in. leaves. Prune out side growth to keep root crown open to air. Winter moisture is a problem; grow plants in pots and turn them on their sides in wet weather.

LEYCESTERIA formosa

HIMALAYAN HONEYSUCKLE, HIMALAYAN PHEASANTBERRY

Caprifoliaceae

DECIDUOUS SHRUB

ZONES 4–6, 14–17, 20–24

FULL SUN OR LIGHT SHADE

REGULAR WATER

Leycesteria formosa

Native to Himalayas and western China. Fast-growing shrub to 6 ft. high and wide; the branches do not become woody until their second year. Stems are a handsome gray green when young, later turning bright green. Paired bright green leaves to 6 in. long.

From summer to early fall, inflorescences form at branch tips and in upper leaf joints; the small white flowers are less conspicuous than the purplish bracts that partially conceal them. Inflorescences are 1–2 in. long at first, then gradually lengthen to 6 in. Blossoms are followed by berries much appreciated by birds; fruit starts out green but rapidly turns deep red, then purplish black (all three colors are present simultaneously). In cold-winter areas, shoots may freeze back; cut them to the ground in late winter or early spring (regrowth is rapid).

LEYMUS

LYME GRASS, WILD RYE

Poaceae (Gramineae)

PERENNIAL GRASSES

ZONES VARY BY SPECIES

FULL SUN OR LIGHT SHADE

LITTLE TO MODERATE WATER

Leymus arenarius

These wild ryes or lyme grasses were formerly assigned to *Elymus* but are now known as *Leymus* (simply an anagram of the former generic name). They are grown principally for their blue-gray or silvery blue foliage. Very drought tolerant; will remain evergreen with some summer water. For other types of blue-leafed grasses, see *Elymus magellanicus, Festuca,* and *Helictotrichon sempervirens.*

L. arenarius (Elymus arenarius). BLUE LYME GRASS. Zones A2, A3; 1–9, 14–24. From coastal northern and western Europe. Low, vigorous clump of gray-blue leaves topped by clusters of inconspicuous flowers. To 3–4 ft. in bloom, spreading widely by thick rhizomes. Good soil binder; may need curbing. Flowers are not especially attractive, and plant looks best when cut back after bloom to stimulate fresh foliage. Does best in cool weather but withstands considerable heat. Grows in sandy soils in the wild; tolerates clay soils. Often sold as 'Glaucus', which is identical to the species. 'Findhorn' is a compact variety.

L. condensatus. Zones 7–12, 14–24. Native to coastal Southern California and Channel Islands. Basic species is usually green leafed, reaching 9 ft. tall and 6 ft. wide in bloom. More commonly grown is 'Canyon Prince', to 4 ft. tall and 3 ft. wide; its foliage is greenish when new, maturing to brilliant silvery blue. Spreads slowly by rhizomes.

FOR DEFINITIONS OF GARDENING TERMS
PLEASE SEE PAGES 746–750

LIATRIS spicata

GAYFEATHER

Asteraceae (Compositae)

PERENNIAL

ZONES A2, A3; 1–10, 14–24

FULL SUN

REGULAR WATER

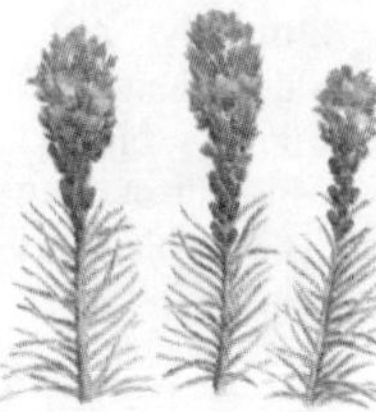

Liatris spicata

From eastern and central North America. Showy bloomer to 4 ft. tall, 1½ ft. wide. Basal tufts of grassy leaves grow from thick, often tuberous rootstocks. In summer, tufts lengthen into tall stems densely set with leaves and topped by "foxtails" of small light purple flowers with prominent stamens. Blossom spikes open from the top downward. Best-known selection is 'Kobold' (2 ft. tall), with bright rosy lilac flowers. 'Floristan White' (3 ft. tall) is a white-flowered selection. 'Silvertips' (2½–3 ft. tall) has lavender flowers with white tips.

Endures heat, cold, aridity, poor soil. Needs moderately fertile, well-drained soil; sensitive to soggy soil during winter dormancy. Plant in spring, in clumps or drifts; you can start from nursery transplants or set out rootstocks 2 in. deep, 6–8 in. apart. When performance declines, divide clumps in early spring. Often sold as *L. callilepis* by Dutch bulb growers.

LIBERTIA

Iridaceae

PERENNIALS

ZONES 8, 9, 14–24

LIGHT SHADE IN HOTTEST CLIMATES

REGULAR WATER

Libertia peregrinans

Iris relatives with swordlike leaves in fans and clusters of white flowers from late spring to midsummer. Blooms consist of three large petals and three much smaller ones, giving them a triangular look.

L. formosa. From Chile. Leathery bright green leaves form a clump 6–18 in. high, 2 ft. wide. Flowering stems to 3 ft. tall carry dense, spikelike clusters of 1¼-in. flowers.

L. grandiflora. From New Zealand. Bright green leaves in a clump 2 ft. high, 1½ ft. wide. Branching clusters of ¾-in. flowers on 2½-ft. stems.

L. peregrinans. From New Zealand. To 2 ft. high, 1 ft. wide; forms colonies by rhizomes. Narrow, stiffly erect olive green leaves have an orange to brownish orange center stripe; especially attractive when backlit. Branching clusters of inch-wide flowers on stems shorter than leaves.

LIBOCEDRUS. See CALOCEDRUS

LICORICE FERN. See POLYPODIUM glycyrrhiza

LICORICE MINT. See AGASTACHE rupestris

LICORICE PLANT. See HELICHRYSUM petiolare

LIGNUM-VITAE. See GUAIACUM officinale

LIGULARIA

Asteraceae (Compositae)

PERENNIALS

ZONES 1–9, 14–17, EXCEPT AS NOTED

PARTIAL OR FULL SHADE, EXCEPT AS NOTED

AMPLE MOISTURE

Ligularia stenocephala 'The Rocket'

Stately perennials from China and Japan. Form 3-ft.-wide clumps of large leaves topped by daisy-type flowers in yellow to orange. All need rich soil, plenty of moisture, and some shade; they do not tolerate heat or low humidity. Good around pools, along stream beds, in bog gardens. Control slugs and snails. Clumps can remain undisturbed for years; if more plants are needed, divide clumps in early spring.

L. dentata. Grown primarily for big, attractive leaves (to more than a foot across), roundish with heart-shaped base. In midsummer to early fall, sends up 3–5-ft. stems topped by large, branching heads of 4-in.-wide, orange-yellow daisies. 'Othello' (grows in Zones A2, A3; 1–9, 14–17) and 'Desdemona' have deep purple leafstalks, veins, and leaf undersides; upper surfaces of leaves are green.

L. 'Gregynog Gold'. Clump of 14–in.-wide, heart-shaped, tooth-edged leaves sends up stems to 6 ft. tall. In late summer and fall, stems bear conical clusters of 4-in. yellow flowers.

L. przewalskii. Deeply lobed and cut leaves grow to 1 ft. wide. Dark purplish flowering stalks rise to about 6 ft., topped with dense, narrow spires of ¾-in. yellow daisy flowers in summer. In the Pacific Northwest, can take full sun.

L. stenocephala. Zones A2, A3; 1–9, 14–17. Especially stunning flower spikes. Usually represented by variety 'The Rocket', with a clump of foot-wide, deeply cut leaves topped by tall (up to 5-ft.), narrow spires of 1½-in. yellow daisies in summer.

L. tussilaginea. See Farfugium japonicum

L. wilsoniana. Zones 2–9, 14–17. Bears kidney-shaped leaves that reach 20 in. wide. Stems grow to 6 ft. tall, carry spikes of inch-wide yellow daisies in summer.

LIGUSTRUM

PRIVET

Oleaceae

EVERGREEN, SEMIEVERGREEN, DECIDUOUS SHRUBS AND TREES

ZONES VARY BY SPECIES

FULL SUN OR PARTIAL SHADE

REGULAR WATER

LEAVES AND FRUITS CAUSE GASTRIC DISTRESS IF INGESTED

Ligustrum lucidum

Most widely used as hedges, though one type is a street tree; can also be clipped into formal shapes and featured in tubs or large pots. All bear abundant, showy clusters of white to creamy white flowers in late spring or early summer (some people find the scent unpleasant). Flowers attract bees. Clipped hedges bloom less heavily, since shearing removes most of the flower-bearing branches. Blossoms are followed by small blue-black berries; birds eat them, thus distributing seeds. Most privets grow well in any soil.

Nurseries sometimes misidentify certain privets. The plant sold as *L. japonicum* very often turns out to be the tree species *L. lucidum*. The true *L. japonicum* is available in two or more forms. The tall, shrubby kind is the true species; the lower-growing and more densely foliaged form is often sold as *L. texanum* but probably should be called *L. japonicum* 'Texanum'.

Smaller-leafed hardy privets used for hedging are also often confused. *L. amurense*, *L. ovalifolium*, and *L. vulgare* look much alike, and any of these is likely to be sold as "common privet"—a name that rightly belongs only to *L. vulgare*.

L. amurense. AMUR PRIVET. Shrub. Zones A2, A3; 1–24. Deciduous in coldest areas, where it is widely used for hedge and screen planting. Partially evergreen in milder climates but seldom planted there. Native to northern China. Much like *L. ovalifolium* in appearance, but foliage is not as glossy.

L. japonicum. JAPANESE PRIVET, WAX-LEAF PRIVET. Evergreen shrub. Zones 4–24; H1, H2. From northern China, Korea, Japan. To 10–12 ft. tall, 8 ft. wide, with dense, compact habit. Roundish oval leaves are 2–4 in. long, with a thick, slightly spongy feel; they are glossy medium to dark

long, with a thick, slightly spongy feel; they are glossy medium to dark green above, distinctly paler to almost whitish beneath. Excellent plant for hedges or screens and for shaping into globes, pyramids, and other shapes. With lower limbs pruned off, also makes an attractive small standard tree. Sunburns in hot spells. In areas where there is hardpan or where Texas root rot prevails, grow it in containers. Often confused with its variety 'Texanum'.

'Rotundifolium' ('Coriaceum'). To 5 ft. tall and 3 ft. wide, with nearly round leaves to 2½ in. long. Give partial shade in hottest climates.

'Silver Star'. To 6–8 ft. tall, 4–6 ft. wide. Deep green leaves with gray-green mottling and startling creamy white edges. Provides a good contrast to deep green foliage.

'Texanum'. Very similar to species but lower growing (to 8–10 ft. tall, 4–6 ft. wide), with somewhat denser, lusher foliage. Useful as a windbreak. This plant is often sold as the species.

L. lucidum. GLOSSY PRIVET. Evergreen tree. Zones 5–24; H1, H2. Native to China, Korea, Japan. Round-headed tree to 20–40 ft. high and wide, with one or several trunks. Glossy, 4–6-in.-long leaves are tapered and pointed, medium to dark green on both sides. They feel leathery but lack the slightly spongy feel of *L. japonicum* leaves. Flowers bloom in especially large, feathery clusters in late spring and early summer; they are followed by a profuse crop of fruit. Can be used as lawn tree or planted 10 ft. apart for tall privacy screen or windbreak. Performs well in large containers.

Before planting this tree, carefully consider its disadvantages. Eventual fruit crop is immense; never plant where fruit will fall on cars, walks, or other paved areas (it stains). Fallen seeds (and those dropped by birds) sprout profusely in ground covers and will need pulling. Many people dislike the flowers' odor, and fruiting clusters are bare and unattractive after fruit drop.

L. ovalifolium. CALIFORNIA PRIVET. Semievergreen shrub; evergreen only in warmest winter climates. Zones 3b–24; H1, H2. Native to Japan. Dark green, oval, 2½-in. leaves. Grows rapidly to 8–15 ft. tall, 6–10 ft. wide, but can be kept sheared as a 4-ft. hedge. For use as a hedge, set plants 9–12 in. apart. Clip early and frequently to encourage low, dense branching. Greedy roots. Well-fed, well-watered plants hold their foliage longest. Tolerates heat. 'Aureum', golden privet, has yellow-edged leaves; it is often sold as 'Variegatum'.

L. 'Suwannee River'. Evergreen shrub. Zones 4–24. Reported to be a hybrid between *L. japonicum* 'Rotundifolium' and *L. lucidum.* Slow-growing, compact plant reaches 1½ ft. tall in 3 years, eventually grows 3–4 ft. high and wide. Leathery, somewhat twisted dark green leaves; no fruit. Use as low hedge, as foundation planting, in containers.

L. 'Vicaryi'. VICARY GOLDEN PRIVET. Deciduous shrub. Zones 2–24. To 8–10 ft. high and wide. Yellow leaves; color is most pronounced on plants in full sun. Best planted alone; color does not develop well under hedge shearing.

L. vulgare. COMMON PRIVET. Deciduous shrub. Zones 2–24; H1. From northern Europe, Mediterranean, Asia Minor. To 15 ft. tall, 12 ft. wide. Dark green leaves are less glossy than those of *L. ovalifolium,* and root system is not as greedy. Clusters of black fruit are conspicuous on unpruned or lightly pruned plants. 'Lodense' ('Nanum') is a dense dwarf that reaches only 4 ft. high and wide.

LILAC. See SYRINGA

LILAC VINE. See HARDENBERGIA

Liliaceae. The lily family contains hundreds of species of ornamental plants, as well as vegetables such as asparagus and the entire onion tribe. Most grow from bulbs, corms, or rhizomes. Flowers are often showy, usually with six petal-like segments of equal size.

A PRACTICAL GUIDE TO GARDENING
PLEASE SEE PAGES 658–731

LILIUM

LILY

Liliaceae

PERENNIALS FROM BULBS

ZONES VARY BY SPECIES OR TYPE

ROOTS COOL, TOPS IN SUN OR FILTERED LIGHT

REGULAR WATER, EXCEPT AS NOTED

Lilium auratum

Most stately and varied of bulbous plants, ranging in height from 1 to 9 ft. For many years, only the species—the same plants growing wild in parts of Asia, Europe, and North America—were available, and many of these were difficult and unpredictable.

Around 1925, lily growers began a significant breeding program. They bred new hybrids from species with desirable qualities and also developed strains and varieties that were healthier, hardier, and easier to grow than the original species. They produced new forms and new colors; what is more important, they developed methods for growing healthy lilies in large quantities. Today, hybrids and strains typically provide the best garden lilies, but it is still possible to get some desirable species.

Plant bulbs as soon as possible after you get them. If you must wait, keep them in a cool place until you plant. If bulbs are dry, place them in moist sand or peat moss until scales plump up and new roots begin to sprout.

Before planting bulbs, remove any injured portions and dust cuts with sulfur. For each bulb, dig a generous planting hole (6–12 in. deeper than height of bulb). Place enough soil at bottom of hole to bring it up to proper level for bulb (see next paragraph). Set bulb with its roots spread, fill in hole with soil, firming it in around bulb to eliminate air pockets. If your area is infested with gophers, you may have to plant each bulb in a 6-in.-square wire basket made of ½-in. hardware cloth. (The depth of the basket will depend on the planting depth.)

Planting depths vary according to size and rooting habit of bulb. General rule is to cover smaller bulbs with 2–3 in. of soil, medium-size bulbs with 3–4 in., and larger bulbs with 4–6 in. (but never cover *L. candidum* bulbs with more than 1 in. of soil). Planting depth can be quite flexible. It is better to err by planting shallowly than too deeply; lily bulbs have contractile roots that draw them down to proper depth. Ideal spacing for lily bulbs is 1 ft. apart, but you can plant as close as 6 in. for densely massed effect.

Lilium candidum

Since most lilies never really enter a dormant period, they need moisture year-round; keep soil moist to at least 6 in. deep. Cut back on watering somewhat after tops turn yellow in fall, but never let roots go completely dry. Exceptions to this rule are *L. candidum* and its hybrids and any other species native to dry-summer areas *(L. columbianum, L. humboldtii, L. pardalinum).*

Flooding is preferable to overhead watering, which can help to spread disease spores and also topple tall lilies when they're in flower. Pull weeds by hand if possible; hoeing may injure roots.

Remove faded flowers to prevent seed formation. Wait until stems and leaves turn yellow before you cut plants back. If clumps become too large and crowded, dig, divide, and transplant them in spring or fall. If you're careful, you can lift lily clumps at any time, even when they are in bloom.

Lilies are fine container plants. Place one bulb in a deep 5–7-in. pot or five in a 14–16-in. pot. First, fill pot one-third full of potting mix. Then place bulb with roots spread and pointing downward; cover with about an inch of soil. Water thoroughly and place in a cool room or garage, a deep cold frame, or a greenhouse that is heated (in colder climates) just enough to keep out frost. During root-forming period, keep soil moderately moist. When top growth appears, add more soil mixture and gradually fill pot as stems elongate. Leave 1-in. space between surface of soil and rim of pot for watering. Move pots to a partially shaded area during blooming period. Later, if you wish to repot bulbs, do so in late fall or early spring. ▸

TOP: Asiatic Hybrid Lily
BOTTOM: *Lilium lancifolium*

TOP: Aurelian Hybrid Lily 'Golden Splendour'
BOTTOM: *Lilium longiflorum*

TOP: Oriental Hybrid Lily 'Casablanca'
BOTTOM: *Lilium martagon*

TOP: *Lilium candidum*
BOTTOM: *Lilium pardalinum*

TOP: *Lilium henryi*
BOTTOM: *Lilium regale*

Incurable viral or mosaic infection is a serious problem in lilies. To avoid the problem, buy healthy bulbs from reliable sources. Dig and destroy any lilies that display mottled leaves or seriously stunted growth. Control aphids, which spread the infection. Reduce risk of botrytis blight (a fungal disease) by maintaining good air circulation around plants; don't let dense foliage surround lilies. Botrytis can be controlled with an appropriate fungicide and by keeping lily foliage dry.

Although the official classification of lilies lists eight divisions of hybrids and a ninth division of species, the following describes the lilies ordinarily available to Western gardeners. Advances in breeding continue to produce new lilies. Consult specialists' catalogs to learn about these wonders, which are reaching the market faster than books can deal with them.

ASIATIC HYBRIDS

Zones A1–A3; 1–9, 14–24. These are the easiest to grow and most reliable for the average garden, and they are also the earliest to bloom (early summer). Flowers are usually unscented. Some of the hybrids have upward-facing flowers, while others have horizontally held or drooping blooms. Stems are strong, erect, and short (1½ ft.) to moderate (4½ ft.) in height. Colors range from white through yellow and orange to pink and red. Many have dark spots or contrasting bands of color. Examples are 'Enchantment', orange red spotted with black; 'Impala', bright yellow; 'Pink Floyd', ivory pink banded with rose pink; and 'Sancerre', pure white and unspotted.

AURELIAN HYBRIDS

Zones 1–9, 14–24. Derived from Asiatic species (but not *L. auratum* and *L. speciosum*). Midsummer bloomers with trumpet- or bowl-shaped, usually scented flowers. Blossoms range in color from white and cream through yellow and pink, many with green, brown, or purple shading on their outer surfaces. Plants are typically 3–6 ft. tall; each stem carries 12–20 flowers. Examples include 'Golden Splendour', deep gold with maroon striping on petal backs; and 'Thunderbolt', soft apricot orange.

WHAT LILIES NEED

EXPOSURE: Where summers are cool and overcast, you can plant in full sun; elsewhere, choose a spot that gets filtered sun, light shade, or afternoon shade. Locating lilies among low-growing plants is a good way to keep their roots shaded.

WIND PROTECTION: In all climates, avoid planting lilies in windy sites.

SOIL: Provide deep, loose, well-drained, fertile soil. Before planting, work in lots of organic matter to 1 ft. deep.

MULCHING: After planting, mulch with 2–3 in. of organic material to conserve moisture, keep soil cool, and reduce weed growth.

WATERING: Because lilies never completely stop growing, provide moisture all year. Lilies native to dry-summer areas are an exception; withhold summer water from these.

Lilium columbianum

ORIENTAL HYBRIDS

Zones 1–9, 14–24. The most exotic of the hybrids. Bloom midsummer to early fall, with big (to 9-in.) fragrant flowers of white or pink, often spotted with gold and shaded or banded with red. Most are tall, with nodding flowers, but a few are dwarf and have upward-facing blooms. Examples are 'Casablanca', pure white; 'Pink Ribbons', light rose banded and spotted with deep rose; and 'Stargazer', rose red with white margins.

SPECIES AND VARIANTS

A number of excellent species lilies are listed below. Those described as having Turk's cap flowers bear blooms with strongly recurved petals.

L. amabile. Zones 2b–9, 14–17. Native to Korea. To 3 ft. tall, with one to five flowers per stem in early summer. Orange-red Turk's cap blossoms with dark purple spots. Scent is slightly unpleasant. Tolerates alkaline soils.

L. auratum. GOLD-BAND LILY. Zones 1–7, 14–17. Native to Japan. To 4–6 ft. tall. Very fragrant white flowers with crimson spots and gold band are carried 6–30 per stem. Blooms in late summer.

L. candidum. MADONNA LILY. Zones 1–9, 14–24; H1. Native to the Balkans and eastern Mediterranean. The lily of medieval romance, a sentimental choice for many gardeners. To 3–4 ft. tall. Fragrant flowers, white with yellow base, borne 5–20 per stem from late spring to early summer. Unlike most lilies, dies down soon after bloom, then makes new growth in fall. Plant in summer, while dormant. Does not have stem roots; set top of bulb only 1–2 in. deep. Bulb quickly makes foliage rosette that lives over winter. Subject to diseases that shorten its life. Cascade strain, grown from seed, is more disease resistant than imported bulbs. Prefers full sun.

L. cernuum. Zones 1–9, 14–24. Native to Korea, Manchuria, Siberia. Summer bloomer only 12–20 in. high, with fragrant lilac-colored flowers often dotted in darker purple. Usually bears up to six blossoms per stem.

L. columbianum. COLUMBIA LILY, TIGER LILY. Zones 2–7, 14–19. Native from British Columbia to Northern California. To 5–6 ft. tall, with one to six small, golden orange, unscented lilies per stem in midsummer.

L. formosanum. Zones 2–7, 14–24. Native to Taiwan. To 4–5 ft. tall, with long, grassy leaves. Narrow, fragrant white trumpets are usually carried one or two per stem; midsummer bloom. Tolerates alkaline soils.

L. henryi. Zones 1–10, 14–21; H1. Native to China. Slender stems to 8–9 ft., each topped by 10–20 barely scented, bright orange Turk's cap flowers. Summer bloom. Does best in light shade in all regions.

L. humboldtii. HUMBOLDT LILY. Zones 3, 7, 14–24. Native to open woodlands of the Sierra Nevadas. To 3–6 ft. tall. Unscented, nodding Turk's cap blooms are bright orange with large maroon dots; early summer bloom. *L. h. ocellatum* is similar, but its maroon dots are margined in red.

L. lancifolium (L. tigrinum). TIGER LILY. Zones 1–10, 14–22. Native to China, Japan, Korea. To 4 ft. or taller. Blooms in late summer, bearing up to 40 pendulous, unscented, black-spotted orange flowers on each stem. An old, easy-to-grow favorite. Newer tiger lilies are available in white, cream, yellow, pink, and red, all with black spots.

L. lankongense. Zones 2b–24. Alpine native of China. To 3–5 ft. tall, spreading by stoloniferous stems. Powerfully fragrant Turk's cap flowers in rose red with purple spots, carried up to 15 per stem. Midsummer bloom. Tolerates alkaline soils.

L. leucanthum centifolium. Zones 2–9, 14–24. Native to China. To 7–8 ft. tall. Up to 18 fragrant, white, midsummer flowers with external purple-red streaks. Funnel-shaped blooms, slightly pendulous.

L. longiflorum. EASTER LILY. Zones 2–9, 14–24; H1. Native to Japan, Taiwan. Up to six trumpet-shaped, very fragrant white flowers on each short stem. Usually purchased in bloom at Easter. Set out in garden after flowers fade—but don't plant forced Easter lilies near other lilies, since they may transmit a virus. Stems will die down. Plant may rebloom in fall; in 1 or 2 years, may flower in midsummer, its normal bloom season. Recent hybridization has yielded pink, red, and yellow types.

L. martagon. TURK'S CAP LILY. Zones 1–10, 14–17. Native from Europe to Mongolia. To 3–5 ft. tall. In midsummer, each stem bears up to 50 pendent flowers with sharply recurved petals. Blossoms are typically purplish pink with darker spots, but darker colored and pure white variants exist. Flowers have an unpleasant scent. Easy to grow but slow to establish; eventually forms big clumps.

L. pardalinum. LEOPARD LILY. Zones 2–7, 14–17. Native from southwestern Oregon to Southern California. To 4–8 ft. tall, with unscented Turk's cap flowers in orange or red orange shading to yellow, with brown spotting in center. Up to 10 flowers per stem. Blooms in late spring or early summer.

L. pumilum. CORAL LILY. Zones 1–10, 14–24. Native to northern China, Mongolia, Siberia. To 1–1½ ft. high, with up to 20 fragrant red Turk's cap flowers per stem. Blooms in early summer. 'Yellow Bunting' has golden yellow blossoms.

L. regale. REGAL LILY. Zones 1–9, 14–24. Native to western China. Superseded in quality by modern hybrids, but still popular and easy to grow. Stems to 6 ft. tall; in midsummer, each bears up to 25 fragrant, funnel-shaped white blossoms flushed purple outside; carried horizontally.

L. speciosum. Zones 1–7, 14–17. Native to China, Japan, Taiwan. To 2½–5 ft. tall. Large, wide, fragrant Turk's cap flowers are white, heavily suffused with rose pink and sprinkled with raised crimson dots. Usually up to 12 flowers per stem. Blooms in late summer. *L. s. album* has pure white blooms, *L. s. rubrum* red ones; there are also other named forms.

L. tigrinum. See L. lancifolium

LILLY-PILLY TREE. See ACMENA smithii

LILY. See LILIUM

LILY-OF-THE-NILE. See AGAPANTHUS

LILY-OF-THE-VALLEY. See CONVALLARIA majalis

LILY-OF-THE-VALLEY SHRUB. See PIERIS japonica

LILY-OF-THE-VALLEY TREE. See CLETHRA arborea, CRINODENDRON patagua

LILY TURF. See LIRIOPE and OPHIOPOGON

LIME. See CITRUS

LIMEQUAT. See CITRUS

LIMNANTHES douglasii

MEADOWFOAM, POACHED EGGS

Limnanthaceae

ANNUAL

ZONES 1–9, 14–24

FULL SUN

REGULAR WATER

Limnanthes douglasii

Native to wet meadows and other damp, sunny locales in California and southwestern Oregon. Produces a blanket of flowers in spring; can be coaxed into a longer bloom period if given some supplemental water as the ground starts drying out later in spring. Grows 6–12 in. tall and broad, with yellowish green, finely divided leaves and clusters of inch-wide flowers. Blossoms may be white or yellow but are most commonly yellow with white petal tips. Sow seeds in fall or earliest spring. Plants self-sow where adapted.

LIMONIUM

STATICE, SEA LAVENDER

Plumbaginaceae

PERENNIALS AND ANNUALS

ZONES VARY BY SPECIES

FULL SUN

MODERATE WATER

Limonium perezii

Large, leathery, green basal leaves contrast with airy clusters of tiny, delicate flowers on nearly leafless, many-branched stems. The flowers consist of two parts: an outer, papery envelope (the calyx) and an inner part (the corolla). Calyx and corolla are often of different colors. Flowers are good for cutting and keep their color when dried. Plants tolerate heat and many kinds of soil but need good drainage. They often self-sow. For spring and summer bloom of annual kinds, sow indoors and move to garden when weather warms up. Or sow outdoors in early spring for later bloom.

L. gmelinii. Zones 1–10, 14–24. From eastern Europe, Siberia. Much like a slightly smaller *L. platyphyllum,* with 5-in. basal leaves and widely branching clusters of blue flowers in mid- to late summer.

L. perezii. Perennial. Zones 13, 15–17, 20–24. Often freezes in Zones 14, 18, 19. To 3 ft. tall, with flower clusters spreading nearly as wide. Calyx is rich purple, corolla white. Long spring and summer bloom. Leaves up to 1 ft. long, including stalks. First-rate beach plant. Often naturalizes in coastal Southern California. Damaged at 25°F/–4°C but useful even where it freezes out occasionally; nursery-grown seedlings develop fast. Needs afternoon shade in Zone 13.

L. platyphyllum (L. latifolium). Perennial. Zones 1–10, 14–24; H1. Native to central and southeastern Europe. Vigorous plant to 2½ ft. tall, covered in a haze of flowers up to 3 ft. wide in summer. Calyx is white, corolla bluish; pure white and pink kinds exist. Smooth-edged leaves to 10 in. long.

L. sinuatum. Annual. All zones. Mediterranean native widely grown for use as a cut flower in both fresh and dried arrangements. To 1½ ft. tall and 1 ft. wide, with basal leaves lobed nearly to midrib and flower stems distinctly winged. Calyx is blue, lavender, or rose; corolla is white. Improved garden strains come in many colors, including yellow, apricot, orange, peach, rose, light blue, deep blue, purple, and white.

L. suworowii. See Psylliostachys

L. tataricum. See Goniolimon tataricum

Linaceae. The flax family of annuals, perennials, and shrubs displays cup- or disk-shaped flowers with four or five petals. Flowers are often showy. Individually short lived, they appear over a long season. Examples are flax *(Linum)* and yellow flax *(Reinwardtia)*.

LINANTHUS grandiflorus

MOUNTAIN PHLOX

Polemoniaceae

ANNUAL

ZONES 1–9, 14–24

FULL SUN

LITTLE OR NO WATER TO MODERATE WATER

Linanthus grandiflorus

Native to Northern California, this phlox relative somewhat resembles annual phlox *(Phlox drummondii)*, bearing heads of inch-wide, pink-tinged white or lavender-pink blossoms with yellow throats. Good cut flower. Plant grows to 2 ft. tall, 1 ft. wide. Sow seeds in fall or earliest spring. In cooler areas, needs little or no water for spring bloom; in warmer regions, give occasional irrigation.

LINARIA

TOADFLAX

Scrophulariaceae

ANNUALS AND PERENNIALS

ZONES 1–24, EXCEPT AS NOTED

FULL SUN OR LIGHT SHADE

REGULAR WATER

Linaria maroccana

Brightly colored blooms like small, spurred snapdragons *(Antirrhinum)*. Medium green, very narrow leaves. Easy to grow. Best in masses; individual plants are rather wispy.

L. cymbalaria. See Cymbalaria muralis

L. Fantasy Hybrids. Annuals. Compact plants 1 ft. tall or less and 6–8 in. wide, with very narrow bluish green leaves. Clusters of small (½–1-in.) flowers in spring and summer. 'Fantasy Blue' has bright blue flowers with a touch of yellow in the throat. Other selections are available in magenta, pink, yellow, and white.

L. maroccana. BABY SNAPDRAGON, TOADFLAX. Annual. From Morocco. To 1½–2 ft. high, 6 in. wide. Summer flowers in red-and-gold, rose, pink, mauve, chamois, blue, violet, or purple, blotched with a different shade on the lip. Spur is longer than flower. Northern Lights strain offers shades of red, orange, and yellow as well as bicolors. Fairy Bouquet strain is only 9 in. tall and has larger flowers in pastel shades. For a showy display, sow seeds in quantity in early spring, after danger of frost is past. In Zones 10–13, sow in fall for winter bloom.

L. purpurea. Perennial. Zones 2–10, 14–24. From southern Europe. Narrow, bushy, erect growth to 2½–3 ft. high, 1 ft. wide. Blue-green foliage; violet-blue flowers from spring to late fall. 'Canon Went' is a pink form.

L. reticulata. Annual. From Portugal, North Africa. To 2–4 ft. tall, 10 in. wide, with very narrow bluish green leaves and showers of small purple-and-orange flowers in late spring and summer. 'Flamenco' (1–1½ ft. high) has yellow flowers with a conspicuous maroon blotch.

LINDEN. See TILIA

LINDERA

SPICEBUSH

Lauraceae

DECIDUOUS SHRUBS OR TREES

ZONES VARY BY SPECIES

FULL SUN OR PART SHADE

REGULAR WATER

Lindera obtusiloba

Spicebushes are grown principally for the beauty of their fall foliage; early spring clusters of small, greenish yellow flowers on leafless shoots are attractive but not conspicuous. On female plants, fruits will follow the blossoms if a male plant is nearby. Best used at woodland edge or as space fillers. Need good drainage; tolerate some drought. The common name refers to the spicy odor of the crushed leaves.

L. benzoin. Zones 2–6. Native to woodlands in eastern U.S. Reaches 6–12 ft. tall and broad. Light green leaves are 3–5 in. long, half as wide. Yellow fall color and plant form are best in full sun; if plants are grown in shade, foliage color isn't as pronounced and habit is loose and open. Fruits (noticeable after leaf fall) are bright red, to ½ in. long.

L. obtusiloba. JAPANESE SPICEBUSH. Zones 3b–6, 14–17. Native to Japan, China, Korea. To 10–20 ft. tall and a little narrower. Leaves are 5 in. long, 4 in. wide, occasionally lobed near the tip to give leaf a mitten shape. Fall color is an exceptionally brilliant yellow that develops even in shade and holds for 2 weeks or more. Small (¼-in.-wide) red fruits eventually turn black.

LINGONBERRY. See VACCINIUM vitis-idaea minus

LINNAEA borealis

TWINFLOWER

Caprifoliaceae

PERENNIAL

ZONES A1–A3; 1, 2, 4–6, 14–17

PARTIAL OR FULL SHADE

REGULAR WATER

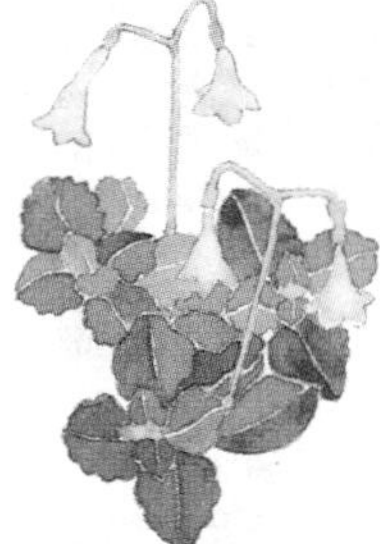

Linnaea borealis

Native to much of North America; in the West, found from Northern California to Alaska and Idaho. Delicate, flat mats of evergreen, 1-in., glossy green leaves spread to about 3 ft. by runners. Blooms in summer, carrying pairs of pale pink or rosy pink, fragrant, trumpet-shaped, ⅓-in.-long flowers on 3–4-in. stems. Collector's item or small-scale ground cover for woodland garden. Keep area around plants mulched with leaf mold to induce spreading. Tolerates sun in cool-summer climates.

LINUM

FLAX

Linaceae

PERENNIALS AND ANNUALS

ZONES VARY BY SPECIES

FULL SUN

MODERATE WATER

Linum perenne

Plants with erect, branching stems and narrow leaves produce an abundance of shallow-cupped, five-petaled flowers over a long bloom period. Each bloom lasts only a day, but others keep coming. The flax of commerce—*L. usitatissimum*—is grown for its fiber and seeds, which yield linseed oil.

Use in borders; some naturalize freely in uncultivated areas. Light, well-drained soil. Most perennial kinds live only 3 or 4 years and should be replaced regularly. Easy to grow from seed; perennials also can be propagated from cuttings. Difficult to divide.

L. flavum. GOLDEN FLAX. Perennial. Zones 2–24. From central and southern Europe. To 12–15 in. high, 1 ft. wide, with somewhat woody base. Grooved branches, green leaves. Spring and summer flowers are golden yellow, about 1 in. wide, carried in branched clusters. Often called yellow flax—a name correctly applied to the closely related *Reinwardtia indica.* 'Compactum' is just 6 in. high and wide.

L. grandiflorum. FLOWERING FLAX. Annual. Zones 1–24. From North Africa. To 1½–2½ ft. tall and 6–12 in. wide, with narrow gray-green leaves. Summer flowers are rose pink, 1–1½ in. wide. Sow seed thickly in place in early spring or (in mild-winter climates) in fall. Self-sows without becoming a pest and is often included in wildflower mixes. Two selections are far more common than the species: 'Rubrum', scarlet flax, with bright red flowers; and 'Bright Eyes', bearing white flowers with a brownish red eye.

L. narbonense. Perennial. Zones 3–24. Wiry-stemmed Mediterranean native to 2 ft. tall, 1½ ft. wide. Narrow blue-green leaves. Open clusters of 1¾-in., azure blue flowers with white eye; blooms in late spring and early summer. 'Six Hills' has rich sky blue blossoms.

L. perenne. PERENNIAL BLUE FLAX. Perennial. Zones 2–24. Native Europe to central Asia. Most vigorous blue-flowered flax, to 2 ft. tall, 1½ ft. wide. Stems are usually leafless on lower part. Profuse bloomer, producing branching clusters of light blue flowers that close in shade or late in the day. Blooms in late spring and summer. Self-sows freely.

LION'S TAIL. See LEONOTIS leonurus

LIPPIA citriodora. See ALOYSIA triphylla

LIPPIA repens. See PHYLA nodiflora

LIQUIDAMBAR

SWEET GUM

Hamamelidaceae

DECIDUOUS TREES

ZONES VARY BY SPECIES

FULL SUN

MODERATE TO REGULAR WATER

Liquidambar styraciflua

Valuable for form, foliage, fall color, easy culture. Moderate growth rate. Young and middle-aged trees are generally upright, somewhat cone shaped; older ones have a more spreading habit. Lobed, maplelike leaves. Flowers are inconspicuous; fruits are spiny balls that ornament trees in winter, must be raked up throughout the year.

Give neutral or slightly acid, well-amended garden soil; chlorosis in strongly alkaline soil is hard to correct (the reason why none of these trees is recommended for desert zones). Trees branch from the ground up and look most natural that way, but lower limbs can be removed to expose a definite trunk. To develop a strong central leader on young trees, pinch back side branches. Without proper training in youth, trees can develop weak branching pattern. Mature trees need little or no pruning.

Good street trees only if given a wide parking strip in which to grow: their surface roots can crack sidewalks, create a nuisance in lawns. Effective planted 6–10 ft. apart to form tall screens or groves. Brilliant fall foliage (color is less effective in mildest climates or in mild, late autumns).

L. formosana. CHINESE SWEET GUM. Zones 4–9, 14–24. Native to China. To 40–60 ft. tall, 25 ft. wide. Free-form outline; sometimes pyramidal, especially when young. Three- to five-lobed leaves are 3–4½ in. across, violet red when expanding, maturing to deep green. Fall color ranges from red in northern part of range to yellow beige in Southern California. Leaves drop late, usually in early winter. 'Afterglow' has lavender-purple new growth, rosy red fall color.

L. orientalis. ORIENTAL SWEET GUM. Zones 5–9, 14–24. Native to Turkey. To 20–30 ft. tall and wide. Leaves 2–3 in. wide, deeply five lobed, each lobe again lobed to give a lacy effect. Leafs out early after short dormant period. Fall color varies from deep gold and bright red in cooler areas to dull brown purple in coastal Southern California. Resistant to oak root fungus.

L. styraciflua. AMERICAN SWEET GUM. Zones 3–9, 14–24. Native to eastern U.S. To about 60 ft. tall in gardens; much taller in the wild. Narrow and erect in youth, with lower limbs eventually spreading to 20–25 ft. Tolerates damp soil; resists oak root fungus. Good looking all year. Branching pattern, furrowed bark, and corky wings on twigs all provide winter interest, as do hanging seedpods—1½-in., spiky spheres reminiscent of tiny medieval maces. On mature trees, seedpods are profuse enough to cause a litter problem (especially on lawns, where they interfere with mowing), and they're painful to walk on in bare feet.

Five- to seven-lobed, 3–7-in.-wide leaves are deep green in spring and summer, turning to purple, yellow, or red in fall. Even seedling trees usually give good fall color, though color may vary somewhat from year to year. To get desired and uniform color, purchase budded trees of a named variety, preferably while they are in fall leaf. Good selections include the following. (Note that 'Burgundy', 'Festival', and 'Palo Alto' were developed in California and color better there than in the Northwest.)

'Burgundy'. Deep purple-red fall color. Foliage hangs on late into winter—or even into early spring if storms are not heavy.

'Cherokee'. Produces very few or no seedpods. Fall color is burgundy red (yellow on trees grown in shade).

'Festival'. Narrow, columnar. Light green foliage turns a combination of yellow, peach, pink, orange, and red in fall.

'Golden Treasure'. Deep green leaves bordered in gold. In fall, gold rim lightens to pale yellow, then white; green center turns burgundy.

'Palo Alto'. Orange-red to bright red fall color.

'Rotundiloba'. Leaves have rounded rather than sharp-pointed lobes. Sets no seedpods. Fall color is yellow, red, burgundy, and purple.

'Variegata'. Green leaves with yellow streaks and splotches. In fall, the yellow variegation turns pink; green part of leaf becomes red.

'Worplesdon'. Narrow-lobed leaves turn orange red in fall.

LIRIODENDRON tulipifera

TULIP TREE

Magnoliaceae

DECIDUOUS TREE

ZONES 2–12, 14–24

FULL SUN

REGULAR WATER

Liriodendron tulipifera

Eastern U.S. native. Fast growth to 60–80 ft., with eventual spread to 40 ft.; considerably larger in the wild. Straight, columnar trunk, with spreading, rising branches that form a tall, pyramidal crown. The 5–6-in. leaves are unique; variously described as lyre shaped, saddle shaped, or truncated, they're like blunt-tipped maple leaves missing the end lobe. Foliage turns from bright yellow green to bright yellow in fall. (This is one of the best deciduous trees for Southern California, where it turns yellow most autumns.) Tulip-shaped, 2-in.-wide flowers in late spring are greenish yellow, orange at base; they are handsome at close range but not showy on the tree, since they are carried high up and well concealed by leaves. Trees usually do not bloom until they are 12 to 15 years old.

Thrives in deep, rich, well-drained, neutral to slightly acid soil. Give this tree plenty of room to grow; it makes a good large shade or lawn tree. Wide-spreading network of shallow, fleshy roots, however, makes it difficult to garden under. Control scale insects and aphids as necessary. Immune to oak root fungus.

Nurseries may carry two selections that are slower growing and somewhat smaller than the species. Columnar 'Arnold' ('Fastigiata') reaches about 10–15 ft. wide; it will bloom just 2 to 3 years after planting. 'Aureomarginatum' ('Majestic Beauty') has yellow-edged leaves.

LIRIOPE and OPHIOPOGON

LILY TURF

Liliaceae

PERENNIALS

ZONES VARY BY SPECIES

SOME SHADE IN HOTTEST CLIMATES

REGULAR WATER

SEE CHART

Liriope muscari

These two Asian plants are similar in appearance: both form clumps or tufts of evergreen grasslike leaves and bear summer flowers in spikelike or branched clusters. Blossoms come in white and various shades of purple and are quite showy in some species. Last well in flower arrangements. Use as casual ground cover in small areas. Also attractive as borders along paths, between flower bed and lawn, among rock groupings, or in rock gardens. Grow well along streams and around garden pools. They compete well with roots of other plants; try them under bamboo or to cover bare soil at bases of trees or shrubs (either in the ground or in large containers). None is satisfactory as mowed lawn. Tolerate indoor conditions.

Provide filtered sun to full shade; can take full sun in cool-summer regions. Plant in well-drained soil. Become ragged and brown with neglect. Cut back shaggy old foliage after new leaves appear. Plants don't need heavy feeding. Protect from snails and slugs. To increase, divide in early spring before new growth starts.

Plants look best from spring until cold winter weather arrives. Extended frosts may cause them to turn yellow; they take quite a while to recover. Can show tip burn on leaves if soil contains excess salts or if plants are kept too wet where drainage is poor.

LISIANTHUS. See EUSTOMA grandiflorum

LITCHI

LITCHI, LITCHI NUT

Sapindaceae

EVERGREEN TREE

ZONES 21–24; H1, H2

FULL SUN

REGULAR WATER

Litchi

From China and known botanically as *Litchi chinensis.* Slow-growing, round-topped tree to 20–40 ft. tall and wide. Leathery leaves are coppery red when new, maturing to dark green; each has three to nine 3–6-in.-long leaflets. Tiny cream-colored flowers bloom in late spring. Usually self-fruitful, though an individual tree may set more male flowers than female ones, reducing fruit production.

Allow fruit to ripen on the tree; when warty, brittle, easy-to-peel rind turns from green to red, fruit is ready to harvest. The smooth, white, edible portion inside looks somewhat like a grape but has a pit in the middle. The most desirable varieties have a small or shriveled seed known as a chicken tongue. Fruit of all types is sweet—juicy when fresh, raisinlike when dried. Varieties include small-pitted 'Groff', 'Kaimana' (the best variety for Hawaii), and 'Kwai Mi' ('Mauritius'). 'Sweet Cliff' has a small to medium-size seed; the slightly more acidic 'Brewster' has a large one.

Litchi needs a frost-free site, acid soil, moist atmosphere, light nitrogen fertilizer. Has fruited in a few coastal areas of Southern California; reliable in Hawaii.

FOR INFORMATION ON YOUR CLIMATE ZONE
PLEASE SEE PAGES 27–63

LITHOCARPUS densiflorus

TANBARK OAK

Fagaceae

EVERGREEN TREE

ZONES 4–7, 14–24

FULL SUN OR LIGHT SHADE

LITTLE OR NO WATER TO MODERATE WATER

Lithocarpus densiflorus

Native to Coast Ranges from southern Oregon to Santa Barbara, California. To 40–80 ft. tall, 30–50 ft. wide. Tree reaches taller end of height range under forest conditions; in the open, it is lower growing and broader, with the lower branches sometimes touching the ground. Leathery, 1½–4-in.-long, sharply toothed leaves are covered with whitish or yellowish wool when they expand, then mature to smooth green above, gray green beneath. Tiny, whitish male flowers in large, branched clusters bloom in summer, giving off an odd odor that some people find offensive. Acorns in burlike cups. As street or lawn tree, it resembles holly oak *(Quercus ilex)* but has lusher foliage. *L. d. echinoides* is a shrub 3–10 ft. tall and wide; its bluish leaves are smaller than those of the species and bear few or no teeth.

Sudden oak death syndrome, caused by a *Phytophthora* fungus, has been attacking tanbark oak trees as well as some oak species in northern and central coastal California, causing quick decline and death. For more information about this disease, see *Quercus*.

LITHODORA diffusa

Boraginaceae

PERENNIAL

ZONES 5–7, 14–17

LIGHT SHADE IN HOTTEST CLIMATES

MODERATE WATER

Lithodora diffusa

Native to southern and western Europe. Forms a prostrate, somewhat woody, slightly mounded mass 6–12 in. high, 3–4 ft. wide. Narrow evergreen leaves are ¾–1 in. long; both foliage and stems are hairy. In late spring (and often later), plant is sprinkled with brilliant blue, tubular, ½-in.-long flowers. Give loose, well-drained, lime-free soil. Use in rock gardens, spilling over walls, as small-scale ground cover. Best suited to mild-summer climates. 'Heavenly Blue' and 'Grace Ward' are the forms most commonly seen. The plant was formerly called *Lithospermum diffusum* or *L. prostratum.*

LITHOPS

STONEFACE

Aizoaceae

SUCCULENT PERENNIALS

ZONES 12, 13; OR INDOORS

FULL SUN; BRIGHT SUNNY WINDOW

LITTLE WATER

Lithops

Of the so-called living rocks or pebble plants of South Africa, these are among the best known. Shaped like inverted cones 2–4 in. high; tops resemble stones with a fissure across the middle. Colors include gray and gray green, often mottled with tan or brown. During bloom season, a single stemless flower emerges from the fissure; blossom resembles an ice plant flower and is typically yellow or white. New leaves also emerge from fissure. Many species are available, all of them interesting. Grow in pots of fast-draining soil mix. Can be grown outdoors year-round in the warmest desert regions. There, they bloom in winter and go dormant in summer. Indoors, they bloom in midsummer to midautumn and are dormant in winter. Give little water during the growing season, none during dormancy.

LIRIOPE and OPHIOPOGON

NAME	ZONES	GROWTH/FORM	LEAVES	FLOWERS	COMMENTS
Liriope muscari BIG BLUE LILY TURF	2b–10, 14–24; H1, H2	To 1–1½ ft. high and wide, with rather loose growth habit. Clump forming; does not spread by underground stems	Dark green; to 2 ft. long, ¾ in. wide	Profuse dark violet blooms in rather dense, 6–8-in., spikelike clusters on 5–12-in. stems; resemble grape hyacinth *(Muscari).* Flowers are held above leaves on young plants, partly hidden on older ones. Round, shiny black fruits follow flowers	'Lilac Beauty' differs only in having paler violet flowers. Many other varieties
L. m. 'Majestic'	2b–10, 14–24; H1, H2	Like *L. muscari,* but clump form is even more open	Like those of *L. muscari*	Clusters of dark violet blossoms on 8–10-in. stems look somewhat like cockscombs. Flowers show up well, held above leaves on young plants	Heavy blooming
L. m. 'Monroe's White'	2b–10, 14–24; H1, H2	Like *L. muscari*	Like those of *L. muscari*	White blossom spikes stand well above foliage	Prefers more shade than most types
L. m. 'Silvery Sunproof'	2b–10, 14–24; H1, H2	Like *L. muscari* in size. Open growth, with strongly vertical leaves that arch somewhat at tips	Foliage has gold stripes that turn white as leaves mature	Lilac blooms in spikelike clusters rise well above foliage	One of the best for full sun and for flower production. Leaves are whiter in sun, greener or yellower in shade
L. m. 'Variegata' (may be sold as **Ophiopogon jaburan 'Variegatus'**)	2b–10, 14–24; H1, H2	Like *L. muscari* but somewhat looser and softer	Foliage is green edged with yellow when young, turning solid dark green in its second season; to 1–1½ ft. long	Violet blooms in spikelike clusters held well above foliage	Best in partial shade. Sometimes sold as *L. exiliflora* 'Vittata'
L. spicata CREEPING LILY TURF	3–10, 14–24; H1, H2	Dense ground cover to 8–9 in. high, spreading at slow to moderate rate by rhizomes	Grows to 1½ ft. long, ¼ in. wide, deep green and grasslike. Softer and less upright than foliage of *L. muscari*	Pale lilac to white blooms in spikelike clusters; blossoms barely reach above leaves	Set plants 1 ft. apart. For best effect, mow annually in spring prior to new growth. Good ground cover for cold areas where *Ophiopogon japonicus* won't grow
L. s. 'Silver Dragon'	3–10, 14–24; H1, H2	Like *L. spicata* in size, but habit is sparser	Striped silvery white	Pale purple flowers on short spikes	Good ground cover in shade, but slower growing than *L. spicata*
Ophiopogon jaburan (often sold as **Liriope gigantea**)	5–9, 14–24; H1, H2	To 2–3 ft. tall, 1–1½ ft. wide. Clump forming; does not spread by underground stems	Dark green, somewhat curved, firm; 1½–3 ft. long, ½ in. wide	Small, chalk white flowers in nodding clusters that are partly hidden by leaves. Metallic violet-blue fruit	Plant produces fruit that is very attractive, good for cutting. 'Vittatus' (sometimes sold as *Liriope exiliflora* 'Vittata' or *L. muscari* 'Variegata') has leaves with lengthwise white stripes when young, later age to solid green. Grows best in part or full shade
O. japonicus MONDO GRASS	5–9, 14–24; H1, H2	Forms a dense clump to 6–8 in. high; plant spreads by underground stems, many of which are tuberlike. Slow to establish as ground cover	Dark green, 8–12 in. long, ⅛ in. wide	Light lilac flowers in short spikes that are usually hidden by leaves. Blue fruit	If plants look shabby, mow or shear before spring growth begins. Easy to divide; set divisions 6–8 in. apart. 'Kyoto Dwarf' and 'Nana' are half the size of species, spread more slowly
O. planiscapus 'Nigrescens' ('Arabicus')	5–9, 14–24; H1, H2	Tuft to 8 in. high, 1 ft. wide	Foliage grows to 14 in. long and ⅛–¼ in.wide. New leaves are green but soon turn black	White (sometimes flushed pink), in loose, spikelike clusters	Spreads slowly and does not make a solid cover. Interesting in containers. Valuable as a novelty

L

LITHOSPERMUM. See LITHODORA

LIVERLEAF. See HEPATICA

LIVINGSTONE DAISY. See DOROTHEANTHUS bellidiformis

LIVISTONA

Livistona australis

Arecaceae (Palmae)

PALMS

ZONES 13–17, 19–24; H1, H2

FULL SUN

REGULAR WATER, EXCEPT AS NOTED

These slow-growing fan palms somewhat resemble *Washingtonia* but generally have shorter, darker, shinier leaves. They are hardy to about 22°F/−6°C. All make good potted plants.

L. australis. From coastal forest of eastern Australia. To 40–50 ft. tall, 15 ft. wide. Has clean, slender trunk with interesting-looking leaf scars. Dark green leaves 3–5 ft. wide.

L. chinensis. CHINESE FOUNTAIN PALM. From Japan, Taiwan. Very slow growing; eventually to 40 ft. tall, 15 ft. wide. Roundish, bright green, 3–6-ft.-wide leaves droop strongly at outer edges.

L. decipiens. From northeastern Australia. To 30–40 ft. tall and 15 ft. wide in 20 years. Stiff, open head of leaves that are green on top, bluish beneath, 2–5 ft. across; leaves are carried on long, spiny stems.

L. mariae. From hot, dry interior Australia. To 10–15 ft. tall after many years (ultimately to as high as 80 or even 100 ft.), 15 ft. wide. Leaves 3–4 ft. wide. Young plants and those grown in containers have attractive reddish leaves and leaf stems. Little to moderate water.

LOBELIA

Campanulaceae (Lobeliaceae)

PERENNIALS AND ANNUALS

ZONES VARY BY SPECIES

EXPOSURE NEEDS VARY BY SPECIES

WATER NEEDS VARY BY SPECIES

MOST CONTAIN POISONOUS ALKALOIDS

Lobelia erinus

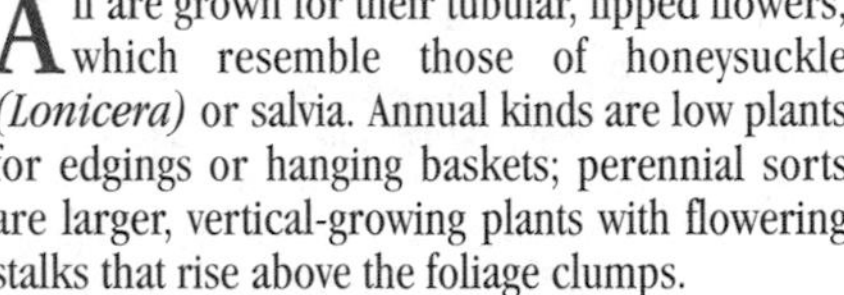

All are grown for their tubular, lipped flowers, which resemble those of honeysuckle *(Lonicera)* or salvia. Annual kinds are low plants for edgings or hanging baskets; perennial sorts are larger, vertical-growing plants with flowering stalks that rise above the foliage clumps.

L. cardinalis. CARDINAL FLOWER. Perennial. Zones 1–7, 14–17. Native to eastern U.S. and to a few sites in mountains of the Southwest. Erect, single-stemmed plant to 2–4 ft. high, 1 ft. wide. Sawtooth-edged leaves are set directly on the stems. Spikes of flame red, inch-long flowers in summer. A bog plant in nature, it needs rich soil and ample moisture throughout the growing season. Full sun or partial shade.

L. erinus. Annual. All zones. From South Africa. Popular and dependable edging plant to 3–6 in. high. Compact forms reach 5–9 in. wide; trailing types spread to 1½ ft. Leafy, branching stems with green or bronzy green foliage. Blooms from early summer to frost, bearing ¾-in.-wide flowers in light blue to violet (sometimes pink, reddish purple, or white) with white or yellowish throats. Lives over winter in mild climates. In mild-winter, hot-summer regions, grow it as a winter-to-spring annual. If started from seed sown in pots, takes about 2 months to reach planting-out size. Give rich soil, regular water. Self-sows where adapted. Can take full sun in cooler climates; needs some shade in warmer regions.

Compact types include 'Cambridge Blue', with pure, soft blue flowers and green leaves; and 'Crystal Palace', with rich deep blue blossoms and bronzy green leaves. Trailing kinds include the Cascade series, with carmine red, violet-blue, blue, pink, or white blooms, and 'Sapphire', with bright blue flowers; both are green leafed. Trailers are well suited to hanging baskets, wall plantings. They also make a graceful underplanting in containers, where the stems, loaded with flowers, can spill over the edges.

L. fulgens (L. splendens). Perennial. Zones 4–9, 14–24. Native to Mexico. Similar to *L. cardinalis* but with narrower leaves; both stems and leaves have deep red undertones. Give same growing conditions as *L. cardinalis.*

L. × gerardii. Perennial. Zones 2–9, 14–17. Group of summer-blooming hybrids between *L. cardinalis* and *L. siphilitica.* Most common is 4-ft. 'Vedrariensis', with coppery green foliage and bright purple flowers. 'Rosea', 2½ ft. tall, has rose pink flowers; 'Ruby Queen', 3 ft. tall, has ruby red blooms. All form clumps about 1 ft. wide. Provide rich soil, regular water, partial shade.

L. laxiflora. Perennial. Zones 7–9, 12–24. Native to Arizona, Mexico. To 3 ft. tall, 3–6 ft. wide. Erect stems set with narrow leaves grow from creeping underground rootstock, bear open clusters of tubular orange-red flowers over a long summer season. Withstands considerable aridity and neglect; often persists in abandoned gardens. Can be invasive. Little water. Full sun or partial shade.

L. siphilitica. Perennial. Zones 1–9, 14–17. Native to eastern U.S. Leafy plant to 2–3 ft. tall and 1 ft. wide. Blue flowers in summer. Ample water, partial shade.

L. × speciosa. Perennial. Zones 2–9, 14–17. Group of hybrids of uncertain ancestry. Can reach 5 ft. tall, 1 ft. wide; many combine red leaves and red flowers. Two 4–5-footers are 'Queen Victoria', with purple-red foliage and scarlet flowers; and 'Dark Crusader', with dark purple leaves and deep magenta flowers. Compliment series, to 2½ ft. high, has dark green leaves; blossoms may be scarlet, deep red, or blue purple. Ample water. Full sun or partial shade.

Lobeliaceae. See Campanulaceae

LOBIVIA, LOBIVOPSIS. See ECHINOPSIS

LOBSTER-CLAW. See HELICONIA

LOBULARIA maritima

Lobularia maritima
'Rosie O'Day'

SWEET ALYSSUM

Brassicaceae (Cruciferae)

ANNUAL

ALL ZONES

BEST IN SUN, TOLERATES LIGHT SHADE

REGULAR WATER

Mediterranean native. Low, branching, trailing plant to 1 ft. high and wide, with narrow or lance-shaped leaves ½–2 in. long. Crowded clusters of tiny, four-petaled white flowers with a sweet honey fragrance. In cold-winter regions, blooms from spring until frost; in mild climates, blooms all year from self-sown seedlings. Seeds are sometimes included in wildflower mixes or erosion-control mixes for bare or disturbed earth.

Easy, quick, dependable. Blooms from seed in 6 weeks; grows in almost any soil. Useful for carpeting, edging, bulb cover; temporary filler in rock garden or perennial border; between flagstones; in window boxes or containers. Flowers attract bees. If you shear plants halfway back 4 weeks after they come into bloom, new growth will make another crop of flowers, and plants won't become rangy.

Garden varieties are better known than the species. These varieties self-sow too, but seedlings tend to revert to taller, looser growth and bear smaller, paler blossoms than the parent. 'Carpet of Snow' (2–4 in. tall), 'Little Gem' (4–6 in.), and 'Tiny Tim' (3 in.) are good compact whites. 'Tetra Snowdrift' (1 ft.) has long stems, large white flowers. 'Rosie O'Day' (2–4 in.) and 'Pink Heather' (6 in.) have lavender pink blooms. 'Oriental Night' (4 in.) and 'Violet Queen' (5 in.) bear rich violet purple flowers.

LOCUST. See ROBINIA

LOGANBERRY. See BLACKBERRY

LOLIUM

RYEGRASS

Poaceae (Gramineae)

ANNUAL AND PERENNIAL GRASSES

ZONES VARY BY SPECIES

FULL SUN

REGULAR WATER

Lolium perenne

These European natives are clumping, not running, grasses. Not considered the choicest lawn grasses, but useful in special conditions and situations (lawns, pasture, soil reclamation). To make tight turf, sow heavily. Ryegrass is often mixed with other lawn grass species for low-cost, large-area coverage in cool-summer climates. In Bermuda grass country, it is often sown in fall on reconditioned Bermuda lawns to give winter green.

L. multiflorum. ANNUAL RYEGRASS, ITALIAN RYEGRASS. Annual. Zones 1–24. Larger, coarser than perennial ryegrass. Some plants live for several seasons in mild climates. Fast growing, deep rooted. Hybrid between *L. multiflorum* and *L. perenne* is common or domestic ryegrass, often used as winter cover on soil or winter-dormant lawns.

L. perenne. PERENNIAL RYEGRASS. Perennial. Zones A2, A3; 1–6, 15–17. Finer in texture than *L. multiflorum;* deep green with high gloss. Sprouts quickly and grows fast. Best in cool-summer climates. Has become the most popular lawn grass in the Northwest, west of the Cascades. 'Manhattan' is finer, more uniform. Other varieties are 'Pennfine', 'Derby', 'Yorktown', 'Loretta'. Mow at 2 in.

LONDON PRIDE. See SAXIFRAGA umbrosa

LONICERA

HONEYSUCKLE

Caprifoliaceae

EVERGREEN, SEMIEVERGREEN, DECIDUOUS SHRUBS AND VINES

ZONES VARY BY SPECIES

FULL SUN OR PARTIAL SHADE, EXCEPT AS NOTED

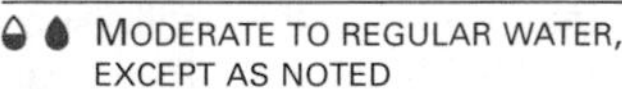

MODERATE TO REGULAR WATER, EXCEPT AS NOTED

Lonicera hildebrandiana

Most honeysuckles are valued for their clustered or paired, often fragrant flowers. Blossoms are tubular in form. Some have two flaring, unequal lips; others are trumpets or straight tubes, sometimes flaring at the mouth into five equal lobes. Flowers attract hummingbirds, and the red or purple berries that follow provide food for many other kinds of birds. Blossoms typically deepen in color after opening, so clusters contain both pale and darker blooms. Vining species climb by twining and need staking until they are tall enough to reach a trellis or other support. As they grow, they may need to be tied to the support here and there to distribute the branches well.

Provide good drainage. Honeysuckles typically need some thinning; ideal time for the job is after bloom. Cut old, straggling honeysuckles to the ground before spring growth begins; they will regrow rapidly. Generally free of serious pests, though aphids sometimes infest them.

L. × brownii. SCARLET TRUMPET HONEYSUCKLE. Deciduous vine. Zones A3; 1–7. Represented in nurseries by its superior selection 'Dropmore Scarlet', which climbs to 9–10 ft. Unscented, bright red flowers that look like trumpets bloom from late spring or early summer until frost. Pairs of triangular blue-green leaves to about 3 in. long appear to be joined at the bases.

L. caerulea edulis. SWEETBERRY HONEYSUCKLE. Deciduous shrub. Zones A1–A3; 1–3. Native to northern Europe and Asia. To 4–6 ft tall and 4–5 ft. wide, with pointed bright green leaves to 3 in. long. Small, unscented, pale yellow flowers are straight tubes ending in five equal lobes. Blooms in early spring. Edible, teardrop-shaped blue berries ripen in mid- to late spring; they resemble highbush blueberries but are not as sweet, though experimentation in Russia is producing improved varieties. Produce crops even north of the Arctic Circle. Early warm spells sometimes induce flowers to open before the last frost; they then suffer cold damage. For best fruiting, set at least two plants in a sunny location and keep soil moist. Watch to see if you need to protect berries from birds. For an ornamental hedge, space plants 3–4 ft. apart; for living snow fence, space 1½–2 ft. apart.

L. fragrantissima. WINTER HONEYSUCKLE. Deciduous shrub, semievergreen in mild-winter areas. Zones 1–9, 14–24. Native to China. Arching, rather stiff growth to about 8 ft. high and wide. Oval, 1–3-in.-long leaves are dull dark green above, blue green beneath. Creamy white, half-inch-long, two-lipped flowers from late winter to early spring; blossoms are richly fragrant (like *Daphne odora*) but not showy. Red berries. Can be used as a clipped hedge or background plant. Bring budded branches indoors for bloom.

Lonicera fragrantissima

L. × heckrottii. GOLDFLAME HONEYSUCKLE, CORAL HONEYSUCKLE. Deciduous or semievergreen vining shrub. Zones 2–24; H1, H2. Vigorous. To 12–15 ft. tall, with 2½-in., oval, blue-green leaves. Free blooming spring to frost. Clusters of coral pink buds open to 1½-in., slightly fragrant, two-lipped flowers that are bright coral pink outside and rich yellow within. Train as espalier or on wire along eaves.

L. hildebrandiana. GIANT BURMESE HONEYSUCKLE. Evergreen vine. Zones 9, 14–17, 19–24; H1, H2. Native to China. Fast-growing to 30 ft., with 4–6 in., oval, glossy dark green leaves on ropelike stems. Bears fragrant, 6–7-in., two-lipped, summer flowers that open white, then turn yellow to dull orange; blossoms slow to drop. May bear dark green berries. Thin out older stems occasionally and remove some of the growth that has bloomed. Striking along eaves, on arbor or wall. Needs sturdy support.

L. japonica. JAPANESE HONEYSUCKLE. Vine. Evergreen in mild-winter climates, semievergreen or deciduous in colder areas. Zones 1–24; H1, H2. Native to eastern Asia. Can reach 30 ft. Rampant (even invasive) plant that can become a weed, since birds spread the seeds; consider planting the similar but less aggressive *L. periclymenum.* Basic species has oval deep green leaves to 3 in. long and sweet-scented, two-lipped, purple-tinged white flowers from spring to fall.

Several varieties are grown, all better known than the species. Better behaved than *L. japonica* is 'Aureo-reticulata', goldnet honeysuckle, with leaves veined in yellow; variegation is especially strong in full sun. 'Halliana', Hall's honeysuckle, is the most vigorous and widely grown variety; it bears pure white flowers that age to yellow and attract bees. 'Purpurea' (probably same as *L. j. chinensis*) has leaves with purple-tinged undersides and flowers that are purplish red outside, white inside.

Of the above, 'Halliana' is the most commonly used as bank and ground cover and for erosion control in large areas; as ground cover, set plants 2–3 ft. apart. Unless curbed, it can become a weed, smothering less vigorous plants. Needs severe pruning once a year to prevent undergrowth from building up and becoming a fire hazard. Cut back almost to framework with hedge shears. Train as privacy or wind screen on chain link or wire fence. Takes dryness pretty well when established; tolerates poor drainage.

L. korolkowii floribunda 'Blue Velvet'. Deciduous shrub. Zones 1–9, 14–21. Native to central Asia. To 12 ft. tall and 8 ft. wide. Tidy-looking, rounded, 2-in. leaves are light blue when young, maturing to gray green. Showy, fragrant, two-lipped light pink flowers open in mid- to late spring and are followed by bright red berries. Does best in full sun but tolerates part shade. Little to moderate water. A choice plant for the high plains and intermountain zones of the West.

L. nitida. BOX HONEYSUCKLE. Evergreen shrub. Zones 4–9, 14–24; H1, H2. Native to southwestern China. To 11 ft. tall, 10 ft. wide. Branches densely clothed in tiny (½-in.), egg-shaped, shiny dark green leaves that may turn an attractive bronze to plum color in winter. Late spring or early summer flowers are straight tubes—fragrant, creamy white, ½ in. long. Translucent blue-purple berries. Grows fast and tends toward untidiness but is easily pruned as specimen plant or hedge. Tolerates salt spray. 'Baggesen's Gold', to 4–6 ft. high and wide, has foliage that is golden in sun (though very strong sun may burn leaves), chartreuse in shade. 'Maigrün', to 3 ft. high and 8 ft. wide, has leaves that are pale green when young, dark green when mature; it can be used as a tall ground cover.

L. periclymenum. WOODBINE. Evergreen or deciduous vine. Zones 1–24. Native to Europe and the Mediterranean region. Grows 10–20 ft. tall. Resembles *L. japonica* but is less rampant. Whorls of 2-in.-long, fragrant, two-lipped flowers in summer and fall. Blooms of 'Serotina' (also known as late Dutch honeysuckle) are purple outside, yellow inside. 'Berries Jubilee' has yellow flowers followed by a profusion of red berries. 'Belgica' (also called early Dutch honeysuckle) is less vining and more bushy than most, with abundant purple-flushed white flowers that fade to yellow and are followed by large red fruit. 'Graham Thomas' has white flowers aging to copper-tinted yellow.

L. pileata. PRIVET HONEYSUCKLE. Semievergreen shrub. Zones 3b–9, 14–24; H1. Native to China. To 2–3 ft. tall and 8 ft. wide. Low and spreading, with stiff, horizontal branches. Dark green, 1½-in. leaves like those of privet *(Ligustrum)*. Small, fragrant white flowers are shaped like straight tubes; they bloom in midspring and are followed by translucent violet berries. Good bank cover. Does well at the seashore. Give partial or full shade in hot climates.

L. sempervirens. TRUMPET HONEYSUCKLE. Evergreen in mild-winter climates, semievergreen or deciduous in colder areas. Zones 2–24. Native to eastern and southern U.S. Can climb 10–20 ft. tall but shrubby if not given support. Showy, unscented, trumpet-shaped flowers are 1½–2 in. long, orange-yellow to scarlet, carried in whorls at branch ends from late spring into summer. Scarlet fruit. Oval, ½–3-in.-long leaves are medium green above, bluish green beneath. 'Cedar Lane' is a vigorous selection with deep red flowers; *L. s. sulphurea* has yellow blooms. Forms with larger flowers may be sold as 'Magnifica' or 'Superba'. For hybrid 'Dropmore Scarlet', see *L. × brownii* (the latter is a hybrid between *L. sempervirens* and *L. hirsuta*).

Lonicera sempervirens

LOOSESTRIFE. See LYSIMACHIA punctata, LYTHRUM virgatum

LOPHOSPERMUM scandens. See ASARINA scandens

LOPHOSTEMON confertus (Tristania conferta)

BRISBANE BOX
Myrtaceae
EVERGREEN TREE
ZONES 15–17, 19–24; H1, H2
FULL SUN
LITTLE TO REGULAR WATER

Australian native somewhat resembling eucalyptus. Erect, moderate to fast growth to 30–45 ft. tall and 25 ft. wide. Trunk and limbs resemble those of madrone *(Arbutus menziesii)*, with reddish brown bark flaking off to reveal smooth, light-colored bark beneath. Oval, leathery bright green leaves are 4–6 in. long, tend to cluster at tips of branchlets; those of 'Variegata' are edged in a strikingly brilliant yellow. White to cream-colored, ¾-in. flowers in clusters of three to seven appear in summer, followed by woody capsules like those of eucalyptus. Takes almost any soil, but young plants get a better start with good soil; chlorosis can be a problem in poor soils. Pinch and prune to get more twiggy growth. Good street or lawn tree.

Lophostemon confertus

LOQUAT. See ERIOBOTRYA

LOROPETALUM chinense

Hamamelidaceae
EVERGREEN SHRUB
ZONES 6–9, 14–24; BORDERLINE IN ZONES 4, 5
PARTIAL SHADE IN HOTTEST CLIMATES
REGULAR WATER

Loropetalum chinense 'Razzleberri'

Native to China, Japan. To 6–10 ft. high and wide. Neat, compact habit, with tiers of arching or drooping branches. Roundish, light green, soft-textured leaves 1–2 in. long; throughout the year, the occasional leaf turns yellow or red, providing a nice touch of color. White to greenish flowers, each with four narrow, twisted, inch-long petals, appear in clusters of four to eight at branch tips. Flowering is heaviest in spring, but some bloom is likely at any time. Subtly beautiful plant; good in foreground, raised beds, woodland garden. Young plants can be grown in hanging baskets. Give rich, well-drained soil. Can take any amount of pruning. In Pacific Northwest, needs protection against hard freezes.

The following varieties all have purple foliage and pink to purple flowers and look much alike: 'Burgundy', 'Fire Dance', 'Pippa's Red', 'Razzleberri', 'Ruby', 'Sizzlin' Pink'. All are attractive, but the species makes a more striking show—white flowers contrast better with green foliage than pink blooms with purple leaves, especially in the shade.

LOTUS

Fabaceae (Leguminosae)
PERENNIALS
ZONES VARY BY SPECIES
FULL SUN OR PARTIAL SHADE
REGULAR WATER

Produces trailing stems that are often completely prostrate. Leaves are divided into leaflets. Flowers are sweet pea shaped, in shades of red to yellow. (For plants with the common name "lotus," see *Nelumbo*.)

Lotus maculatus 'Gold Flash'

L. berthelotii. PARROT'S BEAK. Zones 9, 15–24; H1. Woody-based perennial native to Canary Islands, Cape Verde Islands. To 8–12 in. high, with trailing, 2–3-ft.-long stems thickly covered with silvery gray leaves with three to five leaflets. Very narrow, 1-in., scarlet blossoms in summer. Space plants 2 ft. apart as ground cover; cut back occasionally to induce bushiness. Also very effective in hanging baskets or as cascader over wall or rocks. Dies back in cold weather; suffers root rot where drainage is poor. Not a long-lived plant in Southern California.

L. corniculatus. BIRD'S FOOT TREFOIL. Zones 2–24. From Europe, Asia. Herbaceous plant 6–12 in. high, with prostrate stems; forms a mat of dark green, cloverlike, three-leafleted leaves. Clusters of small yellow flowers in summer and fall. Seedpods at tops of flower stems spread into segments like a bird's foot, hence the common name. Use as ground cover or coarse lawn substitute; sow seeds or set out plants (if they are available). Mow occasionally. Goes dormant where winters are cold. Has become invasive in parts of the Northwest.

L. maculatus. Zones 9, 15–24. Canary Island native resembling *L. berthelotii*. To 8–12 in. high, 2–3 ft. wide. Known mainly through its selections. 'Gold Flash' has bright yellow flowers with striking orange-red markings; needs cool nights to set flower buds. 'New Gold Flash' (flower color similar to that of 'Gold Flash') and 'Amazon Sunset' (bright orange red) are similar in plant and flower form to 'Gold Flash', but they bloom better where nights remain warm.

LOVAGE. See LEVISTICUM officinale

LOVE-IN-A-MIST. See NIGELLA damascena

LOVE-LIES-BLEEDING. See AMARANTHUS caudatus

LUFFA. See GOURD

LUMA apiculata (Myrtus luma)

Myrtaceae

EVERGREEN SHRUB OR TREE

ZONES 14–24

FULL SUN

LITTLE TO REGULAR WATER

Luma apiculata

Native to Chile, Argentina. Fast grower to 6–8 ft. (possibly 20 ft.) tall and wide, densely foliaged in closely set, oval to roundish, dark green leaves ½–1 in. long. Like common myrtle *(Myrtus)* but is denser, deeper green. Old plants develop beautiful smooth bark the color of cinnamon. Blooms in late summer and early fall, with white to pinkish, four-petaled, about ½-in.-wide flowers with a central brush of stamens. Blue-black, ½-in. fruits are edible but not especially tasty.

LUNARIA annua

MONEY PLANT

Brassicaceae (Cruciferae)

BIENNIAL

ZONES 2–10, 14–24

AFTERNOON SHADE IN HOTTEST CLIMATES

LITTLE TO REGULAR WATER

Lunaria annua

Native to Europe. Old-fashioned garden plant grown for the translucent, 1¼-in.-wide circles that hang onto flower stalks; these "coins" are all that remains of the ripened seedpods after the outer coverings have dropped with seeds. Reaches 1½–3 ft. high, 1 ft. wide, with coarse, heart-shaped, tooth-edged leaves. Spring flowers resemble wild mustard blooms but are purple or white. Plant in an out-of-the-way spot in poor soil or in mixed flower bed where shining pods can be admired before they are picked for dried arrangements. Tough and persistent; can reseed and become weedy.

LUNGWORT. See PULMONARIA

LUPINUS

LUPINE

Fabaceae (Leguminosae)

ANNUALS, PERENNIALS, AND EVERGREEN SHRUBS

ZONES VARY BY SPECIES

FULL SUN

WATER NEEDS VARY BY SPECIES

Lupinus Russell hybrids

Leaves are divided into many leaflets that spread out like fingers of a hand. Sweet pea–shaped flowers are borne in dense spikes at ends of stems. There are hundreds of species, many of them native to the western U.S. and found in a wide range of habitats. The most commonly grown lupines are the Russell hybrids. Most lupines are not fussy about soil, though hybrids prefer rich, slightly acidic soil. All need good drainage. Except as noted, start plants from seed sown in fall, winter, or early spring. To hasten germination, soak seeds for a few hours before planting.

L. arboreus. Evergreen shrub. Zones 4, 5, 14–17, 22–24. Native to California coastal areas. To 5–8 ft. tall and wide. Spring flowers, in clusters 4–16 in. long, are usually yellow but may be lilac, bluish, white, or some mixture of those colors. Striking beach plant. Little or no water.

L. argenteus. SILVERSTEM LUPINE. Perennial. Zones 1–7. Native to Southwest, Sierra Nevada, Rocky Mountains. To 2 ft. high, 1 ft. wide, with silvery-haired stems and (usually) smooth leaves. Flowers variable in color—usually blue, sometimes lilac or white. Moderate to regular water.

L. hartwegii. Annual. Zones 1–24. Native to Mexico. To 1½–3 ft. tall, 1 ft. wide. Flowers in shades of blue, white, and pink. Sow seeds in place in spring for summer bloom. Moderate water.

L. hybrids. Perennials. Zones A1–A3; 1–7, 14–17. To 4–5 ft. tall, 2 ft. wide. These English-bred hybrid groups are descended from plants native to western America. Self-sown seedlings won't resemble parents. Regular water.

Russell hybrids—the classic lupines—bloom during late spring or early summer, bearing tall flower spikes in white, cream, yellow, pink, red, orange, blue, purple, or bicolors. Little Lulu and Minarette are small strains—to 1½ ft. high and wide. All Russell hybrids tend to be short lived. They are prone to powdery mildew; provide good air circulation. Grow from seed or buy nursery plants.

New Generation hybrids have all the merits of the Russell hybrids (from which they were developed) but are sturdier, needing no staking; longer lived, requiring replacement only after 7 or 8 years; and mildew resistant. They also come in a wider range of brighter, more intense colors, including interesting bicolors such as yellow-and-orange combinations. Bloom period is longer, too—from late spring to the end of summer, with possible autumn rebloom if plants are deadheaded regularly. Sold as seedling plants.

L. microcarpus densiflorus (L. densiflorus). Annual. Zones 3–24. California native to 1½–2 ft. high and wide, with white, yellow, pink, or lavender-tinged flowers in spikes to 1 ft. long. 'Ed Gedling', a selection of *L. densiflorus aureus,* is a choice form with bright yellow blossoms. Sow in fall for spring bloom. Good roadside decoration. Little or no water to moderate water.

L. nanus. SKY LUPINE. Annual. Zones 3–24. Native from California to British Columbia. To 8–24 in. high, 9–12 in. wide. Spring flowers in rich blue marked with white. Sow seeds in fall or winter; combine California poppies *(Eschscholzia)* with the lupines for contrast. Self-sows readily where it gets little competition. Excellent for barren banks. No irrigation needed except in desert zones.

L. polyphyllus. Perennial. Zones 3–7, 14–21. Native to moist places from California to British Columbia. Grows 1½–4 ft. tall, 2–2½ ft. wide. Blooms in summer, bearing blue, purple, or reddish flowers in clusters 6–24 in. long. One important ancestor of the Russell hybrids. Regular water.

L. succulentus. Annual. Zones 7–24. California native. To 3 ft. tall, 2½ ft. wide; lush and leafy, with 6-in. spikes of blue flowers in spring. Normally found in damp places but adapts to other locations; sometimes used to aid in erosion control. Moderate to ample water.

LYCHEE. See LITCHI

LYCHNIS

Caryophyllaceae

PERENNIALS, SOME TREATED AS ANNUALS

ZONES VARY BY SPECIES

FULL SUN OR LIGHT SHADE

WATER NEEDS VARY BY SPECIES

Lychnis coronaria

Old-fashioned garden flowers. All plants are very tolerant of adverse soils. The different kinds vary in appearance, but all of them offer eye-catching colors.

L. × arkwrightii. Short-lived perennial best treated as annual. Zones 3–9, 14–24. To 1½ ft. tall, 1 ft. wide, with brown-tinted dark green leaves. Clusters of 1½-in. orange-scarlet flowers. Regular water. ▸

L. chalcedonica. MALTESE CROSS. Perennial. Zones A1–A3; 1–10, 14–24. Native to Russia. Loose, open form. Grows to 2–3 ft. high, 1 ft. wide. Leaves and stems are hairy; scarlet, ½-in. flowers with deeply cut petals are borne in dense terminal clusters. Particularly effective in large borders alongside white-flowered or gray-foliaged plants. 'Alba' has white blossoms. Regular water.

L. coeli-rosa. See Silene coeli-rosa

L. coronaria. CROWN-PINK, DUSTY MILLER, MULLEIN PINK, ROSE CAMPION. Perennial. Zones 1–9, 14–24. From southeastern Europe. To 1½–2½ ft. tall, 1½ ft. wide, with attractive, silky white foliage and magenta to crimson flowers a little less than an inch across. Effective massed. 'Alba' produces white flowers; 'Angel's Blush' bears white blooms with a cherry red eye. All self-sow freely if faded blossoms are not removed. Moderate water.

L. flos-cuculi. RAGGED ROBIN. Perennial. Zones 1–7, 14–17. Alpine native to 2½ ft. tall and wide. Bluish green leaves; loose clusters of inch-wide, pale to deep pink or white flowers with fringed petals. Ample water.

L. viscaria 'Splendens'. Perennial. Zones 1–10, 14–24. Selection of a Eurasian native to 1 ft. high and wide. Forms a low, compact, evergreen clump of grasslike leaves to 5 in. long; stalks with clusters of ½-in.-wide, pink to rose blooms rise above the foliage clump. 'Splendens Flore Pleno' is a double-flowered selection. Good rock garden plant; flowers last well when cut. Regular water.

LYCIANTHES rantonnetii. See SOLANUM rantonnetii

LYCIUM

Solanaceae

DECIDUOUS SHRUBS

ZONES VARY BY SPECIES

FULL SUN

LITTLE OR NO WATER TO MODERATE WATER

Lycium fremontii

Though not particularly attractive, these shrubs are useful where climate or poor, infertile soil rules out less rugged plants. Most are spiny; all bear little bell-shaped to tubular blossoms that develop into small bright red or orange-red fruits that are attractive to birds. Tolerate heat; take any kind of soil as long as drainage is good. Need some water in hottest climates.

L. andersonii. WATERJACKET. Zones 2, 3, 7–13. Native from Southern California to Utah, New Mexico, northwestern Mexico. To 3–9 ft. tall and wide, with spiny branches and narrow, ½-in.-long green leaves. White flowers in late winter or early spring; orange-red fruit.

L. brevipes. Zones 7–9, 12–16, 18–24. From Southern California, Mexico. Spiny shrub with tangled branches. Grows 3–12 ft. tall and nearly as wide, with clustered grayish green leaves ¼–1 in. long. Best of the native Western lyciums for landscape use. White to pale lavender flowers in late winter or early spring; red fruit.

L. californicum. Zones 8, 9, 14–17, 19–24. Native from Southern California to Mexico. Intricately tangled, thorny shrub 1½–3 ft. tall, 1½–6 ft. wide, with pale gray bark and tiny (up to ⅜-in.-long), very narrow green leaves. Grayish lavender flowers in late winter or early spring followed by orange-red fruit.

L. chinense. MATRIMONY VINE, BOX THORN. Zones 3, 9, 14, 18–20. Native to China. Vinelike shrub with typically thornless branches to 12 ft. long. Creeps or sprawls unless supported; branches root where they touch ground. Diamond-shaped bright green leaves to 3 in. long. Purplish blue flowers in late spring and summer; orange-red to unshaded red fruit. Can be used as bank cover, clipped hedge. Thrives in poor soil. Can be invasive. There is some confusion in the nursery trade; some plants sold as *L. chinense* may actually be the similar *L. barbarum (L. halimiifolium)*.

L. fremontii. Zones 8–16, 18–24. From Southern California, Arizona, Nevada, Mexico. Dense, tangled, thorny growth to 3–9 ft. tall and wide, with grayish green leaves to 1 in. long. White to lavender flowers in winter; red fruit.

LYCORIS

SPIDER LILY

Amaryllidaceae

PERENNIALS FROM BULBS

ZONES VARY BY SPECIES; OR GROW IN POTS

FULL SUN

REGULAR WATER DURING GROWTH AND BLOOM

Lycoris radiata

Native to China, Japan. Narrow, strap-shaped leaves appear in fall (in mild-winter regions) or in spring; they remain green until some point in summer, then die down completely. Leafless flower stalks emerge after the foliage disappears. In late summer or early fall, each stalk bears a cluster of blooms with narrow, pointed petal-like segments and—in some species—projecting, spidery-looking stamens. Blossoms may be funnel shaped or have segments splayed outward or reflexed.

Grow in a sunny site that can stay dry during summer dormancy. (In areas of summer rainfall, grow in pots that can be protected from moisture.) Plant in late summer, setting bulbs in well-drained soil about 1 ft. apart. Keep tops of bulb necks at or just above soil surface—except in coldest part of range, where tops of necks should be just under surface. Water regularly while plants are growing and again when flower stalks emerge. It's best to withhold water and let soil go dry in summer when foliage begins to wither, though plants can take some summer water if drainage is excellent. Disturb clumps (after bloom) only when you want to move them or divide them to increase a planting. Beyond hardiness range, grow spider lilies in containers and overwinter them indoors.

L. aurea. GOLDEN SPIDER LILY. Zones 16, 17, 19–24; H1. Bright yellow, 3-in. flowers on 2-ft. stems. Slightly protruding stamens.

L. radiata. Zones 4–9, 12–24; H1. Best known and easiest to grow. Stems 1½ ft. tall bear 1½–2-in., coral red flowers with a golden sheen; stamens are very prominent. 'Alba' has white flowers.

L. sanguinea. Zones 4–24. To 2 ft. tall, with 2½-in., bright red to orange-red blooms. Stamens do not protrude.

L. sprengeri. Zones 4–24. Similar to *L. squamigera,* but with slightly smaller flowers in a more purplish pink.

L. squamigera (Amaryllis hallii). Zones 2–24. Fragrant, lilac pink, 3-in. blossoms on 2-ft. stems resemble those of belladonna lily *(Amaryllis belladonna)*. Stamens do not protrude.

LYME GRASS. See LEYMUS

LYONOTHAMNUS floribundus

CATALINA IRONWOOD

Rosaceae

EVERGREEN TREE

ZONES 14–17, 19–24

FULL SUN

MODERATE WATER

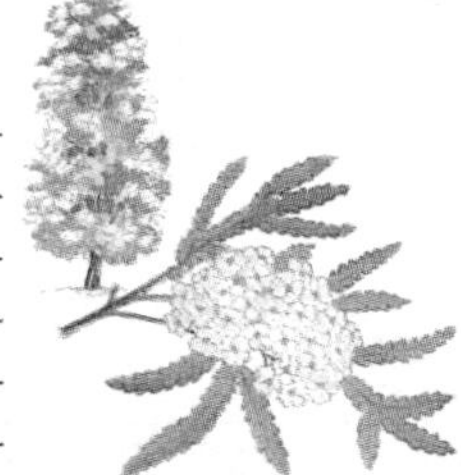
Lyonothamnus floribundus asplenifolius

Native to Channel Islands off coast of Southern California. The species has lobed or scallop-edged leaves that are not divided into leaflets; it is seldom seen in cultivation. Much better known is *L. f. asplenifolius,* fernleaf Catalina ironwood. It grows at a moderate rate to 20–35 ft. high, 15 ft. wide. Red-brown bark peels off in long, thin strips; young twigs are often reddish. Leaves are 4–6 in. long, deep green above, gray and hairy beneath, divided into three to seven deeply notched or lobed leaflets. Blooms in late spring or early summer, bearing small white blossoms in flat, 8–18-in.-wide clusters that contrast well with the dark foliage. Old clusters turn brown; if it is practical to do so, cut them off.

Needs excellent drainage and should be pruned in winter to shape and control growth. Sometimes suffers from chlorosis in heavy soils. Easiest to grow near coast. Handsome in groves.

LYSILOMA microphylla thornberi (L. thornberi)

FEATHER BUSH, FERN-OF-THE-DESERT

Fabaceae (Leguminosae)

EVERGREEN OR DECIDUOUS SHRUB OR TREE

ZONES 12–24; H1, H2

FULL SUN

NO IRRIGATION NEEDED

Lysiloma microphylla thornberi

Native to foothills of Arizona's Rincon Mountains. To 12–15 ft. tall and about as wide, with multiple stems and a broad canopy of finely cut bright green leaves somewhat like those of acacia. Blooms in late spring or early summer, bearing masses of ½–1-in.-wide, creamy white, clustered flowers like little puffballs emerging from round buds. These are followed by flat, ridged brown seedpods 4–8 in. long. Good informal background shrub, patio tree (can be trained to a single stem), or transition plant between garden and desert. To accentuate plant's filmy look, thin out crowded and weak branches in center. Evergreen in frost-free areas; deciduous elsewhere. May be killed to the ground by heavy frosts but usually comes back from the roots.

LYSIMACHIA

Primulaceae

PERENNIALS

ZONES VARY BY SPECIES

FULL SUN OR PARTIAL SHADE

MODERATE TO REGULAR WATER

Lysimachia nummularia

Most are vigorous perennials capable of spreading beyond their allotted space, especially if they receive plenty of water. Police them to be sure they don't invade choicer plantings. Useful for naturalizing at woodland edges or in barely maintained areas. Blossoms are yellow or white; except as noted, they appear in summer.

L. barystachys. Zones 3b–9, 14–21. Native to eastern Russia and Asia. To 2 ft. high, 1½ ft. wide, with narrow green leaves to 3 in. long. Small white flowers in foot-long spikes that start out horizontal and gradually turn upright.

L. ciliata. Zones 1–9, 14–21. Native to northeastern U.S. Erect clump to 4 ft. tall, 2 ft. wide, with narrow green leaves to 6 in. long. Nodding, 1-in., yellow flowers with red-brown centers appear singly or in loose clusters in upper leaf joints. 'Atropurpurea' ('Firecracker') is similar but has reddish leaves.

L. clethroides. GOOSENECK LOOSESTRIFE. Zones A2, A3; 1–9, 14–24. Native to China, Korea, Japan. To 3 ft. tall, quickly spreading as wide or wider. Erect stems are clothed with pointed olive green leaves to 5 in. long. Flower spikes densely packed with tiny white blossoms are 6–8 in. long, arched like a goose's neck.

L. congestiflora. GOLDEN GLOBES. Zones 8, 9, 14–24; H1, H2. Native to China. Mat-forming plant grows to 4 in. high and 1 ft. or wider. Oval green leaves to 2 in. long. Upturned yellow flowers, ½ in. across, grow in leafy terminal clusters. Plant blooms from spring to summer. 'Outback Sunset' produces red-tinged leaves with yellow variegation and bears yellow flowers with red centers.

L. ephemerum. Zones 2b–10, 14–24. Native to southwestern Europe. Leathery gray-green leaves to 6 in. long form a neat clump to 3 ft. tall and 1 ft. wide. Slender clusters of white, ½-in.-wide, long-lasting flowers. Not invasive.

L. nummularia. CREEPING JENNY, MONEYWORT. Zones 1–9, 14–24. Native to Europe; naturalized in eastern North America. To 4–8 in. high, spreading 2 ft. or more, rooting as it goes. Forms attractive mat of roundish, light green, 1-in. leaves. Yellow flowers about 1 in. across appear singly in leaf joints. Best use is in corners or containers where it need not be restrained. Will spill from wall, hanging basket. 'Aurea' has bright yellow leaves; needs shade.

L. punctata. LOOSESTRIFE. Zones 1–9, 14–24. Native to central Europe, Asia Minor. To 3 ft. tall, spreading to 2 ft. or more by underground stems. Narrow green leaves to 3 in. long are borne in whorls on erect stems; inch-wide yellow flowers, also in whorls, appear on top third of stems.

Lythraceae. The loosestrife family is represented by such diverse plants as crape myrtle *(Lagerstroemia)*, purple loosestrife *(Lythrum)*, and *Cuphea*. *Lysimachia punctata*, also commonly called loosestrife, belongs to the primrose family (Primulaceae).

LYTHRUM virgatum

PURPLE LOOSESTRIFE

Lythraceae

PERENNIAL

ZONES 1–9, 14–24

FULL SUN

REGULAR WATER

Lythrum virgatum

Native to Europe, Asia. Showy plant for pond margins, but often escapes its boundaries by freely self-sowing. Has naturalized in many areas, displacing native vegetation; wild populations have clogged waterways in parts of the Northwest and the mountain states. Foliage clumps to 2 ft. wide send up 2½–5-ft.-high stems—the lower portions clothed with narrow leaves, the upper parts densely set with ¾-in., magenta flowers in late summer and fall. Hybrids (often sold as varieties of *L. salicaria*, a similar plant) include 'Morden Gleam', 'Morden Pink', 'Pink Spires', 'Roseum Superbum', and 'Rosy Spires'. They are not self-fertile, but they cross-pollinate with other lythrums and become a nuisance. Planting purple loosestrife and its variants is forbidden in some places and unwise wherever the plants will have reliable moisture through much of the year.

MAACKIA

Fabaceae (Leguminosae)

DECIDUOUS TREES

ZONES 1–10, 14–17

FULL SUN

REGULAR WATER

Maackia amurensis

Related to locust *(Robinia)* and yellow wood *(Cladrastis)*, maackias are small to medium-size trees with leaves divided like feathers into many small, narrow leaflets. They grow at a slow to moderate rate. Summer flowers resemble small sweet peas; creamy to yellowish white, crowded into erect, 4–6-in.-long, spikelike clusters. Flat, 2–3-in.-long seedpods follow the blossoms. Plants are not fussy about soil. Need minimal pruning.

M. amurensis. AMUR MAACKIA. Native to Manchuria, Siberia. Possibly to 60 ft. tall and wide but unlikely to exceed 30 ft. in gardens. Broad, rounded head; dark green leaves. Bark on trunk is an attractive bronze color and peels in curling flakes. *M. a. buergeri* differs only in that its leaves have fuzzy undersides.

M. chinensis. CHINESE MAACKIA. Chinese native reaches 20–30 ft. high and wide. Shrubbier than *M. amurensis*, with leaves divided into more and smaller leaflets. Foliage unfolds silvery grayish green, matures to dark green.

FOR GROWING SYMBOL EXPLANATIONS
PLEASE SEE PAGE 161

MACADAMIA

Proteaceae

EVERGREEN TREES

ZONES 9, 16, 17, 19–24; H1, H2

FULL SUN

REGULAR WATER

Macadamia tetraphylla

Native to Australia. Clean, handsome ornamental trees where frosts are light. Where best adapted (Zones 23, 24, H1, H2), produce clusters of delicious hard-shelled nuts, usually within 3 to 5 years after planting.

Set out macadamias from containers any time of year, but they'll suffer less stress from moisture loss and heat if planted in fall. Avoid windy sites. Perform best in deep, rich soil, with light applications of fertilizer at least twice a year. Trees are weak wooded, so prune young plants to encourage strong structure. New growth that emerges during winter is usually yellow; this is caused by cold, not health problems. Later growth will be green. Macadamias are resistant to oak root fungus.

Though most macadamias are sold under the name *M. ternifolia,* any tree you buy will nearly always be one of the two species (or their hybrids) described below. Trees grow 30–40 ft. tall and almost as wide, with whorls of glossy, leathery, 5–12-in.-long leaves; mature foliage is durable and attractive in arrangements. Look for grafted, named varieties of proven nut-bearing ability. Seedlings take longer to bear nuts, and their quality is unpredictable. Macadamias are self-fruitful, but planting two different varieties often produces bigger harvests. Trees bloom in winter and spring, bearing small, sometimes fragrant white to pink flowers in dense, pendent, 1-ft. clusters. Roundish fruit to 1½ in. wide consists of a leathery husk containing a hard-shelled nut. To harvest nuts, pick them up as they fall from tree (husks of ripe nuts split, making the nuts easy to remove).

M. hybrids. Crosses between *M. integrifolia* and *M. tetraphylla.* 'Beaumont' is one of the best varieties for Southern California, bearing over a very long period. It produces medium to large nuts with moderately thick shells; new leaves are reddish. 'Cooper' has small nuts, also with moderately thick shells. 'Vista' has small to medium-size, very thin-shelled nuts.

M. integrifolia. SMOOTH-SHELL MACADAMIA. Commercial species best adapted to Hawaii. Can be grown near the coast in Southern California. Leaves are smooth edged. Nuts ripen from late fall to late spring. Popular varieties include 'Kakea', 'Kau', 'Keaau', 'Mauka', and 'Purvis'.

M. tetraphylla. ROUGH-SHELL MACADAMIA. More widely grown than *M. integrifolia* in California, where it performs best slightly inland. Differs from *M. integrifolia* in having a more open growth habit, spiny leaves, and thinner-shelled nuts that ripen from fall to midwinter. Varieties include 'Burdick', 'Cate', and 'Fenton'.

MACFADYENA unguis-cati

CAT'S CLAW, YELLOW TRUMPET VINE

Bignoniaceae

EVERGREEN OR DECIDUOUS VINE

ZONES 8–24; H1, H2

FULL SUN OR PARTIAL SHADE

MODERATE WATER

Macfadyena unguis-cati

Vigorous vine formerly known as *Doxantha unguis-cati.* Climbs high (to 25–40 ft.) and fast by hooked, clawlike, forked tendrils. Each leaf consists of two oval, glossy light green leaflets to 2 in. long; a tendril is centered between them. Blooms in early spring, bearing lobed yellow trumpets to 2 in. long, 4 in. across.

Succeeds in cool-summer areas but is faster growing and stronger where summers are hot—even on south walls in Zones 12, 13. Can climb any surface that isn't slick, including stone, wood, chain link fences, tree trunks; vines are even seen clinging to undersides of freeway overpasses. Tends to produce leaves and flowers at stem ends; after bloom, cut back some stems nearly to the ground to stimulate new growth lower down. During growing season, pinch back vigorous shoots as needed. Can be used as a ground cover; it puts down roots where stems touch the ground, making it a good choice for erosion control on slopes. Evergreen where frosts are light or absent; partially to almost completely deciduous in colder areas.

MACHAERANTHERA tanacetifolia

TAHOKA DAISY, PRAIRIE ASTER

Asteraceae (Compositae)

ANNUAL OR BIENNIAL

ZONES 1–24

FULL SUN

LITTLE TO REGULAR WATER

Machaeranthera tanacetifolia

Native to much of central and western North America—from Alberta south to Texas and Mexico, west to California. Much-branched plant to 1–1½ ft. high and wide, with finely divided bright green leaves. Blooms in late spring and summer, bearing 2-in., yellow-eyed, lavender-blue daisies; each blossom is carried on its own inch-long stalk just above the foliage clump. Sow seeds in fall or early spring in well-drained soil. Tolerates drought but performs better with some moisture.

MACHILUS thunbergii. See PERSEA thunbergii

MACKAYA bella

Acanthaceae

EVERGREEN SHRUB

ZONES 15–24

PARTIAL OR FULL SHADE

MODERATE TO REGULAR WATER

Mackaya bella

From South Africa. Grows 4–5 ft. high and wide, sometimes much taller, with glossy dark green leaves to 5 in. long. From spring into early summer, produces loose, 9–10-in.-long clusters of trumpet-shaped, 2-in.-long flowers with flaring lobes; blossoms are lavender with deep purple lines in the throat. Give well-drained soil. Minimal pruning needed.

MACLEAYA

PLUME POPPY

Papaveraceae

PERENNIALS

ZONES VARY BY SPECIES

LIGHT SHADE IN HOTTEST CLIMATES

REGULAR WATER

Macleaya microcarpa

These tall perennials from China and Japan are often still listed under *Bocconia,* a name properly belonging to their shrubby tropical relatives. Tall, branching stems carry clouds of tiny flowers. Leaves are large and deeply lobed. Plants look tropical, and their garden value lies in size and structure rather than floral impact. Spread by creeping rhizomes and can be invasive if not controlled; plant them among sturdy shrubs rather than among delicate perennials.

M. cordata. Zones A2, A3; 1–24. To 7–8 ft. tall and 3 ft. wide, with grayish green, 10-in. leaves. White to beige flowers. Considered less invasive than *M. microcarpa.*

M. microcarpa. Zones 2b–24. Similar to *M. cordata* but has pinkish beige flowers. Blossoms of 'Coral Plume' are more decidedly pink.

MACLURA pomifera

OSAGE ORANGE
Moraceae
DECIDUOUS TREE
ZONES 2, 3, 10–13
FULL SUN
LITTLE OR NO WATER TO REGULAR WATER

Maclura pomifera

Native from Arkansas to Oklahoma and Texas. Fast growth to 60 ft. tall and 40 ft. wide (though often less), with spreading, open habit. Young branches are thornier than mature ones. Wood is orange in color and very hard. Glossy medium green leaves to 5 in. long. If a male plant is present, female plants may bear 4-in.-wide, inedible fruits (so-called hedge-apples) that look like bumpy yellow-green oranges. 'Whiteshield' and 'Wichita' are thornless male selections.

Withstands heat, cold, wind, poor soil, moderate alkalinity, and wet or dry conditions. Immune to oak root fungus. Easily propagated from seed, stem cuttings, or root cuttings; easy to transplant. Useful as big, tough, rough-looking tall hedge or background plant. Prune to any size from 6 ft. up; pruned high, becomes a shade tree.

MADAGASCAR JASMINE. See STEPHANOTIS floribunda

MADAGASCAR PALM. See PACHYPODIUM lamerei

MADAGASCAR PERIWINKLE. See CATHARANTHUS roseus

MADRONE, MADRONA. See ARBUTUS menziesii

MAGELLAN WHEATGRASS. See ELYMUS magellanicus

MAGNOLIA

Magnoliaceae
DECIDUOUS AND EVERGREEN TREES AND SHRUBS
ZONES VARY BY SPECIES
FULL SUN OR PARTIAL SHADE
REGULAR WATER
SEE CHART NEXT PAGE

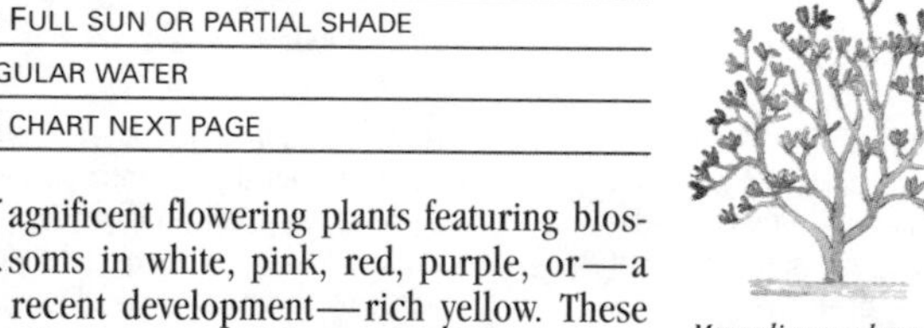

Magnolia × soulangeana

Magnificent flowering plants featuring blossoms in white, pink, red, purple, or—a more recent development—rich yellow. These plants show a remarkable variety of leaf shapes and plant forms. The following text classifies magnolias by general type; the chart lists them alphabetically. New varieties and hybrids appear every year, but distribution is spotty in local nurseries. Many more kinds are available from mail-order specialists.

MAGNOLIA TYPES

Magnolias include both evergreen and deciduous types. Most have large, striking blossoms composed of petal-like segments, but a few are grown for use as foliage plants.

Evergreen magnolias. To gardeners in California and Arizona, "magnolia" usually means *M. grandiflora,* the classic Southern magnolia with glossy leaves and big, fragrant white blossoms. Loved for its foliage and flowers, it also offers the advantages of heat resistance and tolerance for damp soil. On the other hand, it requires a fair amount of maintenance and has limited uses. It's messy, shedding its big, hard leaves (they look almost like plastic) and other litter constantly from late spring into earliest autumn. And though it's generally considered a street or lawn tree, it tends to lift paved walks with its surface roots, and it casts dense, year-round shade that prevents the growth of a healthy lawn beneath. Furthermore, it is slow growing in heavy soil or where root area is restricted. Before planting this tree, carefully consider whether its advantages outweigh its drawbacks. Other evergreen options are *M. delavayi* and *M. virginiana.*

Magnolia grandiflora

Deciduous magnolias with saucer flowers. This group includes saucer magnolia *(M. × soulangeana)* and its many varieties, often called tulip trees because of the shape and bright colors of their flowers. Also included here are yulan magnolia *(M. denudata)* and lily magnolia *(M. liliiflora)*. All are hardy to cold, thriving in various climates throughout the West—but early flowers of all forms are subject to frost damage, and all do poorly in hot, dry, windy areas. Related to these, but more tender to cold (and heat), are the big, spectacular Oriental magnolias from western China and the Himalayas—*M. campbellii, M. dawsoniana, M. sargentiana robusta, M. sprengeri* 'Diva'. Their early flowers are also subject to frost and storm damage.

Deciduous magnolias with star flowers. Included in this group are *M. kobus, M. stellata* and its varieties (the star magnolias), and *M. salicifolia.* All are hardy, slow-growing, early-blooming plants with wide climatic adaptability.

Other magnolias. Less widely planted is a group of magnolias generally considered foliage plants or shade trees; they bloom as leaves appear or after they unfurl. Among them are *M. hypoleuca,* a big tree with large leaves and large (but not especially noticeable) flowers; and *M. fraseri* and *M. macrophylla,* medium-size trees with huge leaves and blooms. *M. acuminata* is a big shade tree with inconspicuous greenish yellow flowers; the similar *M. a. subcordata* is a smaller tree with slightly showier blossoms. Hybrids of the latter are grown for their flowers, which show better yellow color than their parent. Blossoms of some of these hybrids appear on bare branches; others bloom as leaves emerge. *M. sieboldii* and *M. wilsonii* constitute another flowering category; they bear drooping, cup-shaped, fragrant white blossoms after leafout.

MAGNOLIA CULTURE

For any magnolia, choose planting site carefully—virtually all these trees are hard to move once established. Magnolias never look their best when crowded. Larger deciduous types are most effective standing alone against a background that will display their flowers and, in winter, their strongly patterned, typically gray limbs and big, fuzzy flower buds. Smaller deciduous magnolias show up well in large flower or shrub borders and make choice ornaments in Japanese gardens. All magnolias may be used as lawn trees; try to provide a good-size grass-free area around the trunk, and don't plant under the tree. In frost-prone areas, plant early-flowering magnolias in a northern exposure to delay bloom as long as possible and lessen frost damage.

Balled-and-burlapped plants are available in late winter and early spring; container plants are sold any time. Do not set plants lower than their original soil level. In windy locations, stake single-trunked or very heavy plants to keep them from rocking to and fro—the movement would tear the thick, fleshy, sensitive roots. Soggy soil can topple newly planted large magnolias, so stake big specimens if planting them just before the rainy season; to avoid damaging roots, set stakes in planting hole before placing tree. Remove stakes as soon as the tree is firmly rooted.

Magnolias are generally not bothered by pests or diseases. Watch for scale and aphids at any time and for spider mites in hot weather. Protect lower leaves of shrubby types from snails and slugs. Magnolias are not immune to oak root fungus, but they seem somewhat resistant.

More troublesome are problems caused by nutrient deficiencies. (Also see What Magnolias Need, page 455.) Chlorosis from lack of iron in alkaline soils shows up as yellowing between leaf veins; iron chelates will correct this condition. Fertilizer will remedy nitrogen deficiency. Feed trees if new growth is sparse and weak, or if the tree shows a fair amount of dieback despite adequate watering and drainage. Use a slow-release product, since magnolias are very susceptible to salt damage from overfertilizing, resulting in burned leaf edges. The same leaf damage can result

▶ page 455

MAGNOLIA

NAME	ZONES	TYPE	HEIGHT	SPREAD	AGE AT BLOOM	FLOWERS	USES, CHARACTERISTICS, COMMENTS
Magnolia acuminata CUCUMBER TREE	2–9, 14–21	Decid-uous	60–80 ft.	30 ft.	12 yrs.	Greenish yellow, to 3½ in. wide; not conspicuous. Appear after leaves in late spring, summer. Handsome reddish seed capsules with red seeds	Shade or lawn tree. Canopy of glossy, 5–9-in. leaves provides dense shade. Hardy to cold; dislikes hot, dry winds
M. a. subcordata (M. cordata) YELLOW CUCUMBER TREE, YELLOW MAGNOLIA	4–9, 14–21	Decid-uous	25–35 ft.	20–35 ft.	12 yrs.	Yellow to yellow-green flowers larger than those of species (to 4 in.); appear as leaves start to expand. Mild lemon scent	Slow-growing lawn or border tree. Showier, lower, and shrubbier than *M. acuminata.* Not ordinarily a tree you can walk or sit under. 'Miss Honeybee' is a selection with larger, pale yellow flowers
M. 'Apollo'	4–9, 14–24	Decid-uous	To 35 ft.	18–20 ft.	2 yrs. from grafts	Abundant, fragrant, star-shaped flowers to 10 in. across. Blooms in early to midspring, before leaf-out. First blossoms to open are deep violet outside, paler inside; later ones are deep rose pink	Smallish, round-headed tree
M. 'Butterflies'	2b–9, 14–24	Decid-uous	To 20 ft.	To 15 ft.	2 yrs. from grafts	Produces many 4–5-in., light yellow flowers with red stamens. Blooms in midspring, before leaves emerge	Hybrid of *M. acuminata* and *M. denudata.* Upright and pyramidal when young; later spreading. Leaves 8 in. long, medium to dark green, sparsely hairy. Hardy to –29°F/–34°C without injury
M. campbellii	4–9, 14–21 (best in 15–17)	Decid-uous	60–80 ft.	To 40 ft.	20 yrs.; grafts bloom younger, at 4–5 yrs.	Magnificent 6–10-in., bowl-shaped blooms in crimson to rose pink, with central segments cupped over rose-colored stamens. Late winter to spring, before leaves emerge	Plant in lee of evergreens to protect flowers from strong winds. Make it focus of garden and give it room. 'Alba', 'Strybing White' are white forms; 'Hendricks Park', 'Late Pink' are good pinks. 'Charles Raffill' has very large bright pink flowers with white interior
M. dawsoniana DAWSON MAGNOLIA	4–9, 14–21	Decid-uous	40–50 ft.	25–30 ft.	10 yrs. from grafts	Large (8–10-in.), faintly scented white blossoms with rose shading. Narrow, slightly pendulous segments. Profuse early bloom	Good choice for big gardens. Puts on a magnificent show; a little untidy close up. Very dark green leaves. Quite cold hardy when established; needs hardening off in fall. Blooms of 'Chyverton' are deep pink, lighter at tips and within
M. delavayi	7–9, 14–21	Ever-green	20–30 ft.	To 20 ft.	4–5 yrs.	Dull creamy white, 6–8 in. wide. Fragrant, short lived; shatter day they open. Long summer bloom	Foliage is the feature: leaves are 8–14 in. long, 5–8 in. wide, stiff, leathery, gray green, tropical looking. Use as single tree or giant shrub in lawn or large corner. Hard to train as single-stemmed tree
M. denudata (M. conspicua, M. heptapeta) YULAN MAGNOLIA	3b–9, 14–24	Decid-uous	To 35 ft.	To 30 ft.	6–7 yrs.	Fragrant white flowers, some-times tinged purple at base. Blossoms are erect; somewhat tulip shaped, 3–4 in. long, spreading to 6–7 in. Early bloom on base branches; often a few flowers appear in summer	Tends toward irregular form; good in informal garden or at woodland edge. Choose a site where it can be shown off against dark background or sky. Leaves 4–7 in. long. Does well in Southern California
M. 'Elizabeth'	3b–9, 14–24	Decid-uous	To 40 ft. or more	To 20 ft.	2–6 yrs. from grafts	Fragrant soft yellow flowers, 6–7 in. wide. Color is paler in mild-winter areas. Blossoms appear before or with the leaves	Hybrid between *M. acuminata* and *M. denudata.* Grow as single-trunked tree or multitrunked shrub-tree. Hardy to at least –20°F/–29°C

MAGNOLIA

NAME	ZONES	TYPE	HEIGHT	SPREAD	AGE AT BLOOM	FLOWERS	USES, CHARACTERISTICS, COMMENTS
M. fraseri (M. auriculata)	4–9, 14–21	Deciduous	To 30 ft.	To 20 ft.	10–12 yrs.	Creamy to yellowish white, fragrant, 8–10 in. wide. Blooms in late spring, when leaves are full grown. Rose red, 5-in. seed capsules are showy in summer	Single lawn or woodland tree. Thin, stiff, brittle leaves 16–18 in. long, with two earlike lobes at base; borne in whorls at branch ends. Effect is that of parasols. Handsome dark brown fall color
M. 'Galaxy'	3b–9, 14–24	Deciduous	To 40 ft.	To 25 ft.	5 yrs. from grafts	Abundant bright red-purple, slightly fragrant, goblet-shaped blossoms to 5 in. across. Blooms in midspring, before leaves emerge but usually after last frost	Fast-growing, broadly conical tree. Medium green leaves to 8 in. long. Cross between *M. liliiflora* and *M. sprengeri* 'Diva'
M. grandiflora SOUTHERN MAGNOLIA, BULL BAY	4–12, 14–24; H1, H2	Evergreen	To 80 ft.	To 60 ft.	15 yrs., sometimes much less; 2–3 years from grafts or cuttings	Pure white, aging buff; large (8–10 in. across), powerfully fragrant. Usually have six segments. Species and its varieties bloom throughout summer, fall	Street or lawn tree, big container plant, wall or espalier plant. Unpredictable in form and age of bloom. Grafted plants more predictable but need pruning to become single-trunked trees. Can grow as multitrunked tree. Glossy, leathery leaves, 4–8 in. long. Needs warmest location (or warm wall) in Zones 4, 5. Expect breakage, some yearly pruning (see care box, page 455) in Zones 6, 7. Give wind-sheltered spot in desert. In Hawaii, does best in Zone H1 and in inland valleys of H2
M. g. 'D. D. Blanchard'	4–12, 14–24; H1, H2	Evergreen	To 50 ft. or more	25–35 ft.	2 yrs.	Like those of *M. grandiflora*	Handsome pyramidal tree. Lustrous dark green leaves are orange-toned brown on undersides
M. g. 'Edith Bogue'	4–12, 14–24; H1, H2	Evergreen	To 35 ft.	To 20 ft.	2–3 yrs. from grafts	Like those of *M. grandiflora.* Young plants slower to come into heavy bloom than some other varieties	Shapely, vigorous tree. One of hardiest selections of *M. grandiflora;* has withstood –24°F/–31°C. The one to try in coldest regions. Keep it out of strong winds
M. g. 'Little Gem'	4–12, 14–24; H1, H2	Evergreen	Slow to 20–25 ft.	10–15 ft.	2 yrs. from grafts	Small (5–6-in.-wide) flowers from spring through late summer (fewer blooms form during midsummer heat)	Narrow form makes it good in container, as espalier, in confined area. Branches to ground. Half-size leaves are dark green above, rusty beneath
M. g. 'Majestic Beauty'	7–12, 14–24; H1, H2	Evergreen	35–50 ft.	To 20 ft.	2 yrs. from grafts	Very large (to 1 ft. across)	Vigorous, dense-branching street or shade tree of broadly pyramidal form. Leaves are exceptionally long, broad, and heavy
M. g. 'Russet'	4–12, 14–24; H1, H2	Evergreen	Fast to 80 ft.	To 20 ft.	2 yrs. from grafts	Flattish, 10-in.-wide blooms	Useful where fast-growing, narrow evergreen tree is needed. Densely foliaged. Narrow, glossy leaves with russet wool on undersides
M. g. 'Samuel Sommer'	4–12, 14–24; H1, H2	Evergreen	Fairly fast to 30–40 ft.	To 30 ft.	Same as *M. grandiflora*	Full and very large, ranging from 10 to 14 in. wide	Large, leathery, glossy leaves are very dark green above, with heavy rusty red felting on underside
M. g. 'San Marino'	4–12, 14–24; H1, H2	Evergreen	Slow to 25 ft.	To 20 ft.	Same as *M. grandiflora*	Profuse show of 4-in. flowers	Grow this plant as a large shrub, small round-headed tree, or espalier. Densely foliaged to the ground unless shaped

▸

MAGNOLIA

NAME	ZONES	TYPE	HEIGHT	SPREAD	AGE AT BLOOM	FLOWERS	USES, CHARACTERISTICS, COMMENTS
M. grandiflora 'St. Mary'	4–12, 14–24; H1, H2	Ever- green	Usually 20 ft.; much larger in old age	To 20 ft.	Same as *M. grandiflora*	Heavy production of 8–10-in. flowers on small tree	Fine where standard-size magnolia would grow too large and too fast. Left alone, it will form a big, dense bush. Can be trained as a small tree. Good plant for containers and espalier
M. g. 'Victoria'	4–12, 14–24; H1, H2	Ever- green	To 20 ft.	To 15 ft.	2–3 yrs. from grafts	Like those of *M. grandiflora*	Parent plant came from Victoria, British Columbia. Withstands –10°F/–23°C with little damage, but should be located out of wind. Leaves dark green, exceptionally broad and heavy
M. hypoleuca	4–9, 14–21	Decid- uous	To 50 ft.	To 30 ft.	15 yrs.	Strongly perfumed flowers to 8 in. across; creamy white with purplish red stamens. Blooms in early summer, after leaves expand (blossoms are partly concealed by foliage). Red, 5–8-in.-long fruits	For large lawn or garden. Coarse-textured plant with attractive gray bark; leaves to 16 in. long
M. 'Iolanthe'	3b–9, 14–24	Decid- uous	To 25 ft.	To 25 ft.	3–5 yrs.	Abundant, bowl-shaped blossoms 10–12 in. across, in soft pink with paler pink interior; open from large, hairy, outward-facing buds. Blooms in late winter and early spring, before leafout	Small, wide-spreading tree has survived brief periods down to –12°F/–24°C. Outward-facing blooms are more desirable than the more common upturned or downturned magnolia flowers
M. kobus KOBUS MAGNOLIA	2b–9, 14–24	Decid- uous	To 30 ft.	To 20 ft.	15 yrs.	White, slightly fragrant blossoms to 4 in. wide. Blooms in early to midspring, before leaves emerge	Cold-hardy, sturdy tree for planting singly in a lawn or in informal shrub and tree groupings. *M. k. borealis* is much larger (to 75 ft.), with larger leaves
M. k. stellata (see **M. stellata**)							
M. Kosar-De Vos Hybrids (the so-called "Little Girl" series)	2b–9, 14–24	Decid- uous	To 12 ft.	To 15 ft.	4–5 yrs.	Flower color ranges from deep to pale purple (sometimes with pink or white interior), depending on variety. Trees bloom in spring before leafout; sporadic rebloom in summer	Hybrids between *M. liliiflora* 'Nigra' and *M. stellata* 'Rosea'; bred to bloom later than *M. stellata*, thus avoiding frost damage. Erect, shrubby growers bearing girls' names: 'Ann', 'Betty', 'Jane', 'Judy', 'Pinky', 'Randy', 'Ricki', 'Susan'. Use in shrub border or singly in lawn
M. liliiflora (M. quinquepeta) LILY MAGNOLIA	2b–9, 14–24	Decid- uous	To 12 ft.	To 15 ft.	4–5 yrs.	White inside, purplish outside. Blooms over long spring, summer season. Tends to have two distinct bloom periods in Northwest	Good for shrub border; strong vertical effect in big flower border. Spreads slowly by suckering. Leaves 4–6 in. long. Blooms of 'Gracilis', 'Nigra', and 'O'Neill' are dark purplish red outside, pink inside
M. × loebneri	2b–9, 14–24	Decid- uous	Slow to 12–15 ft.; can reach 50 ft.	12–15 ft.	3 yrs.	Narrow, strap-shaped flower segments similar to those of *M. stellata*, but generally fewer and somewhat longer and wider. Blooms appear before leaves in midspring. Some selections are fragrant	Hybrids between *M. kobus* and *M. stellata*. 'Ballerina', white with faint pink blush, and taller, pure white 'Spring Snow' are both fragrant. Very lightly scented are 'Leonard Messel', with pink blooms from darker buds, and 'Merrill' ('Dr. Merrill'), a vigorous, free-flowering white-blossomed form. Use in lawn, shrub border, at woodland edge

MAGNOLIA

NAME	ZONES	TYPE	HEIGHT	SPREAD	AGE AT BLOOM	FLOWERS	USES, CHARACTERISTICS, COMMENTS
M. macrophylla BIGLEAF MAGNOLIA	4–9, 14–21	Decid-uous	Slow to 30 ft.	To 20 ft.	12–15 yrs.	Fragrant white flowers to 16 in. across in late spring and early summer, after leafout	Showy tree with leaves 1–3 ft. long and 9–12 in. wide. Needs to stand alone. Be sure to give it some shade in warm climates
M. officinalis	4–9, 14–21	Decid-uous	To 50 ft.	To 25 ft.	15 yrs.	Fragrant, creamy white flowers to 8 in. wide. Blooms in midspring, after leafout	Much like *M. hypoleuca.* Big and exotic-looking tree for big garden or large lawn
M. quinquepeta (see **M. liliiflora**)							
M. 'Royal Crown'	2b–9, 14–24	Decid-uous	20–25 ft.	20–25 ft.	3–5 yrs.	Candle-shaped pink buds open to upright, 10–12-in. blooms with narrow segments; blossoms dark red to violet outside, white inside. Blooms in early spring, before leafout	Vigorous, densely branched hybrid of *M. liliiflora* and *M.* ×*veitchii*
M. salicifolia ANISE MAGNOLIA	2b–9, 14–21	Decid-uous	Slow to 18–30 ft.	To 12 ft.	2–10 yrs.	White, fragrant, to 4 in. across; narrow segments. Blooms in midspring, before leaves emerge	Usually upright, with slender branches, graceful appearance. Can be used for shrub border. Leaves are 3–6 in. long, have anise scent when crushed; turn bronzy red in fall. 'Kochanakee' and 'W. B. Clarke' are large flowered, bloom young and heavily. Another heavy bloomer is 'Miss Jack'
M. sargentiana robusta	5–9, 14–24	Decid-uous	To 35 ft.	To 35 ft.	10–12 yrs.; 8–10 yrs. from grafts	Huge (8–12-in.), fragrant mauve pink bowls open erect, then nod. Blooms in mid- to late spring, before leaves open	Among most spectacular of flowering plants. Leaves 6–8 in. long. Not for hot, dry areas. Must have ample room
M. sieboldii OYAMA MAGNOLIA	4–9, 14–24	Decid-uous	6–15 ft.	6–15 ft.	5 yrs.	Cup-shaped, fragrant, white flowers centered with crimson stamens. Bloom begins in late spring, continues through late summer. Bright pink seedpods	Good for small gardens. Buds look like white Japanese lanterns. Nice planted upslope or at top of wall so people can look up into somewhat nodding flowers. Leaves 3–6 in. long. Best in part shade
M. ×soulangeana SAUCER MAGNOLIA (often called TULIP TREE)	2b–10, 12–24	Decid-uous	To 25 ft.	To 25 ft. or more	3–5 yrs.	White to pink or purplish red, fragrant, variable in form and size (from 3 to 6 in. wide). Blooms from late winter into spring, both before leaves emerge and as they open	Hybrid of *M. denudata* and *M. liliiflora.* Good lawn plant; good anchor plant in big container plantings. Seedlings highly variable; look for named selections (especially later-blooming ones for frost-prone regions). Medium green, rather coarse-looking leaves 4–6 in. long or longer
M. ×s. 'Alba' ('Amabilis', 'Alba Superba')	2b–10, 12–24	Decid-uous	To 30 ft.	To 25 ft. or more	3–5 yrs.	Purple-suffused buds open to large, nearly pure white flowers. Early	Same uses as for *M.* ×*soulangeana.* Rather more upright in growth than most varieties
M. ×s. 'Alexandrina'	2b–10, 12–24	Decid-uous	To 25 ft.	To 25 ft. or more	3–5 yrs.	Deep purplish pink outside, white inside, large. Midseason, before leaves emerge	Same uses as for *M.* ×*soulangeana.* Large, rather heavy leaves
M. ×s. 'Brozzonii'	2b–10, 12–24	Decid-uous	To 25 ft.	To 25 ft. or more	3–5 yrs.	White blossoms very slightly flushed purplish rose at base; 8 in. across. Late	One of the most handsome white-flowered magnolias. Vigorous tree

▶

MAGNOLIA

NAME	ZONES	TYPE	HEIGHT	SPREAD	AGE AT BLOOM	FLOWERS	USES, CHARACTERISTICS, COMMENTS
M. × soulangeana 'Burgundy'	2b–10, 12–24	Decid-uous	To 25 ft.	To 25 ft. or more	3–5 yrs.	Large, cup- or bowl-shaped flowers are deep purple halfway up from base; then color pales to pink. Early	Earlier bloom than most makes it more susceptible to frost damage. San Francisco's Japanese Tea Garden has many of these, pruned into picturesque shapes
M. ×s. 'Coates'	2b–10, 12–24	Decid-uous	To 25 ft.	To 25 ft. or more	3–5 yrs.	Large, attractive blooms resemble those of *M.* 'Royal Crown'. Midseason	Large, shrubby. Quick grower
M. ×s. 'Lennei' (M. lennei)	2b–10, 12–24	Decid-uous	To 25 ft.	To 25 ft. or more	3–5 yrs.	Very large, globe-shaped blossoms are deep purple outside, white inside. Late	Spreading, vigorous plant. Late bloom helps it escape frosts in cold areas
M. ×s. 'Lennei Alba' (M. lennei 'Alba')	2b–10, 12–24	Decid-uous	To 25 ft.	To 25 ft. or more	3–5 yrs.	Like those of 'Lennei', but white in color, slightly smaller, and earlier (midseason)	Spreading, vigorous plant
M. ×s. 'Lilliputian'	2b–10, 12–24	Decid-uous	To 18 ft.	10–15 ft.	3–5 yrs.	Flowers are pink outside, white inside, somewhat smaller than those of other *M. × soulangeana* selections. Late	Good where a smaller magnolia is called for
M. ×s. 'Norbertii'	2b–10, 12–24	Decid-uous	To 18 ft.	10–15 ft.	3–5 yrs.	White, suffused with purple on outside. Late	Upright, dense habit
M. ×s. 'Pink Superba'	2b–10, 12–24	Decid-uous	To 25 ft.	To 25 ft. or more	3–5 yrs.	Large deep pink blooms are white inside. Early	Best where late frosts are not a problem. Identical to *M. ×s.* 'Alba' except for flower color
M. ×s. 'Rustica Rubra'	2b–10, 12–24	Decid-uous	To 25 ft.	To 25 ft. or more	3–5 yrs.	Large, cup-shaped, deep reddish purple flowers. Blooms somewhat past midseason. Big (6-in.) dark rose seedpods	Vigorous grower for large areas. More treelike than many *M. × soulangeana* varieties
M. ×s. 'San Jose'	2b–10, 12–24	Decid-uous	To 25 ft.	To 25 ft. or more	3–5 yrs.	Large white flowers flushed with pink. Very early	Exceptionally early bloom puts it at risk for frost damage in cold areas
M. sprengeri 'Diva'	5–9, 14–24	Decid-uous	To 40 ft.	To 30 ft.	3 yrs.	Spectacular, erect, sweet-scented blooms to 8 in. wide are bright rose pink outside, pink-suffused white with deeper pink lines inside. Blooms late winter to early spring, before leaves open	Buds more frost resistant than those of *M. sargentiana robusta*. Big shrub that can be trained as tree. Young plants are broad, twiggy
M. 'Star Wars'	3b–9, 14–24	Decid-uous	30–35 ft.	To 20 ft.	4 yrs.	Rich bright pink blossoms (paler inside), 11 in. across. Blooms for 1–2 months, beginning in early spring (before leafout)	Cross between *M. campbellii* and *M. liliiflora*. Especially good magnolia for Southern California and inland areas

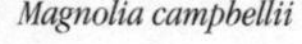

Magnolia campbellii

Magnolia 'Elizabeth'

Magnolia grandiflora

Magnolia grandiflora

MAGNOLIA

NAME	ZONES	TYPE	HEIGHT	SPREAD	AGE AT BLOOM	FLOWERS	USES, CHARACTERISTICS, COMMENTS
M. stellata STAR MAGNOLIA	2b–9, 14–24	Decid-uous	To 10 ft.	To 20 ft.	3 yrs.	White flowers to 3 in. across, with 12–18 narrow, strap-shaped segments. Profuse bloom comes very early—late winter to early spring, before leafout. Some varieties are fragrant	Slow growing, shrubby; use for borders, entryway gardens, edge of woods. Good idea to plant this early bloomer where you can see flowers from indoors. Quite hardy, but flowers often nipped by frost in colder part of range. Fine texture in twig, leaf. Fair yellow-and-brown fall leaf color
M. s. 'Centennial'	2b–9, 14–24	Decid-uous	To 10 ft.	To 20 ft.	3 yrs.	White blossoms faintly marked pink, 5 in. across, with 40–50 segments. Midspring	Same uses as *M. stellata*. Like an improved *M. s.* 'Waterlily'
M. s. 'Dawn'	2b–9, 14–24	Decid-uous	To 10 ft.	To 20 ft.	3 yrs.	White flowers have 25 or more segments, each with a longi-tudinal pink stripe	Same uses as *M. stellata*
M. s. 'Jane Platt'	2b–9, 14–24	Decid-uous	12–15 ft.	10–12 ft.	3–5 yrs.	Rich pink, 4–5-in. blossoms with 40–50 segments. Blooms in early spring	Typical shrubby *M. stellata* plant form
M. s. 'Rosea' PINK STAR MAGNOLIA	2b–9, 14–24	Decid-uous	To 10 ft.	To 20 ft.	3 yrs.	Pink buds; flowers open pink-flushed white, age to plain white. Late winter	Same uses as for *M. stellata*. Various plants are sold under this name
M. s. 'Royal Star'	2b–9, 14–24	Decid-uous	18–20 ft.	To 15 ft.	3 yrs.	Fragrant white blooms with 25–30 segments. Blooms 2 weeks later than species	Same uses as for *M. stellata*. Faster growing
M. s. 'Rubra'	2b–9, 14–24	Decid-uous	To 10 ft.	To 20 ft.	3 yrs.	Rosy pink blooms to 5 in. across	More treelike in form than other *M. stellata* varieties
M. s. 'Waterlily'	2b–9, 14–24	Decid-uous	To 10 ft.	To 20 ft.	3 yrs.	Pink buds open to very fragrant white blossoms to 5 in. across, with 40–50 segments. Blooms late, after most other *M. stellata* varieties	Faster growing than most star magnolias. Various plants are sold under this name
M. 'Timeless Beauty'	4–9, 14–24	Ever-green	15–20 ft.	20–25 ft.	2 yrs.	Creamy white, fragrant flowers to 10 in. wide. Blooms in spring and summer	Extremely dense crown with spreading branches
M. × veitchii VEITCH MAGNOLIA	4–9, 14–24	Decid-uous	30–40 ft.	To 30 ft.	4–5 yrs.	Profuse show of goblet shaped, 8–10-in.-wide blooms in soft white flushed with pink. Blooms in midspring, before leafout	Spectacular tree. Hybrid between *M. campbellii* and *M. denudata*. Fast growing and vigorous. Needs plenty of room. Protect from wind; branches are brittle. Good magnolia for Southern California. Give it afternoon shade in hottest areas

▶

Magnolia kobus

Magnolia kobus

Magnolia 'Randy' (Kosar-De Vos Hybrid)

Magnolia liliiflora

M. × *loebneri* 'Spring Snow'

M

MAGNOLIA

NAME	ZONES	TYPE	HEIGHT	SPREAD	AGE AT BLOOM	FLOWERS	USES, CHARACTERISTICS, COMMENTS
M. × veitchii 'Columbus'	4–9, 14–24	Deciduous	30–35 ft.	15–20 ft.	2 yrs.	Cup-shaped, 4–5-in.-wide, white with purple highlight at base of each segment. Late winter or early spring, before leafout	Has a thicker trunk and stronger branching structure than other magnolias, making it a sturdy choice for urban plantings
M. virginiana (M. glauca) SWEET BAY	4–9, 14–24	Evergreen to deciduous	To 50 ft, usually less	To 20 ft.	8–10 yrs.	Creamy white, fragrant, nearly globular blossoms are 2–3 in. wide. Late spring to late summer	Prefers moist, acid soil. Grows in swamps in eastern U.S. Big evergreen or semievergreen tree in milder climates; deciduous shrub in colder areas. Leaves bright green above, nearly white beneath, 2–5 in. long. Twigs and branches are bright green, adding winter interest if leaves fall
M. 'Vulcan'	4–9, 14–24	Deciduous	To 25 ft.	To 25 ft.	1 yr. from grafts	Showy, ruby red blossoms to 10–12 in. across. Flowers borne in tree's younger years may be smaller and paler than those on older trees. With good care, trees will produce mature flowers in 3 or 4 years. Blooms in spring, before leafout	Open form when young, becoming more rounded with age
M. 'Wada's Memory'	2b–9, 14–24	Deciduous	To 30 ft.	To 20 ft.	3–5 yrs. from grafts	White, slightly fragrant blossoms over 4 in. across. Blooms in early to midspring, before leaves emerge	Also sold as *M. × kewensis* 'Wada's Memory' or as *M. × proctoriana* 'Wada's Memory'. Same uses as *M. kobus;* grows faster than *M. kobus.* Coppery red new leaves
M. wilsonii WILSON MAGNOLIA	4–9, 14–24	Deciduous	To 25 ft.	To 25 ft.	10 yrs.	Fragrant, pendulous, 3–4-in.-wide, white blossoms with red stamens. Late spring	Spreading shrub or tree with rich purple-brown twigs. Leaves 3–6 in. long; may be narrow or somewhat broad. Plant high on bank where you can look up into flowers. Best in light shade. Effect similar to that of *M. sieboldii*
M. 'Yellow Bird'	3b–9, 14–24	Deciduous	To 40 ft.	To 20 ft.	2 yrs. from grafts	Deepest yellow color of the yellow hybrids. Slight green tinge at base of erect, 3-in.-long flower segments. Blooms for 2–3 weeks in early to midspring, as leaves emerge	Hybrid of *M. acuminata* and *M. × bronxensis* 'Evamaria'. Upright and pyramidal when young, broadly oval when mature. Furrowed bark. Sometimes available as a multi-trunked form
M. 'Yellow Lantern'	3b–9, 14–24	Deciduous	To 50 ft.	20–25 ft.	2–3 yrs. from grafts	Clear yellow blossoms (darker than those of *M.* 'Elizabeth', paler than those of *M.* 'Yellow Bird') with upright or slightly spreading segments to 6 in. long. Open from large, furry buds. Midspring, before leafout	Hybrid of *M. acuminata* and *M. × soulangeana* 'Alexandrina'. Upright, single-trunked tree

M

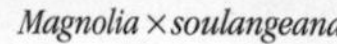

Magnolia × soulangeana

Magnolia × soulangeana

Magnolia salicifolia

Magnolia salicifolia

from excess mineral salts in the soil or salts in irrigation water. The latter is a problem in Southern California and, typically, the factor limiting success of magnolias in desert regions. Frequent heavy waterings will help leach out salts and carry them to lower soil levels—as long as drainage is good. In the Northwest, late frosts may burn edges of new leaves.

WHAT MAGNOLIAS NEED

CAREFUL SITING: Pick a location where the shallow, fleshy roots won't be damaged by digging or by soil compaction from constant foot traffic.

SOIL: Magnolias appreciate fairly rich, well-drained, neutral to slightly acid soil amended with plenty of organic matter at planting time. They will grow in somewhat alkaline soil but may develop chlorosis.

MULCHING: At least in the early years, keep a cooling mulch over the root area.

WATERING: Irrigate deeply and thoroughly, but don't waterlog the soil or the tree will drown. Only *M. virginiana* can take constantly wet soil.

FERTILIZING: Treat chlorosis with iron chelates. Feed trees if new growth is scanty or weak, or if you see significant dieback despite adequate watering and drainage; use a controlled-release product. For more on fertilizing, see text.

PRUNING: For deciduous magnolias, best time is after bloom; for evergreen kinds, do the job before the spring growth flush. Best method is to remove the entire twig or limb right to the base. Cuts on deciduous kinds are often slow to callus over, so prune these only when necessary to correct shape, eliminate or cut back wayward branches, or remove lower branches from trunk as tree gains height.

Magnolia × soulangeana

Magnoliaceae. The magnolia family contains evergreen and deciduous trees and shrubs with large, showy flowers, usually with a large number of petal-like segments (commonly called petals), sepals, and stamens. Tulip tree *(Liriodendron)*, *Magnolia*, and *Michelia* are examples.

MAHONIA

Berberidaceae

EVERGREEN SHRUBS

ZONES VARY BY SPECIES

EXPOSURE NEEDS VARY BY SPECIES

WATER NEEDS VARY BY SPECIES

Mahonia aquifolium

Related to barberry *(Berberis)* and described under that name by some botanists. Easy to grow; good looking all year. Typically spiny-edged leaves are divided into leaflets; foliage can be quite prickly, so avoid setting mahonias too close to walkways or in other areas where they might snag passersby. Yellow flowers are borne in dense, rounded to spikelike clusters and followed by berrylike, typically blue or blue-black (sometimes red or brown) fruit with a powdery bloom. Generally disease resistant, though foliage is sometimes disfigured by a small looper caterpillar. Fruit of all mahonias attracts birds. In general, pruning is needed only to remove old, damaged stems or to correct rank growth; cut those stems all the way to the ground.

M. aquifolium. OREGON GRAPE. Zones 2–12, 14–24. Native from British Columbia to Northern California, mostly west of the Cascades. State flower of Oregon. Dense, bushy plant grows erect to 6 ft. high, spreading by underground stems to 5 ft. wide. Leaves are typically glossy green, 6–12 in. long, with five to nine leaflets that resemble holly leaves. Ruddy or bronze new growth; scattered mature red leaves throughout the year (more pronounced in fall and winter). Leaves turn purplish or bronze in winter, especially in cold-winter areas or where plants are grown in full sun. Early spring flowers appear in 2–3-in. clusters along stems. Edible blue-black fruit with gray bloom (makes good jelly).

'Compacta' grows 2–3 ft. high and spreads to 5 ft. or more. New foliage is a glossy light to coppery green; mature leaves are matte medium green. 'Orange Flame', 2 ft. tall and 3 ft. wide, has bronzy new growth, glossy green mature leaves that turn wine red in winter.

Mass as foundation planting or as low screen or garden barrier; plant in woodland or in tubs. Control height and form by pruning; if any woody stems jut out too far, cut them down to ground (new growth fills in quickly). Can be sheared as a formal hedge. Resistant to oak root fungus. Give wind protection in cold-winter areas. Can take any exposure but performs best with shade in hottest climates (northern exposure recommended in desert). Little to regular water.

M. bealei. LEATHERLEAF MAHONIA. Zones 3b–12, 14–24. Native to China. To 10–12 ft. high and 10 ft. wide, with strong pattern of vertical stems and horizontal leaves. The leaves reach over a foot long, divided into 7–15 broad, thick, leathery leaflets to 5 in. long. Foliage is yellowish green above, gray green below, with a small yellow patch at the base of each leaflet. Blooms in late winter, producing erect, 3–6-in.-long blossom spikes at ends of branches. Powdery blue berries. Truly distinguished plant against background of stone, brick, wood, glass. Plant in rich soil amended with ample organic matter. Takes sun in cool-summer areas; does best in partial shade elsewhere. Regular water.

M. fortunei. Zones 5–9, 14–24. Native to China. To 6 ft. high and 3 ft. wide, with an unusual stiff charm. Erect stems bear 10-in.-long leaves with 7–13 leaflets; matte green above, yellowish green with heavily netted veins on undersides. Short clusters of flowers in late fall. Full sun or light shade. Regular water.

M. fremontii. DESERT MAHONIA. Zones 2b–24. Native to deserts of Southwest. Upright, many-stemmed plant to 3–12 ft. tall, 6 ft. wide. Gray-green to yellowish green leaves, each with three to five thick, inch-long leaflets that are edged with very sharp, tough spines. Flowers in 1–1½-in.-long clusters in late spring; dark blue to brown fruit. Full sun or light shade. Little or no water.

M. 'Golden Abundance'. Zones 2b–12, 14–24. Vigorous, densely foliaged plant reaches 6 ft. high, spreading by underground stems to 5 ft. wide. Glossy green leaves with red midribs. Blooms profusely in early spring with clusters of yellow flowers; later produces an abundant crop of purplish blue berries with gray bloom. Full sun in cooler climates, some shade in hotter ones. Little to regular water.

M. lomariifolia. Zones 6 (borderline), 7–9, 14–24. Native to China. To 6–12 ft. high and 6 ft. wide, with erect stems that branch only slightly. Young plants often have a single, vertical unbranched stem; older ones produce more (almost vertical-growing) branches from near base. Clustered deep green leaves are held horizontally near ends of branches. Each leaf reaches 2 ft. long, has 19–41 barbed leaflets arranged symmetrically along both sides of central leafstalk (with a single leaflet at the tip). Midwinter flowers grow in long, erect clusters at branch tips, just above topmost cluster of leaves. Blue berries. Strong-structured plant for dramatic effect. Partial shade, especially in afternoon. Regular water. ▶

Mahonia lomariifolia

M

M. ×media. Zones 6–9, 14–24. Hybrids between *M. lomariifolia* and a Japanese species similar to *M. bealei.* Plants bear upright clusters of fragrant flowers in late fall and winter; generally resemble *M. lomariifolia* and require the same conditions. 'Buckland' and 'Charity' grow to 15 ft. high, 12 ft. wide; 'Faith' reaches 6–10 ft. high and 6 ft. wide; 'Hope' and 'Lionel Fortescue' both grow to 6 ft. high and wide; and 'Winter Sun' reaches 4–5 ft. high and as wide.

M. nervosa. LONGLEAF MAHONIA. Zones 2b–10, 14–24. Native from British Columbia to Northern California, mostly west of the Cascades. To 2 ft. (occasionally 3–4 ft.) high and 3 ft. wide, spreading by underground stems. Clustered at stem tips are 10–18-in.-long leaves divided into 9–19 leaflets, each 1–3 in. long; plant creates the impression of a stiff, leathery fern. Early spring flowers are borne in upright, 3–6-in.-long clusters. Blue berries. Use as woodland ground cover, facing for taller mahonias, low barrier plant. Partial or full shade; little to moderate water. This plant is an excellent choice for dry shade.

M. nevinii. NEVIN MAHONIA. Zones 7–24. Native to scattered areas in Southern California. Many-branched shrub to 6 ft. high and wide. Gray leaves with three to five 1-in.-long leaflets. Loose, 1–2-in. clusters of spring flowers are followed by red berries. Resistant to oak root fungus. Use individually or as screen, hedge, barrier. Full sun or partial shade. Little or no water to regular water.

M. pinnata. CALIFORNIA HOLLY GRAPE. Zones 4–9, 14–24. Native from southern Oregon to Southern California. To 4–5 ft. high (often taller along the coast) and as wide. Similar to *M. aquifolium* but with spinier, more crinkly leaves; new growth often shows lots of red and orange. Spikelike springtime flower clusters; dark blue berries. 'Ken Hartman' has dense, uniform growth. Full sun in cooler areas, light shade in hottest climates. No irrigation needed (takes aridity better than *M. aquifolium*).

M. repens. CREEPING MAHONIA. Zones 2b–9, 14–24. Native from British Columbia to Northern California, eastward to Rocky Mountains. To 1 ft. high and 3 ft. wide, spreading by underground stems when cold weather arrives. One of the best mahonias for winter color: dull blue-green leaves turn bronzy or pinkish when cold weather arrives. Short clusters of flowers in mid- to late spring are followed by blue berries. Good ground cover. Full sun or partial shade. Little or no water.

M. 'Skylark'. Zones 4–9, 14–24. Grows to 5 ft. high or higher, 5 ft. wide. Shiny leaves to 6 in. long are reddish when new; they mature to deep green, then take on purple tints in winter. Spring flowers in dense, 4–6-in. spikes. Dark blue berries. Full sun in cooler areas, partial shade in hotter ones. No irrigation needed.

M. trifoliolata. Zones 3, 10–13. Native to Arizona, southern New Mexico, Texas. To 8 ft. high and about half as wide. Blue-green leaves with three wavy-edged leaflets. Short flower clusters in spring are followed by orange-red berries sometimes used for jelly. Full sun. Moderate water.

MAIANTHEMUM dilatatum

FALSE LILY-OF-THE-VALLEY
Liliaceae
PERENNIAL
ZONES A2, A3; 2–9, 14–17
PARTIAL SHADE
REGULAR WATER

Maianthemum dilatatum

Native from Northern California to Alaska, Idaho. Also known as *M. bifolium* or as *M. d. kamtschaticum.* To 6–8 in. high; in good growing conditions, spreads rapidly by creeping rootstocks to form broad mats. Stems 2–6 in. high bear neat, roundish to heart-shaped, heavily veined leaves to 8 in. long and half as wide. Bears foamy clusters of white flowers in spring that are followed by red berries in summer. Makes an attractive woodland-type ground cover but is capable of overwhelming more delicate plants growing nearby. Give well-drained, acid soil. Disappears in winter.

MAIDEN GRASS. See MISCANTHUS sinensis 'Gracillimus'

MAIDENHAIR FERN. See ADIANTUM

MAIDENHAIR SPLEENWORT. See ASPLENIUM trichomanes

MAIDENHAIR TREE. See GINKGO biloba

MAIDEN PINK. See DIANTHUS deltoides

MAIDEN'S WREATH. See FRANCOA ramosa

MAILE. See ALYXIA oliviformis

MAJORANA hortensis. See ORIGANUM majorana

MALCOLMIA maritima

VIRGINIAN STOCK
Brassicaceae (Cruciferae)
ANNUAL
ZONES 1–24
FULL SUN
REGULAR WATER

Malcolmia maritima

Low-growing Mediterranean native reaches only 8–15 in. high. Single stemmed or branching from base, with oblong gray-green leaves to 2 in. long. From spring to fall, plant is covered with nearly scentless, four-petaled flowers in white, yellow, pink, lilac, or magenta. Blooms from seed in 6 weeks; sow seed in place (in moderately rich soil) at any time except during hot or very cold weather. Thin seedlings to about 8 in. apart. Does not reseed readily. Good choice as bulb cover. May not flower well in hot, humid conditions.

MALEPHORA (Hymenocyclus)

ICE PLANT
Aizoaceae
SUCCULENT PERENNIALS
ZONES VARY BY SPECIES
FULL SUN
LITTLE OR NO WATER

Malephora lutea

Ground cover plants from South Africa. Dense, smooth, 1–1¾-in.-long fleshy leaves are highly resistant to heat, wind, exhaust fumes, and fire. Widely used in streetside and freeway plantings. Plants bloom over a long season, but their daisylike flowers are scattered rather than in sheets. Attractive to bees.

M. crocea. Zones 11–24. To 6 in.–1 ft. high and 6 ft. wide, with blue-green foliage. Sparse production of reddish yellow flowers nearly year-round, with heaviest bloom in spring. Good choice for moderately steep slopes. *M. c. purpureo-crocea* has bluish green foliage, salmon-colored flowers.

M. lutea. ROCKY POINT ICE PLANT. Zones 12–24. To 1 ft. high and 6 ft. wide, with bright green foliage. Inch-wide yellow flowers bloom during most of year. More vigorous than *M. crocea.*

MALLEE. See EUCALYPTUS

MALLOW. See MALVA

MALOSMA laurina. See RHUS laurina

MALTESE CROSS. See LYCHNIS chalcedonica

FOR INFORMATION ON SELECTING PLANTS
PLEASE SEE PAGES 64–160

MALUS

FLOWERING CRABAPPLE

Rosaceae

DECIDUOUS TREES

ZONES 1–11, 14–21, EXCEPT AS NOTED IN CHART

FULL SUN

MODERATE TO REGULAR WATER

SEE CHART NEXT PAGE

Malus floribunda

From North America, Europe, Asia. Valued for brief, lavish show of white, pink, or red flowers and for fruit that is showy, edible, or both. (Most of the trees listed in the chart bear fruit that is enjoyed primarily by birds. For crabapples used chiefly in cooking, see Crabapple.) Hundreds of different kinds are cultivated, and new varieties appear every year. Most grow about 25 ft. high, though size ranges from as low as 6 ft. to as tall as 40 ft. Leaves are pointed ovals, often fuzzy, varying in color from medium green to nearly purple. Fall foliage is rarely noteworthy. Bloom in spring (usually before leaves unfurl), bearing masses of single, semidouble, or double flowers that sometimes have a musky, sweet scent. Small red, orange, or yellow apples, ranging from under ¾ in. to almost 2 in. wide, ripen from midsummer into autumn; in some varieties, the fruit hangs on well after leaves drop and even into winter. Some varieties bear flowers and fruit more heavily in alternate years.

Plant bare-root trees in winter or early spring; set out container plants any time. Flowering crabapples are hardier, more tolerant of wet soil, and longer lived than flowering cherries and other flowering stone fruits. Take heat but are not at their best in low desert.

Malus sargentii

Flowering crabapple varieties differ widely in disease resistance. Many of the most popular varieties of years past are highly prone to one or more of the diseases that can plague these trees: apple scab, cedar-apple rust, fireblight, powdery mildew. Today, the nursery trade places great emphasis on promoting disease-resistant varieties—thus displacing many of the old favorites. The chart beginning on the following page notes degree of resistance or susceptibility for each variety. In the Pacific Northwest, it's imperative to choose trees that resist cedar-apple rust, scab, and powdery mildew. Fireblight may afflict susceptible trees anywhere when conditions are favorable for its development.

Flowering crabapples are subject to attack from the same pests that affect apple. Scale, aphids, spider mites, and tent caterpillars may require control; codling moths and apple maggots should be controlled if you intend to harvest the fruit.

These are fine lawn trees, good for underplanting with primroses, spring-blooming bulbs, or shade-loving bedding plants. Plant them near fences to heighten the screening effect.

WHAT CRABAPPLES NEED

WINTER CHILL: For best growth and productivity, plants need about 600 hours at 45°F/7°C or lower.

SOIL: They prefer good, well-drained, deep soils but will grow in rocky or gravelly ones. They take acid to slightly alkaline soil.

PROTECTION: Many crabapples are planted in lawns, where their bark is often nicked by mowers. To protect the trees, create a sod-free, mulched area around the trunk.

DISEASE CONTROL: Scab, powdery mildew, and cedar-apple rust are serious problems primarily in the Northwest. Prevention is the best control—grow disease-resistant varieties.

PRUNING: Prune only to build a good framework, remove any suckers, and correct the shape. Crabapple trees can be trained as espaliers.

Malus 'Dorothea'

MALVA

MALLOW

Malvaceae

PERENNIALS OR BIENNIALS

ZONES 1–9, 14–24

FULL SUN

REGULAR WATER

Malva alcea

From Europe; naturalized in U.S. These plants are related to and somewhat resemble hollyhock *(Alcea)*, but they are bushier, with smaller, roundish to heart-shaped leaves. Bloom from summer to fall. Easy to grow; need good drainage, average soil. Grow from seed; usually bloom first year. Use in perennial borders or for a quick tall edging. Not long lived.

M. alcea. Perennial. To 4 ft. tall, 2 ft. wide; upper leaves deeply divided. Saucer-shaped pink flowers to 2 in. wide. Most common form is 'Fastigiata'; it is narrower than the species and looks much like hollyhock.

M. moschata. MUSK MALLOW. Perennial. Erect, branching plant to 3 ft. tall, 2 ft. wide. Finely cut leaves; pink or white flowers to 1 in. wide or somewhat wider. Entire plant emits a mild, musky odor if brushed against or bruised. Named selections are more frequently grown than the species. 'Rosea' has pink blossoms; 'Alba' is 2 ft. tall, bears white flowers.

M. sylvestris. Perennial or biennial. Erect, bushy growth to 2–4 ft. tall, 2 ft. wide. Can become invasive. Flowers 2 in. wide; often bloom until frost. Common variety 'Zebrina' (often sold as *M. zebrina*) has blossoms in pale lavender pink with pronounced deep purple veining. 'Mauritiana' has darker, often semidouble flowers.

Malvaceae. The mallow family contains hundreds of species of mainly herbaceous plants and some shrubs and trees, often with lobed leaves and showy flowers. Ornamentals include flowering maple *(Abutilon)*, hollyhock *(Alcea)*, *Hibiscus*, mallow *(Malva)*, and checkerbloom *(Sidalcea)*. Commercially, the family is important as the source of cotton.

MALVASTRUM lateritium (Modiolastrum lateritium)

TRAILING MALLOW

Malvaceae

PERENNIAL

ZONES 8, 9, 14–24

FULL SUN

LITTLE OR NO WATER

Malvastrum lateritium

From South America. To 8 in. high, 5 ft. wide, with trailing stems that root as they spread. Roundish, 2–3-in.-wide leaves. Blossoms throughout warm weather, bearing saucer-shaped, 1½–2-in.-wide flowers that are salmon pink with pinkish orange center. Useful for holding soil on a bank or for ground cover (but does not tolerate foot traffic). Withstands poor soil, heat, much aridity. Its only drawback is invasiveness; keep it away from more delicate plants.

MALUS

NAME	HABIT, SIZE	FLOWERS	FRUIT	COMMENTS
Malus 'Adams' Zones A2, A3; 1–21	Dense, round headed, to 20 ft. tall and wide	Red buds open to single pink flowers	Dull red, small, long lasting	Orange fall foliage. Good disease resistance
M. 'Adirondack'	Columnar, to 12 ft. by 6 ft.	Red buds; large, red-tinged, single, waxy white flowers	Red to orange red	Formal in appearance. High disease resistance
M. 'Almey' Zones A2, A3; 1–21	Upright, spreading, to 20 ft. (possibly taller) by 30 ft.	Single scarlet flowers, white at base	Maroon; hangs on well	Purplish green foliage. Old-fashioned variety; very prone to disease except where humidity is very low. Newer, more disease-resistant crabapples are a better choice
M. 'Ames White'	Dense, upright, to 25 ft. tall and wide	Pink buds open to single white flowers	Yellow	High disease resistance
M. ×arnoldiana ARNOLD CRABAPPLE	Broad, to 25 ft. by 35 ft.	Red buds open to single pink flowers that fade to white. Fragrant	Red-blushed yellow	Susceptible to scab and fireblight. Bears more heavily in alternate years
M. ×atrosanguinea CARMINE CRABAPPLE	Erect, dense, irregular, to 18 ft. by 25 ft.	Single deep pink to red flowers. Fragrant	Reddish or greenish yellow, turning brown; hangs on all winter	Foliage has a purplish sheen. Moderate disease resistance
M. 'Brandywine'	Vigorous, shapely, to 15–20 ft. tall and wide	Double rose pink. Fragrant	Yellowish green	Leaves have a reddish cast. Fair disease resistance
M. 'Callaway'	Attractive, round headed, to 18 ft. by 16 ft.	Pink buds open to single white flowers	Deep red, large, long lasting	Low chill requirement for bloom; good in warmer-winter areas. High disease resistance
M. 'Centurion'	Oval crowned, to 25 ft. by 15–20 ft.	Red buds open to single red flowers	Shiny deep red, long lasting	Blooms young. High disease resistance
M. 'Coralburst'	Small, dense, to 10–15 ft. by 8–10 ft.	Coral pink buds open to small, double rose pink flowers	Reddish orange, small; scant crop	Usually grafted on a standard; sometimes grown as a shrub. Fair disease resistance
M. coronaria 'Charlottae'	Broadly spreading, to 30 ft. by 35 ft.	Large, double pale pink flowers	Yellowish green, large	Orange-red autumn foliage color. Like the species, blooms late and is susceptible to rust and scab
M. 'Donald Wyman'	Broad, to 20 ft. by 25 ft.	Pink to red buds open to single white flowers	Shiny, bright red, small, long lasting	Lustrous foliage. Good disease resistance
M. 'Dorothea'	Dense, round headed, to 25 ft. tall and wide	Red buds open to large, semidouble pink flowers	Bright yellow, small	Susceptible to scab and fireblight
M. floribunda JAPANESE FLOWERING CRABAPPLE	Broad, dense grower to 12 ft. by 18 ft.	Deep pink buds open to single white flowers. Fragrant, incredibly profuse blooms	Red-blushed yellow, small; does not last long	Moderate disease resistance
M. 'Harvest Gold'	Vigorous, narrow, to 30 ft. by 15 ft.	Pink buds open to single white flowers. Late blooming	Yellow, showy; hangs on until spring	High disease resistance
M. 'Hopa'	Fast growth to 25 ft. by 20 ft.	Single rose red flowers; fragrant	Orange red, large; drops early. Good for jelly	Suckers freely. Old-fashioned variety; very prone to disease except where humidity is very low. Newer, more disease-resistant crabapples are a better choice
M. hupehensis (M. theifera) TEA CRABAPPLE	Broad form; moderate growth to 15 ft. by 25 ft.	Deep pink buds open to single white flowers. Fragrant	Greenish yellow to red, small, not showy	Picturesque form, with branches strongly angled from short trunk. Moderate disease resistance

MALUS

NAME	HABIT, SIZE	FLOWERS	FRUIT	COMMENTS
M. 'Indian Magic'	Round headed, to 15–20 ft. tall and wide	Red buds open to single deep pink flowers	Shiny red to orange, small, long lasting	Moderate susceptibility to disease
M. 'Indian Summer'	Rounded, to 18 ft. tall and wide	Single rose red	Bright red, long lasting	Good orange-red fall leaf color. High disease resistance
M. ioensis 'Plena' BECHTEL CRABAPPLE	Round headed, open, to 30 ft. tall and wide	Double pink flowers. Fragrant	Dull yellow green, large	Highly susceptible to disease. 'Klehm's' is a similar variety that offers better disease resistance
M. 'Jewelberry'	Dwarfish, dense, to 8 ft. by 12 ft.	Pink buds open to single white flowers	Shiny, red, small, long lasting	Bears young. Moderate disease resistance
M. 'Katherine'	Slow growing to 20 ft. tall and wide	Deep pink buds open to large, double pink flowers that quickly fade to white	Red-blushed yellow, very small	Fair disease resistance. Bears more heavily in alternate years
M. 'Liset'	Roundish, dense growth to 15–20 ft. tall and wide	Crimson buds open to single flowers in deep red to crimson	Dark red to maroon; hangs on well	Deep purplish green leaves. Fair disease resistance
M. 'Madonna'	Narrow, erect tree grows to 15–20 ft. by 10–15 ft.	Pink buds open to double white flowers. Long bloom season	Red-blushed yellow, small	Bronzy new growth. Good disease resistance
M. × micromalus (M. kaido) MIDGET CRABAPPLE	Slow growth to 15 ft. by 8–10 ft.	Red buds open to single pink flowers that hold their color. Profuse bloomer	Red or greenish, not showy	Some susceptibility to scab
M. 'Molten Lava'	Spreading, weeping tree to 12 ft. by 15 ft.	Deep red buds open to single white flowers	Red orange, small; lasts well on tree	Attractive yellow winter bark. Good disease resistance
M. 'Narragansett'	Broad, round headed, to 15 ft. tall and wide	Red buds open to single white flowers with faint touch of pink	Bright red, small, showy	High disease resistance
M. 'Oekonomierat Echtermeyer' ('Pink Weeper') WEEPING CRABAPPLE	Grows at moderate rate to 15 ft. by 20 ft., with weeping branches	Red buds open to single purplish red flowers	Purplish to reddish to greenish brown	Foliage is purple when new, turning purplish green by summer. Prune out any erect-growing branches. Disease prone
M. 'Pink Perfection'	Round headed, to 20 ft. tall and wide	Red buds open to large, bicolored double flowers in pale pink and white	Yellow, insignificant	Susceptible to scab
M. 'Pink Princess'	Low, broad, to 15 ft. by 12 ft.	Single rose pink	Deep red, small; lasts well on tree	Reddish green foliage. Good disease resistance
M. 'Pink Spires' Zones A2, A3; 1–21	Narrow, upright, to 25 ft. by 12–15 ft.	Deep rose pink buds open to single flowers in a lighter rose pink	Reddish purple; hangs on well	Foliage is red when new, maturing to bronzy green. Moderate disease resistance
M. 'Prairifire'	Round headed, to 20 ft. tall and wide	Red buds open to single flowers in deep pinkish red	Dark red, small; hangs on well	Leaves emerge reddish maroon, turn dark green. High disease resistance
M. 'Profusion'	Upright, spreading, to 20 ft. tall and wide	Deep red buds, single deep purplish pink flowers	Dark red, long lasting	Foliage is purple when young, matures to bronzy green. Moderate disease resistance
M. 'Purple Wave'	Broad, spreading, to 10–15 ft. tall and wide	Large, single to semidouble rose red flowers fade to purplish pink with age	Dark purple red	Purplish foliage. Susceptible to rust, scab

M

▶

MALUS

NAME	HABIT, SIZE	FLOWERS	FRUIT	COMMENTS
M. × purpurea 'Eleyi'	Irregular, open, to 20 ft. tall and wide	Single wine red flowers	Dark purple red. Profuse	Old-fashioned variety; very susceptible to disease except where humidity is very low. Newer, more disease-resistant crabapples are a better choice
M. 'Radiant' Zones A2, A3; 1–21	Broad, round headed, to 20 ft. tall and wide	Deep red buds open to single deep pink flowers	Bright red; colors early and lasts into winter	Leaves are reddish when they open, later turn green. Susceptible to scab
M. 'Red Barron'	Narrow (to 20 ft. by 12 ft.), growing broader with age	Very deep red buds open to single reddish pink flowers	Shiny dark red	New leaves are purple, mature ones bronzy green. Susceptible to scab
M. 'Red Jade' Zones A2, A3; 1–21	Irregular, weeping form; to 15 ft. tall and wide	Small, single white flowers	Bright red, heavy crop; holds well into fall	Moderate disease resistance
M. 'Red Jewel'	Small, round headed, to 15 ft. by 12 ft.	Large, single white flowers	Bright red, small, long lasting	Fair disease resistance
M. 'Red Silver'	Angular, irregular, to 30 ft. tall and wide	Single deep wine red flowers	Dark purplish red. Good for jelly	Reddish foliage covered with silky hairs that give it a silvery look. Very prone to scab
M. 'Robinson'	Dense, upright, vase-shaped tree to 25 ft. by 15 ft.	Deep red buds open to single deep pink flowers	Dark red	Copper-tinged foliage. High disease resistance
M. 'Royal Fountain'	Weeping form; to 15 ft. tall and wide	Single rose red	Deep red	Leaves start out purple, turn bronze in summer. Moderate disease resistance
M. 'Royalty' Zones A1–A3; 1–21	Upright, to 20 ft. by 18 ft.	Single purplish crimson	Dark red	Foliage is dark purple in spring, purplish green in summer, dark purple again in fall. Susceptible to scab, fireblight
M. sargentii SARGENT CRABAPPLE	Broad, densely branched, to 10 ft. by 20 ft.	Single white flowers. Blooms are small, fragrant, profuse	Red, tiny, long lasting	Good disease resistance. 'Candymint' has pink flowers with petals outlined in red. 'Rosea', a pink-flowered form, may be more disease prone than the species
M. sieboldii 'Calocarpa' (M. × zumi calocarpa)	Densely branched, rounded, to 15 ft. tall and wide	Single flowers open pale pink, then fade to white. Fragrant	Glossy, bright red, small; lasts well on tree	Moderate susceptibility to fireblight
M. 'Snowdrift' Zones A1–A3; 1–21	Rounded, dense, to 20–25 ft. tall and wide	Red buds open to single white flowers. Long bloom season	Orange red, small, long lasting	Good disease resistance
M. 'Strathmore'	Erect, narrow, to 20 ft. by 10 ft.	Single deep pink to reddish pink flowers	Purplish red, small	Reddish leaves turn bright scarlet in fall. Subject to scab
M. 'Strawberry Parfait'	Open, vase shaped, to 20 ft. by 25 ft.	Red buds open to single pink flowers edged in red; profuse bloomer	Red-blushed yellow	High disease resistance
M. 'Sugar Tyme'	Upright, oval, to 18 ft. by 15 ft.	Delicate light pink buds open to single white flowers. Fragrant	Red, abundant, long lasting	High disease resistance
M. 'Thunderchild' Zones A2, A3; 1–21	Erect, oval, to 20 ft. by 18 ft.	Single rose pink	Dark red	Purple foliage. Good disease resistance
M. 'Weeping Candied Apple'	Weeping form; to 10–15 ft. by 20 ft.	Outer petals deep pink, inner petals whitish edged in pink, opening from reddish buds	Bright red, small; persists all winter	Good disease resistance

MAMMILLARIA

Cactaceae

CACTI

ZONES 8–24, EXCEPT AS NOTED

PARTIAL SHADE IN HOTTEST CLIMATES

REGULAR WATER

Mammillaria

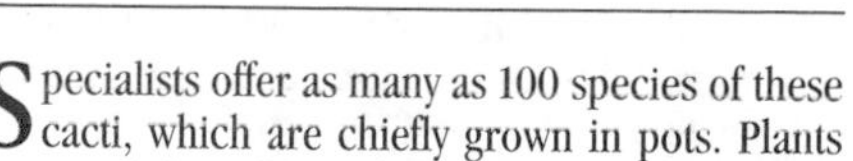

Specialists offer as many as 100 species of these cacti, which are chiefly grown in pots. Plants are small (usually 2–6 in. high), cylindrical or globe shaped, with single or clustered stems. Purple, red, pink, or white flowers (generally small) are arranged in a circle near top of plant. Southwestern natives *M. meiacantha* and *M. wrightii* are hardy to Zone 2. Both are 4 in. high and bear spring flowers; those of *M. meiacantha* are pink or white, those of *M. wrightii* purple or pink.

All mammillarias are easy to grow. Provide some shade in hot desert regions. Give regular moisture during growing season; keep dry in winter to induce bloom. For the plant sold as *M. vivipara*, see *Coryphantha vivipara.*

MANCHURIAN ASH. See FRAXINUS mandshurica 'Mancana'

MANDARIN. See CITRUS

MANDEVILLA

Apocynaceae

EVERGREEN AND DECIDUOUS VINES OR VINING SHRUBS

ZONES VARY BY SPECIES

FULL SUN OR PARTIAL SHADE

REGULAR WATER

Mandevilla 'Alice du Pont'

Grown for showy flowers, the genus *Mandevilla* includes plants formerly called *Dipladenia.* Blossoms feature five broad lobes that flare out from a tubular throat; except as noted, they are unscented. Plants climb by twining. They survive outdoors only in mildest regions. In colder areas, treat as annuals, or grow them in containers and move them indoors or to a greenhouse for the winter. Need heat to bloom; in coastal areas, train against a protected south- or west-facing wall, preferably with additional reflected heat from paving. Watch for spider mites. Growth may need thinning from time to time.

M. boliviensis. Evergreen. Zones 23, 24; H1, H2. Native to Ecuador and Bolivia. Grows to 12 ft. as a vine; reaches 3 ft. tall and 5 ft. wide as a sprawling shrub. Glossy, pointed leaves to 4 in. long, 1½ in. wide. Blooms throughout the year, producing white, 2½-in.-wide flowers with golden yellow throats.

M. hybrids. Evergreen. Zones 21–24; H1, H2. The hybrid mandevillas described here are sometimes sold as selections of *M. ×amabilis* or *M. ×amoena.* Plants grow to 15–20 ft., with glossy dark green, oval leaves 3–8 in. long. Most widely grown is 'Alice du Pont', with clusters of glowing pink, 2–4-in. flowers appearing among the leaves from spring to fall; even very small plants in 4-in. pots will bloom. 'Summer Snow' ('Monte', 'Flora Snow') bears blush pink blossoms that eventually fade to white. 'White Delight' has pale pink buds opening to white blooms with a light yellow throat. 'Ruby Star' is a slightly more compact plant with narrower-lobed, 3-in.-wide flowers; blossoms open deep pink, then mature to magenta with a touch of yellow deep in the throat. 'Rita Marie Green' ('Pink Parfait') has long-lasting, hot pink double flowers. Plant all hybrids in rich soil and provide a frame, trellis, or stake for support. Pinch tips of young plants to induce bushiness.

M. laxa (M. suaveolens). CHILEAN JASMINE. Deciduous; evergreen in frost-free areas. Zones 4–9, 14–24. Native to Chile and Argentina. Grows to 15 ft. or more, with heart-shaped, 2–6-in.-long leaves. Blooms in summer. Clustered flowers are white, 1½–2 in. across, with a powerful perfume like that of gardenia. Requires less heat to bloom than other mandevillas. Provide rich soil. If plant becomes badly tangled, cut to ground in winter; it will resprout and bloom on new growth. Roots hardy to about 5°F/–15°C.

M. splendens (M. sanderi, Dipladenia splendens). Evergreen. Zones 21–24; H1, H2. Native to southeastern Brazil. Compact, shrubby plant to 2 ft. tall, 3 ft. wide; eventually starts to twine (to 15–20 ft. tall with support), but you can keep it bushy by pinching climbing shoots. Deep green leaves are 4–8 in. long, tinged with bronze when new. Flowers are 3–4 in. wide, rose pink with yellow throats; color grows paler as blossoms age. 'Red Riding Hood', with deep cherry red flowers, and white-blooming 'Faire Lady' ('My Fair Lady') are lower growing and shrubbier than the species (to 6–8 ft. as climbers) and superb in hanging baskets. 'Scarlet Pimpernel' is similar in form to the preceding two varieties, but it has scarlet flowers.

MANFREDA maculosa

TEXAS TUBEROSE

Agavaceae

SUCCULENT PERENNIAL

ZONES 4–24

SUN OR SHADE

LITTLE TO REGULAR WATER

Manfreda maculosa

Native to southern Texas, northern Mexico. Fleshy, 6–12-in.-wide leaves grow from a bulblike rootstock to form a 1-ft.-tall, 2-ft.-wide plant that resembles a small, virtually spineless century plant *(Agave americana).* Deep green leaves are strikingly blotched with purple; markings are more pronounced in sun than in shade. In summer, 3–4½-ft. stalks bear fragrant, 2-in.-long, tubular flowers in creamy white aging to purple; long stamens give them a spidery look. Flowers attract hummingbirds. Good in containers or in the ground. Leaves die back in winter but reappear quickly when warm weather arrives. Plants form new clumps by offsets.

MANGLE DULCE. See MAYTENUS phyllanthoides

MANGO

Anacardiaceae

EVERGREEN TREE

ZONES 23, 24; H1, H2

FULL SUN

REGULAR WATER

SAP AND JUICE FROM FRUIT CAUSE SKIN RASH IN SOME PEOPLE

Mango

Tropical Asian native, known botanically as *Mangifera indica.* In Hawaii, mango trees reach upwards of 50 ft. tall and spread to 30 ft. or more. These trees are very long lived and produce heavy crops of fruit. In mildest parts of Southern California, however, plants often remain shrubby and are likely to fruit only in the most favorable frost-free locations. Large (8–16-in.-long), handsome leaves are often coppery red or purple when new; they later turn dark green.

Trees are self-fruitful. Long clusters of yellow to reddish flowers appear at branch ends from spring into summer; these are followed by oval fruits up to 9 in. long, weighing up to 2 lbs. in good growing conditions. Fruit has green to reddish or yellowish skin, a large seed, and very juicy pale yellow to deep orange flesh that tastes somewhat like a peach with flowery overtones. Poorer-quality fruit may be stringy and/or have a flavor reminiscent of varnish or turpentine. In Southern California, skin may not color well, but fruit quality can still be excellent. ▶

Mangoes are most flavorful if allowed to ripen on the tree; they are usually ready to harvest 4 to 5 months after bloom. Many reliable varieties are sold, among them 'Ah Ping', 'Julie', 'Keitt', 'Pope', and 'Rapoza'. Trees tend to bear more heavily in alternate years.

Trees tolerate fairly poor, shallow soil as long as it is well drained. Fertilize as recommended for citrus. Anthracnose, scale, and powdery mildew can be serious problems. Little pruning is needed.

MANZANITA. See ARCTOSTAPHYLOS

MAPLE. See ACER

Marantaceae. The arrowroot family consists of tropical or subtropical herbaceous plants with fleshy rhizomes or tubers and highly asymmetrical flowers. Most are grown for handsome foliage, a few for flowers. An example is *Calathea.*

MARGUERITE. See CHRYSANTHEMUM frutescens

MARIGOLD. See TAGETES

MARIPOSA LILY. See CALOCHORTUS

MARJORAM. See ORIGANUM

MARLBERRY. See ARDISIA

MARMALADE BUSH. See STREPTOSOLEN jamesonii

MARRUBIUM vulgare

HOREHOUND
Lamiaceae (Labiatae)
PERENNIAL
ZONES 1–24
FULL SUN
LITTLE TO MODERATE WATER

Marrubium vulgare

Native to Mediterranean region and western Asia; naturalized throughout Europe and the Americas. Coarse, upright plant to 1–3 ft. tall, 1–1½ ft. wide, with wrinkled, woolly, aromatic gray-green leaves to 2 in. long. Rounded whorls of white flowers (similar to those of mint) bloom on foot-long, branching stems in summer. Flowers in second year from seed. As a garden plant, it is invasive and rather weedy looking, but it makes a serviceable edging in a garden of gray-leafed plants. Used for medicinal purposes and in candy. Foliage lasts well in bouquets. Requires little water but will take more if drainage is good; otherwise not fussy about soil. Give protection from cold, wind.

MARSH MARIGOLD. See CALTHA palustris

MASCAGNIA

ORCHID VINE
Malpighiaceae
DECIDUOUS VINES
ZONES 12–24
FULL SUN
MODERATE WATER

Mascagnia lilacina

Twining vines native to Mexico; useful in desert gardens, where they bloom at the hottest time of year. Bright green leaves in opposite pairs resemble those of honeysuckle *(Lonicera).* Bear clusters of five-petaled blossoms (the petals are shaped like ping-pong paddles); each bloom is centered with ten stamens. Oddly winged seedpods that look something like butterflies follow the flowers; these are sometimes used in dried arrangements.

M. lilacina. LAVENDER ORCHID VINE. To 15–20 ft., with 1½-in. leaves and lilac flowers that are followed by inch-wide seedpods. Plant is hardy to 15 to 18°F/−9 to −8°C.

M. macroptera. YELLOW ORCHID VINE. To 15 ft., with 3-in. leaves. Abundant bright yellow flowers are followed by conspicuous 2-in., yellow-green seedpods. Hardy to 22 to 24°F/−6 to −4°C.

MASTERWORT. See ASTRANTIA

MASTIC. See PISTACIA lentiscus

MATILIJA POPPY. See ROMNEYA coulteri

MATRICARIA recutita (M. chamomilla)

CHAMOMILE
Asteraceae (Compositae)
ANNUAL
ZONES 1–24
FULL SUN
MODERATE WATER

Matricaria recutita

Native to Europe, western Asia; naturalized in North America. Aromatic plant grows to 2 ft. tall and 1½ ft. wide, with finely cut, almost fern-like foliage. White-and-yellow daisy-type flowers to 1 in. wide bloom in summer. Grows easily in ordinary soil; sow seed in late winter or spring. Valued for its herbal use: dried flowers are used in making the familiar, fragrant chamomile tea.

Plants or seeds sold as *Matricaria* 'White Stars', 'Golden Ball', and 'Snowball' are varieties of *Chrysanthemum parthenium.* Chamomile sold as a walk-on ground cover is *Chamaemelum nobile (Anthemis nobilis).*

MATRIMONY VINE. See LYCIUM chinense

MATTEUCCIA struthiopteris

OSTRICH FERN
Polypodiaceae
FERN
ZONES A1–A3; 1–10, 14–17
FULL SUN IN COOLER CLIMATES ONLY
REGULAR TO AMPLE WATER

Matteuccia struthiopteris

Native to northern regions of North America, Europe, Asia. Is hardy to extreme cold and does not grow with full vigor in mild-winter areas. Clump is narrow at base, then spreads out at top like a shuttlecock. Plant can grow 6 ft. tall and 3 ft. wide in moist, moderate climates, but it may reach only a quarter or a third of that size in mountain regions with short growing season, low humidity.

Plant spreads by underground rhizomes. Attractive in woodland or beside pond or stream. Unfolding young fronds (fiddleheads) are edible; they are usually served as a cooked vegetable. Needs rich soil. Also sold as *Matteuccia pensylvanica.*

FOR DEFINITIONS OF GARDENING TERMS
PLEASE SEE PAGES 746–750

MATTHIOLA

STOCK

Brassicaceae (Cruciferae)

BIENNIALS OR PERENNIALS GROWN AS ANNUALS

ZONES 1–24

FULL SUN OR LIGHT SHADE

REGULAR WATER

Matthiola incana

From the Mediterranean region. Old-fashioned favorites, with narrow gray-green leaves and profuse, erect spikes of fragrant flowers. Best in cool weather.

M. incana. Valued for spicy-sweet perfume, cut flowers. Oblong leaves to 4 in. long. Flowers are single or double, 1 in. wide, in colors including white, pink, red, purple, lavender, blue, yellow, and cream.

Many strains are available, ranging from under 1 ft. to as tall as 3 ft., from 10 to 16 in. wide. Earliest bloomer is Trysomic Seven Weeks (flowers in 7 weeks), with branching plants about 12–15 in. tall. Ten Weeks, also branching, reaches 15–18 in. tall. Column and Double Giant Flowering are unbranched plants 2–3 ft. tall; they can be planted 6–8 in. apart in rows and are ideal for cutting. Giant Imperial strain is branching, 2–2½ ft. tall; it comes in solid or mixed colors.

Stock needs light, fertile soil and good drainage. In cold-winter areas, plant in earliest spring to get flowers before hot weather (choose early bloomers). In mild-winter regions, plants set out in early fall will bloom in winter or early spring. Take moderate frost but will not set flower buds if nights are too chilly; late planting means no flowers until spring. Where winter rainfall is heavy, plant in raised beds for good drainage.

M. longipetala bicornis. EVENING SCENTED STOCK. To 1 ft. or a little taller, 9 in. wide, with lance-shaped leaves to 3½ in. long. Small purplish flowers are not showy, but they give off a powerful fragrance at night. In hot-summer, mild-winter climates, grow as a winter annual.

MATTRESS VINE. See MUEHLENBECKIA complexa

MAY APPLE. See PODOPHYLLUM peltatum

MAYBUSH, MAYDAY TREE. See PRUNUS padus

MAYTENUS

Celastraceae

EVERGREEN TREES AND SHRUBS

ZONES VARY BY SPECIES

FULL SUN

WATER NEEDS VARY BY SPECIES

Maytenus boaria

Two species of this genus of primarily South American natives are grown in the West. Both have inconspicuous flowers and fruit, but they are otherwise remarkably dissimilar in appearance.

M. boaria. MAYTEN. Zones 8, 9, 14–24. From Chile. Graceful tree with narrow, 1–2-in.-long, light to medium green leaves. Resembles a small-scale weeping willow *(Salix)*, with long, pendulous branchlets hanging down from branches. Slow to moderate growth to an eventual 30–50 ft. high and wide; 20 ft. tall by 15 ft. wide is typical at 12 years of age. For uniformity, plant cutting-grown trees of 'Green Showers'; its weeping branchlets are densely clad with deep green leaves that are a little broader than those of the species.

Give well-drained soil. Disturbing the roots by cultivating may cause suckers to appear. Tree produces much side growth; remove unwanted branches along trunk, or keep some of them for multiple-trunk effect. May show partial defoliation after a cold snap, but recovery is rapid. Resistant to oak root fungus. Moderate to regular water; irrigate deeply to keep tree from rooting near soil surface and invading planting beds.

M. phyllanthoides. MANGLE DULCE. Zones 12, 13, 23, 24. From Baja California, Mexico, the Caribbean. Like mangroves (*mangle* is Spanish for "mangrove"), this plant grows in or near salt water and in brackish, swampy soils inland. Usually a 6–12 ft. shrub but occasionally a small tree up to 24 ft.; usually as wide as tall. Smooth light gray bark; fleshy dark green to gray-green leaves to 1½ in. long. Little to moderate water.

MAZUS reptans

Scrophulariaceae

PERENNIAL

ZONES 1–9, 14–24

PARTIAL SHADE IN HOTTEST CLIMATES

REGULAR WATER

Mazus reptans

Himalayan native to 2 in. high; spreads 1 ft. or wider by slender stems that creep and root along the ground. Sparsely toothed, rather narrow leaves are bright green, about 1 in. long. Spring and early summer flowers are ¾ in. across, purplish blue with white and yellow markings; they appear in clusters of two to five. In shape, blossoms resemble those of monkey flower *(Mimulus)*. Use in rock garden, as small-scale ground cover, as filler between pavers (takes heavy foot traffic in this last role). Needs rich soil. Evergreen in mild-winter climates; in colder areas, freezes to ground but usually recovers quickly in spring if protected over winter by snow cover or light mulch.

MEADOWFOAM. See LIMNANTHES douglasii

MEADOW RUE. See THALICTRUM

MEADOW SAFFRON. See COLCHICUM

MECONOPSIS

Papaveraceae

PERENNIALS

ZONES VARY BY SPECIES

PARTIAL OR FULL SHADE

REGULAR WATER

Meconopsis betonicifolia

Ardent collectors and shade garden enthusiasts sometimes attempt the many species offered by specialist seed firms. Most of these are difficult to grow, but the choices listed here are not too trying if given loose, acid soil and cool, humid, shady conditions. Plants consist of foliage rosettes with elongated leaves that vary in shape from undivided to lobed or cut; these foliage clumps send up flowering stems at bloom time. Protect seaside plantings from wind. Plants self-sow without becoming invasive. Except as noted, these plants are native to the Himalayas.

M. betonicifolia (M. baileyi). HIMALAYAN POPPY. Zones A1–A3; 1–6, 17. In the right climate, can reach 6 ft. tall and 2 ft. wide. Abundant hairy leaves with serrated edges; silky, 3–4-in., sky blue poppies with yellow stamens. In less favorable locales, it is a much squatter, shorter-lived plant with smaller flowers verging on mauve. Blooms in late spring or early summer.

M. cambrica. WELSH POPPY. Zones 1–9, 14–17. Native to western Europe. To 1–2 ft. tall, 1 ft. wide, with divided leaves. Easier to grow than *M. betonicifolia.* Produces orange or yellow, 3-in. poppies from late spring to fall. In the coolest-summer areas, it tolerates full sun, some drought. *M. c. aurantiaca* 'Flore Pleno' has semidouble flowers.

M. grandis. Zones A2, A3; 1–6, 17. To 4 ft. tall, 2 ft. wide. Tooth-edged basal leaves are up to 10 in. long; leaf size is reduced farther up the stems. Leaves and stems have rusty hairs. In late spring, 4–6-in.-wide flowers in pure blue to purplish red are borne on long (to 16-in.) stalks that rise from the uppermost leaves. May be biennial if moisture is not adequate. ▶

M. ×sheldonii. Zones A2, A3; 1–6, 17. Hybrid of *M. betonicifolia* and *M. grandis.* Plant grows to 4–5 ft. tall, 2 ft. wide, with toothed leaves and 4-in., pure blue poppies on 8–20-in. stalks. Blooms in late spring or early summer.

MEDITERRANEAN FAN PALM. See CHAMAEROPS humilis

MELALEUCA

Myrtaceae

EVERGREEN SHRUBS OR TREES

ZONES VARY BY SPECIES

FULL SUN

LITTLE WATER, EXCEPT AS NOTED

Melaleuca linariifolia

Australia is home to 140 or more species of melaleucas, and many of these show up in Western gardens. All have narrow, sometimes needlelike leaves and bear clustered flowers with prominent stamens; the blossoms attract birds. Since each flower cluster resembles a bottlebrush, some melaleucas are called bottlebrushes, though that name is more generally applied to members of the genus *Callistemon.* Tight clusters of woody seed capsules are attached directly to branches; these hang on for several years, forming odd, decorative cylinders around twigs and branches. Many melaleucas have interestingly contorted branches and bark that peels off in thick, papery layers.

All melaleucas are easy to grow. Most withstand heat, wind, seacoast conditions, poor soil, limited moisture. Most are vigorous and fast growing; for a natural appearance, control by cutting back selected branches to a well-placed side branch. Almost all melaleucas make good screens; some of the larger ones are useful as flowering or shade trees.

M. armillaris. DROOPING MELALEUCA. Shrub or tree. Zones 8, 9, 12–24; H1, H2. As sprawling shrub, grows 12–15 ft. high, 15–30 ft. wide; trained as a tree, reaches 15–30 ft. tall and wide. Branches are drooping. Furrowed gray bark peels off in strips near base of trunk. Light green, needlelike leaves to 1 in. long; fluffy white flowers in 1–3½-in.-long spikes from spring to fall. Tough and adaptable; especially useful in sea winds. Use as clipped hedge or unclipped informal screen; prickly leaves make it a good barrier plant.

M. decussata. LILAC MELALEUCA. Shrub or tree. Zones 9, 12–24; H1. To 8–20 ft. tall and wide. Brown, shredding bark. Tiny (½-in.) bluish leaves closely set on arching, pendulous branches. Lilac to purple flowers in 1-in. spikes from late spring to summer. Withstands some neglect. Use it for big masses of fine-textured foliage in the landscape. Thin to improve appearance, show off trunk and branch character.

M. elliptica. GRANITE BOTTLEBRUSH. Shrub or tree. Zones 9, 12–24. To 8–16 ft. high, 10–15 ft. wide. Brown, shredding bark. Branches are fanlike, with each one producing a number of branchlets that spread outward and upward in a single plane; roundish, ½-in., bluish or grayish green leaves are set mostly at branchlet ends. Blooms from early spring to fall, bearing showy, bright pink to crimson, 2–3½-in.-long bottlebrushes on side branches.

M. ericifolia. HEATH MELALEUCA. Shrub or tree. Zones 9, 12–24; H1. To 18–36 ft. tall, 12–24 ft. wide. Soft, fibrous tan or gray bark. Dark green, needlelike, 1-in. leaves like those of heather *(Calluna)*. Yellowish white flowers in 1-in. spikes bloom in early spring. Grows fast and tolerates alkaline soil, poor drainage; good near beach. Makes an attractive multi-trunked tree.

M. fulgens. SCARLET HONEY MYRTLE. Shrub. Zones 13, 15–24. To 3–9 ft. tall, 5–9 ft. wide, with flat, narrow green to gray-green leaves ¼–1 in. long. Blooms from late winter to early summer, with sporadic rebloom likely; flower clusters are 2 in. long and wide, in pale orange, salmon, or bright scarlet (all with golden anthers). Blossoms appear at ends of branches, and new leafy growth proceeds from center of flower cluster. Showy plant.

M. huegelii. CHENILLE HONEY MYRTLE. Shrub or tree. Zones 9, 12–24. Highly variable species to 3–25 ft. tall, 6–20 ft. wide. Nearly triangular leaves are less than ½ in. long, set close together on branches, usually overlapping. Profuse spring to summer show of 2–4-in.-long flowers that are pink or red in bud, opening to white or cream (rarely pink). Blossoms are good for cutting. Plant can take hard pruning and serve as hedge or windbreak.

M. hypericifolia. DOTTED MELALEUCA. Shrub. Zones 9, 12–24; H1. To 6–12 ft. tall, 3–12 ft. wide, with thin, peeling pale gray bark and drooping branches. Coppery green to dull green, 1¼-in. leaves. Blooms from late spring through winter, producing bright orange-red flowers in dense 2-in. clusters (often hidden by foliage). Can be clipped into a hedge but blooms more profusely as an informal, unclipped screen. Not suitable for planting right at beach, though it takes ocean wind.

M. incana. GRAY HONEY MYRTLE. Shrub or tree. Zones 8, 9, 12–24. Spreading, arching plant with semiweeping branchlets. Gray, furry foliage gives the plant an overall pale, smoky look. Small clusters of yellowish white flowers in spring. Naturally grows as a broad shrub to 9 ft. tall and wide but can be shaped into a handsome small tree.

M. lanceolata. BLACK TEA TREE. Shrub or tree. Zones 8, 9, 12–24. To 18–30 ft. tall, 12–25 ft. wide. Narrow dark green leaves to ½ in. long. White or cream, 2-in. bottlebrush flower clusters bloom from summer into fall, with sporadic bloom the rest of the year. Tolerates most soil types and takes hard frosts. Tends to retain its foliage down to ground level.

M. linariifolia. FLAXLEAF PAPERBARK. Tree. Zones 9, 13–24; H1. To 20–30 ft. tall, 20–25 ft. wide, with dense, umbrellalike crown. White bark sheds in papery flakes. Slender branchlets covered with stiff, bright green or bluish green, needlelike leaves about 1¼ in. long. In summer, numerous fluffy spikes of small white flowers give effect of snow on branches. Young plants are willowy and need staking until trunk firms up.

M. nesophila. PINK MELALEUCA. Tree or shrub. Zones 13, 16–24; H1. Fast growth to 15–20 ft. high (possibly to 30 ft.) and about as wide. Grows naturally as a small tree. Develops gnarled, heavy branches that sprawl or ascend in picturesque patterns. Grayish cream to pale brown bark is thick and spongy; gray-green leaves are thick, roundish, to 1 in. long. Roundish bottlebrush flower clusters to 1 in. wide are produced at branch ends most of the year; they open mauve pink, fade to white with yellow tips. Use as tree or big, informal screen; or shear as hedge. Takes ocean winds and spray; poor, rocky soil; desert heat. Little to regular water.

M. quinquenervia. CAJEPUT TREE, PAPERBARK TREE. Zones 9, 12, 13, 15–17, 20–24; H1, H2. Upright, open growth to 20–40 ft. tall, 15–25 ft. wide; can become twice as large in the tropics. Pendulous young branches. Thick, spongy, light brown to whitish bark peels off in sheets (you can use these sheets to line wire hanging baskets). Stiff, narrowly oval, 2–4-in.-long leaves are shiny pale green, covered with silky hairs when young. The foliage turns purple with light frosts. Yellowish white (sometimes pink or purple) flowers bloom in 2–3-in. spikes in summer and fall. Good street tree. Trees planted 8–10 ft. apart and thinned occasionally make a pleasant grove. Little to regular water. Has been sold as *M. leucadendra.*

Melaleuca quinquenervia

M. rhaphiophylla. SWAMP PAPERBARK. Zones 8, 9, 12–24. Shrub or tree to 12–45 ft. tall and 9–24 ft. wide, with papery gray or tan bark and green or gray-green, needlelike leaves ½–2 in. long. Profuse, showy bloom from spring into summer, with fragrant white or cream, 1½-in.-long flower clusters. Can endure some shade. Regular to ample water.

M. styphelioides. BLACK TEA TREE. Tree. Zones 9, 13–24; H1. To 20–40 ft. tall, 10–20 ft. wide, with lacy, open growth and pendulous branchlets. Thick, spongy bark turns from pale tan to charcoal colored with age, peels off in papery layers. Light green, prickly leaves to ¾ in. long are sometimes twisted. Creamy white flowers in 1–2-in. brushes from summer through fall. Thrives in any soil. Resistant to oak root fungus. Good lawn tree. Best trained with multiple trunks.

M. thymifolia. THYMELEAF MELALEUCA. Shrub. Zones 8, 9, 12–24. Low, spreading bush 2–4 ft. high, 4–8 ft. wide. Bark is corky, flaking, grayish brown. Narrow blue-green leaves to 3/4 in. long are fragrant when crushed. Blooms spring through early summer, with 2–3-in.-wide flower clusters resembling bundles of tiny ostrich feathers in white, pink, deep mauve, or dusky purple. Many different color forms, including 'Pink Lace' and 'White Lace'. Prefers acid soil but tolerates soils that lack fertility, are somewhat alkaline, or have sluggish drainage. Prune after flowering to keep compact. Takes occasional drought; best with regular water.

M. viridiflora. BROAD-LEAFED PAPERBARK. Shrub or tree. Zones 13, 19–24. To 12–25 ft. tall, 6–18 ft. wide, with papery gray or light tan bark. Thick, leathery dark green or gray green leaves less than 1 in. long. Flowering comes sporadically throughout the year; blossoms are narrow brushes to 6 in. long in white, cream, or green. *M. v. rubriflora* has pink to red flowers.

M. wilsonii. VIOLET HONEY MYRTLE. Shrub. Zones 8, 9, 12–24. To 3–10 ft. tall, 5–12 ft. wide, with spreading or arching habit. Leaves very narrow, 1/2 in. long, dark green. Clusters of two to five pink or purplish pink, 1/2-in.-wide flowers line the branches to make spikes that may or may not be interrupted by leaves. Can be pruned as a hedge. Will tolerate hard frost and occasional flooding. Takes extended dry spells but looks best with regular water.

MELAMPODIUM leucanthum

BLACKFOOT DAISY
Asteraceae (Compositae)
PERENNIAL
ZONES 2, 3, 10–13
FULL SUN
MODERATE WATER

Melampodium leucanthum

Short-lived perennial from Arizona, New Mexico, Texas, Mexico. Narrow gray leaves in clumps to 1 ft. tall and wide are topped by clouds of inch-wide, honey-scented white daisies with yellow centers. Showy when in bloom. In mild climates, it flowers off and on during the winter months and more heavily from midspring into early fall—if given some water. Where freezing temperatures are routine, expect bloom in spring and summer only. Grow in fast-draining soil; in nature, blackfoot daisy grows principally in decomposed granite. If plant becomes straggly, cut it back in fall.

For the annual butter daisy, sometimes sold as *M. paludosum,* see *Chrysanthemum paludosum.*

Melastomataceae. The melastoma family consists almost entirely of tropical shrubs and trees with strongly veined leaves and symmetrical flowers. Two members are Spanish shawl *(Heterocentron)* and princess flower *(Tibouchina).*

MELIA azedarach

CHINABERRY
Meliaceae
DECIDUOUS TREE
ZONES 6–24; H1, H2
FULL SUN
MODERATE WATER
FRUIT IS POISONOUS IF INGESTED

Melia azedarach 'Umbraculiformis'

Native to China, northern India. To 30–50 ft. high and wide, with irregular habit. Rich green, 1–3-ft.-long leaves are cut into many toothed, narrow or oval leaflets 1–2 in. long. In spring or early summer, bears loose clusters of lilac flowers that are fragrant in the evening. Blossoms are followed by hard, berrylike yellow fruits about 1/2 in. wide. Tough plant; tolerates heat, wind, poor alkaline soil, drought. In areas with year-round moisture, tends to self-sow and become a pest.

'Umbraculiformis', Texas umbrella tree, is less picturesque but far more common than the species. Grows to 20–25 ft. high, with dense, dome-shaped crown and drooping leaves. Grows true from seed.

Meliaceae. The mahogany family, consisting largely of tropical trees and shrubs, includes two plants grown in the West: *Melia* and *Toona.* Both have finely divided leaves and clustered flowers.

MELIANTHUS major

HONEY BUSH
Melianthaceae
EVERGREEN SHRUB
ZONES 8, 9, 12–24; H1, H2
PARTIAL SHADE IN HOTTEST CLIMATES
LITTLE TO REGULAR WATER

Melianthus major

Native to South Africa. This soft-wooded plant grows rapidly to 6–12 ft. tall and 8–10 ft. wide but is easily kept much shorter. Irregular habit, with stems that may be semierect or sprawling and spreading. Bold-looking foliage: grayish green, foot-long leaves divided into strongly toothed leaflets. Foliage is malodorous when brushed against or bruised. Foot-tall spikes of reddish brown, 1-in. flowers bloom in late winter, early spring. Adapts to most soils. Use for tropical effects; good as accent plant. To get a tall shrub, stake a few stems; for a sprawling, bulkier plant, shorten some stems in early spring before new growth begins.

M. minor is a rare plant occasionally seen at plant sales or in collectors' gardens. Leaves are shorter than those of *M. major* (6–7 in. long), on a shorter (3-ft.-tall) plant. Its flowers are hidden among the leaves.

M

MELISSA officinalis

LEMON BALM, SWEET BALM
Lamiaceae (Labiatae)
PERENNIAL
ZONES 1–24
FULL SUN OR PARTIAL SHADE
REGULAR WATER

Melissa officinalis

From southern Europe. A single plant grows to about 2 ft. tall, 1½ ft. wide—but plants self-sow and spread rapidly, sometimes becoming pests. Lemon-scented, heavily veined foliage is light green in the species. Check catalogs to find 'Aurea' and 'All Gold', with solid yellow leaves, and 'Variegata', with green foliage variegated in yellow. Leaves are used fresh in cold drinks, fruit cups, salads, fish dishes; dried leaves give lemon perfume to sachets, potpourris. Likes rich soil. Shear occasionally to keep compact.

MELON

Cucurbitaceae
ANNUALS
ZONES 2–24; DIFFICULT IN ZONES A2, A3, 1, H1, H2
FULL SUN
REGULAR WATER

Melon

Classified botanically as *Cucumis melo* and thought to have originated in Africa. Principal types cultivated in the West are muskmelons ("cantaloupes") and late melons; the true cantaloupe is a hard-shelled melon rarely grown in North America. Also see Watermelon. ▶

Muskmelons are ribbed, with netted skin and typically salmon-colored flesh; they are more widely adapted than late melons. Varieties include 'Ambrosia', 'Burpee Hybrid', 'Earligold', and 'Sweet 'n Early'. Hybrids are superior to others in disease resistance and uniformity of size and quality. (Growing melons resistant to mildew and other diseases is particularly important in humid, coastal regions.) Seed packets and catalogs will usually tell you if the variety you buy is a hybrid. Other muskmelons include small, tasty, highly perfumed types from the Mediterranean, such as white-fleshed 'Ha-Ogen' and orange-fleshed 'Charmel' and 'Charentais'.

Late melons are a varied group including honeydew, casaba, 'Crenshaw', 'Honey Pearl', 'Persian', and 'Sweet Delight'. Because they need a longer growing season than muskmelons, they are less widely cultivated. They dislike high humidity and grow best in areas with hot, relatively dry summers (Zones 8, 9, 12–14, 18, 19).

To ripen to full sweetness, melons need steady heat for 2½ to 4 months. Sow seeds in light, well-drained soil 2 weeks after average last-frost date; don't rush it, since melons are truly tropical plants and will perish in even a light frost. In regions where summers are cool or relatively short, start plants indoors in pots a few weeks before last-frost date, then plant outdoors in warmest southern exposure. Row covers permit earlier planting outdoors. Clear plastic mulch (in areas where summers are very short) or black plastic mulch under melons warms soil, speeds harvest, and helps keep fruit from rotting.

Though you can grow melons on sun-bathed trellises, the heavy fruit must be supported in individual cloth slings. These plants are best grown in hills or mounded rows a few inches high at center; you will need to provide considerable space. Make hills about 3 ft. in diameter and space them 3–4 ft. apart; encircle each with a furrow for irrigation. Make rows 3 ft. wide and as long as desired, spacing them 3–4 ft. apart; make furrows for irrigation along both sides. Plant seeds 1 in. deep—four or five seeds per hill, two or three seeds every 1 ft. in rows. When plants are well established, thin each hill to the best two plants; thin rows to one strong plant per foot. Fill furrows with water from time to time (furrows let you water plants without wetting foliage), but do not keep soil soaked. Feed (again in furrows) every 6 weeks.

To determine if a cantaloupe is ready for harvest, lift the fruit and twist; it will easily slip off the stem if ripe. A pleasant, perfumy fragrance also indicates ripeness.

Late melons do not slip from stems when ripe. Honeydews are ready to pick when the area where the melon rests on the ground turns from yellow to white. Harvest 'Crenshaw', casaba, and other late melons when the fruit begins to turn yellow and starts to soften at the blossom end. As 'Crenshaw' approaches maturity, protect fruits from sunburn by shading them on the southwest side with a wooden shingle.

MENTHA

MINT

Lamiaceae (Labiatae)

PERENNIALS

ZONES VARY BY SPECIES

FULL SUN OR PARTIAL SHADE

REGULAR WATER

Mentha spicata

These Mediterranean natives spread rapidly by underground stems and can be quite invasive; to keep them in bounds, grow them in pots or boxes. Tough and unfussy, they grow almost anywhere but perform best with light, moist, medium-rich soil; regular water; and full sun or part shade. Plants disappear in winter in colder part of range. Replant about every 3 years; propagate from runners.

M. ×gracilis (M. ×gentilis). GOLDEN APPLE MINT. Zones 3–24. To 2 ft. tall. Smooth deep green leaves with yellow variegation have a spicy apple fragrance and flavor. Inconspicuous flowers. Use in flavoring foods. Foliage is excellent in mixed bouquets.

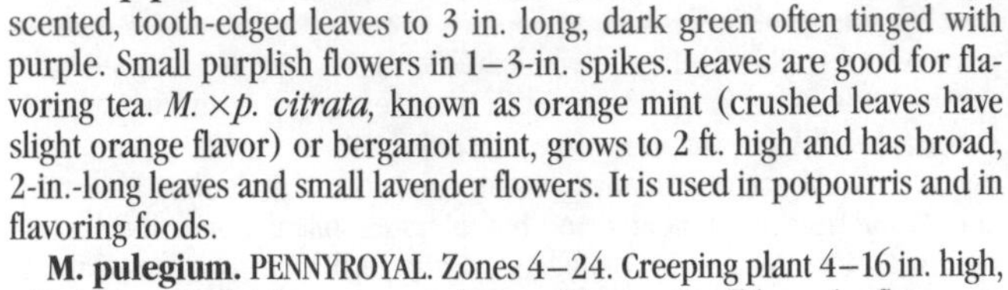

M. ×piperita. PEPPERMINT. Zones A2, A3; 1–24. To 3 ft. tall. Strongly scented, tooth-edged leaves to 3 in. long, dark green often tinged with purple. Small purplish flowers in 1–3-in. spikes. Leaves are good for flavoring tea. *M. ×p. citrata,* known as orange mint (crushed leaves have slight orange flavor) or bergamot mint, grows to 2 ft. high and has broad, 2-in.-long leaves and small lavender flowers. It is used in potpourris and in flavoring foods.

M. pulegium. PENNYROYAL. Zones 4–24. Creeping plant 4–16 in. high, with inch-wide, bright green, nearly round leaves. Small lavender flowers in tight, short whorls. Strong mint fragrance and flavor. Poisonous if consumed in large quantities but safe as a flavoring. Needs a cool, moist site.

M. requienii. JEWEL MINT OF CORSICA. Zones 5–9, 12–24. Creeping, mat-forming mint reaches only ½ in. high. Tiny, round bright green leaves give this plant a mossy appearance; leaves release a delightful minty or sagelike fragrance when bruised. Can be used as an aromatic filler between stepping-stones (won't take heavy foot traffic). Bears tiny, tubular light purple flowers in summer.

M. spicata. SPEARMINT. Zones A2, A3; 1–24. To 1–3 ft. high. Dark green, toothed leaves are slightly smaller than those of *M. ×piperita.* Leafy spikes of pale blue flowers. Use leaves fresh from the garden or dried, as flavoring for foods, cold drinks, jelly.

M. suaveolens (M. rotundifolia). APPLE MINT. Zones 3–24. Stiff stems grow 1½–3 ft. tall, bearing rounded, slightly hairy gray-green leaves 1–4 in. long. Purplish white flowers in 2–3-in. spikes. Foliage has scent combining fragrances of apple and mint. 'Variegata', pineapple mint, has leaves with white markings, faint scent of pineapple.

MENTZELIA

BLAZING STAR

Loasaceae

PERENNIALS, BIENNIALS, AND ANNUALS

ZONES VARY BY SPECIES

FULL SUN

WATER NEEDS VARY BY SPECIES

Mentzelia lindleyi

Native to desert and semidesert areas of western U.S. Tolerate heat, wind, and poor soil, but require good drainage. Star-shaped yellow blossoms are large and showy. Good in naturalistic plantings.

M. laevicaulis. Biennial or short-lived perennial. Zones 1–3, 7–9, 14–24. Rough, ungainly plant to 3–3½ ft. tall and wide, with narrow, 3–7-in.-long leaves. During spring and summer, spectacular pale yellow, 4-in. stars open in the evening; plant is often given the name "evening star" for that reason. Best used on bare banks. Little or no water.

M. lindleyi. Annual. Zones 4–9, 14–24. To 1–4 ft. tall; usually narrow but sometimes spreading to 1½ ft. Rough-textured light green to gray-green leaves. In spring or early summer, produces flowers that are bright yellow with orange or reddish central ring and a big brush of yellow stamens. Use alone or in wildflower mixtures. Sow seed in place in fall, winter, or earliest part of spring. Provide regular water until plants come into bloom, then reduce or stop watering.

MERREMIA

YELLOW MORNING GLORY, WOOD ROSE

Convolvulaceae

EVERGREEN VINES

ZONES VARY BY SPECIES

FULL SUN

REGULAR WATER

Merremia aurea

Twining vines with leaves divided into leaflets and golden, 3-in. flowers like those of morning glory *(Ipomoea).* Flowers are followed by woody, roundish seed capsules surrounded by woody sepals—the "wood roses" admired by flower arrangers. Tolerate some drought.

M. aurea. Zones 12–24. Native to Baja California. Climbs to 25 ft., with a woody base and leaves divided into five 1½-in. leaflets. Blooms during warm months. Drops leaves in summer drought. May be felled by frost but will resprout from the roots.

M. tuberosa (Ipomoea tuberosa). PILIKAI. Zones 23 (borderline), 24; H1, H2. Native to tropical America but naturalized throughout the tropics. Climbs to 50–100 ft., with 6-in. leaves divided into seven lobes. Flowers in late winter and spring.

MERTENSIA

Boraginaceae

PERENNIALS

ZONES VARY BY SPECIES

PARTIAL OR FULL SHADE

REGULAR WATER

Mertensia pulmonarioides

Resemble giant-size forget-me-nots *(Myosotis)* and belong to the same family. Plants emerge and flower early, then go dormant soon after going to seed (usually before midsummer). Typically smooth, gray-green or blue-green leaves. Nodding, bell-shaped flowers are carried in gradually uncoiling clusters. Blooms are pink or lavender in bud, opening to blue flowers that sometimes have a pinkish cast. Good in woodland gardens.

Provide moist, rich soil. Use summer annuals to fill void after plants die back. Clumps can be left in place indefinitely; they will slowly spread. To increase a planting, transplant volunteer seedlings or dig and divide the clump in early fall.

M. ciliata. CHIMING BELLS, MOUNTAIN BLUEBELL. Zones 1–7, 14–17. Native to damp places in the Rocky Mountains and the Blue Mountains of Oregon. To 3 ft. tall and 1 ft. wide, with ½–¾-in. flowers. Several other species, most of them lower growing than *M. ciliata,* also are native to mountainous areas of the West.

M. pulmonarioides (M. virginica). VIRGINIA BLUEBELLS. Zones 1–9, 14–21. From eastern U.S. Most widely planted species. To 1–2 ft. tall and 1½ ft. wide, with 1-in. flowers.

MESCAL BEAN. See SOPHORA secundiflora

MESEMBRYANTHEMUM crystallinum

ICE PLANT

Aizoaceae

SUCCULENT ANNUAL OR BIENNIAL

ALL ZONES

FULL SUN

LITTLE OR NO WATER TO MODERATE WATER

Mesembryanthemum crystallinum

The least ornamental of many plants commonly called *Mesembryanthemum* or ice plant, this native of South Africa is now considered the only true *Mesembryanthemum.* For other, showier ice plants, see listings under Ice Plants.

M. crystallinum is a sprawling plant a few inches tall and several feet wide. Oval, flat, stalked, fleshy leaves grow to 4 in. long, turn red at dry times of year. Leaves are covered with tiny, transparent blisters that glisten like flecks of ice. Foliage is edible and resembles New Zealand spinach in flavor. White to pinkish, 1-in. flowers bloom in summer. Easy to grow from seed. Has naturalized in parts of California. Very drought tolerant plant when grown in the ground. Best use in gardens, though, is in hanging baskets and window boxes—in which locations this plant will need at least moderate watering.

MESQUITE. See PROSOPIS

METASEQUOIA glyptostroboides

DAWN REDWOOD

Taxodiaceae

DECIDUOUS TREE

ZONES A3; 3–10, 14–24

FULL SUN

REGULAR WATER

Metasequoia glyptostroboides

Thought to have been extinct for thousands of years, this plant was found growing in a few isolated sites in its native China during the 1940s. It is a pyramidal tree with small cones and soft, pale green needles that turn light bronze in autumn, then drop to reveal attractive winter silhouette. Branchlets tend to turn upward. Young trees have reddish bark; older ones have darker, fissured bark and rugged, fluted trunk bases. Grows very fast when young—sometimes as much as 4–6 ft. a year in California (less in colder areas). Reaches about 90 ft. tall and about 20 ft. wide at the age of 40 or so (trees haven't been in cultivation long enough to determine the maximum garden size). Looks somewhat like bald cypress *(Taxodium distichum),* another deciduous conifer. While in leaf, it also bears superficial resemblance to coast redwood *(Sequoia sempervirens).*

Grows best in good, well-drained soil with regular moisture. Good lawn tree, though in time surface roots may interrupt smooth flow of turf. Not suited to arid regions or seacoast, since dry heat and salty ocean winds will burn foliage. Resistant to oak root fungus.

M

METROSIDEROS

Myrtaceae

EVERGREEN TREES OR SHRUBS

ZONES VARY BY SPECIES

BEST IN SUN, TOLERATE SOME SHADE

MODERATE WATER

Grown for attractive, leathery foliage and showy flowers with prominent stamens. Best near coast; tolerate wind, salt spray. Grow in well-drained soil. Sensitive to frost.

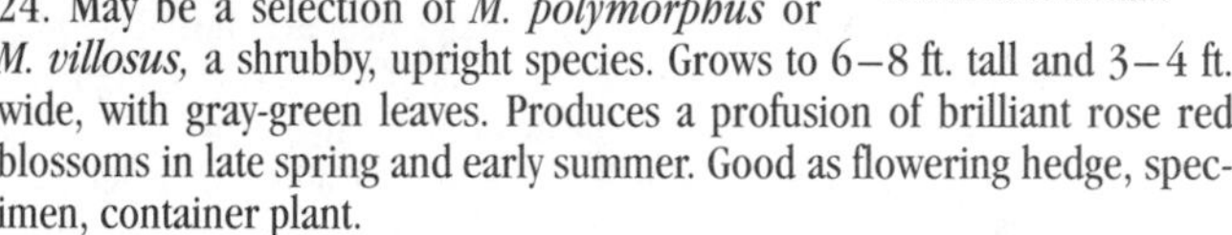

Metrosideros excelsus

M. collinus 'Springfire'. Zones 16, 17, 23, 24. May be a selection of *M. polymorphus* or *M. villosus,* a shrubby, upright species. Grows to 6–8 ft. tall and 3–4 ft. wide, with gray-green leaves. Produces a profusion of brilliant rose red blossoms in late spring and early summer. Good as flowering hedge, specimen, container plant.

M. excelsus. NEW ZEALAND CHRISTMAS TREE, POHUTUKAWA. Zones 16, 17, 23, 24; H1, H2. Native to New Zealand. To 30 ft. tall or more, spreading as wide as tall; prune lower branches to get tree form. On young plants, leaves are glossy green; on older ones, they are dark green above, white and woolly beneath. Big clusters of dark red flowers cover branch ends in late spring and early summer. (Bloom occurs in December in New Zealand, hence common name "New Zealand Christmas tree.") Useful lawn or street tree (if given ample root space) in coastal gardens. 'Aurea' has yellow flowers.

M. polymorphus (M. collinus polymorphus). 'OHI'A LEHUA, LEHUA. Zones H1, H2. Native to Hawaii. Slow-growing, highly variable plant; may form a small, erect to prostrate shrub or grow as tree up to 100 ft. tall. The foliage is also variable—as are the flowers, which are produced throughout the year. Blossoms are commonly red but are also seen in white and shades of orange, pink, and yellow; they are used in leis.

MEXICAN BLUE PALM. See BRAHEA armata

MEXICAN BUSH SAGE. See SALVIA leucantha

MEXICAN DAISY. See ERIGERON karvinskianus

MEXICAN FAN PALM. See WASHINGTONIA robusta

MEXICAN FIRE BUSH. See KOCHIA scoparia trichophylla

MEXICAN FIRE PLANT. See EUPHORBIA heterophylla

MEXICAN FLAME VINE. See SENECIO confusus

MEXICAN GRASS TREE. See DASYLIRION quadrangulatum, NOLINA longifolia

MEXICAN HAT. See RATIBIDA columnifera

MEXICAN HONEYSUCKLE. See JUSTICIA spicigera

MEXICAN ORANGE. See CHOISYA ternata

MEXICAN OREGANO. See ALOYSIA wrightii, POLIOMINTHA maderense

MEXICAN PALO VERDE. See PARKINSONIA aculeata

MEXICAN PIÑON PINE. See PINUS cembroides

MEXICAN POPPY. See ARGEMONE mexicana

MEXICAN SHELL FLOWER. See TIGRIDIA pavonia

MEXICAN SUNFLOWER. See TITHONIA rotundifolia

MEXICAN TARRAGON. See TAGETES lucida

MEXICAN TULIP POPPY. See HUNNEMANNIA fumariifolia

MICHAELMAS DAISY. See ASTER novi-belgii

MICHELIA

Magnoliaceae

EVERGREEN SHRUBS OR TREES

ZONES VARY BY SPECIES

PARTIAL SHADE IN HOTTEST CLIMATES

REGULAR WATER

Michelia doltsopa

Magnolia relatives native to China and the Himalayas. When in flower, they might be mistaken for some kind of magnolia—but unlike magnolias, they bear their blossoms among the leaves rather than singly at branch ends.

M. figo has been in gardens for some 200 years, and *M. doltsopa* has been in cultivation in North America for perhaps half a century. The other species listed here, however, are newcomers about which we have much to learn; they have not yet had time to grow to maturity in North American gardens. All are attractive, with lush foliage and profuse, fragrant blossoms divided into petal-like segments.

M. champaca. CHAMPACA. Shrub or tree. Zones 16–24; H1, H2. To 10–20 ft. tall and broad. Glossy bright green, 10-in. leaves. Orange-yellow, 3-in. flowers with up to 20 segments are borne intermittently throughout the year, most often in winter and summer; their perfume is legendary. 'Alba' *(M. alba)* has white flowers.

M. crassipes. Shrub or tree. Zones 5–9, 14–24. Recently introduced and with no long track record in the West. Rich green foliage. Plants have bloomed at a very young age, bearing a profusion of white flowers. Has succeeded in the Puget Sound area.

M. doltsopa. Tree. Zones 14–24; H1, H2. To 90 ft. tall in its native Himalayas; in San Francisco, it has grown to 25 ft. in as many years. Varies from bushy (nearly as wide as high) to narrow and upright (about half as broad as tall); choose plants for desired form, then prune to shape. Thin-textured, leathery dark green leaves 3–8 in. long, 1–3 in. wide. In winter, furry brown buds open to blossoms ranging from cream colored to white, with a slight green tinge at the base; they are 5–7 in. across, with 12–16 segments, each 1 in. wide.

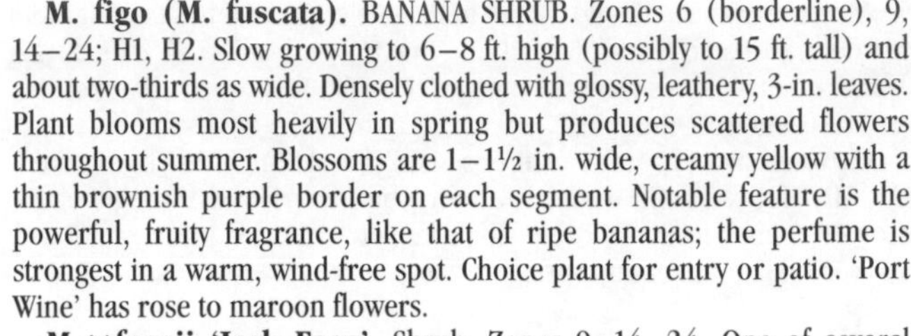

M. figo (M. fuscata). BANANA SHRUB. Zones 6 (borderline), 9, 14–24; H1, H2. Slow growing to 6–8 ft. high (possibly to 15 ft. tall) and about two-thirds as wide. Densely clothed with glossy, leathery, 3-in. leaves. Plant blooms most heavily in spring but produces scattered flowers throughout summer. Blossoms are 1–1½ in. wide, creamy yellow with a thin brownish purple border on each segment. Notable feature is the powerful, fruity fragrance, like that of ripe bananas; the perfume is strongest in a warm, wind-free spot. Choice plant for entry or patio. 'Port Wine' has rose to maroon flowers.

M. ×foggii 'Jack Fogg'. Shrub. Zones 9, 14–24. One of several hybrids between *M. figo* and *M. doltsopa*. To 18 ft. tall, 6–8 ft. wide. Spring flowers are white, with each segment bordered in purplish pink.

M. maudiae. Shrub or tree. Zones 5–9, 14–24. This newcomer is a large shrub or small tree, possibly to 25 ft. tall, with 6-in. leaves that are glossy medium green above, gray green beneath. White, 3–4-in. flowers bloom from late spring to midsummer.

M. sinensis (M. wilsonii). Tree. Zones 5–9, 14–24. To 20 ft. tall, possibly much taller in time, with 6-in., glossy green leaves. Blooms in early summer, bearing white flowers with 9–11 segments.

M. yunnanensis. Shrub or tree. Zones 5–9, 14–24. Another newcomer. To 15 ft. tall. Blooms in early spring, when white flowers burst from dark, velvety buds.

MICKEY MOUSE PLANT. See OCHNA serrulata

MICROBIOTA decussata

SIBERIAN CARPET CYPRESS

Cupressaceae

EVERGREEN SHRUB

ZONES A3; 1–10, 14–17

PARTIAL SHADE IN HOTTEST CLIMATES

MODERATE WATER

Microbiota decussata

Native to Siberian mountains and hardy to any amount of cold. Neat, sprawling shrub that resembles a trailing arborvitae *(Thuja)*. Grows 1½ ft. tall, 7–8 ft. wide, with many plumy, horizontal or trailing branches closely set with scalelike leaves. Foliage is green in summer, turning purplish or reddish brown in winter. More shade tolerant than junipers. Needs excellent drainage. Use as a bank cover.

MICROLEPIA

Polypodiaceae

FERNS

ZONES 17, 23, 24

PARTIAL OR FULL SHADE

MODERATE WATER

Microlepia strigosa

Sturdy plants useful for landscaping in mild climates. Both species described below can take fairly dry soil—drier than is usual for ferns. Both are hardy to 28°F/–2°C.

M. firma. Native to India. Grows to 2½ ft. high and 2 ft. wide. Dull green, delicately cut, triangular fronds to 3 ft. long. Frond surfaces are densely hairy.

M. strigosa. LACE FERN. Native to tropical Asia. Robust fern with delicate dark green fronds. Grows 2–3 ft. tall and wide. Sometimes sold as *M. speluncae*.

MICROMERIA chamissonis. See SATUREJA douglasii

MIGNONETTE. See RESEDA odorata

MILFOIL. See ACHILLEA millefolium

MILIUM effusum 'Aureum'

BOWLES' GOLDEN GRASS
Poaceae (Gramineae)
PERENNIAL GRASS
ZONES 3B–9, 14–17
LIGHT SHADE
REGULAR TO AMPLE WATER

Milium effusum 'Aureum'

Species is native to eastern North America, Eurasia. Its colorful selection 'Aureum' forms a clump to 2 ft. high and wide. Bright greenish gold leaves first grow erect, then take on arching, weeping form. Foliage is brightest in spring, turns light green by summer. Effective for a spot of color in a woodland garden or shaded rock garden. Does best where summers are cool or mild; in hotter regions, goes partially dormant in summer. Seedlings usually have yellow foliage, though color may vary.

MILKBUSH. See EUPHORBIA tirucalli

MILLETTIA reticulata

EVERGREEN WISTERIA
Fabaceae (Leguminosae)
EVERGREEN OR DECIDUOUS VINE
ZONES 8, 9, 14–24; MARGINAL IN ZONES 6, 7
FULL SUN
REGULAR WATER

Millettia reticulata

From China. Vigorous, twining vine, with shiny, leathery, many-leafleted leaves like those of wisteria. In fall, bears tight clusters of dark purple-red flowers with odor of cedar and camphor. Usually described as reaching 15 ft., but—like wisteria—can attain great size. Grows extremely fast and, once established, can overwhelm trees if permitted to climb into them. Best used as cover for large arbor, pergola, or chain-link fence. Evergreen in frost-free areas, deciduous elsewhere.

MILLION BELLS. See CALIBRACHOA

MIMOSA. See ACACIA baileyana, ALBIZIA julibrissin

MIMULUS

MONKEY FLOWER
Scrophulariaceae
PERENNIALS, ONE GROWN AS ANNUAL
ZONES VARY BY SPECIES
EXPOSURE NEEDS VARY BY SPECIES
WATER NEEDS VARY BY SPECIES

Mimulus aurantiacus longiflorus

Wide-ranging group of plants with widely differing needs. All have funnel-shaped, two-lipped flowers said to resemble a grinning monkey face—hence the common name.

M. aurantiacus (Diplacus aurantiacus). STICKY MONKEY FLOWER, SHRUBBY MONKEY FLOWER. Woody-based perennial. Zones 5 and 6 (with protection), 7–9, 14–24. To 4½ ft. tall and wide, with narrow, 1½-in.-long, sticky dark green leaves. Buff-toned orange, 1¾-in. flowers bloom over a long spring-and-summer season. Several subspecies were formerly considered separate species. These include *M. a. bifidus,* with large pale yellow to peach flowers; *M. a. longiflorus,* with cream to orange-yellow blooms; and *M. a. rutilus,* with deep red blossoms. All thrive in full sun or partial shade, with little water.

More important than the subspecies themselves are the showy hybrids derived from them (often called Verity hybrids, after their originator). These plants grow 1–4 ft. tall and wide, with narrow, glossy dark green leaves that are sometimes sticky. Flowers are 1–3 in. long, in colors ranging from white and cream to yellow, orange, copper, salmon, red, and maroon. Plant in full sun or light shade; give good drainage. Prune in spring before growth starts. Pruned again after first flowering, they often rebloom in fall—and, if given moderate water with good drainage, they may flower repeatedly throughout the year. Because plants are not long lived, take cuttings of your favorites; they root easily in moist sand.

M. cardinalis. SCARLET MONKEY FLOWER. Perennial. Zones 2–24. Native to damp or wet locales throughout much of the West. To 2½ ft. high and wide, with upright or sprawling stems and bright green, sticky, 1–3-in. leaves. Tubular, scarlet, 1½–2-in.-long flowers bloom throughout summer. Give full shade in Zones 12 and 13, sun or shade elsewhere. Ample water.

M. × hybridus. Short-lived perennial grown as annual. Zones 1–24. To 1 ft. high and wide, with smooth, succulent leaves. Flowers are 2–2½ in. across, in colors including cream, rose, orange, yellow, scarlet, and brown, usually with heavy brownish maroon spotting or mottling. Mystic Mix series has virtually unspotted flowers. Sow in spring for summer bloom, or set out plants for early spring show. Provide rich soil with high organic content, regular water, partial or full shade.

Mimulus × hybridus

MING ARALIA. See POLYSCIAS fruticosa

MINT. See MENTHA

MINT BUSH. See PROSTANTHERA

MINTLEAF. See PLECTRANTHUS madagascariensis

M

MIRABILIS

FOUR O'CLOCK
Nyctaginaceae
PERENNIALS, ONE OFTEN GROWN AS ANNUAL
ZONES VARY BY SPECIES
FULL SUN
LITTLE WATER
SEEDS AND ROOTS ARE POISONOUS IF INGESTED

Mirabilis jalapa

Strong-looking, mounding plants with the substance and character of shrubs—albeit only seasonal or temporary ones. In summer, branch ends bear clusters of trumpet-shaped, 2-in.-long flowers that open late in the afternoon. Plants are killed to the ground by frost but resprout from their large tuberous roots. Sow seeds in fall or spring. Plants self-sow freely.

M. jalapa. FOUR O'CLOCK, MARVEL OF PERU. Zones 4–24, H1, H2 as perennial. In colder climates, treat as annual; or dig and store like dahlia. Native to Peru. To 3–4 ft. tall and wide, with green leaves 2–6 in. long. Flowers in white and shades of red, pink, or yellow; several colors may appear on the same plant or even the same flower. Blossoms are fragrant at night. Jingles strain is lower growing than old-fashioned kinds, has flowers splashed and stained in two or three colors at once.

M. multiflora. DESERT FOUR O'CLOCK. Zones 1–3, 7–16, 18–24. Native to much of the Southwest. To 1–2 ft. high, 3–5 ft. wide, with magenta flowers and gray-green leaves to 3 in. long.

MIRROR PLANT. See COPROSMA repens

A PRACTICAL GUIDE TO GARDENING
PLEASE SEE PAGES 658–731

MISCANTHUS

EULALIA, SILVER GRASS

Poaceae (Gramineae)

PERENNIAL GRASSES

ZONES VARY BY SPECIES

FULL SUN OR PARTIAL SHADE

MODERATE TO REGULAR WATER

Miscanthus sinensis 'Gracillimus'

Among the showiest and liveliest looking of ornamental grasses, these are clump-forming plants that range from very large kinds to dwarf types good for small gardens and containers. Attractive flower panicles appear atop tall stalks; they open as tassels and gradually expand into silvery to pinkish or bronze plumes that usually last well into winter. Leaves are broad or narrow, always graceful; they may be solid colored, striped lengthwise, or banded crosswise. In fall and winter, foliage of most species turns shades of yellow, orange, or reddish brown; it looks especially showy against snow or a background of dark evergreens.

Need little care. Cut old foliage back to the ground before new leaves sprout in early spring; in climates with a long growing season, cut back again in midsummer to keep compact and to freshen foliage. Some varieties collapse at bloom time unless given support of four or five narrow stakes inserted inconspicuously at edge of clump, concealed by foliage; wind twine or wire around stakes and clump at two levels. Divide every 2 or 3 years to limit clump size and prevent decline in vigor. Stunning accent plants in large pots or tubs.

M. 'Giganteus'. GIANT SILVER GRASS. Zones 1–24. Impressive upright grass to 10–14 ft. tall, 8–10 ft. wide; self-supporting on stems to 2 in. thick. Arching, drooping leaves to 3 ft. long, 1½ in. wide, dark green with white midrib. In cold-winter areas, plant does not bloom. In other regions, however, flower plumes to 1 ft. long rise 1–2 ft. above foliage in very late summer to fall; they emerge tan, open silver. Leaves turn purplish green in fall, then drop to leave tall, bare stalks over winter. Good summer screen or hedge; provides tropical effect. Takes seacoast conditions. Give partial shade in hottest climates.

M. sinensis. EULALIA, JAPANESE SILVER GRASS. Zones 2–24. Native to Japan, Korea, China. Variable in size and foliage. Blooms in late summer or fall. Flowers are usually held well above foliage clumps; they may be cut for fresh or dried arrangements. Many varieties are obtainable, and new ones arrive on the market every year. Here are some of the choicest.

'Adagio'. Very narrow green leaves form a clump 2–3 ft. high and wide. Pink plumes rise to 4–5 ft. Better flower production than similar 'Yaku Jima'. Yellow fall foliage. Good container plant.

M. s. condensatus 'Cabaret'. Boldest variegated miscanthus. Big, upright clump 6–7 ft. tall, 4–5 ft. across; wide (to 1¼-in.), ribbonlike leaves with a broad white center stripe and green edges. Pink-suffused stems to 8–9 ft. bear coppery pink plumes that age to cream. Seed-sterile.

M. s. condensatus 'Cosmopolitan'. Similar in growth and bloom to 'Cabaret', but foliage has the reverse pattern: leaves have a green center (with a white midrib) and white margins.

'Goldfeder' ('Gold Feather'). Clump grows 4–5 ft. high and wide, with ¾-in.-wide leaves edged light golden yellow. Silvery pink flower plumes on lax stems to 7 ft. tall. Stems tend to flop, but do so gracefully; can be staked to keep upright.

'Gracillimus'. MAIDEN GRASS. Narrow dark green leaves with silver midrib; graceful clump to 4–5 ft. high, 6–8 ft. wide. Stems 5–6 ft. tall bear coppery plumes that mature to cream. Tends to flop; divide in spring every year or two to keep compact. Bright orange fall foliage. Seeds profusely and can become a pest.

'Graziella'. Narrow leaves form a clump 4–5 ft. tall, 5–8 ft. wide. Silvery "ostrich" plumes rise to 6–7 ft. Coppery red and orange fall foliage. More refined and upright than 'Gracillimus'.

'Kirk Alexander'. Clump to 3–4 ft. tall and wide, with green leaves horizontally banded in greenish yellow. Pinkish copper plumes on stems to 5 ft. tall.

'Malepartus'. Dark green leaves are broader than those of species, in a clump 3 ft. high and wide. Flower plumes on 6–7-ft. stalks open rose pink, fade to silvery white, finish tan. Orange fall foliage.

'Morning Light'. Sport of 'Gracillimus', with narrow band of white on leaf margins; less vigorous and more compact than 'Gracillimus'. Grows to 3–4 ft. high and as wide; coppery flower plumes reach 5–6 ft. tall. Where the growing season is long, dig and divide clumps yearly to keep plants compact. Seedlings have leaves like those of 'Gracillimus'—deep green with silvery midrib.

'Purpurascens'. FLAME GRASS. Best where summers are not too hot. Upright clump 3–4 ft. high and wide, with green leaves to ½ in. wide. Silvery flower plumes 5–6 ft. tall. Foliage turns orange red in fall, then fades to reddish brown.

'Strictus'. PORCUPINE GRASS. Narrow, erect clump 4–6 ft. tall, 3–4 ft. wide. Spiky, ½-in.-wide leaves are banded horizontally with creamy yellow, suggesting porcupine quills. Coppery plumes on 5–7-ft.- tall stems. Tends to flop with weight of blooms; should be staked.

'Variegatus'. A fountain of silver. Graceful, weeping clump 3–4 ft. high and as wide, with ¾-in. green leaves edged and striped in white. Spikes 5–6 ft. tall, tend to flop, especially on older plants; need staking. Divide every year or two. Give partial shade in hottest climates.

'Yaku Jima'. Compact, fine-leafed selection similar in form to 'Adagio'. Tan flower plumes; reddish brown fall foliage.

'Zebrinus'. ZEBRA GRASS. Like 'Strictus', but broadly arching and lax; certain to flop in bloom unless staked. Most plants sold under this name are 'Strictus'.

M. transmorrisonensis. EVERGREEN MISCANTHUS. Zones 4–24. Native to Taiwan. Forms a compact clump 2½–3½ ft. high and 3–4 ft. wide, with narrow leaves 2–3 ft. long, ½ in. wide. Foliage remains green into early winter (and is evergreen in mildest-winter areas). Slender, silvery flower plumes on stems 5–7 ft. tall.

Plant begins blooming in spring in mild-winter climates; cutting stems back to ground when plumes begin to fade will produce a second bloom flush—sometimes even a third one. Cutting back stems also keeps clump looking fresh. Where winters are cold, bloom time comes in mid- to late summer. Plumes age to tan and drop seed before winter, leaving bare stems. Makes a good large-scale ground cover if given regular moisture and yearly mowing.

MISSION BELLS. See FRITILLARIA biflora

MISS WILLMOTT'S GHOST. See ERYNGIUM giganteum

MISTLETOE FIG. See FICUS deltoidea

MITCHELLA repens

PARTRIDGEBERRY, TWINBERRY

Rubiaceae

PERENNIAL

ZONES 1–6

PARTIAL OR FULL SHADE

REGULAR TO AMPLE WATER

Mitchella repens

Attractive small, creeping evergreen plant native to much of eastern North America. Roundish leaves are less than 1 in. long, borne in pairs along trailing, somewhat woody stems that root where they touch the ground. Paired small white flowers appear in late spring or early summer; these are followed by bright red berries less than ¼ in. across. Use as small-scale ground cover, preferably where it can be seen near eye level—on a shady bank or above a wall. Provide moist, acid soil containing plenty of leaf mold or other organic material.

MIZUNA. See ASIAN GREENS

MOCK ORANGE. See CHOISYA ternata, PHILADELPHUS

MOLE PLANT. See EUPHORBIA lathyris

MOLINIA caerulea

MOOR GRASS

Poaceae (Gramineae)

PERENNIAL GRASSES

ZONES 1–9, 14–17

FULL SUN OR PARTIAL SHADE

REGULAR TO AMPLE WATER

Molinia caerulea 'Variegata'

Native to moist places from the British Isles to Siberia, south to the Caucasus and Turkey; resents dry, alkaline conditions. Long lived but slow growing, taking several years to reach full size. Erect, narrow light green leaves form a neat, dense clump. In summer, spikelike clusters of yellowish to purplish flowers rise above clump; they turn to tan and last well into fall. Inflorescences are profuse but narrow, giving clump a see-through quality. Good cut flowers. In late fall, both leaves and flower clusters detach from bulbous crown, leaving nothing visible above ground. There are two forms of moor grass, each with numerous varieties.

The typical form, often called purple moor grass, produces a leafy clump 1–2 ft. high and wide; flower stalks are 2–3 ft. tall. 'Moorflamme' ('Moor Flame') has airy flower heads held 2 ft. above the foliage, good red-orange autumn foliage color. 'Variegata' has leaves broadly edged in creamy white; yellowish flower stems arch out in all directions, giving perfect fountain effect.

M. c. arundinacea, known as tall moor grass, has broader gray-green leaves that form a clump 2–3 ft. high and wide. Flowering stems are 5–8 ft. tall; they arch to the ground when wet, then straighten up as they dry. Give this one space so you can enjoy its form and motion in the wind. Among its forms are old favorite 'Karl Foerster', still one of the best; it has arching, 2½-ft.-long leaves and semierect flower stalks to 7 ft. tall. 'Skyracer' has erect, 3-ft.-tall leaves and 7–8-ft. stems bearing yellow flowers that sparkle with morning dew. Arching, 6-ft. stems of 'Transparent' have a translucent section between highest leaf and beginning of flower spike; plant bears tiny, airy blossoms and has bright orange-yellow fall foliage. 'Windspiel' ('Windplay') has wiry vertical stems 7–8 ft. tall that sway with the slightest breeze.

MOLUCCELLA laevis

BELLS-OF-IRELAND, SHELL FLOWER

Lamiaceae (Labiatae)

ANNUAL

ZONES 1–24; H1, H2

FULL SUN

REGULAR WATER

Moluccella laevis

Though its common name implies Irish origin, this plant is in fact native to the Mideast. To 2–3 ft. high, 10 in. wide. Flowers are carried almost from base in whorls of six. Showy part of flower is large, apple green, shell- or bell-shaped calyx, very veiny and crisp textured; small white tube of united petals in center is inconspicuous. Calyx-blossom spikes are quite attractive and long lasting in either fresh or dried arrangements; be sure to remove the unattractive leaves.

Needs loose, well-drained soil. Doesn't perform well in hot, humid climates. Sow seed in ground in early spring for summer bloom; in mildest climates, can be sown in fall for winter bloom. Usually grown as winter annual in the desert. If weather is warm, refrigerate seed for a week before planting. For long blossom spikes, fertilize regularly.

MOMORDICA charantia. See BITTER MELON

MONARDA

BEE BALM, OSWEGO TEA, HORSEMINT

Lamiaceae (Labiatae)

PERENNIALS

ZONES VARY BY SPECIES

LIGHT SHADE IN HOTTEST CLIMATES

REGULAR TO AMPLE WATER

Monarda didyma 'Marshall's Delight'

Native to eastern North America. Bushy, leafy clumps to 2–4 ft. high, initially about 1½ ft. wide; spread rapidly at edges but are not really invasive. Dark green, 4–6-in.-long leaves have a strong, pleasant odor like a blend of mint and basil. In summer, upright stems are topped by tight clusters of long-tubed flowers much visited by hummingbirds. Divide every 3 or 4 years. Not long lived in areas with warm winters and long, hot summers.

M. didyma. Zones A2, A3; 1–11, 14–17. Basic species has scarlet flowers surrounded by reddish bracts. Garden selections include scarlet 'Adam'; pink 'Croftway Pink' and 'Granite Pink'; and dark red 'Mahogany'. 'Cambridge Scarlet' is a very old variety that is still widely sold. Mildew-resistant varieties include lavender 'Violet Queen' and pink 'Marshall's Delight'. All bloom over long period of 2 months or more when spent flowers are removed. Don't let soil dry out.

M. fistulosa. Zones A2, A3; 1–10, 14–17. Bears lavender to light pink flowers encircled by whitish bracts; they are less showy than blossoms of *M. didyma.* Best suited to wild garden.

MONARDELLA

Lamiaceae (Labiatae)

PERENNIALS

ZONES VARY BY SPECIES

FULL SUN

LITTLE WATER

Monardella macrantha

Aromatic mint-family perennials native to California and adjacent states. Typically sprawling, with two-lipped flowers in clusters at stem ends. All require excellent drainage. Use in wild gardens or rock gardens.

M. macrantha. Zones 7–9, 14–24. To 6 in. high, 1 ft. wide. Stems of shiny dark green leaves sprawl, turn up at ends to show tight, 1–1½-in. clusters of bright red, 1½-in.-long flowers in late spring and summer.

M. odoratissima. Zones 1–3, 7–10, 14–24. Bushy plant with a sprawling, woody base. Grows from 4 in. to 2 ft. tall, spreading as wide as high. Hairy gray-green leaves; 1-in.-wide heads of small purplish flowers in summer and early fall. Has been used to make a fragrant tea.

M. villosa. COYOTE MINT. Zones 7–9, 14–24. Bushy grower 1–2 ft. tall, 1–1½ ft. wide, with furry gray-green leaves and 1½-in. heads of small purplish, pink, or white flowers in late spring and summer.

MONDO GRASS. See OPHIOPOGON japonicus, under LIRIOPE and OPHIOPOGON

MONEY PLANT. See LUNARIA annua

MONEYWORT. See LYSIMACHIA nummularia

MONKEY FLOWER. See MIMULUS

MONKEY PUZZLE TREE. See ARAUCARIA araucana

MONKSHOOD. See ACONITUM

FOR INFORMATION ON YOUR CLIMATE ZONE PLEASE SEE PAGES 27–63

MONSTERA

Araceae

EVERGREEN VINES

ZONES VARY BY SPECIES; OR INDOORS

FILTERED SUNLIGHT; BRIGHT LIGHT

REGULAR WATER

Monstera deliciosa

Tropical American natives related to philodendrons and resembling them in the glossiness and texture of their foliage. Need rich soil. They can be grown outdoors only in the warmest climates. Indoors, direct sun in winter and bright reflected light the rest of the year are ideal; in dim light, leaves will be small and widely spaced on long, droopy stalks. If a tall potted plant gets bare at the base, replant it in a larger container along with a younger, lower plant to fill in; or cut it back and let it regrow from new shoots.

M. deliciosa. SPLIT-LEAF PHILODENDRON. Zones 16, 17, 22–24; H1, H2. To 30–60 ft. if planted in open bed outdoors or in greenhouse. Protect from frost (recovers fairly quickly from frost damage, though). Long, cordlike roots hang from stems and root when they reach soil; also help support plant on trees or on moss logs. Young foliage is uncut; mature leaves are heavy, leathery, dark green, deeply cut and perforated. Big plants may bear flowers like those of calla *(Zantedeschia),* with a thick, 10-in.-long spike surrounded by a boatlike white bract. If heat, light, and humidity are high, spike may ripen into edible fruit said to combine flavors of banana and pineapple. Eat only when fully ripe (green, caplike rind will knock off easily, exposing sticky fruit kernels); fruit can be painfully caustic before that stage. Allow plenty of room when growing this species as a houseplant; it may reach 15 ft. Often sold as *Philodendron pertusum.*

M. friedrichsthalii. SWISS CHEESE PLANT. Zones 24; H1, H2. Plant sold under this name is probably *M. obliqua.* Can reach 25 ft. outdoors but is more commonly used as indoor plant. Smaller, thinner-textured leaves than those of *M. deliciosa,* with wavy rather than deeply cut edges. Common name comes from oval holes on either side of leaf midrib.

MONTBRETIA. See CROCOSMIA × crocosmiiflora

MOONFLOWER. See IPOMOEA alba

MOOR GRASS. See MOLINIA caerulea

Moraceae. The mulberry family includes deciduous and evergreen trees, shrubs, and vines. Individual fruits are tiny and single-seeded but often aggregated into clusters. Fig *(Ficus)* and mulberry *(Morus)* are examples.

MORAINE LOCUST. See GLEDITSIA triacanthos inermis 'Moraine'

MORETON BAY CHESTNUT. See CASTANOSPERMUM australe

MORINA longifolia

WHORLFLOWER

Morinaceae

PERENNIAL

ZONES 2–9, 14–24

FULL SUN OR LIGHT SHADE

REGULAR WATER

Morina longifolia

This little-known but attractive Himalayan native looks something like a thistle. Forms a foot-wide rosette of glossy dark green, spine-toothed, deeply cut basal leaves to 10 in. long. In midsummer, foliage clump sends up a 2–3-ft. flower spike bearing closely spaced whorls of 1½-in. flowers; blossoms open white and age to pink, then red. Easy to grow in average soil.

MORMON TEA. See EPHEDRA

MORNING GLORY. See CONVOLVULUS, IPOMOEA, MERREMIA

MORUS

MULBERRY

Moraceae

DECIDUOUS TREES

ZONES VARY BY SPECIES

FULL SUN

REGULAR WATER

Morus alba

Deciduous trees with leaves of variable size and shape, often on the same plant. Yellow autumn color ranges from subdued to bright. Fruits somewhat resemble miniature blackberries and are favored by birds. For providing shade in home gardens, the most important kinds are fruitless forms of *M. alba.*

M. alba. WHITE MULBERRY, SILKWORM MULBERRY. Zones 2–24; H1, H2. Native to China. Fast-growing tree can reach 30–50 ft. high and wide, though it's often smaller. Leaves to 6 in. long and nearly as wide, often lobed. Fruit-bearing (female) trees have inconspicuous flowers followed by white, pink, or purple fruit that is sweet but rather insipid; it stains paved surfaces (as well as clothing). 'Pendula' ('Teas' Weeping') is a low-growing, strongly weeping form—but a fruit producer. Fruitless (male) forms are better for home gardens, though they do produce pollen in prodigious amounts. Varieties include 'Chaparral' (weeping), 'Fan-San', 'Fruitless', 'Kingan', and 'Stribling' ('Mapleleaf').

Tolerates desert heat, alkaline soil, seacoast conditions. Resistant to Texas root rot. Subject to sooty canker disease. Stake new plants; they quickly develop large crowns, which may snap from slender young trunks in high winds. For first few years, branches may grow so long that they droop from their own weight; shorten such branches to a well-placed upward-growing bud. Difficult to garden under because of heavy surface roots. Takes some aridity but performs better with regular moisture.

M. australis 'Unryu' (M. bombycis 'Unryu'). CONTORTED MULBERRY. Zones 3–24. To 25 ft. tall and wide, with twisted, contorted branches useful in dried floral arrangements or for winter silhouette. Fast growth means that branches may be cut freely with no harm to the tree. Dark green, broadly oval leaves 6–7 in. long.

M. nigra. BLACK MULBERRY, PERSIAN MULBERRY. Zones 4–24; H1, H2. Likely a native of western Asia. To 30 ft. tall, 35 ft. wide, with short trunk and dense, spreading head. Heart-shaped leaves to 8 in. long. Large, juicy dark red to black fruit. 'Oscar' and 'Wellington' are heavy bearers. 'Black Beauty' is smaller (15 ft. tall). All do best with regular water.

M. rubra. RED MULBERRY. Zones 2–7. Native to eastern and central U.S. Resembles *M. alba* but bears fruit that is somewhat larger and has a better flavor. Fruit is red when immature; it ripens to black. Does best in rich soil. 'Illinois Everbearing' is a hybrid between this species and *M. alba;* its fruit ripens throughout summer.

MOSES-IN-THE-BOAT, MOSES-IN-THE-CRADLE. See TRADESCANTIA spathacea

MOSQUITO GRASS. See BOUTELOUA gracilis

MOSS, IRISH and SCOTCH. See SAGINA

MOSS CAMPION. See SILENE acaulis, S. schafta

MOSS PINK. See PHLOX subulata

MOSS ROSE. See PORTULACA grandiflora

MOTHER FERN. See ASPLENIUM bulbiferum

MOTH ORCHID. See PHALAENOPSIS

MOUNTAIN ASH. See SORBUS

MOUNTAIN GARLAND. See CLARKIA unguiculata

MOUNTAIN IRONWOOD. See CERCOCARPUS betuloides

MOUNTAIN LAUREL. See KALMIA latifolia

MOUNTAIN MAHOGANY. See CERCOCARPUS

MOUNTAIN PHLOX. See LINANTHUS grandiflorus

MOUNTAIN SPRAY. See HOLODISCUS dumosus

MOUNT ATLAS DAISY. See ANACYCLUS depressus

MOURNING BRIDE. See SCABIOSA atropurpurea

MRS. ROBB'S BONNET. See EUPHORBIA amygdaloides robbiae

MUEHLENBECKIA

WIRE VINE

Polygonaceae

EVERGREEN SHRUBS AND VINES

ZONES VARY BY SPECIES

FULL SUN OR PARTIAL SHADE

REGULAR WATER

Muehlenbeckia axillaris

Unusual New Zealand natives with thin, wiry stems, small leaves, and insignificant flowers. Both of the species below spread by rhizomes, but one is a noninvasive creeper, the other a vigorous climber or sprawler that can overrun other plants.

M. axillaris (M. nana). CREEPING WIRE VINE. Shrub. Zones 3–9, 14–24; H1. Small, dense, creeping plant; can grow just a few inches tall or mound to 1 ft. high. Closely spaced leaves are oblong to nearly round, up to 3/8 in. long, glossy dark green. Bears very small (1/8-in.), translucent white fruits with black seeds. Use in rock garden or plant 1½–2 ft. apart for a small-scale ground cover. Can be mowed yearly to keep flat. Deciduous where winter chill is pronounced.

M. complexa. MATTRESS VINE, WIRE VINE. Vine. Zones 8, 9, 14–24. Twining vine can climb to 20–30 ft. or more; sprawls in the absence of support. Used as a ground cover, spreads over a 30-ft.-wide area. Forms a dense tangle of thin black or brown stems. Light green leaves are ½–¾ in. long, variable in shape—may be oval, rounded, fiddle shaped. Good for beach planting, screen. Curb growth by shearing or cutting back as much as desired; plant will regrow vigorously.

MUHLENBERGIA

Poaceae (Gramineae)

PERENNIAL GRASSES

ZONES VARY BY SPECIES

FULL SUN OR LIGHT SHADE

LITTLE OR NO WATER TO MODERATE WATER

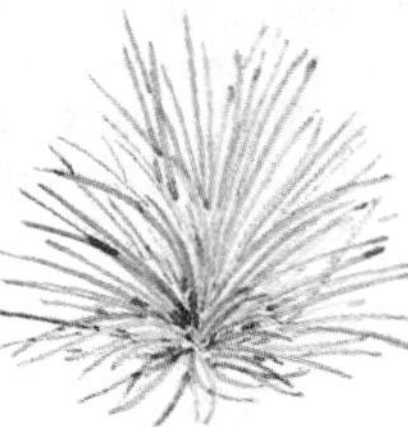
Muhlenbergia rigens

Narrow-leafed grasses large and showy enough to stand out in the garden. Except as noted, evergreen in mild winters but turn tan or brown with hard freezes. They are very drought tolerant plants but look better and grow larger if given some supplemental water.

M. capillaris. PINK MUHLY. Zones 4–24. From eastern U.S. Dark green foliage forms a mound to 3 ft. tall, 6 ft. wide; airy plumes of feathery reddish flowers rise an additional 2½ ft. in fall. Evergreen in low desert. Cut plants back in late winter for fresh new growth in spring. 'Regal Mist' ('Lenca') has deep rosy pink flowers.

M. dumosa. BAMBOO MUHLY. Zones 8–24. Native to Arizona, Mexico. To 3–6 ft. high and wide. Resembles bamboo, with slender, woody stems set with narrow bright green leaves to about 3 in. long. Branching flower clusters appear in spring; blossoms are barely distinguishable from foliage.

M. emersleyi. BULL GRASS. Zones 2–24. Native to Arizona, New Mexico, Texas. Glossy green leaves form a mound 1½ ft. tall, 3–4 ft. wide, with flower spikes rising 2–3 ft. above the foliage from summer into fall. Spikes are purplish or reddish, fading to cream with age.

M. lindheimeri. Zones 6–24. From Texas, Mexico. Clump of soft, arching blue-green leaves grows to 5 ft. tall and wide, with amber flower spikes arching 2 ft. above the foliage in autumn. Blooms of the species fade to gray; those of 'Autumn Glow' are yellow in fall. Attractive in dried arrangements. Semievergreen in mild-winter areas; dies to the ground in colder climates.

M. pubescens. SOFT BLUE MEXICAN MUHLY. Zones 8–24. From central Mexico. Downy blue-green foliage forms a clump 1 ft. tall, 2 ft. wide. In spring or early summer, soft flower spikes rise 1–1½ ft. above the clump; they are light blue, aging to amber. Light frosts turn foliage purplish red; harder freezes kill it to the ground.

M. rigens. DEER GRASS. Zones 4–24. Native from California to Texas and south into Mexico. Bright green leaves form a dense, tight clump to 4 ft. high and wide. Slender yellow or purplish flower spikes in autumn are erect at first, then leaning; rise 2 ft. above the leaves.

M. rigida. PURPLE MUHLY. Zones 6–24. From Texas, New Mexico. Green clump to 2 ft. high and wide, producing 3-ft. spikes of brownish purple to deep purple flowers in late summer and fall. 'Nashville' flowers are an attractive true purple.

MULBERRY. See MORUS

MULLEIN. See VERBASCUM

MULLEIN PINK. See LYCHNIS coronaria

MURRAYA paniculata (M. exotica)

ORANGE JESSAMINE

Rutaceae

EVERGREEN SHRUB

ZONES 21–24; H1, H2

FILTERED SUNLIGHT

REGULAR WATER

Murraya paniculata

Native to Southeast Asia. Open habit; fast grower to 6–15 ft. tall and wide. Good as hedge, filler, foundation plant. Sometimes grown as small single- or multitrunked tree. Has graceful, pendulous branches with glossy dark green leaves divided into three to nine oval, 1–2-in. leaflets. Blooms in late summer and fall (sometimes in spring), with white, ¾-in., bell-shaped blossoms with jasmine fragrance. On mature plants, small red fruits follow flowers. Needs rich soil, frequent feeding. Slowly recovers beauty after cold winters. Blooms attract bees.

A dwarf variety is usually sold as *M. exotica.* It is slower growing, more upright, and more compact than the species, reaching 6 ft. tall, 4 ft. wide. Its leaves are a lighter shade of green and have smaller, stiffer leaflets; bloom is usually less profuse.

MUSA

BANANA

Musaceae

PERENNIALS

ZONES VARY BY SPECIES

FULL SUN OR PARTIAL SHADE

AMPLE WATER

Musa × paradisiaca

For information on fruiting types, see Banana. The ornamental bananas described here include tall, medium-size, and dwarf plants; some of the tall sorts are the size of trees. All are fast growing; all have soft, thickish stems and spread by suckers or underground roots to form clumps that are often as wide as or wider than the plant is tall. Spectacular-looking long, typically broad leaves are easily tattered by strong winds, so choose protected planting sites. Will usually regrow from roots if cut down by frost; in frost-prone areas, locate plants where their absence won't be conspicuous. Attractive near swimming pools. Can be grown in tubs and wintered indoors (cut tops off tall plants). Give rich soil; feed heavily.

M. acuminata. Zones 8, 9, 14–24; H1, H2. From Southeast Asia. Many varieties available. Plants are grown for fruit in warmest gardens, but they also make handsome ornamentals there as well as in cooler areas. Some have especially attractive foliage. Leaves of 6–10-ft.-tall 'Zebrina' ('Roja', 'Rojo', 'Sumatra', 'Sumatrana') are green with maroon stripes; the plant produces tiny, inedible dark maroon fruit.

M. basjoo. JAPANESE BANANA. Zones 2 and 3 (with protection), 4–9, 14–24; H1, H2. From Japan. The hardiest of the banana clan. To 15 ft. tall, with narrow green leaves about 8 ft. long. Terminal spikes of yellow flowers may be followed by small, unpalatable fruit. Where plants freeze to the ground, spring regrowth will be quicker if trunks are heavily mulched in winter.

M. ensete. See Ensete ventricosum

M. lasiocarpa (Musella lasiocarpa). CHINESE YELLOW BANANA. Zones 5–9, 11–24; H1, H2. From mountains of China. To 5–6 ft. tall, with dark green, 3–4-ft.-long leaves. Grown for unusual inflorescence that resembles a giant (8-in.-wide) yellow artichoke and can last all summer. Plant dies after flowering, but new growth sprouts from base. Performs best in cool conditions.

M. ×paradisiaca (M. sapientum). Zones 9, 12–16, 19–24; H1, H2. This is the most common form of the ornamental bananas. Makes a clump to 20 ft. tall and half as wide. Leaves to 9 ft. long. Flower stalks are pendent, bearing large, showy, powdery purple bracts; fruit (usually seedy and inedible) sometimes follows.

M. velutina. Zones 23, 24; H2. From India. To 5–7 ft. tall, with 3-ft.-long leaves that are green above, bronzy beneath. Upright pink bracts, orange flowers, and small, velvety pink bananas that are inedible but highly decorative.

Musaceae. The banana family consists of giant herbaceous plants that resemble palm trees; the bases of the enormous leaves form a false trunk. *Ensete* and *Musa* are grown in the West.

MUSCARI

GRAPE HYACINTH

Liliaceae

PERENNIALS FROM BULBS

ZONES VARY BY SPECIES

FULL SUN OR LIGHT SHADE

REGULAR WATER DURING GROWTH AND BLOOM

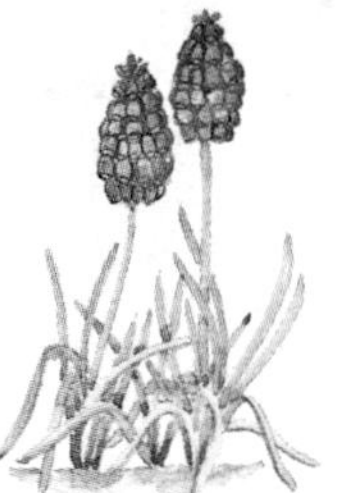

Muscari armeniacum

Native to the Mediterranean and southwestern Asia. Clumps of grassy, fleshy leaves appear in fall and live through cold and snow. Spikes of small, typically urn-shaped blue or white flowers (fragrant, in some species) bloom in early spring. Plant in early fall, setting bulbs about 2 in. deep and 3 in. apart in well-drained soil. Plant in masses or drifts under flowering trees or shrubs; use in edgings and rock gardens; grow in containers. Very long lived. Dig and divide when clumps become crowded. Plants self-sow under favorable conditions.

M. armeniacum. Zones A1–A3; 1–24. Bright blue flowers on 8-in. stems rise above a clump of floppy foliage. 'Blue Spike' has double blue flowers in a tight cluster at top of spike. 'Early Giant' blooms somewhat earlier than the species, has darker blue flowers edged in white. 'Cantab', with light blue blossoms, grows lower than the species and has neater foliage and a later bloom time.

M. aucheri (M. tubergenianum). Zones A1–A3; 1–24. Stems to 8 in. tall. Flowers on lower part of spike are bright blue; those on upper part are paler blue.

M. azureum (Hyacinthella azurea, Hyacinthus azureus). Zones 2–24. Blossom spires are between those of hyacinth and grape hyacinth in appearance. Stalks to 8 in. high bear tight clusters of fragrant sky blue flowers that have a bell shape (rather than the usual urn shape).

M. botryoides. Zones A1–A3; 1–24. Medium blue flowers on stems to 1 ft. tall. 'Album' has white flowers.

M. comosum. FRINGE HYACINTH, TASSEL HYACINTH. Zones 1–24. Bears rather loose clusters of unusual, tattered-looking flowers on 1–1½-ft. stems. In the species, blossoms are greenish brown on lower part of spike, bluish purple on upper part. 'Monstrosum' ('Plumosum'), feathered or plume hyacinth, bears violet-blue to reddish purple flowers that look like shredded coconut.

M. latifolium. Zones 1–24. Possibly the showiest of the grape hyacinths. Each bulb produces just one leaf and a flowering stem to 1 ft. tall. Flowers on lower part of spike are deepest violet, those on upper part vivid indigo blue.

M. neglectum. STARCH HYACINTH. Zones 1–24. Stems about 6 in. tall. Lower part of bloom spike holds tightly crowded, very dark blue blossoms edged in white, while upper part is set with pale blue blooms. Flowers are said to smell like laundry starch.

MUSTARD

Brassicaceae (Cruciferae)

ANNUAL

ALL ZONES

FULL SUN

REGULAR WATER

Mustard

Two kinds of mustard are popular in Western gardens. Curly-leafed mustard somewhat resembles curly-leafed kale in appearance. It is usually cooked like spinach or cabbage; young leaves are sometimes eaten raw in salads or used as garnishes. Mustard spinach (tendergreen mustard) has smooth dark green leaves. It matures earlier than curly-leafed mustard and is more tolerant of hot, dry weather. 'Red Giant' ('Chinese Red') has large, crinkled leaves with strong red shading and is handsome enough for a border. Use young mustard spinach as a salad green; older leaves can be cooked.

Mustard is easy to grow, and it grows fast—it's ready for the table 35 to 60 days after planting. Sow in rows in early spring; make successive sowings when young plants from each previous planting are established. Thrives in cool weather but quickly goes to seed in summer heat. For fall harvest, sow in late summer; in mild-winter areas, plant again in fall and winter. Thin seedlings to 6 in. apart. Harvest outer leaves as needed. To learn about broadleaf mustard and Chinese mustard greens, see Asian Greens.

MYOPORUM

Myoporaceae

EVERGREEN SHRUBS OR TREES

ZONES VARY BY SPECIES

FULL SUN, EXCEPT AS NOTED

LITTLE TO MODERATE WATER, EXCEPT AS NOTED

Myoporum laetum

Bell-shaped flowers attractive at close range but not showy; fruit small but colorful. Shiny dark green leaves with translucent dots. Tough and fast growing.

M. floribundum. Shrub. Zones 15–17, 19–24. Native to Australia. Interesting sculptural form; graceful, open growth to 5–9 ft. tall, 6–12 ft. wide. Sticky, very narrow, 3½-in.-long leaves droop from horizontally held branches. White to cream flowers are borne profusely along branches in spring; they are followed by tiny purplish fruits. Full sun or partial shade. Does best with regular water but takes wetter and drier conditions.

M. insulare. Shrub or tree. Zones 8, 9, 14–17, 19–24. Native to Australia. Varies in height and width, growing from 3 to 20 ft. tall, 6 to 25 ft.

wide. Tends to be shrubby in cooler or coastal areas, more treelike in hot climates. Leaves and flowers are very similar to those of *M. laetum* but somewhat smaller. Bluish purple fruits.

M. laetum. Shrub or tree. Zones 8, 9, 14–17, 19–24. Temperatures below 24°F/–4°C can cause severe damage. Native to New Zealand. Exceptionally fast growth to 30 ft. tall, 20 ft. wide. Densely clothed in rather narrow, 3–4-in.-long leaves. If allowed to grow naturally, it forms a billowing mass, but it can be trained as an attractive multitrunked tree. To use it as a ground cover, peg down branches so they'll root and spread. Clusters of small white summer flowers with purple markings are followed by reddish purple fruits. Good seaside plant. 'Carsonii' is even faster growing than the species, with larger, broader, darker green leaves; branches are leafy all the way to ground.

M. 'Pacificum'. Shrub. Zones 16–24. Extremely fast growing to 2 ft. tall and 30 ft. wide. As ground cover, can cover 100 sq. ft. in a year. Medium green, 1-in.-long leaves have an elongated oval shape. Bears small white flowers in summer. Performs best in cooler regions. Prune as needed; regrowth is rapid.

M. parvifolium (M. p. 'Prostratum'). Shrub. Zones 8, 9, 12–24. Native to Australia. Ground cover to 3–6 in. high, 9 ft. wide, with dense covering of light green leaves ¼–1½ in. long, ¼ in. or less wide. Tiny white summer flowers are followed by purple fruits. Plant 6–8 ft. apart; plants will fill in within 6 months, rooting where stems touch moist soil. Good on banks, slopes. Will not tolerate foot traffic. 'Burgundy Carpet' has red stems, purple new growth; 'Pink' bears pink flowers. 'Putah Creek' is taller than the species and not quite as wide spreading; it grows 1 ft. high, 8 ft. wide.

M. sandwicense. FALSE SANDALWOOD, NAIO. Shrub or tree. Zones H1, H2. Moderately slow-growing Hawaiian native to 30 ft. high and wide; extremely variable in the wild, where it is seen both at tree size and as low as 3 ft. Fragrance of wood is similar to that of sandalwood. Pointed, glossy green leaves 2–6 in. long. Blooms in spring and summer, bearing small white or pink flowers clustered close to the stems; these are followed by small white fruits that shrivel and turn brown with age. Excellent windbreak, hedge, screen, or specimen plant. Good tolerance for wind, salt, and drought. Needs well-drained soil. Normally does not require pruning but can be shaped during growth.

MYOSOTIS

FORGET-ME-NOT

Boraginaceae

PERENNIALS, BIENNIALS, AND ANNUALS

ZONES A1–A3; 1–24

PARTIAL SHADE

REGULAR WATER

Myosotis sylvatica

Both of the forget-me-not species described feature profuse, typically blue springtime flowers, tiny but exquisite. Grow easily and densely as ground covers. Do best in cool, moist areas, as in woodland gardens, at pond edges, along stream banks. They have invaded damp woodlands in some areas.

M. scorpioides. Perennial. Native to Europe, Asia, North America. This species is similar in most respects to *M. sylvatica,* but it grows a little lower, blooms even longer, and has roots that live over from year to year. Flowers are about ¼ in. wide; they come in blue with a yellow eye, white, or pink. Shiny, oblong bright green leaves. Plant spreads by creeping roots.

M. sylvatica. Annual or biennial. Native to Europe. State flower of Alaska. To 6–12 in. high, 2 ft. wide. Soft, hairy foliage; basal leaves reach 4 in. long, while those set higher on stems are ½–2 in. long. Pure blue flowers with a white eye are ⅓ in. wide, set loosely along top portions of stems. Blooms and seeds profusely for a long season, beginning in late winter or early spring. Self-sows and will persist for years unless weeded out. Often sold as *M. alpestris.* Improved varieties include 'Blue Ball' and 'Royal Blue Improved'. Forget-me-nots are attractive beneath pink, rose, and salmon-colored tulips.

MYRICA

Myricaceae

EVERGREEN AND SEMIEVERGREEN OR DECIDUOUS SHRUBS OR TREES

ZONES VARY BY SPECIES

FULL SUN

WATER NEEDS VARY BY SPECIES

Myrica californica

The two species described here are coastal natives: one comes from the Pacific coast, the other from the Atlantic. Both are cultivated for their attractive, pleasantly aromatic foliage. Flowers are inconspicuous, but the fruits that follow are effective in autumn and winter. Plants are useful as screens and as informal or clipped hedges.

M. californica. PACIFIC WAX MYRTLE. Evergreen shrub or tree. Zones 4–9, 14–24. Native to coast and coastal valleys from Southern California to Washington. In windy oceanfront conditions, it can be a low, flattened mass. Grown out of wind, it's a big shrub or tree to 10–30 ft. tall and wide, usually with many upright trunks. One of the best-looking native plants for gardens. Branches are densely clad with tooth-edged, narrow, 2–4½-in.-long leaves that are glossy dark green above, paler beneath, and clean looking throughout the year. Purplish, wax-coated nutlets are attractive to birds. Moderate water.

M. pensylvanica (M. caroliniensis). BAYBERRY. Deciduous to semievergreen shrub. Zones 1–7. Native to coastal eastern North America. Dense, compact growth to 9 ft. tall, 5–12 ft. wide. Narrowish glossy green leaves to 4 in. long are dotted with resin glands. Roundish fruit is covered with white wax—the bayberry wax used for candles. Tolerates poor, sandy soil. Resistant to oak root fungus. Regular water.

MYROBALAN. See PRUNUS cerasifera

Myrsinaceae. This family consists of evergreen shrubs and trees with attractive foliage and habit and (usually) inconspicuous flowers. Fruits are sometimes showy. Two representatives of the group are marlberry *(Ardisia)* and African boxwood *(Myrsine).*

MYRSINE africana

AFRICAN BOXWOOD

Myrsinaceae

EVERGREEN SHRUB

ZONES 8, 9, 14–24

FULL SUN OR PARTIAL SHADE

MODERATE WATER

Myrsine africana

Native to Africa, Himalayas, and China. Shrub grows to 3–8 ft. tall and 2½–6 ft. wide. Form is slightly floppy when young, but plant stiffens as it matures into a dense, rounded bush that is easily kept to 3–4 ft. with pinching and pruning. Erect-growing dark red stems are closely set with very dark green, glossy, rounded, aromatic ½-in. leaves. Insignificant flowers. Good choice for low hedges, topiary, foundation plantings, narrow beds, and containers. Cut foliage is attractive in arrangements. Withstands air pollution.

Myrtaceae. The immense myrtle family of trees and shrubs is largely tropical and subtropical. Leaves are evergreen and often aromatic. Flowers are frequently showy, thanks to their large tufts of stamens. Fruits may be fleshy (as in *Feijoa,* the feijoa or pineapple guava) or dry and capsular (as in *Eucalyptus*). Other family members include bottlebrush *(Callistemon),* myrtle *(Myrtus),* and guava *(Psidium).*

MYRTLE. See MYRTUS communis

MYRTUS communis

MYRTLE

Myrtaceae

EVERGREEN SHRUB

ZONES 8–24; H1, H2

FULL SUN OR PARTIAL SHADE

LITTLE TO MODERATE WATER

Myrtus communis

From the Mediterranean. Rounded plant is bulky and dense but has fine-textured foliage. Reaches 5–6 ft. high and 4–5 ft. wide (as much as 15 ft. by 20 ft. in old age). Glossy bright green leaves are pointed, 2 in. long, pleasantly aromatic when bruised or brushed against. White, sweet-scented, 3/4-in. flowers with many stamens bloom in summer; these are followed by bluish black, 1/2-in. berries. Takes any soil, but good drainage is essential. Makes a good informal hedge or screen, requiring little or no pruning; as a specimen shrub, it can be selectively pruned to reveal limb structure. Withstands shearing into formal hedges and topiary.

Named selections vary in foliage character and overall size. 'Variegata' fits the basic description but has white-edged leaves. 'Boetica' is especially upright, with thick, twisted branches and larger, darker leaves. 'Buxifolia' has small leaves like those of boxwood *(Buxus)*. Dwarf forms include 'Compacta', a small-leafed variety popular for edgings and low formal hedges; 'Compacta Variegata', similar but with white-margined foliage; and 'Microphylla', with tiny, closely set leaves.

M. luma. See Luma apiculata

M. ugni. See Ugni molinae

NAIO. See MYOPORUM sandwicense

NAKED LADY. See AMARYLLIS belladonna

NANDINA domestica

HEAVENLY BAMBOO, SACRED BAMBOO

Berberidaceae

EVERGREEN OR SEMIEVERGREEN SHRUB

ZONES 3 (WITH SOME PROTECTION), 4–24; H1, H2

SOME SHADE IN HOTTEST CLIMATES

LITTLE TO REGULAR WATER

Nandina domestica

From China and Japan. Belongs to the barberry family but is reminiscent of bamboo in its lightly branched, canelike stems and delicate, fine-textured, lacy-looking foliage. Slow to moderate growth to 6–8 ft. tall, 3–4 ft. wide. Old clumps may be wider than tall because of slow, steady spread by suckers. Leaves are divided into many 1–2-in. leaflets shaped like pointed ovals. Foliage emerges pinkish and bronzy red, then turns to soft light green; it takes on purple and bronze tints in fall and often turns fiery crimson in winter, especially in a sunny location and with some frost. A good filler in bouquets. Pinkish white or creamy white blossoms in loose, erect, 6–12-in. clusters bloom at branch ends in late spring or early summer. If plants are grouped, shiny red berries follow the flowers; isolated plants seldom fruit heavily.

In climates where summers are very hot, requires some shade; in milder climates, can take sun or shade. Does best in rich soil with regular water but can even compete with tree roots in dry shade. Subject to chlorosis in alkaline soil. Resistant to oak root fungus. In time, unpruned clumps become top-heavy and bare at base; to encourage denser foliage lower down, cut oldest canes to the ground each year before new growth begins in spring. Loses leaves at 10°F/–12°C; stems are damaged at 5°F/–15°C, but plant usually recovers quickly. Has withstood –12°F/–24°C with some snow cover and little wind; severely damaged at 0°F/–18°C if exposed to strong winds.

Makes a light, airy-looking hedge, screen, or tub plant. Good for bonsai and in narrow, restricted spaces. Dramatic with night lighting. Varieties include the following.

'Compacta'. To 4–5 ft. tall, 3 ft. wide. Very lacy looking, with more canes and narrower, more numerous leaflets than the species.

'Fire Power'. To 2 ft. tall and wide. Red-tinged summer foliage turns bright red in winter.

'Gulf Stream'. To 3–3 1/2 ft. tall, 1 1/2 ft. wide, with blue-green summer foliage and good red winter color.

'Harbour Dwarf'. To 2–3 ft. tall. Rather than forming a discrete clump, it spreads by rhizomes to make a good ground cover. Foliage has orange-red to bronzy red winter color.

N. d. leucocarpa ('Alba'). To 4–6 ft. tall, 2–3 ft. wide, with creamy white berries and light yellow foliage that turns golden in fall. More subject to cold damage than the species.

'Moon Bay'. To 2 1/2 ft. high and wide. Leaves are lighter green than those of the species, and they turn bright red in winter. Not known to flower or fruit.

'Moyers Red'. Standard-size plant with broad leaflets. Brilliant red winter color in regions that get frost. Flowers are pinker than those of the species, and berries ripen a month or two earlier.

'Nana' ('Nana Purpurea', 'Atropurpurea Nana'). To 2 ft. tall, 2–3 ft. wide. Coarse foliage is purplish green in summer, purplish red to bright red in winter. Leaves typically show cupping, curling, and color streaks, though plants sold under the names listed here vary in the degree to which these characteristics are present. A very slow grower, best used as an individual plant in a container or against a background of rock or gravel to emphasize its domed habit. Not known to flower or fruit.

'Plum Passion'. To 4–5 ft. tall and 3 ft. wide. Narrow leaves are deep purplish red when young; turn deep green by summer, then reddish purple in winter.

'Umpqua Chief'. Slow growing to 3 ft. high and 2 ft. wide in 3 years; matures at 5–6 ft. Tallest stems tend to flop. Leaflets are large, give good winter color.

'Umpqua Princess'. To 3–4 ft. high, 2 ft. wide. Narrow leaflets give it an open appearance.

'Woods Dwarf'. Slow, dense grower to 1 1/2 ft. high and wide. Foliage turns crimson-orange to scarlet in winter.

NANKING CHERRY. See PRUNUS tomentosa

NARCISSUS

DAFFODIL, NARCISSUS, JONQUIL

Amaryllidaceae

PERENNIALS FROM BULBS

ZONES A2, A3, 1–24, EXCEPT AS NOTED

FULL SUN DURING BLOOM, PART SHADE AFTER IN HOT CLIMATES

REGULAR WATER DURING GROWTH AND BLOOM

Trumpet Daffodil

Beyond their fascinating variety in flower form and color, these natives of Europe and North Africa offer numerous appealing traits. They are permanent, increasing from year to year; they stand up to cold (most are hardy to –30°F/–34°C) and heat; and they are useful in many garden situations. Given minimum care at planting, they thrive with virtually no further attention. These plants do not require summer watering (but will take it), need only infrequent division (and will even survive without it), and are totally unappetizing to gophers and deer. They bloom in late winter or spring.

All plants known by the names "daffodil," "narcissus," and "jonquil" are properly *Narcissus.* In gardener's terms, however, "daffodil" refers to large-flowered kinds, "narcissus" denotes small-flowered (and usually early-blooming) types bearing blossoms in clusters, and "jonquil" refers to *N. jonquilla* and its hybrids.

All have the same basic flower structure. Each bloom has a perianth (six outer petal-like segments) held at right angles to the corona (also called trumpet or cup, depending on its length) in the blossom's center. Flowers may be borne singly or in clusters. Colors are basically yellow and white, but there are many variations—shades of orange, red, apricot, pink, cream. Some are fragrant. Leaves may be straight and flat (strap shaped) or narrow and rushlike.

Use under trees and flowering shrubs, in ground cover plantings, near water, in rock gardens and on patios, in borders. Naturalize in sweeping drifts where space is available. Good in containers; fine cut flowers. Flowers usually face the sun—a fact to keep in mind when selecting planting locations.

When buying bulbs, look for those that are solid and heavy, with no injury to the basal plate. So-called double-nose bulbs will give you the most and largest flowers the first season after planting. In most climate zones, it's best to plant bulbs in late summer or early fall, as soon as they are available. In regions with long, warm autumns and fairly mild winters, however, put off planting until soil has cooled in midautumn.

After blooms fade, let foliage mature and yellow naturally. Established clumps need dividing only when flower production and bloom quality decline. It's easiest to dig clumps just after foliage dies down, when you can still see where plants are. After digging bulbs, store them as you would gladiolus corms until planting time.

To grow daffodils in containers, set bulbs close together, tips level with soil surface. Place pots in a well-drained trench or cold frame and cover with 6–8 in. of moist peat moss, wood shavings, sawdust, or sand. Look for roots in 8 to 10 weeks (tip from pot carefully). Remove pots with well-started bulbs to a greenhouse, a cool room, or a sheltered garden spot to bloom. Keep well watered until foliage yellows; then plant out in the garden. You can sink containers of bulbs in borders when plants are almost ready to bloom, then lift them when flowers fade.

WHAT DAFFODILS NEED

EXPOSURE: Choose a planting area that will be in full sun while bulbs are blooming. One traditional location is under high-branching deciduous trees. After bloom, partial shade is beneficial, especially in hot-summer regions.

SOIL: They are not fussy about soil as long as it is well drained. To improve drainage in heavy soils, deeply dig in plenty of organic matter prior to planting.

PLANTING: Set bulbs approximately twice as deep as they are tall—typically 5–6 in. deep for large bulbs, 3–5 in. deep for smaller ones. Space bulbs 6–8 in. apart.

WATERING: Water newly planted bulbs thoroughly. In many regions, fall and winter are wet or snowy enough to provide moisture. Keep plantings well watered if precipitation fails; continue until foliage begins to yellow. Plants don't need summer moisture.

DIVIDING: Clumps need dividing only when bloom quantity and/or quality decline. Wait until the leaves die back, then dig the clumps and store the bulbs until planting season.

Triandrus Hybrid 'Hawera'

The most serious pest is the narcissus bulb fly. An adult fly resembles a small bumblebee. The female lays eggs on leaves and on necks of bulbs; when eggs hatch, young grubs eat their way into the bulbs. Check bulbs before planting and destroy any grubs; dust leaves and soil with diazinon as new foliage emerges.

Following are the 12 generally recognized divisions of daffodils and representative varieties in each division.

Trumpet daffodils. Trumpet is as long as or longer than surrounding perianth segments; one flower to each stem. Best known is yellow 'King Alfred', but newer yellow-flowered 'Arctic Gold', 'Hawera', and 'Unsurpassable' are superior. Pure white varieties include 'Mount Hood', 'Empress of Ireland'. Bicolors with white segments and yellow trumpet include "Bravoure', 'Las Vegas', 'Peace Pipe'; among those with yellow segments and white trumpet are 'Honeybird', 'Spellbinder'.

Large-cupped daffodils. Cup is shorter than perianth segments but always more than one-third their length; one flower per stem. Varieties include 'Stainless' (white); 'Carlton' and 'Saint Keverne' (both yellow). Varieties with white perianth segments and colored cup include 'Ice Follies' (yellow cup); 'Romance', 'Salome' (pink cup); 'Johann Strauss', 'Professor Einstein' (orange cup). 'Ambergate', 'Ceylon', and 'Fortissimo' all have yellow perianth segments and pink, orange, or red cup. Those with yellow segments and white cup include 'Daydream', 'June Jungrund'.

Small-cupped daffodils. Cup no more than one-third the length of perianth segments; one flower per stem. Varieties include 'Audubon' (white segments, pale yellow cup banded pink) and 'Barrett Browning' (white segments, orange-red cup).

Double daffodils. Cup has segments that are separate rather than joined together. Flower looks like a peony rather than a typical daffodil. One flower per stem. Examples are 'Christmas Valley' and

Daffodil Divisions

TOP: Trumpet Daffodil 'Bravoure' BOTTOM: Cyclamineus Hybrid 'Phalarope'

TOP: Large-Cupped Daffodil 'Ice Follies' BOTTOM: Jonquilla Hybrid 'Sun Disc'

TOP: Small-Cupped Daffodil 'Barrett Browning' BOTTOM: Tazetta Hybrid 'Early Splendor'

TOP: Double Daffodil 'Christmas Valley' BOTTOM: Poeticus Daffodil 'Actaea'

TOP: Triandrus Hybrid 'Thalia' BOTTOM: Split-Corona Hybrid 'Colblanc'

'Replete' (white perianth segments, pink cup segments), 'Tahiti' (yellow segments, red cup), 'White Lion' (white segments, yellow cup).

Triandrus hybrids. Cup at least two-thirds the length of perianth segments; several flowers to each stem. White 'Thalia' is an old favorite. Others include 'Hawera' (yellow) and 'Silver Chimes' (white segments, yellow cup).

Cyclamineus hybrids. Early bloomers with one flower per stem. Perianth segments are strongly recurved. Yellow 'February Gold' is best known. Yellow 'Peeping Tom' has an especially long trumpet. 'Jack Snipe' and 'Phalarope' have white segments, yellow trumpets.

Jonquilla hybrids. Each stem bears two to four small, very fragrant flowers; foliage is often rushlike. Choices include 'Bell Song' (white perianth segments, pink cup); 'Pipit' (yellow segments, white cup); 'Quail', 'Sun Disc', and 'Trevithian' (solid yellow).

Tazetta and Tazetta hybrids. Zones 5–24. Hardy to about 10°F/–12°C. Early-blooming, cluster-flowering types popularly known by the name "narcissus." Each stem bears four to eight or more highly fragrant flowers with short cup. Many have white perianth segments and yellow cup, but there are other color combinations. *N. tazetta* 'Orientalis', Chinese sacred lily, has light yellow segments and darker yellow cup. 'Paper White' is pure white; 'Early Splendor' has white segments, orange cup; 'Grand Soleil d'Or' has yellow segments, orange cup. Newer varieties include 'Cragford' and 'Geranium' (white segments, orange cup); and 'Falconet' and 'Scarlet Gem' (yellow segments, orange cup). Tazettas are often grown indoors in bowls of pebbles and water (keep dark and cool until growth is well along, then gradually bring into light).

Tazetta Hybrid 'Cragford'

Poeticus daffodils. Perianth segments are white; very short, broad cup is in a contrasting color, usually with red edges. 'Actaea' and 'Pheasant's Eye' are old favorites.

Species, varieties, and hybrids. This category includes species, their naturally occurring forms, and wild hybrids. Included here are many miniature types popular with collectors and rock garden enthusiasts. Prominent among these are the following.

N. asturiensis. Often sold as *N.* 'Miniature'. Very early miniature trumpet daffodil. Pale yellow flowers, only 1 in. long, on 3-in.-tall stems.

N. bulbocodium. HOOP PETTICOAT DAFFODIL. Zones 3–24. Plant is hardy to about –10°F/–23°C. Stems to 6 in. tall bear small yellow flowers that are mostly trumpet, with almost threadlike perianth segments. Foliage is grassy.

N. cyclamineus. Zones 3–24. Hardy to about –10°F/–23°C. Small flowers, one to each 6–12-in. stem, have strongly recurved, lemon yellow perianth segments and narrow, tubular golden cup.

N. jonquilla. JONQUIL. Very fragrant golden yellow flowers with short cups in clusters of two to six on 1-ft. stems. Rushlike foliage.

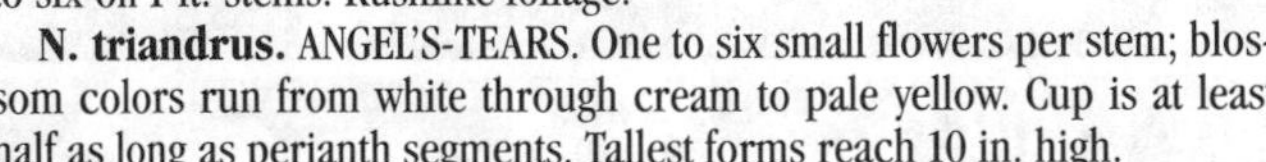
Narcissus bulbocodium

N. triandrus. ANGEL'S-TEARS. One to six small flowers per stem; blossom colors run from white through cream to pale yellow. Cup is at least half as long as perianth segments. Tallest forms reach 10 in. high.

Split-corona hybrids. Cup is split for at least one-third its length into two or more segments. 'Cassata' (white perianth segments, yellow cup), 'Colblanc' (all-white flowers), and 'Palmares' (white segments, pink cup) are three of the more readily available varieties in this small but growing class.

Miscellaneous. This category contains all types that don't fit the other divisions. 'Tête-à-tête' and 'Jumblie' (both yellow) have flowers like those of Cyclamineus hybrids but are rock garden dwarfs to about 6 in. high.

NASSELLA

NEEDLE GRASS

Poaceae (Gramineae)

PERENNIAL GRASSES

ZONES VARY BY SPECIES

FULL SUN

LITTLE OR NO WATER, EXCEPT AS NOTED

Nassella tenuissima

These needle grasses were once included in *Stipa.* All are clump formers characterized by long awns—needlelike or threadlike appendages that give a feathery look to the inflorescence. The first three species described are California natives that look much alike; all are useful for revegetation of wild areas, for stabilizing soil, and for restoring natural meadows. They can be started from seed. Clear area of weeds and other grasses first; *Nassella* species can self-sow once established, but initially they cannot compete with other vegetation.

All these needle grasses are cool-season growers that go dormant during hot, dry summers, reviving with cooler autumn weather and rains.

N. cernua. NODDING NEEDLE GRASS. Zones 7–9, 11, 14–24. To 3 ft. tall, 2 ft. wide, with deep green leaves. Purple-toned awns reach 4½ in. long, age to a silvery color. Blooms in late winter, early spring.

N. lepida. FOOTHILL NEEDLE GRASS. Zones 7–9, 11, 14–24. Similar to *N. cernua* in appearance and bloom season, but awns are shorter (to 2 in. long).

N. pulchra. PURPLE NEEDLE GRASS. Zones 5–9, 11, 14–24. The classic native California bunch grass. Much like the two species listed above, but with 4-in. awns. Same early bloom period.

N. tenuissima. MEXICAN FEATHER GRASS. Zones 2b–24. Native to Texas, New Mexico, Mexico. Among finest textured and most billowy looking of all ornamental grasses. To 2 ft. tall, 2–3 ft. wide, with threadlike bright green leaves. In summer, produces very thin flowering stems that arch outward and downward, ending in a cloud of silvery green, 3-in. awns that age to a light straw color, remain attractive into winter. Remains green where summers are cooler. Thrives with little to regular water. Can self-sow in well-irrigated gardens; to prevent, cut plants back before seeds ripen.

NASTURTIUM. See TROPAEOLUM

NATAL IVY. See SENECIO macroglossus

NATAL PLUM. See CARISSA macrocarpa

NAUPLIUS sericeus. See ASTERISCUS sericeus

NEANTHE bella. See CHAMAEDOREA elegans

NECTARINE. See PEACH and NECTARINE

NECTAROSCORDUM siculum (Allium siculum)

Liliaceae

PERENNIAL FROM BULB

ZONES 2B–9, 14–24

FULL SUN OR LIGHT SHADE

REGULAR WATER DURING GROWTH AND BLOOM

Nectaroscordum siculum

Onion relative from the Mediterranean region and western Asia. Creates an attractive silhouette. Strap-shaped, 12–16-in.-long leaves emerge in spring, give off garlic scent if crushed or bruised. Thick, fleshy stems to 4 ft. tall appear in summer, each carrying a cluster of up to 30 nodding, 1-in., bell-shaped flowers. Blossoms are white, suffused with pink or purple and tinged green at the base. Leaves die back at or just after bloom. Flowers are followed by upright seed capsules that can be dried for winter arrangements. In fall, plant bulbs 1½ ft. apart and 2 in. deep in well-drained soil, or start from seed in early spring.

NEEDLE GRASS. See NASSELLA

NEEDLE PALM. See RHAPIDOPHYLLUM hystrix

NEILLIA

Rosaceae

DECIDUOUS SHRUBS

ZONES 2B–9, 14–24

FULL SUN OR LIGHT SHADE

REGULAR WATER

Neillia affinis

From China. Graceful, arching shrubs related to spiraea and, like it, useful in shrub borders or as space fillers. Attractive green, glossy foliage. Both species described below bear short, nodding clusters of pink blossoms in spring and early summer. To keep shrubs open and graceful, prune them after bloom, cutting branches that have flowered to the base.

N. affinis. To 6 ft. tall and wide, with reddish purple stems; 3½-in., oval to lance-shaped leaves; and 3-in.-long flower clusters.

N. sinensis. To 9 ft. tall and wide, with peeling brown bark; 3-in., lance-shaped leaves; and 2½-in.-long flower clusters.

NELUMBO (Nelumbium)

LOTUS

Nymphaeaceae

AQUATIC PLANTS

ZONES 1–24; H1, H2

FULL SUN OR PARTIAL SHADE

LOCATE IN PONDS, WATER GARDENS

Nelumbo nucifera

Huge, round leaves attached at their centers to leafstalks rise above the water. Large, fragrant summer flowers form above or below leaves. Ornamental woody fruit is perforated like a salt shaker, looks attractive in dried arrangements.

If you buy started plants in containers, put them in a pond, positioned so soil in pots is 8–10 in. below surface of water. If you acquire roots, plant them in spring, setting them horizontally and about 4 in. deep in a 1–1½-ft.-deep container of fairly rich soil; then place container at recommended depth in pond, as described above for started plants. Do not let roots freeze; where freezes are possible, cover the pond or fill it deeper with water. Beware of introducing lotus plants or roots to earth-bottom ponds 3–4 ft. or shallower; plants will eventually fill in pond, and rhizomes are difficult to remove.

N. lutea (Nelumbium luteum). AMERICAN LOTUS. Native to North America. Similar to *N. nucifera* but somewhat smaller in leaf and flower. Flowers are pale yellow.

N. nucifera (Nelumbium nelumbo). INDIAN or CHINESE LOTUS. Native to Asia, Australia. Round leaves, 2 ft. or wider, carried 3–6 ft. above water surface. Pink, 4–10-in.-wide flowers borne singly on stems. Both tubers and seeds are esteemed in Chinese cookery, and the entire plant holds great religious significance for Buddhists: represents human soul rising from mud and aspiring to light and purity. White, rose-colored, and double varieties exist. 'Speciosum' is the classic, single light pink lotus of Oriental art. 'Alba Grandiflora' bears large, very fragrant white flowers. 'Empress' has single white blooms with deep pink edges. Dwarf forms (12–24 in. tall) suitable for tubs or small ponds include 'Tulip' ('Shirokunshi'), single white; and 'Momo Botan', double, deep rose fading to white on 1½–2-ft. stems.

FOR GROWING SYMBOL EXPLANATIONS
PLEASE SEE PAGE 161

NEMATANTHUS gregarius

GOLDFISH PLANT

Gesneriaceae

PERENNIAL

ZONES H1, H2; OR INDOORS

PARTIAL SHADE; BRIGHT INDIRECT LIGHT

REGULAR WATER

Nematanthus gregarius

From tropical South America. Related to African violet *(Saintpaulia)* and has similar cultural needs. Grows to 2½ ft. high, 3 ft. wide, with foot-long, arching branches that are closely set with rich green, oval leaves ¾–1½ in. long. Orange, puffy, roundish flowers are about 1 in. long, pinched at tip into pursed "mouth" like that of a goldfish. Given enough warmth and humidity, this plant will bloom year-round. Easy to root from tip cuttings; stems may root where they contact damp soil mix. Arching, trailing growth makes it best suited to hanging pots or baskets.

NEMESIA

Scrophulariaceae

ANNUALS AND PERENNIALS

ZONES VARY BY SPECIES

FULL SUN

REGULAR WATER

Nemesia strumosa

Colorful South African natives, some with fragrant flowers. None is at its best in hot weather, though new *N. caerulea* hybrids are more heat tolerant than other types. All need well-drained soil. Remove faded flowers to prolong bloom. Use as bedding or rock garden plants, in hanging baskets, as bulb covers.

N. caerulea (N. foetens, N. fruticans). Perennial in Zones 14–24; annual anywhere. To 2 ft. tall, 1 ft. wide, with small bright green leaves and upright stems carrying many intensely fragrant blossoms in blue, pink, or lavender. Flowers are narrower than those of *N. strumosa.* Often blooms for months without special attention (almost all year in cool-summer, mild-winter climates), but if flowers decline, cut plant back to stimulate new growth and more bloom. Tolerates light afternoon shade.

While the species prefers cool weather, the following hybrids, both to 1 ft. high and wide, withstand temperatures as high as 95°F/35°C. 'Compact Innocence' has yellow-centered white flowers; 'Blue Bird' (takes heat a bit better than 'Compact Innocence') bears blue-violet blossoms with yellow centers. Well-established plantings of the species and hybrids are hardy to 15°F/–9° C.

N. strumosa. Annual. Zones 1–24. The true species grows 1½ ft. high and 1 ft. wide, but plants sold under this name are usually more compact hybrids between *N. strumosa* and *N. versicolor;* they remain under a foot high, reach about 6 in. wide, and produce small, unscented flowers in clusters to about 4 in. across. Blossoms are chalice shaped, flaring at the mouth into two unequal lips, the lower one larger than the upper. They come in every color but green. Several mixtures offer a wide range of bright solid colors; bicolors include 'Mello Red and White' and blue-and-white 'KLM'.

Buy started plants or sow seeds in place. Time plantings of this rapid grower to avoid frost but come into bloom during cool weather. In cold-winter climates, sow in early spring for late spring, early summer bloom; in mild-winter areas, sow in fall for bloom in winter and spring. Give rich soil and regular moisture. Pinch to induce bushiness. Good bulb cover or hanging basket plant.

N. versicolor. Annual. Zones 1–24. Grows to 8–10 in. high and as wide. Unscented flowers are similar to those of *N. strumosa,* but color range of *N. versicolor* contains more blue, yellow, and white. Flowers of 'Blue Gem' are a rich pure blue with a white center. Time plantings as for *N. strumosa.*

NEMOPHILA

Hydrophyllaceae
ANNUALS
ZONES VARY BY SPECIES
FULL SUN OR PARTIAL SHADE
REGULAR WATER

Nemophila menziesii

To 6–12 in. high and trailing to 1 ft. wide, with bell-shaped flowers to 1 in. across in spring. Pale green, hairy, ferny leaves give plants a delicate appearance. Often used as bulb cover. Broadcast seed in place. In cold-winter areas, sow as soon as the ground is workable in spring; in mild-winter regions, plant in fall. Plant is quickly killed by heat and humidity. Reseeds when grown in cool, moist conditions.

N. maculata. FIVE-SPOT NEMOPHILA. Zones 1–9, 12–24. Native to California. Flowers are white, marked with fine purple lines and dots; a large purple dot appears at the tip of each of the five lobes.

N. menziesii (N. insignis). BABY BLUE EYES. Zones 1–24. Native to California, southern Oregon. Blooms as freely in gardens as it does in the wild, bearing sky blue blossoms with a white or near-white center. 'Snow Storm' *(N. m. atomaria),* the baby blue eyes variety most commonly grown in Oregon, has white flowers dotted with black. 'Pennie Black' *(N. m. discoidalis)* produces blackish purple flowers rimmed in white.

NEODYPSIS decaryi. See DYPSIS decaryi

NEOLITSEA sericea

JAPANESE SILVER TREE
Lauraceae
EVERGREEN TREE
ZONES 4–9, 14–24
FULL SUN TO LIGHT SHADE
MODERATE TO REGULAR WATER

Neolitsea sericea

Fast-growing tree native to Japan, Korea, China. Related to camphor tree *(Cinnamomum).* Broadly cone shaped, growing 30–45 ft. tall, 25–40 ft. wide. Foliage is aromatic when bruised. New leaves are bronze, drooping, covered with silky white hairs; mature ones are dark green with velvety white undersides, 3–7 in. long. Tiny, inconspicuous flowers are followed by red, ½–¾-in. fruits.

NEOMARICA

Iridaceae
PERENNIALS
ZONES 16, 17, 21–24; H2; OR INDOORS
FULL SUN OR LIGHT SHADE; BRIGHT INDIRECT LIGHT
REGULAR WATER

Neomarica caerulea

Like iris, these perennials produce fans of lance-shaped leaves. Foliage arises from short rhizomes; leaves and flowering stems grow to about the same height. Flowers are intricate, with three large, rounded outer segments surrounding three smaller, curled segments that are banded in contrasting colors. Individual flowers last only a day, but others follow over an extended period.

N. caerulea. From Brazil. To 5–5½ ft. tall, 2–3 ft. wide, with stiffly erect leaves. As plant grows, lower leaves fan out to the side. Branching flower stems carry a succession of 3–4-in. blue blossoms, their centers intricately banded in yellow, white, and brown. Blooms in early summer. Offsets are produced at flowering points on the stems; they detach easily for additional plants.

N. gracilis. WALKING IRIS. From Mexico to Brazil. To 2–2½ ft. tall, 1–1½ ft. wide. Blooms in late spring and summer; flower stems resemble the leaves so closely that blossoms appear to emerge directly from the foliage. Flowers are 2½ in. wide. Outer segments are white; inner ones show a combination of blue, brown, and yellow. As flowers fade, the blossom stalk bends downward and produces plantlets that take root—hence the common name.

NEOREGELIA

Bromeliaceae
PERENNIALS
ZONES 21–24; H2; OR INDOORS
SOME SHADE; BRIGHT INDIRECT LIGHT
KEEP CUP WITHIN ROSETTE FILLED WITH WATER

Neoregelia carolinae 'Tricolor'

From South America. Bromeliads with rosettes of leathery leaves, often strikingly colored or marked; short spikes of typically inconspicuous flowers are buried in hearts of rosettes. Keep central tube or cup within leaf rosette filled with water. Need light, open, fast-draining soil mix that holds moisture but does not exclude air; water the mix when it dries out. Feed lightly. Use outdoors year-round only in frost-free locations; can be grown on tree branches with sphagnum moss around roots.

N. carolinae. To 1 ft. tall, 2½ ft. wide. Many shiny, medium green leaves about 1 ft. long, 1½ in. wide. As plant approaches bloom, leaves turn rich red at base. 'Tricolor' has green leaves with lengthwise white stripes; as is true for the species, center of rosette turns red before bloom.

N. spectabilis. PAINTED FINGERNAIL PLANT. To 1½ ft. tall, 3 ft. wide. Leaves are about 1 ft. long, 2 in. wide, olive green with bright red tips. Foliage takes on a bronzy color in strong light.

NEPETA

Lamiaceae (Labiatae)
PERENNIALS
ZONES 1–24, EXCEPT AS NOTED
FULL SUN OR PARTIAL SHADE
MODERATE WATER

Nepeta cataria

Vigorous, spreading members of the mint family with aromatic foliage. With the exception of catnip *(N. cataria),* these plants are valuable for their spikes of two-lipped blue or blue-violet (or sometimes pink, white, or yellow) flowers. As soon as blossoms fade, shear plants back by half or cut faded flower stems to the ground to encourage rebloom. (Most species seed freely and can become invasive if spent flowers are not removed.) Plants make attractive, informal low hedges or edgings.

In winter or early spring, cut out last year's growth to make way for new stems. At that time, you can also divide clumps for increase, though it's easy to start new plants from cuttings (take them before flower buds form). When buying named varieties, be sure to obtain cutting-grown plants; seedlings vary in flower color and habit. In cold-winter climates, nepetas are occasionally used as a substitute for lavender *(Lavandula)* in borders and edgings. Most species resent heat combined with high humidity. In Zones 12 and 13, most are best treated as winter annuals. Tolerate regular moisture if soil is well drained.

N. cataria. CATNIP. From the Mediterranean and western Asia. To 2–3 ft. high and wide, with downy, heart-shaped, tooth-edged gray-green leaves. Spikes of small (¼–½-in.) whitish or pinkish flowers in late spring, early summer. Not very ornamental but worthy of a place in the herb garden. Grows easily in light soil and self-sows readily. Common name refers to stimulant effect on cats, but their susceptibility to the herb varies: some felines fall into a rapturous frenzy, rolling wildly on the plant, but others ignore it. If necessary, protect crown of plant with an inverted wire basket; stems will grow through. The same tactic also helps preserve potted plants grown outdoors and brought indoors occasionally for cats to enjoy. You can also sprinkle dried leaves over your cat's food or use them to stuff cloth toys. Some people use catnip to flavor tea. 'Citriodora' has lemon-scented foliage.

N. clarkei. Zones 2b–9, 14–24. Himalayan native to 2½–4 ft. tall, 1½–3 ft. wide. Truest blue flowers of all nepetas, with white patch on lower lip. Blooms in summer and early fall. Lance-shaped green leaves are 1–2½ in. long.

N. ×faassenii. CATMINT. Sterile hybrid of *N. racemosa* and a European species; often sold as *N. mussinii.* Soft, silvery gray-green, spreading mound grows to 1 ft. high, 1½–2 ft. wide. Scallop-edged, heart-shaped gray-green leaves to 1 in. long. Attractive to some cats, who enjoy nibbling on and rolling in plantings; insert short sticks in the ground among the foliage to discourage cats and prevent destruction. Loose, lax spikes of ½-in. lavender-blue flowers in late spring, early summer. Set plants 1–1½ ft. apart for ground cover. 'Select Blue' has darker flowers than the species; 'Snowflake' has pure white blooms. 'Dropmore' grows to 1½ ft. high and 3 ft. wide; it may be a hybrid involving another species.

N. grandiflora. Native to Europe, Caucasus. Open clump to 2½ ft. tall, 1½ ft. wide. Gray-green, hairless or sparsely hairy, scallop-edged, egg-shaped leaves to 4 in. long. Violet-blue, ¾-in. flowers in late spring, early summer. 'Bramdean' has lavender-blue blossoms with purple calyxes; 'Dawn to Dusk' has lilac-pink flowers, smoky violet calyxes. Calyxes of both these varieties persist after flowers have faded.

N. hederacea. See Glechoma hederacea

N. nervosa. Zones 3–10, 14–24. Native to Kashmir. Bushy habit to 1–2 ft. tall, 1 ft. wide. Bright green, conspicuously veined, tooth-edged leaves are lance shaped, 2–4 in. long. Brilliant violet-blue (rarely yellow), ½-in. flowers bloom from midsummer to early fall.

N. racemosa (N. mussinii). Native to the Caucasus, Turkey, Iran. Sprawling plant grows from 6 in. to 1 ft. tall and about 2 ft. or more wide. Roundish, scallop-edged, ½–1¼-in.-long leaves can range in shades from medium green to gray green; they are covered with fine hairs. The typical form produces ⅓-in.-long lavender flowers for a short period in midsummer; may rebloom if sheared. Reseeds prodigiously. Inferior to its hybrid *N. ×faassenii,* but there are several worthwhile selections that are more compact than the species and bloom over a longer period. 'Blue Ice' has dense gray-green foliage and pale blue flowers that fade to near-white. 'Superba' has a dense, matlike habit and gray-green leaves that are smaller than those of the species; it bears lavender-blue blossoms from spring through fall. Violet-blue flowers of 'Walker's Low' appear over an equally long season.

N. reichenbachiana. Native to Armenia and the Caucasus. May be a form of *N. racemosa.* Makes a thick, low mound to 1 ft. high, 2–4 ft. wide. Woolly, heart-shaped, deeply veined leaves have pointed tips and scalloped edges; they are pale green above, gray or white beneath, ¾–1¼ in. long. Blooms from late spring through fall, producing 6–8-in.-tall spikes of deep blue flowers with just a hint of violet. Good ground cover; space plants 3 ft. apart.

N. sibirica (N. macrantha, Dracocephalum sibiricum). SIBERIAN CATNIP. Native to Siberia. Sturdy, upright habit to 2–3 ft. tall, 1½–2 ft. wide. Dark green, oblong to lance-shaped, 3-in.-long leaves are softly hairy beneath. Spikes of large (1½-in.) violet-blue blossoms appear for about a month, beginning in early summer.

N. 'Six Hills Giant'. Possibly a hybrid of *N. ×faassenii* and similar to it—but grows taller (reaches 2½–3 ft. high and as wide), has greener foliage, and bears deeper blue flowers. More tolerant of damp climates than other nepetas.

N. 'Souvenir d'André Chaudron' ('Blue Beauty'). Probably a hybrid of *N. sibirica.* Similar to parent but grows only 1½ ft. high and blooms for a longer period, with season extending into late summer.

FOR INFORMATION ON SELECTING PLANTS
PLEASE SEE PAGES 64–160

NEPHROLEPIS

SWORD FERN
Polypodiaceae
FERNS
ZONES VARY BY SPECIES; OR INDOORS
SOME SHADE; BRIGHT INDIRECT LIGHT
REGULAR WATER

Nephrolepis exaltata 'Bostoniensis'

Tough and easy to grow, these are the most widely used of all ferns. For native Western sword fern, see *Polystichum munitum.*

N. cordifolia. SOUTHERN SWORD FERN. Zones 8, 9, 12–24; H1, H2. Native to many tropical regions of the world. To 2–3 ft. tall, 5 ft. wide. Tufts of bright green, narrow (2-in.-wide), upright fronds with closely spaced, finely toothed leaflets. Roots often have small, roundish tubers. Plant spreads by thin, fuzzy runners and can be invasive. Will not take hard frosts but is otherwise adaptable, tolerating poor soil and erratic watering. Good in narrow, shaded beds; can thrive in full sun with adequate water. Effective ground cover; also good in pots and hanging baskets. Often sold as *N. exaltata.*

N. exaltata. Zones 23, 24; H2. Like *N. cordifolia,* this is a tropical species, but it grows larger than *N. cordifolia* (to 7 ft. high and wide) and has broader fronds (to 6 in. wide). Most common are named selections grown as houseplants. Best known is 'Bostoniensis', Boston fern. Growing about 3 ft. high, it is the classic parlor fern, with spreading, arching habit and graceful, eventually drooping fronds broader than those of the species. Among the many forms with more finely cut and feathery fronds are 'Fluffy Ruffles', 'Rooseveltii', and 'Whitmanii'.

N. obliterata. Zones H1, H2. From northwestern Australia. Grows to 3–4½ ft. high and wide. Similar to *N. cordifolia* but has darker green, somewhat narrower fronds. Used mainly as a houseplant. Habit is stiffer and more erect than that of *N. exaltata* 'Bostoniensis', and plant is more tolerant of low humidity and both high and low light conditions. Selections include 'Kimberley Queen' and 'Western Queen'.

NERINE

Amaryllidaceae
PERENNIALS FROM BULBS
ZONES 5, 6, 8, 9, 13–24
PARTIAL SHADE IN HOTTEST CLIMATES
REGULAR WATER DURING GROWTH AND BLOOM

Nerine sarniensis curvifolia fothergillii

South African relatives of spider lily *(Lycoris),* which they closely resemble. Most have strap-shaped leaves to about 1 ft. long; these die back well before bloom time in late summer or early fall, then reappear later in the year (typically around bloom time or shortly afterward). Some types are essentially evergreen. All have broad, funnel-shaped flowers carried in clusters atop leafless stems; each blossom has six spreading segments, recurved at their tips.

Same planting instructions, cultural conditions as for *Lycoris.* Withhold summer water for species that experience summer dormancy, but keep watering the essentially evergreen kinds. As is true for *Lycoris,* these plants can be grown in pots in areas beyond their hardiness range or where soil cannot be kept dry for summer-dormant types.

N. bowdenii. Flowers to 3 in. long, soft pink marked with deeper pink, in clusters of 8–12 on 2-ft. stems. Forms with taller stems and larger flower clusters are available in deeper pink, crimson, and red. 'Crispa' is 1 ft. tall, with pale pink, wavy-edged segments; 'Pink Triumph' is a larger plant that blooms later.

N. filifolia. Essentially evergreen, since new leaves—narrow, grassy, 6–8 in. long—are produced as old ones fade. Inch-wide, rose red flowers with narrow, crinkled segments are carried in clusters of 8–12 on 1-ft. stems. Spreads rapidly.

N. masoniorum. Virtually evergreen species like *N. filifolia,* but it bears its flowers in clusters of 4–12 on 9-in. stems.

N. sarniensis. GUERNSEY LILY. Large clusters of 1½-in., iridescent crimson flowers with prominent stamens, borne on stalks to 2 ft. tall. Pink, orange, scarlet, and pure white varieties. *N. s. curvifolia fothergillii* has scarlet flowers overlaid with shimmering gold.

NERIUM oleander

OLEANDER

Apocynaceae

EVERGREEN SHRUB

ZONES 8–16, 18–24; H1, H2

FULL SUN

LITTLE TO MODERATE WATER

ALL PARTS ARE POISONOUS IF INGESTED. DON'T BURN PRUNINGS; SMOKE CAN CAUSE SEVERE IRRITATION

Nerium oleander

Mediterranean native. Moderate to fast growth to 3–20 ft. tall and 4–12 ft. wide, depending on variety. Larger types can be easily trained into single or multitrunked trees. Narrow, 4–12-in.-long leaves are dark green, leathery, and semiglossy; attractive in all seasons. Blooms from late spring to fall, bearing 2–3-in.-wide, often fragrant flowers clustered at twig or branch ends. Forms with double and single flowers are sold, in colors ranging from white to shades of yellow, pink, salmon, and red. 'Sister Agnes', single white, is the most vigorous oleander, often reaching 20 ft. tall; 'Mrs. Roeding', double salmon pink, grows 6 ft. tall and has smaller leaves, finer-textured foliage than big oleanders. Flowers of double types hang on after bloom and turn brown. Single-flowered 'Hawaii' offers the same rich color as 'Mrs. Roeding', but its flowers drop cleanly.

'Petite Pink' and 'Petite Salmon' grow 3–6 ft. high and nearly as wide; keep at lower end of range with moderate pruning. They make excellent informal flowering hedges, though they are not as cold hardy as standard-size oleanders. Bright red 'Little Red', to 3–4 ft. tall and wide, is completely hardy—as are the following, intermediate in size between dwarfs and full-size plants: deep red 'Algiers', white 'Casablanca', bright red 'Ruby Lace' (with 3-in., wavy-edged flowers), and white 'Morocco'.

Oleanders need little water once established, but they can take moderate amounts. They tolerate poorly drained and relatively salty soils. In shade or ocean fog, they produce weak or leggy growth and few flowers. Routine pruning isn't necessary, but you may need to prune to guide growth. To control size and form, cut oldest stems to the ground before spring growth begins; shorten remaining stems to restrict height. To prevent bushiness at base, pull (don't cut) any unwanted suckers. To renew an old, unattractive, leggy plant, lop it to the ground before new growth begins in spring.

Oleander was once the basic landscaping shrub for regions with hot, dry summers and mild winters, but it is now facing a severe threat from leaf scorch, a bacterial disease spread by the glassy-winged sharpshooter (an insect pest). Leaves of infected plants turn brown and drop, and the plant quickly declines and dies. No cure is known, although the disease's progress may be slowed by pruning out affected parts of the plant (sterilize pruning tools after each cut). The disease is already serious in Southern California and in parts of Arizona and Texas. Efforts are being made to curb its spread by controlling the insect carrier. Previously, chief problems were scale, yellow oleander aphid, and bacterial gall disease (causing deformed flowers and warty growths).

Caution children against eating leaves or flowers; keep prunings and dead leaves away from hay or other animal feed; don't use wood for barbecue fires or skewers. Smoke from burning prunings can cause severe irritation to mucous membranes.

For a plant called yellow oleander, see *Thevetia.*

NEW MEXICAN PRIVET. See FORESTIERA neomexicana

NEW ZEALAND CHRISTMAS TREE. See METROSIDEROS excelsus

NEW ZEALAND FLAX. See PHORMIUM tenax

NEW ZEALAND LACEBARK. See HOHERIA populnea

NEW ZEALAND LAUREL. See CORYNOCARPUS laevigata

NEW ZEALAND TEA TREE. See LEPTOSPERMUM scoparium

NICOTIANA

Solanaceae

PERENNIALS, MOST GROWN AS ANNUALS

ALL ZONES, EXCEPT AS NOTED

FULL SUN OR PARTIAL SHADE

REGULAR WATER

ALL PARTS ARE EXTREMELY POISONOUS IF INGESTED

Nicotiana alata

Tender perennials from South America. All but *N. glauca* are grown as annuals, but they may live over in mild-winter areas. Upright-growing plants with large, soft, oval leaves; both foliage and stems are slightly sticky. Flowers—very fragrant, in some species—are tubular, typically flaring at the mouth into five pointed lobes; they appear near tops of branching stems in summer. They usually open at night or on cloudy days, though some kinds open during the day. Some nicotianas reseed readily.

N. alata (N. affinis). Wild species (for which seed is available) grows 2–4 ft. tall (possibly to 6 ft. under ideal conditions), 1 ft. wide. Bears large, intensely fragrant white flowers that open toward evening. Selection and hybridization with other species have produced many garden strains that stay open day and night and come in colors including white, pink shades, red, and lime green, but their perfume is not as strong as that of the "unimproved" species.

Domino strain grows 12–15 in. high and has upward-facing flowers that take heat and sun better than taller kinds. Nicki strain is taller, to 15–18 in. The older Sensation strain is taller still (to 4 ft.) and looks more at home in informal mixed borders than as a bedding plant. Fragrance in these strains is erratic. If scent (especially during evening) is important to you, plant 3-ft.-tall 'Grandiflora'.

N. glauca. TREE TOBACCO. Zones 7–24. Naturalized in Hawaii and from California to Texas and Mexico. Shrubby or treelike habit to 10–25 ft. tall, 10 ft. wide. Bluish green leaves to 6 in. long; small, unscented yellow-green flowers. Be especially careful with the leaves—they can be deadly if eaten.

N. langsdorffii. To 5 ft. tall, 1½ ft. wide. Branching stems are hung with drooping sprays of bell-shaped bright green flowers. Unusual blossom color blends well with blues, yellows in flower border. No noticeable scent.

N. sylvestris. To 5 ft. tall, 2 ft. wide. Intensely fragrant, long, tubular white flowers are borne in tiers atop a statuesque plant. Striking in a night garden.

NIEREMBERGIA

CUP FLOWER

Solanaceae

PERENNIALS

ZONES VARY BY SPECIES

LIGHT SHADE IN HOTTEST CLIMATES

REGULAR WATER

Nierembergia repens

The first species listed here grows as a spreading mound; the second is a ground-covering mat. Both are blanketed with broadly cup-shaped blooms in summer. Beyond hardiness range, treat as annuals.

N. caerulea (N. hippomanica). DWARF CUP FLOWER. Zones 8–24; H1, H2. To 6–12 in. high and wide. Much-branched, mounding plant, with very small, stiff leaves. Flowers are blue to violet. Trimming back plant after bloom to induce new growth seems to lengthen its life. 'Purple Robe' is a common variety; 'Mont Blanc' bears white flowers.

N. repens (N. rivularis). WHITE CUP. Zones 5–9, 14–24; H1. Mat to 4–6 in. high, 2 ft. wide, with bright green foliage and white blossoms. For best performance, don't crowd it with more aggressive plants. Not as heat tolerant as *N. caerulea.*

NIGELLA damascena

LOVE-IN-A-MIST

Ranunculaceae

ANNUAL

ALL ZONES

FULL SUN OR PARTIAL SHADE

REGULAR WATER

Nigella damascena

Mediterreranean native. Old-fashioned favorite to 1–1½ ft. high, 10 in. wide. All leaves, even those that form under collar beneath each flower, are finely cut into threadlike divisions. Blue, white, or rose-colored blooms, 1–1½ in. across, are borne singly at branch ends in spring. Curious papery-textured, horned seed capsules lend an airy effect to bouquets and mixed borders, look very decorative in dried arrangements. 'Miss Jekyll', to 1½ ft. tall, has semidouble cornflower blue blossoms. Persian Jewels, to 15 in. high, is a superior strain in mixed colors.

Love-in-a-mist comes into bloom quickly in spring, dries up in summer heat. Start from seed in spring, as soon as ground is workable and frost danger is past; can be sown in fall in mild-winter areas. Sow seed where plants are to grow, since long taproot makes transplanting unsatisfactory. Self-sows freely.

NIGHT JESSAMINE. See CESTRUM nocturnum

NIKAU PALM. See RHOPALOSTYLIS sapida

NINEBARK. See PHYSOCARPUS

NIU. See COCOS nucifera

NOBLE FIR. See ABIES procera

NOLANA paradoxa

Nolanaceae

PERENNIAL GROWN AS ANNUAL

ALL ZONES

FULL SUN OR LIGHT SHADE

MODERATE WATER

Nolana paradoxa

Unusual plant from Chile that looks like a trailing, sky blue petunia. To 6–8 in. high and 2 ft. wide, with trailing stems bearing ovate, 2-in.-long leaves. In summer, plant is covered with 2-in., funnel-shaped flowers in bright blue with a white or yellow throat. 'Blue Bird' has deep sky blue blossoms with a white throat. Use as edging or in hanging basket. Withstands wide range of temperatures. Needs good drainage.

NOLINA

Agavaceae

PERENNIALS

ZONES VARY BY SPECIES

FULL SUN

LITTLE OR NO WATER TO MODERATE WATER

Nolina recurvata

Accent plants with tough, grassy leaves, typically on a thick trunk; leaves are usually about 3 ft. long. In spring or summer, 3–4-ft. stalks rise from the center of the foliage rosette, carrying tiny greenish or creamy white flowers. Plants are valued for their strong vertical silhouette rather than their blossoms. Good for desert or other dry landscapes.

N. bigelovii. Zones 7–16, 18–24. Native to California, Arizona. Stout stem to 3 ft. tall is topped by a rosette of gray-green, 3–4-ft. leaves. Plant eventually reaches about 6 ft. wide.

N. longifolia. MEXICAN GRASS TREE. Zones 12–24. Native to central Mexico. In youth, forms a fountain of bright green, grasslike leaves. In time, leafy whorls top trunks 6–10 ft. tall, sometimes with a few branches. Plant can eventually spread to 9 ft.

N. matapensis. TREE BEAR GRASS. Zones 10–13. From Mexico. To 10–25 ft. tall, 10 ft. wide, with a branching trunk that is slow to develop. Each branch ends in a shower of bright green, broad-based leaves with sharp edges; leaves may reach 9 ft. long.

N. microcarpa. Zones 3, 10–13. Native from Arizona to Texas and Mexico. Unlike others, doesn't form a noticeable trunk; instead, branching and slowly spreading underground stems give rise here and there to rosettes of narrow (less than ½-in.-wide) olive green leaves with tips split into tufts. Each foliage clump can reach 3 ft. tall, 6 ft. wide.

N. parryi. Zones 2, 3, 7–24. Native to deserts of Southern California. Resembles *N. bigelovii,* but leaf bases are expanded into a spoonlike shape. Some authorities consider this a subspecies of *N. bigelovii.*

N. recurvata (Beaucarnea recurvata). BOTTLE PALM, PONYTAIL PALM. Zones 13, 16–24, H1, H2; or indoors. Native to Mexico. To 12–15 ft. tall (possibly to 30 ft. in great age), 9–12 ft. wide. One or more trunks rise from greatly swollen base. On young plants, trunk base looks like a big onion sitting on the soil; on old plants, it can measure several feet across. Clusters of bright green leaves arch and droop at ends of branches. Mature outdoor plants may bloom. Does exceptionally well indoors if given bright light and not overwatered.

NORFOLK ISLAND PINE. See ARAUCARIA heterophylla

NORTHERN BEDSTRAW. See GALIUM boreale

NOTHOFAGUS

SOUTHERN BEECH, FALSE BEECH

Fagaceae

EVERGREEN AND DECIDUOUS TREES

ZONES 5, 6, 14–17

FULL SUN

REGULAR WATER

Nothofagus antarctica

Relatives of beech *(Fagus);* native to Southern Hemisphere. Small dark green leaves and open branch structure give these trees a graceful look. Nuts are so tiny as to go unnoticed. Need high humidity, neutral to acid soil, and good drainage. The three species described below, all from Chile, are sold in Western specialty nurseries; evergreen species from Australia and New Zealand are rarely sold and are not covered here.

N. antarctica. Deciduous. To 50 ft. tall, 30 ft. wide. Closely set, oval, ½–1½-in. leaves line long, graceful shoots on young trees. Grows fast in youth; fills out with age, but branches maintain their graceful, fern-frond appearance. Yellow fall foliage. Open growth makes for handsome silhouette against wall or sky.

N. dombeyi. Evergreen. To 50–70 ft. tall, 30 ft. wide. Leaves to 1½ in. long, ½ in. wide. Good tree for shading rhododendrons, azaleas; open structure admits filtered light.

N. obliqua. Deciduous. Fast growing to 70–100 ft. tall, 50 ft. wide. Oblong, 3-in. leaves turn yellow, orange, or red in autumn; several colors may be present on a single tree.

Nyctaginaceae. The four-o'clock family contains annuals, perennials, shrubs, and vines with showy flowers or bracts. Two familiar members are *Bougainvillea* and four o'clock *(Mirabilis).*

N

NYMPHAEA

WATER LILY
Nymphaeaceae
AQUATIC PLANTS
ZONES 1–24; H1, H2
FULL SUN
LOCATE IN PONDS, WATER GARDENS

Nymphaea

Floating leaves are rounded, with deep notch at one side where leafstalk is attached. Showy flowers either float on surface or stand above it on stiff stalks. There are hardy and tropical kinds. Hardy types come in white, yellow, copper, pink, and red. Tropical types add blue and purple to the color range; recent introductions include an unusual greenish blue. Some tropicals in the white-pink-red color range are night bloomers; all others close at night. Many are fragrant.

Hardy kinds are easiest for beginners. Plant them from February to October in mild-winter areas, from April to July in cold-winter regions. Set 6-in.-long pieces of rhizome on soil at pool bottom or in boxes (not redwood ones, since these can discolor the water), placing rhizome in a nearly horizontal position with its bud end up. In either case, top of soil should be 8–12 in. below surface of water. Feed at planting time and monthly thereafter, using a controlled-release product. Groom plants by removing spent leaves and blossoms. They usually bloom throughout warm weather and go dormant in fall, reappearing in spring. In very cold areas, protect plants by covering pond or by adding more water to it.

Tropical kinds begin to grow and bloom later in summer but last longer, often until the first frost. Buy started tropical plants and set them at the same depth as hardy rhizomes. Tropical types go dormant but do not survive really low winter temperatures. Their best chance of long-term survival is in regions where orange trees grow. Where winters are colder, store dormant tubers in damp sand over winter or buy new plants each year.

Nymphaeaceae. The water lily family consists of aquatic plants, usually with floating leaves and flowers. Two examples are lotus *(Nelumbo)* and water lily *(Nymphaea)*.

Nyssaceae. Deciduous trees from Asia and North America. Two grown in the West are dove tree *(Davidia)* and sour gum *(Nyssa)*.

NYSSA sylvatica

SOUR GUM, TUPELO, PEPPERIDGE
Nyssaceae
DECIDUOUS TREE
ZONES 2–10, 14–21
FULL SUN OR PARTIAL SHADE
MODERATE TO REGULAR WATER

Nyssa sylvatica

Native to eastern U.S. Slow to moderate growth to 30–50 ft. or taller, 15–25 ft. wide. Pyramidal when young; spreading, irregular, and rugged in age. Crooked branches and dark, red-tinged bark make dramatic picture against winter sky. Glossy dark green, 2–5-in.-long leaves emerge rather late in spring. Male and female flowers borne on separate plants. Both sexes bear inconspicuous flowers; females will bear fruit if a male is growing nearby (males may set some fruit as well). Fruits are bluish black, shaped like small olives; birds like them. In fall, even in mild-winter regions, leaves turn yellow and orange, then bright red before dropping.

Prefers moist, deep, acid, well-drained soil, but tolerates poor drainage and some drought. Does not thrive in polluted air. Excellent specimen or shade tree; very attractive in naturalized landscapes. Select a permanent location, since this tree's taproot makes it difficult to move later on.

OAK. See **QUERCUS**

OAT GRASS, BLUE. See **HELICTOTRICHON sempervirens**

OAT GRASS, BULBOUS. See **ARRHENATHERUM elatius bulbosum 'Variegatum'**

OCEAN SPRAY. See **HOLODISCUS discolor**

OCHNA serrulata (O. multiflora)

BIRD'S-EYE BUSH, MICKEY MOUSE PLANT
Ochnaceae
EVERGREEN SHRUB
ZONES 14–24
PARTIAL SHADE
MODERATE WATER

Ochna serrulata

From South Africa. Slow, spreading growth to 4–8 ft. high and wide. Oblong leaves, 2–5 in. long, are leathery, fine toothed, bronzy in spring, deep green later. Early summer flowers are the size of buttercups *(Ranunculus)*. After the yellow petals fall, sepals turn vivid red; then five or more green, seedlike fruits protrude from red center. Fruits later turn glossy jet black, in strong contrast to red sepals; at this stage the configuration can be said to resemble eyes, ears, and nose of a mouse. Prefers slightly acid soil. Good in tub or box or as small espalier. Makes an interesting accent in a shrub border.

OCIMUM basilicum

BASIL
Lamiaceae (Labiatae)
ANNUAL
ALL ZONES
FULL SUN
REGULAR WATER

Ocimum basilicum

From tropical and subtropical Asia. Somewhat bushy plant to 2 ft. tall and 1 ft. wide, with green, shiny, 1–2-in.-long leaves and spikes of white flowers. Forms with purple or variegated leaves have purple flowers. Very popular culinary herb. Used fresh or dry, its leaves lend a pleasant, mildly sweet flavor to sauces and cooked dishes of all sorts. The best leaves are from younger stems that have not yet borne flowers. There is a dwarf, small-leafed kind that thrives in containers.

'Dark Opal' has large leaves in a deep bronzy purple and small lavender-pink flowers; it grows 1–1½ ft. high and is attractive enough for borders and mass plantings. Other good purple-leafed varieties include 'Red Rubin', with uniform dark color, and 'Purple Ruffles', with deeply fringed and ruffled leaf edges.

Sow seeds of any basil in early spring; or set out nursery plants after all danger of frost is past. Space plants about 10–12 in. apart or thin to this distance. Fertilize once during the growing season with a complete fertilizer. To prolong leaf production—which will cease when plants come into bloom—pinch out flower spikes as they form. Where the growing season is long, though, flowering will always win out and plants will mature and stop producing new growth. In these regions, make successive sowings about every 2 weeks to ensure a steady supply of leaves throughout the season.

OCONEE BELLS. See **SHORTIA galacifolia**

OCOTILLO. See **FOUQUIERIA**

OCTOPUS TREE. See **SCHEFFLERA actinophylla**

OEMLERIA cerasiformis (Osmaronia cerasiformis)

OSO BERRY, INDIAN PLUM

Rosaceae

DECIDUOUS SHRUB OR TREE

ZONES 4–9, 14–24

FULL SUN IN COOLER CLIMATES ONLY

AMPLE WATER

Oemleria cerasiformis

In damp woodlands and meadows in the Northwest and in parts of California, oso berry's tiny, almond-scented white flowers are among the first signs of spring. Suckering shrub to 3–15 ft. tall spreads into thickets 12 ft. or wider. Lance-shaped leaves to 3½ in. long are dark green on top, gray green and slightly fuzzy beneath. Bell-shaped blooms in drooping clusters 4 in. long appear with the foliage, which emerges very early in the year. Male and female plants are separate; if a male is nearby, females will bear small (less than ½-in.-long) blue-black fruits. To keep the plant open, remove some of the oldest stems after bloom. Or revive an old, overgrown shrub by cutting it back almost to the ground.

OENANTHE javanica

JAPANESE WATERCRESS, FLAMINGO CELERY

Apiaceae (Umbelliferae)

PERENNIAL

ZONES 9, 14–24

FULL SUN

AMPLE WATER

Oenanthe javanica 'Flamingo'

Native to Asia. Stems 8–16 in. long, prostrate or semierect, set with 4-in., bright green leaves divided like celery foliage. Flat, round clusters of whitish flowers bloom in summer. Stems root where they touch damp soil, and plant spreads indefinitely; it will grow even in water. Can be eaten as a vegetable; use leaves raw or shred them into soups.

In North America, the species is rarely grown. More commonly seen is 'Flamingo', with grayish green leaves edged in white; the white border becomes suffused with pink during cool weather, the pink eventually spreading to the whole leaf. Dormant in winter except in the mildest climates. Use as an ornamental around pools and in wet places.

OENOTHERA

EVENING PRIMROSE, SUNDROPS

Onagraceae

PERENNIALS OR BIENNIALS

ZONES VARY BY SPECIES

FULL SUN OR PARTIAL SHADE

LITTLE TO MODERATE WATER, EXCEPT AS NOTED

Oenothera speciosa 'Rosea'

Valued for showy, four-petaled, silky flowers in bright yellow, pink, or white. Some types display their blossoms during the day, but others open in late afternoon and close the following morning. Flowers of some are fragrant. Plants succeed in tough, rough places.

O. berlandieri. See O. speciosa 'Rosea'

O. caespitosa. TUFTED, FRAGRANT, or WHITE EVENING PRIMROSE. Perennial or biennial. Zones 1–3, 7–14, 18–21. Native to western U.S. Clump to 8–12 in. high, 2 ft. wide, with many rosettes of narrow, fuzzy gray-green leaves to 4 in. long. Fragrant, 3–4-in. flowers fade from white to pink; they open in the evening. Blooms heavily in late spring, early summer.

O. elata hookeri (O. hookeri). Perennial or biennial. Zones 5–7, 14–24. Native to moist places in many parts of western U.S. To 3 ft. high and wide. Basal rosette of medium green, lance-shaped, 2–5-in.-long leaves; branching flower stems are hairy, carry smaller leaves. Evening-blooming plant that produces flowers all summer. The 2–3-in. blossoms are carried in terminal spikes; they open pale yellow, later turn orange red. Reseeds heavily; not recommended for orderly, irrigated gardens. Grow in moist area where it can run wild. Tolerates both drought and flooding.

O. fruticosa. SUNDROPS. Perennial or biennial. Zones 1–21. Native to eastern U.S. Erect growth to 2 ft. high and wide. Branching reddish stems are set with medium green, lance-shaped leaves to 4½ in. long; leaves turn dull red with frost. Clusters of 1–2-in.-wide, deep yellow flowers from late spring through summer; open in daytime. 'Fireworks' ('Fyrverkeri') has red flower buds and leaves tinted purplish brown. Foliage of 'Summer Solstice' ('Sonnenwende') turns bright red in summer, darkens to burgundy in fall. *O. f. glauca (O. tetragona)* has light yellow flowers and red stems; its leaves (red tinted when young) are broader than those of species.

O. macrocarpa (O. missouriensis). OZARK SUNDROPS. Perennial. Zones 1–24. Native to south-central U.S. To 6 in. tall and 2 ft. wide, with narrow, lance-shaped leaves to 3 in. long. Late spring to early fall, bears pure yellow, 4-in. flowers that remain open all day. Large winged seedpods follow the flowers. Good in rock gardens. Give partial shade in hottest climates. *O. m. incana* 'Silver Blade' has silvery blue leaves.

O. speciosa. MEXICAN EVENING PRIMROSE. Perennial. Zones 2b–24; H1, H2. Native to southwestern U.S. and Mexico. To 1 ft. high and 3 ft. or more wide, spreading by rhizomes. Forms rosettes of medium green, oblong to lance-shaped, 1–3-in.-long leaves. Fragrant, 2-in. flowers are white to pinkish, aging to pink; despite plant's common name, they open during the day. Blooms spring or early summer into fall, then stems die back. Good ground cover for dry slopes or parking strips, but can be aggressive and is potentially invasive. Varieties include pure white 'Alba', light pink 'Rosea' *(O. berlandieri, O. speciosa childsii)*, pink 'Siskiyou', and 'Woodside White' (white blossoms with a chartreuse eye).

O. stubbei. SALTILLO EVENING PRIMROSE. Perennial. Zones 10–14, 18–24. Native to Mexico. Evening-blooming plant that forms a dark green mat 5 in. high and 4 ft. wide; prostrate stems root along the ground, forming offset plants. Narrow leaves to 2½ in. long. Yellow, 2½-in. flowers rise on individual stems 6–8 in. above foliage. Blooms most heavily in spring, sporadically throughout the rest of the year. Endures heat and drought but does better with occasional water. Often sold as *O. drummondii.*

O. tetragona. See O. fruticosa glauca

OKRA

Malvaceae

ANNUAL

ALL ZONES

FULL SUN

REGULAR WATER

Okra

Warm-season vegetable from tropical Asia; botanical name is *Abelmoschus esculentus.* Large, erect, bushy plant to 6 ft. tall, with big, bold, deeply lobed leaves; the edible pods are produced in leaf joints. Grows well under same conditions as sweet corn. Plant when danger of frost is past and ground has warmed to 70°F/21°C. To speed germination, soak seeds for 24 hours before planting; use only seeds that are swollen. Leave 2½–4 ft. between rows; thin plants to 1–1½ ft. apart. Apply a complete fertilizer when the first pods set, again when plants are shoulder high. Begin picking when pods are 2–4 in. long (wear gloves, since pods are prickly). Pick every 2 days or so; plants stop producing if pods are not harvested. Okra takes 55 to 60 days from planting to harvest.

'Annie Oakley' and 'Cajun Delight' are early varieties that mature in areas with a short growing season. 'Burgundy' has red leaves and pods, looks attractive in containers. Grown in a large tub in a warm spot, a single okra plant can yield a crop large enough to make it worth growing. Okra is used to flavor and thicken soups and gumbos; it can also be sautéed, steamed, or batter-fried.

OLD MAN CACTUS. See **CEPHALOCEREUS senilis**

OLD MAN'S WHISKERS. See **GEUM triflorum**

Oleaceae. The olive family encompasses about 900 species of trees and shrubs with opposite leaves and flower parts that are usually in fours. Members include privet *(Ligustrum)*, olive *(Olea)*, and lilac *(Syringa)*.

OLEA europaea

OLIVE

Oleaceae

EVERGREEN TREE

ZONES 8, 9, 11–24; H1, H2

FULL SUN

LITTLE TO MODERATE WATER

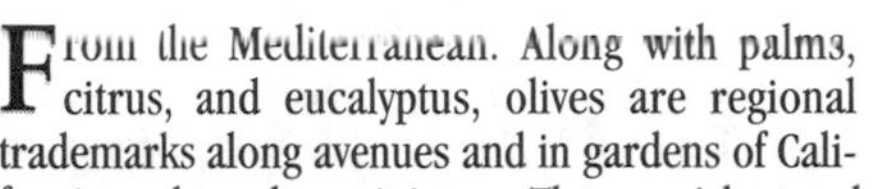

Olea europaea

From the Mediterranean. Along with palms, citrus, and eucalyptus, olives are regional trademarks along avenues and in gardens of California and southern Arizona. The trees' beauty has been appreciated in those areas since they were introduced to mission gardens for the oil their fruit produces.

Willowlike foliage is a soft gray green that goes well with most colors. Smooth gray trunks and branches become gnarled and picturesque in age. Trees grow slowly, typically to 25–30 ft. high and as wide; however, young ones put on height (if not substance) fairly fast. Begin training early. For single trunk, prune out or shorten side branches below point where you want branching to begin; cut off basal suckers. For multiple trunks, stake lower branches or basal suckers to continue growth at desired angles. Large old trees can (with reasonable care) be boxed and transplanted with near certainty of survival.

Olive trees look best when grown in deep, rich soil, but they will also grow in shallow, alkaline, or stony soil and with little fertilizer. They thrive in areas with hot, dry summers but also perform adequately in coastal areas. They take temperatures down to 15°F/–9°C.

Olives withstand heavy pruning. Thinning each year shows off branch pattern and eliminates some flowering/fruiting wood, reducing the fruit crop—which can be a nuisance in ornamental plantings.

On fruiting varieties, olives ripen and drop late in the year. Without processing, the olives are inedible, and they can stain paving and harm lawns if not removed. In addition to pruning, reduce crop by spraying with fruit-control hormones when tiny white flowers appear. Or spread tarpaulin at dropping time, knock off all fruit, and dispose of it. So-called fruitless varieties are not always reliably barren.

'Ascolana'. A variety grown commercially for fruit; available as a specimen tree from landscaping firms. Large fruit, small pit.

'Bonita'. Sold as fruitless; actually, has tiny fruit resembling that of privet *(Ligustrum)*.

'Little Ollie'. Big, dense shrub (to 12 ft. high and wide), very dark green; excellent as hedge or screen. Bears almost no fruit.

'Majestic Beauty'. Airy and fluffy looking; suitable as specimen or as hedge or screen. Bears almost no fruit.

'Manzanillo'. Commercial-grove kind most often sold as specimen tree by landscaping firms. More spreading habit than most. Apple-shaped fruit.

'Mission.' Commercial-grove kind sold as specimen tree by landscaping firms. Taller than 'Manzanillo', 'Sevillano'.

'Sevillano'. Commercial-grove kind sold as specimen tree by landscaping firms. Oaklike form.

'Skylark Dwarf'. Typically a large, compact, multitrunked shrub to 16 ft. high and wide. Sets very small fruit crop in some years.

'Swan Hill'. Leaves are deep green. Bears no fruit. Little or no pollen—a boon to allergy sufferers.

'Wilsoni'. Bears no fruit.

OLEANDER. See **NERIUM oleander**

OLIVE. See **OLEA europaea**

OLNEYA tesota

DESERT IRONWOOD

Fabaceae (Leguminosae)

EVERGREEN TREE

ZONES 8, 9, 11–14, 18–23

FULL SUN

LITTLE OR NO WATER TO MODERATE WATER

Olneya tesota

Thorny native of the Southwest's Sonoran Desert; found in warm-winter areas of California. Grows slowly to 15–30 ft. tall, with equal spread; common name "ironwood" refers to its extremely hard, heavy heartwood. May be single- or multitrunked; prune to maintain desired form. Branches are erect in youth, later spreading. Gray-green leaves, each with two spines at base, are divided into many ¾-in. leaflets. In late spring, clusters of pinkish lavender, ½-in., sweet pea–shaped flowers put on a good show. These are followed by dark brown, fuzzy, 2-in.-long pods. Tree drops leaves heavily around bloom time, but new foliage emerges quickly.

In the wild, this plant grows near washes, where some deep water is usually available. In the garden, it is extremely drought tolerant but will grow faster with occasional summer water. Drops its leaves in hard frosts and cannot endure prolonged freezes.

OMPHALODES

Boraginaceae

PERENNIALS

ZONES VARY BY SPECIES

PARTIAL SHADE

REGULAR WATER

Omphalodes verna

These resemble forget-me-nots *(Myosotis)* but typically have deeper blue, somewhat larger (½-in.) flowers and more restrained behavior—these plants don't have the irritating habit of reseeding themselves all over the place.

Omphalodes thrive in woodland gardens or shaded rock gardens and look especially attractive on a wall or bank, where their flowers may be viewed at eye level.

O. cappadocica. Zones 3–9, 14–21. Native to Turkey. Slowly spreading clump of bright green foliage to 1½ ft. wide. Sends up 1–1½-ft.-high sprays of bright blue, white-eyed flowers in spring. 'Lilac Mist' is shorter (to 10 in.), with grayish lavender flowers. 'Starry Eyes', also to 10 in. high, has pale lilac flowers with dark blue spots at the base of each petal.

O. verna. BLUE-EYED MARY. Zones 2–9, 14–21. Native to mountains of Europe. Forms a foliage mat 3 in. high, 3 ft. or more wide, with dark green, 4-in. leaves. In spring, leafy stalks to 8 in. tall bear clustered deep blue flowers with a white eye.

Onagraceae. Most members of the evening primrose family have flower parts in fours, but otherwise they are diverse in appearance and structure. They include *Fuchsia, Gaura,* and various Western natives such as *Clarkia,* many sundrops and evening primroses *(Oenothera),* and California fuchsia *(Zauschneria).*

FOR INFORMATION ON SELECTING PLANTS
PLEASE SEE PAGES 64–160

ONCIDIUM

Orchidaceae

EPIPHYTIC ORCHIDS

ZONES 17, 20–24, H1, H2; OR INDOORS

PARTIAL SHADE; BRIGHT INDIRECT LIGHT

REGULAR WATER

Oncidium crispum

Orchids native from Florida and Mexico through South America. The several hundred species and countless hybrids range from tiny plants just 1 in. tall to giants with branching flower spikes to 6 ft. or more bearing dozens of blooms. Most produce long spikes of yellow or brown-and-yellow flowers; a few come in white or rose. Some (including the plants described here) have compressed pseudobulbs with one or two large leaves; others are almost without pseudobulbs; still others have cylindrical, pencil-like leaves. Plants typically produce a few large blossoms or many small ones, but some have numerous large flowers and a few bear their blooms singly. In many, flowers have a large, flaring lip reminiscent of a flamenco dancer's skirt; these are sometimes called dancing ladies. Blossoms of some are scented. As outdoor plants, oncidiums are usually grown on tree trunks or in pots on the patio; indoor plants can be brought outdoors during warm weather. Take same houseplant culture as cattleya. Also see Orchidaceae.

O. crispum. Pseudobulbs 4 in. high are topped by 8-in. leaves. In fall, produces a branching, 3-ft.-tall spike carrying many 4-in. flowers in chestnut brown spotted with yellow. Each bloom has a brown lip with a large bright yellow spot.

O. ornithorhynchum. Pseudobulbs 2½ in. tall are topped by leaves to 1 ft. long. In summer, many branching, 8–12-in.-tall spikes carry a cloud of inch-wide pink or purplish pink flowers with yellow markings.

O. Sharry Baby 'Sweet Fragrance'. Powerfully fragrant hybrid selection with 4-in.-high pseudobulbs topped with 8-in. leaves. Bears 2–3-ft. spikes of reddish or purplish brown, inch-wide blossoms in summer and fall. Some liken the flowers' perfume to chocolate, others to vanilla.

ONION

Amaryllidaceae

BIENNIAL GROWN AS ANNUAL

ALL ZONES

FULL SUN

REGULAR WATER

Onion

Botanically, the onion is *Allium cepa,* a species not known in the wild. More so than for other vegetables, growing onions successfully requires proper variety selection, appropriate planting methods, and good timing. Consult an area nursery or your Cooperative Extension Office for advice on varieties that grow well in your area.

Onion varieties differ in size, shape, color, flavor, and storage life. More important, different types form bulbs in response to varying day lengths. If you choose a type inappropriate for your area, it may bolt, form small premature bulbs, or not bulb up at all.

Long-day varieties need 14 to 16 hours of daylight to form bulbs and are best adapted to northern latitudes, such as Alaska and the Pacific Northwest. They tend to be pungent, and they store well; examples include 'Early Yellow Globe', 'Ebenezer', 'Ruby', 'Southport White Globe', 'Sweet Spanish'. Generally, long-day onions are planted in early spring and form bulbs as the days get longer in summer.

Short-day varieties need 10 to 12 hours of daylight and are best adapted to southern latitudes, such as Southern California, the Southwest, and Hawaii. They are typically planted in fall to early winter, grow vegetatively through winter, then begin to bulb up in spring. These onions tend to be sweet and are poor keepers; examples are 'Bermuda', 'California Red', 'Granex', 'Grano', and 'Super Sweet'.

Intermediate-day onions, requiring 12 to 14 hours of daylight, are best suited to interior valleys of central California. They store moderately well. Examples are 'Autumn Spice', 'Red Torpedo', 'Ringmaker'. They are usually planted in early spring.

(True bunching onions, also sold as scallions, are varieties that do not form bulbs and are harvested like scallions or green onions; they can be grown anywhere.)

Onions can be grown from seed, sets (small bulbs), or transplants. Sets and transplants are easiest for beginners, though starting from seed gives a larger crop for a smaller investment and offers a wider choice of varieties.

In mild-winter climates, onions grow well from seed planted in fall to early winter. Sets and transplants can be planted all winter long and through early spring, although sets are generally long-day varieties that will not bulb up well in southern regions. They can, however, be grown for scallions or green onions—standard onions harvested before they form bulbs. In Hawaii, short-day varieties are usually started from seed from earliest part of cool season; intermediate types are planted later in cool season for warm-season harvest. Types called Maui onions are actually any sweet, bulbing onion grown in Hawaii. In cold-winter climates, planting can begin in early spring as soon as the soil is workable; or start seed indoors in late winter and transplant later.

Soil should be loose, rich, and well drained. If planting sets, push them just under the soil surface so the point of the bulb is visible. Space sets and transplants 4–5 in. apart (closer if you want to harvest some as green onions). Sow seed ¼ in. deep, in rows 15–18 in. apart. Thin seedlings to 4–5 in. apart; they can be eaten or transplanted to extend planting. Trim back tops of transplants about halfway.

Onions are shallow rooted and need moisture fairly near the surface. Feed plants regularly, especially early in the season: the larger and stronger the plant, the bigger the bulb it forms. Carefully eliminate weeds. When most of the tops have begun to yellow and fall over, dig bulbs and let them cure and dry on top of the ground for several days. Cover bulbs with tops to prevent sunburn. When tops and necks are completely dry, pull off the tops and brush dirt from bulbs; then store bulbs in dark, cool, airy place.

OPHIOPOGON. See LIRIOPE and OPHIOPOGON

OPUNTIA

Cactaceae

CACTI

ZONES VARY BY SPECIES

FULL SUN

LITTLE OR NO WATER, EXCEPT AS NOTED

Opuntia microdasys

The species described here originate in the desert Southwest and Mexico; other species are native to those areas and/or to other parts of the western U.S., the Great Plains, Canada, and Florida. Many kinds, with varied appearance. Most species fall into one of two sorts: those having flat, broad joints (pads) or those having cylindrical joints. Though the use of common names is somewhat inconsistent, members of the first group are often called prickly pear; those in the second group are frequently known as cholla. Hardiness is variable. Flowers are generally large and showy. The fruit is a berry, often edible.

O. basilaris. BEAVERTAIL CACTUS. Zones 2, 3, 7–24. Low-branching plant to 1 ft. high, 4 ft. wide. Oval to roundish gray-green to purplish pads are 2–12 in. wide and ½ in. thick, set with spines up to 2 in. long. Rich rose purple, 2–3-in. spring flowers.

O. bigelovii. TEDDYBEAR CACTUS. Zones 10–24. Slow growing to 3–6 ft. tall, 3 ft. wide, with treelike form. Woody trunk is covered with black spines, which are less conspicuous than their prominent yellow-gold sheaths. Cylindrical, easily detached joints are covered with vicious silvery yellow spines. Most plants never bloom, though may bear 1–1½-in. pale green, yellow, or white flowers (all with lavender markings) in early spring. Grows freely in hottest, driest deserts.

O. ficus-indica. Zones 8, 9, 12–24; H1, H2. Big, shrubby or treelike cactus to 15 ft. tall, 10 ft. wide, with woody trunks and smooth, flat green joints. Few or no spines; has clusters of bristles. Bears 3–5-in.-wide, yellow to orange flowers in late spring and early summer. Blossoms are followed by roundish, 2–3½-in.-long fruits that ripen from yellow to red; these are the prickly pears you may see sold in grocery stores. Handle fruit carefully—bristles break off easily and irritate the skin. Use rubber gloves when peeling fruit, or impale it on a fork and strip skin carefully, avoiding bristly areas. This plant is very drought tolerant, but in hottest regions it needs regular moisture for best fruit.

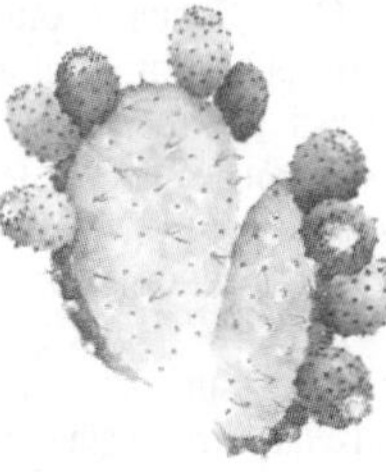

Opuntia ficus-indica

O. leptocaulis. DESERT CHRISTMAS CACTUS, CHRISTMAS CHOLLA, PENCIL CACTUS. Zones 3, 7–24. To 2–3 ft. (rarely to 6 ft.) tall and equally wide. Joints are 1–12 in. long, ¼ in. thick, with 1–2-in.-long spines. Spring flowers, to ¾ in. across, are green to yellow. Fleshy fruits about the size and shape of olives mature from green to red, usually around Christmastime; hang on all winter. Very striking cold-hardy species.

O. macrocentra (O. violacea). Zones 2, 3, 7–24. To 4 ft. tall and 6 ft. wide, with round, 8-in., purplish green pads that turn rich purple in cool weather. Yellow-and-red flowers in spring are 3–3½ in. wide. 'Tubac' is said to hold its purple pad color more consistently throughout the year.

O. microdasys. BUNNY EARS. Zones 12–24; or indoors. Fast growth to 2–3 ft. high, 4–5 ft. wide (much smaller in pots). Flat, thin, nearly round pads to 6 in. across, in a soft, velvety green; neatly spaced tufts of short golden bristles give a polka-dot effect. 'Albispina' has white bristles. New pads atop larger old ones give plant the shape of an animal's head.

ORANGE. See CITRUS

ORANGE CLOCK VINE. See THUNBERGIA gregorii

ORANGE JESSAMINE. See MURRAYA paniculata

ORANGEQUAT. See CITRUS, Kumquat hybrids

Orchidaceae. The orchid family is probably the largest in the plant kingdom, with nearly 800 genera and over 17,000 species. Best known in the West are *Bletilla, Cattleya, Cymbidium, Dendrobium, Epidendrum, Laelia, Oncidium, Paphiopedilum, Phalaenopsis, Pleione,* and *Vanda.*

Orchid growers' terms. Here are definitions of the orchid growers' terms you will encounter in this book.

Epiphytic. In nature, epiphytic orchids cling to high branches of trees in tropical or subtropical jungles, deriving their nourishment from air, rain, and whatever decaying vegetable matter they can trap in their root systems.

Pseudobulb. Epiphytic orchids have thickened stems called pseudobulbs that store food and water and allow the plants to survive drought. These may be short and fat or erect and slender. They vary in color from green to brown. Leaves may grow along pseudobulbs or from their tips.

Terrestrial. Some orchids (including most native North American orchids) are terrestrial and must grow in loose, moist, humus-rich soil. They often occur in wooded areas but sometimes grow in open meadows as well. These orchids require constant moisture and food.

Sepals, petals, and other flower parts. Segments of an orchid flower include three sepals and three petals; stamens, style, and stigma are united into a single organ, the column. One of the petals, usually the lowest one, is called the lip. The lip is usually larger and more brightly colored than the other segments and may be marked with stripes, spots, or streaks. In some orchids, it is unusually shaped (having various appendages) or folded into a slipperlike "pouch."

Rafts, bark. Nearly all orchids, terrestrial or epiphytic, are grown in pots. A few are grown on "rafts" (slabs of bark or wood) or in baskets of wood slats; a few natives are grown in open ground.

Potting and growing orchids. For most epiphytic orchids, the potting materials used for cattleyas (the most commonly grown orchids) work well: osmunda fiber, hapu'u (tree fern stem), or ground bark. Other potting materials suitable for orchids may be available locally. It is sensible to use the ready-made mixes sold by orchid growers; these are blended for proper texture and acidity.

Watering and fertilizing needs vary somewhat depending on the particular orchid. In general, though, water plants when the potting mix dries out and becomes lightweight (usually about once a week), and apply a water-soluble orchid fertilizer every 2 weeks during the growing season. To provide humidity for plants growing in the house, fill a metal or plastic tray with gravel to within an inch of the top (the space is necessary for air circulation), then add just enough water to reach almost to top of gravel. Stretch hardware cloth over the tray. Set pots on top of hardware cloth; check water level periodically, and add more water to tray as needed.

Temperature requirements. The various orchids of the world's tropical regions can be grown outdoors year-round in one or another part of Hawaii; some thrive outdoors in coastal Southern California. Elsewhere, you may be able to grow certain types outdoors all year or just during warm weather; others must be kept indoors.

The following list divides tropical orchids into three classes according to their temperature needs; lowland natives need the warmest conditions, higher-altitude natives the coolest ones. The terms "cool-growing," "intermediate," and "warm-growing" refer to the greenhouse temperatures that approximate ideal conditions for good growth and regular flowering in the plants' native environments. (Most of these orchids will get along fine in somewhat less than ideal situations, though.)

Cool-growing orchids do best with temperatures of 50 to 55°F/10 to 13°C at night, 60 to 75°F/16 to 24°C during the day. This group includes *Cymbidium* (some), *Dendrobium* (some), *Epidendrum* (some), *Laelia* (some), *Paphiopedilum* (green-leafed forms). Some cool growers are thoroughly hardy to many cold-winter zones of the West, and others can withstand winters in mildest parts of California.

Intermediate orchids thrive with temperatures of 55 to 60°F/13 to 16°C at night, 65 to 80°F/18 to 27°C during the day. Members of this group include *Cattleya, Cymbidium* (some), *Dendrobium* (some), *Epidendrum* (some), *Laelia* (some), *Oncidium, Paphiopedilum* (the mottled-leafed forms). These can be grown in pots or on a windowsill with other houseplants but will peform best with additional humidity. An excellent method of supplying humidity is described in "Potting and growing orchids" (above). Most can be moved outdoors in summer; place them in the shade of high-branching trees, on the patio, or in a lathhouse.

Warm-growing orchids do best with temperatures of 60 to 65°F/16 to 18°C at night, 70 to 85°F/21 to 29°C during the day. Warm growers described in this book include *Phalaenopsis* and *Vanda.* These orchids can grow outdoors in warmest parts of Hawaii but need greenhouse conditions (uniform warm temperatures and high humidity) in colder climates.

ORCHID CACTUS. See EPIPHYLLUM

ORCHID TREE. See BAUHINIA

ORCHID VINE. See MASCAGNIA, STIGMAPHYLLON

OREGANO. See ORIGANUM

OREGON BOXWOOD. See PAXISTIMA myrsinites

OREGON GRAPE. See MAHONIA aquifolium

OREGON MYRTLE. See UMBELLULARIA californica

ORGANPIPE CACTUS. See STENOCEREUS thurberi

ORIENTAL ARBORVITAE. See THUJA orientalis

ORIENTAL POPPY. See PAPAVER orientale

ORIGANUM

OREGANO, MARJORAM

Lamiaceae (Labiatae)

PERENNIALS

ZONES VARY BY SPECIES

FULL SUN, EXCEPT AS NOTED

LITTLE TO MODERATE WATER

Origanum majorana

Mint relatives with tight clusters of small flowers. Each blossom has a collar of bracts—large, colorful, and quite decorative in some species—that can overlap to give the inflorescence the look of a small pinecone. Blossoms are especially attractive to bees, butterflies. Many species have pleasantly aromatic foliage, and the leaves of several have culinary use. Some are good as ground covers, as trailers to cascade over rocks or retaining walls, or in hanging baskets. Those with conspicuous bracts are attractive dried and used in wreaths and arrangements; cut and hang just as first flowers open.

Not fussy about soil type but need good drainage. In milder climates, many species can become woody with age, but wood of previous seasons is seldom as productive as new growth from the base. For best results, cut previous year's stems to ground in winter or early spring. Propagate by division or from cuttings taken before flower buds form. The various species hybridize freely, and seedlings may not resemble the parents. Colored-leaf varieties need a half day of direct sun for best color but can burn in afternoon sun in hot-summer areas.

O. amanum. Zones 2b–24. Native to Turkey and the eastern Mediterranean. Low, evergreen mound to 8 in. high, 1 ft. wide, with bright green, hairy, heart-shaped leaves ¾ in. long. Blooms in summer and fall, when arching stems are weighed down by clusters of light green bracts and slender, tubular, five-lobed pink blossoms about 1½ in. long that radiate in all directions. Bracts age to soft purple, making plants decorative even after the flowers fade. Dislikes wet conditions.

O. calcaratum (O. tournefortii). Zones 8, 9, 12–24. Native to Crete and the Aegean islands. Bushy, many-stemmed plant to 1 ft. tall, 2 ft. wide, with pairs of gray-green, densely furry, ¼–1¼-in.-long leaves evenly spaced along radiating stems. Bright pink flowers emerge from pendent, 2-in.-long clusters of gray-green bracts tinged rose; several clusters to each stem. Blooms from spring through fall.

O. dictamnus (Amaracus dictamnus). DITTANY OF CRETE, HOP MARJORAM. Zones 8, 9, 12–24. Native to Crete. Aromatic herb to 8 in. high, 1½–2 ft. wide, with slender, arching stems to 1 ft. long. Thick, roundish, woolly white leaves to ¾ in. long. Pink to purplish flowers emerge from rose-tinted light green bracts; blooms summer to fall. Shows up best when planted individually in rock garden or in hanging basket.

O. ×hybridum. Zones 4–9, 12–24. Resembles parent *O. dictamnus,* but its leaves are gray green and downy rather than woolly.

O. laevigatum. Zones 2–24. Native to Turkey, Cyprus. Sprawling plant with grayish green leaves about 1¼ in. long; reaches 2 ft. tall in bloom. It spreads by rhizomes and arching stems that root at the joints to form a dense clump 2–3 ft. wide. Branching, airy clusters of ½-in., tubular pink or purple flowers and small purplish bracts appear from late spring to fall. Useful as bank or ground cover. 'Herrenhausen' has larger bracts and more compact heads of lilac-pink flowers. 'Hopley's', probably a hybrid with *O. vulgare,* blooms from mid- to late summer, bearing denser heads of purplish pink flowers and purplish bracts; it self-sows freely, producing seedlings with variable foliage and flower color. Both 'Herrenhausen' and 'Hopley's' have purple leaves in cool weather.

O. libanoticum. Zones 2b–24. Native to Lebanon. Attractive trailing plant to 2 ft. high and wide, with small, roundish, smooth green leaves. From midsummer to fall, produces cascades of pale green to pinkish bracts (similar to those of hop, *Humulus*) and small rose pink flowers; heads elongate as the season progresses, ending up several inches long. For best effect, plant at top of wall or in hanging basket.

O. majorana (Majorana hortensis). SWEET MARJORAM, KNOTTED MARJORAM. Zones 8–24; summer annual anywhere. Native to the Mediterranean and Turkey. To 1–2 ft. tall and wide. Oval gray-green leaves to ¾ in. long. Inconspicuous white flowers emerge from clusters of knotlike heads at top of plant. Keep blossoms cut off and plant trimmed to encourage fresh growth. Fresh or dried leaves are used for seasoning meats, scrambled eggs, salads, vinegars, casseroles, tomato dishes. Often grown in pots indoors on sunny windowsill in cold-winter areas. Leaves of 'White Anniversary' have a distinct cream margin.

O. ×majoricum. ITALIAN MARJORAM, SICILIAN MARJORAM. Zones 4–24. Similar to *O. majorana* but with wider, greener leaves. Some gourmet cooks consider this the best marjoram for seasoning.

O. 'Norton Gold'. Zones 2b–24. Hybrid of *O. laevigatum* and *O. vulgare* 'Aureum'. To 1 ft. tall, 1½–2 ft. or more wide, with open habit like that of *O. laevigatum.* Rounded leaves are brilliant gold with a bluish sheen. Foliage is aromatic, with a good flavor; for mealtime color, use sprays of leaves as garnish. Pink flowers bloom in midsummer. Protect from hottest sun.

O. onites. POT MARJORAM, RHIGANI. Zones 8–24. Eastern Mediterranean native. To 2 ft. tall and wide, with bright green, aromatic, inch-long leaves and 2-in.-wide, flattish heads of white or purplish flowers in late summer. Sometimes called Cretan oregano.

O. rotundifolium. Zones 2b–24. Native to Turkey, Armenia, Republic of Georgia. Dense, suckering plant grows 8 in. high, 1 ft. wide, composed of numerous wiry stems set with pairs of virtually stemless, blue-green, 1-in. leaves that have a rounded heart shape. Blooms throughout summer, bearing spikes of small pale pink blossoms and green, 2–3-in.-long bracts like those of hop *(Humulus)* at stem ends (bracts almost obscure the flowers). 'Kent Beauty' is a hybrid with *O. scabrum;* has a more compact habit (4 in. high, 8 in. wide) and bears conspicuous mauve-toned pink blossoms and deep rose bracts in the summer. 'Barbara Tingey' is a hybrid with *O. calcaratum* and similar to 'Kent Beauty'; its rose pink flowers peep out from under light green bracts that age to deep purplish pink.

Origanum rotundifolium
'Kent Beauty'

O. syriacum (O. maru). BIBLICAL HYSSOP, SYRIAN MARJORAM. Zones 7–24. Native to Syria, Turkey, and Cyprus. With its strong, sweet, pungent flavor, this plant is a favorite herb for flavoring Mideastern dishes. Grows to 1½ ft. tall and wide. Soft gray-green leaves to 1½ in. long. Blooms in late spring and early summer, with pale pink, ¼-in. flowers in branching, 2–3-in. clusters.

O. vulgare. OREGANO, WILD MARJORAM. Zones 1–24, except as noted. Native to most of Europe and temperate Asia. Upright growth to 2½ ft. tall, 2–3 ft. wide. Oval dark green leaves to 1½ in. long and ¾ in. wide; white or purplish pink blossoms from midsummer to early fall. Fresh or dried leaves are used in many dishes, especially Spanish and Italian ones.

Most wild forms have scentless leaves; be sure to choose a selected form with a good aroma and a flavor that you like. For best flavor, keep this plant trimmed to prevent flowering—but let some clumps bloom for bees and butterflies to enjoy.

'Aureum' has pinkish flowers and bright golden foliage in spring (with morning sun), turning to green by late summer and fall; 'Thumble's Variety' is similar, with white blossoms. 'Aureum Crispum' has curly golden leaves. 'Compactum' ('Humile') is a wide-spreading plant just a few inches tall, suitable for a ground cover or between paving stones; it seldom flowers, but leaves turn purple in winter. 'Country Cream' (with white flowers) and 'Polyphant' (lilac-pink blooms) are compact growers to 4–6 in. and have leaves with a distinct creamy white edge; they are often confused in commerce (and both are sometimes sold as 'Variegatum'). 'Roseum' has bright rose pink flowers, green leaves.

O. v. hirtum (O. heracleoticum). GREEK OREGANO. Zones 8, 9, 12–24. Native to Greece, Turkey, the Aegean islands. Like the species, but with broader, slightly fuzzy gray-green leaves. Spicy, pungent flavor.

ORNAMENTAL PEAR. See PYRUS

ORNITHOGALUM

Ornithogalum dubium

Liliaceae

PERENNIALS FROM BULBS

ZONES VARY BY SPECIES

FULL SUN OR PARTIAL SHADE

WATER NEEDS VARY BY SPECIES

ALL PARTS, ESPECIALLY BULBS, ARE POISONOUS IF INGESTED

Clusters of typically star-shaped flowers appear in spring; *O. dubium* may start blooming in late winter. Leaves vary from narrow to broad and tend to droop. In mild-winter areas, ornithogalums can fill many different roles. Set them in open woodlands, wild gardens, or rock gardens, where many kinds will naturalize; plant them in containers or mass them in borders. Where cold winters prevent growing ornithogalums outdoors, plant the bulbs in pots and force them to early flowering indoors or in a greenhouse.

Plant bulbs in early fall in well-drained soil amended with plenty of organic matter, setting them 3 in. deep and 3–4 in. apart. Provide regular moisture during growth and bloom (*O. longibracteatum,* however, is drought tolerant and needs only moderate water). *O. arabicum* and *O. dubium* both need a dry dormant period: after flowering has finished and leaves have died down, withhold water until new foliage begins to emerge. In areas with summer rainfall, grow them in pots to keep them dry. *O. nutans* and *O. umbellatum* can take moisture during dormancy. *O. longibracteatum* will remain evergreen with some water. Dig and divide plantings of all species only when plant vigor and bloom quality decline.

O. arabicum. STAR OF BETHLEHEM. Zones 5–24. From the eastern Mediterranean. Stems to 2 ft. tall carry clusters of 2-in., waxy-looking white flowers, each centered with a shiny, beadlike black eye. Bluish green, strap-shaped, inch-wide leaves may reach same length as stems, but they're usually floppy. Best where summers are warm and dry.

O. dubium. Zones 8, 9, 14–24. From South Africa. Stems 8–12 in. high bear blooms resembling those of *O. arabicum,* but petals surrounding the beady black eye come in shades of yellow orange. Dark green to yellowish green, lance-shaped leaves are about 4 in. long, nearly prostrate.

Ornithogalum longibracteatum

O. longibracteatum (O. caudatum). PREGNANT ONION, FALSE SEA ONION. Zones 21–24; or indoors. From South Africa. Grown for bulb and foliage rather than its tall wands of small

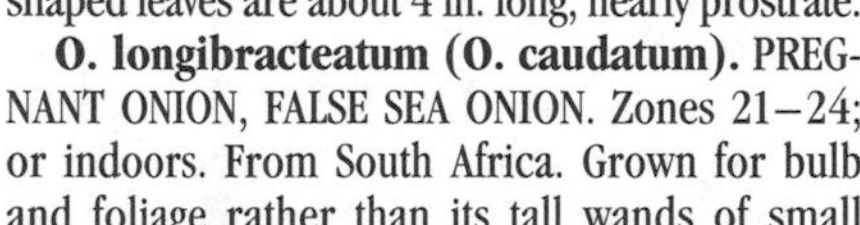

green-and-white flowers. To 3 ft. tall in leaf; flowers increase height to 5 ft. Long, strap-shaped light green leaves droop downward. Gray-green, smooth-skinned bulb is 3–4 in. wide and grows on top of, not in, the soil. Bulblets form under skin and grow quite large before they drop out and root. Hardy to 25°F/–4°C; will lose leaves if not given moderate water.

O. nutans. Zones 3–24. From the eastern Mediterranean. To 1½–2 ft. tall. Starlike to nearly bell-shaped flowers are white striped with green on the outside; they have pronounced central clusters of stamens. Up to 15 blooms are spaced along upper part of each stalk. Narrow, floppy bright green leaves. Spreads rapidly and may become weedy. Sometimes called silver bells.

O. umbellatum. STAR OF BETHLEHEM. Zones 1–24; H1. From the eastern Mediterranean. Stems to 1 ft. tall bear clusters of inch-wide white flowers striped green on the outside. Semierect, grassy-looking leaves about as long as flower stems. Cut flowers last well but close at night. Once established, may naturalize and become weedy.

ORYZOPSIS hymenoides. See ACHNATHERUM speciosum

OSAGE ORANGE. See MACLURA pomifera

OSCULARIA. See LAMPRANTHUS

OSMANTHUS

Osmanthus fragrans

Oleaceae

EVERGREEN SHRUBS

ZONES VARY BY SPECIES

FULL SUN OR PARTIAL SHADE

LITTLE TO REGULAR WATER

All have clean, leathery, attractive foliage and, typically, white flowers that are inconspicuous but fragrant. Fruits (on female plants) are rarely seen. Plants tolerate broad range of soils, including heavy clay. Most are dense shrubs that can eventually reach tree size. To grow them as background shrubs, pinch tips of new growth on young plants to encourage bushiness; on older, established plants, occasionally cut back any wayward branches. These shrubs also make good informal or lightly clipped tall hedges.

O. ×burkwoodii (×Osmarea burkwoodii). Zones 4–9, 14–17. Slow growing to 6–10 ft. tall, 8–12 ft. wide. Densely clothed in 1–2-in., glossy bright green, tooth-edged leaves. Spring bloom. Useful as hedge.

O. delavayi. DELAVAY OSMANTHUS. Zones 4–9, 14–21. From China. Slow-growing, graceful plant with arching branches; reaches 4–6 ft. tall, 6–8 ft. wide. Dark green, oval, tooth-edged leaves to 1 in. long. Blooms profusely in spring, bearing clusters of four to eight blossoms (largest flowers of any osmanthus). Attractive all year. Good choice for foundation plantings, massing. Handsome on retaining walls where branches can hang down. Needs partial shade in hot-summer areas.

O. ×fortunei. Zones 4–10, 14–24. Hybrid between *O. heterophyllus* and *O. fragrans.* Slow, dense growth to an eventual 15–20 ft. tall, 6–8 ft. wide; usually seen at about 6 ft. tall. Oval, 4-in.-long leaves resemble those of holly *(Ilex).* Spring and summer bloom. 'San Jose' blooms in fall, bears flowers ranging in color from cream to orange.

O. fragrans. SWEET OLIVE. Zones 5–7 (with shelter), 8, 9, 12–24; H1. Native to China, Japan, Himalayas. Broad, dense, compact. Grows at a moderate rate to 10 ft. tall, 6–8 ft. wide (though older plants may reach 30 ft. tall, 10–12 ft. wide). Oval, glossy medium green leaves to 4 in. long, toothed or smooth edged. Flowers are powerfully fragrant, with a sweet scent like that of ripe apricots. Bloom is heaviest in spring and early summer, but plants flower sporadically throughout year. Sometimes trained as an esapalier. Give afternoon shade in hottest climates. *O. f. aurantiacus* has narrower, less glossy leaves than the species; its crop of wonderfully fragrant orange flowers is concentrated in early fall.

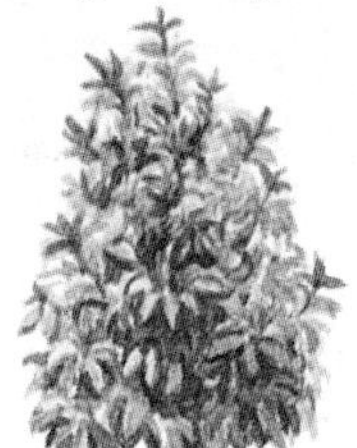
Osmanthus fragrans

O. heterophyllus (O. ilicifolius). HOLLY-LEAF OSMANTHUS. Zones 4–10, 14–24. From Japan. Grows to 10–20 ft. tall and slightly wider, with 2½-in., spiny-edged, glossy green leaves. Resembles English holly *(Ilex aquifolium),* but leaves are opposite one another on stems rather than alternate. Late fall and winter bloom. Useful as hedge.

'Goshiki'. Erect growth to 3½ ft. tall, 5 ft. wide. New leaves have pinkish orange markings; in mature foliage, the variegations are creamy yellow (on a deep green background).

'Gulftide'. Dense grower to 8 ft. tall, 10 ft. wide. May actually be a selection of *O. ×fortunei.*

'Purpureus' ('Purpurascens'). Same growth habit as species. Leaves are dark purple when new, maturing to purple-toned deep green.

'Rotundifolius'. Slow growing to 5 ft. tall and wide. Small, roundish leaves are lightly spined.

'Variegatus'. Slow growing to 8–10 ft. tall and wide, with densely set leaves edged in creamy white. Useful for lighting up shady areas. Foliage is somewhat more prone to freeze damage than that of other species.

FOR DEFINITIONS OF GARDENING TERMS
PLEASE SEE PAGES 746–750

OSMUNDA

Osmundaceae

FERNS

ZONES VARY BY SPECIES

FULL SUN OR LIGHT SHADE

AMPLE WATER

Osmunda regalis

Large deciduous ferns for damp (even wet) soils in regions with cold (or at least chilly) winters. Rather coarse looking but handsome nonetheless. They produce large masses of matted roots; root masses of *O. regalis* provide the osmunda fiber used in potting mixes for orchids. Fronds are twice divided; they turn orange, brown, and yellow as they approach dormancy. Use at woodland edges or in cool, moist or wet areas. Both species described here are native to much of the Northern Hemisphere. *O. cinnamomea* has separate sterile and fertile fronds; in *O. regalis,* each frond has a fertile segment near the tip.

O. cinnamomea. CINNAMON FERN, FIDDLEHEADS. Zones 1–6. To 2–5 ft. tall and 2 ft. wide. This fern has two types of fronds. Sterile fronds are erect, up to 5 ft. tall, and divided in typical fern fashion. Fertile ones are shorter and consist of stalks topped by short, tightly clustered, brown spore-bearing bodies. The unfolding sterile fronds, called fiddleheads, are edible; they are typically served as a cooked vegetable, steamed and lightly buttered.

O. regalis. ROYAL FERN, FLOWERING FERN. Zones 1–9, 14–17. To 6 ft. tall, 3 ft. wide; each frond segment is quite large. Fertile segments are smaller, clustered near frond tips; they look something like flower buds. 'Cristata' has crested fronds; 'Purpurascens' has purplish red new growth and stems that remain purple throughout the season. The species and its varieties love moisture and can even grow in water.

OSO BERRY. See OEMLERIA cerasiformis

OSTEOSPERMUM

AFRICAN DAISY

Asteraceae (Compositae)

PERENNIALS

ZONES 8, 9, 12–24, EXCEPT AS NOTED; ANYWHERE AS ANNUALS

FULL SUN

MODERATE TO REGULAR WATER

Osteospermum fruticosum

Woody-based perennials native to South Africa; closely related to *Dimorphotheca* and often sold as such. Mounded or trailing in habit, bearing a profusion of daisylike flowers over a long season; blossoms are more profuse during cooler parts of bloom period. Grow them as summer annuals in areas beyond hardiness range, as winter annuals in hot desert regions. Narrowish oval leaves are 2–4 in. long, smooth-edged or with a few large teeth. Flowers of most kinds open only in sunlight, but many have a second color on the backs of rays that shows on half-open flowers during overcast weather.

Tolerate drought and neglect but look better with good garden soil and irrigation. Tip-pinch young plants to induce bushiness. Deadheading produces more blooms. Cut back old, sprawling branches to young side growth in late summer to midautumn. Mass along driveways or paths or use in borders, rock gardens, containers. Types that spread by rooting stems are good on slopes.

O. barberae. See O. jucundum

O. ecklonis (Dimorphotheca ecklonis). To 2–5 ft. tall, 2–4 ft. wide. Long stems bear 3-in. flowers with dark blue centers and rays that are white above, lavender blue on backs. Blooms in spring.

'Lavender Mist'. Zones 2b–24. To 1 ft. tall, 15 in. wide; 3-in. flowers open white, age to soft pale purple. Blooms from midspring until fall.

Passion Mix. Compact growth to 1–1½ ft. high and about as wide, with 2–2½-in. flowers in a variety of colors (pink, rose, purple, white), all with sky blue centers. Blooms throughout the year, more heavily in spring and fall. Blossoms stay open in low light better than those of many nonhybrid varieties.

O. fruticosum (Dimorphotheca fruticosa). TRAILING AFRICAN DAISY, FREEWAY DAISY. Zones 8, 9, 12–24; H1, H2. To 6–12 in. tall, spreading rapidly by trailing, rooting stems; will cover a 2–4-ft.-wide circle in a year. Deep lilac buds open to 2-in.-wide flowers with a dark purple center; rays are lilac above (fading nearly to white by second day), deeper lilac beneath. Blooms intermittently all year, more heavily in fall and winter. Needs well-drained soil. Does well near the ocean. Use as ground cover or bank cover; if it gets too tall or weedy, mow or cut back in midsummer. Also good planted at top of a wall or in a hanging basket.

The following hybrids reach 18–20 in. high. 'African Queen' and 'Burgundy' have purple blooms. 'Whirlygig' ('Pinwheel') bears unusual white-and-blue flowers with rays that are white on upper surface, blue on back; each ray is pinched in the middle to reveal its blue underside, giving it the look of a spoon with a blue handle and a white bowl. Blossoms of Side Series stay open on overcast days and at night; selections include 'Brightside' (white with a blue eye), 'Highside' (bicolor blooms in white and dark pink), 'Riverside' (butter yellow), 'Seaside' (bicolor in white and light pink), and 'Wildside' (dark purple).

O. jucundum (O. barberae, Dimorphotheca barberae). Grows to 4–20 in. high; spreads by rooting stems to 2–3 ft. across. Bears long-stalked, 2-in.-wide flowers with purple centers; rays vary in color from mauve pink to magenta, with bronzy purple to purplish pink undersides. Blooms more heavily in spring and fall, generally less profusely in summer.

O. j. compactum 'Purple Mountain'. Zones 2b–24. Choice plant for colder climates. To 10 in. high, 1 ft. wide, with a profusion of bright purple, 2–3-in. flowers from spring to midsummer. If deadheaded, continues to bloom (albeit sparingly) until fall.

O. Symphony Series. Mounding habit to 8–12 in. high, 3 ft. wide (1 ft. as annual). Among the most heat tolerant of osteospermums, flowering throughout moderately hot summers as well as during cool weather. Flowers are 2–2½ in. wide, with dark blue centers. Choices include 'Cream Symphony' (pale yellow rays), 'Lemon Symphony' (medium yellow), 'Orange Symphony' (light orange). Particularly attractive in window boxes and hanging baskets.

OSTRICH FERN. See MATTEUCCIA struthiopteris

OSWEGO TEA. See MONARDA

OTATEA. See BAMBOO

OUR LORD'S CANDLE. See YUCCA whipplei

OXALIS

Oxalidaceae

PERENNIALS

ZONES VARY BY SPECIES

PARTIAL SHADE IN HOTTEST CLIMATES, EXCEPT AS NOTED

REGULAR WATER

Oxalis oregana

Leaves typically divided into three leaflets, giving them the look of clover leaves. Flowers may be pink, white, rose, or yellow.

O. acetosella. WOOD SORREL, SHAMROCK. Zones 1–10, 14–24. From many northern temperate regions of the world. To 5 in. high, spreading widely by rhizomes. Typical clover-type leaves with three heart-shaped leaflets. Blooms in late spring, bearing ¾-in.-wide white flowers with purple to pink veins; blossoms rise just above the foliage. Can be somewhat invasive in its favored woodland conditions (moist, rich soil and partial shade). See also Shamrock. ▶

O. adenophylla. Zones 4–9, 12–24. Native to South America. Dense, compact, leafy tuft 4 in. high, 6 in. wide. Each leaf has 9–22 crinkly gray-green leaflets. In late spring, 4–6-in.-high stalks bear 1-in., bell-shaped flowers in lilac pink with deeper veins. Good rock garden plant or companion to bulbs such as species tulips or smaller kinds of narcissus, either in pots or in the ground. Needs good drainage. Plant tubers in fall, setting 1 in. deep, 3–5 in. apart.

O. hirta. Zones 8, 9, 14–24. Native to South Africa. To 1 ft. high, 1½ ft. wide, with many upright, branching stems that gradually fall over with weight of leaves and flowers. Small pale green leaves are set directly on the stems or on very short stalks. General effect is feathery. Bright rose pink, 1-in. flowers in late fall or winter. Plant is dormant in summer. Grow from bulbs planted in fall; set them 1 in. deep, 3–5 in. apart. Good for rock gardens, hanging baskets.

O. lasiandra. Zones 8, 9, 12–24; H1, H2. Native to Mexico. Taprooted plant forms a clump to 1 ft. high and wide, with reddish leafstalks and medium green, wheel-shaped leaves, each with up to ten narrow leaflets. Dark red, 1-in.-wide flowers through summer and fall.

O. oregana. REDWOOD SORREL, OREGON OXALIS. Zones 4–9, 14–24. Native to coastal forests from Washington to California. Grows to 10 in. high, spreading indefinitely by creeping rhizomes. Medium green, velvety leaves 1½–4 in. wide. Blooms in spring, sometimes again in fall, bearing white (sometimes pink), 1-in.-wide flowers with lavender veining. Makes an attractive ground cover for partial to deep shade in areas with mild winters and cool summers. Plant may outcompete other ground covers. Dies down in winter in colder part of climate range; elsewhere, mow to renovate. Tolerates wet conditions.

O. pes-caprae (O. cernua). BERMUDA BUTTERCUP. Zones 8, 9, 12–24. Native to South Africa. Reaches 1 ft. high, spreading indefinitely by bulbs. Produces clusters of bright green leaves, often spotted with dark brown, that spring directly from soil in fall. Flowering stems rise above the foliage in winter and spring, topped with clusters of 1-in., bright yellow flowers. Can become an invasive pest in an open garden; best grown in pots or baskets.

O. purpurea (O. variabilis). Zones 8, 9, 12–24. Native to South Africa. Grows to 4 in. tall and 6 in. wide; dark green leaves have large (up to 1½-in.-wide) leaflets. Bears 1–2-in., rose red flowers over a long period in fall and winter. Spreads by bulbs and rhizomelike roots but is not aggressive or weedy. Plant bulbs in fall, setting them 1 in. deep, 3–5 in. apart. Improved kinds, sold under the name "Grand Duchess," have larger flowers in rose pink, white, or lavender.

O. versicolor. CANDY CANE SORREL. Zones 6–9, 14–24. Native to South Africa. To 3–6 in. high and 8 in. wide. Medium green leaves have deeply notched leaflets less than ½ in. wide. Funnel-shaped flowers are white, over 1 in. wide, with a crimson margin on the petal backs; buds also show striping. Plant bulbs in fall for spring flowers (set them 1 in. deep, 3–5 in. apart); bloom lasts for months.

OXYDENDRUM arboreum

SOURWOOD, SORREL TREE
Ericaceae
DECIDUOUS TREE
ZONES 2B–9, 14–17
FULL SUN
REGULAR WATER

Oxydendrum arboreum

Native to eastern U.S. Beautiful flowering tree offering year-round interest. Slow growth to 15–30 ft. (eventually to 50 ft.) high, 20 ft. wide. Pyramidal shape with slender trunk, somewhat rounded crown, and slightly pendulous branches; creates a handsome winter silhouette. Narrow, 5–8-in.-long leaves look a bit like peach leaves; they are bronze tinted in early spring, rich green in summer. In fall, leaves turn orange, scarlet, or blackish purple; all colors may be present on the same tree. Vividly colored autumn leaves remain on the tree for a long time, dropping over an extended period much like the leaves of liquidambar. Tree blooms in the summer, bearing fragrant, bell-shaped creamy white flowers in 10-in.-long, drooping clusters at branch tips. In autumn, branching clusters of seed capsules extend outward and downward from branches like fingers; capsules ripen from greenish to light silvery gray and hang on late into winter.

Best known in areas with cool summers, well-defined winters. Needs acid, well-drained soil. Not competitive; doesn't do well in lawns without careful attention (you must remove grass from beneath canopy, mulch well, and irrigate deeply). Avoid underplanting with anything that may need cultivation.

Use as specimen in a woodland garden or as patio shade tree. Young plants make good container subjects.

OZOTHAMNUS rosmarinifolius

Asteraceae (Compositae)
EVERGREEN SHRUB
ZONES 14–24
FULL SUN
REGULAR WATER

Ozothamnus rosmarinifolius

Native to Australia. Dense, erect habit to 6–10 ft. tall, 3–5 ft. wide. Close-set, upright branches are thickly clothed with straight, narrow, 1½-in.-long, dark green leaves that resemble those of rosemary. In early summer, closely packed red buds appear at branch tips; these open into 1½-in. clusters of tiny white daisies. The entire plant has a pleasant aroma, especially in warm weather.

PACHISTIMA. See PAXISTIMA

PACHYPODIUM lamerei

MADAGASCAR PALM
Apocynaceae
SUCCULENT SHRUB
ZONES 13, 21–24; OR INDOORS
FULL SUN OR PARTIAL SHADE; BRIGHT LIGHT
REGULAR WATER

Pachypodium lamerei

From Madagascar. Not a palm, though it looks something like one. Easy-to-grow shrub with impressive silhouette: spiny, succulent, unbranched trunk topped with a circle of strap-shaped leaves to 1 ft. long and 1–4 in. wide. May reach 18 ft. tall and 8 ft. wide in frostless climates. Large, old plants may bloom in summer, bearing fragrant, saucer-shaped white flowers to 4 in. across; smaller, younger plants seldom bloom. Some people think of older, blooming plants as spiny plumerias.

Madagascar palm can survive outdoors year-round in areas that get light frosts, but it will drop its leaves and go dormant there and may never grow higher than 8 ft. If you grow it outdoors in these regions, give it very little moisture during dormancy. Beyond hardiness range, grow it in a pot indoors and summer it outside, or keep it indoors all year as a houseplant.

PACHYRHIZUS erosus. See JICAMA

A PRACTICAL GUIDE TO GARDENING
PLEASE SEE PAGES 658–731

PACHYSANDRA

Pachysandra terminalis

Buxaceae

PERENNIALS

ZONES VARY BY SPECIES

PARTIAL OR FULL SHADE

REGULAR WATER

Spreading slowly but surely by underground runners, these are invaluable ground covers for shady places. Compact growth and clean-looking, attractive foliage are their chief virtues. Spring flowers are not showy when viewed casually but are attractive at close range. Plants have somewhat woody growth, *P. terminalis* more so than *P. procumbens.* Compete successfully with tree roots. Give them moist, somewhat acid soil, well amended with organic material; for good coverage, plant both species 1 ft. apart. Too much sun yellows the foliage and causes poor growth. Hardy to cold.

P. procumbens. ALLEGHENY SPURGE. Zones 2–6, 15–17. From southeastern U.S. To 6–12 in. high. Grayish green, broadly oval to roundish leaves are 2–4 in. long, clustered near stem tips; they are often mottled with gray or brown. Small, fragrant white or pinkish flowers in 2–4-in. spikes. Spreads more slowly than species *P. terminalis.* Deciduous in northern part of range, semievergreen to evergreen farther south.

P. terminalis. JAPANESE SPURGE. Zones 2–10, 14–21; performs better in northern part of range. From Japan, northern China. To 8–12 in. high. Evergreen leaves are shiny dark green, about same length as those of *P. procumbens* but somewhat narrower; upper half of each leaf is shallowly toothed. Small white flowers are borne in 1–2-in. spikes. Withstands heavy shade and is widely used under trees. 'Green Carpet' is shorter (to 4 in.) and denser than the species, with deeper green leaves. Leaves of 'Green Sheen' are especially glossy; those of 'Silver Edge' ('Variegata') have a creamy border. 'Cut Leaf' has deeply dissected foliage.

PAEONIA

Herbaceous Peony, Single

PEONY

Paeoniaceae

PERENNIALS AND DECIDUOUS SHRUBS

ZONES VARY BY TYPE

AFTERNOON SHADE IN HOTTEST CLIMATES

REGULAR WATER

Though a few species peonies may be found on specialists' lists or in seed exchanges, most garden peonies are hybrids. The basic types are herbaceous and tree peonies; both are descended from Chinese species. Herbaceous kinds, largely descendants of the perennial *P. lactiflora,* die to the ground in late fall. Tree (actually shrub) peonies produce flowers on permanent woody branches and are chiefly descendants of *P. suffruticosa,* a 6-ft. shrub. All peonies are extremely long-lived plants of significant size; they provide choice cut flowers and are a mainstay of big perennial borders. They demand more than ordinary care in site preparation—but in return for the effort, they can produce flowers of outstanding beauty for a lifetime.

Herbaceous peonies are planted in fall (preferably) or earliest spring as bare-root plants: compact rhizomes with thick, tuberous roots and several "eyes" (growth buds). Tree peonies, practically all of them grafted onto herbaceous peony roots, are also sold bare-root. Many growers offer them as container plants, as well—from spring to fall in cold-winter areas, all year in mild-winter regions.

Ideally, the planting site for peonies should be deeply dug at least several days before planting. Work in plenty of well-rotted manure or compost and incorporate a high-phosphorus fertilizer; then allow the soil to settle before planting. Position herbaceous peony roots carefully, since planting too deep will prevent flowering: set them with eyes 2 in. deep in cold climates, 1 in. deep in warmer regions. Set tree peonies so the graft line is 3–4 in. below the soil surface (the aim is to get the shrubby top to root on its own). Mulch the first year after the ground has frozen. Plants are unlikely to bloom during their first year, but they should bloom every year thereafter if fertilized after the flowering period and again in fall.

To gather peonies for bouquets, cut them just as buds begin to open. Leave at least three leaves behind on every cut stem, and do not remove more than half the blooms from any clump. The object is to preserve leaf growth so that it nourishes the plant for the following year. Deadhead plants to prevent seed formation.

During humid spells—particularly when weather is cool as well as humid—the fungal disease botrytis is sometimes a problem. Young buds on infected plants blacken and wither; fuzzy brown spots develop on flowers and leaves; stems wilt and collapse. To prevent the problem, provide good air circulation around plants and be sure to clean up the planting in autumn, disposing of all fallen leaves (on herbaceous peonies, also cut back all stems to soil level). As new growth emerges in spring, spray with copper fungicide.

Herbaceous peonies. Perennials. Zones A1–A3; 1–11, 14–20. Bloom well only where they experience a period of pronounced winter chill. Summer heat is not a problem, but flowers do not last well where spring days are hot and dry. In such areas, choose early-blooming varieties and give plants some afternoon shade and adequate water. In Zones 1–7, where these plants grow best, they thrive in full sun.

Well-grown clumps reach 2–4 ft. tall and as wide or wider. Large, deep green, attractively divided leaves are an effective background for the plants' spectacular spring or early summer flowers and look good throughout summer. Flower colors range from pure white through cream to pink and red; some of the reds are very deep, with chocolate brown overtones. Depending on variety, blossoms range from 2 in. to as much as 10 in. across; many have a perfume similar to that of old-fashioned roses. In form, they fall into three basic categories: single or semidouble, with one or two rows of petals; Japanese, with a single row of petals and a large central mass of narrow petal-like segments called staminodes; and double, with full flowers composed of many petals. In hot-summer climates, singles, semidoubles, and Japanese varieties tend to bloom better than doubles (Japanese sorts in particular do well in the warmest zones). Where summers are very hot, all profit from light afternoon shade. Be sure to provide support for types with very large or double flowers, which can become so heavy with water during spring rains that they topple to the ground.

Varieties are too numerous to list. Three fragrant doubles—all introduced more than a century ago and still popular—deserve mention because they are among the peonies most likely to be found in local garden centers and nurseries. These are 'Edulis Superba', bright pink with an outer ring of somewhat lighter petals; 'Felix Krousse', deep red; and 'Festiva Maxima', white with a few crimson flecks near the center. Enthusiasts can choose from dozens of others in catalogs.

A noteworthy species is southeastern European *P. tenuifolia,* called fernleaf peony. Only 1½–2½ ft. high and wide, it has exceedingly finely cut dark green foliage. Deep red, single flowers on short stems seem to be sitting on the foliage. 'Rubra Plena' ('Flore Plena', 'Plena') has long-lasting double flowers.

There is no reason to divide herbaceous peonies except to increase your stock. Dig clumps in early fall, hose off soil, and divide into sections, making sure that each has at least three eyes; these appear at top of root cluster, at or near bases of past season's stems. Plant at once, so that plants will have time to put down roots before the onset of freezing weather. Transplants may take a year or two to establish before blooming.

Tree peonies. Deciduous shrubs. Zones 2–12, 14–23. Slow growth to 3–5 ft. tall and eventually as wide, with handsome, blue-green to bronzy green, divided leaves. Single to double, typically very large flowers (to 10–12 in.) appear in spring. These peonies seldom show their full potential until they have spent several years in your garden,

Tree Peony, Double

but the spectacular results are worth the wait. Small, recently grafted packaged plants are sometimes available. These are a good buy if you are patient—they'll take longer to reach flowering size than older, container-grown or field-grown plants costing much more. Count on 2 or 3 years before they come into flower for the first time.

Catalogs offer named varieties of Japanese origin in white and shades of pink, red, and purple. These are generally semidouble and display their flowers well. Some of the older European hybrids in pink and yellow are fully double, with flowers so heavy they hang their heads. More recent and more expensive are orange, yellow, and copper-colored hybrids resulting from crosses of *P. suffruticosa* with *P. delavayi* and *P. lutea;* these bear semidouble blooms that face outward and upward.

Tree peonies require less winter chill than herbaceous peonies. The large flowers are fragile and should be sheltered from strong winds. Prune only to remove faded flowers and any dead wood. In coldest climates, protect from winter sun and wind with a burlap curtain.

PAGODA FLOWER. See CLERODENDRUM buchananii fallax

PAINTED DAISY. See CHRYSANTHEMUM coccineum

PAINTED FINGERNAIL PLANT. See NEOREGELIA spectabilis

PAINTED TONGUE. See SALPIGLOSSIS sinuata

Palmae. See Arecaceae

PALMETTO. See SABAL

PALMS. Most palms are tropical or subtropical; a few are surprisingly hardy (specimens are seen in Edinburgh, London, and southern Russia, as well as Portland, Seattle, and Denver). These trees offer great opportunity for imaginative planting. In nature, they grow not only in solid stands but also with other plants, notably broad-leafed evergreen trees and shrubs. They are effective near swimming pools.

Most young palms prefer shade, and all tolerate it; this fact makes them good house or patio plants when they are small. As they grow, they can be moved into full sun or partial shade, depending on the species. Growth rates vary, but keeping plants in pots usually slows growth of faster-growing kinds. If temperatures are 60°F/16°C or higher, fertilize potted palms often; also wash them off frequently to provide some humidity and clean the foliage. Washing also dislodges insects, which (indoors, at any rate) are protected from their natural enemies and can increase extremely rapidly.

To pot a palm, supply good potting soil, adequate drainage, and not too big a container. As with all potted plants, pot or repot a palm in a container just slightly larger than the one it is in.

Some shade-tolerant palms such as *Rhapis, Chamaedorea,* and *Howea* may spend decades in pots indoors. Others that later may reach great size—*Phoenix, Washingtonia, Chamaerops*—make charming temporary indoor plants but must eventually be moved.

Planting holes for palms should generally be the same depth as and 1–2 ft. wider than the root ball, and you can use unamended native soil for backfill. If you are planting in very poor, alkaline, or clay soil, however, some experts suggest a different procedure. For a 5-gal.-size palm, dig a 3-ft.-wide hole that is 8 in. deeper than root ball. Place 1–2 cu. ft. of well-rotted manure, nitrogen-fortified sawdust, or other organic amendment in the hole, then mix in a handful or two of blood meal and top with a 6-in. layer of soil. Set in the palm and fill in around it with a mixture of half native soil and half nitrogen-fortified sawdust, ground bark, or peat moss. Water newly planted palms faithfully until established.

Most palms, even big ones, transplant easily in late spring or early summer. Since new roots form from the base of the trunk, the root ball need not be large; a new root system will form and produce lush new growth. When transplanting large palms, contractors usually tie leaves together over the center "bud" or heart, then secure the leaf mass to a length of 2-by-4 tied to the trunk.

Established palms need little maintenance; they thrive in reasonably fertile soil, with the appropriate amount of moisture (see individual entries for recommendations). All tropical palms do their growing during warm times of year. Winter rains wash the foliage down (and, in areas with salty soil, leach out accumulated salts). Palms growing in dry or dusty areas or beyond the reach of rain or dew should be hosed off periodically; this helps control populations of spider mites and sucking insects that find refuge in the long leaf stems. Beach plantings should also be washed off occasionally to keep salt from accumulating on the leaves.

Feather palms and many fan palms look neater when old leaves are removed after they have turned brown. Make neat cuts close to trunk, leaving leaf bases. Some palms shed old leaf bases on their own. Others, including *Syagrus* and *Chamaedorea,* may hold old bases. You can remove them by slicing them off at the very bottom of base (be careful not to cut into trunk).

Many palm admirers say that dead leaves of *Washingtonia* should remain on the tree, the thatch being part of the palm's character. If you agree but prefer a neater look, you can cut lower fronds uniformly close to trunk, but leave leaf bases, which present a rather attractive lattice surface.

Most species are frost sensitive. Frost becomes more damaging to palms as it extends its stay and is repeated. A light frost that lasts for half an hour may not harm plants at all, but if the same degree of frost persists for 4 hours, it may injure some palms, kill others. Hardiness is also a matter of plant size; larger palms may survive severe frosts without harm, while smaller ones perish. At its least serious, frost damage consists simply of burned leaf edges—but frost may affect whole leaves, parts of trunks, or crown. Damage to the crown is usually fatal (though some trees have recovered from it).

Following are nine roles that the right kinds of palms can fill. Palms in each listing are described under their own entries elsewhere in this book.

Sturdy palms for street trees and vertical effects in large gardens. *Archontophoenix, Brahea, Cocos, Jubaea, Livistona, Phoenix canariensis, P. dactylifera, P. loureiri, P. rupicola, Pritchardia, Rhopalostylis, Roystonea, Sabal* (tall species), *Syagrus, Washingtonia.*

Small to medium-size palms for frost-free gardens. *Archontophoenix, Caryota, Chamaedorea, Chamaerops, Dypsis lutescens, Hedyscepe, Howea.*

Small to medium-size palms that tolerate a light, brief frost. *Brahea, Butia, Chamaedorea cataractarum, C. elegans, Chamaerops, Dypsis decaryi, Livistona, Phoenix roebelenii, Trachycarpus.*

Hardiest palms. *Brahea armata, B. edulis, Chamaerops, Jubaea, Livistona, Phoenix canariensis, P. dactylifera, P. loureiri, Rhapidophyllum, Rhapis, Sabal mexicana, S. minor, S. palmetto, Trachycarpus, Washingtonia.*

Salt-tolerant palms for seaside plantings. *Brahea edulis, Butia, Chamaerops, Cocos, Phoenix canariensis, P. dactylifera, P. reclinata, Sabal blackburniana, S. palmetto, Washingtonia robusta.*

Palms for hot, dry climates. *Brahea armata, Butia, Chamaerops, Livistona chinensis, L. mariae, Phoenix canariensis, P. dactylifera, P. loureiri, P. sylvestris, Sabal mexicana, S. minor, Washingtonia.*

Palms to grow under lath, beneath overhangs, or indoors. *Archontophoenix, Caryota mitis, C. ochlandra, C. urens, Chamaedorea, Hedyscepe, Howea, Livistona* (when young), *Phoenix reclinata* (when young), *P. roebelenii, Rhapidophyllum, Rhapis, Rhopalostylis, Trachycarpus* (when young). Indoor palms should occasionally be brought outdoors into soft light.

Palms as underplantings. Young palms, especially slow growers such as *Livistona chinensis* and *Chamaerops,* stay low for 5 to 10 years and can be used effectively as plantings under tall trees. Keep in mind that they may have to be moved if they get too tall, a project you may not want to undertake. Two shrubby palms that remain small are *Rhapidophyllum* (6–8 ft. high) and *Sabal minor* (rarely exceeds 6 ft.).

Palms for night lighting. Thanks to their stateliness and spectacular leaves, all palms are good subjects for this. Light them from behind or below; or direct lights to silhouette them against light-colored walls.

PALO BLANCO. See ACACIA willardiana

PALO VERDE. See CERCIDIUM

PAMPAS GRASS. See CORTADERIA selloana

PANDANUS tectorius

SCREWPINE, HALA
Pandanaceae
EVERGREEN TREE
ZONE H2
FULL SUN
REGULAR WATER

Pandanus tectorius

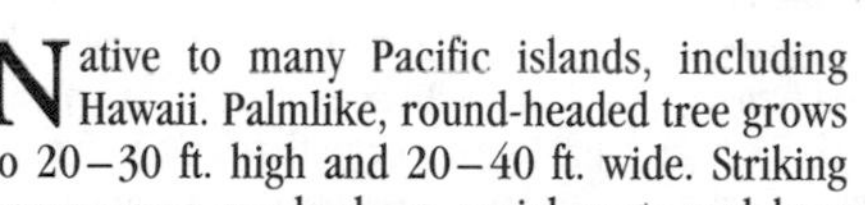

Native to many Pacific islands, including Hawaii. Palmlike, round-headed tree grows to 20–30 ft. high and 20–40 ft. wide. Striking appearance; sends down aerial roots and bears spirals of stiff, spiny, 3-ft.-long leaves at the ends of stubby branches. Female plants develop large fruits resembling pineapples. Has good wind and salt tolerance; thrives in any well-drained soil, even beach sand. Excellent shade or windbreak tree for the beach garden. Produces litter; needs maintenance to remove old leaves. Young plants can be grown in pots on the patio or indoors.

PANDA PLANT. See KALANCHOE tomentosa

PANDOREA

Bignoniaceae
EVERGREEN VINES
ZONES 16–24; H1, H2
PARTIAL SHADE IN HOTTEST CLIMATES
WATER NEEDS VARY BY SPECIES

Pandorea jasminoides

Twining vines noted for clusters of trumpet-shaped flowers and for rich green, glossy, divided leaves; the foliage is so attractive that the plants look lovely even when out of bloom. Perform best in good, organically enriched soil. Blooms are borne on previous year's growth; prune to shape or thin vines after flowering.

P. jasminoides (Bignonia jasminoides, Tecoma jasminoides). BOWER VINE. Native to Australia. Fast growth to 20–30 ft. Each leaf has five to seven oval, 1–2-in.-long leaflets with pointed tips. Typically unscented flowers are white with pink throats, 1½–2 in. long; bloom from late spring to early fall. 'Alba' and the stronger-growing 'Lady Di' have pure white flowers; 'Rosea' produces soft pink blooms with nearly red throats. 'Rosea Superba' and a variety known simply as 'Deep Pink Form' are fragrant. There is a form with variegated leaves. Plant in lee of prevailing wind. Prolonged freezes will kill this species and its varieties. Regular water.

P. pandorana (Bignonia australis, Tecoma australis). WONGA-WONGA VINE. Native to Australia, Pacific islands. More vigorous than *P. jasminoides*, covering twice the space; give it plenty of room. Leaves divided into 8–17 leaflets that are narrower than those of *P. jasminoides* and 1–3 in. long. Small (to ¾-in.-long), unscented spring flowers are typically creamy white, often spotted brownish purple in the throat. 'Golden Showers' has golden yellow blossoms. Tougher, more wind resistant, and less susceptible to freeze damage than *P. jasminoides*. Moderate water.

PANICUM virgatum

SWITCH GRASS
Poaceae (Gramineae)
PERENNIAL GRASS
ZONES 1–11, 14–23
FULL SUN OR LIGHT SHADE
ANY AMOUNT OF WATER

Panicum virgatum

Native to much of the U.S. except the Far West. Upright, 2–4-ft.-wide clump of narrow deep green or gray-green leaves. Bloom begins in midsummer, when slender flower clusters rise above the foliage, increasing height of clump to 4–7 ft.; clusters open into loose, airy clouds of pinkish blossoms that fade to white, then brown. Foliage turns yellow in fall, gradually fades to beige. Both foliage and flowers persist all winter, providing interest in cold-weather gardens. Tolerates coastal winds. Foliage of 'Haense Herms' turns dark red in autumn, while that of 'Rotstrahlbusch' takes on red tones; both selections reach 4 ft. high in bloom. 'Heavy Metal', to 5 ft. tall in flower, has blue-gray leaves that turn bright yellow in fall.

PANSY. See VIOLA

PAPAVER

POPPY
Papaveraceae
PERENNIALS AND ANNUALS
ZONES VARY BY SPECIES
FULL SUN
MODERATE TO REGULAR WATER

Papaver orientale

Poppies provide gay spring and summer color for borders, containers, and bouquets. Give ordinary, well-drained soil (note exception for *P. alpinum*); feed lightly until established. Perennial species tend to be short lived. When using poppies as cut flowers, sear cut stem ends in a flame before placing them in water.

P. alpinum (P. burseri). ALPINE POPPY. Perennial. Zones 1–9, 14–17. In keeping with its origin in the Pyrenees, Alps, and Carpathians, this species is best adapted to colder climates and requires the exceptionally fast-draining soil of a rock garden. Produces 4-in.-wide basal rosette of divided, 2–6-in.-long leaves; foliage is blue green, nearly hairless. In spring or summer, leafless flower stems to 5–8 in. tall bear 1½–2-in. blossoms in white, orange, yellow, or salmon. Blooms first year from seed sown in fall or early spring. Where adapted, self-sows freely.

P. atlanticum. Perennial. Zones 2b–9, 14–24. Native to Morocco. To 2 ft. tall, with downy gray-green leaves in basal rosette 6 in. across. Flowers are soft orange to red, 2–4 in. across, opening in late spring and early summer. Sow seed in fall. To prolong bloom period, remove spent flowers.

P. commutatum 'Lady Bird'. Annual. Zones 1–24. Selection of a species native to Greece, Turkey, the Caucasus, Iran. To 1½ ft. tall and nearly as wide. Blooms profusely for several weeks in midsummer, producing 3-in., bright red flowers with a black blotch in the middle of each petal. Flower stems are softly hairy. Sow in late winter or early spring; or set out plants in midspring.

P. nudicaule. ICELAND POPPY. Short-lived perennial in Zones A2, A3, 1–6, 10; grown as annual in Zones 7–9, 12–24. Native to subarctic regions. Blue-green, coarsely hairy, divided leaves make basal rosettes 6 in. wide. Hairy, 1–2-ft. stalks bear cup-shaped, slightly fragrant flowers to 3 in. across, in yellow, orange, salmon, rose, pink, cream, white. In cold-winter areas, sow seed in earliest spring for summer bloom; or set out plants in fall for bloom the following year. In mild-winter climates, set out plants in fall for winter and early spring bloom. To prolong flowering, pick flowers freely.

Champagne Bubbles (to 1 ft.) and wind-resistant Wonderland (to 10 in.) are widely grown strains. Partyfun hybrids (to 1 ft.) include bright colors, pastels, and bicolors. Oregon Rainbows (to 15–20 in.) produces large (to 8-in.-wide) blooms in pastel colors, including bicolors and picotees; it performs superbly in the Northwest, but in warmer climates it produces many buds that fail to open.

P. orientale. ORIENTAL POPPY. Perennial. Zones A1–A3; 1–11, 14–21. Native to the Caucasus, northeastern Turkey, northern Iran. Needs winter chill for best performance. In mild-winter areas, flowers tend to form without stalks, so they are partly or completely hidden among the leaves. Height is variable; some types are just 16 in. tall, others reach 4 ft. Plants spread by offsets to 2 ft. or more. These are among the leafiest of poppies, forming bushy clumps of hairy, medium green, coarsely cut leaves to 1 ft. long. Blooms are 4–6 in. across; deeply crinkled petals often have a black blotch at the base. Many named varieties are sold, offering single or double flowers in orange, scarlet, red, pink, salmon, or white.

Plants bloom from late spring to early summer, then die back (sometimes not completely) later in summer. Superpoppy hybrids, developed in California, were bred for mild-winter regions of the West; tolerate summer heat. In all types, new leafy growth appears in fall, lasts over winter, and develops rapidly in spring. Set sprawling plants such as baby's breath *(Gypsophila)* nearby to cover the bare areas left after poppies die down. Plant dormant crowns in fall with tops 3 in. deep; or set out container-grown plants. Provide good drainage and room for air circulation. Divide every 3 to 5 years in mid- to late summer, after foliage has died back.

P. rhoeas. FLANDERS FIELD POPPY, SHIRLEY POPPY. Annual. Zones A1–A3; 1–24. Best in cool-summer areas. Native to Eurasia, North Africa. Slender, branching, hairy-stemmed plant to 3 ft. tall, 1 ft. wide, with short, irregularly divided leaves. Single or double flowers are 2 in. or more wide, in white, pink, red, orange, salmon, scarlet, lilac, soft blue, bicolors. Mix seed with an equal amount of fine sand, then broadcast it where plants are to grow. For bloom from spring through summer, make successive sowings starting in early spring. In low and intermediate desert, plant in fall for outstanding early spring show. For cut flowers, pick when buds first show color. Remove seed capsules (old flower bases) weekly to prolong the bloom season. Notorious self-sower.

Selections bearing single scarlet flowers with a black base are sold as 'American Legion' or 'Flanders Field'. Angels' Choir strain offers double flowers in a wide range of colors, including some with creamy picotee edges. Mother of Pearl strain has single flowers, primarily soft pastels and white, with an occasional red; also includes some bicolors and picotees, as well as speckled blooms.

P. somniferum. OPIUM POPPY, BREADBOX POPPY. Annual; may self-sow or even overwinter in mild-winter areas. All zones. Believed to have originated in southeastern Europe and western Asia. To 4 ft. tall. Virtually hairless gray-green leaves have jagged edges. Late spring flowers are 4–5 in. across, in white, pink, red, purple, deep plum, and are sometimes single, usually double; some of the double forms have fringed petals. Blooms are followed by large, decorative seed capsules used in dried arrangements. Opium is derived from the sap of the green capsules. Ripe pods yield large quantities of the poppy seed used in baking. Shake pods over a tray to collect the seeds. Because of its narcotic properties, this species is not as widely offered as many other types.

Papaveraceae. The poppy family of annuals, perennials, and shrubs displays showy flowers, usually borne one per stem. In addition to *Papaver,* members include California poppy *(Eschscholzia)* and Matilija poppy *(Romneya).*

PAPAYA

Caricaceae

PERENNIALS

ZONES VARY BY SPECIES

FULL SUN, EXCEPT AS NOTED

REGULAR WATER

Papaya

They may look like trees or large shrubs, but these members of the genus *Carica* are actually big perennials with hollow stems. All are tall, upright, narrow plants, 3–6 ft. wide at the top. Cream-colored flowers are inconspicuous. Fruit takes 6 to 10 months to ripen, depending on climate; in Hawaii, it is borne throughout the year. Plants produce crops when young. To get most fruit, don't grow papaya as a permanent plant; keep a few plants coming along each year, and destroy old ones. Give regular moisture and fertilizer in warm weather. Grow from seeds saved from fruit or start with purchased plants. Babaco (see following text) is seedless and must be started from transplants. Transplant carefully, disturbing the root ball as little as possible. All need excellent drainage. Papayas grow well in large containers.

C. papaya—the papaya found in markets—is the species grown most frequently. This native of tropical America can be cultivated outdoors in Zones 21–24 and H2, and anywhere in a greenhouse. Needs year-round warmth. Thrives in Hawaii. In California, the key to success is choosing the right location; root rot in cold, wet soil is the principal cause of failure, so locate on south slope or south side of house where winter sun can heat soil. Plant will also benefit from reflected heat in winter

C. papaya grows 20–25 ft. tall in Hawaii, perhaps half that in California, with a straight stem topped by a crown of broad, fanlike, deeply lobed leaves on 2-ft.-long stalks. Grow three to five "trees" in a group; you ordinarily need both male and female plants for fruit production. Some plants are self-fruitful, producing either bisexual flowers or both male and female flowers on the same plant. Varieties with yellow-orange flesh grown primarily in Hawaii include 'Kapoho', 'Solo', and dwarf 'Waimanalo'. Types with pinkish flesh grown in Hawaii and California include 'Sunrise', 'Sunset', and 'Thai Dwarf'. Varieties grown in Hawaii have pear-shaped fruit as large as 1–2 lbs. Mexican varieties bear much bigger fruit (up to 10 lbs., to more than 1 ft. long) with yellow, orange, or pink flesh and a less intense flavor. Harvest papayas of both types when skin begins to turn yellow; let ripen fully at room temperature. Seeds edible, with a somewhat peppery flavor.

Two other papayas, both from highland areas of South America, are less widely grown. Mountain papaya *(C. pubescens),* native to the Andes, can be grown in Zones 21–24, H1, H2. It reaches 10–12 ft. tall; foliage is borne in dense clusters at tops of its multiple trunks. Elaborately lobed, foot-wide leaves are fan shaped, deeply veined, sandpapery in texture; they are dark green above, lighter beneath. Small fruit is edible when cooked (it's unpalatable raw). Male and female plants are needed for fruit set.

Babaco is the common name of Ecuadorean native *C.* ×*heilbornii pentagona,* a self-fruitful, naturally occurring hybrid between *C. pubescens* and another Andean species. It can be grown in Zones 17, 19–24, H1. Resembles a dwarf (5–8-ft.-tall) *C. papaya.* Foot-long, seedless fruit has juicy flesh similar to that of 'Crenshaw' melon in color and texture; the unique sweet-tart flavor combines papaya, pineapple, and strawberry. Needs partial shade in hottest climates. Can be grown as a houseplant.

PAPER BUSH. See EDGEWORTHIA chrysantha

PAPER DAISY. See PSILOSTROPHE cooperi

PAPER MULBERRY. See BROUSSONETIA papyrifera

PAPHIOPEDILUM

LADY'S SLIPPER

Orchidaceae

TERRESTRIAL ORCHIDS

ZONES VARY BY TYPE; OR INDOORS

PARTIAL SHADE; BRIGHT INDIRECT LIGHT

REGULAR WATER

Paphiopedilum insigne

Sometimes sold as *Cypripedium,* these terrestrial orchids are native to tropical and subtropical regions of Asia. Usually grown in greenhouse or as houseplants; can be brought outdoors in warm weather. Some green-leafed forms can stay outdoors all year in mildest parts of the West Coast (Zones 17, 20–24); more tender, mottled-leafed forms can be grown outdoors year-round in Zone H2.

Plants have graceful, arching leaves and no pseudobulbs. Green-leafed types usually flower in winter, mottled-leafed kinds in summer. Most plants obtained from orchid dealers are hybrids rather than species. Blooms are perky, usually one to a stem, occasionally two or more. Many of them shine as if lacquered. Flowers may be white, yellow, green with white stripes, or pure green; or they may show a combination of background colors and markings in tan, mahogany, brown, maroon, green, and white.

A noteworthy species is *P. insigne.* Among the cold hardiest of the green-leafed types, it can withstand brief exposure to 28°F/–2°C. It blooms at any time from early fall through winter, bearing polished-looking flowers on stiff, hairy brown stems. Sepals and petals show a combination of green and white, with brown spots and stripes; pouch is reddish brown.

For indoor culture, green-leafed forms generally require temperatures of 50 to 55°F/10 to 13°C at night, 60 to 75°F/16 to 24°C during the day. Mottled-leafed forms do best with temperatures of about 55 to 60°F/13 to 16°C at night, 65 to 80°F/18 to 27°C during the day. Heat requirements are best met in a greenhouse. The least fussy types can be grown in pots in the house. Lady's slippers have no rest period. Use same potting mix as for cymbidiums. Don't plant in oversize pot; plants thrive when crowded. Flourish with less light than most orchids require.

PAPYRUS. See CYPERUS papyrus, C. prolifer

PARADISE PALM. See HOWEA forsteriana

PARAGUAY NIGHTSHADE. See SOLANUM rantonnetii

PARAHEBE

Scrophulariaceae

SHRUBBY PERENNIALS

ZONES 5, 6, 15–17, 20–24

FULL SUN OR LIGHT SHADE

REGULAR WATER

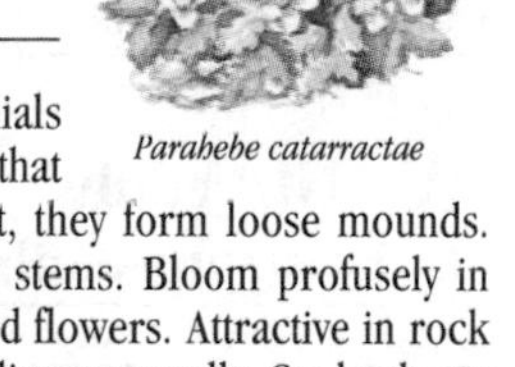
Parahebe catarractae

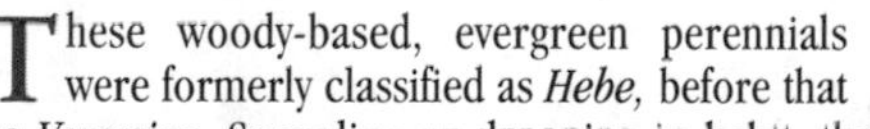

These woody-based, evergreen perennials were formerly classified as *Hebe,* before that as *Veronica.* Sprawling or drooping in habit, they form loose mounds. Leaves are arranged in opposite pairs along stems. Bloom profusely in summer, bearing small (½-in.), saucer-shaped flowers. Attractive in rock gardens, at the front of perennial borders, trailing over walls. Cut back any frost-damaged stems to near base of plant.

P. catarractae. From New Zealand. To 1 ft. high, twice as wide as tall. Narrow dark green leaves to 1¼ in. long. Flowers are white with blue or pink veining and a red eye, carried in narrow clusters to 4 in. long. Stems root where they touch moist soil. If plants begin looking leggy, you can cut them back somewhat, but not as severely as *P. perfoliata.*

P. perfoliata (Derwentia perfoliata). From Australia. To 1½–4 ft. tall, 6 ft. wide. The pairs of 2-in.-long, gray-green leaves clasp the stem completely, so that stem seems to be piercing the foliage. Clusters of deep blue flowers appear at branch ends and in upper leaf joints. To restore an old plant to beauty, cut it back nearly to the ground. Thrives beneath blue gum trees *(Eucalyptus globulus).*

×PARDANCANDA norrisii

CANDY LILY

Iridaceae

PERENNIAL FROM RHIZOME

ZONES 2–24

FULL SUN OR LIGHT SHADE

REGULAR WATER

×Pardancanda norrisii

Group of garden hybrids resulting from a cross between *Belamcanda* (blackberry lily) and *Pardanthopsis,* an iris relative. To 3 ft. tall, 2 ft. wide. Foliage fans are like those of iris. From midsummer to fall, plants produce six-segmented, 3–4-in.-wide flowers in a great range of colors, including yellow, blue, red, purple, pink, white, orange, and bicolors. Each bloom lasts only a day, but new flowers keep the show going. Good cut flowers. Plants are short lived, often blooming themselves to death; they self-sow in areas with warm summers. Grow from seed; in areas where the growing season is long, early sowing results in flowers the first year. Provide good drainage. Drought tolerant.

PARIS

Trilliaceae (Liliaceae)

PERENNIALS

ZONES 4–7, 14–17

PARTIAL OR FULL SHADE

REGULAR WATER

FRUIT IS POISONOUS IF INGESTED

Paris polyphylla

To picture these plants, visualize trilliums that suddenly sprouted four or more leaves instead of the traditional three, then abandoned their traditional flowers for an assemblage of green sepals and narrow yellow petals. These plants bear one blossom per stem; fruit consists of a black or red, berrylike mass of mildly poisonous seeds. Plants spread slowly by rhizomes. Curiosities for woodland or shaded rock garden.

P. polyphylla. Himalayan native to 2–3 ft. tall, 1 ft. wide, with four to ten oblong to lance-shaped, 7-in.-long, medium green leaves. Summer flowers are 4 in. wide, with broad, triangular sepals and threadlike petals as long as or longer than sepals. Fruit (rarely seen) is scarlet.

P. quadrifolia. HERB PARIS. Native to Europe, eastern Asia. To 6–15 in. high, 1 ft. wide, with four (sometimes more) oval, 3–5-in.-long, dark green leaves. Late-spring flowers have four or more leaflike sepals and eight very narrow, almost threadlike petals. Fruit is black.

PARKINSONIA aculeata

JERUSALEM THORN, MEXICAN PALO VERDE

Fabaceae (Leguminosae)

DECIDUOUS TREE

ZONES 8–24; H1, H2

FULL SUN

LITTLE TO MODERATE WATER

Parkinsonia aculeata

Native to southwestern U.S., Mexico. Rapid growth at first, then slowing; eventually reaches 15–30 ft. high and wide. Yellow-green bark, spiny twigs, picturesque form. Sparse foliage; leaves 6–9 in. long, with many tiny leaflets that quickly fall in drought or cold. Numerous yellow flowers in loose, 3–7-in.-long clusters. Long bloom season in spring; intermittent bloom throughout year. Flowers are followed by 2–6-in.-long seedpods that mature in summer.

Tolerates alkaline soil. Requires minimal attention once established. As shade tree, it filters sun rather than blocking it. Litter drop is a problem. Thorns, sparse foliage rule it out of tailored gardens. Reseeds freely in the desert. Flowering branches are attractive in arrangements.

PARROT BEAK. See CLIANTHUS puniceus

PARROTIA persica

PERSIAN PARROTIA

Hamamelidaceae

DECIDUOUS TREE OR SHRUB

ZONES 2B–7, 14–17

FULL SUN OR LIGHT SHADE

MODERATE TO REGULAR WATER

Parrotia persica

Native to Iran. Slow growing to 15–35 ft. tall and wide; naturally multistemmed but can be trained to a single trunk. Oval, 3–6-in.-long leaves have wavy margins; upper half is shallowly toothed. Choice, colorful tree, attractive in all seasons. Most dramatic display comes in autumn: leaves usually turn golden yellow, then orange or rosy pink, and finally scarlet. Smooth gray bark flakes off to reveal white patches; showy when on display in winter. Dense clusters of tiny flowers with red stamens and woolly brown bracts appear in late winter or early spring before leaves open; they give the plant an overall reddish haze. New foliage unfurls reddish purple, matures to lustrous dark green. Prefers slightly acid soil but tolerates alkaline soil.

PARSLEY. See PETROSELINUM crispum

PARSNIP

Apiaceae (Umbelliferae)
BIENNIAL GROWN AS ANNUAL
ALL ZONES
FULL SUN
REGULAR WATER

Parsnip

Carrot relative from Siberia and Europe, known scientifically as *Pastinaca sativa.* Among the most cold hardy of vegetables; grown for its delicately sweet, creamy white to yellowish roots, most often used in stews. For long roots, it needs well-prepared, loose, deep soil (roots of some varieties grow to 15 in.). In cold-winter areas, sow seeds in late spring, harvest in fall; leave surplus in ground to be dug as needed in winter. Cold makes the roots sweeter. In mild-winter climates, sow in fall and harvest in spring; in these areas, mature roots will continue to grow if left in ground, becoming tough and woody. Soak seeds in water for a day before planting to improve germination. Sow ¼–½ in. deep, in rows spaced 2 ft. apart; thin seedlings to 3 in. apart.

PARTHENOCISSUS

Vitaceae
DECIDUOUS VINES
ZONES VARY BY SPECIES
SUN OR SHADE
MODERATE WATER

Parthenocissus quinquefolia

Valued for handsome foliage—green in summer, reliably turning to superb orange or red shades in fall. Blossoms are insignificant; more noticeable are clusters of small blue-black fruits that form in late summer or fall and hang on into winter if not consumed by birds. Vines typically cling to walls by suction disks at ends of tendrils. All but the fairly restrained *P. henryana* are said to grow to 50–60 ft., but they are really limited only by the size of the support.

Thrive in organically enriched soil. Think twice before letting them attach to shingles, clapboard, or mortared brick or stone. At repainting time their clinging tendrils are hard to remove, and vines can creep under siding. They also hasten deterioration of wood and mortar. When vines reach desired size, prune each dormant season to restrain spread and—for those trained on buildings—to keep them away from doors, windows, and eaves. Cut out any wayward branches; likewise cut out any that have pulled away from their support, since disks will not reattach. Trim as needed during the growing season.

P. henryana. SILVERVEIN CREEPER. Zones 4–9, 14–17. Native to China. Grows to 20 ft.; less aggressive growth than the other species listed. Leaves have five leaflets to 2 in. long; they open purplish, then turn dark bronzy green with pronounced silver veining and purple undersides. Color is best in partial or full shade; in strong light, leaves fade to plain green. Foliage turns rich red in autumn. This vine clings to walls, but it needs some support to get started. Also a good choice for spilling over walls or as a small-scale ground cover.

P. inserta. VIRGINIA CREEPER, WOODBINE. Zones 1–24. Native to Rocky Mountains and eastward; the Western form of *P. quinquefolia.* Scrambles rather than clings; tendrils have few or no suction disks.

P. quinquefolia. VIRGINIA CREEPER. Zones A2, A3; 1–24. Native to eastern U.S. Big, vigorous vine that clings or runs over ground, fences, trellises, arbors, trees. Looser growth than *P. tricuspidata;* has a see-through quality. Leaves divided into five 6-in. leaflets with saw-toothed edges. Foliage is bronze tinted when new, matures to semiglossy dark green, turns crimson and burgundy in early fall. Good ground cover on slopes; can control erosion. 'Engelmannii', denser grower with smaller leaves; leaves of 'Star Showers' splashed with white, take on pink tones in fall, then turn red.

P. tricuspidata. BOSTON IVY. Zones 1–24. Native to China, Japan. Semievergreen in mild-winter areas. This species is even more vigorous than *P. quinquefolia.* Foliage color is similar to that of *P. quinquefolia* in spring and summer but covers a broader spectrum in fall. Leaves are glossy, to 8 in. wide, variable in shape; usually three lobed or divided into three leaflets. Autumn color varies from orange to wine red. Clings tightly, grows fast to make a dense, uniform wall cover. This is the "ivy" of the Ivy League; covers brick or stone in areas where English ivy *(Hedera helix)* freezes. In intensely hot regions, plant only on walls with northern or eastern exposure. 'Green Showers' has large (10-in.) leaves that turn burgundy in fall. 'Lowii' and 'Veitchii' produce half-size leaves on less rampant vines.

Parthenocissus tricuspidata

PARTRIDGEBERRY. See MITCHELLA repens

PASANIA edulis (Lithocarpus edulis)

JAPANESE FALSE OAK
Fagaceae
EVERGREEN TREE
ZONES 7, 9, 14–24
FULL SUN OR LIGHT SHADE
MODERATE WATER

Pasania edulis

From Japan. Closely related to Western native tanbark oak *(Lithocarpus densiflorus).* To 25–45 ft. tall and wide, with smooth grayish bark and leathery, 3–6-in.-long, glossy green leaves. Differs from oak *(Quercus)* in having erect male catkins (those of oak are drooping) and acorns that are tightly clustered in groups (acorns are usually solitary or paired in oak). The inch-long acorns have edible kernels. Needs good drainage.

PASPALUM vaginatum

SEASHORE PASPALUM
Poaceae (Gramineae)
PERENNIAL GRASS
ZONES 17, 24; H2
FULL SUN
MODERATE TO REGULAR WATER

Paspalum vaginatum

Native to southeastern U.S. Makes an attractive lawn near coast; tolerates salty soil, heat, wear. Color is close to that of bluegrass, and lawns are pest free. In interior climates, it develops tough stems that turn brown after cutting. Mow to ¾ in. with a reel mower and feed only between midautumn and late spring. Usually sold as sod under names like Adalayd and Excalibre.

PASQUE FLOWER. See PULSATILLA

PASSIFLORA

PASSION VINE
Passifloraceae
EVERGREEN, SEMIEVERGREEN, DECIDUOUS VINES
ZONES VARY BY SPECIES
FULL SUN OR PARTIAL SHADE
MODERATE TO REGULAR WATER

Passiflora × alatocaerulea

All but one of the passion vines listed here are South American natives. All climb by tendrils to 20–30 ft. Foliage is typically rich green. Plants bloom during warm weather. Flower parts can be seen to symbolize elements of the passion of Christ, hence plant's common name: the crown represents a halo or crown of thorns; the five stamens, the five wounds; the ten petal-like segments, the ten faithful apostles. Many species produce edible fruit as a bonus; for the species cultivated specifically for its edible crop, see Passion Fruit.

Train passion vines on trellises or walls for their vigor and bright, showy flowers; or use as a soil-holding bank cover. Vigorous, likely to overgrow and tangle; require rigorous thinning and untangling. Winter and early spring are best times for major pruning, but you can thin excess new growth at any time in the growing season. Tolerate many soil types. These vines are the favorite food of caterpillars of the gulf fritillary butterfly.

P. × alatocaerulea (P. pfordtii). Evergreen or semievergreen. Zones 5–9, 12–24; H1, H2. Dies to ground in colder part of range. Hybrid between *P. caerulea* and *P. alata,* a species not described here. Among the best-known, most widely planted passion vines, and probably least subject to damage from caterpillars. Three-lobed leaves are 3 in. long; fragrant, 4-in. flowers are white shaded pink and lavender, with deep blue or purple crown. Forms no fruit. In colder areas, give it a warm place out of wind, such as against a wall or beneath an overhang; mulch roots in winter.

P. caerulea. BLUE CROWN PASSION FLOWER. Evergreen or semievergreen. Zones 5–9, 12–24; H1, H2. Dies to the ground in colder part of range. Five-lobed leaves are smaller than those of *P. × alatocaerulea;* faintly fragrant flowers in greenish white with white-and-purple crown are also smaller. Egg-shaped, yellow to orange, $2\frac{1}{2}$-in. fruit isn't very tasty. Can be invasive. Has naturalized in Hawaii.

P. edulis. See Passion Fruit

P. × exoniensis. Evergreen. Zones 16, 17, 23, 24; H2. Hybrid descended from *P. mollissima.* Five-lobed, 5-in.-long leaves. Drooping, 5-in., unscented flowers are dark green and brownish red outside, brilliant pink inside, with a touch of purple in the throat and an inconspicuous white crown. Banana-shaped, yellow, 3-in.-long fruit.

P. incarnata. WILD PASSION VINE, MAYPOP. Deciduous. Zones 4–10, 12–24; H1, H2. Native to eastern U.S. Hardiest of the passion flowers, surviving to at least −10°F/−23°C and possibly even lower. Dies to the ground in colder part of range. Three-lobed leaves are 4–6 in. wide. Freely produced fragrant, 3-in. flowers are white or pale lavender, with a showy crown of filaments banded in purple and pink. Egg-shaped, yellow, 2-in. fruit. Spreads vigorously from underground roots and can become an attractive pest. Seldom offered as plants; easy to grow from seed.

P. 'Incense'. Deciduous. Zones 5–24; H1, H2. Hardy to 0°F/−18°C; holds its leaves through short cold spells, dies to the ground when the weather turns colder. Hybrid between *P. incarnata* and an Argentinian species. Flowers are 5 in. wide, violet with lighter crown, with fragrance similar to that of sweet peas *(Lathyrus).* Egg-shaped, 2-in., olive green to yellow-green fruit with fragrant, tasty pulp.

P. jamesonii. Evergreen. Zones 14–24; H1, H2. The true species is probably not in cultivation; plants sold under this name are hybrids of *P. mixta* and other species. Glossy, three-lobed leaves. Profuse, unscented salmon pink flowers lack a conspicuous corona; the floral segments are carried at the end of a long (4-in.) tube. Quick cover for bank or fence. Rampant growth in mild-winter regions has earned these plants an unflattering comparison to kudzu, the vining scourge of the South. 'Coral Glow' and 'Coral Seas' are available selections.

P. 'Lavender Lady'. Evergreen. Zones 16–24; H2. Profuse show of unscented, 4-in., lavender flowers with deep violet crown.

P. mollissima. BANANA PASSION VINE. Evergreen. Zones 13, 15–24; H2. Soft green leaves are three lobed, deeply toothed. Pendulous, unscented rose pink blossoms are similar in shape to those of *P. jamesonii;* they are long tubed, about 3 in. long. Flavorful yellow fruit is oblong, 4–6 in. long. Extremely aggressive grower; useful for covering banks in some areas but a problem if planted among trees or shrubs. In Hawaii, it is a serious pest, smothering trees with its rapid growth.

P. vitifolia. Evergreen. Zones 16, 17, 23, 24; H2. Deep green, 6-in. leaves shaped like grape leaves set off bright red, $3\frac{1}{2}$-in., unscented flowers with red to yellow coronas. Egg-shaped, greenish yellow, 2-in. fruit. Does not attract caterpillars. Has naturalized in Hawaii.

PASSION FRUIT

Passifloraceae
EVERGREEN OR SEMIEVERGREEN VINE
ZONES 15–17, 21–24; H1, H2
FULL SUN
REGULAR WATER

Passion Fruit

Known botanically as *Passiflora edulis,* this vigorous South American native climbs by tendrils to 20–30 ft. Light yellow-green, toothed leaves are three lobed. Blooms during warm weather, bearing white, 2–3-in.-wide flowers with white-and-purple crown (for more on flower form, see *Passiflora*). Doesn't need cross-pollination to bear fruit. Fragrant, roundish fruit $1\frac{1}{2}$–3 in. wide ripens mainly in summer and fall; at maturity, waxy rind turns from green to deep purple, and fruit falls from the tree. Either pick the fruit when it turns color or gather it from the ground every few days. Pulp is orange in color, with an exotic, citruslike flavor; use for juice or cut fruit in half and eat pulp, seeds and all, with a spoon. There is a form with larger, more acidic, yellow-skinned fruit. Sweet-fruited hybrids with good-size fruit include red-skinned 'Red Rover' and 'Frederick', and purple-skinned 'Edgehill' (particularly good in Southern California) and 'Kahuna'.

Grow in well-drained soil; give wind protection. Train on trellis or wall to show off flowers. Withhold water during cold months. Prune yearly after harvest: thin out excess stems by cutting them to the ground and cut back vigorous growth by a third. Semievergreen in colder part of range. Plants are often short lived. Has naturalized in Hawaii.

PASSION VINE. See PASSIFLORA

PATRINIA

Valerianaceae
PERENNIALS
ZONES 2B–6, 15–17
FULL SUN
REGULAR WATER

Patrinia scabiosifolia

Native to eastern Asia. Deeply cut or lobed leaves to 6 in. long form mounds of foliage. In summer, plants produce flowering stems bearing few or no leaves and flat-topped clusters of tiny yellow or white blossoms. Good in perennial borders. Long-lasting cut flowers. Appreciate rich, well-drained soil.

P. scabiosifolia. To 4–6 ft. tall, 2 ft. wide. Flowering stems produce sprays of tiny yellow blossoms. Because stems have a see-through quality, plant can be grown either at front or at rear of border. May need staking.

P. villosa. To 2–3 ft. tall, 2 ft. wide, with leaves that may be divided or uncut. Showers of white blossoms.

P

PAULOWNIA tomentosa

EMPRESS TREE

Bignoniaceae

DECIDUOUS TREE

ZONES 4–9, 11–24

FULL SUN

REGULAR WATER

Paulownia tomentosa

Native to China. Somewhat similar to catalpa in growth habit, leaves. Grows quickly to 40–50 ft., with nearly equal spread. Heavy trunk and heavy, nearly horizontal branches. Foliage gives tropical effect: light green, roughly heart-shaped, sometimes lobed leaves are 5–12 in. long, 4–7 in. wide. Fall color insignificant. Brown flower buds the size of small olives form in autumn and persist over winter, then open in early spring, before leafout. Fragrant, 2-in., trumpet-shaped flowers are lilac blue, marked on the inside with darker spotting and yellow stripes; they appear in 6–12-in.-long, upright clusters. Flowers are followed by 1½–2-in. seed capsules shaped like tops; these are persistent, remaining on the tree along with next season's flower buds. This tree does not bloom well where winters are very cold (buds freeze) or very mild (buds may drop off).

Grows in many soils but does best in deep, moist, well-drained soil. Tolerates air pollution. Protect from strong winds. Plant where falling flowers and leaves are not a problem. Not a tree to garden under due to dense shade, surface roots. If cut back yearly or every other year from an early age, it will produce a mass of giant-size leaves to 2 ft. long but at the expense of flower production. A tree called "sapphire dragon tree" is *P. kawakamii,* similar to *P. tomentosa* but smaller at maturity.

PAWPAW

Annonaceae

DECIDUOUS TREE

ZONES 2–9, 14, 18–21

FULL SUN, EXCEPT AS NOTED

REGULAR WATER

Pawpaw

From eastern North America, the pawpaw *(Asimina triloba)* is the only hardy member of a tropical family that also includes cherimoya. To 30 ft. tall; spreads as wide as high when grown alone but is often seen in thickets of narrow, erect plants that arise from suckering. In hot-summer climates, give it some shade in its first years. Medium green leaves are oval, somewhat drooping, 4–10 in. long; turn bright yellow in fall. Foliage smells unpleasant when crushed. Purplish or brownish (sometimes green) flowers with three prominent petals are large but not showy. Fruits are roughly oval, 3–5 in. long, yellowish green ripening to brown. Soft custardlike flesh has a number of large brown seeds and a flavor somewhat like banana. If possible, get grafted plants of named varieties such as 'Prolific', 'Rebecca's Gold', 'Sunflower', 'Taylor', and 'Wells'; seedlings are highly variable. Plant two varieties for cross-pollination.

PAXISTIMA (Pachystima, Pachistima)

Celastraceae

EVERGREEN SHRUBS

ZONES VARY BY SPECIES

PARTIAL SHADE IN HOTTEST CLIMATES

MODERATE TO REGULAR WATER

Paxistima canbyi

Low-growing shrubs with small, shiny, leathery leaves and insignificant flowers. Hardiness and compact habit make them useful as low hedges, edgings, ground cover in cold-winter areas. Best in well-drained soil.

P. canbyi. Zones 1–10, 14–21. Native to mountains of eastern U.S. Slowly makes a mat to 1 ft. high, 3–5 ft. wide. Narrow dark green leaves to ¾ in. long.

P. myrtifolia (P. myrsinites). OREGON BOXWOOD. Zones 2–7, 15, 16. Native to mountains of the West. Dense plant of variable habit; may be nearly prostrate or as tall as 4 ft. Spreads about 4 ft. Growth is more compact in sun. Leaves to 1¼ in. long are dark green above, paler beneath.

PEA

Fabaceae (Leguminosae)

ANNUAL

ALL ZONES

FULL SUN

REGULAR WATER

Pea

Native to southern Europe; known scientifically as *Pisum sativum.* Some peas are for shelling, some have edible pods, and others can be eaten either way. If you have space and don't mind the bother, grow tall (vining) peas on trellises, strings, or chicken wire; they climb by tendrils to 6 ft. or more and bear heavily. Bush types are more commonly grown in home gardens; they require no support, though they can be grown on short trellises for easy picking.

Among shelling peas, a good tall variety is 'Mr. Big'. Superior bush varieties of shelling peas include 'Green Arrow', 'Maestro', and 'Patriot'. In France, tiny peas called petits pois are considered a delicacy because of their tenderness and sweet flavor. These aren't just immature versions of shelling peas; they're genetically smaller (2–3 in. long at maturity), with six to nine small peas per pod. Two common varieties are 'Waverex' and 'Precovelle'.

An unusually good vegetable (and one popular in Asian cooking) is the edible-pod pea, usually called snow or sugar pea. 'Mammoth Melting Sugar' is a tall variety; 'Manoa Sugar' is a tall type developed for Hawaii gardens. 'Oregon Sugar Pod II' and 'Oregon Giant' are bush varieties.

'Sugar Snap' (tall), 'Super Sugar Snap' (tall), and 'Sugar Ann' (bush) combine the qualities of shelling peas and edible-pod peas. You can eat the immature pods, eat pods and peas together as you would string beans (the most popular way), or wait for the peas to mature and harvest them for shelling.

All peas are easy to grow when conditions are right. They need coolness and humidity and must be planted at just the right time. Where winters are cold, sow as early in spring as the ground can be worked; for a fall crop, sow about 12 weeks before the first frost date. Where winters are mild, plant at any time from fall to early spring—but don't sow after midwinter in areas where spring days quickly become too warm for peas. Successive plantings several days apart will lengthen the bearing season; most varieties are ready to pick 60 to 70 days from planting.

Grow peas in slightly acid to slightly alkaline soil that is water retentive but fast draining. Soak seeds overnight in water before planting them. If planting in winter, sow ½–1 in. deep. At other times of year, sow 2 in. deep in light soil, ½–1 in. deep in heavy soil. Leave 2 ft. between rows for bush types, 5 ft. for tall vines; thin seedlings to 2–4 in. apart. Moisten ground thoroughly before planting; then hold off on watering until seedlings are up. Plants need little fertilizer, but if soil is very light give one application of complete fertilizer about 6 weeks after planting. If weather turns warm and dry, supply water in furrows; overhead watering encourages mildew. Provide support for vining peas as soon as tendrils form.

When peas reach harvesting size, pick all pods that are ready; if seeds are allowed to ripen, plant will stop producing. Begin harvesting peas for shelling when the pods have swelled to almost a cylindrical shape but before they lose their bright green color. Harvest edible-pod peas when they're 2–3 in. long, before the seeds begin to swell. Vines are brittle; steady them with one hand while picking with the other. Refrigerate peas unwashed, and use as soon as possible.

PEACH and NECTARINE

Rosaceae

DECIDUOUS FRUIT TREES

ZONES VARY BY VARIETY

FULL SUN

REGULAR WATER DURING FRUIT DEVELOPMENT

SEE CHART NEXT PAGE

Peach

Native to China. Peach *(Prunus persica)* and nectarine *(P. p. nucipersica)* trees look alike and have the same cultural needs. Where fruit is concerned, both peaches and nectarines may be clingstone (flesh adheres to the pit), freestone (flesh easily separates from pit), or semifreestone (between the two); but other than this, nectarines differ from peaches in several respects. They have smooth rather than fuzzy skin; in some varieties, flavor is slightly different; and many are more susceptible to brown rot of stone fruit (controls described at right). Here we consider fruiting peaches and nectarines. For strictly flowering types, see *Prunus*.

In most regions, crops ripen between June and September, depending on variety. Early varieties grown in mild-winter climates may mature as early as April. For good harvests, trees must be exposed to winter chill (see care box); insufficient chilling results in delayed leafout, a scanty crop, and eventual death of the tree. In extremely mild-winter areas, only low-chill varieties do well (and very few of those are satisfactory in the low desert). A few low-chill peach varieties have been tried successfully at higher elevations in Hawaii; nectarines tend to split in Hawaii and so are not commonly grown there. In areas subject to late frosts, early-blooming varieties are risky. Where spring is particularly cold and rainy, plants set few flowers, pollinate poorly, and get peach leaf curl. They need clear, hot weather during the growing season.

The peach and nectarine varieties listed in the chart are the most widely available and recommended. However, many more are sold, some with local adaptation. For information on the varieties that perform best in your area, consult your Cooperative Extension Office or a local nursery.

A standard-size peach or nectarine tree grows rapidly to 25 ft. tall and wide, but properly pruned trees are usually kept to 10–12 ft. high and a little wider. They start bearing large crops when 3 or 4 years old and reach peak production at 8 to 12 years. Genetic or natural dwarf trees, most of which grow to 5–6 ft. tall and produce medium-size fruit, are useful in tubs and small planting areas. You can also save space by planting three or four full-size varieties in one hole: prune the new bare-root trees so that each retains just one primary branch, and point those branches outward as you plant the trees in the hole. With a few exceptions (see comments in chart), peaches and nectarines are self-fruitful.

Peach and nectarine trees require good drainage, regular fertilizing, and heavier pruning than other fruit trees. Genetic dwarf trees need less pruning than standard ones. When planting a bare-root tree that is an unbranched "whip," cut it back to 2–3½ ft. above ground (the thicker the trunk, the less severe the cutting back). New branches will form below cut. After first year's growth, select three well-placed branches for scaffold limbs. On mature trees, in each dormant season cut off two-thirds of previous year's growth by removing two of every three branches formed that year; or head back each branch to one-third its length; or head back some and cut out others. Trees can be trained as espaliers.

Among the most serious diseases of peaches and nectarines are brown rot of stone fruit and peach leaf curl. The fungus responsible for peach leaf curl causes emerging new leaves to thicken and pucker. Infected foliage may be tinged red, pink, yellow, or white; it usually falls in midsummer. Severely infected trees are weakened and may stop producing. Brown rot fungus causes flowers to wilt and decay, twigs to crack and ooze sap. To control both diseases, practice good sanitation—get rid of diseased plant parts to keep fungus from reinfecting the tree the next year. Also apply fixed copper or lime sulfur dormant sprays once after autumn leaf drop and again just as buds begin to swell but before they open. In coastal areas of the Northwest, where winter and spring are almost always rainy, spray three times, starting in late December and repeating at 2- to 4-week intervals. Some gardeners reduce peach leaf curl by planting the trees under eaves and training them in a fan shape against a south-facing wall. Move potted genetic dwarf peaches and nectarines to a covered location in rainy weather. To control the diseases as well as scale insects, use sprays combining horticultural oil with either lime sulfur or fixed copper.

Peach tree borer, which tends to attack trees stressed by poor growing conditions or wounds, causes defoliation, branch dieback, and possibly death. Jellylike matter exuding from the base of the tree is the first indication of the pest's presence. The insect holes will be evident at or just below ground level. Prevention through good growing conditions is the best control; if a tree is attacked, consult your Cooperative Extension Office for best treatment.

WHAT PEACHES AND NECTARINES NEED

WINTER CHILL: Most varieties need 600 to 900 hours of winter chill (45°F/7°C or lower). Low-chill selections are the best bet for mild-winter regions.

PRUNING: They need more pruning than other fruit trees, since they produce fruit on 1-year-old branches. Severe annual pruning (see text) not only renews fruiting wood—it encourages fruiting throughout the tree rather than at the ends of sagging branches that can easily break.

FRUIT THINNING: Even with good pruning, peaches and nectarines form too much fruit. When fruits are 1 in. wide, thin out (remove some) to 8–10 in. apart.

DISEASE CONTROL: Where peach leaf curl and brown rot of stone fruit are troublesome, apply dormant sprays annually (see text).

'Springtime' Peach

PEANUT

Fabaceae (Leguminosae)

ANNUAL

ZONES 2–24

FULL SUN

REGULAR WATER

Peanut

Known botanically as *Arachis hypogaea,* the peanut originated in South America and bears best where summers are long and warm. It is tender to frost but worth growing even in cool regions. Plants resemble bush sweet peas *(Lathyrus)* 10–20 in. tall. After the bright yellow flowers fade, a "peg" (shootlike structure) develops at each flower's base and grows down into soil; peanuts develop underground. For best performance, give fertile, well-drained soil; sandy or other light-textured soil is ideal for penetration by pegs.

The four basic classes of peanuts are Virginia and Runner types, with two large seeds per pod; Spanish, with two or three small seeds per pod; and Valencia, with three to six small seeds per pod. Buy seeds (unroasted peanuts) from mail-order suppliers. Plant just as soon as soil has warmed in spring, setting seeds (with shells removed but skins intact) 1½–2 in. deep. Sow seeds of Virginia and Runner peanuts 6–8 in. apart; sow Spanish and Valencia peanuts 4–6 in. apart. Fertilize at planting time. In cool-summer areas, grow under floating row covers to hasten growth. In 110 to 120 days after planting, foliage yellows and plants are ready to dig; loosen soil, then pull up plants. Let peanuts dry on vines in a warm, airy, shaded place for 2 to 3 weeks; then strip them from plants.

PEACH and NECTARINE

NAME	ZONES	FRUIT	COMMENTS
PEACHES			
'Arctic Supreme'	7–9, 14, 15, 18	Large. Clingstone. Red-over-cream skin; white flesh. Superb flavor. Midseason	Among the finest flavored of all peaches
'August Pride'	7–9, 14, 15, 18–24	Large. Freestone. Yellow skin with red blush; yellow flesh. Aromatic fruit with rich flavor. Midseason	Low chill requirement
'Babcock'	12, 13, 15, 16, 19–24; H1	Small to medium. Freestone. Light pink skin with red blush; little fuzz. White flesh reddens near pit. Sweet flavor with some tang. Early	Low chill requirement. Old-timer
'Baby Crawford'	7–9, 14, 15, 18	Small. Freestone. Golden orange skin with slight blush; yellow flesh. Intense flavor. Midseason	An exceptionally flavorful variety
'Bonanza II'	2, 3, 7–12, 14–16, 18–23	Large. Freestone. Attractive red-and-yellow skin; deep yellow to orange flesh. Good flavor. Midseason	Genetic dwarf. Showy flowers. Fruit more flavorful than that of 'Bonanza', the original dwarf variety for home gardens
'Bonita'	15–24	Large. Freestone. Yellow skin with medium red blush; firm yellow flesh. Fine flavor. Midseason	Low chill requirement
'Cresthaven'	2, 3, 6–11, 14, 15, 18	Medium to large. Freestone. Golden skin with red blush; yellow flesh. High-quality, firm fruit. Midseason to late	Blooms late. Fruit holds well on tree. Good fresh, frozen, or canned
'Desertgold'	8, 9, 12, 13, 18–24	Medium-size. Semifreestone. Yellow skin and flesh. Good quality. Very early	Very early bloom rules it out wherever spring frosts are likely
'Donut' ('Stark Saturn')	7–9, 13–15, 18–23	Medium-size. Freestone. Shaped like a doughnut, with a sunken middle. White skin with red blush; white flesh. Mildly sweet flavor with a hint of almond. Early	Low chill requirement. Almost evergreen in mild-winter areas
'Early Elberta'	2–11, 14, 15	Like 'Elberta' but has better color and even better flavor; also ripens about 1 week earlier	Needs somewhat less heat and less winter chill than 'Elberta'; less subject to fruit drop
'Elberta'	1–3, 6–11, 14	Medium to large. Freestone. Yellow skin with red blush; yellow flesh. High quality. Midseason	Needs good amount of winter chill, high summer heat to ripen to full flavor
'El Dorado'	2, 3, 7–12, 14, 15, 18	Medium-size. Freestone. Yellow skin with red blush; yellow flesh. Rich flavor. Early	Genetic dwarf
'Eva's Pride'	12, 13, 18–24	Medium to large. Freestone. Yellow skin and flesh. Fine flavor. Early to midseason	Low chill requirement
'Fay Elberta' ('Gold Medal')	2, 3, 6–11, 14, 15, 18, 19	Medium to large. Freestone. Yellow flesh. Has more red blush on skin and keeps better than 'Elberta'. Midseason; ripens with 'Elberta'	Large, handsome single flowers. 'Fantastic Elberta' is a double-flowered sport; its fruit has excellent flavor
'Flordaprince'	12, 13, 18–24; H1	Medium to large. Semifreestone, becoming freestone when fully ripe. Red-blushed yellow skin; yellow flesh. Very good quality. Very early	Low chill requirement
'Fortyniner'	5–9, 14–16, 18	Large. Freestone. Yellow skin with bright red blush; yellow flesh. Fine flavor. Early midseason	Looks like its parent, 'J. H. Hale'; blooms about 1 week earlier
'Frost'	3–9, 14, 15, 18	Medium-size. Freestone. Yellow skin with slight red blush; yellow flesh. Tangy flavor. Midseason to late	Resistant to peach leaf curl
'Gold Dust'	6–9, 11, 14–16	Small to medium. Freestone. Yellow skin, blushed bright red over much of the fruit; yellow flesh. Rich and tangy flavor. Early	Best quality in Zones 8, 9, 14

PEACH and NECTARINE

NAME	ZONES	FRUIT	COMMENTS
'Halehaven'	1–3, 6–11, 14–16	Medium to large. Freestone. Red skin; firm yellow flesh. Juicy and flavorful. Midseason	Flower and leaf buds are very winter hardy. Good fresh or canned
'Harken'	1–7	Large. Freestone. Yellow skin with red blush; yellow flesh. Very sweet. Midseason	Good performer in cold climates and coastal Northwest
'Honey Babe'	3–12, 14–16, 18–20	Small to medium. Freestone. Yellow skin with red blush; yellow flesh. Fine flavor. Midseason	Genetic dwarf. Needs another genetic dwarf peach or nectarine for pollination in the Northwest
'Indian Blood Cling' ('Indian Cling')	1–3, 6–11, 14–16	Medium-size. Clingstone. Red skin; firm yellow flesh streaked with red. Rich flavor. Late	Old-fashioned variety with small but devoted band of enthusiasts. Good for preserves
'Indian Free'	7–11, 14–16	Large. Freestone. Greenish white skin with red blush; red-tinged yellow flesh, deep red at pit. Rich and aromatic when fully ripe. Late midseason	Needs pollinating by any other peach except 'J. H. Hale'. An old favorite with a few loyal supporters
'J. H. Hale'	1–3, 7–11, 14–16	Very large. Freestone. Yellow skin overlaid with deep red; little fuzz. Yellow flesh. High quality; fine keeper. Midseason	Needs pollinating by any other peach except 'Indian Blood Cling' or 'Indian Free'
'July Elberta' ('Kim Elberta')	2, 3, 6–12, 14–16, 18, 19	Medium to large. Freestone. Yellow skin blushed red; yellow flesh. High quality. Early, 3 weeks before 'Elberta'	Prolific bearer
'Loring'	7–9, 14, 15, 18	Large. Freestone. Attractive yellow skin blushed red; little fuzz. Moderately juicy yellow flesh. Good quality. Midseason	Vigorous. Showy flowers appear early; susceptible to frost
'May Pride'	7–9, 14, 15, 18–24	Large. Freestone. Red skin; yellow flesh. Sweet with a slight tang. Early	Low chill requirement
'Midpride'	7–9, 12–16, 18–24	Medium-size. Freestone. Red-blushed yellow skin; yellow flesh. Exceptional flavor. Midseason	Excellent variety with low chill requirement
'Nectar'	7–11, 14–16	Medium to large. Freestone. Creamy white skin with red blush; white flesh. Excellent flavor. Early midseason	Among the best white peaches
'New Haven'	1–7	Large. Freestone. Red-blushed yellow skin; yellow flesh. Good quality. Midseason to late	Good performer in cold climates and coastal Northwest
'O'Henry'	7–10, 14–16, 18	Large. Freestone. Yellow skin with red blush; yellow flesh streaked red. Fine flavor. Midseason	Good commercial and home-garden variety
'Orange Cling' ('Miller Cling')	1–3, 7–12, 14–16, 18	Large. Clingstone. Yellow skin lightly blushed red; firm, deep yellow flesh. Fine flavor. Late	Favorite variety for home canning
'Pix Zee'	2, 3, 7–9, 14, 15, 18	Large. Freestone. Yellow skin with red blush; yellow flesh. Good flavor. Early to midseason	Genetic dwarf
'Polly'	1–3, 10	Medium-size. Freestone. White skin blushed red; juicy white flesh. Excellent flavor. Late midseason	Tree and buds very hardy to cold
'Q 1-8'	3–9, 14, 15, 18	Medium-size. Semifreestone. Yellow skin with red blush; white flesh. Sweet, flavorful. Early	Resistant to peach leaf curl
'Red Baron'	7–9, 14–16, 18–23	Large. Freestone. Yellow skin and flesh. Sweet, rich flavor. Midseason to late	Ornamental tree with double red blossoms
'Redhaven'	3, 5, 12, 14–16	Medium-size. Freestone. Yellow skin with bright red blush; firm yellow flesh. Good flavor. Long ripening season permits numerous harvests. Early	Colors up early, so test for ripeness. One of the best varieties. Good fresh or frozen. 'Early Redhaven' ripens 2 weeks earlier

PEACH and NECTARINE

NAME	ZONES	FRUIT	COMMENTS
'Redskin'	1–3, 6–12, 14–16	Medium to large. Freestone. Yellow skin heavily blushed red; yellow flesh. Excellent quality. Midseason	Productive tree. Good fresh, canned, or frozen
'Reliance'	1–11	Medium to large. Freestone. Yellow skin blushed dull red; soft yellow flesh. Good flavor. Early	Outstanding cold hardiness
'Rio Grande'	8–10, 15, 18–20	Medium to large. Freestone. Yellow skin with red blush; firm yellow flesh. Good flavor. Early	Productive tree with showy flowers
'Rio Oso Gem'	3, 7–11, 14, 15	Medium to large. Freestone. Yellow skin with red blush; firm yellow flesh. Excellent flavor. Late midseason	Small tree; not vigorous. Fruit is excellent fresh or frozen
'Santa Barbara'	18–24; H1	Large. Freestone. Red-blushed yellow skin; yellow flesh. Excellent flavor; best used fresh. Midseason	Low chill requirement. Sport of 'Ventura'
'Snow Beauty'	7–9, 14, 15, 18	Large. Freestone. Red skin, white flesh. Midseason	Among the best flavored of white peaches
'Southern Rose'	2, 3, 7–12, 14–16, 18–23	Medium-size. Freestone. Yellow skin with red blush; yellow flesh. Fair flavor. Midseason	Genetic dwarf with low chill requirement. 'Southern Flame' and 'Southern Sweet' are others in the series
'Springtime'	18–23	Medium-size. Semifreestone. Creamy yellow skin blushed red; white, juicy flesh. Sweet, mild flavor. Very early	One of the earliest peaches
'Strawberry Free'	7–9, 14–16, 18–20	Medium-size. Freestone. Medium red blush on yellow skin; firm white flesh. Excellent flavor. Early midseason	An old favorite among white peaches
'Tropi-berta'	8, 9, 14–16, 18–22; H1	Large. Freestone. Yellow skin blushed red; juicy yellow flesh. Good flavor. Late midseason	Moderately low chill requirement
'Tropic Snow'	12, 13, 18–23; H1	Medium-size. Freestone. Red skin, white flesh. Superb flavor. Early	Best low-chill white peach
'Ventura'	18–23; H1	Medium-size. Freestone. Very smooth yellow skin; yellow flesh. Attractive fruit with fair flavor. Midseason	Low chill requirement. Developed especially for Southern California
NECTARINES			
'Arctic Jay'	7–9, 14–16, 18	Large. Freestone. Deep red skin; white flesh. Excellent, rich flavor. Early to midseason	Among the many excellent white nectarines in the Arctic series; harvest season depends on variety. "Arctic" refers to white color of flesh, not to cold hardiness
'Arctic Rose'	7–9, 14–16, 18	Medium-size. Freestone. White to pale yellow skin with red blush; white flesh. Delicious sweet flavor. Midseason	One of the best-tasting nectarines
'Arctic Star'	7–9, 14, 15, 18–24	Large. Semifreestone. Bright red skin; white flesh. Very sweet, rich flavor. Early	Low chill requirement. One of the best white nectarines for mild-winter areas

'July Elberta' Peach

'Flordaprince' Peach

'Midpride' Peach

Genetic Dwarf Peach Tree

PEACH and NECTARINE

NAME	ZONES	FRUIT	COMMENTS
'Double Delight'	7–9, 14–16, 18–20	Medium-size. Freestone. Dark red skin; yellow flesh. Rich flavor. Midseason	Ornamental double pink flowers
'Fantasia'	3, 7–9, 14–16, 18–22	Large. Freestone. Bright yellow-and-red skin; firm yellow flesh. Sweet, rich flavor. Midseason	Vigorous. Relatively low chill requirement
'Gold Mine'	7–9, 14–16, 18–24	Large. Freestone. Creamy yellow, tough skin with red blush; firm white flesh. Excellent, distinctive flavor. Late midseason	Low chill requirement. Excellent fresh or frozen
'Heavenly White'	7–9, 14–16, 18	Very large. Freestone. Creamy white skin that is heavily blushed with red; white flesh. Especially fine flavor. Midseason	Has been called a connoisseur's delight
'Independence'	7–9, 14–16, 18, 19	Large. Freestone. Red skin, yellow flesh. Good flavor. Early	Moderately vigorous, moderately productive tree
'Juneglo'	3–9, 14–16, 18	Medium-size. Freestone. Red skin, yellow flesh. Fine flavor. Early	One of the most reliable varieties in coastal Northwest
'Le Grand'	7–9, 14–16, 18	Large. Clingstone. Bright yellow-and-red skin; yellow flesh. Delicate, sweet-tart flavor. Late	Fruit holds well on the tree
'Liz's Late'	7–9, 14–16, 18	Medium-size. Freestone. Red-over-yellow skin; yellow flesh. Sprightly, sweet-spicy flavor. Good keeper. Late	Unusual flavor makes this nectarine a favorite
'Mericrest'	1–3, 10, 11, 14–16, 18	Medium-size. Freestone. Bright red skin; yellow flesh. Flavorful. Midseason	May be as cold hardy as 'Reliance' peach. Good resistance to brown rot
'Nectar Babe'	2–12, 14–16, 18–20	Small to medium-size. Freestone. Dark red skin; yellow flesh. Good flavor. Midseason	Genetic dwarf
'Necta Zee'	2–12, 14–16, 18–20	Medium-size. Freestone. Red skin, yellow flesh. Sweet and flavorful. Early to midseason	Genetic dwarf
'Panamint'	7–9, 14–16, 18–24	Medium to large. Freestone. Bright red skin; yellow flesh. Very good flavor. Midseason	Low chill requirement
'Silver Lode'	7–9, 14–16, 18–20	Medium-size. Freestone. Scarlet-and-white skin; white flesh. Good flavor. Early	Low chill requirement
'Snow Queen'	7–9, 14–16, 18–23	Medium-size. Freestone. Red skin; white flesh. Sweet and juicy. Early	Low chill requirement
'Southern Belle'	7–12, 14–16, 18–23	Large. Freestone. Yellow skin with red blush; yellow flesh. Good flavor. Early	Genetic dwarf. Low chill requirement
'Sunred'	18–23	Medium-size. Semifreestone. Bright red skin; yellow flesh. Good flavor. Very early	Low chill requirement

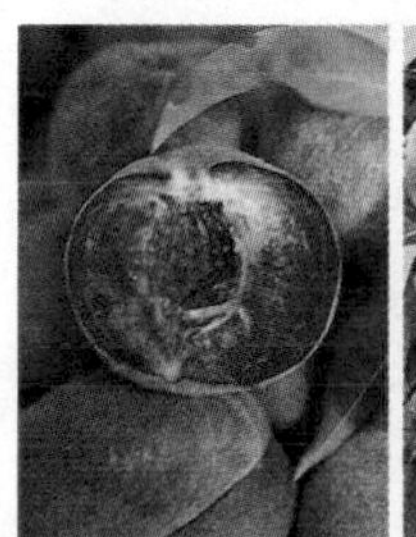
'Indian Free' Peach

'Redhaven' Peach

'Rio Oso Gem' Peach

'Springtime' Peach

'Independence' Nectarine

'Fantasia' Nectarine

PEANUT CACTUS. See ECHINOPSIS chamaecereus

PEAR, ASIAN

Rosaceae

DECIDUOUS FRUIT TREES

ZONES 2–12, 14–21, EXCEPT AS NOTED

FULL SUN

REGULAR WATER

Asian Pear

These pears are descendants of two Asian species: *Pyrus pyrifolia (P. serotina)* and *P. ussuriensis.* Trees grow to 25–30 ft. tall and about half as wide, but they're easily kept to half that size with pruning. Unlike European pears, Asian pears are generally round in shape, with a crisp, gritty, firm to hard texture. Asian pears are often called apple pears because of their roundness and crispness, but they are not hybrids of those two fruits. All pears benefit from pollination by a second variety that flowers at the same time (consult your local nursery). European pears, however, are not reliable pollenizers for Asian types because they generally bloom later. Asian pears should be thinned to one pear per fruiting spur and should be picked ripe.

Fresh Asian pears are excellent combined with other fruits and vegetables in salads. They need the same general culture as European pears but have a lower chill requirement (take as few as 400 hours) and a greater resistance to fireblight. Asian pear varieties include 'Chojuro', 'Hosui', 'Ichiban', 'Kikusui', 'Kosui', 'Mishirasu', 'Seuri', 'Shinko', 'Tsu Li', 'Ya Li', 'Yoinashi', and 'Yongi'. 'Shinseiki' grows in Zones 2–13, 14–21. 'Nijisseki' ('Twentieth Century') is a particularly cold-hardy variety.

PEAR, EUROPEAN

Rosaceae

DECIDUOUS FRUIT TREES

ZONES VARY BY VARIETY

FULL SUN

REGULAR WATER

SEE CHART NEXT PAGE

European Pear

Most pears sold in markets and grown in gardens are varieties of *Pyrus communis,* a European species. The long-lived trees are pyramidal in form, with strongly vertical branching; they grow 30–40 ft. tall (sometimes taller), 15–25 ft. wide. Pears on dwarfing understocks make good small garden trees; they range from one-half to three-fourths the size of standard-size trees. Pears also make excellent espaliers. All types have leathery, glossy bright green leaves and bear handsome clusters of white flowers in early spring. For ornamental relatives, see *Pyrus.*

To produce good crops, pears need winter chill (see care box). In cold climates, their early bloom makes them prone to damage from spring frosts; in such areas, they are often planted in protected locations, such as on slopes. Hybrids between European pears and the hardy species *P. ussuriensis,* such as 'Ure', are worth trying in the coldest regions. Where winters are very mild, choose varieties needing little winter chill. Some low-chill types are Asian hybrids, crosses between European and Asian pears with fruit similar to that of European varieties.

Pears do best in well-drained loam, but they tolerate damp, heavy soil better than other fruit trees. They produce fruit on knobby spurs that remain productive for up to 5 years. Thinning the fruit is not usually necessary. Harvest season is July to late October, depending on variety. Fruit does not ripen properly on the tree; pick it when full size but not yet ripe. Fruit of most kinds should be put in a cool, dark place to ripen; exceptions are 'Anjou', 'Bosc', and 'Comice', which should be put in cold storage (32 to 40°F/0 to 4°C) for about a month after picking, then brought into a warm room to ripen.

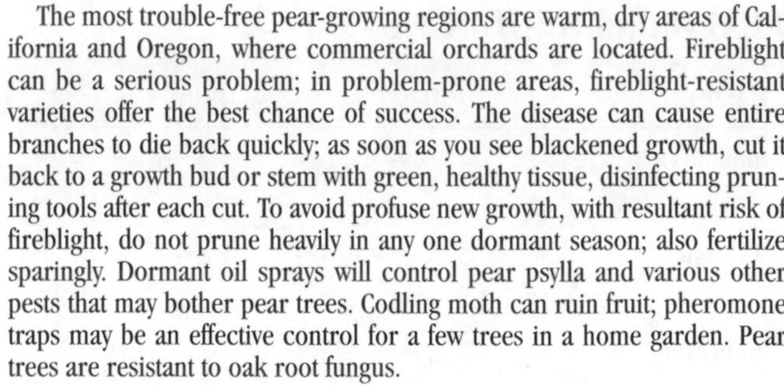

The most trouble-free pear-growing regions are warm, dry areas of California and Oregon, where commercial orchards are located. Fireblight can be a serious problem; in problem-prone areas, fireblight-resistant varieties offer the best chance of success. The disease can cause entire branches to die back quickly; as soon as you see blackened growth, cut it back to a growth bud or stem with green, healthy tissue, disinfecting pruning tools after each cut. To avoid profuse new growth, with resultant risk of fireblight, do not prune heavily in any one dormant season; also fertilize sparingly. Dormant oil sprays will control pear psylla and various other pests that may bother pear trees. Codling moth can ruin fruit; pheromone traps may be an effective control for a few trees in a home garden. Pear trees are resistant to oak root fungus.

WHAT EUROPEAN PEARS NEED

WINTER CHILL: Pears need at least 600 hours of winter chill (45°F/7°C or lower), and most do better still with 900 hours. In warmest-winter climates, choose low-chill varieties.

POLLINATION: They normally need cross-pollination for good fruit set; plant two or more varieties. Some types, notably 'Bartlett' and 'Comice', are self-fruitful in many parts of California but not usually elsewhere.

PRUNING AND TRAINING: Best done when trees are young to establish a good framework of main branches. Prune lightly each year during the dormant season to keep good form, eliminate crowding branches.

HARVESTING: Don't wait for pears to ripen on the tree—they'll be ruined. Pick unripe, when they're green and firm. If a pear is ready to harvest, the stem will snap free from the branch when you lift the fruit so that it is horizontal. If the stem remains connected, check again in a few days.

'Bartlett'

PEARL BUSH. See EXOCHORDA

PEASHRUB. See CARAGANA

PECAN

Juglandaceae

DECIDUOUS TREE

ZONES 2 AND 3 (WARMER PARTS), 6–10, 12–14, 18–20

FULL SUN

REGULAR WATER

Pecan

Native to southern and central U.S.; scientific name is *Carya illinoensis.* Graceful, shapely tree to 70 ft. tall and wide; too large for smaller home plots but attractive where space is available. Foliage is like that of English walnut but prettier; leaves have more (11–17), narrower, longer (4–7-in.) leaflets. Tree has a finer-textured foliage pattern than English walnut and casts lighter shade. Inconspicuous flowers are followed by nuts enclosed in husks. Best nut production is in areas with long, hot summers (Zones 8–10, 12–14, 18–20); crops in other recommended zones are less certain, but possible (see page 508). Mature nuts drop in autumn. To harvest, gather fallen nuts and remove husks right away; then dry and store the nuts.

Most pecans will set light crops without cross-pollination, which may be enough for homeowners who plant these trees primarily for shade.

▶ page 508

PEAR, EUROPEAN

NAME	ZONES	FRUIT	COMMENTS
'Anjou' ('d'Anjou', 'Beurre d'Anjou')	2, 3, 6–9	Medium to large fruit may be round or have a short neck. Yellow to russeted yellow. Fine flavor. Ripens after cold storage. Late	Upright, vigorous tree. Tie down limbs for more consistent bearing. Moderately susceptible to fireblight. 'Red d'Anjou' is a red-skinned form
'Bartlett'	2–11, 14–18	Medium to large, with short but definite neck. Thin skinned, yellow or slightly blushed, very sweet and tender. Midseason	Standard summer pear of fruit markets. Generally self-fruitful but may need a pollenizer in cool California coastal areas and Northwest; use any variety except 'Seckel'. Tree does not have the best form, is susceptible to fireblight; nevertheless a good home variety
'Bosc' ('Beurre Bosc', 'Golden Russet')	2–9, 14–18; best in Northwest and higher elevations farther south	Medium to large, quite long necked, interesting and attractive in form. Heavy russeting on green or yellow skin. Fine flavor; firm, juicy flesh. Holds shape when cooked. Ripens after cold storage. Midseason	Large, upright, vigorous tree. Needs pruning in youth. Highly susceptible to fireblight
'Clapp Favorite'	2–9, 14–18; best in Northwest, inter-mountain areas	Resembles 'Bartlett'. Soft, sweet flesh. Early	Productive, shapely tree; attractive foliage. Highly prone to fireblight. 'Bennett', popular in Northwest, is a red-blushed strain
'Comice' ('Doyenne du Comice', 'Royal Riviera')	2–9, 14–18	Large to very large, roundish to pear shaped. Thick, greenish yellow skin is russeted, sometimes blushed. Superb flavor and texture. Ripens after cold storage. Late	Big, vigorous tree; slow to reach bearing age. Bears good crops when soil, climate, and exposure are right. Generally self-fruitful but does better in Northwest with a pollenizer. Moderately susceptible to fireblight. 'Red Comice' is a red-skinned sport
'Conference'	2–9, 14–18	Large, yellow, elongated fruit borne in clusters. Very juicy, sweet flesh with buttery texture. Late	Very productive. Good resistance to fireblight
'Fan Stil'	2, 3, 7–12, 14–23	Medium-size, bell-shaped yellow fruit with slight red blush. Crisp, juicy; good fresh and cooked. Midseason	Asian pear hybrid. Vigorous, upright growth. Consistently large crops. Needs little winter chill; tolerates heat. Highly resistant to fireblight
'Flordahome'	2, 3, 7–23	Small to medium, light green fruit with short pear shape. Juicy flesh. Early	Resistant to fireblight. Needs little winter chill. Pollinate with 'Hood'
'Harrow Delight'	1b, 2–7	Resembles 'Bartlett' but is smaller. Smooth texture, very good flavor. Early	Cold-hardy variety developed in Canada. Excellent resistance to fireblight
'Hood'	2, 3, 7–24; H1	Large yellow-green fruit with typical pear shape. Ripens a little later than 'Flordahome'	Vigorous tree. Resistant to fireblight. Needs very little winter chill. Pollinate with 'Flordahome'
'Kieffer'	2, 3, 7–23	Medium to large, oval; greenish yellow skin blushed red. Gritty texture; fair flavor. Good for canning, baking. Late	Asian pear hybrid. Low-chill variety. Good for hot or cold climates. Quite resistant to fireblight
'Max-Red Bartlett'	2–11, 14–18	Resembles 'Bartlett' but has bright red skin and a somewhat sweeter flavor. Midseason	Red color extends to twigs and tints leaves. Susceptible to fireblight. Bears better in Northwest with a pollenizer; use any except 'Seckel'

▶

'Anjou' 'Bartlett' 'Bosc' 'Comice' 'Sensation Red Bartlett' 'Red Comice'

PEAR, EUROPEAN

NAME	ZONES	FRUIT	COMMENTS
'Monterrey'	2, 3, 7–12, 14–23	Large, apple shaped; yellow skin. Good flavor; texture not too gritty. Midseason	Probably an Asian pear hybrid. Needs little winter chill. Very resistant to fireblight
'Moonglow'	2, 3, 7–12, 14–23	Somewhat like 'Bartlett' in looks. Juicy, soft fruit with good flavor. Ripens 2 weeks before 'Bartlett'	Upright, vigorous tree; very heavy bearer. Highly resistant to fireblight
'Orcas'	2–7, 14–17	Large. Pear shaped but has a pointier stem end than a typical pear. Yellow skin with red blush. Flavorful, melt-in-the-mouth flesh. Midseason	Vigorous, spreading tree
'Orient'	2–21	Large, bell-shaped fruit with russeting on yellow skin. Firm, juicy, and somewhat sweet; good for canning, baking. Late	Asian pear hybrid. Heavy producer. Highly resistant to fireblight
'Rescue'	2–7, 14–17	Large, traditional shape; yellow skin with red-orange blush. Sweet, juicy, and smooth textured. Good keeper. Midseason	Vigorous, productive, upright tree. Northwest favorite
'Seckel' ('Sugar')	2–11, 14–21	Very small, very sweet, aromatic. Roundish to pear shaped; yellow-brown skin, granular flesh. A favorite for home gardens, preserving. Early midseason	Highly productive. Fairly resistant to fireblight. Self-fruitful but bears more heavily with pollenizer (any except 'Bartlett' and its strains will do)
'Sensation Red Bartlett'	2–9, 14–18	Looks much like 'Bartlett', but skin is bright red over most of fruit. Midseason	Medium-size tree, less vigorous than 'Bartlett'. Susceptible to fireblight
'Summer Crisp'	A2, A3; 1–3	Small, roundish. Red-blushed green skin. Crisp, mildly sweet flesh. Late	Cold-hardy variety from Minnesota. Quite resistant to fireblight
'Sure Crop'	2–9, 14–18	Resembles 'Bartlett' in looks and flavor. Late midseason	Consistent annual bearer. Prolonged bloom makes it safe where spring frosts come late. Fairly resistant to fireblight
'Ure'	A2, A3; 1–3	Small, roundish fruit with greenish yellow skin. Sweet and juicy. Good fresh or canned. Midseason	Cold-hardy Asian hybrid developed in Canada. Small tree. Resistant to fireblight
'Warren'	1b–9, 14–18	Medium to large fruit with teardrop shape; pale green skin, often with a red blush. Buttery, juicy flesh with excellent flavor. Good keeper. Late	Cold-hardy tree. Extremely resistant to fireblight
'Winter Nelis'	2, 3, 7–9, 14–18	Small to medium, roundish fruit with rough, dull green or yellowish skin. Not attractive but has a very fine flavor. Very good keeper, fine for baking. Late	Moderately susceptible to fireblight

P

However, if a good-size crop is desired, plant two varieties (consult a local nursery about the best combination for your area). The best selections include 'Mohawk', 'Pawnee', 'Western Schley' and 'Wichita'. Early-ripening 'Pawnee' is the best choice in areas that normally don't get warm enough to ripen pecans (Zones 6 and 7 and even the warmer parts of Zones 2 and 3). It also has good resistance to scab, which can be a problem in areas with summer rainfall. Other early-ripening varieties that may succeed in these short-season areas include 'Lucas' and scab-resistant 'Kanza'.

Pecan trees need well-drained, deep soil (6–10 ft. deep); they will not take salinity. To plant, set out bare-root trees in winter. Dig planting hole deep to accommodate the long taproot; position bud union above soil level. Firm soil around roots; then water thoroughly. If you're counting on a quality nut crop, don't let soil dry out. Prevent or cure pecan rosette (abnormal clumps of twigs caused by zinc deficiency) with zinc sulfate sprays or soil treatment. Pecan is prone to aphid infestations; it is resistant to oak root fungus. Pruning is needed only to remove suckers from below graft union and to clear out dead, broken, or poorly placed limbs.

PEDILANTHUS

Euphorbiaceae

DECIDUOUS AND EVERGREEN SHRUBS

ZONES VARY BY SPECIES

EXPOSURE NEEDS VARY BY SPECIES

LITTLE WATER

MILKY SAP CAN CAUSE STOMACH UPSET

Pedilanthus tithymaloides smallii

Both species have decorative stems, but those of the first are bare most of the year. Both have inconspicuous red flowers concealed in tubular or slipper-shaped red bracts.

P. macrocarpus. LADY'S SLIPPER. Deciduous. Zones 12, 13, 19–24. Native to Mexico. Grows to 5 ft. tall, and 2–3 ft. wide, with small, scanty leaves that drop soon after they emerge. The fleshy, waxy, whitish, forking, half-inch-thick stems are the main feature. Bears 1-in. bracts in late spring;

may repeat in summer after rainfall. Tolerates light shade, but has best form in full sun.

P. tithymaloides smallii. DEVIL'S BACKBONE, JACOB'S LADDER. Evergreen. Zone H2; or indoors. Caribbean native to 1–2 ft. tall, with somewhat fleshy, zigzagging stems and 2–3-in., oval mid-green leaves. 'Variegatus' is a selection with grayish stems and leaves marked with white and pink; fairly common as a houseplant. Under good growing conditions, may produce ½-in. bracts in summer. Partial shade in Zone H2. Give houseplants bright indirect light; fertilize every couple of months during warm months, and keep soil barely moist.

PELARGONIUM

GERANIUM

Geraniaceae

SHRUBBY PERENNIALS

ZONES 8, 9, 12–24; A2, A3, 1–7, 10, 11 AS ANNUALS; OR INDOORS

SOME SHADE IN HOTTEST CLIMATES; BRIGHT SUNNY WINDOW

MODERATE TO REGULAR WATER

Pelargonium ×domesticum

The common name "geranium" is widely used for *Pelargonium*—but botanically speaking, it is not really accurate. To the botanist, pelargoniums are woody-based perennials (most of them native to South Africa) that endure light frosts but not hard freezes and have slightly asymmetrical flowers in clusters. True geraniums, on the other hand, are annuals and perennials (some woody-based) native mainly to the Northern Hemisphere, bearing symmetrical flowers either singly or in clusters. Some are weeds, while others are valued border or rock garden plants.

In the past, the commonly grown pelargoniums were *P. ×domesticum,* Lady Washington pelargonium; *P. ×hortorum,* common geranium (this group also includes variegated forms usually referred to as fancy-leafed or color-leafed geraniums); and *P. peltatum,* ivy geranium. Today, other kinds are increasingly available, including many with scented leaves.

Plants perform best in areas with warm, dry days and cool nights. They can be grown outdoors year-round where winters are very mild; in these areas, they bloom throughout warm weather. Zones 17 and 24 are ideal climates; next best are Zones 15, 16, 22, 23; possible but not as easy are Zones 8, 9, 12–14, 18–21. Elsewhere, they are summer annuals or houseplants. In cold-winter climates, move plants indoors before the first frost or take cuttings for next year.

Plant in any good, fast-draining soil. Amend poor alkaline soil with plenty of organic matter. Geraniums growing in good garden soil need little fertilizer; those in light sandy soil should receive two or three feedings during active growth. Remove faded flowers regularly to encourage new bloom. Pinch growing tips of young, small plants to force side branches. All geraniums do well in pots; they bloom best when somewhat pot-bound. Common pests include aphids, whiteflies, and spider mites. Geranium (tobacco) budworm may be a problem in some areas; affected flowers look tattered or fail to open at all.

P. cordifolium (P. cordatum). Rounded plant to 4 ft. tall and wide, with 2½-in., dull green, toothed and lobed leaves. Loose clusters of reddish purple, 1-in. flowers. Good for borders.

P. ×domesticum. LADY WASHINGTON PELARGONIUM, MARTHA WASHINGTON PELARGONIUM, REGAL GERANIUM. Erect or somewhat spreading, to 3 ft. tall and wide. Rangier than *P. ×hortorum.* Heart-shaped to kidney-shaped leaves are dark green, 2–4 in. wide, with crinkled margins and unequal sharp teeth. Loose, rounded clusters of large (2-in. or wider), showy flowers; colors include white and many shades of pink, red, lavender, purple, with brilliant blotches and markings of darker colors. Can be planted in beds but tends to get rangy. First-class potted plant. Some varieties are used in hanging baskets.

P. ×hortorum. COMMON GERANIUM, GARDEN GERANIUM. Succulent stemmed; grows to 3 ft. or more high and wide. In mild climates, older plants grown in the open become woody. Round or kidney-shaped leaves are velvety and hairy, soft to the touch, aromatic, edges indistinctly lobed and scallop toothed; most varieties show a zone of deeper color just inside edge of leaf, though some have plain green foliage. Single or double flowers are flatter and smaller than those of *P. ×domesticum,* but clusters bear many more blossoms. Many varieties are sold, in white and shades of pink, rose, red, orange, and violet; flowers are usually solid colored.

Pelargonium ×hortorum

Tough, attractive geraniums for outdoor bedding can be grown from seed, flowering the first summer. Available strains include Elite (quick to reach bloom stage, compact, needs no pinching); Maverick (open habit with many flowering stems); Multibloom (compact, early blooming); and Orbit (distinct leaf zoning; broad, rounded flower clusters). 'Orange Appeal', a seed-grown selection, has blooms in pure bright orange. There are also dwarf, cactus-flowered, and other novelty varieties.

Fancy-leafed or color-leafed varieties have zones, borders, or splashes of brown, gold, red, white, and green in various combinations. Some also have highly attractive flowers. 'Golden Ears', 1 ft. high and wide, has small, deeply cut, almost star-shaped leaves of deep bronzy red with a wide border of chartreuse; flowers are bright coral. 'Vancouver Centennial' is very similar if not identical. 'Mrs. Pollock' has green leaves with a red zone and a creamy yellow margin; it bears vermilion blooms.

P. peltatum. IVY GERANIUM. To 1–1½ ft. tall, trailing to 3–5 ft. wide. Rather succulent, glossy, bright green, 2–3-in.-wide leaves have pointed lobes and look something like those of ivy *(Hedera).* Inch-wide single or double flowers in rounded clusters of five to ten; colors include white, pink, rose, red, and lavender. Upper petals may be blotched or striped. Many named varieties. 'L'Elegante' has white-edged foliage; other varieties are available with white or yellow veins in leaves. Summer Showers strain can be grown from seed, features blossoms in mixed colors (white, pink, red, lavender, magenta). Use ivy geranium in hanging containers, window boxes, or raised beds; it also makes a good bank or ground cover (but not for erosion control).

P. sidoides. Slow-growing; dense mound 1 ft. tall and wide. Silvery gray, heart-shaped leaves to 1½ in. across. Clusters of dark purple, ¾-in. flowers bloom on slender, branching, trailing stems. ▸

P

Pelargonium ×domesticum

Pelargonium peltatum

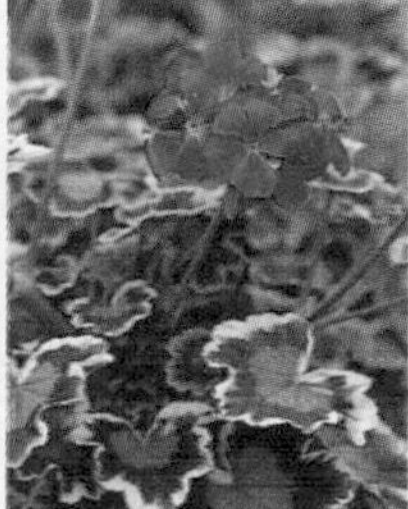

Pelargonium ×hortorum 'Mrs. Pollock'

Scented Geranium *Pelargonium graveolens*

Scented Geranium *Pelargonium ×fragrans*

P. 'Splendide'. To 1–1½ ft. high and wide, with spreading or stiffly trailing stems. Silvery gray, 1–1½-in.-long, oval leaves have slightly toothed edges. Distinctive blossoms, carried a few to a cluster, are 1–1¼ in. wide, have unusual coloring: the two upper petals are dark red, nearly black at the base, while the three lower ones are nearly white. Use in pots, hanging baskets. Often sold as *P. tricolor* or *P. violareum.*

Scented geraniums. Many aromatic species, hybrids, and selections are available. Most grow 1–3 ft. tall, spreading as wide as high. Foliage scent is the main draw; clusters of small, typically white or rosy flowers are secondary in appeal. Leaves vary in shape from nearly round to finely cut and almost ferny; they range in size from minute to 4 in. across. These plants' common names usually refer to the fragrance of their leaves: almond geranium *(P. quercifolium),* apple geranium *(P. odoratissimum),* lime geranium *(P. nervosum),* nutmeg geranium (*P. ×fragrans* 'Nutmeg'), peppermint geranium *(P. tomentosum).* There are several rose geraniums, including *P. capitatum, P. graveolens,* and *P.* 'Lady Plymouth'. Various types offer lemon fragrance, including *P. crispum* and *P.* 'Prince Rupert'. All scented geraniums are good for herb gardens, edgings, front of borders, window boxes, hanging baskets; peppermint geranium makes a good ground cover in frost-free gardens. Use fresh leaves of all types for flavoring jelly and iced drinks; use dried leaves in potpourri and sachets.

Pelargonium tomentosum

Pelargonium graveolens

PELLAEA

CLIFF-BRAKE

Polypodiaceae

FERNS

ZONES VARY BY SPECIES

FILTERED SUNLIGHT

WATER NEEDS VARY BY SPECIES

Pellaea rotundifolia

Though these small plants are not striking in overall appearance, they have charmingly detailed foliage, with leaves divided into little narrow to roundish leaflets.

P. andromedifolia. COFFEE FERN. Zones 7–9, 14–24. Native to California, southern Oregon. Slow growing to 1½–2 ft. high and wide, with thin, wiry stalks holding finely cut gray-green to bluish green fronds divided into oblong leaflets. Give good drainage. Use in native landscapes, rock gardens. Little water.

P. mucronata. BIRD'S FOOT FERN. Zones 4–11, 14–24. Native from California to Texas. To 6–12 in. high and wide, with gray-green, airy-looking fronds and narrow leaflets arranged in groups of three. Little water. Good tucked into rock walls.

P. rotundifolia. ROUNDLEAF FERN. Zones 14–17, 19–24. Native to Australia, New Zealand. Neat little plant grows to 1 ft. high and 2 ft. wide, with spreading fronds divided into nearly round, evenly spaced leaflets. Pretty fern for contrast with finer-textured ferns or to show off in pots, baskets, or raised beds. Regular water. Sometimes used as a houseplant; give bright indirect light.

P. viridis (P. adiantoides). Zones 14–17, 19–24; H2. Native to Africa. Grows to 1 ft. high and wide, with fronds consisting of fresh green, oval to lance-shaped leaflets. Good as ground cover, in rock garden, in containers. Regular water.

PELTIPHYLLUM peltatum. See DARMERA peltata

PENCILBUSH, PENCIL TREE. See EUPHORBIA tirucalli

PENCIL CACTUS. See OPUNTIA leptocaulis

PENNISETUM

FOUNTAIN GRASS

Poaceae (Gramineae)

PERENNIAL GRASSES

ZONES VARY BY SPECIES

FULL SUN OR PARTIAL SHADE, EXCEPT AS NOTED

MODERATE TO REGULAR WATER, EXCEPT AS NOTED

Pennisetum setaceum 'Rubrum'

Growing in fountainlike mounds, these are among the most graceful of ornamental grasses. They have long, narrow leaves and arching stems that bear furry, foxtail-like flower plumes in summer, with bloom often extending into fall. Use them in containers, in perennial or shrub borders, as bank covers.

P. alopecuroides. Zones 2b–24. From eastern Asia. To 5 ft. high and wide. Clump of bright green foliage is topped by pinkish plumes. Leaves turn yellow in fall, brown in winter. The following reach about 3 ft. high and wide: 'Hameln' (white plumes), 'Moudry' (black plumes), 'Cassian' (light brown plumes, gold fall foliage with red tints). 'Little Bunny' is a dwarf form growing just 1½ ft. high and wide. The species and its varieties all can self-sow; 'Moudry' is an especially heavy self-seeder.

P. orientale. Zones 3–10, 14–24. From central and western Asia. To 2 ft. high, 2½ ft. wide, with pinkish plumes standing above a mound of green to gray-green foliage. Plumes mature to light brown; foliage turns straw colored in winter. Seldom self-sows.

P. setaceum. Zones 8–24; H1, H2. Often grown as an annual in colder climates. From tropical Africa, southwestern Asia, Arabian Peninsula. To 5 ft. high and wide. Forms a dense clump of medium green foliage; long plumes of coppery pink or purplish flowers are held within the clump or just above it. Dies back in winter, even in mild climates. Full sun. Can take supplemental irrigation but doesn't need any. In arid climates, thrives in gravel beds and other dry sites. Thanks to its heavy self-sowing, this species will threaten to crowd out native vegetation when planted near open country; it has become a rampant pest in the Hawaiian Islands. To prevent seeding, cut off flower plumes before seeds mature. 'Rubrum' ('Cupreum'), with reddish brown leaves and rose-colored plumes that fade to beige, usually does not set seed.

PENNYROYAL. See MENTHA pulegium

PENSTEMON

BEARD TONGUE

Scrophulariaceae

PERENNIALS

ZONES VARY BY SPECIES

PARTIAL SHADE IN HOTTEST CLIMATES

LITTLE TO MODERATE WATER, EXCEPT AS NOTED

Penstemon ×gloxinioides

There are some 250 species of penstemon. Most are native to the West, ranging from Canada into Mexico; some grow on highest mountains, some in the desert, others in forest glades, in foothills, on plains. A few are widely available, but most are sold only by specialists. Some of the perennials described here have woody-based stems, while others are herbaceous. Most species have narrowish, pointed leaves; those in basal foliage clump are larger, those on flower stems smaller. Narrowly bell-shaped, lipped flowers (usually ¾–1½ in. long) are most commonly seen in bright reds and blues, but they also come in shades from soft pink through salmon and peach to deep rose, lilac, dark purple, white, and, rarely, yellow. Blossoms attract hummingbirds.

Need fast drainage. Species in particular benefit from rock garden conditions. Usually short lived (3 or 4 years). Hybrids and selections tend to be easier to grow than wild species alongside regular garden plants;

wild kinds may die quickly if given too-rich soil and too much water. In dry years or with restricted water, however, plants of wild species may thrive.

P. ambiguus. PRAIRIE PENSTEMON, SAND PENSTEMON. Zones 2, 3, 7–15, 18–21. Native to southwestern U.S. Woody-based growth to 2 ft. high and wide. Grayish green, very narrow leaves. White to pink flowers come in broad (rather than tall) clusters that resemble those of phlox. Blooms from early summer to early fall.

P. baccharifolius. ROCK PENSTEMON. Zones 10–13. Native to southern Texas. Woody-based growth to 1½ ft. high and wide. Small, broad, glossy dark green, toothed leaves have a thick, leathery feel. Coral pink flowers bloom all summer.

P. barbatus. Zones 1–20; needs some winter chill for best performance. Native to mountain regions, from Colorado and Utah south to Mexico. Open, somewhat sprawling habit to 3 ft. or more tall, 1½ ft. wide. Bright green foliage. Long, loose spikes of red flowers over a long period, starting at some point from late spring to midsummer. One of the best penstemons for humid-summer areas. Selections include foot-tall 'Elfin Pink', with clear pink flowers; 2½-ft. 'Rose Elf', with deep rose blooms; and 2-ft. 'Schooley's Yellow', with soft lemon yellow flowers.

P. centranthifolius. SCARLET BUGLER. Zones 7–23. Native to Coast Ranges of California. To 2–3 ft. tall, 1½–2 ft. wide, with waxy gray leaves that vary from lance shaped to oval. Long spikes of narrow bright red flowers in spring or early summer.

P. cordifolius. See Keckiella cordifolia

P. davidsonii (P. menziesii davidsonii). Zones 1–7, 14, 15. Native to high mountains of Sierra Nevada and western Nevada, north to British Columbia. Forms a mat 4–8 in. high, 1½ ft. wide. Small dark green leaves; violet-blue flowers in midsummer. Prefers snow cover in winter; without it, hardy only to about –10°F/–23°C. Regular water.

P. digitalis. Zones 1–9, 14–24. Native to eastern and central U.S. To 3–5 ft. tall, 2–3 ft. wide, with long, medium green leaves and clusters of white or pale pink flowers in summer. Tolerates heat and humidity. Regular water. 'Husker Red' grows to 2½–3 ft. tall and has maroon foliage and pinkish white flowers.

P. eatonii. FIRECRACKER PENSTEMON. Zones 1–3, 7–13, 18–21. Native to mountains of desert Southwest. This scarlet-flowered species is similar to *P. centranthifolius.* Grows 1–3 ft. tall and wide and has lance-shaped, leathery green leaves, sometimes with a whitish bloom (but without a waxy coating). Flowers appear on tall spikes in spring to early summer. Tolerates heat.

P. ×gloxinioides. BORDER PENSTEMON, GARDEN PENSTEMON. Perennials in Zones 6–9, 14–24; treated as annuals elsewhere (grow as winter annual in Zones 12, 13). Specific name has no botanical standing but is widely used to refer to this hybrid group. All are compact, bushy, upright plants to 2–4 ft. tall and 3 ft. wide, with narrow green leaves. Large (to 2-in.) summer flowers in loose spikes at stem ends, in almost all colors but blue and yellow. Mass these plants in borders or group with other summer-flowering plants. Where grown as perennials, set out nursery transplants in fall for bloom in late spring and early summer. After the flowers fade, cut back to side growth for another round of bloom in late summer, early fall. This group of penstemons prefers regular water but is subject to root rot in wet, heavy soils.

Among the many hybrids are pale lilac 'Alice Hindley' ('Lady Hindley'); pale pink 'Apple Blossom'; dark maroon 'Blackbird'; 'Evelyn', with rosy pink blooms marked inside with dark pink; scarlet 'Firebird'; wine red 'Garnet'; 'Holly's White', white with pink tinge; and dark purple 'Midnight'. True 'Sour Grapes' has flowers in a combination of violet and metallic blue, but some plants sold under this name may have bright red-violet blooms. The Kissed series features white-throated blooms with lips in various bright colors: 'Cerise Kissed', 'Coral Kissed', 'Violet Kissed', 'Wine Kissed'.

P. grandiflorus. Zones 1–3, 10. Native to the Great Plains. To 3½ ft. tall, 10 in. wide, with gray-green leaves. Large (to 1¾-in.) pink to lavender-blue flowers in summer. 'Prairie Snow' has pure white blooms. Prairie Jewel is a silvery-leafed strain 1½–3 ft. high, bearing flowers in colors ranging from white through rosy pink to lavender and deep purple. The species and its various forms are excellent plants for Rocky Mountain and Great Plains states.

P. heterophyllus. Zones 7–24. California native of variable appearance, with glossy bluish green foliage and crowded spikes of narrow blossoms ranging from reddish purple to deep blue. Blooms in spring and early summer. The following grow 1½–2 ft. high and 2–3 ft. wide: 'Margarita', with sky blue fowers that fade to purple; 'Blue Bedder', with bright blue blossoms; and *P. h. purdyi,* with darker green foliage than the species and rosy lavender to intense blue flowers.

Penstemon heterophyllus purdyi

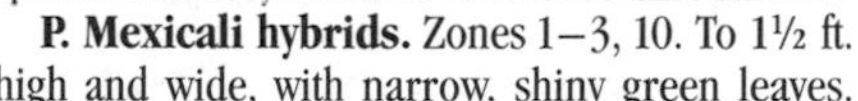

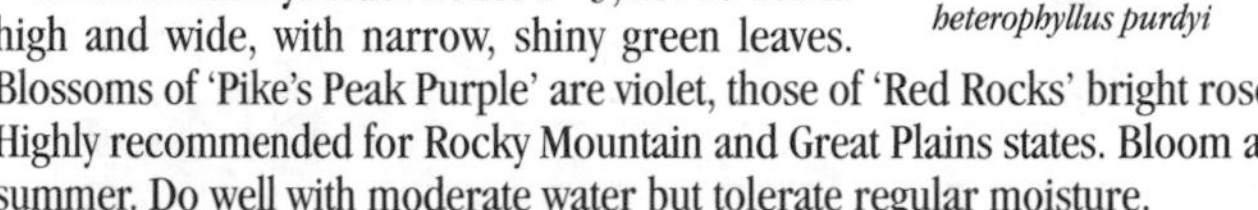

P. Mexicali hybrids. Zones 1–3, 10. To 1½ ft. high and wide, with narrow, shiny green leaves. Blossoms of 'Pike's Peak Purple' are violet, those of 'Red Rocks' bright rose. Highly recommended for Rocky Mountain and Great Plains states. Bloom all summer. Do well with moderate water but tolerate regular moisture.

P. newberryi. MOUNTAIN PRIDE. Zones 1–9, 14–19. Native to higher elevations of the Sierra Nevada. To 1½ ft. high, 3 ft. wide; woody at base. Gray leaves are thick, roundish, tooth-edged, ½–1½ in. long. Rose red, ½-in. flowers in summer. Regular water.

P. palmeri. SCENTED PENSTEMON. Zones 2, 3, 10–13. Native to mountains of desert Southwest. To 4–6 ft. tall and 2–3 ft. wide, with thick grayish leaves. This is among the few scented penstemons, with flower stalks bearing fragrant light pink blossoms in early summer. Will bloom first year from seed. Thrives in hot, dry conditions. Sandy or gravelly soil is essential.

P. parryi. PARRY'S PENSTEMON. Zones 3, 10, 12, 13. Native from Arizona into Mexico. To 2–4 ft. tall, 1–3 ft. wide, with leathery gray-green leaves. Many flower stalks bear reddish pink blossoms in spring. Self-sows.

P. pinifolius. Zones 2–24. Native to southern New Mexico and Arizona. Woody-based growth to 1½ ft. high, 2 ft. wide, with short, needlelike bright green leaves crowded along stems. Red-orange summer flowers. For rock garden, border, small-scale ground cover. Good in dry gardens or regularly watered ones. 'Mersea Yellow', to 1 ft. by 1½ ft., has soft yellow flowers.

P. pseudospectabilis. DESERT BEARD TONGUE. Zones 2, 3, 10, 12–21. Native to mountains of Southern California and Arizona. Shrubby, upright plant 2–4 ft. tall, 2 ft. wide. Large bluish green leaves with bases that clasp the stems. Rosy pink to purple flowers from spring into summer.

P. rupicola. ROCK PENSTEMON. Zones 2–7, 14–17. Native to Cascades and Siskiyou Mountains. Woody-based growth to 4 in. high, 1½ ft. wide, with trailing, much-branched stems. Small, roundish blue-green leaves have finely toothed edges. Bright rose flowers bloom from late spring into summer. Beautiful in rock gardens or chinks in dry stone walls. White-flowered 'Albus' needs partial shade.

P. spectabilis. ROYAL BEARD TONGUE. Zones 7, 14–23. Native to Southern California. To 3–4½ ft. tall and wide, with smooth green or grayish leaves that clasp the stems. Rose-colored to purplish flowers in spring, early summer.

P. strictus. ROCKY MOUNTAIN PENSTEMON. Zones 1–3, 10–13. Native from southern Wyoming to Arizona and New Mexico. To 2–3 ft. tall, 2 ft. wide. Dark green leaves turn purplish in winter. Blooms in early summer, producing large blossoms in near-violet to brilliant bluish purple.

P. superbus. Zones 12, 13. Native to northern Mexico. To 3–4 ft. tall and wide, with gray-green leaves that blacken when they dry out. Deep rose to red flowers in spring or early summer.

PENTAS lanceolata

STAR CLUSTERS

Rubiaceae

PERENNIAL OFTEN GROWN AS ANNUAL

ZONES 23, 24; H1, H2; ANYWHERE AS ANNUAL

FULL SUN

REGULAR WATER

Pentas lanceolata

Woody-based perennial from tropical Africa. In Hawaii, it grows as large as 6 ft. tall, 3 ft. wide; elsewhere, it reaches 2–3 ft. high and wide. Stems are topped by tight, 4-in.-wide

P

clusters of small, star-shaped flowers in white, pink, lilac, or red. As a perennial, it provides nearly year-round color; as an annual, it blooms in summer. Good cut flowers. Green, somewhat hairy leaves are pointed ovals to 6 in. long. Prune plant heavily each year before spring growth begins to keep it compact and encourage flowering. Deadhead regularly for more blooms. Can be used as a houseplant; set in a bright west- or south-facing window.

PEONY. See PAEONIA

PEPINO. See SOLANUM muricatum

PEPPER

Solanaceae

ANNUAL

ALL ZONES

FULL SUN

REGULAR WATER

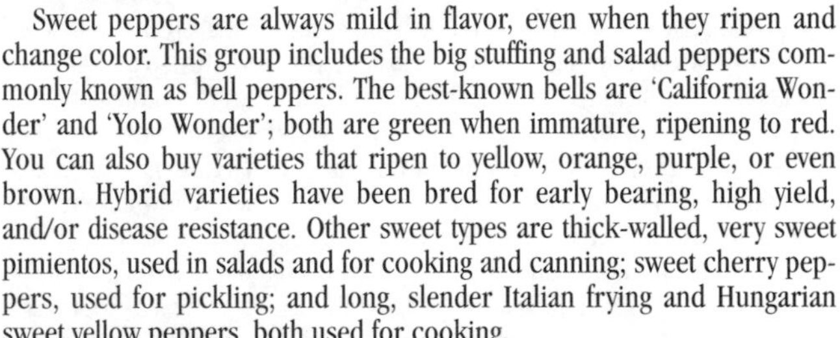
Bell Pepper

The peppers grown in vegetable gardens originated in tropical America and are known botanically as *Capsicum annuum.* They grow on attractive, bushy plants ranging from less than a foot high to 4 ft. tall, depending on variety. The two basic kinds of peppers are sweet and hot.

Sweet peppers are always mild in flavor, even when they ripen and change color. This group includes the big stuffing and salad peppers commonly known as bell peppers. The best-known bells are 'California Wonder' and 'Yolo Wonder'; both are green when immature, ripening to red. You can also buy varieties that ripen to yellow, orange, purple, or even brown. Hybrid varieties have been bred for early bearing, high yield, and/or disease resistance. Other sweet types are thick-walled, very sweet pimientos, used in salads and for cooking and canning; sweet cherry peppers, used for pickling; and long, slender Italian frying and Hungarian sweet yellow peppers, both used for cooking.

Hot peppers vary from pea-size types to narrow, 6–7-in.-long forms, but all are pungent, ranging from mildly hot Italian peperoncini to near-incandescent hot 'Habañero'. 'Anaheim' is a mildly spicy pepper used for making canned green chiles. 'Long Red Cayenne' is used for drying. 'Hungarian Yellow Wax (Hot)', 'Jalapeño', and 'Fresno Chile Grande' are used for pickling. Mexican cooking utilizes a wide variety of hot peppers, among them 'Ancho', 'Mulato', and 'Pasilla'.

Hot Pepper
'Long Red Cayenne'

Peppers need a long, warm growing season, and in most areas they must be planted outdoors as seedlings in order to produce fruit. To grow them successfully in regions with cool or short summers, use floating row covers and clear plastic mulches to extend the season. Buy nursery plants or sow seed indoors 8 to 10 weeks before the average last-frost date. When soil is thoroughly warm and night temperatures remain consistently above 55°F/13°C, set transplants outdoors, spacing them 1½–2 ft. apart. After plants are established (but before blossoms set), fertilize once or twice.

Allow 60 to 95 days from setting out plants to harvest. Sweet peppers are ready to pick when they have reached good size. Pimientos should be picked only when red-ripe, but the other types can be picked green or ripe (flavor typically becomes sweeter as fruit ripens). Pick hot peppers when they reach full size; harvest them still green, or wait until they turn yellow or red for a richer flavor. To harvest any pepper, snip the stem with hand pruners or scissors. Possible pests include aphids, whiteflies, and cutworms. To control pepper weevils (both the larvae and the long-snouted adults attack fruit), destroy plants after harvest.

PEPPERMINT. See MENTHA × piperita

PEPPERMINT TREE. See AGONIS flexuosa

PEPPER TREE. See SCHINUS

PEPPERWOOD. See UMBELLULARIA californica

PERICALLIS × hybrida. See SENECIO × hybridus

PERILLA frutescens

SHISO

Lamiaceae (Labiatae)

ANNUAL

ALL ZONES

FULL SUN OR LIGHT SHADE

REGULAR WATER

Perilla frutescens

Native from the Himalayas to eastern Asia. Sturdy, leafy warm-weather plant grows very quickly to 2–3 ft. tall, 1 ft. wide. Broadly ovate, deeply toothed leaves reach 5 in. long. The kind most commonly seen has bronzy or purple leaves that look much like those of coleus. Fancy Fringe strain has deeply cut and fringed leaves in deep bronzy purple.

Shiso makes an attractive addition to summer borders, but various parts of the plant are also edible. Use leaves as a vegetable or flavoring (they taste something like mint, something like cinnamon); fry the long, thin clusters of flower buds in tempura batter and serve as a vegetable. In Asia, the seeds are pressed for edible oil. Extremely easy to grow; self-sows freely.

PERIWINKLE. See CATHARANTHUS roseus, VINCA

PERNETTYA mucronata (Gaultheria mucronata)

Ericaceae

EVERGREEN SHRUB

ZONES 4–7, 15–17

PARTIAL SHADE IN HOTTEST CLIMATES

REGULAR WATER

Pernettya mucronata

From Chile, Argentina. Compact plant to 2–3 ft. tall, spreading by underground runners to form a 4-ft.-wide clump. Small leaves are glossy dark green; some turn red or bronzy in winter. Tiny, bell-shaped white to pink flowers in late spring are followed by colorful, long-lasting berries in purple, white, red, rose, pink, or near-black, all with a metallic sheen. You'll get more fruit if several plants are grown together to ensure cross-pollination. Grow in moist, acid, well-aerated soil liberally amended with organic matter. Can be invasive; control by trimming roots with a spade. To keep plant compact and attractive, regularly thin it and head it back. Use as informal low hedge or border; plant in tubs or large window boxes.

PEROVSKIA

RUSSIAN SAGE

Lamiaceae (Labiatae)

SHRUBBY PERENNIAL

ZONES 2–24

FULL SUN

LITTLE TO MODERATE WATER

Perovskia 'Blue Spire'

Native to western and central Asia. Woody-based clump with many grayish white, upright-growing stems clothed in gray-green foliage. Leaves on lower part of stem are 2–3 in. long and deeply cut; those toward stem tip are smaller and merely toothed. In late spring and summer, stems are topped with widely branched sprays of small lavender-blue flowers that seem to form a soft haze above the foliage. To extend the bloom season, trim off spent blossoms. Mature clumps may reach 3–4 ft. tall and wide; they often colonize, spreading by underground stems to send up new clumps.

Russian sage is typically marketed as *P. atriplicifolia,* but most plants sold are probably hybrids between *P. atriplicifolia* and *P. abrotanoides.* Widely grown 'Blue Spire', with deep violet blooms, is sometimes sold as *P. atriplicifolia* 'Superba' or *P.* 'Longin'. For lighter blue flowers, grow 'Blue Mist' or 'Blue Haze'. 'Filagran' has silvery, very finely cut leaves. Mass plants or use them individually in borders. Takes any soil as long as drainage is good. Extremely resistant to heat and drought. Performs best in warm summers. Cut nearly to the ground each spring before new growth starts.

PERSEA thunbergii (Machilus thunbergii)

Lauraceae

EVERGREEN TREE

ZONES 8, 9, 14–24

FULL SUN

REGULAR WATER

Persea thunbergii

From Japan, China, and Korea. Related to camphor tree *(Cinnamomum)* and avocado, this large tree grows fairly fast to 60–80 ft. tall, 40–60 ft. wide. Thick, glossy leaves are deep green above, paler beneath, to 6 in. long, 2½ in. wide. Tiny yellowish flowers bloom in spring; these are followed in summer by round, blackish purple fruits less than ½ in. wide. A promising tree for parks, streets, or large gardens.

PERSIAN VIOLET. See EXACUM affine

PERSICARIA

KNOTWEED

Polygonaceae

PERENNIALS

ZONES VARY BY SPECIES

FULL SUN OR PARTIAL SHADE

REGULAR WATER, EXCEPT AS NOTED

Persicaria virginiana 'Painter's Palette'

Sturdy plants with jointed stems and small white or pink flowers. Some kinds tend to get out of hand and need to be controlled.

P. affinis (Polygonum affine). Zones 1–9, 14–17. Himalayan native. Spreading plant to 1 ft. high, 2 ft. or more wide. Deep green, lance-shaped, finely tooth-edged leaves are mostly basal; they grow 2–4½ in. long, turn bronze in winter. Dense, erect, 2–3-in. spikes of bright rosy red flowers bloom in summer, early fall. Informal border or ground cover. 'Darjeeling Red' forms 3-in.-high foliage mats, has 10-in. spikes of deep pink flowers that age to red; its foliage turns red in fall. 'Superba' ('Dimity') has pale pink flowers and larger leaves than the species.

P. amplexicaulis (Polygonum amplexicaule). Zones 2b–9, 14–24. Himalayan native. Forms a big clump—to 4 ft. tall and wide when plants are in flower. Medium green leaves are pointed ovals up to 10 in. long. Blooms profusely from midsummer to fall, bearing narrow, 4-in. blossom spikes similar to those of lavender but in a wider range of colors—pink, purple, red, white.

P. bistorta (Polygonum bistorta). Zones 2–9, 14–24. Native to Eurasia. Makes a clump to 2½ ft. tall, 3 ft. wide, with broadly oval, medium green, 4–12-in.-long leaves. Tight, 2–3-in. spikes of pale pink or white flowers bloom from late spring until well into summer. 'Superba' is a good pink selection.

P. capitata (Polygonum capitatum). Perennial in Zones 8, 9, 12–24; annual in colder climates. Himalayan native. Tough, trailing ground cover 3–6 in. high; spreads indefinitely both by rooting stems and by self-seeding. Oval, 1½-in.-long leaves are dark green when new, take on pinkish overtones when mature. Leaves of all ages have a bronzy cast that deepens in cooler weather; they discolor and die below 28°F/–2°C. Stems and small, round flower heads are pink. Blooms almost all year in mild climates. Best in confined spots (where it won't be able to spread) or in uncultivated areas. No irrigation needed.

P. vacciniifolia (Polygonum vacciniifolium). Zones 4–7, 15–17. Himalayan native. Prostrate plant forms a foliage mat to 3 in. high, trailing to 2 ft. or wider. Slender, branching, reddish stems are clothed in oval, ½-in.-long, shiny green leaves that turn red in fall. In late summer, 6–9-in. flower stalks bear dense, upright, foxtail-like, 2–3-in. spikes of rose pink blossoms. Excellent as a bank cover or for draping over a boulder in a large rock garden.

P. virginiana (Polygonum virginianum, Tovara virginiana). Zones 2–9, 14–17. Native to eastern North America, eastern Asia. To 2–4 ft. tall, spreading indefinitely by creeping rhizomes. Oval green leaves 3–10 in. long; insignificant flowers. The species is rarely found in gardens. More commonly seen is 'Painter's Palette', valued for its flashy foliage: leaves are marbled in green, pale gray green, and ivory, with a ragged chocolate maroon V in the center. On new growth, the ivory patches are closer to yellow, and the central V-shaped mark has a pink cast.

PERSIMMON

Ebenaceae

DECIDUOUS FRUIT TREES

ZONES VARY BY SPECIES

FULL SUN

WATER NEEDS VARY BY SPECIES

Persimmon

Two kinds of persimmons are grown in the West. The native American species is a bigger, more cold-tolerant tree than the Asian species, but the Asian type bears larger fruit (the sort sold in markets). Both species have inconspicuous flowers, and both are tolerant of many soils (as long as drainage is good) and resistant to oak root fungus.

Japanese or Oriental persimmon *(Diospyros kaki)* grows and fruits best in Zones 6–9, 14–16, 18–24, H1 (fruiting may be inconsistent in Hawaii—does best in dry highlands). It reaches 30 ft. tall (or more) and at least as wide. Has a handsome branch pattern and is one of the best fruit trees for ornamental use; makes a good small shade tree and is suitable for espalier. Leaves are light green when new, maturing to dark green, leathery ovals 6–7 in. long. Foliage turns vivid yellow, orange, or red in fall (even in mild climates). After leaves drop, brilliant orange-scarlet, 3–4-in. fruits brighten the tree for weeks and persist until winter unless harvested. Sets fruit without pollination, though pollinated trees often produce tastier, more abundant crops.

Prune trees when they are young to establish a good framework; thereafter, prune only to remove dead wood, shape the tree, or open up a too dense interior. Remove any suckers that shoot up from below the graft line.

Fruit drop is a common problem in young trees. To avoid it, water regularly and feed once in late winter or early spring; too little or inconsistent moisture causes fruit drop, as does overfertilizing (too much fertilizer also causes excessive growth).

Some Japanese persimmon varieties are astringent until soft-ripe—at which stage they become very sweet. To save the crop from birds, pick fruit when fully colored but still hard, then let it ripen off the tree. Eat when the flesh is mushy and puddinglike. Nonastringent varieties are hard (like apples) when ripe, with a mildly sweet flavor; they can be eaten hard, but their flavor improves when they are allowed to soften slightly off the tree.

'Chocolate'. Nonastringent. Medium-size, acorn-shaped fruit. When pollinated, has seeded flesh with dark streaks; when unpollinated, has seedless yellow-orange flesh. Fruit from pollinated trees has best flavor. ▸

'Fuyu'. Nonastringent. Firm fleshed; about the size of a baseball but flattened like a tomato. Favorite variety in Hawaii. Similar but larger is 'Gosho', widely sold as 'Giant Fuyu'.

'Hachiya'. Astringent. Big, slightly pointed fruit. Very shapely tree for ornamental use.

'Izu'. Nonastringent. Medium-size, round fruit borne on a tree about half the standard size. Ripens early.

'Tamopan'. Astringent. Large, acorn-shaped fruit.

American persimmon *(Diospyros virginiana),* native to the eastern U.S., grows best in Zones 3–9, 14–16, 18–23. Can grow to 15–30 ft. high and about as wide, with attractive gray-brown bark that is fissured in a checkered pattern. Glossy green, broadly oval leaves to 6 in. long turn yellow, pink, or reddish purple in fall. Round, 1½–2-in.-wide fruit is yellow to orange (often blushed red); very astringent until soft-ripe, then very sweet. On wild species, fruit ripens in early fall after frost; some varieties do not require winter chill. Both male and female trees are usually needed to get fruit. 'Meader' is self-fruitful; its fruit is seedless if not pollinated. 'Early Golden' has more flavorful fruit; it needs cross-pollination for best crop. Trees usually need pruning only to remove broken or dead branches. Does best with regular moisture but will also perform well with moderate water.

PERUVIAN DAFFODIL. See HYMENOCALLIS narcissiflora

PETALOSTEMON purpureum

PURPLE PRAIRIE CLOVER
Fabaceae (Leguminosae)
PERENNIAL
ZONES 1-3, 10-12
FULL SUN
LITTLE TO MODERATE WATER

Petalostemon purpureum

Native from Saskatchewan to Texas. Attractive perennial for the wild garden. To 1½ ft. high and wide, with many rigid, outward-leaning stems covered with dark green leaves. In summer, stems are tipped with tight heads of small reddish purple flowers. Deep roots supply fertility to the soil through nitrogen-fixing bacteria. This is a tough plant, well suited to the extremes of its native prairies and plains. Tolerates any soil. Botanists are divided as to its exact classification; many include it in the genus *Dalea* and identify it as *D. gattingeri.*

PETASITES japonicus

JAPANESE COLTSFOOT, FUKI
Asteraceae (Compositae)
PERENNIAL
ZONES 2B-9, 14-17
FULL SUN IN COOLER CLIMATES ONLY
AMPLE WATER

Petasites japonicus

Giant perennial for perpetually moist locales near ponds, streams. Creeping rhizomes give rise to big (2½-ft.-wide), round leaves on edible, 3-ft.-long stalks that are used by the Japanese as a vegetable (called fuki). Short, thick spikes of fragrant white daisies appear in early spring before the leaves emerge. Locate this plant with care; its thick rhizomes are invasive, and the plant can be difficult to eradicate. *P. j. giganteus* has leaves to 4 ft. wide on 5-ft. stalks. Its selection 'Variegatus', with 3–4-ft. stalks, has 2–3-ft.-wide leaves with bold white markings.

FOR INFORMATION ON YOUR CLIMATE ZONE
PLEASE SEE PAGES 27–63

PETREA volubilis

QUEEN'S WREATH, SANDPAPER VINE
Verbenaceae
EVERGREEN VINE
ZONES 19–24; H1, H2
FULL SUN
REGULAR WATER

Petrea volubilis

Woody vine native to Mexico, Central America, and the West Indies. Twines to 20–40 ft. but can easily be kept smaller. Elliptical deep green leaves 8 in. long have a sandpapery surface. Stunning floral display: pendent, foot-long clusters of star-shaped, blue-purple, 1½-in.-wide blossoms. Blue calyxes hang on after the petals drop. Main bloom period comes in winter and spring in Hawaii, in late spring and summer in California; lesser displays occur at other times during warm weather.

Beautiful plant trained on arbor or pergola, along eaves, on a high wall. Flowers are sometimes used in leis. Grow this vine in organically enriched, moist but well-drained soil. Provide support for climbing stems. Prune and thin growth as needed in winter. Wind resistant. Frost sensitive; may need some protection in Zones 19–22.

PETROSELINUM crispum

PARSLEY
Apiaceae (Umbelliferae)
BIENNIAL GROWN AS ANNUAL
ZONES A3; 1–24
AFTERNOON SHADE IN HOTTEST CLIMATES
REGULAR WATER

Petroselinum crispum

From southern Europe. Two kinds of parsley are grown, both with finely cut dark green foliage: flat-leafed Italian parsley and curly-leafed French parsley. Leaves are used as a seasoning (both fresh and dried); fresh sprigs and minced leaves are classic garnishes. Flat-leafed parsley grows to 2–3 ft. tall and 2 ft. wide; it is considered more flavorful than curly parsley, which grows to 6–12 in. high and wide and makes a more attractive garnish.

Parsley is best started fresh each year, either from nursery transplants or seed. Set out small plants or sow seed in place—in spring after average last-frost date in cold-winter climates; in fall or early spring where winters are mild; in early fall in low desert. Soak seeds in warm water for 24 hours before planting. (Even after soaking, they may not come up for several weeks; according to an old story, parsley seeds must go to the devil and back before sprouting.) Thin seedlings to 1–1½ ft. apart for flat-leafed parsley, 6–8 in. apart for curly parsley; or space plants at these distances. Attractive edging for herb, vegetable, or flower garden; good in window boxes and pots.

PETUNIA × hybrida

PETUNIA
Solanaceae
PERENNIAL GROWN AS ANNUAL
ALL ZONES
FULL SUN
REGULAR WATER

Petunia × hybrida

Low-growing, bushy to spreading plants with thick, broad leaves that are slightly sticky to the touch. Flowers vary from funnel-shaped single blooms to densely double, heavily ruffled ones (like carnations). The many colors available include pure white, cream, yellow, and the whole range of reds and blues: from soft pink to deepest red, light blue to deepest purple. Bicolors and picotees are also available, as are types that have contrasting veins on the petals and kinds with fluted or fringed edges. In most climate zones, plants bloom throughout summer until frost. In Zones 12 and 13, summer heat kills them; in these areas, grow them for winter and spring color.

Plant in good garden soil. Single-flowered kinds are not particular about soil quality and will tolerate alkalinity, but they must have good drainage. Set 8–18 in. apart, depending on plant size. After plants are established, pinch back halfway for compact growth. Feed monthly with complete fertilizer. Near the end of the main bloom period, cut back rangy plants by half to force new growth. In humid weather, botrytis disease can damage blossoms and foliage of most petunias; Multifloras are somewhat resistant to this disease. Smog damage (spotting on seedling leaves) and geranium (tobacco) budworm (flowers look tattered or fail to open) may be problems in some areas.

Listed below are the various kinds of petunias sold. Grandiflora and Multiflora are older classes that have been popular for a number of years. Great advances in petunia breeding have produced new types and strains, some strikingly different from the older sorts. (The new small-flowered plant sold under the name "million bells" is closely related to petunia and is even considered a petunia by some botanists; see *Calibrachoa*.) Some petunias may be labeled F_1, meaning they are first-generation hybrids. These are more vigorous and uniform in color, height, and growth habit than their offspring, F_2 hybrids.

Hybrid Grandiflora. These hybrid plants bear the largest flowers of all petunia classes but bloom the least profusely. Sturdy plants grow 15–27 in. high, 2–3 ft. across. Flowers are usually single, to 4½ in. across, with ruffled or fringed edges; colors include pink, rose, salmon, red, scarlet, blue, white, pale yellow, and striped combinations.

Fluffy Ruffles strain has the largest blossoms, growing to 6 in. across. Cascade, Countdown, and Supercascade series plants have a trailing habit that makes them good selections for hanging baskets. Magic and Supermagic are compact, heavy-blooming plants bearing large (4–5-in.) single flowers in white, pink, red, blue. Newer strains include weather-tolerant Storm, compact Ultra, cascading Cloud, and Hula Hoop and Frost (both with white-rimmed blossoms). 'Prism Sunshine' is a much-improved yellow. Double Hybrid Grandifloras have heavily ruffled flowers that come in all petunia colors except yellow.

Hybrid Multiflora. This hybrid group is sometimes called Floribunda. Plants are about the same size as Grandifloras, but flowers are single or double, generally smooth edged, and smaller (to 2 in. across). Neat, compact growth makes them ideal for bedding, massing. Many named varieties in pink, rose, salmon, yellow, white, blue. Joy and Plum strains have single, satiny-textured flowers in white, cream, pink, coral, red, blue. 'Summer Sun' has single bright yellow blooms. Celebrity and Prime Time are newer strains with single flowers somewhat larger than those of the typical Hybrid Multiflora.

Hybrid Milliflora. These dwarf petunias form mounds 6–8 in. high and wide; they need no pinching or pruning. Plants cover themselves with small (1–1½-in.) flowers that come in all petunia colors except yellow. Effective planted in groups of a single color; very attractive in containers, hanging baskets, window boxes.

Trailing Petunias. These low, wide-spreading plants are used as ground covers and in tubs, window boxes, hanging baskets. There are seed-grown and cutting-grown types. Plants in the seed-grown Wave series cover themselves with 2½–3-in. flowers in pink, lilac, rose, and purple; among purple choices is the remarkably vigorous 'Purple Wave', the first member of the series. All color selections are fast growers to 6 in. high, spreading to more than 5 ft. across.

The following cutting-grown types grow slightly lower than the Wave series and spread to 4 ft. wide. Surfinias have 1½-in. flowers in pink, violet, purple, blue, or white. Cascadias are very similar to Surfinias but come in more than a dozen colors, including white and various pink, purple, and blue shades. Supertunias have 2½-in. flowers in shades of pink, violet, and purple. Petitunias bear profuse ¾-in. blossoms in colors including pink, purple, and white with darker veins.

PHACELIA campanularia

CALIFORNIA DESERT BLUEBELLS
Hydrophyllaceae
ANNUAL
ZONES 1–3, 7–24
FULL SUN
LITTLE TO MODERATE WATER

Phacelia campanularia

Native to California deserts. To 6–18 in. high and wide, with coarsely toothed gray-green leaves. Clusters of 1-in., bell-shaped deep blue flowers in spring. Takes most well-drained soils. Sow in ground in fall or earliest spring; or sow in pots and transplant while seedlings are very small. Give some water to extend bloom season.

PHAEDRANTHUS buccinatorius. **See DISTICTIS buccinatoria**

PHALAENOPSIS

MOTH ORCHID
Orchidaceae
EPIPHYTIC ORCHIDS
ZONE H2; OR INDOORS
FILTERED SUN; BRIGHT INDIRECT LIGHT
REGULAR WATER

Phalaenopsis

These are tropical orchids with thick, broad, leathery leaves and no pseudobulbs. Leaves are rather flat, to 1 ft. long. From spring to fall, plants bear long (to 3-ft.) sprays of 3–6-in.-wide flowers in white, cream, pale yellow, or light lavender pink; some are spotted or barred or have lips in a contrasting color. Many lovely hybrids are sold. Very popular orchid commercially.

Beyond the tropics, moth orchids are more for advanced amateur orchid growers than for beginners. They are usually greenhouse plants, since they need fairly high humidity and warmer growing conditions than most orchids (minimum of 60 to 65°F/16 to 18°C at night, 70 to 85°F/21 to 29°C during the day). In the house, a good location is near bathroom or kitchen window with light coming through a gauze or other sheer curtain (foliage burns easily in direct sun). Some smaller-flowered new hybrids give promise of being easier to grow, tolerating somewhat lower night temperatures. Give moth orchids same potting medium as cattleya (see Orchidaceae). When cutting flowers, cut back to just above one of the tiny bracts on the stem; secondary sprays may form. To promote stronger new growth, many growers prefer to cut out the entire stem after blossoms fade.

PHALARIS arundinacea picta

RIBBON GRASS, GARDENER'S GARTERS
Poaceae (Gramineae)
PERENNIAL GRASS
ZONES A1–A3; 1–10, 14–24
FULL SUN OR PARTIAL SHADE
REGULAR WATER

Phalaris arundinacea picta

Native to North America, Eurasia. Tough, tenacious grass; forms a 2–3-ft.-high clump that spreads aggressively—and indefinitely—by underground runners. Leaves are deep green with longitudinal white stripes, turn buff colored in autumn. Airy flower clusters are white, aging to pale brown. To keep this plant in-bounds, grow it in large containers or use same control methods as for running kinds of bamboo (see Bamboo). Less invasive selections are 'Woods Dwarf' ('Dwarf Garters'), about half as tall as the species and with brighter white striping; and 'Feesey' ('Strawberries and Cream'), to 1½–2 ft. tall, with white stripes that usually take on pink tints during cool weather.

PHASEOLUS. See BEAN

PHASEOLUS caracalla. See VIGNA caracalla

PHILADELPHUS

MOCK ORANGE

Hydrangeaceae (Philadelphaceae)

DECIDUOUS AND EVERGREEN SHRUBS

ZONES VARY BY SPECIES

PARTIAL SHADE IN HOTTEST CLIMATES

MODERATE TO REGULAR WATER

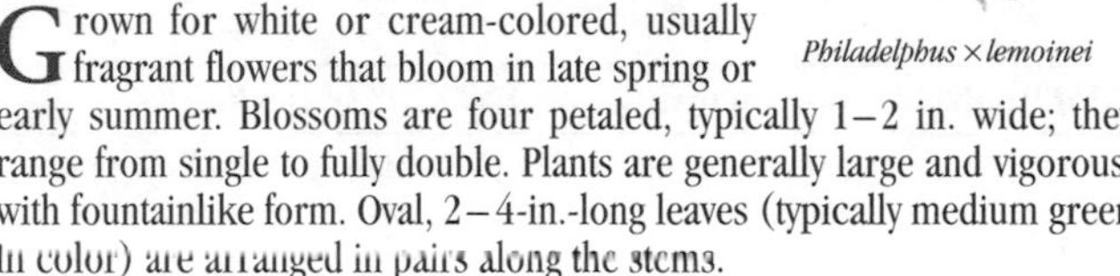

Philadelphus × lemoinei

Grown for white or cream-colored, usually fragrant flowers that bloom in late spring or early summer. Blossoms are four petaled, typically 1–2 in. wide; they range from single to fully double. Plants are generally large and vigorous, with fountainlike form. Oval, 2–4-in.-long leaves (typically medium green in color) are arranged in pairs along the stems.

Prune every year just after bloom, cutting out oldest wood and surplus shoots at base. To rejuvenate, cut to the ground. Taller types are striking planted in lawns and as background and corner plantings; smaller kinds can be planted near foundations or used as low screens or informal hedges. Buy this plant in bloom to check for best fragrance. Not fussy about soil type but must have good drainage.

P. 'Buckley's Quill'. Deciduous. Zones 3–17. Dense, compact grower to 4–5 ft. tall and wide, with clusters of 1-in. double flowers. Petals are narrow and pointed.

P. coronarius. SWEET MOCK ORANGE. Deciduous. Zones A1–A3; 1a, 2–24. From southern Europe, Caucasus. Strong-growing old favorite to 10–12 ft. tall and wide. Clusters of especially fragrant, 1½-in. flowers. 'Aureus', to 8 ft. high, has bright golden foliage that turns yellow green in summer.

P. gordonianus. See P. lewisii

P. × lemoinei. Deciduous. Zones 2b–17. Group of hybrids, most to 5–6 ft. high and wide. All bear clusters of particularly fragrant, 1-in. flowers. Double-flowered 'Enchantment' is a well-known selection.

P. lewisii. WILD MOCK ORANGE. Deciduous. Zones 1–10, 14–24. Native to western North America; the state flower of Idaho. Fountain-shaped, loosely branched shrub 4–10 ft. tall, typically broader than high (tall race from west of the Cascades is often called *P. gordonianus*). Satiny single flowers to 2 in. across. Tolerates some aridity. 'Goose Creek' is a double-flowered selection.

P. mexicanus. EVERGREEN MOCK ORANGE. Zones 8, 9, 14–24. From Mexico. Vining shrub has long, supple stems clothed with evergreen leaves. Creamy white, 1½-in. flowers in small clusters may bloom sporadically throughout year. Can be kept to 6 ft. high and wide as a free-standing shrub. It is best used, however, as a vine or bank cover; can climb 15–20 ft. if given support.

P. microphyllus. Deciduous. Zones 1–3, 7, 10, 14–16, 18. From southwestern U.S., Mexico. To 4–5 ft. tall and wide (often smaller), with small (¾–1½-in.-long) leaves. Extremely fragrant, inch-wide flowers are borne singly or in pairs. Endures some drought.

P. × purpureomaculatus. Deciduous. Zones 2–17. This group of hybrids includes the ever-popular 'Belle Etoile', a compact shrub that grows to 5 ft. tall and 8 ft. wide. This selection bears fringed, purple-centered single flowers to 2½ in. across. Sometimes sold as *P. × lemoinei* 'Belle Etoile'.

P. × virginalis. Deciduous. Zones A3; 1a, 2–17. A hybrid that has produced several garden varieties, most with fragrant double flowers. Large varieties (6–8 ft. high and wide) include 'Minnesota Snowflake' (reputedly hardy to –30°F/–34°C) and 'Virginal', both with 2-in. double flowers; and 'Natchez', with 2-in. single flowers. Lower-growing kinds include 'Glacier' (5 ft. high and wide), with 1¼-in. double blossoms; and 'Dwarf Minnesota Snowflake' ('Dwarf Snowflake', 'Miniature Snowflake'), 3–4 ft. high and wide, with 1–1½-in. double flowers.

PHILODENDRON

Araceae

EVERGREEN VINES AND SHRUBS

ZONES VARY BY TYPE; OR INDOORS

EXPOSURE NEEDS VARY BY TYPE; BRIGHT INDIRECT LIGHT

REGULAR WATER

Philodendron erubescens

From tropical America. Tough, fast-growing plants favored for attractive, leathery, usually glossy leaves. In good conditions, old plants may bloom; the blossoms resemble those of calla *(Zantedeschia)*, with a boatlike bract surrounding a club-shaped structure. Bracts are usually greenish, white, or reddish.

Whether grown in containers or open ground, all philodendrons need rich, loose, well-drained soil. Feed lightly and frequently for good growth and color. Clean dust from leaves of indoor plants. Most philodendrons—especially those grown in containers—tend to drop their lower leaves, leaving a bare stem. Once a plant gets gangly and overgrown, the best course is often simply to discard it and replace it with a new plant. However, you can also cut the plant back to short stub, then let it regrow; or you can air-layer the leafy top, then plant the layer once it roots (and discard the parent). Some philodendrons send down aerial roots. Push these into soil or cut them off (removing them won't hurt plant).

Philodendrons fall into two main classes.

Arborescent; relatively hardy. These are large, shrub-size plants with big leaves and sturdy, self-supporting trunks. They can be grown indoors but need much more space than most houseplants. They grow outdoors in Zones 8, 9, 12–24, H1, H2. As landscape plants, they do best in sun (some shade at midday where light is intense) but can take considerable shade. Use them for tropical effects or as massive silhouettes against walls or glass. Excellent in large containers; effective near swimming pools.

Vining and self-heading; tender. This class includes tender plants of two different habits. They can grow outdoors in Zone H2, where they require partial or full shade; elsewhere, they are houseplants. Many kinds are sold, with many different leaf shapes and sizes. Vining types do not really climb and must be tied to or leaned against a support until they eventually shape themselves to it. The support can be almost anything, but certain water-absorbent columns (sections of tree fern stem, wire and sphagnum "totem poles," slabs of bark) serve especially well, since they can be kept moist. Self-heading types form short, broad plants with leaves radiating out from a central point.

The following list indicates the class of each species and variety. Note that one popular "philodendron"—the so-called split-leaf philodendron—belongs to another genus, *Monstera.*

P. bipinnatifidum (P. selloum). Arborescent. Treelike shrub to 6–15 ft. high and wide, typically with a single, upright trunk that leans with age. Deeply cut leaves to 3 ft. long, on equally long stalks.

P. cordatum. See P. scandens oxycardium

P. erubescens. Vining. Often sold as *P.* 'Hastatum'. To 10–20 ft. high, with foot-long, arrow-shaped deep green leaves. Subject to leaf spot in overly warm, moist conditions. A number of selections and hybrids are available; they are more resistant to leaf spot and tend to be more compact. Some have much red in new foliage and in leafstalks. 'Royal Queen' has bright red new growth; mature leaves are dark green heavily tinged with red. 'Emerald Queen' is a choice deep green form.

Philodendron scandens oxycardium

P. 'Lynette'. Self-heading. To 1 ft. high, 2 ft. wide. Makes tight cluster of foot-long, broadish, bright green leaves that are strongly patterned by deeply sunken veins. Good tabletop plant.

P. oxycardium. See P. scandens oxycardium

P. pertusum. See Monstera deliciosa

P. scandens. Vining. Among the most common philodendrons. Can reach 50 ft. Deep green, heart-shaped leaves; juvenile leaves are 4–6 in. long, while mature ones reach 1 ft. long. *P. s. micans* has velvety young leaves; mature leaves are smooth. *P. s. oxycardium* (often sold as *P. oxycardium* or *P. cordatum*) has glossy leaves throughout its life. Juvenile forms of both are most popular; they are grown on tree trunks, in hanging baskets and window boxes, as houseplants. Indoors, train them on string or wire for a variety of decorative effects; or grow on moisture-retentive columns.

P. wendlandii. Self-heading. To 1 ft. high, 2 ft. wide. Compact clusters of 12 or more deep green, foot-long, broadly lance-shaped leaves on short, broad stalks. Indoors, this species is useful where a tough, compact foliage plant is needed. *P.* 'Lynette' is similar.

PHLOMIS

Lamiaceae (Labiatae)

PERENNIALS AND EVERGREEN SHRUBS

ZONES VARY BY SPECIES

FULL SUN

LITTLE TO MODERATE WATER

Phlomis fruticosa

Mediterranean natives. Erect stems are set with widely spaced whorls of hooded, two-lipped flowers in yellow, purple, or lilac. Moisture-conserving thick, typically furry or hairy leaves are lance shaped to oval, set opposite each other on stems. Not particular about soil but must have good drainage. Need little water where summers are cool; in hot-summer regions, give them more moisture. Cut flowers are striking in mixed arrangements; blooming stems dry well for winter bouquets.

P. 'Edward Bowles' ('Grande Verde', 'Lemon Swirl'). Shrub. Zones 3b–24. To 3–4 ft. tall, 5–6 ft. wide. Hybrid between *P. fruticosa* and *P. russeliana.* Resembles a bulkier *P. fruticosa* and has broader leaves (to 6 in. long, 3 in. wide) and larger, pure yellow flowers. Often sold as *P. fruticosa* and takes the same care.

P. fruticosa. JERUSALEM SAGE. Shrub. Zones 3b–24. To 4 ft. tall and wide, with woolly gray-green leaves to 6–8 in. long, 1¼ in. wide. Deep golden yellow, 1-in. flowers in ball-shaped whorls along upper half of stems. Cut plants back by half in fall to keep them compact. With watering, will produce several waves of bloom in spring and summer if cut back lightly after each flowering. Can tolerate light shade for part of day. Resistant to oak root fungus.

P. italica. Shrub. Zones 5–24. Arching, suckering habit to 3–4 ft. tall, 5–6 ft. or more wide. Gray-green, 2–3-in.-long leaves are covered with silvery wool. Lilac-pink flowers in 1-in. whorls from early to midsummer. To keep plant neat, remove faded flowering stems; cut out basal branches that are more than 3 years old.

P. lanata. Shrub. Zones 7–24. Dense, compact plant to 2½ ft. tall, 4–6 ft. wide. Woolly, wrinkled, 1-in., sage green leaves. Stems and leaf undersides have brownish scales. Whorls of 1-in., deep yellow flowers bloom from spring to fall if faded stems are cut out.

P. purpurea. Shrub. Zones 7–24. Rather lax habit to 4–6 ft. high and wide. Lance-shaped leaves to 4 in. long are gray green and sparsely hairy above, white and woolly beneath; new shoots are also white and woolly. Purplish pink flowers bloom mainly in late spring, but scattered blossoms appear all year long where winters are mild. After each flowering, cut plant back by one-third to keep it neat and compact.

P. russeliana. Perennial. Zones 2–24. Spreads by rhizomes to make a low clump of furry olive green foliage. Leaves are large (to 8 in. long, 6 in. wide) and heart shaped. Creates an effective weed-suppressing ground cover. Sends up 2–3-ft.-tall stems bearing flowers in soft yellow fading to cream. The main bloom period comes in early summer, but some flowers are produced later as well. Flower spikes are attractive even after blossoms fade; they dry out and remain upright throughout the winter. Tolerates partial shade.

P. samia. Perennial. Zones 2–24. Similar in habit to *P. russeliana,* forming a low mat of oval, scallop-edged, 4–8-in.-long leaves that are medium green above, white and woolly below. Blooms throughout summer, sending up 2–3-ft.-tall stems of flowers in purple or purplish pink (greenish or white in some forms).

P. tuberosa. Perennial from tuberous roots. Zones A1–A3; 1–24. Basal rosette of deep green foliage covered with fine hairs; leaves deeply toothed, arrow shaped, to 10 in. long. Late spring into summer, sends up 3–6-ft. stems with purple or pinkish mauve blossoms along upper third; upper lip of each flower is straight rather than hooded. Blooming plants resemble foxgloves *(Digitalis).* Disappears in winter.

PHLOX

Polemoniaceae

PERENNIALS AND ANNUALS

ZONES VARY BY SPECIES

FULL SUN OR LIGHT SHADE, EXCEPT AS NOTED

REGULAR WATER, EXCEPT AS NOTED

Phlox paniculata

Most are natives of North America. With the exception of *P. drummondii* (annual phlox), the species described here are perennial. The many types show wide variation in form, but all have showy flower clusters. Tall kinds are excellent border plants; dwarf ones are mainstays of the rock garden. Unless otherwise noted, grow in ordinary garden soil and provide regular moisture. Two major problems affect phlox: red spider mites (attack almost all species) and powdery mildew (*P. paniculata* is especially susceptible).

P. divaricata. SWEET WILLIAM PHLOX. Zones 1–17. Native to eastern North America. To 1 ft. high, 2 ft. wide, with creeping underground shoots. Slender stems are clothed in oblong, 1½–2-in.-long leaves. Blooms in spring, bearing open clusters of ¾–1½-in.-wide, somewhat fragrant blossoms; color varies from pale blue (sometimes with pinkish tones) to white. Flowers of 'Dirigo Ice' are palest blue, those of *P. d. laphamii* bright blue. Use in rock garden or as bulb cover. Grow in good, deep soil. Light shade.

P. drummondii. ANNUAL PHLOX. Zones A2, A3; 1–24; H1. Native to Texas. To 6–18 in. high, 10–12 in. wide, with erect, leafy stems more or less covered with rather sticky hairs. Lance-shaped to oval, nearly stalkless leaves are 1–3 in. long. Profuse blossoms in tight clusters at tops of stems. Comes in bright and pastel colors (no blue or orange), some with contrasting eye. Tall strains (about 1½ ft. high) in mixed colors include Finest and Fordhook Finest. Dwarf (6–8-in.) strains include Beauty and Globe, both with roundish flowers; and starry-blossomed Petticoat and Twinkle. Bloom period lasts from early summer until frost if faded flowers are removed. Plant in spring in cold-winter regions, in fall in mild climates. Grow in light, rich soil well amended with organic matter. Full sun.

P. maculata. THICK-LEAF PHLOX. Zones 1–14, 18–23. Native to eastern North America. To 3–4 ft. tall, 1½ ft. wide, with thick, narrow, pointed leaves 2–4 in. long. Early summer flowers about ¾ in. wide in 15-in.-long clusters; colors range from white (often with a colored eye) through pink shades to magenta. Shiny, mildew-resistant foliage. Varieties include 'Alpha', rose pink; 'Delta', white with pink eye; 'Omega', white with purplish pink eye; and 'Rosalinde', deep rose pink. Pure white 'Miss Lingard' may be a hybrid between *P. maculata* and another eastern species, *P. carolina.*

P. mesoleuca. See P. nana ensifolia

P. nana. SANTA FE PHLOX. Zones 4–24, except as noted. Native to southwestern U.S., Mexico. To 8 in. high, 1½ ft. wide. Sprawling stems are clothed in grayish green, narrow leaves to 1½ in. long. Blooms from spring into fall, bearing 1½-in. blossoms in bright pink, purple, or white. *P. n. ensifolia (P. mesoleuca),* Chihuahuan phlox, is more cold hardy (Zones 2, 3, 4–24); it grows to 6 in. high, bears blooms in colors ranging from cream to yellow, orange, and red. *P. nana* and *P. n. ensifolia* both like heat; both do well with little water but will take more moisture if soil is well drained. Tip-pinch plants to keep them from getting straggly.

P. nivalis. TRAILING PHLOX. Zones 4–7. Native to central U.S. Trailing plant to 4–6 in. high, 1 ft. wide. Forms loose mat of narrow, inch-long leaves. Pink or white, 1-in. flowers in fairly large clusters, late spring or early summer. Excellent in rock gardens; needs good drainage. ▸

P

P. paniculata. SUMMER PHLOX. Zones 1–14, 18–21. From eastern North America. To 3–5 ft. tall, 2 ft. wide, with narrow, 2–5-in.-long leaves tapering to a slender point. Fragrant, 1-in. flowers in large, dome-shaped clusters throughout summer. Colors include white and shades of lavender, pink, rose, and red; blooms of some varieties have a contrasting eye. Plants do not come true from seed—most seedlings tend toward an uncertain purplish pink, though some may be attractive.

Summer phlox thrives in full sun, but flower color may bleach in hottest areas; performance is better in northern than in southern climates. After setting out young plants, pinch stem tips to induce branching. Mulch to keep roots cool. Divide every few years, replanting young shoots from outside of clump.

Very susceptible to mildew at end of bloom season. To minimize the problem, provide good air circulation: don't crowd plants, and thin mature plants to leave only six to eight stems. Mildew-resistant varieties include 'Bright Eyes', rose pink with darker eye; 'David' and 'Ice Cap', pure white; 'Eva Cullum' and 'Miss Pepper', pink with red eye; 'Franz Schubert', lilac pink; 'Miss Candy', hot pink; 'Miss Marple', white with reddish pink eye; 'Miss Violet', purple; and 'Red Eyes', deep pink with red eye.

P. stolonifera. CREEPING PHLOX. Zones A2, A3; 1–17. From eastern North America. Creeping, mounding plant to 6–8 in. high, 1 ft. wide, with narrow evergreen leaves to 1½ in. long. Profuse springtime show of 1-in., lavender flowers. Varieties include lavender-blue 'Blue Ridge', white 'Bruce's White', and deep lavender 'Sherwood Purple'. Light shade.

P. subulata. MOSS PINK. Zones 1–17. From eastern U.S. Forms a mat to 6 in. high, 1½ ft. or wider, with creeping stems clothed in stiffish, ½-in., needlelike evergreen to semievergreen leaves. Blooms in late spring or early summer, bearing ¾-in. flowers in colors including white, pale to deep shades of pink, and lavender blue. Makes sheets of brilliant color in rock gardens. Plant in loose, not-too-rich soil; give moderate water. After flowering, cut back halfway. Specialists offer two dozen or more varieties; many are actually selections of other low-growing species, or hybrids between those species and *P. subulata.* 'Tamanonagalei' ('Candy Stripe') has rose pink blossoms edged in white; it is more drought tolerant than the average moss pink and has good fall rebloom.

PHOENIX

DATE PALM

Arecaceae (Palmae)

PALMS

ZONES VARY BY SPECIES

FULL SUN, EXCEPT AS NOTED

REGULAR WATER

Phoenix canariensis

These feather palms are mostly large trees, though the following list includes one dwarf. Trunks are patterned with bases of old leafstalks. Small yellowish flowers in large, hanging sprays. On female trees, blossoms are followed by clusters of dates—but only if the tree has been in the ground for at least several years and if a male tree is nearby. Dates of *P. dactylifera* and *P. sylvestris* are used commercially; those of other species don't have as much edible flesh. Date palms hybridize freely, so buy these trees from a reliable nursery that knows the seed or plant source.

P. canariensis. CANARY ISLAND DATE PALM. Zones 9, 12–24; H1, H2. Canary Island native. Hardy to 20°F/–7°C; slow to develop new head of foliage after damage from hard frosts. Big, heavy-trunked plant to 60 ft. tall, with a great many bright green to deep green, gracefully arching fronds that form a crown to 50 ft. wide. Grows slowly until it forms a trunk, then speeds up a little. Young plants do well in pots for many years, looking something like pineapples. Best planted in parks, along wide streets, or in other large spaces; not for small city lots. Takes seacoast conditions.

P. dactylifera. DATE PALM. Zones 9, 12–24; H1, H2. Leaves killed at 20°F/–7°C, but plants have survived 4°F/–16°C. Native to the Mideast. Classic palm of desert oases. Slender-trunked tree to 80 ft., with a crown 20–40 ft. wide; gray-green, waxy leaves have stiff, sharp-pointed leaflets. Sends up suckers from base; natural habit is a clump of several trunks. Bears dates of commerce; principal variety is 'Deglet Noor'. Too large and stiff for most home gardens. Does well at seaside, in desert.

Phoenix dactylifera

P. loureiri (P. humilis). Zones 9, 14–24; H1, H2. Hardy to 20°F/–7°C. Native from India to China. Resembles smaller, slimmer, more refined *P. canariensis.* Slow grower to 10–18 ft. tall and wide, with dark green leaves. Does well in containers.

P. reclinata. SENEGAL DATE PALM. Zones 13, 23, 24; H2. Damaged below 25°F/–4°C. Native to tropical Africa. To 20–30 ft. high and wide. Produces offshoots, forming picturesque clumps with several curving trunks; if you want a single-trunked tree, remove offshoots. Fertilize for fast growth. Good seaside plant.

P. roebelenii. PYGMY DATE PALM. Zones 13, 23, 24; H2; or indoors. Foliage browns at around 26°F/–3°C but recovers rapidly in spring. From Laos. Small, slow-growing, single-trunked palm to 6–10 ft. high. Fine-textured, curving leaves form a dense crown 6–8 ft. across. Good in groves or as a potted plant. Full sun or partial shade. Indoors, provide bright indirect light.

Phoenix roebelenii

P. rupicola. CLIFF DATE PALM. Zones 13, 17, 19–24; H1, H2. Hardy to 26°F/–3°C. Native to India. As stately as *P. canariensis* but slender trunked and much smaller, reaching only 25 ft. high, 15–20 ft. wide. Lower leaves droop gracefully.

P. sylvestris. SILVER DATE PALM. Zones 14–17, 19–24; H1, H2. Hardy to 22°F/–6°C. Native to India. Beautiful single-trunked palm to 30 ft. tall, 20–25 ft. wide. Tapering trunk is wide at base, narrow at top. Dense, rounded crown of gray-green leaves. Fruit is used commercially for making date sugar.

PHORMIUM

Agavaceae

PERENNIALS

ZONES 7–9, 14–24; H1, H2; REGROW AFTER FREEZES IN ZONES 5, 6

FULL SUN OR PARTIAL SHADE

LITTLE TO REGULAR WATER

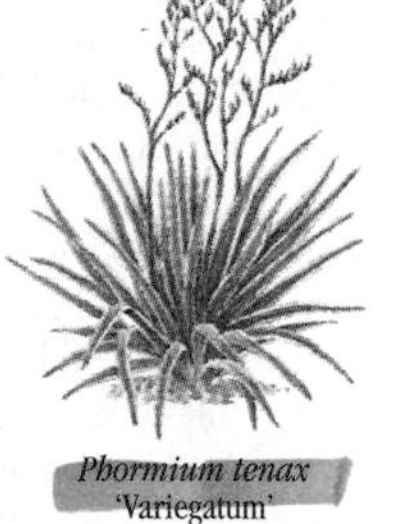

Phormium tenax 'Variegatum'

From New Zealand. Dramatic plants with many swordlike evergreen leaves that grow in a fan pattern; make good garden focal points. The many variegated selections provide year-round color in perennial and shrub borders, on hillsides, in seaside plantings, near swimming pools. Cool weather intensifies foliage colors. On established plants, branched clusters of tubular flowers appear in late spring or early summer, rising to twice the height of the foliage clump in some kinds.

Rugged *P. tenax* varieties are sturdy and fast growing. They take almost any soil, little to regular watering, hot or chilly conditions; do well at seacoast. They will take poor drainage to a point; crown rot can be a problem if they are planted too low in poorly drained soil. Rigid, upright leaves seldom sunburn, even on variegated kinds with light-colored variegation. Subject to summer rot in low desert, but replacement plants set out in fall will grow quickly. Use as windbreak along coast; grow in containers wherever soil doesn't freeze in winter. More finicky than *P. tenax* are forms of *P. cookianium* and the spectacular hybrids between *P. cookianum* and *P. tenax.* To thrive, they require a bit more water; in hot areas, their arching leaves need afternoon shade to prevent burning.

P. tenax, P. cookianum, and their forms and hybrids are all harmed by temperatures below 20°F/–7°C. In cold-winter areas, you can grow smaller sorts indoors or move larger containers to shelter when deep cold threatens.

Nursery plants in containers are deceptively small; when you plant, allow enough room to accommodate a mature specimen. Cut out flower stalks when blossoms wither. As leaves age, colors fade; cut out older ones as close to base as possible to maintain best appearance. On variegated sorts, watch for reversions to solid green or bronze; remove reverted crowns down to root level before they take over the clump. Clumps can remain in place indefinitely. To increase plantings, take individual crowns from clump edges; or divide large clumps (not an easy job).

P. cookianum (P. colensoi). MOUNTAIN FLAX. Medium green leaves (usually pinkish at base) are less rigid than those of *P. tenax;* they arch gracefully, droop at the tips. Leaves are 4–5 ft. long, 2½–3 in. wide; mature clumps are 4–5 ft. high, spreading to 8–10 ft. or more. Yellow flowers on branching, 3–5-ft. stalks; drooping, twisted seedpods. 'Dwarf' is a compact selection only 3 ft. high, 5–6 ft. wide. *P. c. hookeri* 'Tricolor' has green leaves margined in cream and red; foliage is flushed with rose in cool weather. 'Cream Delight' is a sport of 'Tricolor'; its leaves have a broad, creamy yellow central stripe and narrow green margins edged in dark red.

P. hybrids. These are all bird-pollinated, naturally occurring crosses between *P. cookianum* and *P. tenax,* selected for distinctive leaf color.

'Apricot Queen'. To 2½–3 ft. tall, 4–5 ft. wide. Leaves are 2–3 in. wide, light yellow with green margins; blushed with apricot in cool weather.

'Dark Delight'. Arching habit to 3–4 ft. high, 6–8 ft. wide. Leaves are 1–2 in. wide; very dark but vivid reddish brown with a thin orange midrib.

'Dazzler'. To 3 ft. tall, 5–6 ft. wide, with twisting, arching, 1½-in.-wide leaves in scarlet striped with maroon.

'Duet'. To 2½–3½ ft. tall and wide. Stiff leaves to 1¾ in. wide are lime green with creamy yellow stripes at margins.

'Flamingo'. See 'Maori Sunrise'

'Gold Sword'. Fairly stiff, upright plant to 2½–3 ft. tall, 3–5 ft. wide. Bright yellow, 2-in.-wide leaves have green edges and (sometimes) a faint rosy flush in center.

'Guardsman'. To 5–6 ft. tall, 7–8 ft. wide, with rigid, upright leaves to 3 in. wide. Bronzy olive green with red border.

'Maori Chief'. Robust, upright to 6 ft. tall, 6–8 ft. wide. Leaves 2½ in. wide, green with rosy edges. Similar to 'Sundowner' but more refined.

'Maori Maiden'. To 3–4 ft. tall, 4–6 ft. wide. Leaves to 1¾ in. wide are salmon pink (fading to cream) with narrow olive green stripes at edges.

'Maori Queen'. To 3 ft. high, 4–5 ft. wide. Shorter, more upright, narrower-leafed version of 'Sundowner'. Stiff leaves to 2¼ in. wide are bronzy green, with broad marginal streaks of coral fading to cream.

'Maori Sunrise'. To 3 ft. high, 5–6 ft. wide, with stiff leaves to 2½ in. across. Foliage is margined and striped in bronzy green; base color is pinkish orange in younger leaves, aging to cream in older ones. 'Flamingo' is similar or identical.

'Rainbow Warrior'. Similar to 'Maori Maiden' but with leaves in a somewhat darker salmon, fading to cream with age. Foliage turns nearly blood red in winter.

'Red Heart'. Relaxed, arching habit to 3 ft. tall, 4–6 ft. wide. Light red, 1½–2-in.-wide leaves are light green on edges and undersides.

'Sea Jade'. To 4–5 ft. tall, 5–6 ft. wide, with rather stiff leaves to 2½ in. wide. Maroon to bronze in center, with lime green margins and undersides.

'Sundowner'. Erect growth to 5–6 ft. tall, 6–8 ft. wide, with leaves to 3½ in. wide. Olive or bronzy green foliage has stripes of pinkish red (aging to cream) at or near edges and a fine red edge; leaf undersides are grayish green.

'Surfer'. To 3 ft. tall, 5–6 ft. wide. Maroon-bronze, 1½-in.-wide leaves have grayish green undersides and a narrow, gray-green central stripe. Foliage is stiff but arching and twisting.

'Yellow Wave'. To 4–5 ft. high, 5–7 ft. wide, with 2¼-in.-wide leaves in chartreuse with lime green margins. Leaves can burn in hot sun.

P. tenax. NEW ZEALAND FLAX. Large, bold plant with bronzy green leaves to 9 ft. long, 5 in. wide; rigid and mainly upright, curving mainly (if at all) near tips. Mature clumps are about as wide as or a little wider than high. Vertical inflorescences—often to twice the height of foliage clump—contain many dull red or reddish orange flowers; seedpods are twisted but held erect. Many choices, offering great variety in plant size and leaf color. Note that bronze-leafed varieties take on a deeper color in full sun.

'Atropurpureum', 'Bronze', 'Purpureum', 'Rubrum'. These names are used interchangeably in the trade for plants with purplish or brownish red foliage that grow 6–8 ft. tall and wide. Usually grown from seed and somewhat variable; if you want a particular color, make sure you see the actual plant before buying.

'Atropurpureum Compactum' ('Monrovia Red'). To 5 ft. tall and wide, with burgundy-bronze foliage. Uniform; propagated by tissue culture.

'Bronze Baby'. To 3 ft. tall and wide, with 1½-in.-wide leaves. Foliage is deep reddish brown aging to deep bronze; narrow orange leaf edges and midrib (on underside) glow in sunlight.

'Chocolate'. To 4–5 ft. high and wide, with rich brown leaves.

'Dusky Chief'. Dense clump to 6 ft. high and wide. Wine red leaves are 2–3 in. wide and have coral edges that glow when backlit.

'Jack Spratt'. To 1½ ft. high and wide, with ½-in.-wide, twisting, reddish brown leaves.

'Morticia'. To 3–4 ft. high and wide, with stiff, 1½-in.-wide, purple-black leaves.

'Pink Stripe' ('Pink Edge'). To 4–5 ft. high and wide. Gray-green foliage has a purplish tinge. Each leaf has a bright pink margin that is broader at base, gradually narrowing to almost nothing at tip.

'Thumbelina'. Similar to 'Jack Spratt' but more upright growing and a little darker.

'Tiny Tiger' ('Aurea Nana'). Miniature of 'Variegatum', reaching barely 1 ft. high and wide. Leaves are flushed pink in cool weather. 'Toney Tiger' is a 2-ft. version.

'Tom Thumb'. Upright clump to 2–3 ft. high and wide. Green, wavy-edged, ½-in.-wide leaves have red-bronze margins.

'Variegatum'. To 6–8 ft. tall and wide, with ¾-in.-wide, grayish green leaves that have creamy yellow stripes along edges.

'Veitchianum' ('Radiance', 'Williamsii Variegatum'). To 5–6 ft. tall, 7 ft. wide. Green leaves have a central yellow stripe, lime green margins with a thin orange edge.

PHOTINIA

Rosaceae

EVERGREEN AND DECIDUOUS SHRUBS OR TREES

ZONES VARY BY SPECIES

FULL SUN

MODERATE TO REGULAR WATER

Photinia × fraseri 'Birmingham'

Related to hawthorn *(Crataegus),* pyracantha. Densely foliaged plants with elliptical to oval leaves and bright-colored new growth that matures to dark green. In early spring, all bear flattish clusters of small white flowers. In most types, blossoms are followed in fall by red or black berries that may last into winter. Evergreen species may suffer considerable damage if temperatures remain below 10°F/–12°C for prolonged periods. Good for screen and background plantings. Tip-pinch plants to encourage colorful new growth. Prune to shape before spring growth begins or after bloom; don't allow new growth to get away from you and make long, bare switches. Many photinias can be converted to small trees by limbing up; or they can be trained as trees from the beginning. Berries are attractive to birds. All photinias are susceptible to fireblight; all but *P.* ×*fraseri* are subject to powdery mildew.

P. ×fraseri. Evergreen shrub or tree. Zones 3b (with protection), 4–24. 'Birmingham' is the usual selection sold; for many years, it was the only one available and was simply labeled *P.* ×*fraseri.* Moderate to fast growth to 10–15 ft. high and wide. Leaves to 5 in. long; bright bronzy red when new. Flower clusters resemble those of *P. glabra* but are not followed by berries. Good espalier or small single-stemmed tree. Cut branches are excellent in arrangements. Resists mildew and heat. Sometimes suffers from chlorosis in Zones 12, 13. Aphids may be a problem. Often used as a formal hedge, but the large leaves look ragged when sheared; for a more attractive appearance, clip plants more lightly or grow as an informal hedge. ▸

Two newer selections about half the size of 'Birmingham' are useful in smaller spaces: 'Indian Princess', with orange-red new growth, and 'Red Robin', with bright red new leaves.

P. glabra. JAPANESE PHOTINIA. Evergreen shrub. Zones 4–9, 14–24. From Japan. Broad, dense growth to 6–10 ft. high and wide. Leaves to 3 in. long, coppery when new; scattered leaves turn bright red through fall and winter, adding touches of color. Flowers in 4-in. clusters. Berries are red, aging to black.

P. serratifolia (P. serrulata). CHINESE PHOTINIA. Evergreen shrub or tree. Zones 4–16, 18–22; can be grown in Zones 17, 23, 24, but is especially prone to mildew there. From China. Broad, dense grower; can reach 30 ft. high and wide but is easily held to one-third that size. Stiff leaves to 8 in. long are prickly along edges. Bright copper new growth; scattered crimson leaves in fall, winter. Flower clusters to 6 in. across. Bright red berries often last until winter. 'Aculeata' (frequently sold as 'Nova' or 'Nova Lineata') is more compact; its leaf midribs and main veins are ivory yellow.

P. villosa. Deciduous shrub or tree. Zones 3–9, 14–17. From China, Korea, Japan. To 15 ft. tall, 10 ft. wide. Leaves are 1½–3 in. long; they are pale gold with rosy tints when new, green when mature, bright red or yellow in fall. Flower clusters 1–2 in. across; bright red berries.

PHYGELIUS

CAPE FUCHSIA

Scrophulariaceae

PERENNIALS

ZONES 4–9, 14–24; H1, H2

FULL SUN OR LIGHT SHADE

REGULAR WATER

Phygelius capensis

From South Africa. Woody-based perennials that die to the ground in cold climates, remain shrubby in milder areas. Related to snapdragon *(Antirrhinum)* and penstemon, but drooping flowers also suggest fuchsia. Plants grow 3–4 ft. high, spreading about as wide by underground stems or rooting prostrate branches. Bloom from summer into fall, bearing tubular, curved flowers in loosely branched clusters at stem ends. To keep plants neat, cut out old flower stalks after bloom. Mulch roots in cold-winter regions. Species can be started from seed; named varieties should be grown from cuttings or by ground layering.

P. aequalis. Pyramidal clusters of dusty rose flowers. 'Yellow Trumpet' has pale yellow blooms.

P. capensis. More open and sprawling than *P. aequalis,* with loose clusters of orange to red flowers.

P. ×rectus. Hybrids between the previous two species. 'African Queen' has orange flowers with a yellow throat; 'Devil's Tears', scarlet with yellow throat; 'Moonraker', solid pale yellow; 'Tommy Knockers', peach with yellow throat. 'Pink Elf' bears pink flowers on a smaller plant than the usual (2 ft. high, 3 ft. wide).

PHYLA nodiflora (Lippia repens)

LIPPIA

Verbenaceae

PERENNIAL

ZONES 8–24; H1, H2

FULL SUN

LITTLE TO REGULAR WATER

Phyla nodiflora

From many tropical and subtropical regions of the world. Ground-hugging growth and ability to endure foot traffic have established its use as a lawn substitute in some areas where a traditional lawn is impractical. Creeping stems clothed in oval, ¾-in., grayish green leaves form a mat no higher than 2 in. Rounded, ½-in. heads of tiny lavender-pink flowers appear from spring to fall. Blossoms are a magnet for bees; if this bothers you, mow plantings periodically to remove flowers. Set out plants from containers 2 ft. apart; plant rooted sprigs at 1-ft. intervals. Looks shabby in winter, but an early-spring feeding will promote fast new growth. Takes many soils, though performance suffers where nematodes are a problem (in the desert, for example).

PHYLLITIS scolopendrium. See ASPLENIUM scolopendrium

PHYLLOSTACHYS. See BAMBOO

PHYSALIS alkekengi

CHINESE LANTERN PLANT

Solanaceae

PERENNIAL OFTEN GROWN AS ANNUAL

ZONES 1–24

FULL SUN OR LIGHT SHADE

REGULAR WATER

Physalis alkekengi

From Europe, Asia. Grown not for flowers but for the blossoms' decorative, papery, 2-in. calyxes, which look like lanterns and mature to a striking orange red in late summer and fall. Plant grows 1½–3 ft. high and wide, with angular branches set with long-stalked, light green, oval, 2–3-in.-long leaves. Small, star-shaped white flowers appear in leaf joints during summer; these are followed by inedible berries, each enclosed in a colorful inflated husk—the enlarged calyx of the flower. Dry, leafless stalks hung with these gay "lanterns" make choice winter arrangements.

Sow seeds in light soil in spring. Plant is clump forming, spreading widely by long, creeping, whitish underground stems; can become invasive. Increase established plantings by digging and dividing the roots. 'Pygmy' is a dwarf variety just 8 in. high; it makes a good potted plant.

Two other *Physalis* species produce edible fruit within papery husks. See Tomatillo *(P. ixocarpa)* and Poha, Ground Cherry *(P. peruviana).*

PHYSOCARPUS

NINEBARK

Rosaceae

DECIDUOUS SHRUBS

ZONES VARY BY SPECIES

SUN OR SHADE

MODERATE TO REGULAR WATER

Physocarpus capitatus

Ninebarks are so named because of their peeling bark, which strips off to reveal several layers. The plants resemble spiraea and are closely related to it, bearing round clusters of tiny white or pinkish flowers in spring or early summer. All have medium green leaves with lobed edges. Of the species described here, only *P. monogynus* has good fall color. Prune plants as needed after bloom; rejuvenate by cutting old stems to the ground.

P. capitatus. Zones 2b, 3–9, 14–19. Native to mountains of western North America. To 8 ft. tall and wide, with 2-in. leaves and dense clusters of white flowers. Clustered buds are as attractive as the opened blossoms.

P. monogynus. MOUNTAIN NINEBARK. Zones A1–A3; 1–3, 10. Rocky Mountain and High Plains native. To 3–5 ft. high and wide, with 1½-in. leaves and pinkish to white flowers carried just a few to a cluster. Leaves turn brilliant orange and red in fall.

P. opulifolius. COMMON NINEBARK. Zones A1–A3; 1–10, 14–17. Native to eastern and central North America. To 9 ft. tall and 10 ft. wide, with leaves to 3 in. long. Many white or pinkish blossoms in each cluster. Varieties are more attractive than the species. 'Diabolo', to 9–12 ft. high and wide, has intense reddish purple leaves (foliage color can tend toward dark green in very hot summers or when plant is grown in partial shade). Leaves of 'Luteus' are yellow when plant is grown in sunlight, yellow green in shade. Compact varieties to 4–6 ft. tall and broad include 'Dart's Gold', similar to 'Luteus' but brighter; 'Nanus', with small, shallowly lobed dark green leaves; and 'Nugget', with leaves that unfold golden yellow, gradually mature to lime green, and then turn gold again in fall.

PHYSOSTEGIA virginiana

FALSE DRAGONHEAD, OBEDIENT PLANT

Lamiaceae (Labiatae)

PERENNIAL

ZONES A3; 1–9, 14–24

FULL SUN OR PARTIAL SHADE

REGULAR WATER

Physostegia virginiana 'Vivid'

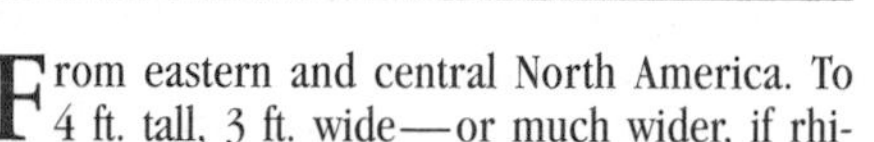

From eastern and central North America. To 4 ft. tall, 3 ft. wide—or much wider, if rhizomes are allowed to spread unchecked. Slender, upright stems carry oblong, toothed, 3–5-in.-long leaves with pointed tips. In summer or early fall, each stem is topped by a 10-in.-long spike densely set with funnel-shaped, 1-in. flowers, typically in bright bluish pink. Blossoms resemble snapdragons (hence the name "false dragonhead") and will remain in place if twisted or pushed out of position (hence the name "obedient plant"). 'Bouquet Rose' reaches 3 ft. high, has rose pink flowers. Varieties growing 2 ft. tall include rose pink 'Vivid', white 'Summer Snow', and 'Variegata', with bluish pink flowers and white-edged leaves.

Attractive in borders; good cut flowers. Bloom stalks may need staking to remain upright. Cut to ground after bloom. Vigorous and notoriously invasive; to keep clumps in-bounds, divide them every 2 years in early spring.

PICEA

SPRUCE

Pinaceae

EVERGREEN TREES

ZONES VARY BY SPECIES

FULL SUN OR LIGHT SHADE

LITTLE TO MODERATE WATER, EXCEPT AS NOTED

Picea pungens glauca

Like firs *(Abies)*, spruces are pyramidal, with branches arranged in neat tiers. Unlike firs, however, they have pendent cones, and their needles are stiffer and attached to branches by small pegs that remain behind after the needles drop. Most spruces are tall timber trees that lose their lower branches fairly early in life as they head upward; their canopies thin out noticeably as they age. Many species have dwarf varieties useful for foundation plantings, in rock gardens, in containers; these plants have shallow root systems and so need a reasonably cool location. Spruces generally grow best where summers are cool or mild; they will not thrive in heat and humidity. *P. pungens* tolerates dry conditions better than the other species. Spruces have no special soil requirements. Birds are attracted to these trees—both for seeds and for shelter.

Check spruces for small, dull green aphids in winter; if they're present, take control measures at that time to prevent defoliation in spring. Pine needle scale (look for flat, white scale insects on needles) may encourage sooty mold. In Rocky Mountain states, spruces may be bothered by spider mites and tussock moths.

Prune only to shape. If a branch grows too long, cut it back to a well-placed side branch. To slow growth and make it denser, remove part of each year's growth to force side branching. When planting larger spruces, don't place them too close to buildings, fences, or walks; they need space. Can be grown in containers for years as living Christmas trees; in coldest climates, move to a protected location in winter.

P. abies (P. excelsa). NORWAY SPRUCE. Zones A2, A3; 1–6, 14–17. Native to northern Europe. Fast growth to 100–150 ft. tall, 20 ft. wide. Doesn't do as well as North American native spruces in Rocky Mountain states. Stiff, deep green, attractive pyramid in youth; in age, branchlets droop strongly, and oldest branchlets (those nearest trunk) die back. Tolerates heat and humidity better than most spruces. Extremely hardy and wind resistant; valued for windbreaks in cold-winter zones. The following slow growers are among the many dwarf varieties available.

'Little Gem'. Dense grower to 1 ft. high and wide, with short needles and flat top.

'Nidiformis'. BIRD'S NEST SPRUCE. Dense growth to 3–5 ft. tall, 4–6 ft. wide. Individual plants vary in form. Some are flat topped; in others, the semierect main branches curve outward, leaving a shallow depression at the plant's top that gives it the look of a bird's nest.

'Pendula'. Grows naturally as a ground cover about 1½ ft. high, 10 ft. wide. Looks attractive cascading downward from rocks or walls. Can be staked to desired height and grown as a short, weeping tree.

'Sherwoodii'. Picturesque shrub with compact but irregular habit. Parent tree was only 5 ft. tall, 10 ft. wide at 60 years of age.

P. breweriana. BREWER'S WEEPING SPRUCE. Zones 2b, 3–7, 14–17. Native to Siskiyou Mountains in California and Oregon. To 30–50 ft. tall and 10–12 ft. wide in cultivation (to 80–120 ft. tall in native habitat). Stiff, upright pyramid in youth; branchlets become pendulous as the tree ages. Very striking form in maturity, with 7–8-ft.-long branchlets hanging vertically from the main branches. Needles are shiny deep green above, gray green beneath. More tender than most spruces. Requires regular water, cool temperatures.

P. engelmanii. ENGELMANN SPRUCE. Zones A2, A3; 1–7, 10, 14–17. Native from British Columbia south to Oregon and northern California, east to the Rockies. To 60–130 ft. tall, 20–25 ft. wide, with densely pyramidal form. Resembles blue-green forms of *P. pungens,* but needles are softer and tree is not as wide at base. Even 25-ft. specimens will be densely branched to ground. Popular lawn tree in Rocky Mountain region.

P. glauca. WHITE SPRUCE. Zones A1–A3, 1–7, 14–17, except as noted. Native to Canada and northern U.S. Cone-shaped, densely foliaged tree to 60–70 ft. tall and 10–12 ft. wide. Broad when young, narrower in age. Pendulous twigs; silver-green needles. Does best where winters are very cold. Many varieties, including the following.

P. g. albertiana 'Conica'. DWARF ALBERTA SPRUCE, DWARF WHITE SPRUCE. Zones A2, A3; 1–7, 14–17. Compact, cone-shaped, bushy shrub grows slowly, reaching 6–8 ft. tall, 4–5 ft. wide in 35 years. Short, soft needles are bright grass green when new, gray green when mature. Needs shelter from drying winds (hot or cold) and from strong, reflected sunlight. Popular tub plant.

P. g. densata. BLACK HILLS SPRUCE. Zones A2, A3; 1–6. Slow-growing, dense pyramid can reach 20–25 ft. tall, 10–12 ft. wide in 35 years. Use in containers; plant in groves for screening or for alpine meadow effect.

'Jean's Dilly'. Pyramidal tree to 8–10 ft. tall and 12–14 ft. wide, with twisted needles.

'Sander's Blue'. To 6 ft. tall and 4 ft. wide. New growth and mature growth differ in color, giving plant a variegated look: young needles are slate blue, mature ones gray green.

P. mariana. BLACK SPRUCE. Zones A1–A3; 1–7. Native to Alaska and other parts of northern North America. Forms an irregular column to 30–50 ft. tall, 6–10 ft. wide. Bluish green needles. Tolerates cold, wet soils. 'Nana' is a compact variety (to 3 ft. high, 4–6 ft. wide) with blue-gray foliage; it is attractive in rock gardens, borders.

P. pungens. COLORADO SPRUCE. Zones A2, A3; 1–10, 14–17. Native to Rocky Mountain region. In gardens, reaches 30–60 ft. tall, 10–20 ft. wide; in the wild, grows to a possible 100 ft. tall, 25–35 ft. wide. Very stiff, regular, horizontal branches form a broad pyramid. Foliage of seedlings varies in color from dark green through all shades of blue green to steely blue. Poor choice for Puget Sound region, where lack of winter cold leads to severe aphid infestations. Throughout its range, subject to an aphid that forms galls. Prefers dry soil. ▶

P. p. glauca. COLORADO BLUE SPRUCE. Like the species but with bluish foliage. Many selections offer good blue color, including the following.

'Fat Albert'. Broad, formal looking. To 10–15 ft. tall, 10–12 ft. wide.

'Hoopsii'. Dense, conical form with spreading branches and blue-white foliage.

'Koster'. Forms a blue-gray cone, though growth habit may be irregular.

'Moerheimii'. Same blue-gray color as 'Koster', but shape is more compact and symmetrical. Needles are longer than in other selections.

'Montgomery'. Slow-growing dwarf that forms a broad, silver-blue cone to 5 ft. high and wide.

'Pendula'. WEEPING BLUE SPRUCE. Gray-blue plant with weeping branchlets. Can be grown as ground cover; can also be trained as small, weeping tree by staking at desired height when young.

'Thomsen'. Similar to 'Hoopsii' in color, but needles are twice as thick. Vigorous, symmetrical habit.

P. sitchensis. SITKA SPRUCE. Zones A2, A3; 4–6, 14–17. Native from Alaska to California. Tall, pyramidal tree to 80–160 ft. high and 20–40 ft. wide, with horizontal branches. Short, prickly needles are glossy dark green above, powder blue beneath. Needs moisture both in atmosphere and in soil to look its best. Subject to Cooley spruce gall—a conelike growth on new shoots that is caused by adelgids, a type of aphid. Control as for scale. 'Papoose' ('Tensa') is a dwarf variety to 4 ft. high and wide.

PICKEREL WEED. See PONTEDERIA cordata

PIERIS

Ericaceae

EVERGREEN SHRUBS

ZONES VARY BY SPECIES

FILTERED SUNLIGHT OR PARTIAL SHADE

REGULAR WATER

LEAVES AND NECTAR ARE POISONOUS IF INGESTED

Pieris japonica

Elegant in foliage and form the year around, these plants make good companions for rhododendron and azalea, to which they are related. They have whorls of leathery, narrowly oval, glossy, medium to dark green leaves and bear clusters of small, urn-shaped, typically white flowers. Most plants form flower buds by autumn; these resemble strings of tiny beads in greenish pink, red, or white and provide a subtle decorative feature in winter. Flowers open from midwinter to midspring. New spring growth is often brightly colored (pink to red or bronze).

Same cultural requirements as rhododendron and azalea. Need acid, well-drained but moisture-retentive soil and summers that are cool to merely warm; do not thrive in hot, dry conditions. Fairly easy to grow in the Pacific Northwest west of the Cascades, but as you move south and inland, they become increasingly fussy and are often less satisfactory. Where water is high in salts, soil needs careful leaching. Choose a planting location sheltered from wind, where plants will get high shade or dappled sunlight at least during the warmest afternoon hours. Where summers are cool or foggy, plants can take more sun. Prune by removing spent flowers. Thin older specimens by taking out whole branches; or limb them up to reveal attractive peeling bark. Splendid in containers, in woodland and Japanese gardens, in entryways where year-round quality is essential.

P. floribunda (Andromeda floribunda). MOUNTAIN PIERIS. Zones 2–9, 14–17. Native to southeastern U.S. Compact, rounded shrub to 6 ft. tall, 10 ft. wide. Differs from the other species—new growth is pale green, mature leaves dull dark green, 1½–3 in. long. Blossoms in upright clusters. Cold hardy; tolerates sun, heat, and low humidity better than the others.

P. 'Forest Flame'. Zones 3b–9, 14–17. Hybrid between *P. japonica* and a form of *P. formosa forrestii.* To 6–10 ft. tall, 3–5 ft. wide. Leaves are about 3½ in. long—brilliant red when new, fading to creamy pink before maturing to dark green. Blooms profusely, bearing broader, heavier flower clusters than those of *P. japonica.*

P. formosa forrestii (P. forrestii). CHINESE PIERIS. Zones 4–9, 14–17. From China. Dense, broad, to 10 ft. tall, 12 ft. wide. Polished-looking leaves to 6 in. long. New growth ranges from brilliant scarlet (in the best forms) to pale salmon pink. To get good color, buy plants when they are producing new growth; the best selections are sometimes offered as 'Bright Red'. Large, drooping flower clusters. Good espalier in shade.

P. japonica (Andromeda japonica). LILY-OF-THE-VALLEY SHRUB. Zones 2b–9, 14–17. Upright, dense, tiered growth to 9–10 ft. high and wide. New leaves are bronzy pink to red; mature ones are glossy green, 3 in. long. Drooping clusters of white, pink, or nearly red flowers; flower buds are often dark red. Many varieties, some rare.

The following are grown for smaller-than-usual size or unusual foliage:

'Bert Chandler'. Salmon pink new foliage ages to cream, then white; then matures to pale green.

'Bisbee Dwarf'. To 1 ft. high and wide, with half-size leaves that are red when young.

'Cavatine'. To 2–3 ft. high and wide, with red new growth.

'Compacta'. Grows to 6 ft. high and wide.

'Crispa'. To 6–7 ft. high and wide, with handsome wavy-edged leaves.

'Flaming Silver'. To 4 ft. high and wide. Young leaves are red with pink margins, mature ones green with white edges.

'Karenoma'. Compact grower to 3–6 ft. high and wide, with upright flower clusters.

'Mountain Fire'. Fiery red new growth.

'Prelude'. To 2–3 ft. high and wide; pink new growth.

'Pygmaea'. Tiny dwarf to 1 ft. high and wide, with very few flowers and narrow leaves to 1 in. long.

'Spring Snow'. Similar to 'Karenoma'.

'Valley Fire'. Brilliant red new growth.

'Variegata'. Slow growing to 6 ft. high and wide. Creamy white leaf variegation; the white markings are tinged pink in spring.

The following varieties are grown principally for their flowers:

'Christmas Cheer'. Early bloomer with bicolored flowers in white and deep rose red; flower stalks are rose red.

'Coleman'. Pink flowers open from red buds.

'Daisen'. Flowers like 'Christmas Cheer', but broader leaves.

'Dorothy Wyckoff'. White flowers open from deep red buds.

'Pink'. Shell pink flowers age to white.

'Purity'. To 3–4 ft. high and wide. Late bloomer with unusually large white flowers.

'Temple Bells'. Slow grower to 3–5 ft. high and wide. Ivory flowers.

'Valley Rose'. Light pink flowers.

'Valley Valentine'. To 5–7 ft. tall and wide. Deep red buds and flowers.

'White Cascade'. Extremely heavy show of pure white blooms.

PIGEON BERRY. See DURANTA erecta

PIGGY-BACK PLANT. See TOLMIEA menziesii

PIKAKE, PIKAKE-HOKU. See JASMINUM sambac, J. multiflorum

PIMPINELLA anisum

ANISE

Apiaceae (Umbelliferae)

ANNUAL

ZONES 1–24; H1, H2

FULL SUN

REGULAR WATER

Pimpinella anisum

Mediterranean native to 2 ft. tall, 1½ ft. wide. First growth produces a clump of bright green, roundish to heart-shaped, tooth-edged leaves. Foliage clumps send up stems set with feathery leaves; in summer, bear umbrellalike clusters of tiny white flowers at stem tips. Use fresh leaves in salads; use seeds for flavoring baked goods, confections.

Plant grows quickly in warm weather, but you'll need to allow about 4 months for a crop of seeds to grow and mature. In coldest regions, sow seeds indoors, then set out young plants when frost danger is past. In mild-winter climates, sow directly in the ground in spring for harvest in summer or early fall. Where summers are very hot, sow in fall for spring harvest. Grow in light, well-drained soil. Plants are fairly wispy and look best in groups. They are taprooted and do not transplant easily once they begin to put on size.

Pinaceae. Members of the pine family are evergreen trees with narrow, usually needlelike leaves and seeds borne on the scales of woody cones. True cedar *(Cedrus)*, larch *(Larix)*, spruce *(Picea)*, pine *(Pinus)*, Douglas fir *(Pseudotsuga)*, and hemlock *(Tsuga)* are examples.

PINCUSHION FLOWER. See SCABIOSA

PINCUSHION TREE. See HAKEA laurina

PINDO PALM. See BUTIA capitata

PINE. See PINUS

PINEAPPLE

Bromeliaceae

PERENNIAL

ZONES 24; H1, H2; OR INDOORS

FULL SUN FOR FRUIT; BRIGHT LIGHT

REGULAR WATER

Pineapple

Native to South America. Well adapted to Hawaii, where it is a commercial crop. Has been cultivated outdoors in Southern California in warm, protected sites; black plastic mulch over soil increases chances of success.

To 2½–5 ft. tall, 3–4 ft. wide, with a short, thick stem topped by a rosette of long (1½–6-ft.), narrow dark green leaves with sawtoothed edges. At bloom time, the stem lengthens and produces a head composed of small red or purple flowers. The blossoms develop into the pineapple fruit. Fruits are typically borne one per stem; in ideal outdoor growing conditions, they reach size and heft of pineapples sold in markets. 'Sugarloaf' ('White Sugarloaf') is a low-acid variety with very sweet white flesh and a soft core.

Whether grown outdoors or as a houseplant, pineapple takes up to 2 years to begin bearing. Fruit should be ready to harvest when it reaches a good size and starts to take on a yellow cast, with bottom turning golden; individual leaves can be pulled out easily. After picking, let ripen fully at room temperature. After the fruit is harvested, the plant will continue to produce for several more years.

Outdoors, plants can be grown in the ground or in pots. Plant in well-drained soil. Start from divisions sold in nurseries; or slice off the leafy top of a market pineapple (cut about an inch below the leaf rosette) and let it dry for a couple of days. Plant 1 ft. apart. Set divisions 3–4 in. deep; set pineapple tops 2 in. deep (base of leaf rosette should be buried). Fertilize frequently.

Pineapple can also be grown indoors in a greenhouse or sunny room where temperature stays above 68°F/20°C. Root the base of a leafy pineapple top in water or in fast-draining but moisture-retentive potting mix. When roots have formed, move pineapple to 7–8-in. pot of rich soil. If you're lucky, a pineapple will form, but it will be much smaller than commercial fruit. A variety with pink, white, and olive green leaves is sometimes sold as a houseplant; it can take reduced light, since it is grown for foliage rather than fruit.

PINEAPPLE FLOWER. See EUCOMIS

PINEAPPLE GUAVA. See FEIJOA

PINK. See DIANTHUS

PINK POLKA-DOT PLANT. See HYPOESTES phyllostachya

PINK SHOWER. See CASSIA grandis

PINK TRUMPET VINE. See PODRANEA ricasoliana

PIÑON. See PINUS cembroides, P. edulis, P. monophylla

PINUS

PINE

Pinaceae

EVERGREEN TREES, RARELY SHRUBS

ZONES VARY BY SPECIES

FULL SUN

LITTLE WATER, EXCEPT AS NOTED

SEE CHART NEXT PAGE

Pinus thunbergii

Pines are the great individualists of the garden, each species differing not only in its characteristics but also in the ways it responds to wind, heat, and other growing conditions. Cone appearance (size and shape) is one identifying feature of these trees. Another is the number of needles in a bundle; most pines carry their long, slender needles in groups of two, three, or five. Young trees tend to be pyramidal, while older ones are more open or round topped. The chart gives typical dimensions for pines in cultivation, but trees often grow much larger in the wild. Seeds of all species attract birds; some species produce the pine nuts enjoyed by people and sold commercially.

All pines can be shaped, and often improved, by some pruning. The best time to prune is in spring, when new growth emerges. Cut the candles (see below) to promote bushiness or limit the plant's size. You can remove unwanted limbs to accent a pine's branching pattern—but before you cut out a branch, remember that a new one won't sprout to take its place. In time, lower limbs of most pines will die naturally; when this happens, cut them off.

▶ page 529

WHAT PINES NEED

DRAINAGE: Well-drained soil is crucial to a pine's good health. In nature, many pines grow on rocky slopes or sandy barrens, where drainage is very fast. Symptoms of excessive moisture are yellowing needles (seen first in older growth) and a generally unhealthy appearance.

WATERING: Most pines are quite drought tolerant; exceptions are noted in the chart.

FERTILIZING: Pines need little if any fertilizer; heavy feeding encourages too rapid, rank growth.

PRUNING: To fatten up a rangy pine or to keep a young one chubby, cut back the spires of new growth (the candles) when they begin to emerge in spring. Cutting back partway will promote bushiness and allow some overall increase in size; cutting out candles entirely will limit size without distorting the natural shape. This kind of careful pruning can even allow you to maintain pines as screens or hedges. For more information about pruning pines, see text.

Pinus muricata

PINUS

NAME, NATIVE HABITAT	ZONES	GROWTH RATE, SIZE	GROWTH HABIT	NEEDLES AND CONES	COMMENTS
Pinus albicaulis WHITEBARK PINE High mountains of Northwest, Northern California, western Nevada, east into Idaho, Wyoming, Montana	A2, A3; 1–7, 15–17	Very slow to 20–40 ft. tall (usually much less), about half as wide	In youth, slender and symmetrical. In nature can become erect tree or prostrate tangle of branches a few feet high and much wider. Densely foliaged; often multitrunked	Needles: in 5s, 1½–3 in., dark green. Cones: 3 in., roundish, purple	Smooth whitish bark in youth. Often dug in mountains by state-licensed collectors and sold under the name "alpine conifer." Good for rock gardens, bonsai
P. aristata BRISTLECONE PINE High mountains of West; widely scattered, very localized	A2, A3; 1–11, 14–19	Very slow to 20 ft. (possibly to 45 ft.) tall, 15 ft. wide	Dense, bushy, heavy-trunked tree with ground-sweeping branches. In youth, symmetrical and narrow crowned	Needles: in 5s, 1–1½ in., dark green flecked with dots of white resin. Cones: 3½ in., narrowly oval, dark purplish brown, bristly	Grows very slowly; good for years in container, rock garden. Good bonsai plant. Needles persist for many years, making crown extremely dense. Protect from wind in cold climates
P. attenuata KNOBCONE PINE Northern and central Cascades in Oregon, Siskiyous, Sierra Nevada foothills in California, south to Baja California	2–10, 14–21	Rapid to 20–80 ft. tall, 20–25 ft. wide	In youth, rounded and regular. In age, typically open and irregular, though some populations are far more densely foliaged and symmetrical; habit depends on seed source	Needles: in 3s, 3–5 in., yellow green. Cones: 4–6 in., narrowly oval, lopsided, light brown, knobby, persistent	Grows well in poor soil
P. balfouriana FOXTAIL PINE Northern Coast Ranges and southern Sierra Nevada in California	2–9, 14–17	Very slow to 20–50 ft. tall, 20–25 ft. wide	In youth, a symmetrical, narrow cone. Spreads more in maturity; lower branches stout and short, upper ones longer, irregular in form	Needles: in 5s, to 1½ in., glossy green; grow in dense tufts at branch tips, last for many years. Cones: 2½–5 in., oblong, purplish brown, drooping	Best planted as shrub; outgrows shrub status only after many years. Good choice for container, bonsai, rock garden
P. banksiana JACK PINE From near the Arctic Circle southward to Minnesota	A1–A3; 1, 2	Slow to moderate, to 30–50 ft. tall (often less), 10–15 ft. wide	Symmetrical pyramid in youth. Irregular, more spreading, picturesque in maturity. Sometimes shrubby	Needles: in 2s, to 2 in., olive green, curved or twisted. Cones: 1–3 in., slender, pointed at tip, yellowish brown	Tolerates poor soil, even sand. Useful for windbreaks, soil conservation
P. brutia (P. halepensis brutia) CALABRIAN PINE Eastern Mediterranean, southern Russia, southern Italy	7–9, 12–24	Rapid, especially in youth, to 30–80 ft. tall, 15–25 ft. wide	Denser and more erect than the related *P. halepensis*, closer to classic pine shape	Needles: in 2s, 5–6½ in., dark green. Cones: like those of *P. halepensis* but not stalked or bent backward	Faster growing and shapelier than *P. halepensis*, though its form is less interesting at maturity. Thrives in heat, wind, poor soil
P. bungeana LACEBARK PINE Northern and central China	2–10, 14–21	Slow to 50–75 ft. tall, 30–50 ft. wide	Starts out pyramidal to rounded, then becomes more open, spreading, picturesque. Often multitrunked; sometimes shrubby	Needles: in 3s, 2–4 in., bright green. Cones: 2–2½ in., oval, yellowish brown	Smooth, dull gray bark on main branches and trunk flakes off like that of sycamore *(Platanus)* to show smooth, creamy white patches. Brittle limbs can break under heavy snow loads
P. canariensis CANARY ISLAND PINE Canary Islands	8, 9, 12–24	Fast to 50–80 ft. tall, 20–35 ft. wide	Grows as a slender, graceful pyramid. Later takes on a tiered look; finally becomes round headed	Needles: in 3s, 9–12 in., bluish green when new, dark green when older. Cones: 4–9 in., oval, glossy brown	Gawky when very young but soon outgrows it. Attractive fissured, reddish brown bark. Resistant to oak root fungus. Drought tolerant but needs irrigation in Southern California
P. cembra SWISS STONE PINE Mountains of central Europe	A1–A3; 1–7, 10	Extremely slow to 50–70 ft. tall (possibly taller), 20–25 ft. wide	Narrow, dense pyramid in youth; becomes broad, open, and round topped in maturity	Needles: in 5s, 3–5 in., dark green. Cones: 3½ in., broad, oval, purplish blue	Slow growth, dense foliage cover; good plant for small gardens. Handsome tree in youth. *P. c. sibirica*, from Siberia, is probably even hardier. Best with regular water

PINUS

NAME, NATIVE HABITAT	ZONES	GROWTH RATE, SIZE	GROWTH HABIT	NEEDLES AND CONES	COMMENTS
P. cembroides MEXICAN PIÑON PINE Arizona to Baja California and northern Mexico	2–24	Slow to 10–25 ft. tall, nearly as wide	Rather rangy in youth; in older trees, stout, spreading branches form a round-topped head	Needles: in 3s or 2s, 1–2 in., dark green. Cones: 1–2 in., rounded, yellowish or reddish brown	Good in desert soils. Cones contain edible seeds (pine nuts)
P. contorta contorta BEACH PINE, SHORE PINE Pacific Coast from Alaska to Northern California	A3; 4–9, 14–24; H1	Fairly fast to 20–35 ft. tall and wide	Nursery trees are compact, pyramidal, somewhat irregular. Trees that are grown along the coast may be dwarfed and contorted by winds	Needles: in 2s, 1¼–2 in., dark green. Cones: 1–2 in., narrow, lopsided, light yellow brown	Good looking in youth; densely foliaged, takes training well. One of the best pines for small gardens. Good in container. Regular water
P. c. murrayana (P. c. latifolia) LODGEPOLE PINE, TAMARACK Mountains of western U.S.	A1–A3; 1–7, 14–17	Slow to 50–80 ft. tall, 20–25 ft. wide (often much smaller)	In cultivation, makes attractive, rather irregular tree with an open habit. Planted close together, trees are tall and slim trunked; solitary trees growing in mountains are typically heavy trunked, narrow, dense	Needles: in 2s, 1½–3 in., yellow green. Cones: 1½ in., shiny brown, oval, persistent	Mountain form of *P. contorta.* Excellent in wild landscape, large rock garden. Regular water
P. coulteri COULTER PINE Dry, rocky California mountain slopes (Mt. Diablo, Mt. Hamilton, Santa Lucia ranges), Southern California, Baja California	3–10, 14–23; H1	Moderate to fast, to 30–80 ft. tall, 20–40 ft. wide	Shapely, open growth, with wide-spreading, persistent lower branches. Sometimes develops several leaders	Needles: in 3s, 5–10 in. (even 14 in.), deep green, stiff. Cones: 10–13 in., oval, buff colored, heavy, persistent	Excellent in gardens, as long as it isn't crowded. Huge cones are attractive but potentially dangerous around play areas, patios, parked cars. Resistant to heat, wind, drought. Good in high desert
P. densiflora JAPANESE RED PINE Japan	2–9, 14–17; H1	Rapid when young. To 40–60 ft. (possibly to 100 ft.) tall, 40 ft. wide	Broad, irregular head, even in youth. Often develops 2 or more trunks at ground level	Needles: in 2s, 2½–5 in., bright green. Cones: 2 in., oval or oblong, tawny brown	Young branches have flaking red-orange bark. Won't take hot, dry, or cold winds. 'Oculus-draconis', dragon eye pine, has 2 yellow bands on each needle; viewed from the tip, each branch has concentric green and yellow bands. 'Pendula' is a dwarf form with a sprawling, weeping habit; good choice for rock gardens. Regular water
P. d. 'Umbraculifera' TANYOSHO PINE Japan	2–10, 14–17	Slow to moderate, 12–20 ft. tall, 18 ft. wide	Broad, flat topped, with many trunks from base. Often grafted onto a short single trunk	Same as for *P. densiflora*	Good for container, rock garden, Asian garden. Young trees have showy bark like that of *P. densiflora.* 'Compacta' is similar in size, denser in habit. Regular water
P. edulis (P. cembroides edulis) PIÑON, NUT PINE California's desert mountains; east to Arizona, New Mexico, and Texas; north to Wyoming	1–11, 14–21	Slow to 10–20 ft. tall, 8–16 ft. wide	Horizontally branching tree is bushy and symmetrical in youth; in age, a spreading tree with a rounded or flat crown	Needles: usually in 2s, ¾–1½ in., dark green, stiff. Cones: 2 in., roundish, light brown	Beautiful, densely foliaged small pine for container, rock garden. Lends look of age to new gardens. Cones contain edible seeds—the pine nuts sold commercially in markets
P. eldarica (P. brutia eldarica) AFGHAN PINE Southern Russia, Afghanistan, Pakistan	7–9, 11–24	Same as for *P. brutia*	Same as for *P. brutia*	Same as for *P. brutia*	One of the best pines for the desert; also thrives near Pacific Coast. Christmas Blue is a blue-green strain

PINUS

NAME, NATIVE HABITAT	ZONES	GROWTH RATE, SIZE	GROWTH HABIT	NEEDLES AND CONES	COMMENTS
P. flexilis LIMBER PINE Mountains of northern Arizona, Utah, Nevada, Southern California; eastern slopes of Rockies from Alberta to Texas. Grows at 5,000–11,000 ft.	A1–A3; 1–11, 14–21	Slow to moderate, reaching 30–55 ft. tall, 15–25 ft.wide	In youth, rather straggly pyramid. In maturity, thick-trunked tree with open, round top; many limber branches may droop at an angle to trunk. Dwarfed, more irregular at higher elevations	Needles: in 5s, to 3 in., slightly curved or twisted, dark green. Cones: 3–5 in., elongated oval, buff to buff orange	Tolerates wind. Good on rocky slopes. Takes well to shearing; can be used for bonsai. 'Vanderwolf's Pyramid' has regular form, blue-green needles
P. halepensis ALEPPO PINE Mediterranean region	8, 9, 11–24	Moderate to fast, to 30–60 ft. tall, 20–40 ft. wide	Already shows rugged character at 5 years; in age, has open, irregular crown of many short, ascending branches	Needles: usually in 2s, 2½–4 in., light green. Cones: 3 in., oval to oblong, reddish brown; stalked and bent backward	Takes poor soils, trying conditions (desert heat, seacoast). Better-looking trees can be found for milder climates. In Southwest, Aleppo blight causes temporary dieback in winter
P. h. brutia (see **P. brutia**)					
P. heldreichii **(P. h. leucodermis)** BOSNIAN PINE Balkans, Greece, Italy	2–11, 14–24	Slow to 50–75 ft. tall, 15–20 ft. wide	Erect, dense, oval to cone shaped	Needles: 2½–3½ in., in 2s, dark green, stiff, persisting 5 or 6 years. Cones: 2–3 in., narrowly oval, blue to bright brown, carried singly or in clusters of 3	Young trees have pale grayish bark on trunk and branches. Slow growth rate, dense habit, and salt tolerance make it a good landscape tree, especially near the ocean. Regular water
P. jeffreyi JEFFREY PINE Mountains of California, southern Oregon, western Nevada, Baja California	2–9, 14–19; H1	Moderate to 60–120 ft. tall, 20–25 ft. wide	Pyramidal, with straight trunk and pendulous branches. Symmetrical in youth; more open in maturity.	Needles: in 3s, 5–8 in., blue green. Cones: 6–12 in., oval, reddish brown; spiny tips of scales curve inward	Attractive in youth, with silvery gray bark and bluish foliage. In older trees, furrows in bark have vanilla odor. High-altitude tree; not at its best in lowlands
P. lambertiana SUGAR PINE Sierra Nevada and California's higher Coast Ranges; high mountains of Southern California, Baja California; north to southwestern Oregon	2–9, 15–17	Slow in youth, then faster; ultimately to 200 ft. or taller, 50 ft. wide	In youth, narrow, open pyramid with spreading, rather pendulous branches. In age, usually flat topped, with wide-spreading, open head	Needles: in 5s, 3–4 in., dark bluish green. Cones: 10–20 in., almost cylindrical, light brown	World's tallest pine. Grows well in Seattle. Huge cones are a potential hazard around play areas, patios, parked cars
P. monophylla SINGLELEAF PIÑON PINE Southeastern California south to Baja California, east to Utah, Arizona	2–12, 14–21	Very slow to 10–25 ft. tall, 10–15 ft. wide	In youth, slender, symmetrical, narrow crowned. Small and round headed in maturity, with crooked trunk; open and broad topped in old age	Needles: ¾–1½ in., gray green, stiff; seemingly carried singly, though "single" needle is two needles pressed together. Cones: 2 in., roundish, brown	Good bonsai or rock garden plant—or shrub of great character in dry, rocky places. Cones contain edible seeds (pine nuts)

Pinus attenuata

Pinus bungeana

Pinus canariensis

Pinus densiflora

Pinus edulis

PINUS

NAME, NATIVE HABITAT	ZONES	GROWTH RATE, SIZE	GROWTH HABIT	NEEDLES AND CONES	COMMENTS
P. monticola WESTERN WHITE PINE Northern California, north to British Columbia, east to Montana	1–7	Fast at first, then slow to moderate; to 60 ft. tall, 20 ft. wide	Attractive, narrow, open crowned in youth; in age, a pyramidal tree with spreading and somewhat drooping branches	Needles: in 5s, 1½–4 in., blue green striped with white beneath, very thin and soft. Cones: 5–11 in., slender, light brown	Bark is purplish, weathering to silvery color; forms plates rather than furrows
P. mugo mugo MUGHO PINE Eastern Alps and Balkan states	A1–A3; 1–11, 14–24	Slow to 4–8 ft. high, 8–15 ft. wide	From the start, a shrubby, symmetrical little pine. Often spreads in old age	Needles: in 2s, 2 in. or less, dark green, crowded on branches. Cones: to 1½ in., oval, tawny to dark brown	Widely used in rock gardens, containers. Pick plants with dense, pleasing form. Pumilio Group includes a number of compact selections
P. mugo uncinata SWISS MOUNTAIN PINE Mountains of Spain, central Europe to Balkans	A1–A3; 1–11, 14–24	Slow; highly variable in size	May be prostrate shrub, low shrub, or pyramidal tree of moderate size (30–80 ft. high and wide)	Needles: in 2s, 2 in., dark green, stout, crowded. Cones: 1–2 in., oval, tawny to dark brown	Nursery plants are generally bushy, twisted, somewhat open
P. muricata BISHOP PINE Northern coast of California, Santa Cruz Island, northwestern Baja California	5, 14–17, 22–24	Rapid to 40–75 ft. tall, 20–40 ft. wide	Open and pyramidal in youth, dense and rounded in middle life, irregular in old age	Needles: in 2s, 4–6 in., dark green. Cones: to 2–3 in., broadly oval, lopsided, brown, in whorls of 3, 4, or 5	Slower growing, denser in youth, better mannered than *P. radiata,* another pine native to California. Takes salt air. First-rate windbreak tree. *P. remorata* (Santa Cruz Island pine) and *P. cedrosensis* (Cedros Island pine) may be forms of this species
P. nigra (P. austriaca) AUSTRIAN BLACK PINE Europe, western Asia	A3; 2–10, 14–21	Slow to moderate, to 40–60 ft. tall, 20–30 ft. wide	Dense, stout, pyramidal tree with uniform crown. Branches grow in regular whorls. In old age, broad and flat topped	Needles: in 2s, 3–6½ in., very dark green, stiff. Cones: to 2–3½ in., oval, brown	Tree of strong character for landscape decoration or as windbreak in cold regions. Tolerant of urban environment and seacoast conditions. Resistant to oak root fungus. Regular water
P. parviflora JAPANESE WHITE PINE Japan and Taiwan	2–9, 14–24	Slow to moderate, to 20–50 ft. tall and wide (or larger)	In youth, a dense pyramid; in age, wide spreading, flat topped	Needles: 1½–2½ in., in 5s, bluish to green. Cones: 2–3 in., oval to oblong, reddish brown	Widely used and popular as bonsai subject, container tree. Grows well in the Seattle area and in Northern California. There are also blue-gray and dwarf forms. Regular water
P. patula JELECOTE PINE Mexico	8, 9, 14–24; H1	Very fast to 60–80 ft. tall, 30–40 ft. wide	Symmetrical pyramid with widely spaced tiers of branches	Needles: in 3s, to 1 ft., grass green, pendent. Cones: to 4½ in., sickle shaped, lustrous pale brown	Graceful tree casts light shade, provides handsome silhouette. One of the fastest-growing pines in the world. Best near coast. Resistant to oak root fungus. Regular water

▶

Pinus halepensis

Pinus mugo mugo

Pinus patula

Pinus pinea

Pinus thunbergii

P

PINUS

NAME, NATIVE HABITAT	ZONES	GROWTH RATE, SIZE	GROWTH HABIT	NEEDLES AND CONES	COMMENTS
P. pinaster CLUSTER PINE, FRENCH TURPENTINE PINE, MARITIME PINE Atlantic coast of France, western Mediterranean, northern Africa	14–24	Very fast to 80–90 ft. tall, 30–35 ft. wide	Pyramidal, with spreading or sometimes pendulous branches	Needles: in 2s, 5–9 in., glossy green, stiff. Cones: 4–7 in., oblong, glossy light brown, borne singly or in clusters	Best near coast, in coastal valleys. Well adapted to ocean exposure. Used in San Francisco's Golden Gate Park to help bind sand dunes. May be weak rooted when young
P. pinea ITALIAN STONE PINE Southern Europe and Turkey	8, 9, 12–24; H1	Moderate to 40–80 ft. tall, 40–60 ft. wide	In youth, grows as a stout, bushy globe; in middle life, develops a thick trunk topped with "umbrella" of many branches. In maturity, tree is broad and flat topped	Needles: in 2s, 5–8 in., bright green to gray green, stiff. Cones: 4–6 in., broadly oval, glossy chestnut brown	Excellent in beach gardens. Eventually too large for small gardens. Heat tolerant. The pine of Renaissance paintings; also a source of edible seeds (pine nuts)
P. ponderosa PONDEROSA PINE, WESTERN YELLOW PINE British Columbia to Mexico and east to Nebraska, Texas, northeast Oklahoma	1–10, 14–21; H1	Moderate to fast, reaching 50–100 ft. tall, 25–30 ft. wide. Grows to more than 200 ft. high in the wild	In youth, straight trunked and well branched. Stately in age, with open branches in spirelike crown	Needles: in 3s, 4–11 in., glossy yellow green to dark green, firm, in clusters at branch ends. Cones: 3–5 in., light brown to red brown, oval, prickly	Important lumber tree. Handsome orange-brown bark in plates. Useful for groves, shelter belt; also for bonsai or containers. Doesn't take desert heat and wind. *P. p. arizonica* has needles in 5s, 4s, or 3s. *P. p. scopulorum,* from Rockies, has shorter needles, drooping branches
P. radiata MONTEREY PINE Central California coast	14–24; H1	Very fast to 80–100 ft. tall, 25–35 ft. wide. Puts on 6 ft. a year when young; reaches 50 ft. in 12 years	Shapely, broad cone in youth; then drops lower branches to develop rounded or flattish crown	Needles: in 3s or 2s, 3–7 in., bright green. Cones: 3–6 in., oval, lopsided, light brown, clustered, persistent	Often shallow rooted, subject to blowing over in wind. Even in ideal climate, suffers many pests and diseases (including pitch canker) that make it a poor risk. Try to keep established plants healthy with occasional deep watering, feeding
P. roxburghii CHIR PINE, INDIAN LONGLEAF PINE Himalaya foothills	5–9, 12–24	Fairly fast to 60–80 ft. (possibly to 150 ft.) tall, 30–40 ft. wide	In youth, slender pyramid; in maturity, broad and spreading, with round-topped head	Needles: in 3s, 8–13 in., light green, slender, drooping. Cones: 4–7 in., egg shaped, lustrous brown	Similar in many respects to *P. canariensis.* Adapted to coastal regions; also succeeds in California's Central Valley as well as in Arizona's Tucson area. Cones contain edible seeds (pine nuts)
P. sabiniana GRAY PINE, FOOTHILL PINE, DIGGER PINE California foothills	3–10, 14–21	Fast to 40–80 ft. tall, 30–50 ft. wide	Irregular to round headed. Trunks are usually forked	Needles: in 3s, 8–12 in., gray green. Cones: 6–10 in., oval, chocolate brown; tips of scales are clawlike	Unusual, very ornamental tree for large gardens. Crown is bulky yet lacy, almost transparent; offers little shade. Though native to dry foothills, thrives in Seattle area. Cones contain edible seeds (pine nuts)
P. strobus WHITE PINE, EASTERN WHITE PINE Newfoundland to Manitoba, south to Georgia, west to Illinois and Iowa	1–6	Slow in seedling stage, then fast to 50–80 ft.tall (or taller), 20–40 ft. wide	Symmetrical pyramid; horizontal branches in regular whorls. Becomes broad, open, irregular with age. Fine textured, handsome	Needles: in 5s, 3–5½ in., blue green, soft. Cones: 3–8 in., slender, often curved, light brown	Intolerant of strong winds. Varieties include 'Contorta', with twisted branches and needles; 'Pendula', with weeping, trailing branches; 'Prostrata', low and trailing
P. s. Nana Group DWARF WHITE PINE	1–6	Very slow to 3–7 ft. tall, 6–12 ft. wide	Broad shrub	Same as for *P. strobus,* but needles are shorter	Useful in rock garden or container, though plants sold under this name have been known to grow into small trees. 'Blue Shag' is a blue-needled form. Regular water

P

PINUS

NAME, NATIVE HABITAT	ZONES	GROWTH RATE, SIZE	GROWTH HABIT	NEEDLES AND CONES	COMMENTS
P. sylvestris SCOTCH PINE Northern Europe, western Asia, northeastern Siberia	A1–A3; 1–9, 14–21	Fast first, then moderate, to 30–70 ft. (possibly to 100 ft.) tall, 25–30 ft. wide	In youth, a narrow, well-branched pyramid. In age, irregular, open, and picturesque, with drooping branches	Needles: in 2s, 1½–3 in., blue green, stiff; often turn yellow green in winter. Cones: 2 in., egg shaped, gray to reddish brown	Popular as a Christmas tree and in gardens. Showy red bark, sparse foliage in maturity. Wind resistant. 'French Blue' keeps its blue color in winter. Other forms include weeping 'Pendula' and dwarf forms 'Nana' and 'Watereri' (both to 12 ft. high). Regular water in hottest areas
P. s. 'Fastigiata'	A1–A3; 1–9, 14–21	Slow to 20–30 ft. tall, 4–6 ft. wide	Dense, narrow column	Same as *P. sylvestris*	Handsome, very densely foliaged
P. thunbergii JAPANESE BLACK PINE Japan	3–12, 14–21	In Northwest, fast to 100 ft. by 40 ft.; in Southern California and desert, slow to moderate, to 20 ft. by 10 ft.	Spreading branches form broad, conical tree; irregular and spreading in age, often with leaning trunk	Needles: in 2s, 3–4½ in., bright green, stiff; new growth (candles) nearly white. Cones: 3 in., oval, brown	Handsome tree that can be sheared as a Christmas tree or pruned as a cascade or giant bonsai. 'Majestic Beauty' tolerates smog. Dwarf 'Thunderhead' (6 ft. tall, 5 ft. wide in 10 years) has dark foliage. Regular water in hottest areas
P. torreyana TORREY PINE California's coastal San Diego area and Santa Rosa Island	8, 9, 14–24	Fast to 40–60 ft. tall (or more), 30–50 ft. wide	Broad, open, irregular, picturesque habit when exposed to ocean winds; tall, upright, symmetrical inland	Needles: in 5s, 8–13 in., light gray green to dark green. Cones: 4–6 in., roundish, chocolate brown	Native to coast but accepts hotter, drier conditions. Less open if grown in heavy soil. Don't prune large branches; they will die back to trunk. Resistant to oak root fungus
P. wallichiana (P. griffithii) HIMALAYAN WHITE PINE Himalayas	A2, A3; 4–6, 15–17	Slow to moderate, to 30–50 ft. tall, 15–30 ft. wide. To 150 ft. high in the wild	Broad, conical. Often retains branches to the ground in age	Needles: in 5s, 6–8 in., blue green, drooping. Cones: 6–10 in., slender, elongated oval, light brown	Good form and color make it fine choice for featured pine in big lawn or garden

Shaping a pine artistically—in the manner of trees in Japanese gardens—requires some skill, but it isn't difficult. Cut out any branches that interfere with the desired effect, shorten others, and create an upswept look by removing all twigs that grow downward. Cut vertical main trunk back to a well-placed side branch to induce side growth; wire or weight branches to produce a cascade effect.

Pines are vulnerable to air pollution, which causes abnormal needle drop and poor growth and may even kill the tree. They are also subject to a number of pests and diseases, but healthy, well-grown plants will usually maintain their vigor with comparatively little attention. Many five-needle pines are subject to a blister rust (a bark disease that can kill the tree) when grown in the vicinity of currants or gooseberries. In the Pacific Northwest, distorted or dead new shoots on two- and three-needle pines indicate an infestation of European pine shoot moth larvae. In California, engraver beetles sometimes bore into bark of Aleppo, beach, Bishop, Coulter, Monterey, ponderosa, and Torrey pines. Sticky secretions, sooty mold, and yellowing needles indicate aphid infestation.

Pinus pinea

It is unlikely that any one nursery will stock most of the pines described in the chart. Bonsai specialists often offer a wide variety. For help in locating rare pines, consult your nursery. Your Cooperative Extension Office can also offer advice concerning each tree's adaptability to your area and any local environmental or pest problems.

PIPESTEMS. See CLEMATIS lasiantha

PISTACHE. See PISTACIA

PISTACHIO NUT

Anacardiaceae

DECIDUOUS TREE

ZONES 7–12, 14, 15, 18–21 (SEE TEXT)

FULL SUN

MODERATE WATER

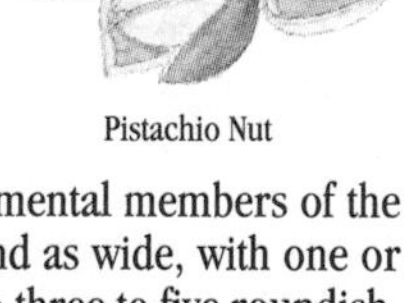

Pistachio Nut

Botanically known as *Pistacia vera,* this native of southwestern and central Asia produces the pistachio nuts sold in markets; for strictly ornamental members of the genus, see *Pistacia.* Tree grows to 25–30 ft. tall and as wide, with one or several trunks. Its gray-green leaves are divided into three to five roundish, 2–4-in.-long leaflets.

Male and female plants are separate; to get fruit, be sure to include a male tree in your planting. 'Peters' is the most commonly grown male; 'Kerman' is the principal female (fruiting) variety. On female trees, small brownish green spring flowers are followed by heavy clusters of soft, wrinkled, reddish husks that contain the hard-shelled pistachio nuts. Harvest nuts in early autumn: spread a tarp beneath tree, then shake tree until nuts fall. Strip off and discard husks; dip nuts in water and dry them in the sun until shells split (dipping in water helps the shells split). Some people like to add flavor by boiling the husked nuts in salted water for a few minutes before drying them.

Nut production is best in Zones 8–11, where trees get just the right amount of summer heat and winter chill. Trees grow well in Zones 7, 12, 14, 15, 18–21, but crops are unpredictable—and when they do appear, nut meats often do not properly fill shells.

When planting, avoid rough handling; budded tops are easily broken away from understock. Susceptible to verticillium wilt and oak root fungus; to lessen disease risk, grow in well-drained soil and water deeply and infrequently.

Trees are inclined to spread and droop; stake them and train to a good framework of four or five limbs beginning 4 ft. or so above ground. Take 5 to 8 years to begin bearing and many years to reach full yield. Tend to bear more heavily in alternate years. Established trees will survive with little water, but nut quality is best if trees receive periodic deep soakings.

PISTACIA

PISTACHE

Anacardiaceae

EVERGREEN, SEMIEVERGREEN, DECIDUOUS TREES AND SHRUBS

ZONES VARY BY SPECIES

FULL SUN

WATER NEEDS VARY BY SPECIES

Pistacia chinensis

These are ornamental species; for the plant grown for edible nuts, see Pistachio Nut. Glossy deep green leaves divided into leaflets; insignificant flowers. If male trees are nearby, female trees will bear clusters of tiny fruits. Verticillium wilt may strike established trees. Minimize susceptibility by planting in well-drained soil, watering deeply but infrequently. Young trees tend to be irregular in form and benefit from early training and pruning.

P. atlantica. MOUNT ATLAS PISTACHE. Semievergreen or deciduous tree. Zones 8–24. From the Mediterranean region. Slow to moderate growth to 45–60 ft. tall and wide. More regular and pyramidal than other pistaches, especially in youth. Leaves have 7–11 narrow leaflets to 2 in. long, rounded at tip. Nearly evergreen in mildest-winter areas of range; holds foliage into late autumn where winters are cold. Dark blue or purple fruit. Needs good drainage. Tolerates desert heat and winds. No irrigation needed. Not widely grown as an ornamental but is much used as understock for pistachio nut .

P. chinensis. CHINESE PISTACHE. Deciduous tree. Zones 4–16, 18–23; little grown in Zones 4–7. From China. Slow to moderate growth to 30–60 ft. tall, with nearly equal spread. Foot-long leaves consist of 10–16 narrow, 2–4-in.-long leaflets. Good fall color, even in mild climates: foliage turns luminous orange to red (sometimes shades of yellow). This is the only tree to color scarlet in the desert. Fruit is red at first, then ripens to blue black. Tolerates a wide range of conditions. Accepts various watering regimes, from no water at all (this only in deep soils) to regular lawn watering (though verticillium wilt is a danger with the latter). Takes moderately alkaline soil. Resistant to oak root fungus. Reliable tree for streetside planting, lawn, patio, or garden.

P. lentiscus. MASTIC. Evergreen shrub or tree. Zones 8, 9, 12–24. From the Mediterranean region. Slow growth to 15–25 ft. high, 20–30 ft. wide. Three to five pairs of leaflets to 1 in. long. Fruit ripens from red to black. Useful as a screen plant for hot, dry locations and poor soil. Sap is the source of mastic, an aromatic resin. Little or no water (monthly soaking is best in Zones 12, 13).

FOR GROWING SYMBOL EXPLANATIONS
PLEASE SEE PAGE 161

PISTIA stratiotes

WATER LETTUCE

Araceae

AQUATIC PERENNIAL

ZONES 24; H2

FULL SUN OR LIGHT SHADE

LOCATE IN PONDS, WATER GARDENS

Pistia stratiotes

Native to many parts of the tropics. Attractive plant that resembles a floating, grayish green loose-head lettuce; each foliage rosette grows to about 4 in. high and wide. The trailing roots provide a refuge for small fish. Inconspicuous flowers. Increases by offsets and can become a pest in open tropical waters.

PITANGA. See EUGENIA uniflora

PITHECELLOBIUM

Fabaceae (Leguminosae)

EVERGREEN, SEMIEVERGREEN, DECIDUOUS TREES

ZONES VARY BY SPECIES

FULL SUN

LITTLE TO MODERATE WATER

Pithecellobium flexicaule

These trees are noted for divided leaves, thorns at leaf bases or along stems, and clusters of small flowers (fragrant, in some species) that develop into brown, flattened, often curved seedpods. Pods are a minor litter problem. Plant where thorns will not snag passersby (or train to a high canopy to eliminate this problem). Prune as needed to shape, watching out for sharp thorns.

P. dulce 'Variegata'. WHITE 'OPIUMA. Evergreen. Zones 13; H1, H2. *P. dulce* itself (from Mexico and Central America) is a pest in Hawaii, but this variegated-leaf form is a desirable tree in Island gardens. To 40 ft. tall, with dense canopy to 30 ft. wide. Leaves are divided into just two pairs of green leaflets marbled with white. Variegation is most pronounced in new growth; leaves may turn solid green by late summer. Inconspicuous whitish, ball-shaped flower heads in summer. Does not usually produce pods. Moderate tolerance to wind, salt spray.

P. flexicaule. TEXAS EBONY. Evergreen to semievergreen. Zones 10–13. From southern Texas, Mexico. Its handsome deep green color is especially welcome in desert landscapes. Slow grower to 15–30 ft. tall and 15–20 ft. wide, with short, smooth gray trunk. Zigzagging thorny branches and twigs are densely set with dark green leaves consisting of three to five pairs of leaflets; tree casts heavy shade. Feathery spikes of creamy yellow, fragrant flowers appear in spring and early summer. Seedpods are 4–6 in. long.

P. mexicanum. MEXICAN EBONY. Deciduous. Zones 12, 13. From Mexico. To 20–30 ft. (possibly to 45 ft.) tall and 30 ft. wide, with sturdy, upright trunk. Small grayish green leaves have three to ten pairs of leaflets. Young bark is grayish green. Canopy and branching pattern are both rather open, creating filtered shade beneath the tree. Little puffballs of white, slightly scented flowers in spring. Pods are 1–3 in. long.

P. pallens. TENAZA, APE'S EARRING. Evergreen. Zones 12, 13. From southern Texas, Mexico. To 10–30 ft. tall, 8–12 ft. wide, with gray bark, small thorns, and medium green leaves with three to ten pairs of leaflets. White flowers in small puffballs from late spring into summer, usually after rains. Pods to 2 in. long.

Pittosporaceae. The pittosporum family consists of evergreen shrubs, trees, and vines from Australia, New Zealand, and eastern Asia. Many have attractive flowers, foliage, or fruit. Sweetshade *(Hymenosporum)*, *Pittosporum*, and Australian bluebell creeper *(Sollya)* are representatives.

PITTOSPORUM

Pittosporaceae

EVERGREEN SHRUBS OR TREES

ZONES VARY BY SPECIES

FULL SUN OR PARTIAL SHADE

MODERATE TO REGULAR WATER, EXCEPT AS NOTED

Pittosporum undulatum

These plants are valued primarily for their foliage and form, though they also bear clusters of small, bell-shaped, often sweetly fragrant flowers followed by fairly conspicuous fruits the size of large peas. All are basic, dependable plants with pleasing outlines when allowed to branch naturally. Prune periodically to enhance form, thinning out weak branches and wayward shoots. Some make good clipped hedges. Excellent for screens, windbreaks. Susceptible to aphids and scale insects; sooty mold on leaves is a sign of infestation. Ripe fruits (usually orange) split open to reveal sticky seeds; fallen fruit can be a nuisance on lawns, paving.

P. brevicalyx. Zones 8, 9, 14–24. Native to China. To 18–20 ft. tall, 16–18 ft. wide. Leathery, glossy dark green leaves have somewhat silvery undersides, reach 4–5 in. long, 1½–2 in. wide. Large clusters of fragrant bright yellow flowers in spring. Produces very little fruit.

P. crassifolium. Zones 9, 14–17, 19–24. From New Zealand. Can reach 25 ft. tall and 20 ft. wide in 8 to 10 years, but yearly pruning easily keeps it to 6–10 ft. tall, 6–8 ft. wide. Branches are densely clothed in gray-green, 1–2-in.-long leaves with rounded ends. Maroon flowers in late spring. Tolerates seaside conditions. 'Compactum' grows to 3 ft. or a bit taller, with equal spread.

P. eugenioides. Zones 9, 14–17, 19–22; H1, H2. From New Zealand. To 20–40 ft. tall, 15–30 ft. wide. Often seen as a high hedge or screen plant; unpruned, becomes a tree with a curving gray trunk. Yellow-green to medium green, wavy-edged, lance-shaped, 2–4-in.-long leaves. Fragrant yellow flowers in spring. Set 1½ ft. apart for a hedge; force bushiness by shearing 2–6 in. from tops of plants several times each year between midwinter and early fall. A form with foliage edged in creamy white grows just 10 ft. tall; it needs partial shade in hottest climates.

P. phillyreoides. WILLOW PITTOSPORUM. Zones 8, 9, 12–24. Native to Australia. Slow grower to 12–20 ft. tall, 10–15 ft. wide. This species differs from other pittosporums in both habit and leaf shape; it is a weeping plant with trailing branches and dark green, very narrow leaves to 3 in. long. Blooms in late winter and early spring, bearing very fragrant yellow flowers. Deep yellow fruit follows the blossoms. Always looks best standing alone; its strong structure should not be diminished by competing foliage. Good by pool or patio. If drainage is poor, water infrequently but very deeply. Tolerates heat and aridity better than other pittosporums and has even naturalized in some desert areas.

P. rhombifolium. QUEENSLAND PITTOSPORUM. Zones 12–24; H1, H2. From Australia. Grows slowly to 15–35 ft. tall, 12–25 ft. wide. Rich green, glossy, nearly diamond-shaped leaves to 4 in. long. White flowers in late spring. Growth is open enough to let you see the showy clusters of round, 1½-in., yellow to orange fruits that decorate the plant from fall through winter. As a small tree, well suited for lawn or patio (as long as sticky fruit won't pose a problem). Or plant several as a not-too-dense screen that needs little pruning. Resistant to oak root fungus.

P. tenuifolium (P. nigricans). Zones 9, 14–17, 19–24. From New Zealand. To 15–25 ft. tall, 10–15 ft. wide. Similar in form to *P. eugenioides* but has darker twigs and leafstalks; purple flowers; shorter, more oval, deeper green leaves with less wavy edges; and greater tolerance for seacoast conditions. 'Silver Sheen' has a somewhat more open habit than the species and smaller, silvery green leaves. 'Marjorie Channon', to about 8 ft. high and wide, has green leaves bordered in creamy white.

P. tobira. TOBIRA. Zones 8–24; H1, H2. Worth trying in Zones 4–7. From Japan. Dense, rounded growth 6–15 ft. (rarely to 30 ft.) tall and wide. You can remove lower limbs from an older plant to make a small tree, or you can hold plant to 6 ft. by careful heading back and thinning (doesn't look good sheared). Whorls of leathery, narrowly elliptical, shiny dark green leaves to 5 in. long. In early spring, creamy white flowers with fragrance of orange blossoms are borne at branch tips. Seldom flowers in Hawaii. Good for screen, tall hedge, multistemmed specimen of interesting, irregular form. Very tolerant of seacoast conditions. 'Variegata' grows 5–10 ft. high and wide, has leaves in gray green and gray with an irregular creamy white margin. It makes a good hedge or foundation plant; sometimes loses many leaves in winter.

Pittosporum tobira

Several compact selections are available. Most common is 'Wheeler's Dwarf', to 2–3 ft. high and 4–5 ft. wide, with the same handsome leaves as *P. tobira.* It is a choice plant for foreground, low boundary, even small-scale ground cover; good near swimming pools. 'Turner's Variegated Dwarf' is the size of 'Wheeler's Dwarf' but has foliage like that of 'Variegata'. 'Cream de Mint' is smaller—just 2–2½ ft. high and wide—and has mint green leaves with a creamy white border.

P. undulatum. VICTORIAN BOX. Zones 14 and 15 (with protection), 16, 17, 21–24; H1, H2. From Australia. Fairly fast to 15 ft., then slow to 30–40 ft. high and wide. Glossy green, lance-shaped, wavy-edged leaves up to 6 in. long. Creamy white, very fragrant flowers in early spring. Makes dense, single- or multitrunked, dome-shaped tree of great beauty. Plants set 5–8 ft. apart can make a thick, 10–15-ft.-tall screen with selective pruning (not shearing). Roots are strong, becoming invasive with age.

P. viridiflorum. CAPE PITTOSPORUM. Zones 15–17, 20–24; H1, H2. From South Africa. To 25 ft. tall and wide. Leaves to 3 in. long are glossy deep green above, paler beneath, often with inrolled edges; tips may be sharp or blunt. Dense clusters of fragrant yellowish green flowers in late spring. Resembles a large *P. tobira.* Use as screen, garden tree, street tree.

PLANE TREE. See PLATANUS

PLANTAIN LILY. See HOSTA

PLATANUS

PLANE TREE, SYCAMORE

Platanaceae

DECIDUOUS TREES

ZONES VARY BY SPECIES

FULL SUN

MODERATE TO REGULAR WATER

Platanus × acerifolia

All are large, with heavy trunk (or trunks) and sculptural branch pattern. Older bark sheds in patches to reveal pale, smooth new bark beneath. Big, rough-surfaced leaves (to 10 in. across) have three to five lobes, resemble maple *(Acer)* leaves. Fall foliage color is yellowish to brown, not striking. Ball-shaped brown seed clusters, usually on threadlike stalks, hang on the bare branches through winter; these are prized for winter arrangements. Best in rich, deep, moist, well-drained soil. All are subject to anthracnose, which causes early leaf drop and twig dieback. Rake up and dispose of dead leaves, since fungus spores can overwinter on them. Chlorosis may be a problem in the desert.

P. × acerifolia (P. × hispanica). LONDON PLANE TREE. Zones 2–24. Hybrid between *P. occidentalis* and *P. orientalis;* often sold under the latter name. Grows fast to 40–80 ft. tall, with 30–40-ft. spread. Creamy new bark weathers to gray. Looks very handsome in winter. Tolerates many soil types and stands up beautifully to smog, soot, dust, and reflected heat. Susceptible to mildew. Good tree for avenue, street, park, large lawn. When pollarded to create a low, dense canopy, it can fit smaller spaces. 'Bloodgood' is resistant to anthracnose; 'Yarwood' is mildew resistant; 'Columbia' is resistant to both diseases. ▸

P. occidentalis. AMERICAN SYCAMORE, BUTTONWOOD. Zones 1–24. Native to eastern U.S. Similar to *P.* ×*acerifolia* but has whiter new bark and a longer leafless period. Irregular habit, contorted branches. Occasionally grows with multiple or leaning trunks. Old trees near streams sometimes reach huge size. Best in a large wild garden.

P. racemosa. CALIFORNIA SYCAMORE. Zones 4–24. Robust native of California foothills and Coast Ranges; grows near streams in the wild. Fast rate of growth to 30–80 ft. tall and 20–50 ft. wide, frequently with multiple or leaning trunks. Smooth branches are often gracefully twisted and contorted. Attractive, patchy bark in brown, gray, white. Deeply lobed leaves turn dusty brown early in autumn; in mild coastal climates, they hang on until new growth starts. In winter, virtually stemless seed balls are carried three to seven along a single stalk. Tolerates much heat, wind. With careful pruning, can be trained into picturesque multitrunked clump. For large informal or wild garden.

P. wrightii (P. racemosa wrightii). ARIZONA SYCAMORE. Zones 10–12. To 80 ft. tall, 55 ft. wide. Native along streams and canyons in mountains of southern and eastern Arizona. Resembles *P. racemosa,* but leaves are more deeply lobed and seed clusters have individual stems branching from common stalk.

PLATYCERIUM

STAGHORN FERN
Polypodiaceae
FERNS
ZONES VARY BY SPECIES; OR INDOORS
PARTIAL SHADE; INDIRECT LIGHT
REGULAR WATER

Platycerium bifurcatum

Native to tropical regions, where they grow on trees; gardeners grow them on slabs of bark or tree fern stem, occasionally in hanging baskets or attached to trees. Do best with regular moisture, though they can dry out briefly without suffering damage. Plants have two kinds of fronds. Sterile ones are flat, pale green, aging to tan and brown; they support the plant and accumulate organic matter to help feed it. Fertile fronds are forked, resembling deer antlers. Give indoor plants light that is filtered through a sheer window covering, or set them in a window shaded by a tree. Flourish in eastern exposures; also do well in north-facing windows.

P. bifurcatum. Zones 15–17, 19–24; H1, H2. From Australia and New Guinea. Surprisingly hardy; has survived 20°F/–6°C with only lath structure for shelter. To 3 ft. high and wide. Gray-green, clustered fertile fronds. Makes numerous offsets that can be used in propagation. Often sold as *P. alcicorne.*

P. superbum. Zones 23, 24; H2. From Australia. To 6 ft. tall, 5 ft. wide. Fertile fronds are gray green, broad but forked; look something like moose antlers. Sterile fronds are also forked. Protect from frosts.

PLATYCODON grandiflorus

BALLOON FLOWER
Campanulaceae (Lobeliaceae)
PERENNIAL
ZONES 1–10, 14–24
LIGHT SHADE IN HOTTEST CLIMATES
REGULAR WATER

Platycodon grandiflorus

From Siberia, northern China, Japan. To 3 ft. tall and 2 ft. wide. Inflated, balloonlike buds are carried on slender stalks at the ends of upright stems clad in broadly oval, 1–3-in.-long, light olive green leaves. Buds open to 2-in.-wide, star-shaped, blue-violet flowers with purple veins. Bloom begins in early summer and continues for 2 months or more if spent blossoms (not entire stems) are removed. Pink, white, and double-flowered varieties are available. Blossoms of 1½–2-ft. 'Komachi' keep their balloon shape, never opening fully. *P. g. mariesii* grows only 1–1½ ft. high and wide; 'Apoyama' reaches 10–12 in. high, 8 in. wide.

Balloon flower is easy to grow from seed, but it is deep rooted and takes 2 or 3 years to get well established. Dies back completely in fall, and new growth appears quite late in spring; mark position to avoid digging up fleshy roots. If you do unearth a root, replace it (or the pieces) right away. Protect roots from gophers. Grow as winter annual in Zones 12, 13.

PLECOSTACHYS serpyllifolia

Asteraceae (Compositae)
PERENNIAL
ZONES 8, 9, 14–24
FULL SUN
MODERATE WATER

Plecostachys serpyllifolia

South African native to 1½ ft. tall, spreading to twice as wide or more. Tiny, furry, whitish leaves are closely packed along sprawling, woody-based stems. Grown for its foliage rather than its clusters of small pinkish flowers. This plant has been sold as a dwarf form of *Helichrysum petiolare,* which it resembles in miniature. Attractive gray plant for ground or bank cover, large rock garden, or border.

PLECTRANTHUS

Lamiaceae (Labiatae)
PERENNIALS AND EVERGREEN SHRUBS
ZONES 22–24; H2; OR INDOORS
PARTIAL SHADE, EXCEPT AS NOTED; BRIGHT INDIRECT LIGHT
REGULAR WATER

Plectranthus oertendahlii

Close relatives of coleus; native to many tropical regions of the world. They have square stems, opposite pairs of fleshy, tooth-edged or scalloped leaves, and whorls of tubular, two-lipped blossoms. Some are highly aromatic, used as seasonings or home remedies. Others are grown for their attractive foliage, yet others for their striking floral displays. Some are good bedding plants for summer color; some make dense, weed-suppressing ground covers for frost-protected areas. Several are trailing plants that drape gracefully from hanging baskets or wall pots. All are superb in containers, either alone or in combination with other plants.

Easy to grow. Stems take root wherever they touch the ground. Cuttings root quickly in soil or water. Remove flower spikes after they fade. *P. argentatus* and *P. fruticosus* are the shrubbiest of the species listed here, but the others get somewhat woody at the base after a year or more. Pinch all types to induce branching; discard old plants when they become leggy or too woody and start new ones.

Confusion reigns in *Plectranthus* nomenclature, with different nurseries selling the same plant under different names. Here are some of the most interesting species.

P. amboinicus (Coleus amboinicus). CUBAN OREGANO, SPANISH THYME, INDIAN MINT. From Africa. Summer-blooming trailer to 1 ft. high, 3 ft. wide, with white, lilac-pink, or light purple flowers in 6-in. spikes. Velvety, ovate gray-green leaves are 3 in. long, with broadly toothed edges. Popular in Cuban cooking, they have a fragrance that falls midway between oregano and thyme but has a sweet note not present in either. Leaves of 'Variegatus' are bordered in cream, with the very edge often tinged bright pink; excellent flavor. 'Well-Sweep' ('Wedgwood'), with extra-sweet flavor, has leaves in chartreuse and gray green with a dark green margin; Wedgwood blue flowers.

P. argentatus. From Australia. Erect to spreading plant to 3 ft. tall, 6 ft. or wider. Densely hairy, scallop-edged, oval leaves to 7 in. long are silvery gray green, with a light purplish flush on growing tips and stems. Pink-tinged white flowers in foot-long spikes in late summer, fall. Best in at least half-day direct sun; will take hot afternoon sun if adequately watered.

P. australis. See P. verticillatus

P. ciliatus. From southern Africa. Handsome, burgundy-stemmed trailer to 6–12 in. high, 3–5 ft. wide. Excellent dense ground cover. Late summer and fall white or purplish flowers in 8–12-in. spikes. Oval leaves to 3½ in. long, with finely toothed edges and pointed tips; leaves have deep green upper surfaces, burgundy undersides and veins. 'Old Gold' leaves are yellow or chartreuse above, burgundy beneath; new leaves are flushed with burgundy. 'Tricolor' is similar, but tops of leaves also have dark green splotches. Both varieties have white blooms.

P. coleoides 'Marginata'. See P. forsteri 'Marginatus'

P. cylindraceus (P. marrubioides). VICK'S PLANT, MENTHOLATO. From Africa. Mounding growth to 1½–3 ft. high, 2–4 ft. wide. Sometimes blooms, bearing blue or lavender flowers in dense, narrow, pointed spikes 12–15 in. long (there may be a pair of shorter spikes near base). Velvety, triangular gray-green leaves 1½–3 in. long, with three to five broad teeth on each side of leaf. Foliage smells like a combination of camphor and menthol and is used medicinally in Mexico.

P. forsteri. From Australia, Fiji, New Caledonia. To 10 in. high, 3 ft. wide; stems actually grow 3 ft. tall, but they arch over from weight of foliage. Tip-pinch early to induce branching; repeat to keep compact. Medium green, ovate, irregularly toothed leaves to 4 in. long. White or pale mauve flowers in 6–8-in. spikes are produced intermittently throughout the year. Leaves of 'Marginatus' (*P. coleoides* 'Marginata') are irregularly edged in creamy white. 'Green and Gold' has lime green leaves with a neat gold margin.

P. fruticosus. From South Africa. Upright growth to 3–5 ft. tall, 2–4 ft. wide. Lance-shaped, coarsely toothed leaves to 4 in. long are olive green above, purplish beneath. Blooms in autumn, bearing mauve pink or bluish blossoms in very showy clusters to 1 ft. long, half as wide.

P. madagascariensis. MINTLEAF. From southern Africa. Vigorous trailer reaches 1 ft. high; spreads 3–4 ft. wide initially, eventually much wider by rooting at leaf joints. Medium green leaves to 2 in. long are hairy, roundish, scallop edged; they smell like mint when crushed. Lavender-blue or white flower spikes in late spring, early summer. 'Variegated Mintleaf', the most commonly grown form, has irregular white leaf margins. Good ground cover to brighten shady areas. Often mistakenly sold as *Iboza,* another genus in the same family.

P. oertendahlii. MOSAIC SWEDISH IVY, ROYAL CHARLIE, CANDLE PLANT. From South Africa. Easy-care specimen for hanging basket or pot; most often grown as houseplant. To 8–12 in. high, with branches trailing to 1½–2 ft. long. Roundish, irregularly toothed, velvety dark green leaves up to 2½ in. long, with purple undersides and intricate network of silver veins. In fall, whitish flowers bloom in loose, 8–12-in.-long spikes. Foliage of 'Uvongo' is more heavily netted with silver than that of the species; leaves of 'Variegatus' are irregularly edged in creamy white.

P. parviflorus. 'ALA 'ALA WAI NUI. From Hawaii, Australia. Occurs naturally in dry, exposed locations. Spreading, trailing plant grows to 6–8 in. or possibly higher; spreads to 3 ft. but can be easily restrained. Light green, toothed leaves are covered with short, silvery fuzz. Short spikes of pale blue flowers bloom all year. Use in hanging baskets, rock garden, or as small-scale ground cover.

P. verticillatus. SWEDISH IVY, CREEPING CHARLIE. From southern Africa. Typically grown in hanging basket or pot in the house or outdoors; also makes a good ground cover in a warm, protected spot. To 4–8 in. high, 4–6 ft. wide, with trailing branches. Waxy, shiny dark green, scallop-edged leaves are roundish, to 1½ in. across. White or pale purplish blossoms in 8-in. spikes bloom intermittently all year. To grow as a ground cover, plant cuttings 1–2 ft. apart for quick coverage. Often incorrectly sold as *P. australis* or *P. nummularis.* 'Marmoratus' produces leaves irregularly marked with ivory.

FOR INFORMATION ON SELECTING PLANTS
PLEASE SEE PAGES 64–160

PLEIOBLASTUS. See BAMBOO

PLEIONE

Orchidaceae

TERRESTRIAL ORCHIDS

ZONES 5–9, 14–24; OR INDOORS

PARTIAL SHADE; BRIGHT INDIRECT LIGHT

REGULAR WATER DURING GROWTH AND BLOOM

Pleione bulbocodioides

Dwarf orchids native to high mountains of India and China. Many species, all deciduous. Each pseudobulb produces one or two narrowly oval, pleated-looking leaves; leaves reach 8 in. long in the biggest species. Flowers are large (3–4 in. wide) for the size of the plant and resemble small cattleyas; they usually appear just as the leaves begin to show in early spring. Blossoms of *P. bulbocodioides* are purple with a white lip marked with reddish spots. Those of *P. formosana* are purple, pink, or white; fringed lip has yellow center with brownish red markings.

Where frosts are rare and summer temperatures moderate, these orchids can be grown outdoors all year—provided they have perfect drainage, rich soil that is moist and well aerated, and some winter protection (shelter from excessive rain). Usually grown in rock gardens or in pots. For a good show, plant pseudobulbs close together. If planting in the ground, bury pseudobulbs, leaving just the tips exposed; or plant in a shallow pot and bury only the bottom quarter of each pseudobulb. Repot yearly before growth begins.

PLUM (including Prune)

Rosaceae

DECIDUOUS FRUIT TREES

ZONES VARY BY VARIETY

FULL SUN

MODERATE WATER

SEE CHART PAGE 535

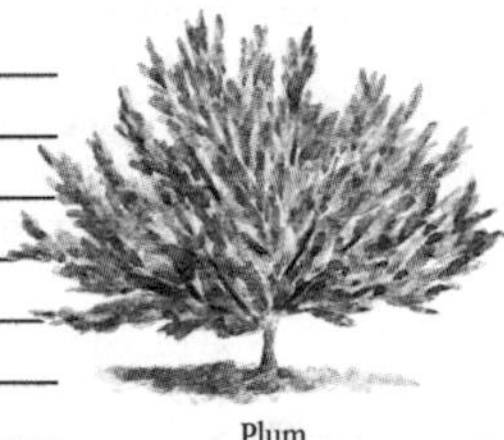

Plum

Like their cherry, peach, and apricot relatives, these are stone fruits of the genus *Prunus.* For flowering plums, see pages 551–552. Three categories of edible plums and prunes are grown in the West: European, Japanese, and hardy. All bloom in late winter or early spring; fruit ripens at some point from May into September, depending on variety and climate.

The two most widely grown groups are European *(Prunus × domestica)* and Japanese *(P. salicina).* 'Damson' plum, which is sometimes considered a separate species *(P. insititia),* is probably a type of European plum *(P. × domestica insititia);* 'Damson' interbreeds freely with other European plums. Prunes are European plum varieties with a high sugar content that makes it possible to sun-dry the fruit without it fermenting at the pit.

European plums and prunes bloom later than Japanese plums and are better adapted to areas with late frosts or cool, rainy spring weather. Most European varieties have a moderately high chill need that excludes them from extremely mild-winter areas. Many European and Japanese varieties are self-fruitful, but others need cross-pollination to produce good crops. The chart lists proven pollenizers, but other choices also exist; consult a knowledgeable local nursery for more information.

Where winters are severe, a third plum category dominates. This is a complex group of hardy hybrids involving Japanese plum, several species of native American wild plums, and the native Western sand cherry *(P. besseyi).* Those with fruit near the size and quality of Japanese plums are sometimes called Japanese-American hybrids; those with smaller fruit closer in flavor to wild species are often called cherry-plum hybrids. The hardy hybrids originated in Canada, the Dakotas, and Minnesota and are exceptionally tolerant of cold and wind. Pollination of hardy hybrids is difficult; ask local nurseries about effective pollenizers. ▶

P

Plums come in many colors—both inside and out. Skin may be yellow, red, purple, green, blue, or almost black; flesh may be yellow, red, or green. Japanese plums are the largest and juiciest of the lot, with a pleasant blend of acid and sugar; they are mainly eaten fresh. European plums have firmer flesh and can be cooked or eaten fresh; prune varieties are largely used for drying or canning, but they can also be eaten fresh if you like the very sweet flavor. Many hardy plums are tasty fresh, while others are better cooked or used in preserves.

Plum

As orchard trees, both Japanese and European plums reach 15–20 ft. tall with somewhat wider spread, but with pruning they are easily kept to 10–15 ft. high and wide. Differences in growth habit are discussed below. There are no truly dwarfing rootstocks for plums, and semidwarf trees are only slightly smaller than standards. Some of the hardy hybrids are trees; others grow as bushes to about 6 ft. high and at least as wide.

Most Japanese plum trees are trained to a vase shape, with five or six main scaffold branches; fruiting laterals grow from these scaffolds. Where space is limited, trees can be trained in a more linear fashion (against a wall or fence, for example). Japanese varieties tend to make tremendous shoot growth, and rather severe pruning is necessary at all ages, regardless of training method. Many varieties produce excessive vertical growth; shorten these shoots to outside branchlets.

European plums do not branch as freely as Japanese types, so selection of framework branches is limited; these plums are usually trained to a central leader. Mature European plums require pruning mainly to thin out annual shoot growth; otherwise, little is needed. If you grow hardy hybrids, prune them to renew unfruitful branches (on shrubby types, remove older shoots to the ground every few years) and to keep the plant's center open.

In the dry-summer West, plums are subject to far fewer problems than peaches or apples. Dormant-season sprays combining horticultural oil with lime sulfur or fixed copper will control the fungal disease brown rot and various insect pests, including scale. Peach tree borer is another potential pest; see Peach and Nectarine.

P

WHAT PLUMS NEED

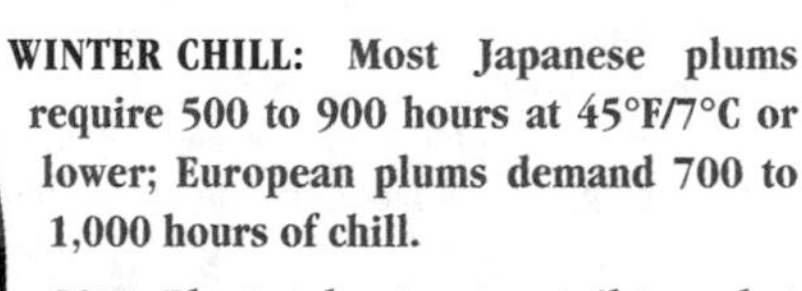
'Green Gage'

WINTER CHILL: Most Japanese plums require 500 to 900 hours at 45°F/7°C or lower; European plums demand 700 to 1,000 hours of chill.

SOIL: Plants tolerate many soil types but do best in fertile, well-drained soil.

FERTILIZING: For larger fruit and vigorous growth, feed heavily. Orchardists give Japanese plums 1–3 lbs. of actual nitrogen a year; they give European plums 1–2 lbs. Home gardeners, however, can usually get by with much less. Hardy hybrids need only light applications of nitrogen.

FRUIT THINNING: Japanese varieties bear very heavily, producing much small fruit. If the entire crop were allowed to ripen, its weight might damage the tree—so thin fruits to 4–6 in. apart as soon as they are large enough to be seen. Other plums usually don't need thinning unless the tree sets a particularly large amount of fruit.

PRUNING: Japanese varieties require heavy annual pruning to ensure fruit set and healthy growth throughout the tree. European plums and hardy hybrids need much less attention.

PLUM, FLOWERING. See PRUNUS

Plumbaginaceae. The leadwort family consists of shrubs and perennials with clusters of funnel-shaped flowers and includes thrift *(Armeria)* and two genera commonly called plumbago *(Ceratostigma* and *Plumbago).*

PLUMBAGO

Plumbaginaceae

EVERGREEN OR SEMIEVERGREEN SHRUBS

ZONES VARY BY SPECIES

FULL SUN OR LIGHT SHADE

LITTLE TO REGULAR WATER

Plumbago auriculata

Sprawling plants that bloom over a long season, bearing phloxlike clusters of blue or white flowers at branch ends. Prune these shrubs back hard in late winter to control their growth and keep them compact. For other plants called plumbago, see *Ceratostigma.*

P. auriculata (P. capensis). CAPE PLUMBAGO. Evergreen or semievergreen. Zones 8, 9, 12–24; H1, H2. Native to South Africa. Makes a mounding shrub to 6 ft. tall, 8–10 ft. wide; or, if tied to a support, grows as a vine to 12 ft. or more. Oblong, 1–2-in, light to medium green leaves. Inch-wide flowers. In seedling plants, blossom color varies from white through pure light blue to sky blue; best way to get good blue color is to buy cutting-grown selections such as 'Royal Cape' or 'Imperial Blue'. 'Alba' is a white selection. Blooms from spring through summer—or nearly all year in warm, frost-free locations. Flowers are used in leis.

Evergreen where frosts are absent or light; heavy frost can burn new growth and blacken leaves, but recovery is fast. Prune out any damaged parts when frost danger is past. In colder part of range, plant in spring to give plants time to become established before cold weather arrives. Not fussy about soil type but must have good drainage. Good cover for bank, fence, wall; good background and filler plant.

P. scandens. Evergreen. Zones 12, 13, 21–24; H1, H2. Native from Florida to Arizona, south to Central America. To 4 ft. or more high and wide. Oblong leaves to 4 in. long are deep red when new, maturing to medium green; nearly all foliage turns red in late fall and winter. Blooms year-round (with a short break during hottest part of summer), bearing typically white (sometimes blue-tinged) flowers nearly 1 in. wide. Particularly striking when white blooms appear in combination with red leaves. With this species, hard pruning both controls size and encourages the growth of colorful new foliage. Accepts most soils. Can get powdery mildew in late summer but doesn't seem to be greatly harmed by it. Attractive ground cover. 'Summer Snow' has pure white blooms.

Plumbago scandens

PLUMBAGO larpentae. See CERATOSTIGMA plumbaginoides

PLUMCOT, PLUOT, APRIUM

Rosaceae

DECIDUOUS FRUIT TREES

ZONES VARY BY TYPE

FULL SUN

MODERATE WATER

'Flavor Delight' Aprium

These hybrids between plum and apricot combine characteristics of both fruits in varying degrees. The differences among them are somewhat blurred. Like their parents, they need winter chill for good fruit production. Not yet widely tested, so zone listings are preliminary.

Plumcot. Zones 2, 3, 7–12, 14–23. This was the original plum-apricot cross made by Luther Burbank. One modern variety, 'Plum Parfait', is widely sold. It has pinkish orange skin, flesh marbled in crimson and amber, and a wonderfully sweet-tart, plumlike flavor; ripens in mid- to late summer. Tree resembles both plum and apricot but is slightly smaller and more compact than either. Treat as for Japanese plum. Self-fruitful but takes 5 years or more to begin bearing.

Pluot. Zones 2, 3, 7–12, 14–23. Enjoys similar conditions and is most likely to succeed where 'Santa Rosa' plum does. Fruit is very sweet, close in flavor to a plum. Mid- to late summer ripeners include 'Dapple Dandy' (often sold in markets under the name "dinosaur egg"), with mottled maroon-and-yellow skin and creamy white flesh streaked with red; 'Flavor King', with purplish red skin and flesh; and 'Flavor Queen', with greenish yellow skin and golden flesh. 'Flavor Supreme' has deep red flesh and skin mottled in green and maroon; it ripens in late spring or early summer. Both 'Dapple Dandy' and 'Flavor Supreme' will pollinate any other pluot; you can also use a Japanese plum that blooms at the same time. Same culture as for Japanese plum.

Aprium. Zones 3–22. Will grow where popular apricot varieties succeed. 'Flavor Delight' has sweet, yellow fruit similar to an apricot, but it's a little juicier and has a touch of plum flavor. Partially self-fruitful, but for best crop pollinate with any apricot that blooms at the same time or with 'Flavor Supreme' pluot. Fruit ripens in late spring or early summer. Tree is similar to apricot and should be maintained as such.

PLUME CEDAR, PLUME CRYPTOMERIA. See CRYPTOMERIA japonica 'Elegans'

PLUME HYACINTH. See MUSCARI comosum 'Monstrosum'

PLUME POPPY. See MACLEAYA

PLUM

NAME	ZONES	POLLINATION	FRUIT	COMMENTS
EUROPEAN VARIETIES				
'Brooks'	2–12, 14–22	Self-fruitful	Large. Yellowish red to blue skin; yellow flesh. Sweet with a little tartness. Midseason	Good canning variety or dried prune. Produces reliably in Pacific Northwest
'Damson' ('Blue Damson')	2–23	Self-fruitful	Small. Purple or blue-black skin; green flesh. Very tart. Late	Variety has low chill requirement. Makes fine jam and jelly. Strains of this variety are sold as 'French Damson', 'Shropshire'
'Early Laxton'	2–12, 14–20	Any other European plum	Medium-size. Pinkish orange skin; yellow flesh. Deliciously sweet flavor. Early	Excellent for cooking. Upright, very productive tree
'French Prune' ('Agen', 'Petite')	2, 3, 7–12, 14–22	Self-fruitful	Small. Red to purplish black skin; greenish yellow flesh. Very sweet and mild. Late	Standard drying prune of California. Also suitable for canning
'Green Gage' ('Reine Claude')	2–22; H1	Self-fruitful	Small to medium. Greenish yellow skin; amber flesh. Very rich, sweet flavor. Midseason	Very old variety; still a favorite for eating fresh, cooking, canning, jam. Selected strains are sold as 'Jefferson'
'Imperial' ('Imperial Epineuse')	3–12, 14–18	Any other European plum	Large. Red-purple to black-purple skin; greenish yellow flesh. Fine-quality fruit with sweet, intense flavor. Late midseason	Excellent fresh. Makes a premium dried prune or canned product
'Italian Prune' ('Fellenburg')	2–12, 14–18	Self-fruitful	Medium-size. Purplish black skin; yellow-green flesh. Sweet flavor. Late midseason	Standard variety for prunes in the Pacific Northwest. Excellent fresh as well as for canning; dries well. 'Early Italian' ripens 2 weeks earlier
'Opal'	A1, A2; 1–3	Self-fruitful	Small. Reddish purple skin; yellow flesh. Good, sweet flavor. Early	Vigorous and hardy
'Reine Claude de Bavay'	2–12, 14–20	Self-fruitful	Large. Yellow skin with white dots; sweet, juicy yellow flesh. Similar to 'Green Gage' in flavor. Late	Compact tree; good choice for smaller gardens
'Seneca'	2–12, 14–20	Any other European plum	Very large. Red skin; yellow flesh. Deliciously sweet. Late	Productive. One of the best for the Pacific Northwest
'Stanley'	2–12, 14–22	Self-fruitful	Large. Purplish black skin; yellow flesh. Sweet and juicy. Midseason	Good canning variety or dried prune. Fruit resembles a larger 'Italian Prune'
'Sugar'	2–12, 14–22	Self-fruitful	Medium-size. Dark blue skin; yellow flesh. Intensely flavored; very sweet. Early midseason	Good fresh as well as canned; good home-drying prune. This variety tends to bear heavily in alternate years

PLUM

NAME	ZONES	POLLINATION	FRUIT	COMMENTS
JAPANESE VARIETIES				
'Autumn Rosa'	7–12, 14–23	Self-fruitful	Medium to large. Purplish red skin; yellow flesh with red streaks. Good, sweet flavor. Very late	Low chill requirement. Ripens over a long period; holds well on tree
'Beauty'	2–24	Self-fruitful; yield improved with 'Santa Rosa'	Medium-size. Bright red skin; amber flesh with scarlet streaks. Good, sweet flavor. Very early	Low chill requirement. Consistent, heavy bearer. Fruit softens quickly and must be harvested promptly
'Burbank'	2–12, 14–20	'Beauty', 'Santa Rosa'	Large. Red skin; amber flesh. Aromatic fruit with excellent, sweet flavor. Midseason	Hardier to cold than most Japanese plums
'Burgundy'	7–12, 14–24	Self-fruitful	Small. Dark red skin and flesh. Excellent, rich flavor. Early to midseason	Low chill requirement. Great fresh or canned. Fruit holds well on the tree
'Casselman'	2, 3, 7–12, 14–22	Self-fruitful	Sport of 'Late Santa Rosa'; skin color is lighter and fruit ripens a few days later	Not subject to cracking of skin
'Catalina'	7–12, 14–24	Self-fruitful	Large. Deep purple skin and flesh. Juicy and sweet. Late	Low chill requirement. Very productive
'Elephant Heart'	2, 3, 7–12, 14–22	'Santa Rosa'	Very large. Dark red skin; rich red flesh. Highly flavored. Midseason to late	Skin is tart until fruit is fully ripe. Long harvest season
'Emerald Beauty'	7–12, 14–20	'Beauty', 'Burgundy', 'Late Santa Rosa'	Medium-size. Light green skin; greenish yellow to orange flesh. Exceptional, sweet, rich flavor. Midseason to late	Fruit holds well on tree without losing quality
'Friar'	2, 3, 7–12, 14–20	'Santa Rosa', 'Late Santa Rosa'	Large. Purplish black skin; amber flesh. Good, sweet flavor. Late midseason	Fruit resists cracking; softens slowly after picking. Very vigorous, productive tree
'Golden Nectar'	2, 3, 7–12, 14–20	Self-fruitful	Very large. Yellow skin and flesh; small pit. Excellent, sweet flavor. Midseason	Fruit keeps well after harvest
'Howard Miracle'	7–10, 14–20	'Santa Rosa', 'Wickson'	Medium-size. Yellow skin with red blush; yellow flesh. Spicy flavor reminiscent of pineapple. Midseason	Very vigorous. Fruit more acid than that of most Japanese plums, but truly distinctive in flavor
'Kelsey'	2, 3, 7–12, 14–18; H1	Self-fruitful	Large. Green to greenish yellow skin splashed red; firm yellow flesh. Sweet but not juicy. Late midseason	Fruit keeps well after harvest
'Laroda'	7–12, 14–22	'Burgundy', 'Santa Rosa', 'Late Santa Rosa'	Large. Red skin; amber flesh (red near skin). Rich and juicy. Midseason	Fruit holds well on the tree
'Late Santa Rosa'	7–12, 14–22	Self-fruitful	Medium to large. Purplish crimson skin; amber flesh (red near skin). Tart-sweet, sprightly flavor. Late	Follows 'Santa Rosa' by a month

'Brooks'

'Damson'

'Green Gage'

'Stanley'

'Beauty'

'Burbank'

P

PLUM

NAME	ZONES	POLLINATION	FRUIT	COMMENTS
'Mariposa' ('Improved Satsuma')	2, 3, 7–12, 14–22; H1	'Autumn Rosa', 'Beauty', 'Santa Rosa', 'Late Santa Rosa', 'Wickson'	Large. Purple-red skin; deep red flesh. Sweet. Midseason	Good for cooking and eating
'Methley'	2–9, 12–24; H1	Self-fruitful	Medium-size. Reddish purple skin; dark red flesh. Sweet and mild. Early	Low chill requirement. Good bloom hardiness
'Nubiana'	2, 3, 7–12, 14–20	Self-fruitful	Large. Deep purple-black skin; amber flesh. Sweet and firm. Midseason	Good for eating fresh and for cooking (flesh turns red when cooked). Good keeper
'Santa Rosa'	2, 3, 7–23	Self-fruitful	Medium to large. Purplish red skin with heavy blue bloom; yellow flesh (dark red near skin). Rich, pleasing, tart flavor. Early	Low chill requirement. Important commercial variety for fresh eating. Good canned if skin is removed. 'Weeping Santa Rosa' has unique drooping habit, grows only 6–8 ft. high
'Satsuma'	2–22	'Beauty', 'Santa Rosa', 'Wickson'	Small to medium. Dull deep red skin; dark red, solid, meaty flesh. Mild, sweet flavor. Small pit. Early midseason	Preferred for jams and jellies. Sometimes called blood plum because of red juice
'Shiro'	2, 3, 7–12, 14–22	Self-fruitful	Medium to large. Yellow skin and flesh. Mild but good flavor. Early midseason	Heavy producer. Fruit good for eating fresh or cooking
'Wickson'	2–12, 14–22	'Beauty', 'Santa Rosa'	Large. Greenish yellow to yellow skin, blushed with red when fruit is ripe. Firm yellow flesh. Mild but fine flavor. Early midseason	Showy fruit that keeps well after harvest. Good for jams and jellies
HARDY HYBRIDS				
'Opata'	A2, A3; 1–3	Check locally	Small. Purple skin; green flesh. Sweet. Late	Cherry-plum hybrid from South Dakota. Bush form. Upper branches often freeze in coldest areas, but lower branches usually fruit well. Fruit is good fresh and for preserves
'Pipestone'	A2, A3; 1–3	Check locally	Large. Tough red skin; yellow flesh. A little stringy but juicy and sweet. Midseason	Vigorous Japanese-American hybrid developed in Minnesota. Tree form. Needs little heat to ripen. Very good for fresh eating and jam; good for jelly
'Sapalta'	A2, A3; 1–3	Check locally	Small. Red-purple skin; almost black flesh. Mildly sweet. Late	Cherry-plum hybrid developed in Canada. Bush form. Good for fresh eating, juice, canning, preserves
'Superior'	A2, A3; 1–3	Check locally	Very large. Dark red, lightly russeted skin. Firm yellow flesh, slightly tart near skin. Dessert quality. Late midseason	Japanese-American hybrid developed in Minnesota. Tree form. Bears at an early age and heavily. Good fresh or for jam, jelly
'Underwood'	A2, A3; 1–3	Check locally	Medium to large. Dark red skin; amber flesh. Tender, juicy, sweet. Early	Vigorous Japanese-American hybrid developed in Minnesota. Tree form. Good for fresh eating and jam; fair for jelly

'Casselman'

'Friar'

'Howard Miracle'

'Santa Rosa'

'Satsuma'

'Wickson'

P

PLUMERIA

FRANGIPANI, PUA MELIA

Apocynaceae

NEARLY EVERGREEN AND DECIDUOUS SHRUBS OR TREES

ZONES VARY BY SPECIES

PARTIAL SHADE IN HOTTEST CLIMATES

MODERATE WATER

Plumeria rubra

Handsome additions to the landscape in the warmest climates, these are natives of tropical America with a spreading to round-headed form. Leathery leaves are clustered near the tips of thick, succulent branches (branches exude caustic sap when injured). Large clusters of showy, waxy, typically fragrant, five-petaled flowers are produced at branch tips much of the year. Widely used in leis.

In Hawaii, plumerias are easy to grow from cuttings. On the mainland, safest method is to begin with container plants (usually sold in leaf and flower in summer). If you want to try cuttings, start with long (15–24-in.) tip sections of stem taken in early spring and allow them to callus over for a week before planting; short cuttings often succumb to rot.

Do best in hot, dry locations in full sun but will grow in light shade. Not fussy about soil type but cannot take cold, wet soils. Some tolerance of salt and wind. Can be pruned at any time of year to maintain desired size and shape; withstands severe pruning (best done in warm season on mainland). Tender to frost. Beyond hardiness range, may be grown in a container and moved indoors in winter to a bright window (for continued bloom) or to a frost-free garage or shed.

P. obtusa. SINGAPORE PLUMERIA, BLUNT-NOSE FRANGIPANI. Nearly evergreen. Zones 24; H2. From Cuba, Hispaniola, Yucatán Peninsula. Fast growing to 30–35 ft. high, 15 ft. wide. Dark green leaves are retained most of the year; they grow to 6 in. or longer, have blunt or rounded tips. Sweet-scented, 3-in.-wide, yellow-centered white flowers spring through fall. On mainland, more difficult to grow than *P. rubra.*

P. rubra. PLUMERIA, TEMPLE TREE, NOSEGAY FRANGIPANI. Deciduous. Zones 12, 13, 19, 21–24; H1, H2. Native from Mexico to Panama. Grows at a moderate rate to 25–35 ft. tall, 15–20 ft. wide. Medium green leaves are 8–16 in. long, with narrow, pointed tips. Bloom begins in spring, often before foliage emerges, and continues for more than 6 months. Well over 100 varieties have been developed; flowers are typically 2–4½ in. wide, in colors from white through yellow, gold, and orange to shades of pink and red; fragrance varies. Dwarf and semidouble-flowered forms (rare on the mainland) are available. The following are full-size varieties with large, very fragrant single flowers.

'Aztec Gold'. Buttercup yellow shading to white at petal edges.

'Daisy Wilcox'. Extra-large blossoms in pale pink shading to white at edges.

'Dean Conklin'. Salmon with orange center.

'Golden Rainbow'. Yellow blending to pink.

'Guillot's Sunset'. Pink-and-white bicolor with orange center.

'Hawaiian Yellow'. Yellow with white margins. Especially sturdy plant.

'Pink Parfait'. Large, reddish pink blooms.

'Smith's Candystripe'. Vibrant pink and white blooms have bright yellow markings on upper surfaces of petals, alternating red and white stripes on undersides. More fragrant than the similar 'Candystripe'.

'Tangerine'. Coral-orange flowers.

TOP: *Plumeria rubra* 'Aztec Gold'
BOTTOM: *Plumeria rubra* 'Daisy Wilcox'

TOP: *Plumeria rubra* 'Candystripe'
BOTTOM: *Plumeria rubra* 'Hawaiian Yellow'

PLUM YEW. See CEPHALOTAXUS harringtonia

POA

BLUEGRASS

Poaceae (Gramineae)

PERENNIAL AND ANNUAL GRASSES

ZONES VARY BY SPECIES

FULL SUN, EXCEPT AS NOTED

REGULAR WATER

Poa pratensis

Native to Europe but naturalized in North America. Of the three species described here, *P. pratensis* is the best-known cool-season lawn grass. Leaves of all have distinctive boat-prow tip.

P. annua. ANNUAL BLUEGRASS. Annual. All zones. Cool-season weed of lawns that often furnishes much of the green in winter lawns. Bright green, soft-textured grass; it would be attractive were it not for its seed heads and propensity to die off in dry-summer regions just when it is needed most—when rain lessens in late spring.To discourage annual bluegrass in lawns, maintain a thick turf of good grasses.

P. pratensis. KENTUCKY BLUEGRASS. Perennial. Best in Zones A1–A3, 1–3; satisfactory with extra care in Zones 4–11, 14–17. Blue-green lawn grass. Many selections available as seed or sod. Mow at 2–2½ in. (dwarf forms can be mowed lower). Use alone or in a mixture with other grasses.

P. trivialis. ROUGH-STALKED BLUEGRASS. Perennial. Zones A1–A3; 1–11, 14–17. Fine-textured bright green grass used in meadow and pasture grass mixes. Can become weedy. Also used in lawn mixtures for shady spots—takes shade and damp soil.

Poaceae. The grass family is undoubtedly the most important plant family in terms of usefulness to humans. All the world's important grain crops are grasses; the bamboos (giant grasses) are useful in building and crafts. Many grasses are used in lawns or as ornamental annual or perennial plants. Some botanists still use Gramineae as the family name for grasses.

POACHED EGGS. See LIMNANTHES douglasii

PODOCARPUS

Podocarpaceae

EVERGREEN SHRUBS OR TREES

ZONES VARY BY SPECIES

FULL SUN OR PARTIAL SHADE

REGULAR WATER

Podocarpus gracilior

Versatile plants grown for their good-looking foliage and interesting form. They are adaptable to many climates and have many garden uses. Make good screens and background plants.

Foliage generally resembles that of related yews *(Taxus),* but leaves of the better-known species are longer, broader, and lighter in color. If a male plant is growing nearby, female plants bear fruit after many years, producing small, fleshy fruits rather than cones. Grow well (if slowly) in most soils, but may develop chlorosis where soil is alkaline or heavy and damp. Some botanists divide the plants into three genera *(Afrocarpus, Nageia, Podocarpus);* where they apply, new names are given in parentheses.

P. elongatus. For plants sold under this name, see P. gracilior

P. falcatus (Afrocarpus falcatus). Tree. Zones 8, 9, 14–24; H2. Slow-growing native of South Africa. Differs from *P. gracilior* in nativity, small botanical details. For uses, see *P. gracilior.*

P. gracilior (Afrocarpus elongatus, Nageia falcatus). FERN PINE. Tree, often grown as espaliered vine or even in hanging baskets. Zones 8, 9, 13–24; H1, H2. From eastern Africa. To 20–60 ft. tall, 10–20 ft. wide. Among the cleanest, most pest-free trees for street, lawn, patio, garden; good as big shrub, as hedge, in container.

Method of propagation determines growth habit. If grown from seed, plants are upright even when young (and stay that way); these plants are usually sold as *P. gracilior.* In youth, they have branches set somewhat sparsely with glossy dark green leaves 2–4 in. long, ½ in. wide. With age, they produce 1–2-in., soft grayish green to bluish green leaves that are more closely spaced on branches. Stake seedling plants until a strong trunk develops.

If grown from cuttings or grafts of a mature tree, plants have the smaller, more closely set leaves just described, but they have very limber branches and are often reluctant to make strong vertical growth. These more willowy plants, suitable for espalier, hanging pots, or growing as vines along fences, are often sold as *P. elongatus.* Given staking and tying, *P. elongatus* types eventually become upright trees, though their foliage mass persists in drooping for some time.

P. henkelii. LONG-LEAFED YELLOWWOOD. Tree. Zones 8, 9, 14–24; H1, H2. From eastern and southern Africa. Handsome, erect tree grows slowly to 30–50 ft. tall, 15–20 ft. wide. Bears masses of drooping, shiny green leaves, pointed at both ends. Young plants have leaves 5–7 in. long, ⅓ in. wide; on older plants, leaves are much smaller, to 1–2 in. long, a little over ⅛ in. wide.

P. latifolius. YELLOWWOOD. Tree. Zones 8, 9, 12 (warmest parts), 13–24; H1, H2. From eastern and southern Africa. This is the true yellowwood, an important timber tree in Africa. Resembles *P. henkelii* in most details. Leaves taper only toward tip.

P. macrophyllus. YEW PINE. Shrub or tree. Zones 4–9, 12–24; H1, H2. Native to eastern China, Japan. Generally narrow and upright; to 15–50 ft. tall, 6–15 ft. wide. Bright green leaves 4 in. long, ½ in. wide. Good as a street or lawn tree, screen, large shrub; limber enough to espalier. Easily pruned as clipped hedge, topiary. Does well in tubs. Very heat tolerant.

P. m. maki. SHRUBBY YEW PINE. Slower growing and smaller than species—to 8–15 ft. tall, 2–4 ft. wide. Dense and upright, with leaves to 3 in. long, ¼ in. wide. A choice shrub; one of the best container plants for outdoor or indoor use.

P. nagi (Nageia nagi). Tree. Zones 8, 9, 14–24; H1, H2. From Japan, where it reaches 80–90 ft. tall. In California, more commonly seen at 15–20 ft. tall, 6–8 ft. wide. Pendulous branchlets; leathery, smooth, dark green, sharp-pointed leaves 1–3 in. long, ½–1½ in. wide. Grows upright in youth without staking; plant in groves for slender sapling effect. Makes a decorative foliage pattern against wood or masonry background. Excellent container plant.

P. nivalis. ALPINE TOTARA. Shrub. Zones 4–9, 14–17. From New Zealand. Broad, low-growing, spreading plant that eventually reaches 2–3 ft. high, 6–10 ft. wide. Branches are densely clothed with dark olive green, ¼–¾-in.-long needles like those of yew. Attractive as ground cover or in large rock garden.

P. totara. TOTARA. Tree. Zones 8, 9, 14–24. From New Zealand. In its native environment, this tree reaches 100 ft. tall. In California, more common size is 25–30 ft. tall and 18–25 ft. wide. Dense and rather narrow. Stiff, leathery gray-green leaves to 1 in. long, pointed at tips. General appearance like that of yew.

PODOPHYLLUM

Berberidaceae

PERENNIALS

ZONES VARY BY SPECIES

PARTIAL OR FULL SHADE

REGULAR TO AMPLE WATER

ALL PARTS (EXCEPT RIPE FRUIT) ARE POISONOUS IF INGESTED

Podophyllum hexandrum

Odd-looking yet striking plants, these herbaceous barberry relatives grow from thick underground rhizomes that send up stalks crowned with large, umbrella-shaped, deeply lobed leaves. Shoots with a single leaf are barren; those with two leaves bear a single 2-in.-wide flower (set between the leaves) in mid- to late spring. Blossoms are followed by juicy, 2-in. berries; these are edible when fully ripe (poisonous until that stage) but can have a powerful laxative effect. Make attractive, slowly spreading deciduous ground covers for shady areas with moist, organically enriched soil.

P. hexandrum. Zones 4–7, 14–17. From Himalayas, western China. To 2–2½ ft. high, 1½–2 ft. wide. Dark green, brown-mottled leaves to 10 in. wide are divided into three or five lobes; each lobe is further divided. White or pink flowers are followed by bright red berries.

P. peltatum. MAY APPLE. Zones 1–7. From eastern North America. To 1–1½ ft. high, 1 ft. wide. Foliage is bronze when new; mature leaves are shiny dark green, to 1 ft. wide, divided into five to nine lobes. White flowers followed by bright yellow berries. Spreads fairly fast in its preferred rich, moist soil. Dies back completely in late summer.

PODRANEA ricasoliana

PINK TRUMPET VINE

Bignoniaceae

EVERGREEN VINE

ZONES 9, 12, 13, 19–24; H1, H2

FULL SUN OR PARTIAL SHADE

MODERATE TO REGULAR WATER

Podranea ricasoliana

Native to South Africa. Sprawling growth to 20 ft.; must be fastened to its support. Glossy dark green leaves consist of two to five opposite pairs of 2-in. leaflets plus one terminal leaflet. Blooms in spring or summer, when tips of new growth produce loose clusters of 2–3-in.-wide, red-veined pink flowers shaped like open trumpets. Grows slowly when young, then speeds up as it matures. Likes heat, good drainage. Use on posts, arbors, trellises, walls, trunks of high-branching trees. Thin out any tangling growth in winter. Light frosts may cause leaves to drop; heavier frosts may kill vine to the ground, but regrowth is almost certain as long as soil doesn't freeze.

POHA, GROUND CHERRY

Solanaceae

PERENNIAL

ZONES H1, H2; ANYWHERE AS ANNUAL

FULL SUN

REGULAR WATER

Poha

From Brazil, but naturalized at higher elevations throughout Hawaiian Islands. Known botanically as *Physalis peruviana* and closely related to tomatillo *(P. ixocarpa)* and Chinese lantern plant *(P. alkekengi).* Bushy plant with heart-shaped, irregularly toothed, somewhat velvety green leaves to 2½–6 in. long. As a perennial, it can reach 6 ft. tall and 4 ft. wide (needs support); as an annual, it is more likely to grow 1½–3 ft. high and wide. Plant produces small, bell-shaped spring flowers that are whitish yellow with brown spots in the throat. After the blossoms fade, the enlarged calyx forms a loose, papery, straw-colored husk around the fruit. The seedy, inch-wide yellow fruit ripens from late summer into autumn; it is smaller and sweeter than tomatillo and can be eaten fresh or used in pies and preserves.

Grow in well-drained soil in a frost-free, wind-protected site. Plant is self-fruitful, but you can help ensure pollination by gently shaking flower stems or spraying them lightly with water. No fertilizer needed. Cut back on watering when fruit is maturing. Harvest fruit when it drops to ground; remove papery husks before using. Plant often self-sows.

POHUTUKAWA. See METROSIDEROS excelsus

POINCIANA. See CAESALPINIA, DELONIX regia

POINSETTIA. See EUPHORBIA pulcherrima

Polemoniaceae. The phlox family consists mostly of annuals and perennials, including many wildflowers; examples are *Gilia, Ipomopsis,* and *Phlox.* Cup-and-saucer vine *(Cobaea)* is another member.

POLEMONIUM

Polemoniaceae

PERENNIALS

ZONES 1–11, 14–17, EXCEPT AS NOTED

PARTIAL OR FULL SHADE

REGULAR WATER

Polemonium caeruleum

Lush rosettes of finely divided, ferny, light to medium green foliage. Blossom stalks are typically leafy and bear clusters of bell-shaped flowers in spring or early summer. Good under trees. Grow from seed or from divisions made after bloom or in spring; give well-drained soil. Many species are choice wildflowers from Western mountains. The following are among those most commonly available in nurseries.

P. caeruleum. JACOB'S LADDER. Native to Europe, Asia. Fairly upright-growing plant to 1–3 ft. high, 1–1½ ft. wide. Lavender-blue, pendulous, 1-in. flowers. 'Brise d'Anjou', with each leaflet neatly outlined in white, is one of the most striking of variegated-foliage plants.

P. carneum. Native from Washington west of the Cascades to California. Sprawls to 1–1½ ft. high, 1 ft. wide. Yellowish buds open to ½–1-in., peachy pink blossoms that age to purplish blue. Use in borders.

P. 'Firmament'. Hybrid between *P. caeruleum* and *P. reptans.* To 20 in. high, 1 ft. wide, with bright blue flowers. Use in borders.

P. pulcherrimum. Zones A1–A3; 1–11, 14–17; H1. Native from Alaska to California. Sprawling or erect, to 1 ft. high and wide. Crowded clusters of ¼-in. flowers in blue shades or white, often with yellow throat. Good in shaded rock gardens.

P. reptans. Native to eastern U.S. Weak-stemmed plant to 1–1½ ft. high, 1 ft. wide; light blue, ¾-in. flowers. Better known than the species is heavy-blooming 'Blue Pearl'; it grows 10 in. high, 1½ ft. wide and bears bright blue blossoms. Good in shaded rock gardens.

POLIANTHES tuberosa

TUBEROSE

Agavaceae

PERENNIAL FROM RHIZOME

ZONES 7–9, 14–24; H1, H2

FULL SUN

REGULAR WATER DURING GROWTH AND BLOOM

Polianthes tuberosa

Native to Mexico. Noted for heady, powerfully sweet fragrance. Each rhizome (actually a modified rhizome with bulblike top and tuberous roots) produces a fountain of narrow, grassy leaves about 1½ ft. tall. Flower spikes rise above the leaves, bearing loose whorls of tubular, glistening white flowers in summer or early fall. Tallest tuberose (to 3½ ft.) is the form sometimes sold as 'Mexican Single'. More widely sold is double-flowered 'The Pearl', to 2½ ft. tall; it is a good garden variety, but single types provide longer-lasting cut flowers.

To bloom year after year, tuberoses need a long warm season (at least 4 months) before flowering. Where this can be provided outdoors, you can plant rhizomes directly in the ground; elsewhere, start them indoors in pots and plant outside after soil warms in spring. Set rhizomes 2 in. deep, 4–6 in. apart. If soil or water is alkaline, apply acid fertilizer when growth begins. When foliage starts to yellow in fall, stop watering. Where winter temperatures remain above 20°F/–7°C, rhizomes can be left in the ground all year (if you do this, divide clumps about every 4 years). However, many gardeners in these areas (and all those living in colder regions) dig rhizomes and store them over the winter. Dig plants in fall after leaves have yellowed; cut off dead foliage, let rhizomes dry for 2 weeks, and store in a cool, dry place until planting time. Tuberoses can also be grown in containers and moved to protection during cold weather.

POLIOMINTHA

Lamiaceae (Labiatae)

EVERGREEN SHRUBS

ZONES VARY BY SPECIES

EXPOSURE NEEDS VARY BY SPECIES

REGULAR WATER

Poliomintha maderensis

These are mint relatives with the family's typical square stems; paired opposite leaves; tubular, two-lipped flowers; and strong, often pleasant aroma. Well-grown plants reach about 3 ft. high and wide. Very tolerant of many soils.

P. incana. HOARY MINT. Zones 10–13. Native to southwestern U.S. Branching gray stems are set with narrow white leaves to ¾ in. long. Blooms profusely in summer, bearing lavender-blue or white flowers less than ½ in. long in spikelike, 2–6-in.-long clusters. Full sun. Can survive with little or no water but looks better with regular moisture.

P. maderensis (P. longiflora). MEXICAN OREGANO. Zones 8–24. Native to eastern Mexico. Habit varies from somewhat cascading to upright. Leaves are shiny deep green, less than ½ in. long, with odor and flavor of true oregano *(Origanum).* Long-tubed (1–1½-in.) flowers open lavender, deepen to purple, and finally fade to white; all three colors are present on the plant at once. Long bloom season, from late spring into fall. Blossoms attract hummingbirds. Give light shade in hottest desert regions, full sun elsewhere.

POLYANTHUS PRIMROSE. See PRIMULA × polyantha

POLYGALA

Polygalaceae

EVERGREEN SHRUBS

ZONES VARY BY SPECIES

FULL SUN OR LIGHT SHADE

REGULAR WATER

Polygala × dalmaisiana

These plants are grown for colorful, asymmetrical flowers that look somewhat like sweet peas *(Lathyrus).* Grow in well-drained soil.

P. chamaebuxus. Zones 4–6. Native to Europe. To 4 in. high, 1 ft. wide; spreads slowly by underground stems. Leathery dark green, 1–1½-in.-long leaves resemble those of boxwood *(Buxus).* Flowers combine bright yellow with creamy yellow or white, sometimes with red; spring or early summer bloom. *P. c. grandiflora* bears flowers in a combination of rosy purple and yellow. Good choice for rock gardens.

P. × dalmaisiana. SWEET-PEA SHRUB. Zones 8, 9, 12–24. To 3–5 ft. high and wide; usually bare at base. Grayish green, oval to lance-shaped leaves to 1 in. long. Blooms nonstop from midsummer to fall, producing flowers in a bright, vivid purplish pink that combines well with blue shades and white. To conceal this plant's legginess, set low, bushy plants in front of it. Cut back hard in late winter to promote more compact, bushy growth. Replace plant if it becomes too lanky. Good filler.

Polygonaceae. The buckwheat family consists of annuals, perennials, shrubs, trees, and vines. Flowers lack petals, but sepals are often showy. Stems are jointed. Fruit is small, dry, single seeded. *Eriogonum* is the best-known Western representative. Other family members include coral vine *(Antigonon)*, knotweed *(Persicaria)*, and rhubarb *(Rheum)*. True buckwheat—the pancake-flour kind—is *Fagopyrum*, a crop plant of no ornamental value.

POLYGONATUM

SOLOMON'S SEAL

Liliaceae

PERENNIALS

ZONES A1–A3; 1–9, 14–17

PARTIAL OR FULL SHADE

REGULAR WATER

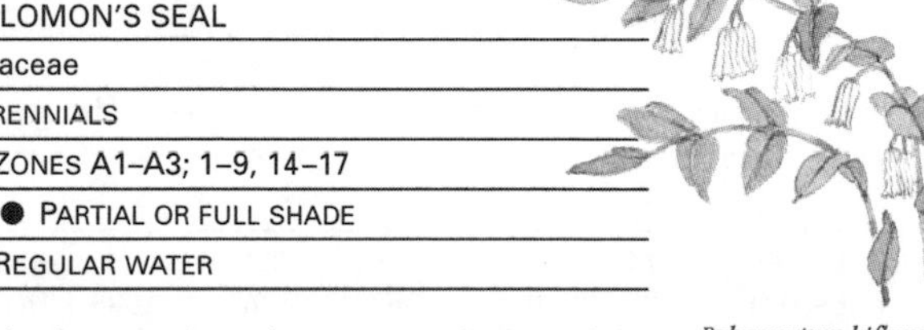

Polygonatum biflorum

Slowly spreading rhizomes send up arching stems clothed in bright green, broadly oval leaves arranged in nearly horizontal planes. Where leaves join stems, pairs or clusters of small, bell-shaped greenish white flowers appear in spring or early summer, hanging beneath the stems on threadlike stalks. Small blue-black berries may follow flowers. Leaves and stems turn bright yellow in autumn before plant dies to the ground. Attractive in woodland gardens. Grow in loose, woodsy soil. Can remain in place for years; to increase your plantings, dig rhizomes from clump edges in early spring and replant. Good in containers. For the Western native called false Solomon's seal, see *Smilacina*.

P. biflorum. Native to eastern North America. To 1–3 ft. tall, 2 ft. wide, with leaves to 4 in. long and flowers usually in pairs or threes. A form sometimes sold as *P. commutatum* or *P. canaliculatum* is much more vigorous, growing 3–7 ft. tall, 3–4 ft. wide. It has leaves to 7 in. long and flowers in groups of two to ten.

P. odoratum (P. japonicum, P. officinale). Native to Europe, Asia. To 1½–3½ ft. tall, 2 ft. wide, with 4–6-in. leaves. Flowers are fragrant, usually borne in pairs but sometimes singly. 'Variegatum' has white-edged leaves; its stems are dark red until fully mature.

POLYGONUM. See FALLOPIA, PERSICARIA

Polypodiaceae. The polypody family contains the vast majority of ferns. Those in other families differ only in technical details concerning spore-bearing bodies (sporangia).

POLYPODIUM

Polypodiaceae

FERNS

ZONES VARY BY SPECIES

PARTIAL OR FULL SHADE

WATER NEEDS VARY BY SPECIES

Polypodium aureum 'Mandaianum'

Widespread, variable group. Some are Western natives suitable for woodland or wild gardens, where they can naturalize. Others are tropical plants most commonly used in hanging baskets, often in the house or greenhouse. Provide bright indirect light for plants grown indoors. As is true for many ferns, reclassification has added new names; these appear in parentheses.

P. aureum (Phlebodium aureum). HARE'S FOOT FERN. Zones 15–17, 19–24; H1, H2; or indoors. From tropical America. To 2½ ft. high, 5 ft. wide, with thick, brown, creeping rhizomes. Coarse blue-green fronds drop after frosts, but plants recover quickly. Fronds of 'Mandaianum', sometimes called lettuce fern, have frilled and wavy edges. Both it and the species are showy. Regular water.

P. glycyrrhiza. LICORICE FERN. Zones A3; 4–6, 14–24. Native to coastal regions from Alaska to California. Mat-forming plant to 1 ft. high, spreading indefinitely by rhizomes. Dark green fronds to 1½ ft. long resemble those of smaller sword ferns *(Polystichum)*. In the wild, tends to grow on rocks or dead logs. In the garden, provide leaf mold or other organic matter and some shade (can take full sun when grown right on the coast). Little to regular water.

P. hesperium. Zones A3; 2–7, 10, 14–19. Native from Alaska to California, east into Rocky Mountains. Smaller than *P. glycyrrhiza* (to 10 in. high) but otherwise similar; takes the same care.

P. scouleri. LEATHERY POLYPODY. Zones 4–6, 15–17, 24. Native along seacoast from British Columbia to Southern California. To about 6 in. high, spreading indefinitely by rhizomes. Thick, glossy deep green fronds are typically about 7 in. long, but may reach 1½ ft. long, 6 in. across at base. Often grows on trees and rocks; when grown in the ground, it tends to form a clump. Same culture as for *P. glycyrrhiza*.

P. subauriculatum 'Knightiae' (Goniophlebium subauriculatum 'Knightiae'). KNIGHT'S POLYPODY. Zones 24; H2; or indoors. Native to tropical Asia. Hanging basket plant with gracefully drooping fronds that reach 3 ft. or longer, have fringed edges. Spectacular plant when well grown. Outdoor plants shed old fronds in spring, then quickly produce new ones. Regular water.

POLYSCIAS

Araliaceae

EVERGREEN SHRUBS OR TREES

ZONES 24; H1, H2; OR INDOORS

FULL SUN OR PARTIAL SHADE; BRIGHT INDIRECT LIGHT

MODERATE TO REGULAR WATER

Polyscias fruticosa

Like many other aralia relatives, these Polynesian natives are grown for their handsomely divided leaves; flowers are unimportant and seldom produced. Foliage is typically olive green with a red tinge. Appreciate warmth, humidity, good drainage.

These plants are grown outdoors in Hawaii, where they often serve as hedges, screens, specimens, tub plants. Elsewhere, they are usually treated as houseplants. As indoor plants, they are considered fussy, demanding fresh, fairly still air (they cannot tolerate drafts) and exactly the right amount of water (enough, but not too much). Overwatering and mite damage are the two main causes of failure. Misting is helpful in maintaining their health, as is light feeding.

P. fruticosa. MING ARALIA, PARSLEY PANAX. To 10 ft. tall, 4–6 ft. wide. Leaves to 2½ ft. long are finely divided and redivided into a multitude of narrow, tooth-edged segments.

P. guilfoylei. Narrowly upright to 12–20 ft. tall, 4–8 ft. wide. Medium green leaves are usually marked with white; they reach 1½ ft. long, have five to nine leaflets. 'Victoriae', to 15 ft. tall, has white-edged leaflets that are deeply slashed and cut.

P. scutellaria 'Balfourii' (P. balfouriana). To 15 ft. tall, 4–8 ft. wide. Leaves usually have up to three roundish, 4-in.-long leaflets in green edged with white. *P.* 'Marginata' is a similar plant.

FOR DEFINITIONS OF GARDENING TERMS
PLEASE SEE PAGES 746–750

POLYSTICHUM

Polystichum munitum

Polypodiaceae

FERNS

ZONES VARY BY SPECIES

PARTIAL OR FULL SHADE

REGULAR WATER

Hardy, symmetrical, easy-to-grow plants with fronds that are evergreen except in the case of *P. braunii* and *P.* ×*setigerum.* Among the most useful and widely planted ferns; combine well with other plants. Do best in rich, well-drained soil. Use in shady beds, along house walls, and in mixed woodland plantings.

P. acrostichoides. CHRISTMAS FERN. Zones 1–9, 14–24. Native to eastern North America. To 1–1½ ft. tall, about 3 ft. wide. Most useful for shaded sites in cold climates, where the dark green foliage makes a fine contrast to snow or to the brown of dead leaves during the winter holiday season. Stiff fronds remain upright until pushed over by heavy snow or hard frost.

P. braunii. BRAUN'S HOLLY FERN. Zones 3–6, 14–17. Native to northern latitudes of America and Asia. To 1–3 ft. high and wide. New growth is silvery green, maturing to dark green. Deciduous in colder areas.

P. californicum. Zones 4–7, 14–24. Native from California north to Washington. To 1½–3 ft. high and wide. Resembles *P. munitum* but has deeply divided leaflets. Needs regular water in warmer areas.

P. dudleyi. Zones 4–7, 14–24. Native to Coast Ranges of Northern California. To 1½–3 ft. high and wide. Resembles *P. munitum* but has shorter, broader fronds that are more finely cut. Choice plant; not always easy to find.

P. munitum. SWORD FERN. Zones A3; 2–9, 14–24. Native from California to Alaska and Montana. Most common fern of Western forests. To 2–4 ft. high and wide. Leathery, shiny dark green fronds are erect, then spreading. Each leaflet is dagger shaped, with toothed edges and a base that looks rather like a sword hilt. Old plants may have 75–100 fronds. Long lasting when cut for arrangements. Established plants get by with reduced moisture.

P. polyblepharum. JAPANESE LACE FERN, TASSEL FERN. Zones 4–9, 14–24. Native to Asia. Handsome, dense, lacy-looking plant to 2–3 ft. tall, 3 ft. wide. Resembles *P. setiferum* but is darker green, somewhat coarser; fronds are a little more upright. Usually sold as *P. setosum* (a name of no botanical standing).

P. setiferum. SOFT SHIELD FERN. Zones 4–9, 14–24. Native to Europe. Many forms, varying from 2 to 4½ ft. high and wide. Finely cut fronds give effect of dark green lace, spread out in flattened vase shape. In 'Proliferum', plantlets form on midribs of older fronds; these can be detached and planted. Fancy varieties with interestingly cut, sometimes fluffy-looking fronds may be sold under the name "English fern." The species and its varieties are splendid in shaded beds or rock gardens.

P. ×setigerum. ALASKA HOLLY FERN. Zones A3; 2–7, 14–17. Native from Alaska to British Columbia. A hybrid between *P. munitum* and *P. braunii.* To 1–3 ft. high and wide. Leaflets near ends of fronds are lobed to deeply cut. Deciduous in colder areas.

P. setosum. See P. polyblepharum

POMEGRANATE

Pomegranate

Punicaceae

DECIDUOUS SHRUB OR TREE

ZONES 5–24 (BUT SEE TEXT); H1, H2

FULL SUN

REGULAR WATER

Native from Iran to the Himalayan region of northern India; naturalized throughout the Mediterranean. Naturally grows as a rounded plant to 15–20 ft. tall and broad, though it is often kept pruned to about 10 ft. high and wide. Showy red flowers at branch tips in spring; thick calyx persists as a projection at base of fruit. Roundish fruit to 5 in. wide is yellow overlaid with pink or red; it contains sacs of seedy, sweet-tart, juicy pulp. Self-fruitful.

Best-known variety is 'Wonderful', with orange-red flowers and burnished red fruit with red pulp. Other varieties are sometimes available, including 'Sweet' (yellow flowers, pink pulp) and 'Fleishman', 'Granada', 'King' (all with pink flowers, pink pulp). 'Eversweet' ripens very early and bears virtually seedless fruit with transparent red pulp and clear, nonstaining juice. 'Utah Sweet' has very sweet, light pinkish pulp and nonstaining pink juice.

Pomegranates ripen in fall; harvest them when they reach full color. Fruit left on the tree is likely to split and rot, especially if weather is rainy. Can be stored for up to 7 months in the refrigerator. To eat fresh, cut into quarters or eighths and pull rind back (starting from the ends) to expose the juicy sacs; eat them, seeds and all. To remove juice for drinking fresh or for use in jams, jellies, or sauces, cut fruit in half and ream with a juicer. Or roll fruit firmly on hard surface; then cut a hole in stem end and squeeze juice into a container.

In Zones 5, 6, and 17, where pomegranate grows and blooms but may not fruit, locate against south or west wall. Tolerates a wide variety of soils, growing well even in alkaline soil. Resistant to oak root fungus. Can take considerable drought but produces better fruit with regular moisture. For ornamental pomegranate varieties, see *Punica granatum.*

Pontederiaceae. The pickerel weed family contains aquatic or marsh plants with showy, usually blue flowers. Members include water hyacinth *(Eichhornia)* and pickerel weed *(Pontederia).*

PONTEDERIA cordata

Pontederia cordata

PICKEREL WEED

Pontederiaceae

AQUATIC PERENNIAL

ZONES 1–24; H1, H2

FULL SUN OR LIGHT SHADE

LOCATE IN PONDS, WATER GARDENS

Native to eastern North America. To 3–4 ft. high, 2–2½ ft. wide. Long-stalked, glossy green leaves stand well above surface of water; these are heart shaped, to 10 in. long and 6 in. wide. Blooms from late spring to fall, bearing short spikes of blue flowers at stem ends. Often grown as a companion to water lilies *(Nymphaea);* plant in pots of rich soil placed in 1 ft. of water. Gives an informal garden pool the look of a wild pond. To use in natural ponds, set plants at shoreline—underwater, directly in the soil. Goes dormant in winter.

PONYTAIL PALM. See NOLINA recurvata

POOR MAN'S ORCHID. See SCHIZANTHUS pinnatus

POOR MAN'S RHODODENDRON. See IMPATIENS sodenii

POPCORN. See CORN

POPLAR. See POPULUS

POPPY. See PAPAVER

POPPY, HIMALAYAN. See MECONOPSIS betonicifolia

POPPY, MEXICAN. See ARGEMONE mexicana

POPPY MALLOW. See CALLIRHOE involucrata

A PRACTICAL GUIDE TO GARDENING
PLEASE SEE PAGES 658–731

POPULUS

POPLAR, COTTONWOOD, ASPEN
Salicaceae
DECIDUOUS TREES
ZONES VARY BY SPECIES
FULL SUN
REGULAR WATER

Populus nigra 'Italica'

Fast-growing, tough trees. Grown primarily—and especially appreciated—in interior regions with hot summers and cold winters. Don't do as well in mild-winter areas and in coastal climates where temperature fluctuation is minimal. Trees have aggressive surface roots that crowd out other plants, heave pavement, and clog sewer and drainage lines; best suited to rural areas and fringes of large properties. Most poplars will sucker if their roots are cut or disturbed. They are subject to many pests and diseases.

Despite their liabilities, some of these trees are beautiful or distinctive enough to be widely sold. Many have good fall color. Leaves of most are roughly triangular, sometimes toothed or lobed. Pendulous catkins (denser on male trees) appear in spring before leafout. Female trees later bear masses of cottony seeds that blow about and become a nuisance; for that reason, male (seedless) varieties are the best choice and are usually offered in nurseries.

P. ×acuminata. LANCELEAF COTTONWOOD. Zones 1–11, 14–21. Hybrid of *P. angustifolia* and another species; like *P. angustifolia,* thrives at high elevations. To 40–60 ft. tall, 35–45 ft. wide. Narrow, triangular leaves to 4 in. long are glossy dark green above, paler dull green beneath. Yellow fall color. Seedless.

P. alba. WHITE POPLAR. Zones A3; 1–11, 14–21. Native to Europe, Asia. To 40–70 ft. high and wide. Common name refers to woolly white leaf undersides and to light-colored young bark. Leaves are 2–5 in. long, usually with three to five lobes.

A "lively" tree with leaves that move even in light breezes, showing flickering white and green highlights. Poor fall color. Tolerates wide range of soils. Suckers profusely—an advantage if it is planted as a windbreak, otherwise a problem. Seedless variety 'Pyramidalis', called Bolleana poplar (often sold as *P. bolleana*), forms a narrow (15-ft.-wide) column and has a white or light gray trunk like that of birch *(Betula)*.

P. angustifolia. NARROWLEAF POPLAR. Zones 1–11, 14–21. Native from Alberta to Mexico, primarily in Rocky Mountains; grows at elevations to 8,000 ft. To 50–60 ft. tall, 35–45 ft. wide, with finely toothed, narrow, willowlike green leaves to 5 in. long. Young bark is green.

P. ×canadensis 'Eugenei'. CAROLINA POPLAR. Zones 1–11, 14–21. Male hybrid to 100 ft. tall, 40 ft. wide. Glossy bright green, tooth-edged leaves to 4 in. long; good yellow fall color.

P. ×canescens 'Macrophylla'. Zones A2, A3; 1–11, 14–21. To 100 ft. tall, 50 ft. wide, with exceptionally large leaves (to 9 in. long on vigorous young shoots) that are glossy dark green above, white beneath. Fine yellow or red fall color. Older trees have creamy gray bark.

P. fremontii. WESTERN COTTONWOOD, FREMONT COTTONWOOD. Zones 1–12, 14–21. Native to California and central Rockies south to Mexico. To 40–60 ft. or taller, 30 ft. wide. Glossy yellow-green, coarsely toothed, virtually triangular leaves are thick textured, 2–4 in. wide; turn bright lemon yellow in fall. Leaves persist almost all winter in Zone 12. 'Nevada' is a male variety.

P. nigra 'Italica'. LOMBARDY POPLAR. Zones A2, A3; 1–11, 14–24. Male selection of a European native. Beautiful columnar tree to 40–100 ft. tall, 15–30 ft. wide, with upward-reaching branches. Bright green, 4-in. leaves turn golden yellow in fall. Excellent along country driveways; valuable both as windbreak and skyline decoration. Healthy and attractive in cold, dry interior climates. Suckers profusely. *P. n. thevestina* has white bark.

P. tremuloides. QUAKING ASPEN. Zones A1–A3; 1–7, 14–19. Native throughout mountains of the West, at elevations to 9,000 ft. Generally performs poorly or grows slowly in lowlands; usually short lived in warmer climates. To 20–60 ft. tall, 15–30 ft. wide; often grows as a multitrunked tree or in a clump. Smooth, pale gray-green to whitish bark. Dainty, roundish, 2–4-in., glossy green leaves flutter with the slightest movement of air. Brilliant golden yellow fall color. Good background tree for native shrubs and wildflowers. Apt to suffer from sudden dieback or borers.

P. trichocarpa. BLACK COTTONWOOD. Zones A2, A3; 1–9, 14–24. Native from Alaska to Southern California. To 30–100 ft. tall, 25–30 ft. wide. Heavy-limbed tree with furrowed dark gray bark, very brittle wood. Leaves are 3–5 in. across, deep green above and distinctly silver beneath; attractive when ruffled by breezes. Good golden yellow fall color.

PORCELAIN BERRY. See AMPELOPSIS brevipedunculata

PORCUPINE GRASS. See MISCANTHUS sinensis 'Strictus'

PORK AND BEANS. See SEDUM rubrotinctum

PORT ORFORD CEDAR. See CHAMAECYPARIS lawsoniana

PORTUGAL LAUREL. See PRUNUS lusitanica

PORTULACA

ROSE MOSS, PURSLANE
Portulacaceae
ANNUALS
ALL ZONES
FULL SUN
MODERATE TO REGULAR WATER

Portulaca grandiflora

Low-growing, fleshy plants. One is called a weed but can be used in cooking and salads. The others are grown for their brilliant flowers, on display from late spring until frost; generally, the blossoms open fully in bright light and close by midafternoon in hot weather. The various plants described here thrive in high temperatures, intense sunlight. Not fussy about soil. Bright-flowered types are attractive in rock gardens, parking strips, hanging baskets, or as edgings and bank covers; they don't require deadheading to prolong bloom.

P. grandiflora. ROSE MOSS. From South America. To 6 in. high, 1½ ft. across. Trailing, branching reddish stems are set with narrow, cylindrical, pointed leaves to 1 in. long. Inch-wide, lustrous-petaled flowers shaped like tiny roses, in white and many bright and pastel shades of red, cerise, rose pink, orange, yellow. Available as single colors or mixes, in either single- or double-flowered strains: Prize, Magic Carpet, Sunglo, Sunkiss are popular. Afternoon Delight and Sundance strains stay open longer in the afternoon. The newer Sundial strain also resists closing and has larger (2-in.), double blossoms; 'Sundial Peach' is especially attractive. All self-sow, but they often fail to come true from seed.

P. oleracea. PURSLANE. Unimproved form is thought to have originated in India; it's an edible weed with tiny yellow flowers and plump, oval leaves to 1¼ in. long. Warm weather and moisture encourage its growth. Control by hoeing or pulling before it goes to seed; don't let pulled plants lie about, since they can reroot or ripen seed. Stems and leaves can be added to salads, soups, sauces; improved garden strains are sold for the vegetable garden. Called *verdolaga* in Mexico, *pourpier* in France.

P. Wildfire hybrids. Sometimes offered as *P. oleracea,* sometimes as *P. grandiflora,* but actually a strain of *P. umbraticola.* Best in hot-summer areas; popular in the Southwest. Plants grow a few inches tall and spread to 2 ft.; they have the broad leaves of *P. oleracea* but bear brightly colored, 1½-in. single flowers in red, pink, lavender, yellow, orange, peach, white, or bicolors. Each flower lasts only a day, but new ones keep the show going. Plants live over in the absence of frost.

Portulacaceae. The portulaca family contains annuals, perennials, and a few shrubs, usually with succulent foliage and frequently with showy flowers. Examples are *Lewisia,* rose moss and purslane *(Portulaca),* and elephant's food *(Portulacaria)*.

P

PORTULACARIA afra

ELEPHANT'S FOOD

Portulacaceae

SUCCULENT SHRUB

ZONES 8, 9, 12–24; H1, H2

SUN OR SHADE

LITTLE TO MODERATE WATER

Portulacaria afra

Native to South Africa. Can be grown outdoors but needs frost protection in Zones 8, 9, 12, 14, 15, 18–21. To 12 ft. tall and nearly as wide, with thick, juicy stems and glossy green leaves. Looks a bit like jade plant *(Crassula ovata)* and is sometimes sold under the name "miniature jade plant," but it's faster growing and more loosely branched, with tapering, more limber branches and smaller (½-in.-long) leaves. In its native land, it bears clusters of tiny pink flowers, but it seldom blooms in North America.

In frost-free or nearly frostless areas, can be used as a fast-growing informal screen or unclipped hedge. Small specimens are good, easy-care potted plants. Forms with variegated leaves ('Foliis Variegatis' and 'Variegata') are slower growing and smaller than the species. Another form has larger (1-in.-long) leaves.

POTATO

Solanaceae

PERENNIAL TREATED AS ANNUAL

ALL ZONES

FULL SUN

REGULAR WATER

GREEN SKIN AND RAW SHOOTS ARE POISONOUS IF INGESTED

Potato

Andean native, botanically known as *Solanum tuberosum.* For ornamental relatives, see *Solanum.* Though other vegetables are more common in home gardens, growing potatoes can be very satisfying: 2 lbs. of seed potatoes can yield 50 lbs. of potatoes for eating. The many pests and diseases that beleaguer commercial growers are not likely to plague home gardeners. To avoid disease problems, plant certified disease-free starter potatoes or disease-resistant varieties.

Can be grown from seed potatoes that you cut into 1½-in. cubes (each with at least two eyes) or from minitubers, which are planted whole and are less likely to rot in the ground. Home gardeners have access to a number of varieties, including types with red, yellow, or bluish purple skins; yellow-fleshed sorts; and even potatoes with blue skin and flesh. Shapes vary from round to fingerlike. Some varieties mature faster than others, but most reach harvesting size about 3 months after planting.

Potatoes need sandy, fast-draining, fertile soil; tubers become deformed in heavy, poorly drained soil. In cold-winter climates, plant as soon as the soil is workable in spring. In mild-winter regions, plant in early spring for a summer crop, in early fall for a winter-into-spring crop. Where frosts are not severe, potatoes can be planted in midwinter—as long as the soil isn't too wet from winter rains. Let seed potato pieces dry for a day or two before planting. Then set minitubers or potato pieces 2 in. deep, 1–1½ ft. apart. Add loose soil as plant grows, taking care not to cover stems completely; developing tubers should always be covered with soil to keep skin from turning green.

The above-ground potato plant is sprawling and bushy, with much-divided dark green leaves somewhat like those of a tomato plant. Clustered inch-wide flowers are pale blue.

Dig early potatoes (so-called new potatoes) when the plants begin to bloom; dig mature potatoes when plants die down. Dig carefully to avoid bruising or cutting the tubers. Well-matured potatoes free of defects are the best keepers; store them in a cool (40°F/4°C), dark, dry place. Where ground doesn't freeze, late potatoes can remain in ground until needed. Dig before warmer temperatures start them growing again.

Another method of growing potatoes is to prepare soil so surface is loose, plant potato pieces or minitubers ½–2 in. deep, and water well. Mound loose soil over plants as directed above; then cover soil with a 1–1½-ft.-thick layer of straw, hay, or dead leaves. Surround the planting with chicken wire to keep loose material from blowing away. Potatoes will form on the soil surface or just beneath it, requiring little digging; you can probe through the mulch with your fingers to harvest them.

POTATO VINE. See SOLANUM jasminoides

POTENTILLA

CINQUEFOIL

Rosaceae

PERENNIALS AND DECIDUOUS SHRUBS

ZONES VARY BY SPECIES

PARTIAL SHADE IN HOTTEST CLIMATES

WATER NEEDS VARY BY TYPE

Potentilla fruticosa 'Tangerine'

Tough, unfussy perennials and small shrubs with flowers in white, cream, and soft to bright shades of pink, red, yellow, orange. Leaves are divided into leaflets; may be green, gray green, or silvery gray.

PERENNIALS

These include sturdy, clumping plants for use in rock gardens or perennial borders and creeping kinds used as ground covers. Leaves are divided fanwise into leaflets and are reminiscent of strawberry foliage. Moderate to regular water.

P. atrosanguinea. Zones 2b–9, 14–24. Sprawling, clump-forming Himalayan native to 1½ ft. high, 2 ft. wide. Leaves divided into three furry, silvery gray leaflets; deep red, 1-in. flowers in summer. A parent of several superior hybrids, including 'Gibson's Scarlet', with scarlet blossoms.

P. nepalensis 'Miss Willmott'. Zones 2b–9, 14–24. Variety of a Himalayan native. Forms a clump to 1 ft. high, 1½ ft. wide. Each leaf consists of five roundish, bright green leaflets. Summer bloomer, bearing branching clusters of ½–1-in.-wide, salmon pink blossoms. For borders, cut flowers. Performs well near coast.

P. neumanniana (P. verna 'Nana'). Zones A1–A3; 1–24. European native. May also be sold as *P. tabernaemontanii.* Dainty-looking yet tough and persistent ground cover to 3–6 in. high; spreads quickly by creeping, rooting stems. Bright green leaves are divided into five leaflets. Butter yellow, ¼-in. flowers bloom in spring and summer. Foliage blankets the ground completely yet is permeable enough to be a good bulb cover; established plantings endure limited foot traffic. Set plants 1 ft. apart in well-drained soil. Plantings look more uniform if mowed annually before spring growth begins; in colder areas, mowing also serves to remove browned winter leaves.

P. recta 'Warrenii'. Zones A2, A3; 1–10, 14–24. Selection of a species from Europe, Siberia. Erect clump to 2 ft. high, 1½ ft. wide, with medium green to gray-green leaves divided into five to seven leaflets. Profuse show of bright yellow, 1-in. flowers in late spring. Tolerates a wide range of soils. Sometimes sold as *P. warrenii.* 'Macrantha' (which may be listed as *P. warrenii* 'Macrantha') is the same or a very similar plant.

P. × tonguei. Zones 2–24. Clumping, to 4 in. high, 1–2 ft. wide; nearly prostrate stems. Dark green leaves are divided into three to five leaflets. Late spring or summer blooms, ½-in.-wide, apricot with a red center.

P. warrenii. See P. recta 'Warrenii'

SHRUBS

The shrubby potentillas, most often sold as named forms of *P. fruticosa,* are native to northern latitudes everywhere, including the Cascades and Olympic and Rocky mountains. They perform well in Zones A1–A3, 1–11, 14–21. All have typically bright green to dark green leaves divided into three to seven leaflets; all bloom cheerfully from late spring to early fall, producing 1½–2-in.-wide blossoms.

These are fairly trouble-free plants that do best in well-drained soil with moderate water but tolerate poor soil, drought, heat. Varieties with red- or orange-tinted blossoms should be grown in light shade; they tend to fade quickly in hot sun. After the bloom period ends, cut out some of the oldest stems from time to time to make room for new growth. Here are some of the many varieties to be found in nurseries.

'Abbotswood'. To 3 ft. high and wide. White flowers.

'Floppy Disc'. To 2–3 ft. tall, 3–4 ft. wide. Deep pink double flowers bleach to pinkish white in high heat.

'Goldfinger'. To 3 ft. tall, 4 ft. wide. Golden yellow flowers.

'Gold Star'. To 2 ft. tall, 2–2½ ft. wide. Bright yellow blooms.

'Jackman's Variety'. To 3–4 ft. tall, 5 ft. wide. Bright yellow blossoms.

'Katherine Dykes'. To 3 ft. tall and wide. Pale yellow flowers.

'Klondike'. Dense grower to 2 ft. high and wide. Deep yellow flowers.

'Mount Everest'. Bushy, upright plant to 4½ ft. high and wide. Pure white blossoms.

'Primrose Beauty'. To 2–3 ft. high and wide, with silvery green foliage and pale yellow flowers.

'Red Ace'. To 2 ft. high, 3–4 ft. wide. Flowers are bright red, with yellow center and yellow petal backs; they fade to solid yellow with age (fading is very rapid in hot-summer climates or under poor growing conditions).

'Sunset'. To 1½ ft. tall, 3 ft. wide. Flowers are red in light shade; in hot sun, they may be reddish orange, orange, or yellow.

'Sutter's Gold'. Grows to 1 ft. high, 3 ft. wide, with soft yellow blooms.

'Tangerine'. To 2½ ft. high and wide, with bright orange-yellow flowers.

POTERIUM. See SANGUISORBA

POTHOS. See EPIPREMNUM pinnatum 'Aureum'

POT MARIGOLD. See CALENDULA officinalis

POWDER PUFF. See CALLIANDRA

PRAIRIE ASTER. See MACHAERANTHERA tanacetifolia

PRATIA

Campanulaceae (Lobeliaceae)

PERENNIALS

ZONES 4–9, 14–24

PARTIAL SHADE IN HOTTEST CLIMATES

REGULAR WATER

Pratia angulata

Small, ground-hugging plants that reach just 2–3 in. high in bloom, with creeping, branching stems that root at the joints. All are useful low ground covers where soil is reasonably rich and well drained. Set plants 8–12 in. apart; fertilize periodically. Small, closely set leaves and tolerance for an occasional footstep make them choice selections for use between stepping-stones. They resemble baby's tears *(Soleirolia)* but offer appealing flowers as well as attractive foliage. Can be invasive where well adapted.

P. angulata. Native to New Zealand. Dark green, ½-in. leaves set off small white to ice blue summer flowers like those of lobelia, with a two-lobed upper lip and a three-lobed lower lip. Small, round fruit is purplish red.

P. pedunculata (Isotoma fluviatilis, Laurentia fluviatilis). BLUE STAR CREEPER. Native to Australia. Bright green, nearly stemless, ¼-in. leaves; in late spring and summer, these form a backdrop for equally tiny, star-shaped pale blue flowers.

PRICKLY PEAR. See OPUNTIA

PRICKLY POPPY. See ARGEMONE

PRIDE OF CALIFORNIA. See LATHYRUS splendens

PRIDE OF MADEIRA. See ECHIUM candicans

PRIMROSE. See PRIMULA

PRIMROSE TREE. See LAGUNARIA patersonii

PRIMULA

PRIMROSE

Primulaceae

PERENNIALS SOMETIMES GROWN AS ANNUALS

ZONES VARY BY SPECIES OR TYPE

FULL SUN IN COOLER CLIMATES ONLY

WATER NEEDS VARY BY TYPE

SEE CHART NEXT PAGE

Primula malacoides

Most primroses are native to the Himalayas and cool regions of Southeast Asia and Europe. Plants form a foliage rosette; at bloom time, typically circular, sometimes fragrant flowers with five petals rise above the leaves. The petals usually overlap and are often indented at the apex, sometimes so deeply that each flower appears to have ten parts. Blossoms may be borne on individual stems, in clusters at stem ends, or in tiered, candelabra-like clusters along the stem. Most primroses are spring blooming, but some start flowering in mid- to late winter in mild climates, and a few bloom in early summer. Some go dormant in late fall or winter; mark their location before they disappear (see chart next page).

Specialists have organized the hundreds of primrose species, selections, named hybrids, and hybrid strains into dozens of groupings called sections. Specialty nurseries, mainly in the Northwest, offer seeds and plants of many kinds, and fanciers exchange seeds and plants through primrose societies. The primroses that are fairly easy to grow in home gardens, however, are relatively few in number.

Primula ×polyantha

The key to success with primroses is the right climate. Almost any primrose flourishes in the cool, humid Pacific Northwest; if given the right amount of moisture and sun protection, these plants can be grown successfully in somewhat warmer, drier regions. Most are quite hardy; many thrive east of the Cascades and in the intermountain regions. Where the climate is less than favorable, they are sometimes treated as annuals. Some will grow indoors. All are subject to slug and snail damage.

WHAT PRIMROSES NEED

CLIMATE: Primroses fare best in areas with chilly winters (*P. malacoides* and *P. obconica* are notable exceptions) and cool summers.

EXPOSURE: In cool-summer regions, especially where foggy or overcast weather is common, primroses can take full sun. In hotter, sunnier areas, they prefer filtered or dappled sunlight or bright shade.

SOIL: Plant in organically enriched, well-drained soil. Mulch to keep roots cool.

WATERING: Some types thrive with regular water; others need damp or even boggy soil.

DIVIDING: Primrose plants form tight clumps that will need dividing when performance declines. When clumps become overcrowded, dig and divide them right after bloom or (in mild-winter areas) in autumn.

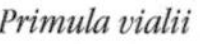

Primula vialii

PRIMULA

NAME, ZONES	SIZE	LEAVES	FLOWERS	COMMENTS
Primula acaulis (see **P. vulgaris**)				
P. alpicola MOONLIGHT PRIMROSE 3–6, 17	To 20 in. high, 1 ft. wide	Elliptical, to 4 in. long, wrinkled, medium green	Clusters of sulfur yellow (sometimes white or purple), bell-shaped blossoms. Powerfully fragrant. Summer	Somewhat tender in coldest zones. Regular water
P. auricula AURICULA A2, A3; 1–6, 15–17, 22–24	To 6–8 in. high,1 ft. wide	Evergreen. Broad, leathery gray-green leaves are toothed or smooth edged, sometimes with mealy, powdery coating that spots and runs in rain	Clustered blooms in white, cream, yellow, orange, pink, rose, red, purple, blue, or brownish, with white or yellow eye. Fragrant. Early spring	Usually grown in pots for display. Some choice named varieties have green or near-black flowers rimmed in mealy powder or in a contrasting color. Regular water
P. beesiana 3–6, 15–17	To 2 ft. high and wide	Oval to lance shaped, toothed, medium green, tapering into leafstalk; to 14 in. long (including stalk)	Tiered blossoms; 2–8 dense whorls per stem. Color is variable but usually reddish purple with yellow eye. Mid to late spring	Very deep rooted. Regular water in the form of deep soakings
P. bulleyana 3–6, 15–17	To 2 ft. high and wide	Like those of *P. beesiana*, but with reddish midribs	Tiered blossoms; 5–7 whorls per stem. Bright yellow, opening from orange buds. Mid- to late spring	Looks showy at woodland edge. Regular water
P. denticulata A2, A3; 1–6	To 1 ft. high and wide	Spoon shaped, medium green, 6–12 in. long. Only half grown at bloom time	Dense, ball-shaped clusters on stout stems. Color ranges from blue violet to purple. Early spring	Sometimes called drumstrick primrose. Pinkish, lavender, and white varieties available. Regular water
P. florindae A2, A3; 3–6, 15–17	To 3 ft. tall, 2 ft. wide	Long-stemmed, toothed, medium green leaves are broadly oval with heart-shaped base, to 9 in. long	Yellow, bell shaped, nodding; carried in clusters of up to 60. Most fragrant primrose and the latest to bloom. Late spring or summer	Ample water; will grow in a few inches of running water or in damp, low spot. Plants are late to appear in spring. Hybrids have red, orange, or yellow flowers
P. helodoxa (see **P. prolifera**)				
P. japonica A3; 2–6, 15–17	To 2½ ft. high, 1½ ft. wide	Spoon shaped, light green, to 9 in. long	Tiered blossoms in purple with yellow eye; up to 5 whorls on each stout stem. Late spring, early summer	'Millie's Crimson' is an excellent red variety. White and pink forms also available. Ample water; will grow at edge of pond, even in very shallow water
P. juliae hybrids (Pruhonicensis hybrids) JULIANA PRIMROSE 2–6, 14–17, 20–23	To 3–4 in. high, 10 in. wide	Rounded, scallop edged, bright green, to 2½ in. long	White, blue, yellow, orange red, pink, or purple, borne singly or in clusters. Early spring	Excellent for edging, woodland, rock garden. Regular water
P. malacoides FAIRY PRIMROSE, BABY PRIMROSE 8, 9, 12–24	To 8–15 in. high, 1 ft. wide	Evergreen. Soft, pale green, oval, 1½–3 in. long, with lobed and cut edges; carried on long stalks	Tiered blossoms in loose, lacy whorls along many upright stems. White, pink, rose, red, lavender. Midwinter to late spring	Perennial in mild-winter areas of California and Arizona, though often grown as annual there. Good under high-branching trees, with spring bulbs. Stands light frost. Treated only as annual, potted plant, or houseplant elsewhere. Regular water
P. obconica 4–9, 14–24	To 1 ft. high and wide	Evergreen. Soft, hairy, medium green, roundish, to 6 in. long; hairy leafstalks. Hairs (except on Freedom and Libre strains) may irritate skin	Large, broad clusters of 1½–2-in.-wide blooms in white, pink, salmon, lavender, reddish purple. Winter, spring; nearly everblooming in cool-summer areas	Perennial, but best treated as annual. Use for bedding where winters are mild, as houseplant in colder regions. Regular water
P. × polyantha POLYANTHUS PRIMROSE, ENGLISH PRIMROSE 1–24	To 8–12 in. high, 9 in. wide	Fresh green, tongue shaped, to 8 in. long; resemble romaine lettuce leaves. Evergreen in milder climates	Large, full clusters of 1–2-in.-wide blossoms (miniature types are smaller). Almost any color; many very brilliant. Winter to early or midspring	Fine large-flowered strains include Barnhaven, Clarke's, Concorde, Pacific, Santa Barbara. Novelties include Gold Laced, with gold-edged mahogany petals. All excellent for massing, with bulbs, in pots. Grow as annuals in hot-summer areas. Regular water

PRIMULA

NAME, ZONES	SIZE	LEAVES	FLOWERS	COMMENTS
P. prolifera (P. helodoxa) 4–6, 15–17	To 2–3 ft. high, 2 ft. wide	Evergreen. Spoon shaped to triangular, deep green, to 14 in. long	Tiered blossoms; up to 7 whorls per stem, each with 3–12 fragrant, light to bright yellow, inch-wide flowers. Late spring, summer	Good beside brooks, in bog gardens. Ample water
P. pulverulenta 3–6, 17	To 3 ft. tall, 2 ft. wide	Elliptical, deep green, wrinkled, to 1 ft. or longer	Tiered blossoms; several to many whorls per stem. Red to red-purple, with purple eye. Flowering stems thickly dusted with white meal. Late spring, summer	Bartley strain has flowers in pink and salmon range. Ample water
P. sieboldii A2, A3; 2–7, 14–17	To 1 ft. high and wide	Oval, light green, deeply lobed and toothed, 2–4 in. long, carried on long leafstalks	White, pink, or purple, all with white eye; 1–1½ in. wide, in clusters of 2–15. Early spring	Many named selections in deep or light colors; flowers of some have fringed petals. Leaves of all types usually die back shortly after flowering. Regular water
P. sinensis CHINESE PRIMROSE Indoors	To 6–8 in. high and wide	Evergreen. Soft, hairy, bright green, roundish, 2–4 in. long, with toothed, lobed edges. Hairs may irritate skin	One or more whorls per stem, each with many 1½-in.-wide blossoms in white, pink, lavender, reddish, or coral. Stellatas have star-shaped flowers. Winter	Tender. Favorite European potted plant; imported seed available from specialists. Regular water
P. veris COWSLIP A3; 2–6, 15–17	To 4–10 in. high, 8 in. wide	Similar to those of polyanthus primrose. Evergreen in milder climates	Clustered flowers are bright yellow, fragrant, ½–1 in. wide. Early spring	Lovely naturalized in wild garden or rock garden. Charming but not as sturdy as polyanthus primrose. Regular water
P. vialii (P. littoniana) 4–6, 15–17	To 1–2 ft. high, 1 ft. wide	Oblong, irregularly toothed, hairy, to 8 in. long	Dense, narrow, 3–5-in.-long spikes of fragrant flowers to ½ in. wide on erect stems. Violet blue, opening from red buds. Late spring or early summer	Not long lived but quite easy to grow from seed. Use in rock garden. Regular to ample water
P. vulgaris (P. acaulis) PRIMROSE, ENGLISH PRIMROSE A3; 2–6, 14–17, 21–24	To 8 in. high, 1 ft. wide	Much like those of *P.* × *polyantha.* Evergreen in milder climates	Borne singly; vigorous garden strains often bear 2 or 3 per stem. White, yellow, red, blue, brown, bronze, or wine colored. Early spring	Sweetheart series is double flowered. Among single types, Gemini and Quantum strains are scented; Nosegay and Biedermeier are heavy bloomers. Good in woodland or rock gardens or as edging. Regular water

Primulaceae. The primrose family of annuals and perennials has single or variously clustered flowers with five-lobed calyxes and corollas. Examples are rock jasmine *(Androsace), Cyclamen,* and primrose *(Primula).*

PRINCE'S FEATHER. See AMARANTHUS hypochondriacus

PRINCESS FLOWER. See TIBOUCHINA urvilleana

PRITCHARDIA

LOULU PALM

Arecaceae (Palmae)

PALM

ZONE H2

FULL SUN

MODERATE WATER

Pritchardia pacifica

Complex genus; comprises 19 native Hawaiian species and about 25 species restricted to various other tropical Pacific islands (Fiji, Samoa, Tonga, and Tuamotus). Erect, medium-size fan palms with straight trunk and regular form. Best in well-drained soil with moderate moisture. Plant in groups or use as specimens. Young plants will tolerate shade and are good container subjects for the patio or indoors.

P. hillebrandii. LOULU LELO. Native to Hawaii. Slow growing to 20 ft. tall, 8 ft. wide. Leaves to 4 ft. long. Full sun brings out the bluish silver color of the foliage. Striking accent in the landscape during the day or under night lighting.

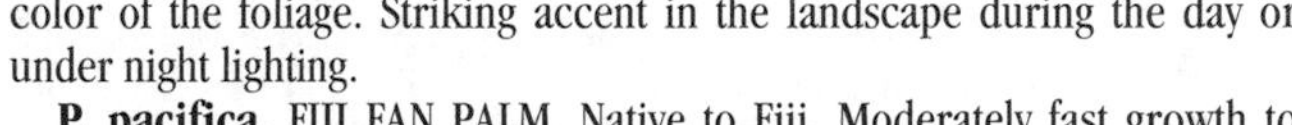

P. pacifica. FIJI FAN PALM. Native to Fiji. Moderately fast growth to 30 ft. tall, 8 ft. wide. Green leaves to about 4 ft. long. Needs protection from drying winds. Moderate salt tolerance.

P. thurstonii. THURSTON FAN PALM. Native to Fiji. Slow-growing, slender-trunked tree to 15–30 ft. tall, 8 ft. wide. Bright green, 5–6-ft.-long leaves. Good salt tolerance.

PRIVET. See LIGUSTRUM

PROSOPIS

MESQUITE

Fabaceae (Leguminosae)

EVERGREEN AND DECIDUOUS TREES OR SHRUBS

ZONES 10–13, 18–24, EXCEPT AS NOTED

FULL SUN

LITTLE TO MODERATE WATER

Prosopis glandulosa torreyana

Native to deserts in the Southwest, Mexico, and South America. Though hardy in other environments, they are most commonly grown in deserts, where they are among the toughest and most useful of trees. Much of their success in these harsh conditions is due to far-reaching roots that will travel great distances to find water (a trait that can cause problems if plants tap into drainage or sewer lines). Once established, these plants are highly drought tolerant, but they easily take regular lawn watering. In poor, rocky soil and without water, mesquites are shrubby; in deep soil where roots can reach groundwater, they grow rapidly to about 30 ft. tall, with a picturesque, spreading canopy approximately as wide.

Because these plants hybridize freely, exact identification is sometimes difficult. They may have one or many trunks; all have dark bark, a thicket of branches, and little leaflets that filter sunlight to cast airy, light shade. Small spikes of tiny greenish yellow flowers in spring and summer are followed by flat, beanlike, 2–6-in.-long pods. Flowers are a source of honey, and the pod contents are edible. Thorniness is variable; thornless varieties are available. Little pruning is needed; do the job only to cut out dead or broken limbs.

P. alba. ARGENTINE MESQUITE. Nearly evergreen. Native to South America. Plants sold under this name are vigorous and fast growing, with an erect single trunk and a rather dense canopy of blue-green leaves and spines. They drop some leaves throughout cold weather. Cutting-grown 'Colorado' is an erect, thornless tree with foliage slightly lighter in color than that of seedling plants. A cutting-grown, thornless form is available, often sold under the name "Chilean mesquite" (even though it is a form of *P. alba,* not of *P. chilensis*).

P. chilensis. CHILEAN MESQUITE. Evergreen in mild-winter climates; deciduous in colder areas. Zones 10–13; H1, H2. Native to South America. Produces a fairly open canopy of deep green leaves. Another tree sold under this name (probably a hybrid) is deciduous, with a denser canopy. In Hawaii, a species thought to be *P. pallida* has been identified as *P. chilensis;* it has naturalized in the Islands, where it reaches 50 ft. tall and nearly as wide.

P. glandulosa. HONEY MESQUITE, TEXAS MESQUITE. Deciduous. Native to southwestern U.S., Texas, Mexico. Often multitrunked. Bright green leaves and drooping branchlets give this tree something of the look of California pepper tree *(Schinus molle)*. Cutting-grown 'Maverick' is a superior, thornless form. *P. g. torreyana* ranges westward as far as California.

P. pubescens. SCREW BEAN. Deciduous. Native to Arizona, Texas, Mexico. Common name refers to the spirally twisted seedpods, which are popular in dried arrangements. Open canopy of bluish green foliage. This is a naturally shrubby plant often used as a barrier planting, but it can be trained as a tree.

P. velutina (P. glandulosa velutina). ARIZONA MESQUITE. Deciduous. Native from southeastern Arizona into Mexico and western Texas. Resembles *P. glandulosa* but may be smaller and shrubbier when grown in poor, dry conditions. Common in Arizona.

PROSTANTHERA

MINT BUSH

Lamiaceae (Labiatae)

EVERGREEN SHRUBS

ZONES 14–17, 19–24

FULL SUN

MODERATE WATER

Prostanthera rotundifolia

Australian natives with minty-smelling foliage and an enormous profusion of small flowers, usually in shades of purplish blue or white. These plants require excellent drainage. Although they tend to be short lived, they grow quickly and put on a good show. Prune them carefully; avoid cutting into bare wood or doing any other hard pruning. There are many species available; look for them at specialists' nurseries or at plant sales held by botanical gardens.

P. nivea induta. Upright, compact form. Grows to 6 ft. tall, 3 ft. wide. Narrow, silvery leaves somewhat longer than 1 in. Produces blue flowers in the spring. *P. nivea* is a larger and more open-growing shrub bearing white flowers.

P. rotundifolia. To 6 ft. tall, 5 ft. wide, with small roundish leaves and purple-blue flowers. Selections include 'Ghost Cave', with grayish green leaves and purple flowers; 'Glen Davis', with an especially profuse showing of dark purple flowers; and 'Rosea', to only 3–4 ft., with dark green leaves and deep rose pink flowers.

PROTEA

Proteaceae

EVERGREEN SHRUBS

ZONES 16, 17, 21–24; H1

FULL SUN

MODERATE WATER

Protea cynaroides

Some 150 species of beautiful flowering plants native to South Africa. Borne at branch ends, the flower heads consist of tight clusters of tubular true flowers surrounded by brightly colored bracts; effect is that of a large, very colorful artichoke or thistle. Superb cut flowers: they hold their color for weeks and retain their shape even after fading. Leaves are leathery, often edged in red.

Widely grown in Hawaii and Southern California for the cut-flower trade. In home gardens, these plants are not for beginners: they need perfect drainage (preferably on slopes), protection from dry winds, good air circulation. Give regular moisture until plants are established; thereafter, water only every 2 to 4 weeks. Most need acid soil, though some accept alkaline soil. Smaller species can be grown in containers. Under any conditions, plants are not long lived.

Young proteas are tender to cold; older ones of most species are hardy to 25 to 27°F/–4 to –3°C. Raised from seed, plants bloom in 3 or 4 years. Fertilize lightly with nitrogen; avoid fertilizers containing phosphorus (plants will glut themselves, then die of the overdose). Small applications of iron can remedy chlorosis. The following species are among the easiest to grow.

P. compacta. PINK PROTEA. Erect grower to 6–10 ft. tall, 4–8 ft. wide. Light green, oval leaves to 4 in. long, with downy, wavy edges. Pure rose pink to carmine, 4-in. flower heads appear from spring to summer.

P. cynaroides. KING PROTEA. To 3–5 ft. high and wide, with open, spreading habit. Dark green, oval leaves to 5½ in. long. Blooms midsummer to winter or early spring; flower heads reach 1 ft. across, with pale pink to crimson bracts surrounding white true flowers. Regular water.

P. eximia. ROSE-SPOON PROTEA. Dense and upright, to 6–8 ft. tall and 3–4 ft. wide. Silvery green, broadly oval leaves to 2½–4 in. long. Profuse bloom in winter; flower heads are rich red, to 5 in. across, with spoon-shaped bracts protruding outward and upward.

P. neriifolia. MINK PROTEA. To 10 ft. tall, 6–8 ft. wide. Leaves are narrow, medium green, to 7 in. long; resemble oleander *(Nerium)* leaves. Blooms in fall and winter; pink to salmon bracts with furry black tips form heads to 5 in. long and 3 in. wide. Withstands temperatures as low as 17°F/ –8°C; will grow in alkaline soil.

P. susannae. SUSANNA PROTEA. To 6–10 ft. high, 9–12 ft. wide. Grayish, elongated oval leaves to 5 in. long. Brownish pink flower heads to 4 in. across in fall and winter. Leaves smell unpleasant; strip them from the stems when cutting flowers for arrangements.

Proteaceae. The protea family of evergreen shrubs and trees is characterized by leathery leaves and irregular, somewhat tubular flowers in spikelike clusters or heads often surrounded by showy colored bracts. Many are attractive *(Grevillea, Protea);* one has edible nuts *(Macadamia).*

PROVENCE BROOM. See CYTISUS purgans

PRUNE. See PLUM

FOR INFORMATION ON YOUR CLIMATE ZONE
PLEASE SEE PAGES 27–63

PRUNELLA

SELF-HEAL, HEAL-ALL

Lamiaceae (Labiatae)

PERENNIALS

ZONES 2–24

FULL SUN OR LIGHT SHADE

REGULAR WATER

Prunella vulgaris

Native to Europe. Creeping perennials that spread by surface and underground runners to form low, dense foliage mats. Upright spikes of hooded flowers rise above the leaves in summer. Though names are much confused, all species are tough, tolerant, and deep rooted. They are useful for small-scale ground covers and can endure the occasional footstep; set 1 ft. apart. Choose location carefully, though: these plants are too invasive to risk near choice, delicate rock garden plants. After bloom, shear off spent flower spikes to keep the planting neat and prevent seed formation.

P. grandiflora. Leaves to 4 in. long; stems to 1½ ft. tall, bearing spikes of 1–1½-in. purple blossoms. Varieties include 'Pink Loveliness', 'Purple Loveliness' (lilac purple touched with white), and 'White Loveliness'.

P. vulgaris. This is the common species. Smaller in all its parts than *P. grandiflora,* with leaves to 2 in. long, 1-ft. stems, and purple or pink flowers just ⅓ in. long. *P. v. incisa* has deeply cut leaves.

PRUNUS

Rosaceae

EVERGREEN AND DECIDUOUS SHRUBS AND TREES

ZONES VARY BY SPECIES

FULL SUN, EXCEPT AS NOTED

MODERATE TO REGULAR WATER, EXCEPT AS NOTED

SEE CHARTS ON FOLLOWING PAGES

Prunus 'Okame' (Flowering Cherry)

Discussed here are ornamental members of the genus *Prunus.* Fruit trees belonging to *Prunus*—collectively known as stone fruits—are described under their common names. See Almond; Apricot; Cherry; Peach and Nectarine; Plum; Plumcot, Pluot, Aprium.

Ornamental species and forms can be divided into two categories: evergreen and deciduous. Evergreen types are used chiefly as hedges, screens, shade trees, street trees. Deciduous flowering trees and shrubs, closely related to the fruit trees mentioned above, are valued for their winter or spring floral display as well as for attractive shape and for foliage form and texture. Many of these deciduous kinds offer a bonus of edible fruit.

EVERGREEN FORMS

These attractive evergreen species are all large shrubs or small trees.

P. caroliniana. CAROLINA LAUREL CHERRY. Zones 5–24. Native from North Carolina to Texas. As an upright shrub, it branches densely from the base and can serve as a clipped hedge or tall screen to 20 ft. high; can be sheared into formal shapes. Trained as a tree, it typically grows 20–30 ft. high and 15–25 ft. wide but can reach 40 ft. tall with a 30–40 ft. spread; it also looks attractive grown with multiple trunks. Plant is thickly clothed in 2–4-in.-long, smooth-edged, glossy green leaves. Small, fragrant creamy white flowers bloom in 1-in. spikes from late winter to midspring; blossoms are followed by black fruit to ½ in. wide that is inconspicuous among the leaves. Flower and fruit litter can be a problem in paved areas.

Carolina laurel cherry looks best in coastal areas. Often shows salt burn and chlorosis in alkaline soils. Withstands desert heat and wind but appreciates a location protected from hottest sun in the low desert. May need moderate water in hottest climates; succeeds with little or no water elsewhere. 'Bright 'n Tight' and 'Compacta' are more densely branched than the species and reach only 8–10 ft. tall, 6–8 ft. wide.

P. ilicifolia. Zones 5–9, 12–24. The two similar forms described below are both useful as small trees, screens, or medium-size to tall clipped hedges. They often hybridize when growing near each other, producing plants with intermediate characteristics. Avoid planting near paved surfaces or parking areas, since fallen fruit causes stains. Unusually high resistance to oak root fungus. Both need good drainage. Can take extreme drought, but look best with occasional deep soakings.

P. i. ilicifolia. HOLLYLEAF CHERRY. Native to California Coast Ranges. To 10–25 ft. high and wide. Glossy, oval to elliptical leaves to 2 in. long are light green when new, maturing to a rich deep green; they are spiny edged like holly *(Ilex)* leaves but not as prickly. Blooms at leafout, bearing fragrant, ½-in., creamy white flowers in narrow, 3–6-in.-long spikes. Round, ¾-in.-wide, dark red or reddish purple fruit is edible but has a large pit and not much flesh.

P. i. lyonii. CATALINA CHERRY. Native to California's Channel Islands. In the wild, plants can grow as trees to 45 ft. tall and over 30 ft. wide, but in gardens they're more often seen as giant shrubs to 15–20 ft. high and wide. Leaves are similar in color and shape to those of *P. i. ilicifolia,* but they are smooth edged or very faintly toothed. Flowers identical to those of *P. i. ilicifolia;* fruit is darker red to almost black.

P. laurocerasus. ENGLISH LAUREL. Zones 4–9, 14–24; best performance in Zones 4–6, 15–17. Native from southeastern Europe to Iran. Fast growing to 15–30 ft. tall and wide. Leathery, oblong, glossy dark green leaves are 3–7 in. long. Blooms in spring or early summer, bearing 3–5-in. spikes of fragrant, creamy white flowers that are often hidden by leaves. Flowers are followed by small black fruit.

Prunus laurocerasus 'Zabeliana'

Needs reasonably good drainage. Can thrive with little to regular water (regular applications of moisture and nutrients will speed growth and keep top dense). Needs some shade in hottest climates; can take sun or shade elsewhere. Tolerates salt spray. Few pests, though it may be troubled occasionally by scale insects. English laurel is often sheared, but doing so mutilates its large leaves; for a better-looking result, make selective cuts back within the plant. Maintaining this plant as a formal hedge is a problem: its fast growth means frequent trimming. It's best used as a tall unclipped screen or trained as a tree. Smaller-growing varieties make lower, easier-to-maintain hedges.

'Marbled White' ('Castlewellan'). To 15 ft. tall and wide; leaves densely speckled with white. Showiest in cool climates.

'Mount Vernon'. Very slow growing. Forms a dense mound to perhaps 1 ft. high in 5 years; eventually attains 3 ft. high and wide. Though very dwarf, it has full-size leaves like those of the species. Can be used as ground cover.

'Nana'. Slow grower to 4–6 ft. tall and wide. Leaves to about 5 in. long.

'Otto Luyken'. To 3–4 ft. high, 5–6 ft. wide (has reportedly reached 6 ft. tall, 10 ft. wide). Leaves to 4½ in. long, exceptionally dark green.

'Schipkaensis'. SCHIPKA LAUREL. Zones 3–9, 14–17. Typically 4–5 ft. tall (possibly to 10 ft.), 7 ft. wide. Narrow, 2–4½-in.-long leaves. There is some variation in plants sold under this name.

'Zabeliana'. Zones 3–9, 14–21. To 4–6 ft. tall, 6–8 ft. wide (wider with age). Branches angle upward and outward from base. Narrow, willow-like leaves 3–5 in. long. Versatile plant; good for low screen, foundation plant, bank cover (with branches pegged down), espalier.

P. lusitanica. PORTUGAL LAUREL. Zones 4–9, 14–24. From Spain and Portugal. Densely branched shrub 10–20 ft. high and wide; or multi-trunked tree to 30 ft. tall and wide. Trained to a single trunk, it is used as a formal street tree. Narrowly oval, glossy dark green leaves to 5 in. long. Small, creamy white flowers in 5–10-in. spikes bloom in spring and early summer; these are followed by clusters of very small, bright red to dark purple fruit. Attractive background plant, screen. Slower grower than *P. laurocerasus* and more tolerant of heat, strong sunlight, wind. Little or no water. 'Variegata' has leaves with narrow, irregular white margins and fruit that ripens from red to black.

P. l. azorica. Native to Azores and Canary Islands, where it grows 60–70 ft. tall. In the West, it is a large, columnar shrub about 20 ft. tall, 10 ft. wide. Glossy, exceptionally deep green foliage.

▶ page 551

P

PRUNUS–FLOWERING CHERRY

NAME	ZONES	GROWTH HABIT, FOLIAGE	HEIGHT, SPREAD	FLOWERS, SEASON, COMMENTS
Prunus 'Accolade'	2–9, 14–17	Small tree with spreading branches, twiggy growth pattern. Very vigorous	To 25 ft. high and wide	Semidouble blush pink, 1½ in. wide, in large, drooping clusters; open from rose pink buds. Early. Hybrid between *P. sargentii* and *P.* × *subhirtella*
P. campanulata TAIWAN FLOWERING CHERRY	6–9, 14–24	Graceful, slender, upright-growing small tree; densely branched	To 20–25 ft. high and wide	Single, bell shaped, drooping, in clusters of 2–5. Striking shade of bright purplish pink. Early. Red fruit about ½ in. long. Good choice for warm-winter areas
P. 'Hally Jolivette'	3–7, 14–20	Dense, shrubby	Slow to 6–8 ft. high and wide; eventually reaches twice that size	Double white blooms open from pink buds. Early; relatively long bloom, lasting several weeks. Can be used in shrub borders. Hybrid between *P.* × *subhirtella* and *P.* × *yedoensis*
P. 'Okame'	4–9, 14–20	Upright, oval habit. Dark green, fine-textured foliage. Good yellow-orange to orange-red fall color	To 25 ft. by 20 ft.	Single carmine pink. Very early. Hybrid between *P. campanulata* and another species
P. sargentii	2–7, 14–17	Upright, spreading branches form rounded crown. Good orange-red fall color	To 40–60 ft. tall and wide	Single blush pink flowers in clusters of 2–4. Midseason. 'Columnaris' is narrower and more erect than species, though more vase shaped than truly columnar
P. serrula	2–7, 14–16	Round-headed tree with narrow, willowlike leaves. Valued for its beautiful, glossy, mahogany red bark	To 30 ft. tall and wide	Bark more notable than small white flowers, which are almost hidden by new leaves. Midseason
P. serrulata		Known through its many varieties. Some are listed here (may be sold by variety name only)		
P. s. 'Amanogawa'	3–7, 14–20	Columnar in youth, becoming vase shaped with age	To 20–25 ft. tall, 4–8 ft. wide	Semidouble light pink with deep pink petal margins. Early midseason
P. s. 'Beni Hoshi' (P. s. 'Pink Star')	3–7, 14–20	Fast grower with arching, spreading branches. Umbrella shaped in outline	To 20–25 ft. tall and wide	Single, vivid pink blooms with long, slightly twisted petals. Flowers hang below branches. Midseason
P. s. 'Kwanzan' ('Kanzan', 'Sekiyama')	3–7, 14–20	Branches stiffly upright, forming narrow, inverted cone that spreads with age	To 30 ft. by 20 ft.	Large, double, deep rosy pink, in pendent clusters. Blossoms appear before or with red young leaves. Midseason
P. s. 'Royal Burgundy'	3–7, 14–20	Habit similar to that of 'Kwanzan'. Leaves are reddish purple	Same as 'Kwanzan'	Like those of 'Kwanzan', but deeper pink and with red stems
P. s. 'Shirofugen'	3–7, 14–20	Wide horizontal branching	To 25 ft. high and wide	Double blooms in pink fading to white; long stalked. Flowers appear at same time as coppery red new leaves. Late
P. s. 'Shirotae' ('Mt. Fuji')	2–7, 14–20	Strong horizontal branching	To 20 ft. by 25 ft.	Semidouble. Pink in bud; white when fully open, aging to purplish pink. Early
P. s. 'Shogetsu' ('Shimidsu Sakura')	3–7, 14–20	Spreading growth, arching branches	To 15 ft. by 25 ft.	Semidouble and fully double pale pink, often with white center. Late
P. s. 'Snow Fountains' ('White Fountain')	3–7, 14–20	Slightly curving trunk; weeping branches reach to ground. Sold as small tree or trunkless ground cover	To 12–15 ft. high and wide as tree; to 1 ft. by 10–15 ft. as ground cover	Single white. Early
P. s. 'Snow Goose'	3–7, 14–20	Erect; narrow at first, eventually becoming broader	To 20 ft. high and wide	Single white. Early

PRUNUS–FLOWERING CHERRY

NAME	ZONES	GROWTH HABIT, FOLIAGE	HEIGHT, SPREAD	FLOWERS, SEASON, COMMENTS
P. s. 'Tai Haku'	2–7, 14–20	Vigorous, with rounded crown. Good orange fall color	To 20–25 ft. high and wide	Extra-large (2½-in.), pure white single blooms. Flowers appear with bronzy new leaves. Late midseason
P. ×subhirtella 'Autumnalis'	2–7, 14–20	Loose-branching, bushy tree with flattened crown	To 25–30 ft. high and wide	Double white or pinkish white. Blooms in fall as well as early spring; may also bloom during warm spells in winter
P. ×s. 'Pendula' SINGLE WEEPING CHERRY, WEEPING HIGAN CHEERY	2–7, 14–20	Usually sold grafted at 5–6 ft. high on upright-growing understock. Graceful branches hang down, often to ground	To 10–12 ft. high and wide	Profuse show of small, pale pink single flowers. Early
P. ×s. 'Rosea'	2–7, 14–20	Wide spreading, horizontally branching	To 20–25 ft. by 30 ft.	Single pink blossoms open from nearly red buds. Profuse, very early bloom. Pacific Northwest favorite
P. ×s. 'Whitcomb'	2–7, 14–20	Same as *P. ×s.* 'Rosea'	To 30 ft. by 35 ft.	Single; pink fading to white. Early
P. ×s. 'Yae-shidare-higan' DOUBLE WEEPING CHERRY	2–7, 14–20	Same as *P. ×s.* 'Pendula'	Same as *P. ×s.* 'Pendula'	Double rose pink. Midseason
P. ×yedoensis YOSHINO FLOWERING CHERRY	3–7, 14–20	Horizontal branches; graceful, open pattern	To 40 ft. by 30 ft.	Single light pink to nearly white. Early. This is the cherry planted around the Tidal Basin in Washington, D.C. Fast growing
P. ×y. 'Akebono' (sometimes called **'Daybreak'**)	3–7, 14–20	Same as *P. ×yedoensis*	To 25 ft. high and wide	Flowers pinker than those of *P. ×yedoensis.* One of the best, most disease-free flowering cherries in the Pacific Northwest. Early

DECIDUOUS FLOWERING FRUIT TREES
Grown for beautiful floral displays in winter, spring. Branches of all types can be cut for indoor decoration; follow proper pruning procedures when you cut, and make your selections with an eye to thinning or shaping the canopy. For longest-lasting bloom, cut branches when buds first begin to show color or when they have just opened. Place branches in a deep container of water; strip off any buds or flowers that will be below water level.

Flowering cherry. For zones, see chart. Early to midspring bloom, depending on variety. Usually blossom before leafout, but some bloom with new leaves. Some flowering cherries have especially good fall color; all are good trees to garden under. Large, sprawling kinds make good shade trees; smaller ones are indispensable in Japanese gardens. Cultural needs of all are identical. They require fast-draining, well-aerated soil; those grown in heavy, poorly drained soil are sometimes subject to root rot, for which there is no cure (an affected tree will usually bloom, then send out new leaves that suddenly collapse). If your soil is substandard, plant in raised beds. Even in good growing conditions, foliage may sustain damage from insect pests. *P. ×subhirtella* varieties are subject to bacterial blight. Best with moderate water. Prune to remove awkward or crossing branches; pinch back the occasional overly ambitious shoot to force branching.

Flowering peach. Zones 3–24 (note, however, that blossoms may suffer frost damage in cold climates and that leafout may be delayed in warm-winter areas). Produces blossoms about 1½ in. wide in late winter and early spring, before leafout. More widely adapted than fruiting peach but identical to it in other respects—plant size, growth habit, cultural needs, pruning requirements, potential problems. Place trees where they will be striking when in bloom yet fairly unobtrusive out of bloom.

Some peach varieties produce both showy blossoms and good fruit; these are described under Peach and Nectarine. The following varieties are strictly "flowering"; that is, they have showy blooms, but fruit is either absent or worthless. In areas with late frosts, choose late bloomers; early bloomers are best in regions with hot, early springs.

'Early Double Pink'. Very early.

'Early Double Red'. Deep purplish red or rose red. Very early. Brilliant color is beautiful but likely to clash with other pinks and reds.

'Early Double White'. Blooms with 'Early Double Pink'.

'Helen Borchers'. Semidouble, pure pink, large (2½-in.) flowers. Late.

'Icicle'. Double white flowers. Late.

'Late Double Red'. Later than 'Early Double Red' by 3 to 4 weeks.

'Peppermint Stick'. Double flowers striped red and white; may also bear all-white and all-red flowers on the same branch. Midseason.

'Weeping Double Pink'. Smaller than other flowering peaches, with weeping branches. Requires staking to develop main stem of suitable height. Midseason.

'Weeping Double Red'. Like above; has deep rose red flowers. Midseason.

'Weeping Double White'. White version of weeping forms listed above.

Flowering plum. For zones, see chart on next page. Flowers appear between midwinter and midspring, usually before leafout. Many flowering plums feature purple foliage. If you are choosing a plum to be planted in a patio or paved area, check its fruiting habit. These trees are less particular about soil than flowering cherry or flowering peach, but they will fail if soil is waterlogged for prolonged periods. Where conditions are boggy, plant in raised beds. Little pruning is needed. Aphids and spider mites are possible pests. Leaf-damaging insects and leaf spot disease are problems in the Pacific Northwest. ▶

PRUNUS—FLOWERING PLUM

NAME	ZONES	GROWTH HABIT, FOLIAGE	HEIGHT, SPREAD	FLOWERS, FRUIT, COMMENTS
Prunus americana WILD PLUM, GOOSE PLUM	1–3, 10	Thicket-forming shrub or small tree. Dark green foliage	To 15–25 ft. by 10–15 ft.	Clusters of 1-in., single white flowers. Fruit yellow to red, to 1 in., sour but good for jelly. Native to Rockies. Very tough
P. × blireiana	3–22	Graceful form. New leaves reddish purple; turn greenish bronze by summer	To 25 ft. by 20 ft.	Double, fragrant pink to rose flowers. Hybrid of *P. cerasifera* 'Atropurpurea' and *P. mume*
P. cerasifera CHERRY PLUM, MYROBALAN	3–22	Most often used as rootstock for various stone fruits. Dark green leaves	To 30 ft. high and wide	Pure white flowers. Red, 1–1¼-in.-wide fruit is sweet but bland. Self-sows freely; some seedlings bear yellow fruit. Purple- and red-leafed varieties are popular
P. c. 'Allred'	3–22	Upright, slightly spreading. Red leaves	To 20 ft. by 12–15 ft.	Single white flowers. Red, 1½-in., tart fruit good for preserves, jelly
P. c. 'Atropurpurea' (P. 'Pissardii') PURPLE-LEAF PLUM	3–22	Rounded habit. Leaves are coppery red when new, later deepen to dark purple; turn red in autumn	Fast to 25–35 ft. high and wide	Single white flowers. Heavy crop of red, 1–1½-in. fruit
P. c. 'Hollywood'	3–22	Upright habit. Leaves dark green above, red beneath	To 30–40 ft. by 25 ft.	Single light pink to white flowers. Good-quality red plums, 2–2½ in. wide. Hybrid of *P. c.* 'Atropurpurea' and a Japanese plum
P. c. 'Krauter Vesuvius'	3–22	Upright, oval form. Darkest foliage (blackish purple) of any flowering plum	To 18 ft. by 12 ft.	Single light pink flowers. Little or no fruit
P. c. 'Mt. St. Helens'	3–22	Upright, spreading, with rounded crown. A sport of *P. c.* 'Newport' but more robust, with larger leaves of a richer purple color	Faster than 'Newport', to 20 ft. high and wide	Same as 'Newport'
P. c. 'Newport'	2–22	Upright and spreading, with rounded crown. Foliage is dark purple all summer, attractively reddish in autumn	To 15–20 ft. by 20 ft.	Fragrant, single white to pale pink flowers. Will bear a little fruit
P. c. 'Purple Pony'	3–22	Naturally semidwarf; available budded low or high. Deep purple foliage holds color throughout season	Usually not taller than 10–12 ft. by 12 ft.	Single pale pink flowers appear with the leaves. No fruit
P. c. 'Thundercloud'	3–22	Rounded in habit (more so than *P. c.* 'Atropurpurea'). Dark coppery leaves	To 20 ft. high and wide	Fragrant, single light pink to white flowers. Sometimes sets good crop of 1-in. red fruit
P. × cistena DWARF RED-LEAF PLUM	A3; 1–22	Dainty multistemmed shrub. Can be trained as single-trunked tree; good for small patios. Intensely red-purple new leaves mature to coppery purple	To 6–10 ft. by 6–8 ft.	Fragrant, single white flowers appear after leafout (unlike flowering plums above); offer striking contrast to foliage. May produce small (½-in.) blackish purple fruit
P. × c. 'Big Cis'	A3; 1–22	Sport of *P. × cistena*. Dense, globular, and more vigorous than *P. × cistena*, with larger purple leaves	Fast to 14 ft. by 12 ft.	Same as *P. × cistena*

ADDITIONAL DECIDUOUS SPECIES

The following shrubs or trees bloom early in the season. In some cases, blossoms are followed by edible fruit.

P. besseyi. WESTERN SAND CHERRY. Shrub. Zones A1–A3; 1–3, 10. Native to the Great Plains. To 3–6 ft. high and wide. Good show of white, ½-in.-wide flowers in mid- to late spring, before leafout, followed by sweet black cherries a little more than ½ in. across. Fruit is used for pies, jams, jellies. Gray-green, 1–2-in.-long leaves. Withstands heat, cold, wind, and drought. A parent of hardy hybrid plums (see Plum).

P. fruticosa. EUROPEAN DWARF CHERRY. Shrub. Zones A1–A3; 1–3, 10. Native from central Europe to Siberia. Similar to *P. besseyi* but grows just 3–4 ft. tall and bears smaller, red-purple fruit that is tart, not sweet (fruit is used in jams, jellies). Sometimes grown as a low hedge. Suckers freely.

P. glandulosa. DWARF FLOWERING ALMOND. Shrub. Zones 2–12, 14–19. Native to China, Japan. To 4–6 ft. high and wide; upright, spreading. Light green, willowlike leaves to 4 in. long. In early spring, the many slender, leafless stems are covered with blossoms. Typically sold are white 'Alboplena' and pink 'Sinensis' ('Rosea Plena'), both with 1–1¼-in. double blooms that look like fluffy pompon chrysanthemums. Prune heavily during or after flowering to promote strong new growth for next year's bloom. Can be used as a flowering hedge. Suckers freely. Fireblight can be a problem. Brown rot causes trouble in the Pacific Northwest.

P. maackii. AMUR CHOKECHERRY. Tree. Zones A1–A3; 1–7, 10. Native to Manchuria and Siberia; extremely hardy to cold and wind. To 25–30 ft. tall, 25 ft. wide. Main feature is handsome bark on trunk; it is yellowish to cinnamon brown and peels off like birch *(Betula)* bark. Strongly veined, rather narrow, pointed leaves to 4 in. long. Blooms after leafout in mid-spring, bearing small, fragrant white flowers in narrow, 2–3-in.- long clusters. Black, ¼-in.-wide fruit.

P. mume. JAPANESE FLOWERING APRICOT, JAPANESE FLOWERING PLUM. Tree. Zones 3–9, 12–22. Blooms may be damaged by frost in coldest areas. From China and Korea. Longer lived, tougher, more trouble-free than other flowering fruit trees; common names notwithstanding, it is neither a true apricot nor a true plum. Leaves to 4½ in. long, broadly oval, pointed. White to dark red, 1–1¼-in. blossoms with a clean, spicy fragrance form on leafless branches in midwinter to early spring. Yellow to green, 1-in. fruit is edible only if pickled.

For profuse bloom on year-old wood, let newly planted trees grow unpruned for their first year. Then prune heavily, as follows. After bloom, prune back all shoots to 6-in. stubs; these stubs will produce long whips that will form next year's flower buds. The next year, cut back half of the young growth to 6-in. stubs; then cut back the other half the following year. Continue this routine in succeeding years. If allowed to develop naturally, Japanese flowering plum grows into a gnarled, picturesque tree 20 ft. tall and wide. Varieties include the following.

'Bonita'. Semidouble rose red.

'Dawn'. Large, ruffled double pink.

'Matsubara Red'. Double, deep red flowers.

'Peggy Clarke'. Double flowers in deep rose, with extremely long stamens and red calyxes.

'Rosemary Clarke'. Double white flowers with red calyxes. Very early; often in bloom on New Year's Day in California.

'W. B. Clarke'. Double pale pink flowers; weeping form. Effective large bonsai or container plant. Bloom and form make it the center of attention in a winter garden.

P. padus. EUROPEAN BIRD CHERRY, MAYDAY TREE, MAYBUSH. Tree. Zones A1–A3; 1–7, 10. Native to Europe, northern Asia. Moderate growth to 15–20 ft. tall and wide, occasionally taller. Rather thin and open in habit when young. Among the first plants to leaf out in spring; leaves are dull dark green, oval, 3–5 in. long. Profuse mid- to late spring show of small, very fragrant white flowers in slender, drooping, 3–6-in. clusters that nearly hide foliage. Small, dark purple fruit follows the flowers; it is bitter but much loved by birds. Fruit is often used for making jelly and wine. Branches are stiff, subject to breakage under heavy snow loads. Older trees tend to sucker.

P. tomentosa. NANKING CHERRY. Shrub. Zones A1–A3; 1–3, 10. From Tibet, China. Like *P. besseyi,* this species is very tough and cold hardy. To 6–8 ft. tall, 10 ft. wide, with shiny reddish brown, peeling bark. Elliptical leaves to 1½ in. long, dull dark green above, woolly beneath. Small, fragrant white flowers open from pinkish buds before leafout in spring; edible, ½-in.-wide, scarlet fruit follows.

P. triloba. FLOWERING ALMOND. Tree or treelike shrub. Zones A1–A3; 1–11, 14–20. Native to China. Slow growth to 8–10 ft. (possibly 15 ft.) tall, with equal spread. May be sold as a single- or multistemmed plant. Rather broad, often three-lobed leaves are 1–2½ in. long, dark green above, lighter green beneath. Pink flowers to 1½ in. wide appear on bare branches in early spring. 'Multiplex' has double pink flowers. A double white form is sometimes available.

P. virginiana. CHOKECHERRY. Shrub or tree. Zones A1–A3, 1–3, 10, except as noted. Native to eastern North America. To 20–30 ft. tall, 18–25 ft. wide, with suckering habit. Broadly elliptical, 2–4-in. leaves. In late spring, very fragrant white flowers appear in slender, 3–6-in. clusters among the leaves; these are followed by astringent, ½-in.-wide, dark red to black fruit. Good fall foliage display; color varies from bright red to pale yellow. 'Canada Red' has leaves that open green, turn red as they mature; it is a sport of 'Schubert', which has mature leaves in a more purplish shade. *P. v. demissa,* Western chokecherry (Zones 2–10, 14–24), is native to the Pacific Coast, Sierra Nevada, Great Basin area, and northern Rockies. It tolerates heat and drought.

PSEUDOLARIX amabilis (P. kaempferi)

GOLDEN LARCH
Pinaceae
DECIDUOUS TREE
ZONES 2–7, 14–17
FULL SUN
REGULAR WATER

Pseudolarix amabilis

Native to China. Slow growing to 40–70 ft. high, often nearly as broad at base; symmetrical, pyramidal form. Wide-spreading branches with pendulous tips grow in whorls. Foliage has a feathery look; 1½–2-in.-long, ⅛-in.-wide needles are clustered in tufts except near branch ends, where they are single. Needles are bluish green during growing season, then turn a magnificent golden yellow very briefly in autumn before dropping. Cones, bare branches present an interesting pattern in winter. Choose a planting spot that is open, but sheltered from cold winds. Best in deep, rich, well-drained, acid soil; performance is better in colder part of range. Fine for spacious lawns.

PSEUDOPANAX

Araliaceae
EVERGREEN SHRUBS OR TREES
ZONES VARY BY SPECIES
SUN OR SHADE
REGULAR WATER

Pseudopanax lessonii

From New Zealand. Typically slow-growing aralia relatives cultivated for their evergreen foliage. In youth, *P. crassifolius* and *P. ferox* are odd looking and very decorative, with long, narrow, spiny-toothed, colorful leaves. Mature plants of all have dark green, divided or undivided leaves of unremarkable shape. Flowers are inconspicuous. No special pruning needs. All make good container plants.

P. crassifolius. LANCEWOOD. Zones 16, 17, 21–24. In time, a tree to 50 ft. tall, 15 ft. wide. Usually seen as single-stemmed plant 3–5 ft. tall, 8–10 in. wide, with rigid, drooping, strongly toothed leaves to 3 ft. long, ½–¾ in. wide. Young leaves are dark green above and dark purple beneath, with an orange or yellow midrib on upper surface. Upright growth habit makes this plant a good choice for narrow areas.

P. ferox. Zones 16, 17, 21–24. To 10–12 ft. tall, 3–4 ft. wide. Young plants produce strongly toothed leaves to 1–1½ ft. long and ½–1 in. wide. Young leaves are dark green to blackish green above and bronzy beneath, with brown, orange, or red midrib on upper surface.

P. lessonii. Zones 17, 22–24. Moderate growth to 12–20 ft. tall, 6–12 ft. wide. Effective multistemmed tree in open ground. Leathery dark green leaves divided into three to five leaflets 2–4 in. long.

PSEUDOSASA. **See BAMBOO**

PSEUDOTSUGA

Pinaceae
EVERGREEN TREES
ZONES VARY BY SPECIES
TOLERATE PARTIAL SHADE IN YOUTH
LITTLE OR NO WATER TO REGULAR WATER

Pseudotsuga menziesii

The two species described here are quite similar, but they differ greatly in status—the first is little known, while the second is the most prominent tree in the Pacific Northwest.

P. macrocarpa. BIGCONE SPRUCE, BIGCONE DOUGLAS FIR. Zones 3–11, 14–23. Native to Southern California. Stout-trunked tree to about 60 ft. tall and 30 ft. wide. Needles are similar to those of *P. menziesii.* Cones are much larger, reaching 4–7½ in. long, 2–3 in. wide; three-pronged bracts on cones barely protrude from each side.

P. menziesii (P. taxifolia). DOUGLAS FIR. Zones A2, A3; 1–10, 14–17. Since pioneer days, Northwesterners have gardened under and near this magnificent native tree. In cultivation, it grows 80–160 ft. tall, 20–30 ft. wide; in forests, it reaches 250 ft. tall. Young trees are sharply pyramidal and foliaged to the ground; they are popular as Christmas trees. As trees age, they lose lower limbs. Branches are densely clothed in soft, 1½-in.-long, deep green or blue-green needles that radiate in all directions. Needles are sweetly fragrant when crushed. Ends of branches turn up. Pointed wine red buds form at branch tips in winter, open to apple green new growth in spring. Reddish brown, oval cones are about 3 in. long, with obvious three-pronged bracts; they are pendent, unlike the upright cones of true firs *(Abies).*

The tree's entire range includes Oregon, Washington, and parts of the Rocky Mountains and extends to Alaska and California (as far south as Monterey and Fresno Counties). In coastal climates, it is fast growing, feathery, dark green, with slightly drooping branchlets. The Rocky Mountain form is *P. m. glauca,* a blue-green tree that is slower growing, more cold tolerant, more compact, and stiffer than the species. Compact, weeping, and other forms exist, but they are grown mostly in arboretums and botanical gardens. All tolerate wind, will grow in all soils except boggy ones. For best success, especially in coldest zones, buy plants raised from seed of trees native to your region. Resistant to oak root fungus.

PSILOSTROPHE cooperi

PAPER DAISY
Asteraceae (Compositae)
PERENNIAL
ZONES 7–14, 18–21
FULL SUN
LITTLE WATER

Psilostrophe cooperi

Native to deserts of the Southwest. To 8–20 in. high and wide, with woody base and open branching habit. Stems are clothed in fuzzy white hairs. Narrow leaves to 2 in. long are woolly when young, becoming greener and less hairy as they mature. Bright yellow daisies appear at branch tips over a long season, even year-round under favorable conditions. Older blossoms hang on and turn white and papery; they are favored for dried arrangements.

PSOROTHAMNUS spinosus (Dalea spinosa)

SMOKE TREE
Fabaceae (Leguminosae)
DECIDUOUS TREE OR SHRUB
ZONES 12, 13
FULL SUN
LITTLE OR NO WATER

Psorothamnus spinosus

Native to deserts of Arizona, Southern California, Baja California. To 10–20 ft. tall, 10–15 ft. wide. Sparsely foliaged in small, hairy white leaves that drop in early spring, revealing an intricate network of silvery gray, spiny branches; the leafless plant is said to resemble a cloud of smoke. In late spring, puts on a good show of fragrant, violet-purple, sweet pea–shaped flowers in 1½–2-in. clusters. Cut branches (in or out of bloom) are good in arrangements. Not always available in nurseries but easily started from seed in warm weather. Provide good drainage. Needs little care.

PSYLLIOSTACHYS suworowii (Limonium suworowii)

Plumbaginaceae
ANNUAL
ZONES 1–24
FULL SUN
REGULAR WATER

Psylliostachys suworowii

Native to Iran, Afghanistan, central Asia. Forms a low, 1-ft.-wide rosette of narrow leaves to 8 in. long. In summer, spikes of tiny lavender-pink blossoms increase the plant's height to 1½ ft. Spikes are branched or unbranched, very slender, and cylindrical; unbranched ones are reminiscent of furry rats' tails. They are excellent in fresh or dried flower arrangements. Sow seeds in ground when danger of frost is past; or start seeds earlier indoors. This plant may be offered as *Statice suworowii.*

PTERIDIUM aquilinum

BRACKEN
Polypodiaceae
FERN
ZONES 1–10, 14–24
FULL SUN OR PARTIAL SHADE
LITTLE TO REGULAR WATER
FRONDS ARE POISONOUS IF INGESTED

Pteridium aquilinum pubescens

Found all over the world, bracken is represented by various subspecies that differ in minor details. *P. a. pubescens* is native to the West. It has coarse, much-divided fronds that rise directly from deep, running rootstocks; grows from as low as 2 ft. high to as tall as 7 ft. under good conditions. Occurs naturally in many places and can be tolerated in untamed gardens, but beware of planting it: deep rootstocks can make it a tough, invasive weed. Do not gather fronds to cook as fiddleheads, since they contain a slow poison.

PTERIS

BRAKE
Polypodiaceae
FERNS
ZONES VARY BY SPECIES
PARTIAL OR FULL SHADE
REGULAR WATER

Pteris cretica

Small evergreen ferns of subtropical or tropical origin. Mostly used in dish gardens or small containers, but some are large enough for landscape use.

P. cretica. Zones 17, 23, 24; H1, H2. To 2½ ft. high, 2 ft. wide, with comparatively few long, narrow leaflets. Numerous varieties exist; some have forked or crested fronds, others are variegated. Light green 'Wimsettii' has fronds that are forked at the tip on mature plants; it is so dense and frilly that it doesn't look like a fern.

P. 'Ouvrardii'. Zones 17, 22–24. To 1–2½ ft. high and wide. Dark green fronds have extremely long, narrow, ribbonlike divisions.

P. quadriaurita 'Argyraea'. SILVER FERN. Zone 24. To 2–4 ft. tall and wide, with rather coarsely divided fronds that are heavily marked in white. Showy, unusual coloring for a fern. Protect from frost; watch for slugs and snails.

P. tremula. AUSTRALIAN BRAKE. Zones 16, 17, 22–24. To 5 ft. tall and 3 ft. wide. Extremely graceful fronds on slender, upright stalks. Good landscape fern with excellent silhouette. Fast growing but tends to be rather short lived.

PTEROCARYA stenoptera

CHINESE WINGNUT

Juglandaceae

DECIDUOUS TREE

ZONES 4–24

FULL SUN

MODERATE TO REGULAR WATER

From China. Fast to 40–90 ft. tall, 30–50 ft. wide, with heavy, wide-spreading limbs. Clearly shows its kinship to walnuts in its leaves: 8–16 in. long and divided into 11–23 finely toothed, oval leaflets. Foot-long clusters of small, single-seeded, winged nuts hang from branches. Good looking but has only one real virtue: it succeeds well in compacted, poorly aerated soil in play yards and other high-traffic areas. Aggressive roots make it unsuitable in garden or lawn. *P. fraxinifolia,* Caucasian wingnut, is similar but has slightly larger leaflets, longer nut clusters.

Pterocarya stenoptera

PTEROSTYRAX hispida

EPAULETTE TREE

Styracaceae

DECIDUOUS TREE

ZONES 3–10, 14–21

FULL SUN

REGULAR WATER

Pterostyrax hispida

Native to Japan. Single- or multitrunked tree to 20–30 ft. (possibly 40 ft.) tall and equally wide. Rather coarse, oval to oblong, 3–8-in.-long leaves are light green above, gray green beneath. Blooms in late spring or early summer, bearing creamy white, lightly fragrant flowers with fringed petal edges in drooping clusters 4–9 in. long, 2–3 in. wide. Pendent clusters of small, furry gray fruits hang on well into winter, are attractive on bare branches. Best planted where you can look up into it—on bank beside path, above a bench, in a raised bed. Choice selection for woodland edge or as focal point in large shrub border. Established trees need little pruning.

PTYCHOSPERMA

Arecaceae (Palmae)

PALMS

ZONES 23, 24; H2

LIGHT SHADE

REGULAR WATER

Ptychosperma macarthuri

Native to Australia and the South Pacific. Small feather palms with slender, ringed trunks and well-defined crown shafts (the smooth, usually green upper portion of the trunk, formed by overlapping bases of newer leaves). Leaflets are toothed at the tip. Often produce red fruit in warmest frost-free climates. Grow in well-drained soil.

P. elegans. ALEXANDER PALM, SOLITAIRE PALM. From Australia. Erect, single-trunked palm to 25 ft. tall, 15 ft. wide. Leaves to 8 ft. long.

P. macarthuri. MACARTHUR PALM. Native to New Guinea. To 10–25 ft. tall, 12–15 ft. wide, with several clustered trunks. Leaves to 6½ ft. long. Good large understory plant. Often grown in tubs.

FOR GROWING SYMBOL EXPLANATIONS PLEASE SEE PAGE 161

PULMONARIA

LUNGWORT

Boraginaceae

PERENNIALS

ZONES 1–9, 14–17

PARTIAL OR FULL SHADE

REGULAR WATER

Pulmonaria saccharata 'Mrs. Moon'

Low-growing shade lovers with quiet charm. In many kinds, foliage is attractively dappled with gray or silver. The long-stalked leaves are mostly in basal clumps, though there are a few on the flower stalks. Plants bloom in later winter or early spring (just before leaves appear or as they emerge), bearing drooping clusters of funnel-shaped, typically blue or purplish flowers. After flowering finishes, more leaves arise from the base of the clump. If plants are well watered, foliage will remain ornamental through the growing season. All have creeping roots and can be used as small-scale ground covers or edgings for beds or woodland paths. Need moist, well-drained, organically enriched soil. Clumps may become crowded after a few years; divide them in early fall.

P. angustifolia. COWSLIP LUNGWORT. Native to Europe. To 8–12 in. high, 1½ ft. wide, with narrowish dark green leaves and bright blue flowers that open from pink buds. *P. a. azurea* has sky blue blossoms.

P. longifolia. Native to the British Isles, western Europe. To 8–12 in. high, 1½ ft. wide. Slender leaves to 20 in. long are deep green spotted with silver. Blooms a little later than other species; flowers are purplish blue. 'Bertram Anderson' has deep blue blossoms.

P. 'Roy Davidson'. Hybrid between *P. saccharata* and *P. longifolia.* Resembles *P. longifolia* 'Bertram Anderson' but has slightly wider leaves and flowers that open pink before deepening to blue.

P. saccharata. BETHLEHEM SAGE. To 1–1½ ft. high, 2 ft. wide, with elliptical, medium green, silver-spotted leaves and blue flowers opening from pink buds. Specialists usually offer named selections, including early-blooming 'Highdown', with deep blue blossoms; old favorite 'Mrs. Moon', with large leaves and pink flowers aging to blue; 'Janet Fisk', with leaves that are silvery almost all over and blossoms that age from pink to blue; and 'Sissinghurst White', with large white flowers.

PULSATILLA

PASQUE FLOWER

Ranunculaceae

PERENNIALS

ZONES VARY BY SPECIES

FULL SUN

REGULAR WATER

Pulsatilla vulgaris

Low-growing, clumping plants. Woody rootstock produces foot-wide rosette of finely cut leaves covered with silky hairs; smaller leaves clothe the short flowering stems. In early spring, each stem is topped by a single large, cup-shaped, erect or nodding blossom with silky hairs on the outside and a mass of yellow stamens within. The fluffy seed clusters are almost as showy as the flowers; each seed is topped by a long, twisting, feathery appendage. Plants reach 5–6 in. high in bloom, rise to about 1½ ft. tall by the time seeds appear. Best in cool conditions. Need well-drained soil. Good rock garden plants. May go dormant in summer.

P. patens. EASTERN PASQUE FLOWER. Zones A1–A3; 1–6, 15–17. From Russia, Siberia, North America. Erect, 2–3½-in. flowers in rich purple, occasionally yellow or white.

P. vulgaris (Anemone pulsatilla). PASQUE FLOWER. Zones 2b–6, 15–17. From central Europe. Blooms are 1½–3½ in. wide; erect, then nodding. Colors range from white through pink shades to purple or red.

PUMMELO. See **CITRUS**

P

PUMPKIN

Cucurbitaceae

ANNUAL

ALL ZONES

FULL SUN

REGULAR WATER

Pumpkin

Member of genus *Cucurbita* thought to have originated in South America; related to squash, gourd, melon. Fruit varies greatly in size, depending on variety. One of the best for a jumbo Halloween pumpkin is 'Atlantic Giant'. 'Small Sugar', a smaller pumpkin with finer-grained, sweeter flesh, is great for pies. 'Jack Be Little' and 'Wee-B-Little' are miniature (3–4-in.) types used for decoration. Novelties with white skin and orange flesh include miniature 'Baby Boo' and 8–10-in. 'Lumina'. Seeds of all are edible, but the easiest to eat are those of hull-less varieties like 'Trick or Treat'.

Giant pumpkins aren't special varieties; they are ordinary full-size pumpkins grown in a special way (though gardeners aiming for colossal fruits do have favorites, such as 'Atlantic Giant'). As plant develops, cut off all but two main stems. After blossom set, remove all but one fruit on each stem. Along the length of each stem, mound a 4-in.-wide hill of soil every 2 ft.; roots will form there.

Pumpkins are available in vining and bush types. Both need lots of room: a single vine can cover 500 sq. ft., and even bush sorts can spread over 20 sq. ft. Where the growing season is short, start plants indoors and use floating row covers early in the season. In most areas, sow seeds outdoors in late spring after soil has warmed; plant in rich soil. For vining pumpkins, sow five or six seeds 1 in. deep in hills 6–8 ft. apart; thin seedlings to two per hill. Plant bush pumpkins in rows spaced 3 ft. apart; plant seeds 1 in. deep in clusters of three or four, spacing clusters 2 ft. apart along the row. Thin seedlings to one or two plants per cluster.

Give periodic fertilizer. Water regularly during rainless periods, but keep foliage dry to prevent leaf diseases. Plants do not perform well in high heat and humidity. In late summer, slide wooden shingles or other protection under fruit to protect it from wet soil and rot (not necessary if soil is sandy). Depending on variety, pumpkins are ready to harvest 90 to 120 days after sowing, when the shell has hardened. Pick after first frost kills the plant. Use a sharp knife or hand pruners to harvest fruit, leaving 1–2 in. of stem. Subject to same pests and diseases as squash.

PUNICA granatum

POMEGRANATE

Punicaceae

DECIDUOUS SHRUB OR TREE

ZONES 5–24; H1, H2

FULL SUN

MODERATE TO REGULAR WATER

Punica granatum

Native from Iran to the Himalayas. For fruiting types, see Pomegranate. The varieties described here either fail to fruit at all or bear fruit that is more decorative than tasty. They make good landscape plants. Taller types can be used as foundation plants, in shrub borders, as tall hedges or small trees; lower-growing varieties are excellent for edgings, in containers. All bear showy single or double summer flowers with ruffled petals surrounding a central cluster of stamens. Narrow leaves are bronzy when new, maturing to glossy bright green or golden green; they turn brilliant yellow in fall except where winters are very mild. Take many soil types, including alkaline soil. In late dormant season, prune as needed to shape. On shrubby types, remove oldest stems occasionally to encourage strong new growth.

'Chico'. DWARF CARNATION-FLOWERED POMEGRANATE. Compact shrub to 3 ft. high and wide. Easily kept to 1½ ft. high with occasional pruning. Double orange-red flowers.

'Legrellei' ('Madame Legrelle', 'California Sunset'). To 8–10 ft. high and wide. Creamy white double flowers heavily striped coral red.

'Nana'. DWARF POMEGRANATE. Dense grower to 3 ft. high, 6 ft. wide. Blooms when a foot tall or less. Orange-red single flowers followed by small, dry red fruit. Nearly evergreen in mild winters.

'Nochi Shibori'. To 8–10 ft. high and wide. Double dark red flowers.

'Tanyosho'. To 8–10 ft. high and wide. Double light apricot flowers.

PURPLE CONEFLOWER. See ECHINACEA purpurea

PURPLE HEART. See TRADESCANTIA pallida 'Purpurea'

PURPLE-LEAF PLUM. See PRUNUS cerasifera 'Atropurpurea'

PURPLE OSIER. See SALIX purpurea

PURPLE PRAIRIE CLOVER. See PETALOSTEMON purpureum

PURSHIA mexicana stansburyana (Cowania mexicana stansburiana)

CLIFF ROSE

Rosaceae

EVERGREEN SHRUB

ZONES 2, 3, 7, 9–11, 14–16, 18–23

FULL SUN

MODERATE WATER

Purshia mexicana stansburyana

Native to much of the Southwest and Mexico. Straggling, much-branched shrub to 6 ft. tall and wide. Tiny (½-in.), deeply toothed leaves. In late spring, bears fragrant creamy yellow or sulfur yellow (rarely white) flowers resembling ½-in.-wide single roses. Moment of glory comes after bloom, when multitudes of very tiny fruits with long, feathery tails cover the plant in a soft haze.

PURSLANE. See PORTULACA oleracea

PUSCHKINIA scilloides

Liliaceae

PERENNIAL FROM BULB

ZONES 1–11, 14

FULL SUN OR LIGHT SHADE

REGULAR WATER DURING GROWTH AND BLOOM

Puschkinia scilloides

Native to Asia Minor. Late winter or early spring bloomer closely related to squill *(Scilla)* and glory-of-the-snow *(Chionodoxa)*. Performs best where ground freezes in winter. Each bulb produces two broad, upright, strap-shaped bright green leaves that are a bit shorter than the 6-in. flower stem. Each stem bears up to 15 star-shaped, inch-wide blossoms in pale blue with a greenish blue stripe down center of each petal. Most widely sold variety is *P. s. libanotica*, which is virtually identical to the species. A white-flowered variant may be offered as *P. s.* 'Alba' or *P. s. libanotica alba.*

Most effective in masses; good choice for naturalizing. Plant from late summer into fall, setting bulbs 3 in. deep, 3 in. apart in well-drained soil. Keep soil slightly moist until foliage appears, then water regularly until leaves start to yellow in early summer. Needs very little water during summer dormant period. Seldom needs dividing.

PUSSY EARS. See CALOCHORTUS

PUSSY TOES. See ANTENNARIA dioica

PUYA berteroniana

Bromeliaceae

PERENNIAL

ZONES 9, 13–17, 19–24

FULL SUN

LITTLE TO MODERATE WATER

Puya berteroniana

Native to Chile. Big, spectacular bromeliad, usually sold as *P. alpestris.* Produces an evergreen foliage clump up to 10 ft. across, crowded with narrow, swordlike gray-green leaves to 2 ft. long; leaves have sharp tips and sharply spined edges. Flower stalks rise from the clump, resembling giant asparagus spears as they develop; they reach 4–6 ft. tall during spring bloom, when they bear massive clusters of 2-in.-wide, bell-shaped blossoms in metallic blue green and steely turquoise, accented with vivid orange anthers. Stiff, spiky branchlet ends protrude from flower clusters. Use in large rock gardens, on banks, in big containers. Good with cacti, succulents. Tolerates poor soil.

PYRACANTHA

FIRETHORN

Rosaceae

EVERGREEN SHRUBS

ZONES VARY BY SPECIES

FULL SUN

MODERATE WATER

Pyracantha coccinea

Grown for bright fruit, evergreen foliage (may be semievergreen in cold climates), versatility in the landscape, ease of culture. All grow fast and vigorously, varying in habit from upright to sprawling. All have glossy green, 1–4-in.-long, ½–1-in.-wide leaves that are generally oval or rounded at ends; all bear flowers and fruit on spurs along wood of last year's growth. Small, spring flowers are dull creamy white, carried in flattish clusters; they're effective thanks to their profusion. Some people find the scent unpleasant. Nearly all species have needlelike thorns.

The real glory of firethorns is in their thick clusters of pea-size, orange-red berries, which light up the garden for months. Depending on variety, berries color up from late summer to midautumn; some types hang on until late winter, when they're cleared out by birds, storms, or decay. Dislodge old, withered or rotted berries with a water jet or an old broom. Selections with red, orange, or yellow berries are available; if color is important to you, buy plants when they are in fruit.

As shrubs and ground covers, firethorns look better and produce more heavily if allowed to grow naturally. Prune to check wayward branches. Plants can be espaliered, or be sheared as hedges (though at the expense of much fruit). To grow low-growing, wide-spreading types as ground covers, set plants 4–5 ft. apart. Firethorns tolerate most soils but should not be overwatered. Subject to fireblight, scale insects, woolly aphids, red spider mites. In coastal areas of the Pacific Northwest, apple scab is sometimes a problem in early spring; it can nearly defoliate plants.

P. angustifolia 'Yukon Belle'. Zones 3–24. Variety of a Chinese native. To 8–10 ft. tall, 6–8 ft. wide. Bright orange berries.

P. coccinea. Zones 3–24. From the eastern Mediterranean. Rounded growth to 8–10 ft. tall and wide (potentially larger trained against a wall). Red-orange fruit. Best known for its varieties.

'Gnome'. Densely branched plant to 6 ft. tall, 8 ft. wide. Orange berries.

'Kasan'. To 8–10 ft. tall, 6–8 ft. wide. Long-lasting orange-red fruit.

'Lalandei' and 'Lalandei Monrovia'. Similar varieties to 10–15 ft. tall and wide. Orange-red berries. Among the hardiest.

'Lowboy'. To 2–3 ft. tall, 6–8 ft. wide. Bright orange berries.

'Wyattii'. To 9–12 ft. high and wide. Orange-red berries.

P. crenatoserrata (P. fortuneana, P. yunnanensis). Zones 4–24. From China. Vase-shaped plant to 15 ft. tall, 10 ft. wide. Limber branches make it a good espalier subject. Pale orange to coral berries persist through winter.

'Cherri Berri'. To 10 ft. tall, 8 ft. wide. Deep red berries.

'Graberi'. More erect than the species; to 10–12 ft. tall, 8–10 ft. wide. Huge clusters of dark red berries.

P. hybrids. These are plants of mixed or uncertain heritage. The group includes many of the most desirable firethorns.

'Harlequin'. Zones 4–24. To 6 ft. tall and wide. New leaves emerge pinkish white, turn green-and-white by summer, take on pink tones again in winter. Orange-red berries.

'Mohave'. Zones 4–24. To 12 ft. tall and wide. Heavy producer of big orange-red berries that color late and hang on for a long time.

'Orange Glow'. Zones 4–24. To 10 ft. tall and wide; erect at first, then spreading. Orange to orange-red berries.

'Red Elf'. Zones 4–9, 12–24. Low-growing, compact plant to 2 ft. high and wide; good in containers. Bright red berries.

'Ruby Mound'. Zones 4–9, 12–24. Among the most graceful of ground cover firethorns. Long, arching, drooping branches make a 2½-ft.-high mound that spreads to about 10 ft. Bright red berries.

'Teton'. Zones 2b–24. Fairly upright growth to 12 ft. tall, 4–6 ft. wide. Yellow-orange berries.

'Tiny Tim'. Zones 4–24. Compact growth to 3 ft. tall and wide. Small leaves, few or no thorns, red berries. Shorten any runaway vertical shoots.

'Watereri'. Zones 4–24. To 8 ft. tall and wide, with long-lasting bright red berries.

P. koidzumii. Zones 4–24. From Taiwan. Loose, unruly grower to 8–12 ft. tall and wide. Best known for its varieties. Among these are 'Santa Cruz' and 'Walderi', both good bank and ground covers.

'Santa Cruz' ('Santa Cruz Prostrata'). Reaches 6 ft. tall but is easily maintained at 3 ft. or lower by pruning out erect-growing branches. Can spread as wide as 10 ft. Red berries.

'Victory'. To 8–10 ft. tall, 6–8 ft. wide. Dark red berries color late but hang on late as well.

'Walderi' ('Walderi Prostrata'). To 3 ft. tall but easily kept to 1½ ft. by pruning out upright branches. Spreads to about 6 ft. wide. Red berries.

PYRETHROPSIS. See CHRYSANTHEMUM gayanum, C. hosmariense

PYRETHRUM. See CHRYSANTHEMUM coccineum, C. pacificum

PYROSTEGIA venusta (P. ignea, Bignonia venusta)

FLAME VINE

Bignoniaceae

EVERGREEN VINE

ZONES 13, 16, 21–24; H1, H2

FULL SUN

MODERATE WATER

Pyrostegia venusta

Native to South America. Climbs rapidly by tendrils and twining to reach 20–40 ft.; where well adapted, grows rampantly. Leaves consist of two or three oval, 2-in. leaflets; two-leafleted leaves have a tendril between the leaflets rather than a third leaflet. Impressive in bloom, when tubular, 3-in., orange flowers appear in clusters of 15–20 at branch ends. Main flower display comes in winter; in warmest gardens, bloom starts in fall and continues into spring. In the mildest climates, a scattering of foot-long seed capsules may form after flowers fade. Striking along fences and eaves, on pergolas and arbors, spilling over the tops of retaining walls, as a bank cover. Tolerates many soils. Revels in heat; in cooler climates, plant in a hot spot such as along a west-facing wall. Do any major pruning in spring or summer, after bloom has finished.

PYRROSIA lingua

JAPANESE FELT FERN
Polypodiaceae
FERN
ZONES 14–17, 19–24
PARTIAL SHADE IN HOTTEST CLIMATES
MODERATE WATER

Pyrrosia lingua

Native to China, Japan. To 1½ ft. high, spreading slowly to 1 ft. wide by creeping rootstocks. Dense clusters of broad, lance-shaped dark green fronds with felty texture. Most often used in hanging baskets but makes choice ground cover for small areas. Crested and sawtooth-edged forms are collectors' items.

PYRUS

ORNAMENTAL PEAR
Rosaceae
EVERGREEN AND DECIDUOUS SHRUBS OR TREES
ZONES VARY BY SPECIES
FULL SUN
MODERATE WATER

Pyrus kawakamii

Fruiting pears are described under Pear, Asian and Pear, European. The following are ornamental species, grown for their profuse late-winter or early-spring show of white flowers and their glossy, attractive leaves. Not at their best in shallow soils but otherwise unfussy about soil, even growing well in heavy clay. Most are subject to fireblight.

P. calleryana. Deciduous tree. Zones 2b–9, 14–21. Chinese native. Needs some winter chill. To 50 ft. tall and wide, with strong horizontal branching pattern; young growth is thorny. Broadly oval, scallop-edged, leathery, 1½–3-in.-long leaves are glossy dark green, turning rich purplish red in fall. Blooms very early; late freezes may destroy flower crop. Very small, round, inedible fruit. Less susceptible to fireblight than most pears.

'Aristocrat'. Essentially pyramidal in form, though somewhat open and rounded; to 35–40 ft. tall, 20 ft. wide. Branches curve upward to form a strong structure. Fall color ranges from yellow to red.

'Bradford'. First variety of *P. calleryana* to be introduced. Pyramidal tree to 50 ft. tall, 30 ft. wide. Strongly vertical limbs (with no central leader); branching pattern spreads with age. Branch crotches in mature trees have a tendency to split.

'Capital'. Columnar. To 40 ft. tall, 15 ft. wide. Coppery fall color.

'Chanticleer' ('Cleveland Select', 'Stone Hill'). Most plants sold under this name are narrowly pyramidal in form; some are more columnar. To 40 ft. tall, 15 ft. wide. Fall color varies from orange to reddish purple.

'Redspire'. Pyramidal; to 30–35 ft. tall, 20 ft. wide. Especially large blossom clusters; yellow to red fall color.

'Trinity'. Round-headed form to 30 ft. tall and wide. Orange-red fall color.

'Whitehouse'. Columnar; to 40 ft. tall, 15 ft. wide. Red to reddish purple fall color.

P. communis. See Pear, European

P. kawakamii. EVERGREEN PEAR. Evergreen shrub or tree; partially deciduous in coldest winters in coldest zones. Zones 8, 9, 12–24. From Taiwan. To 15–30 ft. high and wide, with drooping branchlets and glossy green, oval, 2–4-in. leaves with pointed tips. Masses of flowers in winter and early spring. Small, inedible fruit. Left to its own devices, becomes a broad, sprawling shrub. Can be espaliered but is most often grown as a single- or multitrunked tree. To train as a tree, stake one or several stems and shorten side growth; keep tree staked until it is self-supporting. To build up framework limbs, shorten any overlong, pendent branches to upward-facing growth buds or branchlets. An established, well-shaped tree needs little pruning—and heavily pruned plants seldom bloom. Tolerates many soils. Very prone to fireblight.

P. pyrifolia (P. serotina). SAND PEAR, JAPANESE SAND PEAR. Deciduous tree. Zones 2–9, 14–21. Native to China. To 40 ft. tall, 25 ft. wide. Like European fruiting pear in appearance, but leaves are glossier and more leathery. Fall color ranges from brilliant orange red to reddish purple. Profuse early spring blossoms; small, woody, gritty-textured fruit. This species is involved in the parentage of Asian pear varieties.

P. salicifolia 'Pendula'. WEEPING WILLOW-LEAFED PEAR. Deciduous tree. Zones 2–9, 14–21; performs better in cold climates. Native to southeastern Europe, western Asia. Elegant specimen plant to 12–15 ft. tall, 10–12 ft. wide. Grown for silvery, willowlike foliage and beautiful weeping habit; form is showcased in winter, when branches are bare. Flowers appear as leaves emerge in early spring. Leaves to 3½ in. long; silvery white when new, slowly turning silvery green in summer. Fruit is insignificant. Very susceptible to fireblight. Sometimes sold as 'Silver Frost'.

P. ussuriensis. USSURIAN PEAR. Deciduous tree. Zones A1–A3; 1–3, 10. Native to Manchuria, Siberia. Another parent of Asian pear varieties. Dense, rounded tree to 15–40 ft. tall, 15–25 ft. wide. Roundish, 2–4-in., glossy bright green leaves turn red or purple in fall. Large spring flowers are followed by tiny, hard, inedible fruit. Similar to *P. calleryana* and a good substitute for it in colder climates. 'Korean Sun' is fruitless—which makes it better looking in winter, since the species' fruit tends to blacken and hang on.

QUAIL BUSH. See ATRIPLEX lentiformis

QUAKING ASPEN. See POPULUS tremuloides

QUAKING GRASS. See BRIZA maxima

QUAMOCLIT pennata. See IPOMOEA quamoclit

QUEEN EMMA LILY. See CRINUM augustum

QUEEN OF THE PRAIRIE. See FILIPENDULA rubra

QUEEN PALM. See SYAGRUS romanzoffianum

QUEEN SAGO. See CYCAS circinalis

QUEEN'S TEARS. See BILLBERGIA nutans

QUEEN'S WREATH. See ANTIGONON leptopus, PETREA volubilis

QUERCUS

OAK
Fagaceae
DECIDUOUS AND EVERGREEN TREES AND SHRUBS
ZONES VARY BY SPECIES
FULL SUN
WATER NEEDS VARY; SEE BELOW

Quercus agrifolia

The oaks comprise 600 or so species, all native to the Northern Hemisphere. Their appearance and hardiness vary widely, but all produce acorns preceded by inconspicuous flowers. Single nuts are more or less enclosed in a cuplike cap covered with many closely set scales. In some species, the acorns are edible, with a sweet flavor. Some oaks are widely planted over large areas, while others have a limited range. Many wild-growing species may occur naturally in rural or suburban areas but seldom, if ever, find their way into the nursery trade; these are not described here.

Homeowners acquire oaks either by planting them or by inheriting trees that were present before their land was developed. Oaks that have been planted often thrive with no special care. Those from summer-rainfall areas appreciate moderate to regular summer irrigation during dry spells. Mediterranean natives can take irrigation or leave it, and U.S. natives of the Far West—after they have been watered through the first two dry seasons after planting—are better off without watering. Old, wild oaks from areas without much summer rain must be kept dry during the warm season, since they often succumb to fungal root diseases if given routine summer watering. But don't hesitate to give planted or inherited native oaks monthly soakings in winter if rains fail (and do so every winter in low-rainfall areas like San Diego), applying water at the drip line.

Special treatment for existing native oaks. If possible, do not raise or lower grade level between trunk and drip line. If you must alter grade, put a well around base of trunk so that grade level there is not changed. Never water within 10–15 ft. of trunk, and never let water stand within that area. Protect trunk from earth-moving machinery with cribs of 2-by-4s or heavier timbers. Avoid piling excavated soil around trunk or above root system (which extends somewhat beyond branch spread); or provide drains for aeration and removal of excess water. Do not excavate or pave above the root zone without consulting an arborist. Avoid regular traffic or other ground-compacting activity in root area; when grading and other landscaping have been completed, be sure the tree has access to adequate water and air in the soil.

Quercus lobata

In much of the West, native oaks have adapted their root systems to long, dry summers; heavy summer watering can damage roots by activating oak root fungus (see "Pests and diseases," below). To safeguard such native trees, do not locate plantings (especially those needing regular moisture) too close to the trunk, and use only underplantings that require little or no summer water.

Old native oaks benefit from periodic grooming to remove dead wood, but thick branches should not be cut unless there is a good reason to do so. To avoid stimulating out-of-season new growth that will be susceptible to mildew and other problems, prune trees only when they are dormant. With evergreen oaks in the Far West, this means pruning during the dry season—in mid- to late summer.

Pests and diseases. Oaks and their acorns provide sustenance for a complex network of insects, birds, and other wildlife. Any of a number of sucking and chewing insects and mites feed on these trees, but most of the time such creatures are kept in check by other insects and mites, by birds, or by factors we have not even identified. Many kinds of oaks host several kinds of caterpillars that seldom do enough damage to be considered pests. Occasionally, though, an outbreak of some organism gets bad enough to require artificial control. Oak moth caterpillars can be a serious potential pest: heavy infestations can cause defoliation, and severe attacks for 2 or more years in a row can weaken or even kill a tree. However, oak moths tend to be cyclical, striking perhaps every 7 to 10 years; they may run their course and diminish on their own. If control becomes necessary, consult a professional arborist or tree service. Oak trees are too large for the limited spray equipment available to the home gardener.

Most oaks produce galls of various colors, shapes, and sizes on twigs or leaf surfaces. The galls are swellings that form after insects (mostly wasps) lay eggs in the plant tissue; the larvae develop inside. Depending on the oak species and the type of insect involved, the galls may resemble apples, potatoes, mushrooms, dunce caps, or other objects. They do little harm and normally do not warrant treatment.

Many fungi are associated with the life cycle of oaks. Some are beneficial, but others are harmful. Oak root fungus *(Armillaria)* often is present in neighborhoods that once contained oak forests or walnut groves. This fungus is normally held in check in summer by drought and in winter by cool temperatures. Summer watering, especially close to the trunk, activates it; it grows rapidly in warm, moist conditions. Consult an arborist about infected trees.

Recently, a previously unknown species of *Phytophthora* fungus has killed tens of thousands of coast live oaks *(Quercus agrifolia)*, California black oaks *(Q. kelloggii)*, and closely related tanbark oaks *(Lithocarpus densiflorus)* in coastal California. The condition has been dubbed "sudden oak death syndrome." The responsible fungus can be distributed by beetles, contact with infected roots, or transfer of wood or infected soil on tools, automobile or bicycle tires, or shoes. It flourishes in cool, moist conditions; once it is established, the spores travel in splashing raindrops.

Symptoms of sudden oak death syndrome often begin with oozing of reddish or brownish sap from the afflicted tree's trunk and main limbs. Leaves wilt suddenly, turn dull or yellowish, curl up, and dry. Roots exude a pungent odor of alcohol. The fungus has been accompanied by an epidemic of oak bark beetles and heartwood-boring ambrosia beetles attracted by the fermenting sap of dying trees. These small, black native insects, about the size of a grain of rice, previously were not considered serious pests, since they attack only wounded or stressed trees. But with the sudden oak death epidemic, the beetles are multiplying by the millions, hastening the demise of sick trees. New generations of beetles emerge in spring and early fall.

Avoid pruning in spring, when beetles are most active. Ailing oaks should be cut down as soon as possible after they wilt; they will not revive. Immediately enclose firewood from infected trees in heavy (6-mil) clear plastic sheeting, and leave it wrapped for 6 months to trap and kill beetles. Also cover stumps left in the ground to prevent their becoming nurseries for beetles. Don't transport infected wood. Chip smaller branches into small pieces and heat-treat by enclosing in plastic and leaving in full sun throughout summer; then compost or use as mulch on-site.

How to grow an oak from an acorn. Select shiny, plump fallen acorns, free of worm holes; remove caps. To protect the buried acorn from birds, squirrels, and other creatures, dig the planting hole 6 in. deep, 6 in. wide; then roll an 18-in.-wide length of aluminum screening into a 6-in.-diameter cylinder and insert one end of it into the hole. Refill the screen-lined hole with unamended soil. Plant the acorn sideways and cover it with 1 in. of soil (if a white root has already sprouted, point it downward). Tie screen closed at top. Or plant several acorns in one area and thin to the best seedling. The first summer, give moderate water—just enough to keep soil moist for good root growth. After first summer, remove screen.

Quercus kelloggii

How to transplant an oak. If its root ball is otherwise big and firm enough, an oak seedling up to 5–8 ft. tall seems not to suffer from having its vertical root cut. The tree may wilt or lose leaves after root is cut, but if kept watered it should show new growth within 4 to 6 weeks. Best time to transplant is fall or winter (or early spring, in some cold-winter areas). Oak seedlings in nursery containers should not have a spiraling taproot at the container bottom; better growers cut a seedling's taproot when moving it to a nursery container, so that the young tree will develop a branching root system.

When you dig the tree's planting hole in its new location, mix some oak leaf mold or soil obtained from under an established oak into the hole to inoculate it with beneficial fungi.

How to train a young oak. Many young oaks are twiggy by nature, with growth divided among so many twigs that none elongates quickly. To promote faster vertical growth, pinch off tips of small side branches, but retain as much leaf surface as possible to sustain maximum growth. Western native shrub oaks are adapted to browsing by deer and lend themselves readily to close planting and eventual shearing into handsome formal hedges. They should be used more widely for this purpose in preference to plants with higher water requirements.

BEST OAKS FOR THE WEST

From among the many hundreds of oak species, here are the choices best suited to Western gardens.

Q. acutissima (Q. serrata). SAWTOOTH OAK. Deciduous tree. Zones 2–7, 14–17. From the Himalayas, China, Korea, Japan. Moderate to fast growth to 35–45 ft. (ultimately 50–70 ft.) tall and wide, usually with open, spreading habit. Dark gray bark with red-brown furrows. Shiny dark green, pointed, oblong leaves are 3½–7 in. long, with bristle-toothed, slightly wavy edges; they look like chestnut *(Castanea)* leaves. Foliage is yellowish when new, turns yellow to yellowish brown in fall; may hang on late into winter. Acorns are blunt cylinders to 1 in. long, enclosed for two-thirds of their length in a burlike cap. Prefers well-drained, slightly acid soil but is fairly tolerant of other soils. Good shade or lawn tree. ▶

Q. agrifolia. COAST LIVE OAK. Evergreen tree. Zones 7–9, 14–24. Native to coastal central and Southern California. Round headed and densely foliaged; to 20–70 ft. tall, often with even greater spread. Smooth dark gray bark, deeply fissured in very old trees. Oval, convex, stiff, leathery dark green leaves, tooth edged and hollylike, 1–3 in. long. Foliage is attractive all year (unless devoured by oak moth caterpillars). Conical, ¾–1½-in. acorns are enclosed for one-fourth of their length by a cap with thin, overlapping scales. Has greedy roots; drops almost all its old leaves in early spring. Despite flaws, a handsome and worthwhile shade or street tree. Can be sheared to make a 10–12-ft. hedge.

Q. berberidifolia. SCRUB OAK. Evergreen shrub. Zones 5, 7–10, 14–24. Native to inland slopes and forests of west-central and Southern California. Dense growth to 6–15 ft. tall and wide. Leaves variable in shape but usually ¾–1½ in. long and about two-thirds as wide, with wavy edges; may have smooth, toothed, or quite spiny margins. Medium green on upper surface, grayish green with scattered hairs below. Oval, ½–1-in. acorns, enclosed by one-third to one-half in knobby cap with regular spiral pattern. Good unthirsty clipped hedge, background shrub, informal screen. Long confused with *Q. dumosa,* which is native only near the Southern California coast.

Q. bicolor. SWAMP WHITE OAK. Deciduous tree. Zones A3; 1–3, 10. Native to eastern North America. Slow to moderate growth to 50–60 ft., rarely taller, with equal or greater spread. Bark of trunk and branches flakes off in scales. Shallowly lobed or scalloped leaves are 3–7 in. long, a little more than half as wide, shiny dark green above, silvery white beneath. Fall color is usually yellow but sometimes orange, fiery red, or purple. Oblong to egg-shaped, 1-in. acorns, enclosed by one-third in rounded cap with hairy scales. Tolerates wet soil; also thrives where soil is well drained.

Q. buckleyi (Q. texana). TEXAS OAK, SPANISH OAK. Deciduous tree or shrub. Zones 11–13. Native to central and western Texas, southern Oklahoma. To 35 ft. tall and as wide or wider, with trunk branching almost from the base. Bark is light brown and scaly when young, becoming dark gray with platelike scales and deep fissures at maturity. Leaves are 2½–5½ in. long, with three to seven sharply pointed, bristle-tipped lobes. Foliage is densely hairy and reddish when new, matures to yellowish green, turns bright scarlet in fall. Egg-shaped, ¾-in. acorns with a sharp tip, one-third enclosed in reddish, densely felted cap. Similar to *Q. shumardii.* Takes alkaline soil.

Q. chrysolepis. CANYON LIVE OAK, MAUL OAK, GOLDENCUP OAK. Evergreen tree. Zones 3–11, 14–24. Native to foothills and desert mountains from southwestern Oregon to Baja California, east into Arizona. Handsome, round-headed or somewhat spreading tree to 20–60 ft. tall and wide. Bark is smooth and whitish when young, checked and gray when old. Oval, 1–2-in.-long leaves may be smooth edged or spiny; shiny medium green above, pale blue or grayish beneath, with thin felting of silvery or golden hairs on undersides when new. Oblong, sharp-tipped acorns among largest (to 2 in. long) found on American oaks; they are enclosed by one- to two-thirds in a turbanlike cap covered with golden fuzz. Most widely distributed and variable of all California oaks, and most adaptable to varying conditions.

Quercus coccinea

Q. coccinea. SCARLET OAK. Deciduous tree. Zones 2–10, 14–24. Native to eastern U.S. Grows at moderate rate in deep, rich soil. Can reach 60–80 ft. tall, 40–60 ft. wide. Pyramidal when young, round topped in maturity. Gray-brown bark cracked into irregular plates. Bright green leaves are 3–6 in. long, with pointed, deeply cut lobes; turn scarlet where fall nights are cold. Rounded, ¾–1-in. acorns half-covered in a bowl-like cap. Good street or lawn tree. Deep rooted.

Q. douglasii. BLUE OAK. Deciduous tree. Zones 3–11, 14–24. Native to dry foothills around California's Central Valley and interior valleys of Southern California. Low branching, wide spreading; to 30–50 ft. high, 40–70 ft. wide. Light gray bark is shallowly checked in small squares. Shallowly lobed, oval, decidedly bluish green leaves are 1½–4 in. long, ¾–2 in. wide. Attractive fall colors: pastel pink, orange, yellow. Egg-shaped, ¾–1¼-in. acorns with sharply pointed tip and thin, flat cap. Good in dry, hot situations.

Q. dumosa. COASTAL SCRUB OAK. Evergreen shrub. Zones 15–17, 21–24. Native from coastal bluffs and hillsides near ocean in Southern California and northern Baja California. To 6–10 ft. high and wide. Thin, reddish twigs; small, cupped, usually wavy-edged leaves to ½–1 in. long, ¾ in. wide, with spiny margins often rolled under. Leaves are shiny dark green above, lighter green below; undersides have a hairy coating that is soft, dense, felty. Sharply tapered, ⅓–⅔-in. acorns, enclosed by one-third to one-half in a rust-colored cap. Prefers sandy soil. Takes salt winds.

Q. durata. LEATHER OAK, NUTTALL'S SCRUB OAK. Evergreen shrub. Zones 5, 7–10, 14–24. Native to northern Coast Ranges to San Luis Obispo area and to Sierra Nevada foothills, south to San Gabriel Mountains. In the wild, mostly confined to serpentine soil (a kind of nutrient-poor soil). Dense, rounded growth to 10 ft. tall and 8–12 ft. wide. Bare and somewhat leggy to 3–5 ft. above ground; then forms open-branched tiers of foliage. Tough, oval, convex, ¾–1-in.-long leaves have smooth or prickly edges; dark green above, pale gray beneath, with a dense coating of fine, soft hairs. Acorns variable: ½–1 in. long, often almost cylindrical, half-enclosed in a warty, bowl-shaped cap.

Q. emoryi. EMORY OAK. Evergreen tree. Zones 10–13. Native from Arizona to Texas and adjacent Mexico. Handsome and rounded, to 50 ft. tall, 40 ft. wide. Leathery dark green, oval, sharply toothed leaves to 2–3 in. long are hollylike but flat; turn golden and drop just before new growth begins in late spring. Round-tipped, oblong, edible acorns enclosed by up to one-half in bowl-like cap. Grows well in low desert; tolerates a variety of soils. Needs periodic soakings in summer.

Q. engelmannii. ENGELMANN OAK, MESA OAK, PASADENA OAK. Evergreen tree. Zones 7–9, 14–24. Native to Southern California. Spreading habit to 40–50 ft. high, often twice as wide. Thick, leathery, dull bluish green, oval or oblong leaves to 2 in. long; wavy surfaced or flat, usually smooth edged. Oval to cylindrical, round-tipped acorns to 1¼ in. long half-enclosed in a warty cap. Best with monthly deep soakings in warm season, but don't keep it constantly moist. In its native area, it has the same cherished native status as the more widespread *Q. agrifolia.*

Quercus coccinea

Quercus douglasii

Quercus garryana

Quercus kelloggii

Q. frainetto. HUNGARIAN OAK, ITALIAN OAK. Deciduous tree. Zones 2–12, 14–21. Native to the eastern Mediterranean and south-central Europe. Majestic, fast-growing tree, ultimately to 100 ft. tall by 70 ft. wide. Dark gray, shallowly furrowed bark. Large leaves (to 8 in. long and 4 in. wide) are deeply lobed, glossy deep green; they are covered with silky yellow or white hairs when new, turn yellow brown in fall. Egg-shaped to oblong, ½–1¼-in. acorns, half-enclosed in fuzzy, bowl-shaped cap.

Q. fusiformis (Q. virginiana fusiformis). ESCARPMENT LIVE OAK, PLATEAU OAK. Briefly deciduous tree or shrub. Zones 3, 10–13. Native to plains of central Texas, southern Oklahoma, far eastern New Mexico. To 30–40 ft. tall and about as wide, with dense crown. Rough dark brown bark with scaly ridges. Shiny, leathery, 1½–4-in.-long leaves are oblong to elliptical; margins smooth or with a few sharp teeth, often rolled under. Foliage remains green through winter but turns yellow and drops for 2 to 4 weeks in spring. Acorns are ½–1 in. long, may have an egg shape or look like an elongated spindle; enclosed by one-third to one-half in goblet-shaped cap. Prefers well-drained alkaline soil. Easily endures heat, winter cold from Phoenix to Albuquerque; needs monthly soakings.

Q. gambellii (Q. utahensis). GAMBELL OAK, ROCKY MOUNTAIN WHITE OAK. Deciduous tree or shrub. Zones 1–3, 10. Native to Nevada, Arizona, east to Colorado, New Mexico. Slow to 15–30 ft. (rarely 50 ft.) tall, half as wide. Often forms colonies from root system. Thick, ridged trunk bark is light gray to whitish. Leaves 3–7 in. long, half as wide, with seven to nine deep lobes; dark green above, pale and densely hairy below. Foliage turns yellow, orange, or red in fall. Woolly, egg-shaped or globular, sharp-tipped acorns nearly 1 in. long, half-covered by a knobby cap. Characteristic oak of Arizona's Oak Creek Canyon and Colorado foothills south of Denver. Adaptable to wide range of soils and moisture levels; grows rapidly into a substantial tree in deep, rich soil.

Q. garryana. OREGON WHITE OAK, GARRY OAK. Deciduous tree. Zones 4–11, 14–23. Native from British Columbia to California's Transverse Ranges. Slow to moderate growth to 40–90 ft. tall, 30–60 ft. wide, with rounded crown. Branches are often twisted; bark is gray, scaly, checked. Leathery, 3–6-in.-long, broadly oval leaves with rounded lobes. Foliage is glossy dark green above, rusty or downy beneath; turns reddish brown in fall. Globular, edible acorns to 1¼ in. long, bulging from a small, scale-covered cap. Tree casts moderate shade and has a deep, nonaggressive root system.

Q. ilex. HOLLY OAK, HOLM OAK. Evergreen tree. Zones 4–24. Native to Mediterranean region. To 30–60 ft. tall and wide, with dense, rounded head and smooth dark gray bark. Leaves vary in shape and size but are usually oval to lance shaped, 1–3 in. long, with smooth or prickly edges; rich dark green on top, covered with gray or yellow hairs beneath. Egg-shaped to nearly round, 1–1½-in. acorns are gray brown with darker lines, half-enclosed in deep cap that tapers to stem. Tolerates salt air; will grow in constant sea wind but tends to be shrubby there. Inland, growth rate can be fairly fast but varies with soil and water conditions. Good evergreen street or lawn tree where coast live oak *(Q. agrifolia)* is difficult to maintain, though it lacks that tree's open grace. Can take hard clipping into formal shapes or hedges.

Q. kelloggii. CALIFORNIA BLACK OAK. Deciduous tree. Zones 5 (inland areas), 6, 7, 9, 14–21. Grows in company with conifers in upland locations from southern Oregon to Southern California. To 30–80 ft. tall and wide, with short trunk, ascending branches, and rounded crown. Dark gray, furrowed, checked bark. Handsome foliage: leaves unfold soft pink or dusty rose, mature to dark glossy green, turn yellow or yellow orange in fall. Leaves 4–10 in. long, 2½–6 in. wide, with deep, sharply tapered lobes ending in bristly points. Oblong or almost conical, 1–1½-in. acorns enclosed by about half in bowl-shaped cap. Good moderate-size tree for spring and fall color; attractive winter trunk and branch pattern.

Q. lobata. VALLEY OAK, CALIFORNIA WHITE OAK. Deciduous tree. Zones 3b–9, 12–24. Native to interior valleys, Sierra foothills, and Coast Ranges away from direct coastal influence. California's mightiest oak, often reaching 70 ft. or taller, with equal or greater spread. Massive trunk and limbs with thick, distinctly checked gray bark. Straight and erect during its first several decades of growth; more spreading with age. Limbs often picturesquely twisted; long, drooping outer branches sometimes sweep ground. Deeply cut, round-lobed leaves are 3–4 in. long, 2–3 in. wide; dark green above, paler beneath. Shiny, 1½–2½-in. acorns are conical, enclosed by one-third in warty, bowl-shaped cap.

Possibly the largest North American oak, this species tolerates high heat and moderate alkalinity in its native range. Best in deep soils where it can tap groundwater; in such situations, it can grow fast (2½–3 ft. a year). Magnificent tree for shading a big outdoor living area, though constant rain of debris will create a nuisance on any nearby planting areas or paved surfaces. This is the tree that gives much of California's Central Valley the look of a giant park.

Q. macrocarpa. BURR OAK, MOSSYCUP OAK. Deciduous tree. Zones A2, A3; 1–11, 14–23. Native to eastern North America. Rugged-looking tree to 60–75 ft. tall and about half that wide in youth, equally wide in maturity. Flaky grayish brown bark with flattened, narrow ridges. Leaves are 8–10 in. long, broad at tip, tapered at base, with five to seven deeply cut, rounded lobes; glossy green above, whitish beneath, turning yellow and brown in autumn. Round or egg-shaped, 1–1½-in. acorns are almost completely covered by fringed, mossy-looking cap. Similar to *Q. bicolor* but faster growing and more tolerant of adverse conditions.

Quercus macrocarpa

Q. muehlenbergii. CHINQUAPIN OAK, YELLOW CHESTNUT OAK. Deciduous tree. Zones 2–12, 14–17. Native to central and eastern U.S. To 40–50 ft. tall, 50–60 ft. wide, with wide-spreading, rounded crown. Flaking whitish or gray bark. Deeply toothed, lance-shaped, 4–6-in.-long leaves are shiny green above, whitish and furry below. Foliage turns golden late in fall but hangs on late. Egg-shaped, edible, ½–1-in. acorns are enclosed by one-fourth to one-half in warty cap. Desirable street or shade tree for large area. Long lived but difficult to transplant and establish. Fairly tolerant of alkaline soils.

Q. myrsinifolia. JAPANESE LIVE OAK. Evergreen tree or shrub. Zones 4–7, 14–24. Native to southern China, Japan, Laos; almost extinct in the wild. Reaches 30–50-ft. tall in its native range, but in cultivation it usually

Quercus lobata

Quercus palustris

Quercus suber

Quercus virginiana

grows as a large, round-headed shrub to 20–30 ft. high and as wide (or nearly so). Lance-shaped, glossy dark green leaves 2½–4 in. long, toothed toward tip. Purplish red new foliage. Acorns ¾ in. long, cylindrical with abrupt point, half enclosed in unusual, shallow cap marked with seven to nine concentric rings. Not easily recognized as an oak unless seen with its acorns—unlike most of its relatives, it is wispy and graceful rather than sturdy.

Q. palustris. PIN OAK, SWAMP OAK. Deciduous tree. Zones 2–10, 14–24. Native to eastern U.S. Moderate to fairly rapid growth to 50–80 ft. tall, 30–40 ft. wide. Brownish gray bark with shallow ridges and furrows. Pyramidal in youth, with lower branches sweeping downward. If you remove those branches to gain walking space, the limbs above will simply bend into the same position—so wait to remove lower limbs until tree is mature and has formed an open, rounded top. Glossy dark green leaves are 3–6 in. long, deeply cut into bristle-pointed lobes; in brisk fall weather, leaves turn yellow, red, and finally russet brown. Much of the dead foliage hangs on in winter. Nearly round acorns to ¾ in. across, enclosed by about a third in saucer-shaped, fuzzy cap. Less tolerant of dry conditions than most oaks. Develops chlorosis in alkaline soils. Unlike most native Western oaks, it is a fine tree for lawns.

Quercus palustris

Q. phellos. WILLOW OAK. Deciduous tree. Zones 2–4, 6–16, 18–21. Native to southeastern U.S. To 50–90 ft. tall, 30–50 ft. wide. Pyramidal in youth, spreading wider with age. Smooth gray bark. Leaves look more like those of willow *(Salix)* than those of typical oak—2½–5 in. long, ⅓–1 in. wide, smooth edged. Foliage turns yellowish before falling; in warmer regions, dead leaves may hang on through winter. Has the most delicate foliage pattern of all the oaks. Spherical, ½-in.-wide acorns with a shallow cap enclosing only the end of the nut.

Quercus phellos

Q. phillyreoides. UBAME OAK. Evergreen tree. Zones 4–9, 14–17. Native to China, Japan. Slow to moderately fast growth to 10–15 ft. (possibly to 30 ft.) tall and wide. Dark gray or brownish gray bark with vertical furrows between long, smooth plates. Thick, leathery, glossy dark green leaves 1–2½ in. long and almost as wide; may be rounded or pointed, with short teeth toward tip. Bronzy new foliage. Egg-shaped, ½–¾-in. acorns are enclosed by one-third to one-half in a white, woolly, bowl-shaped cap. Good background for camellias, rhododendrons. Lends itself to elaborate shaping in Japanese gardens. Handsome bonsai plant.

Q. robur. ENGLISH OAK. Deciduous tree. Zones A2, A3; 1–12, 14–21. Native to Europe. Fairly fast grower to 50–60 ft. tall, 30 ft. wide, with rather short trunk and very wide, open head. Dark green, 3–4½-in.-long, 2–3-in.-wide leaves with three to seven pairs of rounded lobes. Leaves hold until late fall without much color change. Acorns are 1–1½ in. long, varying in shape from oval to oblong, coming to an abrupt point at tip; covered by up to one-third in velvety, bowl-shaped cap. *Q. r. fastigiata,* upright English oak, is columnar like Lombardy poplar (*Populus nigra* 'Italica') when young (to 50 ft. tall and 15 ft. wide), then matures to a broad, pyramidal shape. Other varieties include 'Skymaster' (broad pyramid to 50 ft. tall and half as wide) and 'Westminster Globe' (round headed, to about 45 ft. tall and wide).

Q. rubra (Q. r. maxima, Q. borealis). RED OAK, NORTHERN RED OAK. Deciduous tree. Zones 1–10, 14–21. Native to eastern North America. Fast growth to 60–75 ft. tall, 50 ft. wide, with spreading branches and rounded canopy. Bark becomes quite dark and fissured with age. Leaves 5–8 in. long, 4–6 in. wide, with three to seven pairs of sharp-pointed lobes. New leaves and leafstalks are red or bright yellow in spring, dark green in summer, turning dark red, ruddy brown, or orange in fall. Acorns are ¾–1 in. long, shaped like a toy top, enclosed by one-third in shallow cap; often profuse, creating litter on pavement. Needs fertile soil and regular moisture. High-branching habit and reasonably open shade make it a good tree for big lawns, parks, broad avenues. Deep roots make it good to garden under.

Q. shumardii. SHUMARD RED OAK. Deciduous tree. Zones 2–10, 14–17. Native to eastern U.S. Similar to *Q. coccinea* but slightly less hardy. Leaves are bright yellow in spring, dark green in summer, yellow to red in autumn. Acorns to 1¼ in. long are egg shaped, coming to an abrupt point; very shallow cap. Tolerates wide range of soils.

Q. suber. CORK OAK. Evergreen. Zones 5–7 (with occasional winter damage), 8–16, 18–24. Native to western Mediterranean, North Africa. To 30–60 ft. high and wide. Trunk and main limbs covered with handsome, thick, corky bark (the cork of commerce). Toothed, 3-in., oval leaves are shiny dark green above, gray beneath. Egg-shaped acorns with a short point are ¾–1½ in. long, covered by one-third to one-half in bowl-shaped cap.

Good garden shade tree; light-textured foliage contrasts interestingly with massive, fissured trunk. Needs good drainage. Fairly tolerant of various soils, but foliage may turn yellow in highly alkaline conditions. One of best oaks for desert. Value as street or park tree diminishes when children find out how easy it is to carve its bark.

Q. tomentella. ISLAND OAK. Evergreen tree. Zones 7–9, 14–17, 19–24. Native to California's Channel Islands. To 25–40 ft. tall and wide (occasionally to 60 ft. tall in cultivation). Slightly toothed leaves to 2–4 in. long, 1–1½ in. wide, dark green above, matted with fine grayish or tan hairs beneath. Egg-shaped, 1–1½-in. acorns bulge from shallow, woolly cap. Endures seacoast conditions. Needs deep soaking every 2 to 3 weeks outside fog belt. Symmetrical tree when well grown; some consider it the handsomest of California's evergreen oaks.

Q. turbinella. DESERT SCRUB OAK, SHRUB LIVE OAK. Evergreen shrub. Zones 2, 3, 7–24. Native to piñon-juniper belt in desert mountains from Southern California and Baja California east to Colorado, western Texas, adjacent Mexico. To 10 ft. high and as wide, with bushy, stiffly branched form; can be trained as a small tree. Gray, smooth mature bark. Hollylike, oval, dull yellowish green, 1–1½-in.-long leaves with sharp, spine-tipped teeth. Foliage hangs on through winter, drops in spring when replaced by new leaves. Acorns to 1¼ in. long vary in shape but often look like a toy top; they are enclosed by one-fourth to one-half in a bowl-shaped cap with short, papery scales. Tough background plant or hedge for dry, cold-winter inland areas; also does well in the temperate maritime climate of the Pacific Northwest.

Q. vacciniifolia. HUCKLEBERRY OAK. Evergreen shrub. Zones 1–7, 14–23. Native to mountains of Northern California and southern Oregon. Grows to 2–5 ft. high and at least twice as wide, with sprawling branches. Oblong to egg-shaped, smooth-margined, ¾–1¼-in.-long leaves, pointed or round at the tip; shiny gray green above, gray with sparse golden hairs below. Round to oval acorns to ½ in. long, with shallow cap covered in thin, hairy scales. This tree is sometimes planted in wild gardens, large rock gardens, or mountain gardens; it can also be used as an interesting informal hedge.

Q. virginiana. SOUTHERN LIVE OAK. Evergreen tree; partly or wholly deciduous in cold-winter regions. Zones 4–24. Native to coastal plains of southeastern U.S. Grows at a moderate to fast rate, eventually reaching 40–80 ft. tall, with a heavy-limbed crown spreading twice as wide. Long lived; with age, bark becomes very dark and checked. Smooth-edged, narrowly oval, 1½–5-in.-long leaves are shiny dark green above, whitish beneath. Oval acorns to 1 in. long, with sharp spine at tip; enclosed by one-fourth in bowl-shaped cap with hairy scales. Best in deep, rich, moist soil. In hot interior climates, it's the most attractive of all evergreen oaks. Best oak for lawn planting in low desert; fast-growing variety 'Heritage' is recommended for that region.

Q. wislizenii. INTERIOR LIVE OAK. Evergreen tree. Zones 7–9, 14–16, 18–21. Native to Sierra foothills, eastern side of Coast Ranges, interior valleys from southern Oregon to Southern California. To 30–75 ft. tall, often broader than high, with dense, rounded canopy. Elliptical glossy green leaves 1–4 in. long, with smooth or spiny edges and abruptly pointed tip. Slender, conical, sharp-pointed, ¾–1½-in. acorns are enclosed by one-fourth to one-half in a flat-scaled cap. Handsome tree for parks and big lawns. Young plants are sparse and angular, offering little hint of their ultimate beauty.

QUILLAJA saponaria

SOAPBARK TREE
Rosaceae
EVERGREEN TREE
ZONES 8, 9, 14–24
FULL SUN
MODERATE TO REGULAR WATER

Quillaja saponaria

Native to Chile. To 30–45 ft. (occasionally to 60 ft.) tall, half as wide. Young trees are dense columns foliaged right down to ground, with pendulous branches; they give the general effect of a narrow, bushy, weeping coast live oak *(Quercus agrifolia).* Older trees develop a broader, flatter-looking crown; their branchlets are less pendulous than those of young plants. Shiny green, rather leathery, 2-in. leaves are oval to nearly round. White, ½-in.-wide spring flowers are followed by handsome, inch-wide, brown fruit that opens into a star shape. Tends toward multiple trunks and excessive bushiness but responds quickly to pruning. Fairly tolerant of various soils. Drought tolerant but does better with periodic soakings; accepts lawn watering. Good narrow screening tree, tall hedge. The bark contains saponin, a lather-producing chemical; it is used in parts of Chile for washing and cleaning.

QUINCE, FLOWERING. See CHAENOMELES

QUINCE, FRUITING

Rosaceae
DECIDUOUS OR SEMIEVERGREEN SHRUBS OR TREES
ZONES VARY BY SPECIES
FULL SUN
MODERATE TO REGULAR WATER

Fruiting Quince

Two spring-blooming species produce early-fall crops of fragrant yellow fruit; it is typically tart and used for jams and jellies. The fruit can also be made into candy or combined with other fruits in pies. These pear relatives need little winter chill to be productive, and they make good landscape plants (especially the highly ornamental Chinese species). Need good drainage. Do not use high-nitrogen fertilizer, which promotes succulent growth susceptible to fireblight. Fruit is borne on new growth; little pruning is required beyond initial shaping and periodic thinning to keep plant's center open to sunlight. For the thorny shrubs grown mainly for flowers, see *Chaenomeles.*

The deciduous common quince *(Cydonia oblonga),* from western Asia, succeeds in Zones 2–24. Slow grower to 10–25 ft. high and wide, with gnarled, twisted branches that look attractive when leafless in winter. Oval, 2–4-in. leaves are dark green above, whitish beneath; turn yellow in autumn. White or pale pink, 2-in. flowers are followed by 3–4-in., round to pear-shaped fruits. Avoid deep cultivation near trunk; this damages shallow roots and causes suckers. Remove any suckers that sprout around base of tree; they rarely bear fruit and tend to weaken the tree.

Fruiting Quince

'Apple' ('Orange'). This variety is an old favorite. Round fruit with tender orange-yellow flesh.

'Aromatnaya'. Round; sweet yellow flesh that tastes like pineapple. Can be thinly sliced and eaten fresh.

'Cooke's Jumbo'. Pear-shaped fruit with white flesh. Can be nearly twice the size of other quinces.

'Havran'. Large and pear shaped, with very sweet white flesh.

'Pineapple'. Roundish, with tender white flesh that tastes like pineapple.

'Smyrna'. Round to oblong fruit with white flesh; strongly aromatic.

'Van Deman'. Large, oblong fruit; yellow flesh with spicy flavor.

Rarely seen in gardens, Chinese quince *(Pseudocydonia sinensis)* is a deciduous or semievergreen tree that succeeds in Zones 3–10, 14–21. To 15–20 ft. high (rarely taller), from half to equally as wide. Trunk is reason enough to grow this tree: the bark flakes off to reveal a patchwork of brown, green, and gray. Trunks on old trees are often fluted. Roundish oval, dark green leaves to 4½ in. long turn yellow and red in fall. Produces a scattering of pale pink, 1–1½-in. flowers rather than a show. Huge, egg-shaped fruits reach 7 in. long, weigh over 1 lb. each.

QUINOA. See CHENOPODIUM quinoa

RADICCHIO. See CHICORY and RADICCHIO

RADISH

Brassicaceae (Cruciferae)
ANNUAL
ALL ZONES
LIGHT SHADE IN HOTTEST CLIMATES
REGULAR WATER

Radish

Botanically known as *Raphanus sativus;* probably native to eastern Mediterranean region. To grow well, radishes need evenly moist soil and some added nutrients. Supply nutrients by blending well-aged manure into soil at least a month before planting. Or feed about 10 days after planting, applying fertilizer beside rows (as for carrots) or using a liquid fertilizer.

Sow seeds as soon as ground can be worked in spring, then at weekly intervals until warm weather approaches (plants go to seed when temperatures rise, with roots becoming bitter in the process). In mild-winter climates, you can also sow at intervals in fall and winter for harvest during those seasons. Sow seeds ½ in. deep and 1 in. apart; space rows 1–1½ ft. apart. When the tops are up, pull out every other plant; you can eat the thinnings if they are large enough. Radishes are best harvested and eaten as soon as they reach full size; they can become pithy and overly pungent in flavor if left in the ground too long. You can pull them for the table as early as 3 weeks after sowing seeds (the slowest kinds take 2 months to reach table-ready size).

The most familar radishes are short, round, red or red-and-white types like 'Cherry Belle', 'Cherriette', and 'Scarlet White-tipped'. You can also get round radishes in white or pink; 'Easter Egg II' produces a mixture of white, pink, red, and purple. 'French Dressing' and 'Red Flame' are long, narrow, white-tipped types with a sweet flavor; they're known as breakfast radishes. Other long radishes have a more typical radish flavor; white 'Icicle' is the best known of these, but there are also novelties like 'Misato Rose Flesh', which is green outside and pink inside. Some types of long, white radishes with a mildly nippy to hot flavor can be found in markets under the name "daikon."

'French Dressing' Radish

RAINBOW SHOWER. See CASSIA × nealiae

RANGPUR LIME. See CITRUS, Sour-Acid Mandarin

Ranunculaceae. The immense buttercup family numbers nearly 2,000 species, among them numerous ornamental annuals and perennials. Members include *Anemone,* columbine *(Aquilegia), Clematis, Delphinium,* hellebore *(Helleborus),* and *Ranunculus.* Many are poisonous if eaten.

FOR INFORMATION ON SELECTING PLANTS
PLEASE SEE PAGES 64–160

RANUNCULUS

Ranunculaceae

PERENNIALS

ZONES VARY BY SPECIES

EXPOSURE NEEDS VARY BY SPECIES

REGULAR WATER

Ranunculus asiaticus

This very large genus comprises about 250 species of widely different habit and appearance, but the two listed here are the species most commonly grown in gardens.

R. asiaticus. PERSIAN RANUNCULUS, TURBAN RANUNCULUS. All zones; see below. Native to Asia Minor. Tuberous-rooted plant to 1½–2 ft. tall and wide, with fresh green, almost fernlike leaves. Blooms profusely in spring, when each flowering stalk bears one to four 3–5-in.-wide, semidouble to fully double blossoms that some say resemble small peony blooms. Flowers come in white, cream, and many shades of yellow, orange, red, pink. Popular Tecolote Giant strain is available in single colors, mixed colors, and picotees. Bloomingdale strain offers the same variety on dwarf plants 8–10 in. high. All types are good in the ground or in pots.

Tuberous roots are hardy to 10°F/–12°C; in Zones 4–9, 12–24, plant in fall for bloom in winter, early spring. Beyond hardiness range, plant in spring as soon as ground is workable; or start roots indoors 4 to 6 weeks before the usual last-frost date. Nurseries sell tuberous roots of various sizes; all produce equally large blossoms, but bigger roots yield a greater number of flowers.

Grow in full sun, in organically enriched, very well-drained soil (if necessary, plant in raised beds). Set roots with prongs down, 2 in. deep (1 in. deep in heavier soils) and 6–8 in. apart. Water thoroughly, then withhold water until leaves emerge. Birds are fond of ranunculus shoots; protect sprouting plants with netting or wire. Or start plants in pots or flats, then set them in the garden when they're 4–6 in. tall—too mature to appeal to birds. (You can also start with nursery-grown seedlings.) Remove faded flowers to encourage more bloom.

When flowering tapers off and leaves start to yellow, stop watering the plants and allow the foliage to die back. Where tuberous roots are hardy in the ground, they can be left undisturbed—as long as soil can be kept dry during summer. However, most gardeners throughout the West dig plants when foliage turns yellow, cut off the tops, let roots dry for a week or two, and store them in a cool, dry place until planting time.

R. repens pleniflorus. CREEPING BUTTERCUP. Zones 1–10, 14–24. From Eurasia; naturalized in North America. Vigorous plant with thick, fibrous roots and runners that root at the joints. Forms lush, glossy green mat to 1 ft. high, 6 ft. wide; leaves are roundish, deeply cut into three tooth-edged, 2-in.-long leaflets. Fully double, 1-in., button-shaped bright yellow flowers are held above foliage on 1–2-ft. stems in spring. Can be invasive in constantly moist soil. Attractive deciduous ground cover for full sun to deep shade. Basic species is single flowered, as aggressive as *R. r. pleniflorus.*

RAOULIA australis

Asteraceae (Compositae)

PERENNIAL

ZONES 2B–9, 14–24

FULL SUN

MODERATE WATER

Raoulia australis

Ground cover plant from New Zealand. Tiny gray leaves form a very tight carpet to ½ in. high, 1 ft. wide; stems are hidden by the leaves. Inconspicuous pale yellow flowers in spring. Needs sandy soil, perfect drainage. Good in rock gardens.

RAPHIOLEPIS. See RHAPHIOLEPIS

RASPBERRY

Rosaceae

DECIDUOUS SHRUBS

ZONES A1–A3; 1–24; BEST IN 3–6, 15–17

FULL SUN

REGULAR WATER

Red Raspberry

For ornamental species, see *Rubus;* the plants described here are grown for their luscious fruit. Red and yellow raspberries are derived from *R. idaeus,* native to North America, Europe, Asia. Black raspberries (or blackcaps) are varieties of North American species *R. occidentalis.* Purple raspberries are hybrids between black and red types. All bear clusters of white flowers in spring.

Raspberries grow from perennial roots that produce thorny biennial stems called canes. Generally, raspberry canes grow to full size in the first year, then bear fruit in their second summer. Red and yellow varieties known as everbearing (or fall-bearing) produce two crops on the same canes—one in fall of the first year, the second in summer of the next year. In all instances, the canes die after fruiting in the second year.

For raspberry fruit to reach perfection, plants need winter chill and a lingering springtime with slowly warming temperatures. In warmer zones outside of best raspberry climates, satisfactory production may come from plants grown in light shade, mulched heavily to keep soil cool. Good drainage is essential; if you garden in heavy clay, consider planting in raised beds. Rich, slightly acid soil (pH 6 to 6.5) is ideal. Avoid planting where you have previously grown tomatoes, potatoes, peppers, or eggplants, which may have tainted the soil with verticillium wilt.

Plant bare-root stock during the dormant season. Set red and yellow raspberries 2½–3 ft. apart, in rows spaced 6–10 ft. apart. Plant black and purple raspberries in slightly raised mounds 2–3 ft. apart, in rows 6–8 ft. apart; they will develop into clumps of canes. Cut back the cane that rises from the root, leaving only enough (about 6 in.) to serve as a marker. Mulch plantings to discourage weeds and keep soil moist. Water need is greatest during flowering and fruiting. Feed at bloom time.

Red and yellow raspberries are produced on erect plants with long, straight canes; they can be grown as freestanding shrubs and staked, but they are tidier and easier to manage if trained on a trellis or confined to a hedgerow (pairs of parallel wires strung at 3 ft. and 5 ft. above ground along either side of a row of plants).

Summer-bearing varieties should produce three to five canes in first year. Tie these to a trellis or confine them to a hedgerow. Dig or pull out any canes that grow more than 1 ft. away from trellis or outside of hedgerow. In late dormant season, cut canes on trellis to 5–5½ ft. high, those in hedgerow to 4 ft. When growth recommences, new canes will appear all around parent plant and between rows. After the original canes bear fruit, cut them to ground. Then select the best 5–12 new canes and train these (they will bear next summer); cut remaining new canes to ground.

Everbearing red and yellow varieties fruit in first autumn on top third of cane, then again in second summer on lower two-thirds of cane. Cut off upper portion of cane after first harvest; cut out cane entirely after second harvest. As an alternative, you can follow the example of growers who cut everbearing canes to the ground yearly in fall after fruiting has finished (wait until late dormant season in cold-winter regions). You'll sacrifice one of the annual crops but get an extended harvest from late summer into fall. Use a power mower in a large berry patch.

Black and purple raspberries are produced on clump-forming plants with arching canes. No support is needed. In the first summer, force branching by heading back new canes of black varieties to 2 ft., of purple varieties to 2½ ft. If you prefer trellising, cut black varieties to 2–2½ ft., purple ones to 2½–3 ft. In late dormant reason, remove all weak or broken canes. Leave six to eight canes in a hill or spaced 6–8 in. apart in a row. Shorten side branches to 8–10 in. for black raspberries, to 12–14 in. for purple types. The side branches will bear fruit in summer. After harvest, cut to the ground all canes that have fruited and cut back all new canes as described for first summer's growth.

To control anthracnose and other fungal diseases on all raspberries, spray with lime sulfur during dormancy and again as leaf buds begin to open; this also helps control many insect pests, including spider mites and cane borer. If borers attack, prune out and destroy damaged canes below entry points (pinhead-size holes at or near ground level).

A caution to gardeners in Hawaii: the very vigorous *R. niveus,* called Mysore raspberry (ripe fruit is black, but plant is grown like red raspberry), is sometimes grown in Island gardens; however, it can become a troublesome weed, choking out native vegetation.

Red and yellow varieties. Red varieties are the most common; yellow types are mutations of red raspberries.

'Amity'. Everbearing. Large dark red berries of excellent quality. Resists root rot and tolerates somewhat heavier soils than other varieties.

'Autumn Bliss'. Everbearing. Very large red berries with fine flavor. Resists root rot.

'Bababerry'. Everbearing. Large, firm red berries. Needs little winter chill; stands heat well. Best in hot-summer climates.

'Boyne'. Summer-bearing. Very hardy red raspberry bred in Manitoba. Medium-size fruit. Early ripening. Subject to anthracnose.

'Canby'. Summer-bearing. Large bright red berries. Thornless.

'Chilcotin'. Summer-bearing. Very large, firm red berries with excellent flavor. Long harvest season.

'Chilliwack'. Summer-bearing. Very large red berries with fine flavor. Somewhat resistant to root rot.

'Dinkum'. Everbearing. Medium-size, firm red fruit with good flavor.

'Fallgold'. Everbearing. Large yellow fruit with good flavor.

'Fallred'. Everbearing. Large, firm red fruit with outstanding flavor.

'Golden Summit'. Everbearing. Sport of 'Summit' with delicious, medium-size yellow berries.

'Heritage'. Everbearing. Small red berries are tasty but a bit dry.

'Indian Summer'. Everbearing. Small crops of large, tasty red berries. Fall crop is often larger.

'Kiska'. Summer-bearing. Small red berries with good flavor. Hardy; developed for Alaska.

'Latham'. Summer-bearing. Older, very hardy; for coldest regions. Mildews in humid summers. Late. Large red berries are often crumbly.

'Meeker'. Summer-bearing. Large, firm bright red berries on long, willowy branches.

'Newberg'. Summer-bearing. Large light red berries. Late-ripening variety. Takes heavy soil fairly well.

'September'. Everbearing. Small to medium-size red berries of good flavor. Fall crop is heavier.

'Summit'. Everbearing. Large red berries with good flavor. Very productive. Resistant to root rot.

'Sumner'. Summer-bearing. Early-ripening variety with some resistance to root rot in heavy soils. Fine-flavored, large red berries.

'Tulameen'. Summer-bearing. Very large, firm red berries with excellent flavor. Long harvest season.

'Willamette'. Summer-bearing. Large, firm dark red berries that hold color and shape well.

Black and purple varieties. Black raspberries have blue-black fruit that is firmer and seedier than that of red and yellow types, with a more pronounced flavor. Purple raspberries are crosses between black and red kinds.

Black Raspberry

'Brandywine'. Large purple berries. Tart; good for jams, jellies. Ripens late.

'Cumberland'. Large black berries. Old, heavy-bearing variety.

'Jewel'. Large black berries. Vigorous, disease-resistant plant.

'Morrison'. Large black berries. Productive, late-ripening variety.

'Munger'. Medium-size black berries. Most popular commercial black-fruited variety.

'Sodus'. Large purple berries with a white bloom; rich flavored, excellent in pies. Vigorous plant.

RATIBIDA

Asteraceae (Compositae)
PERENNIALS
ALL ZONES
FULL SUN
REGULAR WATER

Ratibida columnifera

Stiffly erect, branched, roughly hairy plants with deeply cut leaves. Flower heads resemble those of black-eyed Susans *(Rudbeckia)* but have fewer ray flowers and a spherical or cylindrical central cone (rather than a flat disk). Use in casual, natural-looking borders with grasses and other minimum-care perennials.

R. columnifera. MEXICAN HAT. From Great Plains. To 2½ ft. tall, 1 ft. wide. Flowers have drooping yellow or brownish purple rays and a tall, columnar brown cone. Effect is that of a sombrero with a drooping brim.

R. pinnata. PRAIRIE or YELLOW CONEFLOWER. Native to central North America. To 4 ft. tall, 1½ ft. wide, with yellow rays and a nearly globular brown cone.

RATTAN PALM. See RHAPIS humilis

RATTLESNAKE GRASS. See BRIZA maxima

RATTLESNAKE MASTER. See ERYNGIUM yuccifolium

RAVENALA madagascariensis

TRAVELER'S TREE, TRAVELER'S PALM
Strelitziaceae
EVERGREEN TREE
ZONES 24; H2
FULL SUN
REGULAR WATER

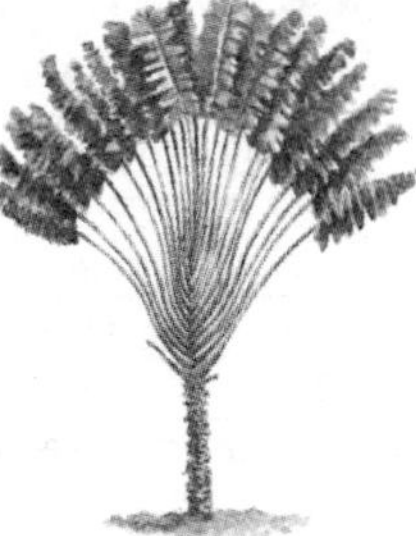

Ravenala madagascariensis

Native to Madagascar. Upright clump to 30–40 ft. tall, 25–30 ft. wide, with numerous large, banana-like leaves held in the shape of a gigantic fan atop an unbranched trunk. Spectacular accent in the garden or displayed against a large building. Protect from strong winds, which will shred the leaves. Small plants have some shade tolerance, can be used as potted specimens.

REDBERRY. See RHAMNUS crocea

REDBIRDS IN A TREE. See SCROPHULARIA macrantha

REDBUD. See CERCIS

RED-FLOWERING GUM. See EUCALYPTUS ficifolia

RED GINGER. See ALPINIA purpurata

RED GUM. See EUCALYPTUS camaldulensis

RED-HOT POKER. See KNIPHOFIA

RED HUCKLEBERRY. See VACCINIUM parvifolium

RED IRONBARK. See EUCALYPTUS sideroxylon

REDONDO CREEPER. See LAMPRANTHUS filicaulis

RED-RIBBONS. See CLARKIA concinna

RED SHANKS. See ADENOSTOMA sparsifolium

RED SPIKE ICE PLANT. See CEPHALOPHYLLUM 'Red Spike'

REDTOP. See AGROSTIS gigantea

RED VALERIAN. See CENTRANTHUS ruber

REDWOOD, COAST REDWOOD. See SEQUOIA sempervirens

R

REDWOOD SORREL. See OXALIS oregana

REED GRASS. See CALAMAGROSTIS

REHMANNIA elata

CHINESE FOXGLOVE
Gesneriaceae
PERENNIAL
ZONES 6 (BORDERLINE), 7–10, 12–24
FULL SUN IN COOLER CLIMATES ONLY
REGULAR WATER

Rehmannia elata

Native to China. To 3 ft. tall, 1½–2 ft. wide. Clump of coarse, deeply toothed leaves (evergreen in mild-winter climates) sends up stalks loosely set with tubular, 3-in.-long flowers that look something like big, gaping foxgloves *(Digitalis)*. Common form bears rosy purple blossoms with a yellow throat dotted in red; there is also a fine white form with cream throat that must be grown from cuttings or divisions. Where winters are mild, blooms from midspring well into fall; in colder climates, bloom comes in summer. Long lasting as a cut flower. Provide rich soil. Easy to grow from seed, root cuttings, divisions.

REINWARDTIA indica (R. trigyna)

YELLOW FLAX
Linaceae
SHRUBBY PERENNIAL
ZONES 8–10, 12–24; H1, H2
FULL SUN OR PARTIAL SHADE
MODERATE TO REGULAR WATER

Reinwardtia indica

Native to mountains from Pakistan to China. To 3–4 ft. high and wide, with elliptical, evergreen leaves 1–3 in. long. Blooms profusely, bearing brilliant yellow, 2-in. flowers like those of flax (*Linum*, to which it is related). Individual blossoms do not last long, but for weeks new ones open daily. In mild-winter regions, blooms in late fall and early winter; in colder areas, bloom comes in summer. Grow in fertile, well-drained soil. Pinch young plants to encourage branching. Cut back hard after bloom to keep compact.

RESEDA odorata

MIGNONETTE
Resedaceae
ANNUAL
ALL ZONES
PARTIAL SHADE IN HOTTEST CLIMATES
REGULAR WATER

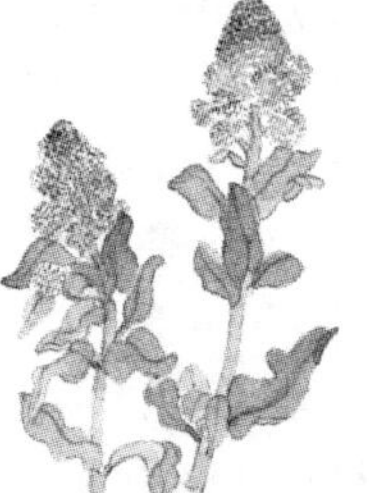
Reseda odorata

Native to North Africa. To 1–1½ ft. tall and wide; rather sprawling. Light green leaves. Not a particularly beautiful plant, but the remarkable spicy-sweet fragrance of its flowers makes it well worth growing. The small blossoms are greenish with a coppery or yellow tinge, carried in dense spikes that become loose and open with age. Flowers dry up quickly in hot weather.

Sow seed in early spring (or in late fall or winter, in mildest climates). Make successive sowings for the longest bloom period. Does best in rich soil. Plant in masses to get full effect of perfume; or locate a few plants in scentless plantings to provide fragrance. Suitable for containers. Strains with longer flower spikes and brighter colors are sold, but they are less fragrant.

Rhamnaceae. The buckthorn family of shrubs and trees has small, usually clustered flowers and fruits that are either drupes (single seeded, juicy) or capsules. Western gardeners grow *Ceanothus*, jujube, and *Rhamnus*.

RHAMNUS

Rhamnaceae
EVERGREEN AND DECIDUOUS SHRUBS OR TREES
ZONES VARY BY SPECIES
EXPOSURE NEEDS VARY BY SPECIES
WATER NEEDS VARY BY SPECIES

Rhamnus californica

Grown for form and foliage; clusters of small flowers are rather inconspicuous. Used chiefly as background plantings, hedges. Berries (typically pea size) are enjoyed by birds; volunteer seedlings may be a nuisance.

R. alaternus. ITALIAN BUCKTHORN. Evergreen shrub. Zones 4–24. Native to Mediterranean region. Fast, dense growth to 10–20 ft. high and wide. Oval, shiny bright green leaves to 2 in. long; small black berries. Easily trained as single- or multitrunked tree. Takes well to shearing and shaping. Tolerates heat; does well with little or no water but also accepts regular watering. Full sun or partial shade. 'John Edwards' is a vigorous, fast-growing, long-lived cutting-grown variety to 15–18 ft. tall, 6–10 ft. wide. Compact 'Variegata' ('Argenteovariegata') grows 6–8 ft. high and equally wide, has cream-edged foliage that looks striking against a dark background (if branches with plain green leaves appear, cut them out or they'll quickly take over).

R. californica. COFFEEBERRY. Evergreen shrub. Zones 4–9, 14–24; H1, H2. Native to California and southwest Oregon. To 3–15 ft. tall, 8 ft. wide. Grown near the ocean, it may have a low, spreading habit; in woodlands, it grows upright. Leaves are 1–3 in. long, variable—shiny or dull, dark green to yellowish green, usually paler on undersides (some forms have gray, hairy leaf undersides). Berries turn from green to red to black as they ripen. Among the many named selections are 'Eve Case', a dense grower to 4–8 ft. high and as wide, with large berries; and 'Seaview', a ground cover variety growing 1½–2 ft. high, 6–8 ft. wide. Both have leaves that are distinctly broader, flatter, and brighter green than those of species. 'Mound San Bruno', to 4–6 ft. tall and wide, has narrower leaves than species. All are tolerant of pruning and shaping. Not fussy about soil. Full sun or partial shade. Established plants need no irrigation, but the broader-leafed types look better with moderate water. 'Mound San Bruno' is especially tolerant where moisture is concerned: it can take regular garden watering or none at all.

R. cathartica. COMMON BUCKTHORN. Deciduous shrub or tree. Zones 1–3. Native to Europe, western and northern Asia. To 15–25 ft. tall and wide. Glossy green, elliptical or oval, 1–2½-in.-long leaves. Foliage turns an unremarkable yellow in fall, drops late in the season. Short twigs near branch ends are often spine tipped. Small black berries. Tolerates poor soil, wind. Useful hedge or small tree in coldest, driest regions. Little or no water. Full sun.

R. crocea. REDBERRY. Evergreen shrub. Zones 7, 14–24. Native to Coast Ranges from Northern California into Baja California. To 2–3 ft. high, 3–6 ft. wide, with many stiff branches, often spiny at tips. Roundish, ½-in.-long leaves, frequently with finely toothed edges; glossy dark to pale green above, golden or brownish beneath. Small bright red fruit. Takes full sun or partial shade in its native territory; does best with some shade in hotter inland areas. Little water.

R. frangula. ALDER BUCKTHORN. Deciduous shrub or tree. Zones 1–7, 10, 11. Native to Europe, western Asia, North Africa. To 10–12 ft. (possibly 18 ft.) tall and wide. Oval to roundish, glossy dark green leaves to 3 in. long; turn yellow in autumn. Berries ripen from red to black. 'Columnaris', tallhedge buckthorn, grows 12–15 ft. tall, 4 ft. wide; set plants 2½ ft. apart for a tight, narrow hedge that can be kept as low as 4 ft. Full sun or partial shade. Moderate water.

R. ilicifolia (R. crocea ilicifolia). HOLLYLEAF REDBERRY. Evergreen shrub. Zones 7–10, 14–23. Native to Coast Ranges and Sierra Nevada foothills, mountains of Southern California, Arizona, Baja California. Bulky shrub or shrubby tree to a possible 15 ft. high, nearly as wide. Roundish, spiny-toothed, ½–1¼-in.-long leaves. Takes heat, drought; makes a good informal screen. Full sun or partial shade. No irrigation needed.

R. purshiana. CASCARA, CHITTAM BARK. Deciduous shrub or tree. Zones 1–9, 14–17. Native from Northern California to British Columbia and Montana. To 20–40 ft. tall, 10–30 ft. wide, with smooth gray or brownish bark that has medicinal value. Picturesque branching pattern. Dark green, prominently veined leaves are elliptical, 1½–8 in. long, usually borne somewhat more heavily (in tufts) at branch ends. Good yellow foliage color in fall. Black berries. Takes full sun to dense shade. Regular water.

RHAPHIOLEPIS

Rosaceae

EVERGREEN SHRUBS

ZONES 8–10, 12–24; H1, H2; WORTH THE RISK IN ZONES 4–7

FULL SUN OR LIGHT SHADE

LITTLE TO REGULAR WATER

Rhaphiolepis indica 'Dancer'

In regions where temperatures never (or very rarely) fall to 0°F/–18°C, these are among the most widely planted shrubs. And for good reason: their glossy, leathery leaves and dense, compact growth habit make them especially attractive background plants and informal hedges. They bloom profusely from late fall or midwinter to late spring, with flowers ranging in color from white to nearly red. Berrylike dark blue fruit follows the flowers (it is not especially showy). New leaves in tones of bronze and red often add more touches of color.

Most are low growers. The taller kinds rarely reach more than 5–6 ft., and pruning can keep them at 3 ft. almost indefinitely. For bushy, compact plants, pinch back branch tips at least once yearly, after flowering. For a more open structure, let plants grow naturally and thin out branches occasionally. Plants in partial shade are less compact and produce fewer flowers than those in full sun. Good seacoast plants; tolerate salt drift. Little bothered by pests, though aphids occasionally attack them. Fireblight and a fungal leaf spot (in cool, wet weather) are possible disease problems. In hot-summer regions, plants will burn in reflected heat; they need some sheltering shade in low desert.

R. ×delacouri. Pink-flowered hybrid of *R. indica* and *R. umbellata.* To 6 ft. tall, 8 ft. wide. Small pink flowers in upright clusters. Leaves are 1¼–2¾ in. long.

R. indica. INDIAN HAWTHORN. Native to China. To 4–5 ft. high, 5–6 ft. wide, with 1½–3-in.-long, pointed leaves and ½-in. flowers in white tinged with pink. The species is seldom seen in gardens, but its varieties are widely grown and sold. They differ mainly in flower color and in plant size and form; there is variation even within a variety. Flower color is especially inconsistent: in warmer climates and exposures, blossoms are usually lighter, and in general blooms are paler in fall than in spring. In the Northwest, subject to a leaf spot fungus, which defoliates the plants. Varieties include the following.

'Ballerina'. To 2 ft. tall, 4 ft. wide. Deep rosy pink flowers. Leaves take on a reddish tinge in winter.

'Clara'. To 3–5 ft. tall and wide. White flowers. Red new growth.

'Dancer'. Reaches 4 ft. tall, 5 ft. wide. Pure pink flowers.

'Enchantress'. To 3 ft. tall, 5 ft. wide, with rose pink blooms. 'White Enchantress' has white blossoms.

'Indian Princess'. Up to 3 ft. high, 5 ft. wide. Light pink flowers.

'Jack Evans'. To 4–5 ft. high, 4 ft. wide. Bright pink flowers. Leaves sometimes have a purplish tinge.

'Spring Rapture'. To 3–4 ft. high and wide. Rose red blossoms.

'Springtime'. Vigorous, upright growth to 4–6 ft. tall and wide. Deep pink flowers.

R. 'Majestic Beauty'. Larger in every detail than the others. Can be trained as a single- or multitrunked tree to 20–25 ft. tall, 8–10 ft. wide; as a shrub, easily kept at 10–12 ft. tall, 6–8 ft. wide. Fragrant light pink flowers in clusters to 10 in. wide. Leaves are 4 in. long. Thought by some to be a hybrid between *Rhaphiolepis* and loquat *(Eriobotrya)*.

R. umbellata (R. u. ovata, R. ovata). Native to Japan, Korea. Vigorous to 4–6 ft. (sometimes to 10 ft.) high and wide. Distinguished from *R. indica* by its leathery dark green, 1–3-in.-long, roundish leaves. White, about ¾-in.- wide flowers. Thick and bushy in full sun. In Northwest, less subject to leaf spot than *R. indica.* Sometimes called Yeddo hawthorn. 'Minor' ('Gulf Green') is a compact, slow-growing form to 3–4 ft. high and wide.

RHAPIDOPHYLLUM hystrix

NEEDLE PALM

Arecaceae (Palmae)

PALM

ZONES 2–24

SUN OR SHADE

MODERATE TO AMPLE WATER

Rhapidophyllum hystrix

Perhaps the hardiest palm in the world, taking temperatures well below 0°F/–18°C. Native to the coastal plains of the southeastern U.S. Shrubby and slow growing, to an eventual 6–8 ft. high and wide; does not have a distinct trunk. Smooth stems bear dramatic fans of lustrous dark green, 3-ft.-wide leaves, each deeply cut into 6–12 segments. Common name refers to the sharp, 4-in.-long black spines on sheaths at bases of leafstalks and on seeds. Tolerates a wide range of soils. Good accent or understory plant. Hard to find in garden centers; available by mail order.

RHAPIS

LADY PALM

Arecaceae (Palmae)

PALMS

ZONES VARY BY SPECIES; OR INDOORS

SOME SHADE; BRIGHT INDIRECT LIGHT

REGULAR WATER

Rhapis excelsa

These choice, slow-growing fan palms form bamboolike clumps. Foliage is deep green; trunks are covered with a net of dark, fibrous leaf sheaths. Several variegated forms exist, and fanciers are willing to pay very high prices for good examples. Good indoor plants.

R. excelsa. LADY PALM. Zones 12–17, 19–24; H1, H2. Hardy to 20°F/ –7°C. From China. To 5–12 ft. tall and wide. One of the finest houseplants. Withstands neglect and poor light but responds quickly to better light, regular watering and fertilizing.

R. humilis. RATTAN PALM, SLENDER LADY PALM. Zones 16, 17, 20–24; H1, H2. Hardy to 22°F/–6°C. To 18 ft. tall, 3 ft. wide, with tall, slender stems. Larger, longer-leafed palm than *R. excelsa.*

RHEUM

ORNAMENTAL RHUBARB

Polygonaceae

PERENNIALS

ZONES 2B–7, 14–17

FULL SUN OR LIGHT SHADE

AMPLE WATER

LEAVES ARE POISONOUS IF INGESTED

Rheum palmatum

The ornamental rhubarbs are stately plants, good focal points in well-watered perennial borders or at woodland edges. The large leaves arise directly from stout rhizomes; flowering stalks produce smaller leaves and prominent bracts. Blossoms are individually

R

inconspicuous but are massed in tall, branching, plumy clusters, making a great show in late spring or early summer. Best in deep, organically enriched soil. For the edible plant, see Rhubarb.

R. australe (R. emodi). From the Himalayas. To 4–10 ft. tall, 6–8 ft. wide. Rounded leaves to 2½ ft. across, with wavy edges and red veins. White flower plumes are 8–12 in. long.

R. palmatum. From China, Tibet. To 6–8 ft. tall, 6 ft. wide. Nearly round, 2–3-ft.-wide leaves are deeply cut into tooth-edged lobes. Red flower plumes to 2 ft. long. In variety 'Atrosanguineum', the entire plant is suffused with red. Leaves of *R. p. tanguticum* are less deeply cut than those of the species and often tinted purple; flowers may be white, pink, or red.

RHIPSALIDOPSIS gaertneri (Schlumbergera gaertneri)

EASTER CACTUS

Cactaceae

CACTUS

ZONES 16, 17, 21–24; H1, H2; OR INDOORS

PARTIAL SHADE; BRIGHT LIGHT

REGULAR WATER

Rhipsalidopsis gaertneri

Native to Brazil. For culture and description, see *Schlumbergera.* Much like *S. ×buckleyi* but initially more upright, then semipendent to 6 in. high, 1 ft. wide (*S. ×buckleyi* is completely drooping). Blooms in spring, often again in late summer or early fall. Many varieties with blossoms in various shades of pink and red. In marginal climates, give protection of lathhouse or covered terrace. Good houseplant; bring outdoors during warm times of year, if desired. Plant has been renamed *Hatiora gaertneri* but is not generally offered as such.

RHODODENDRON (includes Azalea)

Ericaceae

EVERGREEN AND DECIDUOUS SHRUBS, RARELY TREES

FOR ZONES, SEE BELOW

FILTERED SUNLIGHT

REGULAR TO AMPLE WATER

LEAVES ARE POISONOUS IF INGESTED

Rhododendron 'Trude Webster'

Approximately 800 species belong to this huge group. The International Register lists more than 10,000 named varieties, of which perhaps several thousand are currently available. Botanists have arranged species into series and subseries; one of these series includes the plants called azaleas.

With careful selection, gardeners in all climates—even the coldest, hottest, and driest ones—can find ways to grow certain members of this genus (in containers or as houseplants, if need be). Rhododendrons generally do best in Zones 4–6, 15–17, though there are many exceptions. The climate adaptation of azaleas, however, differs greatly from that of rhododendrons. For example, evergreen azaleas are grown extensively in Southern California and Hawaii, while rhododendrons require special attention there. Overall, zones for azaleas vary widely, depending on the hybrid group or species; see the azalea listings on pages 573–575 for specifics.

Rhododendrons and azaleas need more air in the root zone than almost all other garden plants, but they also require a constant supply of moisture. Without excellent drainage, they can succumb to root rot (see care box). Soils rich in organic matter have the desired qualities; if your soil is deficient, amend it liberally with organic material.

In clay or alkaline soil, planting in a raised bed is the simplest way to give these plants the conditions they need. The finished bed should be 1–2 ft. above original soil level. Mix a generous amount of organic material into the top foot of native soil; then fill bed above it with a mixture of 50 percent organic matter, 30 percent native soil, 20 percent sand. This soil mix will be well aerated but moisture retentive and will permit alkaline salts to leach through. Plant azaleas and rhododendrons with top of root ball slightly above soil level. Never allow soil to wash in and bury stems. Plants are surface rooters and benefit from a mulch such as pine needles, oak leaves, or wood by-products (for example, redwood or fir bark or chips). Never cultivate around these plants.

Sun tolerance of azaleas and rhododendrons differs by species and variety. Too much sun causes leaf centers to bleach or burn, though most of these plants can take full sun in cool-summer areas. Ideal location is in filtered shade beneath tall trees; east and north sides of house or fence are next best. Too dense shade results in lanky plants that bloom sparsely.

In areas where dissolved salts accumulate, periodically leach the planting by watering heavily—enough to drain through the soil two or three times. If leaves turn yellow while veins remain green, plants have iron chlorosis; apply iron chelates to soil or spray foliage with iron solution.

Insects and diseases seldom cause well-grown plants much harm. Root weevils are the main problem, especially in the Pacific Northwest. Damage by root weevil adults, which notch leaves, is usually minor, but their larvae can girdle roots. In late May and during summer, spray foliage with acephate to kill adults and prevent new generations; in fall, a soil drench of fresh beneficial nematodes may get rid of larvae.

Both wind and soil salts burn leaf edges; windburn shows up most often on new foliage, salt burn on older leaves. Late frosts often cause deformed leaves.

Pruning rhododendrons is simple; follow these general guidelines. Tip-pinch young plants to make them bushy; prune older, leggy plants to restore shape by cutting back to a side branch, leaf whorl, or cluster of latent buds. Do any extensive pruning in late winter or early spring (wait until danger of frost is past in colder areas). Pruning at this time will sacrifice some flower buds, but the plant's energies will be diverted to latent growth buds, which will then be ready to push out their new growth early in the growing season. (Several varieties will not produce new growth from latent buds.) You can do some shaping while plants are in bloom, using cut branches in arrangements. To prevent seed formation, which can reduce next year's bloom, clip or break off spent flower trusses, taking care not to damage growth buds at base of each truss.

Evergreen azaleas are dense, usually shapely plants; heading back the occasional wayward branch restores symmetry. To keep bushes compact, tip-pinch frequently, starting after flowering ends and continuing until July. Prune deciduous azaleas while they are dormant and leafless (in cold climates, wait until frost danger is past). You don't have to prune azaleas as carefully as you do rhododendrons—the leaves are fairly evenly spaced along the branches, with a bud at base of each leaf, so new growth will sprout from almost anywhere you cut (in either bare or leafy wood). Azaleas can even be sheared into formal hedges.

KINDS OF RHODODENDRONS

Most people know rhododendrons as big, leathery-leafed shrubs with rounded clusters ("trusses") of stunning white, pink, red, or purple blossoms. But there are also dwarfs a few inches high, giants that reach 40 or even 80 ft. tall in their native Southeast Asia, and a host of species and hybrids in every intermediate size, in a color range including scarlet, yellow, near-blue, and a constellation of orange, apricot, salmon, and pink shades. Blossoms of some types are spotted in other colors. In other types, flowers have a blotch or flare in a different color on the upper petal.

The following sections list named varieties by categories, to give you some idea of their adaptability to different climates and garden roles. These varieties are described later. Listed are the generally available kinds, representing only a portion of the best rhododendrons grown in the West.

Ironclad hybrids for coldest winters. These can take temperatures to −25°F/−32°C: 'Calsap', 'Catawbiense Album', 'Crete', 'English Roseum', 'Henry's Red', 'Northern Starburst', 'Nova Zembla', 'PJM', 'Purple Gem', 'Roseum Elegans', and *R. yakushimanum* and its named selections.

Northern California specials. Zones 15–17. The following four rhododendrons, commonly called Maddenii Hybrids, are too tender for Northwest gardens: 'Else Frye', 'Forsterianum', 'Fragrantissimum', 'Mi Amor'. Good performers in Northern California, not highly prized in Northwest: 'Anah Kruschke', 'Antoon Van Welie', 'Rainbow', 'Sappho', 'Van Nes Sensation'.

Vireyas for indoors and frost-free areas. The Vireya rhododendrons, from the tropics of Southeast Asia, manage nicely in frost-free and nearly frostless zones (17, 23, 24; H2). They are also fine container plants (even indoors), so they can be grown in colder zones if brought inside for the winter. They need an especially fast-draining potting mix (many species are epiphytes in the wild); a combination of equal parts peat moss, ground bark, and perlite works well. Typically, plants flower on and off throughout the year rather than in one blooming season. They bear waxy-textured flowers in exciting shades of yellow, gold, orange, vermilion, salmon, and pink, plus cream, white, and bicolors. Species, named hybrids, and unnamed seedlings are offered by some specialty growers.

Among the best ones you are likely to find are *R. aurigeranum* (a hybrid of *R. brookeanum* commonly listed as 'Gracile'), *R. javanicum, R. konori, R. laetum, R. lochae, R. macgregorae,* and the hybrids 'George Budgen' (orange yellow), 'Ne Plus Ultra' (a red-flowering hybrid between *R. laetum* and *R. zoelleri*), and 'Taylori' (pink).

Widely adapted varieties. All of these are highly regarded, dependable, popular, and easy to grow just about anywhere: 'Anna Rose Whitney', 'Blue Ensign', 'Cotton Candy', 'Crest', 'Hallelujah', 'Jean Marie de Montague', 'Loder's White', 'Mrs. G. W. Leak', 'Purple Splendour', 'Ramapo', 'Trude Webster'.

Low-growing species and hybrids. Although they are rhododendrons, these have the charm and general appearance of azaleas: 'Blue Diamond', 'Sapphire', *R. impeditum, R. keiskei, R. moupinense, R. pemakoense, R. rupicola chryseum.*

Dwarfs and low growers. Distinctive foliage and bell-shaped or funnel-shaped flowers, not in typical trusses, mark these varieties: 'Cilpinense', 'Ginny Gee', 'Patty Bee', 'Ramapo', 'Snow Lady'.

WHAT RHODODENDRONS AND AZALEAS NEED

EXPOSURE: Generally, they fare best in filtered sunlight. Where summers are mild or foggy, they can take more sun. In general, however, the sunnier or hotter the climate, the more protection the plants will need. Some individual varieties and hybrid groups have been bred for sun tolerance.

SOIL: Plants need rich, acid soil that is both moisture retentive and fast draining. If plants turn yellow, wilt, or collapse, they are probably suffering from root rot caused by poor drainage.

FERTILIZING: Some experts dig fertilizer into the soil to get new plantings off to a good start. Feed established plants with commercial acid fertilizer well before bloom, as buds swell (in early spring, except for the earliest bloomers). Feed again when new leaves begin to grow, just as blooms are fading. Topdress with compost in early fall.

PINCHING: This is essential for shaping plants and encouraging thick, bushy growth. For other pruning information, see text.

WINTER PROTECTION: In very cold weather, sun and wind can severely damage plants. Protect larger plants in exposed locations with a windbreak of burlap fastened to stakes. Protect roots from damage caused by alternate freezing and thawing by mulching root area after soil has frozen.

Rhododendron 'Mrs. Furnivall'

RHODODENDRON RATINGS AND HARDINESS

For each plant in the following list (hybrids are listed first, followed by species), a three-number rating is given. Flower quality is rated first, plant appearance second, and garden performance third; 5 is superior, 4 above average, 3 average, 2 below average, 1 poor. If two numbers appear in one category, rating authorities disagree. For example, a 4–5/3/3 rating means that judges differ on whether the plant is above average or superior in flower quality, though they agree that plant appearance and garden performance are both average. The list also states hardiness for each plant—the minimum temperature a mature plant can tolerate without serious injury.

The American Rhododendron Society uses average height at 10 years as basis for plant size. Older plants may be taller; crowded or heavily shaded plants may reach the typical 10-year height at a younger age. Low plants (to 3 ft. or less) are usually slow growing and unlikely to exceed the 10-year height by much. Most rhododendrons tend to grow about as wide as high.

Bloom time given is approximate and varies with weather and location. The bloom season starts as early as December or January (in mildest climates) and extends through August; most types are spring bloomers. In the list below, "very early" corresponds to winter; "early" to early spring; "midseason" to midspring; "late" to late spring; and "very late" to summer. All of the following plants are evergreen, unless noted.

'A. Bedford'. 4/3/5. −5°F/−21°C. To 6 ft. Large trusses of lavender-blue blooms with darker flare. Late.

'America'. 3/2–3/3–4. −20°F/−29°C. To 5 ft. Dark red. Late.

'Anah Kruschke'. 4/4/5. −15°F/−26°C. To 6 ft. Lavender blue to reddish purple. Flower color not the best, but plant has good foliage, is very tolerant of heat and sun. Can be sensitive to root rot in warm, wet soils. Midseason to late.

'Anna Rose Whitney'. 4/3/5. −5°F/−21°C. To 6 ft., with excellent foliage. Big trusses of blossoms in rich, deep pink. Late midseason.

'Antoon Van Welie'. 4/3–4/4. −5°F/−21°C. To 6 ft. Tall trusses of carmine pink blooms. Late midseason.

'Autumn Gold'. 3–4/3–4/4. −5°F/−21°C. To 5 ft. Well-branched plant with rather upright growth. Salmon blossoms in flat-topped trusses; blooms from an early age. Very late.

'Baden Baden'. 3–4/4/3–4. −15°F/−26°C. To 2 ft. high, 4 ft. wide. Bright red. Midseason.

'Bambino'. 4/4/4. −5°F/−21°C. To 3 ft. Peach pink suffused with yellow and dotted with red. Large calyx gives effect of a double flower. Midseason.

'Besse Howells'. 3–4/3–4/4. −15°F/−26°C. To 3 ft. Large trusses of rosy red blooms. Early midseason.

'Blaney's Blue'. 4/4/4. −5°F/−21°C. To 4–6 ft., with compact, dense, rounded habit. Profuse pale blue flowers from early age. Midseason.

'Blue Diamond'. 4/4/4. −5°F/−21°C. To 3 ft.; compact, erect. Small leaves. Small lavender-blue flowers cover plant in early midseason. Takes considerable sun in Northwest.

'Blue Ensign'. 4/3/4. −15°F/−26°C. To 4 ft.; compact, well branched, rounded growth. Leaves tend to spot. Lilac-blue flowers with a striking dark blotch. Midseason. Tolerates sun.

'Blue Peter'. 4/2–3/3. −10°F/ −23°C. To 4–5 ft. Broad, sprawling growth; needs regular pruning. Large trusses of lavender-blue flowers with purple blotch. Midseason. Tolerates heat and sun.

'Bow Bells'. 3/4/3. −5°F/−21°C. Forms a 3-ft. mound. Rounded leaves; bronzy new growth. Loose clusters of bright pink, cup-shaped flowers open from deeper pink buds. Early midseason.

'Calsap'. 4/3/4. −25°F/ −32°C. To 4 ft., with broad, dense form. Lavender buds open to white flowers with deep reddish purple blotch. Resembles 'Sappho' but is hardier and has better plant form.

'Cary Ann'. 3/4/4. −5°F/ −21°C. Grows to 3 ft. high, with spreading habit. Foliage looks good all year. Flaring coral red flowers cover plant in midseason.

'Catawbiense Album'. 3/3/4–5. −25°F/−32°C. To 6 ft. Pink buds; white flowers with greenish blotch. Midseason to late. Takes cold and heat.

'Catawbiense Boursault'. 2/3/4–5. −20°F/−29°C. Like 'Catawbiense Album' but has pinkish lavender flowers. Takes cold and heat.

'Chionoides'. 3/4/4. −15°F/−26°C. To 4 ft.; dense, compact, rounded form. White flowers with light yellow spotting. Late midseason. Takes sun.

'Christmas Cheer'. 3/4/4. –10°F/–23°C. Shapely plant to 4 ft. Tight trusses of pink to white flowers; very early. Blooms at Christmas (or earlier) where winters are mild, in March in colder regions. Tolerates sun.

'Cilpinense'. 3–4/3–4/3–4. 5°F/–15°C. To 3 ft., with low, spreading habit. Small leaves. Funnel-shaped flowers in apple blossom pink fading to white; loose clusters nearly cover plant. Easy to grow. Effective massed. Early; protect blossoms from late frosts.

'Cinnamon Bear'. 3–4/5/4. –15°F/–26°C. Dense growth to 3 ft. Rosy pink buds open to pink-tinged white flowers. Midseason. Furry, white new growth; older leaves have furry brown undersides.

'CIS'. 4/3/4. 5°F/–15°C. To 3 ft. Flowers are red in throat, shading to creamy yellow at edges; carried in large trusses. Midseason.

'Cornubia'. 4/3/5. 15°F/–9°C. Strong, upright growth to 7 ft. Blood red flowers in large clusters. Very early.

'Cotton Candy'. 4/4/4. 0°F/–18°C. To 6 ft. Tall trusses of large flowers in soft pink. Midseason.

'Creamy Chiffon'. 4–5/4/2. 0°F/–18°C. To 4 ft.; compact plant with rounded leaves. Salmon buds open to ruffled, creamy yellow double flowers. Midseason.

'Crest'. 5/3/3. –5°F/–21°C. To 6 ft. Tall, open habit; plant tends to be bare toward base. Large trusses of bright yellow flowers. Early midseason. Outstanding blooms.

'Crete'. 4/4–5/4. –25°F/–32°C. To 4 ft. Purplish pink buds open to light purple flowers that age to white. Early midseason.

'Cunningham's Blush'. 2/3/4. –15°F/–26°C. Dependable old variety to 4 ft. Blush pink with white blotch. Late midseason.

'Cunningham's White'. 2/3/4. –15°F/–26°C. May actually be hardier than rated; a plant in Finland has survived –45°F/–43°C. To 4 ft. An old-timer bearing white blooms with greenish yellow blotch. Late midseason.

'Dora Amateis'. 4/4/4. –15°F/–26°C. To 3 ft. Compact, rather small-foliaged plant; good for foreground. Profuse bloomer with green-spotted white flowers. Spicy fragrance. Early midseason.

'Elizabeth'. 4/4/5. 0°F/–18°C. To 3 ft. One of the most popular low-growing red rhododendrons, very widely planted. Attractive foliage sets off large, bright red, waxy, trumpet-shaped flowers that are carried in clusters of three to six at branch ends and in upper leaf joints. Blooms very young. Early midseason; often reblooms in early fall. Very susceptible to fertilizer burn, salts in water or soil.

'Else Frye'. 5/3/4. 15°F/–9°C. To 4 ft. Long, limber growth makes this a natural for informal espalier. Considerable pinching is needed to achieve compact form. Intensely fragrant flowers are pink-flushed white with a gold throat. Early midseason.

'English Roseum' ('Roseum Pink'). 2–3/3/3–4. –25°F/–32°C. Erect habit to 6 ft. Lavender-pink blooms. Midseason. Tough and undemanding.

'Fabia Tangerine'. 3/4/3. 5°F/–15°C. To 3 ft. Compact plant. Leaves covered with reddish brown fuzz. Open trusses of brilliant orange, bell-shaped flowers. Midseason.

'Fantastica'. 4/5/4. –5°F/–21°C. To 3 ft. Compact. Long, elliptical leaves have woolly undersides. Rose pink flowers with white throat, green spotting on petals. Late midseason.

'Fastuosum Flore Pleno'. 3/3/3. –15°F/–26°C. Open, rounded habit to 6 ft. Lavender-blue double flowers marked with gold blotch. Flower center is filled with small, lavender petal-like structures. Midseason. Dependable old-timer. Tolerates heat and sun.

'Forsterianum'. 4/4/4. 15°F/–9°C. To 5 ft. Open, rangy growth. Attractive glossy leaves and red-brown, glossy, peeling bark. Tubular, frilled, fragrant white flowers tinted pink. Very early; buds often damaged by frost in colder areas if plant is not given overhead protection.

'Fragrantissimum'. 4/2–3/4. 15°F/–9°C. Loose, open, rangy growth; bright green, bristly leaves. With hard pinching in youth, a 5-ft. shrub. Easily trained as espalier or vine, reaching 10 ft. or more. Can spill over wall. Large, powerfully fragrant, funnel-shaped white flowers touched with pink. Early midseason. Grow as container plant in Northwest; overwinter indoors in bright but cool room.

Rhododendron 'Fragrantissimum'

'Furnivall's Daughter'. 4–5/4/4. –10°F/–23°C. To 5 ft. Tall trusses of bright pink flowers with cherry red blotch. Midseason.

'Ginny Gee.' 5/5/4. –10°F/–23°C. Striking 2-ft. dwarf with small leaves, dense growth. Small pink bells are dotted inside and out with white. Profuse bloom in early midseason.

'Golfer'. 4/5/4. –15°F/–26°C. Low, broad, to 1½ ft. Leaves densely furred with soft, silvery hairs. Bright pink flowers in tight clusters. Early midseason.

'Gomer Waterer'. 3/4–5/4–5. –15°F/–26°C. To 5 ft. Pink buds open to white flowers with yellowish green blotch. Late midseason. Old-timer. Tolerates sun; endures heat and drought better than most.

'Halfdan Lem'. 4–5/4/4–5. –5°F/–21°C; may be hardier. To 5 ft. Well shaped and vigorous, with heavy stems and large leaves. Big, tight trusses of luminous red flowers. Midseason.

'Hallelujah'. 4–5/5/4–5. –15°F/–26°C. To 4 ft. Rose red flowers stand above thick, beautiful forest green foliage. Very strong grower; fine-looking plant with or without flowers. Midseason. Takes full sun.

'Henry's Red'. 3/3–4/4. –25°F/–32°C. To 5 ft.; broader than tall. Dark red flowers. Midseason.

'Holden'. 3/3–4/4. –15°F/–26°C. To 4 ft. Compact plant. Rose red flowers marked with deeper red. Midseason.

'Hong Kong'. 3/3/3. –20°F/–29°C. To 5 ft. Compact plant. Light yellow flowers. Late midseason. One of the hardiest yellows.

'Hotei'. 5/4/3. 0°F/–18°C. To 3 ft. Compact plant. Canary yellow flowers backed by a prominent calyx come only when plant is 6 to 8 years old. Closest of all varieties to a deep pure yellow. Midseason. Roots can rot easily; needs excellent drainage.

'Janet Blair'. 4/3/4. –15°F/–26°C. To 5 ft.; vigorous and spreading. Large, ruffled flowers blend pastel pink, cream, white, and gold; rounded trusses. Midseason to late.

'Jean Marie de Montague'. 4/4/4. –5°F/–21°C. To 5 ft., with attractive foliage. Brilliant scarlet flowers. Midseason.

Rhododendron 'Autumn Gold'

Rhododendron 'Blue Peter'

Rhododendron 'Catawbiense Album'

Rhododendron 'Fastuosum Flore Pleno'

'Johnny Bender'. 3–4/5/4. –5°F/–21°C. To 4–5 ft. Glossy dark green leaves set off blood red flowers. Midseason.

'Lem's Cameo'. 5/3/3. –5°F/–21°C. To 4–5 ft. Flowers in a blend of apricot, cream, and pink. Midseason.

'Lem's Monarch' ('Pink Walloper'). 4–5/4–5/4–5. –5°F/–21°C. To 6 ft. Big, heavy-branched plant with large leaves. Pink flowers, darker at the edges, bloom in huge, round trusses. Midseason.

'Lem's Stormcloud'. 4/3–4/4. –15°F/–26°C. To 5 ft. Large, erect trusses of bright red flowers; blossoms flare out flat when fully open. Late midseason.

'Leo'. 5/3/3–4. –5°F/–21°C. To 5 ft., well clothed in large dark green leaves. Rounded to dome-shaped trusses packed with rich cranberry red blooms. Midseason to late.

Loderi Hybrids. 4/3–4/4. 5°F/–15°C. Spectacular group with tall trusses of 6–7-in.-wide, extremely fragrant flowers in shades of pink or white. Midseason. Informal, open growth to 6 ft., eventually becoming much larger and nearly treelike; too large for small garden. Slow to reach blooming age, not easy to grow; maintaining good foliage color is difficult. Best known are 'King George', pink quickly fading to white; 'Pink Diamond', blush pink; and 'Venus', deepest pink of the group.

'Loder's White'. 4/3–4/3–4. 0°F/–18°C. Shapely growth to 5 ft. Tall trusses of white flowers with faint yellow throat and light pink picotee edge; blooms turn pure white as they mature. Midseason. Blooms freely even when young. Best white for most regions.

'Lord Roberts'. 2–3/3/4. –15°F/–26°C. To 5 ft. Handsome dark green foliage and rounded trusses of red flowers spotted in black. Midseason. Plants grown in sun are more compact, bloom more profusely.

'Madame Masson'. 3/3/4. –15°F/–26°C. Grows to 5 ft. White with light yellow flare on upper petal. Late midseason. Needs pruning to maintain compact form.

'Mars'. 4/3/3. –15°F/–26°C. To 4 ft. Dark red. Late midseason. Handsome form, foliage, flowers.

'Mi Amor'. 5/3/4. 15°F/–9°C. Striking plant for mild-winter climates. Open, lanky; to 6 ft. Huge (6-in.), powerfully fragrant, bell-shaped white flowers with yellow throat, borne in clusters of three to five. Midseason.

'Molly Ann'. 4/4–5/4. –10°F/–23°C. To 3 ft. Compact grower with roundish leaves. Rose pink flowers in upright trusses. Early midseason.

'Moonstone'. 3–4/4/3. –5°F/–21°C. To 3 ft. Low, compact mound with neat, small, rounded leaves. Flaring bells age from pale pink to creamy yellow. Early midseason. Fine facing taller rhododendrons, as low foundation planting with 'Bow Bells'.

'Mrs. Furnivall'. 5/3–4/3–4. –15°F/–26°C. To 4 ft. Compact-growing plant. Tight, round trusses of light pink flowers with deep red blotch. Late midseason.

'Mrs. G. W. Leak' ('Cottage Gardens Pride'). 4/3/4. 0°F/–18°C. Strong-growing plant to 6 ft. Light pink flowers with showy reddish purple flare. Early midseason.

'Nancy Evans'. 5/4/3–4. 5°F/–15°C. Compact growth to 3 ft., with bronzy new foliage. Orange-tinged buds open to yellow flowers; each bloom is backed by a calyx that makes it look almost double. Midseason.

'Northern Starburst'. Unrated. –30°F/–34°C. To 4 ft. Improved form of 'PJM' with larger flowers and bigger, thicker leaves that turn blackish purple in winter. Early to early midseason.

'Nova Zembla'. 3/3/4. –25°F/–32°C. To 5 ft. Profuse red flowers in midseason. Takes heat.

'Noyo Chief'. 3–4/4–5/4. 10°F/–12°C. To 5 ft. Outstanding glossy green, heavily ribbed leaves. Bright red flowers. Midseason.

'Old Copper'. 4/3–4/4. –5°F/–21°C. Well-shaped plant to 5 ft. Coppery orange flowers. Late. Can take more heat than most rhododendrons.

'Paprika Spiced'. 5/3–4/3–4. 0°F/–18°C. To 3 ft. Flowers in a blend of yellow, pink, and orange, dotted with red. Large yellow calyx. Midseason.

'Patty Bee'. 5/4–5/4–5. –10°F/–23°C. To 1½ ft. Small plant, well clothed with small (1-in.-wide) leaves that turn dark red in winter. Loose trusses of lemon yellow flowers cover even young plants. Early midseason.

'Percy Wiseman'. 4/4/4. –10°F/–23°C. To 3 ft. Compact growth. Peachy yellow flowers fade to white. Midseason. Notably heat resistant.

'Pink Pearl'. 3/3/3. –5°F/–21°C. To 6 ft.; open and rangy if not pruned. Tall trusses of rose pink flowers. Midseason. Grows and blooms dependably in all except coldest climates.

'PJM'. 4/4/4. –25°F/–32°C. Dense, bushy plant to 4 ft. Exceptional purplish pink flowers; profuse bloom. Flowers early, when foliage still has its mahogany winter color. Takes heat as well as cold.

'President Roosevelt'. 4/4/3. 0°F/–18°C. To 4 ft. Dark green leaves marked with golden yellow. Tall trusses of red flowers with white centers. Early midseason. Named for Theodore Roosevelt.

'Purple Gem'. 3/4/3. –25°F/–32°C. To 2 ft. Dwarf with tiny leaves that emerge bluish, take on rust tones. Blue-purple flowers in early midseason.

'Purple Splendour'. 4/3/3. –5°F/–21°C. To 5 ft. Informal habit. Ruffled-looking deep purple blossoms with black-purple blotch. Late midseason. Tolerates sun.

'Rainbow'. 4/3/4. 0°F/–18°C. Strong growth to 6 ft. Heavy-textured foliage. Very showy, tall trusses of large white flowers with deep pink border. Early midseason.

'Ramapo'. 3/4/4. –20°F/–29°C. Dense, spreading growth to 2 ft. in sun, taller in shade. New growth is dusty blue green, maturing to dark green. Pinkish violet flowers cover plant in early midseason. Useful rock garden or low border plant. Good choice in California.

'Rosamundi'. 2/3–4/3–4. –5°F/–21°C. To 4 ft. Slow growing and compact. Ball-like trusses of pink flowers. Very early to early.

'Roseum Elegans'. 2/3/4. –25°F/–32°C. To 6 ft. Olive green foliage. Lilac-pink flowers. Midseason to late. Tolerates both heat and cold.

'Sapphire'. 3/3/3–4. –5°F/–21°C. To 2½ ft. Twiggy, rounded, and dense, with tiny, narrow gray-green leaves. Small, azalea-like light blue flowers. Early midseason.

'Sappho'. 3/2/4. –15°F/–26°C. To 6 ft. Easy to grow; gangly without pruning. Use at back of border. White blossoms, dark purple eye. Midseason.

'Scarlet Wonder'. 4/4/4. –15°F/–26°C. May be hardier than its rating; has survived –45°F/–43°C in Finland (perhaps protected by snow cover). Outstanding, compact dwarf to 2 ft. Shiny, quilted-looking foliage forms backdrop for many bright scarlet blossoms. Midseason. ▸

Rhododendron 'Hotei'

Rhododendron 'Nova Zembla'

Rhododendron 'Percy Wiseman'

Rhododendron 'Pink Pearl'

'Scintillation'. 4/4/4–5. –15°F/–26°C. To 5 ft. Compact plant covered in lustrous dark green leaves. Rounded trusses of pastel pink flowers with deep pink markings in throat; blooms age to brownish pink. Midseason.

'September Song'. 5/4/4. 0°F/–18°C. To 4 ft.; broader than tall. Flowers shade from salmon at edges to golden orange in throat, giving trusses an overall orange look. Blooms young. Midseason.

'Snow Lady'. 3–4/4–5/5. 0°F/–18°C. To 2½ ft. Fuzzy light green leaves. Big show of pure white flowers. Early.

'Susan'. 4/4–5/4. –5°F/–21°C. To 6 ft. Handsome foliage; violet-blue flowers in large trusses. Midseason.

'Taurus'. 4–5/4/4. –5°F/–21°C. To 6 ft. Vigorous and upright; well clothed in forest green leaves. Deep red buds open to large bright red bells with black spotting. Early midseason. Plants bloom only after reaching 4 to 6 years old.

'Top Banana'. 4/4/3–4. 0°F/–18°C. Upright plant to 3 ft. high, wider than tall. Brick red buds open to clear bright yellow flowers. Blooms young. Early midseason.

'Trinidad'. 4–5/4/4. –20°F/–29°C. To 4 ft. Ivory yellow flowers edged in bright red. Late.

'Trude Webster'. 5/4/4. –10°F/–23°C. To 5 ft. Strong-growing plant with large leaves. Huge trusses of pure pink flowers in midseason. One of the best pinks.

'Twilight Pink'. 4/4/4. –5°F/–21°C. To 4 ft. Apricot-and-pink flowers; large calyx makes each bloom look double. Midseason.

'Unique'. 3/4–5/4. –5°F/–21°C. To 4 ft.; oustanding neat, rounded, compact habit. Bright pink buds open to tight, rounded trusses of creamy pale yellow blossoms. Early midseason.

'Unknown Warrior'. 3/3/3–4. 5°F/–15°C. To 4 ft. Blossoms are a pale, soft red, fading quickly in bright sun. Midseason. Easy to grow.

'Van Nes Sensation'. 4/4/4. –5°F/–21°C. To 5 ft. Strong grower. Large trusses of pale lilac flowers. Midseason.

'Vulcan'. 4/4/4. –15°F/–26°C. To 5 ft. Bright brick red flowers. Late midseason. New leaves often grow past flower buds, partially hiding them.

R. augustinii. 4/3/3. –5°F/–21°C. Native to western China, Tibet. Open, moderate growth to 6 ft. Bell-shaped flowers in clusters of up to six. Colors range from white to lavender pink to blue. Early midseason. 'Barto Blue', 'Electra', 'Lackamas Blue', and 'Towercourt' are choice blue forms.

R. brachycarpum. 3/3–4/2–3. –10°F/–12°C. Native to Japan and Korea. Stocky plant to 3 ft. Creamy white flowers flushed pink and spotted green. Very late. *R. b. tigerstedtii* may be the hardiest of all rhododendron species; has withstood –45°F/–43°C. It also tolerates summer heat.

R

R. calophytum. 4/4/3. –15°F/–26°C. Native to southwestern China, Tibet. Becomes a small tree in time; to 6 ft. after 10 years. Noted for big leaves (10–14 in. long, 4 in. wide). Trusses of fragrant pale pink flowers with deep red blotch. Early. Protect from wind.

R. chryseum. See R. rupicola chryseum

R. falconeri. 3/3/2–3. 10°F/–12°C. Native to the Himalayas. Tree to 25 ft. tall. Leathery, 6–12-in.-long leaves with reddish, felted undersides. Clusters of creamy white to pale yellow flowers. Early midseason. Blooms when 15 to 20 years old.

R. forrestii forrestii Repens Group. 3/4/3. 5°F/–15°C. Several prostrate to very low growing plants fall within this group, derived from a species native to China, Myanmar. Bear small clusters of tubular bright red flowers in early midseason. All are useful rock garden plants; require perfect drainage. A plant called simply *R. forrestii forrestii* is actually, according to recent findings, *R. chamaethomsonii chamaethomsonii.*

R. impeditum. 4/4/3–4. –15°F/–26°C. From China. Twiggy, dense dwarf to 1 ft., with tiny, closely packed leaves in light grayish green. Small lavender-blue to purple-blue flowers cover the plant in early midseason. Set 15 in. apart for dense ground cover. Takes full sun in cooler areas. Needs excellent drainage to avoid root rot.

R. keiskei. 4/3–4/4. –5°F/–21°C. Native to Japan. Compact growth to 2 ft. Bears light to bright yellow flowers in clusters of three to five. Early midseason. 'Yaku Fairy' is a selected creeping form reaching just 6 in. high.

R. macrophyllum (R. californicum). 2–3/2–3/2. –5°F/–21°C. COAST RHODODENDRON, WESTERN RHODODENDRON. Native near coast from Northern California to British Columbia. Rangy plant growing 4–10 ft. tall, as high as 20 ft. in some locations. Leathery dark green leaves are 2½–6 in. long. Trusses may hold 20 flowers in pinkish purple to white, spotted with reddish brown. Midseason to late.

R. moupinense. 4/3/3. 0°F/–18°C. From China. To 1½ ft., with open, spreading habit. Small, oval leaves are deep red when new, maturing to green. White or pink flowers with red spots. Very early.

R. mucronulatum. 3–4/3/3. –15°F/–26°C. From China, Mongolia, Korea, Japan. Deciduous rhododendron with open, rather thin growth to 5 ft.; makes up for bare, leggy branches with very early bloom. Small clusters of flowers, usually in bright purple. There is also a pink form, 'Cornell Pink'.

R. pemakoense. 3/4/4. 0°F/–18°C. From the Himalayas, China. To 1½ ft. Compact, spreading plant with small leaves. Very profuse show of pinkish purple blooms. Early. Useful in rock gardens.

R. racemosum. 4/3/4–5. –5°F/–21°C. Native to China. Several forms are available, including a 6-in. dwarf; a compact, upright shrub to 2½ ft.; and a 7-footer. Small pink flowers in clusters of three to six all along stems. Early to early midseason. Easy to grow; sun tolerant in cooler areas.

R. rupicola chryseum (R. chryseum). 4/3/2. –10°F/–23°C. From China, Myanmar. Grows to 1 ft. Dense branching habit; small-leafed dwarf. Bears small, bell-shaped bright yellow blossoms, four or five to a cluster. Early midseason.

R. yakushimanum. 5/5/4. –25°F/–32°C. From Japan. Forms a tight mound to 1–4 ft. high. New growth is covered with a feltlike coat of white hairs; older leaves are glossy dark green above, brown and felted beneath. Clear pink bells age to white. Late midseason. Selections include 'Ken Janeck', a large (to 4-ft.) form with intense pink flowers, and smaller-growing 'Yaku Angel', with pink-tinged buds opening to pure white flowers. There are also a number of hybrids that perform as well in cold climates as they do in milder ones. Among them are 'Mardi Gras', 'Yaku Sunrise', and 'Yaku Princess' (this last selection is part of a good series of hybrids, all with names including royal titles). The three hybrids just mentioned all have blooms in white or pink-tinged white.

Rhododendron 'Unique'

Rhododendron augustinii 'Electra'

Rhododendron impeditum

Rhododendron yakushimanum 'Yaku Angel'

KINDS OF AZALEAS

Azaleas are divided into two broad categories: evergreen and deciduous. Each category includes both hybrid groups and species.

EVERGREEN AZALEAS

Evergreen azaleas fall into more than a dozen groups and species, though an increasing number of hybrids have such mixed parentage that they don't fit into any category. The following list includes some of the most popular groups. Except as noted, bloom season is early (see "Rhododendron ratings and hardiness," page 569, for bloom-season terms). Plants grown in greenhouses can be forced for winter bloom. Plant size tends to vary within a group, but most individual plants are about as wide as high.

Belgian Indica Hybrids. Zones 14–24; H1, H2. These hybrids were originally developed for greenhouse forcing. Where winter lows don't dip below 20°F/–7°C, many of them serve well as landscape plants. They are profuse bloomers with lush, thick foliage and typically semidouble or double, 2–3-in. blossoms. Among the most widely sold are 'Albert and Elizabeth', white with pink edges; 'California Sunset', salmon pink with white border; 'Chimes', dark red; 'Mardi Gras', salmon with white border; 'Mission Bells', red semidouble; 'Mme Alfred Sanders', cherry red; 'Orange Sanders', salmon orange; 'Orchidiflora', orchid pink; 'Paul Schame', salmon. Three choices with pendent growth are 'Red Poppy', deep purple 'Violetta', and orange-red 'William Van Orange'; all are suitable for hanging baskets.

Beltsville Hybrids. Zones 4–9, 14–24. Hardy to 0°F/–18°C. Resemble the Glenn Dale Hybrids. 'Casablanca Improved' has large, white single blossoms. 'Polar Bear' is another white-flowered selection.

Brooks Hybrids. Zones 8, 9, 14–24. Hardy to 20°F/–7°C. Bred in Modesto, California, for heat and drought tolerance, compact form, large flowers. Best known are white 'Madonna'; rose-colored 'My Valentine'; 'Pinkie'; and 'Red Wing'.

Gable Hybrids. Zones 4–9, 14–24. Bred to produce azaleas of Kurume type that take 0°F/–18°C temperatures. In Zones 4–6, they may lose some leaves during winter. Bloom heavily in midseason. Frequently sold are bright pink 'Caroline Gable'; purple 'Herbert'; pink 'Louise Gable', 'Pioneer', and 'Rosebud'; 'Purple Splendor'; 'Purple Splendor Compacta' (less rangy growth than 'Purple Splendor'); and white 'Rose Greeley'.

Girard Hybrids. Zones 4–9, 14–24. Hardy to –5°F/–21°C or somewhat lower. Originated from Gable crosses. 'Girard's Fuchsia' has reddish purple blossoms; 'Girard's Hot Shot', orange-red flowers and orange-red fall and winter foliage, 'Girard's Roberta', 3-in., double pink flowers.

Glenn Dale Hybrids. Zones 4–9, 14–24. Hardy to 0°F/–18°C. Developed primarily for hardiness, though they do drop some leaves in cold winters. Some are tall and rangy, others low and compact. Growth rate varies from slow to rapid. Some have small leaves like Kurume Hybrids; others have large leaves. Familiar varieties are orange 'Anchorite'; pale pink 'Aphrodite'; orange-red 'Buccaneer'; white 'Everest' and 'Glacier'; and 'Geisha', white with red stripes.

Gold Cup Hybrids. Zones 14–24. Members of this group were originally called Mossholder-Bristow Hybrids. Plants combine large flowers of Belgian Indica Hybrids with vigor of Rutherfordiana Hybrids. Good landscape plants where temperatures don't fall below 20°F/–7°C. Some popular varieties are 'Easter Parade', pink blooms mottled in white; 'Sun Valley', white; and 'White Orchid', white with red throat.

Greenwood Hybrids. Zones 4–7, 14–17. Bred in Canby, Oregon. Most of these are compact, hardy plants bearing large double flowers. They were developed to take lows of about 0°F/–18°C but will succeed in colder climates if you keep them from drying out: it's desiccation, not freezing, that does them in. Some of the most popular varieties are 'Greenwood Orange'; 'Greenwood Rosebud', pink with a slight purple blush; 'Sherry', very deep red flowers and maroon winter foliage; 'Silver Streak', reddish purple flowers and white-edged leaves; and 'Sleigh Bells', single white flowers.

Harris Hybrids. Zones 4–7, 15–17. Hardy to 0°F/–18°C. The offspring of Glenn Dale, Kaempferi, and Macrantha azaleas. Grown mainly in the Pacific Northwest, though some gardeners in California use them as well. Most of these hybrids bear extra-large flowers in late midseason. 'Bruce Hancock', to 2 ft. high and spreading to 4 ft., is a good ground cover; it bears 3½-in. white flowers with pink borders. 'Fascination' has 4½-in. red flowers with pink centers; 'Rhonda Stiteler' has double pink, 2½-in. flowers and green leaves lightly variegated with yellow. All of these are worth looking for.

Kaempferi Hybrids. Zones 2–7. Based on *R. kaempferi,* the torch azalea, a cold-hardy plant with orange-red flowers. These are somewhat hardier than Kurume Hybrids (to –15°F/–26°C), with a taller, more open habit. Nearly leafless below 0°F/–18°C. Profuse bloom. Available choices are salmon rose 'Fedora'; 'Holland', a late-season bloomer with large red flowers; orange-red 'John Cairns'; and white 'Palestrina'.

Kurume Hybrids. Zones 5–9, 14–24; H1, H2. Hardy to 5°F/–15°C. Compact, twiggy plants, densely clothed in small, glossy leaves. Small flowers are borne in incredible profusion. Plants have mounded or tiered form, look handsome even out of bloom. Widely used as houseplants. Grow well outdoors but cannot endure hot, dry summer winds. Of the many available varieties, these are among the most widely sold: pink 'Coral Bells', crimson 'Hexe', bright red 'Hino-crimson', cerise red 'Hinodegiri', red-violet 'Sherwood Orchid', orange-red 'Sherwood Red', 'Snow', and dark red 'Ward's Ruby'.

Kurume Hybrid Azalea 'Sherwood Orchid'

Macrantha Hybrids. Zones 5–9, 14–24. Includes plants sometimes referred to as Gumpo and Satsuki azaleas. Hardy to 5°F/–15°C. Low-growing plants, some of them true dwarfs; many are pendent enough for hanging baskets. Large flowers come late. Popular varieties include blush pink 'Bunkwa'; orange-red 'Flame Creeper'; white 'Gumpo'; rose pink 'Gumpo Pink'; bright pink 'Hi Gasa'; rose pink 'Rosaeflora'; and 'Shinnyo-No-Tsuki', bearing violet-red blossoms with white center. ▸

Kurume Hybrid Azalea 'Ward's Ruby'

Southern Indica Hybrid Azalea 'George Lindley Taber'

Northern Lights Hybrid Azalea 'Orchid Lights'

Rhododendron luteum (Deciduous Azalea)

Monrovia Hybrids. Zones 8, 9, 14–24. Hardy to 10°F/–12°C. Developed by Monrovia Nursery in Southern California, using Belgian Indica and Southern Indica azaleas as parents. They resemble Southern Indicas, form 4–6-ft. mounds, and thrive in warm, dry areas. Sun tolerant. 'Imperial Princess' has single pink flowers; 'Imperial Queen' bears double pink blooms. Midseason.

North Tisbury Hybrids. Zones 4–9, 14–24. Hardy to –9°F/–23°C. Most of these hybrids reflect the characteristics of a common prostrate-growing ancestor, *R. nakaharai.* Their dwarf, spreading habit and very late bloom (into midsummer) make them naturals for hanging baskets and ground covers. Some of the best selections are 'Alexander', with red-orange flowers and bronze fall foliage; pink-blossomed 'Pink Cascade'; and 'Red Fountain', with dark red-orange blooms that appear around the Fourth of July.

Pericat Hybrids. Zones 5–9, 14–24. These were originally developed for greenhouse forcing but are as hardy as Kurume Hybrids (5 to 10°F/ –15 to –12°C) and look much the same, though flowers tend to be somewhat larger. Varieties include light pink 'Mme Pericat', blush pink 'Sweetheart Supreme', and rose pink 'Twenty Grand'.

Robin Hill Hybrids. Zones 4–9, 14–24. Hardy to 0°F/–18°, probably lower. A large group with typically large flowers. Most are 2–4-ft. plants; some are more dwarf. Late bloom. There are so many good ones—several with "Robin Hill" in their name—that it's difficult to single out only a few. Try pink 'Betty Ann Voss'; 'Conversation Piece', pink with light center; 'Nancy of Robin Hill', pink with red blotch; red-orange 'Robin Hill Gillie'; and 'Hilda Niblett', with blossoms in a combination of light pink, deep pink, and white.

Rutherfordiana Hybrids. Zones 14–24. Greenhouse plants; also good in garden where temperatures don't go below 20°F/–7°C . Bushy, 2–4-ft. plants with handsome foliage. Medium-size blossoms may be single, semi-double, or double. Available varieties include 'Alaska', white with chartreuse blotch; light orchid pink 'Constance'; brick red 'Dorothy Gish'; rosy red 'Firelight'; orchid pink 'L. J. Bobbink'; white 'Purity'; deep pink 'Rose Queen'; and 'White Gish', very pale pink fading to white.

Southern Indica Hybrids. Zones 8, 9, 14–24. Varieties selected from Belgian Indica Hybrids for vigor and sun tolerance. Most take temperatures of 10 to 20°F/–12 to –7°C, but some are damaged even at the upper end of that range. They generally grow faster, more vigorously, and taller than other kinds of evergreen azaleas. Often sold in California under the name "sun azaleas." Used for massing and as specimens—as shrubs, standards, espaliers. Popular choices include carmine red 'Brilliant'; salmon pink 'Duc de Rohan'; 'Fielder's White'; brilliant rose purple 'Formosa' (also sold as 'Coccinea', 'Phoenicia', 'Vanessa'); light pink 'George Lindley Taber'; 'Iveryana', white with orchid streaks; 'Little John', a dense, rounded bush up to 6 ft. tall (despite the name) bearing burgundy foliage and a few deep red flowers; bright orange 'Orange Pride'; brilliant red 'Pride of Dorking'; watermelon pink 'Southern Charm' (sometimes sold as 'Judge Solomon'); and 'White April'.

Southern Indica Hybrid Azalea 'Formosa'

Vuykiana Hybrids. Zones 2–7. See description of Kaempferi Hybrids. Varieties sold include violet-blue 'Blue Danube', 'Vuyk's Rosy Red', and 'Vuyk's Scarlet'.

R. mucronatum. Zones 4–9, 14–24. Hardy to 5°F/–15°C. Typically listed as a species (*R. mucronatum* or *R. indica alba*) this plant is in fact an old Japanese garden hybrid now properly known as *R.* 'Mucronatum'. It has also been sold as 'Indica Alba' and 'Ledifolia Alba'. Grows 6–10 ft. high, with hairy leaves and large (to 3-in.) white flowers. Two of its sports are 'Sekidera' and 'Indica Rosea'; the former has blossoms flushed or blotched with purplish pink, while the latter bears pink-flushed blooms.

Deciduous azaleas

Very few deciduous shrubs can equal deciduous azaleas for showiness and color range. Evergreen azaleas can't match them for blooms in the yellow, orange, and flame red range, nor for flowers with bicolor contrasts. Foliage often turns brilliant orange red to maroon in autumn. In the following list, hybrid groups are followed by species. Plant size tends to vary within a group, but most individual plants are roughly equal in height and width. For definition of bloom-season terminology, see "Rhododendron ratings and hardiness" (page 569).

Arneson Hybrids. Zones 3–9, 14–17. Hardy to –20°F/–29°C. The azaleas in this group represent further development of the Knap Hill–Exbury Hybrids. Choices available include 'Arneson Gem', a prolific orange-flowered variety; 'Cascade Pink', bearing pink blooms with yellow-orange flare; and deep red 'Red Sunset'.

Ghent Hybrids. Zones 2b–9, 14–17. Many are hardy to –25°F/–32°C. Upright growth. Flowers are generally 1½–2¼ in. wide. Colors include shades of yellow, orange, umber, red, and pink. Midseason.

Knap Hill–Exbury Hybrids. Zones 3–9, 14–17. Hardy to –20°F/ –29°C. These make up perhaps half of all the deciduous azaleas sold in Pacific Northwest. Plants vary from spreading to upright, from 4 to 6 ft. tall. Produce the largest flowers found on deciduous azaleas (up to 5 in. across), borne in clusters of 7–18. Blossoms are sometimes ruffled or fragrant, in colors ranging from white through pink and yellow to orange and red, often with contrasting blotches.

Knap Hill–Exbury Hybrid Azalea 'Old Gold'

Both Knap Hill and Exbury azaleas come from the same original crosses. The first crosses were made at Knap Hill (in England); subsequent improvements were made at both Exbury (also in England) and Knap Hill. The so-called Rothschild azaleas are Exbury plants. Ilam Hybrids are from the same original stock, further improved in New Zealand.

Midseason to late bloom. If you want to be sure of flower color and size, choose named varieties (this does not mean you should dismiss all seedling plants as inferior—but do select them in bloom). Some of the best named forms are pink 'Cannon's Double'; orange 'Gibraltar'; double deep pink 'Homebush'; golden tangerine 'Klondyke'; 'Old Gold', bearing light orange-yellow blossoms flushed pink and blotched deep orange; and 'Oxydol', white flowers with yellow markings.

Mollis Hybrids. Zones A3; 2–9, 14–17. Hardy to –25°F/–32°C. Hybrids of *R. molle* and *R. japonicum.* Upright growth to 4–5 ft. Flowers 2½–4 in. wide, in clusters of 7–13. Colors range from chrome yellow through bright red. Very heavy bloom in midseason. Leaves have a light skunky fragrance when new, but they turn a lovely yellow to orange in autumn.

Northern Lights Hybrids. Zones A2, A3; 1–7. The hardiest of all deciduous azaleas, withstanding –45°F/–43°C. Developed by the University of Minnesota. To 2–4 ft., with ball-shaped trusses of fragrant sterile flowers (no need to deadhead after bloom). Late. Most widely available are 'Apricot Surprise', 'Orchid Lights', 'Rosy Lights', and 'White Lights'. Foliage can have the skunky odor of the Mollis ancestors.

Occidentale Hybrids. Zones 4–7, 14–17. Hardy to –5°F/–21°C. Hybrids between *R. occidentale* and Mollis azaleas. To 8 ft. Flowers 2½–4 in. wide; wide color range—from white blossoms flushed with rose and marked with yellow blotches, to red blooms with orange blotch. Midseason to late. An outstanding example is 'Washington State Centennial' ('Centennial'), with big, fragrant, frilly flowers in light orange-yellow marked with a large yellow flare; blossoms quickly age to white.

Viscosum Hybrids. Zones 3–7. Hardy to –15°F/–26°C. Hybrids between Mollis azaleas and *R. viscosum,* an eastern U.S. native with a powerful clove perfume. Flowers have the colors of Mollis azaleas but the fragrance of *R. viscosum.* Late.

R. japonicum. JAPANESE AZALEA. Zones 3b–7, 14–17. Hardy to –10°F/ –23°C. Native to Japan. Upright, fast growth to 6 ft. Salmon red, 2–3-in.-wide flowers are carried in clusters of 6–12 before leafout. Midseason. *R. j. aureum* has rich yellow flowers.

R. luteum (R. flavum). PONTIC AZALEA. Zones 3–7, 14–17. Hardy to –15°F/–26°C. Native to eastern Europe, Asia Minor. To 8 ft. or more. Blooms before leafout, bearing fragrant, single yellow flowers with darker blotch. Midseason.

R. occidentale. WESTERN AZALEA. Zones 4–7, 14–17, 19–24. Hardy to –5°F/–21°C. Native to mountains and foothills of California and Oregon. Erect growth to 6–10 ft. Clusters of fragrant, funnel-shaped flowers bloom after leafout. Midseason to late. Color varies from white to pinkish white with yellow blotch; some are heavily marked in carmine rose. Superior named cutting-grown plants are scarce but available and worth looking for. 'Leonard Frisbie' is a choice, heavily marked variety.

R. schlippenbachii. ROYAL AZALEA. Zones 3–7, 14–17. Hardy to –20°F/ –29°C. Native to Korea and Manchuria. Densely branched shrub to 6–8 ft. Leaves in whorls of five at tips of branches. Blooms in early midseason as leaves are expanding, producing large (2–4-in.), highly fragrant, pure light pink flowers in clusters of three to six. A white form is also available. Good fall color: yellow, orange, scarlet, crimson. Protect from full sun.

R. vaseyi. PINKSHELL AZALEA. Zones 3–7, 14–17. Hardy to –20°F/ –29°C. Native to mountains of North Carolina. Upright plant with irregular, spreading form. To 10–15 ft. Blooms before leafout, bearing light pink flowers in clusters of five to eight. Midseason.

RHODOHYPOXIS baurii

Hypoxidaceae

PERENNIAL FROM RHIZOMELIKE STRUCTURE

ZONES 4–7, 14–24

FULL SUN

REGULAR WATER DURING GROWTH AND BLOOM

Rhodohypoxis baurii

From mountains of South Africa. Tufts of narrow, 2–3-in. leaves are nearly obscured by masses of inch-wide, six-petaled flowers over a long spring-and-summer bloom period. Typical blossom colors range from pink shades to rosy red, but white varieties are available. Grows from a bulblike structure that is closest to a rhizome but also has characteristics of corm, tuber, and tuberous roots.

Plant roots in early spring, setting them 1 in. deep and 3–5 in. apart in nonalkaline, well-drained soil; choose a location where winter moisture can be kept to minimum. Stop watering when foliage yellows in fall. Divide crowded plantings in early spring, just as growth begins. Good in rock gardens. Often grown in pots to accommodate need for dry winters.

RHODOPHIALA bifida

Amaryllidaceae

PERENNIAL FROM BULB

ZONES 8, 9, 12–24

FULL SUN

REGULAR WATER DURING GROWTH AND BLOOM

Rhodophiala bifida

South American native resembling a small amaryllis *(Hippeastrum)* and considered by some to be *H. advenum.* Puts up a few foot-long leaves and a foot-tall flower stalk that bears two to six bright red, 2-in.-long, narrow-petaled blooms in late summer, early autumn. Plants spread willingly and put on a fine show. Grow as for *Hippeastrum.*

RHOEO spathacea. See TRADESCANTIA spathacea

RHOICISSUS capensis (Cissus capensis)

EVERGREEN GRAPE

Vitaceae

EVERGREEN VINE

ZONES 16, 17, 21–24; H2; OR INDOORS

ROOTS COOL, TOP IN SUN; BRIGHT OR INDIRECT LIGHT

REGULAR WATER

Rhoicissus capensis

Native to Africa. Tuberous-rooted vine, growing slowly to 15 ft. or more. Scallop-toothed leaves are roundish to kidney shaped, something like those of true grape in size and appearance. New stems and leaves are covered with red hairs that give them a rosy rust color. Mature leaves are a bold, coppery-tinged light green on upper surface, hairy and rust colored beneath. Flowers are insignificant.

Makes a good overhead screen or ground cover in frost-free regions. Fine houseplant; tolerates low light.

RHOPALOSTYLIS

Arecaceae (Palmae)

PALMS

ZONES 17, 23, 24; H1, H2

FULL SUN OR PARTIAL SHADE

REGULAR WATER

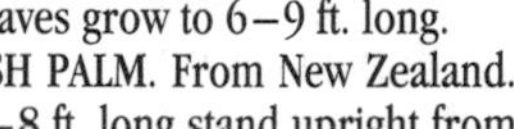
Rhopalostylis sapida

Feather palms with long, clean trunks marked with closely spaced rings. Moderate growth rate. Best in frost-free gardens.

R. baueri. From Norfolk Island. To 50 ft. tall, 20 ft. wide. The beautiful curving, arching leaves grow to 6–9 ft. long.

R. sapida. NIKAU PALM, SHAVING BRUSH PALM. From New Zealand. To 30 ft. high, 15 ft. wide. Feathery leaves 4–8 ft. long stand upright from prominent bulge at top of trunk. Good container plant where small space dictates an upright palm.

RHUBARB

Polygonaceae

PERENNIAL

BEST IN ZONES A1–A3; 1–11; ALSO SUCCEEDS IN ZONES 14–24

PARTIAL SHADE IN HOTTEST CLIMATES

REGULAR WATER

LEAVES ARE POISONOUS IF INGESTED; USE LEAF STEMS ONLY

Rhubarb

Known botanically as *Rheum × cultorum.* Foliage is showy enough to qualify this plant for a display spot in the garden. Bears big, crinkled leaves with an elongated heart shape that are carried on thick, typically red-tinted stalks. Leafstalks have a delicious, tart flavor and are typically used like fruit in sauces and pies. Produces insignificant flowers in spikelike clusters. Preferred varieties include 'Cherry' ('Crimson Cherry'), 'MacDonald', and 'Strawberry', all with red stalks; and 'Victoria', which produces greenish stalks. For strictly ornamental species of rhubarb, see *Rheum.*

Needs some winter chill for thick stems, good red color. Plant divisions (containing at least one bud) in late winter or early spring. In Zones 10 and 11, treat as cool-season annual and plant in fall for winter-into-spring harvest (plants tend to rot in heat of late spring, summer). Set tops of divisions at soil line; space 3–4 ft. apart. Let plants grow for two full seasons before harvesting. In third season, you can pull off leafstalks for 4 or

5 weeks in spring; older, huskier plants can take up to 8 weeks of pulling. To harvest leafstalks, grasp them near base and pull sideways and outward; do not cut with a knife, since cutting leaves a stub that will decay. Never remove all the leaves from a single plant; stop harvesting when slender leafstalks appear. After harvest, feed and water freely; cut out any blossom stalks that appear. In the mildest areas, plants won't die back completely in winter.

RHUS

SUMAC
Anacardiaceae
EVERGREEN AND DECIDUOUS SHRUBS AND TREES
ZONES VARY BY SPECIES
FULL SUN
LITTLE TO MODERATE WATER

Rhus typhina

Of the ornamental sumacs, deciduous kinds are extremely hardy to cold; they are noted for brilliant fall leaf color and, on female plants, showy clusters of (usually) red fruits that attract birds. They tend to produce suckers, especially if their roots are disturbed by cultivation. Evergreen species are less hardy. All sumac species thrive in almost any soil, as long as drainage is good (soggy soils can kill them).

Poison oak and poison ivy were once members of the genus *Rhus,* but they have been reclassified as *Toxicodendron.* For more information on these weedy, rash-causing sumac relatives and recommended controls, see "Poison oak, poison ivy" (page 730).

R. aromatica. FRAGRANT SUMAC. Deciduous shrub. Zones 1–3, 10. Native to eastern North America. Fast-growing plant to 3–5 ft. tall, sprawling 5 ft. or wider. Three-leafleted leaves to 3 in. long are fragrant when brushed against or crushed. Foliage turns red in fall. Tiny yellowish flowers in spring; small red fruit. Coarse bank cover, ground cover for poor or dry soils. 'Gro-Low' grows 2–3 ft. high, 6–8 ft. wide.

R. copallina. SHINING SUMAC. Deciduous shrub or tree. Zones 2–9, 14–18. From eastern U.S. To 10–30 ft. tall, spreading indefinitely by suckers. Foot-long leaves are divided featherwise into 9–12 leaflets, each to 4 in. long; turn brilliant red in fall. Greenish, 6-in. flower spikes in summer are followed by clusters of dark red, fuzzy fruits.

R. glabra. SMOOTH SUMAC. Deciduous shrub or tree. Zones 1–10, 14–17. Native to much of North America. Upright grower to 10 ft., sometimes treelike to 20 ft. Spreads widely by suckers; in the wild, forms large patches. Looks much like *R. typhina* and has the same garden uses, but usually grows lower and does not have velvety branches. Leaves divided into 11–23 tooth-edged, rather narrow, 2–5-in.-long leaflets that are deep green above, whitish beneath; foliage turns scarlet in fall. Inconspicuous flowers in early summer are followed by showy clusters of scarlet fruits that remain on bare branches well into winter. Leaves of 'Laciniata' are deeply cut and slashed, giving the plant a fernlike appearance.

R. integrifolia. LEMONADE BERRY. Evergreen shrub. Zones 8, 9, 14–17, 19–24. Native to coastal Southern California, Channel Islands, Baja California. Generally 3–10 ft. high and wide; rarely treelike to 30 ft. Leathery dark green leaves are oval to nearly round, 1–2½ in. long. White or pinkish flowers in dense clusters from midwinter to spring (sometimes from early winter into summer). Clustered small, flattish fruits are reddish and gummy, with tart pulp that can be used to flavor drinks—hence the common name.

Grows best near coast, where established plants need no irrigation. Makes a wonderful ground cover on rocky slopes exposed to salt-laden winds; one plant eventually sprawls over a wide area, even down cliffs. In less windy places, use as a tall screen or background plant. Excellent for espalier against fences and walls. Can be trimmed to make a dense formal hedge and maintained just under a foot wide. Useful in erosion control. Highly susceptible to verticillium wilt.

R. lancea. AFRICAN SUMAC. Evergreen tree. Zones 8, 9, 12–24. Slow grower to 20–30 ft. tall, 20–35 ft. wide. Open, spreading habit; graceful, weeping outer branchlets. Dark green leaves are divided into three willowlike, 4–5-in.-long leaflets. Inconspicuous early spring flowers are followed by clusters of pea-size yellow or red fruit that can make a mess on pavement. This species can be trained to a single trunk or allowed to grow as a multitrunked tree somewhat resembling olive *(Olea).* Makes a good specimen, background plant, screen; can also be clipped into a hedge. Takes desert heat; susceptible to Texas root rot.

R. laurina (Malosma laurina). LAUREL SUMAC. Evergreen shrub. Zones 14–17, 19–24. Native mostly to coastal foothills of Southern California and Baja California. Grows rapidly to 6–15 ft. tall and wide; sometimes almost treelike in form, with a rounded crown. Attractive reddish branches. Pleasantly aromatic light green leaves often have pink margins and pink leafstalks; they are 2–4 in. long, shaped like those of laurel *(Laurus).* Small whitish flowers in dense, branched, 2–6-in.-long clusters in late spring and early summer, sometimes continuing through autumn. Berrylike white fruit. Gets rangy unless pruned; useful as espalier or clipped hedge. Good bank cover where frosts are rare. More tender to frost than *R. ovata* or *R. integrifolia;* sometimes freezes in its native range but comes back quickly from a stump.

R. microphylla. DESERT SUMAC. Deciduous shrub. Zones 10–13. Native to southwestern U.S. and Mexico. Grows to 8 ft. (possibly 15 ft.) tall, 12 ft. wide. Leaves are divided featherwise into five to nine small (less than ½-in.-long) leaflets. Clusters of little white flowers appear in spring before leafout; these are followed in early summer by tiny, hairy orange or red fruit.

R. ovata. SUGAR BUSH. Evergreen shrub. Zones 9–12, 14–24. Native to dry slopes away from coast in Southern California, Baja California; dry slopes in Arizona. Upright or spreading habit. Typically grows 4–10 ft. high and wide, though it can be shorter or taller. Glossy, leathery leaves are 1½–3 in. long, somewhat trough shaped, pointed at tips. Dense clusters of white or pinkish spring flowers are followed by small, reddish, hairy fruit coated with a sugary secretion. Same landscape uses as species *R. integrifolia* but for inland areas rather than seacoast.

R. trilobata. SQUAWBUSH, SKUNKBUSH. Deciduous shrub. Zones 1–12, 14–21. Native from Illinois westward to Texas and California, north to Washington. Similar in most details to *R. aromatica,* but most people find the scent of the bruised leaves unpleasant. Clumping habit makes it a natural low hedge. Brilliant yellow to red fall color.

R. typhina. STAGHORN SUMAC. Deciduous shrub or tree. Zones A1–A3; 1–10, 14–17. Native to eastern North America. Upright to 15 ft. (sometimes 30 ft.) tall, spreading much wider by suckers. Very similar to species *R. glabra,* but the branches have a velvety coat of short brown hairs—much like antlers of a deer "in velvet." Leaves are divided into 11–31 toothed, 5-in.-long leaflets; foliage is deep green above, grayish beneath, turns yellow orange to rich red in fall. Blooms in early summer, bearing 4–8-in.-long clusters of tiny greenish blossoms followed by clusters of fuzzy crimson fruits that hang on all winter, gradually turning brown. 'Laciniata' is a female selection with deeply cut leaflets; it grows 10–12 ft. tall. 'Dissecta' is similar.

Both *R. typhina* and *R. glabra* take extreme heat and cold. Big, divided leaves give tropical effect; fall show is brilliant (for best effect, plant among evergreens). Bare branches make a fine silhouette in winter; fruit is decorative. Both species colonize aggressively by root suckers—a potential problem, especially in small gardens. They grow well when confined to large containers.

R. virens. EVERGREEN SUMAC. Evergreen shrub. Zones 10–13. Native to southeastern Arizona, New Mexico, Texas, Mexico. To 12 ft. tall and wide, with dark green leaves divided featherwise into five to nine 1½-in. leaflets. White spring and summer flowers (not showy) are followed by small, berrylike red fruit. Tolerates open shade, making it a good choice for an understory plant beneath tall trees.

FOR DEFINITIONS OF GARDENING TERMS
PLEASE SEE PAGES 746–750

RHYNCHELYTRUM (Melinis)

NATAL RUBY GRASS

Poaceae (Gramineae)

PERENNIAL GRASSES

ZONES 2B–24; H1, H2; ALL ZONES AS ANNUALS

FULL SUN

REGULAR WATER

Rhynchelytrum nerviglume 'Pink Crystals'

These short-lived African natives are harmless weeds in the tropics. In mild-winter climates of the West, they can reseed themselves, and plants may live over from year to year. In cold regions, treat as annuals; or pot up divisions and protect them during winter. Narrow blue-green leaves are erect, then arching; form clumps 1 ft. high and slightly wider. From these rise 2-ft. flower spikes that open deep pink to purplish red and gradually fade to light pinkish tan.

R. nerviglume. A strain of this species introduced by the Denver Botanic Garden is sold as 'Pink Crystals'. It blooms in late summer and has survived winters in Pueblo, Colorado.

R. repens. Like the above. Blooms in summer or early autumn; flowering may continue throughout mild winters in Southern California.

RHYNCHOSPERMUM. See TRACHELOSPERMUM

RIBBON GRASS. See PHALARIS arundinacea picta

RIBES

CURRANT, GOOSEBERRY

Grossulariaceae (Saxifragaceae)

EVERGREEN AND DECIDUOUS SHRUBS

ZONES VARY BY SPECIES

FULL SUN OR PARTIAL SHADE

WATER NEEDS VARY BY SPECIES

Ribes sanguineum

Those without spines are called currants; those with spines are known as gooseberries. The following species are grown ornamentally; see Currant and Gooseberry for strictly fruiting types. Members of this genus are alternate hosts to white pine blister rust and are still banned in a few areas where white pines grow.

R. alpinum. ALPINE CURRANT. Deciduous shrub. Zones A2, A3; 1–6, 10. Native to Europe. Dense, twiggy growth to 4–5 ft. (rarely taller) and equally wide. Roundish, ½–1½-in.-wide, deep bright green leaves with toothed, lobed edges appear very early in spring. Flowers and fruit are not showy. Good hedge. 'Green Mound' and yellow-leafed 'Aureum' are dwarf forms about half the size of the species. Regular water.

R. aureum. GOLDEN CURRANT. Deciduous shrub. Zones A2, A3, 1–12, 14–23, except as noted. Native to inland regions of the West. Erect growth to 3–6 ft. tall and wide. Light green leaves with lobed, toothed edges. Small, bright yellow spring flowers, usually with a spicy fragrance, in 1–2½-in.-long clusters. Summer berries turn from yellow to red to black. Moderate to regular water. *R. a. gracillimum,* the more tender California form (Zones 6–10, 14–24), has unscented blooms that age to reddish orange.

R. indecorum. WHITE FLOWERING CURRANT. Deciduous shrub. Zones 7–9, 11, 14–24. Native to Coast Ranges in Southern California. To 6–9 ft. tall, 4–6 ft. wide. Thickish, scallop-edged leaves to 1½ in. long; dark green and roughly hairy above, white and fuzzy beneath. Clusters of small white flowers enclosed in pink bracts put on a good show in winter. Needs no irrigation but will tolerate garden watering.

R. malvaceum. CHAPARRAL CURRANT. Deciduous shrub. Zones 6–9, 14–24. Native to slopes in California's Coast Ranges. To 5 ft. tall and wide, with hairy, roundish, dull green, 2-in. leaves and short clusters of fragrant pink flowers throughout fall, winter. Red fruit. Needs no irrigation, but give it moderate water if you don't want it to go dormant in summer.

R. nigrum. BLACK CURRANT. Deciduous shrub. Zones A1–A3; 1–7. Native to Europe, Asia. To 3–5 ft. high and wide. Deep green, three-lobed, 2–4-in. leaves have an odd scent. Drooping clusters of whitish spring flowers develop into juicy, shiny black fruit with a sweet-tart flavor like that of blackberry. Regular water.

R. odoratum. Deciduous shrub. Zones A2, A3; 1–10, 14–17. Similar to *R. aureum* but native to Midwest and High Plains. Spring flowers have fragrance of carnations *(Dianthus)*. Rust-resistant 'Crandall' has large, shiny black fruit with the rich, sweet-tart flavor of *R. nigrum.* Regular water.

R. sanguineum. PINK WINTER CURRANT, RED FLOWERING CURRANT. Deciduous shrub. Zones A3; 4–9, 14–24. Native to Coast Ranges from California to British Columbia. To 5–12 ft. tall and wide, with maplelike, dark green, 2½-in.-wide leaves. In spring, produces drooping, 2–4-in.-long clusters of 10–30 small deep pink to red flowers. Blue-black fruit has a whitish bloom. Most commonly sold is *R. s. glutinosum* (more southerly in origin than the species); its blossoms are typically deep or pale pink, carried in clusters of 15–40. 'Barrie Coate', 'Elk River Red', and 'King Edward VII' are red-flowering selections. Pink varieties include 'Claremont', with two-tone blossoms aging to red, and 'Spring Showers', with 8-in. flower clusters. 'Album', 'Inverness White', and 'White Icicle' are good white varieties. Little to moderate water.

R. speciosum. FUCHSIA-FLOWERING GOOSEBERRY. Nearly evergreen shrub. Zones 7–9, 14–24. Native near coast, from central coast of California south to Baja California. Erect to 4–8 ft. tall, 6–10 ft. wide, with spiny, often bristly stems. Thick-textured, maplelike, 1-in. leaves are glossy dark green above, lighter beneath. Deep crimson to cherry red flowers, borne from winter to spring, are drooping and fuchsialike, with long, protruding stamens. Gummy, bristly red berries. Excellent barrier. Needs no irrigation, but moderate water keeps it nearly evergreen in summer (it can also take regular moisture). Partial shade in hottest climates.

Ribes speciosum

R. viburnifolium. CATALINA PERFUME, EVERGREEN CURRANT. Evergreen shrub. Zones 5, 7–9, 14–17, 19–24. Native to Catalina Island, Baja California. To 3–6 ft. tall, spreading to 12 ft. wide. Wine red stems are arching or half trailing; they may root in moist soil. Roundish, 1-in., leathery dark green leaves are fragrant after rain or when crushed (some liken the scent to pine, others to apples). Light pink to purplish flowers from midwinter into spring. Red berries. To keep plant low, cut out upright-growing stems. Needs partial shade in hottest climates. Needs no irrigation but can take moderate water. Good on banks or under native oaks where watering is undesirable.

RICE PAPER PLANT. See TETRAPANAX papyriferus

RICINUS communis

CASTOR BEAN

Euphorbiaceae

EVERGREEN SHRUB USUALLY GROWN AS ANNUAL

ZONES 1–24; H1, H2

FULL SUN

REGULAR WATER

SEEDS (OR BEANS) ARE POISONOUS IF INGESTED

Ricinus communis 'Dwarf Red Spire'

Bold, striking plant from Africa, Asia. Can provide tall screen or leafy background in a hurry; grows 6–15 ft. tall and half as wide in a single season. Where winters are mild, will live over and become quite woody and treelike. Has naturalized in small areas in many climates. Should not be planted in areas where small children play—the poisonous seeds are attractive. Foliage and seeds occasionally cause severe contact allergies as well. To prevent seed formation, pinch off the burlike seed capsules while they are small. ▶

Large-lobed leaves are 1–3 ft. across on vigorous young plants, smaller on older plants. Unimpressive, small white flowers are borne in clusters on foot-high stalks in summer, followed by attractive prickly husks that contain seeds. Grown commercially for castor oil extracted from seeds. Many horticultural varieties. 'Zanzibarensis' has very large green leaves; 'Dwarf Red Spire' is lower growing (to 6 ft.), with red leaves and seedpods.

ROBINIA

LOCUST

Fabaceae (Leguminosae)

DECIDUOUS TREES AND SHRUBS

ZONES VARY BY SPECIES

FULL SUN

LITTLE OR NO WATER TO MODERATE WATER

BARK, LEAVES, AND SEEDS ARE POISONOUS IF INGESTED

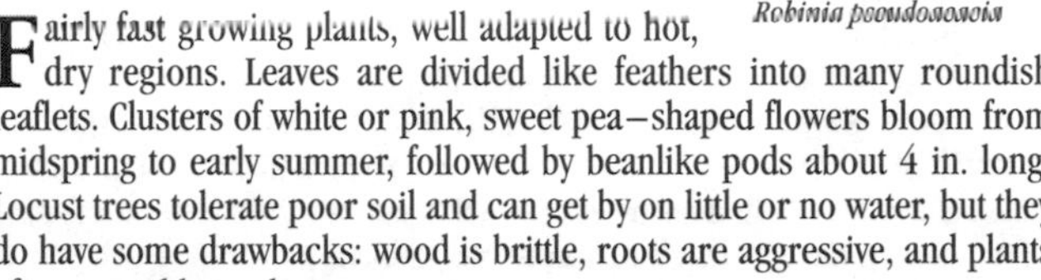

Robinia pseudoacacia

Fairly fast growing plants, well adapted to hot, dry regions. Leaves are divided like feathers into many roundish leaflets. Clusters of white or pink, sweet pea–shaped flowers bloom from midspring to early summer, followed by beanlike pods about 4 in. long. Locust trees tolerate poor soil and can get by on little or no water, but they do have some drawbacks: wood is brittle, roots are aggressive, and plants often spread by suckers.

R. ×ambigua. Tree. Zones 2–24. Hybrid between *R. pseudoacacia* and *R. viscosa,* a seldom-grown pink-flowering locust. The following are the best-known varieties.

'Decaisneana'. To 40–50 ft. tall, 20 ft. wide. Flowers like those of *R. pseudoacacia,* but color is pale pink.

'Idahoensis'. IDAHO LOCUST. Tree of moderately fast growth to a shapely 40 ft. tall, 30 ft. wide. Bright magenta rose flowers in 8-in. clusters; one of showiest of locusts in bloom. Good flowering tree for Rocky Mountain gardens.

'Purple Robe'. Resembles 'Idahoensis' but has darker, purple-pink flowers, reddish bronze new growth; blooms 2 weeks earlier and over a longer period.

R. neomexicana. DESERT LOCUST. Shrub or tree. Zones 2, 3, 7–11, 14, 18–24. Native from California's desert mountains to Arizona, New Mexico. Thorny plant; usually seen as a shrub about 6 ft. high and wide but can become a 30-ft. tree. Drooping, 6-in. clusters of inch-wide pink flowers.

R. pseudoacacia. BLACK LOCUST. Tree. Zones 1–24. Native to eastern and central U.S. Fast growth to 40–75 ft. tall, 30–60 ft. wide, with rather sparse, open branching habit. Deeply furrowed brown bark. Thorny branches. Leaves divided into 7–19 leaflets, each 1–2 in. long. White, fragrant, ½–¾-in.-long flowers are held in dense, pendent clusters 4–8 in. long.

Robinia pseudoacacia

Little valued in its native territory except as a source of honey and fence posts, it has been widely planted (and has subsequently escaped) in much of the western U.S. In California's Gold Country, it has gone native. It manufactures its own fertilizer through nitrogen-fixing root nodule bacteria and can colonize the poorest soil. With some pruning and training in its early years, it can be a truly handsome flowering tree. Has been used as a street tree but is not a good choice for narrow parking strips or under power lines. Wood is extremely hard and tough; suckers are difficult to prune out where soil is not watered. Varieties include the following.

'Frisia'. To 50 ft. tall, 25 ft. wide. New growth is nearly orange; mature leaves are yellow, turning greener in summer heat. Thorns and young wood are red.

'Lace Lady'. Dwarf to 8–10 ft. tall, 12–15 ft. wide. Picturesquely twisted branches; few flowers.

'Pyramidalis' ('Fastigiata'). Narrow, columnar, to 50 ft. tall, 10 ft. wide.

'Tortuosa'. Slow grower to 50 ft. tall, 30 ft. wide, with twisted branches. Few flowers.

'Umbraculifera'. Dense and round headed, to 20 ft. tall and wide. Usually grafted 6–8 ft. high on another locust to create a living green lollipop. Very few flowers.

ROCKCRESS. See ARABIS

ROCKET. See ARUGULA

ROCKROSE. See CISTUS

ROCK SPIRAEA. See HOLODISCUS dumosus

RODGERSIA

Saxifragaceae

PERENNIALS

ZONES 2–9, 14–17

PARTIAL SHADE IN HOTTEST CLIMATES

AMPLE WATER

Rodgersia aesculifolia

Native to China, Japan. Large plants with imposing leaves and clustered tiny flowers in plumes somewhat like those of astilbe; bloom in early to midsummer. Primary feature is handsome foliage, which often takes on bronze tones in late summer. Plants spread by thick rhizomes, need rich soil. The various species hybridize freely. Dormant in winter; provide winter mulch in cold climates. Showy in moist woodland or bog gardens.

R. aesculifolia. To 6 ft. tall, 3 ft. wide. Leaves are divided like fingers of hand into five to seven tooth-edged, 10-in. leaflets; they are similar to those of horsechestnut *(Aesculus).* Shaggy brown hairs on flower stalks, leaf stems, major leaf veins. White flowers.

R. pinnata. To 4 ft. tall, 2½ ft. wide. Leaves have five to nine 8-in. leaflets. Red flowers.

R. podophylla. To 5 ft. tall, 6 ft. wide. Coppery green leaves divided into five 10-in.-long leaflets. Creamy flowers.

R. sambucifolia. To 3 ft. high and wide. Leaves have up to 11 leaflets. Flat-topped clusters of white or pink flowers.

R. tabularis. See Astilboides tabularis

ROMNEYA coulteri

MATILIJA POPPY

Papaveraceae

SHRUBBY PERENNIAL

ZONES 4–12, 14–24; H1

FULL SUN

LITTLE OR NO WATER TO MODERATE WATER

Romneya coulteri

Native from Coast Ranges to coastal valleys of Southern California, Baja California. Spectacular plant to 6–8 ft. or taller, spreading indefinitely by rhizomes. Sends up thick stems clothed in irregularly lobed leaves; stems and foliage are grayish green. Along their upper part, stems bear huge (to 9-in.), slightly scented flowers often likened to giant-size fried eggs: each blossom has five or six crepe-papery petals centered with a cluster of golden stamens. Blooms from late spring into summer, into fall with some watering. Flowers are handsome in arrangements. 'Butterfly' is a profusely branching plant with smaller flowers of rounded, overlapping petals. 'White Cloud' is exceptionally vigorous, with profuse, very large blossoms.

Use on hillsides as soil binder, along roadsides, in marginal areas, in wide borders. Invasive; don't plant near less vigorous plants. Tolerates many soils. Withhold summer irrigation to keep growth in check. Cut nearly to ground in late fall. New shoots emerge after first rains in winter. Although easy to grow once established, the plant is very difficult to propagate. Easiest way to get more plants is to dig up rooted suckers from spreading roots, but you can try taking cuttings from the thickest roots. To make seeds germinate, mix them with potting soil in a foil-lined flat; burn pine needles on top of flat for 30 minutes, then water and hope for sprouting.

ROSA

ROSE

Rosaceae

DECIDUOUS AND EVERGREEN SHRUBS AND VINES

ALL ZONES, EXCEPT AS NOTED

FULL SUN OR LIGHT SHADE

REGULAR WATER, EXCEPT AS NOTED

Grandiflora Rose 'Queen Elizabeth'

The rose is undoubtedly the best-loved flower and most widely planted shrub in the West and all other temperate parts of the world. Although mostly deciduous, roses can be evergreen in mild climates. Centuries of hybridizing have brought us the widest possible range of forms and colors. There are foot-high miniatures, tree-smothering climbers, flowers as tiny as a thumbnail or as large as a salad plate, and all possible variations in between. Red, pink, and white are the traditional colors, but you'll also find flowers in cream, yellow, orange, blends, and bicolors, as well as magenta, purple, lavender, and even tan and brown.

Despite the delicate appearance of their blooms, roses are often quite resilient plants. Growing them is not difficult, provided you choose types suited to your climate, buy healthy plants, locate and plant them properly, and attend to their basic needs—water, nutrients, pest and disease control, and pruning.

CLIMATE

When you're selecting the best roses for your garden, the American Rose Society rating of each plant is one factor to consider. Every year, the ARS rates modern roses (and an increasing number of old roses) on a scale of 1 to 10. The higher the rating, based on a national average of scores, the better the rose. The highest-rated roses are likely to do well in most climates and so are good choices for novice growers. But a rating does not tell the entire story: a rose with a low rating may flourish in certain regions but fail in others. The following tips will help guide your selection.

In cool-summer areas, try to avoid varieties having an unusually great number of petals. Many of these tend to "ball," opening poorly or not at all. Also, in the absence of heat, dark-colored flowers may appear muddy rather than vibrant, while pastel colors are usually clear and attractive. The overcast skies and fog prevalent in many cool-summer areas also encourage foliar diseases—primarily mildew, rust, and black spot. Choose varieties noted for disease resistance; then be sure to plant them in open areas where air circulation is good.

Where summers are hot, roses still grow vigorously, but flowers open rapidly. Varieties with few petals (under 30) may go from bud to flat-open blossom in several hours; those with more petals take longer to open and stay attractive longer. Some colors fade readily, and dark reds may sunburn. To avoid these problems, give roses in hot-summer areas midday or afternoon shade. Avoid planting them where they will receive reflected heat from light-colored walls or fences—especially in southern or western exposures. Best flowering is always in spring and fall (and in winter, in mildest zones); plants approach dormancy during intensely hot weather, so summer flower production may drop markedly.

In cold-winter areas, be especially careful in your choice of varieties, and be prepared to provide winter protection. In Zones 1–3, modern hybrid teas, grandifloras, and floribundas need protection to guarantee survival from year to year (see "Winter protection," page 582). However, the hardy hybrids (bred primarily in Canada and Iowa) can go through winter with little or no special protection. Many old roses (chiefly those that flower only in spring), as well as a number of species and their hybrids, also survive in Zones 1–3 with scant or no winter protection. In Alaska, the only options for rose gardeners are the hardiest species, selections, and hybrids (abundant snow cover, where reliable, can suffice for protection). Hybrid teas and their ilk are usually defeated even in the mildest areas of Zone A3 by damage inflicted by alternating periods of freezing and thawing.

In any region, the best place to see roses suitable for your climate is a municipal or private rose garden. Varieties that are performing well are obviously good choices for you.

BUYING PLANTS

All roses are available as bare-root plants from late fall through early spring. In milder-winter zones, you can plant bare-root roses throughout winter. Where the soil freezes, plant either in fall before ground freezes (then protect plants over winter) or in early spring after soil has thawed.

Most modern roses sold are budded plants: growth eyes of the desired varieties are budded onto understock plants that are carefully selected to promote rapid top growth of the desired roses and to produce root systems capable of thriving in a wide range of soils and climates. However, many old roses, species and their hybrids, and virtually all miniatures are "own-root" plants raised from cuttings. Both budded and own-root roses can grow well and produce fine flowers. Budded plants do offer more uniform root quality and (often) larger size at the time of purchase than own-root plants, but both kinds will be equally husky within a year or two. Own-root roses have one advantage, however: if the plant is killed to the ground by cold (or mowed down by accident), it will regrow from the roots as the rose you want. Regrowth from roots of a budded plant, in contrast, will be the understock rose rather than the desired variety.

Bare-root plants are graded 1, 1½, or 2 according to strict standards. Plants graded 1 and 1½ are the most satisfactory, number 1 being the best. Number 2 plants may take longer to develop into decent bushes than the huskier numbers 1 and 1½. Retail nurseries and mail-order suppliers of modern roses usually offer only number 1 plants, and they will often replace plants that fail to grow. Old roses, shrub roses, and species roses (most commonly available by mail order) may be offered as budded plants that conform to the numbered grading standards, but some growers offer own-root (not budded) plants that may or may not be up to number 1 size. Catalogs usually state what size of plant to expect.

During bare-root planting time, retail nurseries and other stores also may offer a selection of roses with root systems packed in moist material and enclosed in cartons or long, narrow bags. These packaged roses may be a good value, but you should buy them as soon as they appear for sale. Those that are displayed indoors on store shelves may dry out or begin growing prematurely due to the indoor heating. These bargain roses also tend to be mislabeled. ▶

WHAT ROSES NEED

LOCATION: Choose a spot in full sun (light afternoon shade in hottest regions). An open area with good air circulation helps discourage foliage diseases. Don't plant where roots of trees or other shrubs will compete with rose roots.

DRAINAGE: Be sure the soil is reasonably well drained.

WATERING: Regular moisture is essential for good growth and bloom. Mulch soil beneath plants to help conserve moisture.

FERTILIZING: Repeat-flowering roses perform best with repeated feedings throughout the growing season. Once-flowering roses need less fertilizer: feed them once as growth begins, a second time after blooming stops.

PRUNING: All roses will be more productive and attractive with some pruning. Thin out dead, weak, and old growth; reduce plant size according to type of rose and the demands of your climate.

PEST AND DISEASE CONTROL: It may be necessary to thwart various troublemakers (see text), especially if you are growing modern roses.

Shrub Rose 'Sally Holmes' (Miscellaneous Group)

If you wish to plant roses during the growing season, you can buy container-grown plants. These are costlier than bare-root roses, but they let you see unfamiliar varieties before purchase and quickly fill in gaps in your garden. Best time to buy container-grown roses is in mid- to late spring—when plants are fairly well rooted and can be set out before summer heat arrives. For standard bush and climbing roses, look for robust plants growing in large (preferably 5-gal.) containers; this guarantees that root systems were not severely cut back to fit the container. Also try to buy only roses planted in containers toward the end of the most recent dormant season; they generally will be in better condition than plants that have been in containers for a year or more. Avoid plants showing considerable dead or twiggy growth. Miniature roses usually are sold in containers that range from 4-in. pots to 2-gal. cans. Healthy new growth and foliage are signs of a good miniature plant, regardless of container size.

The presence of a plant patent number on a variety's name tag is no assurance of quality. It simply means that for that variety's first 17 years in commerce, the patent holder receives a royalty on each plant sold. Many fine roses that bear no patent number on name tags once were patented but have been in commerce for longer than the 17-year patent life span.

LOCATION AND PLANTING

Hybrid Tea Rose 'Mister Lincoln'

For best results, plant roses where they will receive full sun all day (exceptions are noted under "Climate," page 579). Avoid planting where roots of trees or shrubs will steal water and nutrients intended for roses. To lessen any problem with foliage diseases, plant roses where air circulates freely (but not in the path of regular, strong winds). Generous spacing between plants will also aid air circulation. How far apart to plant depends on the growth habit of the roses and the climate. The colder the winter and the shorter the growing season, the smaller the bushes will be; where the growing season is long and winters are mild, bushes can attain greater size. But some varieties are naturally small, others tall and massive—and those relative size differences will hold in any climate. In the coldest zones, you might plant the most vigorous sorts 3 ft. apart, whereas the same varieties could require 6-ft. spacing in milder climates.

Soil for roses should drain reasonably well; if it does not, the best alternative is to plant in raised beds. Dig soil deeply, incorporating organic matter such as ground bark, peat moss, or compost to help aerate dense clay soils and improve moisture retention in sandy soils. Add a complete fertilizer to soil and dig supplemental phosphorus and potassium into planting holes; this puts nutrients at the level where roots can use them.

Healthy, ready-to-plant bare-root roses should have plump, fresh-looking canes (branches) and roots. Plants that have dried out slightly can be revived by burying them, tops and all, for a few days in moist soil, sand, or sawdust. Before planting any bare-root rose, immerse the entire plant in water for several hours to be certain all canes and roots are plumped up. Plant according to directions for bare-root planting (see page 692), making sure that holes are large enough to let you spread out roots without bending them or cutting them back. Just before planting, cut back broken canes and broken roots. In all but Zones 1–3, set plant in hole so that bud union ("knob" from which canes grow) is just above soil level. In Zones 1–3, some growers set bud union 1–2 in. beneath soil surface for increased cold protection; but because higher planting encourages greater cane production, many growers in coldest zones plant high and pay special attention to winter protection. Water newly planted rose well, then mound soil, damp peat moss, ground bark, or sawdust over bud union and around canes to conserve moisture. Gradually (and carefully) remove soil or other material when leaves begin to expand.

If you plan to plant new roses in ground where existing bushes have been growing for 5 or more years, dig generous planting holes (at least 1½ ft. wide, 1½ ft. deep), and replace old soil with fresh soil from another part of the garden. A condition known as specific replant disease inhibits growth of new roses planted directly in soil of established rose gardens.

ROUTINE CARE

All roses require water, nutrients, pruning, and, at some point, pest and disease control. (Exceptions are some antique and species roses that thrive on little water once established.)

Water. For best performance, the most popular garden roses need watering at all times during the growing season. Inadequate water slows or halts growth and bloom. Water deeply enough to moisten the entire root system. How often to water depends on soil type and weather. Big, well-established plants need more water than newly set plants, but you will need to water new plants more frequently to get them established.

Basin flooding is a simple way to water individual rose plants. If you have a drip irrigation system, you will be able to water many plants at one time. Overhead sprinkling helps remove dust and freshen foliage and provides partial control for aphids and spider mites; on the minus side, it washes off spray residues, may leave mineral deposits on foliage if water is hard, and (in some areas) may encourage foliage diseases. If you sprinkle, do it early in the day to be sure foliage dries off during the daytime. Even if you irrigate in basins, give plants an occasional sprinkling to clean dust off foliage (if rain doesn't do it for you).

A 2–3-in.-thick layer of mulch around the bushes conserves moisture, prevents soil surface from baking hard, deters weed growth, and contributes to healthy soil structure (well aerated, permeable by water and roots). It also helps keep soil cool—a benefit in all but the coolest-summer climates.

Nutrients. Though roses are reputed to be gross feeders, needs vary depending on the particular rose and your soil's natural fertility. Many old roses, shrub roses, and species do not need regular fertilizer if growth is satisfactory. But for many repeat-flowering modern roses, regular fertilizing produces the most gratifying results. In the mildest-winter climates (Zones 8, 9, 12–24, H1, H2), begin feeding established plants with a complete fertilizer in February. Elsewhere, give first feeding just as growth begins. Thereafter, time fertilizer applications according to bloom periods. For roses that flower repeatedly throughout the growing season, the ideal time to fertilize is after each blooming cycle has ended and new growth is just beginning for the next round of flowers. For roses that bloom only in spring, one additional feeding just after flowering ends will encourage vigorous new growth that will bear the next year's flowers. Where winters are cold, stop feeding in late summer or fall, at least 6 weeks before the first expected hard frost. In mild-winter zones experiencing virtually no subfreezing weather, you may continue fertilizing until mid-October for a crop of late-fall flowers.

Dry fertilizer, applied to soil, is most frequently used. A variation on this type is controlled-release fertilizer; follow directions on package for amount and frequency of applications. Liquid fertilizers are useful in smaller gardens utilizing basin watering. Most liquids can also be sprayed on rose leaves, which absorb some nutrients immediately.

Pest and disease control. At some point, you may need to combat certain pests and diseases. Not all the problems mentioned here are certain to strike your roses; these are just the ones to watch for and correct if necessary. Most of these pests and diseases can affect other plants as well; for controls, see "Diseases" (page 664) and "Pests and Pest Management" (page 679). For afflictions specific to roses, controls are suggested below.

The principal rose pests are aphids, spider mites, thrips, and (in some areas) rose midges. Thrips attack petals, ruining flower appearance; the other pests target leaves and stems, stunting or distorting growth.

Aphids feed on new growth; they are more troublesome in early spring and tend to disappear on their own as weather warms. Natural predators can keep these pests in check; various nontoxic sprays can control large populations. Spider mites are hot-weather pests capable of defoliating and weakening plants (especially those that are already debilitated). Controls range from blasting foliage with water to spraying with products specifically targeting spider mites. Thrips do their damage inside flower buds, so contact insecticides can't reach them. You may have some success with insecticidal soaps or horticultural oil, but systemic insecticides typically offer the best control. Adult rose midges are microscopic flying insects so small they are nearly invisible. They lay eggs on rose leaves; when the larvae hatch out, they rasp tender new growth and developing buds, causing them to blacken and shrivel. The larvae then fall to the ground and pupate. This is the best time to attempt control, typically with a soil drench; contact a good local nursery for advice on the best product for the job. New generations appear at roughly 2-week intervals, so repeated applications may be needed for control.

Shrub Rose 'Bonica' (Miscellaneous Group)

Powdery mildew, rust, and black spot are the most widespread and serious foliar diseases of roses; anthracnose and downy mildew can be serious but are less common. If unchecked, infections can weaken plants, especially if defoliation occurs from rust or black spot. Your first line of defense against all diseases is a thorough garden cleanup during the dormant season; rake up and discard all dead leaves and other debris (this is simplest right after you have pruned plants). Then, before new growth begins, spray both plants and soil with dormant-season horticultural oil or lime sulfur (calcium polysulfide). This treatment will destroy many disease organisms (as well as insect eggs) that might live over winter to reinfect plants in spring. During the growing season, apply controls for diseases known to be prevalent in your area.

Black spot and anthracnose are similar in appearance: gray to dark brown or black blotches appear on the leaves and stems. In anthracnose infection, the patches are irregularly shaped; in black spot, they are roughly circular, fringed at the margins, and often encircled in yellow. Anthracnose is primarily a problem in cool, moist spring weather; it vanishes in warmer, dry conditions. Black spot may begin in spring but it is most troublesome in warm summer weather when there is humidity or rainfall to sustain and spread it. If unchecked, both diseases can severely weaken a plant by defoliation and cane dieback. For a nontoxic control, apply a spray made from 2 tsp. baking soda and 2 tsp. fine-grade horticultural oil dissolved in 1 gal. water. Effective chemical controls are sprays containing chlorothalonil or triforine.

Downy mildew begins in the upper reaches of a plant after leaves have fully formed, appearing in moist weather when temperatures are below 80°F/27°C. Foliage shows irregular, purplish blotches, then turns yellow (sometimes with patches of green remaining) and falls off. On stems, the fungus shows as purplish mottling; if not treated, infected stems are likely to die. To combat downy mildew during the growing season, spray infected plants with a fungicide containing zinc or manganese. Where the disease has appeared, use a dormant spray containing zinc or copper after winter pruning and garden cleanup.

Chlorosis—evidenced by leaves turning light green to yellow while veins remain dark green—is not a disease but a symptom, usually of iron deficiency. It can be a major problem in Zones 12 and 13. Iron chelates correct chlorosis most quickly; iron sulfate also is effective but slower to act.

Leaves that show irregular yellow or cream patterning indicate the presence of a mosaic virus. Some plants show symptoms consistently, others just occasionally. Although plants may appear to grow with vigor, the virus does impair overall strength and productivity, and it can make foliage unsightly. Fortunately, it is not transferred from plant to plant by insects or by pruning; it is transmitted in propagation—from infected rootstock or budwood. Commercial rose producers are diligently working to eliminate virus-infected stock. If you have an infected plant that is growing poorly or is unattractive, remove it from the garden.

Pruning. Annual pruning contributes to the health, productivity, and longevity of your roses. The basic objective is to promote strong growth that will bear good flowers. With large-flowered roses, some growers equate flower quality with size; with smaller-flowered and landscape roses, quantity of bloom is more often the goal. In either case, some pruning is beneficial. If left unpruned, a rose can expend its energy in much spindly, twiggy growth that produces only substandard flowers. Thinning out such unproductive growth directs the plant's resources into stronger canes and stems—thus producing a larger, huskier plant with better floral display (the bigger the plant, the more flowers it can produce).

Because nutrients are stored in woody canes, a larger plant is a stronger plant. Prune conservatively: never chop down a vigorous 6-ft. bush to 1½-ft. stubs unless you want only a few huge blooms for exhibition. (Exception: in Zones 1–3, where plant freezes back to its winter protection, you will remove dead wood in spring and may be left with the equivalent of a severely pruned plant.)

The best pruning time for most roses is at the end of the dormant season, when growth buds begin to swell. Exact time will vary according to locality. Where late frosts are common, be sure you don't prune too early—the new growth produced will be vulnerable to freezes.

General pruning guidelines. The following pruning practices apply to all roses except certain shrub and species roses. Special instructions for pruning those roses are included later in this section.

Use sharp pruning shears; make all cuts as shown in "Pruning Cuts" (page 704). Remove wood that is obviously dead and wood that has no healthy growth coming from it, branches that cross through the plant's center and any that rub against larger canes, branches that make bush appear lopsided, and any old and unproductive canes that strong new ones have replaced during past season. Cut back growth produced during previous year, making cuts above outward-facing buds (except for very spreading varieties: some cuts to inside buds will promote more height without producing many crossing branches). As a general rule, remove from one-third to no more than one-half the length of previous season's growth (except in Zones 1–3, as noted above). Ideal result is a V-shaped bush with a relatively open center.

If any suckers (growth produced from understock) are present, completely remove them. Dig down to where suckers grow from understock and pull them off with a downward motion; that removes growth buds that would have produced additional suckers in subsequent years. Let the wound air-dry before you replace soil around it.

Be certain you are removing a sucker rather than a new cane growing from the bud union of the budded variety. Usually you can note a distinct difference in foliage size, shape, and color and in size of thorns on sucker growth. If in doubt, let the presumed sucker grow until you can establish its difference from cane. A sucker's flowers will be different; a flowerless, climbing cane from a bush rose is almost certainly a sucker.

Consider cutting flowers as a form of pruning. Cut off enough stem to support flower in vase, but don't deprive plant of too much foliage; leave a stem with at least two sets of five-leaflet leaves. Prune to an outward-growing bud or to a five-leaflet leaf.

The most widely planted modern roses—hybrid teas and grandifloras—can be pruned successfully according to these guidelines. A few additional tips apply to these other popular types.

Floribunda, polyantha, and many shrub roses. These are grown for amount of bloom rather than quality of individual flowers. Cut back previous season's growth only by one-fourth, and leave as many strong new canes and stems as the plant produced. Most produce more canes per bush than do hybrid teas and grandifloras. If you have a hedge of one variety, cut back all plants to uniform height.

Modern Climbing Rose 'Golden Showers'

Climbing roses. For pruning purposes, climbers fall into two groups: those that bloom in spring only (including a large category known as natural climbers, discussed in "Modern climbing roses," page 583) and those that bloom off and on in other seasons as well as in spring (including climbing sports of hybrid tea roses). All climbers should be left unpruned for the first 2 or 3 years after planting; remove only dead, weak, and twiggy wood, allowing plants to get established and produce their long, flexible canes. Most bloom comes from lateral branches that grow from long canes, and most of those flowering branches develop when long canes are spread out horizontally (as along a fence). Types that bloom only in spring produce strong new growth after they flower, and that new growth bears flowers the following spring. Prune these climbers just after they bloom, removing oldest canes that show

R

no signs of strong new growth. Repeat-flowering climbers (many are climbing sports of bush varieties) are pruned at the same time you'd prune bush roses in your locality. Remove oldest, unproductive canes and any weak, twiggy growth; cut back lateral branches on remaining canes to within two or three buds from main canes.

Pillar roses. Not quite bush or climber, these produce tall, somewhat flexible canes that bloom profusely without having to be trained horizontally. Prune them according to general guidelines for bush roses.

Miniature Rose 'Starina'

Standards. Often called tree roses, standards are an artificial creation: a bush rose budded onto a 2–3-ft.-high understock stem. Be sure to stake trunk securely to keep it from breaking under the weight of the bush it supports. A ½-in. metal pipe makes a good permanent stake; use a tie between stake and trunk to hold them securely. General pruning guidelines apply, with particular attention to maintaining a symmetrical plant.

Miniature roses. Prune these back to at least half the height they attained during the previous year; remove all weak and twiggy stems.

Winter protection. Where winter temperatures regularly drop to 10°F/−12°C or lower, some cold protection is needed for almost all modern roses. Low temperatures can kill exposed canes; repeated freezing and thawing will kill canes by rupturing cells; and winter winds can fatally desiccate exposed canes because plants are unable to draw moisture from frozen soil to replace that lost through transpiration.

A healthy plant that is hardened off before the first hard frost withstands harsh winters better than a weak or actively growing one. Prepare plants for winter by timing your last fertilizer application of the growing season so that bushes will have ceased putting on new growth by expected date of first sharp frost. Leave the last crop of blooms on plants to form hips (fruits), which will aid the ripening process by stopping growth. Keep plants well watered until soil freezes.

After a couple of hard freezes have occurred and nighttime temperatures remain consistently below freezing, mound soil over base of each bush to a height of 1 ft. Collect soil from another part of garden; do not scoop soil from around roses, exposing their surface roots. Cut excessively long canes back to 2–4 ft. (the lower figure applies in Zones 1, 2, and 3a); then, with soft twine, tie canes together to keep them from whipping around in wind. When the mound has frozen, cover it with evergreen boughs, straw, or other fairly lightweight material that will act as insulation to keep the mound frozen. Your objective is to prevent alternate freezing and thawing of mound (and canes it covers), maintaining plant at a constant temperature of 15 to 20°F/−9 to −7°C. A 3–4-ft.-high wire-mesh cylinder filled with noncompacting insulating material (such as straw, hay, oak leaves, or pine needles) may preserve much of the cane growth it encloses.

Remove protection in spring after frost danger is past. Gradually remove soil mounds as they thaw, working carefully to avoid breaking new growth that may have begun sprouting under the soil.

Mound climbing roses in the same manner, but be sure to protect all of their canes. Where winter lows range from −10 to 5°F/−23 to −15°C, wrap canes in burlap stuffed with straw or similar material for insulation. Where temperatures normally go below −10°F/−23°C, remove canes from their support, gently bend them to ground, secure them in that position, and cover with soil. A wiser plan, however, is to plant only climbers known to be hardy in such climates.

Standards (tree roses) may be insulated in the same manner as climbers, but they still may not survive, since the head of the tree is the most exposed. Some rosarians wrap the entire plant with straw and burlap, then construct a plywood box to cover it. Others dig their standards each year, pack the roots loosely in soil or other medium, and store plants in a cool garage, basement, or shed until replanting time in spring. A simpler technique is to grow standards in large containers and move them in fall to a cool shed or garage where temperatures won't drop below 10°F/−12°C.

TYPES OF ROSES

Interest in old and species roses, continued development of large-flowered modern types, and breeding programs geared toward producing landscape shrubs have greatly expanded the number of roses available to the public. The listings below cover six broad categories: modern large-flowered roses, modern climbing roses, miniature roses, modern landscape roses, old roses, and species and species hybrids. In the modern rose categories, the letters AARS indicate All-America Rose Selection varieties—roses that received top scores after several years of testing in nationwide test gardens. Varieties with an asterisk (*) preceding their name have been rated 8.0 or higher by the American Rose Society.

Modern large-flowered roses. Here are the large-blossomed, long-stemmed hybrid teas and grandifloras that dominate the rose market.

Hybrid teas. This, the most popular class of rose, outsells all other types combined. Flowers are large and shapely, generally produced one to a stem on plants that range from 2 ft. to 6 ft. or more, depending on the variety and climate. Many thousands of varieties have been produced since the first rose in the class, 'La France', appeared in 1867; hundreds are cataloged, and new ones appear each year. The most popular choices in each of seven color groups are listed below.

Red. 'Chrysler Imperial' (AARS), 'Ingrid Bergman', *'Mister Lincoln' (AARS), 'Oklahoma', *'Olympiad' (AARS), 'Opening Night' (AARS).

Pink. 'Bewitched' (AARS), 'Brigadoon' (AARS), *'Color Magic' (AARS), *'Dainty Bess' (single), *'First Prize' (AARS), 'Gemini' (AARS), *'Miss All-American Beauty' (AARS), 'Perfume Delight' (AARS), *'Royal Highness' (AARS), 'Secret' (AARS), 'Sheer Bliss' (AARS), *'Tiffany' (AARS), 'Timeless' (AARS), *'Touch of Class' (AARS), 'Tournament of Roses' (AARS).

Multicolors, blends. 'Chicago Peace', *'Double Delight' (AARS), 'Just Joey', 'Medallion' (AARS), 'Perfect Moment' (AARS), 'Rio Samba' (AARS), 'Seashell' (AARS), 'Sunset Celebration' (AARS), 'Voodoo' (AARS).

Orange, orange tones. 'Artistry' (AARS), 'Brandy' (AARS), *'Folklore', *'Fragrant Cloud', 'Tropicana' (AARS).

Yellow. 'Golden Masterpiece', 'Midas Touch' (AARS), 'Oregold' (AARS), *'Peace' (AARS), 'Saint Patrick'.

Hybrid Tea Rose 'Double Delight'

Grandiflora Rose 'Gold Medal'

Modern Climbing Rose 'New Dawn'

Miniature Rose 'Little Artist'

White. *'Garden Party' (AARS), 'Honor' (AARS), 'John F. Kennedy', *'Pascali' (AARS), *'Pristine'.

Lavender. 'Blue Girl', *'Paradise' (AARS), 'Stainless Steel'.

Grandifloras. Vigorous plants, sometimes 8–10 ft. tall, with hybrid tea–type flowers borne singly or in long-stemmed clusters. Some are derived from crosses between hybrid teas and floribundas; others are just extra-vigorous, cluster-flowering segregates from ordinary hybrid tea ancestry. They're good for mass color effect, for number of cuttable flowers produced per plant, and as background or barrier plants.

Red. 'Crimson Bouquet' (AARS), 'Love' (AARS).

Pink, blends. *'Earth Song', *'Fame!' (AARS), *'Pink Parfait' (AARS), *'Queen Elizabeth' (AARS), *'Sonia', *'Tournament of Roses' (AARS).

Orange, blends. 'Arizona' (AARS), 'Candelabra' (AARS), 'Caribbean' (AARS), 'Glowing Peace' (AARS).

Yellow. *'Gold Medal'.

White. 'White Lightnin'' (AARS).

Lavender. 'Lagerfeld'.

Modern climbing roses. These fall into two general categories. One group includes natural climbers (large flowered, except for miniatures); the other comprises climbing sports of bush roses (hybrid teas, grandifloras, floribundas, polyanthas, miniatures).

Here are popular varieties of natural climbers:

Red. *'Altissimo' (single), 'Blaze', *'Don Juan', *'Dublin Bay', 'Fourth of July' (AARS).

Pink. *'Eden' ('Pierre de Ronsard'), *'Jeanne Lajoie' (miniature), 'New Dawn'.

Orange, blends. *'America' (AARS), *'Handel', 'Joseph's Coat', *'Polka', *'Royal Sunset'.

Yellow. 'Golden Showers' (AARS), 'Royal Gold'.

White. 'Lace Cascade', 'White Dawn'.

Here are popular varieties of climbing sports:

Red. *'Cl. Earthquake' (miniature), *'Cl. Etoile de Hollande'.

Pink. 'Cl. Cécile Brunner' (polyantha), 'Cl. First Prize', and 'Cl. Queen Elizabeth'.

Orange, blends. 'Cl. Mrs. Sam McGredy', 'Cl. Peace', 'Cl. Rainbow's End'.

White. *'Cl. Iceberg'.

Miniature roses. These are perfect replicas of modern hybrid teas and floribundas, but plant size is reduced to 1–1½ ft. (grown in the ground), with flowers and foliage in proportion. Derived in part from *R. chinensis minima* (presumably through its forms 'Rouletii' and 'Pompon de Paris'), these are everblooming plants with flowers in all modern hybrid-tea colors. Grow them outdoors in containers, in window boxes, in rock gardens, as border and bedding plants. Or grow indoors: pot in rich soil in 6-in. (or larger) containers and locate in a cool, bright window. Miniatures are hardier than hybrid teas but still need winter protection in Zones 1–3. They are shallow rooted and need regular water and fertilizer; be sure to mulch outdoor plants. Nearly all are own-root, cutting-grown plants.

Many new miniatures appear on the market each year. Among the best are these, all rated 8.5 or higher.

Red, orange. 'Peggy "T"', 'Robin Red Breast', 'Starina'.

Pink. 'Baby Grand', 'Giggles', 'Millie Walters', 'Pierrine'.

Blends. 'Jean Kenneally', 'Little Artist', 'Magic Carrousel', 'Minnie Pearl', 'Party Girl', 'Rainbow's End'.

Yellow. 'My Sunshine', 'Rise 'n' Shine', 'Sunshine Girl', 'Sun Sprinkles' (AARS).

White. 'Gourmet Popcorn', 'Irresistible', 'Simplex', 'Snowbride', 'Whiteout'.

Lavender, purple. 'Ruby Pendant'.

Modern landscape roses. This large and extremely varied group includes all the roses you plant for mass floral effect rather than perfection of individual blooms. Discussed here are the first of the "modern" mass-effect roses, the polyanthas, followed by their descendants, the floribundas, and then the rapidly enlarging group of shrub roses.

Polyanthas. Original members of this class appeared in the late 19th century, the result of crosses involving *R. multiflora.* Small flowers (under 2 in. across) come in large sprays; plants are vigorous, usually low growing, nearly everblooming, and quite disease resistant. 'Margo Koster' has coral orange, very double flowers that resemble ranunculus; it has sported to produce color variants in white, pink, orange scarlet, and red. 'The Fairy' produces huge clusters of small light pink flowers on a plant that can reach 4 ft. high. 'China Doll' is a knee-high plant with larger, deeper pink flowers in smaller clusters. With light pruning, two 19th-century classics make sizable bushes that resemble bushy Noisettes (see page 585). 'Cécile Brunner' (often called Sweetheart Rose) has light pink flowers of perfect hybrid tea form; 'Perle d'Or' (sometimes called Yellow Cécile Brunner) is similar but has apricot orange flowers.

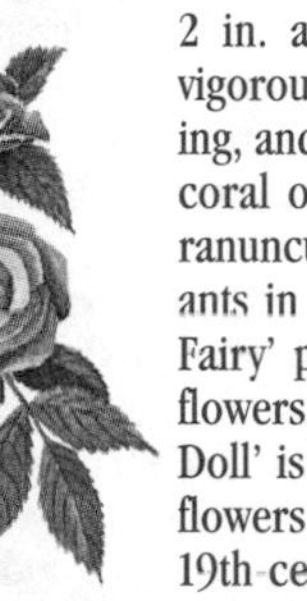
Polyantha Rose 'Margo Koster'

Floribundas. Originally developed from hybrid teas and polyanthas, these are noted for producing quantities of flowers in clusters on vigorous and bushy plants. Plant and flower sizes are smaller than those of most hybrid teas. Some have flowers of elegant hybrid tea shape; others are more informal. These are plants for providing mass color. Use for informal hedges, for low borders and barriers, as container plants.

Red. *'Europeana' (AARS), 'Scentimental' (AARS), *'Showbiz' (AARS).

Pink. *'Betty Prior', *'Sexy Rexy', 'Simplicity'.

Orange, blends. 'Amber Queen' (AARS), 'Betty Boop' (AARS), 'Brass Band' (AARS), 'Gingersnap', 'Livin' Easy' (AARS), 'Marmalade Skies' (AARS), *'Playboy', 'Singin' in the Rain' (AARS).

Yellow. *'Sun Flare' (AARS), *'Sunsprite'.

White. 'French Lace' (AARS), *'Iceberg', *'Margaret Merrill'.

Lavender. *'Angel Face' (AARS), 'Intrigue' (AARS).

Shrub roses. Planting roses for general landscape use is not a new idea; some fine shrub roses date to the early 20th century. Today, however, rose breeders are developing new roses for use purely as flowering shrubs. Many of these are promoted under trademarked group names—the David Austin English roses, for example. In all these roses, both new and older

Polyantha Rose 'Cécile Brunner'

Floribunda Rose 'Iceberg'

Floribunda Rose 'Angel Face'

Shrub Rose 'Ballerina' (Miscellaneous Group)

R

kinds, the emphasis is on plants that bear attractive floral displays (even good-looking individual blossoms) and disease-resistant foliage; some breeders are also developing plants that can survive cold winters with no special attention. Many shrub roses are sold by mail order, and ever more of them are appearing in retail nurseries. Because these roses are highly diverse and numerous, always read descriptions or see actual plants to be sure of choosing individuals that suit you. Here is an overview of available shrub roses, grouped into loosely cohesive categories.

Hybrid musk roses. These were developed in the first 30 years of the 20th century from the multiflora rambler 'Trier', a distant descendant of the musk rose *(R. moschata)* through the Noisettes. Hybrid musks are large (6–8-ft.) shrubs or small climbers that perform well in dappled or partial shade as well as in sun. Most are nearly everblooming, with fragrant, clustered flowers in white, yellow, buff, pink shades, or red. Popular varieties include 'Buff Beauty', buff apricot; 'Cornelia', coral; 'Felicia', pink; 'Kathleen', single pink (like apple blossoms); 'Penelope', salmon; 'Will Scarlet', red.

Hardy roses. Canadian and Midwestern breeding programs have produced many varieties that survive northern and Rocky Mountain winters with virtually no special protection. Some resemble floribundas and grandifloras; ancestries include hardy species plus floribundas and modern hybrid teas. Many of these feature "country" names: 'Country Dancer', 'Hawkeye Belle', 'Maytime', 'Prairie Princess'. Others are mostly larger shrubs to small climbers, derived in part from *R. rugosa;* most are cluster flowered, like large floribundas. Many are named for explorers: 'Alexander Mackenzie', 'Henry Kelsey', 'John Cabot', 'William Baffin'.

Trademark-group roses. Recognizing public loyalty to brand-name products, some rose breeders have taken to fashioning trademark-name "families" to which new varieties can be added over time. The David Austin English roses were the first in this category to make a significant splash. Developed from crosses of various old roses (albas, centifolias, gallicas) with modern roses, they capture the forms and fragrances of old roses in repeat-flowering plants that offer the color range of modern hybrid teas. The group is a varied one, ranging from low shrubs to plants determined to be climbers regardless of pruning; well over 80 such roses are in commerce, with additional varieties expected. Many have names derived from the works of Chaucer and Shakespeare, though three of the most popular—peach-and-orange 'Abraham Darby', yellow 'Graham Thomas', and pink 'Mary Rose'—commemorate, respectively, an English industrialist, a noted English horticulturist, and the flagship of Henry VIII's fleet.

In France, the house of Meilland is releasing the Romantica roses, most of which are named for well-known figures in European arts and letters; the color range is contemporary, but the full-petaled flowers hark back to early hybrid teas and hybrid perpetuals. Another French firm, Guillot (famous for originating the first hybrid tea rose), offers Generosa roses; these are more nearly equivalent to the English roses in variability and old-rose style. The Renaissance roses, developed by the Danish house of Poulsen, are akin to especially healthy floribundas, with an emphasis on vigor, disease resistance, abundance of bloom, and modern flower form.

Ground cover roses. A number of European and American breeders are producing roses that spread their canes widely but build up to no more than 2 ft. high—perfect for covering slopes, forming traffic-proof covers on level ground, and growing in containers. Vigor, disease resistance, and profusion of bloom are the hallmarks of these roses. Examples are 'Essex' (medium pink), 'Flower Carpet' (the original deep pink selection as well as its color variants), 'Nozomi' (white), 'Pink Bells', 'Rosy Carpet' (dark pink).

Miscellaneous shrub roses. Many modern shrub roses of complex (or unknown) ancestry can't be pigeonholed according to species affiliation or specific characteristics. This is truly an "odd-lot" group in size and habit, though most are 3 ft. or more in height, with flowers in small to large clusters. Included are 'Alchymist' (virtually a large-flowered climber, with blossoms in a blend of gold, pink, and apricot), 'Ballerina' (white-centered pink blooms, a hybrid musk but looks like a giant polyantha), 'Erfurt' (pink-edged cream), 'Pearl Drift' (ivory pink), the shrub or small climber 'Sally Holmes' (pinkish ivory), and 'Sea Foam' (white). AARS winners include 'All That Jazz' (coral salmon), 'Bonica' (pure pink), 'Carefree Delight' (white-centered pink), 'Carefree Wonder' (deep pink with cream petal backs), 'First Light' (rose pink), and 'Knock Out' (red); variable 'Kaleidoscope' combines pink, mauve, tan, and yellow, the color depending on the weather. Here also fit the trademarked Meidiland family of roses (including 'Pink Meidiland', 'Red Meidiland', 'Ruby Meidiland', 'White Meidiland'), most of which are somewhat billowy shrubs. So-called patio roses (smaller than floribundas, larger than miniatures) are bushy, profuse-flowering plants usually no taller than 2 ft., such as 'Amorette' and 'Hakuun' (both white) and yellow 'Minilights' and 'Yellow Jacket'.

Old roses. Among rosarians, the dividing line between old and modern roses is 1867—the year that the first hybrid tea was introduced. Old roses are varieties belonging to the rose classes that existed prior to 1867 (though some varieties in these classes were introduced as late as the early 20th century).

Old roses may be divided into two categories. The old European roses comprise the albas, centifolias, damasks, gallicas, and moss roses—the oldest hybrid groups derived from species native to Europe and western Asia. Most flower only in spring; many are hardy in the coldest climates with little or no winter protection. The second group contains classes derived entirely or in part from Asian roses: Chinas, Bourbons, damask perpetuals, hybrid perpetuals, Noisettes, and teas. Original China and tea roses were brought to Europe from eastern Asia; 19th-century hybridizers greatly increased their numbers and also developed the other classes from crosses with European roses. Repeat flowering is a characteristic of these classes; hardiness varies, but nearly all need winter protection in the coldest zones.

Alba roses. Developed from *R. alba,* the White Rose of York, and associated with England's Wars of the Roses. Spring flowers are single to very double, white to delicate pink. These upright plants are vigorous and long lived, with green wood and handsome, disease-resistant gray-green foliage. Varieties include white 'Alba Semiplena' and these in pink: 'Celestial', 'Félicité Parmentier', 'Great Maiden's Blush', 'Königin von Dänemark'.

Centifolia roses. The roses often portrayed by Dutch painters; developed from *R. centifolia,* the cabbage rose. Plants are open growing, with prickly stems that can reach 6 ft. but arch with weight of blossoms. Intensely fragrant spring flowers typically are packed with petals, often with large outer

Alba Rose 'Alba Semiplena'

Rosa centifolia

Gallica Rose 'Rosa Mundi'

Moss Rose 'Mme Louis Lévêque'

petals that cradle a multitude of smaller petals within. Colors include white, pink shades. 'Rose des Peintres' is a typical rich pink cabbage rose; 'Paul Ricault' produces silken deep pink flowers on an upright plant; 'Tour de Malakoff' is a tall, rangy plant with peonylike blossoms of pink fading to grayish mauve. Dwarf varieties (3 ft. or less) are 'Petite de Hollande', 'Pompon de Bourgogne', and 'Rose de Meaux'.

Damask roses. Originating with *R. damascena.* Plants reach 6 ft. or more, typically with long, arching, thorny canes and light or grayish green, downy leaves. The summer damasks flower only in spring; forms of these are cultivated to make attar of roses (used in the perfume industry). Varieties include 'Celsiana', blush pink; 'Leda', white with crimson markings; 'Mme Hardy', white; and 'Versicolor' ('York and Lancaster'), with petals that may be pink, white, or a blend of pink and white. The autumn damask rose, *R. d.* 'Semperflorens' *(R. d. bifera),* flowers more than once in a year; slender buds open to loosely double pure pink blossoms. This is the Rose of Castile of the Spanish missions.

Gallica roses. Cultivated forms of *R. gallica,* the French Rose. Fragrant spring flowers run from pink through red to maroon and purple shades. Plants reach 3–4 ft. tall, with upright to arching canes bearing prickles but few thorns and dark green, often rough-textured leaves. Grown on their own roots, these plants will spread into clumps from creeping rootstocks. Historic 'Officinalis', known as the Apothecary Rose, is presumed to be the Red Rose of Lancaster from the Wars of the Roses; flowers are semidouble, cherry red, on a dense, medium-height plant. Its sport, 'Versicolor'—generally known as 'Rosa Mundi'—has pink petals boldly striped and stippled red. Other gallicas include 'Belle de Crécy', pink aging to violet; 'Cardinal de Richelieu', slate purple; 'Charles de Mills', crimson to purple; and 'Tuscany', dark crimson with gold stamens.

Moss roses. Two old rose classes—centifolia and damask—include variant types that feature mosslike, balsam-scented glands that cover unopened buds, flower stems, sometimes even leaflets. The "moss" of centifolias is soft to the touch; that of damasks is more prickly. Flowers are white, pink, or red, often intensely fragrant. 'Communis' and 'Centifolia Muscosa' ('Muscosa') are typical pink centifolias with moss added; 'White Bath' is 'Centifolia Muscosa' in white. Other varieties are 'Comtesse de Murinais', pale pink to white; 'Gloire des Mousseux', deep pink; 'Mme Louis Lévêque', salmon pink; 'Nuits de Young', dark red; 'William Lobb', dark red to purple. Repeat bloomers include 'Alfred de Dalmas', creamy pink; 'Gabriel Noyelle', apricot; 'Henri Martin', red; and 'Salet', bright pink.

China roses. Best in Zones 4–9, 12–24; H1, H2. The first two China roses to reach Europe (around 1800) were cultivated forms of *R. chinensis* that had been selected and maintained by Chinese horticulturists. Flowers were pink or red, under 3 in. across, borne in small clusters on 2–4-ft. plants. 'Old Blush' ('Parson's Pink China'), one of the original two, is still sold; others include red 'Cramoisi Supérieur' ('Agrippina'), white 'Ducher', and crimson 'Louis Philippe'. China rose ancestry was the primary source of repeat-flowering habit in later-19th- and early-20th-century roses. Modern miniature roses owe their small size to *R. c. minima,* presumably through its forms 'Rouletii' and 'Pompon de Paris'.

Bourbon roses. The original Bourbon rose was a hybrid between *R. chinensis* and the autumn damask (*R. damascena* 'Semperflorens'). Later came shrubs, semiclimbers, and climbers with flowers in white, pink shades, and red, mostly quite fragrant. Best known today are 'La Reine Victoria', 'Mme Ernst Calvat', 'Mme Pierre Oger', and 'Souvenir de la Malmaison' (all pink) and the supremely fragrant 'Mme Isaac Pereire' (magenta red). A famous Bourbon-China hybrid, 'Gloire des Rosomanes', gained widespread distribution as an understock (known popularly as Ragged Robin) in commercial rose production. Occasionally offered as a hedge plant, it is upright to fountainlike, with coarse foliage and semidouble cherry red flowers throughout the growing season.

Damask perpetuals. The first distinct hybrid group to emerge (around 1800), combining China roses with old European types. Ancestries all appear to include China roses and the autumn damask (*R. damascena* 'Semperflorens'); generally the group was known as Portland roses after the first representative, 'Duchess of Portland'. All are fairly short, bushy repeat bloomers with centifolia- and gallica-like flowers. Among those sold are 'Comte de Chambord', cool pink; 'Duchess of Portland', crimson; 'Jacques Cartier', bright pink; and 'Rose du Roi', crimson purple.

Hybrid perpetuals. In the 19th and early 20th centuries, these were *the* garden roses. They are big, vigorous, and hardy to about −30°F/−34°C with minimal winter protection. They need more water and fertilizer than hybrid teas in order to produce repeated bursts of bloom. Prune high, thin out oldest canes, arch over remaining canes to encourage bloom in quantity. Watch for rust. Flowers often are large (to 6–7 in.), full, and strongly fragrant; buds usually are shorter and plumper than standard hybrid tea buds. Colors range from white through pink shades to red and maroon. Varieties still sold include 'Frau Karl Druschki', white; 'Général Jacqueminot', cherry red; 'Mrs. John Laing', rose pink; 'Paul Neyron', with deep pink, peonylike flowers; 'Ulrich Brünner Fils', carmine red.

Noisette roses. The union of a China rose and the musk rose *(R. moschata)* produced the first Noisette rose, 'Champneys' Pink Cluster', a repeat-flowering shrubby climber with small pink flowers in medium-size clusters. Crossed with itself and China roses, it led to a race of similar roses in white, pink shades, and red; crossed with tea roses, it yielded large-flowered, climbing tea-Noisettes. All are best in milder climates (Zones 6–9, 12–24; H1, H2). Small-flowered Noisettes include 'Aimée Vibert Scandens', white; 'Blush Noisette', light pink; and 'Fellenberg', cherry red. Larger-flowered tea-Noisettes are 'Alister Stella Gray', yellow; 'Crepuscule', orange; 'Lamarque', white; 'Maréchal Niel', yellow; 'Mme Alfred Carrière', white; and 'Rêve d'Or', buff apricot.

Tea roses. A race of elegant, virtually everblooming, relatively tender roses; best in Zones 6–9, 12–24, H1, H2. Plants are long lived, building on old wood and disliking heavy pruning. Flowers are in white, cream, light yellow, apricot, buff, pink, or rosy red. Though variable, many resemble hybrid teas. In crosses with hybrid perpetuals, tea roses were parents of the first hybrid teas. Varieties include 'Duchesse de Brabant', warm pink, tuliplike form; 'Lady Hillingdon', saffron; 'Maman Cochet', creamy rose pink; 'Marie van Houtte', soft yellow and pink; 'Mlle Franziska Krüger', pink-and-cream

Bourbon Rose 'Mme Pierre Oger'

Hybrid Perpetual Rose 'Général Jacqueminot'

Tea Rose 'Lady Hillingdon' (Climbing Form)

Rosa foetida 'Bicolor'

Rosa rubiginosa

to orange; 'Monsieur Tillier', warm dark pink with gold and rosy red; and 'White Maman Cochet', creamy white shaded pink. The cross of a tea and the tea ancestor *R. gigantea* produced 'Belle Portugaise' ('Belle of Portugal'), a rampant, spring-flowering climber with large pale pink blooms.

Species and species hybrids. Among this diverse assemblage of wild species and their hybrids are excellent shrub and climbing roses, attractive plants useful for mass floral effect.

R. banksiae. LADY BANKS' ROSE. Evergreen climber (deciduous in cold winters). Zones 4–24; H1, H2. From China. Vigorous grower to 20 feet or more. Aphid resistant, almost immune to disease. Stems have almost no prickles; glossy, leathery leaves have three to five 2½-in.-long leaflets. Large clusters of small yellow or white flowers bloom in early to late spring, depending on zone. Good for covering banks, ground, fence, or arbor. The two forms sold are 'Lutea', with scentless, double yellow flowers; and *R. b. banksiae* ('Alba Plena' or 'White Banksia'), with violet-scented, double white flowers. 'Fortuniana' *(R. fortuniana)* sometimes is sold by the name "double white banksia"; it differs from true *R. b. banksiae* in having thorny canes, larger leaves, and larger flowers that come individually rather than in clusters.

Rosa banksiae 'Lutea'

R. bracteata. MACARTNEY ROSE. Evergreen climber. Zones 4–9, 12–24, H1, H2, except as noted. Native to southeastern China; naturalized in southeastern U.S. Single, 2–3-in., creamy white flowers appear in spring on a plant with brown, thorny stems and glossy dark green leaves. Without support, the plant trails and roots as it spreads, building up to 3 ft. tall; as a climber, it can reach 10–20 ft. Its celebrated offspring 'Mermaid' is a thorny, vigorous evergreen or semievergreen climber, hardy in Zones 7–9, 12–24, H1, H2. It reaches 50 ft., with glossy, leathery dark green leaves. Profuse bloom from spring into fall (and intermittently through winter in the mildest zones); single, creamy yellow, lightly fragrant flowers to 5 in. across. Tough, disease resistant; thrives in sun or partial shade. Plant 8 ft. apart for quick ground cover; or let it climb a wall (will need tying), run along a fence, or scramble into a tree.

R. eglanteria. See R. rubiginosa

R. foetida (R. lutea). AUSTRIAN BRIER. Deciduous shrub. Zones A2, A3; 1–21. From central and western Asia. To 6 ft. tall and wide. Slender, prickly stems are erect or arching. Dark green, smooth or slightly hairy leaves are especially susceptible to black spot; may drop early in fall. Flowers (in mid- to late spring) are single, bright yellow, 2–3 in. across, with odd scent. This species and its well-known variety 'Bicolor', commonly called Austrian Copper, are the source of orange and yellow in modern roses. 'Bicolor' is a 4–5-ft.-tall shrub with brilliant coppery red flowers, their petals backed with yellow. Its form 'Persiana', called Persian Yellow, has fully double yellow blossoms. All forms perform best in warm, fairly dry, well-drained soil and in full sun. Need reflected heat in cool-summer areas. Prune only to remove dead wood.

R. glauca (R. rubrifolia). Deciduous shrub. Zones A1–A3; 1–24. From mountains of central and southern Europe. To 6 ft. tall, 5 ft. wide. This species is valued not so much for its flowers as for its foliage: during the growing season, it is covered in leaves that combine gray green and coppery purple. Small, single pink flowers bloom in spring; these are followed by small, oval hips that turn red in fall.

R. ×harisonii. HARISON'S YELLOW ROSE. Deciduous shrub. Zones 1–24. Hybrid between *R. foetida* and *R. pimpinellifolia;* very old rose that was taken westward by pioneers and still persists in California's Gold Country and around old farmhouses. To 6 ft. tall, 4 ft. wide. Thicket of thorny stems; fine-textured foliage. Flowers (in late spring) are profuse, semi-double, bright yellow, fragrant. Occasionally reblooms in fall in warmer climates. Showy hips. Vigorous, disease free, hardy to cold, and (once established) resistant to aridity. Useful deciduous landscaping shrub.

R. laevigata. CHEROKEE ROSE. Evergreen climber. Zones 4–9, 12–24; H1, H2. Native to Southeast Asia but naturalized in southern U.S. Green stems to 10 ft. tall hold sharp, hooked thorns and lacquered-looking dark green leaves, each with three leaflets. Single white flowers to 3½ in. wide appear only in spring. Crossed with a tea rose, it produced 'Anemone', a mostly spring-flowering climber with single flowers that resemble Japanese anemones in a soft, silvery pink. 'Ramona' is a magenta sport of 'Anemone'.

R. moschata. MUSK ROSE. Deciduous shrub. Zones 4–9, 12–24; H1. Probably from western Asia; not known in the wild. Vigorous, arching plant to 10 ft. high and wide. Densely covered with matte-finish, medium green foliage that turns butter yellow in late fall. Clustered, single ivory white flowers appear in late spring, continue through summer; scent is delicious, somewhat like honey. *R. m. plena* has double blossoms, though their effect is lessened because inner petals wither before outer ones.

R. moyesii. Deciduous shrub. Zones 3–10, 14–21. From western China. Large, loose shrub to 10 ft. high, 8 ft. wide; best as background plant or featured shrub-tree specimen. Spring bloom is a glorious display of single bright red flowers to 2½ in. across, carried singly or in groups of two. A second display comes in fall, when the large, bottle-shaped hips ripen to brilliant scarlet. 'Geranium' is a selection with somewhat shorter, more compact growth and red flowers in clusters of up to five. The hybrid 'Sealing Wax' offers pink flowers, also on a smaller and more compact bush.

'Nevada', resulting from a cross between a hybrid tea and a form of *R. moyesii,* is a large, arching shrub with light green leaves and dark stems. In spring, it is covered with 4-in., pink-tinted, single white flowers; lesser displays follow later in the year. 'Marguerite Hilling' is a pink sport.

R. multiflora. Deciduous shrub. Zones 1–24. From Japan. Dense, vigorous, arching growth to 8–10 ft. tall and wide. Susceptible to mildew, spider mites. Profuse clusters of small white flowers akin in scent to honeysuckle *(Lonicera);* blooms in mid- to late spring. Blossoms are followed in fall by a heavy crop of red, ¼-in. hips that are much loved by birds. (Fruit display has a down side: multitudes of volunteer seedlings, which can put this rose in the "attractive weed" category.) Promoted as hedge but useful for this purpose only on largest properties. Spiny and smooth forms are available. Set plants 2 ft. apart for fast fill-in. Can help control erosion. One of the most widely used understocks in commercial rose production.

Several distinctive climbing roses, known as multiflora ramblers, are hybrids of this species. Best known are several so-called blue ramblers: 'Bleu Magenta', crimson purple fading to gray violet; 'Rose-Marie Viaud', crimson purple to violet and lilac; 'Veilchenblau', maroon purple to gray lilac; and 'Violette', maroon purple to grayish plum.

R. nutkana. NOOTKA ROSE. Deciduous shrub. Zones A1–A3; 1–11, 14–21. Native from Alaska to Northern California and eastward to the Rockies. To 6 ft. by 4 ft., widening into a thicket of dark, sparsely thorned, somewhat arching stems carrying gray-green leaves with sharply toothed margins. Blooms in spring, bearing single deep pink blossoms to 2½ in. wide (primarily borne singly). Showy, rosy red hips follow the flowers.

Rosa nutkana (hips)

R. pimpinellifolia (R. spinosissima). SCOTCH ROSE, BURNET ROSE. Deciduous shrub. Zones A1–A3; 1–24. From western Europe eastward to Korea. To 3–4 ft. tall; equally wide initially, spreading wider by suckers with age. Upright stems covered with needlelike prickles are closely set with small, ferny leaves. White to pink, 1½–2-in.-wide spring flowers; dark brown to blackish hips. Handsome bank cover in good soil; helps prevent erosion. Its form 'Altaica' can reach 6 ft. tall, has larger leaves and garlands of white, 3-in. flowers. Noteworthy hybrids include 'Stanwell Perpetual', with double blush pink blooms spring to fall on a mounding, twiggy plant with small gray-green leaves; 'Golden Wings', a 6-ft. bush with single, 4-in.-wide, light yellow blossoms with red stamens spring to fall. 'Frühlingsmorgen', the best known of several German hybrids, is a 6-ft.-tall, arching plant with large, single yellow flowers edged cherry pink with maroon stamens.

R. roxburghii. CHESTNUT ROSE. Deciduous shrub. Zones 2–24. From western China. To 6 ft. high and wide, with prickly stems and cinnamon-colored, peeling bark. Light green foliage is very fine textured, almost ferny, immune to mildew. Buds and yellow-orange hips are spiny, like chestnut burs. Blooms in mid- to late spring, bearing soft rose pink, very fragrant, typically double blossoms. Normally a big shrub for screen, border, but if stems are pegged down, good for erosion control on bank.

R. rubiginosa (R. eglanteria). SWEET BRIAR, EGLANTINE. Deciduous shrub or climber. Zones 1–24. From Europe, western Asia, North Africa; naturalized in parts of the West. Vigorous to 12 ft. tall, 8 ft. wide. Stems are prickly; dark green leaves have fragrance of green apples, especially after a rain. Single pink flowers to 1½ in. across appear singly or in clusters in late spring. Red-orange hips. Good hedge, barrier, or screen; plant 3–4 ft. apart, prune annually in early spring. Can be held to 3–4 ft. Hybrid forms include 'Lady Penzance', 'Lord Penzance'.

R. rubrifolia. See R. glauca

R. rugosa. RAMANAS ROSE, SEA TOMATO. Deciduous shrub. Zones A1–A3; 1–24. From northern China, Siberia, Korea, Japan. Vigorous, very hardy shrub with prickly stems. To 3–6 ft. tall and wide. Glossy bright green leaves have distinctive heavy veining that gives them a crinkled appearance. Flowers are 3–4 in. across and, in the many varieties, range from single to double and from pure white and creamy yellow through pink to deep purplish red; all are wonderfully fragrant. Blooms in spring, summer, early fall. Bright red, tomato-shaped hips, an inch or more across, are edible but seedy; sometimes used in preserves.

All rugosas are extremely tough and hardy, withstanding hard freezes, wind, aridity, salt spray. They make fine hedges; plants grown on their own roots will make sizable colonies and help prevent erosion. Foliage remains quite free of diseases and insects, except possibly aphids. Among most widely sold rugosas and rugosa hybrids are 'Blanc Double de Coubert', double white; 'Frau Dagmar Hartopp', single pink; 'Hansa', double purplish red; 'Will Alderman', double pink. Two unusual choices are 'F. J. Grootendorst' and 'Grootendorst Supreme'; their double flowers have deeply fringed petals and resemble carnations *(Dianthus)* more than roses.

R. spinosissima. See R. pimpinellifolia

R. wichuraiana. MEMORIAL ROSE. Evergreen or partially evergreen climber (deciduous in cold winters). Zones 3–9, 12–24; H1, H2. From Japan, Korea, eastern China. Trailing stems grow 10–12 ft. long in one season, root in contact with moist soil. Leaves 2–4 in. long, with five to nine smooth, shiny, ¼–1-in. leaflets. Midsummer flowers are white, to 2 in. across, in clusters of six to ten. Good ground cover, even in relatively poor soil. Wichuraiana ramblers, produced in the first 20 years of the 20th century, are hybrids between the species and various garden roses. Pink 'Dorothy Perkins' and red 'Excelsa' bloom heavily in spring; small, formless flowers obscure the often-mildewed leaves. Larger, better-shaped flowers and glossy, healthier leaves are found in 'Albéric Barbier', creamy white; 'Francois Juranville', coral pink; 'Gardenia', light yellow; 'Paul Transon', coppery salmon; and 'Sander's White Rambler', white.

R. xanthina hugonis. FATHER HUGO'S ROSE, GOLDEN ROSE OF CHINA. Deciduous shrub. Zones 2–24. From northern China. Dense growth to 8 ft. tall, 5 ft. wide. Stems arching or straight, with bristles near base. Handsome foliage: deep green, 1–4-in.-long leaves with 5–11 tiny leaflets. Flowers profusely in mid- to late spring, when branches become garlands of 2-in.-wide, bright yellow, faintly scented flowers. Useful in borders, for screen or barrier plantings, against a fence, trained as a fan on trellis. Will take high filtered afternoon shade. Prune oldest wood to ground each year to shape plant, get maximum bloom.

Rosaceae. The rose family contains an immense number of plants of horticultural importance. In addition to roses, family members include strawberry, bramble fruits (blackberry, raspberry), many flowering and fruiting trees (apple, crabapple, pear, plum), *Photinia,* firethorn *(Pyracantha), Spiraea,* and other ornamental trees, shrubs, and perennials.

ROSA DE MONTANA. See ANTIGONON leptopus

ROSARY VINE. See CEROPEGIA woodii

ROSE. See ROSA

ROSE-MALLOW. See HIBISCUS moscheutos

ROSE OF SHARON. See HIBISCUS syriacus

ROSEWOOD. See DALBERGIA sissoo

ROSMARINUS officinalis

ROSEMARY

Lamiaceae (Labiatae)

EVERGREEN SHRUB

ZONES 4–24; H1, H2

FULL SUN

LITTLE TO MODERATE WATER

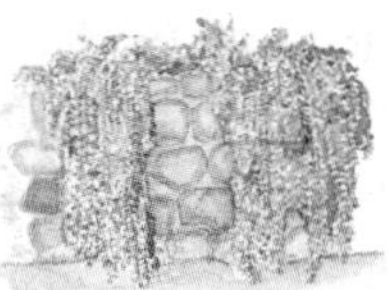

Rosmarinus officinalis 'Prostratus'

The genus name means "dew of the sea," reflecting the plant's native habitat on seaside cliffs in the Mediterranean region. Tough and versatile, rosemary grows most luxuriantly just above the tide line, braving wind and salt spray—but it will thrive inland, even enduring blistering sun and poor alkaline soil, if given moderate water and infrequent light feeding.

The various forms of rosemary vary in habit from stiff, erect types through rounded shrubs and squat, dense tufts to rock-hugging creepers. Height ranges from as low as 1 ft. to as tall as 6 ft. or more. Plants are thickly clothed in narrow, typically 1–1½-in.-long, resinous, aromatic leaves that are usually glossy dark green above, grayish white beneath. Small clusters of ¼–½-in. blossoms in various shades of blue (rarely pink or white) bloom through winter and spring; bloom occasionally repeats in fall. Blossoms attract birds, butterflies, bees; produce excellent honey. Leaves are widely used as a seasoning. Flowers also are edible; add them to salads or use as a garnish.

Good drainage is essential; lighten heavy soils with plenty of organic matter. Heavy feeding and too much water result in rank growth, subsequent woodiness. Control growth by frequent tip-pinching when plants are small. Prune older plants frequently but lightly; cut to side branch or shear. If plants become woody and bare in center, cut back selected branches by half so plant will fill in with new growth (be sure to cut into leafy wood; plants will not regrow from bare wood). Or discard plant and start over with a new one. Branches root wherever they touch the ground; creeping varieties will spread indefinitely, forming extensive colonies. To get new plants, root tip cuttings or dig and replant layered branches.

Cold hardiness varies considerably, depending on selection. In general, upright varieties are hardier, while prostrate ones (originally from Majorca and Corsica) are more tender, suffering damage at 20°F/–7°C or even higher. In cold-winter areas, choose the hardiest types and shelter them from winter winds; wrap upright growers in plastic sheeting (leaving top uncovered) in late fall to prevent branches from breaking under weight of snow. Note that even the hardiest types can succumb to cold if they have wet feet. Beyond hardiness range, grow rosemary in pots and winter indoors on a sunny windowsill; or treat as annual.

Use taller types of rosemary as clipped or informal hedges or in dry borders with native and gray-leafed plants. Lower kinds are good ground or bank covers, useful in erosion control. Set container-grown plants or rooted cuttings 2 ft. apart for moderately quick cover. Foliage of most types has culinary uses, but flavor and fragrance vary; the best have a mildly pungent flavor and a complex aroma with sweet as well as resinous notes. Rosemary is also used in medicines, cosmetics, potpourri, moth repellents.

Rosemary plants sold without names are frequently seedlings, which lack the uniformity of cutting-grown, named selections. Unfortunately, variety names are often confused, and many have synonyms; but named plants are still a better bet than nameless ones.

Rosmarinus officinalis 'Albus'

'Albus' ('Albiflorus'). Semiupright grower, eventually reaching 6 ft. tall and wide. White flowers veined in pale lavender. Hardy to 0°F/–18°C.

'Arp'. The hardiest rosemary, taking temperatures as low as –10°F/ –23°C. Discovered in Arp, Texas. Open grower to 4 ft. tall and wide; best with frequent pruning. Dark green foliage has grayish tinge. Bright medium blue flowers.

'Benenden Blue' ('Balsam'; also called pine-scented rosemary). Semiupright plant to 3 ft. high, 4 ft. or more wide. Especially narrow leaves with strong pine fragrance; light blue flowers. Bitter flavor with turpentine overtones. Tender.

'Blue Boy'. Young plant makes a dense, symmetrical mound 8–12 in. high, 14–18 in. across, reminiscent of a dwarf spruce *(Picea)*. Leaves are just ½ in. long; flowers are light blue. Plant creeps with age, but habit becomes irregular; shear to maintain domed appearance. Good in rock gardens, pots. Pleasant fragrance and flavor. Tender.

'Blue Spires'. Strong vertical grower, to 5–6 ft. tall and as wide or wider with age; can be pruned for narrower form. Deep blue flowers. Superb landscape variety; makes tight sheared hedge. Excellent for seasoning.

'Collingwood Ingram' ('Ingramii', 'Rex #4'). To 2–2½ ft. high, sprawling to 4 ft. or wider; narrower and more upright with pruning. Branches curve gracefully. Flowers in rich, bright deep blue with violet veining. Tallish bank or ground cover that provides excellent color. Not good for seasoning; flavor is too piny. Tender.

'Corsican Prostrate'. Arching, spreading, 1–1½ ft. tall, with dark blue flowers. Tender.

'Golden Rain' ('Joyce DeBaggio'). Bushy, upright growth to 2–3 ft. high and wide. Green leaves with irregular golden edges; variegation is most prominent in cool weather, fades in summer. Deep violet-blue flowers.

'Gorizia'. Vigorous, rigidly upright, to 4–5 ft. high and wide. Reddish brown stems. Leaves to 2 in. long, broader than those of most selections. Light blue flowers. Sweet, gingery fragrance.

'Hill Hardy'. Compact, bushy plant grows semiupright to 5 ft. high and wide. Stiff foliage. Light blue flowers; repeat bloom in fall. Pleasant, light fragrance. Hardy to 0°F/–18°C.

'Huntington Carpet' ('Huntington Blue'). To 1½ ft. high; spreads quickly yet maintains a dense center. Pale blue flowers. Best variety for ground or bank cover.

'Irene'. Vigorous spreader that covers 2–3 ft. or more per year, eventually mounding to 1–1½ ft. high. Deep lavender-blue flowers. Reputedly one of the cold-hardiest prostrate varieties.

'Ken Taylor'. Sport of 'Collingwood Ingram'. Has the same deep blue flower color but is a little lower growing, with a greater tendency to trail. Tender.

'Lockwood de Forest' ('Santa Barbara', 'Lockwoodii', 'Forestii'). Resembles 'Prostratus' but mounds up to 2½ ft. or more; has lighter, brighter green foliage and bluer flowers.

'Majorca Pink'. Initially erect to 2–4 ft. tall and 1½–2 ft. wide; eventually twists into picturesque shape under the weight of its heavy seed crop, flopping to 3–4 ft. wide. Lilac-pink flowers. Slightly fruity fragrance.

'Miss Jessup's Upright' ('Fastigiatus'). Erect growth to 4 ft. or taller, 1½–2 ft. wide, with thin, pointed leaves on slender stems. Pale violet-blue flowers. A little too sparse for a good hedge.

'Prostratus'. To 2 ft. tall, with 4–8-ft. spread. Will trail straight down over wall or edge of raised bed to make a green curtain. Pale lavender-blue flowers come in waves from fall into spring. With age, tends to mound up and become woody and bare in center (except at seashore, where it remains lush throughout). Effective in hanging containers. Tender.

'Severn Sea'. Trails widely; builds up to 1–1½ ft. high. Broader leaves than other trailing types. Profuse show of sky blue flowers. Said to be one of the cold-hardiest trailers.

'Tuscan Blue'. Vita Sackville-West's original, brought to England from Tuscany, had relatively broad (to ¼-in.-wide), 1–1½-in.-long leaves; deep violet-blue flowers; upright habit to 6–7 ft. tall and 1½–2 ft. wide. A plant long sold as 'Tuscan Blue' in the U.S. fits this general description but has light blue flowers; with age, it becomes woody and bare at base. Some nurseries sell 'Blue Spires' under this name.

ROYAL CHARLIE. See PLECTRANTHUS oertendahlii

ROYAL FERN. See OSMUNDA regalis

ROYAL PALM. See ROYSTONEA

ROYAL POINCIANA. See DELONIX regia

ROYAL TRUMPET VINE. See DISTICTIS 'Rivers'

ROYSTONEA

ROYAL PALM

Arecaceae (Palmae)

PALMS

ZONES 24; H2

FULL SUN

REGULAR WATER

Roystonea regia

Stately, symmetrical feather palms. Tall, smooth gray trunk is marked with rings and topped by a green crown shaft formed by the overlapping bases of the feathery fronds. Grow at a moderate to fast rate. Do best in moist, well-drained soil. Good wind and salt resistance. Can be used as street or avenue trees, to frame large buildings, in groups with other palms. Look especially majestic planted in rows.

R. oleracea. CABBAGE PALM, CARIBBEE ROYAL PALM. Native to the Caribbean and South America. May reach over 100 ft. tall, 35 ft. wide. Green fronds grow as long as 20 ft.; they are usually semiupright or spreading.

R. regia. ROYAL PALM, CUBAN ROYAL PALM. Native to Cuba. To 50–75 ft. high, 30 ft. wide. Trunk is swollen at base, tapering toward top, sometimes swollen toward middle. Bright green, 10–20-ft.-long fronds arch gracefully in all directions.

RUBBER TREE. See FICUS elastica

Rubiaceae. The madder family contains herbs, shrubs, and trees with opposite or whorled leaves, usually clustered flowers. Its members include *Bouvardia*, coffee *(Coffea)*, sweet woodruff *(Galium)*, and *Gardenia*.

RUBUS

BRAMBLE

Rosaceae

DECIDUOUS AND EVERGREEN SHRUBS

ZONES VARY BY SPECIES

FULL SUN OR LIGHT SHADE

MODERATE WATER

Rubus deliciosus

Though best known for blackberry and raspberry (see separate entries), the brambles include many ornamental plants, most of them thornless. The species described here differ from blackberry and raspberry not only in their lack of prickles but also in having perennial rather than biennial stems. Spring flowers are followed by small, edible berries that attract birds. Need good drainage; spread widely by rhizomes. Plant ground cover types about 2 ft. apart.

R. arcticus 'Kenai Carpet'. NAGOONBERRY. Deciduous. Zones A1–A3; 1–3. Native to Alaska and other northern climates. Creeping ground cover plant to 6 in. high. Smooth green leaves have three to five ovate, saw-toothed leaflets; foliage turns reddish in fall. Inch-wide hot pink flowers are followed by dark red berries.

R. deliciosus. ROCKY MOUNTAIN THIMBLEBERRY, BOULDER RASPBERRY. Deciduous. Zones 1–6, 10. Native to Rocky Mountains in New Mexico, Colorado, Wyoming. Graceful, arching plant to 3–5 ft. tall, 6 ft. wide. Bright green, lobed, nearly round leaves. White, 2–3-in.-wide flowers resemble single roses. Dark purple berries. Hybrid between this species and *R. trilobus* is *R. tridel* 'Benenden', which grows 8–10 ft. tall.

R. pentalobus (R. calycinoides, R. fockeanus). Evergreen. Zones 4–6, 14–17. Native to mountains of Taiwan. Thickly foliaged stems spread at a moderate rate to form a dense carpet to 1 ft. high. Rounded, 1–1½-in. leaves have three to five broad, ruffled-edged lobes; upper surfaces are lustrous dark green and rough textured, undersides are grayish white and felted. Small white flowers like those of strawberry. Salmon-colored berries. 'Emerald Carpet' is a commonly sold variety with superior foliage.

RUDBECKIA

Asteraceae (Compositae)

PERENNIALS AND BIENNIALS

ZONES 1–24, EXCEPT AS NOTED

FULL SUN

MODERATE TO REGULAR WATER

Rudbeckia hirta

The showy garden rudbeckias that brighten summer and fall borders are descended from wild plants native mainly to the eastern U.S. All are tough and easy to grow. Blossoms have yellow or orange rays and a raised central cone. They make good cut flowers; cutting also encourages rebloom late in season. Divide perennials when they become crowded, usually every few years.

R. fulgida. Perennial. Initially to 3 ft. tall, 2 ft. wide; after a few years, spreads by rhizomes to form a larger clump. Branching stems; broadly lance-shaped, 5-in.-long, hairy dark green leaves. Yellow, 2–2½-in.-wide flowers with black to brown central cone bloom in summer. Varieties are more often grown than the species; among the most popular is *R. f. sullivantii* 'Goldsturm', bearing 3-in., black-eyed yellow flowers on 2–2½-ft. stems. Some nurseries offer the taller, more variable seed-grown Goldsturm strain.

R. hirta. GLORIOSA DAISY, BLACK-EYED SUSAN. Biennial or short-lived perennial; often grown as annual because it blooms the first summer from seed sown in early spring. Grown as winter annual in Zones 12, 13. To 3–4 ft. tall, 1½ ft. wide, with upright, branching habit. Stems and lance-shaped leaves to 4 in. long are rough and hairy. Daisylike, 2–4-in.-wide flowers have orange-yellow rays and a prominent purplish black cone.

Gloriosa Daisy strain has 5–7-in.-wide daisies in yellow, orange, russet, or mahogany, often zoned or banded. Gloriosa Double Daisy strain has somewhat smaller (to 4½-in.) double flowers, nearly all in lighter yellow and orange shades. 'Indian Summer' produces 6–9-in., single to semi-double flowers in golden yellow. 'Irish Eyes' ('Green Eyes') has 2–3-in., golden yellow flowers with a light green central cone that ages to brown. For front of border, try lower-growing selections 'Goldilocks' (double flowers) and 'Toto', both 8–10 in. high; Becky Mix (12–15 in.); 'Sonora' (15 in.); and 'Marmalade' (2 ft.).

R. laciniata. Perennial. The species can reach 10 ft. tall, 4 ft. wide; it has light green, deeply lobed leaves to 4 in. long and blooms from summer to fall, bearing 2–3½-in.-wide flowers with drooping yellow rays and a green cone. More widely grown in gardens are the following two selections. 'Hortensia' ('Golden Glow'), to 6–7 ft. tall, bears bright yellow double flowers 2–3½ in. wide. Good summer screen or tall plant for back of borders. Does not seed, but spreads rapidly (sometimes aggressively) by underground stems. Seems to attract aphids. 'Goldquelle', with double blooms in lemon yellow, is a less aggressive form growing 3 ft. tall, 1½ ft. wide.

R. nitida. Perennial. Zones 2–9, 14–24. Similar to *R. laciniata* but shorter (to 6 ft. tall). More widely grown than the species is 'Herbstsonne' ('Autumn Sun'), which may be a hybrid between *R. laciniata* and *R. nitida.* It grows to 6 ft. tall, 2 ft. wide; bears single, 4–5-in.-wide flowers with yellow rays and a bright green cone that ages to yellow.

RUE. See RUTA graveolens

RUELLIA

Acanthaceae

EVERGREEN SHRUBS AND SHRUBBY PERENNIALS

ZONES VARY BY SPECIES

FULL SUN OR LIGHT SHADE

WATER NEEDS VARY BY SPECIES

Ruellia peninsularis

Ruellias have opposite leaves and flaring, bell-shaped flowers with five shallow lobes. Beyond their hardiness range, they are commonly grown in greenhouses.

R. brittoniana. Shrubby perennial. Zones 8, 9, 12–24; H1, H2. Mexican native naturalized in many areas of the southern and southwestern U.S. To 3 ft. high; initially 1–1½ ft. wide, but can be invasive and should be contained (by an edging, for example). Narrow dark green leaves to 3 in. long, ¾ in. wide; 2-in.-long, lavender-blue flowers throughout warm times of year. 'Chi Chi' has soft pink blossoms; 'Alba' has white flowers. 'Katie' is a dwarf (10–12-in.), noninvasive variety. Regular water.

R. californica. Shrub. Zones 12, 13. Native to Sonoran Desert of Mexico. To 2–4½ ft. tall and wide, with oval light green leaves to 1¼ in. long that drop in cold spells or after protracted dry periods. Deep purple, violet, or pink flowers to 2¼ in. long appear after spring and summer rains. Needs no irrigation but will bloom nearly all year if given little to moderate water.

R. macrantha. Shrub. Zones 21–24; H1, H2. Native to Brazil. To 3 ft. high and wide, with oval dark green leaves to 6 in. long. Clusters of rose pink, 3–4-in. flowers with deeper pink veining. Blooms from earliest winter to spring. Best grown as a container plant and given shelter during frosty weather. Regular water.

R. peninsularis. Shrub. Zones 12, 13, 21–24. Somewhat larger flowered than *R. californica* but otherwise very similar in appearance and bloom season; has same watering needs as *R. californica* and same propensity for dropping leaves in cold or dry periods.

RUMOHRA adiantiformis

LEATHERLEAF FERN

Polypodiaceae

FERN

ZONES 14–17, 19–24; H1, H2

FULL SUN OR PARTIAL SHADE

MODERATE TO REGULAR WATER

Rumohra adiantiformis

From many tropical and subtropical areas of the Southern Hemisphere. To 3 ft. high and wide, spreading wider by rhizomes. Deep glossy green, triangular, finely cut fronds are firm textured, last well in arrangements. Hardy to 24°F/–4°C. Often sold as *Aspidium capense.*

RUPTURE WORT. See HERNIARIA glabra

RUSCUS

BUTCHER'S BROOM

Liliaceae

EVERGREEN SHRUBS

ZONES 4–24; H1

BEST IN SHADE, TOLERATE SOME SUN

LITTLE TO REGULAR WATER

Ruscus hypoglossum

Native to Mediterranean region. Unusual leafless plants with some value as small-scale ground cover, curiosity, or source of material for dried arrangements. Flattened, leaflike branches do work of leaves and bear tiny greenish white flowers in centers of upper surfaces. If male and female plants are present, or if you have a plant with male and female flowers, bright red (sometimes yellow), marble-size fruit follows flowers. Plants spread widely by rhizomes. Tolerate competition from tree roots. Subject to chlorosis in desert.

R. aculeatus. To 1–4 ft. tall, with branched stems. Spine-tipped "leaves" are 1–3 in. long, a third as wide, leathery, dull dark green.

R. hypoglossum. To 1½ ft., with unbranched stems. "Leaves" to 4 in. long, 1½ in. wide, glossy green, not spine tipped. Spreads faster than *R. aculeatus.* Superior as small-scale ground cover.

A PRACTICAL GUIDE TO GARDENING
PLEASE SEE PAGES 658–731

R

RUSSELIA equisetiformis

CORAL FOUNTAIN, FIRECRACKER PLANT

Scrophulariaceae

SHRUBBY PERENNIAL

ZONES 14, 19–24; H1, H2; OR INDOORS

SUN OR PART SHADE; BRIGHT INDIRECT LIGHT

MODERATE TO REGULAR WATER

Russelia equisetiformis

Native to Mexico. To 5 ft. high and wide, with trailing, almost leafless bright green stems that look attractive spilling from a hanging basket or over the top of a wall. Stems can also be fastened to a trellis or other vertical surface. Can be grown in a rock garden. Throughout spring and summer (all year in Hawaii), many side branches bear a profusion of bright red, narrowly tubular flowers that look like little firecrackers. Needs regular fertilizing. Hardy to about 32°F/0°C, but comes back vigorously if cut down by frost. Easy to propagate from pencil-size stem cuttings taken in spring.

RUSSIAN OLIVE. See ELAEAGNUS angustifolia

RUSSIAN SAGE. See PEROVSKIA

RUTABAGA. See TURNIP and RUTABAGA

Rutaceae. Besides rue *(Ruta),* the rue family includes many perennials, shrubs, and trees, the most important of which are the citrus clan. *Boronia,* Mexican orange *(Choisya),* breath of heaven *(Coleonema),* Australian willow *(Geijera),* and *Skimmia* are other notable members. Most are aromatic, thanks to oil glands in leaves or other plant parts.

RUTA graveolens

RUE, HERB-OF-GRACE

Rutaceae

PERENNIAL

ZONES 2–24

FULL SUN

MODERATE TO REGULAR WATER

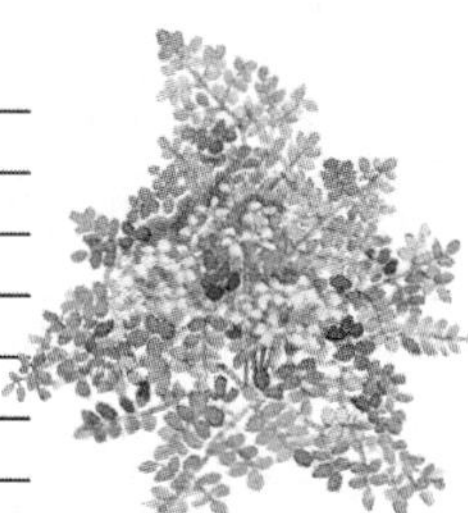
Ruta graveolens 'Jackman's Blue'

To 2–3 ft. high and wide, with aromatic, ferny-looking blue-green leaves. Small greenish yellow flowers are followed by decorative brown seed capsules. 'Jackman's Blue' is dense and compact, with a fine gray-blue color. 'Blue Mound' and 'Curly Girl' are more compact still. Sow seeds in flats; transplant to 1 ft. apart. Rue needs good garden soil; add lime to strongly acid soil. Cut back in early spring to encourage bushiness. Dry seed clusters for use in wreaths or swags. Sap causes dermatitis in some people.

RYEGRASS. See LOLIUM

SABAL

PALMETTO

Arecaceae (Palmae)

PALMS

ZONES 12–17, 19–24; H1, H2

FULL SUN

MODERATE WATER

Sabal palmetto

Slow-growing fan palms; some have trunks, some do not. Mature plants bear large clusters of tiny flowers among the leaves. Tolerate salt spray. All withstand 20°F/–7°C.

S. blackburniana (S. domingensis, S. umbraculifera). HISPANIOLA PALMETTO. Native to the Caribbean. Ultimately 80 ft. or taller, 20 ft. wide, with fan-shaped, immense gray-green leaves to 9 ft. across.

S. mexicana (S. texana). OAXACA PALMETTO. Native from Texas to Guatemala. To 30–50 ft. high, 12 ft. wide. Bright green, 3-ft. leaves. Leaf stems persist on trunk in young trees, later drop to show attractive, slender trunk.

S. minor. Native to southeastern U.S. To 3–6 ft. tall, 10 ft. wide. Green to blue-green, 6-ft. leaves. Tree is usually trunkless but sometimes has a short trunk. Old leaves fold at base, hang down like a closed umbrella.

S. palmetto. CABBAGE PALM. From southeastern U.S. To 20 ft. tall, 10 ft. wide; much taller in its native habitat. Big (5–8-ft.) green leaves form a dense, globular head.

SAFFLOWER. See CARTHAMUS tinctorius

SAGE. See SALVIA

SAGE, RUSSIAN. See PEROVSKIA

SAGEBRUSH. See ARTEMISIA californica, A. tridentata

SAGINA subulata

IRISH MOSS, SCOTCH MOSS

Caryophyllaceae

PERENNIAL

ZONES 1–11, 14–24

FULL SUN OR PARTIAL SHADE

REGULAR WATER

Sagina subulata

Of two different prostrate plants of similar appearance, *Sagina subulata* is the more common. The other is *Arenaria verna,* usually called *A. v. caespitosa.* Both of these European natives make dense, compact, mosslike masses of slender leaves on slender stems. But *A. verna* has tiny white flowers in few-flowered clusters, while *S. subulata* bears flowers singly and differs in other technical details. In common usage, however, green forms of the two species are called Irish moss, and golden green forms (*A. v.* 'Aurea' and *S. s.* 'Aurea') are called Scotch moss.

Both *Sagina* and *Arenaria* are grown primarily as ground covers for limited areas. They're useful for filling gaps between paving blocks. In cool-summer gardens, they can seed themselves and become pests.

These plants won't grow well under conditions that suit true mosses. They need good soil, good drainage, and occasional feeding with controlled-release fertilizer. They take some foot traffic and tend to hump up in time; control humping by occasionally cutting out narrow strips, then pressing or rolling lightly. Control snails, slugs, cutworms. Cut squares from flats and set 6 in. apart for fast cover. To avoid lumpiness, plant so that soil line of squares is at or slightly below planted soil surface.

SAGO PALM. See CYCAS revoluta

SAGUARO. See CARNEGIEA gigantea

ST. AUGUSTINE GRASS. See STENOTAPHRUM secundatum

SAINTPAULIA

AFRICAN VIOLET

Gesneriaceae

PERENNIALS GROWN AS HOUSEPLANTS

FILTERED EARLY SUN, INDIRECT BRIGHT LIGHT

WATERING IS AN ART; SEE BELOW

Saintpaulia

Most popular of all flowering houseplants; given proper care, they bloom almost continuously. Most of the African violets grown are hybrids; they are derived from several species native to East Africa. Form rosettes of velvety green (sometimes variegated) leaves that may be roundish or pointed, with a smooth or quilted surface and scalloped or smooth margins. The original species bear pale blue to lavender and purple blossoms that are typically five petaled—with two smaller petals at the top of the flower, three larger ones below. Hybrids also include flowers in bell, cup, and star shapes, in colors including not only blues and purples but also white, various pink shades, burgundy, and crimson. Creamy yellows exist, but they tend to revert to pink or purple. Some hybrids have bands of color, contrasting veining, or dark accents on paler petals. All have bright yellow centers. Flowers may be single, semi-double, or fully double, sometimes with fringed or ruffled petals.

African violets need a moisture-retentive yet fast-draining potting mix. You can buy packaged mixes; if you prefer to make your own, use 3 parts peat moss to 1 part perlite and 1 part compost or sterilized loam. Don't use too large a pot; plants bloom best when roots are crowded. Choose a location where temperatures average 60 to 70°F/16 to 21°C. Humidity should be high; if house air is quite dry, increase humidity around plant by setting each plant on a saucer filled with wet gravel. Water plants from above or below, but avoid watering root crown or leaves. Wick-irrigated pots work well. Use room-temperature or slightly warmer water; wet potting mix thoroughly, then wait to water again until mix is dry to the touch. Don't let water stand in saucer for more than 2 hours after watering. Feed well-established plants (only when soil is moist) with slightly acid fertilizer once every 2 to 4 weeks. Propagate from seeds, leaf cuttings, or divisions. Common pests are aphids, cyclamen mites, thrips, and mealybugs. Pick off spent leaves and flowers.

Salicaceae. The willow family consists of deciduous trees or shrubs with flowers in catkins and (generally) with silk-tufted seeds that blow about. Besides willow *(Salix),* examples are cottonwood and poplar *(Populus).*

SALIX

WILLOW

Salicaceae

DECIDUOUS TREES AND SHRUBS

ZONES VARY BY SPECIES

FULL SUN

REGULAR TO AMPLE WATER

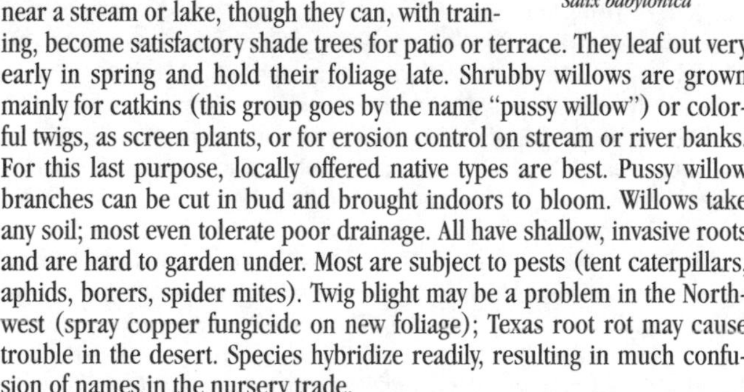

Salix babylonica

Fast-growing, weak-wooded, short-lived plants. Weeping willows are best used as single trees near a stream or lake, though they can, with training, become satisfactory shade trees for patio or terrace. They leaf out very early in spring and hold their foliage late. Shrubby willows are grown mainly for catkins (this group goes by the name "pussy willow") or colorful twigs, as screen plants, or for erosion control on stream or river banks. For this last purpose, locally offered native types are best. Pussy willow branches can be cut in bud and brought indoors to bloom. Willows take any soil; most even tolerate poor drainage. All have shallow, invasive roots and are hard to garden under. Most are subject to pests (tent caterpillars, aphids, borers, spider mites). Twig blight may be a problem in the Northwest (spray copper fungicide on new foliage); Texas root rot may cause trouble in the desert. Species hybridize readily, resulting in much confusion of names in the nursery trade.

S. alba. WHITE WILLOW. Tree. Zones A2, A3; 1–11, 14–24. Native to Europe, North Africa. Upright to 75–100 ft. tall, 50–100 ft. wide. Yellowish brown bark. Narrow, 1½–4-in., bright green leaves are silvery beneath, may turn golden in fall. The following forms are valued for colorful twigs.

S. a. tristis (S. babylonica aurea, S. 'Niobe'*).* GOLDEN WEEPING WILLOW. To 50–70 ft. tall and as wide or wider, with pendulous form. Young stems are bright yellow. Among the most attractive weeping willows.

S. a. vitellina. Upright, with brilliant yellow twigs in winter. Can grow to tree size, but cutting back gives best color display: lop to 1 ft. high yearly, just before spring growth begins. Stems may grow 8 ft. in a season. 'Britzensis' has red or orange-red winter stems; often confused with 'Chermesina'.

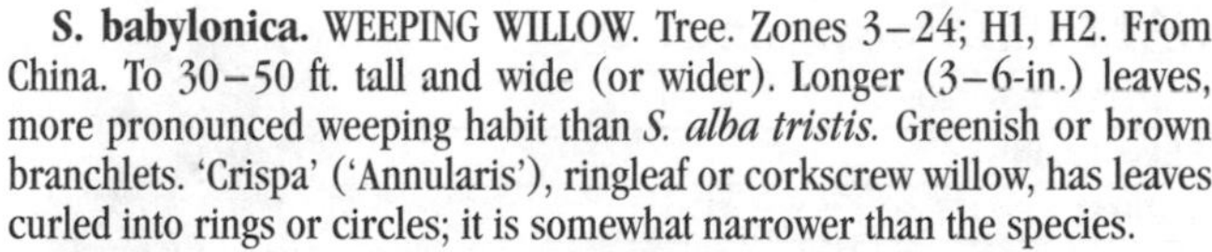

S. babylonica. WEEPING WILLOW. Tree. Zones 3–24; H1, H2. From China. To 30–50 ft. tall and wide (or wider). Longer (3–6-in.) leaves, more pronounced weeping habit than *S. alba tristis.* Greenish or brown branchlets. 'Crispa' ('Annularis'), ringleaf or corkscrew willow, has leaves curled into rings or circles; it is somewhat narrower than the species.

S. caprea. FRENCH PUSSY WILLOW, PINK PUSSY WILLOW. Shrub or tree. Zones 2–11, 14–24. Native from Europe to northeastern Asia. Grows to 15–25 ft. tall, 12–15 ft. wide. Broad, 3–6-in.-long leaves are dark green above, gray and hairy beneath. Before leafout, male plants produce fat, woolly, pinkish gray catkins about 1 in. long. Can be kept to shrub size by cutting to ground every few years. 'Pendula' (a male plant known as Kilmarnock willow) and 'Weeping Sally' (its female counterpart) are two selections that will naturally sprawl on the ground; they are more effective grafted or staked to form small weeping trees 6–8 ft. tall, 6 ft. wide.

S. discolor. PUSSY WILLOW. Shrub or tree. Zones 1–11, 14–24. Native to eastern U.S. To 15–25 ft. tall, 12–15 ft. wide. Slender red-brown stems; bright green, 2–4-in. leaves with bluish undersides. Catkins of male plants are main draw—soft, silky, pearl gray, to 1½ in. long.

S. 'Flame'. Shrub or tree. Zones 2–11, 14–24. To 15–20 ft. high and wide, with compact, dense habit. Branch tips curl upward and inward. Glossy green, lance-shaped leaves to 3 in. long turn a good golden yellow rather late in autumn; twigs turn brilliant orange red in winter. May actually be a variety of *S. alba vitellina.*

S. 'Golden Curls'. Shrub or tree. Zones 3–11, 14–24. To 30 ft. tall and wide, with somewhat weeping and twisting branches. Leaves like those of *S.* 'Flame' but somewhat curled. Bark on new growth is bright yellow. After plant has established a framework, cut it back hard in winter to keep colorful new growth coming on.

S. gracilistyla. ROSE-GOLD PUSSY WILLOW. Shrub. Zones 3–11, 14–24. To 6–10 ft. tall, 12 ft. wide. Narrowly oval, 2–4-in.-long leaves are gray green above, bluish green beneath. Male plants produce plump, gray, furry, 1½-in.-long catkins with numerous stamens with rose-and-gold anthers. Cut branches for arrangements to curb plant's size. Every 3 or 4 years, cut plant back to short stubs; you'll get very vigorous shoots with large catkins. *S. g. melanostachys* has black catkins with red anthers.

S. integra 'Hakuro Nishiki'. DAPPLED WILLOW. Shrub. Zones 3–9, 14–17. Native to Korea, Japan. To 4–6 ft. tall and wide; somewhat weeping. Stems and leaf buds are salmon pink; leaves are 4 in. long, ½–1¼ in. wide, light green mottled with white and pink. Best in partial shade.

S. matsudana. HANKOW WILLOW. Tree. Zones 3–11, 14–24. Upright, pyramidal growth to 40–50 ft. tall, 30–40 ft. wide. Bright green, narrow, 2–4-in.-long leaves. Can thrive on less water than most willows. This species and its varieties are popular in the high desert.

'Navajo'. GLOBE NAVAJO WILLOW. Large, spreading, round-topped tree to 70 ft. tall and wide.

'Tortuosa'. DRAGON-CLAW WILLOW, CORKSCREW WILLOW. To 30 ft. tall, 20 ft. wide; branches fantastically twisted into upright, spiraling patterns. Valued for winter silhouette and cut branches for arrangements.

'Umbraculifera'. GLOBE WILLOW. To 35 ft. high and wide. Umbrella-shaped crown with upright branches, drooping branchlets.

S. ×pendulina. Zones 2–11, 14–24. Hybrid best known for two selections. 'Blanda', Wisconsin weeping willow, grows 40–50 ft. tall or taller, 70 ft. wide; it has a less strongly weeping habit than *S. babylonica,* with broader leaves in a bluer shade of green. The similar 'Fan-Giant', fan giant blue weeping willow, is resistant to borers and twig blight.

S. purpurea. PURPLE OSIER, ALASKA BLUE WILLOW. Shrub. Zones A2, A3; 1–11. From Europe, North Africa, central and eastern Asia. To 15 ft. high and wide, with purple branches. Narrow, 1–3-in.-long leaves are dark green above, bluish beneath. Cut shrub to ground if overgrown. 'Gracilis' ('Nana'), dwarf purple osier, has slimmer branches and narrower leaves; it is usually grown as clipped hedge and kept 1–3 ft. high and wide.

S. udensis 'Sekka' (S. sachalinensis 'Sekka'). JAPANESE FANTAIL. Shrub or tree. Zones 2–11, 14–24. Male selection of a Japanese species. To 10–15 ft. tall, spreading twice as wide. Narrow leaves are 2–4 in. long, green above, silvery beneath. Silvery catkins to 2 in. long. Main feature is the plant's structure: branches are flattened, often 1–2 in. wide, twisted and curled, picturesque in arrangements.

SALPIGLOSSIS sinuata

PAINTED TONGUE

Solanaceae

ANNUAL

ZONES 1–24

FULL SUN

REGULAR WATER

Salpiglossis sinuata

Native to South America. Upright, open habit to 2–3 ft. tall, 1 ft. wide. Stems and narrowly oblong, 4-in.-long leaves are sticky. Flowers are 2–2½ in. wide, resemble petunias in shape but offer more unusual colors—mahogany red, reddish orange, yellow, purple, and pink shades, marbled and penciled with contrasting colors. Plants bloom most heavily in late spring and early summer, but in cool-summer climates they'll carry on until frost if regularly deadheaded. Good background plant for border; handsome cut flower. Bolero (to 2 ft. tall) and Royale (12–16 in.) are compact strains.

Seeds are rather difficult to start, especially when sown directly in garden. A better way to start them is to plant in potting mix in peat pots, several seeds to a pot, in late winter or early spring. Keep pots in a warm, protected location; thin seedlings to one per pot. When young plants are well established and frost danger is past, plant outdoors. Performs best in rich soil. Stake tall types. Tip-pinch growing plants to induce branching.

SALTBUSH. See ATRIPLEX

SALT CEDAR. See TAMARIX chinensis

SALVIA

SAGE

Lamiaceae (Labiatae)

EVERGREEN OR DECIDUOUS SHRUBS, PERENNIALS, BIENNIALS, AND ANNUALS

ZONES VARY BY SPECIES

FULL SUN, EXCEPT AS NOTED

REGULAR WATER, EXCEPT AS NOTED

Salvia officinalis 'Icterina'

Largest genus in the mint family, including some 900 species from throughout the world. In recent years, scores of new species and selections have appeared in Western nurseries; many tender perennials and shrubs are even being offered as annuals in cold-winter climates. All sages have square stems and whorls of two-lipped flowers, either distinctly spaced along flower stalks or so tightly crowded that they look like one dense spike; some species have branched inflorescences. Flower colors range from white and yellow through salmon and pink to scarlet and pure red, from pale lavender to true blue and darkest purple. A few sages have fragrant blossoms. Many have aromatic foliage. Sages attract hummingbirds, bees, butterflies.

Give lax varieties inconspicuous support by letting them grow through a cylinder of green-painted wire mesh. In many sages, aromatic compounds in the foliage repel pests—but this is not true for all species. Some are magnets for slugs and snails; in warm climates, others can be demolished by Mexican giant whitefly. Aphids may be a problem for many. Sages are generally easy to propagate from cuttings or seeds; you can also divide roots of perennial kinds.

Nurseries in the West offer nearly 100 species as well as dozens of selections and hybrids. Those listed here are among the best.

S. africana-lutea (S. aurea). GOLDEN SAGE, BEACH SAGE. Evergreen shrub. Zones 14–17, 19–24. From South Africa. Dense grower to 3–4 ft. high and wide; becomes sparse and woody with age. Young plants thickly covered with elliptical, woolly gray-green leaves to 1¼ in. long. Carried on 2–4-in. stems are whorls of interesting inch-long flowers in bright yellow aging to rusty brown; they emerge from brown, papery calyxes that persist long after blossoms fall. Main bloom in winter, early spring; sporadic through fall. When flowering decreases in late spring, shear plants back by one-third to encourage new basal growth; when plants become too woody (after 3 to 5 years), discard and replace. Prefers sandy soil. Drought tolerant. Top growth hardy to 20°F/–7°C; may resprout from roots in colder temperatures. 'Kirstenbosch' is a dwarf selection 1½–2 ft. high.

S. ambigens. See S. guaranitica

S. apiana. CALIFORNIA WHITE SAGE, BEE SAGE. Evergreen shrub. Zones 7–9, 11, 13–24. From Southern California, Baja California. Coarse plant to 3–5 ft. tall and wide. Aromatic, woolly silvery gray leaves are elliptical, 3–4 in. long. In spring, lavender-tinged white flowers appear in whorls along unbranched, sometimes pinkish stems to 2 ft. long. Attractive at night; reflects moon, garden lighting. To keep neat, shear lightly after flowering. Drought tolerant. 'Vicki Romo' (a hybrid between *S. apiana* and *S. clevelandii*) is more compact, has lavender-blue flowers.

S. argentea. SILVER SAGE. Biennial or short-lived perennial. Zones 1–24. From southern Europe, northwestern Africa. Soft, scallop-edged, silky-haired gray-green leaves grow 6–10 in. long, form a low foliage rosette to 2 ft. wide. In summer, many-branched, 3–4-ft. flowering stems bear 1¼-in.-long, hooded white flowers (sometimes tinged pink or yellow) with silvery calyxes. Cut to ground when flowers fade. Handsome focal point for front of border. Protect from slugs, snails.

S. aurea. See S. africana-lutea

S. azurea grandiflora (S. pitcheri). PRAIRIE SAGE, PITCHER SAGE. Shrubby perennial. Zones 1–24. Native from Colorado and Texas east to Michigan and Georgia. Slender, vertical, usually unbranched stems to 5 ft. form a 2–3-ft.-wide clump. Plant is lax, needs support. Smooth or hairy, medium green to deep green, narrow leaves to 4 in. long. Pure azure blue flowers with white-blotched lower lip on spikes to 1 ft. long; blooms summer to frost. Not always permanent in wet winters.

S. blepharophylla. EYELASH SAGE. Shrubby perennial. Zones 14–24. From northeastern Mexico. To 1½–2 ft. tall, spreading indefinitely by creeping rhizomes. Thin, hairy, purplish stems; oval, glossy dark green leaves to 1½ in. long, edged with fine hairs resembling eyelashes. Inch-long scarlet flowers on stems that lengthen to about 1 ft. as season goes on. Blooms from spring to frost, nearly all year in mild-winter climates. If confined, makes a good ground cover in partial shade.

S. brandegei. BRANDEGEE SAGE. Evergreen shrub. Zones 15–17, 19–24. Native to Santa Rosa Island and coastal Baja California. Sprawling plant to 4–5 ft. high, 5–7 ft. wide. Linear, scalloped, 3–4-in.-long leaves are shiny, rough-textured dark green above, woolly white beneath. Tight, widely spaced whorls of ½-in., pale lavender, broad-lipped flowers on stems to 10 in. long; persistent violet-gray calyxes. Early spring bloom. Shorten branches by one-third during or right after bloom. Long-lasting cut flowers. Drought tolerant.

S. buchananii. BUCHANAN SAGE. Shrubby perennial. Zones 14–24. Thought to be native to Mexico. Rounded growth to 1–2 ft. high and wide, with widely spaced, glossy dark green, oval leaves to 2 in. long. Lax, 8–12-in. stems support drooping, 2-in., brilliant magenta flowers. Blooms in summer and fall, and sporadically in other seasons in milder part of range. Sets no seed; propagate from cuttings. Handsome in containers; winter it indoors in cold climates.

S. cacaliifolia. Perennial. Zones 14–24. From southern Mexico, Guatemala, Honduras. Arching, trailing mass of interlocking stems grows to 2–3 ft. tall, 6–8 ft. or more wide. Will cascade over a bank or retaining wall, rooting where it touches ground. Evergreen, arrow-shaped dark green leaves are 2–3 in. long. Blooms midsummer through fall (continuing all winter, in mild climates), bearing rich blue, ½-in. flowers on 6–8-in.-long stems. Tolerates full sun but blooms better in partial shade.

S. canariensis. CANARY ISLAND SAGE. Evergreen shrub. Zones 9, 12, 14–24. Native to Canary Islands. To 6–7 ft. tall, 8–10 ft. wide; can reach that size in a single season. Angular, arching branches covered with stiff white hairs. Triangular, 4–6-in.-long, gray-green leaves with woolly white undersides. Big (to 8-in.-long, 6-in.-wide), branched flower clusters from spring to late fall. Pinkish violet, ¾-in. blossoms have red-violet calyxes that persist long after flowers fade. In winter, cut to 1 ft. from ground to encourage fresh basal growth. When plant becomes too woody, discard and replace it. 'Alba' has white flowers, pink calyxes.

S

S. chamaedryoides. GERMANDER SAGE. Perennial. Zones 8, 9, 12, 14–24. From eastern Mexico. Rounded plant to 1–2 ft. tall, spreading 2–3 ft. or more by underground runners. Silvery, ¾-in.-long leaves; brilliant true blue, 1-in. flowers on stems to 8 in. long. Heaviest bloom comes in late spring and fall, with intermittent flowering during rest of growing season. Deadhead to encourage rebloom. Elegant front-of-border plant. Drought tolerant but blooms longer and better with more water.

S. chiapensis. CHIAPAS SAGE. Perennial. Zones 17, 23, 24. From cloud forests of Chiapas, Mexico. Many 1½–2-ft. stems form a relaxed clump 3–4 ft. or more wide; growth is taller and laxer in shade. Evergreen, elliptical, glossy dark green leaves up to 3 in. long. Deep hot pink, ¾-in. flowers in widely spaced whorls on stems to 1 ft. long; blooms from early summer through winter in frost-free area or greenhouse. Reseeds freely. Succeeds with moderate water but appreciates frequent wetting of leaves. Good ground cover for dryish shade; good in containers. Needs at least partial shade in hottest climates.

S. clevelandii. CLEVELAND SAGE. CALIFORNIA BLUE SAGE. Evergreen shrub. Zones 8, 9, 12–24. Hardy to 20°F/–7°C. From Southern California, northern Baja California. Rounded, arching growth to 3–5 ft. high, 5–8 ft. wide. Wrinkled, toothed gray-green leaves to 2 in. long are elliptical or lance-shaped, deliciously fragrant. Foliage makes a refreshing tea and is also used as a preservative in potpourri. Fragrant, inch-long, pale lavender to violet-blue flowers in widely spaced whorls along 1½–2-ft. stems. Blooms in early summer; remove faded spikes to encourage rebloom. Drought tolerant. 'Winnifred Gilman' is more compact (3 ft. high and wide), with dark red flower stems and calyx tubes, dark violet-blue flowers. Hybrid 'Allen Chickering' grows like a typical Cleveland sage and bears abundant bright lavender-blue flowers. Hybrid 'Pozo Blue' is similar but hardier; it has endured temperatures to 10°F/–12°C. 'Aromas', also a hybrid, bears larger, darker blue flowers than the species.

WHAT SAGES NEED

LOCATION: Choose a spot in full sun (a few types prefer shade), with good air circulation to help deter mildew and other fungal diseases.

DRAINAGE: Most sages must have good drainage, especially in winter; waterlogged plants seldom make it through hard freezes. If soil is heavy, work in plenty of organic matter and apply a thick mulch of well-rotted compost.

WATERING: "Deep" is the operative word. Most of the plants discussed here come from areas with summer rainfall; they need regular (or, in some cases, moderate) water during dry spells. Plants described as drought tolerant require a deep soaking at least once a month during the heat of summer to retain their foliage and prolong their bloom period.

PRUNING: Most resent severe pruning at any time other than late winter or early spring, when weather is cool and vigorous new growth is emerging from plant base. To shape during the growing season, either tip-pinch shoots or cut them back by no more than one-third (keeping most of the leaves on each stem). Remember: any pruning before the bloom season will delay flowering.

Salvia coccinea 'Lady in Red'

S. coahuilensis. COAHUILA SAGE. Shrubby perennial. Zones 8, 9, 12–24. From mountains of Coahuila, Mexico. To 2½ ft. high and wide. Many slender, upward-sweeping woody branches, sparsely clothed with evergreen, 1-in., linear olive green leaves. Deep violet, 1-in. flowers appear on 3–5-in. stems from early summer to frost, all year in mild-winter climates; heaviest bloom in early summer and fall. Cut back to about 8 in. from ground in late winter. Moderate water.

S. coccinea. TROPICAL SAGE. Perennial in Zones 12–24, H1, H2; usually grown as annual in all zones. From Mexico; naturalized and weedy in Hawaii. Bushy, upright; to 2–3 ft. tall, 2½ ft. wide. Dark green, hairy, oval to heart-shaped leaves to 2½ in. long. In summer, slender stems to 1 ft. long carry many ¾–1-in. flowers with broad lower lip. Colors range from bright red through orange-red to pink and white, including many bicolors. Widely used as bedding plant, border filler. Stems are brittle; shelter from wind. Deadhead to encourage rebloom.

If plant lives over, cut back to 4–6 in. when new spring growth begins, then fertilize. By end of second season, plant will be woody and in decline. Reseeds copiously. Good seed-grown selections include scarlet 'Lady in Red'; salmon 'Brenthurst'('Lady in Pink'); 'Coral Nymph' ('Cherry Blossom'), near white with coral lower lip; and white 'Lactea' ('Lady in White') and 'White Nymph'.

S. confertiflora. Perennial. Zones 16, 17, 22–24. Native to Brazil. Upright grower to 4–6 ft. high and wide (about twice that size in mildest climates). Lance-shaped, scalloped leaves to 8 in. long are dark green with yellowish tinge, densely hairy (especially on undersides); they have an unpleasant odor when bruised. Flowers offer a glowing color combination: flowering stems and calyx tubes are covered with red-brown velvet, and crowded ½-in. blossoms are dark orange. Blooms in fall, continuing through winter in mild areas. Stake plant; shelter from wind. Top growth may burn even in light frosts.

S. 'Costa Rica Blue'. Evergreen shrub. Zones 15–17, 19–24. To 8 ft. tall and wide; can be kept lower by cutting back to 1 ft. in early spring. Broadly oval to heart-shaped, hairy, shiny bright green leaves to 5 in. long. Brilliant true blue, 1–1½-in. flowers on 1–1½-ft. stems. Blooms from the end of summer until frost (through spring in mildest climates). Needs support, shelter from wind and cold. 'Omaha Gold' is a sport with leaves irregularly edged in yellowish green. A violet-flowered form also exists.

S. 'Dara's Choice'. Evergreen shrub. Zones 7, 14–24. A hybrid between *S. sonomensis* and *S. mellifera*. Bushy, spreading, to 2–3 ft. high, 3–6 ft. wide, rooting where it touches ground. Lance-shaped, 2½–3½-in.-long leaves are medium green with a grayish cast. Tight whorls of violet-blue, ½-in. spring, flowers are widely spaced along many 6–12-in. stems. Good as bank cover or draped over a wall. Sometimes subject to verticillium wilt; some branches die, but plant usually survives. Best in areas with coastal influence. Drought tolerant. Hybrid 'Mrs. Beard' has grayer foliage, lower growth (to 2 ft. high), pale lavender flowers; it is not prone to verticillium wilt.

S. darcyi (S. schaffneri, S. oresbia). DARCY SAGE. Perennial. Zones 8, 9, 12, 14–24. From northeastern Mexico. Upright growth to 3–4 ft. tall; spreads by rhizomes to 3 ft. or more. Softly hairy, triangular light green leaves to 1½ in. long have a pleasant, fruity aroma. Widely spaced whorls of 1½-in., coral red blossoms on unbranched stems from early summer to late fall. Stems are 6–12 in. tall, sometimes as high as 2 ft. They are brittle; shelter from wind. Protect from slugs, snails. Dies back to ground in winter. Tolerates partial shade.

S. deserta. See S. × sylvestris

S. dolomitica. DOLOMITE SAGE. Evergreen shrub. Zones 15, 17, 22–24. From mountains of South Africa. Handsome plant to 3–5 ft. tall and wide; may spread wider by short rhizomes. Elliptical, prominently veined gray leaves to 1½ in. long. Unassuming 1-in. summer flowers, arranged in pairs along 4-in. stems, are pale lilac with cream streak extending into throat. Bell-shaped, green or rose-colored, lemon-scented calyxes are persistent. Drought tolerant. Full sun or partial shade.

S. dorisiana. PEACH SAGE, FRUIT-SCENTED SAGE. Perennial. Zones 23, 24. From Honduras. Upright, branching habit to 5 ft. high and wide. Hairy, broadly oval, lime green, 5–7-in.-long leaves emit enticing pineapple-grapefruit scent when touched. Hot pink, 2-in. flowers with lime green calyx tubes on 6–8-in. stems. Blooms in winter and early spring, so must be grown in frost-free site or moved indoors to sunny window or greenhouse to flower. Elegant potted plant. Morning sun or dappled shade.

S. dorrii. DESERT SAGE, GREAT BASIN BLUE SAGE. Evergreen shrub. Zones 2, 3, 10–13, 18, 19. Native to high deserts from Washington and Idaho south to California and Arizona. May have a rounded habit or form a spreading mat; grows 1–3 ft. high, 2–4 ft. wide. Branches densely clothed in gray, linear or spoon-shaped, ¼–1¼-in. leaves. Blooms in late spring; each 1–2-ft.-long stem bears three to five widely spaced whorls of light to deep blue, 1-in. flowers with deep blue bracts and calyxes. Needs sandy soil, perfect drainage. Drought tolerant. Good in dry desert garden.

S. elegans. PINEAPPLE SAGE. Perennial. Zones 8–24. Native to southern Mexico, Guatemala. In the wild, this species is variable in habit, bloom time, leaf fragrance. The most commonly grown form, 'Scarlet Pineapple' *(S. rutilans),* grows upright to 3–4 ft. high and wide, with branching, brittle stems; in part shade, growth is lush and needs support. Densely hairy, bright green leaves to 4 in. long, broadly oval with pointed tip. Foliage has a strong aroma of ripe pineapple; used in cool drinks, fruit salads. Slender, 1½-in., bright red flowers in loose clusters of 8–12 are carried on 6–8-in. stems. In mild-winter areas or indoors, blooms from late fall through spring; elsewhere, it is cut off by frost. Hybrid 'Frieda Dixon' is similar but has pinkish red flowers. 'Honey Melon Sage' grows half as high and spreads rapidly to form a dense ground cover; it has slightly smaller blooms and smaller, more rounded leaves that smell something like ripe honeydew melon. Blooms from early summer through fall (shear off faded flower stems two or three times a season to produce a new crop).

S. farinacea. MEALYCUP SAGE, TEXAS VIOLET. Perennial in Zones 7–10, 12–24, H1, H2; usually grown as annual in all zones. Native to southern New Mexico, Texas, Mexico. Upright growth to 3–4 ft. tall, half as wide. Narrowly lance-shaped leaves to 3 in. long are smooth above, woolly white below. Tall, densely packed spikes of ¾–1-in. flowers on stems 6–12 in. long, late spring to frost. Blossom color varies from deep violet blue to white; cuplike calyxes are covered with white hairs, often have a blue or violet tinge. Many strains are sold for bedding and container use; typically have heavier bloom, better branching, more compact habit. 'Cirrus', to 14 in. high, has silvery white blossoms, calyxes, stems. 'Rhea', 14–16 in. high, has intense deep blue flowers, bluish calyxes; starts blooming earlier in spring. 'Strata', 12–14 in. high, has blue flowers and large, densely woolly, silvery white calyxes. 'Victoria', to 18–20 in. high, has intense violet-blue flowers and calyxes; 'Victoria White' is white flowered.

S. gesneriiflora. Shrubby perennial. Zones 9, 14–17, 19–24. From west-central Mexico. To 4–8 ft. tall and wide. Heart-shaped, yellow-green, heavily felted, strongly aromatic leaves to 6 in. long. Stems 8–12 in. long bear brilliant orange-red, drooping, 2–2½-in. flowers with bell-shaped, usually yellow-green calyxes. Blooms from late fall into spring; to limit growth, cut back to 1–2 ft. after bloom. Best in areas with mild, sunny winters. Prone to damage from wind, rain; grow next to wall and support with stakes if needed. 'Mole Poblano', with chocolate brown calyxes, is more compact and floriferous than the species. 'Tequila' has violet calyxes.

S. greggii. AUTUMN SAGE. Evergreen or deciduous shrub. Zones 8–24. Native to southwest Texas, north-central Mexico. Rounded plant, branching from base; typically grows 1–4 ft. high and wide. Slender, hairy stems are closely set with glossy green, ¾–1¼-in.-long leaves that vary in shape from rounded to linear. Blooms throughout summer and fall, bearing ¼–1-in. flowers on 3–6-in. stems, in colors ranging from deep purplish red through true red to various rose and pink shades to white. To keep plants tidy and free blooming, prune and remove dead flower stems frequently. Before new spring growth begins, shorten and shape plants, removing dead wood. Good low hedge. Replace plants every 4 or 5 years, when they become woody and unproductive. Drought tolerant but does best with moderate water. Full sun or partial shade (be sure to give some shade in hottest climates). A few of the best selections are pure white 'Alba'; hot pink 'Big Pink', with extra-large lower lip; 'Desert Blaze', with brilliant true red flowers and gold-edged leaves; and deep red 'Furman's Red'. (Varieties sold as *S. greggii* with flowers in shades of orange, orange red, or yellow actually belong with *S. ×jamensis.*)

S. guaranitica (S. ambigens). ANISE-SCENTED SAGE. Perennial in Zones 8, 9, 14–24; annual in colder climates. From South America. Upright, branching plant to 4–5 ft. high and nearly as wide. Spreads by short underground runners; roots form tubers resembling small sausages. Narrowly heart-shaped, sparsely hairy, mint green leaves to 5 in. long. Blooms from early summer to frost. Most common form bears 2-in. cobalt blue blossoms, carried several to each foot-long stem; calyxes are bright green, turning purplish on sunny side. Needs support. Where it grows as a perennial, it gets woody by season's end—but that wood dies during winter and must be cut back to ground. Elegant container plant. Can be demolished by Mexican giant whitefly. Tolerates partial shade, especially in hottest climates. 'Argentine Skies' has light blue flowers. 'Black and Blue' bears deep blue blossoms with dark purplish blue calyxes.

S. holwayi. HOLWAY SAGE. Perennial. Zones 9, 14–24. From mountains of southeastern Mexico, Guatemala. Spectacular where it has room to grow. Rambling plant to 4–5 ft. high, spreading to 8–10 ft. in a growing season, rooting wherever its lax stems touch the soil. Triangular, yellowish green, prominently veined leaves to 3 in. long. Bright red, 1-in. flowers in showy pyramidal spikes to 8 in. long; blooms from late fall through early spring. Partial shade under high, open tree canopy suits it well.

S. 'Indigo Spires'. Shrubby perennial. Zones 8, 9, 14–24. Can build up to a sprawling 6–7 ft. by 10 ft. but is easily kept to 3–4 ft. high, 2–3 ft. wide with support and selective pruning. Soft, silky, oval to oblong leaves (to 6 in. long near base of plant, shorter higher up) have a grayish sheen above, are white and woolly beneath. Narrow, twisted spikes of closely spaced, ½-in., violet-blue flowers can reach 3 ft. or longer. Blooms from early summer to frost (almost all year in mildest climates). Indigo calyxes are colorful long after blossoms fall. Excellent cut flowers. Top growth damaged by frost. Full sun or partial shade.

S. involucrata. ROSELEAF SAGE. Shrubby perennial. Zones 8–24; H1, H2. From eastern Mexico. To 5–6 ft. high and wide, often in one season. Oval, minutely toothed, 5–6-in.-long, rich green leaves with purple undersides and midribs. Foot-long stems hold numerous clusters of three purplish red, 2-in. flowers enclosed by a pair of bright purplish rose bracts that fall just as flowers open. Blooms from mid- or late summer to midautumn. Good cut flowers. Usually evergreen in mild-winter climates. Does best with afternoon shade. 'Bethellii' produces an almost spherical cluster of deep pink bracts at the top of its short flower spike. 'Boutin' is more compact (to 4 ft. tall, 5–6 ft. wide), with 6–10-in. flower stems. Hybrid 'Mulberry Jam' is similar to 'Boutin' but narrower (to 2–3 ft. wide).

S. ×jamensis. JAMÉ SAGE. Evergreen shrub. Zones 8–24. Plants sold by this name are hybrids involving *S. greggii, S. microphylla,* an unknown

Salvia argentea

Salvia chamaedryoides

Salvia coccinea 'Coral Nymph'

Salvia farinacea

Salvia 'Maraschino' (*S. microphylla* Hybrid)

S

yellow-flowered species, and possibly other sages; they are found wild in Mexico. Habit varies from upright to horizontal, but plants are usually under 3 ft. tall, with fairly open branching; stems often root where they touch soil. Glossy green, oval to elliptical, toothed leaves ¾–1¼ in. long. Stems 3–6 in. long bear ½–¾-in. flowers in many colors: violet, wine red, orange red, hot pink, coral, salmon, yellow, white, and bicolors. Best in moderate climates without extreme temperature swings. Drought tolerant but perform best with moderate water. Good houseplants for sunny spot. Excellent varieties include 'Cienega de Oro' (creamy yellow flowers) and 'Sierra San Antonio' (light pink blooms with pastel yellow lips); both grow 1½–2 ft. high, 2–3 ft. wide. 'San Isidro Moon' has an open, horizontal habit to 2 ft. high, 2–4 ft. wide; it bears two-tone flowers in peach shades. Varieties often sold as forms of *S. greggii* include soft orange-red 'Coral', pale yellow 'Moonlight', and glowing orange-red 'Wild Thing'.

S. leucantha. MEXICAN BUSH SAGE, VELVET SAGE. Evergreen shrub. Zones 12–24; H1, H2. From central and eastern Mexico. Vigorous, upright, velvety plant to 3–4 ft. tall, 3–6 ft. or more wide; sprawls in bloom. Lance-shaped to linear, 5–6-in.-long leaves are dark grayish green above, whitish below. Stems to 1 ft. long bear whorls of ¾–1¼-in. white flowers with purple calyxes. Bloom period runs from fall through spring in mild-winter areas, stops with frost in colder climates. To limit plant size and renew flowering stems, cut back close to ground before spring growth begins or at end of bloom cycle; where growing season is especially long, cut back again in early to midsummer. Also limit watering to every 2 or 3 weeks and remove blossoms as soon as they fade. 'Eder' has leaves with creamy white edges. 'Midnight' ('Purple Velvet'), considered by many to be the best-looking form, has purple flowers and calyxes.

S. leucophylla. PURPLE SAGE, GRAY SAGE. Evergreen shrub. Zones 8, 9, 14–17, 19–24, except as noted. Native to Coast Ranges of Southern California. Graceful plant to 3–5 ft. high with equal or greater width; arching branches have upturned tips, root where they touch soil. Stems and foliage thickly covered with fine white hairs. Wrinkled, oblong to lance-shaped leaves to 3 in. long are apple green when they emerge, turn whiter as days get hotter. In spring, each 6–8-in. stem carries three to five tightly packed whorls of 1-in., pinkish purple flowers with gray calyxes. Good bank cover. Drought tolerant. 'Point Sal Spreader' (often sold as 'Point Sal') is prostrate, 1–2½ ft. high, 10–12 ft. wide; has broader, grayer leaves than species. 'Figueroa' (Zones 7–9, 14–24), to 3–4 ft. high and twice as wide, is especially silvery and exceptionally tolerant of drought, heat, cold.

S. madrensis. FORSYTHIA SAGE. Perennial. Zones 14–17, 19–24. From west-central Mexico. Strong grower, building up to 5–8 ft. tall and wide. Spreads by rhizomes to make a broad thicket (but stems are easily pulled out). Square stems are very thick—to 2 in. on a side at base. Bright green, elongated heart–shaped, rough-textured leaves reach 6 in. long at bottom of plant, become smaller toward top. Butter yellow, 1-in. flowers on 1–2-ft. stems; good for cutting. Blooms from fall until frost (through spring in mild-winter areas). Top growth damaged by frost.

S. melissodora. GRAPE-SCENTED SAGE. Evergreen or deciduous shrub. Zones 9, 14–17, 19–24. From Mexico. Graceful plant to 6 ft. tall, 4 ft. wide. Medium green, oval leaves to 1½ in. long; veins on leaf undersides are coated with yellowish tan wool. Blooms from late spring to frost; 6–8-in. stems carry ½–¾-in. flowers in lavender with violet upper lip. Fragrance is like that of ripe grapes. Evergreen in mild winters. Worthy addition to a scented garden.

S. mellifera. BLACK SAGE, HONEY SAGE. Evergreen shrub. Zones 7–9, 14–24. Native to coastal California and Baja California. To 3–6 ft. tall, 3–5 ft. or more wide; upright to spreading. Oblong to lance-shaped, deeply veined, aromatic leaves 1–2¼ in. long; olive-tinged dark green above, woolly gray beneath. In late spring, bears tightly packed whorls of whitish or lavender-tinged flowers less than ½ in. long on 8–16-in.-long stems. Not spectacular looking, but butterflies and bees love it. Good cover for dry banks. Drought tolerant. Will stand some shade. 'Repens' is a creeping, cascading form to 1–2 ft. high, 4–6 ft. wide. 'Terra Seca' is an extra-tough variety to 2 ft. high, more than 6 ft. wide; makes a good cascading ground cover if you pinch or shear upward-growing branches to keep foliage in center of plant.

S. mexicana. MEXICAN SAGE. Shrubby perennial. Zones 9, 14–17, 19–24. From central Mexico. Robust, erect growth to 10 ft. or taller, 3–5 ft. wide. Leaves to 6 in. long, typically elongated oval or heart shaped; they may be medium green and smooth above, fuzzy beneath, or gray to gray green and densely hairy on both sides. Pleasant pine fragrance. Tightly spaced whorls of 1–2½-in. flowers on 12–20-in.-long stems; blossoms are dark blue or violet with green or reddish purple calyxes. Blooms from early fall through spring in mild-winter climates; stops with hard frost elsewhere. Protect from wind. To keep compact, remove flower stems and shape plant as blooms are fading. Tolerates some shade; good under high-branching trees. Best with moderate water; more frequent watering produces excessive, brittle growth. 'Black Sepals' has smaller, dark green leaves; its blackish stems and calyxes show best color in full sun. 'Huntington' has gray leaves, attracts butterflies. 'Limelight' ('Chartreuse') has yellow-green stems and calyxes, blue-violet flowers.

S. microphylla. Evergreen shrub. Zones 7–24. Native from southeastern Arizona through southern Mexico. This species grows wild over an enormous geographical area and has many local variants. Drought tolerant but performs best with moderate water. Full sun or partial shade.

S. m. microphylla (S. grahamii). The form most often found in nurseries. Tough, dense, wiry-looking plant to 3–4 ft. high, 3–6 ft. wide. Stems marked with fuzzy white stripes. Triangular to oval, tooth-edged leaves are dark green, ½–1 in. long. Short stems bear pairs of rosy red, 1-in. flowers with small, hooded upper lip, three-lobed lower lip. Blooms most heavily in late spring and fall, sporadically at other times of year.

Forms of *S. m. microphylla* bear flowers in many shades of red, pink, magenta, and violet. 'Alba' is a white-blooming form. 'Belize Form', to 5 ft. tall and 8 ft. wide, is a more tender plant with brighter green leaves; puts on a continuous show of brilliant red flowers. 'Berzerkeley' is more compact (to 2 ft. tall, 3–4 ft. wide), bears glowing pinkish red blossoms. 'San Carlos Festival', 2–3 ft. tall, 4–6 ft. wide, is a nonstop bloomer bearing raspberry pink flowers. Hybrids with *S. greggii* include vigorous 'Maraschino', 3–4 ft. high, 6 ft. wide, bearing bright cherry red flowers; purplish pink 'Plum Wine', to 3–4 ft. high and 2½–3½ ft. wide; and 'Raspberry Royale', to 2½ ft. high and 3–4 ft. wide, with purplish red upper lip, dark red lower lip. ▸

Salvia guaranitica

Salvia officinalis 'Tricolor'

Salvia splendens

Salvia nemorosa 'Ostfriesland'

Salvia uliginosa

S. m. neurepia. 'Kew Red' is the name given to the originally introduced form. To 3–5 ft. tall, 4–6 ft. wide. More open-branched plant than *S. m. microphylla,* with yellowish green leaves, brilliant red flowers.

S. muelleri. ROYAL PURPLE SAGE. Evergreen shrub. Zones 8–24. From northeastern Mexico. Like *S. greggii* but lower, more spreading. Grows 2–3 ft. high, spreads 4–6 ft. by rhizomes. Oval, 1–2-in.-long, shiny green leaves. Violet, inch-long flowers, spaced along 8–12-in. stems, all year in mildest climates, spring to fall in colder ones; most profuse when days are short. Drought tolerant but needs weekly soakings in summer heat.

S. nemorosa. Perennial. Zones 2–10, 14–24. From eastern Europe, eastward to central Asia. To 1½–3 ft. tall, spreading 2–3 ft. wide by rhizomes. Forms tight foliage rosette from which rise erect, branching flower stems. Wrinkled, dull green, finely toothed leaves are oval or lance-shaped. Lower leaves are stalked, to 4 in. long; upper ones are smaller, virtually stalkless, clasping flower stem. Sprawls if not supported. Stems 3–6 in. long hold ¼–½-in. flowers in violet, purple, pink, or white, with persistent violet, purple, or green bracts. Blooms summer through fall if spent stems are removed. 'Lubecca' has grayish green leaves, violet flowers with reddish purple bracts; 'Ostfriesland' ('East Friesland') has intense violet-blue flowers, pink to purple bracts. Both varieties grow 1½ ft. high.

Salvia nemorosa
'Ostfriesland'

S. officinalis. GARDEN SAGE, COMMON SAGE. Shrubby perennial. Zones 2–24; H1, H2. From the Mediterranean region. Traditional culinary and medicinal sage. To 1–3 ft. tall, 1–2½ ft. wide; stems often root where they touch soil. Aromatic, oval to oblong, wrinkled, 2–3-in. leaves are gray green above, white and hairy beneath. Branching, 8–12-in. stems bear loose, spikelike clusters of ½-in. flowers in late spring, summer. Usual color is lavender blue, but violet, red violet, pink, and white forms exist. Delay pruning until new leaves begin to unfurl, then cut just above fresh growth; cutting into bare wood usually causes dieback. Replace plants when woody or leggy (every 3 or 4 years). Subject to root rot where drainage is less than perfect. Give afternoon shade in hottest climates.

'Berggarten' ('Mountain Garden'). Compact; to 16 in. high. Denser growth, rounder leaves, fewer flowers than species; may be longer lived.

'Compacta' ('Nana', 'Minimus'). A half-size (or even smaller) version of the species, with narrower, closer-set leaves.

'Holt's Mammoth'. Leaves (4–5 in. long) used in making condiments.

'Icterina'. Gray-green leaves with golden border. Does not bloom.

'Purpurascens' ('Red Sage'). Leaves are flushed with red violet when new, slowly mature to gray green.

'Tricolor'. Gray-green leaves with irregular cream border; new foliage is flushed with purplish pink.

S. oresbia. See S. darcyi

S. patens. GENTIAN SAGE. Perennial. Zones 9, 14–24; H1, H2. From central Mexico. Upright to 2–3 ft. or taller, 1–2 ft. wide. Spreads slowly by tuberous roots. Arrow-shaped, toothed, softly hairy leaves are bright green, 2–4 in. long. Pairs of brilliant blue, 2-in. blossoms on 6–15-in.-long stems; upper lip is hooded, lower one flared and ruffled. Bloom peaks in early summer but repeats through fall if plant is fertilized and deadheaded. Best in mixed plantings; not showy enough for bedding. Established clumps can be divided. Easy from seed, though color of seedlings may vary. Partial shade in hottest climates. 'Oxford Blue' has deep blue flowers, 'Cambridge Blue' light sky blue ones. 'Guanajuata', to 3 ft. or taller, bears deep blue flowers to 3 in. long; leaves often have a brown central blotch.

S. 'Phyllis's Fancy'. Evergreen shrub. Zones 16, 17, 21–24. Vigorous. Habit like *S. leucantha,* which apparently is involved in its parentage. To 4–5 ft. tall, 6–8 ft. wide; spreads by rhizomes. Wrinkled green leaves to 6 in. long, twice as wide as those of *S. leucantha.* Bluish stems to 1½ ft. or longer bear ¾–1¼-in., lavender-tinged white flowers with blue-violet calyxes, late spring through fall (nearly all year in mildest climates). 'Waverly' ('Mark's Mystery Sage') is a similar but less vigorous hybrid (3 ft. tall, 4–5 ft. wide). Its 1-ft. flower stems are flushed with red violet, as are calyxes; blooms are white tinged pinkish lilac.

S. 'Purple Majesty'. Shrubby perennial. Zones 9, 14–24. To 3 ft. tall, 4 ft. wide. Hybrid of *S. guaranitica,* with leaves of a yellower green; brilliant royal purple flowers with violet-black calyxes. Blooms from summer until frost in colder climates, nearly all year in mild-winter regions (where it is evergreen).

S. recognita. TURKISH SAGE. Perennial. Zones 2–24. Native to Turkey. From a 1½–2-ft.-wide basal clump, densely hairy flowering stems rise 3 ft. or more. Mildly aromatic, 5–8-in.-long leaves have wine red stalks and five to nine grayish green, scalloped, oval to lance-shaped, silky-haired leaflets. Terminal leaflet to 4–5 in. long, others less than half that size. Widely spaced whorls of four to six 1½-in. lilac-pink flowers; hairy calyxes glisten with oil glands. Blooms in early summer, sporadically through fall. Short lived but reseeds freely. Partial shade.

S. regla. MOUNTAIN SAGE. Evergreen or deciduous shrub. Zones 7–10, 14–24. Native to western Texas, central Mexico. Upright stems to 4–6 ft. high; these arch and branch out to form an almost equally wide mass. Scalloped, puckered, fan-shaped leaves (drawn out to sharp points in some forms) are 1 in. across. Orange-scarlet, 1-in. flowers with flaring calyxes appear in short clusters at branch ends; calyxes persist for several weeks after flowers drop. Profuse bloom from fall until frost (through early spring—though less profusely—in mild areas). Prune this plant (if ever) only when it is growing strongly in summer; winter-pruned plants recover slowly, may even die. Loses leaves at 28°F/–2°C. Excellent nectar source for hummingbirds. 'Huntington' has larger flowers, spreading habit (3–4 ft. tall, to 6 ft. wide); 'Royal' is an upright grower to 6–7 ft.

S. roemeriana. CEDAR SAGE. Perennial. Zones 7–24. Native to south-central Texas, northeastern Mexico. To 1–2 ft. high and wide. Reminiscent of coral bells *(Heuchera),* with basal clump of scalloped, rounded leaves to 1 in. long. Foliage has a cedar fragrance. Sparsely branched flowering stalks bear few-flowered whorls of scarlet, 1¼-in. blossoms on 4–8-in. stems. Deadhead to keep the brilliant show going from spring through fall. Reseeds to form colonies. Rich soil, half-day shade.

S. schaffneri. See S. darcyi

S. sclarea. CLARY SAGE. Biennial or short-lived perennial. Zones 2–24. Native to southern Europe, southwestern and central Asia. Foliage clump to 2–3 ft. wide. Oval to lance-shaped, 1–1½-ft.-long, dull grayish green leaves are wrinkled, toothed, unpleasant smelling when bruised. In late spring or early summer, produces much-branched 3–4-ft. flower stalks with 6–12-in. stems bearing whorls of two to six 1¼-in. flowers. Blossoms are typically lilac or lavender blue, with arched upper lip and cream-colored lower lip; large, aromatic, purplish or lilac-pink bracts remain showy for weeks after the flowers drop. Cutting stems before seeds form sacrifices this display, but it often produces rebloom in early fall and may prolong the plant's life. (Allow some seeds to form for replacement plants.) Leaves, flowers, bracts are used to flavor wines and liqueurs; oil is used in perfume, potpourri. Little to moderate water. 'Alba' has white flowers, bracts. 'Turkestanica' is especially vigorous, with creamy white blooms and white bracts flushed deep pink on edges.

S. semiatrata. BICOLOR SAGE. Evergreen shrub. Zones 16, 17, 21–24. Native to cool, high mountains of southern Mexico. Upright growth to 3–6 ft. tall, 2–3 ft. wide, with brittle, woody stems. Wrinkled, velvety, yellowish green leaves to 1¼ in. long are triangular with rounded corners. Whorls of 1–2-in. flowers on 4–6-in. stems. Dusky lavender-blue blooms, with velvety, blackish violet upper lip, throat, and blotch on lower lip. Calyxes are pinkish maroon, velvety. Blooms summer through fall; some winter flowers in mildest areas. Pinch regularly and trim lightly two or three times a year; avoid hard pruning. Protect from slugs, snails. Needs perfect drainage in winter. Give afternoon shade in hottest climates. Elegant container plant.

Salvia semiatrata

S. sinaloensis. SINALOA SAGE. Perennial. Zones 15–17, 20–24. From foothills of western coastal Mexico. Low, mounding, dense plant with slender, 6–12-in.-long, prostrate stems. Spreads to 1–2 ft. or more by rhizomes; stems also root where they touch soil. Good ground cover. Closely spaced, lance-shaped, finely toothed leaves to 1 in. long. Foliage is purple when new, turning green in shade; to preserve purplish color, give full sun (but not in hottest climates unless well watered). Stems 4–6 in. long bear cobalt blue,

¾-in. flowers with two small white patches on lower lip and persistent, wine-colored calyxes. Main bloom in summer; sometimes repeats in fall. Shear back near ground just as new spring growth emerges from base.

S. sonomensis. SONOMA SAGE, CREEPING SAGE. Shrubby perennial. Zones 7, 9, 14–24. Native to dry foothills of California Coast Ranges and Sierra Nevada. Mat-forming creeper grows 8–12 in. high and spreads 3–4 ft. or more, rooting where branches touch soil. Evergreen, rough, irregularly notched leaves are dull green or gray green; they may be narrow and 3–4 in. long or much wider and shorter. Small (less than ½-in.) lavender-blue flowers rise above foliage on leafless, 6-in. stems in late spring or early summer. Needs perfect drainage, gritty soil. Drought tolerant. Best with some high shade in hottest climates.

S. spathacea. HUMMINGBIRD SAGE, PITCHER SAGE. Perennial. Zones 7–9, 14–24. Native to low elevations of Coast Ranges in California. Hardy to 20°F/–7°C. Foliage mass to 1–2 ft. high, 3–4 ft. or more wide, spreading by rhizomes. Evergreen, scalloped, wrinkled leaves are 6–10 in. long, lance shaped or arrow shaped; light green above, paler and hairy beneath. Foliage has a light, fruity aroma. Flower stems rise 2–3 ft. above leaves, carrying many large, ball-shaped whorls of 2-in., magenta or rosy red flowers with maroon bracts and calyxes. Bracts and calyxes remain conspicuous for weeks after flowers fade. Blooms throughout spring, with some repeat in fall. A magnet for hummingbirds. Give rich soil, partial shade. Drought tolerant but performs best with moderate water; tolerates regular garden water. 'Kawatre' has deep magenta flowers that age to orange red; it is hardier than the species (to 10°F/–12°C). 'Powerline Pink' forms a 3-ft.-high foliage mass, with flowering stems rising another 3 ft.; blossoms are rosy pink.

Salvia spathacea

S. splendens. SCARLET SAGE. Perennial in Zones 21–24, H2; usually grown as annual in all zones. Native to Brazil. The traditional bright scarlet bedding sage now comes in a range of colors, from vivid true red through salmon and pink to purple shades. White forms are also available. Plants vary in size from compact 1-ft. dwarfs to 3–4-ft. kinds. Leaves are bright green, heart shaped, 2–4 in. long. Blooms late spring or summer through fall (all year in mild-winter areas); 4–12-in. stems bear 2-in. flowers from 1-in. calyxes of same color. Can be ravaged by Mexican giant whitefly. Give afternoon shade in hottest climates. Seed-grown strains include 'Firecracker', to 1 ft. high and wide, in many single colors and bicolors; and 'Sizzler', an early bloomer offering mixed colors that grows a little taller. 'Van Houttei' is a vigorous old cutting-grown selection to 3 ft. tall, 4 ft. wide (even larger in mild-winter climates). Bears maroon flowers with an orange-scarlet tinge from early fall through spring where temperatures remain above 28°F/–2°C.

S. × superba. Perennial. Zones 2–10, 14–24. Form generally available is 'Superba'. However, many plants sold under this name are seedlings or selections of *S. × sylvestris* or *S. nemorosa.* The real 'Superba' forms a tight foliage clump that spreads 2–3 ft. by rhizomes and sends up erect, much-branched, 3-ft.-tall flowering stems. Smooth, scallop-edged green leaves are lance shaped; basal ones are stalked and 3–4 in. long, upper ones stalkless and smaller. At bloom time, top 6–8 in. of stems bear clusters of ½-in. violet-blue flowers with reddish purple bracts that persist long after flowers fall. (Bracts on most seedlings are green, sometimes with a purple tinge.) Blooms from midsummer to fall if deadheaded. Blooming plant will sprawl 5–6 ft. wide unless staked.

S. × sylvestris (S. deserta). Perennial. Zones 2–10, 14–24. Like its parent *S. nemorosa* but more compact, with stems that are less leafy. Oblong to lance-shaped, medium green, scalloped leaves are wrinkled, softly hairy, to 3 in. long. Typically unbranched or few-branched flowering stems to 6–8 in. long, set with pinkish violet, ½-in. blossoms. Blooms summer through fall if faded flowers are removed. 'Blauhügel' ('Blue Hill'), to 2 ft., has medium blue flowers. 'Mainacht' ('May Night'), 2–2½ ft., bears ¾-in. indigo flowers with green bracts (purplish at base), begins blooming in midspring. Two 1½–2-ft. forms are 'Rosakönigen' ('Rose Queen'), with purplish pink flowers and crimson bracts, and 'Schneehügel' ('Snow Hill'), bearing pure white blossoms with green bracts.

S. uliginosa. BOG SAGE. Perennial. Zones 6–9, 14–24. From moist lowlands in South America. Upright, dense; to 4–6 ft. tall, 3–4 ft. wide, spreading aggressively by rhizomes. Smooth green leaves are lance shaped, toothed; they reach 3½ in. long near plant's base, decrease in size toward top. Branched inflorescence with 5–6-in. stems carries whorls of ½-in., intense sky blue flowers with white throat, wide lower lip. Blooms summer through fall. To restrain spread, give only moderate water or confine roots by planting in 15-gal. nursery can sunk in ground to rim.

S. verticillata (S. regeliana). WHORLED CLARY. Perennial. Zones 2–10, 14–24. From central Europe, western Asia. Foliage clump to 2½ ft. wide sends up branching, 2½–3-ft.-tall flower stems. Wavy-edged, medium green, softly hairy leaves to 5–6 in. long; shape varies from oval to elliptical or oblong. Basal leaves often divided into one or two pairs of smaller leaflets. Widely spaced whorls of 20–40 buds open to violet or lavender-blue flowers nearly ½ in. long, with purple-tinged, persistent calyxes. Blooms from early summer through fall if deadheaded. Protect from slugs, snails. 'Alba' has pure white flowers and calyxes. 'Purple Rain' is 1–2 ft. high, with profuse, showy deep purple blossoms and calyxes.

S. viridis (S. horminum). ANNUAL CLARY. Annual. All zones. Native to the Mediterranean, western Asia. Rapid, upright growth to 1½–2 ft. high, 1 ft. wide. Medium green, 2-in., oval to oblong leaves with blunt ends, notched edges. Inconspicuous cream or pinkish flowers with showy 1½-in., dark-veined bracts in violet, pink, or white. Blooms in early summer; another wave of bloom may follow if stems are cut before flowers go to seed. Bracts remain showy after flowers fade, dry well for winter bouquets. Sow indoors early; sow outdoors in midspring. Claryssa is a mix offering bushy, compact plants (to 16 in.) with bracts in intense shades of the typical colors.

SAMBUCUS

ELDERBERRY

Caprifoliaceae

DECIDUOUS SHRUBS OR TREES

ZONES VARY BY SPECIES

FULL SUN OR LIGHT SHADE

REGULAR WATER, EXCEPT AS NOTED

RAW FRUIT OF RED-BERRIED SPECIES CAN CAUSE NAUSEA, VOMITING, DIARRHEA IF INGESTED

Sambucus mexicana

In their natural state, these are rampant, fast-growing, wild-looking plants—but they can be tamed to a degree. Use as you would spiraea or other large deciduous shrubs. In big gardens, they can be effective as screens or windbreaks. To keep shrubby types dense, prune hard during each dormant season: cut out older stems and head back last year's growth to a few inches. Overgrown plants can be cut to the ground. Types that grow into trees need early training to single or multiple trunks. Botanists tend to assign different names to the same plant. The various elder species have bright to dark green leaves and near-black, blue, or red berries. Birds eat fruit of all types, but the fruit of red-berried species can cause gastric upset in humans if consumed raw in large quantities. (Red-fruited forms of black- and blue-fruited species are not poisonous.)

S. callicarpa. See S. racemosa racemosa

S. canadensis. AMERICAN ELDERBERRY. Zones A1–A3; 1–7, 14–17. Native to central and eastern North America. Seldom grown except in cold-winter climates. Spreading, suckering shrub to 12 ft. tall and wide. Foliage is almost tropical looking; each leaf has seven 2–6-in.-long leaflets. Blooms in early summer, bearing flat, creamy white flower clusters to 10 in. wide; these are followed by tasty purple-black berries. The fruit is used for pies; both flowers and fruit are used for wine. Strictly fruiting varieties include 'Adams', 'Johns', and many more; plant any two for cross-pollination. Ornamental varieties include 'Aurea', with golden green foliage (golden in full sun) and red berries; 'Laciniata', cutleaf or fernleaf elder, with finely cut foliage and near-black berries; and 'Maxima', with leaves to 1–1½ ft. long, flower clusters 10–18 in. wide, and black fruit.

S. mexicana (S. caerulea). BLUE ELDERBERRY. Zones 2–24; H1. Shrub or tree. Native from California north to British Columbia, east to the

S

Rockies. To 10–30 ft. tall, 8–20 ft. wide. Leaves divided into five to nine toothed, 1–6-in.-long leaflets. White or creamy white flowers in flat-topped, 2–8-in.-wide clusters in spring, summer. Clusters of blue to nearly black berries, usually covered with whitish powder, follow the flowers. Fruit is often used in jams, jellies, pies, wine. This species is drought tolerant, but it looks better (and keeps its foliage in summer) if given moderate water.

S. nigra. BLACK ELDER, EUROPEAN ELDER. Shrub or tree. Zones 2–7, 14–17. Native to Europe, North Africa, Asia. Resembles *S. canadensis* but grows larger (to 20–30 ft. high and wide) and bears less flavorful, typically purple-black berries. Blossoms come in flat-topped, 5–8-in.-wide clusters, late spring or early summer. The species is rarely seen, but smaller-growing ornamental forms are available. 'Aurea', 10–20 ft. tall and broad, has yellow new growth maturing to yellow green. 'Guincho Purple', to 15 ft. tall and 10 ft. wide, has green foliage that matures to deep purple, then turns red in fall; purple flower stems bear pink buds that open to pink-tinged white blossoms. Several varieties grow 6–8 ft. tall and wide: 'Aureomarginata', green leaves edged in yellow; 'Laciniata', very finely cut green foliage; and white-fruited 'Marginata' ('Albovariegata', 'Variegata'), green leaves bordered in creamy white. Two smaller selections (4–5 ft. high and wide) are 'Madonna', bearing green leaves that are variegated in light green to chartreuse when young, in cream, yellow, or gray-green when mature; and 'Pulverulenta', with leaves that unfold white, then mature to green splashed and striped with white.

S. pubens. SCARLET ELDER. Shrub. Zones 1–6. Native to northern latitudes in North America. To 12–25 ft. tall and wide. Leaves divided into five or seven 2–4-in.-long leaflets. Blooms in late spring, bearing tall (up to 5-in.), loose flower clusters; inedible bright red berries follow flowers.

S. racemosa. RED ELDERBERRY. Zones A2, A3, 1–6, except as noted. Native to northern latitudes in North America, Europe, Asia. To 8–10 ft. tall and wide. Smooth leaves to 9 in. long are divided into five or seven sharply toothed leaflets. Small, creamy white flowers in dome-shaped clusters to 2½ in. wide, late spring into summer; inedible bright red berries. Leaves of 'Plumosa Aurea' and 'Sutherland Gold' are bright yellow when they unfurl, then turn to green late in the season. A shrub sold as *S. callicarpa* is probably the same as *S. racemosa racemosa;* it grows in Zones 4–7, 14–17, 19–23.

SAND CHERRY. See PRUNUS besseyi

SANDHILL SAGE. See ARTEMISIA pycnocephala

SAN DIEGO MARSH-ELDER. See IVA hayesiana

SANDPAPER VINE. See PETREA volubilis

SAND PEAR. See PYRUS pyrifolia

SAND STRAWBERRY. See FRAGARIA chiloensis

SANGUISORBA

BURNET

Rosaceae

PERENNIALS

ZONES VARY BY SPECIES

LIGHT SHADE IN HOTTEST CLIMATES

REGULAR WATER

Sanguisorba minor

These plants grow from creeping rhizomes. Leaves are divided featherwise into toothed, oval or roundish leaflets. Small flowers are carried in dense, feathery spikes resembling small bottlebrush *(Callistemon)* blossoms. Often sold as *Poterium.*

S. canadensis. GREAT BURNET, CANADIAN BURNET. Zones 1–6, 15–17. Native to eastern North America. To 3–6 ft. tall, 3 ft. wide, with bright green foliage and 8-in. spikes of white flowers in late autumn. Dies to the ground even in mild climates.

S. minor. GARDEN BURNET, SALAD BURNET. Zones 1–10, 14–21. Grown as winter annual in mild-winter desert. Native to Europe, western Asia. Can reach 1½ ft. high and wide but is usually kept clipped to a few inches to maintain a fresh supply of new foliage. Leaves have a mild cucumber flavor and are used in salads, soups, cool drinks. Can be used as an edging for border or herb garden. If not sheared too low, bears roundish, inch-long clusters of red flowers late spring to midsummer. Self-sows prolifically if allowed to go to seed. Evergreen in mild-winter regions.

S. obtusa. Zones 2–6, 15–17. Native to Japan. To 4 ft. tall, 2 ft. wide, with grayish green leaves and pink flower spikes to 4 in. tall in summer. Evergreen in mild-winter regions.

SANSEVIERIA trifasciata

BOWSTRING HEMP, SNAKE PLANT, MOTHER-IN-LAW'S TONGUE

Agavaceae

PERENNIAL

ZONES 13, 23, 24; H1, H2; OR INDOORS

SOME SHADE IN HOTTEST CLIMATES; BRIGHT OR DIM LIGHT

MODERATE WATER

Sansevieria trifasciata 'Laurentii'

From western tropical Africa. Grown outdoors in mildest-winter climates; houseplant anywhere. Often sold as *S. zeylanica.* Appreciated for thick, rigidly upright, patterned leaves that grow from thick rhizomes to form 2-ft.-wide rosettes. Leaves are dark green banded with gray green, grow 4 ft. tall, 2 in. wide. Bears erect, narrow clusters of fragrant greenish white flowers in Hawaii but seldom on mainland. 'Laurentii' is identical to the species but has broad, creamy yellow stripes on leaf edges. Dwarf 'Hahnii' has rosettes of 6-in.-long, broadly triangular, dark green leaves with silvery banding; rosettes pile up to make a mass 1 ft. tall and wide. Other varieties and species are collectors' items; scores can be found in catalogs of succulent plants.

First common name comes from use of tough leaf fibers as bowstrings; second comes from leaf banding or mottling, which resembles some snakeskins; third probably comes from toughness of plants. Outdoors, plants tolerate many soil types, take salt air and drought; indoors, grow in much or little light, seldom need repotting. Withstand dry air, fluctuating temperatures, and scanty, capricious watering.

SANTA BARBARA DAISY. See ERIGERON karvinskianus

SANTOLINA

Asteraceae (Compositae)

EVERGREEN SHRUBS

ZONES VARY BY SPECIES

FULL SUN

LITTLE OR NO WATER TO MODERATE WATER

Santolina chamaecyparissus

These Mediterranean natives are notable for their attractive foliage, profuse summer show of small, round, buttonlike flower heads, and stout constitutions. All are aromatic if bruised. Unpruned plants tend to become sparse and woody in the center. Cut back yearly, before spring growth begins; you can simply trim as needed around the edges (as if giving the plant a haircut) or cut the whole plant back to a few inches high. After blossoms fade, shear or clip off flowering shoots. Remove and replace plants if they become too woody. In coldest part of range, plants may die to the ground, but they should grow back from roots. Good as ground covers, bank covers, edgings for walks or borders, low informal or sheared hedges. Grow in any well-drained soil.

S. chamaecyparissus (S. incana). LAVENDER COTTON. Zones 2–24; H1, H2. To 2 ft. tall, 3 ft. wide. Brittle, woody stems are densely clothed with rough, finely divided, whitish gray leaves. Bright yellow flower heads. Smaller versions of the species include 'Nana', to 1 ft. tall, 2–3 ft. wide;

and 'Pretty Carol', to 16 in. high and wide. 'Lemon Queen', to 2 ft. tall and wide, has creamy yellow flowers.

S. pinnata (S. ericoides). Zones 3–24. To 2–2½ ft. tall, 3 ft. wide; narrow, tooth-edged dark green leaves, cream-colored flowers. *S. p. neapolitana* is 12–15 in. tall, has silvery foliage, bright yellow flowers.

S. rosmarinifolia (S. virens). Zones 3–9, 14–24. To 2 ft. tall, 3 ft. wide, with narrow green leaves like those of rosemary. Leaves may have tiny teeth or none at all. Bright yellow flowers. 'Morning Mist' is similar but more compact.

SANVITALIA procumbens

CREEPING ZINNIA

Asteraceae (Compositae)

ANNUAL

ZONES 1–24

FULL SUN

MODERATE TO REGULAR WATER

Sanvitalia procumbens

This Mexican native is not really a zinnia, but it looks enough like one to fool most people. Grows only 4–6 in. high but spreads or trails to 1½ ft. or wider. Leaves are like miniature (to 2-in.-long) zinnia leaves. Flowers are nearly 1 in. wide, with bright yellow or orange rays around a dark purple-brown center. Blooms from midsummer until frost. Varieties include 'Mandarin Orange' and double-flowered 'Gold Braid'.

Needs good drainage. Resents transplanting, so sow seeds where plants will grow. Plant from earliest spring (in mildest-winter climates) to late spring (where soil is slow to warm up). Heat resistant. Use as temporary filler in borders or edgings, as annual cover for slope or bank; or plant in hanging baskets or pots.

Sapindaceae. Members of the soapberry family are trees and shrubs with (usually) divided leaves, clustered small flowers (sometimes showy), and fruit that is berrylike, often showy. Some have edible fruit. Examples are carrot wood *(Cupaniopsis)*, hop bush *(Dodonaea)*, *Koelreuteria*, and litchi.

SAPIUM sebiferum

CHINESE TALLOW TREE

Euphorbiaceae

DECIDUOUS TREE

ZONES 8, 9, 12–16, 18–21; H1

FULL SUN

MODERATE TO REGULAR WATER

MILKY SAP IS POISONOUS IF INGESTED

Sapium sebiferum

From China, Japan. To 30–40 ft. tall, 25–30 ft. wide, with a dense, round or conical crown. Tends toward shrubbiness, multiple trunks, and suckering but is easily trained to a single trunk. In colder areas, branch tips may freeze back in winter, but new growth will quickly cover damage. Leafs out late in spring. Foliage is dense but flutters in the slightest breeze, giving tree an airy look. Light green leaves are roundish, tapering to a slender point; with moderate autumn chill, they can turn flaming red, plum purple, yellow orange, or mixed colors. For good color, select a tree while it is in fall leaf. Spikes of tiny yellowish flowers at branch tips are followed in fall by clusters of small fruits with a waxy grayish white coating.

Though this tree was once considered suitable for all landscapes, it is best not to plant it if you garden near wetlands, rivers, or native plant habitats. It has become a self-seeding pest in southeastern U.S. and has now naturalized along the American River near Sacramento and in Yolo County, California. Away from areas where it can do damage, it's an attractive tree for lawn, street, patio, terrace; gives light to moderate shade. Good as a screen. Resistant to oak root fungus.

SAPONARIA

Caryophyllaceae

PERENNIALS

ZONES 1–11, 14–24, EXCEPT AS NOTED

FULL SUN

MODERATE TO REGULAR WATER

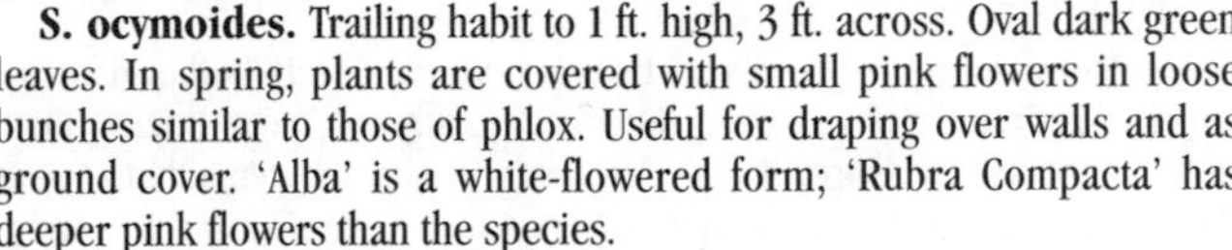

Saponaria ocymoides

Generally low-growing European natives, closely related to *Lychnis* and *Silene*. Easy to grow in well-drained soil. Useful in border or rock garden.

S. ocymoides. Trailing habit to 1 ft. high, 3 ft. across. Oval dark green leaves. In spring, plants are covered with small pink flowers in loose bunches similar to those of phlox. Useful for draping over walls and as ground cover. 'Alba' is a white-flowered form; 'Rubra Compacta' has deeper pink flowers than the species.

S. officinalis. SOAPWORT, BOUNCING BET. To 2 ft. high, spreading by underground runners. Elliptical to ovate, dark green leaves. Loose clusters of inch-wide summer flowers in red, pink, or white. Roots crushed in water produce a sudsy, detergent-like lather. This is a tough plant; before the days of herbicides, it could be seen growing in the cinders along railroad rights-of-way. 'Rosea Plena', with double light pink flowers, is the common garden form. 'Rubra Plena' has crimson blooms that turn paler as they age.

S. pumilio (S. pumila). Zones 2–7, 14–17. Linear, inch-long, bright green leaves form a tight cushion to 2 ft. high and 1 ft. wide. Inch-wide, purplish pink flowers are borne singly at branch ends in spring, making a ring of blossoms around the plant's base.

SAPOTE, WHITE. See WHITE SAPOTE

SARCOCOCCA

SWEET BOX

Buxaceae

EVERGREEN SHRUBS

ZONES 4–9, 14–24, EXCEPT AS NOTED

PARTIAL OR FULL SHADE

MODERATE TO REGULAR WATER

Sarcococca ruscifolia

Native to Himalayas, China. Grown for handsome, waxy dark green leaves and tiny, powerfully fragrant white blossoms that bloom in late winter or early spring, hidden in the foliage. Small berrylike fruit follows the flowers. Useful in shaded areas—under overhangs, in entryways, beneath low-branching evergreen trees. Plants maintain slow, orderly growth and polished appearance in deepest shade. Tolerate sun in cool-summer climates. Grow best in organically enriched soil. Scale insects are the only pests.

S. confusa. Similar to *S. ruscifolia* and generally sold as such. However, *S. ruscifolia* has red fruit, while that of *S. confusa* is black.

S. hookerana humilis (S. humilis). Zones 3–9, 14–24. Low growing, seldom more than 1½ ft. high; spreads by underground runners to 8 ft. or more. Branches are thickly set with pointed leaves 1–3 in. long, ½–¾ in. wide. Glossy blue-black fruit. Good ground cover.

S. ruscifolia. Slow growth to 4–6 ft. high, 3–7 ft. wide. If grown against a wall, it will form a natural espalier, with branches fanning out to create patterns. Oval to elliptical leaves to 2 in. long, densely set on branches. Red fruit.

SASA. See BAMBOO

FOR INFORMATION ON YOUR CLIMATE ZONE
PLEASE SEE PAGES 27–63

S

SATUREJA

Lamiaceae (Labiatae)

ANNUALS AND PERENNIALS

ZONES VARY BY SPECIES

EXPOSURE NEEDS VARY BY SPECIES

REGULAR WATER, EXCEPT AS NOTED

Satureja montana

Two of these aromatic plants are favorite culinary herbs, while the other has a long reputation as a tonic.

S. douglasii (Micromeria chamissonis). YERBA BUENA. Perennial. Zones 4–9, 14–24. Native from Los Angeles area to British Columbia. This is the plant for which San Francisco was given its original name of Yerba Buena. Plant grows to 6 in. high, spreading to 3 ft. wide by slender stems that root as they grow. Roundish, scallop-edged, 1-in. leaves have strong minty scent. Small white or lavender-tinted flowers in spring and summer. Grown as a ground cover. Dried leaves make a pleasant tea, which early settlers drank to treat a variety of ailments, hence the plant's common name (Spanish for "good herb"). Prefers part shade but tolerates full sun in cool-summer climates. Grows best in rich, moist soil but takes drought as well as boggy conditions.

S. hortensis. SUMMER SAVORY. Annual. All zones. From southeastern Europe. Upright to 1½ ft., with loose, open habit. Aromatic, rather narrow leaves to 1½ in. long; use fresh or dried as seasoning for meats, fish, eggs, soups, beans, vegetables. Whorls of tiny, delicate, pinkish white to rose flowers in summer. Grow in light, well-drained, organically enriched soil. Sow seeds in place; thin to 1–1½ ft. apart. Full sun. Good potted plant.

S. montana. WINTER SAVORY. Shrubby perennial. Zones 3–11, 14–24. From southern Europe. To 15 in. high, 2 ft. wide. Stiff, narrow to roundish leaves to 1 in. long; not as delicate in flavor as summer savory. Use leaves fresh or dried; clip at start of flowering season for drying. Blooms profusely in summer, bearing whorls of small white to lilac flowers that are attractive to bees. Use in rock garden, as dwarf clipped hedge in herb garden (space plants 1½ ft. apart). Grow in light, well-drained soil. Cut back as needed to keep compact. Full sun. Moderate water.

SAVORY. See SATUREJA

SAXIFRAGA

SAXIFRAGE

Saxifragaceae

PERENNIALS

ZONES VARY BY SPECIES

EXPOSURE NEEDS VARY BY SPECIES

REGULAR WATER

Saxifraga stolonifera

Some saxifrages are native to mountainous areas of North America; most are from Europe. They do best in rock gardens of the Pacific Northwest, where specialists grow dozens of kinds. Require good drainage and light soil; rot easily in soggy soil. Most grow in full sun or light shade, but those listed here—all evergreen species—are shade plants.

S. decipiens (S. rosacea). Zones 2–7, 14–17. Native to Europe. Confused group generally given the name "mossy saxifrages." Plants form low, compact or loose foliage cushions to 2–4 in. high, 1 ft. wide. Glossy green leaves less than 1 in. long are neatly divided into three to five segments. In spring, wide-open flowers are borne on 2–8-in. stems. The species typically has white flowers, but numerous named forms bear blossoms in cream, pink, or red. Widely sold 'Sternbergii' has white flowers strongly tinged pink. Afternoon shade is best in cool-summer areas; full shade is essential where summers are hot.

S. stolonifera (S. sarmentosa). STRAWBERRY GERANIUM. Zones 2–9, 14–24; or indoors. Native to China, Japan. Creeping plant forms a rosette to 6–8 in. high, 1 ft. wide, but expands fairly rapidly, sending out runners like strawberry. Nearly round green leaves to 4 in. across have white veins, pink undersides. Blooms from late summer to fall, bearing inch-wide white flowers in loose clusters on stems to 2 ft. tall. Good ground cover where hard freezes are infrequent. Partial or full shade. To use as houseplant, grow in hanging basket; give bright indirect light.

S. umbrosa. Zones 2–7, 14–17. Native to the Pyrenees. Tongue-shaped, shiny green leaves to 1½ in. long form a foot-wide rosette only a few inches high. Blooms in spring, bearing open clusters of tiny pink flowers on wine red, 1-ft.-high stalks. Good ground cover for small areas; effective near rocks, stream beds. Best in full shade. This species is often called London pride, a common name correctly belonging to *S.* ×***urbium,*** a hybrid between *S. umbrosa* and the similar *S. hirsuta.*

Saxifraga umbrosa

Saxifragaceae. The saxifrage family once included a number of shrubs, but these now occupy their own families—Grossulariaceae (currants and gooseberries) and Hydrangeaceae. Remaining in Saxifragaceae are a number of herbaceous plants, including *Astilbe, Bergenia,* coral bells *(Heuchera),* and of course saxifrage *(Saxifraga).*

SCABIOSA

PINCUSHION FLOWER

Dipsacaceae

ANNUALS AND PERENNIALS

ZONES VARY BY SPECIES

FULL SUN, EXCEPT AS NOTED

MODERATE TO REGULAR WATER

Scabiosa columbaria

Stamens protrude beyond curved surface of flower head, giving illusion of pins stuck into a cushion. Bloom begins in midsummer, continues until frost if flowers are deadheaded or cut regularly. Good in mixed or mass plantings. Excellent cut flowers.

S. atropurpurea. PINCUSHION FLOWER, MOURNING BRIDE. Annual in Zones 1–24, H1, H2; may persist as perennial where winters are mild. May also be sold as *S. grandiflora.* From southern Europe. To 2½–3 ft. tall, 1 ft. wide. Oblong, coarsely toothed leaves. Many long, wiry stems carry flowers to 2 in. or more wide, in colors ranging from blackish purple to salmon pink, rose, white. Double Mixed strain and 'Salmon Queen' reach 3 ft. tall; Dwarf Double Mixed grows to 1½ ft. high.

S. caucasica. PINCUSHION FLOWER. Perennial. Zones 1–10, 14–24. From the Caucasus, Turkey, Iran. To 1½–2½ ft. high, 1–2 ft. wide. Leaves vary from finely cut to uncut. Flowers 2½–3 in. across, in blue to bluish lavender or white, depending on variety. Needs partial shade in hottest climates. 'Alba' has white blossoms. 'Fama' has branching stalks carrying blue, 3-in. flowers with broad rays. 'Blue Perfection' bears lavender-blue flowers with fringed rays. House's Mix (House's Novelty Mix) contains a mixture of blue shades and white.

S. columbaria. Perennial. Zones 2–11, 14–24. Grown as winter annual in Zones 12, 13. From Europe, Africa, Asia. To 2 ft. high and wide. Finely cut gray-green leaves. Flowers to 3 in., in lavender blue, pink, or white; almost all year in mildest areas. 'Butterfly Blue' (deep lavender blue) and 'Pink Mist' (bright pink) are superior selections.

S. ochroleuca. Biennial or short-lived perennial. Zones 4–24. From Europe, western Asia. To 2 ft. high and wide, with light yellow flowers to 2½ in. across.

S. stellata. Annual. Zones 1–24. From western Mediterranean. To 1½ ft. tall, 1 ft. wide. Many heads of pale blue, 1½-in. flowers; these quickly dry to papery bronze drumsticks, useful in dried arrangements.

SCADOXUS multiflorus katherinae (Haemanthus katherinae)

BLOOD LILY

Amaryllidacaceae

PERENNIAL FROM BULB

ZONES 21–24; OR INDOORS

LIGHT SHADE; BRIGHT INDIRECT LIGHT

REGULAR WATER DURING GROWTH AND BLOOM

Scadoxus multiflorus katherinae

Tender South African plant closely related to amaryllis. Large (4-in.-diameter) white bulb stained red (hence common name). Lance-shaped to ovate, bright green, wavy-edged leaves are 12–15 in. long. In late spring or summer, ball-shaped clusters (to 9 in. wide) of narrow-petaled, salmon-colored flowers are borne atop thick flower stems 1–2 ft. tall. Many threadlike, bright red stamens protrude from each bloom, giving clusters the look of spherical bottlebrushes.

In late winter or early spring, plant in rich, well-drained soil, keeping bulb tip even with soil surface. Can be grown in ground in frost-free regions (set bulbs 2 ft. apart) and the clumps left undisturbed indefinitely, but even there it is usually grown in pots. Choose a pot big enough to leave 2 in. between all sides of bulb and container edges. Place planted pot in fairly warm spot (no cooler than 55°F/13°C at night, around 70°F/21°C during the day). Water sparingly until leaves appear (in about 8 weeks); can be brought outdoors then. Water regularly and feed monthly with liquid fertilizer. After bloom, stop feeding and gradually cut back on water; let plant dry out in a cool, protected place. Do not repot next season; either add new mix on top of original soil or tip out root ball, scrape off some soil, and replace with fresh soil.

SCAEVOLA

Goodeniaceae

PERENNIALS AND EVERGREEN SHRUBS

ZONES 8, 9, 14–24, H1, H2, EXCEPT AS NOTED

FULL SUN

MODERATE TO REGULAR WATER

Scaevola 'Mauve Clusters'

Notable for flower form: blossoms are fan shaped, with all the segments on one side. Named for the Roman hero Mutius Scaevola, who burned off one of his hands to prove his bravery. Most are native to Australia, but some are beach plants from Asia, the Pacific Islands, and the Caribbean. The Australian species are evergreen in mild-winter climates and nearly everblooming as well. In colder regions, where they are often grown as annuals, they bloom from late spring until frost and are useful in hanging baskets, window boxes, and pots.

S. aemula. Perennial. From Australia. Variable. Some forms are prostrate, others upright to 2½ ft.; fleshy stems of some spread to 3 ft. wide, while those of others trail or sprawl to twice that width. Bright green, 1½–2-in.-long leaves; lavender-blue, 1½-in. flowers all along the branches. Species available mainly through its named varieties, including 'Blue Shamrock', 'Blue Wonder', 'Colonial Fan', 'New Wonder', 'Purple Fanfare' ('Diamond Head'). All grow to about 8 in. high, trail to 3 ft. wide, bear lavender-blue blooms. Leaves are less than 1 in. long.

S. 'Mauve Clusters'. Perennial. From Australia. Flowers are smaller and stems less fleshy than those of *S. aemula.* Forms a mat 4–6 in. high, eventually spreading to 3–5 ft. across. Half-inch-wide flowers in lilac-tinged mauve. Often grown as ground cover (set plants 2 ft. apart).

S. taccada (S. sericea). BEACH NAUPAKA, NAUPAKA KAHAKAI. Evergreen shrub. Zone H2. Native to Hawaii. Thick-stemmed plant to 6–10 ft. tall and broad. Fleshy light green leaves to 6 in. long and nearly as wide are clustered near branch ends. Flowers are ¾ in. wide, white with purple markings; followed by fleshy white fruits. Tolerates heat, wind, salt spray. Useful as hedge plant or windbreak, especially at the beach.

SCARLET BUSH. See HAMELIA patens

SCARLET LARKSPUR. See DELPHINIUM cardinale, D. nudicaule

SCHEFFLERA

Araliaceae

EVERGREEN SHRUBS OR TREES

ZONES VARY BY SPECIES; OR INDOORS

SOME SHADE IN HOTTEST CLIMATES; BRIGHT INDIRECT LIGHT

REGULAR WATER

Schefflera actinophylla

Fast-growing, tropical-looking plants; long-stalked leaves are divided into leaflets that spread out like fingers of a hand. Summer flowers (showy in some species) are followed by tiny dark fruits. All need rich, moisture-retentive, well-drained soil. Love humidity but are quite tolerant of drier air. Useful near swimming pools. Good container plants for patio or lanai. As houseplants, they are unlikely to bloom.

S. actinophylla (Brassaia actinophylla). QUEENSLAND UMBRELLA TREE, OCTOPUS TREE, SCHEFFLERA. Zones 21–24, H1, H2; precariously hardy in Zones 16–20 with protection of overhang. Native to Australia. Fast growth to 20–40 ft. tall and wide. The "umbrella" of the common name comes from the foliage form: the long-stalked, glossy bright green leaves are divided into 7–16 large (to 1-ft.-long) leaflets that radiate outward like ribs of an umbrella. Foliage grows in tiers. "Octopus" refers to showy flower heads: narrow, raylike structures to 3 ft. long, set all along their length with little blossoms, radiate from a central point. Flowers age from greenish yellow to pink to dark red. Use for striking tropical effects, for silhouette, for contrast with ferns and other foliage plants. Cut out tips occasionally to keep plant from becoming leggy. Overgrown plants can be cut back nearly to ground level; they will branch and grow back with better form. This species has become a serious pest in some lowland areas of Hawaii.

S. arboricola (Heptapleurum arboricolum). HAWAIIAN ELF SCHEFFLERA. Zones 23, 24; H1, H2. Native to Taiwan. To 20 ft. tall with equal or greater spread, but easily kept smaller with pruning. Dark green leaves are much smaller than those of *S. actinophylla,* with 3-in. leaflets that broaden toward rounded tips. If plants are set into the ground with stems at an angle, they'll continue to grow at that angle—which can give attractive multistemmed effects. Yellowish flowers are clustered in flattened, foot-wide spheres; they turn bronze with age. Overall, produces a denser, darker, less treelike effect than *S. actinophylla.*

Schefflera arboricola

S. elegantissima (Dizygotheca elegantissima). Zones 16, 17, 22–24; H1, H2. Native to New Caledonia. As a juvenile, it is a houseplant; when mature, it's a garden plant to 25 ft. tall and wide. Leaves are divided like fans into leaflets with notched edges. Young plants are unbranched, with narrow (1-in.), lacy-looking leaflets to 9 in. long; foliage is shiny dark green above, reddish beneath. Plant branches as it matures, and leaflets grow slightly longer, broaden to 3 in., and become less glossy. Greenish yellow flowers in clusters to 1 ft. long.

S. pueckleri (Tupidanthus calyptratus). Zones 19–24; H1, H2. Native to southern Asia. Resembles *S. actinophylla* but is a denser plant that branches from the base. May be trained to single trunk. Leaves to nearly 2 ft. wide are divided into seven to nine stalked, glossy bright green leaflets, each to 7 in. long, 2½ in. wide. Flowers are greenish, borne on shorter, fewer "rays" than those of *S. actinophylla.*

FOR GROWING SYMBOL EXPLANATIONS
PLEASE SEE PAGE 161

SCHINUS

PEPPER TREE

Anacardiaceae

EVERGREEN TREES

ZONES VARY BY SPECIES

FULL SUN

WATER NEEDS VARY BY SPECIES

FOLIAGE CAN CAUSE DERMATITIS; BERRIES OF S. TEREBINTHEFOLIUS CAN CAUSE GASTRIC DISTRESS IF INGESTED

Schinus molle

Pepper trees are praised by some gardeners, heartily disliked by others. The two species discussed here differ markedly, though both are tolerant of many soils, and leaves of both can cause dermatitis. Female trees bear fruit that attracts birds.

S. molle. CALIFORNIA PEPPER TREE. Zones 8, 9, 12–24; H1, H2. Native to Peruvian Andes. Fast growth to 25–40 ft. tall and wide. Trunks of old trees are heavy and fantastically gnarled, with knots and burls that often sprout leaves or small branches. Heavy limbs; light, gracefully drooping branchlets. Bright green leaves with many narrow leaflets to 2 in. long. Drooping, 4–6-in. clusters of tiny yellowish white summer flowers; rosy berries in fall, winter. (Some trees have nearly all male flowers; these do not bear fruit.)

This tree produces copious litter, is subject to scale infestation, and has greedy surface roots that make it difficult to garden beneath. Nonetheless, it's handsome when used properly. Plant away from paving, sewers, or drains; give room to spread. A fine choice for shading a play area or gravel-surfaced, outdoor living space. Among the brightest green trees in the desert. Can be planted 2 ft. apart and pruned into a graceful, billowy hedge. Can be killed by root rots, especially Texas root rot. Little or no water to moderate water. In Hawaii, best at higher elevations.

S. terebinthefolius. BRAZILIAN PEPPER TREE. Zones 13, 14 (with shelter), 15–17, 19–24; H1, H2. Native to Brazil; naturalized in Hawaii. Moderate growth to 30 ft. tall and wide; train to single or multiple trunks. Nonpendulous growth. Has darker green, coarser, glossy leaves than *S. molle*, with 5–13 oval leaflets; showy bright red berries in winter.

Individuals of this species show much variation; for best success, select a tree during fruiting season, looking for the largest, showiest berries and best foliage. Dried berries are sold as pink peppercorns; eaten in quantity, they can cause gastric distress. Wood is subject to breakage, so shorten long, lanky limbs and thin canopy to let winds pass through. Prone to verticillium wilt. Attractive shade tree for patio or garden. Self-sown seedlings can be a problem. In Hawaii, the plant has become so invasive that gardeners are advised to forgo the attractive berries and grow male plants only. Moderate to regular water (applied deeply).

SCHIZACHYRIUM scoparium

LITTLE BLUESTEM

Poaceae (Gramineae)

PERENNIAL GRASS

ZONES 1–24

FULL SUN

REGULAR WATER

Schizachyrium scoparium

Native to much of North America; an important grass in the native tall-grass prairie. Formerly known as *Andropogon scoparius.* Clump-forming grass 2–4 ft. tall, 1–2 ft. wide, with narrow leaves that may be erect or arching. Late summer flowers are inconspicuous but age to an attractive silvery shade. Leaf color varies from bright green to distinctly bluish in summer, from light brown to dark red in fall and winter. Types that are bluer in summer take on the deeper cold-weather colors: blue-green leaves of 'Blaze' turn a strong red in fall, while 'The Blues' has striking light blue leaves that turn burgundy red.

SCHIZANTHUS pinnatus

POOR MAN'S ORCHID, BUTTERFLY FLOWER

Solanaceae

ANNUAL

ZONES 1–9, 14–24; BEST IN ZONES 1–6, 15–17, 21–24

FILTERED SUNLIGHT

REGULAR WATER

Schizanthus pinnatus

Chilean native to 1½ ft. high, 1 ft. wide. Profuse, small orchidlike flowers in pink, rose, lilac, purple, or white, all with markings in various colors. Blossoms look quite showy against the ferny foliage, make long-lasting cut flowers. Buy potted plants or start seeds indoors 4 weeks before planting time (germination is slow). Sensitive to frost and heat. Plant in early spring where summers are moderate, in fall where summers are hot and winters are normally frostless. Give well-drained, rich soil in a wind-sheltered site. Good potted plant. Often grown in greenhouses.

SCHIZOCENTRON elegans. See HETEROCENTRON elegans

SCHIZOPHRAGMA hydrangeoides

JAPANESE HYDRANGEA VINE

Hydrangeaceae

DECIDUOUS VINE

ZONES 2–9, 14–17

PARTIAL SHADE

REGULAR WATER

Schizophragma hydrangeoides

Native to Korea, Japan. Resembles climbing hydrangea *(Hydrangea anomala petiolaris).* Climbs by holdfasts to 30 ft. or more. Pointed, tooth-edged dark green leaves are 3–5 in. long. Blooms in summer, producing flat, 8–10-in.-wide clusters of white flowers. Like the bloom clusters of lace cap hydrangeas, these feature tiny fertile flowers surrounded by ring of sterile ones—but the sterile blossoms of this plant have only a single "petal" (those of hydrangea have four). 'Moonlight' has blue-green foliage with a silvery cast. 'Roseum' is a pink-flowered variety. Use species or varieties to climb shaded walls or trees. Plant in good, well-drained soil. Prune only to remove errant growth.

SCHIZOSTYLIS coccinea

CRIMSON FLAG

Iridaceae

PERENNIAL FROM RHIZOME

ZONES 5–9, 14–24; H1, H2

FULL SUN OR LIGHT SHADE

REGULAR TO AMPLE WATER

Schizostylis coccinea

Virtually evergreen South African native. Like gladiolus, it has upright, swordlike leaves and a spike of closely set flowers, but the blossoms themselves—star shaped, bright colored, 2 in. wide—recall another relative, watsonia. Flowers are carried on slender, 1½–2-ft.-tall stems. The species has crimson blooms; color variants include white 'Alba', watermelon red 'Oregon Sunset', and several in pink shades ('Mrs. Hegarty', 'Sunrise', 'Viscountess Byng'). All bloom in autumn. Excellent cut flowers. Plant in spring, in organically enriched, well-drained soil. Set rhizomes ½–1 in. deep, 1 ft. apart. Water generously from planting time until flowering ends; then water more sparingly until growth resumes in spring. If clumps become crowded, divide them in early spring; each division should have at least five shoots. In cold-winter regions, grow in pots and protect in winter.

SCHLUMBERGERA

Cactaceae

CACTI

ZONES 16, 17, 21–24; H1, H2; OR INDOORS

PARTIAL SHADE; BRIGHT INDIRECT LIGHT

REGULAR WATER

Schlumbergera × buckleyi

In nature, these cacti live on trees, as epiphytic orchids do. Need rich, porous soil, such as a mix of equal parts coarse sand, peat moss, and leaf mold. Feed with liquid fertilizer every 7 to 10 days during growth and bloom. Plants are often confused with *Zygocactus.* The many kinds differ principally in flower color.

S. × buckleyi. CHRISTMAS CACTUS. May be labeled *S. bridgesii.* Old favorite to 2 ft. high, 3 ft. wide. Arching, drooping bright green branches of flattened, scallop-edged, smooth, spineless, 1½-in. joints. Can bear hundreds of many-petaled, long-tubed, 3-in.-long, rosy purplish red flowers at Christmastime. To ensure bud set for late December bloom, give plant cool night temperatures (50 to 55°F/10 to 13°C) and 12 to 14 hours of darkness per day during November.

S. gaertneri. See Rhipsalidopsis gaertneri

S. truncata. CRAB CACTUS. Native to Brazil. To 1 ft. high and wide. Bright green, 1–2-in., toothed joints; two large teeth at tip of last joint on each branch. Short-tubed, 3-in.-long, scarlet flowers with spreading, pointed petals from late fall through winter. Many varieties are sold in white, pink, salmon, orange.

Schlumbergera truncata

SCHOENOPLECTUS tabernaemontanus 'Zebrinus'

ZEBRA RUSH

Cyperaceae

PERENNIAL

ZONES 5–24

FULL SUN OR LIGHT SHADE

AMPLE WATER

Variety of a somewhat grasslike species found in many parts of the world. Forms an upright clump to 2–4 ft. high and wide. Hollow, apparently leafless, dark green stems are banded horizontally with light yellow; striping tends to fade late in season and in strong sun. Will grow in several inches of water. Best used at edges of pools and ponds. To increase your planting, divide clumps in spring.

Schoenoplectus tabernaemontanus 'Zebrinus'

SCIADOPITYS verticillata

UMBRELLA PINE

Sciadopityaceae

EVERGREEN TREE

ZONES 4–9, 14–24

AFTERNOON SHADE IN HOTTEST CLIMATES

REGULAR WATER

Sciadopitys verticillata

In its native Japan, this tree reaches 100–120 ft. tall, but in Western gardens it is not likely to exceed 25–40 ft. tall, 25–30 ft. wide. Very slow grower. In youth, it is symmetrical, dense, and rather narrow; with age, it is more open, and limbs tend to droop. Small, scalelike leaves are scattered along branches and bunched at branch ends. Glossy dark green needles grow in whorls of 20–30 at branch and twig ends, radiating out like spokes of an umbrella; they are flattened, firm, fleshy, 3–6 in. long. Woody, 3–5-in. cones may appear on older trees.

Choice decorative tree for open ground or containers. Plant in rich, well-drained, neutral or slightly acid soil. Watch for mites in hot, dry weather. Leave unpruned; or thin to create Oriental effect. Good for bonsai.

SCILLA

SQUILL, BLUEBELL

Liliaceae

PERENNIALS FROM BULBS

ZONES VARY BY SPECIES

FULL SUN DURING BLOOM, PARTIAL SHADE AFTER

REGULAR WATER DURING GROWTH AND BLOOM

ALL PARTS ARE POISONOUS IF INGESTED

Scilla peruviana

The three hardier species are native to cold-winter regions of Europe and Asia and need some winter chill. Gardeners in cold-winter climates know them as harbingers of spring; the earliest ones come into flower with winter aconite *(Eranthis)* and snowdrop *(Galanthus).* Less hardy to cold is Peruvian scilla *(S. peruviana);* despite its name, it is native to Mediterranean region. All squills have bell-shaped or starlike flowers borne on leafless stems that rise from clumps of strap-shaped leaves.

Cold-hardy species look best when naturalized; grow them in small patches or larger drifts. *S. peruviana* is most attractive in clumps along pathways, at edges of mixed plantings, in pots. Plant all types in fall, in well-drained, organically enriched soil. Set bulbs of cold-hardy species 2–3 in. deep, 4 in. apart; set those of *S. peruviana* 3–4 in. deep, 6 in. apart. Reduce watering when foliage yellows after bloom. Hardy kinds will tolerate less moisture during summer dormancy, but don't let soil dry out completely. *S. peruviana* will accept summer moisture but doesn't need any. Divide clumps (during dormancy) only when vigor and bloom quality decline.

S. bifolia. Zones 2–11, 14–21. Each 8-in. stem carries three to eight inch-wide, star-shaped flowers in turquoise blue. White, pale purplish pink, and violet-blue varieties are available. Each bulb produces only two leaves.

S. hispanica. See Hyacinthoides hispanica

S. mischtschenkoana (S. tubergeniana). Zones 1–11, 14–21. Each 6-in. stem bears nodding clusters of three or four starlike flowers in pale blue with darker blue stripes.

S. non-scripta. See Hyacinthoides non-scripta

S. peruviana. PERUVIAN SCILLA. Zones 14–17, 19–24. Large bulb produces numerous, rather floppy leaves; in late spring, 10–12-in. stems appear, each topped with dome-shaped cluster of 50 or more starlike flowers. Most forms have bluish purple blooms, but a white-flowered variety is sometimes sold. Bulbs are dormant only for a short time after leaves wither.

S. siberica. SIBERIAN SQUILL. Zones A2, A3; 1–7, 10. Each 3–6-in. stem bears several flowers shaped like flaring bells. Typical color is intense medium blue, but there are varieties in white, lilac pink, and light to dark shades of violet blue, often with darker stripes. 'Spring Beauty' has brilliant violet-blue blooms that are larger than those of species.

SCIRPUS cernuus (Isolepis cernua)

FIBER OPTICS PLANT

Cyperaceae

PERENNIAL

ZONES 7–24

PARTIAL SHADE

AMPLE WATER

Scirpus cernuus

Grasslike sedge from British Isles, Europe, North Africa. To 6–10 in. high (but usually lower), flopping over to about twice as wide. Blooms all year; small brown flower spikelets appear at ends of the drooping, threadlike green stems. Occasional division and resetting will keep it small. Ideal for edge of shallow pond. Good container plant.

SCOTCH BROOM. See **CYTISUS scoparius**

SCOTCH HEATHER. See **CALLUNA vulgaris**

SCOTCH MOSS. See **SAGINA subulata**

SCOTCH ROSE. See **ROSA pimpinellifolia**

SCRAMBLED EGGS. See **SENNA surattensis**

SCREW BEAN. See **PROSOPIS pubescens**

SCREWPINE. See **PANDANUS tectorius**

SCROPHULARIA

Scrophulariaceae

PERENNIALS

ZONES VARY BY SPECIES

FULL SUN OR PARTIAL SHADE

WATER NEEDS VARY BY SPECIES

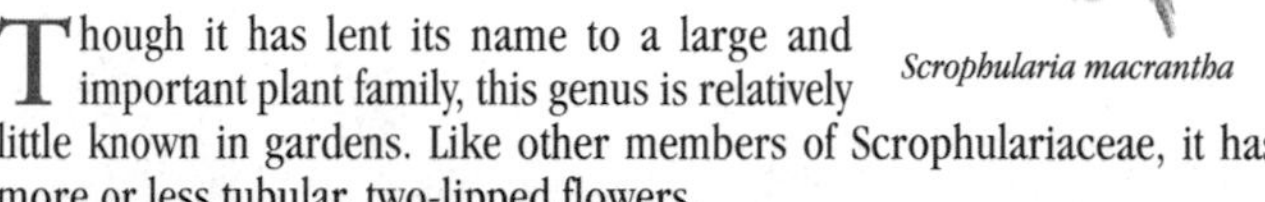

Scrophularia macrantha

Though it has lent its name to a large and important plant family, this genus is relatively little known in gardens. Like other members of Scrophulariaceae, it has more or less tubular, two-lipped flowers.

S. auriculata 'Variegata'. WATER BETONY, WATER FIGWORT. Zones 3–9, 14–24. From western Europe. To 4 ft. tall, 2 ft. wide. Stems have flattened "wings." Wrinkled, toothed, lance-shaped green leaves are strongly marked with cream, grow 2–10 in. long. Green, ½-in.-long flowers with a purplish brown upper lip bloom from summer into early fall. Ample water. Showy plant for waterside plantings or damp borders.

S. macrantha. REDBIRDS IN A TREE. Zones 2b–10, 12–24. From high mountains of the Southwest. To 3–4 ft. tall and 1½ ft. wide, with lance-shaped, glossy dark green, 1–3-in.-long leaves. Stems are leaning, with a tendency to recline; plant with other tall perennials for support. Bright red, puffy, ¾-in.-long flowers in 12–15-in. spires bloom from midsummer until frost. Little to regular water.

Scrophulariaceae. The figwort family consists principally of annuals and perennials. Most have irregular flowers, with four or five lobes often arranged as two lips. Some examples are snapdragon *(Antirrhinum)*, *Calceolaria*, foxglove *(Digitalis)*, *Nemesia*, beard tongue *(Penstemon)*, and wishbone flower *(Torenia)*.

SCUTELLARIA

SKULLCAP

Lamiaceae (Labiatae)

PERENNIALS

ZONES VARY BY SPECIES

FULL SUN OR LIGHT SHADE

REGULAR WATER

Scutellaria baicalensis

Clump-forming mint relatives, with the family's typical square stems and paired leaves. Long, tubular flowers flare out into two lips, the upper one narrow and hooded, the lower one broad. Blossoms are clustered in roundish or elongated inflorescences. Easy to grow if given good drainage.

S. alpina. Zones 1–9, 14–24. Native from southern Europe to Siberia. Sprawling, mat-forming plant to 6 in. high, 1 ft. wide, with dark green, oval, 1-in. leaves. Tight clusters of 1-in., purple or white flowers in late spring, early summer.

S. baicalensis. Zones 1–9, 14–24. Native to Siberia, China, Japan. Stems first spread, then grow upright, forming a clump 1½ ft. tall and wide. Narrowly ovate, 1½-in.-long, medium green leaves. Dense, one-sided clusters of blue-purple, inch-long flowers in summer and fall.

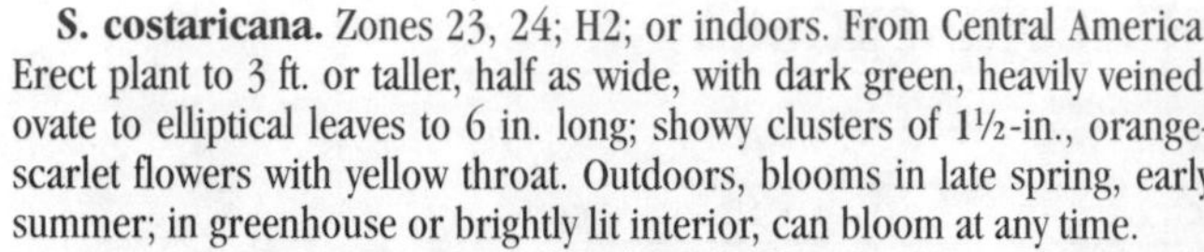

S. costaricana. Zones 23, 24; H2; or indoors. From Central America. Erect plant to 3 ft. or taller, half as wide, with dark green, heavily veined, ovate to elliptical leaves to 6 in. long; showy clusters of 1½-in., orange-scarlet flowers with yellow throat. Outdoors, blooms in late spring, early summer; in greenhouse or brightly lit interior, can bloom at any time.

S. resinosa. Zones 3–10, 14–24. Native from Kansas and Colorado south to Texas and Arizona. Mounding plant 6–8 in. tall, 1 ft. wide, with roundish, resinous, grayish green leaves less than ½ in. long. One-sided, elongated clusters of deep purple-blue, 1-in. flowers in late spring. Deadhead to encourage intermittent bloom through autumn.

SEA BUCKTHORN. See **HIPPOPHAE rhamnoides**

SEAFORTHIA elegans. See **ARCHONTOPHOENIX cunninghamiana**

SEA GRAPE. See **COCCOLOBA uvifera**

SEA HOLLY. See **ERYNGIUM**

SEA KALE. See **CRAMBE maritima**

SEA LAVENDER. See **LIMONIUM**

SEA PINK. See **ARMERIA**

SEA POPPY. See **GLAUCIUM**

SEASIDE DAISY. See **ERIGERON glaucus**

SEA URCHIN. See **HAKEA laurina**

SEDGE. See **CAREX**

SEDUM

STONECROP

Crassulaceae

SUCCULENT PERENNIALS

ZONES VARY BY SPECIES

FULL SUN OR PARTIAL SHADE, EXCEPT AS NOTED

LITTLE TO MODERATE WATER, EXCEPT AS NOTED

Sedum rubrotinctum

Native to many parts of the world. Some are quite hardy to cold, others fairly tender; some are tiny and trailing, others much larger and upright. Fleshy leaves are evergreen (unless otherwise noted) but highly variable in size, shape, and color. Typically small, star-shaped flowers, sometimes brightly colored, are usually borne in fairly large clusters.

Smaller sedums are useful in rock gardens, as ground or bank covers, in small areas where unusual texture is needed. Some are prized by collectors of succulents, who grow them in pots, dish gardens, or miniature gardens. Larger types are good in borders or containers. Most sedums are easy to propagate by stem cuttings; even detached leaves will root and form new plants. Soft and easily crushed, they will not take foot traffic, but they are otherwise tough, low-maintenance plants. Several plants sold as *Sedum* have been reassigned by botanists to the genus *Hylotelephium;* these are noted in the descriptions.

S. acre. GOLDMOSS SEDUM. Zones A2, A3; 1–24. Native to Europe, North Africa, Turkey. To 2–5 in. high, with upright branchlets rising from trailing, rooting stems. Light green leaves to ¼ in. long; clustered yellow flowers in spring. Extremely hardy but can get out of bounds and become a weed. Use as ground cover (set plants 1–1½ ft. apart), between steppingstones, or in chinks of dry walls.

S. album. Zones 1–24. Often sold as *S. brevifolium*. From Europe, Siberia, western Asia, North Africa. Creeping plant grows to 2–6 in. high. Leaves to ½ in. long, light to medium green, sometimes red tinted. White or pinkish summer flowers. Plant 1–1½ ft. apart for ground cover. Roots from the smallest fragment; beware of planting it near choice, delicate rock garden plants. 'Coral Carpet' displays coral pink new growth and turns reddish bronze in winter.

S. altissimum. See S. reflexum, S. sediforme

S. ×amecamecanum. See *S. confusum* for plant sold under this name. True *S. ×amecamecanum (×Sedadia amecamecana)* resembles *S. confusum* but is rare in gardens.

S. anglicum. Zones 1–24. From western Europe. Low, spreading plant 2–4 in. high. Dark green leaves are tiny, to just ⅛ in. long. Pinkish or white spring flowers. For ground cover, set plants 9–12 in. apart.

S. 'Autumn Joy' (Hylotelephium 'Autumn Joy', H. 'Herbstfreude'). Zones 1–10, 14–24. Hybrid of *S. telephium* and *S. spectabile.* To 1–2 ft. tall, 2 ft. wide, with green leaves to 2–3 in. long and about as wide. Rounded clusters of blossoms are pink when they open in late summer or autumn, later age to coppery pink and finally to rust. Dies down in winter.

S. brevifolium. Zones 8, 9, 14–24. Native to the Mediterranean region. Grows just 2–3 in. high, slowly spreading to 1 ft. wide. Gray-white, red-flushed leaves are tiny (less than ⅛ in. long), tightly packed on stems. Pinkish or white summer flowers. Needs good drainage. Best in rock garden or with larger succulents in containers, miniature garden. Sunburns in hot, dry places.

S. cauticolum (Hylotelephium cauticolum). Zones 1–11, 14–24. Native to Japan. Slowly forms a mound 4–6 in. high, 1–1½ ft. wide. Blue-gray, slightly toothed, 1-in. leaves. Clusters of small rose red flowers top stems in late summer or early fall. Dies to ground in winter.

S. confusum. Zones 8, 9, 14–24. Native to Mexico. Spreading, branching plant grows 6–12 in. high and wide. Shiny light green, ¾–1½-in.-long leaves tend to cluster in rosettes toward branch ends. Dense clusters of yellow flowers in spring. Makes a good ground cover but is sometimes plagued by dieback in wet soils, hot weather; looks best during cooler weather. Use in borders or containers, as edging, in miniature garden.

S. dasyphyllum. Zones 2–24; H1, H2. Native to the Mediterranean region. Forms a low (1½–4½-in.-high) mat that spreads to 1 ft. or wider. Gray-green, ⅛–¼-in. leaves are densely packed on stems. Blooms in summer, bearing white flowers with pink streaks. Pink-blossomed 'Riffense' has silver-gray leaves that are especially plump and succulent. Partial shade.

S. dendroideum. Zones 8, 9, 12, 14–24. Native to Mexico. Branching plant to 2 ft. tall and wide. Rounded leaves to 2 in. long are yellow green, often bronze tinted. Deep yellow flowers in spring and summer. For the plant sometimes sold as *S. d. praealtum,* see *S. praealtum.*

S. guatemalense. See S. rubrotinctum

S. kamtschaticum. Zones 1–11, 14–21. Native to Korea, Japan. Variable species to 4–12 in. high, 2 ft. wide, with trailing stems set with thick, somewhat triangular, 1–1½-in., medium green leaves, toothed on the upper third. Summer flowers open yellow, age to red. Useful in colder climates as a rock garden plant or small-space ground cover (set plants 1 ft. apart). 'Variegatum' has cream-edged leaves. *S. k. ellacombianum* (sometimes sold as *S. ellacombianum*) is a shorter plant (4–6 in. high) with more compact growth, unbranched stems, and brighter green leaves. *S. k. floriferum* (sometimes sold as *S. floriferum*) is a more profuse bloomer with smaller flowers in a lighter yellow; its variety 'Weihenstephaner Gold' has abundant golden yellow blossoms that turn orange with age.

S. lineare. Zones 1–24. Often sold as *S. sarmentosum.* Native to China, Japan. To 4 in. high. Trailing, rooting stems to 1 ft. long are closely set with narrow, inch-long light green leaves. Profuse yellow flowers in late spring, early summer. For ground cover, set plants 1–1½ ft. apart. 'Variegatum', with white-edged leaves, is often grown in containers.

S. morganianum. DONKEY TAIL, BURRO TAIL. Zones 17, 22–24; H1, H2; with protection of lath or eaves in Zones 13–16, 18–21; or indoors. Thought to have originated in Mexico. Produces long, trailing stems that reach 3–4 ft. in 6 to 8 years. Thick, ¾-in.-long, light gray-green leaves overlap each other along stems to form braided-looking "tails" less than 1 in. thick. Pink to deep red flowers may appear from spring to summer but are only rarely seen. Because of its long stems, this species is best grown in a hanging basket or wall pot; in mildest climates, try it spilling from top of a wall or in rock garden. Provide rich, fast-draining soil. Protect from wind and give partial shade. Similar relatives include *S.* 'Burro', with fatter (1-in.-thick) tails composed of densely packed, ½-in. leaves; giant donkey tail (often sold as *S. orpetii*), with somewhat shorter, thicker tails; and ×*Sedeveria* 'Super Giant Donkey Tail', with still thicker, shorter tails.

Sedum morganianum

S. oxypetalum. Zones 16, 17, 21–24. Native to Mexico. To 3 ft. tall (usually much less), 1½ ft. wide. Even when tiny, the plant has the look of a gnarled tree. Narrow, 1–1½-in.-long, olive green leaves; dull red, aromatic summer flowers. Evergreen or semievergreen in mildest areas; deciduous elsewhere. Handsome container plant.

S. praealtum. Zones 8, 9, 12, 14–24. Native to Mexico. Similar to *S. dendroideum* (and sometimes sold as *S. d. praealtum*) but larger (up to 3–5 ft. high and wide), with greener leaves and lighter yellow flowers. Blooms in spring and summer.

S. reflexum. Zones 2–24. Native to Europe. Often sold as *S. altissimum.* Much like *S. sediforme* but more vigorous, with shorter leaves and yellow summer flowers. Spreads freely; plant 9–12 in. apart for ground cover.

S. rubrotinctum. PORK AND BEANS. Zones 8, 9, 12, 14–24; H1, H2. Thought to be native to Mexico. Often sold as *S. guatemalense.* Sprawling, leaning, 6–8-in. stems are set with ¾-in. leaves that look like jelly beans; they are green with reddish brown tips, often entirely bronze red in sun. Detach easily and root readily. Reddish yellow spring flowers. Grow in rock garden, in pots, as small-space ground cover (set plants 10 in. apart).

S. sarmentosum. See S. lineare

S. sediforme (S. altissimum). Zones 2–24. Native to the Mediterranean region. Spreading, creeping plant to 16 in. high, 1 ft. wide. Narrow, light blue-gray leaves to 1½ in. long, closely set on stems. Small greenish white to light yellow flowers in summer. Use in rock garden, for blue-green effect in pattern planting, as small-space ground cover (set plants 1 ft. apart).

S. sieboldii (Hylotelephium sieboldii). Zones 2–9, 12, 14–24. Native to Japan. Low-growing plant just 4 in. high, 8–12 in. wide, with spreading, trailing, unbranched stems to 8–9 in. long. Blue-gray leaves with red edges are carried in threes; they are nearly round, stalkless, toothed along upper half. Plant turns coppery red in fall, dies to ground in winter. Each stem bears a broad, dense, flat cluster of dusty pink flowers in autumn. Leaves of 'Variegatum' have yellowish white markings. Species and variety are beautiful in rock gardens, hanging baskets. Light shade.

Sedum sieboldii

S. spathulifolium. Zones 2–9, 14–24. Native from California's Coast Ranges and Sierra Nevada north to British Columbia. Spoon-shaped, ½–1-in. blue-green leaves tinged with reddish purple are packed into rosettes on short, trailing stems. Light yellow flowers bloom in spring and summer. Use as ground cover (set plants 1–1½ ft. apart), in rock garden. Very drought tolerant. 'Cape Blanco' is a selected form with good leaf color; 'Purpureum' has deep purple foliage.

Sedum spathulifolium 'Purpureum'

S. spectabile (Hylotelephium spectabile). Zones 1–24. Native to China, Korea. To 1½ ft. tall and wide, with upright or slightly spreading stems thickly clothed in blue-green, roundish, 3-in. leaves. Dense, 6-in.-wide, dome-shaped flower clusters appear atop stems in late summer and fall; they open pink, mature to dark brown seed heads that put on a long-lasting show. Dies to ground in winter. Full sun. Regular to moderate water. Varieties include 'Brilliant', with deep rose red flowers; 'Carmen', soft rose; 'Indian Chief', coppery red; 'Meteor', carmine red; and 'Ruby Jewel', deep maroon.

S. spurium. Zones 1–10, 14–24. Native to Caucasus. Low-growing plant with trailing stems and dark green or bronze-tinted leaves just an inch or so long; spreads to 2 ft. or wider. In summer, pink flowers appear in dense clusters at ends of 4–5-in. stems. For rock garden, pattern planting, ground cover. 'Bronze Carpet' has bronze leaves and pink flowers; 'Dragon's Blood' ('Schorbuser Blut') bears purplish bronze leaves, dark red blooms. 'Red Carpet' has red leaves and blossoms. Leaves of 'Tricolor' are variegated in green, creamy white, and pink; its flowers are pink. ▶

S. telephium (Hylotelephium telephium). Zones 1–24. To 2 ft. high, 1–2 ft. wide. Native from eastern Europe eastward to Japan. Resembles *S. spectabile* but has gray-green, somewhat narrower leaves. Long-lasting floral display begins in late summer and fall; blossom clusters open purplish pink, age to brownish maroon. Plant dies to ground in winter. 'Matrona' has dark pink–edged gray-green leaves that age to grayish brown (retaining the pink edge), large heads of pink flowers borne on red stems. 'Mohrchen' has purple new growth and rosy pink flowers. *S. t. maximum* 'Atropurpureum' has burgundy foliage all season and dusty pink flowers. Plant in full sun (stems tend to flop in shaded sites). Regular to moderate water.

S. 'Vera Jameson' (Hylotelephium 'Vera Jameson'). Zones 1–9, 14–24. Cross between *S. telephium maximum* 'Atropurpureum' and *S.* 'Ruby Glow' (a low-growing hybrid with purple-gray leaves and ruby red flowers). To 8–12 in. high and 1½ ft. wide, with spreading purple stems clothed in pinkish purple leaves. Rose pink flowers in late summer, fall. Dies to ground in winter.

SEGO LILY. See CALOCHORTUS

SELF-HEAL. See PRUNELLA

SEMIARUNDINARIA. See BAMBOO

SEMPERVIVUM

HOUSELEEK

Crassulaceae

SUCCULENT PERENNIALS

ZONES 2–24

LIGHT SHADE IN HOTTEST CLIMATES

LITTLE TO MODERATE WATER

Sempervivum tectorum

Native to mountains of Europe. Form tightly packed rosettes of fleshy, evergreen leaves; spread by little offsets that cluster around parent rosette. Clustered, star-shaped summer flowers in white, yellowish, pink, red, or greenish; pretty in detail but not showy. Blooming rosettes die after setting seed, but offsets (easily detached and replanted) carry on. Many species, all good in rock gardens, pots, even in pockets in boulders or pieces of porous rock. Need excellent drainage. Water only to prevent shriveling. Protect from full sun in hot desert regions.

S. arachnoideum. COBWEB HOUSELEEK. Gray-green rosettes of many leaves are joined by fine hairs for a cobweb-covered look. Larger rosettes (to 2 in. wide) are surrounded by host of smaller rosettes. Spreads slowly to make dense mat to 1 ft. or wider. Bright red flowers on 4–6-in. stems.

S. tectorum. HEN AND CHICKENS. Gray-green, 2–5-in.-wide rosettes spread quickly to form clumps to 2 ft. or wider. Leaves have red-brown, bristly tips. Red or reddish blossoms are borne on stems to 2 ft. tall.

SENECIO

Asteraceae (Compositae)

PERENNIALS AND EVERGREEN OR DECIDUOUS SHRUBS AND VINES

ZONES VARY BY SPECIES

EXPOSURE NEEDS VARY BY SPECIES

WATER NEEDS VARY BY SPECIES

Senecio cineraria

This group of daisy relatives includes the well-known dusty miller and florist's cineraria as well as less familiar garden plants and even a few weeds. Succulent species are often sold as *Kleinia,* an earlier name.

S. cineraria. DUSTY MILLER. Shrubby perennial. Zones 4–24; H1, H2. From the Mediterranean region. To 2–3 ft. high and wide, with woolly white leaves cut into many blunt-tipped lobes. Blooms at almost any season in mild-winter climates, during summer in colder regions, bearing clustered heads of yellow or creamy yellow flowers. Striking in a night garden. Gets leggy unless sheared occasionally. Full sun. Provide good drainage, little to moderate water. For a plant sometimes sold as *S. cineraria* 'Candissimus', see *S. viravira.*

S. confusus (Pseudogynoxys chenopodioides). MEXICAN FLAME VINE. Evergreen or deciduous vine. Zones 13, 16–24; H1, H2; mild frost kills it to the ground, but it comes back fast from roots. Sometimes grown as a summer annual in colder climates. Native from Mexico to Honduras. Twines to 10–15 ft. in California, as much as 40 ft. in Hawaii. Light green, rather fleshy leaves to 4 in. long are broadly lance shaped, coarsely toothed. Large clusters of ¾–1-in., startling orange-red blooms with golden centers appear at branch ends; blossoms of 'São Paulo' are a deeper orange, almost brick red. Blooms from midspring into fall, sometimes year-round in frostless areas. Provide light soil, moderate to regular water. Full sun or light shade. Use on trellis or column, let cascade over a bank or wall, or plant in a hanging basket.

S. greyi. Evergreen shrub. Zones 5–9, 14–24. Plant commonly sold under this name is actually *Brachyglottis* Dunedin Group 'Sunshine'. To 4–5 ft. high, 6 ft. or more wide. Stiff, slightly curving stems bear 3½-in.-long, leathery gray-green leaves outlined in silvery white. Blooms profusely in summer, producing inch-wide yellow daisies in flattish, 5-in.-wide clusters. Full sun. Moderate to regular water. Prune out oldest growth yearly. Cut branches are long lasting in arrangements.

S. × hybridus (Pericallis × hybrida, S. cruentus). FLORISTS' CINERARIA. Perennial usually grown as an annual; or indoors. Best in Zones 16, 17, 22–24, where it may overwinter or reseed. To 2 ft. high and wide. Valuable for bright colors in cool, shady places; not for hot, dry climates. Most common are large-flowered dwarf kinds generally sold as Multiflora Nana or Hybrida Grandiflora. These are compact, 12–15-in. plants with broad clusters of 3–5-in. daisies in colors ranging from white through pink and purplish red to blue and purple, often with contrasting eyes or bands. Bloom in late winter and early spring in mild-winter areas, spring and early summer elsewhere. Plants sold as *Cineraria stellata* (an invalid botanical name) are taller (to 2½–3 ft.), with clusters of smaller, star-shaped daisies. Grow in loose, rich soil. Plant in fall or spring; protect plants set out in fall from frost by choosing a location under shrubs, trees, overhang, or lath. Effective in mass plantings or combined with other shade-loving plants; excellent in containers on lanai, patio. Even where perennial, usually discarded after bloom. Principal pests are leaf miners, spider mites, slugs, snails. Partial or full shade. Regular water.

Senecio × hybridus

S. leucostachys. See S. viravira

S. macroglossus. KENYA IVY, NATAL IVY, WAX VINE. Evergreen vine. Zones 12 and 13 (if given northern or eastern exposure), 22–24; H1, H2; or indoors. Native to southeastern Africa. Thin, succulent stems twine to 6½ ft. or more. Thick, waxy or rubbery, 2–3-in.-wide leaves are shaped like those of ivy *(Hedera),* with three, five, or seven shallow lobes. Tiny yellow daisies in summer. Leaves of 'Variegatum' are sharply splashed with creamy white. Little to moderate water. Can be grown as a houseplant in a sunny window; water only when soil is dry.

S. mandraliscae (Kleinia mandraliscae). Succulent shrubby perennial. Zones 12, 13, 16, 17, 21–24; H1, H2. Native to South Africa. To 1–1½ ft. high, 2 ft. wide. Cylindrical, slightly curved, striking blue-gray leaves to 3½ in. long. Use as ground cover where blue-gray effect is desired. Partial shade in the desert; full sun elsewhere. Little to moderate water. Beyond hardiness range, sometimes grown in a container and protected in winter.

Senecio mandraliscae

S. mikanioides (Delairea odorata). GERMAN IVY. Evergreen vine; dies to the ground in cold winters. Zones 14–24, H1, H2; or indoors. Native to South Africa. Twines to 18–20 ft. Roundish leaves resemble those of ivy *(Hedera),* have five or seven ½–3-in.-long, sharply pointed lobes. Winter flowers are small yellow "buttons"—daisies without rays. Good screening vine or trailer for window boxes. Full sun or part shade. Little to moderate water. A noxious weed in coastal California and in Hawaii.

S. petasitis. VELVET GROUNDSEL, CALIFORNIA GERANIUM. Shrubby perennial. Zones 15–17, 21–24. From Mexico. Bulky plant to 6–8 ft. or taller, equally wide. Velvety, evergreen leaves have a tropical look: they are large (to 8 in. across), lobed, fanlike. Blooms in midwinter, bearing large clusters of small bright yellow daisies that stand well above the foliage mass. Prune hard after bloom to limit height and sprawl. Can be kept to 2–4 ft. in tubs. Good filler in tropical gardens. Full sun or light shade. Regular water.

S. serpens (Kleinia repens). Succulent perennial. Zones 16, 17, 21–24. From South Africa. This species resembles *S. mandraliscae,* but it is a smaller plant (to 1 ft. high and wide) with smaller (1¼-in.) leaves.

S. viravira (S. leucostachys, S. cineraria 'Candissimus'). DUSTY MILLER. Shrubby perennial. Zones 4–24. Native to Argentina. Sprawling plant to 4 ft. tall and wide. Leaves resemble those of *S. cineraria,* but they are more strikingly white and are cut into much narrower, pointed segments. Creamy white summer flowers are not showy. Grown in full sun, plant is brilliantly white and densely leafy; in part shade, it is looser and more sparsely foliaged, with larger, greener leaves. Tip-pinch young plants to keep them compact. Little to moderate water.

SENNA

Fabaceae (Leguminosae)

EVERGREEN AND DECIDUOUS SHRUBS OR TREES

ZONES VARY BY SPECIES

FULL SUN OR LIGHT SHADE, EXCEPT AS NOTED

LITTLE TO MODERATE WATER, EXCEPT AS NOTED

Senna artemisioides

Previously included in *Cassia* and still often sold as such, these species have been reclassified as *Senna*—a move not accepted by all botanists. Grown for their lavish show of bright yellow, five-petaled flowers that look something like those of potentilla. Blossoms are followed by seedpods that may create litter; to reduce pod production, prune lightly after flowering. Rangy, rank growers should also be cut back periodically to encourage more compact growth. Good for screens, massing, background plantings. Prefer well-drained soil.

S. artemisioides (Cassia artemisioides). FEATHERY CASSIA. Evergreen shrub. Zones 8, 9, 12–16, 18–23. Native to Australia. To 3–5 ft. tall and wide, with attractive, light, airy structure. Gray leaves divided into six to eight needlelike, 1-in.-long leaflets. Bears ¾-in. flowers in clusters of five to eight in winter and spring, with bloom often continuing into summer. In the desert, plants may rest in summer, then resume flowering in fall. Heavy seed production. Very drought tolerant but looks better with moderate to regular water.

S. corymbosa (Cassia corymbosa). FLOWERY SENNA. Evergreen shrub. Zones 12, 13, 21–24; H1, H2. Native to South America. Rangy growth to 10 ft. tall, 10–12 ft. wide. Dark green leaves with six narrow, oblong, 1–2-in. leaflets. Rounded clusters of 1½-in. flowers, spring to fall. Self-seeding can be a problem.

S. didymobotrya (Cassia didymobotrya, C. nairobensis). Evergreen shrub. Zones 13, 22–24; H2. Native to eastern Africa. Rangy growth to 8 ft. tall, 8–10 wide. Blooms from winter into spring, bearing 1½-in.-wide flowers in dense, upright clusters to 1 ft. long. Olive green to dark green leaves made up of 16 to 32 leaflets, each about 2 in. long. Foliage is smelly when cut or bruised, but plant is nonetheless attractive in large wild gardens. Full sun. Moderate to regular water.

S. multiglandulosa (Cassia tomentosa). WOOLLY SENNA. Evergreen shrub. Zones 13, 17, 22–24. Native to many parts of the tropics. Vigorous, rank growth to 12–15 ft. tall and wide. Upright clusters of 1½-in. flowers at branch ends in winter, early spring. Leaves are green above, white and hairy beneath, divided into 12–16 leaflets, each 2½ in. long. Regular water.

S. nemophila (S. artemisiodes filifolia, Cassia eremophila). Evergreen shrub. Zones 12–24. Australian native similar to *C. artemisioides* but with green rather than gray foliage and somewhat greater cold tolerance.

S. phyllodinea (S. artemisioides petiolaris, Cassia phyllodinea). SILVER LEAF CASSIA. Evergreen shrub. Zones 12–24. Native to Australia. Rapid growth to 4–6 ft. tall and wide. Silvery gray leaves are narrow, curved, 1–2 in. long. Flowers are ¾ in. wide, blooming over a long season—from winter (sometimes as early as fall) into spring. Full sun.

S. splendida (Cassia splendida). GOLDEN WONDER SENNA. Evergreen shrub. Zones 12, 13, 21–24; H1, H2. Native to Brazil. Open growth to 9–12 ft. tall, 6–10 ft. wide; habit varies from fairly upright to horizontal. Bright green leaves with four elliptical to oblong leaflets to 3 in. long. Loose clusters of 1½-in. flowers appear at branch ends from autumn into winter. Heavy seed production.

S. sturtii (S. artemisioides sturtii, Cassia sturtii). Evergreen shrub. Zones 12–14. Native to Australia. Bushy growth to 3–6 ft. tall, 3–4 ft. wide. Gray-green leaves with four to ten narrow, 1-in. leaflets. Tidier looking than *S. artemisioides.*

S. surattensis (Cassia surattensis). SCRAMBLED EGGS, KOLOMANA. Evergreen shrub or tree. Zones 19–24; H1, H2. Native to tropical Asia, Polynesia, Australia. In Hawaii, it reaches 25 ft. tall and nearly as wide and is used as a flowering shade or street tree. In California, grows 6–8 ft. high and wide, makes a handsome shrub for a small garden. Blooms nearly year-round, producing small clusters of ¾-in. flowers at branch ends. Each green leaf has 12–20 roundish, 1½-in. leaflets.

S. wislizenii (Cassia wislizenii). Deciduous shrub. Zones 10–13. From southern Arizona into Texas, Mexico. Rounded habit to 5–8 ft. tall, 5–10 ft. wide, with rigid, upright branches. Bright green leaves have four to six leaflets, each to 1¼ in. long. Clusters of 1-in. flowers appear at branch ends from early summer into fall.

SENTRY PALM. See HOWEA belmoreana

SEQUOIA sempervirens

REDWOOD, COAST REDWOOD

Taxodiaceae

EVERGREEN TREE

ZONES 4–9, 14–24

FULL SUN OR LIGHT SHADE

MODERATE TO REGULAR WATER

Sequoia sempervirens

Native to Coast Ranges from southern Oregon to central coastal California. One of the West's most famous native trees (equally famous is its close relative *Sequoiadendron,* called giant sequoia or big tree). Coast redwood is the tallest of the world's trees: some individuals in the wild are over 350 ft. high. Fine landscaping tree—almost entirely pest free and almost always fresh looking and woodsy smelling. In its native range, a redwood tree grows rapidly (3–5 ft. a year in its early years) but will reach only about 70–90 ft. tall, 15–30 ft. wide in 25 years. In less favorable areas, grows more slowly and tops out at perhaps 50 ft. Typically forms a symmetrical pyramid of soft-looking foliage. Flat, pointed, narrow, inch-long leaves are typically medium green on top, grayish beneath; they grow in one plane on both sides of stem, giving stem a featherlike look. Small (½–1½-in.), roundish brown cones. Red-brown, fibrous-barked trunk goes straight up. A trunk with nearly parallel sides indicates a healthy redwood; one with a noticeable taper means the tree is struggling. Habit is somewhat variable, but most redwoods have main branches that grow straight out from trunk and curve up at tips; slightly drooping branchlets grow from these.

The tree's natural variability has led to selection of distinct variants. 'Aptos Blue' has dense blue-green foliage on nearly horizontal branches with drooping branchlets. 'Los Altos' features a thick canopy of dark green leaves on horizontal, arching branches. 'Majestic Beauty' has dense blue-green foliage, horizontal branches with pendulous branchlets. 'Santa Cruz' has soft, light green leaves and slightly downward-angled branches. Fine-textured 'Soquel' bears blue-tinged green foliage on horizontal branches

S

that turn up at tips. 'Filoli' and 'Woodside' are similar if not identical to each other; both are nearly as blue as Colorado blue spruce *(Picea pungens glauca)*. They have an irregular habit, with branches that tend to droop, and need careful training when young to establish good form. 'Simpson's Silver' is somewhat slower growing than other redwood varieties; it has stiffly horizontal branches and silvery blue leaves that fade to blue green with maturity. 'Adpressa' ('Albo-Spica'), to 3 ft. high and 6 ft. wide, is a dwarf variety for rock gardens; it has white-tipped new growth that turns solid green as summer advances.

Grow redwood trees singly or in groves (spaced 7 ft. apart); can also be used for a hedge (plant 3–4 ft. apart and top at least once yearly). One of the best planting locations is in or directly next to a lawn, since the tree thrives on regular moisture (in 10–20 years, however, it may defeat a lawn). Away from lawns, it needs occasional feeding and regular summer watering (at least for first 5 years). Where it is best adapted, an established tree gets all the moisture it needs from fog drip. Resistant to oak root fungus. Troubles the tree encounters are mostly physiological. Inadequate moisture or a hot, dry site will make it sulk and grow slowly; too much competition from bigger trees and structures makes it lanky, thin, and open. Lack of available iron makes needles turn yellow in summer, especially on new growth; solve the problem by applying iron sulfate or chelates. Keep in mind, however, that it is normal for oldest leaves to turn from green to yellow to brown, then drop in late summer and early fall; short twigs also turn brown and drop.

SEQUOIADENDRON giganteum (Sequoia gigantea)

GIANT SEQUOIA, BIG TREE

Taxodiaceae

EVERGREEN TREE

ZONES A1–A3; 1–9, 14–23

FULL SUN

MODERATE WATER

Sequoiadendron giganteum

Native to western slope of central and southern Sierra Nevada. Old specimens reach a towering 325 ft. and have the most massive trunk in the world (to 30 ft. in diameter), yet young trees ("young" in terms of a 3,000-year life span) are neat, handsome trees for larger gardens, reaching 60–100 ft. tall, 30–50 ft. wide. This tree has always shared fame and comparisons with its close relative, coast redwood *(Sequoia)*, but horticulturally the similarities are few.

Giant sequoia is hardier to cold than coast redwood; it grows a little more slowly (2–3 ft. a year) and needs less water. Outside its natural habitat, it is subject to fungal diseases that can disfigure or kill it; seems more successful in colder interior climates than near the coast.

Giant sequoia's dense foliage is bushier than that of coast redwood. It is a somewhat prickly tree to reach into. Branchlets are clothed with short gray-green leaves; each leaf is a pointed scale overlapping the next, like prickly cypress *(Cupressus)* foliage. Dark reddish brown, oval, 2–3-in.-long cones. Lower branches hang on for many years, so that tree is a dense pyramid; lowest branches sometimes root where they touch the ground, forming secondary "trees" that blend into the original. Removing lower branches reveals a fissured, craggy-looking trunk covered in dark red-brown bark. In gardens, giant sequoia is primarily used as a featured tree in a large lawn (roots may surface there) or other open space. Grow in good, deep, well-drained soil. 'Pendulum' has an irregular form and strongly weeping branches; it can be trained into tall pillar to about 25 ft. high, 4 ft. wide or a little wider.

SERVICEBERRY. See AMELANCHIER

SETCREASEA pallida 'Purple Heart'. See TRADESCANTIA pallida 'Purpurea'

SEVEN SONS FLOWER. See HEPTACODIUM miconioides

SHADBLOW. See AMELANCHIER

SHADSCALE. See ATRIPLEX confertifolia

SHALLOT

Liliaceae

PERENNIAL OFTEN GROWN AS ANNUAL

ALL ZONES

FULL SUN

REGULAR WATER

Shallot

Closely related to onion and, like it, a member of the genus *Allium*. Thought to have originated in western or central Asia. The bulb is divided into cloves that grow on a common base; it is prized in cooking for its distinctive flavor, a combination of mild onion and pungent garlic. Young green shoots are also edible. Dutch shallots have golden brown skin and white cloves; red shallots have coppery skin, purple cloves.

In mild climates, you can plant shallots in fall to harvest green tops through winter and early spring, bulbs in late spring and summer. In cold-winter regions, plant them in early spring for green shoots in summer, bulbs in autumn.

Shallots are usually grown from cloves (sections of bulbs). You can purchase these from a seed company or simply buy shallots in the grocery store and separate them into cloves. Plant cloves pointed end up, 4–8 in. apart; cover with ½ in. of soil. You'll have green shoots in about 60 days, new bulbs in 90 to 120 days. Some seed companies sell shallot seeds; plant 12 seeds per foot. Bulbs will be ready to harvest in about 100 days. Nurseries with stocks of herbs may sell growing plants.

When bulbs are mature, shoots yellow and die. To harvest, pull up clumps and separate the bulbs; before using them, let dry for about a month in a cool, dry place. If stored properly, shallots will keep for up to 8 months.

SHAMROCKS. Around St. Patrick's Day, nurseries and florists sell "shamrocks." These are small potted plants of *Medicago lupulina* (hop clover, yellow trefoil, black medick), an annual plant; *Oxalis acetosella* (wood sorrel), a perennial; or *Trifolium repens* (white clover), also a perennial. The last is the most commonly sold. All of these have leaves divided into three leaflets, symbolic of the Trinity. They can be kept on a sunny windowsill or planted out, but they have little ornamental value and are likely to become weeds.

SHASTA DAISY. See CHRYSANTHEMUM maximum

SHELL FLOWER. See ALPINIA zerumbet, MOLUCCELLA laevis

SHELL GINGER. See ALPINIA zerumbet

SHE-OAK. See CASUARINA

SHEPHERDIA

BUFFALOBERRY

Elaeagnaceae

DECIDUOUS SHRUBS

ZONES VARY BY SPECIES

FULL SUN

LITTLE TO REGULAR WATER

Shepherdia argentea

These are tough plants for harsh growing conditions—withstand cold and wind, take most soils, tolerate drought. Related to Russian olive *(Elaeagnus)*, another plant that readily endures difficult situations. If a male plant is nearby, females will bear small, sour bright red or orange berries that can be used for jams and jellies. Birds like the fruit.

S. argentea. SILVER BUFFALOBERRY, SILVERBERRY. Zones 1–3, 7, 10. Native from Canada into intermountain areas of the West. Spreading, suckering plant to 6–12 ft. high and wide, with spine-tipped branchlets. Elongated oval leaves to 1 in. long, silvery on both sides. Looks grayer than *S. canadensis.*

S. canadensis. BUFFALOBERRY, SOAPBERRY. Zones A1–A3; 1–3, 7, 10. Native from Newfoundland west to Alaska, south to Oregon. Rounded habit to 6–8 ft. high and wide, with thornless branches. Leaves reach 2 in. long, half as wide; upper surfaces are green, undersides silvery with brown scales. Two-tone foliage gives the plant an overall grayish green appearance.

SHIBATAEA. See **BAMBOO**

SHIMPAKU. See **JUNIPERUS sargentii**

SHISO. See **PERILLA frutescens**

SHOOTING STAR. See **DODECATHEON**

SHORTIA

Diapensiaceae

PERENNIALS

ZONES 1–7

PARTIAL OR FULL SHADE

REGULAR TO AMPLE WATER

Shortia galacifolia

Beautiful, small, spring-blooming evergreen plants that spread slowly by underground stems. *S. galacifolia* is native to the southeastern U.S.; the other two species are native to Japan. Intolerant of heat. Need acid, organically enriched soil. Grow with azaleas and rhododendrons.

S. galacifolia. OCONEE BELLS. Forms a foot-wide clump of round or oval, glossy green, 1–3-in.-long leaves with scalloped edges. Each of the many 4–6-in.-high stems is topped with a single blossom—a nodding, 1-in.-wide white bell with toothed edges.

S. soldanelloides. FRINGE BELLS. Similar to *S. galacifolia* but has round, coarsely toothed leaves and pink to rose-colored blossoms with deeply fringed edges.

S. uniflora 'Grandiflora'. Like *S. galacifolia* but with somewhat heart-shaped, wavy-edged leaves. Flowers are large, fringed bells in pure soft pink.

SHRIMP PLANT. See **JUSTICIA brandegeeana**

SHUNGIKU. See **CHRYSANTHEMUM coronarium**

SIAM TULIP. See **CURCUMA alismatifolia**

SIDA fallax

'ILIMA

Malvaceae

EVERGREEN SHRUB

ZONES 23, 24; H1, H2

FULL SUN

LITTLE WATER

Sida fallax

Native to Hawaii; widespread in the Pacific Islands and China. There are many forms of this plant, from ground covers to medium-size shrubs to big shrubs (to 10 ft. high and nearly as wide). Roundish, bright green to silvery green leaves to ½ in. long. Blooms all year, producing hibiscuslike, ½–1-in. flowers in colors ranging from yellow and orange to dull red. Blossoms are used in leis. Good wind tolerance. Does best in well-drained, rocky or sandy soil. *'Ilima papa* is a very low-growing form, to just 3 in. high and 2 ft. wide; it is useful as a ground cover. 'Kaneohe Gold', to 3 ft. high and wide, has double blooms in bright golden orange.

SIDALCEA

CHECKERBLOOM, MINIATURE HOLLYHOCK

Malvaceae

PERENNIALS

ZONES 2–10, 14–24, EXCEPT AS NOTED

FULL SUN

REGULAR WATER, EXCEPT AS NOTED

Sidalcea malviflora

All are grown for clusters of five-petaled flowers like little hollyhocks *(Alcea)*. The plants described here range from erect to sprawling; leaves are typically dark green, roundish to kidney-shaped, about 3 in. across. Basal leaves are shallowly lobed, stem leaves more deeply cut.

S. candida. Native to High Plains. To 2–3 ft. high, spreading by rhizomes to 1½ ft. Unbranched stems bear bluish green leaves to 8 in. across. Crowded spikes of white, 1-in. flowers in mid- or late summer.

S. hybrids. Most sidalceas grown in gardens are hybrids between *S. candida* and *S. malviflora.* They form clumps to about 2 ft. wide and bear 1½–2-in. flowers; bloom all summer if deadheaded. Choices include 3-ft. 'Elsie Heugh', with fringed pale pink flowers; 2½-ft. 'Loveliness' (shell pink); and 2–3-ft. 'Party Girl' (deep pink).

S. malviflora. CHECKERBLOOM. Zones 2–9, 14–24. Native to Oregon, California, Baja California. May grow erect to 2 ft. high and wide; or may sprawl and spread more widely by rooting at the nodes. Pink or purplish pink, 2-in. flowers in early spring. Moderate water (without moisture, they go dormant in summer and reappear with fall rains).

S. neomexicana. Zones 2, 3, 10–13, 18–24. Native from eastern Oregon to Wyoming, south to Mexico. To 3 ft. tall, 1–1½ ft. wide; branched or unbranched spikes of white or pinkish, ¾-in., summer flowers.

SILENE

Caryophyllaceae

PERENNIALS AND ANNUALS

ZONES VARY BY SPECIES

FULL SUN OR PARTIAL SHADE

WATER NEEDS VARY BY SPECIES

Silene californica

Many species; some are erect, others cushionlike. Good choices for front of border, rock garden. Flowers are typically single. Need well-drained soil.

S. acaulis. CUSHION PINK, MOSS CAMPION. Perennial. Zones A1–A3; 1–11, 14–16, 18–21. From the Arctic, mountains of North America, Eurasia. Small (¼–½-in.), narrow bright green leaves form a mosslike mat to 2 in. high, 8 in. wide. Reddish purple, ½-in. flowers are borne singly in spring. Good for gravelly, moist but well-drained spot. Regular water.

S. alpestris (S. quadrifolia). Perennial. Zones 2–9, 14–24. From eastern Alps. Creeping plant to 8 in. high and wide. Medium green, very narrow leaves to 1¼ in. Fine spring show of ½-in., double white flowers in loose sprays; scattered bloom later. Moderate water.

S. californica. CALIFORNIA INDIAN PINK. Perennial. Zones 3, 6–9, 14–24. Native to foothills of California and southern Oregon. Loosely branching plant to 1 ft. high and wide. Blooms in spring, producing flaming red, 1½-in. flowers with cleft and fringed petals in clusters of few to many. Gray-green, hairy, lance-shaped to ovate leaves to 3 in. long are somewhat sticky. Occasionally sold in seed packets. In its native range, it receives no moisture during the summer months, but it can take summer water if given excellent drainage.

S. coeli-rosa (Lychnis coeli-rosa, Agrostemma coeli-rosa). VISCARIA. Annual. All zones. Mediterranean native to 1 ft. tall, half as wide, with gray-green, lance-shaped to oblong leaves to 2 in. long. Loose clusters of saucer-shaped, 1-in. flowers in blue, lavender, pink, or white, often with a contrasting eye. Long bloom period. Sow seed in rich soil in early spring for summer bloom; in mild-winter climates, sow in fall for winter and spring bloom. Good cut flower. Regular water. ▸

S. schafta. MOSS CAMPION. Perennial. Zones 2–9, 14–16, 18–21. From western Asia. Upright, wiry stems form a tuft 6–12 in. high, 1 ft. wide. Small (½–¾-in.), tongue-shaped, bright green leaves. Profuse rosy purple, ¾-in. flowers, one or two per stalk, late summer into fall. Moderate water.

S. uniflora (S. vulgaris maritima). Perennial. Zones 1–9, 14–24. From coastal regions of western and northern Europe. Forms a low (6-in.-high, 8-in.-wide) cushion of ¾-in., lance-shaped gray-green leaves. Abundant white, 1-in. summer flowers, each nearly enclosed by a balloonlike calyx; borne one to four per stem. Moderate water.

SILK OAK. See GREVILLEA robusta

SILKTASSEL. See GARRYA

SILK TREE. See ALBIZIA julibrissin

SILVER BELL. See HALESIA carolina

SILVERBERRY. See ELAEAGNUS commutata, E. pungens, SHEPHERDIA argentea

SILVER DOLLAR GUM, SILVER DOLLAR TREE. See EUCALYPTUS polyanthemos, E. cinerea

SILVER FERN. See PTERIS quadriaurita 'Argyraea'

SILVER GRASS. See MISCANTHUS

SILVER LACE VINE. See FALLOPIA baldschuanica

SILVERLEAF. See LEUCOPHYLLUM

SILVER SPEAR. See ASTELIA nervosa chathamica

SILVER TREE. See LEUCADENDRON argenteum

SIMMONDSIA chinensis

JOJOBA, GOATNUT

Simmondsiaceae

EVERGREEN SHRUB

ZONES 7–24

FULL SUN

LITTLE WATER

Simmondsia chinensis

Native to deserts of Southern California, Arizona, Mexico. Dense plant with rigid branches; typically to 3–6 ft. high and wide, occasionally larger. Dull gray-green leaves are leathery, narrowly egg shaped, 1–2 in. long. Inconspicuous flowers. If a male plant is present, females bear edible, nutlike fruit ¾ in. long; flavor is like that of filbert but slightly bitter until fruit is dried or roasted. Fruit's high oil content gives plant commercial value as crop for marginal land, though such plantings are chancy in soil infested with verticillium wilt or Texas root rot. Useful as informal or clipped hedge, foundation planting in desert garden. Young plants are rather tender; established ones will take 15°F/–9°C.

SINARUNDINARIA. See BAMBOO, Fargesia

SINNINGIA speciosa (Gloxinia speciosa)

GLOXINIA

Gesneriaceae

PERENNIAL FROM TUBER; GROWN AS HOUSEPLANT

BRIGHT INDIRECT LIGHT

SEE INSTRUCTIONS BELOW

Sinningia speciosa

Native to Brazil. Squat, full-foliaged plant to 1 ft. high and wide. Broad, oval leaves reach 6 in. or longer, look like quilted green velvet. Blooms in summer, producing showy, velvety-sheened, ruffled bells to 4 in. wide in cluster near top of plant. Colors include white, red, pink, blue, and light to dark shades of purple. Some flowers have dark dots or blotches, others contrasting bands at edges.

Gloxinias need constant warmth and are most often grown in greenhouse or as houseplants; can be taken outdoors in warm weather. Tubers usually available in winter, spring. For each tuber, choose a container big enough to leave 2 in. between all sides of tuber and container edges. Fill with soil mix of equal parts peat moss, perlite, and leaf mold or compost; set tuber ½ in. deep. Place in warm spot (about 72°F/22°C during day, no cooler than 65°F/18°C at night) with plenty of bright light but no direct sun. Water sparingly until first leaves appear, then increase watering as roots and leaves grow. Apply water to soil only, or pour it into drip saucer to be absorbed through pot's drainage holes (pour off any water left unabsorbed after an hour). Apply half-strength liquid fertilizer every 2 weeks, starting when leaves emerge and continuing until flowers fade. After bloom has finished, gradually dry off plants. When leaves have died down completely, move container to dark place where temperatures remain around 60°F/16°C. Mist soil just enough to keep tubers from shriveling. When tubers show signs of resuming growth in midwinter, repot in fresh soil mix. If roots have filled container, move tuber to a larger pot.

SISYRINCHIUM

Iridaceae

PERENNIALS

ZONES 4–9, 14–24, EXCEPT AS NOTED

FULL SUN OR LIGHT SHADE

WATER NEEDS VARY BY SPECIES

Sisyrinchium bellum

Iris relatives with narrow, rather grassy leaves and small, six-segmented flowers that open in sunshine. Pretty but not showy; best suited for informal gardens or naturalizing.

S. bellum (S. idahoense bellum). BLUE-EYED GRASS. Zones 2–9, 14–24. Native to coast of California and Oregon. To 4 in.–2 ft. high, 6 in.–2 ft. wide. Green or bluish green leaves. Purple to bluish purple, ½-in. flowers in spring. Several named forms, many of them dwarf, are available. Plants sold as *S. macounii* (purple blooms) or *S. m.* 'Album' (white blossoms) are probably forms of *S. bellum.* Moderate to regular water.

S. californicum. YELLOW-EYED GRASS. From coastal areas, California to British Columbia. To 6 in.–2 ft. high, 8–10 in. wide. Dull green leaves are broader than those of *S. bellum.* Yellow flowers in late spring or early summer. Succeeds in wet or low spots. Ample water.

S. striatum. Native to Chile, Argentina. To 3 ft. tall, 1 ft. wide, with attractive gray-green leaves. In spring, produces spikelike clusters of many ½-in. flowers in pale yellow streaked with brown; blooms well into summer if old flower clusters are removed (if you don't remove them, you may have hordes of unwanted seedlings the next year). Leaves of 'Aunt May' ('Variegatum') are striped with creamy yellow. Moderate water.

SKIMMIA japonica

Rutaceae

EVERGREEN SHRUB

ZONES 4–9, 14–22

PARTIAL SHADE

REGULAR WATER

Skimmia japonica

Native to Japan, China. Compact, slow grower to 5 ft. tall, 6 ft. wide. Glossy rich green leaves to 3–4 in. long are oval, blunt ended, mostly clustered near twig ends. Blooms in spring, when pinkish to reddish buds held well above the foliage open to tiny, lightly scented white flowers (typically larger and more fragrant on males than on females). In fall and winter, female plants will bear holly-like red berries if a male plant is nearby. Plants tend to be sold simply as "male" or "female" rather than by variety name. A white-berried form is sold. *S. j. reevesiana* (often sold as *S. reevesiana*), a dwarf form to 1½–2 ft. high, 2–3 ft. wide, is self-fruitful and bears dull crimson berries.

Handsome beside shaded walks, under windows, flanking entryways, in containers. Prefers moist, highly organic, acid soil. Grows best in Zones 4–6, 17. Thrips and red spider mites are potential pests throughout its range. In the Northwest, it is prone to attack by several kinds of mites that give leaves a stippled, silvery look. Water mold is a problem in hot regions.

SKULLCAP. See SCUTELLARIA

SKUNKBUSH. See RHUS trilobata

SKY FLOWER. See DURANTA, THUNBERGIA grandiflora

SMILACINA racemosa

FALSE SOLOMON'S SEAL

Liliaceae

PERENNIAL

ZONES 1–7, 14–17

PARTIAL OR FULL SHADE

REGULAR WATER

Smilacina racemosa

Commonly seen in shaded woods from California to British Columbia, east to Rockies. Grows 1–3 ft. tall, spreading by creeping rhizomes to form dense colonies. Each single, arching stalk has several medium green, oval to lance-shaped, 3–10-in.-long leaves with hairy undersides; foliage turns golden yellow in autumn. In spring, stalks are topped by fluffy, conical clusters of small, fragrant, creamy white flowers. Red berries with purple spots ripen in autumn; they are favored by wildlife. Good for naturalizing in wild garden. Needs rich, loose, moist, slightly acid soil. Tolerates full sun in cool-summer climates. Resembles true Solomon's seal *(Polygonatum)*.

SMOKE TREE. See COTINUS, PSOROTHAMNUS spinosus

SNAIL VINE. See VIGNA caracalla

SNAKE PLANT. See SANSEVIERIA trifasciata

SNAKESHEAD. See FRITILLARIA meleagris

SNAPDRAGON. See ANTIRRHINUM majus

SNEEZEWEED. See HELENIUM

SNOWBALL, FRAGRANT. See VIBURNUM × carlcephalum

SNOWBELL. See STYRAX

SNOWBERRY. See SYMPHORICARPOS

SNOW BUSH. See BREYNIA nivosa

SNOWDROP. See GALANTHUS

SNOWDROP TREE. See HALESIA carolina

SNOWFLAKE. See LEUCOJUM

SNOW GUM. See EUCALYPTUS pauciflora niphophila

SNOW-IN-SUMMER. See CERASTIUM tomentosum

SNOW MYRTLE. See CALYTRIX alpestris

SNOW-ON-THE-MOUNTAIN. See EUPHORBIA marginata

SOAPBARK TREE. See QUILLAJA saponaria

SOCIETY GARLIC. See TULBAGHIA violacea

FOR INFORMATION ON SELECTING PLANTS
PLEASE SEE PAGES 64–160

Solanaceae. Members of the potato family bear flowers that are nearly always star or saucer shaped and five petaled; fruits are berries or capsules. Plants are frequently rank smelling or even poisonous, but many are important food crops—eggplant, pepper, potato, tomato. Others are garden annuals, perennials, shrubs, and vines—amethyst flower *(Browallia)*, *Cestrum*, *Nicotiana*, and *Petunia*, to name a few.

SOLANDRA maxima

CUP-OF-GOLD VINE

Solanaceae

EVERGREEN VINE

ZONES 15–24; H2

FULL SUN

REGULAR WATER

Solandra maxima

Native from Mexico to Venezuela and Colombia. Fast-growing, sprawling, rampant vine to 40 ft.; must be tied to its support. Heavy stems bear highly polished, broadly oval, rich green leaves to 6 in. long. Inflated-looking buds open to big (6–8-in.), leathery, bowl-shaped, five-lobed blossoms that are fragrant at night; flowers are golden yellow, with a red-brown stripe running down each lobe to flower center. Main bloom period runs from winter into early spring, but scattered flowering can occur at any time.

Give good, well-drained soil for best growth. Use on big walls and pergolas, along eaves, as bank cover. Spectacular along fence near swimming pool. Cut back long, vigorous shoots to induce branching and more flowers. To make it easy to see inside the big flowers, encourage growth low on plant by tip-pinching. Can be trimmed back to make rough hedge. Takes seacoast conditions, wind, fog. Provide shade for roots in hottest climates; give overhead cold protection in Zones 15, 16, 18–20. Light frost blackens the leaves, but plants usually recover to produce new growth. Often sold as *S. guttata*.

SOLANUM

Solanaceae

EVERGREEN, SEMIEVERGREEN, AND DECIDUOUS SHRUBS, VINES, PERENNIALS

ZONES VARY BY SPECIES

FULL SUN OR PARTIAL SHADE

MODERATE TO REGULAR WATER, EXCEPT AS NOTED

MANY SPECIES ARE POISONOUS WHEN INGESTED; MOST ARE SUSPECT

Solanum pseudocapsicum

In addition to eggplant and potato (described under those names), *Solanum* includes a number of ornamental plants. All have small, star-shaped, five-petaled blue or white flowers with reproductive parts that form a pointed yellow structure in the blossom's center. A few of the species described here produce decorative fruit—edible in the case of *S. muricatum*, but usually poisonous (if fruit is not described as edible, you are better off not sampling it).

S. aviculare. Evergreen shrub. Zones 15–17, 21–24. From Australia, New Zealand. Fast growth to 6–10 ft. tall, 5–8 ft. wide. Lance-shaped deep green leaves are smooth and deeply cut, reach 1 ft. long. Purple, 1-in.-wide flowers in spring and summer are followed by inedible scarlet fruit about 1 in. across.

S. crispum. Evergreen vine. Zones 8, 9, 12–24. From Chile, Peru. Modest (even shrubby) climber to 12 ft., with ovate to lance-shaped, soft green, often wavy-edged leaves to 5 in. long. In summer, bears 4-in. clusters of fragrant lilac-blue flowers with yellow centers. Small, inedible yellowish fruit. Must be fastened to its support; well suited to trellises, walls, posts. May lose leaves in hard frost. 'Glasnevin' has deeper blue flowers in larger clusters. ▶

S. jasminoides. POTATO VINE. Evergreen or semievergreen vine. Zones 8, 9, 12–24; H1, H2. From Brazil. Twines rapidly to 30 ft. Purplish-tinged, arrow-shaped, 1½–3-in.-long leaves. White, 1-in. flowers are carried on threadlike stalks in clusters of up to 12; bloom is almost continuous all year, heaviest in spring. Grown for flowers or for light overhead shade. Cut back severely at any time to prevent tangling, promote vigorous new growth. Control rampant runners that grow along ground.

S. muricatum. PEPINO. Perennial. Zones 17, 23, 24; H2. Thought to have originated in Colombia, Peru, Chile. Grows 2–3 ft. high, sprawling to about 4 ft. wide. Ovate to lance-shaped, bright green leaves to 3 in. long. Bright blue flowers in spring and early summer are not especially showy; they are followed later in summer by football-shaped greenish yellow fruit with purple stripes. Fruit weighs ¼–1 lb. and tastes like a cross between melon and cucumber. Same culture as tomato. Plant is grown as much for ornament as for edible crop. Handsome choice for a hanging basket.

S. pseudocapsicum. JERUSALEM CHERRY. Evergreen shrub. Zones 23, 24; H2; annual or indoor/outdoor plant anywhere. From Madeira; widely naturalized in tropics and subtropics. To 3–4 ft. high and wide (about half that size if grown as an annual). Shiny deep green, smooth, elliptical leaves to 4 in. long. White, ½ in. summer flowers are followed in autumn by a fine show of scarlet (rarely yellow), ½-in. fruits that look like cherry tomatoes but are poisonous. In mildest-winter areas, plant bears flowers and fruit (and self-sows) year-round. More popular than taller kinds are the many dwarf strains, which grow to 1 ft. high and bear larger fruit (to 1 in. across).

Solanum rantonnetii

S. rantonnetii (Lycianthes rantonnetii). Evergreen shrub. Zones 12, 13, 15–24; H1, H2. From Paraguay, Argentina. As freestanding plant, it makes a shrub 8–12 ft. tall and 6–10 ft. wide, but it can be staked into tree form or, with support, grown as a vine to 12–15 ft. or more. Can also be allowed to sprawl and used as a ground cover. Bright green, oval leaves to 4 in. long; violet-blue, ½–1½-in. flowers throughout warm weather, often nearly year-round. Informal, fast growing, not easy to use in tailored landscape; prune hard to keep it neat. In severe cold, leaf drop is heavy and branch tips may die back. The species is seldom seen; common plant in the nursery trade is 'Grandiflorum'. 'Royal Robe' is more compact (to 6–8 ft. high and wide), bears darker purple flowers over a longer season.

S. seaforthianum. BRAZILIAN NIGHTSHADE. Evergreen or semievergreen vine. Zones 16, 21–24; H1, H2. Slender-stemmed plant to 15 ft.; must be fastened to its support. Oval, 4–8-in.-long, medium green leaves are either undivided or quite deeply cleft into three or more lobes. Clusters of violet-blue, 1-in.-wide flowers bloom in summer. Pea-size red fruits are enjoyed by birds but should not be eaten by people.

S. wendlandii. COSTA RICAN NIGHTSHADE. Deciduous vine. Zones 16, 21–24; H1, H2. To 15–20 ft., climbing by twining stems and hooked spines. Glossy green, ovate or (sometimes) lobed leaves 4–10 in. long are corrugated in texture. Foliage forms a lush backdrop for dense, domed clusters of lavender-blue, 2½-in. summer flowers. Somewhat reminiscent of bougainvillea. Let it clamber into tall trees, cover a pergola, decorate eaves of large house. Loses leaves in low temperatures, even without frost; slow to leaf out in spring.

S. xantii. Evergreen shrub. Zones 7–9, 11, 14–24. Native to California. Erect or sprawling to 2–3 ft. high, 3 ft. wide. Ovate green leaves to 1¾ in. long. Purple, 1-in. flowers in late winter, spring. Superior forms are seen in California native plant gardens. Little or no water.

FOR DEFINITIONS OF GARDENING TERMS
PLEASE SEE PAGES 746–750

SOLEIROLIA soleirolii (Helxine soleirolii)

BABY'S TEARS, ANGEL'S TEARS
Urticaceae
PERENNIAL
ZONES 4–24; H1, H2
FULL SUN OR PARTIAL SHADE
REGULAR TO AMPLE WATER

Soleirolia soleirolii

From western Mediterranean. To 2–4 in. high, spreading indefinitely by creeping stems to form a lush, medium green mat. Inconspicuous flowers. Stems and tiny leaves are tender, juicy, easily injured, but aggressive growth repairs damage quickly. Roots easily from pieces of stem and can become an invasive pest. Freezes to black mush in hard frosts but comes back. Cool-looking, neat underplanting for ferns or other shade-loving plants. Can be used to carpet terrariums or space under greenhouse benches. Plant 10 in. apart for small-space ground cover. With enough water, tolerates full sun in cooler climates. There is a golden green variety.

SOLENOSTEMON scutellarioides. **See COLEUS × hybridus**

SOLIDAGO

GOLDENROD
Asteraceae (Compositae)
PERENNIALS
ZONES 1–11, 14–23
FULL SUN OR LIGHT SHADE
MODERATE WATER

Solidago 'Goldenmosa'

From mid- or late summer into fall, these eastern U.S. natives enliven the garden with large, branching clusters of small bright yellow flowers. Blossoms are carried on leafy stems that rise from tough, woody, spreading rootstocks. Leaves are narrow, generally linear to lance shaped. Goldenrods are not as widely grown as they deserve to be, largely due to the mistaken belief that their pollen causes hay fever (in fact, other plants are responsible). All are tough plants that thrive in not-too-rich soil. Use in informal borders or naturalize in meadows.

S. hybrids. The following are among the best garden varieties.

'Crown of Rays'. To 2–3 ft. tall, 1–2 ft. wide, with flattish flower clusters.

'Golden Baby'. To 2 ft. high, 1½ ft. wide; flower clusters are plumelike.

'Goldenmosa'. To 2½ ft. tall, 1½ ft. wide. Very large clusters of blossoms are reminiscent of florists' mimosa *(Acacia baileyana)*.

S. rugosa 'Fireworks'. To 3 ft. tall, 2 ft. wide. Narrow streamers of flowers arch outward and downward like the vapor trails of a skyrocket.

S. sphacelata 'Golden Fleece'. To 1½ ft. tall, 2 ft. wide, with many sprays of flowers. Makes a tough, fast-growing ground cover; set plants 15 in. apart for a solid mat in a year.

SOLLYA heterophylla (S. fusiformis)

AUSTRALIAN BLUEBELL CREEPER
Pittosporaceae
EVERGREEN SHRUB OR VINE
ZONES 8, 9, 14–24; H1, H2
PARTIAL SHADE IN HOTTEST CLIMATES
MODERATE TO REGULAR WATER

Sollya heterophylla

Native to Australia. Loose, spreading shrub to 2–3 ft. high, 4–5 ft. wide. Given support and training, climbs to 6–8 ft. Glossy green foliage has a light, delicate look—leaves are narrow,

1–2 in. long. Clusters of small, bell-shaped, brilliant blue flowers bloom almost all summer. 'Alba' has white blooms; 'Rosea' bears pink flowers. *S. h. parviflora (S. parviflora)* is more vining in habit and has somewhat smaller flowers in a darker blue.

Drought tolerant but prefers some moisture. Good drainage is crucial, however; plant will die in poorly drained soil. Prune frequently to encourage dense habit. Use as ground or bank cover, in borders, along steps, draped over low walls, in containers. Will grow under eucalyptus trees.

SOLOMON'S SEAL. See POLYGONATUM

SOPHORA

Fabaceae (Leguminosae)

EVERGREEN AND DECIDUOUS TREES AND SHRUBS

ZONES VARY BY SPECIES

FULL SUN OR PARTIAL SHADE

WATER NEEDS VARY BY SPECIES

SEEDS OF S. SECUNDIFLORA ARE POISONOUS IF INGESTED

Sophora japonica

Handsome flowering trees with showy, drooping clusters of sweet pea–shaped blossoms. Seedpods are constricted between the seeds, giving them a bead-necklace look. Leaves divided into many leaflets. Provide good drainage.

S. arizonica. Evergreen shrub. Zones 10–13. Native to Arizona. Grows slowly to 3–10 ft. high and wide. Dark gray-green leaves have five to nine ½–1-in.-long leaflets. Clusters of 1–1¼-in., purple to lavender flowers in spring; these are followed by 4–7-in.-long seedpods. Use as an informal hedge, in borders. Takes heat. Tolerates drought but does better with moderate to regular water applied deeply during hot months.

S. japonica. JAPANESE PAGODA TREE, CHINESE SCHOLAR TREE. Deciduous tree. Zones 2–24; bloom is unreliable where summers are cold and damp. Native to China, Korea. Grows at a moderate rate to 50–70 ft. high and wide. Young wood is smooth, dark gray green; old branches and trunk gradually take on rugged look, with rough, deeply furrowed bark. Dark green, 6–10-in. leaves divided into 7–17 leaflets, each 1–2 in. long. Undistinguished yellow fall color. Long (to 1-ft.), open clusters of ½-in., yellowish white flowers in summer; 2–3½-in. pods. 'Regent' is an exceptionally vigorous and uniform grower. This species is one of best trees for shading a lawn or patio, though stains from flowers and pods may be a problem on paved surfaces. Good for Rocky Mountain area, though it is subject to damage from ice storms there. Resistant to oak root fungus. Moderate water.

S. secundiflora. MESCAL BEAN, TEXAS MOUNTAIN LAUREL. Evergreen shrub or tree. Zones 8–16, 18–24. Native to Texas, New Mexico, northern Mexico. To 15–25 ft. tall, 10–15 ft. wide; very slow growing, especially in cool-summer regions. Naturally shrubby but can be trained into tree with short, slender trunk or multiple trunks, narrow crown, upright branches. Leaves 4–6 in. long, divided into seven to nine glossy dark green, 1–2-in.-long leaflets. Blooms from midwinter to early spring, bearing sweet-scented violet-blue flowers in drooping, 4–8-in. clusters reminiscent of wisteria. A white-flowered form is occasionally available. 'Silver Peso' has silvery foliage. Silvery gray or brown, woody, 1–8-in.-long seedpods open when ripe to show poisonous, bright red, ½-in. seeds. If possible, remove pods from plant before they mature. Choice small tree for street, lawn, patio. If left untrained, makes a good large screen or background hedge. Thrives in heat and alkaline soil. Moderate water.

S. tetraptera. KOWHAI, YELLOW KOWHAI. Evergreen or deciduous shrub or tree. Zones 15–17. Native to New Zealand. Slow to 15–20 ft. tall and wide. Slender, open habit. Leaves 3–6 in. long, with 20–40 tiny leaflets; they are silky gray above, reddish beneath. In summer, golden yellow, 2-in.-long flowers appear in hanging clusters of four to eight. Seedpods are 2–8 in. long. Does not take low humidity. Regular water.

SORBARIA

FALSE SPIRAEA

Rosaceae

DECIDUOUS SHRUBS

ZONES VARY BY SPECIES

FULL SUN OR LIGHT SHADE

REGULAR WATER

Sorbaria sorbifolia

Green, ferny-looking leaves are finely divided into many narrow, toothed leaflets. Bloom from mid- to late summer, producing big, plumelike clusters of tiny white or creamy flowers at branch ends. Flowers mature into brown seed clusters; cut off faded blossoms unless you like the look of brown plumes. Use in large shrub borders or at edge of woodland, near water; effect is almost tropical. These shrubs spread by suckering and will cover large areas if not curbed.

S. sorbifolia. Zones A1–A3; 1–10, 14–21. Native to eastern Asia. Grows 3–8 ft. tall, 10 ft. wide. Leaves 6–12 in. long; flower plumes to 1 ft. long.

S. tomentosa angustifolia (S. aitchisonii). Zones 3–10, 14–21. Native to Afghanistan, Pakistan. To 10 ft. tall and wide. Leaves to 1½ ft. long; flower plumes to 16 in. long.

SORBUS

MOUNTAIN ASH

Rosaceae

DECIDUOUS TREES AND SHRUBS

ZONES VARY BY SPECIES

FULL SUN OR LIGHT SHADE

MODERATE TO REGULAR WATER

Sorbus aucuparia

These natives of mountainous areas are valued for showy flowers and showier fruit. Blossoms are grouped in broad, flat clusters that are scattered over the foliage canopy in spring; they develop into hanging clusters of small, berrylike fruit that colors up in late summer or early fall. Most species have red or orange-red fruit, but white, pink, and golden forms are occasionally available. Birds feed on the fruit, but usually not until after leaves have fallen. Foliage is typically finely cut and somewhat fernlike, though some less widely planted species have undivided leaves. Some mountain ashes have good fall color; these are noted below. Plants need good, well-drained soil and some winter chill. Cankers are a problem for trees under stress. Watch for fireblight. Good small garden or street trees, though the fruit can make a mess on paved surfaces.

S. alnifolia. KOREAN MOUNTAIN ASH. Tree. Zones 1–10, 14–17. From China, Korea, Japan. Dense growth to 40–50 ft. tall, 20–30 ft. wide. The specific name *alnifolia* refers to the leaves, which are undivided (like those of alder, *Alnus*); they are 2–4 in. long, toothed, dark green, turning yellow to orange in fall. Reddish pink to orange-red fruit.

S. americana. Tree or shrub. Zones 1–6. From eastern North America. To 10–30 ft. tall and wide. Dark green leaves with paler undersides reach 10 in. long, consist of 11–17 leaflets; turn yellow in fall. Orange-red fruit. This species is very hardy and tolerates damp soil, but it is not the choicest of mountain ashes.

S. aria. WHITEBEAM. Tree. Zones 3–10, 14–17. From Europe. Dense-crowned tree to 30–45 ft. tall, 20–30 ft. wide (probably larger in age). Undivided, 2–4-in.-long leaves are dull green above, whitish beneath. Variable fall color; the best trees turn yellow. Red or orange-red fruit.

S. aucuparia. EUROPEAN MOUNTAIN ASH. Tree. Zones A1–A3; 1–10, 14–17. Native from Europe to western Asia and Siberia; naturalized in North America. To 20–40 ft. tall (or taller), 15–25 ft. wide. Sharply rising branches form a

Sorbus aria

S

dense, oval to round crown. Leaves are 5–9 in. long, with 9–15 leaflets; they are dull green above, gray green below, turning tawny yellow to reddish in autumn. Orange-red fruit. 'Cardinal Royal' has especially large bright red berries. 'Black Hawk' and 'Fastigiata' are slightly narrower, upright forms.

S. hupehensis. Tree. Zones 2–10, 14–17. From China. To 25 ft. tall and wide, eventually much larger. Bluish green leaves to 7 in. long, with 13–17 leaflets; turn orange red in fall. Pure white or pink-tinged white fruit. The form in cultivation is fireblight-resistant 'Coral Cascade', with red fruit and red fall foliage.

S. ×hybrida. Tree. Zones 2–10, 14–17. Erect habit to 20–30 ft. tall and wide. Foliage is blue green above, whitish beneath. Leaves are a little over 5½ in. long, with a large upper portion that is merely lobed (not divided) and one or two pairs of small leaflets at base. Red fruit.

S. reducta. Shrub. Zones 3–6, 14–17. From China. To 1–2 ft. high, 3 ft. wide, spreading by underground runners. Dark green, 4-in.-long leaves with 9–15 leaflets; bronze-red fall color. Pink fruit. For rock garden or bonsai.

S. scopulina. WESTERN MOUNTAIN ASH. Shrub or tree. Zones A1–A3; 1–7. Native to western North America. To 3–15 ft. tall and wide, often with reddish bark. Leaves to 2½ in. long, with up to 15 deeply toothed leaflets; shiny dark green above, paler beneath. Orange-red fall color. Orange to bright red fruit.

S. ×thuringiaca. Tree. Zones 3–6, 14–17. Similar to *S. ×hybrida* but with longer leaves (to 8 in.) and smaller fruit.

S. tianshanica. TURKESTAN MOUNTAIN ASH. Shrub or tree. Zones 3–10, 14–17. Native to central Asia. To 16 ft. tall and wide. Leaves are 5–6 in. long, with 9–15 leaflets; shiny dark green above, grayish beneath. Bright red fruit. Tidy-looking, slow-growing plant, excellent for a small garden. 'Red Cascade' is compact, oval crowned.

SORREL, GARDEN

Polygonaceae

PERENNIAL OFTEN GROWN AS ANNUAL

ZONES VARY BY TYPE; ANYWHERE AS ANNUAL

FULL SUN

REGULAR WATER

Garden Sorrel

Two similar species are grown for their edible leaves, which can be used raw in salads or cooked in soups, sauces, egg dishes. Flavor is like that of a sharp, sprightly spinach, but sorrel is more heat tolerant and produces throughout the growing season. Common sorrel *(Rumex acetosa)* is the larger plant (to 3 ft. tall), with leaves to 6 in. long, many shaped like elongated arrowheads. It is native to northern climates and perennial in Zones A1–A3, 1–9, 14–17. French sorrel *(R. scutatus)* is a somewhat sprawling plant to 1½ ft. high, with shorter, broader leaves and a milder, more lemony flavor than *R. acetosa.* Native to Europe, western Asia, and North Africa, it is perennial in Zones 3–10, 14–24.

Grow sorrel in reasonably good soil. Sow seeds in early spring; thin seedlings to 8 in. apart. Or set out transplants at any time, spacing them 8 in. apart. Pick tender leaves when they are big enough to use; cut out flowering stems to encourage leaf production. Replace (or dig and divide) plants after 3 or 4 years.

SORREL, WOOD or REDWOOD. See OXALIS

SOTOL. See DASYLIRION wheeleri

SOUR GUM. See NYSSA sylvatica

SOURWOOD. See OXYDENDRUM arboreum

SOUTHERNWOOD. See ARTEMISIA abrotanum

SPANISH BAYONET. See YUCCA aloifolia

SPANISH BLUEBELL. See HYACINTHOIDES hispanica

SPANISH BROOM. See GENISTA hispanica, SPARTIUM junceum

SPANISH DAGGER. See YUCCA gloriosa

SPANISH THYME. See PLECTRANTHUS amboinicus

SPARAXIS tricolor

HARLEQUIN FLOWER

Iridaceae

PERENNIAL FROM CORM

ZONES 9, 12–24; OR DIG AND STORE

FULL SUN

REGULAR WATER DURING GROWTH AND BLOOM

Sparaxis tricolor

Native to South Africa. Makes a clump of sword-shaped leaves to 1 ft. high and wide. Blooms over a long period in late spring; 1–1½-ft.-tall flowering stems bear loose, spikelike clusters of small, funnel-shaped blossoms to 2 in. across. Each flower has a yellow center, a dark color surrounding this, and another color—red, pink, orange, or purple—on the rest of the petals. Looks best when naturalized or grouped as accent in border, along pathway. For planting and culture, see *Ixia* (to which *Sparaxis* is closely related).

SPARMANNIA africana

AFRICAN LINDEN

Tiliaceae

EVERGREEN SHRUB OR TREE

ZONES 15–24; H1, H2; OR INDOORS

SUN OR SHADE; BRIGHT INDIRECT LIGHT

REGULAR WATER

Sparmannia africana

Native to South Africa. Dense, coarse-foliaged, fast-growing tree to 10–20 ft. tall, 6–12 ft. wide; usually grows as a thicket, multitrunked from base (especially if frosted back). Heavily veined light green leaves are broad (to 9 in. across), shallowly lobed, covered with coarse hairs that give them a fuzzy texture. Clusters of white, 1–1½-in. flowers centered with a brush of yellow stamens bloom from midwinter to early spring. Prune heavily every few years to control legginess. Best used for furnishing bulk and mass near entryways, for screening, for combining with tropical foliage plants. Good choice near pools—big leaves are easy to clean up when they fall. Susceptible to spider mites.

SPARTINA pectinata

PRAIRIE CORD GRASS

Poaceae (Gramineae)

PERENNIAL GRASS

ZONES 1-9, 14-24

FULL SUN

MODERATE TO AMPLE WATER

Spartina pectinata

Native to wet soils and bogs—even brackish bogs—in the northern U.S. Forms a foliage clump to 5 ft. tall, spreading by rhizomes to 3 ft. wide. Arching, nodding bright green leaves ('Aureomarginata' bears yellow-bordered foliage). Plant can reach 7 ft. tall in bloom; the narrow, 8–10-in., one-sided brown flower spikes are handsome in fresh or dried arrangements. Highly attractive plant grown as aquatic perennial in shallow pond: keep plant in pot to prevent it from spreading, and submerge in water to 6 in. deep. In winter, move plant to garden and bury pot up to rim in soil. When grown directly in the ground in moist locations, it can be invasive, particularly in mild-winter areas. Tolerates drier soil, where rhizomes spread more slowly.

SPARTIUM junceum

SPANISH BROOM

Fabaceae (Leguminosae)

EVERGREEN SHRUB

ZONES 5–24

FULL SUN

LITTLE OR NO WATER

ALL PARTS ARE POISONOUS IF INGESTED

Spartium junceum

Native to the Mediterranean region. To 6–10 ft. high and wide, with many green, almost leafless stems. Fragrant, 1-in., bright yellow flowers in clusters at branch ends over long bloom period—early summer to frost in colder climates, spring to late summer in warmer areas. Hairy seedpods follow flowers. This plant is naturally gaunt, but pruning fattens it up. Takes poor, rocky soil and makes a good rough bank cover. Use it with caution, however; it has naturalized in many places in the West, often crowding out native plants. In Southern California (especially in Zone 24), it is extremely subject to caterpillars in summer; by fall, they often leave the plant without flowers or stems. Stems may resprout at base in winter. Aphids can be a problem at bloom time.

SPATHIPHYLLUM

Araceae

PERENNIALS

ZONES 24; H2; OR INDOORS

SOME SHADE; LOW TO BRIGHT INDIRECT LIGHT

REGULAR TO AMPLE WATER

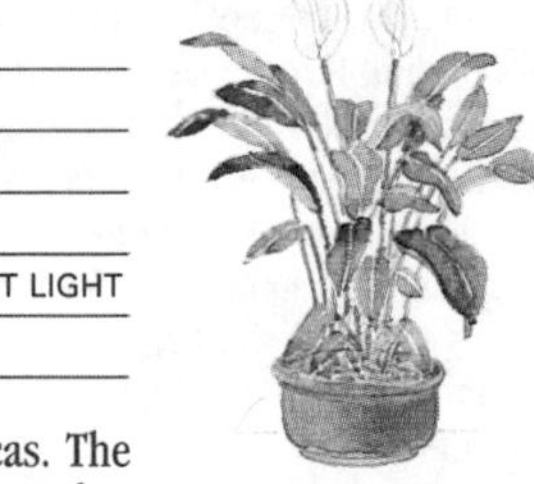

Spathiphyllum 'Mauna Loa'

From the tropics, mainly in the Americas. The various types range from dwarf forms a few inches high to 8-footers; foliage color ranges from light to dark green. Leaves are carried on slender stalks that rise directly from the soil; they are generally large for the plant size, oval or elliptical, narrowed to a point. Flowers—fragrant in some species and varieties—resemble those of calla *(Zantedeschia)* or anthurium, consisting of a leaflike white or greenish white bract surrounding a central club-shaped structure of closely set tiny flowers. Outdoors, use as border plants or accents, for ground cover, in containers on shaded lanai or patio. Provide rich soil, wind protection. Among the few flowering plants that grow and bloom readily indoors; grow in loose, fibrous potting mix and feed weekly with dilute liquid fertilizer. Good choices include *S. wallisii* 'Clevelandii', to 2 ft. high, 20 in. wide; *S.* 'Mauna Loa', 3½ ft. high, 2 ft. wide; and *S.* 'Sensation', 4–6 ft. tall, 3 ft. wide.

SPATHODEA campanulata

AFRICAN TULIP TREE

Bignoniaceae

EVERGREEN TREE

ZONES 21–24; H1, H2

FULL SUN

MODERATE WATER

Spathodea campanulata

From tropical Africa. Very showy, fast-growing tree to 40–75 ft. tall, 20–50 ft. wide. Glossy deep green leaves to 1½ ft. long, divided featherwise into 9–19 oblong to ovate leaflets. Clusters of spectacular, tulip-shaped, 4-in. flowers in scarlet to blood red appear at branch ends. In Hawaii, blossoms come throughout the year; in California, bloom is most profuse in spring, but flowers may appear in any season. Give good drainage and a warm site. This tree grows rapidly and blooms young, but it can be devastated by frosts. Likely to attain size stated above only in truly frost-free locations.

SPEARMINT. See MENTHA spicata

SPEEDWELL. See VERONICA

SPHAERALCEA

GLOBE MALLOW

Malvaceae

PERENNIALS

ZONES VARY BY SPECIES

FULL SUN

LITTLE WATER

Sphaeralcea ambigua

Grown for attractive downy leaves and bright flowers shaped like miniature hollyhocks *(Alcea),* these upright to trailing plants have a persistent woody base with softer stems above. Need well-drained soil. Any more than a little water causes weedy growth and rust. Cut old stems almost to ground before spring growth begins. Colorful accent plants for hot, dry locations.

S. ambigua. APRICOT MALLOW. Zones 3, 7–24. Native to Utah, Arizona, Nevada, California, Mexico. Grows to 3–4 ft. tall, 2–3 ft. wide, with many stems covered in white or yellowish down. Broad, rounded gray-green leaves to 2½ in. long are crinkled and slightly lobed. Each stem bears many inch-wide flowers; usual color is glowing pink or orange, but white-flowered forms are occasionally available.

Blooms in summer and fall; in hot deserts, main bloom season is spring, with a sparse showing of flowers in summer and fall. May become partly deciduous where summers are very hot and dry. Best adapted to desert climates; cannot withstand wet winters. 'Louis Hamilton' has deep orange-red flowers.

S. coccinea. PRAIRIE MALLOW. Zones 1–3, 10–13. Native from Manitoba south to Texas, Arizona. Spreading plant with branching stems and rounded olive green leaves that are deeply lobed, to 1½ in long. Usually grows 2–3 ft. tall and wide but can spread wider if given summer moisture. Produces short wands of cup-shaped, orange to red flowers to 1½ in. across throughout summer.

S. incana. ORANGE MALLOW. Zones 2, 3, 7–13, 18. Native to Arizona, New Mexico, and Texas. Forms slowly spreading clump to 2–4 ft. high, 2 ft. wide, with many upright stems clothed in rounded, 2-in. long, yellowish green leaves. In summer (spring, in desert regions), bears a succession of clustered 1-in., light to deep orange blossoms. More tolerant of wet winters than *S. ambigua.*

S. munroana. Zones 1–3, 7–10, 14–24. Native to intermountain West and Rocky Mountain foothills. Grows to 3 ft. tall and 1½–2 ft. wide, with upright stems and rounded, slightly lobed gray-green leaves to 2 in. long. Bears many wands of inch-wide salmon to reddish orange flowers from midsummer to early fall. Plants sold in California under this name may be the Argentine native *S. philippiana,* which grows to 1½ ft. high and 4–5 ft. wide and has leaves that are more deeply cut than those of *S. munroana.*

SPHAEROPTERIS cooperi. See CYATHEA cooperi

SPICE BUSH. See CALYCANTHUS occidentalis

SPICEBUSH. See LINDERA

SPIDER FLOWER. See CLEOME hasslerana

SPIDER LILY. See CRINUM asiaticum, LYCORIS

SPIDER PLANT. See CHLOROPHYTUM comosum

SPIDERWORT. See TRADESCANTIA virginiana

FOR INFORMATION ON YOUR CLIMATE ZONE
PLEASE SEE PAGES 27–63

SPINACH

Chenopodiaceae, Aizoaceae, Basellaceae

ANNUALS AND PERENNIALS

ZONES VARY BY TYPE

FULL SUN

REGULAR WATER

True Spinach

One of the three plants described here is true spinach *(Spinacia)*; the other two are warm-season vegetables used as substitutes for the real thing, which needs cool weather to succeed. All are grown for their edible leaves, used raw or cooked. All do best in rich, well-drained soil.

True spinach. This is the cool-season annual *Spinacia oleracea,* a member of the goosefoot family (Chenopodiaceae). It is thought to have originated in southwestern Asia. Grows in all zones. Matures slowly during fall, winter, and spring; long days of late spring and heat of summer make it go to seed quickly. To get successive harvests, make small sowings at weekly intervals in fall or early spring. Thin established seedlings to 3–4 in. apart. When plants have reached full size (6–12 in. high; takes about 7 weeks), harvest by cutting entire clump at ground level. Leaf miner is often a pest.

New Zealand spinach. Native to New Zealand and Australia, *Tetragonia tetragonioides* belongs to Aizoaceae, a family of succulent plants. It is an evergreen perennial in mild-winter areas (most likely to live over in Zones 15–17, 21–24; H1, H2) but goes dormant in heavy frosts. In colder climates, it can be grown as a summer annual. Sow seed in early spring after danger of frost is past; thin established seedlings to 1–1½ ft. apart. Mature plants are spreading, 1–2 ft. high. Harvest greens by plucking off top few inches of tender stems and attached leaves; a month later, new shoots will have grown up for another harvest. New Zealand spinach tolerates heat and drought but also thrives in cool, damp conditions.

New Zealand Spinach

Malabar spinach. *Basella alba* is a native of India; it belongs to the family Basellaceae. Perennial vine in H1 and H2; grown as annual in Zones 3–24. It needs night temperatures above 58°F/14°C; it will not survive frost. There is an especially attractive red-stemmed form. Sow seeds in early summer; thin established seedlings to 1 ft. apart. When young plants are about 1 ft. high, train them on wires or a trellis. At 2 ft. high, pinch out a few inches of stem tip (harvesting any young, tender leaves) to encourage the plants to branch and form more stems. Vine grows about 4 ft. tall. As leaves reach full, succulent size, pick them individually. They are bigger and thicker than leaves of true spinach, so you'll need fewer per serving.

SPINDLE TREE. See EUONYMUS europaeus

SPIRAEA

Rosaceae

DECIDUOUS SHRUBS

ZONES VARY BY SPECIES

FULL SUN OR LIGHT SHADE

REGULAR TO MODERATE WATER, EXCEPT AS NOTED

Spiraea japonica 'Anthony Waterer'

There are two distinct kinds of spiraeas: the bridal wreath type, with clusters of white flowers cascading down arching branches in spring or early summer; and the shrubby type, with pink, red, or white flowers clustered at branch ends in summer to fall. Blossoms on both types are usually single.

These are tough, easy-to-grow plants; with few exceptions, they are not fussy about soil. Prune bridal wreath spiraeas after flowers have finished; cut to the ground wood that has produced flowers. Prune shrubby spiraeas in winter or earliest spring, before new growth begins; they generally need less severe pruning than bridal wreaths. If you remove spent flower clusters, plants will produce a second (but less lavish) bloom.

S. × bumalda. See S. japonica 'Bumalda'

S. cantoniensis 'Flore-Pleno'. DOUBLE BRIDAL WREATH. Zones 3–11, 14–23. From China, Japan. To 5–6 ft. tall, 10 ft. wide, with arching branches. Double white flowers wreathe the leafy branches in late spring to early summer. Lance-shaped blue-green leaves to 2½ in. long; they drop late, show no fall color. Plant is nearly evergreen in mildest climates.

S. densiflora. MOUNTAIN SPIRAEA. Zones 1–9, 14–21. Native from central Sierra Nevada to British Columbia. To 1–3 ft. high and wide. Ovate to elliptical, dark green leaves to 2 in. long are woolly white beneath, turn yellow in fall. In summer, branch ends bear rosy pink flowers in dense, flat-topped clusters to 2 in. wide. 'Summer Song', to 2½ ft. high and wide, has bronzy new growth, bronzy fall, leaf color.

S. douglasii. WESTERN SPIRAEA. Zones 1–9, 14–24. Native to Coastal Ranges from Northern California to British Columbia, eastward to Rocky Mountains. Forms a clump 3–6 ft. high and wide; suckers freely and can be invasive. Narrowly oblong, 1–3½-in.-long leaves are dark green above, velvety white beneath; turn yellowish in fall. Pale to deep purplish pink flowers in long (to 8-in.), narrow clusters at branch ends in summer. Needs acid soil, regular to ample water. Useful for wild plantings near streams.

S. japonica. Zones A2, A3; 2–10, 14–21. Native to Japan, China. Upright, shrubby spiraea to 4–6 ft. tall and wide, with flat, 8-in.-wide clusters of pink flowers carried above oval, sharply toothed green leaves. Best known through its selections, which are typically lower than the species and bloom between summer and fall. They include plants formerly classified as hybrids of *S.* × *bumalda,* itself now considered merely a variety.

'Anthony Waterer'. To 3–5 ft. tall and wide. Carmine pink blossoms. Leaves are reddish purple when new, maturing to bright green.

'Bumalda'. To 3 ft. high and wide. Dark pink flowers; bronze-tinted new growth.

'Coccinea'. To 2–3 ft. tall and wide. Maroon-tinged foliage; red flowers.

'Dolchica'. To 3 ft. high, 4 ft. wide. Purplish pink flowers.

'Fortunei'. To 5 ft. tall and wide. Pink flowers.

'Froebelii'. Resembles 'Anthony Waterer' but is somewhat taller.

'Goldflame'. To 2½ ft. high and wide. Bronze new growth matures to yellowish green, turns dark reddish orange in fall. Red flowers.

'Goldmound'. To 3 ft. tall, 4 ft. wide. Leaves emerge golden, mature to pronounced yellow green; hold color well in sun. Pink flowers.

'Limemound'. To 3 ft. tall, 6 ft. wide. Lemon yellow new leaves mature to lime green, then turn orange red in fall. Light pink flowers.

'Little Princess'. To 3 ft. tall, 6 ft. wide. Rose pink blossoms.

'Magic Carpet'. To 1½–2½ ft. tall, slightly wider. Reddish bronze new leaves turn chartreuse to yellow as they mature. Pink flowers.

'Nana' ('Alpina'). ALPINE SPIRAEA. To 2 ft. tall, 5 ft. wide. Pink flowers. Good red fall foliage in some years.

'Neon Flash'. To 3–4 ft. tall, 4–5 ft. wide. Purple-tinted foliage; bright rosy pink flowers.

'Shirobana'. To 2–3 ft. high and wide. Red buds open to bicolored blossoms in white and deep pink.

S. nipponica 'Snowmound'. Zones 1–11, 14–21. From Japan. Compact, spreading bridal wreath spiraea to 2–3 ft. tall, 3–5 ft. wide. Profusion of white flowers in late spring or early summer. Ovate to roundish, dark green leaves to 1¼ in. long; little autumn color.

S. prunifolia 'Plena'. BRIDAL WREATH SPIRAEA, SHOE BUTTON SPIRAEA. Zones A2, A3; 2–11, 14–21. From China, Taiwan. Graceful, arching branches on a suckering, clump-forming plant to 6–7 ft. tall and wide. In early to midspring, bare branches are lined with small, double white flowers resembling tiny roses. Small dark green leaves turn bright shades of red, orange, and yellow in autumn.

S. thunbergii. Zones 1–11, 14–21. From China, Japan. Showy, billowy, graceful bridal wreath species 3–6 ft. or taller, 6 ft. wide, with many slender, arching branches. Round clusters of small white flowers appear all along bare branches in early spring. Blue-green, extremely narrow leaves to 1½ in. long turn soft reddish brown in fall.

S. trilobata 'Swan Lake'. Zones 1–11, 14–17. Native from Siberia to northern China. Like a small version of *S. prunifolia* 'Plena'. To 3–4 ft. tall and wide, with a massive show of tiny white flowers in mid- to late spring. Leaves reach 1 in. long, are often three lobed. 'Fairy Queen' is similar but more compact, seldom exceeding 3 ft.

S. ×vanhouttei. Zones A1–A3; 1–11, 14–21. Widely planted hybrid between *S. cantoniensis* and *S. trilobata.* The classic bridal wreath spiraea. Arching branches form a fountain to about 6 ft. high by 8 ft. or wider. Leafy branches are covered with circular, flattened clusters of white blossoms in mid- to late spring, continuing into early summer in colder regions. Dark green, diamond-shaped leaves to 1½ in. long may turn purplish in fall.

SPLIT-LEAF PHILODENDRON. See MONSTERA deliciosa

SPOROBOLUS airoides

ALKALI SACATON

Poaceae (Gramineae)

PERENNIAL GRASS

ZONES 1–24

FULL SUN

LITTLE TO MODERATE WATER

Sporobolus airoides

Native from South Dakota and Missouri, west to eastern Washington, south to Southern California. Foliage clump grows 3 ft. high and wide; leaves are grayish green during growing season, yellow in fall, beige in winter. At bloom time in summer or fall, showy, erect or arching flower plumes increase plant height to 5 ft.; plumes are pinkish, eventually fading to pale straw color. Extremely tough, deep-rooted plant. Takes a wide range of soils. Good grass for alkaline conditions.

SPOTTED EMU BUSH. See EREMOPHILA maculata

SPREKELIA formosissima

JACOBEAN LILY, ST. JAMES LILY, AZTEC LILY

Amaryllidaceae

PERENNIAL FROM BULB

ZONES 9, 12–24; OR DIG AND STORE

FULL SUN

REGULAR WATER DURING GROWTH AND BLOOM

Sprekelia formosissima

Mexican native often sold as *Amaryllis formosissima.* Foliage looks like that of daffodil *(Narcissus),* but each 1-ft.-tall stem is topped with a dark red, 6-in.-wide bloom resembling an orchid, with three erect upper segments and three drooping lower ones that are united at their bases (near the flower's center) to form a tube. Bloom comes primarily in early summer. In mild climates, foliage may be evergreen and plant may blossom several times a year if you can give it a dry period after flowering, then resume regular watering to trigger a new growth cycle.

Where bulbs are hardy, plant them in fall, setting them 3–4 in. deep and 8 in. apart in good, well-drained soil. Look most effective in groups. Display increases if plants are left undisturbed for several years. Where winters are cold, set out bulbs in spring; lift plants in fall when foliage yellows and store in a cool, dark, dry place over winter (leave dry tops on). Or grow in pots like amaryllis *(Hippeastrum);* repot every 3 to 4 years.

SPRING STAR FLOWER. See IPHEION uniflorum

SPRUCE. See PICEA

SPURGE. See PACHYSANDRA

SPURGE OLIVE. See CNEORUM tricoccon

SQUASH

Cucurbitaceae

ANNUAL

ALL ZONES

FULL SUN

REGULAR WATER

Summer Squash

There are two forms of squash. Types planted for a warm-weather harvest and eaten when immature are called summer squash; this group includes scalloped white squash (pattypan squash), yellow crookneck and straightneck varieties, and cylindrical, green or gray zucchini or Italian squash. The other form is winter squash, grown for harvest in late summer or fall; it stores well and is used for baking and for pies. Varieties come in a many shapes (turban, acorn, and banana are a few), sizes, and colors; all have hard rinds and firm, close-grained, good-tasting flesh. In both forms of squash, blossoms and tiny, developing fruit at base of female flowers can be eaten as delicacies.

Summer squash yields prodigious crops from just a few plants within 50 to 65 days after sowing, and it continues to bear for weeks. Vines are large (2½–4 ft. across at maturity) and need plenty of room; if space is limited, look for bush varieties. There are many vine and bush varieties to choose from.

Winter squash is planted and grown on vines like pumpkins; it typically needs even more space than summer squash. There are a few bush varieties, such as 'Cream of the Crop', a yellow acorn type, and 'All Seasons Hybrid', a buttercup type. Most kinds of winter squash are ready to harvest 60 to 110 days after sowing. Types for storing include small kinds such as 'Table Ace' and other acorn types, butternuts, and buttercups; and the large blue Hubbard varieties and banana squash. Spaghetti squash looks like any other winter squash, but when you cut it open after cooking, you find that the nutty-tasting flesh is made up of long, spaghettilike strands. Winter squash doesn't grow well in high heat and humidity.

Bush varieties of summer squash can be planted 2–4 ft. apart in rows. If planted in circles ("hills"), they need more room; allow a 4-ft. diameter for each. Vining summer or winter squash needs 5-ft. spacing in rows, 8-ft.-diameter hills. The few bush varieties of winter squash can be spaced as for bush varieties of summer squash.

Give all kinds of squash rich soil, periodic fertilizer. Roots need regular moisture, but leaves and stems should be kept as dry as possible to prevent leaf and fruit diseases. Pick summer squash when it is small and tender. Winter squash should stay on vines until thoroughly hardened; harvest with an inch of stem and store in cool place (about 55°F/13°C).

Squash bugs cause leaves to wilt and may damage fruit. To control, destroy yellowish to brown egg clusters on undersides of leaves; trap adults with boards or burlap set in the garden at night, then collect and destroy your catch each morning. Various insecticides are also labeled for control of squash bugs.

SQUAWBUSH. See RHUS trilobata

SQUILL. See SCILLA

SQUIRREL'S FOOT FERN. See DAVALLIA trichomanoides

STACHYS

Lamiaceae (Labiatae)

PERENNIALS

ZONES VARY BY SPECIES

FULL SUN OR LIGHT SHADE

MODERATE WATER

Stachys byzantina

These mint-family members have the typical square stems and leaves in opposite pairs; foliage ranges from rough textured to furry. Except for *S. macrantha,* the species described here have short-stalked or stalkless leaves. Spikelike clusters of small, usually two-lipped flowers bloom in late spring and summer; blossoms are attractive to bees. All are fairly unfussy about soil type, needing only good drainage. Green-leafed species need some shade where summers are hot. Clumps often die out in center; divide and replant outer sections.

S. albotomentosa. HIDALGO. Zones 7–10, 12–24. Native to Mexico. To 2½ ft. tall, sprawling to 5–6 ft. wide. Green, heavily veined leaves have a felty texture, elongated heart shape. Stems and leaf undersides are covered with woolly hairs. Flowers open peach to salmon pink, age to brick red. Sometimes listed as *S. coccinea* 'Hidalgo'.

S. byzantina (S. lanata, S. olympica). LAMB'S EARS. Zones 1–24. Native to the Caucasus, Iran. To 1½ ft. high, spreading freely by surface runners. Dense, ground-hugging rosettes of soft, thick, rather tongue-shaped, woolly white leaves to 4–6 in. long. Blossom stalks 1–1½ ft. high bear small purplish flowers; many gardeners feel that these detract from the foliage and so cut off or pull out flowering stems. Continued rains can mash plants down and make them mushy, and frost can damage foliage, but recovery is strong.

'Silver Carpet' does not produce flower spikes and is somewhat less vigorous than the species. 'Big Ears' ('Countess Helen von Stein') has larger leaves. Flowers of 'Cotton Boll' are like little balls of fluff spaced along the stem. 'Primrose Heron' has furry yellow leaves that mature to chartreuse, then gray green.

Use all forms for contrast with dark green foliage and with leaves of different shapes, such as those of strawberry or some sedums. Good edging for paths, flower beds. Excellent ground cover in high, open shade, such as under tall oaks; space plants 2 ft. apart.

S. coccinea. SCARLET HEDGE NETTLE. Zones 7–10, 12–24. Native to southern Texas, New Mexico, Arizona. Forms a clump to 1½ ft. high and wide, with wrinkled, heavily veined, elongated oval leaves to 3 in. long. Bears short spikes of scarlet flowers. For the form sometimes sold as 'Hidalgo', see *S. albotomentosa.*

S. macrantha (S. grandiflora). BIG BETONY. Zones 1–24. Native to Caucasus, Turkey, Iran. Dense foliage clump to 1 ft. high and wide, with long-stalked, heart-shaped, scallop-edged dark green leaves to 3 in. across; they are wrinkled and roughly hairy. Showy purplish pink blossoms on 1½–2-ft.-tall stems. 'Robusta' and 'Superba' offer larger flowers; 'Alba' has white blooms.

STACHYURUS praecox

Stachyuraceae

DECIDUOUS SHRUB

BEST IN ZONES 4–6; ALSO GROWS IN ZONES 14–17

FULL SUN OR LIGHT SHADE

REGULAR WATER

Stachyurus praecox

Native to Japan. Slow grower to 10 ft. tall and nearly as wide, with slender, polished-looking, chestnut brown branches. Pendulous, 3–4-in.-long flower stalks, each carrying 12–20 buds, hang from branches in fall and winter. In late winter, buds open into bell-shaped, pale yellow or greenish yellow flowers ⅓ in. wide. Greenish yellow, berrylike fruit follows in late summer. Bright green, toothed leaves are 3–7 in. long, tapering to sharp tip; foliage is often somewhat sparse. Rosy red and yellowish fall color is pleasant but not vivid. Grow this plant under a deciduous tree to shelter its winter buds from heavy freezes.

STAGHORN FERN. See PLATYCERIUM

STAR CLUSTERS. See PENTAS lanceolata

STAR JASMINE. See TRACHELOSPERMUM

STAR OF BETHLEHEM. See CAMPANULA isophylla, ORNITHOGALUM arabicum, O. umbellatum

STAR TULIP. See CALOCHORTUS

STATICE. See LIMONIUM

STENOCARPUS sinuatus

FIREWHEEL TREE

Proteaceae

EVERGREEN TREE

ZONES 16, 17, 20–24

FULL SUN

MODERATE TO REGULAR WATER

Stenocarpus sinuatus

Native to Australia. Slow-growing, densely foliaged plant to 30 ft. tall, 15 ft. wide. Shiny deep green leaves; to 1 ft. long and lobed on young plants, smaller and usually unlobed on older ones. Tubular, 2–3-in., scarlet-and-yellow flowers arranged in clusters like spokes of a wheel. Flowering usually is at its peak in early fall, but plant may bloom at any time. Blooms sometimes emerge from bark of trunk—an unusual sight. Plants do not bloom until established for several years.

Rather tender, especially when young. Does best in deep, rich, well-drained, acid soil. Prune to shape in early years. Showy flowering tree near patio or terrace. Also good in lawn or near swimming pool (has little leaf drop). Beautiful juvenile leaves make it an interesting indoor potted plant.

STENOCEREUS thurberi (Lemaireocereus thurberi)

ORGANPIPE CACTUS

Cactaceae

CACTUS

ZONES 12–24

FULL SUN

LITTLE WATER

Stenocereus thurberi

Native to southern Arizona, northern Mexico. Columnar cactus branching from base (also from top, if injured) to form a clump to 12 ft. wide. Dark green or gray-green stems grow slowly to 15–20 ft. tall; each stem reaches 6 in. thick, has 12–19 ribs, and is covered with black spines ½–1 in. long. In old plants, clump may contain 30 or more stems of varying heights; the arrangement is said to resemble a pipe organ. Blooms from mid- to late spring; funnel-shaped, 3-in. flowers in white with a touch of pink to reddish purple open at night. Rounded, 1½-in.-long fruits are olive green, becoming red tinged when ripe. They split open to reveal edible, sweet, bright red pulp with black seeds. Needs excellent drainage.

STENOLOBIUM stans. See TECOMA stans

STENOTAPHRUM secundatum

ST. AUGUSTINE GRASS

Poaceae (Gramineae)

PERENNIAL GRASS

ZONES 12, 13, 18–24; H1, H2

BEST IN SUN, TOLERATES SOME SHADE

REGULAR WATER

Stenotaphrum secundatum

Coarse-textured grass from tropical and subtropical regions. Spreads fast by surface runners that root at joints. Dark green leaves to ⅜ in. wide on coarse, wiry, flattened stems. Turns brown during short winter dormancy, can creep into planting beds, produces thick thatch, must be cut with a power mower. On the plus side, it takes much traffic, has few pest problems, is fairly tolerant of salt and shade, and is easily removed from plantings (roots are shallow). Plant from sod, plugs, or stolons. Mow to 1½–3 in. Needs somewhat less water than bluegrass *(Poa).* A variegated form is sometimes used in hanging baskets.

STEPHANOTIS floribunda

MADAGASCAR JASMINE

Asclepiadaceae

EVERGREEN VINE

ZONES 23, 24; H2; OR INDOORS

ROOTS COOL, TOPS IN FILTERED SUN; BRIGHT LIGHT

REGULAR WATER

Stephanotis floribunda

Native to Madagascar. Twines to 15–30 ft. Waxy, glossy green, oval leaves to 4 in. long. Valued for intense fragrance of its funnel-shaped, 1–2-in.-long, waxy white blossoms. Borne in open clusters, the flowers are a favorite for bridal bouquets and are also used in leis. Blooms in late winter and spring in Hawaii, from late spring through summer in Southern California. Needs warmth. Provide support; train on trellis or fence, along eaves. Give good drainage.

As houseplant, will bloom if given ample light; better suited to greenhouse. Feed liberally; watch for scale, mealybugs. Give indoor plants a rest period by letting them dry out in winter. Can be brought outdoors during warm times of year. May be sold as *Marsdenia floribunda.*

STERCULIA. See BRACHYCHITON

Sterculiaceae. The sterculia family of shrubs and trees has flowers in which the calyx (usually bowl shaped and five lobed) replaces the corolla as the conspicuous element. Examples are *Brachychiton,* Chinese parasol tree *(Firmiana),* and flannel bush *(Fremontodendron).*

STERNBERGIA lutea

Amaryllidaceae

PERENNIAL FROM BULB

ZONES 3–10, 14–24

FULL SUN

REGULAR WATER DURING GROWTH AND BLOOM

Sternbergia lutea

Native from western Mediterranean to central Asia. Golden yellow, 1½-in. flowers, one on each 6–9-in. stem, appear in early fall; they are chalice shaped at first, then open out to a star. Narrow leaves emerge with or just after flowers, reach about 1 ft. long; they remain green through winter, die back in spring. Good alongside paths, in rock gardens or pockets in paved patios.

Plant bulbs in mid- to late summer, as soon as they are available. Set them 4 in. deep, 6 in. apart in well-drained soil. Where winter temperatures drop to 20°F/–7°C or lower, protect planting area with thick layer of mulch. Divide clumps (at normal planting time) only when vigor and flower quality decline. If planting cannot be kept dry during summer dormancy, grow in pots and move to a dry spot in summer. Don't be in a hurry to repot; plant blooms better when pot-bound.

STEWARTIA

Theaceae

DECIDUOUS TREES OR SHRUBS

ZONES 4–6, 14–17, 20, 21

FULL SUN OR PARTIAL SHADE

REGULAR WATER

Stewartia pseudocamellia Koreana Group

Mountain stewartia *(S. ovata)* is from southeastern U.S.; the others are native to Japan, Korea. All are slow-growing, all-season performers that show off fresh green leaves in spring, white flowers resembling single camellias in summer, and colorful foliage in fall. In winter, distinctive pattern of bare branches is on show, as is smooth bark that flakes off in varying degrees, depending on species. All grow best in acid, organically enriched soil. Good in woodland garden and as foreground specimens against backdrop of larger, darker-leafed trees.

S. koreana. See S. pseudocamellia Koreana Group

S. monadelpha. TALL STEWARTIA. Tree. To 25 ft. tall, 20 ft. wide, with slender, upward-angled branches. Leaves are 1½–3 in. long, turn brilliant red in fall. Small (to 1½-in.) flowers. Rich brown, scaly bark when young; smooth cinnamon-colored bark when older.

S. ovata. MOUNTAIN STEWARTIA. Shrub or tree. To 10–15 ft. tall and wide. Leaves grow 2–5 in. long, turn orange to scarlet in fall. Flowers reach 3 in. wide, have frilled petals. Bark not as handsome as that of other species. *S. o. grandiflora* has 4-in. flowers with lavender anthers; it blooms even as a young plant.

S. pseudocamellia. JAPANESE STEWARTIA. Tree. Pyramidal form; may reach 30–40 ft. tall, 20–25 ft. wide after many years. Leaves 2½–3 in. long; turn orange-red to purple in autumn. Cup-shaped, 2½-in.-wide flowers have orange anthers. Very showy bark: it flakes off to show a patchwork of green, gray, brown, rust, terra-cotta, and cream. Members of Koreana Group *(S. koreana, S. pseudocamellia koreana)* have orange or orange-red fall color and 3-in.-wide flowers that open out flatter than the usual.

STIGMAPHYLLON

ORCHID VINE

Malpighiaceae

EVERGREEN OR SEMIEVERGREEN VINES

ZONES VARY BY SPECIES

ROOTS COOL, TOPS IN SUN

REGULAR WATER

Stigmaphyllon ciliatum

From tropical America. Woody, fairly fast-growing twiners with paired leaves and bright yellow, irregularly shaped flowers somewhat like oncidium orchids; blossoms rise in long-stalked clusters from upper portions of stems. Plants bloom most heavily in summer, but they may produce some flowers all year in mildest climates. Grow in organically enriched, well-drained soil. Provide support; prune out dead or straggling growth.

S. ciliatum. Zones 19–24; H1, H2. To 15 ft. Delicate, open foliage cover of heart-shaped, medium green, 1–3-in.-long leaves with a few long, bristly teeth on edges. Clusters of three to seven flowers, each 1½ in. across. Easy to keep small; good on posts, trellises, walls.

S. littorale (S. floribundum). Zones 15–24; H1, H2. Larger vine than *S. ciliatum* (to 20–30 ft. or even higher), with a coarser texture. Oval dark green leaves to 5 in. long; inch-wide flowers in clusters of 10–20. Extremely vigorous; can climb to tops of tall trees. Good for covering arbors, pergolas, heavy wire fencing.

STIPA

FEATHER GRASS

Poaceae (Gramineae)

PERENNIAL GRASSES

ZONES VARY BY SPECIES

FULL SUN

REGULAR WATER, EXCEPT AS NOTED

Stipa gigantea

These clump-forming grasses produce large, open, airy inflorescences that can add lightness and motion to the garden. The genus has undergone much revision by botanists, and some of its former members are now known by other names; see *Nassella* for descriptions of California native needle grasses and the highly ornamental Mexican feather grass.

S. arundinacea (Anemanthele lessoniana). PHEASANT'S-TAIL GRASS. Zones 14–24. From New Zealand. Arching, semievergreen foliage in clump to 2 ft. tall and wide. Medium green leaves have a coppery tinge

S

(strongest in fall, winter). Feathery green flowers with purple tints appear in early summer, rising barely higher than leaves. Tolerates light shade.

S. gigantea. GIANT FEATHER GRASS. Zones 4–9, 14–24. From Spain, Portugal, Morocco. Narrow, arching, evergreen leaves in clump growing 2–3 ft. tall and slightly wider. Open, airy sheaves of yellowish flowers bloom in summer, forming a broad, shimmering cloud that rises 6 ft. tall and as wide or slightly wider. Little to moderate water.

S. ramosissima (Austrostipa ramosissima). PILLAR OF SMOKE. Zones 14–24. From Australia. To 6–7 ft. tall, 3 ft. wide. The erect column of evergreen foliage and blossoms does somewhat resemble a pillar of smoke. Flowering is almost continuous; the airy, light tan inflorescences make up half (or a little more) of the plant's total height.

STOCK. See MATTHIOLA

STOKESIA laevis

STOKES ASTER

Asteraceae (Compositae)

PERENNIAL

ZONES 2–10, 12–24

FULL SUN

REGULAR WATER

Stokesia laevis
'Bluestone'

Native to southeastern U.S. Rugged, adaptable plant. Evergreen in warmer part of range; semievergreen in cold climates. To 2 ft. tall, 1½ ft. wide, with stiff, erect, much-branched stems. Smooth, firm-textured, medium green leaves, 2–8 in. long, sometimes toothed at base. Leafy, curved, finely toothed bracts surround tight flower buds; in summer or early fall, these open to 3–4-in., asterlike blooms in blue, purplish blue, or white. Long-lasting cut flowers. Performs best in well-drained soil. Provide winter cover of evergreen boughs in coldest regions. Good in pots. Selections include lavender 'Blue Danube' (blooms into winter in the mildest climates); white 'Silver Moon'; deep purple 'Wyoming'; and 10-in.-high, medium blue 'Bluestone'.

STONECRESS. See AETHIONEMA

STONECROP. See SEDUM

STONEFACE. See LITHOPS

STRAWBERRY

Rosaceae

PERENNIALS

ZONES A1–A3; 1–9, 14–24; H1, H2; DIFFICULT IN ZONES 10–13

FULL SUN, EXCEPT AS NOTED

REGULAR WATER

Strawberry

Standard market strawberries are hybrids *(Fragaria × ananassa)*. Plants have toothed, roundish, medium green leaves and white flowers. They grow 6–8 in. tall, spreading by long runners to about 1 ft. across.

June-bearing types produce one crop per year in late spring or early summer; in general, they are the highest-quality strawberries you can grow. Everbearing or day-neutral kinds flower and set fruit over a longer season. Their harvest tends to peak in early summer, then continue (often unevenly) through fall; the exact fruiting pattern depends on the variety. Everbearers put out fewer runners than June bearers.

Strawberries of one variety or another can be grown in every part of the West, though it is hard to succeed with them where soil and water salinity are very high. Plant on flat ground if soil drains well or is high in salts, on a mound (5–6 in. high) if soil is heavy or poorly drained. (If soil is both high in salts and poorly drained, plant in containers.) For a small harvest, you can grow a dozen or so plants in a sunny patch in a flower or vegetable garden, or put them in boxes or tubs on the patio. For a big crop of berries, set plants 14–18 in. apart, in rows 2–2½ ft. apart.

Planting season is usually determined by when local nurseries offer plants. In mild-winter areas, set out June bearers in late summer or fall for a crop the next spring; in colder climates, plant in early spring for harvest the following year. Set out everbearing plants in spring for summer and fall berries (in mild-winter areas, they may be available for fall planting). Plant carefully (see care box on facing page). Mulch to deter weeds, conserve moisture, keep berries clean. To hasten spring growth, use clear or black plastic mulch and floating row covers (remove or vent to allow pollinating insects access to plants). Pinch off the earliest blossoms to increase plants' vigor. Don't let plants dry out. Drip irrigation is ideal to help reduce disease problems, but overhead irrigation is satisfactory.

Most varieties reproduce by runners, though some make few or no offsets. Pinch off all runners to get large plants with smaller yields of big berries; let offsets grow 7–10 in. apart for heavy yields of smaller berries. When your plants have made enough offsets, pinch off additional runners.

Most June bearers benefit greatly from renovation if grown as perennials. After the harvest is over, cut off the foliage; you can use a lawn mower set high so it won't injure the crowns. If diseases were a problem, dispose of the leaves. Water and fertilize to encourage new growth. This is also a good time to reduce a dense planting by removing the old "mother" plants and leaving the younger, more productive "daughter" plants.

Some home gardeners are following the example of commercial growers, who treat strawberries as annuals. Plants are installed in summer or early fall, usually with a plastic mulch; they are not allowed to make offsets. After harvest, the plants are removed and a new planting made. Benefits are healthier plants, fewer weeds, and bigger fruit. June-bearing 'Chandler' is especially well adapted to this system, but almost any variety can be grown this way if planted at just the right time (you may have to experiment). In Alaska, home gardeners are treating some everbearing varieties, particularly 'Quinault', as spring-planted annuals.

Strawberries need a winter mulch in cold climates. Cover the planting with a 4–6-in. layer of straw or other light, weed-free, organic material. When temperatures warm in spring, rake the mulch between the plants.

Plants are subject to many diseases: fruit rots (botrytis, anthracnose, leather rot), leaf diseases (leaf spot, leaf scorch, leaf blight), crown diseases (anthracnose), root diseases (verticillium wilt, red stele, black root rot), and—especially in the Pacific Northwest—viruses. Root weevils, aphids, mites, slugs, and snails are among potential pests. To reduce problems, use certified disease-free plants; also remove diseased foliage and ripe or rotten fruit. Replace plants with new ones as they begin to decline, usually after 3 years; or start a new bed with new plants.

Varieties tend to be regionally adapted; check the selections listed here and look for other good choices in local nurseries. Also consider musk strawberries; these come from Italy and are renowned for intense aroma and flavor (strawberry with hints of raspberry and pineapple). They spread by runners and produce one crop in late spring; do best in partial or full shade. 'Profumata di Tortona' and 'Capron' are most common musk varieties. For information on alpine strawberry or fraise du bois, which produces tiny, delectable berries and is a popular edging for flower or herb beds, see *Fragaria vesca.* The *Fragaria* entry also contains descriptions of strictly ornamental strawberries.

JUNE-BEARING VARIETIES

'Benton'. Good crop of firm, flavorful berries. Virus tolerant, mildew resistant. Outstanding in Northwest, especially in mountain and intermountain areas.

'Camarosa'. Huge, conical berries of excellent quality over a long season. Susceptible to mildew. Adapted to California, especially southern areas.

'Chandler'. Large, juicy berries over long period. Excellent flavor, good texture. Some resistance to leaf spot. Grows well in California, particularly Santa Barbara area and southward. Good as an annual elsewhere.

'Douglas'. Heavy producer of flavorful berries. Grows and flowers in low temperatures. Resistant to viruses and leaf spot but prone to botrytis. Prone to red stele in Pacific Northwest. At its best in California.

WHAT STRAWBERRIES NEED

SOIL: Be sure it is well-drained and acidic (most varieties do not tolerate alkalinity).

PROPER PLANTING: The crown should be above soil level (a buried crown will rot); topmost roots should be ¼ in. beneath soil (exposed roots will dry out).

WATERING: Plants need consistent moisture during bearing season.

FERTILIZING: Feed June bearers twice a year—very lightly when growth begins and again, more heavily, after fruiting. Everbearing types prefer consistent light feedings. Heavy feeding of either type in spring leads to excessive plant growth, soft fruit, and fruit rot.

THINNING AND RENEWING: Crowding leads to diseases and lower yields of poorer-quality fruit. To keep a planting from becoming too dense, remove runners as needed. Get rid of older plants every few years and replace with offsets.

'Camarosa'

'Hood'. Large, conical berries for fresh eating, jam. Not the best variety for freezing. Resists mildew. Good in Pacific Northwest.

'Pajaro'. Large, conical berries with good flavor. Long fruiting period. Best in California.

'Puget Reliance'. Large crop of big, tasty berries; excellent flavor when processed. Vigorous plant. Tolerant of viruses. Adapted to Pacific Northwest.

'Rainier'. Good-size berries that hold size throughout long season. Fine flavor. Vigorous plant. Fair tolerance to root rot. Best in Pacific Northwest, west of Cascades.

'Sequoia'. One of the tastiest strawberries. Bears for many months. Resistant to alkalinity, yellows, and most leaf diseases. Developed for coastal California, but widely adapted, even to cold winters.

'Shuksan'. Soft, mealy berries. Excellent frozen; good fresh. Tolerant of alkalinity. Resistant to botrytis, viruses, red stele. Good in Pacific Northwest, east of Cascades.

'Sumas'. Consistent producer of large, attractive berries. Resists fruit rot. Well adapted to Pacific Northwest.

'Toklat'. Large, sweet berries. Susceptible to botrytis. Well suited to Alaska.

EVERBEARING VARIETIES

'Aromas'. Large, sweet, high-quality berries. Excellent vigor. Resists mites and mildew. For California.

'Brighton'. Showy flowers and big, beautiful berries make this good for hanging baskets. Fruit not as intense in flavor as many others. Resists verticillium wilt and viruses. Some mildew resistance. Best in California but hardy enough for cold-winter climates.

'Fern'. Medium-size, wedge-shaped, sweet berries. Susceptible to viruses and red stele. Good throughout West, except in coldest regions.

'Fort Laramie'. Good yield of berries over long season. Excellent flavor. Tolerates −30°F/ −34°C without mulch. Hardy in mountain states, High Plains, milder parts of Alaska. Also good in Southern California.

'Hecker'. Smallish berries are very flavorful, a little soft. Good resistance to viruses and verticillium wilt; gets red stele. Developed on the mild California coast, but like 'Fort Laramie', it can handle extreme cold.

'Ozark Beauty'. Large, long-necked berries with mild, sweet flavor. Produces many runners. Tolerates much cold. Widely adapted.

'Quinault'. Large, attractive berries are tasty, rather soft. Good producer of runners. Resists viruses and red stele. Susceptible to botrytis. Developed for the Pacific Northwest but is widely adapted. This variety is grown as an annual in Alaska.

'Seascape'. Good producer of large berries. Very good for eating fresh; also good for jam and freezing. Excellent virus resistance. For California, the Pacific Northwest, Hawaii. Good choice for annual production in colder climates.

'Selva'. First flush of fruit comes as late as July, but produces heavily through fall. Very sweet berries; huge for everbearing variety. Gets red spider mite, leaf spotting in mild parts of Pacific Northwest, but has good resistance to red stele. Does best in California.

'Sunset'. Large berries with fine flavor. Productive over long season. Prone to mildew. Well suited to California and Hawaii.

'Tillikum'. Because it's such a heavy producer, its soft berries are small. Good flavor. Good virus tolerance, no problem with mildew. Best in Pacific Northwest.

'Tribute.' Medium to large berries with excellent flavor. Resists red stele and verticillium wilt. Prone to viruses in Pacific Northwest. Widely adapted.

'Tristar'. Large berries with excellent flavor. Bears well the first year. Resists red stele and mildew but is moderately susceptible to viruses. Widely adapted.

STRAWBERRY, ORNAMENTAL. See FRAGARIA

STRAWBERRY BUSH. See EUONYMUS americanus

STRAWBERRY GERANIUM. See SAXIFRAGA stolonifera

STRAWBERRY GUAVA. See GUAVA

STRAWBERRY TREE. See ARBUTUS unedo

STRAWFLOWER. See HELICHRYSUM bracteatum

STRELITZIA

BIRD OF PARADISE

Strelitziaceae

PERENNIALS

ZONES VARY BY SPECIES

LIGHT SHADE IN HOTTEST CLIMATES

REGULAR WATER

Strelitzia reginae

From South Africa. Evergreen plants with long-stalked, leathery leaves and highly individual flowers. Blossoms are produced intermittently throughout year; they are long lasting on plant and as cut flowers. Both species are good for poolside plantings; they produce no litter and withstand some splashing. Hardy to about 28°F/−2°C.

S. nicolai. GIANT BIRD OF PARADISE. Zones 22–24; H1, H2; with protection in Zones 12, 13. Clumping, treelike plant to 30 ft. tall and wide. Grown mainly for its dramatic foliage (similar to that of banana plants): gray-green, 5–10-ft.-long leaves arranged fanwise on erect or curving trunks. Flowers are larger than those of *S. reginae* but not as colorful. Floral envelope is purplish gray; flower is white with dark blue "tongue." Feed young plants frequently until they reach full dramatic size; then give little or no fertilizer.

S. reginae. BIRD OF PARADISE. Zones 22–24, H1, H2; under overhangs where heat can be trapped in Zones 9, 12–21. Grown for spectacular flowers, which bear a startling resemblance to the heads of crested tropical birds. Flowers combine orange, blue, and white, are borne on long, stiff stems. Flowering is best in cooler seasons (though blooms appear year-round). Trunkless plant grows 5–6 ft. high and about as wide; blue-green leaves are 1½ ft. long. This species benefits greatly from frequent, heavy feeding.

Divide infrequently, since large, crowded clumps bloom best. Good in containers. Recovers slowly from frost damage.

A PRACTICAL GUIDE TO GARDENING
PLEASE SEE PAGES 658–731

STREPTOCARPUS

CAPE PRIMROSE

Gesneriaceae

PERENNIALS

ZONES 17, 22–24; H2; OR INDOORS

SOME SHADE; BRIGHT INDIRECT LIGHT

REGULAR TO AMPLE WATER

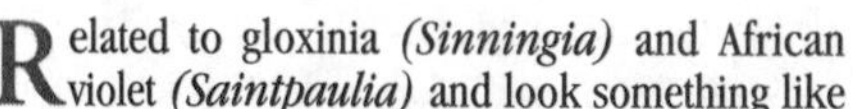

Streptocarpus
'Constant Nymph'

Related to gloxinia *(Sinningia)* and African violet *(Saintpaulia)* and look something like a cross between the two. Fleshy, sometimes velvety leaves; trumpet-shaped flowers with long tube and spreading mouth. Long bloom season; some kinds flower intermittently all year. Many species and hybrids of interest to fanciers; most widely available kinds are hybrids. All types are typically grown in containers. When grown indoors, take same care as African violet.

Large-flowered hybrids. Form 2-ft.-wide clump of long, narrow leaves. Foot-tall stems carry 1½–2-in. flowers in white, blue, pink, rose, red, purple, often with blotches in a contrasting color. Medium blue 'Constant Nymph' is best known of the cutting-grown Nymph series.

S. saxorum (Streptocarpella saxorum). From eastern Africa. Unlike others, this species forms a shrubby, much-branched, spreading mound to 6 in. high, 2 ft. wide. Furry, fleshy gray-green leaves to 1½ in. long. Bloom comes in waves over much of the year; the two-tone flowers are pale blue and white, 1½ in. wide, carried on long, slender stems. Splendid in hanging baskets. Hybrids developed from *S. saxorum* include 'Concord Blue', a nonstop bloomer with medium blue flowers.

STREPTOSOLEN jamesonii

MARMALADE BUSH

Solanaceae

EVERGREEN VINING SHRUB

ZONES 13, 16, 17, 23, 24; H2

PARTIAL SHADE IN HOTTEST CLIMATES

REGULAR WATER

Streptosolen jamesonii

From South America. To 4–6 ft. tall and as wide; to 10–15 ft. trained against a wall, on a bank or trellis. Ribbed, oval bright green leaves to 1½ in. long. Large, loose clusters of 1-in., orange (sometimes yellow) flowers are carried at branch ends from spring to early fall (nearly all year in frost-free areas). Grow in warm spot; give fast-draining soil. Provide protection from frosts; cut back dead wood after last frost. Effective spilling over a wall, lining garden stairs, in hanging basket.

Styracaceae. The storax family includes trees and shrubs with bell-shaped, usually white flowers. Members include *Halesia,* epaulette tree *(Pterostyrax),* and *Styrax.*

STYRAX

Styracaceae

DECIDUOUS TREES AND SHRUBS

ZONES 4–9, 14–21

FULL SUN OR PARTIAL SHADE

REGULAR WATER

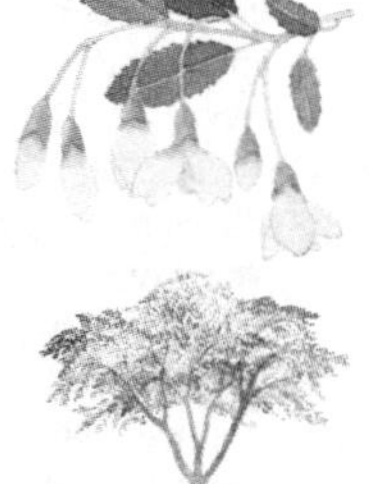

Styrax japonicus

These plants deserve to be better known for their subtly attractive springtime show of white, bell-shaped flowers in hanging clusters. Blossoms are fragrant (only faintly so in *S. japonicus*). Nonaggressive roots. Provide reasonably good, well-drained, nonalkaline soil. Prune to control shape; tend to be shrubby unless lower side branches are suppressed.

S. japonicus. JAPANESE SNOWDROP TREE, JAPANESE SNOWBELL. Tree. Native to eastern Asia. Grows to 30 ft. tall; often narrower than high in youth, but spreads as wide or wider than tall in maturity. Slender, graceful trunk. The branches are often strongly horizontal, giving the tree a broad, flat top. Oval, scallop-edged dark green leaves to 3 in. long; may turn a good red or yellow in fall. Small clusters of ¾-in.-wide flowers hang on short side branches; leaves angle upward from branches while flowers hang down, giving effect of parallel green and white tiers. Splendid tree to look up into; plant it in raised beds near outdoor entertaining area or on high bank above path. 'Pendula' ('Carillon') is a shrubby variety with weeping branches. 'Pink Chimes', also shrubby, is a more upright form with pink flowers.

S. obassia. FRAGRANT SNOWBELL. Tree. From eastern Asia. To 20–30 ft. tall, about two-thirds as wide. Oval to round, deep green, 3–8-in.-long leaves. Where frosts come very late, leaves may color yellow in autumn. Flowers to 1 in. long are carried in drooping, 6–8-in. clusters at branch ends. Good against background of evergreens, or for height and contrast above border of rhododendrons and azaleas. Same culture as for *S. japonicus.*

SUCCULENTS. Strictly speaking, a succulent is any plant that stores water in juicy leaves, stems, or roots to withstand periodic drought. Practically speaking, fanciers of succulents exclude such fleshy plants as epiphytic orchids and include in their collections many desert plants that are not fleshy, such as yuccas and puyas. Although cacti are succulents, common consent sets them up as a separate category (see Cactaceae).

Most succulents come from desert or semidesert areas in warmer parts of the world. Mexico and South Africa are two very important sources. Some (notably sedums and sempervivums) come from colder climates, where they grow on sunny, rocky slopes and ledges.

Succulents are grown everywhere as houseplants; in milder Western climates, many are useful and decorative as landscaping plants, either in open ground or in containers. When well grown and well groomed, they are attractive all year, in bloom or out. Although considered low-maintenance plants, they look shabby if neglected; they may live through extended drought but will drop leaves, shrivel, or lose color. Amount of irrigation needed depends on summer heat, humidity of atmosphere, rainfall level. Give plants just enough water to keep them plump leafed and attractive.

One light feeding at start of growing season should be enough for plants in open ground. Larger and later-blooming kinds may benefit from additional fertilizing.

Some succulents make good ground covers. Some are sturdy and quick growing enough for erosion control on large banks. Other, smaller kinds are useful between stepping-stones or for creating patterns in small gardens. Most of these are easily started from stem or leaf cuttings, and a stock can quickly be grown from a few plants. See *Echeveria,* Ice Plants, *Sedum, Senecio.*

Large succulents have great decorative value. See *Aeonium, Agave, Aloe, Cotyledon, Crassula, Dudleya, Echeveria, Kalanchoe, Portulacaria.* Some smaller succulents are primarily collectors' items, grown for odd form or flowers. See smaller species of *Aloe, Ceropegia, Crassula, Echeveria, Euphorbia, Lithops.*

Many succulents have showy flowers. For some of the best, see *Aloe,* some species of *Crassula, Hoya,* Ice Plants, *Kalanchoe.*

A few words of caution to growers of succulents: Variety of forms, colors, textures offers many possibilities for handsome combinations, but be sure you don't end up with a jumbled medley. Don't use too many kinds in one planting; mass a few species instead of putting in one of each.

You can combine succulents with other types of plants, but plan combinations carefully. Not all plants look right with them. Consider also different cultural requirements. For example, not all succulents like hot sun; read species descriptions carefully. Some do not thrive in summer heat of interior valleys or deserts, even if given some shade.

SUGAR BUSH. See RHUS ovata

SUGAR CANE

Sugar Cane

Poaceae (Gramineae)

PERENNIAL GRASS

ZONES 24; H2

FULL SUN

AMPLE WATER

From Southeast Asia, Polynesia; botanically known as *Saccharum officinarum.* A commercial crop in Hawaii. Sometimes grown as an edible novelty or a bamboo substitute by gardeners in Hawaii and mild-winter parts of Southern California. Plants are rarely sold in nurseries; ethnic markets are a good source for cuttings. Choose plump sections with several nodes (thick, ringlike ridges). In late spring, when ground is warm, place each cutting horizontally in a furrow and cover it with 2 in. of soil. Shoots will sprout from each node. By the end of summer, plants will be 4–8 ft. tall, with ¼–2-in.-thick, yellowish green canes and long, arching, rich green leaves.

To harvest canes for a sweet treat, cut with a machete or snap off at the base. Use a sharp knife to strip away tough skin. Peeled cane is creamy white to yellow, with fibrous, stringy texture. Chew and suck cane to get juice; don't swallow the fibers. If left uncut, plant flops over at the end of season; new ones start from each node touching the ground. Expands slowly; to enlarge planting, divide in spring (roots are easy to cut with a shovel).

SULFUR FLOWER. See ERIOGONUM umbellatum

SUMAC. See RHUS

SUMMER CYPRESS. See KOCHIA scoparia

SUMMER FORGET-ME-NOT. See ANCHUSA capensis

SUMMER HOLLY. See COMAROSTAPHYLIS diversifolia

SUMMER HYACINTH. See GALTONIA candicans

SUMMER LILAC. See BUDDLEJA davidii

SUMMERSWEET. See CLETHRA alnifolia

SUNDROPS. See CALYLOPHUS, OENOTHERA

SUNFLOWER. See HELIANTHUS

SUNROSE. See HALIMIUM, HELIANTHEMUM nummularium

SURINAM CHERRY. See EUGENIA uniflora

SUTERA cordata

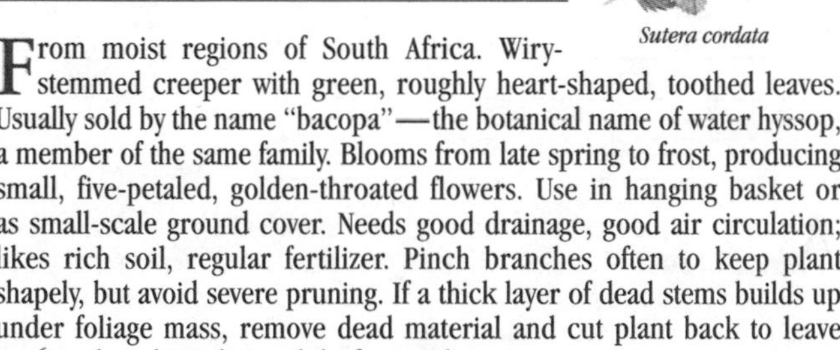

Sutera cordata

Scrophulariaceae

PERENNIAL

ZONES 15–17, 21–24, H2; ANYWHERE AS ANNUAL

AFTERNOON SHADE IN HOTTEST CLIMATES

REGULAR WATER

From moist regions of South Africa. Wiry-stemmed creeper with green, roughly heart-shaped, toothed leaves. Usually sold by the name "bacopa"—the botanical name of water hyssop, a member of the same family. Blooms from late spring to frost, producing small, five-petaled, golden-throated flowers. Use in hanging basket or as small-scale ground cover. Needs good drainage, good air circulation; likes rich soil, regular fertilizer. Pinch branches often to keep plant shapely, but avoid severe pruning. If a thick layer of dead stems builds up under foliage mass, remove dead material and cut plant back to leave 5–6-in.-long branches with leafy growth.

Original variety (sold as 'Snowflake') has ¼-in. white flowers and grows 1–2 in. high, spreading 1–2 ft. in a growing season; eventually covers 3–4 ft. or more in mild climates. 'Giant Snowflake' is more vigorous, reaching 6–8 in. high, 3–4 ft. wide in a season; its white flowers are ½ in. wide. 'Snowstorm' resembles 'Giant Snowflake' but blooms more profusely and has greater heat tolerance. 'Olympic Gold' has leaves irregularly splotched with golden yellow but is otherwise identical to 'Snowstorm' (to which it sometimes reverts). 'Lavender Showers', with ¼-in. lavender-blue flowers, is a small grower like 'Snowflake'; flower color notwithstanding, it is sometimes sold as 'Mauve Mist' or 'Pink Diamond'.

SWAN PLANT. See ASCLEPIAS fruticosa

SWAN RIVER DAISY. See BRACHYSCOME

SWEDISH IVY. See PLECTRANTHUS verticillatus

SWEET ALYSSUM. See LOBULARIA maritima

SWEET BALM. See MELISSA officinalis

SWEET BAY. See LAURUS nobilis, MAGNOLIA virginiana

SWEET BOX. See SARCOCOCCA

SWEET BRIAR. See ROSA rubiginosa

SWEET GUM. See LIQUIDAMBAR

SWEET OLIVE. See OSMANTHUS fragrans

SWEET PEA. See LATHYRUS

SWEET-PEA SHRUB. See POLYGALA × dalmaisiana

SWEET POTATO

Sweet Potato

Convolvulaceae

PERENNIAL GROWN AS ANNUAL

ZONES 8–10, 12–15, 18–24; H1, H2

FULL SUN

REGULAR WATER

Not a potato, but the thickened root of a trailing tropical vine closely related to morning glory *(Convovulus, Ipomoea);* scientific name is *Ipomoea batatas* (see that entry for ornamental varieties of sweet potato). Bush and short vine varieties are also available. Needs long, hot, frost-free growing season; easiest to grow in Hawaii. Also requires well-drained soil (preferably sandy loam) and plenty of room. Start with certified disease-free slips (rooted cuttings) from a garden center or mail-order nursery. Look for disease-resistant varieties. To avoid buildup of disease organisms in the soil, don't grow sweet potatoes in the same location 2 years in a row.

There are two classes of sweet potatoes. One has soft, sugary, yellow-orange flesh (examples are 'Centennial', 'Jewel', 'Kona-B', 'Vineless Puerto Rico'); the other has firm, dry, whitish flesh (examples are 'Onokeo', 'Waimanalo Red', 'Yellow Jersey'). The sweet yellow-orange type is incorrectly sold under the name "yam" in grocery stores. Most varieties of both classes are ready to harvest 110 to 120 days after planting.

Plant in late spring, when soil temperature has warmed to 70°F/21°C. (You can plant year-round in Hawaii, but spring-planted crops mature faster.) Work in a low-nitrogen fertilizer before planting; too much nitrogen produces leafy growth at expense of roots. Set slips so only stem tips and leaves are exposed; space 1 ft. apart, in rows 3 ft. apart. To ensure good drainage, mark off rows and ditch between them to form planting ridges. Row covers provide added heat and keep out many pests.

Harvest before first frost; if tops are killed by sudden frost, harvest immediately. Dig carefully to avoid cutting or bruising roots. Flavor improves in storage (starch is converted to sugar). Let roots dry in the sun until soil can be brushed off; then cure by storing 10 to 14 days in warm (about 85°F/29°C), humid place. Store in a cool, dry environment (not below 55°F/13°C).

SWEETSHADE. See HYMENOSPORUM flavum

SWEET SULTAN. See CENTAUREA moschata

SWEET WILLIAM. See DIANTHUS barbatus

SWISS CHARD

Chenopodiaceae

BIENNIAL GROWN AS ANNUAL

ALL ZONES

FULL SUN

REGULAR WATER

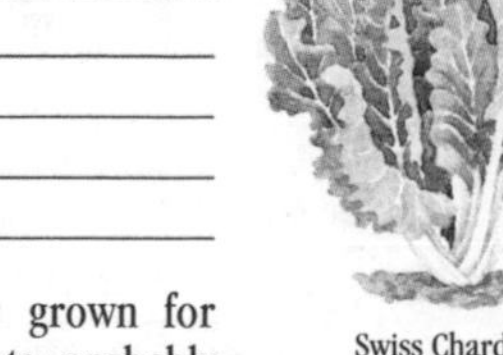
Swiss Chard

A form of beet *(Beta vulgaris)* grown for leaves and stalks instead of roots; probably originated in the Mediterranean area. One of the easiest-to-grow vegetables for home gardens. Sow big, crinkly, tan seeds in spaded soil, any time from spring to early summer. Thin seedlings to 1 ft. apart. About 2 months after sowing (plants will generally have reached 1–1½ ft. tall), you can begin to cut outer leaves as needed for the table. New leaves grow up in center of plants. Plants yield all summer and seldom bolt to seed (if one does, pull it up and throw it away or add it to the compost pile). Where winters are mild, can be grown as fall-into-spring crop.

Regular green-and-white chard looks presentable in flower garden, but 'Bright Lights' is more decorative; it has leaves ranging from green to burgundy, stalks in various shades of yellow, orange, pink, red, purple, green (and in white). Red stems and reddish green leaves of 'Rhubarb' are very decorative in the garden and in floral arrangements. Cook leaves and leafstalks of all types separately, since stalks take longer.

SWISS CHEESE PLANT. See MONSTERA friedrichsthalii

SWITCH GRASS. See PANICUM virgatum

SWORD FERN. See NEPHROLEPIS, POLYSTICHUM munitum

SYAGRUS romanzoffianum (Arecastrum romanzoffianum)

QUEEN PALM

Arecaceae (Palmae)

PALM

ZONES 12, 13, 15–17, 19–24; H1, H2

FULL SUN

REGULAR WATER

Syagrus romanzoffianum

Brazilian native to 50 ft. tall, 20–25 ft. wide, with exceptionally straight trunk. Arching, glossy bright green, 10–15-ft.-long leaves (they break in high winds). May produce decorative orange dates. Give well-drained soil. Grows quickly with fertilizer. Subject to mites; wash young plants frequently. Damaged at 25°F/–4°C but has recovered from 16°F/–9°C freezes.

SYCAMORE. See PLATANUS

SYDNEY BLUE GUM. See EUCALYPTUS saligna

SYMPHORICARPOS

SNOWBERRY, CORALBERRY

Caprifoliaceae

DECIDUOUS SHRUBS

ZONES VARY BY SPECIES

EXPOSURE NEEDS VARY BY SPECIES

LITTLE TO MODERATE WATER

Symphoricarpos albus

North American natives. The various plants described here are upright or arching, typically 2–6 ft. high and wide, often spreading by root suckers. Most are best used as wild thicket for erosion control on steep banks. Clusters of small pink or white flowers in spring or early summer. Attractive round, berrylike fruit remains on stems after leaves drop in autumn; looks nice in winter arrangements, attracts birds.

S. albus (S. racemosus). COMMON SNOWBERRY. Zones A3; 1–11, 14–21. Native from California to Alaska, east to Montana. Roundish, dull green, ¾–2-in.-long leaves (to 4 in. and often lobed on sucker shoots). Pink flowers are followed by white fruit from late summer to winter. Produces most fruit in full sun but takes shade. Not a first-rate shrub but useful for its tolerance of poor soil, lower light, general neglect.

S. × chenaultii. Zones 1–11, 14–21. Hybrid of *S. orbiculatus.* Has larger leaves than its parent, greenish white flowers, and red fruit lightly spotted with white. Can take full sun in cooler climates; needs partial or full shade in hot areas. 'Hancock' is foot-high dwarf valued as woodland ground or bank cover.

S. mollis. CREEPING SNOWBERRY, SPREADING SNOWBERRY. Zones 2–10, 14–24. Native to western North America. Like *S. albus* but usually less than 1½ ft. high, with earlier, sparser bloom, smaller fruit. Spreads like a ground cover, its trailing branches rooting where they touch soil. Partial shade.

S. orbiculatus (S. vulgaris). CORALBERRY, INDIAN CURRANT. Zones 1–11, 14–21. From eastern U.S. Resembles *S. albus* but bears white or sometimes pink-tinged flowers that are followed by small purplish red fruit. Fruit is bright and plentiful enough to provide a good fall-into-winter show. Full sun.

SYMPHYTUM officinale

COMFREY

Boraginaceae

PERENNIAL

ZONES 1–24

PARTIAL SHADE IN HOTTEST CLIMATES

REGULAR WATER

LEAVES CAN BE HARMFUL IF INGESTED

Symphytum officinale

From Eurasia. Deep-rooted plant forms a clump to 3–4 ft. high, 2 ft. wide. Furry leaves set with stiff hairs; basal leaves 8 in. or longer, upper leaves smaller. Small (½-in.-long), unshowy flowers are usually dull rose in color but sometimes white, cream, or purple. In virtually frost-free climates, plant remains leafy through winter; elsewhere, it dies to the ground in fall.

Comfrey has a long history as a folk remedy. Leaves can be dried and brewed to make a medicinal tea, though this use is no longer recommended (leaves have been found to contain potentially carcinogenic substances). Herb enthusiasts claim that the plant adds minerals to compost, but think hard before establishing it in your garden: it spreads freely from roots and is difficult to eradicate.

SYRINGA

LILAC

Oleaceae

DECIDUOUS SHRUBS, RARELY TREES

ZONES VARY BY SPECIES

LIGHT SHADE IN HOTTEST CLIMATES

REGULAR WATER

Syringa vulgaris

A garden staple in cold-winter regions, cherished for big, flamboyant, fragrant flower clusters at branch tips. Best known are common lilac *(S. vulgaris)* and its many named varieties, but there are other species of great usefulness. All are medium-size to large shrubs with medium to deep green foliage and no special appeal when out of bloom. Floral show comes from number of small flowers packed into dense pyramidal to conical clusters; individual flowers are tubular, flaring into four petal-like lobes (in single types) or into a clutch of "petals" (in double kinds). Depending on climate, bloom comes from early spring (in the earliest kinds) to early summer, always after leaves have formed.

Most lilacs bloom on wood formed the previous year, so prune just after flowering ends. Remove spent blossom clusters, cutting back to a pair of leaves; growth buds at that point will make flowering stems for next year. For the few types that bloom on new growth, prune in late dormant season, cutting previous year's growth to varying lengths. Leaf miner, scale, and stem borer are the only important pests; bacterial blight, leaf spot, downy mildew may be problems.

S. ×chinensis. CHINESE LILAC. Zones A2, A3; 1–11, 14–16, 18–21. Hybrid between *S. vulgaris* and *S. ×persica.* To 15 ft. high and wide, usually much less. More graceful than *S. vulgaris,* with finer-textured foliage. Profuse, open clusters of fragrant, rosy purple flowers. Does well in mild-winter, hot-summer climates. 'Alba' has white blossoms.

S. ×hyacinthiflora. Zones 1–12, 14–16, 18–22. Group of hybrids between *S. vulgaris* and *S. oblata,* a Chinese species. Resemble *S. vulgaris* but generally bloom 7 to 10 days earlier. 'Assessippi' (lavender) and 'Mount Baker' (white) are earliest. Other varieties include 'Alice Eastwood' (double magenta), 'Blue Hyacinth' (lavender), 'Clarke's Giant' (lavender; larger flowers than others), 'Esther Staley' (magenta), 'Excel' (light lavender), 'Gertrude Leslie' (double white), 'Pocahontas' (purple), 'Purple Heart' (purple), and 'White Hyacinth' (white).

S. josikaea. HUNGARIAN LILAC. Zones 1–11, 14–16, 18–21. From Hungary. Dense, upright growth to 12 ft. tall and wide. Leaves 2–5 in. long. Lilac purple, slightly fragrant flowers in narrow, 4–7-in.-long clusters.

S. ×laciniata (S. ×persica laciniata). Zones 3–12, 14–16, 18–22. Open-structured plant to 8 ft. tall, 10 ft. wide. Leaves to 2½ in. long, divided nearly to midrib into three to nine segments; good rich green color. Many small clusters of fragrant, lilac-colored blooms.

S. meyeri 'Palibin'. Zones A2, A3; 1–9, 14–16. Dense, twiggy growth to a possible 5 ft. tall and wide; often stays at about 3 ft. Sometimes grafted high to make a standard tree with 3–4-ft. trunk. Produces 5-in. clusters of faintly fragrant flowers in purple fading to pink. Leaves to 1¾ in. long.

S. ×persica. PERSIAN LILAC. Zones A2, A3; 2–12, 14–16, 18–22. Graceful, loose form to 6 ft. high and wide; leaves 2½ in. long. Many clusters of fragrant, pale violet flowers appear all along arching branches.

S. ×prestoniae. Zones A1–A3; 1–11, 14–16. Group of extra-hardy hybrids developed in Canada. To 12 ft. tall and wide. Flowers come on new growth at the end of the lilac season, after *S. vulgaris* has bloomed. Bulky, dense plants resemble *S. vulgaris,* but individual flowers are smaller and are not particularly fragrant. Good selections include 'Donald Wyman' (dark rosy purple), 'Isabella' (lilac), 'Jessica' (violet), 'Minuet' (pale lilac), 'Miss Canada' (bright pink), 'Nocturne' (bluish lilac), and 'Royalty' (purple to violet). For 'James MacFarlane', sometimes sold as member of this group, see *S. ×swegiflexa.*

S. pubescens patula 'Miss Kim'. Zones A2, A3; 1–9, 14–16. Dense, twiggy, rounded; to 8–9 ft. high and wide. Sometimes grafted high to make a standard tree. Purple buds open to very fragrant ice blue flowers. Leaves to 2–4½ in. long; may turn burgundy in fall.

S. reticulata. JAPANESE TREE LILAC. Zones A2, A3; 1–12, 14–16. From Japan. To 30 ft. tall, 20 ft. wide; can be grown as large shrub or easily trained as single-stemmed tree. Smooth, glossy red-brown bark. Leaves to 5 in. long. Blooms on new growth late in the lilac season, bearing white, musky-scented flowers in showy clusters to 1 ft. long. Useful small shade or street tree in cold climates. 'Ivory Silk' is a compact tree to 20 ft. tall, with cream-colored flowers borne in profusion even at a young age.

S. ×swegiflexa. Zones 3–9, 14–16. Hybrid between two Chinese species, *S. reflexa* and *S. sweginzowii;* sometimes called pink pear lilac. To 12 ft. tall, 8 ft. wide. Deep reddish buds; pink flowers in clusters to 8 in. on new growth, about 3 weeks after *S. vulgaris.* 'James MacFarlane' is best-known variety.

S. villosa. LATE LILAC. Zones A1–A3; 1–11, 14–16. From northern China. Stiff, erect bush 6–10 ft. tall and wide. Pinkish lilac to white flowers have a somewhat musky scent, appear on new growth late in the lilac season. Important chiefly as one parent of the *S. ×prestoniae* hybrids.

S. vulgaris. COMMON LILAC. Zones A1–A3; 1–11, 14. In Zones 12–16, 18–22, the standard varieties bloom irregularly after mild winters; gradually discontinue watering near end of summer to force dormancy. From eastern Europe. Can eventually reach 20 ft. tall, with nearly equal spread. Suckers strongly; prune out suckers on grafted plants (no need to do so on own-root plants.) Leaves to 5 in. long, roundish oval with pointed tips. Needs 2 to 5 years to bear flowers of full size and true color. Pinkish or bluish lavender flowers in clusters to 10 in. or longer ('Alba' has pure white flowers) in midspring. Fragrance is legendary; lilac fanciers say species and its older varieties are more fragrant than newer types. Superb cut flowers.

Varieties, often called French hybrids, number in the hundreds. They generally flower a little later than the species and have larger clusters of single or double flowers in wide range of colors. Singles are often as showy as doubles, sometimes more so. Choices include: 'Charles Joly' (double dark purplish red), 'Miss Ellen Willmott' (double pure white), 'Ludwig Spaeth' (reddish purple to dark purple), 'President Lincoln' (Wedgwood blue), 'President Poincaré' (double two-tone purple), 'Sensation' (wine red with white picotee edge), 'William Robinson' (double pink).

Newer varieties include 'Adelaide Dunbar', double purple; 'Krasavitsa Moskvy' ('Beauty of Moscow'), double white from pink buds; 'Nadezhda' ('Hope'), double deep lilac blue from purple buds; 'Primrose', unusual creamy yellow.

Descanso Hybrids, developed for mild winters, excel in Zones 18–22. Try 'Lavender Lady' (best known), 'Blue Skies' and 'Blue Boy' (both blue), 'Chiffon' (lavender), 'Forrest K. Smith' (light lavender), 'Sylvan Beauty' (rose lavender), and 'White Angel' ('Angel White').

WHAT LILACS NEED

WINTER CHILL: Most lilacs bloom best in regions with decidedly chilly winters, but some do well with only light winter chill.

SOIL: Give well-drained, neutral to slightly alkaline soil. If soil is strongly acid, dig lime into it before planting.

PRUNING: Until plants are established, just pinch back any overlong stems. Once they begin blooming, prune yearly for best flower production (see text for details). To encourage young shoots, cut out a few of the oldest stems yearly.

Syringa pubescens patula 'Miss Kim'

Syringa ×chinensis

Syringa ×hyacinthiflora 'Excel'

Syringa meyeri 'Palibin'

Syringa ×prestoniae

Syringa reticulata

Syringa vulgaris 'Primrose'

SYZYGIUM paniculatum

BRUSH CHERRY, AUSTRALIAN BRUSH CHERRY

Myrtaceae

EVERGREEN SHRUB OR TREE

ZONES 16, 17, 20–24; H1, H2

BEST IN SUN, TOLERATES SOME SHADE

MODERATE TO REGULAR WATER

Syzygium paniculatum

Australian native often sold as *Eugenia myrtifolia* or *E. paniculata.* If unclipped, makes a single- or multitrunked tree to 30–60 ft. tall, 10–20 ft. wide, with dense foliage crown. Often clipped into formal shapes and hedges; also used as background or screen plant. Oblong, 1½–3-in.-long leaves in rich glossy green, often bronze tinged; reddish bronze new growth. Small, creamy white summer flowers have conspicuous tufts of stamens that look like little brushes. Blossoms are followed by showy, edible, ¾-in., rosy purple fruit that is insipid raw but good in jellies. Several named varieties selected for good leaf color or dwarf form are sold.

Will not stand heavy frost; foliage burns at 25°F/–4°C, and even old plants may die if temperature drops much lower. Thrives in well-drained soil. Heavy root system makes it difficult to grow other plants nearby. Hedges need frequent clipping to stay neat. Eugenia psyllid can cause defoliation; control is a predatory wasp.

TABEBUIA

TRUMPET TREE

Bignoniaceae

DECIDUOUS, EVERGREEN, SEMIEVERGREEN TREES

ZONES 15, 16, 20–24, H1, H2, EXCEPT AS NOTED

FULL SUN

REGULAR WATER

Tabebuia chrysotricha

Native to tropical America. Showy, trumpet-shaped flowers are borne in rounded clusters that become larger and more profuse as trees mature. Leaves are typically green; may be simple (undivided) or divided into as many as seven leaflets arranged like fingers of hand. Number of leaflets is often variable within a species.

Tend to be gangly or irregular when young; benefit from training in early years. Need well-drained soil; respond well to regular fertilizing. All are useful as color accents, stand-alone flowering trees for display. Larger types are excellent as street or park plantings; smaller species make beautiful patio trees or container plants.

T. chrysotricha. GOLDEN TRUMPET TREE. Briefly deciduous. Zones 13, 15, 16, 20–24; H1, H2. To 25–50 ft. high and wide. Young twigs, leaf undersides covered with tawny fuzz. Golden yellow flowers are 3–4 in. long, often with maroon stripes in throat. Blooms most heavily in spring, when tree loses leaves for brief period. May also bloom lightly at other times, when in leaf. Sometimes sold as *T. pulcherrima.*

T. donnell-smithii (Cybistax donnell-smithii). GOLD TREE, PRIMAVERA. Deciduous. Zones H1, H2. Upright grower to 75–100 ft. high, 30–50 ft. wide. Bloom season is variable: spectacular clusters of yellow blossoms to 1½ in. long are commonly produced in winter or spring before leafout, but occasionally they appear later in the year.

T. heterophylla. PINK TECOMA, PINK TRUMPET TREE. Evergreen to semievergreen. Slender habit to 40 ft. tall, 20 ft. wide; sometimes grown as a large shrub. Flowers 2–3 in. long, in colors ranging from pinkish purple through pink shades to white. Blossoms appear abundantly in spring but may also be seen occasionally throughout the rest of the year.

T. impetiginosa (T. ipe). PURPLE or PINK TRUMPET TREE. Semievergreen. Slow to 25–50 ft. high and wide. In late winter or spring, bears 2–3-in. flowers in white to light pink and purple. Sometimes reblooms in late summer or fall. Does not bloom as a young tree.

TAGETES

MARIGOLD

Asteraceae (Compositae)

ANNUALS AND PERENNIALS

ZONES VARY BY SPECIES

FULL SUN

REGULAR WATER, EXCEPT AS NOTED

Tagetes erecta

Native to Mexico, Central America. Robust, free-branching, nearly trouble-free plants ranging from 6 in. to 6 ft. tall, with flowers from pale yellow through gold to orange and brownish maroon. Finely divided, ferny, usually strongly scented leaves. Annuals will bloom early summer to frost if old flowers are picked off; in the desert, they bloom best from fall until frost. Handsome, long-lasting cut flowers; strong aroma from leaves, stems, and flowers permeates a room (some odorless varieties are available). Easy to grow from seed, which sprouts in a few days in warm soil; to get earlier bloom, start seeds in containers indoors or buy nursery plants. Smog will damage tender young plants, but they soon toughen up.

T. erecta. AMERICAN MARIGOLD, AFRICAN MARIGOLD. Annual. All zones. Original strains were single-flowered plants to 3–4 ft. tall, 2 ft. wide. Modern strains are more varied; most have fully double flowers. They range from dwarf Guys and Dolls and Inca series (12–14 in.) through Galore, Lady, and Perfection (16–20 in.) to Climax (2½–3 ft.). Novelty tall strains include Odorless (2½ ft.). Sweet Cream has creamy white flowers on 16-in. stems. Triploid hybrids, crosses between *T. erecta* and *T. patula,* have exceptional vigor, bear profuse 2-in. flowers over a long bloom season; they are generally shorter than other *T. erecta* strains. Examples are Trinity Mix and Nugget, both 10–12 in. high.

Avoid overhead sprinkling on taller kinds; stems will sag and even break under weight of water. To make tall types stand as firmly as possible (perhaps stoutly enough to do without staking), dig planting hole extra deep, strip any leaves off lower 1–3 in. of stem, and plant with stripped portion below soil line.

T. filifolia. IRISH LACE. Annual. All zones. Forms a mound of bright green, finely divided foliage to 6 in. high and wide; resembles an unusually fluffy, rounded fern. Used primarily as edging plant for its foliage effect, but tiny white flowers are attractive.

T. lemmonii (T. palmeri). COPPER CANYON DAISY. Shrubby perennial. Zones 8–10, 12–24; H1. To 3–6 ft. tall and wide. Finely divided, 2–4-in.-long leaves are strongly fragrant when brushed against or rubbed—they smell like a blend of marigold, mint, and lemon. Golden orange flowers are carried at branch ends sporadically all year, peaking in winter and spring. Damaged by frost in open situations; cut back to remove damaged growth or to correct shape. Tends to be short lived. Moderate to regular water.

T. lucida. MEXICAN MARIGOLD, MEXICAN TARRAGON. Perennial in Zones 8–10, 12–24; often grown as an annual in all zones. To 3 ft. high and wide, typically with unbranched stems. Narrow, uncut, smooth dark green leaves have strong scent and flavor of tarragon or licorice (stems and roots are similarly fragrant). Unimpressive yellow flowers, produced in fall and spring, are less than ½ in. wide. Moderate to regular water.

T. patula. FRENCH MARIGOLD. Annual. All zones. Varieties from 6 in. to 1½ ft. high and wide, in flower colors from yellow to rich maroon brown. Blossoms may be fully double or single; many are strongly bicolored. Excellent for edging are dwarf, very double strains such as Janie (8 in.), Bonanza (10 in.), and Hero (10–12 in.), with 2-in. flowers in a range of colors from yellow through orange to red and brownish red. Aurora and Sophia strains have flowers that are larger (2½ in. wide) but not as double.

T. tenuifolia (T. signata). SIGNET MARIGOLD. Annual. All zones. Infrequently grown species. Flowers are small (just 1 in. wide) and single, but bloom is incredibly profuse. Finely cut foliage. Gem strain offers golden yellow, lemon yellow, and tangerine orange blossoms on 10–12-in.-tall plants.

TAHOKA DAISY. See MACHAERANTHERA tanacetifolia

TALLHEDGE BUCKTHORN. See RHAMNUS frangula 'Columnaris'

TAM. See JUNIPERUS sabina 'Tamariscifolia'

TAMARACK. See LARIX occidentalis, PINUS contorta murrayana

TAMARILLO. See TREE TOMATO

TAMARIX

TAMARISK

Tamaricaceae

DECIDUOUS SHRUBS OR TREES

ZONES VARY BY SPECIES

FULL SUN

LITTLE OR NO WATER TO MODERATE WATER

Tamarix aphylla

In desert regions, tamarisks have no equal in resistance to wind and aridity, and they will grow in saline soils that are toxic to other plants. Also useful in other areas where wind, salt, and poor soil pose challenges, such as seacoast gardens. They demand only a full-sun location with good drainage. Because these trees form deep taproots, nurseries can't keep them in containers long, but they are easy to grow from ½–1-in.-thick cuttings set in the soil where the plant is to grow and kept watered until roots are established.

Tamarisks are difficult to classify, which has led to much confusion in labeling among botanists and in nurseries. Leaves are tiny, as are flowers (a hand lens is necessary to see flower details). However, you don't have to know a tamarisk's identity for pruning purposes. If it blooms only in the earlier part of spring, prune after bloom. If it starts bloom later in spring or in summer, prune just before new spring growth begins. The first two species described here can be kept shrubby by cutting back to ground yearly. If you are growing them as trees, prune only to remove dead or broken branches.

T. aphylla (T. articulata). ATHEL TREE. Zones 7–24. Native to eastern Mediterranean. Cuttings grow fast after planting, to 10 ft. or more in 3 years; with deep soil and some water, reach 30–50 ft. tall, 25–50 ft. wide in 15 years. True leaves are minute; the plant's evergreen appearance is due to greenish, jointed branchlets. Where soils are saline, takes on grayish look in late summer due to secretions of salt. White to pinkish, very small flowers grow in clusters at ends of branches in late summer. Tree is not as spectacular in bloom as other tamarisks. Heavily damaged at 0°F/–18°C but recovers rapidly. Can be sheared into a hedge. Excellent windbreak. Has invasive roots; not a good choice for highly cultivated gardens.

T. chinensis. SALT CEDAR. Zones 4–24. Native to eastern Asia; naturalized in southwestern U.S. To 6–20 ft. tall, 4–10 ft. wide. Blue-green foliage. Flowers ranging from white to pink and deep purple appear mainly at branch ends. Blooms from late spring through summer. Resists heat and cold. Widely seen in desert regions but disliked there: its aggressive spreading and deep, thirsty roots displace native vegetation. Efforts are being made to remove it from many desert areas. *T. ramosissima* may be the same plant.

T. parviflora. Zones 2–24. Native to southeastern Europe. Variable habit; typically a graceful, arching large shrub to 6–15 ft. tall and wide. Profuse spring-only display of pink flowers that turn to tan, then brown. Prune to emphasize arching habit; or remove lower branches to achieve a treelike plant. Often sold as *T. tetrandra;* sold as *T. africana* in California.

TAMPALA. See AMARANTHUS tricolor

FOR INFORMATION ON YOUR CLIMATE ZONE
PLEASE SEE PAGES 27–63

TANACETUM

Asteraceae (Compositae)

PERENNIALS

ZONES VARY BY SPECIES

FULL SUN

MODERATE TO REGULAR WATER

Tanacetum vulgare

Most species have finely divided leaves (often highly aromatic) and clusters of daisylike flower heads. Some have gray to nearly white foliage.

T. balsamita. See Chrysanthemum balsamita

T. coccineum. See Chrysanthemum coccineum

T. densum amanii. Zones 3–24. Native to Turkey. Sometimes sold as *Chrysanthemum haradjanii.* Low-growing (6–8-in.-high) plant, spreading slowly to make mat about 1½ ft. wide. Leaves are finely cut, silvery white, featherlike in appearance. Small yellow flower heads appear a few inches above foliage in late spring. Use in rock garden, as small-scale ground cover in bright, sunny area with good drainage. Can withstand some dry spells when established. One of the whitest-looking plants.

T. parthenium. See Chrysanthemum parthenium

T. ptarmiciflorum. See Chrysanthemum ptarmiciflorum

T. vulgare. TANSY. Zones 1–24. Native to Europe. Coarse, rather weedy garden plant to 3 ft. tall, 2 ft. wide, with finely divided, bright green, aromatic (some say smelly) leaves. Small, buttonlike yellow flowers appear in late summer. Thin clumps yearly to keep in bounds. This plant is no longer used medicinally, though it is still grown in herb gardens. *T. v. crispum,* fern-leaf tansy, grows 2½ ft. tall; it has finely cut foliage and is more decorative than the species.

TANBARK OAK. See LITHOCARPUS densiflorus

TANGELO, TANGOR. See CITRUS

TANGERINE. See CITRUS, Mandarin

TANSY. See TANACETUM vulgare

TARO. See COLOCASIA esculenta

TARRAGON, FRENCH or TRUE. See ARTEMISIA dracunculus

TARRAGON, MEXICAN. See TAGETES lucida

TASMANIAN TREE FERN. See DICKSONIA antarctica

TASSEL FERN. See POLYSTICHUM polyblepharum

Taxodiaceae. The taxodium family includes evergreen (and some deciduous) coniferous trees, usually with small cones containing two to six seeds on each scale. Members include *Cryptomeria,* dawn redwood *(Metasequoia),* redwood *(Sequoia),* giant sequoia *(Sequoiadendron),* and *Taxodium.*

TAXODIUM

Taxodiaceae

DECIDUOUS AND EVERGREEN TREES

ZONES VARY BY SPECIES

FULL SUN

ANY AMOUNT OF WATER

Taxodium distichum

Very tough, tolerant conifers of great size, with shaggy, cinnamon-colored bark and graceful sprays of short, narrow, flat, needlelike leaves. Small, roundish cones.

T. distichum. BALD CYPRESS. Deciduous. Zones 2–10, 12–24. From southeastern U.S. Can grow into 100-ft.-tall, broad-topped tree in the wild, but young and middle-aged garden trees are pyramidal to 50–70 ft. high, 20–30 ft. wide. Feathery, delicate foliage sprays with narrow, ½-in.-long leaves in a pale, delicate, yellow-tinged green. Foliage turns orange-toned brown before dropping. Interesting winter silhouette. Takes any except strongly alkaline soils. Tolerates extremely wet conditions (even grows in swamps) but also takes rather dry soil. Trunk is buttressed near base. When growing in waterlogged soil, develops knobby growths called knees. No particular pests or diseases. Requires only corrective pruning to remove dead wood and unwanted branches. Outstanding tree for stream bank or edge of lake or pond.

T. mucronatum. MONTEZUMA CYPRESS. Evergreen in mild climates; partially or wholly deciduous in cold regions. Zones 5–9, 12–24. From Mexico. Given regular moisture, it quickly attains 40 ft. in 14 years, then grows at a more moderate rate to an eventual 75 ft. tall, 50 ft. wide. Under dry conditions, growth is uniformly slow. Extremely graceful tree with strongly weeping branches. Foliage is finer in texture, lighter in color than that of *T. distichum;* in colder part of range, it turns dull gold in autumn (color change and leaf drop both come very late). Beautiful tree for large lawns.

TAXUS

YEW

Taxaceae

EVERGREEN SHRUBS OR TREES

ZONES VARY BY SPECIES

SUN OR SHADE

MODERATE TO REGULAR WATER

FRUIT (SEEDS) AND FOLIAGE ARE POISONOUS IF INGESTED

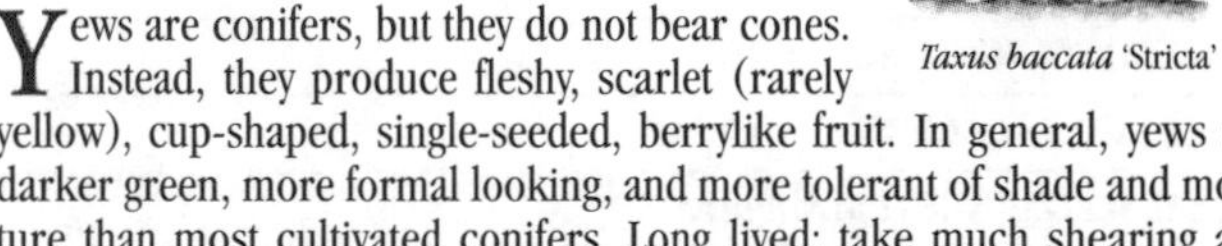

Taxus baccata 'Stricta'

Yews are conifers, but they do not bear cones. Instead, they produce fleshy, scarlet (rarely yellow), cup-shaped, single-seeded, berrylike fruit. In general, yews are darker green, more formal looking, and more tolerant of shade and moisture than most cultivated conifers. Long lived; take much shearing and pruning, since they sprout from bare wood. Excellent for hedges, screens.

Yews can be moved without harm even when large, but since they grow at a slow to moderate rate, big plants are luxury items. They take many soils but do not thrive in strongly alkaline or strongly acid conditions. Do not take extreme heat, and reflected heat from a hot south or west wall will burn foliage. Even cold-hardy kinds show needle damage when exposed to dry winds, very low temperatures. Only female plants produce berries, and many do so without male plants nearby. Subject to vine weevils, scale insects, spider mites. During prolonged spells of hot, dry weather, hose off plants every 2 weeks.

T. baccata. ENGLISH YEW. Tree or shrub. Zones A3; 3–9, 14–24. From Europe, North Africa, western Asia. To 25–40 ft. or taller, 15–25 ft. wide, with broad, low crown. Needles ½–1½ in. long, dark green and glossy above, pale beneath; spirally arranged. Far more common than the species are garden varieties, including the following.

'Adpressa'. Usually sold as *T. brevifolia,* a name correctly belonging to the native Western yew. Wide-spreading, dense shrub to 4–5 ft. high, 6–8 ft. wide.

'Aurea'. Broad pyramid to 25 ft. tall, 12 ft. wide after many years. New foliage is golden yellow from spring to fall, then turns green.

'Repandens'. SPREADING ENGLISH YEW. Long, horizontal, spreading branches make 2–4-ft.-high ground cover; extend to 8–10 ft. after many years. Useful low foundation plant. Will arch over wall.

'Stricta' ('Fastigiata'). IRISH YEW. Dark green column to 15–30 ft. tall, 3–10 ft. wide. Has larger needles and more crowded, upright branches than the species. Branches tend to spread near top, especially in snowy regions or where moisture is plentiful. Branches can be tied together with wire. Plants that outgrow their space can be reduced by heading back and thinning; old wood sprouts freely. There is a form with yellowish white variegation.

T. brevifolia. WESTERN YEW, OREGON YEW. Zones A3; 3–7, 14–17. Native to moist places, California northward to Alaska, inland to Montana. Tree. Loose, open growth to 50–60 ft. tall, 30–40 ft. wide, with peeling red bark and dark yellowish green needles. Not common in nature and difficult to grow; not a garden tree. Most plants sold under this name are actually *T. cuspidata* 'Nana'.

T. cuspidata. JAPANESE YEW. Tree or shrub. Zones A2, A3; 2–6, 14–17. In its native Japan, a tree to 50 ft. tall; in North America, usually seen as a compact, pyramidal tree to 10–25 ft. (possibly taller), half as wide. Can be kept lower by pinching new growth. Fruits heavily. Most useful yew in cold-winter areas east of Cascades. Will succeed in shaded areas of Rocky Mountain gardens. Needles ½–1 in. long, dark green above, tinged yellowish beneath; usually arranged in two rows along twigs to make a flat or V-shaped spray. The following two varieties are commonly sold.

'Capitata'. Plants sold under this name are probably ordinary *T. cuspidata.*

'Nana'. Often sold as *T. brevifolia.* Grows 1–4 in. a year; can reach 3 ft. tall, 6 ft. wide in 20 years. Serves as a good low barrier or foundation plant for many years.

T. × media. Shrubs. Zones 2–6, 14–17. Group of hybrids between *T. baccata* and *T. cuspidata;* intermediate between the two in color and texture. Of the dozens of selections available, these (all with dark green foliage) are among the most widely offered.

'Brownii'. Compact, rounded plant to 6–8 ft. tall, 8–10 ft. wide. Good dense hedge.

'Hatfieldii'. Broad column or pyramid. Reaches 12 ft. tall, 10 ft. wide after 20 years.

'Hicksii'. Upright-growing variety to 10–12 ft. tall, 3–4 ft. wide; grows larger with age.

TEA. See CAMELLIA sinensis

TEABERRY. See GAULTHERIA procumbens

TEA TREE. See LEPTOSPERMUM

TECOMA

Bignoniaceae

EVERGREEN SHRUBS, TREES, VINES

ZONES VARY BY SPECIES

FULL SUN OR LIGHT SHADE

MODERATE WATER, EXCEPT AS NOTED

Tecoma stans

Various trumpet vines once lumped together as *Tecoma* now have different names. Remaining in this genus are several showy shrubs, one of which can be grown as a vine, another as a tree. All have 2-in.-long, trumpet-shaped flowers in the yellow-orange-red range and leaves divided featherwise into many leaflets. Heat tolerant. Take drought but look best with periodic soakings. Tip-pinch young growth to induce branching, reduce tendency toward legginess. Cut faded flowers to prolong bloom and lessen production of seedpods. Prune to remove unwanted seedpods and freeze-damaged wood.

T. × alata (T. × smithii). ORANGE BELLS. Shrub. Zones 12, 13, 21–24. To 8 ft. tall, 4–5 ft. wide, with bright green foliage and orange flowers throughout warm weather. Tolerates light frost; may die to ground in a hard freeze but recovers quickly in warm weather. Some consider 'Orange Jubilee' to be a selection of this plant; others identify it as a hybrid between *T. capensis* and *T. stans.*

T. australis. See Pandorea pandorana

T. capensis (Tecomaria capensis). CAPE HONEYSUCKLE. Vine or shrub. Zones 12, 13, 20–24, H1, H2; with protection in 14, 15, 18, 19. From South Africa. If tied to a support, can scramble to 15–30 ft.; with hard pruning, makes an upright shrub 6–8 ft. tall, 4–5 ft. wide. Shiny dark green leaflets give it a fine-textured look. Brilliant orange-red flowers in compact clusters appear from fall into spring (almost all year in Hawaii). Takes wind, salt air. Use as espalier, bank cover (especially good on hot, steep slopes), coarse barrier hedge. Little water. 'Aurea' has lighter green foliage and yellow flowers; it is somewhat less vigorous than the species. 'Buff Gold' has golden orange blossoms.

T. garrocha. ARGENTINE TECOMA. Shrub. Zones 12, 13, 21–24. From Argentina. To 5 ft. (possibly 10 ft.) tall and wide. Clusters of salmon to orange blossoms throughout warm weather. Reacts to freezes like *T.* ×*alata.*

T. jasminoides. See Pandorea jasminoides.

T. stans (Stenolobium stans). YELLOW BELLS, YELLOW TRUMPET FLOWER, YELLOW ELDER. Zones 12, 13, 21–24, H1, H2, except as noted. Native from southern U.S. to Guatemala. In mildest climates, can be trained as a tree. Where frosts are common, it is usually a large shrub. Wood may die back in hard freezes, but new growth comes on quickly. Can reach 25 ft. tall, 10–20 ft. wide. Large clusters of bright yellow flowers from late spring to early winter. Good for boundary planting, big shrub border, screening. Needs heat, deep soil, fairly heavy feeding.

Tecoma stans

T. s. angustata. Zones 12, 13. Native from Arizona to Texas and adjoining Mexico. To 4–10 ft. tall, 3–8 ft. wide. Narrow leaflets. Blooms from midspring to late fall. Needs less water and fertilizer than the species.

TEDDYBEAR CACTUS. See OPUNTIA bigelovii

TELLIMA grandiflora

FRINGE CUPS
Saxifragaceae
PERENNIAL
ZONES 2–9, 14–17
PARTIAL OR FULL SHADE
REGULAR WATER

Tellima grandiflora

Native from central California to southern Alaska. To 2½ ft. tall, 1½ ft. wide. Often confused with *Tiarella.* Creeping rootstock sends up leafstalks to 8 in. long set with rounded to triangular, lobed, light green, softly hairy leaves to 4 in. across. Foliage is evergreen where winters are mild. Small, urn-shaped spring flowers with tiny fringed petals open green, age to deep red; though not showy, they are attractively arranged along tall, slender stems. Provide rich, moist soil. Choice plant to combine with ferns in a woodland garden.

TENAZA. See PITHECELLOBIUM pallens

TERNSTROEMIA gymnanthera (T. japonica)

Theaceae
EVERGREEN SHRUB
ZONES 4–9, 12–24
PARTIAL OR FULL SHADE
REGULAR TO AMPLE WATER

Ternstroemia gymnanthera

Camellia relative from China, Japan. May eventually reach 6–8 ft. but is usually seen as a rounded plant 3–4 ft. tall, 4–6 ft. wide. This plant's appeal lies in its glossy, leathery foliage. Red-stalked leaves are rounded oval to narrowly oval, 1½–3 in. long, bronzy red when new; color at maturity varies. In deep shade, mature foliage tends to be dark green; with some sun, it may be bronzy green to purplish red. Red tints are deeper in cold weather. Creamy yellow, ½-in. summer flowers are fragrant but not showy. Fruits (uncommon on small plants) resemble small yellow to red-orange holly berries or cherries; they split to reveal black seeds.

Grow in well-drained soil. Leaves turn yellow if soil isn't acid enough; fertilize with acid plant food if necessary. Tip-pinch to encourage compact growth. Use as basic landscaping shrub, informal hedge, tub or poolside plant. Cut foliage keeps well. Good companion for shade-loving plants. Tolerates full sun in cool-summer climates.

TETRANEURIS (Hymenoxys)

Asteraceae (Compositae)
PERENNIALS
ZONES VARY BY SPECIES
FULL SUN
LITTLE TO MODERATE WATER

Tetraneuris acaulis

Taprooted plants with narrow, grassy, aromatic leaves that form small, evergreen foliage tufts about 8 in. high, 1 ft. wide. Somewhat reminiscent of thrift *(Armeria).* Blooms during warm months (nearly all year in mild-winter climates). Yellow daisies to 1½ in. wide have rays with notched edges; blossoms are usually carried singly on stems. Give well-drained soil. Cut off faded flower spikes to neaten plants and prolong bloom. Tolerant of heat, cold, drought. With some moisture, will reseed. Attractive in containers.

T. acaulis. ANGELITA DAISY. Zones 1–3, 7–14, 18–24. Native to plains from Canada to Texas. Golden yellow flowers on stems to 1 ft. high.

T. scaposa. CLUSTERED GOLDFLOWER. Zones 2, 3, 10–14, 18–24. Native from Colorado to Kansas, south to New Mexico, Texas. Leaves are sometimes lobed. Bright yellow flowers on stems to 16 in. high; rays may have red-brown veins on undersides.

TETRAPANAX papyriferus (Aralia papyrifera)

RICE PAPER PLANT
Araliaceae
EVERGREEN SHRUB
ZONES 15–24; H1, H2
AFTERNOON SHADE IN HOTTEST CLIMATES
REGULAR WATER

Tetrapanax papyriferus

From China. Fast growing to 10–15 ft. tall and wide; often multitrunked. Big, bold, long-stalked leaves are 1–2 ft. wide, deeply lobed, gray green above, white and felted beneath, carried in clusters at ends of stems. Fuzz on new growth can irritate eyes or skin. Tan trunks often curve or lean. Big, branched clusters of creamy white flowers on furry tan stems appear in winter.

Young plants sunburn easily; older ones adapt. Seems to suffer only from high winds, which break or tatter leaves, and from frost—foliage is severely damaged at 22°F/–6°C (however, it recovers fast and often puts up suckers to form thickets). Digging around roots stimulates sucker formation; suckers may arise 20 ft. from parent plant. Use for silhouette against walls, on patios; combine with other sturdy, bold-leafed plants for tropical effect. Name comes from the thick pith of the stems, which is used to make Chinese rice paper.

TETRASTIGMA voinieranum (Cissus voinierana)

Vitaceae
EVERGREEN VINE
ZONES 13, 17, 20–24; H1, H2
ROOTS COOL, TOPS IN SUN, EXCEPT AS NOTED
REGULAR WATER

Tetrastigma voinieranum

Native to Laos. Climbs quickly by tendrils to 50–60 ft. Thick, fleshy stems carry glossy, leathery dark green leaves to 1 ft. across, divided fanwise into three to five oval leaflets with toothed edges. New growth is covered with silvery fuzz. Flowers and fruit rarely seen. Good growing along eaves, near swimming pools. Makes a large-scale bank or ground cover in milder part of range. Feed until well established. Needs shade in Zone 13.

TEUCRIUM

GERMANDER

Lamiaceae (Labiatae)

SHRUBBY PERENNIALS

ZONES VARY BY SPECIES

FULL SUN

MODERATE WATER

Teucrium × lucidrys

Mediterranean natives with aromatic foliage and whorls of little flowers. These are tough plants that endure poor, rocky soils; they can't stand wet or poorly drained soils but will tolerate regular watering where drainage is good.

T. chamaedrys. See T. × lucidrys

T. cossonii majoricum (T. majoricum). Zones 7–9, 14–24. Narrow, silvery gray leaves to 1 in. long form a mound to 8 in. high, 1½ ft. wide. Virtually continuous show of small, rosy purple, honey-scented flowers in dense heads (most profuse in late spring, early summer). Good rock garden plant or small-scale ground cover. Also sold as *T. majoricum* and *T. cussonii;* a very similar plant is *T. polium pii-fontanii.*

T. fruticans. BUSH GERMANDER. Zones 4–24. Loose, silvery-stemmed plant to 4–8 ft. tall and wide (or wider). Gray-green, 1¼-in.-long leaves have silvery white undersides, giving plant an overall silvery gray appearance. Blooms almost year-round, bearing lavender-blue flower spikes at branch ends. Thin and cut back before spring growth begins. 'Azureum' has deeper blue flowers than the species; 'Compactum', also with dark blue blooms, grows just 3 ft. high and wide.

T. × lucidrys (T. chamaedrys). Zones 2–24. To 1 ft. tall and 2 ft. wide, with many upright, woody-based stems densely clothed in toothed, dark green, ¾-in.-long leaves. Red-purple or white summer flowers in loose spikes (white-flowered form is looser). Attracts bees. Use as edging, foreground, low clipped hedge, or small-scale ground cover. Shear back once or twice a year to keep neat and force side branching. 'Prostratum' is 4–6 in. high, spreading to 3 ft. or more.

T. marum. CAT THYME. Zones 3–9, 14–24. To 1½ ft. high and wide. Upright, densely clustered stems are closely set with tiny gray-green leaves. Blooms profusely in summer, when stems are covered with many deep pink or purplish flowers in 2-in. spikes. Attracts cats.

TEXAS MOUNTAIN LAUREL. See SOPHORA secundiflora

TEXAS RANGER, TEXAS SAGE. See LEUCOPHYLLUM

THALICTRUM

MEADOW RUE

Ranunculaceae

PERENNIALS

ZONES 2–10, 14–17

LIGHT SHADE

REGULAR WATER

Thalictrum aquilegifolium

Foliage clumps resemble those of columbine *(Aquilegia).* Plants typically bloom in late spring or summer, sending up sparsely leafed stems topped by puffs of small flowers, each consisting of four sepals and a prominent cluster of stamens. Superb for airy effect; delicate tracery of leaves and flowers is particularly effective against dark green background. Offers a pleasing contrast to sturdier perennials. Foliage good in arrangements. Most meadow rues need some winter chill; all thrive in dappled sunlight at woodland edges, tolerate full sun in cooler climates. Protect from wind. Divide clumps every 4 or 5 years.

T. aquilegifolium. From Europe, northern Asia. To 2–3 ft. tall, 1 ft. wide, with bluish green foliage. Earliest of the meadow rues to bloom: clouds of fluffy stamens (the white or greenish sepals drop off) appear for a couple of weeks in mid- to late spring. Rosy lilac is the usual color, but white and purple selections are available. If left in place, spent flowers are followed by attractive, long-lasting seed heads. Heat tolerant.

T. delavayi (T. dipterocarpum). CHINESE MEADOW RUE. From western China. To 3–4 ft. (even 6 ft.) tall, 1½–2 ft. wide, with thin, dark purple stems that need support. Green foliage. Lavender to violet sepals, yellow stamens. 'Hewitt's Double' has double lilac-colored flowers (one row of sepals, another of modified stamens that resemble petals); bloom continues for 2 months or longer.

T. rochebrunianum. From Japan. To 4–6 ft. tall, 1½–2 ft. wide, with sturdy stems that don't need staking. Flowers consist of white or lavender sepals and pale yellow stamens. 'Lavender Mist', with violet sepals, is a superior selection.

Theaceae. The tea family consists of evergreen or deciduous trees and shrubs with leathery leaves and five-petaled flowers that have a large number of stamens. *Camellia, Franklinia,* and *Stewartia* are important representatives.

THEVETIA

Apocynaceae

EVERGREEN SHRUBS OR TREES

ZONES VARY BY SPECIES

FULL SUN

REGULAR WATER

ALL PARTS ARE POISONOUS IF INGESTED

Thevetia peruviana

Fast-growing plants with narrow, glossy deep green leaves and clusters of showy, funnel-shaped flowers at branch ends. Thrive in heat; can take very little frost.

T. peruviana (T. neriifolia). YELLOW OLEANDER, LUCKY NUT. Zones 13, 21–24; H1, H2. From tropical America. In frostless areas, it can be trained as a tree to 20–30 ft. tall and wide. Where frosts are light or rare, an 8-ft. (or larger) shrub; makes a good hedge, screen, or background plant. Leaves 3–6 in. long, with edges rolled under. Fragrant, 2–3-in., yellow to apricot flowers bloom from early summer into fall (all year where winters are warm). Small (1-in.), squat, four-angled fruits are red at first; age to black. Provide good drainage, wind protection. In colder part of range, mound sand 6–12 in. deep around base of stem. Dies back in freezes but recovers quickly; new growth will bloom same year.

T. thevetioides. GIANT THEVETIA. Zones 22–24, H2; with protection in 12, 13. From Mexico. Open growth to 12 ft. or more tall and wide. Leaves are darker green than those of *T. peruviana;* they resemble oleander *(Nerium)* leaves but are corrugated, heavily veined beneath. Large clusters of brilliant yellow, 4-in. flowers bloom from late spring through fall. Desert heat wilts flowers in summer. Makes an attractive patio tree, but fruit (2½ in. wide, green ripening to black) can be a litter problem.

THRIFT. See ARMERIA

THUJA

ARBORVITAE

Cupressaceae

EVERGREEN TREES OR SHRUBS

ZONES VARY BY SPECIES

PARTIAL SHADE IN HOTTEST CLIMATES

MODERATE TO REGULAR WATER

Thuja orientalis
'Aurea Nana'

Neat, symmetrical plants often trimmed into geometrical forms—globes, cones, cylinders. Juvenile foliage is feathery, with small, needlelike leaves; mature foliage is scalelike, carried in flat sprays. Foliage in better-known varieties is often yellow green or bright golden yellow. Small

(½–¾-in.-long) cones are green or bluish green, turning to brownish. Although arborvitaes will take both damp and fairly dry soils, they grow best in well-drained soil. Generic name is sometimes spelled *Thuya.*

T. occidentalis. AMERICAN ARBORVITAE. Zones A2, A3; 1–9, 15–17, 21–24; H1, H2. Native to eastern U.S. Upright, open growth to 30–60 ft. tall, 10–15 ft. wide, with branches that tend to turn up at ends. Bright green to yellowish green leaf sprays. Foliage turns brown in severe cold, will scorch badly in winter in coldest, windiest Rocky Mountain gardens unless plants are shaded, watered. Needs moist air to look its best. Spider mites may cause trouble. Basic species is seldom seen, but smaller garden varieties are common. Among these, the taller ones make good informal or clipped screens, while lower kinds are often used around foundations, along walks or walls, as hedges. The following are some good varieties.

'Brandon'. Fast growth to 12–15 ft. tall, 6–8 ft wide. Useful as screen.

'Douglasii Pyramid'. Vigorous-growing pyramid to 15 ft. tall (or taller), 10 ft. wide.

'Emerald' ('Emerald Green', 'Smaragd'). Neat, dense-growing, narrow cone to 10–15 ft. tall, 3–4 ft. wide. Holds its color throughout winter.

'Fastigiata' ('Pyramidalis', 'Columnaris'). Dense, columnar growth to 25 ft. tall, 5 ft. wide. Tends to get a bit unruly as it puts on size, with branches spreading out; they can be tied together to keep plant looking neat. Set 4 ft. apart for screen. Especially valuable in damp soils and cold regions, where few other columnar choices are available.

'Globosa' ('Little Gem', 'Little Giant', and 'Nana' are similar varieties). GLOBE ARBORVITAE, TOM THUMB ARBORVITAE. Dense and rounded, with bright green foliage. To about 4 ft. high and wide in 10 years; eventually larger.

'Hetz Midget'. Globe shaped, with rich green foliage. Not likely to exceed 3–4 ft. tall and wide.

'Nigra'. Dense dark green cone to 20–30 ft. tall, 4–5 ft. wide.

'Rheingold' ('Improved Ellwangeriana Aurea'). Cone-shaped, slow-growing, bright golden plant with a mixture of scale and needle foliage. Even very old plants seldom exceed 6 ft. tall and wide.

'Woodwardii'. Widely grown dense, globe-shaped shrub with rich green color. May attain considerable size with age but stays small over a reasonably long period; to 4 ft. high and wide in 10 years.

'Yellow Ribbon'. To 8–10 ft. tall, 2–3 ft. wide, with bright yellow foliage throughout the year.

T. orientalis (Platycladus orientalis). ORIENTAL ARBORVITAE. Native to northern China, Manchuria, Korea. Zones 2–24; H1, H2. Species (to 25 ft. tall, 15 ft. wide) is rarely grown; nurseries offer more attractive, shrubbier selections. Widely used around foundations, by doorways or gates, in formal rows. Less hardy to cold than *T. occidentalis* but tolerates heat and low humidity better. In Rocky Mountains, grows best in partial shade; shade during winter is especially helpful. Has survived well in nematode-infested soils. Give good drainage; protect from reflected heat of light-colored walls or pavement. Blight of leaves and twigs in Northwest is easily controlled by copper sprays in early fall and by pruning out and destroying diseased growth. Watch for spider mites.

'Aurea Nana' ('Berckmanii'). DWARF GOLDEN ARBORVITAE, BERCKMAN DWARF ARBORVITAE. Golden-foliaged, compact globe. Usually 3 ft. tall and 2 ft. wide but can grow as high as 5 ft.

'Bakeri'. Compact, cone shaped, bright green. To 5–8 ft. high, 4 ft. wide in 10 years.

'Beverlyensis'. BEVERLY HILLS ARBORVITAE, GOLDEN PYRAMID ARBORVITAE. Upright, globe shaped to conical; somewhat open habit. Golden yellow branchlet tips. In time, can reach 10 ft. tall and wide; give it room.

'Blue Cone'. Dense, upright, conical; good blue-green color. To 8 ft. tall, 4 ft. wide.

'Bonita' ('Bonita Upright', 'Bonita Erecta'). Rounded, full, dense cone to 3 ft. tall, 2 ft. wide. Dark green with slight golden tinting at branch tips.

'Fruitlandii'. FRUITLAND ARBORVITAE. Compact, upright, cone shaped, with deep green foliage.

'Minima Glauca'. DWARF BLUE ARBORVITAE. To 3–4 ft. tall and wide. Blue-green foliage.

'Raffles'. Resembles 'Aurea Nana' but is smaller, denser in growth, brighter in color.

'Westmount'. To 3 ft. tall, 2 ft. wide. Green foliage has yellow tips throughout the growing season.

T. plicata. WESTERN RED CEDAR. Zones A3; 1–9, 14–24. Native from coastal Northern California northward to Alaska and inland to Montana. Plants grown from inland seed are hardy anywhere in the West; those from coastal seed are less hardy to cold. Can reach over 200 ft. high in coastal belt of Washington, but more typical garden size is 50–100 ft. tall, 25–60 ft. wide. Slender, drooping branchlets are closely set with dark green leaf sprays. Single trees are magnificent in large lawns, but bear in mind that their lower branches spread quite broadly—and that the trees lose their characteristic beauty if these are cut off.

Thuja plicata

Varieties include the following.

'Fastigiata'. HOGAN CEDAR. Very dense, narrow, erect to 80–90 ft. tall, 20–25 ft. wide. Fine for tall screen.

'Green Giant'. Hybrid between *T. plicata* and *T. standishii,* a Japanese species. Can grow 3–5 ft. a year, ultimately reaching 30–50 ft. tall, 10–20 ft. wide. Shear as a tall hedge or use as a tall screen.

'Hillieri'. Irregularly shaped, dense plant to 6–10 ft. high and wide, eventually larger.

'Spring Grove'. To 8–10 ft. high in 5 years; ultimately reaches 40–60 ft. tall, 10–15 ft. wide. Can be sheared as a hedge.

'Stoneham Gold'. Dense, slow-growing dwarf to 6 ft. tall, 2 ft. wide. Orange-yellow new growth.

'Zebrina'. Slow grower; same size as species. Foliage is banded in green and golden yellow. Often sold as 'Aurea', a less commonly seen variety with green foliage tinted golden.

THUJOPSIS dolabrata

FALSE ARBORVITAE, DEERHORN CEDAR, HIBA CEDAR

Cupressaceae

EVERGREEN TREE

ZONES 3B–7, 14–17

PARTIAL SHADE IN HOTTEST CLIMATES

MODERATE TO REGULAR WATER

Thujopsis dolabrata

Native to Japan. Pyramidal, coniferous, often shrubby; very slow growing to 30–50 ft. tall, 10–20 ft. wide. Foliage resembles that of *Thuja,* but sprays are coarser, glossy, branching in staghorn effect. Best where summers are cool and humid. Plant as single tree where foliage details can be appreciated. Slow growth makes it a good container plant. 'Nana' is a dwarf variety to 3 ft. high and wide; 'Variegata' has white branch tips that tend to revert to green.

THUNBERGIA

Acanthaceae

PERENNIAL VINE IN ZONES 23, 24, H1, H2; USUALLY GROWN AS AN ANNUAL IN ALL ZONES

ZONES VARY BY SPECIES

PARTIAL SHADE IN HOTTEST CLIMATES

REGULAR WATER

Thunbergia alata

Tropical, typically twining plants noted for showy flowers. Some of the perennial sorts grow fast enough to bloom the first season and can be treated as annuals. Those grown as perennials are evergreen in mildest climates. In cooler part of range, tops may be killed by light frost, but roots usually stay alive to send up new stems. Provide rich, well-drained soil. Good greenhouse plants.

T. alata. BLACK-EYED SUSAN VINE. Perennial vine grown as annual. May live over in Zones 23, 24, H2. To 10 ft., with triangular, 3-in., medium

T

green leaves. Blooms all summer long; tubular flowers flare out to 1 in. wide, come in orange, yellow, or white, all with purple-black throat. Start seed indoors; set plants out in good soil in a sunny spot as soon as weather warms. Display in hanging basket or window box, use as ground cover, or train on strings or low trellis.

T. erecta. KING'S MANTLE. Vining shrub. Zones 16, 21–24; H1, H2. To 6 ft. tall and wide. Erect, sometimes twining, with dark green, ovate to oblong leaves to 3 in. long. Velvety dark blue flowers with orange or cream throats resemble those of gloxinia *(Sinningia);* they appear in joints of upper leaves throughout summer and fall (much of the year in Hawaii). 'Alba' is a white-flowered form.

T. grandiflora. SKY FLOWER. Perennial vine. Zones 16, 21–24; H1, H2. Vigorous growth to 20 ft. or more (as much as 80 ft. in Hawaii), with 8-in., heart-shaped, medium to dark green leaves. Slightly drooping clusters of tubular, flaring, sky blue flowers to 3 in. across appear through summer and into fall (throughout much of the year in Hawaii). Use on arbor, large tellis, or wire fence; casts dense shade. There is a white variety.

T. gregorii (T. gibsonii). ORANGE CLOCK VINE. Perennial vine. Zones 21–24, H1, H2; with protection in Zones 13, 16, 17; anywhere as annual. Twines to 6 ft. high or sprawls over ground to cover a 12-ft. circle. Gray-green, triangular, tooth-edged leaves to 3 in. long. Tubular, flaring, bright orange flowers are borne singly on 4-in. stems. Blooms nearly all year long in mildest climates, in summer where winters are cool. Set plants 3–4 ft. apart to cover a wire fence, about 6 ft. apart as ground cover. Plant it above a wall and let it cascade down; or grow in hanging basket. Showy and easy to grow.

T. mysorensis. Perennial vine. Zones 16, 21–24; H1, H2. Tall climber (15–35 ft.), with narrow, elliptical dark green leaves to 6 in. long. Spectacular, pendent, 1–1½-ft.-long clusters of gaping flowers that are red on the outside, yellow within. Blooms much of the year, most heavily in spring. Train on pergola, arbor, or other overhead structure to permit flowers to dangle. Protect from frost.

THYME. See THYMUS

THYMOPHYLLA (Dyssodia)

Asteraceae (Compositae)
PERENNIALS, SOME GROWN AS ANNUALS
ZONES 8–14, 18–23
FULL SUN
MODERATE WATER

Thymophylla tenuiloba

These low-growing plants with little yellow daisies start easily and quickly from seed planted in flats or sown in place. Not particular about soil type but must have good drainage.

T. acerosa. PRICKLY-LEAF DOGWEED. Shrubby perennial. Native from Nevada and Utah to Texas and Mexico. Much-branched, mounding plant to 6–8 in. high, 1 ft. wide. Covers itself with daisies from late spring to fall. Sharp-pointed, needle-thin, medium green leaves to ½ in. long. Good in beds, in cactus gardens, as edging, as informal ground cover. Especially useful for erosion control on slopes.

T. pentachaeta. GOLDEN DYSSODIA, FIVE-NEEDLE DOGWEED. Perennial. Native from California and Nevada to southern Texas, Mexico. To 4–6 in. high and wide, with open, sparse appearance. Needlelike dark green leaves are ½–1 in. long; stems are covered with fine silky hairs. Blooms most profusely in late spring, sporadically later in the year. Short lived. Use like *T. acerosa.*

T. tenuiloba. DAHLBERG DAISY, GOLDEN FLEECE. Short-lived perennial usually grown as annual. Heat-loving plant native from Texas to Florida and Mexico. Mounding growth to 1 ft. high, 1½ ft. wide. Divided, threadlike leaves make dark green background for flowers that look like miniature golden marguerites *(Anthemis).* Blooms from early summer to fall. Use for mass display or pockets of color. When plants become ragged with age, pull them out. In warm-winter areas, can be planted in fall for winter-to-spring bloom.

THYMUS

THYME
Lamiaceae (Labiatae)
SHRUBBY PERENNIALS
ZONES 1–24, EXCEPT AS NOTED
LIGHT SHADE IN HOTTEST CLIMATES
MODERATE WATER

Thymus vulgaris

Diminutive Mediterranean members of the mint family with tiny, usually heavily scented leaves and masses of little flowers in whorls. Well suited to herb garden, rock garden; prostrate, mat-forming types make good small-space ground covers. Attractive to bees. Provide light, well-drained soil. Shear or cut back established plants to keep them compact. Easy to propagate from cuttings taken in early summer. Botanical names are constantly undergoing revision.

T. camphoratus. CAMPHOR THYME. Zones 7–9, 14–24. To 1½ ft. high and wide, with narrow gray-green leaves that smell like camphor. Blooms in late spring, early summer; flower clusters consist of woolly, rosy purplish bracts and tiny white flowers.

T. × citriodorus. LEMON THYME. Variable hybrid with erect or spreading growth to 1 ft. high, 2 ft. wide. Ovate to lance-shaped, medium green leaves with lemon fragrance. Pale lilac flowers in summer. Leaves of 'Argenteus' are splashed with silver, those of 'Aureus' with gold. 'Lime' has lime green foliage. 'Doone Valley', with yellow-spotted leaves, reaches only 5 in. high.

T. herba-barona. CARAWAY-SCENTED THYME. Fast growing to 2–4 in. high, 2 ft. or more wide; stems root as they spread. Forms a dense mat of wiry stems set with widely spaced ovate to lance-shaped, dark green leaves with caraway fragrance. Clusters of rose pink flowers in midsummer.

T. lanuginosus. See T. pseudolanuginosus

T. praecox arcticus. See T. serpyllum

T. pseudolanuginosus (T. lanuginosus). WOOLLY THYME. Zones A2, A3; 1–24. Forms a flat to undulating mat 2–3 in. high, 3 ft. wide. Stems are densely clothed with elliptical, woolly gray leaves. Blooms seldom and sparsely; when it does, produces pinkish flowers in leaf joints in midsummer. Becomes slightly rangy in winter. Use in rock crevices, between stepping-stones, spilling over bank or raised bed, covering small patches of ground. 'Hall's Woolly' is a profuse bloomer.

T. pulegioides. Fast-growing plant to 3 in. high, 1 ft. wide, with shiny green, oval, lemon-scented leaves. Purplish pink flowers in summer.

T. serpyllum (T. praecox arcticus, T. drucei). MOTHER-OF-THYME, CREEPING THYME. Zones A2, A3; 1–24. Variable species to 3 in. high, 3 ft. wide, with roundish dark green leaves and purplish summer flowers. Good for small areas or as filler between stepping-stones where foot traffic is light. Soft and fragrant underfoot. Leaves can be used in seasoning and in potpourris.

The many varieties include the following. 'Album' ('Albus') has light green leaves and white flowers; 'Coccineum' produces purplish red flowers. Nonblooming 'Elfin' grows 2 in. high and 5 in. wide. 'Minus' is extremely fine textured, forming a carpet to ½ in. high, 1 ft. wide. 'Pink Chintz' (may actually be a variety of *T. polytrichus*) grows 1 in. high and 1½ ft. wide, bears salmon pink flowers; 'Pink Ripple' has lemon-scented leaves and pink flowers. 'Reiter's', with lavender blooms, is a tough, vigorous ground cover for sun or shade; it grows 3 in. high and 2½ ft. wide. 'Reiter's Red', to 1 in. high and 1½ ft. wide, has red flowers; its leaves are smaller than those of 'Reiter's'.

T. vulgaris. COMMON THYME. Variable plant to 1 ft. high, 2 ft. wide, with gray-green, narrow to oval leaves. White to lilac flowers in late spring, early summer. Low edging for flower, vegetable, or herb garden. Good container plant. Use leaves fresh or dried for seasoning fish, shellfish, poultry stuffing, soups, vegetables. 'Argenteus', called silver thyme, has leaves variegated with silver. 'Orange Balsam' has narrow, orange-scented leaves.

FOR GROWING SYMBOL EXPLANATIONS
PLEASE SEE PAGE 161

TIARELLA

FOAMFLOWER, SUGAR-SCOOP

Saxifragaceae

PERENNIALS

ZONES VARY BY SPECIES

PARTIAL OR FULL SHADE

REGULAR WATER

Tiarella wherryi

Clump-forming plants to about 1½ ft. tall (in bloom) and 1½–2 ft. wide; spread by rhizomes (and by aboveground runners, in the case of *T. cordifolia*). Leaves arise directly from rhizomes; they are evergreen but may change color in autumn. Selections with year-round colorful foliage are becoming popular; look for new introductions in addition to those described below. Narrow, erect flower stems carry many small white or pink flowers. Useful in shady rock gardens; make pretty ground covers but will not bear foot traffic.

T. cordifolia. FOAMFLOWER. Zones A3; 1–9, 14–24. Rapid spreader from eastern North America. Light green, lobed, 4-in. leaves show red-and-yellow fall color. Creamy white flowers on foot-tall stalks. Leaves of 'Eco Red Heart' have dark red centers and veins; those of 'Oak Leaf' are deeply lobed. Both selections have pink blossoms.

T. selections and hybrids. Zones 1–9, 14–21. Many of the choicest foamflowers are of uncertain origin. 'Cygnet' has star-shaped leaves with purple markings along the veins; its white flowers open from pink buds. In 'Mint Chocolate', deeply lobed leaves have a central zone of deep brownish purple; flowers are pinkish white. 'Ninja', also with pinkish white blooms, has leaves that are marbled with blackish purple and turn almost entirely purple in winter. 'Skeleton Key' has very deeply cut leaves with deep purple midrib; blooms are white.

T. trifoliata unifoliata (T. unifoliata). SUGAR-SCOOP, WESTERN FOAMFLOWER. Zones A3; 1–7, 14–17. Native from Alaska to Northern California, east to Rocky Mountains. Dark green leaves divided into three tooth-edged leaflets. Tiny white flowers on 1½-ft. stalks are followed by little fruits that look like sugar scoops.

T. wherryi (T. cordifolia collina). Zones 2–9, 14–21. From southeastern U.S. Like *T. cordifolia* but lacks aboveground runners, is slower to spread. Flower clusters are somewhat more slender, often tinged pink.

TIBOUCHINA

Melastomataceae

EVERGREEN SHRUBS

ZONES VARY BY SPECIES

PARTIAL SHADE IN HOTTEST CLIMATES

REGULAR WATER

Tibouchina urvilleana

Brazilian natives with showy flowers at branch ends and broadly oval, prominently veined, velvety leaves. Prefer slightly acid, fast-draining soil. Protect from strong winds, hard frosts. Pinch young growth to induce branching; prune out damaged or badly placed branches before new growth begins. If flower buds fail to open, check for geranium (tobacco) budworm.

T. heteromalla. Zones 16, 17, 21–24; H1, H2. Shrub. To 4–6 ft. tall and wide. Silvery green leaves with silver undersides to 6 in. or longer. Dark purple, 1–1½-in. flowers in 1½-ft.-long clusters from early fall into winter.

T. urvilleana (T. semidecandra). PRINCESS FLOWER. Zones 16, 17, 21–24, H1, H2; with protection in 14, 15. The only species widely available. Fast, rather open growth to 5–18 ft. tall, 3–10 ft. wide. Branch tips, buds, new growth shaded with satiny hairs in orange and bronzy red. Green, 3–6-in.-long leaves, often edged red. Older leaves add spots of orange, red, or yellow, especially in winter. Brilliant royal purple, 3-in. flowers appear intermittently from late spring into winter. Prune lightly and feed after each bloom cycle. Has naturalized in Hawaii, forming thickets in wet areas. Can be used as indoor/outdoor plant in colder climates.

TIGRIDIA pavonia

TIGER FLOWER, MEXICAN SHELL FLOWER

Iridaceae

PERENNIAL FROM BULB

ZONES 4–24; H1; OR DIG AND STORE

PARTIAL SHADE IN HOTTEST CLIMATES

REGULAR WATER DURING GROWTH AND BLOOM

Tigridia pavonia

Mexican native with flashy summertime flowers. Fans of narrow, swordlike, ribbed leaves to 1½ ft. long send up erect, 2½-ft. flower stems bearing triangular blossoms to 6 in. across. Flowers have three large outer segments in red, orange, pink, yellow, or white; cuplike center and three small inner segments are usually boldly blotched with contrasting color. (Immaculata strain is unspotted.) Each flower lasts only one day, but the bloom period lasts for several weeks.

Plant in spring, after weather warms up (night temperatures should not fall below 60°F/16°C). Plant in well-drained soil, setting bulbs 2–4 in. deep, 4–8 in. apart. Stop watering after flowering is finished and when leaves turn yellow. Can be left in ground where hardy; divide every 3 or 4 years, digging in fall and waiting until spring planting time to separate bulbs and replant. Spider mites are main pest (they cause yellowish or whitish streaks on foliage); begin control when leaves are several inches long. Gophers are fond of the bulbs. Beyond hardiness range, dig bulbs after leaves yellow and store as for gladiolus; or grow in pots and protect in winter.

TILIA

LINDEN

Tiliaceae

DECIDUOUS TREES

ZONES 1–17, EXCEPT AS NOTED

FULL SUN

REGULAR WATER

Tilia cordata

Dense trees. Stately good looks, moderate growth rate. All have irregularly heart-shaped leaves and small, fragrant, yellowish white flowers in drooping clusters in late spring, early summer. Flowers develop into nutlets, each with an attached papery bract. Best in deep, rich, moist soil. In cold-winter areas, fall color varies from negligible to good yellow. Young trees need shaping, older ones only corrective pruning. Aphids can cause honeydew, which drips disagreeably and encourages sooty mold.

T. americana. AMERICAN LINDEN, BASSWOOD. Native to eastern North America. To 40–60 ft. tall, 20–25 ft. wide. Straight-trunked tree with a narrow crown. Dull dark green leaves to 4–6 in. long, nearly as wide. 'Redmond' is a pyramidal form with glossy foliage.

T. cordata. LITTLE-LEAF LINDEN. Native to Europe. Dense pyramid to 30–50 ft. tall, 15–30 ft. wide. Leaves 1½–3 in. long and as wide (or wider), dark green above, silvery beneath. Excellent lawn or street tree. Given room to develop its crown, it can be a fine patio shade tree (but expect bees in flowering season). Can be sheared into hedges. Very tolerant of city conditions. Selected forms include 'Chancellor', 'Glenleven', 'Greenspire', 'June Bride' (especially heavy bloomer), and 'Olympic'.

T. × euchlora. CRIMEAN LINDEN. Hybrid derived from *T. cordata.* To 25–35 ft. (perhaps eventually to 50 ft.) tall, almost as wide. Slightly pendulous branches. Rich glossy green leaves have paler undersides, reach 2–4 in. long and wide. Casts more open shade than *T. cordata.*

T. tomentosa. SILVER LINDEN. Zones 2–21. Native to Europe, western Asia. To 40–50 ft. tall, 20–30 ft. wide. Leaves are 3–5 in. long and about as wide, light green above, silvery beneath; they turn and ripple in the slightest breeze. More tolerant of heat, drought than other species. 'Sterling' has silvery young leaves and an especially handsome winter silhouette.

Tiliaceae. The linden family of trees and shrubs includes lavender starflower *(Grewia)*, African linden *(Sparmannia)*, and of course linden *(Tilia)*.

TIPUANA tipu

TIPU TREE

Fabaceae (Leguminosae)

SEMIEVERGREEN OR DECIDUOUS TREE

ZONES 12 (WARMEST AREAS), 13–16, 18–24; H1, H2

FULL SUN

REGULAR WATER

Tipuana tipu

From South America. Grows to 25–40 ft. tall, 30–60 ft. wide (or larger). Has broad, flattened crown that is wider than high, but can be pruned to make a denser, narrower, umbrella-shaped crown. Light green leaves divided into 11–21 oblong, 1½-in.-long leaflets. Blooms from late spring to early summer, bearing clusters of apricot to yellow, sweet pea–shaped flowers; 2½-in. seedpods follow the flowers. Will not take strongly alkaline conditions but is otherwise not particular about soil. Flowers best in warm-summer areas out of immediate ocean influence. Good street tree or lawn tree. Useful as a shade tree for patio or terrace, though litter from flowers can be a slight nuisance. Hardy to 25°F/–4°C; well-ripened wood will take 18°F/–8°C with minor damage.

TITHONIA rotundifolia (T. speciosa)

MEXICAN SUNFLOWER

Asteraceae (Compositae)

PERENNIAL GROWN AS ANNUAL

ALL ZONES

FULL SUN

REGULAR WATER

Tithonia rotundifolia

Native from Mexico to Central America. Husky, rather coarse plant with velvety green leaves, spectacular gaudy flowers. Grows rapidly to 6 ft. tall, 4 ft. wide. Blooms from summer to frost, bearing 3–4-in.-wide blossoms with orange-scarlet rays and tufted yellow centers. Use as a temporary screen. Arcadian Blend grows 2–2½ ft. tall, produces gold, orange, and yellow flowers. 'Aztec Sun', to 4 ft. tall, has apricot gold flowers. 'Fiesta del Sol', to 2½ ft. high, bears 2–3-in. orange flowers, starts blooming earlier than the others. 'Goldfinger', a bushy 4-footer with deep orange flowers, makes a good temporary summer hedge. All have hollow stems; cut carefully for bouquets to avoid bending stalks. Sow seed in place in spring, in well-drained, not-too-rich soil. Tolerates intense heat, some drought. Attractive to butterflies, hummingbirds.

TOADFLAX. See LINARIA

TOBIRA. See PITTOSPORUM tobira

TOLMIEA menziesii

PIGGY-BACK PLANT

Saxifragaceae

PERENNIAL

ZONES 4–9, 14–17, 20–24; OR INDOORS

SOME SHADE; INDIRECT LIGHT

REGULAR TO AMPLE WATER

Tolmiea menziesii

Native to Coast Ranges from Northern California northward to Alaska. Chief asset is abundant production of attractive, triangular to heart-shaped, shallowly lobed leaves of variable size (up to 5 in. long), carried at ends of leafstalks that also vary in length. Leaves are covered in ⅛-in.-long hairs. Typical foliage color is solid medium green, but there is a form irregularly mottled in yellow to chartreuse. Tiny, rather inconspicuous reddish brown flowers top 1–2-ft.-high stems.

Good ground cover for shade. Spreads indefinitely by producing new plantlets at junction of leafstalk and leaf blade; plantlets root in the soil. Handsome in hanging basket. Start new plants any time of year; take leaf with plantlet and insert in moist potting mix so base of plantlet contacts soil. As houseplant, needs cool temperatures, filtered light (bright light is fine if it's indirect). Mealybugs, spider mites are occasional pests.

TOMATILLO

Solanaceae

ANNUAL

ALL ZONES

FULL SUN

REGULAR WATER

Tomatillo

From Mexico. Easy-to-grow, summer-fruiting tomato relative known botanically as *Physalis ixocarpa.* Bushy, sprawling growth to 4 ft. high and at least as wide. Fruit swells to fill—and eventually split—the loose, papery husk (calyx) that surrounds it. When fully ripe, fruit is yellow to purple, about 2 in. wide, and very sweet, but it is usually picked when green and tart and used in sauces and other dishes.

Sow seeds directly in fertile soil 4 to 6 weeks after last frost, when soil has warmed; in moist, warm soil, seeds will germinate in 5 days. Thin seedlings to 10 in. apart. Or start plants indoors and set out in the garden; plant deep, as for tomatoes. Use floating row covers in short-summer areas. Tomatillos can be trained to a trellis like tomatoes but are usually left to sprawl. Once fruiting begins, cut back on water but don't let plants become stressed. Harvest fruit when walnut size (or smaller, if it seems fully developed) and deep green. Don't remove the papery husk until you are ready to use the fruit.

TOMATO

Solanaceae

PERENNIAL GROWN AS ANNUAL

ALL ZONES

FULL SUN

REGULAR WATER

Tomato

Andean native classified as *Lycopersicon esculentum.* Easy to grow and prolific, tomatoes are just about the most widely grown of all garden plants, edible or otherwise. Amateur and commercial growers have varying ideas about how best to raise tomatoes. If you've developed a successful method, continue to follow it—but if you're a novice or are dissatisfied with previous attempts, you may find the following information useful.

Choose varieties suited to your climate that will yield the kind of tomatoes you like on plants you can handle. Some varieties are determinate, others indeterminate. Determinate types are bushier, need little or no staking or trellising. Indeterminate ones are more vinelike, need more training, and generally bear over a longer period. (Though the tomato plant is really a sprawling plant incapable of climbing, you'll often see it referred to as a vine.) Plant a few each of early, midseason, and late varieties for longest possible production. (Or plant in spring and again in summer where growing season is long.) Typically, six plants can supply a family of four with enough fruit to enjoy fresh and to use for canning or sauce.

Set out tomato plants after frost danger is past and the soil has warmed. Plant in February or early March in Zones 12, 13; in April, May, or early June in Zones 7–9, 14–24; in May or early June in Zones A1–A3, 1–6, 10, 11. In Hawaii, tomatoes can be planted year-round in most locations. To grow tomatoes from seed, sow seeds in pots of light soil mix 5 to 7 weeks before you intend to set out plants. Cover seeds with ½ in. of fine soil; firm soil over seeds and keep surface damp. Place seed container in cold frame or sunny window—a temperature of 65 to 70°F/18 to 21°C is ideal, although a range of 50°F/10°C at night to as warm as 85°F/29°C in the day will give acceptable results. When seedlings are 2 in. tall, transplant each into a 3- or 4-in. pot; keep seedlings in sunny area until they reach planting size. When buying tomato plants, look for compact ones with sturdy stems; avoid those that are tall for the pot or have flowers or fruit.

Plant in a sunny site in well-drained soil. Tomato plants prefer neutral to slightly acid soil; add lime to very acid soil or sulfur to alkaline soil the autumn before setting out plants. Space plants 1½–3 ft. apart (staked or trained) to 3–4 ft. apart (untrained). Make planting holes extra deep and set in seedlings so lowest leaves are just above soil level. Additional roots will form on buried stem and provide a stronger root system.

If you live in an area where summers are cool or short (such as the Pacific Northwest, Alaska, or high-elevation regions), or if you want to get an early start, take steps to speed growth and protect tomatoes from frost. A combination of plastic mulch and floating row covers is probably most effective. Individual plants can be protected with paper or plastic caps known as hotcaps (some have water-filled cylinders that trap heat effectively to provide maximum protection).

Tomato management and harvest will be most satisfying if you train plants to keep them off the ground as much as possible. Untrained plants will sprawl, and some fruit will lie on soil, where it often suffers from rot, pest damage, and discoloration. For training indeterminate varieties, the usual practice is to drive a 6-ft.-long stake (at least 1 by 1 in.) into ground a foot from each plant. Use soft ties to hold the plant to the stake as it grows.

Slightly easier in the long run—but more work at planting time—is to grow each plant in a wire cylinder made of concrete reinforcing screen (6-in. mesh). The screen is 7 ft. wide, which is just right for cylinder height. Put stakes at opposite sides of cylinder and tie cylinder firmly to them. As the vine grows, poke protruding branches back inside the cylinder.

Tomato plants need regular moisture at root level; they are deep rooted, so water heavily each time you water. If soil is fairly rich, you won't need to fertilize at all. In ordinary soils, feed lightly every 2 weeks from the time first blossoms set until the end of harvest; or give a single application of controlled-release fertilizer when planting.

Whiteflies are common pests of tomato plants. Large green caterpillars with diagonal white stripes that feed upside down on leaf undersides are hornworms; handpick them. In Hawaii, wrap developing fruit clusters in paper or cloth bags to protect from melon flies. Tomatoes are subject to a long list of diseases, some common only in certain regions. Your Cooperative Extension Office is the best source of control measures for most tomato diseases. If plants are growing strongly, then suddenly wilt and die, they may have been sabotaged by gophers. If you can find no evidence of these rodents, plants probably are suffering from verticillium wilt, fusarium wilt, or both; pull them out and discard them. Diseases live over in soil, so plant in a different location every year and try varieties resistant to wilt or certain other diseases (see introduction to "Tomato varieties," below).

In Pacific Northwest, lessen chance of late blight (which spots leaves and stems, rots fruit) by avoiding overhead sprinkling. Blight declines as weather warms; destroy plant debris after harvest.

Some tomato problems—leaf roll, blossom-end rot, cracked fruit—are physiological and can usually be corrected (or prevented) by maintaining uniform soil moisture. Mulching will help conserve moisture in very hot or dry climates.

If you have done everything right and your tomatoes fail to set fruit in the spring, use hormone spray on blossoms. Tomatoes often fail to set fruit when night temperatures drop below 55°F/13°C. In chilly-night areas, select cold-tolerant varieties (especially small-fruited strains). Fruit-setting hormone often speeds up bearing in the earlier part of the season. Tomatoes can also fail to set fruit when temperatures rise above 100°F/38°C, but hormones are not effective under those conditions.

Harvest fruit when it is fully red and juicy; keep ripe fruit picked to extend season. When frost is predicted, harvest all fruit, both green and partly ripe. Store in a dry place away from direct sunlight at 60 to 70°F/16 to 21°C; check often for ripening.

TOMATO VARIETIES

Following are types of tomatoes you can buy as seeds or started plants. The number of varieties is enormous and increases every year; there are choices for every taste and every region. It's wise to consult a knowledgeable nursery, your Cooperative Extension Office, and other gardeners to find out which varieties flourish in your local climate and soil.

If certain diseases or nematodes cause trouble locally, you may be able to grow varieties that resist one or more problems. Keys to resistance you may see on plant labels or in catalog descriptions include V (verticillium wilt), F (fusarium wilt), FF (Race 1 and Race 2 fusarium), T (tobacco mosaic virus), N (nematodes), A (alternaria leaf spot), and L (septoria leaf spot). For example, a variety labeled VFFNT means that it resists verticillium wilt, two races of fusarium wilt, nematodes, and tobacco mosaic virus.

Main crop or standard tomatoes. 'Celebrity', 'Big Boy', and 'Better Boy' are widely grown. 'Heatwave' is popular in extremely hot climates. 'Ace' and 'Pearson' are local favorites in California.

Early tomatoes. These tomatoes set fruit at lower night temperatures than other tomatoes do; 'Early Girl', 'Burpee's Early Pick', and 'Quick Pick' are standards. Very short-season regions, such as Alaska and high-elevation areas, have their own very early varieties, which set fruit at surprisingly low temperatures; 'Early Tanana' and 'Subarctic Maxi' are examples.

Cool-summer tomatoes. These will ripen fruit where accumulated heat is too low for most tomatoes. Nurseries in cool-summer areas usually offer locally adapted varieties, such as 'San Francisco Fog', 'Oregon Pride', and 'Seattle Best of All'. Many early varieties, especially 'Early Girl' and 'Stupice', also do well where summers are cool.

Hawaiian tomatoes. Varieties developed especially for Hawaii resist nematodes and common diseases found there. They include 'N-5', 'N-52', 'N-65', 'N-69', 'Anahu', 'Healani', 'Kalohi', and 'Puunui'.

Hybrid tomatoes. Some suppliers tout certain tomatoes as hybrids. They are usually referring to first-generation offspring of controlled parent lines, sometimes indicated by F1 after the name. These varieties are more predictable and uniform in growth and fruit quality. Some are giants like 'Beefmaster' and 'Big Beef', but hybrid paste tomatoes are also available.

Novelty tomatoes. Among these are yellow and orange varieties such as 'Orange Queen', 'Mountain Gold', 'Husky Gold', and 'Lemon Boy'. 'Caro Rich' is very high in vitamin A and beta carotene. There are also deep reddish brown tomatoes ('Black Prince'), white tomatoes ('New Snowball', 'White Beauty'), tomatoes with striped fruit ('Green Zebra', 'Tigerella'), and even one with fruit that is green when fully ripe ('Evergreen'). 'Long Keeper' will stay fresh in storage for 3 months. 'Stuffer' and 'Yellow Stuffer' yield large, nearly hollow fruits that resemble bell peppers.

Large-fruited tomatoes. These grow to full size in areas where both days and nights are warm. Fruits can weigh a pound or even more. 'Beefsteak', 'Beefmaster', and 'Big Beef' are typical. 'Burpee's Supersteak Hybrid' can produce 2-lb. fruits; 'Delicious' has borne a 7¾-lb. tomato.

Paste tomatoes. Bears huge crops of small, oval, thick-meated fruits with small seed cavities. Sometimes called plum tomatoes. Favorites for canning, sauces, and tomato paste; also good for drying. 'Roma', 'San Marzano', 'Viva Italia', and yellow 'Italian Gold' are examples.

Small-fruited tomatoes. Bear fruits ranging from very tiny (currant size) to the size of large marbles. Shapes and colors are indicated by names: 'Red Cherry', 'Red Pear', 'Yellow Cherry', 'Yellow Pear'. Those with very small fruits include 'Sweet 100', 'Supersweet 100', 'Sweet Million', and 'Gardener's Delight'. Grape tomatoes, such as 'Juliet', produce large grapelike clusters of smallish fruit. Small-fruiting types that grow on small plants suitable for pots or hanging baskets include 'Tiny Tim', 'Small Fry', and 'Patio'.

'Yellow Pear' Tomato

Heirloom tomatoes. Varying in size, appearance, and plant habit, these represent old varieties that have been maintained by enthusiasts in different parts of the country. Most are grown for excellent flavor. 'Brandywine' is a currently popular heirloom variety.

T

TOONA sinensis (Cedrela sinensis)

Meliaceae

DECIDUOUS TREE

ZONES 2B–9, 14–24

FULL SUN

REGULAR WATER

Toona sinensis

Native to China. Slow to medium growth to 50 ft. tall, 30 ft. wide. Leaves have many leaflets (up to 26) and somewhat resemble those of tree of heaven *(Ailanthus)*. Prized for beauty of new growth, which is tinted in shades of cream, soft pink, and rose. Long, pendulous clusters of white flowers appear in spring. These are followed by woody, star-shaped seed capsules that contain winged seeds and are attractive in dried arrangements. Suckers freely.

TORCH LILY. See KNIPHOFIA

TORENIA fournieri

WISHBONE FLOWER

Scrophulariaceae

ANNUAL

ZONES 1–24; H1, H2

PARTIAL SHADE IN HOTTEST CLIMATES

REGULAR WATER

Torenia fournieri

From tropical Asia. Compact, bushy, to 1 ft. high and wide. Blooms from summer into fall; flowers look like miniature gloxinias *(Sinningia)*, have stamens arranged in wishbone shape. Species has pale lavender blossoms with deeper purple markings and bright yellow throats; a white-flowered form is also sold. Sow seeds in pots and transplant to garden after frost danger is past; or buy nursery plants. Use as edging or in pots and window boxes. If grown in sun, keep roots cool with a mulch. Summer Wave hybrids thrive in heat; their spreading habit makes them a good choice for hanging baskets. Duchess strain is more compact (6–8 in. tall and wide), offers blooms in four color combinations: light blue with blue throat, blue with white throat, deep blue with blue throat, and pink with white throat.

TORREYA californica

CALIFORNIA NUTMEG

Cephalotaxaceae

EVERGREEN TREE

ZONES 4–9, 14–24

FULL SUN OR PARTIAL SHADE

MODERATE WATER

Torreya californica

Native to cool, shaded canyons in California mountain regions below 4,500 ft. Slow-growing conifer to 15–20 ft. tall, 12–15 ft. wide, with trunk 1–3 ft. in diameter. Wide, open pyramidal crown, domelike with age. Branches are horizontal, slender, somewhat drooping at tips. Flat sprays of rigid, sharp-pointed, flat, dark green leaves with two whitish bands underneath; 1¼–2½ in. long, ⅛ in. wide. Plumlike fruit is pale green with purplish markings.

TOTARA. See PODOCARPUS nivalis, P. totara

TOVARA virginiana. See PERSICARIA virginiana

TOYON. See HETEROMELES arbutifolia

TRACHELIUM caeruleum

Campanulaceae (Lobeliaceae)

PERENNIAL

ZONES 7–9, 14–24; ELSEWHERE AS ANNUAL

FULL SUN

REGULAR WATER

Trachelium caeruleum

Tough, undemanding Mediterranean native to 2½ ft. tall and wide. Forms a clump of stems clothed with narrow, sharply toothed, dark green leaves. Blooms over a long summer season, when sparsely foliaged flowering stems are topped by broad, dome-shaped clusters of tiny blossoms in blue, mauve, pink, or white. Good cut flowers. If sown early, will bloom first year (and so can be treated as a summer annual in colder climates or as a winter annual in mild-winter desert).

TRACHELOSPERMUM

STAR JASMINE

Apocynaceae

EVERGREEN SHRUBS OR VINES

ZONES VARY BY SPECIES

LIGHT SHADE IN HOTTEST CLIMATES

REGULAR WATER

Trachelospermum jasminoides

Ground covers, trailers, or climbers bearing delightfully fragrant, pinwheel-shaped blossoms in spring or early summer. Among the most versatile and useful of plants. Prefer well-drained soil. For lush growth, fertilize once before spring growth begins, again after flowering. Prune back as needed to shape. Cut stems exude a milky sap. Formerly sold as *Rhynchospermum*.

T. asiaticum. Zones 6–24. From Japan, Korea. Like *T. jasminoides* but has smaller leaves in darker, duller green and smaller flowers in creamy yellow or yellowish white.

T. jasminoides. STAR JASMINE, CONFEDERATE JASMINE, MAILE HAOLE. Zones 8–24; H1, H2. From China. Given support, a twining vine to 20–30 ft.; without support and with some tip-pinching, a spreading shrub or ground cover to 2 ft. tall, 10 ft. wide. Oval leaves to 3 in. long are glossy light green when new, mature to lustrous dark green. Profusion of white, inch-wide flowers in small clusters on short side branches. Attractive to bees. If grown as shrubby plant, it is good in raised beds or entry gardens, for edging walk or drive, as extension of lawn, spilling over walls, as ground cover under trees and shrubs. Set plants 5 ft. apart for ground cover. 'Variegatum' has leaves bordered and blotched with white.

TRACHYCARPUS fortunei

WINDMILL PALM

Arecaceae (Palmae)

PALM

ZONES 4–24

FULL SUN OR LIGHT SHADE

REGULAR WATER

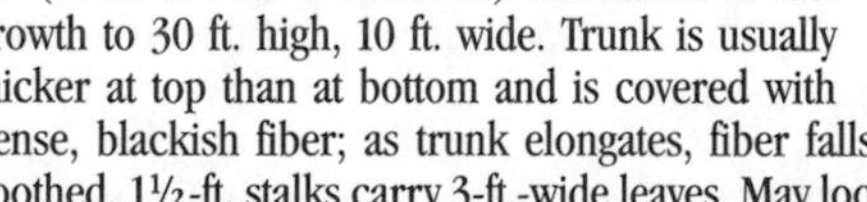
Trachycarpus fortunei

From China. Medium-size, very hardy fan palm (to 10°F/–12°C or lower). Moderate to fast growth to 30 ft. high, 10 ft. wide. Trunk is usually thicker at top than at bottom and is covered with dense, blackish fiber; as trunk elongates, fiber falls off its lower portion. Toothed, 1½-ft. stalks carry 3-ft.-wide leaves. May look untidy in high winds. May be sold as *Chamaerops excelsa*. Young plants can be grown indoors in bright indirect light; plant them outdoors when they become too big.

TRACHYMENE coerulea

BLUE LACE FLOWER

Apiaceae (Umbelliferae)

ANNUAL

ZONES 1–24

FULL SUN

REGULAR WATER

Trachymene coerulea

From Australia. Upright growth to 2 ft. tall and 10 in. wide. Finely divided leaves. Numerous small lavender-blue flowers are borne in 2–3-in.-wide, flat-topped clusters that are quite lacy in appearance. Good cut flowers. Grow in light, rich, well-drained soil. Sow seeds in place; taproot makes transplanting difficult. Does not perform well in heat. Where summers are mild, sow in early spring for summer bloom; in hot-summer, mild-winter regions, sow in fall for winter and spring bloom. Once sold as *Didiscus coeruleus.*

TRADESCANTIA

Commelinaceae

PERENNIALS

ZONES 12–24, H1, H2, EXCEPT AS NOTED; OR INDOORS

EXPOSURE NEEDS VARY BY SPECIES; BRIGHT INDIRECT LIGHT

WATER NEEDS VARY BY SPECIES

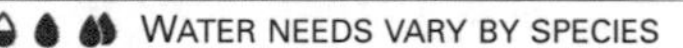

Tradescantia pallida 'Purpurea'

Most are virtually indestructible plants with long, trailing stems. Usually seen in pots or hanging baskets, but can be used as ground covers—though the most vigorous, rambling types are likely to be invasive. On variegated forms, pinch out any growth that reverts to solid green.

T. × andersoniana. See T. virginiana

T. fluminensis. WANDERING JEW. From South America. Rapid grower to 2 in. high, with indefinite spread. Succulent stems have swollen joints where dark green, oval or oblong, 2½-in.-long leaves are attached. Tiny, unshowy white flowers. Easy to grow. Excellent for window boxes and dish gardens. If plants are overgrown, renovate by cutting back severely; or discard them and start new plants with fresh tip growth. Partial or full shade. Regular to ample water. Stems will live a long time in water, rooting quickly and easily. Variegated forms include 'Albovittata', leaves finely and evenly streaked with white; 'Aurea' ('Gold Leaf'), bright yellow-green foliage; 'Laekenensis' ('Rainbow'), leaves banded in white and pale lavender; and 'Variegata', yellow- or white-striped foliage.

T. pallida 'Purpurea' (Setcreasea pallida 'Purple Heart'). PURPLE HEART, PURPLE QUEEN. From Mexico. Creeping plant to 1–1½ ft. high, 1 ft. wide; stems tend to flop. Pointed, rather narrowly oval leaves are strongly shaded with purple, particularly on undersides. Pale or deep purple flowers (not showy). Pinch back after bloom. Generally unattractive in winter. Frost may kill tops, but recovery is fast in warm weather. Use as ground cover, for bedding, in pots. Full sun or light shade. Moderate water.

T. spathacea (Rhoeo spathacea). MOSES-IN-THE-CRADLE, MOSES-IN-THE-BOAT. From Mexico, Central America. To 2 ft. tall, 1 ft. wide. Each plant has a dozen or so broad, sword-shaped, rather erect leaves that are dark green above, deep purple beneath. Small, white, three-petaled blooms are interesting rather than beautiful, crowded into boat-shaped bracts borne down among leaves. There is also a dwarf form. 'Variegata' has leaves striped in red and yellowish green. Most often used as a pot plant or in hanging baskets; grown as a ground cover and edging in Hawaii. Tough plant; takes heat, low humidity, sun or shade. Best with regular moisture but withstands inconsistent watering. Try to keep water out of leaf joints when irrigating.

Tradescantia spathacea

T. virginiana. SPIDERWORT. Zones 1–24; H1. From eastern U.S. Clump-forming border plant to 1½ ft. high and wide. Long, grassy-looking, deep green, erect or arching leaves. Three-petaled flowers last for only a day, but buds come in large clusters and plants are seldom out of bloom in summer. May self-sow and become somewhat invasive. Divide clumps when crowded. Sun or shade. Regular to ample water. Named garden varieties come in white, blue shades, lavender, purple, shades of pink from pale to near-red; these plants are often sold as *T.* × *andersoniana.*

T. zebrina (Zebrina pendula). WANDERING JEW. Zones 24; H1, H2. From southern Mexico. Similar to *T. fluminensis* but not as hardy; bears pinkish or bluish flowers. Most widely grown are forms with colorful leaves, including 'Quadricolor', purplish green leaves with longitudinal bands of silver, pink, and red; and 'Purpusii', dark red or greenish red foliage. Attractive ground covers for shady, frost-free sites. Partial or full shade. Regular water.

TRANSVAAL DAISY. See GERBERA jamesonii

TREE FERN. See BLECHNUM, CYATHEA cooperi, DICKSONIA

TREE MALLOW. See LAVATERA

TREE-OF-HEAVEN. See AILANTHUS altissima

TREE TOMATO, TAMARILLO

Solanaceae

EVERGREEN OR SEMIEVERGREEN SHRUB

ZONES 14–24; H1, H2

FULL SUN OR PARTIAL SHADE

REGULAR WATER

Tree Tomato

Treelike Andean native known botanically as *Cyphomandra betacea.* Fast growth to 10–18 ft. tall, about two-thirds as wide. Pointed oval, 4–10-in.-long leaves; small pinkish flowers in summer and fall. In winter, bears egg-shaped, 2–3-in.-long red fruit (there are also yellow varieties). Grow from seed like tomato. Harvest fruit when it is fully colored; pluck from tree by snapping off, leaving stem attached. Fruit has acid flavor somewhat like that of tomato—if you find it too tart, try stewing it with a little sugar. Bears on new growth. In late winter, prune back branches that have fruited by one-fourth to one-third (this will prevent fruit from developing ever farther out from center of plant). Control sucking insects. Frost sensitive; give overhead protection in Zones 14, 15, 18–21. Fruiting is more reliable in warmer part of range.

TRICHOSTEMA lanatum

WOOLLY BLUE CURLS

Lamiaceae (Labiatae)

EVERGREEN SHRUB

ZONES 14–24

FULL SUN

NO IRRIGATION NEEDED

Trichostema lanatum

Native to dry, sunny slopes of California Coast Ranges. Much-branched, neat plant to 3–5 ft. high, 4–8 ft. wide. Narrow, 1¼–2-in.-long leaves, pungently aromatic when bruised, are shiny dark green on upper surface, white and woolly beneath; leaf edges are rolled under. Flowers, in separated clusters on a long stalk, are blue with conspicuous, arching stamens. Stalks and flowers are covered with blue, pink, or whitish wool. Blooms in spring; continues throughout summer and early fall if old flower stems are cut back. Temperamental plant; needs perfect drainage.

TRICUSPIDARIA dependens. See CRINODENDRON patagua

T

TRICYRTIS

TOAD LILY

Liliaceae

PERENNIALS

ZONES VARY BY SPECIES

PARTIAL SHADE

AMPLE WATER

Tricyrtis hirta

Woodland plants that resemble false Solomon's seal *(Smilacina)* in foliage. Interesting, heavily spotted, inch-long flowers appear at leaf joints and in terminal clusters in late summer and fall. They are complex in structure, somewhat orchidlike: each blossom has three petals and three sepals, with a column of decorative stamens and styles rising from the center. Need soil enriched with plenty of organic matter.

T. formosana (T. stolonifera). Zones 3–9, 14–17. From Taiwan. To 2½ ft. tall. Spreads by aboveground runners to form a clump 1½ ft. or wider (but is not invasive). More erect than *T. hirta,* with flowers mostly in terminal clusters. Leaves are green, mottled with deeper green; brown or maroon buds open to white to pale lilac flowers spotted with purple. 'Amethystina' blooms several weeks earlier than species, bears lavender-blue blossoms with red-spotted white throat.

T. hirta. Zones 2–9, 14–17. From Japan. To 3 ft. tall, 2 ft. wide; it lacks runners. Arching stems bear pale green, softly hairy foliage. White to pale lilac blossoms peppered with purple; appear in leaf joints all along the stems. 'Miyazaki' bears pink to white flowers with crimson spots; 'Miyazaki Gold' is similar but has gold-edged leaves.

TRIFOLIUM repens

WHITE CLOVER, WHITE DUTCH CLOVER

Fabaceae (Leguminosae)

PERENNIAL

ZONES 2–24

FULL SUN OR PARTIAL SHADE

REGULAR WATER

Trifolium repens

Sometimes mixed with lawn grass or dichondra seed. Prostrate stems root freely, send up lush cover of leaves with three ¾-in. leaflets. Can stain clothing; white flowers attract bees. These colored-leaf varieties grow 4 in. high, spread indefinitely, and are used as ground covers or at front of borders: 'Atropurpureum', blackish purple leaves edged in green; 'Green Ice', lime green with dark green margin; 'Purpurascens', maroon outlined in green. *T. r. minus* is one of the shamrocks. All take nitrogen from air and fix it in soil through action of bacteria on their roots.

TRILLIUM

WAKE ROBIN

Liliaceae

PERENNIALS

ZONES VARY BY SPECIES

PARTIAL OR FULL SHADE

REGULAR WATER

Trillium ovatum

Bloom in early spring; need some winter chill. Each stem is topped with a whorl of three leaves; a single three-petaled flower appears in the center of the whorl (sometimes on a stalk, sometimes virtually stalkless). Plant in shady, woodsy site. Left undisturbed, plants will gradually increase by rhizomes. Die to ground in mid- to late summer. In addition to species listed below, many others are offered by specialists in native plants.

T. chloropetalum (T. sessile californicum). Zones 4–9, 14–17. Native to California. To 1–1½ ft. high, 1 ft. wide, with 6-in.-long leaves mottled in maroon. Stalkless flowers have greenish white to yellowish petals about 2½ in. long. *T. c. giganteum* has deep maroon petals.

T. erectum. PURPLE TRILLIUM. Zones 1–6. From eastern North America. To 2 ft. tall, 1 ft. wide, with 7-in.-long leaves. Erect, 2–3-in. flowers are dark reddish purple, carried on stalks; they have an odd odor.

T. grandiflorum. Zones 1–6. From eastern North America. To 1½ ft. tall, 1 ft. wide, with stout stems and 2½–6-in.-long leaves. Nearly stalkless flowers are nodding, to 3 in. across, white aging to rose. There are several choice double-flowered forms.

T. ovatum (T. californicum). Zones 2–7, 14–17. Western native. Resembles *T. grandiflorum* but has narrower petals; flowers are usually upright and are borne on stalks.

TRISTANIA conferta. See LOPHOSTEMON confertus

TRISTANIOPSIS laurina (Tristania laurina)

WATER GUM

Myrtaceae

EVERGREEN TREE OR SHRUB

ZONES 15–24

FULL SUN

REGULAR WATER

Tristaniopsis laurina

From eastern Australia. Slow-growing, rather formal-looking plant with conical, dense crown. To 10 ft. tall, 5 ft. wide at 8 years old; may eventually reach 45 ft. or taller, 30 ft. wide. Mahogany-colored bark peels off, revealing satiny white new bark beneath. Glossy green, narrow leaves to 4 in. long. Clusters of small, faintly fragrant yellow flowers appear in late spring or early summer, borne profusely enough to put on a good show. Seedpods like those of eucalyptus but much smaller (to ¼ in. wide); they don't create a litter problem. 'Elegant' has broad leaves that are red when they emerge, turn green only when shaded by later growth.

Water gum is densely shrubby when young and can be kept that way with a little pinching. Can be trained as a single- or multistemmed tree; once established, trees need only light shaping. Excellent tall screen, boundary, background planting. Good tub plant.

TRITELEIA

Liliaceae

PERENNIALS FROM CORMS

ZONES 3–9, 14–24, EXCEPT AS NOTED

FULL SUN

NO IRRIGATION NEEDED

Triteleia laxa

Plants of this name were formerly known as *Brodiaea.* General descriptions and culture are same as for *Brodiaea,* which differs only in technical details. Spring and early summer bloom.

T. grandiflora (Brodiaea grandiflora). Flowering stalk to 2 ft. tall; many 1¼-in.-long, blue to white trumpets.

T. hyacinthina (B. hyacinthina, B. lactea). WHITE BRODIAEA. Zones 2–9, 14–24. Clusters of 10–40 papery-textured white, purple-tinged flowers with greenish veins. Flowering stalk is 9–20 in. high.

T. ixioides (B. ixioides, B. lutea). PRETTY FACE, GOLDEN BRODIAEA. Flower stalk to 2 ft.; flowers 1 in. long, golden yellow with purple-black midrib and veins.

T. laxa (B. laxa). GRASS NUT, ITHURIEL'S SPEAR. Zones 5–9, 14–24. Flower stalk to 2½ ft.; purple-blue, 1½-in. trumpets.

T. 'Queen Fabiola'. Flower stalk to 2½ ft. tall; deep violet flowers.

T. tubergenii. Flower stalk to 2½ ft. tall; light blue flowers.

T. uniflora. See Ipheion uniflorum

TRITONIA

Iridaceae

PERENNIALS FROM CORMS

ZONES 9, 13–24; OR DIG AND STORE

FULL SUN

REGULAR WATER DURING GROWTH AND BLOOM

Tritonia crocata

South African native related to freesia, harlequin flower *(Sparaxis)*, ixia, montbretia *(Crocosmia)*. Fans of swordlike leaves grow in early spring. Branched spikes of broad, funnel-shaped, brightly colored blossoms appear in late spring; make long-lasting cut flowers. Foliage dies down after bloom, re-emerges the next spring.

Plant corms in well-drained soil, setting them 2–3 in. deep, 3 in. apart. Plant in fall where winter temperatures remain above 20°F/–7°C; wait until spring in colder areas. Corms can remain in the ground where hardy, but they are likely to rot unless planting area is kept fairly dry during summer dormancy. Divide overcrowded plantings during dormant period. Where corms cannot be protected and in colder regions, dig and store over winter or grow in pots. Good in rock gardens, borders.

T. crocata. Often called flame freesia. To 1½ ft. high; orange-red, 2-in. flowers. *T. c. miniata* has bright red blooms; 'Princess Beatrix' has deep orange flowers. Others may be offered in white, yellow, and pink shades.

T. hyalina. To 1 ft. high. Bright orange flowers. Blossom segments are narrower than those of *T. crocata* and have a transparent area near base.

TROCHODENDRON aralioides

WHEEL TREE

Trochodendraceae

EVERGREEN TREE OR SHRUB

ZONES 4–9, 14–24

FULL SUN OR LIGHT SHADE

REGULAR WATER

Trochodendron aralioides

From Japan, Korea. Handsome foliage plant to 30 ft. tall, 25 ft. wide, with horizontal branching pattern. Oval, 5-in.-long, glossy dark green leaves cluster near branch tips. In late spring, elongated (to 5-in.) clusters of 10–20 bright green flowers appear at branch ends. Each ¾-in. blossom is made up of a flat disk surrounded by stamens. Blossoms are followed by fruits consisting of small pods clustered around the disk. Prefers organically enriched soil.

TROLLIUS

GLOBEFLOWER

Ranunculaceae

PERENNIALS

ZONES A2, A3; 1–6

FULL SUN IN COOLER CLIMATES ONLY

REGULAR TO AMPLE WATER

Trollius chinensis

Clumps of finely cut, shiny dark green leaves put up 2–3-ft.-tall stems terminating in yellow to orange flowers typically shaped like globes or rounded cups. Deadhead to prolong bloom. Excellent cut flowers. Cannot take drought, heat; constantly damp area near a pond or stream is an ideal planting site. If growing globeflowers in a regular garden bed, liberally amend soil with organic matter and keep well watered. Divide clumps only when they thin out in center.

T. chinensis (T. ledebouri). From China, Siberia. To 3 ft. tall, 1½ ft. wide. Light orange-yellow, 2-in. flowers with open bowl shape; summer bloom. 'Golden Queen' has pure orange flowers.

T. ×cultorum. Group of hybrids includes 'Earliest of All' (pale orange yellow; midspring) and 'Lemon Queen' (light yellow; late spring, early summer). Both bear 3-in. blooms, reach 2 ft. tall and 1½ ft. wide.

TROPAEOLUM

NASTURTIUM

Tropaeolaceae

ANNUALS AND PERENNIALS

ZONES VARY BY SPECIES

EXPOSURE NEEDS VARY BY SPECIES

REGULAR WATER

Tropaeolum majus

Old-fashioned favorites from South America. Distinctive appearance, rapid growth, and easy culture are three of their many strong points.

T. majus. GARDEN NASTURTIUM. Annual. All zones. Two main kinds: climbing types, which trail over ground or climb to 6 ft. by coiling leafstalks; and compact, bushy, dwarf kinds to 1½ ft. high and wide (dwarf types are more widely sold). Both have round bright green leaves on long stalks. Long-spurred flowers to 2½ in. across have a refreshing fragrance, come in colors including maroon, red brown, orange, yellow, red, creamy white. You can get seeds of mixed colors in several strains; some single colors are also sold. Both single- and double-flowered forms are available. Good cut flowers. Young leaves, flowers, and unripe seedpods have peppery flavor and may be used in salads.

Easy to grow in most well-drained soils, but does best in sandy soil. Sow in early spring; plant grows and blooms quickly, reseeds (it has naturalized in parts of Zone 17). In mild-winter, hot-summer areas, sow in fall for winter and spring bloom. Use climbing types to cover fences, banks, stumps, rocks; use dwarf kinds for bedding, to hide fading bulb foliage, for quick color. Somewhat drought tolerant. Full sun or light shade.

T. peregrinum. CANARY BIRD FLOWER. Perennial in Zones 15–24; H1, H2; annual elsewhere. Climbs to 10–15 ft. Deeply five-lobed leaves. Frilled, fringed, ¾–1-in.-wide, canary yellow flowers with curved green spur. Sow in spring for bloom from summer until frost. Provide support such as stakes or netting; or let plant climb into a shrub. Light shade.

TRUMPET CREEPER, TRUMPET VINE. See CAMPSIS, DISTICTIS

TSUGA

HEMLOCK

Pinaceae

EVERGREEN TREES

ZONES VARY BY SPECIES

FULL SUN OR PARTIAL SHADE, EXCEPT AS NOTED

REGULAR WATER

Tsuga canadensis

These are mostly big, shallow-rooted trees with unusually graceful appearance. Horizontal to drooping branches bear needlelike leaves that are banded with white beneath, flattened and narrowed at the base to form distinct, short stalks. Small, oval brown cones hang down from branches. Deeply furrowed bark. Need some winter chill. Do best with acid soil, summer humidity, protection from hot sun and wind. Take well to heavy pruning; make excellent clipped hedges, screens. Easily damaged by salt and drought. In the Northwest, the hemlock woolly aphid can weaken these plants, especially those grown as hedges; it affects mainly *T. heterophylla.*

T. canadensis. CANADA HEMLOCK. Zones A3; 2–7, 17. From eastern North America. Dense, pyramidal tree to 40–70 ft. or taller, half as wide. Tends to produce two or more trunks. Outer branchlets droop gracefully. Dark green, ½-in.-long needles, mostly arranged in opposite rows. Fine lawn tree, good background plant, outstanding clipped hedge. 'Pendula',

Sargent weeping hemlock, grows slowly to 5 ft. tall and 10 ft. wide, has pendulous branches. 'Cole's Prostrate' is 1 ft. tall (usually less) and spreads to 3 ft. or more. 'Gentsch White', to 2 ft. high and 1½ ft. wide, has white-tipped new growth. Many other dwarf, weeping, and variegated selections are sold.

T. heterophylla. WESTERN HEMLOCK. Zones A2, A3; 2–7, 14–17. Native along coast from Alaska to Northern California, inland to northern Idaho and Montana. Handsome tree with narrow, pyramidal crown. Grows fairly fast to 70–130 ft. tall, 20–30 ft. wide. Somewhat drooping branchlets; fine-textured, dark green to yellowish green foliage with a fernlike quality. Needles are ¼–¾ in. long, grow in two rows. Picturesque large conifer for background, screens, hedges.

T. mertensiana. MOUNTAIN HEMLOCK. Zones A1–A3; 1–7, 14–17. Native to high mountains, from Alaska south through higher Sierra Nevada in California and to northern Idaho, Montana. To 50–90 ft. in the wild but is slow growing, smaller (20–30 ft. tall, half as wide) in gardens. Needles are ½–1 in. long, blue green with a silvery cast; grow all around stems to give branchlets a plump, tufty appearance. Trees at timberline frequently grow in horizontal or twisted fashion. Thrives on cool slopes with highly organic soil. Least adapted to lowland, hot-summer areas. Needs partial shade in Zone 14. Somewhat resistant to hemlock woolly aphid. Good for large rock gardens, containers, bonsai.

TUBEROSE. See POLIANTHES tuberosa

TULBAGHIA

Amaryllidaceae

PERENNIALS FROM RHIZOMES

ZONES 13–24; H1, H2

FULL SUN

REGULAR WATER

Tulbaghia violacea

From South Africa. Dense clumps of straight, narrow, evergreen leaves send up slim, 1–2-ft. stems topped by clusters of small, trumpet-shaped, pinkish lavender flowers. Suffer frost damage at 20 to 25°F/–7 to –4°C but recover quickly. Start plants from containers or divisions at any time (though early spring or early fall is best in hot-summer areas). Give well-drained, organically enriched soil. Divide clumps to increase plantings.

T. simmleri (T. fragrans). Gray-green, 1-in.-wide leaves. Lightly fragrant flowers in clusters of 20–30 in winter or early spring. Good cut flower. 'Alba' has white blossoms.

T. violacea. SOCIETY GARLIC. Bluish green, very narrow leaves. Clusters of 8–20 flowers; bloom is heaviest in spring and summer. Leaves and flower stems have onion or garlic odor if cut or crushed; leaves can be used in cooking. 'Variegata' has a creamy stripe down the middle of each leaf; in 'Silver Lace', each leaf is edged in white. Leaves of 'Tricolor' have white edges with a pinkish cast that intensifies in cool weather.

TULIPA

TULIP

Liliaceae

PERENNIALS FROM BULBS

ZONES 1–24, EXCEPT AS NOTED

FULL SUN DURING BLOOM, PART SHADE AFTER IN HOT CLIMATES

REGULAR WATER DURING GROWTH AND BLOOM

Darwin Hybrid Tulip

Tulips vary considerably. Some are stately and formal, others dainty and whimsical; a few look decidedly bizarre. Bloom comes at some time from March to May, depending on type.

Use larger tulips in colonies or masses, in company with low, spring-blooming plants. Use smaller, shorter types for close-up viewing—in rock gardens, near paths, in raised beds, in patio insets. Tulips are superb container plants; unusual kinds such as Rembrandt and Parrot are especially suited to this use.

Nearly all hybrid tulips and most species (wild) tulips need an extended period of winter cold for best performance. In mild climates, provide the necessary chill by refrigerating bulbs for 6 weeks (not near ripening fruit) before planting; then treat the plants as annuals.

Even in cold-winter regions, there's no guarantee of consistent performance after the first year. Tulip bulbs form offsets that take a few years to reach blooming size, but as offsets mature, they draw energy from the mother bulb. The result is a decline in flowering. For this reason, most tulips are often treated as short-lived perennials in cold climates, though you can encourage repeat flowering by fertilizing with nitrogen before bloom and by letting foliage wither before removing it after bloom.

Some species tulips are exceptions to the above; they give good repeat bloom even where winters are mild.

Plant as described in care box (facing page). To protect tulips from gophers and other burrowing animals, plant in baskets of ¼-in. wire mesh. Thwart ground squirrels and other animals who like to dig up bulbs by securing chicken wire over new plantings. Aphids are another pest.

If tulips do persist from year to year, they will eventually need separating. Dig and divide clumps in late summer; replant at best time for your climate. Species tulips can be left undisturbed for many years.

Tulips have been classified into many divisions, defined mainly by flower type. For the convenience of gardeners, we have arranged the divisions into additional groupings; the first three groupings are by bloom season, while the fourth contains species and their hybrids.

EARLY TULIPS

Single Early tulips. Single flowers on 10–16-in. stems. Colors include white, yellow, salmon, pink, red, dark purple. Popular for forcing and growing indoors in pots. Not adapted to mild-winter areas.

Double Early tulips. Peonylike double flowers, often measuring 4 in. across, on 6–12-in. stems. Same color range as Single Early tulips. Effective massed in borders. In rainy areas, mulch around plants or surround with ground cover to keep mud from splashing the short-stemmed flowers.

MIDSEASON TULIPS

Triumph tulips. Single flowers on sturdy stems to 20 in. tall. Wide range of solid colors, including red, white, and yellow, and bicolors.

Darwin hybrids. Spectacular group with brightly colored flowers on 24–28-in. stems. Most are in scarlet-orange to red range; some have contrasting eyes or penciling. Some reach 7 in. across. Pink, yellow, and white varieties exist.

LATE TULIPS

Single Late. Graceful plants with large, oval or egg-shaped blooms on 1½–3-ft. stems. Clear, beautiful colors: white, yellow, orange, pink, red, mauve, lilac, purple, maroon. May have contrasting margins. Includes old Darwin and Cottage groups.

Lily-flowered tulips. Graceful, lilylike flowers with recurved, pointed segments; come in white and shades of yellow, pink, red, and magenta, often with contrasting markings. Stems 20–26 in. high.

Fringed tulips. Flowers have finely fringed edges. Colors include white, yellow, pink, red, and violet; fringing is often in a different color than rest of flower. Stems 16–24 in. high

Viridiflora tulips. Flowers edged in green or colored in blends of green with other hues—white, yellow, rose, red, buff. Stems 10–20 in. high.

Rembrandt tulips. Streaks and variegation on the original Rembrandts were caused by a transmittable virus; these infected bulbs can no longer be imported and should not be planted. Tulips now sold as Rembrandts have patterning of genetic, not viral, origin. The division now includes other variegated types and the old Bizarre and Bybloem groups.

Parrot tulips. Large, long, deeply fringed and ruffled flowers atop 16–20-in. stems are striped, feathered, and flamed in various colors, including green. They once had weak, floppy stems, but modern types are stouter.

Double Late tulips. Often called peony-flowered tulips, these have very large (to 5-in.-wide), heavy-textured double blossoms on 14–20-in. stems. Colors include orange, rose, yellow, and white.

SPECIES TULIPS

Kaufmanniana tulips. Often called waterlily tulip, *T. kaufmanniana* is a very early bloomer with 3-in., creamy yellow flowers (marked red on petal backs) with dark yellow centers; the flowers open flat in sun. Stems 6–8 in. high. Hybrids come in various colors, usually with flower centers in a contrasting color; many have mottled leaves like Greigii tulips.

Fosteriana tulips. Early-blooming *T. fosteriana* has the largest flowers—to 8 in. wide—of any tulip. The huge red blossoms appear atop 8–10-in. stems. Hybrids include varieties with flowers in red, orange, yellow, pink, and white. The 16-in.-high 'Red Emperor' ('Mme Lefeber') has fiery red flowers.

Greigii tulips. Midseason-blooming *T. greigii* has big (6-in.) flowers borne on 10-in. stems; leaves are heavily spotted and streaked with brown. Hybrids have flowers in white, pink, orange, red; many feature several colors in a single blossom.

Other species. Sold mainly by bulb specialists. Most are native to western and central Asia. They tend to be simpler looking than large hybrid tulips, with a wildflower charm. Generally best in rock gardens or wild gardens, where plantings can remain undisturbed for many years; plant 4 in. apart. Also good in pots. Species that will persist from year to year in mild-winter areas are noted.

T. acuminata. Flowers have long, twisted, spidery segments of red and yellow on 1½-ft.-tall stems. Late.

WHAT TULIPS NEED

CLIMATE: Most tulips do best in areas with a distinct winter chill, but even there they may be short lived. Species tulips are more likely to persist year after year; some will even succeed where winters are mild.

EXPOSURE: Tulips need sunshine at least while in bloom; they will lean toward the source of light if planting area is partly shaded. It's fine to plant under deciduous trees if the trees won't leaf out until after bloom is finished (this is a good practice in hot-summer areas).

SOIL: Rich, sandy soil is ideal, though tulips will grow in any good, fast-draining soil. They perform poorly if planted in soil where other tulips were recently growing; choose a new site or dig out soil to the requisite planting depth and replace it with fresh soil from elsewhere in the garden.

PROPER PLANTING: Set bulbs three times as deep as they are wide (a little shallower in heavy soils). Space 4–8 in. apart, depending on eventual size of plant. Where temperatures regularly dip below 32°F/0°C, plant in October or November, after soil has cooled. In warmer regions, plant in December or January.

Parrot Tulip 'Apricot Parrot'

T. bakeri. Zones 2–24. Similar to and often listed as *T. saxatilis*. Lilac to purple flowers with a yellow base open to a wide, flat star; they are borne in clusters of three or four on stems to 1 ft. high. 'Lilac Wonder', to 6–7 in. high, has rosy purple flowers with a large, circular lemon yellow base. Midseason. Good in mild-winter areas.

T. batalinii. Soft yellow flowers on 6–10-in. stems. Very narrow leaves. 'Yellow Jewel' has lemon yellow blossoms tinged with rose. Midseason.

T. clusiana. LADY or CANDY TULIP. Slender flowers on 9-in. stems are rosy red outside, white inside. Blossoms of 6-in.-high *T. c. chrysantha (T. stellata chrysantha)* are star shaped when fully open; they have rose carmine outer segments (shading to buff at base), bright yellow inner segments. *T. clusiana* and *T. c. chrysantha* both bloom in midseason, make good permanent tulips in mild-winter areas.

T. eichleri. Foot-tall stems bear shining scarlet flowers with jet black centers outlined in yellow. Early.

T. humilis (T. pulchella). One to three pale pink or purplish pink flowers with a yellow center atop each 4–6-in. stem. Early. 'Violacea' has deep violet flowers, usually with a yellow base.

T. praestans. Up to six orange-red flowers on each 2-ft. stem. Midseason. 'Fusilier' is an improved selection growing 10–14 in. high.

T. pulchella. See T. humilis

T. saxatilis. Zones 2–24. Fragrant, yellow-based pale lilac flowers open nearly flat, are carried one to three to each 1-ft. stem. Early bloom. Good in mild-winter areas.

T. stellata chrysantha. See T. clusiana chrysantha

T. sylvestris. Yellow, 2-in. flowers, one or two to each 1-ft. stem. Late. Good in mild-winter areas.

T. tarda (T. dasystemon). Zones A1–A3; 1–24. Each 3–5-in. stem has three to six upward-facing, starlike flowers with golden centers, white-tipped segments. Early.

TOP: Fringed Tulips
BOTTOM: *Tulipa kaufmanniana*

TOP: Lily-flowered Tulips
BOTTOM: *Tulipa greigii*

TOP: *Tulipa fosteriana* Hybrids
BOTTOM: Darwin Hybrid Tulip 'Daydream'

TOP: *Tulipa batalinii* 'Yellow Jewel'
BOTTOM: Double Late Tulip 'Angelique'

TOP: *Tulipa tarda*
BOTTOM: Parrot Tulip 'Orange Parrot'

TULIP TREE. See LIRIODENDRON, MAGNOLIA × soulangeana

TUPELO. See NYSSA sylvatica

TURNIP and RUTABAGA

Turnip

Brassicaceae (Cruciferae)

BIENNIALS GROWN AS ANNUALS

ALL ZONES

FULL SUN

REGULAR WATER

These Mediterranean natives are cabbage relatives and, like cabbage, belong to the genus *Brassica.* Turnips are best known for roots, though foliage is also edible (some varieties are grown for leaves only). Roots come in various colors (white, white with purple on upper part, creamy yellow) and shapes (globe, flattened globe). Rutabaga is a tasty turnip relative with large yellowish roots; its leaves are palatable only when very young. Turnip roots grow fast and should be harvested and used as soon as they are big enough to eat. Rutabaga is a late-maturing crop that stores well in the ground; its flavor improves with light frost.

Grow turnip and rutabaga in rich, loose, well-drained soil. In cold-winter areas, plant in early spring (for early summer harvest) or in summer (for fall harvest). Where winters are mild, plant in fall for winter crop. Sow seeds 1 in. apart. Thin turnips to 2–6 in. apart for roots, 1–4 in. apart for greens. Thin rutabaga plants to 5–8 in. apart; each one needs ample space for root to reach full weight of 3–5 lbs. Roots of turnip and rutabaga are milder if soil is kept moist, become more pungent under drier conditions. Turnip roots are ready to harvest about 75 days after sowing, rutabaga in 90 to 120 days. Root maggot is a pest of turnip (less likely to infest rutabaga); see Cabbage for control.

TURTLEHEAD. See CHELONE lyonii

TWINBERRY. See MITCHELLA repens

TWINFLOWER. See LINNAEA borealis

TWINSPUR. See DIASCIA

UGNI molinae (Myrtus ugni)

Ugni molinae

CHILEAN GUAVA

Myrtaceae

EVERGREEN SHRUB

ZONES 14–24

PARTIAL SHADE IN HOTTEST CLIMATES

REGULAR WATER

South American native grown for foliage, flowers, and fruit. Slow to moderate growth to 3–6 ft. high and wide. Scraggly and open in youth but has a compact, rounded form when mature. Small, oval, leathery leaves are dark green with bronze tints above, whitish beneath; edges are slightly rolled under. Rose-tinted white flowers resembling little bottlebrushes appear in late spring, early summer. These are followed by purplish or reddish, ½-in., pleasant-tasting fruit that smells like apples and can be eaten fresh or used in jams and jellies. Tidy, restrained plant for patios, terraces, near walks and paths. Give neutral to acid soil. For related plants that are grown primarily for fruit, see Feijoa and Guava.

Ulmaceae. The elm family contains trees and shrubs, usually deciduous, with inconspicuous flowers and fruit that may be nutlike, single-seeded and fleshy, or winged. Elm *(Ulmus),* hackberry *(Celtis),* and *Zelkova* are representative.

ULMUS

Ulmus parvifolia

ELM

Ulmaceae

DECIDUOUS OR SEMIEVERGREEN TREES

ZONES VARY BY SPECIES

FULL SUN

REGULAR WATER

Once highly prized shade trees, elms have fallen on hard times. Dutch elm disease (spread by a bark beetle) has killed millions of American elms throughout North America and can attack most other elm species. Many of the larger elms are appealing fare for various beetles, leafhoppers, aphids, and scale, making them time consuming to care for, messy, or both. Elms have other problems not related to pests. They have aggressive, shallow root systems, so you'll have trouble growing other plants beneath them. Many types produce suckers; branch crotches are often narrow, splitting easily in storms. Still, elms are widely planted and researchers continue to devote much effort to finding disease-resistant varieties. All elms are fairly soil tolerant, have handsome oval leaves. Poor yellow fall color, except as noted.

U. americana. AMERICAN ELM. Deciduous. Zones 1–11, 14–21. Native to eastern North America. This majestic, arching tree once graced lawns and streets throughout its range, but it has been decimated by Dutch elm disease. Fast growth to 100 ft. or taller with nearly equal—sometimes greater—spread. Main branches upright, outer ones pendulous. Rough surfaced, 3–6-in.-long, toothed dark green leaves; great variation in shade of yellow fall color. Leafs out very late where winters are mild. Pale green, papery seeds make a mess in spring. 'Liberty' has been promoted as disease resistant—but because plants are produced by seed, performance is variable. Most trees show resistance only when young.

U. glabra. SCOTCH ELM. Deciduous. Zones 2–11, 14–21. Native to Europe. Fairly upright habit to 120 ft. tall, 80 ft. wide. Sharply toothed, rough-surfaced, 3–6-in.-long leaves on very short stalks. Rarely planted now, but old trees are sometimes seen. 'Camperdownii', Camperdown elm, generally 10–20 ft. tall and wide, has weeping branches that reach to ground, making a tent of shade.

U. hybrids. Many institutions have been carrying on breeding experiments to produce trees resistant to Dutch elm disease. Deciduous 'Homestead', a cross of *U. pumila* with two elm hybrids, grows to 55 ft. tall, 35 ft. wide, has pyramidal to oval form. 'Frontier', a deciduous hybrid between *U. parvifolia* and another elm, reaches 40 ft. tall, 30 ft. wide; its glossy green leaves turn reddish purple in fall. Both varieties grow in Zones 2–9, 14–21.

U. parvifolia. CHINESE ELM, CHINESE EVERGREEN ELM. Semievergreen or deciduous, according to winter temperatures and individual tree's heredity. Zones 3–24. From China, Korea, Japan. Fast growth to 40–60 ft. tall, 50–70 ft. wide; often reaches 30 ft. in 5 years. Form is extremely variable, but trees are generally spreading, with long, arching, eventually weeping branchlets. On older trees, bark of trunk sheds in patches (somewhat like bark of sycamore, *Platanus*), often creating beautiful mottling. Leathery dark green, ¾–2½-in.-long, evenly toothed leaves. Round fruit produced in fall. Patio tree, sun screen, or (with careful pruning) street tree. Rub or cut out small branches along trunk for first few years; shorten overlong branches or strongly weeping branches to strengthen scaffolding. Older trees may need thinning to lessen chance of storm damage. Subject to Texas root rot in desert but otherwise little bothered by pests or diseases.

Forms that hold their leaves are often sold as 'Sempervirens', but that is not a true variety. Two commonly offered, more or less evergreen varieties are 'Brea', with larger leaves and more upright habit than the species; and 'Drake', with smaller leaves, weeping habit. A more reliably evergreen variety is round-headed 'True Green', with small, deep green leaves. Newer selections include 'Allee' ('Emer II'), vase-shaped tree to 70 ft. tall, 60 ft. wide; 'Athena' ('Emer I'), moderately fast grower to 35 ft. tall, 50 ft. wide; and 'Dynasty', to 40 ft. by 40 ft., vaselike when young, later rounded. Novelty selections include 'Corticosa', with thick, corky bark; it can reach tree size but usually doesn't get the chance—it's a favorite for bonsai.

Dwarf varieties suitable for bonsai include 'Frosty', 3-ft. shrub with leaves edged in tiny white teeth; 'Hokkaido', tiny-leafed, very slow-growing but shapely miniature tree (1 ft. tall in 20 years); and 'Seiju', a sport of 'Hokkaido' with larger leaves and corky bark. A note of caution: A less desirable species, *U. pumila* (Siberian elm) is sometimes sold as Chinese elm.

U. pumila. SIBERIAN ELM. Deciduous. Zones A1–A3; 1–11, 14–21; used chiefly in Zones A1–A3, 1, 2, 10, 11, where climate limits tree choices. From Russia, northern China. To 50 ft. tall, 40 ft. wide. Smooth dark green leaves are $\frac{3}{4}$–2 in. long. Resists Dutch elm disease and endures cold, heat, aridity, and poor soil—but has brittle wood and weak crotches and is not a desirable tree. Possibly useful in holding soil against erosion; fast growth also makes it suitable for windbreak or shelterbelt. Papery, winged seeds disperse seedlings over wide area.

U. wilsoniana 'Prospector'. Zones 3–9, 14–21. Fairly new variety from western China; similar in shape to *U. americana.* Likely ultimate size is 40 ft. tall, 30 ft. wide. Leaves are orange red when new, mature to deep shiny green, turn yellow in fall. Resistant to Dutch elm disease and elm leaf beetles.

UMBELLULARIA californica

CALIFORNIA LAUREL, CALIFORNIA BAY, OREGON MYRTLE, PEPPERWOOD

Lauraceae

EVERGREEN TREE

ZONES 4–9, 14–24

SUN OR SHADE

LITTLE TO REGULAR WATER

Umbellularia californica

Native to southwestern Oregon, California Coast Ranges, lower elevations of Sierra Nevada. In the wild, form varies. On windy hillsides near coast, it is a huge, gumdrop-shaped shrub; in forests, it's a tree to 75 ft. tall, over 100 ft. wide. In gardens, it tends to grow slowly (about 1 ft. a year) to 20–25 ft. high and wide. Lance-shaped, 2–5-in.-long leaves are medium to deep yellow green and glossy above, dull light green beneath. Leaves can be substituted for sweet bay *(Laurus nobilis)* in cooking, but they have a more pungent flavor. Clusters of tiny yellowish flowers give plant a yellowish cast in spring. Blossoms are followed by olivelike, purplish, inedible fruit.

Grows best and fastest in deep soil with regular water but tolerates many other conditions, including aridity. Will grow in deep shade and ultimately get big enough to become shade maker itself (casts very dense shade unless thinned). Though often afflicted with sooty mold resulting from aphid or scale infestation, it is nonetheless useful for screen, background planting, tall hedge. Heavy drop of yellow to tan leaves in autumn.

UMBRELLA PINE. See SCIADOPITYS verticillata

UMBRELLA PLANT. See CYPERUS alternifolius

UMBRELLA TREE, QUEENSLAND. See SCHEFFLERA actinophylla

VACCINIUM

Ericaceae

EVERGREEN OR DECIDUOUS SHRUBS

ZONES VARY BY SPECIES

EXPOSURE NEEDS VARY BY SPECIES

WATER NEEDS VARY BY SPECIES

Vaccinium ovatum

Excellent ornamental shrubs. Clusters of bell-shaped flowers in spring; colorful, edible berries that attract birds. Provide organically enriched, acid soil. Good for woodland gardens. For species grown largely for fruit, see Blueberry.

V. macrocarpon. CRANBERRY. Evergreen. Zones 1–6, 17. Native to northeastern U.S., eastern Canada. To 2–6 in. high, spreading and rooting from stems to indefinite width. Narrow, dark green, $\frac{1}{2}$–$\frac{3}{4}$-in. leaves turn coppery or purplish in winter. Tiny pinkish flowers; tart red berries in autumn. Commercial growers raise this plant in bogs—beds that can be flooded to control weeds and pests and make harvesting easier. Gardeners can use cranberry as an attractive small-scale ground cover in full sun (space plants 2 ft. apart). Ample water.

V. ovatum. EVERGREEN HUCKLEBERRY. Zones 4–7, 14–17, 22–24. Native to Pacific coastal region, from Santa Barbara area of Southern California north to British Columbia. Erect growth to 2–3 ft. high and wide in sun, 8–10 ft. tall and broad in shade. Leathery, lustrous dark green leaves to 1$\frac{1}{4}$ in. long; bronzy or reddish when new. White or pinkish flowers are followed by black berries good in pies, jams, jellies, syrups. Can be trimmed as a hedge or grown in containers. Cut branches are popular for arrangements. Sun or shade. Moderate to regular water.

V. parvifolium. RED HUCKLEBERRY. Deciduous. Zones A3; 2–7, 14–17. Native to Sierra Nevada, Coast Ranges from Northern California to Alaska. Slow-growing plant, eventually reaching 4–12 ft. (rarely 18 ft.) tall, 6 ft. wide. Thin green branches with spreading or cascading habit provide an intricate winter silhouette. Oval, thin-textured light green leaves are $\frac{1}{2}$–$\frac{3}{4}$ in. long. Greenish or whitish flowers are good in arrangements. Showy bright red berries can be used in jams, jellies, pies. Partial or full shade. Regular water.

V. vitis-idaea. COWBERRY, FOXBERRY. Evergreen. Zones 2–7, 14–17, except as noted. Native to Europe. Slow growth to 1 ft. high; spreads widely by rhizomes if grown in highly organic or thickly mulched soil. Glossy dark green leaves to 1 in. long; new growth often tinged bright red or orange. White or pinkish flowers followed by sour red berries something like tiny cranberries; these are valued for preserves, syrups. Handsome little plant for informal edging around larger plantings; good small-scale ground cover (space plants 2–3 ft. apart). Best without potassium fertilizer. Regular to ample water. Prefers partial or full shade, but if given ample water will take full sun in cool-summer areas. European varieties grown for fruit production are sometimes seen. 'Erntdank' produces one crop in spring, another in summer. 'Koralle' also bears two crops; its berries are darker red and somewhat larger than those of the species, and the later crop (if not harvested) can remain on the plant all winter.

V. v. minus. LINGONBERRY. Zones A1–A3; 1–7, 14–17. Cold-hardier form from arctic North America. Has smaller leaves (to $\frac{1}{2}$ in.), is attractive in rock gardens, containers.

Valerianaceae. The valerian family of perennial herbs (rarely shrubs) has clustered small flowers. In addition to *Valeriana,* members include Jupiter's beard *(Centranthus)* and *Patrinia.*

VALERIANA officinalis

VALERIAN, GARDEN HELIOTROPE

Valerianaceae

PERENNIAL

ZONES 1–24

FULL SUN OR PARTIAL SHADE

REGULAR WATER

Valeriana officinalis

From Europe and western Asia. To 5 ft. tall in bloom, spreading to 4 ft. wide. Most of the foliage remains fairly close to ground. Light green leaves, each with eight to ten pairs of narrow, jagged-edged leaflets. Tall, straight flowering stems carry tiny, fragrant pink blossoms in rounded clusters at stem ends in summer; useful for cut flowers. White- and red-flowered forms exist. Strong-smelling roots are widely used in herbal preparations said to have sedative qualities. Roots also attract cats. Start new plants from seed or divisions. Grow in mixed herb or flower borders, but be aware that it can become invasive; don't let it crowd other plants.

VALLOTA speciosa. See CYRTANTHUS elatus

V

VANCOUVERIA

Berberidaceae

PERENNIALS

ZONES VARY BY SPECIES

PARTIAL SHADE

MODERATE TO REGULAR WATER

Vancouveria planipetala

Closely related to *Epimedium* and likewise used as ground covers in shady spots. Wiry leafstalks grow directly from creeping underground stems; leaves have numerous broad leaflets that resemble small ivy *(Hedera)* leaves. Threadlike flower stalks rise above foliage in late spring or early summer, bearing drooping clusters of small blossoms. Petals and sepals are sharply reflexed, giving flowers a windswept look. Plants spread slowly from ever-enlarging mat of roots, forming sizable patches in time. Set plants about 1½ ft. apart. Need cool, moist, acid conditions.

V. chrysantha. Zones 5, 6, 14–17. Native to mountains of southwestern Oregon and extreme northwestern California. To 16 in. high, with bronzy gray-green, ½-in.-long, evergreen leaflets and yellow, ½-in. flowers.

V. hexandra. Zones 4–7, 14–17, 19–24. Native to coastal forests from Northern California to Washington. To 1 ft. high, with light green, 2½-in. leaflets and white, ½-in. flowers. Dies back in winter.

V. planipetala (V. parviflora). INSIDE-OUT FLOWER. Zones 4–7, 14–17. Native to coastal areas of California and southwestern Oregon. To 2 ft. tall, with light to medium green, 1½-in., shallowly lobed leaflets. White flowers are tiny—only about ⅛ in. wide—but are carried in clusters of 25–50. May die back in colder part of range.

VANDA

Orchidaceae

EPIPHYTIC ORCHIDS

ZONE H2; OR INDOORS

FILTERED SUNLIGHT; BRIGHT INDIRECT LIGHT

REGULAR WATER

Vanda

About 60 species of warm-growing orchids native from India to New Guinea. In the wild, they grow on trees or rock outcroppings. They produce stout stems without pseudobulbs. Stems may be short or tall; tall stems are either self-supporting or climbing. Leaves are arranged in two rows, enveloping stem at base; showy flowers are produced in clusters at leaf joints. Hybrid 'Miss Joaquim' *(V. teres × V. hookeriana)* is widely grown for its attractive lavender blooms, which are popular in Hawaii for orchid leis. It has self-supporting stems, may reach 3–4 ft. or taller.

Vandas are generally too demanding to make good houseplants; they do better in a greenhouse. Best grown on a coarse medium that provides complete drainage (tree fern fiber, for example). See also Orchidaceae.

VAUQUELINIA

Rosaceae

EVERGREEN SHRUBS OR TREES

ZONES 10–13

FULL SUN OR PARTIAL SHADE

LITTLE TO MODERATE WATER

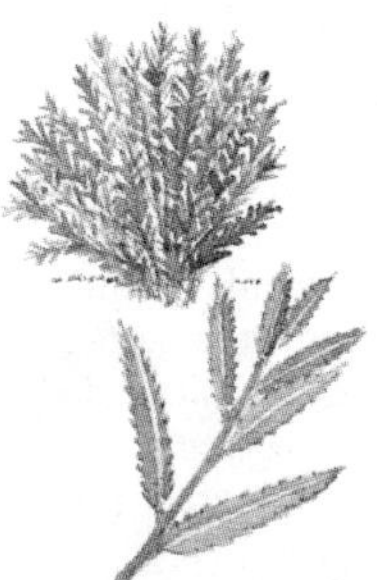

Vauquelinia californica

Rather open-growing plants to 20 ft. tall, 15 ft. wide, with upright, sometimes twisted branches. Somewhat reminiscent of oleander *(Nerium)* in habit. Narrow, leathery, typically tooth-edged leaves are dark green above, grayish beneath. Small white flowers in 2–3-in. clusters decorate branch tips in spring. Blossoms are followed by woody seed capsules that last through fall and winter. Grow as large shrubs or train as single- or multitrunked trees. Very drought tolerant but look best with some water during hot months.

V. californica. ARIZONA ROSEWOOD. Native to southern Arizona, Baja California, Mexico. Leaves to 4 in. long.

V. corymbosa angustifolia. SLIMLEAF VAUQUELINIA. Native to western Texas, northern Mexico. Has longer (6-in.), usually narrower leaves and showier flower clusters than *V. californica.* Often sold as *V. corymbosa.*

VELTHEIMIA bracteata

Liliaceae

PERENNIAL FROM BULB

ZONES 13, 16–24; OR INDOORS

PARTIAL SHADE; BRIGHT INDIRECT LIGHT

REGULAR WATER DURING GROWTH AND BLOOM

Veltheimia bracteata

Handsome foliage is reason enough to grow this South African native. Each bulb produces a fountainlike rosette of wavy-edged, glossy green leaves to 1 ft. long, 3 in. wide. In winter or early spring, brown-mottled flower stems to about 1 ft. tall are topped by elongated clusters of tubular, drooping, pinkish purple flowers tipped in green. Leaves turn yellow and die back in late spring; new growth resumes in fall. Most plants sold as *V. capensis* are actually *V. bracteata;* the true *V. capensis* has nonglossy blue-green leaves and green-tipped, pale pink flowers.

In virtually frostless areas, veltheimia can be grown in the ground, but even there it is usually grown in pots. For each bulb, use a pot large enough to allow about 3 in. between all sides of bulb and container edges. Plant in fall, in fast-draining soil, set top of bulb neck just above soil surface. Fertilize every 2 weeks throughout growing season. Keep soil dry during summer dormancy. Can remain outdoors where temperatures stay above 25°F/–4°C; where light frosts are possible, give overhead protection.

VELVET GROUNDSEL. See SENECIO petasitis

VERBASCUM

MULLEIN

Scrophulariaceae

BIENNIALS AND PERENNIALS

ZONES VARY BY SPECIES

FULL SUN

MODERATE WATER

Verbascum bombyciferum 'Arctic Summer'

Large group of rosette-forming, summer-blooming plants that send up spikes closely set with nearly flat, five-petaled, circular flowers about an inch across. Both foliage and stems are often covered in woolly hairs. Taller mulleins make striking vertical accents. Grow all in well-drained soil. Cut off spent flowers to encourage a second round of blooming. Mulleins self-sow freely—and some are downright weedy, such as the attractive roadside weed *V. thapsus.*

V. blattaria. MOTH MULLEIN. Biennial. Zones 1–11, 14–24. Native from Europe to central Asia. To 6 ft. tall, 2 ft. wide, with smooth-textured, dark green, cut or toothed leaves to 10 in. long. Yellow flowers. 'Rose Form' has rose pink flowers opening from red buds.

V. bombyciferum 'Arctic Summer'. Biennial. Zones 2–11, 14–24. Selection of a species native to Turkey. To 6 ft. tall, 2 ft. wide, with furry gray-green leaves to 1½ ft. long. Yellow flowers on powdery white stems.

V. chaixii. Perennial. Zones 2–11, 14–24. From Europe. To 3 ft. tall and 2 ft. wide, with hairy green leaves to 6 in. long. Red-eyed, pale yellow flowers in narrow, often branching spikes. 'Album' has white flowers with purple centers.

V. dumulosum. Perennial. Zones 7–9, 14–24. Dwarf to 1 ft. high, 1½ ft. wide, with velvety white leaves. Short, branching spikes of lemon yellow blossoms with purple centers. Hybrid 'Letitia' has a longer summer bloom season than the species.

V. hybrids. Zones 3–10, 14–24. Many hybrids are obtainable, either as blends or in single colors. Most must be grown from seed.

'Banana Custard'. Biennial. To 5–6 ft. tall, 2 ft. wide. Bright yellow flowers.

Benary Hybrids, Cotswold Hybrids. Perennials. These resemble *V. phoeniceum* but come in white, cream, pink, and purple. Named varieties are sometimes seen; these include 'Helen Johnson' (peach pink) and 'Pink Domino' (bright pink).

'Copper Rose'. Perennial. To 4–6 ft. high, 2 ft. wide, with flowers in buff, apricot, rose, or tan. Bloom first year from seed sown in late winter, earliest spring.

V. olympicum. Perennial. Zones 3–10, 14–24. From Greece. To 5 ft. high, 3 ft. wide, with soft, downy white leaves to over 2 ft. long. Bright yellow flowers; many flowering stems.

V. phoeniceum. PURPLE MULLEIN. Perennial. Zones 1–10, 14–24. To 2–4 ft. high, 1½ ft. wide. Dark green leaves to 6 in. long are smooth on top, hairy beneath. Slender spikes of purple flowers.

VERBENA

Verbenaceae

PERENNIALS, SOME GROWN AS ANNUALS

ZONES VARY BY SPECIES

FULL SUN

WATER NEEDS VARY BY SPECIES

Verbena peruviana hybrid

Bear clusters of small, tubular, five-petaled flowers, usually in summer. Most are fast-growing ground covers, good in parking strips, along driveways, on dry banks; also attractive in wall crevices, hanging baskets. Best in hot weather. Need good air circulation (to avoid mildew) and well-drained soil, especially in winter.

V. bipinnatifida. Perennial. Zones 1–24. Native from western Great Plains to Mexico. To 8–16 in. high, 1½ ft. or wider. Finely divided leaves and blue flowers. Self-sows. Little water.

V. bonariensis. Perennial in Zones 8–24; annual in colder climates. Native to South America; naturalized in California. Border plant to 3–6 ft. tall, 1½–3 ft. wide, with airy, branching stems carrying purple flowers. Leaves are mostly basal. Plant's see-through quality makes it suited for foreground as well as back of border. Self-sows freely. Little water.

V. gooddingii. Short-lived perennial. Zones 7–24. Native to Southwest deserts. To 1½–2 ft. tall, 3–4 ft. wide, with small, deeply cut leaves. Pinkish lavender flowers at ends of short spikes. Blooms first summer from seed sown in spring. Can reseed where moisture is present. Little to moderate water.

V. 'Homestead Purple'. Perennial in Zones 2–24; often treated as annual. To 1–2 ft. high, 2–3 ft. wide, with dark green leaves and deep purple flowers. Resistant to mildew. Regular water.

V. × hybrida (V. × hortensis). GARDEN VERBENA. Short-lived perennial in Zones 8–24, H1, H2; often treated as annual in all zones. Many-branched plant 6–12 in. high, 1½–3 ft. wide. Oblong, 2–4-in., bright green or gray-green leaves with toothed margins. Flowers in flat, compact clusters to 3 in. wide. Colors include white, pink, bright red, purple, blue, and combinations. Superior strains include Romance (6 in.) and Showtime (10 in.). Deep rose pink 'Showtime Trinidad' can withstand light frosts. 'Coral Red' grows only a few inches high, bears coral to rosy red flowers. 'Peaches 'N Cream' has blooms in a combination of pastel pink and cream. If growing these plants as perennials, prune severely before spring growth begins. Good ground covers in Zones 12, 13. Moderate water.

V. lilacina. CEDROS ISLAND VERBENA. Perennial. Zones 12–24. Native to Baja California. To 1 ft. high, 3 ft. or wider. Light green, deeply cut leaves. Lilac-colored flowers bloom from spring to fall (nearly all year, in mildest areas). Useful ground cover for hot, dry sites. 'De La Mina' forms a 3-ft. mound, has darker purple flowers. Little to moderate water.

V. peruviana (V. chamaedrifolia). Perennial in Zones 8–24; usually treated as annual in all zones. Native to South America. Forms a flat mat that spreads rapidly by aboveground runners. Set out plants 2 ft. apart for a solid cover in one season. Neat, small, closely set dark green leaves. Flat-topped clusters of scarlet-and-white flowers on slender stems cover foliage. Hybrids aren't as flat, spread more slowly, have slightly larger leaves and stouter stems, are available in several colors. They include many purplish varieties, a fine pure white, 'Starfire' (red), and these in pink and rose tones: 'Appleblossom', 'Cherry Pink', 'Little Pinkie', 'Princess Gloria', 'Raspberry Rose', 'St. Paul'. Especially popular in Southern California and the desert. Moderate water.

V. pulchella gracilior (V. tenuisecta). MOSS VERBENA. Perennial in Zones 7–9, 14–24; annual in colder climates. From South America. To 6–12 in. high and 2–5 ft. wide, with finely cut dark green leaves. Blue, purple, or violet flowers. 'Alba' is a white-flowered form. Moderate water.

V. rigida. (V. venosa). Perennial in Zones 3–24; can be grown as annual (blooms in 4 months from seed). Native to South America. To 1–2 ft. high, 3–4 ft. wide. Rough, strongly toothed dark green leaves to 2–4 in. long. Lilac to purple-blue flowers in cylindrical clusters on tall, upright stems in summer and fall. Useful in low-maintenance gardens. Moderate to regular water. 'Flame', to just 4 in. high, is a cutting-grown selection with bright scarlet flowers.

V. 'Sissinghurst'. Perennial. Zones 3–24. To a few inches high, 4 ft. wide. Dark green, finely cut leaves. Bright red flowers. Regular water.

V. stricta. Perennial. Zones 2–24. Native from Massachusetts to Montana, south to Mexico. Upright growth to 3 ft. tall, 1½ ft. or wider. Hairy stems bear narrow to rounded, tooth-edged leaves to 4 in. long; medium green above, whitish beneath. Flower stems are also densely hairy, bear deep lavender or purple flowers. Regular water.

V. Tapien hybrids. Perennials in Zones 4–9, 12–24, H1, H2; annuals anywhere. Prostrate plants to 4 in. high, 1–1½ ft. wide, with finely cut dark green leaves. Wide range of colors, including pink, lavender, pale blue, deep purple, red. Resistant to mildew. Regular water.

V. Temari hybrids. Perennials in Zones 4–9, 12–24, H1, H2; annuals anywhere. Low, spreading plants to 3 in. high, 2½ ft. wide. Broad dark green leaves. Bright pink, burgundy, or violet flowers. Regular water.

VERBENA, LEMON. See ALOYSIA triphylla

Verbenaceae. The immense verbena family contains annuals, perennials, shrubs, and a few trees and vines. Leaves are usually opposite or in whorls, flowers in spikes or spikelike clusters. Fruits may be berries or nutlets. *Clerodendrum, Lantana, Verbena,* and chaste tree *(Vitex)* are examples.

VERONICA

SPEEDWELL

Scrophulariaceae

PERENNIALS

ZONES VARY BY SPECIES

FULL SUN, EXCEPT AS NOTED

WATER NEEDS VARY BY SPECIES

Veronica 'Sunny Border Blue'

Handsome plants ranging from less than an inch tall to 2 ft. in height. Masses of small (¼–½-in.-wide) flowers in white, rose, pink, or pale to deep blue make an effective display. Use in borders and rock gardens. Prostrate kinds are good between stepping-stones, as bulb covers. Named varieties are not easily assigned to a species; authorities differ. For shrubby plants sometimes sold as *Veronica,* see *Hebe.*

V. alpina. Zones 1–7, 14–17. From Europe, Eurasia, North America. Creeping rootstock forms low foliage rosette 4–8 in. high, 1 ft. wide; oval to elliptical leaves to 1 in. long, ½ in. wide. Spikelike clusters of blue flowers in spring or early summer; in warmer parts of range, often reblooms in fall. White-flowered 'Alba' grows 10 in. high. Regular water. ▶

V. austriaca teucrium 'Crater Lake Blue'. Zones 1–9, 14–21. Selection of a species native to Europe. To 12–15 in. high and wide, with tooth-edged, 1½-in.-long leaves. Short spikes of intensely blue flowers in midsummer. Regular water.

V. gentianoides. GENTIAN SPEEDWELL. Zones 1–9, 14–21. From the Caucasus. Creeping rootstock forms a dense mat to 1–2 ft. high and wide. Oblong, glossy dark green, 2–3-in.-long leaves. In spring, foliage is topped by leafy stems carrying 10-in. spikes of ice blue flowers with darker veining. 'Variegata' has leaves marked with white. Regular water.

V. hybrids. The following are among the best varieties. Regular water, except as noted.

'Blue Reflection'. Zones 2–9, 14–21. Forms a gray-green foliage mat to 3 in. high and 1½ ft. wide, covered with blue flowers in midspring. Little to moderate water.

'Goodness Grows'. Zones 1–7, 14–17. To 1 ft. tall and wide. Violet-blue blossoms over long bloom period—from late spring to frost, if old flowers are removed.

'Sunny Border Blue'. Zones 1–9, 14–21. Compact, clump-forming plant to 1½–2 ft. tall, 1 ft. wide, with crinkled dark green leaves. Spires of dark violet-blue flowers appear in late spring or early summer; deadheading prolongs the show until frost.

'Waterperry Blue' ('Waterperry'). Zones 2–9, 14–21. Low, trailing plant to 4–6 in. high and 1½ ft. or more wide; roots as it spreads. Small, rounded, bronze-tinted leaves. Loose clusters of pale blue flowers veined in deeper blue; main bloom in spring, with sporadic flowering throughout summer and fall.

V. liwanensis. Zones 3–9, 14–24. From Turkey. Creeping ground cover to 1–2 in. tall, 1½ ft. wide. In spring, the tiny, waxy deep green leaves are concealed by bright blue flowers. Foliage takes on purplish tints in hot sun. Little to regular water.

V. pectinata. Zones 1–9, 14–24. Western Mediterranean native. Forms prostrate mat of foliage to 3 in. high and 1 ft. wide; spreads by creeping stems that root at joints. Small grayish leaves have scalloped or deeply cut edges. Profuse spring or early summer show of deep blue flowers with white centers; blossoms are borne on 5–6-in. spikes among the leaves. Little to moderate water.

V. peduncularis 'Georgia Blue'. Zones 2–9, 14–24. From Georgia, in the former Soviet Union. Forms a 6–8-in.-high mat that spreads to several feet wide; small dark green leaves turn bronze in cool weather. Profuse, white-eyed cobalt blue flowers in spring, with a few flowers appearing throughout summer and fall. Regular water.

V. prostrata (V. rupestris). Zones 1–9, 14–24. Stems are hairy and tufted. Some are prostrate and form 1–1½-ft.-wide foliage mat; other stems grow erect to 8 in. high and are topped by short clusters of pale blue flowers in late spring or early summer. 'Heavenly Blue' is almost entirely prostrate, with flower stems reaching 6 in. high. 'Mrs. Holt' has pale pink flowers. 'Trehane' has golden yellow leaves, bright blue flowers. Little to moderate water.

Veronica prostrata

V. repens. Zones 3–9, 14–24. Mediterranean native. Flat mat to ½ in. high, 1 ft. or wider. Small, shiny green leaves clothe the prostrate stems, give plant a mossy look. Clusters of tiny lavender to white flowers in spring. Tolerates some shade. Little to moderate water.

V. spicata. Zones A2, A3, 1–9, 14–21, except as noted. From Europe, Asia. Rounded, 1½–2-ft.-wide clump sends up 2-ft.-tall stems clothed in pointed oval, glossy green leaves and topped in summer with spikes of bright blue flowers. Long bloom season if faded flowers are removed. 'Icicle', to 15–18 in. high, has white flower spikes. 'Nana' grows only 6 in. high, bears violet-blue blossoms. 'Red Fox' ('Rotfuchs'), to 15 in. tall and wide, has deep rosy red blooms. Regular water.

V. s. incana (V. incana). SILVER SPEEDWELL. Zones A1–A3; 1–7, 14–17. Furry, silvery white foliage forms a 1–1½-ft.-wide mat. Blooms in summer, producing deep blue blossoms on stems to about 1 ft. high. Little to moderate water.

VIBURNUM

Caprifoliaceae

DECIDUOUS AND EVERGREEN SHRUBS OR TREES

ZONES VARY BY SPECIES

FULL SUN OR PARTIAL SHADE, EXCEPT AS NOTED

REGULAR WATER, EXCEPT AS NOTED

Viburnum opulus 'Roseum'

Large, diverse group of plants with generally oval, often handsome leaves and clusters of typically white, sometimes fragrant flowers. Blossoms are usually followed by single-seeded, often brilliantly colored fruit much appreciated by birds. Many viburnums are grown for their flower display, a few for their showy fruit. Many evergreen types are valuable as foliage plants. Several species (noted below) can be grown as small trees.

V. davidii needs acid soil, but the other viburnums are very soil tolerant. Prune to prevent legginess; some evergreen species can be sheared. Aphids, thrips, spider mites, scale, and root weevils are potential pests. Keep sulfur sprays off foliage.

V. awabukii. SWEET VIBURNUM. Evergreen. Zones 15–24; at some risk of frost damage in Zones 8, 9, 14. From Asia. Often sold as *V. odoratissimum.* Shrub or small tree to 12 ft. tall, 8 ft. wide. Glossy dark green leaves to 8 in. long. Conical, 3–6-in. clusters of fragrant flowers in spring. Pendulous clusters of red fruit that ripens to black. 'Chindo' has smaller leaves, denser habit; makes a good tall hedge or screen.

V. × bodnantense. Deciduous. Zones 4–9, 14–24. To 10 ft. (or more) tall, 6 ft. wide. Dark green, 1½–4-in.-long leaves are deeply veined, turn dark scarlet in fall. Blooms from fall to spring, bearing loose clusters of very fragrant deep pink flowers that age to paler pink. Red fruit is not showy. Best known is 'Dawn' ('Pink Dawn'). Flower buds freeze in coldest Northwest winters.

V. × burkwoodii. Deciduous in coldest areas, nearly evergreen elsewhere. Zones 2–12, 14–24, except as noted. To 6–12 ft. tall, 4–8 ft. wide. Glossy dark green leaves reach 3½ in. long, have white, hairy undersides; turn purplish red in cold weather. Dense, 4-in. clusters of pink buds open to very fragrant flowers in late winter or early spring. Blue-black fruit is not showy. Early growth is straggly, but mature plants are dense. Can be espaliered.

'Chenault' *(V. chenaultii).* Denser, more compact, slightly later blooming, more deciduous in mild climates than the species.

'Mohawk'. Zones 1–12, 14–24. To 7 ft. tall, 5 ft. wide. Red buds are showy long before they open into white flowers. Orange-red fall color.

V. × carlcephalum. FRAGRANT SNOWBALL. Deciduous. Zones 3–11, 14–24. To 6–10 ft. tall and wide. Dull grayish green, 2–3½-in.-long leaves are downy beneath; turn reddish purple in autumn. Long-lasting, waxy, sweetly perfumed spring flowers in dense, 4–5-in. clusters. No fruit. As showy as *V. opulus* 'Roseum' but has the bonus of fragrance.

V. carlesii. KOREAN SPICE VIBURNUM. Deciduous. Zones A3; 2–11, 14–24. From Korea, Japan. Loose, open habit to 4–8 ft. tall and wide. Leaves like those of *V. × carlcephalum;* inconsistent reddish fall color. Pink buds in 2–3-in. clusters open to sweetly fragrant white flowers in spring. Blue-black fruit is not showy. Does best with part shade during hottest months.

V. davidii. Evergreen. Zones 4–9, 14–24. From western China. Compact mound to 3–4 ft. high and wide. Handsome, glossy dark green, deeply veined leaves to 6 in. long. White spring flowers in 3-in. clusters open from dull pinkish red buds; they are not showy but are followed by an arresting show of metallic turquoise blue fruit. Grow with acid-loving plants. Partial shade. Especially good viburnum for Zones 4–6, 17.

V. dentatum. ARROWWOOD. Deciduous. Zones 1–11, 14–21. From eastern and central North America. To 6–10 ft. or taller, equally wide. Cream-colored flowers in late spring are followed by blue-black fruit. Dark green, oval to rounded, 4-in. leaves turn yellow, orange, or deep red in fall.

V. edule. HIGHBUSH CRANBERRY. Deciduous. Zones A1–A3; 1–11. Native to northern Asia and America, including Alaska. Coarse-looking plant to 4–8 ft. tall, 2–4 ft. wide. Roundish dark green leaves are three lobed toward the tip, turn reddish maroon in fall. Inch-wide clusters of flowers in late spring or early summer are followed by small, musty-smelling red fruits that are tart but edible.

V. farreri (V. fragrans). Deciduous. Zones 3–9, 14–24. From northern China. Loose habit to 10 ft. tall, 8 ft. wide. Smooth, heavily veined, 1½–3-in.-long green leaves turn soft russet red to reddish purple in fall. Fragrant white to pink flowers in 2-in. clusters on bare stems at some point between late fall and spring. Blooms survive to 20 to 22°F/–7 to –6°C but freeze at lower temperatures. Bright red fruit. Prune to prevent leggy growth. 'Candidissimum' ('Album') has pure white flowers, pale yellow fruit. 'Nanum' is pink flowered, grows 2½ ft. high, 3 ft. wide.

V. hybrids. These spring-blooming viburnums all have complex ancestry.

'Cayuga'. Deciduous. Zones 2–11, 14–24. To 5 ft. tall and wide. Dark green, 1–3-in.-long leaves. White flowers open from pink buds.

'Chesapeake'. Semievergreen. Zones 3–11, 14–24. To 8 ft. tall, 10 ft. wide, with wavy-edged, glossy dark green leaves. Two-inch clusters of fragrant white flowers open from pink buds; dull red fruit ages to black.

'Conoy'. Evergreen. Zones 3–12, 14–24. Dense growth to 5 ft. high and wide. Lustrous dark green, 2–2½-in. leaves are whitish beneath; take on maroon tinge in cold winters. Slightly fragrant flowers are followed by long-lasting red berries. Tolerates shearing.

'Eskimo'. Semievergreen. Zones 3–12, 14–24. Dense, compact habit to 5 ft. tall and wide. Shiny dark green leaves to 4 in. long; unscented flowers in 3–4-in., snowball-like clusters.

V. japonicum. Evergreen. Zones 5–10, 12, 14–24. From Japan. To 10–15 ft. tall, 8–12 ft. wide; can be trained as a small tree. Leathery, glossy dark green leaves to 6 in. long. Sparse spring show of fragrant flowers in 4-in. clusters. Red fruit is likewise sparse—but very attractive. Best with some shade in hottest climates.

V. ×juddii. Deciduous. Zones 2–9, 14–24. To 4–8 ft. tall, 6–10 ft. wide. More spreading and bushy than *V. carlesii* but similar to it in other respects, including fragrance.

V. lantana. WAYFARING TREE. Deciduous. Zones A3; 2–9, 14–17. From Europe, Asia Minor. Rounded habit to 10–20 ft. tall and wide; can be trained as a small tree. Dark green, 2–5-in.-long leaves turn an inconsistent purplish red in fall. Flat, 3–5-in. clusters of midspring flowers develop into yellow fruits that gradually age to red, then black; all colors are sometimes present at once. 'Mohican' is more compact (to 9 ft. high and wide), with fruit that holds its red color longer.

V. macrocephalum (V. m. 'Sterile'). CHINESE SNOWBALL. Deciduous in coldest areas, nearly evergreen elsewhere. Zones 3–9, 14–24. This species originated in cultivation (not in the wild). Rounded habit to 12–20 ft. tall and wide. Dull green, oval to oblong, 2–4-in.-long leaves. Spectacular big, rounded, 6–8-in. flower clusters bloom in spring (or any time during warm weather); they are composed of sterile flowers that start out lime green, change to white. No fruit. Can be espaliered. *V. m. keteleeri,* wild form from China, has sterile and fertile flowers in lace cap effect; may produce fruit.

V. odoratissimum. See V. awabukii

V. opulus. EUROPEAN CRANBERRY BUSH. Deciduous. Zones A2, A3; 1–9, 14–24. From Europe, North Africa, central Asia. To 8–15 ft. tall and wide, with arching branches. Lobed, maplelike dark green leaves to 2–4 in. long and as wide or wider. Fall foliage color may be yellow, bright red, or reddish purple. Blooms in spring; flower heads have a lace cap look, with a 2–4-in. cluster of small fertile blossoms ringed with larger sterile blossoms. Large, showy red fruit persists from fall into winter. Takes moist to boggy soils. Control aphids.

'Aureum'. Golden yellow foliage. Give some shade to prevent sunburn.

'Compactum'. Like the species but smaller—to 4–5 ft. high and wide.

'Nanum'. To 2 ft. high and wide. Needs no trimming as low, informal hedge. Cannot take poorly drained, wet soils. No flowers or fruit.

'Roseum' ('Sterile'). COMMON SNOWBALL. Resembles the species but has snowball-like flower clusters 2–2½ in. across, composed entirely of sterile flowers (so bears no fruit). Aphids are especially troublesome.

V. plicatum (V. tomentosum 'Sterile'). JAPANESE SNOWBALL. Deciduous. Zones 3–9, 14–24. From China, Japan. To 8–15 ft. tall and wide; horizontal branching pattern gives plant a tiered look. Strongly veined, 3–6-in.-long, dull dark green leaves turn purplish red in autumn. Showy, 3-in., snowball-like clusters of sterile flowers look like those of *V. opulus* 'Roseum', but this plant is less bothered by aphids. Midspring bloom. No fruit.

V. p. tomentosum. DOUBLEFILE VIBURNUM. Deciduous. From China, Japan. A truly beautiful viburnum. Resembles the species but has lace cap flower heads: flat, 2–4-in. clusters of small fertile flowers edged with 1–1½-in. sterile flowers. Fruit is red aging to black; showy but not always profuse. 'Mariesii' grows 6–8 ft. tall, 8–10 ft. wide, has larger sterile flowers. 'Shasta' has a very wide-spreading habit (6 ft. tall, 12 ft. wide). Varieties blooming from spring to the end of the growing season include 'Nanum Semperflorens' ('Watanabe'), 'Summer Snowflake', and 'Summer Stars'; all grow 4–6 ft. tall and wide.

V. ×pragense. PRAGUE VIBURNUM. Evergreen. Zones 3–11, 14–24. Fast-growing, rounded plant to 10 ft. tall and broad. Shiny dark green, 2–4-in.-long leaves. Faintly fragrant white flowers in 3–6-in. clusters open from pink buds in early spring.

V. ×rhytidophylloides. Zones 3–9, 14–24. These are hybrids between *V. rhytidophyllum* and *V. lantana.* Among the best is 'Allegheny', a dense, rounded plant 6–8 ft. tall and broad; it is evergreen in most winters. Leaves resemble those of *V. rhytidophyllum* but are broader and less wrinkled. Flowers and fruit are also similar.

V. rhytidophyllum. LEATHERLEAF VIBURNUM. Evergreen. Zones 3–9, 14–24. Upright to 8–15 ft. tall, 6–12 ft. wide. Narrowish, 4–10-in.-long leaves are deep green and wrinkled above, fuzzy beneath. Yellowish white spring flowers in 4–8-in. clusters; scarlet fruit that ages to black. Leaves droop in cold weather, and plant looks tattered where cold winds blow. Tolerates deep shade. Some find this plant striking; others consider it coarse.

Viburnum rhytidophyllum

V. sargentii. Deciduous. Zones 1–9, 14–21. From northeastern Asia. Erect, rounded growth to 12–15 ft. tall and wide. Lobed, somewhat maplelike, 2–5-in.-long leaves. Foliage is bronze purple when new, matures to dark green by summer, may turn yellow or red in fall. Lace cap flower heads in late spring: 2–4-in. clusters of small fertile flowers edged with 1-in. sterile flowers. Bright red fruit colors up in late summer and fall, hangs on into winter. 'Onondaga', to 6 ft. tall and broad (or larger), has foliage that emerges deep maroon and maintains its purple tinge throughout summer; its flowers are pink-tinged white.

V. setigerum. TEA VIBURNUM. Deciduous. Zones 3–9, 14–21. From China. To 8–12 ft. tall, 6–8 ft. wide. Multistemmed, rather erect; often bare at base (plant lower-growing shrubs around it for concealment). Leaves were once used for making tea; they are 3–6 in. long, dark green or blue green turning to purplish in fall. Spring flowers in 1–2 in. clusters are not striking, but heavy production of scarlet fruit makes this the showiest of fruiting viburnums.

V. suspensum. SANDANKWA VIBURNUM. Evergreen. Zones 12–24; possible in Zones 8–10 but risky in cold winters there. From Japan. To 8–10 ft. tall and broad. Leathery, 2–4-in.-long leaves are glossy deep green above, paler beneath. Blooms in early spring; loose, 2–4-in. clusters of flowers have a scent that some people find objectionable. Red fruit ages to black, is not long lasting. Serviceable screen or hedge. Watch for thrips, spider mites, aphids. Little to moderate water.

V. tinus. LAURUSTINUS. Evergreen. Zones 4–10, 12–24, except as noted. Mediterranean native. To 6–12 ft. tall, half as wide. Leathery dark green, 2–3-in.-long leaves with edges slightly rolled under. Wine red new stems. Blooms from fall to spring; tight clusters of pink buds open to lightly fragrant white flowers. Bright metallic blue fruits last through summer. Dense foliage right to ground makes it good for screens, hedges, clipped topiary shapes. Can be trained as a small tree. Susceptible to mites; prone to mildew near ocean. Varieties include the following.

'Dwarf'. To 3–5 ft. tall and wide. Good for low screens, hedges, foundation plantings.

'Lucidum'. SHINING LAURUSTINUS. Zones 8, 9, 12–24. Less hardy than the species, with larger leaves. Less prone to mildew. ▶

'Robustum'. ROUNDLEAF LAURUSTINUS. Leaves are coarser, rougher than those of species; flower buds are almost white. Less prone to mildew. Excellent small, narrow tree.

'Spring Bouquet' ('Compactum'). Upright to 4–6 ft. high and wide; good for hedges. Leaves are deeper green, slightly smaller than those of the species.

'Variegatum'. Zones 4–9, 14–24. Leaves are marbled with white and pale yellow.

V. trilobum. CRANBERRY BUSH. Deciduous. Zones A1–A3; 1–11, 14–20. Native to Canada, northern U.S. To 15 ft. tall, 12 ft. wide. Leaves look much like those of *V. opulus;* they emerge reddish tinged, mature to dark green, turn yellow to red-purple in fall. Lace cap flowers appear in midspring. Fruit is similar to that of *V. opulus* but is used for preserves and jellies. Less susceptible to aphid damage than *V. opulus.* 'Wentworth' has larger berries and bright red fall foliage. 'Compactum' is a smaller form, to 6 ft. high and wide.

VICK'S PLANT. See PLECTRANTHUS cylindraceus

VICTORIAN BOX. See PITTOSPORUM undulatum

VIGNA caracalla (Phaseolus caracalla)

SNAIL VINE

Fabaceae (Leguminosae)

PERENNIAL VINE SOMETIMES GROWN AS ANNUAL

ZONES 12–24, H1, H2; ELSEWHERE AS ANNUAL

FULL SUN

REGULAR WATER

Vigna caracalla

Tropical American native that generally resembles pole bean in form and foliage. The flowers are different, though: fragrant, cream to pale purple spring and summer blossoms have lilac or purple markings, twisted keel petals that are coiled like a snail shell—odd and pretty. Twines rapidly to 10–20 ft.; good summer screen or bank cover. Evergreen in frostless areas; in colder regions, cut plant to the ground if frost kills top. Sometimes sold as *Phaseolus gigantea.*

VIGUIERA

GOLDENEYE

Asteraceae (Compositae)

SHRUBBY PERENNIALS

ZONES VARY BY SPECIES

FULL SUN

LITTLE WATER

Viguiera multiflora

Desert plants with yellow daisies that are borne singly or in loose clusters at stem ends. Cut plants back after bloom or before new growth begins to encourage bushiness and good looks. Useful in restoring native vegetation and in stabilizing soil.

V. deltoidea (V. parishii). Zones 10–24. Native to California, Arizona, Nevada, Mexico. Freely branching, sprawling plant to 3 ft. high and wide (possibly larger), with triangular, toothed, densely hairy, green to gray-green leaves ½–2 in. long. Spring flowers are 1–1½ in. wide.

V. multiflora. Zones 2, 3, 10–13. Native from Montana to California, Arizona. To 1–3 ft. tall, 1½ ft. wide, with hairy, lance-shaped green leaves 1–2 in. long. Spring or summer flowers to 2 in. wide; blooms first year from seed.

FOR GROWING SYMBOL EXPLANATIONS
PLEASE SEE PAGE 161

VINCA

PERIWINKLE

Apocynaceae

PERENNIALS

ZONES VARY BY SPECIES

FULL SUN IN COOLER CLIMATES ONLY

LITTLE TO MODERATE WATER

Vinca minor

Trailing, arching stems that root where they touch soil make these plants useful as ground and bank covers. Shiny dark green, oval to oblong leaves. Lavender-blue, five-petaled, pinwheel-shaped flowers appear in leaf joints in early spring. Plant the larger species and its varieties 2–2½ ft. apart, dwarf kinds 1½ ft. apart. When plantings mound up or are layered with old stems, shear or mow before new spring growth begins. Very soil tolerant. Compete successfully with surface tree roots.

V. major. Zones 5–24. The larger, more aggressive species. Leaves to 3 in. long, flowers to 2 in. across; mounds to 1–2 ft. high. Spreads rapidly; can be extremely invasive in sheltered, forested areas. 'Variegata', probably as common as the green form, has leaves strongly edged in white.

V. minor. DWARF PERIWINKLE. Zones 1–24. Miniature version of *V. major,* with ¾–1¾-in.-long leaves, flowers to 1 in. wide, and a height of just 4–6 in. More restrained, less likely to invade adjacent plantings. Varieties include 'Alba', with white flowers; 'Atropurpurea', deep purple flowers, small leaves; 'Bowles' Variety' ('La Grave'), deeper blue flowers, larger leaves; 'Green Carpet', with dense foliage and few flowers; 'Gertrude Jekyll' ('Miss Jekyll'), smaller grower with white flowers; 'Ralph Shugert', white-edged leaves, blue flowers, repeat autumn bloom; and 'Sterling Silver', blue flowers, white-edged leaves speckled with pale green.

V. rosea. See Catharanthus roseus

VINE MAPLE. See ACER circinatum

VIOLA

VIOLA, VIOLET, PANSY

Violaceae

ANNUALS AND PERENNIALS, SOME TREATED AS ANNUALS

ZONES VARY BY SPECIES

EXPOSURE NEEDS VARY BY SPECIES

REGULAR WATER

Viola × wittrockiana

Botanically speaking, violas, pansies, and almost all violets are perennials belonging to the genus *Viola.* However, violas and pansies are usually treated as annuals, invaluable for winter and spring bloom in mild-winter areas, for spring-through-summer color in colder climates. Typically used for mass color in borders and edgings, as covers for spring-flowering bulbs, in containers. Violets are more often used as woodland or rock garden plants. Violas and pansies take sun or partial shade; violets grow in part or full shade (except as noted), but most are natives of deciduous forests and bloom best with at least some sun during the flowering season.

Almost all violets have two kinds of flowers: normal, conspicuous ones that rise above the foliage and may be pollinated and set seed, and short-stemmed, inconspicuous cleistogamous (Greek for "closed mouth") flowers that set copious seed without pollination and produce offspring identical to the parent. Many violets also spread by aboveground runners. Some reproduce so freely they can crowd out other small plants.

In cold-winter climates, set out nursery plants of pansies and violas in spring for summer bloom; in mild climates, plant in autumn for winter-to-spring (or longer) bloom. Or start from seed: in cold climates, sow in mid- to late summer and overwinter seedlings in cold frame until spring; or sow indoors in winter, plant in spring. In mild-winter areas, sow in mid- to late summer, plant out in fall. To prolong bloom, pick flowers (with some foliage) regularly and remove faded blooms before they set seed. In hot areas, plants get ragged by midsummer and should be removed.

Violas and pansies have such complex ancestries that many botanists are unwilling to assign them to species, preferring to list them by variety name. However, we believe it will avoid confusion if we retain these plants under their former names, invalid though they now may be.

V. adunca. CALIFORNIA SWEET VIOLET, WESTERN DOG VIOLET. Zones 1–9, 14–24. Native to coastal bluffs and Sierra foothills in central California, Pacific Northwest east to New England. To 3–6 in. high, spreading indefinitely by stolons and seeds. Dark green, heart-shaped leaves to 3 in. long. Half-inch or larger flowers in lavender blue with white petal bases and conspicuous bright orange stigmas. Extremely fragrant. Blooms in spring in cold climates, fall to spring in mild-winter areas. Best with at least half-day winter sun, summer shade. Takes various soils and exposures, tolerates some drought. Can be invasive. Often sold as *V. odorata.*

V. blanda. SWEET WHITE VIOLET. Zones 1–10, 14–24. From eastern North America. To 2–3 in. high, spreading indefinitely by runners. Fragrant white flowers with purple veining have sharply reflexed petals. Likes moist soil with lots of organic material.

V. cornuta. VIOLA, TUFTED PANSY. All zones as annuals; Zones 1–10, 14–24 for kinds grown as perennials. To 6–8 in. high and 8 in. wide, with smooth, wavy-edged leaves. Purple, pansylike, slender-spurred flowers about 1½ in. across. Modern strains and varieties are complex hybrids with larger, shorter-spurred flowers; they come in solid colors (purple, blue, yellow, apricot, ruby red, white) or with elaborate markings ("faces"). Crystal strain has extra-large flowers in pure, unshaded colors. Sorbet strain, which comes in pastel bicolors, is especially hardy to cold.

Some nurseries offer English violas—named varieties propagated by cuttings or division. These form 2-ft.-wide clumps and are reliably perennial. Varieties include 'Better Times', 2-in. yellow flowers; 'Columbine', creamy white liberally splashed with purple; 'Etain', pale yellow with purple border; 'Mt. Spokane', white with a shading of palest blue; and 'Whiskers', cream marked with thin purple lines.

V. cucullata (V. obliqua). MARSH BLUE VIOLET. Zones 1–9, 14–24. From eastern and central North America. To 6 in. high, 10 in. wide. Toothed, heart-shaped leaves to 4 in. across. Blue, ¾-in.-wide flowers are held well above the leaves in early spring. Good ground cover; no runners, but self-sows liberally and can become a pest. The violet often sold as 'White Czar'—white, with yellow throat veined in black— is a selection of this species; the name correctly belongs to an old variety of *V. odorata,* however.

V. grypoceras exilis (V. koreana). Zones 1–10, 14–24. From Japan. Unlike most other violets, an annual, but will maintain itself by self-sowing once established. To 2 in. high, 6–8 in. wide. Deep green, 1–1½-in.-long leaves have heavy silver gray veining, maroon red undersides. Small light purple flowers in spring, with a scattering of summer bloom. Attractive small-scale ground cover for shady, moist places. Sometimes sold as *V. koreana* 'Syletta'.

V. hederacea. AUSTRALIAN VIOLET. Zones 7–9, 14–24. From Australia. To 1–4 in. high; eventually covers several feet, spreading by runners at slow to moderate rate. Kidney-shaped leaves to 1½ in. long. Nearly spurless, ¼–¾-in. flowers—broader than high and rather flat—in summer. They come in violet, blue, or white; commonly seen form is white with heavy blue-violet veining in throat. 'Baby Blue' has pure sky blue flowers. Plants go dormant at about 30°F/–1°C. Use as ground cover in light shade or (with abundant water) in sun.

V. koreana. See V. grypoceras exilis

V. labradorica. Zones A3; 1–6. From northeastern U.S., Canada, Greenland. An infrequently cultivated deciduous species with tiny (¾-in.-long), purple-tinged leaves and pale purple flowers in summer. Most plants sold under this name are *V. riviniana* 'Purpurea'.

V. odorata. SWEET VIOLET. Zones 1–24. The violet of song and story. To 8 in. high, 1½ ft. wide. In cool, mild climates, can spread widely by seeds and runners, possibly becoming a pest. Dark green, heart-shaped, 2½-in.-long leaves with toothed margins. Fragrant, short-spurred flowers ¾ in. or wider in deep violet, bluish rose, or white. Selections include 'Rosina' (pink), 'Royal Elk' (violet), and 'Royal Robe' (deep violet). Clump-forming 'Charm' has small white flowers. Tolerates full sun in cool-summer areas. For better spring display, remove runners and shear rank growth in late fall, then apply complete fertilizer in earliest spring.

V. Parma Violets. Zones 4–9, 14–24. Hybrids of uncertain parentage with small, usually double, intensely fragrant flowers. They resemble *V. odorata* in form and growth habit, but are far less vigorous and less inclined to spread; they advance slowly by runners. Give them rich soil, cool location. 'Duchesse de Parme' (lavender), 'Marie Louise' (deep violet), and 'Swanley White' are sometimes available. Beyond hardiness range, grow in pots and winter in a cool greenhouse or indoor room.

V. pedata. BIRD'S-FOOT VIOLET. Zones 1–7. From eastern North America. So named because its finely divided leaves resemble a bird's foot. Forms a clump to 2 in. high, 4 in. wide; does not spread by runners. Blooms from early spring to early summer; 4-in. stems bear inch-wide, typically two-tone violet-blue flowers with darker veining. Not as easy to grow as other violets; likes excellent drainage, filtered sun or high shade, and acidic soil.

V. riviniana. Zones 1–24. From southern Europe, North Africa. Tiny violet to 3 in. high or less, spreading (sometimes aggressively) by runners and seed. Heart- or kidney-shaped, 1-in. leaves; tiny lavender-blue flowers in spring (fall through late spring in mild-winter areas). Useful for small-scale ground cover in partial shade or morning sun (away from choice small perennials) or as filler between stepping-stones or paving blocks. Most often seen is 'Purpurea', with leaves that emerge deep maroon and eventually mature to dusky green. Succeeds with moderate water if shaded from summer heat.

V. sororia. DOORYARD VIOLET. Zones 1–11, 14–24. From eastern and central North America. To 4–6 in. high, 8 in. wide; does not spread by runners but self-sows freely. Leaves are somewhat heart shaped, to 5 in. wide, vary from densely hairy to almost smooth. Good ground cover under woodland shrubs. Nearly scentless, ½–¾-in. flowers in spring to early summer are held close to leaves; colors range from red-violet to blue-violet to white. Most commonly seen are the following smooth-leafed varieties (all come true from seed): 'Albiflora', pure white with yellow in throat; 'Freckles', white liberally spotted with blue; 'Priceana' (popularly known as Confederate violet), white with blue-violet veining in throat.

V. tricolor. JOHNNY-JUMP-UP. All zones. From Europe, Asia. Spring bloomer to 6–12 tall and broad; spreads widely by profuse self-sowing. Oval, deeply lobed leaves to 1¼ in. long. Pert, ½–¾-in., velvety purple-and-yellow or blue-and-yellow flowers are the original wild pansies. Same planting and care as pansy. Crosses with closely related small-flowered species have produced forms with flowers in violet, blue, white, yellow, lavender, mauve, apricot, orange, red—with or without markings ("faces"). Flowers of 'Molly Sanderson' are very dark purple—almost black.

V. × wittrockiana. PANSY. All zones. To 6–10 in. high, 9–12 in. wide. Many strains with 2–4-in. flowers in white, blue, mahogany red, rose, yellow, apricot, purple; also bicolors. Most have dark blotches on the lower three petals; such flowers are often said to resemble faces. Shiny green leaves are oval to nearly heart shaped, slightly lobed, 1½ in. or longer.

Strains are almost too numerous to mention; here are just a few. Accord/Banner and Universal Plus produce 2–2½-in. flowers in a wide range of solid and blotched colors. Clear Sky, Crystal Bowl (Clear Crystal), and Delta strains bear flowers without blotches or other markings. Contessa has ruffled, 2-in. blooms. Flowers of Ghost Mix are 2½ in. wide, carried on long stems good for cutting. Imperial Hybrids and Majestic Giants offer extra-large (to 4-in.-wide) flowers. Unlike the others, Sprite Mix is a ground cover pansy—4–5 in. high, 1½ ft. wide, with 2-in. blossoms. A few named selections deserve mention. Flowers of 'Jolly Joker' show striking contrast between bright orange lower petals and deep purple upper petals; 'Padparadja' has flowers of pure reddish orange; 'Springtime Black' has 2-in., velvety black blooms.

VIOLET. See VIOLA

VIOLET TRUMPET VINE. See CLYTOSTOMA callistegioides

VIRGINIA BLUEBELLS. See MERTENSIA pulmonarioides

VIRGINIA CREEPER. See PARTHENOCISSUS inserta, P. quinquefolia

VIRGINIAN STOCK. See MALCOLMIA maritima

VISCARIA. See SILENE coeli-rosa

Vitaceae. The grape family contains vines that climb by tendrils and produce berries. Besides grape, best-known representatives are Boston ivy and Virginia creeper (both species of *Parthenocissus*).

VITEX

CHASTE TREE

Verbeneaceae

DECIDUOUS AND EVERGREEN SHRUBS OR TREES

ZONES VARY BY SPECIES

FULL SUN

MODERATE TO REGULAR WATER

Vitex agnus-castus

One is a shrub or tree and the other a shrubby ground cover, but both have handsome foliage and clustered flowers. Prefer well-drained soil.

V. agnus-castus. CHASTE TREE. Deciduous shrub or small tree. Zones 4–24; H1, H2. Native from Mediterranean region to central Asia. In warmest part of range, grows fast to make a tree to 25 ft. tall and wide, typically with multiple trunks; train high to make a good small shade tree. In colder areas, growth is slower and ultimate size is smaller—to 8–10 ft. high and wide. Where it usually freezes to the ground in winter, it is a shrubby perennial about 3–5 ft. high and wide.

Aromatic leaves are divided fanwise into five to seven narrow, 2–6-in.-long leaflets, grayish green above, gray beneath. No real fall color. Blooms summer to fall; small, fragrant lavender-blue flowers held in 6–12-in. spikes at branch ends and in leaf joints. Varieties include 'Alba' and 'Silver Spire', with white flowers; 'Latifolia' (sometimes sold as *V. macrophylla*), a sturdy plant with large leaflets; and 'Rosea', with pink flowers.

Thrives in heat, resists oak root fungus. Good in shrub border. Cut plants treated as perennials to 1 ft. high in spring; they will bloom on new growth.

V. rotundifolia. BEACH VITEX, POHINAHINA. Evergreen shrub. Zones 13–24; H1, H2. Native to coastal areas of Hawaii, Australia, Asia. Sprawls to 1½–4 ft. high, 6–8 ft. wide; roots as it spreads to make a dense ground cover. Aromatic, medium green, broadly oblong to roundish leaves to 2½ in. long. Short spikes of bluish purple, ½-in. flowers (popular in leis) appear all year in warmest areas, in summer in colder part of range. Tiny bluish black fruits. Thrives at seacoast or inland.

VITIS

GRAPE

Vitaceae

DECIDUOUS VINES

ZONES VARY BY SPECIES

FULL SUN OR PARTIAL SHADE

WATER NEEDS VARY BY SPECIES

Vitis coignetiae

For grapes grown for edible fruit, see Grape. Those plants are handsome in leaf and fruit, but the following species produce tiny fruit of no value and are grown instead for ornament. All climb by tendrils and have large, roundish, slightly lobed leaves that turn attractive colors in autumn. Prune as needed before spring growth begins.

V. californica. CALIFORNIA WILD GRAPE. Zones 4–24. From California, Oregon. To 30 ft., with 2–4-in. leaves that emerge grayish, mature to green, and turn red or yellow in autumn. 'Roger's Red' holds its gray-green leaf color all summer, turns brilliant red in fall. 'Walker Ridge', to 6–10 ft., has brilliant red and orange fall color. *V. girdiana* is a nearly identical species native to Southern California. Little or no water.

V. coignetiae. CRIMSON GLORY VINE. Zones 3–10, 14–21. From Japan, Korea. Vigorous vine to 50 ft. tall, with foot-wide deep green leaves that turn brilliant red in fall. Moderate to regular water.

V. vinifera 'Purpurea'. Zones 4–9, 14–23. To 20 ft. or more. Leaves to 6 in. across emerge downy green, mature to deep purple, turn deeper purple in fall. Moderate to regular water.

WAKE ROBIN. See TRILLIUM

WALLFLOWER. See ERYSIMUM

WALNUT

Juglandaceae

DECIDUOUS TREE

ZONES 4–9, 14–23; SOME VARIETIES IN ZONES 1–3

FULL SUN

REGULAR WATER

For walnut species grown mainly as landscape trees producing bonus crops of nuts, see *Juglans*. The species described here, English walnut (*J. regia*), is a widely grown orchard plant native to southeast Europe, southwest Asia; its nuts are the familiar ones sold commercially.

Walnut

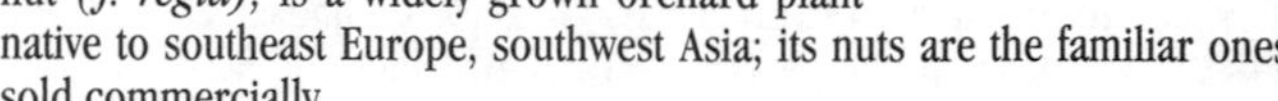

Species is hardy to –5°F/–21°C, but certain varieties are injured by late and early frosts. Reaches 60 ft. high and wide; grows fast, especially when young. Trunk and heavy, horizontal or upward-angled branches have smooth gray bark; leaves have five to seven (rarely more) 3–6-in.-long leaflets. Walnut husks open in fall, dropping nuts to ground; to hasten drop, knock nuts from tree. Gather fallen nuts immediately, remove any adhering husks, and dry in single layer in airy shade until kernels are brittle (crack a nut open to test); then store.

Plant English walnut as a landscape tree only on large lots. It's out of leaf a long time, messy in leaf (honeydew drip and sooty mold due to aphid infestations), and messy in fruit (husks can stain). Many people are allergic to the wind-borne pollen. Grow in deep soil. Established plants survive with no supplemental moisture but need deep watering for top-quality nuts. Keep other plants beyond drip line, where feeder roots grow. Train young trees to a central leader; mature ones need pruning only to remove dead wood or correct shape. In addition to aphids, pests include scale, codling moths, spider mites. Walnut husk fly attacks husks, causing them to turn black and adhere to shell. Husks are difficult to remove and shell is stained, but nutmeats are not damaged.

In Zones 1–3, grow walnuts described as Carpathian or Hardy Persian. Varieties include 'Ambassador', 'Cascade', 'Chopaka', 'Hansen', 'Russian', and 'Somers'; these range in hardiness from –25°F/–32°C to –35°F/–37°C. Here are best choices for other zones. In Zones 4–7, 'Chambers', 'Cooke's Giant Sweet', 'Franquette', and 'Spurgeon' bloom late enough to escape spring frosts, yield high-quality nuts. In Zones 8, 9, grow 'Carmelo', 'Chandler', 'Cooke's Giant Sweet', 'Hartley', 'Idaho', 'Payne', 'Pedro', or 'Serr'. In Zones 14–16 and warm parts of 17, try 'Carmelo', 'Chandler', 'Cooke's Giant Sweet', 'Franquette', 'Hartley', 'Payne', 'Pedro', and 'Serr'. In Zones 18–20, grow 'Payne', 'Pedro', or 'Placentia'. In Zones 21–23, best choices are 'Pedro' and 'Placentia'.

WANDERING JEW. See TRADESCANTIA

WARMINSTER BROOM. See CYTISUS × praecox

WASHINGTONIA

Arecaceae (Palmae)

PALMS

ZONES 8, 9, 10 (WARMER PARTS), 11–24; H1, H2

FULL SUN

LITTLE TO REGULAR WATER

Washingtonia filifera

These fast-growing fan palms are too tall for most suburban gardens; they are best suited to large properties, avenues, parkways. The two species often hybridize if growing near each other.

W. filifera. CALIFORNIA FAN PALM. From California, Arizona. Hardy to 18°F/−8°C. To 60 ft. tall, 20 ft. wide, with thicker trunk than *W. robusta.* Long-stalked, 3–6-ft., light green leaves stand well apart in open crown. As leaves mature, they bend down to form a "skirt" of thatch. In native stands in desert, this species always grows near springs or other moist spots.

W. robusta. MEXICAN FAN PALM. From Mexico. Hardy to 20°F/−7°C. To 100 ft. tall, 10 ft. wide; trunk is slightly curved or bent, slimmer than that of *W. filifera.* Head of bright green foliage is more compact; leafstalks are shorter, with a red streak on the undersides.

WASHINGTON THORN. See CRATAEGUS phaenopyrum

WATER LILY. See NYMPHAEA

WATERMELON

Cucurbitaceae

ANNUAL

ZONES 1–24; H1, H2

FULL SUN

REGULAR WATER

Watermelon

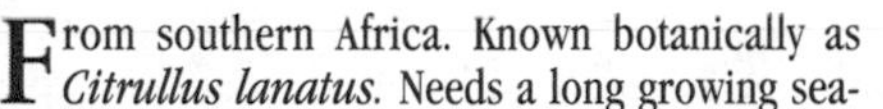

From southern Africa. Known botanically as *Citrullus lanatus.* Needs a long growing season, more heat than most other melons, and more space than other vine crops—about 8 ft. by 8 ft. for each hill (circle of seed). Other than that, culture is as described under Melon. If you garden where watermelons are grown commercially (Zones 8, 9, 12–14, 18–21), choose any variety you like. If your summers are short or cool (Zones 1–7, 10, 11, 15–17, 22–24), choose a fast-maturing ("early") variety (described in catalogs and on seed packets as taking 70 to 75 days from seed to harvest). Also plant through clear plastic mulch and cover planting with floating row covers. In Hawaii, grow proven varieties such as 'Sugar Baby', 'Summer Festival', and 'Top Yield'. Watermelon does not become sweeter after harvest—it must be picked ripe. To check for ripeness, thump the melon (it should produce a "thunk"); check to see that underside has turned from white to pale yellow; and make sure tendrils where melon attaches to stem have darkened and withered. Cut (do not pull) melon from vine.

WATSONIA

Iridaceae

PERENNIALS FROM CORMS

ZONES 4–9, 12–24; OR DIG AND STORE DECIDUOUS TYPE

FULL SUN

REGULAR WATER DURING GROWTH AND BLOOM

Watsonia borbonica

Native to South Africa. Somewhat similar to gladiolus, but there are differences. Watsonia's sword-shaped, 2½-ft.-long leaves are less rigid, and it has taller, slimmer flower spikes set with smaller, more trumpetlike, fragrant blossoms. Tolerates many soils but prefers good drainage. Plant in early fall, setting corms 4 in. deep, 6 in. apart. Where hardy, corms can be left undisturbed for many years. In colder areas, you can grow *W. borbonica* as you would gladiolus: plant in spring for late spring and early summer bloom, then dig and store after foliage dies down. Because *W. pillansii* is evergreen, it cannot be dug and stored.

W. borbonica (W. pyramidata). Deciduous. Blooms in late spring, bearing 2½-in. flowers in pink, rosy red, or white on 4–6-ft. stems. Hybrid forms have pink, red, or lavender blooms. Foliage dies back after bloom, reappearing in fall. Does not need regular moisture during summer dormancy but accepts it if soil is well drained.

W. pillansii (W. beatricis). Evergreen. Blooms in midsummer, with slightly branched, 3½-ft. stems bearing 3-in., bright reddish apricot flowers. Hybrids come in colors ranging from peach to nearly red. Can take less moisture in summer after bloom is over.

WATTLE. See ACACIA

WAX FIG. See FICUS microcarpa crassifolia

WAX FLOWER, WAX PLANT. See HOYA

WAX VINE. See SENECIO macroglossus

WEDELIA trilobata

Asteraceae (Compositae)

PERENNIAL

ZONES 12, 13, 21–24; H1, H2

FULL SUN OR LIGHT SHADE

REGULAR WATER

Wedelia trilobata

From Central and South America. Trailing evergreen plant to 1½–2 ft. high, spreading to 6 ft. or more by stems that root where they touch damp earth. Fleshy, dark glossy green leaves to 4 in. long, half as wide, with a few coarse teeth or shallow lobes toward tips. Inch-wide flowers resembling tiny yellow zinnias or marigolds *(Tagetes)* bloom almost year-round. Spreads fast; easily propagated by lifting rooted pieces or placing tip cuttings in moist soil. Best in sandy, fast-draining soils but takes heavier soils if drainage is good. If killed to ground by frost, it makes a fast comeback. Tolerates desert heat, seaside conditions. Can take lower light but blooms more sparsely in shady conditions. Good for erosion control on slopes: plant 1½ ft. apart, feed lightly. Shear close to ground if planting mounds up or becomes stemmy.

WEIGELA

Caprifoliaceae

DECIDUOUS SHRUBS

ZONES 1–11, 14–21

FULL SUN OR LIGHT SHADE

REGULAR WATER

Weigela florida

From China, Korea, Japan. Weigelas are valued for lavish springtime display of funnel-shaped, 1-in.-long flowers. They aren't attractive out of bloom, have no real fall color. Most are rather coarse leafed and stiff, becoming rangy unless pruned. After flowering, cut back stems that have bloomed to side shoots that have not flowered; leave only one or two of these to each stem. Cut some of the oldest stems to ground. Thin new suckers to a few of the most vigorous. Another method is to cut back entire plant about halfway just after blooms fade; do this every other year. Resulting dense new growth will provide plenty of flowers the next spring. Use as background plants for flower borders, as summer screens, in mixed borders.

W. coraeensis. WHITE WEIGELA. To 12–15 ft. tall and wide, with leaves to 6 in. long. Flowers are 1½ in. long, white or light pink aging to red.

W. florida (W. rosea). Fast growth to 6–10 ft. tall, 9–12 ft. wide, with branches often arching to the ground. Leaves 2–4½ in. long. Pink to rose red flowers. The following selections grow about 6 ft. high and wide: 'Bristol Snowflake', white flowers opening from pinkish buds; 'Java Red', red-tinted foliage, red buds opening to deep pink flowers; 'Pink Princess', lilac-pink flowers.

W. hybrids. These are hybrids between *W. florida, W. praecox,* and other species.

'Briant Rubidor' ('Rubidor', 'Olympiade'). A sport of 'Bristol Ruby' with yellow foliage. To 6 ft. high and wide.

'Bristol Ruby'. To 6–7 ft. tall and nearly as wide, with ruby red flowers. Some repeat bloom in midsummer and fall.

'Candida' ('Alba'). To 5 ft. tall and wide, with white flowers that are tinged with green.

'Minuet'. Dwarf variety to 3 ft. tall, 5 ft. wide. Purplish leaves. Flowers blend red, purple, and yellow. ▸

'Newport Red' ('Cardinal', 'Rhode Island Red', 'Vanicek'). To 6 ft. tall and wide, with bright red flowers. Young stems are bright green in winter.

'Red Prince'. To 5–6 ft. tall and wide, with red flowers, some summer rebloom.

'Variegata'. Compact growth to 4–6 ft. tall and wide, with deep rosy red flowers and creamy yellow to white leaf edges. 'Variegata Nana' is 3 ft. tall and wide.

'Wine and Roses' ('Alexandra'). To 5 ft. tall and wide. Deep purple new leaves are highlighted by bright pink flowers. Foliage matures to purplish green, turns blackish purple in autumn.

WELSH POPPY. See MECONOPSIS cambrica

WESTERN RED CEDAR. See THUJA plicata

WESTRINGIA fruticosa

COAST ROSEMARY

Lamiaceae (Labiatae)

EVERGREEN SHRUB

ZONES 8, 9, 14–24

FULL SUN

LITTLE TO MODERATE WATER

Westringia fruticosa

From Australia. Spreading, rather loose growth to 3–6 ft. tall, 5–10 ft. wide. Medium green to gray-green leaves have white undersides, are slightly finer and filmier in texture than rosemary leaves. Small white flowers bloom from midwinter through spring in colder areas, all year in milder climates. Needs light, well-drained soil. Good near coast; wind tolerant. Often sold as *W. rosmariniformis.* 'Wynyabbie Gem' has light lavender flowers. 'Morning Light' grows 3 ft. tall and wide, has white flowers and white-edged leaves.

WHEATGRASS. See AGROPYRON

WHITE CEDAR. See CHAMAECYPARIS thyoides

WHITE SAPOTE

Rutaceae

EVERGREEN OR DECIDUOUS TREE

ZONES 8, 9, 14–16, 18–24; H1, H2

FULL SUN

REGULAR WATER

White Sapote

Beautiful tropical tree, botanically known as *Casimiroa edulis.* Native to Mexico; withstands more cold than most avocados, does well wherever lemons are grown. To 25–50 ft. tall, 25–30 ft. wide, with luxuriant glossy green leaves divided fanwise into three to seven oval, 3–5-in.-long leaflets. To keep tree lower and create a wide, umbrellalike crown, pinch out terminal bud. Roots are invasive; choose planting location carefully.

Heavy crop of round, 3–4-in. fruit with pale green to yellow skin and white or creamy yellow flesh with custardlike consistency and tropical flavor. Fruit tastes best when allowed to ripen on tree, but it usually drops before reaching ripeness. Pick it when firm-ripe, at which point the flavor is mellow and sweet. (Some varieties become sweeter if left to stand at room temperature; others turn bitter.) To harvest, cut from tree, leaving a small piece of stem attached; pick carefully to avoid bruising. Eat with a spoon. California varieties include 'Bravo!', 'Lemon Gold', 'Louise', 'McDill', 'Suebelle', and 'Vernon'. 'Denzler' is grown in Hawaii.

Needs consistent feeding. Mature tree may produce several hundred pounds of fruit, far more than any one family can use. Cleanup becomes a chore, so plant where dropping fruit can be raked up or disappear into a ground cover. May become partially deciduous in frosty or very hot weather.

WHORLFLOWER. See MORINA longifolia

WILD GINGER. See ASARUM

WILD INDIGO. See BAPTISIA

WILD LILAC. See CEANOTHUS

WILD RYE. See LEYMUS

WILGA. See GEIJERA parviflora

WILIWILI. See ERYTHRINA sandwicensis

WILLOW. See SALIX

WINDFLOWER. See ANEMONE

WINDMILL PALM. See TRACHYCARPUS fortunei

WINTER ACONITE. See ERANTHIS hyemalis

WINTER CREEPER. See EUONYMUS fortunei

WINTERGREEN. See GAULTHERIA procumbens

WINTER HAZEL. See CORYLOPSIS

WINTERSWEET. See CHIMONANTHUS praecox

WIRE VINE. See MUEHLENBECKIA

WISHBONE FLOWER. See TORENIA fournieri

WISTERIA

Fabaceae (Leguminosae)

DECIDUOUS VINES

ZONES VARY BY SPECIES

FULL SUN, EXCEPT AS NOTED

LITTLE TO MODERATE WATER

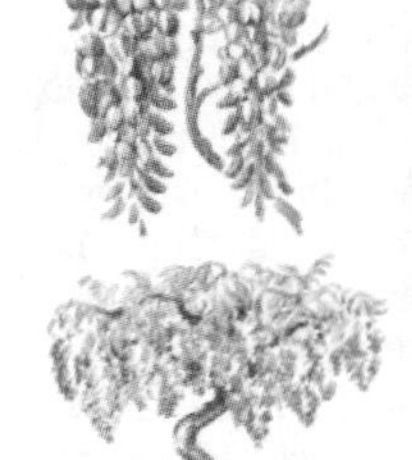

Wisteria sinensis

Twining, woody vines of great size, long life, and exceptional beauty in flower. Very adaptable; can be grown as trees, shrubs, or vines. All have large, fresh green leaves divided into many leaflets, spectacular clusters of blue, white, or pinkish springtime blossoms, and velvety, pealike pods to about 6 in. long. Subdued fall color in shades of yellow. To get off to a good start, buy a cutting-grown or grafted wisteria; seedlings may not bloom for many years. If you start with grafted plants, keep suckers removed or they may take over. Wisteria is not fussy about soil, but it does need good drainage. In alkaline soil, watch for chlorosis.

Pruning and training are important to control size and shape and encourage bloom production. Let newly planted wisteria grow to establish the framework you want, with either single or multiple trunks. Remove stems that interfere with desired framework; pinch back side stems and long streamers. For single-trunked specimens, rub off buds that develop on trunk; for multiple trunks, select as many vigorous stems as you wish and let them develop. If the plant has only one stem, pinch it back to encourage others to develop. Remember that main stem will become good-size trunk, and that weight of mature vine is considerable.

Tree wisterias can be bought already trained; or you can train your own. Remove all but one main stem and stake this one securely. Tie stem to stake at frequent intervals, using plastic tape to prevent girdling. When plant has reached height at which you wish head to form, pinch or prune out tip to force branching. Shorten branches to beef them up. Pinch back long streamers and rub off all buds that form below head. Replace stakes and ties as needed. Wisterias can be trained as big shrubs or multistemmed, small, semiweeping trees; permit well-spaced branches to form the framework, shorten side branches, and nip long streamers. Unsupported plants make a vigorous bank cover.

In general, wisterias do not need fertilizer. Prune blooming plants every winter; cut back or thin out side shoots from main or structural stems and shorten back to two or three buds the flower-producing spurs that grow from these shoots. You'll have no trouble recognizing fat flower buds on these spurs.

In summer, cut back long streamers before they tangle up in main body of vine; save those you want to use to extend height or length of vine and tie them to support—eaves, wall, trellis, arbor. If old plants grow rampantly but fail to bloom (and you have been fertilizing), withhold all nitrogen fertilizers for an entire growing season (buds for the next season's bloom are started in early summer). If that fails to produce bloom the next year, you can try pruning roots in spring—after you're sure no flowers will be produced—by cutting vertically with spade into plant's root zone.

W. brachybotrys (W. venusta). SILKY WISTERIA. Zones 3–24. Often sold as *W. venusta* 'Alba'. Silky-haired, 8–14-in.- long leaves divided into 9–13 leaflets. White, very large, long-stalked, highly fragrant flowers in short (4–6-in.) clusters that open all at once during leafout. 'Violacea' has purple-blue flowers. Older plants (especially in tree form) have remarkably profuse bloom.

W. floribunda. JAPANESE WISTERIA. Zones 2–24. Often sold as *W. multijuga.* Leaves are 12–16 in. long, divided into 15–19 leaflets. Fragrant, 1½-ft. clusters of violet or violet-blue flowers during leafout. Clusters open gradually, starting from the base; this prolongs bloom season but makes for a less spectacular burst of color than that provided by *W. sinensis.* Many varieties in white, pink, and shades of blue, purple, and lavender, usually marked with yellow and white. 'Longissima' ('Macrobotrys') has long (1½–3-ft.) clusters of violet flowers. 'Longissima Alba' bears white flowers in 2-ft. clusters; 'Issai Perfect' and 'Ivory Tower' are similar. 'Rosea' is a good lavender-pink variety. 'Plena' has very full clusters of double, deep blue-violet flowers. 'Texas Purple' blooms at an early age.

W. sinensis. CHINESE WISTERIA. Zones 3–24. Most common wisteria in the West. Leaves are 10–12 in. long, divided into 7–13 leaflets. Blooms before leafout. Clusters of violet-blue, slightly fragrant flowers are shorter (to 1 ft.) than those of *W. floribunda*—but they make quite a show, since flowers open all at once nearly all along the cluster. 'Alba' has white flowers. 'Caroline' and 'Cooke's Special' are grafted forms. 'Prolific' blooms at an early age. Plants will bloom in sun or considerable shade.

WITCH HAZEL. See HAMAMELIS

WONGA-WONGA VINE. See PANDOREA pandorana

WOODBINE. See LONICERA periclymenum, PARTHENOCISSUS inserta

WOOD FERN. See DRYOPTERIS

WOOD ROSE. See MERREMIA

WOODRUFF, SWEET. See GALIUM odoratum

WOODWARDIA fimbriata

GIANT CHAIN FERN
Polypodiaceae
FERN
ZONES 2B–9, 14–24
PARTIAL OR FULL SHADE
REGULAR TO AMPLE WATER

Woodwardia fimbriata

Native from British Columbia to Mexico. Among the largest native Western ferns, this plant can reach 9 ft. tall in wet coastal forests, but it is more typically seen in gardens at 4–5 ft. tall, 3 ft. wide. Spreads by woody rhizomes. Thick, leathery, medium green fronds are erect but spreading toward the top, twice cut but still somewhat coarse. Use near pool or brook, against shaded wall, in woodland garden. Sometimes seen in desert areas where some shade and seepage exist. Slow to get going if dug from existing clumps; nursery plants are vigorous, fast growing. Withstands neglect once well established. Can take full sun in wet spots. Often sold as *W. chamissoi* or *W. radicans.*

WOOLLY BLUE CURLS. See TRICHOSTEMA lanatum

WOOLLY SENNA. See SENNA multiglandulosa

WORMWOOD. See ARTEMISIA

XANTHORRHOEA

GRASS TREE
Liliaceae
PERENNIALS
ZONES 12–24
FULL SUN
LITTLE OR NO WATER

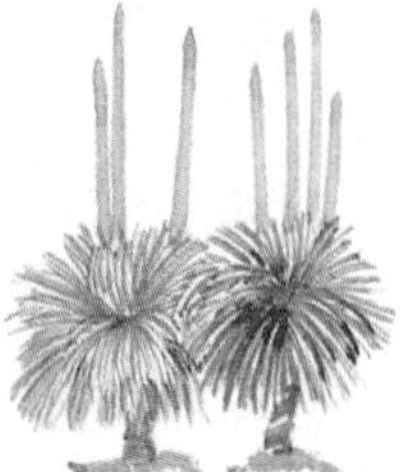
Xanthorrhoea preisii

Native to Australia. Dense tufts of narrow, grasslike, 2–4-ft.-long leaves radiate from top of thick, woody, nearly black, slow-growing stem. Foliage mass stays at about 3–5 ft. tall, 3 ft. wide for many years, but as stem gradually lengthens, plant height eventually increases to 12–15 ft. Sometimes blooms; white flowers are borne in a dense, narrow spike on a tall stem that increases the plant's height further. *X. preisii* and *X. quadrangulata* are similar species. Best used with yuccas or with agaves or other succulents in dry, loose, sandy soil.

XANTHOSOMA

Araceae
PERENNIALS
ZONES 12, 13, 16, 17, 21–24; H1, H2; OR INDOORS
FILTERED SUNLIGHT; BRIGHT INDIRECT LIGHT
AMPLE WATER

Xanthosoma sagittifolium

Tropical plants related to *Alocasia.* Both species are stemless, grow to 6 ft. tall and wide, produce big, arrow-shaped leaves on long stalks. Flowers more curious than attractive; resemble those of calla *(Zantedeschia),* with a central spike surrounded by a usually greenish or yellowish bract. These plants need moist, rich soil for best performance. They can grow in standing water or in pots submerged in a pond or pool. Protect from hard frosts.

X. sagittifolium. Dark green, 3-ft.-long leaves on 3-ft. stalks. Greenish white, 7–9-in.- long bracts.

X. violaceum (X. nigrum). Grows from edible tubers. Dark green leaves to 2 ft. long have paler undersides, purplish veins and margins, powdery appearance. Purple, 2½-ft. leafstalks have a heavy, waxy, bluish or grayish coating. Yellowish white bracts to 1 ft. long.

XERANTHEMUM annuum

COMMON IMMORTELLE
Asteraceae (Compositae)
ANNUAL
ALL ZONES
FULL SUN
REGULAR WATER

Xeranthemum annuum

Mediterranean native to 2½ ft. high, 1½ ft. wide. Bears so-called everlasting flowers, with daisylike heads of papery bracts to 1½ in. across in pink, lavender, white, shades of purple. Scanty foliage is silvery green.

Sow seeds directly in garden beds where plants are to grow; sow in spring for summer and fall bloom. Accepts almost any soil. Cut flowers are often dried for use in winter bouquets.

XYLOSMA congestum

Flacourtiaceae

EVERGREEN OR DECIDUOUS SHRUB OR TREE

ZONES 8–24

FULL SUN OR PARTIAL SHADE

MODERATE WATER

Xylosma congestum

From China. Basic landscape foliage plant. Loose, spreading growth to 8–10 ft. tall and as wide or wider. Shiny yellowish green leaves are ovate with pointed tips, 1½–3 in. long; new growth is bronzy. Flowers are insignificant and rarely seen. Some plants are spiny. Left alone, xylosma develops an angular main stem that takes its time zigzagging upward. Meanwhile, long, graceful side branches develop; these are arching or drooping, sometimes lying on the ground. Can be trained as single or multitrunked small tree, espaliered on wall or fence, used as clipped or unclipped hedge. 'Compacta' grows slowly to half the size of species.

Hardy to 10°F/–12°C but may lose many (or all) leaves in hard frosts. Normally sheds many old leaves when new spring growth begins; frost at that time will kill new growth. This is a useful and versatile plant, though its unattractive appearance in nursery cans (especially in winter, when stems may be nearly bare) and slow start in ground may discourage gardeners. Tolerates heat, most soils. Scale, spider mites are occasional pests. Chlorosis may be a problem.

YARROW. See ACHILLEA

YAUPON. See ILEX vomitoria

YELLOW BELLS, YELLOW ELDER, YELLOW TRUMPET FLOWER. See TECOMA stans

YELLOW-EYED GRASS. See SISYRINCHIUM californicum

YELLOW FLAX. See LINUM flavum, REINWARDTIA indica

YELLOW MORNING GLORY. See MERREMIA

YELLOW OLEANDER. See THEVETIA peruviana

YELLOW TRUMPET VINE. See MACFADYENA unguis-cati

YELLOW WAXBELLS. See KIRENGESHOMA palmata

YELLOW WOOD. See CLADRASTIS kentukea

YELLOWWOOD. See PODOCARPUS henkelii, P. latifolius

YERBA BUENA. See SATUREJA douglasii

YESTERDAY-TODAY-AND-TOMORROW. See BRUNFELSIA pauciflora 'Floribunda'

YEW. See TAXUS

YEW PINE. See PODOCARPUS macrophyllus

YUCCA

Agavaceae

EVERGREEN TREES, SHRUBS, PERENNIALS

ZONES VARY BY SPECIES

FULL SUN, EXCEPT AS NOTED

LITTLE TO MODERATE WATER, EXCEPT AS NOTED

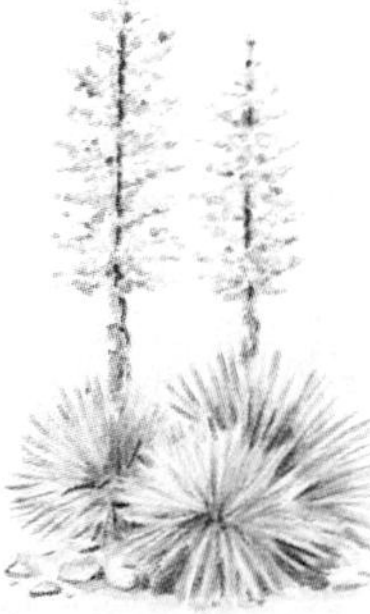

Yucca whipplei

Yuccas grow over much of North America. All have tough, sword-shaped leaves and large clusters of typically white or whitish, rounded to bell-shaped flowers. Some are stemless clumps; others have trunks and reach tree size. Best in well-drained soil. Most need only occasional deep soakings. Group yuccas with cacti or with agaves or other succulents; or grow them with softer-leafed tropical foliage plants. Taller kinds have striking silhouettes, and even stemless species provide important vertical accents when in bloom. Keep those with stiff, sharp-pointed leaves away from walks, terraces, and other well-traveled areas. (Some people clip off the sharp tips with nail clippers.)

Young plants of some species can be used as indoor plants; they tolerate dry air and grow well in hot, sunny windows. For this use, buy plants at gallon-can size or smaller; transplant them outside when they become too large for the house. The following are successful indoors: *Y. aloifolia* (but beware of its sharp-pointed leaves), *Y. elephantipes, Y. filamentosa, Y. gloriosa, Y. recurvifolia.*

Y. aloifolia. SPANISH BAYONET. Zones 7–24; H1, H2. From southern U.S., Mexico. Slow to 10 ft. by 5 ft. or larger. Single or branching trunk; sometimes sprawls for picturesque effect. Stems densely clothed in sharp-pointed dark green leaves to 2½ ft. long, 2 in. wide. Foliage of 'Variegata' is marked with yellowish white. White (sometimes purple-tinged) flowers to 4 in. across are carried in dense, erect clusters to 2 ft. tall in late spring or summer.

Y. baccata. BANANA YUCCA, DATIL. Zones 1–3, 7, 9–14, 18–24. From southwestern U.S., Mexico. Slow to 3 ft. high, 5 ft. wide. Foliage clump may have no stem or several short, prostrate ones. Sharp-tipped, light bluish green or yellowish green leaves to 2 ft. long, 2 in. wide, with fibers along the edges. Large (2–6-in.), fleshy flowers from spring into summer are red brown outside, white inside, carried in dense, 2-ft.-long clusters. Fleshy, edible, bananalike fruits to 6 in. long.

Y. brevifolia. JOSHUA TREE. Zones 7, 9–16, 18–23. From deserts of Southern California, Nevada, Utah, Arizona. Few-branched, slow-growing plant to 15–30 ft. by 30 ft.; both trunk and branches are heavy. Gray-green, spiny-tipped leaves to 16 in. long, 1 in. wide, clustered near branch ends. Old, dead leaves hang on. Dense, foot-long clusters of greenish white, about 3-in. flowers in late winter and spring. Collected plants are sometimes sold; nursery plants are very slow to form trunks. Best in dry, well-drained soil in desert gardens. Difficult under ordinary garden conditions.

Y. elata. SOAPTREE YUCCA. Zones 7–24. From southwestern U.S., northern Mexico. Slow to 6–20 ft. tall, 8–10 ft. wide; single or branched trunk. Pale green, sharp-pointed leaves to 4 ft. long, ½ in. wide. Dead leaves hang on to form a straw-colored, shaggy "skirt" on trunk. Tall stems are topped by white, 2¼-in. flowers in spikes to 3 ft. long; blooms late spring into summer. May not bloom every year.

Y. elephantipes (Y. gigantea). GIANT YUCCA. Zones 12, 13 (protected from afternoon sun, hard frosts), 16, 17, 19–24; H1, H2. From Mexico, Central America. Fast growing (to 2 ft. per year) to an eventual 15–30 ft. by 8 ft. Usually has several trunks. Rich deep green, soft-tipped leaves to 4 ft. long, 3 in. wide. Striking silhouette alone or combined with other big foliage plants; looks out of proportion in smaller gardens. Tall (3–6-ft.) spikes of creamy white, 1½-in. flowers in spring. Does best in good, well-drained soil with moderate to regular water.

Y. filamentosa. ADAM'S NEEDLE. Zones 1–24. From southeastern U.S. To 2½ ft. tall, 5 ft. wide; stemless. Stiff dark green leaves to 1½ ft. long, 1 in. wide, with long, loose fibers at edges. In late spring and summer, bears yellowish white, 2–3-in. flowers (lightly fragrant in evening) in narrow clusters to 4–7 ft. or taller. One of the hardiest, most widely planted yuccas in colder regions. Varieties include 'Bright Edge', yellow-striped leaves; 'Color Guard', leaves striped white and cream. Regular water.

Y. flaccida. Zones 1–9, 14–24. From southeastern U.S. Resembles *Y. filamentosa,* but flower clusters are somewhat shorter and leaves are less rigid, with straight fibers on edges. 'Golden Sword' has yellow-variegated foliage; 'Ivory Tower' bears outward-facing rather than drooping flowers. Regular water.

Y. glauca. SOAPWEED. Zones 1–13. Native from New Mexico and Texas to South Dakota. To 3–4 ft. high and wide or larger, with short or prostrate trunk. May remain in a single rosette or form clumps. Stiff leaves, 2 ft. long, 2 in. wide, grayish green edged with a hairline of white and a few thin threads. White, 2½-in. flowers on 3-ft. stalks in spring or early summer.

Y. gloriosa. SPANISH DAGGER, SOFT-TIP YUCCA. Zones 7–9, 12–24; H1, H2. True species is native to southeastern U.S. Plants sold under this name in the West are most likely a form of *Y. elephantipes* or a hybrid between that form and *Y. gloriosa.* Much like *Y. aloifolia* in appearance. To 10 ft. tall, 8 ft. wide, generally with multiple trunks—except in colder part of range, where it is usually a smaller, stemless plant. Soft-tipped leaves with good green color that blends well with lush, tropical-looking plants. Summer bloom. Moderate to regular water; too much moisture may produce black areas on leaf margins.

Y. recurvifolia (Y. pendula). Zones 7–10, 12–24. From southeastern U.S. To 6–10 ft. tall, 6–8 ft. wide, with single, unbranched trunk (may be lightly branched in age). Can be cut back to keep single trunked. Spreads by offsets to make large groups. Beautiful blue-gray leaves are 2–3 ft. long, 2 in. wide, sharply bent downward. Leaf tips are spined but bend to the touch; they won't cause injury. Not as stiff and metallic looking as most yuccas. White, about 3-in. flowers in late spring or early summer are borne in loose, open, 3–5-ft.-tall clusters. Easy to grow under all garden conditions. Moderate to regular water.

Y. rigida. BLUE YUCCA. Zones 10 (with protection), 11–13. From Chihuahuan Desert of Mexico. To 12 ft. by 5 ft.; trunk may branch with age. Each stem is topped with rosette of stiff, spiny-tipped, blue-green leaves to 2 ft. long, 1½ in. wide. Old leaves form tan thatch on trunk. Dense spikes of white, 2¼-in. flowers appear in spring or early summer.

Y. rostrata (Y. thompsoniana). Zones 7–24. Native from extreme southwestern Texas into Chihuahuan Desert of Mexico. Treelike yucca to 12 ft. by 9 ft. or larger. Notable feature is the trunk, which is covered with soft gray fuzz (fibers remaining from old leaf bases). Needle-pointed leaves to 2 ft. long, ½ in. wide. Blooms in late spring, bearing 2-ft. clusters of white, 2½-in. flowers on a 2-ft. stalk.

Y. schidigera (Y. mohavensis). Zones 7–16, 18–24. From deserts of California, Nevada, Arizona, Baja California. Short-stemmed plant to 3–12 ft. tall, 3 ft. wide (or wider if stem branches). Tough, sharp-tipped, medium green leaves 2–3 ft. long, 1–2½ in. wide. Purple-tinted white flowers about 1¾ in. wide, in 2-ft. clusters. Spring bloom.

Y. schottii. MOUNTAIN YUCCA. Zones 10–13. Native from Arizona and New Mexico to northern Mexico. To 6–15 ft. tall, 3–4 ft. wide, with single (rarely branching) trunk. Gray-green, sharp-tipped leaves 1½–3 ft. long, 2 in. wide. Dead leaves hang on for a long time. Clusters of white, 1½-in. flowers from spring to midsummer. Full sun or light shade.

Y. whipplei. OUR LORD'S CANDLE. Zones 2–24. From California coast, Southern California mountains, Baja California. Dense, trunkless rosette to 3 ft. tall, 6 ft. wide. Gray-green leaves are 1–2 ft. long, ¾ in. wide, with sharply toothed edges, needlelike tips; don't locate this plant where people can walk into it. Blooms in summer; 6–14-ft.-long stems carry drooping, 1–2-in., creamy white blossoms in large, branched, 3–6-ft.-long spikes. Plant dies after flowering; new plants come from seeds or offsets.

YUSHANIA aztecorum. See BAMBOO, Otatea

ZABEL LAUREL. See PRUNUS laurocerasus 'Zabeliana'

Zamiaceae. This family is closely related to Cycadaceae, differing only in technical details; both families are generally considered to be cycads. *Dioon* and *Zamia* are representatives.

ZAMIA

Zamiaceae (Cycadaceae)

CYCADS

ZONES 21–24; H1, H2; OR INDOORS

EXPOSURE NEEDS VARY BY SPECIES

REGULAR WATER

Zamia pumila

Of 100 or so species, only the following two are generally seen. Slow-growing plants. Short trunks (may be completely or partially beneath soil level) are usually marked with scars from old leaf bases. Circular crowns of leaves resembling stiff fern fronds or small palm fronds. Need organically enriched, fast-draining soil.

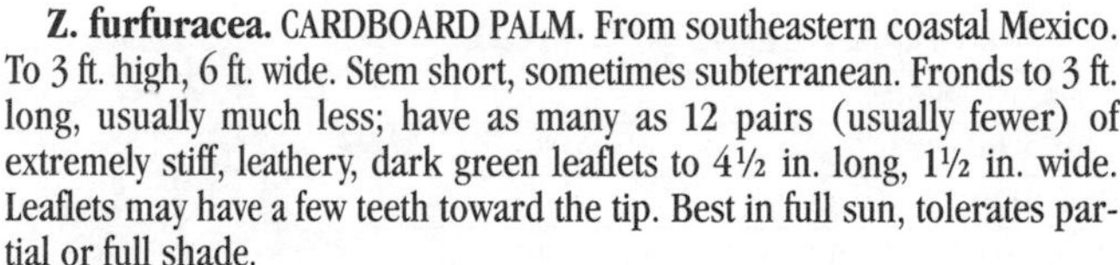

Z. furfuracea. CARDBOARD PALM. From southeastern coastal Mexico. To 3 ft. high, 6 ft. wide. Stem short, sometimes subterranean. Fronds to 3 ft. long, usually much less; have as many as 12 pairs (usually fewer) of extremely stiff, leathery, dark green leaflets to 4½ in. long, 1½ in. wide. Leaflets may have a few teeth toward the tip. Best in full sun, tolerates partial or full shade.

Z. pumila (Z. integrifolia). COONTIE. From Florida, Cuba, West Indies. To 4 ft. high, 6 ft. wide. Short trunk is largely below soil level. Fronds to 3 ft. long, with as many as 30 pairs of dark green leaflets to 5 in. long, 1¼ in. wide. Partial shade.

ZANTEDESCHIA

CALLA

Araceae

PERENNIALS FROM RHIZOMES

ZONES 5, 6, 8, 9, 12–24; H1, H2; OR DIG AND STORE ALL BUT Z. AETHIOPICA

EXPOSURE NEEDS VARY BY SPECIES

WATER NEEDS VARY BY SPECIES

Zantedeschia aethiopica

From South Africa. Clumps of long-stalked, shiny rich green, usually arrow-shaped leaves, sometimes spotted in white. Flower bract (spathe) surrounds a central spike (spadix) tightly covered with tiny true flowers.

Common calla *(Z. aethiopica)* has different cultural needs than other callas. It is soil tolerant and thrives in moist, even boggy, soil all year. Where summers are hot, grow in light shade; in milder climates, give full sun or light shade. Plant fall through early spring; set rhizomes 4 in. deep, 1 ft. apart. Needs year-round moisture. Dig and divide only when performance declines. Plants are evergreen to semievergreen and cannot be dug and stored over winter in cold climates. Beyond hardiness range, grow in pots and protect in winter.

The other callas described here die to the ground in fall, reappear in spring. Need regular water during growth and bloom, less during dormancy. In fall, set rhizomes 2 in. deep, 8–12 in. apart, in organically enriched, well-drained, and (ideally) slightly acid soil. Grow in full sun; in hot-summer areas, give light shade. As for *Z. aethiopica,* dig and divide when overcrowded. Beyond hardiness limits, plant in spring for summer bloom; then dig when leaves die back, store over winter in cool, dark place, replant in spring.

Z. aethiopica. COMMON CALLA. To 2–4 ft. tall, with unspotted leaves to 1½ ft. long, 10 in. wide. In spring (sometimes continuing into summer), pure or creamy white spathes to 8 in. long appear on stems slightly taller than foliage.

Varieties include robust 'Green Goddess', with large spathes that are white at base, green toward tip; and 'Hercules', larger than species, with big spathes that open flat, curve backward. Dwarf types include 'Childsiana' (to 1 ft.) and 'Minor' (to 1½ ft.).

Z. albomaculata. SPOTTED CALLA. To 2 ft. tall, with bright green, white-spotted leaves 1–1½ ft. long, 10 in. wide. Creamy yellow or white spathes to 5 in. long, with red-purple blotch at base. Blooms from spring into summer.

Z. elliottiana. GOLDEN CALLA. To 2 ft. tall, with bright green, white-spotted leaves to 10 in. long, 6 in. wide. Spathes to 6 in. long, greenish yellow aging to rich golden yellow. Summer bloom. Tolerates full sun, even in hot climates.

Z. hybrids. Plants are usually about the size of *Z. rehmanii* and bloom in late spring and summer. Leaves are typically unspotted, though some selections have spots on foliage. Spathe colors include cream, buff, orange, pink shades, lavender, purple.

Z. pentlandii. Resembles *Z. albomaculata,* but leaves are unspotted and spathes are deep golden yellow with purple throat. Summer bloom.

Z. rehmanii. RED or PINK CALLA. To 1½–2 ft., with narrow, lance-shaped, unspotted green leaves to 1 ft. long, 2½ in. wide. Pink or rosy pink spathes to 5 in. long in midspring. 'Superba' has dark pink spathes.

ZANTHOXYLUM piperitum

JAPAN PEPPER
Rutaceae
DECIDUOUS SHRUB OR TREE
ZONES 6–9, 14–17
FULL SUN
MODERATE WATER

Zanthoxylum piperitum

Native to China, Japan, Korea. Dense growth to 8–20 ft. tall and wide. Handsome dark green, 3–6-in.-long leaves with 11–23 oval, 2-in.-long leaflets; may turn yellow in autumn. Flat, ½-in.-long spines in pairs along stems. Inconspicuous green flowers. Small, aromatic red fruits ripen in fall; they have black seeds that are pulverized and used as seasoning in Japan. Peppery-tasting leaves are slightly numbing to the tongue; they too are used in Japanese cuisine.

ZAUSCHNERIA (Epilobium)

CALIFORNIA FUCHSIA
Onagraceae
SHRUBBY PERENNIALS
ZONES 2–11, 14–24, EXCEPT AS NOTED
FULL SUN, EXCEPT AS NOTED
LITTLE TO MODERATE WATER, EXCEPT AS NOTED

Zauschneria californica

Botanists assign California fuchsias to *Epilobium,* while horticulturists prefer to call them *Zauschneria,* as do wildflower enthusiasts and home gardeners. We come down on the side of horticulturists, but with a nod to botanists. Plants are typically low and spreading, with narrow, ½–1½-in.-long, gray-green or gray leaves. In late summer or fall, put on a profuse show of orange or scarlet (rarely white or pink) flowers that are very attractive to hummingbirds. Best in informal gardens, on banks or hillsides—most are a bit rangy, spread into other garden beds by invasive roots, go to seed and reseed themselves, and become twiggy and untidy looking in winter. For better form and flowering, cut back after bloom or before new growth begins.

Z. arizonica. See Z. californica latifolia

Z. californica (Epilobium canum canum). From California, Oregon, Wyoming, New Mexico, northern Mexico. Upright or arching growth to 1–2 ft. high. Leaves generally grayish, evergreen in mild-winter areas. Scarlet flowers. Improved varieties include erect 'Bowman'; semitrailing 'Calistoga'; 'Catalina', with silvery white leaves; mounding 'Cloverdale'; compact 'Dublin'; and light pink–flowered 'Solidarity Pink'. 'Etteri', possibly a hybrid between *Z. californica* and *Z. septentrionalis,* makes low mats of silvery foliage.

Z. c. garrettii (E. canum garrettii). From Utah, Wyoming. The subspecies itself blooms only sparsely, but 'Orange Carpet' is a profuse bloomer with bright orange flowers. Compact habit to 4 in. high. Prefers afternoon shade and regular water.

Z. c. latifolia (E. canum latifolium). Range like that of *Z. californica,* but distribution is more southerly. Differs from *Z. californica* mainly in somewhat shorter habit (1–1½ ft. high) and broader, greener leaves. 'Everett's Choice' is an improved variety. 'Arizonica' *(Z. arizonica)* grows 3 ft. tall, has bright orange flowers.

Z. septentrionalis (E. septentrionale). HUMBOLDT COUNTY FUCHSIA. Zones 5–7, 14–17, 19–24. From northern Coast Ranges of California. Mat-forming species to 8 in. high. Gray-green to silvery leaves; bright scarlet flowers. Needs afternoon shade in hottest climates. 'Wayne's Silver' is a cutting-grown selection with uniform, dense habit and silvery foliage.

ZEBRA PLANT. See CALATHEA zebrina

ZEBRINA pendula. See TRADESCANTIA zebrina

ZELKOVA serrata

SAWLEAF ZELKOVA
Ulmaceae
DECIDUOUS TREE
ZONES 3–21
FULL SUN
MODERATE TO REGULAR WATER

Zelkova serrata

Eastern Asian relative of elm *(Ulmus).* Good shade tree; sometimes used as a substitute for American elm *(U. americana),* which is highly prone to Dutch elm disease (zelkova is also susceptible but rarely succumbs). Grows at moderate to fast rate to 60 ft. or higher, equally wide. Silhouette ranges from vase shaped to quite spreading. Has smooth gray bark. Narrowly oval, sawtoothed, 2–3½-in.-long leaves are similar to those of elm but rougher in texture. Fall color varies from yellow to dark red to dull reddish brown. Among vase-shaped varieties, 'Halka' is the fastest growing and the best American elm mimic; 'Green Vase' has a narrower vase shape than vigorous 'Village Green'.

Takes wide range of soils. Fairly tolerant of drought, wind. You may need to train and prune young trees to establish a good framework; thin out crowded ascending branches.

ZEPHYRANTHES

ZEPHYR FLOWER, FAIRY LILY
Amaryllidaceae
PERENNIALS FROM BULBS
ZONES VARY BY SPECIES
FULL SUN OR PARTIAL SHADE
REGULAR WATER DURING GROWTH AND BLOOM

Zephyranthes candida

Clumps of foot-long, bright green, grassy leaves give rise to slender, hollow stems, each bearing a single funnel-shaped blossom with six segments. In their native Central and South America, often bloom after rains (hence another common name, rain lily). Species described here bloom in late summer and early fall.

Plant bulbs in well-drained soil at any time (though fall planting is ideal), setting them 1–2 in. deep, 3 in. apart. In mild-winter areas with a long growing season, plants may bloom several times a year if you provide a short dry period after bloom, then resume watering to initiate another growth cycle. In other regions, give little or no water after foliage dies back. Can remain undisturbed for many years. Pretty in rock garden or foreground of border. Excellent pot plant for patio or greenhouse.

Z. candida. Zones 4–9, 12–24; H1, H2. White, 2-in. flowers, sometimes stained pink in throat. Evergreen in warmer part of range. Usually sold as potted plants; can be planted out at any time.

Z. citrina. Zones 7–9, 12–24; H1, H2. Similar to *Z. candida* but has bright yellow flowers.

Z. grandiflora. Zones 7–9, 12–24; H1, H2. Extra-large flowers (to 4 in. across). Rose pink blossoms have a lily shape in the morning, open out flat by midday, close in late afternoon.

ZEXMENIA hispida

Asteraceae (Compositae)
SHRUBBY PERENNIAL
ZONES 10–13
FULL SUN OR LIGHT SHADE
LITTLE TO MODERATE WATER

Zexmenia hispida

Native to Texas, Mexico. Compact, rounded plant to 2–3 ft. tall and wide; puts on a good show of bright orange-yellow daisies from late spring into autumn. Rough-textured, somewhat sticky dark green leaves, 1–2 in. long, are oval to lance shaped. In cold winters, plant can lose leaves or even die to the ground, but it recovers quickly in spring. In light shade, it blooms less and sprawls more, making an attractive ground cover. Give well-drained soil.

Zingiberaceae. The ginger family contains tropical or subtropical perennials with fleshy rhizomes, canelike stems, and (usually) large leaves. Flowers are irregular in form, in spikes or heads, often showy or with showy bracts. Many are aromatic or have fragrant flowers. Includes *Alpinia*, ginger lily *(Hedychium)*, and true ginger *(Zingiber)*.

ZINGIBER officinale

TRUE GINGER

Zingiberaceae

PERENNIAL FROM RHIZOME

ZONES 9, 14–24; H1, H2

PARTIAL SHADE

REGULAR TO AMPLE WATER

Zingiber officinale

This tropical Asian plant's rhizomes are the source of the ginger root used in cooking. To 2–4 ft. tall, with indefinite spread. Narrow, glossy bright green leaves to 1 ft. long. Summer flowers are yellowish green, with purple lip marked yellow; they are only rarely seen and not especially showy. Needs heat and humidity. Buy roots (fresh, not dried) at grocery store in early spring; cut into 1–2-in.-long sections, each with well-developed growth buds. Let cut ends of sections dry, then plant just below surface of rich, moist soil (pot culture is common). Water cautiously until top and root growth are active. Feed once a month. Plants are dormant in winter; rhizomes may rot in cold, wet soil. Harvest roots at any time—but allow several months after planting for them to reach some size. Grown commercially in Hawaii.

ZINNIA

Asteraceae (Compositae)

ANNUALS AND PERENNIALS

ZONES 1–24, H1, H2, EXCEPT AS NOTED

FULL SUN

REGULAR WATER, EXCEPT AS NOTED

Zinnia elegans

Longtime favorites for colorful, round flowers, typically in summer and early fall. These are hot-weather plants that do not gain from being planted early; they merely stand still until weather warms up. Subject to mildew in foggy places, if given overhead water, and when autumn brings longer nights, more dew and shade. Sow seeds where plants are to grow (or set out nursery plants) from late spring to early summer. Give good garden soil, feed generously. Most garden zinnias belong to *Z. elegans*.

Z. acerosa. Perennial. Zones 10–24. From southern Arizona, Texas, Mexico. To 6–10 in. high, 2 ft. wide, with hairy, needlelike, ¾-in.-long leaves. Flowers are 1½ in. wide, with relatively large, creamy white rays veined in green on underside. Blooms sporadically from spring through fall, whenever moisture is present; goes dormant during extended periods of drought.

Z. angustifolia. Annual. Compact growth to 16 in. high and wide, with very narrow leaves to 2½ in. long. Orange, inch-wide flowers; each ray has a paler stripe. Blooms in 6 weeks from seed, continues late into fall. 'Classic' grows to 1 ft. high and 2 ft. wide, has 1½-in. flowers. The Star series, also to 1 by 2 ft., has 2-in. blooms in orange, yellow, and white. 'Golden Eye' is much like 'Star White': both have white rays, yellow centers.

Hybrids between *Z. angustifolia* and *Z. elegans* include 'Profusion Orange' and 'Profusion Cherry Pink'. These grow 1–1½ ft. high and wide, with 2½-in. flower heads containing more than one row of rays.

Z. elegans. Annual. From Mexico. The common zinnia, sold in strains ranging from less than a foot high and wide to 4 ft. tall, half as wide. Oval to lance-shaped leaves to 5 in. long; summer flowers from less than 1 in. to as much as 5–7 in. across. Forms include full double, cactus flowered (with quilled rays), and crested (cushionlike center surrounded by rows of broad rays); the many colors available include white, pink, salmon, rose, red, yellow, orange, lavender, and purple. 'Envy' is a novelty type with lime green flowers.

Among smaller strains (to about 1 ft.) for edging or foreground are Dasher Hybrid Mixed, very quick to bloom; Peter Pan Hybrid Improved; and mildew-resistant Small World. All have 3-in. blooms.

Intermediate types include 2-ft.-tall 'Candy Stripe', with 4-in. white flowers striped with pink, rose, or red; 2½-ft. Ruffles Hybrids, 3½-in. blossoms with ruffled rays; and 18–20-in. Sun Bow, with fully double, 1½-in. flowers. Sun Hybrids, 2–2½ ft., have 5-in. flowers; Giant Cactus-flowered Mix, to 3 ft., has 4–5-in. semidouble blooms.

Tall plants for cutting and back-of-border planting include 4-ft. Benary's Giants (also sold as Park's Picks, Blue Point) and 3-ft., double-blossomed Dahlia-flowered Mix; both have 4–5-in. blooms. 'Big Red Hybrid', to 3 ft., has bright red, 5–6-in. flowers.

Z. grandiflora. Perennial in Zones 14–24; annual elsewhere. Native to Rocky Mountains, south into Mexico. To 1 ft. high and wide. Bright green leaves to 1 in. long, ⅛ in. wide. Spring-into-fall flowers are 1½ in. wide, bright yellow with orange eye. Survives with no supplemental moisture but needs regular water to bloom satisfactorily.

Z. haageana. Annual. From southeastern U.S., Mexico. To 2 ft. tall, 1 ft. wide. Narrow, 3-in. leaves. Persian Carpet (1 ft. tall) and Old Mexico (16 in. tall) have double blossoms in mahogany red, yellow, and orange, with all three colors usually mixed in the same flower. Long summer bloom season.

Z. peruviana. Annual. Native from southern U.S. to Argentina. Grows to 3 ft. tall and as wide; leaves to 3 in. long, 1¼ in. wide. In summer, bears profuse, 1½-in. flowers in brick red or soft gold. Blossoms dry well for arrangements, either in a vase or on the plant. Also called Bonita zinnia or *Z. pauciflora*.

ZIZIPHUS jujuba. See JUJUBE

ZOYSIA

Poaceae (Gramineae)

PERENNIAL GRASSES

ZONES VARY BY SPECIES

BEST IN SUN, TOLERATE SOME SHADE

MODERATE TO REGULAR WATER

Zoysia tenuifolia

These Asian natives tend to spread slowly, are fairly deep rooted. Dormant and straw colored during the winter; turn green in spring. Use for lawns, ground covers. Plant using sod, sprigs, stolons, or plugs. Mow lawns 1–2 in. high.

Z. 'Emerald'. EMERALD ZOYSIA. Zones 8, 9, 12–14, 18–24; H1, H2. Hybrid between *Z. japonica* and *Z. tenuifolia.* Makes wiry, dark green, prickly-looking turf. Dense blades are hard to cut. More frost tolerant than other zoysias.

Z. japonica 'Meyer'. MEYER ZOYSIA. Zones 12, 13. Resembles bluegrass *(Poa)*. Turns brown earliest in winter, turns green latest in spring.

Z. matrella. MANILA GRASS. Zones 8, 9, 12–14, 18–24; H1, H2. Also similar to bluegrass in appearance. Holds color a little better than *Z. japonica* 'Meyer'.

Z. tenuifolia. KOREAN GRASS. Hardy in Zones 8, 9, 12–24; H1, H2. Creeping, fine textured, bumpy. Makes a beautiful grassy meadow or gives mossy Oriental effect in areas impossible to mow or water often. The farther inland, the longer the dormant season.

ZUCCHINI. See SQUASH

ZYGOCACTUS. See SCHLUMBERGERA

A Practical Guide to GARDENING

Success in gardening, as in any other endeavor, involves a good understanding of certain basic principles and procedures. In these pages, you'll find the fundamental information and step-by-step instructions you need to plant and care for your garden. Arranged in an easy-to-use alphabetical format, this guide offers advice on topics such as making compost, choosing and using fertilizers, plant propagation and planting techniques, pruning, soil management, watering and water conservation, and buying and caring for tools. You'll also find help in dealing with garden problems—plant diseases, insects, animal pests, and weeds—based on the principles of Integrated Pest Management, with emphasis on the least-toxic means of control. You can look to these pages, too, for information on selecting and growing the major categories of plants, from annuals and biennials through grasses and perennials to shrubs, trees, vegetables, and vines.

Annuals

Annuals are plants that germinate, grow shoots and leaves, flower, set seed, and die within a period of less than a year. Biennials (page 659), in contrast, take two growing seasons to complete their life cycle, while perennials (page 678) live for more than 2 (and sometimes for many) years. Though the annual-biennial-perennial distinction seems clear on paper, in the garden it is somewhat blurred. For example, some tender perennials (those that cannot survive freezing temperatures), such as geranium *(Pelargonium)* and some kinds of salvia and verbena, flower year after year in mild-winter climates but are grown as annuals where winters are cold. A few of the hardier perennials, such as snapdragon *(Antirrhinum majus),* are grown as annuals because older plants don't perform as well as young ones.

Favorite annuals are listed in "Annuals for Seasonal Color" in A Guide to Plant Selection, beginning on page 64.

Flanders field poppies *(Papaver rhoeas)* and corn cockles *(Agrostemma githago)*

PLANTING ANNUALS. The best planting time for annuals depends on your climate and the specific plant. *Cool-season annuals,* such as calendula, sweet pea *(Lathyrus odoratus),* and some primroses *(Primula),* grow best in the cool soil and mild temperatures of fall and early spring. Also called hardy annuals, these plants can withstand fairly heavy frosts. Indeed, if they are to bloom vigorously, they must develop roots and foliage during cool weather. Gardeners in cold-winter areas should plant them in very early spring, as soon as the soil can be worked. Where winters are mild, they can be planted in fall for bloom in winter and early spring. To ensure winter flowers, timing is important: plant while the days are still warm enough to encourage growth but when day length is decreasing. Plant too soon, and the plants will rush into bloom before they have become established; plant too late, and you probably won't get flowers until spring. In mild-winter regions, cool-season annuals can also be planted in late winter or very early spring for spring bloom.

Warm-season annuals are a large group of plants that includes cosmos, sunflower *(Helianthus annuus)*, and zinnia. These plants grow and flower best in the warm months of late spring, summer, and early fall. They are cold tender and may perish in a late frost if planted too early in spring. In cold-winter climates, set them out after all danger of frost has passed; in mild-winter climates, plant in midspring. (However, in desert regions of the Southwest, some warm-season annuals, such as petunias, are planted in early fall for winter bloom.)

You can start annuals from seed sown in containers or, in many cases, directly in the garden (see page 694 for more on starting seeds). Many annuals are also sold as started plants in nurseries; for best results, choose those that are relatively small, with healthy foliage and few or no flowers. Plants with yellowing leaves and those that are leggy, root-bound, too big for their pots, or already in full bloom will establish very slowly in the garden, and they'll usually flower poorly. (See page 691 for directions on planting from containers.)

To get your annuals off to a good start, prepare the garden soil carefully before setting out transplants or sowing seed. You'll find information on preparing planting beds on page 690.

CARING FOR ANNUALS. The key to success with annuals is to keep them growing steadily, through attention to watering, fertilizing, and deadheading, that is, removing dead flowers and any seedpods.

Water the bed thoroughly after you plant; thereafter, water enough to keep soil moist, but not soggy. Young seedlings or transplants may need water once a day in warm weather, but as they become established they will be able to get by with less. Apply a 1- to 2-inch-thick layer of mulch (such as compost, ground bark, or pine needles) to conserve water and discourage weeds from establishing.

Mixing a complete fertilizer into the soil before planting will generally supply annuals with nutrients sufficient for at least half the growing season. In cold-winter areas, an additional feeding after bloom begins will carry the plants through their season. Where winters are warmer and the growing season is correspondingly longer, give supplemental feedings both after flowering starts and again in late summer.

As their flowers fade, annuals focus their energy into ripening seeds. If you regularly deadhead a plant, it will usually bear more flowers in a continued effort to produce seeds. Deadheading also keeps the garden tidy. To do the job, just pinch or cut off individual, spent flowers or shear the flower heads with pruning or hedge shears, being careful not to remove any more than one-third of the plant.

Biennials

Biennials typically complete their life cycle in 2 years—in contrast to annuals (page 658), which live for less than a year, and perennials (page 678), which live for more than 2 years. During their first year, biennials grow from seed into leafy but nonblooming plants. They live through the winter (experiencing the period of cold temperatures that most require for bloom); then, in the following year, they flower, set seed, and die. This is the life cycle you'll observe if you start seeds yourself. Biennials sold in nurseries, though, usually bloom the year you buy them, since the grower has taken the plants through their first phase of growth for you.

Familiar biennials include common foxglove *(Digitalis purpurea)*, hollyhock *(Alcea rosea)*, and Canterbury bell *(Campanula medium)*, as well as vegetables such as carrot and onion. Breeders have developed strains of some biennials (including hollyhock and foxglove) that grow as annuals; these bloom the first year from seed, assuming the seed is sown early in spring. You'll also find hollyhock and foxglove strains that grow as short-lived perennials.

To grow biennials, sow seeds in containers or directly in the garden at the time indicated on the seed packet, typically mid- to late spring or summer. (For more on starting seeds, see page 694.) Transplant young plants into the garden in early fall, setting them in well-prepared soil; water as needed. Where the ground freezes, place a protective mulch of straw or chopped leaves around the plants, taking care not to smother the foliage rosettes. In spring, feed with a complete fertilizer as soon as new growth begins.

Bulbs

Commonly grouped together as "bulbs" are a multitude of plants with underground structures (specialized roots or stem bases) that serve as storage organs, accumulating nutrient reserves that will ensure the plant's survival through dormancy and supply energy for its growth and bloom in the year to come. The five bulb types recognized by botanists—true bulbs, corms, tubers, rhizomes, and tuberous roots—are described on page 660.

SELECTING AND PLANTING BULBS. Choose plump, firm bulbs that feel heavy for their size; avoid any that are soft, squashy, or shriveled.

HOW DEEP?

This ruler shows the depth for planting some common winter- and spring-blooming bulbs. Spacing is also noted.

1" **Anemone** (4 in. apart)

2" **Grape hyacinth** (*Muscari;* 3 in. apart); **Freesia** (2–3 in. apart); **Ranunculus** (6–8 in. apart)

Grape hyacinth

Watsonia

3" **Crocus** (3–4 in. apart)

4" **Dutch iris** (3–4 in. apart); **Watsonia** (6 in. apart)

5" **Daffodil** (*Narcissus,* large; 6–8 in. apart); **Calla** (*Zantedeschia aethiopica,* 1–2 ft. apart); **Tulip** (*Tulipa,* large; 4–6 in. apart)

6" **Hyacinth** (*Hyacinthus,* large; 4–6 in. apart)

Tulip and hyacinth

Many kinds of bulbs are graded by size. Larger-size bulbs generally yield more flowers, but they are also the priciest. If you're planting a large quantity, it's more economical to buy midsize specimens (they'll build up after a year or two to bloom as lavishly as larger bulbs).

Like most plants, bulbs need good drainage. If your soil drains very poorly, plant on a slope or in raised beds.

You can plant bulbs in a separate bed or set them among other plants, digging an individual hole for each bulb. (See page 690 for information on preparing a planting bed.) Work a complete fertilizer into the soil in the bed; or, if you are planting bulbs in individual holes, dig up to a tablespoon of fertilizer into the bottom of each hole, add about 2 inches of compost or soil over that, then plant the bulb. ▸

AVOID WILD BULBS

Certain bulbs have been dug so extensively in the wild that they are fast vanishing from their native habitats; many of these are considered endangered species. Wild-dug sorts that have been offered for sale in the U.S. include species anemones and narcissus (rather than named varieties or hybrids) as well as various species of cyclamen, winter aconite *(Eranthis hymelis)*, fritillary *(Fritillaria)*, snowdrop *(Galanthus)*, snowflake *(Leucojum)*, and sternbergia. To avoid contributing to the disappearance of such plants from the wild, buy only bulbs labeled "commercially propagated" or "from cultivated stock." If the bulbs are not labeled, ask about their origin before purchasing.

B

THE FIVE BULB TYPES AND WAYS TO DIVIDE THEM

The characteristics of each bulb type are summarized below, along with advice on how to divide each type. For information on the best time to divide and replant specific bulbs, consult the Western Plant Encyclopedia. The photos show bulbs oriented the way they should be planted.

True bulb. A true bulb is an underground stem base containing an embryonic plant surrounded by scales—modified leaves that overlap each other. A basal plate at the bottom of the bulb holds the scales together and produces roots. Most true bulbs have a protective papery outer skin called a tunic. Lilies, however, lack a tunic, making them more susceptible to drying and damage than other true bulbs; be sure to handle them with care. Most true bulbs produce offsets (also called increases). To divide, simply separate these from the mother bulb.

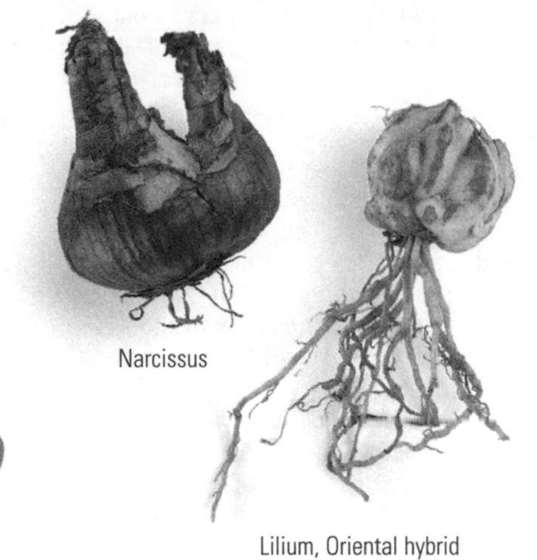

Narcissus

Lilium, Oriental hybrid

Muscari

Iris (bulbous)

Leucojum

Corm. A corm is a swollen underground stem base, but unlike a true bulb, it's composed of solid tissue rather than scales. Roots grow from a basal plate at the corm's bottom; the growth point is at the top. Many corms have a tunic formed from the dried bases of the previous season's leaves. Each corm lasts for a single year; as it shrinks away, a new corm and, in many species, small increases *(cormels)* form on top of it. To divide, separate healthy new corms and any cormels from the old corms (cormels may take as long as 2 to 3 years to reach flowering size).

Crocus

Watsonia

Freesia

In most soils, true bulbs and most corms should be planted about three times as deep as the bulb is wide. In hot climates or sandy soils, plant slightly deeper; in heavy soils, plant a bit shallower. The chart on page 659 shows how deep and how far apart to plant some widely grown winter- and spring-blooming bulbs; for depth and spacing for other bulbs, check the entries in the Western Plant Encyclopedia.

CARING FOR BULBS. Bulbs need water while they're growing actively. For most sorts, this period begins after planting and continues until the foliage dies back, until flowering is finished, or—for some types—until autumn. If you must supplement rainfall, water deeply enough to penetrate the root zone; the roots grow beneath the bulb.

When growth begins, apply a high-nitrogen fertilizer to enhance the quality of the current season's flowers. After bloom ends, much or all of a bulb's stored nutrients are depleted; to ensure a good show next year, those nutrients must be replenished. As long as the leaves are green and growing, they will continue to manufacture food for the coming year, so it's vital to leave them on the plant—bedraggled and weary though they may appear!—until they yellow and pull away easily. (If you want to hide the dying foliage, try overplanting with annuals or a ground cover.) After flowering is finished, it's also important to apply a complete fertilizer such as a 10-10-10 formula or a "bulb food" high in phosphorus and potassium. For these last two nutrients to be effective, they must reach the root zone (see "Fertilizers," page 668); scratch the fertilizer into the soil or apply it in narrow trenches dug near the bulbs, then water thoroughly.

NATURALIZING BULBS

A number of bulbous plants can be planted in meadows, fields, or light woodlands, where they'll form a carpet of wildflower-like blooms year after year. Consult the Western Plant Encyclopedia to see if the bulbs you want to naturalize are good candidates for this treatment and to check their climate, exposure, and moisture needs. If they aren't likely to receive enough water naturally, be prepared to supply it through irrigation.

The traditional naturalizing method is to broadcast a handful of bulbs over the desired planting area, then plant them where they fall. To achieve the most realistic effect, you may need to adjust the pattern slightly: the drift should be denser at one end or toward the center, as if the bulbs began to grow in one spot, then gradually spread to colonize outlying territory. Once you have the pattern you want, use a trowel or bulb planter to set the bulbs at their preferred depths.

Following bloom, fertilize the bulbs and allow the foliage to remain until it withers. After a number of years, overcrowding may cause a decrease in the number of flowers; when this happens, it's time to dig, divide, and replant.

Rhizome. A rhizome is a thickened stem growing partially or entirely belowground. Its roots grow directly from the underside. The primary growing point is at one end of the rhizome; additional growing points form along the sides. To divide, cut into sections that have visible growing points.

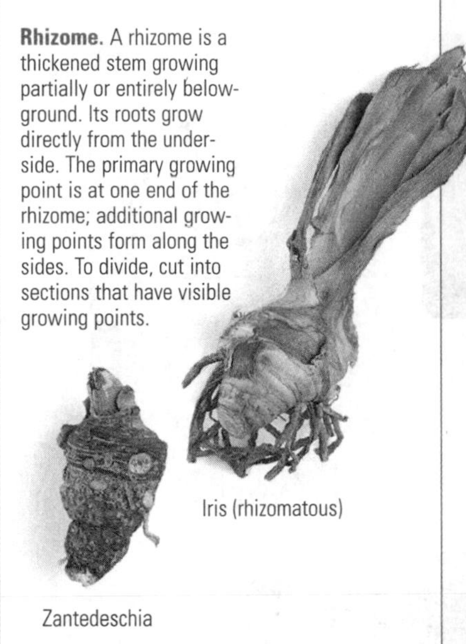

Iris (rhizomatous)

Zantedeschia

Tuber. Tubers, like corms, are swollen underground stem bases, but they lack the corm's distinct organization. There is no basal plate, so roots can grow from all sides. Instead of just one (or a few) growing points, a tuber has multiple growth points scattered over its surface; each is a scalelike leaf with a growth bud *(eye)* in its axil. Some tubers, such as cyclamen and begonia, are perennial; they increase in size each year. Others (the potato is the best-known example) are annual; as new tubers grow, the old ones disintegrate. To divide either kind of tuber, cut it into sections, making sure each has one or more growing points.

Begonia

Cyclamen

Tuberous roots. While the other four bulb types are specialized stems, a tuberous root is a true root, thickened to store nutrients. Fibrous roots for the uptake of water and nutrients develop from its sides and tip. Tuberous roots grow in a cluster, with the swollen portions radiating out from a central point. The growth buds are at the bases of old stems rather than on the roots themselves. To divide, cut the root cluster apart so each division contains both roots and part of a stem base with one or more growth buds.

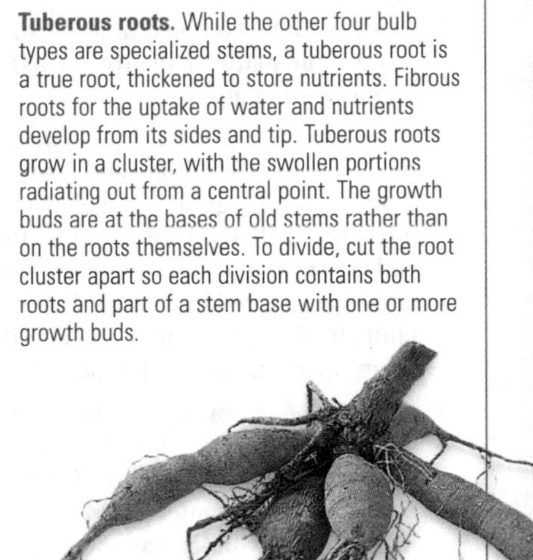

Dahlia

Composting

Composting is a natural process that converts raw organic materials into a valuable soil conditioner you can use to improve a soil's texture, boost its nutrient content, and make it more water retentive. Besides being good for your garden, composting lightens the load at the landfill: you recycle garden debris at home rather than consigning it to the dump.

A pile of leaves, branches, and other garden trimmings will eventually decompose with no intervention on your part. This type of composting is called *slow* or *cold composting.* With a little effort, however, you can speed up the process. If you create optimum conditions for the organisms responsible for decay (by giving them the mixture of air, water, and the carbon- and nitrogen-rich nutrients they need), the compost pile will heat up quickly and decompose in a few months. Such *hot composting* also destroys many (though not all) weeds and disease pathogens.

You can make compost in a freestanding pile or use some sort of enclosure (see page 662). Regardless of the method, though, the fundamentals of composting are the same.

GATHER MATERIALS. You'll need approximately equal amounts by volume of brown matter and green matter. *Brown matter* is high in carbon and includes dry leaves, hay, sawdust, straw, wood chips, and woody prunings. *Green matter* is high in nitrogen; it includes grass

COMPOSTING WITH WORMS

Worm composting, or vermicomposting, is an efficient way to compost fruit and vegetable scraps from the kitchen in a small amount of space. Red wiggler worms and bins for housing them are sold in many nurseries; you can also use a covered homemade wooden bin (about 2 feet square and 8 to 16 inches deep). Fill the bin with bedding made from shredded newspaper, then place it in a shaded, rain-protected location where it won't freeze or overheat from sun exposure. Feed the worms kitchen scraps; 2 pounds of worms will process about 7 pounds of fruit and vegetable scraps each week. After 3 to 6 months, you can begin harvesting the compost, which looks like dark, rich soil.

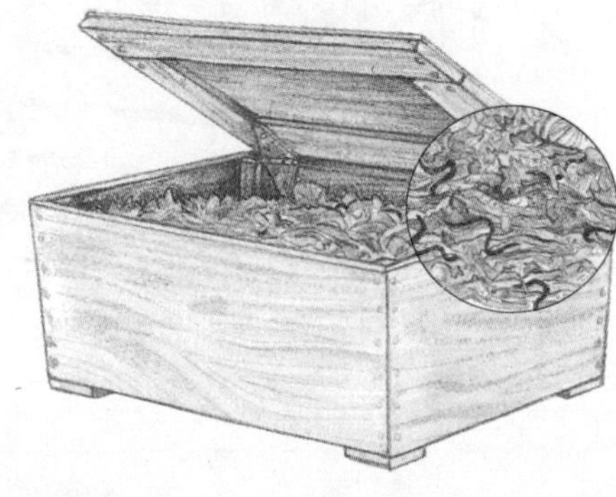

COMPOSTING SYSTEMS

You can make compost in a freestanding pile or in a homemade structure, or use a purchased manufactured composter.

Freestanding pile

Wire cylinder

- **Freestanding compost piles.** These piles should be at least 3 feet high and wide; at this size, their mass is great enough to generate the microbial activity needed for heating the materials. The upper size limit is about 5 feet high and wide; a pile larger than that may not receive enough air at its center. When siting the pile, allow space alongside for turning.
- **Wire cylinders or hoops.** For these, use welded wire, chicken wire, or snow fencing, supporting it with stakes if necessary. The cylinder or hoop should be about 4 feet in diameter and 3 to 4 feet tall. To turn the pile, lift the cylinder and move it to one side; then fork the materials back into it.
- **Three-bin systems.** Bin systems are more complex than freestanding piles or those corralled with wire, but they also offer a more flexible way to make compost. The left bin holds new green and brown material; the center one contains partly decomposed material; while the right bin holds finished or nearly finished compost. Turn the material in each bin weekly, moving decomposed material to the right. (The right bin will be empty for a few weeks at the start.)
- **Manufactured composters.** These include various sorts of ***tumblers***, systems that make it easier to turn materials and produce finished compost quickly. Most are turned with a crank, but some roll on the ground or are turned with foot treads. Such devices provide a tidy way to make compost, especially in small gardens.

  Another manufactured composter is the ***static compost bin***, in which the contents sit without turning (though occasional aerating with a spading fork is helpful). You add new materials at the top; the finished compost is removed through a door at the base. Though tidy, these units produce only fairly small amounts of compost—and they do so rather slowly.

Static bin

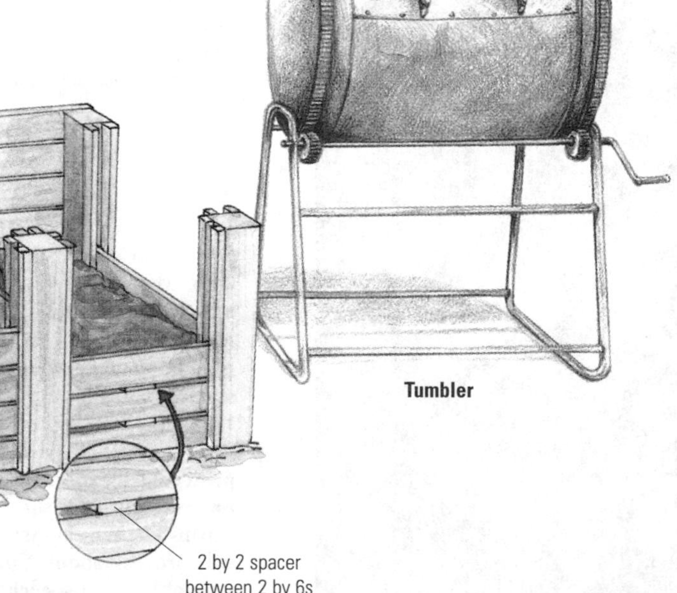

Tumbler

4 by 4 1 by 1 2 by 6

2 by 2 spacer between 2 by 6s

Three-bin system

clippings, fruit and vegetable scraps, coffee grounds, tea bags, crushed eggshells, and manure from cows, horses, goats, poultry, and rabbits. The compost will heat up faster if you collect all the ingredients in advance and assemble the pile all at once. Don't use bones, cat or dog waste, dairy products, meat scraps, badly diseased or insect-infested plants, or pernicious weeds that might survive composting (such as bindweed, quackgrass, and oxalis).

CHOP MATERIALS. Shredding or chopping large, rough materials into smaller pieces (ideally no larger than ¾ inch to 2 inches) allows decay-producing organisms to reach more surfaces and thus speeds up the entire composting process. Shredder-chippers and lawn mowers are good tools to use for this purpose. You can also chop the materials with a machete on a large wooden block. Shredding dry leaves is a good idea, too; collect leaves in an open area and just run a lawn mower over them.

BUILD THE PILE. Building the pile like a layer cake makes it easier to judge the ratio of brown to green materials. Start by spreading a 4- to 8-inch layer of brown material over an area at least 3 feet square; then add a layer of green material about 2 to 8 inches deep. (Layers of grass clippings should be only 2 inches deep; less-dense green materials can be layered more thickly.) Add another layer of brown material and sprinkle the pile with water. Mix these first three layers with a spading fork. Continue adding layers, watering, and mixing. To heat up efficiently, the pile should be about 3 feet tall, giving it a volume of one cubic yard.

TURN THE PILE. In just a few days, the pile should have heated up dramatically. In time, it will decompose on its own, but you can hurry things along by turning the contents to introduce more oxygen—which is needed by the organisms responsible for decomposition. Using a spading fork or pitchfork, restack the pile, redistributing it so that the materials originally on the outside are moved to the pile's center, where they'll be exposed to higher heat. If necessary, add water; the pile should be as moist as a wrung-out sponge. Turn the pile weekly, if possible, until it is no longer generating internal heat and most of the materials have decomposed.

USE THE COMPOST. Finished compost is dark and crumbly, with a pleasant, earthy aroma. Mix it into your planting beds or use it as a mulch. If some of the material from the compost pile's exterior is still coarser than you prefer for either a soil amendment or mulch, simply incorporate it into your next compost pile. To obtain a finer-textured compost to use as potting soil for containers or for starting seeds, sift the finished compost through a screen with ½-inch mesh.

COMPOST TROUBLESHOOTING

PROBLEM	POSSIBLE CAUSES	SOLUTIONS
Rotten odor	Too wet Lacks oxygen	Turn pile to aerate; layer in dry material such as sawdust, dry leaves.
Ammonia odor	Excess nitrogen (green material)	Turn pile; layer in dry material such as sawdust, dry leaves.
Pile not heating up	Too dry Too much dry or woody material	Turn pile, adding water. Add fresh green material such as grass clippings, fruit or vegetable scraps; bury scraps in pile.
Pile is attracting rodents and flies	Fruit or vegetable scraps are on the surface Meat or dairy scraps have been added	Always bury kitchen scraps inside the pile. If meat or dairy scraps are present, remove them. Turn pile to increase temperature. If a rodent problem continues, use a covered bin made of fine-mesh wire.

Container Gardening

Growing plants in containers lets you have a garden even when the space for one is limited or nonexistent: you can install a planter box below a window or use containers to turn a tiny balcony or patio into a leafy haven. Gardeners with plenty of room appreciate containers, too, valuing the versatility they offer. Blooming pot plants bring seasonal color to garden beds, a porch, or the front steps and are easily replaced with new ones when their flowers fade. In addition, containers give you the chance to experiment with new plant combinations and with kinds not suited to the native conditions. For instance, if your soil is alkaline or claylike but you are longing to raise acid-loving plants or those that demand fast drainage, just fill their pots with the sort of soil they need. Plants too tender for your winters can be moved to shelter when cold weather hits.

A SUBSTITUTE FOR PEAT

For potting mixes, many gardeners prefer sphagnum peat moss over ground bark: peat breaks down more slowly, and, unlike bark, it won't compact in the container and limit aeration. There are, however, concerns over the ecological damage that may result from the overmining of some peat bogs. A good alternative to peat is coir dust. A by-product of the coconut fiber industry, it's sold in bales and in compressed "bricks" that expand when soaked in water to make about 9 quarts of fluffy material. Used in potting mixes, it breaks down slowly and retains moisture and air well; it's also useful as a soil additive or mulch in the garden. Keep in mind, though, that coir dust won't help acidify the soil the way peat does, since its pH is closer to neutral (5.7 to 6.2).

PREPARING CONTAINERS. Choose containers with at least one drainage hole, so water won't accumulate around plant roots. Submerge terra-cotta pots in clean water and let them soak thoroughly; if the pots are too dry, they can initially draw water away from the potting mix. Scrub used containers with a solution of 1 part household bleach to 9 parts hot water. Cover the drainage hole(s) with a small piece of fine wire screen to keep soil from washing out.

CHOOSING A POTTING MIX. A good potting soil allows roots to grow easily; it should be fast draining yet moisture retentive. Quick drainage means roots won't run the risk of suffocating in soggy soil, while good water retention saves you from having to water too often. Regular garden soil, even good loam, is too dense for container use. For best success, most gardeners turn to packaged potting mixes, which don't contain soil; they're soilless mixtures of organic materials (such as ground bark, sphagnum peat moss, and/or compost) plus mineral matter such as perlite, pumice, or sand. Limestone may be added to balance the acidity of peat moss; fertilizers and wetting agents (see "Soil Polymers," page 709) may also be included. Before planting, flush the mix with water once or twice to eliminate excess salts.

A 2-cubic-foot bag of potting mix holds enough to transplant 8 to 10 plants from 1-gallon nursery cans into individual 10- to 12-inch pots or to fill a 36- by 8- by 10-inch planter box. For large planting projects, though, you may want to make your own mix. For a basic no-soil mix, combine ⅔ cubic yard nitrogen-stabilized ground bark, coir dust, or sphagnum peat moss; ⅓ cubic yard washed 20-grit sand; 6 pounds 0-10-10 granular fertilizer; and 10 pounds dolomite or dolomite limestone. Mix all ingredients in a wheelbarrow.

WATERING. Because they have only a limited area from which to draw moisture, container plants must be watered more often than those

C

grown in the ground. In hot or windy weather, some (especially those in hanging baskets) may need watering several times a day; in cool weather, it may be sufficient to water weekly or even less often. Test with your finger: if the soil is dry beneath the surface, it's time to water.

Apply water over the entire soil surface until it flows from the pot's drainage holes. This moistens the entire soil mass and prevents any potentially harmful salts from accumulating in the mix. If the water drains out too fast—virtually the instant you pour it in—there's probably air space between the soil and the container walls. In this case, completely submerge the container in a tub of water for about half an hour; or, for large pots, set a hose on the soil surface near plant's base and let water trickle slowly into the mix.

A drip irrigation system (see page 723) can make watering container plants almost effortless. Kits designed for this purpose are widely available.

FERTILIZING. Container plants need regular feeding, since the necessary frequent watering leaches nutrients from the potting mix. Apply a liquid fertilizer every 2 weeks during the growing season, following the directions on the label. Or mix a controlled-release type (see page 668) into the potting mix before planting.

REPOTTING. If roots are crowded and protruding from the drainage holes, the plant has outgrown its container and needs a roomier home. Because you want to keep the soil mass fairly well filled with roots, it's best to shift the plant to a slightly larger container rather than a much bigger one. If the pot is too large, the ratio of soil to roots will be too great for the roots to absorb all the moisture after watering—a situation that often leads to root rot. Select a new container that allows just an inch or two of fresh mix on all sides of the root mass. If the root ball is compacted (with tightly twined roots), make four shallow vertical cuts down its sides with a sharp knife to encourage the roots to move out into the new soil.

If you want to keep an older plant in the same large pot indefinitely, you can root-prune the plant periodically. Gently turn it out of its container and use a sharp knife to shave off an inch or two from all four sides and the bottom of the root ball. Place fresh potting mix in the bottom of the container, put in the plant, and add fresh mix around the sides.

Cover Crops

Also known as green manure, cover crops are legumes or grasses planted expressly to improve garden soil. They also help prevent erosion and effectively loosen soil compacted by heavy equipment during the construction of new homes. Most cover crops are planted in fall (after the rains begin in mild-winter climates; 6 to 8 weeks before the first hard frost in cold

TOP: Buckwheat is a fast-growing cover crop that needs warm weather to grow well; its flowers attract beneficial insects. BOTTOM: Nitrogen-containing nodules on fava bean roots.

regions) and dug into the soil in spring. As they decay, they form humus, which improves the soil's structure and increases its ability to hold moisture. Legumes such as fava beans, bell beans, Austrian peas, clovers, and vetch also add extra nitrogen, thanks to their association with so-called nitrogen-fixing bacteria (genus *Rhizobium*). These bacteria draw nitrogen from air in the soil and "fix" it in nodules on a legume's roots; when the plants eventually decompose, the nitrogen is released back into the soil.

Grass or cereal cover crops such as rye, barley, buckwheat, and mustard don't contribute extra nitrogen to the soil; however, they do produce plenty of organic matter. Gardeners often combine legumes and grasses as cover crops to enjoy the benefits of both.

Before planting, till or dig the area and rake it smooth. Treat legume seeds with an inoculant powder (available from seed companies selling cover-crop seeds) to be certain that *Rhizobium* bacteria are present. Broadcast seeds at the rate recommended by the supplier and rake again to cover them. In spring, dig in the cover crop by hand (for small areas) or with a tiller, then wait until most of the stems and leaves have decayed before planting the garden. You can also cut the stems and leaves and add them to your compost pile, then dig just the lower stems and roots into the soil.

Diseases

Although few gardens escape diseases entirely, the advice and photos in this section will help you prevent the most common plant diseases and, if problems do occur, assist you in identifying them and taking action.

The Integrated Pest Management (IPM) approach discussed on page 679 applies to dealing with diseases as well as with other kinds of pests. IPM aims to maintain an attractive, productive garden with only minimal use of synthetic (chemical) controls; its goal is to reduce diseases and pest populations to tolerable levels, not to eradicate them entirely (which is rarely possible in any case).

PLANT PATHOGENS. Covered here are plant diseases caused by several kinds of organisms. Bacteria, fungi, and viruses are responsible for most leaf, stem, and flower diseases; the most widespread soilborne diseases are due to fungi. Plant problems brought on by other factors are sometimes mistaken for diseases; this is true of iron-deficiency chlorosis, sunburn, and sunscald (page 689).

Fungi are microscopic, typically multicellular organisms. Some obtain their food parasitically from green plants, causing diseases in the process. Many produce multitudinous tiny reproductive bodies called spores, which can be disseminated in numerous ways—by wind, insects, splashing water from rain or irrigation, garden equipment, and handling. Given the right conditions, each spore will germinate and grow, producing a new infection.

A number of diseases resulting from fungal infection are described on the following pages.

Bacteria are single-celled organisms. Like fungi, they cannot create their own food supply, so they feed on organic matter, including plants. Unlike fungi, however, the bacteria that afflict plants must remain inside their host or in plant debris to survive. They do not produce spores but multiply rapidly by cell division. Since they require both moisture and warmth for reproduction, the diseases they cause are generally less prevalent in dry-summer areas than in rainy or humid regions. Nonetheless, garden watering can provide the moisture they need to flourish. Bacteria are spread by insects, splashing water, garden equipment, and handling.

The bacterial disease fireblight is described on this page.

Viruses are ultramicroscopic particles capable of invading plant tissue and reproducing in it, usually at the expense of the host plant. They produce a variety of symptoms, including stunting and other abnormalities in growth; spots or discoloration on leaves; and damaged fruit. (Some attractive plants, such as variegated-leaf abutilon and certain tulips with bizarrely striped flowers, owe their variegation to a virus.) Most garden plants are susceptible to at least one viral disease; especially prone to attack are a number of vegetables, including beans, cucumbers, squash, tomatoes, and peppers.

Viral diseases are commonly spread by plant-eating insects such as aphids, leafhoppers, and whiteflies. Depending on the virus, spread can occur via infected seeds and pollen; through pruning, grafting, budding, and other forms of vegetative propagation; and, in some cases, by contaminated hands, clothing, and tools.

To prevent viral diseases, plant resistant varieties (if available) and buy certified virus-free stock. Control virus-spreading insects; remove weeds, which are hosts for some viruses. If you find a virus-infected plant, the best course of action is to destroy it. There are no chemical controls at this time.

PREVENTING DISEASES. Because many diseases cannot effectively be controlled once their symptoms become apparent, prevention is of prime importance. Whenever possible, plant resistant varieties; many are noted in the entries in the Western Plant Encyclopedia, and your Cooperative Extension Office can also give you information on this score. Choose certified and disease-free plants and seeds to avoid introducing pathogens into your garden.

Give your plants the climate, exposure, and amount of moisture they prefer: a sun-loving plant sited in the shade may be more susceptible to fungal diseases, and one that does best in dry conditions may succumb to certain root and foliage diseases if overwatered. Allow plenty of space between plants to ensure good air circulation. Also fertilize according to each plant's needs; too much or too little fertilizer can increase susceptibility to some diseases.

Use soil solarization (see page 726) to help destroy soil-dwelling pathogens. Control weeds, since they may harbor pathogens; control insects that spread diseases. Clean up the garden each fall so disease organisms can't overwinter in plant debris.

MANAGEMENT OPTIONS. If diseases do appear in your garden, immediately remove diseased annuals and vegetables to keep the problem from spreading. On larger plants (including perennials), remove diseased flowers, leaves, and, if possible, branches. Discard all infected material in the trash, not the compost heap. Disinfecting tools used on afflicted plants by dipping them between cuts in a solution of 1 part household bleach to 9 parts water may help prevent the spread of some diseases.

PLANT DISEASES. Discussed on the following three pages are some of the plant diseases you're most likely to encounter in your garden. Many diseases that affect only one kind of plant—such as peach, rose, or elm *(Ulmus)*, for example—are treated in the appropriate entry in the Western Garden Encyclopedia. For lawn diseases, see page 675.

Anthracnose. Caused by a number of fungi, anthracnose appears early in the growing season. It affects many different plants but seldom kills them. Symptoms depend on the particular plant, but you'll typically see sunken, gray or tan to dark brown spots on leaves, stems, fruit, or twigs. Leaves may wither and drop.

The spores that cause anthracnose are spread by rain and garden sprinkling. To discourage the disease, avoid overhead watering and use a mulch to decrease splashing of rain or sprinkler water. Give plants sufficient space for good air circulation; grow vining plants on trellises to keep them dry. Whenever possible, plant resistant varieties. Remove infected leaves, fruit, twigs, and branches, then destroy them to prevent reinfection.

To prevent anthracnose, you may use fungicides containing lime sulfur (during the dormant season), copper compounds, or chlorothalonil. Consult your Cooperative Extension Office or a commercial sprayer for information on the best chemical spray for your area and the appropriate time to apply it.

TOP TO BOTTOM: Anthracnose, Damping off, Fireblight

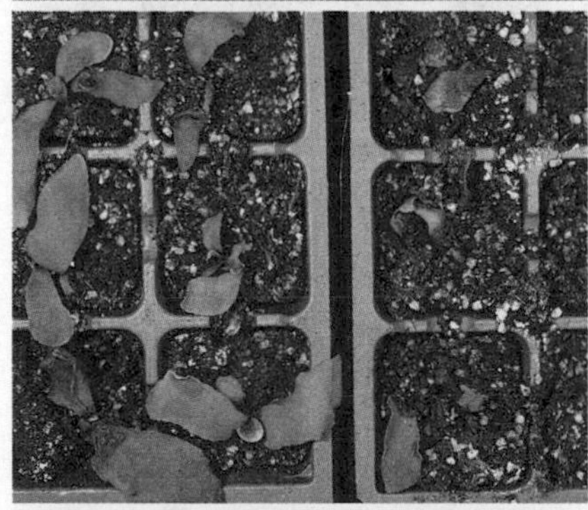

Damping off. A variety of fungi may be responsible for this disease, which affects young seedlings, causing them to collapse at or near the soil surface. In some cases, seeds rot before they can sprout.

To prevent damping off, use pasteurized potting soil for containers; thoroughly clean and disinfect used containers before planting in them (scrub them with a solution of 1 part household bleach to 9 parts hot water). Provide good air circulation around seedlings, thinning them if necessary to eliminate crowding, and do not overwater. You can buy some seeds pretreated with fungicides. A biological fungicide containing live strains of the soil bacterium *Streptomyces griseoviridis* (Mycostop), which protects against damping-off fungi, can also be used to treat seeds, potting soil, or seedlings. (Mycostop may not be registered in all states.)

Fireblight. Resulting from infection by a bacterium, this disease attacks only members of the rose family that produce pomes (applelike fruits), including apple, cotoneaster, crabapple, hawthorn, pear, pyracantha, quince, and toyon. Fireblight causes shoots (and sometimes the entire plant) to blacken and die suddenly; affected parts look as though they have been scorched by fire.

In moist weather, especially in early spring when temperatures are above 60°F/16°C, the bacteria are carried to blossoms by splashing water and by flies and other insects. Once in the blossoms, they're transported to other flowers by honeybees; the infection then spreads to the shoots and limbs. The bacteria survive in infected twigs and cankers, ready to infect blossoms again the following spring.

Whenever possible, plant resistant varieties. To protect blossoms from infection, spray at 3- or 5-day intervals during the bloom season with copper compounds. A product containing fosetyl-al (Aliette) can be used on ornamentals.

To control the pathogen once it has appeared, prune out and discard diseased branches, making pruning cuts at least 6 to 8 inches below blighted tissue. Disinfecting tools between cuts with a solution of 1 part household bleach to 9 parts water may help to keep the disease from spreading. ▸

Oak root fungus. The result of infection by the fungus *Armillaria mellea,* oak root fungus destroys a variety of woody plants by gradually decaying their roots and then moving into the main stem, where it girdles the plant by killing the cells that conduct water. The first symptoms may be dull or yellowed leaves and/or sparse foliage. Later, leaves may wilt and branches die; eventually, the entire plant dies. To check for oak root fungus, look under the bark of stems, trunk (at or below the soil line), or large roots; if the plant is infected, you'll see a layer of whitish fungal tissue. In late autumn or early winter, clumps of tan mushrooms may appear around the bases of diseased plants.

Where oak root fungus is a common problem, choose resistant plants (see A Guide to Plant Selection, page 64). Avoid placing susceptible plants in locations where the fungus is likely to be present—on the site of an old orchard, for example. When clearing infected trees, remove as many roots larger than ½ inch in diameter as possible, since these can harbor the fungus. There is no chemical control.

Powdery mildews. These diseases are caused by fungi that can infect leaves, buds, flowers, and/or stems, depending on the host plant and the particular fungus. The disease first appears as small, white or gray circular patches on plant tissue, then spreads rapidly to form powdery areas of fungal filaments and spores. New growth may be stunted; blossoms may fail to set fruit or may produce fruit covered with powdery fungus. Most powdery mildews thrive in humid air, but the spores—unlike those of other fungi—need dry surfaces, such as leaves, stems, and flowers, to become established.

To prevent powdery mildews, plant resistant varieties; many are noted in the entries in the Western Plant Encyclopedia. Be sure to give plants sufficient light and air circulation.

To control the fungi, first spray infected plants with jets of water; this washes spores from the plant and kills some of them. (To avoid encouraging other fungal diseases, spray plants with water early in the day, so they can dry before nightfall.) Pick off and destroy infected leaves and flowers. If necessary, spray with sulfur, copper soap fungicide, neem oil, potassium bicarbonate, triadimefon, or triforine. Rose growers have had some success controlling powdery mildews with baking soda mixtures, potassium bicarbonate, or antitranspirants such as Cloud Cover or Wilt-Pruf.

Root rots, water molds. Certain fungi (notably *Pythium* and *Phytophthora*) produce mobile spores that can swim short distances through water in the soil and attack plant roots. The fungi kill roots and also invade the crowns of plants, sometimes girdling them. Diseased plants wilt, and their leaves discolor, become stunted, and drop prematurely. Branches or even the entire plant may die. Root rot and water mold fungi are most active in warm soils (55 to 80°F/13 to 27°C), but they can survive in dry, cold ones, becoming active when favorable conditions arise. Many plants are susceptible, especially if they are overwatered or planted in heavy, poorly drained soils.

To prevent the problem, improve drainage (see page 707) or plant in raised beds. Do not overwater. Select disease-resistant plants.

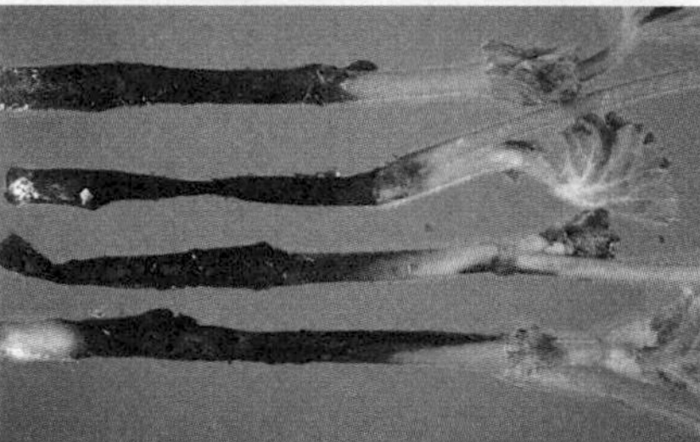

TOP TO BOTTOM: Oak root fungus, Powdery mildew, Pythium root rot, Rust

Rust. Most strains of the 4,000 or so types of these fungi are specific to particular plants; rose rust will not infect hollyhocks, for example, and hollyhock rust will not infect roses. The first sign of infection is the appearance of powdery pustules on leaf undersides; these are usually yellow to rusty brown but may be purple or another color. As the disease progresses, leaf undersides become covered with powdery masses of spores, and the upper surfaces may be spotted with yellow; eventually, the whole leaf may turn yellow, then drop.

Prevent rust by planting resistant varieties. Give plants the best possible air circulation. Remove infected leaves immediately; in winter, clean up all fallen leaves and debris. If watering from overhead, be sure plants will dry before dusk.

Sprays that may be effective (depending on the kind of rust and the infected plant) include copper soap fungicide, sulfur, triadimefon, and triforine.

Sooty mold. Commonly seen on the leaves and twigs of many trees and shrubs, sooty mold is caused by a fungus that grows on honeydew produced by sap-sucking insects such as scale, aphids, mealybugs, and whiteflies. Sooty mold is considered fairly harmless (since it does not feed on plants), but extremely heavy infestations can block sun from reaching leaves, which may then turn yellow and drop prematurely. To prevent the problem, control honeydew-excreting insects. Wash or wipe the fungus from leaves.

Texas root rot. Also known as cotton root rot, this fungal disease is found in the arid Southwest at elevations below 3,500 feet. The fungus destroys the outer portion of the roots, thus cutting off the water supply to the upper part of the plant. Leaves become slightly yellow or bronze and soon wilt; they remain firmly attached to the plant. Small plants may die within a few days; trees and shrubs may be stunted but survive for several years.

Avoid infestation by buying disease-free plants. Replace diseased plants with resistant types. Incorporate organic matter and acidify the soil (see page 708).

Verticillium wilt. A widespread and destructive disease, verticillium wilt results from infection by a fungus that invades and plugs the water-conducting tissues in the roots and stems of plants. It can affect crops such as tomatoes and strawberries, as well as roses and some trees. A common symptom is wilting or death of one side of the plant. Leaves turn yellow or brown, then die; as the disease progresses, entire branches die. Small plants may be destroyed in one season, but mature trees may live on (though in compromised health) for long periods. The fungus can survive in the soil for years, even in the absence of host plants.

Plant resistant selections when these are available. In areas where verticillium wilt is present, grow susceptible crops in containers filled with pasteurized potting mix. Soil solarization can be effective in destroying the fungus.

Mildly affected trees or shrubs may recover from an attack. You can aid recovery by deep but infrequent irrigation. If a plant has been neglected, apply fertilizer; do not, however, fertilize infected trees and shrubs that show lush growth, since excess nitrogen may favor the disease's development. Prune out dead branches. Clean tools of any soil, which can carry the fungus to other parts of the garden.

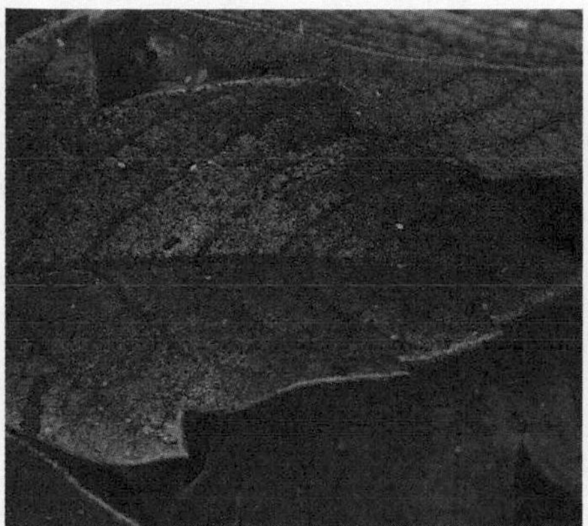
Sooty mold

Texas root rot

Verticillium wilt

D

PRODUCTS FOR DISEASE PREVENTION AND CONTROL

You'll find a number of products aimed at disease prevention or control. These include *preventatives*, products that prevent diseases from occurring but cannot control them once they become established; *eradicants*, which help control diseases once they have appeared (many simply protect new growth); and *systemics*, materials that are taken up by plant roots and act as preventatives, eradicants, or both. Controls described here are the most useful and commonly available ones; other, generally less widely sold products are mentioned in the descriptions of specific plant diseases beginning on page 665.

Synthetic fungicides are manufactured compounds that do not normally occur in nature. *Natural fungicides and bactericides* are products whose active ingredients originate in a plant, animal, or mineral, or whose action results from a biological process (as in a product containing live bacteria that combat harmful fungi; see page 665). "Natural," however, does not mean "harmless"; some of these products can harm people or plants if not used properly. Sources for some less-common natural fungicides are listed on page 679.

When using any product, *read label directions carefully and follow them exactly*. The package will clearly state the plants and diseases for which the control product is registered for use, and it is illegal to use it on a plant or to control a disease not so listed.

The following products are listed by the accepted common name of the *active ingredient*—the actual chemical that prevents or controls the disease or diseases listed on the package label. Some widely used trade names, if they differ from the common name, are noted in parentheses. Before you buy, read the label to make sure you're getting the active ingredient you want. (For more on understanding pesticide labels, see page 686.) Always dispose of pesticides in a safe manner (see page 684).

NATURAL FUNGICIDES AND BACTERICIDES

- **Baking soda, sodium bicarbonate.** You can buy baking soda sprays, but it's easy to make your own by mixing 2 teaspoons each of baking soda and fine-grade horticultural oil with 1 gallon of water. This solution helps to control powdery mildew on roses. Commercial versions contain a "sticker" ingredient to help keep the spray on the plant.
- **Copper compounds (Bordeaux mixture).** General-purpose fungicides and bactericides used to prevent fireblight, peach leaf curl, shot hole, brown rot, and other foliar diseases. Toxic to fish.
- **Copper soap fungicide.** Broad-spectrum fungicide used to control many plant diseases, including rust, black spot, and powdery mildews.
- **Lime sulfur, calcium polysulfide.** Used as a spray in winter (when plants are dormant) to prevent various leaf spots and peach leaf curl. Very caustic; wear goggles and plastic gloves when applying.
- **Neem oil (Rose Defense and others).** Used to prevent and control black spot, powdery mildews, and some other foliar diseases. (Also used as an insecticide and miticide.) Toxic to fish.
- **Potassium bicarbonate (Remedy, others).** Used to control powdery mildews. May not be registered in all states.
- **Sulfur (Sulfur Dust, others).** Controls powdery mildews, rust, and other diseases. Do not use in conjunction with horticultural oil sprays or when the outdoor temperature is above 85°F/29°C.

SYNTHETIC FUNGICIDES

- **Chlorothalonil (Daconil, others).** Broad-spectrum liquid fungicide used to prevent powdery mildews, leaf spots, gray mold, scab, and a variety of lawn and other diseases. Toxic to fish.
- **Triadimefon (Fungi-Fighter; formerly Bayleton).** Wettable powder; systemic used for the prevention or eradication of powdery mildews, rust, and some lawn diseases. Toxic to fish.
- **Triforine (Funginex).** Liquid systemic for prevention and eradication of powdery mildews, rust, black spot, and a variety of other diseases. You must wear goggles and a face mask during application. Keep animals out of treated areas.

Fertilizers

When plants are actively growing, they need a steady supply of nutrients. Though many of these are present in soil, water, and air, the gardener may need to supply others. Most likely to require supplemental feeding are fast-growing annuals (such as vegetables and flowering plants), lawns, perennials, fruit trees, and immature plants of numerous kinds. Mature trees and shrubs, on the other hand, may need little or no fertilizing. The entries in the Western Plant Encyclopedia cover fertilizing needs and schedules for many plants. General guidelines are also given in the listings for annuals (page 658), bulbs (page 659), ground covers (page 671), herbs (page 672), lawns (page 673), perennials (page 678), shrubs (page 705), trees (page 712), and vegetables (page 714). A soil test (see page 708) is a good way to determine any nutrient deficiencies in your soil; test results will also give advice on correcting problems. Your Cooperative Extension Office is another excellent source of information on nutrient needs specific to your area.

FERTILIZER TYPES AND FORMS. Visit almost any nursery and you'll encounter a bewildering array of fertilizers in different forms and formulas. To decide which ones to buy, start by reading the labels. Every fertilizer label states the percentage by weight that the product contains of the three macronutrients used in mineral form: nitrogen (N), phosphorus (P), and potassium (K). These nutrients are always listed in the order N-P-K. For example, a fertilizer labeled 10-8-6 contains 10 percent nitrogen, 8 percent phosphorus, and 6 percent potassium. The label also tells you the source of each nutrient.

Nitrogen is often listed on fertilizer labels as nitrate or some form of ammonium (many products contain both forms). Fertilizers containing nitrogen in the nitrate form are water soluble and fast acting, especially in cool soils, but are easily leached away by rain or irrigation (thus requiring fairly frequent replenishment) and can pollute surface and ground water if used to excess. Fertilizers in the form of ammonium, those from organic sources (such as blood meal), and IBDU (isobutylidene diurea, a synthetic organic fertilizer) are released more slowly and last longer in the soil, because they must be converted into nitrate form by soil microbes before plant roots can absorb them.

Phosphorus is expressed on product labels as phosphate, P_2O_5, and listed as "available phosphoric acid." Potassium is expressed as potash, K_2O, and may be described in various ways, including "available phosphate" and "water-soluble potash." It is important to note that, unlike nitrogen, phosphorus and potassium do not move readily through the soil in solution. They must therefore be applied near plant roots to do the most good. Dig these nutrients into the soil when planting or scratch them into the soil around existing plants.

Complete fertilizers contain the three macronutrients N, P, and K; some may also include secondary and/or micronutrients (which will be listed on the label). *Simple fertilizers* supply just one macronutrient. Most familiar are the nitrogen-only types, such as ammonium sulfate (21-0-0), and phosphorus-only superphosphate (0-20-0). Falling between complete and simple types are *incomplete fertilizers,* which contain two of the three major elements; an example is 0-10-10, providing phosphorus and potassium but no nitrogen.

Fertilizer forms, clockwise from left: soluble crystals (dry and dissolved), dry granules, organic fish meal, and controlled-release pellets.

Natural and chemical fertilizers. You can buy fertilizers in either natural (organic) or synthetic (chemical) form.

Natural fertilizers, derived from dead organisms, include fish emulsion, all kinds of animal manures including bat and seabird guano, and meals made from blood, bone, fish, alfalfa, cottonseed, and soybeans. Most contain lower levels of nutrients than chemical products. They release their nutrients more slowly, as well: rather than dissolving in water, they are broken down by microorganisms in the soil, providing nutrients as they decay (decomposition proceeds more quickly in warm, moist soils than in cold or dry ones). Thanks to this slow nutrient release, natural fertilizers are much less likely to burn roots than are chemical types.

Many natural fertilizers are high in just one major nutrient. Blood meal, for example, supplies only nitrogen (N-P-K ratio 12-0-0), while bonemeal (0-10-0) provides only phosphorus. Some manufacturers combine several natural fertilizers in a single package to produce a complete fertilizer.

Chemical fertilizers are derived from the chemical sources listed on the product label. Compared to natural fertilizers, they usually provide higher levels of nutrients and are faster acting, especially in cold soils; they typically cost less, too. They're a good choice for greening up lawns in spring and giving plants suffering from nutrient deficiencies a quick tonic. Keep in mind that chemical products can burn roots if applied too heavily.

Liquids or solids? Both natural and chemical fertilizers are sold in liquid or solid forms.

Liquid fertilizers, including fish emulsion and water-soluble crystals, deliver nutrients to the roots immediately. They're easy to use, especially on container plants, and if you follow label directions for dilution you'll run no risk of burning roots. Liquid fertilizers must be reapplied frequently, since their nutrients leach through the root zone rapidly.

Solid fertilizers are usually sold as powders, granules, or pellets. Solid fertilizers can be broadcast or spread over lawns and ground covers, scratched or dug into the soil around other plants, and dug into the soil when preparing new planting beds.

Other solids include *controlled-release fertilizers,* sold as spikes, tablets, or beadlike granules that release nutrients gradually over a fairly long period—typically 3 to 9 months—if the soil receives regular moisture. Dig granules into soil at planting time or scratch them into the soil surface (they're useful for fertilizing container plants). Use a mallet to pound spikes into the ground; dig holes for tablets.

General- and special-purpose fertilizers. The various fertilizers labeled "general-purpose" or "all-purpose" contain equal or nearly equal amounts of the macronutrients N, P, and K (a 10-10-10 formula, for example). They are intended to meet most plants' requirements throughout the growing season.

Other fertilizers are formulated for specific needs. High-nitrogen blends (such as 29-3-4) help keep lawns green and growing quickly, while higher-phosphorus mixes (6-10-4, for example) are intended to promote flowering and fruiting. Some packaged fertilizers are formulated for particular types of plants. Those designed for acid lovers such as camellias, rhododendrons, and azaleas are especially useful, as are fertilizers for citrus.

Another special kind of fertilizer is *foliar fertilizer.* Such products are liquids applied to leaves, which can absorb nutrients through stomata (see page 688)—small openings in leaves. Some solutions are high in the macronutrients, while others offer an effective way to apply micronutrients. To avoid burning leaves, water plants thoroughly before spraying them, follow dilution directions, and don't apply the fertilizer at all if outdoor temperatures will rise above 85°F/29°C.

You can also buy formulas that combine fertilizers with insecticides (chiefly for roses) or with weed killers, fungicides, or moss killers (all for lawns). These products are appropriate if you need the extra ingredient every time you fertilize; if not, it's more economical to buy it separately. Before using any such products, read the label carefully, as you would for any fertilizer. The herbicides included in some combination products, for example, can damage plants with roots growing into the application area, such as a lawn.

PLANT NUTRIENTS

The nutrients plants need are divided into three groups: macronutrients, secondary nutrients, and micronutrients.

Macronutrients. These are nutrients that plants need in fairly large quantities. Three—carbon, oxygen, and hydrogen—are found in air and water; plants use the others in mineral form.

***Nitrogen* (chemical symbol N) is used in the synthesis of proteins, chlorophyll, and enzymes—all substances that plant cells require to live and reproduce. Nitrogen is the nutrient most likely to be inadequate in garden soils. When it's in short supply, the plant yellows from the bottom upward, with its leaves yellowing from the tips toward the stem, and growth is stunted (see photograph above).**

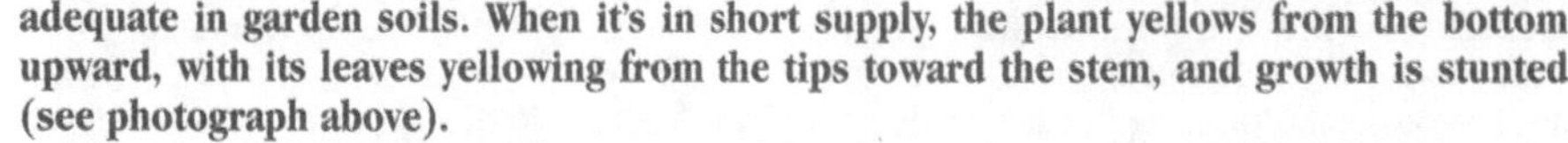

***Phosphorus* (P) promotes flowering and fruiting, strong root growth, and the transfer of energy from one point in the plant to another. Plants deficient in phosphorus show stunted growth and reduced yield of fruit; in some, you may see purplish areas on the leaf undersides.**

***Potassium* (K) is important for regulating the synthesis of proteins and starches that make sturdy plants. It also helps increase resistance to diseases, heat, and cold. Symptoms of deficiency include reduced flowering and fruiting, spotted or curled older leaves, and weak stems and roots.**

Secondary nutrients. Plants need these in about the same amounts as they do the macronutrients. However, since they're less likely to be deficient in most soils than are the macronutrients, they're commonly called secondary nutrients.

***Calcium* (Ca) plays a fundamental role in cell formation and growth, and most roots require some calcium right at the growing tips.**

***Magnesium* (Mg) forms the core of the chlorophyll molecules in the cells of green leaves.**

***Sulfur* (S) acts with nitrogen in the manufacture of protoplasm for plant cells.**

Micronutrients. Also known as trace elements, micronutrients are required in very small quantities; in fact, excess amounts can be toxic. Among them are *zinc* (Zn) and *manganese* (Mn), both thought to function as catalysts in the utilization of other nutrients; and *iron* (Fe), essential for chlorophyll formation (see page 689 for information on iron-deficiency chlorosis).

APPLYING FERTILIZERS

Before planting a new bed, work in a fertilizer containing phosphorus and potassium. This puts these essential nutrients at the level in the soil where they are readily available to plant roots.

Using a cultivator, gently scratch the soil beneath plants with roots growing close to the surface. Apply a granular fertilizer and water thoroughly. Roots of larger plants may extend several feet beyond the reach of the foliage, so be sure to spread fertilizer widely enough to reach all the roots.

Liquid fertilizers can be applied with a watering can. You can also use an injector device to run the fertilizer through a drip watering system. A simple siphon attachment (above) draws a measured amount of fertilizer from concentrate in a pail and dilutes it as it is mixed with water from a hose.

F

Fire, Landscaping to Prevent

Wildfires are common in many parts of the arid West, particularly in foothill and mountainous areas. In wild plant communities such as chaparral, oak woodland, and forest, these burns are part of the natural cycle, clearing out dead and diseased plants and helping some seeds germinate. However, as more homes are built in these ecosystems and as fires are routinely suppressed, the natural burn process is interrupted. The fuel load of living and dead plants builds up, and when fires do occur, they are larger and more damaging. To reduce the chances of fire destroying your home, make sure that roofing, siding, and fencing materials are fire-resistant. Practicing fire-safe landscaping is important, too. Consider the following pointers:

Maintain a greenbelt around your home. Establish a strip about 30 feet wide (wider on steep slopes) of low-growing plants; keep them watered to maintain a high moisture content. Pay special attention to trees, which pose a greater risk to homes than shrubs or ground covers. Remove any trees growing close to the house; thin crowns of others and trim limbs so the lowest ones are 10 to 20 feet above ground. Cut back branches of large specimens to 15 to 20 feet from the house (or simply remove those trees entirely).

Eliminate fire ladders. Plants of different heights that grow adjacent to each other provide a continuous fuel supply from the ground up into the tree canopy. To eliminate such "ladders," remove midsize plants that would let flames jump easily from lower plants to trees.

Eliminate fire pathways. Horizontal bands of foliage provide pathways for fires to move quickly from plant to plant. Interrupt these pathways by separating plants.

Reduce fuel load. Prune and thin trees and shrubs, cut grasses back to 4 inches when they turn brown, remove brush, and cut back ground covers and native chaparral annually. Clear leaf litter from the ground, rooftops, and gutters.

When you plant, choose low-fuel-volume herbaceous perennials such as common yarrow *(Achillea millefolium)*, gazania, and poppy *(Papaver)*, or low-growing ground covers (to 1½ feet tall). Keep them well watered; or, if you must let them dry out due to drought, be sure to cut them back. Avoid highly flammable woody shrubs such as California sagebrush *(Artemisia californica)*, junipers *(Juniperus)*, and California buckwheat *(Eriogonum fasciculatum)*. Check with your Cooperative Extension Office for more information on locally adapted fire-resistant plants; the staff can also direct you to any nearby display gardens that demonstrate fire-safe landscaping practices.

Create a transition zone beyond the greenbelt. Make this zone about 70 feet wide. Separate plants, spacing clumps of shrubs at least 18 to 20 feet from each other and from structures (be sure, however, to leave enough plants to stabilize slopes and prevent erosion). Leave only a few widely spaced trees.

Ease fire truck access to your property. Clear out overhanging tree branches and prune shrubs along driveways and access roads. Also make sure that driveways and roads are wide enough to allow fire trucks to maneuver easily.

A FIRE-RESISTANT LANDSCAPE

Frost and Cold Protection

Wherever you garden, the best defense against cold damage is to choose trees, shrubs, and screen and hedge plants that are hardy in your climate zone. Use tender plants for summer display in borders, or plant them in containers that can be moved to shelter when the weather turns frigid.

It's also helpful to know your garden's microclimates—that is, to learn which areas tend to be warmer, which colder. For marginally hardy plants, the riskiest spots are stretches of open ground exposed to air from all sides (particularly from the north). Other high-risk locations include hollows and low, enclosed areas that catch cold air as it sinks, then hold it motionless. The warmest part of any garden—and the one offering maximum frost protection—is usually the area beside a south-facing wall with an overhang. Lath structures and the branches of evergreen trees also provide some shelter from frost.

To some extent, you can condition plants and soil for cold weather. Water and fertilize as needed in late spring and early summer, while plants are growing the fastest. In late summer, taper off nitrogen feeding: actively growing plants are more susceptible to frost than dormant and semidormant ones, so you don't want to stimulate new growth that won't have time to mature (harden off) before cold weather arrives. Reducing water also helps harden growth—but keep soil moist through the onset of the frost season, since moist soil holds and releases more heat than dry soil.

A frost that hits in early fall (before the growing season ends) or in spring (after growth is under way) is much more damaging than one striking when plants are semidormant or dormant. At these dangerous times of year, be alert for signs of an impending freeze: still air, clear skies, low humidity, and, of course, low temperatures. It's wise to check TV and radio weather bulletins and web sites as well. If you notice danger signals late in the afternoon, move at-risk container plants under a porch roof or into the garage. Give in-ground plants temporary shelter; two types of shelters are shown on the facing page. Remove coverings during the day unless the threat of frost continues. (For ways to protect vegetables from frost and extend their productivity, see page 715.)

Don't hurry to prune frost-damaged plants. Cutting them back too soon can stimulate tender new growth that will be nipped by later frosts, and you may mistake leafless but living stems for dead ones. When new growth begins in spring, remove wood that is clearly dead.

PROTECTING PLANTS FROM OCCASIONAL FROST

1 Make a frame of four strong stakes around the plant. Lay plastic or burlap over tops of stakes; make sure it does not touch the leaves, since this would cause them to freeze. If you need more heat, place one or two trouble lights or small spotlights or a string of holiday lights in the shelter. Plug the lights into an extension cord or outlet intended for outdoor use; do not let them contact the plastic or burlap.

2 For a quick cover for smaller plants, use a large cardboard box. Cut the bottom on three sides to make a lid you can open and close as needed.

ALL-WINTER PROTECTION. In cold climates where the soil freezes hard and temperatures drop below 0°F/–18°C, tender plants will not survive outdoors. However, many gardeners in these areas do grow roses and broad-leafed evergreens such as boxwood *(Buxus)*, euonymus, holly *(Ilex)*, pieris, and rhododendron. All of these plants need some help to survive harsh winters.

With many roses, the aim is to keep the roots and bud union alive and to preserve as many live canes as possible; see the Western Plant Encyclopedia for more information.

Broad-leafed evergreens suffer in winter because the leaves continue to transpire and thus lose moisture (particularly on relatively warm, windy days). And if the soil is frozen, the roots cannot take up water to replace what has been lost, and the plant becomes desiccated. To minimize damage to these plants, water thoroughly before the ground freezes, then apply a thick mulch of oak leaves, pine needles, wood chips, or ground bark. The mulch layer limits the penetration of frost into the ground, allowing the deepest roots to continue absorbing moisture; it also protects surface roots from alternate freezing and thawing. Careful siting is important as well: when you plant broad-leafed evergreens, avoid locations where bright sun—especially in early morning—will strike frozen plants. To avoid rupturing plant tissues, thawing should be gradual.

PROTECTING BROAD-LEAFED EVERGREENS

To protect plants in exposed locations, spray them with an antitranspirant (such as Cloud Cover or Wilt-Pruf) near the time of the first hard freeze. These products form a thin film on the leaves, sealing in moisture and helping prevent desiccation. Make a protective structure by driving three or four stakes into the ground around the plants, then nailing or stapling burlap to the stakes. Don't use plastic film for the structure, since it hinders proper air circulation.

Grasses. See Lawns; Ornamental Grasses pp. 673, 677

Greenhouses

For avid gardeners, a greenhouse is an essential outdoor room for plants, where temperature, humidity, and day length are all under human control. Greenhouses are useful for a number of purposes:

Providing winter shelter for plants too tender to endure the normal outdoor temperatures. Potted citrus trees, for example, often spend the winter in a greenhouse in cold climates.

Starting seeds of annuals and vegetables in early spring so that plants will be growing vigorously and ready to set out in the garden as soon as weather permits.

Starting cuttings that need a protected, moist location.

Raising vegetables and flowers to mature out of season, particularly when outdoor conditions are too cold for them to develop fully.

Growing specialty crops (such as orchids and tropical plants) that require controlled temperatures and humidity.

Greenhouses vary widely in size and complexity, ranging from small bay windows attached to the house to simple lean-tos to more elaborate freestanding structures. Greenhouse frame materials include wood, aluminum, and PVC pipe. The glazing used for the building's walls and roof may be single- or double-walled glass, fiberglass, double-walled polycarbonate plastic, double-walled polyethylene, or acrylic. Double-walled glazing holds heat more efficiently. If you garden where heavy snowfalls are common, be sure the greenhouse can stand up to the snow load.

Ground Covers

Gardeners rely on ground covers to blanket the soil with dense foliage, adding beauty and variety to the garden and suppressing weeds at the same time. Though lawn grasses (see page 673) are doubtless the best-known cover for bare ground, the term "ground cover" is typically used to refer to other, nongrassy plants, among them shrubs, vines, and many perennials. If chosen carefully, they require considerably less maintenance and water than lawns do. Ground cover plants usually create a relatively even surface, though heights range from a few inches to knee-high or even taller.

Japanese spurge *(Pachysandra terminalis)* is an invaluable ground cover for shady places.

CHOOSING GROUND COVERS. When selecting ground covers, start by considering your site. Is it level or sloping, sunny or shady? How much water will be available for the plants? Also decide if you want a ground cover you can walk across or one that will serve as a traffic barrier. Settle on a deciduous cover or an evergreen one; decide if you want flowers or prefer just foliage. Ask yourself how the ground cover will

PLANTING GROUND COVERS ON A SLOPE

When setting plants on a steep slope where erosion may occur, arrange them in staggered rows. Make an individual terrace for each plant and create a basin or low spot behind each one to catch water. Set the crowns of the plants high, so they won't become saturated and rot after watering.

fit in with the garden's other plants and hardscape. As you consider these questions and issues, you'll zero in on the right plants for your situation. For ideas on plant choices, consult "Ground Covers" in A Guide to Plant Selection, beginning on page 64.

PLANTING AND CARING FOR GROUND COVERS. In most of the West, fall planting is preferred, since it gives plants time to establish their roots over winter. In the coldest areas, wait until spring to plant. Most ground covers grow best in well-prepared soil; for these, ready the planting area as directed on page 690, adding plenty of organic matter. Some kinds of ground covers, however, can be planted directly in native soil with little or no amendment. This group includes various tough, shrubby types, many of them Western natives.

Before planting, install landscape fabric (see page 676) to help control weeds, if desired.

When planting ground covers purchased in small pots or flats, set them in holes the same depth as and slightly wider than the root ball. For directions on setting out plants from gallon-size containers, see page 693. The required spacing varies with the plant; check entries in the Western Plant Encyclopedia for details.

Water thoroughly after planting, then keep soil moist (but not soggy) as the plants settle in. Apply a mulch to help conserve moisture and to prevent weed seeds from growing.

Once ground covers are established, their water needs vary depending on the particular plant and the soil in which it is growing. Fertilizer requirements differ, too. As a rule of thumb, though, most woody, shrubby ground covers (especially drought-tolerant sorts) have fairly low nutrient needs; many get along with little or no fertilizing. Perennial ground covers with softer, lusher growth generally have higher nutrient requirements and should receive an annual feeding in spring.

Herbs

The word "herb" applies to any plant that, at some time in history, has been valued for seasoning, medicine, fragrance, or general household use. Within this broad category, you will find tall, willowy plants like dill as well as low, fine-textured creepers (some kinds of thyme, for example) that spread along the ground to form a fragrant carpet. Many herbs are annuals and biennials grown for their leaves and seeds; others, such as French tarragon and oregano, are perennials; still others are tough shrubs like rosemary, as useful in the landscape as in the kitchen.

Herbs have numerous garden uses. They can, of course, be grouped in an all-herb garden, be it a sunny corner of the vegetable plot, a special raised bed, or a traditional circular planting centered with a birdbath or sundial. They are excellent container plants—and pot culture is a good way to grow them near the kitchen door, handy for snipping. And many herbs add interest to the perennial or shrub border.

PLANTING AND CARING FOR HERBS. Choose a planting spot that receives 6 to 8 hours of full sun each day. Well-drained soil is essential; if drainage is poor, dig in plenty of organic matter or plant in raised beds. Work in a complete fertilizer before planting. Herbs aren't heavy feeders, so this should suffice for the entire season.

15 CULINARY HERBS

Many cooks consider these herbs essential: basil *(Ocimum basilicum)*, chives *(Allium schoenoprasum)*, cilantro *(Coriandrum sativum)*, dill *(Anethum graveolens)*, fennel *(Foeniculum vulgare)*, French tarragon *(Artemisia dracunculus)*, mint *(Mentha)*, oregano *(Origanum vulgare)*, parsley *(Petroselinum crispum)*, rosemary *(Rosmarinus officinalis)*, sage *(Salvia officinalis)*, sweet bay *(Laurus nobilis)*, sweet marjoram *(Origanum majorana)*, thyme *(Thymus vulgaris)*, and winter savory *(Satureja montana)*.

'Dark Op basil

Most perennial and shrubby herbs are easier to start from transplants than from seed. Nurseries offer many kinds, typically in 2- or 4-inch pots; some are also sold in gallon containers. Annual and biennial herbs (such as basil, dill, and parsley), on the other hand, can easily be started from seed; see page 694.

After planting herbs from containers, water regularly until the plants are growing steadily; thereafter, most will need only occasional irrigation. Exceptions are basil, chives, mint, and parsley, which prefer evenly moist soil.

When perennial herbs resume growth in early spring, feed them lightly with a complete fertilizer or spread compost around the base of each plant, taking care not to cover the crown.

DRYING HERBS

Harvest herbs for drying just as the first flower buds begin to open. The oils in the leaves are most concentrated at this time, and the herbs will maintain their flavor when preserved. Cut sprigs or branches in the morning, after dew has evaporated. Tie them together at the cut ends and hang them upside down in a warm, dry, well-ventilated place out of direct sunlight. When the leaves are crisp and crumble readily, strip them from the stems and store them whole in airtight jars. Another way to dry herbs is to remove the leaves from the stems and spread them on screens placed in a warm, dry, airy place out of direct sun; stir them every few days as they dry. Once they feel crisp, they're ready to store in airtight containers.

For herbs grown for their seeds, harvest seed heads or pods when they turn brown. Dry them in paper bags until you can shake the seeds loose; then store seeds in airtight containers.

Lawns

The classic lawn—lush, green, and crisply mowed—became a basic landscaping element in the arid West early in the 20th century, when dams, pipelines, and electric pumps made water easily available to homeowners. Today, however, a burgeoning population is straining the water supply in much of the region. Conservation is an important issue, and attention has naturally focused on the huge amount of water needed to keep lawns alive and green. Research has shown that grasses traditionally favored for turf (Kentucky bluegrass, bent grasses, fine fescues, perennial ryegrass) require more water per square foot than almost any other kind of garden plant. Moreover, up to half the water used by a typical single-family household is applied outdoors, primarily to lawns—and most homeowners give the lawn more water than it really needs.

Responding to these findings, some communities now restrict the amount of lawn that can be planted around new homes. Many gardeners, too, have reconsidered the value of a lawn. Some have eliminated it entirely, replacing it with one of the alternatives discussed under "Water Conservation" (page 720); others have sharply reduced its size. Besides demanding less water than a large expanse does, a small lawn requires less labor, time, and money to maintain.

If you plan to include a lawn in your landscape, you can do more to save on time and water than just keep it small. Opt for a simple geometric shape; it will allow you to irrigate without overspray, and it's easier to mow. Keeping the lawn fairly level makes good sense, too, since it minimizes runoff and makes mowing safer. Finally, be sure you choose the right grass for your climate, prepare and plant the site carefully, and maintain the lawn properly.

CHOOSING THE RIGHT LAWN GRASS FOR YOUR REGION

Lawn grasses fall into two basic categories: *cool-season* and *warm-season* (subtropical). Each group comprises a variety of plants with varying water needs. For more information on specific grasses, consult the individual listings in the Western Plant Encyclopedia.

Buffalo grass lawn

COOL-SEASON GRASSES withstand winter cold but typically languish in hot, dry summers. Most grow best in the Northwest; in parts of the Rocky Mountains with (usually) abundant summer rainfall; and in areas where marine influence tempers summer heat. When planted in other regions, most require extensive summer watering. Cool-season grasses are often sold as mixes of several kinds; even if one of them is not adapted to the soil or sun and shade conditions in your garden, chances are that others in the package will do well.

Bent grasses *(Agrostis).* Fine-textured grasses requiring ample water and more care than other lawn grasses. Grow in acid soil, in sun or light shade. Mow at ½ to ¾ inch. Sold as seed, sod.

Crested wheatgrass *(Agropyron cristatum).* Light bluish green grass makes for a tough, very drought-tolerant lawn. Grow in sunny areas; adapted to Rocky Mountains and High Plains. Goes dormant and turns brown in hot weather. Mow at 2 inches. Sold as seed.

Fine fescue (*Festuca rubra* and others). Fine-bladed grasses that succeed in well-drained soil in shaded sites. Fairly drought tolerant. Sometimes blended with Kentucky bluegrass or perennial ryegrass or to overseed warm-season grasses. Mow at 1½ to 2 inches. Sold as seed.

Tall fescue (*Festuca elatior;* also called coarse fescue). Tough grass that tolerates heat and some drought and flourishes in sun or shade. It freezes out in the coldest climates. Newer selections (dwarf tall fescue) are finer bladed, deeper green. Mow at 2 to 3 inches. Sold as seed, sod.

Kentucky bluegrass *(Poa pratensis).* Classic grass for cooler regions. Needs regular water. Takes sun, light shade. Mow at 1 to 2½ inches. Sold as seed, sod.

Perennial ryegrass *(Lolium perenne).* Deep green grass that does best in sun. Needs frequent watering. Used as year-round lawn in cooler regions or to overseed winter-dormant grasses. Mow at 2 inches. Sold as seed, sod.

WARM-SEASON GRASSES thrive in hot weather but turn brown in cold winter weather. Gardeners who want a year-round green lawn sometimes overseed these warm-season grasses with some types of cool-season grasses for the colder months.

Common Bermuda grass *(Cynodon dactylon).* Good, drought-tolerant lawn for large, sunny areas. Invades shrub plantings and flower beds by seed and spreading roots if not contained. Mow at 1 inch. Sold as seed.

Hybrid Bermuda grass *(Cynodon).* Hybrid Bermuda is similar to common Bermuda, but it's finer textured and does not self-sow. Mow at ½ to ¾ inch. Sold as sod, sprigs, plugs.

Blue grama *(Bouteloua gracilis).* Tolerates drought, extremes of temperature, and a wide range of soils. Does best in sun. Makes a better-quality turf when blended with buffalo grass. Mow at 2 to 3 inches. Sold as seed.

Buffalo grass *(Buchloe dactyloides).* Very drought-tolerant lawn for sun; slow growing. Mow at 3 inches. Sold as seed, sod, plugs.

St. Augustine grass *(Stenotaphrum secundatum).* Adapted to wide range of soils but does best along coast. Grows best in sun but tolerates shade. Needs regular water. Stolons can invade other parts of the garden. Mow at 1½ to 3 inches. Sold as sod, sprigs, plugs.

Zoysia *(Zoysia).* Tolerates drought and heat; takes sun or shade. Mow at 1 to 2 inches. Sold as sod, sprigs, plugs.

SEED, SOD, SPRIGS, OR PLUGS?

Lawn grass is sold in several forms. All except sod require diligent weed control after planting.

Seed is the least expensive way to start a lawn, and it's offered for a wide variety of grasses. Read the package label carefully. It should list the named varieties of the grass or grasses included and indicate a high rate of germination for those grasses; it should also show a low percentage of crop or weed seeds in relation to the percentage of lawn grass seeds.

Fall seeding is recommended for most grasses, since fall and winter rains help establish the lawn. In the coldest climates, seed in early fall, so the lawn can grow before winter.

Sod is the most expensive way to start a lawn, but it does give instant coverage with almost no weed problems. Local suppliers offer varieties adapted to your area. The lawn will establish itself most quickly in the cooler weather of spring or fall.

Plugs are small rooted plants. Usually sold in trays, they're used for warm-season grasses that spread as they grow, such as buffalo, hybrid Bermuda, St. Augustine, and zoysia. Plant them in spring, following the supplier's directions.

Sprigs are pieces of grass stem and root; like plugs, they're used to plant spreading warm-season grasses. Plant in spring, following the supplier's directions.

SOWING GRASS SEED

1 After preparing the area, scatter seed. A mechanical spreader helps sow seed evenly.

2 Lightly rake seed into the soil.

3 Spread a 1/16-inch layer of mulch, such as aged or nitrogen-fortified sawdust, over the area; roll with an empty roller to press seed into soil. Water thoroughly. Keep the seedbed moist with frequent, light watering until the seed sprouts.

LAYING SOD

1 After preparing the site, moisten the soil. Unroll the strips and lay them out with their ends staggered, pressing the edges together firmly.

2 Use a knife to trim sod so it fits snugly around paving and other obstacles.

3 To press roots firmly into the soil, roll the lawn with a roller half-filled with water. Water the new lawn once daily (more often in hot weather) for 6 weeks.

PLANTING PLUGS AND SPRIGS

Two-inch plugs of buffalo grass and some other spreading warm-season grasses are sold in trays. Planted at 8-inch intervals, they'll grow together in a year.

Sprigs of hybrid Bermuda grass root and spread quickly in well-prepared soil. Be sure to water plugs or sprigs often until roots take hold.

Bermuda grass sprig

Buffalo grass plug

L

PLANTING A NEW LAWN. When you plant a new lawn—whether you start it from seed, sod, sprigs, or plugs—proper site preparation is essential. Remove any existing sod with a sod cutter (available from rental yards); for easier removal, you can kill the sod with an herbicide such as glyphosate before using the cutter. It's wise to have the soil's pH tested (see page 708) before you plant.

Till the site to a depth of about 8 inches and spread it with a 3- to 4-inch layer of an organic amendment, such as commercial compost or aged or nitrogen-fortified sawdust. Also apply a complete fertilizer and any materials recommended by the soil test lab to adjust the pH. Till again; rake the area smooth and water it thoroughly. Let the soil settle for a few days; then sow seed, lay sod, or set out plugs or sprigs as shown on the facing page.

CARING FOR LAWNS. To look their best, lawns require consistent watering and fertilizing as well as regular mowing.

Watering. To encourage deep rooting and conserve water, irrigate lawns as deeply and infrequently as possible. In mild climates, once or twice a week should be adequate during warm weather; in hotter regions, you'll probably have to water more often. During cooler times of year, you can cut back on watering. Check with local water agencies or your Cooperative Extension Office for guidelines, which are often based on evapotranspiration (ET)—a localized, weather-based, measurement of how much water a plant uses and how much evaporates from the soil.

To determine how thirsty the lawn really is, you can also perform a few informal tests. First, just step on the grass: if the blades don't spring back from your footprint, it's time to water. Or push a screwdriver into the soil; if it doesn't penetrate easily, the lawn probably needs water. A soil sampling tube (see page 721) will give a more accurate indication of the soil's moisture content.

Many sprinklers apply water faster than the soil can absorb it. To prevent runoff, water in cycles; sprinkle until just before runoff or puddling occurs (typically 10 to 15 minutes), then repeat the cycle in an hour. Adjust sprinklers so they don't overshoot onto paving.

To improve water penetration and reduce runoff, aerate and dethatch your lawn once a year. Local nurseries offer information and equipment to help you with these tasks.

Fertilizing. Most lawns are heavy feeders, requiring regular applications of high-nitrogen fertilizer. In the desert, iron may also be beneficial. Give cool-season lawns two applications of fertilizer in spring and two in fall. Fertilize warm-season lawns monthly in late spring and summer (Bermuda grass only lightly in summer, to restrain its growth). Numerous bagged lawn fertilizers, both synthetic and natural, are sold; check the packages for recommended application rates.

If you cut back on watering because of drought, hold back on fertilizer as well.

Mowing. To keep a lawn healthy, mow it regularly; grass is weakened if allowed to grow too long between mowings. When the blades are about one-third taller than the recommended growing height (see the descriptions of lawn grasses on page 673), it's time to mow. Unless the clippings are quite long, leave them on the lawn to decompose and add nutrients to the soil (long clippings might smother the grass).

LAWN PROBLEMS. To avoid lawn problems, plant grass that's well adapted to your area and care for it properly. If you do encounter problems, the following information will help you identify and correct them. (For a discussion of weeds that grow in lawns, see page 724.)

Chinch bugs. These small ($^1/_6$-inch-long), grayish black insects suck sap from grass blades (particularly in hot weather), attacking St. Augustine and sometimes Bermuda, buffalo, and zoysia grasses. Symptoms are brown or yellow patches, especially in dry locations; these patches eventually die. To confirm the presence of these pests, push a can with both ends removed into the soil just where grass is beginning to brown and fill it with water; if present, chinch bugs will float to the surface.

To control, eliminate thatch. Keep lawn moist to promote beneficial fungi that attack chinch bugs. For chemical control, use diazinon.

Fairy ring. This fungal disease is common in lawns growing in soil high in organic matter or containing wood debris (such as boards or old roots). Symptoms include small circular patches of dark green grass surrounding areas of dead or light-colored grass. Mushrooms may or may not be present.

To control, apply a nitrogen fertilizer and keep the lawn wet for 3 to 5 days. Also aerate the lawn. There are no chemical controls.

Rust. Rust fungi can afflict Kentucky bluegrass, perennial ryegrass, tall fescue, and zoysia lawns. Infected lawns have an overall yellowish to reddish color; small, reddish pustules form in circular or elongated patches on older leaf blades and stems. Blades eventually shrivel and die.

To control, apply adequate (but not excessive) nitrogen fertilizer. For rust spores to germinate, leaf surfaces must be wet for 4 hours; water in the morning so that grass will dry out during the day. The fungicides triadimefon and chlorothalonil may be effective.

Sod webworms. The larvae of several kinds of moths, these pests attack all turf grasses. Small dead patches appear in spring and gradually enlarge during summer. Pale moths fly close to the lawn in a zigzag pattern at dusk. To confirm presence of sod webworms, drench an affected patch of lawn with a solution of 1 tablespoon dishwashing soap and 1 gallon water. Larvae will float to the surface; if you find 15 or more per square yard, treat the lawn. To control these pests, try parasitic nematodes (see page 680). For chemical control, use a product containing permethrin (a pyrethroid).

White grubs. These 1- to 1½-inch grubs are the larvae of several species of beetles; they have three pairs of legs and curl into a C shape when exposed. White grubs feed on the roots of all turf grasses. Distinct, irregularly shaped brown patches appear in afflicted lawns; symptoms are most severe in late summer. Sections of dead turf pull up easily.

To control, apply parasitic nematodes (see page 680), first checking to be sure the species you buy is recommended for use against white grubs. Chemical controls include carbaryl and imidacloprid; these controls work best if you first dethatch the lawn.

TOP TO BOTTOM: Chinch bug, Fairy ring, Rust, Sod webworms, White grubs

Mulching

Mulching is the practice of applying organic or inorganic materials to the surface of the soil around plants. Mulches help hold moisture in the soil, and they insulate it from extreme or rapid changes of temperature. They prevent most weed seedlings from becoming established (and make it easier to remove any that do grow); keep mud from splashing up onto foliage, flowers, fruit, and surfaces such as house walls; help prevent erosion; and make your garden beds look tidy. Before applying any mulch, clear away existing weeds.

ORGANIC MULCHES. Derived from once-living matter, organic mulches break down slowly, improving the soil and adding nutrients as they decompose. Choices include chopped leaves, compost, grass clippings (be sure to apply clippings in thin layers, letting each layer dry before applying another), pine needles, shredded bark, ground bark, wood chips, sawdust, straw, and coir dust (see page 663). Other good organic mulches are agricultural by-products such as crushed nut hulls or shells and pomace, the pulpy remains of grapes or apples that have been pressed to make wine or juice. (Let pomace dry before using it.)

Apply organic mulches in a 2- to 4-inch-thick layer on paths and around plants, but take care not to cover the plants' crowns: too much moisture near the crown can cause rot.

INORGANIC MULCHES. Inorganic mulches include gravel and other kinds of rock, plastic sheeting, and landscape fabrics. Stones make permanent mulches that can discourage weeds effectively; check with the supplier for the amount you need. Plastic warms the soil and black plastic suppresses weeds.

Landscape fabrics—unlike plastic—are porous, allowing air, water, and dissolved nutrients to reach the soil. Sold in nurseries and garden supply centers, these fabrics are best used in permanent plantings around trees and shrubs; they aren't really suited for beds of vegetables or annuals, where you change plants often. Install them as shown at right (you can lay them around existing plants or cut slits in them to accommodate new ones). After installation, cover the fabric with a 2- to 3-inch layer of a weed-free organic mulch.

LAYING LANDSCAPE FABRIC

Unroll fabric, then use scissors or a knife to cut X-shaped slits for plants. Tuck the flaps back in around the plants' bases.

HOW MUCH ORGANIC MULCH SHOULD YOU BUY?

Bulk quantities of organic mulch are sold by the cubic yard. Determine how many square feet you want to cover (multiply the area's length by its width), then consult the chart below to determine the approximate amount of mulch you need.

HOW MUCH MULCH TO USE

To cover this area	2 inches deep	3 inches deep	4 inches deep
100 square feet	2/3 cubic yard	1 cubic yard	1 1/3 cubic yards
250	1 2/3	2 1/2	3 1/3
500	3 1/3	5	6 1/3
1,000	6 2/3	10	13 1/3

Native Plants, Gardening with

Native plants give your garden a sense of place, making it part of the overall landscape of the region where you live. They attract wildlife, drawing birds, butterflies, lizards, and insects to the garden. And because they're naturally suited to the climate, they're generally self-sufficient, needing little care once established.

The West is home to a number of native plant communities, including desert, chaparral, oak woodland, coniferous forest, and various kinds of wetlands. Local native plant societies, demonstration gardens at botanical gardens and parks, and field guides can all teach you more about groups of plants indigenous to your area. For a list of plants native to several Western regions, see "Native Plants" in A Guide to Plant Selection, beginning on page 64.

Your garden may offer enough diversity in growing conditions to accommodate natives from different communities. A hot, dry, well-drained slope is an excellent site for chaparral plants. A damp, low-light spot will suit shade-loving natives adapted to moist locales; a little-watered area beneath trees is right for those that prefer dry shade. A permanently wet, even boggy area is ideal for moisture-loving species.

PLANTING AND CARING FOR NATIVE PLANTS. Native plants will thrive in your garden if you take care in getting them established. When setting out container-grown plants, start with young ones that are not root-bound—they may not be much to look at when first planted, but they'll adapt more successfully than larger plants. Water immediately after planting, being sure to saturate the soil. Then water carefully and steadily for the first summer or two: don't inundate the plants, but don't let them dry out, either. Once you've taken care to establish your natives through their first 2 years (and assuming you have planted them where the natural conditions suit them), they should do well with little or no supplemental watering. In general, Western natives don't require fertilizing (and some are actually weakened by it). A light mulch is beneficial, but to avoid rot, keep it away from the plants' crowns.

'Julia Phelps' is a selected form of California native wild lilac *(Ceanothus)*.

Organic Gardening

Also known as chemical-free or natural gardening, organic gardening is often associated with raising crops that are safer to eat, but its principles apply to any sort of garden, not just the vegetable plot and the fruit orchard. Organic gardeners (and farmers) strive to produce the healthiest plants possible with minimal impact on the environment and minimal risk to all creatures—human and otherwise—who enjoy the garden. They avoid using chemical fertilizers and pesticides, focusing instead on creating healthy soil, which in turn promotes healthy plants that are less susceptible to disease and insects. Organic gardeners aim for biological diversity in their gardens, choosing plants that will attract a wide variety of organisms, including the beneficial creatures that help keep damaging pests under control.

ELEMENTS OF AN ORGANIC GARDEN. As noted below, many aspects of organic gardening are covered in greater detail elsewhere in this guide to gardening.

Building healthy soil. Healthy garden soil is home to earthworms and numerous other beneficial creatures. Its structure is hospitable to plant roots—neither too dense nor too loose, fast draining yet moisture retentive. To achieve this kind of soil, amend your planting beds with organic amendments such as compost and manure (see pages 661 and 708 for more on composting and soil amendments). Cover crops (page 664) offer an easy way to add large amounts of organic material into the soil. Fertilizers, too, can increase the soil's store of organic matter. Organic gardeners prefer natural fertilizers (page 668), which, though slower acting than chemical ones, provide a more sustained release of nutrients and encourage beneficial soil-dwelling organisms.

Controlling pests and diseases. Be diligent about monitoring the garden, so you know which problems are present and what natural controls (beneficial insects, for example) may already be at work. Physical controls such as barriers, handpicking, and spraying water jets (page 679) can curtail insect damage. Choosing plant varieties that are resistant to specific diseases and pests is important; you will find many such varieties listed in the Western Plant Encyclopedia. Crop rotation (page 715) prevents diseases and insects that are specific to certain plants from building up in any one part of the garden.

For more specific information on disease control, see page 664. Pest control, including a discussion of beneficial insects and biological controls, begins on page 679.

Controlling weeds. To keep weeds down, use mulches (see facing page; organic mulches also help improve the soil). Physical management techniques such as pulling and hoeing (page 725) are also effective.

Organic gardening practices are designed to protect beneficials such as bees, the primary pollinators of many flowering plants.

Ornamental Grasses

Grown for their graceful form and varying textures, ornamental grasses provide a handsome foil to shrubs and perennials. Many are excellent container plants, too. Like lawn grasses, ornamental sorts can be divided into warm- and cool-season types. *Warm-season grasses* include most species of *Miscanthus, Molinia, Panicum,* and *Pennisetum;* they grow from spring through summer, bloom in fall, and then go dormant. Their foliage and flowering plumes remain attractive—albeit dry and brown—through the winter.

Cool-season grasses are typically evergreen, though some may die back in cold climates. They begin new growth in fall, then flower in spring and summer. This group includes *Calamagrostis, Deschampsia, Festuca, Helictotrichon sempervirens,* and *Sesleria,* as well as the sedges *(Carex).*

For help in choosing these plants, see "Ornamental Grasses" in A Guide to Plant Selection, beginning on page 64. Be aware that a few ornamental grasses can be invasive, spreading too extensively in the garden or into wild lands; these are noted in the entries in the Western Plant Encyclopedia.

PLANTING AND CARING FOR ORNAMENTAL GRASSES. Garden care for ornamental grasses is more or less the same as you would give perennials. Most should be planted in spring, though cool-season sorts can also be set out in autumn. Before planting, work organic matter (such as compost) and a complete fertilizer into the soil. Don't bury the plants' crowns when you set them in, as this can lead to rot. A mulch will help keep down weeds and conserve soil moisture, but again, be careful not to let it pile up around the grasses' crowns.

Ornamental grasses vary greatly in their moisture requirements—some need water regularly, others only rarely. Check the listings in the Western Plant Encyclopedia for details. If planted in well-prepared beds and mulched, most ornamental grasses can do without feeding, but if they're growing poorly it's wise to give them an application of general-purpose fertilizer in early spring.

These plants all benefit from an annual cleanup in late winter. Cut back warm-season grasses just as you see new growth emerging at the plants' bases, using pruning shears to trim dead foliage and flowering stems to within a few inches of the ground. (If you have a number of large clumps, electric hedge shears or a mechanical weed trimmer will make quick work of this project.) Evergreen cool-season grasses needn't be cut back every year. Instead, clean them up by removing dead foliage; you can often simply "comb" out old growth by running your fingers through the clumps. After a few years, however, the grasses may develop a great deal of unattractive or dead leaves; at this point, cut them back by two-thirds in fall or early spring to encourage fresh new growth.

Divide ornamental grasses every few years or so, when the clump's center dies out. Divide warm-season kinds in spring. For cool-season sorts, do the job in fall or early spring. To divide, dig up the clump; if it's very large, you may first need to cut it into sections with a sharp spade or an ax. Then cut off and replant vigorous sections from the outside of the clump.

TOP: *Pennisetum orientale*
BOTTOM: A mechanical weed trimmer with a blade can be used to cut back ornamental grasses.

O

Perennials

The general category of perennials encompasses plants with widely varying habits of growth, but all have at least one thing in common: they live for more than 2 years, in contrast to annuals and biennials (pages 658 and 659), which complete their life cycles within 1 and 2 years, respectively. Some perennials die down to the ground at the end of each growing season, then reappear at the start of the next. These include hosta and peony *(Paeonia)* and are often called "herbaceous" plants. Others, such as Shasta daisy *(Chrysanthemum maximum)* and coral bells *(Heuchera)*, go through winter as low tufts of leaves, ready to grow when spring arrives. A third type of perennial is truly evergreen, its foliage persisting almost unchanged throughout the winter months. Thrift *(Armeria maritima)* and yucca are two examples.

PLANTING PERENNIALS. Perennials are sold both bare-root and in containers. Nurseries and garden centers offer them in containers ranging from cell-packs to 1-gallon pots; for information on planting these, see page 691.

Nurseries and mail-order catalogs also sell some perennials bare-root during their dormant period. As the name implies, bare-root plants have had most or all of the soil removed from around their roots, which are then surrounded with organic packing material and enclosed in plastic bags. If you'll be planting bare-root perennials within a day or two after purchase or receipt, open the bags slightly, add a little water, and hold them in a cool place. If planting must be delayed by more than a few days, however, pot up the plants in small containers or heel them in—plant them temporarily in a shallow trench in the garden. Before setting out bare-root perennials in their permanent location, prepare the soil as described on page 690. Then plant as shown below.

STAKING PERENNIALS

Some perennials are naturally inclined to sprawl or flop over. To display their blooms most effectively and to keep them from smothering neighboring plants, you'll need to prop them up. These illustrations show three useful staking techniques.

Bamboo stake and tie; cork at tip of stake protects eyes from injury

Metal hoop support

Stakes and string

CARING FOR PERENNIALS. Routine watering during growth and bloom will satisfy most perennials. There are, of course, exceptions—some plants prefer drier soil, while others demand lots of moisture. These are noted in the Western Plant Encyclopedia. Keep in mind that young plants require more frequent watering than older ones with deeper, more extensive root systems. A layer of mulch helps conserve water as well as suppressing weeds and improving the soil as it decomposes. Once perennials are established in the garden, feed them once annually in late winter or early spring, using a complete fertilizer.

Throughout the bloom season, deadhead your perennials (that is, remove the spent flowers), both to keep the plants tidy and to prevent them from diverting energy to seed production. Of course, you may not want to deadhead in all cases. Certain perennials, for example, have attractive seedheads that many gardeners prefer to leave in place until winter or early spring, both for decoration and to provide food for seed-eating birds.

Later in the year (in fall or winter), it's a good idea to clean up most perennials by removing old, dead, and fallen foliage, flowers, and stems. Besides neatening up the garden, such a cleanup deprives pests (especially snails and slugs) of hiding places and helps eliminate any disease organisms that may be living on garden debris.

Many gardeners in cold-winter climates mulch perennials over the winter to protect them from alternate freezing and thawing. As soon as the ground freezes, apply a lightweight mulch that won't pack down into an airtight mass; evergreen boughs, salt hay, marsh hay, and pine needles are all good choices.

Over time, many perennials form such thick clumps that the plants are too crowded to turn in a good performance. When this happens, dig and divide as described on page 700.

PLANTING BARE-ROOT PERENNIALS

1 Remove organic packing material and soak the roots in water for about 30 minutes.

2 Dig a hole about twice as wide as the root system. Then make a cone of soil in the center to support the roots.

3 Set the plant on the cone of soil and spread the roots evenly. Fill with soil so that the crown of the plant is level with or slightly above the soil, then water well.

Pests and Pest Management

Chemical-based pesticides were introduced in the 1940s, ushering in a long era of pest control through attempted eradication. Beyond being generally unsuccessful, this approach has often been actively harmful to a wide range of nontarget organisms, including humans and other animals, birds, and beneficial insects. In recent years, recognizing that gardens are complex and interdependent systems, more and more gardeners have rejected the "elimination" method: far from solving a problem, wiping out a particular pest simply upsets the garden's natural balance. The focus today has shifted to maintaining a diversified garden, where pests are largely kept in check by natural forces. If one or more pests do cause excessive damage, gardeners first attempt to manage the situation by using physical or biological controls. Chemicals are employed only as a last resort.

The balanced, safety-conscious approach described above reflects the goals and methods of Integrated Pest Management (IPM) first developed for commercial agriculture but just as appropriate for the home garden. Its primary aim is to prevent problems. When diseases or pest infestations do arise, a number of integrated techniques are brought into play to reduce them to tolerable levels—not to eliminate them completely.

PREVENTING AND IDENTIFYING PROBLEMS. To thwart problems before they start, IPM begins with good cultural practices. Choose healthy plants adapted to your climate and garden conditions; whenever possible, select varieties resistant to diseases and pests prevalent in your area. Plant carefully and follow up with proper watering, fertilizing, garden cleanup, and other care as needed. Use soil solarization (page 726), a technique that reduces or eliminates some soil-dwelling pests and weed seeds. In the vegetable garden, rotate crops to prevent the buildup of specific pests (page 715).

Another basic aspect of IPM is regular garden monitoring. If you check your plants frequently, you're more likely to spot problems before they get out of hand. Note the general condition of each plant; then look for fungal growth, holes in leaves or fruit, sap oozing from bark, and wilted branches. Check for insects hiding on leaf undersides, in bark fissures, or beneath fallen leaves. A hand lens is useful for spotting tiny pests like spider mites.

Because beneficial or harmless creatures sometimes resemble damaging pests, it's important to identify the organisms you find accurately. For help with identification, check the photos and descriptions beginning on page 680 or consult your Cooperative Extension Office.

MANAGEMENT OPTIONS. Even if your garden inspection reveals a few pest problems, you may not need or want to employ controls. Keep in mind that the truly pest-free garden does not exist, and learn to accept some marred fruit, flowers, or foliage. More extensive damage doesn't automatically require control, either. Sometimes it may be better simply removing and replacing an afflicted plant than attempting to remedy the situation.

If you decide that a problem is serious enough to warrant action on your part, it's time to formulate a pest management strategy. Within the guidelines of IPM, you'll begin with physical and biological controls, turning to chemicals only when all else fails.

Physical controls. These nontoxic controls include a number of techniques.

Handpicking. Remove and destroy slugs, snails, caterpillars, and other pests. To get rid of some pests, you may need to pluck and destroy entire leaves (a tactic that can also help control some foliage diseases).

Pruning. Prune and destroy entire branches infested with a pest or disease.

Spraying with water. A jet of water can knock pests from plants and often kill them.

Erecting barriers. Certain physical structures can prevent pests from reaching susceptible plants. These include row covers (page 715); more permanent plant cages made by fastening screening to frames of wood or PVC pipe; and plant collars (paper cups, plastic cartons, or empty cans with the ends cut out) that protect seedlings from cutworms and other insects. Other barriers are discussed in the descriptions of individual pests.

Using traps. You can trap pests in various ways. Colored sticky traps are designed to catch specific insects; some are attracted to the color red, others to white or yellow, for example. Pheromone traps are also used. Pheromones are chemicals involved in communication between insects of the same species; they're placed in traps with sticky materials and used in commercial farming to monitor the presence of particular pests, thus helping to time sprayings precisely. Some pheromone traps are used to control pest caterpillars (notably codling moth) by mass trapping of males.

LOCATING BIOLOGICAL PEST AND DISEASE CONTROLS

Many biological pest and disease control products are sold by mail-order companies specializing in gardening products. These include Harmony Farm Supply, Graton, CA; M & R Durango Inc., Bayfield, CO; Peaceful Valley Farm Supply, Grass Valley, CA; and Rincon-Vitova Insectaries Inc., Ventura, CA. In addition, the California Environmental Protection Agency publishes a free guide, *Suppliers of Beneficial Organisms in North America*. To obtain the guide, write to the California Department of Pesticide Regulation, Environmental Monitoring and Pest Management Branch, 830 K Street, Sacramento, CA 95814-3510; or call (916) 324-4100. The Bio-Integral Resource Center publishes a *Directory of Least-toxic Pest-control Products*, updated yearly; write to P.O. Box 7414, Berkeley, CA 94707; or call (510) 524-2567.

TOP: Plant collars made from plastic cartons prevent cutworms from reaching vegetable seedlings.
BOTTOM: Yellow sticky cards attract and trap whiteflies.

Biological controls. When you use biological controls, you're relying on living organisms—beneficial insects, for example—to destroy garden pests. This sort of control occurs naturally in the garden all the time. To draw beneficials to your garden and encourage them to remain, provide food in the form of nectar-producing flowering plants and be sure to avoid chemical sprays that will indiscriminately destroy both helpful and harmful creatures. You can purchase and release some beneficial insects. See pages 680, 681 for more information on beneficials and plants that attract them.

Certain microorganisms are also classed as biological controls. The best-known of these is *Bacillus thuringiensis (Bt)*, a bacterium that, once ingested by susceptible pest larvae, causes them to stop feeding and eventually die. Many different strains have been identified, each effective against specific types of larvae. *Bt* does not affect other, nontarget creatures.

Chemical controls. As a last resort, IPM turns to various sorts of pesticides, first selecting the least toxic ones (products such as insecticidal soap, for example). If these are not successful, the use of stronger chemicals (synthetics) may be warranted. For lists of both natural and synthetic pesticides, see page 685. ▶

BENEFICIALS

Some of the beneficial creatures described here are naturally present in Western gardens; others, as noted, can be introduced to reduce various pest populations. Beneficials that attack specific pests are noted in the descriptions beginning on page 681. Spiders and centipedes are also important predators, as are toads, frogs, and birds.

Assassin bugs. These slim, ½- to ¾-inch-long insects have long legs and even longer, angled antennae. Some species are brilliant red or black; others are brown or gray. They prey on many insects, stabbing their victims with a long, curved beak.

Damsel bugs are dull gray or brown, about ½ inch long, and very slender, with a long, narrow head. Nymphs resemble the adults, but they're smaller and have no wings. Both adults and nymphs feed on aphids, leafhoppers, and small caterpillars.

Ground beetles range from ½ to 1 inch long; most are shiny black, though some are also marked with bright colors. The smaller species eat other insects, caterpillars, cutworms, and soil-dwelling maggots and grubs. Some larger species eat slugs and snails and their eggs.

Lacewings. An adult lacewing is an inch-long, flying insect with lacy, netted wings and long antennae. The immature or larval form looks something like a ½-inch-long alligator; it has visible legs and is equipped with pincers at the mouth end. Lacewing larvae devour aphids, leafhoppers, mealybugs, mites, psyllids, thrips, whiteflies, and other insects; adults of most species feed only on nectar, pollen, and honeydew from garden plants. Larvae are commercially available.

Lady beetles. Also known as ladybugs, these familiar garden helpers and their larvae (which look like ¼-inch-long, six-legged alligators with orange and black spots or stripes) feed on aphids, mealybugs, and the eggs of many insects. Mail-order and garden centers sell lady beetles, but once released they often fly away rather than staying in your garden. Freeing them at night or keeping them in cages for the first few days may encourage them to remain.

Minute pirate bugs. Both the adults (⅛-inch-long, black-and-white bugs) and pale orange nymphs feed on thrips, spider mites, and insect eggs. Also called flower bugs, they occur naturally in gardens; they can also be purchased for release.

Parasitic nematodes. Parasitic nematodes include several species of microscopic worms. Also known as beneficial or predatory nematodes, they're effective against several hundred kinds of insects, including cucumber beetles, cutworms, flea beetles, grubs, root weevils, and sod webworms. They attack the larvae, releasing a toxic bacterium that kills the host. Can be purchased. Read directions; effectiveness depends on proper soil conditions and release techniques.

Parasitic wasps. Many species of naturally occurring parasitic wasps lay their eggs in the larvae, pupae, or eggs of other insects, thus destroying them. These tiny wasps are not harmful to humans. One type offered in many garden catalogs is the trichogramma wasp, which lays its eggs within the eggs of many moths and butterflies. Several species are sold; check with the seller to get the one best adapted to your situation.

Soldier beetles are narrow, ¾-inch-long, typically red or orange insects with leathery-looking black, gray, or brown wing covers. The adults eat aphids and other soft-bodied insects; the tiny soil-dwelling larvae attack smaller insects. Adults also feed on pollen and nectar.

Syrphid flies. Also known as flower or hover flies, these insects are important naturally occurring beneficials. Adults have bodies banded with yellow; they look a bit like bees but have only one set of wings. While adults feed only on nectar and pollen, the larvae (tapered green or gray maggots with small fangs) consume dozens of aphids each day.

Tachinid flies. The gray, bristled adults look something like houseflies. They feed only on nectar, but their tiny, spined, green larvae parasitize pests such as armyworms, cutworms, stinkbugs, and smaller beetle larvae. There are many species, each attacking specific insects.

TOP: Assassin bug
BOTTOM: Parasitic wasp

TOP: Damsel bug
BOTTOM: Soldier beetle

TOP: Ground beetle
BOTTOM: Syrphid fly

TOP: Lacewing
BOTTOM: Tachinid fly

P

PLANTS THAT ATTRACT BENEFICIAL INSECTS

Certain flowering plants provide sources of food that many beneficials need at various times during their life cycle. Integrate these plants into a border or plant them in swaths around the garden. Mix many kinds: the wider the range of food and shelter you provide, the more varieties of insects you'll attract (and the more likely they are to stay). Plan your garden so that some plants are in flower throughout the year.

Buckwheat *(Eriogonum)*
Clovers (*Trifolium* and other species)
Coriander *(Coriandrum sativum)*
Coreopsis
Corn cockle *(Agrostemma githago)*
Cosmos *(Cosmos bipinnatus)*
Dill *(Anethum graveolens)*
Fennel *(Foeniculum vulgare)*
Feverfew *(Chrysanthemum parthenium)*
Mustard *(Brassica)*
Sweet alyssum *(Lobularia maritima)*
Tansy *(Tanacetum vulgare)*
Tidytips *(Layia platyglossa)*
Yarrow *(Achillea)*

Plant a wide variety of flowers to attract beneficials.

PLANT PESTS. Some of the pests most commonly encountered in Western gardens are discussed here. A number of pests that afflict only one kind of plant—ash trees *(Fraxinus)*, apples, or tomatoes, for example—are treated in the appropriate entry in the Western Plant Encyclopedia.

The controls mentioned for each pest are discussed in order of toxicity, from least to most toxic. Bear in mind that whenever you use chemical controls, you risk killing beneficials along with the target pests.

Ants. On their own, most ants aren't serious pests; some are even important natural enemies of harmful insects. Certain species, however, nurture and protect sap-sucking insects such as aphids, mealybugs, soft scales, and whiteflies. These sap-sucking pests in turn produce honeydew; a fungus grows on the honeydew, causing sooty mold (page 666).

To prevent ants from tending sap-sucking insects on trees, place sticky barriers (commercial brands include Tree Tanglefoot Pest Barrier and Stickum) around the trunks; also prune off any branches that touch the ground to eliminate alternate paths up into the plant. Diatomaceous earth can also be effective in deterring ants. Bait or ant stakes can be effective if used on the ground near trails or nests.

Aphids. These soft, oval insects range from pinhead to matchhead size and may be black, white, pink, or pale green. They cluster together on young shoots, buds, and leaves. Both adult and immature aphids (nymphs) damage a wide variety of plants by piercing the leaves and stems and sucking out plant juices. Some aphids also transmit viral diseases.

Prevent aphids from damaging vegetables by planting under row covers (page 715). Reflective aluminum mulches (available from nurseries and mail-order sources) deter flying adult aphids from laying eggs.

Because numerous creatures keep aphid populations in check, the best control tactic is often to do nothing and leave the pests to natural controls: lady beetles, lacewing larvae, soldier beetles, syrphid flies, predatory midges, parasitic wasps, and even lizards and some small birds. Encourage beneficials by growing plants that attract them (see facing page).

You can blast aphids from plants with strong jets of water; they can also be killed by spraying with insecticidal soap.

Horticultural oil, used as a dormant spray in winter, will kill the overwintering eggs of aphids on deciduous trees. Natural pesticides containing pyrethrins can be used. Other pesticides are also effective in controlling aphids but should be called upon only when infestations are severe. These include diazinon, malathion, and (on nonedible plants) acephate.

Cucumber beetles. Two kinds of cucumber beetles—both about ¼ inch long—cause trouble in Western gardens. The western spotted cucumber beetle looks a bit like a lady beetle with 12 black spots on its back; the western striped cucumber beetle is yellowish orange and marked with three black stripes. Adult beetles chew holes in leaves and flowers and damage stems of cucumbers, melons, squash, and other vegetables; the spotted kind also feeds on roses and other garden plants. Both kinds can spread diseases. The larvae, which live underground, may damage roots.

Protect young plants by using row covers (page 715). Natural controls include birds and tachinid flies. You can handpick these beetles, dropping them into a bucket of soapy water. For major infestations, spray with a natural insecticide containing pyrethrins. Parasitic nematodes will reduce larval populations. Chemical controls include malathion and carbaryl.

Cutworms. A large variety of hairless larvae of night-flying moths make up the diverse group called cutworms. They feed at night and on overcast days; during the daylight hours, they hide underground, curled up in a C shape. Most cut off young plants at ground level—hence their name.

TOP TO BOTTOM: Ants, Aphids, Western spotted cucumber beetle, Cutworm

To help prevent cutworm damage, clear and till garden beds to destroy the eggs, larvae, and pupae before you sow seeds. To protect transplants, encircle each with a can (with both ends removed) or a paper cup or plastic carton with the bottom cut out; it should extend 1 to 2 inches both into the soil and above ground.

Encourage or introduce natural predators such as ground beetles and parasitic nematodes. Spreading diatomaceous earth around young seedlings may deter cutworms. ▸

TOP: Earwig
BOTTOM: Flea beetles

TOP: Galls caused by insects or mites
BOTTOM: Geranium (tobacco) budworm

TOP: Grasshopper
BOTTOM: Leaf miner trails

P

Earwigs. These familiar pests aren't all bad—they prey on aphids and other insects. On the negative side, they destroy young seedlings and damage flower petals, some soft fruits, and corn silks. To prevent earwig damage, keep the garden clean, removing hiding places such as weedy areas and dead foliage.

Several kinds of traps are effective. At night, when earwigs are active, place moistened rolled-up newspapers, rolls of corrugated cardboard, or short sections of garden hose in the garden; in the morning, dispose of the insects that have crept inside. You can also trap earwigs in a short (no larger than 6-ounce) cat food or tuna can containing ½ inch of vegetable oil. Place several such cans around the garden and dispose of them as they fill with the corpses of earwigs unable to resist the lure of the drink.

Flea beetles. These tiny (1/10-inch-long), oval, and shiny beetles may be blue black, brown, or bronze; they jump like fleas when disturbed. Adult flea beetles riddle leaves with small holes. They feed on many vegetable crops and are especially damaging to seedlings; they also spread diseases. Dichondra lawns are attacked by flea beetle larvae.

Adult flea beetles overwinter in weeds and garden debris; a fall cleanup will remove these havens. Protect seedlings with row covers. To control flea beetles, use azadirachtin (neem extract) or diazinon.

Gall-forming insects and mites. Galls—distorted swellings on plant leaves, stems, or flowers—are caused by the larvae of several hundred different species of wasps, midges, mites, aphids, and other invertebrates.

Despite their unsightliness, most leaf galls are harmless. Prune off those on smaller branches or simply remove the whole branch. Large galls (and large branches) are usually better left in place, since pruning them out may harm the plant.

Geranium (tobacco) budworm. A striped caterpillar that may be greenish, tan, or reddish up to ¾ inch long, the geranium (tobacco) budworm is a close relative of the corn earworm (see entry for Corn in the Western Plant Encyclopedia). Besides geraniums, it attacks petunias, roses, and other flowers, burrowing into the buds and feeding from the inside. It also eats leaves and stems. Budworms overwinter as pupae in the soil, then hatch into moths.

Remove dried-up buds and flowers that may harbor the caterpillars. At the end of the growing season, clear away dead annual flowers and infested parts of other plants to remove eggs. *Bt* will kill budworms if dusted or sprayed on plants before the caterpillars enter the buds. Pyrethrins and chemicals such as permethrin (a pyrethroid) and carbaryl must also be applied at this point.

Grasshoppers. During their periodic outbreaks, grasshoppers can cause severe damage, especially in hot-summer areas. They generally lay their eggs in dry, undisturbed areas—along roadsides, in empty lots, on rangeland—but they will also do so in gardens. Eggs hatch from late winter to early summer, depending on temperature and climate. Newly hatched nymphs resemble adults, but they are wingless and smaller in size, and they feed voraciously. Once mature, they fly out to find new feeding areas.

Cultivating the soil in fall, winter, and early spring destroys grasshopper egg clusters. Keep the garden clear of weeds, which can harbor grasshoppers. Row covers (page 715) can be effective, though in severe outbreaks grasshoppers will chew through them.

Grasshoppers are most vulnerable to chemical control in spring and early summer, while they are still young and wingless. Diatomaceous earth deters them. For chemical control, use a bran-and-carbaryl bait, acephate (on nonedibles), or permethrin (a pyrethroid). A biological control, *Nosema locustae* (sold as Nolo bait or Semaspore) targets only grasshoppers. Like the sprays and baits just mentioned, it should be applied early in the season, when the pests are immature. It works best when used over large areas, such as ranchland or a weedy field bordering several gardens.

Leaf miners are the larvae of certain moths, beetles, and flies. They tunnel within foliage, leaving twisting trails on the surface. Adult leaf miners are rarely seen. Various species attack vegetables, ornamental and fruit trees, annuals, and perennials. The damage is mostly cosmetic, although yield of some crops may be reduced.

Protect vegetables by planting under row covers (page 715), thus preventing the adult insects from reaching the plants to lay eggs. Handpicking infested leaves is helpful. Parasitic wasps are natural enemies of leaf miners and

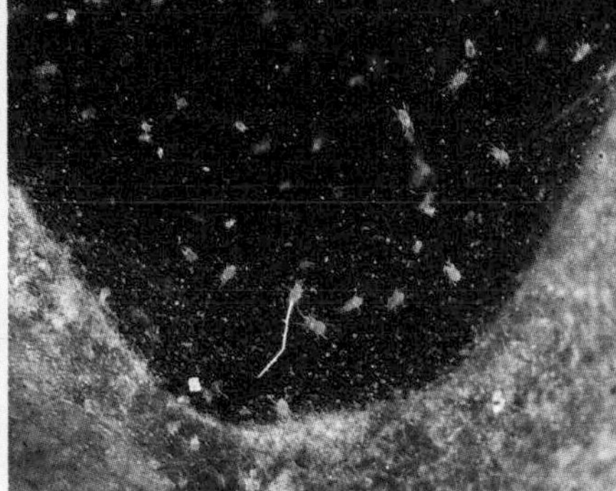

TOP: Mealybugs
BOTTOM: Mites

TOP: Pillbug (left), Sowbug (right)
BOTTOM: Black vine weevil (a root weevil)

lay their eggs on larvae or near leaf miner egg sites. Azadirachtin (neem extract) may discourage adults from laying eggs on leaf surfaces. Once the insect is inside the leaf, chemical control is difficult; the systemic insecticide acephate can be used on nonedibles.

Mealybugs have an oval body with overlapping soft plates and a white, cottony covering. They are closely related to scale insects—but unlike scales, most mealybugs can move around (slowly). They suck plant juices, causing stunting and, in some cases, kill the plant. Sooty mold (page 666) may grow on the honeydew they excrete. Mealybugs are houseplant pests everywhere; outdoors, they are troublesome in warm-winter areas.

For any infestation inside and for minor infestations outside, daub the pests with a cotton swab dipped in rubbing alcohol. Outdoors, hose plants with water jets (or insecticidal soap sprays) every 2 to 4 weeks to remove adult and immature mealybugs and their eggs as well as sooty mold. Control ants (page 681), which nurture mealybugs for their honeydew.

Beneficial insects, including lacewings, lady beetles, and syrphid flies, help control these pests. You can release the mealybug destroyer *(Cryptolaemus montrouzieri)*, a lady beetle relative whose adults and larvae both consume mealybugs; it needs warm temperatures, so it's most effective in greenhouses and during the warmer months outdoors. For severe infestations, spray with horticultural oil, azadirachtin (neem extract), pyrethrins, acephate (on nonedibles), diazinon, or malathion.

Mites. To the naked eye, these tiny spider relatives look like flecks of red, yellow, or green. Signs of mite infestation include yellow-stippled leaves (where the pests have sucked plant juices) and a tan or bronze cast to the foliage. Heavily infested plants are weakened and may eventually die.

To check plants for the presence of mites, hold a piece of white paper under the affected foliage and briskly tap the plant: the disturbed pests will drop down onto the paper, looking much like specks of pepper, then try to crawl away. Of the many kinds of mites, some are host-specific (such as clover and citrus bud mites), but others—notably spider mites—attack a variety of outdoor and indoor plants.

Dust that settles on leaves encourages mites, so hose off plants frequently to keep the pest population down. Increased humidity also helps. Drought-stressed plants are more susceptible to mites.

Many natural predators help keep mites in check. You can purchase lacewing larvae and several species of predatory mites that prey on spider mites.

Mites can often be washed from foliage with water jets; insecticidal soap is also effective. Spraying with horticultural oil in late winter smothers mites and eggs (it can be applied in summer as well). On some plants (check the product label for listings), you can control mites with sulfur dusted on leaf undersides. (Do not use sulfur in combination with oil sprays or when the temperature is above 85°F/29°C.) Neem oil is a miticide. Chemical miticides are available in some areas.

Pillbugs and sowbugs. These familiar creatures are soil-dwelling crustaceans, not insects. Pillbugs roll up when disturbed into black balls about the size of a large pea; sowbugs are usually gray and don't roll up. Both pests' principal food is decaying vegetation (which they help break down into humus), but they also eat very young seedlings, the skins of melons and cucumbers, and berries.

To limit these pests' populations, remove hiding places, such as boards lying on the ground and weedy areas with decaying foliage. Lift ripening fruit off the ground with pebbles or strawberry baskets. Plastic mulch is helpful, because the soil under it gets too hot for the pests' comfort. Chemical control is generally not required.

Root weevils. A number of root weevils and their larvae can harm plants. In some species, such as the black vine weevil, both adults and larvae are harmful; the adults feed on leaves, flowers, and bark of rhododendron, yew, grape, and other plants, while the larvae consume roots, especially those of young plants. Billbugs are root weevil larvae that damage lawns.

Parasitic nematodes help control root weevil larvae. Azadirachtin (neem extract) and some pyrethroids are effective against adults. Acephate can be used to control adults on nonedible plants.

Scales can cause garden problems throughout the West. Though related to mealybugs and aphids, they differ in having a waxy, shell-like covering that camouflages them and protects them from some natural enemies (and insecticides). Scales are classified as "armored" (hard) or soft; soft scales are more mobile and excrete a sticky honeydew.

An adult scale lives under its waxy shell, which sticks to the host plant. Running from the underside of the insect into the plant tissue is a tiny filamentous mouth part, through which the scale sucks plant juices. Scale eggs hatch beneath the shell; in spring or summer, the young scales ("crawlers") leave the protective cover to seek their own feeding sites.

Many naturally occurring parasites and predators, including several species of small, dark lady beetles, control or limit scale populations; a few of these are sold for release in the garden

Scales

or greenhouse. In dry regions, you can help scale-infested plants by hosing them off frequently, since dust inhibits the various scale parasites and predators. Get rid of ants (page 681), which tend and protect soft scales.

You can control light infestations by picking scales off the plant or scraping them off with a plastic scouring pad. On deciduous plants, you can kill some adult scales in winter with horticultural oil. Scales are vulnerable to insecticides when they are in the crawler stage. To check for crawlers, wrap double-sided sticky tape around branches; if you find trapped crawlers, apply controls. Horticultural oil, insecticidal soap, and insecticides such as diazinon or malathion may be effective against crawlers.

Slugs and snails. Often considered the West's worst garden pests, slugs and snails are similar creatures; a slug is simply a snail without a shell. These mollusks have toothlike jaws that rasp large, ragged holes in leaves and flowers. Seedlings and new transplants may be eaten entirely. For the most part, they hide by day and feed at night, though they may be active on gray or rainy days.

Try to eliminate these pests' favorite daytime hiding places—weedy areas, boards, stones, unused flower pots. You can protect newly planted seedlings by encircling them with a 3- to 4-inch-high "fence" made from copper strips; such strips can also be stapled to raised beds and wrapped around tree trunks and containers. Wood ashes and diatomaceous earth also make good barriers.

If done regularly, handpicking is effective. Go hunting after dark (with a flashlight) or early in the morning. You can also trap these creatures. A wide plank elevated about an inch off the ground offers a daytime hiding place from which you can collect and dispatch the pests. Shallow containers filled with beer or a simple solution of 1 teaspoon each active baking yeast and sugar with 1 cup water may lure slugs and snails to their deaths.

Commercial baits containing iron phosphate (Sluggo, Escar-Go) are fairly effective, causing the mollusks to stop feeding and die within a few days. These baits are considered nonhazardous to humans, pets, and wildlife. Commercial baits containing metaldehyde are sold as pellets, meal, or emulsion. Set them out in late evening and clear them away (along with dead pests) in the morning, since they can be toxic to birds and pets.

Snail

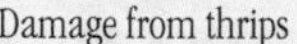
Damage from thrips

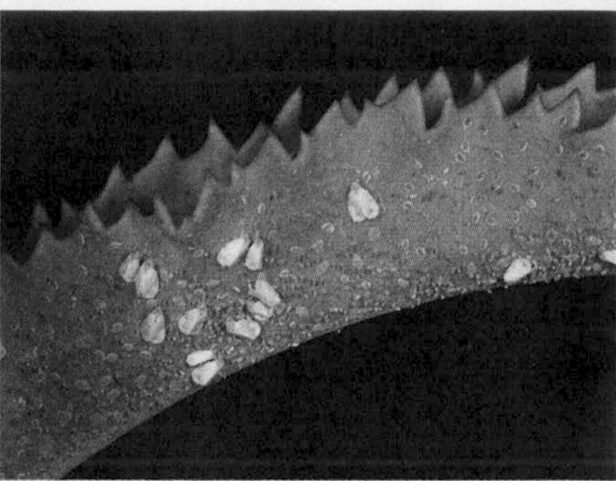
Whiteflies

Thrips are almost microscopic—the light or dark brown adults less than $\frac{1}{20}$ inch long, with narrow, feathery wings; the wingless, light green or pale yellow nymphs are even smaller. Both adults and nymphs feed by rasping soft flower and leaf tissue, then sucking plant juices. Besides damaging foliage and blossoms, they may spread plant diseases.

In heavy infestations, both flowers and leaves are discolored and fail to open normally, looking twisted or stuck together. If you look closely, you will see stippled, puckered areas on flowers and foliage. Leaves may take on a silvery or tan cast similar to that caused by mites—but if thrips are present, you'll see numerous small, black, varnishlike fecal pellets on leaf undersides.

Natural enemies include lacewing larvae, minute pirate bugs, predaceous thrips and mites, and spiders. Insecticidal soaps and horticultural oil help control thrips. Acephate (on nonedibles) and malathion can be effective.

DISPOSING OF PESTICIDES

You may need to dispose of pesticides (including fungicides and herbicides) if you have mixed up more solution than you need or if you have a product that is no longer considered safe due to changes in its registration status. (Until you can dispose of such pesticides properly, keep them—and all others—secured in a locked cabinet.)

Never pour any pesticide down any type of drain, including a storm drain; it could pollute the water supply and harm the environment. Instead, contact your city or county public works department, garbage company, or Cooperative Extension Office to find out where you can discard such products. Many communities sponsor hazardous waste disposal sites, which typically accept used motor oil and leftover paint as well as undiluted pesticides in their original containers and diluted solutions that you have mixed. Since federal law requires that products containing hazardous ingredients be labeled, carefully pour leftover solutions into a glass or plastic container with a tight-fitting lid; write the product name (name of active ingredient and trade name) and its dilution ratio on the container. Empty any powdered or granular pesticide (such as a lawn-care product applied with a spreader) into a heavy-duty garbage bag; then seal and label the bag.

Whiteflies are quite small (about $\frac{1}{8}$-inch-long) winged insects that fly up in clouds when you brush or touch an infested plant. The immature form is a nearly transparent wingless nymph; it excretes honeydew as it feeds, attracting ants and promoting the growth of sooty mold (page 666). Both adults and nymphs suck plant juices. Affected foliage may first show yellow stippling, then curl and turn brown.

Whiteflies thrive in the warm, still air of greenhouses. In warm climates, they're also found outdoors all year, but in colder regions they cause outdoor problems only during summer. In such chilly-winter zones, they do not overwinter outside; garden infestations originate from indoor plants or purchased transplants. To protect your garden, inspect greenhouse and indoor plants and eliminate any whiteflies you find. And no matter what your climate, when you buy new garden plants—particularly bedding plants, which may have started their lives in a greenhouse—carefully examine leaf undersides for adults and nymphs.

Natural enemies, which can be attracted to or introduced into the garden, include lacewing larvae and *Delphastus pusillus,* a species of lady beetle known as whitefly predator. Two species of tiny parasitic wasps, *Encarsia formosa* and *Eretmocerus californicus,* can be released to help control whiteflies in greenhouses.

Handpicking heavily infested leaves helps reduce whitefly populations. Yellow sticky traps (available commercially) can trap significant numbers of the pests. Water jets work well; hose off infested plants every few days, hitting both sides of all leaves. Insecticidal soap can be more effective than water and is less hazardous to natural enemies than other insecticides. Other controls include azadirachtin (neem extract), horticultural oil, and pyrethrins.

▶ page 686

PRODUCTS FOR PEST CONTROL

Sold in liquid, powder, or granular form, pesticides carry one or more active ingredients. Their availability is constantly shifting: new products continue to arrive on the market, while older ones may be withdrawn if research reveals them to be health or environmental hazards.

The lists below cover the most useful and widely available natural and synthetic pesticides for the Western gardener. Others, generally targeting only one kind of pest, are mentioned in the individual pest descriptions beginning on page 681. *Synthetic pesticides* are manufactured compounds that do not normally occur in nature. *Natural pesticides,* in contrast, are products whose active ingredients originate in a plant, animal, or mineral, or whose action results from a biological process (as in the case of *Bacillus thuringiensis;* see page 679). Be aware that "natural" does not mean "harmless"; some natural products can still harm people or plants if they are used incorrectly. Sources for some less-common natural pesticides are given on page 679.

When using any pesticide, *read the label directions carefully and follow them exactly.* The package will clearly state the plants and pests on which the control is registered for use, and it is illegal to apply it to a plant or pest not so listed.

The following products are listed by the accepted common name of the *active ingredient*—the chemical that controls the pest or pests listed on the package label. Some widely used trade names, if they differ from the common name, are noted in parentheses. Before you buy, read the label to make sure you're getting the active ingredient you want. (For more on reading and understanding pesticide labels, see page 686.) Always dispose of pesticides in a safe manner (see facing page).

NATURAL PESTICIDES

- **Azadirachtin, neem oil** (Bioneem; Fruit, Nut, and Vegetable Spray; Rose Defense; others). Azadirachtin (neem extract) is derived from a tropical tree *(Azadirachta indica).* It repels pests and, once ingested, interrupts their growth cycle, killing larvae as well as adults. Effective against aphids, beetles, caterpillars, grasshoppers, leaf miners, mealybugs, root weevils, whiteflies, others. Neem oil (primarily the oil of the neem seed) controls insects in egg, larval, and adult stages; it also controls mites and some plant diseases. Mix with warm water before spraying. Both azadirachtin and neem oil can kill nontarget insects such as honeybees and lady beetles. Toxic to fish.
- ***Bacillus thuringiensis, Bt.*** A bacterium that controls many pest larvae. *Bt kurstaki* is lethal to certain caterpillars, including cabbageworm, geranium budworm, and tomato hornworm; other *Bt* strains are effective against the larvae of mosquitoes, fungus gnats, Colorado potato beetles, and elm leaf beetles.
- **Diatomaceous earth.** A powdery substance made from the skeletons of microscopic marine organisms. Effective against pests such as ants, aphids, cutworms, slugs, snails. Works by matting on the insect and damaging its protective coat (not by lacerating its exoskeleton or membrane and causing death by desiccation, as is widely thought). Be sure to use the insecticidal product, not the one intended for swimming pool filters. Wear a breathing mask during application to avoid inhaling the dust. Diatomaceous earth can kill nontarget insects.
- **Horticultural oils.** These are highly refined petroleum oils that smother pests, pest eggs, and disease spores. In winter, during the dormant season, they are applied to control insect eggs, some overwintering insects, and certain diseases. In summer, these oils are used at a lower rate, sprayed on foliage of many plants to combat insects such as aphids, mealybugs, mites, scales, thrips, and whiteflies. Before using these products on plants in leaf, test-spray a small portion of the plant to be sure foliage will not be damaged.
- **Insecticidal soap.** Made not from detergent, but from potassium salts of fatty acids found in plants and animals. Effective against pests such as aphids, mealybugs, mites, scales, thrips, and whiteflies. Hard water inactivates it, so mix the concentrate with soft water, distilled water, or rainwater. Toxic to earthworms.
- **Pyrethrins** (Bug Buster-O, others). Derived from compounds found in the dried flowers of *Tanacetum cinerariifolium.* Both a contact and a stomach poison; lethal to many pests. Breaks down quickly in sunlight; to give it more time to act, apply after sundown. Some products combine pyrethrins with other pesticides. Toxic to fish. The dried flowers, known as pyrethrum, are also sold as an insecticide.
- **Sulfur.** Dusted or sprayed over plants to control mites and psyllids as well as some plant diseases. Do not use sulfur in conjunction with horticultural oil spray or when air temperature is above 85°F/29°C. Can irritate the eyes.

SYNTHETIC PESTICIDES

- **Acephate** (Orthene). A systemic poison (one absorbed by the plant and incorporated into its tissues), this broad-spectrum product is used against aphids, beetles, caterpillars, grasshoppers, leaf miners, mealybugs, thrips, root weevils, whiteflies, other pests. Do not use on edible crops. Toxic to honeybees and birds.
- **Carbaryl** (Sevin). Broad-spectrum contact insecticide. Controls most chewing insects but is not effective against many sucking types—in fact, it often increases problems with the latter by destroying natural predators. Registered for use on edible crops. Highly toxic to honeybees, fish, and earthworms.
- **Diazinon.** Broad-spectrum contact insecticide that controls ants, aphids, beetles, caterpillars, mealybugs, scales, white grubs, other pests. Often used on lawn pests. Highly toxic to birds, moderately toxic to honeybees and fish. Future registration limitations are possible.
- **Imidacloprid** (Merit). Controls a variety of pests of lawns and ornamentals. Toxic to fish.
- **Malathion.** Broad-spectrum contact insecticide that controls aphids, beetles, caterpillars, mealybugs, scales, thrips, whiteflies, other pests. Registered for use on edible crops. Toxic to honeybees, birds, and fish. Future registration limitations are possible.
- **Pyrethroids.** Synthetic versions of plant-based pyrethrins, pyrethroids are increasingly being used in pesticides and are effective against many garden and household pests. Active ingredients include **permethrin, cyfluthrin,** and others. Less hazardous to humans, birds, and mammals than many other pesticides; toxic to honeybees and fish.

READING A PESTICIDE LABEL

Precautionary statements: This section may start with the headline "Precautionary statements" or with a repeat of the signal word found on the front of the label. Information is customized for product type and its associated toxicity-level category. It tells you of known hazards to humans, domestic animals, and the environment.

First aid instructions: Indicates the immediate action required if the product is ingested or inhaled or comes into contact with the skin or eyes.

Directions for use: Indicates how much of the product to use and how to mix and apply it.

Plants: Lists the plants that can safely be treated by the pesticide. If it can be used on edible crops, also tells you how many days before harvest the product can be applied.

Note to physicians: Specifies the action a physician should take in the event the product is ingested or inhaled or comes into contact with the skin or eyes.

Controls: Lists the pests that the product is formulated to control.

PRECAUTIONARY STATEMENTS
NOTE TO PHYSICIANS
FIRST AID INSTRUCTIONS
DIRECTIONS FOR USE
CONTROLS
PLANTS
STORAGE & DISPOSAL
BRAND
Pesticide
ACTIVE INGREDIENTS
Signal word
Product code identification

Storage & disposal: Specifies how to safely store and dispose of the product.

Product code identification: Provides the number assigned to the product by the manufacturer and the Environmental Protection Agency (EPA) to identify it. Use this number when contacting the manufacturer or EPA about the pesticide.

Product name: Provides the pesticide's trade name, often includes marketing information that positions the product against its competitors and attracts the eye of potential buyer. Sometimes the accepted common name of the active ingredient is included as part of the brand name, especially if that name has become familiar to the public.

Active ingredients: Lists the accepted common name of the pesticide's active ingredient. Learn to identify pesticides by their common names and look here first to find out exactly what is in the pesticide before purchasing it. The chemical name of the pesticide may also be included in this section.

Signal word: Look for words such as *Caution, Warning, Danger,* or *Poison.* These words signal the toxicity-level category associated with the pesticide. Additional information will be found on the back of the container, under the section "Precautionary statements."

BIRDS AND MAMMALS. Most gardeners welcome some—though not all—wildlife into their gardens. (See page 730 for ways to draw wildlife to your yard.) Certain birds and animals, however, can cause significant damage to plants. Some of the West's worst troublemakers are discussed below, along with suggestions for controlling them.

Birds. For the most part, gardeners see birds as friends who can play a significant role in controlling pests such as caterpillars (including cutworms and sod webworms), grasshoppers, and scales. Some kinds of birds, however, can be a nuisance at certain times, eating newly planted seeds (including lawn seed), tender seedlings, transplants, fruits, nuts, or berries.

Providing alternate foods can sometimes reduce damage to the fruits and berries you want to harvest; try planting elderberries *(Sambucus),* fruiting mulberries *(Morus),* or hawthorns *(Crataegus).* Reflectors, fluttering objects, and scarecrows may reduce damage briefly, but birds soon become accustomed to them. The best solution is to use netting or screen. Broad-mesh (¾-inch) nylon or plastic netting is popular for fruit trees, since it readily admits air, water, and sunlight. Enclose trees with netting 2 to 3 weeks before fruit ripens, tying it around the trunk beneath the lowest branches or securing it to the ground so birds can't find an opening.

Row covers (page 715) are the easiest way to protect sprouting seedlings and maturing vegetables, because they require no support. You can also make wooden or plastic pipe frames with screen, aviary wire, or netting attached to cover the top and all sides. Such frames are mobile and reusable, and they can be designed to make harvesting easy.

TOP: Starling
BOTTOM: Netting over strawberries

Deer. As wild vegetation becomes less available during droughts or winter snows, deer move into gardens to forage. They develop feeding patterns, visiting tasty gardens regularly (most often in the evening). Fond of many flowering plants, especially roses, they'll also eat the foliage or fruit of nearly anything you grow for the table. For a list of plants that deer usually ignore, see "Deer-Resistant Plants" in A Guide to Plant Selection, beginning on page 64.

Fencing is the most certain protection. On level ground, a 7- to 8-foot woven wire fence will usually keep deer out; on slopes, you may need to erect a 10- to 11-foot barrier to guard against animals jumping from higher ground. A horizontal "outrigger" extension on a fence makes it harder for deer to clear. Because deer cannot high-jump and broad-jump at the same time, double fencing has worked for many gardeners: construct a pair of parallel 4- to 5-foot fences spaced 4 to 5 feet apart. Low-growing plants can be set out in the area between the fences.

If fencing your entire garden is impractical, put chicken-wire cages around young plants and cylinders of wire fencing around larger specimens. Cover raised beds with mesh or row covers (page 715).

Commercial deer repellents can work if sprayed often enough to keep new growth covered with repellent and to replace what rain and irrigation wash away. Changing the type of repellent may be helpful, since deer get used to smells. Do not apply repellents to edible plants unless the label indicates you can do so.

Moles. Notorious pests in good soils throughout the West, moles are primarily insectivorous; they subsist largely on earthworms, soil insects, and grubs, only occasionally (if at all) nibbling greens and roots. Irrigation and rain keep them near the soil surface, where they do the most damage as they tunnel—heaving plants from the ground, severing tender roots, and disfiguring lawns. A mole's main runways, which are used repeatedly, are usually 6 to 10 inches underground and are frequently punctuated with volcano-shaped mounds of excavated soil, plugged in the center.

Trapping is the most efficient way to control moles. The spear- or harpoon-type trap is the easiest to set, since you simply position it above the soil. A scissor-jaw trap must be carefully positioned in a main runway (probe with a sharp stick to find it), and if it's improperly set, a wily mole will spring it, heave it out, or walk around it.

Due to their feeding habits, moles are very difficult to control with poison baits. They, like pocket gophers, are also hard to kill with toxic gas (fumigants). To be successful with the latter method, place gas "mole bombs" directly in the main runways and block all holes. Be persistent with follow-up treatments.

Pocket gophers, named for the external, fur-lined cheek pouches they use to carry food to storage areas, are serious pests in much of the West. They use their strong, long-clawed forefeet to dig out a network of tunnels, usually 6 to 18 inches below the surface. They eat roots, bulbs, and sometimes entire plants by pulling them down into their burrows.

The first sign of gophers is often a fan-shaped mound of fresh, finely pulverized earth in a lawn or flower bed; a plug of earth is used to close the hole, which is off to one side. (Mole mounds, in contrast, are conical and plugged in the center.)

Trapping is the most efficient method of control. Avoid the temptation to place a single trap down a hole; your chances of catching a gopher are much greater when you dig down to the main horizontal runway connecting with the surface hole and place two traps in it, one on either side of your excavation. Use chain or wire to attach each trap to a stake on the surface (this prevents a trapped gopher from dragging the trap farther into a burrow). The Macabee trap is the most effective. Box-type traps also work and are easier to set, but they require a larger hole for insertion.

When the traps are in place, plug the hole with a ball of carrot tops, fresh grass, or other tender greens; their scent attracts gophers. Next, place a board or soil over the greens to block all light. Check the traps frequently; clear the tunnels if the gopher has pushed soil into the traps. Be persistent: a clever gopher may avoid your first traps.

Poison baits are effective for the control of trapwise gophers. Probe for the deep burrows with a rod or sharp stick, insert the bait, and close the hole. Be aware that these baits are hazardous to other animals; take care not to spill any on the ground. Also keep in mind that dogs and cats may be poisoned by eating poisoned gophers, though incidences are rare.

TOP TO BOTTOM: Mole, Pocket gopher, Ground squirrel, Tree squirrel, Vole

If your garden is subject to ongoing invasion by gophers from neighboring fields or orchards—or if all your trapping efforts fail—you can protect roots of young plants by lining the sides and bottom of planting holes with hardware cloth. Raised beds lined on the bottom with hardware cloth offer a secure way to grow vegetables in gopher country.

Squirrels. Both ground and tree squirrels can cause trouble in gardens.

Ground squirrels. Most troublesome in areas that border fields or wild lands, ground squirrels live in underground burrows, where they store food, raise their young, and hide from predators such as foxes and hawks. They are most active in midmorning or late afternoon (except in very hot weather); most hibernate in winter. When they're up and about, they feed on fruits, nuts, and vegetables as well as eating roots and bark.

Keep ground squirrels out of trees with metal rodent guards around the trunks. Poison baits and traps can be effective; check with your local Cooperative Extension Office for methods legal in your area, or hire a pest-control professional.

Tree squirrels. Familiar pests in much of the West, tree squirrels include several native and introduced species. They behave differently from ground squirrels when alarmed, heading for the safety of a tree rather than retreating to a burrow. And unlike ground squirrels, they do not hibernate in winter. Tree squirrels eat fruits, nuts, vegetables, and some kinds of bulbs; they also raid bird feeders and birds' nests.

To control tree squirrels, clean up fallen fruits and nuts to eliminate some of their food sources. Use squirrel-proof bird feeders. To protect vulnerable trees, use metal rodent guards; prune low branches (if practical) and try to place the guards a minimum of 6 feet from the ground up, since the squirrels can leap at least that high. (Bear in mind, however, that if there are structures or other trees nearby, the agile pests will still be able to jump into trees you wish to protect.) Cover bulb beds with fine-mesh chicken wire. Before resorting to traps or poison baits, check with your local Cooperative Extension Office, since some squirrel species are protected by law.

Voles. Also known as meadow mice, voles are small rodents (just 5 to 8 inches long when mature) with short ears and tails. They feed on a wide variety of vegetables, grasses, bulbs, and tubers and gnaw on the bark of trees, sometimes girdling them; damage to bark may occur just above or below ground. Voles travel in aboveground runways, usually hidden beneath tall grasses or ground covers, that connect the openings to their short, shallow burrows.

You can control voles by managing the vegetation they use for cover: mow weeds, remove heavy mulches (especially those close to trees), and cut back ground covers. Also mow or use herbicides to clear the edges of fields near gardens. Protect the lower trunks of shrubs and young trees with hardware cloth cylinders, being sure to bury the bottom edges so voles can't dig beneath them.

Trapping can be an effective control. Use simple wooden mouse traps, baited with peanut butter or apple slices. Place these along the runways and check them daily. Keep small children and pets away from areas where you have set traps. Baits are sometimes used; check with your Cooperative Extension Office for types available in your area.

Plant Anatomy and Growth

Understanding a plant's basic structure and the role each of its parts plays in growth and reproduction is one of the fundamentals of successful gardening. The box below describes the functions of flowers, leaves, roots, and stems. Though we often think of these elements as separate, their functions are interrelated—and all must work as they should if the plant is to thrive.

Integrally involved in the function of every plant part is the surrounding environment—air, water, light, and soil. A good knowledge of the relationship between a plant's growth and its environment helps gardeners provide the best possible conditions for each plant in its location in the garden.

For illustration and more about flowers, see Glossary (page 746). Seed germination is illustrated on page 694.

HOW PLANTS GROW

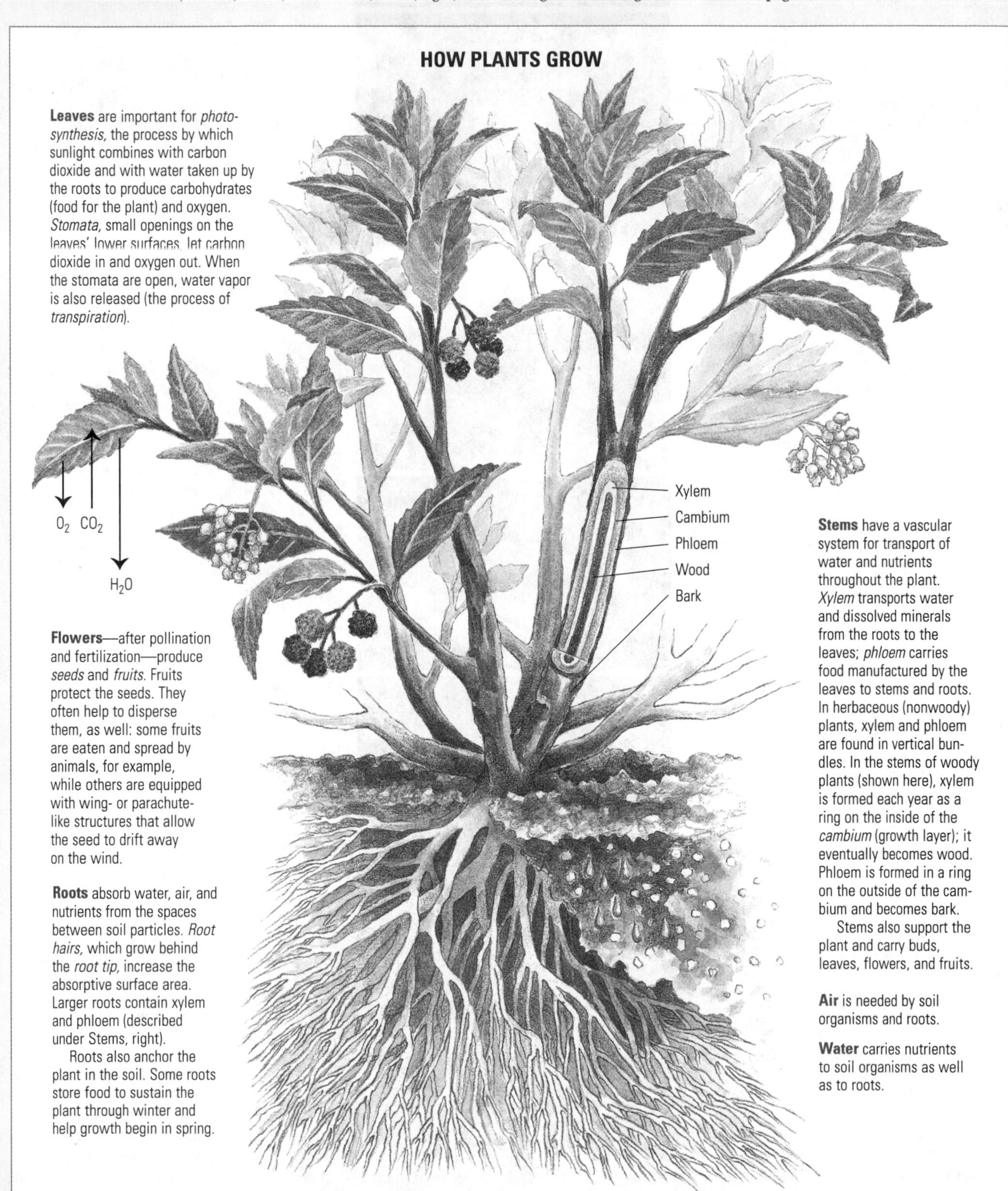

Leaves are important for *photosynthesis,* the process by which sunlight combines with carbon dioxide and with water taken up by the roots to produce carbohydrates (food for the plant) and oxygen. *Stomata,* small openings on the leaves' lower surfaces, let carbon dioxide in and oxygen out. When the stomata are open, water vapor is also released (the process of *transpiration*).

Flowers—after pollination and fertilization—produce *seeds* and *fruits.* Fruits protect the seeds. They often help to disperse them, as well: some fruits are eaten and spread by animals, for example, while others are equipped with wing- or parachute-like structures that allow the seed to drift away on the wind.

Roots absorb water, air, and nutrients from the spaces between soil particles. *Root hairs,* which grow behind the *root tip,* increase the absorptive surface area. Larger roots contain xylem and phloem (described under Stems, right).

Roots also anchor the plant in the soil. Some roots store food to sustain the plant through winter and help growth begin in spring.

Stems have a vascular system for transport of water and nutrients throughout the plant. *Xylem* transports water and dissolved minerals from the roots to the leaves; *phloem* carries food manufactured by the leaves to stems and roots. In herbaceous (nonwoody) plants, xylem and phloem are found in vertical bundles. In the stems of woody plants (shown here), xylem is formed each year as a ring on the inside of the *cambium* (growth layer); it eventually becomes wood. Phloem is formed in a ring on the outside of the cambium and becomes bark.

Stems also support the plant and carry buds, leaves, flowers, and fruits.

Air is needed by soil organisms and roots.

Water carries nutrients to soil organisms as well as to roots.

Plant Conservation

Plants, both wild and cultivated, supply food for humans and other creatures; habitats for insects and wildlife; and medicines, timber, and other essential products. However, it is estimated that more than 34,000 species—some 12.5 percent of all known higher plants (ferns, conifers, and flowering plants)—are either extinct in the wild or threatened with extinction. Concerned gardeners can take some steps to help preserve such plants.

Avoid buying plants dug from their native habitat. Though most plants available to gardeners are commercially propagated, some rare species are still routinely dug in the wild, especially those that are slow growing or difficult to propagate. Bulbs falling into this group are listed on page 659. Other plants threatened by wild collection include the saguaro cacti *(Carnegiea gigantea)* and some other cacti and succulents; trilliums; orchids; Jack-in-the-pulpit (*Arisaema* species); several kinds of carnivorous plants; and various palms and ferns.

Saguaro cacti *(Carnegiea gigantea)*

Don't include invasive plants in your garden if you live near wild lands. Such plants may escape and take over the habitat of natives, crowding them out. For more on invasive plants, see page 725.

Support the conservation of plants in their natural habitats, botanical gardens, and seed banks. Various preserves and other protected areas in the U.S. and abroad practice *in situ* (on-site) conservation: they maintain plants along with the insects, birds, animals, and soil and disease organisms normally associated with them in the wild, preserving the natural diversity of the ecosystem. Such sanctuaries include nature preserves, wildlife refuges, and state and national parks.

Botanical gardens feature *ex situ* (off-site) conservation. They are important repositories of samples of rare and endangered plants and also maintain some that have already become extinct in the wild.

Seeds, especially those of crop plants and their wild relatives, are conserved in special seed banks. They are first dried, then stored at low temperatures, remaining viable for many years.

Plant Disorders, Environmental and Cultural

Some plant problems are caused by environmental or cultural factors rather than by disease organisms or pests. Drying winds and extremes of temperature may hinder plant growth, for example. Other plant problems may be related to soil conditions such as hardpan (see page 707); under- or overfertilizing (see page 669 for information on nitrogen deficiency); and too much or too little water (see page 721). Besides damaging plants directly, such cultural and environmental problems can stress plants, making them more vulnerable to insects and diseases.

If you aren't certain why a plant is languishing, get help before you act. Simply assuming that a pest or disease is the culprit can result in the needless—and useless—application of pesticides. Regular garden monitoring and, when necessary, consultation with nursery personnel or your Cooperative Extension Office can assist you in identifying the precise causes of problems in your garden.

TRAVELERS' ALERT: BRINGING PLANTS HOME

Think twice before packing those plants. The U.S. government regulates the importation of plants, seeds, fruits, and vegetables from foreign countries to America, as well as from Hawaii, Puerto Rico, and the U.S. Virgin Islands to the mainland. The regulations are intended to prevent the introduction of insects, diseases, and potentially invasive plants. Thus, plants must be free of leaf mold and of sand or other soil, and seeds must be cleaned. For more information on bringing home plants or seeds, contact the Animal and Plant Health Inspection Service of the U.S. Department of Agriculture: USDA APHIS, Plant Protection and Quarantine, 4700 River Road, Unit 136, Riverdale, MD 20737-1236, Attn: Permit Unit. You can also call (301) 734-8645 or visit the service's web site (www.aphis.usda.gov).

In addition, the Convention on International Trade in Endangered Species of Wild Fauna and Flora (CITES) regulates international trade in species deemed threatened or likely to be threatened by commercial exploitation. If you want to bring back any plant listed under CITES, you will need permits from the country of origin as well as from the U.S. Department of Interior's Fish and Wildlife Service (FWS), which regulates CITES in the U.S. For more information, contact the U.S. Fish and Wildlife Service, Office of Management Authority, 4401 North Fairfax Drive, Arlington, VA 22203. Or call (703) 358-2095 or visit the web site at www.fws.gov.

CHLOROSIS. This disorder (shown above) affects citrus and some other fruit trees; rhododendron and azalea; and some vegetables and annuals. Leaves lose their green color from the edges inward; leaf veins usually remain green. The newest leaves are the most noticeably affected; they may be unusually small and either white or bright yellow in color. Chlorosis is usually caused by a deficiency of iron (though it occasionally results from lack of another mineral, such as zinc or manganese). When plants are chlorotic, the soil itself is not necessarily iron poor; it may simply be alkaline, a condition under which iron becomes unavailable to roots. Soggy, poorly aerated soils also delay or hinder the release of iron to plant roots.

Adjusting soil pH by adding organic matter or, if necessary, sulfur, is the best long-term solution to chlorosis. Improving drainage is also helpful. Chelated iron, applied according to the directions on the label, can temporarily correct the problem.

SUNBURN, SUNSCALD. Overexposure to sunlight can harm leaves, fruits, or bark. Symptoms include bleached-out, yellowish, or brown foliage; pale, sunken, often wrinkled areas on fruits; and bark that turns dark brown, splits, and dies. Damaged tissue may be invaded by disease-causing organisms.

Plants most likely to experience sunburn or sunscald are those moved into the sun from shaded locations (such as from a nursery to a home garden) and those that have been heavily pruned, reducing the leafy cover that shades and protects bark and fruits.

To prevent sunburn and sunscald, transplant in cool weather, if possible. If conditions are warm, shade new transplants with shade cloth, burlap stapled to wooden frames, or broad, flat pieces of wood placed on end in the ground on the sunny side of the plants. Use burlap or tree-wrapping paper (available at nurseries) to wrap trunks of newly planted or heavily pruned trees. Or protect exposed tree trunks by painting them with water-based interior white latex paint, diluted by half with water. Finally, note that plants adapted to shaded conditions will sunburn if planted in a too-bright location. Always be sure to select plants suited to the site.

Planting Beds, Raised Beds

Before sowing seeds or setting out annuals, perennials, or vegetables, you will want to prepare a planting bed. In most gardens, the simple sort of bed described below will suffice. In some cases, however—notably when soil or drainage is poor—constructing raised beds may be a better choice.

MAKING A PLANTING BED. Good soil preparation is the first step toward success with seeds sown directly in the garden as well as with small plants set out from pots or flats. Begin by eliminating weeds (see page 725). Then loosen the soil with a spading fork or tiller; it should be slightly damp when you work it, not wet or bone-dry. Dig down 10 to 12 inches if you can, breaking up clods and removing stones as you go. Spread a 3- to 4-inch-thick layer of organic matter (such as compost or nitrogen-fortified ground bark or sawdust) over the area. As noted in "Fertilizers" (page 668), both phosphorus and potassium benefit plants most when placed near the roots; work a fertilizer high in these nutrients (such as a 5-10-10 or similar formula) into the soil before planting, rather than applying it to the surface afterward. Also add any amendments needed to alter soil pH at this time.

These raised beds contain a mix of flowering plants, vegetables, and herbs.

Incorporate all the amendments evenly with spading fork or tiller, then level out the planting bed with a rake.

MAKING RAISED BEDS. Besides solving problems involving poor soil and poor drainage, raised beds have other advantages. Their soil warms earlier in spring, and because it is typically not walked upon, it remains loose and easier for roots to penetrate. You can also fill these beds with particular types of soil to suit specific plants—acid soil for blueberries, for example. The simplest raised beds are made by piling amended soil, either purchased or dug from pathways or other parts of your garden, on the area you want to plant. It's a good idea to loosen the area's existing soil as much as possible first, to ease penetration by water and roots.

Many gardeners enclose their raised beds with a low border. Two-inch-thick wood is most common, but rocks or cinder blocks can also be used. Plan to make enclosed beds at least 8 inches high; a height of 12 inches gives roots even more growing space. The bed can be any length that fits the space and available building materials, but it's usually best to limit its width to about 4 feet, so that you can reach the center from either side. If pocket gophers are a problem, line the bottom of the bed with hardware cloth, fastening it to the sides. Fill the raised beds with good topsoil amended with plenty of organic matter, such as nitrogen-fortified ground bark or sawdust or compost.

DOUBLE DIGGING

This soil-preparation technique helps amend soil in the upper level of a planting bed and breaks up soil on the lower level to allow roots to grow deeper. It's hard work, but the results last for years. Before double digging, remove weeds from the plot.

1 Dig a trench one spade-blade deep along one side of the plot. Mound the soil from this trench nearby.

2 Loosen soil in the bottom of the trench with a spade; mix organic matter in with this loosened soil.

3 Dig a second trench one spade-blade deep alongside the first. Shovel the excavated soil into the first trench, along with organic matter and a fertilizer high in phosphorus and potassium (such as a 5-10-10 product).

4 Loosen the soil in the bottom of the second trench; mix in organic matter. Continue to dig trenches across the plot in the same way. Fill the last trench with soil saved from the first.

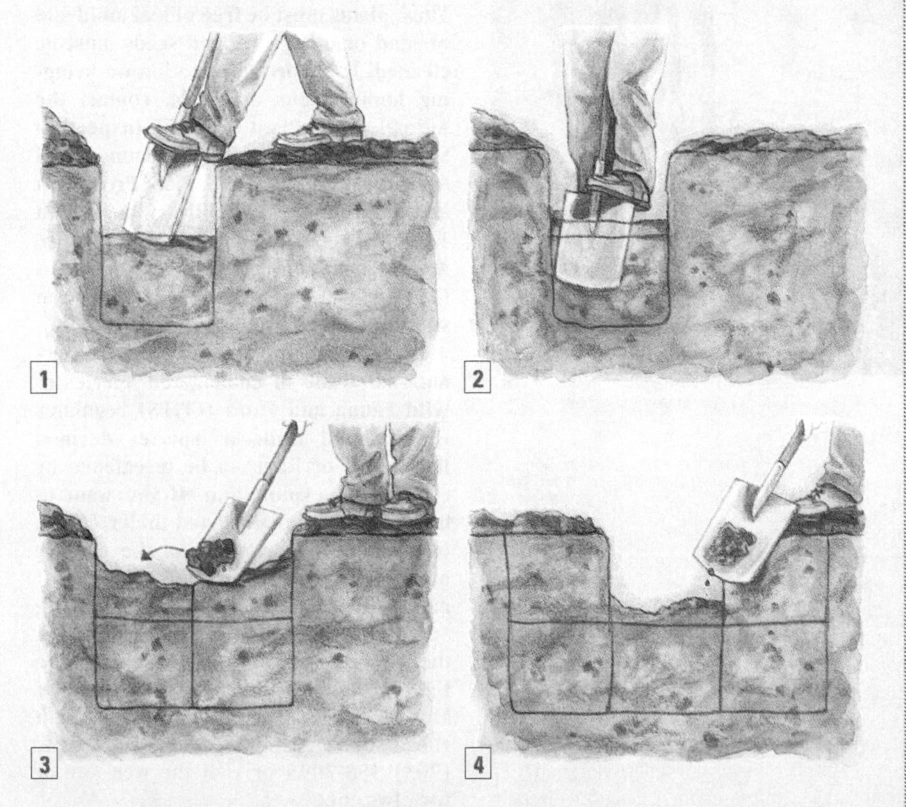

Planting Techniques

Proper planting techniques depend on the plant and how it is sold. Many plants—annuals, vegetables, and some perennials and ground covers—are sold as seedlings in small containers or flats during the growing season. Larger plants, such as shrubs, trees, and certain vines and more mature perennials, may be offered in several ways: in containers of various sizes during the growing season; as bare-root plants in the dormant season; or with the root ball enclosed in burlap, typically from late fall to early spring. The following pages discuss planting all of the above types. For information on planting seeds and bulbs, see pages 694 and 659.

PLANTING ANNUALS AND PERENNIALS. Nurseries offer seedlings of both annuals and perennials, giving you a head start over raising the plants from seed yourself. Many of these, as well as vegetables and some ground covers, are sold in plastic cell-packs, individual plastic pots, peat pots, and flats. (Some perennials, perennial vegetables, and strawberries may also be sold bare-root during their dormant season; for planting instructions, see page 678.) Before planting annuals and perennials, make a planting bed as described on facing page.

At the nursery, choose stocky young plants with good leaf color and a root ball that holds together but is not tangled or matted. Rootbound plants won't grow as well as younger ones, even if you cut or loosen coiled roots. ▶

PLANTING ANNUALS AND PERENNIALS

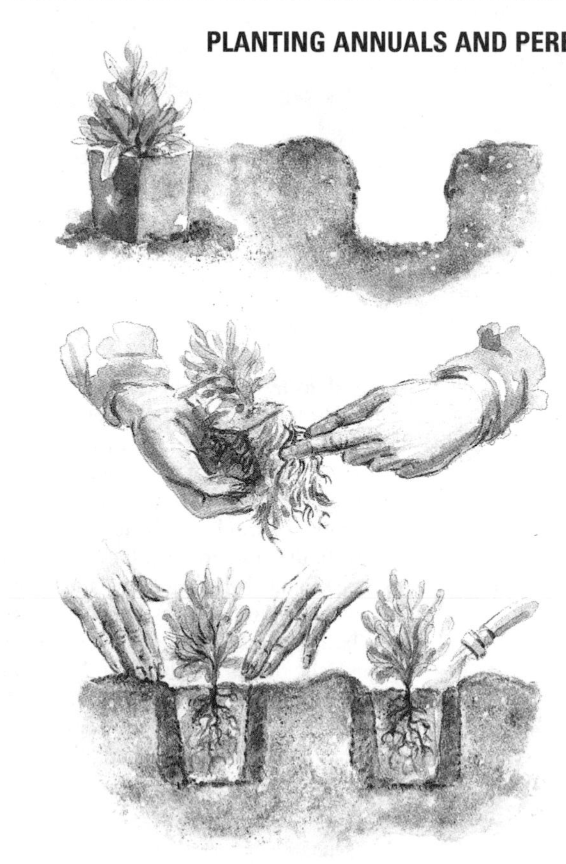

1 Dig a hole for each plant, making it the same depth as the container and an inch or two wider.

2 With your fingers, lightly separate matted roots. If there is a pad of coiled roots at the bottom of the pot, cut or pull it off so that new roots will form and grow into the soil.

3 Place each plant in its hole so that the top of the root ball is even with the soil surface. Firm soil around the roots; then water each plant with a gentle flow that won't disturb soil or roots.

REMOVING PLANTS FROM CONTAINERS

SMALL POTS. To remove plants from small pots, turn pot upside-down, holding plant in place with your fingers. The plant should slip out easily.

FLATS. Separate the plants in a flat by cutting straight down around each one with a putty knife or spatula. Or gently separate the plants from each other with your fingers.

CELL-PACKS. Plants in plastic cell-packs are easy to remove from the container, since each plant is in an individual cube of soil. Turn the cell-pack over and push down on the bottom of each cell with your thumbs.

PEAT POTS. These plants are not removed from their pots, but go into the ground pot and all; the roots then grow through the pot into the soil, while the pot eventually decomposes. Make sure the pots are moist before planting by letting them stand in a shallow container of water for several minutes. If they're dry, they'll absorb moisture too slowly from the soil and the roots may have trouble breaking through them, resulting in a stunted plant. It's also important to cover the tops of the pots with soil, since exposed peat acts as a wick, drawing moisture from the soil. If covering the peat would bury the plant too deeply, break off the pot's rim to slightly below the soil level inside it.

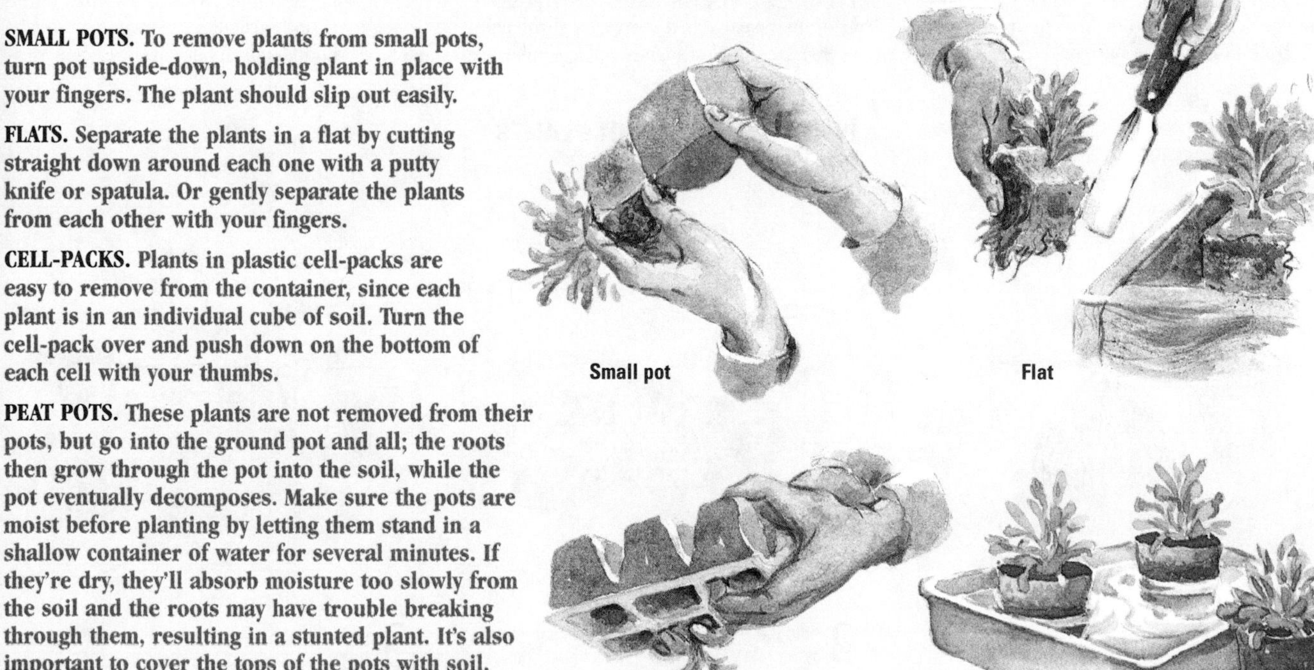

Small pot

Flat

Cell-pack

Peat pots

PLANTING BARE-ROOT SHRUBS AND TREES. Bare-root plants are sold in late winter and early spring by retail nurseries and mail-order companies. Many deciduous plants are available this way, including fruit and shade trees, flowering shrubs, roses, grapes, and cane fruits.

Though venturing out in the cold and wet of winter to set out bare-root plants takes a certain amount of determination, the effort is worthwhile. Such plants typically cost only 40 to 70 percent as much as the same varieties purchased in containers later in the year; beyond that, they usually establish more quickly and grow better initially than containerized plants. This faster growth is in part due to the fact that when you set out a bare-root plant, you refill the planting hole with soil dug from that hole—and the plant's roots thus grow in just one kind of soil. When you plant a containerized or balled-and-burlapped plant, on the other hand, you put two soils, usually with different textures, in contact with each other. The juxtaposition of two different soils can make it difficult for water to penetrate uniformly into the rooting area.

When buying from a local nursery, select bare-root plants with strong stems and fresh-looking, well-formed roots. Avoid any with slimy roots or dry, withered ones; also reject any that have already leafed out.

It's always best to plant bare-root plants as soon as possible after purchase. If bad weather prevents immediate planting, heel in the plants by laying them temporarily in a trench dug in a shady spot in the garden and covering the roots with moist soil or potting mix; it's important not to let the roots dry out. Before planting, soak the roots for a minimum of 4 hours (or preferably overnight) in a bucket of water. Just before planting, be sure to cut any broken or damaged roots back to healthy tissue.

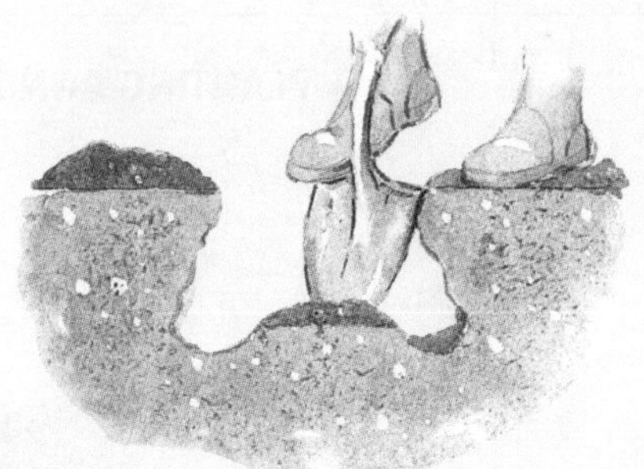

DIGGING THE PLANTING HOLE

To plant trees and shrubs, dig a planting hole with sides that taper outward into the soil. Make the hole at least twice as wide as the roots of the plant. Roughen the sides with a spading fork; if the sides are smooth, it can be difficult for roots to penetrate the soil. To keep the plant from settling too much after planting and watering, make the hole a bit shallower than the root ball or root system, then dig deeper around the edges of the hole's bottom. This leaves a firm plateau of undug soil to support the plant at the proper depth.

Dig a planting hole as shown above. In heavy clay or hardpan, make the hole somewhat wider; this lets the plant establish faster by providing a larger area of loosened soil that's easier for roots to penetrate. Set in the plant as shown below.

SETTING OUT PLANTS FROM CONTAINERS. Most of the broad-leafed evergreen shrubs and trees that are the West's landscaping staples are only offered in containers. But that's not the main reason containerized plants are popular. You can buy them throughout the growing season, choosing from a variety of sizes and prices; they're relatively easy to transport; and they needn't be planted immediately. Furthermore, because you can buy these plants with flowers, fruit, or autumn leaf color on display, you're able to see exactly what you are getting.

When selecting container-grown plants, look for healthy foliage and strong shoots. Check the leaves and stems to be sure no insects are present. Do your best to avoid root-bound plants. Two common signs of this condition are roots protruding above the container's soil level and husky roots growing through the drainage holes; additional indicators are plants that are large for the size of the container, leggy plants, and dead twigs or branches. If you do end up with a root-bound plant, be sure to loosen the roots before planting as shown on facing page.

To remove plants from 1-gallon or larger plastic containers, tap sharply on the bottom and sides to loosen the root ball. The plant should slide out easily. With fiber or pulp pots, tear the pot away from the root ball, taking care not to damage the roots. Plant as shown on facing page.

PLANTING BALLED-AND-BURLAPPED SHRUBS AND TREES. Some kinds of woody plants have root systems that won't survive bare-root transplanting; others are evergreen and cannot be bare-rooted. Instead, such plants are dug from the field with a ball of soil around their roots, and the soil ball is then wrapped in burlap or a synthetic material and tied with twine or wire. These are called balled-and-burlapped (B-and-B) plants. Some deciduous trees and shrubs (large specimens, in particular), evergreen shrubs such as rhododendrons and azaleas, and vari-

PLANTING BARE-ROOT PLANTS

1 Make a firm cone of soil in the planting hole. Spread the roots over the cone, positioning the plant at the same depth as (or slightly higher than) it was in the growing field. Use a shovel handle or yardstick to check the depth.

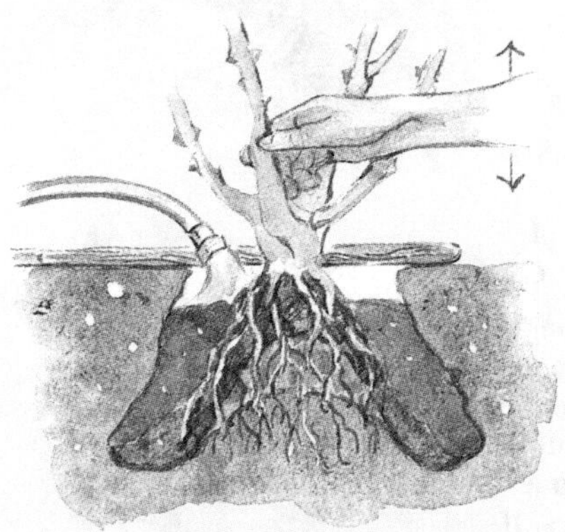

2 Hold the plant upright as you firm soil around its roots. When backfilling is almost complete, add water. This settles the soil around the roots, eliminating any air pockets. If the plant settles below the level of the surrounding soil, pump it up and down while soil is saturated to raise it to the proper level.

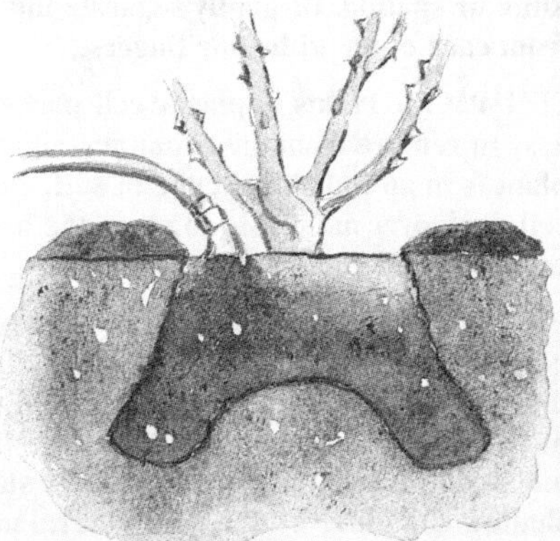

3 Finish filling the hole with soil; then water again. Take care not to overwater while the plant is still dormant, since soggy soil may inhibit the formation of new roots. When the growing season begins, make a ridge of soil around the planting site to form a watering basin; water when the top 2 inches of soil are dry.

ous conifers are sold this way from late fall to early spring.

When buying B-and-B plants, look for healthy foliage and an even branching structure. The covering should be intact (so that the roots are not exposed), and the root ball should feel firm and moist.

B-and-B plants can be damaged if handled roughly. Always support the bottom of the root ball when moving the plant; don't pick the plant up by the trunk or drop it, which might shatter the root ball. Because a B-and-B plant is usually quite heavy, it's a good idea to have the nursery deliver it or have a friend help you move it to and from your vehicle in a sling of stout canvas. Once home, you can move the plant by sliding it onto a piece of plywood and pulling it to the planting spot. For planting directions, see page 694.

Note: Most shrubs and trees grow best if planted in the soil native to your garden rather than in amended soil, but B-and-B plants are sometimes an exception. They are generally grown in clay or heavy soil that holds together well when the plants are dug up and wrapped. If you have medium- to heavy-textured garden soil (such as fairly heavy loam or clay), there's no need to amend the soil you return to the planting hole. If the B-and-B soil is denser than your garden's soil, however, the plant may have a hard time getting established. The heavy soil around its roots will absorb water more slowly than the surrounding garden soil—so the B-and-B's soil can be dry even if the garden soil is kept moist. To avoid this problem, mix an organic amendment such as compost or nitrogen-fortified ground bark or sawdust into the soil removed from the planting hole, using about one shovelful of amendment for every three shovelfuls of soil. Use this blend to fill in around the roots. ▶

DEALING WITH ROOT-BOUND PLANTS

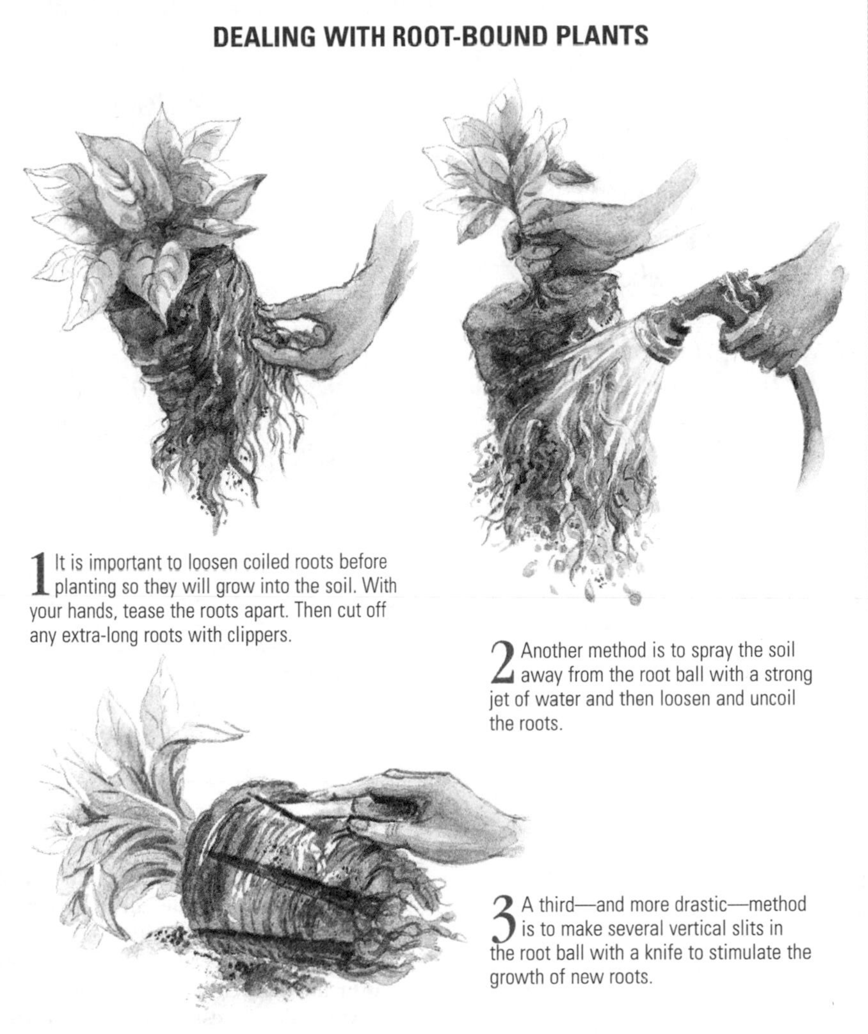

1 It is important to loosen coiled roots before planting so they will grow into the soil. With your hands, tease the roots apart. Then cut off any extra-long roots with clippers.

2 Another method is to spray the soil away from the root ball with a strong jet of water and then loosen and uncoil the roots.

3 A third—and more drastic—method is to make several vertical slits in the root ball with a knife to stimulate the growth of new roots.

PLANTING FROM A CONTAINER

1 Dig a hole as shown at top of facing page. Spread roots out over the central plateau of firm soil. The top of the root ball should be 1 to 2 inches above the surrounding soil.

2 Backfill with the unamended soil you dug from the hole, adding the soil in stages and firming it around the roots with your hands as you work.

3 Make a berm of soil to form a watering basin. Irrigate gently. Spread a layer of mulch around the plant, keeping it several inches away from the stem or trunk.

P

PLANTING BALLED-AND-BURLAPPED PLANTS

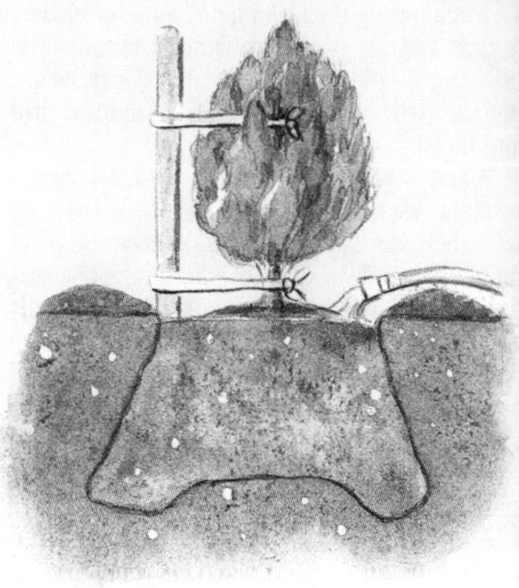

1 Measure the root ball from top to bottom. The planting hole should be a bit shallower than this distance, so that the top of the root ball is about 2 inches above the surrounding soil. Adjust the hole to the proper depth; then set in the plant.

2 Untie the covering. If it's burlap, it will eventually rot; just spread it out to uncover about half the root ball. If it's a synthetic material, however, remove it entirely. If you are planting in a windy site, drive a stake in alongside the root ball. Fill the hole with soil to within 4 inches of the top and water gently.

3 Continue to fill the hole, firming the soil as you go. Make a berm of soil to form a watering basin; then water the plant. If you staked the plant, loosely tie it to the stake. As the plant becomes established, keep the soil moist but not soggy.

Plant Propagation

In gardening usage, "propagation" refers to the various ways of starting new plants. Plants can be propagated either sexually or asexually. *Sexual propagation* involves the union of male and female parts of a flower to produce seed. Plants grown from seed reflect the characteristics of both their parents. In *asexual (vegetative) propagation,* the new plant is produced from a vegetative part (root, stem, bud, or leaf) of just one plant. This new plant is a *clone,* genetically identical to its single parent. Asexual propagation maintains uniformity—assuring, for example, that each plant of the rose 'Queen Elizabeth' is like every other. Methods of asexual propagation include taking cuttings, dividing plants, layering, budding, and grafting.

SOWING SEEDS. Starting plants from seed is an economical way to get lots of plants. It also gives you many choices, since most seed catalogs offer more varieties of flowering plants and vegetables than you're likely to find at the local nursery. Increase your chances of success by making sure you understand what seeds need in order to germinate.

How seeds germinate. To sprout, all seeds require the favorable environmental conditions described under "Seed Germination" (at right). Beyond these needs, the seeds of some plants have specialized requirements. For example, seeds of plants native to areas with cold winters normally need a period of low temperatures before they will sprout. In the wild, this happens naturally: the seeds mature in late summer or

SEED GERMINATION

Seeds cannot germinate until certain favorable environmental conditions are met. These include adequate moisture, a preferred temperature, and a loose-textured soil that provides oxygen to the sprouting seed. Seeds of some species also require light, meaning that no newspaper or other covering should be placed over the planted seeds; seed packets note this requirement.

Once the necessary conditions are met, the *radicle*—the embryonic root—emerges from the seed and begins growing downward, with root hairs and lateral roots developing from it. The lower part of the stem (the *hypocotyl*) pulls the seed leaves or *cotyledons* upward and into the light. Food stored in the cotyledons nourishes the seedling until first true leaves begin photosynthesis process (see page 688). (In some species, like peas, the cotyledons remain underground during germination.)

Some plants—grasses, corn, onions, lilies—have only one cotyledon and are called *monocots.* Plants with two cotyledons, such as beans, are called *dicots.*

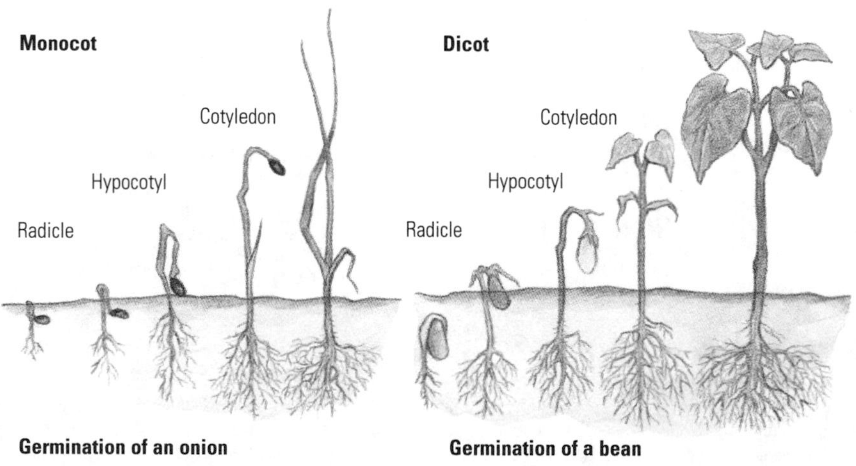

Germination of an onion

Germination of a bean

autumn, are moistened by rain in fall and chilled throughout the winter, then sprout in spring. Gardeners can mimic this cold period by stratifying the seeds—either sowing them in containers that are set outdoors for the winter, or placing them between layers of moist paper towels enclosed in a plastic bag, then refrigerating them for a month or two.

Some seeds—including those of acacia, false indigo *(Baptisia)*, lupine *(Lupinus)*, and locust *(Robinia)*—have a hard seed coat that does not allow water to penetrate. Before they can germinate, they must be scarified. In nature, scarification may be accomplished by soil fungi and bacteria that partially decompose the seed coat; it also occurs when birds or animals consume and then excrete the seeds. Gardeners can scarify seeds by nicking the seed coat with a file or scratching it with sandpaper.

Planting the seeds. Many annuals, wildflowers, and vegetables can be seeded directly in the garden, either broadcast over a bed to give a planted-by-nature look or in the traditional rows of a vegetable or cutting garden. Many other kinds of plants, however, are best raised from seed sown in containers. These include slow-growing types as well as warm-season vegetables and annuals that may need to be started when the soil is still too cold and wet for in-ground planting.

Sowing seeds outdoors. Whether you are planting rows of vegetables, broadcasting a wildflower mixture, or sowing several kinds of annuals for a showy border, start by preparing a planting bed (see page 690).

Planting seeds in rows. Make furrows following seed packet instructions for their depth and spacing. If possible, lay out the rows in a north-south direction, so that both sides will receive an equal amount of sunlight. Form the furrows with a hoe, rake, or stick; for perfectly straight rows, use a board or taut string as a guide, as shown at left.

BROADCASTING SEEDS IN A PREPARED BED

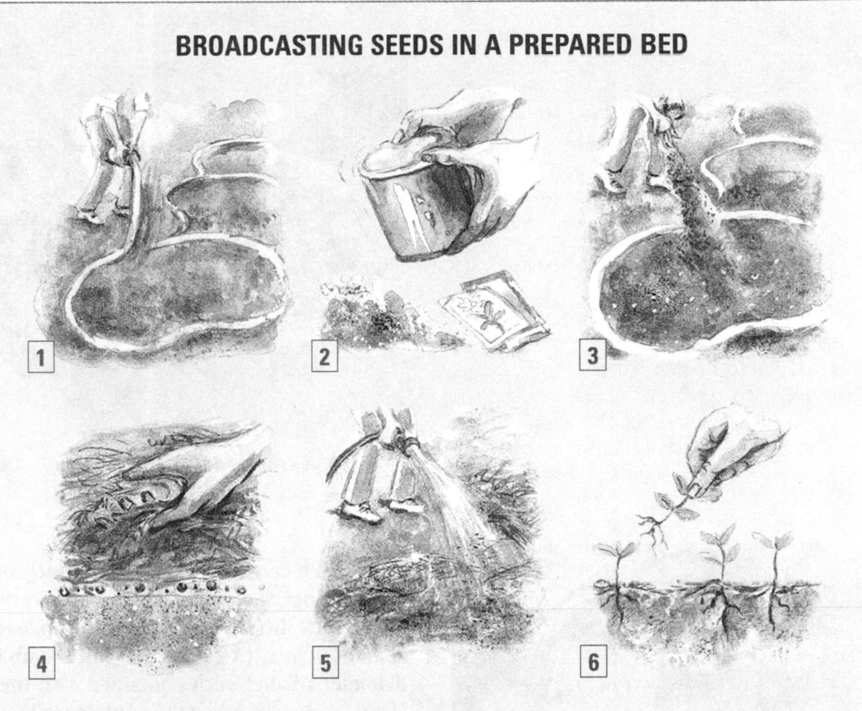

1 For a patterned planting, outline the areas for each kind of seed with gypsum, flour, or stakes and string. You may want to put a label in each area.

2 To achieve a more even distribution, shake each kind of seed (or an entire wildflower seed mixture) in a covered can with several times its bulk of sand.

3 Scatter the seed-sand mixture as evenly as possible over the bed or individual planting areas; then rake lightly, barely covering the seeds with soil. Take care not to bury them too deeply.

4 Spread a very thin layer of mulch (such as sifted compost) over the bed to help retain moisture, keep the surface from crusting, and hide the seeds from birds.

5 Water with a fine spray. Keep the soil surface barely damp until the seeds sprout; once seedlings are up, gradually decrease watering frequency.

6 When seedlings have two sets of true leaves, thin seedlings that are too closely spaced. Transplant the thinned seedlings to fill empty spaces in the bed.

For straight rows, stretch a string between two stakes and plant beneath it. Or lay a board on the surface of the soil, then plant along its edge.

Sow seeds evenly, spacing them as the packet directs. You can tear off a small corner of the packet and tap the seeds out as you move along, or pour a small quantity into your palm and scatter pinches of seed as evenly as possible. Place larger seeds, such as beans, individually.

Water the furrows with a fine spray; then keep the soil surface moist but not dripping wet until seeds sprout. After the seedlings are up and growing, gradually cut back on watering, being sure to keep the root zone moist. Thin seedlings once they've developed two sets of true leaves. Thinned plants can be transplanted into any empty spaces in the rows.

Broadcasting seeds. This technique (shown above) is the best way to plant beds of wildflowers. It also makes natural-looking plantings of other easy-to-grow annuals, such as sweet alyssum *(Lobularia maritima)* and nasturtium *(Tropaeolum majus)*. ▸

BUYING AND STORING SEEDS

Be sure the seeds you buy are fresh; they should be dated for the current year. For many plants, seed may be sold in three different forms: loose, pelletized, and in tapes. Loose seeds, traditionally sold in packets, are familiar to all gardeners. Pelletized seeds, also sold in packets, are individually coated (like small pills) to make handling and proper spacing easier. Seed tapes are strips of biodegradable paper with seeds embedded in them, properly spaced for growing to maturity (which makes thinning unnecessary). You just unroll the tape in a prepared furrow and cover it with soil.

Store extra seeds in an airtight jar or other container in a cool, dry place. With proper storage, many kinds of seeds remain viable for a year, and some stay good for several years.

Sowing seeds in containers. Many plants get off to a better start when sown in containers and transplanted to garden beds later in the season. It's easier to provide plants in containers with the warm temperatures and bright light they need for quick growth; it's easier to protect them from insects and birds as well. The information on the seed packet will help you decide when to plant. Most annual flowers and vegetables should be sown 4 to 8 weeks before it's time to transplant them outdoors.

Container choices. Convenience, cost, and reusability all determine which containers you select. If you're reusing old containers, scrub them out and soak them for 30 minutes in a solution of 1 part household bleach to 9 parts hot water to prevent infection by damping-off fungi (page 665), which destroy seedlings.

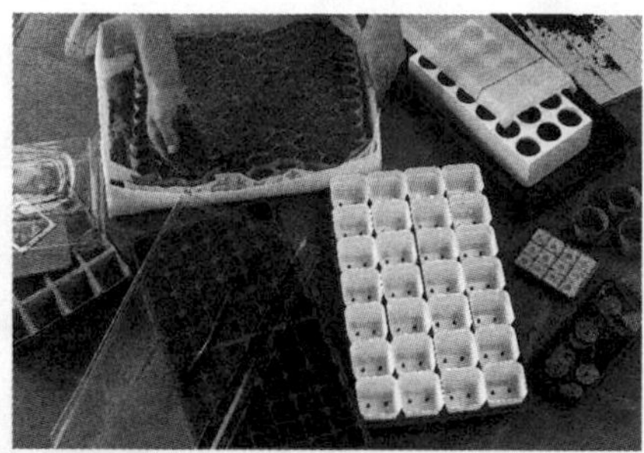

ABOVE, TOP: Various seed-starting trays and pots are available at nurseries and through mail-order catalogs.

ABOVE, BOTTOM: Plant two seeds in each cell of a plastic foam flat; later thin seedlings to one in each cell.

BELOW: To help peat pots retain moisture after seeding, set them in a flat filled with 1½ inches of moist potting mix.

SOWING SEEDS IN CONTAINERS

1 Fill each container to within ½ inch of the rim with damp mix, firming it gently with your fingers or a block of wood. Scatter seeds thinly over the surface of the planting mix. Check the seed packet for recommended planting depth and cover with the proper amount of mix. (A general rule of thumb is to cover seeds to a depth equal to twice their diameter.) Label each container with the plant name and sowing date. Moisten lightly. Many gardeners cover the containers loosely with damp newspaper; this helps keep soil moist but still allows air to get in, preventing the growth of fungi. (Don't cover if the seeds need light to germinate, however; see page 694.)

Place the containers in a warm spot. When the seeds germinate, uncover the containers, if necessary; then move them to a spot where they'll be in bright light, such as a greenhouse or a sunny window. (Or give them 12 to 14 hours of fluorescent light each day, setting the light 6 to 8 inches above the tops of the plants.) Water when the surface of the soil feels dry, spraying with a fine mist.

2 When the seedlings develop their second set of true leaves, it's time to transplant them. (If you don't need many plants, just thin the seedlings to one plant per pot—or thin flat-grown seedlings to a distance of 2 inches apart—and skip transplanting them to larger containers.) To transplant, fill the new containers such as 4-inch plastic pots with dampened potting mix. Remove the seedlings from their original pot by squeezing its sides and turning it upside down, making sure to keep one hand around the soil ball. Once the soil ball is out of the pot, carefully pull it apart with both hands and set it down on a flat surface.

3 Separate the fragile root balls with a toothpick or skewer, or tease them apart with your fingers.

4 Poke a hole in the new container's planting mix. Handle each seedling by the leaves to avoid damaging the tender stem; support the root ball with your finger. Place each seedling in its new container and firm the mix around it. Water immediately, then set pots in bright light; keep them out of direct sunlight for a few days to let the seedlings recover from transplanting. Fertilize weekly with a fertilizer sold for starting seeds or a liquid type diluted to half-strength.

About 10 days before the seedlings are ready to plant outdoors, they'll need to harden off as follows so they can withstand the bright outdoor sun and cooler temperatures. Stop fertilizing them and set them outside for several hours each day in a wind-sheltered spot receiving filtered light. Over the next week or so, gradually increase exposure until the plants are in full sun all day (shade lovers are an exception; they should not be exposed to day-long sun). Then set the young plants out in the garden as illustrated on page 691.

Plastic flats with no dividers are an old favorite. They are readily available from garden supply stores and mail-order catalogs, and free when you buy seedlings at nurseries.

Plastic cell-packs and 2- to 4-inch plastic pots (recycled from nursery purchases) are easy to obtain and use.

Peat pots are inexpensive but not reusable. However, because you plant seedlings pot and all, such pots minimize disturbance to roots. Keep them moist after seeding (so roots can penetrate them easily) as shown on facing page.

Plastic foam flats with tapered individual cells are sold by nurseries and through mail-order catalogs. They come in several cell sizes; some have capillary matting that draws water from a reservoir, making seedling care easier.

You can also use recycled household items—plastic cups, cut-down milk cartons, foil baking pans. Be sure to punch several drainage holes in any container that lacks them, since seedlings will die if water collects around their roots.

ROOT CUTTINGS

To start a few root cuttings, insert them upright in a pot. For a larger number, lay the cuttings in a flat.

Growing medium. Buy a seed-starting mix or potting soil at the nursery, or make your own by combining 1 part peat moss or finely shredded bark with 1 part perlite. Before using purchased mixes, flush them with water to eliminate excess salts. The mix should be moist but not soggy when you plant seeds.

Note: Vermiculite is sometimes recommended as an ingredient in homemade growing mixes. However, the Environmental Protection Agency has warned that some brands of vermiculite may be contaminated with small amounts of potentially cancer-causing asbestos. If you use vermiculite, follow these pointers: mix it with other ingredients outdoors or in a well-ventilated area; keep it damp; and avoid bringing dust from the product indoors on your clothing.

CUTTINGS. Plants can be propagated from cuttings in several ways, depending on the plant part used for propagation. Any plant that produces sprouts from its roots will grow from root cuttings. Some kinds of plants will root successfully from a leaf or a portion of a leaf. Stem cuttings—in which roots are induced to grow from stem sections—are described as softwood, semihardwood, or hardwood, depending on the maturity of the stems; see pages 698 and 699 for details.

Root cuttings. Numerous perennials and other plants can be propagated by root cuttings. A few examples are Japanese anemone, globe thistle *(Echinops)*, trumpet vine *(Campsis)*, Oriental poppy *(Papaver orientale)*, blackberry, and raspberry.

Make root cuttings when the plant is dormant—in late fall or early winter, for most species. You can dig up an entire plant or just a section of its roots. With a sharp knife, remove vigorous, healthy pieces of root 2 to 4 inches long; those growing close to the crown will form new plants most quickly. (Note that rooting hormone is not needed and may actually delay rooting.) If you have only a few cuttings, place them upright in a container filled with damp potting mix, with the top cut ends (those that were closest to the crown on the parent plant) at soil level (see above). For larger numbers of cuttings, fill a flat to within an inch of the top with potting mix; lay the cuttings flat on top of the mix, then cover them with ½ inch more mix.

Water the planted containers well. Then place them in a growing area such as a greenhouse or cold frame; protect from direct sun. Once stems and leaves have formed, move the containers into full light and water as needed. When the young shoots are several inches tall and new roots have formed (check by gently digging up a cutting), transplant them to individual pots and feed with liquid fertilizer.

Leaf cuttings. Some plants can form roots from a leaf or a portion of one. Three examples are shown below. For rooting medium, use a mix of 1 part peat moss and 1 part perlite or coarse builder's sand.

THREE TYPES OF LEAF CUTTINGS

Rex begonias are propagated by making cuts in the large veins on underside of a mature leaf. Lay the leaf flat, cut side down, on the rooting medium; then enclose the container in a plastic bag. In time, new plants will grow at the point where each vein was cut.

To root leaf cuttings of African violet *(Saintpaulia ionantha)*, insert a young leaf with an inch or two of stem into rooting medium. Enclose the container in a plastic bag to retain humidity. New plants form at the base of the stem.

To root leaf cuttings of mother-in-law's tongue *(Sansevieria)*, cut a leaf into 3- to 4-inch-long sections. Insert these into the rooting medium, covering as much as three-fourths of their length. A new plant will eventually form at the base of each cutting.

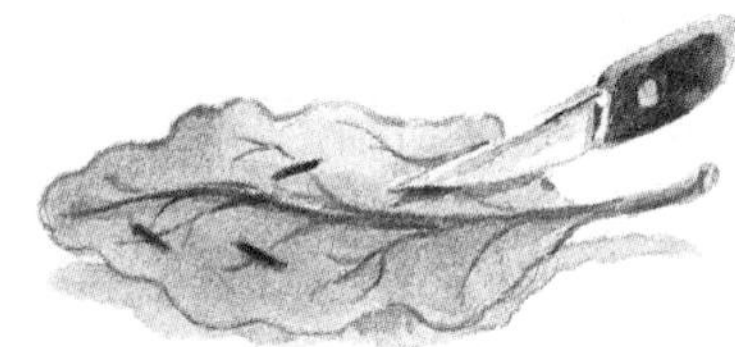

Rex begonia

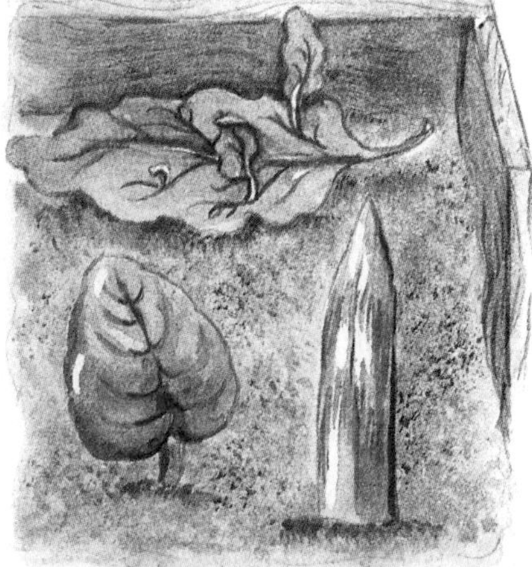

African violet　Mother-in-law's tongue

SOFTWOOD AND SEMIHARDWOOD STEM CUTTINGS

Taken during the active growing season from spring until late summer, softwood cuttings are the easiest stem cuttings to take and the fastest to root. They are made from relatively soft, flexible new growth. Semihardwood cuttings are taken somewhat later in the growing season, usually in summer or early autumn. A suitable semihardwood stem is firm enough to snap if bent sharply; if it just bends, it's too mature for satisfactory rooting.

In addition to deciduous and evergreen shrubs and trees, many perennials may be propagated by semihardwood cuttings and softwood.

ROOTING THE CUTTINGS

1 Prepare containers first. Use clean pots or flats with drainage holes. Fill them with a half-and-half mixture of perlite and peat moss, or with perlite alone. Dampen the mixture.

2 Gather cuttings early in the day, when plants are fresh and full of moisture. The parent plant should be healthy and growing vigorously. With a sharp knife or bypass pruners, cut off an 8- to 12-inch length of stem.

Prepare the cuttings by removing and discarding any flower buds, flowers, and side shoots. Then slice the stem into 3- to 4-inch pieces, each with at least two nodes (growing points). Make each cut just below a node, since new roots will form at this point. Strip the lower leaves from each cutting.

3 Dip the lower cut ends of the cuttings in liquid or powdered rooting hormone; shake off any excess. (Many plants will root without the use of hormones.)

Using a pencil or thin dowel, make holes in the rooting medium an inch or two apart; then insert the cuttings. Firm the medium around the cuttings and water with a fine spray. Label each container with the name of the plant and the date. Set containers in a warm spot that's shaded but not dark.

Enclose each container in a plastic bag; fasten the bag closed to maintain humidity. Open the bag for a few minutes every day to provide ventilation.

4 Once the cuttings have taken hold and are growing roots, they will begin to send out new leaves. To test for rooting, gently pull on a cutting; if you feel resistance, roots are forming. At this point, expose the cuttings to drier air by opening the bags; if the cuttings wilt, close the bags again for a few days.

When the plants seem acclimated to open air, transplant each to its own pot of lightweight potting soil. By the next planting season, the new plants should be ready to go out in the garden.

HARDWOOD CUTTINGS

Take hardwood cuttings during the dormant season (when plants are leafless), from late fall to early spring. Most deciduous shrubs and trees can be propagated by this method. Candidates include dogwood *(Cornus)*, forsythia, crape myrtle *(Lagerstroemia)*, honeysuckle *(Lonicera)*, privet *(Ligustrum)*, elderberry *(Sambucus)*, willow *(Salix)*, and spiraea. Some fruit species, such as fig, grape, mulberry *(Morus)*, and some plums, are easily propagated by hardwood cuttings.

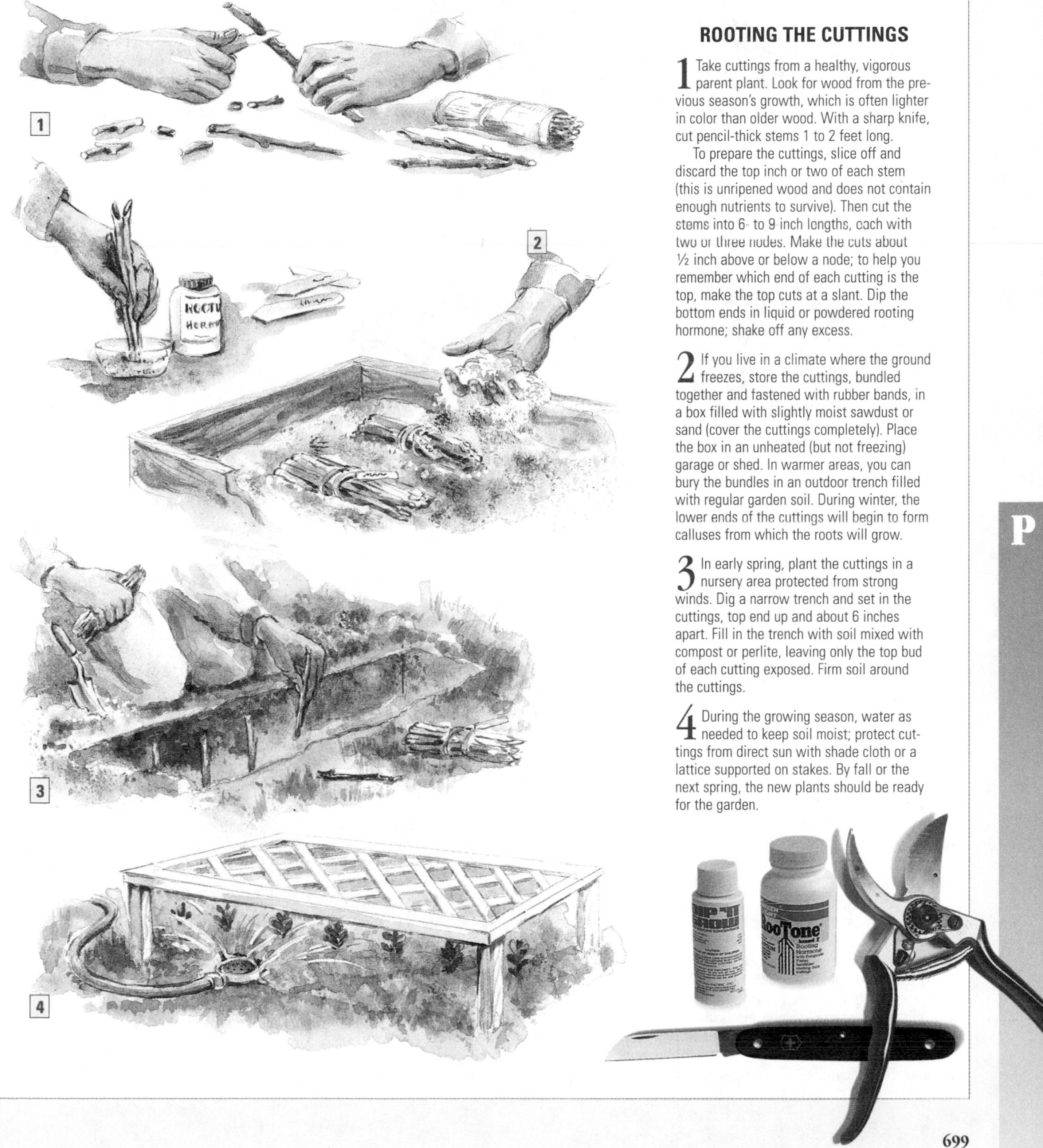

ROOTING THE CUTTINGS

1 Take cuttings from a healthy, vigorous parent plant. Look for wood from the previous season's growth, which is often lighter in color than older wood. With a sharp knife, cut pencil-thick stems 1 to 2 feet long.

To prepare the cuttings, slice off and discard the top inch or two of each stem (this is unripened wood and does not contain enough nutrients to survive). Then cut the stems into 6- to 9-inch lengths, each with two or three nodes. Make the cuts about ½ inch above or below a node; to help you remember which end of each cutting is the top, make the top cuts at a slant. Dip the bottom ends in liquid or powdered rooting hormone; shake off any excess.

2 If you live in a climate where the ground freezes, store the cuttings, bundled together and fastened with rubber bands, in a box filled with slightly moist sawdust or sand (cover the cuttings completely). Place the box in an unheated (but not freezing) garage or shed. In warmer areas, you can bury the bundles in an outdoor trench filled with regular garden soil. During winter, the lower ends of the cuttings will begin to form calluses from which the roots will grow.

3 In early spring, plant the cuttings in a nursery area protected from strong winds. Dig a narrow trench and set in the cuttings, top end up and about 6 inches apart. Fill in the trench with soil mixed with compost or perlite, leaving only the top bud of each cutting exposed. Firm soil around the cuttings.

4 During the growing season, water as needed to keep soil moist; protect cuttings from direct sun with shade cloth or a lattice supported on stakes. By fall or the next spring, the new plants should be ready for the garden.

DIVIDING PERENNIALS

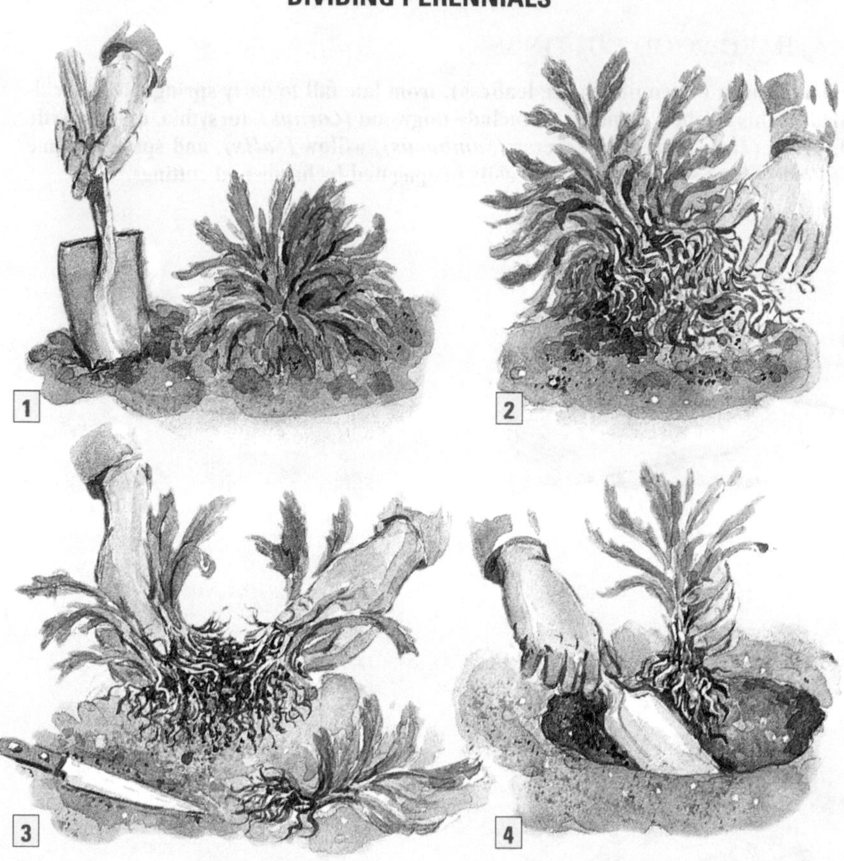

1 Loosen the soil in a circle around the clump, cutting 6 to 12 inches beyond the plant's perimeter with a shovel or spading fork. Then dig under the roots to free them from the soil. Lift the whole clump out of the ground; or, if it's too heavy to lift, cut it into sections. Set the clump (or pieces) in a convenient working spot such as a path.

2 Gently tease some soil from the root ball so you can see what you are doing. For larger, fibrous-rooted perennials such as daylilies *(Hemerocallis)*, hose off as much of the soil as possible.

3 Now make the divisions. Note natural dividing points between stems or sections. You can divide some perennials by pulling the clumps apart by hand. Those with mats of small, fibrous roots can be cut with a knife, small pruning saw, or trowel; types with thick, tough roots may require a sharp-bladed shovel or an ax. Divide clumps into good-sized sections. Trim any damaged roots, stems, or leaves.

4 Replant the divisions as soon as possible, then keep them well watered while they get established. You can also plant divisions in containers (a good idea if they're very small) to set out later or share with other gardeners.

DIVISION. Division is the easiest way to propagate many perennials, bulbs, and shrubs that form suckers or clumps of stems with rooted bases. In essence, dividing a plant involves separating it into several rooted, self-supporting plants. Besides giving you new plants, division rejuvenates overgrown plants, improving bloom and overall appearance.

Most plants can be divided either in fall or early spring. If you plan to divide in fall and you live in a cold-winter climate, do the job early enough in the season to let roots get established before freezing weather arrives (generally 6 to 8 weeks before the first hard frost). Avoid dividing plants in the heat of summer, since it is difficult for divisions to become established then.

A day or two before dividing, thoroughly moisten the soil around the clump to be divided. To make the plants easier to handle, cut back the stems of larger perennials, leaving about 6 inches of foliage. (When dividing shrubs, cut stems back to 6 to 12 inches long.) If you'll be planting in a new bed, prepare the soil (see page 690) before you divide, so the divisions won't have to spend too long out of the ground. If you're replanting in the same location as the parent clump, keep the divisions in a shady spot covered with damp newspapers while you replenish the soil.

For division of bulbous plants, see page 660. For information on dividing ornamental grasses, turn to page 677.

LAYERING. Layering is a technique that encourages new roots to form on branches still attached to the parent plant. The parent plant supplies the layer—the new plant—with water and nutrients during the rooting process.

Ground layering. Also called simple layering, ground layering is an easy way to produce a few new plants, though it may take as long as a year. This technique can be used to propagate many shrubs and perennials that have low-growing or trailing branches. To ground layer, follow the steps below.

GROUND LAYERING

1 In spring, select a young, healthy, pliable shoot growing low on the plant to be layered. Loosen the soil where the shoot will be buried and work in a shovelful of compost. Dig a shallow hole in the prepared area.

With a sharp knife, make a cut where the shoot will touch the soil; cut about halfway through the shoot, starting from the underside. Dust the cut with rooting hormone powder and insert a pebble or wooden matchstick to hold it open.

Lay the shoot (the layer) in the hole and fasten it down with a piece of wire or a forked stick. Some gardeners tie the layer's tip to a stake to help it grow upward.

2 Fill in the hole, firming the soil around the layer. A rock or brick can be placed on top to help hold the layer in place.

During the growing season, keep the soil around the layer moist. Adding a few inches of mulch will help retain moisture.

When you are sure roots have formed (this may take anywhere from a few months to possibly more than a year; gently dig into the soil to check), cut the new plant free from the parent. Dig it up, keeping plenty of soil around the roots, and move it to its intended location.

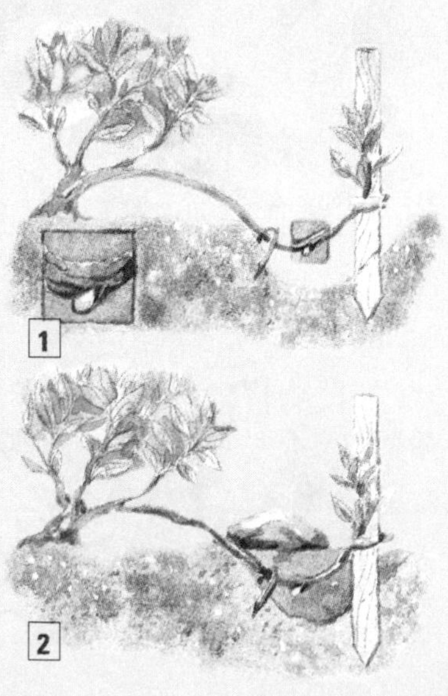

AIR LAYERING

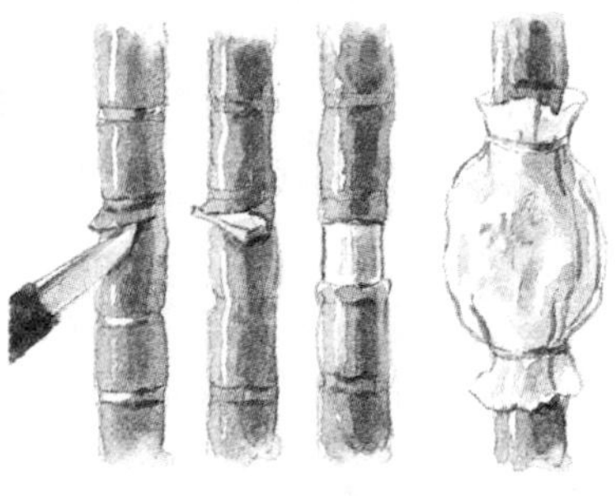

Air layering is most successful if done while a plant is growing actively. To encourage such growth in houseplants, fertilize the plant to be layered, then place it in a sunny window. When new leaves appear, proceed with layering.

Begin below a node. Make a slanting cut (insert a wooden matchstick to keep it open) in bark or remove a ring of bark. Dust cut with rooting hormone, encase in damp sphagnum moss, and then cover with plastic wrap to keep the moss moist.

If layering succeeds, roots will appear in the moss after a few months; you can then sever the rooted stem from the parent and pot it. At this point, it's usually a good idea to remove about half the new plant's leaves to prevent excessive moisture loss through transpiration while it gets established.

If no roots form, the cut you made will form a callus, and new bark will eventually grow over it.

Air layering. This process involves the same principle as ground layering, but air layering is used for branches higher on a plant. It is often employed to propagate large house plants—overgrown rubber plants *(Ficus elastica)*, for example, but it's also successful in some outdoor trees and shrubs, including citrus, witch hazel *(Hamamelis)*, magnolia, and rhododendron. To air layer, follow the steps above.

BUDDING AND GRAFTING. These methods involve joining parts of two different—but closely related—plants so that they will grow as one. With a steady hand and a little practice, you can learn to use budding and grafting to propagate roses, grapes, and fruit and ornamental trees or to add one or more new varieties to an existing fruit or nut tree. The part that becomes the upper or aboveground portion of the plant is known as the *scion;* it may be a piece of a branch or a single bud. The scion gives the new plant the desired qualities of flowering, fruiting, or form. The part that provides the roots is called the *stock, rootstock,* or *understock.* In some cases, the stock is a young plant chosen because it causes the new plant to be hardier, more disease resistant, or smaller in size (as in dwarf fruit trees, for instance). In other cases, the stock may be a mature tree that you want to graft over to a new variety.

Successful budding and grafting depend upon uniting the *cambium* layers of scion and stock—the thin layer of growing cells just inside the bark. When these layers join with each other, new growth can occur. Use a very sharp knife to make all cuts: the cleaner the cut, the better the chance for a successful union. T-budding and cleft grafting are illustrated here. Other methods include chip budding, patch budding, whip grafting, and side grafting; consult a plant propagation manual for details on these.

Budding. Also called bud-grafting, this operation is carried out in summer or early fall when plants are actively growing. Roses and some other flowering shrubs, as well as grapes and fruit trees, are propagated by this method. Budding involves inserting a growth bud (the scion) from one plant beneath the bark of a related plant (the stock). The stock is either a pencil-thick rooted cutting of a sort known to produce a strong root system or a seedling plant of such a species. Usually, buds are inserted just a few inches above the soil. (They are also occasionally placed in small branches in the upper portion of a tree.) If the plants are compatible and budding is successful, the bud will unite with the stem into which it was inserted. It will stay plump but dormant through fall and winter, then begin to grow in spring, when all the plant's buds burst into growth. At this point, the stem is cut back to just above the new,

T-BUDDING

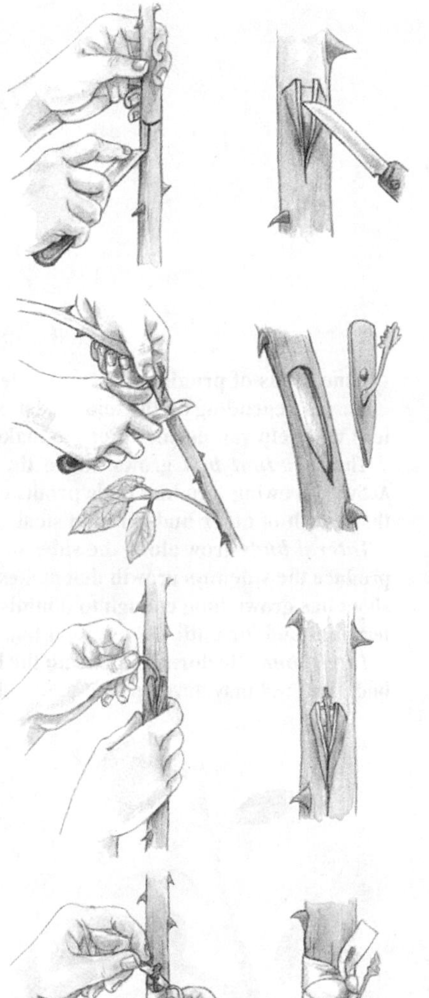

1 Choose a stock stem ¼ to ½ inch in diameter. Make a T-shaped cut in the bark; the top of the T should extend about a third of the way around the stem. Gently pry up the corners of the T. If the bark does not pull away easily, it may be too early in the season; try again in a week or two.

2 Select a bud (located at the base of a leaf) from the budwood plant; remove the leaf but retain its stalk to use as a handle. Be sure to take a vegetative bud, which is usually small and pointed, rather than a larger, plumper flower bud. Cut a shield-shaped patch containing the bud, starting about ½ inch below the bud and finishing about 1 inch above it; leave a bit of wood attached to the back of the bud shield.

3 Push the bud shield down between the flaps of the T-cut, being careful not to damage the bud. Cut off the top of the shield to make it even with the horizontal cut of the T. All of the shield should fit between the bark flaps.

4 Bind the budding site snugly with plastic grafting tape or rubber budding strips, starting beneath the bud and finishing above it. Cover the top of the T, but leave the bud exposed.

P

growing bud. The flowers, fruit, and leaves arising from the implanted bud will have the characteristics of the plant from which it was taken.

Grafting. This technique unites a short length of stem—the scion—with a stock. The stock plant may be a slim seedling to be grafted near ground level or an old fruit tree to be grafted on its major limbs. Cleft grafting (illustrated at right) is popular for converting fruit and nut trees to new varieties. Cleft grafts are made in early spring, when the growth buds of the stock are beginning to swell. However, the scion wood should be dormant when the graft is made—so gather it in late fall or winter. Cut ¼- to ½-inch-thick tip growth, making sure each piece has three or four buds. Bundle the cut stems together, label them, and place in a sealed plastic bag in the refrigerator. Some mail-order companies offer scion wood in winter.

Pruning

Pruning tasks vary in scope—from removing large tree limbs to pinching out new growth on perennials—and your goals in pruning will differ, too. Here are a few reasons why you may need or want to prune.

To maintain the health of your plants. Trees and shrubs will be healthier and more attractive if you remove branches that are badly diseased, dead, or rubbing together. Plants that have become too densely branched should be thinned to allow air and sunlight to reach their inner leaves and stems, helping to discourage some diseases.

To direct growth. Each time you make a pruning cut, you stop growth in one direction and encourage it in another, since growth continues in the buds and branches left behind.

To remove undesirable growth. Prune out wayward branches and remove suckers (stems growing up from the roots) and water sprouts (upright shoots growing from the trunk and branches). It should not, however, be necessary to cut back a plant continually to keep it in bounds. If it requires such treatment, it was probably a poor choice for its location and should be replaced with a plant that will naturally remain smaller.

To increase quality or yield of flowers or fruit. Most fruit trees and many flowering trees and shrubs need regular pruning to produce a good annual crop of fruit or blossoms. Specifics of pruning these plants are given in the Western Plant Encyclopedia.

To maintain safety. Remove split or broken branches that threaten to fall, injuring people or damaging buildings or cars. Also prune away any branches that obscure oncoming traffic from view.

To create hedges or topiary. Suitable plants can be shaped through regular shearing.

CLEFT GRAFTING

1 Prepare the stock by splitting it several inches down into a smooth, straight-grained section (so the split will be even). Shape the bottom end of the scion into a long, gradually tapering wedge; the outside edge of the wedge should be slightly thicker than the inside (as shown in the cross-section diagram).

2 Use a wedge or large screwdriver to hold open the split stock while you work. Insert the scion (or two, as illustrated) into the stock, carefully placed so that the cambium layers of stock and scion match. After the scion is properly placed, remove the wedge and cover the entire union with grafting wax. Also coat the top of the scion so it won't dry out. If the graft is successful, buds on the scion wood will show growth during spring.

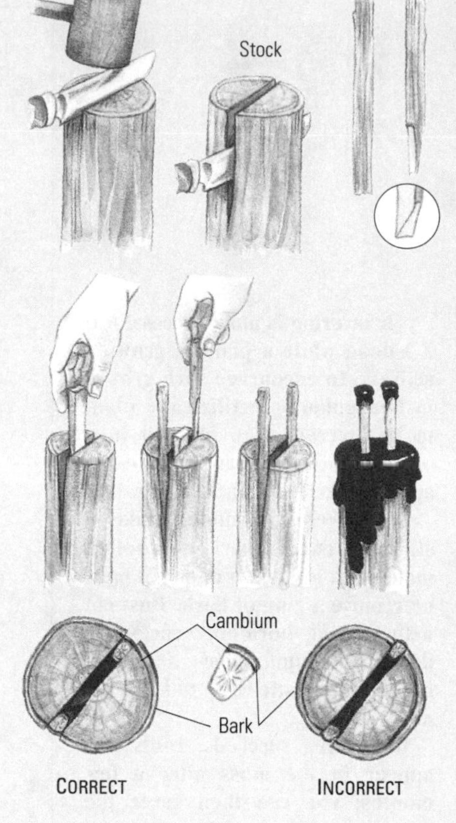

PRUNING AND PLANT GROWTH

Some kinds of pruning cuts are made near a growth bud. Because subsequent growth varies depending on the bud's location, learning about growth buds (shown below, far left) will help you decide where to make cuts.

The *terminal bud* grows at the tip of a shoot, causing that shoot to grow longer. Actively growing terminal buds produce hormones that move down the stem and inhibit the growth of other buds on that stem.

***Lateral buds* grow along the sides of the shoot at leaf attachment points (nodes); they produce the sideways growth that makes a plant bushy. These buds stay dormant until the shoot has grown long enough to diminish the influence of the hormones produced by the terminal bud, or until the terminal bud is pruned off; then they begin to grow.**

***Latent buds* lie dormant beneath the bark. If a branch breaks or is cut off near a latent bud, that bud may develop into a new shoot.**

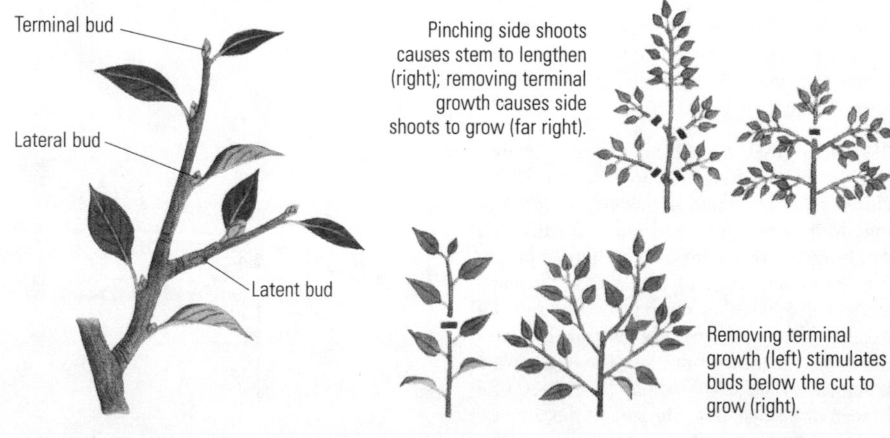

Pinching side shoots causes stem to lengthen (right); removing terminal growth causes side shoots to grow (far right).

Removing terminal growth (left) stimulates buds below the cut to grow (right).

FOUR TYPES OF PRUNING CUTS. Most pruning involves four basic techniques: thinning, heading, shearing, and pinching. What sets these methods apart is where you cut in relation to growth buds and side branches.

Thinning. Most of the cuts you make when pruning should be thinning cuts. Such cuts can direct growth, eliminate competing or old stems, reduce overall size, and open up a plant's structure.

To thin, you remove an entire stem or branch, taking it back to its point of origin or to its junction with another branch. You might cut a branch back to the trunk, to the parent branch from which it arose, or (in the case of plants that send up stems directly from the roots) all the way to the ground. When removing one branch at a branch junction, be sure the remaining branch is at least one-third the diameter of the one being removed. If it's any smaller than that, it will be unable to assume the terminal role, and the effect will be more like that resulting from a heading cut (see below).

When you remove a branch, you of course also remove the buds on that branch. Thinning cuts can cause bud growth elsewhere on the plant, but they're much less likely than heading cuts to stimulate clusters of shoots. Thus, thinning lets you reduce the bulk of a plant with minimal regrowth.

Heading. Heading cuts remove just part of a stem or branch—not the whole thing, as thinning cuts do. Such cuts can be made back to a bud or to a twig or branch too small to take over the terminal role (less than one-third the diameter of the branch you're removing). Heading stimulates the growth of lateral buds just below the cut. (Shearing and pinching, discussed below, are also forms of heading.)

For maintenance pruning of most woody plants, heading is less desirable than thinning. Though it may initially make a plant smaller and more compact, this situation won't last for long: once headed, the plant will produce vigorous new growth from lateral buds. If you head a wayward shoot instead of thinning it out, you can expect a candelabra of shoots to grow in its place. Continual heading thus ruins the natural shape of most woody plants. It is, however, useful when your goal is precisely to induce vigorous growth beneath a cut—when you want to force branching at a particular point on a branch or stem to train young fruit trees; fill a hole in the tree's crown; increase bloom production in roses or other flowering shrubs; or rejuvenate old or neglected shrubs.

Shearing. An indiscriminate form of heading, shearing does not involve careful, precise cutting just above a growing point. Instead, you simply clip a plant's outer foliage to create an even surface, as in hedges or topiary. However, because the plants best suited to shearing have main and lateral branches bearing closely spaced buds, almost every cut ends up near a growing point.

Pinching. This is the simplest, most basic pruning cut. Using your thumb and forefinger or a pair of hand shears, you nip off the tips of new growth, removing the terminal bud. This stops the shoot from growing longer and stimulates branching. Pinching is used primarily on annuals and perennials to make them bushy and encourage the production of more flowers.

TYPES OF PRUNING CUTS

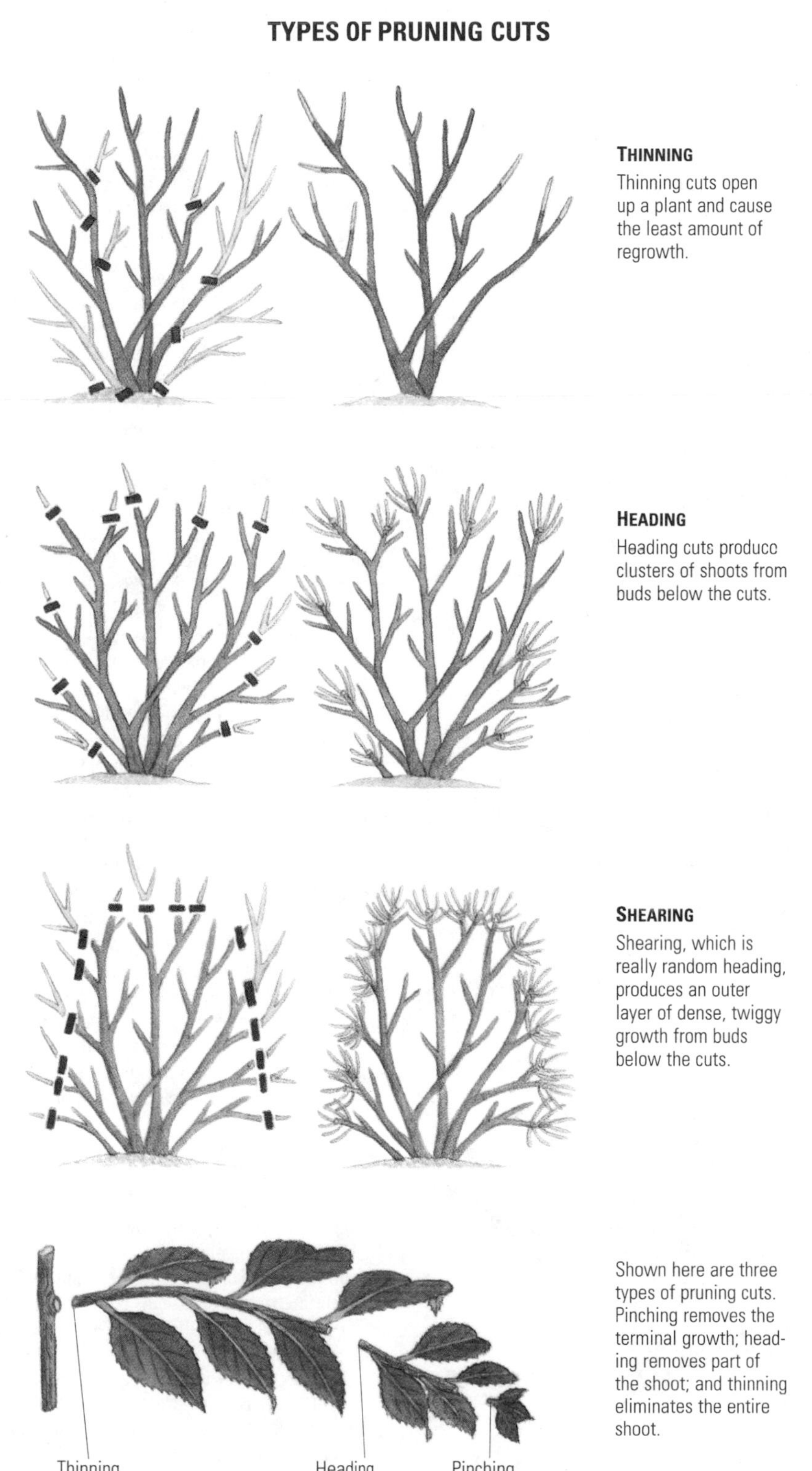

THINNING
Thinning cuts open up a plant and cause the least amount of regrowth.

HEADING
Heading cuts produce clusters of shoots from buds below the cuts.

SHEARING
Shearing, which is really random heading, produces an outer layer of dense, twiggy growth from buds below the cuts.

Shown here are three types of pruning cuts. Pinching removes the terminal growth; heading removes part of the shoot; and thinning eliminates the entire shoot.

MAKING PRUNING CUTS. When pruning, always cut back to a part that will continue to grow—to the trunk, another branch, a bud, or even to the plant's base, if it sends up stems from the roots. At these points of active growth, callus tissue will start to grow inward from cells at the end of the cut; in time, the wound will seal off. Clean cuts callus over faster than ragged ones, so it's important to use an appropriate, well-sharpened pruning tool (for more on tools, see page 709). Forcing a tool to cut a branch bigger than it is designed to handle can result in ragged, uneven cuts (and can damage the tool).

The precise placement of a cut is usually also important. If you cut too close to a bud, the bud is likely to die. If you cut too far away from it, on the other hand, you'll leave a stub that, though still attached to the plant, is no longer involved in its active metabolism. In time, the stub will wither and die, then decay and drop off to leave an open patch of dead tissue—an invitation to disease or insect infestation.

When cutting back to a bud, look for a healthy specimen pointing in the direction you want the new shoot to grow. A proper cut will be about ¼ inch away from the bud, sloping away at approximately a 45° angle. Its lowest point should be opposite the bud and even with it, and it should slant upward in the direction the bud is pointing (see illustration below).

CUTTING ABOVE A BUD

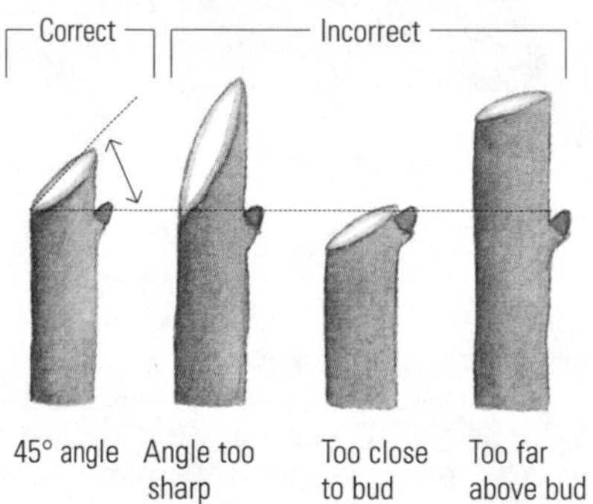

POSITIONING PRUNING SHEARS

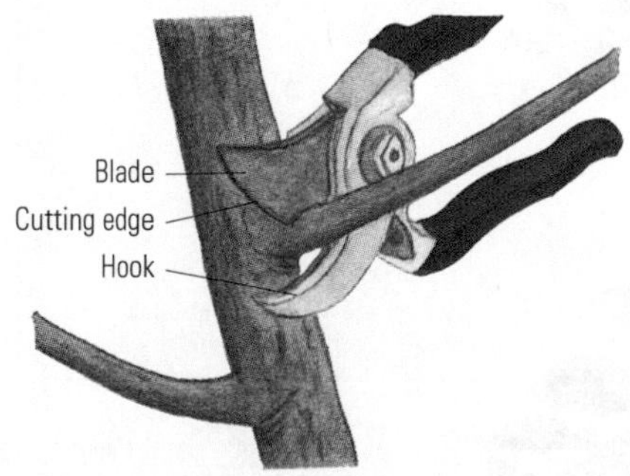

To make a proper close pruning cut, hold shears with the blade closer to the growth that will remain on the plant. A stub results when you reverse the position and place the hook closer to the plant.

When removing a branch, don't make a flush cut. Position your shears or saw just outside the *branch collar,* the wrinkled area (or bulge) at the branch's base where it meets another branch or the trunk. Also refrain from cutting into the *branch bark ridge* (raised bark in the branch crotch). Leaving these areas intact keeps decay to a minimum.

If you need to remove larger branches (any that are too big to support in one hand while sawing with the other), make the cut in three steps to avoid ripping the bark and tearing the tissue around the collar, as shown at right. If the limb in question is very heavy or high in a tree, however, it's wisest to hire a professional arborist. This is also the best course for repairing storm-damaged trees and for pruning around power lines.

WHEN TO PRUNE. In general, pruning is best done in late winter (when plants are dormant) or during mid- to late summer; specific pruning times are given for many plants described in the Western Plant Encyclopedia. Dead or badly diseased wood is an exception: it should be removed as soon as you notice it. (Be sure, however, that dead-looking wood truly is dead. For example, freeze-damaged tissue that looks beyond help is sometimes in fact still alive; see page 670.) The best time to prune also depends in part on whether the plant is deciduous or evergreen.

Deciduous trees and shrubs—those that drop their leaves in fall—are typically pruned in late winter or early spring, just before or just as they resume growth. When the plants are leafless, it's easier to see their overall shape and to spot broken and awkwardly placed branches. To avoid cold damage to exposed tissues, prune after the danger of heavy frost is past.

Flowering trees and shrubs demand a little extra attention to timing—you'll need to know whether they bloom on old or new wood before you decide just when to prune. Plants that bear flowers in spring on wood that grew the preceding year should be pruned only after the flowering season is finished; if you prune in late winter, you'll eliminate the flower buds. Woody plants that produce flowers later in the growing season on the current season's growth, however, can be pruned in late winter without sacrificing blossoms, since the new (flowering) wood will grow after pruning. Check to see which category your plants belong to—older branches are usually darker, less pliable, and woodier looking than new growth.

Many deciduous plants can also be pruned in midsummer, after the growth flush of spring and early summer has slowed. This is a good time to thin out excess growth; moreover, vigorous shoots such as suckers and water sprouts are less likely to regrow if removed in summer. In cold-winter areas, be sure to complete such summer pruning no later than a month before the usual first-frost date, since pruning may stimulate tender new growth susceptible to cold damage.

REMOVING A BRANCH

When removing larger branches, avoid ripping the bark by shortening the branch to a stub before cutting it off just outside the branch collar. Using a sharp pruning saw, make three cuts, as shown below.

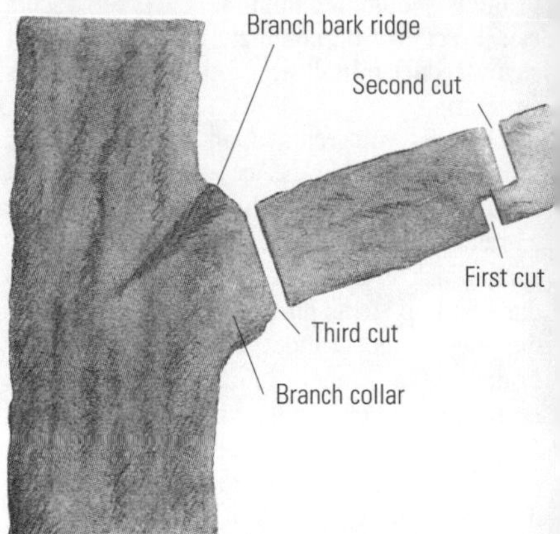

1 About a foot from the branch base, make a cut from the underside approximately a third of the way through.

2 About an inch farther out on the branch, cut through the top until the branch rips off. The branch should split cleanly between the two cuts.

3 Make the final cut by placing your saw just outside the branch bark ridge and cutting downward and just outside of the branch collar. (If the crotch is very narrow, cut upward from the bottom to avoid cutting into the branch collar.)

Broad-leafed evergreen trees and shrubs don't drop their foliage, but growth of most slows down to a level approaching dormancy during the coldest time of year. Most can be pruned during this dormant period (late winter or early spring) or in summer. For flowering broad-leafed evergreens, however, timing is more precise; for deciduous flowering plants, you'll need to prune with an eye toward preserving flower buds. For evergreens flowering on last season's growth, prune after bloom; for those that bloom on new wood, prune before spring growth begins.

Conifers, in many cases, don't require any pruning. For those that do, timing depends on the growth habit of the conifer in question. These typically evergreen plants (which bear needles or scalelike leaves) fall into two broad classes: those with branches radiating out from the trunk in whorls and those that sprout branches in a random fashion.

Fir *(Abies),* spruce *(Picea),* and most pines *(Pinus)* are examples of whorl-type conifers. They produce all their new growth in spring, with buds appearing at the tips of new shoots as well as along their length and at their bases. (On pines, the new shoots are called candles, since that's what they look like until the needles grow.) Prune these conifers in early spring. You can cut new shoots back about halfway to induce more branching, making sure to cut above growth buds; or you can cut them out entirely to force branching from buds at their bases. Cutting back into an old stem—even one that bears foliage—won't necessarily force branching unless you happen to cut back to a latent bud.

Random-branching conifers, including cedar *(Cedrus),* cypress *(Cupressus),* juniper *(Juniperus),* arborvitae *(Thuja)*, yew *(Taxus),* and hemlock *(Tsuga),* grow in spurts throughout the growing season rather than just in spring. They can be pruned much as deciduous and broad-leafed evergreens are. New growth will sprout from the branches below your cuts as long as the remaining part of the branch bears some foliage; most won't develop new growth from bare branches (hemlock and yew are exceptions). You usually have more leeway in timing for pruning random-branching conifers than you do for whorl-branching types, though the best time for the job is usually right before spring growth begins.

ESPALIER

This is a method of training a tree or shrub so that its branches grow in a flat pattern against a wall or fence. The branches are tied to a support—usually a trellis made of wire. The illustration shows several espalier forms.

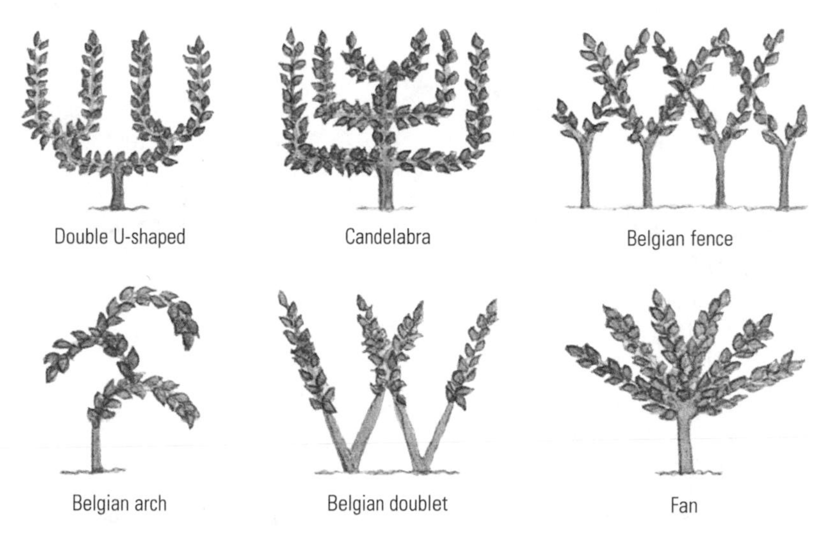

Shrubs

Shrubs are woody plants that live for many years. They are typically planted to provide long-lasting features in a landscape, forming a framework to help unite the garden's various elements. Many establish a permanent woody structure in their youth, then increase in size by growing new branches from older ones. Others produce shorter-lived woody stems (canes) each year from the roots, with a few to many new stems emerging as the older ones decline.

In form, shrubs may be rounded, vase shaped, conical, or columnar; in size, they range from ankle-high dwarfs to plants as tall as small trees. In contrast to trees, though, most have foliage all the way to the ground, rather than only at the top of a bare trunk.

Weigela *(Weigela florida)* is a fast-growing shrub that bears pink to rose-red flowers in late spring.

SELECTING SHRUBS. So many different shrubs are available that you may have some difficulty choosing the best ones for your garden. Start by considering adaptability: select plants that will thrive in your climate and soil conditions. (Check the Western Plant Encyclopedia for specific information on the shrubs you're considering.) It's also important to think about mature size. That little tuft of greenery from a gallon can may look cute in a 4- by 4-foot space for a while, but if it ultimately will reach 12 feet in all directions, it's the wrong plant for the spot. In the same vein, bear in mind that the most attractive shrubs are those allowed to grow according to their natural inclinations, without excessive pruning. (Shrubs intended for hedges are an exception; in this case you can control size by pruning. For a list of good shrubs for hedges as well as those that can serve as privacy screens, see "Plants for Hedges and Screens" in A Guide to Plant Selection, beginning on page 64.) You will also want to decide whether a deciduous or an evergreen shrub best suits your purposes. Finally, consider ornamental features such as foliage texture, variegated or unusually colored leaves, attractive flowers, and colorful fruits.

PLANTING AND CARING FOR SHRUBS. Shrubs may be sold bare-root, in containers, or balled-and-burlapped (B-and-B). See pages 692–694 for planting directions for each type. How the plant is sold also affects the best time of year for planting. Bare-root plants must be set out soon after you purchase them; this is also true of B-and-B shrubs, available from late fall to early spring. You can plant container-grown shrubs at any time during the growing season, but to avoid stressing them, it's best to plant in spring or fall rather than in the heat of summer.

Water newly planted shrubs immediately, then keep the soil moist but not soggy as the plants settle in. Mulching will help conserve water and prevent weed growth around shrubs. Future watering needs depend on the particular shrub. Once established (after a year or two in the garden), many native shrubs and others well adapted to Western climates may survive on rainfall alone, while those that hail from damper regions will need supplemental water in the dry season.

Fertilizer needs vary, too. Some shrubs (notably roses) do best with regular fertilizing, and other flowering sorts may also benefit from at least an annual application of fertilizer. But many shrubs grow well with no supplemental nutrients. If the shrub puts out strong new growth with good color each year, it's doing well without feeding—but if new growth is scant, pale, or weak, it should be fertilized.

To prune shrubs, follow the principles outlined on pages 703–705. Shrubs that have become overgrown—with long, straggling, tangled branches—may require rejuvenation, a rather severe form of pruning (illustrated on page 706). This method works best on shrubs that send up stems (canes) from the roots. Some can even take drastic rejuvenation, which involves cutting back all stems almost to the ground before new spring growth begins. Shrubs so pruned may need several seasons to recover fully, but in the long run they will be more compact and attractive. Plants amenable to this treatment include glossy abelia *(Abelia ×grandiflora),* barberry *(Berberis),* common butterfly bush *(Buddleja davidii),* forsythia,

S

REJUVENATING SHRUBS THAT GROW FROM THE BASE

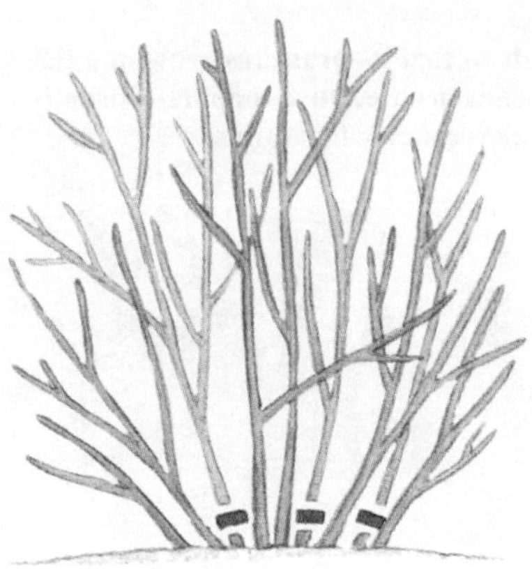

GRADUALLY
Remove about a third of the oldest growth annually for 3 years.

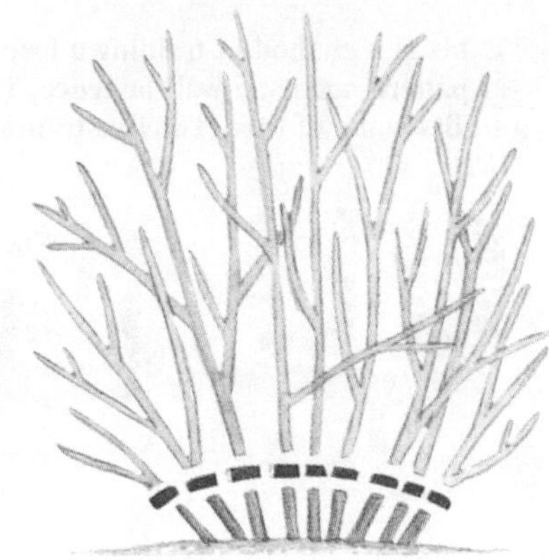

DRASTICALLY
If the shrub withstands severe pruning (as mentioned in the text, page 705), cut back the whole plant before new spring growth begins.

mock orange *(Philadelphus),* shrubby willows *(Salix),* and spiraea.

On most other cane-producing shrubs, it's safest to proceed much more gradually with rejuvenation, spreading the pruning over a period of 3 years. In any case, once you have gotten rid of the old stems, keep the shrub under control by continuing to remove just a few of the oldest stems each spring.

Soils and Soil Management

Understanding your soil and learning how to improve it will help make the garden more productive. Soil texture affects watering and fertilizing schedules, and in some cases, it determines the kinds of plants you'll be able to grow.

Soil supports roots and gives them access to nutrients, water, and air. Most roots grow in the uppermost soil layer, called *topsoil,* which is relatively active biologically and is most directly affected by weather. Below the topsoil is the *subsoil.* It is less affected by microorganisms and weather, and while it may contain plant nutrients, it is not as hospitable to roots as topsoil. Discussions of soil quality and improvement generally focus on topsoil.

Soil is composed of mineral particles, living and dead organic matter, and pore spaces containing water and air. Good garden soil is approximately 45 percent minerals, 5 percent (or more) organic matter, and 50 percent pore spaces. The *mineral* portion is composed of rock broken down into tiny particles, while *organic matter* includes roots, decaying leaves and stems, materials added by gardeners, and myriad soil-dwelling organisms.

The network of *pore spaces* determines the permeability of the soil to water and air, and its water-holding capacity. This network includes large pores *(macropores)* and small ones *(micropores).* Macropores permit water and air to enter the soil easily and allow excess water to drain away. Micropores are responsible for a soil's water-holding capacity: they hold water against the force of gravity, making it available when needed by plants. The proportion of macro- to micropores affects soil quality. Soils that contain a preponderance of large pores are loose in texture; they are well aerated but cannot retain water for long and need more frequent irrigation. Soils with many small pores, on the other hand, are dense types that can hold a lot of water but not much air.

SOIL TEXTURE. Texture describes the size of a soil's mineral particles. These include large, coarse sand particles; smaller silt particles; and tiny particles of clay.

Clay soils. Also called adobe, gumbo, or simply "heavy" soils, clay soils are composed of flattened, platelike, microscopic particles that pack closely together, leaving little pore space for either water or air. But because these particles offer the largest surface area per volume of all soil particles, clay soils can hold the greatest volume of nutrients in soluble form. They also hold water for a longer time after getting wet. Drainage (the downward movement of water) is slow in clay soils, so the loss of soluble nutrients through leaching is slow as well. Due to their high density, clay soils are the slowest to warm in spring.

Sandy soils. Sand particles are comparatively large, and they're irregularly rounded rather than flattened. Their size and shape allow for much larger pore spaces between particles than in clay soils; consequently, sandy soils contain lots of air and drain well. In a given volume of sandy soil, the surface area of the particles is less than in the same volume of clay—so that the volume of soluble nutrients in sandy soil is correspondingly lower. And because sandy soil drains quickly and thus loses nutrients faster than clay, plants in sand need watering and feeding more often than those growing in clay. Sandy soils warm more quickly in spring than clay soils.

Loam. Loam is considered the ideal garden soil. It contains a mix of all three particle types—clay, silt, and sand—but none predominates. With a combination of large and small pore spaces, it drains well (but doesn't dry out too fast), loses nutrients at only a moderate rate, and contains enough air for healthy root growth.

Determining soil texture. To identify the texture of your garden soil, thoroughly wet a patch of soil, then let it dry out for a day. Now pick up a handful of soil and squeeze it firmly in your fist. If it forms a tight ball and has a slippery feel, it's predominantly clay. If it feels gritty and doesn't hold its shape at all but simply crumbles apart when you open your hand, it's sandy. If it is slightly crumbly but still holds a loose ball, it's closer to loam.

SOIL TEXTURE AND TYPE

The size of a soil's mineral particles determines its texture and designates its type: clay, sand, or loam. Clay has the smallest particles, sand the largest; silt particles are intermediate in size. Loam, the ideal garden soil, contains a mix of all three types of particles.

SOIL PARTICLES

Clay
Less than $\frac{1}{12,500}$ in.

Silt
Up to $\frac{1}{500}$ in.

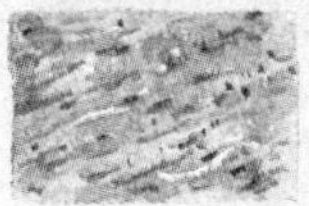

Fine sand
Up to $\frac{1}{250}$ in.

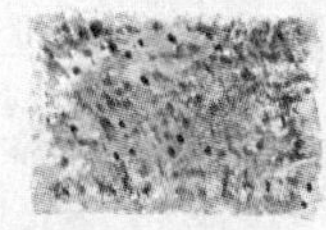

Medium sand
Up to $\frac{1}{50}$ in.

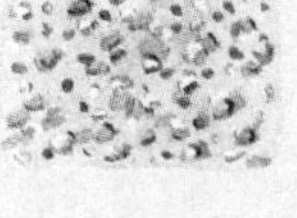

Coarsest sand
$\frac{1}{12}$ in.

SOIL STRUCTURE. A soil's *texture* is defined by the size of its primary particles; its *structure* is determined by the way those particles bind together to form small clumps, called *aggregates.* In soil with a good structure, the pores between and within the aggregates are large enough to contain air and allow water to drain through easily, yet small enough to retain some water for roots to use.

Though you can't change a soil's basic texture, you *can* improve its structure by adding organic matter. Such improvement is especially important in fine-textured (clay) soils, since it increases porosity: organic matter helps bind the small particles together into larger aggregates. Gypsum and lime, both inorganic amendments, are sometimes used to improve structure in clay soils; for advice on using them, consult soil professionals or your Cooperative Extension Office.

In sandy soils, organic matter lodges in the pore spaces and acts like a sponge, holding water and nutrients.

Be aware that soil structure can be damaged, especially in soils high in clay. Running heavy machinery over the soil or even walking on planting areas compresses the pore spaces, as does tilling soil when it's too wet. Always let soil dry out until it's barely moist before working it.

SOIL PROBLEMS. Some of the soil problems that result in poor plant growth may be due to factors other than basic soil texture or structure. Here are a few of the most common such problems—and practical ways to deal with them.

Poor drainage. For most plants, good drainage is essential for healthy growth. If the soil drains poorly, water remains in the pore spaces rather than draining away, and air, necessary both to roots and beneficial soil-dwelling organisms, is thus unable to enter the soil. Soil texture, a low-lying location, and hardpan (see below) can all contribute to poor drainage.

As noted earlier, clay soils often drain poorly. To improve the situation, work in plenty of organic matter. Planting in raised beds filled with good, well-drained soil is another option.

Poor drainage may also occur naturally in the garden's low spots. Solving the problem may require installing drainage tiles to carry away excess water. If this is impractical, consider adapting your garden to the site and growing plants suited to moist areas.

A simple way to check drainage in various parts of your garden is shown above right.

Hardpan is an impervious layer of soil that can cause trouble when it lies near the surface. Hardpan is found naturally in some regions—in the Southwest, for example, where the most common natural hardpan layer is called caliche. Hardpan can also be created, as when builders spread excavated subsoil over the soil surface and then repeatedly drive heavy equipment over it. In either case, though a thin layer of topsoil may conceal the hardpan, roots cannot penetrate it nor water drain through it.

To check drainage, dig a 2-foot-deep hole and fill it with water. After it drains, fill it again. If this second amount of water drains away quickly (in an hour or less), the drainage is good. If it remains for several hours or longer, the soil drains poorly.

If the hardpan layer is thin and close to the surface, it may be possible to break it up by having the soil plowed to a depth of 1 foot or more. If plowing is impractical, you may be able to drill through the hardpan with a soil auger when planting, creating a drainage chimney as shown below. Thick hardpan, however, may require the installation of a subsurface drainage system, a project that usually requires hiring a contractor. Growing plants in raised beds filled with good soil is another alternative.

If hardpan is close enough to the soil surface to interfere with root growth and impede drainage, you can form a "chimney"—a narrow passage to the more porous soil beneath—when planting trees and shrubs. Drill through the hardpan with a soil auger; in severe cases, a jackhammer may be needed.

Soil pH. Soil ranges from acid through neutral to alkaline. This characteristic is stated as a pH number. Soil with a pH of 7 is neutral—neither acid nor alkaline. A pH below 7 indicates acidity, while one above 7 indicates alkalinity. The soil's degree of acidity or alkalinity primarily affects the availability of certain nutrients. If the pH is extreme in either direction, key nutrients are chemically "tied up" in the soil and not available to plant roots. The best way to determine your soil's pH is to have the soil tested (see "Testing Your Soil," page 708).

THE pH SCALE

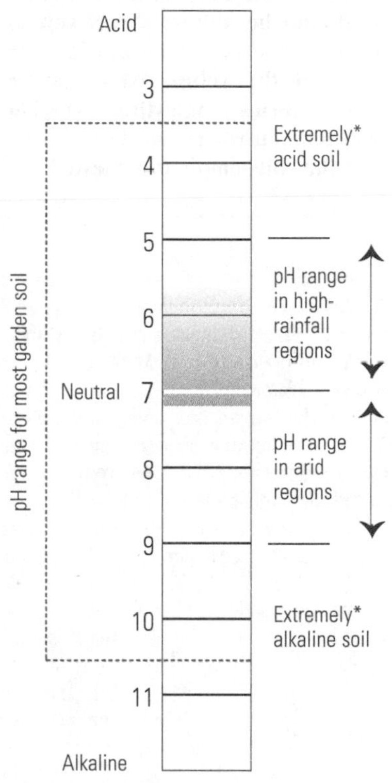

*Soils nearing extremes require professional intervention to modify pH.

Acid soil is most common in regions where rainfall is heavy and is often associated with sandy soils and those high in organic matter. In the West, overly acid soil typically occurs in Alaska, western Washington, Oregon, British Columbia, along the northern coast of California, and in parts of Hawaii. Though most plants grow well in mildly acid soil, highly acid soils are inhospitable. Adding calcium carbonate (lime) is often suggested to raise pH. Follow the recommendations of your soil test lab for amounts to apply.

S

TESTING YOUR SOIL

A soil test and analysis will determine your soil's pH (acidity or alkalinity) and can also reveal nutrient deficiencies. The simple test kits sold at nurseries can give you a general indication of your soil's condition; for a more precise reading, have the test done at a laboratory. In some Western states, the Cooperative Extension Office will test your soil, but even if it does not, it should be able to direct you to commercial soil laboratories. Or look in the yellow pages under "Laboratories—Analytical." The lab will tell you where and how to collect the soil sample to be tested.

To use this pH soil test kit, mix the provided solution with a bit of soil; the resulting color is compared with the color chart that indicates pH.

Alkaline soil, found in many regions of the West where rainfall is typically light, is high in calcium carbonate (lime). Many plants grow well in moderately alkaline soil; others, notably camellias, rhododendrons, and azaleas, do not, because the alkalinity reduces the availability of certain elements (including iron and zinc) necessary for their growth.

Sulfur can be used to lower soil pH; follow the testing lab's recommendation for amounts to apply. You can also lower the pH of alkaline soil over time with regular (at least annual) applications of organic amendments such as compost or well-composted (aged) manure. Another option for growing plants that need acid soil is to plant them in containers or raised beds filled with an appropriate soil mix. (However, if your water is alkaline, the remedies just described are unlikely to be effective.)

Salty soils. Salty soils are found near the seashore and in arid regions. They can also result from the overuse of fertilizers and fresh manures. Excess salts in the soil affect plants by "pulling" water from the roots, making it difficult for plants to take up enough moisture or nutrients; symptoms include scorched and yellowed leaves or browned and withered leaf margins. Seed germination is also inhibited. Salty soils include *saline* and *sodic* types.

Saline soils contain unusually large quantities of any of several soluble salts, such as compounds of calcium, sulfate, chloride, or sodium. To correct the condition, you can improve drainage by adding organic matter and leach the soil periodically with water to wash the salts below the plants' root zones.

Sodic soils, on the other hand, are specifically high in insoluble sodium, which bonds to soil particles; such soils are alkaline and poorly drained (they're also known as black alkali). To correct the problem, you must displace the sodium. In many areas, it's effective to incorporate calcium sulfate (gypsum), then leach the soil to wash away the sodium. However, if the calcium level of your soil is already high (a soil test can tell you this), a better course is to lower the alkalinity by incorporating organic amendments or through the use of sulfur. Check with a soil-testing laboratory or with your Cooperative Extension Office for advice specific to your area's soils.

ORGANIC SOIL AMENDMENTS. The decaying remains of plants and animals, organic matter is vital to maintaining the fertility of all soils and is especially necessary in soils high in clay and sand. Gardeners incorporate organic soil amendments to improve or maintain a soil's structure and to encourage healthy populations of beneficial soil-dwelling microorganisms.

As organic matter decomposes, it releases nutrients that increase fertility. However, the nitrogen released by decaying organic matter isn't immediately available to plants. It must first be converted by various microorganisms (such as bacteria, fungi, actinomycetes) into ammonia, then into nitrites, and, finally, into nitrates, which can be absorbed by plant roots. The final product of the breakdown of organic matter is humus, a soft, sticky material that decomposes slowly and improves soil structure.

The microorganisms that ultimately produce humus require a certain amount of soil moisture, air, and warmth. Soils high in organic matter tend to contain relatively high populations of these organisms. Earthworms are also plentiful in soils rich in organic matter; as they tunnel along, they improve drainage and aeration, while their castings add nutrients.

Many types of organic amendments are available in the West, either commercially packaged or sold in bulk. One choice is manure, which contains more nutrients than most other amendments (manures should be aged well to avoid adding excess salts to the soil). Compost is an excellent amendment; see page 661 for more on homemade compost. Municipal compost is made from grass clippings, leaves, and tree prunings gathered and composted by municipal agencies, then sold or given to local residents. Mushroom compost, a by-product of mushroom farming, is available in some areas; it tends to be high in salts, so use it in smaller quantities than other composts.

Peat moss increases acidity and is thus often used to amend soils around acid-loving plants. There is, however, concern over the ecological damage that may result from the depletion of this natural resource. Some gardeners prefer to use coir dust—a by-product of the coconut fiber industry—instead. For more on this renewable resource, see page 663.

If you add raw (green or uncomposted) organic matter to your soil as an amendment, it may be proportionally higher in carbon than in nitrogen. During the time soil organisms are breaking down high-carbon materials, they require nitrogen and may temporarily compete with plants for nitrogen available in the soil. (Of course, once the organic material has had time

Shown here are some common soil amendments and mulches. *From left to right:* The first two bags hold organic compost, an excellent soil amendment. The next three bags contain mulching materials: shredded bark, redwood mulch, and forest bark. The last bag holds peat moss, often used to amend soil around acid-loving plants.

to decompose, it will release extra nitrogen into the soil.) For this reason, high-carbon soil amendments such as sawdust, wood shavings, and ground bark should be bolstered with nitrogen before use. Some materials can be purchased already fortified with nitrogen; an example is redwood soil conditioner made from the bark and sawdust of redwood trees and treated with nitrogen. If you use unfortified amendments, mix a nitrogen fertilizer into them.

Using organic amendments. Be generous when adding organic amendments. When preparing a new planting bed, spread a 3- to 4-inch layer of amendment over the soil and dig or till it into the top 9 to 12 inches.

Around established plantings, you can add organic material to the soil by spreading it over the soil surface as a mulch; earthworms, microorganisms, and water will help mix it into the top layer of soil. (Note that peat moss is not very effective as a mulch; once it dries out, it's hard to moisten again, and it may blow away. To use peat as an amendment, always mix it into the top few inches of soil.) If the established plants are deep rooted—as are most mature trees and shrubs, for example—you can gently work the amendment into the top inch or so of soil, using a three-pronged cultivator.

SOIL POLYMERS

When added to soil, tiny gel-like soil polymers absorb hundreds of times their weight in rain or irrigation water that would otherwise drain away—holding it (and the dissolved nutrients it contains) for plants to use. The gel's ability to retain water means that plants still have a steady source of moisture when the soil itself is dry. This helps them grow better—since they don't suffer from wide fluctuations in moisture—and lets you stretch the time between waterings. Soil polymers are most often used in potting mixes; in fact, some kinds come with a polymer already incorporated. However, they're also useful in outdoor planting beds in areas with limited rainfall.

Various brands of polymers are available. Sorts containing polyacrylamide are the longest lasting, staying effective for up to 10 years. To do their job, polymers must be mixed into the soil, since root hairs have to grow into the particles to extract water. Mix the dry gel with water to expand the particles, then blend them evenly into the soil at the rate recommended by the manufacturer. Note that if you add too great an amount of gel, the particles will ooze to the surface when the soil is moistened by rain or irrigation. Too much gel can also result in overly wet soil, leading to root rot.

Tools

Stores, nurseries, and specialized mail-order catalogs offer gardening tools in bewildering array. This section describes a number of useful tools—many of them quite versatile—and offers tips for selecting them and using them comfortably and efficiently.

SHOVELS. With their wide, dished heads, *round-point shovels* are efficient soil movers. Use them to loosen soil, pick it up, and transfer it to a pile or wheelbarrow; they're also a good choice for digging planting holes. Select a larger round-point shovel (such as one with a 9-inch-long, 12-inch-wide head) for general digging. If you're working in a confined space, you may find it more convenient to use a smaller model (a *floral shovel*), which has a 6- by 8-inch head and a shorter handle.

Round-point shovels vary in lift—the angle formed between the ground and the shovel handle when the shovel head is laid flat on the ground. To make digging easier by minimizing the amount of bending you'll have to do, choose a tool with generous lift.

Square-nose shovels and *scoops* are not meant for digging. They're used to scoop up loose material such as compost or gravel from a flat surface and move it to a different spot. They come in various sizes; choose one that will pick up the greatest amount of material you can lift repeatedly without tiring.

SPADES. In contrast to shovels, spades have longer, narrower, relatively flat heads. They're used to prepare soil for planting, to dig narrow, straight-sided trenches, and (sometimes) to prune roots.

Most familiar and most generally useful is the *English garden spade*, which has an almost flat blade (about 7 inches wide by 11 inches long) and forward-turned steps (the ledge at the top of the blade where you place your foot when you dig). The handle—often a short D type—extends almost straight up from the blade with little or no lift.

Border spades are smaller, with blades about 6 inches wide and 8 inches long. As the name indicates, they're handy in confined spaces such as flower beds and borders. At the opposite extreme in size are various spades with long, narrow blades, such as *transplanting spades,* which have slightly dished blades about 5 inches wide and 14 or 16 inches long.

SPADING FORKS. Substitutes for spades in clay or rocky soils, spading forks (also called digging forks) help fracture large clods of soil, breaking them into smaller clumps. Like spades, they come with shorter D handles or longer straight handles.

When you shop for a spading fork, look for one that has four tines that are square or rectangular in cross-section and about ½ inch wide. Tines this thick help concentrate your pulling strength, and they don't bend easily.

MANURE FORKS. These tools (as well as pitch forks and compost forks) aren't for spading. Instead, they're used to move manure or piles of prunings or to turn compost. Various styles in a range of sizes and weights are available; they have four or more tines. For a long-lasting fork, look for one with forged tines rather than welded ones. A T-shaped handle makes turning compost easier.

HOES. You'll find hoes designed for a variety of jobs, including cultivating, moving soil, digging furrows, and removing weeds. *Conventional* or *American-style garden hoes* have flat front edges to cut weeds off at ground level and sharp corners that work like small picks. The most common kind has a 6-inch-wide blade. Narrower (2½-inch-wide) blades are useful for light jobs in tight spots; a wider (8-inch) blade is ideal for paths and driveways.

So-called V hoes come in blade sizes varying from 1 by 3 inches to 4 by 6 inches. The most common is the *Warren hoe,* which is especially useful in vegetable gardens. Use the point to make small furrows, and the sides—well sharpened—to slice weeds.

Eye hoes and *grape hoes* are heavy-duty hoes with wide, deep blades set perpendicular to the handle. They are used for breaking ground, chopping tough weeds, scraping away dense growth, and moving soil.

A number of hoes are intended specifically for weeding. These hoes have little or no blade surface and are used with the blade parallel to the ground (or nearly so). They come in a variety of sizes and shapes, such as circle, diamond, stirrup, rectangle, arrowhead, and scuffle. However, there are only three variables in the way they function: they may be push hoes, draw hoes, or scuffle hoes (which cut on both the push and draw strokes). When using any of these hoes, the idea is to run the blade just under the soil surface to cut off weeds at ground level. Disturb the soil as little as possible to avoid bringing more weed seeds to the surface, where they will be able to germinate.

RAKES. *Garden* or *soil rakes* have thick steel tines, either straight or curved. The tines may be attached to the handle directly by a tang or socket, or indirectly by a curving bow. The bow type has more spring or resilience. These types of rakes are used to break up clods of dirt, level the soil, tamp seedbeds to make them firm, and work amendments into the top few inches of a planting bed.

Soil rakes are available with 6, 8, 14, or 16 tines. Select a rake with some weight in its head; if it's too light, you'll have to work harder to provide the downward force needed to break clods or move soil.

Leaf rakes have wide, thin, flat, springy tines. In the best ones, the tines are closely spaced and curve downward and slightly inward at the tip; they're arranged in a curving fan with a stabilizing brace about 8 inches up from the tip of the tines. Metal tines will last longer than those

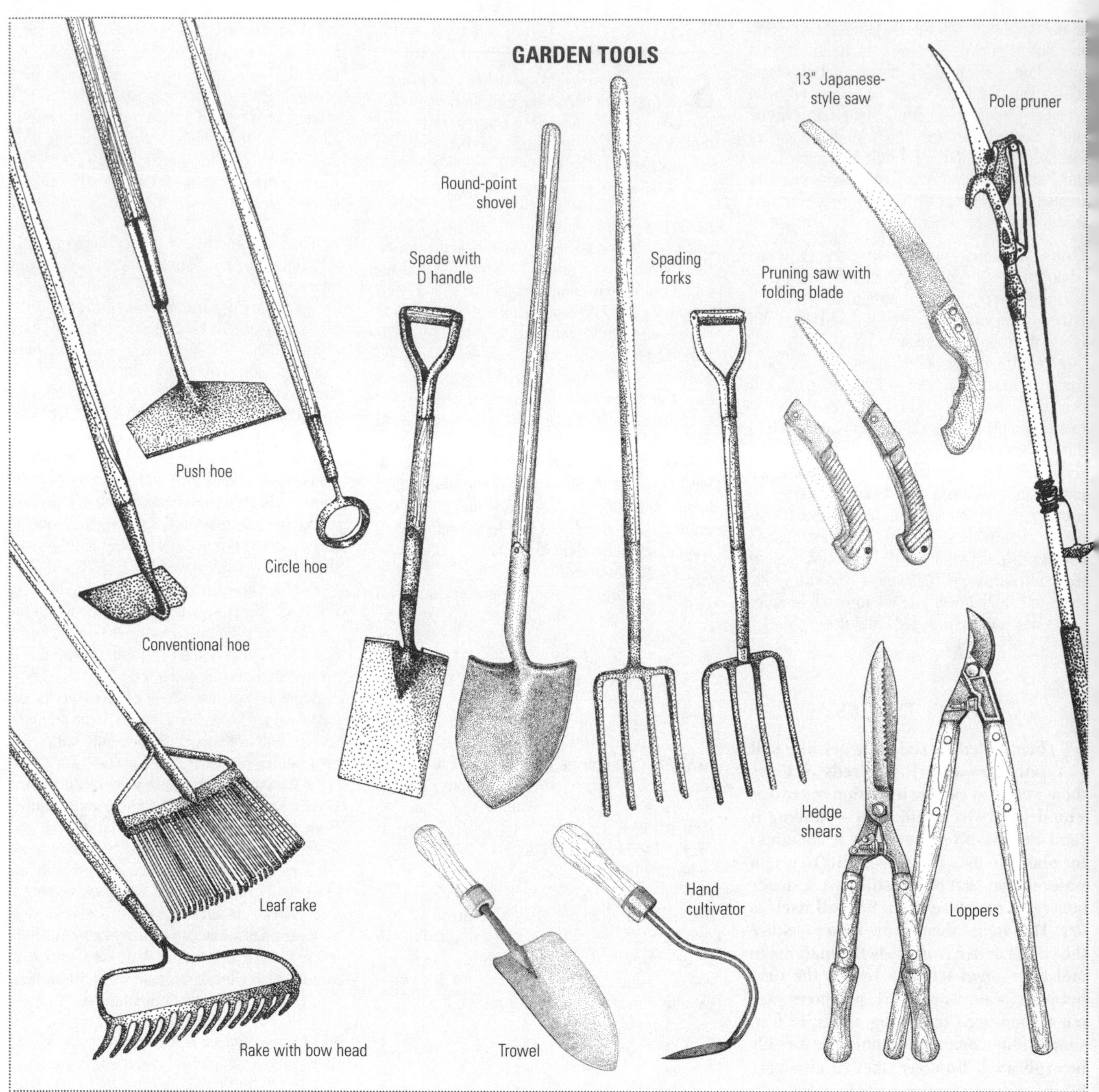

SELECTING TOOLS: HANDLES AND HEADS

When choosing tools for your garden, look for high-quality tools that fit your body type. For example, shovels, spades, and spading forks are available with either shorter D-type handles or long handles. D handles are best for shorter, smaller gardeners (though they're also useful in confined spaces), but tall people are usually more comfortable using long-handled tools. If possible, buy hoes, cultivators, and rakes that are at least as tall (preferably an inch taller) than you are; this allows you to use them in a standing rather than a stooping position.

Handles made of straight-grained, knot-free wood are generally the best choice for most garden tools (make sure handle and head are attached with a rivet that passes all the way through the handle). Tubular aluminum handles are easily bent, while tubular fiberglass ones can be shattered, especially on heavily used digging tools. What's more, these handles are usually narrower in diameter than wooden ones and thus more tiring to grasp for long periods.

Forging—heating metal until it is almost molten, then pounding it into shape—produces a denser tool head that is less likely to bend or break and takes an edge better than less-expensive stamped steel. Highly polished, forged stainless steel tools are preferred by some gardeners because they don't rust and they slide easily into the soil. However, they're somewhat more brittle than tools made of conventional carbon steel, which makes them more difficult to sharpen and more likely to fracture if they are used improperly.

made of bamboo or polypropylene. In addition to raking leaves, these rakes are useful for gathering grass clippings and other lightweight materials into piles.

A leaf rake should be light but sturdy, allowing you to apply firm pressure to the ground with a minimum of effort. Widths may be as great as 4 feet—ideal for large properties with lots of deciduous trees. Smaller versions (only 8 or 10 inches wide) are useful for raking between shrubs and perennials.

A *thatching rake* is used to clear thatch out of lawn grasses. It has semicircular metal tines that are attached with the rounded edge facing forward. When you use this rake, you keep the head on the ground. Pulled through dense grass, the tines rip out thatch; the push or forward stroke clears material from the tines.

CULTIVATORS. These tools may have only one tine or two to five tines, spaced 1½ to 2 inches apart. The tines may be long or short, curved or straight; the tine ends are pointed in some models, flattened to form a lozenge-shaped tooth in others. Use cultivators to break up compacted soil around plants, keeping it loose and friable, and to work amendments into the upper few inches of soil; they are also effective for weeding.

Select a narrow cultivator if you plan to cultivate between closely spaced plants or if your soil is heavy; the fewer the tines, the more concentrated your pulling force will be. A cultivator with tines arranged in a V shape rather than lined up in a row is also easier to pull through heavy soils. If plants are widely spaced, a four- or five-tine cultivator is more practical; it also works best in sandy or well-amended soils.

A single-tine cultivator is known as a *finger hoe.* If you sharpen the sides of its tooth or tine, you can use it both for nicking weeds out of small spaces and for cultivating.

HALF-MOON EDGER. This tool is used to maintain a neat edge between lawn and adjacent beds of flowers or ground covers. You can also use it to edge between lawn and paving.

HAND TOOLS. In addition to scaled-down versions of hoes and cultivators, hand tools include knives, dibbles, specialized weeders—and, of course, the indispensable trowel.

Trowels. Though principally planting tools, trowels are also useful for cultivating, weeding, and scooping fertilizers and other soil amendments from bags.

A trowel should be both strong and sharp; the best ones are made of forged steel and have a wooden handle driven and pinned into a socket at the base of the blade. For general use, select one with a shallowly dished blade about 4 inches wide and 6 inches long. *Transplanting trowels* are narrower (about 3 inches wide), tapered, and deeply dished; they may have marks on the blade to help you gauge planting depth. *Potting trowels* are even narrower—about 2½ inches wide—and only shallowly dished. *Crevice* or rockery trowels are just 1 inch wide; they are invaluable for weeding as well as for planting a rock garden.

DIGGING AND HOEING

Learning to dig and hoe properly can literally save your back. When digging with a shovel, don't drive the tool into the ground at a low angle, bend over to lever the soil loose, and then lift with your back bent. Instead, drive the shovel blade straight down, as close to your body as you can manage comfortably. The shovel handle will angle away from you. When you've driven the blade in as far as possible, step back with the foot that is not on the shovel's step or tread and pull the handle toward the center of your chest. Then, grasping the handle at the top with one hand and sliding the other hand toward the bottom, bend your knees and lower your body, keeping your back straight. Lift the shovelful of soil, using the strength of your legs, not your back.

Using a spade involves the same techniques, except that you'll usually be turning the soil over in a bed instead of lifting and moving it.

When using a hoe, rake, or cultivator, stand sideways to the work—as if you were using a kitchen broom. Grasp the handle with your thumbs wrapped around it near the top. As you work, flex your knees slightly and pull the tool across the front of your body. This position keeps your back straight and, if you hit a buried rock or large root, you'll naturally pull with the strong muscles in your upper legs instead of straining your lower back.

Knives. A sturdy knife comes in handy for diverse tasks: dividing roots of plants, opening bags of soil or soil amendments, carving points on the ends of wooden stakes. The *Japanese farmer's knife* (Hori Hori) features a slightly dished blade that can be used as a trowel; one side of the blade is saw-toothed, while the other has a sharp edge that can cut roots and burlap.

Dibbles. These are used to poke holes in prepared soil to plant bulbs, bedding plants, and vegetable starts. They are usually carrot shaped, with an iron point and a rounded or T-shaped handle.

Weeders. Look for a hand weeder with a bent shaft or with a ball attached to the shaft to serve as a fulcrum, giving you leverage to pop weeds out of the ground. The weeder's head should be small and forked.

PRUNING TOOLS. Shears and saws for pruning come in many different forms and sizes—not surprising, when you consider that pruning cuts and techniques (not to mention the plants being pruned) vary, too (see "Pruning," page 702).

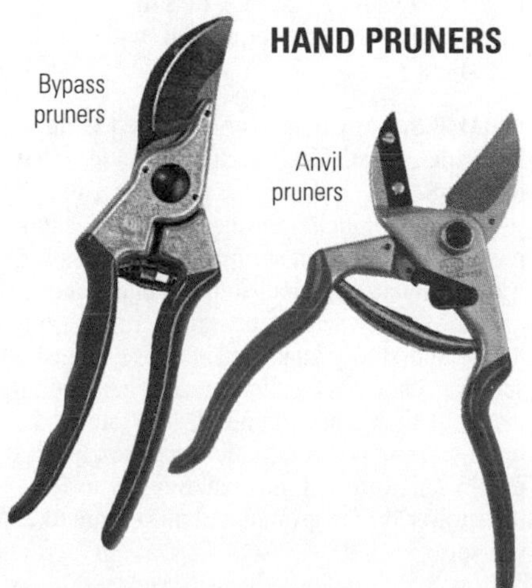

Hand pruners. Many gardeners take this tool with them whenever they go into the garden, carrying it in a leather case that clips to a belt or pants pocket. There are two basic types. *Bypass pruners* have a curved hook and a curved blade. The branch to be cut rests against the hook; the blade cuts it, passing the hook as it slices through the branch. In some models, the cutting blade bends away from the handle at an angle up to 45°; this gives you more cutting power and minimizes strain on your wrists. *Anvil pruners* have a flat anvil (instead of a hook) and a straight blade; the blade cuts through the branch until it hits the anvil.

Hand pruners should not be used on any branch thicker than your little finger; doing so risks damaging the plant, the tool, or both. Use a lopper or a saw instead.

Loppers. These powerful branch cutters have long handles that give you much more leverage than the short handles of hand pruners. They range from 1 to 3 feet in length and may have either bypass or anvil construction. Smaller loppers can substitute for hand pruners if you lack the hand strength needed to operate the latter; they're also good for cutting among thorny branches without scratching your hands and arms. The cutting capacity of loppers (that is, the diameter of branch they can cut) is the distance between the center of the blade and the center of the hook or anvil when the blades are opened at right angles to each other. The largest loppers will cut 3-inch-thick branches. A good in-between size for most garden jobs, capable of cutting branches up to 2 inches thick, is a 26-inch model. Be sure to select loppers with strong handles, preferably bolted on. A shock absorber, located below the pivot point, saves wear on your arms.

Pruning saws. If a branch is too large to cut with hand pruners or loppers, use a pruning saw. In contrast to carpenter's saws, most modern pruning types cut on the pull rather than the push stroke. They may have straight or

CARING FOR GARDEN TOOLS

Given proper care, well-made tools not only make gardening easier but will last for generations. All tools need cleaning after use, and any tool with an edge—be it a shovel, spade, hoe, or pruning tool—should be kept sharp. When blades eventually become dull, it's easiest to have a professional restore them; many garden supply and hardware stores can recommend a reliable sharpening service.

Cleaning tools. To remove accumulated sap and rust from pruning shears, use a little oil and steel wool; you can also buy special oil/solvent mixtures (such as CLP Shear Oil) to clean sap and dirt from pruning tools and to lubricate them. To maintain the smoothest operation, occasionally disassemble the tool and work a dab of synthetic white lithium grease onto the pivot bolt and into the area around the bolt hole.

Clean the sawdust from pruning saws after each use and remove any sap and rust with steel wool and oil. Apply a thin coat of paraffin to the blade before using.

A barbecue brush (with scraper) is handy for cleaning digging tools. Use the scraper to remove layers of dirt and mud as you work in the garden. The bristles give a final cleanup before you store the tool.

Give tool heads a thorough cleaning annually. Remove rust with medium steel wool and a little oil; then use paint thinner to clean off the oily residue. Finally, apply a rust-proofing paint.

Maintaining wooden handles. Wooden handles on all types of garden tools last for many years if kept clean and oiled. Wipe them off after every use. Once a year or so, sand them lightly and apply a coat of boiled linseed oil with a cloth; if the oil soaks in completely, apply another coat. Then buff the handles.

curved blades; a curved one fits more easily into tight spots between branches. They may also have fixed or folding blades. Some models come with gullets—deep slots about every fourth tooth that accumulate and release sticky sawdust, so cutting teeth don't get gummed up.

Older-style saws have teeth bent slightly to right and left. When used, such a saw makes a wide kerf (slot), preventing binding. Newer types omit this feature; instead, each tooth is ground on three edges. These models (sometimes referred to as *Japanese-style saws*) cut much more rapidly and give a smoother cut. They can snap if you apply too much force or try to cut on the push stroke, and they cannot be resharpened, but most gardeners feel that their ease of use and cutting speed more than make up for any drawbacks. A 13-inch Japanese-style saw with a fixed blade is a good choice for most gardens; it easily cuts branches 1 to 5 inches in diameter. Call an arborist if you need to cut larger branches.

Pole pruning tools. Look to these when you need extra reach for cutting high branches. They typically come with both shears and a saw, which you attach to a pole. To make the shears work, pull a cord or press a lever to draw the blade through the branch; most will cut through branches ¾ to 1 inch thick. The saw is usually a standard pull-cut curved saw. The poles are available in various lengths; some are telescoping, while others fit together in sections. In either case, the pruners will be easiest to use if the poles are fairly stiff.

Hedge shears. In addition to trimming hedges, these are useful for shearing flowering shrubs and cutting back perennials. For heavy-duty pruning of hedges with dense, woody growth, select shears with a short (7-inch) blade. One blade will often be serrated and notched; the notch helps to hold the bigger twigs in place while you cut. Hedge shears with longer blades (up to 11 inches) are meant for light-duty shearing of leafy tip growth; the longer blades shear a larger area with each stroke. Be sure any hedge shears you buy are equipped with shock absorbers.

SPRAYERS. Garden sprayers are used to apply fungicides, pesticides, herbicides, and foliar fertilizers. Many styles and sizes are available. If you don't do much spraying, a 1-quart, hand-pumped compression sprayer is a good choice; it allows you to mix small amounts of chemicals, avoiding waste. Select one with a brass spray nozzle and sturdy innards. For more extensive spraying, choose a 2-gallon capacity hand pump model. It should have a polyethylene tank and a brass valve wand, adjustable brass nozzle, and pump. An extra-long hose allows you to leave the sprayer on the ground and move around as you spray.

Trees

Trees are the backbone of the garden, providing shade and shelter and bringing year-round beauty through their foliage, flowers, fruits, bark, and branch structure. The distinction between a tree and a large shrub is sometimes blurred, but trees typically are tall plants with one dominant trunk (though some kinds may have several trunks) topped by a crown of foliage. In contrast, most shrubs are smaller and have foliage all the way to the ground.

SELECTING TREES. Because trees are so important to the landscape and are generally slow growing, it's worth taking the time to choose them carefully. Start by considering the points below; also consult local nursery personnel and look at the trees in your neighborhood to see which ones perform particularly well. "Garden Trees" in A Guide to Plant Selection (beginning on page 64) lists trees suitable for many situations.

Landscape function. What role should the tree play in your garden? If you need a source of shade, choose a tree with a wide canopy. Deciduous trees give you shade (and can significantly reduce air-conditioning expenses) in summer, then admit sun to warm the house after their leaves drop in fall. If you want to block views into your home or garden, choose relatively tall, dense trees. If you're looking for a specimen tree to serve as a garden focal point, search for interesting foliage or a striking display of blossoms or berries. Fruit trees have special appeal, providing delicious fruit as well as lovely form and flowers.

Climate adaptability. Be sure that any tree you consider planting is well adapted to your climate zone.

Cultural preferences. Match the needs of each tree to the conditions in your garden. Select those that will grow well in the soil you have, with the amount of water they'll receive naturally or that you can provide.

Deciduous versus evergreen. Deciduous trees start their growth with a burst of new leaves (and often flowers) in early spring, then remain in leaf through summer. In autumn, the foliage drops to reveal bare limbs, often changing color before it falls.

Evergreen trees include both broad-leafed evergreens and conifers (though there are a few deciduous conifers); both kinds serve well as screens and windbreaks. Broad-leafed evergreens have the same sort of foliage as deciduous plants, but they keep their leaves all year. Older leaves may fall intermittently throughout the year or in one season, but there's always enough foliage on the branches to give the tree a well-clothed look. Most conifers have leaves that are narrow and needlelike or tiny and scalelike; they may drop some of their leaves year-round.

STAKING YOUNG TREES

A young tree will develop a sturdier trunk if it grows unsupported and can sway in the breeze. Stake it only if it is planted in an extremely windy location or if the main trunk is too weak to stay upright on its own. Use ties that won't bind or cut into the bark, such as wide strips of canvas or rubber; fasten each tie around the tree and both stakes in a figure-8 pattern, as shown at right. The tree should be able to move an inch in either direction.

To figure out where to attach the ties to a weak trunk, run your hand up the trunk, holding it firmly, and stop when you find the point where the top of the tree no longer flops over. This is the point where you will attach the ties. Cut off the stakes an inch or so above the ties. In a windswept site, a young tree's roots may need anchoring to keep them in firm contact with the soil; use stakes and ties only a foot above ground level for this kind of staking. In both cases, sink stakes at right angles to the prevailing wind. Remove them after a year or as soon as the tree appears to be self-supporting.

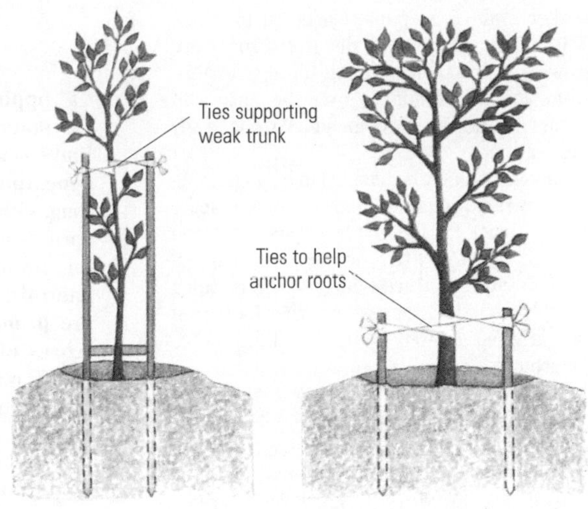

Growth rate and size. Different trees grow at different rates. If you need a tree to shade a south-facing window or provide privacy, select a fast-growing sort for quick results—but take care not to choose one that will outgrow its site. In fact, it's important to visualize the ultimate height and spread of a tree you consider for any role: not only is an overly large one out of scale in most gardens, but it will eventually crowd structures and other plants and may ultimately have to be removed.

Root system. A tree with a network of greedy surface roots is a poor candidate for planting in a lawn or garden, since it will hog most of the water and nutrients. The same tree may be just right, however, at the garden's fringes or along a country drive. Some trees have surface roots that can lift and crack nearby pavement, making them less-than-ideal choices for a patio, entryway, or parking strip.

Maintenance. Trees that produce a fair amount of litter from falling leaves, flowers, or fruits shouldn't be planted beside a patio, in a lawn, or near a swimming pool—you'd be spending far too much time cleaning up. Such trees are better candidates for background areas, where the litter can remain where it falls. In regions with regular high winds or heavy annual snowfall, avoid trees with weak or brittle wood: they can be hazardous to people and property, and removing broken limbs can both ruin the tree's beauty and cost you a tidy sum.

Pest and disease problems. Make sure the trees you're considering aren't overly susceptible to pests or diseases. Keep in mind that a particular tree may be trouble free in one climate but plagued with problems in another.

Longevity. Some trees can be planted for future generations to enjoy; others grow quickly but also decline quickly. Trees that are planted for screening or shade should be long lived, but for specimen planting, shorter-lived kinds may be an excellent choice. Plant the latter, however, only where removal will be relatively easy and won't compromise your overall landscape. Many attractive flowering trees, for example, run their course in about 20 years, but when they die you can fill the resulting gap with another tree of the same sort.

PLANTING AND CARING FOR TREES. Many deciduous trees are sold bare-root during the dormant season from late fall through early spring. Deciduous trees as well as conifers and broad-leafed evergreens may also be sold balled-and-burlapped from early fall into the following spring, or in containers throughout the year. For instructions on planting all types, see pages 692–694.

The exposed trunk of a newly planted tree needs protection from drying winds, hot sun, freezing temperatures, gnawing animals (such as rabbits, deer, and rodents), and damage from lawn mowers or string trimmers. To keep a trunk free from harm, wrap it loosely in burlap or a manufactured trunk-wrapping material. Remove the wrapping after a year, when the bark has become thicker and tougher (don't leave wrapping in place longer than this, since it can eventually girdle the tree).

All trees, even drought-tolerant kinds, need regular water during the first several years after planting, until their roots have grown deep enough to carry them through dry periods. Once established, however, many kinds require only infrequent irrigation.

Regular fertilizing, too, is needed for a few years after planting. By ensuring a good supply of nitrogen for the springtime growth surge, you'll encourage young trees to get established quickly. Once a tree is well settled in, though, it may grow satisfactorily with no further feeding—and in fact, fertilizing a tree that continues to put out healthy, vigorous new growth is a waste of both time and fertilizer. Feeding may be in order, however, if a tree's new growth is weak, sparse, or unusually pale, or if it has a fair amount of dieback that cannot be ascribed to over- or underwatering.

TRAINING AND PRUNING. Most young trees benefit from some early training or pruning. The idea is to encourage the development of a sturdy trunk from which radiate strong, well-placed main limbs (scaffold branches). Conifers are an exception: they seldom need training unless they develop more than one leader (central upward-growing stem). If that occurs, remove the weaker of the two stems. Deciduous and broad-leafed evergreen trees, on the other hand, are more likely to require training, but don't rush the job. Prune newly planted trees as little as possible: just remove dead, broken, or rubbing branches and the

FORMING A STRONG TREE TRUNK

Young trees develop a strong trunk more quickly if their lower branches are left in place for the first few years after planting; these branches also help shade the trunk. During this time, shorten the side branches only if they become too long or vigorous, pruning during the dormant season or just before spring growth begins. Once the trunk is at least 2 inches thick, begin removing the lower branches gradually, over a period of several years.

weaker limb of a double leader (if present). Wait a full year—until the tree's roots are growing well—before doing more than this. Prune the tree gradually over the next 3 to 5 years, but don't remove too much wood in any one year.

Though you may be tempted to begin training a tree by removing lower limbs, it's best to leave these in place for the first few years, as shown on page 713. Don't remove the lower limbs of conifers such as spruces, firs, and others with a strongly pyramidal shape at all. They look most natural when allowed to branch all the way to the ground.

As the tree grows, encourage well-placed scaffold branches by selecting shoots at fairly evenly spaced intervals, both up the trunk and spiraling around it. Whenever possible, favor wide-angled branches forming more-or-less U-shaped crotches over narrow-angled ones that have V-shaped crotches. If the angle is very narrow, branches tend to be weakly attached to the trunk and split off easily. Remove badly placed and superfluous branches before they become too large, keeping the ultimate shape of the tree in mind. Also remove suckers, water sprouts, and lateral branches growing toward the center of the tree.

For more information on pruning methods, including instructions for removing large limbs, see page 704.

WHAT'S WRONG WITH TOPPING?

Topping—reducing the height of a mature tree by sawing off its top limbs—is the fastest way to ruin a tree's appearance. It doesn't reduce height for long, either. Unlike a bushy hedge that soon sprouts new growth even after severe shearing, an older tree does not grow back in a natural-looking way when its upper limbs are pruned to stubs. Instead, it sends out scores of weak shoots from buds near the cutoff points, and these shoots are often taller, coarser, denser, and more weakly attached than the natural top was. Topping may also shorten a tree's life, both because the resultant large wounds are exposed to decay and insect attack and because the process removes much of the leafy growth needed to manufacture food for the plant.

Though some topped trees can eventually recover their form, it may take decades. A good professional arborist will not top a tree that has grown too large for its space, but instead will gradually scale it back by making thinning cuts to groups of branches in the upper part of the canopy.

Vegetable Gardening

Growing your own vegetables is rewarding and enjoyable. In return for your efforts, you'll harvest food that's fresh and bursting with flavor. To make your vegetable patch a success, plan before you plant. If you're new to vegetable gardening, start small: an area of just 100 to 130 square feet can provide a substantial harvest. As you gain experience, you may elect to expand the plot.

To decide which vegetables to plant, first list the kinds your family really enjoys. Then consider how much room each type requires. If space is limited, raise those that give a good yield for the area they occupy. Beans, tomatoes, and some summer squash, for example, can overwhelm you with produce from a postage stamp–size plot. At the other extreme are melon and squash varieties that grow on long vines; these, as well as corn, require a great deal of space relative to their yield.

Because vegetables grow best with at least 6 hours of full sun each day, be sure to choose a sunny planting area. To avoid both shade and root competition, locate the garden away from trees and large shrubs. It's also important to choose a spot protected from cold winds in spring and hot, dry winds in summer. Steer clear of "frost pockets"—low-lying areas that may experience frosts later in spring and earlier in fall than other parts of the garden. To make watering and other routine tasks easier, aim for a level site; if only sloping land is available, try to find a south- or southeast-facing slope to take full advantage of the sun. Lay out rows along the slope's contours to minimize water runoff and erosion. On very steep sites, constructing terraces will make gardening much easier.

PLANTING VEGETABLES. The first step toward a satisfying vegetable garden is careful soil preparation: you'll be rewarded with faster growth and a substantially larger harvest. Follow the steps on page 690 for preparing your planting bed.

The size and shape of the bed (or beds) will depend on several factors. You may choose to plant vegetables in *rows,* separated by paths that give you access to the plants and let you easily till or hoe the soil. This layout works well for tall-growing plants like corn and for those that need support, such as tomatoes and pole beans. Other plants, however, grow best in *hills*—that is, grouped in a cluster (though not necessarily on a mound). This method is useful for sprawling plants such as most varieties of melons and winter squash. Smaller-growing vegetables, such as beets, carrots, spinach, and lettuce, can be grown efficiently in *wide beds.* In this arrangement, you prepare a bed about 3 feet wide, then broadcast the seeds over it rather than sowing them in rows. Paths on either side allow access to the plants.

If your soil is very poor or does not drain well, you may elect to grow your vegetables in raised beds (see page 690) filled with a mixture of compost and good topsoil.

You can start vegetables by planting seeds outdoors in the garden or by setting out transplants you have either started yourself or purchased from a nursery. Vegetables requiring a long growing season—peppers and tomatoes, for example—need many weeks of warm temperatures before they produce fruit and are best set out as transplants. But other types, including beans, carrots, corn, and peas, do not transplant well and grow best if started from seed sown directly in the garden. For more on sowing seeds and on starting and setting out transplants, see pages 695 and 696.

CARING FOR VEGETABLES. For the best harvest, keep your vegetables growing steadily throughout the season, trying to avoid any checks in their development. Those started from seed sown in the ground usually require thinning, so that each plant will have enough space to develop properly. Thin plants when they're a few inches tall, making sure that you space them as indicated in descriptions provided in the Western Plant Encyclopedia or on the seed packet.

Provide a steady supply of moisture from planting until harvest. Until they're well established, transplants will need frequent watering—enough to keep the soil moist but not soggy. Rows or beds of seeds and young seedlings likewise need steady moisture, sometimes requiring sprinkling as often as two or three times a day in hot weather. As transplants and seedlings grow and their roots reach deeper, you can water less often—but when you do, be sure to moisten the entire root zone thoroughly. To water the garden, use sprinklers, furrows, or a drip system (see "Watering Methods," page 722).

Mulching the garden is important: it conserves moisture and suppresses weed growth. An organic mulch such as straw or compost also improves soil structure as it decomposes, making the top few inches looser and more crumbly. However, because organic mulches also keep the soil cool, it's best not to apply them until warm weather arrives; don't put them down too early in spring. A mulch of plastic sheeting, on the other hand, helps warm the soil quickly—making it especially useful for growing heat-loving crops such as melons and eggplant in regions with cool or short summers. After preparing the soil, cover it with black plastic; then cut small holes where you want to sow seeds or set out plants.

For many vegetables, the fertilizer applied when you prepare the bed at planting time will be sufficient for the entire season. However, heavy feeders (such as corn) and those requiring a long growing season, including tomatoes and some varieties of cabbage and broccoli, may need one or two follow-up feedings. Lightly scratch dry granular fertilizer into the soil (keep it off plant foliage), then water it in thoroughly; or use a water-soluble fertilizer.

As is true for the garden as a whole, caring for a vegetable plot involves preventing pest and disease damage. You'll find information on many diseases and pests and advice for controlling them on pages 664–667, 679–687, and in the entries for specific vegetables in the Western Plant Encyclopedia. The following measures will also help keep your garden productive and healthy.

Keep the garden clean. Composting or discarding spent plants and tilling the soil (especially in fall) can help you avoid trouble, since some insects and diseases overwinter or spend certain developmental stages on plant debris.

Plant resistant varieties when available. Seed packets and plant tags may bear code letters noting inbred resistance to certain serious problems. Tomatoes, for example, may be designated V, F, N, and/or T, indicating resistance to verticillium wilt, fusarium wilt, harmful nematodes (which cause root knots), and tobacco mosaic virus, respectively.

Mix different kinds of plants. Expanses of just one sort can result in large populations of pests fond of that particular plant. Mixed plantings encourage more kinds of insects, including beneficial species that prey on the troublemakers.

Encourage natural controls. Toads, lizards, many birds, and beneficial insects (see page 680) all prey on pests. Avoid chemical sprays, if possible—and be aware that even sprays made from natural ingredients can harm helpful creatures as well as pests, leaving the garden vulnerable to new attack.

Rotate crops from season to season. This tactic prevents the buildup of diseases and insects specific to certain kinds of vegetables in any one part of the garden.

ROW COVERS AND OTHER SEASON EXTENDERS

Warm-season vegetables may need protection from frost when they are first planted in spring, then again as temperatures begin to dip in fall. In spring, individual plants can be protected with various plastic or paper caps known as hotcaps. Also available is a special plastic hotcap for tomatoes; it consists of water-filled cylinders that trap heat effectively.

Floating row covers (shown above) made of polyethylene, polyester, or polypropylene are one of the most useful tools for protecting plants from cold temperatures (and from certain insect pests and birds, as well). Sold in rolls, these fabric-type covers can be laid directly over seeded beds or plants or propped on stakes; they serve as miniature greenhouses. They are extremely lightweight, transmit 80 to 95 percent of the sunlight that strikes them, and allow both water and air to pass through. Burying the cover's edges in the soil will seal out insect pests, though any pests already on the plants may proliferate (remove covers when plants begin to bloom, to admit pollinating insects).

WARM-SEASON AND COOL-SEASON VEGETABLES

Depending on the weather they need for best growth, vegetables are classed as warm-season or cool-season. *Cool-season* crops grow best at temperatures an average of 10 to 15°F/6 to 8°C below those needed by warm-season types. Most will endure short spells of frost. Many familiar cool-season vegetables have edible leaves or roots (lettuce, spinach, carrots, and radishes, for example), while others (such as broccoli, cauliflower, and artichokes) are grown for their immature flowers. A few—peas and broad beans—produce edible seeds. Success depends on bringing plants to maturity in cool weather; in hot conditions, many become bitter tasting and may bolt to seed rather than producing edible parts. Plant them in very early spring—so the crop will mature before summer heat settles in—or in the late part of summer, for a crop in fall or winter. In the West's warmer regions, cool-season vegetables can be planted from late summer to early fall to provide harvests in late fall, winter, and early spring.

For planting schedules for cool-season crops by climate zone, see pages 716–717.

***Warm-season* vegetables require both warm soil and high temperatures (with little cooling at night) to grow steadily and produce a harvest. They include traditional summer crops such as snap beans, corn, cucumbers, melons, peppers, tomatoes, and squash. So-called winter squashes such as acorn, hubbard, and banana are warm-season crops; the name refers not to the planting season, but to the fact that the fruits can be stored for winter consumption. For almost all of these vegetables, the fruit (rather than the leaves or roots) is the edible part. Warm-season vegetables are killed by frost, so don't plant them until after the last frost in spring unless you give them cold protection; see box at left. For planting schedules for warm-season crops by climate zone, see pages 718–719.**

The charts below and on the following pages indicate approximate planting times for annual cool-season and warm-season vegetables. Find the crop you want to grow on the following charts; then check the recommended times for your climate zone. (For information on your climate zones, see pages 27–63). If you garden in a colder part of your zone, choose the later month in the recommended spring planting times; if you are planting in late summer or fall, use the earlier month in the range. Also keep in mind that microclimates may influence planting time. Keeping year-to-year records of specific planting dates will help you pinpoint the best dates for your garden.

PLANTING SCHEDULE FOR COOL-SEASON VEGETABLES

VEGETABLE	ZONES A1–A3	ZONES 1, 2	ZONE 3	ZONES 4, 5	ZONE 6	ZONE 7	ZONES 8, 9	ZONE 10
BEETS (S)	Late May–June	Apr–June	Mar–July	Mar–June, July–Aug	Mar–June	Feb–May, Aug–Sep	Feb–Mar, Aug–Sep	Feb–mid-Apr, July–mid-Aug
BROCCOLI (T)	Late May–June	Apr–June	Apr–July	Mar–June, Aug–Sep	Mar–Aug	Mar–Apr, Aug–Sep	Feb–Mar, Aug–Sep	Mid-Feb–Mar, mid-June–mid-July
BRUSSELS SPROUTS (T)	Late May–June	Apr–June	Apr–July	Mar–June, Aug	May–July	Mar–Apr, Aug	Feb, Aug	Late May–early June
CABBAGE (T)	Late May–June	Apr–June	Apr–July	Mar–June, July–Aug	Apr–June, Aug	Mar–Apr, Aug–Sep	Feb–Mar, Aug–Sep	Mid-Feb–Mar, June–July
CARROTS (S)	Late May–June	Apr–June	Mar–July	Mar–June, Sep–Oct	Mar–July	Mar–May, Aug–Sep	Feb–Apr, Aug–Sep	Mid-Jan–Mar, June–Aug
CAULIFLOWER (T)	Late May–June	Apr–May	Apr–July	Mar–June, Aug	Apr–July	Mar–Apr, Aug–Sep	Feb–Mar, Aug–Sep	Mid-Feb–Mar, mid-June–mid-July
CELERY (T)	Late May–June	May–June	June–Aug	Mar–June	Mar–July	May–July	June–Aug	Mar, Sep
CHARD (S, T)	Late May–June	Mar–June	Feb–May	Feb–May, Aug	Apr–July	Mar–May, Aug–Sep	Feb–Mar, Aug	Feb–mid-Apr, July–mid-Aug
KOHLRABI (S)	Late May–June	Apr–May	Apr–Aug	Mar–June, July–Aug	Apr–Aug	Mar–May, Aug–Sep	Feb–Apr, Aug–Sep	Feb–mid-Apr, July–mid-Aug
LETTUCE (S, T)	Late May–June	Apr–Aug	Feb–Aug	Feb–Aug	Apr–Aug	Mar–May, Aug–Sep	Feb–Mar, Aug–Sep	Dec–Mar, July–Aug
ONIONS, BULBING (S, T)	Late May–June	May–June	Feb–Apr	Mar–May, Aug–Oct	Mar–May, Aug–Oct	Feb–Apr	Dec–Feb, Sep–Oct	Mid-Jan–mid-Mar, early Oct
PEAS (S)	Late May–June	Apr–June	Mar–June	Mar–Aug	Mar–May	Feb–Apr, Aug–Oct	Feb–Mar, Aug–Nov	Mid-Jan–mid-Apr
POTATOES (eyes)	Late May–June	May–June	Mar–June	Feb–Aug	Apr–Aug	Mar–May	Dec–Mar	Feb–Apr
RADISHES (S)	Late May–June	Apr–July	Mar–Sep	Mar–Aug	Mar–Sep	Feb–Apr, Sep–Oct	Feb–Apr, Aug–Oct	Feb–Apr
SPINACH (S)	Late May–June	Apr, July	Feb–Mar, Sep	Feb–Mar, Aug	Apr, Sep	Feb–Apr, Sep–Oct	Sep–Apr	Mid-Jan–mid-Mar, Aug–Sep

S = Plant from seed; T = Plant from transplants; + = Can be planted year-round in some parts of zone.

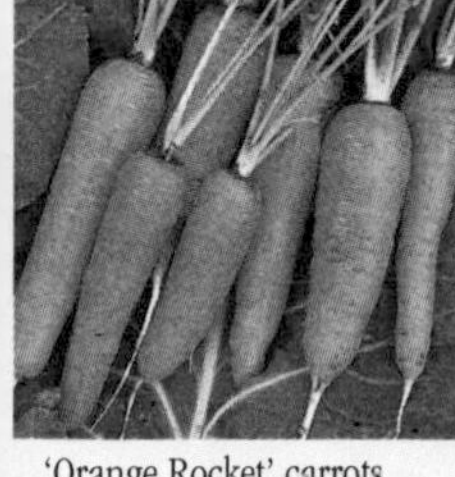
'Orange Rocket' carrots

'Sultan' cabbage

Romaine lettuce

'Green Arrow' peas

Pink new potatoes

Red and white radishes

ZONE 11	ZONE 12	ZONE 13	ZONE 14	ZONES 15, 16	ZONE 17	ZONES 18, 19	ZONES 20, 21	ZONES 22–24	ZONES H1, H2
Feb–Mar, Sep	Feb, mid-Sep–Nov	Feb, Oct–mid-Dec	Feb–Apr, Aug–Sep	Feb–Aug+	Feb–Aug+	Feb–Apr, Aug	Jan–June	Jan–Sep	Year-round
Feb, Sep	Mid-Sep–Oct	Sep–Nov	Feb–Mar, Aug–Sep	Feb–Mar, Aug–Sep	Feb–Apr, Aug–Sep+	Jan–Feb, Sep–Oct	Jan–Mar, July–Nov	Aug–Apr	Oct–Mar+
Feb, Sep	Mid-Sep–Oct	Sep–Nov	Feb, Aug	Feb, Aug	Apr–July	Sep–Oct	Sep–Nov	Feb–Mar, Sep–Nov	Nov–Feb (H1 only)
Feb, Sep	Mid-Sep–Oct	Sep–Nov	Feb–Mar, Aug–Sep	Feb–Mar, Aug–Sep	Feb–Apr, Aug–Sep+	Jan–Feb, Sep–Oct	Aug–Feb	Aug–Mar	Oct–Mar+
Feb–Mar, Sep	Sep–Jan	Sep–Jan	Feb–Apr, Aug–Sep	Feb–Apr, Aug–Sep+	Mar–Oct+	Feb–Apr, Sep	Jan–Sep	Feb–Apr	Nov–Feb+
Feb, Sep	Mid-Sep–Oct	Aug–Nov	Feb–Mar, Aug–Sep	Feb–Mar, Aug–Sep	Feb–Apr, Aug–Sep+	Sep	Jan–Feb, July–Oct	Jan–Feb, July–Aug	Oct–Jan+
Mid-March, Sep	Sep–Oct	Mid-Sep–mid-Oct	June–Aug	Feb–Apr, July–Sep	Feb–Aug+	Feb–Apr, June–Aug	Apr–Aug	Apr–Aug	Nov–Feb
Feb–Mar, Sep	Feb–Mar, Sep–Oct	Jan–Mar, Oct–Nov	Feb–Apr, Aug–Sep	Mar–Apr, Aug+	Year-round	Feb–May, Sep	Jan–May	Year-round	Year-round
Feb–mid-Mar, Sep	Sep–Oct	Mid-Sep–Nov	Feb–Apr, Aug–Sep	Feb–Apr, Aug–Sep	Feb–May, July–Aug+	Jan, Sep–Oct	July–Sep	Year-round	Year-round
Feb, Sep	Feb, Sep–mid-Nov	Mid-Jan–mid-Feb, Sep–mid-Nov	Feb–Apr, Aug–Sep	Feb–Apr, Aug–Sep+	Feb–Nov+	Mar, Oct	Sep–May	Sep–May	Nov–Jan
Mid-Sep–early Oct	Sep–Oct	Mid-Sep–Oct	Jan–Feb, Sep–Oct	Jan–Feb, Sep–Oct	Jan–Mar	Nov–Mar	Nov–Mar	Oct–Nov	Sep–Feb
Mid-Sep–mid-Oct, Feb–mid-Mar	Sep–mid-Nov	Mid-Sep–Nov	Feb–Apr, Aug–Sep	Feb–Mar, Aug–Sep	Feb–Apr, Aug–Nov+	Sep–Jan	Aug, Dec–Mar	Sep–Apr	Oct–Feb+
Mid-Feb–mid-Mar	Jan–Feb	Jan–Feb	Dec–Mar, Aug	Mar–June, Aug	Mar–June, Aug	Feb–Mar, Aug	Feb–May	Feb–May	Oct–Jan
Feb–mid-Apr, mid-Sep–Oct	Mid-Sep–Feb	Oct–mid-Feb	Jan–Mar, Sep–Nov	Feb–Mar, Aug–Sep+	Year-round	Sep–Apr	Sep–Apr	Sep–Apr	Oct–Mar+
Feb–Mar, mid-Sep–Oct	Sep–mid-Feb	Oct–Jan	Feb–Mar, Oct–Nov	Sep–Apr	Feb–Apr, July–Sep+	Sep–Jan	Sep–Mar	Sep–Mar	Nov–Jan+

V

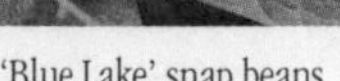
'Blue Lake' snap beans

'Silver Bullet' corn

Lemon cucumbers

Eggplant

'Charentais' melon

PLANTING SCHEDULE FOR WARM-SEASON VEGETABLES

VEGETABLE	ZONES A1–A3	ZONES 1, 2	ZONE 3	ZONES 4, 5	ZONE 6	ZONE 7	ZONES 8, 9	ZONE 10
BEANS (S)	June	May–June	May–June	May–June	May–July	Apr–June	Mar–Aug	Mid-Apr–May, July–mid-Aug
CORN (S)	June	May	May	May	Apr–June	Apr–June	Mar–July	Late Mar–July
CUCUMBERS (S, T)	June	May–June	Mid-Apr–June	May–June	May–June	Apr–June	Mar–June	Apr–mid-June
EGGPLANT (T)	June	May	May	May*	May	Apr–June	Apr–June	Apr–mid-May
MUSKMELONS (S, T)	June	May*	May	May	May	Apr–May	Mar–June	Apr–mid-June
PEPPERS (T)	June	May	May	May	May	May–June	Apr–June	Apr–May
SQUASH, SUMMER (S, T)	June	May–June	Mid-Apr–May	May–June	May–June	Apr–July	Mar–July	Apr–July
SQUASH, WINTER (S, T)	June	May	Mid-Apr–May	May	May	May–June	Apr–June	Apr–May
TOMATOES (T)	June	May	Apr–May	May	May	Apr–June	Mar–July	Apr–May
WATERMELONS (S, T)	June	May*	May	May*	May	Apr–May	Mar–June	Apr–mid-June

S = Plant from seed; T = Plant from transplants; * = Succeeds only in warmest locations or with season extenders.

Vines

Versatile additions to almost any landscape, vines can be used to frame entryways, decorate bare walls and fences, and cover arbors with foliage and flowers. Defined in the most basic terms, a vine is simply a flexible shrub that doesn't stop extending its growth—it just keeps getting taller or longer, depending on whether you train it vertically or horizontally. If unsupported, it won't climb at all; it will sprawl across the ground (some vines are grown in this manner for use as ground covers).

SELECTING VINES. Like trees and shrubs, vines vary widely. They may be deciduous, semievergreen, or evergreen. Some provide greenery alone; others bear decorative fruits or blossoms.

Think about ultimate size and weight, too: some vines are lightweight enough to adorn a flimsy trellis without damaging it, but others eventually become weighty enough to pull down all but the sturdiest supports. As noted below, the vine's method of attachment will also determine the kind of support needed.

Once you have a good idea of what you're looking for—an evergreen flowering vine for a delicate trellis, say—narrow the list to just those plants suited to your climate zone. For ideas, see "Vines" in A Guide to Plant Selection, beginning on page 64.

METHODS OF ATTACHMENT. Some vines twine around their supports with stems, others with tendrils; some cling with special growths such as suction disks, while others need to be tied to their support to climb along it.

Twining vines. New growth twists or spirals as it elongates, coiling around a support or even around growth on the same or nearby plants. Nearly all twiners make too tight a spiral to encircle a post; support them with cord or wire.

Vines with tendrils. Specialized growths along stems or at leaf tips reach out and wrap around anything within reach—a wire, another stem of the same vine, an adjoining plant. The tendrils grow out straight until they make contact, then contract into a spiral; supply narrow supports that they can easily grasp.

Clinging vines. Special growths along the stems of these vines attach to flat surfaces. Some clingers have tendrils equipped at their tips with suction disks that grip the support; others have "claws" that hook into small irregularities or

'Yellow Banana' sweet pepper

'Golden Scallop' summer squash

'Emerald Buttercup' winter squash

'Enchantress' tomatoes

'Cherokee Moon and Stars' watermelon

ZONE 11	ZONE 12	ZONE 13	ZONE 14	ZONES 15, 16	ZONE 17	ZONES 18, 19	ZONES 20, 21	ZONES 22–24	ZONES H1, H2
Mid-Mar–Apr, early Aug	Mid-Mar–Apr, Aug	Mar–mid-Apr, mid-Aug–Sep	Apr–Aug	Apr–Aug	Mid-Apr–mid-July	Mar–May	Mar–July	Apr–Aug	Year-round
Mid-Mar–Apr, July–mid-Aug	Mid-Mar–mid-Apr, early Aug	Feb–Mar, late Aug–mid-Sep	Apr–July	Apr–July	Apr–July	Mar–July	Mar–July	Apr–July	Year-round
Mid-Mar–mid-Aug	Apr, Aug	Feb–mid-Apr, mid-Aug–Sep	Mid-Mar–June	Apr–June	May–mid-July	Apr–May	Apr–May	Apr–June	Year-round
Mid-Mar–mid-May	Apr–mid-May	Mar–April	Apr–June	May–June	May*	Apr	Apr	Apr	Year-round
Mid-Mar–mid-June	Mar–Apr, early July	Feb–Mar, mid-July–Aug	Apr–June	May–June	May*	Apr–June	Apr–June	May–June	Year-round
Mid-Mar–early May	Apr–May	Mid-Mar–Apr	Apr–June	May–June	May*	Apr–May	Apr–May	May	Year-round
Mid-Mar–early July	Mar–May	Mid-Feb–Apr, Aug	Mar–July	Apr–July	Apr–July	Apr–July	Apr–June	May	Year-round
Mid-May–June	June	July	Apr–June	May–June	May–June	Apr–June	Apr–June	May–June	Year-round
Mid-Mar–Apr	Mid-Mar–mid-Apr	Mid-Feb–mid-Mar	Apr–July	Apr–June	Apr–June	Apr–May	Apr–July	Apr–May	Year-round
Mid-Mar–June	Mar–Apr	Feb–Mar	Apr–June	May–June	May*	Apr–June	Apr–June	May–June	Year-round

VINE ATTACHMENTS

Twining stems
Tendrils
Suction (holdfast) disks
Aerial rootlets
Scrambles; no means of attachment

crevices of a flat surface. Another type of clinger has aerial rootlets along its stems that tenaciously grip all but absolutely smooth, slick surfaces. Bear in mind that all of these clinging devices—known collectively as holdfasts—can damage brick, wood, concrete, and other building materials.

Vines that require tying. Some vines have no means of attachment. They simply thread their way through and over other plants, depending on this living support to hold their stems in place. A few (climbing roses, for example) have thorns on their stems; these help secure the stems in place as they scramble but offer no permanent support. In the garden, these sorts of plants must be tied to their supports.

PLANTING AND CARING FOR VINES. Most vines are sold in containers; a few deciduous kinds (roses and grapes, for example) are available bare-root. See pages 692 and 693 for container and bare-root planting guidelines.

Many vines grow well in ordinary soil with an annual feeding in spring; likewise, many require only average amounts of water. To look their best, almost all require yearly pruning. Check the Western Plant Encyclopedia for comments on the specific needs of each vine.

CONSERVING WATER ON SLOPES

Plants on slopes are often challenging to irrigate, since water can run downhill faster than it can seep into the root zone. To prevent wasteful runoff, make basins or terracing to channel water directly to plant roots, as shown below.

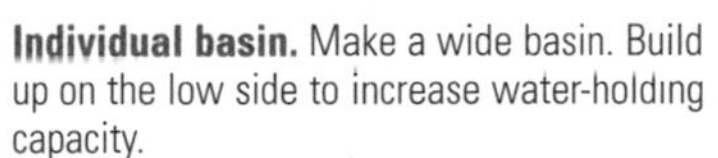

Individual basin. Make a wide basin. Build up on the low side to increase water-holding capacity.

Terracing. Headers help control runoff. Because surface reservoir is small, water must be applied slowly.

Water Conservation

Most of the West's climates are characterized by low rainfall, a long dry season, or both. Thus, Western gardeners typically spend a good part of the year watering plants. (Only those living in Alaska, the higher-rainfall parts of Hawaii, California's northern coastal fog belt, and the area north of the Siskiyous and west of the Cascades are spared this task.) And although each region's overall water supply remains virtually fixed, the demand for water continues to rise. In the years to come, water management will present an ever greater challenge. Here are some ways to meet that challenge.

LOCATE PLANTS WISELY. If you mix plants that require little or no irrigation with those that require regular moisture, you'll be wasting water on the undemanding plants (and may even harm them). To avoid this situation, try to organize your garden into *hydrozones*—groups of plants with similar water needs. Doing so will simplify irrigation while giving each plant the right amount of moisture. The concept of hydrozoning was developed for arid and semiarid climates, but it can be applied anywhere that gardeners need to supplement rainfall. High-water-use plants are typically located nearest the house, while those needing less water are planted progressively farther away. (For a list of drought-tolerant plants, see "Plants for Dry Areas" in A Guide to Plant Selection, beginning on page 64.) This scheme frees you from dragging hoses to the far reaches of the garden or extending an irrigation system farther than necessary.

RECONSIDER YOUR LAWN. Most conventional lawn grasses use water at a rate disproportionate to other plants, largely because they have a shallow root system that dries out quickly (especially in sandy soil). Consider reducing the size of your lawn or choosing a lawn alternative such as an unthirsty ground cover, gravel, or hard surface such as brick, other paving, or a wooden deck. If you feel that a lawn is a necessary component of your garden, select a grass requiring less water than the more familiar types; see page 673 for less-thirsty turf grasses adapted to your climate.

MULCH YOUR PLANTINGS. An organic mulch spread several inches thick over planting beds acts as an insulating blanket, slowing evaporation from the soil and keeping it cooler than it would be if unprotected. Rocks and gravel also do the job. Black plastic sheeting, sold in rolls, conserves moisture and suppresses weeds. You can also buy rolls of various plastic materials, known collectively as landscape fabrics. For more information on all these mulches, see page 676.

ELIMINATE RUNOFF. Don't waste water by irrigating paved surfaces. If your sprinkler system showers water over a sidewalk, patio, or driveway, replace the heads with models that deliver water only where it is needed; or, if necessary, redesign the system.

Sloping land and heavy clay soils invite runoff—due to gravity in the first case, slow water penetration in the second. To avoid runoff in such sites, adjust the rate at which water is applied. If you use sprinklers, you can improve penetration by watering in successive short intervals, giving the water time to soak in between each spell of sprinkling. On slopes, terraces and basins can also help prevent runoff (see above).

USE LOW-VOLUME WATERING DEVICES. Soaker hoses are effective and easy to install. Drip irrigation (see page 723) offers an excellent way to reduce water use. You can also upgrade an existing underground sprinkler system: install low-volume sprinkler heads or convert the system to a drip setup, using the parts and kits available at hardware stores.

USE TIMERS. With the simplest timers, you set the dial for the length of time you want the water to run; then you turn on the water. The timer turns the faucet off for you.

More sophisticated timers operate on batteries or household current. You set them to a schedule; they turn the water on and off as programmed. Such timers assure that your garden will be watered whether you're at home or away. What's more, you can select a schedule that will give your plants the precise amount of water they need to thrive.

The flaw of automatic controllers is that they follow your schedule regardless of weather: they'll turn on the water during a deluge or apply amounts of water appropriate for hot summer temperatures on a cool fall day. To solve this problem, reset the controller so that it takes seasonal rainfall and weather conditions into account. Or use electronic attachments that function as weather sensors. By linking a soil moisture sensor to the controller, for example, you can trigger the sprinklers to switch on only when the sensor indicates that soil moisture has dropped to the point where water is needed. Another useful attachment is a rain shutoff device; it accumulates rainwater in a special collector pan, turning off the controller when the pan is filled to a prescribed depth and triggering it to resume watering when the collected water has evaporated. Before installing either of these sensors, be sure that they are compatible with the automatic controller.

Watering

Plants, like animals, need water to live. A seed must absorb water before it can germinate. Roots can take up nutrients only when water is present in the soil, and water transports nutrients throughout plants. Water is also essential for photosynthesis.

WATERING GUIDELINES. A number of interrelated factors—including soil texture, the particular plants and their ages and root depths, and the weather—determine how much water your plants need and how often they need it.

A soil's ability to absorb and retain water is closely related to its composition. Clay soils absorb water slowly and drain slowly too, retaining water longer than other soils. Sandy soils, in contrast, absorb water quickly and drain just as rapidly. Loam soils absorb water fairly quickly and drain well, but not too fast. Absorption patterns vary, too: though water moves primarily downward, it also moves laterally to some extent. Lateral movement is greatest in clay soils; in sandy ones, most water seeps straight down and there is little horizontal movement.

To improve absorption and drainage in clay and to make sandy soils more moisture retentive, work in organic amendments. (For more on soil texture and organic amendments, see pages 706–709.)

Once their roots are established, different plants have widely differing water needs. Those native to semiarid and arid climates, called *xerophytes,* have evolved features that allow them to survive with little water and low relative humidity. They may have deep root systems, for example, or water-retaining leaves that are small, hairy, or waxy. Many familiar garden plants, however, are adapted to moist soil and high relative humidity. Called *mesophytes,* they usually have broad, thin leaves that lose moisture readily.

Keep in mind that *all* young plants, including xerophytes, need more frequent watering than mature ones until their root systems become well established. And many annuals and vegetables require regular moisture throughout the growing season if they are to bloom well or produce a good crop.

The depth of a plant's root zone also influences watering practices; typical root depths of trees, shrubs, and other plants are shown above. Applying enough water to moisten the entire root zone encourages roots to grow throughout that area, while shallow watering keeps them near the soil surface. Deeper roots have access to more moisture, thus letting the plant go longer between waterings. They're also less subject to stress from heat and drying winds than shallow roots are.

Root hairs of underwatered plants will dry out and die, causing the plant to slow its growth, wilt, and eventually die. But you don't want to overdo it, either. It's important to learn how often you must water to keep the root zone moist. Watering below the root zone is wasteful, since the water is not used—and beyond that, keeping the soil too moist can cause as many problems as letting it get too dry. Roots need air as well as water, and they absorb both from the pore spaces between soil particles. When water penetrates the soil, it displaces the air in the pores; then, as it drains away, evaporates, and is taken up by roots, the pore spaces fill with air again. If water is applied too often, the pore spaces never have a chance to drain. They remain filled with water, cutting off the roots' air supply. This lack of oxygen makes roots susceptible to various water-mold fungi, which in turn can lead to rot.

To check how far water penetrates your soil, water for a set amount of time (say, 30 minutes). Wait for 24 hours, then use a soil sampling tube (shown below) or dig a hole to check for moisture. Sampling tubes are especially useful in lawns or around established trees and shrubs; they let you test moisture at deeper levels without digging a hole that might disturb roots. A metal rod or a long screwdriver pushed into the ground can also serve as a soil probe. It will move easily through moist soil but slow down or stop when it reaches dry soil, allowing you to estimate how deeply the moist area extends. You'll soon learn to judge how long to water each plant or group of plants to soak the root zone thoroughly.

COMPARATIVE ROOT DEPTHS

Lawn grasses
Annuals and other nonwoody plants
Small and medium-size shrubs
Trees and large shrubs
6 in.
12 in.
18 in.
24 in.

The rooting depths illustrated here will help you determine the amount of water needed to supply moisture to your plants' root zones. Even in the case of large trees, most of the feeder roots are within the top 2 feet of soil, though taproots (which serve to anchor the tree) may penetrate farther. It's also important to note that the feeder roots of trees and shrubs extend well beyond the plant's leafy top or canopy; be sure to apply water to all of the root area.

SOIL TEXTURE AND WATER PENETRATION

Applied to sand (left), 1 inch of water penetrates about 12 inches. Applied to loam (center), 1 inch of water reaches about 7 inches. Applied to clay (right), 1 inch of water soaks only 4 to 5 inches.

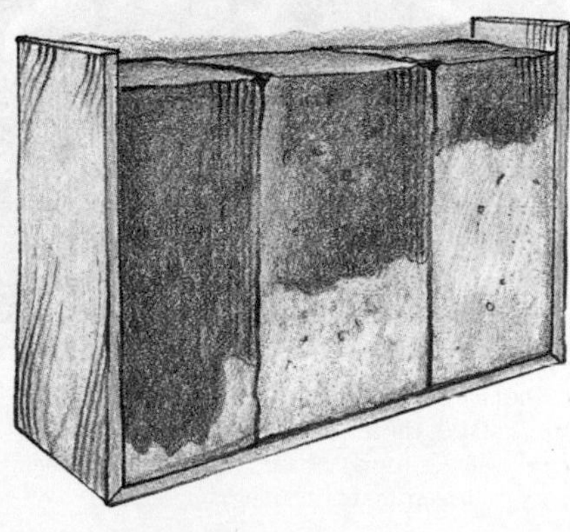

USING A SOIL SAMPLING TUBE

This device allows you to check soil moisture at deeper levels than you can reach with a trowel, without disturbing plant roots too much. Push the tube into the ground, pull it out, and examine the soil in the sample. If it is dry or only slightly moist, it's time to water. If the top layer is damp and the rest is dry, you need to water for a longer time to ensure deeper penetration. A soil sampling tube is also useful for detecting compacted layers of soil, checking depth of root penetration, and taking samples for soil tests.

MEASURING SPRINKLER DELIVERY RATE AND DISPERSION

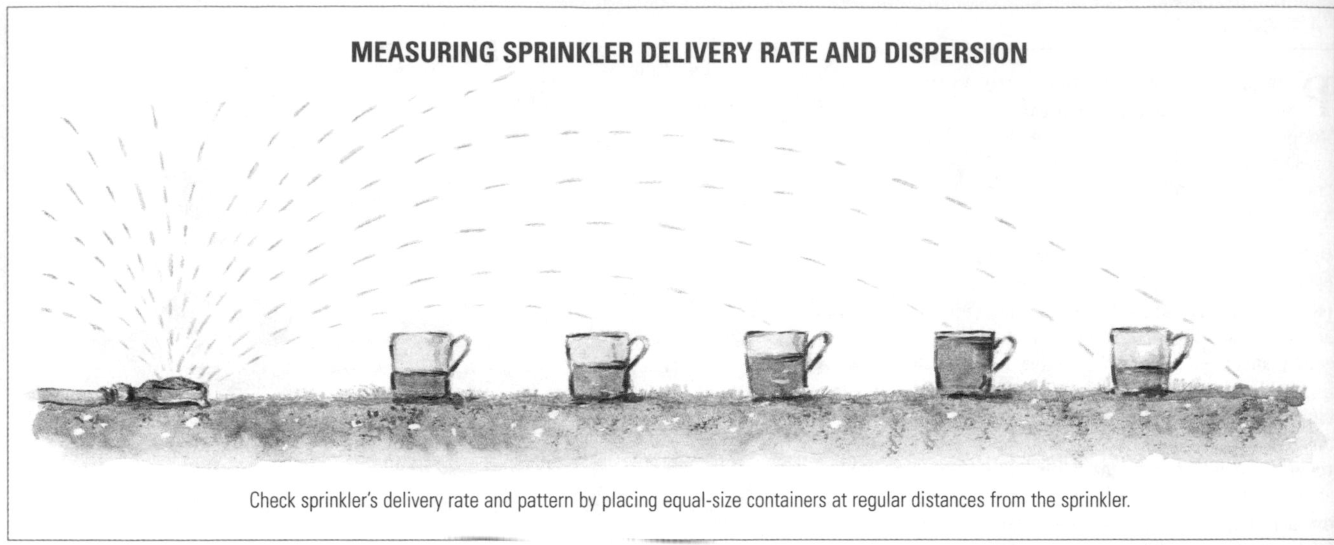

Check sprinkler's delivery rate and pattern by placing equal-size containers at regular distances from the sprinkler.

Weather affects water needs as well. When it's hot, dry, and windy, plants use water quickly, and young or shallow-rooted ones sometimes cannot absorb it fast enough to keep foliage from wilting. Such plants need frequent watering to keep moisture around their roots. During cool, damp weather, on the other hand, plants require much less water.

Because the factors just discussed—soil texture, plant characteristics and age, and weather—are variable, following a fixed watering schedule year-round (or even all summer) isn't the most efficient way to meet your plant's needs. Before you water, always test the soil for moisture content (see page 721) and look at plants for signs of wilting.

WATERING METHODS. Methods for applying water range from simple hand-held sprayers to hose-end sprinklers to more complex underground rigid-pipe systems and drip systems. The method or methods appropriate for your garden depend on how often you need to water, the size of your garden, and how much equipment you want to buy.

Hand watering. Watering with a hand-held nozzle may be a relaxing pastime, but it's usually inadequate for plants; it takes too long to truly soak the soil. Hand watering is, however, useful for new transplants, seedlings, and container plants, since you can apply the water gently and put it exactly where it's needed.

Sprinkling. Water can be applied through sprinklers attached to the end of a hose or via an in-ground sprinkler system. In either case, the sprinklers apply a high volume of water over a large surface. Many plants, particularly those that like a cool, humid atmosphere, thrive with overhead sprinkling. This method also rinses dust from foliage and discourages certain pests (especially spider mites). But sprinkling has some negative aspects as well. It can be wasteful: wind may carry off some water before it even reaches the ground, and water that falls on or runs off onto pavement is lost too. In humid climates, sprinkling encourages some foliage diseases such as black spot and rust—though you can minimize this risk by sprinkling early in the morning, so that leaves dry as the day warms. Another potential drawback is that plants with weak stems and/or heavy flowers may collapse under a heavy load of water.

The wide assortment of portable, hose-end sprinklers includes stationary models that resemble salt shakers or rings; oscillating, rotating, and impulse sprinklers; and "walking" types that slowly roll through the area to be watered. When selecting a sprinkler, look for one with a coverage pattern that most closely matches the area to be irrigated; the shape and size of the space the sprinkler covers should be listed on the package.

Permanent underground sprinkler systems—the traditional watering method in low-rainfall areas—offer some advantages over hose-end watering. They free you from moving hoses and sprinklers and can be automated to operate even if you're away from home for an extended period. And recent refinements in the design of the sprinklers have improved such systems' efficiency: the newer sprinklers produce less runoff and overspray onto buildings, walkways, and fences and distribute water more evenly. For such a system to work properly, though, it must be well designed; consult with a licensed landscape contractor or a company specializing in irrigation systems.

Sprinkler application rates. To sprinkle effectively with a portable or an underground system, you need to know how fast water penetrates your soil and the delivery rate of your sprinklers. As the illustration on page 721 shows, 1 inch of water (from sprinkling or rainfall) moistens about 12 inches in sandy soil, 7 inches in loam, and 4 to 5 inches in clay. Thus, if you want to water to a depth of 12 inches, you'll need to apply about an inch of water to sandy soil, 2½ to 3 inches to clay soil.

To determine delivery rate, place a number of equal-size containers (straight-sided coffee cups, for example) at regular intervals outward from the sprinkler, as shown above. (If you are testing an underground system, place the containers among the sprinkler heads.) Then turn on the water and note how long it takes to fill a container with an inch of water. This test will also show you the delivery pattern. If the containers fill unevenly, move portable sprinklers to achieve more even coverage, or check the sprinkler heads of underground systems to see if they need adjusting or replacing.

Root irrigators. This device—which resembles a giant hypodermic needle—is useful for getting water to root zones of trees growing near sidewalks, patios, or other areas with a minimum of open soil. It also helps get water deep into the soil on sloping land, where deep penetration without runoff can be a problem. Attach the tool to the end of a garden hose; then insert it into the ground as you turn the water on. Water travels down a hollow probe and shoots out of holes at the tip. Some models also supply fertilizer as they water.

The basin around this newly planted conifer has been flooded to deliver water to the roots. As the tree grows, enlarge the basin. To avoid overwatering, remove the basin during rainy seasons.

Flooding. Flooding or soaking is an effective way to supply sufficient water to the deep, extensive root systems of large shrubs and trees. Form two concentric rings of soil and flood the outer ring as shown on facing page. For freshly planted trees and shrubs, make the outer ring just outside the outer edge of the rootball; move it farther out as the plant grows.

If you grow vegetables or flowers in rows, you can build adjoining basins for large plants like squash or make furrows between rows (shown at right). To minimize damage to roots, construct the furrows when the plants are young, before their root systems have spread. Broad, shallow furrows are generally better than deep, narrow ones: the wider the furrow, the wider the root area you can soak, since water moves primarily downward rather than laterally. And a shallow furrow is safer for plants—nearby roots are less likely to be disturbed when you scoop out the furrow.

WATERING IN FURROWS AND BASINS

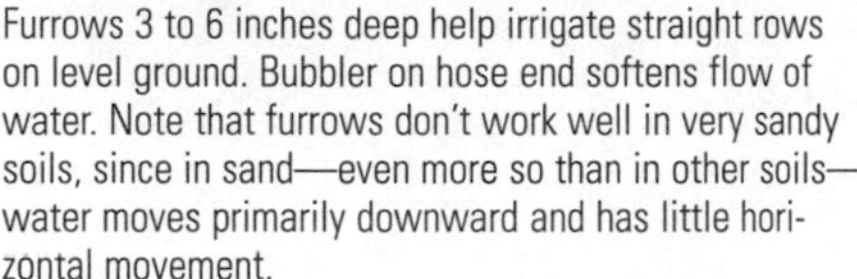

Furrows 3 to 6 inches deep help irrigate straight rows on level ground. Bubbler on hose end softens flow of water. Note that furrows don't work well in very sandy soils, since in sand—even more so than in other soils—water moves primarily downward and has little horizontal movement.

Basins with sides 3 inches high hold water around large plants such as tomatoes and peppers. On level ground, link basins to make watering easier.

Soil soaker hoses. Soaker hoses, the forerunners of drip irrigation systems, are still useful for slow, steady delivery of water. They are long tubes made of perforated or porous plastic or rubber, with hose fittings at one or both ends. When you attach a soaker to a regular hose and turn on the water supply, water seeps or sprinkles from the soaker along its entire length. You can also water wide beds by snaking soakers back and forth around the plants; trees and shrubs can be watered with a soaker coiled over the outermost edges of the root zone. You'll probably need to leave soakers on longer than you would sprinklers; to determine timing, check water penetration with a trowel or soil sampling tube.

Drip irrigation. The term "drip irrigation" describes the application of water by drip emitters and microsprays. Both devices operate at low pressure, and both deliver a low volume of water compared to standard sprinklers. Because the water is applied slowly on or near the ground, there should be no waste from runoff and little or no loss to evaporation. You position the emitters to deliver water just where plants need it; you control penetration by varying the time the system runs and/or the emitters' delivery capacity (rated in gallons per hour—gph). You can also regulate the volume of water delivered to each plant by varying the type and number of emitters you set up for each.

In addition to water conservation, drip systems offer the advantage of flexibility. You can tailor them to water individual plants by providing each with its own emitter(s), or distribute water over larger areas with microsprays. A standard layout might include hookups to two or more valves and several kinds of parts. Because the lines are aboveground (they are easily concealed with mulch) and are made of limber plastic, changing the system is simple: just add or subtract lines or emitters as needed.

A drip system can be attached to a hose end or provided with fittings to allow it to be screwed into a hose bibb. Or you can connect it permanently to your main water source. Like

DRIP IRRIGATION COMPONENTS

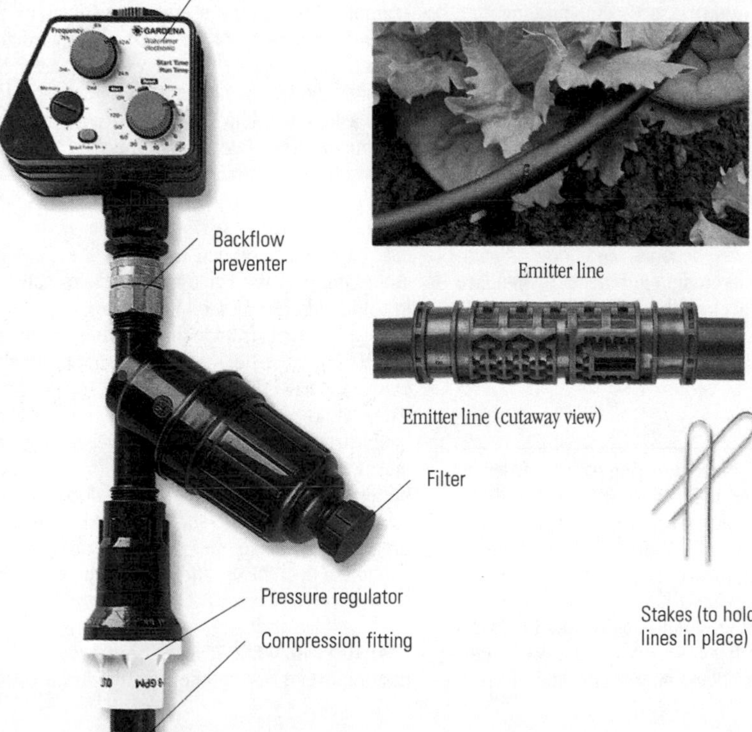

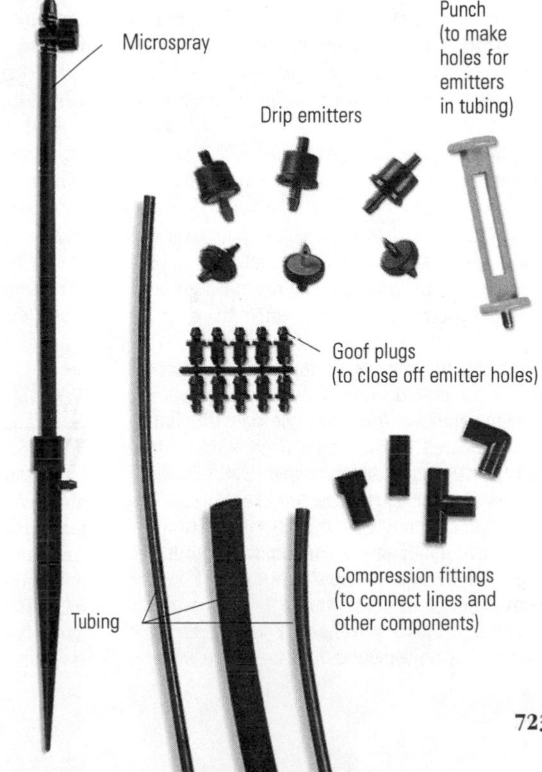

W

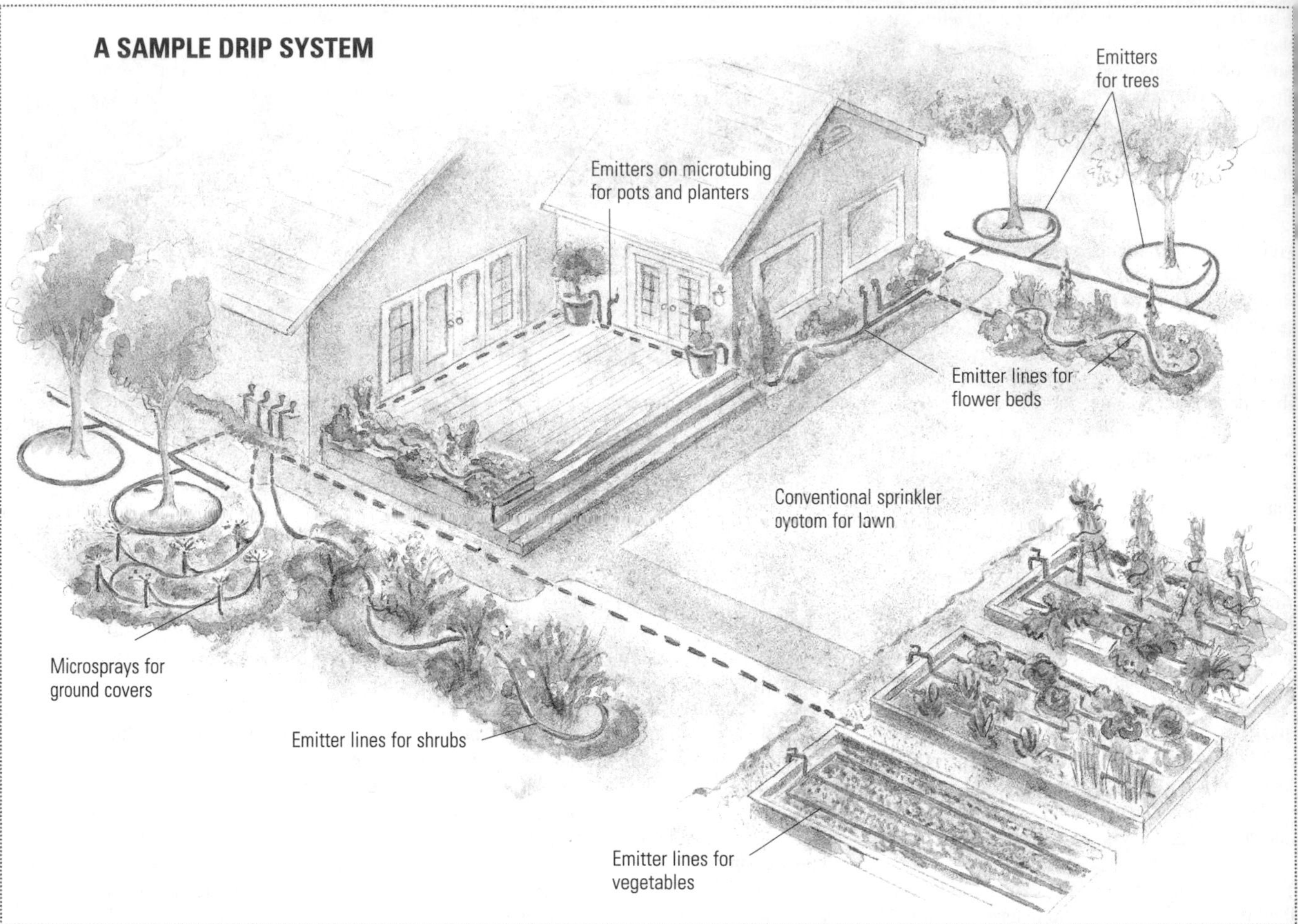

A SAMPLE DRIP SYSTEM

Emitters for trees

Emitters on microtubing for pots and planters

Emitter lines for flower beds

Conventional sprinkler system for lawn

Microsprays for ground covers

Emitter lines for shrubs

Emitter lines for vegetables

underground irrigation systems, drip systems should be outfitted with a backflow preventer. In addition, a filter is necessary (even when you're using municipal supplies of clean water) to keep the small openings on drip emitters and microsprays from becoming clogged. A pressure regulator is also needed—drip systems are designed to run best at a much lower pressure than is found in most household water supplies. The regulator protects the fittings from blowing apart under excess force and allows the watering devices to work properly.

Emitters for drip systems. Emitters vary in shape, size, and internal mechanism, but all operate on the principle of dispensing water slowly; flow rates of most range from ½ to 2 gph. Insert the emitters directly into ½- or ⅜-inch drip irrigation tubing or thinner microtubing positioned to run from the larger tubing to each plant. Non-pressure-compensating emitters work well on flat or relatively level ground and with lines that are less than 200 feet long. But when water pressure will be lowered by gravity or friction (on hillsides or with long lines), opt for pressure-compensating emitters. These deliver the same amount of water throughout the system.

You can also purchase emitters factory-installed in polyethylene tubing. These may be referred to as "in-line" emitters or emitter lines. Spaced 1, 1½, 2, or 3 feet apart along the tubing, they deliver ½, 1, or 2 gph and are available in non-pressure-compensating and pressure-compensating versions. Some emitter lines are infused with a small amount of herbicide to prevent root intrusion; these can be buried to water lawns.

While the standard emitters simply drip, types that deliver water in other ways are available as well. *Misters* produce a fine spray—a good way to increase humidity for plants like fuchsia, tuberous begonia, and ferns. *Microsprays* are low-volume equivalents of standard sprinklers, particularly useful for irrigating closely spaced or dense plantings such as ground covers and flower beds.

Weeds

Weeds are plants growing where gardeners don't want them to grow. They rob desirable plants of water, nutrients, and sunlight; they may harbor insects and diseases—and they're frequently unattractive.

Whether a plant is labeled a weed depends on several factors. Some plants, like bindweed and yellow oxalis, are regarded as weeds wherever they grow. Others may be considered weeds in some situations, garden plants in others: common yarrow *(Achillea millefolium)* is an annoying weed when it invades a lawn, for example, but a very useful ornamental as a ground cover in a hot, dry part of the garden. Certain plants spread so aggressively that they are often thought of as weeds; examples include some asters, bamboo, mint *(Mentha)*, Mexican evening primrose (*Oenothera speciosa* 'Rosea', often sold as *O. berlandieri*), sweet woodruff *(Galium odoratum)*, and Jerusalem artichoke *(Helianthus tuberosus)*. And some ornamentals have gone beyond invading the garden alone, jumping the fence to overwhelm natives in wild lands (see box on facing page).

Despite their frankly undesirable qualities (from the gardener's point of view), weedy plants do have their positive side. An assemblage of weeds can hold the soil on a steep bank, preventing erosion. Some weeds provide nectar and shelter for beneficial insects and butterflies. When they die and decompose, weeds add humus to the soil. And even the dreaded poison oak and poison ivy are important to the deer, birds, and rabbits who eat their berries.

CLASSIFYING WEEDS. Identifying weeds is the first important step in choosing the best way to manage these pests. They are often classified by the length of their life cycle. *Annual weeds* (like annual garden plants) grow shoots and leaves, flower, set seed, and die within a period of less than a year. Most members of this group are summer annuals, germinating in spring or summer and dying by fall. Winter annual weeds begin growth in fall or early winter, then set seed in early spring while the weather is still cool. *Biennial weeds* produce a cluster or rosette of leaves in their first year of growth; in the following year, they flower, set seed, and die. Both annuals and biennials reproduce by seed. Almost all *perennial weeds,* which live for several years, also reproduce by seed. Once they mature, however, most produce spreading roots, stolons, rhizomes, bulbs, or tubers as well, making control more difficult.

You'll find descriptions of some of the most common Western weeds in each of these groups on pages 727–730, along with suggestions for controlling them. You can also consult your Cooperative Extension Office or a local nursery expert for advice on identifying and controlling troublesome weeds in your area.

MANAGEMENT OPTIONS. As is true for other kinds of pests, it is rarely possible to eradicate weeds entirely. You can, however, substantially reduce infestations and prevent further problems through physical controls—employing methods that range from hand pulling through mowing, flaming, and mulching—as well as soil solarization (see page 726). If these measures are unsuccessful, chemical management may be needed.

Physical controls. When you're confronted with a weed problem, turn to these methods first.

Hand pulling or hoeing is your first line of defense against most weeds. If you're diligent for several consecutive years about pulling or hoeing out annual and biennial weeds before they set seed, their numbers will decline significantly. These methods will also help control perennial weeds, as long as you catch the plants while they're young. Once perennials have passed the seedling stage, though, it's usually necessary to dig out their roots; if you just pull up or cut off the tops, the pests can resprout from fragments left behind. Even with assiduous digging, you'll probably need to repeat the process several times to manage perennial weeds. Some useful tools for weeding are discussed on pages 709–711.

Don't leave pulled or hoed-out weeds on bare ground, since they may take root again. Leafy annual or biennial types that do not yet have flowers or seeds can safely be relegated to the compost pile, as can the top growth of perennial weeds (before seeding). But roots of perennials (dandelions and quack grass, for example) should be tossed in the trash rather than composted—as should any weeds that have set seed.

Rototilling or disking will do the job on annual and biennial weeds in larger areas, such as orchards, vacant lots, roadsides, and plots intended for future gardens. These methods not only knock down weeds but also incorporate them into the soil, where they eventually decay to form humus. However, perennial weeds usually sprout again from the roots or crowns—and some kinds even grow more abundantly after tilling.

Using rotary mowers or weed eaters is another good choice for seasonal weed control in larger areas. Both tools cut the weeds: weed eaters leave the severed tops behind, while mowers grind them up as they cut them. These methods are also effective for reducing weeds in fire-prone areas.

Smothering effectively kills weeds in areas earmarked for future planting. After mowing or cutting off the top growth, put down a layer of heavy cardboard, newspapers (in a layer at least three dozen sheets thick), or black plastic. Overlap these materials so weeds can't grow through the cracks. Anchor the covering with a layer of bark chips or other organic mulch. Leave these smothering materials in place for at least a full growing season; allow a year or more for tough or perennial weeds.

Flaming offers another way to knock down weeds. Powered by propane or a mixture of propane and butane, flamers are not meant to burn weeds; instead, they heat them to the point at which their cell walls burst. Though this damage is drastic enough to kill many young weeds, types with deep perennial roots usually regrow; destroying these requires several treatments. Take care when using flamers around mulches, wooden fences, or wood-bordered raised beds, and never use them in dry, fire-prone areas.

Presprouting is a useful technique for preparing planting areas for vegetables, perennial beds, or new lawns in parts of the garden plagued by weeds. Add needed amendments, till the soil, water, and then wait a week or two for

WEEDS OF WILD LANDS

While most of the plants brought from other parts of the world to ornament gardens (or provide timber or food) are welcome and well behaved, some have escaped from cultivation and invaded wild lands throughout the West. Unchecked by the natural forces, such as diseases, insects, or animals, that helped control them in their homelands, they thrive, displacing local native plants; they change the structure of the ecosystems they enter, threatening diversity and destroying wildlife habitats. Native plant societies maintain lists of problem plants in each state; a few of the worst offenders are noted here.

Giant reed *(Arundo donax)* has become a serious invader of riparian areas in California and Hawaii. Jubata grass *(Cortaderia jubata)* as well as pampas grass *(C. selloana)* are so common in some coastal habitats that they are sometimes thought to be natives, as is Scotch broom *(Cytisus scoparius)*, an invader of coastal scrub and oak woodlands. Blackberry (page 728) is another well-known weed infesting wild areas as well as gardens. Several species of tamarisk or salt cedar *(Tamarix)* take water from more shallowly rooted native plants, altering the ecology of large areas of the arid Southwest. Purple loosestrife (*Lythrum salicaria, L. virgatum,* and related hybrids) has overrun thousands of acres of wetlands. Lantana, ginger lily *(Hedychium coronarium)*, ivy gourd *(Coccinia grandis)*, and miconia *(Miconia calvescens)* are just a few of the plant invaders causing problems in Hawaii.

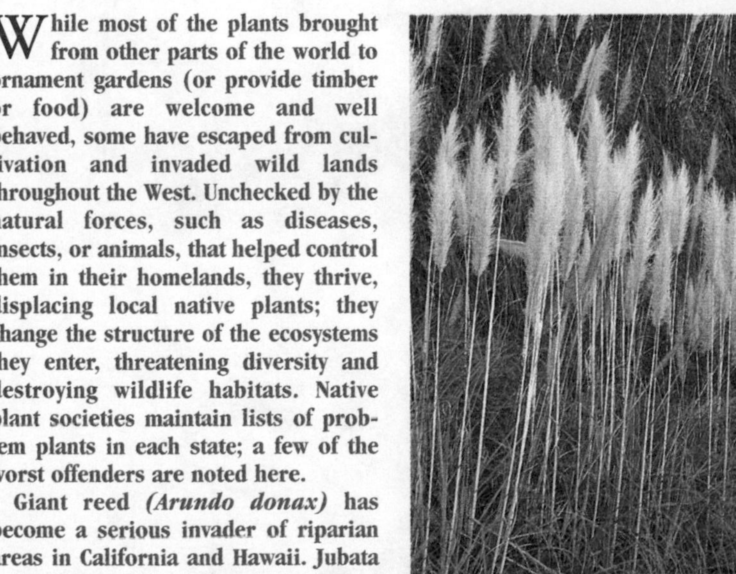

Jubata grass *(Cortaderia jubata)*

Gardeners can help stem the spread of invasive plants by not using them near natural areas, as in gardens of rural or vacation homes. Native plant societies as well as other organizations, such as garden clubs and volunteer groups at state and national parks, sponsor weed eradication programs and plant restoration projects in many areas.

weed seeds to germinate. When they're only a few inches high, scrape them away. Then sow or transplant your vegetables, flowers, or lawn, disturbing the soil as little as possible to avoid bringing more weed seeds to the surface.

Soil solarization (see below) controls many kinds of weed seeds as well as harmful fungi, bacteria, and some nematodes.

Once you've destroyed weeds in a garden area, take steps to prevent their reappearance. Mulching bare soil is an effective deterrent to weed growth; see page 676 for information on choosing and using mulches, including landscape fabrics. Ground covers, sometimes called living mulches, are effective in preventing weed growth: like organic and inorganic mulches, they keep sunlight from reaching weeds and their seeds. You'll usually have to do some hand weeding or apply a mulch for the first few seasons after you plant a ground cover, but as it grows and spreads to form a tight carpet, weed growth is much reduced. For more on ground covers, see page 671.

Chemical controls. Synthetic herbicides are not recommended for food gardens. In home ornamental gardens, use them only when all other methods have failed. Beyond the risks they may pose to health and the environment, many of these chemicals can damage desirable plants if they drift through the air or run off in irrigation or rainwater. Some persist in the soil for long periods, injuring later plantings. And often the entire process of herbicide use—selecting a product, mixing and applying it, cleaning up—takes more effort than pulling or digging out the weeds.

If you use herbicides, always make sure the product is safe for the desirable plants growing in and near the areas to be treated. Also keep in mind that you can be held responsible for any damage to neighboring properties resulting from herbicides you use (do not apply them on windy days). See page 729 for lists of natural and synthetic herbicides as well as explanations of terms used in describing herbicides, such as pre-emergence and postemergence.

ANNUAL WEEDS. Most of these weeds can be controlled by diligent hand weeding and hoeing. This should be carried out before the weeds go to seed, since most annual weeds produce prodigious amounts of seed. To discourage the growth of these weeds in lawns, maintain a thick turf (for more on lawns, see pages 673–675). Mulches are effective in reducing the germination of annual weeds in garden areas; most such weeds can also be destroyed by soil solarization. If chemical control is required, use a pre-emergence herbicide labeled for the weed in question. Apply it in fall for winter annual weeds, in early spring for summer annuals. For postemergence treatment, spot-treat annual weeds with herbicidal soaps or products containing glufosinate-ammonium or glyphosate (don't get these chemicals on desirable plants). Selective postemergence herbicides effective on particularly troublesome annual weeds are included in the following descriptions.

Biennial weeds such as mallows are controlled in the same way as annual ones.

SOIL SOLARIZATION

Soil solarization takes advantage of the sun's heat, trapped under clear plastic sheeting, to control many kinds of weed seeds as well as harmful fungi, bacteria, and some nematodes. The process is carried out in summer and works best in regions that have hot, sunny weather for 4 to 8 weeks straight; daytime temperatures above 80°F/27°C are ideal. Solarization isn't very effective in coastal climates with summer fog, nor does it work well in very windy areas.

Plan to solarize areas you intend to use for fall vegetables, ornamental beds, or lawn. Follow these steps.

1 Cultivate soil, clearing it of weeds, debris, and large clods of earth. It is important to get rid of growing weeds, because clear plastic—unlike black plastic—doesn't halt growth of plants in the soil beneath it.

2 Make a bed at least 2½ feet wide (narrower beds make it difficult to build up enough heat to have much effect). Carve a small ditch around perimeter and rake to level surface. Soak soil to a depth of 1 foot: moist soil conducts heat better than dry soil and initiates germination of weed seeds. Both seeds and any seedlings will then be killed by heat.

3 Cover soil with 1- to 4-mil clear plastic; use UV-resistant plastic if it's available, since it won't break down during solarization. Stretch plastic tightly so that it is in contact with the soil. Bury the edges in the perimeter ditch. An optional second layer of plastic increases heat and makes solarization more effective; use soda cans as spacers between the two sheets (see inset at right). Leave plastic in place for 4 to 6 weeks (8 weeks for really persistent weeds); then remove it. Don't leave it down longer than 8 weeks, or soil structure may suffer. You can now plant. After planting, avoid cultivating more than the upper 2 inches of soil, since weed seeds at deeper levels may still be viable.

TOP: Annual bluegrass; BOTTOM: Burclover

TOP: Crabgrass; BOTTOM: Mallow

TOP: Nettleleaf goosefoot; BOTTOM: Purslane

Annual bluegrass *(Poa annua)*. A winter annual, though there are also perennial forms. Forms a bright light green tuft of softly textured grass. Bluegrass is a weed in lawns; it is also troublesome in flower borders and winter vegetable crops.

Burclover *(Medicago polymorpha)*. Winter annual in most areas. Low, spreading, broad-leafed weed with yellow flowers and spiny burs. Common in lawns and garden beds that lack nitrogen (high phosphorus encourages this weed). It is also troublesome in gravel paths and driveways. To help control burclover, increase nitrogen fertilizing.

Crabgrass (*Digitaria* species). Summer annual. This shallow-rooted weed thrives in hot, moist areas. Seeds germinate in early spring in warmer climates, later in colder areas. As the plant grows, it branches out at the base; stems can root where they touch the soil. It is typically found in lawns and flower beds that receive frequent surface watering; infrequent deep watering can dry out crabgrass roots, killing the weeds or diminishing their vigor.

Corn gluten meal is used as a pre-emergence herbicide to control crabgrass; it also acts as a fertilizer, thickening lawns and thus suppressing weed growth. For postemergence treatment around ornamental plants, use herbicides that kill grasses, such as fluazifop-butyl or sethoxydim.

Mallows (*Malva* species). Winter or summer annual or biennial, depending on climate. Also known as cheeseweed (thanks to the fruits, which resemble a round of cheese), these broad-leafed weeds have rounded, lobed leaves and pinkish white flowers. They grow quickly, ranging in height from a few inches to 4 feet tall, and are found in lawns, in gardens, and on roadsides. They're easiest to pull when young; older plants develop a deep taproot.

Nettleleaf goosefoot *(Chenopodium murale)*. Summer annual. Coarse, leafy weed grows 1 to 2 feet high; its dark green, fleshy leaves have a mealy texture. It is common in gardens and orchards and on roadsides.

Purslane *(Portulaca oleracea)*. Summer annual. A prostrate broad-leafed weed with small yellow flowers and fleshy stems and leaves (which are edible, with a tart, lemony flavor), purslane thrives in moist conditions but can withstand considerable drought. Though it's easy to pull or hoe, pieces of stem reroot readily, so be sure to remove them from the garden. Do not compost these weeds. Related to the bright-blossomed garden flowers rose moss *(Portulaca grandiflora)* and ornamental purslane (*P.* Wildfire hybrids).

Scarlet pimpernel *(Anagallis arvensis)*. Winter or summer annual, depending on climate. Scarlet pimpernel is a summer weed in cold climates, but in milder regions it can germinate and grow at any time of year. Sometimes given the common name "poor man's weather glass" (because the pretty salmon-colored flowers open only on sunny days and close at the approach of bad weather), it is a low-growing plant with many branching, four-angled stems.

Sowthistles (*Sonchus* species). Summer annual. These upright, 1- to 4-foot-tall weeds have stout taproots, hollow stems, and milky sap that oozes out when a leaf or stem is broken. The yellow flowers look like those of dandelions. Common in gardens, they may grow in lawns as well.

Spotted spurge *(Chamaesyce maculata;* also listed as *Euphorbia maculata)*. Summer annual, though seeds can germinate in February in warm regions. This weed is particularly

Scarlet pimpernel

Sowthistle

Spotted spurge

aggressive: not only does it produce large quantities of seed, it also sets seed just a few weeks after germination—and the seeds may germinate immediately. It grows from a shallow taproot and forms a low mat of branching stems that exude a milky juice when cut or broken.

PERENNIAL WEEDS. Described below are some of the West's most troublesome perennial weeds. Management options are described from least to most toxic—physical controls first, then chemical ones. In general, growth of perennial weeds can be controlled with landscape fabrics installed so that no light reaches the soil (note that these must be applied *after* clearing the area of weeds; see page 676). Organic mulches are not as effective, since seeds or plants sprouting from roots left in the ground often grow through them.

Bermuda grass *(Cynodon dactylon).* A fine-textured and fast-growing perennial, Bermuda grass is frequently planted as a lawn in warm climates. It spreads by underground stems (rhizomes), aboveground runners (stolons), and, in common Bermuda grass, by seed—and easily becomes a difficult-to-control weed in shrub borders, flower beds, and lawns planted with other kinds of grasses. If you have a Bermuda lawn, use 8-inch-deep barriers or edging to prevent it from advancing into other parts of the garden.

Dig up stray clumps before they form sod, being sure to remove all the underground stems; any left behind can start new shoots. Repeated pulling and digging are usually necessary to eliminate this weed. Seeds and shallow-growing rhizomes of Bermuda grass are destroyed by soil solarization, but deeply buried rhizomes will survive.

For chemical control, you can use a preemergence herbicide containing pendimethalin or oryzalin to prevent seeds from growing. Postemergence products include herbicides that kill grasses, such as fluazifop-butyl or sethoxydim; these are effective against most grasses and can be sprayed over some broadleafed ornamentals without harming them (check the product label). Bermuda grass growing in cool-season lawn grasses can be treated with some products containing triclopyr, as indicated on the label. Spot-treat actively growing Bermuda grass with glyphosate, taking care not to get it on desirable plants.

Bindweed *(Convolvulus arvensis).* Also called wild morning glory or field bindweed, this weed grows in open spaces throughout the West, usually in loam to heavy clay soil. Its 1- to 4-foot-long stems crawl over the ground and twine over and around other plants. The trumpet-shaped flowers are white to pink.

Once established, bindweed forms a deep, extensive root system, so hand-pulling seldom controls it—the stems break off, but the weed returns from the root. To kill it, cultivate or hoe every 6 weeks throughout the growing season; this eventually weakens the root system. Don't let bindweed set seed: the hard-coated seeds can sprout even after lying dormant in the soil for 50 years. Seeds (but not roots) can be killed by soil solarization.

TOP TO BOTTOM: Bermuda grass, Bindweed, Blackberry, Dandelion, Kikuyu grass

An herbicide containing trifluralin may provide pre-emergence control around many ornamentals. In midsummer, when bindweed is growing vigorously but has not yet set seed, spot-treat isolated patches with glyphosate, taking care to avoid contact with desirable plants.

Blackberry (*Rubus* species). Several species of blackberries or brambles are pests in various parts of the West. Himalaya blackberry *(Rubus discolor),* an escapee from cultivation, is the most vigorous of these, thriving in the mild, moist climates of Northern California and western Oregon and Washington. The roots are perennial, the canes biennial, growing one year, then blooming, fruiting, and dying the next. Plants spread by underground stems that send up new shoots. Birds enjoy the berries and scatter the seeds, thus sowing the weed in pastures, along roads, and in gardens, where it turns up in lawns, paths, flower and shrub borders, and ground covers.

Pull young plants in spring before they develop a perennial root system. To kill established clumps, repeatedly prune back the stems as they sprout; this eventually exhausts the roots. Or mow the tops and dig out the roots; repeat the process as new canes grow from roots left behind in the soil.

For chemical control, cut the stems to the ground and apply glyphosate to the stubs as soon as possible after cutting. Spot-treat any new shoots with glyphosate as they appear; or spray triclopyr or glyphosate on mature leaves. Take care to avoid contacting desirable plants with these herbicides. Repeated spraying is usually required.

Dandelion *(Taraxacum officinale).* Familiar as a lawn weed throughout the West, dandelions are particularly troublesome in the Northwest and mountain states. As the plants mature, they form a deep, fleshy taproot. They spread by windborne seeds that appear in fluffy heads after the familiar yellow blossoms fade.

If dandelions are growing in your lawn, the turf is probably thin and undernourished. A healthy lawn can outcompete this weed, so thicken the turf by overseeding and proper fertilizing, watering, and mowing. Pull dandelions from lawns and gardens while they're small, before they produce a deep taproot and set seed. Once the taproot has formed, it's necessary to remove all of it to get rid of the plant, since new plants can sprout from even a small piece. A dandelion weeder with a forked blade is helpful. A hand weeder with a bent shaft (or a ball attached to the shaft) to serve as a fulcrum increases leverage, helping to pop dandelions out of the ground.

For chemical control in lawns, use a postemergence product labeled for dandelions in turf; these typically combine several herbicides. Spot-treating with glyphosate will partially control dandelions in gardens, but take care not to get the chemical on desirable plants.

Kikuyu grass *(Pennisetum clandestinum).* A native of tropical Africa, kikuyu grass is used as a lawn grass in some coastal areas, but it has escaped cultivation to become a serious pest in lawns and ornamental beds. Spreading rapidly by rhizomes and stolons, it eventually forms an impenetrable mat of wiry stems. Both the stems and the medium green leaves are covered with fine hairs. In Southern California, kikuyu grass also spreads by seed.

If you plant this grass as a turf, contain its spread with a strong barrier that extends 6 to 8 inches into the soil. Dig any invading kikuyu

PRODUCTS FOR WEED CONTROL

Herbicides are classified according to what stage of weed growth they affect, as well as by how they damage weeds.

Pre-emergence herbicides work by inhibiting the growth of germinating weed seeds and very young seedlings; they do not affect established plants. To be effective, they must thus be applied before the seeds sprout. Before applying these chemicals in ornamental gardens, remove any existing weeds. Some pre-emergence products are formulated to kill germinating weeds in lawns; these may be sold in combination with fertilizers, which increase the vigor of the lawn and improve its ability to compete against weeds. (Such dual-purpose products should not, however, be treated solely as fertilizers and reapplied whenever the lawn needs feeding—for that purpose, use a regular lawn fertilizer.) Some pre-emergence products must be watered into the soil, while others are incorporated into it. Some may also harm seeds you sow later in the season. Check the label to learn how long the product remains active in the soil.

Postemergence herbicides act on growing weeds rather than on seeds. They damage plants in different ways. Those that are ***translocated*** must be absorbed by the plant through its leaves or stems; they then kill it by interfering with its metabolism. ***Contact*** herbicides kill only the plant parts on which they are sprayed; regrowth can still occur from roots or unsprayed buds.

The natural and synthetic herbicides listed here are widely available to Western gardeners. ***Synthetic herbicides*** are manufactured compounds that do not normally occur in nature. ***Natural herbicides,*** in contrast, are products whose active ingredients originate in a plant or mineral.

When using any herbicide, ***read the label directions carefully and follow them exactly.*** The package will clearly state the weeds the product controls and the other plants, if any, around which it can be safely used; it is illegal to apply it to any plant not designated as a target. Always dispose of pesticides in a safe manner (see page 684).

The following products are listed alphabetically by the accepted common name of the ***active ingredient***—the actual chemical that controls the weed or weeds listed on the package label. Some widely used trade names, if they differ from the common name, are noted in parentheses. Before you buy, read the label to make sure you're getting the active ingredient you want. (For more on reading and understanding pesticide labels, see page 686.)

NATURAL HERBICIDES

- **Corn gluten meal (Suppressa, others).** Pre-emergence. Used to control some germinating weed seeds in lawns. This product is also a fertilizer, serving to thicken lawns and thus suppress weed growth (some research shows that this may be its primary contribution to weed control).
- **Herbicidal soap (Superfast, others).** Postemergence. Contact herbicides that degrade quickly. Kill top growth of young, actively growing weeds; work most effectively on annual weeds. Made from selected fatty acids (as are insecticidal soaps).

SYNTHETIC HERBICIDES

- **Fluazifop-butyl.** Postemergence. A translocated herbicide that controls actively growing grasses. Can be sprayed over many broad-leafed ornamentals without damaging them; check the label.
- **Glufosinate-ammonium (Finale).** Postemergence. Contact herbicide that damages or kills many kinds of weeds. Take care not to apply to desirable plants.
- **Glyphosate (Roundup).** Postemergence. Translocated herbicide that kills or damages any plant it contacts. Effective on a broad range of troublesome weeds, but must be used with care to avoid contacting desirable plants.
- **Oryzalin (Surflan).** Pre-emergence. Used to control annual grasses and many broad-leafed weeds in warm-season turf grasses and in gardens.
- **Pendimethalin (Prowl).** Pre-emergence. Used to control many grasses and broad-leafed weeds in turf and in ornamental plantings. Toxic to fish.
- **Sethoxydim (Grass-Getter).** Postemergence. Translocated herbicide that controls many grasses growing in ornamental plantings; check the label.
- **Triclopyr (Brush-B-Gon, Turflon Ester).** Postemergence. Translocated herbicide. Depending on formulation, used on cool-season turf to control broad-leafed weeds and Bermuda grass; also used to control hard-to-kill woody plants. Use with care to avoid damaging desirable plants.
- **Trifluralin.** Pre-emergence. Controls many grasses and broad-leafed weeds in turf and ornamental plantings. Toxic to fish.

grass out of garden beds, removing as much of the root system as possible. Plan on repeating this process, since the grass will resprout from any rhizomes left in the soil.

For chemical treatment, spray with a postemergence herbicide that controls grassy weeds, such as fluazifop-butyl or sethoxydim. Or spot-treat with an herbicide containing triclopyr or glyphosate, taking care not to contact desirable plants.

Nutsedge, yellow *(Cyperus esculentus).* Yellow nutsedge resembles a grass, but its stems are solid and triangular in cross-section, and its leaves grow from the base in groups of three. True grasses, in contrast, have hollow stems that are oval or flat in cross-section, and their leaves grow in sets of two. Yellow nutsedge forms small, roundish tubers (nutlets) at tips of roots; it spreads by these tubers as well as by seed.

Yellow nutsedge

Remove plants when they are young and still small. Older, taller plants are mature enough to produce tubers; when you dig or pull the plant, the tubers remain in the soil to sprout. Repeatedly removing top growth eventually weakens tubers. Soil solarization provides only partial control.

TOP TO BOTTOM: Yellow oxalis, Poison oak, Quack grass

For postemergence chemical control, try glyphosate, being careful not to get the chemical on desirable plants. It is most effective on young plants; it will not kill mature tubers or those that have become detached from the treated plant.

Oxalis, yellow *(Oxalis corniculata)*. Also called yellow wood sorrel, this aggressive weed thrives throughout the West. Happy in sun or shade, it spreads quickly by seed. Seedlings start from a single taproot, which soon develops into a shallow, spreading, knitted root system. Tiny, five-petaled yellow flowers are followed by elongated seed capsules that can propel seed as far as 6 feet.

Dig out small plants before they have a chance to set seed. Keep lawns vigorous to provide tough competition; water deeply but infrequently, since frequent shallow watering encourages this shallow-rooted weed.

For chemical control, use a pre-emergence herbicide containing oryzalin or pendimethalin on the turf grasses and around the ornamental plants listed on the label. Oxalis growing in cool-season lawn grasses can be treated with some products containing triclopyr, as indicated on the label. Spot-treat oxalis with glyphosate, taking care to keep the chemical from contacting desirable plants.

Poison oak, poison ivy *(Toxicodendron diversilobum, T. radicans)*. Poison oak is most common in California, western Oregon, and western Washington. In the open or in filtered sun, it forms a dense, leafy shrub; in the shade, it's a tall-growing vine. Its leaves are divided into three leaflets with scalloped, toothed, or lobed edges. (Leaves of true oaks, in contrast, are not divided; they grow singly, with each leaf on a separate stem.) Poison ivy, common east of the Rockies and also in eastern Oregon, eastern Washington, and parts of British Columbia and Alberta, is quite similar in appearance. Usually found in shady areas and at the edges of woodlands, it sprawls along the ground until it finds something to climb; then it becomes a vine.

A resin on the leaves, stems, fruits, and roots of both plants causes severe contact dermatitis in most people. Leaves turn red in fall, then drop—but plants are just as poisonous in winter as when in leaf. Never burn poison oak or ivy; the smoke is toxic.

Poison oak and poison ivy are most effectively controlled with an appropriately labeled herbicide, such as triclopyr or glyphosate; take care to avoid getting these chemicals on desirable plants. Repeated applications are needed as new leaves grow.

Quack grass *(Elytrigia repens)*. Also known as couch grass or devil's grass, this aggressive weed invades both lawns and gardens. It can reach 3 feet tall but stays much lower in mowed areas. It produces an extensive network of long, slender, branching, yellowish white rhizomes that can spread laterally 3 to 5 feet. The rhizomes are able to penetrate hard soil and grow into tubers and rhizomes of other plants such as potatoes and iris.

Because it reproduces readily from even small pieces of rhizome left in the soil, quack grass is difficult to manage. Before planting, thoroughly dig the area and remove all visible pieces of rhizome; this will slow the weed's growth for a few years.

For chemical control, use herbicides that control grassy weeds, such as fluazifop-butyl or sethoxydim. Or spot-treat with an herbicide containing glyphosate, taking care to avoid contact with desirable plants.

Wildlife, Gardening to Attract

Making your garden attractive to wildlife—songbirds, hummingbirds, butterflies, toads, lizards, frogs, and other creatures—is primarily a matter of providing shelter, water, and food. It's also important to avoid using pesticides. Try to emphasize native plants, since they're familiar to the local wildlife and adapted to your climate. Also remember that a garden teeming with wildlife is not overly tidy; parts of it are left to grow naturally, providing safe havens for creatures of all sorts. See A Guide to Plant Selection (beginning on page 64) for lists of plants attractive to butterflies and hummingbirds, including kinds that provide food for butterfly larvae (caterpillars).

A GARDEN FOR WILDLIFE

Tall trees. Provide shelter, food (seeds or fruits), and nesting places; also protect the garden from strong winds.

Hummingbird feeder. To prepare feeder solution, combine 1 part granulated sugar and 4 parts water and bring to a boil; let cool. Keep feeder clean; hummers can develop a deadly infection from dirty feeders.

Birdbath. To provide some protection from cats and other predators, place in an open area; a location 10 to 20 feet from shrubs offers a safety zone. In freezing weather, thaw water with boiling water or use a birdbath heater.

Hedgerow. Provides food, shelter, and nesting sites for birds. Plant a selection of small trees and low to medium-tall shrubs; include fruit-bearing types as well as kinds that feed butterfly larvae.

Brush pile. Instead of hauling away or shredding tree prunings and other brush, make piles to shelter birds and other wildlife.

Flower borders. Include a wide selection of plants that provide nectar for butterflies, beneficial insects, and hummingbirds; also plant species whose foliage feeds butterfly larvae. Let plants go to seed to furnish food for songbirds.

Nesting boxes. Install away from the activity around feeders and face away from prevailing weather. Mount on metal poles to keep cats and raccoons at bay.

Meadow. Plant native grasses, wildflowers, and low shrubs for food, shelter, and nest-building materials.

Pond. Provides water for birds and a habitat for frogs and turtles. Birds are especially attracted to the splashing water of a small fountain. Make a "beach" at one side to provide shallow water. An "island" (a large rock) in the center provides refuge for turtles and frogs. Water plants add more shelter.

Vines. Flowering vines provide shelter, nesting sites, and nectar; many also bear berries and foliage that are sources of food for birds and butterfly larvae.

Rocky area. Shelters lizards and toads.

Bird feeders. Locate feeders near trees or shrubs so birds can fly to cover; keep them off the ground to protect the clientele from cats. Set up feeders in fall and maintain them through winter when natural foods are scarce. Keep feeders clean. Besides seeds (sunflower, millet, safflower, thistle, and so on), birds enjoy suet, offered in mesh bags or special feeders.

RESOURCE DIRECTORY

Many resources are available to inspire and help Western gardeners. Since the 1800s, the West's fertile valleys and mild coastal plains have attracted enthusiastic gardeners and plant collectors who have started successful nurseries, created distinctly Western garden styles, and left as legacies great gardens. Today, growers from New Mexico to Alaska offer a vast array of plants—everything from native grasses to roses, plumerias, and poinsettias. But with these many choices comes the difficulty of zeroing in on the best plants for your garden. The following pages list resources to help you choose plants.

Public and Historic Gardens

There are many fine gardens throughout the West that are open to the public, ranging in size from a city block to hundreds of acres. Some are part of historic estates. Some recreate wild lands. Others are formal gardens or displays of plants in labeled collections. They may have demonstration gardens packed with flowers, fruits, and vegetables or gardens featuring plants that attract wildlife, plants well suited to dry areas, or plants for fire-prone areas. Many offer classes or seminars, demonstrate gardening techniques, operate horticultural libraries, and sell hard-to-find plants.

If you're planting a new garden or adding to an established one, a visit to a public garden can give you ideas to work with in your garden, such as plants well suited to your climate, show-stopping flower combinations, innovative ways to plant vegetable beds, and interesting container plantings. Before you purchase new plants, you can see which fit best with your natural landscape and what they look like when fully grown. You'll find listings of these gardens by state on pages 733–741.

Scientific Plant Names

In public gardens, nurseries, and catalogs, you'll most likely encounter scientific plant names (also referred to as botanical or Latin names). To learn about their significance and meaning, see pages 742–743. How do you pronounce them? For guidelines, see pages 744–745.

Flowering vines and ground covers enhance the natural beauty of Glacier Gardens Rainforest Adventure in Juneau, Alaska. Visitors to this public garden can gather ideas for use in their own gardens in similar climate zones.

PUBLIC AND HISTORIC GARDENS

An important resource for home gardeners, public and historic gardens display plants from around the world and from their own regions, often in landscape situations. Some are living plant laboratories that oversee the propagation and preservation of endangered plants. Historic gardens often include grand old estates left to posterity by pioneering gardeners and plant collectors as well as living museums that celebrate plants of the region and beyond. Such gardens are often rich in ideas that gardeners can take home, and they offer the opportunity to view plants tested by time and local climate. Below we list public and historic gardens we have visited around the West. Hours listed are subject to change.

ALASKA

Alaska Botanical Garden
Campbell Airstrip Road
Anchorage, AK 99520
(907) 770-3692

http://www.alaska.net/~garden

Daily 9 to 9

Specialty: plants for south-central Alaska

More than 480 varieties of plants are displayed on 11 acres of this 110-acre site. A perennial demonstration garden features raised beds made of recycled construction materials, and a wildflower trail winds around moss- and lichen-covered boulders, remnants of glacial activity. Nature trails lead visitors through forests, bogs, and meadows. Recent additions to the gardens include a formal herb garden and an alpine rock garden.

Georgeson Botanical Garden
West Tanana Drive
University of Alaska
Fairbanks, AK 99775
(907) 474-1959

http://www.lter.uaf.edu/salrm/gbg

Daily 8 to 8 May through September

Specialty: research and testing of plants for the far north

This 5-acre facility is the northernmost botanical garden in the Western Hemisphere. Paths wind through flower gardens, water and bog gardens, perennial trial gardens, a fern garden, and a garden featuring Alaska's world-famous giant vegetables.

Glacier Gardens Rainforest Adventure
7600 Glacier Highway
Juneau, AK 99801
(907) 790-3377

http://www.ptialaska.net/~ggardens

Daily 9 to 6 May through September

Specialty: garden plants in natural settings

This 50-acre site in southeast Alaska's Mendenhall Valley, home to an active glacier, enhances a rain forest setting with Japanese maples, dogwoods, rhododendrons, azaleas, ferns, and mosses. Visitors can take a motorized tour.

ARIZONA

The Arboretum at Flagstaff
4001 S. Woody Mountain Road
Flagstaff, AZ 86001
(520) 774-1442

http://www.thearb.org

Daily 9 to 5 April 1 through December 15

Specialty: high-elevation, low-rainfall plants

Ten acres of beautiful gardens, surrounded by 200 acres of ponderosa pine forest, display plants native to the alpine tundra, coniferous forest, and high desert of the Colorado Plateau. Located near the San Francisco Peaks, the arboretum (elevation 7,150 feet) conducts programs and classes as well as daily guided tours of the 11 display gardens, passive solar greenhouse, constructed wetlands, and nature trail.

The Arizona-Sonora Desert Museum
2021 N. Kinney Road
Tucson, AZ 85743
(520) 883-2702 (recording)
(520) 883-1380

http://www.desertmuseum.org

Daily 8:30 to 5 October through February, 7:30 to 5 March through September

Specialty: plants of the Sonoran Desert

This living museum encompasses more than 25 developed acres on a total of 88 acres, including demonstration gardens where you can see plants such as palo verdes and salvias that are well adapted to desert gardens. An enclosed garden contains hummingbirds and is landscaped with plants that attract them.

The Boyce Thompson Arboretum
37615 Highway 60
Superior, AZ 85273
(520) 689-2811 (recording)

http://arboretum.ag.arizona.edu

Daily 8 to 5; closed Christmas Day

Specialty: desert plants

Set against the steep red cliffs of Magma Ridge 60 miles east of Phoenix, the arboretum's 323 acres feature plants adapted to southern Arizona's Sonoran Desert as well as plants native to the Chihuahuan Desert.

The Boyce Thompson Arboretum

The Desert Botanical Garden
1201 N. Galvin Parkway
Phoenix, AZ 85008
(480) 941-1225

http://www.dbg.org

Daily 8 to 8 October through April, 7 a.m. to 8 p.m. May through September; closed Christmas Day

Specialty: plants of the Sonoran Desert

Displays on 145 acres focus on plants and ecology of the Sonoran Desert, featuring many kinds of cacti including giant saguaros. Display gardens showcase plants native to the deserts of Mexico, Australia, and Africa. October through May is the best time to visit. Wildflowers add seasonal color.

Tucson Botanical Gardens
2150 N. Alvernon Way
Tucson, AZ 85712
(520) 326-9686

http://www.tucsonbotanical.org

Daily 8:30 to 4:30; closed major holidays

Specialty: ideas for desert gardeners

Five acres of display areas and gardens include a Sensory Garden, to be explored by touch, smell, and taste; a Spring Wildflower Garden; and a Backyard Bird Garden. In the Xeriscape Garden plants are grouped by water needs. March and April are the gardens' most colorful months.

CALIFORNIA

The Arboretum of Los Angeles County
301 N. Baldwin Avenue
Arcadia, CA 91007
(626) 821-3222

http://www.arboretum.org

Daily 9 to 4:30; closed Christmas Day

Specialties: plants from around the world, demonstration gardens

Demonstration gardens and greenhouses are scattered throughout these 127 acres around the former estate of plant collector Elia J. Baldwin. Plants are grouped according to regions of origin; many are being tested for suitability to Southern California's climate. Palm-edged Baldwin Lake and an 1880s Queen Anne cottage are popular backdrops for films and television.

Blake Garden
70 Rincon Road
Kensington, CA 94707
(510) 524-2449 (recording)

Monday through Friday 8 to 4:30; closed university holidays

Specialty: Mediterranean plants

This garden surrounds an Italianate house used by the president of the University of California at Berkeley. The garden on the 10.5-acre site is run by the university's Department of Landscape Architecture and Environmental Planning. Formal gardens surround a reflecting pool shaded by magnolia trees. Dryland plants from the Mediterranean, South Africa, and South America thrive on a sunny, west-facing slope against the backdrop of San Francisco Bay.

Descanso Gardens
1418 Descanso Drive
La Cañada, CA 91011
(818) 952-4400

http://www.descansogardens.org

Daily 9 to 4:30; closed Christmas Day

Specialties: camellias, roses

Many camellias the size of large trees bloom mostly January through March on this site, which began as a private estate called Rancho del Descanso, "Ranch of Rest." The garden's 165 acres, about half of which are cultivated, also contain an international rosarium, a California native plant garden on 15 acres, and a Japanese garden where azaleas and wisteria bloom beside streams and a teahouse. Bulbs are another spring highlight: the tulip display typically includes 20,000 bulbs.

Filoli
86 Cañada Road
Woodside, CA 94062
About 25 miles south of San Francisco
(650) 364-8300 ext. 507

http://www.filoli.org

Tuesday through Saturday 10 to 2 mid-February through October. Docent-led tours available; call for reservations

Specialties: spring bulbs, roses, rhododendrons

Magnificent formal gardens surround a stately Georgian manor house. Walls and hedges divide the 16-acre gardens into individual garden rooms, including a sunken garden with lily pond; the Woodland Garden, where tall oaks shelter rhododendrons; and the Rose Garden, with more than 500 plants. Spectacular spring display of 40,000 bulbs, annuals, flowering fruit trees, and a huge, old wisteria.

Fullerton Arboretum
California State University, Fullerton
1900 Associated Road
Fullerton, CA 92831
(714) 278-3579

http://arboretum.fullerton.edu

Daily 8 to 4:45; closed major holidays

The Living Desert

Specialties: plants from around the world, rare fruit trees
A 26-acre oasis that displays plants from around the world arranged by climate. Gardens include the Rare Fruit Grove and Orchard, Desert Garden, Thorn Forest, Chaparral Hill (featuring California native plants), a bog garden of carnivorous plants, and a subtropical woodland containing a rain forest section and a collection of rare and unusual cycads and palms. Tours and workshops are offered throughout the year.

The Huntington Botanical Gardens
1151 Oxford Road
San Marino, CA 91108
(626) 405-2141

http://www.huntington.org

Tuesday through Friday noon to 4:30, Saturday and Sunday 10:30 to 4:30; closed major holidays

Specialty: plants from around the world
More than 150 meticulously landscaped acres, showcasing one of the country's finest collections of plants, surround the former mansion of the late railroad tycoon Henry E. Huntington. The plants—many of them rare—are displayed in separate gardens: the Jungle Garden, the Palm Garden, the 12-acre Desert Garden (which contains a large collection of cacti and succulents), and the Camellia Garden, Rose Garden, and Japanese Garden. A Shakespeare Garden features many of the plants mentioned in the playwright's works.

The Living Desert
47900 Portola Avenue
Palm Desert, CA 92260
(760) 346-5694

http://www.livingdesert.org

Daily 9 to 4 September 1 through June 15, 8 to 1:30 June 16 through August 31

Specialty: plants and animals of the Southwest deserts
More than 1,200 acres include protected, preserved natural desert; some 20 acres of developed gardens; demonstration gardens; trails; a plant nursery; and live desert animals in realistic settings. Plants on display include palms from around the world and groves of smoke trees.

Lotusland
695 Ashley Road
Santa Barbara, CA 93108
(805) 969-9990 weekdays 9 to noon (reservation office)

http://www.lotusland.org

Limited-space tours by reservation only, Wednesday through Saturday at 10 and 1:30 mid-February to mid-November

Specialty: rare and exotic subtropical plants in novel settings
This 37-acre estate was the home of the late Ganna Walska, an eccentric Polish opera diva and a passionate plant collector. Hosts 13 gardens, including gardens that feature plants with bluish foliage, aloes, a cycad garden containing more than 370 plant specimens, a Japanese garden, and a water garden featuring lotuses, papyrus, and water lilies.

Lummis Home State Historic Monument
200 E. Avenue 43
Los Angeles, CA 90031
(323) 222-0546

http://www.socalhistory.org

Friday through Sunday noon to 4

Specialty: Mediterranean and California native plants
Mature sycamore trees, oaks, and California bay trees create a leafy backdrop for this historic stone house built by Charles Lummis and called El Alisal, "The Place of the Sycamores." The 1.8-acre site includes a garden that Lummis began and tended until his death in 1928; the garden now displays dry-climate plants from around the world. Most colorful in spring, when ceanothus and wildflowers bloom, and in summer, when crape myrtles bear their papery flowers.

Luther Burbank Home & Gardens
Santa Rosa Avenue at Sonoma Avenue
Santa Rosa, CA 95402
(707) 524-5445

http://www.lutherburbank.org

Daily 8:00 a.m. until sunset

The home, greenhouse, and gardens where pioneer horticulturist Luther Burbank worked for most of his 50-year career. Intimate gardens include many of his introductions. Special events and tours are offered throughout the year.

Mendocino Coast Botanical Gardens
18220 N. Highway 1
Fort Bragg, CA 95437
(707) 964-4352

http://www.gardenbythesea.org

Daily 9 to 5 March through October, 9 to 4 November through February; closed Christmas Day, Thanksgiving, and the Saturday after Labor Day

Specialty: tender plants from around the world
The only public garden in the continental U.S. situated directly on the ocean. This 47-acre site includes canyons, wetlands, a pine forest, and coastal bluffs overlooking the Pacific. Formal gardens showcase old-fashioned roses, heaths, heathers, and rarely seen plants from Australia and New Zealand. Rare native species can be viewed in natural plant communities.

Mendocino Coast Botanical Gardens

Mildred E. Mathias Botanical Garden
University of California, Los Angeles
Los Angeles, CA 90095
(310) 825-1260

http://www.botgard.ucla.edu

Monday through Friday 8 to 5,
Saturday and Sunday 8 to 4

Specialty: plants from around the world, emphasizing tropicals and subtropicals

Named in honor of the renowned botanist, taxonomist, and conservationist Mildred E. Mathias, this 7-acre garden features plants that thrive in frost-free climates. More than 5,000 species displayed, with specialty collections of rhododendrons, palms, bromeliads, cycads, ferns, and shrubby plants of Mediterranean climates.

Mourning Cloak Ranch and Botanical Garden
22101 Old Town Road
Tehachapi, CA 93561
(661) 822-1661

http://tehachapi.com/mourningcloak

By appointment only

Specialties: plants from around the world, host and food plants for butterflies

At 4,000 feet in the Tehachapi Mountains, this garden comprises 22 acres on a private ranch named for the Mourning Cloak butterfly native to the area. More than 2,200 plant species are displayed along a meandering path. Seminars and guided tours are offered.

Quail Botanical Gardens
230 Quail Gardens Drive
Encinitas, CA 92024
(760) 436-3036

http://qbgardens.org

Daily 9 to 5; closed Thanksgiving,
Christmas Day, and New Year's Day

Specialties: bamboos, cycads, and palms

Over 30 acres of trails, gardens, and pools. Frost-free conditions favor the growth of tropical fruits. Focus on native people and plants and landscaping for fire safety. Two desert gardens are sited alongside a tropical rain forest garden.

Quarryhill Botanical Garden
12841 Sonoma Highway
Glen Ellen, CA 95442
(707) 996-3802

March through October by appointment only

Specialty: new garden plants from Asia

This 40-acre garden is dedicated to the conservation and study of Asian plants grown from seed collected in the wild. Since 1987, yearly expeditions to China, Japan, India, and Nepal have yielded plants that now constitute one of the largest collections of Asian plants in North America. Oaks, maples, dogwoods, and roses are particularly well represented among the garden's more than 17,000 plants.

Rancho Los Alamitos
6400 Bixby Hill Road
Long Beach, CA 90815
(562) 431-3541

http://www.ci.long-beach.ca.us/park/rancho

Wednesday through Sunday 1 to 5

The gardens of this 7.5-acre estate were designed and planted in the 1920s and consist of two bands of outdoor rooms encircling an adobe-style ranch house. The inner circle of terraces and paths provides a gentle transition from house to garden; outer beds are divided into theme gardens, including roses, native plants, and cacti.

Rancho Santa Ana Botanic Garden
1500 N. College Avenue
Claremont, CA 91711
(909) 625-8767

http://www.rsabg.org

Daily 8 to 5; closed major holidays

Specialty: California native plants

Quail Botanical Gardens

California native trees, shrubs, perennials, and bulbs grow throughout the garden's 86 acres in residential, chaparral, forest, woodland, and desert settings.

San Diego Zoo
2920 Zoo Drive
San Diego, CA 92103
(619) 231-1515

http://www.sandiegozoo.org

Daily hours vary

Specialty: exotic plants

This is one of the finest zoological gardens in the world, containing more than 6,500 plant species. Organized according to bioclimatic zones, the gardens present impressive collections of orchids, cycads, fig trees, palms, acacias, and coral trees.

Santa Barbara Botanic Garden
1212 Mission Canyon Road
Santa Barbara, CA 93105
(805) 682-4726

http://www.sbbg.org

Weekdays 9 to 5, weekends 9 to 6,
March through October; closes an hour earlier November through February

Specialty: California native plants

This 65-acre garden at the foot of the Santa Ynez Mountains has more than a thousand species of California native plants in habitats from oak woodland to wildflower meadow. A home demonstration garden displays native plants well suited to dry, fire-prone areas. Self-guided and docent-led tours are available.

Sherman Library and Garden
2647 E. Pacific Coast Highway
Corona Del Mar, CA 92625
(949) 673-2261

Daily 10:30 to 4; closed Thanksgiving,
Christmas Day, and New Year's Day

Specialty: flowering annuals

Colorful annuals, hanging baskets, and plants from around the world populate this garden, which covers a city block. Shaded patios spotlight grand collections of begonias and fuchsias. Ferns, orchids, and bromeliads thrive in the Tropical Conservatory.

South Coast Botanic Garden
26300 Crenshaw Boulevard
Palos Verdes Peninsula, CA 90274
(310) 544-6815

http://www.palosverdes.com/botanicgardens

Daily 9 to 5; closed Christmas Day

Specialties: ideas for home gardeners; plants from around the world

More than 87 acres of gardens on the site of a former diatomite mine. Trails wind through a diverse collection of trees, flowering plants, and demonstration gardens, with a particular emphasis on plants from Australia and South America.

Strybing Arboretum & Botanical Gardens
Golden Gate Park
Ninth Avenue at Lincoln Way
San Francisco, CA 94122
(415) 661-1316

http://www.strybing.org

Weekdays 8 to 4:30, weekends and holidays 10 to 5

Specialty: plants from around the world

In this 55-acre arboretum, plants are displayed in 17 theme gardens with labeled collections of plants from Asia, Australia, South Africa, Chile, Mexico, Central America, New Zealand, and California. Highlights include a redwood trail, a moon-viewing garden, and a garden of primitive plants. A 3.5-acre native plant section uses rocks, plant groupings, and low soil undulations to simulate creek beds and craggy terrain. In spring it's carpeted with blooming poppies, Pacific Coast irises, and meadowfoam.

Theodore Payne Foundation
10459 Tuxford Street
Sun Valley, CA 91352
(818) 768-1802; (818) 768-3533 (wildflower hotline March through June)

http://www.theodorepayne.org

Wednesday through Saturday 8:30 to 4:30, Sunday 11 to 4:30 October through June; Friday and Saturday 8:30 to 4:30, Sunday 12 to 4:30 July through September; closed major holidays

Specialties: native plants, wildflowers

This nonprofit organization dedicated to the preservation and use of wildflowers and native plants oversees a nursery and garden on the site's 21 acres. In spring Wildflower Hill is in brilliant bloom; demonstration gardens provide landscaping ideas.

UC Botanical Garden
200 Centennial Drive
Berkeley, CA 94720
(510) 643-2755

http://www.mip.berkeley.edu/garden

Daily 9 to 4:45; closed Christmas Day

Specialty: plants from around the world

A notably diverse collection of more than 13,000 kinds of plants from six continents naturalistically displayed according to region of origin on this hilly 34-acre site. Special features include some 11 acres devoted to California natives, a garden of old roses, a garden of Chinese medicinal herbs, and a glass house filled with economically important tropical plants.

UC Davis Arboretum
University of California at Davis
Davis, CA 95616
(530) 752-4880

http://arboretum.ucdavis.edu

Daily

Specialty: trees, shrubs, and perennials for dry gardens

Native and exotic trees—especially species that thrive in the Central Valley's hot, dry climate—provide plenty of shade throughout the 100-acre grounds. Plants from Mexico, Argentina, and Australia are featured in separate gardens. In the central section, native plants such as lupines and poppies put on a bloom show in spring.

UC Irvine Arboretum
North Campus
University of California at Irvine
Irvine, CA 92697
(949) 824-5833

http://darwin.bio.uci.edu/arboretum

Monday through Saturday 9 to 3; closed holidays

Specialty: plants from Mediterranean-climate regions

This 12-acre garden has a fine collection of plants from South Africa, California, and other dry-climate regions. Individual gardens display California wildflowers and shrubs, succulents from Baja California, ferns, South African bulbs and perennials, aloes, and Old World succulents.

UC Riverside Botanic Gardens
University of California at Riverside
Riverside, CA 92521
(909) 787-4650 or (909) 784-6962

Daily 8 to 5; closed major holidays

Specialty: plants from around the world

Plants from various regions arranged by microclimates and plant communities. Among them are rare fruits and desert plants like yuccas and jojobas. Visitors can take a self-guided tour along 4½ miles of scenic trails.

UC Santa Cruz Arboretum
University of California at Santa Cruz
1500 High Street
Santa Cruz, CA 95064
(831) 427-2998

http://www2.ucsc.edu/arboretum

Daily 9 to 5

Specialty: plants from Australia, New Zealand, South Africa, and California

This arboretum is a repository for plants from Mediterranean climates. In the Australian section, paths wind through tall trees (including many eucalypts) and shrubs such as grevilleas and banksias. Colorful proteas highlight the South African section.

Hudson Gardens, Littleton, Colorado

COLORADO

Betty Ford Alpine Gardens
530 S. Frontage Road East
Vail, CO 81657
(970) 476-0103

http://www.bettyfordalpinegardens.org

Dawn to dusk, snowmelt to snowfall

Specialty: alpine and rock garden plants

When the ski season ends, the growing season begins here, one of the highest alpine gardens (elevation 8,200 feet) in North America. Displayed among large rocks and water features is an extensive collection of alpine plants. A sunken garden demonstrates perennials suitable for the region, and a meditation garden is enclosed by a stand of Colorado blue spruces. The Alpine Rock Garden showcases hundreds of plants native to the Rocky Mountains.

Denver Botanic Garden
1005 York Street
Denver, CO 80206
(303) 331-4000

http://www.botanicgardens.org

Daily 9 to 5 October through April; Wednesday through Friday 9 to 5 and Saturday through Tuesday 9 to 8 May through September

Specialty: plants from around the world

Set in the heart of the city in view of the Rocky Mountains, this 23-acre landscape is a year-round haven for plant enthusiasts. In the Tropical Botanica conservatory, brilliant bougainvilleas and orchids challenge winter doldrums. Theme gardens include a Japanese garden, a plains garden, an extensive shade garden, a Western cottage garden, and a renowned rock garden. Lectures and workshops are offered.

Hudson Gardens
6115 S. Santa Fe Drive
Littleton, CO 80120
(303) 797-8565

http://www.hudsongardens.org

Daily 9 to 5 May through September, 10 to 2 October through April

Specialty: Colorado landscape plants

This 30-acre garden is known for its beautiful displays of trees, grasses, and flowers that thrive in the dry Colorado climate. Sixteen garden rooms contain rose gardens, wildflower and prairie-grass meadows, perennial display gardens, conifer groves, and water gardens. The site includes a natural wetlands habitat.

Western Colorado Botanical Garden and Butterfly House
641 Struthers Avenue
Grand Junction, CO 81501
(970) 245-3288

http://www.wcbotanic.org

Tuesday through Sunday 10 to 5 March through October, 10 to 4:30 November through February

Specialty: community education

Located on the bank of the Colorado River, this 12.3-acre facility encompasses a butterfly house and a greenhouse in addition to several outdoor gardens including a children's garden and areas devoted to native plants, roses, and dahlias. The greenhouse contains more than 600 tropical plants and houses in a separate area 24 species of butterflies in a climate-controlled enclosure. Seminars and workshops.

Hawaii Tropical Botanical Garden

HAWAII

Amy B. H. Greenwell Ethnobotanical Garden
Route 11
Captain Cook, HI 96704
12 miles south of Kailua-Kona on the Big Island
(808) 323-3318

http://www.bishopmuseum.org/greenwell

Monday through Friday 8:30 to 5

Specialty: Hawaiian plants

This 15-acre landscaped plant collection and archaeological site demonstrates traditional uses of Hawaiian plants and land. More than 250 types of native and Polynesian introduced plants are displayed, including major collections of taro, sugar cane, and rare plants native to the dry forest. Guided tours available.

Hawaii Tropical Botanical Garden
27-717 Old Mamalahoa Highway
Papaikou, HI 96781
On the 4-Mile Scenic Route, 8 miles north of Hilo on the Big Island
(808) 964-5233

http://www.htbg.com

Daily 9 to 5; closed Thanksgiving, Christmas Day, and New Year's Day

Specialty: tropical plants

This 40-acre garden tucked into the Onomea Valley hosts an international collection of more than 2,500 species of tropical plants, including world-class collections of palms, heliconias, and orchids. Century-old mango and palm trees tower above trails cut into lava rock, and a three-tiered waterfall is regarded as one of Hawaii's most beautiful.

Honolulu Botanical Gardens
Head Office: Foster Botanical Garden
50 N. Vineyard Boulevard
Honolulu, HI 96817
(808) 522-7060

http://www.co.honolulu.hi.us/parks/hbg

Daily 9 to 4; closed Christmas and New Year's Day

Specialties: vary according to site

Five gardens in separate locations of Oahu are operated by Honolulu Botanical Gardens. Foster Botanical Garden, on 13 acres in downtown Honolulu, displays orchids and large, old tropical trees like Mindanao gum. Koko Crater Botanical Garden showcases dryland plants in a wild setting, occupying the crater of an extinct volcano. Wahiawa Botanical Garden, a cool rain forest habitat, straddles a 27-acre wooded gulch in Wahiawa, 13 miles northwest of Honolulu, and features native Hawaiian plants, palms, heliconias, and epiphytic orchids, ferns, and cacti. Ho'omaluhia, tucked against Oahu's windward cliffs, is a 400-acre garden of trees (including one of the world's largest mango trees) and shrubs of Hawaii, Polynesia, and wet, lowland tropics. Lili'uokalani Botanical Garden, on 7 acres near downtown Honolulu, features native Hawaiian plants and a popular urban waterfall.

Lyon Arboretum
3860 Manoa Road
Honolulu, HI 96822
(808) 988-0456

http://www.hawaii.edu/lyonarboretum

Monday through Saturday 9 to 3

Specialty: plants from the world's tropical regions

A lush 194-acre garden in the upper Manoa Valley hosts exotics from around the world. Paths wind among towering palms and majestic trees and vines. An ethnobotanical garden displays plants used by the earliest Hawaiians for food, medicine, and building materials. Conservation of endangered native plants is an important focus.

National Tropical Botanical Garden Headquarters
3530 Papalina Road
Kalaheo, HI 96741
(808) 332-7324

http://www.ntbg.org

Call locations for hours

Specialties: tropicals and native Hawaiian plants

The nation's sole congressionally chartered tropical botanical garden has four locations in Hawaii. McBryde Garden, on the south shore of Kauai, features the world's largest collection of native Hawaiian plants, including some that are extinct in the wild. Reservations are required; call 808-742-2623. Adjacent to this site is the Allerton Garden, a former estate, where statuary, fountains, and pools are tucked among tropical plants. Reservations are required; call 808-742-2623. Limahuli Garden is situated on the north shore of Kauai. A pristine stream transects the garden and feeds the taro growing in terraces built by the island's first settlers. Call 808-826-1053 for more information. On the east shore of Maui, Kahanu Garden sits among jagged volcanic lava flows and a forest of native *hala* (screwpine). It hosts the world's largest collection of breadfruit, a staple in the Polynesian diet, and an ancient *heau* (stone temple). Call 808-248-8912 for more information.

Waimea Arboretum and Botanical Garden
59-864 Kamehameha Highway
Haleiwa, HI 96712
(808) 638-8655

Daily 10 to 5:30

Specialties: tropicals and native Hawaiian plants

This 100-acre garden straddles a coastal valley on Oahu's windward side. Paths wander among 36 small gardens featuring regional collections of tropical plants, mostly from islands such as Guam, Fiji, and the Mascarenes, as well as Hawaiian native plants. This garden hosts one of the world's largest collections of coral trees.

IDAHO

The Idaho Botanical Garden
2355 N. Penitentiary Road
Boise, ID 83712
(208) 343-8649

http://www.idahobotanicalgarden.org

Weekdays 9 to 5, weekends 10 to 6, spring through fall; call for winter hours.

Specialty: plants for Idaho gardens

Built on the former site of a state penitentiary, this 12-acre garden is divided into 13 specialty gardens devoted to herbs, roses, irises, alpines, cacti, Idaho native plants, and plants that attract butterflies and hummingbirds.

NEVADA

Desert Demonstration Gardens
3701 W. Alta Drive
Las Vegas, NV 89153
(702) 258-3205

http://www.lvvwd.com/conservation/ddg/ddg.html

Daily 8 to 5; closed major holidays

Specialty: water-conserving gardens

Developed in cooperation with the Las Vegas Valley Water District, these demonstration gardens showcase plants and designs for water-efficient landscaping. The 2.4-acre grounds include a children's vegetable garden, an herb garden, a wildflower garden, and an area devoted to cacti. Simulated residential landscapes illustrate water-efficient designs, and a sloping wash is planted with Joshua trees, creosote bushes, mesquites, and other native plants.

Wilbur D. May Arboretum and Botanical Garden
1502 Washington Street
Reno, NV 89503
(775) 785-4153

http://www.maycenter.com

Daily 8 a.m. to sunset

Specialty: plants for the high desert

Twelve-acre high-desert (4,600 feet) garden sited between the Sierra Nevada and the Great Basin desert. Snowmelt feeds a creek that runs past groves of trees, outdoor courtyards, and small secluded gardens before ending in a wetland habitat. The Songbird Garden is filled with plants that offer birds food and shelter.

NEW MEXICO

Rio Grande Botanic Garden
2601 Central Avenue N.W.
Albuquerque, NM 87104
(505) 764-6200

http://www.cabq.gov/biopark/garden

Tuesday through Sunday 9 to 5 (Saturday and Sunday 9 to 6 June through August)

Specialty: diverse plants in a beautiful setting

Part of the Albuquerque Biological Park, this garden includes a glass conservatory hosting year-round blooms, desert species, and aromatic Mediterranean plants. Three walled gardens display herbs and roses among tiled fountains. The Butterfly Pavilion houses blooming plants and butterflies.

OREGON

Hoyt Arboretum
400 S.W. Fairview Boulevard
Portland, OR 97221
(503) 228-8733

http://www.parks.ci.portland.or.us/parks/hoytarboretum.htm

Daily dawn to dusk

Specialties: conifers, flowering trees and shrubs

Trails crisscross this 175-acre site through collections of trees from around the world as well as the Pacific Northwest. In spring, flowering cherries and magnolias are cloaked in blooms. Fall brings flaming glory to the arboretum's poplars, persimmons, and maples.

Japanese Garden Society of Portland
611 S.W. Kingston Avenue
Portland, OR 97201
(503) 223-1321

http://www.japanesegarden.com

Hours vary with seasons; closed holidays

Specialty: Japanese garden design

Set on a hilly 5.5 acres, this garden is filled with formal Japanese garden designs. Evergreen and deciduous plants offer striking textural contrasts alongside ponds and winding paths. The Natural Garden features waterfalls and bamboo fences; the Strolling Pond Garden incorporates Japanese maples, weeping cherries, and conifers in its design. Visit in October and November to see maples in vibrant color, in March and April for cherries in bloom.

Japanese Garden Society of Portland

Leach Botanical Garden
6704 S.E. 122nd Avenue
Portland, OR 97236
(503) 761-9503

http://www.parks.ci.portland.or.us/parks/leachbotanicalgar.htm

Tuesday through Saturday 9 to 4,
Sunday 1 to 4

Specialty: Pacific Northwest natives

More than 2,000 plant species and varieties, including some 125 Northwest natives, grow in this 5-acre garden started in the 1930s by botanist Lilla Leach and her husband, John. Most of the native plants are arranged in habitat groupings, such as a dry woodland, a riparian area, and a rock garden. To see azaleas, camellias, and wildflowers in bloom, visit in spring. Self-guided and curator-led tours.

Mount Pisgah Arboretum
33735 Seavey Loop Road
Eugene, OR 97405
(541) 747-3817

http://www.efn.org/~mtpisgah

Daily sunrise to sunset

Specialty: wildflowers of the Northwest

The arboretum occupies 208 acres within the 2,300-acre Howard Buford Recreation Area bordering the coast fork of the Willamette River on the slope of Mount Pisgah. Seven miles of all-weather trails and 23 bridges lead visitors through diverse ecological habitats—from riparian meadow to oak savanna, from open plateaus to forested hillsides. A 2-acre wildflower garden is planted with Western native (some indigenous) and introduced trees, shrubs, ferns, perennials, and annuals adapted to mesic and riparian habitats. Nature walks and weekend workshops.

Oregon Garden
879 W. Main Street
Silverton, OR 97381
(877) 674-2733 (toll-free)

http://www.oregongarden.org

Daily 9 to 6 April through October, 9 to 3 November through March; closed Thanksgiving, Christmas Day, and New Year's Day

Specialty: display gardens

This beautifully designed site 15 miles east of Salem contains more than a dozen specialty gardens, including a wetlands area, a native oak woodland, a conifer garden, a rose garden, tulips and annuals, and a children's garden. Guided tours, classes, and seminars are offered.

Red Butte Garden and Arboretum/State Arboretum of Utah

UTAH

Red Butte Garden and Arboretum/ State Arboretum of Utah
University of Utah
300 Wakara Way
Salt Lake City, UT 84108
(801) 581-4747

http://www.redbutte.utah.edu

Monday through Saturday 9 to 8,
Sunday 9 to 5 May through September;
Tuesday through Sunday 10 to 5
October through April

Specialty: gardening in the intermountain West

With more than 150 acres of gardens, this is the largest botanical and ecological center in the intermountain West that tests, displays, and interprets regional horticulture. Plants are displayed among fountains and waterfalls. Programs include workshops, nature outings, and children's events.

WASHINGTON

Bellevue Botanical Garden
12001 Main Street
Bellevue, WA 98005
(425) 452-2750

http://www.bellevuebotanical.org

Daily dawn to dusk; visitor center
open daily 10 to 4

Specialties: perennials, alpine rock garden, water-wise garden

This 36-acre garden offers plenty of garden and plant ideas for Northwest gardeners. It is organized into separate garden rooms, which include a water-wise garden, dahlia and fuchsia display gardens, and a native plant garden, joined by a half-mile loop trail. A 300-foot-long perennial border is at its peak bloom in late spring.

Bloedel Reserve
7571 N.E. Dolphin Drive
Bainbridge Island, WA 98110
(206) 842-7631

http://www.bloedelreserve.org

Wednesday through Sunday; closed on national holidays; reservations required

Specialty: garden rooms

Native woodland and meadows crisscross this 150-acre site. The moss garden, reflection pool, bird marsh, English landscape, and Japanese garden reflect styles that influence garden design in the Pacific Northwest.

Lakewold
Lakewood, WA 98498
On Gravelly Lake, 8 miles south of Tacoma
(253) 584-4106

http://lakewold.org

Thursday and Saturday through Monday
10 to 4, Friday noon to 8, April through
September; Friday and Saturday only
10 to 3 October through March;
reservations required for guided tours

Specialty: plants in formal settings

Started in the 1920s and developed over more than a half century, this 10-acre lakeside garden includes boxwood parterres, a rose-covered teahouse, and a knot garden of handsomely interwoven herbs.

Ohme Gardens
3327 Ohme Road
Wenatchee, WA 98801
Just north of Wenatchee near junction
of Highways 2 and 97A
(509) 662-5785

http://www.ohmegardens.com

Daily 9 to 6 April 15 through October 15,
9 to 7 Memorial Day through Labor Day

Specialty: alpine rock garden plants

This 9-acre garden reflects the commitment of two generations of the Ohme family, who have created a natural-looking landscape of beauty and tranquility. Paths wind among rocky outcrops and up hillsides that are most colorful when sweeps of thyme and sedum bloom (beginning in April).

Rhododendron Species Botanical Garden
2525 S. 336th Street
Federal Way, WA 98003
(253) 838-4646; (253) 661-9377
for guided tours

http://www.halcyon.com/rsf/

Saturday through Thursday 10 to 4 March through May, Saturday through Wednesday 11 to 4 June through February

Specialty: species rhododendrons

These 22 woodland acres host one of the most expansive collections of rhododendron species in North America, with more than 10,000 plants representing 450 species. Many of them are rare. Companion plantings include ferns, primroses, irises, heathers, maples, and conifers, as well as many exotic and unusual plants.

Washington Park Arboretum
2300 Arboretum Drive East
Seattle, WA 98112
Just off Lake Washington Boulevard East
(206) 543-8800

Daily 7 a.m. to dusk

Specialty: landscape plants for western Washington

This 230-acre arboretum, founded in 1934, demonstrates the wealth of landscape plants well-suited to the Puget Sound area. Azalea Way is a promenade lined with flowering cherries, azaleas, and dogwoods. A waterfront wildlife habitat features alders, birches, oaks, and pines. In January, plants such as wintersweet and witch hazel add winter color and spice the air with fragrance. Japanese maples and other deciduous trees in the Woodland Garden offer fall color. Guided tours are offered.

Rhododendron Species Botanical Garden

WYOMING

Cheyenne Botanic Gardens
710 S. Lions Park Drive
Cheyenne, WY 82001
(307) 637-6458

http://www.botanic.org

Daily dawn to dusk; conservatory open Monday through Friday 8 to 4:30, weekends and most holidays 11 to 3:30

Specialty: outreach and education

Seniors, youth, and disabled volunteers provide the labor force for this garden. Seven acres of grounds feature perennials, annuals, roses, herbs, and cacti, as well as xeriscape and community gardens. A conservatory houses tropical and subtropical plants as well as garden crops. Flowers for municipal displays are grown on site.

ALBERTA

Devonian Botanic Garden
University of Alberta at Edmonton
Edmonton, AB, Canada T6G 2E1
(780) 987-3054

http://www.discoveredmonton.com/devonian

Call for hours

Specialty: cold-hardy plants

This is the northernmost botanical garden in Canada, with 80 acres of gardens and 110 acres of pine forest and wetland preserves. Features a Japanese garden, a primula dell, a butterfly house, and a native people's garden where plants used by the first people of Alberta are displayed.

BRITISH COLUMBIA

The Butchart Gardens
800 Benvenuto Avenue
Brentwood Bay, BC, Canada V8M 1J8
(250) 652-4422

http://www.butchartgardens.com

Call for hours

Specialty: flowering plants

This 50-acre garden, started in 1904, is considered one of the top tourist destinations in the Northwest. The Sunken Garden, once a limestone quarry, was originally planted by Jennie Butchart. In spring thousands of bulbs bloom; in summer hanging baskets overflow with flowers, and beds blaze with color against a backdrop of trees and shrubs. The vivid colors of Japanese maples steal the show in autumn.

The Horticulture Centre of the Pacific
505 Quayle Road
Victoria, BC, Canada V9E 2J7
(250) 479-6162

http://www.islandnet.com/~hcp

Daily 8 to 8 April 1 through October 31, 9 to 4:30 November 1 through March 31

Specialty: research and education

This site consists of 5 acres of demonstration gardens and 90 acres of mostly undeveloped land, including unspoiled wetlands and mature stands of Garry oak. Paths lead visitors through a winter garden and a Japanese garden, and around beds of lilies, herbs, rhododendrons, heathers, and dahlias, all maintained by local garden clubs. Monthly workshops and guided seasonal walks are offered.

University of British Columbia Botanical Garden
6804 Southwest Marine Drive
Vancouver, BC, Canada V6T 1Z4
(604) 822-3928

http://www.hedgerows.com

Daily 10 to 6 mid-March through mid-October, 10 to 2:30 mid-October through mid-March

Specialties: alpine plants, rhododendrons, and magnolias

On the shores of the Straits of Georgia, this 100-acre site includes a botanical garden and the Nitobe Memorial Garden, an authentic Japanese tea and stroll garden. The botanical garden hosts a food garden, an apothecary's garden, a garden for winter interest, an alpine rock garden, a garden displaying woody climbers on arbors, a British Columbia native garden, and an Asian garden that contains a renowned collection of rhododendrons.

VanDusen Botanical Garden
5251 Oak Street
Vancouver, BC, Canada V6M 4H1
(604) 878-9274

http://www.vandusengarden.org

Daily 10 a.m. to various closing times; closed Christmas Day

Specialty: plants from around the world

This 55-acre garden in the heart of Vancouver features more than 7,500 different kinds of plants from six continents. Garden areas, such as the Rhododendron Walk, illustrate botanical relationships or geographical origins, as in the Sino-Himalayan Garden. Seminars, lectures, and gardening classes are offered throughout the year.

DEMYSTIFYING
Scientific Plant Names

Campsis radicans

Scientific plant names can be intimidating to gardeners. So why have they been used around the world for hundreds of years? Why do we use them in this book? And why do the plants sold at nurseries most often have scientific names printed somewhere on their labels? There's good reason: common names for plants are often confusing and misleading. A single common name can apply to different plants in different parts of the country or the world. It can be used for two or more plants that not only look different but vary tremendously in growth habit, needs, and bloom season.

Scientific Names Are Precise

Scientific names are more precise than common ones. If you tell a nursery you want to buy a dusty miller, for example, you might be asked: "Which one?" A number of plants answer to the name. They are all perennials with silvery foliage, but *Centaurea cineraria* has big, yellow thistlelike flowers; *Senecio cineraria* has small yellow flowers; *Senecio vira-vira* has creamy white flowers; and *Lychnis coronaria* has magenta to crimson flowers.

Other plants with the same common name often are not at all similar. "Black-eyed Susan," for example, applies to a golden-flowered perennial *(Rudbeckia hirta)* and to a vine most often planted as a summer annual *(Thunbergia alata)*. "Angel's tears" is a bulb grown for its clusters of white flowers *(Narcissus triandrus)* and is also a ground cover with inconspicuous flowers *(Soleirolia soleirolii)*.

Rudbeckia hirta

Thunbergia alata

Ornamentals and weeds may bear the same common name. "Spanish broom" is either a tidy, 2-foot shrub with yellow flowers *(Genista hispanica)* or a rangy, 6- to 10-foot shrub *(Spartium junceum)* that runs wild across many parts of the West.

So the real reason for learning scientific names is a practical one: they provide the most accurate means we have for putting a verbal handle on a plant. You can't be sure what you are getting unless you order a plant by its scientific name.

Scientific Names Offer Clues

Scientific names, if you break them down, can tell you something about the plants. The first part of a scientific name is the genus name, which is usually a classical name. The second part is the species name, which is usually a descriptive word and often simple to decipher.

Descriptive words used again and again in species names are listed opposite. When you know the meanings of these words, many names become easy to understand and helpful in identifying plants. *Sollya heterophylla*, for example, combines *hetero* (heterogeneous or various) with *phylla* (leaves) to mean "various-size leaves." Some of the leaves are lanceolate and others are oblong.

The common names that are direct translations are among the easiest to remember. Bigleaf hydrangea *(Hydrangea macrophylla)* does have large leaves. *Macro* means large, *phylla* means leaves.

Some of the scientific names are so much like English words that there is no question as to their meaning. *Prostratum, compacta, deliciosa, fragrans,* and *pendula* all say something immediately recognizable.

A GUIDE TO BOTANICAL NAMES

Color of Flowers or Foliage

albus—white
argenteus—silvery
aureus—golden
azureus—azure, sky blue
caeruleus—dark blue
caesius—blue-gray
candidus—pure white, shiny
canus—ashy gray, hoary
cereus—waxy
citrinus—yellow
coccineus—scarlet
concolor—one color
croceus—yellow
cruentus—bloody
discolor—two colors, separate colors
glaucus—covered with gray bloom
incanus—gray, hoary
luteus—yellow
pallidus—pale
purpureus—purple
rubens, ruber—red, ruddy
rufus—ruddy

Dodonaea viscosa 'Purp

Form of Leaf (*folius*—leaves or foliage)

acerifolius—maplelike
angustifolius—narrow
aquifolius—spiny
buxifolius—boxwood-like
ilicifolius—hollylike
laurifolius—laurel-like
parvifolius—small
populifolius—poplarlike
salicifolius—willowlike

Lavandula angustifolia 'Hidcote'

Shape of Plant

adpressus—pressing against, hugging
altus—tall
arboreus—treelike
capitatus—headlike
compactus—compact, dense
confertus—crowded, pressed together

contortus—twisted
decumbens—trailing, with tips upright
depressus—pressed down
elegans—elegant, slender, willowy
fastigiatus—branches erect and close together
humifusus—sprawling on the ground
humilis—low, small, humble
impressus—sunken
nanus—dwarf
procumbens—trailing
prostratus—prostrate
pumilus—dwarf, small
pusillus—puny, insignificant
repens—creeping
reptans—creeping
scandens—climbing

Where It Came From

The suffix *-ensis* (of a place) is added to place names to specify the habitat where the plant was first discovered.

africanus—of Africa
alpinus—of the Alps
australis—southern
borealis—northern
campestris—of the field or plains
canadensis—of Canada
canariensis—of the Canary Islands
capensis—of the Cape of Good Hope area
chilensis—of Chile
chinensis—of China
hispanicus—of Spain
hortensis—of gardens
indicus—of India
insularis—of the island
japonicus—of Japan
littoralis—of the seashore

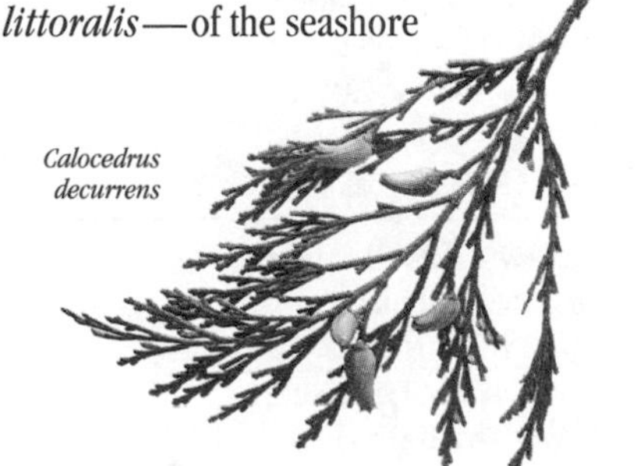

Calocedrus decurrens

montanus—of the mountains
riparius—of riverbanks
rivalis, rivularis—of brooks
saxatilis—inhabiting rocks

Plant Parts

dendron—tree
flora, florum, flori, florus—flowers
phyllus, phylla—leaf or leaves

Cestrum elegans

Zephyranthes grandiflora

Elaeagnus pungens

Ligustrum japonicum

Passiflora caerulea

Brachychiton acerifolius

Plant Peculiarities

armatus—armed
augusta—majestic, notable
baccatus—berried, berrylike
barbatus—barbed or bearded
campanulatus—bell or cup shaped
ciliaris—fringed
cordatus—heart shaped
cornutus—horned
crassus—thick, fleshy
decurrens—running down the stem
diversi—varying
edulis—edible
floridus—free flowering

Hydrangea macrophylla

fruticosus—shrubby
fulgens—shiny
gracilis—slender, thin, graceful
grandi—large, showy
-ifer, -iferus—bearing or having; e.g., *stoloniferus,* having stolons
imperialis—showy
laciniatus—fringed or with torn edges
laevigatus—smooth
lobatus—lobed
longus—long
macro—large
maculatus—spotted
micro—small
mollis—soft, soft-haired
mucronatus—pointed
nutans—nodding, swaying
obtusus—blunt or flattened
officinalis—medicinal
-oides—like or resembling; e.g., *jasminoides,* like a jasmine
patens—open, spreading growth
pinnatus—constructed like a feather
platy—broad
plenus—double, full
plumosus—feathery
praecox—early
pungens—piercing
radicans—rooting, especially along the stem

Gardenia augusta

reticulatus—net-veined
retusus—notched at blunt apex
rugosus—wrinkled, rough
saccharatus—sweet, sugary
sagittalis—arrowlike
scabrus—rough feeling
scoparius—broomlike

OUR SPELLING	AS IN
a	hat, hand
ay	baby
ah	hall
ai	air
e	met, bed
ee	we
i	tin
ye	wine
o	hot
oe	romance
u	must, burr
oo	rumor
ew	human
uh	comma, consider, sinister, vapor, minus

PRONUNCIATION GUIDE

Scientific names are the universal language for plants, but they are pronounced differently in various parts of the world, even among English-speaking countries. Because these names come from Latin and Greek, there is no absolute, approved, obligatory pronunciation for them—we say them as we choose. What follows is a list of the most-often-used ways to say many scientific plant names.

Abutilon

A

Abelia—uh-BEE-lee-uh
Abutilon—uh-BEW-tuh-lon

Acacia—uh-KAY-shuh
Acer—AY-sir
Achillea—ak-il-LEE-uh
Achimenes—uh-KIM-muh-neez
Aconitum—ak-oe-NYE-tuhm
Actinidia—AK-ti-NID-ee-uh
Adiantum—ad-ee-AN-tuhm
Aesculus—ES-keew-luhs
Agapanthus—ag-uh-PAN-thuhs
Agave—ah-GAH-vay
Ageratum—ah-JER-ah-tum (usually pronounced ad-juh-RAY-tuhm)
Ailanthus—uh-LAN-thuhs
Ajuga—uh-JEW-guh
Alstroemeria—al-struh-MEE-ree-uh
Amaryllis—am-uh-RIL-is
Anemone—uh-NEM-uh-nee
Anthurium—an-THU-ree-uhm

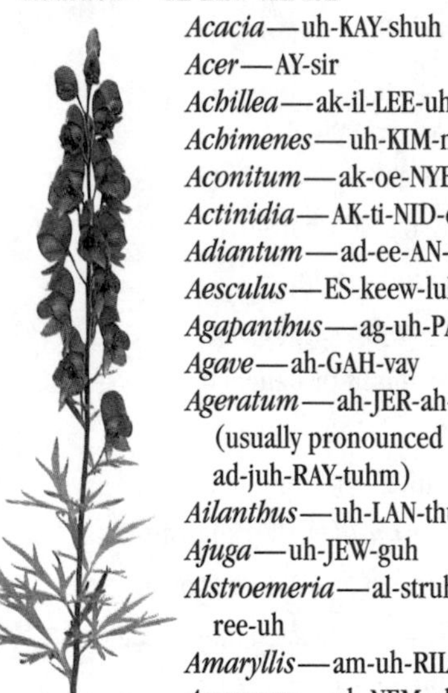
Aconitum

Aquilegia—ak-wuh-LEE-jee-uh
Arabis—AIR-uh-bis
Aralia—uh-RAY-lee-uh
Arctostaphylos—ark-toe-STAF-i-luhs
Arctotheca—ark-toe-THEE-kuh
Artemisia—AHR-tuh-MEE-zee-uh
Aspidistra—as-puh-DIS-truh
Astilbe—as-STIL-bee
Atriplex—AT-rip-lex

B

Babiana—bab-ee-AN-uh
Baccharis—BAK-uh-ris
Bauhinia—boe-HIN-ee-uh
Berberis—BUR-buh-ris
Bergenia—bur-GEN-ee-uh
Betula—BET-ew-luh

Bougainvillea

Bougainvillea—boo-guhn-VIL-ee-uh
Buddleja—BUD-lee-uh

C

Caladium—kuh-LAY-dee-uhm
Calceolaria—kal-see-oe-LAIR-ee-uh
Calendula—kuh-LEN-dew-luh
Callistemon—ka-lis-STEE-muhn
Callistephus—ka-LIS-tee-fuhs
Calochortus—kal-oh-COR-tuhs
Campanula—kam-PAN-ew-luh
Carpenteria—CAHR-pen-TEER-ee-a
Cattleya—KAT-lee-uh
Ceanothus—see-uh-NO-thuhs
Celosia—see-LOW-she-uh
Centaurea—sen-tah-REE-uh
Ceratonia—sair-uh-TONE-ee-uh
Ceratostigma—sair-uh-toe-STIG-muh
Cercidium—sir-CID-ee-uhm
Cercis—SIR-suhs
Chamaecyparis—kam-uh-SIP-uh-ris
Cheiranthus—kye-RAN-thuhs
Chionanthus—kye-oe-NAN-thuhs
Chlorophytum—klor-oe-FYE-tum
Choisya—SHOY-zee-uh
Clematis—KLEM-uh-tis
Cleome—KLEE-oe-mee
Clivia—KLYE-vee-uh
Cocculus—COC-ew-lus
Colchicum—KAHL-chik-uhm
Convallaria—con-va-LAIR-ee-uh
Convolvulus—kon-VOL-vew-luhs
Coreopsis—kor-ee-OP-suhs
Cotinus—koe-TYE-nuhs
Cotoneaster—koe-toe-nee-AS-tuhr
Crataegus—kruh-TEE-guhs
Crocosmia—kroe-KOZ-mee-uh
Cuphea—KEW-fee-uh
Cymbidium—sim-BID-ee-uhm
Cynoglossum—sin-oh-GLOS-uhm

D

Daboecia—dab-EE-shee-uh
Daphne—DAFF-nee
Deutzia—DOOT-zee-uh or DOYT-zee-uh
Dieffenbachia—deef-uhn-BAK-ee-uh
Dizygotheca—diz-uh-GOTH-ik-uh or diz-uh-goe-THEE-kah
Dracaena—druh-SEE-nuh
Dryopteris—drye-OP-ter-uhs
Duchesnea—dew-KEZ-nee-uh

E

Echeveria—ek-uh-VAIR-ee-uh
Echinacea—ek-uh-NAY-see-uh
Echinops—EK-uh-nops
Echium—EK-ee-uhm
Elaeagnus—el-ee-AG-nuhs
Epidendrum—ep-uh-DEN-druhm
Epiphyllum—ep-uh-FIL-uhm
Equisetum—ek-wuh-SEE-tuhm
Eremurus—er-uh-MEWR-uhs
Erica—ee-RYE-kuh (correct, but universally pronounced AIR-ik-uh)
Erigeron—ee-RIJ-uh-ron
Erythrina—air-i-THRYE-nuh
Eschscholzia—eh-SCHOELT-see-uh
Eucalyptus—ew-kuh-LIP-tuhs
Euonymus—ew-ON-uh-mus
Exacum—EK-suh-kuhm
Exochorda—ek-so-KOR-duh

F

Fatshedera—fats-HED-uh-ruh
Feijoa—fay-HOE-uh
Ficus—FYE-kuhs
Forsythia—for-SITH-ee-uh
Fragaria—fra-GAIR-ee-uh
Fraxinus—FRAK-suh-nuhs
Fuchsia—FEW-shee-uh

G

Gaillardia—gay-LAHR-dee-uh
Gazania—guh-ZAY-nee-uh
Genista—jen-NIS-tuh
Gentiana—jen-shee-AY-nah
Gerbera—GUR-bur-uh
Geum—JEE-uhm
Gleditsia—gluh-DIT-see-uh
Gomphrena—gom-FREE-nuh
Grevillea—gruh-VIL-ee-uh
Gypsophila—jip-SOF-uh-luh

H

Hamamelis—ham-uh-MEE-luhs
Hebe—HEE-bee
Hedera—HED-uh-ruh
Helianthemum—hee-lee-AN-thuh-muhm
Helianthus—hee-lee-AN-thuhs
Heliopsis—hee-lee-OP-suhs
Heliotropium—hee-lee-oe-TROE-pee-uhm
Hemerocallis—hem-uh-roe-KAL-uhs
Heteromeles—het-uh-roe-MEE-leez
Heuchera—HEW-kuh-ruh
Hibiscus—hye-BIS-kuhs
Hippeastrum—hip-ee-AS-truhm
Hosta—HAHST-uh
Hydrangea—hye-DRAIN-jee-uh
Hymenocallis—hye-muh-noe-KAL-uhs
Hypericum—hye-PEER-ik-uhm

I

Iberis—eye-BEE-ruhs
Ilex—EYE-lex
Impatiens—im-PAY-shuns
Ipomoea—ip-oe-MEE-uh
Iresine—ir-uh-SYE-nee

Ilex

J

Jacaranda—jak-uh-RAN-duh
Jasminum—JAZ-muh-nuhm
Juniperus—joo-NIP-uh-ruhs

K

Kalanchoe—kal-an-KO-ee
Kniphofia—nip-HOE-fee-uh
Kochia—KO-kee-uh
Koelreuteria—kell-rew-TEE-ree-uh
Kolkwitzia—koel-KWIT-zee-uh

L

Lagerstroemia—lay-gur-STREE-mee-uh
Lathyrus—LATH-uh-ruhs
Leptospermum—lep-toe-SPUR-muhm
Liatris—lie-AT-ruhs
Liriodendron—lear-ee-oe-DEN-druhn
Liriope—leer-EYE-oh-pee
Lobelia—loe-BEE-lee-uh
Lonicera—lo-NIS-uh-ruh
Lychnis—LIK-nis
Lysimachia—lye-suh-MAY-kee-uh

M

Malus—MAY-lus
Mandevilla—man-duh-VIL-uh
Matthiola—ma-thee-OE-luh
Maytenus—MAY-te-nuhs
Melaleuca—mel-uh-LOO-kuh
Metrosideros—MET-roe-SID-uh-ruhs
Mimulus—MIM-ew-luhs
Musa—MEW-zuh
Myosotis—mye-oh-SO-tuhs
Myrica—mi-RYE-kuh

N

Nandina—nan-DEE-nuh
Narcissus—nahr-SIS-uhs
Nerine—nuh-RYE-nee
Nerium—NEE-ree-uhm
Nicotiana—ni-koe-shee-AY-nuh
Nierembergia—nee-rem-BURG-ee-uh
Nyssa—NIS-uh

O

Olea—O-lee-uh
Osmanthus—oz-MAN-thuhs
Osteospermum—os-tee-oe-SPUR-muhm
Oxalis—OK-sal-uhs
Oxydendrum—OK-see-DEN-druhm

P

Pachysandra—pak-ee-SAN-druh
Papaver—puh-PAY-vur
Parthenocissus—PAHR-thuh-noe-SIS-uhs
Pelargonium—pel-ahr-GOE-nee-uhm
Pennisetum—pen-uh-SEE-tuhm
Penstemon—PEN-stuh-muhn
Philadelphus—fil-uh-DEL-fuhs
Photinia—foe-TIN-ee-uh
Phyla—FYE-luh
Phyllostachys—FIL-oe-STACK-ees
Physalis—FYE-suh-luhs
Picea—pye-SEE-uh
Pieris—pee-AIR-uhs
Pinus—PYE-nuhs
Pittosporum—pit-TOS-poe-ruhm, pit-toe-SPOER-uhm
Platanus—PLAT-uh-nuhs
Platycladus—plat-i-CLAD-uhs
Podocarpus—poe-doe-KAR-puhs
Polianthes—pol-ee-AN-thez
Polygonatum—pol-ee-GON-uh-tuhm
Portulaca—por-tew-LAK-a
Potentilla—poe-ten-TIL-uh
Primula—PRIM-ew-luh
Protea—PROE-tee-uh or proe-TEE-uh
Pseudotsuga—soo-doe-TSOO-guh
Pyrostegia—pye-roe-STEE-jee-uh
Pyrus—PYE-ruhs

Q

Quercus—KWER-kuhs

R

Ranunculus—ra-NUN-kew-luhs
Rhaphiolepis—raf-ee-OL-uh-pis or raf-ee-o-LEP-uhs
Rhoeo—REE-oe
Romneya—ROM-nee-uh
Rosmarinus—ros-muh-RYE-nuhs
Rudbeckia—rud-BECK-ee-uh

Rosmarinus

S

Salpiglossis—sal-pi-GLOS-sis
Sanvitalia—san-vi-TALE-ee-uh
Scabiosa—skay-bee-OH-suh
Schefflera—SHEF-luh-ruh
Schizanthus—ski-ZAN-thuhs
Scilla—SIL-luh
Sempervivum—sem-per-VYE-vuhm
Senecio—suh-NEE-shee-oe
Sequoia—suh-QUOY-uh
Sinningia—si-NIN-jee-uh
Solandra—soe-LAN-druh
Soleirolia—soe-lee-uh-ROE-lee-uh
Spiraea—spye-REE-uh
Strelitzia—stre-LIT-see-uh
Syngonium—sin-GOE-nee-uhm

T

Tagetes—tuh-JEE-teez
Taxodium—taks-OE-dee-uhm
Thuja—THOO-yuh
Thymus—TYE-muhs
Tibouchina—tib-oo-KYE-nuh
Tigridia—tye-GRID-ee-uh
Tolmiea—tol-MEE-uh
Trachelospermum—tra-kee-lo-SPER-muhm
Tradescantia—trad-es-KAN-shee-uh
Trichostema—trik-oe-STEE-mah
Tropaeolum—tro-PEE-oh-luhm
Tsuga—TSOO-guh

V

Vaccinium—vak-SIN-ee-uhm
Vancouveria—van-koo-VEE-ree-uh
Verbascum—vur-BAS-kuhm
Verbena—ver-BEE-nuh
Vinca—VING-kuh
Vitex—VEE-teks

Vinca minor

W–Z

Weigela—wye-JEE-luh
Xylosma—zye-LOZ-muh
Zantedeschia—zan-tuh-DES-kee-uh
Zephyranthes—zef-i-RAN-theez
Zizyphus—ZIZ-uh-fuhs
Zoysia—ZOY-see-uh

GLOSSARY

Gardening Terms

Acid soil. A soil with a pH below 7. See "Soil pH" (page 707).

Alkaline soil. A soil with a pH above 7. See "Soil pH" (page 707).

Alternate leaves. See Opposite leaves.

Annual. A plant that completes its life cycle in 1 year or less. For information on planting and caring for annuals, see page 658.

Anther. See Flower.

Axil. The inner angle between a leaf (or other organ of a plant) and the stem from which it springs. Organs in the axil, such as flowers and buds, are called *axillary.*

Balled-and-burlapped (B-and-B). Refers to specimen shrubs and trees sold for planting with a large ball of soil around the roots, wrapped in burlap or a synthetic material to hold the soil together. Usually available from late fall to early spring. For planting instructions, see page 692.

Bare-root. Refers to deciduous shrubs and trees and some perennials sold for planting with the soil removed from their roots. Usually sold in winter and early spring. For information on planting bare-root shrubs and trees, see page 692; for perennials, see page 678.

Bedding plant. Any plant suitable for massing in beds for its colorful flowers or foliage. Most bedding plants are annuals or perennials that are grown as annuals.

Biennial. A plant that germinates and produces foliage and roots during its first growing season, then blooms, produces seed, and dies during its second growing season. For information on planting and caring for biennials, see page 659.

Blanching. The process of blocking light from parts of certain vegetables to keep them paler in color or milder in flavor (or both). In the case of heads of cauliflower and the central leaves of endive or cardoon (an artichoke relative), the outer leaves are tied over the inner head or leaves. Asparagus is blanched by mounding soil over the emerging spears.

Bolt. To produce seeds or flowers prematurely; the term usually refers to annual flowers and vegetables. Bolting most frequently occurs when plants that prefer cool weather (lettuce, for example) are set out too late in the year or when unseasonably hot weather rushes growth.

Bonsai. Bonsai (the word is Japanese for "tray planting") is one of the fine arts of gardening: growing and carefully training dwarf plants in containers selected to harmonize with them. The objective is to create a tree or landscape in miniature; often the dwarfed trees take on the appearance of very old, gnarled specimens.

Bracts. Modified leaves growing just below a flower or flower cluster; not all plants have them. Bracts are usually green, but in some cases they are conspicuous and colorful, constituting what people often mistake for flowers or petals. Bougainvillea, dogwood *(Cornus),* and poinsettia *(Euphorbia pulcherrima)* all have showy bracts.

Broad-leafed. Used to describe evergreen shrubs or trees, this term refers to plants that have foliage year-round—boxwood *(Buxus)* and camellia, for example—but are not conifers (such as juniper), which have needlelike or scalelike leaves. When used to categorize weeds, "broad-leafed" refers to any weed that is not a grass.

Bud. An undeveloped or rudimentary organ or shoot of a plant. A flower bud develops into a blossom, while a growth bud produces shoots of leafy growth. Terminal buds (also called apical buds) are produced at the end of a shoot. Lateral buds (also called axillary buds) are produced in the axil of a plant. Latent buds lie dormant beneath the bark; if a branch breaks or is cut off near a latent bud, that bud may develop into a new shoot. For an illustration of growth buds, see page 702.

Budding. A method of propagation in which a bud (the scion) from one plant is inserted beneath the bark of another related plant. See "Budding and Grafting" (page 701).

Bud union. The point at which a shoot or bud (scion) unites with the rootstock. See "Budding and Grafting" (page 701).

Bulb. In layman's terms, any plant that grows from a thickened underground structure may be referred to as a bulb. Botanically speaking, however, not all such underground structures are really bulbs. A true bulb consists of an underground stem base that contains an embryonic plant surrounded by scales—modified leaves that overlap each other. Bulblike structures include corms, rhizomes, tubers, and tuberous roots. See "The Five Bulb Types" (page 660).

Calyx. Collectively, the sepals of a flower.

Cambium. The layer of growing cells between the xylem and phloem. See "Plant Anatomy and Growth" (page 688).

Cane. An elongated flowering or fruiting stem, usually arising directly from the roots. Examples of cane-producing plants include barberry *(Berberis),* forsythia, rose, raspberry, and grape.

Cane pruning. A method of pruning grapevines. During winter pruning, selected canes that grew the previous summer are cut back to two buds (called renewal spurs). Two to four other canes are retained (often tied to a permanent trellis); buds on these canes produce fruit the following summer or fall. Meanwhile, buds on the renewal spurs grow into new canes that will be retained to fruit the following year. For details, see Grape (page 370) in the Western Plant Encyclopedia.

Catkin. A slender, spikelike, often drooping flower cluster. Alder *(Alnus),* birch *(Betula),* and oak *(Quercus)* are three familiar trees that produce catkins.

Chill requirement. Many bulbs, perennials, and deciduous shrubs and trees (fruit trees in particular) need a certain amount of cold weather—measured in hours required at temperatures below 45°F/7°C—in order to grow and bloom well in the following year. In mild-winter areas where these plants do not receive the necessary winter chill, their performance is often disappointing: they leaf out late, fail to flower or fruit well, and often decline in health and vigor. For certain such plants—apples and lilacs *(Syringa),* for example—varieties have been developed that require less winter chill. In milder-winter areas, bulbs that require winter chilling can be stored in the vegetable bin of the refrigerator prior to planting; chill them for as long as the supplier recommends.

Composite head. See Inflorescence.

Compound leaf. See Leaf.

Conifer. A more precise term for some of the plants many people simply call evergreens, such as cedar *(Cedrus),* juniper *(Juniperus),* and pine *(Pinus).* Leaves of most are usually narrow and needlelike or tiny and scalelike. A few conifers, including larch *(Larix)* and dawn redwood *(Metasequoia),* are deciduous. All conifers bear seeds in cones or in modified conelike structures (juniper berries, for example). Yew *(Taxus)* and *Podocarpus* bear single seeds on fleshy bases, but thanks to their needlelike foliage, they are sometimes grouped with conifers.

Corm. A swollen underground stem base composed of solid tissue (unlike the scales of a true bulb). See "The Five Bulb Types" (page 660).

Corolla. Collectively, the petals of a flower.

Crown. This word has two meanings. A tree's crown is its entire branch structure, including foliage. "Crown" also refers to the point at which a plant's roots and top structure join, usually at or near the soil line.

Cultivar. This coined word is shorthand for "cultivated variety." Cultivars are genetically distinct plants, maintained in cultivation by human effort; they may be of hybrid origin or simply selected varieties of plants that occur in the wild. Cultivars are propagated by divisions, cuttings, or (in some cases) seed. Cultivar names are enclosed in single quotation marks and are not italicized, as in *Lobelia erinus* 'Crystal Palace'. In general usage and throughout this book, the term "variety" (see also Variety) refers both to cultivars and to varieties found in nature.

Deadhead. To remove spent flowers. By preventing a plant from setting seed, deadheading both prolongs the bloom season and eliminates unwanted seedlings. It also keeps the garden looking tidy.

Deciduous. This term describes any plant that naturally sheds all of its leaves at any one time (usually in fall).

Defoliation. Refers to the unnatural loss of foliage, usually to the detriment of the plant's health. Defoliation may result from high winds that strip foliage away; intense heat (especially if accompanied by wind) that critically wilts leaves; drought; unusually early or late frosts that strike a plant in active growth; or severe damage caused by chemicals, insects, or diseases.

Dieback. This occurs when a plant's stems die for part of their length, beginning at the tips. Causes of dieback include inadequate moisture, nutrient deficiency, poor climate adaptation, and severe injury from pests or diseases.

Dormancy. The annual period when a plant's growth processes greatly slow down. For many plants, dormancy commences with the onset of winter, as days grow shorter and temperatures colder.

Double flower. See Flower forms.

Drainage. The downward movement of water through the soil. When this process happens quickly, the soil is well drained; when it occurs slowly, it is poorly drained. See "Soils and Soil Management" (page 706) for more information on soils and drainage.

Drip line. The circle you would draw on the soil around a tree directly under its outermost branch tips is called the drip line; rainwater tends to drip from the tree at this point. The roots of established trees usually extend beyond the drip line.

Epiphyte. Epiphytes grow on another plant for support but take no nourishment from the host plant. Examples include cattleya orchids and staghorn ferns *(Platycerium)*. Epiphytes are sometimes mistakenly considered parasites, but true parasites draw nourishment from the host, while epiphytes live on nutrients drawn from the air, rainwater, and organic debris on the supporting plant.

Espalier. A tree or shrub trained so that its branches grow in a flat pattern—against a wall or fence, on a trellis, along horizontal wires. For espalier patterns, see page 705.

BASIC FLOWER FORMS

Single

Semidouble

Double

Established plant. A plant that is firmly rooted and producing good foliage growth.

Evergreen. Unlike deciduous plants, evergreens never lose all their leaves at one time. See also Broad-leafed; Conifer.

Family. Every plant belongs to a family whose members share certain broad characteristics that set them apart from plants in other families. Family names are in Latin and typically end in "-aceae"; examples include *Rosaceae* (the rose family) and *Iridaceae* (the iris family). A few family names formerly ended simply in "-ae", among them *Compositae,* the daisy family; *Palmae,* the palm family; and *Leguminosae,* the pea family. Botanists have renamed these, giving them the "-aceae" ending: *Asteraceae* (formerly *Compositae*), *Arecaceae* (formerly *Palmae*), *Fabaceae* (formerly *Leguminosae*). However, some reference works still use the former names.

Fertilization. The fusion of male and female gametes (fertile reproductive cells) following pollination.

Fertilize. To apply nutrients (fertilizer) to a plant; see "Fertilizers" (page 668).

Flower. The part of a seed-bearing plant that contains the reproductive organs.

COMPLETE FLOWER

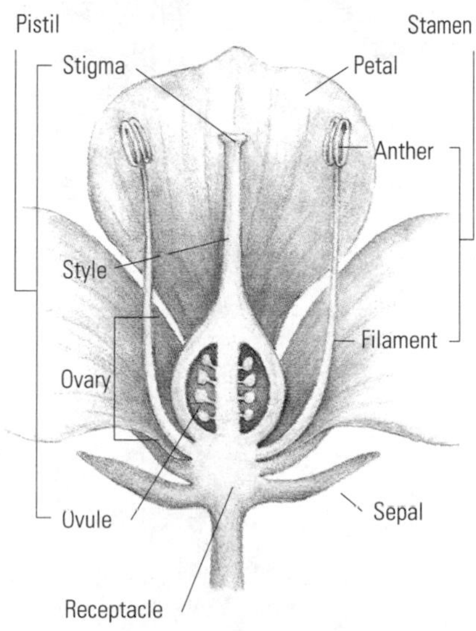

Flower forms: single, semidouble, double. The basic flower forms are single, with one row of petals containing the minimum number of petals for the blossoms of that particular species (usually four, five, or six); semidouble, with two or three times the minimum number of petals, usually in two or three rows; and double, with multitudinous densely packed petals that typically produce a rounded blossom shape. See also Inflorescence.

Forcing. The process of hastening a plant to maturity or a marketable state or of growing it to the flowering or fruiting stage out of its normal season. Forcing usually occurs in a greenhouse, where temperature, light, and humidity can be controlled.

Foundation plant. This term originally described a plant used to hide the foundation of a house. Since many of today's homes lack high or even visible foundations, the term has come to refer to any shrub planted near house walls.

Frond. In the strictest sense, fronds are the foliage of ferns. Often, however, the word is applied to the leaves of palms or used to describe any foliage that looks fernlike.

Fruit. A general term used to describe the mature ovary of a plant, containing one to many seeds. Fruits may be soft and fleshy, as in the case of peaches or apples, or dry, like an acorn or dried pea pod.

Genus (plural: Genera). Plant families are subdivided into groups of more closely related plants called genera. Some families contain only a single genus: for example, the family *Ginkgoaceae* includes only the genus *Ginkgo.* Others contain hundreds of genera; *Asteraceae* (the daisy family), for instance, comprises around 950 genera. The first word in a plant's botanical name is its genus—such as *Rosa,* which comprises all the roses, and *Hemerocallis,* which includes all the daylilies. The second word is the species (see also Species). Both genus and species are written in italics, with just the name of the genus capitalized—as in *Rosa moschata,* musk rose; and *Hemerocallis lilioasphodelus,* lemon daylily.

Girdling. The removal of bark all around a stem or branch, cutting off the flow of water and nutrients. Girdling often occurs when a woody plant has been tied tightly to a stake or support;

as the plant grows, the tie constricts the stem. If girdling goes unnoticed, the part of the plant above the constriction will die. Carelessly used string trimmers can also girdle plants, as can damage from insects or gnawing rodents. Girdling is done deliberately in some cases; a gardener may remove a narrow ring of bark to reduce overly vigorous growth or to kill an unwanted plant.

Growing season. In technical terms, "growing season" refers to the number of days between the average dates of the last killing frost in spring and the first killing frost in fall. The term is also used to describe the period of time a plant is actively growing and not dormant. For information on the growing season in each Western climate zone, see pages 27–63.

Harden off. To adapt a plant that has been grown indoors or in a greenhouse or other shelter to outdoor conditions. Over a week or more, the plant is exposed to increasing periods of time outside, so that when it is planted in the garden it can make the transition with a minimum of shock.

Hardy. In horticultural terms, a plant's hardiness is its resistance to, or tolerance of, frosts or freezing temperatures. A plant hardy to −20°F/−29°C will survive undamaged to a temperature that low, for example. The word does not mean tough, pest resistant, or disease resistant.

Herbaceous. The opposite of "woody," the word "herbaceous" describes a plant with soft or fleshy (nonwoody) tissue. In the strictest sense, the term refers to plants that die to the ground each year and regrow stems the following growing season. In common parlance, it refers to any nonwoody plant—annual, perennial, or bulb.

Humus. The soft brown or black substance formed in the last stages of decomposition of animal or vegetable matter. Common usage, however, incorrectly applies the term to almost all organic materials that will eventually decompose into humus—sawdust, ground bark, leaf mold, and animal manures, for example.

Hybrid. A distinct plant resulting from a cross between two species, subspecies, varieties, cultivars, strains, or any combination of the above; or, less commonly, between two plants from different genera. Hybrids sometimes occur in the wild, but more often they are produced by plant breeders. In botanical nomenclature, hybrids are indicated with the symbol ×, as in *Buddleja* ×*weyeriana,* a cross between the two butterfly bush species *B. davidii* and *B. globosa.*

Hydroponics. A method of gardening without soil. Nutrients are provided in a water-based solution; in some systems, an inert medium is used to anchor plant roots. One such medium is rockwool, a material made from fibers spun from molten mineral rock and formed into planting blocks.

INFLORESCENCES

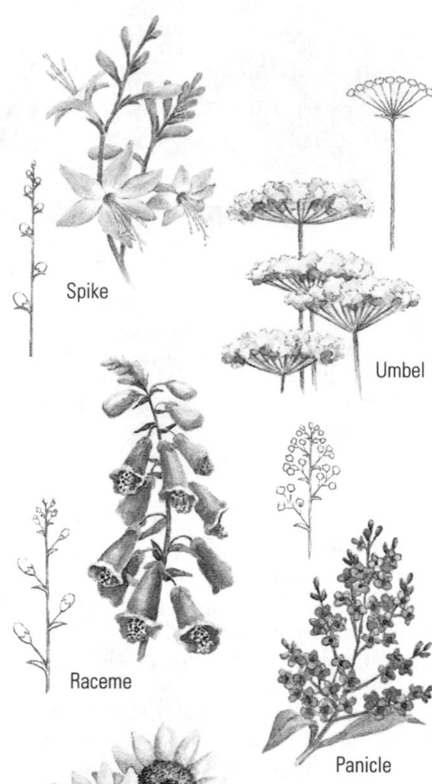

LEAF TYPES

Inflorescence. A group of individual flowers borne on a single stem. Inflorescences can take many forms. For example, a spike refers to flowers attached to the main stem without stalks, as in bottlebrush *(Callistemon)* or montbretia *(Crocosmia)*. In an umbel, all the individual flowers spring from approximately the same point, as in the blossoms of dill *(Anethum graveolens)*. In a raceme, flowers are formed on stalks arising from the main stem, as in foxglove *(Digitalis)*. A panicle refers to groups of flowers borne on stalks (racemes) arising from the main stem; the flowers of lilac *(Syringa)* and privet *(Ligustrum)* are panicles. A composite head refers to small, closely packed, stalkless flowers of the sort found in the daisy family; these may include central disk flowers and outer ray flowers, as in sunflower *(Helianthus)*. See also Flower forms.

Internode. See Node.

Lath. Any overhead structure (originally a roof of spaced laths) that reduces the amount of sunlight reaching plants beneath its cover or protects them from frost.

Leader. The central upward-growing stem of a single-trunked tree or shrub.

Leaf. The main photosynthetic organ of most plants. A simple leaf is a single unit, while a compound leaf is divided into separate segments called leaflets. In a palmately compound leaf, the leaflets grow from one point at the end of a stem. In a pinnately compound (once-divided) leaf, the leaflets are arranged along a central axis; a bipinnately compound leaf is twice pinnate or twice-divided.

Leafburn. Results from damage to or destruction of a leaf's tissues from sunlight, chemicals (in the soil or on the leaves), strong wind, or lack of water. Leafburn usually starts as brownish, dried-out tissue around the edges of the leaves. In bad cases, the whole leaf can dry out. Leafburn often occurs in Japanese maples *(Acer palmatum)* and azaleas *(Rhododendron)*.

Leaflet. A division or segment of a compound leaf. See also Leaf.

Leaf mold. Partially decomposed leaves dug into the soil as an organic amendment or used in potting soil mixes.

Leaf scar. A leaf scar indicates where a leafstalk was once attached. It is usually a rounded or crescent-shaped mark on a branch.

Lip. Irregular flowers (those in which the segments are not equal in size and arrangement) often show two divisions, an upper and a lower, each bearing one or more segments. Each division is known as a lip. Examples are honeysuckle *(Lonicera)* and snapdragon *(Antirrhinum majus)*.

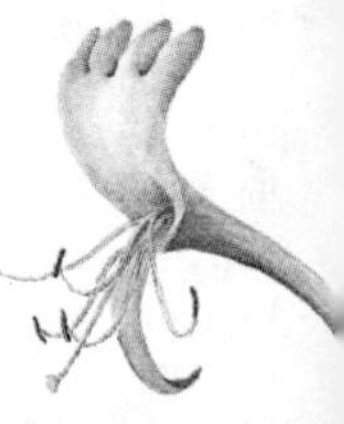

Microclimate. The climate of a small area or locality (such as a backyard or even just a portion of it) as opposed to that of a larger region. Microclimates are determined by such factors as hills, hollows, and the location of houses and other structures. They influence which plants you choose for a particular area and how well they grow there. See "Frost and Cold Protection" (page 670).

Naturalize. To set out plants or bulbs randomly, without a precise pattern, and leave them in place to spread at will, as they would in the wild (see "Naturalizing Bulbs," page 660). The term also refers to a plant's becoming established in an area to which it is not native. Common foxglove *(Digitalis purpurea)*, for example, has naturalized in parts of the Pacific Northwest.

Node. The joint in a stem where a bud, branch, or leaf starts to grow. The area of stem between nodes is the internode.

Offset. A young plant that develops by natural vegetative reproduction, usually at or near the base of the parent plant. Hen and chicks *(Echeveria)* and strawberry readily produce offsets. The word also refers to the increases of bulbs and corms.

Open-pollinated plants. Varieties or cultivars of plants produced from natural, random pollination. These are in contrast to hybrids, which are the result of deliberate crosses (controlled pollination).

Opposite leaves; alternate leaves. Leaves are opposite when they spring from the same node on a stem, but on opposite sides. Alternate leaves arise from different nodes on opposite sides of the stem.

Organic matter. Any material originating from a living organism—peat moss, ground bark, compost, or manure, for example—that can be dug into soil to improve its condition. See "Organic Soil Amendments" (page 708).

Ovary. See Flower; Fruit.

Panicle. See Inflorescence.

Peat moss. A highly water-retentive, spongy organic soil amendment, peat moss is the partially decomposed remains of any of several mosses. It increases soil acidity. Sphagnum peat moss is generally considered the highest in quality. See also "A Substitute for Peat" (page 663).

Perennial. A perennial is a nonwoody plant that lives for more than 2 years and sometimes for many years. For information on planting and caring for perennials, see page 678.

Petal. See Flower.

Pistil. See Flower.

Pleaching. A method of training plants in which branches are interwoven and plaited together to form a hedge or arbor. Subsequent pruning keeps a neat, rather formal pattern.

Pollarding. In this pruning style, the main limbs of a young tree are drastically cut back to short lengths. In each subsequent dormant season, the growth from these branch stubs is cut back to one or two buds. In time, the branch ends become large and knobby. The result is a compact, leafy dome during the growing season and a somewhat grotesque branch structure during the dormant months. London plane tree *(Platanus × acerifolia)* is the tree most often subjected to this treatment.

STEM NODES

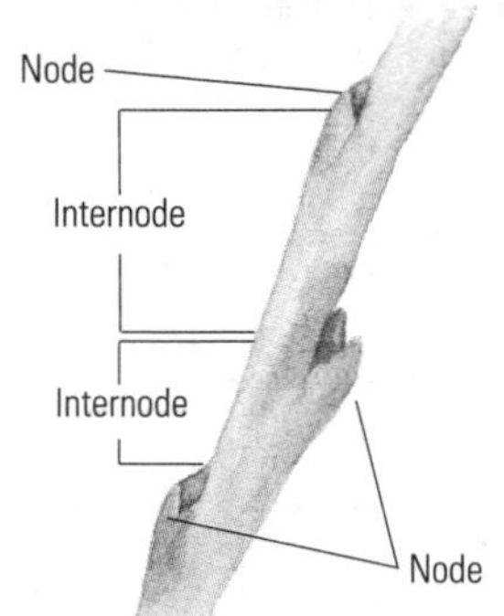

OPPOSITE/ALTERNATE LEAVES

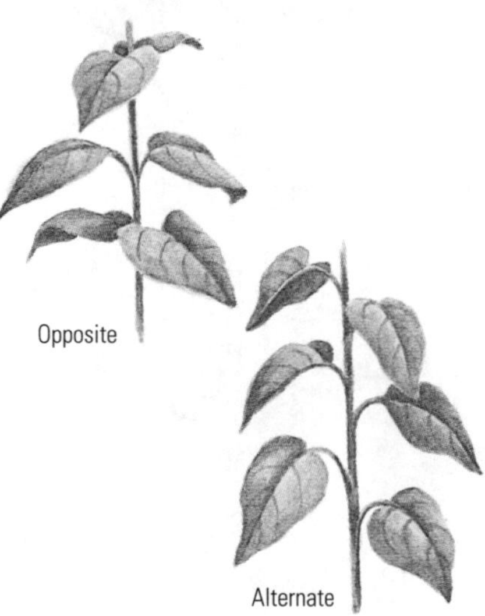

Pollenizer. A plant used to provide pollen for another plant. An example is an apple variety planted to provide pollen for a nearby second variety that does not produce fertile pollen.

Pollination. The transfer of pollen from the male reproductive organs to the female ones, which leads to fertilization and seed production.

Pollinator. An insect or animal that transfers pollen from one part of a flower to another or from flowers on one plant to flowers on another.

Pseudobulb. A modified aboveground stem that serves as a storage organ; variable in size and shape. Some orchids have pseudobulbs; see *Orchidaceae* (page 488) in the Western Plant Encyclopedia.

Raceme. See Inflorescence.

Rhizome. A modified stem growing horizontally under or at the soil surface. It may be long and slender, as in some perennials (and in perennial weeds like blackberry), or thick and fleshy, as in many irises. See "The Five Bulb Types"(page 660).

Root-bound. Plants suffer from this condition when they grow in the same container for too long. The roots become tangled and matted and grow in circles. See "Dealing with Root-bound Plants" (page 693).

Rootstock. The part of a budded or grafted plant that furnishes the root system and sometimes part of the branch structure. Understock has the same meaning. See "Budding and Grafting" (page 701).

Rosette. Leaves closely set around a crown or center, usually at or close to ground level. Hen and chicks *(Echeveria)* and partridge-breast aloe *(Aloe variegata)* both grow in rosettes.

Runner. See Stolon.

Scion. A shoot or bud cut from one plant to be grafted or budded onto the rootstock of another. See "Budding and Grafting" (page 701).

Self-seed, self-sow. Refers to a plant shedding fertile seeds that produce seedlings, usually near the parent plant.

Semidouble flower. See Flower forms.

Sepal. See Flower.

Simple leaf. See Leaf.

Single flower. See Flower forms.

Species. Each genus is subdivided into groups of individuals called species. Each species is generally a distinct entity (though it may closely resemble other species in the genus), reproducing from seed with only a small amount of variation. The second word in a plant's botanical name designates the species; the first word designates the genus. Both genus and species are italicized; the name of the genus is capitalized. For example, French marigold is, in botanical terms, *Tagetes patula*—genus *Tagetes*, species *patula*. See also Genus.

Specimen. A tree or shrub large or striking enough to make an immediate, significant impact in a planting. The term may also refer to a single large plant in a conspicuous location in the garden.

Sphagnum. Various mosses native to bogs. Much of the peat moss sold in the West is composed partly or entirely of decomposed sphagnum. These mosses also are collected live and packaged in whole pieces, fresh or dried. In this form, they are used for lining hanging baskets and for air layering (page 701).

Spike. See Inflorescence.

Spore. A simple type of reproductive cell capable of producing a new plant. Certain kinds of plants, including algae, fungi, mosses, and ferns, reproduce by spores.

Sport. A mutation: a spontaneous variation from the normal pattern. In horticulture, a sport is usually seen as a branch that differs notably from the rest of the plant. Examples include the spurred apple varieties that occur as limb sports on standard apple varieties, and camellias propagated from branches that have shown changes in flower color or form.

Spur. This term has two meanings. Used in relation to grapevines and fruit trees (particularly apples and cherries), it refers to a specialized short twig that bears the plant's blossoms and, later, its fruit. Used to describe flowers, "spur" refers to short and saclike or long and tubular projections from a blossom's petals or sepals; most species of columbine *(Aquilegia)*, for example, have flowers with pronounced spurs.

Spur pruning. A method of pruning grapevines. During winter pruning, canes that grew and fruited in the past season are removed from a framework of permanent arms, leaving a series of spurs (short twigs, each with two buds). These buds will produce fruit in the following summer or fall. For details, see Grape (page 370) in the Western Plant Encyclopedia.

Stamen. See Flower.

Standard. A plant trained to resemble a small tree, with a single, upright trunk topped by a rounded crown of foliage. In some standards, the trunk and top are joined by grafting. The "tree rose" is a familiar example of a standard.

Stolon. A stem that creeps along the soil surface, taking root at intervals and forming new plants where it roots. Bermuda and St. Augustine grasses spread by stolons.

Strain. Many popular annuals and some perennials are sold as strains (sometimes referred to as series). Examples include State Fair zinnias, Super Elfin impatiens, and Pacific delphiniums. Plants in a strain generally share similar growth characteristics but are variable in some respect—usually in flower color.

Stress. A condition (or conditions) endangering a plant's health. Stress may result from inadequate or excess water, wind, or excessively high or low temperatures. Wilting, dulling or loss of foliage color, and browning of leaf edges are typical symptoms of stress.

Subshrub. This term can refer to a low-growing plant with woody stems—a small shrub. It also describes a plant, usually classified as a perennial, with a woody base but soft, herbaceous stems in its upper part.

Subspecies. A simple botanical name consists of two words in italics, denoting genus and species. When a third name in italics appears, it may denote a subspecies—a major division within a species, indicating geographical or other variations. An example is *Eucalyptus mannifera maculosa,* red-spotted gum. (The name of the subspecies may be preceded by the abbreviation "ssp.": *Eucalyptus mannifera* ssp. *maculosa.*) A third italicized name may also denote a variety (see also Variety).

Sucker. In a grafted or budded plant, sucker growth originates from the rootstock rather than from the desired grafted or budded part of the plant. See also Water sprout.

Taproot. A thick central root that may penetrate deeply into the ground. In some plants, such as carrots and parsnips, taproots are storage organs.

Tender. The opposite of hardy plants, tender plants have a low tolerance for frost or freezing temperatures.

SUCKER AND WATER SPROUT

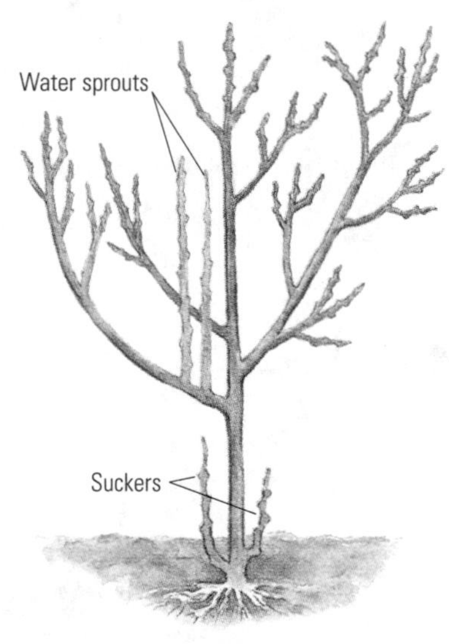

WHORL

Tendrils. Specialized growths along the stems or at the ends of leaves on some vines. Tendrils wrap around supports, enabling the vine to climb. See "Vines" (page 718).

Thin. With regard to pruning, to thin is to remove entire branches, large or small, cutting back to the main trunk, a side branch, or the ground; see "Pruning" (page 702). Seedlings or developing fruits may also be thinned; in this case, the term refers to removing excess plants or fruits so that the remaining ones are spaced far enough apart to grow well.

Topiary. The technique of pruning and training shrubs and trees into formal shapes. Some topiary plants are shaped to resemble animals; others are trained to geometric forms such as cones, spheres, pyramids, and rectangles.

Truss. A cluster of flowers, usually rather compact, at the end of a stem, branch, or stalk. Many rhododendrons bear their flowers in trusses.

Tuber. A swollen underground stem with multiple growth points scattered over its surface. The potato is a familiar example. See "The Five Bulb Types" (page 660).

Tuberous root. A true root, thickened to store nutrients. Unlike tubers, tuberous roots carry their growth buds at the bases of old stems rather than on the roots themselves. See "The Five Bulb Types" (page 660).

Umbel. See Inflorescence.

Underplanting. Planting one plant beneath another, such as setting out a ground cover under a tree.

Understock. See Rootstock.

Variegation. Striping, edging, or other markings in a color different from the primary color of a leaf or petal.

Variety. Like a subspecies (see Subspecies), a botanical variety is a variant of the basic species as it occurs in nature. For example, it may be a type whose leaves are narrow rather than broad. Like a subspecies name, a botanical variety name is written in italics as the third word in a plant's botanical name; it may be preceded by the abbreviation "var." (such as *Ilex pernyi veitchii* or *Ilex pernyi* var. *veitchii*). The word "variety" is also used in a general sense to include cultivated varieties (see also Cultivar).

Water sprout. In trees, any strong vertical shoot growing from the main framework of trunk and branches is properly called a water sprout, though the word "sucker" may also be used.

Whorl. Three or more leaves, branches, or flowers growing in a circle from a node on a stem or trunk.

Woody. This word describes a plant with hardened (woody) stems or trunks. An herbaceous plant, in contrast, has soft stems.

INDEX

Gardening Terms and Topics

INDEX

Scientific and Common Names

Italic page numbers refer to pages on which there are relevant photographs. The **boldface** page number after a scientific name—or common name, in the case of edibles—refers to the plant's encyclopedia entry. Listings for common names of ornamentals are followed by a scientific name; use it to find further page references to the plant.

A

B

C

D

E

F

G

H

I

J

K

L

M

Q

R

S

T

U

V

W

X

Y

Z

Acknowledgments

Syringa × laciniata

SPECIAL CONSULTANTS

Alaska: Donald Dinkel, Sarah McClellan, Mel Monsen

Northwest: Sam Benowitz, Wilbur Bluhm, George Taylor, Sue Thomas

Mountain States: Whitney Cranshaw, Marcia Tatroe

Southwest: Dusty Eiker, Mary Irish

California and Nevada: Steve Brigham, Clyde Elmore, Vincent Lanzaneo, Craig Minor, Kurt Peacock, Robert Raabe

Hawaii: Norman Bezona, Richard Criley, Fred D. Rauch, Tom Shea

A special thanks to those consultants who contributed to the development of previous editions of the Sunset Western Garden Book. *Much of their work lives on in this edition.*

Our thanks also to the many experts around the West who go unnamed but nonetheless contributed to this New Century Edition, and to Britta Swartz, Joyce Reeder, the Anchorage National Weather Service Office, Richard Dufresne, Joan Head, and Rexford H. Talbert.

CONSULTANTS

Alaska:
Pat Holloway
Dave Vonderheide

Northwest:
Charles Brun
Tonie Fitzgerald
Harold Greer
Warren Manhart
Fran McFarland
Gary Moulton
George Pinyuh
Lon Rombough

Mountain States:
John Inness Hetzler
Chris Moritz
Richard D. Rifkind
Curtis Swift
Diane Wilson

Southwest:
Tom Brodt
Chris Broughton
George Hull
Joyce Maschinski
Judith Phillips
Janet Rademacher
Troy Towne

Hawaii:
Heidi Bornhorst
Melanie Chapin
Paul Cox
Steven Fukuda
Charles Lamoureux
Tom Loffman
Dave Lorence
Leland Miyano
Diane Ragone
Peter Van Dyke
Paul Weissich

California and Nevada:
Christine Altermann
Harry Andris
Bruce Asakawa
Karminder Aulakh
Randy Baldwin
Carol Bornstein
Fredrick C. Boutin
Betsy Clebsch
Barrie Coate
Larry Costello
Joan DeFato
Bob Denman
Karen Dyka
Pam Elam
John Etheridge
Mike Evans
Susan Frommer
Janet Gerland
Liz Hartley
George Hull
Ted King
Robert Ludekens
Gary Lyons
Jim Marshall
Gary Matsuoka
Kenneth Montgomery
Robert Morris
Bart O'Brien
Sean A. O'Hara
Wendy Proud
Kelly Redmond
Warren Roberts
Jeff Rosendale
M. Nevin Smith
Janet Smithen
Dennis Swartzell
Ernie Wasson
Celeste Wilson
Jack Zunino

Photography Credits

Photographs are listed sequentially either in horizontal or vertical order. For additional clarification, the following position indicators may be used: Left (L), Center (C), Right (R); Top (T), Middle (M), Bottom (B).

Academy of Natural Sciences, Philadelphia/Vireo: 83 L1. **Rollo Adams/Rhododendron Species Botanical Gdn.:** 741. **Wayne Aldridge:** 40 BR, T. **William H. Allen, Jr.:** 273 T1. **Curtis Anderson:** 189 L, R; 193 BR, BRC. **Scott Atkinson:** 123 L1; 708 T. **Max Badgley:** 675 2, L5; 680 T4. **Bill Beatty/Visuals Unlimited:** 681 R3. **Brad Bertagnole/Red Butte Gdn.:** 740. **Paul Black:** 403 1. **David Boyton/Photo Resource Hawaii:** 115 R6. **Marion Brenner:** 23 T; 48 TL, TR; 65 L2, R2; 66 L5; 67 L2; 70 L2; 72 L2; 73 R5; 75 L1, L3, L4, L5; 76 L1, L2, R4; 77 R4; 80 L3, R4; 84 L3; 86 L1, L5; 87 L1, R2; 91 L1, L2, L3; 93 L4; 94 L3, L4, L5, R1; 95 R1, R5; 98 L3, L4; 99 L4, L5, R1, R5; 103 L2; 108 L3; 109 L2; 110 R2; 111 L2, R2, R4; 112 L3, LC2, R2; 113 L4, R1; 117 L3, R1; 118 L3, R2; 121 L2, R3; 133 R1, R4; 135 L2; 136 L2, R3, R4, R5; 137 L5; 143 L2; 144 R2; 145 R1; 146 L2, L3, R2; 147 L4; 148 L1, L2, L3, L5, R1, R2, R3, R4; 149 R3; 151 R1, R2, R4, R5; 152 L2, L3, R4; 153 L2, L3, R3, R5, R6; 154 L1, L2, L3, L5, R2, R3, R4, R5; 155 L4, L5, R1, R3, R4, R5; 156 L1, L2, L4, R1, R2, R3, R4; 157 L1, L2, L3, L4, R4, R5; 160 L2; 743 LC1, RC2; 744 LT. **Kathleen Norris Brenzel:** 4 BR; 63 B; 83 R4. **R. Bridges/Hudson Gardens:** 737. **Richard Brown:** 59 BL. **Lisa Butler:** 107 L2; 109 L6, R1, R2, R3; 110 L1, L2, L4; 117 R3. **Ralph S. Byther:** 665 C. **John B. Callahan/Photo Resource Hawaii:** 115 R1. **James Carrier:** 89 R1; 90 L5; 104 L1; 123 L3. **David Cavagnaro:** 6 B; 14 B; 21 B; 66 L1; 67 R4; 70 L4; 78 L1; 79 L1; 83 R1; 84 R4; 85 R1; 98 R1; 105 R1; 106 L4; 121 R2; 122 L1; 126 L1, L5; 127 L4, R2; 128 L1; 129 L4, R1, R5; 139 R2; 158 L1; 159 L2; 402 3; 434 M2, T4, T5; 527 1, 3; 560 2, 3, 4; 625 B6; 690; 715; 717 1, 2; 718 5; 719 2, 3, 5. **VanChaplin/Southern Living:** 434 M1. **Peter Christiansen:** 193 R; 659 B; 676 T. **Glenn Christiansen:** 708 B. **Steven Cohan:** 52 BR. **Albert Cohen:** 538 BL. **Ed Cooper:** 41 B; 45 T; 48 B; 60 T. **Richard Cowles:** 675 R5; 689 R; 727 BR. **Crandall & Crandall:** 94 L2; 102 R4; 125 L3; 126 R5; 127 R3; 128 R1; 135 R2; 138 L3; 158 L4; 159 L1; 277; 279 B2; 337; 452 3, 4; 504 2; 536 5; 537 5; 675 L4, R4; 679 T. **Rosalind Creasy:** 717 5; 718 2; 719 4. **Claire Curran:** 11 B; 52 T; 53 BL, BR; 55 T; 60 BL; 66 L3, R2; 68 R4; 69 R2; 70 L3, R1; 71 L2, L5, R5; 72 L3; 73 R1; 74 L4, L5, R3, R4, R5; 75 R1, R2; 76 R3; 77 L1, L2, L4; 78 L3, L4; 79 L2, L3, R1; 80 L4; R2; 81 L3, L4, R1, R3, R4; 82 L2, L3, L4, L5, R1, R2, R3;

83 L4; 84 L2, R2; 85 R4; 88 L2, L3; 91 R3; 92 L2, L3, R2, R3; 93 L1; 94 R3; 96 R1, R2, R4, R5; 97 L1, L3, L4, R1, R2, R3, R4, R5, R6; 98 R3; 99 L1, R4; 103 R3; 106 R3; 111 L1, L3, L4, R3; 112 L1, L5, LC1, LC3, R4; 113 L1; 114 L5; 116 R2; 117 L5; 118 R4; 119 L4, R5; 120 L1; 130 L2, L4, R2, R3, R4; 131 L1, L2, R1, R2, R4; 133 L2; 136 L3, L6; 138 L5; 140 L2, L3, R3, R5; 141 L2, R5, R6; 142 L1, L2, R2, R4; 143 L1, L4, L5, R4; 144 L1; 146 R4, R5; 147 L2, R5; 149 L5, R5; 154 R1; 155 R2; 156 L5; 157 R1; 244 6; 434 T3; 582 3; 583 2; 677 B; 742 BL1, BL2; 743 LC3, RC1, RC3. **Robin B. Cushman:** 9 C; 12 T; 18 T; 19 B, TR; 75 R4; 77 R2; 88 R6; 116 L1; 126 R3; 151 R3. **R. Todd Davis:** 100 R3; 102 L3; 104 L2; 116 L2; 571 3. **Descat/M.A.P.:** 99 R3. **Alan & Linda Detrick:** 4 BLC; 64 B; 65 L4, L5; 86 R5; 106 R4; 116 R1; 118 L1; 146 L1; 454 3; Back CL. **William Dewey:** 42; 49 T; 52 BL; 53 T; 56 B, T; 119 L1, L5; 120 L3, L4; 121 L3, L5, R1, R4, R5; 138 L2; 142 R1; 143 R3; 144 R4; 595 3. **Ken Druse:** 68 L1. **Jack Dykinga:** 27 C; 689 L. **Philip Edinger:** 402 4; 404 2. **Clyde Elmore:** 727 BC, BL, MC. **Thomas E. Eltzroth:** 371; 374 2; 666 2, 4. **Linda Enger:** 7 B; 16 T. **Craig Engle:** 92 L5; 136 R2. **M. Essler/Natural Selection:** 9 B. **Derek Fell:** 74 L1; 80 R5; 81 L1; 93 R2; 100 L2; 103 R4; 106 L3, R1; 117 L1, L2; 119 L3; 120 R5; 123 L2; 124 R4; 128 R2; 129 R3; 132 R1; 140 L4; 141 R1; 193 BLC; 210; 216 BR, TR; 279 T5; 527 5; 536 6; 583 1; 585 4; 641 M3. **William E. Ferguson:** 687 1. **Christopher Gallagher/The Garden Picture Library:** 527 4. **Gardener's Supply Co.:** 699 BL, R, TL. **Fiona Gilsenan:** 106 L2; 147 L1; 505 3; 728 3. **Nicholas Gitts/Swan Island Dahlias:** 308 M1, T4. **John Glover/The Garden Picture Library:** 330 3; 331 4; 536 2; 641 B1. **David Goldberg:** 10 B; 25 B; 66 R4; 82 R4; 101 R3; 120 R2; 122 R3; 123 R5; 124 R1; 125 L4, R3; 130 L1; 131 R3; 139 R5; 145 R5; 152 L1; 156 R5; 402 1; 725; 728 1; 729; 730 B. **Jay Graham:** 12 C. **Harold E. Greer:** 126 L4; 132 R4; 141 R3; 244 4; 330 2; 331 5; 454 4; 504 4; 570 1, 2, 3, 4; 571 2, 4; 572 2, 3, 4; 573 1, 3, 4; 625 B5. **Steven Gunther:** 13; 26 T; 59 BR. **Todd Gustafson/Natural Selection:** 687 3. **Joe K. Hale:** 55 MR. **Pamela Harper:** 84 R6; 561 4. **Jerry Harpur:** 11 T; 22 B. **Jessie M. Harris:** 66 R3; 119 R3; 139 L3. **Lynne Harrison:** 69 R1; 308 M6; 405 2; 477 M4; 572 1; 584 3; 585 5; 641 B5. **Philip Harvey:** 707. **Tom Hertz/AG Stock USA, Inc.:** 374 5. **Fred Hirschmann:** 27 R; 29 T; 31 B, M; 107 L1, R1, R2; 115 R2; 732. **W. H. Hodge/Peter Arnold, Inc.:** 84 R5. **Robert Holmes:** 63 M. **Neil Holmes/The Garden Picture Library:** 534. **Gary Holscher/AG Stock USA, Inc.:** 372 3; Back TL. **Saxon Holt:** 6 T; 41 TR; 65 L1; 69 L3, L4; 71 L1, L3; 72 L1, L4, R4; 73 L2, L3, L4, R4; 76 R2; 77 L5, R1, R3, R5; 79 R2, R3; 80 R1; 83 L2, L3, R3; 84 L4, L5; 87 L3, R4; 88 R4; 89 L1, L2, L4, R2, R4; 90 L1, L4, R3; 95 R4; 104 L3; 105 L2, R5; 107 R3; 117 L4, R4; 122 L2, L3, R2; 123 R2; 124 L2; 126 L2, R4; 129 L3; 133 L3; 134 R4, R5; 136 L1; 138 R1; 139 L4, R4; 140 R1; 141 R2; 143 R2; 146 L4, R1; 147 R1; 150 L1, L2, R1, R4; 152 R1; 153 L1; 159 R2; 229 B3; 273 M2, M3, T2, T4; 279 B5; 374 3; 412 4; 452 1; 509 2; 560 1; 561 1; 584 2; 585 1; 595 4; 669 BL; 676 B; 735 T; Back BL. **Verna Johnston:** 41 TL. **Andrea Jones/The Garden Picture Library:** 331 3. **Dency Kane:** 4 BCR; 88 R5; 98 L1; 105 R3; 128 R3; 273 B, M5; 330 6; 405 1; 477 B5, M5; 509 5; 641 B2. **David Karp:** 505 1. **Ted King/King's Mums:** 273 M4. **Dwight Kuhn:** 664 T. **Michael Landis:** 89 L5. **G. Brad Leeves/Photo Resource Hawaii:** 63 T. **Kirsten Leitner/Friends of the Urban Forest:** 714. **A. M. Leonard:** 711 R. **George Lepp/AG Stock USA, Inc.:** 537 4. **Lightworker/GardenIMAGE:** 24 T. **Janet Loughrey:** 4 TR; 16 B; 21 L; 72 R1; 139 L1; 158 L2; 229 B4; 256; 593. **Maggie MacLaren:** 24 B. **Raymond R. Maleike:** 669 TR. **Allan Mandell:** 19 TL; 37 B; 64 T; 105 L4; Back BR. **Mandell/Japan. Gdn. Soc.:** 739. **Charles Mann:** 1; 9 T; 10 T; 25 T; 37 TL, TR; 59 TL, TR; 60 BR; 66 L2; 67 L1, L3, L5, R3; 72 R3; 74 L2; 76 L5; 77 L3; 78 L5, R3; 80 L2; 81 R5; 83 R2; 85 L2, R3; 86 L2, L3, L4, R1, R3; 88 L5; 90 L2, L3, R5; 91 L4, R2, R4; 92 L1, R4; 93 L2, R3, R4; 94 R4, R5; 95 L2, L4, R3; 96 L3; 100 R1; 101 R4; 102 L2, R3; 105 L1, L5; 109 R4, R5; 110 R1, R3, R4; 111 R5; 112 L2; 113 R2, R3, R4, R5; 114 L1, L2, L3, L4, R1, R2, R3, R4, R5; 115 L1, L2, L3, L4, L5; 116 R4; 118 L2, L4, R3; 120 R4; 123 R3; 129 R4; 132 L2, L3, L4; 138 R3; 140 R4; 141 L3, R4; 142 L3, L4; 144 L4, R3, R5; 145 L4, L5, R4; 149 L3, R4; 155 L3; 158 R1, R2; 160 L3, R1; 526 5; 594 1; 686 B; 705. **Steve W. Marley:** 719 1. **John Marshall/AG Stock USA, Inc.:** 193 TRC. **James Marshall:** 29 B. **Ells Marugg:** 144 L2; 244 2; 569; 571 1; 582 1; 583 3; 717 3; 718 3. **Stephanie Massey:** 244 3. **J. R. Mau/Photo Resource Hawaii:** 538 TR. **Mayer/Le Scanff/The Garden Picture Library:** 561 2. **Jim McCausland:** 434 T1. **David McDonald/PhotoGarden, Inc.:** 38 B; 66 L4; 70 R3; 73 L1, R2, R3; 74 L3; 78 R2; 85 R2; 87 L2, L5, R1; 88 R1, R2; 93 L3; 98 R5; 100 L3, L4, L5, R2; 101 L1, L2, L3, R1, R2, R5; 102 L4, L5, R1, R2; 107 L3, R4; 108 L1, L2, L4, R1, R2, R3, R4; 109 L1, L4; 110 L3; 112 R1, R3; 118 R1; 130 L3; 132 R2, R3; 133 L1, R3, R5; 134 L1, L2, L3, L4, R2; 136 L4, L5, R1; 137 L1, L3, L4, R1, R2, R4; 145 L2, R2; 147 R4; 149 L2, L6, R1, R2; 153 R4; 155 L2; 216 TLC; 453 2; 526 1; 641 T; 743 LC2. **Joe McDonald/Natural Selection:** 7 T. **Mendecino Coast Botanical Gdn:** 735 B. **Anthony Mercieca/Natural Selection:** 687 4. **Scott Millard:** 55 B. **Kevin Miller:** 404 3. **Terrence Moore:** 17; 18 B; 21 TR; 23 B. **Princely Nesadurai/Boyce Thompson:** 734. **Netherlands Flowers:** 641 M2. **Bart O'Brien:** 49 B. **Arthur N. Orans/Horticultural Photography:** 373 3; 537 6. **Orion Press/Natural Selection:** 20 B. **Jerry Pavia:** 81 L2; 85 L1; 87 R5; 89 L3; 90 R1; 103 L1; L4, L5; 104 R3; 105 L3, R2; 106 L1; 109 L3, L5; 112 LC4; 125 L2, R2; 127 L1, R4; 128 L3, L4, L5; 129 L2; 135 R4; 139 R3; 144 L3; 145 L1; 150 R2, R3, R5; 151 L2; 159 R1, R4; 160 R2, R3; 207 R; 216 BLC; 229 B1; 279 B4; 330 4; 331 2; 403 4; 405 4; 412 1, 2, 3, 5; 413 2, 3, 4; 434 M3, T2; 455; 477 B3; 509 4; 523; 536 3; 561 3; 573 2; 579; 582 2, 4; 585 3; 594 4, 5; 625 B2, B3; 660 B. **Joanne Pavia:** 71 L4; 157 R2. **Pamela K. Peirce:** 68 R3; 665 B; 682 TC; 683 BC; 684 TL; 727 ML, MR, TC, TL, TR; 728 2. **Norman A. Plate:** 8 B; 14 T; 15 B, T; 20 T; 22 T; 66 R1; 68 R1; 69 L2, R3, R4; 84 L1; 88 R3; 113 L3; 124 L1; 145 L3; 168 R; 193 L; 273 T3, T5; 308 B, M2, M3, M4, M5, T1, T2, T3, T5; 403 2; 452 2; 477 M2; 506; 507 1, 3, 6; 595 1; 621; 658 B, T; 659 C, T; 660 1, 2, 3, 4, 5, 6, 7, 8; 661 1, 2, 3; 662; 664 B; 668; 669 BC, BR; 672 B, T; 674 BCL, BCR, BL, BR, MC, ML, MR, TC, TL, TR; 676 M; 695; 696 BL, BR, MB, MT, TC, TL, TR; 717 6; 718 1, 4; 721; 722; 723. **Rob Proctor:** 12 B. **Jay Pscheidt:** 665 T. **Quail Botanical Gardens:** 736. **Ian Reeves:** 711 L; 712. **Sandra Lee Reha:** 38 T. **Ed Reschke/Peter Arnold, Inc.:** 135 L3. **Howard Rice/The Garden Picture Library:** 244 5. **Susan A. Roth:** 71 R3; 74 R2; 78 R1; 104 R1, R2; 119 R2; 121 L4, L5, R1; 123 L4, R1; 124 L4; 125 R1, R4; 126 L3, R1; 129 R2; 141 L1; 152 R3; 158 L3; 159 L3, R3; 207 C; 216 L; 273 M1; 404 5; 453 3; 454 1, 2; 457; 477 B2, B4, M1, M3, T; 507 4; 526 2; 527 2; 536 4; 584 1; 625 T; 641 B3, M1. **E. S. Ross:** 681 Rl. **Mark Rutherford:** 3; 65 R1; 70 L1, R2. **Marc Schecter/Photo Resource Hawaii:** 115 R5. **Scotts Company:** 675 3 L1, R1. **Richard Shiell:** 4 TL; 8 T; 26 B; 84 R1; 103 R1, R5; 104 L4; 115 R3, R4; 120 L2; 124 L5, R2, R3; 125 L1; 126 R2; 127 L2; 128 L2; 138 R2, R4; 151 L3; 153 R1; 160 L1; 216 RC; 228; 229 B2, T, T2, T3, T4; 244 1; 279 B3, T1, T3; 329; 331 1; 405 3; 413 1; 509 1, 3; 526 3; 538 TL; 595 2; 625 B4; 681 L; 687 2; 730 T; Back TR. **Malcolm C. Shurtleff:** 666 3. **Steve Sibbet:** 667 R; 666 1. **Rob & Ann Simpson/Visuals Unlimited:** 687 5. **J. S. Sira/Garden Picture Library:** Back CR. **John J. Smith:** 728 4. **Joe Solem/Photo Resource Hawaii:** 538 BR. **Southern Living:** 673; 679 B. **Lauren Springer:** 2. **Randy & Kara Stephens-Flemming:** 677 M. **Joseph G. Strauch, Jr.:** 89 R3; 95 L1; 105 R4; 122 L4; 123 L5, R4; 135 L1; 148 L4; 158 R3; 410. **Friedrich Strauss/The Garden Picture Library:** 625 B1. **Dan Suzio:** 728 5. **Eric Tankesley-Clark:** 403 3; 404 4. **Texas A & M University:** 667 C. **Michael S. Thompson:** 4 BL; 40 BL; 67 R1, R5; 68 L2, R2; 69 L5; 75 R5; 76 L3; 78 R4; 85 L4; 90 R2; 96 L2; 98 R2; 99 L2, L3; 104 R4; 106 R2; 127 R1; 129 L1; 135 R3; 138 L4, R5; 139 L2; 143 R5; 151 L1, L4; 153 L4; 157 R3; 158 R4; 160 L4; 193 TLC; 194; 207 L; 243; 330 1, 5; 372 1, 2, 4; 373 1, 2, 4; 402 2; 404 1; 413 5; 434 B, M4, M5; 453 1, 4, 5; 477 B1; 504 1; 505 2, 5, 6; 507 2, 5; 536 1; 537 3; 545; 584 4; 585 2; 594 2, 3; 595 5; 641 B4, M5; 671; 717 4. **Larry Ulrich:** 27 L; 31 T; 35 T. **G. Vaughn/Hawaii Tropical Botanical Gdn.:** 738. **Randy Vaughn Dotta/AG Stock USA, Inc.:** 374 4. **Juliette Wade /The Garden Picture Library:** 526 4. **Lance Walheim:** 279 B1, T2. **Darrow Watt:** 45 B, M; 716. **Randy Wells:** 32 B; 35 BL, BR. **Ron West:** 667 L; 677 T; 680 B1, B2, B3, B4, T1, T2, T3; 681 R2, R4; 682 BC, BL, BR, TL, TR; 683 BL, BR, TC, TL; 684 BL, TR; 686 T; 730 M. **Stephen Whalen/Zephyr Pictures:** 55 ML. **Peter O. Whiteley:** 130 R1; 641 M4. **Michael Wickes:** 32 T. **Doug Wilson:** 65 L3, R3, R4; 67 L4; 68 L3; 72 R2; 75 R3; 88 L4; 116 L3; 119 R1; 120 R1; 134 R1; 137 R3; 146 R3; 147 R2. **Dave Wilson Nursery:** 501; 504 3; 505 4. **Tom Woodward:** 67 R2; 68 L4; 71 R2, R4; 74 R1; 75 L2; 76 L4, R1, R5; 78 R5; 79 R4; 80 L1, L5, R3; 81 R2; 82 L1; 84 R3; 85 L3, R5; 87 L4, R3; 88 L1; 90 R4; 91 R1; 92 L4, R1, R5; 93 R1; 94 L1, R2; 95 L3, R2; 96 L1, L4; 97 L2; 98 L2, R4; 99 R2; 100 L1, R4; 102 L1, R5; 103 L3, R2; 107 L4; 108 R5; 111 R1; 112 L4; 113 L2; 116 L4, R3; 117 R2, R5; 118 R5; 119 L2, R4; 120 L5; 121 L1; 124 L3; 127 L3; 131 L3; 132 L1, L5; 133 R2; 134 R3; 135 L4, R1; 136 R6; 137 L2, R5; 138 L1; 140 L1, L5, R2; 142 R3; 143 L3, R1; 144 L5, R1; 145 R3; 146 L5; 147 L3, R3; 149 L1, L4; 150 L3; 152 L4; 153 R2; 154 L4; 155 L1; 156 L3; 742 CT, RB, RT; 743 BL, BR, TR; 744 LB, R; 745 L, RB, RT; 86 R2, R4. **Cynthia Woodyard:** 71 R1; 78 L2; 96 R3; 120 R3; 129 L5; 139 R1. **Tom Wyatt:** 69 L1; 583 4. **Ed Young/AG Stock USA, Inc.:** 279 T4; 374 1; 537 1, 2. **Josephine Zeitlin:** 160 R4.

Illustration Credits

A Practical Guide to Gardening; Glossary

Denman & Company: 710; **Lois Lovejoy:** 713 bottom; **Jane McCreary:** 661, 662, 663, 670, 690, 694 bottom, 701 middle, 702 top, 723; **Rik Olson:** 707, 721; **Mimi Osborne:** 671 top, 692 top; **Erin O'Toole:** 659, 671 bottom, 672, 678, 691, 692, 693, 694 top, 695, 697, 698, 699, 700, 701 left, 706 bottom, 720, 722, 724, 726; **Mark Pechenik:** 730–731; **Jenny Speckels:** 688, 747–750; **Catherine M. Watters:** 702 bottom, 703, 704, 705, 706 top, 713 top, 719